THE

VEDAS

The Saṃhitās of the Ṛig, Yajur (White and Black), Sāma, and Atharva Vedas

Single Volume, Unabridged

TRANSLATIONS INTO ENGLISH

BY

RALPH T. H. GRIFFITH

(Ṛig, White Yajur, Sāma, and Atharva)

AND

ARTHUR BERRIEDALE KEITH

(Black Yajur)

COMPILED AND EDITED BY

JON WILLIAM FERGUS

First Editions: Ṛig, 1889; White Yajur, 1899; Black Yajur, 1914; Sāma, 1895; Atharva, 1895.

Compiled, Edited and Re-formatted, 2017.

KSHETRA BOOKS
IDEAS EMBODIED.
www.kshetrabooks.com

Editions used in this volume:

The Rig Veda
First Edition, 1889
Second (revised) Edition, 1896

The Texts of the White Yajurveda
First Edition, 1899

The Veda of the Black Yajus School
First Edition, 1914

The Hymns of the Sāmaveda
First Edition, 1895

The Hymns of the Atharva-Veda
First Edition, 1895-6
Second Edition, 1916

Compiled, Edited and Re-formatted

ISBN: 978-1541294714

Contents

Hymns of the Atharvaveda

Foreword

The Vedas (from the root *vid*, "to know," or "divine knowledge") are the most ancient of all the Hindu scriptures. There were originally three Vedas—the *Laws of Manu* always speaks of the three, as do the oldest (Mukhya) Upaniṣhads—but a later work called the Atharvaveda has been added to these, to now constitute the fourth. The name Ṛigveda signifies "Veda of verses," from *rig*, a spoken stanza; Sāmaveda, the "Veda of chants," from *sāman*, a song or chant; Yajurveda, the "Veda of sacrificial formulas," from *yajus*, a sacrificial text. The Atharvaveda derives its name from the sage Atharvan, who is represented as a Prajāpati, the edlest son of Brahmā, and who is said to have been the first to institute the fire-sacrifices. The complex nature of the Vedas and the array of texts associated with them may be briefly outlined as follows:

> "The *Rig-Veda* is the original work, the *Yajur-Veda* and *Sama-Veda* in their mantric portions are different arrangements of its hymns for special purposes. The Vedas are divided into two parts, the Mantra and Brahmana. The Mantra part is composed of *suktas* (hymns in verse); the Brahmana part consists of liturgical, ritualistic, exegetical, and mystic treatises in prose. The Mantra or verse portion is considered more ancient than the prose works; and the books in which the hymns are collected are called *saṃhitās* (collections). More or less closely connected with the Brahmanans (and in a few exceptional cases with the Mantra part) are two classes of treatises in prose and verse called Aranyaka and Upaniṣhad. The Vedic writings are again divided into two great divisions, exoteric and esoteric, the former called the *karma-kanda* (the section of works) and the latter the *jnana-kanda* (section of wisdom)." (Encyclopedic Theosophical Glossary)

The great antiquity of the Vedas is sufficiently proven by the fact that they are written in such an ancient form of Sanskrit, so different from the Sanskrit now used, that there is no other work like them in the literature of this "eldest sister" of all the known languages, as Prof. Max Müller calls it. Only the most learned of the Brahman Pundits can read the Vedas in their original. Furthermore, the Vedas cannot be viewed as singular works by singular authors, but rather as compilations, assembled over a great and unknown period of time.

> "Almost every hymn or division of a Veda is ascribed to various authors. It is generally believed that these subdivisions were revealed orally to the rishis or sages whose respective names they bear; hence the body of the Veda is known as *sruti* (what was heard) or divine revelation. The very names of these Vedic sages, such as Vasishtha, Visvamitra, and Narada, all of which belong to men born in far distant ages, shows that millennia must have elapsed between the different dates of their composition." (Encyclopedic Theosophical Glossary)

It is generally agreed that the Vedas were finally arranged and compiled around fourteen centuries before our era; but this interferes in no way with their great antiquity, as they are acknowledged to have been long taught and passed down orally, perhaps for thousands of years, perhaps for far longer, before being finally compiled and recorded (the latter is traditionally said to have occurred on the shores of Lake Manasarovara, beyond the Himalayas).

The following, from Vedanta scholar Paul Deussen's *The System of the Vedanta*, will provide a general overview and outline of the Vedas, their divisions, history and influence on Indian life.

Some Remarks on the Veda

1. General view.

The great and not yet fully accessible complex of writings which bears the name of *Veda*, that is, "(theological) knowledge," and whose extent exceeds that of the Bible more than six times over, falls in the first place into four divisions, the Ṛigveda, Sāmaveda, Yajurveda and Atharvaveda. In each of these four Vedas we have to distinguish between three different classes of writings, according to content, form and age: 1) The Saṃhitā, 2) The Brāhmaṇam, 3) The Sūtram. Moreover, the greater part of these twelve divisions exists in different, more or less divergent recensions, as used by the different schools for whose study they served, and these are commonly spoken of as the *Śākhā's*, that is, "the branches," of the Veda-tree. For an understanding of this complicated organism it will be useful to distinguish between the form in which the Veda exists at present, and the historical development through which it has grown to this form.

2. The literary materials of the Veda.

In the first place the four Vedas, in the form in which they come to us, are nothing else than the Manuals of the Brahmanical Priests (*ṛitvij*), providing them with the materials of hymns and sentences necessary for the sacrificial cult, as well as teaching them their right use. To each complete sacrificial ceremony belong, in fact, four chief-priests distinguished according to their courses of studies, and their functions: 1) the Hotar, who recites the verses *(ṛic)* of the hymns, in order to invite the Gods to the enjoyment of the Soma or other offerings, 2) the Udgātar, who accompanies the preparation and presentation of the Soma with his chants (*sāman*), 3) the Adhvaryu, who performs the sacred rite, while he mutters the corresponding verses and sacrificial sentences (*yajus*), 4) the Brahman, to whom is confided the superintending and guiding of the whole. The canonical book for the Hotar is the Ṛigveda (though the Ṛigveda-saṃhitā has from the outset a wider import, not merely ritual but also literary): that for the Udgātar is the Sāmaveda, that for the Adhvaryu the Yajurveda, while on the contrary the Atharvaveda has nothing to do with the Brahman, who must know all the three Vedas, and to whom the Atharvaveda is only referred for the sake of appearance, in order to help to raise it to the dignity of a fourth Veda, which was for a long time refused to it. It finds its practical application on the one hand in the domestic cult (birth, marriage, burial, sicknesses, blessing the harvest, incantations over cattle and so forth), on the other hand in certain official acts (inauguration of the king, blessing before a battle, cursing of the enemy and so on); in the latter aspect it is the Veda of the Kṣhatriya caste, as the three others are of the Brahman caste, and might stand in the same relation to the *Purohita* (prince's family priest) as that which the others hold to the *Ṛitvijs* (cf. Yājñavalkya 1, 312).

Each of the priests named required in his duties, first, a collection of prayer-formulas (*mantra*) and, second, directions for the right liturgical and ritual application of these (*brāhmaṇam*). With the exception of the black Yajurveda, we find these two more or less completely separated and relegated to two different divisions.

1. The Saṃhitā of each Veda, as the name indicates, is a "collection" of the Mantras belonging to it, which are either verses (*ṛic*) or chants (*sāman*) or sacrificial sentences (*yajus*). Thus the Ṛigveda-saṃhitā consists of 1,017 hymns in 10,580 verses, from which the Hotar has to select the required invocation for the purpose in view; the Sāmav ed a-saṃhitā contains a selection of 1,549 verses (or with repetitions 1,810), either from the Ṛigveda-saṃhitā, or from the materials on which it is based; all these excepting only 75, are also found in the Ṛigveda. They are modulated in numerous ways, for the purposes of the chant (*sāman*); the Samhita of the white Yajurveda contains both prose sacrificial sentences (*yajus*) and verses, the latter of which are in great measure taken from the materials of the Ṛigveda; on the other hand, the Atharvaveda-saṃhitā consists merely of 760 Hymns, only about one sixth of which are common to it and the Ṛigveda, while the remainder occupy an independent and in many respects quite peculiar position in the total of the Vedic Mantra literature. Each of these four Saṃhitās, according to the *Śākhās* or Schools, in which it is studied, is extant in different recensions, which, however, do not, as a rule, differ materially from one another. It is otherwise, as will presently be shown, with the second division of Vedic literature.

2. The Brāhmaṇam, whose most direct purpose generally is, to teach the practical use of the materials presented in the Saṃhitā, in its widest scope often goes far beyond this immediate purpose, and draws within its sphere what (with Madhusādana) we may include in the three categories of *vidhi*, *arthavāda* and *vedānta*. 1) As *vidhi* (*i.e.*, precept) the Brāhmaṇam enjoins the ceremonies, explains the occasions of their use, as well as the means for carrying them out, and finally describes the process of the sacred rite itself. 2) With this, under the name of *arthavāda* (*i.e.*, explanation) are linked the most various discussions, whose purpose is, to support the content of the precept by exegesis, polemic, mythology, dogma, and so forth. 3) The consideration of the subject here and there rises to thoughts of a philosophical character, which, as they are found for the most part towards the end of the Brāhmaṇas, are called *vedānta* (*i.e.*, Veda-end). They are the chief content of the appendixes to the Brāhmaṇas which are called *Āraṇyakas*, and whose original purpose (though not strictly maintained) was to serve for the life in the forest (*araṇyam*), which was enjoined upon the Brahmans in old age, to serve as a substitute for the ritual which, if not completely left behind, was yet very much limited. However this may be, it is the fact that in them we meet abundantly a wonderful spiritualising of the sacrificial cult: in place of the practical carrying out of the ceremonies, comes meditation upon them, and with it a symbolical change of meaning, which then leads on farther to the loftiest thoughts.

The most important parts of these Āraṇyakas were later detached from them under the name Upanishad, and were brought together from the different Vedas into a single whole; but originally, as we must admit, each Vedic school had its special ritual textbook, and together with this a more or less rich dogmatic textbook, and if there were in reality, as the Muktikā Upanishad (Ind. St. III, 324) affirms, 21 + 1000 + 109 + 50 = 1,180 Śākhās, it follows that there must have been 1,180 Upanishads. In reality, however, the matter is much simpler, since the number of the Śākhās, which we really know, is limited for each Veda to a very small number, whose textbooks present the common ritual and dogmatic material in differing order, treatment and elaboration. Thus we are acquainted with only two Śākhās of the Ṛigveda, that of the *Aitareyins* and that of the *Kaushītakins*, each of which possesses one *Brāhmaṇam* and one *Āraṇyakam*, the latter containing the Upanishad of the school. For the Sāmaveda we know up to the present for the Brāhmaṇa section only one Śākhā accurately and completely, that of the *Tāṇḍins,* to which belong the following writings: a) the *Pañchaviṃśa-brahmaṇam*; b) the *Ṣhaḍviṃśa-brāhmaṇam*, whose name already characterizes it as an addition to the former; c) we must also attribute to the school of the Tāṇḍins the hitherto incompletely known *Chāndogya-brāhmaṇam*, since Śaṅkara under this name quotes a passage, which according to Rājendralāla Mitra (The Chāndogya-Up., Introduction, p. 17 N.) forms the beginning of the Chāndogya-brāhmaṇam; d) finally Śaṅkara repeatedly quotes the *Chāndogya-upanishad* as belonging to the Tāṇḍins. A second independent book of ritual for the Sāmaveda is possibly the *Talavakāra-brāhmanam* of the Jaiminīya-śākhā, according to Burnell in five Adhyāyas, the last but one of which contains the well-known short *Kena-Upanishad*, while the last consists of the *Ārsheya-brāhmaṇam*. The four remaining Brahmaṇas of the Sāmaveda (*Sāmavidhāna*, *Vaṃśa*, *Devatādhyāya*, *Saṃhitopanṣhad*) can make no claim to the name of independent text-books of the school. For the Yajurveda we have to distinguish two forms, the black (that is, unarranged) and the white (arranged) Yajurveda. The former contains Brāhmaṇa-like materials mingled with the Mantras in the Saṃhitā; in this form the schools of the *Taittirīyakas* (whose Brāhmaṇam and Āraṇyakam are merely continuations of the Saṃhitā), the *Kaṭhas* and the *Maitrāyaṇīyas* have handed the Yajurveda down to us. The *Taittirīya-āraṇyakam* contains at its close two Upanishads, the *Taittirīya Upanishad* (Book VII. VIII. IX.) and the *Nārāyaṇīya Upanishad* (Book X). To the school of the Kaṭhas belongs the *Kāṭhaka Upanishad*, which we now possess only in an Atharvan recension, whereas in Śaṅkara's time it seems to have formed a whole with the other texts of the Kaṭhas; under the name *Maitri Upanishad* we have received a late product of very apocryphal character;s the name of a fourth Śākhā of the black Yajurveda, the *Śvetāśvataras*, is that of a metrical Upanishad of secondary origin, which, however, is largely quoted by Śaṅkara as "Śvetāśvatarāṇāṃ mantropanishad" and seemingly also already by Bādarāyaṇa.

In contrast to the Śākhās of the black Yajurveda, the *Vājasaneyins*, the chief school of the white Yajurveda, separated the Mantras and Brahmaṇas after the manner of the remaining Vedas; the former are collected in the *Vājasaneyi-saṃhitā*, the latter form the content of the *Śatapatha-brāhmaṇam*, the concluding part (B. XIV.) of which contains the greatest and most beautiful of all the Upanishads, the *Bṛihad-āraṇyakam*. A piece closely related to it (probably only on account of its metrical form) has been added to the Vājasaneyi-saṃhitā as Adhyāya (Book) 40, and is called, from its first word the *Īśā Upanishad;* in the version of Anquetil Duperron four additional sections of the same Saṃhitā, *Śatarudriyam* (B. XVI.), *Purushasūktam* (XXXI.), *Tadeva* (XXXII.), and *Śivasaṃkalpa* (XXXIV, the beginning) are classed as Upanishads. Besides the Vājasaneyins Śaṅkara thirteen times quotes another school of the White Yajurveda, the *Jābālas*; nine of these quotations are found, with important variants, in the *Jābāla Upanishad*, which is today included among the Atharva Upanishads, four others are not, so that, as it seems, Śaṅkara had a more complete work of this school before him. Whether Bādarāyaṇa quotes the same work (1, 2, 32. 4, 1, 3) remains uncertain. To the Atharvaveda belongs the *Gopatha-brāhmaṇam*, a work which has preponderatingly the character of a compilation and is without close relation to the Atharva-saṃhitā. We find no quotations from it in Śaṅkara; the circumstance that at 3, 3, 24, p. 889ff., he does not also consider Gopatha-br. II, 5, 4, increases the probability that he did not know or did not recognize this work. Finally, to the Atharvaveda, which could most probably not be guarded against new invasions by supervision of the guild as were the other Vedas, has been attached a long series of Upanishads for the most part short, many of which have a wholly apocryphal character and are nothing more than the text-books of later Indian sects. Two Upanishads of the Atharvan are of special significance for the Vedanta, the *Muṇḍaka* and the *Praśna Upanishads*, both of which are frequently quoted by Bādarayaṇa and Śaṅkara, while we strangely find no certain quotation from the *Māṇḍūkya Upanishad* which is so abundantly used in the Vedāntasāra.

3. A third and last stage of the Vedic literature is formed by the Sūtras, likewise divided according to Vedas and Śākhās (whose relations however seem to be somewhat unfixed); they bring together the contents of the Brāhmaṇas, on which they are based, condensing, systematizing and completing them, for the purpose of practical life, in very compendious form, and in the lapidary style which is often quite incomprehensible without a commentary, a style to which also the grammatical, and the philosophical literature of India has adapted itself. There are three classes of Vedic Sūtras: 1) the *Śrauta-sūtras*, which regulate public worship, 2) the *Gṛihya-sūtras*, which regulate domestic ceremonies (at birth, marriage, and the funeral), and 3) the *Dharma-sūtras*, in which the duties of the Castes and *Āśramas* are set forth in detail, and from which the later lawbooks of Manu and so on are derived. The Śrauta-sūtras are based on the *Śruti* (that is, Divine Revelation), while the two other classes in like manner rest on the *Smṛiti* (that is, Tradition) and *Āchāra* (that is, Custom).

3. Of the Genesis of the Veda.

The most ancient monument in this extensive circle of literature (and perhaps also the most ancient literary monument of the human race) is formed by the Hymns of the Ṛigveda, since, as regards the great bulk of them, they go back to a time when their possessors were not yet in the valley of the Ganges, but lived among the tributaries of the Indus, had as yet no Castes, no privileged worship, no Brahmanical system of government and life, but belonged to small tribes (*viś*) under kings most of whom were hereditary, tilling their fields, pasturing their herds, fighting among themselves, and enjoying a primitive life. The Hymns of the Ṛigveda unfold a graphic picture of all these relations, but especially we can follow in them the genesis of the primitive nature religion of India through its different phases, in part even from the moment when the Gods are crystallizing under the hand of the poet out of the phenomena of nature, to the point at which belief in them for the thinking part of the nation begins to grow dim, and is being replaced by the first stirrings of philosophical speculation, the latter especially in the later hymns chiefly found in the last Maṇḍala, many of which, as for example the Hymn of Purusha, Ṛigv. 10, 90, already show an immigration into the Ganges valley with the consequent development of the Caste system.

For after the Indians through many battles and struggles, whose poetical reflections are contained for us in the Mahābhāratam, had won a permanent dwelling place for themselves in the paradise-like plain between the Himālaya and the Vindhya, their manner of life took on a form essentially different from the earlier one, owing to its altered external relations: an insurmountable barrier was in the first place erected between the *Śūdras*, the repressed population of the aborigines, and the immigrant Āryas; then further, above the *Vāiśyas*, that is, the collective mass of Ārya tribes, were raised on the one side, as possessors of material might, the *Kṣhatriyas* the warrior-nobility with the kings at their head, and on the other side the real or pretended descendants of the old Vedic poet-families, who called themselves *Brāhmaṇas* (offerers of prayer, priests), and succeeded in making their family privilege not only the Vedic hymns and the worship bound up with them, but by and by also the whole national education. It is true that, as before, all members of the three upper castes, so far as they were *Dvijas* ("twice-born," reborn through the sacrament of the *Upanayanam*, the admission into the Brahmanical church) had to offer, and in part also to perform sacrifices, but only the Brahmans could eat the sacrificial food, drink the Soma, and receive the sacrificial gift without which the sacrifice was not efficacious; they only could be *Ṛitvijs* (sacrificial priests for another for hire) and *Purohitas* (permanent family priests of the princes). Of these caste privileges the Brahmans were able in time to make a more and more extended use. In proportion as, through the consolidation of their settlements, the prosperity of the princes and the people grew, the external pageantry of worship increased; the number of the participating priests augmented, the names Brahman, Hotar, Adhvaryu, Udgātar, which we see emerging in the Ṛigveda at first sporadically and without strict distinction, were bound up into a system, and by the side of each of these Ṛitvijs at a great sacrifice stood a series of accolytes.

Now the more complex the system of worship became, the more imperatively it demanded a special training, and this practical need was the decisive factor in the arrangement of the Vedic literature,—if indeed this word can be employed for a condition of things in which no written record is to be thought of. Little by little, a firm tradition grew up about the verses and sentences with which the Adhvaryu had to accompany his manipulations (*Yajurveda*), as about the songs which the Udgātar chanted at the sacred operations (*Sāmaveda*), and lastly it was no longer enough for the Hotar to know the songs hereditary in his own family; the separate collections of hymns were gathered into circles (*maṇḍalam*), the circles into a single whole (*Ṛigveda*), which then for a certain further period still remained open for additional new productions. Not all the old hymns were admitted into this canon; many had to be excluded, because their contents were thought to be offensive or otherwise unsuited; others because, sprung from the people, they were not supported by the authority of some famous bardic family. To these were continually added new blossoms which the old stem of Vedic lyrics bore in the Brāhmaṇa Period, and which bear clear testimony to the altered consciousness of the time. From these materials, which had to be handed down for a long time outside the schools in the mouths of the people (to which fact their frequent and especially metrical negligence bears testimony), there came into being in course of time a fourth collection (*Atharvaveda*), which had to struggle long before gaining a recognition which always remained conditional.

Meanwhile the other older collections had become the basis of a certain course of study, which in course of time took a more and more regular form. Originally it was the father who initiated his son into the sacred lore handed down by the family, as best he could (Brih. 6, 2, 4. Chand. 5, 3, 5), soon, through the growing difficulty of understanding the old texts, the more and more complicated form of the ritual, the perpetually extending circle of studies, this became too difficult for him; it became necessary to look for the most approved authorities for each of the theories (*vidyā*) that had to be learned, travelling scholars (*charaka*) went further afield (Brih. 3, 3, 1), celebrated wandering teachers moved from place to place (Kaush. 4, 1), and to many teachers pupils streamed, "like the waters to the deep" (Taitt. 1, 4, 3). Later custom demanded that every Ārya should spend a series of years (according to Āpast. dharma-sūtra 1, 1, 2, 16 at least twelve) in the house of a teacher, the Brāhmaṇas, to prepare themselves for their future calling, the Kṣhatriyas and Vaiśyas, to receive the influences which were to mould their later thought and life. We must assume (even if we have no quotation at hand to prove it) that the imparting of this instruction became in course of time the exclusive privilege of the Brahmans: only thus can be explained the unparalleled influence over the life of the Indian peoples which the Brahmans succeeded in winning and maintaining. As the outward apparel of the scholars of the different castes differed, so also probably did their instruction. As payment for it, the scholars performed the household and field labour of the teacher; they tended the sacred fire (Chand. 4, 10, 1), herded the teacher's cattle (Chand. 4, 4, 5), collected the customary gifts for him in the village and brought him presents at the conclusion of the course. In the time left free by these manifold obligations (*guroḥ karma-atiśeṣheṇa*, Chand. 8, 15) the Veda was studied. On the whole, it was less a time of study than a time of discipline, as the name *Āśrama* implies, intended for the practice of obedience to the teacher (of which extravagant examples are handed down) and strenuous self-abnegating activity. It was the tendency of Brahmanism to mould the whole life to such an *Āśrama*. Not all, after the termination of the time of study, set themselves to found a family: many remained in the teacher's house to the end of their lives (*naishṭhika*);

others betook themselves to the forest to devote themselves to privations and penance; others again disdained even this form of regular existence, and cast away every thing (*saṃnyāsin*), to roam about (*parivrājaka*) as beggars (*bhikshu*). The different kinds of "*Āśrama*," or "religious exercise," were further bound together in a whole, in which what appears as an abrupt command in St. Matthew's Gospel XIX, 21, seems to have been expanded into a vast system embracing the whole of life. Accordingly the life of every Brāhmaṇa, and even the life of every Dvija, was to be divided into four stages, or *Āśramas*; he was (1), as *Brahmachārin*, to dwell in the house of a teacher, then (2), as *Gṛihastha*, to fulfil the duty of founding a family, then (3) to leave it in old age, as a *Vānaprastha* (forest hermit), to give himself up more and more to increasing penances, and lastly (4), towards the end of his life, as a *Saṃnyāsin* (*Bhikṣhu, Parivrājaka*) to wander free from all earthly ties and live on alms. We do not know how far the reality corresponded to these ideal claims.

While Brahmanical teaching and conduct of life were surrounding the existence of the Indian peoples in ever denser toils, we see ripening on the branch of Brahmanism itself a world concept which, though outwardly bound up with it, was inwardly opposed to it in its very basis. Already in the Ṛigveda strong movements of a certain philosophical tendency make themselves manifest. We perceive a special seeking and asking after the Unity which finally lies at the basis of all diversity; we see many attempts being made to solve the riddle of creation; to grasp through the motley changes of the world of appearances, through the more and more richly developed variety of the Vedic pantheon, the one formless principle of all that has form,—until at last the soul finds and lays hold of unity where alone unity is to be found—in th e soul its elf. Here, in the mysterious depths of his own heart, the seeker, raised above his own individuality by the fervour of aspiration (*brāhman*) discovered a power which he felt to transcend all the other powers of creation, a God-like might which, as he felt, dwells within all earthly and celestial beings as inner ruling principle (*antaryāmin*) on which all worlds and all Gods rest, through fear of which fire burns, the sun shines, the storm, wind and death perform their work (Kath. 6, 3), and without which not a straw can be burned by Agni, or carried away by Vāyu (Kena 3, 19. 23). A poetic formative power had clothed Agni, Indra and Vayu with personality; this power it was by which that power of fervour, "that which in the narrow sphere expanding to all sides grows mightily, as a delight of the great Gods, that which extends as a God to the Gods from afar and embraces this universe" (Ṛigv. II, 24, 11) was raised above all Gods first in a very transparent personification as *Bṛihaspati, Brahmaṇaspati*, but afterwards more truly, boldly, philosophically as *Brāhman* (prayer), as *Ātman* (Self), and from this power the Gods and the whole world besides were derived in endlessly varied play of phantasy. We may hope that thanks to the wealth of texts preserved in the Ṛigveda, Atharvaveda, and Brāhmaṇas, we may be able to trace step by step how the sparks of philosophic light appearing in the Ṛigveda shine out brighter and brighter until, at last, in the Upaniṣhads, they burst out in that bright flame which is able to light and warm us today.

Numerous indications intimate that the real guardians of these thoughts were originally not the priestly caste, absorbed in their ceremonial, but rather the caste of the Kṣhatriyas. Again and again, in the Upaniṣhads, we meet the situation that the Brahman begs the Kṣhatriya for instruction which the latter, after several representations of the unseemliness of such a proceeding, imparts to him (cf. Brih. 2, 1. Kaush. 4, 1. Brih. 6, 2. Chand. 5, 3. Chand. 5, 11. Kaush. 1, 1). However this may be, the Brahmans appropriated this new teaching of Brahman and its identity with the Self, and attached it, as best they could, to their own system of justification by works. Both systems, the ritual and the philosophic, were propagated in the Vedic schools, became inside and outside the school (at public festivals, at the courts of kings and so forth) the subject of keen debate and a not seldom vehement polemic; both suffered manifold transformations and exchanges in these contests and mutual accommodations; at last, as the precipitate of this rich spiritual life, the *Brahmaṇas* and the *Upaniṣhads*, in which they issue, were formed and brought into their present shape and finally (probably after their practical meaning had already long been transferred to the Sūtras) recorded in writing. It is to be hoped that in time it will be possible to reconstruct from them, even if not in every detail, the course of development which found its conclusion in them.

We have already seen how to the older Upaniṣhads, which are the philosophical text-books of the different Śākhās, were added a long series of younger products of the same name; in these we can follow the further extension of religious concepts, and, hand in hand with it, the development of a special tendency to accomplish even in this life the union with the All-spirit, through a certain practical process (called *Yoga*), down to the time of the Indian sects. These texts, as it seems, have a purely external connection with the Atharvaveda.

Students interested in further exploring the historical development of Vedanta thought—from the Vedas through the Brāhmaṇas and Upaniṣhads, and on through to Śaṅkaracharya's works—with explanations of the philosophical, metaphysical and theological nature of the system, are encouraged to begin with the remainder of Paul Deussen's *The System of the Vedanta*, along with Charles Johnston's translations of, and commentaries on, the *Mukhya Upanishads* and the *Vedanta Philosophy of Sankaracharya*.

Editor's Notes

Throughout these translations of the Vedas, the reader will come across several verses, and occasionally entire hymns, where the translation has been rendered in Latin instead of English. A surface (*i.e.* non-symbolical) reading of these hymns and verses reveal topics generally erotic or sexual in nature, which on occasion deal with quite inappropriate subject matter. An example of this is found in Ṛigveda 10:61, where verses 5-9 are rendered in Latin. These verses deal with an incestual event between Prajāpati and his daughter Sarasvatī. The Śatapatha Brāhmaṇa of the Śukla (White) Yajurveda, 1:7:4, provides some commentary on the event in question. As in other examples, a surface reading of these verses is indeed quite troubling and inappropriate, but as is the case with stories of the exploits of gods from other traditions, a symbolical reading may reveal a different meaning.

A second, perhaps simpler, example of such a case is that of two verses omitted from Ṛigveda 10:86, where Griffith chose not to present even a Latin rendering, but instead simply noted: "I pass over stanzas 16 and 17, which I cannot translate into decent English." The Oxford (Jamison, Brereton) rendering of these verses is as follows:

16. [Indra:] "He is not master, whose penis hangs (limp) between his thighs. He is master, for whose (penis) the hairy (vulva) gapes when it [=erect penis] has sat down." Above all Indra!

17. [Indrāṇī:] "He is not master, for whose (penis) the hairy (vulva) gapes when it [=erect penis] hangs (limp) between his thighs." Above all Indra!

One may understand Griffith's hesitation, particularly given the quite reserved western mindset towards sex and sexuality during the late 19th and early 20th century. The same general tendency occurs throughout such omitted verses in each of the following translations.

In regards to the utilization of Latin, it is a language that was widely understood among the more educated classes at the time of these translations, thus the choice to render such verses into Latin made them available to scholars, who would be more likely to understand the symbolical meaning, but not to laymen, who may tend towards a more surface reading. It is also clear from some of Griffith's and Keith's notes that they omitted or rendered in Latin several verses at least in part simply because they found them to be offensive to their sensibilities. The sincere and dedicated student is encouraged to seek the symbolic meaning in such verses and hymns in favour of a mere surface reading (advice that is applicable to the whole of the Vedas).

The serious student may wish to consult the original editions of both Griffith's and Keith's translations, as they contain copious notes by the translators, with explanations of terms, verses, etc.

Note: in this volume, romanized Sanskrit terms are given in modern IAST standard, except for three deviations meant to aid in proper pronunciation (*i.e.* Ṛ or ṛ is given as Ṛi or ṛi, Ş or ş is given as Şh or şh, and C or c is given as Ch or ch). Pluralizations of Sanskrit nouns use the standard English addition of an *s* to the end of the term.

Hymns of the Ṛigveda

Translated by Ralph T.H. Griffith, 1896

Preface

"What can be more tedious than the Veda, and yet what can be more interesting, if once we know that it is the first word spoken by the Ārya man?"

"The Veda has a two-fold interest: it belongs to the history of the world and to the history of India. As long as man continues to take an interest in the history of his race, and as long as we collect in libraries and museums the relics of former ages, the first place in that long row of books which contains the records of the Ārya branch of mankind, will belong forever to the Ṛigveda." F. Max Müller.

This work is an attempt to bring within easy reach of all readers of English a translation of the Hymns of the Ṛigveda which, while aiming especially at close fidelity to the letter and the spirit of the original, shall be as readable and intelligible as the nature of the subject and other circumstances permit.

Veda, meaning literally knowledge, is the name given to certain ancient works which formed the foundation of the early religious belief of the Hindus. These are the Ṛigveda, the Sāmaveda, the Yajurveda, and the Atharvaveda; and of these the Ṛigveda—so called because its *Saṃhitā* or collection of mantras or hymns consists of *Ṛichas* or verses intended for loud recitation—is the oldest, the most important, and the most generally interesting, some of its hymns being rather Indo-European than Hindu, and representing the condition of the Āryas before their final settlement in India.

These four Vedas are [traditionally] considered to be of divine origin and to have existed from all eternity, the Ṛishis or sacred poets to whom the hymns are ascribed being merely inspired seers who saw or received them by sight directly from the Supreme Creator. In accordance with this belief these sacred books have been preserved and handed down with the most reverential care from generation to generation, and have accompanied the great army of Ārya immigrants in their onward march from the Land of the Seven Rivers to the Indian Ocean and the Bay of Bengal. Each of these four Vedas is divided into two distinct parts, one the Mantra containing prayer and praise, the other the Brāhmaṇa containing detailed directions for the performance of the ceremonies at which the Mantras were to be used, and explanations of the legends connected with them, the whole forming a vast body of sacred literature in verse and in prose, devotional, ceremonial, expository and theosophic.

The *Saṃhitā* of the Ṛigveda is a collection of hymns and songs brought by the remote ancestors of the present Hindus from their ancient homes on the banks of the Indus where they had been first used in adoration of the Father of Heaven, of the Sun, of Dawn, of Agni or the God of fire, in prayers for health, wealth, long life, offspring, cattle, victory in battle, and freedom from the bonds of sin; and in celebration of the ever-renewed warfare between the beneficent thunder-wielding Indra, the special champion of the Āryas, and the malevolent powers of darkness and the demons of drought who withheld the rain of heaven.

Of these hymns there are more than a thousand, arranged in ten Maṇḍalas, Circles, or Books,[1] in accordance with an ancient tradition of what we should call authorship, the hymns ascribed to the same Ṛishi, inspired poet or seer, or to the same school or family of Ṛishis being placed together. Within these divisions the hymns are generally arranged more or less in the order of the deities to whom they are addressed. Agni and Indra are the Gods most frequently invoked. Hymns to Agni generally come first, next come those addressed to Indra, and after them those in honour of other deities or deified objects of adoration. The ninth Maṇḍala is devoted almost entirely to Soma, the deified juice used in pouring libations to the Gods, and the tenth forms a sort of appendix of peculiar and miscellaneous materials. Independently of the evidence afforded by Indian tradition, there can be no reasonable doubt of the great antiquity of the Ṛigveda Saṃhitā which, with the exception of the Egyptian monumental records and papyrus rolls, and the recently discovered Assyrian literature, is probably the oldest literary document in existence. But it seems impossible to fix, with anything approaching to certainty, any date for the composition of the hymns. In the first Hymn of Maṇḍala 1, ancient and recent or modern Ṛishis or seers are spoken of, and there is other internal evidence that some hymns are much older than others. Colebrooke came to the conclusion, from astronomical calculations, that a certain Vedic calendar was composed in the fourteenth century before the Christian era; from which it would follow, that as this calendar must have been prepared after the arrangement of the Ṛigveda and the inclusion of the most modern hymn, the date of the earliest hymn might be carried back, perhaps, some thousand years. The correctness of Colebrooke's conclusions, however, has been questioned, and some recent scholars consider that his calculations are of a very vague character, and do not yield any such definite date. In the absence of any direct evidence, the opinions of scholars vary and must continue to vary with regard to the age of the Hymns of the Ṛigveda.

"The reasons, however," (to quote Professor Weber) "by which we are fully justified in regarding the literature of India as the most ancient literature of which written records on an extensive scale have been handed down to us are these:—In the more ancient parts of the Ṛigveda Saṃhitā, we find the Indian race settled on the north-western borders of India, in the Punjab, and even beyond the Punjab, on the Kubhi, or Κωφήν, in Kabul. The gradual spread of the race from these seats towards the east, beyond the Sarasvatī and over Hindustan as far as the Ganges, can be traced in the later portions of the Vedic writings almost step by step. The writings of the following period, that of the epic, consists of accounts of the internal conflicts among the conquerors of Hindustan themselves, as, for instance, the Mahabharata; or of the farther spread of Brahmanism towards the south, as, for instance, the Ramayana. If we connect with this the first fairly accurate information about India which

---

1. Maṇḍala 1 comprises 191 hymns; Maṇḍala 2 comprises 43 hymns; Maṇḍala 3 comprises 62 hymns; Maṇḍala 4 comprises 58 hymns; Maṇḍala 5 comprises 87 hymns; Maṇḍala 6 comprises 75 hymns; Maṇḍala 7 comprises 104 hymns; Maṇḍala 8 comprises 103 hymns (92 + the 11 vālakhilya hymns); Maṇḍala 9 comprises 114 hymns; and Maṇḍala 10 comprises 191 hymns. The whole of the work, then, is composed of 1,028 hymns, made up of approximately 10,580 verses, a monumental compilation by any standard. (Ed.)

we have from a Greek source, *viz.*, from Megasthenes, it becomes clear that at the time of this writer the Brahmanising of Hindustan was already completed, while at the time of the Periplus the very southern-most point of the Dekhan had already become the seat of the worship of the wife of Siva. What a series of years, of centuries, must necessarily have elapsed before this boundless tract of country, inhabited by wild and vigorous tribes, could have been brought over to Brahmanism?"

. . . My translation, which follows the text of Max Müller's splendid six-volume edition, is partly based on the work of the great scholiast Sāyaṇa, who was Prime Minister at the court of the King of Vijayanagar—in what is now the Madras District of Bellary—in the fourteenth century of our era. Sāyaṇa's Commentary has been consulted and carefully considered for the general sense of every verse and for the meaning of every word, and his interpretation has been followed whenever it seemed rational, and consistent with the context, and with other passages in which the same word or words occur. With regard to Sāyaṇa's qualifications as an interpreter of the Veda there is, or was, a conflict of opinion among European scholars. Professor Wilson—whose translation of the Ṛigveda is rather a version of Sāyaṇa's paraphrase—was firmly persuaded that he had a "knowledge of his text far beyond the pretensions of any European scholar, and must have been in possession of all the interpretations which had been perpetuated by traditional teaching from the earliest times." Yet, as Dr. J. Muir has pointed out, Professor Wilson in the notes to his translation admits that he "occasionally failed to find in Sāyaṇa a perfectly satisfactory guide," that "the scholiast is evidently puzzled," and that his explanations are obscure. On the other hand Professor Roth—the author of the Vedic portion of the great St. Petersburg Lexicon—says in his preface to that work:

"so far as regards one of the branches of Vedic literature, the treatises on theology and worship, we can desire no better guides then these commentators, so exact in all respects, who follow their texts word-by -word, who, so long as even the semblance of a misconception might arise, are never weary of repeating what they have frequently said before, and who often appear as if they had been writing for us foreigners rather than for their own priestly alumni who had grown up in the midst of these conceptions and impressions. Here . . . they are in their proper ground. The case, however, is quite different when the same men assume the task of interpreting the ancient collections of hymns . . . Here were required not only quite different qualifications for interpretation but also a greater freedom of judgment and a greater breadth of view and of historical intuitions. Freedom of judgment, however, was wanting to priestly learning, whilst in India no one has ever had any conception of historical development. The very qualities which have made those commentators excellent guides to an understanding of the theological treatises, render them unsuitable conductors on that far older and quite differently circumstanced domain. As the so-called classical Sanskrit was perfectly familiar to them, they sought its ordinary idiom in the Vedic hymns also. Since any difference in the ritual appeared to them inconceivable and the present forms were believed to have existed from the beginning of the world, they fancied that the patriarchs of the Indian religion must have sacrificed in the very same manner. As the recognized mythological and classical systems of their own age appeared to them unassailable and revealed verities, they must necessarily (so the commentators thought) be discoverable in that centre point of revelation, the hymns of the ancient Ṛishis, who had, indeed, lived in familiar intercourse with the Gods, and possessed far higher wisdom than the succeeding generations . . . It has never occurred to any one to make our understanding of the Hebrew books of the Old Testament depend on the Talmud and the Rabbins, while there are not wanting scholars who hold it as the duty of a conscientious interpreter of the Veda to translate in conformity with Sāyaṇa, Mahīdhara, etc. Consequently, we do not believe like H. H. Wilson, that Sāyaṇa, for instance, understood the expressions of the Veda better than any European interpreter; but we think that a conscientious European interpreter may understand the Veda far better and more correctly than Sāyaṇa. We do not esteem it our first task to arrive at that understanding of the Veda which was current in India some centuries ago, but to search out the sense which the poets themselves have put into their hymns and utterances, Hence we are of opinion that the writings of Sāyaṇa and the other commentators do not form a rule for the interpreter, but are merely one of those helps of which the latter will avail himself for the execution of his undoubtedly difficult task, a task which is not to be accomplished at the first onset, or by any single individual. . . . We have, therefore, endeavoured to follow the path prescribed by philology, to derive from the texts themselves the sense which they contain, by a juxtaposition of all the passages which are cognate in diction or contents;—a tedious and laborious path, in which neither the commentators nor the translators have preceded us. The double duty of exegete and lexicographer has thus devolved upon us. A simple etymological procedure, practised as it must be by those who seek to divine the sense of a word from the sole consideration of the passage before them without regard to the ten or twenty other passages in which it recurs, cannot possibly lead to a correct result."

Professor Max Müller says:

"As the authors of the Brāhmaṇas were blinded by theology, the authors of the still later Niruktas were deceived by etymological fictions, and both conspired to mislead by their authority later and more sensible commentators, such as Sāyaṇa. Where Sāyaṇa has no authority to mislead him, his commentary is at all events rational; but still his scholastic notions would never allow him to accept the free interpretation which comparative study of these venerable documents forces upon the unprejudiced scholar. We must therefore discover ourselves the real vestiges of these ancient poets."

Professor Benfey says:

"Every one who has carefully studied the Indian interpretations is aware that absolutely no continuous tradition extending from the composition of the Veda to their explanation by Indian scholars, can be assumed; that, on the contrary, between the genuine poetic remains of Vedic antiquity and their interpretations a long-continued break in tradition must have intervened, out of which at most the comprehension of some particulars may have been rescued and handed down to later times by means of liturgical usages and words, formulae, and perhaps, also, poems connected therewith. Besides these remains of tradition, which must be estimated as very scanty, the interpreters of the Veda had, in the main, scarcely any other helps than those which, for the most part, are still at our command, the usage of the classical speech, and the grammatical and etymological-lexicographical investigation of words. At the utmost, they found some aid in materials preserved in local dialects; but this advantage is almost entirely outweighed by the comparison which we are able to institute with the Zend, and that which we can make (though here we must of course proceed with caution and prudence) with the languages cognate to the Sanskrit,—a comparison which has already supplied so many helps to a clearer understanding of the Vedas. But quite irrespectively of all particular aids, the Indian method of interpretation becomes in its whole essence an entirely false one, owing to the prejudice with which it chooses to conceive the ancient circumstances and ideas which have become quite strange to it, from its own religious stand-point, so many centuries more recent, whilst, on the other hand, an advantage for the comprehension of the whole is secured to us by the acquaintance (drawn from analogous relations) with the life, the conceptions, the wants, of ancient peoples and popular songs, which we possess,—an advantage which, even if the Indians owed more details than they actually do owe, to tradition, would not be eclipsed by their interpretation."

A very different opinion of the value of the Indian commentators was held and expressed by Professor Goldstücker:

"Without the vast information," he says, "which those commentators have disclosed to us,—without their method of explaining the obscurest text,—in one word, without their scholarship, we should still stand at the outer doors of Hindu antiquity."

He ridicules the assertion that a European scholar can understand the Veda more correctly than Sāyaṇa, or arrive more nearly at the meaning which the Ṛishis gave to their own hymns, and yet even this staunch champion of the Indian commentators "cannot be altogether acquitted (as Dr. J. Muir says and shows) of a certain heretical tendency to deviate in practice from the interpretations of Sāyaṇa."

The last quotation which I shall make in connection with this question is from Professor E. B. Cowell's Preface to his edition of Vol. V. of Wilson's Translation of the Rig-Veda Saṃhitā:

> "This work does not pretend to give a complete translation of the Rig Veda, but only a faithful image of that particular phase of its interpretation which the mediaeval Hindus, as represented by Sāyaṇa, have preserved. This view is in itself interesting and of an historical value; but far wider and deeper study is needed to pierce to the real meaning of these old hymns. Sāyaṇa's commentary will always retain a value of its own,—even its mistakes are often interesting,—but his explanations must not for a moment bar the progress of scholarship. We can be thankful to him for any real help; but let us not forget the debt which we owe to modern scholars, especially to those of Germany. The great St. Petersburg Dictionary is indeed a monument of triumphant erudition, and it has inaugurated a new era in the interpretation of the Rig Veda."

My translation, then, is partly based on the commentary of Sāyaṇa, corrected and regulated by rational probability, context, and intercomparison of similar words and passages. For constant and most valuable assistance in my labour I am deeply indebted to the works of many illustrious scholars, some departed, and some, happily, still flourishing. I am thankful to Sāyaṇa, my first guide to the hymns of the Ṛigveda; to my revered Master, Professor H. H. Wilson; to Professors Roth, Benfey, Weber, Ludwig, Max Müller, Grassmann, and Monier Williams, and Dr. John Muir and Mr. Wallis. I have also consulted, and shall probably make more use hereafter of, the works of M. Bergaigne and Dr. Oldenberg; nor can I omit to mention the *Siebenaig Lieder des Ṛigveda* by Geldner and Kaegi, *Der Ṛigveda* by Kaegi, and *Hymns from the Ṛigveda* by Professor Peterson of Bombay, all of which I have read with pleasure and profit.

But it must not be supposed that European students and interpreters of the Veda claim anything like infallibility, completeness, or finality for the results to which their researches have led them. All modern scholars will allow that many hymns are dark as the darkest oracle, that, as Professor Max Müller says, there are whole verses which, as yet, yield no sense whatever, and words the meaning of which we can only guess. As in the interpretation of the more difficult books of the Old Testament and the Homeric poems, so in the explanation of the Veda complete success, if ever attainable, can be attained only by the labours of generations of scholars.

The Hymns are composed in various metres, some of which are exceedingly simple and others comparatively complex and elaborate, and two or more different metres are frequently found in the same Hymn; one Hymn, for instance, in Maṇḍala 1, shows nine distinct varieties in the same number of verses. The verses or stanzas consist of three or more—generally three or four—*pādas*, semi-hemistichs or lines, each of which contains eight, eleven, or twelve syllables, sometimes, but rarely, five, and still less frequently four or more than twelve. As regards quantity, the first syllables of the line are not strictly defined, but the last four are regular, the measure being iambic in the eight and twelve syllable verses and trochaic in these of eleven syllables. Partly by way of safeguard against the besetting temptation to paraphrase and expand, and partly in the hope of preserving, however imperfectly, something of the form of the Hymns, I have translated each verse by a verse syllabically commensurate with the original and generally divided into corresponding hemistichs.

The verses consisting of three or four octosyllabic lines are tolerably well represented by the common octosyllabic or dimeter iambic metre which I have employed. In other verses I have not attempted to reproduce or imitate the rhythm or metre of the original: such a task, supposing its satisfactory completion to be possible, would require more time and labour than I could spare for the purpose. All that I have done, or tried to do, is to show to some extent the original external form of the Hymns by rendering them in syllabically commensurate hemistichs and verses, as Benfey and the translators of the *Seventy Hymns* have done for a portion of the Ṛigveda, and Grassmann for nearly the whole of the Collection.

. . . To conclude, my reasons for publishing this work are chiefly these: there is at present no complete translation of the Ṛigveda in English, Professor Wilson's version—of which the last two volumes have only lately appeared—being "only a faithful image of that particular phase of its interpretation which the mediaeval Hindus, as represented by Sāyaṇa, have preserved."

I can hardly hope that my work will find acceptance with Pundits and Indian scholars inasmuch as I venture to deviate both widely and frequently from Sāyaṇa whom they have been taught to regard as infallible. No arguments are likely to shake this belief. Nothing short of a course of study similar to that to which the leaders of the modern school of Vedic interpretation have devoted half their lives will enable them to see with our eyes and accept our views. I trust, however, that they will at any rate give the leaders and the followers of this modern school credit for deep devotion to ancient Indian literature and due admiration of the great Indian scholars who have expounded it; and will acknowledge that these modern scholars—however mistaken their views may appear to be—are labouring sincerely and solely to discover and declare the spirit and the truth of the most ancient and venerated literary records that are the heritage of Ārya man.

R. T. H. GRIFFITH.
Kotaoiri, Nilgiri:, May 25th 1889.

Maṇḍala 1.

Hymn 1:1. Agni.

1. I laud Agni, the chosen Priest, God, minister of sacrifice, | The Hotar, lavishest of wealth. || 2. Worthy is Agni to be praised by living as by ancient seers. | He shall bring hitherward the Gods. || 3. Through Agni man obtaineth wealth, yea, plenty waxing day by day, | Most rich in heroes, glorious. || 4. Agni, the perfect sacrifice which thou encompassest about | Verily goeth to the Gods. || 5. May Agni, sapient-minded Priest, truthful, most gloriously great, | The God, come hither with the Gods. || 6. Whatever blessing, Agni, thou wilt grant unto thy worshipper, | That, Aṅgiras, is indeed thy truth. || 7. To thee, dispeller of the night, O Agni, day by day with prayer | Bringing thee reverence, we come || 8. Ruler of sacrifices, guard of Law eternal, radiant One, | Increasing in thine own abode. || 9. Be to us easy of approach, even as a father to his son: | Agni, be with us for our weal.

Hymn 1:2. Vāyu.

1. Beautiful Vāyu, come, for thee these Soma drops have been prepared: | Drink of them, hearken to our call. || 2. Knowing the days, with Soma juice poured forth, the singers glorify | Thee, Vāyu, with their hymns of praise. || 3. Vāyu, thy penetrating stream goes forth unto the worshipper, | Far-spreading for the Soma draught. || 4. These, Indra-Vāyu, have been shed; come for our offered dainties' sake: | The drops are yearning for you both. || 5. Well do ye mark libations, ye Vāyu and Indra, rich in spoil | So come ye swiftly hitherward. || 6. Vāyu and Indra, come to what the Soma. presser hath prepared: | Soon, Heroes, thus I make my prayer. || 7. Mitra, of holy strength, I call, and foe-destroying Varuṇa, | Who make the oil-fed rite complete. || 8. Mitra and Varuṇa, through Law, lovers and cherishers of Law, | Have ye obtained your might power. || 9. Our Sages, Mitra-Varuṇa, wide dominion, strong by birth, | Vouchsafe us strength that worketh well.

Hymn 1:3. Aśvins.

1. Ye Aśvins, rich in treasure, Lords of splendour, having nimble hands, | Accept the sacrificial food. || 2. Ye Aśvins, rich in wondrous deeds, ye heroes worthy of our praise, | Accept our songs with mighty thought. || 3. Nāsatyas, wonder-workers, yours are these libations with clipt grass: | Come ye whose paths are red with flame. || 4. O Indra marvellously bright, come, these libations long for thee, | Thus by fine fingers purified. || 5. Urged by the holy singer, sped by song, come, Indra, to the prayers, | Of the libation-pouring priest. || 6. Approach, O Indra, hasting thee, Lord of Bay Horses, to the prayers. | In our libation take delight. || 7. Ye Viśvedevas, who protect, reward, and cherish men, approach | Your worshipper's drink-offering. || 8. Ye Viśvedevas, swift at work, come hither quickly to the draught, | As milch-kine hasten to their stalls. || 9. The Viśvedevas, changing shape like serpents, fearless, void of guile, | Bearers, accept the sacred draught || 10. Wealthy in spoil, enriched with hymns, may bright Sarasvatī desire, | With eager love, our sacrifice. || 11. Inciter of all pleasant songs, inspirer o all gracious thought, | Sarasvatī accept our rite || 12. Sarasvatī, the mighty flood,—she with be light illuminates, | She brightens every pious thought.

Hymn 1:4. Indra.

1. As a good cow to him who milks, we call the doer of fair deeds, | To our assistance day by day. || 2. Come thou to our libations, drink of Soma; Soma-drinker thou! | The rich One's rapture giveth kine. || 3. So may we be acquainted with thine innermost benevolence: | Neglect us not, come hitherward. || 4. Go to the wise unconquered One, ask thou of Indra, skilled in song, | Him who is better than thy friends. || 5. Whether the men who mock us say, Depart unto another place, | Ye who serve Indra and none else; || 6. Or whether, God of wondrous deeds, all our true people call us blest, | Still may we dwell in Indra's care. || 7. Unto the swift One bring the swift, man-cheering, grace of sacrifice, | That to the Friend gives wings and joy. || 8. Thou, Śatakratu, drankest this and wast the Vṛitras' slayer; thou | Helpest the warrior in the fray. || 9. We strengthen, Śatakratu, thee, yea, thee the powerful in fight, | That, Indra, we may win us wealth. || 10. To him the mighty stream of wealth, prompt friend of him who pours the juice, | yea, to this Indra sing your song.

Hymn 1:5. Indra.

1. O Come ye hither, sit ye down: to Indra sing ye forth, your song, | companions, bringing hymns of praise. || 2. To him the richest of the rich, the Lord of treasures excellent, | Indra, with Soma juice outpoured. || 3. May he stand by us in our need and in abundance for our wealth: | May he come nigh us with his strength. || 4. Whose pair of tawny horses yoked in battles foemen challenge not: | To him, to Indra sing your song. || 5. Nigh to the Soma-drinker come, for his enjoyment, these pure drops, | The Somas mingled with the curd. || 6. Thou, grown at once to perfect strength, wast born to drink the Soma juice, | Strong Indra, for preeminence. || 7. O Indra, lover of the song, may these quick Somas enter thee: | May they bring bliss to thee the Sage. || 8. Our chants of praise have strengthened thee, O Śatakratu, and our lauds | So strengthen thee the songs we sing. || 9. Indra, whose succour never fails, accept these viands thousandfold, | Wherein all manly powers abide. || 10. O Indra, thou who lovest song, let no man hurt our bodies, keep | Slaughter far from us, for thou canst.

Hymn 1:6. Indra.

1. They who stand round him as he moves harness the bright, the ruddy Steed | The lights are shining in the sky. || 2. On both sides to the car they yoke the two bay coursers dear to him, | Bold, tawny, bearers of the Chief. || 3. Thou, making light where no light was, and form, O men: where form was not, | Wast born together with the Dawns. || 4. Thereafter they, as is their wont, threw off the state of babes unborn, | Assuming sacrificial names. || 5. Thou, Indra, with the Tempest-Gods, the breakers down of what is firm, | Foundest the kine even in the cave. || 6. Worshipping even as they list, singers laud him who findeth wealth, | The far-renowned, the mighty One. || 7. Mayest thou verily be seen coming by fearless Indra's side: | Both joyous, equal in your sheen. || 8. With Indra's well beloved hosts, the blameless, hastening to heaven, | The sacrificer cries aloud. || 9. Come from this place, O Wanderer, or downward from the light of heaven: | Our songs of praise all yearn for this. || 10. Indra we seek to give us help, from here, from heaven above the earth, | Or from the spacious firmament.

Hymn 1:7. Indra.

1. Indra the singers with high praise, Indra reciters with their lauds, | Indra the choirs have glorified. || 2. Indra hath ever close to him his two bay steeds and word-yoked car, | Indra the golden, thunder-armed. || 3. Indra hath raised the Sun on high in heaven, that he may see afar: | He burst the mountain for the kine. || 4. Help us, O Indra, in the frays, yea, frays, where thousand spoils are gained, | With awful aids, O awful One. || 5. In mighty battle we invoke Indra, Indra in lesser fight, | The Friend who bends his bolt at fiends. || 6. Unclose, our manly Hero, thou for ever bounteous, yonder cloud, | For us, thou irresistible. || 7. Still higher, at each strain of mine, thunder-armed Indra's praises rise: | I find no laud worthy of him. || 8. Even as the bull drives on the herds, he drives the people with his might, | The Ruler irresistible: || 9. Indra who rules with single sway men, riches, and the fivefold race | Of those who dwell upon the earth. || 10. For your sake from each side we call Indra away from other men: | Ours, and none others, may he be.

Hymn 1:8. Indra.

1. Indra, bring wealth that gives delight, the victor's ever-conquering wealth, | Most excellent, to be our aid; || 2. By means of which we may repel our foes in battle hand to hand, | By thee assisted with the car. || 3. Aided by thee, the thunder-armed, Indra, may we lift up the bolt, | And conquer all our foes in fight. || 4. With thee, O India, for ally with missile-darting heroes, may | We conquer our embattled foes. || 5. Mighty is Indra, yea supreme; greatness be his, the Thunderer: | Wide as the heaven extends his power || 6. Which aideth those to win them sons, who come as heroes to the fight, | Or singers loving holy thoughts. || 7. His belly, drinking deepest draughts of Soma, like an ocean swells, | Like wide streams from the cope of heaven. || 8. So also is his excellence, great, vigorous, rich in cattle, like | A ripe branch to the worshipper. || 9. For verily thy mighty powers, Indra, are saving helps at once | Unto a worshipper like me. || 10. So are his lovely gifts; let lauds and praises be to Indra sung, | That he may drink the Soma juice.

Hymn 1:9. Indra.

1. Come, Indra, and delight thee with the juice at all the Soma feasts, | Protector, mighty in thy strength. || 2. To Indra pour ye forth the juice, the active gladdening juice to him | The gladdening, omnific God. || 3. O Lord of all men, fair of cheek, rejoice thee in the gladdening lauds, | Present at these drink-offerings. || 4. Songs have outpoured themselves to thee, Indra, the strong, the guardian Lord, | And raised themselves unsatisfied. || 5. Send to us bounty manifold, O Indra, worthy of our wish, | For power supreme is only thine. || 6. O Indra, stimulate thereto us emulously fain for wealth, | And glorious, O most splendid One. || 7. Give, Indra, wide and lofty fame, wealthy in cattle and in strength, | Lasting our life-time, failing not. || 8. Grant us high fame, O Indra, grant riches bestowing thousands, those | Fair fruits of earth borne home in wains. || 9. Praising with songs the praise-worthy who cometh to our aid, we call | Indra, the Treasure-Lord of wealth. || 10. To lofty Indra, dweller by each libation, the pious man | Sings forth aloud a strengthening hymn.

Hymn 1:10. Indra.

1. The chanters hymn thee, they who say the word of praise magnify thee. | The priests have raised thee up on high, O Śatakratu, like a pole. || 2. As up he climbed from ridge to ridge and looked upon the toilsome task, | Indra observes this wish of his, and the Rain hastens with his troop. || 3. Harness thy pair of strong bay steeds, long-maned, whose bodies fill the girths, | And, Indra, Soma-drinker, come to listen to our songs of praise. || 4. Come hither, answer thou the song, sing in approval, cry aloud. | Good Indra, make our prayer succeed, and prosper this our sacrifice. || 5. To Indra must a laud be said, to strengthen him who freely gives, | That Śakra may take pleasure in our friendship and drink-offerings. || 6. Him, him we seek for friendship, him for riches and heroic might. | For Indra, he is Śakra, he shall aid us while he gives us wealth. || 7. Easy to turn and drive away, Indra, is spoil bestowed by thee. | Unclose the stable of the kine, and give us wealth O Thunder-armed || 8. The heaven and earth contain thee not, together, in thy wrathful mood. | Win us the waters of the sky, and send us kine abundantly. || 9. Hear, thou whose ear is quick, my call; take to thee readily my songs | O Indra, let this laud of mine come nearer even than thy friend. || 10. We know thee mightiest of all, in battles hearer of our cry. | Of thee most mighty we invoke the aid that giveth thousandfold. || 11. O Indra, Son of Kuśika, drink our libation with delight. | Prolong our life anew, and cause the seer to win a thousand gifts. || 12. Lover of song, may these our songs on every side encompass thee: | Strengthening thee of lengthened life, may they be dear delights to thee.

Hymn 1:11. Indra.

1. All sacred songs have magnified Indra expansive as the sea, | The best of warriors borne on cars, the Lord, the very Lord of strength. || 2. Strong in thy friendship, Indra, Lord of power and might, we have no fear. | We glorify with praises thee, the never-conquered conqueror. || 3. The gifts of Indra from of old, his saving succours, never fail, | When to the praise-singers he gives the boon of substance rich in kine. || 4. Crusher of forts, the young, the wise, of strength unmeasured, was he born | Sustainer of each sacred rite, Indra, the Thunderer, much-extolled. || 5. Lord of the thunder, thou didst burst the cave of Vala rich in cows. | The Gods came pressing to thy side, and free from terror aided thee, || 6. I, Hero, through thy bounties am come to the flood addressing thee. | Song-lover, here the singers stand and testify to thee thereof. || 7. The wily Śuṣhṇa, Indra! thou o'er-threwest with thy wondrous powers. | The wise beheld this deed of thine: now go beyond their eulogies. || 8. Our songs of praise have glorified Indra who ruleth by his might, | Whose precious gifts in thousands come, yea, even more abundantly.

Hymn 1:12. Agni.

1. We choose Agni the messenger, the herald, master of all wealth, | Well skilled in this our sacrifice. || 2. With callings ever they invoke Agni, Agni, Lord of the House, | Oblation-bearer, much beloved. || 3. Bring the Gods hither, Agni, born for him who strews the sacred grass: | Thou art our herald, meet for praise. || 4. Wake up the willing Gods, since thou, Agni, performest embassage: | Sit on the sacred grass with Gods. || 5. O Agni, radiant One, to whom the holy oil is poured, burn up | Our enemies whom fiends protect. || 6. By Agni Agni is inflamed, Lord of the House, wise, young, who bears | The gift: the ladle is his mouth. || 7. Praise Agni in the sacrifice, the Sage whose ways are ever true, | The God who driveth grief away. || 8. God, Agni, be his strong defence who lord of sacrificial gifts, | Worshippeth thee the messenger. || 9. Whoso with sacred gift would fain call Agni to the feast of Gods, | O Purifier, favour him. || 10. Such, Agni, Purifier, bright, bring hither to our sacrifice, | To our oblation bring the Gods. || 11. So lauded by our newest song of praise bring opulence to us, | And food, with heroes for our sons. || 12. O Agni, by effulgent flame, by all invokings of the Gods, | Show pleasure in this laud of ours.

Hymn 1:13. Agni.

1. Agni, well-kindled, bring the Gods for him who offers holy gifts. | Worship them, Purifier, Priest. || 2. Son of Thyself, present, O Sage, our sacrifice to the Gods today. | Sweet to the taste, that they may feast. || 3. Dear Narāśaṃsa, sweet of tongue, the giver of oblations, I | Invoke to this our sacrifice. || 4. Agni, on thy most easy car, glorified, hither bring the Gods: | Manu appointed thee as Priest. || 5. Strew, O ye wise, the sacred grass that drips with oil, in order due, | Where the Immortal is beheld. || 6. Thrown open be the Doors Divine, unfailing, that assist the rite, | For sacrifice this day and now. || 7. I call the lovely Night and Dawn to seat them on the holy grass | At this our solemn sacrifice. || 8. The two Invokers I invite, the wise, divine and sweet of tongue, | To celebrate this our sacrifice. || 9. Ilā, Sarasvatī, Mahī, three Goddesses who bring delight, | Be seated, peaceful, on the grass. || 10. Tvaṣhṭar I call, the earliest born, the wearer of all forms at will: | May he be ours and curs alone. || 11. God, Sovereign of the Wood, present this our oblation to the Gods, | And let the giver be renowned. || 12. With Svāhā pay the sacrifice to Indra in the offerer's house: | Thither I call the Deities.

Hymn 1:14. Viśvedevas.

1. To drink the Soma, Agni, come, to our service and our songs. | With all these Gods; and worship them. || 2. The Kaṇvas have invoked thee; they, O Singer, sing thee songs of praise | Agni, come hither with the Gods; || 3. Indra, Vāyu, Bṛihaspati, Mitra, Agni, Pūṣhan, Bhaga, | Ādityas, and the Marut host. || 4. For you these juices are poured forth that gladden and exhilarate, | The meath-drops resting in the cup. || 5. The sons of Kaṇva fain for help adore thee, having strewn the grass, | With offerings and all things prepared. || 6. Let the swift steeds who carry thee, thought-yoked and dropping holy oil, | Bring the Gods to the Soma draught. || 7. Adored, the strengtheners of Law, unite them, Agni, with their Dames: | Make them drink meath, O bright of tongue. || 8. Let them, O Agni, who deserve worship and praise drink with thy tongue | The meath in solemn sacrifice. || 9. Away, from the Sun's realm of light, the wise invoking Priest shall bring | All Gods awaking with the dawn. || 10. With all the Gods, with Indra, with Vāyu, and Mitra's splendours, drink, | Agni, the pleasant Soma juice. || 11. Ordained by Manu as our Priest, thou sittest, Agni, at each rite: | Hallow thou this our sacrifice. || 12. Harness the Red Mares to thy car, the Bays, O God, the flaming ones: | With those bring hitherward the Gods.

Hymn 1:15. Ṛitu.

1. O Indra drink the Soma juice with Ṛitu; let the cheering drops | Sink deep within, which settle there. || 2. Drink from the Purifier's cup, Marutas, with Ṛitu; sanctify | The rite, for ye give precious gifts. || 3. O Neṣhṭar, with thy Dame accept our sacrifice; with Ṛitu drink, | For thou art he who giveth wealth. || 4. Bring the Gods, Agni; in the three appointed places set them down: | Surround them, and with Ṛitu drink. || 5. Drink Soma after the Ṛitus, from the Brāhmaṇa's bounty: undissolved, | O Indra, is thy friendship's bond. || 6. Mitra, Varuṇa, ye whose ways are firm—a Power that none deceives— | With Ṛitu ye have reached the rite. || 7. The Soma-pressers, fain for wealth, praise the Wealth-giver in the rite, | In sacrifices praise the God. || 8. May the Wealth-giver grant to us riches that shall be far renowned. | These things we gain, among the Gods. || 9. He with the Ṛitu fain would drink, Wealth-giver, from the Neṣhṭar's bowl. | Haste, give your offering, and depart. || 10. As we this fourth time, Wealth-giver, honour thee with the Ṛitus, be | A Giver bountiful to us. || 11. Drink ye the meath, O Aśvins bright with flames, whose acts are pure, who with | Ṛitus accept the sacrifice. || 12. With Ṛitu, through the house-fire, thou, kind Giver, guidest sacrifice: | Worship the Gods for the pious man.

Hymn 1:16. Indra.

1. Let thy Bay Steeds bring thee, the Strong, hither to drink the Soma draught— | Those, Indra, who are bright as suns. || 2. Here are the grains

bedewed with oil: hither let the Bay Coursers bring | Indra upon his easiest car. || 3. Indra at early morn we call, Indra in course of sacrifice, | Indra to drink the Soma juice. || 4. Come hither, with thy long-maned Steeds, O Indra, to the draught we pour | We call thee when the juice is shed. || 5. Come thou to this our song of praise, to the libation poured for thee | Drink of it like a stag athirst. || 6. Here are the drops of Soma juice expressed on sacred grass: thereof | Drink, Indra, to increase thy might. || 7. Welcome to thee be this our hymn, reaching thy heart, most excellent: | Then drink the Soma juice expressed. || 8. To every draught of pressed-out juice Indra, the Vṛitra-slayer, comes, | To drink the Soma for delight. || 9. Fulfil, O Śatakratu, all our wish with horses and with kine: | With holy thoughts we sing thy praise.

Hymn 1:17. Indra-Varuṇa

1. I Crave help from the Imperial Lords, from Indra-Varuṇa; may they | Both favour one of us like me. || 2. Guardians of men, ye ever come with ready succour at the call | Of every singer such as I. || 3. Sate you, according to your wish, O Indra-Varuṇa, with wealth: | Fain would we have you nearest us. || 4. May we be sharers of the powers, sharers of the benevolence | Of you who give strength bounteously. || 5. Indra and Varuṇa, among givers of thousands, meet for praise, | Are Powers who merit highest laud. || 6. Through their protection may we gain great store of wealth, and heap it up | Enough and still to spare, be ours. || 7. O Indra-Varuṇa, on you for wealth in many a form I call: | Still keep ye us victorious. || 8. O Indra-Varuṇa, through our songs that seek to win you to ourselves, | Give us at once your sheltering help. || 9. O Indra-Varuṇa, to you may fair praise which I offer come, | Joint eulogy which ye dignify.

Hymn 1:18. Brahmaṇaspati.

1. O Brahmaṇaspati, make him who presses Soma glorious, | Even Kakṣhīvant Auśija. || 2. The rich, the healer of disease, who giveth wealth, increaseth store, | The prompt,—may he be with us still. || 3. Let not the foeman's curse, let not a mortal's onslaught fall on us | Preserve us, Brahmaṇaspati. || 4. Ne'er is the mortal hero harmed whom Indra, Brahmaṇaspati, | And Soma graciously inspire. || 5. Do, thou, O Brahmaṇaspati, and Indra, Soma, Dakṣhiṇā, | Preserve that mortal from distress. || 6. To the Assembly's wondrous Lord, to Indra's lovely Friend who gives | Wisdom, have I drawn near in prayer. || 7. He without whom no sacrifice, e'en of the wise man, prospers; he | Stirs up the series of thoughts. || 8. He makes the oblation prosper, he promotes the course of sacrifice: | Our voice of praise goes to the Gods. || 9. I have seen Narāśaṃsa, him most resolute, most widely famed, | As 'twere the Household Priest of heaven.

Hymn 1:19. Agni, Marutas.

1. To this fair sacrifice to drink the milky draught thou art invoked: | O Agni, with the Marutas come. || 2. No mortal man, no God exceeds thy mental power, O Mighty one: | O Agni, with the Marutas come: || 3. All Gods devoid of guile, who know the mighty region of mid-air: | O Agni, with those Marutas come. || 4. The terrible, who sing their song, not to be overcome by might: | O Agni, with those Marutas come. || 5. Brilliant, and awful in their form, mighty, devourers of their foes: | O Agni, with those Marutas come. || 6. Who sit as Deities in heaven, above the sky-vault's luminous sphere: | O Agni, with those Marutas come. || 7. Who scatter clouds about the sky, away over the billowy sea: | O Agni, with those Marutas come. || 8. Who with their bright beams spread them forth over the ocean in their might | O Agni, with those Marutas come. || 9. For thee, to be thine early draught, I pour the Soma-mingled meath: | O Agni, with the Marutas come.

Hymn 1:20. Ṛibhus.

1. For the Celestial Race this song of praise which gives wealth lavishly | Was made by singers with their lips. || 2. They who for Indra, with their mind, formed horses harnessed by a word, | Attained by works to sacrifice. || 3. They for the two Nāsatyas wrought a light car moving every way: | They formed a nectar-yielding cow. || 4. The Ṛibhus with effectual prayers, honest, with constant labour, made | Their Sire and Mother young again. || 5. Together came your gladdening drops with Indra by the Marutas girt, | With the Ādityas, with the Kings. || 6. The sacrificial ladle, wrought newly by the God Tvaṣhṭar's hand— | Four ladles have ye made thereof. || 7. Vouchsafe us wealth, to him who pours thrice seven libations, yea, to each | Give wealth, pleased with our eulogies. || 8. As ministering Priests they held, by pious acts they won themselves, | A share in sacrifice with Gods.

Hymn 1:21. Indra-Agni.

1. Indra and Agni I invoke fain are we for their song of praise: | Chief Soma-drinkers are they both. || 2. Praise ye, O men, and glorify Indra-Agni in the holy rites: | Sing praise to them in sacred songs. || 3. Indra and Agni we invite, the Soma-drinkers, for the fame | Of Mitra, to the Soma-draught. || 4. Strong Gods, we bid them come to this libation that stands ready here: | Indra and Agni, come to us. || 5. Indra and Agni, mighty Lords of our assembly, crush the fiends: | Childless be the devouring ones. || 6. Watch ye, through this your truthfulness, there in the place of spacious view | Indra and Agni, send us bliss.

Hymn 1:22. Aśvins and Others.

1. Waken the Aśvin Pair who yoke their car at early morn: may they | Approach to drink this Soma juice. || 2. We call the Aśvins Twain, the Gods borne in a noble car, the best | Of charioteers, who reach the heavens. || 3. Dropping with honey is your whip, Aśvins, and full of pleasantness | Sprinkle therewith the sacrifice. || 4. As ye go thither in your car, not far, O Aśvins, is the home | Of him who offers Soma juice. || 5. For my protection I invoke the golden-handed Savitar. | He knoweth, as a God, the place. || 6. That he may send us succour, praise the Waters' Offspring Savitar: | Fain are we for his holy ways. || 7. We call on him, distributor of wondrous bounty and of wealth, | On Savitar who looks on men. || 8. Come hither, friends, and seat yourselves Savitar, to be praised by us, | Giving good gifts, is beautiful. || 9. O Agni, hither bring to us the willing Spouses of the Gods, | And Tvaṣhṭar, to the Soma draught. || 10. Most youthful Agni, hither bring their Spouses, Hotrā, Bhāratī, | Varūtrī, Dhiṣhaṇā, for aid. || 11. Spouses of Heroes, Goddesses, with whole wings may they come to us | With great protection and with aid. || 12. Indrāṇī, Varuṇānī, and Agnāyī hither I invite, | For weal, to drink the Soma juice. || 13. May Heaven and Earth, the Mighty Pair, bedew for us our sacrifice, | And feed us full with nourishments. || 14. Their water rich with fatness, there in the Gandharva's steadfast place, | The singers taste through sacred songs. || 15. Thornless be thou, O Earth, spread wide before us for a dwelling-place: | Vouchsafe us shelter broad and sure. || 16. The Gods be gracious unto us even from the place whence Viṣhṇu strode | Through the seven regions of the earth! || 17. Through all this world strode Viṣhṇu; thrice his foot he planted, and the whole | Was gathered in his footstep's dust. || 18. Viṣhṇu, the Guardian, he whom none deceiveth, made three steps; thenceforth | Establishing his high decrees. || 19. Look ye on Viṣhṇu's works, whereby the Friend of Indra, close-allied, | Hath let his holy ways be seen. || 20. The princes evermore behold that loftiest place where Viṣhṇu is, | Laid as it were an eye in heaven. || 21. This, Viṣhṇu's station most sublime, the singers, ever vigilant, | Lovers of holy song, light up.

Hymn 1:23. Vāyu and Others.

1. Strong are the Somas; come thou nigh; these juices have been mixed with milk: | Drink, Vāyu, the presented draughts. || 2. Both Deities who touch the heaven, Indra and Vāyu we invoke | To drink of this our soma juice. || 3. The singers' for their aid, invoke Indra and Vāyu, swift as mind, | The thousand-eyed, the Lords of thought. || 4. Mitra and Varuṇa, renowned as Gods of consecrated might, | We call to drink the Soma juice. || 5. Those who by Law uphold the Law, Lords of the shining light of Law, | Mitra I call, and Varuṇa. || 6. Let Varuṇa be our chief defence, let Mitra guard us with all aids | Both make us rich exceedingly. || 7. Indra, by Marutas girt, we call to drink the Soma juice: may he | Sate him in union with his troop. || 8. Gods, Marut hosts whom Indra leads, distributors of Pūṣhan's gifts, | Hearken ye all unto my cry. || 9. With conquering Indra for ally, strike Vṛitra down, ye bounteous Gods | Let not the wicked master us. || 10. We call the Universal Gods, and Marutas to the Soma draught, | For passing strong are Pṛiśni's Sons. || 11. Fierce comes the Marutas' thundering voice, like that of conquerors, when ye go | Forward to victory, O Men. || 12. Born of the laughing lightning. may the Marutas guard us everywhere | May they be gracious unto Us. || 13. Like some lost animal, drive to us, bright Pūṣhan, him who bears up heaven, | Resting on many-coloured grass. || 14. Pūṣhan the Bright has found the King, concealed and hidden in a cave, | Who rests on grass of many hues. || 15. And may he. duly bring to me the six bound closely, through these drops, | As one who ploughs with steers brings corn. || 16. Along their paths the Mothers go, Sisters of priestly

ministrants, | Mingling their sweetness with the milk. || 17. May Waters gathered near the Sun, and those wherewith the Sun is joined, | Speed forth this sacrifice of ours. || 18. I call the Waters, Goddesses, wherein our cattle quench their thirst; | Oblations to the Streams be given. || 19. Amṛita is in the Waters in the Waters there is healing balm | Be swift, ye Gods, to give them praise. || 20. Within the Waters—Soma thus hath told me—dwell all balms that heal, | And Agni, he who blesseth all. The Waters hold all medicines. || 21. O Waters, teem with medicine to keep my body safe from harm, | So that I long may see the Sun. || 22. Whatever sin is found in me, whatever evil I have wrought. | If I have lied or falsely sworn, Waters, remove it far from me. || 23. The Waters I this day have sought, and to their moisture have we come: | O Agni, rich in milk, come thou, and with thy splendour cover me. || 24. Fill me with splendour, Agni; give offspring and length of days; the Gods | Shall know me even as I am, and Indra with the Ṛiṣhis, know.

Hymn 1:24. Varuṇa and Others.

1. Who now is he, what God among Immortals, of whose auspicious name we may bethink us? | Who shall to mighty Aditi restore us, that I may see my Father and my Mother? || 2. Agni the God the first among the Immortals,—of his auspicious name let us bethink us. | He shall to mighty Aditi restore us, that I may see my Father and my Mother. || 3. To thee, O Savitar, the Lord of precious things, who helpest us | Continually, for our share we come— ||4. Wealth, highly lauded ere reproach hath fallen on it, which is laid, | Free from all hatred, in thy hands || 5. Through thy protection may we come to even the height of affluence | Which Bhaga hath dealt out to us. || 6. Ne'er have those birds that fly through air attained to thy high dominion or thy might or spirit; | Nor these the waters that flow on for ever, nor hills, abaters of the wind's wild fury. || 7. Varuṇa, King, of hallowed might, sustaineth erect the Tree's stem in the baseless region. | Its rays, whose root is high above, stream downward. Deep may they sink within us, and be hidden. || 8. King Varuṇa hath made a spacious pathway, a pathway for the Sun wherein to travel. | Where no way was he made him set his footstep, and warned afar whate'er afflicts the spirit. || 9. A hundred balms are thine, O King, a thousand; deep and wide-reaching also be thy favours. | Far from us, far away drive thou Destruction. Put from us e'en the sin we have committed. || 10. Whither by day depart the constellations that shine at night, set high in heaven above us? | Varuṇa's holy laws remain unweakened, and through the night the Moon moves on in splendor. || 11. I ask this of thee with my prayer adoring; thy worshipper craves this with his oblation. | Varuṇa, stay thou here and be not angry; steal not our life from us, O thou Wide-Ruler. || 12. Nightly and daily this one thing they tell me, this too the thought of mine own heart repeateth. | May he to whom prayed fettered Śunaḥśepa, may he the Sovereign Varuṇa release us. || 13. Bound to three pillars captured Śunaḥśepa thus to the Āditya made his supplication. | Him may the Sovereign Varuṇa deliver, wise, ne'er deceived, loosen the bonds that bind him. || 14. With bending down, oblations, sacrifices, O Varuṇa, we deprecate thine anger: | Wise Asura, thou King of wide dominion, loosen the bonds of sins by us committed. || 15. Loosen the bonds, O Varuṇa, that hold me, loosen the bonds above, between, and under. | So in thy holy law may we made sinless belong to Aditi, O thou Āditya.

Hymn 1:25. Varuṇa.

1. Whatever law of thine, O God, O Varuṇa, as we are men, | Day after day we violate. || 2. give us not as a prey to death, to be destroyed by thee in wrath, | To thy fierce anger when displeased. || 3. To gain thy mercy, Varuṇa, with hymns we bind thy heart, as binds | The charioteer his tethered horse. || 4. They flee from me dispirited, bent only on obtaining wealths | As to their nests the birds of air. || 5. When shall we bring, to be appeased, the Hero, Lord of warrior might, | Him, the far-seeing Varuṇa? || 6. This, this with joy they both accept in common: never do they fail | The ever-faithful worshipper. || 7. He knows the path of birds that fly through heaven, and, Sovereign of the sea, | He knows the ships that are thereon. || 8. True to his holy law, he knows the twelve moons with their progeny: | He knows the moon of later birth. || 9. He knows the pathway of the wind, the spreading, high, and mighty wind: | He knows the Gods who dwell above. || 10. Varuṇa, true to holy law, sits down among his people; he, | Most wise, sits there to govern all. || 11. From thence perceiving he beholds all wondrous things, both what hath been, | And what hereafter will be done. || 12. May that Āditya, very wise, make fair paths for us all our days: | May he prolong our lives for us. || 13. Varuṇa, wearing golden mail, hath clad him in a shining robe. | His spies are seated found about. || 14. The God whom enemies threaten not, nor those who tyrannize o'er men, | Nor those whose minds are bent on wrong. || 15. He who gives glory to mankind, not glory that is incomplete, | To our own bodies giving it. || 16. Yearning for the wide-seeing One, my thoughts move onward unto him, | As kine unto their pastures move. || 17. Once more together let us speak, because my meath is brought: priest-like | Thou eatest what is dear to thee. || 18. Now saw I him whom all may see, I saw his car above the earth: | He hath accepted these my songs. || 19. Varuṇa, hear this call of mine: be gracious unto us this day | Longing for help I cried to thee. || 20. Thou, O wise God, art Lord of all, thou art the King of earth and heaven | Hear, as thou goest on thy way. || 21. Release us from the upper bond, untie the bond between, and loose | The bonds below, that I may live.

Hymn 1:26. Agni.

1. O worthy of oblation, Lord of prospering powers, assume thy robes, | And offer this our sacrifice. || 2. Sit ever to be chosen, as our Priest, most youthful, through our hymns, | O Agni, through our heavenly word. || 3. For here a Father for his son, Kinsman for kinsman worshippeth, | And Friend, choice-worthy, for his friend. || 4. Here let the foe-destroyers sit, Varuṇa, Mitra, Aryaman, | Like men, upon our sacred grass. || 5. O ancient Herald, be thou glad in this our rite and fellowship: | Hearken thou well to these our songs. || 6. Whate'er in this perpetual course we sacrifice to God and God, | That gift is offered up in thee || 7. May he be our dear household Lord, Priest, pleasant and, choice-worthy may | We, with bright fires, be dear to him. || 8. The Gods, adored with brilliant fires. have granted precious wealth to us | So, with bright fires, we pray to thee. || 9. And, O Immortal One, so may the eulogies of mortal men | Belong to us and thee alike. || 10. With all thy fires, O Agni, find pleasure in this our sacrifice, | And this our speech, O Son of Strength.

Hymn 1:27. Agni.

1. With worship will I glorify thee, Agni, like a long-tailed steed, | Imperial Lord of sacred rites. || 2. May the far-striding Son of Strength, bringer of great felicity, | Who pours his gifts like rain, be ours. || 3. Lord of all life, from near; from far, do thou, O Agni evermore | Protect us from the sinful man. || 4. O Agni, graciously announce this our oblation to the Gods, | And this our newest song of praise. || 5. Give us a share of strength most high, a share of strength that is below, | A share of strength that is between. || 6. Thou dealest gifts, resplendent One; nigh, as with waves of Sindhu, thou | Swift streamest to the worshipper. || 7. That man is lord of endless strength whom thou protectest in the fight, | Agni, or urgest to the fray. || 8. Him, whosoever he may be, no man may vanquish, mighty One: | Nay, very glorious power is his. || 9. May he who dwells with all mankind bear us with war-steeds through the fight, | And with the singers win the spoil. || 10. Help, thou who knowest lauds, this work, this eulogy to Rudra, him | Adorable in every house. || 11. May this our God, great, limitless, smoke-bannered excellently bright, | Urge us to strength and holy thought. || 12. Like some rich Lord of men may he, Agni the banner of the Gods, | Refulgent, hear us through our lauds. || 13. Glory to Gods, the mighty and the lesser glory to Gods the younger and the elder! | Let us, if we have power, pay the God worship: no better prayer than this, ye Gods, acknowledge.

Hymn 1:28. Indra, etc.

1. There where the broad-based stone raised on high to press the juices out, | O Indra, drink with eager thirst the droppings which the mortar sheds. || 2. Where, like broad hips, to hold the juice the platters of the press are laid, | O Indra, drink with eager thirst the droppings which the mortar sheds. || 3. There where the woman marks and leans the pestle's constant rise and fall, | O Indra, drink with eager thirst the droppings which the mortar sheds. || 4. Where, as with reins to guide a horse, they bind the churning-staff with cords, | O Indra, drink with eager thirst the droppings which the mortar sheds. || 5. If of a truth in every house, O Mortar thou art set for work, | Here give thou forth thy clearest sound, loud as the drum of conquerors. || 6. O Sovereign of the Forest, as the wind blows soft in front of thee, | Mortar, for Indra press thou forth the Soma juice that he may drink. || 7. Best

strength-givers, ye stretch wide jaws, O Sacrificial Implements, | Like two bay horses champing herbs. || 8. Ye Sovereigns of the Forest, both swift, with swift pressers press today | Sweet Soma juice for Indra's drink. || 9. Take up in beakers what remains: the Soma on the filter pour, | and on the ox-hide set the dregs.

Hymn 1:29. Indra.

1. O Soma-drinker, ever true, utterly hopeless though we be, | Do thou, O Indra, give us hope of beauteous horses and of kine, | In thousands, O most wealthy One. || 2. O Lord of Strength, whose jaws are strong, great deeds are thine, the powerful: | Do thou, O Indra, give us hope of beauteous horses and of kine, | In thousands, O most wealthy One. || 3. Lull thou asleep, to wake no more, the pair who on each other look | Do thou, O Indra, give us hope of beauteous horses and of kine, | In thousands, O most wealthy One. || 4. Hero, let hostile spirits sleep, and every gentler genius wake: | Do thou, O Indra, give us hope of beauteous horses and of kine, | In thousands, O most wealthy One. || 5. Destroy this ass, O Indra, who in tones discordant brays to thee: | Do thou, O Indra, give us hope of beauteous horses and of kine, | In thousands, O most wealthy One. || 6. Far distant on the forest fall the tempest in a circling course! | Do thou, O Indra, give us hope of beauteous horses and of kine, | In thousands, O most wealthy One. || 7. Slay each reviler, and destroy him who in secret injures us: | Do thou, O Indra, give us hope of beauteous horses and of kine | In thousands, O most wealthy One.

Hymn 1:30. Indra.

1. We seeking strength with Soma-drops fill full your Indra like a well, | Most liberal, Lord of Hundred Powers, || 2. Who lets a hundred of the pure, a thousand of the milk-blent draughts | Flow, even as down a depth, to him; || 3. When for the strong, the rapturous joy he in this manner hath made room | Within his belly, like the sea. || 4. This is thine own. Thou drawest near, as turns a pigeon to his mate: | Thou carest too for this our prayer. || 5. O Hero, Lord of Bounties, praised in hymns, may power and joyfulness | Be his who sings the laud to thee. || 6. Lord of a Hundred Powers, stand up to lend us succour in this fight | In others too let us agree. || 7. In every need, in every fray we call as friends to succour us | Indra the mightiest of all. || 8. If he will hear us let him come with succour of a thousand kinds, | And all that strengthens, to our call. || 9. I call him mighty to resist, the Hero of our ancient home, | Thee whom my sire invoked of old. || 10. We pray to thee, O much-invoked, rich in all precious gifts, O Friend, | Kind God to those who sing thy praise. || 11. O Soma-drinker, Thunder-armed, Friend of our lovely-featured dames | And of our Soma-drinking friends. || 12. Thus, Soma-drinker, may it be; thus, Friend, who wieldest thunder, act | To aid each wish as we desire. || 13. With Indra splendid feasts be ours, rich in all strengthening things wherewith, | Wealthy in food, we may rejoice. || 14. Like thee, thyself, the singers' Friend, thou movest, as it were, besought, | Bold One, the axle of the car. || 15. That, Śatakratu, thou to grace and please thy praisers, as it were, | Stirrest the axle with thy strength. || 16. With champing, neighing loudly-snorting horses Indra hath ever won himself great treasures | A car of gold hath he whose deeds are wondrous received from us, and let us too receive it. || 17. Come, Aśvins, with enduring strength wealthy in horses and in kine, | And gold, O ye of wondrous deeds. || 18. Your chariot yoked for both alike, immortal, ye of mighty acts, | Travels, O Aśvins, in the sea. || 19. High on the forehead of the Bull one chariot wheel ye ever keep, | The other round the sky revolves. || 20. What mortal, O immortal Dawn, enjoyeth thee? Where lovest thou? | To whom, O radiant, dost thou go? || 21. For we have had thee in our thoughts whether anear or far away, | Red-hued and like a dappled mare. || 22. Hither, O Daughter of the Sky, come thou with these thy strengthenings, | And send thou riches down to us.

Hymn 1:31. Agni.

1. Thou, Agni, wast the earliest Aṅgiras, a Seer; thou wast, a God thyself, the Gods' auspicious Friend. | After thy holy ordinance the Marutas, sage, active through wisdom, with their glittering spears, were born. || 2. O Agni, thou, the best and earliest Aṅgiras, fulfillest as a Sage the holy law of Gods. | Sprung from two mothers, wise, through all existence spread, resting in many a place for sake of living man. || 3. To Mātariśvan first thou, Agni, wast disclosed, and to Vivasvat through thy noble inward power. | Heaven and Earth, Vasu! shook at the choosing of the Priest: the burthen thou didst bear, didst worship mighty Gods. || 4. Agni thou madest heaven to thunder for mankind; thou, yet more pious, for pious Purūravas. | When thou art rapidly freed from thy parents, first eastward they bear thee round, and, after, to the west. || 5. Thou, Agni, art a Bull who makes our store increase, to be invoked by him who lifts the ladle up. | Well knowing the oblation with the hallowing word, uniting all who live, thou lightenest first our folk || 6. Agni, thou savest in the synod when pursued e'en him, farseeing One! who walks in evil ways. | Thou, when the heroes fight for spoil which men rush, round, slayest in war the many by the hands of few. || 7. For glory, Agni, day by day, thou liftest up the mortal man to highest immortality, | Even thou who yearning for both races givest them great bliss, and to the prince grantest abundant food. || 8. O Agni, highly lauded, make our singer famous that he may win us store of riches: | May we improve the rite with new performance. O Earth and Heaven, with all the Gods, protect us. || 9. O blameless Agni lying in thy Parents' lap, a God among the Gods, be watchful for our good. | Former of bodies, be the singer's Providence: all good things hast thou sown for him, auspicious One! || 10. Agni, thou art our Providence, our Father thou: we are thy brethren and thou art our spring of life. | In thee, rich in good heroes, guard of high decrees, meet hundred, thousand treasures, O infallible! || 11. Thee, Agni, have the Gods made the first living One for living man, Lord of the house of Nahuṣha. | Iḷā they made the teacher of the sons of men, what time a Son was born to the father of my race. || 12. Worthy to be revered, O Agni, God, preserve our wealthy patrons with thy succours, and ourselves. | Guard of our seed art thou, aiding our cows to bear, incessantly protecting in thy holy way. || 13. Agni, thou art a guard close to the pious man; kindled art thou, four-eyed! for him who is unarmed. | With fond heart thou acceptest e'en the poor man's prayer, when he hath brought his gift to gain security. || 14. Thou, Agni gainest for the loudly-praising priest the highest wealth, the object of a man's desire. | Thou art called Father, caring even for the weak, and wisest, to the simple one thou teachest lore. || 15. Agni, the man who giveth guerdon to the priests, like well-sewn armour thou guardest on every side. | He who with grateful food shows kindness in his house, an offerer to the living, is the type of heaven. || 16. Pardon, we pray, this sin of ours, O Agni,—the path which we have trodden, widely straying, | Dear Friend and Father, caring for the pious, who speedest nigh and who inspirest mortals. || 17. As erst to Manus, to Yayāti, Aṅgiras, so Aṅgiras! pure Agni! come thou to our hall | Bring hither the celestial host and seat them here upon the sacred grass, and offer what they love. || 18. By this our prayer be thou, O Agni, strengthened, prayer made by us after our power and knowledge. | Lead thou us, therefore, to increasing riches; endow us with thy strength-bestowing favour.

Hymn 1:32. Indra.

1. I will declare the manly deeds of Indra, the first that he achieved, the Thunder-wielder. | He slew the Dragon, then disclosed the waters, and cleft the channels of the mountain torrents. || 2. He slew the Dragon lying on the mountain: his heavenly bolt of thunder Tvaṣhṭar fashioned. | Like lowing kine in rapid flow descending the waters glided downward to the ocean. || 3. Impetuous as a bull, he chose the Soma and in three sacred beakers drank the juices. | Maghavan grasped the thunder for his weapon, and smote to death this firstborn of the dragons. || 4. When, Indra, thou hadst slain the dragon's firstborn, and overcome the charms of the enchanters, | Then, giving life to Sun and Dawn and Heaven, thou foundest not one foe to stand against thee. || 5. Indra with his own great and deadly thunder smote into pieces Vṛitra, worst of Vṛitras. | As trunks of trees, what time the axe hath felled them, low on the earth so lies the prostrate Dragon. || 6. He, like a mad weak warrior, challenged Indra, the great impetuous many-slaying Hero. | He, brooking not the clashing of the weapons, crushed—Indra's foe—the shattered forts in falling. || 7. Footless and handless still he challenged Indra, who smote him with his bolt between the shoulders. | Emasculate yet claiming manly vigour, thus Vṛitra lay with scattered limbs dissevered. || 8. There as he lies like a bank-bursting river, the waters taking courage flow above him. | The Dragon lies beneath the feet of torrents which Vṛitra with his greatness had encompassed. || 9. Then humbled was the strength of Vṛitra's mother: Indra hath cast his deadly bolt against her. | The mother was above, the son

was under and like a cow beside her calf lay Danu. || 10. Rolled in the midst of never-ceasing currents flowing without a rest for ever onward. | The waters bear off Vṛitra's nameless body: the foe of Indra sank to during darkness. || 11. Guarded by Ahi stood the thralls of Dāsas, the waters stayed like kine held by the robber. | But he, when he had smitten Vṛitra, opened the cave wherein the floods had been imprisoned. || 12. A horse's tail wast thou when he, O Indra, smote on thy bolt; thou, God without a second, | Thou hast won back the kine, hast won the Soma; thou hast let loose to flow the Seven Rivers. || 13. Nothing availed him lightning, nothing thunder, hailstorm or mist which had spread around him: | When Indra and the Dragon strove in battle, Maghavan gained the victory for ever. || 14. Whom sawest thou to avenge the Dragon, Indra, that fear possessed thy heart when thou hadst slain him; | That, like a hawk affrighted through the regions, thou crossedst nine-and-ninety flowing rivers? || 15. Indra is King of all that moves and moves not, of creatures tame and horned, the Thunder-wielder. | Over all living men he rules as Sovereign, containing all as spokes within the felly.

Hymn 1:33. Indra.

1. Come, fain for booty let us seek to Indra: yet more shall he increase his care that guides us. | Will not the Indestructible endow us with perfect knowledge of this wealth, of cattle? || 2. I fly to him invisible Wealth-giver as flies the falcon to his cherished eyrie, | With fairest hymns of praise adoring Indra, whom those who laud him must invoke in battle. || 3. Mid all his host, he bindeth on the quiver: he driveth cattle from what foe he pleaseth: | Gathering up great store of riches, Indra. be thou no trafficker with us, most mighty. || 4. Thou slewest with thy bolt the wealthy Dasyu, alone, yet going with thy helpers, Indra! | Far from the floor of heaven in all directions, the ancient riteless ones fled to destruction. || 5. Fighting with pious worshippers, the riteless turned and fled, Indra! with averted faces. | When thou, fierce Lord of the Bay Steeds, the Stayer, blewest from earth and heaven and sky the godless. || 6. They met in fight the army of the blameless: then the Navagvas put forth all their power. | They, like emasculates with men contending, fled, conscious, by steep paths from Indra, scattered. || 7. Whether they weep or laugh, thou hast o'erthrown them, O Indra, on the sky's extremest limit. | The Dasyu thou hast burned from heaven, and welcomed the prayer of him who pours the juice and lauds thee. || 8. Adorned with their array of gold and jewels, they o'er the earth a covering veil extended. | Although they hastened, they o'ercame not Indra: their spies he compassed with the Sun of morning. || 9. As thou enjoyest heaven and earth, O Indra, on every side surrounded with thy greatness, | So thou with priests bast blown away the Dasyu, and those who worship not with those who worship. || 10. They who pervaded earth's extremest limit subdued not with their charms the Wealth-bestower: | Indra, the Bull, made his ally the thunder, and with its light milked cows from out the darkness. || 11. The waters flowed according to their nature; he raid the navigable streams waxed mighty. | Then Indra, with his spirit concentrated, smote him for ever with his strongest weapon. || 12. Indra broke through Ilībiśa's strong castles, and Śuṣhṇa with his horn he cut to pieces: | Thou, Maghavan, for all his might and swiftness, slewest thy fighting foeman with thy thunder || 13. Fierce on his enemies fell Indra's weapon: with. his sharp bull he rent their forts in pieces. | He with his thunderbolt dealt blows on Vṛitra; and conquered, executing all his purpose. || 14. Indra, thou helpest Kutsa whom thou lovedst, and guardedst brave Daśadyu when he battled, | The dust of trampling horses rose to heaven, and Śvitrā's son stood up again for conquest. || 15. Śvitrā's mild steer, O Maghavan thou helpest in combat for the land, mid Tugra's houses. | Long stood they there before the task was ended: thou wast the master of the foemen's treasure.

Hymn 1:34. Aśvins.

1. Ye who observe this day be with us even thrice: far-stretching is you bounty, Aśvins and your course. | To you, as to a cloak in winter, we cleave close: you are to be drawn nigh unto us by the wise. || 2. Three are the fellies in your honey-bearing car, that travels after Soma's loved one, as all know. | Three are the pillars set upon it for support: thrice journey ye by night, O Aśvins, thrice by day. || 3. Thrice in the self-same day, ye Gods who banish want, sprinkle ye thrice today our sacrifice with meath; | And thrice vouchsafe us store of food with plenteous strength, at evening, O ye Aśvins, and at break of day. || 4. Thrice come ye to our home, thrice to the righteous folk, thrice triply aid the man who well deserves your help. | Thrice, O ye Aśvins, bring us what shall make us glad; thrice send us store of food as nevermore to fail. || 5. Thrice, O ye Aśvins, bring to us abundant wealth: thrice in the Gods' assembly, thrice assist our thoughts. | Thrice, grant ye us prosperity, thrice grant us fame; for the Sun's daughter hath mounted your three-wheeled car. || 6. Thrice, Aśvins, grant to us the heavenly medicines, thrice those of earth and thrice those that the waters hold, | Favour and health and strength bestow upon my son; triple protection, Lords of Splendour, grant to him. || 7. Thrice are ye to be worshipped day by day by us: thrice, O ye Aśvins, ye travel around the earth. | Car-borne from far away, O ye Nāsatyas, come, like vital air to bodies, come ye to the three. || 8. Thrice, O ye Aśvins, with the Seven Mother Streams; three are the jars, the triple offering is prepared. | Three are the worlds, and moving on above the sky ye guard the firm-set vault of heaven through days and nights. || 9. Where are the three wheels of your triple chariot, where are the three seats thereto firmly fastened? | When will ye yoke the mighty ass that draws it, to bring you to our sacrifice. Nāsatyas? || 10. Nāsatyas, come: the sacred gift is offered up; drink the sweet juice with lips that know the sweetness well. | Savitar sends, before the dawn of day, your car, fraught with oil, various-coloured, to our sacrifice. || 11. Come, O Nāsatyas, with the thrice-eleven Gods; come, O ye Aśvins, to the drinking of the meath. | Make long our days of life, and wipe out all our sins: ward off our enemies; be with us evermore. || 12. Borne in your triple car, O Aśvins, bring us present prosperity with noble offspring. | I cry to you who hear me for protection be ye our helpers where men win the booty.

Hymn 1:35. Savitar.

1. Agni I first invoke for our prosperity; I call on Mitra, Varuṇa, to aid us here. | I call on Night who gives rest to all moving life; I call on Savitar the God to lend us help. || 2. Throughout the dusky firmament advancing, laying to rest the immortal and the mortal, | Borne in his golden chariot he cometh, Savitar, God who looks on every creature. || 3. The God moves by the upward path, the downward; with two bright Bays, adorable, he journeys. | Savitar comes, the God from the far distance, and chases from us all distress and sorrow. || 4. His chariot decked with pearl, of various colours, lofty, with golden pole, the God hath mounted, | The many-rayed One, Savitar the holy, bound, bearing power and might, for darksome regions. || 5. Drawing the gold-yoked car his Bays, white-footed, have manifested light to all the peoples. | Held in the lap of Savitar, divine One, all men, all beings have their place for ever. || 6. Three heavens there are; two Savitar's, adjacent: in Yama's world is one, the home of heroes, | As on a linch-pin, firm, rest things immortal: he who hath known it let him here declare it. || 7. He, strong of wing, hath lightened up the regions, deep-quivering Asura, the gentle Leader. | Where now is Sūrya, where is one to tell us to what celestial sphere his ray hath wandered? || 8. The earth's eight points his brightness hath illumined, three desert regions and the Seven Rivers. | God Savitar the gold-eyed hath come hither, giving choice treasures unto him who worships. || 9. The golden-handed Savitar, far-seeing, goes on his way between the earth and heaven, | Drives away sickness, bids the Sun approach us, and spreads the bright sky through the darksome region. || 10. May he, gold-handed Asura, kind Leader, come hither to us with his help and favour. | Driving off Rākṣhasas and Yātudhānas, the God is present, praised in hymns at evening. || 11. O Savitar, thine ancient dustless pathways are well established in the air's mid-region: | O God, come by those paths so fair to travel, preserve thou us from harm this day, and bless us.

Hymn 1:36. Agni.

1. With words sent forth in holy hymns, Agni we supplicate, the Lord | Of many families who duly serve the Gods, yea, him whom others also praise. || 2. Men have won Agni, him who makes their strength abound: we, with oblations, worship thee. | Our gracious-minded Helper in our deeds of might, be thou, O Excellent, this day. || 3. Thee for our messenger we choose, thee, the Omniscient, for our Priest. | The flames of thee the mighty are spread wide around: thy splendour reaches to the sky. || 4. The Gods enkindle thee their ancient messenger,—Varuṇa, Mitra, Aryaman. | That mortal man, O Agni, gains through thee all wealth, who hath poured offerings unto thee. || 5. Thou, Agni, art a cheering Priest, Lord of

the House, men's messenger: | All constant high decrees established by the Gods, gathered together, meet in thee. || 6. In thee, the auspicious One, O Agni, youthfullest, each sacred gift is offered up: | This day, and after, gracious, worship thou our Gods, that we may have heroic sons. || 7. To him in his own splendour bright draw near in worship the devout. | Men kindle Agni with their sacrificial gifts, victorious o'er the enemies. || 8. Vṛitra they smote and slew, and made the earth and heaven and firmament a wide abode. | The glorious Bull, invoked, hath stood at Kaṇva's side: loud neighed the Steed in frays for kine. || 9. Seat thee, for thou art mighty; shine, best entertainer of the Gods. | Worthy of sacred food, praised Agni! loose the smoke, ruddy and beautiful to see. || 10. Bearer of offerings, whom, best sacrificing Priest, the Gods for Manu's sake ordained; | Whom Kaṇva, whom Medhātithi made the source of wealth, and Vṛiṣhan and Upastuta. || 11. Him, Agni, whom Medhātithi, whom Kaṇva kindled for his rite, | Him these our songs of praise, him, Agni, we extol: his powers shine out preeminent. || 12. Make our wealth perfect thou, O Agni, Lord divine: for thou hast kinship with the Gods. | Thou rulest as a King o'er widely-famous strength: be good to us, for thou art great. || 13. Stand up erect to lend us aid, stand up like Savitar the God: | Erect as strength-bestower we call aloud, with unguents and with priests, on thee. || 14. Erect, preserve us from sore trouble; with thy flame burn thou each ravening demon dead. | Raise thou us up that we may walk and live: so thou shalt find our worship mid the Gods. || 15. Preserve us, Agni, from the fiend, preserve us from malicious wrong. | Save us from him who fain would injure us or slay, Most Youthful, thou with lofty light. || 16. Smite down as with a club, thou who hast fire for teeth, smite thou the wicked, right and left. | Let not the man who plots against us in the night, nor any foe prevail o'er us. || 17. Agni hath given heroic might to Kaṇva, and felicity: | Agni hath helped our friends, hath helped Medhātithi, hath helped Upastuta to win. || 18. We call on Ugrādeva, Yadu, Turvaśa, by means of Agni, from afar; | Agni, bring Navavāstva and Bṛihadratha, Turvīti, to subdue the foe. || 19. Manu hath established thee a light, Agni, for all the race of men: | Sprung from the Law, oil-fed, for Kaṇva hast thou blazed, thou whom the people reverence. || 20. The flames of Agni full of splendour and of might are fearful, not to be approached. | Consume for ever all demons and sorcerers, consume thou each devouring fiend.

Hymn 1:37. Marutas.

1. Sing forth, O Kaṇvas, to your band of Marutas unassailable, | Sporting, resplendent on their car || 2. They who, self-luminous, were born together, with the spotted deer, | Spears, swords, and glittering ornaments. || 3. One hears, as though 'twere close at hand, the cracking of the whips they hold | They gather glory on their way. || 4. Now sing ye forth the God-given hymn to your exultant Marut host, | The fiercely-vigorous, the strong. || 5. Praise ye the Bull among the cows; for 'tis the Marutas' sportive band: | It strengthened as it drank the rain. || 6. Who is your mightiest, Heroes, when, O shakers of the earth and heaven, | Ye shake them like a garment's hem? || 7. At your approach man holds him down before the fury of your wrath: | The rugged-jointed mountain yields. || 8. They at whose racings forth the earth, like an age-weakened lord of men, | Trembles in terror on their ways. || 9. Strong is their birth: vigour have they to issue from their Mother; strength, | Yea, even twice enough, is theirs. || 10. And these, the Sons, the Singers, in their racings have enlarged the bounds, | So that the kine must walk knee-deep. || 11. Before them, on the ways they go, they drop this offspring of the cloud, | Long, broad, and inexhaustible. || 12. O Marutas, as your strength is great, so have ye cast men down on earth, | So have ye made the mountains fall. || 13. The while the Marutas pass along, they talk together on the way: | Doth any hear them as they speak? || 14. Come quick with swift steeds, for ye have worshippers among Kaṇva's sons | May you rejoice among them well. || 15. All is prepared for your delight. We are their servants evermore, | To live as long as life may last.

Hymn 1:38. Marutas.

1. What now? When will ye take us by both hands, as a dear sire his son, | Gods, for whom sacred grass is clipped? || 2. Now whither? To what goal of yours go ye in heaven, and not on earth? | Where do your cows disport themselves? || 3. Where are your newest favours shown? Where, Marutas, your prosperity? | Where all your high felicities? || 4. If, O ye Marutas, ye the Sons whom Pṛiśni bore, were mortal, and | Immortal he who sings your praise. || 5. Then never were your praiser loathed like a wild beast in pasture-land, | Nor should he go on Yama's path. || 6. Let not destructive plague on plague hard to be conquered, strike its down: | Let each, with drought, depart from us. || 7. Truly, they the fierce and mighty Sons of Rudra send their windless | Rain e'en on the desert places. || 8. Like a cow the lightning lows and follows, mother-like, her youngling, | When their rain-flood hath been loosened. || 9. When they inundate the earth they spread forth darkness e'en in day time, | With the water-laden rain-cloud. || 10. O Marutas, at your voice's sound this earthly habitation shakes, | And each man reels who dwells therein. || 11. O Marutas, with your strong-hoofed steeds, unhindered in their courses, haste | Along the bright embanked streams. || 12. Firm be the fellies of your wheels, steady your horses and your cars, | And may your reins be fashioned well. || 13. Invite thou hither with this song, for praise, Agni the Lord of Prayer, | Him who is fair as Mitra is. || 14. Form in thy mouth the hymn of praise expand thee like, a rainy cloud | Sing forth the measured eulogy. || 15. Sing glory to the Marut host, praiseworthy, tuneful, vigorous: | Here let the Strong Ones dwell with us.

Hymn 1:39. Marutas.

1. When thus, like flame, from far away, Marutas, ye cast your measure forth, | To whom go Ye, to whom, O shakers of the earth, moved by whose wisdom, whose design? || 2. Strong let your weapons be to drive away your foes, firm for resistance let them be. | Yea, passing glorious must be your warrior might, not as a guileful mortal's strength. || 3. When what is strong ye overthrow, and whirl about each ponderous thing, | Heroes, your course is through the forest trees of earth, and through the fissures of the rocks. || 4. Consumers of your foes, no enemy of yours is found in heaven or on the earth: | Ye Rudras, may the strength, held in this bond, be yours, to bid defiance even now. || 5. They make the mountains rock and reel, they rend the forest-kings apart. | Onward, ye Marutas, drive, like creatures drunk with wine, ye, Gods with all your company. || 6. Ye to your chariot have yoked the spotted deer: a red deer, as a leader, draws. | Even the Earth herself listened as ye came near, and men were sorely terrified. || 7. O Rudras, quickly we desire your succour for this work of ours. | Come to us with your aid as in the days of old, so now for frightened Kaṇva's sake. || 8. Should any monstrous foe, O Marutas, sent by you or sent by mortals threaten us, | Tear ye him from us with your power and with your might, and with the succours that are yours. || 9. For ye, the worshipful and wise, have guarded Kaṇva perfectly. | O Marutas, come to us with full protecting help, as lightning flashes seek the rain. || 10. Whole strength have ye, O Bounteous Ones; perfect, earth-shakers, is your might. | Marutas, against the poet's wrathful enemy send ye an enemy like a dart.

Hymn 1:40. Brahmaṇaspati.

1. O Brahmaṇaspati, stand up: God-serving men we pray to thee. | May they who give good gifts, the Marutas, come to us. Indra, most swift, be thou with them. || 2. O Son of Strength, each mortal calls to thee for aid when spoil of battle waits for him. | O Marutas, may this man who loves you well obtain wealth of good steeds and hero might. || 3. May Brahmaṇaspati draw nigh, may Sūnṛitā the Goddess come, | And Gods bring to this rite which gives the five-fold gift the Hero, lover of mankind. || 4. He who bestows a noble guerdon on the priest wins fame that never shall decay. | For him we offer sacred hero-giving food, peerless and conquering easily. || 5. Now Brahmaṇaspati speaks forth aloud the solemn hymn of praise, | Wherein Indra and Varuṇa, Mitra, Aryaman, the Gods, have made their dwelling place. || 6. May we in holy synods, Gods! recite that hymn, peerless, that brings felicity. | If you, O Heroes, graciously accept this word, may it obtain all bliss from you. || 7. Who shall approach the pious? who the man whose sacred grass is trimmed? | The offerer with his folk advances more and more: he fills his house with precious things. || 8. He amplifies his lordly might, with kings he slays: e'en mid alarms he dwells secure | In great or lesser fight none checks him, none subdues,—the wielder of the thunderbolt.

Hymn 1:41. Varuṇa, Mitra, Aryaman.

1. Ne'er is he injured whom the Gods Varuṇa, Mitra, Aryaman, | The excellently wise, protect. || 2. He prospers ever, free from scathe, whom they, as with full hands, enrich, | Whom they preserve from every foe. || 3. The Kings drive far away from him his troubles and his enemies, | And lead him safely o'er distress. || 4. Thornless, Ādityas, is the path, easy for him

who seeks the Law: | With him is naught to anger you. || 5. What sacrifice, Ādityas, ye Heroes guide by the path direct,— | May that come nigh unto your thought. || 6. That mortal, ever unsubdued, gains wealth and every precious thing, | And children also of his own. || 7. How, my friends, shall we prepare Aryaman's and Mitra's laud, | Glorious food of Varuṇa? || 8. I point not out to you a man who strikes the pious, or reviles: | Only with hymns I call you nigh. || 9. Let him not love to speak ill words: but fear the One who holds all four | Within his hand, until they fall.

Hymn 1:42. Pūṣhan.

1. Shorten our ways, O Pūṣhan, move aside obstruction in the path: | Go close before us, cloud-born God. || 2. Drive, Pūṣhan, from our road the wolf, the wicked inauspicious wolf, | Who lies in wait to injure us. || 3. Who lurks about the path we take, the robber with a guileful heart: | Far from the road chase him away. || 4. Tread with thy foot and trample out the firebrand of the wicked one, | The double-tongued, whoe'er he be. || 5. Wise Pūṣhan, Wonder-Worker, we claim of thee now the aid wherewith | Thou furtheredst our sires of old. || 6. So, Lord of all prosperity, best wielder of the golden sword, | Make riches easy to be won. || 7. Past all pursuers lead us, make pleasant our path and fair to tread: | O Pūṣhan, find thou power for this. || 8. Lead us to meadows rich in grass: send on our way no early heat: | O Pūṣhan, find thou power for this. || 9. Be gracious to us, fill us full, give, feed us, and invigorate: | O Pūṣhan, find thou power for this. || 10. No blame have we for Pūṣhan; him we magnify with songs of praise: | We seek the Mighty One for wealth.

Hymn 1:43. Rudra.

1. What shall we sing to Rudra, strong, most bounteous, excellently wise, | That shall be dearest to his heart? || 2. That Aditi may grant the grace of Rudra to our folk, our kine, | Our cattle and our progeny; || 3. That Mitra and that Varuṇa, that Rudra may remember us, | Yea, all the Gods with one accord. || 4. To Rudra Lord of sacrifice, of hymns and balmy medicines, | We pray for joy and health and strength. || 5. He shines in splendour like the Sun, refulgent as bright gold is he, | The good, the best among the Gods. || 6. May he grant health into our steeds, well-being to our rams and ewes, | To men, to women, and to kine. || 7. O Soma, set thou upon us the glory of a hundred men, | The great renown of mighty chiefs. || 8. Let not malignities, nor those who trouble Soma, hinder us. | Indu, give us a share of strength. || 9. Soma! head, central point, love these; Soma! know these as serving thee, | Children of thee Immortal, at the highest place of holy law.

Hymn 1:44. Agni.

1. Immortal Jātavedas, thou many-hued fulgent gift of Dawn, | Agni, this day to him who pays oblations bring the Gods who waken with the morn. || 2. For thou art offering-bearer and loved messenger, the charioteer of sacrifice: | Accordant with the Aśvins and with Dawn grant us heroic strength and lofty fame. || 3. As messenger we choose today Agni the good whom many love, | Smoke-bannered spreader of the light, at break of day glory of sacrificial rites. || 4. Him noblest and most youthful, richly worshipped guest, dear to the men who offer gifts, | Him, Agni Jātavedas, I beseech at dawn that he may bring the Gods to us. || 5. Thee, Agni, will I glorify, deathless nourisher of the world, | Immortal, offering-bearer, meet for sacred food, preserver, best at sacrifice. || 6. Tell good things to thy praiser, O most youthful God, as richly worshipped, honey-tongued, | And, granting to Praskaṇva lengthened days of life, show honour to the Heavenly Host. || 7. For the men, Agni, kindle thee as all possessor and as Priest; | So Agni, much-invoked, bring hither with all speed the Gods, the excellently wise, || 8. At dawn of day, at night, Uṣhas and Savitar, the Aśvins, Bhaga, Agni's self: | Skilled in fair rites, with Soma poured, the Kaṇvas light thee, the oblation-wafting God. || 9. For, Agni, Lord of sacrifice and messenger of men art thou: | Bring thou the Gods who wake at dawn who see the light, this day to drink the Soma juice. || 10. Thou shonest forth, O Agni, after former dawns, all visible, O rich in light. | Thou art our help in battle-strife, the Friend of man, the great high priest in sacrifice. || 11. Like Manu, we will establish thee, Agni, performer of the rite, | Invoker, ministering Priest, exceeding wise, the swift immortal messenger. || 12. When as the Gods' High Priest, by many loved, thou dost their mission as their nearest Friend, | Then, like the far-resounding billows of the flood, thy flames, O Agni, roar aloud. || 13. Hear, Agni, who hast ears to hear, with all thy train of escort Gods; | Let Mitra, Aryaman, seeking betimes our rite, seat them upon the sacred grass. || 14. Let those who strengthen Law, who bountifully give, the life-tongued Marutas, hear our praise. | May Law-supporting Varuṇa with the Aśvins twain and Uṣhas, drink the Soma juice.

Hymn 1:45. Agni.

1. Worship the Vasus, Agni! here, the Rudras, the Ādityas, all | Who spring from Manu, those who know fair rites, who pour their blessings down. || 2. Agni, the Gods who understand give ear unto the worshipper: | Lord of Red Steeds, who lovest song, bring thou those Three-and-Thirty Gods. || 3. O Jātavedas, great in act, hearken thou to Praskaṇva's call, | As Priyamedha erst was heard, Atri, Virūpa, Aṅgiras. || 4. The sons of Priyamedha skilled in lofty praise have called for help | On Agni who with fulgent flame is Ruler of all holy rites. || 5. Hear thou, invoked with holy oil, bountiful giver of rewards, | These eulogies, whereby the sons of Kaṇva call thee to their aid. || 6. O Agni, loved by many, thou of fame most wondrous, in their homes | Men call on thee whose hair is flame, to be the bearer of their gifts. || 7. Thee, Agni, best to find out wealth, most widely famous, quick to hear, | Singers have established in their rites Herald and ministering Priest. || 8. Singers with Soma pressed have made thee, Agni, hasten to the feast, | Great light to mortal worshipper, what time they bring the sacred gift. || 9. Good, bounteous, Son of Strength, this day seat here on sacred grass the Gods | Who come at early morn, the host of heaven, to drink the Soma juice || 10. Bring with joint invocations thou, O Agni, the celestial host: | Here stands the Soma, bounteous Gods drink this expressed ere yesterday.

Hymn 1:46. Aśvins.

1. Now Morning with her earliest light shines forth, dear Daughter of the Sky: | High, Aśvins, I extol your praise, || 2. Sons of the Sea, mighty to save discoverers of riches, ye | Gods with deep thought who find out wealth. || 3. Your giant coursers hasten on over the region all in flames, | When your car flies with winged steeds. || 4. He, liberal, lover of the flood, Lord of the House, the vigilant, | Chiefs! with oblations feeds you full. || 5. Ye have regard unto our hymns, Nāsatyas, thinking of our words: | Drink boldly of the Soma juice. || 6. Vouchsafe to us, O Aśvin Pair, such strength as, with attendant light, | May through the darkness carry us. || 7. Come in the ship of these our hymns to bear you to the hither shore | O Aśvins, harness ye the car. || 8. The heaven's wide vessel is your own on the flood's shore your chariot waits | Drops, with the hymn, have been prepared. || 9. Kaṇvas, the drops are in the heaven; the wealth is at the waters' place: | Where will ye manifest your form? || 10. Light came to lighten up the branch, the Sun appeared as it were gold: | And with its tongue shone forth the dark. || 11. The path of sacrifice was made to travel to the farther goal: | The road of heaven was manifest. || 12. The singer of their praise awaits whatever grace the Aśvins give, | who save when Soma gladdens them. || 13. Ye dwellers with Vivasvat come, auspicious, as to Manu erst; | come to the Soma and our praise. || 14. O circumambient Aśvins, Dawn follows the brightness of your way: | Approve with beams our solemn rites. || 15. Drink ye of our libations, grant protection, O ye Aśvins Twain, | With aids which none may interrupt.

Hymn 1:47. Aśvins.

1. Aśvins, for you who strengthen Law this sweetest Soma hath been shed. | Drink this expressed ere yesterday and give riches to him who offers it. || 2. Come, O ye Aśvins, mounted on your triple car three-seated, beautiful of form | To you at sacrifice the Kaṇvas send the prayer: graciously listen to their call. || 3. O Aśvins, ye who strengthen Law, drink ye this sweetest Soma juice. | Borne on your wealth-fraught car come ye this day to him who offers, ye of wondrous deeds. || 4. Omniscient Aśvins, on the thrice-heaped grass bedew with the sweet juice the sacrifice. | The sons of Kaṇva, striving heavenward, call on you with draughts of Soma juice out-poured. || 5. O Aśvins, with those aids wherewith ye guarded Kaṇva carefully, | Keep us, O Lords of Splendour: drink the Soma juice, ye strengtheners of holy law. || 6. O Mighty Ones, ye gave Sudās abundant food, brought on your treasure-laden car; | So now vouchsafe to us the wealth which many crave, either from heaven or from the sea. || 7. Nāsatyas, whether ye be far away or close to Turvaśa, | Borne on your lightly-rolling chariot come to us, together with the sunbeams come. || 8. So let your coursers, ornaments of

sacrifice, bring you to our libations here. | Bestowing food on him who acts and gives aright, sit, Chiefs, upon the sacred grass. || 9. Come, O Nāsatyas, on your car decked with a sunbright canopy, | Whereon ye ever bring wealth to the worshipper, to drink the Soma's pleasant juice. || 10. With lauds and songs of praise we call them down to us, that they, most rich, may succour us; | For ye have ever in the Kaṇvas' well-loved house, O Aśvins, drunk the Soma juice.

Hymn 1:48. Dawn.

1. Dawn on us with prosperity, O Uṣhas, Daughter of the Sky, | Dawn with great glory, Goddess, Lady of the Light, dawn thou with riches, Bounteous One. || 2. They, bringing steeds and kine, boon-givers of all wealth, have oft sped forth to lighten us. | O Uṣhas, waken up for me the sounds of joy: send us the riches of the great. || 3. Uṣhas hath dawned, and now shall dawn, the Goddess, driver forth of cars | Which, as she cometh nigh, have fixed their thought on her, like glory-seekers on the flood. || 4. Here Kaṇva, chief of Kaṇva's race, sings forth aloud the glories of the heroes' names,— | The. princes who, O Uṣhas, as thou comest near, direct their thoughts to liberal gifts. || 5. Like a good matron Uṣhas comes carefully tending everything: | Rousing all life she stirs all creatures that have feet, and makes the birds of air fly up. || 6. She sends the busy forth, each man to his pursuit: delay she knows not as she springs. | O rich in opulence, after thy dawning birds that have flown forth no longer rest. || 7. This Dawn hath yoked her steeds afar, beyond the rising of the Sun: | Borne on a hundred chariots she, auspicious Dawn, advances on her way to Men. || 8. To meet her glance all living creatures bend them down: Excellent One, she makes the light. | Uṣhas, the Daughter of the Sky, the opulent, shines foes and enmities away. || 9. Shine on us with thy radiant light, O Uṣhas, Daughter of the Sky, | Bringing to us great store of high felicity, and beaming on our solemn rites. || 10. For in thee is each living creature's breath and life, when, Excellent! thou dawnest forth. | Borne on thy lofty car, O Lady of the Light, hear, thou of wondrous wealth, our call. || 11. O Uṣhas, win thyself the strength which among men is wonderful. | Bring thou thereby the pious unto holy rites, those who as priests sing praise to thee. || 12. Bring from the firmament, O Uṣhas, all the Gods, that they may drink our Soma juice, | And, being what thou art, vouchsafe us kine and steeds, strength meet for praise and hero might. || 13. May Uṣhas whose auspicious rays are seen resplendent round about, | Grant us great riches, fair in form, of all good things, wealth which light labour may attain. || 14. Mighty One, whom the Ṛiṣhis of old time invoked for their protection and their help, | O Uṣhas, graciously answer our songs of praise with bounty and with brilliant light. || 15. Uṣhas, as thou with light to day hast opened the twin doors of heaven, | So grant thou us a dwelling wide and free from foes. O Goddess, give us food with kine. || 16. Bring us to wealth abundant, sent in every shape, to plentiful refreshing food, | To all-subduing splendour, Uṣhas, Mighty One, to strength, thou rich in spoil and wealth.

Hymn 1:49. Dawn.

1. E'en from above the sky's bright realm come, Uṣhas, by auspicious ways: | Let red steeds bear thee to the house of him who pours the Soma, juice. || 2. The chariot which thou mountest, fair of shape, O Uṣhas light to move,— | Therewith, O Daughter of the Sky, aid men of noble fame today. || 3. Bright Uṣhas, when thy times return, all quadrupeds and bipeds stir, | And round about flock winged birds from all the boundaries of heaven. || 4. Thou dawning with thy beams of light illumest all the radiant realm. | Thee, as thou art, the Kaṇvas, fain for wealth, have called with sacred songs.

Hymn 1:50. Sūrya.

1. His bright rays bear him up aloft, the God who knoweth all that lives, | Sūrya, that all may look on him. || 2. The constellations pass away, like thieves, together with their beams, | Before the all-beholding Sun. || 3. His herald rays are seen afar refulgent o'er the world of men, | Like flames of fire that burn and blaze. || 4. Swift and all beautiful art thou, O Sūrya, maker of the light, | Illuming all the radiant realm. || 5. Thou goest to the hosts of Gods, thou comest hither to mankind, | Hither all light to be beheld. || 6. With that same eye of thine wherewith thou lookest brilliant Varuṇa, | Upon the busy race of men, || 7. Traversing sky and wide mid-air, thou metest with thy beams our days, | Sun, seeing all things that have birth. || 8. Seven Bay Steeds harnessed to thy car bear thee, O thou farseeing One, | God, Sūrya, with the radiant hair. || 9. Sūrya hath yoked the pure bright Seven, the daughters of the car; with these, | His own dear team, he goeth forth. || 10. Looking upon the loftier light above the darkness we have come | To Sūrya, God among the Gods, the light that is most excellent. || 11. Rising this day, O rich in friends, ascending to the loftier heaven, | Sūrya remove my heart's disease, take from me this my yellow hue. || 12. To parrots and to starlings let us give away my yellowness, | Or this my yellowness let us transfer to Haritāla trees. || 13. With all his conquering vigour this Āditya hath gone up on high, | Giving my foe into mine hand: let me not be my foeman's prey.

Hymn 1:51. Indra.

1. Make glad with songs that Ram whom many men invoke, worthy of songs of praise, Indra, the sea of wealth; | Whose gracious deeds for men spread like the heavens abroad: sing praise to him the Sage, most liberal for our good. || 2. As aids the skilful Ṛibhus yearned to Indra strong to save, who fills mid-air, encompassed round with might, | Rushing in rapture; and o'er Śatakratu came the gladdening shout that urged him on to victory. || 3. Thou hast disclosed the kine's stall for the Aṅgirasas, and made a way for Atri by a hundred doors. | On Vimada thou hast bestowed both food and wealth, making thy bolt dance in the sacrificer's fight. || 4. Thou hast unclosed the prisons of the waters; thou hast in the mountain seized the treasure rich in gifts. | When thou hadst slain with might the dragon Vṛitra, thou, Indra, didst raise the Sun in heaven for all to see. || 5. With wondrous might thou blewest enchanter fiends away, with powers celestial those who called on thee in jest. | Thou, hero-hearted, hast broken down Pipru's forts, and helped Ṛijiśvan when the Dasyus were struck dead. || 6. Thou savedst Kutsa when Śuṣhṇa was smitten down; to Atithigva gavest Śambara for a prey. | E'en mighty Arbuda thou troddest under foot: thou from of old wast born to strike the Dasyus dead. || 7. All power and might is closely gathered up in thee; thy bounteous spirit joys in drinking Soma juice. | Known is the thunderbolt that lies within thine arms: rend off therewith all manly prowess of our foe. || 8. Discern thou well Āryas and Dasyus; punishing the lawless give them up to him whose grass is strewn. | Be thou the sacrificer's strong encourager all these thy deeds are my delight at festivals. || 9. Indra gives up the lawless to the pious man, destroying by the Strong Ones those who have no strength. | Vamra when glorified destroyed the gathered piles of the still waxing great one who would reach the heaven. || 10. The might which Uśanā hath formed for thee with might rends in its greatness and with strength both worlds apart. | O Hero-souled, the steeds of Vāta, yoked by thought, have carried thee to fame while thou art filled with power. || 11. When Indra hath rejoiced with Kāvya Uśanā, he mounts his steeds who swerve wider and wider yet. | The Strong hath loosed his bolt with the swift rush of rain, and he hath rent in pieces Śuṣhṇa's firm-built forts. || 12. Thou mountest on thy car amid strong Soma draughts: Śāryāta brought thee those in which thou hast delight. | Indra, when thou art pleased with men whose Soma flows thou risest to unchallenged glory in the sky. || 13. To old Kakṣhīvant, Soma-presser, skilled in song, O Indra, thou didst give the youthful Vṛichayā. | Thou, very wise, wast Menā, Vṛiṣhaṇaśva's child: those deeds of thine must all be told at Soma feasts. || 14. The good man's refuge in his need is Indra, firm as a doorpost, praised among the Pajras. | Indra alone is Lord of wealth, the Giver, lover of riches, chariots, kine, and horses. || 15. To him the Mighty One, the self-resplendent, verily strong and great, this praise is uttered. | May we and all the heroes, with the princes, be, in this fray, O Indra, in thy keeping.

Hymn 1:52. Indra.

1. I glorify that Ram who finds the light of heaven, whose hundred nobly-natured ones go forth with him. | With hymns may I turn hither Indra to mine aid,—the Car which like a strong steed hasteth to the call. || 2. Like as a mountain on firm basis, unremoved, he, thousandfold protector, waxed in mighty strength, | When Indra, joying in the draughts of Soma juice, forced the clouds, slaying Vṛitra stayer of their flow. || 3. For he stays e'en the stayers, spread o'er laden cloud, rooted in light, strengthened in rapture by the wise. | Indra with thought, with skilled activity, I call, most liberal giver, for he sates him with the juice. || 4. Whom those that flow in heaven on sacred grass, his own assistants, nobly-natured, fill full like the sea,— | Beside that Indra when he smote down Vṛitra stood his helpers,

straight in form, mighty, invincible. ‖ 5. To him, as in wild joy he fought with him who stayed the rain, his helpers sped like swift streams down a slope, | When Indra, thunder-armed, made bold by Soma draughts, as Trita cleaveth Vala's fences, cleft him through. ‖ 6. Splendour encompassed thee, forth shone thy warrior might: the rain-obstructor lay in mid-air's lowest deep, | What time, O Indra, thou didst cast thy thunder down upon the jaws of Vṛitra hard to be restrained. ‖ 7. The hymns which magnify thee, Indra, reach to thee even as water-brooks flow down and fill the lake. | Tvashṭar gave yet more force to thine appropriate strength, and forged thy thunderbolt of overpowering might. ‖ 8. When, Indra, thou whose power is linked with thy Bay Steeds hadst smitten Vṛitra, causing floods to flow for man, | Thou heldst in thine arms the metal thunderbolt, and settest in the heaven the Sun for all to see. ‖ 9. In fear they raised the lofty self-resplendent hymn, praise giving and effectual, leading up to heaven, | When Indra's helpers fighting for the good of men, the Marutas, faithful to mankind, joyed in the light. ‖ 10. Then Heaven himself, the mighty, at that Dragon's roar reeled back in terror when, Indra, thy thunderbolt | In the wild joy of Soma had struck off with might the head of Vṛitra, tyrant of the earth and heaven. ‖ 11. O Indra, were this earth extended forth tenfold, and men who dwell therein multiplied day by day, | Still here thy conquering might, Maghavan, would be famed: it hath waxed vast as heaven in majesty and power. ‖ 12. Thou, bold of heart, in thine own native might, for help, upon the limit of this mid-air and of heaven, | Hast made the earth to be the pattern of thy strength: embracing flood and light thou reachest to the sky. ‖ 13. Thou art the counterpart of earth, the Master of lofty heaven with all its mighty Heroes: | Thou hast filled all the region with thy greatness: yea, of a truth there is none other like thee. ‖ 14. Whose amplitude the heaven and earth have not attained, whose bounds the waters of mid-air have never reached,— | Not, when in joy he fights the stayer of the rain: thou, and none else, hast made all things in order due. ‖ 15. The Marutas sang thy praise in this encounter, and in thee all the Deities delighted, | What time thou, Indra, with thy spiky weapon, thy deadly bolt, smotest the face of Vṛitra.

Hymn 1:53. Indra.

1. We will present fair praise unto the Mighty One, our hymns to Indra in Vivasvat's dwelling-place; | For he hath ne'er found wealth in those who seem to sleep: those who give wealth to men accept no paltry praise. ‖ 2. Giver of horses, Indra, giver, thou, of kine, giver of barley, thou art Lord and guard of wealth: | Man's helper from of old, not disappointing hope, Friend of our friends, to thee as such we sing this praise. ‖ 3. Indra, most splendid, powerful, rich in mighty deeds, this treasure spread around is known to be thine own. | Gather therefrom, O Conqueror, and bring to us: fail not the hope of him who loves and sings to thee. ‖ 4. Well pleased with these bright flames and with these Soma drops, take thou away our poverty with seeds and kine. | With Indra scattering the Dasyu through these drops, freed from their hate may we obtain abundant food. ‖ 5. Let us obtain, O Indra, plenteous wealth and food, with strength exceeding glorious, shining to the sky: | May we obtain the Goddess Providence, the strength of heroes, special source of cattle, rich in steeds. ‖ 6. These our libations strength-inspiring, Soma draughts, gladdened thee in the fight with Vṛitra, Hero Lord, | What time thou slewest for the singer with trimmed grass ten thousand Vṛitras, thou resistless in thy might. ‖ 7. Thou goest on from fight to fight intrepidly, destroying castle after castle here with strength. | Thou, Indra, with thy friend who makes the foe bow down, slewest from far away the guileful Namuchi. ‖ 8. Thou hast struck down in death Karañja, Parṇaya, in Atithigva's very glorious going forth. | Unyielding, when Ṛijiśvan compassed them with siege, thou hast destroyed the hundred forts of Vaṅgṛida. ‖ 9. With all-outstripping chariot-wheel, O Indra, thou far-famed, hast overthrown the twice ten Kings of men, | With sixty thousand nine-and-ninety followers, who came in arms to fight with friendless Suśravas. ‖ 10. Thou hast protected Suśravas with succour, and Tūrvayāṇa with thine aid, O Indra. | Thou madest Kutsa, Atithigva, Āyu, subject unto this King, the young, the mighty. ‖ 11. May we protected by the Gods hereafter remain thy very prosperous friends, O Indra. | Thee we extol, enjoying through thy favour life long and joyful and with store of heroes.

Hymn 1:54. Indra.

1. Urge us not, Maghavan, to this distressful fight, for none may comprehend the limit of thy strength. | Thou with fierce shout hast made the woods and rivers roar: did not men run in crowds together in their fear? ‖ 2. Sing hymns of praise to Śakra, Lord of power and might; laud thou and magnify Indra who heareth thee, | Who with his daring might, a Bull exceeding strong in strength, maketh him master of the heaven and earth. ‖ 3. Sing forth to lofty Dyaus a strength-bestowing song, the Bold, whose resolute mind hath independent sway. | High glory hath the Asura, compact of strength, drawn on by two Bay Steeds: a Bull, a Car is he. ‖ 4. The ridges of the lofty heaven thou madest shake; thou, daring, of thyself smotest through Śambara, | When bold with gladdening juice, thou warredst with thy bolt, sharp and two-edged, against the banded sorcerers. ‖ 5. When with a roar that fills the woods, thou forcest down on wind's head the stores which Śushṇa kept confined, | Who shall have power to stay thee firm and eager-souled from doing still this day what thou of old hast done? ‖ 6. Thou helpest Nārya, Turvaśa, and Yadu, and Vayya's son Turvīti, Śatakratu! | Thou helpest horse and car in final battle thou breakest down the nine-and-ninety castles. ‖ 7. A hero-lord is he, King of a mighty folk, who offers free oblations and promotes the Law, | Who with a bounteous guerdon welcomes hymns of praise: for him flows down the abundant stream below the sky. ‖ 8. His power is matchless, matchless is his wisdom; chief, through their work, be some who drink the Soma, | Those, Indra, who increase the lordly power, the firm heroic strength of thee the Giver. ‖ 9. Therefore for thee are these abundant beakers Indra's drink, stone-pressed juices held in ladles. | Quaff them and satisfy therewith thy longing; then fix thy mind upon bestowing treasure. ‖ 10. There darkness stood, the vault that stayed the waters' flow: in Vṛitra's hollow side the rain-cloud lay concealed. | But Indra smote the rivers which the obstructor stayed, flood following after flood, down steep declivities. ‖ 11. So give us, Indra, bliss-increasing glory give us great sway and strength that conquers people. | Preserve our wealthy patrons, save our princes; vouchsafe us wealth and food with noble offspring.

Hymn 1:55. Indra.

1. Though e'en this heaven's wide space and earth have spread them out, nor heaven nor earth may be in greatness Indra's match. | Awful and very mighty, causing woe to men, he whets his thunderbolt for sharpness, as a bull. ‖ 2. Like as the watery ocean, so doth he receive the rivers spread on all sides in their ample width. | He bears him like a bull to drink of Soma juice, and will, as Warrior from of old, be praised for might. ‖ 3. Thou swayest, Indra, all kinds of great manly power, so as to bend, as't were, even that famed mountain down. | Foremost among the Gods is he through hero might, set in the van, the Strong One, for each arduous deed. ‖ 4. He only in the wood is praised by worshippers, when he shows forth to men his own fair Indra-power. | A friendly Bull is he, a Bull to be desired when Maghavan auspiciously sends forth his voice. ‖ 5. Yet verily the Warrior in his vigorous strength stirreth up with his might great battles for mankind; | And men have faith in Indra, the resplendent One, what time he hurleth down his bolt, his dart of death. ‖ 6. Though, fain for glory, and with strength increased on earth, he with great might destroys the dwellings made with art, | He makes the lights of heaven shine forth secure, he bids, exceeding wise, the floods flow for his worshipper. ‖ 7. Drinker of Soma, let thy heart incline to give; bring thy Bays hitherward, O thou who hearest praise. | Those charioteers of' thine, best skilled to draw the rein, the rapid sunbeams, Indra, lead thee not astray. ‖ 8. Thou bearest in both hands treasure that never fails; the famed One in his body holds unvanquished might. | O Indra, in thy members many powers abide, like wells surrounded by the ministering priests.

Hymn 1:56. Indra.

1. For this man's full libations held in ladles, he hath roused him, eager, as a horse to meet the mare. | He stays his golden car, yoked with Bay Horses, swift, and drinks the Soma juice which strengthens for great deeds. ‖ 2. To him the guidance-following songs of praise flow full, as those who seek gain go in company to the flood. | To him the Lord of power, the holy synod's might, as to a hill, with speed, ascend the loving ones. ‖ 3. Victorious, great is he; in manly battle shines, unstained with dust, his might, as shines a mountain peak; | Wherewith the iron one, fierce e'en

against the strong, in rapture, fettered wily Śushṇa fast in bonds. || 4. When Strength the Goddess, made more strong for help by thee, waits upon Indra as the Sun attends the Dawn, | Then, he who with his might unflinching kills the gloom stirs up the dust aloft, with joy and triumphing. || 5. When thou with might, upon the framework of the heaven, didst fix, across, air's region firmly, unremoved, | In the light-winning war, Indra, in rapturous joy, thou smotest Vṛitra dead and broughtest floods of rain. || 6. Thou with thy might didst grasp, the holder-up of heaven, thou who art mighty also in the seats of earth. | Thou, gladdened by the juice, hast set the waters free, and broken Vṛitra's stony fences through and through.

Hymn 1:57. Indra.

1. To him most liberal, lofty Lord of lofty wealth, verily powerful and strong, I bring my hymn,— | Whose checkless bounty, as of waters down a slope, is spread abroad for all that live, to give them strength. || 2. Now all this world, for worship, shall come after thee—the offerer's libations like floods to the depth, | When the well-loved one seems to rest upon the hill, the thunderbolt of Indra, shatterer wrought of gold. || 3. To him the terrible, most meet for lofty praise, like bright Dawn, now bring gifts with reverence in this rite, | Whose being, for renown, yea, Indra-power and light, have been created, like bay steeds, to move with speed. || 4. Thine, Indra, praised by many, excellently rich! are we who trusting in thy help draw near to thee. | Lover of praise, none else but thou receives our laud: as earth loves all her creatures, love thou this our hymn. || 5. Great is thy power, O Indra, we are thine. Fulfil, O Maghavan, the wish of this thy worshipper. | After thee lofty heaven hath measured out its strength: to thee and to thy power this earth hath bowed itself. || 6. Thou, who hast thunder for thy weapon, with thy bolt hast shattered into pieces this broad massive cloud. | Thou hast sent down the obstructed floods that they may flow: thou hast, thine own for ever, all victorious might.

Hymn 1:58. Agni.

1. Ne'er waxeth faint the Immortal, Son of Strength, since he, the Herald, hath become Vivasvat's messenger. | On paths most excellent he measured out mid-air: he with oblation calls to service of the Gods. || 2. Never decaying, seizing his appropriate food, rapidly, eagerly through the dry wood he spreads. | His back, as he is sprinkled, glistens like a horse: loud hath he roared and shouted like the heights of heaven? || 3. Set high in place o'er all that Vasus, Rudras do, immortal, Lord of riches, seated as High Priest; | Hastening like a car to men, to those who live, the God without delay gives boons to be desired. || 4. Urged by the wind be spreads through dry wood as he lists, armed with his tongues for sickles, with a mighty roar. | Black is thy path, Agni, changeless, with glittering waves! when like a bull thou rushest eager to the trees. || 5. With teeth of flame, wind-driven, through the wood he speeds, triumphant like a bull among the herd of cows, | With bright strength roaming to the everlasting air: things fixed, things moving quake before him as he flies. || 6. The Bhṛigus established thee among mankind for men, like as a treasure, beauteous, easy to invoke; | Thee, Agni, as a herald and choice-worthy guest, as an auspicious Friend to the Celestial Race. || 7. Agni, the seven tongues' deftest Sacrificer, him whom the priests elect at solemn worship, | The Herald, messenger of all the Vasus, I serve with dainty food, I ask for riches. || 8. Grant, Son of Strength, thou rich in friends, a refuge without a flaw this day to us thy praisers. | O Agni, Son of Strength, with forts of iron preserve thou from distress the man who lauds thee. || 9. Be thou a refuge, Bright One, to the singer, a shelter, Bounteous Lord, to those who worship. | Preserve the singer from distress, O Agni. May he, enriched with prayer, come soon and early.

Hymn 1:59. Agni.

1. The other fires are, verily, thy branches; the Immortals all rejoice in thee, O Agni. | Centre art thou, Vaiśvānara, of the people, sustaining men like a deep-founded pillar. || 2. The forehead of the sky, earth's centre, Agni became the messenger of earth and heaven. | Vaiśvānara, the Deities produced thee, a God, to be a light unto the Ārya. || 3. As in the Sun firm rays are set for ever, treasures are in Vaiśvānara, in Agni. | Of all the riches in the hills, the waters, the herbs, among mankind, thou art the Sovereign. || 4. As the great World-halves, so are their Son's praises; skilled, as a man, to act, is he the Herald. | Vaiśvānara, celestial, truly mighty, most manly One, hath many a youthful consort. || 5. Even the lofty heaven, O Jātavedas Vaiśvānara, hath not attained thy greatness. | Thou art the King of lands where men are settled, thou hast brought comfort to the Gods in battle. || 6. Now will I tell the greatness of the Hero whom Pūru's sons follow as Vṛitra's slayer: | Agni Vaiśvānara struck down the Dasyu, cleave Śambara through and shattered down his fences. || 7. Vaiśvānara, dwelling by his might with all men, far-shining, holy mid the Bharadvājas, | Is lauded, excellent, with hundred praises by Purunītha, son of Śatavani.

Hymn 1:60. Agni.

1. As 'twere Some goodly treasure Mātariśvan brought, as a gift, the glorious Priest to Bhṛigu, | Banner of sacrifice, the good Protector, child of two births, the swiftly moving envoy. || 2. Both Gods and men obey this Ruler's order, Gods who are worshipped, men who yearn and worship. | As Priest he takes his seat ere break of morning, House-Lord, adorable with men, Ordainer. || 3. May our fair praise, heart-born, most recent, reach him whose tongue, e'en at his birth, is sweet as honey; | Whom mortal priests, men, with their strong endeavour, supplied with dainty viands, have created. || 4. Good to mankind, the yearning Purifier hath among men been placed as Priest choice-worthy. | May Agni be our Friend, Lord of the Household, protector of the riches in the dwelling. || 5. As such we Gotamas with hymns extol thee, O Agni, as the guardian Lord of riches, | Decking thee like a horse, the swift prizewinner. May he, enriched with prayer, come soon and early.

Hymn 1:61. Indra.

1. Even to him, swift, strong and high. exalted, I bring my song of praise as dainty viands, | My thought to him resistless, praise-deserving, prayers offered most especially to Indra. || 2. Praise, like oblation, I present, and utter aloud my song, my fair hymn to the Victor. | For Indra, who is Lord of old, the singers have decked their lauds with heart and mind and spirit. || 3. To him then with my lips mine adoration, winning heaven's light, most excellent, I offer, | To magnify with songs of invocation and with fair hymns the Lord, most bounteous Giver. || 4. Even for him I frame a laud, as fashions the wright a chariot for the man who needs it,— | Praises to him who gladly hears our praises, a hymn well-formed, all-moving, to wise Indra. || 5. So with my tongue I deck, to please that Indra, my hymn, as 'twere a horse, through love of glory, | To reverence the Hero, bounteous Giver, famed far and wide, destroyer of the castles. || 6. Even for him hath Tvashṭar forged the thunder, most deftly wrought, celestial, for the battle, | Wherewith he reached the vital parts of Vṛitra, striking-the vast, the mighty with the striker. || 7. As soon as, at libations of his mother, great Vishṇu had drunk up the draught, he plundered. | The dainty cates, the cooked mess; but One stronger transfixed the wild boar, shooting through the mountain. || 8. To him, to Indra, when he slew the Dragon, the Dames, too, Consorts of the Gods, wove praises. | The mighty heaven and earth hath he encompassed: thy greatness heaven and earth, combined, exceed not. || 9. Yea, of a truth, his magnitude surpasseth the magnitude of earth, mid-air, and heaven. | Indra, approved by all men, self-resplendent, waxed in his home, loud-voiced and strong for battle. || 10. Through his own strength Indra with bolt of thunder cut piece-meal Vṛitra, drier up of waters. | He let the floods go free, like cows imprisoned, for glory, with a heart inclined to bounty. || 11. The rivers played, through his impetuous splendour, since with his bolt he compassed them on all sides. | Using his might and favouring him who worshipped, he made a ford, victorious, for Turvīti. || 12. Vast, with thine ample power, with eager movement, against this Vṛitra cast thy bolt of thunder. | Rend thou his joints, as of an ox, dissevered, with bolt oblique, that floods of rain may follow. || 13. Sing with new lauds his exploits wrought aforetime, the deeds of him, yea, him who moveth swiftly, | When, hurling forth his weapons in the battle, he with impetuous wrath lays low the foemen. || 14. When he, yea, he, comes forth the firm. Set mountains and the whole heaven and earth, tremble for terror. | May Nodhas, ever praising the protection of that dear Friend, gain quickly strength heroic. || 15. Now unto him of these things hath been given what he who rules alone o'er much, electeth. | Indra hath helped Etaśa, Soma-presser, contending in the race of steeds with Sūrya. || 16. Thus to thee, Indra, yoker of Bay Coursers, the Gotamas have brought their prayers to please thee. | Bestow upon them thought, decked with all beauty. May he, enriched with prayer, come soon and early.

Hymn 1:62. Indra.

1. Like Aṅgiras a gladdening laud we ponder to him who loveth song, exceeding mighty. | Let us sing glory to the far-famed Hero who must be praised with fair hymns by the singer. || 2. Unto the great bring ye great adoration, a chant with praise to him exceeding mighty, | Through whom our sires, Aṅgirasas, singing praises and knowing well the places, found the cattle. || 3. When Indra and the Aṅgirasas desired it, Saramā found provision for her offspring. | Bṛihaspati cleft the mountain, found the cattle: the heroes shouted with the kine in triumph. || 4. Mid shout, loud shout, and roar, with the Navagvas, seven singers, hast thou, heavenly, rent the mountain; | Thou hast, with speeders, with Daśagvas, Indra, Śakra, with thunder rent obstructive Vala. || 5. Praised by Aṅgirasas, thou, foe-destroyer, hast, with the Dawn, Sun, rays, dispelled the darkness. | Thou Indra, hast spread out the earth's high ridges, and firmly fixed the region under heaven. || 6. This is the deed most worthy of all honour, the fairest marvel of the Wonder-Worker, | That, nigh where heaven bends down, he made four rivers flow full with waves that carry down sweet water. || 7. Unwearied, won with lauding hymns, he parted of old the ancient Pair, united ever. | In highest sky like Bhaga, he the doer of marvels set both Dames and earth and heaven. || 8. Still born afresh, young Dames, each in her manner, unlike in hue, the Pair in alternation | Round heaven and earth from ancient time have travelled, Night with her dark limbs, Dawn with limbs of splendour. || 9. Rich in good actions, skilled in operation, the Son with might maintains his perfect friendship. | Thou in the raw cows, black of hue or ruddy, storest the ripe milk glossy white in colour. || 10. Their paths, of old connected, rest uninjured; they with great might preserve the immortal statutes. | For many thousand holy works the Sisters wait on the haughty Lord like wives and matrons. || 11. Thoughts ancient, seeking wealth, with adoration, with newest lauds have sped to thee, O Mighty. | As yearning wives cleave to their yearning husband, so cleave our hymns to thee, O Lord most potent. || 12. Strong God, the riches which thy hands have holden from days of old have perished not nor wasted. | Splendid art thou, O Indra, wise, unbending: strengthen us with might, O Lord of Power. || 13. O mighty Indra, Gotama's son Nodhas hath fashioned this new prayer to thee Eternal, | Sure leader, yoker of the Tawny Coursers. May he, enriched with prayer, come soon and early.

Hymn 1:63. Indra.

1. Thou art the Mighty One; when born, O Indra, with power thou terrifiedst earth and heaven; | When, in their fear of thee, all firm-set mountains and monstrous creatures shook like dust before thee. || 2. When thy two wandering Bays thou drawest hither, thy praiser laid within thine arms the thunder, | Wherewith, O Much-invoked, in will resistless, thou smitest foemen down and many a castle. || 3. Faithful art thou, these thou defiest, Indra; thou art the Ṛibhus' Lord, heroic, victor. | Thou, by his side, for young and glorious Kutsa, with steed and car in battle slewest Śushṇa, || 4. That, as a friend, thou furtheredst, O Indra, when, Thunderer, strong in act, thou crushedst Vṛitra; | When, Hero, thou, great-souled, with easy conquest didst rend the Dasyus in their | distant dwelling. || 5. This doest thou, and art not harmed, O Indra, e'en in the anger of the strongest mortal. | Lay thou the race-course open for our horses: as with a club, slay, Thunder-armed! our foemen. || 6. Hence men invoke thee, Indra, in the tumult of battle, in the light-bestowing conflict. | This aid of thine, O Godlike One, was ever to be implored in deeds of might in combat. || 7. Warring for Purukutsa thou, O Indra, Thunder-armed! breakest down the seven castles; | Easily, for Sudās, like grass didst rend them, and out of need, King, broughtest gain to Pūru. || 8. O Indra, God who movest round about us, feed us with varied food plenteous as water— | Food wherewithal, O Hero, thou bestowest vigour itself to flow to us for ever. || 9. Prayers have been made by Gotamas, O Indra, addressed to thee, with laud for thy Bay Horses. | Bring us in noble shape abundant riches. May he, enriched with prayer, come soon and early.

Hymn 1:64. Marutas.

1. Bring for the manly host, wise and majestical, O Nodhas, for the Marutas bring thou a pure gift. | I deck my songs as one deft-handed, wise in mind prepares the water that hath power in solemn rites. || 2. They spring to birth, the lofty Ones, the Bulls of Heaven, divine, the youths of Rudra, free from spot and stain; | The purifiers, shining brightly even as suns, awful of form like giants, scattering rain-drops down. || 3. Young Rudras, demon-slayers, never growing old, they have waxed, even as mountains, irresistible. | They make all beings tremble with their mighty strength, even the very strongest, both of earth and heaven. || 4. With glittering ornaments they deck them forth for show; for beauty on their breasts they bind their chains of gold. | The lances on their shoulders pound to pieces; they were born together, of themselves, the Men of Heaven. || 5. Loud roarers, giving strength, devourers of the foe, they make the winds, they make the lightnings with their powers. | The restless shakers drain the udders of the sky, and ever wandering round fill the earth full with milk. || 6. The bounteous Marutas with the fatness dropping milk fill full the waters which avail in solemn rites. | They lead, as 'twere, the Strong Horse forth, that it may rain: they milk the thundering, the never-failing spring. || 7. Mighty, with wondrous power and marvellously bright, selfstrong like mountains, ye glide swiftly on your way. | Like the wild elephants ye eat the forests up when ye assume your strength among the bright red flames. || 8. Exceeding wise they roar like lions mightily, they, all-possessing, are beauteous as antelopes; | Stirring the darkness with lances and spotted deer, combined as priests, with serpents' fury through their might. || 9. Heroes who march in companies, befriending man, with serpents' ire through strength, ye greet the earth and heaven. | Upon the seats, O Marutas, of your chariots, upon the cars stands lightning visible as light. || 10. Lords of all riches, dwelling in the home of wealth, endowed with mighty vigour, singers loud of voice, | Heroes, of powers infinite, armed with strong men's rings, the archers, they have laid the arrow on their arms. || 11. They who with golden fellies make the rain increase drive forward the big clouds like wanderers on the way. | Self-moving, brisk, unwearied, they o'erthrow the firm; the Marutas with bright lances make all things to reel. || 12. The progeny of Rudra we invoke with prayer, the brisk, the bright, the worshipful, the active Ones | To the strong band of Marutas cleave for happiness, the chasers of the sky, impetuous, vigorous. || 13. Marutas, the man whom ye have guarded with your help, he verily in strength surpasseth all mankind. | Spoil with his steeds he gaineth, treasure with his men; he winneth honourable strength and prospereth. || 14. O Marutas, to the worshippers give glorious strength invincible in battle, brilliant, bringing wealth, | Praiseworthy, known to all men. May we foster well, during a hundred winters, son and progeny. || 15. Will ye then, O ye Marutas, grant us riches, durable, rich in men, defying onslaught. | A hundred, thousandfold, ever increasing? May he, enriched with prayer, come soon and early.

Hymn 1:65. Agni.

1. One-minded, wise, they tracked thee like a thief lurking in dark cave with a stolen cow: | Thee claiming worship, bearing it to Gods: there nigh to thee sate all the Holy Ones. || 2. The Gods approached the ways of holy Law; there was a gathering vast as heaven itself. | The waters feed with praise the growing Babe, born nobly in the womb, the seat of Law. || 3. Like grateful food, like some wide dwelling place, like a fruit-bearing hill, a wholesome stream. | Like a steed urged to run in swift career, rushing like Sindhu, who may check his course? || 4. Kin as a brother to his sister floods, he eats the woods as a King eats the rich. | When through the forest, urged by wind, he spreads, verily Agni shears the hair of earth. || 5. Like a swan sitting in the floods he pants wisest in mind mid men he wakes at morn. | A Sage like Soma, sprung from Law, he grew like some young creature, mighty, shining far.

Hymn 1:66. Agni.

1. Like the Sun's glance, like wealth of varied sort, like breath which is the life, like one's own son, | Like a swift bird, a cow who yields her milk, pure and refulgent to the wood he speeds. || 2. He offers safety like a pleasant home, like ripened corn, the Conqueror of men. | Like a Seer lauding, famed among the folk; like a steed friendly he vouchsafes us power. || 3. With flame insatiate, like eternal might; caring for each one like a dame at home; | Bright when he shines forth, whitish mid the folk, like a car, gold-decked, thundering to the fight. || 4. He strikes with terror like a dart shot forth, e'en like an archer's arrow tipped with flame; | Master of present and of future life, the maidens' lover and the matrons' Lord. || 5. To him lead all your ways: may we attain the kindled God as cows their home at eve. | He drives the flames below as floods their swell: the rays rise up to the

fair place of heaven.

Hymn 1:67. Agni.

1. Victorious in the wood, Friend among men, ever he claims obedience as a King. | Gracious like peace, blessing like mental power, Priest was he, offering-bearer, full of thought. || 2. He, bearing in his hand all manly might, crouched in the cavern, struck the Gods with fear. | Men filled with understanding find him there, when they have sting prayers formed within their heart. || 3. He, like the Unborn, holds the broad earth up; and with effective utterance fixed the sky. | O Agni, guard the spots which cattle love: thou, life of all, hast gone from lair to lair. || 4. Whoso hath known him dwelling in his lair, and hath approached the stream of holy Law,— | They who release him, paying sacred rites,—truly to such doth he announce great wealth. || 5. He who grows mightily in herbs, within each fruitful mother and each babe she bears, | Wise, life of all men, in the waters' home,—for him have sages built as 'twere a seat.

Hymn 1:68. Agni.

1. Commingling, restless, he ascends the sky, unveiling nights and all that stands or moves, | As he the sole God is preeminent in greatness among all these other Gods. || 2. All men are joyful in thy power, O God, that living from the dry wood thou art born. | All truly share thy Godhead while they keep, in their accustomed ways, eternal Law. || 3. Strong is the thought of Law, the Law's behest; all works have they performed; he quickens all. | Whoso will bring oblation, gifts to thee, to him, bethinking thee, vouchsafe thou wealth. || 4. Seated as Priest with Manu's progeny, of all these treasures he alone is Lord. | Men yearn for children to prolong their line, and are not disappointed in their hope. || 5. Eagerly they who hear his word fulfil his wish as sons obey their sire's behest. | He, rich in food, unbars his wealth like doors: he, the House-Friend, hath decked heaven's vault with stars.

Hymn 1:69. Agni.

1. Bright, splendid, like Dawn's lover, he hath filled the two joined worlds as with the light of heaven. | When born, with might thou hast encompassed them: Father of Gods, and yet their Son wast thou. || 2. Agni, the Sage, the humble, who discerns like the cow's udder, the sweet taste of food, | Like a bliss-giver to be drawn to men, sits gracious in the middle of the house. || 3. Born in the dwelling like a lovely son, pleased, like a strong steed, he bears on the folk. | What time the men and I, with heroes, call, may Agni then gain all through Godlike power. || 4. None breaks these holy laws of thine when thou hast granted audience to these chieftains here. | This is thy boast, thou smotest with thy peers, and joined with heroes dravest off disgrace. || 5. Like the Dawn's lover, spreading light, well-known as hued like morn, may he remember me. | They, bearing of themselves, unbar the doors: they all ascend to the fair place of heaven.

Hymn 1:70. Agni.

1. May we, the pious, win much food by prayer, may Agni with fair light pervade each act,— | He the observer of the heavenly laws of Gods, and of the race of mortal man. || 2. He who is germ of waters, germ of woods, germ of all things that move not and that move,— | To him even in the rock and in the house: Immortal One, he cares for all mankind. || 3. Agni is Lord of riches for the man who serves him readily with sacred songs. | Protect these beings thou with careful thought, knowing the races both of Gods and men. || 4. Whom many dawns and nights, unlike, make strong, whom, born in Law, all things that move and stand,— | He hath been won, Herald who sits in light, making effectual all our holy works. || 5. Thou settest value on our cows and woods: all shall bring tribute to us to the light. | Men have served thee in many and sundry spots, parting, as 'twere, an aged father's wealth. || 6. Like a brave archer, like one skilled and bold, a fierce avenger, so he shines in fight.

Hymn 1:71. Agni.

1. Loving the loving One, as wives their husband, the sisters of one home have urged him forward, | Bright-coloured, even, as the cows love morning, dark, breaking forth to view, and redly beaming. || 2. Our sires with lauds burst e'en the firm-set fortress, yea, the Aṅgirasas, with roar, the mountain. | They made for us a way to reach high heaven, they found us day, light, day's sign, beams of morning. || 3. They established order, made his service fruitful; then parting them among the longing faithful, | Not thirsting after aught, they come, most active, while with sweet food the race of Gods they strengthen. || 4. Since Mātariśvan, far-diffused, hath stirred him, and he in every house grown bright and noble, | He, Bhṛigu-like I hath gone as his companion, as on commission to a greater Sovereign. || 5. When man poured juice to Heaven, the mighty Father, he knew and freed himself from close embracement. | The archer boldly shot at him his arrow, and the God threw his splendour on his Daughter. || 6. Whoso, hath flames for thee within his dwelling, or brings the worship which thou lovest daily, | Do thou of double might increase his substance: may he whom thou incitest meet with riches. || 7. All sacrificial viands wait on Agni as the Seven mighty Rivers seek the ocean. | Not by our brethren was our food discovered: find with the Gods care for us, thou who knowest. || 8. When light hath filled the Lord of men for increase, straight from the heaven descends the limpid moisture. | Agni hath brought to light and filled with spirit the youthful host blameless and well providing. || 9. He who like thought goes swiftly on his journey, the Sun, alone is ever Lord of riches. | The Kings with fair hands, Varuṇa and Mitra, protect the precious nectar in our cattle. || 10. O Agni, break not our ancestral friendship, Sage as thou art, endowed with deepest knowledge. | Old age, like gathering cloud, impairs the body: before that evil be come nigh protect me.

Hymn 1:72. Agni.

1. Though holding many gifts for men, he humbleth the higher powers of each wise ordainer. | Agni is now the treasure-lord of treasures, for ever granting all immortal bounties. || 2. The Gods infallible all searching found not him, the dear Babe who still is round about us. | Worn weary, following his track, devoted, they reached the lovely highest home of Agni. || 3. Because with holy oil the pure Ones, Agni, served thee the very pure three autumn seasons, | Therefore they won them holy names for worship, and nobly born they dignified their bodies. || 4. Making them known to spacious earth and heaven, the holy Ones revealed the powers of Rudra. | The mortal band, discerning in the distance, found Agni standing in the loftiest station. || 5. Nigh they approached, one-minded, with their spouses, kneeling to him adorable paid worship. | Friend finding in his own friend's eye protection, they made their own the bodies which they chastened. || 6. Soon as the holy beings had discovered the thrice-seven mystic things contained within thee, | With these, one-minded, they preserve the Amṛita: guard thou the life of all their plants and cattle. || 7. Thou, Agni, knower of men's works, hast sent us good food in constant course for our subsistence: | Thou deeply skilled in paths of Gods becamest an envoy never wearied, offering-bearer. || 8. Knowing the Law, the seven strong floods from heaven, full of good thought, discerned the doors of riches. | Saramā found the cattle's firm-built prison whereby the race of man is still supported. || 9. They who approached all noble operations making a path that leads to life immortal, | To be the Bird's support, the spacious mother, Aditi, and her great Sons stood in power. || 10. When Gods immortal made both eyes of heaven, they gave to him the gift of beauteous glory. | Now they flow forth like rivers set in motion: they knew the Red Steeds coming down, O Agni.

Hymn 1:73. Agni.

1. He who gives food, like patrimonial riches and guides aright like some wise man's instruction, | Loved like a guest who lies in pleasant lodging,—may he, as Priest, prosper his servant's dwelling. || 2. He who like Savitar the God, true-minded protecteth with his power. all acts of vigour, | Truthful, like splendour, glorified by many, like breath joy-giving,—all must strive to win him. || 3. He who on earth dwells like a king surrounded by faithful friends, like a God all-sustaining, | Like heroes who preside, who sit in safety: like as a blameless dame dear to her husband. || 4. Thee, such, in settlements secure, O Agni, our men serve ever kindled in each dwelling. | On him have they laid splendour in abundance: dear to all men, bearer be he of riches. || 5. May thy rich worshippers win food, O Agni, and princes gain long life who bring oblation. | May we get booty from our foe in battle, presenting to the Gods their share for glory. || 6. The cows of holy law, sent us by Heaven, have swelled with laden udders, loudly lowing; | Soliciting his favour, from a distance the rivers to the rock have flowed together. || 7. Agni, with thee, soliciting thy favour, the holy Ones have gained glory in heaven. | They made the Night and Dawn of different colours, and set the black and purple hues together. || 8. May we and those

who worship be the mortals whom thou, O Agni, leadest on to riches. | Thou hast filled earth and heaven and air's mid-region, and followest the whole world like a shadow. || 9. Aided by thee, O Agni, may we conquer steeds with steeds, men with men, heroes with heroes, | Lords of the wealth transmitted by our fathers: and may our princes live a hundred winters. || 10. May these our hymns of praise, Agni, Ordainer, be pleasant to thee in thy heart and spirit. | May we have power to hold thy steeds of riches, laying on thee the God-sent gift of glory.

Hymn 1:74. Agni.

1. As forth to sacrifice we go, a hymn to a hymn let us say, | Who hears us even when afar; || 2. Who, from of old, in carnage, when the people gathered, hath preserved | His household for the worshipper. || 3. And let men say, Agni is born, e'en he who slayeth Vṛitra, he | Who winneth wealth in every fight. || 4. Him in whose house an envoy thou lovest to taste his offered gifts, | And strengthenest his sacrifice, || 5. Him, Aṅgiras, thou Son of Strength, all men call happy in his God, | His offerings, and his sacred grass. || 6. Hitherward shalt thou bring these Gods to our laudation and to taste. | These offered gifts, fair-shining One. || 7. When, Agni, on thine embassage thou goest not a sound is heard of steed or straining of thy car. || 8. Aided by thee uninjured, strong, one after other, goes he forth: | Agni, the offerer forward steps. || 9. And splendid strength, heroic, high, Agni, thou grantest from the Gods, | Thou God, to him who offers gifts.

Hymn 1:75. Agni.

1. Accept our loudest-sounding hymn, food most delightful to the Gods, | Pouring our offerings in thy mouth. || 2. Now, Agni, will we say to thee, O wisest and best Aṅgiras, | Our precious, much-availing prayer. || 3. Who, Agni, is thy kin, of men? who is thy worthy worshipper? | On whom dependent? who art thou? || 4. The kinsman, Agni, of mankind, their well beloved Friend art thou, | A Friend whom friends may supplicate. || 5. Bring to us Mitra, Varuṇa, bring the Gods to mighty sacrifice. | Bring them, O Agni, to thine home.

Hymn 1:76. Agni.

1. How may the mind draw nigh to please thee, Agni? What hymn of praise shall bring us greatest blessing? | Or who hath gained thy power by sacrifices? or with what mind shall we bring thee oblations? || 2. Come hither, Agni; sit thee down as Hotar; be thou who never wast deceived our leader. | May Heaven and Earth, the all-pervading, love thee: worship the Gods to win for us their favour. || 3. Burn thou up all the Rākṣhasas, O Agni; ward thou off curses from our sacrifices. | Bring hither with his Bays the Lord of Soma: here is glad welcome for the Bounteous Giver. || 4. Thou Priest with lip and voice that bring us children hast been invoked. Here with the Gods be seated. | Thine is the task of Cleanser and Presenter: waken us, Wealth-bestower and Producer. || 5. As with oblations of the priestly Manus thou worshippedst the Gods, a Sage with sages, | So now, O truthfullest Invoker Agni, worship this day with joy-bestowing ladle.

Hymn 1:77. Agni.

1. How shall we pay oblation unto Agni? What hymn, God-loved, is said to him refulgent? | Who, deathless, true to Law, mid men a herald, bringeth the Gods as best of sacrificers? || 2. Bring him with reverence hither, most propitious in sacrifices, true to Law, the herald; | For Agni, when he seeks the Gods for mortals, knows them full well and worships them in spirit. || 3. For he is mental power, a man, and perfect; he is the bringer, friend-like, of the wondrous. | The pious Ārya tribes at sacrifices address them first to him who doeth marvels. || 4. May Agni, foe-destroyer, manliest Hero, accept with love our hymns and our devotion. | So may the liberal lords whose strength is strongest, urged by their riches, stir our thoughts with vigour. || 5. Thus Agni Jātavedas, true to Order, hath by the priestly Gotamas been lauded. | May he augment in them splendour and vigour: observant, as he lists, he gathers increase.

Hymn 1:78. Agni.

1. O Jātavedas, keen and swift, we Gotamas with sacred song exalt thee for thy glories' sake. || 2. Thee, as thou art, desiring wealth Gotama worships with his song: | We laud thee for thy glories' sake. || 3. As such, like Aṅgiras we call on thee best winner of the spoil: | We laud thee for thy glories' sake. || 4. Thee, best of Vṛitra-slayers, thee who shakest off our Dasyu foes: | We laud thee for thy glories' sake. || 5. A pleasant song to Agni we, sons of Rahūgaṅa, have sung: | We laud thee for thy glories' sake.

Hymn 1:79. Agni.

1. He in mid-air's expanse hath golden tresses; a raging serpent, like the rushing tempest: | Purely refulgent, knowing well the morning; like honourable dames, true, active workers. || 2. Thy well-winged flashes strengthen in their manner, when the black Bull hath bellowed round about us. | With drops that bless and seem to smile he cometh: the waters fall, the clouds utter their thunder. || 3. When he comes streaming with the milk of worship, conducting by directest paths of Order | Aryaman, Mitra, Varuṇa, Parijman fill the hide full where lies the nether press-stone. || 4. O Agni, thou who art the lord of wealth in kine, thou Son of Strength, | Vouchsafe to us, O Jātavedas, high renown. || 5. He, Agni, kindled, good and wise, must be exalted in our song: | Shine, thou of many forms, shine radiantly on us. || 6. O Agni, shining of thyself by night and when the morning breaks, | Burn, thou whose teeth are sharp, against the Rākṣhasas. || 7. Adorable in all our rites, favour us, Agni, with thine aid, | When the great hymn is chanted forth. || 8. Bring to us ever-conquering wealth, wealth, Agni, worthy of our choice, | In all our frays invincible. || 9. Give us, O Agni, through thy grace wealth that supporteth all our life, | Thy favour so that we may live. || 10. O Gotama, desiring bliss present thy songs composed with care | To Agni of the pointed flames. || 11. May the man fall, O Agni, who near or afar assaileth us: | Do thou increase and prosper us. || 12. Keen and swift Agni, thousand-eyed, chaseth the Rākṣhasas afar: | He singeth, herald meet for lauds.

Hymn 1:80. Indra.

1. Thus in the Soma, in wild joy the Brahman hath exalted thee: | Thou, mightiest thunder-armed, hast driven by force the Dragon from the earth, lauding thine own imperial sway. || 2. The mighty flowing Soma-draught, brought by the Hawk, hath gladdened thee, | That in thy strength, O Thunderer, thou hast struck down Vṛitra from the floods, lauding thine own imperial sway. || 3. Go forward, meet the foe, be bold; thy bolt of thunder is not checked. | Manliness, Indra, is thy might: stay Vṛitra, make the waters thine, lauding thine own imperial sway. || 4. Thou smotest Vṛitra from the earth, smotest him, Indra, from the sky. | Let these life-fostering waters flow attended by the Marut host, lauding thine own imperial sway. || 5. The wrathful Indra with his bolt of thunder rushing on the foe, | Smote fierce on trembling Vṛitra's back, and loosed the waters free to run, lauding his own imperial sway. || 6. With hundred-jointed thunderbolt Indra hath struck him on the back, | And, while rejoicing in the juice, seeketh prosperity for friends, lauding his own imperial sway. || 7. Indra, unconquered might is thine, Thunderer, Caster of the Stone; | For thou with thy surpassing power smotest to death the guileful beast, lauding thine own imperial sway. || 8. Far over ninety spacious floods thy thunderbolts were cast abroad: | Great, Indra, is thy hero might, and strength is seated in thine arms, lauding thine own imperial sway. || 9. Laud him a thousand all at once, shout twenty forth the hymn of praise. | Hundreds have sung aloud to him, to Indra hath the prayer been raised, lauding his own imperial sway. || 10. Indra hath smitten down the power of Vṛitra,—might with stronger might. | This was his manly exploit, he slew Vṛitra and let loose the floods, lauding his own imperial sway. || 11. Yea, even this great Pair of Worlds trembled in terror at thy wrath, | When, Indra, Thunderer, Marut-girt, thou slewest Vṛitra in thy strength, lauding thine own imperial sway. || 12. But Vṛitra scared not Indra with his shaking or his thunder roar. | On him that iron thunderbolt fell fiercely with its thousand points, lauding his own imperial sway. || 13. When with the thunder thou didst make thy dart and Vṛitra meet in war, | Thy might, O Indra, fain to slay the Dragon, was set firm in heaven, lauding thine own imperial sway. || 14. When at thy shout, O Thunder-armed, each thing both fixed and moving shook, | E'en Tvaṣhṭar trembled at thy wrath and quaked with fear because of thee, lauding thine own imperial sway. || 15. There is not, in our knowledge, one who passeth Indra in his strength: | In him the Deities have stored manliness, insight, power and might, lauding his own imperial sway. || 16. Still as of old, whatever rite Atharvan, Manus sire of all, | Dadhyach performed, their prayer and praise united in that Indra meet, lauding his own imperial sway.

Hymn 1:81. Indra.

1. The men have lifted Indra up, the Vṛitra slayer, to joy and strength: | Him, verily, we invocate in battles whether great or small: be he our aid in deeds of might. || 2. Thou, Hero, art a warrior, thou art giver of abundant spoil. | Strengthening e'en the feeble, thou aidest the sacrificer, thou givest the offerer ample wealth. || 3. When war and battles are on foot, booty is laid before the bold. | Yoke thou thy wildly-rushing Bays. Whom wilt thou slay and whom enrich? Do thou, O Indra, make us rich. || 4. Mighty through wisdom, as he lists, terrible, he hath waxed in strength. | Lord of Bay Steeds, strong-jawed, sublime, he in joined hands for glory's sake hath grasped his iron thunderbolt. || 5. He filled the earthly atmosphere and pressed against the lights in heaven. | None like thee ever hath been born, none, Indra, will be born like thee. Thou hast waxed mighty over all. || 6. May he who to the offerer gives the foeman's man-sustaining food, | May Indra lend his aid to us. Deal forth—abundant is thy wealth—that in thy bounty I may share. || 7. He, righteous-hearted, at each time of rapture gives us herds of kine. | Gather in both thy hands for us treasures of many hundred sorts. Sharpen thou us, and bring us wealth. || 8. Refresh thee, Hero, with the juice outpoured for bounty and for strength. | We know thee Lord of ample store, to thee have sent our hearts' desires: be therefore our Protector thou. || 9. These people, Indra, keep for thee all that is worthy of thy choice. | Discover thou, as Lord, the wealth of men who offer up no gifts: bring thou to us this wealth of theirs.

Hymn 1:82. Indra.

1. Graciously listen to our songs, Maghavan, be not negligent. | As thou hast made us full of joy and lettest us solicit thee, now, Indra, yoke thy two Bay Steeds. || 2. Well have they eaten and rejoiced; the friends have risen and passed away. | The sages luminous in themselves have. praised thee with their latest hymn. Now, Indra, yoke thy two Bay Steeds. || 3. Maghavan, we will reverence thee who art so fair to look upon. | Thus praised, according to our wish come now with richly laden car. Now, Indra, yoke thy two Bay Steeds. || 4. He will in very truth ascend the powerful car that finds the kine, | Who thinks upon the well-filled bowl, the Tawny Coursers' harnesser. Now, Indra, yoke thy two Bay Steeds. || 5. Let, Lord of Hundred Powers, thy Steeds be harnessed on the right and left. | Therewith in rapture of the juice, draw near to thy beloved Spouse. Now, Indra, yoke thy two Bay Steeds. || 6. With holy prayer I yoke thy long-maned pair of Bays: come hitherward; thou holdest them in both thy hands. | The stirring draughts of juice outpoured have made thee glad: thou, Thunderer, hast rejoiced with Pūṣhan and thy Spouse.

Hymn 1:83. Indra.

1. Indra, the mortal man well guarded by thine aid goes foremost in the wealth of horses and of kine. | With amplest wealth thou fillest him, as round about the waters clearly seen afar fill Sindhu full. || 2. The heavenly Waters come not nigh the priestly bowl: they but look down and see how far mid-air is spread: | The Deities conduct the pious man to them: like suitors they delight in him who loveth prayer. || 3. Praiseworthy blessing hast thou laid upon the pair who with uplifted ladle serve thee, man and wife. | Unchecked he dwells and prospers in thy law: thy power brings blessing to the sacrificer pouring gifts. || 4. First the Aṅgirasas won themselves vital power, whose fires were kindled through good deeds and sacrifice. | The men together found the Paṇi's hoarded wealth, the cattle, and the wealth in horses and in kine. || 5. Atharvan first by sacrifices laid the paths then, guardian of the Law, sprang up the loving Sun. | Uśanā Kāvya straightway hither drove the kine. Let us with offerings honour Yama's deathless birth. || 6. When sacred grass is trimmed to aid the auspicious work, or the hymn makes its voice of praise sound to the sky. | Where the stone rings as 'twere a singer skilled in laud,—Indra in truth delights when these come near to him.

Hymn 1:84. Indra.

1. The Soma hath been pressed for thee, O Indra; mightiest, bold One, come. | May Indra-vigour fill thee full, as the Sun fills mid-air with rays. || 2. His pair of Tawny Coursers bring Indra of unresisted might | Hither to Ṛiṣhis' songs of praise and sacrifice performed by men. || 3. Slayer of Vṛitra, mount thy car; thy Bay Steeds have been yoked by prayer. | May, with its voice, the pressing-stone draw thine attention hitherward. || 4. This poured libation, Indra, drink, immortal, gladdening, excellent. | Streams of the bright have flowed to thee here at the seat of holy Law. || 5. Sing glory now to Indra, say to him your solemn eulogies. | The drops poured forth have made him glad: pay reverence to his might supreme. || 6. When, Indra, thou dost yoke thy Steeds, there is no better charioteer: | None hath surpassed thee in thy might, none with good steeds o'ertaken thee. || 7. He who alone bestoweth on mortal man who offereth gifts, | The ruler of resistless power, is Indra, sure. || 8. When will he trample, like a weed, the man who hath no gift for him? | When, verily, will Indra hear our songs of praise? || 9. He who with Soma juice prepared amid the many honours thee, — | Verily Indra gains thereby tremendous might. || 10. The juice of Soma thus diffused, sweet to the taste, the bright cows drink, | Who for the sake of splendour close to mighty Indra's side rejoice, good in their own supremacy. || 11. Craving his touch the dappled kine mingle the Soma with their milk. | The milch-kine dear to Indra send forth his death-dealing thunderbolt, good in their own supremacy. || 12. With veneration, passing wise, honouring his victorious might, | They follow close his many laws to win them due preeminence, good in their | own supremacy. || 13. With bones of Dadhyach for his arms, Indra, resistless in attack, | Struck nine-and-ninety Vṛitras dead. || 14. He, searching for the horse's head, removed among the mountains, found | At Śaryaṇāvat what he sought. || 15. Then verily they recognized the essential form of Tvaṣhṭar's Bull, | Here in the mansion of the Moon. || 16. Who yokes today unto the pole of order the strong and passionate steers of checkless spirit, | With shaft-armed mouths, heart-piercing, health-bestowing? | Long shall he live who richly pays their service. || 17. Who fleeth forth? who suffereth? who feareth? Who knoweth Indra present, Indra near us? | Who sendeth benediction on his offspring, his household, wealth and person, and the People? || 18. Who with poured oil and offering honours Agni, with ladle worships at appointed seasons? | To whom to the Gods bring oblation quickly? What offerer, God-favoured, knows him thoroughly? || 19. Thou as a God, O Mightiest, verily blessest mortal man. | O Maghavan, there is no comforter but thou: Indra, I speak my words to thee. || 20. Let not thy bounteous gifts, let not thy saving help fail us, good Lord, at any time; | And measure out to us, thou lover of mankind, all riches hitherward from men.

Hymn 1:85. Marutas.

1. They who are glancing forth, like women, on their way, doers of mighty deeds, swift racers, Rudra's Sons, | The Marutas have made heaven and earth increase and grow: in sacrifices they delight, the strong and wild. || 2. Grown to their perfect strength greatness have they attained; the Rudras have established their abode in heaven. | Singing their song of praise and generating might, they have put glory on, the Sons whom Pṛiśni bare. || 3. When, Children of the Cow, they shine in bright attire, and on their fair limbs lay their golden ornaments, | They drive away each adversary from their path, and, following their traces, fatness floweth down, || 4. When, mighty Warriors, ye who glitter with your spears, o'erthrowing with your strength e'en what is ne'er o'erthrown, | When, O ye Marutas, ye the host that send the rain, had harnessed to your cars the thought-fleet spotted deer. || 5. When ye have harnessed to your cars the spotted deer, urging the thunderbolt, O Marutas, to the fray, | Forth rush the torrents of the dark red stormy cloud, and moisten, like a skin, the earth with water-floods. || 6. Let your swift-gliding coursers bear you hitherward with their fleet pinions. Come ye forward with your arms. | Sit on the grass; a wide seat hath been made for you: delight yourselves, O Marutas, in the pleasant food. || 7. Strong in their native strength to greatness have they grown, stepped to the firmament and made their dwelling wide. | When Viṣhṇu saved the Soma bringing wild delight, the Marutas sate like birds on their dear holy grass. || 8. In sooth like heroes fain for fight they rush about, like combatants fame-seeking have they striven in war. | Before the Marutas every creature is afraid: the men are like to Kings, terrible to behold. || 9. When Tvaṣhṭar deft of hand had turned the thunderbolt, golden, with thousand edges, fashioned more skilfully, | Indra received it to perform heroic deeds. Vṛitra he slew, and forced the flood of water forth. || 10. They with their vigorous strength pushed the well up on high, and clove the cloud in twain though it was passing strong. | The Marutas, bounteous Givers, sending forth their voice, in the wild joy of Soma wrought their glorious deeds. || 11. They drave the cloud transverse directed hitherward, and poured the fountain forth for thirsting Gotama. | Shining with varied

light they come to him with help: they with their might fulfilled the longing of the sage. ‖ 12. The shelters which ye have for him who lauds you, bestow them threefold on the man who offers. | Extend the same boons unto us, ye Marutas. Give us, O Heroes, wealth with noble offspring.

Hymn 1:86. Marutas.

1. The best of guardians hath that man within whose dwelling place ye drink, | O Marutas, giants of the sky. ‖ 2. Honoured with sacrifice or with the worship of the sages' hymns, | O Marutas, listen to the call. ‖ 3. Yea, the strong man to whom ye have vouchsafed to give a sage, shall move | Into a stable rich in kine. ‖ 4. Upon this hero's sacred grass Soma is poured in daily rites: | Praise and delight are sung aloud. ‖ 5. Let the strong Marutas hear him, him surpassing all men: strength be his | That reaches even to the Sun. ‖ 6. For, through the swift Gods' loving help, in many an autumn, Marutas, we | Have offered up our sacrifice. ‖ 7. Fortunate shall that mortal be, O Marutas most adorable, | Whose offerings ye bear away. ‖ 8. O Heroes truly strong, ye know the toil of him who sings your praise, | The heart's desire of him who loves. ‖ 9. O ye of true strength, make this thing manifest by your greatness: strike | The demon with your thunderbolt. ‖ 10. Conceal the horrid darkness, drive far from us each devouring fiend. | Create the light for which we long.

Hymn 1:87. Marutas.

1. Loud Singers, never humbled, active, full of strength, immovable, impetuous, manliest, best-beloved, | They have displayed themselves with glittering ornaments, a few in number only, like the heavens with stars. ‖ 2. When, Marutas, on the steeps ye pile the moving cloud, ye are like birds on whatsoever path it be. | Clouds everywhere shed forth the rain upon your cars. Drop fatness, honey-hued, for him who sings your praise. ‖ 3. Earth at their racings trembles as if weak and worn, when on their ways they yoke their cars for victory. | They, sportive, loudly roaring, armed with glittering spears, shakers of all, themselves admire their mightiness. ‖ 4. Self-moving is that youthful band, with spotted steeds; thus it hath lordly sway, endued with power and might. | Truthful art thou, and blameless, searcher out of sin: so thou, Strong Host, wilt be protector of this prayer. ‖ 5. We speak by our descent from our primeval Sire; our tongue, when we behold the Soma, stirs itself. | When, shouting, they had joined Indra in toil of fight, then only they obtained their sacrificial names. ‖ 6. Splendours they gained for glory, they who wear bright rings; rays they obtained, and men to celebrate their praise. | Armed with their swords, impetuous and fearing naught, they have possessed the Marutas' own beloved home.

Hymn 1:88. Marutas.

1. Come hither, Marutas, on your lightning laden cars, sounding with sweet songs, armed with lances, winged with steeds. | Fly unto us with noblest food, like birds, O ye of mighty power. ‖ 2. With their red-hued or, haply, tawny coursers which speed their chariots on, they come for glory. | Brilliant like gold is he who holds the thunder. Earth have they smitten with the chariot's felly. ‖ 3. For beauty ye have swords upon your bodies. As they stir woods so may they stir our spirits. | For your sake, O ye Marutas very mighty and well-born, have they set the stone, in motion. ‖ 4. The days went round you and came back O yearners, back, to this prayer and to this solemn worship. | The Gotamas making their prayer with singing have pushed the well's lid up to drink the water. ‖ 5. No hymn way ever known like this aforetime which Gotama sang forth for you, O Marutas, | What time upon your golden wheels he saw you, wild boars rushing about with tusks of iron. ‖ 6. To you this freshening draught of Soma rusheth, O Marutas, like the voice of one who prayeth. | It rusheth freely from our hands as these libations wont to flow.

Hymn 1:89. Viśvedevas.

1. May powers auspicious come to us from every side, never deceived, unhindered, and victorious, | That the Gods ever may be with us for our gain, our guardians day by day unceasing in their care. ‖ 2. May the auspicious favour of the Gods be ours, on us descend the bounty of the righteous Gods. | The friendship of the Gods have we devoutly sought: so may the Gods extend our life that we may live. ‖ 3. We call them hither with a hymn of olden time, Bhaga, the friendly Dakṣha, Mitra, Aditi, | Aryaman, Varuṇa, Soma, the Aśvins. May Sarasvatī, auspicious, grant felicity. ‖ 4. May the Wind waft to us that pleasant medicine, may Earth our Mother give it, and our Father Heaven, | And the joy-giving stones that press the Soma's juice. Aśvins, may ye, for whom our spirits long, hear this. ‖ 5. Him we invoke for aid who reigns supreme, the Lord of all that stands or moves, inspirer of the soul, | That Pūṣhan may promote the increase of our wealth, our keeper and our guard infallible for our good. ‖ 6. Illustrious far and wide, may Indra prosper us: may Pūṣhan prosper us, the Master of all wealth. | May Tārkṣhya with uninjured fellies prosper us: Bṛihaspati vouchsafe to us prosperity. ‖ 7. The Marutas, Sons of Pṛiśni, borne by spotted steeds, moving in glory, oft visiting holy rites, | Sages whose tongue is Agni, brilliant as the Sun,—hither let all the Gods for our protection come. ‖ 8. Gods, may we with our ears listen to what is good, and with our eyes see what is good, ye Holy Ones. | With limbs and bodies firm may we extolling you attain the term of life appointed by the Gods. ‖ 9. A hundred autumns stand before us, O ye Gods, within whose space ye bring our bodies to decay; | Within whose space our sons become fathers in turn. Break ye not in the midst our course of fleeting life. ‖ 10. Aditi is the heaven, Aditi is mid-air, Aditi is the Mother and the Sire and Son. | Aditi is all Gods, Aditi five-classed men, Aditi all that hath been born and shall be born.

Hymn 1:90. Viśvedevas.

1. May Varuṇa with guidance straight, and Mitra lead us, he who knows, | And Aryaman in accord with Gods. ‖ 2. For they are dealers forth of wealth, and, not deluded, with their might | Guard evermore the holy laws. ‖ 3. Shelter may they vouchsafe to us, Immortal Gods to mortal men, | Chasing our enemies away. ‖ 4. May they mark out our paths to bliss, Indra, the Marutas, Pūṣhan, | and Bhaga, the Gods to be adored. ‖ 5. Yea, Pūṣhan, Viṣhṇu, ye who run your course, enrich our hymns with kine; | Bless us with all prosperity. ‖ 6. The winds waft sweets, the rivers pour sweets for the man who keeps the Law | So may the plants be sweet for us. ‖ 7. Sweet be the night and sweet the dawns, sweet the terrestrial atmosphere; | Sweet be our Father Heaven to us. ‖ 8. May the tall tree be full of sweets for us, and full of sweets the Sun: | May our milch-kine be sweet for us. ‖ 9. Be Mitra gracious unto us, and Varuṇa and Aryaman: | Indra, Bṛihaspati be kind, and Viṣhṇu of the mighty stride.

Hymn 1:91. Soma.

1. Thou, Soma, art preeminent for wisdom; along the straightest path thou art our leader. | Our wise forefathers by thy guidance, Indu, dealt out among the Gods their share of treasure. ‖ 2. Thou by thine insight art most wise, O Soma, strong by thine energies and all possessing, | Mighty art thou by all thy powers and greatness, by glories art thou glorious, guide of mortals. ‖ 3. Thine are King Varuṇa's eternal statutes, lofty and deep, O Soma, is thy glory. | All-pure art thou like Mitra the beloved, adorable, like Aryaman, O Soma. ‖ 4. With all thy glories on the earth, in heaven, on mountains, in the plants, and in the waters,— | With all of these, well-pleased and not in anger, accept, O royal Soma, our oblations. ‖ 5. Thou, Soma, art the Lord of heroes, King, yea, Vṛitra-slayer thou: | Thou art auspicious energy. ‖ 6. And, Soma, let it be thy wish that we may live and may not die: | Praise-loving Lord of plants art thou. ‖ 7. To him who keeps the law, both old and young, thou givest happiness, | And energy that he may live. ‖ 8. Guard us, King Soma, on all sides from him who threatens us: never let | The friend of one like thee be harmed. ‖ 9. With those delightful aids which thou hast, Soma, for the worshipper,— | Even with those protect thou us. ‖ 10. Accepting this our sacrifice and this our praise, O Soma, come, | And be thou nigh to prosper us. ‖ 11. Well-skilled in speech we magnify thee, Soma, with our sacred songs: | Come thou to us, most gracious One. ‖ 12. Enricher, healer of disease, wealth-finder, prospering our store, | Be, Soma, a good Friend to us. ‖ 13. Soma, be happy in our heart, as milch-kine in the grassy meads, | As a young man in his own house. ‖ 14. O Soma, God, the mortal man who in thy friendship hath delight, | Him doth the mighty Sage befriend. ‖ 15. Save us from slanderous reproach, keep us, O Soma, from distress: | Be unto us a gracious Friend. ‖ 16. Soma, wax great. From every side may vigorous powers unite in thee: | Be in the gathering-place of strength. ‖ 17. Wax, O most gladdening Soma, great through all thy rays of light, and be | A Friend of most illustrious fame to prosper us. ‖ 16. In thee be juicy nutriments united, and powers and mighty foe-subduing vigour, | Waxing to immortality, O Soma: win highest glories for thyself in heaven. ‖ 19. Such of thy glories as with poured

oblations men honour, may they all invest our worship. | Wealth-giver, furtherer with troops of heroes, sparing the brave, come, Soma, to our houses. || 20. To him who worships Soma gives the milch-cow, a fleet steed and a man of active knowledge, | Skilled in home duties, meet for holy synod, for council meet, a glory to his father. || 21. Invincible in fight, saver in battles, guard of our camp, winner of light and water, | Born amid hymns, well-housed, exceeding famous, victor, in thee will we rejoice, O Soma. || 22. These herbs, these milch-kine, and these running waters, all these, O Soma, thou hast generated. | The spacious firmament bast thou expanded, and with the light thou hast dispelled the darkness. || 23. Do thou, God Soma, with thy Godlike spirit, victorious, win for us a share of riches. | Let none prevent thee: thou art Lord of valour. Provide for both sides in the fray for booty.

Hymn 1:92. Dawn.

1. These Dawns have raised their banner; in the eastern half of the mid-air they spread abroad their shining light. | Like heroes who prepare their weapons for the war, onward they come bright red in hue, the Mother Cows. || 2. Readily have the purple beams of light shot up; the Red Cows have they harnessed, easy to be yoked. | The Dawns have brought distinct perception as before: red-hued, they have attained their fulgent brilliancy. || 3. They sing their song like women active in their tasks, along their common path hither from far away, | Bringing refreshment to the liberal devotee, yea, all things to the worshipper who pours the juice. || 4. She, like a dancer, puts her broidered garments on: as a cow yields her udder so she bares her breast. | Creating light for all the world of life, the Dawn hath laid the darkness open as the cows their stall. || 5. We have beheld the brightness of her shining; it spreads and drives away the darksome monster. | Like tints that deck the Post at sacrifices, Heaven's Daughter hath attained her wondrous splendour. || 6. We have o'erpast the limit of this darkness; Dawn breaking forth again brings clear perception. | She like a flatterer smiles in light for glory, and fair of face hath wakened to rejoice us. || 7. The Gotamas have praised Heaven's radiant Daughter, the leader of the charm of pleasant voices. | Dawn, thou conferrest on us strength with offspring and men, conspicuous with kine and horses. || 8. O thou who shinest forth in wondrous glory, urged onward by thy strength, auspicious Lady, | Dawn, may I gain that wealth, renowned and ample, in brave sons, troops of slaves, far-famed for horses. || 9. Bending her looks on all the world, the Goddess shines, widely spreading with her bright eye westward. | Waking to motion every living creature, she understands the voice of each adorer. || 10. Ancient of days, again again born newly, decking her beauty with the self-same raiment. | The Goddess wastes away the life of mortals, like a skilled hunter cutting birds in pieces. || 11. She hath appeared discovering heaven's borders: to the far distance she drives off her Sister. | Diminishing the days of human creatures, the Lady shines with all her lover's splendour. || 12. The bright, the blessed One shines forth extending her rays like kine, as a flood rolls his waters. | Never transgressing the divine commandments, she is beheld visible with the sunbeams. || 13. O Dawn enriched with ample wealth, bestow on us the wondrous gift | Wherewith we may support children and children's sons. || 14. Thou radiant mover of sweet sounds, with wealth of horses and of kine | Shine thou on us this day, O Dawn auspiciously. || 15. O Dawn enriched with holy rites, yoke to thy car thy purple steeds, | And then bring thou unto us all felicities. || 16. O Aśvins wonderful in act, do ye unanimous direct | Your chariot to our home wealthy in kine and gold. || 17. Ye who brought down the hymn from heaven, a light that giveth light to man, | Do ye, O Aśvins, bring strength hither unto us. || 18. Hither may they who wake at dawn bring, to drink Soma both the Gods | Health-givers Wonder-Workers, borne on paths of gold.

Hymn 1:93. Agni-Soma.

1. Agni and Soma, mighty Pair, graciously hearken to my call, | Accept in friendly wise my hymn, and prosper him who offers gifts. || 2. The man who honours you today, Agni and Soma, with this hymn, | Bestow on him heroic strength, increase of kine, and noble steeds. || 3. The man who offers holy oil and burnt oblations unto you, | Agni and Soma, shall enjoy great strength, with offspring, all his life. || 4. Agni and Soma, famed is that your. prowess wherewith ye stole the kine, his food, from Paṇi. | Ye caused the brood of Bṛisaya to perish; ye found the light, the single light for many. || 5. Agni and Soma, joined in operation ye have set up the shining lights in heaven. | From curse and from reproach, Agni and Soma, ye freed the rivers that were bound in fetters. || 6. One of you Mātariśvan brought from heaven, the Falcon rent the other from the mountain. | Strengthened by holy prayer Agni and Soma have made us ample room for sacrificing. || 7. Taste, Agni, Soma, this prepared oblation; accept it, Mighty Ones, and let it please you. | Vouchsafe us good protection and kind favour: grant to the sacrificer health and riches. || 8. Whoso with oil and poured oblation honours, with God-devoted heart, Agni and Soma,— | Protect his sacrifice, preserve him from distress, grant to the sacrificer great felicity. || 9. Invoked together, mates in wealth, Agni-Soma, accept our hymns: | Together be among the Gods. || 10. Agni and Soma, unto him who worships you with holy oil | Shine forth an ample recompense. || 11. Agni and Soma, be ye pleased with these oblations brought to you, | And come, together, nigh to us. || 12. Agni and Soma, cherish well our horses, and let our cows be fat who yield oblations. | Grant power to us and to our wealthy patrons, and cause our holy rites to be successful.

Hymn 1:94. Agni.

1. For Jātavedas worthy of our praise will we frame with our mind this eulogy as 'twere a car. | For good, in his assembly, is this care of ours. Let us not, in thy friendship, Agni, suffer harm. || 2. The man for whom thou sacrificest prospereth, dwelleth without a foe, gaineth heroic might. | He waxeth strong, distress never approacheth him. Let us not, in thy friendship, Agni, suffer harm. || 3. May we have power to kindle thee. Fulfil our thoughts. In thee the Gods eat the presented offering, | Bring hither the Ādityas, for we long for them. Let us not in thy friendship, Agni, suffer harm. || 4. We will bring fuel and prepare burnt offerings, reminding thee at each successive festival. | Fulfil our thought that so we may prolong our lives. Let us not in thy friendship, Agni, suffer harm. || 5. His ministers move forth, the guardians of the folk, protecting quadruped and biped with their rays. | Mighty art thou, the wondrous herald of the Dawn. Let us not in thy friendship, Agni, suffer harm. || 6. Thou art Presenter and the chief Invoker, thou Director, Purifier, great High Priest by birth. | Knowing all priestly work thou perfectest it, Sage. Let us not in thy friendship, Agni, suffer harm. || 7. Lovely of form art thou, alike on every side; though far, thou shinest brightly as if close at hand. | O God, thou seest through even the dark of night. Let us not in thy friendship, Agni, suffer harm. || 8. Gods, foremost be his car who pours libations out, and let our hymn prevail o'er evil-hearted men. | Attend to this our speech and make it prosper well. Let us not in thy friendship, Agni, suffer harm. || 9. Smite with thy weapons those of evil speech and thought, devouring demons, whether near or tar away. | Then to the singer give free way for sacrifice. Let us not in thy friendship, Agni, suffer harm. || 10. When to thy chariot thou hadst yoked two red steeds and two ruddy steeds, wind-sped, thy roar was like a bull's. | Thou with smoke-bannered flame attackest forest trees. Let us not in thy friendship, Agni, suffer harm. || 11. Then at thy roar the very birds are terrified, when, eating-up the grass, thy sparks fly forth abroad. | Then is it easy for thee and thy car to pass. Let us not in thy friendship, Agni, suffer harm. || 12. He hath the Power to soothe Mitra and Varuṇa: wonderful is the Marutas' wrath when they descend. | Be gracious; let their hearts he turned to us again. Let us not in thy friendship, Agni, suffer harm. || 13. Thou art a God, thou art the wondrous Friend of Gods, the Vasu of the Vasus, fair in sacrifice. | Under, thine own most wide protection may we dwell. Let us not in thy friendship, Agni, suffer harm. || 14. This is thy grace that, kindled in thine own abode, invoked with Soma thou soundest forth most benign, | Thou givest wealth and treasure to the worshipper. Let us not in thy friendship, Agni, suffer harm. || 15. To whom thou, Lord of goodly riches, grantest freedom from every sin with perfect wholeness, | Whom with good strength thou quikenest, with children and wealth—may we be they, Eternal Being. || 16. Such, Agni, thou who knowest all good fortune, God, lengthen here the days of our existence. | This prayer of ours may Varuṇa grant, and Mitra, and Aditi and Sindhu, Earth and Heaven.

Hymn 1:95. Agni.

1. To fair goals travel Two unlike in semblance: each in succession nourishes an infant. | One bears a Godlike Babe of golden colour; bright

and fair-shining, is he with the other. ‖ 2. Tvaṣhṭar's ten daughters, vigilant and youthful, produced this Infant borne to sundry quarters. | They bear around him whose long flames are pointed, fulgent among mankind with native splendour. ‖ 3. Three several places of his birth they honour, in mid-air, in the heaven, and in the waters. | Governing in the east of earthly regions, the seasons hath he established in their order. ‖ 4. Who of you knows this secret One? The Infant by his own nature hath brought forth his Mothers. | The germ of many, from the waters' bosom he goes forth, wise and great, of Godlike nature. ‖ 5. Visible, fair, he grows in native brightness uplifted in the lap of waving waters. | When he was born both Tvaṣhṭar's worlds were frightened: they turn to him and reverence the Lion. ‖ 6. The Two auspicious Ones, like women, tend him: like lowing cows they seek him in their manner. | He is the Lord of Might among the mighty; him, on the right, they balm with their oblations. ‖ 7. Like Savitar his arms with might he stretches; awful, he strives grasping the world's two borders. | He forces out from all a brilliant vesture, yea, from his Mothers draws he forth new raiment. ‖ 8. He makes him a most noble form of splendour, decking him in his home with milk and waters. | The Sage adorns the depths of air with wisdom: this is the meeting where the Gods are worshipped. ‖ 9. Wide through the firmament spreads forth triumphant the far-resplendent strength of thee the Mighty. | Kindled by us do thou preserve us, Agni, with all thy self-bright undiminished succours. ‖ 10. In dry spots he makes stream, and course, and torrent, and inundates the earth with floods that glisten. | All ancient things within his maw he gathers, and moves among the new fresh-sprouting grasses. ‖ 11. Fed with our fuel, purifying Agni, so blaze to us auspiciously for glory. | This prayer of ours may Varuṇa grant, and Mitra, and Aditi and Sindhu, Earth and Heaven.

Hymn 1:96. Agni.

1. He in the ancient way by strength engendered, lo! straight hath taken to himself all wisdom. | The waters and the bowl have made him friendly. The Gods possessed the wealth bestowing Agni. ‖ 2. At Āyu's ancient call he by his wisdom gave all this progeny of men their being, | And, by refulgent light, heaven and the waters. The Gods possessed the wealth. bestowing Agni. ‖ 3. Praise him, ye Ārya folk, as chief performer of sacrifice adored and ever toiling, | Well-tended, Son of Strength, the Constant Giver. The Gods possessed the wealth bestowing Agni. ‖ 4. That Mātariśvan rich in wealth and treasure, light-winner, finds a pathway for his offspring. | Guard of our folk, Father of earth and heaven. The Gods possessed the wealth bestowing Agni. ‖ 5. Night and Dawn, changing each the other's colour, meeting together suckle one same Infant: | Golden between the heaven and earth he shineth. The Gods possessed the wealth bestowing Agni. ‖ 6. Root of wealth, gathering-place of treasures, banner of sacrifice, who grants the suppliant's wishes: | Preserving him as their own life immortal, the Gods possessed the wealth-bestowing Agni. ‖ 7. Now and of old the home of wealth, the mansion of what is born and what was born aforetime, | Guard of what is and what will be hereafter,—the Gods possessed the wealth bestowing Agni. ‖ 8. May the Wealth-Giver grant us conquering riches; may the Wealth-Giver grant us wealth with heroes. | May the Wealth-Giver grant us food with offspring, and length of days may the Wealth-Giver send us. ‖ 9. Fed with our fuel, purifying Agni, so blaze to us auspiciously for glory. | This prayer of ours may Varuṇa grant, and Mitra, and Aditi and Sindhu, Earth and Heaven.

Hymn 1:97. Agni.

1. Chasing with light our sin away, O Agni, shine thou wealth on us. | May his light chase our sin away. ‖ 2. For goodly fields, for pleasant homes, for wealth we sacrifice to thee. | May his light chase our sin away. ‖ 3. Best praiser of all these be he; foremost, our chiefs who sacrifice. | May his light chase our sin away. ‖ 4. So that thy worshippers and we, thine, Agni, in our sons may live. | May his light chase our sin away. ‖ 5. As ever-conquering Agni's beams of splendour go to every side, | May his light chase our sin away. ‖ 6. To every side thy face is turned, thou art triumphant everywhere. | May his light chase our sin away. ‖ 7. O thou whose face looks every way, bear us past foes as in a ship. | May his light chase our sin away. ‖ 8. As in a ship, convey thou us for our advantage o'er the flood. | May his light chase our sin away.

Hymn 1:98. Agni.

1. Still in Vaiśvānara's grace may we continue: yea, he is King supreme o'er all things living. | Sprung hence to life upon this All he looketh. Vaiśvānara hath rivalry with Sūrya. ‖ 2. Present in heaven, in earth, all-present Agni, —all plants that grow on ground hath he pervaded. | May Agni, may Vaiśvānara with vigour, present, preserve us day and night from foemen. ‖ 3. Be this thy truth, Vaiśvānara, to us-ward: let wealth in rich abundance gather round us. | This prayer of ours may Varuṇa grant, and Mitra, and Aditi and Sindhu, Earth and Heaven.

Hymn 1:99. Agni.

1. For Jātavedas let us press the Soma: may he consume the wealth of the malignant. | May Agni carry us through all our troubles, through grief as in a boat across the river.

Hymn 1:100. Indra.

1. May he who hath his home with strength, the Mighty, the King supreme of earth and spacious heaven, | Lord of true power, to he invoked in battles,—may Indra, girt by Marutas, be our succour. ‖ 2. Whose way is unattainable like Sūrya's: he in each fight is the strong Vṛitra-slayer, | Mightiest with his Friends in his own courses. May Indra, girt by Marutas, be our succour. ‖ 3. Whose paths go forth in their great might resistless, forthmilking, as it were, heaven's genial moisture. | With manly strength triumphant, foe-subduer,—may Indra, girt by Marutas, be our succour. ‖ 4. Among Aṅgirasas he was the chiefest, a Friend with friends, mighty amid the mighty. | Praiser mid praisers, honoured most of singers. May Indra, girt by Marutas, be our succour. ‖ 5. Strong with the Rudras as with his own children, in manly battle conquering his foemen | With his close comrades doing deeds of glory,—may Indra, girt by Marutas, be our succour. ‖ 6. Humbler of pride, exciter of the conflict, the Lord of heroes, God invoked of many, | May he this day gain with our men the sunlight. May Indra, girt by Marutas, be our succour. ‖ 7. His help hath made him cheerer in the battle, the folk have made him guardian of their comfort. | Sole Lord is he of every holy service. May Indra, girt by Marutas, be our succour. ‖ 8. To him the Hero, on high days of prowess, heroes for help and booty shall betake them. | He hath found light even in the blinding darkness. May Indra, girt by Marutas, be our succour. ‖ 9. He with his left hand checketh even the mighty, and with his right hand gathereth up the booty. | Even with the humble he acquireth riches. May Indra, girt by Marutas, be our succour. ‖ 10. With hosts on foot and cars he winneth treasures: well is he known this day by all the people. | With manly might he conquereth those who hate him. May Indra, girt by Marutas, be our succour. ‖ 11. When in his ways with kinsmen or with strangers he speedeth to the fight, invoked of many, | For gain of waters, and of sons and grandsons, may Indra, girt by Marutas, be our succour. ‖ 12. Awful and fierce, fiend-slayer, thunder-wielder, with boundless knowledge, hymned by hundreds, mighty, | In strength like Soma, guard of the Five Peoples, may Indra, girt by Marutas, be our succour. ‖ 13. Winning the light, hitherward roars his thunder like the terrific mighty voice of Heaven. | Rich gifts and treasures evermore attend him. May Indra, girt by Marutas, be our succour. ‖ 14. Whose home eternal through his strength surrounds him on every side, his laud, the earth and heaven, | May he, delighted with our service, save us. May Indra, girt by Marutas, be our succour. ‖ 15. The limit of whose power not Gods by Godhead, nor mortal men have reached, nor yet the Waters. | Both Earth and Heaven in vigour he surpasseth. May Indra, girt by Marutas, he our succour. ‖ 16. The red and tawny mare, blaze-marked, high standing, celestial who, to bring Ṛijrāśva riches, | Drew at the pole the chariot yoked with stallions, joyous, among the hosts of men was noted. ‖ 17. The Vārṣhāgiras unto thee, O Indra, the Mighty One, sing forth this laud to please thee, | Ṛijrāśva with his fellows, Ambarīṣha, Surādhas, Sahadeva, Bhayamāna. ‖ 18. He, much invoked, hath slain Dasyus and Śimyus, after his wont, and laid them low with arrows. | The mighty Thunderer with his fair-complexioned friends won the land, the sunlight, and the waters. ‖ 19. May Indra evermore be our protector, and unimperilled may we win the booty. | This prayer of ours may Varuṇa grant, and Mitra, and Aditi and Sindhu, Earth and Heaven.

Hymn 1:101. Indra.

1. Sing, with oblation, praise to him who maketh glad, who with Ṛijiśvan drove the dusky brood away. | Fain for help, him the strong whose right

hand wields the bolt, him girt by Marutas we invoke to be our Friend. || 2. Indra, who with triumphant wrath smote Vyaṃsa down, and Śambara, and Pipru the unrighteous one; | Who extirpated Śuṣhṇa the insatiate,—him girt by Marutas we invoke to be our Friend. || 3. He whose great work of manly might is heaven and earth, and Varuṇa and Sūrya keep his holy law; | Indra, whose law the rivers follow as they flow,—him girt by Marutas we invoke to be our Friend. || 4. He who is Lord and Master of the steeds and kine, honoured—the firm and sure—at every holy act; | Stayer even of the strong who pours no offering out,—him girt by Marutas we invoke to be our Friend. || 5. He who is Lord of all the world that moves and breathes, who for the Brahman first before all found the Cows; | Indra who cast the Dasyus down beneath his feet,—him girt by Marutas we invoke to be our Friend. || 6. Whom cowards must invoke and valiant men of war, invoked by those who conquer and by those who flee; | Indra, to whom all beings turn their constant thought,—him girt by Marutas we invoke to be our Friend. || 7. Refulgent in the Rudras' region he proceeds, and with the Rudras through the wide space speeds the Dame. | The hymn of praise extols Indra the far-renowned: him girt by Marutas we invoke to be our Friend. || 8. O girt by Marutas, whether thou delight thee in loftiest gathering-place or lowly dwelling, | Come thence unto our rite, true boon-bestower: through love of thee have we prepared oblations. || 9. We, fain for thee, strong Indra, have pressed Soma, and, O thou sought with prayer, have made oblations. | Now at this sacrifice, with all thy Marutas, on sacred grass, O team-borne God, rejoice thee. || 10. Rejoice thee with thine own Bay Steeds, O Indra, unclose thy jaws and let thy lips be open. | Thou with the fair cheek, let thy Bay Steeds bring thee: gracious to us, he pleased with our oblation. || 11. Guards of the camp whose praisers are the Marutas, may we through Indra, get ourselves the booty. | This prayer of ours may Varuṇa grant, and Mitra, and Aditi and Sindhu, Earth and Heaven.

Hymn 1:102. Indra.

1. To thee the Mighty One I bring this mighty hymn, for thy desire hath been gratified by my laud. | In Indra, yea in him victorious through his strength, the Gods have joyed at feast and when the Soma flowed. || 2. The Seven Rivers bear his glory far and wide, and heaven and sky and earth display his comely form. | The Sun and Moon in change alternate run their course, that we, O Indra, may behold and may have faith. || 3. Maghavan, grant us that same car to bring us spoil, thy conquering car in which we joy in shock of fight. | Thou, Indra, whom our hearts praise highly in the war, grant shelter, Maghavan, to us who love thee well. || 4. Encourage thou our side in every fight: may we, with thee for our ally, conquer the foeman's host. | Indra, bestow on us joy and felicity break down, O Maghavan, the vigour of our foes. || 5. For here in divers ways these men invoking thee, holder of treasures, sing hymns to win thine aid. | Ascend the car that thou mayest bring spoil to us, for, Indra, thy fixt winneth the victory. || 6. His arms win kine, his power is boundless in each act best, with a hundred helps waker of battle's din | Is Indra: none may rival him in mighty strength. Hence, eager for the spoil the people call on him. || 7. Thy glory, Maghavan, exceeds a hundred yea, more than a hundred, than a thousand mid the folk, | The great bowl hath inspirited thee boundlessly: so mayst thou slay the Vṛitras breaker-down of forts! || 8. Of thy great might there is a three counterpart, the three earths, Lord men and the three realms of light. | Above this whole world, Indra, thou hast waxen great: without a foe art thou, nature, from of old. || 9. We invocate thee first among the Deities: thou hast become a mighty Conquer in fight. | May Indra fill with spirit this our singer's heart, and make our car impetuous, foremost in attack. || 10. Thou hast prevailed, and hast not kept the booty back, in trifling battles in those of great account. | We make thee keen, the Mighty One, succour us: inspire us, Maghavan, when we defy the foe. || 11. May Indra evermore be our Protector, and unimperilled may we win the booty. | This prayer of ours may Varuṇa grant and Mitra, and Aditi and Sindhu, Earth and Heaven.

Hymn 1:103. Indra.

1. That highest Indra-power of thine is distant: that which is here sages possessed aforetime. | This one is on the earth, in heaven the other, and both unite as flag with flag in battle. || 2. He spread the wide earth out and firmly fixed it, smote with his thunderbolt and loosed the waters. | Maghavan with his puissance struck down Ahi, rent Rauhiṇa to death and slaughtered Vyaṃsa. || 3. Armed with his bolt and trusting in his prowess he wandered shattering the forts of Dāsas. | Cast thy dart, knowing, Thunderer, at the Dasyu; increase the Ārya's might and glory, Indra. || 4. For him who thus hath taught these human races, Maghavan, bearing a fame-worthy title, | Thunderer, drawing nigh to slay the Dasyus, hath given himself the name of Son for glory. || 5. See this abundant wealth that he possesses, and put your trust in Indra's hero vigour. | He found the cattle, and he found the horses, he found the plants, the forests and the waters. || 6. To him the truly strong, whose deeds are many, to him the strong Bull let us pour the Soma. | The Hero, watching like a thief in ambush, goes parting the possessions of the godless. || 7. Well didst thou do that hero deed, O Indra, in waking with thy bolt the slumbering Ahi. | in thee, delighted, Dames divine rejoiced them, the flying Marutas and all Gods were joyful. || 8. As thou hast smitten Śuṣhṇa, Pipru, Vṛitra and Kuyava, and Śambara's forts O Indra. | This prayer of ours may Varuṇa grant, and Mitra, and Aditi and Sindhu, Earth and Heaven.

Hymn 1:104. Indra.

1. The altar hath been made for thee to rest on: come like a panting courser and be seated. | Loosen thy flying Steeds, set free thy Horses who bear thee swiftly nigh at eve and morning. || 2. These men have come to Indra for assistance: shall he not quickly come upon these pathways? | May the Gods quell the fury of the Dāsa, and may they lead our folk to happy fortune. || 3. He who hath only wish as his possession casts on himself, casts foam amid the waters. | Both wives of Kuyava in milk have bathed them: may they be drowned within the depth of Śiphā. || 4. This hath his kinship checked who lives beside us: with ancient streams forth speeds and rules the Hero, | Añjasī, Kuliśī, and Vīrapatnī, delighting him, bear milk upon their waters. || 5. Soon as this Dasyu's traces were discovered, as she who knows her home, he sought the dwelling. | Now think thou of us, Maghavan, nor cast us away as doth a profligate his treasure. || 6. Indra, as such, give us a share of sunlight, of waters, sinlessness, and reputation. | Do thou no harm to our yet unborn offspring: our trust is in thy mighty Indra-power. || 7. Now we, I think, in thee as such have trusted: lead us on, Mighty One, to ample riches. | In no unready house give us, O Indra invoked of many, food and drink when hungry. || 8. Slay us not, Indra; do not thou forsake us: steal not away the joys which we delight in. | Rend not our unborn brood, strong Lord of Bounty! our vessels with the life that is within them. || 9. Come to us; they have called thee Soma-lover: here is the pressed juice. Drink thereof for rapture. | Widely-capacious, pour it down within thee, and, invocated, hear us like a Father.

Hymn 1:105. Viśvedevas.

1. Within the waters runs the Moon, he with the beauteous wings in heaven. | Ye lightnings with your golden wheels, men find not your abiding-place. Mark this my woe, ye Earth and Heaven. || 2. Surely men crave and gain their wish. Close to her husband clings the wife. | And, in embraces intertwined, both give and take the bliss of love. Mark this my woe, ye Earth and Heaven. || 3. O never may that light, ye Gods, fall from its station in the sky. | Ne'er fail us one like Soma sweet, the spring of our felicity. Mark this my woe ye Earth and Heaven. || 4. I ask the last of sacrifice. As envoy he shall tell it forth. | Where is the ancient law divine? Who is its new diffuser now? Mark this my woe, ye Earth and Heaven. || 5. Ye Gods who yonder have your home in the three lucid realms of heaven, | What count ye truth and what untruth? Where is mine ancient call on you? Mark this my woe, ye Earth and Heaven. || 6. What is your firm support of Law? What Varuṇa's observant eye? | How may we pass the wicked on the path of mighty Aryaman? Mark this my woe, ye Earth and Heaven. || 7. I am the man who sang of old full many a laud when Soma flowed. | Yet torturing cares consume me as the wolf assails the thirsty deer. Mark this my woe, ye Earth and Heaven. || 8. Like rival wives on every side enclosing ribs oppress me sore. | O Śatakratu, biting cares devour me, singer of thy praise, as rats devour the weaver's threads. Mark this my woe, ye Earth and Heaven. || 9. Where those seven rays are shining, thence my home and family extend. | This Trita Āptya knoweth well, and speaketh out for brotherhood. Mark this my woe, ye Earth and Heaven. || 10. May those five Bulls which stand on high full in the midst of mighty heaven, | Having together swiftly borne my praises to the Gods, return. Mark this

my woe, ye Earth and Heaven. || 11. High in the mid ascent of heaven those Birds of beauteous pinion sit. | Back from his path they drive the wolf as he would cross the restless floods. Mark this my woe, ye Earth and Heaven. || 12. Firm is this new-wrought hymn of praise, and meet to be told forth, O Gods. | The flowing of the floods is Law, Truth is the Sun's extended light. Mark this my woe, ye Earth and Heaven. || 13. Worthy of laud, O Agni, is that kinship which thou hast with Gods. | Here seat thee like a man: most wise, bring thou the Gods for sacrifice. Mark this my woe, ye Earth and Heaven. || 14. Here seated, man-like as a priest shall wisest Agni to the Gods | Speed onward our oblations, God among the Gods, intelligent. Mark this my woe, ye Earth and Heaven. || 15. Varuṇa makes the holy prayer. To him who finds the path we pray. | He in the heart reveals his thought. Let sacred worship rise anew. Mark this my woe, ye Earth and Heaven. || 16. That pathway of the Sun in heaven, made to be highly glorified, | Is not to be transgressed, O Gods. O mortals, ye behold it not. Mark this my woe, ye Earth and Heaven. || 17. Trita, when buried in the well, calls on the Gods to succour him. | That call of his Bṛihaspati heard and released him from distress. Mark this my woe, ye Earth and Heaven. || 18. A ruddy wolf beheld me once, as I was faring on my path. | He, like a carpenter whose back is aching crouched and slunk away. Mark this my woe, ye Earth and Heaven. || 19. Through this our song may we, allied with Indra, with all our heroes conquer in the battle. | This prayer of ours may Varuṇa grant, and Mitra, and Aditi and Sindhu, Earth and Heaven.

Hymn 1:106. Viśvedevas.

1. Call we for aid on Indra, Mitra, Varuṇa and Agni and the Marut host and Aditi. | Even as a chariot from a difficult ravine, bountiful Vasus, rescue us from all distress. || 2. Come ye Ādityas for our full prosperity, in conquests of the foe, ye Gods, bring joy to us. | Even as a chariot from a difficult ravine, bountiful Vasus, rescue us from all distress. || 3. May the most glorious Fathers aid us, and the two Goddesses, Mothers of the Gods, who strengthen Law. | Even as a chariot from a difficult ravine, bountiful Vasus, rescue us from all distress. || 4. To mighty Narāśaṃsa, strengthening his might, to Pūṣhan, ruler over men, we pray with hymns. | Even as a chariot from a difficult ravine, bountiful Vasus, rescue us from all distress. || 5. Bṛihaspati, make us evermore an easy path: we crave what boon thou hast for men in rest and stir. | Like as a chariot from a difficult ravine, bountiful Vasus, rescue us from all distress. || 6. Sunk in the pit the Ṛishi Kutsa called, to aid, Indra the Vṛitra-slayer, Lord of power and might. | Even as a chariot from a difficult ravine, bountiful Vasus, rescue us from all distress. || 7. May Aditi the Goddess guard us with the Gods: may the protecting God keep us with ceaseless care. | This prayer of ours may Varuṇa grant, and Mitra, and Aditi and Sindhu, Earth and Heaven.

Hymn 1:107. Viśvedevas.

1. The sacrifice obtains the Gods' acceptance: be graciously inclined to us, Ādityas. | Hitherward let your favour be directed, and be our best deliverer from trouble. || 2. By praise-songs of Aṅgirasas exalted, may the Gods come to us with their protection. | May Indra with his powers, Marutas with Marutas, Aditi with Ādityas grant us shelter. || 3. This laud of ours may Varuṇa and Indra, Aryaman Agni, Savitar find pleasant. | This prayer' of ours may Varuṇa grant, and Mitra, and Aditi and Sindhu, Earth and Heaven.

Hymn 1:108. Indra-Agni.

1. On that most wondrous car of yours, O Indra and Agni, which looks round on all things living, | Take ye your stand and come to us together, and drink libations of the flowing Soma. || 2. As vast as all this world is in its compass, deep as it is, with its far-stretching surface, | So let this Soma be, Indra and Agni, made for your drinking till your soul be sated. || 3. For ye have won a blessed name together: yea, with one aim ye strove, O Vṛitra-slayers. | So Indra-Agni, seated here together, pour in, ye Mighty Ones, the mighty Soma. || 4. Both stand adorned, when fires are duly kindled, spreading the sacred grass, with lifted ladles. | Drawn by strong Soma juice poured forth around us, come, Indra-Agni, and display your favour. || 5. The brave deeds ye have done, Indra and Agni, the forms ye have displayed and mighty exploits, | The ancient and auspicious bonds of friendship,—for sake of these drink of the flowing Soma. || 6. As first I said when choosing you, in battle we must contend with Asuras for this Soma. | So came ye unto this my true conviction, and drank libations of the flowing Soma. || 7. If in your dwelling, or with prince or Brahman, ye, Indra-Agni, Holy Ones, rejoice you, | Even from thence, ye mighty Lords, come hither, and drink libation of the flowing Soma. || 8. If with, the Yadus, Turvaśas, ye sojourn, with Druhyus, Anus, Pūrus, Indra-Agni! | Even from thence, ye mighty Lords, come hither, and drink libations of the flowing Soma. || 9. Whether, O Indra-Agni, ye be dwelling in lowest earth, in central, or in highest. | Even from thence, ye mighty Lords, come hither, and drink libations of the flowing Soma. || 10. Whether, O Indra-Agni, ye be dwelling in highest earth, in central, or in lowest, | Even from thence, ye mighty Lords, come hither, and drink libations of the flowing Soma. || 11. Whether ye be in heaven, O Indra-Agni, on earth, on mountains, in the herbs, or waters, | Even from thence, ye mighty Lords, come hither, and drink libations of the flowing Soma. || 12. If, when the Sun to the mid-heaven hath mounted, ye take delight in food, O Indra-Agni, | Even from thence, ye mighty Lords, come hither, and drink libations of the flowing Soma. || 13. Thus having drunk your fill of our libation, win us all kinds of wealth, Indra and Agni. | This prayer of ours may Varuṇa grant, and Mitra, and Aditi and Sindhu, Earth and Heaven.

Hymn 1:109. Indra-Agni.

1. Longing for weal I looked around, in spirit, for kinsmen, Indra-Agni, or for brothers. | No providence but yours alone is with me so have I wrought for you this hymn for succour. || 2. For I have heard that ye give wealth more freely than worthless son-in-law or spouse's brother. | So offering to you this draught of Soma, I make you this new hymn, Indra and Agni, || 3. Let us not break the cords: with this petition we strive to gain the powers of our forefathers. | For Indra-Agni the strong drops are joyful, for here in the bowl's lap are both the press-stones. || 4. For you the bowl divine, Indra and Agni, presses the Soma gladly to delight you. | With hands auspicious and fair arms, ye Aśvins, haste, sprinkle it with sweetness in the waters. || 5. You, I have heard, were mightiest, Indra-Agni, when Vṛitra fell and when the spoil was parted. | Sit at this sacrifice, ye ever active, on the strewn grass, and with the juice delight you. || 6. Surpassing all men where they shout for battle, ye Twain exceed the earth and heaven in greatness. | Greater are ye than rivers and than mountains, O Indra-Agni, and all things beside them. || 7. Bring wealth and give it, ye whose arms wield thunder: Indra and Agni, with your powers protect us. | Now of a truth these be the very sunbeams wherewith our fathers were of old united. || 8. Give, ye who shatter forts, whose hands wield thunder: Indra and Agni, save us in our battles. | This prayer of ours may Varuṇa grant, and Mitra, and Aditi and Sindhu, Earth and Heaven.

Hymn 1:110. Ṛibhus.

1. The holy work I wrought before is wrought again: my sweetest hymn is sung to celebrate your praise. | Here, O ye Ṛibhus, is this sea for all the Gods: sate you with Soma offered with the hallowing word. || 2. When, seeking your enjoyment onward from afar, ye, certain of my kinsmen, wandered on your way, | Sons of Sudhanvan, after your long journeying, ye came unto the home of liberal Savitar. || 3. Savitar therefore gave you immortality, because ye came proclaiming him whom naught can hide; | And this the drinking-chalice of the Asura, which till that time was one, ye made to be fourfold. || 4. When they had served with zeal at sacrifice as priests, they, mortal as they were, gained immortality. | The Ṛibhus, children of Sudhanvan, bright as suns, were in a year's course made associate with prayers. || 5. The Ṛibhus, with a rod measured, as 'twere a field, the single sacrificial chalice. wide of mouth, | Lauded of all who saw, praying for what is best, desiring glorious fame among Immortal Gods. || 6. As oil in ladles, we through knowledge will present unto the Heroes of the firmament our hymn,— | The Ṛibhus who came near with this great Father's speed, and rose to heaven's high sphere to eat the strengthening food. || 7. Ṛibhu to us is Indra freshest in his might, Ṛibhu with powers and wealth is giver of rich gifts. | Gods, through your favour may we on the happy day quell the attacks of those who pour no offerings forth. || 8. Out of a skin, O Ṛibhus, once ye formed a cow, and brought the mother close unto her calf again. | Sons of Sudhanvan, Heroes, with surpassing skill ye made your aged Parents youthful as before. || 9. Help us with strength where spoil is won, O Indra: joined with the Ṛibhus give us varied bounty. | This prayer of ours may Varuṇa grant, and Mitra, and Aditi and Sindhu, Earth and Heaven.

Hymn 1:111. Ṛibhus.

1. Working with skill they wrought the lightly rolling car: they wrought the Bays who bear Indra and bring great gifts. | The Ṛibhus for their Parents made life young again; and fashioned for the calf a mother by its side. || 2. For sacrifice make for us active vital power for skill and wisdom food with noble progeny. | Grant to our company this power most excellent, that with a family all-heroic we may dwell. || 3. Do ye, O Ṛibhus, make prosperity for us, prosperity for car, ye Heroes, and for steed. | Grant us prosperity victorious evermore, | conquering foes in battle, strangers or akin. || 4. Indra, the Ṛibhus' Lord, I invocate for aid, the Ṛibhus, Vājas, Marutas to the Soma draught. | Varuṇa, Mitra, both, yea, and the Aśvins Twain: let them speed us to wealth, wisdom, and victory. || 5. May Ṛibhu send prosperity for battle, may Vāja conquering in the fight protect us. | This prayer of ours may Varuṇa grant, and Mitra, and Aditi and Sindhu, Earth and Heaven.

Hymn 1:112. Aśvins.

1. To give first thought to them, I worship Heaven and Earth, and Agni, fair bright glow, to hasten their approach. | Come hither unto us, O Aśvins, with those aids wherewith in fight ye speed the war-cry to the spoil. || 2. Ample, unfailing, they have mounted as it were an eloquent car that ye may think of us and give. | Come hither unto us, O Aśvins, with those aids wherewith ye help our thoughts to further holy acts. || 3. Ye by the might which heavenly nectar giveth you are in supreme dominion Lords of all these folk. | Come hither unto us, O Aśvins, with those aids wherewith ye, Heroes, made the barren cow give milk. || 4. The aids wherewith the Wanderer through his offspring's might, or the Two-Mothered Son shows swiftest mid the swift; | Wherewith the sapient one acquired his triple lore, —Come hither unto us, O Aśvins, with those aids. || 5. Wherewith ye raised from waters, prisoned and fast bound, Rebha, and Vandana to look upon the light; | Wherewith ye succoured Kaṇva as he strove to win,—Come hither unto us, O Aśvins, with those aids. || 6. Wherewith ye rescued Antaka when languishing deep in the pit, and Bhujyu with unfailing help. | And comforted Karkandhu, Vayya, in their woe,—Come hither unto us, O Aśvins, with those aids. || 7. Wherewith ye gave Śuchanti wealth and happy home, and made the fiery pit friendly for Atri's sake; | Wherewith ye guarded Purukutsa, Pṛiśnigu,—Come hither unto us, O Aśvin;, with those aids. || 8. Mighty Ones, with what powers ye gave Parāvṛij aid what time ye made the blind and lame to see and walk; | Wherewith ye set at liberty the swallowed quail,—Come hither unto us, O Aśvins, with those aids. || 9. Wherewith ye quickened the most sweet exhaustless flood, and comforted Vasiṣhṭha, ye who ne'er decay; | And to Śrutarya, Kutsa, Nārya gave your help,—Come hither unto us, O Aśvins, with those aids. || 10. Wherewith ye helped, in battle of a thousand spoils, Viśpalā seeking booty, powerless to move. | Wherewith ye guarded friendly Vaśa, Aśva's son,— Come hither unto us, O Aśvins, with those aids. || 11. Whereby the cloud, ye Bounteous Givers, shed sweet rain for Dīrghaśravas, for the merchant Auśija, | Wherewith ye helped Kakṣhīvant, singer of your praise,—Come hither unto us, O Aśvins, with those aids. || 12. Wherewith ye made Rasā swell full with water-floods, and urged to victory the car without a horse; | Wherewith Triśoka drove forth his recovered cows,—Come hither unto us, O Aśvins, with those aids. || 13. Wherewith ye, compass round the Sun when far away, strengthened Mandhātar in his tasks as lord of lands, | And to sage Bharadvāja gave protecting help,—Come hither unto us, O Aśvins, with those aids. || 14. Wherewith, when Śambara was slain, ye guarded well great Atithigva, Divodāsa, Kaśoju, | And Trasadasyu when the forts were shattered down,—Come hither unto us, O Aśvins, with those aids. || 15. Wherewith ye honoured the great drinker Vamra, and Upastuta and Kali when he gained his wife, | And lent to Vyaśva and to Pṛithi favouring help, —Come hither unto us, O Aśvins, with those aids. || 16. Wherewith, O Heroes, ye vouchsafed deliverance to Śayu, Atri, and to Manu long ago; | Wherewith ye shot your shafts in Syūmaraśmi's cause.—Come hither unto us, O Aśvins, with those aids. || 17. Wherewith Paṭharvā, in his majesty of form, shone in his course like to a gathered kindled fire; | Wherewith ye helped Śaryāta in the mighty fray,—Come hither unto us, O Aśvins, with those aids. || 18. Wherewith, Aṅgirasas! ye triumphed in your heart, and onward went to liberate the flood of milk; | Wherewith ye helped the hero Manu with new strength,—Come hither unto us, O Aśvins, with those aids. || 19. Wherewith ye brought a wife for Vimada to wed, wherewith ye freely gave the ruddy cows away; | Wherewith ye brought the host of kind Gods to Sudās—Come hither unto us, O Aśvins, with those aids. || 20. Wherewith ye bring great bliss to him who offers gifts, wherewith ye have protected Bhujyu, Adhrigu, | And good and gracious Subharā and Ṛitastubh,—Come hither unto us, O Aśvins, with those aids. || 21. Wherewith ye served Kṛiśānu where the shafts were shot, and helped the young man's horse to swiftness in the race; | Wherewith ye bring delicious honey to the bees,—Come hither unto us, O Aśvins, with those aids. || 22. Wherewith ye speed the hero as he fights for kine in hero battle, in the strife for land and sons, | Wherewith ye safely guard his horses and his car, —Come hither unto us, O Aśvins with those aids. || 23. Wherewith ye, Lords of Hundred Powers, helped Kutsa, son of Ārjuni, gave Turvīti and Dabhīti strength, | Favoured Dhvasanti and lent Puruṣhanti help,—Come hither unto us, O Aśvins, with those aids. || 24. Make ye our speech effectual, O ye Aśvins, and this our hymn, ye mighty Wonder-Workers. | In luckless game I call on you for succour: strengthen us also on the field of battle. || 25. With, undiminished blessings, O ye Aśvins, for evermore both night and day protect us. | This prayer of ours may Varuṇa grant, and Mitra, and Aditi and Sindhu, Earth and Heaven.

Hymn 1:113. Dawn.

1. This light is come, amid all lights the fairest; born is the brilliant, far-extending brightness. | Night, sent away for Savitar's uprising, hath yielded up a birth-place for the Morning. || 2. The Fair, the Bright is come with her white offspring; to her the Dark One hath resigned her dwelling. | Akin, immortal, following each other, changing their colours both the heavens move onward. || 3. Common, unending is the Sisters' pathway; taught by the Gods, alternately they travel. | Fair-formed, of different hues and yet one-minded, Night and Dawn clash not, neither do they travel. || 4. Bright leader of glad sounds, our eyes behold her; splendid in hue she hath unclosed the portals. | She, stirring up the world, hath shown us riches: Dawn hath awakened every living creature. || 5. Rich Dawn, she sets afoot the coiled-up sleeper, one for enjoyment, one for wealth or worship, | Those who saw little for extended vision. All living creatures hath the Dawn awakened. || 6. One to high sway, one to exalted glory, one to pursue his gain, and one his labour: | All to regard their different vocations, all moving creatures hath the Dawn awakened. || 7. We see her there, the Child of Heaven apparent, the young Maid, flushing in her shining raiment. | Thou sovereign Lady of all earthly treasure, flush on us here, auspicious Dawn, this morning. || 8. She first of endless morns to come hereafter, follows the path of morns that have departed. | Dawn, at her rising, urges forth the living him who is dead she wakes not from his slumber. || 9. As thou, Dawn, hast caused Agni to be kindled, and with the Sun's eye hast revealed creation. | And hast awakened men to offer worship, thou hast performed, for Gods, a noble service. || 10. How long a time, and they shall be together,—Dawns that have shone and Dawns to shine hereafter? | She yearns for former Dawns with eager longing, and goes forth gladly shining with the others. || 11. Gone are the men who in the days before us looked on the rising of the earlier Morning. | We, we the living, now behold her brightness and they come nigh who shall hereafter see her. || 12. Foe-chaser, born of Law, the Law's protectress, joy-giver, waker of all pleasant voices, | Auspicious, bringing food for Gods' enjoyment, shine on us here, most bright, O Dawn, this morning. || 13. From days eternal hath Dawn shone, the Goddess, and shows this light today, endowed with riches. | So will she shine on days to come immortal she moves on in her own strength, undecaying. || 14. In the sky's borders hath she shone in splendour: the Goddess hath thrown off the veil of darkness. | Awakening the world with purple horses, on her well-harnessed chariot Dawn approaches. || 15. Bringing all life-sustaining blessings with her, showing herself she sends forth brilliant lustre. | Last of the countless mornings that have vanished, first of bright morns to come hath Dawn arisen. || 16. Arise! the breath, the life, again hath reached us: darkness hath passed away and light approacheth. | She for the Sun hath left a path to travel we have arrived where men prolong existence. || 17. Singing the praises of refulgent Mornings with his hymn's web the priest, the poet rises. | Shine then today, rich Maid, on him who lauds thee, shine down on us the gift of life and offspring. || 18. Dawns giving sons all heroes, kine and

horses, shining upon the man who brings oblations,— | These let the Soma-presser gain when ending his glad songs louder than the voice of Vāyu. || 19. Mother of Gods, Aditi's form of glory, ensign of sacrifice, shine forth exalted. | Rise up, bestowing praise on our devotion all-bounteous, make us chief among the people. || 20. Whatever splendid wealth the Dawns bring with them to bless the man who offers praise and worship, | Even that may Mitra, Varuṇa vouchsafe us, and Aditi and Sindhu, Earth and Heaven.

Hymn 1:114. Rudra.

1. To the strong Rudra bring we these our songs of praise, to him the Lord of Heroes with the braided hair, | That it be well with all our cattle and our men, that in this village all be healthy and well-fed. || 2. Be gracious unto us, O Rudra, bring us joy: thee, Lord of Heroes, thee with reverence will we serve. | Whatever health and strength our father Manu won by sacrifice may we, under thy guidance, gain. || 3. By worship of the Gods may we, O Bounteous One, O Rudra, gain thy grace, Ruler of valiant men. | Come to our families, bringing them bliss: may we, whose heroes are uninjured, bring thee sacred gifts, || 4. Hither we call for aid the wise, the wanderer, impetuous Rudra, perfecter of sacrifice. | May he repel from us the anger of the Gods: verily we desire his favourable grace. || 5. Him with the braided hair we call with reverence down, the wild-boar of the sky, the red, the dazzling shape. | May he, his hand filled full of sovereign medicines, grant us protection, shelter, and a home secure. || 6. To him the Marutas' Father is this hymn addressed, to strengthen Rudra's might, a song more sweet than sweet. | Grant us, Immortal One, the food which mortals eat: be gracious unto me, my seed, my progeny. || 7. O Rudra, harm not either great or small of us, harm not the growing boy, harm not the full-grown man. | Slay not a sire among us, slay no mother here, and to our own dear bodies, Rudra, do not harm. || 8. Harm us not, Rudra, in our seed and progeny, harm us not in the living, nor in cows or steeds, | Slay not our heroes in the fury of thy wrath. Bringing oblations evermore we call to thee. || 9. Even as a herdsman I have brought thee hymns of praise: O Father of the Marutas, give us happiness, | Blessed is thy most favouring benevolence, so, verily, do we desire thy saving help. || 10. Far be thy dart that killeth men or cattle: thy bliss be with us, O thou Lord of Heroes. | Be gracious unto us, O God, and bless us, and then vouchsafe us doubly-strong protection. || 11. We, seeking help, have spoken and adored him: may Rudra, girt by Marutas, hear our calling. | This prayer of ours may Varuṇa grant, and Mitra, and Aditi and Sindhu, Earth and Heaven.

Hymn 1:115. Sūrya.

1. The brilliant presence of the Gods hath risen, the eye of Mitra, Varuṇa and Agni. | The soul of all that moveth not or moveth, the Sun hath filled the air and earth and heaven. || 2. Like as a young man followeth a maiden, so doth the Sun the Dawn, refulgent Goddess: | Where pious men extend their generations, before the Auspicious One for happy fortune. || 3. Auspicious are the Sun's Bay-coloured Horses, bright, changing hues, meet for our shouts of triumph. | Bearing our prayers, the sky's ridge have they mounted, and in a moment speed round earth and heaven. || 4. This is the Godhead, this might of Sūrya: he hath withdrawn what spread o'er work unfinished. | When he hath loosed his Horses from their station, straight over all Night spreadeth out her garment. || 5. In the sky's lap the Sun this form assumeth that Varuṇa and Mitra may behold it. | His Bay Steeds well maintain his power eternal, at one time bright and darksome at another. || 6. This day, O Gods, while Sūrya is ascending, deliver us from trouble and dishonour. | This prayer of ours may Varuṇa grant, and Mitra, and Aditi and Sindhu, Earth and Heaven.

Hymn 1:116. Aśvins.

1. I trim like grass my song for the Nāsatyas and send their lauds forth as the wind drives rain-clouds, | Who, in a chariot rapid as an arrow, brought to the youthful Vimada a consort. || 2. Borne on by rapid steeds of mighty pinion, or proudly trusting in the Gods' incitements. | That stallion ass of yours won, O Nāsatyas, that thousand in the race, in Yama's contest. || 3. Yea, Aśvins, as a dead man leaves his riches, Tugra left Bhujyu in the cloud of waters. | Ye brought him back in animated vessels, traversing air, unwetted by the billows. || 4. Bhujyu ye bore with winged things, Nāsatyas, which for three nights, three days full swiftly travelled, | To the sea's farther shore, the strand of ocean, in three cars, hundred-footed, with six horses. || 5. Ye wrought that hero exploit in the ocean which giveth no support, or hold or station, | What time ye carried Bhujyu to his dwelling, borne in a ship with hundred oars, O Aśvins. || 6. The white horse which of old ye gave Aghāśva, Aśvins, a gift to be his wealth for ever,— | Still to be praised is that your glorious present, still to be famed is the brave horse of Pedu. || 7. O Heroes, ye gave wisdom to Kakṣhīvant who sprang from Pajra's line, who sang your praises. | Ye poured forth from the hoof of your strong charger a hundred jars of wine as from a strainer. || 8. Ye warded off with cold the fire's fierce burning; food very rich in nourishment ye furnished. | Atri, cast downward in the cavern, Aśvins ye brought, with all his people, forth to comfort. || 9. Ye lifted up the well, O ye Nāsatyas, and set the base on high to open downward. | Streams flowed for folk of Gotama who thirsted, like rain to bring forth thousandfold abundance. || 10. Ye from the old Chyavāna, O Nāsatyas, stripped, as 'twere mail, the skin upon | his body, | Lengthened his life when all had left him helpless, Dasras! and made him lord of youthful maidens. || 11. Worthy of praise and worth the winning, Heroes, is that your favouring succour O Nāsatyas, | What time ye, knowing well his case, delivered Vandana from the pit like hidden treasure. || 12. That mighty deed of yours, for gain, O Heroes, as thunder heraldeth the rain, I publish, | When, by the horse's head, Atharvan's offspring Dadhyach made known to you the Soma's sweetness. || 13. In the great rite the wise dame called, Nāsatyas, you, Lords of many treasures, to assist her. | Ye heard the weakling's wife, as 'twere an order, and gave to her a son Hiraṇyahasta. || 14. Ye from the wolf's jaws, as ye stood together, set free the quail, O Heroes, O Nāsatyas. | Ye, Lords of many treasures, gave the poet his perfect vision as he mourned his trouble. || 15. When in the time of night, in Khela's battle, a leg was severed like a wild bird's pinion, | Straight ye gave Viśpalā a leg of iron that she might move what time the conflict opened. || 16. His father robbed Ṛijrāśva of his eyesight who for the she-wolf slew a hundred wethers. | Ye gave him eyes, Nāsatyas, Wonder-Workers, Physicians, that he saw with sight uninjured. || 17. The Daughter of the Sun your car ascended, first reaching as it were the goal with coursers. | All Deities within their hearts assented, and ye, Nāsatyas, are close linked with glory. || 18. When to his house ye came, to Divodāsa, hasting to Bharadvāja, O ye Aśvins, | The car that came with you brought splendid riches: a porpoise and a bull were yoked together. || 19. Ye, bringing wealth with rule, and life with offspring, life rich in noble heroes; O Nāsatyas, | Accordant came with strength to Jahnu's children who offered you thrice every day your portion. || 20. Ye bore away at night by easy pathways Jāhuṣha compassed round on every quarter, | And, with your car that cleaves the toe asunder, Nāsatyas never decaying! rent the mountains. || 21. One morn ye strengthened Vaśa for the battle, to gather spoils that might be told in thousands. | With Indra joined ye drove away misfortunes, yea foes of Pṛithuśravas, O ye mighty. || 22. From the deep well ye raised on high the water, so that Ṛichatka's son, Śara, should drink it; | And with your might, to help the weary Śayu, ye made the barren cow yield milk, Nāsatyas. || 23. To Viśvaka, Nāsatyas! son of Kṛiṣhṇa, the righteous man who sought your aid and praised you, | Ye with your powers restored, like some lost creature, his son Viṣhṇāpū for his eyes to look on. || 24. Aśvins, ye raised, like Soma in a ladle Rebha, who for ten days and ten nights, fettered. | Had lain in cruel bonds, immersed and wounded, suffering sore affliction, in the waters. || 25. I. have declared your wondrous deeds, O Aśvins: may this be mine, and many kine and heroes. | May I, enjoying lengthened life, still seeing, enter old age as 'twere the house I live in.

Hymn 1:117. Aśvins.

1. Aśvins, your ancient priest invites you hither to gladden you with draughts of meath of Soma. | Our gift is on the grass, our song apportioned: with food and strength come hither, O Nāsatyas. || 2. That car of yours, swifter than thought, O Aśvins, which drawn by brave steeds cometh to the people, | Whereon ye seek the dwelling of the pious,—come ye thereon to our abode, O Heroes. || 3. Ye freed sage Atri, whom the Five Tribes honoured, from the strait pit, ye Heroes with his people, | Baffling the guiles of the malignant Dasyu, repelling them, ye Mighty in succession. || 4. Rebha the sage, ye mighty Heroes, Aśvins! whom, like a horse, vile men had sunk in water,— | Him, wounded, with your wondrous power ye rescued: your exploits of old time endure for ever. || 5. Ye

brought forth Vandana, ye Wonder-Workers, for triumph, like fair gold that hath been buried, | Like one who slumbered in destruction's bosom, or like the Sun when dwelling in the darkness. || 6. Kakshīvant, Pajra's son, must laud that exploit of yours, Nāsatyas, Heroes, ye who wander! | When from the hoof of your strong horse ye showered a hundred jars of honey for the people. || 7. To Kṛishṇa's son, to Viśvaka who praised you, O Heroes, ye restored his son Vishṇāpū. | To Ghoshā, living in her father's dwelling, stricken in years, ye gave a husband, Aśvins. || 8. Rushatī, of the mighty people, Aśvins, ye gave to Śyāva of the line of Kaṇva. | This deed of yours, ye Strong Ones should be published, that ye gave glory to the son of Nṛishad. || 9. O Aśvins, wearing many forms at pleasure, on Pedu ye bestowed a fleet-foot courser, | Strong, winner of a thousand spoils, resistless the serpent slayer, glorious, triumphant. || 10. These glorious things are yours, ye Bounteous Givers; prayer, praise in both worlds are your habitation. | O Aśvins, when the sons of Pajra call you, send strength with nourishment to him who knoweth. || 11. Hymned with the reverence of a son, O Aśvins ye Swift Ones giving booty to the singer, | Glorified by Agastya with devotion, established Viśpalā again, Nāsatyas. || 12. Ye Sons of Heaven, ye Mighty, whither went ye, sought ye, for his fair praise the home of Kāvya. | When, like a pitcher full of gold, O Aśvins, on the tenth day ye lifted up the buried? || 13. Ye with the aid of your great powers, O Aśvins, restored to youth the ancient man Chyavāna. | The Daughter of the Sun with all her glory, O ye Nāsatyas, chose your car to bear her. || 14. Ye, ever-youthful Ones, again remembered Tugra, according to your ancient manner: | With horses brown of hue that flew with swift wings ye brought back Bhujyu from the sea of billows. || 15. The son of Tugra had invoked you, Aśvins; borne on he went uninjured through the ocean. | Ye with your chariot swift as thought, well-harnessed, carried him off, O Mighty Ones, to safety. || 16. The quail had invocated you, O Aśvins, when from the wolf's devouring jaws ye freed her. | With conquering car ye cleft the mountain's ridges: the offspring of Viśvāch ye killed with poison. || 17. He whom for furnishing a hundred wethers to the she-wolf, his wicked father blinded,— | To him, Ṛijrāśva, gave ye eyes, O Aśvins; light to the blind ye sent for perfect vision. || 18. To bring the blind man joy thus cried the she-wolf: O Aśvins, O ye Mighty Ones, O Heroes, | For me Ṛijrāśva, like a youthful lover, hath. cut piecemeal one and a hundred wethers. || 19. Great and weal-giving is your aid, O Aśvins, ye, objects of all thought, made whole the cripple. | Purandhi also for this cause invoked you, and ye, O mighty, came to her with succours. || 20. Ye, Wonder-Workers, filled with milk for Śayu the milkless cow, emaciated, barren; | And by your powers the child of Purumitra ye brought to Vimada to be his consort. || 21. Ploughing and sowing barley, O ye Aśvins, milking out food for men, ye Wonder-Workers, | Blasting away the Dasyu with your trumpet, ye gave far-spreading light unto the Ārya. || 22. Ye brought the horse's head, Aśvins, and gave it unto Dadhyach the offspring of Atharvan. | True, he revealed to you, O Wonder-Workers, sweet Soma, Tvashṭar's secret, as your girdle. || 23. O Sages, evermore I crave your favour: be gracious unto all my prayers, O Aśvins. | Grant me, Nāsatyas, riches in abundance, wealth famous and accompanied with children. || 24. With liberal bounty to the weakling's consorts ye, Heroes, gave a son Hiraṇyahasta; | And Śyāva, cut into three several pieces, ye brought to life again, O bounteous Aśvins. || 25. These your heroic exploits, O ye Aśvins, done in the days. of old, have men related. | May we, addressing prayer to you, ye Mighty, speak with brave sons about us to the synod.

Hymn 1:118. Aśvins.

1. Flying, with falcons, may your chariot, Aśvins, most gracious, bringing friendly | help, come hither,— | Your chariot, swifter than the mind of mortal, fleet as the wind, three-seated O ye Mighty. || 2. Come to us with your chariot triple seated, three-wheeled, of triple form, that rolleth lightly. | Fill full our cows, give mettle to our horses, and make each hero son grow strong, O Aśvins. || 3. With your well-rolling car, descending swiftly, hear this the press-stone's song, ye Wonder-Workers. | How then have ancient sages said, O Aśvins, that ye most swiftly come to stay affliction? || 4. O Aśvins, let your falcons bear you hither, yoked to your chariot, swift, with flying pinions, | Which, ever active, like the airy eagles, carry you, O Nāsatyas, to the banquet. || 5. The youthful Daughter of the Sun, delighting in you, ascended there your chariot, Heroes. | Borne on their swift wings let your beauteous horses, your birds of ruddy hue, convey you near us. || 6. Ye raised up Vandana, strong Wonder-Workers! with great might, and with power ye rescued Rebha. | From out the sea ye saved the son of Tugra, and gave his youth again unto Chyavāna. || 7. To Atri, cast down to the fire that scorched him, ye gave, O Aśvins, strengthening food and favour. | Accepting his fair praises with approval, ye gave his eyes again to blinded Kaṇva. || 8. For ancient Śayu in his sore affliction ye caused his cow to swell with milk, O Aśvins. | The quail from her great misery ye delivered, and a new leg for Viśpalā provided. || 9. A white horse, Aśvins, ye bestowed on Pedu, a serpent-slaying steed sent down by Indra, | Loud-neighing, conquering the foe, high-mettled, firm-limbed and vigorous, winning thousand treasures. || 10. Such as ye are, O nobly born, O Heroes, we in our trouble call on you for succour. | Accepting these our songs, for our well-being come to us on your chariot treasure-laden. || 11. Come unto us combined in love, Nāsatyas come with the fresh swift vigour of the falcon. | Bearing oblations I invoke you, Aśvins, at the first break of everlasting morning.

Hymn 1:119. Aśvins.

1. Hither, that I may live, I call unto the feast your wondrous car, thought-swift, borne on by rapid steeds. | With thousand banners, hundred treasures, pouring gifts, promptly obedient, bestowing ample room. || 2. Even as it moveth near my hymn is lifted up, and all the regions come together to sing praise. | I sweeten the oblations; now the helpers come. Ūrjānī hath, O Aśvins, mounted on your car. || 3. When striving man with man for glory they have met, brisk, measureless, eager for victory in fight, | Then verily your car is seen upon the slope when ye, O Aśvins, bring some choice boon to the prince. || 4. Ye came to Bhujyu while he struggled in the flood, with flying birds, self-yoked, ye bore him to his sires. | Ye went to the far-distant home, O Mighty Ones; and famed is your great aid to Divodāsa given. || 5. Aśvins, the car which you had yoked for glorious show your own two voices urged directed to its goal. | Then she who came for friendship, Maid of noble birth, elected you as Husbands, you to be her Lords. || 6. Rebha ye saved from tyranny; for Atri's sake ye quenched with cold the fiery pit that compassed him. | Ye made the cow of Śayu stream refreshing milk, and Vandana was holpen to extended life. || 7. Doers of marvels, skilful workers, ye restored Vandana, like a car, worn out with length of days. | From earth ye brought the sage to life in wondrous mode; be your great deeds done here for him who honours you. || 8. Ye went to him who mourned in a far distant place, him who was left forlorn by treachery of his sire. | Rich with the light of heaven was then the help ye gave, and marvellous your succour when ye stood by him. || 9. To you in praise of sweetness sang the honey-bee: Auśija calleth you in Soma's rapturous joy. | Ye drew unto yourselves the spirit of Dadhyach, and then the horse's head uttered his words to you. || 10. A horse did ye provide for Pedu, excellent, white, O ye Aśvins, conqueror of combatants, | Invincible in war by arrows, seeking heaven worthy of fame, like Indra, vanquisher of men.

Hymn 1:120. Aśvins.

1. Aśvins, what praise may win your grace? Who may be pleasing to you both? | How shall the ignorant worship you? || 2. Here let the ignorant ask the means of you who know—for none beside you knoweth aught— | Not of a spiritless mortal man. || 3. Such as ye: are, all-wise, we call you. Ye wise, declare to us this day accepted prayer. | Loving you well your servant lauds you. || 4. Simply, ye Mighty Ones, I ask the Gods of that wondrous oblation hallowed by the mystic word. | Save us from what is stronger, fiercer than ourselves. || 5. Forth go the hymn that shone in Ghoshā Bhṛigu's like, the song wherewith the son of Pajra worships you, | Like some wise minister. || 6. Hear ye the song of him who hastens speedily. O Aśvins, I am he who sang your praise. | Hither, ye Lords of Splendour, hither turn your eyes. || 7. For ye were ever nigh to deal forth ample wealth, to give the wealth that ye had gathered up. | As such, ye Vasus, guard us well, and keep us safely from the wicked wolf. || 8. Give us not up to any man who hateth us, nor let our milch-cows stray, whose udders give us food, | Far from our homes without their calves. || 9. May they who love you gain you for their Friends. Prepare ye us for opulence with strengthening food, | Prepare us for the food that floweth from our cows || 10. I have obtained the horseless car of Aśvins rich in sacrifice, | And I am well content therewith. || 11. May it convey me

evermore: may the light chariot pass from men | To men unto the Soma draught. || 12. It holdeth slumber in contempt, and the rich who enjoyeth not: | Both vanish quickly and are lost.

Hymn 1:121. Indra.

1. When will men's guardians hasting hear with favour the song of Aṅgiras's pious children? | When to the people of the home he cometh he strideth to the sacrifice, the Holy. || 2. He established heaven; he poured forth, skilful worker, the wealth of kine, for strength, that nurtures heroes. | The Mighty One his self-born host regarded, the horse's mate, the mother of the heifer. || 3. Lord of red dawns, he came victorious, daily to the Aṅgirasas' former invocation. | His bolt and team hath he prepared, and established the heaven for quadrupeds and men two-footed. || 4. In joy of this thou didst restore, for worship, the lowing company of hidden cattle. | When the three-pointed one descends with onslaught he opens wide the doors that cause man trouble. || 5. Thine is that milk which thy swift-moving Parents brought down, a strengthening genial gift for conquest; | When the pure treasure unto thee they offered, the milk shed from the cow who streameth nectar. || 6. There is he born. May the Swift give us rapture, and like the Sun shine forth from yonder dawning, | Indu, even us who drank, whose toils are offerings, poured from the spoon, with praise, upon the altar. || 7. When the wood-pile, made of good logs, is ready, at the Sun's worship to bind fast the Bullock, | Then when thou shinest forth through days of action for the Car-borne, the Swift, the Cattle-seeker. || 8. Eight steeds thou broughtest down from mighty heaven, when fighting for the well that giveth splendour, | That men might press with stones the gladdening yellow, strengthened with milk, fermenting, to exalt thee. || 9. Thou hurledst forth from heaven the iron missile, brought by the Skilful, from the sling of leather, | When thou, O Much-invoked, assisting Kutsa with endless deadly darts didst compass Śuṣhṇa. || 10. Bolt-armed, ere darkness overtook the sunlight, thou castest at the veiling cloud thy weapon, | Thou rentest, out of heaven, though firmly knotted, the might of Śuṣhṇa that was thrown around him. || 11. The mighty Heaven and Earth, those bright expanses that have no wheels, joyed, Indra, at thine exploit. | Vṛitra, the boar who lay amid the waters, to sleep thou sentest with thy mighty thunder. || 12. Mount Indra, lover of the men thou guardest, the well-yoked horses of the wind, best bearers. | The bolt which Kāvya Uśanā erst gave thee, strong, gladdening, Vṛitra-slaying, hath he fashioned. || 13. The strong Bay Horses of the Sun thou stayedst: this Etaśa drew not the wheel, O Indra. | Casting them forth beyond the ninety rivers thou dravest down into the pit the godless. || 14. Indra, preserve thou us from this affliction Thunder-armed, save us from the misery near us. | Vouchsafe us affluence in chariots, founded on horses, for our food and fame and gladness. || 15. Never may this thy loving-kindness fail us; mighty in strength, may plenteous food surround us. | Maghavan, make us share the foeman's cattle: may we be thy most liberal feast companions.

Hymn 1:122. Viśvedevas.

1. Say, bringing sacrifice to bounteous Rudra, This juice for drink to you whose wrath is fleeting! | With Dyaus the Asura's Heroes I have lauded the Marutas as with prayer to Earth and Heaven. || 2. Strong to exalt the early invocation are Night and Dawn who show with varied aspect. | The Barren clothes her in wide-woven raiment, and fair Morn shines with Sūrya's golden splendour. || 3. Cheer us the Roamer round, who strikes at morning, the Wind delight us, pourer forth of waters! | Sharpen our wits, O Parvata and Indra. May all the Gods vouchsafe to us this favour. || 4. And Auśija shall call for me that famous Pair who enjoy and drink, who come to brighten. | Set ye the Offspring of the Floods before you; both Mothers of the Living One who beameth. || 5. For you shall Auśija call him who thunders, as, to win Arjuna's assent, cried Ghoṣhā. | I will invoke, that Pūṣhan may be bounteous to you, the rich munificence of Agni. || 6. Hear, Mitra-Varuṇa, these mine invocations, hear them from all men in the hall of worship. | Giver of famous gifts, kind hearer, Sindhu who gives fair fields, listen with all his waters! || 7. Praised, Mitra, Varuṇa! is your gift, a hundred cows to the Pṛikṣhayāmas and the Pajra. | Presented by car-famous Priyaratha, supplying nourishment, they came directly. || 8. Praised is the gift of him the very wealthy: may we enjoy it, men with hero children: | His who hath many gifts to give the Pajras, a chief who makes me rich in cars and horses. || 9. The folk, O Mitra-Varuṇa, who hate you, who sinfully hating pour you no libations, | Lay in their hearts, themselves, a wasting sickness, whereas the righteous gaineth all by worship. || 10. That man, most puissant, wondrously urged onward, famed among heroes, liberal in giving, | Moveth a warrior, evermore undaunted in all encounters even with the mighty. || 11. Come to the man's, the sacrificer's calling: hear, Kings of Immortality, joy-givers! | While ye who speed through clouds decree your bounty largely, for fame, to him the chariot rider. || 12. Vigour will we bestow on that adorer whose tenfold draught we come to taste, so spake they. | May all in whom rest splendour and great riches obtain refreshment in these sacrifices. || 13. We will rejoice to drink the tenfold present when the twicefive come bearing sacred viands. | What can he do whose steeds and reins are choicest? These, the all-potent, urge brave men to conquest. || 14. The sea and all the Deities shall give us him with the golden ear and neck bejewelled. | Dawns, hasting to the praises of the pious, be pleased with us, both offerers and singers. || 15. Four youthful sons of Maśarśāra vex me, three, of the king, the conquering Āyavasa. | Now like the Sun, O Varuṇa and Mitra, your car hath shone, long-shaped and reined with splendour.

Hymn 1:123. Dawn.

1. The Dakṣhiṇā's broad chariot hath been harnessed: this car the Gods Immortal have ascended. | Fain to bring light to homes of men the noble and active Goddess hath emerged from darkness. || 2. She before all the living world hath wakened, the Lofty One who wins and gathers treasure. | Revived and ever young on high she glances. Dawn hath come first unto our morning worship. || 3. If, Dawn, thou Goddess nobly born, thou dealest fortune this day to all the race of mortals, | May Savitar the God, Friend of the homestead, declare before the Sun that we are sinless. || 4. Showing her wonted form each day that passeth, spreading the light she visiteth each dwelling. | Eager for conquest, with bright sheen she cometh. Her portion is the best of goodly treasures. || 5. Sister of Varuṇa, sister of Bhaga, first among all sing forth, O joyous Morning. | Weak be the strength of him who worketh evil: may we subdue him with our car the guerdon. || 6. Let our glad hymns and holy thoughts rise upward, for the flames brightly burning have ascended. | The far-refulgent Mornings make apparent the lovely treasures which the darkness covered. || 7. The one departeth and the other cometh: unlike in hue day's, halves march on successive. | One hides the gloom of the surrounding Parents. Dawn on her shining chariot is resplendent. || 8. The same in form today, the same tomorrow, they still keep Varuṇa's eternal statute. | Blameless, in turn they traverse thirty regions, and dart across the spirit in a moment. || 9. She who hath knowledge Of the first day's nature is born refulgent white from out the darkness. | The Maiden breaketh not the law of Order, day by day coming to the place appointed. || 10. In pride of beauty like a maid thou goest, O Goddess, to the God who longs to win thee, | And smiling youthful, as thou shinest brightly, before him thou discoverest thy bosom. || 11. Fair as a bride embellished by her mother thou showest forth thy form that all may see it. | Blessed art thou O Dawn. Shine yet more widely. No other Dawns have reached what thou attainest. || 12. Rich in kine, horses, and all goodly treasures, in constant operation with the sunbeams, | The Dawns depart and come again assuming their wonted forms that promise happy fortune. || 13. Obedient to the rein of Law Eternal give us each thought that more and more shall bless us. | Shine thou on us today, Dawn, swift to listen. With us be riches and with chiefs who worship.

Hymn 1:124. Dawn.

1. The Dawn refulgent when the fire is kindled, and the Sun rising, far diffuse their brightness. | Savitar, God, hath sent us forth to labour, each quadruped, each biped, to be active. || 2. Not interrupting heavenly ordinances, although she minisheth human generations. | The last of endless morns that have departed, the first of those that come, Dawn brightly shineth. || 3. There in the eastern region she, Heaven's Daughter, arrayed in garments all of light, appeareth. | Truly she followeth the path of Order, nor faileth, knowing well, the heavenly quarters. || 4. Near is she seen, as 'twere the Bright One's bosom: she showeth sweet things like a new song-singer. | She cometh like a fly awaking sleepers, of all returning dames most true and constant. || 5. There in the east half of the watery region the Mother of the Cows hath shown her ensign. | Wider and wider still she spreadeth onward, and filleth full the laps of both heir Parents. || 6.

She, verily, exceeding vast to look on debarreth from her light nor kin nor stranger. | Proud of her spotless form she, brightly shining, turneth not from the high nor from the humble. || 7. She seeketh men, as she who hath no brother, mounting her car, as 'twere to gather riches. | Dawn, like a loving matron for her husband, smiling and well attired, unmasks her beauty. || 8. The Sister quitteth, for the elder Sister, her place, and having looked on her departeth. | She decks her beauty, shining forth with sunbeams, like women trooping to the festal meeting. || 9. To all these Sisters who ere now have vanished a later one each day in course succeedeth. | So, like the past, with days of happy fortune, may the new Dawns shine forth on us with riches. || 10. Rouse up, O Wealthy One, the liberal givers; let niggard traffickers sleep on unwakened: | Shine richly, Wealthy One, on those who worship, richly, glad. | Dawn while wasting, on the singer. || 11. This young Maid from the east hath shone upon us; she harnesseth her team of bright red oxen. | She will beam forth, the light will hasten hither, and Agni will be present in each dwelling. || 12. As the birds fly forth from their resting places, so men with store of food rise at thy dawning. | Yea, to the liberal mortal who remaineth at home, O Goddess Dawn, much good thou bringest. || 13. Praised through my prayer be ye who should be lauded. Ye have increased our wealth, ye Dawns who love us. | Goddesses, may we win by your good favour wealth to be told by hundreds and by thousands.

Hymn 1:125. Svanaya.

1. Coming at early morn he gives his treasure; the prudent one receives and entertains him. | Thereby increasing still his life and offspring, he comes with brave sons to abundant riches. || 2. Rich shall he be in gold and kine and horses. Indra bestows on him great vital power, | Who stays thee, as thou comest, with his treasure, like game caught in the net, O early comer. || 3. Longing, I came this morning to the pious, the son of sacrifice, with car wealth-laden. | Give him to drink juice of the stalk that gladdens; prosper with pleasant hymns the Lord of Heroes. || 4. Health-bringing streams, as milch-cows, flow to profit him who hath worshipped, him who now will worship. | To him who freely gives and fills on all sides full streams of fatness flow and make him famous. || 5. On the high ridge of heaven he stands exalted, yea, to the Gods he goes, the liberal giver. | The streams, the waters flow for him with fatness: to him this guerdon ever yields abundance. || 6. For those who give rich meeds are all these splendours, for those who give rich meeds suns shine in heaven. | The givers of rich meeds are made immortal; the givers of rich fees prolong their lifetime. || 7. Let not the liberal sink to sin and sorrow, never decay the pious chiefs who worship! | Let every man besides be their protection, and let affliction fall upon the niggard.

Hymn 1:126. Bhāvayavya.

1. With wisdom I present these lively praises of Bhāvya dweller on the bank of Sindhu; | For he, unconquered King, desiring glory, hath furnished me a thousand sacrifices. || 2. A hundred necklets from the King, beseeching, a hundred gift-steeds I at once accepted; | Of the lord's cows a thousand, I Kakṣhīvant. His deathless glory hath he spread to heaven. || 3. Horses of dusky colour stood beside me, ten chariots, Svanaya's gift, with mares to draw them. | Kine numbering sixty thousand followed after. Kakṣhīvant gained them when the days were closing. || 4. Forty bay horses of the ten cars' master before a thousand lead the long procession. | Reeling in joy Kakṣhīvant's sons and Pajra's have grounded the coursers decked with pearly trappings. || 5. An earlier gift for you have I accepted eight cows, good milkers, and three harnessed horses, | Pajras, who with your wains with your great kinsman, like troops of subjects, have been fain for glory. || [see the appendix for two additional verses]

Hymn 1:127. Agni.

1. Agni I hold as herald, the munificent, the gracious, Son of Strength, who knoweth all that live, as holy Singer, knowing all, | Lord of fair rites, a God with form erected turning to the Gods, | He, when the flame hath sprung forth from the holy oil, the offered fatness, longeth for it with his glow. || 2. We, sacrificing, call on thee best worshipper, the eldest of Aṅgirasas, Singer, with hymns, thee, brilliant One! with singers' hymns; | Thee, wandering round as 't were the sky, who art the invoking Priest of men, | Whom, Bull with hair of flame the people must observe, the people that he speed them on. || 3. He with his shining glory blazing far and wide, he verily it is who slayeth demon foes, slayeth the demons like an axe: | At whose close touch things solid shake, and what is stable yields like trees. | Subduing all, he keeps his ground and flinches not, from the skilled archer flinches not. || 4. To him, as one who knows, even things solid yield: unrough fire-sticks heated hot he gives his gifts to aid. Men offer Agni gifts for aid. | He deeply piercing many a thing hews it like wood with fervent glow. | Even hard and solid food he crunches with his might, yea, hard and solid food with might. || 5. Here near we place the sacrificial food for him who shines forth fairer in the night than in the day, with life then stronger than by day. | His life gives sure and firm defence as that one giveth to a son. | The during fires enjoy things given and things not given, the during fires enjoy as food. || 6. He, roaring very loudly like the Marutas' host, in fertile cultivated fields adorable, in desert spots adorable, | Accepts and eats our offered gifts, ensign of sacrifice by desert; | So let all, joying, love his path when he is glad, as men pursue a path for bliss. || 7. Even as they who sang forth hymns, addressed to heaven, the Bhṛigus with their prayer and praise invited him, the Bhṛigus rubbing, offering gifts. | For radiant Agni, Lord of all these treasures, is exceeding strong. | May he, the wise, accept the grateful coverings, the wise accept the coverings. || 8. Thee we invoke, the Lord of all our settled homes, common to all, the household's guardian, to enjoy, bearer of true hymns, to enjoy. | Thee we invoke, the guest of men, by whose mouth, even as a sire's, | All these Immortals come to gain their food of life, oblations come to Gods as food. || 9. Thou, Agni, most victorious with thy conquering strength, most Mighty One, art born for service of the Gods, like wealth for service of the Gods. | Most mighty is thine ecstasy, most splendid is thy mental power. | Therefore men wait upon thee, undecaying One, like vassals, undecaying One. || 10. To him the mighty, conquering with victorious strength, to Agni walking with the dawn, who sendeth kine, be sung your laud, to Agni sung; | As he who with oblation comes calls him aloud in every place. | Before the brands of fire he shouteth singer-like, the herald, kindler of the brands. || 11. Agni, beheld by us in nearest neighbourhood, accordant with the Gods, bring us, with gracious love, great riches with thy gracious love. | Give us O Mightiest, what is great, to see and to enjoy the earth. | As one of awful power, stir up heroic might for those who praise thee, Bounteous Lord!

Hymn 1:128. Agni.

1. By Manu's law was born this Agni, Priest most skilled, born for the holy work of those who yearn therefore, yea, born for his own holy work. | All ear to him who seeks his love and wealth to him who strives for fame, | Priest ne'er deceived, he sits in Iḷā's holy place, girt round in Iḷā's holy place. || 2. We call that perfecter of worship by the path or sacrifice; with reverence rich in offerings, with worship rich in offerings. | Through presentation of our food he grows not old in this his from; | The God whom Mātariśvan brought from far away, for Manu brought from far away. || 3. In ordered course forthwith he traverses the earth, swift-swallowing, bellowing Steer, bearing the genial seed, bearing the seed and bellowing. | Observant with a hundred eyes the God is conqueror in the wood: | Agni, who hath his seat in broad plains here below, and in the high lands far away. || 4. That Agni, wise High-Priest, in every house takes thought for sacrifice and holy service, yea, takes thought, with mental power, for sacrifice. | Disposer, he with mental power shows all things unto him who strives; | Whence he was born a guest enriched with holy oil, born as Ordainer and as Priest. || 5. When through his power and in his strong prevailing flames the Marutas' gladdening boons mingle with Agni's roar, boons gladdening for the active One, | Then he accelerates the gift, and by the greatness of his wealth, | Shall rescue us from overwhelming misery, from curse and overwhelming woe. || 6. Vast, universal, good he was made messenger; the speeder with his right hand hath not loosed his hold, through love of fame not loosed his hold. | He bears oblations to the Gods for whosoever supplicates. | Agni bestows a blessing on each pious man, and opens wide the doors for him. || 7. That Agni hath been set most kind in camp of men, in sacrifice like a Lord victorious, like a dear Lord in sacred rites. | His are the oblations of mankind when offered up at Iḷā's place. | He shall preserve us from Varuṇa's chastisement, yea, from the great God's chastisement. || 8. Agni the Priest they supplicate to grant them wealth: him, dear, most

thoughtful, have they made their messenger, him, offering-bearer have they made, | Beloved of all, who knoweth all, the Priest, the Holy one, the Sage— | Him, Friend, for help, the Gods when they are fain for wealth, him, Friend, with hymns, when fain for wealth.

Hymn 1:129. Indra.

1. The car which Indra, thou, for service of the Gods though it be far away, O swift One, bringest near, which, Blameless One, thou bringest near, | Place swiftly nigh us for our help: be it thy will that it be strong. | Blameless and active, hear this speech of orderers, this speech of us like orderers. || 2. Hear, Indra, thou whom men in every fight must call to show thy strength, for cry of battle with the men, with men of war for victory. | He who with heroes wins the light, who with the singers gains the prize, | Him the rich seek to gain even as a swift strong steed, even as a courser fleet and strong. || 3. Thou, Mighty, pourest forth the hide that holds the rain, thou keepest far away, Hero, the wicked man, thou shuttest out the wicked man. | Indra, to thee I sing, to Dyaus, to Rudra glorious in himself, | To Mitra, Varuṇa I sing a far-famed hymn to the kind God a far-famed hymn. || 4. We wish our Indra here that he may further you, the Friend, beloved of all, the very strong ally, in wars the very strong ally | In all encounters strengthen thou our prayer to be a help to us. | No enemy—whom thou smitest down—subdueth thee, no enemy, whom thou smitest down. || 5. Bow down the overweening pride of every foe with succour like to kindling-wood in fiercest flame, with mighty succour, Mighty One. | Guide us, thou Hero, as of old, so art thou counted blameless still. | Thou drivest, as a Priest, all sins of man away, as Priest, in person, seeking us. || 6. This may I utter to the present Soma-drop, which, meet to be invoked, with power, awakes the prayer, awakes the demon-slaying prayer. | May he himself with darts of death drive far from us the scorner's hate. | Far let him flee away who speaketh wickedness and vanish like a mote of dust. || 7. By thoughtful invocation this may we obtain, obtain great wealth, O Wealthy One, with Hero sons, wealth that is sweet with hero sons. | Him who is wroth we pacify with sacred food and eulogies, | Indra the Holy with our calls inspired and true, the Holy One with calls inspired. || 8. On, for your good and ours, come Indra with the aid of his own lordliness to drive the wicked hence, to rend the evil-hearted ones! | The weapon which devouring fiends cast at us shall destroy themselves. | Struck down, it shall not reach the mark; hurled forth, the fire-brand shall not strike. || 9. With riches in abundance, Indra, come to us, come by an unobstructed path, come by a path from demons free. | Be with us when we stray afar, be with us when our home is nigh. | Protect us with thy help both near and far away: protect us ever with thy help. || 10. Thou art our own, O Indra, with victorious wealth: let might accompany thee, the Strong, to give us aid, like Mitra, to give mighty aid. | O strongest saviour, helper thou, Immortal! of each warrior's car. | Hurt thou another and not us, O Thunder-armed, one who would hurt, O Thunder-armed! || 11. Save us from injury, thou who art well extolled: ever the warder-off art thou of wicked ones, even as a God, of wicked ones; | Thou slayer of the evil fiend, saviour of singer such as I. | Good Lord, the Father made thee slayer of the fiends, made thee, good Lord, to slay the fiends.

Hymn 1:130. Indra.

1. Come to us, Indra, from afar, conducting us even as a lord of heroes to the gatherings, home, like a King, his heroes' lord. | We come with gifts of pleasant food, with juice poured forth, invoking thee, | As sons invite a sire, that thou mayst get thee strength thee, bounteousest, to get thee strength. || 2. O Indra, drink the Soma juice pressed out with stones. poured from the reservoir, as an ox drinks the spring, a very thirsty bull the spring. | For the sweet draught that gladdens thee, for mightiest freshening of thy strength. | Let thy Bay Horses bring thee hither as the Sun, as every day they bring the Sun. || 3. He found the treasure brought from heaven that lay concealed, close-hidden, like the nestling of a bird, in rock, enclosed in never-ending rock. | Best Aṅgiras, bolt-armed, he strove to win, as 'twere, the stall of kine; | So Indra hath disclosed the food concealed, disclosed the doors, the food that lay concealed. || 4. Grasping his thunderbolt with both hands, Indra made its edge most keen, for hurling, like a carving-knife for Ahi's slaughter made it keen. | Endued with majesty and strength, O Indra, and with lordly might, | Thou crashest down the trees, as when a craftsman fells, crashest them down as with an axe. || 5. Thou, Indra, without effort hast let loose the floods to run their free course down, | like chariots, to the sea, like chariots showing forth their strength. | They, reaching hence away, have joined their strength for one eternal end, | Even as the cows who poured forth every thing for man, Yea, poured forth all things for mankind. || 6. Eager for riches, men have formed for thee this song, like as a skilful craftsman fashioneth a car, so have they wrought thee to their bliss; | Adorning thee, O Singer, like a generous steed for deeds of might, | Yea, like a steed to show his strength and win the prize, that he may bear each prize away. || 7. For Pūru thou hast shattered, Indra ninety forts, for Divodāsa thy boon servant with thy bolt, O Dancer, for thy worshipper. | For Atithigva he, the Strong, brought Śambara. from the mountain down, | Distributing the mighty treasures with his strength, parting all treasures with his strength. || 8. Indra in battles help his Ārya worshipper, he who hath hundred helps at hand in every fray, in frays that win the light of heaven. | Plaguing the lawless he gave up to Manu's seed the dusky skin; | Blazing, 'twere, he burns each covetous man away, he burns, the tyrannous away. || 9. Waxed strong in might at dawn he tore the Sun's wheel off. Bright red, he steals away their speech, the Lord of Power, their speech he steals away from them, | As thou with eager speed, O Sage, hast come from far away to help, | As winning for thine own all happiness of men, winning all happiness each day. || 10. Lauded with our new hymns, O vigorous in deed, save us with strengthening help, thou Shatterer of the Forts! | Thou, Indra, praised by Divodāsa's clansmen, as heaven grows great with days, shalt wax in glory.

Hymn 1:131. Indra.

1. To Indra Dyaus the Asura hath bowed him down, to Indra mighty Earth with wide-extending tracts, to win the light, with wide-spread tracts. | All Gods of one accord have set Indra in front preeminent. | For Indra all libations must be set apart, all man's libations set apart. || 2. In all libations men with hero spirit urge the Universal One, each seeking several light, each fain to win the light apart. | Thee, furthering like a ship, will we set to the chariot-pole of strength, | As men who win with sacrifices Indra's thought, men who win Indra with their lauds. || 3. Couples desirous of thine aid are storming thee, pouring their presents forth to win a stall of kine, pouring gifts, Indra, seeking thee. | When two men seeking spoil or heaven thou bringest face to face in war, | Thou showest, Indra, then the bolt thy constant friend, the Bull that ever waits on thee. || 4. This thine heroic power men of old time have known, wherewith thou breakest down, Indra, autumnal forts, breakest them down with conquering might. | Thou hast chastised, O Indra, Lord of Strength, the man who worships not, | And made thine own this great earth and these water-floods; with joyous heart these water-floods. || 5. And they have bruited far this hero-might when thou, O Strong One, in thy joy helpest thy suppliants, who sought to win thee for their Friend. | Their battle-cry thou madest sound victorious in the shocks of war. | One stream after another have they gained from thee, eager for glory have they gained. || 6. Also this morn may he be well inclined to us, mark at our call our offerings and our song of praise, our call that we may win the light. | As thou, O Indra Thunder-armed, wilt, as the Strong One, slay the foe, | Listen thou to the prayer of me a later sage, hear thou a later sage's prayer. || 7. O Indra, waxen strong and well-inclined to us, thou very mighty, slay the man that is our foe, slay the man, Hero! with thy bolt. | Slay thou the man who injures us: hear thou, as readiest, to hear. | Far be malignity, like mischief on the march, afar be all malignity.

Hymn 1:132. Indra.

1. Helped, Indra Maghavan, by thee in war of old, may we subdue in fight the men who strive with us, conquer the men who war with us. | This day that now is close at hand bless him who pours the Soma juice. | In this our sacrifice may we divide the spoil, showing our strength, the spoil of war. || 2. In war which wins the light, at the free-giver's call, at due oblation of the early-rising one, oblation of the active one, | Indra slew, even as we know—whom each bowed head must reverence. | May all thy bounteous gifts be gathered up for us, yea, the good gifts of thee the Good. || 3. This food glows for thee as of old at sacrifice, wherein they made thee chooser of the place, for thou choosest the place of sacrifice. | Speak thou and make it known to us: they see within with beams of light. | Indra, indeed, is found a seeker after spoil, spoil-seeker for his own allies. || 4. So now must thy great deed

be lauded as of old, when for the Aṅgirasas thou openedst the stall, openedst, giving aid, the stall. | In the same manner for us here fight thou and be victorious: | To him who pours the juice give up the lawless man, the lawless who is wroth with us. || 5. When with wise plan the Hero leads the people forth, they conquer in the ordered battle, seeking fame, press, eager, onward seeking fame. | To him in time of need they sing for life with offspring and with strength. | Their hymns with Indra find a welcome place of rest: the hymns go forward to the Gods. || 6. Indra and Parvata, our champions in the fight, drive ye away each man who fain would war with us, drive him far from us with the bolt. | Welcome to him concealed afar shall he the lair that he hath found. | So may the Render rend our foes on every side, rend them, O Hero, everywhere.

Hymn 1:133. Indra.

1. With sacrifice I purge both earth and heaven: I burn up great she-fiends who serve not Indra, | Where throttled by thy hand the foes were slaughtered, and in the pit of death lay pierced and mangled. || 2. O thou who castest forth the stones crushing the sorceresses' heads, | Break them with thy wide-spreading foot, with thy wide-spreading mighty foot. || 3. Do thou, O Maghavan, beat off these sorceresses' daring strength. | Cast them within the narrow pit. within the deep and narrow pit. || 4. Of whom thou hast ere now destroyed thrice-fifty with thy fierce attacks. | That deed they count a glorious deed, though small to thee, a glorious deed. || 5. O Indra, crush and bray to bits the fearful fiery-weaponed fiend: | Strike every demon to the ground. || 6. Tear down the mighty ones. O Indra, hear thou us. For heaven hath glowed like earth in fear, O Thunder-armed, as dreading fierce heat, Thunder-armed! | Most Mighty mid the Mighty Ones thou speedest with strong bolts of death, | Not slaying men, unconquered Hero with the brave, O Hero, with the thrice-seven brave. || 7. The pourer of libations gains the home of wealth, pouring his gift conciliates hostilities, yea, the hostilities of Gods. | Pouring, he strives, unchecked and strong, to win him riches thousandfold. | Indra gives lasting wealth to him who pours forth gifts, yea, wealth he gives that long shall last.

Hymn 1:134. Vāyu.

1. Vāyu, let fleet-foot coursers bring thee speedily to this our feast, to drink first of the juice we pour, to the first draught of Soma juice. | May our glad hymn, discerning well, uplifted, gratify thy mind. | Come with thy team-drawn car, O Vāyu, to the gift, come to the sacrificer's gift. || 2. May the joy-giving drops, O Vāyu gladden thee, effectual, well prepared, directed to the heavens, strong, blent with milk and seeking heaven; | That aids, effectual to fulfil, may wait upon our skilful power. | Associate teams come hitherward to grant our prayers: they shall address the hymns we sing. || 3. Two red steeds Vāyu yokes, Vāyu two purple steeds, swift-footed, to the chariot, to the pole to draw, most able, at the pole, to draw. | Wake up intelligence, as when a lover wakes his sleeping love. | Illumine heaven and earth, make thou the Dawns to shine, for glory make the Dawns to shine. || 4. For thee the radiant Dawns in the far-distant sky broaden their lovely garments forth in wondrous beams, bright-coloured in their new-born beams. | For thee the nectar-yielding Cow pours all rich treasures forth as milk. | The Marut host hast thou engendered from the womb, the Marutas from the womb of heaven. || 5. For thee the pure bright quickly-flowing Soma-drops, strong in their heightening power, hasten to mix themselves, hasten to the water to be mixed. | To thee the weary coward prays for luck that he may speed away. | Thou by thy law protectest us from every world, yea, from the world of highest Gods. || 6. Thou, Vāyu, who hast none before thee, first of all hast right to drink these offerings of Soma juice, hast right to drink the juice out-poured, | Yea, poured by all invoking tribes who free themselves from taint of sin, | For thee all cows are milked to yield the Soma-milk, to yield the butter and the milk.

Hymn 1:135. Vāyu, Indra-Vāyu.

1. Strewn is the sacred grass; come Vāyu, to our feast, with team of thousands, come, Lord of the harnessed team, with hundreds, Lord of harnessed steeds! | The drops divine are lifted up for thee, the God, to drink them first. | The juices rich in sweets have raised them for thy joy, have raised themselves to give thee strength. || 2. Purified by the stones the Soma flows for thee, clothed with its lovely splendours, to the reservoir, flows clad in its refulgent light. | For thee the Soma is poured forth, thy portioned share mid Gods and men. | Drive thou thy horses, Vāyu, come to us with love, come well-inclined and loving us. || 3. Come thou with hundreds, come with thousands in thy team to this our solemn rite, to taste the sacred food, Vāyu, to taste the offerings. | This is thy seasonable share, that comes co-radiant with the Sun. | Brought by attendant priests pure juice is offered up, Vāyu, pure juice is offered up. || 4. The chariot with its team of horses bring you both, to guard us and to taste the well-appointed food, Vāyu, to taste the offerings! | Drink of the pleasant-flavoured juice: the first draught is assigned to you. | O Vāyu, with your splendid bounty come ye both, Indra, with bounty come ye both. || 5. May our songs bring you hither to our solemn rites: these drops of mighty vigour have they beautified, like a swift steed of mighty strength. | Drink of them well-inclined to us, come hitherward to be our help. | Drink, Indra-Vāyu, of these Juices pressed with stones, Strength-givers! till they gladden you. || 6. These Soma juices pressed for you in waters here, borne by attendant priests, are offered up to you: bright, Vāyu, are they offered up. | Swift through the strainer have they flowed, and here are shed for both of you, | Soma-drops, fain for you, over the wether's fleece, Somas over the wether's fleece. || 7. O Vāyu, pass thou over all the slumberers, and where the press-stone rings enter ye both that house, yea, Indra, go ye both within. | The joyous Maiden is beheld, the butter flows. With richly laden team come to our solemn rite, yea, Indra, come ye to the rite. || 8. Ride hither to the offering of the pleasant juice, the holy Fig-tree which victorious priests surround: victorious be they still for us. | At once the cows yield milk, the barley-meal is dressed. For thee, | O Vāyu, never shall the cows grow thin, never for thee shall they be dry. || 9. These Bulls of thine, O Vāyu with the arm of strength, who swiftly fly within the current of thy stream, the Bulls increasing in their might, | Horseless, yet even through the waste swift-moving, whom no shout can stay, | Hard to be checked are they, like sunbeams, in their course. hard to be checked by both the hands.

Hymn 1:136. Mitra-Varuṇa.

1. Bring adoration ample and most excellent, hymn, offerings, to the watchful Twain, the bountiful, your sweetest to the bounteous Ones. | Sovereigns adored with streams of oil and praised at every sacrifice. | Their high imperial might may nowhere be assailed, ne'er may their Godhead be assailed. || 2. For the broad Sun was seen a path more widely laid, the path of holy law hath been maintained with rays, the eye with Bhaga's rays of light. | Firm-set in heaven is Mitra's home, and Aryaman's and Varuṇa's. | Thence they give forth great vital strength which merits praise, high power of life that men shall praise. || 3. With Aditi the luminous, the celestial, upholder of the people, come ye day by day, ye who watch sleepless, day by day. | Resplendent might have ye obtained, Ādityas, Lords of liberal gifts. | Movers of men, mild both, are Mitra, Varuṇa, mover of men is Aryaman. || 4. This Soma be most sweet to Mitra, Varuṇa: he in the drinking-feasts, shall have a share thereof, sharing, a God, among the Gods. | May all the Gods of one accord accept it joyfully today. | Therefore do ye, O Kings, accomplish what we ask, ye Righteous Ones, whate'er we ask. || 5. Whoso, with worship serves Mitra and Varuṇa, him guard ye carefully, uninjured, from distress, guard from distress the liberal man. | Aryaman guards him well who acts uprightly following his law, | Who beautifies their service with his lauds, who makes it beautiful with songs of praise. || 6. Worship will I profess to lofty Dyaus, to Heaven and Earth, to Mitra and to bounteous Varuṇa, the Bounteous, the Compassionate. | Praise Indra, praise thou Agni, praise Bhaga and heavenly Aryaman. | Long may we live and have attendant progeny, have progeny with Soma's help. || 7. With the Gods' help, with Indra still beside us, may we be held self-splendid with the Marutas. | May Agni, Mitra, Varuṇa give us shelter this may we gain, we and our wealthy princes.

Hymn 1:137. Mitra-Varuṇa.

1. With stones have we pressed out: O come; these gladdening drops are blent with milk, these Soma-drops which gladden you. | Come to us, Kings who reach to heaven, approach us, coming hitherward. | These milky drops are yours, Mitra and Varuṇa, bright Soma juices blent with milk. || 2. Here are the droppings; come ye nigh the Soma-droppings blent with curd, juices expressed and blent with curd. | Now for the wakening of your Dawn together with the Sun-God's rays, | juice waits for Mitra and for Varuṇa to drink, fair juice for drink, for sacrifice. || 3. As 'twere a radiant-

coloured cow, they milk with stones the stalk for you, with stones they milk the Soma-plant. | May ye come nigh us, may ye turn hither to drink the Soma juice. | The men pressed out this juice, Mitra and Varuṇa, pressed out this Soma for your drink.

Hymn 1:138. Pūṣhan.

1. Strong Pūṣhan's majesty is lauded evermore, the glory of his lordly might is never faint, his song of praise is never faint. | Seeking felicity I laud him nigh to help, the source, of bliss, | Who, Vigorous one, hath drawn to him the hearts of all, drawn them, the Vigorous One, the God. || 2. Thee, then, O Pūṣhan, like a swift one on his way, I urge with lauds that thou mayst make the foemen flee, drive, camel-like, our foes afar. | As I, a man, call thee, a God, giver of bliss, to be my Friend, | So make our loudly-chanted praises glorious, in battles make them glorious. || 3. Thou, Pūṣhan, in whose friendship they who sing forth praise enjoy advantage, even in wisdom, through thy grace, in wisdom even they are advanced. | So, after this most recent course, we come to thee with prayers for wealth. | Not stirred to anger, O Wide-Ruler, come to us, come thou to us in every fight. || 4. Not stirred to anger, come, Free-giver, nigh to us, to take this gift of ours, thou who hast goats for steeds, Goat-borne! their gift who long for fame. | So, Wonder-Worker! may we turn thee hither with effectual lauds. | I slight thee not, O Pūṣhan, thou Resplendent One: thy friendship may not be despised.

Hymn 1:139. Viśvedevas.

1. Heard be our prayer! In thought I honour Agni first: now straightway we elect this heavenly company, Indra and Vāyu we elect. | For when our latest thought is raised and on Vivasvat centred well, | Then may our holy songs go forward on their way, our songs as 'twere unto the Gods. || 2. As there ye, Mitra, Varuṇa, above the true have taken to yourselves the untrue with your mind, with wisdom's mental energy, | So in the seats wherein ye dwell have we beheld the Golden One, | Not with our thoughts or spirit, but with these our eyes, yea, with the eyes that Soma gives. || 3. Aśvins, the pious call you with their hymns of praise, sounding their loud song forth to you, these living men, to their oblations, living men. | All glories and all nourishment, Lords of all wealth! depend on you. | The fellies of your golden chariot scatter drops, Mighty Ones! of your golden car. || 4. Well is it known, O Mighty Ones: ye open heaven; for you the chariot-steeds are yoked for morning rites, unswerving steeds for morning rites, | We set you on the chariot-seat, ye Mighty, on the golden car. | Ye seek mid-air as by a path that leads aright, as by a path that leads direct. || 5. O Rich in Strength, through your great power vouchsafe us blessings day and night. | The offerings which we bring to you shall never fail, gifts brought by us shall never fail. || 6. These Soma-drops, strong Indra! drink for heroes, poured, pressed out by pressing-stones, are welling forth for thee, for thee the drops are welling forth. | They shall make glad thy heart to give, to give wealth great and wonderful. | Thou who acceptest praise come glorified by hymns, come thou to us benevolent. || 7. Quickly, O Agni, hear us: magnified by us thou shalt speck for us to the Gods adorable yea, to the Kings adorable: | When, O ye Deities, ye gave that Milch-cow to the Aṅgirasas, | They milked her: Aryaman, joined with them, did the work: he knoweth her as well as I. || 8. Ne'er may these manly deeds of yours for us grow old, never may your bright glories fall into decay, never before our time decay. | What deed of yours, new every age, wondrous, surpassing man, rings forth, | Whatever, Marutas! may be difficult to gain, grant us, whate'er is hard to gain. || 9. Dadhyach of old, Aṅgiras, Priyamedha these, and Kaṇva, Atri, Manu knew my birth, yea, those of ancient days and Manu knew. | Their long line stretcheth to the Gods, our birth-connections are with them. | To these, for their high station, I bow down with song, to Indra, Agni, bow with song. || 10. Let the Invoker bless: let offerers bring choice gifts; Bṛihaspati the Friend doth sacrifice with Steers, Steers that have many an excellence. | Now with our ears we catch the sound of the press-stone that rings afar. | The very Strong hath gained the waters by himself, the strong gained many a resting-place. || 11. O ye Eleven Gods whose home is heaven, O ye Eleven who make earth your dwelling, | Ye who with might, Eleven, live in waters, accept this sacrifice, O Gods, with pleasure.

Hymn 1:140. Agni.

1. To splendid Agni seated by the altar, loving well his home, I bring the food as 'twere his place of birth. | I clothe the bright One with my hymn as with a robe, him with the car of light, bright-hued, dispelling gloom. || 2. Child of a double birth he grasps at triple food; in the year's course what he hath swallowed grows anew. | He, by another's mouth and tongue a noble Bull, with other, as an elephant, consumes the trees. || 3. The pair who dwell together, moving in the dark bestir themselves: both parents hasten to the babe, | Impetuous-tongued, destroying, springing swiftly forth, one to be watched and cherished, strengthener of his sire. || 4. For man, thou Friend of men, these steeds of thine are yoked, impatient, lightly running, ploughing blackened lines, | Discordant-minded, fleet, gliding with easy speed, urged onward by the wind and rapid in their course. || 5. Dispelling on their way the horror of black gloom, making a glorious show these flames of his fly forth, | When o'er the spacious tract he spreads himself abroad, and rushes panting on with thunder and with roar. || 6. Amid brown plants he stoops as if adorning them, and rushes bellowing like a bull upon his wives. | Proving his might, he decks the glory of his form, and shakes his horns like one terrific, hard to stay. || 7. Now covered, now displayed he grasps as one who knows his resting-place in those who know him well. | A second time they wax and gather Godlike power, and blending both together change their Parents' form. || 8. The maidens with long, tresses hold him in embrace; dead, they rise up again to meet the Living One. | Releasing them from age with a loud roar he comes, filling them with new spirit, living, unsubdued. || 9. Licking the mantle of the Mother, far and wide he wanders over fields with beasts that flee apace. | Strengthening all that walk, licking up all around, a blackened path, forsooth, he leaves where'er he goes. || 10. O Agni, shine resplendent with our wealthy chiefs, like a loud-snorting bull, accustomed to the house. | Thou casting off thine infant wrappings blazest forth as though thou hadst put on a coat of mail for war. || 11. May this our perfect prayer be dearer unto thee than an imperfect prayer although it please thee well. | With the pure brilliancy that radiates from thy form, mayest thou grant to us abundant store of wealth. || 12. Grant to our chariot, to our house, O Agni, a boat with moving feet and constant oarage, | One that may further well our wealthy princes and all the folk, and be our certain refuge. || 13. Welcome our laud with thine approval, Agni. May earth and heaven and freely flowing rivers | Yield us long life and food and corn and cattle, and may the red Dawns choose for us their choicest.

Hymn 1:141. Agni.

1. Yea, verily, the fair effulgence of the God for glory was established, since he sprang from strength. | When he inclines thereto successful is the hymn: the songs of sacrifice have brought him as they flow || 2. Wonderful, rich in nourishment, he dwells in food; next, in the seven auspicious Mothers is his home. | Thirdly, that they might drain the treasures of the Bull, the maidens brought forth him for whom the ten provide. || 3. What time from out the deep, from the Steer's wondrous form, the Chiefs who had the power produced him with their strength; | When Mātariśvan rubbed forth him who lay concealed, for mixture of the sweet drink, in the days of old. || 4. When from the Highest Father he is brought to us, amid the plants he rises hungry, wondrously. | As both together join to expedite his birth, most youthful he is born resplendent in his light. || 5. Then also entered he the Mothers, and in them pure and uninjured he increased in magnitude. | As to the first he rose, the vigorous from of old, so now he runs among the younger lowest ones. || 6. Therefore they choose him Herald at the morning rites, pressing to him as unto Bhaga, pouring gifts, | When, much-praised, by the power and will of Gods, he goes at all times to his mortal worshipper to drink. || 7. What time the Holy One, wind-urged, hath risen up, serpent-like winding through the dry grass unrestrained, | Dust lies upon the way of him who burneth all, black-winged and pure of birth who follows sundry paths. || 8. Like a swift chariot made by men who know their art, he with his red limbs lifts himself aloft to heaven. | Thy worshippers become by burning black of hue: their strength flies as before a hero's violence. || 9. By thee, O Agni, Varuṇa who guards the Law, Mitra and Aryaman, the Bounteous, are made strong; | For, as the felly holds the spokes, thou with thy might pervading hast been born encompassing them round. || 10. Agni, to him who toils and pours libations, thou, Most Youthful! sendest wealth and all the host of Gods. | Thee, therefore, even as Bhaga, will we set anew, young Child of Strength, most wealthy! in our battle-song. || 11. Vouchsafe us riches turned to worthy

ends, good luck abiding in the house, and strong capacity, | Wealth that directs both worlds as they were guiding-reins, and, very Wise, the Gods' assent in sacrifice. || 12. May he, the Priest resplendent, joyful, hear us, he with the radiant car and rapid horses. | May Agni, ever wise, with best directions to bliss and highest happiness conduct us. || 13. With hymns of might hath Agni now been lauded, advanced to height of universal kingship. | Now may these wealthy chiefs and we together spread forth as spreads the Sun above the rain-clouds.

Hymn 1:142. Āprīs.

1. Kindled, bring, Agni, Gods today for him who lifts the ladle up. | Spin out the ancient thread for him who sheds, with gifts, the Soma juice. || 2. Thou dealest forth, Tanūnapāt, sweet sacrifice enriched with oil, | Brought by a singer such as I who offers gifts and toils for thee. || 3. He wondrous, sanctifying, bright, sprinkles the sacrifice with mead, | Thrice, Narāśaṃsa from the heavens, a God mid Gods adorable. || 4. Agni, besought, bring hitherward Indra the Friend, the Wonderful, | For this my hymn of praise, O sweet of tongue, is chanted forth to thee. || 5. The ladle-holders strew trimmed grass at this well-ordered sacrifice; | A home for Indra is adorned, wide, fittest to receive the Gods. || 6. Thrown open be the Doors Divine, unfailing, that assist the rite, | High, purifying, much-desired, so that the Gods may enter in. || 7. May Night and Morning, hymned with lauds, united, fair to look upon, | Strong Mothers of the sacrifice, seat them together on the grass. || 8. May the two Priests Divine, the sage, the sweet-voiced lovers of the hymn, | Complete this sacrifice of ours, effectual, reaching heaven today. || 9. Let Hotrā pure, set among Gods, amid the Marutas Bhāratī, Iḷā, Sarasvatī, Mahī, rest on the grass, adorable. || 10. May Tvaṣhṭar send us genial dew abundant, wondrous, rich in gifts, | For increase and for growth of wealth, Tvaṣhṭar our kinsman and our Friend. || 11. Vanaspati, give forth, thyself, and call the Gods to sacrifice. | May Agni, God intelligent, speed our oblation to the Gods. || 12. To Vāyu joined with Pūṣhan, with the Marutas, and the host of Gods, | To Indra who inspires the hymn cry Glory! and present the gift. || 13. Come hither to enjoy the gifts prepared with cry of Glory! Come, | O Indra, hear their calling; they invite thee to the sacrifice.

Hymn 1:143. Agni.

1. To Agni I present a newer mightier hymn, I bring my words and song unto the Son of Strength, | Who, Offspring of the Waters, bearing precious things sits on the earth, in season, dear Invoking Priest. || 2. Soon as he sprang to birth that Agni was shown forth to Mātariśvan in the highest firmament. | When he was kindled, through his power and majesty his fiery splendour made the heavens and earth to shine. || 3. His flames that wax not old, beams fair to look upon of him whose face is lovely, shine with beauteous sheen. | The rays of Agni, him whose active force is light, through the nights glimmer sleepless, ageless, like the floods. || 4. Send thou with hymns that Agni to his own abode, who rules, one Sovereign Lord of wealth, like Varuṇa, | Him, All-possessor, whom the Bhṛigus with their might brought to earth's central point, the centre of the world. || 5. He whom no force can stay, even as the Marutas' roar, like to a dart sent forth, even as the bolt from heaven, | Agni with sharpened jaws chews up and eats the trees, and conquers them as when the warrior smites his foes. || 6. And will not Agni find enjoyment in our praise, will not the Vasu grant our wish with gifts of wealth? | Will not the Inspirer speed our prayers to gain their end? Him with the radiant glance I laud with this my song. || 7. The kindler of the flame wins Agni as a Friend, promoter of the Law, whose face is bright with oil. | Inflamed and keen, refulgent in our gatherings, he lifts our hymn on high clad in his radiant hues. || 8. Keep us incessantly with guards that cease not, Agni, with guards auspicious, very mighty. | With guards that never slumber, never heedless, never beguiled. O Helper, keep our children.

Hymn 1:144. Agni.

1. The Priest goes forth to sacrifice, with wondrous power sending aloft the hymn of glorious brilliancy. | He moves to meet the ladles turning to the right, which are the first to kiss the place where he abides. || 2. To him sang forth the flowing streams of Holy Law, encompassed in the home and birth-place of the God. | He, when he dwelt extended in the waters' lap, absorbed those Godlike powers for which he is adored. || 3. Seeking in course altern to reach the selfsame end the two co-partners strive to win this beauteous form. | Like Bhaga must he be duly invoked by us, as he who drives the car holds fast the horse's reins. || 4. He whom the two co-partners with observance tend, the pair who dwell together in the same abode, | By night as in the day the grey one was born young, passing untouched by eld through many an age of man. || 5. Him the ten fingers, the devotions, animate: we mortals call on him a God to give us help. | He speeds over the sloping surface of the land: new deeds hath he performed with those who gird him round. || 6. For, Agni, like a herdsman, thou by thine own might rulest o'er all that is in heaven and on the earth; | And these two Mighty Ones, bright, golden closely joined, rolling them round are come unto thy sacred grass. || 7. Agni, accept with joy, be glad in this our prayer, joy-giver, self-sustained, strong, born of Holy Law! | For fair to see art thou turning to every side, pleasant to look on as a dwelling filled with food.

Hymn 1:145. Agni.

1. Ask ye of him for he is come, he knoweth it; he, full of wisdom, is implored, is now implored. | With him are admonitions and with him commands: he is the Lord of Strength, the Lord of Power and Might. || 2. They ask of him: not all learn by their questioning what he, the Sage, hath grasped, as 'twere, with his own mind. | Forgetting not the former nor the later word, he goeth on, not careless, in his mental power. || 3. To him these ladles go, to him these racing mares: he only will give ear to all the words I speak. | All-speeding, victor, perfecter of sacrifice, the Babe with flawless help hath mustered vigorous might. || 4. Whate'er he meets he grasps and then runs farther on, and straightway, newly born, creeps forward with his kin. | He stirs the wearied man to pleasure and great joy what time the longing gifts approach him as he comes. || 5. He is a wild thing of the flood and forest: he hath been laid upon the highest surface. | He hath declared the lore of works to mortals, Agni the Wise, for he knows Law, the Truthful.

Hymn 1:146. Agni.

1. I laud the seven-rayed, the triple-headed, Agni all-perfect in his Parents' bosom, | Sunk in the lap of all that moves and moves not, him who hath filled all luminous realms of heaven. || 2. As a great Steer he grew to these his Parents; sublime he stands, untouched by eld, far-reaching. | He plants his footsteps on the lofty ridges of the broad earth: his red flames lick the udder. || 3. Coming together to their common youngling both Cows, fair-shaped, spread forth in all directions, | Measuring out the paths that must be travelled, entrusting all desires to him the Mighty. || 4. The prudent sages lead him to his dwelling, guarding with varied skill the Ever-Youthful. | Longing, they turned their eyes unto the River: to these the Sun of men was manifested. || 5. Born noble in the regions, aim of all mens' eyes to be implored for life by great and small alike, | Far as the Wealthy One hath spread himself abroad, he is the Sire all-visible of this progeny.

Hymn 1:147. Agni.

1. How, Agni, have the radiant ones, aspiring, endued thee with the vigour of the living, | So that on both sides fostering seed and offspring, the Gods may joy in Holy Law's fulfilment? || 2. Mark this my speech, Divine One, thou, Most Youthful! offered to thee by him who gives most freely. | One hates thee, and another sings thy praises: I thine adorer laud thy form, O Agni. || 3. Thy guardian rays, O Agni, when they saw him, preserved blind Māmateya from affliction. | Lord of all riches, he preserved the pious the foes who fain would harm them did no mischief. || 4. The sinful man who worships not, O Agni, who, offering not, harms us with double-dealing, — | Be this in turn to him a heavy sentence may he distress himself by his revilings. || 5. Yea, when a mortal knowingly, O Victor, injures with double tongue a fellow-mortal, | From him, praised Agni! save thou him that lauds thee: bring us not into trouble and affliction.

Hymn 1:148. Agni.

1. What Mātariśvan, piercing, formed by friction, Herald of all the Gods. in varied figure, | Is he whom they have set mid human houses, gay-hued as light and shining forth for beauty. || 2. They shall not harm the man who brings thee praises: such as I am, Agni my help approves me. | All acts of mine shall they accept with pleasure, laudation from the singer who presents it. || 3. Him in his constant seat men skilled in worship have taken and with praises have established. | As, harnessed to a chariot fleet-foot horses, at his command let bearers lead him forward. || 4. Wondrous, full many a thing he chews and crunches: he shines amid the wood with

spreading brightness. | Upon his glowing flames the wind blows daily, driving them like the keen shaft of an archer. || 5. Him, whom while yet in embryo the hostile, both skilled and fain to harm, may never injure, | Men blind and sightless through his splendour hurt not: his never-failing lovers have preserved him.

Hymn 1:149. Agni.

1. Hither he hastens to give, Lord of great riches, King of the mighty, to the place of treasure. | The pressing-stones shall serve him speeding near us. || 2. As Steer of men so Steer of earth and heaven by glory, he whose streams all life hath drunken, | Who hasting forward rests upon the altar. || 3. He who hath lighted up the joyous castle, wise Courser like the Steed of cloudy heaven, | Bright like the Sun, with hundredfold existence. || 4. He, doubly born, hath spread in his effulgence through the three luminous realms, through all the regions, | Best sacrificing Priest where waters gather. || 5. Priest doubly born, he through his love of glory hath in his keeping all things worth the choosing, | The man who brings him gifts hath noble offspring.

Hymn 1:150. Agni.

1. Agni, thy faithful servant I call upon thee with many a gift, | As in the keeping of the great inciting God; || 2. Thou who ne'er movest thee to aid the indolent, the godless man, | Him who though wealthy never brings an offering. || 3. Splendid, O Singer, is that man, mightiest of the great in heaven. | Agni, may we be foremost, we thy worshippers.

Hymn 1:151. Mitra and Varuṇa.

1. Heaven and earth trembled at the might and voice of him, whom, loved and Holy One, helper of all mankind, | The wise who longed for spoil in fight for kine brought forth with power, a Friend, mid waters, at the sacrifice. || 2. As these, like friends, have done this work for you, these prompt servants of Purumīḷha Soma-offerer, | Give mental power to him who sings the sacred song, and hearken, Strong Ones, to the master of the house. || 3. The folk have glorified your birth from Earth and Heaven, to be extolled, ye Strong Ones, for your mighty power. | Ye, when ye bring to singer and the rite, enjoy the sacrifice performed with holy praise and strength. || 4. The people prospers, Asuras! whom ye dearly love: ye, Righteous Ones, proclaim aloud the Holy Law. | That efficacious power that comes from lofty heaven, ye bind unto the work, as to the pole an ox. || 5. On this great earth ye send your treasure down with might: unstained by dust, the crowding kine are in the stalls. | Here in the neighbourhood they cry unto the Sun at morning and at evening, like swift birds of prey. || 6. The flames with curling tresses serve your sacrifice, whereto ye sing the song, Mitra and Varuṇa. | Send down of your free will, prosper our holy songs: ye are sole Masters of the singer's hymn of praise. || 7. Whoso with sacrifices toiling brings you gifts, and worships, sage and priest, fulfilling your desire,— | To him do ye draw nigh and taste his sacrifice. Come well-inclined to us unto our songs and prayer. || 8. With sacrifices and with milk they deck you first, ye Righteous Ones, as if through stirrings of the mind. | To you they bring their hymns with their collected thought, while ye with earnest soul come to us gloriously. || 9. Rich strength of life is yours: ye, Heroes, have obtained through your surpassing powers rich far-extending might. | Not the past days conjoined with nights, not rivers, not the Paṇis have attained your Godhead and your wealth.

Hymn 1:152. Mitra-Varuṇa.

1. The robes which ye put on abound with fatness: uninterrupted courses are your counsels. | All falsehood, Mitra-Varuṇa! ye conquer, and closely cleave unto the Law Eternal. || 2. This might of theirs hath no one comprehended. True is the crushing word the sage hath uttered, | The fearful four-edged bolt smites down the three-edged, and those who hate the Gods first fall and perish. || 3. The Footless Maid precedeth footed creatures. Who marketh, Mitra-Varuṇa, this your doing? | The Babe Unborn supporteth this world's burthen, fulfilleth Law and overcometh falsehood. || 4. We look on him the darling of the Maidens, always advancing, never falling downward, | Wearing inseparable, wide-spread raiment, Mitra's and Varuṇa's delightful glory. || 5. Unbridled Courser, born but not of horses, neighing he flieth on with back uplifted. | The youthful love mystery thought-surpassing, praising in Mitra-Varuṇa, its glory. || 6. May the milch-kine who favour Māmateya prosper in this world him who loves devotion. | May he, well skilled in rites, be food, and calling Aditi with his lips give us assistance. || 7. Gods, Mitra-Varuṇa, with love and worship, let me make you delight in this oblation. | May our prayer be victorious in battles, may we have rain from heaven to make us prosper.

Hymn 1:153. Mitra-Varuṇa.

1. We worship with our reverence and oblations you, Mitra Varuṇa, accordant, mighty, | So that with us, ye Twain whose backs are sprinkled with oil, the priests with oil and hymns support you. || 2. Your praise is like a mighty power, an impulse: to you, Twain Gods, a well-formed hymn is offered, | As the priest decks yon, Strong Ones, in assemblies, and the prince fain to worship you for blessings. || 3. O Mitra-Varuṇa, Aditi the Milch-cow streams for the rite, for folk who bring oblation, | When in the assembly he who worships moves you, like to a human priest, with gifts presented. || 4. So may the kine and heavenly Waters pour you sweet drink in families that make you joyful. | Of this may he, the ancient House-Lord, give us. Enjoy, drink of the milk the cow provideth.

Hymn 1:154. Viṣhṇu

1. I will declare the mighty deeds of Viṣhṇu, of him who measured out the earthly regions, | Who propped the highest place of congregation, thrice setting down his footstep, widely striding. || 2. For this his mighty deed is Viṣhṇu lauded, like some wild beast, dread, prowling, mountain-roaming; | He within whose three wide-extended paces all living creatures have their habitation. || 3. Let the hymn lift itself as strength to Viṣhṇu, the Bull far-striding, dwelling on the mountains, | Him who alone with triple step hath measured this common dwelling-place, long, far extended. || 4. Him whose three places that are filled with sweetness, imperishable, joy as it may list them, | Who verily alone upholds the threefold, the earth, the heaven, and all living creatures. || 5. May I attain to that his well-loved mansion where men devoted to the Gods are happy. | For there springs, close akin to the Wide-Strider, the well of meath in Viṣhṇu's highest footstep. || 6. Fain would we go unto your dwelling-places where there are many-horned and nimble oxen, | For mightily, there, shineth down upon us the widely-striding Bull's sublimest mansion.

Hymn 1:155. Viṣhṇu-Indra.

1. To the great Hero, him who sets his mind thereon, and Viṣhṇu, praise aloud in song your draught of juice,— | Gods ne'er beguiled, who borne as 'twere by noble steed, have stood upon the lofty ridges of the hills. || 2. Your Soma-drinker keeps afar your furious rush, Indra and Viṣhṇu, when ye come with all your might. | That which hath been directed well at mortal man, bow-armed Kṛiśānu's arrow, ye turn far aside. || 3. These offerings increase his mighty manly strength: he brings both Parents down to share the genial flow. | He lowers, though a son, the Father's highest name; the third is that which is high in the light of heaven. || 4. We laud this manly power of him the Mighty One, preserver, inoffensive, bounteous and benign; | His who strode, widely pacing, with three steppings forth over the realms of earth for freedom and for life. || 5. A mortal man, when he beholds two steps of him who looks upon the light, is restless with amaze. | But his third step doth no one venture to approach, no, nor the feathered birds of air who fly with wings. || 6. He, like a rounded wheel, hath in swift motion set his ninety racing steeds together with the four. | Developed, vast in form, with those who sing forth praise, a youth, no more a child, he cometh to our call.

Hymn 1:156. Viṣhṇu.

1. Far-shining, widely famed, going thy wonted way, fed with the oil, be helpful. Mitra-like, to us. | So, Viṣhṇu, e'en the wise must swell thy song of praise, and he who hath oblations pay thee solemn rites. || 2. He who brings gifts to him the Ancient and the Last, to Viṣhṇu who ordains, together with his Spouse, | Who tells the lofty birth of him the Lofty One, shall verily surpass in glory e'en his peer. || 3. Him have ye satisfied, singers, as well as ye know, primeval germ of Order even from his birth. | Ye, knowing e'en his name, have told it forth: may we, Viṣhṇu, enjoy the grace of thee the Mighty One. || 4. The Sovereign Varuṇa and both the Aśvins wait on this the will of him who guides the Marut host. | Viṣhṇu hath power supreme and might that finds the day, and with his Friend unbars the stable of the kine. || 5. Even he the Heavenly One who came for fellowship, Viṣhṇu to Indra, godly to the godlier, | Who Maker, throned in three worlds, helps the Ārya man, and gives the worshipper his share of Holy Law.

Hymn 1:157. Aśvins.

1. Agni is wakened: Sūrya riseth from the earth. Mighty, refulgent Dawn hath shone with all her light. | The Aśvins have equipped their chariot for the course. God Savitar hath moved the folk in sundry ways. ‖ 2. When, Aśvins, ye equip your very mighty car, bedew, ye Twain, our power with honey and with oil. | To our devotion give victorious strength in war: may we win riches in the heroes' strife for spoil. ‖ 3. Nigh to us come the Aśvins' lauded three-wheeled car, the car laden with meath and drawn by fleet-foot steeds, | Three-seated, opulent, bestowing all delight. may it bring weal to us, to cattle and to men. ‖ 4. Bring hither nourishment for us, ye Aśvins Twain; sprinkle us with your whip that drops with honey-dew. | Prolong our days of life, wipe out our trespasses; destroy our foes, be our companions and our Friends. ‖ 5. Ye store the germ of life in female creatures, ye lay it up within all living beings. | Ye have sent forth, O Aśvins passing mighty, the fire, the sovereigns of the wood, the waters, ‖ 6. Leeches are ye with medicines to heal us, and charioteers are ye with skill in driving. | Ye Strong, give sway to him who brings oblation and with his heart pours out his gift before you.

Hymn 1:158. Aśvins.

1. Ye Vasus Twain, ye Rudras full of counsel, grant us, Strong Strengtheners, when ye stand beside us, | What wealth Auchathya craves of you, great Helpers when ye come forward with no niggard succour. ‖ 2. Who may give you aught, Vasus, for your favour, for what, at the Cow's place, ye grant through worship? | Wake for us understanding full of riches, come with a heart that will fulfil our longing. ‖ 3. As erst for Tugra's son your car, sea-crossing, strong, was equipped and set amid the waters, | So may I gain your shelter and protection as with winged course a hero seeks his army. ‖ 4. May this my praise preserve Uchathya's offspring: let not these Twain who fly with wings exhaust me. | Let not the wood ten times up-piled consume me, when fixed for you it bites the ground it stands on. ‖ 5. The most maternal streams, wherein the Dāsas cast me securely bound, have not devoured me. | When Traitana would cleave my head asunder, the Dāsa wounded his own breast and shoulders. ‖ 6. Dīrghatamas the son of Mamatā hath come to length of days in the tenth age of human kind. | He is the Brahman of the waters as they strive to reach their end and aim: their charioteer is he.

Hymn 1:159. Heaven and Earth.

1. I praise with sacrifices mighty Heaven and Earth at festivals, the wise, the Strengtheners of Law. | Who, having Gods for progeny, conjoined with Gods, through wonder-working wisdom bring forth choicest boons. ‖ 2. With invocations, on the gracious Father's mind, and on the Mother's great inherent power I muse. | Prolific Parents, they have made the world of life, and for their brood all round wide immortality. ‖ 3. These Sons of yours well skilled in work, of wondrous power, brought forth to life the two great Mothers first of all. | To keep the truth of all that stands and all that moves, ye guard the station of your Son who knows no guile. ‖ 4. They with surpassing skill, most wise, have measured out the Twins united in their birth and in their home. | They, the refulgent Sages, weave within the sky, yea, in the depths of sea, a web for ever new. ‖ 5. This is today the goodliest gift of Savitar: this thought we have when now the God is furthering us. | On us with loving-kindness Heaven and Earth bestow riches and various wealth and treasure hundredfold!

Hymn 1:160. Heaven and Earth.

1. These, Heaven and Earth, bestow prosperity on all, sustainers of the region, Holy Ones and wise, | Two Bowls of noble kind: between these Goddesses the God, the fulgent Sun, travels by fixed decree. ‖ 2. Widely-capacious Pair, mighty, that never fail, the Father and the Mother keep all creatures safe: | The two world-halves, the spirited, the beautiful, because the Father hath clothed them in goodly forms. ‖ 3. Son of these Parents, he the Priest with power to cleanse, Sage, sanctifies the worlds with his surpassing power. | Thereto for his bright milk he milked through all the days the party-coloured Cow and the prolific Bull. ‖ 4. Among the skilful Gods most skilled is he, who made the two world-halves which bring prosperity to all; | Who with great wisdom measured both the regions out, and established them with pillars that shall ne'er decay. ‖ 5. Extolled in song, O Heaven and Earth, bestow on us, ye mighty Pair, great glory and high lordly sway, | Whereby we may extend ourselves ever over the folk; and send us strength that shall deserve the praise of men.

Hymn 1:161. Ṛibhus.

1. Why hath the Best, why hath the Youngest come to us? Upon what embassy comes he? What have we said? | We have not blamed the chalice of illustrious birth. We, Brother Agni, praised the goodness of the wood. ‖ 2. The chalice that is single make ye into four: thus have the Gods commanded; therefore am I come. | If, O Sudhanvan's Children, ye will do this thing ye shall participate in sacrifice with Gods. ‖ 3. What to the envoy Agni in reply ye spake, A courser must be made, a chariot fashioned here, | A cow must be created, and the Twain made young. When we have done these things, Brother, we turn to you. ‖ 4. When thus, O Ṛibhus, ye had done ye questioned thus, Whither went he who came to us a messenger? | Then Tvaṣhṭar, when he viewed the four wrought chalices, concealed himself among the Consorts of the Gods. ‖ 5. As Tvaṣhṭar thus had spoken, Let us slay these men who have reviled the chalice, drinking-cup of Gods, | They gave themselves new names when Soma juice was shed, and under these new names the Maiden welcomed them. ‖ 6. Indra hath yoked his Bays, the Aśvins' car is horsed, Bṛihaspati hath brought the Cow of every hue. | Ye went as Ṛibhus, Vibhvan, Vāja to the Gods, and skilled in war, obtained your share in sacrifice. ‖ 7. Ye by your wisdom brought a cow from out a hide; unto that ancient Pair ye gave again their youth. | Out of a horse, Sudhanvan's Sons, ye formed a horse: a chariot ye equipped, and went unto the Gods. ‖ 8. Drink ye this water, were the words ye spake to them; or drink ye this, the rinsing of the Muñja-grass. | If ye approve not even this, Sudhanvan's Sons, then at the third libation gladden ye yourselves. ‖ 9. Most excellent are waters, thus said one of you; most excellent is Agni, thus another said. | Another praised to many a one the lightning cloud. Then did ye shape the cups, speaking the words of truth. ‖ 10. One downward to the water drives the crippled cow, another trims the flesh brought on the carving-board. | One carries off the refuse at the set of sun. How did the Parents aid their children in their task! ‖ 11. On the high places ye have made the grass for man, and water in the valleys, by your skill, O Men. | Ṛibhus, ye iterate not today that act of yours, your sleeping in the house of him whom naught can hide. ‖ 12. As, compassing them round, ye glided through the worlds, where had the venerable Parents their abode? | Ye laid a curse on him who raised his arm at you: to him who spake aloud to you ye spake again. ‖ 13. When ye had slept your fill, ye Ṛibhus, thus ye asked, O thou whom naught may hide, who now hath wakened us? | The goat declared the hound to be your wakener. That day, in a full year, ye first unclosed our eyes. ‖ 14. The Marutas move in heaven, on earth this Agni; through the mid-firmament the Wind approaches. | Varuṇa comes in the sea's gathered waters, O Sons of Strength, desirous of your presence.

Hymn 1:162. The Horse.

1. Slight us not Varuṇa, Aryaman, or Mitra, Ṛibhukṣhan, Indra, Āyu, or the Marutas, | When we declare amid the congregation the virtues of the strong Steed, God-descended. ‖ 2. What time they bear before the Courser, covered with trappings and with wealth, the grasped oblation, | The dappled goat goeth straightforward, bleating, to the place dear to Indra and to Pūṣhan. ‖ 3. Dear to all Gods, this goat, the share of Pūṣhan, is first led forward with the vigorous Courser, | While Tvaṣhṭar sends him forward with the Charger, acceptable for sacrifice, to glory. ‖ 4. When thrice the men lead round the Steed, in order, who goeth to the Gods as meet oblation, | The goat precedeth him, the share of Pūṣhan, and to the Gods the sacrifice announceth. ‖ 5. Invoker, ministering priest, atoner, fire-kindler Soma-presser, sage, reciter, | With this well ordered sacrifice, well finished, do ye fill full the channels of the rivers. ‖ 6. The hewers of the post and those who carry it, and those who carve the knob to deck the Horse's stake; | Those who prepare the cooking-vessels for the Steed,—may the approving help of these promote our work. ‖ 7. Forth, for the regions of the Gods, the Charger with his smooth back is come my prayer attends him. | In him rejoice the singers and the sages. A good friend have we won for the Gods' banquet. ‖ 8. May the fleet Courser's halter and his heel-ropes, the head-stall and the girths and cords about him. | And the grass put within his mouth to bait him,—among the Gods, too, let all these be with thee. ‖ 9. What part of the Steed's flesh the fly hath eaten, or is left sticking to the post or hatchet, | Or to the slayer's hands and nails

adhereth,—among the Gods, too, may all this be with thee. ‖ 10. Food undigested steaming from his belly, and any odour of raw flesh remaining, | This let the immolators set in order and dress the sacrifice with perfect cooking. ‖ 11. What from thy body which with fire is roasted, when thou art set upon the spit, distilleth, | Let not that lie on earth or grass neglected, but to the longing Gods let all be offered. ‖ 12. They who observing that the Horse is ready call out and say, the smell is good; remove it; | And, craving meat, await the distribution,—may their approving help promote labour. ‖ 13. The trial-fork of the flesh-cooking cauldron, the vessels out of which the broth is sprinkled, | The warming-pots, the covers of the dishes, hooks, carving-boards,—all these attend the Charger. ‖ 14. The starting-place, his place of rest and rolling, the ropes wherewith the Charger's feet were fastened, | The water that he drank, the food he tasted,—among the Gods, too, may all these attend thee. ‖ 15. Let not the fire, smoke-scented, make thee crackle, nor glowing cauldron smell and break to pieces. | Offered, beloved, approved, and consecrated,—such Charger do the Gods accept with favour. ‖ 16. The robe they spread upon the Horse to clothe him, the upper covering and the golden trappings, | The halters which restrain the Steed, the heel-ropes,—all these, as grateful to the Gods, they offer. ‖ 17. If one, when seated, with excessive urging hath with his heel or with his whip distressed thee, | All these thy woes, as with the oblations' ladle at sacrifices, with my prayer I banish. ‖ 18. The four-and-thirty ribs of the. Swift Charger, kin to the Gods, the slayer's hatchet pierces. | Cut ye with skill, so that the parts be flawless, and piece by piece declaring them dissect them. ‖ 19. Of Tvashṭar's Charger there is one dissector,—this is the custom-two there are who guide him. | Such of his limbs as I divide in order, these, amid the balls, in fire I offer. ‖ 20. Let not thy dear soul burn thee as thou comest, let not the hatchet linger in thy body. | Let not a greedy clumsy immolator, missing the joints, mangle thy limbs unduly. ‖ 21. No, here thou diest not, thou art not injured: by easy paths unto the Gods thou goest. | Both Bays, both spotted mares are now thy fellows, and to the ass's pole is yoked the Charger. ‖ 22. May this Steed bring us all-sustaining riches, wealth in good kine, good horses, manly offspring. | Freedom from sin may Aditi vouchsafe us: the Steed with our oblations gain us lordship!

Hymn 1:163. The Horse.

1. What time, first springing into life, thou neighedst, proceeding from the sea or upper waters, | Limbs of the deer hadst thou, and eagle pinions. O Steed, thy birth is nigh and must be lauded. ‖ 2. This Steed which Yama gave hath Trita harnessed, and him, the first of all, hath Indra mounted. | His bridle the Gandharva grasped. O Vasus, from out the Sun ye fashioned forth the Courser. ‖ 3. Yama art thou, O Horse; thou art Āditya; Trita art thou by secret operation. | Thou art divided thoroughly from Soma. They say thou hast three bonds in heaven | that hold thee. ‖ 4. Three bonds, they say, thou hast in heaven that bind thee, three in the waters, | three within the ocean. | To me thou seemest Varuṇa, O Courser, there where they say is thy sublimest birth-place. ‖ 5. Here-, Courser, are the places where they groomed thee, here are the traces of thy hoofs as winner. | Here have I seen the auspicious reins that guide thee, which those who guard the holy Law keep safely. ‖ 6. Thyself from far I recognized in spirit,—a Bird that from below flew through the heaven. | I saw thy head still soaring, striving upward by paths unsoiled by dust, pleasant to travel. ‖ 7. Here I beheld thy form, matchless in glory, eager to win thee food at the Cow's station. | Whene'er a man brings thee to thine enjoyment, thou swallowest the plants most greedy eater. ‖ 8. After thee, Courser, come the car, the bridegroom, the kine come after, and the charm of maidens. | Full companies have followed for thy friendship: the pattern of thy vigour Gods have copied. ‖ 9. Horns made of gold hath he: his feet are iron: less fleet than he, though swift as thought, is Indra. | The Gods have come that they may taste the oblation of him who mounted, first of all, the Courser. ‖ 10. Symmetrical in flank, with rounded haunches, mettled like heroes, the Celestial Coursers | Put forth their strength, like swans in lengthened order, when they, the Steeds, have reached the heavenly causeway. ‖ 11. A body formed for flight hast thou, O Charger; swift as the wind in motion is thy spirit. | Thy horns are spread abroad in all directions: they move with restless beat in wildernesses. ‖ 12. The strong Steed hath come forward to the slaughter, pondering with a mind directed God-ward. | The goat who is his kin is led before him the sages and the singers follow after. ‖ 13. The Steed is come unto the noblest mansion, is come unto his Father and his Mother. | This day shall he approach the Gods, most welcome: then he declares good gifts to him who offers.

Hymn 1:164. Viśvedevas.

1. Of this benignant Priest, with eld grey-coloured, the brother midmost of the three is lightning. | The third is he whose back with oil is sprinkled. Here I behold the Chief with seven male children. ‖ 2. Seven to the one-wheeled chariot yoke the Courser; bearing seven names the single Courser draws it. | Three-naved the wheel is, sound and undecaying, whereon are resting all these worlds of being. ‖ 3. The seven who on the seven-wheeled car are mounted have horses, seven in tale, who draw them onward. | Seven Sisters utter songs of praise together, in whom the names of the seven Cows are treasured. ‖ 4. Who hath beheld him as he sprang to being, seen how the boneless One supports the bony? | Where is the blood of earth, the life, the spirit? Who may approach the man who knows, to ask it? ‖ 5. Unripe in mind, in spirit undiscerning, I ask of these the Gods' established places; | For up above the yearling Calf the sages, to form a web, their own seven threads have woven. ‖ 6. I ask, unknowing, those who know, the sages, as one all ignorant for sake of knowledge, | What was that ONE who in the Unborn's image hath established and fixed firm these worlds' six regions. ‖ 7. Let him who knoweth presently declare it, this lovely Bird's securely founded station. | Forth from his head the Cows draw milk, and, wearing his vesture, with their foot have drunk the water. ‖ 8. The Mother gave the Sire his share of Order: with thought, at first, she wedded him in spirit. | She, the coy Dame, was filled with dew prolific: with adoration men approached to praise her. ‖ 9. Yoked was the Mother to the boon Cow's car-pole: in the dank rows of cloud the Infant rested. | Then the Calf lowed, and looked upon the Mother, the Cow who wears all shapes in three directions. ‖ 10. Bearing three Mothers and three Fathers, single he stood erect: they never make him weary. | There on the pitch of heaven they speak together in speech all-knowing but not all-impelling. ‖ 11. Formed with twelve spokes, by length of time, unweakened, rolls round the heaven this wheel of during Order. | Herein established, joined in pairs together, seven hundred Sons and twenty stand, O Agni. ‖ 12. They call him in the farther half of heaven the Sire five-footed, of twelve forms, wealthy in watery store. | These others say that he, God with far-seeing eyes, is mounted on the lower seven-wheeled, six-spoked car. ‖ 13. Upon this five-spoked wheel revolving ever all living creatures rest and are dependent. | Its axle, heavy-laden, is not heated: the nave from ancient time remains unbroken. ‖ 14. The wheel revolves, unwasting, with its felly: ten draw it, yoked to the far-stretching car-pole. | The Sun's eye moves encompassed by the region: on him dependent rest all living creatures. ‖ 15. Of the co-born they call the seventh single-born; the six twin pairs are called Ṛishis, Children of Gods. | Their good gifts sought of men are ranged in order due, and various in their form move for the Lord who guides. ‖ 16. They told me these were males, though truly females: he who hath eyes sees this, the blind discerns not. | The son who is a sage hath comprehended: who knows this rightly is his father's father. ‖ 17. Beneath the upper realm, above this lower, bearing her calf at foot the Cow hath risen. | Witherward, to what place hath she departed? Where calves she? Not amid this herd of cattle. ‖ 18. Who, that the father of this Calf discerneth beneath the upper realm, above the lower, | Showing himself a sage, may here declare it? Whence hath the Godlike spirit had its rising? ‖ 19. Those that come hitherward they call departing, those that depart they call directed hither. | And what so ye have made, Indra and Soma, steeds bear as 'twere yoked to the region's car-pole. ‖ 20. Two Birds with fair wings, knit with bonds of friendship, in the same sheltering tree have found a refuge. | One of the twain eats the sweet Fig-tree's fruitage; the other eating not regardeth only. ‖ 21. Where those fine Birds hymn ceaselessly their portion of life eternal, and the sacred synods, | There is the Universe's mighty Keeper, who, wise, hath entered into me the simple. ‖ 22. The, tree whereon the fine Birds eat the sweetness, where they all rest and procreate their offspring,— | Upon its top they say the fig is luscious none gaineth it who knoweth not the Father. ‖ 23. How on the Gāyatrī the Gāyatrī was based, how from the Trishṭubh they fashioned the Trishṭubh forth, | How on the Jagatī was based the Jagatī,—they who know this have won themselves

immortal life. ‖ 24. With Gāyatrī he measures out the praise-song, Sāman with praise-song, triplet with the Trishṭubh. | The triplet with the two or four-foot measure, and with the syllable they form seven metres. ‖ 25. With Jagatī the flood in heaven he established, and saw the Sun in the Rathantara Sāman. | Gāyatrī hath, they say, three brands for kindling: hence it excels in majesty and vigour. ‖ 26. I invocate the milch-cow good for milking so that the milker, deft of hand, may drain her. | May Savitar give goodliest stimulation. The cauldron is made hot; I will proclaim it. ‖ 27. She, lady of all treasure, is come hither yearning in spirit for her calf and lowing. | May this cow yield her milk for both the Aśvins, and may she prosper to our high advantage. ‖ 28. The cow hath lowed after her blinking youngling; she licks his forehead, as she lows, to form it. | His mouth she fondly calls to her warm udder, and suckles him with milk while gently lowing. ‖ 29. He also snorts, by whom encompassed round the Cow laws as she clings unto the shedder of the rain. | She with her shrilling cries hath humbled mortal man, and, turned to lightning, hath stripped off her covering robe. ‖ 30. That which hath breath and speed and life and motion lies firmly established in the midst of houses. | Living, by offerings to the Dead he moveth Immortal One, the brother of the mortal. ‖ 31. I saw the Herdsman, him who never stumbles, approaching by his pathways and departing. | He, clothed with gathered and diffusive splendour, within the worlds continually travels. ‖ 32. He who hath made him cloth not comprehend him: from him who saw him surely is he hidden. | He, yet enveloped in his Mother's bosom, source of much life, hath sunk into destruction. ‖ 33. Dyaus is my Father, my begetter: kinship is here. This great earth is my kin and Mother. | Between the wide-spread world-halves is the birth-place: the Father laid the Daughter's germ within it. ‖ 34. I ask thee of the earth's extremest limit, where is the centre of the world, I ask thee. | I ask thee of the Stallion's seed prolific, I ask of highest heaven where Speech abideth. ‖ 35. This altar is the earth's extremest limit; this sacrifice of ours is the world's centre. | The Stallion's seed prolific is the Soma; this Brahman highest heaven where Speech abideth. ‖ 36. Seven germs unripened yet are heaven's prolific seed: their functions they maintain by Vishṇu's ordinance. | Endued with wisdom through intelligence and thought, they compass us about present on every side. ‖ 37. What thing I truly am I know not clearly: mysterious, fettered in my mind I wander. | When the first-born of holy Law approached me, then of this speech I first obtain a portion. ‖ 38. Back, forward goes he, grasped by strength inherent, the Immortal born the brother of the mortal | Ceaseless they move in opposite directions: men mark the one, and fail to mark the other. ‖ 39. Upon what syllable of holy praise-song, as twere their highest heaven, the Gods repose them,— | Who knows not this, what will he do with praise-song? But they who know it well sit here assembled. ‖ 40. Fortunate mayst thou be with goodly pasture, and may we also be exceeding wealthy. | Feed on the grass, O Cow, at every season, and coming hitherward drink limpid water. ‖ 41. Forming the water-floods, the buffalo hath lowed, one-footed or two-footed or four-footed, she, | Who hath become eight-footed or hath got nine feet, the thousand-syllabled in the sublimest heaven. ‖ 42. From her descend in streams the seas of water; thereby the world's four regions have their being, | Thence flows the imperishable flood and thence the universe hath life. ‖ 43. I saw from far away the smoke of fuel with spires that rose on high o'er that beneath it. | The Mighty Men have dressed the spotted bullock. These were the customs in the days aforetime, ‖ 44. Three with long tresses show in ordered season. One of them sheareth when the year is ended. | One with his powers the universe regardeth: Of one, the sweep is seen, but his figure. ‖ 45. Speech hath been measured out in four divisions, the Brahmans who have understanding know them. | Three kept in close concealment cause no motion; of speech, men speak only the fourth division. ‖ 46. They call him Indra, Mitra, Varuṇa, Agni, and he is heavenly nobly-winged Garutmān. | To what is One, sages give many a title they call it Agni, Yama, Mātariśvan. ‖ 47. Dark the descent: the birds are golden-coloured; up to the heaven they fly robed in the waters. | Again descend they from the seat of Order, and all the earth is moistened with their fatness. ‖ 48. Twelve are the fellies, and the wheel is single; three are the naves. What man hath understood it? | Therein are set together spokes three hundred and sixty, which in nowise can be loosened. ‖ 49. That breast of thine exhaustless, spring of pleasure, wherewith thou feedest all things that are choicest, | Wealth-giver, treasure. finder, free bestower,—bring that, Sarasvatī, that we may drain it. ‖ 50. By means of sacrifice the Gods accomplished their sacrifice: these were the earliest ordinances. | These Mighty Ones attained the height of heaven, there where the Sādhyas, Gods of old, are dwelling. ‖ 51. Uniform, with the passing days, this water mounts and fails again. | The tempest-clouds give life to earth, and fires re-animate the heaven. ‖ 52. The Bird Celestial, vast with noble pinion, the lovely germ of plants, the germ of waters, | Him who delighteth us with rain in season, Sarasvat I invoke that he may help us.

Hymn 1:165. Indra. Marutas.

1. With what bright beauty are the Marutas jointly invested, peers in age, who dwell together? | From what place have they come? With what intention? Sing they their strength through love of wealth, these Heroes? ‖ 2. Whose prayers have they, the Youthful Ones, accepted? Who to his sacrifice hath turned the Marutas? | We will delay them on their journey sweeping—with what high spirit!—through the air like eagles. ‖ 3. Whence comest thou alone, thou who art mighty, Indra, Lord of the Brave? What is thy purpose? | Thou greetest us when meeting us the Bright Ones. Lord of Bay Steeds, say what thou hast against us. ‖ 4. Mine are devotions, hymns; sweet are libations. Strength stirs, and hurled forth is my bolt of thunder. | They call for me, their lauds are longing for me. These my Bay Steeds bear me to these oblations. ‖ 5. Therefore together with our strong companions, having adorned our bodies, now we harness, | Our spotted deer with might, for thou, O Indra, hast learnt and understood our Godlike nature. ‖ 6. Where was that nature then of yours, O Marutas, that ye charged me alone to slay the Dragon? | For I in truth am fierce and strong and mighty. I bent away from every foeman's weapons. ‖ 7. Yea, much hast thou achieved with us for comrades, with manly valour like thine own, thou Hero. | Much may we too achieve, O mightiest Indra, with our great power, we Marutas, when we will it. ‖ 8. Vṛitra I slew by mine own strength, O Marutas, having waxed mighty in mine indignation. | I with the thunder in my hand created for man these lucid softly flowing waters. ‖ 9. Nothing, O Maghavan, stands firm before thee; among the Gods not one is found | thine equal. | None born or springing into life comes nigh thee. Do what thou hast to do, exceeding mighty? ‖ 10. Mine only be transcendent power, whatever I, daring in my spirit, may accomplish. | For I am known as terrible, O Marutas I, Indra, am the Lord of what I ruined. ‖ 11. Now, O ye Marutas, hath your praise rejoiced me, the glorious hymn which ye have made me, Heroes! | For me, for Indra, champion strong in battle, for me, yourselves, as lovers for a lover. ‖ 12. Here, truly, they send forth their sheen to meet me, wearing their blameless glory and their vigour. | When I have seen you, Marutas, in gay splendour, ye have delighted me, so now delight me. ‖ 13. Who here hath magnified you, O ye Marutas? speed forward, O ye lovers, to your lovers. | Ye Radiant Ones, assisting their devotions, of these my holy rites he ye regardful. ‖ 14. To this hath Mānya's wisdom brought us, so as to aid, as aids the poet him who worships. | Bring hither quick! On to the sage, ye Marutas! These prayers for you the singer hath recited. ‖ 15. May this your praise, may this your song, O Marutas, sung by the poet, Māna's son, Māndārya, | Bring offspring for ourselves with food to feed us. May we find strengthening food in full abundance!

Hymn 1:166. Marutas.

1. Now let us publish, for the vigorous company the herald of the Strong One, their primeval might. | With fire upon your way, O Marutas loud of voice, with battle, Mighty Ones, achieve your deeds of strength. ‖ 2. Bringing the pleasant meath as 'twere their own dear son, they sport in sportive wise gay at their gatherings. | The Rudras come with succour to the worshipper; self-strong they fail not him who offers sacrifice. ‖ 3. To whomsoever, bringer of oblations, they immortal guardians, have given plenteous wealth, | For him, like loving friends, the Marutas bringing bliss bedew the regions round with milk abundantly. ‖ 4. Ye who with mighty powers have stirred the regions up, your coursers have sped forth directed by themselves. | All creatures of the earth, all dwellings are afraid, for brilliant is your coming with your spears advanced. ‖ 5. When they in dazzling rush have made the mountains roar, and shaken heaven's high back in their heroic strength, | Each sovereign of the forest fears as ye drive near, aid the shrubs fly before you swift as whirling wheels. ‖ 6. Terrible

Marutas, ye with ne'er-diminished host, with great benevolence fulfil our heart's desire. | Where'er your lightning bites armed with its gory teeth it crunches up the cattle like a well-aimed dart. || 7. Givers of during gifts whose bounties never fail, free from ill-will, at sacrifices glorified, | They sing their song aloud that they may drink sweet juice: well do they know the Hero's first heroic deeds. || 8. With castles hundredfold, O Marutas, guard ye well the man whom ye have loved from ruin and from sin,— | The man whom ye the fierce, the Mighty ones who roar, preserve from calumny by cherishing his seed. || 9. O Marutas, in your cars are all things that are good: great powers are set as 'twere in rivalry therein. | Rings are upon your shoulders when ye journey forth: your axle turns together both the chariot wheels. || 10. Held in your manly arms are many goodly things, gold chains are on your chests, and glistering ornaments, | Deer-skins are on their shoulders, on their fellies knives: they spread their glory out as birds spread out their wings. || 11. Mighty in mightiness, pervading, passing strong, visible from afar as 'twere with stars of heaven, | Lovely with pleasant tongues, sweet singers with their mouths, the Marutas, joined with Indra, shout forth all around. || 12. This is your majesty, ye Marutas nobly born, far as the sway of Aditi your bounty spreads. | Even Indra by desertion never disannuls the boon bestowed by you upon the pious man. || 13. This is your kinship, Marutas, that, Immortals, ye were oft in olden time regardful of our call, | Having vouchsafed to man a hearing through this prayer, by wondrous deeds the Heroes have displayed their might. || 14. That, O ye Marutas, we may long time flourish through your abundant riches, O swift movers, | And that our men may spread in the encampment, let me complete the rite with these oblations. || 15. May this your laud, may this your song, O Marutas, sung by the poet, Māna's son, Māndārya, | Bring offspring for ourselves with food to feed us. May we find strengthening food in full abundance.

Hymn 1:167. Indra. Marutas.

1. A thousand are thy helps for us, O Indra: a thousand, Lord of Bays, thy choice refreshments. | Wealth of a thousand sorts hast thou to cheer us: may precious goods come nigh to us in thousands. || 2. May the most sapient Marutas, with protection, with best boons brought from lofty heaven, approach us, | Now when their team of the most noble horses speeds even on the sea's extremest limit. || 3. Close to them clings one moving in seclusion, like a man's wife, like a spear carried rearward, | Well grasped, bright, decked with gold there is Vāk also, like to a courtly, eloquent dame, among them. || 4. Far off the brilliant, never-weary Marutas cling to the young Maid as a joint possession. | The fierce Gods drave not Rodasī before them, but wished for her to grow their friend and fellow. || 5. When chose immortal Rodasī to follow—she with loose tresses and heroic spirit— | She climbed her servant's chariot, she like Sūrya with cloud-like motion and refulgent aspect. || 6. Upon their car the young men set the Maiden wedded to glory, mighty in assemblies, | When your song, Marutas, rose, and, with oblation, the Soma-pourer sang his hymn in worship. || 7. I will declare the greatness of these Marutas, their real greatness, worthy to be lauded, | How, with them, she though firm, strong-minded, haughty, travels to women happy in their fortune. || 8. Mitra and Varuṇa they guard from censure: Aryaman too, discovers worthless sinners Firm things are overthrown that ne'er were shaken: he prospers, Marutas, who gives choice oblations. || 9. None of us, Marutas, near or at a distance, hath ever reached the limit of your vigour. | They in courageous might still waxing boldly have compassed round their foemen like an ocean. || 10. May we this day be dearest friends of Indra, and let us call on him in fight tomorrow. | So were we erst. New might attend us daily! So be with us! Ṛibhukṣhan of the Heroes! || 11. May this your laud, may this your song, O Marutas, sung by the poet, Māna's | son, Māndārya, | Bring offspring for ourselves with. food to feed us. May we find strengthening food in full abundance.

Hymn 1:168. Marutas.

1. Swift gain is his who hath you near at every rite: ye welcome every song of him who serves the Gods. | So may I turn you hither with fair hymns of praise to give great succour for the weal of both the worlds. || 2. Surrounding, as it were, self-born, self-powerful, they spring to life the shakers-down of food and light; | Like as the countess undulations of the floods, worthy of praise when near, like bullocks and like kine. || 3. They who, like Somas with their well-grown stalks pressed out, imbibed within the heart, dwell there in friendly wise. | Upon their shoulders rests as 'twere a warrior's spear and in their hand they hold a dagger and a ring. || 4. Self-yoked they have descended lightly from the sky. With your own lash, Immortals, urge yourselves to speed. | Unstained by dust the Marutas, mighty in their strength, have cast down e'en firm things, armed with their shining spears. || 5. Who among you, O Marutas armed with lightning-spears, moveth you by himself, as with the tongue his jaws? | Ye rush from heaven's floor as though ye sought for food, on many errands like the Sun's diurnal Steed. || 6. Say where, then, is this mighty region's farthest bound, where, Marutas, is the lowest depth that ye have reached, | When ye cast down like chaff the firmly established pile, and from the mountain send the glittering water-flood? || 7. Your winning is with strength, dazzling, with heavenly light, with fruit mature, O Marutas, fall of plenteousness. | Auspicious is your gift like a free giver's meed, victorious, spreading far, as of immortal Gods. || 8. The rivers roar before your chariot fellies when they are uttering the voice of rain-clouds. | The lightnings laugh upon the earth beneath them, what time the Marutas scatter forth their fatness. || 9. Pṛiśni brought forth, to fight the mighty battle, the glittering army of the restless Marutas. | Nurtured together they begat the monster, and then looked round them for the food that strengthens. || 10. May this your laud, may this your song O Marutas, sung by the poet Māna's son, | Māndārya, | Bring offspring for ourselves with food to feed us. May we find strengthening food in full abundance.

Hymn 1:169. Indra.

1. As, Indra, from great treason thou protectest, yea, from great treachery these who approach us, | So, marking well, Controller of the Marutas grant us their blessings, for they are thy dearest. || 2. The various doings of all mortal people by thee are ordered, in thy wisdom, Indra. | The host of Marutas goeth forth exulting to win the light-bestowing spoil of battle. || 3. That spear of thine sat firm for us, O Indra: the Marutas set their whole dread power in motion. | E'en Agni shines resplendent in the brush-wood: the viands hold him as floods hold an island. || 4. Vouchsafe us now that opulence, O Indra, as guerdon won by mightiest donation. | May hymns that please thee cause the breast of Vāyu to swell as with the mead's refreshing sweetness. || 5. With thee, O Indra, are most bounteous riches that further every one who lives uprightly. | Now may these Marutas show us loving-kindness, Gods who of old were ever prompt to help us. || 6. Bring forth the Men who rain down boons, O Indra: exert thee in the great terrestrial region; | For their broad-chested speckled deer are standing like a King's armies on the field of battle. || 7. Heard is the roar of the advancing Marutas, terrific, glittering, and swiftly moving, | Who with their rush o'erthrow as 'twere a sinner the mortal who would fight with those who love him || 8. Give to the Mānas, Indra with Marutas, gifts universal, gifts of cattle foremost. | Thou, God, art praised with Gods who must be lauded. May we find strengthening food in full abundance.

Hymn 1:170. Indra. Marutas.

1. Naught is today, tomorrow naught. Who comprehends the mystery? | We must address ourselves unto another's thought, and lost is then the hope we formed. || 2. The Marutas are thy brothers. Why, O Indra, wouldst thou take our lives? | Agree with them in friendly wise, and do not slay us in the fight. || 3. Agastya, brother, why dost thou neglect us, thou who art our friend? | We know the nature of thy mind. Verity thou wilt give us naught. || 4. Let them prepare the altar, let them kindle fire in front: we two | Here will spread sacrifice for thee, that the Immortal may observe. || 5. Thou, Lord of Wealth, art Master of all treasures, thou, Lord of friends, art thy friends' best supporter. | O Indra, speak thou kindly with the Marutas, and taste oblations in their proper season.

Hymn 1:171. Marutas.

1. To you I come with this mine adoration, and with a hymn I crave the Strong Ones' favour | A hymn that truly makes you joyful, Marutas. Suppress your anger and unyoke your horses. || 2. Marutas, to you this laud with prayer and worship, formed in the mind and heart, ye Gods, is offered. | Come ye to us, rejoicing in your spirit, for ye are they who make our prayer effective. || 3. The Marutas, praised by us, shall show us favour; Maghavan, lauded, shall be most propitious. | Marutas,, may all our days that are to follow be very pleasant, lovely and triumphant. || 4. I fled in

terror from this mighty Indra, my body trembling in alarm, O Marutas. | Oblations meant for you had been made ready; these have we set aside: for this forgive us. || 5. By whom the Mānas recognize the day-springs, by whose strength at the dawn of endless mornings, | Give us, thou Mighty, glory with Marutas. fierce with the fierce, the Strong who givest triumph. || 6. Do thou, O Indra, guard the conquering Heroes, and rid thee of thy wrath against the Marutas, | With them, the wise, victorious and bestowing. May we find strengthening food in full abundance.

Hymn 1:172. Marutas.

1. Wonderful let your coming be, wondrous with help, ye Bounteous Ones, | Marutas, who gleam as serpents gleam. || 2. Far be from us, O Marutas, ye free givers, your impetuous shaft; | Far from us be the stone ye hurl. || 3. O Bounteous Givers, touch ye not, O Marutas, Tṛiṇaskanda's folk; | Lift ye us up that we may live.

Hymn 1:173. Indra.

1. The praise-song let him sing forth bursting bird-like: sing we that hymn which like heaven's light expandeth, | That the milk-giving cows may, unimpeded call to the sacred grass the Gods' assembly. || 2. Let the Bull sing with Bulls whose toil is worship, with a loud roar like some wild beast that hungers. | Praised God! the glad priest brings his heart's devotion; the holy youth presents twofold oblation. || 3. May the Priest come circling the measured stations, and with him bring the earth's autumnal fruitage. | Let the Horse neigh led near, let the Steer bellow: let the Voice go between both worlds as herald, || 4. To him we offer welcomest oblations, the pious bring their strength-inspiring praises. | May Indra, wondrous in his might, accept them, car-borne and swift to move like the Nāsatyas. || 5. Praise thou that Indra who is truly mighty, the car-borne Warrior, Maghavan the Hero; | Stronger in war than those who fight against him, borne by strong steeds, who kills enclosing darkness; || 6. Him who surpasses heroes in his greatness: the earth and heavens suffice not for his girdles. | Indra endues the earth to be his garment, and, God-like, wears the heaven as 'twere a frontlet, || 7. Thee, Hero, guardian of the brave in battles, who roamest in the van,—to draw thee hither, | Indra, the hosts agree beside the Soma, and joy, for his great actions, in the Chieftain. || 8. Libations in the sea to thee are pleasant, when thy divine Floods come to cheer these people. | To thee the Cow is sum of all things grateful when with the wish thou seekest men and princes. || 9. So may we in this One be well befriended, well aided as it were through praise of chieftains, | That Indra still may linger at our worship, as one led swift to work, to hear our praises. || 10. Like men in rivalry extolling princes, our Friend be Indra, wielder of the thunder. | Like true friends of some city's lord within them held in good rule with sacrifice they help him. || 11. For every sacrifice makes Indra stronger, yea, when he goes around angry in spirit; | As pleasure at the ford invites the thirsty, as the long way brings him who gains his object. || 12. Let us not here contend with Gods, O Indra, for here, O Mighty One, is thine own portion, | The Great, whose Friends the bounteous Marutas honour, as with a stream, his song who pours oblations. || 13. Addressed to thee is this our praise, O Indra: Lord of Bay Steeds, find us hereby advancement. | So mayst thou lead us on, O God, to comfort. May we find strengthening food in full abundance.

Hymn 1:174. Indra.

1. Thou art the King of all the Gods, O Indra: protect the men, O Asura, preserve us. | Thou Lord of Heroes, Maghavan, our saver, art faithful, very rich, the victory-giver. || 2. Indra, thou humbledst tribes that spake with insult by breaking down seven autumn forts, their refuge. | Thou stirredst, Blameless! billowy floods, and gavest his foe a prey to youthful Purukutsa. || 3. With whom thou drivest troops whose lords are heroes, and bringest daylight now, much worshipped Indra, | With them guard lion-like wasting active Agni to dwell in our tilled fields and in our homestead. || 4. They through the greatness of thy spear, O Indra, shall, to thy praise, rest in this earthly station. | To loose the floods, to seek, for kine, the battle, his Bays he mounted boldly seized the booty. || 5. Indra, bear Kutsa, him in whom thou joyest: the dark-red horses of the Wind are docile. | Let the Sun roll his chariot wheel anear us, and let the Thunderer go to meet the foemen. || 6. Thou Indra, Lord of Bays, made strong by impulse, hast slain the vexers of thy friends, who give not. | They who beheld the Friend beside the living were cast aside by thee as they rode onward. || 7. Indra, the bard sang forth in inspiration: thou madest earth a covering for the Dāsa. | Maghavan made the three that gleam with moisture, and to his home brought Kuyavāch to slay him. || 8. These thine old deeds new bards have sung, O Indra. Thou conqueredst, boundest many tribes for ever. | Like castles thou hast crushed the godless races, and bowed the godless scorner's deadly weapon. || 9. A Stormer thou hast made the stormy waters flow down, O Indra, like the running rivers. | When o'er the flood thou broughtest them, O Hero, thou keptest Turvaśa and Yadu safely. || 10. Indra, mayst thou be ours in all occasions, protector of the men, most gentle-hearted, | Giving us victory over all our rivals. May we find strengthening food in full abundance.

Hymn 1:175. Indra.

1. Glad thee: thy glory hath been quaffed, Lord of Bay Steeds, as 'twere the bowl's enlivening mead. | For thee the Strong there is strong drink, mighty, omnipotent to win. || 2. Let our strong drink, most excellent, exhilarating, come to thee, | Victorious, Indra! bringing gain, immortal conquering in fight, || 3. Thou, Hero, winner of the spoil, urgest to speed the car of man. | Burn, like a vessel with the flame, the lawless Dasyu, Conqueror! || 4. Empowered by thine own might, O Sage, thou stolest Sūrya's chariot wheel. | Thou barest Kutsa with the steeds of Wind to Śuṣhṇa as his death. || 5. Most mighty is thy rapturous joy, most splendid is thine active power, | Wherewith, foe-slaying, sending bliss, thou art supreme in gaining steeds. || 6. As thou, O Indra, to the ancient singers wast ever joy, as water to the thirsty, | So unto thee I sing this invocation. May we find strengthening food in full abundance.

Hymn 1:176. Indra.

1. Cheer thee with draughts to win us bliss: Soma, pierce Indra in thy strength. | Thou stormest trembling in thy rage, and findest not a foeman nigh. || 2. Make our songs penetrate to him who is the Only One of men; | For whom the sacred food is spread, as the steer ploughs the barley in. || 3. Within whose hands deposited all the Five Peoples' treasures rest. | Mark thou the man who injures us and kill him like the heavenly bolt. || 4. Slay everyone who pours no gift, who, hard to reach, delights thee not. | Bestow on us what wealth he hath: this even the worshipper awaits. || 5. Thou helpest him the doubly strong whose hymns were sung unceasingly. | When Indra fought, O Soma, thou helpest the mighty in the fray. || 6. As thou, O Indra, to the ancient singers wast ever joy, like water to the thirsty, | So unto thee I sing this invocation. May we find strengthening food in full abundance.

Hymn 1:177. Indra.

1. The Bull of men, who cherishes all people, King of the Races, Indra, called of many, | Fame-loving, praised, hither to me with succour turn having yoked both vigorous Bay Horses! || 2. Thy mighty Stallions, yoked by prayer, O Indra, thy. Coursers to thy mighty chariot harnessed,— | Ascend thou these, and borne by them come hither: with Soma juice out. poured, Indra, we call thee. || 3. Ascend thy mighty car: the mighty Soma is poured for thee and sweets are sprinkled round us. | Come down to us-ward, Bull of human races, come, having harnessed them, with strong Bay Horses. || 4. Here is God-reaching sacrifice, here the victim; here, Indra, are the prayers, here is the Soma. | Strewn is the sacred grass: come hither, Śakra; seat thee and drink: unyoke thy two Bay Coursers. || 5. Come to us, Indra, come thou highly lauded to the devotions of the singer Māna. | Singing, may we find early through thy succour, may we find strengthening food in full abundance.

Hymn 1:178. Indra.

1. If, Indra, thou hast given that gracious hearing where with thou helpest those who sang thy praises. | Blast not the wish that would exalt us may I gain all from thee, and pay all man's devotions. || 2. Let not the Sovereign Indra disappoint us in what shall bring both Sisters to our dwelling. | To him have run the quickly flowing waters. May Indra come to us with life and friendship. || 3. Victorious with the men, Hero in battles, Indra, who hears the singer's supplication, | Will bring his car nigh to the man who offers, if he himself upholds the songs that praise him. || 4. Yea, Indra, with the men, through love of glory consumes the sacred food which friends have offered. | The ever-strengthening song of him who worships is sung in fight amid the clash of voices. || 5. Aided by thee, O Maghavan, O Indra, may we subdue our foes who count them mighty. | Be our protector,

strengthen and increase us. May we find strengthening food in full abundance.

Hymn 1:179. Rāti.

[see the appendix for notes on this hymn]

1. Through many autumns have I toiled and laboured, at night and morn, through age-inducing dawnings. | Old age impairs the beauty of our bodies. Let husbands still come near unto their spouses. || 2. For even the men aforetime, law-fulfillers, who with the Gods declared eternal statutes, — | They have decided, but have not accomplished: so now let Wives come near unto their husbands. || 3. Non inutilis est labor cui Dii favent: nos omnes aemulos et aemulas vincamus. | Superemus in hac centum artium pugna in qua duas partes convenientes utrinque commovemus. || 4. Cupido me cepit illius tauri [viri] qui me despicit, utrum hinc utrum illinc ab aliqua parte nata sit. | Lopāmudrā taurum [maritum suum] ad se detrahit: insipiens illa sapientem anhelantem absorbet. || 5. This Soma I address that is most near us, that which hath been imbibed within the spirit, | To pardon any sins we have committed. Verily mortal man is full of longings. || 6. Agastya thus, toiling with strong endeavour, wishing for children, progeny and power, | Cherished—a sage of mighty strength—both classes, and with the Gods obtained his prayer's fulfilment.

Hymn 1:180. Aśvins.

1. Lightly your coursers travel through the regions when round the sea of air your car is flying. | Your golden fellies scatter drops of moisture: drinking the sweetness ye attend the Mornings. || 2. Ye as ye travel overtake the Courser who flies apart, the Friend of man, most holy. | The prayer is that the Sister may convey you, all praised, meath-drinkers! to support and strengthen. || 3. Ye have deposited, matured within her, in the raw cow the first milk of the milch-cow, | Which the bright offerer, shining like a serpent mid trees, presents to you whose form is perfect. || 4. Ye made the fierce heat to be full of sweetness for Atri at his wish, like streaming water. | Fire-offering thence is yours, O Aśvins, Heroes: your car-wheels speed to us like springs of honey. || 5. Like Tugra's ancient son may I, ye Mighty, bring you to give your gifts with milk-oblations. | Your greatness compasseth Earth, Heaven, and Waters: decayed for you is sorrow's net, ye Holy. || 6. When, Bounteous Ones, ye drive your yoked team downward, ye send, by your own natures, understanding. | Swift as the wind let the prince please and feast you: he, like a pious man, gains strength for increase. || 7. For verily we truthful singers praise you the niggard trafficker is here excluded. | Now, even now do ye O blameless Aśvins, ye Mighty, guard the man whose God is near him. || 8. You of a truth day after day, O Aśvins, that he might win the very plenteous torrent, | Agastya, famous among mortal heroes, roused with a thousand lauds like sounds of music. || 9. When with the glory of your car ye travel, when we go speeding like the priest of mortals, | And give good horses to sacrificers, may we, Nāsatyas! gain our share of riches. || 10. With songs of praise we call today, O Aśvins, that your new chariot, for our own well-being, | That circles heaven with never-injured fellies. May we find strengthening food in full abundance.

Hymn 1:181. Aśvins.

1. What, dearest Pair, is this in strength and riches that ye as Priests are bring from the waters? | This sacrifice is your glorification, ye who protect mankind and give them treasures. || 2. May your pure steeds, rain-drinkers, bring you hither, swift as the tempest, your celestial coursers, | Rapid as thought, with fair backs, full of vigour, resplendent in their native light, O Aśvins. || 3. Your car is like a torrent rushing downward: may it come nigh, broad-seated, for our welfare,— | Car holy, strong, that ever would be foremost, thought-swift, which ye, for whom we long, have mounted. || 4. Here sprung to life, they both have sung together, with bodies free from stain, with signs that mark them; | One of you Prince of Sacrifice, the Victor, the other counts as Heaven's auspicious offspring. || 5. May your car-seat, down-gliding, golden-coloured, according to your wish approach our dwellings. | Men shall feed full the bay steeds of the other, and, Aśvins they with roars shall stir the regions. || 6. Forth comes your strong Bull like a cloud of autumn, sending abundant food of liquid sweetness. | Let them feed with the other's ways and vigour: the upper streams have come and do us service. || 7. Your constant song hath been sent forth, Disposers! that flows threefold in mighty strength, O Aśvins. | Thus lauded, give the suppliant protection moving or resting hear mine invocation. || 8. This song of bright contents for you is swelling in the men's hall where threefold grass is ready. | Your strong rain-cloud, ye Mighty Ones, hath swollen, honouring men as 'twere with milk's outpouring. || 9. The prudent worshipper, like Pūṣhan, Aśvins! praises you as he praises Dawn and Agni, | When, singing with devotion, he invokes you. May we find strengthening food in full abundance.

Hymn 1:182. Aśvins.

1. This was the task. Appear promptly, ye prudent Ones. Here is the chariot drawn by strong steeds: be ye glad. | Heart-stirring, longed for, succourers of Viśpalā, here are Heaven's Sons whose sway blesses the pious man. || 2. Longed for, most Indra-like, mighty, most Marut-like, most wonderful in deed, car-borne, best charioteers, | Bring your full chariot hither heaped with liquid sweet: thereon, ye Aśvins, come to him who offers gifts. || 3. What make ye there, ye Mighty? Wherefore linger ye with folk who, offering not, are held in high esteem? | Pass over them; make ye the niggard's life decay: give light unto the singer eloquent in praise. || 4. Crunch up on. every side the dogs who bark at us: slay ye our foes, O Aśvins this ye understand. | Make wealthy every word of him who praises you: accept with favour, both Nāsatyas, this my laud. || 5. Ye made for Tugra's son amid the water-floods that animated ship with wings to fly withal, | Whereon with God-devoted mind ye brought him forth, and fled with easy flight from out the mighty surge. || 6. Four ships most welcome in the midst of ocean, urged by the Aśvins, save the son of Tugra, | Him who was cast down headlong in the waters, plunged in the thick inevitable darkness. || 7. What tree was that which stood fixed in surrounding sea to which the son of Tugra supplicating clung? | Like twigs, of which some winged creature may take hold, ye, Aśvins, bore him off safely to your renown. || 8. Welcome to you be this the hymn of praises uttered by Mānas, O Nāsatyas, Heroes, | From this our gathering where we offer Soma. May we find strengthening food in full abundance.

Hymn 1:183. Aśvins.

1. Make ready that which passes thought in swiftness, that hath three wheels and triple seat, ye Mighty, | Whereon ye seek the dwelling of the pious, whereon, threefold, ye fly like birds with pinions. || 2. Light rolls your easy chariot faring earthward, what time, for food, ye, full of wisdom, mount it. | May this song, wondrous fair, attend your glory: ye, as ye travel, wait on Dawn Heaven's Daughter. || 3. Ascend your lightly rolling car, approaching the worshipper who turns him to his duties,— | Whereon ye come unto the house to quicken man and his offspring, O Nāsatyas, Heroes. || 4. Let not the wolf, let not the she-wolf harm you. Forsake me not, nor pass me by or others. | Here stands your share, here is your hymn, ye Mighty: yours are these vessels, full of pleasant juices. || 5. Gotama, Purumīḷha, Atri bringing oblations all invoke you for protection. | Like one who goes straight to the point directed, ye Nāsatyas, to mine invocation. || 6. We have passed o'er the limit of this darkness: our praise hath been bestowed on you, O Aśvins. | Come hitherward by paths which Gods have travelled. May we find strengthening food in full abundance.

Hymn 1:184. Aśvins.

1. Let us invoke you both this day and after the priest is here with lauds when morn is breaking: | Nāsatyas, wheresoe'er ye be, Heaven's Children, for him who is more liberal than the godless. || 2. With us, ye Mighty, let yourselves be joyful, glad in our stream of Soma slay the niggards. | Graciously hear my hymns and invitations, marking, O Heroes, with your cars my longing. || 3. Nāsatyas, Pūṣhans, ye as Gods for glory arranged and set in order Sūrya's bridal. | Your giant steeds move on, sprung from the waters, like ancient times of Varuṇa the Mighty. || 4. Your grace be with us, ye who love sweet juices: further the hymn sung by the poet Māna, | When men are joyful in your glorious actions, to win heroic strength, ye Bounteous Givers. || 5. This praise was made, O liberal Lords, O Aśvins, for you with fair adornment by the Mānas. | Come to our house for us and for our children, rejoicing, O Nāsatyas, in Agastya. || 6. We have passed o'er the limit of this darkness: our praise hath been bestowed on you, O Aśvins. | Come hitherward by paths which Gods have travelled. may we find strengthening food in full abundance.

Hymn 1:185. Heaven and Earth.

1. Whether of these is elder, whether later? How were they born? Who knoweth it, ye sages? | These of themselves support all things existing: as on

a car the Day and Night roll onward. || 2. The Twain uphold, though motionless and footless, a widespread offspring having feet and moving. | Like your own son upon his parents' bosom, protect us, Heaven and Earth, from fearful danger. || 3. I call for Aditi's unrivalled bounty, perfect, celestial, deathless, meet for worship. | Produce this, ye Twain Worlds, for him who lauds you. Protect us, Heaven and Earth, from fearful danger. || 4. May we be close to both the Worlds who suffer no pain, Parents of Gods, who aid with favour, | Both mid the Gods, with Day and Night alternate. Protect us, Heaven and Earth, from fearful danger. || 5. Faring together, young, with meeting limits, Twin Sisters lying in their Parents' bosom, | Kissing the centre of the world together. Protect us, Heaven and Earth, from fearful danger. || 6. Duly I call the two wide seats, the mighty, the general Parents, with the God's protection. | Who, beautiful to look on, make the nectar. Protect us, Heaven and Earth, from fearful danger. || 7. Wide, vast, and manifold, whose bounds are distant,—these, reverent, I address at this our worship, | The blessed Pair, victorious, all-sustaining. Protect us, Heaven and Earth, from fearful danger. || 8. What sin we have at any time committed against the Gods, our friend, our house's chieftain, | Thereof may this our hymn be expiation. Protect us, Heaven and Earth, from fearful danger. || 9. May both these Friends of man, who bless, preserve me, may they attend me with their help and favour. | Enrich the man more liberal than the godless. May we, ye Gods, be strong with food rejoicing. || 10. Endowed with understanding, I have uttered this truth, for all to hear, to Earth and Heaven. | Be near us, keep us from reproach and trouble. Father and Mother, with your help preserve us. || 11. Be this my prayer fulfilled, O Earth and Heaven, wherewith, Father and Mother, I address you. | Nearest of Gods be ye with your protection. May we find strengthening food in full abundance.

Hymn 1:186. Viśvedevas.

1. Loved of all men, may Savitar, through praises offered as sacred food, come to our synod, | That you too, through-our hymn, ye ever-youthful, may gladden, at your visit, all our people. || 2. To us may all the Gods come trooped together, Aryaman, Mitra, Varuṇa concordant, | That all may be promoters of our welfare, and with great might preserve our strength from slackness. || 3. Agni I sing, the guest you love most dearly: the Conqueror through our lauds is friendly-minded. | That he may be our Varuṇa rich in glory and send food like a prince praised by the godly. || 4. To you I seek with reverence, Night and Morning, like a cow good to milk, with hope to conquer, | Preparing on a common day the praise. song with milk of various hues within this udder. || 5. May the great Dragon of the Deep rejoice us: as one who nourishes her young comes Sindhu, | With whom we will incite the Child of Waters whom vigorous course swift as thought bring hither. || 6. Moreover Tvaṣhṭar also shall approach us, one-minded with the princes at his visit. | Hither shall come the Vṛitra-slayer Indra, Ruler of men, as strongest of the Heroes. || 7. Him too our hymns delight, that yoke swift horses, like mother cows who lick their tender youngling. | To him our songs shall yield themselves like spouses, to him the most delightful of the Heroes. || 8. So may the Marutas, armed with mighty weapons, rest here on heaven and earth with hearts in concord, | As Gods whose cars have dappled steeds like torrents, destroyers of the foe allies of Mitra. || 9. They hasten on to happy termination their orders when they are made known by | glory. | As on a fair bright day the arrow flieth o'er all the barren soil their missiles sparkle. || 10. Incline the Aśvins to show grace, and Pūṣhan, for power and might have they, their own possession. | Friendly are Viṣhṇu, Vāta, and Ṛibhukṣhan so may I bring the Gods to make us happy. || 11. This is my reverent thought of you, ye Holy; may it inspire you, make you dwell among us,— | Thought, toiling for the Gods and seeking treasure. May we find strengthening food in full abundance.

Hymn 1:187. Praise of Food.

1. Now will I glorify Food that upholds great strength, | By whose invigorating power Trita rent Vṛitra limb from limb. || 2. O pleasant Food, O Food of meath, thee have we chosen for our own, | So be our kind protector thou. || 3. Come hitherward to us, O Food, auspicious with auspicious help, | Health-bringing, not unkind, a dear and guileless friend. || 4. These juices which, O Food, are thine throughout the regions are diffused. | like winds they have their place in heaven. || 5. These gifts of thine, O Food, O Food most sweet to taste, | These savours of thy juices work like creatures that have mighty necks. || 6. In thee, O Food, is set the spirit of great Gods. | Under thy flag brave deeds were done he slew the Dragon with thy help. || 7. If thou be gone unto the splendour of the clouds, | Even from thence, O Food of meath, prepared for our enjoyment, come. || 8. Whatever morsel we consume from waters or from plants of earth, O Soma, wax thou fat thereby. || 9. What Soma, we enjoy from thee in milky food or barley-brew, Vātāpi, grow thou fat thereby. || 10. O Vegetable, Cake of meal, he wholesome, firm, and strengthening: Vātāpi, grow thou fat thereby. || 11. O Food, from thee as such have we drawn forth with lauds, like cows, our sacrificial gifts, | From thee who banquetest with Gods, from thee who banquetest with us.

Hymn 1:188. Āprīs.

1. Winner of thousands, kindled, thou shinest a God with Gods today. | Bear out oblations, envoy, Sage. || 2. Child of Thyself the sacrifice is for the righteous blent with meath, | Presenting viands thousandfold. || 3. Invoked and worthy of our praise bring Gods whose due is sacrifice: | Thou, Agni, givest countless gifts. || 4. To seat a thousand Heroes they eastward have strewn the grass with might, | Whereon, Ādityas, ye shine forth. || 5. The sovereign all-imperial Doors, wide, good, many and manifold, | Have poured their streams of holy oil. || 6. With gay adornment, fair to see, in glorious beauty shine they forth: | Let Night and Morning rest them here. || 7. Let these two Sages first of all, heralds divine and eloquent, | Perform for us this sacrifice. || 8. You I address, Sarasvatī, and Bhāratī, and Iḷā, all: | Urge ye us on to glorious fame. || 9. Tvaṣhṭar the Lord hath made all forms and all the cattle of the field | Cause them to multiply for us. || 10. Send to the Gods, Vanaspati, thyself, the sacrificial draught: | Let Agni make the oblations sweet. || 11. Agni, preceder of the Gods, is honoured with the sacred song: | He glows at offerings blest with Hail!

Hymn 1:189. Agni.

1. By goodly paths lead us to riches, Agni, God who knowest every sacred duty. | Remove the sin that makes us stray and wander. most ample adoration will we bring thee. || 2. Lead us anew to happiness, O Agni; lead us beyond all danger and affliction. | Be unto us a wide broad ample castle bless, prosper on their way our sons and offspring. || 3. Far from us, Agni, put thou all diseases let them strike lauds that have no saving Agni. | God, make our home again to be a blessing, with all the Immortal Deities, O Holy. || 4. Preserve us, Agni, with perpetual succour, refulgent in the dwelling which thou lovest. | O Conqueror, most youthful, let no danger touch him who praises thee today or after. || 5. Give not us up a prey to sin, O Agni, the greedy enemy that brings us trouble; | Not to the fanged that bites, not to the toothless: give not us up, thou Conqueror, to the spoiler. || 6. Such as thou art, born after Law, O Agni when lauded give protection to our bodies, | From whosoever would reproach or injure: for thou, God, rescuest from all oppression. || 7. Thou, well discerning both these classes, comest to men at early morn, O holy Agni. | Be thou obedient unto man at evening, to be adorned, as keen, by eager suitors. || 8. To him have we addressed our pious speeches, I, Māna's son, to him victorious Agni. | May we gain countless riches with the sages. May we find strengthening food in full abundance.

Hymn 1:190. Bṛihaspati

1. Glorify thou Bṛihaspati, the scatheless, who must be praised with hymns, sweet-tongued and mighty, | To whom as leader of the song, resplendent, worthy of lauds, both Gods and mortals listen. || 2. On him wait songs according to the season even as a stream of pious men set moving. | Bṛihaspati—for he laid out the expanses—was, at the sacrifice, vast Mātariśvan. || 3. The praise, the verse that offers adoration, may he bring forth, as the Sun sends his arms out, | He who gives daily light through this God's wisdom, strong as a dread wild beast, and inoffensive. || 4. His song of praise pervades the earth and heaven: let the wise worshipper draw it, like a courser. | These of Bṛihaspati, like hunters' arrows, go to the skies that change their hue like serpents. || 5. Those, God, who count thee as a worthless bullock, and, wealthy sinners, live on thee the Bounteous,— | On fools like these no blessing thou bestowest: Bṛihaspati, thou punishest the spiteful. || 6. Like a fair path is he, where grass is pleasant, though hard to win, a Friend beloved most early. | Those who unharmed by enemies behold us, while they would make them bare, stood closely compassed. || 7. He to whom songs of praise go forth like torrents, as rivers eddying under

banks flow sea-ward— | Bṛihaspati the wise, the eager, closely looks upon both, the waters and the vessel. || 8. So hath Bṛihaspati, great, strong and mighty, the God exceeding powerful, been brought hither. | May he thus lauded give us kine and horses. May we find strengthening food in full abundance.

Hymn 1:191. Water. Grass. Sun.

1. Venomous, slightly venomous, or venomous aquatic worm,— | Both creatures, stinging, unobserved, with poison have infected me. || 2. Coming, it kills the unobserved; it kills them as it goes away, | It kills them as it drives them off, and bruising bruises them to death. || 3. Śara grass, Darbha, Kuśara, and Sairya, Muñja, Vīraṇa, | Where all these creatures dwell unseen, with poison have infected me. || 4. The cows had settled in their stalls, the beasts of prey had sought their lairs, | Extinguished were the lights of men, when things unseen infected me. || 5. Or these, these reptiles, are observed, like lurking thieves at evening time. | Seers of all, themselves unseen: be therefore very vigilant. || 6. Heaven is your Sire, your Mother Earth, Soma your Brother, Aditi | Your Sister: seeing all, unseen, keep still and dwell ye happily. || 7. Biters of shoulder or of limb, with needle-stings, most venomous, | Unseen, whatever ye may be, vanish together and be gone. || 8. Slayer of things unseen, the Sun, beheld of all, mounts, eastward, up, | Consuming all that are not seen, and evil spirits of the night. || 9. There hath the Sun-God mounted up, who scorches much and everything. | Even the Āditya from the hills, all-seen, destroying things unseen. || 10. I hang the poison in the Sun, a wine-skin in a vintner's house, | He will not die, nor shall we die: his path is far: he whom Bay Horses bear hath turned thee to sweet meath. || 11. This little bird, so very small, hath swallowed all thy poison up. | She will not die, nor shall we die: his path is far: he whom Bay Horses bear hath turned thee to sweet meath. || 12. The three-times-seven bright sparks of fire have swallowed up the poison's strength. | They will not die, nor shall we die: his path is far: he whom Bay Horses bear hath turned thee to sweet meath. || 13. Of ninety rivers and of nine with power to stay the venom's course,— | The names of all I have secured: his path is far: he whom Bay Horses bear hath turned thee to sweet meath. || 14. So have the peahens three-times-seven, so have the maiden Sisters Seven | Carried thy venom far away, as girls bear water in their jars. || 15. The poison-insect is so small; I crush the creature with a stone. | I turn the poison hence away, departed unto distant lands. || 16. Forth issuing from the mountain's side the poison-insect spake and said: | Scorpion, they venom is but weak.

Maṇḍala 2

Hymn 2:1. Agni.

1. Thou, Agni, shining in thy glory through the days, art brought to life from out the waters, from the stone: | From out the forest trees and herbs that grow on ground, thou, Sovereign Lord of men art generated pure. || 2. Thine is the Herald's task and Cleanser's duly timed; Leader art thou, and Kindler for the pious man. | Thou art Director, thou the ministering Priest: thou art the Brahman, Lord and Master in our home. || 3. Hero of Heroes, Agni! Thou art Indra, thou art Vishṇu of the Mighty Stride, adorable: | Thou, Brahmaṇaspati, the Brahman finding wealth: thou, O Sustainer, with thy wisdom tendest us. || 4. Agni, thou art King Varuṇa whose laws stand fast; as Mitra, Wonder-Worker, thou must be implored. | Aryaman, heroes' Lord, art thou, enriching all, and liberal Aṃśa in the synod, O thou God. || 5. Thou givest strength, as Tvashṭar, to the worshipper: thou wielding Mitra's power hast kinship with the Dames. | Thou, urging thy fleet coursers, givest noble steeds: a host of heroes art thou with great store of wealth. || 6. Rudra art thou, the Asura of mighty heaven: thou art the Marutas' host, thou art the Lord of food, | Thou goest with red winds: bliss hast thou in thine home. As Pūshan thou thyself protectest worshippers. || 7. Giver of wealth art thou to him who honours thee; thou art God Savitar, granter of precious things. | As Bhaga, Lord of men! thou rulest over wealth, and guardest in his house him who hath served thee well. || 8. To thee, the people's Lord within the house, the folk press forward to their King most graciously inclined. | Lord of the lovely look, all things belong to thee: ten, hundred, yea, a thousand are outweighed by thee. || 9. Agni, men seek thee as a Father with their prayers, win thee, bright-formed, to brotherhood with holy act. | Thou art a Son to him who duly worships thee, and as a trusty Friend thou guardest from attack. || 10. A Ṛibhu art thou, Agni, near to be adored thou art the Sovereign Lord of foodful spoil and wealth. | Thou shinest brightly forth, thou burnest to bestow: pervading sacrifice, thou lendest us thine help. || 11. Thou, God, art Aditi to him who offers gifts: thou, Hotrā, Bhāratī, art strengthened by the song. | Thou art the hundred-wintered Iḷā to give strength, Lord of Wealth! Vṛitra-slayer and Sarasvatī. || 12. Thou, Agni, cherished well, art highest vital power; in thy delightful hue are glories visible. | Thou art the lofty might that furthers each design: thou art wealth manifold, diffused on every side. || 13. Thee, Agni, have the Ādityas taken as their mouth; the Bright Ones have made thee, O Sage, to be their tongue. | They who love offerings cling to thee at solemn rites: by thee the Gods devour the duly offered food. || 14. By thee, O Agni, all the Immortal guileless Gods cat with thy mouth the oblation that is offered them. | By thee do mortal men give sweetness to their drink. Bright art thou born, the embryo of the plants of earth. || 15. With these thou art united, Agni; yea thou, God of noble birth, surpassest them in majesty, | Which, through the power of good, here spreads abroad from thee, diffused through both the worlds, throughout the earth and heaven. || 16. The princely worshippers who send to those who sing thy praise, O Agni, guerdon graced with kine and steeds,— | Lead thou both these and us forward to higher bliss. With brave men in the assembly may we speak aloud.

Hymn 2:2. Agni.

1. With sacrifice exalt Agni who knows all life; worship him 'with oblation and the song of praise, | Well kindled, nobly fed; heaven's Lord, Celestial Priest, who labours at the pole where deeds of might are done. || 2. At night and morning, Agni, have they called to thee, like milch-kine in their stalls lowing to meet their young. | As messenger of heaven thou lightest all night long the families of men. Thou Lord of precious boons. || 3. Him have the Gods established at the region's base, doer of wondrous deeds, Herald of heaven and earth; | Like a most famous car, Agni the purely bright, like Mitra. to be glorified among the folk. || 4. Him have they set in his own dwelling, in the vault, like the Moon waxing, fulgent, in the realm of air. | Bird of the firmament, observant with his eyes, guard of the place as 'twere, looking to Gods and men. || 5. May he as Priest encompass all the sacrifice. men throng to him with offerings and with hymns of praise. | Raging with jaws of gold among the growing plants, like heaven with all the stars, he quickens earth and sky. || 6. Such as thou art, brilliantly kindled for our weal, a liberal giver, send us riches in thy shine, | For our advantage, Agni, God, bring Heaven and Earth hither that they may taste oblation brought by man. || 7. Agni, give us great wealth, give riches thousandfold. unclose to us, like doors, strength that shall bring renown. | Make Heaven and Earth propitious through the power of prayer, and like the sky's bright sheen let mornings beam on us. || 8. Enkindled night by night at every morning's dawn, may he shine forth with red flame like the realm of light,— | Agni adored in beauteous rites with lauds of men, fair guest of living man and King of all our folk. || 9. Song chanted by us men, O Agni, Ancient One, has swelled unto the deathless Gods in lofty heaven— | A milch-cow yielding to the singer in the rites wealth manifold, in hundreds, even as he wills. || 10. Agni, may we show forth our valour with the steed or with the power of prayer beyond all other men; | And over the Five Races let our glory shine high like the realm of light and unsurpassable. || 11. Such, Conqueror! be to us, be worthy of our praise, thou for whom princes nobly born exert themselves; | Whose sacrifice the strong seek, Agni, when it shines for never-failing offspring in thine own abode. || 12. Knower of all that lives, O Agni may we both, singers of praise and chiefs, be in thy keeping still. | Help us to wealth exceeding good and glorious, abundant, rich in children and their progeny. || 13. The princely worshippers who send to those who sing thy praise, O Agni, guerdon, graced with kine and steeds,— | Lead thou both these and us forward to higher bliss. With brave men in the assembly may we speak aloud.

Hymn 2:3. Āprīs.

1. Agni is set upon the earth well kindled; he standeth in the presence of all beings. | Wise, ancient, God, the Priest and Purifier, let Agni serve the Gods for he is worthy. || 2. May Narāśaṃsa lighting up the chambers, bright in his majesty through threefold heaven, | Steeping the gift with oil diffusing purpose, bedew the Gods at chiefest time of worship. || 3. Adored

in heart, as is thy right, O Agni, serve the Gods first today before the mortal. | Bring thou the Marut host. Ye men do worship to Indra seated on the grass, eternal. || 4. O Grass divine, increasing, rich in heroes, strewn for wealth' sake, well laid upon this altar,— | On this bedewed with oil sit ye, O Vasus, sit all ye Gods, ye Holy, ye Ādityas. || 5. Wide be the Doors, the Goddesses, thrown open, easy to pass, invoked, through adorations, | Let them unfold, expansive, everlasting, that sanctify the class famed, rich in heroes. || 6. Good work for us, the glorious Night and Morning, like female weavers, waxen from aforetime, | Yielders of rich milk, interweave in concert the long-extended thread, the web of worship. || 7. Let the two heavenly Heralds, first, most wise, most fair, present oblation duly with the sacred verse, | Worshipping God at ordered seasons decking them at three high places at the centre of the earth. || 8. Sarasvatī who perfects our devotion, Iḷā divine, Bhāratī all surpassing,— | Three Goddesses, with power inherent, seated, protect this holy Grass, our flawless refuge! || 9. Born is the pious hero swift of hearing, like gold in hue, well formed, and full of vigour. | May Tvaṣhṭar lengthen our line and kindred, and may they reach the place which Gods inhabit. || 10. Vanaspati shall stand anear and start us, and Agni with his arts prepare oblation. | Let the skilled heavenly Immolator forward unto the Gods the offering thrice anointed. || 11. Oil has been mixed: oil is his habitation. In oil he rests: oil is his proper province. | Come as thy wont is: O thou Steer, rejoice thee; bear off the oblation duly consecrated.

Hymn 2:4. Agni.

1. For you I call the glorious refulgent Agni, the guest of men, rich in oblations | Whom all must strive to win even as a lover, God among godly people, Jātavedas. || 2. Bhṛigus who served him in the home of waters set him of old in houses of the living. | Over all worlds let Agni be the Sovereign, the messenger of Gods with rapid coursers. || 3. Among the tribes of men the Gods placed Agni as a dear Friend when they would dwell among them. | Against the longing nights may he shine brightly, and show the offerer in the house his vigour. || 4. Sweet is his growth as of one's own possessions; his look when rushing fain to burn is lovely. | He darts his tongue forth, like a harnessed courser who shakes his flowing tail, among the bushes. || 5. Since they who honour me have praised my greatness,—he gave, as 'twere, his hue to those who love him. | Known is he by his bright delightful splendour, and waxing old renews his youth for ever. || 6. Like one athirst, he lighteth up the forests; like water down the chariot ways he roareth. | On his black path he shines in burning beauty, marked as it were the heaven that smiles through vapour. || 7. Around, consuming the broad earth, he wanders, free roaming like an ox without a herdsman,— | Agni refulgent, burning up the bushes, with blackened lines, as though the earth he seasoned. || 8. I, in remembrance of thine ancient favour have sung my hymn in this our third assembly. | O Agni, give us wealth with store of heroes and mighty strength in food and noble offspring. || 9. May the Gṛitsamadas, serving in secret, through thee, O Agni, overcome their neighbours, | Rich in good heroes and subduing foemen. That vital power give thou to chiefs and singers.

Hymn 2:5. Agni.

1. Herald and teacher was he born, a guardian for our patrons' help, | Earner by rites of noble wealth. That Strong One may we grasp and guide; || 2. In whom, Leader of sacrifice, the seven reins, far extended, meet; | Who furthers, man-like, eighth in place, as Cleanser, all the work divine. || 3. When swift he follows this behest, bird-like he chants the holy prayers. | He holds all knowledge in his grasp even as the felly rounds the wheel. || 4. Together with pure mental power, pure, as Director, was he born. | Skilled in his own unchanging laws he waxes like the growing boughs. || 5. Clothing them in his hues, the kine of him the Leader wait on him. | Is he not better than the Three, the Sisters who have come to us? || 6. When, laden with the holy oil, the Sister by the Mother stands, | The Priest delights in their approach, as corn at coming of the rain. || 7. For his support let him perform as ministrant his priestly task; | Yea, song of praise and sacrifice: we have bestowed, let us obtain. || 8. That so this man well skilled, may pay worship to all the Holy Ones. | And, Agni, this our sacrifice which we have here prepared, to thee.

Hymn 2:6. Agni.

1. Agni, accept this flaming brand, this waiting with my prayer on thee: | Hear graciously these songs of praise. || 2. With this hymn let us honour thee, seeker of horses, Son of Strength, | With this fair hymn, thou nobly born. || 3. As such, lover of song, with songs, wealth-lover, giver of our wealth! | With reverence let us worship thee. || 4. Be thou for us a liberal Prince, giver and Lord of precious things. | Drive those who hate us far away. || 5. Such as thou art, give rain from heaven, give strength which no man may resist: | Give food exceeding plentiful. || 6. To him who lauds thee, craving help, most youthful envoy! through our song, | Most holy Herald! come thou nigh. || 7. Between both races, Agni, Sage, well skilled thou passest to and fro, | As envoy friendly to mankind. || 8. Befriend us thou as knowing all. Sage, duly worship thou the Gods, | And seat thee on this sacred grass.

Hymn 2:7. Agni.

1. Vasu, thou most youthful God, Bhārata, Agni, bring us wealth, | Excellent, splendid, much-desired. || 2. Let no malignity prevail against us, either God's or man's. | Save us from this and enmity. || 3. So through thy favour may we force through all our enemies a way, | As 'twere through streaming water-floods. || 4. Thou, Purifier Agni, high shinest forth, bright, adorable, | When worshipped with the sacred oil. || 5. Ours art thou, Agni, Bhārata, honoured by us with barren cows, | With bullocks and with kine in calf || 6. Wood-fed, bedewed with sacred oil, ancient, Invoker, excellent, | The Son of Strength, the Wonderful.

Hymn 2:8.Agni.

1. Now praise, as one who strives for strength, the harnessing of Agni's car, | The liberal, the most splendid One; || 2. Who, guiding worshippers aright, withers, untouched by age, the foe: | When worshipped fair to look upon; || 3. Who for his glory is extolled at eve and morning in our homes, | Whose statute is inviolate; || 4. Who shines refulgent like the Sun, with brilliance and with fiery flame, | Decked with imperishable sheen. || 5. Him Atri, Agni, have our songs Strengthened according to his sway: | All glories hath he made his own. || 6. May we with Agni's, Indra's help, with Soma's, yea, of all the Gods, | Uninjured dwell together still, and conquer those who fight with us.

Hymn 2:9. Agni.

1. Accustomed to the Herald's place, the Herald hath seated him, bright, splendid, passing mighty, | Whose foresight keeps the Law from violation, excellent, pure-tongued, bringing thousands, Agni. || 2. Envoy art thou, protector from the foeman, strong God, thou leadest us to higher blessings. | Refulgent, be an ever-heedful keeper, Agni, for us and for our seed offspring. || 3. May we adore thee in thy loftiest birthplace, and, with our praises, in thy lower station. | The place whence thou issued forth I worship: to thee well kindled have they paid oblations. || 4. Agni, best Priest, pay worship with oblation; quickly commend the gift to be presented; | For thou art Lord of gathered wealth and treasure. of the bright song of praise thou art inventor. || 5. The twofold opulence, O Wonder-Worker, of thee new-born each day never decreases. | Enrich with food the man who lauds thee, Agni: make him the lord of wealth with noble offspring. || 6. May he, benevolent with this fair aspect, best sacrificer, bring the Gods to bless us. | Sure guardian, our protector from the foemen, shine, Agni, with thine affluence and splendour.

Hymn 2:10. Agni.

1.Agni, first, loudly calling, like a Father, kindled by man upon the seat of worship. | Clothed in his glory, deathless, keen of insight, must be adorned by all, the Strong, the Famous. || 2. May Agni the resplendent hear my calling through all my songs, Immortal, keen of insight. | Dark steeds or ruddy draw his car, or carried in sundry ways he makes them red of colour. || 3. On wood supine they got the well-formed Infant: a germ in various-fashioned plants was Agni; | And in the night, not compassed round by darkness, he dwells exceeding wise, with rays of splendour. || 4. With oil and sacred gifts I sprinkle Agni who makes his home in front of all things living, | Broad, vast, through vital power o'er all expanded, conspicuous, strong with all the food that feeds him. || 5. I pour to him who looks in all directions: may he accept it with a friendly spirit. | Agni with bridegroom's grace and lovely colour may not be touched when all his form is fury. || 6. By choice victorious, recognize thy portion: with thee for envoy may we speak like Manu. | Obtaining wealth, I call on perfect Agni who with an eloquent tongue dispenses sweetness.

Hymn 2:11. Indra.

1. Hear thou my call, O Indra; be not heedless: thine may we be for thee to give us treasures; | For these presented viands, seeking riches, increase thy strength like streams of water flowing. || 2. Floods great and many, compassed by the Dragon, thou badest swell and settest free, O Hero. | Strengthened by songs of praise thou rentest piecemeal the Dāsa, him who deemed himself immortal. || 3. For, Hero, in the lauds wherein thou joyedst, in hymns of praise, O Indra, songs of Rudras, | These streams in which is thy delight approach thee, even as the brilliant ones draw near to Vāyu. || 4. We who add strength to thine own splendid vigour, laying within thine arms the splendid thunder— | With us mayst thou, O Indra, waxen splendid, with Sūrya overcome the Dāsa races. || 5. Hero, thou slewest in thy valour Ahi concealed in depths, mysterious, great enchanter, | Dwelling enveloped deep within the waters, him who checked heaven and stayed the floods from flowing. || 6. Indra, we laud thy great deeds wrought aforetime, we laud thine exploits later of achievement; | We laud the bolt that in thine arms lies eager; we laud thy two Bay Steeds, heralds of Sūrya. || 7. Indra, thy Bay Steeds showing forth their vigour have sent a loud cry out that droppeth fatness. | The earth hath spread herself in all her fullness: the cloud that was about to move hath rested. || 8. Down, never ceasing, hath the rain-cloud settled: bellowing, it hath wandered with the Mothers. | Swelling the roar in the far distant limits, they have spread wide the blast sent forth by Indra. || 9. Indra hath hurled down the magician Vṛitra who lay beleaguering the mighty river. | Then both the heaven and earth trembled in terror at the strong Hero's thunder when he bellowed. || 10. Loud roared the mighty Hero's bolt of thunder, when he, the Friend of man, burnt up the monster, | And, having drunk his fill of flowing Soma, baffled the guileful Dānava's devices. || 11. Drink thou, O Hero Indra, drink the Soma; let the joy-giving juices make thee joyful. | They, filling both thy flanks, shall swell thy vigour. The juice that satisfies hath helped Indra. || 12. Singers have we become with thee, O Indra: may we serve duly and prepare devotion. | Seeking thy help we meditate thy praises: may we at once enjoy thy gift of riches. || 13. May we be thine, such by thy help, O Indra, as swell thy vigour while they seek thy favour. | Give us, thou God, the riches that we long for, most powerful, with stare of noble children. || 14. Give us a friend, give us an habitation; Indra, give us the company of Marutas, | And those whose minds accord with theirs, the Vāyus, who drink the first libation of the Soma. || 15. Let those enjoy in whom thou art delighted. Indra, drink Soma for thy strength and gladness. | Thou hast exalted us to heaven, Preserver, in battles, through the lofty hymns that praise thee. || 16. Great, verily, are they, O thou Protector, who by their songs of praise have won the blessing. | They who strew sacred grass to be thy dwelling, helped by thee have got them strength, O Indra. || 17. Upon the great Trikadruka days, Hero, rejoicing thee, O Indra, drink the Soma. | Come with Bay Steeds to drink of libation, shaking the drops from out thy beard, contented. || 18. Hero, assume the might wherewith thou clavest Vṛitra piecemeal, the Dānava Aurṇavābha. | Thou hast disclosed the light to light the Ārya: on thy left hand, O Indra, sank the Dasyu. || 19. May we gain wealth, subduing with thy succour and with the Ārya, all our foes, the Dasyus. | Our gain was that to Trita of our party thou gavest up Tvashṭar's son Viśvarūpa. || 20. He cast down Arbuda what time his vigour was strengthened by libations poured by Trita. | Indra sent forth his whirling wheel like Sūrya, and aided by the Aṅgirasas rent Vala. || 21. Now let that wealthy Cow of thine, O Indra, yield in return a boon to him who lauds thee. | Give to thy praisers: let not fortune fail us. Loud may we speak, with brave men, in the assembly.

Hymn 2:12. Indra.

1. He who, just born, chief God of lofty spirit by power and might became the Gods' protector, | Before whose breath through greatness of his valour the two worlds trembled, He, O men, is Indra. || 2. He who fixed fast and firm the earth that staggered, and set at rest the agitated mountains, | Who measured out the air's wide middle region and gave the heaven support, He, men, is Indra. || 3. Who slew the Dragon, freed the Seven Rivers, and drove the kine forth from the cave of Vala, | Begat the fire between two stones, the spoiler in warriors' battle, He, O men, is Indra. || 4. By whom this universe was made to tremble, who chased away the humbled brood of demons, | Who, like a gambler gathering his winnings seized the foe's riches, He, O men, is Indra. || 5. Of whom, the Terrible, they ask, Where is He? or verily they say of him, He is not. | He sweeps away, like birds, the foe's possessions. Have faith in him, for He, O men, is Indra. || 6. Stirrer to action of the poor and lowly, of priest, of suppliant who sings his praises; | Who, fair-faced, favours him who presses Soma with stones made ready, He, O men, is Indra. || 7. He under whose supreme control are horses, all chariots, and the villages, and cattle; | He who gave being to the Sun and Morning, who leads the waters, He, O men, is Indra. || 8. To whom two armies cry in close encounter, both enemies, the stronger and the weaker; | Whom two invoke upon one chariot mounted, each for himself, He, O ye men, is Indra. || 9. Without whose help our people never conquer; whom, battling, they invoke to give them succour; | He of whom all this world is but the copy, who shakes things moveless, He, O men, is Indra. || 10. He who hath smitten, ere they knew their danger, with his hurled weapon many grievous sinners; | Who pardons not his boldness who provokes him, who slays the Dasyu, He, O men, is Indra. || 11. He who discovered in the fortieth autumn Śambara as he dwelt among the mountains; | Who slew the Dragon putting forth his vigour, the demon lying there, He, men, is Indra. || 12. Who with seven guiding reins, the Bull, the Mighty, set free the Seven great Floods to flow at pleasure; | Who, thunder-armed, rent Rauhiṇa in pieces when scaling heaven, He, O ye men, is Indra. || 13. Even the Heaven and Earth bow down before him, before his very breath the mountains tremble. | Known as the Soma-drinker, armed with thunder, who wields the bolt, He, O ye men, is Indra. || 14. Who aids with favour him who pours the Soma and him who brews it, sacrificer, singer. | Whom prayer exalts, and pouring forth of Soma, and this our gift, He, O ye men, Is Indra. || 15. Thou verily art fierce and true who sendest strength to the man who brews and pours libation. | So may we evermore, thy friends, O Indra, speak loudly to the synod with our heroes.

Hymn 2:13. Indra.

1. The Season was the parent, and when born therefrom it entered rapidly the floods wherein it grows. | Thence was it full of sap, streaming with milky juice: the milk of the plant's stalk is chief and meet for lauds. || 2. They come trooping together bearing milk to him, and bring him sustenance who gives support to all. | The way is common for the downward streams to flow. Thou who didst these things first art worthy of our lauds. || 3. One priest announces what the instituter gives: one, altering the forms, zealously plies his task, | The third corrects the imperfections left by each. Thou who didst these things first art worthy of our lauds. || 4. Dealing out food unto their people there they sit, like wealth to him who comes, more than the back can bear. | Greedily with his teeth he eats the master's food. Thou who didst these things first art worthy of our lauds. || 5. Thou hast created earth to look upon the sky: thou, slaying Ahi, settest free the river's paths. | Thee, such, a God, the Gods have quickened with their lauds, even as a steed with waters: meet for praise art thou. || 6. Thou givest increase, thou dealest to us our food: thou milkest from the moist the dry, the rich in sweets. | Thou by the worshipper layest thy precious store: thou art sole Lord of all. Meet for our praise art thou. || 7. Thou who hast spread abroad the streams by established law, and in the field the plants that blossom and bear seed; | Thou who hast made the matchless lightnings of the sky,—vast, compassing vast realms, meet for our praise art thou. || 8. Who broughtest Nārmara with all his wealth, for sake of food, to slay him that the fiends might be destroyed, | Broughtest the face unclouded of the strengthening one, performing much even now, worthy art thou of praise. || 9. Thou boundest up the Dāsa's hundred friends and ten, when, at one's hearing, thou helpest thy worshipper. | Thou for Dabhīti boundest Dasyus not with cords; Thou wast a mighty help. Worthy of lauds art thou. || 10. All banks of rivers yielded to his manly might; to him they gave, to him, the Strong, gave up their wealth. | The six directions hast thou fixed, a five-fold view: thy victories reached afar. Worthy of lauds art thou. || 11. Meet for high praise, O Hero, is thy power, that with thy single wisdom thou obtainest wealth, | The life-support of conquering Jātūshṭhira. Indra, for all thy deeds, worthy of lauds art thou. || 12. Thou for Turvīti heldest still the flowing floods, the river-stream for Vayya easily to pass | Didst raise the outcast from the depths, and gavest fame unto the halt and blind. Worthy of lauds art thou. || 13. Prepare thyself to grant us that great bounty, O Vasu, for abundant is thy treasure. | Snatch

up the wonderful, O Indra, daily. Loud may we speak, with heroes, in assembly.

Hymn 2:14. Indra.

1. Ministers, bring the Soma juice for Indra, pour forth the gladdening liquor with the beakers. | To drink of this the Hero offer it to the Bull, for this he willeth. || 2. Ye ministers, to him who with the lightning smote, like a tree, the rain-withholding Vṛitra— | Bring it to him, him who is fain to taste it, a draught of this which Indra here deserveth. || 3. Ye ministers, to him who smote Dṛibhīka who drove the kine forth, and discovered Vala, | Offer this draught, like Vāta in the region: clothe him with Soma even as steeds with trappings. || 4. Him who did Uraṇa to death, Adhvaryus! though showing arms ninety-and-nine in number; | Who cast down headlong Arbuda and slew him,—speed ye that Indra to our offered Soma. || 5. Ye ministers, to him who struck down Svaśna, and did to death Vyaṃsa and greedy Śuṣhṇa, | And Rudhikrās and Namuchi and Pipru,—to him, to Indra, pour ye forth libation. || 6. Ye ministers, to him who as with thunder demolished Śambara's hundred ancient castles; | Who cast down Varchin's sons, a hundred thousand,—to him, to Indra, offer ye the Soma. || 7. Ye ministers, to him who slew a hundred thousand, and cast them down upon earth's bosom; | Who quelled the valiant men of Atithigva, Kutsa, and Āyu,—bring to him the Soma. || 8. Ministers, men, whatever thing ye long for obtain ye quickly bringing gifts to Indra. | Bring to the Glorious One what bands have cleansed; to Indra bring, ye pious ones, the Soma. || 9. Do ye, O ministers, obey his order: that purified in wood, in wood uplift ye. | Well pleased he longs for what your hands have tended: offer the gladdening Soma juice to Indra. || 10. As the cow's udder teems with milk, Adhvaryus, so fill with Soma Indra, liberal giver. | I know him: I am sure of this, the Holy knows that I fain would give to him more largely. || 11. Him, ministers, the Lord of heavenly treasure and all terrestrial wealth that earth possesses, | Him, Indra, fill with Soma as a garner is filled with barley full: be this your labour. || 12. Prepare thyself to grant us that great booty, O Vasu, for abundant is thy treasure. | Gather up wondrous wealth, O Indra, daily. Loud may we speak, with heroes, in assembly.

Hymn 2:15. Indra

1. Now, verily, will I declare the exploits, mighty and true, of him the True and Mighty. | In the Trikadrukas he drank the Soma then in its rapture Indra slew the Dragon. || 2. High heaven unsupported in space he established: he filled the two worlds and the air's mid-region. | Earth he upheld, and gave it wide expansion. These things did Indra in the Soma's rapture. || 3. From front, as 'twere a house, he ruled and measured; pierced with his bolt the fountains of the rivers, | And made them flow at ease by paths far-reaching, These things did Indra in the Soma's rapture. || 4. Compassing those who bore away Dabhīti, in kindled fire he burnt up all their weapons. | And made him rich with kine and cars and horses. These things did Indra in the Soma's rapture. || 5. The mighty roaring flood he stayed from flowing, and carried those who swam not safely over. | They having crossed the stream attained to riches. These things did Indra in the Soma's rapture. || 6. With mighty power he made the stream flow upward, crushed with his thunderbolt the car of Uṣhas, | Rending her slow steeds with his rapid coursers. These things did Indra in the Soma's rapture. || 7. Knowing the place wherein the maids were hiding, the outcast showed himself and stood before them. | The cripple stood erect, the blind beheld them. These things did Indra in the Soma's rapture. || 8. Praised by the Aṅgirasas he slaughtered Vala, and burst apart the bulwarks of the mountain. | He tore away their deftly-built defences. These things did Indra in the Soma's rapture. || 9. Thou, with sleep whelming Chumuri and Dhuni, slewest the Dasyu, keptest safe Dabhīti. | There the staff-bearer found the golden treasure. These things did Indra in the Soma's rapture. || 10. Now let that wealthy Cow of thine, O Indra, yield in return a boon to him who lauds thee. | Give to thy praisers: let not fortune fail us. Loud may we speak, with brave men, in assembly.

Hymn 2:16. Indra.

1. To him, your own, the best among the good, I bring eulogy, like oblation in the kindled fire. | We invocate for help Indra untouched by eld, who maketh all decay, strengthened, for ever young. || 2. Without whom naught exists, Indra the Lofty One; in whom alone all powers heroic are combined. | The Soma is within him, in his frame vast strength, the thunder in his hand and wisdom in his head. || 3. Not by both worlds is thine own power to be surpassed, nor may thy car be stayed by mountains or by seas. | None cometh near, O Indra, to thy thunderbolt, when with swift steeds thou fliest over many a league. || 4. For all men bring their will to him the Resolute, to him the Holy One, to him the Strong they cleave. | Pay worship with oblation, strong and passing wise. Drink thou the Soma, Indra, through the mighty blaze. || 5. The vessel of the strong flows forth, the flood of meath, unto the Strong who feeds upon the strong, for drink, | Strong are the two Adhvaryus, strong are both the stones. They press the Soma that is strong for him the Strong. || 6. Strong is thy thunderbolt, yea, and thy car is strong; strong are thy Bay Steeds and thy weapons powerful. | Thou, Indra, Bull, art Lord of the strong gladdening drink, with the strong Soma, Indra, satisfy thyself. || 7. I, bold by prayer, come near thee in thy sacred rites, thee like a saving ship, thee shouting in the war. | Verily he will hear and mark this word of ours: we will pour Indra forth as 'twere a spring of wealth. || 8. Turn thee unto us ere calamity come nigh, as a cow full of pasture turns her to her calf. | Lord of a Hundred Powers, may we once firmly cling to thy fair favours even as husbands to their wives. || 9. Now let that wealthy Cow of thine, O Indra, yield in return a boon to him who lauds thee. | Give to thy praisers: let not fortune fail us. Loud may we speak, with heroes, in assembly.

Hymn 2:17. Indra.

1. Like the Aṅgirasas, sing this new song forth to him, for, as in ancient days, his mighty powers are shown, | When in the rapture of the Soma he unclosed with strength the solid firm-shut stables of the kine. || 2. Let him be even that God who, for the earliest draught measuring out his power, increased his majesty; | Hero who fortified his body in the wars, and through his greatness set the heaven upon his head. || 3. Thou didst perform thy first great deed of hero might what time thou showedst power, through prayer, before this folk. | Hurled down by thee the car-borne Lord of Tawny Steeds, the congregated swift ones fled in sundry ways. || 4. He made himself by might Lord of all living things, and strong in vital power waxed great above them all. | He, borne on high, o'erspread with light the heaven and earth, and, sewing up the turbid darkness, closed it in. || 5. He with his might made firm the forward-bending hills, the downward rushing of the waters he ordained. | Fast he upheld the earth that nourisheth all life, and stayed the heaven from falling by his wondrous skill. || 6. Fit for the grasping of his arms is what the Sire hath fabricated from all kind of precious wealth. | The thunderbolt, wherewith, loud-roaring, he smote down, and striking him to death laid Krivi on the earth. || 7. As she who in her parents' house is growing old, I pray to thee as Bhaga from the seat of all. | Grant knowledge, mete it out and bring it to us here: give us the share wherewith thou makest people glad. || 8. May we invoke thee as a liberal giver thou givest us, O Indra, strength and labours. | Help us with manifold assistance, Indra: Mighty One, Indra, make us yet more wealthy. || 9. Now may that wealthy Cow of thine, O Indra, give in return a boon to him who lauds thee. | Give to thy praisers: let not fortune fail us. Loud may we speak, with heroes, in assembly.

Hymn 2:18. Indra

1. The rich new car hath been equipped at morning; four yokes it hath, three whips, seven reins to guide it: | Ten-sided, friendly to mankind, light-winner, that must be urged to speed with prayers and wishes. || 2. This is prepared for him the first, the second, and the third time: he is man's Priest and Herald. | Others get offspring of another parent he goeth, as a noble Bull, with others. || 3. To Indra's car the Bay Steeds have I harnessed, that new well-spoken words may bring him hither. | Here let not other worshippers detain thee, for among us are many holy singers. || 4. Indra, come hitherward with two Bay Coursers, come thou with four, with six when invocated. | Come thou with eight, with ten, to drink the Soma. Here is the juice, brave Warrior: do not scorn it. || 5. O Indra, come thou hither having harnessed thy car with twenty, thirty, forty horses. | Come thou with fifty well trained coursers, Indra, sixty or seventy, to drink the Soma. || 6. Come to us hitherward, O Indra, carried by eighty, ninety, or an hundred horses. | This Soma juice among the Śunahotras hath been poured out, in love, to glad thee, Indra. || 7. To this my prayer, O Indra, come thou hither: bind to thy car's pole all thy two Bay Coursers. | Thou

art to be invoked in many places Hero, rejoice thyself in this libation. || 8. Ne'er be my love from Indra disunited still may his liberal Milch-cow yield us treasure. | So may we under his supreme protection, safe in his arms, succeed in each forth-going. || 9. Now may that wealthy Cow Of thine, O Indra, give in return a boon to him who lauds thee. | Give to thy praisers: let not fortune fail us. Loud may we speak, with heroes, in assembly.

Hymn 2:19. Indra.

1. Draughts of this sweet juice have been drunk for rapture, of the wise Soma-presser's offered dainty, | Wherein, grown mighty in the days aforetime, Indra hath found delight, and men who worship. || 2. Cheered by this meath Indra, whose hand wields thunder, rent piecemeal Ahi who barred up the waters, | So that the quickening currents of the rivers flowed forth like birds unto their resting-places. || 3. Indra, this Mighty One, the Dragon's slayer, sent forth the flood of waters to the ocean. | He gave the Sun his life, he found the cattle, and with the night the works of days completed. || 4. To him who worshippeth hath Indra given many and matchless gifts. He slayeth Vṛitra. | Straight was he to be sought with supplications by men who struggled to obtain the sunlight. || 5. To him who poured him gifts he gave up Sūrya,—Indra, the God, the Mighty, to the mortal; | For Etaśa with worship brought him riches that keep distress afar, as 'twere his portion. || 6. Once to the driver of his chariot, Kutsa, he gave up greedy Sūrya, plague of harvest; | And Indra, for the sake of Divodāsa demolished Śambara's nine-and-ninety castles. || 7. So have we brought our hymn to thee, O Indra, strengthening thee and fain ourselves for glory. | May we with best endeavours gain this friendship, and mayst thou bend the godless scorner's weapons. || 8. Thus the Gṛitsamadas for thee, O Hero, have wrought their hymn and task as seeking favour. | May they who worship thee afresh, O Indra, gain food and strength, bliss, and a happy dwelling. || 9. Now may that wealthy Cow of thine, O Indra, give in return a boon to him who lauds thee, | Give to thy praisers: let not fortune fail us. Loud may we speak, with heroes, in assembly.

Hymn 2:20. Indra.

1. As one brings forth his car when fain for combat, so bring we power to thee—regard us, Indra— | Well skilled in song, thoughtful in spirit, seeking great bliss from one like thee amid the Heroes. || 2. Indra, thou art our own with thy protection, a guardian near to men who love thee truly, | Active art thou, the liberal man's defender, his who draws near to thee with right devotion. || 3. May Indra, called with solemn invocations. the young, the Friend, be men's auspicious keeper, | One who will further with his aid the singer, the toiler, praiser, dresser of oblations. || 4. With laud and song let me extol that Indra in whom of old men prospered and were mighty. | May he, implored, fulfil the prayer for plenty of him who worships, of the living mortal. || 5. He, Indra whom the Aṅgirasas' praise delighted, strengthened their prayer and made their goings prosper. | Stealing away the mornings with the sunlight, he, lauded, crushed even Aśna's ancient powers. || 6. He verily, the God, the glorious Indra, hath raised him up for man, best Wonder-Worker. | He, self-reliant, mighty and triumphant, brought low the dear head of the wicked Dāsa. || 7. Indra the Vṛitra-slayer, Fort-destroyer, scattered the Dāsa hosts who dwelt in darkness. | For men hath he created earth and waters, and ever helped the prayer of him who worships. || 8. To him in might the Gods have ever yielded, to Indra in the tumult of the battle. | When in his arms they laid the bolt, he slaughtered the Dasyus and cast down their forts of iron. || 9. Now may that wealthy Cow of thine, O Indra, give in return a boon to him who lauds thee. | Give to thy praisers: let not fortune fail us. Loud may we speak, with heroes, in assembly.

Hymn 2:21.

1. To him the Lord of all, the Lord of wealth, of light; him who is Lord for ever, Lord of men and tilth, | Him who is Lord of horses, Lord of kine,of floods, to Indra, to the Holy bring sweet Soma juice. || 2. To him the potent One, who conquers and breaks down, the Victor never vanquished who disposes all, | The mighty-voiced, the rider, unassailable, to Indra ever-conquering speak your reverent prayer. || 3. Still Victor, loved by mortals, ruler over men, o'erthrower, warrior, he hath waxen as he would; | Host-gatherer, triumphant, honoured mid the folk. Indra's heroic deeds will I tell forth to all. || 4. The strong who never yields, who slew the furious fiend, the deep, the vast, of wisdom unattainable; | Who speeds the good, the breaker-down, the firm, the vast,—Indra whose rites bring joy hath made the light of Dawn. || 5. By sacrifice the yearning sages sending forth their songs found furtherance from him who speeds the flood. | In Indra seeking help with worship and with hymn, they drew him to themselves and won them kine and wealth. || 6. Indra, bestow on us the best of treasures, the spirit of ability and fortune; | Increase of riches, safety of our bodies, charm of sweet speech, and days of pleasant weather.

Hymn 2:22. Indra.

1. At the Trikadrukas the Great and Strong hath drunk drink blent with meal. With Vishṇu hath he quaffed the poured out Soma juice, all that he would. | That hath so heightened him the Great, the Wide, to do his mighty work. | So may the God attain the God, true Indu Indra who is true. || 2. So he resplendent in the battle overcame Krivi by might. He with his majesty hath filled the earth and heaven, and waxen strong. | One share of the libation hath he swallowed down: one share he left. | So may the God attend the God, true Indu Indra who is true. || 3. Brought forth together with wisdom and mighty power thou grewest great; with hero deeds subduing the malevolent, most swift in act; | Giving prosperity, and lovely wealth to him who praiseth thee. So may the God attend the God, true Indu Indra who is true. || 4. This, Indra, was thy hero deed, Dancer, thy first and ancient work, worthy to be told forth in heaven, | What time thou sentest down life with a God's own power, freeing the floods. | All that is godless may he conquer with his might, and, Lord of Hundred Powers, find for us strength and food.

Hymn 2:23. Brahmaṇaspati.

1. We call thee, Lord and Leader of the heavenly hosts, the wise among the wise, the famousest of all, | The King supreme of prayers, O Brahmaṇaspati: hear us with help; sit down in place of sacrifice. || 2. Bṛihaspati, God immortal! verily the Gods have gained from thee, the wise, a share in holy rites. | As with great light the Sun brings forth the rays of morn, so thou alone art Father of all sacred prayer. || 3. When thou hast chased away revilers and the gloom, thou mountest the refulgent car of sacrifice; | The awful car, Bṛihaspati, that quells the foe, slays demons, cleaves the stall of kine, and finds the light. || 4. Thou leadest with good guidance and preservest men; distress o'ertakes not him who offers gifts to thee. | Him who hates prayer thou punishest, Bṛihaspati, quelling his wrath: herein is thy great mightiness. || 5. No sorrow, no distress from any side, no foes, no creatures double-tongued have overcome the man,— | Thou drivest all seductive fiends away from him whom, careful guard, thou keepest Brahmaṇaspati. || 6. Thou art our keeper, wise, preparer of our paths: we, for thy service, sing to thee with hymns of praise. | Bṛihaspati, whoever lays a snare for us, him may his evil fate, precipitate, destroy. || 7. Him, too, who threatens us without offence of ours, the evil-minded, arrogant, rapacious man,— | Him turn thou from our path away, Bṛihaspati: give us fair access to this banquet of the Gods. || 8. Thee as protector of our bodies we invoke, thee, saviour, as the comforter who loveth us. | Strike, O Bṛihaspati, the Gods' revilers down, and let not the unrighteous come to highest bliss. || 9. Through thee, kind prosperer, O Brahmaṇaspati, may we obtain the wealth of Men which all desire: | And all our enemies, who near or far away prevail against us, crush, and leave them destitute. || 10. With thee as our own rich and liberal ally may we, Bṛihaspati, gain highest power of life. | Let not the guileful wicked man be lord of us:-still may we prosper, singing goodly hymns of praise. || 11. Strong, never yielding, hastening to the battle-cry, consumer of the foe, victorious in the strife, | Thou art sin's true avenger, Brahmaṇaspati, who tamest e'en the fierce, the wildly passionate. || 12. Whoso with mind ungodly seeks to do us harm, who, deeming him a man of might mid lords, would slay,— | Let not his deadly blow reach us, Bṛihaspati; may we humiliate the strong ill-doer's wrath. || 13. The mover mid the spoil, the winner of all wealth, to be invoked in fight and reverently adored, | Bṛihaspati hath overthrown like cars of war all wicked enemies who fain would injure us. || 14. Burn up the demons with thy fiercest flaming brand, those who have scorned thee in thy manifested might. | Show forth that power that shall deserve the hymn of praise: destroy the evil speakers, O Bṛihaspati. || 15. Bṛihaspati, that which the foe deserves not which shines among the folk effectual, splendid, | That, Son of Law I which is with might refulgent-that treasure wonderful bestow thou on us. || 16. Give us not up to those who, foes in ambuscade, are greedy

for the wealth of him who sits at ease, | Who cherish in their heart abandonment of Gods. Bṛihaspati, no further rest shall they obtain. || 17. For Tvashṭar, he who knows each sacred song, brought thee to life, preeminent o'er all the things that be. | Guilt-scourger, guilt-avenger is Bṛihaspati, who slays the spoiler and upholds the mighty Law. || 18. The mountain, for thy glory, cleft itself apart when, Aṅgiras! thou openedst the stall of kine. | Thou, O Bṛihaspati, with Indra for ally didst hurl down water-floods which gloom had compassed round. || 19. O Brahmaṇaspati, be thou controller of this our hymn and prosper thou our children. | All that the Gods regard with love is blessed. Loud may we speak, with heroes, in assembly.

Hymn 2:24. Brahmaṇaspati.

1. Be pleased with this our offering, thou who art the Lord; we will adore thee with this new and mighty song. | As this thy friend, our liberal patron, praises thee, do thou, Bṛihaspati, fulfil our hearts' desire. || 2. He who with might bowed down the things that should be bowed, and in his fury rent the holds of Śambara: | Who overthrew what shook not, Brahmaṇaspati, he made his way within the mountain stored with wealth. || 3. That was a great deed for the Godliest of the Gods: strong things were loosened and the firmly fixed gave way. | He drave the kine forth and cleft Vala through by prayer, dispelled the darkness and displayed the light of heaven. || 4. The well with mouth of stone that poured a flood of meath, which Brahmaṇaspati hath opened with his might— | All they who see the light have drunk their fill thereat: together they have made the watery fount flow forth. || 5. Ancient will be those creatures, whatsoe'er they be; with moons, with autumns, doors unclose themselves to you. | Effortless they pass on to perfect this and that, appointed works which Brahmaṇaspati ordained. || 6. They who with much endeavour searching round obtained the Paṇis' noblest treasure hidden in the cave,— | Those sages, having marked the falsehoods, turned them back whence they had come, and sought again to enter in. || 7. The pious ones when they had seen the falsehoods turned them back, the sages stood again upon the lofty ways. | Cast down with both their arms upon the rock they left the kindled fire, and said, No enemy is he. || 8. With his swift bow, strung truly, Brahmaṇaspati reaches the mark whate'er it be that he desires. | Excellent are the arrows wherewithal he shoots, keen-eyed to look on men and springing from his ear. || 9. He brings together and he parts, the great High Priest; extolled is he, in battle Brahmaṇaspati | When, gracious, for the hymn he brings forth food and wealth, the glowing Sun untroubled sends forth fervent heat. || 10. First and preeminent, excelling all besides are the kind gifts of liberal Bṛihaspati. | These are the boons of him the Strong who should be loved, whereby both classes and the people have delight. || 11. Thou who in every way supreme in earthly power, rejoicing, by thy mighty strength hast waxen great,— | He is the God spread forth in breadth against the Gods: he, Brahmaṇaspati, encompasseth this All. || 12. From you, twain Maghavans, all truth proceedeth: even the waters break not your commandment. | Come to us, Brahmaṇaspati and Indra, to our oblation like yoked steeds to fodder. || 13. The sacrificial flames most swiftly hear the call: the priest of the assembly gaineth wealth for hymns. | Hating the stern, remitting at his will the debt, strong in the shock of fight is Brahmaṇaspati. || 14. The wrath of Brahmaṇaspati according to his will had full effect when he would do a mighty deed. | The kine he drave forth and distributed to heaven, even as a copious flood with strength flows sundry ways. || 15. O Brahmaṇaspati, may we be evermore masters of wealth well-guided, full of vital strength. | Heroes on heroes send abundantly to us, when thou omnipotent through prayer seekest my call. || 16. O Brahmaṇaspati, be thou controller of this our hymn, and prosper thou our children. | All that the Gods regard with love is blessed. Loud may we speak, with heroes, in assembly.

Hymn 2:25. Brahmaṇaspati.

1. He lighting up the flame shall conquer enemies: strong shall he be who offers prayer and brings his gift. | He with his seed spreads forth beyond another's seed, whomever Brahmaṇaspati takes for his friend. || 2. With heroes he shall overcome his hero foes, and spread his wealth by kine wise by himself is be. | His children and his children's children | grow in strength, whomever Brahmaṇaspati takes for his friend. || 3. He, mighty like a raving river's billowy flood, as a bull conquers oxen, overcomes with strength. | Like Agni's blazing rush he may not be restrained, whomever Brahmaṇaspati takes for his friend. || 4. For him the floods of heaven flow never failing down: first with the heroes he goes forth to war for kine. | He slays in unabated vigour with great might, whomever Brahmaṇaspati takes for his friend. || 5. All roaring rivers pour their waters down for him, and many a flawless shelter hath been granted him. | Blest with the happiness of Gods he prospers well, whomever Brahmaṇaspati takes for his friend.

Hymn 2:26. Brahmaṇaspati.

1. The righteous singer shall o'ercome his enemies, and he who serves the Gods subdue the godless man. | The zealous man shall vanquish the invincible, the worshipper share the food of him who worships not. || 2. Worship, thou hero, chase the arrogant afar: put on auspicious courage for the fight with foes. | Prepare oblation so that thou mayst have success. we crave the favouring help of Brahmaṇaspati. || 3. He with his folk, his house, his family, his sons, gains booty for himself, and, with the heroes, wealth,believing | Who with oblation and a true heart serves Brahmaṇaspati the Father of the Gods. || 4. Whoso hath honoured him with offerings rich in oil, him Brahmaṇaspati leads forward on his way, | Saves him from sorrow, frees him from his enemy, and is his wonderful deliverer from woe.

Hymn 2:27. Ādityas.

1. These hymns that drop down fatness, with the ladle I ever offer to the Kings Ādityas. | May Mitra, Aryaman, and Bhaga hear us, the mighty Varuṇa Dakṣha, and Aṃśa. || 2. With one accord may Aryaman and Mitra and Varuṇa this day accept this praise-song— | Ādityas bright and pure as streams of water, free from all guile and falsehood, blameless, perfect. || 3. These Gods, Ādityas, vast, profound, and faithful, with many eyes, fain to deceive the wicked, | Looking within behold the good and evil near to the Kings is even the thing most distant. || 4. Upholding that which moves and that which moves not, Ādityas, Gods, protectors of all being, | Provident, guarding well the world of spirits, true to eternal Law, the debt-exactors. || 5. May I, Ādityas, share m this your favour which, Aryaman, brings profit e'en in danger. | Under your guidance, Varuṇa and Mitra, round troubles may I pass, like rugged places. || 6. Smooth is your path, O Aryaman and Mitra; excellent is it, Varuṇa, and thornless. | Thereon, Ādityas, send us down your blessing: grant us a shelter hard to be demolished. || 7. Mother of Kings, may Aditi transport us, by fair paths Aryaman, beyond all hatred. | May we uninjured, girt by many heroes, win Varuṇa's and Mitra's high protection. || 8. With their support they stay three earths, three heavens; three are their functions in the Gods' assembly. | Mighty through Law, Ādityas, is your greatness; fair is it, Aryaman, Varuṇa, and Mitra. || 9. Golden and splendid, pure like streams of water, they hold aloft the three bright heavenly regions. | Ne'er do they slumber, never close their eyelids, faithful, far-ruling for the righteous mortal. || 10. Thou over all, O Varuṇa, art Sovereign, be they Gods, Asura! or be they mortals. | Grant unto us to see a hundred autumns ours be the blest long lives of our forefathers. || 11. Neither the right nor left do I distinguish, neither the cast nor yet the west, Ādityas. | Simple and guided by your wisdom, Vasus! | may I attain the light that brings no danger. || 12. He who bears gifts unto the Kings, true Leaders, he whom their everlasting blessings prosper, | Moves with his chariot first in rank and wealthy, munificent and lauded in assemblies. || 13. Pure, faithful, very strong, with heroes round him, he dwells beside the waters rich with pasture. | None slays, from near at hand or from a distance, him who is under the Ādityas' guidance. || 14. Aditi, Mitra, Varuṇa, forgive us however we have erred and sinned against you. | May I obtain the broad light free from peril: O Indra, let not during darkness seize us. || 15. For him the Twain united pour their fullness, the rain from heaven: he thrives most highly favoured. | He goes to war mastering both the mansions: to him both portions of the world are gracious. || 16. Your guiles, ye Holy Ones, to quell oppressors, your snares spread out against the foe, Ādityas, | May I car-borne pass like a skilful horseman: uninjured may we dwell in spacious shelter. || 17. May I not live, O Varuṇa, to witness my wealthy, liberal, dear friend's destitution. | King, may I never lack well-ordered riches. Loud may we speak, with heroes, in assembly.

Hymn 2:28. Varuṇa

1. This laud of the self-radiant wise Āditya shall be supreme o'er all that is

in greatness. | 1 beg renown of Varuṇa the Mighty, the God exceeding kind to him who worships. | 2, Having extolled thee. Varuṇa, with thoughtful care may we have high fortune in thy service, | Singing thy praises like the fires at coming, day after day, of mornings rich in cattle. || 3. May we be in thy keeping, O thou Leader wide-ruling Varuṇa, Lord of many heroes. | O sons of Aditi, for ever faithful, pardon us, Gods, admit us to your friendship. || 4. He made them flow, the Āditya, the Sustainer: the rivers run by Varuṇa's commandment. | These feel no weariness, nor cease from flowing: swift have they flown like birds in air around us. || 5. Loose me from sin as from a bond that binds me: may we swell, Varuṇa, thy spring of Order. | Let not my thread, while I weave song, be severed, nor my work's sum, before the time, be shattered. || 6. Far from me, Varuṇa, remove all danger accept me graciously, thou Holy Sovereign. | Cast off, like cords that hold a calf, my troubles: I am not even mine eyelid's lord without thee. || 7. Strike us not, Varuṇa, with those dread weapons which, Asura, at thy bidding wound the sinner. | Let us not pass away from light to exile. Scatter, that we may live, the men who hate us || 8. O mighty Varuṇa, now and hereafter, even as of old, will we speak forth our worship. | For in thyself, invincible God, thy statutes ne'er to be moved are fixed as on a mountain. || 9. Move far from me what sins I have committed: let me not suffer, King, for guilt of others. | Full many a morn remains to dawn upon us: in these, O Varuṇa, while we live direct us. || 10. O King, whoever, be he friend or kinsman, hath threatened me affrighted in my slumber—| If any wolf or robber fain would harm us, therefrom, O Varuṇa, give thou us protection. | 11May I not live O Varuṇa, to witness my wealthy, liberal dear friend's destitution. | King, may I never lack well-ordered riches. Loud may we speak, with heroes, in assembly.

Hymn 2:29. Viśvedevas.

1. Upholders of the Law, ye strong Ādityas, remove my sin like her who bears in secret. | You, Varuṇa, Mitra and all Gods who listen, I call to help me, I who know your goodness. || 2. Ye, Gods, are providence and ye are power: remove ye utterly all those who hate us. | As givers of good things deal with us kindly: this day be gracious to us and hereafter. || 3. What service may we do you with our future, what service, Vasus, with our ancient friendship? | O Aditi, and Varuṇa and Mitra, Indra and Marutas, make us well and happy. || 4. Ye, O ye Gods, are verily our kinsmen as such be kind to me who now implore you. | Let not your car come slowly to our worship: of kinsmen such as you ne'er let us weary. || 5. I singly have sinned many a sin against you, and ye chastised me as a sire the gambler. | Far be your nets, far, Gods, be mine offences: seize me not like a bird upon her offspring. || 6. Turn yourselves hitherward this day, ye Holy, that fearing in my heart I may approach you. | Protect us, God; let not the wolf destroy us. Save us, ye Holy, from the pit and falling. || 7. May I not live, O Varuṇa, to witness my wealthy, liberal, dear friend's destitution. | King, may I never lack well-ordered riches. Loud may we speak, with heroes, in assembly.

Hymn 2:30. Indra and Others.

1. The streams unceasing flow to Indra, slayer of Ahi, Savitar, God, Law's fulfiller, | Day after day goes on the sheen of waters. What time hath past since they were first set flowing? || 2. His Mother—for she knew—spake and proclaimed him who was about to cast his bolt at Vṛitra. | Cutting their paths according to his pleasure day after day flow to their goal the rivers. || 3. Aloft he stood above the airy region, and against Vṛitra shot his deadly missile. | Enveloped in a cloud he rushed upon him. Indra subdued the foe with sharpened weapons. || 4. As with a bolt, Bṛihaspati, fiercely flaming, pierce thou Vṛikadvaras, the Asura's, heroes. | Even as in time of old with might thou slewest, so slay even now our enemy, O Indra. || 5. Cast down from heaven on high thy bolt of thunder wherewith in joy thou smitest dead the foeman. | For gain of children make us thine, O Indra, of many children's children and of cattle. || 6. Whomso ye love, his power ye aid and strengthen; ye Twain are the rich worshipper's advancers. | Graciously favour us, Indra and Soma; give us firm standing in this time of danger. || 7. Let it not vex me, tire me, make me slothful, and never let us say, Press not the Soma; | For him who cares for me, gives gifts, supports me, who comes with kine to me who pour libations. || 8. Sarasvatī, protect us: with the Marutas allied thou boldly conquerest our foemen, | While Indra does to death the daring chieftain of Śaṇḍikas exulting in his prowess. || 9. Him who waylays, yea, him who would destroy us,—aim at him, pierce him with thy sharpened weapon. | Bṛihaspati, with arms thou slayest foemen O King, give up the spoiler to destruction. || 10. Perform, O Hero, with our valiant heroes the deeds heroic which thou hast to finish. | Long have they been inflated with presumption: slay them, and bring us hither their possessions. || 11. I craving joy address with hymn and homage your heavenly host, the company of Marutas, | That we may gain wealth with full store of heroes, each day more famous, and with troops of children.

Hymn 2:31. Viśvedevas.

1. Help, Varuṇa and Mitra, O ye Twain allied with Vasus, Rudras, and Ādityas, help our car, | That, as the wild birds of the forest from their home, our horses may fly forth, glad, eager for renown. || 2. Yea, now ye Gods of one accord speed on our car what time among the folk it seeks an act of might; | When, hasting through the region with the stamp of hoofs, our swift steeds trample on the ridges of the earth. || 3. Or may our Indra here, the Friend of all mankind, coming from heaven, most wise, girt by the Marut host, | Accompany, with aid untroubled by a foe, our car to mighty gain, to win the meed of strength. || 4. Or may this Tvashṭar, God who rules the world with power, one-minded with the Goddesses speed forth our car; | Ilā and Bhaga the celestial, Earth and Heaven, Pūshan, Purandhi, and the Aśvins, ruling Lords. || 5. Or, seen alternate, those two blessed Goddesses, Morning and Night who stir all living things to act: | While with my newest song I praise you both, O Earth, that from what moves not ye may spread forth threefold food. || 6. Your blessing as a boon for suppliants we desire: the Dragon of the Deep, and Aja-Ekapāda, | Trita, Ṛibhukṣhan, Savitar shall joy in us, and the Floods' swift Child in our worship and our prayer. || 7. These earnest prayers I pray to you, ye Holy: to pay you honour, living men have formed them, | Men fain to win the prize and glory. May they win, as a car-horse might the goal, your notice.

Hymn 2:32. Various Deities.

1. Graciously further, O ye Heaven and Earth, this speech striving to win reward, of me your worshipper. | First rank I give to you, Immortal, high extolled! I, fain to win me wealth, to you the mighty Pair. || 2. Let not man's guile annoy us, secret or by day: give not us up a prey to these calamities. | Sever not thou our friendship: think thereon for us. This, with a heart that longs for bliss, we seek from thee. || 3. Bring hither with benignant mind the willing Cow teeming with plenteous milk, full, inexhaustible. | O thou invoked by many, day by day I urge thee with my word, a charger rapid in his tread. || 4. With eulogy I call on Rākā swift to hear may she, auspicious, hear us, and herself observe. | With never-breaking needle may she sew her work, and give a hero son most wealthy, meet for praise. || 5. All thy kind thoughts, O Rākā, lovely in their form, wherewith thou grantest wealth to him who offers gifts— | With these come thou to us this day benevolent, O Blessed One, bestowing food of thousand sorts. || 6. O broad-tressed Sinīvālī, thou who art the Sister of the Gods, | Accept the offered sacrifice, and, Goddess, grant us progeny. || 7. With lovely fingers, lovely arms, prolific Mother of many sons— | Present the sacred gifts to her, to Sinīvālī Queen of men. || 8. Her, Sinīvālī, her, Guṅgū, her, Rākā, her, Sarasvatī, Indrāṇī to mine aid I call, and Varuṇānī for my weal.

Hymn 2:33. Rudra.

1. Father of Marutas, let thy bliss approach us: exclude us not from looking on the sunlight. | Gracious to our fleet courser be the Hero may we transplant us, Rudra, in our children. || 2. With the most saving medicines which thou givest, Rudra, may I attain a hundred winters. | Far from us banish enmity and hatred, and to all quarters maladies and trouble. || 3. Chief of all born art thou in glory, Rudra, armed with the thunder, mightiest of the mighty. | Transport us over trouble to well-being repel thou from us all assaults of mischief. || 4. Let us not anger thee with worship, Rudra, ill praise, Strong God! or mingled invocation. | Do thou with strengthening balms incite our heroes: I hear thee famed as best of all physicians. || 5. May I with praise-songs win that Rudra's favour who is adored with gifts and invocations. | Ne'er may the tawny God, fair-checked, and gracious, swift-hearing, yield us to this evil purpose. || 6. The Strong, begirt by Marutas, hath refreshed me, with most invigorating food, imploring. | As he who finds a shade in fervent sunlight may I, uninjured, win the bliss of Rudra. || 7. Where is that gracious hand of thine,

O Rudra, the hand that giveth health and bringeth comfort, | Remover of the woe that Gods have sent us? O Strong One, look thou on me with compassion. || 8. To him the strong, great, tawny, fair-complexioned, I utter forth a mighty hymn of praises. | We serve the brilliant God with adorations, we glorify, the splendid name of Rudra. || 9. With firm limbs, multiform, the strong, the tawny adorns himself with bright gold decorations: | The strength of Godhead ne'er departs from Rudra, him who is Sovereign of this world, the mighty. || 10. Worthy, thou carriest thy bow and arrows, worthy, thy many-hued and honoured necklace. | Worthy, thou cuttest here each fiend to pieces: a mightier than thou there is not, Rudra. || 11. Praise him the chariot-borne, the young, the famous, fierce, slaying like a dread beast of the forest. | O Rudra, praised, be gracious to the singer. let thy hosts spare us and smite down another. || 12. I bend to thee as thou approachest, Rudra, even as a boy before the sire who greets him. | I praise thee Bounteous Giver, Lord of heroes: give medicines to us as thou art lauded. || 13. Of your pure medicines, O potent Marutas, those that are wholesomest and health-bestowing, | Those which our father Manu hath selected, I crave from. Rudra for our gain and welfare. || 14. May Rudra's missile turn aside and spare us, the great wrath of the impetuous One avoid us. | Turn, Bounteous God, thy strong bow from our princes, and be thou gracious to our seed and offspring. || 15. O tawny Bull, thus showing forth thy nature, as neither to be wroth, O God, nor slay us. | Here, Rudra, listen to our invocation. Loud may we speak, with heroes, in assembly.

Hymn 2:34. Marutas

1. The Marutas of resistless might who love the rain, resplendent, terrible like wild beasts in their strength, | Glowing like flames of fire, impetuous in career, blowing the wandering rain-cloud, have disclosed the kine. || 2. They gleam with armlets as the heavens are decked with stars, like cloud-born lightnings shine the torrents of their rain. | Since the strong Rudra, O Marutas with brilliant chests, sprang into life for you in Pṛiśni's radiant lap. || 3. They drip like horses in the racings of swift steeds; with the stream's rapid cars they hasten on their way. | Marutas with helms of gold, ye who make all things shake, come with your spotted deer, one-minded, to our food. || 4. They have bestowed of Mitra all that live, to feed, they who for evermore cause their swift drops to flow; | Whose steeds are spotted deer, whose riches never fail, like horses in full speed, bound to the pole in work. || 5. With brightly-flaming kine whose udders swell with milk, with glittering lances on your unobstructed paths, | O Marutas, of one mind, like swans who seek their nests, come to the rapturous enjoyment of the meath. || 6. To these our prayers, O Marutas, come unanimous, come ye to our libations like the praise of men. | Make it swell like a mare, in udder like a cow, and for the singer grace the song with plenteous strength. || 7. Give us a steed, O Marutas mighty in the car; prevailing prayer that brings remembrance day by day; | Food to your praisers, to your bard in deeds of might give winning wisdom, power uninjured, unsurpassed. || 8. When the bright-chested Marutas, lavish of their gifts, bind at the time bliss their horses to the cars, | Then, as the milch-cow feeds her calf within the stalls, they pour forth food for all oblation-bringing men. || 9. Save us, O Marutas, Vasus, from the injurer, the mortal foe who makes us looked upon as wolves. | With chariot all aflame compass him round about: O Rudras, cast away the foeman's deadly bolt. || 10. Well-known, ye Marutas, is that wondrous course of yours, when they milked Pṛiśni's udder, close akin to her. | Or when to shame the bard who lauded, Rudra's Sons, ye O infallible brought Trita to decay. || 11. We call you such, great Marutas, following wonted ways, to the oblation paid to Vishṇu Speeder-on. | With ladles lifted up, with prayer, we seek of them preeminent, golden-hued, the wealth which all extol. || 12. They, the Daśagvas, first of all brought sacrifice: they at the break of mornings shall inspirit us. | Dawn with her purple beams uncovereth the nights, with great light glowing like a billowy sea of milk. || 13. The Rudras have rejoiced them in the gathered bands at seats of worship as in purple ornaments. | They with impetuous vigour sending down the rain have taken to themselves a bright and lovely hue. || 14. Soliciting their high protection for our help, with this our adoration we sing praise to them, | Whom, for assistance, like the five terrestrial priests. Trita hath brought to aid us hither on his car. || 15. So may your favouring help be turned to us-ward, your kindness like a lowing cow approach us, | Wherewith ye bear your servant over trouble, and free your worshipper from scoff and scorning.

Hymn 2:35. Son of Waters.

1. Eager for spoil my flow of speech I utter: may the Floods' Child accept my songs with favour. | Will not the rapid Son of Waters make them lovely, for he it is who shall enjoy them? || 2. To him let us address the song well-fashioned, forth from the heart. Shall he not understand it' | The friendly Son of Waters by the greatness of Godhead hath produced all things existing. || 3. Some floods unite themselves and others join them: die sounding rivers fill one common storehouse. | On every side the bright Floods have encompassed the bright resplendent Offspring of the Waters. || 4. The never-sullen waters, youthful Maidens, carefully decking, wait on him the youthful. | He with bright rays shines forth in splendid beauty, unfed with wood. in waters, oil-enveloped. || 5. To him three Dames are offering food to feed him, Goddesses to the God whom none may injure. | Within the waters hath he pressed, as hollows, and drinks their milk who now are first made mothers. || 6. Here was the horse's birth; his was the sunlight. Save thou our princes from the oppressor's onslaught. | Him, indestructible, dwelling at a distance in forts unwrought lies and ill spirits reach not. || 7. He, in whose mansion is the teeming Milch-cow, swells the Gods' nectar and cats noble viands. | The Son of Waters, gathering strength in waters, shines for his worshipper to give him treasures. || 8. He who in waters with his own pure Godhead shines widely, law-abiding, everlasting— | The other worlds are verily his branches, and plants are born of him with all their offspring. || 9. The Waters' Son hath risen, and clothed in lightning ascended up unto the curled cloud's bosom; | And bearing with them his supremest glory the Youthful Ones, gold-coloured, move around him. || 10. Golden in form is he, like gold to look on, his colour is like gold, the Son of Waters. | When he is seated fresh from golden birthplace those who present their gold give food to feed him. || 11. This the fair name and this the lovely aspect of him the Waters' Son increase in secret. | Whom here the youthful Maids together kindle, his food is sacred oil of golden colour. || 12. Him, nearest Friend of many, will we worship with sacrifice. and reverence and oblation. | I make his back to shine, with chips provide him; t offer food and with my songs exalt him. || 13. The Bull hath laid his own life-germ Within them. He sucks them as an infant, and they kiss him. | He, Son of Waters, of unfading colour, had entered here as in another's body. || 14. While here he dwelleth in sublimest station, resplendent with the rays that never perish, | The Waters, bearing oil to feed their offspring, flow, Youthful Ones, in wanderings about him. || 15. Agni, I gave good shelter to the people, and to the princes goodly preparation. | Blessed is all that Gods regard with favour. Loud may we speak, with heroes, in assembly.

Hymn 2:36. Various Gods.

1. Water and milk hath he endued, sent forth to thee: the men have drained him with the filters and the stones. | Drink, Indra, from the Hotar's bowl-first right is thine-Soma hallowed and poured with Vashaṭ and Svāhā. || 2. Busied with sacrifice, with spotted deer and spears, gleaming upon your way with ornaments, yea, our Friends, | Sitting on sacred grass, ye Sons of Bhārata, drink Soma from the Potar's bowl, O Men of heaven. || 3. Come unto us, ye swift to listen: as at home upon the sacred grass sit and enjoy yourselves. | And, Tvashṭar, well-content be joyful in the juice with Gods and Goddesses in gladsome company. || 4. Bring the Gods hither, Sage, and offer sacrifice: at the three altars seat thee willingly, O Priest. | Accept for thy delight the proffered Soma meath: drink from the Kindler's bowl and fill thee with thy share. || 5. This is the strengthener of thy body's manly might: strength, victory for all time are placed within thine arms. | Pressed for thee, Maghavan, it is offered unto thee: drink from the chalice of this Brahman, drink thy fill. || 6. Accept the sacrifice; mark both of you, my call: the Priest hath seated him after the ancient texts. | My prayer that bids them come goes forth to both the Kings: drink ye the Soma meath from the Director's bowl.

Hymn 2:37. Various Gods.

1. Enjoy thy fill of meath out of the Hotar's cup: Adhvaryus he desires a full draught poured for him. | Bring it him: seeking this he gives. Granter of Wealth, drink Soma with the Ṛitus from the Hotar's cup. || 2. He whom of old I called on, him I call on now. He is to be invoked; his name is He who

Gives, | Here brought by priests is Soma meath. Granter of Wealth, drink Soma with the Ṛitus from the Potar's cup. || 3. Fat may the horses be wherewith thou speedest on: Lord of the Wood, unharming, strengthen thou thyself. | Drawing and seizing, Bold One, thou who grantest wealth, drink Soma with the Ṛitus from the Neshṭar's cup. || 4. From Hotar's cup and Potar's he hath drunk and joyed: the proffered food hath pleased him from the Neshṭar's bowl. | The fourth cup undisturbed, immortal, let him drink who giveth wealth, the cup of the wealth-giving God. || 5. Yoke, O ye Twain, today your hero-bearing car, swift-moving hitherward: your loosing-place is here. | Mix the oblations, then come hither with the meath, and drink the Soma, ye rich in abundant strength. || 6. Agni, accept the fuel and our offered gift: accept the prayer of man, accept our eulogy, | Do thou with all, with Ṛitu, O thou Excellent, fain, make the great Gods all fain taste the gift we bring.

Hymn 2:38. Savitar.

1. Uprisen is Savitar, this God, to quicken, Priest who neglects not this most constant duty. | To the Gods, verily, he gives rich treasure, and blesses him who calls them to the banquet. || 2. Having gone up on high, the God broad-handed spreads his arms widely forth that all may mark him. | Even the waters bend them to his service: even this wind rests in the circling region. || 3. Though borne by swift steeds he will yet unyoke them: e'en the fleet chariot hath he stayed from going. | He hath checked e'en their haste who glide like serpents. Night closely followed Savitar's dominion. || 4. What was spread out she weaves afresh, re-weaving: the skilful leaves his labour half-completed. | He hath arisen from rest, and parted seasons: Savitar hath approached, God, holy-minded. || 5. Through various dwellings, through entire existence, spreads, manifest, the household light of Agni. | The Mother gives her Son the goodliest portion, and Savitar hath sped to meet his summons. || 6. He comes again, unfolded, fain for conquest: at home was he, the love of all things moving. | Each man hath come leaving his evil doings, after the Godlike Savitar's commandment. || 7. The wild beasts spread through desert places seeking their watery share which thou hast set in waters. | The woods are given to the birds. These statutes of the God Savitar none disobeyeth. || 8. With utmost speed, in restless haste at sunset Varuṇa seeks his watery habitation. | Then seeks each bird his nest, each beast his lodging. In due place Savitar hath set each creature. || 9. Him whose high law not Varuṇa nor Indra, not Mitra, Aryaman, nor Rudra breaketh, | Nor evil-hearted fiends, here for my welfare him I invoke, God Savitar, with worship. || 10. May they who strengthen bliss, and thought and wisdom, and the Dames' Lord and Narāśaṃsa aid us. | That good may come to us and wealth be gathered, may we be Savitar the God's beloved. || 11. So come to us our hearts' desire, the bounty bestowed by thee, from heaven and earth and waters, | That it be well with friends and those who praise thee, and, Savitar, with the loud-lauding singer.

Hymn 2:39. Aśvins.

1. Sing like the two press-stones for this same purpose; come like two misers to the tree of treasure; | Like two laud-singing Brahmans in the assembly, like the folk's envoys called in many places. || 2. Moving at morning like two car-borne heroes, like to a pair of goats ye come electing; | Like two fair dames embellishing their bodies, like a wise married pair among the people. || 3. Like to a pair of horns come first to us-ward, like to a pair of hoofs with rapid motion; | Come like two Chakravākas in the grey of morning, come like two chariot wheels at dawn, ye Mighty. || 4. Bear us across the rivers like two vessels, save us as ye were yokes, naves, spokes and fellies. | Be like two dogs that injure not our bodies; preserve us, like two crutches, that we fall not. || 5. Like two winds ageing not, two confluent rivers, come with quick vision like two eyes before us. | Come like two hands most helpful to the body, and guide us like two feet to what is precious. || 6. Even as two lips that with the mouth speak honey, even as two breasts that nourish our existence, | Like the two nostrils that protect our being, be to us as our ears that hear distinctly. || 7. Like two hands give ye us increasing vigour; like heaven and earth constrain the airy regions. | Aśvins, these hymns that struggle to approach you, sharpen ye like an axe upon a whetstone. || 8. These prayers of ours exalting you, O Aśvins, have the Gṛitsamadas, for a laud, made ready. | Welcome them, O ye Heroes, and come hither. Loud may we speak. with brave men, in assembly.

Hymn 2:40. Soma and Pūṣhan.

1. Soma and Pūṣhan, Parents of all riches, Parents of earth and Parents of high heaven, | You Twain, brought forth as the whole world's protectors, the Gods have made centre of life eternal. || 2. At birth of these two Gods all Gods are joyful: they have caused darkness, which we hate, to vanish. | With these, with Soma and with Pūṣhan, India generates ripe warm milk in the raw milch-cows. || 3. Soma and Pūṣhan, urge your chariot hither, the seven-wheeled car that measures out the region, | That stirs not all, that moves to every quarter, five-reined and harnessed by the thought, ye Mighty. || 4. One in the heaven on high hath made his dwelling, on earth and in the firmament the other. | May they disclose to us great store of treasure, much-longed for, rich in food, source of enjoyment. || 5. One of you Twain is Parent of all creatures, the other journeys onward all-beholding. | Soma and Pūṣhan, aid my thought with favour: with you may we o'ercome in all encounters. || 6. May Pūṣhan stir our thought, the all-impelling, may Soma Lord of riches grant us riches. | May Aditi the perfect Goddess aid us. Loud may we speak, with heroes, in assembly.

Hymn 2:41. Various Deities.

1. O Vāyu, come to us with all the thousand chariots that are thine, | Team-borne, to drink the Soma juice. || 2. Drawn by thy team, O Vāyu, come; to thee is offered this, the pure. | Thou visitest the presser's house. || 3. Indra and Vāyu, drawn by teams, ye Heroes, come today and drink. | Of the bright juice when blent with milk. || 4. This Soma hath been shed for you, Law strengtheners, Mitra-Varuṇa! | Listen ye here to this my call. || 5. Both Kings who never injure aught seat them in their supremest home, | The thousand-pillared, firmly-based. || 6. Fed with oblation, Sovereign Kings, Ādityas, Lords of liberal gifts. | They wait on him whose life is true. || 7. With kine, Nāsatyas, and with steeds, come, Aśvins, Rudras, to the house | That will protect its heroes well; || 8. Such, wealthy Gods! as none afar nor standing nigh to us may harm, | Yea, no malicious mortal foe. || 9. As such, O longed-far Aśvins, lead us on to wealth of varied sort, | Wealth that shall bring us room and rest. || 10. Verily Indra, conquering all, driveth e'en mighty fear away, | For firm is he and swift to act. || 11. Indra be gracious unto us: sin shall not reach us afterward, | And good shall be before us still. || 12. From all the regions of the world let Indra send security, | The foe-subduer, swift to act. || 13. O all ye Gods, come hitherward: hear this mine invocation, seat | Yourselves upon this sacred grass. || 14. Among the Śunahotras strong for you is this sweet gladdening draught. | Drink ye of this delightsome juice. || 15. Ye Marutas led by Indra, Gods with Pūṣhan for your bounteousest, | Hear all of you this call of mine. || 16. Best Mother, best of Rivers, best of Goddesses, Sarasvatī, We are, as 'twere, of no repute and dear Mother, give thou us renown. || 17. In thee, Sarasvatī, divine, all generations have their stay. | Be, glad with Śunahotra's sons: O Goddess grant us progeny. || 18. Enriched with sacrifice, accept Sarasvatī, these prayers of ours, | Thoughts which Gṛitsamadas beloved of Gods bring, Holy One,to thee. || 19. Ye who bless sacrifice, go forth, for verily we choose you both, | And Agni who conveys our gifts. || 20. This our effectual sacrifice, reaching the sky, shall Heaven and Earth | Present unto the Gods today. || 21. In both your laps, ye guileless Ones, the Holy Gods shall sit them down | today to drink the Soma here.

Hymn 2:42. Kapiñjala.

1. Telling his race aloud with cries repeated, he sends his voice out as his boat a steersman. | O Bird, be ominous of happy fortune from no side may calamity befall thee. || 2. Let not the falcon kill thee, nor the eagle let not the arrow-bearing archer reach thee. | Still crying in the region of the Fathers, speak here auspicious, bearing joyful tidings. || 3. Bringing good tidings, Bird of happy omen, call thou out loudly southward of our dwellings, | So that no thief, no sinner may oppress us. Loud may we speak, with heroes, in assembly.

Hymn 2:43. Kapiñjala.

1. Here on the right sing forth chanters of hymns of praise, even the winged birds that in due season speak. | He, like: a Sāman-chanter utters both the notes, skilled in the mode of Trishṭubh and of Gāyatrī. || 2. Thou like the chanter-priest chantest the Sāman, Bird; thou singest at libations like a Brahman's son. | Even as a vigorous horse when he comes near the mare, announce to us good fortune, Bird, on every side, proclaim in all directions happy luck, O Bird. || 3. When singing here, O Bird. announce

good luck to us, and when thou sittest still think on us with kind thoughts. | When flying off thou singest thou art like a lute. With brave sons in assembly may we speak aloud.

Maṇḍala 3

Hymn 3:1. Agni.

1. Thou, Agni, who wilt have the strong, hast made me the Soma's priest, to worship in assembly. | Thou shinest to the Gods, I set the press-stones I toil; be joyful in thyself, O Agni. || 2. East have we turned the rite; may the hymn aid it. With wood and worship shall they honour Agni. | From heaven the synods of the wise have learnt it: e'en for the quick and strong they seek advancement. || 3. The Prudent, he whose will is pure, brought welfare, allied by birth to Heaven and Earth in kinship. | The Gods discovered in the midst of waters beautiful Agni with the Sisters' labour. || 4. Him, Blessed One, the Seven strong Floods augmented, him white at birth and red when waxen mighty. | As mother mares run to their new-born you ling, so at his birth the Gods wondered at Agni. || 5. Spreading with radiant limbs throughout the region, purging his power with wise purifications, | Robing himself in light, the life of waters, he spreads abroad his high and perfect glories. || 6. He sought heaven's Mighty Ones, the unconsuming, the unimpaired, not clothed and yet not naked. | Then they, ancient and young, who dwell together, Seven sounding Rivers, as one germ received him. || 7. His piles, assuming every form, are scattered where flow sweet waters, at the spring of fatness; | There stood the milch-kine with full-laden udders, and both paired Mighty Mothers of the Wondrous. || 8. Carefully cherished, Son of Strength, thou shonest assuming lasting and refulgent beauties. | Full streams of fatness and sweet juice descended, there where the Mighty One grew strong by wisdom. || 9. From birth he knew even his Father's bosom, he set his voices and his streams in motion; | Knew him who moved with blessed Friends in secret, with the young Dames of heaven. He stayed not hidden. || 10. He nursed the Infant of the Sire and Maker: alone the Babe sucked many a teeming bosom. | Guard, for the Bright and Strong, the fellow-spouses friendly to men and bound to him in kinship. || 11. The Mighty One increased in space unbounded; full many a glorious flood gave strength to Agni. | Friend of the house, within the lap of Order lay Agni, in the Sister Rivers' service. || 12. As keen supporter where great waters gather, light-shedder whom the brood rejoice to look on; | He who begat, and will beget, the dawn-lights, most manly, Child of Floods, is youthful Agni. || 13. Him, varied in his form, the lovely Infant of floods and plants the blessed wood hath gendered. | Gods even, moved in spirit, came around him, and served him at his birth, the Strong, the Wondrous. || 14. Like brilliant lightnings, mighty luminaries accompany the light-diffusing Agni, | Waxen, as 'twere in secret, in his dwelling, while in the boundless stall they milk out Amṛita. || 15. I sacrificing serve thee with oblations and crave with longing thy good-will and friendship. | Grant, with the Gods, thy grace to him who lauds thee, protect us with thy rays that guard the homestead. || 16. May we, O Agni, thou who leadest wisely, thy followers and masters of all treasures, | Strong in the glory of our noble offspring, subdue the godless when they seek the battle. || 17. Ensign of Gods hast thou become, O Agni, joy-giver, knower of all secret wisdom. | Friend of the homestead, thou hast lightened mortals: car-borne thou goest to the Gods, fulfilling. || 18. Within the house hath sate the King immortal of mortals, filling full their sacred synods. | Bedewed with holy oil he shineth widely, Agni, the knower of all secret wisdom. || 19. Come unto us with thine auspicious friendship, come speeding, Mighty, with thy mighty succours. | Grant us abundant wealth that saves from danger, that brings a good repute, a glorious portion. || 20. To thee who art of old these songs, O Agni, have I declared, the ancient and the later. | These great libations to the Strong are offered: in every birth is Jātavedas established. || 21. Established in every birth is Jātavedas, kindled perpetual by the Viśvāmitras. | May we rest ever in the loving-kindness, in the auspicious grace of him the Holy. || 22. This sacrifice of ours do thou, O Mighty, O truly Wise, bear to the Gods rejoicing. | Grant us abundant food, thou priestly Herald, vouchsafe to give us ample wealth, O Agni. || 23. As holy food, Agni, to thine invoker give wealth in cattle, lasting, rich in marvels. | To us he born a son, and spreading offspring. Agni, be this thy gracious will to us-ward.

Hymn 3:2. Agni.

1. To him, Vaiśvānara, who strengthens Holy Law, to Agni we present our praise like oil made pure. | With thoughtful insight human priests bring him anear, our Herald from of old, as an axe forms a car. || 2. He made the heaven and earth resplendent by his birth: Child of two Mothers he was meet to be implored, | Agni, oblation-bearer, gracious, ever-young, infallible, rich in radiant light, the guest of men. || 3. Within the range of their surpassing power, by might, the Gods created Agni with inventive thought. | I, eager to win strength, address him, like a steed, resplendent with his brilliance, with his ample light. || 4. Eager to gain, we crave from him the friendly God strength confident, choice-worthy meet to be extolled: | The Bhṛigus' bounty, willing, strong with sages' lore, even Agni shining forth with light that comes from heaven. || 5. For happiness, men, having trimmed the sacred grass, set Agni glorious for his strength before them here; | Yea, with raised ladles, him bright, dear to all the Gods, perfecting aims of works, Rudra of solemn rites. || 6. Around thy dwelling-place, O brightly-shining Priest, are men at sacrifice, whose sacred grass is trimmed. | Wishing to do thee service, Agni, they are there, desirous of thy friendship grant them store of wealth. || 7. He hath filled heaven and earth and the great realm of light, when at his birth the skilful held him in their hold. | He like a horse is led forth to the sacrifice Sage, graciously inclined, that he may win us strength. || 8. Honour the oblation-bearer, him who knows fair rites, serve ye the Household Friend who knows all things that be. | He drives the chariot of the lofty ordinance: Agni most active, is the great High Priest of Gods. || 9. They who are free from death, fain for him, purified three splendours of the mighty Agni, circling all. | To man, for his enjoyment, one of these they gave: the other two have passed into the sister sphere. || 10. Man's sacrificial food hath sharpened like an axe, for brightness, him the Sage of men, the people's Lord, | Busied with sacred rites he mounts and he descends. He hath laid down his vital germ within these worlds. || 11. He stirs with life in wombs dissimilar in kind, born as a Lion or a loudly-bellowing Bull: | Vaiśvānara immortal with wide-reaching might, bestowing goods and wealth on him who offers gifts. || 12. Vaiśvānara, as of old, mounted the cope of heaven, heaven's ridge, well greeted, by those skilled in noble songs. | He, as of old, producing riches for the folk, still watchful, traverses the common way again. || 13. For new prosperity we seek to Agni, him whose course is splendid, gold-haired, excellently bright, | Whom Mātariśvan established, dweller in the heaven, meet for high praise and holy, sage and true to Law. || 14. As pure and swift of course, beholder of the light, who stands in heaven's bright sphere a sign, who wakes at dawn, | Agni, the head of heaven, whom none may turn aside-to him the Powerful with mighty prayer we seek. || 15. The cheerful Priest, the pure, in whom no guile is found, Friend of the House, praise-worthy, dear to all mankind, | Fair to behold for beauty like a splendid car,—Agni the Friend of men we ever seek for wealth.

Hymn 3:3. Agni.

1. To him who shines afar, Vaiśvānara, shall bards give precious things that he may go on certain paths: | For Agni the Immortal serves the Deities, and therefore never breaks their everlasting laws. || 2. He, wondrous envoy, goes between the earth and heaven, firm seated as the Herald, great High Priest of men. | He compasseth with rays the lofty dwelling-place, Agni, sent forward by the Gods, enriched with prayer. || 3. Sages shall glorify Agni with earnest thoughts, ensign of sacrifice, who fills the synod full: | In whom the singers have stored up their holy acts to him the worshipper looks for joy and happiness. || 4. The Sire of sacrifice, great God of holy bards, Agni, the measure and the symbol of the priests, | Hath entered heaven and earth that show in varied form: the Sage whom many love rejoiceth in his might. || 5. Bright Agni with the bright car, Lord of green domains, Vaiśvānara dweller in the floods, who finds the light, | Pervading, swift and wild, encompassed round with powers, him very glorious have the Gods established here. || 6. Agni, together with the Gods and Manu's folk by thought extending sacrifice in varied form, | Goes, car-borne, to and fro with those who crown each rite, the fleet, the Household Friend, who turns the curse aside. || 7. Sing, Agni, for long life to us and

noble sons: teem thou with plenty, shine upon us store of food. | Increase the great man's strength, thou ever-vigilant: thou, longing for the Gods, knowest their hymns full well. || 8. The Mighty One, Lord of the people and their guest, the leader of their thoughts, devoted Friend of priests, | Our solemn rites' announcer, Jātavedas, men with worship ever praise, with urgings for their weal. || 9. Agni the God resplendent, giver of great joy, hath on his lovely car compassed the lands with, might. | Let us with pure laudations in his house approach the high laws of the nourisher of multitudes. || 10. I celebrate thy glories, O Vaiśvānara, wherewith thou, O far-sighted God, has found the light. | Thou filledst at thy birth both worlds, the earth and heaven: all this, O Agni, hast thou compassed of thyself. || 11. By his great skill the Sage alone hath brought to pass a great deed, mightier than Vaiśvānara's wondrous acts. | Agni sprang into being, magnifying both his Parents, Heaven and Earth, rich in prolific seed.

Hymn 3:4. Āprīs.

1. Be friendly with each kindled log of fuel, with every flash bestow the boon of riches. | Bring thou the Gods, O God, unto our worship: serve, well-inclined, as Friend thy friends, O Agni. || 2. Agni whom daily Varuṇa and Mitra the Gods bring thrice a day to this our worship, | Tanūnapāt, enrich with meath our service that dwells with holy oil, that offers honour. || 3. The thought that bringeth every boon proceedeth to worship first the Priest of the libation, | That we may greet the Strong One with our homage. Urged, may he bring the Gods, best Sacrificer. || 4. On high your way to sacrifice was made ready; the radiant flames went upward to the regions. | Full in the midst of heaven the Priest is seated: strew we the sacred grass where Gods may rest them. || 5. Claiming in mind the seven priests' burnt oblations, inciting all, they came in settled order. | To this our sacrifice approach the many who show in hero beauty at assemblies. || 6. Night and Dawn, lauded, hither come together, both smiling, different are their forms in colour, | That Varuṇa and Mitra may accept us, and Indra, girt by Marutas, with his glories. | 7. I crave the grace of heaven's two chief Invokers: the seven swift steeds joy in their wonted manner. | These speak of truth, praising the truth eternal, thinking on Order as the guards of Order. || 8. May Bhāratī with all her Sisters, Iḷā accordant with the Gods, with mortals Agni, | Sarasvatī with all her kindred Rivers, come to this grass, Three Goddesses, and seat them. || 9. Well pleased with us do thou O God, O Tvaṣhṭar, give ready issue to our procreant vigour, | Whence springs the hero, powerful, skilled in action, lover of Gods, adjuster of the press-stones. || 10. Send to the Gods the oblation, Lord of Forests; and let the Immolator, Agni, dress it. | He as the truer Priest shall offer worship, for the Gods' generations well he knoweth. || 11. Come thou to us, O Agni, duly kindled, together with the potent Gods and Indra. | On this our grass sit Aditi, happy Mother, and let our Hail delight the Gods Immortal.

Hymn 3:5. Agni.

1. Agni who shines against the Dawns is wakened. The holy Singer who precedes the sages. | With far-spread lustre, kindled by the pious, the Priest hath thrown both gates of darkness open. || 2. Agni hath waxen mighty by laudations, to be adored with hymns of those who praise him. | Loving the varied shows of holy Order at the first flush of dawn he shines as envoy. || 3. Amid men's homes hath Agni been established, fulfilling with the Law, Friend, germ of waters. | Loved and adored, the height he hath ascended, the Singer, object of our invocations. || 4. Agni is Mitra when enkindled duly, Mitra as Priest, Varuṇa, Jātavedas; | Mitra as active minister, and House-Friend, Mitra of flowing rivers and of mountains. || 5. The Earth's, the Bird's dear lofty place he guardeth, he guardeth in his might the course of Sūrya, | Guardeth the Seven-headed in the centre, guardeth sublime the Deities enjoyment. || 6. The skilful God who knows all forms of knowledge made for himself a fair form, meet for worship. | This Agni guards with care that never ceases the Soma's skin, the Bird's place rich in fatness. || 7. Agni hath entered longingly the longing shrine rich with fatness, giving easy access. | Resplendent, pure, sublime and purifying, again, again he renovates his Mothers. || 8. Born suddenly, by plants he grew to greatness, when tender shoots with holy oil increased him, | Like waters lovely when they hasten downward may Agni in his Parents' lap protect us. || 9. Extolled, the Strong shone forth with kindled fuel to the earth's centre, to the height of heaven. | May Agni, Friend, adorable Mātariśvan, as envoy bring the Gods unto our worship. || 10. Best of all luminaries lofty Agni supported with his flame the height of heaven, | When, far from Bhṛigus, Mātariśvan kindled the oblation-bearer where he lay in secret. || 11. As holy food, Agni to thine invoker give wealth in cattle, lasting, rich in marvels. | To us be born a son and spreading offspring. Agni, be this thy gracious will to us-word.

Hymn 3:6. Agni.

1. Urged on by deep devotion, O ye singers, bring, pious ones, the God-approaching ladle. | Borne onward to the right it travels eastward, and, filled with oil, to Agni bears oblation. || 2. Thou at thy birth didst fill both earth and heaven, yea, Most Adorable, thou didst exceed them. | Even through the heaven's and through the earth's expanses let thy swift seven-tongued flames roll on, O Agni. || 3. Both Heaven and Earth and Gods who should be worshipped establish thee as Priest for every dwelling, | Whenever human families, God-devoted, bringing oblations; laud thy splendid lustre. || 4. Firm in the Gods' home is the Mighty seated, between vast Heaven and Earth the well-beloved— | Those Cows who yield, unharmed, their nectar, Spouses of the Far-Strider, ever-young, united. || 5. Great are the deeds of thee, the Great, O Agni: thou by thy power hast spread out earth and heaven. | As soon as thou wast born thou wast an envoy, thou, Mighty One, was Leader of the people. || 6. Bind to the pole with cords of holy Order the long-maned ruddy steeds who sprinkle fatness. | Bring hither, O thou God, all Gods together: provide them noble worship, Jātavedas. || 7. Even from the sky thy brilliant lights shone hither: still hast thou beamed through many a radiant morning, | That the Gods praised their joyous Herald's labour eagerly burning, Agni, in the forests. || 8. The Gods who take delight in air's wide region, or those the dwellers in heaven's realm of brightness, | Or those, the Holy, prompt to hear, our helpers, who, car-borne, turn their horses hither, Agni— || 9. With these, borne on one ear, Agni, approach us, or borne on many, for thy steeds are able. | Bring, with their Dames, the Gods, the Three and-Thirty, after thy Godlike nature, and be joyful. || 10. He is the Priest at whose repeated worship even wide Heaven and Earth sing out for increase. | They fair and true and holy coming forward stand at his sacrifice who springs from Order. || 11. As holy food, Agni, to thine invoker give wealth in cattle, lasting, rich in marvels. | To us be born a son and spreading offspring. Agni, be this thy gracious will to us-ward.

Hymn 3:7.

1. The seven tones risen from the white-backed viand have made their way between the pair of Mothers. | Both circumjacent Parents come together to yield us length of days they hasten forward. || 2. The Male who dwells in heaven hath Mares and Milchkine: he came to Goddesses who bring sweet treasure. | To thee safe resting in the seat of Order the Cow alone upon her way proceedeth. || 3. Wise Master, wealthy finder-out of riches, he mounted those who may with case be guided. | He, dark-backed, manifold with varied aspect, hath made them burst forth from their food the brush-wood. || 4. Strength-giving streams bear hither him eternal, fain to support the mighty work. of Tvaṣhṭar. | He, flashing in his home with all his members, hath entered both the worlds as they were single. || 5. They know the red Bull's blessing, and are joyful under the flaming-coloured Lord's dominion: | They who give shine from heaven with fair effulgence, whose lofty song like Iḷā must be honoured. || 6. Yea, by tradition from the ancient sages they brought great strength from the two mighty Parents, | To where the singer's Bull, the night's dispeller, after his proper law hath waxen stronger. || 7. Seven holy singers guard with five Adhvaryus the Bird's beloved firmly-settled station. | The willing Bulls, untouched by old, rejoice them: as Gods themselves the ways of Gods they follow. || 8. I crave the grace of heaven's two chief Invokers: the seven swift steeds joy in their wonted manner. | These speak of truth, praising the Truth Eternal, thinking on Order as the guards of Order. || 9. The many seek the great Steed as a stallion: the reins obey the Lord of varied colour. | O heavenly Priest, most pleasant, full of wisdom, bring the great Gods to us, and Earth and Heaven. || 10. Rich Lord, the Mornings have gleamed forth in splendour, fair-rayed, fair-speaking, worshipped with all viands, | Yea, with the glory of the earth, O Agni. Forgive us, for our weal, e'en sin committed. || 11. As holy food, Agni, to thine invoker, give wealth in cattle, lasting, rich in marvels. | To us be born a son, and spreading offspring Agni, be this thy gracious will to us-ward.

Hymn 3:8. Sacrificial Post.

1. God-Serving men, O Sovereign of the Forest, with heavenly meath at sacrifice anoint thee. | Grant wealth to us when thou art standing upright as when reposing on this Mother's bosom. || 2. Set up to eastward of the fire enkindled, accepting prayer that wastes not, rich in hero. | Driving far from us poverty and famine, lift thyself up to bring us great good fortune. || 3. Lord of the Forest, raise. thyself up on the loftiest spot of earth. | Give splendour, fixt and measured well, to him who brings the sacrifice. || 4. Well-robed, enveloped he is come, the youthful: springing to life his glory waxeth greater. | Contemplative in mind and God-adoring, sages of high intelligence upraise him. || 5. Sprung up he rises in the days' fair weather, increasing in the men-frequented synod. | With song the wise and skilful consecrate him: his voice the God-adoring singer utters. | 6, Ye whom religious men have firmly planted; thou Forest Sovereign whom the axe hath fashioned,— | Let those the Stakes divine which here are standing be fain to grant us wealth with store of children. || 7. O men who lift the ladles up, these hewn and planted in the ground, | Bringing a blessing to the field, shall bear our precious gift to Gods. || 8. Ādityas, Rudras, Vasus, careful leaders, Earth, Heaven, and Pṛithivī and Air's mid-region, | Accordant Deities shall bless our worship and make our sacrifice's ensign lofty. || 9. Like swan's that flee in lengthened line, the Pillars have come to us arrayed in brilliant colour. | They, lifted up on high, by sages, eastward, go forth as Gods to the God's dwelling-places. || 10. Those Stakes upon the earth with rings that deck them seem to the eye like horns of horned creatures; | Or, as upraised by priests in invocation, let them assist us in the rush to battle. || 11. Lord of the Wood, rise with a hundred branches. with thousand branches may we rise to greatness, | Thou whom this hatchet, with an edge well whetted for great felicity, hath brought before us.

Hymn 3:9.

1. We as thy friends have chosen thee, mortals a God, to be our help, | The Waters' Child, the blessed, the resplendent One, victorious and beyond compare. || 2. Since thou delighting in the woods hast gone unto thy mother streams, | Not to be scorned, Agni, is that return of thine when from afar thou now art here. || 3. O'er pungent smoke host thou prevailed, and thus art thou benevolent. | Some go before, and others round about thee sit, they in whose friendship thou hast place. || 4. Him who had passed beyond his foes, beyond continual pursuits, Him the unerring Ones, observant, found in floods, couched like a lion in his lair. || 5. Him wandering at his own free will, Agni here hidden from our view, | Him Mātariśvan brought to us from far away produced by friction, from the Gods. || 6. O Bearer of Oblations, thus mortals received thee from the Gods, | Whilst thou, the Friend of man, guardest each sacrifice with thine own power, Most Youthful One. || 7. Amid thy wonders this is good, yea, to the simple is it clear, | When gathered round about thee, Agni, lie the herds where thou art kindled in the morn. || 8. Offer to him who knows fair rites, who burns with purifying glow, | Swift envoy, active, ancient, and adorable: serve ye the God attentively. || 9. Three times a hundred Gods and thrice a thousand, and three times ten and nine have worshipped Agni, | For him spread sacred grass, with oil bedewed him, and established him as Priest and Sacrificer.

Hymn 3:10. Agni.

1. Thee Agni, God, Imperial Lord of all mankind, do mortal men | With understanding kindle at the sacrifice. || 2. They laud thee in their solemn rites, Agni, as Minister and Priest, | Shine forth in thine own home as guardian of the Law. || 3. He, verily, who honours thee with fuel, Knower of all life, | He, Agni! wins heroic might, he prospers well. || 4. Ensign of sacrifices, he, Agni, with Gods is come to us, | Decked by the seven priests, to him who bringeth gifts. || 5. To Agni, the Invoking Priest, offer your best, your lofty speech, | To him Ordainer-like who brings the light of songs. || 6. Let these our hymns make Agni grow, whence, meet for laud, he springs to life, | To mighty strength and great possession, fair to see. || 7. Best Sacrificer, bring the Gods, O Agni, to the pious man: | A joyful Priest, thy splendour drive our foes afar || 8. As such, O Purifier, shine on us heroic glorious might: | Be nearest Friend to those who laud thee, for their weal. || 9. So, wakeful, versed in sacred hymns, the holy singers kindly thee. | Oblation-bearer, deathless, cherisher of strength.

Hymn 3:11. Agni.

1. Agni is Priest, the great High Priest of sacrifice, most swift in act: | He knows the rite in constant course. || 2. Oblation-bearer, deathless, well inclined, an eager messenger, | Agni comes nigh us with the thought. || 3. Ensign of sacrifice from of old, Agni well knoweth with his thought | To prosper this man's aim and hope. || 4. Agni, illustrious from old time, the Son of Strength who knows all life, | The Gods have made to their Priest. || 5. Infallible is Agni, he who goes before the tribes of men, | A chariot swift and ever new. || 6. Strength of the Gods which none may harm, subduing all his enemies, | Agni is mightiest in fame. || 7. By offering sacred food to him the mortal worshipper obtains. | A home from him whose light makes pure. || 8. From Agni, by our hymns, may we gain all things that bring happiness, | Singers of him who knows all life. || 9. O Agni, in our deeds of might may we obtain all precious things: | The Gods are centred all in thee.

Hymn 3:12. Indra-Agni.

1. Moved, Indra-Agni, by our hymn, come to the juice, the precious dew: | Drink ye thereof, impelled by song. || 2. O Indra-Agni, with the man who lauds you comes the wakening rite: | So drink ye both this juice assured. || 3. Through force of sacrifice I choose Indra-Agni who love the wise: | With Soma let these sate them here. || 4. Indra and Agni I invoke, joint-victors, bounteous, unsubdued, | Foe-slayers, best to win the spoil. || 5. Indra and Agni, singers skilled in melody hymn you, bringing lauds: | I choose you for the sacred food. || 6. Indra and Agni, ye cast down the ninety forts which Dāsas held, | Together, with one mighty deed. || 7. To Indra-Agni reverent thoughts go forward from the holy task | Along the path of sacred Law. || 8. O Indra-Agni, powers are yours, and dwellings and delightful food | Good is your readiness to act. || 9. Indra and Agni, in your deeds of might ye deck heaven's lucid realms: | Famed is that hero strength of yours.

Hymn 3:13. Agni.

1. To Agni, to this God of yours I sing aloud with utmost power. | May he come to us with the Gods, and sit, best Offerer, on the grass. || 2. The Holy, whose are earth and heaven, and succour waits upon his strength; | Him men who bring oblations laud, and they who wish to gain, for grace. || 3. He is the Sage who guides these men, Leader of sacred rites is he. | Him your own Agni, serve ye well, who winneth and bestoweth wealth. || 4. So may the gracious Agni grant most goodly shelter for our use; | Whence in the heavens or in the floods he shall pour wealth upon our lands. || 5. The singers kindle him, the Priest, Agni the Lord of tribes of men, | Resplendent and without a peer through his own excellent designs. || 6. Help us, thou Brahman, best of all invokers of the Gods in song. | Beam, Friend of Marutas, bliss on us, O Agni, a most liberal God. || 7. Yea, grant us treasure thousandfold with children and with nourishment, | And, Agni, splendid hero strength, exalted, wasting not away.

Hymn 3:14. Agni.

1 The pleasant Priest is come into the synod, true, skilled in sacrifice, most wise, Ordainer. | Agni, the Son of Strength, whose car is lightning, whose hair is flame, hath shown on earth his lustre. || 2. To thee I offer reverent speech: accept it: to thee who markest it, victorious, faithful! | Bring, thou who knowest, those who know, and seat thee amid the sacred grass, for help, O Holy. || 3. The Two who show their vigour, Night and Morning, by the wind's paths shall haste to thee O Agni. | When men adorn the Ancient with oblations, these seek, as on two chariot-seats, the dwelling. || 4. To thee, strong Agni! Varuṇa and Mitra and all the Marutas sang a song of triumph, | What time unto the people's lands thou camest, spreading them as the Sun of men, with lustre. || 5. Approaching with raised hands and adoration, we have this day fulfilled for thee thy longing. | Worship the Gods with most devoted spirit, a Priest with no unfriendly thought, O Agni. || 6. For, Son of Strength, from thee come many succours, and powers abundant that a God possesses. | Agni, to us with speech that hath no falsehood grant riches, real, to be told in thousands. || 7. Whatever, God, in sacrifice we mortals have wrought is all for thee, strong, wise of purpose! | Be thou the Friend of each good chariot's master. All this enjoy thou here, immortal Agni.

Hymn 3:15. Agni.

1. Resplendent with thy wide-extending lustre, dispel the terrors of the

fiends who hate us | May lofty Agni be my guide and shelter, the easily-invoked, the good Protector. || 2. Be thou To us, while now the morn is breaking, be thou a guardian when the Sun hath mounted. | Accept, as men accept a true-born infant, my laud, O Agni nobly born in body. || 3. Bull, who beholdest men, through many mornings, among the dark ones shine forth red, O Agni. | Lead us, good Lord, and bear us over trouble: Help us who long, Most Youthful God, to riches. || 4. Shine forth, a Bull invincible, O Agni, winning by conquest all the forts and treasures, | Thou Jātavedas who art skilled in guiding, the chief high saving sacrifice's Leader. || 5. Lighting Gods hither, Agni, wisest Singer, bring thou to us many and flawless shelters. | Bring vigour, like a car that gathers booty: bring us, O Agni, beauteous Earth and Heaven. || 6. Swell, O thou Bull and give those powers an impulse, e'en Earth and Heaven who yield their milk in plenty, | Shining, O God, with Gods in clear effulgence. Let not a mortal's evil will obstruct us. || 7. Agni, as holy food to thine invoker, give wealth in cattle, lasting, rich in marvels. | To us be born a son and spreading offspring. Agni, be this thy gracious will to us-ward.

Hymn 3:16. Agni.

1. This Agni is the Lord of great felicity and hero Strength; | Lord of wealth in herds of kine; Lord of the battles with the foe. || 2. Wait, Marutas, Heroes, upon him the Prosperer in whom is bliss-increasing wealth; | Who in fights ever conquer evil-hearted men, who overcome the enemy. || 3. As such, O Agni, deal us wealth and hero might, O Bounteous One! | Most lofty, very glorious, rich in progeny, free from disease and full of power. || 4. He who made all that lives, who passes all in might, who orders service to the Gods, | He works among the Gods, he works in hero strength, yea, also in the praise of men. || 5. Give us not up to indigence, Agni, nor want of hero sons, | Nor, Son of Strength, to lack of cattle, nor to blame. Drive thou our enemies away. || 6. Help us to strength, blest Agni! rich in progeny, abundant, in our sacrifice. | Flood us with riches yet more plenteous, bringing weal, with high renown, most Glorious One!

Hymn 3:17. Agni.

1. Duly enkindled after ancient customs, bringing all treasures, he is balmed with unguents,— | Flame-haired, oil-clad, the purifying Agni, skilled in fair rites, to bring the Gods for worship. || 2. As thou, O Agni, skilful Jātavedas, hast sacrificed as Priest of Earth, of Heaven, | So with this offering bring the Gods, and prosper this sacrifice today as erst for Manu. || 3. Three are thy times of life, O Jātavedas, and the three mornings are thy births, O Agni. | With these, well-knowing, grant the Gods' kind favour, and help in stir and stress the man who worships. || 4. Agni most bright and fair with song we honour, yea, the adorable, O Jātavedas. | Thee, envoy, messenger, oblation-bearer, the Gods have made centre of life eternal. || 5. That Priest before thee, yet more skilled in worship, established of old, health-giver by his nature,— | After his custom offer, thou who knowest, and lay our sacrifice where Gods may taste it.

Hymn 3:18. Agni.

1. Agni, be kind to us when we approach thee good as a friend to friend, as sire and mother. | The races of mankind are great oppressors burn up malignity that strives against us. || 2. Agni, burn up the unfriendly who are near us, burn thou the foeman's curse who pays no worship. | Burn, Vasu, thou who markest well, the foolish: let thine eternal nimble beams surround thee. || 3. With fuel, Agni, and with oil, desirous, mine offering I present for strength and conquest, | With prayer, so far as I have power, adoring—this hymn divine to gain a hundred treasures. || 4. Give with thy glow, thou Son of Strength, when lauded, great vital power to those who toil to serve thee. | Give richly, Agni, to the Viśvāmitras in rest and stir. Oft have we decked thy body. || 5. Give us, O liberal Lord, great store of riches, for, Agni, such art thou when duly kindled. | Thou in the happy singer's home bestowest, amply with arms extended, things of beauty.

Hymn 3:19. Agni.

1. Agni, quick, sage, infallible, all-knowing, I choose to be our Priest at this oblation. | In our Gods' service he, best skilled, shall worship: may he obtain us boons for strength and riches. || 2. Agni, to thee I lift the oil-fed ladle, bright, with an offering, bearing our oblation. | From the right hand, choosing the Gods' attendance, he with rich presents hath arranged the worship. || 3. Of keenest spirit is the man thou aidest give us good offspring, thou who givest freely. | In power of wealth most rich in men. O Agni, of thee, the Good, may we sing forth fair praises. || 4. Men as they worship thee the God, O Agni, have set on thee full many a brilliant, aspect. | So bring Most Youthful One, the Gods' assembly, the Heavenly Host which thou today shalt honour. || 5. When Gods anoint thee Priest at their oblation, and seat thee for thy task as Sacrificer, | O Agni, be thou here our kind defender, and to ourselves vouchsafe the gift of glory.

Hymn 3:20. Agni.

1. With lauds at break of morn the priest invoketh Agni, Dawn, Dadhikrās, and both the Aśvins. | With one consent the Gods whose light is splendid, longing to taste our sacrifice, shall hear us. || 2. Three are thy powers, O Agni, three thy stations, three are thy tongues, yea, many, Child of Order! | Three bodies hast thou which the Gods delight in: with these protect our hymns with care unceasing. || 3. O Agni, many are the names thou bearest, immortal, God, Divine, and Jātavedas. | And many charms of charmers, All-Inspirer! have they laid in thee, Lord of true attendants! || 4. Agni, like Bhaga, leads the godly people, he who is true to Law and guards the seasons. | Ancient, all-knowing, he the Vṛitra-slayer shall bear the singer safe through every trouble. || 5. I call on Savitar the God, on Morning, Bṛihaspati, and Dadhikrās, and Agni, | On Varuṇa and Mitra, on the Aśvins, Bhaga, the Vasus, Rudras and Ādityas.

Hymn 3:21. Agni.

1. Set this our sacrifice among the Immortals: be pleased with these our presents, Jātavedas. | O Priest, O Agni, sit thee down before us, and first enjoy the drops of oil and fatness. || 2. For thee, O Purifier, flow the drops of fatness rich in oil. | After thy wont vouchsafe to us the choicest boon that Gods may feast. || 3. Agni, Most Excellent! for thee the Sage are drops that drip with oil. | Thou art enkindled as the best of Seers. Help thou the sacrifice. || 4. To thee, O Agni, mighty and resistless, to thee stream forth the drops of oil and fatness. | With great light art thou come, O praised by poets! Accept our offering, O thou Sage. || 5. Fatness exceeding rich, extracted from the midst,—this as our gift we offer thee. | Excellent God, the drops run down upon thy skin. Deal them to each among the Gods.

Hymn 3:22. Agni.

1 This is that Agni whence the longing Indra took the pressed Soma deep within his body. | Winner of spoils in thousands, like a courser, with praise art thou exalted, Jātavedas. || 2. That light of thine in heaven and earth, O Agni, in plants, O Holy One, and in the waters, | Wherewith thou hast spread wide the air's mid-region-bright is that splendour, wavy, man-beholding. || 3. O Agni, to the sea of heaven thou goest: thou hast called hither Gods beheld in spirit. | The waters, too, come hither, those up yonder in the Sun's realm of light, and those beneath it. || 4. Let fires that dwell in mist, combined with those that have their home in floods, | Guileless accept our sacrifice, great viands free from all disease. || 5. Agni, as holy food to thine invoker give wealth in cattle, lasting, rich in marvels. | To us be born a son and spreading offspring. Agni, be this thy gracious will to us-ward.

Hymn 3:23. Agni.

1. Rubbed into life, well established in the dwelling, Leader of sacrifice, the Sage, the youthful, | Here in the wasting fuel Jātavedas, eternal, hath assumed immortal being. || 2. Both Bhāratas, Devaśravas, Devavāta, have strongly rubbed to life effectual Agni. | O Agni, look thou forth with ample riches: be, every day, bearer of food to feed us. || 3. Him nobly born of old the fingers ten produced, him whom his Mothers counted dear. | Praise Devavāta's Agni, thou Devaśravas, him who shall be the people's Lord. || 4. He set thee in the earth's most lovely station, in Iḷā's place, in days of fair bright weather. | On man, on Āpayā, Agni! on the rivers Dṛiṣhadvatī, Sarasvatī, shine richly. || 5. Agni, as holy food to thine invoker give wealth in cattle, lasting, rich in marvels. | To us be born a son and spreading offspring Agni, be this thy gracious will to us-ward

Hymn 3:24. Agni.

1. Agni, subdue opposing bands, and drive our enemies away. | Invincible, slay godless foes: give splendour to the worshipper. || 2. Lit with libation, Agni, thou, deathless, who callest Gods to feast, | Accept our sacrifice with joy. || 3. With splendour, Agni, Son of Strength, thou who art worshipped, wakeful One. | Seat thee on this my sacred grass. || 4. With all thy fires, with all the Gods, Agni, exalt the songs we sing. | And living men in holy rites. ||

5. Grant, Agni, to the worshipper wealth rich in heroes, plenteous store, | Make thou us rich with many sons.

Hymn 3:25. Agni.

1. Thou art the sapient Son of Dyaus, O Agni, yes and the Child of Earth, who knowest all things. | Bring the Gods specially, thou Sage, for worship. | 2. Agni the wise bestows the might of heroes grants strengthening food, preparing it for nectar. | Thou who art rich in food bring the Gods hither. || 3. Agni, infallible, lights Earth and Heaven, immortal Goddesses gracious to all men,— | Lord through his strength, splendid through adorations. || 4. Come to the sacrifice, Agni and Indra come to the offerer's house who hath the Soma. | Come, friendly-minded, Gods, to drink the Soma. || 5. In the floods' home art thou enkindled, Agni, O Jātavedas, Son of Strength, eternal, | Exalting with thine help the gathering places.

Hymn 3:26. Agni.

1. Revering in our heart Agni Vaiśvānara, the finder of the light, whose promises are true, | The liberal, gladsome, car-borne God we Kuśikas invoke him with oblation, seeking wealth with songs. || 2. That Agni, bright, Vaiśvānara, we invoke for help, and Mātariśvan worthy of the song of praise; | Bṛihaspati for man's observance of the Gods, the Singer prompt to hear, the swiftly-moving guest. || 3. Age after age Vaiśvānara, neighing like a horse, is kindled with the women by the Kuśikas. | May Agni, he who wakes among Immortal Gods, grant us heroic strength and wealth in noble steeds. || 4. Let them go forth, the strong, as flames of fire with might. Gathered for victory they have yoked their spotted deer. | Pourers of floods, the Marutas, Masters of all wealth, they who can ne'er be conquered, make the mountains shake. || 5. The Marutas, Friends of men, are glorious as the fire: their mighty and resplendent succour we implore. | Those storming Sons of Rudra clothed in robes of rain, boon-givers of good gifts, roar as the lions roar. || 6. We, band on band and troop following troop, entreat with fair lauds Agni's splendour and the Marutas' might, | With spotted deer for steeds, with wealth that never fails, they, wise Ones, come to sacrifice at our gatherings. || 7. Agni am I who know, by birth, all creatures. Mine eye is butter, in my mouth is nectar. | I am light threefold, measurer of the region exhaustless heat am I, named burnt-oblation. || 8. Bearing in mind a thought with light accordant, he purified the Sun with three refinings; | By his own nature gained the highest treasure, and looked abroad over the earth and heaven. || 9. The Spring that fails not with a hundred streamlets, Father inspired of' prayers that men should utter, | The Sparkler, joyous in his Parents' bosom, him, the Truth-speaker, sate ye, Earth and Heaven.

Hymn 3:27. Agni.

1. In ladle dropping oil your food goes in oblation up to heaven, | Goes to the Gods in search of bliss. || 2. Agni I laud, the Sage inspired, crowner of sacrifice through song, | Who listens and gives bounteous gifts. || 3. O Agni, if we might obtain control of thee the potent God, | Then should we overcome our foes. || 4. Kindled at sacrifices he is Agni, hallower, meet for praise, | With flame for hair: to him we seek. || 5. Immortal Agni, shining far, enrobed with oil, well worshipped, bears | The gifts of sacrifice away. || 6. The priests with ladles lifted up, worshipping here with holy thought, | Have brought this Agni for our aid. || 7. Immortal, Sacrificer, God, with wondrous power he leads the way, | Urging the great assembly on. || 8. Strong, he is set on deeds of strength. In sacrifices led in front, | As Singer he completes the rite. || 9. Excellent, he was made by thought. The Germ of beings have I gained, | Yea, and die Sire of active strength. || 10. Thee have I established, Excellent, O strengthened by the sage's prayer, | Thee, Agni, longing, nobly bright. || 11. Agni, the swift and active One, singers, at time of sacrifice, | Eagerly kindle with their food. || 12. Agni the Son of Strength who shines up to the heaven in solemn rites, | The wise of heart, I glorify. || 13. Meet to be lauded and adored, showing in beauty through the dark, | Agni, the Strong, is kindled well. || 14. Agni is kindled as a bull, like a horse-bearer of the Gods: | Men with oblations worship him. || 15. Thee will we kindle as a bull, we who are Bulls ourselves, O Bull. | Thee, Agni, shining mightily.

Hymn 3:28. Agni.

1. Agni who knowest all, accept our offering and the cake of meal, | At dawn's libation, rich in prayer! || 2. Agni, the sacrificial cake hath been prepared and dressed for thee: | Accept it, O Most Youthful God. || 3. Agni, enjoy the cake of meal and our oblation three days old: | Thou, Son of Strength, art established at our sacrifice. || 4. Here at the midday sacrifice enjoy thou the sacrificial cake, wise, Jātavedas! | Agni, the sages in assemblies never minish the portion due to thee the Mighty. || 5. O Agni, at the third libation take with joy the offered cake of sacrifice, thou, Son of Strength. | Through skill in song bear to the Gods our sacrifice, watchful and fraught with riches, to Immortal God. || 6. O waxing Agni, knower, thou, of all, accept our gifts, the cake, | And that prepared ere yesterday.

Hymn 3:29. Agni.

1. Here is the gear for friction, here tinder made ready for the spark. | Bring thou the Matron: we will rub Agni in ancient fashion forth. || 2. In the two fire-sticks Jātavedas lieth, even as the well-set germ in pregnant women, | Agni who day by day must be exalted by men who watch and worship with oblations. || 3. Lay this with care on that which lies extended: straight hath she borne the Steer when made prolific. | With his red pillar-radiant is his splendour -in our skilled task is born the Son of Iḷā. || 4. In Iḷā's place we set thee down, upon the central point of earth, | That, Agni Jātavedas, thou mayst bear our offerings to the Gods. || 5. Rub into life, ye men, the Sage, the guileless, Immortal, very wise and fair to look on. | O men, bring forth the most propitious Agni, first ensign of the sacrifice to eastward. || 6. When with their arms they rub him straight he shineth forth like a strong courser, red in colour, in the wood. | Bright, checkless, as it were upon the Aśvins' path, lie passeth by the stones and burneth up the grass. || 7. Agni shines forth when born, observant, mighty, the bountiful, the Singer praised by sages; | Whom, as adorable and knowing all things, Gods set at solemn rites as offering-bearer || 8. Set thee, O Priest, in, thine own place, observant: lay down the sacrifice in the home of worship. | Thou, dear to Gods, shalt serve them with oblation: Agni, give long life to the sacrificer. || 9. Raise ye a mighty smoke, my fellow-workers! Ye shall attain to wealth without obstruction. | This Agni is the battle-winning Hero by whom the Gods have overcome the Dasyus. || 10. This is thine ordered place of birth whence sprung to life thou shonest forth. | Knowing this, Agni, sit thee down, and prosper thou the songs we sing. || 11. As Germ Celestial he is called Tanūnapāt, and Narāśaṃsa born diffused in varied shape. | Formed in his Mother he is Mātariśvan; he hath, in his course, become the rapid flight of wind. || 12. With strong attrition rubbed to life, laid down with careful hand, a Sage, | Agni, make sacrifices good, and for the pious bring the Gods. || 13. Mortals have brought to life the God Immortal, the Conqueror with mighty jaws, unfailing. | The sisters ten, unwedded and united, together grasp the Babe, the new-born Infant. || 14. Served by the seven priests, he shone forth from ancient time, when in his Mother's bosom, in her lap, he glowed. | Giving delight each day he closeth not his eye, since from the Asura's body he was brought to life. || 15. Even as the Marutas, onslaughts who attack the foe, those born the first of all knew the full power of prayer. | The Kuśikas have made the glorious hymn ascend, and, each one singly in his home, have kindled fire. || 16. As we, O Priest observant, have elected thee this day, what time the solemn sacrifice began, | So surely hast thou worshipped, surely hast thou toiled: come thou unto the Soma, wise and knowing all.

Hymn 3:30. Indra.

1. The friends who offer Soma long to find thee: they pour forth Soma and present their viands. | They bear unmoved the cursing of the people, for all our wisdom comes from thee, O Indra. || 2. Not far for thee are mid-air's loftiest regions: start hither, Lord of Bays, with thy Bay Horses. | Made for the Firm and Strong are these libations. The pressing-stones are set and fire is kindled. || 3. Fair cheeks hath Indra, Maghavan, the Victor, Lord of a great host, Stormer, strong in action. | What once thou didst in might when mortals vexed thee,—where now, O Bull, are those thy hero exploits? || 4. For, overthrowing what hath ne'er been shaken, thou goest forth alone destroying Vṛitras. | For him who followeth thy Law the mountains and heaven and earth stand as if firmly established. || 5. Yea, Much-invoked! in safety through thy glories alone thou speakest truth as Vṛitra's slayer. | E'en these two boundless worlds to thee, O Indra, what time thou graspest them, are but a handful. || 6. Forthwith thy Bay steeds down the steep, O Indra, forth, crushing foemen, go thy bolt of thunder! | Slay those who meet thee, those who flee, who follow: make all thy promise true; be all completed. || 7. The man to whom thou givest as

Provider enjoys domestic plenty undivided. | Blest, Indra, is thy favour dropping fatness: thy worship, Much-invoked! brings gifts in thousands. || 8. Thou, Indra, Much-invoked! didst crush to pieces Kuṇāru handless fiend who dwelt with Danu. | Thou with might, Indra, smotest dead the scorner, the footless Vṛitra as he waxed in vigour. || 9. Thou hast established in her seat, O Indra, the level earth, vast, vigorous, unbounded. | The Bull hath propped the heaven and air's mid-region. By thee sent onward let the floods flow hither. || 10. He who withheld the kine, in silence I yielded in fear before thy blow, O Indra. | He made paths easy to drive forth the cattle. Loud-breathing praises helped the Much-invoked One. || 11. Indra alone filled full the earth and heaven, the Pair who meet together, rich in treasures. | Yea, bring thou near us from the air's mid-region strength, on thy car, and wholesome food, O Hero. || 12. Sūrya transgresses not the ordered limits set daily by the Lord of Tawny Coursers. | When to the goal he comes, his journey ended, his Steeds he looses: this is Indra's doing. || 13. Men gladly in the course of night would look on the broad bright front of the refulgent Morning; | And all acknowledge, when she comes in glory, the manifold and goodly works of Indra. || 14. A mighty splendour rests upon her bosom: bearing ripe milk the Cow, unripe, advances. | All sweetness is collected in the Heifer, sweetness which Indra made for our enjoyment. || 15. Barring the way they come. Be firm, O Indra; aid friends to sacrifice and him who singeth. | These must be slain by thee, malignant mortals, armed with ill arts, our quiver-bearing foemen. || 16. A cry is beard from enemies most near us: against them send thy fiercest-flaming weapon. | Rend them from under, crush them and subdue them. Slay, Maghavan, and make the fiends our booty. || 17. Root up the race of Rākṣhasas, O Indra rend it in front and crush it in the middle. | How long hast thou behaved as one who wavers? Cast thy hot dart at him who hates devotion: || 18. When borne by strong Steeds for our weal, O Leader, thou seatest thee at many noble viands. | May we be winners of abundant riches. May Indra be our wealth with store of children. || 19. Bestow on us resplendent wealth. O Indra let us enjoy thine overflow of bounty. | Wide as a sea our longing hath expanded, fulfil it, O thou Treasure-Lord of treasures. || 20. With kine and horses satisfy this longing with very splendid bounty skill extend it. | Seeking the light, with hymns to thee, O Indra, Kuśikas have brought their gift, the singers. || 21. Lord of the kine, burst the kine's stable open: cows shall be ours, and strength that wins the booty. | Hero, whose might is true, thy home is heaven: to us, O Maghavan, grant gifts of cattle. || 22. Call we on Maghavan, auspicious Indra, best Hero in this fight where spoil is gathered, | The Strong who listens, who gives aid in battles, who slays the Vṛitras, wins and gathers riches.

Hymn 3:31. Indra.

1. Wise, teaching, following the thought of Order, the sonless gained a grandson from his daughter. | Fain, as a sire, to see his child prolific, he sped to meet her with an eager spirit. || 2. The Son left not his portion to the brother, he made a home to hold him who should gain, it. | What time his Parents gave the Priest his being, of the good pair one acted, one promoted. || 3. Agni was born trembling with tongue that flickered, so that the Red's great children should be honoured. | Great is their germ, that born of them is mighty, great the Bays' Lord's approach through sacrifices. || 4. Conquering bands upon the Warrior waited: they recognized great light from out the darkness. | The conscious Dawns went forth to meet his coming, and the sole Master of the kine was Indra. || 5. The sages freed them from their firm-built prison: the seven priests drove them forward with their spirit. | All holy Order's pathway they discovered he, full of knowledge, shared these deeds through worship. || 6. When Saramā had found the mountain's fissure, that vast and ancient place she plundered thoroughly. | In the floods' van she led them forth, light-footed: she who well knew came first unto their lowing. || 7. Longing for friendship came the noblest singer: the hill poured forth its treasure for the pious. | The Hero with young followers fought and conquered, and straightway Aṅgiras was singing praises, || 8. Peer of each noble thing, yea, all excelling, all creatures doth he know, he slayeth Śuṣhṇa. | Our leader, fain for war, singing from heaven, as Friend he saved his lovers from dishonour. || 9. They sate them down with spirit fain for booty, making with hymns a way to life eternal. | And this is still their place of frequent session, whereby they sought to gain the months through Order. || 10. Drawing the milk of ancient seed prolific, they joyed as they beheld their own possession. | Their shout of triumph heated earth and heaven. When the kine showed, they bade the heroes rouse them. || 11. Indra drove forth the kine, that Vṛitra-slayer, while hymns of praise rose up and gifts were offered. | For him the Cow, noble and far-extending, poured pleasant juices, bringing oil and sweetness. || 12. They made a mansion for their Father, deftly provided him a great and glorious dwelling; | With firm support parted and stayed the Parents, and, sitting, fixed him there erected, mighty. || 13. What time the ample chalice had impelled him, swift waxing, vast, to pierce the earth and heaven,— | Him in whom blameless songs are all united: all powers invincible belong to Indra. || 14. I crave thy powers, I crave thy mighty friendship: full many a team goes to the Vṛitra-slayer. | Great is the laud, we seek the Princes' favour. Be thou, O Maghavan, our guard and keeper. || 15. He, having found great, splendid, rich dominion, sent life and motion to his friends and lovers. | Indra who shone together with the Heroes begot the song, the fire, and Sun and Morning. || 16. Vast, the House-Friend, he set the waters flowing, all-lucid, widely spread, that move together. | By the wise cleansings of the meath made holy, through days, and nights they speed the swift streams onward. || 17. To thee proceed the dark, the treasure-holders, both of them sanctified by Sūrya's bounty. | The while thy ovely storming Friends, O Indra, fail to attain the measure of thy greatness. || 18. Be Lord of joyous songs, O Vṛitra-slayer, Bull dear to all, who gives the power of living. | Come unto us with thine auspicious friendship, hastening, Mighty One, with mighty succours. || 19. Like Aṅgiras I honour him with worship, and renovate old song for him the Ancient. | Chase thou the many godless evil creatures, and give us, Maghavan, heaven's light to help m. || 20. Far forth are spread the purifying waters convey thou us across them unto safety. | Save us, our Charioteer, from harm, O Indra, soon, very soon, make us win spoil of cattle. || 21. His kine their Lord hath shown, e'en Vṛitra's slayer, through the black hosts he passed with red attendants. | Teaching us pleasant things by holy Order, to, us hath he thrown open all his portals. || 22. Call we on Maghavan, auspicious Indra, best Hero in this fight where spoil is gathered. | The Strong who listens, who gives aid in battles, who slays the Vṛitras, wins and gathers riches.

Hymn 3:32. Indra

1. Drink thou this Soma, Indra, Lord of Soma; drink thou the draught of noonday which thou lovest. | Puffing thy cheeks, impetuous, liberal Giver, here loose thy two Bay Horses and rejoice thee. || 2. Quaff it pure, meal-blent, mixed with milk, O Indra; we have poured forth the Soma for thy rapture. | Knit with the prayer-fulfilling band of Marutas, yea, with the Rudras, drink till thou art sated; || 3. Those who gave increase to thy strength and vigour; the Marutas singing forth thy might, O Indra. | Drink thou, O fair of cheek, whose hand wields thunder, with Rudras banded, at our noon libation. || 4. They, even the Marutas who were there, excited with song the meath-created strength of Indra. | By them impelled to act he reached the vitals Of Vṛitra, though he deemed that none might wound him. || 5. Pleased, like a man, with our libation, Indra, drink, for enduring hero might, the Soma. | Lord of Bays, moved by sacrifice come hither: thou with the Swift Ones stirrest floods and waters. || 6. When thou didst loose the streams to run like racers in the swift contest, having smitten Vṛitra | With flying weapon where he lay, O Indra, and, godless, kept the Goddesses encompassed. || 7. With reverence let us worship mighty Indra, great and sublime, eternal, ever youthful, | Whose greatness the dear world-halves have not measured, no, nor conceived the might of him the Holy. || 8. Many are Indra's nobly wrought achievements, and none of all the Gods transgress his statutes. | He beareth up this earth and heaven, and, doer of marvels, he begot the Sun and Morning. || 9. Herein, O Guileless One, is thy true greatness, that soon as born thou drankest up the Soma. | Days may not check the power of thee the Mighty, nor the nights, Indra, nor the months, nor autumns. || 10. As soon as thou wast born in highest heaven thou drankest Soma to delight thee, Indra; | And when thou hadst pervaded earth and heaven thou wast the first supporter of the singer. || 11. Thou, puissant God, more mighty, slewest. Ahi showing his strength when couched around the waters. | The heaven itself attained not to thy greatness when with one hip of thine the earth was shadowed. || 12. Sacrifice, Indra, made thee wax so mighty, the dear oblation with the flowing Soma. | O Worshipful, with worship help our worship, for worship

helped thy bolt when slaying Ahi. ‖ 13. With sacrifice and wish have I brought Indra; still for new blessings may I turn him hither, | Him magnified by ancient songs and praises, by lauds of later time and days yet recent. ‖ 14. I have brought forth a song when longing seized me: ere the decisive day will I laud Indra; | Then may lie safely bear us over trouble, as in a ship, when both sides invocate him. ‖ 15. Full is his chalice: Glory! Like a pourer I have filled up the vessel for his drinking. | Presented on the right, dear Soma juices have brought us Indra, to rejoice him, hither. ‖ 16. Not the deep-flowing flood, O Much-invoked One! not hills that compass thee about restrain thee, | Since here incited, for thy friends, O Indra, thou breakest e'en the firm built stall of cattle. ‖ 17. Call we on Maghavan, auspicious Indra, best Hero in this fight where spoil is gathered, | The Strong who listens, who gives aid in battles, who slays the Vṛitras, wins and gathers riches.

Hymn 3:33. Indra.

1. Forth from the bosom of the mountains, eager as two swift mares with loosened rein contending, | Like two bright mother cows who lick their youngling, Vipāś and Śutudrī speed down their waters. ‖ 2. Impelled by Indra whom ye pray to urge you, ye move as 'twere on chariots to the ocean. | Flowing together, swelling with your billows, O lucid Streams, each of you seeks the other. ‖ 3. I have attained the most maternal River, we have approached Vipāś, the broad, the blessed. | Licking as 'twere their calf the pair of Mothers flow onward to their common home together. ‖ 4. We two who rise and swell with billowy waters move forward to the home which Gods have made us. | Our flood may not be stayed when urged to motion. What would the singer, calling to the Rivers? ‖ 5. Linger a little at my friendly bidding rest, Holy Ones, a moment in your journey. | With hymn sublime soliciting your favour Kuśika's son hath called unto the River. ‖ 6. Indra who wields the thunder dug our channels: he smote down Vṛitra, him who stayed our currents. | Savitar, God, the lovely-handed, led us, and at his sending forth we flow expanded. ‖ 7. That hero deed of Indra must be lauded for ever that he rent Ahi in pieces. | He smote away the obstructors with his thunder, and eager for their course forth flowed the waters. ‖ 8. Never forget this word of thine, O singer, which future generations shall re-echo | In hymns, O bard, show us thy loving kindness. Humble us not mid men. To thee be honour! ‖ 9. List quickly, Sisters, to the bard who cometh to you from far away with car and wagon. | Bow lowly down; be easy to be traversed stay, Rivers, with your floods below our axles. ‖ 10. Yea, we will listen to thy words, O singer. With wain and car from far away thou comest. | Low, like a nursing mother, will I bend me, and yield me as a maiden to her lover. ‖ 11. Soon as the Bhāratas have fared across thee, the warrior band, urged on and sped by Indra, | Then let your streams flow on in rapid motion. I crave your favour who deserve our worship. ‖ 12. The warrior host, the Bhāratas, fared over the singer won the favour of the Rivers. | Swell with your billows, hasting, pouring riches. Fill full your channels, and roll swiftly onward. ‖ 13. So let your wave bear up the pins, and ye, O Waters, spare the thongs; | And never may the pair of Bulls, harmless and sinless, waste away.

Hymn 3:34. Indra.

1. Fort-render, Lord of Wealth, dispelling foemen, Indra with lightnings hath o'ercome the Dāsa. | Impelled by prayer and waxen great in body, he hath filled earth and heaven, the Bounteous Giver. ‖ 2. I stimulate thy zeal, the Strong, the Hero decking my song of praise forth; Immortal. | O Indra, thou art equally the Leader of heavenly hosts and human generations. ‖ 3. Leading, his band Indra encompassed Vṛitra; weak grew the wily leader of enchanters. | He who burns fierce in forests slaughtered Vyaṃsa, and made the Milch-kine of the nights apparent. ‖ 4. Indra, light-winner, days' Creator, conquered, victorious, hostile bands with those who loved him. | For man the days' bright ensign he illumined, and found the light for his joy and gladness. ‖ 5. Forward to fiercely falling blows pressed Indra, hero-like doing many hero exploits. | These holy songs he taught the bard who gaised him, and widely spread these Dawns' resplendent colour. ‖ 6. They laud the mighty acts of him the Mighty, the many glorious deeds performed by Indra. | He in his strength, with all-surpassing prowess, through wondrous arts crushed the malignant Dasyus. ‖ 7. Lord of the brave, Indra who rules the people gave freedom to the Gods by might and battle. | Wise singers glorify with chanted praises these his achievements in Vivasvat's dwelling. ‖ 8. Excellent, Conqueror, the victory-giver, the winner of the light and Godlike Waters, | He who hath won this broad earth and this heaven, in Indra they rejoice who love devotions. ‖ 9. He gained possession of the Sun and Horses, Indra obtained the Cow who feedeth many. | Treasure of gold he won; he smote the Dasyus, and gave protection to the Ārya colour. ‖ 10. He took the plants and days for his possession; he gained the forest trees and air's mid-region. | Vala he cleft, and chased away opponents: thus was he tamer of the overweening. ‖ 11. Call we on Maghavan, auspicious Indra, best Hero in the fight where spoil is gathered, | The Strong, who listens, who gives aid in battles, who slays the Vṛitras, wins and gathers treasures.

Hymn 3:35. Indra.

1. Mount the Bay Horses to thy chariot harnessed, and come to us like Vāyu with his coursers. | Thou, hastening to us, shalt drink the Soma. Hail, Indra. We have poured it for thy rapture. ‖ 2. For him, the God who is invoked by many, the two swift Bay Steeds to the pole I harness, | That they in fleet course may bring Indra hither, e'en to this sacrifice arranged completely. ‖ 3. Bring the strong Steeds who drink the warm libation, and, Bull of Godlike nature, be thou gracious. | Let thy Steeds eat; set free thy Tawny Horses, and roasted grain like this consume thou daily. ‖ 4. Those who are yoked by prayer I harness, fleet friendly Bays who take their joy together. | Mounting thy firm and easy car, O Indra, wise and all-knowing come thou to the Soma. ‖ 5. No other worshippers must stay beside them thy Bays, thy vigorous and smooth-backed Coursers. | Pass by them all and hasten onward hither: with Soma pressed we will prepare to feast thee. ‖ 6. Thine is this Soma: hasten to approach it. Drink thou thereof, benevolent, and cease not. | Sit on the sacred grass at this our worship, and take these drops into thy belly, Indra. ‖ 7. The grass is strewn for thee, pressed is the Soma; the grain is ready for thy Bays to feed on. | To thee who lovest them, the very mighty, strong, girt by Marutas, are these gifts presented. ‖ 8. This the sweet draught, with cows, the men, the mountains, the waters, Indra, have for thee made ready. | Come, drink thereof, Sublime One, friendly-minded, foreseeing, knowing well the ways thou goest. ‖ 9. The Marutas, they with whom thou sharedst Soma, Indra, who made thee strong and were thine army,— | With these accordant, eagerly desirous drink thou this Soma with the tongue of Agni. ‖ 10. Drink, Indra, of the juice by thine own nature, or by the tongue of Agni, O thou Holy. | Accept the sacrificial gift, O Śakra, from the Adhvaryu's hand or from the Hotar's. ‖ 11. Call we on Maghavan, auspicious Indra, best Hero in the fight where spoil is gathered, | The Strong, who listens, who gives aid in battles, who slays the Vṛitras, wins and gathers riches.

Hymn 3:36. Indra.

1. With constant succours, fain thyself to share it, make this oblation which we bring effective. | Grown great through strengthening gifts at each libation, he hath become renowned by mighty exploits. ‖ 2. For Indra were the Somas erst—discovered, whereby he grew strong-jointed, vast, and skilful. | Indra, take quickly these presented juices: drink of the strong, that which the strong have shaken. ‖ 3. Drink and wax great. Thine are the juices, Indra, both Somas of old time and these we bring thee. | Even as thou drankest, Indra, earlier Somas, so drink today, a new guest, meet for praises. ‖ 4. Great and impetuous, mighty-voiced in battle, surpassing power is his, and strength resistless. | Him the broad earth hath never comprehended when Somas cheered the Lord of Tawny Coursers. ‖ 5. Mighty and strong he waxed for hero exploit: the Bull was furnished a Sage's wisdom. | Indra is our kind Lord; his steers have vigour; his cows are many with abundant offspring. ‖ 6. As floods according to their stream flow onward, so to the sea, as borne on cars, the waters. | Vaster is Indra even than his dwelling, what time the stalk milked out, the Soma, fills him. ‖ 7. Eager to mingle with the sea, the rivers carry the well-pressed Soma juice to Indra. | They drain the stalk out with their arms, quick-handed, and cleanse it with a stream of mead and filters. ‖ 8. Like lakes appear his flanks filled full with Soma: yea, he contains libations in abundance. | When Indra had consumed the first sweet viands, he, after slaying Vṛitra, claimed the Soma. ‖ 9. Then bring thou hither, and let none prevent it: we know thee well, the Lord of wealth and treasure. | That splendid gift which is thine own, O Indra, vouchsafe to us, Lord of the Tawny Coursers. ‖ 10. O Indra, Maghavan, impetuous mover, grant us

abundant wealth that brings all blessings. | Give us a hundred autumns for our lifetime: give us, O fair-checked Indra, store of heroes. || 11. Call we on Indra, Maghavan, auspicious, best Hero in the fight where spoil is gathered, | The Strong, who listens, who gives aid in battles, who slays the Vṛitras, wins and gathers riches.

Hymn 3:37. Indra.

1. O Indra, for the strength that slays Vṛitra and conquers in the fight, | We turn thee hitherward to us. || 2. O Indra, Lord of Hundred Powers, may those who praise thee hitherward. | Direct thy spirit and thine eye. || 3. O Indra, Lord of Hundred Powers, with all our songs we invocate | Thy names for triumph over foes. || 4. We strive for glory through the powers immense of him whom many praise, | Of Indra who supports mankind. || 5. For Vṛitra's slaughter I address Indra whom many invocate, | To win us booty in the wars. || 6. In battles be victorious. We seek thee, Lord of Hundred Powers, | Indra, that Vṛitra may be slain. || 7. In splendid combats of the hosts, in glories where the fight is won. | Indra, be victor over foes. || 8. Drink thou the Soma for our help, bright, vigilant, exceeding strong, | O Indra, Lord of Hundred Powers. || 9. O Śatakratu, powers which thou mid the Five Races hast displayed— | These, Indra, do I claim of thee. || 10. Indra, great glory hast thou gained. Win splendid fame which none may mar | We make thy might perpetual. || 11. Come to us either from anear, Or, Śakra, come from far away. | Indra, wherever be thy home, come to us thence, O Thunder-armed.

Hymn 3:38. Indra.

1. Hasting like some strong courser good at drawing, a thought have I imagined like a workman. | Pondering what is dearest and most noble, I long to see the sages full of wisdom. || 2. Ask of the sages' mighty generations firm-minded and devout they framed the heaven. | These are thy heart-sought strengthening directions, and they have come to be sky's upholders. || 3. Assuming in this world mysterious natures, they decked the heaven and earth for high dominion, | Measured with measures, fixed their broad expanses, set the great worlds apart held firm for safety. || 4. Even as he mounted up they all adorned him: self-luminous he travels clothed in splendour. | That is the Bull's, the Asura's mighty figure: he, omniform, hath reached the eternal waters. || 5. First the more ancient Bull engendered offspring; these are his many draughts that lent him vigour. | From days of old ye Kings, two Sons of Heaven, by hymns of sacrifice have won dominion. || 6. Three seats ye Sovereigns, in the Holy synod, many, yea, all, ye honour with your presence. | There saw I, going thither in the spirit, Gandharvas in their course with wind-blown tresses. || 7. That same companionship of her, the Milch-cow, here with the strong Bull's divers forms they established. | Enduing still some new celestial figure, the skilful workers shaped a form around him. || 8. Let no one here debar me from enjoying the golden light which Savitar diffuses. | He covers both all-fostering worlds with praises even as a woman cherishes her children. || 9. Fulfil, ye twain, his work, the Great, the Ancient: as heavenly blessing keep your guard around us. | All the wise Gods behold his varied actions who stands erect, whose voice is like a herdsman's. || 10. Call we on Indra, Maghavan, auspicious, best Hero in the fight where spoil is gathered, | The Strong, who listens, who gives aid in battles, who slays the Vṛitras, wins and gathers riches.

Hymn 3:39. Indra.

1. To Indra from the heart the hymn proceedeth, to him the Lord, recited, built with praises; | The wakening song sung forth in holy synod: that which is born for thee, O Indra, notice. || 2. Born from the heaven e'en in the days aforetime, wakening, sting aloud in holy synod, | Auspicious, clad in white and shining raiment, this is the ancient hymn of our forefathers. || 3. The Mother of the Twins hath borne Twin Children: my tongue's tip raised itself and rested silent. | Killing the darkness at the light's foundation, the Couple newly born attain their beauty. || 4. Not one is found among them, none of mortals, to blame our sires who fought to win the cattle. | Their strengthener was Indra the Majestic he spread their stalls of kine the Wonder-Worker. || 5. Where as a Friend with friendly men, Navagvas, with heroes, on his knees he sought the cattle. | There, verily with ten Daśagvas Indra found the Sun lying hidden in the darkness. || 6. Indra found meath collected in the milch-cow, by foot and hoof, in the cow's place of pasture. | That which lay secret, hidden in the waters, he held in his right hand, the rich rewarder. || 7. He took the light, discerning it from darkness: may we be far removed from all misfortune. | These songs, O Soma-drinker, cheered by Soma, Indra, accept from thy most zealous poet. || 8. Let there be light through both the worlds for worship: may we be far from most overwhelming evil. | Great woe comes even from the hostile mortal, piled up; but good at rescue are the Vasus. || 9. Call we on Maghavan, auspicious Indra, best Hero in the fight where spoil is gathered, | The Strong, who listens, who gives aid in battles, who slays the Vṛitras, wins and gathers riches.

Hymn 3:40. Indra.

1. Thee, Indra, we invoke, the Bull, what time the Soma is expressed. | So drink thou of the savoury juice. || 2. Indra, whom many laud, accept the strength-conferring Soma juice: | Quaff, pour down drink that satisfies. || 3. Indra, with all the Gods promote our wealth-bestowing sacrifice, | Thou highly-lauded Lord of men. || 4. Lord of the brave, to thee proceed these drops of Soma juice expressed, | The bright drops to thy dwelling-place. || 5. Within thy belly, Indra, take juice, Soma the most excellent: Thine are the drops celestial. || 6. Drink our libation, Lord of hymns: with streams of meath thou art bedewed | Our glory, Indra, is thy gift. || 7. To Indra go the treasures of the worshipper, which never fail: | He drinks the Soma and is strong || 8. From far away, from near at hand, O Vṛitra-slayer, come to us: | Accept the songs we sing to thee. || 9. When from the space between the near and far thou art invoked by us, | Thence, Indra. come thou hitherward.

Hymn 3:41. Indra.

1. Invoked to drink the Soma juice, come with thy Bay Steeds, Thunder-armed | Come, Indra, hitherward to me. || 2. Our priest is seated, true to time; the grass is regularly strewn; | The pressing-stones were set at morn. || 3. These prayers, O thou who hearest prayer are offered: seat thee on the grass. | Hero, enjoy the offered cake. || 4. O Vṛitra-slayer, be thou pleased with these libations, with these hymns, | Song-loving Indra, with our lauds. || 5. Our hymns caress the Lord of Strength, vast, drinker of the Soma's juice, | Indra, as mother-cows their calf. || 6. Delight thee with the juice we pour for thine own great munificence: | Yield not thy singer to reproach. || 7. We, Indra, dearly loving thee, bearing oblation, sing thee hymns | Thou, Vasu, dearly lovest us. || 8. O thou to whom thy Bays are dear, loose not thy Horses far from us: | Here glad thee, Indra, Lord divine. || 9. May long-maned Coursers, dropping oil, bring thee on swift car hitherward, | Indra, to seat thee on the grass.

Hymn 3:42. Indra.

1. Come to the juice that we have pressed, to Soma, Indra, bleat with milk: | Come, favouring us, thy Bay-drawn car! || 2. Come, Indra, to this gladdening drink, placed on the grass, pressed out with stones: | Wilt thou not drink thy fill thereof? || 3. To Indra have my songs of praise gone forth, thus rapidly sent hence, | To turn him to the Soma-draught. || 4. Hither with songs of praise we call Indra to drink the Soma juice: | Will he not come to us by lauds? || 5. Indra, these Somas are expressed. Take them within thy belly, Lord | Of Hundred Powers, thou Prince of Wealth. || 6. We know thee winner of the spoil, and resolute in battles, Sage! | Therefore thy blessing we implore. || 7. Borne hither by thy Stallions, drink, Indra, this juice which we have pressed, | Mingled with barley and with milk. || 8. Indra, for thee, in thine own place, I urge the Soma for thy draught: | Deep in thy heart let it remain, || 9. We call on thee, the Ancient One, Indra, to drink the Soma juice, | We Kuśikas who seek thine aid.

Hymn 3:43. Indra.

1. Mounted upon thy chariot-seat approach us: thine is the Soma-draught from days aforetime. | Loose for the sacred grass thy dear companions. These men who bring oblation call thee hither. || 2. Come our true Friend, passing by many people; come with thy two Bay Steeds to our devotions; | For these our hymns are calling thee, O Indra, hymns formed for praise, soliciting thy friendship. || 3. Pleased, with thy Bay Steeds, Indra, God, come quickly to this our sacrifice that heightens worship; | For with my thoughts, presenting oil to feed thee, I call thee to the feast of sweet libations. || 4. Yea, let thy two Bay Stallions bear thee hither, well limbed and good to draw, thy dear companions. | Pleased with the corn-blent offering which we bring thee, may Indra, Friend, hear his friend's adoration. || 5. Wilt thou not make me guardian of the people, make me,

impetuous Maghavan, their ruler? | Make me a Ṛishi having drunk of Soma? Wilt thou not give me wealth that lasts for ever? ‖ 6. Yoked to thy chariot, led thy tall Bays, Indra, companions of thy banquet, bear thee hither, | Who from of old press to heaven's farthest limits, the Bull's impetuous and well-groomed Horses. ‖ 7. Drink of the strong pressed out by strong ones, Indra, that which the Falcon brought thee when thou longedst; | In whose wild joy thou stirrest up the people, in whose wild joy thou didst unbar the cow-stalls. ‖ 8. Call we on Indra, Maghavan, auspicious, best Hero in the fight where spoil is gathered; | The Strong, who listens, who gives aid in battles, who slays the Vṛitras, wins and gathers riches.

Hymn 3:44. Indra.

1. May this delightsome Soma be expressed for thee by tawny stones. | Joying thereat, O Indra, with thy Bay Steeds come:. ascend thy golden-coloured car. ‖ 2. In love thou madest Uṣhas glow, in love thou madest Sūrya shine. | Thou, Indra, knowing, thinking, Lord of Tawny Steeds, above all glories waxest great. ‖ 3. The heaven with streams of golden hue, earth with her tints of green and gold— | The golden Pair yield Indra plenteous nourishment: between them moves the golden One. ‖ 4. When born to life the golden Bull illumines all the realm of light. | He takes his golden weapon, Lord of Tawny Steeds, the golden thunder in his arms. ‖ 5. The bright, the well-loved thunderbolt, girt with the bright, Indra disclosed, | Disclosed the Soma juice pressed out by tawny stones, with tawny steeds drave forth the kine.

Hymn 3:45. Indra.

1. Come hither, Indra, with Bay Steeds, joyous, with tails like peacocks' plumes. | Let no men cheek thy course as fowlers stay the bird: pass o'er them as o'er desert lands. ‖ 2. He who slew Vṛitra, burst the cloud, brake the strongholds and drave the floods, | Indra who mounts his chariot at his Bay Steeds' cry, shatters e'en things that stand most firm. ‖ 3. Like pools of water deep and full, like kine thou cherishest thy might; | Like the milch-cows that go well-guarded to the mead, like water-brooks that reach the lake. ‖ 4. Bring thou us wealth with power to strike, our share, 'gainst him who calls it his. | Shake, Indra, as with hooks, the tree for ripened fruit, for wealth to satisfy our wish. ‖ 5. Indra, self-ruling Lord art thou, good Leader, of most glorious fame. | So, waxen in thy strength, O thou whom many praise, be thou most swift to hear our call.

Hymn 3:46. Indra.

1. Of thee, the Bull, the Warrior, Sovereign Ruler, joyous and fierce, ancient and ever youthful, | The undecaying One who wields the thunder, renowned and great, great are the exploits, Indra. ‖ 2. Great art thou, Mighty Lord, through manly vigour, O fierce One, gathering spoil, subduing others, | Thyself alone the universe's Sovereign: so send forth men to combat and to rest them. ‖ 3. He hath surpassed all measure in his brightness, yea, and the Gods, for none may be his equal. | Impetuous Indra in his might exceedeth wide vast mid-air and heaven and earth together. ‖ 4. To Indra, even as rivers to the ocean, flow forth from days of old the Soma juices; | To him wide deep and mighty from his birth-time, the well of holy thoughts, all-comprehending. ‖ 5. The Soma, Indra, which the earth and heaven bear for thee as a mother bears her infant, | This they send forth to thee, this, vigorous Hero! Adhvaryus purify for thee to drink of.

Hymn 3:47. Indra.

1. Drink, Indra, Marut-girt, as Bull, the Soma, for joy, for rapture even as thou listest. | Pour down the flood of meath within thy belly: thou from of old art King of Soma juices. ‖ 2. Indra, accordant, with the banded Marutas, drink Soma, Hero, as wise Vṛitra-slayer. | Slay thou our foemen, drive away assailants and make us safe on every side from danger. ‖ 3. And, drinker at due seasons, drink in season, Indra, with friendly Gods, our pressed-out Soma. | The Marutas following, whom thou madest sharers, gave thee the victory, and thou slewest Vṛitra. ‖ 4. Drink Soma, Indra, banded with the Marutas who, Maghavan, strengthened thee at Ahi's slaughter, | 'gainst Śambara, Lord of Bays! in winning cattle, and now rejoice in thee, the holy Singers. ‖ 5. The Bull whose strength hath waxed, whom Marutas follow, free-giving Indra, the celestial Ruler, | Mighty, all-conquering, the victory-giver, him let us call to grant us new protection.

Hymn 3:48. Indra.

1. Soon as the young Bull sprang into existence he longed to taste the pressed-out Soma's liquor. | Drink thou thy fill, according to thy longing, first, of the goodly mixture blent with Soma. ‖ 2. That day when thou wast born thou, fain to taste it, drankest the plant's milk which the mountains nourish. | That milk thy Mother first, the Dame who bare thee, poured for thee in thy mighty Father's dwelling. ‖ 3. Desiring food he came unto his Mother, and on her breast beheld the pungent Soma. | Wise, he moved on, keeping aloof the others, and wrought great exploits in his varied aspects. ‖ 4. Fierce, quickly conquering, of surpassing vigour, he framed his body even as he listed. | E'en from his birth-time Indra conquered Tvaṣhṭar, bore off the Soma and in beakers drank it. ‖ 5. Call we on Maghavan, auspicious Indra, best Hero in the fight where spoil is gathered; | The Strong, who listens, who gives aid in battles, who slays the Vṛitras, wins and gathers riches.

Hymn 3:49. Indra.

1. Great Indra will I laud, in whom all people who drink the Soma have attained their longing; | Whom, passing wise, Gods, Heaven and Earth, engendered, formed by a Master's hand, to crush the Vṛitras. ‖ 2. Whom, most heroic, borne by Tawny Coursers, verily none subdueth in the battle; | Who, reaching far, most vigorous, hath shortened the Dasyu's life with Warriors bold of spirit. ‖ 3. Victor in fight, swift mover like a warhorse, pervading both worlds, rainer down of blessings, | To he invoked in war like Bhaga, Father, as 'twere, of hymns, fair, prompt to hear, strength-giver. ‖ 4. Supporting heaven, the high back of the region, his car is Vāyu with his team of Vasus. | Illumining the nights, the Sun's creator, like Dhiṣhaṇā he deals forth strength and riches. ‖ 5. Call we on Maghavan, auspicious Indra, best Hero in the fight where spoil is gathered; | The Strong, who listens, who gives aid in battles, who slays the Vṛitras, wins and gathers treasure.

Hymn 3:50. Indra.

1. Let Indra drink, All-hail! for his is Soma,—the mighty Bull come, girt by Marutas, hither. | Far-reaching, let him fill him with these viands, and let our offering sate his body's longing. ‖ 2. I yoke thy pair of trusty Steeds for swiftness, whose faithful service from of old thou lovest. | Here, fair of cheek! let thy Bay Coursers place thee: drink of this lovely well-effused libation. ‖ 3. With milk they made Indra their good Preserver, lauding for help and rule the bounteous rainer. | Impetuous God, when thou hast drunk the Soma, enraptured send us cattle in abundance. ‖ 4. With kine and horses satisfy this longing with very splendid bounty still extend it. | Seeking the light, with hymns to thee, O Indra, the Kuśikas have brought their gift, the singers. ‖ 5. Call we on Maghavan, auspicious Indra, best Hero in the fight where spoil is gathered; | The Strong, who listens, who gives aid in battles, who slays the Vṛitras, wins and gathers riches.

Hymn 3:51. Indra.

1. High hymns have sounded forth the praise of Maghavan, supporter of mankind, of Indra meet for lauds; | Him who hath waxen great, invoked with beauteous songs, Immortal One, whose praise each day is sung aloud. ‖ 2. To Indra from all sides go forth my songs of praise, the Lord of Hundred Powers, strong, Hero, like the sea, | Swift, winner of the booty, breaker-down of forts, faithful and ever-glorious, finder of the light. ‖ 3. Where battle's spoil is piled the singer winneth praise, for Indra taketh care of matchless worshippers. | He in Vivasvat's dwelling findeth his delight: praise thou the ever-conquering slayer of the foe. ‖ 4. Thee, valorous, most heroic of the heroes, shall the priests glorify with songs and praises. | Full of all wondrous power he goes to conquest: worship is his, sole Lord from days aforetime. ‖ 5. Abundant are the gifts he gives to mortals: for him the earth bears a rich store of treasures. | The heavens, the growing plants, the living waters, the forest trees preserve their wealth for Indra. ‖ 6. To thee, O Indra, Lord of Bays, for ever are offered prayers and songs: accept them gladly. | As Kinsman think thou of some fresh assistance; good Friend, give strength and life to those who praise thee. ‖ 7. Here, Indra, drink thou Soma with the Marutas, as thou didst drink the juice beside Śāryāta. | Under thy guidance, in thy keeping, Hero, the singers serve, skilled in fair sacrifices. ‖ 8. So eagerly desirous drink the Soma, our juice, O Indra, with thy friends the Marutas, | Since at thy birth all Deities adorned thee for the great fight, O thou invoked of many. ‖ 9. He was your

comrade in your zeal, O Marutas: they, rich in noble gifts, rejoiced in Indra. | With them together let the Vṛitra-slayer drink in his home the worshipper's libation. || 10. So, Lord of affluent gifts, this juice hath been pressed for thee with strength | Drink of it, thou who lovest song. || 11. Incline thy body to this juice which suits thy Godlike nature well: | May it cheer thee who lovest it. || 12. Brave Indra, let it work through both thy flanks, and through thy head by prayer, | And through thine arms, to prosper us.

Hymn 3:52. Indra.

1. Indra, accept at break of day our Soma mixed with roasted corn, | With groats with cake, with eulogies. || 2. Accept, O Indra, and enjoy the well-dressed sacrificial cake: Oblations are poured forth to thee. || 3. Consume our sacrificial cake, accept the songs of praise we sing, | As he who woes accepts his bride. || 4. Famed from of old, accept the cake at our libation poured at dawn, | For great, O Indra, is thy power. || 5. Let roasted corn of our midday libation, and sacrificial cake here please thee, Indra, | What time the lauding singer, keen of purpose and eager as a bull, with hymns implores thee. || 6. At the third sacrifice, O thou whom many praise, give glory to the roasted corn and holy cake. | With offered viands and with songs may we assist thee, Sage, whom Vāja and the Ṛibhus wait upon. || 7. The groats have we prepared for thee with Pūṣhan, corn for thee, Lord of Bay Steeds, with thy horses. | Eat thou the meal-cake, banded with the Marutas, wise Hero, Vṛitra-slayer, drink the Soma. || 8. Bring forth the roasted corn to meet him quickly, cake for the bravest Hero mid the heroes. | Indra, may hymns accordant with thee daily strengthen thee, Bold One, for the draught of Soma.

Hymn 3:53. Indra, Parvata, etc.

1. On a high car, O Parvata and Indra, bring pleasant viands, with brave heroes, hither. | Enjoy the gifts, Gods, at our sacrifices wax strong by hymns, rejoice in our oblation. || 2. Stay still, O Maghavan, advance no farther. a draught of well-pressed Soma will I give thee. | With sweetest song I grasp, O Mighty Indra, thy garment's hem as a child grasps his father's. || 3. Adhvaryu, sing we both; sing thou in answer: make we a laud acceptable to Indra. | Upon this sacrificer's grass he seated: to Indra shall our eulogy be uttered. || 4. A wife, O Maghavan is home and dwelling: so let thy Bay Steeds yoked convey thee hither. | Whenever we press out for thee the Soma, let Agni as our Herald speed to call thee. || 5. Depart, O Maghavan;again come hither: both there and here thy goat is Indra, Brother, | Where thy tall chariot hath a place to rest in, and where thou loosest thy loud-neighing Courser. || 6. Thou hast drunk Soma, Indra, turn thee homeward; thy joy is in thy home, thy racious Consort; | Where thy tall chariot hath a place to rest in, and thy strong Courser is set free with guerdon. || 7. Bounteous are these, Aṅgirasas, Virūpas: the Asura's Heroes and the Sons of Heaven. | They, giving store of wealth to Viśvāmitra, prolong his life through countless Soma-pressings. || 8. Maghavan weareth every shape at pleasure, effecting magic changes in his body, | Holy One, drinker out of season, coming thrice, in a moment, through fit prayers, from heaven. || 9. The mighty sage, God-born and God-incited, who looks on men, restrained the billowy river. | When Viśvāmitra was Sudās's escort, then Indra through the Kuśikas grew friendly. || 10. Like swans, prepare a song of praise with pressing-stones, glad in your hymns with juice poured forth in sacrifice. | Ye singers, with the Gods, sages who look on men, ye Kuśikas drink up the Soma's savoury meath. || 11. Come forward, Kuśikas, and be attentive; let loose Sudās's horse to win him riches. | East, west, and north, let the King slay the foeman, then at earth's choicest place perform his worship. || 12. Praises to Indra have I sung, sustainer of this earth and heaven. This prayer of Viśvāmitra keeps secure the race of Bhāratas. || 13. The Viśvāmitras have sung forth this prayer to Indra Thunder-aimed: | So let him make us prosperous. || 14. Among the Kīkaṭas what do thy cattle? They pour no milky draught, they heat no cauldron | Bring thou to us the wealth of Pramaganda; give up to us, O Maghavan, the low-born. || 15. Sasarparī, the gift of Jamadagnis, hath lowed with mighty voice dispelling famine. | The Daughter of the Sun hath spread our glory among the Gods, imperishable, deathless. || 16. Sasarparī brought glory speedily to these, over the generations of the Fivefold Race; | Daughter of Pakṣha, she bestows new vital power, she whom the ancient Jamadagnis gave to me. || 17. Strong be the pair of oxen, firm the axles, let not the pole slip nor the yoke be broken. | May Indra, keep the yoke-pins from decaying: attend us, thou whose fellies are uninjured. || 18. O Indra, give our bodies strength, strength to the bulls who draw the wains, | Strength to our seed and progeny that they may live, for thou art he who giveth strength. || 19. Enclose thee in the heart of Khadira timber, in the car wrought of Śiṃśapā put firmness. | Show thyself strong, O Axle, fixed and strengthened: throw us not from the car whereon we travel. || 20. Let not this sovereign of the wood leave us forlorn or injure us. | Safe may we be until we reach our homes and rest us and unyoke. || 21. With various aids this day come to us, Indra, with best aids speed us, Maghavan, thou Hero. | Let him who hateth us fall headlong downward: him whom we hate let vital breath abandon. || 22. He heats his very axe, and then cuts a mere Śimbala (Śālmali blossom) off. | O Indra, like a cauldron cracked and seething, so he pours out foam. || 23. Men notice not the arrow, O ye people; they bring the red beast deeming it a bullock. | A sluggish steed men run not with the courser, nor ever lead an ass before a charger. || 24. These men, the sons of Bhārata, O Indra, regard not severance or close connection. | They urge their own steed as it were another's, and take him, swift as the bow's string, to battle.

Hymn 3:54. Viśvedevas.

1. To him adorable, mighty, meet for synods, this strengthening hymn, unceasing, have they offered. | May Agni hear us with his homely splendours, hear us, Eternal One, with heavenly lustre. || 2. To mighty Heaven and Earth I sing forth loudly: my wish goes out desirous and well knowing | Both, at whose laud in synods, showing favour, the Gods rejoice them with the living mortal. || 3. O Heaven and Earth, may your great law he faithful: he ye our leaders for our high advantage. | To Heaven and Earth I offer this my homage, with food, O Agni, as I pray for riches. || 4. Yea, holy Heaven and Earth, the ancient sages whose word was ever true had power to find you; | And brave men in the fight where heroes conquer, O Earth, have known you well and paid you honour. || 5. What pathway leadeth to the Gods? Who knoweth this of a truth, and who will now declare it? | Seen are their lowest dwelling-places only, but they are in remote and secret regions. || 6. The Sage who looketh on mankind hath viewed them bedewed, rejoicing in the seat of Order. | They make a home as for a bird, though parted, with one same will finding themselves together. || 7. Partners though parted, with far-distant limits, on one firm place both stand for ever watchful, | And, being young for evermore, as sisters, speak to each other names that are united. || 8. All living things they part and keep asunder; though bearing up the mighty Gods they reel not. | One All is Lord of what is fixed and moving, that walks, that flies, this multiform creation. || 9. Afar the Ancient from of old I ponder, our kinship with our mighty Sire and Father,— | Singing the praise whereof the Gods by custom stand on the spacious far-extended pathway. || 10. This laud, O Heaven and Earth, to you I utter: let the kind-hearted hear, whose tongue is Agni, | Young, Sovereign Rulers, Varuṇa and Mitra, the wise and very glorious Ādityas. || 11. The fair-tongued Savitar, the golden-handed, comes thrice from heaven as Lord in our assembly. | Bear to the Gods this song of praise, and send us, then, Savitar, complete and perfect safety. || 12. Deft worker, skilful-handed, helpful, holy, may Tvaṣhṭar, God, give us these things to aid us, | Take your delight, Ye Ṛibhus joined with Pūṣhan: ye have prepared the rite with stones adjusted. || 13. Borne on their flashing car, the spear-armed Marutas, the nimble Youths of Heaven, the Sons of Order, | The Holy, and Sarasvatī, shall hear us: ye Mighty, give us wealth with noble offspring. || 14. To Viṣhṇu rich in marvels, songs And praises shall go as singers on the road of Bhaga,— | The Chieftain of the Mighty Stride, whose Mothers, the many young Dames, never disregard him. || 15. Indra, who rules through all his powers heroic, hath with his majesty filled earth and heaven. | Lord of brave hosts, Fort-crusher, Vṛitra-slayer, gather thou up and bring us store of cattle. || 16. My Sires are the Nāsatyas, kind to kinsmen: the Aśvins' kinship is a glorious title. | For ye are they who give us store of riches: ye guard your gift uncheated by the bounteous. || 17. This is, ye Wise, your great and glorious title, that all ye Deities abide in Indra. | Friend, Much-invoked! art thou with thy dear Ṛibhus: fashion ye this our hymn for our advantage. || 18. Aryaman, Aditi deserve our worship: the laws of Varuṇa remain unbroken. | The lot of childlessness remove ye from us, and let our course be rich in kine and offspring. || 19. May the Gods' envoy, sent to many a quarter, proclaim us sinless for our perfect safety. |

May Earth and Heaven, the Sun, the waters, hear us, and the wide firmament and constellations. || 20. Hear us the mountains which distil the rain-drops, and, resting firm, rejoice in freshening moisture. | May Aditi with the Ādityas hear us, and Marutas grant us their auspicious shelter. || 21. Soft be our path for ever, well-provisioned: with pleasant meath, O Gods, the herbs besprinkle. | Safe be my bliss, O Agni, in thy friendship: may I attain the seat of foodful. riches, || 22. Enjoy the offering: beam thou strength upon us; combine thou for our good all kinds of glory. | Conquer in battle, Agni, all those foemen, and light us every day with loving kindness.

Hymn 3:55. Viśvedevas.

1. At the first shining of the earliest Mornings, in the Cow's home was born the Great Eternal. | Now shall the statutes of the Gods be valid. Great is the Gods' supreme and sole dominion— || 2. Let not the Gods here injure us, O Agni, nor Fathers of old time who know the region, | Nor the sign set between two ancient dwellings. Great is the Gods' supreme and sole dominion. || 3. My wishes fly abroad to many places: I glance back to the ancient sacrifices. | Let us declare the truth when fire is kindled. Great is the Gods' supreme and sole dominion. || 4. King Universal, born to sundry quarters, extended through the wood be lies on couches. | One Mother rests: another feeds the Infant. Great is the Gods' supreme and sole dominion. || 5. Lodged in old plants, he grows again in younger, swiftly within the newly-born and tender. | Though they are unimpregned, he makes them fruitful. Great is the Gods' supreme and sole dominion. || 6. Now lying far away, Child of two Mothers, he wanders unrestrained, the single youngling. | These are the laws of Varuṇa and Mitra. Great is the Gods' supreme and sole dominion. || 7. Child of two Mothers, Priest, sole Lord in synods, he still precedes while resting as foundation. | They who speak sweetly bring him sweet addresses. Great is the Gods' supreme and sole dominion. || 8. As to a friendly warrior when he battles, each thing that comes anear is seen to meet him. | The hymn commingles with the cow's oblation. Great is the Gods' supreme and sole dominion. || 9. Deep within these the hoary envoy pierceth; mighty, he goeth to the realm of splendour, | And looketh on us, clad in wondrous beauty. Great is the Gods' supreme and sole dominion. || 10. Vishṇu, the guardian, keeps the loftiest station, upholding dear, immortal dwelling-places. | Agni knows well all these created beings. Great is the Gods' supreme and sole dominion. || 11. Ye, variant Pair, have made yourselves twin beauties: one of the Twain is dark, bright shines the other; | And yet these two, the dark, the red, are Sisters. Great is the Gods' supreme and sole dominion. || 12. Where the two Cows, the Mother and the Daughter, meet and give suck yielding their lordly nectar, | I praise them at the seat of law eternal. Great is the Gods' supreme and sole dominion. || 13. Loud hath she lowed, licking the other's youngling. On what world hath the Milch-cow laid her udder? | This Iḷā streameth with the milk of Order. Great is the Gods' supreme and sole dominion. || 14. Earth weareth beauties manifold: uplifted, licking her Calf of eighteen months, she standeth. | Well-skilled I seek the seat of law eternal. Great is the Gods' supreme and sole dominion. || 15. Within a wondrous place the Twain are treasured: the one is manifest, the other hidden. | One common pathway leads in two directions. Great is the Gods' supreme and sole dominion. || 16. Let the milch-kine that have no calves storm downward, yielding rich nectar, streaming, unexhausted, | These who are ever new and fresh and youthful. Great is the Gods' supreme and sole dominion. || 17. What time the Bull bellows in other regions, another herd receives the genial moisture; | For he is Bhaga, King, the earth's Protector. Great is the Gods' supreme and sole dominion. || 18. Let us declare the Hero's wealth in horses, O all ye folk: of this the Gods have knowledge. | Sixfold they bear him, or by fives are harnessed. Great is the Gods' supreme and sole dominion. || 19. Tvashṭar the God, the omniform. Creator, begets and feeds mankind in various manner. | His, verily, arc all these living creatures. Great is the Gods' supreme dominion. || 20. The two great meeting Bowls hath he united: each of the Pair is laden with his treasure. | The Hero is renowned for gathering riches. Great is the Gods' supreme and sole dominion. || 21. Yea, and on this our earth the All-Sustainer dwells like a King with noble friends about him. | In his protection heroes rest in safety. Great is the Cods' supreme and sole dominion. || 22. Rich in their gifts for thee are herbs and waters, and earth brings all her wealth for thee, O Indra. | May we as friends of thine share goodly treasures. Great is the Gods' supreme and sole dominion.

Hymn 3:56. Viśvedevas.

1. Not men of magic skill, not men of wisdom impair the Gods' first steadfast ordinances. | Ne'er may the earth and heaven which know not malice, nor the fixed hills, be bowed by sage devices. || 2. One, moving not away, supports six burthens: the Cows proceed to him the true, the Highest. | Near stand three Mighty Ones who travel swiftly: two are concealed from sight, one is apparent. || 3. The Bull who wears all shapes, the triple-breasted, three-uddered, with a brood in many places, | Ruleth majestic with his triple aspect, the Bull, the Everlasting Ones' impregner. || 4. When nigh them, as their tracer he observed them: he called aloud the dear name of Ādityas. | The Goddesses, the Waters, stayed to meet him: they who were wandering separate enclosed him. || 5. Streams! the wise Gods have thrice three habitations. Child of three Mothers, he is Lord in synods. | Three are the holy Ladies of the Waters, thrice here from heaven supreme in our assembly. || 6. Do thou, O Savitar, from heaven thrice hither, three times a day, send down thy blessings daily. | Send us, O Bhaga, triple wealth and treasure; cause the two worlds to prosper us, Preserver! || 7. Savitar thrice from heaven pours down abundance, and the fair-handed Kings Varuṇa, Mitra; | And spacious Heaven and Earth, yea, and the Waters, solicit wealth that Savitar may send us. || 8. Three are the bright realms, best, beyond attainment, and three, the Asura's Heroes, rule as Sovereigns, | Holy and vigorous, never to be injured. Thrice may the Gods from heaven attend our synod.

Hymn 3:57. Viśvedevas.

1. My thought with fine discernment hath discovered the Cow who wanders free without a herdsman, | Her who hath straightway poured me food in plenty: Indra and Agni therefore are her praisers. || 2. Indra and Pūshan, deft of hand and mighty, well-pleased have drained the heaven's exhaustless udder. | As in this praise the Gods have all delighted, may I win blessing here from you, O Vasus. || 3. Fain to lend vigour to the Bull, the sisters with reverence recognize the germ within him. | The Cows come lowing hither to the Youngling, to him endued with great and wondrous beauties. || 4. Fixing with thought, at sacrifice, the press-stones, I bid the well-formed Heaven and Earth come hither; | For these thy flames, which give men boons in plenty, rise up on high, the beautiful, the holy. || 5. Agni, thy meath-sweet tongue that tastes fair viands, which among Gods is called the far-extended,— | Therewith make all the Holy Odes be seated here for our help, and feed them with sweet juices. || 6. Let thy stream give us drink, O God, O Agni, wonderful and exhaustless like the rain-clouds. | Thus care for us, O Vasu Jātavedas, show us thy loving-kindness, reaching all men.

Hymn 3:58. Aśvins.

1. The Ancient's Milch-cow yields the things we long for: the Son of Dakshiṇā travels between them. | She with the splendid chariot brings refulgence. The praise of Ushas hath awoke the Aśvins. || 2. They bear you hither by well-ordered statute: our sacred offerings rise as if to parents. | Destroy in us the counsel of the niggard come hitherward, for we have shown you favour. || 3. With lightly-rolling car and well-yoked horses hear this, the press-stone's song, ye Wonder-Workers. | Have not the sages of old time, ye Aśvins, called you most prompt to come and stay misfortune? || 4. Remember us, and come to us, for ever men, as their wont is, invocate the Aśvins. | Friends as it were have offered you these juices, sweet, blent with milk at the first break of morning. || 5. Even through many regions, O ye Aśvins high praise is yours among mankind, ye Mighty— | Come, helpers, on the paths which Gods have travelled: here your libations of sweet meath are ready. || 6. Ancient your home, auspicious is your friendship: Heroes, your wealth is with the house of Jahnu. | Forming again with you auspicious friendship, let us rejoice with draughts of meath together. || 7. O Aśvins, Very Mighty ones, with Vāyu and with his steeds, one-minded, ever-youthful, | Nāsatyas, joying in the third day's Soma, drink it, not hostile, Very Bounteous Givers. || 8. Aśvins, to you are brought abundant viands in rivalry with sacred songs, unceasing. | Sprung from high Law your car, urged on by press-stones, goes round the earth and heaven in one brief moment. || 9. Aśvins, your Soma sheds delicious sweetness: drink ye thereof and come unto our dwelling. | Your car,

assuming many a shape, most often goes to the Soma-presser's place of meeting.

Hymn 3:59. Mitra.

1. Mitra, when speaking, stirreth men to labour: Mitra sustaineth both the earth and heaven. | Mitra beholdeth men with eyes that close not. To Mitra bring, with holy oil, oblation. || 2. Foremost be he who brings thee food, O Mitra, who strives to keep thy sacred Law, Āditya. | He whom thou helpest ne'er is slain or conquered, on him, from near or far, falls no affliction. || 3. joying in sacred food and free from sickness, with knees bent lowly on the earth's broad surface, | Following closely the Āditya's statute, may we remain in Mitra's gracious favour. || 4. Auspicious and adorable, this Mitra was born with fair dominion, King, Disposer. | May we enjoy the grace of him the Holy, yea, rest in his propitious loving-kindness. || 5. The great Āditya, to be served with worship, who stirreth men, is gracious to the singer. | To Mitra, him most highly to be lauded, offer in fire oblation that he loveth. || 6. The gainful grace of Mitra, God, supporter of the race of man, | Gives splendour of most glorious fame. || 7. Mitra whose glory spreads afar, he who in might surpasses heaven, | Surpasses earth in his renown. || 8. All the Five Races have repaired to Mitra, ever strong to aid, | For he sustaineth all the Gods. || 9. Mitra to Gods, to living men, to him who strews the holy grass, | Gives food fulfilling sacred Law.

Hymn 3:60. Ṛibhus.

1. Here is your ghostly kinship, here, O Men: they came desirous to these holy rites with store of wealth, | With wondrous arts, whereby, with schemes to meet each need, Ye gained, Sudhanvan's Sons! your share in sacrifice. || 2. The mighty powers wherewith. ye formed the chalices, the thought by which ye drew the cow from out the hide, | The intellect wherewith ye wrought the two Bay Steeds,—through these, O Ṛibhus, ye attained divinity. || 3. Friendship with Indra have the Ṛibhus, fully gained: grandsons of Manu, they skilfully urged the work. | Sudhanvan's Children won them everlasting life, serving with holy rites, pious with noble acts. || 4. In company with Indra come ye to the juice, then gloriously shall your wishes be fulfilled. | Not to be paragoned, ye Priests, are your good deeds, nor your heroic acts, Ṛibhus, Sudhanvan's Sons. || 5. O Indra, with the Ṛibhus, Mighty Ones, pour down the Soma juice effused, well-blent, from both thy hands. | Maghavan, urged by song, in the drink-offerer's house rejoice thee with the Heroes, with Sudhanvan's Sons. || 6. With Ṛibhu near, and Vāja, Indra, here exult, with Sachi, praised of many, in the juice we pour. | These homes wherein we dwell have turned themselves to thee, -devotions to the Gods, as laws of men ordain. || 7. Come with the mighty Ṛibhus, Indra, come to us, strengthening with thy help the singer's holy praise; | At hundred eager calls come to the living man, with thousand arts attend the act of sacrifice.

Hymn 3:61. Uṣhas.

1. O Uṣhas, strong with strength, endowed with knowledge, accept the singer's praise, O wealthy Lady. | Thou, Goddess, ancient, young, and full of wisdom, movest, all-bounteous! as the Law ordaineth. || 2. Shine forth, O Morning, thou auspicious Goddess, on thy bright car awaking pleasant voices. | Let docile horses of far-reaching splendour convey thee hitherward, the golden-coloured || 3. Thou, Morning, turning thee to every creature, standest on high as ensign of the Immortal, | To one same goal ever and ever wending now, like a wheel, O newly-born, roll hither. || 4. Letting her reins drop downward, Morning cometh, the wealthy Dame, the Lady of the dwelling; | Bringing forth light, the Wonderful, the Blessed hath spread her from the bounds of earth and heaven. || 5. Hither invoke the radiant Goddess Morning, and bring with reverence your hymn to praise her. | She, dropping sweets, hath set in heaven her brightness, and, fair to look on, hath beamed forth her splendour. || 6. From heaven, with hymns, the Holy One was wakened: brightly to both worlds came the wealthy Lady. | To Morning, Agni, when she comes refulgent, thou goest forth soliciting fair riches. || 7. On Law's firm base the speeder of the Mornings, the Bull, hath entered mighty earth and heaven. | Great is the power of Varuṇa and Mitra, which, bright, hath spread in every place its splendour.

Hymn 3:62. Indra and Others.

1. Your well-known prompt activities aforetime needed no impulse from your faithful servant. | Where, Indra-Varuṇa, is now that glory wherewith ye brought support to those who loved you? || 2. This man, most diligent, seeking after riches, incessantly invokes you for your favour. | Accordant, Indra-Varuṇa, with Marutas, with Heaven and Earth, hear ye mine invocation. || 3. O Indra-Varuṇa, ours be this treasure ours be wealth, Marutas, with full store of heroes. | May the Varūtrīs with their shelter aid us, and Bhāratī and Hotrā with the Mornings. || 4. Be pleased! with our oblations, thou loved of all Gods, Bṛihaspati: | Give wealth to him who brings thee gifts. || 5. At sacrifices, with your hymns worship the pure Bṛihaspati— | I pray for power which none may bend— || 6. The Bull of men, whom none deceive, the wearer of each shape at will, | Bṛihaspati Most Excellent. || 7. Divine, resplendent Pūṣhan, this our newest hymn of eulogy, | By us is chanted forth to thee. || 8. Accept with favour this my song, be gracious to the earnest thought, | Even as a bridegroom to his bride. || 9. May he who sees all living things, see, them together at a glance,— | May lie, may Pūṣhan be our help. || 10. May we attain that excellent glory of Savitar the God: | So May he stimulate our prayers. || 11. With understanding, earnestly, of Savitar the God we crave | Our portion of prosperity. || 12. Men, singers worship Savitar the God with hymn and holy rites, | Urged by the impulse of their thoughts. || 13. Soma who gives success goes forth, goes to the gathering place of Gods, | To seat him at the seat of Law. || 14. To us and to our cattle may Soma give salutary food, | To biped and to quadruped. || 15. May Soma, strengthening our power of life, and conquering our foes, | In our assembly take his seat. || 16. May Mitra-Varuṇa, sapient Pair, bedew our pasturage with oil, | With meath the regions of the air. || 17. Far-ruling, joyful when adored, ye reign through majesty of might, | With pure laws everlastingly. || 18. Lauded by Jamadagni's song, sit in the place of holy Law: | Drink Soma, ye who strengthen Law.

Maṇḍala 4

Hymn 4:1. Agni.

1, Thee Agni, have the Gods, ever of one accord, sent hither down, a God, appointed messenger, yea, with their wisdom sent thee down. | The Immortal, O thou Holy One, mid mortal men, the God-devoted God, the wise, have they brought forth, brought forth the omnipresent God-devoted Sage. || 2. As such, O Agni, bring with favour to the Gods thy Brother Varuṇa who loveth sacrifice, | True to the Law, the Āditya who supporteth men, the King, supporter of mankind. || 3. Do thou, O Friend, turn hither him who is our Friend, swift as a wheel, like two car-steeds in rapid course, Wondrous! to us in rapid course. | O Agni, find thou grace for us with Varuṇa, with Marutas who illumine all. | Bless us, thou Radiant One, for seed and progeny, yea, bless us, O thou Wondrous God. || 4. Do thou who knowest Varuṇa, O Agni, put far away from us the God's displeasure. | Best Sacrificer, brightest One, refulgent remove thou far from us all those who hate us. || 5. Be thou, O Agni, nearest us with succour, our closest Friend while now this Morn is breaking. | Reconcile to us Varuṇa, be bounteous enjoy the gracious juice; be swift to hear us. || 6. Excellent is the glance, of brightest splendour, which the auspicious God bestows on mortals— | The God's glance, longed-for even as the butter, pure, heated, of the cow, the milch-cow's bounty. || 7. Three are those births, the true, the most exalted, eagerly longed-for, of the God, of Agni. | He came invested in the boundless region, pure, radiant, friendly, mightily resplendent. || 8. This envoy joyeth in all seats of worship, borne on his golden car, sweet-tongued Invoker: | Lovely to look on, with red steeds, effulgent, like a feast rich in food, joyous for ever. || 9. Allied by worship, let him give man knowledge: by an extended cord they lead him onward. | He stays, effectual in this mortal's dwelling, and the God wins a share in his possessions. || 10. Let Agni -for he knows the way—conduct us to all that he enjoys of God-sent riches, | What all the Immortals have prepared with wisdom, Dyaus, Sire, Begetter, raining down true blessings. || 11. In houses first he sprang into existence, at great heaven's base, and in this region's bosom; | Footless and headless, both his ends concealing, in his Bull's lair drawing himself together. || 12. Wondrously first he rose aloft, defiant, in the Bull's lair, the home of holy Order, | Longed-for, young, beautiful, and far-resplendent: and seven dear friends sprang up unto the Mighty. || 13. Here did our human fathers take their places, fain to fulfil the sacred Law of worship. | Forth drave they, with loud call, Dawn's teeming Milch-kine bid in the mountain stable, in the cavern. || 14. Splendid were they when they had rent the mountain: others, around, shall tell forth this their exploit. | They sang their song, prepared to free the cattle: they found the light; with holy hymns they worshipped. || 15. Eager, with thought intent upon the booty, the men with their celestial speech threw open, | The solid mountain firm, compact, enclosing, confining Cows, the stable full of cattle. || 16. The Milch-cow's earliest name they comprehended: they found the Mother's thrice-seven noblest titles. | This the bands knew, and sent forth acclamation:with the Bull's sheen the Red One was apparent. || 17. The turbid darkness fled, the heaven was splendid! up rose the bright beam of celestial Morning. | Sūrya ascended to the wide expanses, beholding deeds of men both good and evil. || 18. Then, afterwards they looked around, awakened, when first they held that Heaven allotted treasure. | Now all the Gods abide in all their dwellings. Varuṇa, Mitra, be the prayer effective. || 19. I will call hither brightly-beaming Agni, the Herald, all-supporting, best at worship. | He hath disclosed, like the milch cows' pure udder, the Soma's juice when cleansed and poured from beakers. || 20. The freest God of all who should be worshipped, the guest who is received in all men's houses, | Agni who hath secured the Gods' high favour,—may he be gracious, to us Jātavedas.

Hymn 4:2. Agni.

1. The, Faithful One, Immortal among mortals, a God among the Gods, appointed envoy, | Priest, best at worship, must shine forth in glory. Agni shall be raised high with man's oblations. || 2. Born for us here this day, O Son of Vigour, between both races of born beings, Agni, | Thou farest as an envoy, having harnessed, Sublime One! thy strong-muscled radiant stallions. || 3. I laud the ruddy steeds who pour down blessing, dropping oil, fleetest through the thought of Order. | Yoking red horses to and fro thou goest between you Deities and mortal races. || 4. Aryaman, Mitra, Varuṇa, and Indra with Viṣhṇu, of the Gods, Marutas and Aśvins— | These, Agni, with good car and steeds, bring hither, most bountiful, to folk with fair oblations. || 5. Agni, be this our sacrifice eternal, with brave friends, rich in kine and sheep and horses, | Rich, Asura! in sacred food and children, in full assembly, wealth broad-based and during. || 6. The man who, sweating, brings for thee the fuel, and makes his head to ache, thy faithful servant, — | Agni, to him be a self-strong Protector guard him from all who seek to do him mischief. || 7. Who brings thee food, though thou hast food in plenty, welcomes his cheerful guest and speeds him onward, | Who kindles thee devoutly in his dwelling, to him be wealth secure and freely giving. || 8. Whoso sings praise to thee at eve or morning, and, with oblation, doth the thing thou lovest,— | In his own home, even as a gold-girt courser, rescue him from distress, the bounteous giver. || 9. Whoso brings gifts to thee Immortal, Agni, and doth thee service with uplifted ladle,— | Let him not, sorely toiling, lose his riches; let not the sinner's wickedness enclose him. || 10. Whose well-wrought worship thou acceptest, Agni, thou God a mortal's gift, thou liberal Giver,— | Dear be his sacrifice to thee, Most Youthful! and may we strengthen him when he adores thee. || 11. May he who knows distinguish sense and folly of men, like straight and crooked backs of horses. | Lead us, O God, to wealth and noble offspring: keep penury afar and grant us plenty. || 12. This Sage the Sages, ne'er deceived, commanded, setting him down in dwellings of the living. | Hence mayst thou, friendly God, with rapid footsteps behold the Gods, wonderful, fair to look on. || 13. Good guidance hast thou for the priest, O Agni, who, Youngest God! with outpoured Soma serves thee. | Ruler of men, thou joyous God, bring treasure splendid and plentiful to aid the toiler. || 14. Now all that we, thy faithful servants, Agni, have done with feet, with hands, and with our bodies, | The wise, with toil, the holy rite have guided, as those who frame a car with manual cunning. || 15. May we, seven sages first in rank, engender, from Dawn the Mother, men to be ordainers. | May we, Aṅgirasas, be sons of Heaven, and, radiant, burst the wealth-containing mountain. || 16. As in the days of old our ancient Fathers, speeding the work of holy worship, Agni, | Sought pure light and devotion, singing praises; they cleft the ground and made red Dawns apparent. || 17. Gods, doing holy acts, devout, resplendent, smelting like ore their human generations. | Enkindling Agni and exalting Indra, they came encompassing the stall of cattle. || 18. Strong One! he marked them-and the Gods before them-like herds of cattle in a foodful pasture. | There they moaned forth their strong desire for mortals, to aid the True, the nearest One, the Living. || 19. We have worked for thee, we have laboured nobly-bright Dawns have shed their light upon our worship— | Adding a beauty to the perfect Agni, and the God's beauteous eye that shines for ever. || 20. Agni, Disposer, we have sung these praises to thee the Wise: do thou accept them gladly. | Blaze up on high and ever make us richer. Give us great wealth, O thou whose boons are many.

Hymn 4:3. Agni.

1. Win, to assist you, Rudra, Lord of worship, Priest of both worlds, effectual | Sacrificer, | Agni, invested with his golden colours, before the thunder strike and lay you senseless. || 2. This shrine have we made ready for thy coming, as the fond dame attires her for her husband. | Performer of good work, sit down before us, invested while these flames incline to meet thee. || 3. A hymn, O Priest, to him who hears, the gentle, to him who looks on men, exceeding gracious, | A song of praise sing to the God Immortal, whom the stone, presser of the sweet juice, worships. || 4. Even as true knower of the Law, O Agni, to this our solemn rite he thou attentive. | When shall thy songs of festival be sung thee? When is thy friendship shown within our dwelling? || 5. Why this complaint to Varuṇa, O Agni? And why to Heaven? for what is our transgression? | How wilt thou speak to Earth and bounteous Mitra? What wilt thou say to Aryaman and Bhaga? || 6. What, when thou blazest on the lesser altars, what to the mighty Wind who comes to bless us, | True, circumambient? what to Earth, O Agni, what wilt thou say to man-destroying Rudra? || 7. How to great Pūṣhan who promotes our welfare,—to honoured Rudra what, who gives oblations? | What sin of ours to the far-striding Viṣhṇu, what, Agni, wilt thou tell the Lofty Arrow. || 8. What wilt thou tell the truthful band of Marutas, how answer the great Sun when thou art questioned? | Before the Free, before the Swift, defend us: fulfil heaven's work, all-knowing Jātavedas. || 9. I crave the cow's true gift arranged by Order: though raw, she hath the sweet ripe juice, O Agni. | Though she is black of hue with milk she teemeth, nutritious, brightly shining, all-sustaining. || 10. Agni the Bull, the manly, hath been sprinkled with oil upon his back, by Law eternal. | He who gives vital power goes on unswerving. Pṛiśni the Bull hath milked the pure white udder. || 11. By Law the Aṅgirasas cleft the rock asunder, and sang their hymns together with the cattle. | Bringing great bliss the men encompassed Morning: light was apparent at the birth of Agni. || 12. By Law the Immortal Goddesses the Waters, with meath-rich waves, O Agni, and uninjured, | Like a strong courser lauded in his running, sped to flow onward swiftly and for ever. || 13. Go never to the feast of one who harms us, the treacherous neighbour or. unworthy kinsman. | Punish us not for a false brother's trespass. Let us riot feel the might of friend or foeman. || 14. O Agni, keep us safe with thy protection, loving us, honoured God! and ever guarding. | Beat thou away, destroy severe affliction slay e'en the demon when he waxes mighty. || 15. Through these our songs of praise be gracious, Agni; moved by our prayers, O Hero, touch our viands. | Accept, O Aṅgiras, these our devotions, and let the praise which Gods desire address thee. || 16. To thee who knowest, Agni, thou Disposer, all these wise secret speeches have I uttered, | Sung to thee, Sage, the charming words of wisdom, to thee, O Singer, with. my thoughts and Praises.

Hymn 4:4. Agni.

1. Put forth like a wide-spreading net thy vigour; go like a mighty King with his attendants. | Thou, following thy swift net, shootest arrows: transfix the fiends with darts that burn most fiercely. || 2. Forth go in rapid flight thy whirling weapons: follow them closely, glowing in thy fury. | Spread with thy tongue the winged flames, O Agni; unfettered, cast thy firebrands all around thee. || 3. Send thy spies forward, fleetest in thy motion; be, ne'er deceived, the guardian of this people | From him who, near or far, is bent on evil, and let no trouble sent from thee o'ercome us. || 4. Rise up, O Agni, spread thee out before us: burn down our foes, thou who hast sharpened arrows. | Him, blazing Agni! who hath worked us mischief, consume thou utterly like dried-up stubble. || 5. Rise, Agni, drive off those who fight against us: make manifest thine own celestial vigour. | Slacken the strong bows of the demon-driven: destroy our foemen whether kin or stranger. || 6. Most Youthful God, he knoweth well thy

favour who gave an impulse to this high devotion. | All fair days and magnificence of riches hast thou beamed forth upon the good man's portals. || 7. Blest, Agni, be the man, the liberal giver, who with his lauds and regular oblation | Is fain to please thee for his life and dwelling. May all his days be bright: be this his longing. || 8. I praise thy gracious favour: sing in answer. May this my song sing like a loved one with thee. | Lords of good steeds and cars may we adorn thee, and day by day vouchsafe thou us dominion. || 9. Here of free choice let each one serve thee richly, resplendent day by day at eve and morning. | So may we honour thee, content and joyous, passing beyond the glories of the people. || 10. Whoso with good steeds and fine gold, O Agni, comes nigh thee on a car laden with treasure, | His Friend art thou, yea, thou art his Protector whose joy it is to entertain thee duly. || 11. Through words and kinship I destroy the mighty: this power I have from Gotama my father. | Mark thou this speech of ours, O thou Most Youthful, Friend of the House, exceeding wise, Invoker. || 12. Knowing no slumber, speedy and propitious, alert and ever friendly, most unwearied, | May thy protecting powers, unerring Agni, taking their places here, combined, preserve us. || 13. Thy guardian rays, O Agni, when they saw him, preserved blind Māmateya from affliction. | Lord of all riches, he preserved the pious: the fees who fain would harm them did no mischief || 14. Aided by thee with thee may we be wealthy, may we gain strength with thee to guide us onward. | Fulfil the words of both, O Ever Truthful: straightway do this, thou God whom power emboldens. || 15. O Agni, with this fuel will we serve thee; accept the laud we sing to thee with favour | Destroy the cursing Rākṣhasas: preserve us, O rich in friends, from guile and scorn and slander.

Hymn 4:5. Agni.

1. How shall we give with one accord oblation to Agni, to Vaiśvānara the Bounteous? | Great light, with full high growth hath he uplifted, and, as a pillar bears the roof, sustains it. || 2. Reproach not him who, God and self-reliant, vouchsafed this bounty unto me a mortal,— | Deathless, discerner, wise, to me the simple, Vaiśvānara most manly, youthful Agni. || 3. Sharp-pointed, powerful, strong, of boundless vigour, Agni who knows the lofty hymn, kept secret | As the lost milch-cow's track, the doubly Mighty,—he hath declared to me this hidden knowledge. || 4. May he with sharpened teeth, the Bounteous Giver, Agni, consume with flame most fiercely glowing. | Those who regard not Varuṇa's commandments and the dear steadfast laws of sapient Mitra. || 5. Like youthful women without brothers, straying, like dames who hate their lords, of evil conduct, | They who are full of sin, untrue, unfaithful, they have engendered this abysmal station. || 6. To me, weak, innocent, thou, luminous Agni, bast boldly given as 'twere a heavy burthen, | This Pṛiṣhṭha hymn, profound and strong and mighty, of seven elements, and with offered dainties. || 7. So may our song that purifies, through wisdom reach in a moment him the Universal, | Established on the height, on earth's best station, above the beauteous grassy skin of Pṛiśni. || 8. Of this my speech what shall I utter further? They indicate the milk stored up in secret | When they have thrown as 'twere the cows' stalls open. The Bird protects earths' best and well-loved station. || 9. This is the Great Ones' mighty apparition which from of old the radiant Cow hath followed. | This, shining brightly in the place of Order, swift, hasting on in secret, she discovered. || 10. He then who shone together with his Parents remembered Pṛiśni's fair and secret treasure, | Which, in the Mother Cow's most lofty station, the Bull's tongue, of the flame bent forward, tasted. || 11. With reverence I declare the Law, O Agni; what is, comes by thine order, Jātavedas. | Of this, whate'er it be, thou art the Sovereign, yea, all the wealth that is in earth or | heaven. || 12. What is our wealth therefrom, and what our treasure? Tell us O Jātavedas, for thou | knowest, | What is our best course in this secret passage: we, unreproached, have reached a t)lace far distant. || 13. What is the limit, what the rules, the guerdon? Like fleet-foot coursers speed we to the contest. | When will the Goddesses, the Immortal's Spouses, the Dawns, spread over us the Sun-God's splendour? || 14. Unsatisfied, with speech devoid of vigour, scanty and frivolous and inconclusive, | Wherefore do they address thee here, O Agni? Let these who have no weapons suffer sorrow. || 15. The majesty of him the Good, the Mighty, aflame, hath shone for glory in the dwelling. | He, clothed in light, hath shone most fair to look on, wealthy in boons, as a home shines with riches.

Hymn 4:6. Agni.

1. Priest of our rite, stand up erect, O Agni, in the Gods' service best of sacrificers, | For over every thought thou art the Ruler: thou furtherest e'en the wisdom of the pious. || 2. He was set down mid men as Priest unerring, Agni, wise, welcome in our holy synods. | Like Savitar he hath lifted up his splendour, and like a builder raised his smoke to heaven. || 3. The glowing ladle, filled with oil, is lifted; choosing Gods' service to the right he circles. | Eager he rises like the new-wrought pillar which, firmly set and fixed, anoints the victims. || 4. When sacred grass is strewn and Agni kindled, the Adhvaryu rises to, his task rejoicing. | Agni the Priest, like one who tends the cattle, goes three times round, as from of old he wills it. || 5. Agni himself, the Priest, with measured motion, goes round, with sweet speech, cheerful, true to Order. | His fulgent flames run forth like vigorous horses; all creatures are affrighted when he blazes. || 6. Beautiful and auspicious is thine aspect, O lovely Agni, terrible when spreading. | Thy splendours are not covered by the darkness: detraction leaves no stain upon thy body. || 7. Naught hindered his production, Bounteous Giver: his Mother and his Sire were free to send him. | Then as Friend benevolent, refulgent, Agni shone forth in human habitations. || 8. He, Agni, whom the twice-five sisters, dwelling together, in the homes of men engendered, | Bright like a spear's tooth, wakened in the morning, with powerful mouth and like an axe well-sharpened. || 9. These thy Bay Coursers, Agni, dropping fatness, ruddy vigorous, speeding straightly forward, | And red steeds, wonderful, of mighty muscle, are to this service of the Gods invited: || 10. These brightly-shining games of thine, O Agni, that move for ever restless, all-subduing, | Like falcons hasting eagerly to the quarry, roar loudly like the army of the Marutas. || 11. To thee, O flaming God, hath prayer been offered. Let the priest laud thee: give to him who worships. | Men have established Agni as Invoker, fain to adore the glory of the living.

Hymn 4:7. Agni.

1. Here by ordainers was this God appointed first Invoker, best at worship, to be praised at rites: | Whom Apnavāna, and the Bhṛigus caused to shine bright-coloured in the wood, spreading from home to home. || 2. When shall thy glory as a God, Agni, be suddenly shown forth. | For mortal men have held thee fast, adorable in all their homes, || 3. Seeing thee faithful to the Law, most sapient, like the starry heaven, | Illumining with cheerful ray each solemn rite in every house. || 4. Vivasvat's envoy living men have taken as their ensign, swift, | The ruler over all mankind, moving like Bhṛigu in each home. || 5. Him the intelligent have they placed duly as Invoking Priest, | Welcome, with sanctifying flame, best worshipper, with sevenfold might; || 6. In his Eternal Mothers, in the wood, concealed and unapproached, | Kept secret though his flames are bright seeking on all sides, quickly found. || 7. That as food spreads forth in this earthly udder, Gods may rejoice them in the home of Order, | Great Agni, served with reverence and oblation, flies ever to the sacrifice, the Faithful. || 8. Bird of each rite, skilled in an envoy's duties, knowing both worlds and that which lies between them, | Thou goest from of old a willing Herald, knowing full well heaven's innermost recesses. || 9. Bright God, thy path is black: light is before thee: thy moving splendour is the chief of wonders. | When she, yet unimpregnate, hath conceived thee, even when newly born thou art an envoy. || 10. Yet newly born, his vigour is apparent when the wind blows upon his fiery splendour, | His sharpened tongue he layeth on the brushwood, and with his teeth e'en solid food consumeth. || 11. When he hath borne off food with swift flame swiftly, strong Agni makes himself a speedy envoy, | Follows the rustling of the wind, consuming, and courser-like, speeds, drives the swift horse onward.

Hymn 4:8. Agni.

1. Your envoy who possesses all, Immortal, bearer of your gifts, | Best worshipper, I woo with song. || 2. He, Mighty, knows the gift of wealth, he knows the deep recess of heaven: | He shall bring hitherward the Gods. || 3. He knows, a God himself, to guide Gods to the righteous in his home: | He gives e'en treasures that we love. || 4. He is the Herald: well-informed, he doth his errand to and fro, | Knowing the deep recess of heaven. || 5. May we be they who gratify Agni with sacrificial gifts, | Who cherish and enkindle him. || 6. Illustrious for wealth are they, and hero deeds, victorious, | Who have served Agni reverently. || 7. So unto us, day after day, may riches craved by many come, | And power and might spring up for us. || 8. That

holy Singer in his strength shoots forth his arrows swifter than | The swift shafts of the tribes of men.

Hymn 4:9. Agni.

1. Agni, show favour: great art thou who to this pious man art come, | To seat thee on the sacred grass. || 2. May he the Immortal, Helper, bard to be deceived among mankind, | Become the messenger of all. || 3. Around the altar is he led, welcome Chief Priest at solemn rites, | Or as the Potar sits him down. || 4. Agni in fire at sacrifice, and in the house as Lord thereof, | And as a Brahman takes his seat. || 5. Thou comest as the guide of folk who celebrate a sacrifice, | And to oblations brought by men. || 6. Thou servest as his messenger whose sacrifice thou lovest well, | To bear the mortal's gifts to heaven. || 7. Accept our solemn rite; be pleased, Aṅgiras, with our sacrifice: | Give ear and listen to our call. || 8. May thine inviolable car, wherewith thou guardest those who give, | Come near to us from every side.

Hymn 4:10. Agni.

1. This day with praises, Agni, we bring thee that which thou lovest. | Right judgment, like a horse, with our devotions. || 2. For thou hast ever been the Car-driver, Agni, of noble | Strength, lofty sacrifice, and rightful judgment. || 3. Through these our praises come thou to meet us, bright as the sunlight, | O Agni, well disposed, with all thine aspects. || 4. Now may we serve thee singing these lauds this day to thee, Agni. | Loud as the voice of Heaven thy blasts are roaring. || 5. just at this time of the day and the night thy look is the sweetest. | It shineth near us even as gold for glory. || 6. Spotless thy body, brilliant as gold, like clarified butter: | This gleams like gold on thee, O Self. dependent. || 7. All hate and mischief, yea, if committed, Agni, thou turnest, | Holy One, from the man who rightly worships. || 8. Agni, with you Gods, prosperous be our friendships and kinships. | Be this our bond here by this place, thine al tar.

Hymn 4:11. Agni.

1. Thy blessed majesty, victorious Agni, shines brightly in the neighbourhood of Sūrya. | Splendid to see, it shows even at night-time, and food is fair to look on in thy beauty. || 2. Agni, disclose his thought for him who singeth, the well, Strong God! while thou art praised with fervour. | Vouchsafe to us that powerful hymn, O Mighty, which, Radiant One! with all the Gods thou lovest. || 3. From thee, O Agni, springs poetic wisdom, from thee come thoughts and hymns of praise that prosper; | From thee flows wealth, with heroes to adorn it, to the true-hearted man who gives oblation. || 4. From thee the hero springs who wins the booty, bringer of help, mighty, of real courage. | From thee comes wealth, sent by the Gods, bliss-giving; Agni, from thee the fleet impetuous charger. || 5. Immortal Agni, thee whose voice is pleasant, as first in rank, as God, religious mortals | Invite with hymns; thee who removest hatred, Friend of the Home, the household's Lord, unerring. || 6. Far from us thou removest want and sorrow, far from us all ill-will when thou protectest. | Son of Strength, Agni, blest is he at evening, whom thou as God attendest for his welfare.

Hymn 4:12. Agni.

1. Whoso enkindles thee, with lifted ladle, and thrice this day offers thee food, O Agni, | May he excel, triumphant through thy splendours, wise through thy mental power, O Jātavedas. || 2. Whoso with toil and trouble brings thee fuel, serving the majesty of mighty Agni, | He, kindling thee at evening and at morning, prospers, and comes to wealth, and slays his foemen. || 3. Agni is Master of sublime dominion, Agni is Lord of strength and lofty riches. | Straightway the self-reliant God, Most Youthful, gives treasures to the mortal who adores him. || 4. Most Youthful God, whatever sin, through folly, we here, as human beings, have committed, | In sight of Aditi make thou us sinless remit, entirely, Agni, our offences. || 5. Even in the presence of great sin, O Agni, free us from prison of the Gods or mortals. | Never may we who are thy friends be injured: grant health and strength unto our seed and offspring. || 6. Even as ye here, Gods Excellent and Holy, have loosed the cow that by the foot was tethered, | So also set us free from this affliction long let our life, O Agni, be extended.

Hymn 4:13. Agni.

1. Agni hath looked, benevolently-minded, on the wealth-giving spring of radiant Mornings. | Come, Aśvins, to the dwelling of the pious: Sūrya the God is rising with his splendour. || 2. Savitar, God, hath spread on high his lustre, waving his flag like a spoil-seeking hero. | Their established way go Varuṇa and Mitra, what time they make the Sun ascend the heaven. || 3. Him whom they made to drive away the darkness, Lords of sure mansions, constant to their object, | Him who beholds the universe, the Sun-God, seven strong and youthful Coursers carry onward. || 4. Spreading thy web with mightiest Steeds thou comest, rending apart, thou God, the black-hued mantle. | The rays of Sūrya tremulously shining sink, like a hide, the darkness in the waters. || 5. How is it that, unbound and not supported, he falleth not although directed downward? | By what self power moves he? Who liath seen it? He guards the vault of heaven, a close-set pillar.

Hymn 4:14. Agni.

1. The God hath looked, even Agni Jātavedas, to meet the Dawns refulgent in their glories. | Come on your chariot, ye who travel widely, come to this sacrifice of ours, Nāsatyas. || 2. Producing light for all the world of creatures, God Savitar hath raised aloft his banner. | Making his presence known by sunbeams, Sūrya hath filled the firmament and earth and heaven. || 3. Red Dawn is come, riding with brightness onward, distinguished by her beams, gay-hued and mighty. | Dawn on her nobly-harnessed car, the Goddess, awaking men to happiness, approacheth. || 4. May those most powerful steeds and chariot bring you, O Aśvins, hither at the break of morning. | Here for your draught of meath are Soma juices: at this our sacrifice rejoice, ye Mighty. || 5. How is it that, unbound and unsupported, he falleth not although directed downward? | By what self-power moves he? Who hath seen it? He guards the vault of heaven, a close-set pillar?

Hymn 4:15. Agni.

1. Agni the Herald, like a horse, is led forth at our solemn rite, | God among Gods adorable. || 2. Three times unto our solemn rite comes Agni like a charioteer, | Bearing the viands to the Gods. || 3. Round the oblations hath he paced, Agni the Wise, the Lord of Strength, | Giving the offerer precious boons. || 4. He who is kindled eastward for Sṛñjaya, Devavāta's son, | Resplendent, tamer of the foe. || 5. So mighty be the Agni whom the mortal hero shall command, | With sharpened teeth and bountiful. || 6. Day after day they dress him, as they clean a horse who wins the prize. | Dress the red Scion of the Sky. || 7. When Sahadeva's princely son with two bay horses thought of me, | Summoned by him I drew not back. || 8. And truly those two noble bays I straightway took when offered me, | From Sahadeva's princely son. || 9. Long, O ye Aśvins, may he live, your care, ye Gods, the princely son. | Of Sahadeva, Somaka. || 10. Cause him the youthful prince, the son of Sahadeva, to enjoy | Long life, O Aśvins, O ye Gods.

Hymn 4:16. Indra.

1. Impetuous, true, let Maghavan come hither, and let his Tawny Coursers speed to reach us. | For him have we pressed juice exceeding potent: here, praised with song, let him effect his visit. || 2. Unyoke, as at thy journey's end, O Hero, to gladden thee today at this libation. | Like Uśanā, the priest a laud shall utter, a hymn to thee, the Lord Divine, who markest. || 3. When the Bull, quaffing, praises our libation, as a sage paying holy rites in secret, | Seven singers here from heaven hath he begotten, who e'en by day have wrought their works while singing. || 4. When heaven's fair light by hymns was made apparent (they made great splendour shine at break of morning), | He with his succour, best of Heroes, scattered the blinding darkness so that men saw clearly. || 5. Indra, Impetuous One, hath waxed immensely: he with his vastness hath filled earth and heaven. | E'en beyond this his majesty extendeth who hath exceeded all the worlds in greatness. || 6. Śakra who knoweth well all human actions hath with his eager Friends let loose the waters. | They with their songs cleft e'en the mountain open and willingly disclosed the stall of cattle. || 7. He smote away the floods' obstructer, Vṛtra; Earth, conscious, lent her aid to speed thy thunder. | Thou sentest forth the waters of the ocean, as Lord through power and might, O daring Hero. || 8. When, Much-invoked! the water's rock thou cleftest, Saramā showed herself and went before thee. | Hymned by Aṅgirasas, bursting the cow-stalls, much strength thou foundest for us as our leader. || 9. Come, Maghavan, Friend of Man, to aid the singer imploring thee in battle for the sunlight. | Speed him with help in his inspired invokings: down sink the sorcerer, the prayerless Dasyu. || 10.

Come to our home resolved to slay the Dasyu: Kutsa longed eagerly to win thy friendship. | Alike in form ye both sate in his dwelling the faithful Lady was in doubt between you. || 11. Thou comest, fain to succour him, with Kutsa,—a goad that masters both the Wind-God's horses, | That, holding the brown steeds like spoil for capture, the sage may on the final day be present. || 12. For Kutsa, with thy thousand, thou at day-break didst hurl down greedy Śuṣhṇa, foe of harvest. | Quickly with Kutsa's friend destroy the Dasyus, and roll the chariot-wheel of Sūrya near us. || 13. Thou to the son of Vidathin, Ṛijiśvan, gavest up mighty Mṛigaya and Pipru. | Thou smotest down the swarthy fifty thousand, and rentest forts as age consumes a garment. || 14. What time thou settest near the Sun thy body, thy form, Immortal One, is seen expanding: | Thou a wild elephant with might invested. like a dread lion as thou wieldest weapons. || 15. Wishes for wealth have gone to Indra, longing for him in war for light and at libation, | Eager for glory, labouring with praise songs: he is like home, like sweet and fair nutrition. || 16. Call we for you that Indra, prompt to listen, him who hath done so much for men's advantage; | Who, Lord of envied bounty, to a singer like me brings quickly booty worth the capture. || 17. When the sharp-pointed arrow, O thou Hero, flieth mid any conflict of the people, | When, Faithful One, the dread encounter cometh, then be thou the Protector of our body. || 18. Further the holy thoughts of Vāmadeva be thou a guileless Friend in fight for booty. | We come to thee whose providence protects us: wide be thy sway for ever for thy singer. || 19. O Indra, with these men who love thee truly, free givers, Maghavan, in every battle, | May we rejoice through many autumns, quelling our foes, as days subdue the nights with splendour. || 20. Now, as the Bhṛigus wrought a car, for Indra the Strong, the Mighty, we our prayer have fashioned, | That he may, ne'er withdraw from us his friendship, but be our bodies' guard and strong defender. || 21. Now, Indra! lauded, glorified with praises, let power swell. high like rivers for the singer. | For thee a new hymn, Lord of Bays, is fashioned. May we, car-borne, through song be victors ever.

Hymn 4:17. Indra.

1. Great art thou, Indra; yea, the earth, with gladness, and heaven confess to thee thine high dominion. | Thou in thy vigour having slaughtered Vṛitra didst free the floods arrested by the Dragon. || 2. Heaven trembled at the birth of thine effulgence; Earth trembled at the fear of thy displeasure. | The steadfast mountains shook in agitation, the waters flowed, and desert spots were flooded. || 3. Hurling his bolt with might he cleft the mountain, while, putting forth his strength, he showed his vigour. | He slaughtered Vṛitra with his bolt, exulting, and, their lord slain, forth flowed the waters swiftly. || 4. Thy Father Dyaus esteemed himself a hero: most noble was the work of Indra's Maker, | His who begat the strong bolt's Lord who roareth, immovable like earth from her foundation. || 5. He who alone o'erthrows the world of creatures, Indra the peoples' King, invoked of many— | Verily all rejoice in him, extolling the boons which Maghavan the God hath sent them. || 6. All Soma juices are his own for ever, most gladdening draughts are ever his, the Mighty, | Thou ever wast the Treasure-Lord of treasures: Indra, thou lettest all folk share thy bounty. || 7. Moreover, when thou first wast born, O Indra, thou struckest terror into all the people. | Thou, Maghavan, rentest with thy bolt the Dragon who lay against the water-floods of heaven. || 8. The ever-slaying, bold and furious Indra, the bright bolt's Lord, infinite, strong and mighty, | Who slayeth Vṛitra and acquireth booty, giver of blessings, Maghavan the bounteous: || 9. Alone renowned as Maghavan in battles, he frighteneth away assembled armies. | He bringeth us the booty that he winneth may we, well-loved, continue in his friendship. || 10. Renowned is he when conquering and when slaying: 'tis he who winneth cattle in the combat. | When Indra hardeneth his indignation all that is fixed and all that moveth fear him. || 11. Indra hath won all kine, all gold, all horses,—Maghavan, he who breaketh forts in pieces; | Most manly with these men of his who help him, dealing out wealth and gathering the treasure. || 12. What is the care of Indra for his Mother, what cares he for the Father who begat him? | His care is that which speeds his might in conflicts, like wind borne onward by the clouds that thunder. || 13. Maghavan makes the settled man unsettled: he scatters dust that he hath swept together, | Breaking in pieces like Heaven armed with lightning: Maghavan shall enrich the man who lauds h;m. || 14. He urged the chariot-wheel of Sūrya forward: Etaśa, speeding on his way, he rested. | Him the black undulating cloud bedeweth, in this mid-air's depth, at the base of darkness, || 15. As in the night the sacrificing priest. || 16. Eager for booty, craving strength and horses, we-singers stir Indra, the strong, for friendship, | Who gives the wives we seek, whose succour fails not, to hasten, like a pitcher to the fountain. || 17. Be thou our guardian, show thyself our kinsman, watching and blessing those who pour the Soma; | As Friend, as Sire, most fatherly of fathers giving the suppliant vital strength and freedom. || 18. Be helping Friend of those who seek thy friendship give life, when lauded, Indra, to the singer. | For, Indra, we the priests have paid thee worship, exalting thee with these our sacrifices. || 19. Alone, when Indra Maghavan is lauded, he slayeth many ne'er-resisted Vṛitras. | Him in whose keeping is the well-loved singer never do Gods or mortals stay or hinder. || 20. E en so let Maghavan, the loud-voiced Indra, give us true blessings, foeless, men's upholder. | King of all creatures, give us glory amply, exalted glory due to him who lauds thee. || 21. Now, Indra! lauded, glorified with praises, let power swell high like rivers for the singer. | For thee a new hymn, Lord of Bays! is fashioned. May we, car-borne, through song be victors ever.

Hymn 4:18. Indra and Others.

1. This is the ancient and accepted pathway by which all Gods have come into existence. | Hereby could one be born though waxen mighty. Let him not, otherwise, destroy his Mother. || 2. Not this way go I forth: hard is the passage. Forth from the side obliquely will I issue. | Much that is yet undone must I accomplish; one must I combat and the other question. || 3. He bent his eye upon the dying Mother: My word I now withdraw. That way I follow. | In Tvaṣhṭar's dwelling India drank the Soma, a hundred worth of juice pressed from the mortar. || 4. What strange act shall he do, he whom his Mother bore for a thousand months and many autumns? | No peer hath he among those born already, nor among those who shall be born hereafter. || 5. Deeming him a reproach, his mother hid him, Indra, endowed with all heroic valour. | Then up he sprang himself, assumed his vesture, and filled, as soon as born, the earth and heaven. || 6. With lively motion onward flow these waters, the Holy Ones, shouting, as 'twere, together. | Ask them to. tell thee what the floods are saying, what girdling rock the waters burst asunder. || 7. Are they addressing him with words of welcome? Will the floods take on them the shame of Indra? | With his great thunderbolt my Son hath slaughtered Vṛitra, and set these rivers free to wander. || 8. I cast thee from me, mine,—thy youthful mother: thee, mine own offspring, Kuṣhavā hath swallowed. | To him, mine infant, were the waters gracious. Indra, my Son, rose up in conquering vigour. || 9. Thou art mine own, O Maghavan, whom Vyaṃsa struck to the ground and smote thy jaws in pieces. | But, smitten through, the mastery thou wonnest, and with thy bolt the Dāsa's head thou crushedst. || 10. The Heifer hath brought forth the Strong, the Mighty, the unconquerable Bull, the furious Indra. | The Mother left her unlicked Calf to wander, seeking himself, the path that he would follow. || 11. Then to her mighty Child the Mother turned her, saying, My son, these Deities forsake thee. | Then Indra said, about to slaughter Vṛitra, O my friend Vṛitra, stride full boldly forward. || 12. Who was he then who made thy Mother widow? Who sought to stay thee lying still or moving? | What God, when by the foot thy Sire thou tookest and slewest, was at hand to give thee comfort? || 13. In deep distress I cooked a dog's intestines. Among the Gods I found not one to comfort. | My consort I beheld in degradation. The Falcon then brought me the pleasant Soma.

Hymn 4:19. Indra.

1. Thee, verily, O Thunder-wielding Indra, all the Gods here, the Helpers swift to listen, | And both the worlds elected, thee the Mighty, High, waxen strong, alone to slaughter Vṛitra. || 2. The Gods, as worn with eld, relaxed their efforts: thou, Indra, born of truth, wast Sovereign Ruler. | Thou slewest Ahi who besieged the waters, and duggest out their all-supporting channels. || 3. The insatiate one, extended, hard to waken, who slumbered in perpetual sleep, O Indra,— | The Dragon stretched against the seven prone rivers, where no joint was, thou rentest with thy thunder. || 4. Indra with might shook earth and her foundation as the wind stirs the water with its fury. | Striving, with strength he burst the firm asunder, and tore away the summits of the mountains. || 5. They ran to thee as mothers to their offspring: the clouds, like chariots, hastened forth together. | Thou

didst refresh the streams and force the billows: thou, Indra, settest free obstructed rivers. || 6. Thou for the sake of Vayya and Turvīti didst stay the great stream, flowing, all-sustaining: | Yea, at their prayer didst check the rushing river and make the floods easy to cross, O Indra. || 7. He let the young Maids skilled in Law, unwedded, like fountains, bubbling, flow forth streaming onward. | He inundated thirsty plains and deserts, and milked the dry Cows of the mighty master. || 8. Through many a morn and many a lovely autumn, having slain Vṛitra, lie set free the rivers. | Indra hath set at liberty to wander on earth the streams encompassed pressed together. || 9. Lord of Bay Steeds, thou broughtest from the ant-hill the unwedded damsel's son whom ants were eating. | The blind saw clearly, as he grasped the serpent, rose, brake the jar: his joints again united. || 10. To the wise man, O Sage and Sovereign Ruler, the man who knoweth all thine ancient exploits. | Hath told these deeds of might as thou hast wrought them, great acts, spontaneous, and to man's advantage. || 11. Now, Indra! lauded, glorified with praises, let powers swell high, like rivers, for the singer. | For thee a new hymn, Lord of Bays! is fashioned. May we, car-borne, through song be victors ever.

Hymn 4:20. Indra.

1. From near or far away may mighty Indra giver of succour, come for our protection | Lord of men, armed with thunder, with the Strongest, slaying his foes in conflict, in the battles. || 2. May Indra come to us with Tawny Coursers, inclined to us, to favour and enrich us. | May Maghavan, loud-voiced and wielding thunder, stand by us at this sacrifice, in combat. || 3. Thou, honouring this our sacrifice, O Indra, shalt give us strength and fill us full of courage. | To win the booty, Thunder-armed! like hunters may we with thee subdue in fight our foemen. || 4. Loving us well, benevolent, close beside us, drink, Godlike Indra, of the well-pressed Soma. | Drink of the meath we offer, and delight thee with food that cometh from the mountain ridges. || 5. Him who is sung aloud by recent sages, like a ripe-fruited tree, a scythe-armed victor,— | I, like a bridegroom thinking of his consort, call hither Indra, him invoked of many; || 6. Him who in native strength is like a mountain, the lofty Indra born or old for conquest, | Terrific wielder of the ancient thunder. filled full with splendour as a jar with water. || 7. Whom from of old there is not one to hinder, none to curtail the riches of his bounty. | Pouring forth freely, O thou Strong and Mighty, vouchsafe us riches, God invoked of many! || 8. Of wealth and homes of men thou art the ruler, and opener of the stable of the cattle. | Helper of men, winner of spoil in combats, thou leadest to an ample heap of riches. || 9. By what great might is he renowned as strongest, wherewith the Lofty One stirs up wild battles? | Best soother of the worshipper's great sorrow, he gives possessions to the man who lauds him. || 10. Slay us not; bring, bestow onus the ample gift which thou hast to give to him who offers. | At this new gift, with this laud sung before thee, extolling thee, we, Indra, will declare it. || 11. Now, Indra! lauded, glorified with praises, let power swell high, like rivers, for the singer. | A new hymn, Lord of Bays! for thee is fashioned. May we, car-born, through song be victors ever.

Hymn 4:21. Indra.

1. May Indra come to us for our protection; here be the Hero, praised, our feast-companion. | May he whose powers are many, waxen mighty, cherish, like Dyaus, his own supreme dominion. || 2. Here magnify his great heroic exploits, most glorious One, enriching men with bounties, | Whose will is like a Sovereign in assembly, who rules the people, Conqueror, all-surpassing. || 3. Hither let Indra come from earth or heaven, hither with speech from firmament or ocean; | With Marutas, from the realm of light to aid us, or from a distance, from the seat of Order. || 4. That Indra will we laud in our assemblies, him who is Lord of great and lasting riches, | Victor with Vāyu where the herds are gathered, who leads with boldness on to higher fortune. || 5. May the Priest, Lord of many blessings, striving,—who fixing reverence on reverence, giving | Vent to his voice, inciteth men to worship with lauds bring Indra hither to our dwellings. || 6. When sitting pondering in deep devotion in Auśija's abode they ply the press-stone, | May he whose wrath is fierce, the mighty bearer, come as the house-lord's priest within our chambers. || 7. Surely the power of Bhārvara the mighty for ever helpeth to support the singer; | That which in Auśija's abode lies hidden, to come forth for delight and for devotion. || 8. When he unbars the spaces of the mountains, and quickens with his floods the water-torrents, | He finds in lair the buffalo and wild-ox when the wise lead him on to vigorous exploit. || 9. Auspicious are thy hands, thine arms well-fashioned which proffer bounty, Indra, to thy praiser. | What sloth is this? Why dost thou not rejoice thee? Why dost thou not delight thyself with giving? || 10. So Indra is the truthful Lord of treasure. Freedom he gave to man by slaying Vṛitra. | Much-lauded! help us with thy power to riches: may I be sharer of thy Godlike favour. || 11. Now, Indra! lauded, glorified with praises, let power swell high, like rivers, for,the singer. | For thee a new hymn, Lord of Bays! is fashioned. May we, care-borne, through song be victors ever.

Hymn 4:22. Indra.

1. That gift of ours which Indra loves and welcomes, even that he makes for us, the Great and Strong One. | He who comes wielding in his might the thunder, Maghavan, gives prayer, praise, and laud, and Soma. || 2. Bull, hurler of the four-edged rain-producer with both his arms, strong, mighty, most heroic; | Wearing as wool Parushṇī for adornment, whose joints for sake of friendship he hath covered. || 3. God who of all the Gods was born divinest, endowed with ample strength and mighty powers, | And bearing in his arms the yearning thunder, with violent rush caused heaven and earth to tremble. || 4. Before the High God, at his birth, heaven trembled, earth, many floods and all the precipices. | The Strong One bringeth nigh the Bull's two Parents: loud sing the winds, like men, in air's mid-region. || 5. These are thy great deeds, Indra, thine, the Mighty, deeds to be told aloud at all libations, | That thou, O Hero, bold and boldly daring, didst with thy bolt, by strength, destroy the Dragon. || 6. True are all these thy deeds, O Most Heroic. The Milch-kine issued from the streaming udder. | In fear of thee, O thou of manly spirit, the rivers swiftly set themselves in motion. || 7. With joy, O Indra, Lord of Tawny Coursers, the Sisters then, these Goddesses, extolled thee, | When thou didst give the prisoned ones their freedom to wander at their will in long succession. || 8. Pressed is the gladdening stalk as 'twere a river: so let the rite, the toiler's power, attract thee | To us-ward, of the Bright One, as the courser strains his. exceedingly strong leather bridle. || 9. Ever by us perform thy most heroic, thine highest, best victorious deeds, O Victor. | For us make Vṛitras easy to be conquered: destroy the weapon of our mortal foeman. || 10. Graciously listen to our prayer, O Indra, and strength of varied sort bestow thou on us. | Send to us all intelligence arid wisdom O Maghavan, be he who gives us cattle. || 11. Now, Indra! lauded, glorified with praises, let wealth swell high like rivers to the singer. | For thee a new hymn, Lord of Bays, is fashioned. May we, car-borne, through song be victors ever.

Hymn 4:23. Indra.

1. How, what priest's sacrifice hath he made mighty, rejoicing in the Soma and its fountain? | Delighting in juice, eagerly drinking, the Lofty One hath waxed for splendid riches. || 2. What hero hath been made his feast-companion? Who hath been partner in his loving-kindness? | What know we of his wondrous acts? How often comes he to aid and speed the pious toiler? || 3. How heareth Indra offered invocation? How, hearing, marketh he the invoker's wishes? | What are his ancient acts of bounty? Wherefore call they him One who filleth full the singer? || 4. How doth the priest who laboureth, ever longing, win for himself the wealth which he possesseth? | May he, the God, mark well my truthful praises, having received the homage which he loveth. || 5. How, and what bond of friendship with a mortal hath the God chosen as this morn is breaking? | How, and what love hath he for those who love him, who have entwined in him their firm affection? || 6. Is then thy friendship with thy friends most mighty? Thy brotherhood with us, -when may we tell it? | The streams of milk move, as most wondrous sunlight, the beauty of the Lovely One for glory. || 7. About to stay the Indra-less destructive spirit he sharpens his keen arms to strike her. | Whereby the Strong, although our debts' exactor, drives in the distant mornings that we know not. || 8. Eternal Law hath varied food that strengthens; thought of eternal Law, removes transgressions. | The praise-hymn of eternal Law, arousing, glowing, hath opened the deaf ears of the living. || 9. Firm-seated are eternal Law's foundations in its fair form are many splendid beauties. | By holy Law long lasting food they bring us; by holy Law have cows come to our worship. || 10. Fixing eternal Law he, too, upholds it swift moves the might of Law and wins the booty. | To Law belong the vast deep Earth and Heaven: Milch-kine supreme, to Law their

milk they render. ‖ 11. Now, Indra! lauded,—glorified with praises, let power swell high like rivers to the singer. | For thee a new hymn, Lord of Bays, is fashioned. May we, car-borne, through song be victors ever.

Hymn 4:24. Indra.

1. What worthy praise will bring before us Indra, the Son of Strength, that he may grant us riches; | For he the Hero, gives the singer treasures: he is the Lord who sends us gifts, ye people. ‖ 2. To be invoked and hymned in fight with Vṛitra, that well-praised Indra gives us real bounties. | That Maghavan brings comfort in the foray to the religious man who pours libations. ‖ 3. Him, verily, the men invoke in combat; risking their lives they make him their protector, | When heroes, foe to foe, give up their bodies, fighting, each side, for children and their offspring. ‖ 4. Strong God! the folk at need put forth their vigour, striving together in the whirl of battle. | When warrior bands encounter one another some in the grapple quit themselves like Indra. ‖ 5. Hence many a one worships the might of Indra: hence let the brew succeed the meal-oblation. | Hence let the Soma banish those who pour not: even hence I joy to pay the Strong One worship. ‖ 6. Indra gives comfort to the man who truly presses, for him who longs for it, the Soma, | Not disaffected, with devoted spirit this man he takes to be his friend in battles. ‖ 7. He who this day for Indra presses Soma, prepares the brew and fries the grains of barley— | Loving the hymns of that devoted servant, to him may Indra give heroic vigour. ‖ 8. When the impetuous chief hath sought the conflict, and the lord looked upon the long-drawn battle, | The matron calls to the Strong God whom pressers of Soma have encouraged in the dwelling. ‖ 9. He bid a small price for a thing of value: I was content, returning, still unpurchased. | He heightened not his insufficient offer. Simple and clever, both milk out the udder. ‖ 10. Who for ten milch-kine purchaseth from me this Indra who is mine? | When he hath slain the Vṛitras let the buyer give him back to me. ‖ 11. Now, Indra! lauded, glorified with praises, let wealth swell high like rivers for the singer. | For thee a new hymn, Lord of Bays, is fashioned. May we, car-borne, through song be victors ever.

Hymn 4:25. Indra.

1. What friend of man, God-loving, hath delighted, yearning therefore, this day in Indra's friendship? | Who with enkindled flame and flowing Soma laudeth him for his great protecting favour? ‖ 2. Who hath with prayer bowed to the Soma-lover? What pious man endues the beams of morning? | Who seeks bond, friendship, brotherhood with Indra? Who hath recourse unto the Sage for succour? ‖ 3. Who claims today the Deities' protection, asks Aditi for light, or the Ādityas? | Of whose pressed stalk of Soma drink the Aśvins, Indra, and Agni, well-inclined in spirit? ‖ 4. To him shall Agni Bhārata give shelter: long shall he look upon the Sun uprising, | Who sayeth, Let us press the juice for Indra, man's Friend, the Hero manliest of heroes. ‖ 5. Him neither few men overcome, nor many to him shall Aditi give spacious shelter. | Dear is the pious, the devout, to Indra dear is the zealous, dear the Soma-bringer. ‖ 6. This Hero curbs the mighty for the zealous: the presser's brew Indra possesses solely: | No brother, kin, or friend to him who pours not, destroyer of the dumb who would resist him. ‖ 7. Not with the wealthy churl who pours no Soma doth Indra, Soma-drinker, bind alliance. | He draws away his wealth and slays him naked, own Friend to him who offers, for oblation. ‖ 8. Highest and lowest, men who stand between diem, going, returning, dwelling in contentment, | Those who show forth their strength when urged to battle-these are the men who call for aid on Indra.

Hymn 4:26. Indra.

1. I was aforetime Manu, I was Sūrya: I am the sage Kakṣhīvant, holy singer. | Kutsa the son of Ārjuni I master. I am the sapient Uśanā behold me. ‖ 2. I have bestowed the earth upon the Ārya, and rain upon the man who brings oblation. | I guided forth the loudly-roaring waters, and the Gods moved according to my pleasure. ‖ 3. In the wild joy of Soma I demolished Śambara's forts, ninety-and-nine, together; | And, utterly, the hundredth habitation, when helping Divodāsa Atithigva. ‖ 4. Before all birds be ranked this Bird, O Marutas; supreme of falcons be this fleet-winged Falcon, | Because, strong—pinioned, with no car to bear him, he brought to Manu the God-loved oblation. ‖ 5. When the Bird brought it, hence in rapid motion sent on the wide path fleet as thought he hurried. | Swift he returned with sweetness of the Soma, and hence the Falcon hath acquired his glory. ‖ 6. Bearing the stalk, the Falcon speeding onward, Bird bringing from afar the draught that gladdens, | Friend of the Gods, brought, grasping fast, the Soma which be bad taken from yon loftiest heaven. ‖ 7. The Falcon took and brought the Soma, bearing thousand libations with him, yea, ten thousand. | The Bold One left Malignities behind him, wise, in wild joy of Soma, left the foolish.

Hymn 4:27. The Falcon.

1. I, As I lay within the womb, considered all generations of these Gods in order. | A hundred iron fortresses confined me but forth I flew with rapid speed a Falcon. ‖ 2. Not at his own free pleasure did he bear me: he conquered with his strength and manly courage. | Straightway the Bold One left the fiends behind him and passed the winds as he grew yet more mighty. ‖ 3. When with loud cry from heaven down sped the Falcon, thence hasting like the wind he bore the Bold One. | Then, wildly raging in his mind, the archer Kṛiśānu aimed and loosed the string to strike him. ‖ 4. The Falcon bore him from heaven's lofty summit as the swift car of Indra's Friend bore Bhujyu. | Then downward hither fell a flying feather of the Bird hasting forward in his journey. ‖ 5. And now let Maghavan accept the beaker, white, filled with milk, filled with the shining liquid; | The best of sweet meath which the priests have offered: that Indra to his joy may drink, the Hero, that he may take and drink it to his rapture.

Hymn 4:28. Indra-Soma.

1. Allied with thee, in this thy friendship, Soma, Indra for man made waters flow together, | Slew Ahi, and sent forth the Seven Rivers, and opened as it were obstructed fountains. ‖ 2. Indu, with thee for his confederate, Indra swiftly with might pressed down the wheel of Sūrya. | What rolled, all life's support, on heaven's high summit was separated from the great oppressor. ‖ 3. Indra smote down, Agni consumed, O Indu, the Dasyus ere the noontide in the conflict. | Of those who gladly sought a hard-won dwelling he cast down many a thousand with his arrow. ‖ 4. Lower than all besides hast thou, O Indra, cast down the Dasyus, abject tribes of Dāsas. | Ye drave away, ye put to death the foemen, and took great vengeance with your murdering weapons. ‖ 5. So, of a truth, Indra and Soma, Heroes, ye burst the stable of the kine and horses, | The stable which the bar or stone obstructed; and piercing through set free the habitations.

Hymn 4:29. Indra.

1. Come, lauded, unto us with powers and succours, O Indra, with thy Tawny Steeds; exulting, | Past even the foeman's manifold libations, glorified with our hymns, true Wealth-bestower. ‖ 2. Man's Friend, to this our sacrifice he cometh marking how he is called by Soma-pressers. | Fearless, and conscious that his Steeds are noble, he joyeth with the Soma-pouring heroes. ‖ 3. Make his cars hear, that he may show his vigour and may be joyful in the way he loveth. | May mighty Indra pouring forth in bounty bestow on us good roads and perfect safety; ‖ 4. He who with succour comes to his implorer, the singer here who with his song invites him; | He who himself sets to the pole swift Coursers, he who hath hundreds, thousands, Thunder-wielder. ‖ 5. O Indra Maghavan, by thee protected may we be thine, princes and priests and singers, | Sharing the riches sent from lofty heaven which yields much food, and all desire its bounty.

Hymn 4:30. Indra.

1. O Indra, Vṛitra-slayer, none is better, mightier than thou: | Verily there is none like thee. ‖ 2. Like chariot-wheels these people all together follow after thee: | Thou ever art renowned as Great. ‖ 3. Not even all the gathered Gods conquered thee, Indra, in the war, | When thou didst lengthen days by night. ‖ 4. When for the sake of those oppressed, and Kutsa as he battled, | Thou stolest away the Sun's car-wheel. ‖ 5. When, fighting singly, Indra. thou o'ercamest all the furious Gods, thou slewest those who strove with thee. ‖ 6. When also for a mortal man, Indra, thou speddest forth the Sun, | And holpest Etaśa with might. ‖ 7. What? Vṛitra-slayer, art not thou, Maghavan, fiercest in thy wrath? | So hast thou quelled the demon too. ‖ 8. And this heroic deed of might thou, Indra, also hast achieved, | That thou didst smite to death the Dame, Heaven's Daughter, meditating ill. ‖ 9. Thou, Indra, Mighty One, didst crush Uṣhas, though Daughter of the Sky. | When lifting up herself in pride. ‖ 10. Then from her chariot Uṣhas fled, affrighted, from her ruined car. | When the strong God had shattered it. ‖ 11. So there this car of Uṣhas lay, broken to pieces, in Vipāś, | And she herself

fled far away. || 12. Thou, Indra, didst. with magic power resist the overflowing stream | Who spread her waters o'er the land. || 13. Valiantly didst thou seize and take the store which Śushṇa had amassed, | When thou didst crush his fortresses. || 14. Thou, Indra, also smotest down Kulitara's son Śambara, | The Dāsa, from the lofty hill. || 15. Of Dāsa Varchin's thou didst slay the hundred thousand and the five, | Crushed like the fellies, of a car. || 16. So Indra, Lord of Heroes, Powers, caused the unwedded damsel's son, | The castaway, to share the lauds. || 17. So sapient Indra, Lord of Might, brought Turvaśa and Yadu, those | Who feared the flood, in safety o'er. || 18. Arṇa and Chitraratha, both Āryas, thou, Indra, slewest swift, | On yonder side of Sarayu, || 19. Thou, Vṛitra-slayer, didst conduct those two forlorn, the blind, the lame. | None may attain this bliss of thine. || 20. For Divodāsa, him who brought oblation, Indra overthrew | A hundred fortresses of stone. || 21. The thirty thousand Dāsas he with magic power and weapons sent | To slumber, for Dabhīti's sake. || 22. As such, O Vṛitra-slayer, thou art general Lord of kine for all, | Thou Shaker of all things that be. || 23. Indra, whatever deed of might thou hast this day to execute, | None be there now to hinder it. || 24. O Watchful One, may Aryaman the God give thee all goodly things. | May Pūshan, Bhaga, and the God Karūḷatī give all things fair.

Hymn 4:31. Indra.

1. With what help will he come to us, wonderful, ever-waxing Friend; | With what most mighty company? || 2. What genuine and most liberal draught will spirit thee with juice to burst | Open e'en strongly-guarded wealth? || 3. Do thou who art Protector of us thy friends who praise thee | With hundred aids approach us. || 4. Like as a courser's circling wheel, so turn thee hitherward to us, | Attracted by the hymns of men. || 5. Thou seekest as it were thine own stations with swift descent of powers: | I share thee even with the Sun. || 6. What time thy courage and his wheels together, Indra, run their course | With thee and with the Sun alike, || 7. So even, Lord of Power and Might, the people call thee Maghavan, | Giver, who pauses not to think. || 8. And verily to him who toils and presses Soma juice for thee | Thou quickly givest ample wealth. || 9. No, not a hundred hinderers can check thy gracious bounty's flow, | Nor thy great deeds when thou wilt act. || 10. May thine assistance keep us safe, thy hundred and thy thousand aids: | May all thy favours strengthen us. || 11. Do thou elect us this place for friendship and prosperity, | And great celestial opulence. || 12. Favour us, Indra, evermore with overflowing store of wealth: | With all thy succours aid thou us. || 13. With new protections, Indra, like an archer, open thou for us | The stables that are filled with kine. || 14. Our chariot, Indra, boldly moves endued with splendour, ne'er repulsed, | Winning for us both kine and steeds. || 15. O Sūrya, make our fame to be most excellent among the Gods, | Most lofty as the heaven on high.

Hymn 4:32. Indra.

1. O thou who slewest Vṛitra, come, O Indra, hither to our side, | Mighty One with thy mighty aids. || 2. Swift and impetuous art thou, wondrous amid the well-dressed folk: | Thou doest marvels for our help. || 3. Even with the weak thou smitest down him | who is stronger, with thy strength | The mighty, with the Friends thou hast. || 4. O Indra, we are close to thee; to thee we sing aloud our songs: | Help and defend us, even us. || 5. As such, O Caster of the Stone, come with thy succours wonderful, | Blameless, and irresistible. || 6. May we be friends of one like thee, O Indra, with the wealth of kine, | Comrades for lively energy. || 7. For thou, O Indra, art alone the Lord of strength that comes from kine | So grant thou us abundant food. || 8. They turn thee not another way, when, lauded, Lover of the Song, | Thou wilt give wealth to those who praise. || 9. The Gotamas have sung their song of praise to thee that thou mayst give, | Indra, for lively energy. || 10. We will declare thy hero deeds, what Dāsa forts thou brakest down, | Attacking them in rapturous joy. || 11. The sages sing those manly deeds which, Indra, Lover of the Song, | Thou wroughtest when the Soma flowed. || 12. Indra, the Gotamas who bring thee praises have grown strong by thee. | Give them renown with hero sons. || 13. For, Indra, verily thou art the general treasure even of all. | Thee, therefore, do we invocate. || 14. Excellent Indra, turn to us: glad thee among us with the juice | Of Somas, Soma-drinker thou. || 15. May praise from us who think on thee, O Indra, bring thee near to us. | Turn thy two Bay Steeds hitherward. || 16. Eat of our sacrificial cake: rejoice thee in the songs we sing. | Even as a lover in his bride. || 17. To India for a thousand steeds well-trained and fleet of foot we pray, | And hundred jars of Soma juice. || 18. We make a hundred of thy kine, yea, and a thousand, hasten nigh: | So let thy bounty come to us. || 19. We have obtained, a gift from thee, ten water-ewers wrought of gold: | Thou, Vṛitra-slayer, givest much. || 20. A bounteous Giver, give us much, bring much and not a trifling gift: | Much, Indra, wilt thou fain bestow. || 21. O Vṛitra-slayer, thou art famed in many a place as bountiful | Hero, thy bounty let us share. || 22. I praise thy pair of Tawny Steeds, wise Son of him who giveth kine | Terrify not the cows with these. || 23. Like two slight images of girls, unrobed, upon a new-wrought post, | So shine the Bay Steeds in their course. || 24. For me the Bays are ready when I start, or start not, with the dawn, Innocuous in the ways they take.

Hymn 4:33. Ṛibhus.

1. I send my voice as herald to the Ṛibhus; I crave the white cow for the overspreading. | Wind-sped, the Skillful Ones in rapid motion have in an instant compassed round the heaven. || 2. What time the Ṛibhus had with care and marvels done proper service to assist their Parents, | They won the friendship of the Gods; the Sages carried away the fruit of their devotion. || 3. May they who made their Parents, who were lying like posts that moulder, young again for ever,— | May Vāja, Vibhvan, Ṛibhu, joined with Indra, protect our sacrifice, the Soma-lovers. || 4. As for a year the Ṛibhus kept the Milch-cow, throughout a year fashioned and formed her body, | And through a year's space still sustained her brightness, through these their labours they were made immortal. || 5. Two beakers let us make,— thus said the eldest. Let us make three,—this was the younger's sentence. | Four beakers let us make,—thus spoke the youngest. Tvashṭar approved this rede of yours, O Ṛibhus. || 6. The men spake truth and even so they acted: this Godlike way of theirs the Ṛibhus followed. | And Tvashṭar, when he looked on the four beakers resplendent as the day, was moved with envy. || 7. When for twelve days the Ṛibhus joyed reposing as guests of him who never may be hidden, | They made fair fertile fields, they brought the rivers. Plants spread o'er deserts, waters filled the hollows. || 8. May they who formed the swift car, bearing Heroes, and the Cow omniform and all-impelling, | Even may they form wealth for us,—the Ṛibhus, dexterous-handed, deft in work and gracious. || 9. So in their work the Gods had satisfaction, pondering it with thought and mental insight. | The Gods' expert artificer was Vāja, Indra's Ṛibhukshan, Varuṇa's was Vibhvan. || 10. They who, made glad with sacrifice and praises, wrought the two Bays, his docile Steeds, for Indra,— | Ṛibhus, as those who wish a friend to prosper, bestow upon us gear and growth of riches. || 11. This day have they set gladdening drink before you. Not without toil are Gods inclined to friendship. | Therefore do ye who are so great, O Ṛibhus, vouchsafe us treasures at this third libation.

Hymn 4:34. Ṛibhus.

1. To this our sacrifice come Ṛibhu, Vibhvan, Vāja, and Indra with the gift of riches, | Because this day hath Dhishaṇā the Goddess set drink for you: the gladdening draughts have reached you. || 2. Knowing your birth and rich in gathered treasure, Ṛibhus, rejoice together with the Ṛitus. | The gladdening draughts and wisdom have approached you: send ye us riches with good store of heroes. || 3. For you was made this sacrifice, O Ṛibhus, which ye, like men, won for yourselves aforetime. | To you come all who find in you their pleasure: ye all were-even the two elder-Vājas. || 4. Now for the mortal worshipper, O Heroes, for him who served you, was the gift of riches. | Drink, Vājas, Ṛibhus! unto you is offered, to gladden you, the third and great libation. || 5. Come to us, Heroes, Vājas and Ṛibhukshans, glorified for the sake of mighty treasure. | These draughts approach you as the day is closing, as cows, whose calves are newly-born, their stable. || 6. Come to this sacrifice of ours, ye Children of Strength, invoked with humble adoration. | Drink of this meath, Wealth-givers, joined with Indra with whom ye are in full accord, ye Princes. || 7. Close knit with Varuṇa drink the Soma, Indra; close-knit, hymn-lover! with the Marutas drink it: | Close-knit with drinkers first, who drink in season; close-knit with heavenly Dames who give us treasures. || 8. Rejoice in full accord with the Ādityas, in concord with the Parvatas, O Ṛibhus; | In full accord with Savitar, Divine One; in full accord with floods that pour forth riches. || 9. Ṛibhus, who helped their Parents and the Aśvins, who formed the Milch-cow and the pair of horses, | Made armour, set the heaven and earth

asunder,—far-reaching Heroes, they have made good offspring. || 10. Ye who have wealth in cattle and in booty, in heroes, in rich sustenance and treasure, | Such, O ye Ṛibhus, first to drink, rejoicing, give unto us and those who laud our present. || 11. Ye were not far: we have not left you thirsting, blameless in this our sacrifice, O Ṛibhus. | Rejoice you with the Marutas and with Indra, with the Kings, Gods! that ye may give us riches.

Hymn 4:35. Ṛibhus.

1. Come hither, O ye Sons of Strength, ye Ṛibhus; stay not afar, ye Children of Sudhanvan. | At this libation is your gift of treasure. Let gladdening draughts approach you after Indra's. || 2. Hither is come the Ṛibhus' gift of riches; here was the drinking of the well-pressed Soma, | Since by dexterity and skill as craftsmen ye made the single chalice to be fourfold || 3. Ye made fourfold the chalice that wag single: ye spake these words and said, O Friend, assist us; | Then, Vājas! gained the path of life eternal, deft-handed Ṛibhus, to the Gods' assembly. || 4. Out of what substance was that chalice fashioned which ye made fourfold by your art and wisdom? | Now for the gladdening draught press out the liquor, and drink, O Ṛibhus, of die meath of Soma. || 5. Ye with your cunning made your Parents youthful; the cup, for Gods to drink, ye formed with cunning; | With cunning, Ṛibhus, rich in treasure, fashioned the two swift Tawny Steeds who carry Indra. || 6. Whoso pours out for you, when days are closing, the sharp libation for your joy, O Vājas, | For him, O mighty Ṛibhus, ye, rejoicing, have fashioned wealth with plenteous store of heroes. || 7. Lord of Bay Steeds, at dawn the juice thou drankest: thine, only thine, is the noonday libation. | Now drink thou with the wealth-bestowing Ṛibhus, whom for their skill thou madest friends, O Indra. || 8. Ye, whom your artist skill hath raised to Godhead have set you down above in heaven like falcons. | So give us riches, Children of Sudhanvan, O Sons of Strength; ye have become immortal. || 9. The third libation, that bestoweth treasure, which ye have won by skill, ye dexterous-handed,— | This drink hath been effused for you, O Ṛibhus, drink it with high delight, with joy like Indra's.

Hymn 4:36. Ṛibhus.

1. This car that was not made for horses or for reins, three-wheeled, worthy of lauds, rolls round the firmament. | That is the great announcement of your Deity, that, O ye Ṛibhus, ye sustain the earth and heaven. || 2. Ye Sapient Ones who made the lightly-rolling car out of your mind, by thought, the car that never errs, | You, being such, to drink of this drink-offering, you, O ye Vājas, and ye Ṛibhus, we invoke. || 3. O Vājas, Ṛibhus, reaching far, among the Gods this was your exaltation gloriously declared, | In that your aged Parents, worn with length of days, ye wrought again to youth so that they moved at will. || 4. The chalice that wag single ye have made fourfold, and by your wisdom brought the Cow forth from the hide. | So quickly, mid the Gods, ye gained immortal life. Vājas and Ṛibhus, your great work must be extolled. || 5. Wealth from the Ṛibhus is most glorious in renown, that which the Heroes, famed for vigour, have produced. | In synods must be sung the car which Vibhvan wrought: that which ye favour, Gods! is famed among mankind. || 6. Strong is the steed, the man a sage in eloquence, the bowman is a hero hard to beat in fight, | Great store of wealth and manly power hath he obtained whom Vāja, Vibhvan, Ṛibhus have looked kindly on. || 7. To you hath been assigned the fairest ornament, the hymn of praise: Vājas and Ṛibhus, joy therein; | For ye have lore and wisdom and poetic skill: as such, with this our prayer we call on you to come. || 8. According to the wishes of our hearts may ye, who have full knowledge of all the delights of men, | Fashion for us, O Ṛibhus, power and splendid wealth, rich in high courage, excellent, and vital strength. || 9. Bestowing on us here riches and offspring, here fashion fame for us befitting heroes. | Vouchsafe us wealth of splendid sort, O Ṛibhus, that we may make us more renowned than others.

Hymn 4:37. Ṛibhus.

1. Come to our sacrifice, Vājas, Ṛibhukṣhans, Gods, by the paths which Gods are wont to travel, | As ye, gay Gods, accept in splendid weather the sacrifice among these folk of Manus. || 2. May these rites please you in your heart and spirit; may the drops clothed in oil this day approach you. | May the abundant juices bear you onward to power and strength, and, when imbibed, delight you. || 3. Your threefold going near is God-appointed, so praise is given you, Vājas and Ṛibhukṣhans. | So, Manus-like, mid younger folk I offer, to you who are aloft in heaven, the Soma. || 4. Strong, with fair chains of gold and jaws of iron, ye have a splendid car and well-fed horses. | Ye Sons of Strength, ye progeny of Indra, to you the best is offered to delight you. || 5. Ṛibhukṣhans! him, for handy wealth, the mightiest comrade in the fight, | Him, Indra's equal, we invoke, most bounteous ever, rich in steeds. || 6. The mortal man whom, Ṛibhus, ye and Indra favour with your help, | Must be successful, by his thoughts, at sacrifice and with the steed. || 7. O Vājas and Ṛibhukṣhans, free for us the paths to sacrifice, | Ye Princes, lauded, that we may press forward to each point of heaven. || 8. O Vājas and Ṛibhukṣhans, ye Nāsatyas, Indra, bless this wealth, | And, before other men's, the steed, that ample riches may be won.

Hymn 4:38. Dadhikrās.

1. From you two came the gifts in days aforetime which Trasadasyu granted to the Pūrus. | Ye gave the winner of our fields and plough-lands, and the strong smiter who subdued the Dasyus. || 2. And ye gave mighty Dadhikrās, the giver of many gifts, who visiteth all people, | Impetuous hawk, swift and of varied colour, like a brave King whom each true man must honour. || 3. Whom, as 'twere down a precipice, swift rushing, each Pūru praises and his heart rejoices,— | Springing forth like a hero fain for battle, whirling the car and flying like the tempest. || 4. Who gaineth precious booty in the combats and moveth, winning spoil, among the cattle; | Shown in bright colour, looking on the assemblies, beyond the churl, to worship of the living. || 5. Loudly the folk cry after him in battles, as 'twere a thief who steals away a garment; | Speeding to glory, or a herd of cattle, even as a hungry falcon swooping downward. || 6. And, fain to come forth first amid these armies, this way and that with rows of cars he rushes, | Gay like a bridesman, making him a garland, tossing the dust, champing the rein that holds him. || 7. And that strong Steed, victorious and faithful, obedient with his body in the combat, | Speeding straight on amid the swiftly pressing, casts o'er his brows the dust he tosses upward. || 8. And at his thunder, like the roar of heaven, those who attack tremble and are affrighted; | For when he fights against embattled thousands, dread is he in his striving; none may stay him. || 9. The people praise the overpowering swiftness of this fleet Steed who giveth men abundance. | Of him they say when drawing back from battle. Dadhikrās hath sped forward with his thousands. || 10. Dadhikrās hath o'erspread the Fivefold People with vigour, as the Sun lightens the waters. | May the strong Steed who winneth hundreds, thousands, requite with sweetness these my words and praises.

Hymn 4:39. Dadhikrās.

1. Now give we praise to Dadhikrās the rapid, and mention in our laud the Earth and Heaven. | May the Dawns flushing move me to exertion, and bear me safely over every trouble. || 2. I praise the mighty Steed who fills my spirit, the Stallion Dadhikrāvan rich in bounties, | Whom, swift of foot and shining bright as Agni, ye, Varuṇa and Mitra, gave to Pūrus. || 3. Him who hath honoured, when the flame is kindled at break of dawn, the Courser Dadhikrāvan, | Him, of one mind with Varuṇa and Mitra may Aditi make free from all transgression. || 4. When we remember mighty Dadhikrāvan our food and strength, then the blest name of Marutas, | Varuṇa, Mitra, we invoke for welfare, and Agni, and the thunder-wielding Indra. || 5. Both sides invoke him as they call on Indra when they stir forth and turn to sacrificing. | To us have Varuṇa and Mitra granted the Courser Dadhikrās, a guide for mortals. || 6. So have I glorified with praise strong Dadhikrāvan, conquering Steed. | Sweet may he make our mouths; may he prolong the days we have to live.

Hymn 4:40. Dadhikrāvan.

1. Let us recite the praise of Dadhikrāvan: may all the Mornings move me to exertion; | Praise of the Lord of Waters, Dawn, and Agni, Bṛihaspati Son of Aṅgiras, and Sūrya. || 2. Brave, seeking war and booty, dwelling with the good and with the swift, may he hasten the food of Dawn. | May he the true, the fleet, the lover of the course, the bird-like Dadhikrāvan, bring food, strength, and light. || 3. His pinion, rapid runner, fans him m his way, as of a bird that hastens onward to its aim, | And, as it were a falcon's gliding through the air, strikes Dadhikrāvan's side as he speeds on with might. || 4. Bound by the neck and by the flanks and by the mouth, the vigorous Courser lends new swiftness to his speed. | Drawing himself together, as his strength allows, Dadhikrās springs along the windings of the paths. || 5. The Haṃsa homed in light, the Vasu in mid-air, the priest

beside the altar, in the house the guest, | Dweller in noblest place, mid men, in truth, in sky, born of flood, kine, truth, mountain, he is holy Law.

Hymn 4:41. Indra-Varuṇa.

1. What laud, O Indra-Varuṇa, with oblation, hath like the Immortal Priest obtained your favour? | Hath our effectual laud, addressed with homage, touched you, O Indra-Varuṇa, in spirit? || 2. He who with dainty food hath won you, Indra and Varuṇa, Gods, as his allies to friendship, | Slayeth the Vṛitras and his foes in battles, and through your mighty favours is made famous. || 3. Indra and Varuṇa are most liberal givers of treasure to the men who toil to serve them, | When they, as Friends inclined to friendship, honoured with dainty food, delight in flowing Soma. || 4. Indra and Varuṇa, ye hurl, O Mighty, on him your strongest flashing bolt of thunder | Who treats us ill, the robber and oppressor: measure on him your overwhelming vigour. || 5. O Indra-Varuṇa, be ye the lovers of this my song, as steers who love the milch-Cow. | Milk may it yield us as, gone forth to pasture, the great Cow pouring out her thousand rivers. || 6. For fertile fields, for worthy sons and grandsons, for the Sun's beauty and for steer-like vigour, | May Indra-Varuṇa with gracious favours work marvels for us in the stress of battle. || 7. For you, as Princes, for your ancient kindness, good comrades of the man who seeks for booty, | We choose to us for the dear bond of friendship, most liberal Heroes bringing bliss like parents. || 8. Showing their strength, these hymns for grace, Free-givers I have gone to you, devoted, as to battle. | For glory have they gone, as milk to Soma, to Indra-Varuṇa my thoughts and praises. || 9. To Indra and to Varuṇa, desirous of gaining wealth have these my thoughts proceeded. | They have come nigh to you as treasure-lovers, like mares, fleet-footed, eager for the glory. || 10. May we ourselves be lords of during riches, of ample sustenance for car and hones. | So may the Twain who work with newest succours bring yoked teams hitherward to us and riches. || 11. Come with your mighty succours, O ye Mighty; come, Indra-Varuṇa, to us in battle. | What time the flashing arrows play in combat, may we through you be winners in the contest.

Hymn 4:42. Indra-Varuṇa.

1. I am the royal Ruler, mine is empire, as mine who sway all life are all Immortals. | Varuṇa's will the Gods obey and follow. I am the King of men's most lofty cover. || 2. I am King Varuṇa. To me were given these first existing high celestial powers. | Varuṇa's will the Gods obey and follow. I am the King of men's most lofty cover. || 3. I Varuṇa am Indra: in their greatness, these the two wide deep fairly-fashioned regions, | These the two world-halves have I, even as Tvashṭar knowing all beings, joined and held together. || 4. I made to flow the moisture-shedding waters, and set the heaven firm in the scat of Order. | By Law the Son of Aditi, Law Observer, hath spread abroad the world in threefold measure. || 5. Heroes with noble horses, fain for battle, selected warriors, call on me in combat. | I Indra Maghavan, excite the conflict; I stir the dust, Lord of surpassing vigour. || 6. All this I did. The Gods' own conquering power never impedeth me whom none opposeth. | When lauds and Soma juice have made me joyful, both the unbounded regions are affrighted. || 7. All beings know these deeds of thine thou tellest this unto Varuṇa, thou great Disposer! | Thou art renowned as having slain the Vṛitras. Thou madest flow the floods that were obstructed. || 8. Our fathers then were these, the Seven his, what time the son of Durgaha was captive. | For her they gained by sacrifice Trasadasyu, a demi-God, like Indra, conquering foemen. || 9. The spouse of Purukutsa gave oblations to you, O Indra-Varuṇa, with homage. | Then unto her ye gave King Trasadasyu, the demi-God, the slayer of the foeman. || 10. May we, possessing much, delight in riches, Gods in oblations and the kine in pasture; | And that Milch-cow who shrinks not from the milking, O Indra-Varuṇa, give to us daily.

Hymn 4:43. Aśvins.

1. Who will hear, who of those who merit worship, which of all Gods take pleasure in our homage? | On whose heart shall we lay this laud celestial, rich with fair offerings, dearest to Immortals? || 2. Who will be gracious? Who will come most quickly of all the Gods? Who will | bring bliss most largely? | What car do they call swift with rapid coursers? That which the Daughter of the Sun elected. || 3. So many days do ye come swiftly hither, as Indra to give help in stress of battle. | Descended from the sky, divine, strong-pinioned, by which of all your powers are ye most mighty? || 4. What is the prayer that we should bring you, Aśvins, whereby ye come to us when invocated? | Whether of you confronts e'en great betrayal? Lovers of sweetness, Dasras, help and save us. || 5. In the wide space your chariot reacheth heaven, what time it turneth hither from the ocean. | Sweets from your sweet shall drop, lovers of sweetness! These have they dressed for you as dainty viands. || 6. Let Sindhu with his wave bedew your horses: in fiery glow have the red birds come hither. | Observed of all was that your rapid going, whereby ye were the Lords of Sūrya's Daughter. || 7. Whene'er I gratified you here together, your grace was given us, O ye rich in booty. | Protect, ye Twain, the singer of your praises: to you, Nāsatyas, is my wish directed.

Hymn 4:44. Aśvins.

1. We will invoke this day your car, far spreading, O Aśvins, even the gathering, of the sunlight,— | Car praised in hymns, most ample, rich in treasure, fitted with seats, the car that beareth Sūrya. || 2. Aśvins, ye gained that glory by your Godhead, ye Sons of Heaven, by your own might and power. | Food followeth close upon your bright appearing when stately horses in your chariot draw you. || 3. Who bringeth you today for help with offered oblation, or with hymns to drink the juices? | Who, for the sacrifice's ancient lover, turneth you hither, Aśvins, offering homage? || 4. Borne on your golden car, ye omnipresent! come to this sacrifice of ours, Nāsatyas. | Drink of the pleasant liquor of the Soma give riches to the people who adore you. || 5. Come hitherward to us from earth, from heaven, borne on your golden chariot rolling lightly. | Suffer not other worshippers to stay you here are ye bound by earlier bonds of friendship. || 6. Now for us both, mete out, O Wonder-workers, riches exceeding great with store of heroes, | Because the men have sent you praise, O Aśvins, and Ajamīḷhas come to the laudation. || 7. Whene'er I gratified you here together, your grace was given us, O ye rich in booty. | Protect, ye Twain, the singer of your praises: to you, Nāsatyas, is my wish directed.

Hymn 4:45. Aśvins

1. Yonder goes up that light: your chariot is yoked that travels round upon the summit of this heaven. | Within this car are stored three kindred shares of food, and a skin filled with meath is rustling as the fourth. || 2. Forth come your viands rich with store of pleasant meath, and cars and horses at the flushing of the dawn, | Stripping the covering from the surrounded gloom, and spreading through mid-air bright radiance like the Sun. || 3. Drink of the meath with lips accustomed to the draught; harness for the meath's sake the chariot that ye love. | Refresh the way ye go, refresh the paths with meath: hither, O Aśvins, bring the skin that holds the meath. || 4. The swans ye have are friendly, rich in store of meath, gold-pinioned, strong to draw, awake at early morn, | Swimming the flood, exultant, fain for draughts that cheer: ye come like flies to our libations of the meath. || 5. Well knowing solemn rites and rich in meath, the fires sing to the morning Aśvins at the break of day, | When with pure hands the prudent energetic priest hath with the stones pressed out the Soma rich in meath. || 6. The rays advancing nigh, chasing with day the gloom, spread through the firmament bright radiance like the Sun; | And the Sun harnessing his horses goeth forth: ye through your Godlike nature let his paths be known. || 7. Devout in thought I have declared, O Aśvins, your chariot with good steeds, which lasts for ever, | Wherewith ye travel swiftly through the regions to the prompt worshipper who brings oblation.

Hymn 4:46. Vāyu. Indra-Vāyu.

1. Drink the best draught of Soma-juice, O Vāyu, at our holy rites: | For thou art he who drinketh first. || 2. Come, team-drawn, with thy hundred helps, with Indra, seated in the car, | Vāyu, and drink your fill of juice. || 3. May steeds a thousand bring you both, Indra. and Vāyu, hitherward | To drink the Soma, to the feast. || 4. For ye, O Indra-Vāyu, mount the golden-seated car that aids | The sacrifice, that reaches heaven. || 5. On far-refulgent chariot come unto the man who offers gifts: | Come, Indra-Vāyu, hitherward. || 6. Here, Indra-Vāyu, is the juice: drink it, accordant with the Gods, | Within the giver's dwelling-place. || 7. Hither, O Indra-Vāyu, be your journey here unyoke your steeds, | Here for your draught of Soma juice.

Hymn 4:47. Vāyu. Indra-Vāyu.

1. Vāyu, the bright is offered thee, best of the meath at holy rites. | Come

thou to drink the Soma juice, God, longed-for, on thy team-drawn car. ‖ 2. O Vāyu, thou and Indra are meet drinkers of these Soma-draughts, | For unto you the drops proceed as waters gather to the vale. ‖ 3. O Indra-Vāyu, mighty Twain, speeding together, Lords of Strength, | Come to our succour with your team, that ye may drink the Soma juice. ‖ 4. The longed-for teams which ye possess, O Heroes, for the worshipper, | Turn to us, Indra-Vāyu, ye to whom the sacrifice is paid.

Hymn 4:48. Vāyu.

1. Taste offerings never tasted yet, as bards enjoy the foeman's wealth. | O Vāyu, on refulgent car come to the drinking of the juice. ‖ 2. Removing curses, drawn by teams, with indra, seated by thy side, | O Vāyu, on refulgent car come to the drinking of the juice. ‖ 3. The two dark treasuries of wealth that wear | all beauties wait on thee. | O Vāyu, on refulgent car come to the drinking of the juice. ‖ 4. May nine-and-ninety harnessed steeds who yoke them at thy will bring thee. | O Vāyu, on refulgent car come to the drinking of the juice. ‖ 5. Harness, O Vāyu, to thy car a hundred well-fed tawny steeds, | Yea, or a thousand steeds, and let thy chariot come to us with might.

Hymn 4:49. Indra-Bṛihaspati.

1. Dear is this offering in your mouth, O Indra and Bṛihaspati: | Famed is the laud, the gladdening draught. ‖ 2. This lovely Soma is effused, O Indra and Bṛihaspati, | For you, to drink it and rejoice. ‖ 3. As Soma-drinkers to our house come, Indra and Bṛihaspati—and Indra—to drink Soma juice. ‖ 4. Vouchsafe us riches hundredfold, O Indra, and Bṛihaspati, | With store of horses, thousandfold. ‖ 5. O Indra. and Bṛihaspati, we call you when the meath is shed, | With songs, to drink the Soma juice. ‖ 6. Drink, Indra and Bṛihaspati, the Soma in the giver's house: | Delight yourselves abiding there.

Hymn 4:50. Bṛihaspati.

1. Him who with might hath propped earth's ends, who sitteth in threefold seat, Bṛihaspati, with thunder, | Him of the pleasant tongue have ancient sages, deep-thinking, holy singers, set before them. ‖ 2. Wild in their course, in well-marked wise rejoicing were they, Bṛihaspati, who pressed around us. | Preserve Bṛihaspati, the stall uninjured, this company's raining, ever-moving birthplace. ‖ 3. Bṛihaspati, from thy remotest distance have they sat down who love the law eternal. | For thee were dug wells springing from the mountain, which murmuring round about pour streams of sweetness. ‖ 4. Bṛihaspati, when first he had his being from mighty splendour in supremest heaven, | Strong, with his sevenfold mouth, with noise of thunder, with his seven rays, blew and dispersed the darkness. ‖ 5. With the loud-shouting band who sang his praises, with thunder, he destroyed obstructive Vala. | Bṛihaspati thundering drave forth the cattle, the lowing cows who make oblations ready. ‖ 6. Serve we with sacrifices, gifts, and homage even thus the Steer of all the Gods, the Father. | Bṛihaspati, may we be lords of riches, with noble progeny and store of heroes. ‖ 7. Surely that King by power and might heroic hath made him lord of all his foes' possessions, | Who cherishes Bṛihaspati well-tended, adorns and worships him as foremost sharer. ‖ 8. In his own house he dwells in peace and comfort: to him for ever holy food flows richly. | To him the people with free will pay homage—the King with whom the Brahman hath precedence. ‖ 9. He, unopposed, is master of the riches of his own subjects and of hostile people. | The Gods uphold that King with their protection who helps the Brahman when he seeks his favour. ‖ 10. Indra, Bṛihaspati, rainers of treasure, rejoicing at this sacrifice drink the Soma. | Let the abundant drops sink deep within you: vouchsafe us riches with full store of heroes. ‖ 11. Bṛihaspati and Indra, make us prosper may this be your benevolence to us-ward. | Assist our holy thoughts, wake up our spirit: weaken the hatred of our foe and rivals.

Hymn 4:51. Dawn.

1. Forth from the darkness in the region eastward this most abundant splendid light hath mounted. | Now verily the far-refulgent Mornings, Daughters of Heaven, bring welfare to the people. ‖ 2. The richly-coloured Dawns have mounted eastward, like pillars planted at our sacrifices, | And, flushing far, splendid and purifying, unbarred the portals of the fold of darkness. ‖ 3. Dispelling gloom this day the wealthy Mornings urge liberal givers to present their treasures. | In the unlightened depth of darkness round them let niggard traffickers sleep unawakened. ‖ 4. O Goddesses, is this your car, I ask you, ancient this day, or is it new, ye Mornings, | Wherewith, rich Dawns, ye seek with wealth Navagva, Daśagva Aṅgira, the seven-toned singer? ‖ 5. With horses harnessed by eternal Order, Goddesses, swiftly round the worlds ye travel, | Arousing from their rest, O Dawns, the sleeping, and all that lives, man, bird, and beast, to motion. ‖ 6. Which among these is eldest, and where is she through whom they fixed the Ṛibhus' regulations? | What time the splendid Dawns go forth for splendour, they are not known apart, alike, unwasting. ‖ 7. Blest were these Dawns of old, shining with succour, true with the truth that springs from holy Order; | With whom the toiling worshipper, by praises, hymning and lauding, soon attained to riches. ‖ 8. Hither from eastward all at once they travel, from one place spreading in the selfsame manner. | Awaking, from the seat of holy Order the Godlike Dawns come nigh like troops of cattle. ‖ 9. Thus they go forth with undiminished colours, these Mornings similar, in self-same fashion, | Concealing the gigantic might of darkness with radiant bodies bright and pure and shining. ‖ 10. O Goddesses, O Heaven's refulgent Daughters, bestow upon us wealth with store of children. | As from our pleasant place of rest ye rouse us may we be masters of heroic vigour. ‖ 11. Well-skilled in lore of sacrifice, ye Daughters of Heaven, refulgent Dawns, I thus address you. | May we be glorious among the people. May Heaven vouchsafe us this, and Earth the Goddess.

Hymn 4:52. Dawn.

1. This Lady, giver of delight, after her Sister shining forth, Daughter of Heaven, hath shown herself.— ‖ 2. Unfailing, Mother of the Kine, in colour like a bright red mare, | The Dawn became the Aśvins' Friend. ‖ 3. Yea, and thou art the Aśvins' Friend, the Mother of the Kine art thou: | O Dawn thou rulest over wealth. ‖ 4. Thinking of thee, O joyous One, as her who driveth hate away, | We woke to meet thee with our lauds. ‖ 5. Our eyes behold thy blessed rays like troops of cattle loosed to feed. | Dawn hath filled full the wide expanse. ‖ 6. When thou hast filled it, Fulgent One! thou layest bare the gloom with light. | After thy nature aid us, Dawn. ‖ 7. Thou overspreadest heaven with rays, the dear wide region of mid-air. | With thy bright shining lustre, Dawn.

Hymn 4:53. Savitar.

1. Of Savitar the God, the sapient Asura, we crave this great gift which is worthy of our choice, | Wherewith he freely grants his worshipper defence. This with his rays the Great God hath vouchsafed to us. ‖ 2. Sustainer of the heaven, Lord of the whole world's life, the Sage, he putteth on his golden-coloured mail. | Clear-sighted, spreading far, filling the spacious realm, Savitar hath brought forth bliss that deserveth laud. ‖ 3. He hath filled full the regions of the heaven and earth: the God for his own strengthening waketh up the hymn. | Savitar hath stretched out his arms to cherish life, producing with his rays and lulling all that moves. ‖ 4. Lighting all living creatures, ne'er to be deceived, Savitar, God, protects each holy ordinance. | He hath stretched out his arms to all the folk of earth, and, with his laws observed, rules his own mighty course. ‖ 5. Savitar thrice surrounding with his mightiness mid-air, three regions, and the triple sphere of light, | Sets the three heavens in motion and the threefold earth, and willingly protects us with his triple law. ‖ 6. Most gracious God, who brings to life and lulls to rest, he who controls the world, what moves not and what moves, | May he vouchsafe us shelter, Savitar the God,—for tranquil life, with triple bar against distress. ‖ 7. With the year's seasons hath Savitar, God, come nigh: may he prosper our home, give food and noble sons. | May he invigorate us through the days and nights, and may he send us opulence with progeny.

Hymn 4:54. Savitar.

1. Now must we praise and honour Savitar the God: at this time of the day the men must call to him, | Him who distributes wealth to Manu's progeny, that he may grant us here riches most excellent. ‖ 2. For thou at first producest for the holy Gods the noblest of all portions, immortality: | Thereafter as a gift to men, O Savitar, thou openest existence, life succeeding life. ‖ 3. If we, men as we are, have sinned against the Gods through want of thought, in weakness, or through insolence, | Absolve us from the guilt and make us free from sin, O Savitar, alike among both Gods and men. ‖ 4. None may impede that power of Savitar the God whereby he will maintain the universal world. | What the fair-fingered God brings forth on earth's expanse or in the height of heaven, that work

of his stands sure. || 5. To lofty hills thou sendest those whom Indra leads, and givest fixed abodes with houses unto these. | However they may fly and draw themselves apart, still, Savitar, they stand obeying thy behest. || 6. May the libations poured to thee thrice daily, day after day, O Savitar, bring us blessing. | May Indra, Heaven, Earth, Sindhu with the Waters, Aditi with Ādityas, give us shelter.

Hymn 4:55. Viśvedevas.

1. Who of you, Vasus, saveth? who protecteth? O Heaven and Earth and Aditi, preserve us, | Varuṇa, Mitra, from the stronger mortal Gods, which of you at sacrifice giveth comfort? || 2. They who with laud extol the ancient statutes, when they shine forth infallible dividers, | Have ordered as perpetual Ordainers, and beamed as holy-thoughted Wonder-workers || 3. The Housewife Goddess, Aditi, and Sindhu, the Goddess Svasti I implore for friendship: | And may the unobstructed Night and Morning both, day and night, provide for our protection. || 4. Aryaman, Varuṇa have disclosed the pathway, Agni as Lord of Strength the road to welfare. | Lauded in manly mode may Indra-Vishṇu grant us their powerful defence and shelter. || 5. I have besought the favour of the Marutas, of Parvata, of Bhaga God who rescues. | From trouble caused by man the Lord preserve us; from woe sent by his friend let Mitra save us. || 6. Agree, through these our watery oblations, Goddesses, Heaven and Earth, with Ahirbudhnya. | As if to win the sea, the Gharma-heaters have opened, as they come anear, the rivers. || 7. May Goddess Aditi with Gods defend us, save us the saviour God with care unceasing. | We dare not stint the sacred food of Mitra and Varuṇa upon the back of Agni. || 8. Agni is Sovereign Lord of wealth, Agni of great prosperity: | May he bestow these gifts on us. || 9. Hither to us, rich pleasant Dawn, bring many things to be desired, | Thou who hast ample store of wealth. || 10. So then may Bhaga, Savitar, Varuṇa, Mitra, Aryaman, Indra, with bounty come to us.

Hymn 4:56. Heaven and Earth.

1. May mighty Heaven and Earth, most meet for honour, be present here with light and gleaming splendours; | When, fixing them apart, vast, most extensive, the Steer roars loudly in far-reaching courses. || 2. The Goddesses with Gods, holy with holy, the Two stand pouring out their rain, exhaustless: | Faithful and guileless, having Gods for children, leaders of sacrifice with shining splendours. || 3. Sure in the worlds he was a skilful Craftsman, he who produced these Twain the Earth and Heaven. | Wise, with his power he brought both realms, together spacious and deep, well-fashioned, unsupported. || 4. O Heaven and Earth, with one accord promoting, with high protection as of Queens, our welfare, | Far-reaching, universal, holy, guard us. May we, car-borne, through song be victors ever. || 5. To both of you, O Heaven and Earth, we bring our lofty song of praise, | Pure Ones! to glorify you both. || 6. Ye sanctify each other's form, by your own proper might ye rule, | And from of old observe the Law. || 7. Furthering and fulfilling, ye, O Mighty, perfect Mitra's Law. | Ye sit around our sacrifice.

Hymn 4:57. Kṣhetrapati, etc.

1. We through the Master of the Field, even as through a friend, obtain | What nourisheth our kine and steeds. In such may he be good to us. || 2. As the cow yieldeth milk, pour for us freely, Lord of the Field, the wave that beareth sweetness, | Distilling meath, well-purified like butter, and let the. Lords of holy Law be gracious. || 3. Sweet be the plants for us. the heavens, the waters, and full of sweets for us be air's mid-region. | May the Field's Lord for us be full of sweetness, and may we follow after him uninjured. || 4. Happily work our steers and men, may the plough furrow happily. | Happily be the traces bound; happily may he ply the goad. || 5. Śuna and Sīra, welcome ye this laud, and with the milk which ye have made in heaven | Bedew ye both this earth of ours. || 6. Auspicious Sītā, come thou near: we venerate and worship thee | That thou mayst bless and prosper us and bring us fruits abundantly. || 7. May Indra press the furrow down, may Pūṣhan guide its course aright. | May she, as rich in milk, be drained for us through each succeeding year. || 8. Happily let the shares turn up the ploughland, happily go the ploughers with the oxen. | With meath and milk Parjanya make us happy. Grant us prosperity, Śuna and Sīra.

Hymn 4:58. Ghṛita.

1. Forth from the ocean sprang the wave of sweetness: together with the stalk it turned to Amṛita, | That which is holy oil's mysterious title: but the Gods' tongue is truly Amṛita's centre. || 2. Let us declare aloud the name of Ghṛita, and at this sacrifice hold it up with homage. | So let the Brahman hear the praise we utter. This hath the four-horned Buffalo emitted. || 3. Four are his horns, three are the feet that bear him; his heads are two, his hands are seven in number. | Bound with a triple bond the Steer roars loudly: the mighty God hath entered in to mortals. || 4. That oil in triple shape the Gods discovered laid down within the Cow, concealed by Paṇis. | Indra produced one shape, Sūrya another: by their own power they formed the third from Vena. || 5. From inmost reservoir in countless channels flow down these rivers which the foe beholds not. | I look upon the streams of oil descending, and lo! the Golden Reed is there among them. || 6. Like rivers our libations flow together, cleansing themselves in inmost heart and spirit. | The streams of holy oil pour swiftly downward like the wild beasts that fly before the bowman. || 7. As rushing down the rapids of a river, flow swifter than the wind the vigorous currents, | The streams of oil in swelling fluctuation like a red courser bursting through the fences. | 8. Like women at a gathering fair to look on and gently smiling, they incline to Agni. | The streams of holy oil attain the fuel, and Jātavedas joyfully receives them. || 9. As maidens dock themselves with gay adornment to join the bridal feast, I now behold them. | Where Soma flows and sacrifice is ready, thither the streams of holy oil are running. || 10. Send to our eulogy a herd of cattle bestow upon us excellent possessions. | Bear to the Gods the sacrifice we offer the streams of oil flow pure and full of sweetness. || 11. The universe depends upon thy power and might within the sea, within the heart, within all life. | May we attain that sweetly-flavoured wave of thine, brought, at its gathering, o'er the surface of the floods.

Maṇḍala 5

Hymn 5:1. Agni

1. Agni is wakened by the people's fuel to meet the Dawn who cometh like a milch-cow. | Like young trees shooting up on high their branches, his flames are rising to the vault of heaven. || 2. For worship of the Gods the Priest was wakened: at morning gracious Agni hath arisen. | Kindled, his radiant might is made apparent, and the great Deity set free from darkness. || 3. When he hath stirred the line of his attendants, with the pure milk pure Agni is anointed. | The strength-bestowing gift is then made ready, which spread in front, with tongues, erect, he drinketh. || 4. The spirits of the pious turn together to Agni, as the eyes of all to Sūrya. | He, when both Dawns of different hues have borne him, springs up at daybreak as a strong white charger. || 5. The noble One was born at days' beginning, laid red in colour mid the well-laid fuel. | Yielding in every house his seven rich treasures, Agni is seated, Priest most skilled in worship. || 6. Agni hath sat him down, a Priest most skilful, on a sweet-smelling place, his Mother's bosom. | Young, faithful, sage, preeminent o'er many, kindled among the folk whom he sustaineth. || 7. This Singer excellent at sacrifices, Agni the Priest, they glorify with homage. | Him who spread out both worlds by Law Eternal they balm with oil, strong Steed who never faileth. | 8. He, worshipful House-Friend, in his home is worshipped, our own auspicious guest, lauded by sages. | That strength the Bull with thousand horns possesses. In might, O Agni, thou excellest others. || 9. Thou quickly passest by all others, Agni, for him to whom thou hast appeared most lovely, | Wondrously fair, adorable, effulgent, the guest of men, the darling of the people. || 10. To thee, Most Youthful God! to thee, O Agni from near and far the people bring their tribute. | Mark well the prayer of him who best extols thee. Great, high, auspicious, Agni, is thy shelter. || 11. Ascend today thy splendid car, O Agni, in splendour, with the Holy Ones around it. | Knowing the paths by mid-air's spacious region bring hither Gods to feast on our oblation. || 12. To him adorable, sage, strong and mighty we have sung forth our song of praise and homage. | Gavishṭhira hath raised with prayer to Agni this laud far-reaching, like gold light to heaven.

Hymn 5:2. Agni.

1. The youthful Mother keeps the Boy in secret pressed to her close, nor yields him to the Father. | But, when he lies upon the arm, the people see his unfading countenance before them. || 2. What child is this thou carriest

as handmaid, O Youthful One? The Consort-Queen hath borne him. | The Babe unborn increased through many autumns. I saw him born what time his Mother bare him. || 3. I saw him from afar gold-toothed, bright-coloured, hurling his weapons from his habitation, | What time I gave him Amṛita free from mixture. How can the Indraless, the hymnless harm me? || 4. I saw him moving from the place he dwells in, even as with a herd, brilliantly shining. | These seized him not: he had been born already. They who were grey with age again grow youthful. || 5. Who separate my young bull from the cattle, they whose protector was in truth no stranger? | Let those whose hands have seized upon them free them. May he, observant, drive the herd to us-ward. || 6. Mid mortal men godless have secreted the King of all who live, home of the people. | So may the prayers of Atri give him freedom. Reproached in turn be those who now reproach him. || 7. Thou from the stake didst loose e'en Śunaḥśepa bound for a thousand; for he prayed with fervour. | So, Agni, loose from us the bonds that bind us, when thou art seated here, O Priest who knowest. || 8. Thou hast sped from me, Agni, in thine anger: this the protector of Gods' Laws hath told me. | Indra who knoweth bent his eye upon thee: by him instructed am I come, O Agni. || 9. Agni shines far and wide with lofty splendour, and by his greatness makes all things apparent. | He conquers godless and malign enchantments, and sharpens both his horns to gore the Rakṣhas. || 10. Loud in the heaven above be Agni's roarings with keen-edged weapons to destroy the demons. | Forth burst his splendours in the Soma's rapture. The godless bands press round but cannot stay him. || 11. As a skilled craftsman makes a car, a singer I, Mighty One! this hymn for thee have fashioned. | If thou, O Agni, God, accept it gladly, may we obtain thereby the heavenly Waters. || 12. May he, the strong-necked Steer, waxing in vigour, gather the foeman's wealth with none to check him. | Thus to this Agni have the Immortals spoken. To man who spreads the grass may he grant shelter, grant shelter to the man who brings oblation.

Hymn 5:3. Agni.

1. Thou at thy birth art Varuṇa, O Agni; when thou art kindled thou becomest Mitra. | In thee, O Son of Strength, all Gods are centred. Indra art thou to man who brings oblation. || 2. Aryaman art thou as regardeth maidens mysterious, is thy name, O Self-sustainer. | As a kind friend with streams of milk they balm thee what time thou makest wife and lord one-minded. || 3. The Marutas deck their beauty for thy glory, yea, Rudra! for thy birth fair, brightly-coloured. | That which was fixed as Viṣhṇu's loftiest station-therewith the secret of the Cows thou guardest. || 4. Gods through thy glory, God who art so lovely! granting abundant gifts gained life immortal. | As their own Priest have men established Agni; and serve him fain for praise from him who liveth. || 5. There is no priest more skilled than thou in worship; none Self-sustainer pass thee in wisdom. | The man within whose house as guest thou dwellest, O God, by sacrifice shall conquer mortals. || 6. Aided by thee, O Agni may we conquer through our oblation, fain for wealth, awakened: | May we in battle, in the days' assemblies,O Son of Strength, by riches conquer mortals. || 7. He shall bring evil on the evil-plotter whoever turns against us sin and outrage. | Destroy this calumny of him, O Agni, whoever injures us with double-dealing. || 8. At this dawn's flushing, God! our ancient fathers served thee with offerings, making thee their envoy, | When, Agni, to the store of wealth thou goest, a God enkindled with good things by mortals. || 9. Save, thou who knowest, draw thy father near thee, who counts as thine own son, O Child of Power. | O sapient Agni, when wilt thou regard us? When, skilled in holy Law, wilt thou direct us? || 10. Adoring thee he gives thee many a title, when thou, Good Lord! acceptest this as Father. | And doth not Agni, glad in strength of Godhead, gain splendid bliss when he hath waxen mighty? || 11. Most Youthful Agni, verily thou bearest thy praiser safely over all his troubles. | Thieves have been seen by us and open foemen: unknown have been the plottings of the wicked. || 12. To thee these eulogies have been directed: or to the Vasu hath this sin been spoken. | But this our Agni, flaming high, shall never yield us to calumny, to him who wrongs us.

Hymn 5:4. Agni.

1. O Agni, King and Lord of wealth and treasures, in thee is my delight at sacrifices. | Through thee may we obtain the strength we long for, and overcome the fierce attacks of mortals. || 2. Agni, Eternal Father, offering —bearer, fair to behold, far-reaching, far-refulgent, | From well-kept household fire beam food to feed us, and measure out to us abundant glory. || 3. The Sage of men, the Lord of human races, pure, purifying Agni, balmed with butter, | Him the Omniscient as your Priest ye establish: he wins among the Gods things worth the choosing. || 4. Agni, enjoy, of one accord with Iḷā, striving in rivalry with beams of Sūrya, | Enjoy, O Jātavedas, this our fuel, and bring the Gods to us to taste oblations. || 5. As dear House-Friend, guest welcome in the dwelling, to this our sacrifice come thou who knowest. | And, Agni, having scattered all assailants, bring to us the possessions of our foemen. || 6. Drive thou away the Dasyu with thy weapon. As, gaining vital power for thine own body, | O Son of Strength, the Gods thou satisfiest, so in fight save us, most heroic Agni. || 7. May we, O Agni, with our lauds adore thee, and with our gifts, fair-beaming Purifier! | Send to us wealth containing all things precious: bestow upon us every sort of riches. || 8. Son of Strength, Agni, dweller in three regions, accept our sacrifice and our oblation. | Among the Gods may we be counted pious: protect us with a triply-guarding shelter. || 9. Over all woes and dangers, Jātavedas, bear us as in a boat across a river. | Praised with our homage even as Atri praised thee, O Agni, be the guardian of our bodies. || 10. As I, remembering thee with grateful spirit, a mortal, call with might on thee Immortal, | Vouchsafe us high renown, O Jātavedas, and may I be immortal by my children. || 11. The pious man, O Jātavedas Agni, to whom thou grantest ample room and pleasure, | Gaineth abundant wealth with sons and horses, with heroes and with kine for his well-being.

Hymn 5:5. Āprīs.

1. To Agni, Jātavedas, to the flame, the well-enkindled God, | Offer thick sacrificial oil. || 2. He, Narāśaṃsa, ne'er beguiled, inspiriteth this sacrifice: | For sage is he, with sweets in hand. || 3. Adored, O Agni, hither bring Indra the Wonderful, the Friend, | On lightly-rolling car to aid. || 4. Spread thyself out, thou soft as wool The holy hymns have sung to thee. | Bring gain to us, O beautiful! || 5. Open yourselves, ye Doors Divine, easy of access for our aid: | Fill, more and more, the sacrifice. || 6. Fair strengtheners of vital power, young Mothers of eternal Law, | Morning and Night we supplicate. || 7. On the wind's flight come, glorified, ye two celestial Priests of man | Come ye to this our sacrifice. || 8. Iḷā, Sarasvatī, Mahī, three Goddesses who bring us weal, | Be seated harmless on the grass. || 9. Rich in all plenty, Tvaṣhṭar, come auspicious of thine own accord | Help us in every sacrifice. || 10. Vanaspati, wherever thou knowest the Gods' mysterious names, | Send our oblations thitherward. || 11. To Agni and to Varuṇa, Indra, the Marutas, and the Gods, | With Svāhā be oblation brought.

Hymn 5:6. Agni.

1. I value Agni that good Lord, the home to which the kine return: | Whom fleet-foot coursers seek as home, and strong enduring steeds as home. Bring food to those who sing thy praise. || 2. 'tis Agni whom we laud as good, to whom the milch-kine come in herds, | To whom the chargers swift of foot, to whom our well-born princes come. Bring food to those who sing thy praise. || 3. Agni the God of all mankind, gives, verily, a steed to man. | Agni gives precious gear for wealth, treasure he gives when he is pleased. Bring food to those who sing thy praise. || 4. God, Agni, we will kindle thee, rich in thy splendour, fading not, | So that this glorious fuel may send forth by day its light for thee. Bring food to those who sing thy praise. || 5. To thee the splendid, Lord of flame, bright, wondrous, Prince of men, is brought. | Oblation with the holy verse, O Agni, bearer of our gifts. | Bring food to those who sing thy praise. || 6. These Agnis in the seats of the fire nourish each thing most excellent. | They give delight, they spread abroad, they move themselves continually. Bring food to those who sing thy praise. || 7. Agni, these brilliant flames of thine wax like strong chargers mightily, | Who with the treadings of their hoofs go swiftly to the stalls of kine. Bring food to those who sing thy praise. || 8. To us who laud thee, Agni, bring fresh food and safe and happy homes. | May we who have sung hymns to thee have thee for envoy in each house. Bring food to those who sing thy praise. || 9. Thou, brilliant God, within thy mouth warmest both ladies of the oil. | So fill us also, in our hymns, abundantly, O Lord of Strength. Bring food to those who sing thy praise. || 10. Thus Agni have we duly served with sacrifices and with hymns. | So may he give us what we crave, store of brave sons and fleet-foot steeds. Bring food to those who sing thy praise.

Hymn 5:7. Agni.

1. Offer to Agni, O my friends, your seemly food, your seemly praise; | To him supremest o'er the folk, the Son of Strength, the mighty Lord: || 2. Him in whose presence, when they meet in full assembly, men rejoice; | Even him whom worthy ones inflame, and living creatures bring to life. || 3. When we present to him the food and sacrificial gifts of men, | He by the might of splendour grasps the holy Ordinance's rein. || 4. He gives a signal in the night even to him who is afar, | When he, the Bright, unchanged by eld, consumes the sovereigns of the wood. || 5. He in whose service on the ways they offer up their drops of sweat, | On him is their high kin have they mounted, as ridges on the earth. || 6. Whom, sought of many, mortal man hath found to be the Stay of all; | He who gives flavour to our food, the home of every man that lives. || 7. Even as a herd that crops the grass he shears the field and wilderness, | With flashing teeth and beard of gold, deft with his unabated might. || 8. For him, to whom, bright as an axe he, as to Atri, hath flashed forth, | Hath the well-bearing Mother borne, producing when her time is come. || 9. Agni to whom the oil is shed by him thou lovest to support, | Bestow upon these mortals fame and splendour and intelligence. || 10. Such zeal hath he, resistless one: he gained the cattle given by thee. | Agni, may Atri overcome the Dasyus who bestow no gifts, subdue the men who give no food.

Hymn 5:8. Agni.

1. O Agni urged to strength, the men of old who loved the Law enkindled thee, | the Ancient, for their aid, | Thee very bright, and holy, nourisher of all, most excellent, the Friend and Master of the home. || 2. Thee, Agni, men have 'established as their guest of old, as Master of the household, thee, with hair of flame; | High-bannered, multiform, distributor of wealth, kind helper, good protector, drier of the floods. || 3. The tribes of men praise thee, Agni, who knowest well burnt offerings, the Discerner, lavishest of wealth, | Dwelling in secret, Blest One! visible to all, loud-roaring, skilled in worship, glorified with oil. || 4. Ever to thee, O Agni, as exceeding strong have we drawn nigh with songs and reverence singing hymns. | So be thou pleased with us, Aṅgiras! as a God enkindled by the noble with man's goodly light. || 5. Thou, Agni! multiform, God who art lauded much! givest in every house subsistence as of old. | Thou rulest by thy might o'er food of many a sort: that light of thine when blazing may not be opposed. || 6. The Gods, Most Youthful Agni, have made thee, inflamed, the bearer of oblations and the messenger. | Thee, widely-reaching, homed in sacred oil, invoked, effulgent, have they made the Eye that stirs the thought. || 7. Men seeking joy have lit thee worshipped from of old, O Agni, with good fuel and with sacred oil. | So thou, bedewed and waxing mighty by the plants, spreadest thyself abroad over the realms of earth.

Hymn 5:9. Agni.

1. Bearing; oblations mortal men, O Agni, worship thee the God. | I deem thee Jātavedas: bear our offerings, thou, unceasingly. || 2. In the man's home who offers gifts, where grass is trimmed, Agni is Priest, | To whom all sacrifices come and strengthenings that win renown. || 3. Whom, as an infant newly-born, the kindling-sticks have brought to life, | Sustainer of the tribes of men, skilled in well-ordered sacrifice. || 4. Yea, very hard art thou to grasp, like offspring of the wriggling snakes, | When thou consumest many woods like an ox, Agni, in the mead. || 5. Whose flames, when thou art sending forth the smoke, completely reach the mark, | When Trita in the height of heaven, like as a smelter fanneth thee, e'en as a smelter sharpeneth thee. || 6. O Agni, by thy succour and by Mitra's friendly furtherance, | May we, averting hate, subdue the wickedness of mortal men. || 7. O Agni, to our heroes bring such riches, thou victorious God. | May he protect and nourish us, and help in gaining strength: be thou near us in fight for our success.

Hymn 5:10. Agni.

1. Bring us most mighty splendour thou, Agni, resistless on thy way. | With overflowing store of wealth mark out for us a path to strength. || 2. Ours art thou, wondrous Agni, by wisdom and bounteousness of power. | The might of Asuras rests on thee, like Mitra worshipful in act. || 3. Agni, increase our means of life, increase the house and home of these, | The men, the princes who have won great riches through our hymns of praise. || 4. Bright Agni, they who deck their songs for thee have horses as their meed. | The men are mighty in their might, they whose high laud, as that of heaven, awakes thee of its own accord. || 5. O Agni, those resplendent flames of thine go valorously forth, | Like lightnings flashing round us, like a rattling car that seeks the spoil. || 6. Now, Agni, come to succour us; let priests draw nigh to offer gifts; | And let the patrons of our rites subdue all regions of the earth. || 7. Bring to us, Agni, Aṅgiras, lauded of old and lauded now, | Invoker! wealth to quell the strong, that singers may extol thee. Be near us in fight for our success.

Hymn 5:11. Agni.

1. The watchful Guardian of the people hath been born, Agni, the very strong, for fresh prosperity. | With oil upon his face, with high heaven-touching flame, he shineth splendidly, pure, for the Bhāratas. || 2. Ensign of sacrifice, the earliest Household-Priest, the. men have kindled Agni in his threefold seat, | With Indra and the Gods together on the grass let the wise Priest sit to complete the sacrifice. || 3. Pure, unadorned, from thy two Mothers art thou born: thou camest from Vivasvat as a charming Sage. | With oil they strengthened thee, O Agni, worshipped God: thy banner was the smoke that mounted to the sky. || 4. May Agni graciously come to our sacrifice. The men bear Agni here and there in every house. | He hath become an envoy, bearer of our gifts: electing Agni, men choose one exceeding wise. || 5. For thee, O Agni, is this sweetest prayer of mine: dear to thy spirit be this product of my thought. | As great streams fill the river so our song of praise fill thee, and make thee yet more mighty in thy strength. || 6. O Agni, the Aṅgirasas discovered thee what time thou layest hidden, fleeing back from wood to wood. | Thou by attrition art produced as conquering might, and men, O Aṅgiras, call thee the Son of Strength.

Hymn 5:12. Agni.

1. To Agni, lofty Asura, meet for worship, Steer of eternal Law, my prayer I offer; | I bring my song directed to the Mighty like pure oil for his mouth at sacrifices. || 2. Mark the Law, thou who knowest, yea, observe it: send forth the full streams of eternal Order. | I use no sorcery with might or falsehood the sacred Law of the Red Steer I follow. || 3. How hast thou, follower of the Law eternal, become the knower of a new song, Agni? | The God, the Guardian of the seasons, knows me: the Lord of him who won this wealth I know not. || 4. Who, Agni, in alliance with thy foeman, what splendid helpers won for them their riches? | Agni, who guard the dwelling-place of falsehood? Who are protectors of the speech of liars? || 5. Agni, those friends of thine have turned them from thee: gracious of old, they have become ungracious. | They have deceived themselves by their own speeches, uttering wicked words against the righteous. || 6. He who pays sacrifice to thee with homage, O Agni, keeps the Red Steer's Law eternal; | Wide is his dwelling. May the noble offspring of Nahuṣha who wandered forth come hither.

Hymn 5:13. Agni.

1. With songs of praise we call on thee, we kindle thee with songs of praise, | Agni, -with songs of praise, for help. || 2. Eager for wealth, we meditate Agni's effectual praise today, | Praise of the God who touches heaven. || 3. May Agni, Priest among mankind, take pleasure in our songs of praise, | And worship the Celestial Folk. || 4. Thou, Agni, art spread widely forth, Priest dear and excellent; through thee | Men make the sacrifice complete. || 5. Singers exalt thee, Agni, well lauded, best giver of our strength: | So grant thou us heroic might. || 6. Thou Agni, as the felly rings the spokes, encompassest the Gods. | I yearn for bounty manifold.

Hymn 5:14. Agni.

1. Enkindling the Immortal, wake Agni with song of praise: may he bear our oblations to the Gods. || 2. At high solemnities mortal men glorify him the Immortal, best | At sacrifice among mankind. || 3. That he may bear their gifts to heaven, all glorify him Agni, God, | With ladle that distilleth oil. || 4. Agni shone bright when born, with light killing the Dasyus and the dark: | He found the Kine, the Floods, the Sun. || 5. Serve Agni, God adorable, the Sage whose back is balmed with oil: | Let him approach, and hear my call. || 6. They have exalted Agni, God of all mankind, with oil and hymns | Of praise, devout and eloquent.

Hymn 5:15. Agni.

1. To him, the far-renowned, the wise Ordainer, ancient and glorious, a song I offer. | Enthroned in oil, the Asura, bliss-giver, is Agni, firm support

of noble, riches. ‖ 2. By holy Law they kept supporting Order, by help of sacrifice, in loftiest heaven,— | They who attained with born men to the unborn, men seated on that stay, heaven's firm sustainer. ‖ 3. Averting woe, they labour hard to bring him, the ancient, plenteous food as power resistless. | May he, born newly, conquer his assailants: round him they stand as round an angry lion. ‖ 4. When, like a mother, spreading forth to nourish, to cherish and regard each man that liveth,— | Consuming all the strength that thou hast gotten, thou wanderest round, thyself, | in varied fashion. ‖ 5. May strength preserve the compass of thy vigour, God! that broad stream of thine that beareth riches. | Thou, like a thief who keeps his refuge secret, hast holpen Atri to great wealth, by teaching.

Hymn 5:16. Agni.

1. Great power is in the beam of light, sing praise to, Agni, to the God | Whom men have set in foremost place like Mitra with their eulogies. ‖ 2. He by the splendour of his arms is Priest of every able man. | Agni conveys oblation straight, and deals, as Bhaga deals, his boons. ‖ 3. All rests upon the laud and love of him the rich, high-flaming God, | On whom, loud-roaring, men have laid great strength as on a faithful friend. ‖ 4. So, Agni, be the Friend of these with liberal gift of hero strength. | Yea, Heaven and Earth have not surpassed this Youthful One in glorious fame. ‖ 5. O Agni, quickly come to us, and, glorified, bring precious wealth. | So we and these our princes will assemble for the good of all. Be near in fight to prosper us.

Hymn 5:17. Agni.

1. God, may a mortal call the Strong hither, with solemn rites, to aid, | A man call Agni to protect when sacrifice is well prepared. ‖ 2. Near him thou seemest mightier still in native glory, set to hold | Apart yon flame-hued vault of heaven, lovely beyond the thought of man. ‖ 3. Yea, this is by the light of him whom powerful song hath bound to act, | Whose beams of splendour flash on high as though they sprang from heavenly seed. ‖ 4. Wealth loads the Wonder-Worker's car through his, the very wise One's power. | Then, meet to be invoked among all tribes, is Agni glorified. ‖ 5. Now, too, the princes shall obtain excellent riches by our lips. | Protect us for our welfare: lend thy succour, O thou Son of Strength. Be near in fight to prosper us.

Hymn 5:18. Agni.

1. At dawn let: Agni, much-beloved guest of the house, be glorified; | Immortal who delights in all oblations brought by mortal men. ‖ 2. For Dvita who receives through wealth of native strength maimed offerings, | Thy praiser even gains at once the Soma-drops, Immortal Gods! ‖ 3. Nobles, with song I call that car of yours that shines with lengthened life, | For, God who givest steeds! that car hither and thither goes unharmed. ‖ 4. They who have varied ways of thought, who guard, the lauds within their lips, | And strew the grass before the light, have decked themselves with high renown. ‖ 5. Immortal Agni, give the chiefs, heroes who institute the rite, | Heroes' illustrious, lofty fame, who at the synod met for praise presented me with fifty steeds.

Hymn 5:19. Agni.

1. One state begets another state: husk is made visible from husk: | Within his Mother's side he speaks. ‖ 2. Discerning, have they offered gifts: they guard the strength that never wastes. | To a strong fort have they pressed in. ‖ 3. Śvaitreya's people, all his men, have gloriously increased in might. | A gold chain Bṛihaduktha wears, as, through this Soma, seeking spoil. ‖ 4. I bring, as 'twere, the longed-for milk, the dear milk of the Sister-Pair. | Like to a cauldron filled with food is he, unconquered, conquering all. ‖ 5. Beam of light, come to us in sportive fashion, finding thyself close to the wind that fans thee. | These flames of his are wasting flames, like arrows keen-pointed, sharpened, on his breast.

Hymn 5:20. Agni.

1. Agni, best winner of the spoil, cause us to praise before the Gods | As our associate meet for lauds, wealth which thou verily deemest wealth. ‖ 2. Agni, the great who ward not off the anger of thy power and might | Stir up the wrath and hatred due to one who holds an alien creed. ‖ 3. Thee, Agni, would we choose as Priest, the perfecter of strength and skill; | We who bring sacred food invoke with song thee Chief at holy rites. ‖ 4. Here as is needful for thine aid we toil, O Conqueror, day by day, | For wealth, for Law. May we rejoice, Most Wise One! at the feast, with kine, rejoice, with heroes, at the feast.

Hymn 5:21. Agni.

1. We establish thee as Manus used, as Manus used we kindle thee. | Like Manus, for the pious man, Aṅgiras, Agni, worship Gods. ‖ 2. For well, O Agni, art thou pleased when thou art kindled mid mankind. | Straight go the ladles unto thee, thou high-born God whose food is oil. ‖ 3. Thee have all Gods of one accord established as their messenger. | Serving at sacrifices men adore thee as a God, O Sage. ‖ 4. Let mortal man adore your God, Agni, with worship due to Gods. | Shine forth enkindled, Radiant One. Sit in the chamber of the Law, sit in the chamber of the food.

Hymn 5:22. Agni.

1. Like Atri, Viśvasāman! sing to him of purifying light, | Who must be praised in holy rites, the Priest most welcome in the house. ‖ 2. Set Jātavedas in his place, Agni the God and Minister. | Let sacrifice proceed today duly, comprising all the Gods. ‖ 3. All mortals come to thee for aid, the God of most observant mind. | Of thine excelling favour we bethink us as we long for it. ‖ 4. Mark with attention this our speech, O Agni, thou victorious One. | Thee, Strong-jawed! as the homestead's Lord, the Atris with their lauds exalt, the Atris beautify with songs.

Hymn 5:23. Agni.

1. By thy fair splendour's mighty power, O Agni, bring victorious wealth, | Wealth that o'ercometh all mankind, and, near us, conquereth in fight. ‖ 2. Victorious Agni, bring to us the wealth that vanquisheth in war; | For thou art wonderful and true, giver of strength in herds of kine. ‖ 3. For all the folk with one accord, whose sacred grass is trimmed and strewn, | Invite thee to their worship-halls, as a dear Priest, for choicest wealth. ‖ 4. For he, the God of all men, hath gotten him might that quelleth foes. | O Agni, in these homes shine forth, bright God! for our prosperity, shine, Purifier! splendidly.

Hymn 5:24. Agni.

1. O Agni, be our nearest Friend, be thou a kind deliverer and a gracious Friend. ‖ 2. Excellent Agni, come thou nigh to us, and give us wealth most splendidly renowned. ‖ 3. So hear us, listen to this call of ours, and keep us far from every sinful man. ‖ 4. To thee then, O Most Bright, O Radiant God, we come with prayer for happiness for our friends.

Hymn 5:25. Agni.

1. I will sing near, for grace, your God Agni, for he is good to us. | Son of the Brands, may he give gifts, and, righteous, save us from the foe. ‖ 2. For be is true, whom men of old enkindled, and the Gods themselves, | The Priest with the delicious tongue, rich with the light of glorious beams. ‖ 3. With wisdom that surpasseth all, with gracious will most excellent, | O Agni, worthy of our choice, shine wealth on us through hymns of praise. ‖ 4. Agni is King, for he extends to mortals and to Gods alike. | Agni is bearer of our gifts. Worship ye Agni with your thoughts. ‖ 5. Agni gives to the worshipper a son, the best, of mightiest fame, | Of deep devotion, ne'er subdued, bringer of glory to his sire. ‖ 6. Agni bestows the hero-lord who conquers with the men in fight. | Agni bestows the fleet-foot steed, the victor never overcome. ‖ 7. The mightiest song is Agni's: shine on high, thou who art rich in light. | Like the Chief Consort of a King, riches and strength proceed from thee. ‖ 8. Resplendent are thy rays of light: loud is thy voice like pressing-stones. | Yea, of itself thy thunder goes forth like the roaring of the heaven. ‖ 9. Thus, seeking riches, have we paid homage to Agni Conqueror. | May he, most wise, as with a ship, carry us over all our foes.

Hymn 5:26. Agni.

1. O Agni, Holy and Divine, with splendour and thy pleasant tongue | Bring hither and adore the Gods. ‖ 2. We pray thee, thou who droppest oil, bright-rayed! who lookest on the Sun, | Bring the Gods hither to the feast. ‖ 3. We have enkindled thee, O Sage, bright caller of the Gods to feast. | O Agni, great in Sacrifice. ‖ 4. O Agni, come with all the Gods, come to our sacrificial gift: | We choose thee as Invoking Priest. ‖ 5. Bring, Agni, to the worshipper who pours the juice, heroic strength: | Sit with the Gods upon the grass. ‖ 6. Victor of thousands, Agni, thou, enkindled, cherishest the laws, | Laud-worthy, envoy of the Gods. ‖ 7. Set Agni Jātavedas down, the bearer of our sacred gifts, | Most-youthful, God and Minister. ‖ 8. Duly proceed our sacrifice, comprising all the Gods, today: | Strew holy grass to

be their seat. || 9. So may the Marutas sit thereon, the Aśvins, Mitra, Varuṇa: | The Gods with all their company.

Hymn 5:27. Agni.

1. The Godlike hero, famousest of nobles, hath granted me two oxen with a wagon. | Traivṛishṇa's son Tryaruṇa hath distinguished himself, Vaiśvānara Agni! with ten thousands. || 2. Protect Tryaruṇa, as thou art waxing strong and art highly praised, Vaiśvānara Agni! | Who granteth me a hundred kine and twenty, and two bay horses, good at draught, and harnessed. || 3. So Trasadasyu served thee, God Most Youthful, craving thy favour for the ninth time, Agni; | Tryaruṇa who with attentive spirit accepteth many a song from me the mighty. || 4. He who declares his wish to me, to Aśvamedha, to the Prince, | Pays him who with his verse seeks gain, gives power to him who keeps the Law. || 5. From whom a hundred oxen, all of speckled hue, delight my heart, | The gifts of Aśvamedha, like thrice-mingled draughts of Soma juice. || 6. To Aśvamedha who bestows a hundred gifts grant hero power, | O Indra-Agni! lofty rule like the unwasting Sun in heaven.

Hymn 5:28. Agni.

1. Agni inflamed hath sent to heaven his lustre: he shines forth widely turning unto Morning. | Eastward the ladle goes that brings all blessing, praising the Gods with homage and oblation. || 2. Enkindled, thou art King of the immortal world: him who brings offerings thou attendest for his weal. | He whom thou urgest on makes all possessions his: he sets before thee, Agni, gifts that guests may claim. || 3. Show thyself strong for mighty bliss, O Agni, most excellent be thine effulgent splendours. | Make easy to maintain our household lordship, and overcome the might of those who hate us. || 4. Thy glory, Agni, I adore, kindled, exalted in thy strength. | A Steer of brilliant splendour, thou art lighted well at sacred rites. || 5. Agni, invoked and kindled, serve the Gods, thou skilled in sacrifice: | For thou art bearer of our gifts. || 6. Invoke and worship Agni while the sacrificial rite proceeds: | For offering-bearer choose ye him.

Hymn 5:29. Agni.

1. Man's worship of the Gods hath three great lustres, and three celestial lights have they established | The Marutas gifted with pure strength adore thee, for thou, O Indra, art their sapient Ṛishi. || 2. What time the Marutas sang their song to Indra, joyous when he had drunk of Soma juices, | He grasped his thunderbolt to slay the Dragon, and loosed, that they might flow, the youthful Waters. || 3. And, O ye Brahmans, Marutas, so may Indra drink draughts of this my carefully pressed Soma; | For this oblation found for man the cattle, and Indra, having quaffed it, slew the Dragon. || 4. Then heaven and earth he sundered and supported: wrapped even in these he struck the Beast with terror. | So Indra forced the Engulfer to disgorgement, and slew the Dānava. panting against him. || 5. Thus all the Gods, O Maghavan, delivered to thee of their free will the draught of Soma; | When thou for Etaśa didst cause to tarry the flying mares of Sūrya racing forward. || 6. When Maghavan with the thunderbolt demolished his nine-and-ninety castles all together, | The Marutas, where they met, glorified Indra: ye with the Trishṭubh hymn obstructed heaven. || 7. As friend to aid a friend, Agni dressed quickly three hundred buffaloes, even as he willed it. | And Indra, from man's gift, for Vṛitra's slaughter, drank off at once three lakes of pressed-out Soma. || 8. When thou three hundred buffaloes' flesh hadst eaten, and drunk, as Maghavan, three lakes of Soma, | All the Gods raised as 'twere a shout of triumph to Indra praise because he slew the Dragon. || 9. What time ye came with strong steeds swiftly speeding, O Uśanā and Indra, to the dwelling, | Thou camest thither—conquering together with Kutsa and the Gods: thou slewest Śushṇa. || 10. One car-wheel of the Sun thou rolledst forward, and one thou settest free to move for Kutsa. | Thou slewest noseless Dasyus with thy weapon, and in their home o'erthrewest hostile speakers. || 11. The lauds of Gaurivīti made thee mighty to Vidathin's son, as prey, thou gavest Pipru. | Ṛijiśvan drew thee into friendship dressing the sacred food, and thou hast drunk his Soma. || 12. Navagvas and Daśagvas with libations of Soma juice sing hymns of praise to Indra. | Labouring at their task the men laid open the stall of Kine though firmly closed and fastened. || 13. How shall I serve thee, Maghavan, though knowing full well what hero deeds thou hast accomplished? | And the fresh deeds which thou wilt do, Most Mighty! these, too, will we tell forth in sacred synods. || 14. Resistless from of old through hero courage, thou hast done all these many acts, O Indra. | What thou wilt do in bravery, Thunder-wielder! none is there who may hinder this thy prowess. || 15. Indra, accept the prayers which now are offered, accept the new prayers, Mightiest! which we utter. | Like fair and well-made robes, I, seeking riches, as a deft craftsman makes a car, have wrought them.

Hymn 5:30. Indra.

1. Where is that Hero? Who hath looked on Indra borne on light-rolling car by Tawny Coursers, | Who, Thunderer, seeks with wealth the Soma-presser, and to his house goes, much-invoked, to aid him? || 2. I have beheld his strong and secret dwelling, longing have sought the Founder's habitation. | I asked of others, and they said in answer, May we, awakened men, attain to Indra. || 3. We will tell, Indra, when we pour libation, what mighty deeds thou hast performed to please us. | Let him who knows not learn, who knows them listen: hither rides Maghavan with all his army. || 4. Indra, when born, thou madest firm thy spirit: alone thou seekest war to fight with many. | With might thou clavest e'en the rock asunder, and foundest out the stable of the Milch-kine. || 5. When thou wast born supremest at a distance, bearing a name renowned in far-off regions, | Since then e'en Gods have been afraid of Indra: he conquered all the floods which served the Dāsa. || 6. These blissful Marutas sing their psalm to praise thee, and pour to thee libation of the Soma. | Indra with wondrous powers subdued the Dragon, the guileful lurker who beset the waters. || 7. Thou, Maghavan, from the first didst scatter foemen, speeding, while joying in the milk, the Giver. | There, seeking man's prosperity, thou torest away the head of Namuchi the Dāsa. || 8. Pounding the head of Namuchi the Dāsa, me, too thou madest thine associate, Indra! | Yea, and the rolling stone that is in heaven both worlds, as on a car, brought to the Marutas. || 9. Women for weapons hath the Dāsa taken, What injury can his feeble armies To me? | Well he distinguished his two different voices, and Indra then advanced to fight the Dasyu. || 10. Divided from their calves the Cows went lowing around, on every side, hither and thither. | These Indra re-united with his helpers, what time the well-pressed Soma made him joyful. || 11. What time the Somas mixed by Babhru cheered him, loud the Steer bellowed in his habitations. | So Indra drank thereof, the Fort-destroyer, and gave him guerdon, in return, of milch-kine. || 12. This good deed have the Ruśamas done, Agni! that they have granted me four thousand cattle. | We have received Ṛiṇaṃchaya's wealth, of heroes the most heroic, which was freely offered. || 13. The Ruśamas, O Agni, sent me homeward with fair adornment and with kine in thousands. | The strong libations have made Indra joyful, when night, whose course was ending, changed to morning. || 14. Night, well-nigh ended, at Ṛiṇaṃchaya's coming, King of the Ruśamas, was changed to morning. | Like a strong courser, fleet of foot, urged onward, Babhru hath gained four thousand as his guerdon. || 15. We have received four thousand head of cattle presented by the Ruśamas, O Agni. | And we, the singers, have received the cauldron of metal which was heated for Pravargya.

Hymn 5:31. Indra.

1. Maghavan Indra turns his chariot downward, the strength-displaying car which he hath mounted. | Even as a herdsman driveth forth his cattle, he goeth, first, uninjured, fain for treasure. | 2. Haste to us, Lord of Bays; be not ungracious: visit us, lover of gold-hued oblation. | There is naught else better than thou art, Indra: e'en to the wifeless hast thou given spouses. || 3. When out of strength arose the strength that conquers, Indra displayed all powers that he possesses. | Forth from the cave he drove the milky mothers, and with the light laid bare investing darkness. | 4. Anus have wrought a chariot for thy Courser, and Tvashṭar, Much-invoked! thy bolt that glitters. | The Brahmans with their songs exalting Indra increased his strength that he might slaughter Ahi. || 5. When heroes sang their laud to thee the Hero, Indra! and stones and Aditi accordant, | Without or steed or chariot were the fellies which, sped by Indra, rolled upon the Dasyus. || 6. I will declare thine exploits wrought aforetime, and, Maghavan, thy deeds of late achievement, | When, Lord of Might, thou sunderedst earth and heaven, winning for man the moistly-gleaming waters. || 7. This is thy deed, e'en this, Wonderful! Singer! that, slaying Ahi, here thy strength thou showedst, | Didst check and stay e'en Shusṇa's wiles and magic, and, drawing nigh, didst chase away the Dasyus. || 8. Thou, Indra, on the farther

bank for Yadu and Turvaśa didst stay the gushing waters. | Ye both assailed the fierce: thou barest Kutsa: when Gods and Uśanā came to you together. || 9. Let the steeds bring you both, Indra and Kutsa, borne on the chariot within hearing-distance. | Ye blew him from the waters, from his dwelling, and chased the darkness from the noble's spirit. || 10. Even this sage hath come looking for succour even to Vāta's docile harnessed horses. | Here are the Marutas, all, thy dear companions: prayers have increased thy power and might, O Indra. || 11. When night was near its close he carried forward e'en the Sun's chariot backward in its running. | Etaśa brought his wheel and firmly stays it: setting it eastward he shall give us courage. || 12. This Indra, O ye men, hath come to see you, seeking a friend who hath expressed the Soma. | The creaking stone is laid upon the altar, and the Adhvaryus come to turn it quickly. || 13. Let mortals who were happy still be happy; let them not come to sorrow, O Immortal. | Love thou the pious, and to these thy people-with whom may we be numbered-give thou vigour.

Hymn 5:32. Indra.

1. The well thou clavest, settest free the fountains, and gavest rest to floods that were obstructed. | Thou, Indra, laying the great mountain open, slaying the Dānava, didst loose the torrents. || 2. The fountain-depths obstructed in their seasons, thou, Thunderer! madest flow, the mountain's udder. | Strong Indra, thou by slaying e'en the Dragon that lay extended there hast shown thy vigour. || 3. Indra with violence smote down the weapon, | yea, even of that wild and mighty creature. | Although he deemed himself alone unequalled, another had been born e'en yet more potent. || 4. Him, whom the heavenly food of these delighted, child of the mist, strong waxing, couched in darkness, | Him the bolt-hurling Thunderer with his lightning smote down and slew, the Dānava's wrath-fire, Śushṇa. || 5. Though he might ne'er be wounded still his vitals felt that, the God's bolt, which his powers supported, | When, after offered draughts, Strong Lord, thou laidest him, fain to battle, in the pit in darkness. || 6. Him as he lay there huge in length extended, still waxing in the gloom which no sun lightened, | Him, after loud-voiced threats, the Hero Indra, rejoicing in the poured libation, slaughtered. || 7. When 'gainst the mighty Dānava his weapon Indra uplifted, power which none could combat, | When at the hurling of his bolt he smote him, he made him lower than all living creatures. || 8. The fierce God seized that huge and restless coiler, insatiate, drinker of the sweets, recumbent, | And with his mighty weapon in his dwelling smote down the footless evil-speaking ogre. || 9. Who may arrest his strength or cheek his vigour? Alone, resistless, he bears off all riches. | Even these Twain, these Goddesses, through terror of Indra's might, retire from his dominion. || 10. E'en the Celestial Axe bows down before him, and the Earth, lover-like, gives way to Indra. | As he imparts all vigour to these people, straightway the folk bend them to him the Godlike. || 11. I hear that thou wast born sole Lord of heroes of the Five Races, famed among the people. | As such my wishes have most lately grasped him, invoking Indra both at eve and morning. || 12. So, too, I hear of thee as in due season urging to action and enriching singers. | What have thy friends received from thee, the Brahmans who, faithful, rest their hopes on thee, O Indra?

Hymn 5:33. Indra.

1. Great praise to Indra, great and strong mid heroes, I ponder thus, the feeble to the Mighty, | Who with his band shows favour to this people, when lauded, in the fight where spoil is gathered. || 2. So made attentive by our hymns, Steer! Indra! thou fastenedst the girth of thy Bay Coursers, | Which, Maghavan, at thy will thou drivest hither. With these subdue for us the men who hate us. || 3. They were not turned to us-ward, lofty Indra! while yet through lack of prayer they stood unharnessed. | Ascend this chariot, thou whose hand wields thunder, and draw the rein, O Lord of noble horses. || 4. Thou, because many lauds are thine, O Indra, wast active warring in the fields | for cattle. | For Sūrya in his own abode thou, Hero, formedst in fights even a Dāsa's nature. || 5. Thine are we, Indra; thine are all these people, conscious of might, whose cars are set in motion. | Some hero come to us, O Strong as Ahi beauteous in war, to be invoked like Bhaga. || 6. Strength much to be desired is in thee, Indra: the Immortal dances forth his hero exploits. | Such, Lord of Treasure, give us splendid riches. I praise the Friend's gift, his whose wealth is mighty. || 7. Thus favour us, O Indra, with thy succour; Hero, protect the bards who sing thy praises. | Be friendly in the fray to those who offer the skin of beautiful and well-pressed Soma. || 8. And these ten steeds which Trasadasyu gives me, the gold-rich chief, the son of Purukutsa, | Resplendent in their brightness shall convey me. Gairikṣhita willed it and so came I hither. || 9. And these, bestowed as sacrificial guerdon, the powerful tawny steeds of Mārutāśva; | And thousands which kind Chyavatāna gave me, abundantly bestowed for my adornment. || 10. And these commended horses, bright and active, by Dhvanya son of Lakṣhmaṇa presented, | Came unto me, as cows into the Ṛiṣhi Saṃvaraṇa's stall, with magnitude of riches.

Hymn 5:34. Indra.

1. Boundless and wasting not, the heavenly food of Gods goes to the foeless One, doer of wondrous deeds. | Press out, make ready, offer gifts with special zeal to him whom many laud, accepter of the prayer. || 2. He who filled full his belly with the Soma's juice, Maghavan, was delighted with the meath's sweet draught, | When Uśanā, that he might slay the monstrous beast, gave him the mighty weapon with a thousand points. || 3. Illustrious is the man whoever presseth out Soma for him in sunshine or in cloud and rain. | The mighty Maghavan who is the sage's Friend advanceth more and more his beauteous progeny. || 4. The Strong God doth not flee away from him whose sire, whose mother or whose brother he hath done to death. | He, the Avenger, seeketh this man's offered gifts: this God, the source of riches, doth not flee from sin. || 5. He seeks no enterprise with five or ten to aid, nor stays with him who pours no juice though prospering well. | The Shaker conquers or slays in this way or that, and to the pious gives a stable full of kine. || 6. Exceeding strong in war he stays the chariot wheel, and, hating him who pours not, prospers him who pours. | Indra the terrible, tamer of every man, as Ārya leads away the Dāsa at his will. || 7. He gathers up for plunder all the niggard s gear: excellent wealth he gives to him who offers gifts. | Not even in wide stronghold may all the folk stand firm who have provoked to anger his surpassing might. || 8. When Indra Maghavan hath marked two wealthy men fighting for beauteous cows with all their followers, | He who stirs all things takes one as his close ally, and, Shaker, with his Heroes, sends the kine to him. || 9. Agni! I laud the liberal Āgniveśi Śatri the type and standard of the pious. | May the collected waters yield him plenty, and his be powerful and bright dominion.

Hymn 5:35. Indra.

1. Indra, for our assistance bring that most effectual power of thine, | Which conquers men for us, and wins the spoil, invincible in fight. || 2. Indra, whatever aids be thine, four be they, or, O Hero, three, | Or those of the Five Tribes of men, bring quickly all that help to us. || 3. The aid most excellent of thee the Mightiest hitherward we call, | For thou wast born with hero might, conquering, Indra, with the Strong. || 4. Mighty to prosper us wast thou born, and mighty is the strength thou hast. | In native power thy soul is firm: thy valour, Indra, slays a host. || 5. O Śatakratu, Lord of Strength, O Indra, Caster of the Stone. | With all thy chariot's force assail the man who shows himself thy foe. || 6. For, Mightiest Vṛitra-slayer, thee, fierce, foremost among many, folk | Whose sacred grass is trimmed invite to battle where the spoil is won. || 7. Indra, do thou protect our car that mingles foremost in the fights, | That bears its part in every fray, invincible and seeking spoil. || 8. Come to us, Indra, and protect our car with thine intelligence. | May we, O Mightiest One, obtain excellent fame at break of day, and meditate our hymn at dawn.

Hymn 5:36. Indra.

1. May Indra come to us, he who knows rightly to give forth treasures from his store of riches. | Even as a thirsty steer who roams the deserts may he drink eagerly the milked-out Soma. || 2. Lord of Bay Horses, Hero, may the Soma rise to thy cheeks and jaws like mountain-ridges. | May we, O King, as he who driveth coursers, all joy in thee with hymns, invoked of many! || 3. Invoked of many, Caster of the Stone my heart quakes like a rolling wheel for fear of penury. | Shall not Purūvasu the singer give thee praise, O ever-prospering Maghavan, mounted on thy car? || 4. Like the press-stone is this thy praiser, Indra. Loudly he lifts his voice with strong endeavour. | With thy left hand, O Maghavan, give us riches: with thy right, Lord of Bays, be not reluctant. || 5. May the strong Heaven make thee the Strong wax stronger: Strong, thou art borne by thy two strong Bay Horses. | So,

fair of cheek, with mighty chariot, mighty, uphold us, strong-willed, thunder-armed, in battle. ‖ 6. Marutas, let all the people in obeisance bow down before this youthful Śrutaratha, | Who, rich in steeds, gave me two dark red horses together with three hundred head of cattle.

Hymn 5:37. Indra.

1. Bedewed with holy oil and meetly worshipped, the Swift One vies with Sūrya's beam in splendour. | For him may mornings dawn without cessation who saith, Let us press Soma out for Indra. ‖ 2. With kindled fire and strewn grass let him worship, and, Soma-presser, sing with stones adjusted: | And let the priest whose press-stones ring forth loudly, go down with his oblation to the river. ‖ 3. This wife is coming near who loves her husband who carries to his home a vigorous consort. | Here may his car seek fame, here loudly thunder, and his wheel make a thousand revolutions. ‖ 4. No troubles vex that King in whose home Indra drinks the sharp Soma juice with milk commingled. | With heroes he drives near, he slays the foeman: Blest, cherishing that name, he guards his people. ‖ 5. May he support in peace and win in battle: he masters both the hosts that meet together. | Dear shall he be to Sūrya, dear to Agni, who with pressed Soma offers gifts to India.

Hymn 5:38. Indra.

1. Wide, Indra Śatakratu, spreads the bounty of thine ample grace: | So, Lord of fair dominion, Friend of all men, give us splendid wealth. ‖ 2. The food which, Mightiest Indra, thou possessest worthy of renown | Is bruited as most widely famed, invincible, O Golden-hued! ‖ 3. O Darter of the Stone, the powers which readily obey thy will,— | Divinities, both thou and they, ye rule, to guard them, earth and heaven. ‖ 4. And from whatever power of thine, O Vṛitra-slayer, it may be, | Bring thou to us heroic strength: thou hast a man's regard for us. ‖ 5. In thy protection, with these aids of thine, O Lord of Hundred Powers, | Indra, may we be guarded well, Hero, may we be guarded well.

Hymn 5:39. Indra.

1. Stone-darting Indra. Wondrous One, what wealth is richly given from thee, | That bounty, Treasure-Finder! bring filling both thy hands, to us. ‖ 2. Bring what thou deemest worth the wish, O Indra, that which is in heaven. | So may we know thee as thou art, boundless in thy munificence. ‖ 3. Thy lofty spirit, far-renowned as fain to give and prompt to win,— | With this thou rendest e'en the firm, Stone-Darter! so to gain thee strength. ‖ 4. Singers with many songs have made Indra propitious to their fame, | Him who is King of human kind, most liberal of your wealthy ones. ‖ 5. To him, to Indra must be sung the poet's word, the hymn of praise. | To him, accepter of the prayer, the Atris raise their songs on high, the Atris beautify their songs.

Hymn 5:40. Indra. Sūrya. Atri.

1. Come thou to what the stones have pressed, drink Soma, O thou Soma's Lord, | Indra best Vṛitra-slayer Strong One, with the Strong. ‖ 2. Strong is the stone, the draught is strong, strong is this Soma that is pressed, | Indra, best Vṛitra-slayer, Strong One with the Strong. ‖ 3. As strong I call on thee the Strong, O Thunder-armed, with various aids, | Indra, best Vṛitra-slayer, Strong One with the Strong. ‖ 4. Impetuous, Thunderer, Strong, quelling the mighty, King, potent, Vṛitra-slayer, Soma-drinker, | May he come hither with his yoked Bay Horses; may Indra gladden him at the noon libation. ‖ 5. O Sūrya, when the Asura's descendant Svarbhānu, pierced thee through and through with darkness, | All creatures looked like one who is bewildered, who knoweth not the place where he is standing. ‖ 6. What time thou smotest down Svarbhānu's magic that spread itself beneath the sky, O Indra, | By his fourth sacred prayer Atri discovered Sūrya concealed in gloom that stayed his function. ‖ 7. Let not the oppressor with this dread, through anger swallow me up, for I am thine, O Atri. | Mitra art thou, the sender of true blessings: thou and King Varuṇa be both my helpers. ‖ 8. The Brahman Atri, as he set the press-stones, serving the Gods with praise and adoration, | Established in the heaven the eye of Sūrya, and caused Svarbhānu's magic arts to vanish. ‖ 9. The Atris found the Sun again, him whom Svarbhānu of the brood | Of Asuras had pierced with gloom. This none besides had power to do.

Hymn 5:41. Viśvedevas

1. Who, Mitra-Varuṇa, is your pious servant to give you gifts from earth or mighty heaven? | Preserve us in the seat of holy Order, and give the offerer power that winneth cattle. ‖ 2. May Mitra, Varuṇa, Aryaman, and Āyu, Indra Ṛibhukṣhan, and the Marutas, love us, | And they who of one mind with bounteous Rudra accept the hymn and laud with adorations. ‖ 3. You will I call to feed the car-horse, Aśvins, with the wind's flight swiftest of those who travel: | Or also to the Asura of heaven, Worshipful, bring a hymn as 'twere libation. ‖ 4. The heavenly Victor, he whose priest is Kaṇva, Trita with Dyaus accordant, Vāta, Agni, | All-feeding Pūṣhan, Bhaga sought the oblation, as they whose steeds are fleetest seek the contest. ‖ 5. Bring ye your riches forward borne on horses: let thought be framed for help and gain of treasure. | Blest he the priest of Auśija through courses, the courses which are yours the fleet, O Marutas. ‖ 6. Bring hither him who yokes the car, your Vāyu, who praises with his songs, the God and Singer; | And, praying and devout, noble and prudent, may the Gods' Spouses in their thoughts retain us. ‖ 7. I speed to you with powers that should be honoured, with songs distinguishing Heaven's mighty Daughters, | Morning and Night, the Two, as 'twere all-knowing: these bring the sacrifice unto the mortal. ‖ 8. You I extol, the nourishers of heroes bringing you gifts, Vāstoṣhpati and Tvaṣhṭar— | Rich Dhiṣhaṇā accords through our obeisance—and Trees and Plants, for the swift gain of riches. ‖ 9. Ours be the Parvatas, even they, for offspring, free-moving, who are Heroes like the Vasus. | May holy Āptya, Friend of man, exalted, strengthen our word for ever and be near us. ‖ 10. Trita praised him, germ of the earthly hero, with pure songs him the Offspring of the Waters. | Agni with might neighs loudly like a charger: he of the flaming hair destroys the forests. ‖ 11. How shall we speak to the great might of Rudra? How speak to Bhaga who takes thought for riches? | May Plants, the Waters, and the Sky preserve us, and Woods and Mountains with their trees for tresses. ‖ 12. May the swift Wanderer, Lord of refreshments listen to our songs, who speeds through cloudy heaven: | And may the Waters, bright like castles, hear us, as they flow onward from the cloven mountain. ‖ 13. We know your ways, ye Mighty Ones receiving choice meed, ye Wonderful, we will proclaim it. | Even strong birds descend not to the mortal who strives to reach them with swift blow and weapons. ‖ 14. Celestial and terrestrial generations, and Waters will I summon to the feasting. | May days with bright dawns cause my songs to prosper, and may the conquered streams increase their waters. ‖ 15. Duly to each one hath my laud been offered. Strong be Varūtrī with her powers to succour. | May the great Mother Rasā here befriend us, straight-handed, with the princes, striving forward. ‖ 16. How may we serve the Liberal Ones with worship, the Marutas swift of course in invocation, the Marutas far-renowned in invocation? | Let not the Dragon of the Deep annoy us, and gladly may he welcome our addresses. ‖ 17. Thus thinking, O ye Gods, the mortal wins you to give him increase of his herds of cattle: the mortal wins him, O ye Gods, your favour. | Here he wins wholesome food to feed this body: as for mine old age, Nirṛiti consume it ‖ 18. O Gods, may we obtain from you this favour, strengthening food through the Cow's praise, ye Vasus. | May she who gives good gifts, the gracious Goddess, come speeding nigh to us for our well-being. ‖ 19. May Iḷā, Mother of the herds of cattle, and Urvaśī with all the streams accept us; | May Urvaśī in lofty heaven accepting, as she partakes the oblation of the living, ‖ 20. Visit us while she shares Ūrjavya's food.

Hymn 5:42. Viśvedevas.

1. Now may our sweetest song with deep devotion reach Varuṇa, Mitra, Aditi, and Bhaga. | May the Five Priests' Lord, dwelling in oblations, bliss-giving Asura, hear, whose paths are open. ‖ 2. May Aditi welcome, even as a mother her dear heart-gladdening son, my song that lauds her. | The prayer they love, bliss-giving, God-appointed, I offer unto Varuṇa and Mitra. ‖ 3. In spirit him, the Sagest of the Sages; with sacrificial oil and meath bedew him | So then let him, God Savitar, provide us excellent, ready, and resplendent treasures. ‖ 4. With willing mind, Indra, vouchsafe us cattle, prosperity, Lord of Bays! and pious patrons; | And, with the sacred prayer by Gods appointed, give us the holy Deities' loving kindness. ‖ 5. God Bhaga, Savitar who deals forth riches, Indra, and they who conquer Vṛitra's treasures, | And Vāja and Ṛibhukṣhan and Purandhi, the Mighty and Immortal Ones, protect us! ‖ 6. Let us declare his deeds, the undecaying unrivalled Victor whom the Marutas follow. | None of old times, O Maghavan, nor later, none of these days hath reached thy hero

prowess. || 7. Praise him the Chief who gives the boon of riches, Brihaspati distributor of treasures, | Who, blessing most the man who sings and praises, comes with abundant wealth to his invoker. || 8. Tended, Brihaspati, with thy protections, the princes are unharmed and girt by heroes. | Wealth that brings bliss is found among the givers of horses and of cattle and of raiment. || 9. Make their wealth flee who, through our hymns enjoying their riches, yield us not an ample guerdon. | Far from the sun keep those who hate devotion, the godless, prospering in their vocation. || 10. With wheelless chariots drive down him, O Marutas, who at the feasts of Gods regards the demons. | May he, though bathed in sweat, form empty wishes, who blames his sacred rite who toils to serve you. || 11. Praise him whose bow is strong and sure his arrow, him who is Lord of every balm that healeth. | Worship thou Rudra for his great good favour: adore the Asura, God, with salutations. || 12. May the House-friends, the cunning-handed Artists, may the Steer's Wives, the streams carved out by Vibhvan, | And may the fair Ones honour and befriend us, Sarasvatī, Brihaddiva, and Rākā. || 13. My newest song, thought that now springs within me, I offer to the Great, the Sure Protector, | Who made for us this All, in fond love laying each varied form within his Daughter's bosom. || 14. Now, even now, may thy fair praise, O Singer, attain Iḍaspati who roars and thunders, | Who, rich in clouds and waters with his lightning speeds forth bedewing both the earth and heaven. || 15. May this my laud attain the troop of Marutas, those who are youths in act, the Sons of Rudra. | The wish calls me to riches and well-being: praise the unwearied Ones whose steeds are dappled. || 16. May this my laud reach earth and air's mid-region, and forest trees and plants to win me riches. | May every Deity be swift to listen, and Mother Earth with no ill thought regard me. || 17. Gods, may we dwell in free untroubled bliss. || 18. May we obtain the Aśvins' newest favour, and gain their health-bestowing happy guidance. | Bring riches hither unto us, and heroes, and all felicity and joy, Immortals!

Hymn 5:43. Viśvedevas.

1. May the Milch-cows who hasten to their object come harmless unto us with liquid sweetness. | The Singer, lauding, calls, for ample riches, the Seven Mighty Ones who bring enjoyment. || 2. With reverence and fair praise will I bring hither, for sake of strength, exhaustless Earth and Heaven. | Father and Mother, sweet of speech, fair-handed, may they, far-famed, in every fight protect us. || 3. Adhvaryus, make the sweet libations ready, and bring the beautiful bright juice to Vāyu. | God, as our Priest, be thou the first to drink it: we give thee of the mead to make thee joyful. || 4. Two arms—the Soma's dexterous immolators—and the ten fingers set and fix the press-stone. | The stalk hath poured, fair with its spreading branches, the mead's bright glittering juice that dwells on mountains. || 5. The Soma hath been pressed for thee, its lover, to give thee power and might and high enjoyment. | Invoked, turn hither in thy car, O Indra, at need, thy two well-trained and dear Bay Horses. || 6. Bring by God-traversed paths, accordant, Agni, the great Aramati, Celestial Lady, | Exalted, worshipped with our gifts and homage, who knoweth holy Law, to drink sweet Soma. || 7. As on his father's lap the son, the darling, so on the fire is set the sacred cauldron, | Which holy singers deck, as if extending and heating that which holds the fatty membrane. || 8. Hither, as herald to invite the Aśvins, come the great lofty song, most sweet and pleasant! | Come in one car, joy-givers! to the banquet, like the bolt binding pole and nave, come hither. || 9. I have declared this speech of adoration to mightiest Pūṣhan and victorious Vāyu, | Who by their bounty are the hymns' inspirers, and of themselves give power as a possession. || 10. Invoked by us bring hither, Jātavedas the Marutas all under their names and figures. | Come to the sacrifice with aid all Marutas, all to the songs and praises of the singer! || 11. From high heaven may Sarasvatī the Holy visit our sacrifice, and from the mountain. | Eager, propitious, may the balmy Goddess hear our effectual speech, our invocation. || 12. Set in his seat the God whose back is dusky, Brihaspati the lofty, the Disposer. | Him let us worship, set within the dwelling, the red, the golden-hued, the all-resplendent || 13. May the Sustainer, high in heaven, come hither, the Bounteous One, invoked, with all his favours, | Dweller with Dames divine, with plants, unwearied, the Steer with triple horn, the life-bestower. || 14. The tuneful eloquent priests of him who liveth have sought the Mother's bright and loftiest station. | As living men, with offered gifts and homage they deck the most auspicious Child to clothe him. || 15. Agni, great vital power is thine, the mighty: pairs waxing old in their devotion seek thee. | May every Deity be swift to listen, and Mother Earth with no ill thought regard me. || 16. Gods, may we dwell in free untroubled bliss. || 17. May we obtain the Aśvins' newest favour, and gain their health-bestowing happy guidance. | Bring riches hither unto us, and heroes, and all felicity and joy, Immortals!

Hymn 5:44. Viśvedevas.

1. As in the first old times, as all were wont, as now, he draweth forth the power turned hitherward with song, | The Princedom throned on holy grass, who findeth light, swift, conquering in the' plants wherein he waxeth strong. || 2. Shining to him who leaves heaven's regions undisturbed, which to his sheen who is beneath show fair in light, | Good guardian art thou, not to be deceived, Most Wise! Far from deceits thy name dwelleth in holy Law. || 3. Truth waits upon oblation present and to come: naught checks him in his way, this victory—bringing Priest: | The Mighty Child who glides along the sacred grass, the undecaying Youth set in the midst of plants. || 4. These come, well-yoked, to you for furtherance in the rite: down come the twin-born strengtheners of Law for him, | With reins easily guided and commanding all. In the deep fall the hide stealeth away their names. || 5. Thou, moving beauteously in visibly pregnant ones, snatching with trees the branching plant that grasps the juice, | Shinest, true Singer! mid the upholders of the voice. Increase thy Consorts thou, lively at sacrifice. || 6. Like as he is beheld such is he said to be. | They with effectual splendour in the floods have made | Earth yield us room enough and amply wide extent, great might invincible, with store of hero sons. || 7. Sūrya the Sage, as if unwedded, with a Spouse, in battle-loving spirit moveth o'er the foes. | May he, self-excellent, grant us a sheltering home, a house that wards the fierce heat off on every side. || 8. Thy name, sung forth by Rishis in these hymns of ours, goes to the loftier One with this swift mover's light. | By skill he wins the boon whereon his heart is set: he who bestirs himself shall bring the thing to pass. || 9. The chief and best of these abideth in the sea, nor doth libation fail wherein it is prolonged. | The heart of him who praiseth trembleth not in fear there where the hymn is found connected with the pure. || 10. For it is he: with though to of Kṣhatra, Manasa, of Yajata, and Sadhri, and Evāvada, | With Avatsāra's sweet songs will we strive to win the mightiest strength which even he who knows should gain. || 11. The Hawk is their full source, girth-stretching rapturous drink of Viśvavāra, of Māyin, and Yajata. | They ever seek a fresh draught so that they may come, know when thy time to halt and drink thy fill is near. || 12. Sadāpriṇa the holy, Tarya, Śrutavit, and Bāhuvrikta, joined with you, have slain the foes. | He gains his wish in both the worlds and brightly shines-when he adores the host with well-advancing steeds. || 13. The worshipper's defender is Sutambhara, producer and uplifter of all holy thoughts. | The milch-cow brought, sweet-flavoured milk was dealt around. Who speaks the bidding text knows this, not he who sleeps. || 11. The sacred hymns love him who wakes and watches: to him who watches come the Sāman verses. | This Soma saith unto the man who watches, I rest and have my dwelling in thy friendship. || 15. Agni is watchful, and the Richas love him; Agni is watchful, Sāman verses seek him. | Agni is watchful, to him saith this Soma, I rest and have my dwelling in thy friendship.

Hymn 5:45. Viśvedevas.

1. Bards of approaching Dawn who know the heavens are come with hymns to throw the mountain open. | The Sun hath risen and opened the stable portals: the doors of men, too, hath the God thrown open. || 2. Sūrya hath spread his light as splendour: hither came the Cows' Mother, conscious, from the stable, | To streams that flow with biting waves to deserts; and heaven is established like a firm-set pillar. || 3. This laud hath won the burden of the mountain. To aid the ancient birth of mighty waters | The mountain parted, Heaven performed his office. The worshippers were worn with constant serving. || 4. With hymns and God-loved words will I invoke you, Indra and Agni, to obtain your favour, | For verily sages, skilled in sacrificing, worship the Marutas and with lauds invite them. || 5. This day approach us: may our thoughts be holy, far from us let us cast away misfortune. | Let us keep those who hate us at a distance, and haste to meet the man who sacrifices. || 6. Come, let us carry out, O

friends, the purpose wherewith the Mother threw the Cow's stall open, | That wherewith Manu conquered Viśiśipra, wherewith the wandering merchant gained heaven's water. || 7. Here, urged by hands, loudly hath rung the press-stone wherewith Navagvas through ten months sang praises. | Saramā went aright and found the cattle. Aṅgiras gave effect to all their labours. || 8. When at the dawning of this mighty Goddess, Aṅgirasas all sang forth with the cattle,— | Their spring is in the loftiest place of meeting,—Saramā found the kine by Order's pathway. || 9. Borne by his Coursers Seven may Sūrya visit the field that spreadeth wide for his long journey. | Down on the Soma swooped the rapid Falcon. Bright was the young Sage moving mid his cattle. || 10. Sūrya hath mounted to the shining ocean when he hath yoked his fair-backed Tawny Horses. | The wise have drawn him like a ship through water: the floods obedient have descended hither. || 11. I lay upon the Floods your hymn, light-winning, wherewith Navagvas their ten months completed. | Through this our hymn may we have Gods to guard us: through this our hymn pass safe beyond affliction.

Hymn 5:46. Viśvedevas.

1. Well knowing I have bound me, horselike, to the pole: I carry that which bears as on and gives us help. | I seek for no release, no turning back therefrom. May he who knows the way, the Leader, guide me straight. || 2. O Agni, Indra, Varuṇa, and Mitra, give, O ye Gods, and Marut host, and Vishṇu. | May both Nāsatyas, Rudra, heavenly Matrons, Pūshan, Sarasvatī, Bhaga, accept us. || 3. Indra and Agni, Mitra, Varuṇa, Aditi, the Waters, Mountains, Marutas, Sky, and Earth and Heaven, | Vishṇu I call, Pūshan, and Brahmaṇaspati, and Bhaga, Śaṃsa, Savitar that they may help. || 4. May Vishṇu also and Vāta who injures none, and Soma granter of possessions give us joy; | And may the Ṛibhus and the Aśvins, Tvashṭar and Vibhvan remember us so that we may have wealth. || 5. So may the band of Marutas dwelling in the sky, the holy, come to us to sit on sacred grass; | Bṛihaspati and Pūshan grant us sure defence, Varuṇa, Mitra, Aryaman guard and shelter us. || 6. And may the Mountains famed in noble eulogies, and the fair-gleaming Rivers keep us safe from harm. | May Bhaga the Dispenser come with power and grace, and far-pervading Aditi listen to my call. || 7. May the Gods' Spouses aid us of their own freewill, aid us to offspring and the winning of the spoil. | Grant us protection, O ye gracious Goddesses, ye who are on the earth or in the waters' realm. || 8. May the Dames, wives of Gods, enjoy our presents, Rāṭ, Aśvinī, Agnāyī, and Indrāṇī. | May Rodasī and Varuṇānī hear us, and Goddesses come at the Matrons' season.

Hymn 5:47. Viśvedevas.

1. Urging to toil and making proclamation, seeking Heaven's Daughter comes the Mighty Mother: | She comes, the youthful Hymn, unto the Fathers, inviting to her home and loudly calling. || 2. Swift in their motion, hasting to their duty, reaching the central point of life immortal, | On every side about the earth and heaven go forth the spacious paths without a limit. || 3. Steer, Sea, Red Bird with strong wings, he hath entered the dwelling-place of the Primeval Father. | A gay-hued Stone set in the midst of heaven, he hath gone forth and guards mid-air's two limits. || 4. Four bear him up and give him rest and quiet, and ten invigorate the Babe for travel. | His kine most excellent, of threefold nature, pass swiftly round the boundaries of heaven. || 5. Wondrous, O people, is the mystic knowledge that while the waters stand the streams are flowing: | That, separate from his Mother, Two support him, closely-united, twins, here made apparent. || 6. For him they lengthen prayers and acts of worship: the Mothers weave garments for him their offspring. | Rejoicing, for the Steer's impregning contact, his Spouses move on paths or heaven to meet him. || 7. Be this our praise, O Varuṇa and Mitra may this be health and force to us, O Agni. | May we obtain firm ground and room for resting: Glory to Heaven, the lofty habitation!

Hymn 5:48. Viśvedevas.

1. What may we meditate for the beloved Power, mighty in native strength and glorious in itself, | Which as a magic energy seeking waters spreads even to the immeasurable middle region's cloud? || 2. O'er all the region with their uniform advance these have spread out the lore that giveth heroes strength. | Back, with their course reversed, the others pass away: the pious lengthens life with those that are before. || 3. With pressing-stones and with the bright beams of the day he hurls his broadest bolt against the Guileful One. | Even he whose hundred wander in his own abode, driving the days afar and bringing them again. || 4. I, to enjoy the beauty of his form, behold that rapid rush of his as 'twere an axe's edge, | What time he gives the man who calls on him in fight wealth like a dwelling-house filled full with store of food. || 5. Four-faced and nobly clad, Varuṇa, urging on the pious to his task, stirs himself with the tongue. | Naught by our human nature do we know of him, him from whom Bhaga Savitar bestows the boon.

Hymn 5:49. Viśvedevas.

1. This day I bring God Savitar to meet you, and Bhaga who allots the wealth of mortals. | You, Aśvins, Heroes rich in treasures, daily seeking your friendship fain would I turn hither. || 2. Knowing full well the Asura's time of coming, worship God Savitar with hymns and praises. | Let him who rightly knoweth speak with homage to him who dealeth out man's noblest treasure. || 3. Not for reward doth Pūshan send his blessings, Bhaga, or Aditi: his garb is splendour. | May Indra, Vishṇu, Varuṇa, Mitra, Agni produce auspicious days, the Wonder-Workers. || 4. Sending the shelter which we ask, the foeless Savitar and the Rivers shall approach us. | When I, the sacrifice's priest, invite them, may we he lords of wealth and rich possessions. || 5. They who devote such worship to the Vasus, singing their hymns to Varuṇa and Mitra, | Vouchsafe them ample room, far off be danger. Through grace of Heaven and Earth may we be happy.

Hymn 5:50. Viśvedevas.

1. Let every mortal man elect the friendship of the guiding God. | Each one solicits him for wealth and seeks renown to prosper him. || 2. These, leading God, are thine, and these here ready to speak after us. | As such may we attain to wealth and wait with services on thee. || 3. So further honour as our guests the Hero Gods and then the Dames. | May he remove and keep afar our foes and all who block our path. || 4. Where fire is set, and swiftly runs the victim dwelling in the trough, | He wins, with heroes in his home, friendly to man, like constant streams. || 5. May these thy riches, Leader God! that rule the car, be blest to us, | Yea, blest to us for wealth and weal. This will we ponder praising strength, this ponder as we praise the God.

Hymn 5:51. Viśvedevas.

1. With all assistants, Agni, come hither to drink the Soma-juice; | With Gods unto our sacred gifts. || 2. Come to the sacrifice, O ye whose ways are right, whose laws are true, | And drink the draught with Agni's tongue. || 3. O Singer, with the singers, O Gracious, with those who move at dawn, | Come to the Soma-draught with Gods. || 4. To Indra and to Vāyu dear, this Soma, by the mortar pressed, | Is now poured forth to fill the jar. || 5. Vāyu, come hither to the feast, well pleased unto our sacred gifts: | Drink of the Soma juice effused come to the food. || 6. Ye, Indra, Vāyu, well deserve to drink the juices pressed by us. | Gladly accept them, spotless Pair come to the food. || 7. For Indra and for Vāyu pressed are Soma juices blent with curd, | As rivers to the lowland flow: come to the food. || 8. Associate with all the Gods, come, with the Aśvins and with Dawn, | Agni, as erst with Atri, so enjoy the juice. || 9. Associate with Varuṇa, with Mitra, Soma, Vishṇu, come, | Agni, as erst with Atri, so enjoy the juice. || 10. Associate with Vasus, with Ādityas, Indra, Vāyu, come, Agni as erst with Atri, so enjoy the juice. || 11. May Bhaga and the Aśvins grant us health and wealth, and Goddess Aditi and he whom none resist. | The Asura Pūshan grant us all prosperity, and Heaven and Earth most wise vouchsafe us happiness. || 12. Let us solicit Vāyu for prosperity, and Soma who is Lord of all the world for weal; | For weal Bṛihaspati with all his company. May the Ādityas bring us health and happiness. || 13. May all the Gods, may Agni the beneficent, God of all men, this day be with us for our weal. | Help us the Ṛibhus, the Divine Ones, for our good. May Rudra bless and keep us from calamity. || 14. Prosper us, Mitra, Varuṇa. O wealthy Pathyā, prosper us. | Indra and Agni, prosper us; prosper us thou, O Aditi. || 15. Like Sun and Moon may we pursue in full prosperity our path, | And meet with one who gives again,— who knows us well and slays us not.

Hymn 5:52. Marutas.

1. Sing boldly forth, Śyāvāśva, with the Marutas who are loud in song, | Who, holy, as their wont is, joy in glory that is free from guile. || 2. For in their boldness they are friends of firm and sure heroic strength. | They in their course, bold-spirited, guard all men of their own accord. || 3. Like steers in rapid motion they advance and overtake the nights; | And thus the

Marutas' power in heaven and on the earth we celebrate. || 4. With boldness to your Marutas let us offer laud and sacrifice: | Who all, through ages of mankind, guard mortal man from injury. || 5. Praiseworthy, givers of good gifts, Heroes with full and perfect strength— | To Marutas, Holy Ones of heaven, will I extol the sacrifice. || 6. The lofty Heroes cast their spears and weapons bright with gleaming gold. | After these Marutas followed close, like laughing lightning from the sky, a splendour of its own accord. || 7. They who waxed mighty, of the earth, they who are in the wide mid-air, | Or in the rivers' compass, or in the abode of ample heaven. || 8. Praise thou the Marutas' company, the valorous and truly strong, | The Heroes, hasting, by themselves have yoked their deer for victory. || 9. Fair-gleaming, on Parushṇī they have clothed themselves in robes of wool, | And with their chariot tires they cleave the rock asunder in their might. || 10. Whether as wanderers from the way or speeders on or to the path, | Under these names the spreading band tend well the sacrifice for me. || 11. To this the Heroes well attend, well do their teams attend to this. | Visible are their varied forms. Behold, they are Pārāvatas. || 12. Hymn-singing, seeking water, they, praising, have danced about the spring. | What are they unto me? No thieves, but helpers, splendid to behold. || 13. Sublime, with lightnings for their spears, Sages and Orderers are they. | Ṛishi, adore that Marut host, and make them happy with thy song. || 14. Ṛishi, invite the Marut band with offerings, as a maid her friend. | From heaven, too, Bold Ones, in your might haste hither glorified with songs. || 15. Thinking of these now let him come, as with the escort of the Gods, | And with the splendid Princes, famed for rapid courses, to the gifts. || 16. Princes, who, when I asked their kin, named Pṛiśni as their Mother-cow, | And the impetuous Rudra they, the Mighty Ones, declared their Sire. || 17. The mighty ones, the seven times seven, have singly given me hundred gifts. | I have obtained on Yamunā famed wealth in kine and wealth in steeds.

Hymn 5:53. Marutas.

1. Who knows the birth of these, or who lived in the Marutas' favour in the days of old | What time their spotted deer were yoked? || 2. Who, when they stood upon their cars, hath heard them tell the way they went? | Who was the bounteous man to whom their kindred rains flowed down with food of sacrifice? || 3. To me they told it, and they came with winged steeds radiant to the draught, | Youths, Heroes free from spot or stain: Behold us here and praise thou us; || 4. Who shine self-luminous with ornaments and swords, with breastplates, armlets, and with wreaths, | Arrayed on chariots and with bows. || 5. O swift to pour your bounties down, ye Marutas, with delight I look upon your cars, | Like splendours coming through the rain. || 6. Munificent Heroes, they have cast heaven's treasury down for the worshipper's behoof: | They set the storm-cloud free to stream through both the worlds, and rain floods flow o'er desert spots. || 7. The bursting streams m billowy flood have spread abroad, like milch-kine, o'er the firmament. | Like swift steeds hasting to their journey's resting-place, to every side run glittering brooks. || 8. Hither, O Marutas, come from heaven, from mid-air, or from near at hand | Tarry not far away from us. || 9. So let not Rasā, Krumu, or Anitabhā, Kubhā, or Sindhu hold you back. | Let not the watery Sarayu obstruct your way. With us be all the bliss ye give. || 10. That brilliant gathering of your cars, the company of Marutas, of the Youthful Ones, | The rain-showers, speeding on, attend. || 11. With eulogies and hymns may we follow your army, troop by troop, and band by band, | And company by company. || 12. To what oblation-giver, sprung of noble ancestry, have sped | The Marutas on this course today? || 13. Vouchsafe to us the bounty, that which we implore, through which, for child and progeny, | Ye give the seed of corn that wasteth not away, and bliss that reacheth to all life. || 14. May we in safety pass by those who slander us, leaving behind disgrace and hate. | Marutas, may we be there when ye, at dawn, in rest and toil, rain waters down and balm. || 15. Favoured by Gods shall he the man, O Heroes, Marutas! and possessed of noble sons, | Whom ye protect. Such may we be. || 16. Praise the Free-givers. At this liberal patron's rite they joy like cattle in the mead. | So call thou unto them who come as ancient Friends: hymn those who love thee with a song.

Hymn 5:54. Marutas.

1. This hymn will I make for the Marut host who bright in native splendour cast the mountains down. | Sing the great strength of those illustrious in renown, who stay the heat, who sacrifice on heights of heaven. || 2. O Marutas, rich in water, strengtheners of life are your strong bands with harnessed steeds, that wander far. | Trita roars out at him who aims the lightning-flash. The waters sweeping round are thundering on their way. || 3. They gleam with lightning, Heroes, Casters of the Stone, wind-rapid Marutas, overthrowers of the bills, | Oft through desire to rain coming with storm of hail, roaring in onset, violent and exceeding strong. || 4. When, mighty Rudras, through the nights and through the days, when through the sky and realms of air, shakers of all, | When over the broad fields ye drive along like ships, e'en to strongholds ye come, Marutas, but are not harmed. || 5. Marutas, this hero strength and majesty of yours hath, like the Sun, extended o'er a lengthened way, | When in your course like deer with splendour unsubdued ye bowed the hill that gives imperishable rain. || 6. Bright shone your host, ye Sages, Marutas, when ye smote the waving tree as when the worm consumeth it. | Accordant, as the eye guides him who walks, have ye led our devotion onward by an easy path. || 7. Never is he, O Marutas, slain or overcome, never doth he decay ne'er is distressed or harmed; | His treasures, his resources, never waste away, whom. whether he be prince or Ṛishi, ye direct. || 8. With harnessed team like heroes overcoming troops, the friendly Marutas, laden with their water-casks, | Let the spring flow, and when impetuous' they roar they inundate the earth with floods of pleasant meath. || 9. Free for the Marutas is the earth with sloping ways, free for the rushing Ones is heaven with steep descents. | The paths of air's mid-region are precipitous, precipitous the mountains with their running streams. || 10. When, as the Sun hath risen up, ye take delight, O bounteous radiant Marutas, Heroes of the sky, | Your coursers weary not when speeding on their way, and rapidly ye reach the end of this your path. || 11. Lances are on your shoulders, anklets on your feet, gold chains are on your breasts, gems, Marutas, on your car. | Lightnings aglow with flame are flashing in your hands, and visors wrought of gold are laid upon your heads. || 12. Marutas, in eager stir ye shake the vault of heaven, splendid beyond conception, for its shining fruit. | They gathered when they let their deeds of might flash forth. The Pious Ones send forth a far-resounding shout. || 13. Sage Marutas, may we be the drivers of the car of riches full of life that have been given by you. | O Marutas, let that wealth in thousands dwell with us which never vanishes like Tishya from the sky. || 14. Marutas, ye further wealth with longed for heroes, further the Ṛishi skilled in chanted verses. | Ye give the Bhārata as his strength, a charger, and ye bestow a king who quickly listens. || 15. Of you, most swift to succour! I solicit wealth wherewith we may spread forth mid men like as the Sun. | Accept, O Marutas, graciously this hymn of mine that we may live a hundred winters through its power.

Hymn 5:55. Marutas.

1. With gleaming lances, with their breasts adorned with gold, the Marutas, rushing onward, hold high power of life. | They hasten with swift steeds easy to be controlled. Their cars moved onward as they went to victory. || 2. Ye, as ye wish, have gained of your own selves your power: high, O ye Mighty Ones, and wide ye shine abroad. | They with their strength have even measured out the sky. | Their cars moved onward as they went to victory. || 3. Strong, born together, they together have waxed great: the Heroes more and more have grown to majesty | Resplendent as the Sun's beams in their light are they. Their cars moved onward as they went to victory. || 4. Marutas, your mightiness deserves to be adored, sight to be longed for like the shining of the Sun. | So lead us with your aid to immortality. | Their cars moved onward as they went to victory. || 5. O Marutas, from the Ocean ye uplift the rain, and fraught with vaporous moisture pour the torrents down. | Never, ye Wonder-Workers, are your Milch-kine dry. Their cars moved onward as they went to victory. || 6. When to your car-poles ye have yoked your spotted deer to be your steeds, and put your golden mantles on, | O Marutas, ye disperse all enemies abroad. Their cars moved onward as they went to victory. || 7. Neither the mountains nor the rivers keep you back: whither ye have resolved thither ye, Marutas, go. | Ye compass round about even the heaven and earth. Their cars moved onward as they went to victory. | Whate'er is ancient, Marutas, what of recent time, whate'er is spoken, Vasus, what is chanted forth, | They who take cognizance of all of this are ye. Their cars moved onward as

they went to victory. || 9. Be gracious unto us, ye Marutas, slay us not extend ye unto us shelter of many a sort. | Pay due regard unto our friendship and our praise. Their cars moved onward as they went to victory. || 10. O Marutas, lead us on to higher fortune deliver us, when lauded, from afflictions. | Accept, ye Holy Ones, the gifts we bring you. May we be masters of abundant riches.

Hymn 5:56. Marutas.

1. Agni, that valorous company adorned with ornaments of gold, | The people of the Marutas, I call down today even from the luminous realm of heaven. || 2. Even as thou thinkest in thy heart, thither my wishes also tend. | Those who have come most near to thine invoking calls, strengthen them fearful to behold. || 3. Earth, like a bounteous lady, liberal of her gifts, struck down and shaken, yet exultant, comes to us. | Impetuous as a bear, O Marutas, is your rush terrible as a dreadful bull. || 4. They who with mighty strength o'erthrow like oxen difficult to yoke, | Cause e'en the heavenly stone to shake yea, shake the rocky mountain as they race along. || 5. Rise up! even now with lauds I call the very numerous company, | Unequalled, of these Marutas, like a herd of kine, grown up together in their strength. || 6. Bind to your car the bright red mares, yoke the red coursers to your car. | Bind to the pole, to draw, the fleet-foot tawny steeds, the best at drawing, to the pole. || 7. Yea, and this loudly-neighing bright red vigorous horse who hath been stationed, fair to see, | Let him not cause delay, O Marutas,, in your course, urge ye him onward in your cars. || 8. The Marutas' chariot, ever fain to gather glory, we invoke, | Which Rodasī hath mounted, bringing pleasant gifts, with Marutas in her company. || 9. I call that brilliant band of yours, adorable, rapid on the car | Whereon the bounteous Dame, auspicious, nobly born, shows glorious with the Marut host.

Hymn 5:57. Marutas.

1. Of one accord, with Indra, O ye Rudras, come borne on your golden car for our prosperity. | An offering from us, this hymn is brought to you, as, unto one who thirsts for water, heavenly springs. || 2. Armed with your daggers, full of wisdom, armed with spears, armed with your quivers, armed with arrows, with good bows, | Good horses and good cars have ye, O Pṛiśni's Sons: ye, Marutas, with good weapons go to victory. || 3. From hills and heaven ye shake wealth for the worshipper: in terror at your coming low the woods bow down. | Ye make the earth to tremble, Sons of Pṛiśni, when for victory ye have yoked, fierce Ones! your spotted deer. || 4. Bright with the blasts of wind, wrapped in their robes of rain, like twins of noble aspect and of lovely form, | The Marutas, spotless, with steeds tawny-hued and red, strong in their mightiness and spreading wide like heaven. || 5. Rich in adornment, rich in drops, munificent, bright in their aspect, yielding bounties that endure, | Noble by birth, adorned with gold upon their breasts, the Singers of the sky have won immortal fame. || 6. Borne on both shoulders, O ye Marutas, are your spears: within your arms is laid your energy and 3trength. | Bold thoughts are in your heads, your weapons in your cars, all glorious majesty is moulded on your forms. || 7. Vouchsafe to us, O Marutas, splendid bounty in cattle and in steeds, in cars and heroes. | Children of Rudra, give us high distinction: may I enjoy your Godlike help and favour. || 8. Ho! Marutas, Heroes, skilled in Law, immortal, be gracious unto us, ye rich in treasures, | Ye hearers of the truth, ye sage and youthful, grown mighty, dwelling on the lofty mountains.

Hymn 5:58. Marutas.

1. Now do I glorify their mighty cohort, the company of these the youthful Marutas, | Who ride impetuous on with rapid horses, and radiant in themselves, are Lords of Amṛita. || 2. The mighty glittering band, arm-bound with bracelets, givers of bliss, unmeasured in their greatness, | With magical powers, bountiful, ever-roaring,—these, liberal Heroes, venerate thou singer. || 3. This day may all your water-bringers, Marutas, they who impel the falling rain, approach us. | This fire, O Marutas, hath been duly kindled; let it find favour with you, youthful Sages. || 4. Ye raise up for the folk an active ruler whom, Holy Ones! a Master's hand hath fashioned. | Ye send the fighter hand to hand, arm mighty, and the brave hero, Marutas with good horses. || 5. They spring forth more and more, strong in their glories, like days, like spokes where none are last in order. | Highest and mightiest are the Sons of Pṛiśni. Firm to their own intention cling the Marutas. || 6. When ye have hastened on with spotted coursers, O Marutas, on your cars with strong-wrought fellies, | The waters are disturbed, the woods are shattered. Let Dyaus the Red Steer send his thunder downward. || 7. Even Earth hath spread herself wide at their coming, and they as husbands have with power impregned her. | They to the pole have yoked the winds for coursers: their sweat have they made rain, these Sons of Rudra. || 8. Ho! Marutas, Heroes, skilled in Law, immortal, be gracious unto us, ye rich in treasures, | Ye hearers of the truth, ye sage and youthful, grown mighty, dwelling on the lofty mountains.

Hymn 5:59. Marutas.

1. Your spy hath called to you to give prosperity. I sing to Heaven and Earth and offer sacrifice. | They bathe their steeds and hasten through the firmament: they spread abroad their radiance through the sea of cloud. || 2. Earth shakes and reels in terror at their onward rush, like a full ship which, quivering, lets the water in. | Marked on their ways are they, visible from afar: the Heroes press between in mighty armament. || 3. As the exalted horn of bulls for splendid might, as the Sun's eye set in the firmament's expanse, | Like vigorous horses ye are beauteous to behold, and for your glory show like bridegrooms, O ye Men. || 4. Who, O ye Marutas, may attain the mighty lore of you the mighty, who may reach your manly deeds? | Ye, verily, make earth tremble like a ray of light what time ye bring your boons to give prosperity, || 5. Like steeds of ruddy colour, scions of one race, as foremost champions they have battled in the van. | The Heroes have waxed strong like well-grown manly youths; with floods of rain they make the Sun's eye fade away, || 6. Having no eldest and no youngest in their band, no middle-most, preeminent they have waxed in might, | These Sons of Pṛiśni, sprung of noble ancestry: come hitherward to us, ye bridegrooms of the sky. || 7. Like birds of air they flew with might in lengthened lines from heaven's high ridges to the borders of the sky. | The steeds who carry them, as Gods and mortals know, have caused the waters of the mountains to descend. || 8. May Dyaus, the Infinite, roar for our banquet: may Dawns toil for us, glittering with moisture. | Lauded by thee, these Marutas, Sons o Rudra, O Ṛishi, have sent down the heavenly treasure.

Hymn 5:60. Marutas.

1. I laud with reverence the gracious Agni: here may he sit and part our meed among us. | As with spoil-seeking cars I bring oblation: turned rightward I will swell the Marut's, praise-song. || 2. The Marutas, yea, the Rudras, who have mounted their famous spotted deer and cars swift-moving,— | Before you, fierce Ones! woods bow down in terror: Earth, even the mountain, trembles at your coming. || 3. Though vast and tall, the mountain is affrighted, the height of heaven is shaken at your roaring | When, armed with lances, ye are sporting, Marutas, and rush along together like the waters. || 4. They, like young suitors, sons of wealthy houses, have with their golden natures decked their bodies. | Strong on their cars, the lordly Ones, for glory, have set their splendours on their forms for ever. || 5. None being eldest, none among them youngest, as brothers they have grown to happy fortune. | May their Sire Rudra, young and deft, and Pṛiśni pouring much milk, bring fair days to the Marutas. || 6. Whether, O blessed Marutas, ye be dwelling in highest, midmost, or in lowest heaven, | Thence, O ye Rudras, and thou also, Agni, notice the sacrificial food we offer. || 7. O Marutas, Lords of all, when Agni and when ye drive downward from sublimest heaven along the heights, | Shakers of all, rejoicing, slayers of the foe, give riches to the Soma-pressing worshipper. || 8. O Agni, with the Marutas as they gleam and sing, gathered in troop, rejoicing drink the Soma juice; | With these the living ones who cleanse and further all, joined with thy banner, O Vaiśvānara, from of old.

Hymn 5:61. Marutas.

1. O Heroes lordliest of all, who are ye that have singly come | Forth from a region most remote? | 2. Where are your horses, where the reins? How came ye? how had ye the power? | Rein was on nose and seat on back. || 3. The whip is laid upon the flank. The heroes stretch their thighs apart, | Like women when the babe is born. || 4. Go ye, O Heroes, far away, ye bridegrooms with a lovely Spouse | That ye may warm you at the fire. || 5. May she gain cattle for her meed, hundreds of sheep and steeds and kine, | Who threw embracing arms around the hero whom Śyāvāśva praised. || 6. Yea, many a woman is more firm and better than the man who turns | Away from Gods, and offers not. || 7. She who discerns the weak and worn,

the man who thirsts and is in want | She sets her mind upon the Gods. || 8. And yet full many a one, unpraised, mean niggard, is entitled man, | Ever the same in enmity. || 9. And she, the young, the joyous-spirited, divulged the path to Śyāva, yea, to me. | Two red steeds carried me to Purumīḷha's side, that sage of far-extended fame, || 10. Him who, like Vaidadaśvi, like Taranta, hath bestowed on me | A hundred cows in liberal gift. || 11. They who are borne by rapid steeds, drinking the meath that gives delight, | They have attained high glories here. || 12. They by whose splendour both the worlds are over-spread they shine on cars | As the gold gleams above in heaven. || 13. That Marut band is ever young, borne on bright cars, unblamable, | Moving to victory, checked by none. || 14. Who knoweth, verily, of these where the All-shakers take delight, | Born, spotless, after sacred Law? || 15. Guides are ye, lovers of the song to mortal man through holy hymn, | And hearers when he cries for help. || 16. Do ye, destroyers of the foe, worshipful and exceeding bright, | Send down the treasures that we crave. || 17. O Ūrmyā, bear thou far away to Dārbhya this my hymn of praise, | Songs, Goddess, as if chariot-borne. || 18. From me to Rathavīti say, when he hath pressed the Soma juice, | The wish I had departeth not. || 19. This wealthy Rathavīti dwells among the people rich in kine, | Among the mountains, far withdrawn.

Hymn 5:62. Mitra-Varuṇa

1. By your high Law firm order is established there where they loose for travel Sūrya's horses. | Ten hundred stood together: there I looked on this the most marvellous Deities' one chief glory. || 2. This, Mitra-Varuṇa, is your special greatness: floods that stood there they with the days attracted. | Ye cause to flow all voices of the cowpen: your single chariot-felly hath rolled hither. || 3. O Mitra-Varuṇa, ye by your greatness, both Kings, have firmly established earth and heaven, | Ye caused the cows to stream, the plants to flourish, and, scattering swift drops, sent down the rain-flood. || 4. Let your well-harnessed horses bear you hither: hitherward let them come with reins drawn tightly. | A covering cloud of sacred oil attends you, and your streams flow to us from days aforetime. || 5. To make the lustre wider and more famous, guarding the sacred grass with veneration, | Ye, Mitra-Varuṇa, firm, strong, awe-inspiring, are seated on a throne amid oblations. || 6. With hands that shed no blood, guarding the pious, whom, Varuṇa, ye save amid oblations. | Ye Twain, together, Kings of willing spirit, uphold dominion based on thousand pillars. || 7. Adorned with gold, its columns are of iron. in heaven it glitters like a whip for horses; | Or established on a field deep-spoiled and fruitful. So may we share the meath that loads your car-seat. || 8. Ye mount your car gold-hued at break of morning, and iron-pillared when the Sun is setting, | And from that place, O Varuṇa and Mitra, behold infinity and limitation. || 9. Bountiful guardians of the world! the shelter that is impenetrable, strongest, flawless, | Aid us with that, O Varuṇa and Mitra, and when we long to win may we be victors.

Hymn 5:63. Mitra-Varuṇa.

1. Guardians of Order, ye whose Laws are ever true, in the sublimest heaven your chariot ye ascend. | O Mitra-Varuṇa whomsoe'er ye: favour, here, to him the rain with sweetness streameth down from heaven. || 2. This world's imperial Kings, O Mitra-Varuṇa, ye rule in holy synod, looking on the light. | We pray for rain, your boon, and immortality. Through heaven and over earth the thunderers take their way. || 3. Imperial Kings, strong, Heroes, Lords of earth and heaven, Mitra and Varuṇa, ye ever active Ones, | Ye wait on thunder with the many-tinted clouds, and by the Asura's magic power cause Heaven to rain. || 4. Your magic, Mitra-Varuṇa, resteth in the heaven. The Sun, the wondrous weapon, cometh forth as light. | Ye hide him in the sky with cloud and flood of rain, and water-drops, Parjanya! full of sweetness flow. || 5. The Marutas yoke their easy car for victory, O Mitra-Varuṇa, as a hero in the wars. | The thunderers roam through regions varied in their hues. Imperial Kings, bedew us with the milk of heaven. || 6. Refreshing is your voice, O Mitra-Varuṇa: Parjanya sendeth out a wondrous mighty voice. | With magic power the Marutas clothe them with the clouds. Ye Two cause Heaven to rain, the red, the spotless One. || 7. Wise, with your Law and through the Asura's magic power ye guard the ordinances, Mitra-Varuṇa. | Ye by eternal Order govern all the world. Ye set the Sun in heaven as a refulgent car.

Hymn 5:64. Mitra-Varuṇa

1. You, foeman-slaying Varuṇa and Mitra, we invoke with song, | Who, as with penfold of your arms, encompass round the realm of light. || 2. Stretch out your arms with favouring love unto this man who singeth hymns, | For in all places is sung forth your ever-gracious friendliness. || 3. That I may gain a refuge now, may my steps be on Mitra's path. | Men go protected in the charge of this dear Friend who harms us not. || 4. Mitra and Varuṇa, from you may I, by song, win noblest meed. | That shall stir envy in the homes of wealthy chiefs and those who praise. || 5. With your fair splendours, Varuṇa and Mitra, to our gathering come, | That in their homes the wealthy chiefs and they who are your friends may thrive. || 6. With those, moreover, among whom ye hold your high supremacy, | Vouchsafe us room that we may win strength for prosperity and wealth. || 7. When morning flushes, Holy Ones! in the Gods' realm where white Cows shine, | Supporting Archanānas, speed, ye Heroes, with your active feet hither to my pressed Soma juice.

Hymn 5:65. Mitra-Varuṇa.

1. Full wise is he who hath discerned: let him speak to us of the Gods,— | The man whose praise-songs Varuṇa the beautiful, or Mitra, loves. || 2. For they are Kings of noblest might, of glorious fame most widely spread; | Lords of the brave, who strengthen Law, the Holy Ones with every race. || 3. Approaching you with prayer for aid, together I address you first | We who have good steeds call on you, Most Sage, to give us strength besides. || 4. E'en out of misery Mitra gives a way to dwelling at our case, | For he who worships hath the grace of Mitra, fighter in the van. || 5. In Mitra's shelter that extends to utmost distance may we dwell, | Unmenaced, guarded by the care, ever as sons of Varuṇa. || 6. Ye, Mitra, urge this people on, and to one end direct their ways. | Neglect not ye the wealthy chiefs, neglect not us the Ṛishis: be our guardians when ye quaff the milk.

Hymn 5:66. Mitra-Varuṇa.

1. O sapient man, call the Two Gods, the very wise, who slay the foe. | For Varuṇa, whose form is Law, place offerings for his great delight. || 2. For they have won unbroken sway in full perfection, power divine. | And, like high laws, the world of man hath been made beautiful as light. || 3. Therefore we praise you that your cars may travel far in front of ours— | You who accept the eulogy of Rātahavya with his hymns. || 4. And ye show wisdom, Wondrous Gods with fullness of intelligence. | By men's discernment are ye marked, O ye whose might is purified. || 5. This is the Law sublime, O Earth: to aid the Ṛishis' toil for fame | The Two, wide-spreading, are prepared. They come with ample overflow. || 6. Mitra, ye Gods with wandering eyes, would that the worshippers and we | Might strive to reach the realm ye rule, most spacious and protected well,

Hymn 5:67. Mitra-Varuṇa.

1. Ye Gods, Ādityas, Varuṇa, Aryaman, Mitra, verily | Have here obtained supremest sway, high, holy, set apart for you. || 2. When, Varuṇa and Mitra, ye sit in your golden dwelling-place, | Ye Twain, supporters of mankind, foe-slayers, give felicity. || 3. All these, possessors of all wealth, Varuṇa, Mitra, Aryaman, | Follow their ways, as if with feet, and guard from injury mortal man. || 4. For they are true, they cleave to Law, held holy among every race, | Good leaders, bounteous in their gifts, deliverers even from distress. || 5. Which of your persons, Varuṇa or Mitra, merits not our praise? | Therefore our thought is turned to you, the Atris' thought is turned to you.

Hymn 5:68. Mitra-Varuṇa.

1. Sing forth unto your Varuṇa and Mitra with a song inspired. | They, Mighty Lords, are lofty Law || 2. Full springs of fatness, Sovereign Kings, Mitra. and Varuṇa, the Twain, | Gods glorified among the Gods. || 3. So help ye us to riches, great terrestrial and celestial wealth: | Vast is your sway among the Gods. || 4. Carefully tending Law with Law they have attained their vigorous might. | The two Gods wax devoid of guile. || 5. With rainy skies and streaming floods, Lords of the strength that bringeth gifts, | A lofty seat have they attained.

Hymn 5:69. Mitra-Varuṇa.

1. Three spheres of light, O Varuṇa, three heavens, three firmaments ye comprehend, O Mitra: | Waxed strong, ye keep the splendour of dominion, guarding the Ordinance that lasts for ever. || 2. Ye, Varuṇa, have

kine who yield refreshment; Mitra, your floods pour water full of sweetness. | There stand the Three Steers, splendid in their brightness, who fill the three world-bowls with genial moisture. || 3. I call at dawn on Aditi the Goddess, I call at noon and when the Sun is setting. | I pray, O Mitra-Varuṇa, for safety, for wealth and progeny, in rest and trouble. || 4. Ye who uphold the region, sphere of brightness, ye who support earth's realm Divine Ādityas, | The Immortal Gods, O Varuṇa and Mitra, never impair your everlasting statutes.

Hymn 5:70. Mitra-Varuṇa.

1. Even far and wide, O Varuṇa and Mitra, doth your grace extend. | May I obtain your kind good-will. || 2. From you, benignant Gods, may we gain fully food for sustenance. | Such, O ye Rudras, my we be. || 3. Guard us, O Rudras. with your guards, save us, ye skilled to save, may we | Subdue the Dasyus, we ourselves, || 4. Or ne'er may we, O wondrous Strong, enjoy another's solemn feast, | Ourselves, our sons, or progeny.

Hymn 5:71. Mitra-Varuṇa.

1. O Varuṇa and Mitra, ye who slay the foemen, come with might | To this our goodly sacrifice. || 2. For, Varuṇa and Mitra, ye Sages are Rulers over all. Fill full our songs, for this ye can. || 3. Come to the juice that we have pressed. Varuṇa, Mitra, come to drink | This Soma of the worshipper.

Hymn 5:72. Mitra-Varuṇa.

1 To Varuṇa and Mitra we offer with songs, as Atri did. Sit on the sacred grass to drink the Soma juice. || 2. By Ordinance and Law ye dwell in peace secure, bestirring men. | Sit on the sacred grass to drink the Soma juice. || 3. May Varuṇa and Mitra, for our help, accept the sacrifice. | Sit on the sacred grass to drink the Soma juice.

Hymn 5:73. Aśvins.

1. Whether, O Aśvins, ye this day be far remote or near at hand, | In many spots or in mid-air, come hither, Lords of ample wealth. || 2. These here, who show o'er widest space, bringing full many a wondrous act, | Resistless, lovingly I seek, I call the Mightiest to enjoy. || 3. Another beauteous wheel have ye fixed there to decorate your car. | With others through the realms ye roam in might unto the neighbouring tribes. || 4. That deed of yours that is extolled, Viśvas! hath all been done with this. | Born otherwise, and spotless, ye have entered kinship's bonds with us. || 5. When Sūrya mounted on your car that rolls for ever rapidly, | Birds of red hue were round about and burning splendours compassed you. || 6. Atri bethinks himself of you, O Heroes, with a friendly mind, | What time, Nāsatyas, with his mouth he stirs the spotless flame for you. || 7. Strong is your swiftly moving steed, famed his exertion in the course | When by your great deeds, Aśvins, Chiefs, Atri is brought to us again. || 8. Lovers of sweetness, Rudras, she who streams with sweetness waits on you. | When ye have travelled through the seas men bring you gifts of well-dressed food. || 9. Aśvins, with truth they call you Twain bestowers of felicity; | At sacrifice most prompt to hear, most gracious ye at sacrifice. || 10. Most pleasing to the Aśvins be these prayers which magnify their might, | Which we have fashioned, even as cars high reverence have we spoken forth.

Hymn 5:74. Aśvins.

1. Where in the heavens are ye today, Gods, Aśvins, rich in constancy? | Hear this, ye excellent as Steers: Atri inviteth you to come. || 2. Where are they now? Where are the Twain, the famed Nāsatyas, Gods in heaven? | Who is the man ye strive to reach? Who of your suppliants is with you? || 3. Whom do ye visit, whom approach? to whom direct your harnessed car? | With whose devotions are ye pleased? We long for you to further us. || 4. Ye, Strengtheners, for Paura stir the filler swimming in the flood, | Advancing to be captured like a lion to the ambuscade. || 5. Ye from Chyavāna worn with age removed his skin as 'twere a robe. | So, when ye made him young again, he stirred the longing of a dame. || 6. Here is the man who lauds you both: to see your glory are we here. | Now bear me, come with saving help, ye who are rich in store of wealth. || 7. Who among many mortal men this day hath won you to himself? | What bard, accepters of the bard? Who, rich in wealth! with sacrifice? || 8. O Aśvins, may your car approach, most excellent of cars for speed. | Through many regions may our praise pass onward among mortal men. || 9. May our laudation of you Twain, lovers of meath! be sweet to you. | Fly hitherward, ye wise of heart, like falcons with your winged steeds. || 10. O Aśvins, when at any time ye listen to this call of mine, | For you is dainty food prepared: they mix refreshing food for you.

Hymn 5:75. Aśvins.

1. To meet your treasure-bringing car, the mighty car most dear to us, | Aśvins, the Ṛishi is prepared, your raiser, with his song of praise. Lovers of sweetness, hear my call. || 2. Pass, O ye Aśvins, pass away beyond all tribes of selfish men, | Wonderful, with your golden paths, most gracious, bringers of the flood. Lovers of sweetness, hear my call. || 3. Come to us, O ye Aśvin Pair, bringing your precious treasures, come | Ye Rudras, on your paths of gold, rejoicing, rich in store of wealth. Lovers of sweetness, hear my call. || 4. O strong and Good, the voice of him who lauds you well cleaves to your car. | And that great beast, your chariot-steed, fair, wonderful, makes dainty food. Lovers of sweetness, hear my call. || 5. Watchful in spirit, born on cars, impetuous, listing to his cry, | Aśvins, with winged steeds ye speed down to Chyavāna void of guile. Lovers of sweetness, hear my call. || 6. Hither, O Heroes, let your steeds, of dappled hue, yoked at the thought, | Your flying steeds, O Aśvins, bring you hitherward, with bliss, to drink. Lovers of sweetness, hear my call. || 7. O Aśvins, hither come to us; Nāsatyas, be not disinclined. | Through longing for the pious turn out of the way to reach our home. Lovers of sweetness, bear my call. || 8. Ye Lords of Splendour, free from guile, come, stand at this our sacrifice. | Beside the singer, Aśvins, who longs for your grace and lauds you both. Lovers of sweetness, hear my call. || 9. Dawn with her white herd hath appeared, and in due time hath fire been placed. | Harnessed is your immortal car, O Wonder-workers, strong and kind. Lovers of sweetness, bear my call.

Hymn 5:76. Aśvins

1. Agni, the bright face of the Dawns, is shining; the singers' pious voices have ascended. | Borne on your chariot, Aśvins, turn you hither and come unto our full and rich libation. || 2. Most frequent guests, they scorn not what is ready: even now the lauded Aśvins are beside us. | With promptest aid they come at morn and evening, the worshipper's most blessed guards from trouble. || 3. Yea, come at milking-time, at early morning, at noon of day and when the Sun is setting, | By day, by night, with favour most auspicious. Not only now the draught hath drawn the Aśvins. || 4. For this place, Aśvins, was of old your dwelling, these were your houses, this your habitation. | Come to us from high heaven and from the mountain. Come from the waters bringing food and vigour. || 5. May we obtain the Aśvins' newest favour, and gain their health-bestowing happy guidance. | Bring riches hither unto us, and heroes, and all felicity and joy, Immortals!

Hymn 5:77. Aśvins.

1. First worship those who come at early morning: let the Twain drink before the giftless niggard. | The Aśvins claim the sacrifice at daybreak: the sages yielding the first share extol them. || 2. Worship at dawn and instigate the Aśvins:nor is the worshipper at eve rejected. | Besides ourselves another craves and worships: each first in worship is most highly favoured. || 3. Covered with gold, meath-tinted, dropping fatness, your chariot with its freight of food comes hither, | Swift as thought, Aśvins, rapid as the tempest, wherewith ye travel over all obstructions. || 4. He who hath served most often the Nāsatyas, and gives the sweetest food at distribution, | Furthers with his own holy works his offspring, and ever passes those whose flames ascend not. || 5. May we obtain the Aśvins' newest favour, and gain their health-bestowing happy guidance. | Bring riches hither unto us, and heroes, and all felicity and joy, Immortals!

Hymn 5:78. Aśvins.

1. Ye Aśvins, hither come to us: Nāsatyas, be not disinclined. | Fly hither like two swans unto the juice we shed. || 2. O Aśvins, like a pair of deer, like two wild cattle to the mead: | Fly hither like two swans unto the juice we shed. || 3. O Aśvins rich in gifts, accept our sacrifice to prosper it: | Fly hither like two swans unto the juice we shed. || 4. As Atri when descending to the cavern called on you loudly like a wailing woman. | Ye came to him, O Aśvins, with the freshest and most auspicious fleetness of a falcon. || 5. Tree, part asunder like the side of her who bringeth forth a child. | Ye Aśvins, listen to my call: loose Saptavadhri from his bonds. || 6. For Saptavadhri, for the seer affrighted when he wept and wailed, | Ye, Aśvins, with your magic powers rent up the tree and shattered it. || 7. Like as the wind on every side ruffles a pool of lotuses, | So stir in thee the babe unborn, so may the ten-month babe descend. || 8. Like as the wind, like as the wood, like as the sea is set astir, | So also, ten-month babe, descend together with the after-

birth. ‖ 9. The child who hath for ten months' time been lying in his mother's side,— | May he come forth alive, unharmed, yea, living from the living dame.

Hymn 5:79. Dawn.

1. O Heavenly Dawn, awaken us to ample opulence today | Even as thou hast wakened us with Satyaśravas, Vayya's son, high-born! delightful with thy steeds! ‖ 2. Daughter of Heaven, thou dawnedst on Sunītha Śuchadratha's son, | So dawn thou on one mightier still, on Satyaśravas, Vayya's son, high-born! delightful with thy steeds! ‖ 3. So, bringing treasure, dawn today on us thou Daughter of the Sky, | As thou, O mightier yet. didst shine for Satyaśravas, Vayya's son, high-born! delightful with thy steeds! ‖ 4. Here round about thee are the priests who laud thee, Bright One, with their hymns, | And men with gifts, O Bounteous Dame, splendid with wealth and offering much, high-born! delightful with thy steeds! ‖ 5. Whatever these thy bands perform to please thee or to win them wealth, | E'en fain they gird us round and give rich gifts which ne'er are reft away, high-born! delightful with thy steeds! ‖ 6. Give to these wealthy patrons fame, O affluent Dawn, with hero sons, | To these our princes who have brought rich gifts ne'er to be reft away, high-born! delightful with thy steeds! ‖ 7. Bring lofty and resplendent fame, O thou munificent Dawn, to these | Our wealthy patrons who bestow rich gifts on us of steeds and kine, high-born! delightful with thy steeds! ‖ 8. Bring us, O Daughter of the Sky, subsistence in our herds of kine, | Together with the sunbeams, with the shine of pure refulgent flames, high-born! delightful with thy steeds! ‖ 9. O Daughter of the Sky, shine forth; delay not to perform thy task. | Let not the Sun with fervent heat consume thee like a robber foe, high-born! delightful with the steeds! ‖ 10. So much, and more exceedingly, O Dawn, it suits thee to bestow, | Thou Radiant One who ceasest not to shine for those who sing thy praise, high-born! delightful with thy steeds!

Hymn 5:80. Dawn.

1. The singers welcome with their hymns and praises the Goddess Dawn who bringeth in the sunlight, | Sublime, by Law true to eternal Order, bright on her path, red-tinted, far-refulgent. ‖ 2. She comes in front, fair, rousing up the people, making the pathways easy to be travelled. | High, on her lofty chariot, all-impelling, Dawn gives her splendour at the days' beginning. ‖ 3. She, harnessing her car with purple oxen. injuring none, hath brought perpetual riches. | Opening paths to happiness, the Goddess shines, praised by all, giver of every blessing. ‖ 4. With changing tints she gleams in double splendour while from the eastward she displays her body. | She travels perfectly the path of Order, nor fails to reach, as one who knows, the quarters. ‖ 5. As conscious that her limbs are bright with bathing, she stands, as 'twere, erect that we may see her. | Driving away malignity and darkness, Dawn, Child of Heaven, hath come to us with lustre. ‖ 6. The Daughter of the Sky, like some chaste woman, bends, opposite to men, her forehead downward. | The Maid, disclosing boons to him who worships, hath brought again the daylight as aforetime.

Hymn 5:81. Savitar.

1. The priests of him the lofty Priest well-skilled in hymns harness their spirit, yea, harness their holy thoughts. | He only knowing works assigns their priestly tasks. Yea, lofty is the praise of Savitar the God. ‖ 2. The Sapient One arrays himself in every form: for quadruped and biped he hath brought forth good. | Excellent Savitar hath looked on heaven's high vault, and shineth after the outgoing of the Dawn. ‖ 3. Even he, the God whose going-forth and majesty the other Deities have followed with their might, | He who hath measured the terrestrial regions out by his great power, he is the Courser Savitar. ‖ 4. To the three spheres of light thou goest, Savitar, and with the rays of Sūrya thou combinest thee. | Around, on both sides thou encompassest the night: yea, thou, O God, art Mitra through thy righteous laws. ‖ 5. Over all generation thou art Lord alone: Pūṣhan art thou, O God, in all thy goings-forth. | Yea, thou hast domination over all this world. Śyāvāśva hath brought praise to thee, O Savitar,

Hymn 5:82. Savitar.

1. We crave of Savitar the God this treasure much to be enjoyed. | The best, all-yielding, conquering gift of Bhaga we would gladly win. ‖ 2. Savitar's own supremacy, most glorious and beloved of all, | No one diminisheth in aught. ‖ 3. For Savitar who is Bhaga shall send riches to his worshipper. | That wondrous portion we implore. ‖ 4. Send us this day, God Savitar, prosperity with progeny. | Drive thou the evil dream away. ‖ 5. Savitar, God, send far away all sorrows and calamities, | And send us only what is good. ‖ 6. Sinless in sight of Aditi through the God Savitar's influence, | May we obtain all lovely things. ‖ 7. We with our hymns this day elect the general God, Lord of the good, | Savitar whose decrees are true. ‖ 8. He who for ever vigilant precedes these Twain, the Day and Night, | Is Savitar the thoughtful God. ‖ 9. He who gives glory unto all these living creatures with the song, | And brings them forth, is Savitar.

Hymn 5:83. Parjanya.

1. Sing with these songs thy welcome to the Mighty, with adoration praise and call Parjanya. | The Bull, loud roaring, swift to send his bounty, lays in the plants the seed. for germination. ‖ 2. He smites the trees apart, he slays the demons: all life fears him who wields the mighty weapon. | From him exceeding strong flees e'en the guiltless, when thundering Parjanya smites the wicked. ‖ 3. Like a car-driver whipping on his horses, he makes the messengers of rain spring forward. | Far off resounds the roaring of the lion, what time Parjanya fills the sky with rain-cloud. ‖ 4. Forth burst the winds, down come the lightning-flashes: the plants shoot up, the realm of light is streaming. | Food springs abundant for all living creatures, what time Parjanya quickens earth with moisture. ‖ 5. Thou at whose bidding earth bows low before thee, at whose command hoofed cattle fly in terror, | At whose behest the plants assume all colours, even thou Parjanya, yield us great protection. ‖ 6. Send down for us the rain of heaven, ye Marutas, and let the Stallion's flood descend in torrents. | Come hither with this thunder while thou pourest the waters down, our heavenly Lord and Father. ‖ 7. Thunder and roar: the germ of life deposit. Fly round us on thy chariot water-laden | Thine opened water-skin draw with thee downward, and let the hollows and the heights be level. ‖ 8. Lift up the mighty vessel, pour down water, and let the liberated streams rush forward. | Saturate both the earth and heaven with fatness, and for the cows let there be drink abundant. ‖ 9. When thou, with thunder and with roar, Parjanya, smitest sinners down, | This universe exults thereat, yea, all that is upon the earth. ‖ 10. Thou hast poured down the rain-flood now withhold it. Thou hast made desert places fit for travel. | Thou hast made herbs to grow for our enjoyment: yea, thou hast won thee praise from living creatures.

Hymn 5:84. Pṛithivī.

1. Thou, of a truth,O Pṛithivī, bearest the tool that rends the hills: | Thou rich in torrents, who with might quickenest earth, O Mighty One. ‖ 2. To thee, O wanderer at will, ring out the lauds with beams of day, | Who drivest, like a neighing steed, the swelling cloud, O bright of hue. ‖ 3. Who graspest with thy might on earth. e'en the strong sovereigns of the wood, | When from the lightning of thy cloud the rain-floods of the heaven descend.

Hymn 5:85. Varuṇa.

1. Sing forth a hymn sublime and solemn, grateful to glorious. Varuṇa, imperial Ruler, | Who hath struck out, like one who slays the victim, earth as a skin to spread in front of Sūrya. ‖ 2. In the tree-tops the air he hath extended, put milk in kine and vigorous speed in horses, | Set intellect in hearts, fire in the waters, Sūrya in heaven and Soma on the mountain. ‖ 3. Varuṇa lets the big cask, opening downward, flow through the heaven and earth and air's mid-region. | Therewith the universe's Sovereign waters earth as the shower of rain bedews the barley. ‖ 4. When Varuṇa is fain for milk he moistens the sky, the land, and earth to her foundation. | Then straight the mountains clothe them in the rain-cloud: the Heroes, putting forth their vigour, loose them. ‖ 5. I will declare this mighty deed of magic, of glorious Varuṇa the Lord Immortal, | Who standing in the firmament hath meted the earth out with the Sun as with a measure. ‖ 6. None, verily, hath ever let or hindered this the most wise God's mighty deed of magic, | Whereby with all their flood, the lucid rivers fill not one sea wherein they pour their waters. ‖ 7. If we have sinned against the man who loves us, have ever wronged a brother, friend, or comrade, | The neighbour ever with us, or a stranger, O Varuṇa, remove from us the trespass. ‖ 8. If we, as gamesters cheat at play, have cheated, done wrong unwittingly or sinned of purpose, | Cast all these sins away like loosened fetters, and, Varuṇa let us be thine own beloved.

Hymn 5:86. Indra-Agni.

1. The mortal man whom ye, the Twain, Indra and Agni, help in fight, | Breaks through e'en strongly-guarded wealth as Trita burst his way through reeds. || 2. The Twain invincible in war, worthy to be renowned in frays, | Lords of the Fivefold. People, these, Indra and Agni, we invoke. || 3. Impetuous is their strength, and keen the lightning of the mighty Pair, | Which from their arms speeds with the car to Vṛitra's slayer for the kine. || 4. Indra and Agni, we invoke you both, as such, to send your cars: | Lords of quick-coming bounty, ye who know, chief lovers of the song. || 5. These who give increase day by day, Gods without guile for mortal man, | Worthy themselves, I honour most, Two Gods as partners, for my horse. || 6. The strength-bestowing offering thus to Indra-Agni hath been paid, as butter, purified by stones. | Deal to our princes high renown, deal wealth to those who sing your praise, deal food to those who sing your praise.

Hymn 5:87. Marutas.

1. To Vishṇu, to the Mighty whom the Marutas follow let your hymns born in song go forth, Evayāmarut; | To the impetuous, strong band, adorned with bracelets, that rushes on in joy and ever roars for vigour. || 2. They who with might were manifest, and who willingly by their own knowledge told it forth, Evayāmarut. | Marutas, this strength of yours no wisdom comprehendeth: through their gifts' greatness they are moveless as the mountains. || 3. Who by the psalm they sing are heard, from lofty heaven, the strong, the brightly shining Ones, Evayāmarut; | In whose abode there is no mightier one to move them, whose lightnings are as fires, who urge the roaring rivers. || 4. He of the Mighty Stride forth strode, Evayāmarut, out of the spacious dwelling-place, their home in common. | When he, himself, hath yoked his emulous strong horses on heights, he cometh forth, joy-giving, with the Heroes. || 5. Like your tremendous roar, the rainer with light flashing, strong, speeding, hath made all tremble, Evayāmarut, | Wherewith victorious ye, self-luminous, press onward, with strong reins, decked with gold, impetuous and well-weaponed. || 6. Unbounded is your greatness, ye of mighty power: may your bright vigour be our aid, Evayāmarut; | For ye are visible helpers in the time of trouble: like fires, aglow with light, save us from shame and insult. || 7. So may the Rudras, mighty warriors, Evayāmarut, with splendid brilliancy, like fires, be our protectors; | They whose terrestrial dwelling-place is wide-extended, whom none suspect of sin, whose bands have lofty courage. || 8. Come in a friendly spirit, come to us, O Marutas, and hear his call who praises you, Evayāmarut. | Like car-borne men, one-minded with the mighty Vishṇu, keep enmity far from us with your deeds of wonder. || 9. Come to our sacrifice, ye Holy Ones, to bless it, and, free from demons, hear our call, Evayāmarut. | Most excellent, like mountains in the air's raid-region, be irresistible, ye, Wise, to this man's hater.

Maṇḍala 6

Hymn 6:1. Agni.

1. Thou, first inventor of this prayer, O Agni, Worker of Marvels, hast become our Herald. | Thou, Bull, hast made us strength which none may conquer, strength that shall overcome all other prowess. || 2. As Priest thou sattest at the seat of worship, furthering us, best Offerer, meet for honour. | So first to thee have pious men resorted, turning thy mind to thoughts of ample riches. || 3. In thee, still watching, they have followed riches, who goest with much wealth as with an army, | The radiant Agni, lofty, fair to look on, worshipped with marrow, evermore resplendent. || 4. They who approached the God's abode with homage, eager for glory, won them perfect glory: | Yea, they gained even sacrificial titles, and found delight in thine auspicious aspect. || 5. On earth the people magnify thee greatly, thee their celestial and terrestrial riches. | Thou, Helper, must be known as our Preserver, Father and Mother of mankind for ever. || 6. Dear priest among mankind, adorable Agni hath seated him, joy-giver, skilled in worship. | Let us approach thee shining in thy dwelling, kneeling upon our knees, with adoration. || 7. Longing for bliss, pure-minded, God-devoted, Agni, we seek thee, such, meet to be lauded. | Thou, Agni, leddest forth our men to battle, refulgent with the heaven's exalted splendour. || 8. Sage of mankind, all peoples' Lord and Master, the Bull of men, the sender down of blessings, | Still pressing on, promoting, purifying, Agni the Holy One, the Lord of riches. || 9. Agni, the mortal who hath toiled and worshipped, brought thee oblations with his kindled fuel, | And well knows sacrifice with adoration, gains every joy with thee to guard and help him. || 10. Mightily let us worship thee the Mighty, with reverence, Agni! fuel and oblations, | With songs, O Son of Strength, with hymns, with altar: so may we strive for thine auspicious favour. || 11. Thou who hast covered heaven and earth with splendour and with thy glories, glorious and triumphant. | Continue thou to shine on us, O Agni, with strength abundant, rich, and long enduring. || 12. Vouchsafe us ever, as man needs, O Vasu, abundant wealth of kine for son and offspring. | Food noble, plenteous, far from sin and evil, he with us, and fair fame to make us happy. || 13. May I obtain much wealth in many places by love of thee and through thy grace, King Agni; | For in thee Bounteous One, in thee the Sovereign, Agni, are many boons for him who serves thee.

Hymn 6:2. Agni.

1. Thou, Agni, even as Mitra, hast a princely glory of thine own. | Thou, active Vasu, makest fame increase like full prosperity. || 2. For, verily, men pray to thee with sacrifices and with songs. | To thee the Friendly Courser, seen of all, comes speeding through the air. || 3. Of one accord men kindle thee Heaven's signal of the sacrifice, | When, craving bliss, this race of man invites thee to the solemn rite. || 4. Let the man thrive who travails sore, in prayer, far thee the Bountiful. | He with the help of lofty Dyaus comes safe through straits of enmity. || 5. The mortal who with fuel lights thy flame and offers unto thee, | Supports a house with many a branch, Agni, to live a hundred years. || 6. Thy bright smoke lifts itself aloft, and far-extended shines in heaven. | For, Purifier! like the Sun thou beamest with thy radiant glow. || 7. For in men's houses thou must be glorified as a well-loved guest, | Gay like an elder in a fort, claiming protection like a son. || 8. Thou, Agni, like an able steed, art urged by wisdom in the wood. | Thou art like wind; food, home art thou, like a young horse that runs astray. || 9. E'en things imperishable, thou, O Agni, like a gazing ox, | Eatest, when hosts, Eternal One! of thee the Mighty rend the woods. || 10. Agni, thou enterest as Priest the home of men who sacrifice. | Lord of the people, prosper them. Accept the offering, Aṅgiras! || 11. O Agni, God with Mitra's might, call hither the favour of the Gods from earth and heaven. | Bring weal from heaven, that men may dwell securely. May we o'ercome the foe's malign oppressions, may we o'ercome them, through thy help o'ercome them.

Hymn 6:3. Agni.

1. True, guardian of the Law, thy faithful servant wins ample light and dwells in peace, O Agni, | Whom thou, as Varuṇa in accord with Mitra, guardest, O God, by banishing his trouble. || 2. He hath paid sacrifices, toiled in worship, and offered gifts to wealth-increasing Agni. | Him the displeasure of the famous moves not, outrage and scorn affect not such a mortal. || 3. Bright God, whose look is free from stain like Sūrya's, thou, swift, what time thou earnestly desirest, | Hast gear to give us. Come with joy at evening, where, Child of Wood, thou mayest also tarry. || 4. Fierce is his gait and vast his wondrous body: he champeth like a horse with bit and bridle, | And, darting forth his tongue, as 'twere a hatchet, burning the woods, smelteth them like a smelter. || 5. Archer-like, fain to shoot, he sets his arrow, and whets his splendour like the edge of iron: | The messenger of night with brilliant pathway, like a tree-roosting bird of rapid pinion. || 6. In beams of morn he clothes him like the singer, and bright as Mitra with his splendour crackles. | Red in the night, by day the men's possession: red, he belongs to men by day, Immortal. || 7. Like Heaven's when scattering beams his voice was uttered: among the plants the radiant Hero shouted, | Who with his glow in rapid course came hither to fill both worlds, well-wedded Dames, with treasure. || 8. Who, with supporting streams and rays that suit him, hath flashed like lightning with his native vigour. | Like the deft Maker of the band of Marutas, the bright impetuous One hath shone refulgent.

Hymn 6:4. Agni.

1. As at man's service of the Gods, Invoker, thou, Son of Strength, dost sacrifice and worship, | So bring for us today all Gods together, bring willingly the willing Gods, O Agni. || 2. May Agni, radiant Herald of the morning, meet to be known, accept our praise with favour. | Dear to all life, mid mortal men Immortal, our guest, awake at dawn, is Jātavedas. || 3. Whose might the very heavens regard with wonder: bright as the Sun he

clothes himself with lustre. | He who sends forth, Eternal Purifier, hath shattered e'en the ancient works of Aśna. || 4. Thou art a Singer, Son! our feast-companion: Agni at birth prepared his food and pathway. | Therefore vouchsafe us strength, O Strength-bestower. Win like a King: foes trouble not thy dwelling. || 5. Even he who cats his firm hard food with swiftness,and overtakes the nights as Vāyu kingdoms. | May we o'ercome those who resist thine orders, like a steed casting down the flying foemen. || 6. Like Sūrya with his fulgent rays, O Agni, thou overspreadest both the worlds with splendour. | Decked with bright colour he dispels the darkness, like Auśija, with clear flame swiftly flying. || 7. We have elected thee as most delightful for thy beams' glow: hear our great laud, O Agni. | The best men praise thee as the peer of Indra in strength, mid Gods, like Vāyu in thy bounty. || 8. Now, Agni, on the tranquil paths of riches come to us for our weal: save us from sorrow. | Grant chiefs and bard this boon. May we live happy, with hero children, through a hundred winters.

Hymn 6:5. Agni.

1. I invocate your Son of Strength, the Youthful, with hymns, the Youngest God, whose speech is guileless; | Sage who sends wealth comprising every treasure, bringer of many boons, devoid of malice. || 2. At eve and morn thy pious servants bring thee their precious gifts, O Priest of many aspects, | On whom, the Purifier, all things living as on firm. ground their happiness have established. || 3. Thou from of old hast dwelt among these people, by mental power the charioteer of blessings. | Hence sendest thou, O sapient Jātavedas, to him who serves thee treasures in succession. || 4. Agni, whoever secretly attacks us, the neighbour, thou with Mitra's might! who harms us, | Burn him with thine own Steers for ever youthful, burning with burning heat, thou fiercest burner. || 5. He who serves thee with sacrifice and fuel, with hymn, O Son of Strength, and chanted praises, | Shines out, Immortal! in the midst of mortals, a sage, with wealth, with splendour and with glory. || 6. Do this, O Agni, when we urge thee, quickly, triumphant in thy might subdue our foemen. | When thou art praised with words and decked with brightness, accept this chanted hymn, the singer's worship. || 7. Help us, that we may gain this wish, O Agni, gain riches, Wealthy One! with store of heroes. | Desiring strength from thee may we be strengthened, and win, Eternal! thine eternal glory.

Hymn 6:6. Agni.

1. He who seeks furtherance and grace to help him goes to the Son of Strength with newest worship, | Calling the heavenly Priest to share the banquet, who rends the wood, bright, with his blackened pathway. || 2. White-hued and thundering he dwells in splendour, Most Youthful, with the loud-voiced and eternal— | Agni, most variform, the Purifier, who follows crunching many ample forests. || 3. Incited by the wind thy flames, O Agni, move onward, Pure One! pure, in all directions. | Thy most destructive heavenly Navagvas break the woods down and devastate them boldly. || 4. Thy pure white horses from their bonds are loosened: O Radiant One, they shear the ground beneath them, | And far and wide shines out thy flame, and flickers rapidly moving over earth's high ridges. || 5. Forth darts the Bull's tongue like the sharp stone weapon discharged by him who fights to win the cattle. | Agni's fierce flame is like a hero's onset: dread and resistless he destroys the forests. || 6. Thou with the sunlight of the great Impeller hast boldly over-spread the earth's expanses. | So drive away with conquering might all perils. fighting out foemen burn up those who harm us. || 7. Wondrous! of wondrous power! give to the singer wealth wondrous, marked, most wonderful, life-giving. | Wealth bright, O Bright One, vast, with many heroes, give with thy bright flames to the man who lauds thee.

Hymn 6:7. Agni.

1. Him, messenger of earth and head of heaven, Agni Vaiśvānara, born in holy Order, | The Sage, the King, the guest of men, a vessel fit for their mouths, the Gods have generated. || 2. Him have they praised, mid-point of sacrifices, great cistern of libations, seat of riches. | Vaiśvānara, conveyer of oblations, ensign of worship, have the Gods engendered. || 3. From thee, O Agni, springs the mighty singer, from thee come heroes who subdue the foeman. | O King, Vaiśvānara, bestow thou on us excellent treasures worthy to belonged for. || 4. To thee, Immortal! when to life thou springest, all the Gods sing for joy as to their infant. | They by thy mental powers were made immortal, Vaiśvānara, when thou shonest from thy Parents. || 5. Agni Vaiśvānara, no one hath ever resisted these thy mighty ordinances, | When thou, arising from thy Parents' bosom, foundest the light for days' appointed courses. || 6. The summits of the heaven are traversed through and through by the Immortal's light, Vaiśvānara's brilliancy. | All creatures in existence rest upon his head. The Seven swift-flowing Streams have grown like branches forth, || 7. Vaiśvānara, who measured out the realms of air, Sage very wise who made the lucid spheres of heaven, | The Undeceivable who spread out all the worlds, keeper is he and guard of immortality.

Hymn 6:8. Agni.

1. At Jātavedas' holy gathering I will tell aloud the conquering might of the swift red-hued Steer. | A pure and fresher hymn flows to Vaiśvānara, even as for Agni lovely Soma is made pure. || 2. That Agni, when in loftiest heaven he sprang to life, Guardian of Holy Laws, kept and observed them well. | Exceeding wise, he measured out the firmament. Vaiśvānara attained to heaven by mightiness. || 3. Wonderful Mitra propped the heaven and earth apart, and covered and concealed | the darkness with his light. | He made the two bowls part asunder like two skins. Vaiśvānara put forth all his creative power. || 4. The Mighty seized him in the bosom of the floods: the people waited on the King who should be praised. | As envoy of Vivasvat Mātariśvan brought Agni Vaiśvānara hither from far away. || 5. In every age bestow upon the singers wealth, worthy of holy synods, glorious, ever new. | King, undecaying, as it were with sharpened bolt, smite down the sinner like a tree with lightning-flash. || 6. Do thou bestow, O Agni, on our wealthy chiefs, rule, with good heroes, undecaying, bending not. | So may we win for us strength. O Vaiśvānara, hundredfold, thousandfold, O Agni, by thy help. || 7. O thou who dwellest in three places, Helper, keep with effective guards our princely patrons. | Keep our band, Agni, who have brought thee presents. Lengthen their lives, Vaiśvānara, when lauded.

Hymn 6:9. Agni.

1. One half of day is dark, and bright the other: both atmospheres move on by sage devices. | Agni Vaiśvānara, when born as Sovereign, hath with his lustre overcome the darkness. || 2. I know not either warp or woof, I know not the web they weave when moving to the contest. | Whose son shall here speak words that must be spoken without assistance from the Father near him? || 3. For both the warp and woof he understandeth, and in due time shall speak what should be spoken, | Who knoweth as the immortal world's Protector, descending, seeing with no aid from other. || 4. He is the Priest, the first of all: behold him. Mid mortal men he is the light immortal. | Here was he born, firm-seated in his station Immortal, ever waxing in his body. || 5. A firm light hath been set for men to look on: among all things that fly the mind is swiftest. | All Gods of one accord, with one intention, move unobstructed to a single purpose. || 6. Mine ears unclose to hear, mine eye to see him; the light that harbours in my spirit broadens. | Far roams my mind whose thoughts are in the distance. What shall I speak, what shall I now imagine? || 7. All the Gods bowed them down in fear before thee, Agni, when thou wast dwelling in the darkness. | Vaiśvānara be gracious to assist us, may the Immortal favour us and help us.

Hymn 6:10. Agni.

1. Install at sacrifice, while the rite advances, your pleasant, heavenly Agni, meet for praises. | With hymns—for he illumines us—install him. He, Jātavedas, makes our rites successful. || 2. Hear this laud, Radiant Priest of many aspects, O Agni with the fires of man enkindled, | Laud which bards send forth pure as sacred butter, strength to this man, as 'twere for self-advantage. || 3. Mid mortal men that singer thrives in glory who offers gifts with hymns of praise to Agni, | And the God, wondrous bright, with wondrous succours helps him to win a stable filled with cattle. || 4. He, at his birth, whose path is black behind him, filled heaven and earth with far-apparent splendour: | And he himself hath been. through night's thick darkness, made manifest by light, the Purifier. || 5. With thy most mighty aid, confer, O Agni, wonderful wealth on us and on our princes, | Who stand preeminent, surpassing others in liberal gifts, in fame, and hero virtues. || 6. Agni, accept this sacrifice with gladness, which, seated here, the worshipper presenteth. | Fair hymns hadst thou among the Bharadvājas, and holpest them to gain abundant vigour. || 7. Scatter our foes, increase our store. May we he glad a hundred winters with brave sons.

Hymn 6:11. Agni.

1. Eagerly Sacrifice thou, most skilful, Agni! Priest, pressing on as if the Marutas sent thee. | To our oblation bring the two Nāsatyas, Mitra and Varuṇa and Earth and Heaven. || 2. Thou art our guileless, most delightful Herald, the God, among mankind, of holy synods. | A Priest with purifying tongue, O Agni, sacrifice with thy mouth to thine own body. || 3. For even the blessed longing that is in thee would bring the Gods down to the singer's worship, | When the Aṅgirasas' sagest Sage, the Poet, sings the sweet measure at the solemn service. || 4. Bright hath he beamed, the wise, the far-refulgent. Worship the two wide-spreading Worlds, O Agni, | Whom as the Living One rich in oblations the Five Tribes, bringing gifts, adorn with homage. || 5. When I with reverence clip the grass for Agni, when the trimmed ladle, full of oil, is lifted, | Firm on the seat of earth is based the altar: eye-like, the sacrifice is directed Sun-ward. || 6. Enrich us, O thou Priest of many aspects, with the Gods, Agni, with thy fires, enkindled. | O Son of Strength, clad in the robe of riches, may we escape from woe as from | a prison.

Hymn 6:12. Agni.

1. King of trimmed grass, Herald within the dwelling, may Agni worship the Impeller's World-halves. | He, Son of Strength, the Holy, from a distance hath spread himself abroad with light like Sūrya. || 2. In thee, most wise, shall Dyaus, for full perfection, King! Holy One! pronounce the call to worship. | Found in three places, like the Speeder's footstep, come to present men's riches as oblations! || 3. Whose blaze most splendid, sovereign in the forest, shines waxing on his way like the Impeller. | He knows himself, like as a guileless smelter, not to be stayed among the plants, Immortal. || 4. Our friends extol him like a steed for vigour even Agni in the dwelling, Jātavedas. | Tree-fed, he fights with power as doth a champion, like Dawn's Sire to be praised with sacrifices. || 5. Men wonder at his shining glows when, paring the woods with case, o'er the broad earth he goeth, | And, like a rushing flood, loosed quickly, burneth, swift as a guilty thief, o'er desert places. || 6. So mighty thou protectest us from slander, O Champion, Agni! with all fires enkindled. | Bring opulence and drive away affliction. May brave sons gladden us through a hundred winters.

Hymn 6:13. Agni.

1. From thee, as branches from a tree, O Agni, from thee, Auspicious God! spring all our blessings— | Wealth swiftly, strength in battle with our foemen, the rain besought of heaven, the flow of waters. || 2. Thou art our Bhaga to send wealth thou dwellest, like circumambient air, with wondrous splendour. | Friend art thou of the lofty Law, like Mitra, Controller, Agni! God! of many a blessing. || 3. Agni! the hero slays with might his foeman; the singer bears away the Paṇi's booty— | Even he whom thou, Sage, born in Law, incitest by wealth, accordant with the Child of Waters. || 4. The man who, Son of Strength 1 with sacrifices, hymns, lauds, attracts thy fervour to the altar, | Enjoys each precious thing, O God, O Agni, gains wealth of corn and is the lord of treasures. || 5. Grant, Son of Strength, to men for their subsistence such things as bring high fame and hero children. | For thou with might givest much food in cattle even to the wicked wolf when he is hungry. || 6. Eloquent, Son of Strength, Most Mighty, Agni, vouchsafe us seed and offspring, full of vigour. | May I by all my songs obtain abundance. May brave sons gladden us through a hundred winters.

Hymn 6:14. Agni.

1. Whoso to Agni hath endeared his thought and service by his hymns, | That mortal cats before the rest, and finds sufficiency of food. || 2. Agni, in truth, is passing wise, most skilled in ordering, a Seer. | At sacrifices Manus' sons glorify Agni as their Priest. || 3. The foeman's wealth in many a place, Agni, is emulous to help. | Men fight the fiend, and seek by rites to overcome the riteless foe. || 4. Agni bestows the hero chief, winner of waters, firm in fray. | Soon as they look upon his might his enemies tremble in alarm. || 5. For with his wisdom Agni, God, protects the mortal from reproach, | Whose conquering wealth is never checked, is never checked in deeds of might. || 6. O Agni, God with Mitra's might call hither the favour of the Gods from earth and heaven. | Bring weal from heaven that men may dwell securely. May we o'ercome the foe's malign oppressions, may we o'ercome them, through thy help o'ercome them.

Hymn 6:15. Agni.

1. With this my song I strive to reach this guest of yours, who wakes at early morn, the Lord of all the tribes. | Each time he comes from heaven, the Pure One from of old: from ancient days the Child cats everlasting food. || 2. Whom, tended well, the Bhṛigus established as a friend, whom men must glorify, high-flaming in the wood. | As such, most friendly, thou art every day extolled in lauds by Vītahavya, O thou wondrous God. || 3. Be thou the foeless helper of the skilful man, subduer of the enemy near or far away. | Bestow a wealthy home on men, O Son of Strength. Give Vītahavya riches spreading far and wide, give Bharadvāja wide-spread wealth. || 4. Him, your refulgent guest, Agni who comes from heaven, the Herald of mankind, well-skilled in sacred rites, | Who, like a holy singer, utters heavenly words, oblation-bearer, envoy, God, I seek with hymns. || 5. Who with his purifying, eye-attracting form hath shone upon the earth as with the light of Dawn; | Who speeding on, as in the fight of Etaśa, cometh, untouched by age, as one athirst in heat. || 6. Worship ye Agni, Agni, with your log of wood; praise your beloved, your beloved guest with songs. | Invite ye the Immortal hither with your hymns. A God among the Gods, he loveth what is choice, loveth our service, God mid Gods. || 7. Agni inflamed with fuel in my song I sing, pure, Cleanser, steadfast, set in front at sacrifice. | Wise Jātavedas we implore with prayers for bliss the Priest, the holy Singer, bounteous, void of guile. || 8. Men, Agni, in each age have made thee, Deathless One, their envoy, offering-bearer, guard adorable. | With reverence Gods and mortals have established thee, the ever-watchful, omnipresent Household Lord. || 9. Thou, Agni, ordering the works and ways of both, as envoy of the Gods traversest both the worlds. | When we lay claim to thy regard and gracious fare, be thou to us a thrice-protecting friendly guard. || 10. Him fair of face, rapid, and fair to look on, him very wise may we who know not follow. | Let him who knows all rules invite for worship, Agni announce our offering to the Immortals. || 11. Him, Agni, thou deliverest and savest who brings him prayer to thee the Wise, O Hero, | The end of sacrifice or its inception; yea, thou endowest him with power and riches. || 12. Guard us from him who would assail us, Agni; preserve us, O thou Victor, from dishonour. | Here let the place of darkening come upon thee: may wealth be ours, desirable in thousands. || 13. Agni, the Priest, is King, Lord of the homestead, he, Jātavedas, knows all generations. | Most skilful worshipper mid Gods and mortals, may he begin the sacrifice, the Holy. || 14. Whate'er today thou, bright-flamed Priest, enjoyest from the man's rite-for thou art sacrificer— | Worship, for duly dost thou spread in greatness: bear off thine offerings of today, Most Youthful. || 15. Look thou upon the viands duly laid for thee. Fain would he set thee here to worship Heaven and,Earth. | Help us, O liberal Agni, in the strife for spoil, so that we may o'ercome all things that trouble us, o'ercome, o'ercome them with thy help. || 16. Together with all Gods, O fair-faced Agni, be seated first upon the wool-lined altar, | Nest-like, bedewed with oil. Bear this our worship to Savitar who sacrifices rightly. || 17. Here the arranging priests, as did Atharvan, rub this Agni forth, | Whom, not bewildered, as he moved in winding ways, they brought from gloom. || 18. For the Gods' banquet be thou born, for full perfection and for weal. | Bring the Immortal Gods who strengthen holy Law: so let our sacrifice reach the Gods. || 19. O Agni, Lord and Master of men's homesteads, with kindled fuel we have made thee mighty. | Let not our household gear be found defective. Sharpen us with thy penetrating splendour.

Hymn 6:16. Agni.

1. Priest of all sacrifices hast thou been appointed by the Gods, | Agni, amid the race of man. || 2. So with thy joyous tongues for us sacrifice nobly in this rite. | Bring thou the Gods and worship them. || 3. For well, O God, Disposer, thou knowest, straight on, the paths and ways, | Agni, most wise in sacrifice. || 4. Thee, too, hath Bhārata of old, with mighty men, implored for bliss. | And worshipped thee the worshipful. || 5. Thou givest these abundant boons to Divodāsa pouring forth, | To Bharadvāja offering gifts. || 6. Do thou, Immortal Messenger, bring hither the Celestial Folk; | Hearing the singer's eulogy. || 7. Mortals with pious thought implore thee, Agni, God, at holy rites, | To come unto the feast of Gods. || 8. I glorify thine aspect and the might of thee the Bountiful. | All those who love shall joy in thee, || 9. Invoker placed by Manus, thou, Agni, art near, the wisest

Priest: | Pay worship to the Tribes of Heaven. || 10. Come, Agni, lauded, to the feast; come to the offering of the gifts. | As Priest be seated on the grass. || 11. So, Aṅgiras, we make thee strong with fuel and with holy oil. | Blaze high, thou youngest of the Gods. || 12. For us thou winnest, Agni, God, heroic strength exceeding great, | Far-spreading and of high renown. || 13. Agni, Atharvan brought thee forth, by rubbing, from the lotus-flower, | The head of Viśva, of the Priest. || 14. Thee. Vṛitra's slayer, breaker down of castles, hath Atharvan's son, | Dadhyach the Ṛishi, lighted up. || 15. The hero Pāthya kindled thee the Dasyus. most destructive foe, | Winner of spoil in every fight. || 16. Come, here, O Agni, will I sing verily other songs to thee, | And with these drops shalt thou grow strong. || 17. Where'er thy mind applies itself, vigour preeminent bast thou: | There wilt thou gain a dwelling-place. || 18. Not for a moment only lasts thy bounty, good to many a one! | Our service therefore shalt thou gain. || 19. Agni, the Bhārata, hath been sought, the Vṛitra-slayer, marked of all, | Yea, Divodāsa's Hero Lord. || 20. For he gave riches that surpass in greatness all the things of earth, | Fighting untroubled, unsubdued. || 21. Thou, Agni, as in days of old, with recent glory, gathered light, | Hast overspread the lofty heaven. || 22. Bring to your Agni, O my friends, boldly your laud and sacrifice: | Give the Disposer praise and song. || 23. For as sagacious Herald he hath sat through every age of man, | Oblation-bearing messenger. || 24. Bring those Two Kings whose ways are pure, Ādityas, and the Marut host, | Excellent God! and Heaven and Earth. || 25. For strong and active mortal man, excellent, Agni, is the look Of thee Immortal, Son of Strength || 26. Rich through his wisdom, noblest be the giver serving thee today: | The man hath brought his hymn of praise. || 27. These, Agni, these are helped by thee, who strong and active all their lives, | O'ercome the malice of the foe, fight down the malice of the foe. || 28. May Agni with his pointed blaze cast down each fierce devouring fiend | May Agni win us wealth by war. || 29. O active Jātavedas, bring riches with store of hero sons: | Slay thou the demons, O Most Wise. || 30. Keep us, O Jātavedas, from the troubling of the man of sin: | Guard us thou Sage who knowest prayer. || 31. Whatever sinner, Agni, brings oblations to procure our death, | Save us from woe that he would work. || 32. Drive from us with thy tongue, O God, the man who doeth evil deeds, | The mortal who would strike us dead. || 33. Give shelter reaching far and wide to Bharadvāja, conquering Lord! | Agni, send wealth most excellent. || 34. May Agni slay the Vṛitras,—fain for riches, through the lord of song, | Served with oblation, kindled, bright. || 35. His Father's Father, shining in his Mother's everlasting side, | Set on the seat of holy Law. || 36. O active Jātavedas, bring devotion that wins progeny, Agni, that it may shine to heaven. || 37. O Child of Strength, to thee whose look is lovely we with dainty food, | O Agni, have poured forth our songs. || 38. To thee for shelter are we come, as to the shade from fervent heat | Agni, who glitterest like gold. || 39. Mighty as one who slays with shafts, or like a bull with sharpened horn, | Agni, thou breakest down the forts. || 40. Whom, like an infant newly born, devourer, in their arms they bear, | Men's Agni, skilled in holy rites. || 41. Bear to the banquet of the Gods the God best finder-out of wealth, | Let him he seated in his place. || 42. In Jātavedas kindle ye the dear guest who hath now appeared | In a soft place, the homestead's Lord. || 43. Harness, O Agni, O thou God, thy steeds which are most excellent: | They bear thee as thy spirit wills. || 44. Come hither, bring the Gods to us to taste the sacrificial feast, | To drink the draught of Soma juice. || 45. O Agni of the Bhāratas, blaze high with everlasting might, | Shine forth and gleam, Eternal One. || 46. The mortal man who serves the God with banquet, and, bringing gifts at sacrifice, lauds Agni, | May well attract, with prayer and hands uplifted, the Priest of Heaven and Earth, true Sacrificer. || 47. Agni, we bring thee, with our hymn, oblation fashioned in the heart. | Let these be oxen unto thee, let these be bulls and kine to thee. || 48. The Gods enkindle Agni, best slayer of Vṛitra, first in rank, | The Mighty, One who brings us wealth and crushes down the Rākṣhasas.

Hymn 6:17. Indra.

1. Drink Soma, Mighty One, for which, when lauded, thou breakest through the cattle-stall, O Indra; | Thou who, O Bold One, armed with thunder smotest Vṛitra with might, and every hostile being. || 2. Drink it thou God who art impetuous victor, Lord of our hymns, with beauteous jaws, the Hero, | Render of kine-stalls, car-borne, thunder-wielding, so pierce thy way to wondrous strength, O Indra. || 3. Drink as of old, and let the draught delight thee. hear thou our prayer and let our songs exalt thee. | Make the Sun visible, make food abundant, slaughter the foes, pierce through and free the cattle. || 4. These gladdening drops, O Indra, Self-sustainer, quaffed shall augment thee in thy mighty splendour. | Yea, let the cheering drops delight thee greatly, great, perfect, strong, powerful, all-subduing. || 5. Gladdened whereby, bursting the firm enclosures, thou gavest splendour to the Sun and Morning. | The mighty rock that compassed in the cattle, ne'er moved, thou shookest from its seat, O Indra. || 6. Thou with thy wisdom, power, and works of wonder, hast stored the ripe milk in the raw cows' udders | Unbarred the firm doors for the kine of Morning, and, with the Aṅgirasas, set free the cattle. || 7. Thou hast spread out wide earth, a mighty marvel, and, high thyself, propped lofty heaven, O Indra. | Both worlds, whose Sons are Gods, thou hast supported, young, Mothers from old time of holy Order. || 8. Yea, Indra, all the Deities installed thee their one strong Champion in the van for battle. | What time the godless was the Gods' assailant, Indra they chose to win the light of heaven. || 9. Yea, e'en that heaven itself of old bent backward before thy bolt, in terror of its anger, | When Indra, life of every living creature, smote down within his lair the assailing Dragon. || 10. Yea, Strong One! Tvaṣhṭar turned for thee, the Mighty, the bolt with thousand spikes and hundred edges, | Eager and prompt at will, wherewith thou crushedst the boasting Dragon, O impetuous Hero. || 11. He dressed a hundred buffaloes, O Indra, for thee whom all accordant Marutas strengthen. | He, Pūṣhan Viṣhṇu, poured forth three great vessels to him, the juice that cheers, that slaughters Vṛitra. || 12. Thou settest free the rushing wave of waters, the floods' great swell encompassed and obstructed. | Along steep slopes their course thou turnedst, Indra, directed downward, speeding to the ocean. || 13. So may our new prayer bring thee to protect us, thee well-armed Hero with thy bolt of thunder, | Indra, who made these worlds, the Strong, the mighty, who never groweth old, the victory-giver. || 14. So, Indra, form us brilliant holy singers for strength, for glory, and for food and riches. | Give Bharadvāja hero patrons, Indra Indra, be ours upon the day of trial. || 15. With this may we obtain strength God-appointed, and brave sons gladden us through a hundred winters.

Hymn 6:18. Indra.

1. Glorify him whose might is all-surpassing, Indra the much-invoked who fights uninjured. | Magnify with these songs the never-vanquished, the Strong, the Bull of men, the Mighty Victor. || 2. He, Champion, Hero, Warrior, Lord of battles, impetuous, loudly roaring, great destroyer, | Who whirls the dust on high, alone, o'erthrower, hath made all races of mankind his subjects. || 3. Thou, thou alone, hast tamed the Dasyus; singly thou hast subdued the people for the Ārya. | In this, or is it not, thine hero exploit, Indra? Declare it at the proper season. || 4. For true, I deem, thy strength is, thine the Mighty, thine, O Most Potent, thine the Conquering Victor; | Strong, of the strong, Most Mighty, of the mighty, thine, driver of the churl to acts of bounty. || 5. Be this our ancient bond of friendship with you and with Aṅgirasas here who speak of Vala. | Thou, Wondrous, Shaker of things firm, didst smite him in his fresh strength, and force his doors and castles. || 6. With holy thoughts must he be called, the Mighty, showing his power in the great fight with Vṛitra. | He must be called to give us seed and offspring, the Thunderer must he moved and sped to battle. || 7. He in his might, with name that lives for ever, hath far surpassed all human generations. | He, most heroic, hath his home with splendour, with glory and with riches and with valour. || 8. Stranger to guile, who ne'er was false or faithless, bearing a name that may be well remembered, | Indra crushed Chumuri, Dhuni, Śambara, Pipru, and Śuṣhṇa, that their castles fell in ruin. || 9. With saving might that must be praised and lauded, Indra, ascend thy car to smite down Vṛitra. | In thy right hand hold fast thy bolt of thunder, and weaken, Bounteous Lord, his art and magic. || 10. As Agni, as the dart burns the dry forest, like the dread shaft burn down the fiends, O Indra; | Thou who with high deep-reaching spear hast broken, hast covered over mischief and destroyed it. || 11. With wealth, by thousand paths come hither, Agni, paths that bring ample strength, O thou Most Splendid. | Come, Son of Strength, o'er whom, Invoked of many! the godless hath no power to keep thee distant. || 12. From heaven, from earth is bruited forth the greatness of him the firm,

the fiery, the resplendent. | No foe hath he, no counterpart, no refuge is there from him the Conqueror full of wisdom || 13. This day the deed that thou hast done is famous, when thou, for him, with many thousand others | Laidest low Kutsa, Āyu, Atithigva, and boldly didst deliver Tūrvayāṇa. || 14. In thee, O God, the wisest of the Sages, all Gods were joyful when thou slewest Ahi. | When lauded for thyself, thou gavest freedom to sore-afflicted Heaven and to the people. || 15. This power of thine both heaven and earth acknowledge, the deathless Gods acknowledge it, O Indra. | Do what thou ne'er hast done, O Mighty Worker: beget a new hymn at thy sacrifices.

Hymn 6:19. Indra.

1. Great, hero-like controlling men is Indra, unwasting in his powers, doubled in vastness. | He, turned to us, hath grown to hero vigour: broad, wide, he hath been decked by those who serve him. || 2. The bowl made Indra swift to gather booty, the High, the Lofty, Youthful, Undecaying, | Him who hath waxed by strength which none may conquer, and even at once grown to complete perfection. || 3. Stretch out those hands of thine, extend to us-ward thy wide capacious arms, and grant us glory. | Like as the household herdsman guards the cattle, so move thou round about us in the combat. || 4. Now, fain for strength, let us invite your Indra hither, who lieth hidden with his Heroes,— | Free from all blame, without reproach, uninjured, e'en as were those who sang, of old, his praises. || 5. With steadfast laws, wealth-giver, strong through Soma, he hath much fair and precious food to feed us. | In him unite all paths that lead to riches, like rivers that commingle with the ocean. || 6. Bring unto us the mightiest might, O Hero, strong and most potent force, thou great Subduer! | All splendid vigorous powers of men vouchsafe us, Lord of Bay Steeds, that they may make us joyful. || 7. Bring us, grown mighty in its strength, O Indra, thy friendly rapturous joy that wins the battle, | Wherewith by thee assisted and triumphant, we may laud thee in gaining seed and offspring. || 8. Indra, bestow on us the power heroic skilled and exceeding strong, that wins the booty, | Wherewith, by thine assistance, we may conquer our foes in battle, be they kin or stranger. || 9. Let thine heroic strength come from behind us, before us, from above us or below us. | From every side may it approach us, Indra. Give us the glory of the realm of splendour. || 10. With most heroic aid from thee, like heroes Indra, may we win wealth by deeds glory. | Thou, King, art Lord of earthly, heavenly treasure: vouchsafe us riches vast, sublime, and lasting. || 11. The Bull, whose strength hath waxed, whom Marutas follow, free-giving Indra, the Celestial Ruler, | Mighty, all-conquering, the victory-giver, him let us call to grant us new protection. || 12. Give up the people who are high and haughty to these men and to me, O Thunder-wielder! | Therefore upon the earth do we invoke thee, where heroes win, for sons and kine and waters. || 13. Through these thy friendships, God invoked of many! may we be victors over every foeman. | Slaying both kinds of foe, may we, O Hero, be happy, helped by thee, with ample riches.

Hymn 6:20. Indra.

1. Give us wealth, Indra, that with might, as heaven o'ertops the earth, o'ercomes our foes in battle | Wealth that brings thousands and that wins the corn-lands, wealth, Son of Strength! that vanquishes the foeman. || 2. Even as the power of Dyaus, to thee, O Indra, all Asura sway was by the Gods entrusted, | When thou, Impetuous! leagued with Vishṇu, slewest Vṛitra the Dragon who enclosed the waters. || 3. Indra, Strong, Victor, Mightier than the mighty, addressed with prayer and perfect in his splendour, | Lord of the bolt that breaketh forts in pieces, became the King of the sweet juice of Soma. || 4. There, Indra, while the light was won, the Paṇis fied, 'neath a hundred blows, for wise Daśoṇi, | And greedy Śushṇa's magical devices nor left he any of their food remaining. || 5. What time the thunder fell and Śushṇa perished, all life's support from the great Druh was taken. | Indra made room for his car-driver Kutsa who sate beside him, when he gained the sunlight. || 6. As the Hawk rent for him the stalk that gladdens, he wrenched the head from Namuchi the Dāsa. | He guarded Namī, Sāpya's son, in slumber, and sated him with food, success, and riches. || 7. Thou, thunder-armed, with thy great might hast shattered Pipru's strong forts who knew the wiles of serpents. | Thou gavest to thy worshipper Ṛijiśvan imperishable Wealth, O Bounteous Giver. || 8. The crafty Vetasu, the swift Daśoṇi, and Tugra speedily with all his servants, | Hath Indra, gladdening with strong assistance, forced near as 'twere to glorify the Mother. || 9. Resistless, with the hosts he battles, bearing in both his arms the Vṛitra-slaying thunder. | He mounts his Bays, as the car-seat an archer: yoked at a word they bear the lofty Indra. || 10. May we, O Indra, gain by thy new favour: so Pūrus laud thee, with their sacrifices, | That thou hast wrecked seven autumn forts, their shelter, slain Dāsa tribes and aided Purukutsa. || 11. Favouring Uśanā the son of Kavi, thou wast his ancient strengthener, O Indra. | Thou gavest Navavāstva. as a present, to the great father gavest back his grandson. || 12. Thou, roaring Indra, drovest on the waters that made a roaring sound like rushing rivers, | What time, O Hero, o'er the sea thou broughtest, in safety broughtest Turvaśa and Yadu. || 13. This Indra, was thy work in war: thou sentest Dhuni and Chumuri to sleep and slumber. | Dabhīti lit the flame for thee, and worshipped with fuel, hymns, poured Soma, dressed oblations.

Hymn 6:21. Indra. Viśvedevas.

1. These the most constant singer's invocations call thee who art to be invoked, O Hero; | Hymns call anew the chariot-borne, Eternal: by eloquence men gain abundant riches. || 2. I praise that Indra, known to all men, honoured with songs, extolled with hymns at sacrifices, | Whose majesty, rich in wondrous arts, surpasseth the magnitude of earth, and heaven in greatness. || 3. He hath made pathways, with the Sun to aid him, throughout the darkness that extended pathless. | Mortals who yearn to worship ne'er dishonour, O Mighty God, thy Law who art Immortal. || 4. And he who did these things, where is that Indra? among what tribes? what people doth he visit? | What sacrifice contents thy mind, and wishes? What priest among them all? what hymn, O Indra? || 5. Yea, here were they who, born of old, have served thee, thy friends of ancient time, thou active Worker. | Bethink thee now of these, Invoked of many! the midmost and the recent, and the youngest. || 6. Inquiring after him, thy later servants, Indra, have gained thy former old traditions. | Hero, to whom the prayer is brought, we praise thee as great for that wherein we know thee mighty. || 7. The demon's strength is gathered fast against thee: great as that strength hath grown, go forth to meet it. | With thine own ancient friend and companion, the thunderbolt, brave Champion! drive it backward. || 8. Hear, too, the prayer of this thy present beadsman, O Indra, Hero, cherishing the singer. | For thou wast aye our fathers' Friend aforetime, still swift to listen to their supplication. || 9. Bring to our help this day, for our protection, Varuṇa, Mitra, Indra, and the Marutas, | Pūshan and Vishṇu, Agni and Purandhi, Savitar also, and the Plants and Mountains. || 10. The singers here exalt with hymns and praises thee who art very Mighty and Most Holy. | Hear, when invoked, the invoker's invocation. Beside thee there is none like thee, Immortal! || 11. Now to my words come quickly thou who knowest, O Son of Strength, with all who claim our worship, | Who visit sacred rites, whose tongue is Agni, Gods who made Manu stronger than the Dasyu. || 12. On good and evil ways be thou our Leader, thou who art known to all as Path-preparer. | Bring power to us, O Indra, with thy Horses, Steeds that are best to draw, broad-backed, unwearied.

Hymn 6:22. Indra.

1. With these my hymns I glorify that Indra who is alone to be invoked by mortals, | The Lord, the Mighty One, of manly vigour, victorious, Hero, true, and full of wisdom. || 2. Our sires of old, Navagvas, sages seven, while urging him to show his might, extolled him, | Dwelling on heights, swift, smiting down opponents, guileless in word, and in his thoughts most mighty. || 3. We seek that Indra to obtain his riches that bring much food, and men, and store of heroes. | Bring us, Lord of Bay Steeds, to make us joyful, celestial wealth, abundant, undecaying. || 4. Tell thou us this, if at thy hand aforetime the earlier singers have obtained good fortune, | What is thy share and portion, Strong Subduer, Asura-slayer, rich, invoked of many? || 5. He who for car-borne Indra, armed with thunder, hath a hymn, craving, deeply-piercing, fluent, | Who sends a song effectual, firmly-grasping, and strength-bestowing, he comes near the mighty. || 6. Strong of thyself, thou by this art hast shattered, with thought-swift Parvata, him who waxed against thee, | And, Mightiest! roaring! boldly rent in pieces things that were firmly fixed and never shaken. || 7. Him will we fit for you with new devotion, the strongest Ancient One, in ancient manner. | So may that Indra, boundless, faithful Leader, conduct us o'er all places hard to traverse. || 8. Thou for the people who oppress hast kindled the earthly

firmament and that of heaven. | With heat, O Bull, on every side consume them: heat earth and flood for him who hates devotion. || 9. Of all the Heavenly Folk, of earthly creatures thou art the King, O God of splendid aspect. | In thy right hand, O Indra, grasp die thunder: Eternal! thou destroyest all enchantments. || 10. Give us confirmed prosperity, O Indra, vast and exhaustless for the foe's subduing. | Strengthen therewith the Ārya's hate and Dāsa's, and let the arms of Nahushas be mighty. || 11. Come with thy team which brings all blessings hither, Disposer, much-invoked, exceeding holy. | Thou whom no fiend, no God can stay or hinder, come swiftly with these Steeds in my direction.

Hymn 6:23. Indra.

1. Thou art attached to pressed-out Soma, Indra, at laud, at prayer, and when the hymn is chanted; | Or when with yoked Bays, Maghavan, thou comest, O Indra, bearing in thine arms the thunder. || 2. Or when on that decisive day thou holpest the presser of the juice at Vṛitra's slaughter; | Or when thou, while the strong one feared, undaunted, gavest to death, Indra, the daring Dasyus. || 3. Let Indra drink the pressed-out Soma, Helper and mighty Guide of him who sings his praises. | He gives the hero room who pours oblations, and treasure even to the lowly singer. || 4. E'en humble rites with his Bay steeds he visits: he wields the bolt, drinks Soma, gives us cattle. | He makes the valiant rich in store of heroes, accepts our praise and hears the singer's calling. || 5. What he hath longed for we have brought to Indra, who from the days of old hath done us service. | While Soma flows we will sing hymn, and laud him, so that our prayer may strengthen Indra's vigour. || 6. Thou hast made prayer the means of thine exalting, therefore we wait on thee with hymns, O Indra. | May we, by the pressed Soma, Soma-drinker! bring thee, with sacrifice, blissful sweet refreshment. || 7. Mark well our sacrificial cake, delighted Indra, drink Soma and the milk commingled. | Here on the sacrificer's grass be seated: give ample room to thy devoted servant. || 8. O Mighty One, be joyful as thou willest. Let these our sacrifices reach and find thee; | And may this hymn and these our invocations turn thee, whom many men invoke, to help us. || 9. Friends, when the juices flow, replenish duly your own, your bounteous Indra with the Soma. | Will it not aid him to support us? Indra. spares him who sheds the juice to win his favour. || 10. While Soma flowed, thus Indra hath been lauded, Ruler of nobles, mid the Bharadvājas, | That Indra may become the singer's patron and give him wealth in every kind of treasure.

Hymn 6:24. Indra.

1. Strong rapturous joy, praise, glory are with Indra: impetuous God, he quaffs the juice of Soma: | That Maghavan whom men must laud with singing, Heaven-dweller, King of songs, whose help is lasting. || 2. He, Friend of man, most wise, victorious Hero, hears, with far-reaching aid, the singer call him. | Excellent, Praise of Men, the bard's Supporter, Strong, he gives strength, extolled in holy synod. || 3. The lofty axle of thy wheels, O Hero, is not surpassed by heaven and earth in greatness. | Like branches of a tree, Invoked of many manifold aids spring forth from thee, O Indra. || 4. Strong Lord, thine energies, endowed with vigour, are like the paths of kine converging homeward. | Like bonds of cord, Indra, that bind the younglings, no bonds are they, O thou of boundless bounty. || 5. One act today, another act tomorrow oft Indra makes what is not yet existent. | Here have we Mitra, Varuṇa, and Pūshan to overcome the foeman's domination. || 6. By song and sacrifice men brought the waters from thee, as from a mountain's ridge, O Indra. | Urging thy might, with these fair lauds they seek thee, O theme of song, as horses rush to battle. || 7. That Indra whom nor months nor autumn seasons wither with age, nor fleeting days enfeeble,— | Still may his body Wax, e'en now so mighty, glorified by the lauds and hymns that praise him. || 8. Extolled, he bends not to the strong, the steadfast, nor to the bold incited by the Dasyu. | High mountains are as level plains to Indra: even in the deep he finds firm ground to rest on. || 9. Impetuous Speeder through all depth and distance, give strengthening food, thou drinker of the juices. | Stand up erect to help us, unreluctant, what time the gloom of night brightens to morning. || 10. Hasting to help, come hither and protect him, keep him from harm when he is here, O Indra. | At home, abroad, from injury preserve him. May brave sons gladden us through a hundred winters.

Hymn 6:25. Indra.

1. With thine assistance, O thou Mighty Indra, be it the least, the midmost, or the highest,— | Great with those aids and by these powers support us, Strong God! in battle that subdues our foemen. || 2. With these discomfit hosts that fight against us, and check the opponent's wrath, thyself uninjured. | With these chase all our foes to every quarter: subdue the tribes of Dāsas to the Ārya. || 3. Those who array themselves as foes to smite us, O Indra, be they kin or be they strangers,— | Strike thou their manly strength that it be feeble, and drive in headlong flight our foemen backward. || 4. With strength of limb the hero slays the hero, when bright in arms they range them for the combat. | When two opposing hosts contend in battle for seed and offspring, waters, kine, or corn-lands. || 5. Yet no strong man hath conquered thee, no hero, no brave, no warrior trusting in his valour. | Not one of these is match for thee, O Indra. Thou far surpassest all these living creatures. || 6. He is the Lord of both these armies' valour when the commanders call them to the conflict: | When with their ranks expanded they are fighting with a great foe or for a home with heroes. || 7. And when the people stir themselves for battle, be thou their saviour, Indra, and protector, | And theirs, thy manliest of our friends, the pious, the chiefs who have installed us priests, O Indra. || 8. To thee for high dominion hath been for evermore, for slaughtering the Vṛitras, | All lordly power and might, O Holy Indra, given by Gods for victory in battle. || 9. So urge our hosts together in the combats: yield up the godless bands that fight against us. | Singing, at morn may we find thee with favour, yea, Indra, and e'en now, we Bharadvājas.

Hymn 6:26. Indra.

1. O Indra, hear us. Raining down the Soma, we call on thee to win us mighty valour. | Give us strong succour on the day of trial, when the tribes gather on the field of battle. || 2. The warrior, son of warrior sire, invokes thee, to gain great strength that may be won as booty: | To thee, the brave man's Lord, the fiends' subduer, he looks when fighting hand to hand for cattle. || 3. Thou didst impel the sage to win the daylight, didst ruin Śushṇa for the pious Kutsa. | The invulnerable demon's head thou clavest when thou wouldst win the praise of Atithigva. || 4. The lofty battle-car thou broughtest forward; thou holpest Daśadyu the strong when fighting. | Along with Vetasu thou slewest Tugra, and madest Tuji strong, who praised thee, Indra. || 5. Thou madest good the laud, what time thou rentest a hundred thousand fighting foes, O Hero, | Slewest the Dāsa Śambara of the mountain, and with strange aids didst succour Divodāsa. || 6. Made glad with Soma-draughts and faith, thou sentest Chumuri to his sleep, to please Dabhīti. | Thou, kindly giving Raji to Piṭhīnas, slewest with might, at once, the sixty thousand. || 7. May I too, with the liberal chiefs, O Indra, acquire thy bliss supreme and domination, | When, Mightiest! Hero-girt! Nahusha heroes boast them in thee, the triply-strong Defender. || 8. So may we he thy friends, thy best beloved, O Indra, at this holy invocation. | Best be Prātardani, illustrious ruler, in slaying foemen and in gaining riches.

Hymn 6:27. Indra.

1 What deed hath Indra done in the wild transport, in quaffing or in friendship with, the Soma? | What joys have men of ancient times or recent obtained within the chamber of libation? || 2. In its wild joy Indra hath proved him faithful, faithful in quaffing, faithful in its friendship. | His truth is the delight that in this chamber the men of old and recent times have tasted. || 3. All thy vast power, O Maghavan, we know not, know not the riches of thy full abundance. | No one hath seen that might of thine, productive of bounty every day renewed, O Indra. || 4. This one great power of thine our eyes have witnessed, wherewith thou slewest Varaśikha's children, | When by the force of thy descending thunder, at the mere sound, their boldest was demolished. || 5. In aid of Abhyāvartin Chāyamāna, Indra destroyed the seed of Varaśikha. | At Hariyūpīyā he smote the vanguard of the Vṛichīvats, and the rear fled frighted. || 6. Three thousand, mailed, in quest of fame, together, on the Yavyāvatī, O much-sought Indra, | Vṛichīvat's sons, falling before the arrow, like bursting vessels went to their destruction. || 7. He, whose two red Steers, seeking goodly pasture, plying their tongues move on 'twixt earth and heaven, | Gave Turvaśa to Sṛiñjaya, and, to aid him, gave the Vṛichīvats up to Daivavāta. || 8. Two wagon-teams, with damsels, twenty oxen, O Agni, Abhyāvartin Chāyamāna, | The liberal Sovereign, giveth me. This guerdon

of Pṛithu's seed is hard to win from others.

Hymn 6:28. Cows.

1. The Kine have come and brought good fortune: let them rest in the cow-pen and be happy near us. | Here let them stay prolific, many-coloured, and yield through many morns their milk for Indra. || 2. Indra aids him who offers sacrifice and gifts: he takes not what is his, and gives him more thereto. | Increasing ever more and ever more his wealth, he makes the pious dwell within unbroken bounds. || 3. These are ne'er lost, no robber ever injures them: no evil-minded foe attempts to harass them. | The master of the Kine lives many a year with these, the Cows whereby he pours his gifts and serves the Gods. || 4. The charger with his dusty brow o'ertakes them not, and never to the shambles do they take their way. | These Cows, the cattle of the pious worshipper, roam over widespread pasture where no danger is. || 5. To me the Cows seem Bhaga, they seem Indra, they seem a portion of the first-poured Soma. | These present Cows, they, O ye Indra. I long for Indra with my heart and spirit. || 6. O Cows, ye fatten e'en the worn and wasted, and make the unlovely beautiful to look on. | Prosper my house, ye with auspicious voices. Your power is glorified in our assemblies. || 7. Crop goodly pasturage and be prolific drink pure sweet water at good drinking places. | Never be thief or sinful man your matter, and may the dart of Rudra still avoid you. || 8. Now let this close admixture be close intermigled with these Cows, | Mixt with the Steer's prolific flow, and, Indra, with thy hero might.

Hymn 6:29. Indra.

1. Your men have followed Indra for his friendship, and for his loving-kindness glorified him. | For he bestows great wealth, the Thunder-wielder: worship him, Great and Kind, to win his favour. || 2. Him to whose hand, men closely cling, and drivers stand on his golden chariot firmly stationed. | With his firm arms he holds the reins; his Horses, the Stallions, are yoked ready for the journey. || 3. Thy devotees embrace thy feet for glory. Bold, thunder-armed, rich, through thy strength, in guerdon, | Robed in a garment fair as heaven to look on, thou hast displayed thee like an active dancer. || 4. That Soma when effused hath best consistence, for which the food is dressed and grain is mingled; | By which the men who pray, extolling Indra chief favourites of Gods, recite their praises. || 5. No limit of thy might hath been appointed, which by its greatness sundered earth and heaven. | These the Prince filleth full with strong endeavour, driving, as 'twere, with help his flocks to waters. || 6. So be the lofty Indra prompt to listen, Helper unaided, golden-visored Hero. | Yea, so may he, shown forth in might unequalled, smite down the many Vṛitras and the Dasyus.

Hymn 6:30. Indra.

1. Indra hath waxed yet more for hero prowess, alone, Eternal, he bestoweth treasures. | Indra transcendeth both the worlds in greatness: one half of him equalleth earth and heaven. || 2. Yea, mighty I esteem his Godlike nature: none hindereth what he hath once determined. | Near and afar he spread and set the regions, and every day the Sun became apparent. || 3. E'en now endures thine exploit of the Rivers, when, Indra, for their floods thou clavest passage. | Like men who sit at meat the mountains settled: by thee, Most Wise! the regions were made steadfast. || 4. This is the truth, none else is like thee, Indra, no God superior to thee, no mortal. | Thou slewest Ahi who besieged the waters, and lettest loose the streams to hurry seaward. || 5. Indra, thou breakest up the floods and portals on all sides, and the firmness of the mountain. | Thou art the King of men, of all that liveth, engendering at once Sun, Heaven, and Morning.

Hymn 6:31. Indra.

1. Sole Lord of wealth art thou, O Lord of riches: thou in thine hands hast held the people, Indra! | Men have invoked thee with contending voices for seed and waters, progeny and sunlight. || 2. Through fear of thee, O Indra, all the regions of earth, though naught may move them, shake and tremble. | All that is firm is frightened at thy coming, -the earth, the heaven, the mountain, and the forest. || 3. With Kutsa, Indra! thou didst conquer Śuṣhṇa, voracious, bane of crops, in fight for cattle. | In the close fray thou rentest him: thou stolest the Sun's wheel and didst drive away misfortunes. || 4. Thou smotest to the ground the hundred castles, impregnable, of Śambara the Dasyu, | When, Strong, with might thou holpest Divodāsa who poured libations out, O Soma-buyer, and madest Bharadvāja rich who praised thee. || 5. As such, true Hero, for great joy of battle mount thy terrific car, O Brave and Manly. | Come with thine help to me, thou distant Roamer, and, glorious God, spread among men my glory.

Hymn 6:32. Indra.

1. I with my lips have fashioned for this Hero words never matched, most plentiful and auspicious, | For him the Ancient, Great, Strong, Energetic, the very mighty Wielder of the Thunder. || 2. Amid the sages, with the Sun he brightened the Parents: glorified, he burst the mountain; | And, roaring with the holy-thoughted singers, he loosed the bond that held the beams of Morning. || 3. Famed for great deeds, with priests who kneel and laud him, he still hath conquered in the frays for cattle, | And broken down the forts, the Fort-destroyer, a Friend with friends, a Sage among the sages. || 4. Come with thy girthed mares, with abundant vigour and plenteous strength to him who sings thy praises. | Come hither, borne by mares with many heroes, Lover of song! Steer! for the people's welfare. || 5. Indra with rush and might, sped by his Coursers, hath swiftly won the waters from the southward. | Thus set at liberty the rivers daily flow to their goal, incessant and exhaustless.

Hymn 6:33. Indra.

1. Give us the rapture that is mightiest, Indra, prompt to bestow and swift to aid, O Hero, | That wins with brave steeds where brave steeds encounter, and quells the Vṛitras and the foes in battle. || 2. For with loud voice the tribes invoke thee, Indra, to aid them in the battlefield of heroes. | Thou, with the singers, hast pierced through the Paṇis: the charger whom thou aidest wins the booty. || 3. Both races, Indra, of opposing foemen, O Hero, both the Ārya and the Dāsa, | Hast thou struck down like woods with well-shot lightnings: thou rentest them in fight, most manly Chieftain! || 4. Indra, befriend us with no scanty succour, prosper and aid us, Loved of all that liveth, | When, fighting for the sunlight, we invoke thee, O Hero, in the fray, in war's division. || 5. Be ours, O Indra, now and for the future, be graciously inclined and near to help us. | Thus may we, singing, sheltered by the Mighty, win many cattle on the day of trial.

Hymn 6:34. Indra.

1. Full Many songs have met in thee, O Indra, and many a noble thought from thee proceedeth. | Now and of old the eulogies of sages, their holy hymns and lauds, have yearned for Indra. || 2. He, praised of many, bold, invoked of many, alone is glorified at sacrifices. | Like a car harnessed for some great achievement, Indra must be the cause of our rejoicing. || 3. They make their way to Indra and exalt him, him whom no prayers and no laudations trouble; | For when a hundred or a thousand singers. laud him who loves the song their praise delights him. || 4. As brightness mingles with the Moon in heaven, the offered Soma yearns to mix with Indra. | Like water brought to men in desert places, our gifts at sacrifice have still refreshed him. || 5. To him this mighty eulogy, to Indra hath this our laud been uttered by the poets, | That in the great encounter with the foemen, Loved of all life, Indra may guard and help us.

Hymn 6:35. Indra.

1. When shall our prayers rest in thy car beside thee? When dost thou give the singer food for thousands? | When wilt thou clothe this poet's laud with plenty, and when wilt thou enrich our hymns with booty? || 2. When wilt thou gather men with men, O Indra, heroes with heroes, and prevail in combat? | Thou shalt win triply kine in frays for cattle, so, Indra, give thou us celestial glory. || 3. Yea, when wilt thou, O Indra, thou Most Mighty, make the prayer all-sustaining for the singer? | When wilt thou yoke, as we yoke songs, thy Horses, and come to offerings that bring wealth in cattle? || 4. Grant to the Singer food with store of cattle, splendid with horses and the fame of riches. | Send food to swell the milch-cow good at milking: bright be its shine among the Bharadvājas. || 5. Lead otherwise this present foeman, Śakra! Hence art thou praised as Hero, foe destroyer | Him who gives pure gifts may I praise unceasing. Sage, quicken the Aṅgirasas by devotion.

Hymn 6:36. Indra.

1. Thy raptures ever were for all men's profit: so evermore have been thine earthly riches. | Thou still hast been the dealer-forth of vigour, since among Gods thou hast had power and Godhead. || 2. Men have obtained

his strength by sacrificing, and ever urged him, on to hero valour. | For the rein-seizing, the impetuous Charger they furnished power even for Vṛitra's slaughter. ‖ 3. Associate with him, as teams of horses, help, manly might, and vigour follow Indra. | As rivers reach the sea, so, strong with praises, our holy songs reach him the Comprehensive. ‖ 4. Lauded by us, let flow the spring, O Indra, of excellent and brightly-shining riches. | For thou art Lord of men, without an equal: of all the world thou art the only Sovereign. ‖ 5. Hear what thou mayst hear, thou who, fain for worship, as heaven girds earth, guardest thy servant's treasure; | That thou mayst be our own, joying in power, famed through thy might in every generation.

Hymn 6:37. Indra.

1. Let thy Bay Horses, yoked, O mighty Indra, bring thy car hither fraught with every blessing. | For thee, the Heavenly, e'en the poor invoketh: may we this day, thy feast-companions, prosper. ‖ 2. Forth to the vat the brown drops flow for service, and purified proceed directly forward. | May Indra drink of this, our guest aforetime, Celestial King of the strong draught of Soma. ‖ 3. Bringing us hitherward all-potent Indra on well-wheeled chariot, may the Steeds who bear him | Convey him on the road direct to glory, and ne'er may Vāyu's Amṛita cease and fail him. ‖ 4. Supreme, he stirs this man to give the guerdon,—Indra, most efficacious of the princes, — | Wherewith, O Thunderer, thou removest sorrow, and, Bold One! partest wealth among the nobles. ‖ 5. Indra is he who gives enduring vigour: may our songs magnify the God Most Mighty. | Best Vṛitra-slayer be the Hero Indra these things he gives as Prince, with strong endeavour.

Hymn 6:38. Indra.

1. He hath drunk hence, Most Marvellous, and carried away our great and splendid call on Indra. | The Bounteous, when we serve the Gods, accepteth song yet more famous and the gifts we bring him. ‖ 2. The speaker filleth with a cry to Indra his ears who cometh nigh e'en from a distance. | May this my call bring Indra to my presence, this call to Gods composed in sacred verses. ‖ 3. Him have I sung with my best song and praises, Indra of ancient birth and Everlasting. | For prayer and songs in him are concentrated: let laud wax mighty when addressed to Indra: ‖ 4. Indra, whom sacrifice shall strengthen, Soma, and song and hymn, and praises and devotion, | Whom Dawns shall strengthen when the night departeth, Indra whom days shall strengthen, months, and autumns. ‖ 5. Him, born for conquering might in full perfection, and waxen strong for bounty and for glory, | Great, Powerful, will we today, O singer, invite to aid. us and to quell our foemen.

Hymn 6:39. Indra.

1. Of this our charming, our celestial Soma, eloquent, wise, Priest, with inspired devotion, | Of this thy close attendant, hast thou drunken. God, send the singer food with milk to grace it. ‖ 2. Craving the kine, rushing against the mountain led on by Law, with holy-minded comrades, | He broke the never-broken ridge of Vala. With words of might Indra subdued the Paṇis. ‖ 3. This Indu lighted darksome nights, O Indra, throughout the years, at morning and at evening. | Him have they established as the days' bright ensign. He made the Mornings to be born in splendour. ‖ 4. He shone and caused to shine the worlds that shone not. By Law he lighted up the host of Mornings. | He moves with Steeds yoked by eternal Order, contenting men with nave that finds the sunlight. ‖ 5. Now, praised, O Ancient King! fill thou the singer with plenteous food that he may deal forth treasures. | Give waters, herbs that have no poison, forests, and kine, and steeds, and men, to him who lauds thee.

Hymn 6:40. Indra

1. Drink, Indra; juice is shed to make thee joyful: loose thy Bay Steeds and give thy friends their freedom. | Begin the song, seated in our assembly. Give strength for sacrifice to him who singeth. ‖ 2. Drink thou of this whereof at birth, O Indra, thou drankest, Mighty One for power and rapture. | The men, the pressing-stones, the cows, the waters have made this Soma ready for thy drinking. ‖ 3. The fire is kindled, Soma pressed, O Indra: let thy Bays, best to draw, convey thee hither. | With mind devoted, Indra, I invoke thee. Come, for our great prosperity approach us. ‖ 4. Indra, come hither: evermore thou camest through our great strong desire to drink the Soma. | Listen and hear the prayers which now we offer, and let this sacrifice increase thy vigour. ‖ 5. Mayst thou, O Indra, on the day of trial, present or absent, wheresoe'er thou dwellest, | Thence, with thy team, accordant with the Marutas, Song-lover! guard our sacrifice, to help us.

Hymn 6:41. Indra.

1. Come gracious to our sacrifice, O Indra: pressed Soma-drops are purified to please thee. | As cattle seek their home, so Thunder-wielder, come, Indra, first of those who claim our worship. ‖ 2. With that well-formed most wide-extending palate, wherewith thou ever drinkest streams of sweetness, | Drink thou; the Adhvaryu standeth up before thee: let thy spoil-winning thunderbolt attend thee. ‖ 3. This drop, steer-strong and omniform, the Soma, hath been made ready for the Bull, for India. | Drink this, Lord of the Bays, thou Strong Supporter, this that is thine of old, thy food for ever. ‖ 4. Soma when pressed excels the unpressed Soma, better, for one who knows, to give him pleasure. | Come to this sacrifice of ours, O Victor replenish all thy powers with this libation. ‖ 5. We call on thee, O Indra: come thou hither: sufficient be the Soma for thy body. | Rejoice thee, Śatakratu! in the juices guard us in wars, guard us among our people.

Hymn 6:42. Indra.

1. Bring sacrificial gifts to him, Omniscient, for he longs to drink, | The Wanderer who comes with speed, the Hero ever in the van. ‖ 2. With Soma go ye nigh to him chief drinker of the Soma's juice: | With beakers to the Impetuous God, to Indra with the drops effused. ‖ 3. What time, with Soma, with the juice effused, ye come before the God, | Full wise he knows the hope of each, and, Bold One, strikes this foe and that. ‖ 4. To him, Adhvaryu! yea, to him give offerings of the juice expressed. | Will he not keep us safely from the spiteful curse of each presumptuous high-born foe?

Hymn 6:43. Indra

1. In whose wild joy thou madest once Śambara Divodāsa's prey, | This Soma is pressed out for thee, O Indra: drink! ‖ 2. Whose gladdening draught, shed from the points, thou guardest in the midst and end, | This Soma is pressed out for thee, O Indra drink! ‖ 3. In whose wild joy thou settest free the kine held fast within the rock, | This Soma is pressed out for thee, O Indra: drink! ‖ 4. This, in whose juice delighting thou gainest the might of Maghavan, | This Soma is pressed out for thee, O Indra drink!

Hymn 6:44. Indra.

1. That which is wealthiest, Wealthy God in splendours most illustrious, | Soma is pressed: thy gladdening draught, Indra! libation's Lord! is this. ‖ 2. Effectual, Most Effectual One! thine, as bestowing wealth of hymns, | Soma is pressed: thy gladdening draught, Indra! libation's Lord! is this. ‖ 3. Wherewith thou art increased in strength, and conquerest with thy proper aids, | Soma is pressed: thy gladdening draught, Indra! libation's Lord! is this. ‖ 4. Him for your sake I glorify as Lord of Strength who wrongeth none, | The Hero Indra, conquering all, Most Bounteous, God of all the tribes. ‖ 5. Those Goddesses, both Heaven and Earth, revere the power and might of him, | Him whom our songs increase in strength, the Lord of bounty swift to come. ‖ 6. To seat your Indra, I will spread abroad with power this song of praise. | The saving succours that abide in him, like songs, extend and grow. ‖ 7. A recent Friend, he found the skilful priest: he drank, and showed forth treasure from the Gods. | He conquered, borne by strong all-shaking mares, and was with far-spread power his friends' Protector. ‖ 8. In course of Law the sapient juice was quaffed: the Deities to glory turned their mind. | Winning through hymns a lofty title, he, the Lovely, made his beauteous form apparent. ‖ 9. Bestow on us the most illustrious strength ward off men's manifold malignities. | Give with thy might abundant vital force, and aid us graciously in gaining riches. ‖ 10. We turn to thee as Giver, liberal Indra. Lord of the Bay Steeds, be not thou ungracious. | No friend among mankind have we to look to: why have men called thee him who spurs the niggard? ‖ 11. Give us not up, Strong Hero! to the hungry: unharmed be we whom thou, so rich, befriendest. | Full many a boon hast thou for men demolish those who present no gifts nor pour oblations. ‖ 12. As Indra thundering impels the rain-clouds, so doth he send us store of kine and horses. | Thou art of old the Cherisher of singers let not the rich who bring no gifts deceive thee. ‖ 13. Adhvaryu, hero, bring to mighty Indra—for he is King thereof—the pressed-out juices; | To him exalted by the hymns and praises, ancient and modern, of the singing Ṛishis. ‖ 14. In the wild joy of this hath Indra, knowing full many a form, struck down resistless Vṛitras. | Proclaim aloud to him the savoury Soma so that the Hero, strong of jaw, may drink it. ‖ 15. May Indra

drink this Soma poured to please him, and cheered therewith slay Vṛitra with his thunder. | Come to our sacrifice even from a distance, good lover of our songs, the bard's Supporter. || 16. The cup whence Indra drinks the draught is present: the Amṛita dear to Indra hath been drunken, | That it may cheer the God to gracious favour, and keep far from us hatred and affliction. || 17. Therewith enraptured, Hero, slay our foemen, the unfriendly, Maghavan be they kin or strangers, | Those who still aim their hostile darts to smite us, turn them to flight, O Indra, crush and kill them. || 18. O Indra Maghavan, in these our battles win easy paths for us and ample freedom. | That we may gain waters and seed and offspring, set thou our princes on thy side, O Indra. || 19. Let thy Bay Stallions, harnessed, bring thee hither, Steeds with strong chariot and strong reins to hold them, | Strong Horses, speeding hither, bearing thunder, well-harnessed, for the strong exciting potion. || 20. Beside the vat, Strong God! stand thy strong Horses, shining with holy oil, like waves exulting. | Indra, they bring to thee, the Strong and Mighty, Soma of juices shed by mighty press-stones. || 21. Thou art the Bull of earth, the Bull of heaven, Bull of the rivers, Bull of standing waters. | For thee, the Strong, O Bull, hath Indu swollen. juice pleasant, sweet to drink, for thine election. || 22. This God, with might, when first he had his being, with Indra for ally, held fast the Paṇi. | This Indu stole away the warlike weapons, and foiled the arts of his malignant father. || 23. The Dawns he wedded to a glorious Consort, and set within the Sun the light that lights him. | He found in heaven, in the third lucid regions, the threefold Amṛita in its close concealment. || 24. He stayed and held the heaven and earth asunder: the chariot with the sevenfold reins he harnessed. | This Soma Set with power within the milch-kine a spring whose ripe contents ten fingers empty.

Hymn 6:45. Indra.

1. That Indra is our youthful Friend, who with his trusty guidance led | Turvaśa, Yadu from afar. || 2. Even to the dull and uninspired Indra, gives vital power, and wins | Even with slow steed the offered prize. || 3. Great are his ways of guiding us, and manifold are his eulogies: | His kind protections never fail. || 4. Friends, sing your psalm and offer praise to him to whom the prayer is brought: | For our great Providence is he. || 5. Thou, Slaughterer of Vṛitra, art Guardian and Friend of one and two, | Yea, of a man like one of us. || 6. Beyond men's hate thou leadest us, and givest cause to sing thy praise: | Good hero art thou called by men. || 7. I call with hymns, as 'twere a cow to milk, the Friend who merits praise, | The Brahman who accepts the prayer. || 8. Him in whose hands they say are stored all treasures from the days of old, | The Hero, conquering in the fight. || 9. Lord of Strength, Caster of the Stone, destroy the firm forts built by men, | And foil their arts, unbending God! || 10. Thee, thee as such, O Lord of Power, O Indra, Soma-drinker, true, | We, fain for glory, have invoked. || 11. Such as thou wast of old, and art now to be called on when the prize | lies ready, listen to our call. || 12. With hymns and coursers we will gain, Indra, through thee, both steeds and spoil | Most glorious, and the proffered prize. || 13. Thou, Indra, Lover of the Song, whom men must stir to help, hast been | Great in the contest for the prize. || 14. Slayer of foes, whatever aid of thine imparts the swiftest course, | With that impel our car to speed. || 15. As skilfullest of those who drive the chariot, with our art and aim, | O Conqueror, win the proffered prize. || 16. Praise him who, Matchless and Alone, was born the Lord of living men, | Most active, with heroic soul. || 17. Thou who hast been the singers' Friend, a Friend auspicious with thine aid, | As such, O Indra, favour us. || 18. Grasp in thine arms the thunderbolt, O Thunder-armed, to slay the fiends: | Mayst thou subdue the foemen's host. || 19. I call the ancient Friend, allied with wealth, who speeds the lowly man, | Him to whom chiefly prayer is brought. || 20. For he alone is Lord of all the treasures of the earth: he speeds | Hither, chief Lover of the Song. || 21. So with thy yoked teams satisfy our wish with power and wealth in steeds | And cattle, boldly, Lord of kine! || 22. Sing this, what time the juice is pressed, to him your Hero, Much-invoked, | To please him as a mighty Steer. || 23. He, Excellent, withholdeth not his gift of power and wealth in kine, | When he hath listened to our songs. || 24. May he with might unclose for us the cow's stall, whosesoe'er it be, | To which the Dasyu-slayer goes. || 25. O Indra Śatakratu, these our songs have called aloud to thee, | Like mother cows to meet their calves. || 26. Hard is thy love to win: thou art a Steer to him who longs for steers: | Be to one craving steeds a Steed. || 27. Delight thee with the juice we pour for thine own great munificence: | Yield not thy singer to reproach. || 28. These songs with every draught we pour come, Lover of the Song, to thee, | As milch-kine hasten to their young || 29. To thee most oft invoked, amid the many singers' rivalry | Who beg with all their might for wealth. || 30. Nearest and most attractive may our laud, O Indra come to thee. | Urge thou us on to ample wealth. || 31. Bṛibu hath set himself above the Paṇis, o'er their highest head, | Like the wide bush on Gaṅgā's bank. || 32. He whose good bounty, thousandfold, swift as the rushing of the wind, | Suddenly offers as a gift. || 33. So all our singers ever praise the pious Bṛibu's noble deed, | Chief, best to give his thousands, best to give a thousand liberal gifts.

Hymn 6:46. Indra.

1. That we may win us wealth and power we poets, verily, call on thee: | In war men call on thee, Indra, the hero's Lord, in the steed's race-course call on thee. || 2. As such, O Wonderful, whose hand holds thunder, praised as mighty, Caster of the Stone! | Pour on us boldly, Indra, kine and chariot steeds, ever to be the conqueror's strength. || 3. We call upon that Indra, who, most active, ever slays the foe: | Lord of the brave, Most Manly, with a thousand powers, help thou and prosper us in fight. || 4. Ṛichīṣhama, thou forcest men as with a bull, with anger, in the furious fray. | Be thou our Helper in the mighty battle fought for sunlight, water, and for life. || 5. O Indra, bring us name and fame, enriching, mightiest, excellent, | Wherewith, O Wondrous God, fair-visored, thunder-armed, thou hast filled full this earth and heaven. || 6. We call on thee, O King, Mighty amid the Gods, Ruler of men, to succour us. | All that is weak in us, Excellent God, make firm: make our foes easy to subdue. || 7. All strength and valour that is found, Indra, in tribes of Nahuṣhas, and all the splendid fame that the Five Tribes enjoy | Bring, yea, all manly powers at once. || 8. Or, Maghavan, what vigorous strength in Tṛikṣhi lay, in Druhyus or in Pūru's folk, | Fully bestow on us, that, in the conquering fray, we may subdue our foes in fight. || 9. O Indra, grant a happy home, a triple refuge triply strong. | Bestow a dwelling-place on the rich lords and me, and keep thy dart afar from these. || 10. They who with minds intent on spoil subdue the foe, boldly attack and smite him down,— | From these, O Indra Maghavan who lovest song, be closest guardian of our lives. || 11. And now, O Indra, strengthen us: come near and aid us in the fight, | What time the feathered shafts are flying in the air, the arrows with their sharpened points. || 12. Give us, where heroes strain their bodies in the fight, the shelter that our fathers loved. | To us and to our sons give refuge: keep afar all unobserved hostility. || 13. When, Indra, in the mighty fray thou urgest chargers to their speed, | On the uneven road and on a toilsome path, like falcons, eager for renown, || 14. Speeding like rivers rushing down a steep descent, responsive to the urging call, | That come like birds attracted to the bait, held in by reins in both the driver's hands.

Hymn 6:47. Indra, etc.

1. Yea, this is good to taste and full of. sweetness, verily it is strong and rich in flavour. | No one may conquer Indra in the battle when he hath drunken of the draught we offer. || 2. This sweet juice here had mightiest power to gladden: it boldened Indra when he slaughtered Vṛitra, | When he defeated Śambara's many onslaughts, and battered down his nine and ninety ramparts. || 3. This stirreth up my voice when I have drunk it: this hath aroused from sleep my yearning spirit. | This Sage hath measured out the six expanses from which no single creature is excluded. || 4. This, even this, is he who hath created the breadth of earth, the lofty height of heaven. | He formed the nectar in three headlong rivers. Soma supports the wide mid-air above us. || 5. He found the wavy sea of brilliant colours in forefront of the Dawns who dwell in brightness. | This Mighty One, the Steer begirt by Marutas, hath propped the heavens up with a mighty pillar. || 6. Drink Soma boldly from the beaker, Indra, in war for treasures, Hero, Vṛitra-slayer! | Fill thyself full at the mid-day libation, and give us wealth, thou Treasury of riches. || 7. Look out for us, O Indra, as our Leader, and guide us on to gain yet goodlier treasure. | Excellent Guardian, bear us well through peril, and lead us on to wealth with careful guidance. || 8. Lead us to ample room, O thou who knowest, to happiness, security, and sunlight. | High, Indra, are the arms of thee the Mighty: may we betake us to their lofty shelter. || 9. Set us on widest chariot-seat, O Indra, with two steeds best to draw, O Lord of Hundreds! | Bring us the best among all sorts of viands:

let not the foe's wealth, Maghavan, subdue us. ‖ 10. Be gracious, Indra, let my days be lengthened: sharpen my thought as 'twere a blade of iron | Approve whatever words I speak, dependent on thee, and grant me thy divine protection. ‖ 11. Indra the Rescuer, Indra the Helper, Hero who listens at each invocation, | Śakra I call, Indra invoked of many. May Indra Maghavan prosper and bless us. ‖ 12. May helpful Indra as our good Protector, Lord of all treasures, favour us with succour, | Baffle our foes, and give us rest and safety, and may we be the lords of hero vigour. ‖ 13. May we enjoy the grace of him the Holy, yea, may we dwell in his auspicious favour. | May helpful Indra as our good Preserver drive from us, even from afar, our foemen. ‖ 14. Like rivers rushing down a slope, O Indra, to thee haste songs and prayers and linked verses. | Thou gatherest, Thunderer! like widespread bounty, kine, water, drops, and manifold libations. ‖ 15. Who lauds him, satisfies him, pays him worship? E'en the rich noble still hath found him mighty. | With power, as when one moves his feet alternate, he makes the last precede, the foremost follow. ‖ 16. Famed is the Hero as each strong man's tamer, ever advancing one and then another. | King of both worlds, hating the high and haughty, Indra protects the men who are his people. ‖ 17. He loves no more the men he loved aforetime: he turns and moves away allied with others. | Rejecting those who disregard his worship, Indra victorious lives through many autumns. ‖ 18. In every figure he hath been the mode: this is his only form for us to look on. | Indra moves multiform by his illusions; for his Bay Steeds are yoked, ten times a hundred. ‖ 19. Here Tvaṣṭar, yoking to the car the Bay Steeds, hath extended sway. | Who will for ever stand upon the foeman's side, even when our princes sit at ease? ‖ 20. Gods, we have reached a country void of pasture the land, though spacious, was too small to hold us. | Bṛihaspati, provide in war for cattle; find a path, Indra, for this faithful singer. ‖ 21. Day after day far from their seat he drove them, alike, from place to place, those darksome creatures. | The Hero slew the meanly-huckstering Dāsas, Varchin and Śambara, where the waters gather. ‖ 22. Out of thy bounty, Indra, hath Prastoka bestowed ten coffers and ten mettled horses. | We have received in turn from Divodāsa Śambara's wealth, the gift of Atithigva. ‖ 23. Ten horses and ten treasure-chests, ten garments as an added gift, | These and ten lumps of gold have I received from Divodāsa's hand. ‖ 24. Ten cars with extra steed to each, for the Atharvans hundred cows, | Hath Aśvattha to Pāyu given. ‖ 25. Thus Sṛiñjaya's son honoured the Bharadvājas, recipients of all noble gifts and bounty. ‖ 26. Lord of the wood, be firm and strong in body: be, bearing us, a brave victorious hero | Show forth thy strength, compact with straps of leather, and let thy rider win all spoils of battle. ‖ 27. Its mighty strength was borrowed from the heaven and earth: its conquering force was brought from sovereigns of the wood. | Honour with holy gifts the Car like Indra's bolt, the Car bound round with straps, the vigour of the floods. ‖ 28. Thou Bolt of Indra, Vanguard of the Marutas, close knit to Varuṇa and Child of Mitra,— | As such, accepting gifts which here we offer, receive, O Godlike Chariot, these oblations. ‖ 29. Send forth thy voice aloud through earth and heaven, and let the world in all its breadth regard thee; | O Drum, accordant with the Gods and Indra, drive thou afar, yea, very far, our foemen. ‖ 30. Thunder out strength and fill us full of vigour: yea, thunder forth and drive away all dangers. | Drive hence, O War-drum, drive away misfortune: thou art the Fist of Indra: show thy firmness. ‖ 31. Drive hither those, and these again bring hither: the War-drum speaks aloud as battle's signal. | Our heroes, winged with horses, come together. Let our car-warriors, Indra, be triumphant.

Hymn 6:48. Agni and Others.

1. Sing to your Agni with each song, at every sacrifice, for strength. | Come, let us praise the Wise and Everlasting God, even as a well-beloved Friend, ‖ 2. The Son of Strength; for is he not our gracious Lord? Let us serve him who bears our gifts. | In battle may he be our help and strengthener, yea, be the saviour of our lives. ‖ 3. Agni, thou beamest forth with light, great Hero, never changed by time. | Shining, pure Agni! with a light that never fades, beam with thy fair beams brilliantly. ‖ 4. Thou worshippest great Gods: bring them without delay by wisdom and thy wondrous power. | O Agni, make them turn hither to succour us. Give strength, and win it for thyself. ‖ 5. He whom floods, stones, and trees support, the offspring of eternal Law; | He who when rubbed with force is brought to life by men

upon the lofty height of earth; ‖ 6. He who hath filled both worlds full with his brilliant shine, who hastens with his smoke to heaven; | He made himself apparent through the gloom by night, the Red Bull in the darksome nights, the Red Bull in the darksome nights. ‖ 7. O Agni, with thy lofty beams, with thy pure brilliancy, O God, | Kindled, Most Youthful One! by Bharadvāja's hand, shine on us, O pure God, with wealth, shine, Purifier! splendidly. ‖ 8. Thou art the Lord of house and home of all the tribes, O Agni, of all tribes of men. | Guard with a hundred forts thy kindler from distress, through hundred winters, Youngest God! and those who make thy singers rich. ‖ 9. Wonderful, with thy favouring help, send us thy bounties, gracious Lord. | Thou art the Charioteer, Agni, of earthly wealth: find rest and safety for our seed. ‖ 10. With guards unfailing never negligent speed thou our children and our progeny. | Keep far from us, O Agni, all celestial wrath and wickedness of godless men. ‖ 11. Hither, O friends, with newest song drive her who freely pours her milk; ‖ Loose her who never turns away; ‖ 12. Who, for the host of Marutas bright with native sheen, hath shed immortal fame like milk; | Whom the impetuous Marutas look upon with love, who moves in splendour on their ways. ‖ 13. For Bharadvāja she poured down in days of old | The milch-cow yielding milk for all, and food that gives all nourishment. ‖ 14. Your friend like Indra passing wise, with magic power like Varuṇa. | Like Aryaman joy-giving, bringing plenteous food like Viṣṇu for my wish, I praise, ‖ 15. Bright as the host of Marutas mighty in their roar. May they bring Pūṣhan free from foes; | May they bring hither hundreds, thousands for our men: may they bring hidden stores to light, and make wealth easy to be found. ‖ 16. Haste to me, Pūṣhan, in thine car, bright Deity: I fain would speak: | Most sinful is our foeman's hate. ‖ 17. Tear not up by the roots the Kākambīra tree: destroy thou all malignity. | Let them not snare by day the neck of that Celestial Bird the Sun. ‖ 18. Uninjured let thy friendship be, like the smooth surface of a skin, | A flawless skin, containing curds, full to the mouth, containing curds. ‖ 19. For thou art high above mankind, in glory equal to the Gods. | Therefore, O Pūṣhan, look upon us in the fight: now help us as in days of old. ‖ 20. May the kind excellence of him the Kind, loud Roarers! be our guide, | Be it the God's, O Marutas, or a mortal man's who worships, ye impetuous Ones! ‖ 21. They whose high glory in a moment like the God, the Sun, goes round the space of heaven, | The Marutas have obtained bright strength, a sacred name, strength that destroys the Vṛitras, strength Vṛitra-destroying excellent. ‖ 22. Once, only once, the heaven was made, once only once, the earth was formed— | Once, only Pṛiśni's milk was shed: no second, after this, is born.

Hymn 6:49. Viśvedevas.

1. I laud with newest songs the Righteous People, Mitra and Varuṇa who make us happy. | Let them approach, here let them listen, Agni, Varuṇa, Mitra, Lords of fair dominion. ‖ 2. Him, to be praised at each tribe's sacrifices, the Two young Matrons' sober-minded Herald, | The Son of Strength, the Child of Heaven, the signal of sacrifice, red Agni will I worship. ‖ 3. Unlike in form are the Red God's two Daughters: one is the Sun's, and stars bedeck the other. | Apart, the Sanctifiers, in succession, come to the famed hymn, praised in holy verses. ‖ 4. I with a lofty song call hither Vāyu, all-bounteous, filler of his car, most wealthy. | Thou, Sage, with bright path, Lord of harnessed horses, impetuous, promptly honourest the prudent. ‖ 5. That chariot of the Aśvins, fair to look on, pleaseth me well, yoked with a thought, refulgent, | Wherewith, Nāsatyas, Chiefs, ye seek our dwelling, to give new strength to us and to our children. ‖ 6. Bulls of the Earth, O Vāta and Parjanya, stir up for us the regions of the water. | Hearers of truth, ye, Sages, World-Supporters, increase his living wealth whose songs delight you. ‖ 7. So may Sarasvatī, the Hero's Consort, brisk with rare life, the lightning's Child, inspire us, | And, with the Dames accordant, give the singer a refuge unassailable and flawless. ‖ 8. I praise with eloquence him who guards all pathways. He, when his love impelled him, went to Arka. | May he vouchsafe us gear with gold to grace it: may Pūṣhan make each prayer of ours effective. ‖ 9. May Herald Agni, fulgent, bring for worship Tvaṣṭar adored, in homes and swift to listen, | Glorious, first to share, the life-bestower, the ever active God, fair-armed, fair-handed. ‖ 10. Rudra by day, Rudra at night we honour with these our songs, the Universe's Father. | Him great and lofty, blissful, undecaying let us call specially as the Sage impels us. ‖ 11. Ye who are

youthful, wise, and meet for worship, come, Marutas, to the longing of the singer. | Coming, as erst to Aṅgiras, O Heroes, ye animate and quicken e'en the desert. || 12. Even as the herdsman driveth home his cattle, I urge my songs to him the strong swift Hero | May he, the glorious, lay upon his body the singer's hymns, as stars bedeck the heaven. || 13. He who for man's behoof in his affliction thrice measured out the earthly regions, Vishṇu— | When one so great as thou affordeth shelter, may we with wealth and with ourselves be happy. || 14. Sweet be this song of mine to Ahirbudhnya, Parvata, Savitar, with Floods and Lightnings; | Sweet, with the Plants, to Gods who seek oblations. May liberal Bhaga speed us on to riches. || 15. Give riches borne on cars, with many heroes, contenting men, the guard of mighty Order. | Give us a lasting home that we may battle with godless bands of men who fight against us, and meet with tribes to whom the Gods are gracious.

Hymn 6:50. Viśvedevas.

1. I call with prayers on Aditi your Goddess, on Agni, Mitra, Varuṇa for favour, | On Aryaman who gives unasked, the gracious, on Gods who save, on Savitar and Bhaga. || 2. Visit, to prove us free from sin, O Sūrya Lord of great might, the bright Gods sprung from Dakṣha, | Twice-born and true, observing sacred duties, Holy and full of light, whose tongue is Agni. || 3. And, O ye Heaven and Earth, a wide dominion, O ye most blissful Worlds, our lofty shelter, | Give ample room and freedom for our dwelling, a home, ye Hemispheres, which none may rival. || 4. This day invited may the Sons of Rudra, resistless, excellent, stoop down to meet us; | For, when beset with slight or sore affliction, we ever call upon the Gods, the Marutas; || 5. To whom the Goddess Rodasī clings closely, whom Pūṣhan follows bringing ample bounty. | What time ye hear our call and come, O Marutas, upon your separate path all creatures tremble. || 6. With a new hymn extol, O thou who singest, the Lover of the Song, the Hero Indra. | May he, exalted, hear our invocation, and grant us mighty wealth and strength when lauded. || 7. Give full protection, Friends of man, ye Waters, in peace and trouble, to our sons and grandsons. | For ye are our most motherly physicians, parents of all that standeth, all that moveth. || 8. May Savitar come hither and approach us, the God who rescues, Holy, golden-handed, | The God who, bounteous as the face of Morning, discloses precious gifts for him who worships. || 9. And thou, O Son of Strength, do thou turn hither the Gods today to this our holy service. | May I for evermore enjoy thy bounty and, Agni, by thy grace be rich in heroes. || 10. Come also to my call, O ye Nāsatyas, yea, verily, through my prayers, ye Holy Sages. | As from great darkness ye delivered Atri, protect us, Chiefs, from danger in the conflict. || 11. O Gods, bestow upon us riches, splendid with strength and heroes, bringing food in plenty. | Be gracious, helpful Gods of earth, of heaven, born of the Cow, and dwellers in the waters. || 12. May Rudra and Sarasvatī, accordant, Vishṇu and Vāyu, pour down gifts and bless us; | Ṛibhukṣhan, Vāja, and divine Vidhātar, Parjanya, Vāta make our food abundant. || 13. May this God Savitar, the Lord, the Offspring of Waters, pouring down his dew be gracious, | And, with the Gods and Dames accordant, Tvaṣhṭar; Dyaus with the Gods and Pṛithivī with oceans. || 14. May Aja-Ekapāda and Ahirbudhnya, and Earth and Ocean hear our invocation; | All Gods who strengthen Law, invoked and lauded, and holy texts uttered by sages, help us. || 15. So with my thoughts and hymns of praise the children of Bharadvāja sing aloud to please you. | The Dames invoked, and the resistless Vasus, and all ye Holy Ones have been exalted.

Hymn 6:51. Viśvedevas.

1. That mighty eye of Varuṇa and Mitra, infallible and dear, is moving upward. | The pure and lovely face of holy Order hath shone like gold of heaven in its arising. || 2. The Sage who knows these Gods' three ranks and orders, and all their generations near and distant, | Beholding good and evil acts of mortals, Sūra marks well the doing of the pious. || 3. I praise you Guards of mighty Law eternal, Aditi, Mitra, Varuṇa, the noble, | Aryaman, Bhaga, all whose thoughts are faithful: hither I call the Bright who share in common. || 4. Lords of the brave, infallible, foe-destroyers, great Kings, bestowers of fair homes to dwell in, | Young, Heroes, ruling heaven with strong dominion, Ādityas, Aditi I seek with worship. || 5. O Heaven our Father, Earth our guileless Mother, O Brother Agni, and ye Vasus, bless us. | Grant us, O Aditi and ye Ādityas, all of one mind, your manifold protection. || 6. Give us not up to any evil creature, as spoil to wolf or she-wolf, O ye Holy. | For ye are they who guide aright our bodies, ye are the rulers of our speech and vigour. || 7. Let us not suffer for the sin of others, nor do the deed which ye, O Vasus, punish. | Ye, Universal Gods! are all-controllers: may he do harm unto himself who hates Me. || 8. Mighty is homage: I adopt and use it. Homage hath held in place the earth and heaven. | Homage to Gods! Homage commands and rules them. I banish even committed sin by homage || 9. You Furtherers of Law, pure in your spirit, infallible, dwellers in the home of Order, | To you all Heroes mighty and far-seeing I bow me down, O Holy Ones, with homage. || 10. For these are they who shine with noblest splendour; through all our troubles these conduct us safely— | Varuṇa, Mitra, Agni, mighty Rulers, true minded, faithful to the hymn's controllers. || 11. May they, Earth, Aditi, Indra, Bhaga, Pūṣhan increase our laud, increase the Fivefold people. | Giving good help, good refuge, goodly guidance, be they our good deliverers, good protectors. || 12. Come now, O Gods, to your celestial station: the Bharadvājas' priest entreats your favour. | He, sacrificing, fain for wealth, hath honoured the Gods with those who sit and share oblations. || 13. Agni, drive thou the wicked foe, the evil-hearted thief away, | Far, far, Lord of the brave I and give us easy paths. || 14. Soma, these pressing-stones have called aloud to win thee for our Friend. | Destroy the greedy Paṇi, for a wolf is he. || 15. Ye, O most bountiful, are they who, led by Indra, seek the sky. | Give us good paths for travel: guard us well at home. || 16. Now have we entered on the road that leads to bliss, without a foe, | The road whereon a man escapes all enemies and gathers wealth.

Hymn 6:52. Viśvedevas.

1. This I allow not in the earth or heaven, at sacrifice or in these holy duties. | May the huge mountains crush him down: degraded be Atiyāja's sacrificing patron. || 2. Or he who holds us in contempt, O Marutas, or seeks to blame the prayer that we are making, | May agonies of burning be his portion. May the sky scorch the man who hates devotion. || 3. Why then, O Soma, do they call thee keeper of prayer? Why then our guardian from reproaches? | Why then beholdest thou how men revile us? Cast thy hot dart at him who hates devotion. || 4. May Mornings as they spring to life, protect me, and may the Rivers as they swell preserve me. | My guardians be the firmly-seated mountains: the Fathers, when I call on Gods, defend me! || 5. Through all our days may we be healthy-minded, and look upon the Sun when he arises. | Grant this the Treasure-Lord of treasures, coming, observant, oftenest of Gods, with succour! || 6. Most near, most oft comes Indra with protection, and she Sarasvatī, who swells with rivers— | Parjanya, bringing health with herbs, and Agni, well lauded swift to listen, like a father. || 7. Hear this mine invocation; come hither, O Universal Gods, | Be seated on this holy grass. || 8. To him who comes to meet you, Gods, with offerings bathed in holy oil— | Approach ye, one and all, to him. || 9. All Sons of Immortality shall listen to the songs we sing, | And be exceeding good to us. || 10. May all the Gods who strengthen Law, with Ṛitus, listening to our call, | Be pleased with their appropriate draught. || 11. May ındra, with the Marut host, with Tvaṣhṭar, Mitra, Aryaman, | Accept the laud and these our gifts. || 12. O Agni, Priest, as rules ordain, offer this sacrifice of ours, | Remembering the Heavenly Folk. || 13. Listen, All-Gods, to this mine invocation, Ye who inhabit heaven, and air's mid-regions, | All ye, O Holy Ones, whose tongue is Agni, seated upon this sacred grass, be joyful. || 14. May the All-Gods who claim our worship hear my thought; may the two World-halves hear it, and the Waters' Child. | Let me not utter words that ye may disregard. Closely allied with you may we rejoice in bliss. || 15. And those who, Mighty, with the wiles of serpents, were born on earth, in heaven, where waters gather— | May they vouchsafe us life of full duration. May the Gods kindly give us nights and mornings. || 16. At this my call, O Agni and Parjanya, help, swift to hear, my thought and our laudation. | One generates holy food, the other offspring, so grant us food enough with store of children. || 17. When holy grass is strewn and fire enkindled, with hymn and lowly homage I invite you. | All-Gods, to day in this our great assembly rejoice, ye Holy, in the gifts we offer.

Hymn 6:53. Pūṣhan.

1. Lord of the path, O Pūṣhan, we have yoked and bound thee to our hymn, | Even as a car, to win the prize. || 2. Bring us the wealth that men

require, a manly master of a house, | Free-handed with the liberal meed. || 3. Even him who would not give, do thou, | O glowing Pūṣhan, urge to give, | And make the niggard's soul grow soft. || 4. Clear paths that we may win the prize; scatter our enemies afar. | Strong God, be all our thoughts fulfilled. || 5. Penetrate with an awl, O Sage, the hearts of avaricious churls, | And make them subject to our will. || 6. Thrust with thine awl, O Pūṣhan: seek that which the niggard's heart holds dear, | And make him subject to our will. || 7. Tear up and read in pieces, Sage, the hearts of avaricious churls, | And make them subject to our will. || 8. Thou, glowing Pūṣhan, carriest an awl that urges men to prayer; | Therewith do thou tear up and rend to shreds the heart of every one. || 9. Thou bearest, glowing Lord! a goad with horny point that guides the cows | Thence do we seek thy gift of bliss. || 10. And make this hymn of ours produce kine, horses, and a store of wealth | For our delight and use as men.

Hymn 6:54. Pūṣhan.

1. O Pūṣhan, bring us to the man who knows, who shall direct us straight, | And say unto us, It is here. || 2. May we go forth with Pūṣhan who shall point the houses out to us, | And say to us, These same are they. || 3. Unharmed is Pūṣhan's chariot wheel; the box ne'er falleth to the ground, | Nor doth the loosened felly shake. || 4. Pūṣhan forgetteth not the man who serveth him with offered gift: | That man is first to gather wealth. || 5. May Pūṣhan follow near our kine; may Pūṣhan keep our horses safe: | May Pūṣhan gather gear for us. || 6. Follow the kine of him who pours libations out and worships thee; | And ours who sing thee songs of praise. || 7. Let none be lost, none injured, none sink in a pit and break a limb. | Return with these all safe and sound. || 8. Pūṣhan who listens to our prayers, the Strong whose wealth is never lost, | The Lord of riches, we implore. || 9. Secure in thy protecting care, O Pūṣhan, never may we fail. | We here are they who sing thy praise. || 10. From out the distance, far and wide, may Pūṣhan stretch his right hand forth, | And drive our lost again to us.

Hymn 6:55. Pūṣhan.

1. Son of Deliverance, come, bright God! | Let us twain go together: be our charioteer of sacrifice. || 2. We pray for wealth to thee most skilled of charioteers, with braided hair, | Lord of great riches, and our Friend. || 3. Bright God whose steeds are goats, thou art a stream of wealth, a treasure-heap, | The Friend of every pious man. || 4. Pūṣhan, who driveth goats for steeds, the strong and Mighty, who is called | His Sister's lover, will we laud. || 5. His Mother's suitor I address. May he who loves his Sister hear, | Brother of Indra, and my Friend. || 6. May the sure-footed goats come nigh, conveying Pūṣhan on his car, | The God who visiteth mankind.

Hymn 6:56. Pūṣhan.

1. Whoso remembers Pūṣhan as cater of mingled curd and meal | Need think no more upon the God. || 2. And he is best of charioteers. Indra, the hero's Lord, allied | With him as Friend, destroys the foes. || 3. And there the best of charioteers hath guided through the speckled cloud | The golden wheel of Sūra's car. || 4. Whate'er we speak this day to thee, Wise, Wondrous God whom many praise, | Give thou fulfilment of our thought. || 5. Lead on this company of ours, that longs for kine, to win the spoil: | Thou, Pūṣhan, art renowned afar. || 6. Prosperity we crave from thee, afar from sin and near to wealth, | Tending to perfect happiness both for tomorrow and today.

Hymn 6:57. Indra and Pūṣhan.

1. Indra and Pūṣhan will we call for friend ship and prosperity | And for the winning of the spoil. || 2. One by the Soma sits to drink juice which the mortar hath expressed: | The other longs for curd and meal. || 3. Goats are the team that draws the one: the other hath Bay Steeds at hand; | With both of these he slays the fiends. || 4. When Indra, wondrous strong, brought down the streams, the mighty water-floods, | Pūṣhan was standing by his side. || 5. To this, to Pūṣhan's favouring love, and Indra's, may we closely cling, | As to a tree's extended bough. || 6. As one who drives a car draws in his reins, may we draw Pūṣhan near, | And Indra, for our great success.

Hymn 6:58. Pūṣhan.

1. Like heaven art thou: one form is bright, one holy, like Day and Night dissimilar in colour. | All magic powers thou aidest, self-dependent! Auspicious be thy bounty here, O Pūṣhan. || 2. Goat-borne, the guard of cattle, he whose home is strength, inspirer of the hymn, set over all the world; | Brandishing here and there his lightly. moving goad, beholding every creature, Pūṣhan, God, goes forth. || 3. O Pūṣhan, with thy golden ships that travel across the ocean, in the air's mid-region, | Thou goest on an embassy to Sūrya, subdued by love, desirous of the glory. || 4. Near kinsman of the heaven and earth is Pūṣhan, liberal, Lord of food, of wondrous lustre, | Whom strong and vigorous and swiftly moving, subdued by love, the Deities gave to Sūrya.

Hymn 6:59. Indra-Agni.

1. I will declare, while juices flow, the manly deeds that ye have done: | Your Fathers, enemies of Gods, were smitten down, and, Indra-Agni, ye survive. || 2. Thus, Indra-Agni, verily your greatness merits loftiest praise, | Sprung from one common Father, brothers, twins are ye; your Mother is in every place. || 3. These who delight in flowing juice, like fellow horses at their food, | Indra and Agni, Gods armed with the thunderbolt, we call this day to come with help. || 4. Indra and Agni, Friends of Law, served with rich gifts, your speech is kind | To him who praises you while these libations flow: that man, O Gods, ye ne'er consume. || 5. What mortal understands, O Gods, Indra and Agni, this your way? | One of you, yoking Steeds that move to every side, advances in your common car. || 6. First, Indra-Agni, hath this Maid come footless unto those with feet. | Stretching her head and speaking loudly with her tongue, she hath gone downward thirty steps. || 7. E'en now, O Indra-Agni, men hold in their arms and stretch their bows. | Desert us not in this great fray, in battles for the sake of kine. || 8. The foeman's sinful enmities, Indra and Agni, vex me sore. | Drive those who hate me far away, and keep them distant from the Sun. || 9. Indra and Agni, yours are all the treasures of the heavens and earth. | Here give ye us the opulence that prospers every living man. || 10. O Indra-Agni, who accept the laud, and hear us for our praise, | Come near us, drawn by all our songs, to drink of this our Soma juice.

Hymn 6:60. Indra-Agni.

1. He slays the foe and wins the spoil who worships Indra and Agni, strong and mighty Heroes, | Who rule as Sovereigns over ample riches, victorious, showing forth their power in conquest. || 2. So battle now, O Indra and thou, Agni, for cows and waters, sunlight, stolen Mornings. | Team-borne, thou makest kine thine own, O Agni: thou, Indra, light, Dawns, regions, wondrous waters. || 3. With Vṛitra-slaying might, Indra and Agni, come, drawn by homage, O ye Vṛitra-slayers. | Indra and Agni, show yourselves among us with your supreme and unrestricted bounties. || 4. I call the Twain whose deeds of old have all been famed in ancient days | O Indra-Agni, harm us not. || 5. The Strong, the scatterers of the foe, Indra and Agni, we invoke; | May they be kind to one like me. || 6. They slay our Ārya foes, these Lords of heroes, slay our Dasyu foes | And drive our enemies away. || 7. Indra and Agni, these our songs of praise have sounded forth to you: | Ye who bring blessings! drink the juice. || 8. Come, Indra-Agni, with those teams, desired of many, which ye have, | O Heroes, for the worshipper. || 9. With those to this libation poured, ye Heroes, Indra-Agni, come: | Come ye to drink the Soma juice. || 10. Glorify him who compasses all forests with his glowing flame, | And leaves them blackened with his tongue. || 11. He who gains Indra's bliss with fire enkindled finds an easy way | Over the floods to happiness. || 12. Give us fleet coursers to convey Indra and Agni, and bestow | Abundant strengthening food on us. || 13. Indra and Agni, I will call you hither and make you joyful with the gifts I offer. | Ye Twain are givers both of food and riches: to win me strength and vigour I invoke you. || 14. Come unto us with riches, come with wealth in horses and in kine. | Indra and Agni, we invoke you both, the Gods, as Friends for friendship, bringing bliss. || 15. Indra and Agni, hear his call who worships. with libations poured. | Come and enjoy the offerings, drink the sweetly-flavoured Soma juice.

Hymn 6:61. Sarasvatī.

1. To Vadhryaśva when. be worshipped her with gifts she gave fierce Divodāsa, canceller of debts. | Consumer of the churlish niggard, one and all, thine, O Sarasvatī, are these effectual boons. || 2. She with her might, like one who digs for lotus-stems, hath burst with her strong waves the ridges of the hills. | Let us invite with songs and holy hymns for help Sarasvatī who slayeth the Pārāvatas. || 3. Thou castest down, Sarasvatī, those who scorned the Gods, the brood of every Bṛisaya skilled in magic arts. |

Thou hast discovered rivers for the tribes of men, and, rich in wealth! made poison flow away from them. || 4. May the divine Sarasvatī, rich in her wealth, protect us well, | Furthering all our thoughts with might || 5. Whoso, divine Sarasvatī, invokes thee where the prize is set, | Like Indra when he smites the foe. || 6. Aid us, divine Sarasvatī, thou who art strong in wealth and power | Like Pūṣhan, give us opulence. || 7. Yea, this divine Sarasvatī, terrible with her golden path, | Foe-slayer, claims our eulogy. || 8. Whose limitless unbroken flood, swift-moving with a rapid rush, | Comes onward with tempestuous roar. || 9. She hath spread us beyond all foes, beyond her Sisters, Holy One, | As Sūrya spreadeth out the days. || 10. Yea, she most dear amid dear stream, Seven-sistered, graciously inclined, | Sarasvatī hath earned our praise. || 11. Guard us from hate Sarasvatī, she who hath filled the realms of earth, | And that wide tract, the firmament! || 12. Seven-sistered, sprung from threefold source, the Five Tribes' prosperer, she must be | Invoked in every deed of might. || 13. Marked out by majesty among the Mighty Ones, in glory swifter than the other rapid Streams, | Created vast for victory like a chariot, Sarasvatī must be extolled by every sage. || 14. Guide us, Sarasvatī, to glorious treasure: refuse us not thy milk, nor spurn us from thee. | Gladly accept our friendship and obedience: let us not go from thee to distant countries.

Hymn 6:62. Aśvins.

1. I laud the Heroes Twain, this heaven's Controllers: singing with songs of praise I call the Aśvins, | Fain in a moment, when the morns are breaking, to part the earth's ends and the spacious regions. || 2. Moving to sacrifice through realms of lustre they light the radiance of the car that bears them. | Traversing many wide unmeasured spaces, over the wastes ye pass, and fields, and waters. || 3. Ye to that bounteous path of yours, ye mighty, have ever borne away our thoughts with horses, | Mind-swift and full of vigour, that the trouble of man who offers gifts might cease and slumber. || 4. So ye, when ye have yoked your chariot-horses, come to the hymn of the most recent singer. | Our true and ancient Herald Priest shall bring you, the Youthful, bearing splendour, food, and vigour. || 5. With newest hymn I call those Wonder-Workers, ancient and brilliant, and exceeding mighty, | Bringers of bliss to him who lauds and praises, bestowing varied bounties on the singer. || 6. So ye, with birds, out of the sea and waters bore Bhujyu, son of Tugra, through the regions. | Speeding with winged steeds through dustless spaces, out of the bosom of the flood they bore him. || 7. Victors, car-borne, ye rent the rock asunder: Bulls, heard the calling of the eunuch's consort. | Bounteous, ye filled the cow with milk for Śayu: thus, swift and zealous Ones, ye showed your favour. || 8. Whate'er from olden time, Heaven, Earth! existeth great object of the wrath of Gods and mortals, | Make that, Ādityas, Vasus, sons of Rudra, an evil brand to one allied with demons. || 9. May he who knows, as Varuṇa and Mitra, air's realm, appointing both the Kings in season, | Against the secret fiend cast forth his weapon, against the lying words that strangers utter. || 10. Come to our home with friendly wheels, for offspring; come on your radiant chariot rich in heroes. | Strike off, ye Twain, the heads of our assailants who with man's treacherous attack approach us. || 11. Come hitherward to us with teams of horses, the highest and the midmost and the lowest. | Bountiful Lords, throw open to the singer doors e'en of the firm-closed stall of cattle.

Hymn 6:63. Aśvins.

1. Where hath the hymn with reverence, like an envoy, found both fair Gods today, invoked of many— | Hymn that hath brought the two Nāsatyas hither? To this man's thought be ye, both Gods, most friendly. || 2. Come readily to this mine invocation, lauded with songs, that ye may drink the juices. | Compass this house to keep it from the foeman, that none may force it, either near or distant. || 3. Juice in wide room hath been prepared to feast you: for you the grass is strewn, most soft to tread on. | With lifted hands your servant hath adored you. Yearning for you the press-stones shed the liquid. || 4. Agni uplifts him at your sacrifices: forth goes the oblation dropping oil and glowing. | Up stands the grateful-minded priest, elected, appointed to invoke the two Nāsatyas. || 5. Lords of great wealth! for glory, Sūrya's Daughter mounted your car that brings a hundred succours. | Famed for your magic arts were ye, magicians! amid the race of Gods, ye dancing Heroes! || 6. Ye Twain, with these your glories fair to look on, brought, to win victory, rich gifts for Sūrya. | After you flew your birds, marvels of beauty: dear to our hearts! the song, well lauded, reached you. || 7. May your winged coursers, best to draw. Nāsatyas! convey you to the object of your wishes. | Swift as the thought, your car hath been sent onward to food of many a sort and dainty viands. || 8. Lords of great wealth, manifold is your bounty: ye filled our cow with food that never faileth. | Lovers of sweetness! yours are praise and singers, and poured libations which have sought your favour. || 9. Mine were two mares of Puraya, brown, swift-footed; a hundred with Sumīḷha, food with Peruka | Śāṇḍa gave ten gold-decked and well-trained horses, tame and obedient and of lofty stature. || 10. Nāsatyas! Purupanthā offered hundreds, thousands of steeds to him who sang your praises, | Gave, Heroes! to the singer Bharadvāja. Ye-Wonder-Workers, let the fiends be slaughtered. || 11. May I with princes share your bliss in freedom.

Hymn 6:64. Dawn.

1. The radiant Dawns have risen up for glory, in their white splendour like the waves of waters. | She maketh paths all easy, fair to travel, and, rich, hath shown herself benign and friendly. || 2. We see that thou art good: far shines thy lustre; thy beams, thy splendours have flown up to heaven. | Decking thyself, thou makest bare thy bosom, shining in majesty, thou Goddess Morning. || 3. Red are the kine and luminous that bear her the Blessed One who spreadeth through the distance. | The foes she chaseth like a valiant archer, like a swift warrior she repelleth darkness. || 4. Thy ways are easy on the hills: thou passest Invincible! Self-luminous! through waters. | So lofty Goddess with thine ample pathway, Daughter of Heaven, bring wealth to give us comfort. || 5. Dawn, bring me wealth: untroubled, with thine oxen thou bearest riches at thy will and pleasure; | Thou who, a Goddess, Child of Heaven, hast shown thee lovely through bounty when we called thee early. || 6. As the birds fly forth from their resting places, so men with store of food rise at thy dawning. | Yea, to the liberal mortal who remaineth at home, O Goddess Dawn, much good thou bringest.

Hymn 6:65. Dawn.

1. Shedding her light on human habitations this Child of Heaven hath called us from our slumber; | She who at night-time with her argent lustre hath shown herself e'en through the shades of darkness. || 2. All this with red-rayed steeds have they divided: the Dawns on bright cars shine in wondrous fashion. | They, bringing near the stately rite's commencement, drive far away the night's surrounding shadows. || 3. Dawns, bringing hither, to the man who worships, glory and power and might and food and vigour, | Opulent, with imperial sway like heroes, favour your servant and this day enrich him. || 4. Now is there treasure for the man who serves you, now for the hero, Dawns! who brings oblation; | Now for the singer when he sings the praise-song. Even to one like me ye brought aforetime. || 5. O Dawn who standest on the mountain ridges, Aṅgirasas now praise thy stalls of cattle. | With prayer and holy hymn they burst them open: the heroes' calling on the Gods was fruitful. || 6. Shine on us as of old, thou Child of Heaven, on him, rich Maid! who serves like Bharadvāja. | Give to the singer wealth with noble heroes, and upon us bestow wide-spreading glory.

Hymn 6:66. Marutas.

1. E'en to the wise let that be still a wonder to which the general name of Cow is given. | The one hath swelled among mankind for milking: Pṛiśni hath drained but once her fair bright udder. || 2. They who like kindled flames of fire are glowing, the Marutas, twice and thrice have waxen mighty. | Golden and dustless were their cars, invested with their great strength and their heroic vigour. || 3. They who are Sons of the rain-pouring Rudra, whom the long-lasting One had power to foster: | The Mighty Ones whose germ great Mother Pṛiśni is known to have received for man's advantage. || 4. They shrink not from the birth; in this same manner still resting there they purge away reproaches. | When they have streamed forth, brilliant, at their pleasure, with their own splendour they bedew their bodies. || 5. Even those who bear the brave bold name of Marutas, whom not the active quickly wins for milking. | Even the liberal wards not off those fierce ones, those who are light and agile in their greatness. || 6. When, strong in strength and armed with potent weapons, they had united well-formed earth and heaven, | Rodasī stood among these furious Heroes like splendour shining with her native brightness. || 7. No team of goats shall draw your car, O Marutas, no horse no charioteer

be he who drives it. | Halting not, reinless, through the air it travels, speeding alone its paths through earth and heaven. || 8. None may obstruct, none overtake, O Marutas, him whom ye succour in the strife of battle | For sons and progeny, for kine and waters: he bursts the cow-stall on the day of trial. || 9. Bring a bright hymn to praise the band of Marutas, the Singers, rapid, strong in native vigour, | Who conquer mighty strength with strength more mighty: earth shakes in terror at their wars, O Agni. || 10. Bright like the flashing flames of sacrifices, like tongues of fire impetuous in their onset, | Chanting their psalm, singing aloud, like heroes, splendid from birth, invincible, the Marutas. || 11. That swelling band I call with invocation, the brood of Rudra, armed with glittering lances. | Pure hymns are meet for that celestial army: like floods and mountains have the Strong Ones battled.

Hymn 6:67. Mitra-Varuṇa.

1. Now Mitra-Varuṇa shall be exalted high by your songs, noblest of all existing; | They who, as 'twere with reins are best Controllers, unequalled with their arms to check the people. || 2. To you Two Gods is this my thought extended, turned to the sacred grass with loving homage. | Give us, O Mitra-Varuṇa, a dwelling safe from attack, which ye shall guard, Boon-Givers! || 3. Come hither, Mitra-Varuṇa, invited with eulogies and loving adoration, | Ye who with your might, as Work-Controllers, urge even men who quickly hear to labour. || 4. Whom, of pure origin, like two strong horses, Aditi bore as babes in proper season, | Whom, Mighty at your birth, the Mighty Goddess brought forth as terrors to the mortal foeman. || 5. As all the Gods in their great joy and gladness gave you with one accord your high dominion, | As ye surround both worlds, though wide and spacious your spies are ever true and never bewildered. || 6. So, through the days maintaining princely power. ye prop the height as 'twere from loftiest heaven. | The Star of all the Gods, established, filleth the heaven and earth with food of man who liveth. || 7. Take the strong drink, to quaff till ye are sated, when he and his attendants fill the chamber. | The young Maids brook not that none seeks to win them, when, Quickeners of all! they scatter moisture. || 8. So with your tongue come ever, when your envoy, faithful and very wise, attends our worship. | Nourished by holy oil! be this your glory: annihilate the sacrificer's trouble. || 9. When, Mitra-Varuṇa, they strive against you and break the friendly laws ye have established, | They, neither Gods nor men in estimation, like Apī's sons have godless sacrifices. || 10. When singers in their song uplift their voices, some chant the Nivid texts with steady purpose. | Then may we sing you lauds that shall be fruitful: do ye not rival all the Gods in greatness? || 11. O Mitra-Varuṇa, may your large bounty come to us hither, near to this our dwelling, | When the kine haste to us, and when they harness the fleet-foot mettled stallion for the battle.

Hymn 6:68. Indra-Varuṇa.

1. His honouring rite whose grass is trimmed is offered swiftly to you, in Manu's wise, accordant, | The rite which Indra-Varuṇa shall carry this day to high success and glorious issue. || 2. For at Gods' worship they are best through vigour; they have become the strongest of the Heroes; | With mighty strength, most liberal of the Princes, Chiefs of the host, by Law made Vṛitra's slayers. || 3. Praise those Twain Gods for powers that merit worship, Indra and Varuṇa, for bliss, the joyous. | One with his might and thunderbolt slays Vṛitra; the other as a Sage stands near in troubles. || 4. Though dames and men have waxen strong and mighty, and all the Gods self-praised among the Heroes, | Ye, Indra-Varuṇa, have in might surpassed them, and thus were ye spread wide, O Earth and Heaven. || 5. Righteous is he, and liberal and helpful who, Indra-Varuṇa, brings you gifts with gladness. | That bounteous man through food shall conquer foemen, and win him opulence and wealthy people. || 6. May wealth which ye bestow in food and treasure on him who brings you gifts and sacrifices, | Wealth, Gods! which breaks the curse of those who vex us, be, Indra-Varuṇa, e'en our own possession. || 7. So also, Indra-Varuṇa, may our princes have riches swift to save, with Gods to guard them— | They whose great might gives victory in battles, and their triumphant glory spreads with swiftness. || 8. Indra. and Varuṇa, Gods whom we are lauding, mingle ye wealth with our heroic glory. | May we, who praise the strength of what is mighty, pass dangers, as with boats we cross the waters. || 9. Now will I sing a dear and far-extending hymn to Varuṇa the God, sublime, imperial Lord, | Who, mighty Governor, Eternal, as with flame, illumines both wide worlds with majesty and power. || 10. True to Law, Indra-Varuṇa, drinkers of the juice, drink this pressed Soma which shall give you rapturous joy. | Your chariot cometh to the banquet of the Gods, to sacrifice, as it were home, that ye may drink. || 11. Indra and Varuṇa, drink your fill, ye Heroes, of this invigorating sweetest Soma. | This juice is shed by us that ye may quaff it: on this trimmed grass be seated, and rejoice you

Hymn 6:69. Indra-Vishṇu

1. Indra and Vishṇu, at my task's completion I urge you on with food and sacred service. | Accept the sacrifice and grant us riches, leading us on by unobstructed pathways. || 2. Ye who inspire all hymns, Indra and Vishṇu, ye vessels who contain the Soma juices, | May hymns of praise that now are sung address you, the lauds that are recited by the singers. || 3. Lords of joy-giving draughts, Indra and Vishṇu, come, giving gifts of treasure, to the Soma. | With brilliant rays of hymns let chanted praises, repeated with the lauds, adorn and deck you. || 4. May your foe-conquering horses bring you hither, Indra and Vishṇu, sharers of the banquet. | Of all our hymns accept the invocations list to my prayers and hear the songs I sing you. || 5. This your deed, Indra-Vishṇu, must be lauded: widely ye strode in the wild joy of Soma. | Ye made the firmament of larger compass, and made the regions broad for our existence. || 6. Strengthened with sacred offerings, Indra-Vishṇu, first eaters, served with worship and oblation, | Fed with the holy oil, vouchsafe us riches ye are the lake, the vat that holds the Soma. || 7. Drink of this meath, O Indra, thou, and Vishṇu; drink ye your fill of Soma, Wonder-Workers. | The sweet exhilarating juice hath reached you. Hear ye my prayers, give ear unto my calling. || 8. Ye Twain have conquered, ne'er have ye been conquered: never hath either of the Twain been vanquished. | Ye, Indra-Vishṇu, when ye fought the battle, produced this infinite with three divisions.

Hymn 6:70. Heaven and Earth.

1. Filled full of fatness, compassing all things that be, wide, spacious, dropping meath, beautiful in their form, | The Heaven and the Earth by Varuṇa's decree, unwasting, rich in germs, stand parted each from each. || 2. The Everlasting Pair, with full streams, rich in milk, in their pure rule pour fatness for the pious man. | Ye who are Regents of this world, O Earth and Heaven, pour into us the genial flow that prospers men. || 3. Whoso, for righteous life, pours offerings to you, O Heaven and Earth, ye Hemispheres, that man succeeds. | He in his seed is born again and spreads by Law: from you flow things diverse in form, but ruled alike. || 4. Enclosed in fatness, Heaven and Earth are bright therewith: they mingle with the fatness which they still increase. | Wide, broad, set foremost at election of the priest, to them the singers pray for bliss to further them. || 5. May Heaven and Earth pour down the balmy rain for us, balm-dropping, yielding balm, with balm upon your path, | Bestowing by your Godhead sacrifice and wealth, great fame and strength for us and good heroic might. || 6. May Heaven and Earth make food swell plenteously for us, all-knowing father, mother, wondrous in their works. | Pouring out bounties, may, in union, both the Worlds, all beneficial, send us gain, and power, and wealth.

Hymn 6:71. Savitar.

1. Full of effectual wisdom Savitar the God hath stretched out golden arms that he may bring forth life. | Young and most skilful, while he holds the region up, the Warrior sprinkles fatness over both his hands. || 2. May we enjoy the noblest vivifying force of Savitar the God, that he may give us wealth: | For thou art mighty to produce and lull to rest the world of life that moves on two feet and on four. || 3. Protect our habitation, Savitar, this day, with guardian aids around, auspicious, firm and true. | God of the golden tongue, keep us for newest bliss: let not the evil-wisher have us in his power. || 4. This Savitar the God, the golden-handed, Friend of the home, hath risen to meet the twilight. | With cheeks of brass, with pleasant tongue, the Holy, he sends the worshipper rich gifts in plenty. || 5. Like a Director, Savitar hath extended his golden arms, exceeding fair to look on. | He hath gone up the heights of earth and heaven, and made each monster fall and cease from troubling. || 6. Fair wealth, O Savitar, today, tomorrow, fair wealth produce for us each day that passes. | May we through this our song be happy gainers, God, of a fair and spacious habitation.

Hymn 6:72. Indra-Soma.

1. Great is this might of yours, Indra and Soma: the first high exploits were your own achievements. | Ye found the Sun ye found the light of heaven: ye killed all darkness and the Gods' blasphemers. || 2. Ye, Indra-Soma, gave her light to Morning, and led the Sun on high with all his splendour. | Ye stayed the heaven with a supporting pillar, and spread abroad apart, the Earth, the Mother. || 3. Ye slew the flood-obstructing serpent Vṛitra, Indra and Soma: Heaven approved your exploit. | Ye urged to speed the currents of the rivers, and many seas have ye filled full with waters. || 4. Ye in the unripe udders of the milch-kine have set the ripe milk, Indra, thou, and Soma. | Ye have held fast the unimpeded whiteness within these many-coloured moving creatures. || 5. Verily ye bestow, Indra and Soma, wealth, famed, victorious, passing to our children. | Ye have invested men, ye Mighty Beings, with manly strength that conquers in the battle.

Hymn 6:73. Bṛihaspati.

1. Served with oblations, first-born, mountain-render, Aṅgiras' son, Bṛihaspati, the Holy, | With twice-firm path, dwelling in light, our Father, roars loudly, as a bull, to Earth and Heaven. || 2. Bṛihaspati, who made for such a people wide room and verge when Gods were invocated, | Slaying his enemies, breaks down their castles, quelling his foes and conquering those who hate him. || 3. Bṛihaspati in war hath won rich treasures, hath won, this God, the great stalls filled with cattle. | Striving to win waters and light, resistless, Bṛihaspati with lightning smites the foeman.

Hymn 6:74. Soma-Rudra.

1. Hold fast your Godlike sway, O Soma-Rudra: let these our sacrifices quickly reach you. | Placing in every house your seven great treasures, bring blessing to our quadrupeds and bipeds. || 2. Soma and Rudra, chase to every quarter the sickness that hath visited our dwelling. | Drive Nirṛiti away into the distance, and give us excellent and happy glories. || 3. Provide, O Soma-Rudra, for our bodies all needful medicines to heal and cure us. | Set free and draw away the sin committed which we have still inherent in our persons. || 4. Armed with keen shafts and weapons, kind and loving, be gracious unto us, Soma and Rudra. | Release us from the noose of Varuṇa; keep us from sorrow, in your tender loving-kindness.

Hymn 6:75. Weapons of War.

1. The warrior's look is like a thunderous rain-cloud's, when, armed with mail, he seeks the lap of battle. | Be thou victorious with unwounded body: so let the thickness of thy mail protect thee. || 2. With Bow let us win kine, with Bow the battle, with Bow be victors in our hot encounters. | The Bow brings grief and sorrow to the foeman: armed with the Bow may we subdue all regions. || 3. Close to his car, as fain to speak, She presses, holding her well-loved Friend in her embraces. | Strained on the Bow, She whispers like a woman-this Bowstring that preserves us in the combat. || 4. These, meeting like a woman and her lover, bear, mother-like, their child upon their bosom. | May the two Bow-ends, starting swift asunder, scatter, in unison, the foes who hate us. || 5. With many a son, father of many daughters, He clangs and clashes as he goes to battle. | Slung on the back, pouring his brood, the Quiver vanquishes all opposing bands and armies. || 6. Upstanding in the Car the skilful Charioteer guides his strong Horses on whithersoe'er he will. | See and admire the strength of those controlling Reins which from behind declare the will of him who drives. || 7. Horses whose hoofs rain dust are neighing loudly, yoked to the Chariots, showing forth their vigour, | With their forefeet descending on the foemen, they, never flinching, trample and destroy them. || 8. Car-bearer is the name of his oblation, whereon are laid his Weapons and his Armour. | So let us here, each day that passes, honour the helpful Car with hearts exceeding joyful. || 9. In sweet association lived the fathers who gave us life, profound and strong in trouble, | Unwearied, armed with shafts and wondrous weapons, free, real heroes, conquerors of armies. || 10. The Brahmans, and the Fathers meet for Soma-draughts, and, graciously inclined, unequalled Heaven and Earth. | Guard us from evil, Pūṣhan, guard us strengtheners of Law: let not the evil-wisher master us. || 11. Her tooth a deer, dressed in an eagle's feathers, bound with cow-hide, launched forth, She flieth onward. | There where the heroes speed hither and thither, there may the Arrows shelter and protect us. || 12. Avoid us thou whose flight is straight, and let our bodies be as stone. | May Soma kindly speak to us, and Aditi protect us well. || 13. He lays his blows upon their backs, he deals his blows upon their thighs. | Thou, Whip, who urgest horses, drive sagacious horses in the fray. || 14. It compasses the arm with serpent windings, fending away the friction of the bowstring: | So may the Brace, well-skilled in all its duties, guard manfully the man from every quarter. || 15. Now to the Shaft with venom smeared, tipped with deer-horn, with iron mouth, | Celestial, of Parjanya's seed, be this great adoration paid. || 16. Loosed from the Bowstring fly away, thou Arrow, sharpened by our prayer. | Go to the foemen, strike them home, and let not one be left alive. || 17. There where the flights of Arrows fall like boys whose locks are yet unshorn. | Even there may Brahmaṇaspati, and Aditi protect us well, protect us well through all our days. || 18. Thy vital parts I cover with thine Armour: with immortality King Soma clothe thee. | Varuṇa give thee what is more than ample, and in thy triumph may the Gods be joyful. || 19. Whoso would kill us, whether he be a strange foe or one of us, | May all the Gods discomfit him. My nearest, closest Mail is prayer.

Maṇḍala 7

Hymn 7:1. Agni.

1. The men from fire-sticks, with their hands' swift movement, have, in deep thought, engendered glorious Agni, | Far-seen, with pointed flame, Lord of the homestead. || 2. The Vasus set that Agni in the dwelling, fair to behold, for help from every quarter: | Who, in the home for ever, must be honoured. || 3. Shine thou before us, Agni, well-enkindled, with flame, Most Youthful God, that never fadeth. | To thee come all our sacrificial viands. || 4. Among all fires these fires have shone most brightly, splendid with light, begirt by noble heroes, | Where men of lofty birth sit down together. || 5. Victorious Agni, grant us wealth with wisdom, wealth with brave sons, famous and independent, | Which not a foe who deals in magic conquers. || 6. To whom, the Strong, at morn and eve comes, maid-like, the ladle dropping oil, with its oblation. | Wealth-seeking comes to him his own devotion. || 7. Burn up all malice with those flames, O Agni, wherewith of old thou burntest up Jarūtha, | And drive away in silence pain and sickness. || 8. With him who lighteth up thy splendour, Agni, excellent, pure, refulgent, Purifier, | Be present, and with us through these our praises. || 9. Agni, the patriarchal men, the mortals who have in many places spread thy lustre,— | Be gracious to us here for their sake also. || 10. Let these men, heroes in the fight with foemen, prevail against all godless arts of magic,— | These who approve the noble song I sing thee. || 11. Let us not sit in want of men, O Agni, without descendants, heroless, about thee: | But, O House-Friend, in houses full of children. || 12. By sacrifice which the Steeds' Lord ever visits, there make our dwelling rich in seed and offspring, | Increasing still with lineal successors. || 13. Guard us, O Agni, from the hated demon, guard us from malice of the churlish sinner: | Allied with thee may I subdue assailants. || 14. May this same fire of mine surpass all others, this fire where offspring, vigorous and firm-handed, | Wins, on a thousand paths, what ne'er shall perish. || 15. This is that Agni, saviour from the foeman, who guards the kindler of the flame from sorrow: | Heroes of noble lineage serve and tend him. || 16. This is that Agni, served in many places, whom the rich lord who brings oblation kindles, | And round him goes the priest at sacrifices. || 17. Agni, may we with riches in possession bring thee continual offerings in abundance, | Using both means to draw thee to our worship. || 18. Agni, bear thou, Eternal, these most welcome oblations to the Deities' assembly: | Let them enjoy our very fragrant presents. || 19. Give us not up, Agni, to want of heroes, to wretched clothes, to need, to destitution. | Yield us not, Holy One, to fiend or hunger; injure us not at home or in the forest. || 20. Give strength and power to these my prayers, O Agni; O God, pour blessings on our chiefs and nobles. | Grant that both we and they may share thy bounty. Ye Gods, protect us evermore with blessings. || 21. Thou Agni, swift to hear, art fair of aspect: beam forth, O Son of Strength, in full effulgence. | Let me not want, with thee, a son for ever: let not a manly hero ever fail us. || 22. Condemn us not to indigence, O Agni, beside these flaming fires which Gods have kindled; | Nor, even after fault, let thy displeasure, thine as a God, O Son of Strength, o'ertake us. || 23. O Agni, fair of face, the wealthy mortal who to the Immortal offers his oblation. | Hath him who wins him treasure by his Godhead, to whom the prince, in need, goes supplicating. || 24. Knowing our chief felicity, O Agni, bring hither ample riches to our nobles, |

Wherewith we may enjoy ourselves, O Victor, with undiminished life and hero children. || 25. Give strength and power to these my prayers, O Agni; O God, pour blessings on bur chiefs and nobles. | Grant that both we and they may share thy bounty. Ye Gods, protect us evermore with blessings.

Hymn 7:2. Āprīs.

1. Gladly accept, this day, our fuel, Agni: send up thy sacred smoke and shine sublimely. | Touch the celestial summits with thy columns, and overspread thee with the rays of Sūrya. || 2. With sacrifice to these we men will honour the majesty of holy Narāśaṃsa— | To these the pure, most wise, the thought. inspirers, Gods who enjoy both sorts of our oblations. || 3. We will extol at sacrifice for ever, as men may do, Agni whom Manu kindled, | Your very skilful Asura, meet for worship, envoy between both worlds, the truthful speaker. || 4. Bearing the sacred grass, the men who serve him strew it with reverence, on their knees, by Agni. | Calling him to the spotted grass, oil-sprinkled, adorn him, ye Adhvaryus, with oblation. || 5. With holy thoughts the pious have thrown open Doors fain for chariots in the Gods' assembly. | Like two full mother cows who lick their youngling, like maidens for the gathering, they adorn them. || 6. And let the two exalted Heavenly Ladies, Morning and Night, like a cow good at milking, | Come, much-invoked, and on our grass be seated wealthy, deserving worship, for our welfare. || 7. You, Bards and Singers at men's sacrifices, both filled with wisdom, I incline to worship. | Send up our offerings when we call upon you, and so among the Gods obtain us treasures. || 8. May Bhāratī with all her Sisters, Iḷā accordant with the Gods, with mortals Agni, | Sarasvatī with all her kindred Rivers, come to this grass, Three Goddesses, and seat them. || 9. Well pleased with us do thou, O God, O Tvaṣhṭar, give ready issue to our procreant vigour, | Whence springs the hero, powerful, skilled in action, lover of Gods, adjuster of the press-stones. || 10. Send to the Gods the oblation, Lord of Forests, and let the Immolator, Agni, dress it. | He as the truer Priest shall offer worship, for the God's generations well he knoweth. || 11. Come thou to us, O Agni, duly kindled, together with the potent Gods and Indra. | On this our grass sit Aditi, happy Mother, and let our Hail! delight the Gods Immortal.

Hymn 7:3. Agni.

1. Associate with fires, make your God Agni envoy at sacrifice, best skilled in worship, | Established firm among mankind, the Holy, flame-crowned and fed with oil, the Purifier. || 2. Like a steed neighing eager for the pasture, when he hath stepped forth from the great enclosure: | Then the wind following blows upon his splendour, and, straight, the path is black which thou hast travelled. || 3. From thee a Bull but newly born, O Agni, the kindled everlasting flames rise upward. | Aloft to heaven thy ruddy smoke ascendeth: Agni, thou speedest to the Gods as envoy. || 4. Thou whose fresh lustre o'er the earth advanceth when greedily with thy jaws thy food thou eatest. | Like a host hurried onward comes thy lasso: fierce, with thy tongue thou piercest, as 'twere barley. || 5. The men have decked him both at eve and morning, Most Youthful Agni, as they tend a courser. | They kindle him, a guest within his dwelling: bright shines the splendour of the worshipped Hero. || 6. O fair of face, beautiful is thine aspect when, very near at hand, like gold thou gleamest, | Like Heaven's thundering roar thy might approaches, and like the wondrous Sun thy light thou showest. || 7. That we may worship, with your Hail to Agni! with sacrificial cakes and fat oblations, | Guard us, O Agni, with those boundless glories as with a hundred fortresses of iron. || 8. Thine are resistless songs for him who offers, and hero-giving hymns wherewith thou savest; | With these, O Son of Strength, O Jātavedas, guard us, preserve these princes and the singers. || 9. When forth he cometh, like an axe new-sharpened, pure in his form, resplendent in his body, | Sprung, sought with eager longing, from his Parents, for the Gods' worship, Sage and Purifier: || 10. Shine this felicity on us, O Agni: may we attain to perfect understanding. | All happiness be theirs who sing and praise thee. Ye Gods, preserve us evermore with blessings.

Hymn 7:4. Agni.

1. Bring forth your gifts to his refulgent splendour, your hymn as purest offering to Agni, | To him who goes as messenger with knowledge between all songs of men and Gods in heaven. || 2. Wise must this Agni be, though young and tender, since he was born, Most Youthful, of his Mother; | He who with bright teeth seizeth fast the forests, and eats his food, though plenteous, in a moment. || 3. Before his presence must we all assemble, this God's whom men have seized in his white splendour. | This Agni who hath brooked that men should seize him hath shone for man with glow insufferable. || 4. Far-seeing hath this Agni been established, deathless mid mortals, wise among the foolish. | Here, O victorious God, forbear to harm us: may we forever share thy gracious favour. || 5. He who hath occupied his God-made dwelling, Agni, in wisdom hath surpassed Immortals. | A Babe unborn, the plants and trees support him, and the earth beareth him the All-sustainer. || 6. Agni is Lord of Amṛita. in abundance, Lord of the gift of wealth and hero valour, | Victorious God, let us not sit about thee like men devoid of strength, beauty, and worship. || 7. The foeman's treasure may be won with labour: may we be masters of our own possessions. | Agni, no son is he who springs from others: lengthen not out the pathways of the foolish. || 8. Unwelcome for adoption is the stranger, one to be thought of as another's offspring, | Though grown familiar by continual presence. May our strong hero come, freshly triumphant. || 9. Guard us from him who would assail us, Agni; preserve us O thou Victor, from dishonour. | Here let the place of darkening come upon thee: may wealth be ours, desirable, in thousands. || 10. Shine this felicity on us, O Agni: may we attain to perfect understanding. | All happiness be theirs who sing and praise thee. Ye Gods, preserve us evermore with blessings.

Hymn 7:5. Agni.

1. Bring forth your song of praise to mighty Agni, the speedy messenger of earth and heaven, | Vaiśvānara, who, with those who wake, hath waxen great in the lap of all the Gods Immortal. || 2. Sought in the heavens, on earth is Agni established, leader of rivers, Bull of standing waters. | Vaiśvānara when he hath grown in glory, shines on the tribes of men with light and treasure. || 3. For fear of thee forth fled the dark-hued races, scattered abroad, deserting their possessions, | When, glowing, O Vaiśvānara, for Pūru, thou Agni didst light up and rend their castles. || 4. Agni Vaiśvānara, both Earth and Heaven submit them to thy threefold jurisdiction. | Refulgent in thine undecaying lustre thou hast invested both the worlds with splendour. || 5. Agni, the tawny horses, loudly neighing our resonant hymns that drop with oil, attend thee; | Lord of the tribes, our Charioteer of riches, Ensign of days, Vaiśvānara of mornings. || 6. In thee, O bright as Mitra, Vasus seated the might of Asuras, for they loved thy spirit. | Thou dravest Dasyus from their home, O Agni, and broughtest forth broad light to light the Ārya. || 7. Born in the loftiest heaven thou in a moment reachest, like wind, the place where Gods inhabit. | Thou, favouring thine offspring, roaredst loudly when giving life to creatures, Jātavedas. || 8. Send us that strength, Vaiśvānara, send it, Agni, that strength, O Jātavedas, full of splendour, | Wherewith, all-bounteous God, thou pourest riches, as fame wide-spreading, on the man who offers. || 9. Agni, bestow upon our chiefs and nobles that famous power, that wealth which feedeth many. | Accordant with the Vasus and the Rudras, Agni, Vaiśvānara, give us sure protection.

Hymn 7:6. Agni.

1. Praise of the Asura, high imperial Ruler, the Manly One in whom the folk shall triumph— | I laud his deeds who is as strong as Indra, and lauding celebrate the Fort-destroyer. || 2. Sage, Sing, Food, Light,—they bring him from the mountain, the blessed Sovereign of the earth and heaven. | I decorate with songs the mighty actions which Agni, Fort-destroyer, did aforetime. || 3. The foolish, faithless, rudely-speaking niggards, without belief or sacrifice or worship,— | Far far sway hath Agni chased those Dasyus, and, in the cast, hath turned the godless westward. || 4. Him who brought eastward, manliest with his prowess, the Maids rejoicing in the western darkness, | That Agni I extol, the Lord of riches, unyielding tamer of assailing foemen. || 5. Him who brake down the walls with deadly weapons, and gave the Mornings to a noble Husband, | Young Agni, who with conquering strength subduing the tribes of Nahus made them bring their tribute. || 6. In whose protection all men rest by nature, desiring to enjoy his gracious favour— | Agni Vaiśvānara in his Parents, bosom hath found the choicest seat in earth and heaven. || 7. Vaiśvānara the God, at the sun's setting, hath taken to himself deep-hidden treasures: | Agni hath taken them from earth and heaven, from the sea under and the sea above us.

Hymn 7:7. Agni.

1. I send forth even your God, victorious Agni, like a strong courser, with mine adoration. | Herald of sacrifice be he who knoweth he hath reached Gods, himself, with measured motion. || 2. By paths that are thine own come hither, Agni, joyous, delighting in the Gods' alliance, | Making the heights of earth roar with thy fury, burning with eager teeth the woods and forests. || 3. The grass is strewn; the sacrifice advances adored as Priest, Agni is made propitious, | Invoking both All-boon-bestowing Mothers of whom, Most Youthful! thou wast born to help us. || 4. Forthwith the men, the best of these for wisdom, have made him leader in the solemn worship. | As Lord in homes of men is Agni established, the Holy One, the joyous, sweetly speaking. || 5. He hath come, chosen bearer, and is seated in man's home, Brahman, Agni, the Supporter, | He whom both Heaven and Earth exalt and strengthen whom, Giver of all boons, the Hotar worships. || 6. These have passed all in glory, who, the manly, have wrought with skill the hymn of adoration; | Who, listening, have advanced the people's welfare, and set their thoughts on this my holy statute. || 7. We, the Vasiṣhṭhas, now implore thee, Agni, O Son of Strength, the Lord of wealth and treasure. | Thou hast brought food to singers and to nobles. Ye Gods, preserve us evermore with blessings.

Hymn 7:8. Agni

1. The King whose face is decked with oil is kindled with homage offered by his faithful servant. | The men, the priests adore him with oblations. Agni hath shone forth when the dawn is breaking. || 2. Yea, he hath been acknowledged as most mighty, the joyous Priest of men, the youthful Agni. | He, spreading o'er the earth, made light around him, and grew among the plants with blackened fellies. || 3. How dost thou decorate our hymn, O Agni? What power dost thou exert when thou art lauded? | When, Bounteous God, may we be lords of riches, winners of precious wealth which none may conquer? || 4. Far famed is this the Bhārata's own Agni he shineth like the Sun with lofty splendour. | He who hath vanquished Pūru in the battle, the heavenly guest hath glowed in full refulgence. || 5. Full many oblations are in thee collected: with all thine aspects thou hast waxen gracious. | Thou art already famed as praised and lauded, yet still, O nobly born, increase thy body. || 6. Be this my song, that winneth countless treasure, engendered with redoubled force for Agni, | That, splendid, chasing sickness, slaying demons, it may delight our friend and bless the singers. || 7. We, the Vasiṣhṭhas, now implore thee, Agni, O Son of Strength, the Lord of wealth and riches. | Thou hast brought food to singers and to nobles. Ye Gods, preserve us evermore with blessings.

Hymn 7:9. Agni.

1. Roused from their bosom is the Dawns' beloved, the joyous Priest, most sapient, Purifier. | He gives a signal both to Gods and mortals, to Gods oblations, riches to the pious. || 2. Most wise is he who, forcing doors of Paṇis, brought the bright Sun to us who feedeth many. | The cheerful Priest, men's Friend and home-companion, through still night's darkness he is made apparent. || 3. Wise, ne'er deceived, uncircumscribed, refulgent, our gracious guest, a Friend with good attendants, | Shines forth with wondrous light before the Mornings; the young plants hath he entered, Child of Waters. || 4. Seeking our gatherings, he, your Jātavedas, hath shone adorable through human ages, | Who gleams refulgent with his lovely lustre: the kine have waked to meet him when enkindled. || 5. Go on thy message to the Gods, and fail not, O Agni, with their band who pray and worship. | Bring all the Gods that they may give us riches, Sarasvatī, the Marutas, Aśvins, Waters. || 6. Vasiṣhṭha, when enkindling thee, O Agni, hath slain Jarūtha. Give us wealth in plenty. | Sing praise in choral song, O Jātavedas. Ye Gods, preserve us evermore with blessings.

Hymn 7:10. Agni.

1. He hath sent forth, bright, radiant, and refulgent, like the Dawn's Lover, his far-spreading lustre. | Pure in his splendour shines the golden Hero: our longing thoughts hath he aroused and wakened. || 2. He, like the Sun, hath shone while Morn is breaking, and priests who weave the sacrifice sing praises, | Agni, the God, who knows their generations and visits Gods, most bounteous, rapid envoy. || 3. Our songs and holy hymns go forth to Agni, seeking the God and asking him for riches, | Him fair to see, of goodly aspect, mighty, men's messenger who carries their oblations. || 4. joined with the Vasus, Agni, bring thou Indra bring hither mighty Rudra with the Rudras, | Aditi good to all men with Ādityas, Bṛihaspati All-bounteous, with the Singers. || 5. Men eagerly implore at sacrifices Agni, Most Youthful God, the joyous Herald. | For he is Lord and Ruler over riches, and for Gods' worship an unwearied envoy.

Hymn 7:11. Agni.

1. Great art thou, Agni, sacrifice's Herald: not without thee are deathless Gods made joyful. | Come hither with all Deities about thee here take thy seat, the first, as Priest, O Agni. || 2. Men with oblations evermore entreat thee, the swift, to undertake an envoy's duty. | He on whose sacred grass with Gods thou sittest, to him, O Agni, are the days propitious. || 3. Three times a day in thee are shown the treasures sent for the mortal who presents oblation. | Bring the Gods hither like a man, O Agni: be thou our envoy, guarding us from curses. || 4. Lord of the lofty sacrifice is Agni, Agni is Lord of every gift presented. | The Vasus were contented with his wisdom, so the Gods made him their oblation-bearer || 5. O Agni, bring the Gods to taste our presents: with Indra leading, here let them be joyful. | Convey this sacrifice to Gods in heaven. Ye Gods, preserve us evermore with blessings.

Hymn 7:12. Agni.

1. We with great reverence have approached The Youngest who hath shone forth well-kindled in his dwelling, | With wondrous light between wide earth and heaven, well-worshipped, looking forth in all directions. || 2. Through his great might o'ercoming all misfortunes, praised in the house is Agni Jātavedas. | May he protect us from disgrace and trouble, both us who laud him and our noble patrons. || 3. O Agni, thou art Varuṇa and Mitra: Vasiṣhṭhas with their holy hymns exalt thee. | With thee be most abundant gain of treasure. Ye Gods, preserve us evermore with blessings.

Hymn 7:13. Agni.

1. Bring song and hymn to Agni, Asura-slayer, enlightener of all and thought-bestower. | Like an oblation on the grass, to please him, I bring this to Vaiśvānara, hymn-inspirer. || 2. Thou with thy flame, O Agni, brightly glowing, hast at thy birth filled full the earth and heaven. | Thou with thy might, Vaiśvānara Jātavedas, settest the Gods free from the curse that bound them. || 3. Agni, when, born thou lookedst on all creatures, like a brisk herdsman moving round his cattle. | The path to prayer, Vaiśvānara, thou foundest. Ye Gods, preserve us evermore with blessings.

Hymn 7:14. Agni.

1. With reverence and with offered gifts serve we the God whose flame is bright: | Let us bring Jātavedas fuel, and adore Agni when we invoke the Gods. || 2. Agni, may we perform thy rites with fuel, and honour thee, O Holy one, with praises: | Honour thee, Priest of sacrifice! with butter, thee, God of blessed light! with our oblation. || 3. Come, Agni, with the Gods to our invoking, come, pleased, to offerings sanctified with Vaṣhaṭ. | May we be his who pays thee, God, due honour. Ye Gods, preserve us evermore with blessings.

Hymn 7:15. Agni.

1. Offer oblations in his mouth, the bounteous God's whom we must serve. | His who is nearest kin to us: || 2. Who for the Fivefold People's take hath seated him in every home | Wise, Youthful, Master of the house. || 3. On all sides may that Agni guard our household folk and property; | May he deliver us from woe. || 4. I have begotten this new hymn for Agni, Falcon of the sky: | Will he not give us of his wealth? || 5. Whose glories when he glows in front of sacrifice are fair to see, | Like wealth of one with hero sons. || 6. May he enjoy this hallowed gift, Agni accept our songs, who bears | Oblations, best of worshippers. || 7. Lord of the house, whom men must seek, we set thee down, O Worshipped One! | Bright, rich in heroes, Agni! God || 8. Shine forth at night and morn: through thee with fires are we provided well. | Thou, rich in heroes, art our Friend. || 9. The men come near thee for their gain, the singers with their songs of praise: | Speech, thousandfold, comes near to thee. || 10. Bright, Purifier, meet for praise, Immortal with refulgent glow, | Agni drives Rākṣhasas away. || 11. As such, bring us abundant wealth, young Child of Strength, for this thou canst | May Bhaga give us what is choice. || 12. Thou, Agni, givest hero fame: Bhaga and Savitar the God, | And Did give us what is good. || 13. Agni, preserve us from distress: consume our enemies, O God, | Eternal, with the hottest flames. || 14. And, irresistible, be thou a mighty iron fort to us, |

With hundred walls for man's defence. ‖ 15. Do thou preserve us, eve and morn, from sorrow, from the wicked men, | Infallible! by day and night.

Hymn 7:16. Agni.

1. With this my reverent hymn I call Agni for you, the Son of Strength, | Dear, wisest envoy, served with noble sacrifice, immortal messenger of all. ‖ 2. His two red horses, all-supporting, let him yoke: let him, well-worshipped, urge them fast. | Then hath the sacrifice good prayers and happy end, and heavenly gift of wealth to men. ‖ 3. The flame of him the Bountiful, the Much-invoked, hath mounted up, | And his red-coloured smoke-clouds reach and touch the sky: the men are kindling Agni well. ‖ 4. Thee, thee Most Glorious One we make our messenger. Bring the Gods hither to the feast. | Give us, O Son of Strength, all food that feedeth man: give that for which we pray to thee. ‖ 5. Thou, Agni, art the homestead's Lord, our Herald at the sacrifice. | Lord of all boons, thou art the Cleanser and a Sage. Pay worship, and enjoy the good. ‖ 6. Give riches to the sacrificer, O Most Wise, for thou art he who granteth wealth. | Inspire with zeal each priest at this our solemn rite; all who are skilled in singing praise. ‖ 7. O Agni who art worshipped well, dear let our princes he to thee, | Our wealthy patrons who are governors of men, who part, as gifts, their stalls of kine. ‖ 8. They in whose home, her hand bearing the sacred oil, Iḷā sits down well-satisfied— | Guard them, Victorious God, from slander and from harm. give us a refuge famed afar. ‖ 9. Do thou, a Priest with pleasant tongue, most wise, and very near to us, | Agni, bring riches hither to our liberal chiefs, and speed the offering of our gifts. ‖ 10. They who bestow as bounty plenteous wealth of steeds, moved by desire of great renown— | Do thou with saving help preserve them from distress, Most Youthful! with a hundred forts. ‖ 11. The God who gives your wealth demands a full libation poured to him. | Pour ye it forth, then fill the vessel full again: then doth the God pay heed to you. ‖ 12. Him have the Gods appointed Priest of sacrifice, oblation-bearer, passing wise. | Agni gives wealth and valour to the worshipper, to folk who offer up their gifts.

Hymn 7:17. Agni.

1. Agni, be kindled well with proper fuel, and let the grass be scattered wide about thee. ‖ 2. Let the impatient Portals be thrown open bring thou the Gods impatient to come hither. ‖ 3. Taste, Agni: serve the Gods with our oblation. Offer good sacrifices, Jātavedas! ‖ 4. Let Jātavedas pay fair sacrifices, worship and gratify the Gods Immortal. ‖ 5. Wise God, win for us things that are all-goodly, and let the prayers, we pray today be fruitful. ‖ 6. Thee, even thee, the Son of Strength, O Agni, those Gods have made the bearer of oblations. ‖ 7. To thee the God may we perform our worship: do thou, besought, grant us abundant riches.

Hymn 7:18. Indra.

1. All is with thee, O Indra, all the treasures which erst our fathers won who sang thy praises. | With thee are milch-kine good to milk, and horses: best winner thou of riches for the pious. ‖ 2. For like a King among his wives thou dwellest: with glories, as a Sage, surround and help us. | Make us, thy servants, strong for wealth, and honour our songs with kine and steeds and decoration. ‖ 3. Here these our holy hymns with joy and gladness in pious emulation have approached thee. | Hitherward come thy path that leads to riches: may we find shelter in thy favour, Indra. ‖ 4. Vasiṣhṭha hath poured forth his prayers, desiring to milk thee like a cow in goodly pasture. | All these my people call thee Lord of cattle: may Indra. come unto the prayer we offer. ‖ 5. What though the floods spread widely, Indra made them shallow and easy for Sudās to traverse. | He, worthy of our praises, caused the Śimyu, foe of our hymn, to curse the rivers' fury. ‖ 6. Eager for spoil was Turvaśa Puroḍās, fain to win wealth, like fishes urged by hunger. | The Bhṛigus and the Druhyus quickly listened: friend rescued friend mid the two distant peoples. ‖ 7. Together came the Pakthas, the Bhalānas, the Alinas, the Śivas, the Viṣhāṇins. | Yet to the Tṛitsus came the Ārya's Comrade, through love of spoil and heroes' war, to lead them. ‖ 8. Fools, in their folly fain to waste her waters, they parted inexhaustible Paruṣhṇī. | Lord of the Earth, he with his might repressed them: still lay the herd and the affrighted herdsman. ‖ 9. As to their goal they sped to their destruction: they sought Paruṣhṇī; e'en the swift returned not. | Indra abandoned, to Sudās the manly, the swiftly flying foes, unmanly babblers. ‖ 10. They went like kine unherded from the pasture, each clinging to a friend as chance directed. | They who drive spotted steeds, sent down by Pṛiśni, gave ear, the Warriors and the harnessed horses. ‖ 11. The King who scattered one-and-twenty people of both Vaikarṇa tribes through lust of glory— | As the skilled priest clips grass within the chamber, so hath the Hero Indra, wrought their downfall. ‖ 12. Thou, thunder-armed, o'erwhelmedst in the waters famed ancient Kavaṣha and then the Druhyu. | Others here claiming friendship to their friendship, devoted unto thee, in thee were joyful. ‖ 13. Indra at once with conquering might demolished all their strong places and their seven castles. | The goods of Anu's son he gave to Tṛitsu. May we in sacrifice conquer scorned Pūru. ‖ 14. The Anavas and Druhyus, seeking booty, have slept, the sixty hundred, yea, six thousand, | And six-and-sixty heroes. For the pious were all these mighty exploits done by Indra. ‖ 15. These Tṛitsus under Indra's careful guidance came speeding like loosed waters rushing downward. | The foemen, measuring exceeding closely, abandoned to Sudās all their provisions. ‖ 16. The hero's side who drank the dressed oblation, Indra's denier, far o'er earth he scattered. | Indra brought down the fierce destroyer's fury. He gave them various roads, the path's Controller. ‖ 17. E'en with the weak he wrought this matchless exploit: e'en with a goat he did to death a lion. | He pared the pillar's angles with a needle. Thus to Sudās Indra gave all provisions. ‖ 18. To thee have all thine enemies submitted: e'en the fierce Bheda hast thou made thy subject. | Cast down thy sharpened thunderbolt, O Indra, on him who harms the men who sing thy praises. ‖ 19. Yamunā and the Tṛitsus aided Indra. There he stripped Bheda bare of all his treasures. | The Ajas and the Śigrus and the Yakṣhus brought in to him as tribute heads of horses. ‖ 20. Not to be scorned, but like Dawns past and recent, O Indra, are thy favours and thy riches. | Devaka, Mānyamāna's son, thou slewest, and smotest Śambara from the lofty mountain. ‖ 21. They who, from home, have gladdened thee, thy servants Parāśara, Vasiṣhṭha, Śatayātu, | Will not forget thy friendship, liberal Giver. So shall the days dawn prosperous for the princes. ‖ 22. Priest-like, with praise, I move around the altar, earning Paijavana's reward, O Agni, | Two hundred cows from Devavāta's descendant, two chariots from Sudās with mares to draw them. ‖ 23. Gift of Paijavana, four horses bear me in foremost place, trained steeds with pearl to deck them. | Sudās's brown steeds, firmly-stepping, carry me and my son for progeny and glory. ‖ 24. Him whose fame spreads between wide earth and heaven, who, as dispenser, gives each chief his portion, | Seven flowing Rivers glorify like Indra. He slew Yudhyāmadhi in close encounter. ‖ 25. Attend on him O ye heroic Marutas as on Sudās's father Divodāsa. | Further Paijavana's desire with favour. Guard faithfully his lasting firm dominion.

Hymn 7:19. Indra.

1. He like a bull with sharpened horns, terrific, singly excites and agitates all the people: | Thou givest him who largely pours libations his goods who pours not, for his own possession. ‖ 2. Thou, verily, Indra, gavest help to Kutsa, willingly giving car to him in battle, | When, aiding Ārjuneya, thou subduedst to him both Kuyava and the Dāsa Śuṣhṇa. ‖ 3. O Bold One, thou with all thine aids hast boldly holpen Sudās whose offerings were accepted, | Pūru in winning land and slaying foemen, and Trasadasyu son of Purukutsa. ‖ 4. At the Gods' banquet, hero-souled! with Heroes, Lord of Bay Steeds, thou slewest many foemen. | Thou sentest in swift death to sleep the Dasyu, both Chumuri and Dhuni, for Dabhīti. ‖ 5. These were thy mighty powers that, Thunder-wielder, thou swiftly crushedst nine-and-ninety castles: | Thou capturedst the hundredth in thine onslaught; thou slewest Namuchi, thou slewest Vṛitra. ‖ 6. Old are the blessings, Indra, which thou gavest Sudās the worshipper who brought oblations. | For thee, the Strong, I yoke thy strong Bay Horses: may our prayers reach thee and win strength, Most Mighty! ‖ 7. Give us not up, Lord of Bay Horses, Victor, in this thine own assembly, to the wicked. | Deliver us with true and faithful succours: dear may we be to thee among the princes. ‖ 8. May we men, Maghavan, the friends thou lovest, near thee be joyful under thy protection. | Fain to fulfil the wish of Atithigva humble. the pride of Turvaśa and Yādva. ‖ 9. Swiftly, in truth, O Maghavan, about thee men skilled in hymning sing their songs and praises. | Elect us also into their assembly who by their calls on thee despoiled the niggards. ‖ 10. Thine are these lauds, O manliest of heroes, lauds which revert to us and give us riches. | Favour these, Indra, when they fight with foemen, as Friend and Hero and the heroes' Helper. ‖ 11. Now, lauded for thine aid, Heroic Indra,

sped by our prayer, wax mighty in thy body. | Apportion to us strength and habitations. Ye Gods, protect us evermore with blessings.

Hymn 7:20. Indra.

1. Strong, Godly-natured, born for hero exploit, man's Friend, he doth whatever deed he willeth. | Saving us e'en from great transgression, Indra, the Youthful, visiteth man's home with favour. || 2. Waxing greatness Indra slayeth Vṛitra: the Hero with his aid hath helped the singer. | He gave Sudās wide room and space, and often hath granted wealth to him who brought oblations. || 3. Soldier unchecked, war-rousing, battling Hero, unconquered from of old, victorious ever, | Indra the very strong hath scattered armies; yea, he hath slain each foe who fought against him. || 4. Thou with thy greatness hast filled full, O Indra, even both the worlds with might, O thou Most Mighty. | Lord of Bays, Indra, brandishing his thunder, is gratified with Soma at the banquet. || 5. A Bull begat the Bull for joy of battle, and a strong Mother brought forth him the manly. | He who is Chief of men, their armies' Leader, is strong Hero, bold, and fain for booty. || 6. The people falter not, nor suffer sorrow, who win themselves this God's terrific spirit. | He who with sacrifices worships Indra is lord of wealth, law-born and law's protector. || 7. Whene'er the elder fain would help the younger the greater cometh to the lesser's present. | Shall the Immortal sit aloof, inactive? O Wondrous Indra, bring us wondrous riches. || 8. Thy dear folk, Indra, who present oblations, are, in chief place, thy friends, O Thunder-wielder. | May we be best content in this thy favour, sheltered by One who slays not, but preserves us. || 9. To thee the mighty hymn hath clamoured loudly, and, Maghavan, the eloquent hath besought thee. | Desire of wealth hath come upon thy singer: help us then, Śakra, to our share of riches. || 10. Place us by food which thou hast given, O Indra, us and the wealthy patrons who command us. | Let thy great power bring good to him who lauds thee. Ye Gods, preserve us evermore with blessings.

Hymn 7:21. Indra.

1. Pressed is the juice divine with milk commingled: thereto hath Indra ever been accustomed. | We wake thee, Lord of Bays, with sacrifices: mark this our laud in the wild joy of Soma. || 2. On to the rite they move, the grass they scatter, these Soma-drinkers eloquent in synod. | Hither, for men to grasp, are brought the press-stones, far-thundering, famous, strong, that wait on heroes. || 3. Indra, thou settest free the many waters that were encompassed, Hero, by the Dragon. | Down rolled, as if on chariots borne, the rivers: through fear of thee all things created tremble. || 4. Skilled in all manly deeds the God terrific hath with his weapons mastered these opponents. | Indra in rapturous joy shook down their castles he slew them in his might, the Thunder-wielder. || 5. No evil spirits have impelled us, Indra, nor fiends, O Mightiest God, with their devices. | Let our true God subdue the hostile rabble: let not the lewd approach our holy worship. || 6. Thou in thy strength surpassest Earth and Heaven: the regions comprehend not all thy greatness. | With thine own power and might thou slewest Vṛitra: no foe hath found the end of thee in battle. || 7. Even the earlier Deities submitted their powers to thy supreme divine dominion. | Indra wins wealth and deals it out to other's: men in the strife for booty call on Indra. || 8. The humble hath invoked thee for protection, thee, Lord of great felicity, O Indra. | Thou with a hundred aids hast been our Helper: one who brings gifts like thee hath his defender. || 9. May we, O Indra, be thy friends for ever, eagerly, Conqueror, yielding greater homage. | May, through thy grace, the strength of us who battle quell in the shock the onset of the foeman. || 10. Place us by food which thou hast given, O Indra, us and the wealthy patrons who command us. | Let thy great power bring good to him who lauds thee. Ye Gods, preserve us evermore with blessings.

Hymn 7:22. Indra.

1. Drink Soma, Lord of Bays, and let it cheer thee: Indra, the stone, like a well guided courser, | Directed by the presser's arms hath pressed it. || 2. So let the draught of joy, thy dear companion, by which, O Lord of Bays, thou slayest foemen, | Delight thee, Indra, Lord of princely treasures. || 3. Mark closely, Maghavan, the words I utter, this eulogy recited by Vasiṣhṭha: | Accept the prayers I offer at thy banquet. || 4. Hear thou the call of the juice-drinking press-stone: hear thou the Brahman's hymn who sings and lauds thee. | Take to thine inmost self these adorations. || 5. I know and ne'er forget the hymns and praises of thee, the Conqueror, and thy strength immortal. | Thy name I ever utter. Self-Refulgent || 6. Among mankind many are thy libations, and many a time the pious sage invokes thee. | O Maghavan, be not long distant from us. || 7. All these libations are for thee, O Hero: to thee I offer these my prayers. that strengthen. | Ever, in every place, must men invoke thee. || 8. Never do men attain, O Wonder-Worker, thy greatness, Mighty One, who must be lauded, | Nor, Indra, thine heroic power and bounty. || 9. Among all Ṛiṣhis, Indra, old and recent, who have engendered hymns as sacred singers, | Even with us be thine auspicious friendships. Ye Gods, preserve us evermore with blessings.

Hymn 7:23. Indra.

1. Prayers have been offered up through love of glory: Vasiṣhṭha, honour Indra in the battle. | He who with might extends through all existence hears words which I, his faithful servant, utter. || 2. A cry was raised which reached the Gods, O Indra, a cry to them to send us strength in combat. | None among men knows his own life's duration: bear us in safety over these our troubles. || 3. The Bays, the booty-seeking car I harness: my prayers have reached him who accepts them gladly. | Indra, when he had slain resistless foemen, forced with his might the two world-halves asunder. || 4. Like barren cows, moreover, swelled the waters: the singers sought thy holy rite, O Indra. | Come unto us as with his team comes Vāyu: thou, through our solemn hymns bestowest booty. || 5. So may these gladdening draughts rejoice thee, Indra, the Mighty, very bounteous to the singer. | Alone among the Gods thou pitiest mortals: O Hero, make thee glad at this libation. || 6. Thus the Vasiṣhṭhas glorify with praises Indra, the Powerful whose arm wields thunder. | Praised, may he guard our wealth in kine and heroes. Ye Gods, preserve us evermore with blessings.

Hymn 7:24. Indra.

1. A home is made for thee to dwell in, Indra: O Much-invoked, go thither with the heroes. | That thou, to prosper us, mayst be our Helper, vouchsafe us wealth, rejoice with draughts of Soma. || 2. Indra, thy wish, twice-strong, is comprehended: pressed is the Soma, poured are pleasant juices. | This hymn of praise, from loosened tongue, made perfect, draws Indra to itself with loud invoking. || 3. Come, thou Impetuous; God, from earth or heaven; come to our holy grass to drink the Soma. | Hither to me let thy Bay Horses bring thee to listen to our hymns and make thee joyful. || 4. Come unto us with all thine aids, accordant, Lord of Bay Steeds, accepting our devotions, | Fair-helmeted, o'ercoming with the mighty, and lending us the strength of bulls, O Indra. || 5. As to the chariot pole a vigorous courser, this laud is brought to the great strong Upholder. | This hymn solicits wealth of thee: in heaven, as 'twere above the sky, set thou our glory. || 6. With precious things. O Indra, thus content us: may we attain to thine exalted favour. | Send our chiefs plenteous food with hero children. Preserve us evermore, ye Gods, with blessings.

Hymn 7:25. Indra.

1. When with thy mighty help, O potent Indra, the armies rush together in their fury. | When from the strong man's arm the lightning flieth, let not the mind go forth to side with others. || 2. O Indra, where the ground is hard to traverse, smite down our foes, the mortals who assail us, | Keep far from us the curse of the reviler: bring us accumulated store of treasures. || 3. God of the fair helm, give Sudās a hundred succours, a thousand blessings, and thy bounty. | Strike down the weapon of our mortal foeman: bestow upon us splendid fame and riches. || 4. I wait the power of one like thee, O Indra, gifts of a Helper such as thou art, Hero. | Strong, Mighty God, dwell with me now and ever: Lord of Bay Horses, do not thou desert us. || 5. Here are the Kutsas supplicating Indra for might, the Lord of Bays for God-sent conquest. | Make our foes ever easy to be vanquished: may we, victorious, win the spoil, O Hero. || 6. With precious things, O Indra, thus content us: may we attain to thine exalted favour. | Send our chiefs plenteous food with hero children. Preserve us evermore, ye Gods, with blessings.

Hymn 7:26. Indra.

1. Soma unpressed ne'er gladdened liberal Indra, no juices pressed without a prayer have pleased him. | I generate a laud that shall delight him, new and heroic, so that he may hear us. || 2. At every laud the Soma gladdens Indra: pressed juices please him as each psalm is chanted, | What time the priests with one united effort call him to aid, as sons invoke their father. || 3. These deeds he did; let him achieve new exploits, such as the priests declare at

their libations. | Indra hath taken and possessed all castles, like as one common husband doth his spouses. || 4. Even thus have they declared him. Famed is Indra as Conqueror, sole distributor of treasures; | Whose many succours come in close succession. May dear delightful benefits attend us. || 5. Thus, to bring help to men, Vasiṣhṭha laudeth Indra, the peoples' Hero, at libation. | Bestow upon us strength and wealth in thousands. Preserve us evermore, ye Gods, with blessings.

Hymn 7:27. Indra.

1. Men call on Indra in the armed encounter that he may make the hymns they sing decisive. | Hero, rejoicing in thy might, in combat give us a portion of the stall of cattle, || 2. Grant, Indra Maghavan, invoked of many, to these my friends the strength which thou possessest. | Thou, Maghavan, hast rent strong places open: unclose for us, Wise God, thy hidden bounty. || 3. King of the living world, of men, is Indra, of all in varied form that earth containeth. | Thence to the worshipper he giveth riches: may he enrich us also when we laud him. || 4. Maghavan Indra, when we all invoke him, bountiful ever sendeth strength to aid us: | Whose perfect guerdon, never failing, bringeth wealth to the men, to friends the thing they covet. || 5. Quick, Indra, give us room and way to riches, and let us bring thy mind to grant us treasures, | That we may win us cars and Steeds and cattle. Preserve us evermore, ye Gods, with blessings.

Hymn 7:28. Indra.

1. Come to our prayers, O Indra, thou who knowest: let thy Bay Steeds be yoked and guided hither. | Though mortal men on every side invoke thee, still give thine ear to us, O All-impeller. || 2. Thy greatness reacheth to our invocation, the sages' prayer which, Potent God, thou guardest. | What time thy hand, O Mighty, holds the thunder, awful in strength thou hast become resistless. || 3. What time thou drewest both world-halves together, like heroes led by thee who call each other— | For thou wast born for strength and high dominion-then e'en the active overthrew the sluggish. || 4. Honour us in these present days, O Indra, for hostile men are making expiation. | Our sin that sinless Varuṇa discovered, the Wondrous-Wise hath long ago forgiven. || 5. We will address this liberal Lord, this Indra, that he may grant us gifts of ample riches, | Best favourer of the singer's prayer and praises. Preserve us evermore, ye Gods, with blessings.

Hymn 7:29. Indra.

1. This Soma hath been pressed for thee, O Indra: come hither, Lord of Bays, for this thou lovest. | Drink of this fair, this well-effused libation: Maghavan, give us wealth when we implore thee. || 2. Come to us quickly with thy Bay Steeds, Hero, come to our prayer, accepting our devotion. | Enjoy thyself aright at this libation, and listen thou unto the prayers we offer. || 3. What satisfaction do our hymns afford thee? When, Maghavan? Now let us do thee service. | Hymns, only hymns, with love for thee, I weave thee: then hear, O Indra, these mine invocations. || 4. They, verily, were also human beings whom thou wast wont to hear, those earlier sages. | Hence I, O Indra Maghavan, invoke thee: thou art our Providence, even as a Father. || 5. We will address this liberal Lord, this Indra, that he may grant us gifts of ample riches, | Best favourer of the singer's prayer and praises. Preserve us evermore, ye Gods, with blessings.

Hymn 7:30. Indra.

1. With power and strength, O Mighty God, approach us: be the augmenter, Indra, of these riches; | Strong Thunderer, Lord of men, for potent valour, for manly exploit and for high dominion. || 2. Thee, worth invoking, in the din of battle, heroes invoke in fray for life and sunlight. | Among all people thou art foremost fighter: give up our enemies to easy slaughter. || 3. When fair bright days shall dawn on us, O Indra, and thou shalt bring thy banner near in battle, | Agni the Asura shall sit as Herald, calling Gods hither for our great good fortune. || 4. Thine are we, Indra, thine, both these who praise thee, and those who give rich gifts, O God and Hero. | Grant to our princes excellent protection, may they wax old and still be strong and happy. || 5. We will address this liberal Lord, this Indra that he may grant us gifts of ample riches: | Best favourer of the singer's prayer and praises. Preserve us evermore, ye Gods, with blessings.

Hymn 7:31. Indra.

1. Sing ye a song, to make him glad, to Indra, Lord of Tawny Steeds, | The Soma-drinker, O my friends. || 2. To him the Bounteous say the laud, and let us glorify, as men May do, the Giver of true gifts. || 3. O Indra, Lord of boundless might, for us thou winnest strength and kine, | Thou winnest gold for us, Good Lord. || 4. Faithful to thee we loudly sing, heroic Indra, songs to thee: Mark, O Good Lord, this act of ours. || 5. Give us not up to man's reproach, to foeman's hateful calumny: In thee alone is all my strength. || 6. Thou art mine ample coat of mail, my Champion, Vṛitra-slayer, thou: | With thee for Friend I brave the foe. || 7. Yea, great art thou whose conquering might two independent Powers confess. | The Heaven, O India, and the Earth. || 8. So let the voice surround thee, which attends the Marutas on their way, | Reaching thee with the rays of light. || 9. Let the ascending drops attain to thee, the Wondrous God, in heaven: | Let all the folk bow down to thee. || 10. Bring to the Wise, the Great, who waxeth mighty, your offerings, and make ready your devotion; | To many clans he goeth, man's controller. || 11. For Indra, the sublime, the far-pervading, have singers generated prayer and praises: | The sages never violate his statutes. || 12. The choirs have established Indra King for ever, for victory, him whose anger is resistless: | And, for the Bays' Lord, strengthened those he loveth.

Hymn 7:32. Indra.

1. Let none, no, not thy worshippers, delay thee far away from us. | Even from far away come thou unto our feast, or listen if already here. || 2. For here, like flies on honey, these who pray to thee sit by the juice that they have poured. | Wealth-craving singers have on Indra set their hope, as men set foot upon a car. || 3. Longing for wealth I call on him, the Thunderer with the strong right hand, | As a son calleth on his sire. || 4. These Soma juices, mixed with curd, have been expressed for Indra here. | Come with thy Bay Steeds, Thunder-wielder, to our home, to drink them till they make thee glad. || 5. May he whose ear is open hear us. He is asked for wealth: will he despise our prayer? | Him who bestows at once a hundred thousand gifts none shall restrain when he would give. || 6. The hero never checked by men hath gained his strength through Indra, he | Who presses out and pours his deep libations forth, O Vṛitra-slayer, unto thee. || 7. When thou dost drive the fighting men together be, thou Mighty One, the mighty's shield. | May we divide the wealth of him whom thou hast slain: bring us, Unreachable, his goods. || 8. For Indra, Soma-drinker, armed with thunder, press the Soma juice. | Make ready your dressed meats: cause him to favour us. The Giver blesses him who gives. || 9. Grudge not, ye Soma pourers; stir you, pay the rites, for wealth, to the great Conqueror. | Only the active conquers dwells in peace, and thrives: not for the niggard are the Gods. || 10. No one hath overturned or stayed the car of him who freely gives. | The man whom Indra and the Marut host defend comes to a stable full of kine. || 11. Indra, that man when fighting shall obtain the spoil, whose strong defender thou wilt be. | Be thou the gracious helper, Hero I of our cars, be thou the helper of our men. || 12. His portion is exceeding great like a victorious soldier's spoil. | Him who is Indra, Lord of Bays, no foes subdue. He gives the Soma-pourer strength. || 13. Make for the Holy Gods a hymn that is not mean, but well-arranged and fair of form. | Even many snares and bonds subdue not him who dwells with Indra through his sacrifice. || 14. Indra, what mortal will attack the man who hath his wealth in thee? | The strong will win the spoil on the decisive day through faith in thee, O Maghavan. || 15. In battles with the foe urge on our mighty ones who give the treasures dear to thee, | And may we with our princes, Lord of Tawny Steeds! pass through all peril, led by thee. || 16. Thine, Indra, is the lowest wealth, thou cherishest the mid-most wealth, | Thou ever rulest all the highest: in the fray for cattle none resisteth thee. || 17. Thou art renowned as giving wealth to every one in all the battles that are fought. | Craving protection, all these people of the earth, O Much-invoked, implore thy name. || 18. If I, O Indra, were the Lord of riches ample as thine own, | I should support the singer, God. who givest wealth! and not abandon him to woe. || 19. Each day would I enrich the man who sang my praise, in whatsoever place he were. | No kinship is there better, Maghavan, than thine: a father even is no more. || 20. With Plenty for his true ally the active man will gain the spoil. | Your Indra, Much-invoked, I bend with song, as bends a wright his wheel of solid wood. || 21. A moral wins no riches by unworthy praise: wealth comes not to the niggard churl. | Light is the task to give, O Maghavan, to one like me on the decisive day. || 22. Like kine unmilked we call aloud, Hero, to thee, and sing thy praise, |

Looker on heavenly light, Lord of this moving world, Lord, Indra, of what moveth not. || 23. None other like to thee, of earth or of the heavens, hath been or ever will be born. | Desiring horses, Indra Maghavan! and kine, as men of might we call on thee. || 24. Bring, Indra, the Victorious Ones; bring, elder thou, the younger host. | For, Maghavan, thou art rich in treasures from of old, and must be called in every fight. || 25. Drive thou away our enemies, O Maghavan: make riches easy to be won. | Be thou our good Protector in the strife for spoil: Cherisher of our friends be thou. || 26. O Indra, give us wisdom as a sire gives wisdom to his sons. | Guide us, O Much-invoked, in this our way may we still live and look upon the light. || 27. Grant that no mighty foes, unknown, malevolent, unhallowed, tread us to the ground. | With thine assistance, Hero, may we ass through all the waters that are rushing down.

Hymn 7:33. Vasiṣhṭha.

1. These who wear hair-knots on the right, the movers of holy thought, white-robed, have won me over. | I warned the men, when from the grass I raised me, Not from afar can my Vasiṣhṭhas help you. || 2. With soma they brought Indra from a distance, Over Vaiśanta, from the strong libation. | Indra preferred Vasiṣhṭhas to the Soma pressed by the son of Vāyata, Pāśadyumna. || 3. So, verily, with these he crossed the river, in company with these he slaughtered Bheda. | So in the fight with the Ten Kings, Vasiṣhṭhas! did Indra help Sudās through your devotions. || 4. I gladly, men I with prayer prayed by our fathers have fixed your axle: ye shall not be injured: | Since, when ye sang aloud the Śakvarī verses, Vasiṣhṭhas! ye invigorated Indra. || 5. Like thirsty men they looked to heaven, in battle with the Ten Kings, surrounded and imploring. | Then Indra heard Vasiṣhṭha as he praised him, and gave the Tṛitsus ample room and freedom. || 6. Like sticks and staves wherewith they drive the cattle, Stripped bare, the Bhāratas were found defenceless: | Vasiṣhṭha then became their chief and leader: then widely. were the Tṛitsus' clans extended. || 7. Three fertilize the worlds with genial moisture: three noble Creatures cast a light before them. | Three that give warmth to all attend the morning. All these have they discovered, these Vasiṣhṭhas. || 8. Like the Sun's growing glory is their splendour, and like the sea's is their unflathomed greatness. | Their course is like the wind's. Your laud, Vasiṣhṭhas, can never be attained by any other. || 9. They with perceptions of the heart in secret resort to that which spreads a thousand branches. | The Apsarases brought hither the Vasiṣhṭhas wearing the vesture spun for them by Yama. || 10. A form of lustre springing from the lightning wast thou, when Varuṇa and Mitra saw thee. | Thy one and only birth was then, Vasiṣhṭha, when from thy stock Agastya brought thee hither. || 11. Born of their love for Urvaśī, Vasiṣhṭha thou, priest, art son of Varuṇa and Mitra; | And as a fallen drop, in heavenly fervour, all the Gods laid thee on a lotus-blossom. || 12. He thinker, knower both of earth and heaven, endowed with many a gift, bestowing thousands, | Destined to wear the vesture spun by Yama, sprang from the Apsaras to life, Vasiṣhṭha. || 13. Born at the sacrifice, urged by adorations, both with a common flow bedewed the pitcher. | Then from the midst thereof there rose up Māna, and thence they say was born the sage Vasiṣhṭha. || 14. He brings the bearer of the laud and Sāman: first shall he speak bringing the stone for pressing. | With grateful hearts in reverence approach him: to you, O Pratṛidas, Vasiṣhṭha cometh.

Hymn 7:34. Viśvedevas.

1. May our divine and brilliant hymn go forth, like a swift chariot wrought and fashioned well. || 2. The waters listen as they flow along: they know the origin of heaven and earth. || 3. Yea, the broad waters swell their flood for him: of him strong heroes think amid their foes. || 4. Set ye for him the coursers to the pole: like Indra Thunderer is the Golden-armed. || 5. Arouse you, like the days, to sacrifice speed gladly like a traveller on the way. || 6. Go swift to battles, to the sacrifice: set up a flag, a hero for the folk. || 7. Up from his strength hath risen as 'twere a light: it bears the load as earth bears living things. || 8. Agni, no demon I invoke the Gods: by law completing it, I form a hymn. || 9. Closely about you lay your heavenly song, and send your voice to where the Gods abide. || 10. Varuṇa, Mighty, with a thousand eyes, beholds the paths wherein these rivers run. || 11. He, King of kings, the glory of the floods, o'er all that liveth hath resistless sway. || 12. May he assist us among all the tribes, and make the envier's praise devoid of light. || 13. May the foes' threatening arrow pass us by: may he put far from us our bodies' sin. || 14. Agni, oblation-cater, through our prayers aid us: to him our dearest laud is brought. || 15. Accordant with the Gods choose for our Friend the Waters' Child: may he be good to us. || 16. With lauds I sing the Dragon born of floods: he sits beneath the streams in middle air. || 17. Ne'er may the Dragon of the Deep harm us: ne'er fail this faithful servant's sacrifice. || 18. To these our heroes may they grant renown: may pious men march boldly on to wealth. || 19. Leading great hosts, with fierce attacks of these, they burn their foes as the Sun burns the earth. || 20. What time our wives draw near to us, may he, left-handed Tvaṣhṭar, give us hero sons. || 21. May Tvaṣhṭar find our hymn acceptable, and may Aramati, seeking wealth, be ours. || 22. May they who lavish gifts bestow those treasures: may Rodasī and Varuṇānī listen. | May he, with the Varūtrīs, be our refuge, may bountiful Tvaṣhṭar give us store of riches. || 23. So may rich Mountains and the liberal Waters, so may all Herbs that grow on ground, and Heaven, | And Earth accordant with the Forest-Sovereigns, and both the World-halves round about protect us. || 24. To this may both the wide Worlds lend approval, and Varuṇa in heaven, whose Friend is Indra. | May all the Marutas give consent, the Victors, that we may hold great wealth in firm possession. || 25. May Indra, Varuṇa, Mitra, and Agni, Waters, Herbs, Trees accept the praise we offer. | May we find refuge in the Marut's bosom. Protect us evermore, ye Gods, with blessings.

Hymn 7:35. Viśvedevas.

1. Befriend us with their aids Indra and Agni, Indra and Varuṇa who receive oblations! | Indra and Soma give health, strength and comfort, Indra and Pūṣhan be our help in battle. || 2. Auspicious Friends to us be Bhaga, Śaṃsa, auspicious be Purandhi aid all Riches; | The blessing of the true and well-conducted, and Aryaman in many forms apparent. || 3. Kind unto us he Maker and Sustainer, and the far-reaching Pair with God-like natures. | Auspicious unto us be Earth and Heaven, the Mountain, and the Gods' fair invocations. || 4. Favour us Agni with his face of splendour, and Varuṇa and Mitra and the Aśvins. | Favour us noble actions of the pious, impetuous vita blow on us with favour. || 5. Early invoked, may Heaven and Earth be friendly, and Air's mid-region good for us to look on. | To us may Herbs and Forest-Trees be gracious, gracious the Lord Victorious of the region. || 6. Be the God Indra with the Vasus friendly, and, with Ādityas, Varuṇa who blesseth. | Kind, with the Rudras, be the Healer Rudra, and, with the Dames, may Tvaṣhṭar kindly listen. || 7. Blest unto us be Soma, and devotions, blest be the Sacrifice, the Stones for pressing. | Blest be the fixing of the sacred Pillars, blest be the tender Grass and blest the Altar. || 8. May the far-seeing Sun rise up to bless us: be the four Quarters of the sky auspicious. | Auspicious be the firmly-seated Mountains, auspicious be the Rivers and the Waters. || 9. May Aditi through holy works be gracious, and may the Marutas, loud in song, be friendly. | May Viṣhṇu give felicity, and Pūṣhan, the Air that cherisheth our life, and Vāyu. || 10. Prosper us Savitar, the God who rescues, and let the radiant Mornings be propitious. | Auspicious to all creatures be Parjanya, auspicious be the field's benign Protector. || 11. May all the fellowship of Gods befriend us, Sarasvatī, with Holy Thoughts, be gracious. | Friendly be they, the Liberal Ones who seek us, yea, those who dwell in heaven, on earth, in waters. || 12. May the great Lords of Truth protect and aid us: blest to us be our horses and our cattle. | Kind be the pious skilful-handed Ṛibhus, kind be the Fathers at our invocations. || 13. May Aja-Ekapāda, the God, be gracious, gracious the Dragon of the Deep, and Ocean. | Gracious be he the swelling Child of Waters, gracious be Pṛiśni who hath Gods to guard her. || 14. So may the Rudras, Vasus, and Ādityas accept the new hymn which we now are making. | May all the Holy Ones of earth and heaven, and the Cow's offspring hear our invocation. || 15. They who of Holy Gods are very holy, Immortal, knowing Law, whom man must worship,— | May these today give us broad paths to travel. Preserve us evermore, ye Gods, with blessings.

Hymn 7:36. Viśvedevas

1. Let the prayer issue from the seat of Order, for Sūrya with his beams hath loosed the cattle. | With lofty ridges earth is far extended, and Agni's flame hath lit the spacious surface. || 2. O Asuras, O Varuṇa and Mitra, this hymn to you, like food, anew I offer. | One of you is a strong unerring Leader, and Mitra, speaking, stirreth men to labour. || 3. The movements of the gliding wind come hither: like cows, the springs are filled to overflowing. |

Born in the station e'en of lofty heaven the Bull hath loudly bellowed in this region. ‖ 4. May I bring hither with my song, O Indra, wise Aryaman who yokes thy dear Bay Horses, | Voracious, with thy noble car, O Hero, him who defeats the wrath of the malicious. ‖ 5. In their own place of sacrifice adorers worship to gain long life and win his friendship. | He hath poured food on men when they have praised him; be this, the dearest reverence, paid to Rudra. ‖ 6. Coming together, glorious, loudly roaring—Sarasvatī, Mother of Floods, the seventh— | With copious milk, with fair streams, strongly flowing, full swelling with the volume of their water; | 7. And may the mighty Marutas, too, rejoicing, aid our devotion and protect our offspring. | Let not swift-moving Akṣharā neglect us: they have increased our own appropriate riches, ‖ 8. Bring ye the great Aramati before you, and Pūṣhan as the Hero of the synod, | Bhaga who looks upon this hymn with favour, and, as our strength, the bountiful Purandhi. ‖ 9. May this our song of praise reach you, O Marutas, and Viṣhṇu guardian of the future infant. | May they vouchsafe the singer strength for offspring. Preserve us evermore, ye Gods, with blessings.

Hymn 7:37. Viśvedevas.

1. Let your best-bearing car that must be lauded, ne'er injured, bring you Vājas and Ṛibhukṣhans. | Fill you, fair-helmeted! with mighty Soma, thrice-mixed, at our libations to delight you. ‖ 2. Ye who behold the light of heaven, Ṛibhukṣhans, give our rich patrons unmolested riches. | Drink, heavenly-natured. at our sacrifices, and give us bounties for the hymns we sing you. ‖ 3. For thou, O Bounteous One, art used to giving, at parting treasure whether small or ample. | Filled full are both thine arms with great possessions: thy goodness keeps thee not from granting riches. ‖ 4. Indra, high-famed, as Vāja and Ṛibhukṣhans, thou goest working, singing to the dwelling. | Lord of Bay Steeds, this day may we Vasiṣhṭhas offer our prayers to thee and bring oblations. ‖ 5. Thou winnest swift advancement for thy servant, through hymns, Lord of Bay Steeds, which thou hast favoured. | For thee with friendly succour have we battled, and when, O Indra, wilt thou grant us riches? ‖ 6. To us thy priests a home, as 'twere, thou givest: when, Indra wilt thou recognize our praises? | May thy strong Steed, through our ancestral worship, bring food and wealth with heroes to our dwelling. ‖ 7. Though Nirṛiti the Goddess reigneth round him, Autumns with food in plenty come to Indra. | With three close Friends to length of days he cometh, he whom men let not rest at home in quiet. ‖ 8. Promise us gifts, O Savitar: may riches come unto us in Parvata's full bounty. | May the Celestial Guardian still attend us. Preserve us evermore, ye Gods, with blessings.

Hymn 7:38. Savitar.

1. On high hath Savitar, this God, extended the golden lustre which he spreads around him. | Now, now must Bhaga be invoked by mortals, Lord of great riches who distributes treasures. ‖ 2. Rise up, O Savitar whose hands are golden, and hear this man while sacrifice is offered, | Spreading afar thy broad and wide effulgence, and bringing mortal men the food that feeds them. ‖ 3. Let Savitar the God he hymned with praises, to whom the Vasus, even, all sing glory. | Sweet be our lauds to him whose due is worship: may he with all protection guard our princes. ‖ 4. Even he whom Aditi the Goddess praises, rejoicing in God Savitar's incitement: | Even he who praise the high imperial Rulers, Varuṇa, Mitra, Aryaman, sing in concert. ‖ 5. They who come emulous to our oblation, dispensing bounty, from the earth and heaven. | May they and Ahirbudhnya hear our calling: guard us Varūtrī with the Ekadhenus. ‖ 6. This may the Lord of Life, entreated, grant us,—the wealth which Savitar the God possesses. | The mighty calls on Bhaga for protection, on Bhaga calls the weak to give him riches. ‖ 7. Bless us the Vājins when we call, while slowly they move, strong Singers, to the Gods' assembly. | Crushing the wolf, the serpent, and the demons, may they completely banish all affliction. ‖ 8. Deep-skilled in Law eternal, deathless, Singers, O Vājins, help us in each fray for booty. | Drink of this meath, he satisfied, be joyful: then go on paths which Gods are wont to travel.

Hymn 7:39. Viśvedevas.

1. Agni, erect, hath shown enriching favour: the flame goes forward to the Gods' assembly. | Like car-borne men the stones their path have chosen: let the priest, quickened, celebrate our worship. ‖ 2. Soft to the tread, their sacred grass is scattered: these go like Kings amid the band around them, | At the folks early call on Night and Morning,—Vāyu, and Pūṣhan with his team, to bless us. ‖ 3. Here on their path the noble Gods proceeded: in the wide firmament the Beauteous decked them. | Bend your way hither, ye who travel widely: hear this our envoy who hath gone to meet you. ‖ 4. For they are holy aids at sacrifices: all Gods approach the place of congregation. | Bring these, desirous, to our worship, Agni, swift the Nāsatyas, Bhaga, and Purandhi. ‖ 5. Agni, to these men's hymns, from earth, from heaven, bring Mitra, Varuṇa, Indra, and Agni, | And Aryaman, and Aditi, and Viṣhṇu. Sarasvatī be joyful, and the Marutas. ‖ 6. Even as the holy wish, the gift is offered: may he, unsated, come when men desire him. | Give never-failing ever-conquering riches: with Gods for our allies may we be victors. ‖ 7. Now have both worlds been praised by the Vasiṣhṭhas; and holy Mitra, Varuṇa, and Agni. | May they, bright Deities, make our song supremest. Preserve us evermore, ye Gods, with blessings.

Hymn 7:40. Viśvedevas.

1. Be gathered all the audience of the synod: let us begin their praise whose course is rapid. | Whate'er God Savitar this day produces, may we be where the Wealthy One distributes. ‖ 2. This, dealt from heaven may both the Worlds vouchsafe us, and Varuṇa, Indra, Aryaman, and Mitra. | May Goddess Aditi assign us riches, Vāyu and Bhaga make them ours for ever. ‖ 3. Strong be the man and full of power, O Marutas, whom ye, borne on by spotted coursers, favour. | Him, too, Sarasvatī and Agni further, and there is none to rob him of his riches. ‖ 4. This Varuṇa is guide of Law, he, Mitra, and Aryaman, the Kings, our work have finished. | Divine and foeless Aditi quickly listens. May these deliver us unharmed from trouble. ‖ 5. With offerings I propitiate the branches of this swift-moving God, the bounteous Viṣhṇu. | Hence Rudra gained his Rudra-strength: O Aśvins, ye sought the house that hath celestial viands. ‖ 6. Be not thou angry here, O glowing Pūṣhan, for what Varūtrī and the Bounteous gave us. | May the swift-moving Gods protect and bless us, and Vāta send us rain, who wanders round us. ‖ 7. Now have both worlds been praised by the Vasiṣhṭhas, and holy Mitra, Varuṇa, and Agni. | May they, bright Deities, make our song supremest. Preserve us evermore, ye Gods, with blessings.

Hymn 7:41. Bhaga.

1. Agni at dawn, and Indra we invoke at dawn, and Varuṇa and Mitra, and the Aśvins twain. | Bhaga at dawn, Pūṣhan, and Brahmaṇaspati, Soma at dawn, Rudra we will invoke at dawn. ‖ 2. We will invoke strong, early-conquering Bhaga, the Son of Aditi, the great supporter: | Thinking of whom, the poor, yea, even the mighty, even the King himself says, Give me Bhaga. ‖ 3. Bhaga our guide, Bhaga whose gifts are faithful, favour this song, and give us wealth, O Bhaga. | Bhaga, augment our store of kine and horses, Bhaga, may we be rich in men and heroes. ‖ 4. So may felicity be ours at present, and when the day approaches, and at noontide; | And may we still, O Bounteous One, at sunset be happy in the Deities' loving-kindness. ‖ 5. May Bhaga verily be bliss-bestower, and through him, Gods! may happiness attend us. | As such, O Bhaga, all with might invoke thee: as such be thou our Champion here, O Bhaga. ‖ 6. To this our worship may all Dawns incline them, and come to the pure place like Dadhikrāvan. | As strong steeds draw a chariot may they bring us hitherward Bhaga who discovers treasure. ‖ 7. May blessed Mornings dawn on us for ever, with wealth of kine, of horses, and of heroes, | Streaming with all abundance, pouring fatness. Preserve us evermore, ye Gods, with blessings.

Hymn 7:42. Viśvedevas.

1. Let Brahmans and Aṅgirasas come forward, and let the roar of cloudy heaven surround us. | Loud low the Milch-kine swimming in the waters: set be the stones that grace our holy service. ‖ 2. Fair, Agni, is thy long-known path to travel: yoke for the juice thy bay, thy ruddy horses, | Or red steeds, Hero-bearing, for the chamber. Seated, I call the Deities' generations. ‖ 3. They glorify your sacrifice with worship, yet the glad Priest near them is left unequalled. | Bring the Gods hither, thou of many aspects: turn hitherward Aramati the Holy. ‖ 4. What time the Guest hath made himself apparent, at ease reclining in the rich man's dwelling, | Agni, well-pleased, well-placed within the chamber gives to a house like this wealth worth the choosing. ‖ 5. Accept this sacrifice of ours, O Agni; glorify it with Indra and the Marutas. | Here on our grass let Night and Dawn be seated: bring longing Varuṇa and Mitra hither. ‖ 6. Thus hath Vasiṣhṭha praised victorious Agni, yearning for wealth that giveth all subsistence. | May he

bestow on us food, strength, and riches. Preserve us evermore, ye Gods, with blessings.

Hymn 7:43. Viśvedevas.

1. Sing out the pious at your sacrifices to move with adorations Earth and Heaven— | The Holy Singers, whose unmatched devotions, like a tree's branches, part in all directions. || 2. Let sacrifice proceed like some fleet courser: with one accord lift ye on high the ladles. | Strew sacred grass meet for the solemn service: bright flames that love the Gods have mounted upward. || 3. Like babes in arms reposing on their mother, let the Gods sit upon the grass's summit. | Let general fire make bright the flame of worship: scorn us not, Agni, in the Gods' assembly. || 4. Gladly the Gods have let themselves be honoured, milking the copious streams of holy Order. | The highest might today is yours, the Vasus': come ye, as many as ye are, one-minded. || 5. So, Agni, send us wealth among the people: may we be closely knit to thee, O Victor, | Unharmed, and rich, and taking joy together. Preserve us evermore, ye Gods, with blessings.

Hymn 7:44. Dadhikrās.

1. I call on Dadhikrās, the first, to give you aid, the Aśvins, Bhaga, Dawn, and Agni kindled well, | Indra, and Vishṇu, Pūshan, Brahmaṇaspati, Ādityas, Heaven and Earth, the Waters, and the Light. || 2. When, rising, to the sacrifice we hasten, awaking Dadhikrās with adorations. | Seating on sacred grass the Goddess Iḷā. let us invoke the sage swift-hearing Aśvins. || 3. While I am thus arousing Dadhikrāvan I speak to Agni, Earth, and Dawn, and Sūrya, | The red, the brown of Varuṇa ever mindful: may they ward off from us all grief and trouble. || 4. Foremost is Dadhikrāvan, vigorous courser; in forefront of the cars, his way he knoweth, | Closely allied with Sūrya and with Morning, Ādityas, and Aṅgirasas, and Vasus. || 5. May Dadhikrās prepare the way we travel that we may pass along the path of Order. | May Agni bear us, and the Heavenly Army: hear us all Mighty Ones whom none deceiveth.

Hymn 7:45. Savitar.

1. May the God Savitar, rich in goodly treasures, filling the region, borne by steeds, come hither, | In his hand holding much that makes men happy, lulling to slumber and arousing creatures. || 2. Golden, sublime, and easy in their motion, his arms extend unto the bounds of heaven. | Now shall that mightiness of his he lauded: even Sūrya yields to him in active vigour. || 3. May this God Savitar, the Strong and Mighty, the Lord of precious wealth, vouchsafe us treasures. | May he, advancing his far-spreading lustre, bestow on us the food that feedeth mortals. || 4. These songs praise Savitar whose tongue is pleasant, praise him whose arms are full, whose hands are lovely. | High vital strength, and manifold, may he grant us. Preserve us evermore, ye Gods, with blessings.

Hymn 7:46. Rudra.

1. To Rudra bring these songs, whose bow is firm and strong, the self-dependent God with swiftly-flying shafts, | The Wise, the Conqueror whom none may overcome, armed with sharp-pointed weapons: may he hear our call. || 2. He through his lordship thinks on beings of the earth, on heavenly beings through his high imperial sway. | Come willingly to our doors that gladly welcome thee, and heal all sickness, Rudra, in our families. || 3. May thy bright arrow which, shot down by thee from heaven, flieth upon the earth, pass us uninjured by. | Thou, very gracious God, bast thousand medicines: inflict no evil on our sons or progeny. || 4. Slay us not, nor abandon us, O Rudra let not thy noose, when thou art angry, seize us. | Give us trimmed grass and fame among the living. Preserve us evermore, ye Gods, with blessings.

Hymn 7:47. Waters.

1. May we obtain this day from you, O Waters, that wave of pure refreshment, which the pious | Made erst the special beverage of Indra, bright, stainless, rich in sweets and dropping fatness. || 2. May the Floods' Offspring, he whose course is rapid, protect that wave most rich in sweets, O Waters, | That shall make Indra and the Vasus joyful. This may we gain from you today, we pious. || 3. All-purifying, joying in their nature, to paths of Gods the Goddesses move onward. | They never violate the laws of Indra. Present the oil-rich offering to the Rivers. || 4. Whom Sūrya with his bright beams hath attracted, and Indra dug the path for them to travel, | May these Streams give us ample room and freedom. Preserve us evermore, ye Gods, with blessings.

Hymn 7:48. Ṛibhus.

1. Ye liberal Heroes, Vājas and Ṛibhukshans, come and delight you with our flowing Soma. | May your strength, Vibhus, as ye come to meet us, turn hitherward your car that brings men profit. || 2. May we as Ṛibhu with your Ṛibhus conquer strength with our strength, as Vibhus with the Vibhus. | May Vāja aid us in the fight for booty, and helped by Indra may we quell the foeman. || 3. For they rule many tribes with high dominion, and conquer all their foes in close encounter. | May Indra, Vibhvan, Vāja, and Ṛibhukshan destroy by turns the wicked foeman's valour. || 4. Now, Deities, give us ample room and freedom: be all of you, one-minded, our protection. | So let the Vasus grant us strength and vigour. Preserve us evermore, ye Gods, with blessings.

Hymn 7:49. Waters.

1. Forth from the middle of the flood the Waters—their chief the Sea—flow cleansing, never sleeping. | Indra, the Bull, the Thunderer, dug their channels: here let those Waters, Goddesses, protect me. || 2. Waters which come from heaven, or those that wander dug from the earth, or flowing free by nature, | Bright, purifying, speeding to the Ocean, here let those Waters. Goddesses, protect me. || 3. Those amid whom goes Varuṇa the Sovereign, he who discriminates men's truth and falsehood— | Distilling meath, the bright, the purifying, here let those Waters, Goddesses, protect me. || 4. They from whom Varuṇa the King, and Soma, and all the Deities drink strength and vigour, | They into whom Vaiśvānara Agni entered, here let those Waters, Goddesses, protect Me.

Hymn 7:50. Various Deities.

1. O Mitra-Varuṇa, guard and protect me here: let not that come to me which nests within and swells. | I drive afar the scorpion hateful to the sight: let not the winding worm touch me and wound my foot. || 2. Eruption that appears upon the twofold joints, and that which overspreads the ankles and the knees, | May the refulgent Agni banish far away let not the winding worm touch me and wound my foot. || 3. The poison that is formed upon the Śalmali, that which is found in streams, that which the plants produce, | All this may all the Gods banish and drive away: let not the winding worm touch me and wound my foot. || 4. The steep declivities, the valleys, and the heights, the channels full of water, and the waterless— | May those who swell with water, gracious Goddesses, never afflict us with the Śipadā disease, may all the rivers keep us free from Śimidā.

Hymn 7:51. Ādityas.

1. Through the Ādityas' most auspicious shelter, through their most recent succour may we conquer. | May they, the Mighty, giving ear, establish this sacrifice, to make us free and sinless. || 2. Let Aditi rejoice and the Ādityas, Varuṇa, Mitra, Aryaman, most righteous. | May they, the Guardians of the world, protect us, and, to show favour, drink this day our Soma. || 3. All Universal Deities, the Marutas, all the Ādityas, yea, and all the Ṛibhus, | Indra, and Agni, and the Aśvins, lauded. Preserve us evermore, ye Gods, with blessings.

Hymn 7:52. Ādityas.

1. May we be free from every bond, Ādityas! a castle among Gods and men, ye Vasus. | Winning, may we win Varuṇa and Mitra, and, being, may we be, O Earth and Heaven. || 2. May Varuṇa and Mitra grant this blessing, our Guardians, shelter to our seed and offspring. | Let us not suffer for another's trespass. nor do the thing that ye, O Vasus, punish. || 3. The ever-prompt Aṅgirasas, imploring riches from Savitar the God, obtained them. | So may our Father who is great and holy, and all the Gods, accordant, grant this favour.

Hymn 7:53. Heaven and Earth.

1. As priest with solemn rites and adorations I worship Heaven and Earth, the High and Holy. | To them, great Parents of the Gods, have sages of ancient time, singing, assigned precedence. || 2. With newest hymns set in the seat of Order, those the Two Parents, born before all others, | Come, Heaven and Earth, with the Celestial People, hither to us, for strong is your protection. || 3. Yea, Heaven and Earth, ye hold in your possession full many a treasure for the liberal giver. | Grant us that wealth which comes in free abundance. Preserve us evermore, ye Gods, with blessings.

Hymn 7:54. Vāstoṣhpati.

1. Acknowledge us, O Guardian of the Homestead: bring no disease, and give us happy entrance. | Whate'er we ask of thee, be pleased to grant it, and prosper thou quadrupeds and bipeds. || 2. Protector of the Home, be our promoter: increase our wealth in kine and steeds, O Indu. | May we be ever-youthful in thy friendship: be pleased in us as in his sons a father. || 3. Through thy dear fellowship that bringeth welfare, may we be victors, Guardian of the Dwelling! | Protect our happiness in rest and labour. Preserve us evermore, ye Gods, with blessings.

Hymn 7:55. Vāstoṣhpati.

1. Vāstoṣhpati, who killest all disease and wearest every form, | Be an auspicious Friend to us. || 2. When, O bright Son of Saramā, thou showest, tawny-hued! thy teeth, | They gleam like lances' points within thy mouth when thou wouldst bite; go thou to steep. || 3. Saramā's Son, retrace thy way: bark at the robber and the thief. | At Indra's singers barkest thou? Why dust thou seek to terrify us? Go to sleep. || 4. Be on thy guard against the boar, and let the boar beware of thee. | At Indra's singers barkest thou? Why dost thou seek to terrify us? Go to sleep. || 5. Sleep mother, let the father sleep, sleep dog and master of the house. | Let all the kinsmen sleep, sleep all the people who are round about. || 6. The man who sits, the man who walks, and whosoever looks on us, | Of these we closely shut the eyes, even as we closely shut this house. || 7. The Bull who hath a thousand horns, who rises up from out the sea,— | By him the Strong and Mighty One we lull and make the people sleep. || 8. The women sleeping in the court, lying without, or stretched on beds, | The matrons with their odorous sweets these, one and all, we lull to sleep.

Hymn 7:56. Marutas.

1. Who are these radiant men in serried rank, Rudra's young heroes borne by noble steeds? || 2. Verily no one knoweth whence they sprang: they, and they only, know each other's birth. || 3. They strew each other with their blasts, these Hawks: they strove together, roaring like the wind. || 4. A sage was he who knew these mysteries, what in her udder mighty Pṛiśni bore. || 5. Ever victorious, through the Marutas, be this band of Heroes, nursing manly strength, || 6. Most bright in splendour, fleetest on their way, close-knit to glory, strong with varied power. || 7. Yea, mighty is your power and firm your strength: so, potent, with the Marutas, be the band. || 8. Bright is your spirit, wrathful are your minds: your bold troop's minstrel is like one inspired. || 9. Ever avert your blazing shaft from us, and let not your displeasure reach us here || 10. Your dear names, conquering Marutas, we invoke, calling aloud till we are satisfied. || 11. Well-armed, impetuous in their haste, they deck themselves, their forms, with oblations: to you, the pure, ornaments made of gold. || 12. Pure, Marutas, pure yourselves, are your oblations: to you, the pure, pure sacrifice I offer. | By Law they came to truth, the Law's observers, bright by their birth, and pure, and sanctifying. || 13. Your rings, O Marutas, rest upon your shoulders, and chains of gold are twined upon your bosoms. | Gleaming with drops of rain, like lightning-flashes, after your wont ye whirl about your weapons. || 14. Wide in the depth of air spread forth your glories, far, most adorable, ye bear your titles. | Marutas, accept this thousandfold allotment of household sacrifice and household treasure. || 15. If, Marutas, ye regard the praise recited here at this mighty singer invocation, | Vouchsafe us quickly wealth with noble heroes, wealth which no man who hateth us may injure. || 16. The Marutas, fleet as coursers, while they deck them like youths spectators of a festal meeting, | Linger, like beauteous colts, about the dwelling, like frisking calves, these who pour down the water. || 17. So may the Marutas help us and be gracious, bringing free room to lovely Earth and Heaven. | Far be your bolt that slayeth men and cattle. Ye Vasus, turn yourselves to us with blessings. || 18. The priest, when seated, loudly calls you, Marutas, praising in song your universal bounty. | He, Bulls! who hath so much in his possession, free from duplicity, with hymns invokes you. || 19. These Marutas bring the swift man to a stand-still, and strength with mightier strength they break and humble | These guard the singer from the man who hates him and lay their sore displeasure on the wicked. || 20. These Marutas rouse even the poor and needy: the Vasus love him as an active champion. | Drive to a distance, O ye Bulls, the darkness: give us full store of children and descendants. || 21. Never, O Marutas, may we lose your bounty, nor, car-borne Lords! be hindmost when ye deal it. | Give us a share in that delightful treasure, the genuine wealth that, Bulls! is your possession. || 22. What time the men in fury rush together for running streams, for pastures, and for houses. | Then, O ye Marutas, ye who spring from Rudra, be our protectors in the strife with foemen. || 23. Full many a deed ye did for our forefathers worthy of lauds which, even of old, they sang you. | The strong man, with the Marutas, wins in battle, the charger, with the Marutas, gains the booty. || 24. Ours, O ye Marutas, be the vigorous Hero, the Lord Divine of men, the strong Sustainer, | With whom to fair lands we may cross the waters, and dwell in our own home with you beside us. || 25. May Indra, Mitra, Varuṇa and Agni, Waters, and Plants, and Trees accept our praises. | May we find shelter in the Marut's bosom. Preserve us evermore, ye Gods, with blessings.

Hymn 7:57. Marutas.

1. Yea, through the power of your sweet juice, ye Holy! the Marut host is glad at sacrifices. | They cause even spacious heaven and earth to tremble, they make the spring flow when they come, the Mighty. || 2. The Marutas watch the man who sings their praises, promoters of the thought of him who worships. | Seat you on sacred grass in our assembly, this day, with friendly minds, to share the banquet. || 3. No others gleam so brightly as these Marutas with their own forms, their golden gauds, their weapons. | With all adornments, decking earth and heaven, they heighten, for bright show, their common splendour. || 4. Far from us be your blazing dart, O Marutas, when we, through human frailty, sin against you. | Let us not he exposed to that, ye Holy! May your most loving favour still attend us. || 5. May even what we have done delight the Marutas, the blameless Ones, the bright, the purifying. | Further us, O ye Holy, with your kindness: advance us mightily that we may prosper. || 6. And may the Marutas, praised by all their titles, Heroes, enjoy the taste of our oblations. | Give us of Amṛita for the sake of offspring: awake the excellent fair stores of riches. || 7. Hither, ye Marutas, praised, with all your succours, with all felicity come to our princes, | Who, of themselves, a hundredfold increase us. Preserve us evermore, ye Gods, with blessings.

Hymn 7:58. Marutas.

1. Sing to the troop that pours down rain in common, the Mighty Company of celestial nature. | They make the world-halves tremble with their greatness: from depths of earth and sky they reach to heaven. || 2. Yea, your birth, Marutas, was with wild commotion, ye who move swiftly, fierce in wrath, terrific. | Ye all-surpassing in your might and vigour, each looker on the light fears at your coming. || 3. Give ample vital power unto our princes let our fair praises gratify the Marutas. | As the way travelled helpeth people onward, so further us with your delightful succours. || 4. Your favoured singer counts his wealth by hundreds: the strong steed whom ye favour wins a thousand. | The Sovereign whom ye aid destroys the foeman. May this your gift, ye Shakers, be distinguished. || 5. I call, as such, the Sons of bounteous Rudra: will not the Marutas turn again to us-ward? | What secret sin or open stirs their anger, that we implore the Swift Ones to forgive us. || 6. This eulogy of the Bounteous hath been spoken: accept, ye Marutas, this our hymn of praises. | Ye Bulls, keep those who hate us at a distance. Preserve us evermore, ye Gods, with blessings.

Hymn 7:59. Marutas.

1. Whomso ye rescue here and there, whomso ye guide, O Deities, | To him give shelter, Agni, Mitra, Varuṇa, ye Marutas, and thou Aryaman. || 2. Through your kind favour, Gods, on some auspicious day, the worshipper subdues his foes. | That man increases home and strengthening ample food who brings you offerings as ye list. || 3. Vasiṣhṭha will not overlook the lowliest one among you all. | O Marutas, of our Soma juice effused today drink all of you with eager haste. || 4. Your succour in the battle injures not the man to whom ye, Heroes, grant your gifts. | May your most recent favour turn to us again. Come quickly, ye who fain would drink. || 5. Come hitherward to drink the juice, O ye whose bounties give you joy. | These offerings are for you, these, Marutas, I present. Go not to any place but this. || 6. Sit on our sacred grass, be graciously inclined to give the wealth for which we long, | To take delight, ye Marutas, Friends of all, with Svāhā, in sweet Soma juice. || 7. Decking the beauty of their forms in secret the Swans with purple backs have flown down hither. | Around me all the Company hath settled, like joyous Heroes glad in our libation. || 8. Marutas, the man whose wrath is hard to master, he who would slay us ere we think, O Vasus,

| May he be tangled in the toils of mischief; smite ye him down with your most flaming weapon. || 9. O Marutas, ye consuming Gods, enjoy this offering brought for you, | To help us, ye who slay the foe. || 10. Sharers of household sacrifice, come, Marutas, stay not far away, | That ye may help us, Bounteous Ones. || 11. Here, Self-strong Marutas, yea, even here. ye Sages with your sunbright skins | I dedicate your sacrifice. || 12. Tryambaka we worship, sweet augmenter of prosperity. | As from its stem the cucumber, so may I be released from death, not reft of immortality.

Hymn 7:60. Mitra-Varuṇa.

1. When thou, O Sun, this day, arising sinless, shalt speak the truth to Varuṇa and Mitra, | O Aditi, may all the Deities love us, and thou, O Aryaman, while we are singing. || 2. Looking on man, O Varuṇa and Mitra, this Sun ascendeth up by both the pathways, | Guardian of all things fixt, of all that moveth, beholding good and evil acts of mortals. || 3. He from their home hath yoked the Seven gold Coursers who, dropping oil and fatness, carry Sūrya. | Yours, Varuṇa and Mitra, he surveyeth the worlds and living creatures like a herdsman. || 4. Your coursers rich in store of sweets have mounted: to the bright ocean Sūrya hath ascended, | For whom the Ādityas make his pathway ready, Aryaman, Mitra, Varuṇa, accordant. || 5. For these, even Aryaman, Varuṇa and Mitra, are the chastisers of all guile and falsehood. | These, Aditi's Sons, infallible and mighty, have waxen in the home of law Eternal. || 6. These, Mitra, Varuṇa whom none deceiveth, with great power quicken even the fool to wisdom, | And, wakening, moreover, thoughtful insight, lead it by easy paths o'er grief and trouble. || 7. They ever vigilant, with eyes that close not, caring for heaven and earth, lead on the thoughtless. | Even in the river's bed there is a shallow. across this broad expanse may they conduct us. || 8. When Aditi and Varuṇa and Mitra, like guardians, give Sudās their friendly shelter, | Granting him sons and lineal succession, let us not, bold ones! move the Gods to anger. || 9. May he with offerings purify the altar from any stains of Varuṇa's reviler. | Aryaman save us us all those who hate us: give room and freedom to Sudās, ye Mighty. || 10. Hid from our eyes is their resplendent meeting: by their mysterious might they hold dominion. | Heroes! we cry trembling in fear before you, even in the greatness of your power have mercy. || 11. He who wins favour for his prayer by worship, that he may gain him strength and highest riches, | That good man's mind the Mighty Ones will follow: they have brought comfort to his spacious dwelling. || 12. This priestly task, Gods! Varuṇa and Mitra! hath been performed for you at sacrifices. | Convey us safely over every peril. Preserve us evermore, ye Gods, with blessings.

Hymn 7:61. Mitra-Varuṇa.

1. O Varuṇa and Mitra, Sūrya spreading the beauteous light of you Twain Gods ariseth. | He who beholdeth all existing creatures observeth well the zeal that is in mortals. || 2. The holy sage, renowned afar, directeth his hymns to you, O Varuṇa and Mitra,— | He whose devotions, sapient Gods, ye favour so that ye fill, as 'twere, with power his autumns. || 3. From the wide earth, O Varuṇa and Mitra from the great lofty heaven, ye, Bounteous Givers,— | Have in the fields and houses set your warder-, who visit every spot and watch unceasing. || 4. I praise the strength of Varuṇa and Mitra that strength, by mightiness, keeps both worlds asunder. | Heroless pass the months of the ungodly he who loves sacrifice makes his home enduring. || 5. Steers, all infallible are these your people in whom no wondrous thing is seen, no worship. | Guile follows close the men who are untruthful: no secrets may be hidden from your knowledge. || 6. I will exalt your sacrifice with homage: as priest, I, Mitra-Varuṇa, invoke you. | May these new hymns and prayers that I have fashioned delight you to the profit of the singer. || 7. This priestly task, Gods! Varuṇa and Mitra! hath been performed for you at sacrifices. | Convey us safely over every peril. Preserve us evermore, ye Gods, with blessings.

Hymn 7:62. Mitra-Varuṇa.

1. Sūrya hath sent aloft his beams of splendour o'er all the tribes of men in countless places. | Together with the heaven he shines apparent, formed by his Makers well with power and wisdom. || 2. So hast thou mounted up before us, Sūrya, through these our praises, with fleet dappled horses. | Declare us free from all offence to Mitra, and Varuṇa, and Aryaman, and Agni. || 3. May holy Agni, Varuṇa, and Mitra send down their riches upon us in thousands. | May they, the Bright Ones, make our praise-song perfect, and, when we laud them, grant us all our wishes. || 4. O undivided Heaven and Earth, preserve us, us, Lofty Ones! your nobly-born descendants. | Let us not anger Varuṇa, nor Vāyu, nor him, the dearest Friend of mortals, Mitra. || 5. Stretch forth your arms and let our lives be lengthened: with fatness dew the pastures of our cattle. | Ye Youthful, make us famed among the people: hear, Mitra-Varuṇa, these mine invocations. || 6. Now Mitra, Varuṇa, Aryaman vouchsafe us freedom and room, for us and for our children. | May we find paths all fair and good to travel. Preserve us evermore, ye Gods, with blessings.

Hymn 7:63. Mitra-Varuṇa.

1. Common to all mankind, auspicious Sūrya, he who beholdeth all, is mounting upward; | The God, the eye of Varuṇa and Mitra, who rolled up darkness like a piece of leather. || 2. Sūrya's great ensign, restless as the billow, that urgeth men to action, is advancing: | Onward he still would roll the wheel well-rounded, which Etaśa, harnessed to the car-pole, moveth. || 3. Refulgent from the bosom of the Mornings, he in Whom singers take delight ascendeth. | This Savitar, God, is my chief joy and pleasure, who breaketh not the universal statute. || 4. Golden, far-seeing, from the heaven he riseth: far is his goal, he hasteth on resplendent. | Men, verily, inspirited by Sūrya speed to their aims and do the work assigned them. || 5. Where the immortals have prepared his pathway he flieth through the region like a falcon. | With homage and oblations will we serve you, O Mitra-Varuṇa, when the Sun hath risen. || 6. Now Mitra, Varuṇa, Aryaman vouchsafe us freedom and room, for us and for our children. | May we find paths all fair and good to travel. Preserve us evermore, ye Gods, with blessings.

Hymn 7:64. Mitra-Varuṇa.

1. Ye Twain who rule, in heaven and earth, the region, clothed be your clouds in robes of oil and fatness. | May the imperial Varuṇa, and Mitra, and high-born Aryaman accept our presents. || 2. Kings, guards of mighty everlasting Order, come hitherward, ye Princes, Lords of Rivers. | Send us from heaven, O Varuṇa and Mitra, rain and sweet food, ye who pour down your bounties. || 3. May the dear God, and Varuṇa and Mitra conduct us by the most effective pathways, | That foes may say unto Sudās our chieftain, May, we, too, joy in food with Gods to guard us. || 4. Him who hath wrought for you this car in spirit, who makes the song rise upward and sustains it, | Bedew with fatness, Varuṇa and Mitra ye Kings, make glad the pleasant dwelling-places. || 5. To you this laud, O Varuṇa and Mitra is offered like bright Soma juice to Vāyu. | Favour our songs of praise, wake thought and spirit. Preserve us evermore, ye Gods, with blessings.

Hymn 7:65. Mitra-Varuṇa.

1. With hymns I call you, when the Sun hath risen, Mitra, and Varuṇa whose thoughts are holy, | Whose Power Divine, supreme and everlasting, comes with good heed at each man's supplication. || 2. For they are Asuras of Gods, the friendly make, both of you, our lands exceeding fruitful. | May we obtain you, Varuṇa and Mitra, wherever Heaven and Earth and days may bless us. || 3. Bonds of the sinner, they bear many nooses: the wicked mortal hardly may escape them. | Varuṇa-Mitra, may your path of Order bear us o'er trouble as a boat o'er waters. || 4. Come, taste our offering, Varuṇa and Mitra: bedew our pasture with sweet food and fatness. | Pour down in plenty here upon the people the choicest of your fair celestial water. || 5. To you this laud, O Varuṇa and Mitra, is offered, like bright Soma juice to Vāyu. | Favour our songs of praise, wake thought and spirit. Preserve us evermore, ye Gods, with blessings.

Hymn 7:66. Mitra-Varuṇa.

1. Let our strong hymn of praise go forth, the laud of Mitra-Varuṇa, | With homage to that high-born Pair; || 2. The Two exceeding wise, the Sons of Dakṣha, whom the Gods ordained | For lordship, excellently great. || 3. Such, Guardians of our homes and us, O Mitra-Varuṇa, fulfil | The thoughts of those who sing your praise. || 4. So when the Sun hath risen today, may sinless Mitra, Aryaman, | Bhaga, and Savitar send us forth. || 5. May this our home be guarded well forward, ye Bounteous, on the way, | Who bear us safely o'er distress. | 6. And those Self-reigning, Aditi, whose statute is inviolate, | The Kings who rule a vast domain. || 7. Soon as the Sun hath risen, to you, to Mitra-Varuṇa, I sing, | And Aryaman who slays the foe. || 8. With wealth of gold may this my song bring unmolested power and might, | And, Brahmans, gain the sacrifice. || 9. May we be thine, God

Varuṇa, and with our princes, Mitra, thine. | Food and Heaven's light will we obtain. || 10. Many are they who strengthen Law, Sun-eyed, with Agni for their tongue, | They who direct the three great gatherings with their thoughts, yea, all things with surpassing might. || 11. They who have established year and month and then the day, night, sacrifice and holy verse, | Varuṇa, Mitra, Aryaman, the Kings, have won dominion which none else may gain. || 12. So at the rising of the Sun we think of you with hymns today, | Even as Varuṇa, Mitra, Aryaman deserve: ye are the charioteers of Law. || 13. True to Law, born in Law the strengtheners of Law, terrible, haters of the false, | In their felicity which gives the best defence may we men and our princes dwell. || 14. Uprises, on the slope of heaven, that marvel that attracts die sight | As swift celestial Etaśa bears it away, prepared for every eye to see. || 15. Lord of each single head, of fixt and moving things, equally through the whole expanse, | The Seven sister Bays bear Sūrya on his car, to bring us wealth and happiness. || 16. A hundred autumns may we see that bright Eye, God-ordained, arise | A hundred autumns may we live. || 17. Infallible through your wisdom, come hither, resplendent Varuṇa, | And Mitra, to the Soma draught. || 18. Come as the laws of Heaven ordain, Varuṇa, Mitra, void of guile: | Press near and drink the Soma juice. || 19. Come, Mitra, Varuṇa, accept, Heroes, our sacrificial gift: | Drink Soma, ye who strengthen Law.

Hymn 7:67. Aśvins.

1. I with a holy heart that brings oblation will sing forth praise to meet your car, ye Princes, | Which, Much-desired! hath wakened as your envoy. I call you hither as a son his parents. || 2. Brightly hath Agni shone by us enkindled: the limits even of darkness were apparent. | Eastward is seen the Banner of the Morning, the Banner born to give Heaven's Daughter glory. || 3. With hymns the deft priest is about you, Aśvins, the eloquent priest attends you now, Nāsatyas. | Come by the paths that ye are wont to travel, on car that finds the light, laden with treasure. || 4. When, suppliant for your help, Lovers of Sweetness! I seeking wealth call you to our libation, | Hitherward let your vigorous horses bear you: drink ye with us the well-pressed Soma juices. || 5. Bring forward, Aśvins, Gods, to its fulfilment my never-wearied prayer that asks for riches. | Vouchsafe us all high spirit in the combat, and with your powers, O Lords of Power, assist us. || 6. Favour us in these prayers of ours, O Aśvins. May we have genial vigour, ne'er to fail us. | So may we, strong in children and descendants, go, wealthy, to the banquet that awaits you. || 7. Lovers of Sweetness, we have brought this treasure to you as 'twere an envoy sent for friendship. | Come unto us with spirits free from anger, in homes of men enjoying our oblation. || 8. With one, the same, intention, ye swift movers, o'er the Seven Rivers hath your chariot travelled. | Yoked by the Gods, your strong steeds never weary while speeding forward at the pole they bear you. || 9. Exhaustless be your bounty to our princes who with their wealth incite the gift of riches, | Who further friendship with their noble natures, combining wealth in kine with wealth in horses. || 10. Now hear, O Youthful Twain, mine invocation: come, Aśvins, to the home where food aboundeth. | Vouchsafe us wealth, do honour to our nobles. Preserve us evermore, ye Gods, with blessings.

Hymn 7:68. Aśvins.

1. Come, radiant Aśvins, with your noble horses: accept your servant's hymns, ye Wonder-Workers: | Enjoy oblations which we bring to greet you. || 2. The gladdening juices stand prepared before you: come quickly and partake of mine oblation. | Pass by the calling of our foe and bear us. || 3. Your chariot with a hundred aids, O Aśvins, beareth you swift as thought across the regions, | Speeding to us, O ye whose wealth is Sūrya. || 4. What time this stone of yours, the Gods' adorer, upraised, sounds forth for you as Soma-presser, | Let the priest bring you, Fair Ones, through oblations. || 5. The nourishment ye have is, truly, wondrous: ye gave thereof a quickening store to Atri, | Who being dear to you, receives your favour. || 6. That gift, which all may gain, ye gave Chyavāna, when he grew old, who offered you oblations, | When ye bestowed on him enduring beauty. || 7. What time his wicked friends abandoned Bhujyu, O Aśvins, in the middle of the ocean, | Your horse delivered him, your faithful servant. || 8. Ye lent your aid to Vṛika when exhausted, and listened when invoked to Śayu's calling. | Ye made the cow pour forth her milk like water, and, Aśvins, strengthened with your strength the barren. || 9. With his fair hymns this singer, too, extols you, waking with glad thoughts at the break of morning. | May the cow nourish him with milk to feed him. Preserve us evermore, ye Gods, with blessings.

Hymn 7:69. Aśvins.

1. May your gold chariot, drawn by vigorous horses, come to us, blocking up the earth | and heaven, | Bright with its fellies while its way drops fatness, food-laden, rich in coursers, man's protector. || 2. Let it approach, yoked by the will, three-seated, extending far and wide o'er fivefold beings, | Whereon ye visit God-adoring races, bending your course whither ye will, O Aśvins. || 3. Renowned, with noble horses, come ye hither: drink, Wondrous Pair, the cup that holds sweet juices. | Your car whereon your Spouse is wont to travel marks with its track the farthest ends of heaven. || 4. When night was turning to the grey of morning the Maiden, Sūrya's Daughter, chose your splendour. | When with your power and might ye aid the pious he comes through heat to life by your assistance. || 5. O Chariot-borne, this car of yours invested with rays of light comes harnessed to our dwelling. | Herewith, O Aśvins, while the dawn is breaking, to this our sacrifice bring peace and blessing. || 6. Like the wild cattle thirsty for the lightning, Heroes, come nigh this day to our libations. | Men call on you with hymns in many places, but let not other worshippers detain you. || 7. Bhujyu, abandoned in the midst of ocean, ye raised from out the water with your horses, | Uninjured, winged, flagging not, undaunted, with deeds of wonder saving him, O Aśvins. || 8. Now hear, O Youthful Twain, mine invocation: come, Aśvins, to the home where food aboundeth. | Vouchsafe us wealth, do honour to our nobles. Preserve us evermore, ye Gods, with blessings.

Hymn 7:70. Aśvins.

1. Rich in all blessings, Aśvins come ye hither: this place on earth is called your own possession, | Like a strong horse with a fair back it standeth, whereon, as in a lap, ye seat you firmly. || 2. This most delightful eulogy awaits you in the man's house drink-offering hath been heated, | Which bringeth you over the seas and rivers, yoking as 'twere two well-matched shining horses. || 3. Whatever dwellings ye possess, O Aśvins, in fields of men or in the streams of heaven, | Resting upon the summit of the mountain, or bringing food to him who gives oblation, || 4. Delight yourselves, ye Gods, in plants and waters when Ṛishis give them and ye find they suit You. | Enriching us with treasures in abundance ye have looked back to former generations. || 5. Aśvins, though ye have heard them oft aforetime, regard the many prayers which Ṛishis offer. | Come to the man even as his heart desireth: may we enjoy your most delightful favour. || 6. Come to the sacrifice offered you, Nāsatyas, with men, oblations, and prayer duly uttered. | Come to Vasiṣhṭha as his heart desireth, for unto you these holy hymns are chanted. || 7. This is the thought, this is the song, O Aśvins: accept this hymn of ours, ye Steers, with favour. | May these our prayers addressed to you come nigh you. Preserve us evermore, ye Gods, with blessings.

Hymn 7:71. Aśvins.

1. The Night retireth from the Dawn her Sister; the Dark one yieldeth to the Red her pathway. | Let us invoke you rich in steeds and cattle—by day and night keep far from us the arrow. || 2. Bearing rich treasure in your car, O Aśvins, come to the mortal who presents oblation. | Keep at a distance penury and sickness; Lovers of Sweetness, day and night preserve us. || 3. May your strong horses, seeking bliss, bring hither your chariot at the earliest flush of morning. | With coursers yoked by Law drive hither, Aśvins, your car whose reins are light, laden with treasure. || 4. The chariot, Princes, that conveys you, moving at daylight, triple-seated, fraught with riches, | Even with this come unto us, Nāsatyas, that laden with all food it may approach us. || 5. Ye freed Chyavāna from old age and weakness: ye brought the courser fleet of food to Pedu. | Ye rescued Atri from distress and darkness, and loosed for Jāhuṣha the bonds that bound him. || 6. This is the thought, this is the song, O Aśvins: accept this hymn of ours, ye Steers, With favour. | May these our prayers addressed to you come nigh you. Preserve us evermore, ye Gods, with blessings.

Hymn 7:72. Aśvins.

1. Come, O Nāsatyas, on your car resplendent, rich in abundant wealth of kine and horses. | As harnessed steeds, all our laudations follow you whose forms shine with most delightful beauty. || 2. Come with the Gods associate, come ye hither to us, Nāsatyas, with your car accordant. | 'twixt

you and us there is ancestral friendship and common kin: remember and regard it. ‖ 3. Awakened are the songs that praise the Aśvins, the kindred prayers and the Celestial Mornings. | Inviting those we long for, Earth and Heaven, the singer calleth these Nāsatyas hither. ‖ 4. What time the Dawns break forth in light, O Aśvins, to you the poets offer their devotions. | God Savitar hath sent aloft his splendour, and fires sing praises with the kindled fuel. ‖ 5. Come from the west, come from the cast, Nāsatyas, come, Aśvins, from below and from above us. | Bring wealth from all sides for the Fivefold People. Preserve us evermore, ye Gods, with blessings.

Hymn 7:73. Aśvins.

1. We have o'erpassed the limit of this darkness while, worshipping the Gods, we sang their praises. | The song invoketh both Immortal Aśvins far-reaching, born of old, great Wonder-workers. ‖ 2. And, O Nāsatyas, man's dear Priest is seated, who brings to sacrifice and offers worship, | Be near and taste the pleasant juice, O Aśvins: with food, I call you to the sacrifices. ‖ 3. We choosing you, have let our worship follow its course: ye Steers, accept this hymn with favour. | Obeying you as your appointed servant, Vasiṣhṭha singing hath with lauds aroused you. ‖ 4. And these Two Priests come nigh unto our people, united, demon-slayers, mighty-handed. | The juices that exhilarate are mingled. Injure us not, but come with happy fortune. ‖ 5. Come from the west, come from the cast, Nāsatyas, come, Aśvins, from below and from above us. | Bring wealth from all sides for the Fivefold People. Preserve us evermore, ye Gods, with blessings.

Hymn 7:74. Aśvins.

1. These morning sacrifices call you, Aśvins, at the break of day. | For help have I invoked you rich in power and might: for, house by house ye visit all. ‖ 2. O Heroes, ye bestow wonderful nourishment. send it to him whose songs are sweet | Accordant, both of you, drive your car down to us, and drink the savoury Soma juice. ‖ 3. Approach ye and be near to us. drink, O ye Aśvins, of the meath. | Draw forth the milk, ye Mighty, rich in genuine wealth: injure us not, and come to us. ‖ 4. The horses that convey you in their rapid flight down to the worshipper's abode, | With these your speedy coursers, Heroes, Aśvins, come, ye Gods, come well-inclined to us. ‖ 5. Yea, verily, our princes seek the Aśvins in pursuit of food. | These shall give lasting glory to our liberal lords, and, both Nāsatyas, shelter us. ‖ 6. Those who have led the way, like cars, offending none, those who are guardians of the men— | Also through their own might the heroes have grown strong, and dwell in safe and happy homes.

Hymn 7:75. Dawn.

1. Born in the heavens the Dawn hath flushed, and showing her majesty is come as Law ordaineth. | She hath uncovered fiends and hateful darkness; best of Aṅgirasas, hath waked the pathways. ‖ 2. Rouse us this day to high and happy fortune: to great felicity, O Dawn, promote us. | Vouchsafe us manifold and splendid riches, famed among mortals, man-befriending Goddess! ‖ 3. See, lovely Morning's everlasting splendours, bright with their varied colours, have approached us. | Filling the region of mid-air, producing the rites of holy worship, they have mounted. ‖ 4. She yokes her chariot far away, and swiftly visits the lands where the Five Tribes are settled, | Looking upon the works and ways of mortals, Daughter of Heaven, the world's Imperial Lady. ‖ 5. She who is rich in spoil, the Spouse of Sūrya, wondrously opulent, rules all wealth and treasures. | Consumer of our youth, the seers extol her: lauded by priests rich Dawn shines out refulgent. ‖ 6. Apparent are the steeds of varied colour, the red steeds carrying resplendent Morning. | On her all-lovely car she comes, the Fair One, and brings rich treasure for her faithful servant. ‖ 7. True with the True and Mighty with the Mighty, with Gods a Goddess, Holy with the Holy, | She brake strong fences down and gave the cattle: the kine were lowing as they greeted Morning. ‖ 8. O Dawn, now give us wealth in kine and heroes, and horses, fraught with manifold enjoyment. | Protect our sacred grass from man's reproaches. Preserve us evermore, ye Gods, with blessings.

Hymn 7:76. Dawn.

1. Savitar God of all men hath sent upward his light, designed for all mankind, immortal. | Through the Gods' power that Eye was first created. Dawn hath made all the universe apparent. ‖ 2. I see the paths which Gods are wont to travel, innocuous paths made ready by the Vasus. | Eastward the flag of Dawn hath been uplifted; she hath come hither o'er the tops of houses. ‖ 3. Great is, in truth, the number of the Mornings which were aforetime at the Sun's uprising. | Since thou, O Dawn, hast been beheld repairing as to thy love, as one no more to leave him. ‖ 4. They were the Gods' companions at the banquet, the ancient sages true to Law Eternal. | The Fathers found the light that lay in darkness, and with effectual words begat the Morning. ‖ 5. Meeting together in the same enclosure, they strive not, of one mind, one with another. | They never break the Gods' eternal statutes, and injure none, in rivalry with Vasus. ‖ 6. Extolling thee, Blest Goddess, the Vasiṣhṭhas, awake at early morn, with lauds implore thee. | Leader of kine and Queen of all that strengthens, shine, come as first to us, O high-born Morning. ‖ 7. She bringeth bounty and sweet charm of voices. The flushing Dawn is sung by the Vasiṣhṭhas, | Giving us riches famed to distant places. Preserve us evermore, ye Gods, with blessings.

Hymn 7:77. Dawn.

1. She hath shone brightly like a youthful woman, stirring to motion every living creature. | Agni hath come to feed on mortal? fuel. She hath made light and chased away the darkness. ‖ 2. Turned to this All, far-spreading, she hath risen and shone in brightness with white robes about her. | She hath beamed forth lovely with golden colours, Mother of kine, Guide of the days she bringeth. ‖ 3. Bearing the Gods' own Eye, auspicious Lady, leading her Courser white and fair to look on, | Distinguished by her beams Dawn shines apparent, come forth to all the world with wondrous treasure. ‖ 4. Draw nigh with wealth and dawn away the foeman: prepare for us wide pasture free from danger. | Drive away those who hate us, bring us riches: pour bounty, opulent Lady, on the singer. ‖ 5. Send thy most excellent beams to shine and light us, giving us lengthened days, O Dawn, O Goddess, | Granting us food, thou who hast all things precious, and bounty rich in chariots, kine, and horses. ‖ 6. O Uṣhas, nobly-born, Daughter of Heaven, whom the Vasiṣhṭhas with their hymns make mighty, | Bestow thou on us vast and glorious riches. Preserve us evermore, ye Gods, with blessings.

Hymn 7:78. Dawn.

1. We have beheld her earliest lights approaching: her many glories part, on high, asunder. | On car sublime, refulgent, wending hither, O Uṣhas, bring the Wealth that makes us happy. ‖ 2. The fire well-kindled sings aloud to greet her, and with their hymns the priests are chanting welcome. | Uṣhas approaches in her splendour, driving all evil darkness far away, the Goddess. ‖ 3. Apparent eastward are those lights of Morning, sending out lustre, as they rise, around them. | She hath brought forth Sun, sacrifice, and Agni, and far away hath fled detested darkness. ‖ 4. Rich Daughter of the Sky, we all behold her, yea, all men look on Dawn as she is breaking. | Her car that moves self-harnessed hath she mounted, the car drawn onward by her well-yoked horses. ‖ 5. Inspired with loving thoughts this day to greet thee, we and our wealthy nobles have awakened. | Show yourselves fruitful, Dawns, as ye are rising. Preserve us evermore, ye Gods, with blessings.

Hymn 7:79. Dawn.

1. Rousing the lands where men's Five Tribes are settled, Dawn hath disclosed the pathways of the people. | She hath sent out her sheen with beauteous oxen. The Sun with light hath opened earth and heaven. ‖ 2. They paint their bright rays on the sky's far limits. the Dawns come on like tribes arrayed for battle. | Thy cattle, closely shutting up the darkness, as Savitar spreads his arms, give forth their lustre. ‖ 3. Wealthy, most like to Indra, Dawn hath risen, and brought forth lauds that shall promote our welfare. | Daughter of Heaven, a Goddess, she distributes, best of Aṅgirasas, treasures to the pious. ‖ 4. Bestow on us, O Dawn, that ample bounty which thou didst send to those who sang thy praises; | Thou whom with bellowings of a bull they quickened: thou didst unbar the firm-set mountain's portals. ‖ 5. Impelling every God to grant his bounty sending to us the charm of pleasant voices, | Vouchsafe us thoughts, for profit, as thou breakest. Preserve us evermore, ye Gods, with blessings.

Hymn 7:80. Dawn.

1 The priests, Vasiṣhṭhas, are the first awakened to welcome Uṣhas with their songs and praises, | Who makes surrounding regions part asunder, and shows apparent all existing creatures. ‖ 2. Giving fresh life when she hath hid the darkness, this Dawn hath wakened there with new-born

lustre. | Youthful and unrestrained she cometh forward: she hath turned thoughts to Sun and fire and worship. || 3. May blessed Mornings shine on us for ever, with wealth of kine, of horses, and of heroes, | Streaming with all abundance, pouring fatness. Preserve us evermore, ye Gods, with blessings.

Hymn 7:81. Dawn.

1. Advancing, sending forth her rays, the Daughter of the Sky is seen. | Uncovering, that we may see, the mighty gloom, the friendly Lady makes the light. || 2. The Sun ascending, the refulgent Star, pours down his beams together with the Dawn. | O Dawn, at thine arising, and the Sun's, may we attain the share allotted us. || 3. Promptly we woke to welcome thee, O Uṣhas, Daughter of the Sky, | Thee, Bounteous One, who bringest all we long to have, and to the offerer health and wealth. || 4. Thou, dawning, workest fain to light the great world, yea, heaven, Goddess! that it may be seen. | We yearn to be thine own, Dealer of Wealth: may we be to this Mother like her sons. || 5. Bring us that wondrous bounty, Dawn, that shall be famed most far away. | What, Child of Heaven, thou hast of nourishment for man, bestow thou on us to enjoy. || 6. Give to our princes opulence and immortal fame, and strength in herds of kine to us. | May she who prompts the wealthy, Lady of sweet strains, may Uṣhas dawn our foes away.

Hymn 7:82. Indra-Varuṇa

1. Grant us your strong protection, Indra-Varuṇa, our people, and our family, for sacrifice. | May we subdue in fight our evil-hearted foes, him who attacks the man steadfast in lengthened rites. || 2. O Indra-Varuṇa, mighty and very rich One of you is called Monarch and One Autocrat. | All Gods in the most lofty region of the air have, O ye Steers, combined all power and might in you. || 3. Ye with your strength have pierced the fountains of the floods: the Sun have ye brought forward as the Lord in heaven. | Cheered by this magic draught ye, Indra-Varuṇa, made the dry places stream, made songs of praise flow forth. || 4. In battles and in frays we ministering priests, kneeling upon our knees for furtherance of our weal, | Invoke you, only you, the Lords of twofold wealth, you prompt to hear, we bards, O Indra-Varuṇa. || 5. O Indra-Varuṇa, as ye created all these creatures of the world by your surpassing might, | In peace and quiet Mitra waits on Varuṇa, the Other, awful, with the Marutas seeks renown. || 6. That Varuṇa's high worth may shine preeminent, these Twain have measured each his proper power and might. | The One subdueth the destructive enemy; the Other with a few furthereth many a man. || 7. No trouble, no misfortune, Indra-Varuṇa, no woe from any side assails the mortal man | Whose sacrifice, O Gods, ye visit and enjoy: ne'er doth the crafty guile of mortal injure him. || 8. With your divine protection, Heroes, come to us: mine invocation hear, if ye be pleased therewith. | Bestow ye upon us, O Indra-Varuṇa, your friendship and your kinship and your favouring grace. || 9. In battle after battle, Indra-Varuṇa, be ye our Champions, ye who are the peoples' strength, | When both opposing bands invoke you for the fight, and men that they may gain offspring and progeny. || 10. May Indra, Varuṇa, Mitra, and Aryaman vouchsafe us glory and great shelter spreading far. | We think of the beneficent light of Aditi, and Savitar's song of praise, the God who strengthens Law.

Hymn 7:83. Indra-Varuṇa.

1. Looking to you and your alliance, O ye Men, armed with broad axes they went forward, fain for spoil. | Ye smote and slew his Dāsa and his Ārya enemies, and helped Sudās with favour, Indra-Varuṇa. || 2. Where heroes come together with their banners raised, in the encounter where is naught for us to love, | Where all things that behold the light are terrified, there did ye comfort us, O Indra-Varuṇa. || 3. The boundaries of earth were seen all dark with dust: O Indra-Varuṇa, the shout went up to heaven. | The enmities of the people compassed me about. Ye heard my calling and ye came to me with help. || 4. With your resistless weapons, Indra-Varuṇa, ye conquered Bheda and ye gave Sudās your aid. | Ye heard the prayers of these amid the cries of war: effectual was the service of the Tṛitsus' priest. || 5. O Indra-Varuṇa, the wickedness of foes and mine assailants' hatred sorely trouble me. | Ye Twain are Lords of riches both of earth and heaven: so grant to us your aid on the decisive day. || 6. The men of both the hosts invoked you in the fight, Indra and Varuṇa, that they might win the wealth, | What time ye helped Sudās, with all the Tṛitsu folk, when the Ten Kings had pressed him down in their attack. || 7. Ten Kings who worshipped not, O Indra-Varuṇa, confederate, in war prevailed not o'er Sudās. | True was the boast of heroes sitting at the feast: so at their invocations Gods were on their side. || 8. O Indra-Varuṇa, ye gave Sudās your aid when the Ten Kings in battle compassed him about, | There where the white-robed Tṛitsus with their braided hair, skilled in song worshipped you with homage and with hymn. || 9. One of you Twain destroys the Vṛitras in the fight, the Other evermore maintains his holy Laws. | We call on you, ye Mighty, with our hymns of praise. Vouchsafe us your protection, Indra-Varuṇa. || 10. May Indra, Varuṇa, Mitra, and Aryaman vouchsafe us glory and great shelter spreading far. | We think of the beneficent light of Aditi, and Savitar's song of praise, the God who strengthens Law.

Hymn 7:84. Indra-Varuṇa.

1. Kings, Indra-Varuṇa, I would turn you hither to this our sacrifice with gifts and homage. | Held in both arms the ladle, dropping fatness, goes of itself to you whose forms are varied. || 2. Dyaus quickens and promotes your high dominion who bind with bonds not wrought of rope or cordage. | Far from us still be Varuṇa's displeasure may Indra give us spacious room to dwell in. || 3. Make ye our sacrifice fair amid the assemblies: make ye our prayers approved among our princes. | May God-sent riches come for our possession: further ye us with your delightful succours. || 4. O Indra-Varuṇa, vouchsafe us riches with store of treasure, food, and every blessing; | For the Āditya, banisher of falsehood, the Hero, dealeth wealth in boundless plenty. || 5. May this my song reach Varuṇa and Indra, and, strongly urging, win me sons and offspring. | To the Gods' banquet may we go with riches. Preserve us evermore, ye Gods, with blessings.

Hymn 7:85. Indra-Varuṇa.

1. For you I deck a harmless hymn, presenting the Soma juice to Varuṇa and Indra— | A hymn that shines like heavenly Dawn with fatness. May they be near us on the march and guard us. || 2. Here where the arrows fall amid the banners both hosts invoke the Gods in emulation. | O Indra-Varuṇa, smite back those-our foemen,yea, smite them with your shaft to every quarter. || 3. Self-lucid in their seats, e'en heavenly Waters endowed with Godhead Varuṇa and Indra. | One of these holds the folk distinct and sundered, the Other smites and slays resistless foemen. || 4. Wise be the priest and skilled in Law Eternal, who with his sacred gifts and oration. | Brings you to aid us with your might, Ādityas: let him have viands to promote his welfare. || 5. May this my song reach Varuṇa and Indra, and, strongly urging, win me sons and offspring. | To the Gods' banquet may we go with riches. Preserve us evermore, ye Gods with blessings.

Hymn 7:86. Varuṇa.

1. Wise, verily, are creatures through his greatness who stayed ever, spacious heaven and earth asunder; | Who urged the high and mighty sky to motion, the Star of old, and spread the earth before him. || 2. With mine own heart I commune on the question how Varuṇa and I may be united. | What gift of mine will he accept unangered? When may I calmly look and find him gracious? || 3. Fain to know this in in I question others: I seek the wise, O Varuṇa, and ask them. | This one same answer even the sages gave me, 'Surely this Varuṇa is angry with thee.' || 4. What, Varuṇa, hath been my chief transgression, that thou wouldst slay the friend who sings thy praises? | Tell me, Unconquerable Lord, and quickly sinless will I approach thee with mine homage. || 5. Free us from sins committed by our fathers, from those wherein we have ourselves offended. | O King, loose, like a thief who feeds the cattle, as from the cord a calf, set free Vasiṣhṭha. || 6. Not our own will betrayed us, but seduction, thoughtlessness, Varuṇa wine, dice, or anger. | The old is near to lead astray the younger: even sleep removeth not all evil-doing. || 7. Slave-like may I do service to the Bounteous, serve, free from sin, the God inclined to anger. | This gentle Lord gives wisdom to the simple: the wiser God leads on the wise to riches. || 8. O Lord, O Varuṇa, may this laudation come close to thee and lie within thy spirit. | May it be well with us in rest and labour. Preserve us ever-more, ye Gods, with blessings.

Hymn 7:87. Varuṇa.

1. Varuṇa cut a pathway out for Sūrya, and led the watery floods of rivers onward. | The Mares, as in a race, speed on in order. He made great channels for the days to follow. || 2. The wind, thy breath, hath sounded

through the region like a wild beast that seeks his food in pastures. | Within these two, exalted Earth and Heaven, O Varuṇa, are all the forms thou lovest. || 3. Varuṇa's spies, sent forth upon their errand, survey the two world-halves well formed and fashioned. | Wise are they, holy, skilled in sacrifices, the furtherers of the praise-songs of the prudent. || 4. To me who understand hath Varuṇa spoken, the names borne by the Cow are three times seven. | The sapient God, knowing the place's secret, shall speak as 'twere to teach the race that cometh. || 5. On him three heavens rest and are supported, and the three earths are there in sixfold order. | The wise King Varuṇa hath made in heaven that Golden Swing to cover it with glory. || 6. Like Varuṇa from heaven he sinks in Sindhu, like a white-shining spark, a strong wild creature. | Ruling in depths and meting out the region, great saving power hath he, this world's Controller. || 7. Before this Varuṇa may we be sinless him who shows mercy even to the sinner— | While we are keeping Aditi's ordinances. Preserve us evermore, ye Gods, with blessings.

Hymn 7:88. Varuṇa.

1. Present to Varuṇa thine hymn, Vasiṣhṭha, bright, most delightful to the Bounteous Giver, | Who bringeth on to us the Bull, the lofty, the Holy, laden with a thousand treasures. || 2. And now, as I am come before his presence, I take the face of Varuṇa for Agni's. | So might he bring-Lord also of the darkness-the light in heaven that I may see its beauty! || 3. When Varuṇa and I embark together and urge our boat into the midst of ocean, | We, when we ride o'er ridges of the waters, will swing within that swing and there be happy. || 4. Varuṇa placed Vasiṣhṭha in the vessel, and deftly with his might made him a Ṛishi. | When days shone bright the Sage made him a singer, while the heavens broadened and the Dawns were lengthened. || 5. What hath become of those our ancient friendships, when without enmity we walked together? | I, Varuṇa, thou glorious Lord, have entered thy lofty home, thine house with thousand portals. || 6. If he, thy true ally, hath sinned against thee, still, Varuṇa, he is the friend thou lovedst. | Let us not, Living One, as sinners I know thee: give shelter, as a Sage, to him who lauds thee. || 7. While we abide in these fixed habitations, and from the lap of Aditi win favour, | May Varuṇa untie the bond that binds us. Preserve us evermore, ye Gods, with blessings.

Hymn 7:89. Varuṇa.

1. Let me not yet, King Varuṇa, enter into the house of clay: | Have mercy, spare me, Mighty Lord. || 2. When, Thunderer! I move along tremulous like a wind-blown skin, | Have mercy, spare me, Mighty Lord. || 3. O Bright and Powerful God, through want of strength I erred and went astray | Have mercy, spare me, Mighty Lord. || 4. Thirst found thy worshipper though he stood in the midst of water-floods: | Have mercy, spare me, Mighty Lord. || 5. O Varuṇa, whatever the offence may be which we as men commit against the heavenly host, | When through our want of thought we violate thy laws, punish us not, O God, for that iniquity.

Hymn 7:90. Vāyu.

1. To you pure juice, rich in meath, are offered by priest: through longing for the Pair of Heroes. | Drive, Vāyu, bring thine harnessed horses hither: drink the pressed Soma till it make thee joyful. || 2. Whoso to thee, the Mighty, brings oblation, pure Soma unto thee, pure-drinking Vāyu, | That man thou makest famous among mortals: to him strong sons are born in quick succession. || 3. The God whom both these worlds brought forth for riches, whom heavenly Dhiṣhaṇā for our wealth appointeth, | His team of harnessed horses waits on Vāyu, and, foremost, on the radiant Treasure-bearer. || 4. The spotless Dawns with fair bright days have broken; they found the spacious light when they were shining. | Eagerly they disclosed the stall of cattle: floods streamed for them as in the days aforetime. || 5. These with their truthful spirit, shining brightly, move on provided with their natural insight. | Viands attend the car that beareth Heroes, your car, ye Sovereign Pair, Indra and Vāyu. || 6. May these who give us heavenly light, these rulers, with gifts of kine and horses, gold and treasures. | These princes, through full life, Indra and Vāyu! o'ercome in battle with their steeds and heroes. || 7. Like coursers seeking fame will we Vasiṣhṭhas, O Indra-Vāyu, with our fair laudations. | Exerting all our power call you to aid us. Preserve us evermore, ye Gods, with blessings.

Hymn 7:91. Vāyu.

1. Were not in sooth, the Gods aforetime blameless, whose pleasure was increased by adoration? | For Vāyu and for man in his affliction they caused the Morning to arise with Sūrya. || 2. Guardians infallible, eager as envoys' preserve us safe through many months and autumns. | Addressed to you, our fair praise, Indra-Vāyu, implores your favour and renewed well-being. || 3. Wise, bright, arranger of his teams, he. seeketh men with rich food whose treasures are abundant. | They have arranged them of one mind with Vāyu: the men have wrought all noble operations. || 4. So far as native power and strength permit you, so far as men behold whose eyes have vision, | O ye pure-drinkers, drink with us pure Soma: sit on this sacred grass, Indra and Vāyu. || 5. Driving down teams that bear the lovely Heroes, hitherward, Indra-Vāyu, come together. | To you this prime of savoury juice is offered: here loose your horses and be friendly-minded. || 6. Your hundred and your thousand teams, O Indra and Vāyu, all-munificent, which attend you, | With these most gracious-minded come ye hither, and drink, O Heroes of the meath we offer. || 7. Like coursers seeking fame will we Vasiṣhṭhas, O Indra-Vāyu, with our fair laudations, | Exerting all our power, call you to aid us. Preserve us evermore, ye Gods, with blessings.

Hymn 7:92. Vāyu

1. O Vāyu, drinker of the pure, be near us: a thousand teams are thine, All-bounteous Giver. | To thee the rapture-bringing juice is offered, whose first draught, God, thou takest as thy portion. || 2. Prompt at the holy rites forth came the presser with Soma-draughts for Indra and for Vāyu, | When ministering priests with strong devotion bring to you Twain the first taste of the Soma. || 3. The teams wherewith thou seekest him who offers, within his home, O Vāyu, to direct him, | Therewith send wealth: to us with full enjoyment, a hero son and gifts of kine and horses. || 4. Near to the Gods and making Indra joyful, devout and offering precious gifts to Vāyu, | Allied with princes, smiting down the hostile, may we with heroes conquer foes in battle. || 5. With thy yoked teams in hundreds and in thousands come to our sacrifice and solemn worship. | Come, Vāyu, make thee glad at this libation. Preserve us evermore, ye Gods, with blessings.

Hymn 7:93. Indra-Agni.

1. Slayers of enemies, Indra and Agni, accept this day our new-born pure laudation. | Again, again I call you prompt to listen, best to give quickly strength to him who craves it. || 2. For ye were strong to gain, exceeding mighty, growing together, waxing in your vigour. | Lords of the pasture filled with ample riches, bestow upon us strength both fresh and lasting. || 3. Yea when the strong have entered our assembly, and singers seeking with their hymns your favour, | They are like steeds who come into the race-course, those men who call aloud on Indra-Agni. || 4. The singer, seeking with his hymns your favour, begs splendid riches of their first possessor. | Further us with new bounties, Indra-Agni, armed with strong thunder, slayers of the foeman. || 5. When two great hosts, arrayed against each other, meet clothed with brightness, in the fierce encounter | Stand ye beside the godly, smite the godless; and still assist the men who press the Soma. || 6. To this our Soma-pressing, Indra-Agni, come ye prepared to show your loving-kindness, | For not at any time have ye despised us. So may I draw you with all strengthenings hither. || 7. So Agni, kindled mid this adoration, invite thou Mitra, Varuṇa, and Indra. | Forgive whatever sin we have committed may Aryaman and Aditi remove it. || 8. While we accelerate these our sacrifices, may we win strength from both of you, O Agni: | Ne'er may the Marutas, Indra, Viṣhṇu slight us. Preserve us evermore, ye Gods, with blessings.

Hymn 7:94. Indra-Agni.

1. As rain from out the cloud, for you, Indra and Agni, from my soul | This noblest praise hath been produced. || 2. Do ye, O Indra-Agni, hear the singer's call: accept his songs. | Ye Rulers, grant his heart's desire. || 3. Give us not up to poverty, ye Heroes, Indra-Agni, nor | To slander and reproach of men. || 4. To Indra and to Agni we bring reverence, high and holy hymn, | And, craving help, soft words with prayer. || 5. For all these holy singers here implore these Twain to succour them, | And priests that they may win them strength. || 6. Eager to laud you, we with songs invoke you, bearing sacred food, | Fain for success in sacrifice. || 7. Indra and Agni, come to us with favour, ye who conquer men: | Let not the wicked master us. || 8. At no time let the injurious blow of hostile mortal fall on us: | O Indra-Agni, shelter us. || 9. Whatever wealth we crave of you, in gold, in cattle, or in steeds, | That, Indra-Agni, let us gain; || 10. When heroes prompt in worship call Indra and Agni, Lords of steeds, | Beside the Soma juice

effused. || 11. Call hither with the song and lauds those who best slay the foemen, those | Who take delight in hymns of praise. || 12. Slay ye the wicked man whose thought is evil of the demon kind. | Slay him who stays the waters, slay the Serpent with your deadly dart.

Hymn 7:95. Sarasvatī.

1. This stream Sarasvatī with fostering current comes forth, our sure defence, our fort of iron. | As on a car, the flood flows on, surpassing in majesty and might all other waters. || 2. Pure in her course from mountains to the ocean, alone of streams Sarasvatī hath listened. | Thinking of wealth and the great world of creatures, she poured for Nahuṣha her milk and fatness. || 3. Friendly to man he grew among the women, a strong young Steer amid the Holy Ladies. | He gives the fleet steed to our wealthy princes, and decks their bodies for success in battle. || 4. May this Sarasvatī be pleased and listen at this our sacrifice, auspicious Lady, | When we with reverence, on our knees, implore her close-knit to wealth, most kind to those she loveth. || 5. These offerings have ye made with adoration: say this, Sarasvatī, and accept our praises; | And, placing us under thy dear protection, may we approach thee, as a tree, for shelter. || 6. For thee, O Blest Sarasvatī, Vasiṣhṭha hath here unbarred the doors d sacred Order. | Wax, Bright One, and give strength to him who lauds thee. Preserve us evermore, ye Gods, with blessings.

Hymn 7:96. Sarasvatī.

1. I sing a lofty song, for she is mightiest, most divine of Streams. | Sarasvatī will I exalt with hymns and lauds, and, O Vasiṣhṭha, Heaven and Earth. || 2. When in the fullness of their strength the Pūrus dwell, Beauteous One, on thy two grassy banks, | Favour us thou who hast the Marutas for thy friends: stir up the bounty of our chiefs. || 3. So may Sarasvatī auspicious send good luck; she, rich in spoil, is never niggardly in thought, | When praised in Jamadagni's way and lauded as Vasiṣhṭha lauds. || 4. We call upon Sarasvat, as unmarried men who long for wives, | As liberal men who yearn for sons. || 5. Be thou our kind protector, O Sarasvat, with those waves of thine | Laden with sweets and dropping oil. || 6. May we enjoy Sarasvat's breast, all-beautiful, that swells with streams, | May we gain food and progeny.

Hymn 7:97. Bṛihaspati.

1. Where Heaven and Earth combine in men's assembly, and those who love the Gods delight in worship, | Where the libations are effused for Indra, may he come first to drink and make him stronger. || 2. We crave the heavenly grace of Gods to guard us-so may Bṛihaspati, O friends, exalt us— | That he, the Bounteous God, may find us sinless, who giveth from a distance like a father. || 3. That Brahmaṇaspati, most High and Gracious, I glorify with offerings and with homage. | May the great song of praise divine, reach Indra who is the King of prayer the Gods' creation. || 4. May that Bṛihaspati who brings all blessings, most dearly loved, be seated by our altar. | Heroes and wealth we crave; may he bestow them, and bear us safe beyond the men who vex us. || 5. To us these Deathless Ones, erst born, have granted this laud of ours which gives the Immortal pleasure. | Let us invoke Bṛihaspati, the foeless, the clear-voiced God, the Holy One of households || 6. Him, this Bṛihaspati, his red-hued horses, drawing together, full of strength, bring hither. | Robed in red colour like the cloud, they carry the Lord of Might whose friendship gives a dwelling. || 7. For he is pure, with hundred wings, refulgent, with sword of gold, impetuous, winning sunlight. | Sublime Bṛihaspati, easy of access granteth his friends most bountiful refreshment. || 8. Both Heaven and Earth, divine, the Deity's Parents, have made Bṛihaspati increase in grandeur. | Glorify him, O friends, who merits glory: may he give prayer fair way and easy passage. || 9. This, Brahmaṇaspati, is your laudation prayer hath been made to thunder-wielding Indra. | Favour our songs, wake up our thought and spirit: destroy the godless and our foemen's malice. || 10. Ye Twain are Lords of wealth in earth and heaven, thou, O Bṛihaspati, and thou, O Indra. | Mean though he be, give wealth to him who lauds you. Preserve us evermore, ye Gods, with blessings.

Hymn 7:98. Indra.

1. Priests, offer to the Lord of all the people the milked-out stalk of Soma, radiant-coloured. | No wild-bull knows his drinking-place like Indra who ever seeks him who hath pressed the Soma, || 2. Thou dost desire to drink, each day that passes, the pleasant food which thou hast had aforetime, | O Indra, gratified in heart and spirit, drink eagerly the Soma set before thee. || 3. Thou, newly-born, for strength didst drink the Soma; the Mother told thee of thy future greatness. | O Indra, thou hast filled mid-air's wide region, and given the Gods by battle room and freedom. || 4. When thou hast urged the arrogant to combat, proud in their strength of arm, we will subdue them. | Or, Indra, when thou fightest girt by heroes, we in the glorious fray with thee will conquer. || 5. I will declare the earliest deeds of Indra, and recent acts which Maghavan hath accomplished. | When he had conquered godless wiles and magic, Soma became his own entire possession. || 6. Thine is this world of flocks and herds around thee, which with the eye of Sūrya thou beholdest. | Thou, Indra, art alone the Lord of cattle; may we enjoy the treasure which thou givest. || 7. Ye Twain are Lords of wealth in earth and heaven, thou, O Bṛihaspati, and thou, O Indra. | Mean though he be, give wealth to him who lauds you. Preserve us evermore, ye Gods, with blessings.

Hymn 7:99. Viṣhṇu.

1. Men come not nigh thy majesty who growest beyond all bound and measure with thy body. | Both thy two regions of the earth, O Viṣhṇu, we know: thou God, knowest the highest also. || 2. None who is born or being born, God Viṣhṇu, hath reached the utmost limit of thy grandeur. | The vast high vault of heaven hast thou supported, and fixed earth's eastern pinnacle securely. || 3. Rich in sweet food be ye, and rich in milch-kine, with fertile pastures, fain to do men service. | Both these worlds, Viṣhṇu, hast thou stayed asunder, and firmly fixed the earth with pegs around it. || 4. Ye have made spacious room for sacrificing by generating Sūrya, Dawn, and Agni. | O Heroes, ye have conquered in your battles even the bull-jawed Dāsa's wiles and magic. || 5. Ye have destroyed, thou, Indra, and thou Viṣhṇu, Śambara's nine-and-ninety fenced castles. | Ye Twain smote down a hundred times a thousand resistless heroes of the royal Varchin. || 6. This is the lofty hymn of praise, exalting the Lords of Mighty Stride, the strong and lofty. | I laud you in the solemn synods, Viṣhṇu: pour ye food on us in our camps, O Indra. || 7. O Viṣhṇu, unto thee my lips cry Vaṣhaṭ! Let this mine offering, Śipiviṣhṭa, please thee. | May these my songs of eulogy exalt thee. Preserve us evermore, ye Gods, with blessings.

Hymn 7:100. Viṣhṇu.

1 Ne'er doth the man repent, who, seeking profit, bringeth his gift to the far-striding Viṣhṇu. | He who adoreth him with all his spirit winneth himself so great a benefactor. || 2. Thou, Viṣhṇu, constant in thy courses, gavest good-will to all men, and a hymn that lasteth, | That thou mightst move us to abundant comfort of very splendid wealth with store of horses. || 3. Three times strode forth this God in all his grandeur over this earth bright with a hundred splendours. | Foremost be Viṣhṇu, stronger than the strongest: for glorious is his name who lives for ever. || 4. Over this earth with mighty step strode Viṣhṇu, ready to give it for a home to Manu. | In him the humble people trust for safety: he, nobly born, hath made them spacious dwellings. || 5. today I laud this name, O Śipiviṣhṭa, I, skilled in rules, the name of thee the Noble. | Yea, I the poor and weak praise thee the Mighty who dwellest in the realm beyond this region. || 6. What was there to be blamed in thee, O Viṣhṇu, when thou declaredst, I am Śipiviṣhṭa? | Hide not this form from us, nor keep it secret, since thou didst wear another shape in battle. || 7. O Viṣhṇu, unto thee my lips cry Vaṣhaṭ! Let this mine offering, Śipiviṣhṭa, please thee. | May these my songs of eulogy exalt thee. Preserve us evermore, ye Gods, with blessings.

Hymn 7:101. Parjanya.

1. Speak forth three words, the words which light precedeth, which milk this udder that produceth nectar. | Quickly made manifest, the Bull hath bellowed, engendering the germ of plants, the Infant. || 2. Giver of growth to plants, the God who ruleth over the waters and all moving creatures, | Vouchsafe us triple shelter for our refuge, and threefold light to succour and befriend us. || 3. Now he is sterile, now begetteth offspring, even as he willeth doth he change his figure. | The Father's genial flow bedews the Mother; therewith the Sire, therewith the son is nourished. || 4. In him all living creatures have their being, and the three heavens with triply-flowing waters. | Three reservoirs that sprinkle down their treasure shed their sweet streams around him with a murmur. || 5. May this my song to Sovereign Lord Parjanya come near unto his heart and give him pleasure. | May we obtain the showers that bring enjoyment, and God-protected

plants with goodly fruitage. || 6. He is the Bull of all, and their impregner lie holds the life of all things fixed and moving. | May this rite save me till my hundredth autumn. Preserve us evermore, ye Gods, with blessings.

Hymn 7:102. Parjanya.

1. Sing forth and laud Parjanya, son of Heaven, who sends the gift of rain | May he provide our pasturage. || 2. Parjanya is the God who forms in kine, in mares, in plants of earth, | And womankind, the germ of life. || 3. Offer and pour into his mouth oblation rich in savoury juice: | May he for ever give us food.

Hymn 7:103. Frogs.

1. They who lay quiet for a year, the Brahmans who fulfil their vows, | The Frogs have lifted up their voice, the voice Parjanya hath inspired. || 2. What time on these, as on a dry skin lying in the pool's bed, the floods of heaven descended, | The music of the Frogs comes forth in concert like the cows lowing with their calves beside them. || 3. When at the coming of the Rains the water has poured upon them as they yearned and thirsted, | One seeks another as he talks and greets him with cries of pleasure as a son his father. || 4. Each of these twain receives the other kindly, while they are revelling in the flow of waters, | When the Frog moistened by the rain springs forward, and Green and Spotty both combine their voices. || 5. When one of these repeats the other's language, as he who learns the lesson of the teacher, | Your every limb seems to be growing larger as ye converse with eloquence on the waters. || 6. One is Cow-bellow and Goat-bleat the other, one Frog is Green and one of them is Spotty. | They bear one common name, and yet they vary, and, talking, modulate the voice diversely. || 7. As Brahmans, sitting round the brimful vessel, talk at the Soma-rite of Atirātra, | So, Frogs, ye gather round the pool to honour this day of all the year, the first of Rain-time. || 8. These Brahmans with the Soma juice, performing their year-long rite, have lifted up their voices; | And these Adhvaryus, sweating with their kettles, come forth and show themselves, and none are hidden. || 9. They keep the twelve month's God-appointed order, and never do the men neglect the season. | Soon as the Rain-time in the year returneth, these who were heated kettles gain their freedom. || 10. Cow-bellow and Goat-bleat have granted riches, and Green and Spotty have vouchsafed us treasure. | The Frogs who give us cows in hundreds lengthen our lives in this most fertilizing season.

Hymn 7:104. Indra-Soma.

1. Indra and Soma, burn, destroy the demon foe, send downward, O ye Bulls, those who add gloom to gloom. | Annihilate the fools, slay them and burn them up: chase them away from us, pierce the voracious ones. || 2. Indra and Soma, let sin round the wicked boil like as a cauldron set amid the flames of fire. | Against the foe of prayer, devourer of raw flesh, the vile fiend fierce of eye, keep ye perpetual hate. || 3. Indra and Soma, plunge the wicked in the depth, yea, cast them into darkness that hath no support, | So that not one of them may ever thence return: so may your wrathful might prevail and conquer them. || 4. Indra and Soma, hurl your deadly crushing bolt down on the wicked fiend from heaven and from the earth. | Yea, forge out of the mountains your celestial dart wherewith ye burn to death the waxing demon race. || 5. Indra and Soma, cast ye downward out of heaven your deadly darts of stone burning with fiery flame, | Eternal, scorching darts; plunge the voracious ones within the depth, and let them sink without a sound. || 6. Indra and Soma, let this hymn control you both, even as the girth encompasses two vigorous steeds— | The song of praise which I with wisdom offer you: do ye, as Lords of men, animate these my prayers. || 7. In your impetuous manner think ye both thereon: destroy these evil beings, slay the treacherous fiends. | Indra and Soma, let the wicked have no bliss who evermore assails us with malignity. || 8. Whoso accuses me with words of falsehood when I pursue my way with guileless spirit, | May he, the speaker of untruth, be, Indra, like water which the hollowed hand compresses. || 9. Those who destroy, as is their wont, the simple, and with their evil natures harm the righteous, | May Soma give them over to the serpent, or to the lap of Nirṛiti consign them. || 10. The fiend, O Agni, who designs to injure the essence of our food, kine, steeds, or bodies, | May he, the adversary, thief, and robber, sink to destruction, both himself and offspring || 11. May he be swept away, himself and children: may all the three earths press him down beneath them. | May his fair glory, O ye Gods, be blighted, who in the day or night would fain destroy us. || 12. The prudent finds it easy to distinguish the true and false: their words oppose each other. | Of these two that which is the true and honest, Soma protects, and brings the false to nothing. || 13. Never doth Soma aid and guide the wicked or him who falsely claims the Warrior's title. | He slays the fiend and him who speaks untruly: both lie entangled in the noose of Indra. || 14. As if I worshipped deities of falsehood, or thought vain thoughts about the Gods, O Agni. | Why art thou angry with us, Jātavedas? Destruction fall on those who lie against thee! || 15. So may I die this day if I have harassed any man's life or if I be a demon. | Yea, may he lose all his ten sons together who with false tongue hath called me Yātudhāna. || 16. May Indra slay him with a mighty weapon, and let the vilest of all creatures perish, | The fiend who says that he is pure, who calls me a demon though devoid of demon nature. || 17. She too who wanders like an owl at night-time, hiding her body in her guile and malice, | May she fall downward into endless caverns. May press-stones with loud ring destroy the demons. || 18. Spread out, ye Marutas, search among the people: seize ye and grind the Rākṣhasas to pieces, | Who fly abroad, transformed to birds, at night-time, or sully and pollute our holy worship. || 19. Hurl down from heaven thy bolt of stone, O Indra: sharpen it, Maghavan, made keen by Soma. | Forward, behind, and from above and under, smite down the demons with thy rocky weapon. || 20. They fly, the demon dogs, and, bent on mischief, fain would they harm indomitable Indra. | Śakra makes sharp his weapon for the wicked: now, let him cast his bolt at fiendish wizards. || 21. Indra hath ever been the fiends' destroyer who spoil oblations of the Gods' invokers: | Yea, Śakra, like an axe that splits the timber, attacks and smashes them like earthen vessels. || 22. Destroy the fiend shaped like an owl or owlet, destroy him in the form of dog or cuckoo. | Destroy him shaped as eagle or as vulture as with a stone, O Indra, crush the demon. || 23. Let not the fiend of witchcraft-workers reach us: may Dawn drive off the couples of Kimīdins. | Earth keep us safe from earthly woe and trouble: from grief that comes from heaven mid-air preserve us. || 24. Slay the male demon, Indra! slay the female, joying and triumphing in arts of magic. | Let the fools' Gods with bent necks fall and perish, and see no more the Sun when he arises. || 25. Look each one hither, look around Indra and Soma, watch ye well. | Cast forth your weapon at the fiends against the sorcerers hurt your bolt.

Maṇḍala 8

Hymn 8:1. Indra.

1. Glorify naught besides, O friends; so shall no sorrow trouble you. | Praise only mighty Indra when the juice is shed, and say your lauds repeatedly: || 2. Even him, eternal, like a bull who rushes down, men's Conqueror, bounteous like a cow; | Him who is cause of both, of enmity and peace, to both sides most munificent. || 3. Although these men in sundry ways invoke thee to obtain thine aid, | Be this our prayer, addressed, O Indra, unto thee, thine exaltation every day. || 4. Those skilled in song, O Maghavan among these men o'ercome with might the foeman's songs. | Come hither, bring us strength in many a varied form most near that it may succour us. || 5. O Caster of the Stone, I would not sell thee for a mighty price, | Not for a thousand, Thunderer! nor ten thousand, nor a hundred, Lord of countless wealth! || 6. O Indra, thou art more to me than sire or niggard brother is. | Thou and my mother, O Good Lord, appear alike, to give me wealth abundantly. || 7. Where art thou? Whither art thou gone? For many a place attracts thy mind. | Haste, Warrior, Fort-destroyer, Lord of battle's din, haste, holy songs have sounded forth. || 8. Sing out the psalm to him who breaks down castles for his faithful friend, | Verses to bring the Thunderer to destroy the forts and sit on Kaṇva's sacred grass. || 9. The Horses which are thine in tens, in hundreds, yea, in thousands thine, | Even those vigorous Steeds, fleet-footed in the course, with those come quickly near to us. || 10. This day I call Sabardughā who animates the holy song, | Indra the richly-yielding Milch-cow who provides unfailing food in ample stream. || 11. When Sūra wounded Etaśa, with Vāta's rolling winged car. | Indra bore Kutsa Ārjuneya off, and mocked Gandharva. the unconquered One. || 12. He without ligature, before making incision in the neck, | Closed up the wound again, most wealthy Maghavan, who maketh whole the injured part. || 13. May we be never cast aside, and strangers, as it

were, to thee. | We, Thunder-wielding Indra, count ourselves as trees rejected and unfit to bum. || 14. O Vṛitra-slayer, we were thought slow and unready for the fray. | Yet once in thy great bounty may we have delight, O Hero, after praising thee. || 15. If he will listen to my laud, then may out Soma-drops that flow | Rapidly through the strainer gladden Indra, drops due to the Tugryas' Strengthener. || 16. Come now unto the common laud of thee and of thy faithful friend. | So may our wealthy nobles' praise give joy to thee. Fain would I sing thine eulogy. || 17. Press out the Soma with the stones, and in the waters wash it clean. | The men investing it with raiment made of milk shall milk it forth from out the stems. || 18. Whether thou come from earth or from the lustre of the lofty heaven, | Wax stronger in thy body through my song of praise: fill full all creatures, O most Wise. || 19. For India press the Soma out, most gladdening and most excellent. | May Śakra make it swell sent forth with every prayer and asking, as it were, for strength. || 20. Let me not, still beseeching thee with earnest song at Soma rites, | Anger thee like soma wild beast. Who would not beseech him who hath power to grant his prayer? || 21. The draught made swift with rapturous joy, effectual with its mighty strength, | All-conquering, distilling transport, let him drink: for he in ecstasy gives us gifts. || 22. Where bliss is not, may he, All-praised, God whom the pious glorify, | Bestow great wealth upon the mortal worshipper who sheds the juice and praises him. || 23. Come, Indra, and rejoice thyself, O God, in manifold affluence. | Thou fillest like a lake thy vast capacious bulk with Soma and with draughts besides. || 24. A thousand and a hundred Steeds are harnessed to thy golden car. | So may the long-maned Bays, yoked by devotion, bring Indra to drink the Soma juice. || 25. Yoked to thy chariot wrought of gold, may thy two Bays with peacock tails, | Convey thee hither, Steeds with their white backs, to quaff sweet juice that makes us eloquent. || 26. So drink, thou Lover of the Song, as the first drinker, of this juice. | This the outpouring of the savoury sap prepared is good and meet to gladden thee. || 27. He who alone by wondrous deed is Mighty, Strong by holy works, | May he come, fair of cheek; may he not stay afar, but come and turn not from our call. || 28. Śushṇa's quick moving castle thou hast crushed to pieces with thy bolts. | Thou, Indra, from of old, hast followed after light, since we have had thee to invoke. || 29. My praises when the Sun hath risen, my praises at the time of noon, | My praises at the coming of the gloom of night, O Vasu, have gone forth to thee. || 30. Praise yea, praise him. Of princes these are the most liberal of their gifts, | These, Paramajyā, Ninditāśva, Prapathī, most bounteous, O Medhātithi. || 31. When to the car, by faith, I yoked the horses longing for the way— | For skilled is Yadu's son in dealing precious wealth, he who is rich in herds of kine. || 32. May he who gave me two brown steeds together with their cloths of gold, | May he, Āsaṅga's son Svanadratha, obtain all joy and high felicities. || 33. Playoga's son Āsaṅga, by ten thousand, O Agni, hath surpassed the rest in giving. | For me ten bright-hued oxen have come forward like lotus-stalks from out a lake upstanding. || 34. What time her husband's perfect restoration to his lost strength and manhood was apparent, | His consort Śaśvatī with joy addressed him, Now art thou well, my lord, and shalt be happy.

Hymn 8:2. Indra.

1. Here is the Soma juice expressed; O Vasu, drink till thou art full: | Undaunted God, we give it thee. || 2. Washed by the men, pressed out with stones, strained through the filter made of wool, | 'tis like a courser bathed in stream. || 3. This juice have we made sweet for thee like barley, blending it with milk. | Indra, I call thee to our feast. || 4. Beloved of all, Indra alone drinks up the flowing Soma juice | Among the Gods and mortal men. || 5. The Friend, whom not the brilliant-hued, the badly-mixed or bitter draught, | Repels, the far-extending God; || 6. While other men than we with milk chase him as hunters chase a deer, | And with their kine inveigle him. || 7. For him, for Indra, for the God, be pressed three draughts of Soma juice | In the juice-drinker's own abode. || 8. Three reservoirs exude their drops, filled are three beakers to the brim, | All for one offering to the God. || 9. Pure art thou, set in many a place, and blended in the midst with milk | And curd, to cheer the Hero best. || 10. Here, Indra, are thy Soma-draughts pressed out by us, the strong, the pure: | They crave admixture of the milk. || 11. O Indra, pour in milk, prepare the cake, and mix the Soma-draught. | I hear them say that thou art rich. || 12. Quaffed juices fight within the breast. The drunken praise not by their wine, | The naked praise not when it rains. || 13. Rich be the praiser of one rich, munificent and famed like thee: | High rank be his, O Lord of Bays. || 14. Foe of the man who adds no milk, he heeds not any chanted hymn | Or holy psalm that may he sung. || 15. Give us not, Indra, as a prey unto the scornful or the proud: | Help, Mighty One, with power and might. || 16. This, even this, O Indra, we implore. as thy devoted friends, | The Kaṇvas praise thee with their hymns. || 17. Naught else, O Thunderer, have I praised in the skilled singer's eulogy: | On thy land only have I thought. || 18. The Gods seek him who presses out the Soma; they desire not sleep | They punish sloth unweariedly. || 19. Come hither swift with gifts of wealth—be not thou angry with us—like | A great man with a youthful bride. || 20. Let him not, wrathful with us, spend the evening far from us today, | Like some unpleasant son-in-law. || 21. For well we know this Hero's love, most liberal of the boons he gives, | His plans whom the three worlds display. || 22. Pour forth the gift which Kaṇvas bring, for none more glorious do we know | Than the Strong Lord with countless aids. || 23. O presser, offer Soma first to Indra, Hero, Śakra, him | The Friend of man, that he may drink; || 24. Who, in untroubled ways, is best provider, for his worshippers. | Of strength in horses and in kine. || 25. Pressers, for him blend Soma juice, each draught most excellent, for him | The Brave, the Hero, for his joy. || 26. The Vṛitra-slayer drinks the juice. May he who gives a hundred aids | Approach, nor stay afar from us. || 27. May the strong Bay Steeds, yoked by prayer, bring hither unto us our Friend, | Lover of Song, renowned by songs. || 28. Sweet are the Soma juices, come! Blent are the Soma juices, come! | Ṛishi-like, mighty, fair of cheek, come hither quickly to the feast. || 29. And lauds which strengthen thee for great bounty and valour, and exalt | Indra who doeth glorious deeds, || 30. And songs to thee who lovest song, and all those hymns addressed to thee— | These evermore confirm thy might. || 31. Thus he, sole doer of great deeds whose hand holds thunder, gives us strength, | He who hath never been subdued. || 32. Vṛitra he slays with his right hand, even Indra, great with mighty power, | And much-invoked in many a place. || 33. He upon whom all men depend, all regions, all achievements, he | Takes pleasure in our wealthy chiefs. || 34. All this hath he accomplished, yea, Indra, most gloriously renowned, | Who gives our wealthy princes strength. || 35. Who drives his chariot seeking spoil, from afar, to him he loves: | For swift is he to bring men wealth. || 36. The Sage who, winning spoil with steeds, slays Vṛitra, Hero with the men, | His servant's faithful succourer. || 37. O Priyamedhas, worship with collected mind this Indra whom | The Soma hath full well inspired. || 38. Ye Kaṇvas, sing the Mighty One, Lord of the Brave, who loves renown, | All-present, glorified by song. || 39. Strong Friend, who, with no trace of feet, restores the cattle to the men, | Who rest their wish and hope on him. || 40. Shaped as a Ram, Stone-hurler I once thou camest hither to the son | Of Kaṇva, wise Medhātithi. || 41. Vibhindu, thou hast helped this man, giving him thousands four times ten, | And afterward eight thousand more. || 42. And these twain pouring streams of milk, creative, daughters of delight, | For wedlock sake I glorify.

Hymn 8:3. Indra.

1. Drink, Indra, of the savoury juice, and cheer thee with our milky draught. | Be, for our weal, our Friend and sharer of the feast, and let thy wisdom guard us well. || 2. In thy kind grace and favour may we still be strong: expose us not to foe's attack. | With manifold assistance guard and succour us, and bring us to felicity. || 3. May these my songs of praise exalt thee, Lord, who hast abundant wealth. | Men skilled in holy hymns, pure, with the hues of fire, have sung them with their lauds to thee. || 4. He, with his might enhanced by Ṛishis thousandfold, hath like an ocean spread himself. | His majesty is praised as true at solemn rites, his power where holy singers rule. || 5. Indra for worship of the Gods, Indra while sacrifice proceeds, | Indra, as worshippers in battle-shock, we call, Indra that we may win the spoil. || 6. With might hath Indra spread out heaven and earth, with power hath Indra lighted up the Sun. | In Indra are all creatures closely held; in him meet the distilling Soma-drops. || 7. Men with their lauds are urging thee, Indra, to drink the Soma first. | The Ṛibhus in accord have lifted up their voice, and Rudras sung thee as the first. || 8. Indra increased his manly strength at sacrifice, in the wild rapture of this juice. | And living men today, even as of old, sing forth their praises to his majesty. || 9. I crave of thee that hero strength, that thou mayst first regard

this prayer, | Wherewith thou holpest Bhṛigu and the Yatis and Praskaṇva when the prize was staked. || 10. Wherewith thou sentest mighty waters to the sea, that, Indra, is thy manly strength. | For ever unattainable is this power of him to whom the worlds have cried aloud. || 11. Help us, O Indra, when we pray to thee for wealth and hero might. | First help thou on to strength the man who strives to win, and aid our laud, O Ancient One. || 12. Help for us, Indra, as thou holpest Paura once, this man's devotions bent on gain. | Help, as thou gavest Ruśama and Śyāvaka and Svarṇara and Kṛipa aid. || 13. What newest of imploring prayers shall, then, the zealous mortal sing? | For have not they who laud his might, and Indra-power won for themselves the light of heaven? || 14. When shall they keep the Law and praise thee mid the Gods? Who counts as Ṛishi and as sage? | When ever wilt thou, Indra Maghavan, come nigh to presser's or to praiser's call? || 15. These songs of ours exceeding sweet, these hymns of praise ascend to thee, | Like ever-conquering chariots that display their strength, gain wealth, and give unfailing aid. || 16. The Bhṛigus are like Suns, like Kaṇvas, and have gained all that their thoughts were bent upon. | The living men of Priyamedha's race have sung exalting Indra with their lauds. || 17. Best slayer of the Vṛitras, yoke thy Bay Steeds, Indra, from afar. | Come with the High Ones hither, Maghavan, to us, Mighty, to drink the Soma juice. || 18. For these, the bards and singers, have cried out to thee with prayer, to gain the sacrifice. | As such, O Maghavan, Indra, who lovest song, even as a lover bear my call. || 19. Thou from the lofty plains above, O Indra, hurledst Vṛitra down. | Thou dravest forth the kine of guileful Mṛigaya and Arbuda from the mountain's hold. || 20. Bright were the flaming fires, the Sun gave forth his shine, and Soma, Indra's juice, shone clear. | Indra, thou blewest the great Dragon from the air -. men must regard that valorous deed. || 21. The fairest courser of them all, who runneth on as 'twere to heaven. | Which Indra and the Marutas gave, and Pākasthāman Kaurayāṇa. || 22. To me hath Pākasthāman given, a ruddy horse,good at the pole, | Filling is girth and rousing wealth; || 23. Compared with whom no other ten strong coursers, harnessed to the pole, | Bear Tugrya to his dwelling place. || 24. Raiment is body, food is life, and healing ointment giveth strength. | As the free-handed giver of the ruddy steed, I have named Pākasthāman fourth.

Hymn 8:4. Indra.

1. Though, Indra, thou art called by men eastward and westward, north and south, | Thou chiefly art with Anava and Turvaśa, brave Champion I urged by men to Come. || 2. Or, Indra, when with Ruma, Ruśama, Śyāvaka, and Kṛipa thou rejoicest thee, | Still do the Kaṇvas, bringing praises, with their prayers, O Indra, draw thee hither: come. || 3. Even as the wild-bull, when he thirsts, goes to the desert's watery pool, | Come hither quickly both at morning and at eve, and with the Kaṇvas drink thy fill. || 4. May the drops gladden thee, rich Indra, and obtain bounty for him who pours the juice. | Soma pressed in the mortar didst thou take and drink, and hence hast won surpassing might. || 5. With mightier strength he conquered strength, with energy he crushed their wrath. | O Indra, Strong in youth, all those who sought the fray bent and bowed down to thee like trees. || 6. He who wins promise of thine aid goes girt as with a thousand mighty men of war. | He makes his son preeminent in hero might—he serves with reverential prayer. || 7. With thee, the Mighty, for our Friend, we will riot fear or feel fatigue. | May we see Turvaśa and Yadu: thy great deed, O Hero, must be glorified. || 8. On his left hip the Hero hath reclined himself: the proffered feast offends him not. | The milk is blended with the honey of the bee: quickly come hither, baste, and drink. || 9. Indra, thy friend is fair of form and rich in horses, cars, and kine. | He evermore hath food accompanied by wealth, and radiant joins the company. || 10. Come like a thirsty antelope to the drinking-place: drink Soma to thy heart's desire. | Raining it down, O Maghavan, day after day, thou gainest thy surpassing might. || 11. Priest, let the Soma juice flow forth, for Indra longs to drink thereof. | He even now hath yoked his vigorous Bay Steeds: the Vṛitra-slayer hath come near. || 12. The man with whom thou fillest thee with Soma deems himself a pious worshipper. | This thine appropriate food is here poured out for thee: come, hasten forward. drink of it, || 13. Press out the Soma juice, ye priests, for Indra borne upon his car. | The pressing-stones speak loud of Indra, while they shed the juice which, offered, honours him. || 14. To the brown juice may his dear vigorous Bay Steeds bring Indra, to our holy task. | Hither let thy Car-steeds who seek the sacrifice bring thee to our drink-offerings. || 15. Pūṣhan, the Lord of ample wealth, for firm alliance we elect. | May he with wisdom, Śakra! Looser! Much-invoked! aid us to riches and to seed. || 16. Sharpen us like a razor in the barber's hands: send riches thou who settest free. | Easy to find with thee are treasures of the Dawn for mortal man whom thou dost speed. || 17. Pūṣhan, I long to win thy love, I long to praise thee, Radiant God. | Excellent Lord, 'tis strange tome, no wish have I to sing the psalm that Pajra sings. || 18. My kine, O Radiant God, seek pasture where they will, my during wealth, Immortal One. | Be our protector, Pūṣhan! be, most liberal Lord, propitious to our gathering strength. || 19. Rich was the gift Kuruṅga gave, a hundred steeds at morning rites. | Among the gifts of Turvaśas we thought of him, the opulent, the splendid King. || 20. What by his morning songs Kaṇva, the powerful, hath, with the Priyamedhas, gained — | 71 The herds of sixty thousand pure and spotless kine, have I, the Ṛishi, driven away. || 21. The very trees were joyful at my coming: kine they obtained in plenty, steeds in plenty.

Hymn 8:5. Aśvins.

1. When, even as she were present here, red Dawn hath shone from far away, | She spreadeth light on every side. || 2. Like Heroes on your will-yoked car far-shining, Wonder-Workers! ye | Attend, O Aśvins, on the Dawn. || 3. By you, O Lords of ample wealth our songs of praise have been observed: | As envoy have I brought the prayer. || 4. Kaṇvas must praise the Aśvins dear to many, making many glad, | Most rich, that they may succour us. || 5. Most liberal, best at winning strength, inciters, Lords of splendour who | Visit the worshipper's abode. || 6. So for devout Sudeva dew with fatness his unfailing mead, | And make it rich for sacrifice. || 7. Hitherward running speedily with horses, as with rapid hawks, | Come, Aśvins, to our song of praise || 8. Wherewith the three wide distances, and all the lights that are in heaven. | Ye traverse, and three times of night. || 9. O Finders of the Day, that we may win us food of kine and wealth, | Open the paths for us to tread. || 10. O Aśvins, bring us wealth in kine, in noble heroes, and in cars: | Bring us the strength that horses give. || 11. Ye Lords of splendour, glorified, ye Wonder-Workers borne on paths | Of gold, drink sweets with Soma juice. || 12. To us, ye Lords of ample wealth, and to our wealth chiefs extend | Wide shelter, ne'er to be assailed. || 13. Come quickly downward to the prayer of people whom ye favour most: | Approach not unto other folk. || 14. Ye Aśvins whom our minds perceive, drink of this lovely gladdening draught, | The meath which we present to you. || 15. Bring riches hither unto us in hundreds and in thousands, source | Of plenteous food, sustaining all. || 16. Verily sages call on you, ye Heroes, in full many a place. | Moved by the priests, O Aśvins, conic. || 17. Men who have trimmed the sacred grass, bringing oblations and prepared, | O Aśvins, are invoking you. || 18. May this our hymn of praise today, most powerful to bring you, be, | O Aśvins, nearest to your hearts. || 19. The skin filled full of savoury meath, laid in the pathway of your car— | O Aśvins, drink ye both therefrom. || 20. For this, ye Lords of ample wealth, bring blessing for our herd, our kine, | Our progeny, and plenteous food. || 21. Ye too unclose to us like doors the strengthening waters of the sky, | And rivers, ye who find the day. || 22. When did the son of' Tugra serve you, Men? Abandoned in the sea, | That with winged steeds your car might fly. || 23. Ye, O Nāsatyas, ministered to Kaṇva with repeated aid, | When cast into the heated pit. || 24. Come near with those most recent aids of yours which merit eulogy, | When I invoke you, Wealthy Gods. || 25. As ye protected Kaṇva erst, Priyamedha and Upastuta, | Atri, Śiñjāra, Aśvins Twain || 26. And Aṃśu in decisive fight, Agastya in the fray for kine. | And, in his battles, Sobhari. || 27. For so much bliss, or even more, O Aśvins, Wealthy Gods, than this, | We pray white singing hymns to you. || 28. Ascend your car with golden seat, O Aśvins, and with reins of gold, | That reaches even to the sky. || 29. Golden is its supporting shaft, the axle also is of gold, | And both the wheels are made of gold. || 30. Thereon, ye Lords of ample wealth, come to us even from afar, | Come ye to this mine eulogy. || 31. From far away ye come to us, Aśvins, enjoying plenteous food | Of Dāsas, O Immortal Ones. || 32. With splendour, riches, and renown, O Aśvins, hither come to us, | Nāsatyas, shining brilliantly. || 33. May dappled horses, steeds who fly with pinions, bring you hitherward | To people skilled in sacrifice. || 34. The wheel delayeth not that car of yours accompanied by song, | That cometh

with a store of food. || 35. Borne on that chariot wrought of gold, with coursers very fleet of foot, | Come, O Nāsatyas, swift as thought. || 36. O Wealthy Gods, ye taste and find the brisk and watchful wild beast good. | Associate wealth with food for us. || 37. As such, O Aśvins, find for me my share of new-presented gifts, | As Kaśu, Chedi's son, gave me a hundred head of buffaloes, and ten thousand kine. || 38. He who hath given me for mine own ten Kings like gold to look upon. | At Chaidya's feet are all the people round about, all those who think upon the shield. || 39. No man, not any, goes upon the path on which the Chedis walk. | No other prince, no folk is held more liberal of gifts than they.

Hymn 8:6. Indra

1. Indra, great in his power and might, and like Parjanya rich in rain, | Is magnified by Vatsa's lauds. || 2. When the priests, strengthening the Son of Holy Law, present their gifts, | Singers with Order's hymn of praiser. || 3. Since Kaṇvas with their lauds have made Indra complete the sacrifice. | Words are their own appropriate arms. || 4. Before his hot displeasure all the peoples, all the men, bow down, | As rivers bow them to the sea. || 5. This power of his shone brightly forth when Indra brought together, like | A skin, the worlds of heaven and earth. || 6. The fiercely-moving Vṛitra's head he severed with his thunderbolt, | His mighty hundred-knotted bolt. || 7. Here are-we sing them loudly forth-our thoughts among-the best of songs. | Even lightnings like the blaze of fire. || 8. When bidden thoughts, spontaneously advancing, glow, and with the stream | Of sacrifice the Kaṇvas shine. || 9. Indra, may we obtain that wealth in horses and in herds of cows, | And prayer that may be noticed first. || 10. I from my Father have received deep knowledge of the Holy Law | I was born like unto the Sun. || 11. After the lore of ancient time I make, like Kaṇva, beauteous songs, | And Indra's self gains strength thereby. || 12. Whatever Ṛishis have not praised thee, Indra, or have lauded thee, | By me exalted wax thou strong. || 13. When his wrath thundered, when he rent Vṛitra to pieces, limb by limb, | He sent the waters to the sea. || 14. Against the Dasyu Śushṇa thou, Indra, didst hurl thy during bolt: | Thou, Dread one, hast a hero's fame. || 15. Neither the heavens nor firmaments nor regions of the earth contain | Indra, the Thunderer with his might. || 16. O Indra him who lay at length staying thy copious waters thou, | In his own footsteps, smotest down || 17. Thou hiddest deep in darkness him, O Indra, who had set his grasp | On spacious heaven and earth conjoined. || 18. Indra, whatever Yatis and Bhṛigus have offered praise to thee, | Listen, thou Mighty, to my call. || 19. Indra, these spotted cows yield thee their butter and the milky draught; | Aiders, thereby, of sacrifice; || 20. Which, teeming, have received thee as a life-germ, Indra, with their mouth, | Like Sūrya who sustaineth all. || 21. O Lord of Might, with hymns of praise the Kaṇvas have increased thy power, | The drops poured forth have strengthened thee. || 22. Under thy guidance, Indra, mid thy praises, Lord of Thunder, shall | The sacrifice be soon performed. || 23. Indra, disclose much food for us, like a stronghold with store of kine: | Give progeny and heroic strength. || 24. And, Indra, grant us all that wealth of fleet steeds which shone bright of old | Among the tribes of Nahushas. || 25. Hither thou seemest to attract heaven's fold which shines before our eyes, | When, Indra, thou art kind to us. || 26. Yea, when thou puttest forth thy power, Indra, thou governest the folk. | Mighty, unlimited in strength. || 27. The tribes who bring oblations call to thee, to thee to give them help, | With drops to thee who spreadest far. || 28. There where the mountains downward slope, there by the meeting of the streams | The Sage was manifest with song. || 29. Thence, marking, from his lofty place downward he looks upon the sea, | And thence with rapid stir he moves. || 30. Then, verify, they see the light refulgent of primeval seed, | Kindled on yonder side of heaven. || 31. Indra, the Kaṇvas all exalt thy wisdom and thy manly power, | And, Mightiest! thine heroic strength. || 32. Accept this eulogy of mine, Indra, and guard me carefully: | Strengthen my thought and prosper it. || 33. For thee, O Mighty, Thunder-armed, we singers through devotion have | Fashioned the hymn that we may live. || 34. To Indra have the Kaṇvas sung, like waters speeding down a slope: | The song is fain to go to him. || 35. As rivers swell the ocean, so our hymns of praise make Indra strong, | Eternal, of resistless wrath. || 36. Come with thy lovely Bay Steeds, come to us from regions far away | O Indra, drink this Soma juice. || 37. Best slayer of Vṛitras, men whose sacred grass is ready trimmed | Invoke thee for the gain of spoil. || 38. The heavens and earth come after thee as the wheel follows Etaśa: | To thee flow Soma-drops effused. || 39. Rejoice, O Indra, in the light, rejoice in Śaryaṇāvat, be Glad in the sacrificer's hymn. || 40. Grown strong in heaven, the Thunder-armed hath bellowed, Vṛitra-slayer, Bull, | Chief drinker of the Soma juice. || 41. Thou art a Ṛishi born of old, sole Ruler over all by might: | Thou, Indra, guardest well our wealth. || 42. May thy Bay Steeds with beauteous backs, a hundred, bring thee to the feast, | Bring thee to these our Soma-draughts. || 43. The Kaṇvas with their hymns of praise have magnified this ancient thought | That swells with streams of meath and oil. || 44. Mid mightiest Gods let mortal man choose Indra at the sacrifice, | Indra, whoe'er would win, for help. || 45. Thy steeds, by Priyamedhas praised, shall bring thee, God whom all invoke, | Hither to drink the Soma juice. || 46. A hundred thousand have I gained from Parśu, from Tirindira, | And presents of the Yādavas. || 47. Ten thousand head of kine, and steeds three times a hundred they bestowed | On Pajra for the Sāman-song. || 48. Kakuha hath reached up to heaven, bestowing buffaloes yoked in fours, | And matched in fame the Yādavas.

Hymn 8:7. Marutas.

1. O Marutas, when the sage hath poured the Trishṭubh forth as food for you, | Ye shine amid the mountain-clouds. || 2. When, Bright Ones, fain to show your might ye have determined on your course, | The mountain-clouds have bent them down. || 3. Loud roaring with the winds the Sons of Pṛiśni have upraised themselves: | They have poured out the streaming food. || 4. The Marutas spread the mist abroad and make mountains rock and reel, | When with the winds they go their way || 5. What time the rivers and the hills before your coming bowed them down, | So to sustain your mighty force. || 6. We call on you for aid by night, on you for succour in the day, | On you while sacrifice proceeds. || 7. These, verily, wondrous, red of hue, speed on their courses with a roar | Over the ridges of the sky. || 8. With might they drop the loosened rein so that the Sun may run his course, | And spread themselves with beams of light. || 9. Accept, ye Marutas, this my song, accept ye this mine hymn of praise, | Accept, Ṛibhukshans, this my call. || 10. The dappled Cows have poured three lakes, meath for the Thunder-wielding God, | From the great cask, the watery cloud. || 11. O Marutas, quickly come to us when, longing for felicity, | We call you hither from the sky. || 12. For, Rudras and Ṛibhukshans, ye, Most Bountiful, are in the house, | Wise when the gladdening draught is drunk. || 13. O Marutas, send us down from heaven riches distilling rapturous joy, | With plenteous food, sustaining all. || 14. When, Bright Ones, hither from the hills ye have resolved to take your way, | Ye revel in the drops effused. || 15. Man should solicit with his lauds happiness which belongs to them, | So great a band invincible. || 16. They who like fiery sparks with showers of rain blow through the heaven and earth, | Milking the spring that never fails. || 17. With chariots and tumultuous roar, with tempests and with hymns of praise | The Sons of Pṛiśni hurry forth. || 18. For wealth, we think of that whereby ye aided Yadu, Turvaśa, | And Kaṇva who obtained the spoil. || 19. May these our viands Bounteous Ones I that flow in streams like holy oil, | With Kaṇva's hymns, increase your might. || 20. Where, Bounteous Lords for whom the grass is trimmed, are ye rejoicing now? | What Brahman is adoring you? || 21. Is it not there where ye of old, supplied with sacred grass, for lauds | Inspired the strong in sacrifice? || 22. They brought together both the worlds, the mighty waters, and the Sun, | And, joint by joint, the thunderbolt. || 23. They sundered Vṛitra limb from limb and split the gloomy mountain-clouds, | Performing a heroic deed. || 24. They reinforced the power and strength of Trita as he fought, and helped | Indra in battle with the foe. || 25. They deck themselves for glory, bright, celestial, lightning in their hands, | And helms of gold upon their heads. || 26. When eagerly ye from far away came to the cavern of the Bull, | He bellowed in his fear like Heaven. || 27. Borne by your golden-footed steeds, O Gods, come hither to receive | The sacrifice we offer you. || 28. When the red leader draws along their spotted deer yoked to the car. | The Bright Ones come, and shed the rain. || 29. Sushoma, Śaryaṇāvat, and Ārjīka full of homes, have they. | These Heroes, sought with downward car. || 30. When, Marutas, ye come to him, the singer who invokes you thus, | With favours to your suppliant? || 31. What now? where have ye still a friend since ye left Indra all alone? | Who counteth on your friendship now? || 32. The Kaṇvas sing forth Agni's praise together with our Marutas' who | Wield thunder

and wear swords of gold. || 33. Hither for new felicity may I attract the Impetuous Ones, | The Heroes with their wondrous strength || 34. Before them sink the very hills deeming themselves abysses: yea, | Even the mountains bend them down. || 35. Steeds flying on their tortuous path through mid-air carry them, and give | The man who lauds them strength and life. || 36. Agni was born the first of all, like Sūrya lovely with his light: | With lustre these have spread abroad.

Hymn 8:8. Aśvins.

1. With all the succours that are yours, O Aśvins, hither come to us: | Wonderful, borne on paths of gold, drink ye the meath with Soma juice. || 2. Come now, ye Aśvins, on your car decked with a sun-bright canopy, | Bountiful, with your golden forms, Sages with depth of intellect. || 3. Come hither from the Nahushas, come, drawn by pure hymns, from mid-air. | O Aśvins, drink the savoury juice shed in the Kaṇvas' sacrifice. || 4. Come to us hither from the heavens, come from mid-air, well-loved by us: | Here Kaṇva's son hath pressed for you the pleasant meath of Soma juice. || 5. Come, Aśvins, to give car to us, to drink the Soma, Aśvins, come. | Hail, Strengtheners of the praise-song speed onward, ye Heroes, with your thoughts. || 6. As, Heroes, in the olden time the Ṛishis called you to their aid, | So now, O Aśvins, come to us, come near to this mine eulogy. || 7. Even from the luminous sphere of heaven come to us, ye who find the light, | Carers for Vatsa, through our prayers and lauds, O ye who hear our call. || 8. Do others more than we adore the Aśvins with their hymns of praise? | The Ṛishi Vatsa, Kaṇva's son, hath magnified you with his songs. || 9. The holy singer with his hymns hath called you, Aśvins, hither-ward; | Best Vṛitra-slayers, free from stain, as such bring us felicity. || 10. What time, ye Lords of ample wealth, the Lady mounted on your car, | Then, O ye Aśvins, ye attained all wishes that your hearts desired. || 11. Come thence, O Aśvins, on your car that hath a thousand ornaments: | Vatsa the sage, the sage's son, hath sung a song of sweets to you. || 12. Cheerers of many, rich in goods, discoverers of opulence, | The Aśvins, Riders through the sky, have welcomed this my song of praise. || 13. O Aśvins, grant us all rich gifts wherewith no man may interfere. | Make us observe the stated times: give us not over to reproach. || 14. Whether, Nāsatyas, ye be nigh, or whether ye be far away, | Come thence, O Aśvins, on your car that hath a thousand ornaments. || 15. Vatsa the Ṛishi with his songs, Nāsatyas, hath exalted you: | Grant him rich food distilling oil, graced with a thousand ornaments. || 16. Bestow on him, O Aśvins, food that strengthens, and that drops with oil, | On him who praises you for bliss, and, Lords of bounty, prays for wealth. || 17. Come to us, ye who slay the foe, Lords of rich treasure, to this hymn. | O Heroes, give us high renown and these good things of earth for help. || 18. The Priyamedhas have invoked you with all succours that are yours, | You, Aśvins, Lords of solemn rites, with calls entreating you to come. || 19. Come to us, Aśvins, ye Who bring felicity, auspicious Ones, | To Vatsa who with prayer and hymn, lovers of song, hath honoured you. || 20. Aid us, O Heroes, for those hymns for which ye helped Gośarya erst, | Gave Vaśa, Daśavraja aid, and Kaṇva and Medhātithi: || 21. And favoured Trasadasyu, ye Heroes, in spoil-deciding fray: | For these, O Aśvins, graciously assist us in acquiring strength. || 22. O Aśvins, may pure hymns of ours, and songs and praises, honour you: | Best slayers everywhere of foes, as such we fondly yearn for you. || 23. Three places of the Aśvins, erst concealed, are made apparent now. | Both Sages, with the flight of Law come hither unto those who live.

Hymn 8:9. Aśvins.

1. To help and favour Vatsa now, O Aśvins, come ye hitherward. | Bestow on him a dwelling spacious and secure, and keep malignities away. || 2. All manliness that is in heaven, with the Five Tribes, or in mid-air, | Bestow, ye Aśvins, upon us. || 3. Remember Kaṇva first of all among the singers, Aśvins, who | Have thought upon your wondrous deeds. || 4. Aśvins, for you with song of praise this hot oblation is effused, | This your sweet Soma juice, ye Lords of ample wealth, through which ye think upon the foe. || 5. Whatever ye have done in floods, in the tree, Wonder-Workers, and in growing plants, | Therewith, O Aśvins, succour me. || 6. What force, Nāsatyas, ye exert, whatever, Gods, ye tend and heal, | This your own Vatsa gains not by his hymns alone: ye visit him who offers gifts. || 7. Now hath the Ṛishi splendidly thought out the Aśvins' hymn of praise. | Let the Atharvan pour the warm oblation forth, and Soma very rich in sweets. || 8. Ye Aśvins, now ascend your car that lightly rolls upon its way. | May these my praises make you speed hitherward like a cloud of heaven. || 9. When, O Nāsatyas, we this day make you speed hither with our hymns, | Or, Aśvins, with our songs of praise, remember Kaṇva specially. || 10. As erst Kakshīvant and the Ṛishi Vyaśva, as erst Dīrghatamas invoked your presence, | Or, in the sacrificial chambers, Vainya Pṛithi, so be ye mindful of us here, O Aśvins. || 11. Come as home-guardians, saving us from foemen, guarding our living creatures and our bodies, | Come to the house to give us seed and offspring, || 12. Whether with Indra ye be faring, Aśvins, or resting in one dwelling-place with Vāyu, | In concord with the Ṛibhus or Ādityas, or standing still in Vishṇu's striding-places. || 13. When I, O Aśvins, call on you today that I may gather strength, | Or as all-conquering might in war, be that the Aśvins' noblest grace. || 14. Now come, ye Aśvins, hitherward: here are oblations set for you; | These Soma-draughts to aid Yadu and | Turvaśa, these offered you mid Kaṇva's Sons. || 15. Whatever healing balm is yours, Nāsatyas, near or far away, | Therewith, great Sages, grant a home to Vatsa and to Vimada. || 16. Together with the Goddess, with the Aśvins' Speech have I awoke. | Thou, Goddess, hast disclosed the hymn, and holy gift from mortal men. || 17. Awake the Aśvins, Goddess Dawn! Up Mighty Lady of sweet strains! | Rise, straightway, priest of sacrifice! High glory to the gladdening draught! || 18. Thou, Dawn, approaching with thy light shinest together with the Sun, | And to this man-protecting home the chariot of the Aśvins comes. || 19. When yellow stalks give forth the juice, as cows from udders pour their milk, | And voices sound the song of praise, the Aśvins' worshippers show first. || 20. Forward for glory and for strength, protection that shall conquer men, | And power and skill, most sapient Ones! || 21. When Aśvins, worthy of our lauds, ye seat you in the father's house. | With wisdom or the bliss ye bring.

Hymn 8:10. Aśvins.

1. Whether ye travel far away or dwell in yonder light of heaven, | Or in a mansion that is built above the sea, come thence, ye Aśvins, hitherward. || 2. Or if for Manu ye prepared the sacrifice, remember also Kaṇva's son. | I call Bṛihaspati, Indra, Vishṇu, all the Gods, the Aśvins borne by rapid steeds. || 3. Those Aśvins I invoke who work marvels, brought hither to receive, | With whom our friendship is most famed, and kinship passing that of Gods. || 4. On whom the solemn rites depend, whose worshippers rise without the Sun: | These who foreknow the holy work of sacrifice, and by their Godhead drink the sweets of Soma juice. || 5. Whether ye, Lords of ample wealth, now linger in the cast or west, | With Druhyu, or with Anu, Yadu, Turvaśa, I call you hither; come to me. || 6. Lords of great riches, whether through the firmament ye fly or speed through heaven and earth, | Or with your Godlike natures stand upon your cars, come thence, O Aśvins, hitherward.

Hymn 8:11. Agni.

1. Thou Agni, God mid mortal men, art guard of sacred rites, thou art | To be adored at sacrifice. || 2. O Mighty Agni, thou must be glorified at our festivals, | Bearing our offerings to the Gods. || 3. O Jātavedas Agni, fight and drive our foes afar from us, | Them and their godless enmities. || 4. Thou, Jātavedas, seekest not the worship of a hostile man, | However nigh it be to thee. || 5. We sages, mortals as we are, adore the mighty name of thee, | Immortal Jātavedas' name. || 6. Sages, we call the Sage to help, mortals, we call the God to aid: | We call on Agni with our songs. || 7. May Vatsa draw—thy mind away even from thy loftiest dwelling-place, | Agni, with song that yearns for thee. || 8. Thou art the same in many a place: mid all the people thou art Lord. | In fray and fight we call on thee. || 9. When we are seeking strength we call Agni to help us in the strife, | The giver of rich gifts in war. || 10. Ancient, adorable at sacrifices, Priest from of old, meet for our praise, thou sittest. | Fill full and satisfy thy body, Agni, and win us happiness by offering worship.

Hymn 8:12. Indra.

1. Joy, mightiest Indra, known and marked, sprung most from Soma-draughts, wherewith | Thou smitest down the greedy fiend, for that we long. || 2. Wherewith thou holpest Adhrigu, the great Daśagva, and the God | Who stirs the sunlight, and the sea, for that we long. || 3. Wherewith thou dravest forth like cars Sindhu and all the mighty floods | To go the way ordained by Law, for that we long. || 4. Accept this laud for aid, made pure like oil, thou Caster of the Stone, | Whereby even in a moment thou

hast waxen great. ‖ 5. Be pleased, Song-lover, with this song it flows abundant like the sea. | Indra, with all thy succours thou hast waxen great. ‖ 6. The God who from afar hath sent gifts to maintain our friendship's bond, | Thou. spreading them like rain from heaven, hast waxen great. ‖ 7. The beams that mark him have grown strong, the thunder rests between his arms, | When, like the Sun, he hath increased both Heaven and Earth. ‖ 8. When, Mighty Lord of Heroes, thou didst cat a thousand buffaloes, | Then grew and waxed exceeding great thine Indra-power. ‖ 9. Indra consumeth with the rays of Sūrya the malicious man: | Like Agni conquering the woods, he hath grown strong. ‖ 10. This newest thought of ours that suits the time approaches unto thee: | Serving, beloved in many a place it metes and marks. ‖ 11. The pious germ of sacrifice directly purifies the soul. | By Indra's lauds it waxes great, it metes and marks. ‖ 12. Indra who wins the friend hath spread himself to drink the Soma-draught: | Like worshipper's dilating praise; it metes and marks. ‖ 13. He whom the sages, living men, have gladdened, offering up their hymns, | Hath swelled like oil of sacrifice in Agni's mouth. ‖ 14. Aditi also hath brought forth a hymn for Indra, Sovereign Lord: | The work of sacrifice for help is glorified. ‖ 15. The ministering priests have sung their songs for aid and eulogy: | God, thy Bays turn not from the rite which Law ordains. ‖ 16. If, Indra, thou drink Soma by Vishṇu's or Trita Āptya's side, | Or with the Marutas take delight in flowing drops; ‖ 17. Or, Śakra, if thou gladden thee afar or in the sea of air, | Rejoice thee in this juice of ours, in flowing drops. ‖ 18. Or, Lord of Heroes if thou aid the worshipper who shed; the, juice, | Or him whose laud delights thee, and his flowing drops. ‖ 19. To magnify the God, the God, Indra, yea, Indra for your help, | And promptly end the sacrifice-this have they gained. ‖ 20. With worship, him whom men adore, with Soma, him who drinks it most, | Indra with lauds have they increased this have they gained. ‖ 21. His leadings are with power and might and his instructions manifold: | He gives the worshipper all wealth: this have they gained. ‖ 22. For slaying Vṛitra have the Gods set Indra in the foremost place. | Indra the choral bands have sung, for vigorous strength. ‖ 23. We to the Mighty with our might, with lauds to him who hears our call, | With holy hymns have sung aloud, for vigorous strength. ‖ 24. Not earth, nor heaven, nor firmaments contain the Thunder-wielding God: | They shake before his violent rush and vigorous strength. ‖ 25. What time the Gods, O Indra, get thee foremost in the furious fight, | Then thy two beautiful Bay Steeds carried thee on. ‖ 26. When Vṛitra, stayer of the floods, thou slewest, Thunderer with might, | Then thy two beautiful Bay Steeds carried thee on. ‖ 27. When Vishṇu, through thine energy, strode wide those three great steps of his, | Then thy two beautiful Bay Steeds carried thee on. ‖ 28. When thy two beautiful Bay Steeds grew great and greater day by day, | Even then all creatures that had life bowed down to thee. ‖ 29. When, Indra, all the Marut folk humbly submitted them to thee, | Even then all creatures that had life bowed down to thee. ‖ 30. When yonder Sun, that brilliant light, thou settest in the heaven above, | Even then all creatures that had life bowed down to thee. ‖ 31. To thee, O Indra, with this thought the sage lifts up this eulogy, | Akin and leading as on foot to sacrifice. ‖ 32. When in thine own dear dwelling all gathered have lifted up the voice | Milk-streams at worship's central spot, for sacrifice, ‖ 33. As Priest, O Indra, give us wealth in brave men and good steeds and kine | That we may first remember thee for sacrifice.

Hymn 8:13. Indra.

1. Indra, when Soma juices flow, makes his mind pure and meet for lauds. | He gains the power that brings success, for great is he. ‖ 2. In heaven's first region, in the seat of Gods, is he who brings success, | Most glorious, prompt to save, who wins the water-floods. ‖ 3. Him, to win strength, have I invoked, even Indra mighty for the fray. | Be thou most near to us for bliss, a Friend to aid. ‖ 4. Indra, Song -lover, here for thee the worshipper's libation flows. | Rejoicing in this sacred grass thou shinest forth. ‖ 5. Even now, O Indra, give us that which, pressing juice, we crave of thee. | Bring us wealth manifold which finds the light of heaven. ‖ 6. What time the zealous worshipper hath boldly sung his songs to thee, | Like branches of a tree up-grows what they desire. ‖ 7. Generate songs even as of old, give car unto the singer's call. | Thou for the pious hast grown great at each carouse. ‖ 8. Sweet strains that glorify him play like waters speeding down a slope, | Yea, him who in this song is called the Lord of Heaven; ‖ 9. Yea, who alone is called the Lord, the single Ruler of the folk, | By worshippers seeking aid: may he joy in the draught. ‖ 10. Praise him, the Glorious, skilled in song, Lord of the two victorious Bays: | They seek the worshipper's abode who bows in prayer. ‖ 11. Put forth thy strength: with dappled Steeds come, thou of mighty intellect, | With swift Steeds to the sacrifice, for 'tis thy joy. ‖ 12. Grant wealth to those who praise thee, Lord of Heroes, Mightiest Indra: give | Our princes everlasting fame and opulence. ‖ 13. I call thee when the Sun is risen, I call thee at the noon of day: | With thy car-horses, Indra, come well-pleased to us. ‖ 14. Speed forward hither, come to us, rejoice thee in the milky draught: | Spin out the thread of ancient time, as well is known. ‖ 15. If, Śakra, Vṛitra-slayer, thou be far away or near to us. | Or in the sea, thou art the guard of Soma juice. ‖ 16. Let songs we sing and Soma-drops expressed by us make Indra strong: | The tribes who bring oblations find delight in him. ‖ 17. Him sages longing for his aid, with offerings brought in eager haste, | Him. even as branches, all mankind have made to grow. ‖ 18. At the Trikadrukas the Gods span sacrifice that stirred the mind: | May our songs strengthen him who still hath strengthened us. ‖ 19. When, true to duty, at due times the worshipper offers lauds to thee, | They call him Purifier, Pure, and Wonderful. ‖ 20. That mind of Rudra, fresh and strong, moves conscious in the ancient ways, | With reference whereto the wise have ordered this. ‖ 21. If thou elect to be my Friend drink of this sacrificial juice, | By help whereof we may subdue all enemies. ‖ 22. O Indra, Lover of the song, when shall thy praiser be most blest? | When wilt thou grant us wealth in herds of kine and steeds? ‖ 23. And thy two highly-lauded Bays, strong stallions, draw thy car who art | Untouched by age, most gladdening car for which we pray. ‖ 24. With ancient offerings we implore the Young and Strong whom many praise. | He from of old hath sat upon dear sacred grass. ‖ 25. Wax mighty, thou whom many laud for aids which Ṛishis have extolled. | Pour down for us abundant food and guard us well. ‖ 26. O Indra, Caster of the Stone, thou helpest him who praises thee: | From sacrifice I send to thee a mind-yoked hymn. ‖ 27. Here, yoking for the Soma-draught these Horses, sharers of thy feast, | Thy Bay Steeds, Indra, fraught with wealth, consent to come. ‖ 28. Attendants on thy glory, let the Rudras roar assent to thee, | And all the Marut companies come tithe feast. ‖ 29. These his victorious followers bold in the heavens the place they love, | Leagued in the heart of sacrifice, as well we know. ‖ 30. That we may long behold the light, what time the ordered rite proceeds, | He duly measures, as he views, the sacrifice. ‖ 31. O Indra, strong is this thy car, and strong are these Bay Steeds of thine: | O Śatakratu, thou art strong, strong is our call. ‖ 32. Strong is the press-stone, strong thy joy, strong is the flowing Soma juice: | Strong is the rite thou furtherest, strong is our call. ‖ 33. As strong I call on thee the Strong, O Thunderer with thy thousand aids: | For thou hast won the hymn of praise. Strong is our call.

Hymn 8:14. Indra.

1. If I, O Indra, were, like thee, the single Sovereign of all wealth, | My worshipper should be rich in kine. ‖ 2. I should be fain, O Lord of Power, to strengthen and enrich the sage, | Were I the Lord of herds of kine. ‖ 3. To worshippers who press the juice thy goodness, Indra, is a cow | Yielding in plenty kine and steeds. ‖ 4. None is there, Indra, God or man, to hinder thy munificence, | The wealth which, lauded, thou wilt give. ‖ 5. The sacrifice made Indra strong when he unrolled the earth, and made | Himself a diadem in heaven. ‖ 6. Thine aid we claim, O Indra, thine who after thou hast waxen great | Hast won all treasures for thine own. ‖ 7. In Soma's ecstasy Indra spread the firmament and realms of light, | When he cleft Vala limb from limb. ‖ 8. Showing the hidden he drave forth the cows for the Aṅgirasas, | And Vala he cast headlong down. ‖ 9. By Indra were the luminous realms of heaven established and secured, | Firm and immovable from their place. ‖ 10. Indra, thy laud moves quickly like a joyous wave of water-floods: | Bright shine the drops that gladden thee. ‖ 11. For thou, O Indra, art the God whom hymns and praises magnify: | Thou blessest those who worship thee. ‖ 12. Let the two long-maned Bay Steeds bring Indra to drink the Soma juice, | The Bountiful to our sacrifice. ‖ 13. With waters' foam thou torest off, Indra, the head of Namuchi, | Subduing all contending hosts. ‖ 14. The Dasyus, when they fain would climb | by magic arts and mount to heaven, | Thou, Indra, castest down to earth. ‖ 15. As Soma-drinker conquering all, thou scatteredst to every side | Their settlement who poured no gifts.

Hymn 8:15. Indra.

1. Sing forth to him whom many men invoke, to him whom many laud. | Invite the powerful Indra with your songs of praise. || 2. Whose lofty might-for doubly strong is he-supports the heavens and earth, | And hills and plains and floods and light with manly power. || 3. Such, Praised by many! thou art King alone thou smitest Vṛitras dead, | To gain, O Indra, spoils of war and high renown. || 4. We sing this strong and wild delight of thine which conquers in the fray, | Which, Caster of the Stone! gives room and shines like gold. || 5. Wherewith thou also foundest lights for Āyu and for Manu's sake: | Now joying in this sacred grass thou beamest forth. || 6. This day too singers of the hymn praise, as of old, this might of thine: | Win thou the waters day by day, thralls of the strong. || 7. That lofty Indra-power of thine, thy strength and thine intelligence, | Thy thunderbolt for which we long, the wish makes keen. || 8. O Indra, Heaven and Earth augment thy manly power and thy renown; | The waters and thy mountains stir and urge thee on. || 9. Vishṇu the lofty ruling Power, Varuṇa, Mitra sing thy praise: | In thee the Marutas' company have great delight. || 10. O Indra, thou wast born the Lord of men, most liberal of thy gifts: | Excellent deeds for evermore are all thine own. || 11. Ever, alone, O highly-praised, thou sendest Vṛitras to their rest: | None else than Indra executes the mighty deed. || 12. Though here and there, in varied hymns, Indra, men call on thee for aid, | Still with our heroes fight and win the light of heaven. || 13. Already have all forms of him entered our spacious dwelling-place: | For victory stir thou Indra, up, the Lord of Might.

Hymn 8:16. Indra.

1. Praise Indra whom our songs must laud, sole Sovereign of mankind, the Chief | Most liberal who controlleth men. || 2. In whom the hymns of praise delight, and all the glory-giving songs. | Like the floods' longing for the sea. || 3. Him I invite with eulogy, best King, effective in the fight, | Strong for the gain of mighty spoil. || 4. Whose perfect ecstasies are wide, profound, victorious, and give | joy in the field where heroes win. || 5. Him, when the spoils of war are staked, men call to be their advocate: | They who have Indra win the day. || 6. Men honour him with stirring songs and magnify with solemn rites: | Indra is he who giveth case. || 7. ındra is priest and Ṛishi, he is much invoked by many men, | And mighty by his mighty powers. || 8. Meet to be lauded and invoked, true Hero with his deeds of might, | Victorious even when alone. || 9. The men, the people magnify that Indra with their Sāman songs, | With hymns and sacred eulogies || 10. Him who advances them to wealth, sends light to lead them in the war, | And quells their foemen in the fray. || 11. May he, the saviour much-invoked, may Indra bear us in a ship | Safely beyond all enemies. || 12. As such, O Indra, honour us with gifts of booty, further us, | And lead us to felicity.

Hymn 8:17. Indra.

1. Come, we have pressed the juice for thee; O Indra, drink this Soma here | Sit thou on this my sacred grass. || 2. O Indra, let thy long-maned Bays, yoked by prayer, bring thee hitherward | Give car and listen to our prayers. || 3. We Soma-bearing Brahmans call thee Soma-drinker with thy friend, | We, Indra, bringing Soma juice. || 4. Come unto us who bring the juice, come unto this our eulogy, | Fair-visored! drink thou of the juice. || 5. I pour it down within thee, so through all thy members let it spread: | Take with. thy tongue the pleasant drink. || 6. Sweet to thy body let it be, delicious be the savoury juice: | Sweet be the Soma to thine heart. || 7. Like women, let this Soma-draught, invested with its robe, approach, | O active Indra, close to thee. || 8. Indra, transported with the juice, vast in his bulk, strong in his neck | And stout arms, smites the Vṛitras down. || 9. O Indra, go thou forward, thou who rulest over all by might: | Thou Vṛitra-slayer slay the fiends, || 10. Long be thy grasping-hook wherewith thou givest ample wealth to him | Who sheds the juice and worships thee. || 11. Here, Indra, is thy Soma-draught, made pure upon the sacred grass: | Run hither, come and drink thereof. || 12. Famed for thy radiance, worshipped well this juice is shed for thy delight | Thou art invoked, Ākhaṇḍala! || 13. To Kuṇḍapāyya, grandson's son, grandson of Śṛiṅgavṛiṣh! to thee, | To him have I addressed my thought. || 14. Strong pillar thou, Lord of the home armour of Soma-offerers: | The drop of Soma breaketh all the strongholds down, and Indra is the Ṛishis' Friend. || 15. Holy Pṛidākusānu, winner of the spoil, one eminent o'er many men, | Lead on the wild horse Indra with his vigorous grasp forward to drink the Soma juice.

Hymn 8:18. Ādityas.

1. Now let the mortal offer prayer to win the unexampled grace | Of these Ādityas and their aid to cherish life. || 2. For not an enemy molests the paths which these Ādityas tread: | Infallible guards, they strengthen us in happiness. || 3. Now soon may Bhaga, Savitar, Varuṇa, Mitra, Aryaman | Give us the shelter widely spread which we implore. || 4. With Gods come thou whose fostering care none checks, O Goddess Aditi: | Come, dear to many, with the Lords who guard us well. || 5. For well these Sons of Aditi know to keep enmities aloof, | Unrivalled, giving ample room, they save from woe. || 6. Aditi guard our herd by day, Aditi, free from guile, by night, | Aditi, ever strengthening, save us from grief! || 7. And in the day our hymn is this: May Aditi come nigh to help, | With loving-kindness bring us weal and chase our foes. || 8. And may the Aśvins, the divine Pair of Physicians, send us health: | May they remove iniquity and chase our foes. || 9. May Agni bless us with his fires, and Sūrya warm us pleasantly: | May the pure Wind breathe sweet on us, and chase our foes. || 10. Drive ye disease and strife away, drive ye away malignity: | Ādityas, keep us ever far from sore distress. || 11. Remove from us the arrow, keep famine, Ādityas! far away: | Keep enmities afar from us, Lords of all wealth! || 12. Now, O Ādityas, grant to us the shelter that lets man go free, | Yea, even the sinner from his sin, ye Bounteous Gods ı || 13. Whatever mortal with the power of demons fain would injure us, | May he, impetuous, suffer harm by his own deeds. || 14. May sin o'ertake our human foe, the man who speaketh evil thing, | Him who would cause our misery, whose heart is false. || 15. Gods, ye are with the simple ones, ye know each mortal in your hearts; | Ye, Vasus, well discriminate the false and true. || 16. Fain would we have the sheltering aid of mountains and of water-floods: | Keep far from us iniquity, O Heaven and Earth. || 17. So with auspicious sheltering aid do ye, O Vasus, carry us | Beyond all trouble and distress, borne in your ship. || 18. Ādityas, ye Most Mighty Ones, grant to our children and their seed | Extended term of life that they may live long days. || 19. Sacrifice, O Ādityas, is your inward monitor: be kind, | For in the bond of kindred we are bound to you. || 20. The Marutas' high protecting aid, the Aśvins, and the God who saves, | Mitra and Varuṇa for weal we supplicate. || 21. Grant us a home with triple guard, Aryaman, Mitra, Varuṇa! | Unthreatened, Marutas! meet for praise, and filled with men. || 22. And as we human beings, O Ādityas, are akin to death, | Graciously lengthen ye our lives that we may live.

Hymn 8:19. Agni.

1. Sing praise to him, the Lord of Light. The Gods have made the God to be their messenger, | And sent oblation to Gods. || 2. Agni, the Bounteous Giver, bright with varied flames, laud thou, O singer Sobhari— | Him who controls this sacred food with Soma blent, who hath first claim to sacrifice. || 3. Thee have we chosen stillest in sacrifice, Immortal Priest among the Gods, | Wise finisher of this holy rite: || 4. The Son of Strength, the blessed, brightly shining One, Agni whose light is excellent. | May be by sacrifice win us in heaven the grace of Mitra, Varuṇa, and the Floods. || 5. The mortal who hath ministered to Agni with oblation, fuel, ritual lore, | And reverence, skilled in sacrifice. || 6. Verily swift to run are his fleet-footed steeds, and most resplendent fame is his. | No trouble caused by Gods or wrought by mortal man from any side o'ertaketh him. || 7. May we by thine own fires be well supplied with fire, O Son of Strength, O Lord of Might: | Thou as our Friend hast worthy men. || 8. Agni, who praises like a guest of friendly mind, is as a car that brings us gear. | Also in thee is found perfect security thou art the Sovereign Lord of wealth. || 9. That man, moreover, merits praise who brings, auspicious Agni, sacrificial gifts | May he win riches by his thoughts. || 10. He for whose sacrifice thou standest up erect is prosperous and rules o'er men. | He wins with coursers and with singers killed in song: with heroes he obtains the prize. || 11. He in whose dwelling Agni is chief ornament, and, all-desired, loves his laud well, | And zealously tends his offerings— || 12. His, or the lauding sage's word, his, Son of Strength! who Is most prompt with sacred gifts, | Set thou beneath the Gods, Vasu, above mankind, the speech of the intelligent. || 13. He who with sacrificial gifts or homage bringeth very skilful Agni nigh, | Or him who flashes fast with song, || 14. The mortal who with blazing fuel, as his laws command, adores the Perfect God, | Blest with his thoughts in splendour shall exceed all men, as though he overpassed the floods. || 15.

Give us the splendour, Agni, which may overcome each greedy fiend in our abode, | The wrath of evil-hearted folk. || 16. That, wherewith Mitra, Varuṇa, and Aryaman, the Aśvins, Bhaga give us light, | That may we, by thy power finding best furtherance, worship, O Indra, helped by thee. || 17. O Agni, most devout are they, the sages who have set thee Sage exceeding wise, | O God, for men to look upon: || 18. Who have arranged thine altar Blessed God, at morn brought thine oblation, pressed the juice. | They by their deeds of strength have won diem, mighty wealth, who have set all their hope in thee. || 19. -May Agni worshipped bring us bliss, may the gift, Blessed One, and sacrifice bring bliss; | Yea, may our praises bring us bliss. || 20. Show forth the mind that brings success in war with fiends, wherewith thou conquerest in fight. | Bring down the many firm hopes of our enemies, and let us vanquish with thine aid. || 21. I praise with song the Friend of man, whom Gods sent down to be herald and messenger, | Best worshipper, bearer of our gifts. || 22. Thou unto sharp-toothed Agni, Young and Radiant God, proclaimest with thy song the feast— | Agni, who for our sweet strains moulds heroic strength when sacred oil is offered him, || 23. While, served with sacrificial oil, now upward and now downward Agni moves his sword, | As doth the Asura his robe. || 24. The God, the Friend of man, who bears our gifts to heaven, the God with his sweet-smelling mouth, | Distributes, skilled in sacrifice, his precious things, Invoking Priest, Immortal God. || 25. Son of Strength, Agni, if thou wert the mortal, bright as Mitra, I worshipped with our gifts! | And I were the Immortal God || 26. I would not give thee up, Vasu, to calumny, or misery, O Bounteous One. | My worshipper should feel no hunger or distress, nor, Agni, should he live in sin. || 27. Like a son cherished in his father's house, let our oblation rise unto the Gods. || 28. With thine immediate aid may I, excellent Agni, ever gain my wish | A mortal with a God to help. || 29. O Agni, by thy wisdom, by thy bounties, by thy leading may I gather wealth. | Excellent Agni, thou art called my Providence: delight thou to be liberal. || 30. Agni, he conquers by thine aid that brings him store of noble heroes and great strength, | Whose bond of friendship is thy choice. || 31. Thy spark is black and crackling, kindled in due time, O Bounteous, it is taken up. | Thou art the dear Friend of the mighty Mornings: thou shinest in glimmerings of the night. || 32. We Sobharis have come to him, for succour, who is good to help with thousand powers, | The Sovereign, Trasadasyu's Friend. || 33. O Agni, thou on whom all other fires depend, as branches on the parent stem, | I make the treasures of the folk, like songs, mine own, while I exalt thy sovereign might. || 34. The mortal whom, Ādityas, ye, guileless, lead to the farther bank | Of all the princes, Bounteous Ones || 35. Whoe'er he be, Man-ruling Kings! the Regent of the race of men— | May we, O Mitra, Varuṇa, and Aryaman, like him be furtherers of your law. || 36. A gift of fifty female slaves hath Trasadasyu given me, Purukutsa's son, | Most liberal, kind, lord of the brave. || 37. And Śyāva too for me led forth a strong steed at Suvāstu's ford: | A herd of three times seventy kine, good lord of gifts, he gave to me.

Hymn 8:20. Marutas.

1. Let none, Swift Travellers! check you: come hither, like-spirited, stay not far away, | Ye benders even of what is firm. || 2. Marutas, Ṛibhukṣhans, Rudras come ye with your cars strong-fellied and exceeding bright. | Come, ye for whom we long, with food, to sacrifice, come ye with love to Sobhari. || 3. For well we know the vigorous might of Rudra's Sons, the Marutas, who are passing strong, | Swift Vishṇu's band, who send the rain. || 4. Islands are bursting forth and misery is stayed: the heaven and earth are joined in one. | Decked with bright rings, ye spread the broad expanses out, when ye, Self-luminous, stirred yourselves. || 5. Even things immovable shake and reel, the mountains and the forest trees at your approach, | And the earth trembles as ye come. || 6. To lend free course, O Marutas, to your furious rush, heaven high and higher still gives way, | Where they, the Heroes mighty with their arms, display their gleaming ornaments on their forms. || 7. After their Godlike nature they, the bull. like Heroes, dazzling and impetuous, wear | Great splendour as they show erect. || 8. The pivot of the Sobharis' chariot within the golden box is balmed with milk. | May they the Well-born, Mighty, kindred of the Cow, aid us to food and to delight. || 9. Bring, ye who sprinkle balmy drops. oblations to your vigorous Marut company, | To those whose leader is the Bull. || 10. Come hither, O ye Mares, on your strong-horsed car, solid in look, with solid naves. | Lightly like winged falcons, O ye Heroes, come, come to enjoy our offerings || 11. Their decoration is the same: their ornaments of gold are bright upon their arms; | Their lances glitter splendidly. || 12. They toil not to defend their bodies from attack, strong Heroes with their mighty arms. | Strong are your bows and strong the weapons in your cars, and glory sits on every face. || 13. Whose name extendeth like a sea, alone, resplendent, so that all have joy in it, | And life-power like ancestral might. || 14. Pay honour to these Marutas and sing praise to them, for of the wheel-spokes of the car | Of these loud roarers none is last: this is their power, this moves them to give mighty gifts. || 15. Blest by your favouring help was he, O Marutas, at the earlier flushings of the morn, | And even now shall he be blest. || 16. The strong man to whose sacrifice, O Heroes, ye approach that ye may taste thereof, | With glories and with war that winneth spoil shall gain great bliss, ye Shakers of the world. || 17. Even as Rudra's Sons, the brood of the Creator Dyaus, the Asura, desire, | O Youthful Ones, so shall it be: || 18. And these the bounteous, worthy of the Marutas who move onward pouring down the rain— | Even for their sake, O Youthful Ones, with kindest heart take us to you to be your own. || 19. O Sobhari, with newest song sing out unto the youthful purifying Bulls, | Even as a plougher to his steers. || 20. Who, like a celebrated boxer, overcome the challengers in every fight: | They who, like shining bulls, are most illustrious-honour those Marutas with thy song. || 21. Allied by common ancestry, ye Marutas, even the Cows, alike in energy, | Lick, all by turns, each other's head. || 22. Even mortal man, ye Dancers breast adorned with gold, attains to brotherhood with you. | Mark ye and notice us, O Marutas; evermore your friendship is secured to us. || 23. O Marutas, rich in noble gifts, bring us a portion of the Marutas' medicine, | Ye Coursers who are Friends to us. || 24. Haters of those who serve you not, bliss-bringers, bring us bliss with those auspicious aids | Wherewith ye are victorious and guard Sindhu well, and succour Krivi in his need. || 25. Marutas, who rest on fair trimmed grass, what balm soever Sindhu or Asiknī hath, | Or mountains or the seas contain. || 26. Ye carry on your bodies, ye who see it all: so bless us graciously therewith. | Cast, Marutas, to the ground our sick man's malady: replace the dislocated limb.

Hymn 8:21. Indra.

1. We call on thee, O Matchless One! We seeking help, possessing nothing firm ourselves, | Call on thee wonderful in fight || 2. On thee for aid in sacrifice. This youth of ours, the bold, the mighty, hath gone forth. | We therefore, we thy friends, Indra, have chosen thee, free-giver, as our Guardian God. || 3. Come hither, for the drops are here, O Lord of corn-lands. Lord of horses, Lord of kine: | Drink thou the Soma, Soma's Lord! || 4. For we the kinless singers have drawn hither thee, O Indra, who hast numerous kin. | With all the forms thou hast, comic thou of bull-like strength, come near to drink the Soma juice. || 5. Sitting like birds beside thy meath, mingled with milk, that gladdeneth and exalteth thee, | Indra, to thee we sing aloud. || 6. We speak to thee with this our reverential prayer. Why art thou pondering yet awhile? | Here are our wishes; thou art liberal, Lord of Bays: we and our hymns are present here. || 7. For not in recent times alone, O Indra, Thunder-armed, have we obtained thine aid. | Of old we knew thy plenteous wealth. || 8. Hero, we knew thy friendship and thy rich rewards: these, Thunderer, now we crave of thee. | O Vasu, for all wealth that cometh of the kine, sharpen our powers, fair-visored God. || 9. Him who of old hath brought to us this and that blessing, him I magnify for you, | Even Indra, O my friends, for help || 10. Borne by Bay Steeds, the Lord of heroes, ruling men, for it is he who takes; delight. | May Maghavan bestow on us his worshippers hundreds of cattle and of steeds. || 11. Hero, may we, with thee for Friend, withstand the man who pants against us in his wrath, | In fight with people rich in kine. || 12. May we be victors in the singer's battle-song, and meet the wicked, Much invoked! | With heroes smite the foeman and show forth our strength. O Indra, further thou our thoughts. || 13. O Indra, from all ancient time rival-less ever and companionless art thou: | Thou seekest comradeship in war. || 14. Thou findest not the wealthy man to be thy friend: those scorn thee who are flown with wine. | What time thou thunderest and gatherest, then thou, even as a Father, art invoked. || 15. O Indra, let us not, like fools who waste their lives at home, with friendship such as thine | Sit idly by the poured-out juice. || 16. Giver of kine, may we not miss thy gracious gifts: let us not

rob thee of thine own. | Strip even the strong places of the foe, and bring: thy gifts can never be made vain. || 17. Indra or blest Sarasvatī alone bestows such wealth, treasure so great, or thou, | O Chitra, on the worshipper. || 18. Chitra is King, and only kinglings are the rest who dwell beside Sarasvatī. | He, like Parjanya with his rain, hath spread himself with thousand, yea, with myriad gifts.

Hymn 8:22. Aśvins.

1. Hitherward have I called today, for succour, that most wondrous car | Which ye ascended, Aśvins, ye whose paths are red, swift to give Car, for Sūrya's sake. || 2. Car ever young, much longed-for, easily invoked, soon guided, first in deeds of might, | Which waits and serves, O Sobhari, with benevolence, without a rival or a foe. || 3. These Aśvins with our homage, these Two Omnipresent Deities | Hitherward will we bring for kind help, these who seek the dwelling of the worshipper. || 4. One of your chariot wheels is moving swiftly round, one speeds for you its onward course. | Like a milch-cow, O Lords of splendour, and with haste let your benevolence come to us. || 5. That chariot of yours which hath a triple seat and reins of gold, | The famous car that traverseth the heaven and earth, thereon Nāsatyas, Aśvins, come. || 6. Ye with your plough, when favouring Manu with your help, ploughed the first harvest in the sky. | As such will we exalt you, Lords of splendour, now, O Aśvins, with our prayer and praise. || 7. Come to us, Lords of ample wealth, by paths of everlasting Law, | Whereby to high dominion ye with mighty strength raised Tṛikṣhi, Trasadasyu's son. || 8. This Soma pressed with stones is yours, ye Heroes, Lords of plenteous wealth. | Approach to drink the Soma, come, drink in the worshipper's abode. || 9. O Aśvins, mount the chariot, mount the golden seat, ye who are Lords of plenteous wealth, | And bring to us abundant food. || 10. The aids wherewith ye helped Paktha and Adhrigu, and Babhru severed from his friends,— | With those, O Aśvins, come hither with speed and soon, and heal whatever is diseased. || 11. When we continually invoke the Aśvins, the resistless, at this time of day, | We lovers of the song, with songs. || 12. Through these, ye Mighty Ones, come hither to my call which brings all blessings, wears all forms,— | Through which, All-present Heroes, lavishest of food ye strengthened Krivi, come through these. || 13. I speak to both of these as such, these Aśvins whom I reverence at this time of day: | With homage we entreat them both. || 14. Ye who are Lords of splendour, ye whose paths are red, at eve, at morn, at sacrifice, | Give us not utterly as prey to mortal foe, ye Rudras, Lords of ample wealth. || 15. For bliss I call. the blissful car, at morn the inseparable Aśvins with their car | I call, like Sobhari our sire. || 16. Rapid as thought, and strong, and speeding to the joy, bringing your swiftly-coming help, | Be to us a protection even from far away Lords of great wealth, with many aids. || 17. Come, Wonder-Workers, to our home, our home, O Aśvins, rich in cattle, steeds, and gold, | Chief drinkers of the Soma's juice || 18. Choice-worthy strength, heroic, firm and excellent, uninjured by the Rakṣhas foe, | At this your coming nigh, ye Lords of ample wealth and all good things, may we obtain.

Hymn 8:23. Agni.

1. Worship thou Jātavedas, pray to him who willingly accepts, | Whose smoke wanders at will, and none may grasp his flame. || 2. Thou, all men's friend, Viśvamanas, exaltest Agni with thy song, | The Giver, and his flames with which no cars contend. || 3. Whose resolute assault, to win vigour and food, deserves our praise,— | Through whose discovering power the priest obtaineth wealth. || 4. Up springs the imperishable flame, the flame of the Refulgent One | Most bright, with glowing jaws and glory in his train. || 5. Skilled in fair sacrifice, extolled, arise in Godlike loveliness, | Shining with lofty splendour, with effulgent light. || 6. Called straight to our oblations, come, O Agni, through our eulogies, | As thou hast been our envoy bearing up our gifts. || 7. I call your Agni, from of old Invoking Priest of living men: | Him with this song I laud and magnify for you. || 8. Whom, wondrous wise, they animate with solemn rites and his fair form, | Kind as a friend to men who keep the holy Law. || 9. Him, true to Law, who perfecteth the sacrifice, Law-loving ones! | Ye with your song have gratified in the place of prayer. || 10. May all our sacrifices go to him the truest Aṅgiras, | Who is among mankind the most illustrious Priest. || 11. Imperishable Agni, thine are all these high enkindled lights, | Like horses and like stallions showing forth their strength. || 12. So give us, Lord of Power and Might, riches combined with hero strength, | And guard us with our sons and grand. sons in our frays. || 13. Soon as the eager Lord of men is friendly unto Manu's race, | Agni averteth from us all the demon host. || 14. O Hero Agni, Lord of men, on hearing this new laud of mine, | Burn down the Rākṣhasas, enchanters, with thy flame. || 15. No mortal foe can e'er prevail by arts of magic over him | Who serveth Agni well with sacrificial gifts. || 16. Vyaśva the sage, who sought the Bull, hath won thee, finder of good things: | As such may we enkindle thee for ample wealth. || 17. Uśanā Kāvya established thee, O Agni, as Invoking Priest: | Thee, Jātavedas, Sacrificing Priest for man. || 18. All Deities of one accord appointed thee their messenger: | Thou, God, through hearing, hadst first claim to sacrifice. || 19. Him may the mortal hero make his own immortal messenger. | Far-spreading, Purifier, him whose path is black. || 20. With lifted ladles let us call him splendid with his brilliant flame, | Men's ancient Agni, wasting not, adorable. || 21. The man who pays the worship due to him with sacrificial gifts | Obtains both plenteous nourishment and hero fame. || 22. To Jātavedas Agni, chief in sacrifices, first of all | With homage goes the ladle rich with sacred gifts. || 23. Even as Vyaśva did, may we with these most high and liberal hymns | Pay worship unto Agni of the splendid flame. || 24. Now sing, as Sthūrayūpa sang, with lands to him who spreadeth far, | To Agni of the home, O Ṛiṣhi, Vyaśva's son. || 25. As welcome guest of human kind, as offspring of the forest kings, | The sages worship ancient Agni for his aid. || 26. For men's oblations brought to him who is the mighty Lord of all, | Sit, Agni, mid our homage, on the sacred grass. || 27. Grant us abundant treasures, grant the opulence which many crave, | With store of heroes, progeny, and high renown. || 28. Agni, Most Youthful of the Gods, send evermore the gift of wealth | Unto Varosuṣhāman and to all his folk. || 29. A mighty Conqueror art thou, O Agni, so disclose to us | Food in our herds of kine and gain of ample wealth. || 30. Thou, Agni, art a glorious God: bring hither Mitra, Varuṇa, | Imperial Sovereigns, holy-minded, true to Law.

Hymn 8:24. Indra.

1. Companions, let us learn a prayer to Indra. whom the thunder arms, | To glorify your bold and most heroic Friend. || 2. For thou by slaying Vṛitra art the Vṛitra-slayer, famed for might. | Thou, Hero, in rich gifts surpassest wealthy chiefs. || 3. As such, when glorified, bring us riches of very wondrous fame, | Set in the highest rank, Wealth-giver, Lord of Bays! || 4. Yea, Indra, thou disclosest that preeminent dear wealth of men: | Boldly, O Bold One, glorified, bring it to us. || 5. The workers of destruction stay neither thy right hand nor thy left: | Nor hosts that press about thee, Lord of Bays, in fight. || 6. O Thunder-armed, I come with songs to thee as to a stall with kine: | Fulfil the wish and thought of him who sings thy praise. || 7. Chief Vṛitra-slayer, through the hymn of Viśvamanas think of all, | All that concerneth us, Excellent, Mighty Guide. || 8. May we, O Vṛitra-slayer, O Hero, find this thy newest boon, Longed-for, and excellent, thou who art much invoked! || 9. O Indra, Dancer, Much-invoked! as thy great power is unsurpassed, | So be thy bounty to the worshipper unchecked. || 10. Most Mighty, most heroic One, for mighty bounty fill thee full. | Though strong, strengthen thyself to win wealth, Maghavan! || 11. O Thunderer, never have our prayers gone forth to any God but thee: | So help us, Maghavan, with thine assistance now. || 12. For, Dancer, verily I find none else for bounty, saving thee, | For splendid wealth and power, thou Lover of the Song. || 13. For Indra pour ye out the drops meath blent with Soma let him drink | With bounty and with majesty will he further us. || 14. I spake to the Bay Coursers' Lord, to him who gives ability: | Now hear the son of Aśva as he praises thee. || 15. Never was any Hero born before thee mightier than thou: | None certainly like thee in goodness and in wealth. || 16. O ministering priest, pour out of the sweet juice what gladdens most: | So is the Hero praised who ever prospers us. || 17. Indra, whom Tawny Coursers bear, praise such as thine, preeminent, | None by his power or by his goodness hath attained. || 18. We, seeking glory, have invoked this Master of all power and might | Who must be glorified by constant sacrifice. || 19. Come, sing we praise to Indra, friends, the Hero who deserves the laud, | Him who with none to aid o'ercomes all tribes of men. || 20. To him who wins the kine, who keeps no cattle back, Celestial God, | Speak wondrous speech more sweet than butter and than meath. || 21. Whose hero powers are measureless, whose bounty ne'er may be surpassed, | Whose liberality,

like light, is over all. || 22. As Vyaśva did, praise Indra, praise the Strong unfluctuating Guide, | Who gives the foe's possessions to the worshipper. || 23. Now, son of Vyaśva, praise thou him who to the tenth time still is new, | The very Wise, whom living men must glorify || 24. Thou knowest, Indra, Thunder-armed, how to avoid destructive powers, | As one secure from pitfalls each returning day. || 25. O Indra, bring that aid wherewith of old, Most Wondrous! thou didst slay | His foes for active Kutsa: send it down to us. || 26. So now we seek thee fresh in might, Most Wonderful in act! for gain: | For thou art he who conquers all our foes for us. || 27. Who will set free from ruinous woe, or Ārya on the Seven Streams: | O valiant Hero, bend the Dāsa's weapon down. || 28. As to Varosushāman thou broughtest great riches, for their gain, | To Vyaśva's sons, Blest Lady, rich in ample wealth! || 29. Let Nārya's sacrificial meed reach Vyaśva's Soma-bearing sons: | In hundreds and in thousands be the great reward. || 30. If one should ask thee, Where is he who sacrificed? Whither lookest thou? | Like Vala he hath passed away and dwelleth now on Gomatī.

Hymn 8:25. Mitra-Varuṇa.

1. I worship you who guard this All, Gods, holiest among the Gods, | You, faithful to the Law, whose power is sanctified. || 2. So, too, like charioteers are they, Mitra and sapient Varuṇa, | Sons high-born from of old, whose holy laws stand fast. || 3. These Twain, possessors of all wealth, most glorious, for supremest sway | Aditi, Mighty Mother, true to Law, brought forth. || 4. Great Varuṇa and Mitra, Gods, Asuras and imperial Lords, | True to Eternal Law proclaim the high decree. || 5. The offspring of a lofty Power, Dakṣha's Two Sons exceeding strong, | Who, Lords of flowing rain, dwell in the place of food. || 6. Ye who have gathered up your gifts, celestial and terrestrial food, | Let your rain come to us fraught with the mist of heaven. || 7. The Twain, who from the lofty sky seem to look down on herds below, | Holy, imperial Lords, are set to be revered. || 8. They, true to Law, exceeding strong, have sat them down for sovereign rule: | Princes whose laws stand fast, they have obtained their sway. || 9. Pathfinders even better than the eye, with unobstructed sight, | Even when they close their lids, observant, they perceive. || 10. So may the Goddess Aditi, may the Nāsatyas guard us well, | The Marutas guard us well, endowed with mighty strength. || 11. Do ye, O Bounteous Gods, protect our dwelling lace by day and night: | With you for our defenders may we go unharmed. || 12. May we, unharmed, serve bountiful Viṣhṇu, the God who slayeth none: | Self-moving Sindhu hear and be the first to mark. || 13. This sure protection we elect, desirable and reaching far, | Which Mitra, Varuṇa, and Aryaman afford. || 14. And may the Sindhu of the floods, the Marutas, and the Aśvin Pair, | Boon Indra, and boon Viṣhṇu have one mind with us. || 15. Because these warring Heroes stay the enmity of every foe, | As the fierce water-flood repels the furious ones. || 16. Here this one God, the Lord of men, looks forth exceeding far and wide: | And we, for your advantage, keep his holy laws. || 17. We keep the old accustomed laws, the statutes of supremacy, | The long-known laws of Mitra and of Varuṇa. || 18. He who hath measured with his ray the boundaries of heaven and earth, | And with his majesty hath filled the two worlds full, || 19. Sūrya hath spread his light aloft up to the region of the sky, | Like Agni all aflame when gifts are offered him. || 20. With him who sits afar the word is lord of food that comes from kine, | Controller of the gift of unempoisoned food. || 21. So unto Sūrya, Heaven, and Earth at morning and at eve I speak. | Bringing enjoyments ever rise thou up for us. || 22. From Ukṣhaṇyāyana a bay, from Harayāṇa a white steed, | And from Suṣhāman we obtained a harnessed car. || 23. These two shall bring me further gain of troops of tawny-coloured steeds, | The carriers shall they be of active men of war. || 24. And the two sages have I gained who hold the reins and bear the whip, | And the two great strong coursers, with my newest song.

Hymn 8:26. Aśvins.

1. I call your chariot to receive united praise mid princely men, | Strong Gods who pour down wealth, of never vanquished might! || 2. Ye to Varosuṣhāman come, Nāsatyas, for this glorious rite. | With your protecting aid. Strong Gods, who pour down wealth. || 3. So with oblations we invoke you, rich in ample wealth, today, | When night hath passed, O ye who send us plenteous food. | O Aśvins, Heroes, let your car, famed, best to travel, come to us, | And, for his glory, mark your zealous servant's lauds. || 5. Aśvins, who send us precious gifts, even when offended, think of him: | For ye, O Rudras, lead us safe beyond our foes. || 6. For, Wonder-Workers, with fleet steeds ye fly completely round this All, | Stirring our thoughts, ye Lords of splendour, honey-hued. || 7. With all-sustaining opulence, Aśvins, come hitherward to us, | Ye rich and noble Heroes, ne'er to be o'erthrown. || 8. To welcome this mine offering, O ye Indra-like Nāsatyas, come | As Gods of best accord this day with other Gods. || 9. For we, like Vyaśva, lifting up our voice like oxen, call on you: | With all your loving kindness, Sages, come to us. || 10. O Ṛiṣhi, laud the Aśvins well. Will they not listen to thy call? | Will they not bum the Paṇis who are nearer them? || 11. O Heroes, listen to the son of Vyaśva, and regard me here, | Varuṇa, Mitra, Aryaman, of one accord. || 12. Gods whom we yearn for, of your gifts, of what ye bring to us, bestow | By princes' hands on me, ye Mighty, day by day. || 13. Him whom your sacrifices clothe, even as a woman with her robe, | The Aśvins help to glory honouring him well. || 14. Whoso regards your care of men as succour widest in its reach, | About his dwelling go, ye Aśvins, loving us. || 15. Come to us ye who pour down wealth, come to the home which men must guard: | Like shafts, ye are made meet for sacrifice by song. || 16. Most fetching of all calls, the laud, as envoy, Heroes, called to you | Be it your own, O Aśvin Pair. || 17. Be ye in yonder sea of heaven, or joying in the home of food, | Listen to me, Immortal Ones. || 18. This river with his lucid flow attracts you, more than all the streams,— | Even Sindhu with his path of gold. || 19. O Aśvins, with that glorious fame come hither, through our brilliant song, | Come ye whose ways are marked with light. || 20. Harness the steeds who draw the car, O Vasu, bring the well-fed pair. | O Vāyu, drink thou of our meath: come unto our drink-offerings. || 21. Wonderful Vāyu, Lord of Right, thou who art Tvaṣhṭar's son-in-law, | Thy saving succour we elect. || 22. To Tvaṣhṭar's son-in-law we pray for wealth whereof he hath control: | For glory we seek Vāyu, men with juice effused. || 23. From heaven, auspicious Vāyu, come drive hither with thy noble steeds: | Come on thy mighty car with wide-extending seat. || 24. We call thee to the homes of men, thee wealthiest in noble food, | And liberal as a press-stone with a horse's back. || 25. So, glad and joyful in thine heart, do thou, God, Vāyu, first of all | Vouchsafe us water, strength, and thought.

Hymn 8:27. Viśvedevas.

1. Chief Priest is Agni at the laud, as stones and grass at sacrifice: | With song I seek the Marutas, Brahmaṇaspati, Gods for help much to be desired. || 2. I sing to cattle and to Earth, to trees, to Dawns, to Night, to plants. | O all ye Vasus, ye possessors of all wealth, be ye the furtherers of our thoughts. || 3. Forth go, with Agni, to the Gods our sacrifice of ancient use, | To the Ādityas, Varuṇa whose Law stands fast, and the all-lightening Marut troop. || 4. Lords of all wealth, may they be strengtheners of man, destroyers of his enemies. | Lords of all wealth, do ye, with guards which none may harm, preserve our dwelling free from foes. || 5. Come to us with one mind today, come to us all with one accord, | Marutas with holy song, and, Goddess Aditi, Mighty One, to our house and home. || 6. Send us delightful things, ye Marutas, on your steeds: come ye, O Mitra, to our gifts. | Let Indra, Varuṇa, and the Ādityas sit, swift Heroes, on our sacred grass. || 7. We who have trimmed the grass for you, and set the banquet in array, | And pressed the Soma, call you, Varuṇa, like men, with sacrificial fires aflame. || 8. O Marutas, Viṣhṇu, Aśvins, Pūṣhan, haste away with minds turned hitherward to Me. | Let the Strong Indra, famed as Vṛitra's slayer, come first with the winners of the spoil. || 9. Ye Guileless Gods, bestow on us a refuge strong on every side, | A sure protection, Vasus, unassailable from near at hand or from afar. || 10. Kinship have I with you, and close alliance O ye Gods, destroyers of our foes. | Call us to our prosperity of former days, and soon to new felicity. || 11. For now have I sent forth to you, that I may win a fair reward, | Lords of all wealth, with homage, this my song of praise. like a milch-cow that faileth not. || 12. Excellent Savitar hath mounted up on high for you, ye sure and careful Guides. | Bipeds and quadrupeds, with several hopes and aims, and birds have settled to their tasks. || 13. Singing their praise with God-like thought let us invoke each God for grace, | Each God to bring you help, each God to strengthen you. || 14. For of one spirit are the Gods with mortal man, co-sharers all of gracious gifts. | May they increase our strength hereafter and today, providing case and ample room. || 15. I laud you, O ye Guileless Gods, here where we meet to render praise. | None, Varuṇa and Mitra, harms the mortal, man who honours and obeys your laws. || 16. He makes his house

endure, he gathers plenteous food who pays obedience to your will. | Born in his sons anew he spreads as Law commands, and prospers every way unharmed. || 17. E'en without war he gathers wealth, and goes his way on pleasant paths, | Whom Mitra, Varuṇa and Aryaman protect, sharing the gift,of one accord. || 18. E'en on the plain for him ye make a sloping path, an easy way where road is none: | And far away from him the ineffectual shaft must vanish, shot at him in vain. || 19. If ye appoint the rite today, kind Rulers, when the Sun ascends, | Lords of all wealth, at sunset or at waking time, or be it at the noon of day, || 20. Or, Asuras, when ye have sheltered the worshipper who goes to sacrifice, at eve | may we, O Vasus, ye possessors of all wealth, come then into the midst of You. || 21. If ye today at sunrise, or at noon, or in the gloom of eve, | Lords of all riches, give fair treasure to the man, the wise man who hath sacrificed, || 22. Then we, imperial Rulers, claim of you this boon, your wide protection, as a son. | May we, Ādityas, offering holy gifts, obtain that which shall bring us greater bliss.

Hymn 8:28. Viśvedevas.

1. The Thirty Gods and Three besides, whose seat hath been the sacred grass, | From time of old have found and gained. || 2. Varuṇa, Mitra, Aryaman, Agnis, with Consorts, sending boons, | To whom our Vaṣhaṭ! is addressed: || 3. These are our guardians in the west, and northward here, and in the south, | And on the cast, with all the tribe. || 4. Even as the Gods desire so verily shall it be. None minisheth this power of theirs, | No demon, and no mortal || 5. The Seven carry seven spears; seven are the splendours they possess, | And seven the glories they assume.

Hymn 8:29. Viśvedevas.

1. One is a youth brown, active, manifold he decks the golden one with ornament. || 2. Another, luminous, occupies the place of sacrifice, Sage, among the Gods. || 3. One brandishes in his hand an iron knife, firm, in his seat amid the Deities. || 4. Another holds the thunderbolt, wherewith he slays the Vṛitras, resting in his hand. || 5. Another bears a pointed weapon: bright is he, and strong, with healing medicines. || 6. Another, thief-like, watches well the ways, and knows the places where the treasures lie. || 7. Another with his mighty stride hath made his three steps thither where the Gods rejoice. || 8. Two with one Dame ride on with winged steeds, and journey forth like travellers on their way. || 9. Two, highest, in the heavens have set their seat, worshipped with holy oil, imperial Kings. || 10. Some, singing lauds, conceived the Sāman-hymn, great hymn whereby they caused the Sun to shine.

Hymn 8:30. Viśvedevas.

1. Not one of you, ye Gods, is small, none of you is a feeble child: | All of you, verily, are great. || 2. Thus be ye lauded, ye destroyers of the foe, ye Three-and-Thirty Deities, | The Gods of man, the Holy Ones. || 3. As such defend and succour us, with benedictions speak to us: | Lead us not from our fathers' and from Manu's path into the distance far away. || 4. Ye Deities who stay with us, and all ye Gods of all mankind, | Give us your wide protection, give shelter for cattle and for steed.

Hymn 8:31. Various Deities.

1. That Brahman pleases Indra well, who worships, sacrifices, pours Libation, and prepares the meal. || 2. Śakra protects from woe the man who gives him sacrificial cake. | And offers Soma blent with milk. || 3. His chariot shall be glorious, sped by Gods, and mighty shall he be, | Subduing all hostilities. || 4. Each day that passes, in his house flows his libation, rich in milk, | Exhaustless, bringing progeny. || 5. O Gods, with constant draught of milk, husband and wife with one accord | Press out and wash the Soma juice. || 6. They gain sufficient food: they come united to the sacred grass, | And never do they fail in strength. || 7. Never do they deny or seek to hide the favour of the Gods: | They win high glory for themselves. || 8. With sons and daughters by their side they reach their full extent of life, | Both decked with ornaments of gold. || 9. Serving the Immortal One with gifts of sacrificial meal and wealth, | They satisfy the claims of love and pay due honour to the Gods. || 10. We claim protection from the Hills, we claim protection of the Floods, | Of him who stands by Viṣhṇu's side. || 11. May Pūṣhan come, and Bhaga, Lord of wealth, All-bounteous, for our weal | Broad be the path that leads to bliss: || 12. Aramati, and, free from foes, Viśva with spirit of a God, | And the Ādityas' peerless might. || 13. Seeing that Mitra, Aryaman, and Varuṇa are guarding us, | The paths of Law are fair to tread. || 14. I glorify with song, for wealth, Agni the God, the first of you. | We honour as a well-loved Friend the God who prospereth our fields. || 15. As in all frays the hero, so swift moves his car whom Gods attend. | The man who, sacrificing, strives to win the heart of Deities will conquer those who worship not. || 16. Ne'er are ye injured, worshipper, presser of juice, or pious man. | The man who, sacrificing, strives to win the heart of Deities will conquer those who worship not. || 17. None in his action equals him, none holds him far or keeps him off. | The man who, sacrificing, strives to win the heart of Deities will conquer those who worship not. || 18. Such strength of heroes shall be his, such mastery of fleet-foot steeds. | The man who, sacrificing, strives to win the heart of Deities will conquer those who worship not.

Hymn 8:32. Indra.

1. Kaṇvas, tell forth with song the deeds of Indra, the Impetuous, | Wrought in the Soma's wild delight. || 2. Strong God, he slew Anarśani, Sṛibinda, Pipru, and the fiend, | Ahīśuva, and loosed the floods. | 3. Thou broughtest down the dwelling-place, the height of lofty Arbuda. | That exploit, Indra, must be famed. || 4. Bold, to your famous Soma I call the fair-visored God for aid, | Down like a torrent from the hill. || 5. Rejoicing in the Soma-draughts, Hero, burst open, like a fort, | The stall of horses and of kine. || 6. If my libation gladdens, if thou takest pleasure in my laud, | Come with thy Godhead from afar. || 7. O Indra, Lover of the Song, the singers of thy praise are we: | O Soma-drinker, quicken us. || 8. And, taking thy delight with us bring us still undiminished food: | Great is thy wealth, O Maghavan. || 9. Make thou us rich in herds of kine, in steeds, in gold: let us exert | Our strength in sacrificial gifts. || 10. Let us call him to aid whose hands stretch far, to whom high laud is due. | Who worketh well to succour us. || 11. He, Śatakratu, even in fight acts as a Vṛitra-slayer s,till: | He gives his worshippers much wealth. || 12. May he, this Śakra, strengthen us, Boon God who satisfies our needs, | Indra, with all his saving helps. || 13. To him, the mighty stream of wealth, the Soma-presser's rescuing Friend, | To Indra sing your song of praise; || 14. Who bringeth what is great and firm, who winneth glory in his wars, | Lord of vast wealth through power and might. || 15. There liveth none to cheek or stay his energies and gracious deeds: | None who can say, He giveth not. || 16. No debt is due by Brahmans now, by active men who press the juice: | Well hath each Soma-draught been paid. || 17. Sing ye to him who must be praised, say lauds to him who must be praised, | Bring prayer to him who must be praised. || 18. May be, unchecked, strong, meet for praise, bring hundreds, thousands forth to light, | Indra who aids the worshipper. || 19. Go with thy God-like nature forth, go where the folk are calling thee: | Drink, Indra, of the drops we pour. || 20. Drink milky draughts which are thine own, this too which was with Tugrya once, | This is it, Indra, that is thine. || 21. Pass him who pours libations out in angry mood or after sin: | Here drink the juice we offer thee. || 22. Over the three great distances, past the Five Peoples go thy way, | O Indra, noticing our voice. || 23. Send forth thy ray like Sūrya: let my songs attract thee hitherward, | Like waters gathering to the vale. || 24. Now to the Hero fair of cheek, Adhvaryu, pour the Soma forth: | Bring of the juice that he may drink || 25. Who cleft the water-cloud in twain, loosed rivers for their downward flow, | And set the ripe milk in the kine. || 26. He, meet for praise, slew Vṛitra, slew Ahīśuva, Ūrṇavābha's son, | And pierced through Arbuda with frost. || 27. To him your matchless Mighty One, unconquerable Conqueror, | Sing forth the prayer which Gods have given: || 28. Indra, who in the wild delight of Soma juice considers here | All holy Laws among the Gods. || 29. Hither let these thy Bays who share thy banquet, Steeds with golden manes, | Convey thee to the feast prepared. || 30. Hither, O thou whom many laud, the Bays whom Priyamedha praised, | Shall bring thee to the Soma-draught.

Hymn 8:33. Indra.

1. We compass thee like waters, we whose grass is trimmed and Soma pressed. | Here where the filter pours its stream, thy worshippers round thee, O Vṛitra-slayer, sit. || 2. Men, Vasu! by the Soma, with lauds call thee to the foremost place: | When comest thou athirst unto the juice as home, O Indra, like a bellowing bull? || 3. Boldly, Bold Hero, bring us spoil in thousands for the Kaṇvas' sake. | O active Maghavan, with eager prayer we crave the yellow-hued with store of kine. || 4. Medhātithi, to Indra sing, drink of the juice to make thee glad. | Close-knit to his Bay Steeds, bolt-

armed, beside the juice is he: his chariot is of gold. ‖ 5. He Who is praised as strong of hand both right and left, most wise and hold: | Indra who, rich in hundreds, gathers thousands up, honoured as breaker-down of forts. ‖ 6. The bold of heart whom none provokes, who stands in bearded confidence; | Much-lauded, very glorious, overthrowing foes, strong Helper, like a bull with might. ‖ 7. Who knows what vital power he wins, drinking beside the flowing juice? | This is the fair-checked God who, joying in the draught, breaks down the castles in his strength. ‖ 8. As a wild elephant rushes on this way and that way, mad with heat. | None may compel thee, yet come hither to the draught: thou movest mighty in thy power. ‖ 9. When he, the Mighty, ne'er o'erthrown, steadfast, made ready for the fight, | When Indra Maghavan lists to his praiser's call, he will not stand aloof, but come. ‖ 10. Yea, verily, thou art a Bull, with a bull's rush. whom none may stay: | Thou Mighty One, art celebrated as a Bull, famed as a Bull both near and far. ‖ 11. Thy reins are very bulls in strength, bulls' strength is in thy golden whip. | Thy car, O Maghavan, thy Bays are strong as bulls: thou, Śatakratu, art a Bull. ‖ 12. Let the strong presser press for thee. Bring hither, thou straight-rushing Bull. | The mighty makes the mighty run in flowing streams for thee whom thy Bay Horses bear. ‖ 13. Come, thou most potent Indra, come to drink the savoury Soma juice. | Maghavan, very wise, will quickly come to hear the songs, the prayer, the hymns of praise. ‖ 14. When thou hast mounted on thy car let thy yoked Bay Steeds carry thee, | Past other men's libations, Lord of Hundred Powers, thee, Vṛitra-slayer, thee our Friend. ‖ 15. O thou Most Lofty One, accept our laud as nearest to thine heart. | May our libations be most sweet to make thee glad, O Soma-drinker, Heavenly Lord. ‖ 16. Neither in thy decree nor mine, but in another's he delights,— | The man who brought us unto this. ‖ 17. Indra himself hath said, The mind of woman brooks not discipline, | Her intellect hath little weight. ‖ 18. His pair of horses, rushing on in their wild transport, draw his car: | High-lifted is the stallion's yoke. ‖ 19. Cast down thine eyes and look not up. More closely set thy feet. Let none | See what thy garment veils, for thou, a Brahman, hast become a dame.

Hymn 8:34. Indra.

1. Come hither, Indra, with thy Bays, come thou to Kaṇva's eulogy. | Ye by command of yonder Dyaus, God bright by day! have gone to heaven. ‖ 2. May the stone draw thee as it speaks, the Soma-stone with ringing voice. | Ye by command of yonder Dyaus, God bright by day! have gone to heaven. ‖ 3. The stones' rim shakes the Soma here like a wolf worrying a sheep. | Ye by command of yonder Dyaus, God bright by day! have gone to heaven. ‖ 4. The Kaṇvas call thee hitherward for succour and to win the spoil. | Ye by command of yonder Dyaus, God bright by day! have gone to heaven. ‖ 5. I set for thee, as for the Strong, the first draught of the juices shed. ‖ 6. Come with abundant blessings, come with perfect care to succour us. ‖ 7. Come, Lord of lofty thought, who hast infinite wealth and countless aids. ‖ 8. Adorable mid Gods, the Priest good to mankind shall bring thee near. ‖ 9. As wings the falcon, so thy Bays rushing in joy shall carry thee. ‖ 10. Come from the enemy to us, to Svāhā! and the Soma-draught. ‖ 11. Come hither with thine car inclined to hear, take pleasure in our lauds. ‖ 12. Lord of well-nourished Horses, come with well-fed Steeds alike in hue. ‖ 13. Come hither from the mountains, come from regions of the sea of air. ‖ 14. Disclose to us O Hero, wealth in thousands both of kine and steeds. ‖ 15. Bring riches hitherward to us in hundreds, thousands, myriads. | Ye by command of yonder Dyaus, God bright by day! have gone to heaven. ‖ 16. The thousand steeds, the mightiest troop, which we and Indra have received | From Vasurochis as a gift, ‖ 17. The brown that match the wind in speed, and bright bay coursers fleet of foot, | Like Suns, resplendent are they all. ‖ 18. Mid the Pārāvata's rich gifts, swift steeds whose wheels run rapidly, | I seemed to stand amid a wood.

Hymn 8:35. Aśvins.

1. With Agni and with Indra, Vishṇu. Varuṇa, with the Ādityas, Rudras, Vasus, closely leagued; | Accordant, of one mind with Sūrya and with Dawn, O Aśvins, drink the Soma juice. ‖ 2. With all the Holy Thoughts, all being Mighty Ones! in close alliance with the Mountains, Heaven, and Earth; | Accordant. of one mind with Sūrya and with Dawn, O Aśvins, drink the Soma juice. ‖ 3. With all the Deities, three times eleven, here, in close alliance with the Marutas, Bhṛigus, Floods; | Accordant, of one mind with Sūrya and with Dawn, O Aśvins, drink the Soma juice. ‖ 4. Accept the sacrifice, attend to this my call: come nigh, O ye Twain Gods, to all libations here. | Accordant, of one mind with Sūrya and with Dawn, O Aśvins, bring us strengthening food. ‖ 5. Accept our praise-song as a youth accepts a maid. Come nigh, O ye Twain Gods, to all libations here. | Accordant, of one mind with Sūrya and with Dawn O Aśvins, bring us strengthening food. ‖ 6. Accept the songs we sing, accept the solemn rite. Come nigh, O ye Twain Gods, to all libations here. | Accordant, of one mind with Sūrya and with Dawn, O Aśvins, bring us strengthening food. ‖ 7. Ye fly as starlings fly unto the forest trees; like buffaloes ye seek the Soma we have shed. | Accordant, of one mind with Sūrya and with Dawn, come thrice, O Aśvins, to our home. ‖ 8. Ye fly like swans, like those who travel on their way; like buffaloes ye seek the Soma we have shed. | Accordant, of one mind with Sūrya and with Dawn, come thrice, O Aśvins, to our home. ‖ 9. Ye fly to our oblation like a pair of hawks; like buffaloes ye seek the Soma we have shed. | Accordant, of one mind with Sūrya and with Dawn, come thrice, O Aśvins, to our home. ‖ 10. Come hitherward and drink and satisfy yourselves, bestow upon us progeny and affluence. | Accordant, of one mind with Sūrya and with Dawn, O Aśvins, grant us vigorous strength. ‖ 11. Conquer your foes, protect us, praise your worshippers; bestow upon us progeny and affluence. | Accordant, of one mind with Sūrya and with Dawn, O Aśvins, grant us vigorous strength. ‖ 12. Slay enemies, animate men whom ye befriend; bestow upon us progeny and affluence. | Accordant, of one mind with Sūrya and with Dawn, O Aśvins, grant us vigorous strength. ‖ 13. With Mitra, Varuṇa, Dharma, and the Marutas in your company approach unto your praiser's call. | Accordant, of one mind with Sūrya and with Dawn, and with the Ādityas, Aśvins! come. ‖ 14. With Vishṇu and the Aṅgirasas attending you, and with the Marutas come unto your praiser's call. | Accordant, of one mind with Sūrya and with Dawn, and with the Ādityas, Aśvins! come. ‖ 15. With Ṛibhus and With Vājas. O ye Mighty Ones, leagued with the Marutas come ye to your praiser's call. | Accordant, of one mind with Sūrya and with Dawn, and with the Ādityas, Aśvins! come. ‖ 16. Give spirit to our prayer and animate our thoughts; slay ye the Rākshasas and drive away disease. | Accordant, of One mind with Sūrya and with Dawn, the presser's Soma, Aśvins drink. ‖ 17. Strengthen the Ruling Power, strengthen the men of war; slay ye the Rākshasas and drive away disease. | Accordant, of one mind with Sūrya and with Dawn, the presser's Soma, Aśvins drink. ‖ 18. Give strength unto the milch-kine, give the people strength, slay ye the Rākshasas and drive away disease. | Accordant, of one mind with Sūrya and with Dawn, the presser's Soma, Aśvins drink. ‖ 19. As ye heard Atri's earliest eulogy, so hear Śyāvāśva, Soma-presser, ye who reel in joy. | Accordant, of one mind with Sūrya and with Dawn, drink juice, O Aśvins, three days old. ‖ 20. Further like running streams Śyāvāśva's eulogies who presses out the Soma, ye who reel in joy. | Accordant, of one mind with Sūrya and with Dawn, drink juice, O Aśvins, three days old. ‖ 21. Seize, as ye grasp the reins, Śyāvāśva's solemn rites who presses out the Soma, ye who reel in joy. | Accordant, of one mind with Sūrya and with Dawn, drink juice, O Aśvins, three days old. ‖ 22. Drive down your chariot hitherward drink ye the Soma's savoury juice. | Approach, ye Aśvins, come to us: I call you, eager for your aid. Grant treasures to the worshipper. ‖ 23. When sacrifice which tells our reverence hath begun. Heroes! to drink the gushing juice, | Approach, ye Aśvins, come to us: I call you, eager for your aid. Grant treasures to the worshipper. ‖ 24. Sate you with consecrated drink, with juice effused, ye Deities. | Approach, ye Aśvins, come to us: I call you, eager for your aid. Grant treasures to the worshipper.

Hymn 8:36. Indra.

1. Thou helpest him whose grass is trimmed, who sheds the juice, O Śatakratu, drink Soma to make thee glad. | The share which they have fixed for thee, thou, Indra, Victor o'er all hosts and space, begirt with Marutas, Lord of Heroes, winner of the floods. ‖ 2. Maghavan, help thy worshipper: let him help thee. O Śatakratu, drink Soma to make thee glad. | The share which they have fixed for thee, etc. ‖ 3. Thou aidest Gods with food, and that with might aids thee, | O Śatakratu, drink Soma to make thee glad. ‖ 4. Creator of the heaven, creator of the earth, O Śatakratu, drink Soma to make thee glad. ‖ 5. Father of cattle, father of all steeds art thou. O Śatakratu, drink Soma to make thee glad. ‖ 6. Stone-hurler,

glorify the Atris' hymn of praise. O Śatakratu, drink Soma to make thee glad. || 7. Hear thou Śyāvāśva while he pours to thee, as erst thou heardest Atri when he wrought his holy rites. | Indra, thou only gavest Trasadasyu aid in the fierce fight with heroes, strengthening his prayers.

Hymn 8:37. Indra.

1. This prayer, and those who shed the juice, in wars with Vṛitra thou holpest, Indra, Lord of Strength, with all thy succours. | O Vṛitra-slayer, from libation poured at noon, drink of the Soma juice, thou blameless Thunderer. || 2. Thou mighty Conqueror of hostile armaments, O Indra, Lord of Strength, with all thy saving help. || 3. Sole Ruler, thou art Sovereign of this world of life, O Indra, Lord of Strength, with all thy saving help. || 4. Thou only sunderest these two consistent worlds, O Indra, Lord of Strength, with all thy saving help. || 5. Thou art the Lord supreme o'er rest and energy, O Indra, Lord of Strength, with all thy saving help. || 6. Thou helpest one to power, and one thou hast not helped, O Indra, Lord of Strength, with all thy saving aid. || 7. Hear thou Śyāvāśva while he sings to thee, as erst thou heardest Atri when he wrought his holy rites. | Indra, thou only gavest Trasadasyu aid in the fierce fight with heroes, strengthening his powers.

Hymn 8:38. Indra-Agni.

1. Ye Twain are Priests of sacrifice, winners in war and holy works: | Indra and Agni, mark this well. || 2. Ye bounteous riders on the car, ye Vṛitra-slayers unsubdued: | Indra and Agni, mark this well. || 3. The men with pressing-stones have pressed this meath of yours which gives delight: | Indra, and Agni, mark this well. || 4. Accept our sacrifice for weal, sharers of praise! the Soma shed: | Indra and Agni, Heroes, come. || 5. Be pleased with these libations which attract you to our sacred gifts | Indra and Agni, Heroes, come. || 6. Accept this eulogy of mine whose model is the Gāyatrī: | Indra and Agni, Heroes, Come. || 7. Come with the early-faring Gods, ye who are Lords of genuine wealth: | Indra-Agni, to the Soma-draught || 8. Hear ye the call of Atris, hear Śyāvāśva as he sheds the juice: | Indra-Agni to the Soma-draught || 9. Thus have I called you to our aid as sages called on you of old: | Indra-Agni to the Soma draught! || 10. Indra's and Agni's grace I claim, Sarasvatī's associates | To whom this psalm of praise is sung.

Hymn 8:39. Agni.

1. The glorious Agni have I praised, and worshipped with. the sacred food. | May Agni deck the Gods for us. Between both gathering-places he goes on his embassy, the Sage. May all the others die away. || 2. Agni, burn down the word within their bodies through our newest speech, | All hatreds of the godless, all the wicked man's malignities. Away let the destroyers go. May all the others die away. || 3. Agni, I offer hymns to thee, like holy oil within thy mouth. | Acknowledge them. among the Gods, for thou art the most excellent, the worshipper's blissful messenger. Let all the others die away. || 4. Agni bestows all vital power even as each man supplicates. | He brings the Vasus strengthening gifts, and grants delight, in rest and stir, for every calling on the Gods. Let all the others die away. || 5. Agni hath made himself renowned by wonderful victorious act. | He is the Priest of all the tribes, chosen with sacrificial meeds. He urges Deities to receive. Let all the others die away. || 6. Agni knows all that springs from Gods, he knows the mystery of men. | Giver of wealth is Agni, he uncloses both the doors to us when worshipped with our newest gift. Let all the others die away. || 7. Agni inhabiteth with Gods and men who offer sacrifice. | He cherisheth with great delight much wisdom, as all things that be, God among Gods adorable. May all the others die away. || 8. Agni who liveth in all streams, Lord of the Sevenfold Race of men, | Him dweller in three homes we seek, best slayer of the Dasyus for Mandhātar, first in sacrifice. Let all the others die away. || 9. Agni the Wise inhabiteth three gathering-places, triply formed. | Decked as our envoy let the Sage bring hither and conciliate the Thrice Eleven Deities. Let all the others die away. || 10. Our Agni, thou art first among the Gods, and first mid living men. | Thou only rulest over wealth. Round about thee, as natural dams, circumfluous the waters run. Let all the others die away.

Hymn 8:40. Indra-Agni.

1. Indra and Agni, surely ye as Conquerors will give us wealth, | Whereby in fight we may o'ercome that which is strong and firmly fixed, as Agni burns the woods with wind. Let all the others die away. || 2. We set no snares to tangle you; Indra we worship and adore, Hero of heroes mightiest. | Once may he come unto us with his Steed, come unto us to win us strength, and to complete the sacrifice. || 3. For, famous Indra-Agni, ye are dwellers in the midst of frays. | Sages in wisdom, ye are knit to him who seeketh you as friends. Heroes, bestow on him his wish. || 4. Nabhāka-like, with sacred song Indra's and Agni's praise I sing, | Theirs to whom all this world belongs, this heaven and this mighty earth which bear rich treasure in their lap. || 5. To Indra and to Agni send your prayers, as was Nabhāka's wont,— | Who opened with sideway opening the sea with its foundations seven—Indra all powerful in his might. || 6. Tear thou asunder, as of old, like tangles of a creeping plant, | Demolish thou the Dāsa's might. May we with Indra's help divide the treasure he hath gathered up. || 7. What time with this same song these men call Indra-Agni sundry ways, | May we with our own heroes quell those who provoke us to the fight, and conquer those who strive with us. || 8. The Two refulgent with their beams rise and come downward from the sky. | By Indra's and by Agni's hest, flowing away, the rivers, run which they released from their restraint. || 9. O Indra, many are thine aids, many thy ways of guiding us, | Lord of the Bay Steeds, Hinva's Son. To a Good Hero come our prayers, which soon shall have accomplishment. || 10. Inspire him with your holy hymns, the Hero bright and glorious, | Him who with might demolisheth even the brood of Śuṣhṇa, and winneth for us the heavenly streams. || 11. Inspire him worshipped with fair rites, the glorious Hero truly brave. | He brake in pieces Śuṣhṇa's brood who still expected not the stroke, and won for us the heavenly streams. Let all the others die away. || 12. Thus have we sung anew to Indra-Agni, as sang our sires, Aṅgirasas, and Mandhātar. | Guard us with triple shelter and preserve us: may we be masters of a store of riches.

Hymn 8:41. Varuṇa.

1. To make this Varuṇa come forth sing thou a song unto the band of Marutas wiser than thyself,— | This Varuṇa who guardeth well the thoughts of men like herds of kine. | Let all the others die away. || 2. Him altogether praise I with the song and hymns our fathers sang, and with Nabhāka's eulogies,— | Him dwelling at the rivers' source, surrounded by his Sisters Seven. || 3. The nights he hath encompassed, and established the morns with magic art visible over all is he. | His dear Ones, following his Law, have prospered the Three Dawns for him. || 4. He, visible o'er all the earth, established the quarters of the sky: | He measured out the eastern place, that is the fold of Varuṇa: like a strong herdsman is the God. || 5. He who supports the worlds of life, he who well knows the hidden names mysterious of the morning beams, | He cherishes much wisdom, Sage, as heaven brings forth each varied form. || 6. In whom all wisdom centres, as the nave is set within the wheel. | Haste ye to honour Trita, as kine haste to gather in the fold, even as they muster steeds to yoke. || 7. He wraps these regions as a robe; he contemplates the tribes of Gods and all the works of mortal men. | Before the home of Varuṇa all the Gods follow his decree. || 8. He is an Ocean far-removed, yet through the heaven to him ascends the worship which these realms possess. | With his bright foot he overthrew their magic, and went up to heaven. || 9. Ruler, whose bright far-seeing rays, pervading all three earths, have filled the three superior realms of heaven. | Firm is the seat of Varuṇa: over the Seven he rules as King. || 10. Who, after his decree, o'erspread the Dark Ones with a robe of light; | Who measured out the ancient seat, who pillared both the worlds apart as the Unborn supported heaven. Let all the others die away.

Hymn 8:42. Varuṇa.

1. Lord of all wealth, the Asura propped the heavens, and measured out the broad earth's wide expanses. | He, King supreme, approached all living creatures. All these are Varuṇa's holy operations. || 2. So humbly worship Varuṇa the Mighty revere the wise Guard of World Immortal. | May he vouchsafe us triply-barred protection. O Earth and Heaven, within your lap preserve us. || 3. Sharpen this song of him who strives his utmost, sharpen, God Varuṇa, his strength and insight; | May we ascend the ship that bears us safely, whereby we may pass over all misfortune. || 4. Aśvins, with songs the singer stones have made you hasten hitherward, | Nāsatyas, to the Soma-draught. Let all the others die away. || 5. As the sage Atri with his hymns, O Aśvins, called you eagerly, | Nāsatyas, to the Soma-draught. Let all the others die away. || 6. So have I called you to our aid, even as the wise have called of old, | Nāsatyas, to the Soma-draught. Let all the others die away.

Hymn 8:43. Agni.

1. These songs of mine go forth as lauds of Agni, the disposing Sage, | Whose worshipper is ne'er o'erthrown. || 2. Wise Agni Jātavedas, I beget a song of praise for thee. | Who willingly receivest it. || 3. Thy sharpened flames, O Agni, like the gleams of light that glitter through, | Devour the forests with their teeth. || 4. Gold-coloured, bannered with the smoke, urged by the wind, aloft to heaven | Rise, lightly borne, the flames of fire. || 5. These lightly kindled fiery flames are all around made visible, | Even as the gleanings of the Dawns. || 6. As Jātavedas speeds along, the dust is black beneath his feet, | When Agni spreads upon the earth. || 7. Making the plants his nourishment, Agni devours and wearies not, | Seeking the tender shrubs again. || 8. Bending him down with all his tongues, he flickers with his fiery glow | Splendid is Agni in the woods. || 9. Agni, thine home is in the floods: into the plants thou forcest way, | And as their Child art born anew. || 10. Worshipped with offerings shines thy flame, O Agni, from the sacred oil, | With kisses on the ladle's mouth. || 11. Let us serve Agni with our hymns, Disposer, fed on ox and cow, | Who bears the Soma on his back. || 12. Yea, thee, O Agni, do we seek with homage and with fuel, Priest | Whose wisdom is most excellent. || 13. O worshipped with oblations, pure Agni, we call on thee as erst, | Did Bhṛigu, Manus, Aṅgiras. || 14. For thou, O Agni, by the fire, Sage by the Sage, Good by the Good, | Friend by the Friend, art lighted up. || 15. So wealth in thousands, food with store of heroes give thou to the sage, | O Agni, to the worshipper. || 16. O Agni, Brother, made by strength, Lord of red steeds and brilliant sway, | Take pleasure in this laud of mine. || 17. My praises, Agni, go to thee, as the cows seek the stall to meet, | The lowing calf that longs for milk. || 18. Agni, best Aṅgiras, to thee all people who have pleasant homes, | Apart, have turned as to their wish. || 19. The sages skilled in holy song and thinkers with their thoughts have urged | Agni to share the sacred feast. || 20. So, Agni, unto thee the Priest, Invoker, strong in forays, pray | 'nose who spin out the sacrifice. || 21. In many a place, the same in look art thou, a Prince o'er all the tribes | In battles we invoke thine aid. || 22. Pray thou to Agni, pray to him who blazes served with sacred oil: | Let him give ear to this our call. || 23. We call on thee as such, as one who hears, as Jātavedas, one, | Agni! who beats away our foes. || 24. I pray to Agni, King of men, the Wonderful, the President | Of holy Laws: may he give ear. || 25. Him like a bridegroom, him who stirs all people, like a noble horse, | Like a fleet steed, we instigate. || 26. Slaying things deadly, burning up foes, Rākṣhasas, on every side, | Shine, Agni, with thy sharpened flame. || 27. Thou whom the people kindle even as Manus did, best Aṅgiras! | O Agni, mark thou this my speech. || 28. O Agni, made by strength! be thou born in the heavens or born in floods, | As such we call on thee with songs. || 29. Yea, all the people, all the folk who have good dwellings, each apart, | Send food for thee to eat thereof. || 30. O Agni, so may we, devout, gazed at by men, throughout our days, | Pass lightly over all distress. || 31. We venerate with cheerful hearts the cheerful Agni, dear to all, | Burning, with purifying flame. || 32. So thou, O Agni rich in light, beaming like Sūrya with thy rays | Boldly demolishest the gloom, || 33. We pray to thee for this thy gift, Victor the gift that faileth not, | O Agni, choicest wealth from thee.

Hymn 8:44. Agni.

1. Pay service unto Agni with your fuel, rouse your Guest with oil: | In him present your offerings. || 2. Agni, do thou accept my laud, be magnified by this my song: | Welcome my sweetly-spoken words. || 3. Agni, envoy, I place in front; the oblation-bearer I address: | Here let him seat the Deities. || 4. Agni, the lofty flames of' thee enkindled have gone up on high, | Thy bright flames, thou Refulgent One. || 5. Beloved! let my ladles full of sacred oil come near to thee: | Agni, accept our offerings. || 6. I worship Agni—may he hear!—the cheerful, the Invoker, Priest, | Of varied splendour, rich in light. || 7. Ancient Invoker, meet for praise, beloved Agni, wise and strong, | The visitant of solemn rites. || 8. Agni, best Aṅgiras, accept straightway these offerings, and guide | The seasonable sacrifice. || 9. Excellent God, with brilliant flames, enkindled bring thou hitherward, | Knowing the way, the Heavenly Host. || 10. Him, Sage and Herald, void of guile, ensign of sacrifices, him | Smoke-bannered, rich in light, we seek. || 11. O Agni, be our Guardian thou, God, against those who injure us: | Destroy our foes, thou Son of Strength. || 12. Making his body beautiful, Agni the Sage hath waxen by | The singer and his ancient hymn. || 13. I invocate the Child of Strength, Agni with purifying flame, | At this well-ordered sacrifice. || 14. So Agni, rich in many friends, with fiery splendour, seat thyself | With Gods upon our sacred grass. || 15. The mortal man who serves the God Agni within his own abode, | For him he causes wealth to shine. || 16. Agni is head and height of heaven, the Master of the earth is he: | He quickeneth the waters' seed. || 17. Upward, O Agni, rise thy flames, pure and resplendent, blazing high, | Thy lustres, fair effulgences. || 18. For, Agni, thou as Lord of Light rulest o'er choicest gifts: may I, | Thy singer, find defence in thee. || 19. O Agni, they who understand stir thee to action with their thoughts: | So let our songs enhance thy might. || 20. We ever claim the friendship of Agni, the singing messenger, | Of God-like nature, void of guile. || 21. Agni who bears most holy sway, the holy Singer, holy Sage, | Shines holy when we worship him. || 22. Yea, let my meditations, let my songs exalt thee evermore. | Think, Agni, of our friendly bond, || 23. If I were thou and thou wert I, O Agni, every prayer of thine | Should have its due fulfilment here. || 24. For Excellent and Lord of wealth. art thou O Agni, rich in light: | May we enjoy thy favouring grace. || 25. Agni, to thee whose laws stand fast our resonant songs of praise speed forth, | As rivers hasten to the sea. || 26. Agni, the Youthful Lord of men, who stirreth much and eateth all, | The Sage, I glorify with hymns. || 27. To Agni let us haste with lauds, the Guide of sacrificial rites, | Armed with sharp teeth, the Mighty One. || 28. And let this man, good Agni, be with thee the singer of thy praise: | Be gracious, Holy One, to him. || 29. For thou art sharer of our feast, wise, ever watchful as a Sage: | Agni, thou shinest in the sky. || 30. O Agni, Sage, before our foes, before misfortunes fall on us, | Excellent Lord, prolong our lives.

Hymn 8:45. Indra

1. Hitherward! they who light flame and straightway trim the sacred grass. | Whose Friend is Indra ever young. || 2. High is their fuel, great their laud, wide is their splinter from the stake, | Whose Friend is Indra ever young. || 3. Unequalled in fight the hero leads his army with the warrior chiefs. | Whose Friend is Indra ever young. || 4. The new-born Vṛitra-slayer asked his Mother, as he seized his shaft, | Who are the fierce? Who are renowned? || 5. Śavasī answered, He who seeks thine enmity will battle like | A stately elephant on a hill. || 6. And hear, O Maghavan; to him who craves of thee thou grantest all | Whate'er thou makest firm is firm. || 7. What time the Warrior Indra goes to battle, borne by noble steeds, | Best of all charioteers is he. || 8. Repel, O Thunder-armed, in all directions all attacks on us: | And be our own most glorious God. || 9. May Indra set our car in front, in foremost Place to win the spoil, | He whom the wicked injure not. || 10. Thine enmity may we escape, and, Śakra, for thy bounty, rich | In kine, may we come near to thee || 11. Softly approaching, Thunder-armed wealthy by hundreds, rich in steeds, | Unrivalled, ready with our gifts. || 12. For thine exalted excellence gives to thy worshippers each day | Hundreds and thousands of thy boons. || 13. Indra, we know thee breaker-down even of tong forts, winner of spoil, | As one who conquers wealth for us. || 14. Though thou art highest, Sage and Bold let the drops cheer thee when we come | To thee as to a trafficker. || 15. Bring unto us the treasure of the opulent man who, loth to give, | Hath slighted thee for gain of wealth. || 16. Indra, these friends of ours, supplied with Soma, wait and look to thee, | As men with fodder to the herd. || 17. And thee who art not deaf, whose ears are quick to listen, for our aid, | We call to us from far away. || 18. When thou hast listened, make our call one which thou never wilt forget, | And be our very nearest Friend. || 19. When even now, when we have been in trouble, we have thought of thee, | O Indra, give us gifts of kine. || 20. O Lord of Strength, we rest on thee, as old men rest upon a staff: | We long to have. thee dwell with us. || 21. To Indra sing a song of praise, Hero of mighty valour, him | Whom no one challenges to war. || 22. Hero, the Soma being shed, I pour the juice for thee to drink: | Sate thee and finish thy carouse. || 23. Let not the fools, or those who mock beguile thee when they seek thine aid | Love not the enemies of prayer. || 24. Here let them with rich milky draught cheer thee to great munificence: | Drink as the wild-bull drinks the lake. || 25. Proclaim in our assemblies what deeds, new and ancient, far away, | The Vṛitra-slayer hath achieved. || 26. In battle of a thousand arms Indra drank Kadrū's Soma juice: | There he displayed his manly might. || 27. True undeniable strength he found in Yadu and in Turvaśa, | And conquered through the sacrifice. || 28. Him have I

magnified, our Lord in, common, Guardian of your folk, | Discloser of great wealth in kine; || 29. Ṛibhukṣhan, not to be restrained, who strengthened Tugra's son in lauds, | Indra beside the flowing juice; || 30. Who for Triśoka clave the hill that formed a wide receptacle, | So that the cows might issue forth. || 31. Whate'er thy plan or purpose be, whate'er, in transport, thou wouldst do, | Do it not, Indra, but be kind. || 32. But little hath been heard of done upon the earth by one like thee: | Let thine heart, Indra, turn to us. || 33. Thine then shall be this high renown, thine shall these lofty praises be, | When, Indra, thou art kind to us. || 34. Not for one trespass, not for two, O Hero, slay us, nor for three, | Nor yet for many trespasses. || 35. I fear one powerful like thee, the crusher down of enemies, | Mighty, repelling all attacks. || 36. O wealthy God, ne'er may I live to see my friend or son in need: | Hitherward let thy heart be turned. || 37. What friend, O people, unprovoked, hath ever said unto a friend, | He turns and leaves us in distress? || 38. Hero, insatiate enjoy this Soma juice so near to thee, | Even as a hunter rushing down. || 39. Hither I draw those Bays of thine yoked | by our hymn, with splendid car, | That thou mayst give unto the priests. || 40. Drive all our enemies away, smite down the foes who press around, | And bring the wealth for which we long: || 41. O Indra, that which is concealed in strong firm place precipitous: | Bring us the wealth for which we long || 42. Great riches which the world of men shall recognize as sent by thee: | Bring us the wealth for which we long.

Hymn 8:46. Indra.

1. We, Indra, Lord of ample wealth, our Guide, depend on one like thee, | Thou driver of the Tawny Steeds. || 2. For, Hurler of the Bolt, we know thee true, the giver of our food, | We know the giver of our wealth. || 3. O thou whose majesty the bards celebrate with their songs, thou Lord, | Of hundred powers and hundred aids. || 4. Fair guidance hath the mortal man whom Aryaman, the Marut host, | And Mitra, void of guile, protect. || 5. Kine, steeds, and hero strength he gains, and prospers, by the Ādityas sped, | Ever in wealth which all desire. || 6. We pray to Indra for his gift, to him the Fearless and the Strong, | We pray to him the Lord of wealth. || 7. For verily combined in him are all the fearless powers of aid. | Him, rich in wealth, let swift Steeds bring to us, his Bays, to Soma juice for his carouse: || 8. Yea, that most excellent carouse, Indra, which slays most enemies, | With Heroes wins the light of heaven, and is invincible in war: || 9. Which merits fame, all-bountiful! and, unsubdued, hath victory in deeds of might. | So come to our libations, Strongest! Excellent! May we obtain a stall of kine. || 10. Responding to our wish for cows, for steeds, and chariots, as of old, | Be gracious, Greatest of the Great || 11. For, Hero, nowhere can I find the bounds of thy munificence. | Still do thou favour us, O Bolt-armed Maghavan: with strength hast thou rewarded hymns. || 12. High, glorifier of his friend, he knows all generations, he whom many praise. | All races of mankind with ladies lifted up invoke that Mighty Indra's aid. || 13. Be he our Champion and Protector in great deeds, rich in all wealth, the Vṛitra-slayer, Maghavan. || 14. In the wild raptures of the juice sing to your Hero with high laud, to him the Wise, | To Indra, glorious in his name, the Mighty One, even as the hymn alloweth it. || 15. Thou givest wealth to me myself, thou givest treasure, Excellent! and the strong steed, | O Much-invoked, in deeds of might, yea, even now. || 16. Him, Sovereign Ruler of all precious things, who even hath power o'er this fair form of his, | As now it taketh shape, and afterward, || 17. We praise, so that the Mighty One may speed to you, Pourer of bounties, Traveller, prepared to go. | Thou favourest the Marutas known to all, by song and sacrifice. | With song and praise I sing to thee. || 18. We in the sacrifice perform their will whose voice is lifted high, | The worship of those Thundering ones who o'er the ridges of these mountains fly in troops. || 19. O Indra, Mightiest, bring us that which crushes men of evil minds, | Wealth suited to our needs, O Stirrer of the thought, best wealth, O thou who stirrest thought. || 20. O Winner, noble winner, strong, wondrous, most splendid, excellent, | Sole Lord of victory, bring all-overpowering wealth, joy-giving, chief in deeds of might. || 21. Now let the godless man approach who hath received reward so great | As Vaśa, Aśvya, when this light of morning dawned, received from Pṛithuśravas, from Kanīta's son. || 22. Steeds sixty thousand and ten thousand kine, and twenty hundred camels I obtained; | Ten hundred brown in hue, and other ten red in three spots: in all, ten thousand kine. || 23. Ten browns that make my wealth increase, fleet steeds whose tails are long and fair, | Turn with swift whirl my chariot wheel; || 24. The gifts which Pṛithuśravas gave, Kanīta's son munificent. | He gave a chariot wrought of gold: the prince was passing bountiful, and won himself most lofty fame. || 25. Come thou to this great rite of ours, Vāyu! to give us vigorous light. | We have served thee that thou mightest give much to us, yea, mightest quickly give great wealth. || 26. Who with thrice seven times seventy horses comes to us, invested with the rays of morn, | Through these our Soma-draughts and those who press, to give, drinker of pure bright Soma Juice. || 27. Who hath inclined this glorious one, bounteous himself, to give me gifts. | Borne on firm chariot with the prosperous Nahuṣha, wise, to a man yet more devout. || 28. Sole Lord in beauty meet for praise, O Vāyu, dropping fatness down, | Hurried along by steeds, by camels, and by hounds, spreads forth thy train: even this it is. || 29. So, as a prize dear to the strong, the sixty thousand have I gained, | Bulls that resemble vigorous steeds. || 30. To me come oxen like a herd, yea, unto me the oxen come. || 31. And in the grazing herd he made a hundred camels bleat for me, | And twenty hundred mid the white. || 32. A hundred has the sage received, Dāsa Balbūtha's and Tarukṣha's gifts. | These are thy people, Vāyu, who rejoice with Indra for their guard, rejoice with Gods for guards. || 33. And now to Vaśa Aśvya here this stately woman is led forth, | Adorned with ornaments of gold.

Hymn 8:47. Ādityas.

1. Great help ye give the worshipper, Varuṇa, Mitra, Mighty Ones! No sorrow ever reaches him whom ye, Ādityas, keep from harm. Yours are incomparable aids, and good the succour they afford. || 2. O Gods, Ādityas, well ye know the way to keep all woes afar. | As the birds spread their sheltering wings, spread your protection over us. || 3. As the birds spread their sheltering wings let your protection cover us. | We mean all shelter and defence, ye who have all things for your own. || 4. To whomsoever they, Most Wise, have given a home and means of life, | O'er the whole riches of this man they, the Ādityas, have control. || 5. As drivers of the car avoid ill roads, let sorrows pass us by. | May we be under Indra's guard, in the Ādityas' favouring grace. || 6. For verily men sink and faint through loss of wealth which ye have given. | Much hath he gained from you, O Gods, whom ye, Ādityas, have approached. || 7. On him shall no fierce anger fall, no sore distress shall visit him, | To whom, Ādityas, ye have lent your shelter that extendeth far. || 8. Resting in you, O Gods, we are like men who fight in coats of mail. | Ye guard us from each great offence, ye guard us from each lighter fault. || 9. May Aditi defend us, may Aditi guard and shelter us, | Mother of wealthy Mitra and of Aryaman and Varuṇa. || 10. The shelter, Gods, that is secure, auspicious, free from malady, | A sure protection, triply strong, even that do ye extend to us. || 11. Look down on us, Ādityas, as a guide exploring from the bank. | Lead us to pleasant ways as men lead horses to an easy ford. || 12. Ill be it for the demons' friend to find us or come near to us. | But for the milch-cow be it well, and for the man who strives for fame. || 13. Each evil deed made manifest, and that which is concealed, O Gods, | The whole thereof remove from us to Trita Āptya far away. || 14. Daughter of Heaven, the dream that bodes evil to us or to our kine, | Remove, O Lady of the Light, to Trita Āptya far away. || 15. Even if, O Child of Heaven, it make a garland or a chain of gold, | The whole bad dream, whate'er it be, to Trita Āptya we consign. || 16. To him whose food and work is this, who comes to take his share therein, | To Trita, and to Dvita, Dawn! bear thou the evil dream away. || 17. As we collect the utmost debt, even the eighth and sixteenth part, | So unto Āptya we transfer together all the evil dream. || 18. Now have we conquered and obtained, and from our trespasses are free. | Shine thou away the evil dream, O Dawn, whereof we are afraid. Yours are incomparable aids, and good the succour they afford.

Hymn 8:48. Soma.

1. Wisely have I enjoyed the savoury viand, religious-thoughted, best to find out treasure, | The food to which all Deities and mortals, calling it meath, gather themselves together. || 2. Thou shalt be Aditi as thou hast entered within, appeaser of celestial anger. | Indu, enjoying Indra's friendship, bring us—as a swift steed the car—forward to riches. || 3. We have drunk Soma and become immortal; we have attained the light, the Gods discovered. | Now what may foeman's malice do to harm us? What, O Immortal, mortal man's deception? || 4. Absorbed into the heart, be sweet,

O Indu, as a kind father to his son, O Soma, | As a wise Friend to friend: do thou, wide-ruler, O Soma, lengthen out our days for living. || 5. These glorious drops that give me freedom have I drunk. Closely they knit my joints as straps secure a car. | Let them protect my foot from slipping on the way: yea, let the drops I drink preserve me from disease. || 6. Make me shine bright like fire produced by friction: give us a clearer sight and make us better. | For in carouse I think of thee, O Soma, Shall I, as a rich man, attain to comfort? || 7. May we enjoy with an enlivened spirit the juice thou givest, like ancestral riches. | O Soma, King, prolong thou our existence as Sūrya makes the shining days grow longer. || 8. King Soma, favour us and make us prosper: we are thy devotees; of this be mindful. | Spirit and power are fresh in us, O Indu give us not up unto our foeman's pleasure. || 9. For thou hast settled in each joint, O Soma, aim of men's eyes and guardian of our bodies. | When we offend against thine holy statutes, as a kind Friend, God, best of all, be gracious. || 10. May I be with the Friend whose heart is tender, who, Lord of Bays! when quaffed will never harm me— | This Soma now deposited within me. For this, I pray for longer life to Indra. || 11. Our maladies have lost their strength and vanished: they feared, and passed away into the darkness. | Soma hath risen in us, exceeding mighty, and we are come where men prolong existence. | 12, Fathers, that Indu which our hearts have drunken, Immortal in himself, hath entered mortals. | So let us serve this Soma with oblation, and rest securely in his grace and favour. || 13. Associate with the Fathers thou, O Soma, hast spread thyself abroad through earth and heaven. | So with oblation let us serve thee, Indu, and so let us become the lords of riches, || 14. Give us your blessing, O ye Gods' preservers. Never may sleep or idle talk control us. | But evermore may we, as friends of Soma, speak to the synod with brave sons around us. || 15. On all sides, Soma, thou art our life-giver: aim of all eyes, light-finder, come within us. | Indu, of one accord with thy protections both from behind and from before preserve us.

Note: "I place at the end of this Maṇḍala the eleven spurious or apocryphal hymns, called the Vālakhilya, which are usually inserted after Hymn 48. These hymns are not reckoned in the division of the Ṛigveda into Maṇḍalas and Anuvākas (chapters), and Sāyaṇa does not notice them in his Commentary (see Wilson's Translation, Note by Professor Cowell). Eleven must be added to the number of the following hymn and of all that follow in this Maṇḍala to make them correspond with the numbers in Professor Max Müller's edition of the text."—Griffith

Hymn 8:49. Agni.

1. Agni, come hither with thy fires; we choose thee as Invoking Priest. | Let the extended ladle full of oil balm thee, best Priest, to sit on sacred grass. || 2. For unto thee, O Aṅgiras, O Son of Strength, move ladles in the sacrifice. | To Agni, Child of Force, whose locks drop oil, we seek, foremost in sacrificial rites. || 3. Agni, thou art Disposer, Sage, Herald, bright God! and worshipful, | Best offerer, cheerful, to be praised in holy rites, pure Lord! by singers with their hymns. || 4. Most Youthful and Eternal, bring the longing Gods to me, the guileless, for the feast. | Come, Vasu, to the banquet that is well-prepared: rejoice thee, gracious, with our songs. || 5. Famed art thou, Agni, far and wide, Preserver, righteous, and a Sage. | The holy singers, O refulgent kindled God! arrangers, call on thee to come— || 6. Shine, Most Resplendent! blaze, send bliss unto the folk, and to thy worshipper | Great art thou. | So may my princes, with good fires, subduing foes, rest in the keeping of the Gods. || 7. O Agni, as thou burnest down to earth even high-grown underwood, | So, bright as Mitra is, burn him who injures us, him who plots ill against thy friend. || 8. Give us not as a prey to mortal enemy, nor to the wicked friend of fiends. | With conquering guards, auspicious, unassailable, protect us, O Most Youthful God. || 9. Protect us, Agni, through the first, protect us through the second hymn, | Protect us through three hymns, O Lord of Power and Might, through four hymns, Vasu, guard thou us. || 10. Preserve us from each fiend who brings the Gods no gift, preserve thou us in deeds of strength: | For we possess in thee the nearest Friend of all, for service of the Gods and weal. || 11. O Holy Agni, give us wealth renowned with men and strengthening life. | Bestow on us, O Helper, that which many crave, more glorious still by righteousness; || 12. Wherewith we may o'ercome our rivals in the war, o'erpowering the foe's designs. | So wax thou by our food, O Excellent in strength. Quicken our thoughts that find out wealth. || 13. Agni is even as a bull who whets and brandishes his horns. | Well-sharpened are his jaws which may not be withstood: the Child of Strength hath powerful teeth. || 14. Not to be stayed, O Bull, O Agni, are thy teeth when thou art spreading far and wide. | Make our oblations duly offered up, O Priest, and give us store of precious things. || 15. Thou liest in the wood: from both thy Mothers mortals kindle thee. | Unweariedly thou bearest up the offerer's gifts, then shinest bright among the Gods. || 16. And so the seven priests, O Agni, worship thee, Free-giver, Everlasting One. | Thou cleavest through the rock with heat and fervent glow. Agni, rise up above the men. || 17. For you let us whose grass is trimmed call Agni, Agni, restless God. | Let us whose food is offered call to all the tribes Agni the Invoking Priest of men. || 18. Agni, with noble psalm that tells his wish he dwells, thinking on thee who guardest him. | Speedily bring us strength of many varied sorts to be most near to succour us. || 19. Agni, Praise-singer! Lord of men, God burner-up of Rākṣhasas, | Mighty art thou, the ever-present Household-Lord, Home-friend and Guardian from the sky. || 20. Let no fiend come among us, O thou rich in light, no spell of those who deal in spells. | To distant pastures drive faint hunger: far away, O Agni, chase the demons' friends.

Hymn 8:50. Indra.

1. Both boons, may Indra, hitherward turned, listen to this prayer of ours, | And mightiest Maghavan with thought inclined to us come near to drink the Soma juice. || 2. For him, strong, independent Ruler, Heaven and Earth have fashioned forth for power and might. | Thou seatest thee as first among thy peers in place, for thy soul longs for Soma juice. || 3. Fill thyself full, O Lord of wealth, O Indra, with the juice we shed. | We know thee, Lord of Bay Steeds victor in the fight, vanquishing e'en the invincible. || 4. Changeless in truth, O Maghavan Indra, let it be as thou in wisdom willest it. | May we, O fair of check, win booty with thine aid, O Thunderer, swiftly seeking it. || 5. Indra, with all thy saving helps give us assistance, Lord of power. | For after thee we follow even as glorious bliss, thee, Hero, finder-out of wealth. || 6. Increaser of our steeds and multiplying kine, a golden well, O God, art thou, | For no one may impair the gifts laid up in thee. Bring me whatever thing I ask. || 7. For thou,—come to the worshipper!-wilt find great wealth to make us rich. | Fill thyself full, O Maghavan, for gain of kine, full, Indra, for the gain of steeds. || 8. Thou as thy gift bestowest many hundred herds, yea, many thousands dost thou give. | With singers' hymns have we brought the Fort-render near, singing to Indra for his grace. || 9. Whether the simple or the sage, Indra, have offered praise to thee, | He Śatakratu! by his love hath gladdened thee, ambitious! ever pressing on! || 10. If he the Strong of arm, the breaker-down of forts, the great Destroyer, hear my call, | We, seeking riches cry to Indra, Lord of wealth, to Śatakratu with our lauds. || 11. We count not then as sinners, nor as niggardly or foolish men, | When with the Soma juice which we have shed we make Indra, the Mighty One, our Friend. || 12. Him have we yoked in fight, the powerful Conqueror, debt-claimer, not to be deceived. | Best charioteer, the Victor marks each fault, he knows the strong to whom he will come near. || 13. Indra, give us security from that whereof we are afraid. | Help us, O Maghavan, let thy succour give us this: drive away foes and enemies. || 14. For thou, O liberal Lord of bounty, strengthenest his ample home who worships thee. | So Indra, Maghavan, thou Lover of the Song, we with pressed Soma call on thee, || 15. Indra is Vṛitra-slayer, guard, our best defender from the foe. | May he preserve our last and middle-most, and keep watch from behind us and before. || 16. Defend us from behind, below, above, in front, on all sides, Indra, shield us well. | Keep far away from us the terror sent from heaven: keep impious weapons far away. || 17. Protect us, Indra, each today, each morrow, and each following day. | Our singers, through all days, shalt thou, Lord of the brave, keep safely both by day and night. || 18. A crushing Warrior, passing rich is Maghavan, endowed with all heroic might. | Thine arms, O Śatakratu, are exceeding strong, arms which have grasped the thunderbolt.

Hymn 8:51. Indra.

1. Offer ye up as praise to him that wherein Indra takes delight. | The Soma-bringers magnify Indra's great energy with hymns. Good are the gifts that Indra gives. || 2. Sole among chiefs, companionless, impetuous, and peerless, he | Hath waxen great o'er many folk, yea, over all things

born, in might. || 3. Lord of swift bounty, he will win e'en with a steed of worthless sort. | This, Indra, must be told of thee who wilt perform heroic deeds. || 4. Come to us hither: let us pay devotions that enhance thy might, | For which, Most Potent! thou wouldst fain bless the man here who strives for fame. || 5. For thou, O Indra, makest yet more bold the spirit of the bold | Who with strong Soma serveth thee, still ready with his reverent prayers. || 6. Worthy of song, he looketh down as a man looketh into wells. | Pleased with the Soma-bringer's skill he maketh him his mate and friend. || 7. In strength and wisdom all the Gods, Indra, have yielded unto thee. | Be thou the Guard of all, O thou whom many praise. || 8. Praised, Indra, is this might of thine, best for the service of the Gods, | That thou with power dost slay Vṛitra, O Lord of Strength. || 9. He makes the races of mankind like synods of the Beauteous One. | Indra knows this his manifest deed, and is renowned. || 10. Thy might, O Indra, at its birth, thee also, and thy mental power, | In thy care, Maghavan rich in kine! they have increased exceedingly. || 11. O Vṛitra-slayer, thou and I will both combine for winning spoil. | Even malignity will consent, O Bolt-armed Hero, unto us. || 12. Let us extol this Indra as truthful and never as untrue. | Dire is his death who pours no gifts great light hath he who offers them. Good are the gifts that Indra gives.

Hymn 8:52. Indra.

1. With powers of Mighty Ones hath he, Ancient, Beloved, been equipped, | Through whom the Father Manu made prayers efficacious with the Gods. || 2. Him, Maker of the sky, let stones wet with the Soma ne'er forsake, | Nor hymns and prayer that must be said. || 3. Indra who knew full well disclosed the kine to the Aṅgirasas. | This his great deed must be extolled. || 4. Indra, promoter of the song, the sage's Strengthener as of old, | Shall come to bless and succour us at presentation of this laud. || 5. Now after their desire's intent the pious singers with the cry | Of Hail! have sung loud hymns to thee, Indra, to gain a stall of kine. || 6. With Indra rest all deeds of might, deeds done and yet to be performed, | Whom singers know devoid of guile. || 7. When the Five Tribes with all their men to Indra have sent out their voice, | And when the priest hath strewn much grass, this is the Friend's own dwelling-place. || 8. This praise is verily thine own: thou hast performed these manly deeds, | And sped the wheel upon its way. || 9. At the o'erflowing of this Steer, boldly he strode for life, and took | Soma as cattle take their corn. || 10. Receiving this and craving help, we, who with you are Dakṣha's sons, | Would fain exalt the Marutas' Lord. || 11. Yea, Hero, with the singers we sing to the duly-coming Band. | Allied with thee may we prevail. || 12. With us are raining Rudras, clouds accordant in call to battle, at the death of Vṛitra, | The strong assigned to him who sings and praises. May Gods with Indra at their head protect us.

Hymn 8:53. Indra.

1. May our hymns give thee great delight. Display thy bounty, Thunderer. | Drive off the enemies of prayer. || 2. Crush with thy foot the niggard churls who bring no gifts. Mighty art thou | There is not one to equal thee. || 3. Thou art the Lord of Soma pressed, Soma impressed is also thine. | Thou art the Sovereign of the folk. || 4. Come, go thou forth, dwelling in heaven and listening to the prayers of men: | Thou fillest both the heavens and earth. || 5. Even that hill with rocky heights, with hundreds, thousands, held within. | Thou for thy worshippers brakest through. || 6. We call on thee both night and day to taste the flowing Soma juice: | Do thou fulfil our heart's desire. || 7. Where is that ever-youthful Steer, strong. necked and never yet bent down? | What Brahman ministers to him? || 8. To whose libation doth the Steer, betake him with delight therein? | Who takes delight in Indra now? || 9. Whom, Vṛitra-slayer, have thy gift and hero powers accompanied? | Who is thy dearest in the laud? || 10. For thee among mankind, among the Pūrus is this Soma shed. | Hasten thou hither: drink thereof. || 11. This, growing by Soma and by Śaryaṇāvat, dear to thee, | In Ārjīkīya, cheers thee best. || 12. Hasten thou hitherward, and drink this for munificence today, | Delightful for thine eager draught.

Hymn 8:54. Indra.

1. Though, Indra, thou art called by men from east and west, from north and south, | Come hither quickly with fleet steeds || 2. If in the effluence of heaven, rich in its light, thou takest joy, | Or in the sea in Soma juice. || 3. With songs I call thee, Great and Wide, even as a cow to profit us, | Indra, to drink the Soma-draught. || 4. Hither, O Indra, let thy Bays bear up and, bring upon thy car | Thy glory, God! and majesty. || 5. Thou, Indra, wouldst be sung and praised as great, strong, lordly in thy deeds | Come hither, drink our Soma juice. || 6. We who have shed the Soma and prepared the feast are calling thee. | To sit on this our sacred grass. || 7. As, Indra, thou art evermore the common Lord of all alike, | As such we invocate thee now. || 8. The men with stones have milked for thee this nectar of the Soma juice: | Indra, be pleased with it, and drink. || 9. Neglect all pious men with skill in sacred song: come hitherward, | With speed, and give us high renown. || 10. Gods, may the mighty rest unharmed, the King who gives me spotted kine, | Kine decked with golden ornaments. || 11. Beside a thousand spotted kine I have received a gift of gold, | Pure, brilliant, and exceeding great. || 12. Durgaha's grandsons, giving me a thousand kine, munificent, | Have won renown among the Gods.

Hymn 8:55. Indra.

1. Loud singing at the sacred rite where Soma flows we priests invoke | With haste, that he may help, as the bard's Cherisher, Indra who findeth wealth for you. | 2. Whom with fair helm, in rapture of the juice, the firm resistless slayers hinder not: | Giver of glorious wealth to him who sing a his praise, honouring him who toils and pours: || 3. Śakra, who like a curry-comb for horses or a golden goad, | Indra, the Vṛitra-slayer, urges eagerly the opening of the stall of kine: || 4. Who for the worshipper scatters forth ample wealth, even though buried, piled in heaps: | May Indra, Lord of Bay Steeds, fair-helmed Thunderer, act at his pleasure, as he lists. || 5. Hero whom many praise, what thou hast longed for, oven of old, from men. | All that we offer unto thee, O Indra, now, sacrifice, laud, effectual speech. || 6. To Soma, Much-invoked, Bolt-armed! for thy carouse, Celestial, Soma-drinker come. | Thou to the man who—prays and pours the juice hast been best giver of delightful wealth. || 7. Here, verily, yesterday we let the Thunder-wielder drink his fill. | So in like manner offer him the juice today. Now range you by the Glorious One. || 8. Even the wolf, the savage beast that rends the sheep, follows the path of his decrees. | So graciously accepting, Indra, this our praise, with wondrous thought come forth to us. || 9. What manly deed of vigour now remains that Indra hath not done? | Who hath not heard his glorious title and his fame, the Vṛitra-slayer from his birth? || 10. How great his power resistless! how invincible the Vṛitra-slayer's matchless might! | Indra excels all usurers who see the day, excels all traffickers in strength. || 11. O Indra, Vṛitra-slayer, we, thy very constant worshippers, | Bring prayers ne'er heard before to thee, O Much-invoked, O Thunder-armed, to be thy meed. || 12. O thou of mighty acts, the aids that are in thee call forward many an eager hope. | Past the drink-offerings, Vasu, even of the good, hear my call, Strongest God, and come. || 13. Verily, Indra, we are thine, we worshippers depend on thee. | For there is none but only thou to show us race, O Maghavan, thou much invoked. || 14. From this our misery and famine set us free, from this dire curse deliver us. | Succour us with thine help and with thy wondrous thought. Most Mighty, finder of the way. || 15. Now let your Soma juice be poured; be not afraid, O Kali's sons. | This darkening sorrow goes away; yea, of itself it vanishes.

Hymn 8:56. Ādityas.

1. Now pray we to these Kṣhatriyas, to the Ādityas for their aid, | These who are gracious to assist. || 2. May Mitra bear us o'er distress, and Varuṇa and Aryaman, | Yea, the Ādityas, as they know. || 3. For wonderful and meet for praise is these Ādityas' saving help | To him who offers and prepares. || 4. The mighty aid of you, the Great, Varuṇa, Mitra, Aryaman, | We claim to be our sure defence. || 5. Guard us, Ādityas, still alive, before the deadly weapon strike: | Are ye not they who hear our call? || 6. What sheltering defence ye have for him who toils in pouring gifts, | Graciously bless ye us therewith. || 7. Ādityas, Gods, from sorrow there is freedom; for the sinless, wealth, | O ye in whom no fault is seen. || 8. Let not this fetter bind us fast: may he release us for success; | For strong is Indra and renowned. || 9. O Gods who fain would lend your aid, destroy not us as ye destroy | Your enemies who go astray. || 10. And thee too, O Great Aditi, thee also, Goddess, I address, | Thee very gracious to assist. || 11. Save us in depth and shallow from the foe, thou Mother of Strong Sons | Let no one of our seed be harmed. || 12. Far-spread! wide-ruling! grant that we, unharmed by envy, may expand | Grant that our progeny may live. || 13. Those who, the Princes of the folk, in native glory, ne'er deceived, | Maintain their statutes, void of

guilt— || 14. As such, from mouth of ravening wolves, O ye Ādityas, rescue us, | Like a bound thief, O Aditi. || 15. Ādityas, let this arrow, yea, let this malignity depart | From us or e'er it strike us dead. || 16. For, Bountiful Ādityas, we have evermore enjoyed your help, | Both now and in die days of old. || 17. To every one, O ye Most Wise, who turneth even from sin to you, | Ye Gods vouchsafe that he may live. || 18. May this new mercy profit us, which, ye Ādityas, frees like one, | Bound from his bonds, O Aditi. || 19. O ye Ādityas, this your might is not to be despised by us: | So be ye graciously inclined. || 20. Let not Vivasvat's weapon nor the shaft, Ādityas, wrought with skill, | Destroy us ere old age be nigh. || 21. On every side dispel all sin, Ādityas, all hostility, | Indigence, and combined attack.

Hymn 8:57. Indra.

1. Even as a car to give us aid, we draw thee hither for our bliss, | Strong in thy deeds, checking assault, Lord, Mightiest Indra, of the brave! || 2. Great in thy power and wisdom, Strong, with thought that comprehendeth all | Thou hast filled full with majesty. || 3. Thou very Mighty One, whose hands by virtue of thy greatness grasp, | The golden bolt that breaks its way. || 4. Your Lord of might that ne'er hath bent, that ruleth over all mankind, | I call, that he, as he is wont, may aid the chariots and the men. || 5. Whom, ever furthering, in frays that win the light, in both the hosts | Men call to succour and to help. || 6. Indra, the Strong, the measureless, worthy of praise, Most Bountiful, | Sole Ruler even over wealth. || 7. Him, for his ample bounty, him, this Indra do I urge to drink, | Who, as his praise was sung of old, the Dancer, is the Lord of men. || 8. Thou Mighty One, whose friendship none of mortals ever hath obtained | None will attain unto thy might. || 9. Aided by thee, with thee allied, in frays for water and for sun, | Bolt-armed! may we win ample spoil. || 10. So seek we thee with sacrifice and songs, chief Lover of the Song, | As, in our battles Indra, thou to Purumāyya gavest help. || 11. O Thunderer, thou whose friendship and whose onward guidance both are sweet, | Thy sacrifice must be prepared. || 12. To us, ourselves, give ample room, give for our dwelling ample room | Give ample room to us to live. || 13. We count the banquet of the Gods a spacious pathway for the men, | And for the cattle, and the car. || 14. Six men, yea, two and two, made glad with Soma juice, come near to me | With offerings pleasant to the taste. || 15. Two brown-hued steeds, Indrota's gift, two bays from Ṛiksha's son were mine, | From Aśvamedha's son two red. || 16. From Atithigva good car-steeds; from Ārksha rein-obeying steeds, | From Aśvamedha beauteous ones. || 17. Indrota, Atithigva's son, gave me six horses matched with mares | And Pūtakratu gave besides. || 18. Marked above all, amid the brown, is the red mare Vṛishaṇvatī, | Obedient to the rein and whip. || 19. O bound to me by deeds of might, not even the man who loves to blame. | Hath found a single fault in you.

Hymn 8:58. Indra.

1. I send you forth the song of praise for Indu, hero-gladdener. | With hymn and plenty he invites you to complete the sacrifice. || 2. Thou wishest for thy kine a bull, for those who long for his approach, | For those who turn away from him, lord of thy cows whom none may kill. || 3. The dappled kine who stream with milk prepare his draught of Soma juice: | Clans in the birth-place of the Gods, in the three luminous realms of heaven. || 4. Praise, even as he is known, with song Indra the guardian of the kine, | The Son of Truth, Lord of the brave. || 5. Hither his Bay Steeds have been sent, red Steeds are on the sacred grass,, | Where we in concert sing our songs. || 6. For Indra Thunder-armed the kine have yielded mingled milk and meath, | What time he found them in the vault. || 7. When I and Indra mount on high up to the Bright One's place and home, | We, having drunk of meath, will reach his seat whose Friends are three times seven. || 8. Sing, sing ye forth your songs of praise, ye Priyamedhas, sing your songs: | Yea, let young children sing their lauds as a strong castle praise ye him. || 9. Now loudly let the viol sound, the lute send out its voice with might, | Shrill be, the music of the string. To Indra. is the hymn upraised. || 10. When hither speed the dappled cows, unflinching, easy to be milked, | Seize quickly, as it bursts away, the Soma juice for Indra's drink. || 11. Indra hath drunk, Agni hath drunk. all Deities have drunk their fill. | Here Varuṇa shall have his home, to whom the floods have sung aloud as mother kine unto their calves. || 12. Thou, Varuṇa, to whom belong Seven Rivers, art a glorious God. | The waters flow into thy throat as 'twere a pipe with ample mouth. || 13. He who hath made the fleet steeds spring, well-harnessed, to the worshipper, | He, the swift Guide, is that fair form that loosed the horses near at hand. || 14. Indra, the very Mighty, holds his enemies in utter scorn. | He, far away, and yet a child, cleft the cloud smitten by his voice. || 15. He, yet a boy exceeding small, mounted his newly-fashioned car. | He for his Mother and his Sire cooked the wild mighty buffalo. || 16. Lord of the home, fair-helmeted, ascend thy chariot wrought of gold. | We will attend the Heavenly One, the thousand-footed, red of hue, matchless, who blesses where he goes. || 17. With reverence they come hitherward to him as to. a Sovereign lord, | That they may bring him near for this man's good success, to prosper and bestow his gifts. || 18. The Priyamedhas have observed the offering of the men of old, | Of ancient custom, while they strewed the sacred grass, and spread their sacrificial food.

Hymn 8:59. Indra.

1. He who, as Sovereign Lord of men, moves with his chariots unrestrained, | The Vṛitra-slayer vanquisher, of fighting hosts, preeminent, is praised with song. || 2. Honour that Indra, Puruhanman! for his aid, in whose sustaining hand of old, | The splendid bolt of thunder was deposited, as the great Sun was set in heaven. || 3. No one by deed attains to him who works and strengthens evermore: | No, not by sacrifice, to Indra. praised o all, resistless, daring, bold in might. || 4. The potent Conqueror, invincible in war, him at whose birth the Mighty Ones, | The Kine who spread afar, sent their loud voices out, heavens, earths seat their loud voices out, || 5. O Indra, if a hundred heavens and if a hundred earths were thine — | No, not a thousand Suns could match thee at thy birth, not both the worlds, O Thunderer. || 6. Thou, Hero, hast performed thy hero deeds with might, yea, all with strength, O Strongest One. | Maghavan, help us to a stable full of kine, O Thunderer, with wondrous aids. || 7. Let not a godless mortal gain this food, O thou whose life is long! | But one who yokes the bright-hued steeds, the Etaśas, even Indra yoker of the Bays. || 8. Urge ye the Conqueror to give, your Indra greatly to be praised, | To be invoked in shallow waters and in depths, to be invoked in deeds of might. || 9. O Vasu, O thou Hero, raise us up to ample opulence. | Raise us to gain of mighty wealth, O Maghavan, O Indra, to sublime renown. || 10. Indra, thou justifiest us, and tramplest down thy slanderers. | Guard thyself, valiant Hero, in thy vital parts: strike down the Dāsa with thy blows. || 11. The man who brings no sacrifice, inhuman, godless, infidel, | Him let his friend the mountain cast to rapid death, the mountain cast the Dasyu down. || 12. O Mightiest Indra, loving us, gather thou up, as grains of corn, | Within thine hand, of these their kine, to give away, yea, gather twice as loving us. || 13. O my companions, wish for power. How may we perfect Śara's praise, | The liberal princely patron, never to be harmed? || 14. By many a sage whose grass is trimmed thou art continually praised, | That thou, O Śara, hast bestowed here one and here another calf. || 15. The noble, Śūradeva's son, hath brought a calf, led by the car to three of us. | As a chief brings a goat to milk.

Hymn 8:60. Agni.

1. O Agni, with thy mighty wealth guard us from all malignity, | Yea, from all hate of mortal man. || 2. For over thee, O Friend from birth, the wrath of man hath no control: | Nay, Guardian of the earth art thou. || 3. As such, with all the Gods, O Son of Strength, auspicious in thy flame. | Give us wealth bringing all things good. || 4. Malignities stay not from wealth the mortal man whom, Agni, thou | Protectest while he offers gifts. || 5. Sage Agni, be whom thou dost urge, in worship of the Gods, to wealth, | With thine assistance winneth kine. || 6. Riches with many heroes thou hast for the man who offers gifts: | Lead thou us on to higher bliss. || 7. Save us, O Jātavedas, nor abandon us to him who sins, | Unto the evil-hearted man. || 8. O Agni, let no godless man avert thy bounty as a God: | Over all treasures thou art Lord. || 9. So, Son of Strength, thou aidest us to what is great and excellent. | Those, Vasu! Friend! who sing thy praise. || 10. Let our songs come anear to him beauteous and bright with piercing flame | Our offerings, with our homage, to the | Lord of wealth, to him whom many praise, for help: || 11. To Agni Jātavedas, to the Son of Strength, that he may give us precious gifts, | Immortal, from of old Priest among mortal men, the most delightful in the house. || 12. Agni, made yours by sacrifice, Agni, while holy rites advance; | Agni, the first in songs, first with the warrior steed; Agni, to win the land for us. || 13. May Agni who is Lord of wealth

vouchsafe us food for friendship sake. | Agni we ever seek for seed and progeny, the Vasu who protects our lives. || 14. Solicit with your chants, for help, Agni the God with piercing flame, | For riches famous Agni, Purumīlha and ye men! Agni to light our dwelling well. || 15. Agni we laud that he may keep our foes afar, Agni to give us health and strength. | Let him as Guardian be invoked in all the tribes, the lighter-up of glowing brands.

Hymn 8:61. Agni.

1. Prepare oblation: let him come; and let the minister serve again | Who knows the ordering thereof, || 2. Rejoicing in his friendship, let the priest be seated over man, | Beside the shoot of active power. || 3. Him, glowing bright beyond all thought, they seek among the race of man; | With him for tongue they seize the food. || 4. He hath inflamed the twofold plain: life-giving, he hath climbed the wood, | And with his tongue hath struck the rock. || 5. Wandering here the radiant Calf finds none to fetter him, and seeks | The Mother to declare his praise. || 6. And now that great and mighty team, the team of horses that are his, | And traces of his car, are seen. || 7. The seven milk a single cow; the two set other five to work, | On the stream's loud-resounding bank. || 8. Entreated by Vivasvat's ten, Indra cast down the water-jar | With threefold hammer from the sky. || 9. Three times the newly-kindled flame proceeds around the sacrifice: | The priests anoint it with the meath. || 10. With reverence they drain the fount that circles with its wheel above, | Exhaustless, with the mouth below. || 11. The pressing-stones are set at work: the meath is poured into the tank, | At the out-shedding of the fount. || 12. Ye cows, protect the fount: the two Mighty Ones bless the sacrifice. | The handles twain are wrought of gold. || 13. Pour on the juice the ornament which reaches both the heaven and earth | Supply the liquid to the Bull. || 14. These know their own abiding-place: like calves beside the mother cows | They meet together with their kin. || 15. Devouring in their greedy jaws, they make sustaining food in heaven, | To Indra, Agni light and prayer. || 16. The Pious One milked out rich food, sustenance dealt in portions seven, | Together with the Sun's seven rays. || 17. I took some Soma when the Sun rose up, O Mitra, Varuṇa. | That is the sick man's medicine. || 18. From where oblations must be laid, which is the Well-beloved's home, | He with his tongue hath compassed heaven.

Hymn 8:62. Aśvins.

1. Rouse ye for him who keeps the Law, yoke your steeds, Aśvins, to your car | Let your protecting help be near. || 2. Come, Aśvins, with your car more swift than is the twinkling of an eye | Let your protecting help be near. || 3. Aśvins, ye overlaid with cold the fiery pit for Atri's sake: | Let your protecting help be near. || 4. Where are ye? whither are ye gone? whither, like falcons, have ye flown? | Let your protecting help be near. || 5. If ye at any time this day are listening to this my call, | Let your protecting help be near. || 6. The Aśvins, first to hear our prayer, for closest kinship I approach: | Let your protecting help be near. || 7. For Atri ye, O Aśvins, made a dwelling-place to shield him well, | Let your protecting help be near. || 8. Ye warded off the fervent heat for Atri when he sweetly spake: | Let your protecting help be near. || 9. Erst Saptavadhri by his prayer obtained the trenchant edge of fire: | Let your protecting help be near. || 10. Come hither, O ye Lords of wealth, and listen to this call of mine: | Let your protecting help be near. || 11. What is this praise told forth of you as Elders in the ancient way? | Let your protecting help be near. || 12. One common brotherhood is yours, Aśvins your kindred is the same: | Let your protecting help be near. || 13. This is your chariot, Aśvins, which speeds through the regions, earth and heaven | Let your protecting aid be near. || 14. Approach ye hitherward to us with thousands both of steeds and kine: | Let your protecting help be near. || 15. Pass us not by, remember us with thousands both of kine and steeds: | Let your protecting help be near. || 16. The purple-tinted Dawn hath risen, and true to Law hath made the light | Let your protecting help be near. || 17. He looked upon the Aśvins, as an axe-armed man upon a tree: | Let your protecting help be near. || 18. By the black band encompassed round, break it down, bold one, like a fort. | Let your protecting help be near.

Hymn 8:63. Agni.

1. Exerting all our strength with thoughts of power we glorify in speech | Agni your dear familiar Friend, the darling Guest in every home. || 2. Whom, served with sacrificial oil like Mitra, men presenting gifts | Eulogize with their songs of praise || 3. Much-lauded Jātavedas, him who bears oblations up to heaven | Prepared in service of the Gods. || 4. To noblest Agni, Friend of man, best Vṛitra-slayer, are we come, | Him in whose presence Ṛikṣha's son, mighty Śrutarvan, waxes great; || 5. To deathless Jātavedas, meet for praise, adored, with sacred oil, | Visible through the gloom of night || 6. Even Agni whom these priestly men worship with sacrificial gifts, | With lifted ladles offering them. || 7. O Agni, this our newest hymn hath been addressed from us to thee, | O cheerful Guest, well-born, most wise, worker of wonders, ne'er deceived. || 8. Agni, may it be dear to thee, most grateful, and exceeding sweet: | Grow mightier, eulogized therewith. || 9. Splendid with splendours may it be, and in the battle with the foe | Add loftier glory to thy fame. || 10. Steed, cow, a lord of heroes, bright like Indra, who shall fill the car. | Whose high renown ye celebrate, and people praise each glorious deed. || 11. Thou whom Gopavana made glad with song, O Agni Aṅgiras, | Hear this my call, thou Holy One. || 12. Thou whom the priestly folk implore to aid the gathering of the spoil, | Such be thou in the fight with foes. || 13. I, called to him who reels with joy, Śrutarvan, Ṛikṣha's son, shall stroke | The heads of four presented steeds, like the long wool of fleecy rams. || 14. Four coursers with a splendid car, Śaviṣhṭha's horses, fleet of foot, | Shall bring me to the sacred feast, as flying steeds brought Tugra's son. || 15. The very truth do I declare to thee, Paruṣhṇī, mighty flood. | Waters! no man is there who gives more horses than Śaviṣhṭha gives.

Hymn 8:64. Agni.

1. Yoke, Agni, as a charioteer, thy steeds who best invite the Gods: As ancient Herald seat thyself. || 2. And, God, as skilfullest of all, call for us hitherward the Gods: | Give all our wishes sure effect. || 3. For thou, Most Youthful, Son of Strength, thou to whom sacrifice is paid, | Art holy, faithful to the Law. || 4. This Agni, Lord of wealth and spoil hundredfold, thousandfold, is head | And chief of riches and a Sage. || 5. As craftsmen bend the felly, so bend at our general call: come nigh, | Aṅgiras, to the sacrifice. || 6. Now, O Virūpa, rouse for him, Strong God who shines at early morn, | Fair praise with voice that ceases not. || 7. With missile of this Agni, his who looks afar, will we lay low | The thief in combat for the kine. || 8. Let not the Companies of Gods fail us, like Dawns that float away, | Like cows who leave the niggardly. || 9. Let not the sinful tyranny of any fiercely hating foe | Smite us, as billows smite a ship. || 10. O Agni, God, the people sing reverent praise to thee for strength: | With terrors trouble thou the foe. || 11. Wilt thou not, Agni, lend us aid in winning cattle, winning wealth? | Maker of room, make room for us. || 12. In this great battle cast us not aside as one who bears a load: | Snatch up the wealth and win it all. || 13. O Agni, let this plague pursue and fright another and not us: | Make our impetuous strength more strong. || 14. The reverent or unwearied man whose holy labour he accepts, | Him Agni favours with success. || 15. Abandoning the foeman's host pass hither to this company: | Assist the men with whom I stand. || 16. As we have known thy gracious help, as of a Father, long ago, | So now we pray to thee for bliss.

Hymn 8:65. Indra.

1. Not to forsake me, I invoke this Indra girt by Marutas, | Lord Of magic power who rules with might. || 2. This Indra with his Marut Friends clave into pieces Vṛitra's bead | With hundred-knotted thunderbolt. || 3. Indra, with Marut Friends grown strong, hath rent asunder Vṛitra, and | Released the waters of the sea. || 4. This is that Indra who, begirt by Marutas, won the light of heaven | That he might drink the Soma juice. || 5. Mighty, impetuous, begirt by Marutas, him who loudly roars, | Indra we invocate with songs. || 6. Indra begirt by Marutas we invoke after the ancient plan, | That he may drink the Soma juice. || 7. O liberal Indra, Marut-girt, much-lauded Śatakratu, drink | The Soma at this sacrifice. || 8. To thee, O Indra, Marut-girt, these Soma juices, Thunderer! | Are offered from the heart with lauds. || 9. Drink, Indra, with thy Marut Friends, pressed Soma at the morning rites, | Whetting thy thunderbolt with strength. || 10. Arising in thy might, thy jaws thou shookest, Indra, having quaffed | The Soma which the mortar pressed. || 11. Indra, both worlds complained to thee when uttering thy fearful roar, | What time thou smotest Dasyus dead. || 12. From Indra have I measured out a song eight-footed with nine parts, | Delicate, faithful to the Law.

Hymn 8:66. Indra.

1. Scarcely was Śatakratu, born when of his Mother he inquired, | Who are the mighty? Who are famed? | 2. Then Śavasī declared to him Aurṇavābha, Ahīśuva: | Son, these be they thou must o'erthrow || 3. The Vṛitra-slayer smote them all as spokes are hammered into naves: | The Dasyu-killer waxed in might. || 4. Then Indra at a single draught drank the contents of thirty pails, | Pails that were filled with Soma juice. || 5. Indra in groundless realms of space pierced the Gandharva through, that he | Might make Brahmans' strength increase. || 6. Down from the mountains Indra shot hither his well-directed shaft: | He gained the ready brew of rice. || 7. One only is that shaft of thine, with thousand feathers, hundred barbs, | Which, Indra, thou hast made thy friend. || 8. Strong as the Ṛibhus at thy birth, therewith to those who praise thee, men, | And women, bring thou food to eat. || 9. By thee these exploits were achieved, the mightiest deeds, abundantly: | Firm in thy heart thou settest them. || 10. All these things Vishṇu brought, the Lord of ample stride whom thou hadst sent— | A hundred buffaloes, a brew of rice and milk: and Indra, slew the ravening boar || 11. Most deadly is thy bow, successful, fashioned well: good is thine arrow, decked with gold. | Warlike and well equipped thine arms are, which increase sweetness for him who drinks the sweet.

Hymn 8:67. Indra.

1. Bring us a thousand, Indra, as our guerdon for the Soma juice: | Hundreds of kine, O Hero, bring. || 2. Bring cattle, bring us ornament, bring us embellishment and steeds, | Give us, besides, two rings of gold. || 3. And, Bold One, bring in ample store rich jewels to adorn the ear, | For thou, Good Lord, art far renowned. || 4. None other is there for the priest, Hero! but thou, to give him gifts, | To win much spoil and prosper him. || 5. Indra can never be brought low, Śakra can never be subdued: | He heareth and beholdeth all. || 6. He spieth out the wrath of man, he who can never be deceived: | Ere blame can come he marketh it. || 7. He hath his stomach full of might, the Vṛitra-slayer, Conqueror, | The Soma-drinker, ordering all. || 8. In thee all treasures are combined, Soma all blessed things in thee, | Uninjured, easy to bestow. || 9. To thee speeds forth my hope that craves the gift of corn, and kine and gold, | Yea, craving horses, speeds to thee. || 10. Indra, through hope in thee alone even this sickle do I grasp. | Fill my hand, Maghavan, with all that it can hold of barley cut or gathered up.

Hymn 8:68. Soma.

1. This here is Soma, ne'er restrained, active, all-conquering bursting forth, | Ṛishi and Sage by sapience, || 2. All that is bare he covers o'er, all that is sick he medicines; | The blind man sees, the cripple walks. || 3. Thou, Soma, givest wide defence against the hate of alien men, | Hatreds that waste and weaken us. || 4. Thou by thine insight and thy skill, Impetuous One, from heaven and earth | Drivest the sinner's enmity. || 5. When to their task they come with zeal, may they obtain the Giver's grace, | And satisfy his wish who thirsts. || 6. So may he find what erst was lost, so may be speed the pious man, | And lengthen his remaining life. || 7. Gracious, displaying tender love, unconquered, gentle in thy thoughts, | Be sweet, O Soma, to our heart. || 8. O Soma, terrify us not; strike us not with alarm, O King: | Wound not our heart with dazzling flame. || 9. When in my dwelling-place I see the wicked enemies of Gods, | King, chase their hatred far away, thou Bounteous One, dispel our foes.

Hymn 8:69. Indra

1. O Śatakratu! truly I have made none else my Comforter. | Indra; be gracious unto us. || 2. Thou who hast ever aided us kindly of old to win the spoil, | As such, O Indra, favour us. || 3. What now? As prompter of the poor thou helpest him who sheds the juice. | Wilt thou not, Indra, strengthen us? || 4. O Indra, help our chariot on, yea, Thunderer, though it lag behind: | Give this my car the foremost place. || 5. Ho there! why sittest thou at ease? Make thou my chariot to be first | And bring the fame of victory near. || 6. Assist our car that seeks the prize. What can be easier for thee? | So make thou us victorious. || 7. Indra, be firm: a fort art thou. To thine appointed place proceeds | The auspicious hymn in season due. || 8. Let not our portion be disgrace. Broad is the course, the prize is set, | The barriers are opened wide. || 9. This thing we wish. that thou mayst take thy fourth, thy sacrificial name. | So art thou held to be our Lord. || 10. Ekadyū hath exalted you, Immortals: both Goddesses and Gods hath he delighted. | Bestow upon him bounty meet for praises. May he, enriched with prayer, come soon and early.

Hymn 8:70. Indra.

1. Indra, God of the mighty arm, gather for us with thy right hand | Manifold and nutritious spoil. || 2. We know thee mighty in thy deeds, of mighty bounty, mighty wealth, | Mighty in measure, prompt to aid. || 3. Hero, when thou art fain to give, neither may Gods nor mortal men | Restrain thee like a fearful Bull. || 4. Come, let us glorify Indra, Lord supreme of wealth, Self-ruling King: | In bounty may he harm us not. || 5. Let prelude sound and following chant so let him hear the Sāman sung, | And with his bounty answer us. || 6. O Indra, with thy right hand bring, and with thy left remember us. | Let us not lose our share of wealth. || 7. Come nigh, O Bold One, boldly bring hither the riches of the churl | Who giveth least of all the folk. || 8. Indra, the booty which thou hast with holy singers to receive, | Even that booty win with us. || 9. Indra, thy swiftly-coming spoil, the booty which rejoices all, | Sounds quick in concert with our hopes.

Hymn 8:71. Indra.

1. Haste forward to us from afar, or, Vṛitra-slayer, from anear, | To meet the offering to the meath. || 2. Strong are the Soma-draughts; come nigh: the juices fill thee with delight: | Drink boldly even as thou art wont. || 3. Joy, Indra, in the strengthening food et it content thy wish and thought, | And be delightful to thine heart. || 4. Come to us thou who hast no foe: we call thee down to hymns of praise, | In heaven's sublimest realm of light. || 5. This Soma here expressed with stones and dressed with milk for thy carouse, | Indra, is offered up to thee. || 6. Graciously, Indra, hear my call. Come and obtain the draught, and sate | Thyself with juices blent with milk. || 7. The Soma, Indra, which is shed in chalices and vats for thee, | Drink thou, for thou art Lord thereof. || 8. The Soma seen within the bowls, as in the flood the Moon is seen, | Drink thou, for thou art Lord thereof. || 9. That which the Hawk brought in his claw, inviolate, through the air to thee, | Drink thou, for thou art Lord thereof.

Hymn 8:72. Viśvedevas.

1. We choose unto ourselves that high protection of the Mighty Gods | That it may help and succour us. || 2. May they be ever our allies, Varuṇa, Mitra, Aryaman, | Far-seeing Gods who prosper us. || 3. Ye furtherers of holy Law, transport us safe o'er many woes, | As over water-floods in ships. || 4. Dear wealth be Aryaman to us, Varuṇa dear wealth meet for praise: | Dear wealth we choose unto ourselves. || 5. For Sovereigns of dear wealth are ye, Ādityas, not of sinner's wealth, | Ye sapient Gods who slay the foe. || 6. We in our homes, ye Bounteous Ones, and while we journey on the road, | Invoke you, Gods, to prosper us. || 7. Regard us, Indra, Vishṇu, here, ye Aśvins and the Marut host, | Us who are kith and kin to you. || 8. Ye Bounteous Ones, from time of old we here set forth our brotherhood, | Our kinship in. the Mother's womb. || 9. Then come with Indra for your chief, as early day, ye Bounteous Gods | Yea, I address you now for this.

Hymn 8:73. Agni.

1. Agni, your dearest Guest, I laud, him who is loving as a friend, | Who brings us riches like a car. || 2. Whom as a far-foreseeing Sage the Gods have, from the olden time, | Established among mortal men. || 3. Do thou, Most Youthful God, protect the men who offer, hear their songs, | And of thyself preserve their seed. || 4. What is the praise wherewith, O God, Aṅgiras, Agni, Son of Strength, | We, after thine own wish and thought, || 5. May serve thee, O thou Child of Power, and with what sacrifice's plan? | What prayer shall I now speak to thee? || 6. Our God, make all of us to dwell in happy habitations, and | Reward our songs with spoil and wealth. || 7. Lord of the house, what plenty fills the songs which thou inspirest now, | Thou whose hymn helps to win the kine? || 8. Him Wise and Strong they glorify, the foremost Champion in the fray, | And mighty in his dwelling-place. || 9. Agni, he dwells in rest and peace who smites and no one smites again: | With hero sons he prospers well.

Hymn 8:74. Aśvins.

1. To this mine invocation, O ye Aśvins, ye Nāsatyas, come, | To drink the savoury Soma juice. || 2. This laud of mine, ye Aśvins Twain, and this mine invitation hear, | To drink the savoury Soma juice. || 3. Here Kṛishṇa is invoking you, O Aśvins, Lords of ample wealth. | To drink the savoury Soma juice. || 4. List, Heroes, to the singer's call, the call of Kṛishṇa lauding

you, | To drink the savoury Soma juice. || 5. Chiefs, to the sage who sings your praise grant an inviolable home, | To drink the savoury Soma juice. || 6. Come to the worshipper's abode, Aśvins, who here is lauding you, | To drink the savoury Soma juice. || 7. Yoke to the firmly jointed car the ass which draws you, Lords of wealth. | To drink the savoury Soma juice. || 8. Come hither, Aśvins, on your car of triple form with triple seat, | To drink the savoury Soma juice. || 9. O Aśvins, O Nāsatyas, now accept with favouring grace my songs, | To drink the savoury Soma juice.

Hymn 8:75. Aśvins.

1. Ye Twain are wondrous strong, well-skilled in arts that heal, both bringers of delight, ye both won Dakṣha's praise. | Viśvaka calls on you as such to save his life. Break ye not off our friendship, come and set me free. || 2. How shall he praise you now who is distraught in mind? Ye Twain give wisdom for the gain of what is good. | Viśvaka calls on you as such to save his life. Break ye not off our friendship, come and set me free. || 3. Already have ye Twain, possessors of great wealth, prospered Viṣhṇāpū thus for gain of what is good. | Viśvaka calls on you as such to save his life. Break ye not off our friendship, come and set me free. || 4. And that Impetuous Hero, winner of the spoil, though he is far away, we call to succour us, | Whose gracious favour, like a father's, is most sweet. Break ye not off our friendship, come and set me free. || 5. About the holy Law toils Savitar the God the horn of holy Law hath he spread far and wide. | The holy Law hath quelled even mighty men of war. Break ye not off our friendship, come and act me free.

Hymn 8:76. Aśvins.

1. Splendid, O Aśvins, is your praise. Come fountain-like, to pour the stream. | Of the sweet juice effused-dear is it, Chiefs, in heaven-drink like two wild bulls at a pool. || 2. Drink the libation rich in sweets, O Aśvins Twain: sit. Heroes, on the sacred grass. | Do ye with joyful heart in the abode of man preserve his life by means of wealth. || 3. The Priyamedhas bid you come with all the succours that are yours. | Come to his house whose holy grass is trimmed, to dear sacrifice at the morning rites. || 4. Drink ye the Soma rich in meath, ye Aśvins Twain: sit gladly on the sacred grass. | So, waxen mighty, to our eulogy from heaven come ye as wild-bulls to the pool. || 5. Come to us, O ye Aśvins, now with steeds of many a varied hue, | Ye Lords of splendour, wondrous, borne on paths of gold, drink Soma, ye who strengthen Law. || 6. For we the priestly singers, fain to hymn your praise, invoke you for the gain of strength. | So, wondrous, fair, and famed for great deeds come to us, through our hymn, Aśvins, when ye hear.

Hymn 8:77. Indra.

1. As cows low to their calves in stalls, so with our songs we glorify | This Indra, even your Wondrous God who checks attack, who joys in the delicious juice. || 2. Celestial, bounteous Giver, girt about with might, rich, mountain-like, in precious things, | Him swift we seek. for foodful booty rich in kine, brought hundredfold and thousandfold. || 3. Indra, the strong and lofty hills are powerless to bar thy way. | None stay that act of thine when thou wouldst fain give wealth to one like me who sings thy praise. || 4. A Warrior thou by strength, wisdom, and wondrous deed, in might excellest all that is. | Hither may this our hymn attract thee to our help, the hymn which Gotamas have made. || 5. For in thy might thou stretchest out beyond the boundaries of heaven. | The earthly region, Indra, comprehends thee not. After thy Godhead hast thou waxed. || 6. When, Maghavan, thou honourest the worshipper, no one is there to stay thy wealth. | Most liberal Giver thou, do thou inspire our song of praise, that we may win the spoil.

Hymn 8:78. Indra.

1. To Indra sing the lofty hymn, Marutas that slays the Vṛitras best. | Whereby the Holy Ones created for the God the light divine that ever wakes. || 2. Indra who quells the curse blew curses far away, and then in splendour came to us. | Indra, refulgent with thy Marut host! the Gods strove eagerly to win thy love. || 3. Sing to your lofty Indra, sing, Marutas, a holy hymn of praise. | Let Śatakratu, Vṛitra-slayer, kill the foe with hundred-knotted thunderbolt. || 4. Aim and fetch boldly forth, O thou whose heart is bold: great glory will be thine thereby. | In rapid torrent let the mother waters spread. Slay Vṛitra, win the light of heaven. || 5. When thou, unequalled Maghavan, wast born to smite the Vṛitras dead, | Thou spreadest out the spacious earth and didst support and prop the heavens. || 6. Then was the sacrifice produced for thee, the laud, and song of joy, | Thou in thy might surpassest all, all that now is and yet shall be. || 7. Raw kine thou filledst with ripe milk. Thou madest Sūrya rise to heaven, | Heat him as milk is heated with pure Sāman hymns, great joy to him who loves the song.

Hymn 8:79. Indra.

1. May Indra, who in every fight must be invoked, be near to us. | May the most mighty Vṛitra-slayer, meet for praise, come to libations and to hymns. || 2. Thou art the best of all in sending bounteous gifts, true art thou, lordly in thine act. | We claim alliance with the very Glorious One, yea, with the Mighty Son of Strength. || 3. Prayers unsurpassed are offered up to thee the Lover of the Song. | Indra, Lord of Bay Steeds, accept these fitting hymns, hymns which we have thought out for thee. || 4. For thou, O Maghavan, art truthful, ne'er subdued and bringest many a Vṛitra low. | As such, O Mightiest Lord, Wielder of Thunder, send wealth hither to the worshipper. || 5. O Indra, thou art far-renowned, impetuous, O Lord of Strength. | Alone thou slayest with the guardian of mankind resistless never-conquered foes. || 6. As such we seek thee now, O Asura, thee most wise, craving thy bounty as our share. | Thy sheltering defence is like a mighty cloak. So may thy glories reach to us.

Hymn 8:80. Indra.

1. Down to the stream a maiden came, and found the Soma by the way. | Bearing it to her home she said, For Indra will I press thee out, for Śakra will I press thee out. || 2. Thou roaming yonder, little man, beholding every house in turn, | Drink thou this Soma pressed with teeth, accompanied with grain and curds, with cake of meal and song of praise. || 3. Fain would we learn to know thee well, nor yet can we attain to thee. | Still slowly and in gradual drops, O Indu, unto Indra flow. || 4. Will he not help and work for us? Will he not make us wealthier? | Shall we not, hostile to our lord, unite ourselves to Indra now? || 5. O Indra, cause to sprout again three places, these which I declare,— | My father's head, his cultured field, and this the part below my waist. || 6. Make all of these grow crops of hair, you cultivated field of ours, | My body, and my father's head. || 7. Cleansing Apālā, Indra! thrice, thou gavest sunlike skin to her, | Drawn, Śatakratu! through the hole of car, of wagon, and of yoke.

Hymn 8:81. Indra

1. Invite ye Indra with a song to drink your draught of Soma juice, | All-conquering Śatakratu, most munificent of all who live. || 2. Lauded by many, much-invoked, leader of song, renowned of old: | His name is Indra, tell it forth. || 3. Indra the Dancer be to us the giver of abundant strength: | May he, the mighty, bring it near. || 4. Indra whose jaws are strong hath drunk of worshipping Sudakṣha's draught, | The Soma juice with barley mixed. || 5. Call Indra loudly with your songs of praise to drink the Soma juice. | For this is what augments his strength. || 6. When he hath drank its gladdening drops, the God with vigour of a God | Hath far surpassed all things that are. || 7. Thou speedest down to succour us this ever-conquering God of yours, | Him who is drawn to all our songs || 8. The Warrior not to he restrained, the Soma-drinker ne'er o'erthrown, | The Chieftain of resistless might. || 9. O Indra, send us riches, thou Omniscient, worthy of our praise: | Help us in the decisive fray. || 10. Even thence, O Indra, come to us with food that gives a hundred powers, | With food that gives a thousand powers. || 11. We sought the wisdom of the wise. Śakra, Kine-giver, Thunder-armed! | May we with steeds o'ercome in fight. || 12. We make thee, Śatakratu, find enjoyment in the songs we sing. | Like cattle in the pasture lands. || 13. For, Śatakratu, Thunder-armed, all that we craved, as men are wont, | All that we hoped, have we attained. || 14. Those, Son of Strength, are come to thee who cherish wishes in their hearts | O Indra, none excelleth thee. || 15. So, Hero, guard us with thy care, with thy most liberal providence, | Speedy, and terrible to foes. || 16. O Śatakratu Indra, now rejoice with that carouse of thine | Which is most splendid of them all || 17. Even, Indra, that carouse which slays the Vṛitras best, most widely famed, | Best giver of thy power and might. || 18. For that which is thy gift we know, true Soma-drinker, Thunder-armed, | Mighty One, amid all the folk. || 19. For Indra, Lover of Carouse, loud be our songs about the juice: | Let poets sing the song of praise. || 20. We summon Indra to the draught, in whom all glories rest, in whom | The seven

communities rejoice. || 21. At the Trikadrukas the Gods span sacrifice that stirs the mind: | Let our songs aid and prosper it. || 22. Let the drops pass within thee as the rivers flow into the sea: | O Indra, naught excelleth thee. || 23. Thou, wakeful Hero, by thy might hast taken food of Soma juice, | Which, Indra, is within thee now. || 24. O Indra, Vṛitra-slayer, let Soma be ready for thy maw, | The drops be ready for thy forms. || 25. Now Śrutakakṣha sings his song that cattle and the steed may come, | That Indra's very self may come. || 26. Here, Indra, thou art ready by our Soma juices shed for thee, | Śakra, at hand that thou mayst give. || 27. Even from far away our songs reach thee, O Caster of the Stone: | May we come very close to thee. || 28. For so thou art the hero's Friend, a Hero, too, art thou, and strong: | So may thine heart be won to us. || 29. So hath the offering, wealthiest Lord, been paid by all the worshippers: | So dwell thou, Indra, even with me. || 30. Be not thou like a slothful priest, O Lord of spoil and wealth: rejoice | In the pressed Soma blent with milk. || 31. O Indra, let not ill designs surround us in the sunbeams' light: | This may we gain with thee for Friend. || 32. With thee to help us, Indra, let us answer all our enemies: | For thou art ours and we are thine. || 33. Indra, the poets and thy friends, faithful to thee, shall loudly sing | Thy praises as they follow thee.

Hymn 8:82. Indra.

1. Sūrya, thou mountest up to meet the Hero famous for his wealth, | Who hurls the bolt and works for man || 2. Him who with might of both his arms brake nine-and-ninety castles down, | Slew Vṛitra and smote Ahi dead. || 3. This Indra is our gracious Friend. He sends us in a full broad stream | Riches in horses, kine, and corn. || 4. Whatever, Vṛitra-slayer! thou, Sūrya, hast risen upon today, | That, Indra, all is in thy power. || 5. When, Mighty One, Lord of the brave, thou thinkest thus, I shall not die, | That thought of thine is true indeed. || 6. Thou, Indra, goest unto all Soma libations shed for thee, | Both far away and near at hand. || 7. We make this Indra very strong to strike the mighty Vṛitra dead: | A vigorous Hero shall he be. || 8. Indra was made for giving, set, most mighty, o'er the joyous draught. | Bright, meet for Soma, famed in song. || 9. By song as 'twere, the powerful bolt which none may parry was prepared | Lofty, invincible he grew. || 10. Indra, Song-lover, lauded, make even in the wilds fair ways for us, | Whenever, Maghavan, thou wilt. || 11. Thou whose commandment and behest of sovereign sway none disregards, | Neither audacious man nor God. || 12. And both these Goddesses, Earth, Heaven, Lord of the beauteous helm! revere | Thy might which no one may resist. || 13. Thou in the black cows and the red and in the cows with spotted skin | This white milk hast deposited. || 14. When in their terror all the Gods shrank from the Dragon's furious might, | Fear of the monster fell on them. || 15. Then he was my Defender, then, Invincible, whose foe is not, | The Vṛitra-slayer showed his might. || 16. Him your best Vṛitra-slayer, him the famous Champion of mankind | I urge to great munificence, || 17. To come, Much-lauded! Many-named with this same thought that longs for milk, | Whene'er the Soma juice is shed. || 18. Much-honoured by libations, may the Vṛitra-slayer wake for us: | May Śakra listen to our prayers. || 19. O Hero, with that aid dost thou delight us, with what succour bring | Riches to those who worship thee? || 20. With whose libation joys the Strong, the Hero with his team who quells | The foe, to drink the Soma juice? || 21. Rejoicing in thy spirit bring thousandfold opulence to us: | Enrich thy votary with gifts. || 22. These juices with their wedded wives flow to enjoyment lovingly: | To waters speeds the restless one. || 23. Presented strengthening gifts have sent Indra away at sacrifice, | With might, onto the cleansing bath. || 24. These two who share his feast, Bay Steeds with golden manes, shall bring him to | The banquet that is laid for him. || 25. For thee, O Lord of Light, are shed these Soma-drops, and grass is strewn | Bring Indra to his worshippers. || 26. May Indra give thee skill, and lights of heaven, wealth to his votary | And priests who praise him: laud ye him. || 27. O Śatakratu, wondrous strength and all our lauds I bring to thee: | Be gracious to thy worshippers. || 28. Bring to us all things excellent, O Śatakratu, food and strength: | For, Indra, thou art kind to us. || 2. O Śatakratu, bring to us all blessings, all felicity: | For, Indra, thou art kind to us. || 30. Bearing the Soma juice we call, best Vṛitra-slayer, unto thee: | For, Indra, thou art kind to us. || 31. Come, Lord of rapturous, joys, to our libation with thy Bay Steeds, come | To our libation with thy Steeds. || 32. Known as best Vṛitra-slayer erst, as Indra Śatakratu, come | With Bay Steeds to the juice we shed. || 33. O Vṛitra-slayer, thou art he who drinks these drops of Soma: come | With Bay Steeds to the juice we shed. || 34. May Indra give, to aid us, wealth handy that rules the Skilful Ones: | Yea, may the Strong give potent wealth.

Hymn 8:83. Marutas.

1. The Cow, the famous Mother of the wealthy Marutas, pours her milk: | Both horses of the cars are yoked,— || 2. She in whose bosom all the Gods, and Sun and Moon for men to see, | Maintain their everlasting Laws. || 3. This all the pious sing to us, and sacred poets evermore: | The Marutas to the Soma-draught || 4. Here is the Soma ready pressed of this the Marutas drink, of this | Self-luminous the Aśvins drink. || 5. Of this, moreover, purified, set in three places, procreant, | Drink Varuṇa, Mitra, Aryaman. || 6. And Indra, like the Herald Priest, desirous of the milky juice, | At early morn will quaff thereof. || 7. When have the Princes gleamed and shone through waters as through troops of foes? | When hasten they whose might is pure? || 8. What favour do I claim this day of you | great Deities, you who are | Wondrously splendid in yourselves? || 9. I call, to drink the Soma, those Marutas who spread all realms of earth | And luminous regions of the sky. || 10. You, even such, pure in your might, you, O ye Marutas, I invoke | From heaven to drink this Soma juice. || 11. The Marutas, those who have sustained and propped the heavens and earth apart, | I call to drink this Soma juice. || 12. That vigorous band of Marutas that abideth in the mountains, | I invoke to drink this Soma juice.

Hymn 8:84. Indra.

1. Song-lover! like a charioteer come songs to thee when Soma flows. | O Indra, they have called to thee as mother-kine unto their calves. || 2. Bright juices hitherward have sped thee, Indra, Lover of the Song. | Drink, Indra, of this flowing sap: in every house 'tis set for thee. || 3. Drink Soma to inspirit thee, juice, Indra, which the Falcon brought: | For thou art King and Sovereign Lord of all the families of men. || 4. O Indra, hear Tiraśchi's call, the call of him who serveth thee. | Satisfy him with wealth of kine and valiant offspring: Great art thou. || 5. For he, O Indra, hath produced for thee the newest gladdening song, | A hymn that springs from careful thought, ancient, and full of sacred truth. || 6. That Indra will we laud whom songs and hymns of praise have magnified. | Striving to win, we celebrate his many deeds of hero might. || 7. Come now and let us glorify pure Indra with pure Sāman hymns. | Let the pure milky draught delight him strengthened by pure songs of praise. || 8. O Indra, come thou pure to us, with pure assistance, pure thyself. | Pure, send thou riches down to us, and, meet for Soma, pure, be glad. || 9. O Indra, pure, vouchsafe us wealth, and, pure, enrich the worshipper. | Pure, thou dost strike the Vṛitras dead, and strivest, pure, to win the spoil.

Hymn 8:85. Indra.

1. For him the Mornings made their courses longer, and Nights with pleasant voices spake to Indra. | For him the Floods stood still, the Seven Mothers, Streams easy for the heroes to pass over. || 2. The Darter penetrated, though in trouble, thrice-seven close-pressed ridges of the mountains. | Neither might God nor mortal man accomplish what the Strong Hero wrought in full-grown vigour. || 3. The mightiest force is Indra's bolt of iron when firmly grasped in both the arms of Indra. | His head and mouth have powers that pass all others, and all his people hasten near to listen. || 4. I count thee as the Holiest of the Holy, the caster-down of what hath ne'er been shaken. | I count thee as the Banner of the heroes, I count thee as the Chief of all men living. || 5. What time, O Indra, in thine arms thou tookest thy wildly rushing bolt to Slay the Dragon, | The mountains roared, the cattle loudly bellowed, the Brahmans with their hymns drew nigh to Indra. || 6. Let us praise him who made these worlds and creatures, all things that after him sprang into being. | May we win Mitra with our songs, and Indra, and wait upon our Lord with adoration. || 7. Flying in terror from the snort of Vṛitra, all Deities who were thy friends forsook thee. | So, Indra, be thy friendship with the Marutas: in all these battles thou shalt be the victor. || 8. Thrice-sixty Marutas, waxing strong, were with thee, like piles of beaming light, worthy of worship. | We come to thee: grant us a happy portion. Let us adore thy might with this oblation. || 9. A sharpened weapon is the host of Marutas. Who, Indra, dares withstand thy bolt of thunder? | Weaponless are the Asuras, the godless: scatter them with thy wheel, Impetuous Hero. || 10. To him the

Strong and Mighty, most auspicious, send up the beauteous hymn for sake of cattle. | Lay on his body many songs for Indra invoked with song, for will not he regard. them? || 11. To him, the Mighty, who accepts laudation, send forth thy thought as by a boat o'er rivers, | Stir with thy hymn the body of the Famous and Dearest One, for will not he regard it? || 12. Serve him with gifts of thine which Indra welcomes: praise with fair praise, invite him with thine homage. | Draw near, O singer, and refrain from outcry. Make thy voice heard, for will not he regard it? || 13. The Black Drop sank in Aṃśumatī's bosom, advancing with ten thousand round about it. | Indra with might longed for it as it panted: the hero-hearted laid aside his weapons. || 14. I saw the Drop in the far distance moving, on the slope bank of Aṃśumatī's river, | Like a black cloud that sank into the water. Heroes, I send you forth. Go, fight in battle. || 15. And then the Drop in Aṃśumatī's bosom, splendid with light, assumed its proper body; | And Indra, with Bṛihaspati to aid him, conquered the godless tribes that came against him. || 16. Then, at thy birth, thou wast the foeman, Indra, of those the seven who ne'er had met a rival. | The hidden Pair, the Heaven and Earth, thou foundest, and to the mighty worlds thou gavest pleasure. || 17. So, Thunder-armed! thou with thy bolt of thunder didst boldly smite that power which none might equal; | With weapons broughtest low the might of Śushṇa, and, Indra, foundest by thy strength the cattle. || 18. Then wast thou, Chieftain of all living mortals, the very mighty slayer of the Vṛitras. | Then didst thou set the obstructed rivers flowing, and win the floods that were enthralled by Dāsas. || 19. Most wise is he, rejoicing in libations, splendid as day, resistless in his anger. | He only doth great deeds, the only Hero, sole Vṛitra-slayer he, with none beside him. || 20. Indra is Vṛitra's slayer, man's sustainer: he must be called; with fair praise let us call him. | Maghavan is our Helper, our Protector, giver of spoil and wealth to make us famous. || 21. This Indra, Vṛitra-slayer, this Ṛibhukshan, even at his birth, was meet for invocation. | Doer of many deeds for man's advantage, like Soma quaffed, for friends we must invoke him.

Hymn 8:86. Indra.

1. O Indra, Lord of Light, what joys thou broughtest from the Asuras, | Prosper therewith, O Maghavan, him who lauds that deed, and those whose grass is trimmed for thee. || 2. The unwasting share of steeds and kine which, Indra, thou hast fast secured, | Grant to the worshipper who presses Soma and gives guerdon, not unto the churl. || 3. The riteless, godless man who sleeps, O Indra, his unbroken steep,— | May he by following his own devices die. Hide from him wealth that nourishes. || 4. Whether, O Śakra, thou be far, or, Vṛitra-slayer, near at hand, | Thence by heaven-reaching songs he who hath pressed the juice invites thee with thy long-maned Steeds. || 5. Whether thou art in heaven's bright sphere, or in the basin of the sea; | Whether, chief Vṛitra-slayer, in some place on earth, or in the firmament, approach. || 6. Thou Soma-drinker, Lord of Strength, beside our flowing Soma juice | Delight us with thy bounty rich in pleasantness, O Indra, with abundant wealth. || 7. O Indra, turn us not away: be the companion of our feast. | For thou art our protection, yea, thou art our kin: O Indra, turn us not away. || 8. Sit down with us, O Indra, sit beside the juice to drink the meath. | Show forth great favour to the Singer, Maghavan; Indra, with us, beside the juice. || 9. O Caster of the Stone, nor Gods nor mortals have attained to thee. | Thou in thy might surpassest all that hath been made: the Gods have not attained to thee. || 10. Of one accord they made and formed for kingship Indra, the Hero who in all encounters overcometh, | Most eminent for power, destroyer in the conflict, fierce and exceeding strong, stalwart and full of vigour. || 11. Bards joined in song to Indra so that he might drink the Soma juice, | The Lord of Light, that he whose laws stand fast might aid with power and with the help he gives. || 12. The holy sages form a ring, looking and singing to the Ram. | Inciters, full of vigour, not to he deceived, are with the chanters, nigh to bear. || 13. Loudly I call that Indra, Maghavan the Mighty, who evermore possesses power, ever resistless. | Holy, most liberal, may he lead us on to riches, and, Thunder-armed, make all our pathways pleasant for us. || 14. Thou knowest well, O Śakra, thou Most Potent, with thy strength, Indra, to destroy these castles. | Before thee, Thunder-armed! all beings tremble: the heavens and earth before thee shake with terror, || 15. May thy truth, Indra, Wondrous Hero be my guard: bear me o'er much woe, Thunderer! as over floods. | When, Indra, wilt thou honour us with opulence, all-nourishing and much-to-be. desired, O King?

Hymn 8:87. Indra.

1. To Indra sing a Sāman hymn, a lofty song to Lofty Sage, | To him who guards the Law, inspired, and fain for praise. || 2. Thou, Indra, art the Conqueror: thou gavest splendour to the Sun. | Maker of all things, thou art Mighty and All-God. || 3. Radiant with light thou wentest to the sky, the luminous realm of heaven. | The Deities, Indra strove to win thee for their Friend. || 4. Come unto us, O Indra, dear, still conquering, unconcealable, | Vast as a mountain spread on all sides, Lord of Heaven. || 5. O truthful Soma-drinker, thou art mightier than both the worlds. | Thou strengthenest him who pours libation, Lord of Heaven. || 6. For thou art he, O Indra, who stormeth all castles of the foe, | Slayer of Dasyus, man's Supporter, Lord of Heaven. || 7. Now have we, Indra, Friend of Song, sent our great wishes forth to thee, | Coming like floods that follow floods. || 8. As rivers swell the ocean, so, Hero, our prayers increase thy might, | Though of thyself, O Thunderer, waxing day by day. || 9. With holy song may bind to the broad wide-yoked car the Bay Steeds of the rapid God, | Bearers of Indra, yoked by word. || 10. O Indra, bring great strength to us, bring valour, Śatakratu, thou most active, bring | A hero conquering in war. || 11. For, gracious Śatakratu, thou hast ever been a Mother and a Sire to us, | So now for bliss we pray to thee. || 12. To thee, Strong, Much-invoked, who showest forth thy strength, O Śatakratu, do I speak: | So grant thou us heroic strength.

Hymn 8:88. Indra.

1. O Thunderer, zealous worshippers gave thee drink this time yesterday. | So, Indra, listen here to those who bring the laud: come near unto our dwelling-place || 2. Lord of Bay Steeds, fair-helmed, rejoice thee: this we crave. Here the disposers wait on thee. | Thy loftiest glories claim our lauds beside the juice, O Indra, Lover of the Song. || 3. Turning, as 'twere, to meet the Sun, enjoy from Indra all good things. | When he who will be born is born with power we look to treasures as our heritage. || 4. Praise him who sends us wealth, whose bounties injure none: good are the gifts which Indra. grants. | He is not worth with one who satisfies his wish: he turns his mind to giving boons. || 5. Thou in thy battles, Indra, art subduer of all hostile bands. | Father art thou, all-conquering, cancelling the curse, thou victor of the vanquisher. || 6. The Earth and Heaven clung close to thy victorious might as to their calf two mother-cows. | When thou attackest Vṛitra all the hostile bands shrink and faint, Indra, at thy wrath. || 7. Bring to your aid the Eternal One, who shoots and none may shoot at him, | Inciter, swift, victorious, best of Charioteers. Tugrya's unvanquished Strengthener; || 8. Arranger of things unarranged, e'en Śatakratu, source of might, | Indra, the Friend of all, for succour we invoke, Guardian of treasure, sending wealth.

Hymn 8:89. Indra. Vāk.

1. I move before thee here present in person, and all the Deities follow behind me. | When, Indra, thou securest me my portion, with me thou shalt perform heroic actions. || 2. The food of meath in foremost place I give thee, thy Soma shall be pressed, thy share appointed. | Thou on my right shalt be my friend and comrade: then shall we two smite dead full many a foeman. || 3. Striving for strength bring forth a laud to Indra, a truthful hymn if he in truth existeth. | One and another say, There is no Indra. Who hath beheld him? Whom then shall we honour? || 4. Here am I, look upon me here, O singer. All that existeth I surpass in greatness. | The Holy Law's commandments make me mighty. Rending with strength I rend the worlds asunder. || 5. When the Law's lovers mounted and approached me as I sate lone upon the dear sky's summit. | Then spake my spirit to the heart within me, My friends have cried unto me with their children. || 6. All these thy deeds must be declared at Soma-feasts, wrought, Indra, Bounteous Lord, for him who sheds the juice, | When thou didst open wealth heaped up by many, brought from far away to Śarabha, the Ṛishi's kin. || 7. Now run ye forth your several ways: he is not here who kept you back. | For hath not Indra sunk his bolt deep down in Vṛitra's vital part? || 8. On-rushing with the speed of thought within the iron fort he pressed: | The Falcon went to heaven and brought the Soma to the Thunderer. || 9. Deep in the ocean lies the bolt with waters compassed round about, | And in continuous onward flow the floods their tribute bring to it. || 10. When, uttering words which no one comprehended, Vāk,

Queen of Gods, the Gladdener, was seated, | The heaven's four regions drew forth drink and vigour: now whither hath her noblest portion vanished? || 11. The Deities generated Vāk the Goddess, and animals of every figure speak her. | May she, the Gladdener, yielding food and vigour, the Milch-cow Vāk, approach us meetly lauded. || 12. Step forth with wider stride, my comrade Vishṇu; make room, Dyaus, for the leaping of the lightning. | Let us slay Vṛitra, let us free the rivers let them flow loosed at the command of Indra.

Hymn 8:90. Various.

1. Yea, specially that mortal man hath toiled for service of the Gods, | Who quickly hath brought near Mitra and Varuṇa. to share his sacrificial gifts. || 2. Supreme in sovereign power, far-sighted, Chiefs and Kings, most swift to hear from far away, | Both, wondrously, set them in motion as with arms, in company with Sūrya's beams. || 3. The rapid messenger who runs before you, Mitra-Varuṇa, with iron head, swift to the draught, || 4. He whom no man may question, none may summon back, who stands not still for colloquy,— | From hostile clash with him keep ye us safe this day: keep us in safety with your arms. || 5. To Aryaman and Mitra sing a reverent song, O pious one, | A pleasant hymn that shall protect to Varuṇa: sing forth a laud unto the Kings. || 6. The true, Red Treasure they have sent, one only Son born of the Three. | They, the Immortal Ones, never deceived, survey the families of mortal men. || 7. My songs are lifted up, and acts most splendid are to be performed. | Come hither, ye Nāsatyas, with accordant mind, to meet and to enjoy my gifts. || 8. Lords of great wealth, when we invoke your bounty which no demon checks, | Both of you, furthering our eastward-offered praise, come, Chiefs whom Jamadagni lauds! || 9. Come, Vāyu, drawn by fair hymns, to our sacrifice that reaches heaven. | Poured on the middle of the straining-cloth, and cooked, this bright drink hath been offered thee. || 10. He comes by straightest paths, as ministering Priest, to taste the sacrificial gifts. | Then, Lord of harnessed teams I drink of the twofold draught, bright Soma mingled with the milk. || 11. Verily, Sūrya, thou art great; truly, Āditya, thou art great. | As thou art great indeed, thy greatness is admired: yea, verily, thou, God, art great. || 12. Yea, Sūrya, thou art great in fame thou evermore, O God, art great. | Thou by thy greatness art the Gods' High Priest, divine, far-spread unconquerable light. || 13. She yonder, bending lowly down, clothed in red hues and rich in rays, | Is seen, advancing as it were with various tints, amid the ten surrounding arms. || 14. Past and gone are three mortal generations: the fourth and last into the Sun hath entered. | He mid the worlds his lofty place hath taken. Into green plants is gone the Purifying. || 15. The Rudras' Mother, Daughter of the Vasus, centre of nectar, the Ādityas' Sister— | To folk who understand will I proclaim it-injure not Aditi, the Cow, the sinless. || 16. Weak-minded men have as a cow adopted me who came hither from the Gods, a Goddess, | Who, skilled in eloquence, her voice uplifteth, who standeth near at hand with all devotions.

Hymn 8:91. Agni.

1. Lord of the house, Sage, ever young, high power of life, O Agni, God, | Thou givest to thy worshipper. || 2. So with our song that prays and serves, attentive, Lord of spreading light, | Agni, bring hitherward the Gods. || 3. For, Ever-Youthful One, with thee, best Furtherer, as our ally, | We overcome, to win the spoil. || 4. As Aurva Bhṛigu used, as Apnavāna used, I call the pure | Agni who clothes him with the sea. || 5. I call the Sage who sounds like wind, the Might that like Parjanya roars, | Agni who clothes him with the sea. || 6. As Savitar's productive Power, as him who sends down bliss, I call | Agni who clothes him with the sea. || 7. Hither, for powerful kinship, I call Agni, him Who prospers you, | Most frequent at our solemn rites || 8. That through this famed One's power, he may stand by us even as Tvashṭar comes | Unto the forms that must he shaped. || 9. This Agni is the Lord supreme above all glories mid the Gods: | May he come nigh to us with strength. || 10. Here praise ye him the most renowned of all the ministering Priests, | Agni, the Chief at sacrifice; || 11. Piercing, with purifying flame, enkindled in our homes, most high, | Swiftest to hear from far away. || 12. Sage, laud the Mighty One who wins the spoil of victory like a steed, | And, Mitra like, unites the folk. || 13. Still turning to their aim in thee, the oblation-bearer's sister hymns | Have come to thee before the wind. || 14. The waters find their place in him, for whom the threefold sacred grass | Is spread unbound, unlimited. || 15. The station of the Bounteous God hath, through his aid which none impair, | A pleasant aspect like the Sun. || 16. Blazing with splendour, Agni, God, through pious gifts of sacred oil, | Bring thou the Gods and worship them. || 17. The Gods as mothers brought thee forth, the Immortal Sage, O Aṅgiras, | The bearer of our gifts to heaven. || 18. Wise Agni, Gods established thee, the Seer, noblest messenger, | As bearer of our sacred gifts. || 19. No cow have I to call mine own, no axe at hand wherewith to work, | Yet what is here I bring to thee. || 20. O Agni, whatsoever be the fuel that we lay for thee, | Be pleased therewith, Most Youthful God || 21. That which the white-ant eats away, that over which the emmet crawls— | May all of this be oil to thee. || 22. When he enkindles Agni, man should with his heart attend the song: | I with the priests have kindled him.

Hymn 8:92. Agni

1. That noblest Furtherer hath appeared, to whom men bring their holy works. | Our songs of praise have risen aloft to Agni who was barn to give the Ārya strength. || 2. Agni of Divodāsa turned, as 'twere in majesty, to the Gods. | Onward he sped along the mother earth, and took his station in the height of heaven. || 3. Him before whom the people shrink when he performs his glorious deeds, | Him who wins thousands at the worship of the Gods, himself, that Agni, serve with sons. || 4. The mortal man whom thou wouldst lead to opulence, O Vasu, he who brings thee gifts. | He, Agni, wins himself a hero singing lauds, yea, one who feeds a thousand men. || 5. He with the steed wins spoil even in the fenced fort, and gains imperishable fame. | In thee, O Lord of wealth, continually we lay all precious offerings to the Gods. || 6. To him who dealeth out all wealth, who is the cheerful Priest of men, | To him, like the first vessels filled with savoury juice, to Agni go the songs of praise. || 7. Votaries, richly-gifted, deck him with their songs, even as the steed who draws the car. | On both, Strong Lord of men! on child and grandson pour the bounties which our nobles give. || 8. Sing forth to him, the Holy, most munificent, sublime with his refulgent glow, | To Agni, ye Upastutas. || 9. Worshipped with gifts, enkindled, splendid, Maghavan shall win himself heroic fame. | And will not his most newly shown benevolence come to us with abundant strength? || 10. Priest, presser of the juice! praise now the dearest Guest of all our friends, | Agni, the driver of the cars. || 11. Who, finder-out of treasures open and concealed, bringeth them hither, Holy One; | Whose waves, as in a cataract, are hard to pass, when he, through song, would win him strength. || 12. Let not the noble Guest, Agni, be wroth with us: by many a man his praise is sung, | Good Herald, skilled in sacrifice. || 13. O Vasu, Agni, let not them be harmed who come in any way with lauds to thee. | Even the lowly, skilled in rites, with offered gifts, seeketh thee for the envoy's task. || 14. Friend of the Marutas, Agni, come with Rudras to the Soma-draught, | To Sobhari's fair song of praise, and be thou joyful in the light.

Vālakhilya Hymns.

Hymn 1. Indra.

1. To you will I sing Indra's praise who gives good gifts as well we know; | The praise of Maghavan who, rich in treasure, aids his singers with wealth thousandfold. || 2. As with a hundred hosts, he rushes boldly on, and for the offerer slays his foes. | As from a mountain flow the water-brooks, thus flow his gifts who feedeth many a one. || 3. The drops effused, the gladdening draughts, O Indra, Lover of the Son | As waters seek the lake where they are wont to rest, fill thee, for bounty, Thunderer. || 4. The matchless draught that strengthens and gives eloquence, the sweetest of the meath drink thou, | That in thy joy thou mayst scatter thy gifts o'er us, plenteously, even as the dust. || 5. Come quickly to our laud, urged on by Soma-pressers like a horse— | Laud, Godlike Indra, which milch-kine make sweet for thee: with Kaṇva's sons are gifts for thee. || 6. With homage have we sought thee as a Hero, strong, preeminent, with unfailing wealth. | O Thunderer, as a plenteous spring pours forth its stream, so, Indra, flow our songs to thee. || 7. If now thou art at sacrifice, or if thou art upon the earth, | Come thence, high-thoughted! to our sacrifice with the Swift, come, Mighty with the Mighty Ones. || 8. The active, fleet-foot, tawny Coursers that are thine are swift to victory, like the Wind, | Wherewith thou goest round to visit Manus' seed, wherewith all heaven is visible. || 9. Indra, from thee so great we crave prosperity in wealth of kine, | As, Maghavan, thou favouredst Medhātithi, and, in the fight, Nīpātithi. || 10.

As, Maghavan, to Kaṇva, Trasadasyu, and to Paktha and Daśavraja; | As, Indra, to Gośarya and Ṛijiśvan, thou vouchsafedst wealth in kine and gold.

Hymn 2. Indra.

1. Śakra I praise, to win his aid, far-famed, exceeding bountiful, | Who gives, as 'twere in thousands, precious wealth to him who sheds the juice and worships him. ‖ 2. Arrows with hundred points, unconquerable, are this Indra's mighty arms in war. | He streams on liberal worshippers like a hill with springs, when juices poured have gladdened him. ‖ 3. What time the flowing Soma-drops have gladdened with their taste the Friend, | Like water, gracious Lord! were my libations made, like milch-kine to the worshipper. ‖ 4. To him the peerless, who is calling you to give you aid, forth flow the drops of pleasant meath. | The Soma-drops which call on thee, O gracious Lord, have brought thee to our hymn of praise. ‖ 5. He rushes hurrying like a steed to Soma that adorns our rite, | Which hymns make sweet to thee, lover of pleasant food. The call to Paura thou dost love. ‖ 6. Praise the strong, grasping Hero, winner of the spoil, ruling supreme o'er mighty wealth. | Like a full spring, O Thunderer, from thy store hast thou poured on the worshipper evermore. ‖ 7. Now whether thou be far away, or in the heavens, or on the earth, | O Indra, mighty—thoughted, harnessing thy Bays, come Lofty with the Lofty Ones. ‖ 8. The Bays who draw thy chariot, Steeds who injure none, surpass the wind's impetuous strength— | With whom thou silencest the enemy of man, with whom; thou goest round the sky. ‖ 9. O gracious Hero, may we learn anew to know thee as thou art: | As in decisive fight thou holpest Etaśa, or Vaśa 'gainst Daśavraja, ‖ 10. As, Maghavan, to Kaṇva at the sacred feast, to Dīrghanītha thine home-friend, | As to Gośarya thou, Stone-darter, gavest wealth, give me a gold-bright stall of kine.

Hymn 3. Indra.

1. As with Manu Sāṃvaraṇa, Indra, thou drankest Soma juice, | And, Maghavan, with Nīpātithi, Medhātithi, with Puṣṭigu and Śruṣṭigu,— ‖ 2. The son of Pārṣadvāna was Praskaṇva's host, who lay decrepit and forlorn. | Aided by thee the Ṛiṣhi Dasyave-vṛika strove to obtain thousands of kine. ‖ 3. Call hither with thy newest song Indra who lacks not hymns of praise, | Him who observes and knows, inspirer of the sage, him who seems eager to enjoy. ‖ 4. He unto whom they sang the seven-headed hymn, three-parted, in the loftiest place, | He sent his thunder down on all these living things, and so displayed heroic might. ‖ 5. We invoke that Indra who bestoweth precious things on us. | Now do we know his newest favour; may we gain a stable that is full of kine. ‖ 6. He whom thou aidest, gracious Lord, to give again, obtains great wealth to nourish him. | We with our Soma ready, Lover of the Song! call, Indra Maghavan, on thee. ‖ 7. Ne'er art thou fruitless, Indra ne'er dost thou desert the worshipper | But now, O Maghavan, thy bounty as a God is poured forth ever more and more. ‖ 8. He who hath. overtaken Krivi with his might, and silenced Śuṣhṇa with death-bolts,— | When he supported yonder heaven and spread it out, then first the son of earth was born. ‖ 9. Good Lord of wealth is he to whom all Āryas, Dāsas here belong. | Directly unto thee, the pious Ruśama Pavīru, is that wealth brought nigh. ‖ 10. In zealous haste the singers have sung forth a song distilling oil and rich in sweets. | Riches have spread among us and heroic strength, with us are flowing Soma-drops.

Hymn 4. Indra.

1. As, Śakra, thou with Manu called Vivasvat drankest Soma juice, | As, Indra, thou didst love the hymn by Trita's side, so dost thou joy with Āyu now. ‖ 2. As thou with Mātariśvan, Medhya, Prishadhra, hast cheered thee Indra, with pressed juice, | Drunk Soma with Ṛijūnas, Syūmaraśmi, by Daśonya's Daśaśipra's side. ‖ 3. 'tis he who made the lauds his own and boldly drank the Soma juice, | He to whom Viṣhṇu came striding his three wide steps, as Mitra's statutes ordered it. ‖ 4. In whose laud thou didst joy, Indra, at the great deed, O Śatakratu, Mighty One! | Seeking renown we call thee as the milkers call the cow who yields abundant milk. ‖ 5. He is our Sire who gives to us, Great, Mighty, ruling as he wills. | Unsought, may he the Strong, Rich, Lord of ample wealth, give us of horses and of kine. ‖ 6. He to whom thou, Good Lord, givest that he may give increases wealth that nourishes. | Eager for wealth we call on Indra, Lord of wealth, on Śatakratu with our lauds. ‖ 7. Never art thou neglectful: thou guardest both

races with thy care. | The call on Indra, fourth Āditya! is thine own. Amṛita is established in the heavens. ‖ 8. The offerer whom thou, Indra, Lover of the Song, liberal Maghavan, favourest,— | As at the call of Kaṇva so, O gracious Lord, hear, thou our songs and eulogy. ‖ 9. Sung is the song of ancient time: to Indra have ye said the prayer. | They have sung many a Bṛihatī of sacrifice, poured forth the worshipper's many thoughts. ‖ 10. Indra hath tossed together mighty stores of wealth, and both the worlds, yea, and the Sun. | Pure, brightly-shining, mingled with the milk, the draughts of Soma have made Indra glad.

Hymn 5. Indra.

1. As highest of the Maghavans, preeminent among the Bulls, | Best breaker-down of forts, kine-winner, Lord of wealth, we seek thee, Indra Maghavan. ‖ 2. Thou who subduedst Āyu, Kutsa, Atithigva, waxing daily in thy might, | As such, rousing thy power, we invocate thee now, thee Śatakratu, Lord of Bays. ‖ 3. The pressing-stones shall pour for us the essence of the meath of all, | Drops that have been pressed out afar among the folk, and those that have been pressed near us. ‖ 4. Repel all enmities and keep them far away: let all win treasure for their own. | Even among Śiṣhṭas are the stalks that make thee glad, where thou with Soma satest thee. ‖ 5. Come, Indra, very near to us with aids of firmly-based resolve; | Come, most auspicious, with thy most auspicious help, good Kinsman, with good kinsmen, come! ‖ 6. Bless thou with progeny the chief of men, the lord of heroes, victor in the fray. | Aid with thy powers the men who sing thee lauds and keep their spirits ever pure and bright. ‖ 7. May we be such in battle as are surest to obtain thy grace: | With holy offerings and invocations of the Gods, we mean, that we may win the spoil. ‖ 8. Thine, Lord of Bays, am I. Prayer longeth for the spoil. Still with thy help I seek the fight. | So, at the raiders' head, I, craving steeds and kine, unite myself with thee alone.

Hymn 6. Indra.

1. Indra, the poets with. their hymns extol this hero might of thine: | They strengthened, loud in song, thy power that droppeth oil. With hymns the Pauras came to thee. ‖ 2. Through piety they came to Indra for his aid, they whose libations give thee joy. | As thou with, Kṛiśa and Saṃvarta hast rejoiced, so, Indra, be thou glad with us. ‖ 3. Agreeing in your spirit, all ye Deities, come nigh to us. | Vasus and Rudras shall come near to give us aid, and Marutas listen to our call. ‖ 4. May Pūṣhan, Viṣhṇu, and Sarasvatī befriend, and the Seven Streams, this call of mine: | May Waters, Wind, the Mountains, and the Forest-Lord, and Earth give ear unto my cry. ‖ 5. Indra, with thine own bounteous gift, most liberal of the Mighty Ones, | Be our boon benefactor, Vṛitra-slayer, be our feast-companion for our weal. ‖ 6. Leader of heroes, Lord of battle, lead thou us to combat, thou Most Sapient One. | High fame is theirs who win by invocations, feasts and entertainment of the Gods. ‖ 7. Our hopes rest on the Faithful One: in Indra is the people's life. | O Maghavan, come nigh that thou mayst give us aid: make plenteous food stream forth for us. ‖ 8. Thee would we worship, Indra, with our songs of praise: O Śatakratu, be thou ours. | Pour down upon Praskaṇva bounty vast and firm, exuberant, that shall never fail.

Hymn 7. Praskaṇva's Gift.

1. Great, verily, is Indra's might. I have beheld, and hither comes | Thy bounty, Dasyave-vṛika! ‖ 2. A hundred oxen white of hue are shining like the stars in heaven, | So tall, they seem to prop the sky. ‖ 3. Bamboos a hundred, a hundred dogs, a hundred skins of beasts well-tanned, | A hundred tufts of Balbaja, four hundred red-hued mares are mine. ‖ 4. Blest by the Gods, Kāṇvāyanas! be ye who spread through life on life: | Like horses have ye stridden forth. ‖ 5. Then men extolled the team of seven not yet full-grown, its fame is great. | The dark mares rushed along the paths, so that no eye could follow them.

Hymn 8. Praskaṇva's Go.

1. Thy bounty, Dasyave-vṛika, exhaustless hath displayed itself: | Its fullness is as broad as heaven. ‖ 2. Ten thousand Dasyave-vṛika, the son of Pūtakratā, hath | From his own wealth bestowed on me. ‖ 3. A hundred asses hath he given, a hundred head of fleecy sheep, | A hundred slaves, and wreaths besides. ‖ 4. There also was a mare led forth, picked out for Pūtakratā's sake, | Not of the horses of the herd. ‖ 5. Observant Agni hath appeared, oblation-bearer with his car. | Agni with his resplendent flame hath shone on high as shines the Sun, hath shone like Sūrya in the

heavens.

Hymn 9. Aśvins.

1. Endowed, O Gods, with your primeval wisdom, come quickly with your chariot, O ye Holy. | Come with your mighty powers, O ye Nāsatyas; come hither, drink ye this the third libation. || 2. The truthful Deities, the Three-and-Thirty, saw you approach before the Ever-Truthful. | Accepting this our worship and libation, O Aśvins bright with fire, drink ye the Soma. || 3. Aśvins, that work of yours deserves our wonder,—the Bull of heaven and earth and air's mid region; | Yea, and your thousand promises in battle, to all of these come near and drink beside us. || 4. Here is your portion laid for you, ye Holy: come to these songs of ours, O ye Nāsatyas. | Drink among us the Soma full of sweetness, and with your powers assist the man who worships.

Hymn 10. Viśvedevas.

1. He whom the priests in sundry ways arranging the sacrifice, of one accord, bring hither, | Who was appointed as a learned Brahman,—what is the sacrificer's knowledge of him? || 2. Kindled in many a spot, still One is Agni; Sūrya is One though high o'er all he shineth. | Illumining this All, still One is Uṣhas. That which is One hath into All developed. || 3. The chariot bright and radiant, treasure-laden, three-wheeled, with easy seat, and lightly rolling, | Which She of Wondrous Wealth was born to harness, —this car of yours I call. Drink what remaineth.

Hymn 11. Indra-Varuṇa.

1. In offerings poured to you, O Indra-Varuṇa, these shares of yours stream forth to glorify your state. | Ye haste to the libations at each sacrifice when ye assist the worshipper who sheds the juice. || 2. The waters and the plants, O Indra-Varuṇa, had efficacious vigour, and attained to might: | Ye who have gone beyond the path of middle air,—no godless man is worthy to be called your foe. || 3. True is your Kṛiśa's word, Indra and Varuṇa: The seven holy voices pour a wave of meath. | For their sake, Lords of splendour! aid the pious man who, unbewildered, keeps you ever in his thoughts. || 4. Dropping oil, sweet with Soma, pouring forth their stream, are the Seven Sisters in the seat of sacrifice. | These, dropping oil, are yours, O Indra-Varuṇa: with these enrich with gifts and help the worshipper. || 5. To our great happiness have we ascribed to these Two Bright Ones truthfulness, great strength, and majesty. | O Lords of splendour, aid us through the Three-times-Seven, as we pour holy oil, O Indra-Varuṇa. || 6. What ye in time of old Indra and Varuṇa, gave Ṛiṣhis revelation, thought, and power of song, | And places which the wise made, weaving sacrifice,—these through my spirit's fervid glow have I beheld. || 7. O Indra-Varuṇa, grant to the worshippers cheerfulness void of pride, and wealth to nourish them. | Vouchsafe us food, prosperity, and progeny, and lengthen out our days that we may see long life.

Maṇḍala 9

Hymn 9:1. Soma Pavamāna.

1. In sweetest and most gladdening stream | flow pure, O Soma, on thy way, | Pressed out for Indra, for his drink. || 2. Fiend-queller, Friend of all men, he hath with the wood attained unto | His place, his iron-fashioned home. || 3. Be thou best Vṛitra-slayer, best granter of bliss, most liberal: | Promote our wealthy princes' gifts. || 4. Flow onward with thy juice unto the banquet of the Mighty Gods: | Flow hither for our strength and fame. || 5. O Indu, we draw nigh to thee, with this one object day by day: | To thee alone our prayers are said || 6. By means of this eternal fleece may Sūrya's Daughter purify | Thy Soma that is foaming forth. || 7. Ten sister maids of slender form seize him within the press and hold | Him firmly on the final day. || 8. The virgins send him forth: they blow the the skin musician-like and fuse | The triple foe-repelling meath. || 9. Inviolable milch-kine round about him blend for Indra's drink, | The fresh young Soma with their milk. || 10. In the wild raptures of this draught, Indra slays all the Vṛitras: he, | The Hero, pours his wealth on us.

Hymn 9:2. Soma Pavamāna.

1. Soma, flow on, inviting Gods, speed to the purifying cloth: | Pass into Indra, as a Bull. || 2. As mighty food speed hitherward, Indu, as a most splendid Steer: | Sit in thy place as one with strength. || 3. The well-loved meath was made to flow, the stream of the creative juice | the Sage drew waters to himself. || 4. The mighty waters, yea, the floods accompany thee Mighty One, | When thou wilt clothe thee with the milk. || 5. The lake is brightened in the floods. Soma, our Friend, heaven's prop and stay, | Falls on the purifying cloth. || 6. The tawny Bull hath bellowed, fair as mighty Mitra to behold: | He shines together with the Sun. || 7. Songs, Indu, active in their might are beautified for thee, wherewith | Thou deckest thee for our delight. || 8. To thee who givest ample room we pray, to win the joyous draught: | Great are the praise& due to thee. || 9. Indu as, Indra's Friend, on us pour with a stream of sweetness, like | Parjanya sender of the rain. || 10. Winner of kine, Indu, art thou, winner of heroes, steeds, and strength | Primeval Soul of sacrifice.

Hymn 9:3. Soma Pavamāna.

1. Here present this Immortal God flies, like a bird upon her wings, | To settle in the vats of wood. || 2. This God, made ready with the hymn, runs swiftly through the winding ways, | Inviolable as he flows. || 3. This God while flowing is adorned, like a bay steed for war, by men | Devout and skilled in holy songs. || 4. He, like a warrior going forth with heroes, as he flows along | Is fain to win all precious boons. || 5. This God, as he is flowing on, speeds like a car and gives his gifts: | He lets his voice be heard of all || 6. Praised by the sacred bards, this God dives into waters, and bestows | Rich gifts upon the worshipper. || 7. Away he rushes with his stream, across the regions, into heaven, | And roars as he is flowing on. || 8. While flowing, meet for sacrifice, he hath gone up to heaven across | The regions, irresistible. || 9. After the way of ancient time, this God, pressed out for Deities, | Flows tawny to the straining-cloth. || 10. This Lord of many Holy Laws, even at his birth engendering strength, | Effused, flows onward in a stream.

Hymn 9:4. Soma Pavamāna.

1. O Soma flowing on thy way, win thou and conquer high renown; | And make us better than we are. || 2. Win thou the light, win heavenly light, and, Soma, all felicities; | And make us better than we are. || 3. Win skilful strength and mental power. O Soma, drive away our foes; | And make us better than we are. || 4. Ye purifiers, purify Soma for Indra, for his drink: | Make thou us better than we are. || 5. Give us our portion in the Sun through thine own mental power and aids; | And make us better than we are. || 6. Through thine own mental power and aid long may we look upon the Sun; | Make thou us better than we are. || 7. Well-weaponed Soma, pour to us a stream of riches doubly great; | And make us better than we are. || 8. As one victorious unsubdued in battle pour forth wealth to us; | And make us better than we are. || 9. By worship, Pavamāna! men have strengthened thee to prop the Law: | Make thou us better than we are. || 10. O Indu, bring us wealth in steeds, manifold. quickening all life; | And mate us better than we are.

Hymn 9:5. Āprīs.

1. Enkindled, Pavamāna, Lord, sends forth his light on, every side | In friendly show, the bellowing Bull. || 2. He, Pavamāna, Self-produced, speeds onward sharpening his horns: | He glitters through the firmament. || 3. Brilliant like wealth, adorable, with splendour Pavamāna shines, | Mightily with the streams of meath. || 4. The tawny Pavamāna, who strews from of old the grass with might, | Is worshipped, God amid the Gods. || 5. The golden, the Celestial Doors are lifted with their frames on high, | By Pavamāna glorified. || 6. With passion Pavamāna longs for the great lofty pair, well-formed | Like beauteous maidens, Night and Dawn || 7. Both Gods who look on men I call, Celestial Heralds: Indra's Self | Is Pavamāna, yea, the Bull. || 8. This, Pavamāna's sacrifice, shall the three beauteous Goddesses, | Sarasvatī and Bhāratī and Iḷā, Mighty One, attend. || 9. I summon Tvaṣhṭar hither, our protector, champion, earliest-born, | Indu is Indra, tawny Steer; Pavamāna is Prajāpati. || 10. O Pavamāna, with the meath in streams anoint Vanaspati, | The ever-green. the golden-hued, refulgent, with a thousand boughs. || 11. Come to the consecrating rite of Pavamāna, all ye Gods,— | Vāyu, Sūrya, Bṛihaspati, Indra, and Agni, in accord.

Hymn 9:6. Soma Pavamāna.

1. Soma, flow on with pleasant stream, a Bull devoted to the Gods, | Our Friend, unto the woollen sieve. || 2. Pour hitherward, as Indra's Self, Indu, that gladdening stream of thine, | And send us coursers full of strength. || 3.

Flow to the filter hitherward, pouring that ancient gladdening juice, | Streaming forth power and high renown. || 4. Hither the sparkling drops have flowed, like waters down a steep descent | They have reached Indra purified. || 5. Whom, having passed the filter, ten dames cleanse, as 'twere a vigorous steed, | While he disports him in the wood,— || 6. The steer-strong juice with milk pour forth, for feast and service of the Gods, | To him who bears away the draught. | 7. Effused, the God flows onward with his stream to Indra, to the God, | So that his milk may strengthen him. || 8. Soul of the sacrifice, the juice effused flows quickly on: he keeps | His ancient wisdom of a Sage. || 9. So pouring forth, as Indra's Friend, strong drink, best Gladdener! for the feast, | Thou, even in secret, storest hymns.

Hymn 9:7. Soma Pavamāna.

1. Forth on their way the glorious drops have flowed for maintenance of Law, | Knowing this sacrifice's course. || 2. Down in the mighty waters sinks the stream of meath, most excellent, | Oblation best of all in worth. || 3. About the holy place, the Steer true, guileless, noblest, hath sent forth | Continuous voices in the wood. || 4. When, clothed in manly strength, the Sage flows in celestial wisdom round, | The Strong would win the light of heaven. || 5. When purified, he sits as King above the hosts, among his folk, | What time the sages bring him nigh. || 6. Dear, golden-coloured, in the fleece he sinks and settles in the wood: | The Singer shows his zeal in hymns. || 7. He goes to Indra, Vāyu, to the Aśvins, as his custom is, | With gladdening juice which gives them joy. || 8. The streams of pleasant Soma flow to Bhaga, Mitra-Varuṇa,— | Well-knowing through his mighty powers. | Heaven and Earth, riches of meath to win us wealth: | Gain for us treasures and renown.

Hymn 9:8. Soma Pavamāna.

1. Obeying Indra's dear desire these Soma juices have flowed forth, | Increasing his heroic might. || 2. Laid in the bowl, pure-flowing on to Vāyu and the Aśvins, may | These give us great heroic strength. || 3. Soma, as thou art purified, incite to bounty Indra's heart, | To sit in place of sacrifice. || 4. The ten swift fingers deck thee forth, seven ministers impel thee on: | The sages have rejoiced in thee. || 5. When through the filter thou art poured, we clothe thee with a robe of milk | To be a gladdening draught for Gods. || 6. When purified within the jars, Soma, bright-red and golden-hued, | Hath clothed him with a robe of milk. || 7. Flow on to us and make us rich. Drive all our enemies away. | O Indu, flow into thy Friend. | Send down the rain from heaven, a stream of opulence from earth. Give us, | O Soma, victory in war. || 9. May we obtain thee, Indra's drink, who viewest men and findest light, | Gain thee, and progeny and food.

Hymn 9:9. Soma Pavamāna.

1. The Sage of Heaven whose heart is wise, when laid between both hands and pressed, | Sends us delightful powers of life. || 2. On, onward to a glorious home; dear to the people void of guile, | With excellent enjoyment, flow. || 3. He, the bright Son, when born illumed his Parents who had sprung to life, | Great Son great Strengtheners of Law. || 4. Urged by the seven devotions he hath stirred the guileless rivers which | Have magnified the Single Eye. || 5. These helped to might the Youthful One, high over all, invincible, | Even Indu, Indra! in thy law. || 6. The immortal Courser, good to draw, looks down upon the Seven: the fount | Hath satisfied the Goddesses || 7. Aid us in holy rites, O Man: O Pavamāna, drive away | Dark shades that must be met in fight. || 8. Make the paths ready for a hymn newer and newer evermore: | Make the lights shine as erst they shone. || 9. Give, Pavamāna, high renown, give kine and steeds and hero sons: | Win for us wisdom, win the light.

Hymn 9:10. Soma Pavamāna.

1. Like cars that thunder on their way, like coursers eager for renown, | Have Soma-drops flowed forth for wealth. || 2. Forth have they rushed from holding hands, like chariots that are urged to speed, | Like joyful songs of singing-men. || 3. The Somas deck themselves with milk, as Kings are graced with eulogies, | And, with seven priests, the sacrifice. || 4. Pressed for the gladdening draught, the drops flow forth abundantly with song, | The Soma juices in a stream. || 5. Winning Vivasvat's glory and producing Morning's light, the Suns | Pass through the openings of the cloth. || 6. The singing-men of ancient time open the doors of sacred songs,— | Men, for the mighty to accept. || 7. Combined in close society sit the seven priests, the brother-hood, | Filling the station of the One. || 8. He gives us kinship with the Gods, and with the Sun unites our eye: | The Sage's offspring hath appeared. || 9. The Sun with his dear eye beholds that quarter of the heavens which priests | Have placed within the sacred cell.

Hymn 9:11. Soma Pavamāna.

1. Sing forth to Indu, O ye men, to him who is purified, | Fain to pay worship to the Gods. || 2. Together with thy pleasant juice the Atharvans have commingled milk, | Divine, devoted to the God. || 3. Bring, by thy flowing, weal to kine, weal to the people, weal to steeds. | Weal, O thou King, to growing plants || 4. Sing a praise-song to Soma brown of hue, of independent might. | The Red, who reaches up to heaven. || 5. Purify Soma when effused with stones which bands move rapidly, | And pour the sweet milk in the meath. || 6. With humble homage draw ye nigh; blend the libation with the curds: | To Indra offer Indu up. || 7. Soma, foe-queller, chief o'er men, doing the will of pour forth | Prosperity upon our kine. || 8. Heart-knower, Sovereign of the heart, thou art effused, O Soma, that Indra may drink thee and rejoice. || 9. O Soma Pavamāna, give us riches and heroic strength,— | Indu! with. Indra for ally.

Hymn 9:12. Soma Pavamāna.

1. To Indra have the Soma drops, exceeding rich in sweets, been poured, | Shed in the seat of sacrifice. || 2. As mother kine low to their calves, to Indra have the sages called, | Called him to drink the Soma juice. || 3. In the stream's wave wise Soma dwells, distilling rapture, in his seat, | Resting upon a wild-cow's hide. || 4. Far-sighted Soma, Sage and Seer, is worshipped in the central point | Of heaven, the straining-cloth of wool. || 5. In close embraces Indu holds Soma when | poured within the jars. | And on the. purifying sieve. || 6. Indu sends forth a voice on high to regions of the sea of air, | Shaking the vase that drops with meath. || 7. The Tree whose praises never fail yields heavenly milk among our hymns, | Urging men's generations on. || 8. The Wise One, with the Sage's stream, the Soma urged to speed, flows on | To the dear places of the sky. || 9. O Pavamāna, bring us wealth bright with a thousand splendours. Yea. | O Indu, give us ready help.

Hymn 9:13. Soma Pavamāna.

1. Passed through, the fleece in thousand streams the Soma, purified, flows on | To Indra's, Vāyu's special place. || 2. Sing forth, ye men who long for help, to Pavamāna, to the Sage, | Effused to entertain the Gods. || 3. The Soma-drops with thousand powers are purified for victory, | Hymned to become the feast of Gods. || 4. Yea, as thou flowest bring great store of food that we may win the spoil | Indu, bring splendid manly might. || 5. May they in flowing give us wealth in thousands, and heroic power,— | These Godlike Soma-drops effused. || 6. Like coursers by their drivers urged, they were poured forth, for victory, | Swift through the woollen straining-cloth. || 7. Noisily flow the Soma-drops, like milch-kine lowing to their calves: | They have run forth from both the hands. || 8. As Gladdener whom Indra loves, O Pavamāna, with a roar | Drive all our enemies away. || 9. O Pavamānas, driving off the godless, looking on the light, | Sit in the place of sacrifice.

Hymn 9:14. Soma Pavamāna.

1. Reposing on the river's wave the Sage hath widely flowed around, | Bearing the hymn which many love. || 2. When the Five kindred Companies, active in duty, with the song | Establish him, the Powerful, || 3. Then in his juice whose strength is great, have all the Gods rejoiced themselves, | When he hath clothed him in the milk. || 4. Freeing himself he flows away, leaving his body's severed limbs, | And meets his own Companion here. || 5. He by the daughters of the priest, like a fair youth, hath been adorned, | Making the milk, as 'twere, his robe. || 6. O'er the fine fingers, through desire of milk, in winding course he goes, | And utters voice which he hath found. || 7. The nimble fingers have approached, adorning him the Lord of Strength: | They grasp the vigorous Courser's back. || 8. Comprising all the treasures that are in the heavens and on the earth, | Come, Soma, as our faithful Friend.

Hymn 9:15. Soma Pavamāna.

1. Through the fine fingers, with the song, this Hero comes with rapid ears, | Going to Indra's special place. || 2. In holy thought he ponders much for the great worship of the Gods. | Where the Immortals have their seat. || 3. Like a good horse is he led out, when on the path that shines with light | The mettled steeds exert their strength. || 4. He brandishes his horns on

high, and whets them Bull who leads the herd, | Doing with might heroic deeds. || 5. He moves, a vigorous Steed, adorned with beauteous rays of shining gold, | Becoming Sovereign of the streams. || 6. He, over places rough to pass, bringing rich treasures closely packed. | Descends into the reservoirs. || 7. Men beautify him in the vats, him worthy to be beautified, | Him who brings forth abundant food. || 8. Him, even him, the fingers ten and the seven songs make beautiful, | Well-weaponed, best of gladdeners.

Hymn 9:16. Soma Pavamāna.

1. The pressers from the Soma-press send forth thy juice for rapturous joy | The speckled sap runs like a flood. || 2. With strength we follow through the sieve him who brings might and wins the kine, | Enrobed in water with his juice. || 3. Pour on the sieve the Soma, ne'er subdued in waters, waterless, | And make it pure for Indra's drink. || 4. Moved by the purifier's thought, the Soma flows into the sieve: | By wisdom it hath gained its home. || 5. With humble homage, Indra, have the Soma-drops flowed forth to thee, | Contending for the glorious prize. || 6. Purified in his fleecy garb, attaining every beauty, he | Stands, hero-like, amid the kine. || 7. Swelling, as 'twere, to heights of heaven, the stream of the creative juice | Falls lightly on the cleansing sieve. || 8. Thus, Soma, purifying him who knoweth song mid living men, | Thou wanderest through the cloth of wool.

Hymn 9:17. Soma Pavamāna.

1. Like rivers down a steep descent, slaying the Vṛitras, full of zeal, | The rapid Soma-streams have flowed. || 2. The drops of Soma juice effused fall like the rain upon the earth: | To Indra flow the Soma-streams. || 3. With swelling wave the gladdening drink, the Soma, flows into the sieve, | Loving the Gods and slaying fiends. || 4. It hastens to the pitchers, poured upon the sieve it waxes strong | At sacrifices through the lauds. || 5. Soma, thou shinest mounting heaven as 'twere above light's triple realm, | And moving seem'st to speed the Sun. || 6. To him, the head of sacrifice, singers and bards have sung their songs, | Offering what he loves to see. || 7. The men, the sages with their hymns, eager for help, deck thee strong &teed, | Deck thee for service of the Gods. || 8. Flow onward to the stream of meath rest efficacious in thy home, | Fair, to be drunk at sacrifice.

Hymn 9:18. Soma Pavamāna.

1. Thou, Soma, dweller on the hills, effused, hast flowed into the sieve,: | All-bounteous art thou in carouse. || 2. Thou art a sacred Bard, a Sage; the meath is offspring of thy sap: | All-bounteous art thou in carouse. || 3. All Deities of one accord have come that they may drink of thee: | All-bounteous art thou in carouse. || 4. He who containeth in his hands all treasures much to be desired: | All-bounteous art thou in carouse. || 5. Who milketh out this mighty Pair, the Earth and Heaven, like mother kine | All-bounteous art thou in carouse. || 6. Who in a moment mightily floweth around these two world-halves: | All-bounteous art thou in carouse. || 7. The Strong One, being purified, hath in the pitchers cried aloud: | All-bounteous art thou in carouse.

Hymn 9:19. Soma Pavamāna.

1. O Soma, being purified bring us the wondrous treasure, meet | For lauds, that is in earth and heaven. || 2. For ye Twain, Indra, Soma, are Lords of the light, Lords of the kine: | Great Rulers, prosper ye our songs. || 3. The tawny Steer, while cleansed among the living, bellowing on the grass, | Hath sunk and settled in his home. || 4. Over the Steer's productive flow the sacred songs were resonant, | The mothers of the darling Son. || 5. Hath he not, purified, impregned the kine who long to meet their Lord, | The kine who yield the shining milk? || 6. Bring near us those who stand aloof strike fear into our enemies: | O Pavamāna, find us wealth. || 7. Soma, bring down the foeman's might, his vigorous strength and vital power, | Whether he be afar or near.

Hymn 9:20. Soma Pavamāna.

1. Forth through the straining-cloth the Sage flows to the banquet of the Gods, | Subduing all our enemies. || 2. For he, as Pavamāna, sends thousandfold treasure in the shape | Of cattle to the singing-men. || 3. Thou graspest all things with thy mind, and purifiest thee with thoughts | As such, O Soma, find us fame. || 4. Pour lofty glory on us, send sure riches to our liberal lords, | Bring food to those who sing thy praise. || 5. As thou art cleansed, O Wondrous Steed, O Soma, thou hast entered, like | A pious King, into the songs. || 6. He, Soma, like a courser in the floods invincible, made clean | With hands, is resting in the jars. || 7. Disporting, like a liberal chief, thou goest, Soma, to the sieve, | Lending the laud a Hero's strength.

Hymn 9:21. Soma Pavamāna.

1. To Indra flow these running drops, these Somas frolicsome in mood. | Exhilarating, finding light; || 2. Driving off foes, bestowing room upon the presser, willingly | Bringing their praiser vital-force. || 3. Lightly disporting them, the drops flow to one common reservoir, | And fall into the river's wave. || 4. These Pavamānas have obtained all blessings much to be desired, | Like coursers harnessed to a car. || 5. With view to us, O Soma-drops, bestow his manifold desire | On him who yet hath given us naught. || 6. Bring us our wish with this design, as a wright brings his new-wrought wheel: | Flow pure and shining with the stream. || 7. These drops have cried with resonant voice: like swift steeds they have run the course, | And roused the good man's hymn to life.

Hymn 9:22. Soma Pavamāna.

1. These rapid Soma-streams have stirred themselves to motion like strong steeds, | Like cars, like armies hurried forth. || 2. Swift as wide winds they lightly move, like rain-storms of Parjanya, like | The flickering flames of burning fire. || 3. These Soma juices, blent with curds, purified, skilled in sacred hymns, | Have gained by song their hearts' desire. || 4. Immortal, cleansed, these drops, since first they flowed, have never wearied, fain | To reach the regions and their paths. || 5. Advancing they have travelled o'er the ridges of the earth and heaven, | And this the highest realm of all. || 6. Over the heights have they attained the highest thread that is spun out, | And this which must be deemed most high. || 7. Thou, Soma, boldest wealth in kine which thou hast seized from niggard churls: | Thou calledst forth the outspun thread.

Hymn 9:23. Soma Pavamāna.

1. Swift Soma drops have been effused in streams of meath, the gladdening drink, | For sacred lore of every kind. || 2. Hither to newer. resting-place the ancient Living Ones are come. | They made the Sun that he might shine. || 3. O Pavamāna, bring to us the unsacrificing foeman's wealth, | And give us food with progeny. || 4. The living Somas being cleansed diffuse exhilarating drink, | Turned to the vat which drips with meath. || 5. Soma flows on intelligent, possessing sap and mighty strength, | Brave Hero who repels the curse. || 6. For Indra, Soma! thou art cleansed, a feast-companion for the Gods: | Indu, thou fain wilt win us strength || 7. When he had drunken draughts of this, Indra smote down resistless foes: | Yea, smote them, and shall smite them still.

Hymn 9:24. Soma Pavamāna.

1. Hitherward have the Soma streamed, | the drops while they are purified: | When blent, in waters they are rinsed. || 2. The milk hath run to meet them like floods rushing down a precipice: | They come to Indra, being cleansed. || 3. O Soma Pavamāna, thou art flowing to be Indra's drink: | The men have seized and lead thee forth. || 4. Victorious, to be hailed with joy, O Soma, flow, delighting men, | To him who ruleth o'er mankind. || 5. Thou, Indu, when, effused by stones, thou runnest to the filter, art, | Ready for Indra's high decree. || 6. Flow on, best Vṛitra-slayer; flow meet to be hailed with joyful lauds. | Pure, purifying, wonderful. || 7. Pure, purifying is he called the Soma of the meath effused, | Slayer of sinners, dear to Gods.

Hymn 9:25. Soma Pavamāna.

1. Green-hued! as one who giveth strength flow on for Gods to drink, a draught | For Vāyu and the Marut host. || 2. O Pavamāna, sent by song, roaring about thy dwelling-place, | Pass into Vāyu as Law bids. || 3. The Steer shines with the Deities, dear Sage in his appointed home, | Foe-Slayer, most beloved by Gods. || 4. Taking each beauteous form, he goes, desirable, while purified, | Thither where—the Immortals sit. || 5. To Indra Soma flows, the Red, engendering song, exceeding wise, | The visitor of living men. || 6. Flow, best exhilarator, Sage, flow to the filter in a stream | To seat thee in the place of song.

Hymn 9:26. Soma Pavamāna.

1. The sages with the fingers' art have dressed and decked that vigorous Steed | Upon the lap of Aditi, || 2. The kine have called aloud to him exhaustless with a thousand streams, | To Indu who supporteth heaven. || 3. Him, nourisher of many, Sage, creative Pavamāna, they | Have sent, by

wisdom, to the sky. || 4. Him, dweller with Vivasvat, they with use of both arms have sent forth, | The Lord of Speech infallible. || 5. Him, green, beloved, many eyed, the Sisters with pressing stones | Send down to ridges of the sieve. || 6. O Pavamāna, Indu, priests hurry thee on to Indra, thee | Who aidest song and cheerest him.

Hymn 9:27. Soma Pavamāna.

1. This Sage, exalted by our lauds, flows to the purifying cloth, | Scattering foes as he is cleansed. || 2. As giving power and winning light, for Indra and for Vāyu he | Is poured upon the filtering-cloth. || 3. The men conduct him, Soma, Steer, Omniscient, and the Head of Heaven, | Effused into the vats of wood. || 4. Longing for kine, longing for gold hath Indu Pavamāna lowed, | Still Conqueror, never overcome. || 5. This Pavamāna, gladdening draught, drops on the filtering cloth, and then | Mounts up with Sūrya to the sky. || 6. To Indra in the firmament this mighty tawny Steer hath flowed, | This Indu, being purified.

Hymn 9:28. Soma Pavamāna.

1. Urged by the men, this vigorous Steed, Lord of the mind, Omniscient, | Runs to the woollen straining-cloth. || 2. Within the filter hath he flowed, this Soma for the Gods effused, | Entering all their essences. || 3. He shines in beauty there, this God Immortal in his dwelling-place, | Foe-slayer, dearest to the Gods. || 4. Directed by the Sisters ten, bellowing on his way this Steer | Runs onward to the wooden vats. || 5. This Pavamāna, swift and strong, Omniscient, gave splendour to | The Sun and all his forms of light. || 6. This Soma being purified, flows mighty and infallible, | Slayer of sinners, dear to Gods.

Hymn 9:29. Soma Pavamāna.

1. Forward with mighty force have flowed the currents of this Steer effused, | Of him who sets him by the Gods. || 2. The singers praise him with their song, and learned priests adorn the Steed, | Brought forth as light that merits laud. || 3. These things thou winnest lightly while purified, Soma, Lord of wealth: | Fill full the sea that claims our praise. || 4. Winning all precious things at once, flow on, O Soma, with thy stream | Drive to one place our enemies. || 5. Preserve us from the godless, from ill-omened voice of one and all, | That so we may be freed from blame. || 6. O Indu, as thou flowest on bring us the wealth of earth and heaven, | And splendid vigour, in thy stream.

Hymn 9:30. Soma Pavamāna.

1. Streams of this Potent One have flowed easily to the straining-cloth: | While he is cleansed he lifts his voice. || 2. Indu, by pressers urged to speed, bellowing out while beautified. | Sends forth a very mighty sound. || 3. Pour on us, Soma, with thy stream man-conquering might which many crave, | Accompanied with hero sons. || 4. Hither hath Pavamāna flowed, Soma flowed hither in a stream, | To settle in the vats of wood. || 5. To waters with the stones they drive thee tawny-hued, most rich in sweets, | O Indu, to be Indra's drink. || 6. For Indra, for the Thunderer press the Soma very rich in sweets, | Lovely, inspiriting, for strength.

Hymn 9:31. Soma Pavamāna.

1. The, Soma-drops, benevolent, come forth as they are purified, | Bestowing wealth which all may see. || 2. O Indu, high o'er heaven and earth be thou, increaser of our might: | The Master of all strength be thou. || 3. The winds are gracious in their love to thee, the rivers flow to thee | Soma, they multiply thy power. || 4. Soma, wax great. From every side may vigorous powers unite in thee: | Be in the gathering-Place of strength. || 5. For thee, brown-hued! the kine have poured imperishable oil and milk. | Aloft on the sublimest height. || 6. Friendship, O Indu, we desire with thee who bearest noble arms, | With thee, O Lord of all that is.

Hymn 9:32. Soma Pavamāna.

1. The rapture-shedding Soma-drops, effused in our assembly, have | Flowed forth to glorify our prince. || 2. Then Trita's Maidens onward urge the Tawny-coloured with the stones, | Indu for Indra, for his drink. || 3. Now like a swan he maketh all the company sing each his hymn: | He, like a steed, is bathed in milk. || 4. O Soma, viewing heaven and earth, thou runnest like a darting deer | Set in the place of sacrifice. || 5. The cows have sung with joy to him, even as a woman to her love | He came as to a settled race. || 6. Bestow illustrious fame on us, both on our liberal lords and me, | Glory, intelligence, and wealth.

Hymn 9:33. Soma Pavamāna.

1. Like waves of waters, skilled in song the juices of the Soma speed | Onward, as buffaloes to woods. || 2. With stream of sacrifice the brown bright drops have flowed with strength in store | Of kine into the wooden vats. || 3. To Indra, Vāyu, Varuṇa, to Vishṇu, and the Marutas, flow | The drops of Soma juice effused. || 4. Three several words are uttered: kine are] owing, cows who give their milk: | The Tawny-hued goes bellowing on. || 5. The young and sacred mothers of the holy rite have uttered praise: | They decorate the Child of Heaven. || 6. From every side, O Soma, for our profit, pour thou forth four seas | Filled full of riches thousandfold.

Hymn 9:34. Some Pavamāna.

1. The drop of Soma juice effused flows onward with this stream impelled. | Rending strong places with its might. || 2. Poured forth to Indra, Varuṇa, to Vāyu and the Marut hosts, | To Vishṇu, flows the Soma juice. || 3. With stones they press the Soma forth, the Strong conducted by the strong: | They milk the liquor out with skill. || 4. 'tis he whom Trita must refine, 'tis he who shall make Indra glad: | The Tawny One is decked with tints. || 5. Him do the Sons of Pṛiśni milk, the dwelling-place of sacrifice, | Oblation lovely and most dear. || 6. To him in one united stream these songs flow on straight forward. he, | Loud voiced, hath made the milch-kine low.

Hymn 9:35. Soma Pavamāna.

1. Pour forth on us abundant wealth, O Pavamāna, with thy stream. | Wherewith thou mayest find us light || 2. O Indu, swayer of the sea, shaker of all things, flow thou on, | Bearer of wealth to us with might. || 3. With thee for Hero, Valiant One! may we subdue our enemies: | Let what is precious flow to us. || 4. Indu arouses strength the Sage who strives for victory, winning power, | Discovering holy works and means. || 5. Mover of speech, we robe him with our songs as he is purified | Soma, the Guardian of the folk; || 6. On whose way, Lord of Holy Law, most rich, as he is purified. | The people all have set their hearts.

Hymn 9:36. Soma Pavamāna.

1. Forth from the mortar is the juice sent, like a car-horse, to the sieve: | The Steed steps forward to the goal. || 2. Thus, Soma, watchful, bearing well, cheering the Gods, flow past the sieve, | Turned to the vat that drops with meath. || 3. Excellent Pavamāna, make the lights shine brightly out for us. | Speed us to mental power and skill. || 4. He, beautified by pious men, and coming from their hands adorned, | Flows through the fleecy straining-cloth. || 5. May Soma pour all treasures of the heavens, the earth, the firmament | Upon the liberal worshipper. || 6. Thou mountest to the height of heaven, O Soma, seeking steeds and kine, | And seeking heroes, Lord of Strength!

Hymn 9:37. Soma Pavamāna.

1. Soma, the Steer, effused for draught, flows to the purifying sieve, | Slaying the fiends, loving the Gods. || 2. Far-sighted, tawny-coloured, he flows to the sieve, intelligent, | Bellowing, to his place of rest. || 3. This vigorous Pavamāna runs forth to the luminous realm of heaven, | Fiend-slayer, through the fleecy sieve. || 4. This Pavamāna up above Trita's high ridge hath made the Sun, | Together with the Sisters, shine. || 5. This Vṛitra-slaying Steer, effused, Soma room-giver, ne'er deceived, | Hath gone, as 'twere, to win the spoil. || 6. Urged onward by the sage, the God speeds forward to the casks of wood, | Indu to Indra willingly.

Hymn 9:38. Soma Pavamāna.

1. This Steer, this Chariot, rushes through the woollen filter, as he goes | To war that wins a thousand spoils. || 2. The Dames of Trita with the stones onward impel this Tawny One | Indu to Indra for his drink. || 3. Ten active fingers carefully adorn him here; they make him bright | And beauteous for the gladdening draught. || 4. He like a falcon settles down amid the families of men. | Speeding like lover to his love. || 5. This young exhilarating juice looks downward from its place in heaven, | This Soma-drop that pierced the sieve. || 6. Poured for the draught, this tawny juice | flows forth, intelligent, crying out, | Unto the well-beloved place.

Hymn 9:39. Soma Pavamāna.

1. Flow on, O thou of lofty thought, flow swift in thy beloved form, | Saying, I go where dwell the Gods. || 2. Preparing what is unprepared, and bringing store of food to man, | Make thou the rain descend from heaven. || 3. With might, bestowing power, the juice enters the purifying sieve, | Far-

seeing, sending forth its light. ‖ 4. This is it which in rapid course hath with the river's wave flowed down | From heaven upon the straining cloth. ‖ 5. Inviting him from far away, and even from near at hand, the juice | For Indra is poured forth as meath. ‖ 6. In union they have sung the hymn: with stones they urge the Tawny One. | Sit in the place of sacrifice.

Hymn 9:40. Soma Pavamāna.

1. The Very Active hath assailed, while purified, all enemies: | They deck the Sage with holy songs. ‖ 2. The Red hath mounted to his place; to India, goes the mighty juice: | He settles in his firm abode. ‖ 3. O Indu, Soma, send us now great opulence from every side, Pour on us treasures thousandfold. ‖ 4. O Soma Pavamāna, bring, Indu, all splendours hitherward: | Find for us food in boundless store. ‖ 5. As thou art cleansed, bring hero strength and riches to thy worshipper, | And prosper thou the singer's hymns. ‖ 6. O Indu, Soma, being cleansed, bring hither riches doubly-piled, | Wealth, mighty Indu, meet for lauds.

Hymn 9:41. Soma Pavamāna.

1. Active and bright have they come forth, impetuous in speed like bulls, | Driving the black skin far away. ‖ 2. Quelling the riteless Dasyu, may we think upon the bridge of bliss, | Leaving the bridge of woe behind. ‖ 3. The mighty Pavamāna's roar is heard as 'twere the rush of rain | Lightnings are flashing to the sky. ‖ 4. Pour out on us abundant food, when thou art pressed, O Indu wealth | In kine and gold and steeds and spoil. ‖ 5. Flow on thy way, Most Active, thou. fill full the mighty heavens and earth, | As Dawn, as Sūrya with his beams. ‖ 6. On every side, O Soma, flow round us with thy protecting stream, | As Rasā flows around the world.

Hymn 9:42. Soma Pavamāna.

1. Engendering the Sun in floods, engendering heaven's lights, green-hued, | Robed in the waters and the milk, ‖ 2. According to primeval plan this Soma, with his stream, effused | Flows purely on, a God for Gods. ‖ 3. For him victorious, waxen great, the juices with a thousand powers | Are purified for winning spoil. ‖ 4. Shedding the ancient fluid he is poured into the cleansing sieve: | He, thundering, hath produced the Gods. ‖ 5. Soma, while purifying, sends hither all things to be desired, | He sends the Gods who strengthen Law. ‖ 6. Soma, effused, pour on us wealth in kine, in heroes, steeds, and spoil, | Send us abundant store of food.

Hymn 9:43. Soma Pavamāna.

1. We will enrobe with sacred song the Lovely One who, as a Steed, | Is decked with milk for rapturous joy. ‖ 2. All songs of ours desiring grace adorn him in the ancient way, | Indu for Indra, for his drink. ‖ 3. Soma flows on when purified, beloved and adorned with songs, | Songs of the sage Medhātithi. ‖ 4. O Soma Pavamāna, find exceeding glorious wealth for us, | Wealth, Indu, fraught with boundless might. ‖ 5. Like courser racing to the prize Indu, the lover of the Gods, | Roars, as he passes, in the sieve. ‖ 6. Flow on thy way to win us strength, to speed the sage who praises thee: | Soma, bestow heroic power.

Hymn 9:44. Soma Pavamāna.

1. Indu, to us for this great rite, bearing as 'twere thy wave to Gods, | Unwearied, thou art flowing forth. ‖ 2. Pleased with the hymn, impelled by prayer, Soma is hurried far away, | The Wise One in the Singer's stream. ‖ 3. Watchful among the. Gods, this juice advances to the cleansing sieve | Soma, most active, travels on. ‖ 4. Flow onward, seeking strength for us, embellishing the sacrifice: | The priest with trimmed grass calleth thee. ‖ 5. May Soma, ever bringing power to Bhaga and to Vāyu, Sage | And Hero, lead us to the Gods. ‖ 6. So, to increase our wealth today, Inspirer, best of Furtherers, | Win for us strength and high renown.

Hymn 9:45. Soma Pavamāna.

1. Flow, thou who viewest men, to give delight, to entertain the Gods, | Indu, to Indra for his drink. ‖ 2. Stream to thine embassy for us: thou hastenest, for Indra, to | The Gods, O better than our friends. ‖ 3. We balm thee, red of hue, with milk to fit thee for the rapturous joy: | Unbar for us the doors of wealth. ‖ 4. He through the sieve hath passed, as comes a courser to the pole, to run | Indu belongs unto the Gods. ‖ 5. All friends have lauded him as he sports in the wood, beyond the fleece: | Singers have chanted Indu's praise. ‖ 6. Flow, Indu, with that stream wherein steeped thou announcest to the man | Who worships thee heroic strength.

Hymn 9:46. Soma Pavamāna.

1. Like able coursers they have been sent forth to be the feast of Gods, | joying in mountains, flowing on. ‖ 2. To Vāyu flow the Soma-streams, the drops of juice made beautiful | Like a bride dowered by her sire. ‖ 3. Pressed in the mortar, these, the drops of | juice, the Somas rich in food, | Give strength to Indra with their work. ‖ 4. Deft-handed men, run hither, seize the brilliant juices blent with meal, | And cook with milk the gladdening draught. ‖ 5. Thus, Soma, Conqueror of wealth! flow, finding furtherance for us, | Giver of ample opulence. ‖ 6. This Pavamāna, meet to be adorned, the fingers ten adorn, | The draught that shall make Indra glad.

Hymn 9:47. Soma Pavamāna.

1. Great as he was, Soma hath gained strength by this high solemnity: | joyous he riseth like a bull. ‖ 2. His task is done: his crushings of the Dasyus are made manifest: | He sternly reckoneth their debts. ‖ 3. Soon as his song of praise is born, the Soma, Indra's juice, becomes | A thousand-winning thunderbolt. ‖ 4. Seer and Sustainer, he himself desireth riches for the sage | When he embellisheth his songs. ‖ 5. Fain would they both win riches as in races of the steeds. In war | Thou art upon the conquerors' side.

Hymn 9:48. Soma Pavamāna.

1. With sacrifice we seek to thee kind Cherisher of manly might | In mansions of the lofty heavens; ‖ 2. Gladdening crusher of the bold, ruling with very mighty sway, | Destroyer of a hundred forts. ‖ 3. Hence, Sapient One! the Falcon, strong of wing, unwearied, brought thee down, | Lord over riches, from the sky. ‖ 4. That each may see the light, the Bird brought us the guard of Law, the Friend | Of all, the speeder through the air. ‖ 5. And now, sent forth, it hath attained to mighty power and majesty, | Most active, ready to assist.

Hymn 9:49. Soma Pavamāna.

1. Pour down the rain upon us, pour a wave of waters from the sky, | And plenteous store of wholesome food. ‖ 2. Flow onward with that stream of thine, whereby the cows have come to us, | The kine of strangers to our home. ‖ 3. Chief Friend of Gods in sacred rites, pour on us fatness with thy stream, | Pour down on us a flood of rain. ‖ 4. To give us vigour, with thy stream run through the fleecy straining-cloth | For verily the Gods will bear. ‖ 5. Onward hath Pavamāna flowed and beaten off the Rākṣhasas, | Flashing out splendour as of old.

Hymn 9:50. Soma Pavamāna.

1. Loud as a river's roaring wave thy powers have lifted up themselves: | Urge on thine arrow's sharpened point. ‖ 2. At thine effusion upward rise three voices full of joy, when thou | Flowest upon the fleecy ridge. ‖ 3. On to the fleece they urge with stone the tawny well-beloved One, | Even Pavamāna, dropping meath. ‖ 4. Flow with thy current to the sieve, O Sage most powerful to cheer, | To seat thee in the place of song. ‖ 5. Flow, Most Exhilarating! flow anointed with the milk for balm, | Indu, for Indra, for his drink.

Hymn 9:51. Soma Pavamāna.

1. Adhvaryu, on the filter pour the Soma juice expressed with stones, | And make it pure for Indra's drink. ‖ 2. Pour out for Indra, Thunder-armed, the milk of heaven,, the Soma's juice, | Most excellent, most rich in sweets. ‖ 3. These Gods and all the Marut host, Indu enjoy this juice of thine, | This Pavamāna's flowing meath. ‖ 4. For, Soma, thou hast been effused, strengthening for the wild carouse, | O Steer, the singer, for our help. ‖ 5. Flow with thy stream, Far-sighted One, effused, into the cleansing sieve: | Flow on to give us strength and fame.

Hymn 9:52. Soma Pavamāna.

1. Wealth-winner, dwelling in the sky, bringing us vigour with the juice, | Flow to the filter when effused. ‖ 2. So, in thine ancient ways, may he, beloved, with a thousand streams | Run o'er the fleecy straining-cloth. ‖ 3. Him who is like a cauldron shake: O Indu, shake thy gift to us | Shake it, armed Warrior! with thine arms. ‖ 4. Indu, invoked with many a prayer, bring down the vigour of these men, | Of him who threatens us with war. ‖ 5. Indu, Wealth-giver, with thine help pour out for us a hundred, yea, | A thousand of thy pure bright streams.

Hymn 9:53. Soma Pavamāna.

1. O thou with stones for arms, thy powers, crushing the fiends, have raised themselves: | Chase thou the foes who compass us. ‖ 2. Thou conquerest thus

with might when car meets car, and when the prize is staked: | With fearless heart will I sing praise. || 3. No one with evil thought assails this Pavamāna's holy laws: | Crush him who fain would fight with thee. || 4. For Indra to the streams they drive the tawny rapture-dropping Steed, | Indu the bringer of delight.

Hymn 9:54. Soma Pavamāna.

1. After his ancient splendour, they, the bold, have drawn the bright milk from | The Sage who wins a thousand gifts. || 2. In aspect he is like the Sun; he runneth forward to the lakes, | Seven currents flowing through the sky. || 3. He, shining in his splendour, stands high over all things that exist— | Soma, a God as Sūrya is. || 4. Thou, Indu, in thy brilliancy, pourest on us, as Indra's Friend, | Wealth from the kine to feast the Gods.

Hymn 9:55. Soma Pavamāna.

1. Pour on us with thy juice all kinds of corn, each sort of nourishment, | And, Soma, all felicities. || 2. As thine, O Indu, is the praise, and thine what springeth from the juice, | Seat thee on the dear sacred grass. || 3. And, finding for us kine and steeds, O Soma, with thy juice flow on | Through days that fly most rapidly. || 4. As one who conquers, ne'er subdued, attacks and stays the enemy, | Thus, Vanquisher of thousands! flow.

Hymn 9:56. Soma Pavamāna.

1. Swift to the purifying sieve flows Soma as exalted Law, | Slaying the fiends, loving the Gods. || 2. When Soma pours the strengthening food a hundred ever-active streams | To Indra's friendship win their way. || 3. Ten Dames have sung to welcome thee, even as a maiden greets her love: | O Soma, thou art decked to win. || 4. Flow hitherward, O Indu, sweet to Indra and to Vishṇu: guard | The men, the singers, from distress.

Hymn 9:57. Soma Pavamāna.

1. Thy streams that never fail or waste flow forth like showers of rain from heaven, | To bring a thousand stores of strength. || 2. He flows beholding on his way all well-beloved sacred lore, | Green-tinted, brandishing his, arms. || 3. He, when the people deck him like a docile king of elephants. | Sits as a falcon in the, wood. || 4. So bring thou hitherward to us, Indu, while thou art purified, | All treasures both of heaven and earth.

Hymn 9:58. Soma Pavamāna.

1. Swift runs this giver of delight, even the stream of flowing juice: | Swift runs this giver of delight. || 2. The Morning knows all precious things, the Goddess knows her grace to man: | Swift runs this giver of delight. || 3. We have accepted thousands from Dhvasra's and Purushanti's hands: | Swift runs this giver of delight. || 4. From whom we have accepted thus thousands and three times ten beside: | Swift runs this giver of delight.

Hymn 9:59. Soma Pavamāna.

1. Flow onward, Soma, winning kine, and steeds, and all that gives delight: | Bring hither wealth with progeny. || 2. Flow onward from the waters, flow, inviolable, from the plants: | Flow onward from the pressing-boards. || 3. Soma, as Pavamāna, pass over all trouble and distress: | Sit on the sacred grass, a Sage. || 4. Thou, Pavamāna, foundest light; thou at thy birth becamest great: | O Indu, thou art over all.

Hymn 9:60. Soma Pavamāna.

1. Sing forth and laud with sacred song most active Pavamāna, laud | Indu who sees with thousand eyes. || 2. Thee who hast thousand eyes to see, bearer of thousand burthens, they | Have filtered through the fleecy cloth. || 3. He, Pavamāna, hath streamed through the fleece then: he runs into the jars, | Finding his way to Indra's heart. || 4. That Indra may be bounteous, flow, most active Soma, for our weal: | Bring genial seed with progeny.

Hymn 9:61. Soma Pavamāna.

1. Flow onward, Indu, with this food for him who in thy wild delight | Battered the nine-and-ninety down, || 2. Smote swiftly forts, and Śambara, then Yadu and that Turvaśa, | For pious Divodāsa's sake. || 3. Finder of horses, pour on us horses and | wealth in kine and gold, | And, Indu, food in boundless store. || 4. We seek to win thy friendly love, even Pavamāna's flowing o'er | The limit of the cleansing sieve. || 5. With those same waves which in their stream overflow the purifying sieve, | Soma; be gracious unto us. || 6. O Soma, being purified, bring us from all sides,—for thou canst,— | Riches and food with hero sons. || 7. Him here, the Child whom streams have borne, the ten swift fingers beautify | With the Ādityas is he seen. || 8. With Indra and with Vāyu he, effused, flows onward with,the beams | Of Sūrya to the cleansing sieve. || 9. Flow rich in sweets and lovely for our Bhaga, Vāyu, Pūshan flow | For Mitra and for Varuṇa. || 10. High is thy juice's birth: though set in heaven, on earth it hath obtained | Strong sheltering power and great renown. || 11. Striving to win, with him we gain all wealth from the ungodly man, | Yea, all the glories of mankind. || 12. Finder of room and freedom, flow for Indra whom we must adore, | For Varuṇa and the Marut host. || 13. The Gods have come to Indu well-descended, beautified with milk, | The active crusher of the foe. || 14. Even as mother cows their calf, so let our praise-songs strengthen him, | Yea, him who winneth Indra's heart. || 15. Soma, pour blessings on our kine, pour forth the food that streams with milk | Increase the sea that merits laud. || 16. From heaven hath Pavamāna made, as 'twere, the marvellous thunder, and | The lofty light of all mankind. || 17. The gladdening and auspicious juice of thee, of Pavamāna, King! | Flows o'er the woollen straining-cloth. || 18. Thy juice, O Pavamāna, sends its rays abroad like splendid skill, | Like lustre, all heaven's light, to see. || 19. Flow onward with that juice of thine most excellent, that brings delight, | Slaying the wicked, dear to Gods. || 20. Killing the foeman and his hate, and winning booty every day, | Gainer art thou of steeds and kine. || 21. Red-hued, be blended with the milk that seems to yield its lovely breast, | Falcon-like resting in thine home. || 22. Flow onward thou who strengthenedst Indra to slaughter Vṛitra who | Compassed and stayed the mighty floods. || 23. Soma who rainest gifts, may we win riches with our hero sons: | Strengthen, as thou art cleansed, our hymns. || 24. Aided by thee, and through thy grace, may we be slayers when we war: | Watch, Soma, at our solemn rites. || 25. Chasing our foemen, driving off the godless, Soma floweth on, | Going to Indra's special place. || 26. O Pavamāna, hither bring great riches, and destroy our foes: | O Indu, grant heroic fame. || 27. A hundred obstacles have ne'er checked | thee when fain to give thy boons, | When, being cleansed, thou combatest. || 28. Indu, flow on, a mighty juice; glorify us among the folk: | Drive all our enemies away. || 29. Indu, in this thy friendship most lofty and glorious may we | Subdue all those who war with us. || 30. Those awful weapons that thou hast, sharpened at point to strike men down— | Guard us therewith from every foe.

Hymn 9:62. Soma Pavamāna.

1. These rapid Soma-drops have been poured through the purifying sieve | To bring us all felicities. || 2. Dispelling manifold mishap, giving the courser's progeny, | Yea, and the warrior steed, success. || 3. Bringing prosperity to kine, they make perpetual Iḷā flow | To us for noble eulogy. || 4. Strong, mountain-born, the stalk hath been | pressed in the streams for rapturous joy: | Hawk-like he settles in his home. || 5. Fair is the God-loved juice; the plant is washed in waters, pressed by men | The milch-kine sweeten it with milk. || 6. As drivers deck a courser, so have they adorned the meath's juice for | Ambrosia, for the festival. || 7. Thou, Indu, with thy streams that drop sweet juices, which were poured for | help, | Hast settled in the cleansing sieve. || 8. So flow thou onward through the fleece, for Indra flow, to be his drink, | Finding thine home in vats of wood. || 9. As giving room and freedom, as most sweet, pour butter forth and milk, | O Indu, for the Aṅgirasas. || 10. Most active and benevolent, this Pavamāna, sent to us | For lofty friendship, meditates. || 11. Queller of curses, mighty, with strong sway, this Pavamāna shall | Bring treasures to the worshipper. || 12. Pour thou upon us thousandfold possessions, both of kine and steeds, | Exceeding glorious, much-desired. || 13. Wandering far, with wise designs, the juice here present is effused, | Made beautiful by living men. || 14. For Indra flows the gladdening drink, the measurer of the region, Sage, | With countless wealth and endless help. || 15. Born on the mountain, lauded here, Indu for Indra is set down, | As in her sheltering nest a bird. || 16. Pressed by the men, as 'twere to war hath Soma Pavamāna sped, | To test with might within the vats. || 17. That he may move, they yoke him to the three-backed triple-seated car | By the Seven Ṛishis' holy songs. || 18. Drive ye that Tawny Courser, O ye pressers, on his way to war, | Swift Steed who carries off the spoil. || 19. Pouring all glories hither, he, effused and entering the jar, | Stands like a hero mid the kine. || 20. Indu, the living men milk out the juice to make the rapturous draught: | Gods for the Gods milk out the meath. || 21. Pour for the Gods into the sieve our Soma very rich in sweets, | Him whom the Gods most gladly hear. || 22. Into his stream who gladdens best these Soma juices have been poured, | Lauded with songs for lofty

fame. || 23. Thou flowest to enjoy the milk, and bringest valour, being cleansed: | Winning the spoil flow hitherward. || 24. And, hymned by Jamadagnis, let all nourishment that kine supply, | And general praises, flow to us. || 25. Soma, as leader of the song flow onward with thy wondrous aids, | For holy lore of every kind. || 26. Do thou as leader of the song, stirring the waters of the sea, | Flow onward, thou who movest all. || 27. O Soma, O thou Sage, these worlds stand ready to attest thy might: | For thy behoof the rivers flow. || 28. Like showers of rain that fall from heaven thy streams perpetually flow | To the bright fleece spread under them. || 29. For potent Indra purify Indu effectual and strong, | Enjoyment-giver, Mighty Lord. || 30. Soma, true, Pavamāna, Sage, is seated in the cleansing sieve, | Giving his praiser hero strength.

Hymn 9:63. Soma Pavamāna.

1. Pour hitherward, O Soma, wealth in thousands and heroic strength, | And keep renown secure for us. || 2. Thou makest food and vigour swell for Indra, best of gladdeners! | Within the cups thou seatest thee. || 3. For Indra and for Vishṇu poured, Soma hath flowed into the jar: | May Vāyu find it rich in sweets. || 4. These Somas swift and brown of hue, in stream of solemn sacrifice | Have flowed through twisted obstacles, || 5. Performing every noble work, active, augmenting Indra's strength, | Driving away the godless ones. || 6. Brown Soma-drops, effused that seek Indra, to their appropriate place | Flow through the region hitherward. || 7. Flow onward with that stream of thine wherewith thou gavest Sūrya light, | Urging on waters good to men. || 8. He, Pavamāna, high o'er man yoked the Sun's courser Etaśa | To travel through the realm of air. || 9. And those ten Coursers, tawny-hued, he harnessed that the Sun might come | Indu, he said, is Indra's self. || 10. Hence, singers, pour the gladdening juice to Vāyu and to Indra, pour | The drops upon the fleecy cloth. || 11. O Soma Pavamāna, find wealth for us not to be assailed, | Wealth which the foeman may not win. || 12. Send riches hither with thy stream in thousands, both of steeds and kine, | Send spoil of war and high renown. || 13. Soma the God, expressed with stones, like Sūrya, floweth on his way, | Pouring the juice within the jar. || 14. These brilliant drops have poured for us, in stream of solemn sacrifice, | Worshipful laws and strength in kine. || 15. Over the cleansing sieve have flowed the Somas, blent with curdled milk, | Effused for Indra Thunder-armed. || 16. Soma, do thou most rich in sweets, a gladdening drink most dear to Gods, | Flow to the sieve to bring us wealth. || 17. For Indra, living men adorn the Tawny Courser in the streams, Indu, the giver of delight. || 18. Pour for us, Soma, wealth in gold, in horses and heroic sons, | Bring hither strength in herds of kine. || 19. For Indra pour ye on the fleece him very sweet to taste, who longs. | For battle as it were in war. || 20. The singers, seeking help, adorn the Sage who must be decked with songs: | Loud bellowing the Steer comes on, || 21. The singers with their thoughts and hymns have, in the stream of sacrifice, | Caused Soma, active Steer, to roar. || 22. God, working with mankind, flow on; to Indra go thy gladdening juice: | To Vāyu mount as Law commands || 23. O Soma, Pavamāna, thou pourest out wealth that brings renown: | Enter the lake, as one we love. || 24. Soma thou flowest chasing foes and bringing wisdom and delight: | Drive off the folk who love not Gods. || 25. The Pavamānas have been poured, the brilliant drops of Soma juice, | For holy lore of every kind. || 26. The Pavamānas have been shed, the beautiful swift Soma-drops, | Driving all enemies afar. || 27. From, heaven, from out the firmament, hath Pavamāna been effused | Upon the summit of the earth. || 28. O Soma, Indu, very wise, drive, being purified, with thy stream | All foes, all Rākshasas away. || 29. Driving the Rākshasas afar, O Soma, bellowing, pour for us | Most excellent and splendid strength. || 30. Soma, do thou secure for us the treasures of the earth and heaven, | Indu, all boons to be desired.

Hymn 9:64. Soma Pavamāna.

1. Soma, thou art a splendid Steer, a Steer, O God, with steer-like sway: | Thou as a Steer ordainest laws. || 2. Steer-strong thy might is as a steer's, steer-strong thy wood, steer-like thy drink | A Steer indeed, O Steer, art thou. || 3. Thou, Indu, as a vigorous horse, hast neighed together steeds and kine: | Unbar for us the doors to wealth. || 4. Out of desire of cows and steeds and horses. potent Soma-drops, | Brilliant and swift, have been effused. || 5. They purified in both the hands, made beautiful by holy men, | Flow onward to the fleecy cloth. || 6. These Soma juices shall pour forth all treasures for the worshipper | From heaven and earth and firmament. || 7. The streams of Pavamāna, thine, Finder of all, have been effused, | Even as Sūrya's rays of light. || 8. Making the light that shines from heaven thou flowest on to every form | Soma, thou swellest like a sea. || 9. Urged on thou sendest out thy voice, O Pavamāna; thou hast moved, | Like the God Sūrya, to the sieve. || 10. Indu, Enlightener, Friend, hath been purified by the sages' hymns: | So starts the charioteer his steed— || 11. Thy God-delighting wave which hath flowed to purifying sieve, | Alighting in the home of Law. || 12. Flow to our sieve, a gladdening draught that hath most intercourse with Gods, | Indu, to Indra for his drink. || 13. Flow onward with a stream for food, made beautiful by sapient men: | Indu with sheen approach the milk. || 14. While thou art cleansed, Song-Lover, bring comfort and vigour to the folk, | Poured, Tawny One! on milk and curds. || 15. Purified for the feast of Gods, go thou to Indra's special place, | Resplendent, guided by the strong. || 16. Accelerated by the hymn, the rapid drops of Soma juice | Have flowed, urged onward, to the lake. || 17. Easily have the living drops, made beautiful, approached the lake, | Yea, to the place of sacrifice. || 18. Compass about, our faithful Friend, all our possessions with thy might: | Guard, hero like, our sheltering home. || 19. Loud neighs the Courser Etaśa, with singers, harnessed for the place, | Guided for travel to the lake. || 20. What time the Swift One resteth in the golden place of sacrifice, | He leaves the foolish far away. || 21. The friends have sung in unison, the prudent wish to sacrifice: | Down sink the unintelligent. || 22. For Indra girt by Marutas, flow, thou Indu, very rich in sweets, | To sit in place of sacrifice. || 23. Controlling priests and sages skilled in holy song adorn thee well: | The living make thee beautiful. || 24. Aryaman, Mitra, Varuṇa drink Pavamāna's juice, yea, thine: | O Sage, the Marutas drink thereof. || 25. O Soma, Indu, thou while thou art purified urgest onward speech. | Thousandfold, with the lore of hymns. || 26. Yea, Soma, Indu, while thou art purified do thou bring to us | Speech thousandfold that longs for war. || 27. O Indu, Much-invoked, while thou art purifying, as the Friend. | Of these men enter thou the lake. || 28. Bright are these Somas blent with milk, with light that flashes brilliantly. And form that utters loud acclaim. || 29. Led by his drivers, and sent forth, the Strong Steed hath come nigh for spoil, | Like warriors when they stand arrayed. || 30. Specially, Soma, coming as a Sage from heaven to prosper us, | Flow like the Sun for us to see.

Hymn 9:65. Soma Pavamāna.

1. The, glittering maids send Sūra forth, the glorious sisters, close-allied, | Send Indu forth, their mighty Lord. || 2. Pervade, O Pavamāna, all our treasures with repeated light, | God, coming hither from the Gods. || 3. Pour on us, Pavamāna, rain, as service and rain praise for Gods: | Pour all to be our nourishment. || 4. Thou art a Steer by lustre: we, O Pavamāna, faithfully | Call upon thee the Splendid One. || 5. Do thou, rejoicing, nobly-armed! pour upon us heroic strength: | O Indu, come thou hitherward. || 6. When thou art cleansed with both the hands and dipped in waters, with the wood. | Thou comest to the gathering-place. || 7. Sing forth your songs, as Vyaśva sang, to Soma Pavamāna, to, | The Mighty One with thousand eyes; || 8. Whose coloured sap they drive with stones, the yellow death-dealing juice, | Indu for Indra, for his drink. || 9. We seek to gain the friendly love of thee that Strong and Mighty One, | Of thee the winner of all wealth. || 10. Flow onward with thy stream, a Steer, inspiriting the Marutas' Lord, | Winning all riches by thy might. || 11. I send thee forth to battle from the press, O Pavamāna, Strong, | Sustainer, looker on the light. || 12. Acknowledged by this song of mine, flow, tawny-coloured, with thy stream | Incite to battle thine ally. || 13. O Indu, visible to all pour out for us abundant food: | Soma, be thou our prosperer. || 14. The pitchers, Indu, with thy streams have sung aloud in vigorous might | Enter them, and let Indra drink. || 15. O thou whose potent gladdening juice they milk out with the stones, flow on, | Destroyer of our enemies. || 16. King Pavamāna is implored with holy songs, on man's behalf, | To travel through the firmament. || 17. Bring us, O Indu, hundredfold increase of kine, and noble steeds, | The gift of fortune for our help. || 18. Pressed for the banquet of the Gods, O Soma, bring us might, and speed, | Like beauty for a brilliant show. || 19. Soma, flow on exceeding bright with loud roar to the wooden vats, | Falcon-like resting in thine home. || 20. Soma, the Water-winner flows to Indra, Vāyu, Varuṇa, | To Vishṇu and the Marut host. || 21. Soma, bestowing food upon our progeny, from every sides, | Pour on us riches

thousandfold || 22. The Soma juices which have been expressed afar or near at hand, | Or there on Śaryaṇāvat's bank, || 23. Those pressed among Ārjīkas, pressed among the active, in men's homes, | Or pressed among the Races Five— || 24. May these celestial drops, expressed, pour forth upon us, as they flow, | Rain from the heavens and hero strength. || 25. Urged forward o'er the ox-hide flows the Lovely One of tawny hue, | Lauded by Jamadagni's song. || 26. Like horses urged to speed, the drops, bright, stirring vital power, when blent | With milk, are beautified in streams. || 27. So they who toil with juices send thee forward for the Gods' repast: | So with this splendour flow thou on. || 28. We choose today that chariot-steed of thine, the Strong, that brings us bliss, | The Guardian, the desire of all, || 29. The Excellent, the Gladdener, the Sage with heart that understands, | The Guardian, the desire of all; || 30. Who for ourselves, O thou Most Wise, is wealth and fair intelligence, | The Guardian, the desire of all.

Hymn 9:66. Soma Pavamāna.

1. For holy lore of every sort, flow onward thou whom all men love. | A Friend to be besought by friends. || 2. O'er all thou rulest with these Two which, Soma Pavamāna, stand, | Turned, as thy stations, hitherward. || 3. Wise Soma Pavamāna, thou encompassest on every side | Thy stations as the seasons come. || 4. Flow onward, generating food, for precious boons of every kind, | A Friend for friends, to be our help. || 5. Upon the lofty ridge of heaven thy bright rays with their essences, | Soma, spread purifying power. || 6. O Soma, these Seven Rivers flow, as being thine, to give command: | The Streams of milk run forth to thee. || 7. Flow onward, Soma in a stream, effused to gladden Indra's heart, | Bringing imperishable fame. || 8. Driving thee in Vivasvat's course, the Seven Sisters with their hymns | Made melody round thee the Sage. || 9. The virgins deck thee o'er fresh streams to drive thee to the sieve when thou, | A singer, bathest in the wood. || 10. The streams of Pavamāna, thine, Sage, Mighty One, have poured them forth. | Like coursers eager for renown. || 11. They have been poured upon the fleece towards the meath-distilling vat: | The holy songs have sounded forth. || 12. Like milch-kine coming home, the drops of Soma juice have reached the lake, | Have reached the place of sacrifice. || 13. O Indu, to our great delight the running waters flow to us, | When thou wilt robe thyself in milk. || 14. In this thy friendship, and with thee to help us, fain to sacrifice, | Indu, we crave thy friendly love. || 15. Flow on, O Soma, for the great Viewer of men, for gain of kine | Enter thou into Indra's throat. || 16. Best art thou, Soma, of the great, Strongest of strong ones, Indu: thou | As Warrior ever hast prevailed. || 17. Mightier even than the strong, more valiant even than the brave, | More liberal than the bountiful, || 18. Soma, as Sūra, bring us food, win offspring of our bodies: we | Elect thee for our friendship, we elect thee for companionship. || 19. Agni, thou pourest life; send down upon us food and vigorous strength; | Drive thou misfortune far away, || 20. Agni is Pavamāna, Sage, Chief Priest of all the Races Five: | To him whose wealth is great we pray. || 21. Skilled in thy task, O Agni, pour splendour with hero strength on us, | Granting me wealth that nourishes. || 22. Beyond his enemies away to sweet praise Pavamāna flows, | Like Sūrya visible to all. || 23. Adorned by living men, set forth for entertainment, rich in food, | Far-sighted Indu is a Steed. || 24. He, Pavamāna, hath produced the lofty Law, the brilliant light, | Destroying darkness black of hue. || 25. From tawny Pavamāna, the Destroyer, radiant streams have sprung, | Quick streams from him whose gleams are swift. || 26. Best rider of the chariot, praised with fairest praise mid beauteous ones, | Gold-gleaming with the Marut host, || 27. May Pavamāna, best to win the booty, penetrate with rays, | Giving the singer hero strength. || 28. Over the fleecy sieve hath flowed the drop effused: to Indra comes | Indu while he is purified || 29. This Soma, through the pressing-stones, is sporting on the ox-hide, and | Summoning Indra to the draught. || 30. O Pavamāna, bless us, so that we may live, with that bright milk | Of thine which hath been brought from heaven.

Hymn 9:67. Soma and Others.

1. Thou, Soma, hast a running stream, joyous, most strong at sacrifice: | Flow bounteously bestowing wealth. || 2. Effused as cheerer of the men, flowing best gladdener, thou art | A Prince to Indra with thy juice. || 3. Poured forth by pressing-stones, do thou with loud roar send us in a stream | Most excellent illustrious might. || 4. Indu, urged forward, floweth through the fleecy cloth: the Tawny One | With his loud roar hath brought as strength. || 5. Indu, thou flowest through the fleece, bringing felicities and fame, | And, Soma, spoil and wealth in kine. || 6. Hither, O Indu, bring us wealth in steeds and cattle hundredfold: | Bring wealth, O Soma, thousandfold. || 7. In purifying, through the sieve the rapid drops of Soma juice | Come nigh to Indra in their course. || 8. For Indra floweth excellent Indu, the noblest Soma juice | The Living for the Living One. || 9. The glittering maids send Sūra forth they with their song have sung aloud | To Pavamāna dropping meath. || 10. May Pūṣhan, drawn by goats, be our protector, and on all his paths | Bestow on us our share of maids. || 11. This Soma flows like gladdening oil for him who wears the braided locks: | He shall give us our share of maids. || 12. This Soma juice, O glowing God, flows like pure oil, effused for thee: | He shall give us our share of maids. || 13. Flow onward, Soma, in thy stream, begetter of the sages' speech: | Wealth-giver among Gods art thou. || 14. The Falcon dips within the jars: he wrap him in his robe and goes | Loud roaring to the vats of wood. || 15. Soma, thy juice hath been effused and poured into the pitcher: like | A rapid hawk it rushes on. || 16. For Indra flow most rich in sweets, O Soma, bringing him delight. || 17. They were sent forth to feast the Gods, like chariots that display their strength. || 18. Brilliant, best givers of delight, these juices have sent Vāyu forth. || 19. Bruised by the press-stones and extolled, Soma, thou goest to the sieve, | Giving the worshipper hero strength. || 20. This juice bruised by the pressing-stones and lauded passes through the sieve, | Slayer of demons, through the fleece. || 21. O Pavamāna, drive away the danger, whether near at hand | Or far remote, that finds me here. || 22. This day may Pavamāna cleanse us with his purifying power, | Most active purifying Priest. || 23. O Agni, with the cleansing light diffused through all thy fiery glow, | Purify thou this prayer of ours. || 24. Cleanse us with thine own cleansing power, O Agni, that is bright with flame, | And by libations poured to thee. || 25. Savitar, God, by both of these, libation, purifying power, | Purify me on every side. || 26. Cleanse us, God Savitar, with Three, O Soma, with sublimest forms, | Agni, with forms of power and might. || 27. May the Gods' company make me clean, and Vasus make rue pure by song. | Purify me, ye General Gods; O Jātavedas, make me pure. || 28. Fill thyself full of juice, flow forth, O Soma, thou with all thy stalks, | The best oblation to the Gods. || 29. We with our homage have approached the Friend who seeks our wondering praise, | Young, strengthener of the solemn rite. || 30. Lost is Alayya's axe. O Soma, God do thou send it back hither in thy flow | Even, Soma, God, if 'twere a mole. || 31. The man who reads the essence stored by saints, the Pavamāna hymns, | Tastes food completely purified, made sweet by Mātariśvan's touch. || 32. Whoever reads the essence stored by saints, the Pavamāna hymns, | Sarasvatī draws forth for him water and butter, milk and meath.

Hymn 9:68. Soma Pavamāna.

1. The drops of Soma juice like cows who yield their milk have flowed forth, rich in meath, unto the Shining One, | And, seated on the grass, raising their voice, assumed the milk, the covering robe wherewith the udders stream. || 2. He bellows with a roar around the highest twigs: the Tawny One is sweetened as he breaks them up. | Then passing through the sieve into the ample room, the God throws off the dregs according to his wish. || 3. The gladdening drink that measured out the meeting Twins fills full with milk the Eternal Ever-waxing Pair. | Bringing to light the Two great Regions limitless, moving above them he gained sheen that never fades. || 4. Wandering through, the Parents, strengthening the floods, the Sage makes his place swell with his own native might. | The stalk is mixed with grain: he comes led by the men together with the sisters, and preserves the Head. || 5. With energetic intellect the Sage is born, deposited as germ of Law, far from the Twins. | They being young at first showed visibly distinct the Creature that is half-concealed and half-exposed. || 6. The sages knew the form of him the Gladdener, what time the Falcon brought the plant from far away. | Him who assures success they beautified in streams, the stalk who yearned therefore, mighty and meet for praise. || 7. Together with the Ṛishis, with their prayers and hymns ten women deck thee, Soma, friendly when effused. | Led by the men, with invocations of the Gods, through the fleece, thou hast given us strength to win the spoil. || 8. Songs resonant with praise have celebrated him. Soma, Friend, springing forth with his fair company. | Even him who rich in

meath, with undulating stream, Winner of Wealth, Immortal, sends his voice from heaven, ‖ 9. He sends it into all the region forth from heaven. Soma, while he is filtered, settles in the jars. | With milk and waters is he decked when pressed with stones: Indu, when purified, shall find sweet rest and room. ‖ 10. Even thus poured forth How on thy way, O Soma, vouchsafing us most manifold lively vigour. | We will invoke benevolent Earth and Heaven. Give us, ye Gods, riches with noble heroes.

Hymn 9:69. Soma Pavamāna.

1. Laid like an arrow on the bow the hymn hath been loosed like a young calf to the udder of its dam. | As one who cometh first with full stream she is milked the Soma is impelled to this man's holy rites. ‖ 2. The thought is deeply fixed; the savoury juice is shed; the tongue with joyous sound is stirring in the mouth; | And Pavamāna, like the shout of combatants, the drop rising in sweet juice, is flowing through the fleece. ‖ 3. He flows about the sheep-skin, longing for a bride: he looses Aditi's Daughters for the worshipper. | The sacred drink hath come, gold-tinted, well-restrained: like a strong Bull he shines, whetting his manly might. ‖ 4. The Bull is bellowing; the Cows are coming nigh: the Goddesses approach the God's own resting-place. | Onward hath Soma passed through the sheep's fair bright fleece, and hath, as 'twere, endued a garment newly washed. ‖ 5. The golden-hued, Immortal, newly bathed, puts on a brightly shining vesture that is never harmed. | He made the ridge of heaven to be his radiant robe, by sprinkling of the bowls from moisture of the sky. ‖ 6. Even as the beams of Sūrya, urging men to speed, that cheer and send to sleep, together rush they forth, | These swift outpourings in long course of holy rites: no form save only Indra shows itself so pure. ‖ 7. As down the steep slope of a river to the vale, drawn from the Steer the swift strong draughts have found a way. | Well be it with the men and cattle in our home. May powers, O Soma, may the people stay with us. ‖ 8. Pour out upon us wealth in goods, in gold, in steeds, in cattle and in corn, and great heroic strength. | Ye, Soma, are my Fathers, lifted up on high as heads of heaven and makers of the strength of life. ‖ 9. These Pavamānas here, these drops of Soma, to Indra have sped forth like cars to booty. | Effused, they pass the cleansing fleece, while, gold-hued, they cast their covering off to pour the rain down. ‖ 10. O Indu, flow thou on for lofty Indra, flow blameless, very gracious, foe-destroyer. | Bring splendid treasures to the man who lauds thee. O Heaven and Earth, with all the Gods protect. us.

Hymn 9:70. Soma Pavamāna.

1. The three times seven Milch-kine in the eastern heaven have for this Soma poured the genuine milky draught. | Four other beauteous Creatures hath he made for his adornment, when he waxed in strength through holy rites. ‖ 2. Longing for lovely Amṛita, by his wisdom he divided, each apart from other, earth and heaven. | He gladly wrapped himself in the most lucid floods, when through their glory they found the God's resting-place. ‖ 3. May those his brilliant rays he ever free from death, inviolate, for both classes of created things,— | Rays wherewith powers of men and Gods are purified. Yea, even for this have sages welcomed him as King. ‖ 4. He, while he is adorned by the ten skilful ones, that he too in the Midmost Mothers may create, | While he is watching o'er the lovely Amṛita's ways, looks on both races as Beholder of mankind. ‖ 5. He, while he is adorned to stream forth mighty strength, rejoices in his place between the earth and heaven. | The Steer dispels the evil-hearted with his might, aiming at offerings as an archer at the game. ‖ 6. Beholding, as it were, Two Mother Cows, the Steer goes roaring on his way even as the Marutas roar. | Knowing Eternal Law, the earliest light of heaven, he, passing wise, was chosen out to tell it forth. ‖ 7. The fearful Bull is bellowing with violent might, far-sighted, sharpening his yellow-coloured horns. | Soma assumes his seat in the well-fashioned place: the cowhide and the sheepskin are his ornament. ‖ 8. Bright, making pure his body free from spot and stain, on the sheep's back the Golden-coloured hath flowed down. | Acceptable to Mitra, Vāyu, Varuṇa, he is prepared as threefold meal by skilful men. ‖ 9. Flow on for the God's banquet, Soma, as a Steer, and enter Indra's heart, the Soma's reservoir. | Bear us beyond misfortune ere we be oppressed: the man who knows the land directs the man who asks. ‖ 10. Urged like a car-steed flow to strength, O Soma: Indu, flow onward to the throat of Indra. | Skilled, bear us past, as in a boat o'er water: as battling Hero save us from the foeman.

Hymn 9:71. Soma Pavamāna.

1. The guerdon is bestowed: the Mighty takes his Seat, and, ever-Watchful, guards from fiend and evil sprite. | Gold-hued, he makes the cloud his diadem, the milk his carpet in both worlds, and prayer his robe of state. ‖ 2. Strong, bellowing, he goes, like one who slays the folk; he lets this hue of Asuras flow off from him, | Throws off his covering, seeks his father's meeting-place, and thus makes for himself the bright robe he assumes. ‖ 3. Onward he flows, from both the hands, pressed out with stones: excited by the prayer, the water makes him wild. | He frolics and draws near, completes his work with song, and bathes in streams to satisfy the worshipper. ‖ 4. They pour out meath around the Master of the house, Celestial Strengthener of the mountain that gives might; | In whom, through his great powers, oblation-eating cows in their uplifted udder mix their choicest milk. ‖ 5. They, the ten sisters, on the lap of Aditi, have sent him forward like a car from both the arms. | He wanders and comes near the Cow's mysterious place, even the place which his inventions have produced. ‖ 6. Like as a falcon to his home, so speeds the God to his own golden wisely-fashioned place to rest. | With song they urge the darling to the sacred grass: the Holy One goes like a courser to the Gods. ‖ 7. From far away, from heaven, the red-hued noted Sage, Steer of the triple height, hath sung unto the kine. | With thousand guidings he, leading this way and that, shines, as a singer, splendidly through many a morn. ‖ 8. His covering assumes a radiant hue; where'er he comes into the fight he drives the foe afar. | The Winner of the Floods, with food he seeks the host of heaven, he comes to praises glorified with milk. ‖ 9. Like a bull roaming round the herds he bellows: he hath assumed the brilliancy of Sūrya. | Down to the earth hath looked the heavenly Falcon: Soma with wisdom views all living creatures.

Hymn 9:72. Soma Pavamāna.

1. They cleanse the Gold-hued: like a red Steed is he yoked, and Soma in the jar is mingled with the milk. | He sendeth out his voice, and many loving friends of him the highly lauded hasten with their songs. ‖ 2. The many sages utter words in unison, while into Indra's throat they pour the Soma juice, | When, with the ten that dwell together closely joined, the men whose hands are skilful cleanse the lovely meath. ‖ 3. He goes upon his way, unresting, to the cows, over the roaring sound which Sūrya's Daughter loves. | The Falcon brought it to him for his own delight: now with the twofold kindred sisters is his home. ‖ 4. Washed by the men, stone-pressed, dear on the holy grass, faithful to seasons, Lord of cattle from of old, | Most liberal, completing sacrifice for men, O Indra, pure bright Soma, Indu, flows for thee. ‖ 5. O Indra, urged by arms of men and poured in streams, Soma flows on for thee after his Godlike kind. | Plans thou fulfillest, gatherest thoughts for sacrifice: in the bowls sits the Gold-hued like a roosting bird. ‖ 6. Sages well-skilled in work, intelligent, drain out the stalk that roars, the Sage, the Everlasting One. | The milk, the hymns unite them with him in the place of sacrifice, his seat who is produced anew. ‖ 7. Earth's central point, sustainer of the mighty heavens, distilled into the streams, into the waters' wave, | As Indra's thunderbolt, Steer with far-spreading wealth, Soma is flowing on to make the heart rejoice. ‖ 8. Over the earthly region flow thou on thy way, helping the praiser and the pourer, thou Most Wise. | Let us not lack rich treasure reaching to our home, and may we clothe ourselves in manifold bright wealth. ‖ 9. Hither, O Indu, unto us a hundred gifts of steeds, a thousand gifts of cattle and of gold, | Measure thou forth, yea, splendid ample strengthening food do thou, O Pavamāna, heed this laud of ours.

Hymn 9:73. Soma Pavamāna.

1. They from the spouting drop have sounded at the rim: naves speed together to the place of sacrifice. | That Asura hath formed, to seize, three lofty heights. The ships of truth have borne the pious man across. ‖ 2. The strong Steers, gathering, have duly stirred themselves,and over the stream's wave the friends sent forth the song. | Engendering the hymn, with flowing streams of meath, Indra's dear body have they caused to wax in strength. ‖ 3. With sanctifying gear they sit around the song: their ancient Father guards their holy work from harm. | Varuṇa hath o'erspread the mighty sea of air. Sages had power to hold him in sustaining floods. ‖ 4. Sweet-tongued, exhaustless, they have sent their voices down together, in heaven's vault that pours a thousand streams. | His wildly-restless warders

never close an eye: in every place are found the bonds that bind man fast. || 5. O'er Sire and Mother they have roared in unison bright with the verse of praise, burning up riteless men, | Blowing away with supernatural might from earth and from the heavens the swarthy skin which Indra hates. || 6. Those which, as guides of song and counsellors of speed, were manifested from their ancient dwelling place,— | From these the eyeless and the deaf have turned aside: the wicked travel not the pathway of the Law. || 7. What time the filter with a thousand streams is stretched, the thoughtful sages purify their song therein. | Bright-coloured are their spies, vigorous, void of guile, excellent, fair to see, beholders of mankind. || 8. Guardian of Law, most wise, he may not be deceived: three Purifiers hath he set within his heart. | With wisdom he beholds all creatures that exist: he drives into the pit the hated riteless ones. || 9. The thread of sacrifice spun in the cleansing sieve, on Varuṇa's tongue-tip, by supernatural might,— | This, by their striving, have the prudent ones attained: he who hath not this power shall sink into the pit.

Hymn 9:74. Soma Pavamāna

1. Born like a youngling he hath clamoured in the wood, when he, the Red, the Strong, would win the light of heaven. | He comes with heavenly seed that makes the water swell: him for wide-spreading shelter we implore with prayer. || 2. A far-extended pillar that supports the sky the Soma-stalk, filled full, moves itself every way. | He shall bring both these great worlds while the rite proceeds: the Sage holds these who move! together and all food. || 3. Wide space hath he who follows Aditi's right path, and mighty, well-made food, meath blent with Soma juice; | He who from hence commands the rain, Steer of the kine, Leader of floods, who helps us hence, who claims our laud. || 4. Butter and milk are drawn from animated cloud; thence Amṛita is produced, centre of sacrifice. | Him the Most Bounteous Ones, ever united, love; him as our Friend the Men who make all swell rain down. || 5. The Soma-stalk hath roared, following with the wave: he swells with sap for man the skin which Gods enjoy. | Upon the lap of Aditi he lays the germ, by means whereof we gain children and progeny. || 6. In the third region which distils a thousand streams, may the Exhaustless Ones descend with procreant power. | The kindred Four have been sent downward from the heavens: dropping with oil they bring Amṛita and sacred gifts. || 7. Soma assumes white colour when he strives to gain: the bounteous Asura knows full many a precious boon. | Down the steep slope, through song, he comes to sacrifice, and he will burst the water-holding cask of heaven, || 8. Yea, to the shining milk-anointed beaker, as to his goal, hath stepped the conquering Courser. | Pious-souled men have sent their gifts of cattle unto Kakṣhīvant of the hundred winters. || 9. Soma, thy juice when thou art blended with the streams, flows, Pavamāna, through the long wool of the sheep. | So, cleansed by sages. O best giver of delight, grow sweet for Indra, Pavamāna! for his drink.

Hymn 9:75. Soma Pavamāna.

1. Graciously-minded he is flowing on his way to win dear names o'er which the Youthful One grows great. | The Mighty and Far-seeing One hath mounted now the mighty Sūrya's car which moves to every side. || 2. The Speaker, unassailable Master of this hymn, the Tongue of sacrifice pours forth the pleasant meath. | Within the lustrous region of the heavens the Son makes the third secret name of Mother and of Sire. || 3. Sending forth flashes he hath bellowed to the jars, led by the men into the golden reservoir. | The milky streams of sacrifice have sung to him: he of the triple height shines brightly through the morns. || 4. Pressed by the stones, with hymns, and graciously inclined, illuminating both the Parents, Heaven and Earth, | He flows in ordered season onward through the flee, a current of sweet juice still swelling day by day. || 5. Flow onward, Soma, flow to bring prosperity: cleansed by the men, invest thee with the milky draught. | What gladdening drinks thou hast, foaming, exceeding strong, even with these incite Indra to give us wealth.

Hymn 9:76. Soma Pavamāna.

1. On flows the potent juice, sustainer of the heavens, the strength of Gods, whom men must hail with shouts of joy. | The Gold-hued, started like a courser by brave men, impetuously winneth splendour in the streams. || 2. He takes his weapons, like a hero, in his hands, fain to win light, car-borne, in forays for the kine. | Indu, while stimulating India's might, is urged forward and balmed by sages skilful in their task. || 3. Soma, as thou art purified with flowing wave, exhibiting thy strength enter thou Indra's throat. | Make both worlds stream for us, as lightning doth the clouds: mete out exhaustless powers for us, as 'twere through song. || 4. Onward he flows, the King of all that sees the light: the Ṛishis' Lord hath raised the song of sacrifice; | Even he who is adorned with Sūrya's arrowy beam, Father of hymns, whose wisdom is beyond our reach. || 5. Like as a bull to herds, thou flowest to the pail, bellowing as a steer upon the water's lap. | So, best of Cheerers, thou for Indra flowest on that we, with thy protection, may o'ercome in fight.

Hymn 9:77. Soma Pavamāna.

1. More beauteous than the beautiful, as Indra's bolt, this Soma, rich in sweets, hath clamoured in the vat. | Dropping with oil, abundant, streams of sacrifice flow unto him like milch-kine, lowing, with their milk. || 2. On flows that Ancient One whom, hitherward, from heaven, sped through the region of the air, the Falcon snatched. | He, quivering with alarm and terrified in heart before bow-armed Kṛiśānu, holdeth fast the sweet. || 3. May those first freshest drops of Soma juice effused flow on, their way to bring us mighty strength in kine. | Beauteous as serpents, worthy to be looked upon, they whom each sacred gift and all our prayers have pleased. || 4. May that much-lauded Indu, with a heart inclined to us, well-knowing, fight against our enemies. | He who hath brought the germ beside the Strong One's seat moves onward to the widely-opened stall of kine. || 5. The active potent juice of heaven is flowing on, great Varuṇa whom the forward man can ne'er deceive. | Mitra, the Holy, hath been pressed for troubled times, neighing like an impatient horse amid the herd.

Hymn 9:78. Soma Pavamāna.

1. Raising his voice the King hath flowed upon his way: invested with the waters he would win the kine. | The fleece retains his solid parts as though impure, and bright and cleansed he seeks the special place of Gods. || 2. Thou, Soma, art effused for Indra by the men, balmed in the wood as wave, Sage, Viewer of mankind. | Full many are the paths whereon thou mayest go: a thousand bay steeds hast thou resting in the bowls. || 3. Apsarases who dwell in waters of the sea, sitting within, have flowed to Soma wise of heart. | They urge the Master of the house upon his way, and to the Eternal Pavamāna pray for bliss. || 4. Soma flows on for us as winner of the kine, winner of thousands, cars, water, and light, and gold; | He whom the Gods have made a gladdening draught to drink, the drop most sweet to taste, weal-bringing, red of hue. || 5. Soma, as Pavamāna thou, our faithful Friend, making for us these real treasures, flowest on. | Slay thou the enemy both near and,far away: grant us security and ample pasturage.

Hymn 9:79. Soma Pavamāna.

1. Spontaneous let our drops of Soma juice flow on, pressed, golden-hued, among the Gods of lofty heaven. | Perish among us they who give no gifts of food! perish the godless! May our prayers obtain success. || 2. Forward to us the drops, distilling meath, shall flow, like riches for whose sake we urge the horses on. | Beyond the crafty hindering of all mortal men may we continually bear precious wealth away. || 3. Yea, verily, foe of hate shown to himself is he, yea, verity, destroyer too of other hate. | As thirst subdueth in the desert, conquer thou, O Soma Pavamāna, men of evil thoughts. || 4. Near kin to thee is he, raised loftiest in the heavens: upon the earth's high ridge thy scions have grown forth. | The press-stones chew and crunch thee on the ox's hide: sages have milked thee with their hands into the streams. || 5. So do they hurry on thy strong and beauteous juice, O Indu, as the first ingredient of the draught. | Bring low, thou Pavamāna, every single foe, and be thy might shown forth as sweet and gladdening drink.

Hymn 9:80. Soma Pavamāna.

1. On flows the stream of Soma who beholds mankind: by everlasting Law he calls the Gods from heaven. | He lightens with the roaring of Bṛihaspati: the lakes have not contained the pourings of juice. || 2. Thou, powerful Soma, thou to whom the cows have lowed, ascendest bright with sheen, thine iron-fashioned home. | Thou, lengthening our princes' life and high renown, flowest for Indra as his might to gladdening drink. || 3. Best giver of delight, he flows to Indra's throat, robing himself in might, Auspicious One, for fame. | He spreads himself abroad to meet all things that be: the vigorous Tawny Steed flows sporting on his way. || 4. The men, the ten swift fingers, milk thee out for Gods, even thee most rich in meath, with

thousand flowing streams. | Soma who winnest thousands, driven by the men, expressed with stones, bring, as thou flowest, all the Gods. || 5. Deft-handed men with stones, the ten swift fingers, drain thee into waters, thee, the Steer enriched with sweets. | Thou, Soma, gladdening Indra, and the Heavenly Host, flowest as Pavamāna like a river's wave.

Hymn 9:81. Soma Pavamāna.

1. Onward to Indra's throat move, beauteously adorned, the waves of Soma as he purifies himself, | When they, brought forward with the lovely curd of kine, effused, have cheered the Hero to bestow his gifts. || 2. Hither hath Soma flowed unto the beakers, like a chariot-horse, a stallion swift upon his way. | Thus, knowing both the generations, he obtains the rights and dues of Gods from yonder and from hence. || 3. While thou art cleansed, O Soma, scatter wealth on us; Indu, bestow great bounty as a liberal Prince. | Giver of life, with wisdom help to opulence; strew not our home possessions far away from us. || 4. Hither let Pūshan Pavamāna come to us, Varuṇa, Mitra, bountiful, of one accord, | The Marutas, Aśvins, Vāyu, and Bṛihaspati, Savitar, Tvashṭar, tractable Sarasvatī. || 5. Both Heaven and Earth, the all-invigorating Pair, Vidhātar, Aditi, and Aryaman the God, | Bhaga who blesses men, the spacious Firmament,—let all the Gods in Pavamāna take delight.

Hymn 9:82. Soma Pavamāna.

1. Even as a King hath Soma, red and tawny Bull, been pressed: the Wondrous One hath bellowed to the kine. | While purified he passes through the filtering fleece to seat him hawk-like on the place that drops with oil. | 2. To glory goest thou, Sage with disposing skill, like a groomed steed thou rushest forward to the prize. | O Soma, be thou gracious, driving off distress: thou goest, clothed in butter, to a robe of state. || 3. Parjanya is the Father of the Mighty Bird: on mountains, in earth's centre hath he made his home. | The waters too have flowed, the Sisters, to the kine: he meets the pressing-stones at the beloved rite. || 4. Thou givest pleasure as a wife delights her lord. Listen, O Child of Pajra, for to thee I speak. | Amid the holy songs go on that we may live: in time of trouble, Soma, watch thou free from blame. || 5. As to the men of old thou camest, Indu unharmed, to strengthen, winning hundreds, thousands, | So now for new felicity flow onward: the waters follow as thy law ordaineth.

Hymn 9:83. Soma Pavamāna.

1. Spread is thy cleansing filter, Brahmaṇaspati: as Prince, thou enterest its limbs from every side. | The raw, whose mass hath not been heated gains not this: they only which are dressed, which bear, attain to it. || 2. High in the seat of heaven is spread the Scorcher's sieve: its threads are standing separate, glittering with light. | The Swift Ones favour him who purifieth this: with consciousness they stand upon the height of heaven. || 3. The foremost spotted Steer hath made the Mornings shine, and yearning after strength sustains all things that be. | By his high wisdom have the mighty Sages wrought: the Fathers who behold mankind laid down the germ, || 4. Gandharva verily protects his dwelling-place; Wondrous, he guards the generations of the Gods. | Lord of the snare, he takes the foeman with the snare: those who are most devout have gained a share of meath. || 5. Rich in oblations! robed in cloud, thou corapassest oblation, sacrifice, the mighty seat of Gods. | King, on thy chariot-sieve thou goest up to war, and with a thousand weapons winnest lofty fame.

Hymn 9:84. Soma Pavamāna.

1. Flow, cheering Gods, most active, winner of the flood, for Indra, and for Vāyu, and for Varuṇa. | Bestow on us today wide room with happiness, and in thine ample dwelling laud the Host of Heaven. || 2. He who hath come anear to creatures that have life, Immortal Soma flows onward to all of them. | Effecting, for our aid, both union and release, Indu, like Sūrya, follows closely after Dawn. || 3. He who is poured with milk, he who within the plants hastes bringing treasure for the happiness of Gods, | He, poured forth in a stream flows with the lightning's flash, Soma who gladdens Indra and the Host of Heaven. || 4. Winner of thousands, he, this Soma, flows along, raising a vigorous voice that wakens with the dawn. | Indu with winds drives on the ocean of the air, he sinks within the jars, he rests in Indra's heart. || 5. The kine with milk dress him who makes the milk increase, Soma, amid the songs, who finds the light of heaven. | Winner of wealth, the effectual juice is flowing on, Singer and Sage by wisdom, dear as heaven itself.

Hymn 9:85. Soma Pavamāna.

1. Flow on to Indra, Soma, carefully effused: let sickness stay afar together with the fiends. | Let not the double-tongued delight them with thy juice. here be thy flowing drops laden with opulence. || 2. O Pavamāna, urge us forward in the fight thou art the vigour of the Gods, the well-loved drink. | Smite thou our enemies who raise the shout of joy: Indra, drink Soma juice, and drive away our foes. || 3. Unharmed, best Cheerer, thou, O Indu, flowest on: thou, even thou thyself, art Indra's noblest food. | Full many a wise man lifts to thee the song of praise, and hails thee with a kiss as Sovereign of this world. || 4. Wondrous, with hundred streams, hymned in a thousand songs, Indu pours out for Indra his delightful meath. | Winning us land and waters, flow thou hitherward: Rainer of bounties, Soma, make broad way for us. || 5. Roaring within the beaker thou art balmed with milk: thou passest through the fleecy filter all at once. | Carefully cleansed and decked like a prizewinning steed, O Soma, thou hast flowed down within Indra's throat. || 6. Flow onward sweet of flavour for the Heavenly Race, for Indra sweet, whose name is easily invoked: | Flow sweet for Mitra, Varuṇa, and Vāyu, rich in meath, inviolable for Bṛihaspati. || 7. Ten rapid fingers deck the Courser in the jar: with hymns the holy singers send their voices forth. | The filtering juices hasten to their eulogy, the drops that gladden find their way to Indra's heart. || 8. While thou art purified pour on us hero strength, great, far-extended shelter, spacious pasturage. | Let no oppression master this our holy work: may we, O Indu, gain all opulence through thee. || 9. The Steer who sees afar hath risen above the sky: the Sage hath caused the lights of heaven to give their shine. | The. King is passing through the filter with a roar: they drain the milk of heaven from him who looks on men. || 10. High in the vault of heaven, unceasing, honey-tongued, the Loving Ones drain out the mountain-haunting Steer,— | The drop that hath grown great in waters, in the lake meath-rich, in the stream's wave and in the cleansing sieve. || 11. The Loving Ones besought with many voices the Eagle who had flown away to heaven. | Hymns kiss the Youngling worthy of laudation, resting on earth, the Bird of golden colour. || 12. High to heaven's vault hath the Gandharva risen, beholding all his varied forms and figures. | His ray hath shone abroad with gleaming splendour: pure, he hath lighted both the worlds, the Parents.

Hymn 9:86. Soma Pavamāna.

1. Thy gladdening draughts, O Pavamāna, urged by song flow swiftly of themselves like sons of fleet-foot mares. | The drops of Soma juice, those eagles of the heavens, most cheering, rich in meath, rest in the reservoir. || 2. As rapid chariot-steeds, so turned in several ways have thine exhilarating juices darted forth, | Soma-drops rich in meath, waves, to the Thunder-armed, to Indra, like milch-kine who seek their calf with milk. || 3. Like a steed urged to battle, finder of the light; speed onward to the cloud-born reservoir of heaven, | A Steer that o'er the woolly surface seeks the sieve, Soma while purified for Indra's nourishment. || 4. Fleet as swift steeds, thy drops, divine, thought-swift, have been, O Pavamāna, poured with milk into the vat. | The Ṛishis have poured in continuous Soma drops, ordainers who adorn thee, Friend whom Ṛishis love. || 5. O thou who seest all things, Sovereign as thou art and passing strong, thy rays encompass all abodes. | Pervading with thy natural powers thou flowest on, and as the whole world's Lord, O Soma, thou art King. || 6. The beams of Pavamāna, sent from earth and heaven, his ensigns who is ever steadfast, travel round. | When on the sieve the Golden-hued is cleansed, he rests within the vats as one who seats him in his place. || 7. Served with fair rites he flows, ensign of sacrifice: Soma advances to the special place of Gods. | He speeds with thousand currents to the reservoir, and passes through the filter bellowing as a bull. || 8. The Sovereign dips him in the sea and in the streams, and set in rivers with the waters' wave moves on. | High heaven's Sustainer at the central point of earth, raised on the fleecy surface Pavamāna stands. || 9. He on whose high decree the heavens and earth dependeth roared and thundered like the summit of the sky. | Soma flows on obtaining Indra's friendly love, and, as they purify him, settles in the jars. || 10. He, light of sacrifice distils delicious meath, most wealthy, Father and begetter of the Gods. | He, gladdening, best of Cheerers, juice!hat Indra loves, enriches with mysterious treasure earth and heaven. || 11. The vigorous and far-seeing one, the Lord of heaven, flows, shouting to the beaker, with his thousand

streams. | Coloured like gold he rests in seats where Mitra dwells, the Steer made beautiful by rivers and by sheep. || 12. In forefront of the rivers Pavamāna speeds, in forefront of the hymn, foremost among the kine. | He shares the mighty booty in the van of war: the well-armed Steer is purified by worshippers. || 13. This heedful Pavamāna, like a bird sent forth, hath with his wave flowed onward to the fleecy sieve. | O Indra, through thy wisdom, b thy thought, O Sage, Soma flows bright and pure between the earth and heaven. || 14. He, clad in mail that reaches heaven, the Holy One, filling the firmament stationed amid the worlds, | Knowing. the realm of light, hath come to us in rain: he summons to himself his own primeval Sire. || 15. He who was first of all to penetrate his form bestowed upon his race wide shelter and defence. | From that high station which he hath in loftiest heaven he comes victorious to all encounters here. || 16. Indu hath started for Indra's special place and slights not as a Friend the promise of his Friend. | Soma speeds onward like a youth to youthful maids, and gains the beaker by a course of hundred paths. || 17. Your songs, exhilarating, tuneful, uttering praise, are come into the places where the people meet. | Worshippers have exalted Soma with their hymns, and milch kine have come near to meet him with their milk. || 18. O Soma, Indu, while they cleanse thee, pour on us accumulated, plentiful, nutritious food, | Which, ceaseless, thrice a day shall yield us hero power enriched with store of nourishment, and strength, and Meath. || 19. Far-seeing Soma flows, the Steer, the Lord of hymns, the Furtherer of day, of morning, and of heaven. | Mixt with the streams he caused the beakers to resound, and with the singers' aid they entered Indra's heart. || 20. On, with the prudent singers, flows the ancient Sage and guided by the men hath roared about the vats. | Producing Trita's name, may he pour forth the meath, that Vāyu and that Indra may become his Friends. || 21. He, being purified, hath made the Mornings shine: this, even this is he who gave the rivers room. | He made the Three Times Seven pour out the milky flow: Soma, the Cheerer, yields whate'er the heart finds sweet. || 22. Flow, onward, Soma, in thine own celestial forms, flow, Indu, poured within the beaker and the sieve. | Sinking into the throat of Indra with a roar, led by the men thou madest Sūrya mount to heaven. || 23. Pressed out with stones thou flowest onward to the sieve, O Indu, entering the depths of Indra's throat. | Far-sighted Soma, now thou lookest on mankind: thou didst unbar the cow-stall for the Aṅgirasas. || 24. In thee, O Soma, while thou purifiedst thee, high-thoughted sages, seeking favour, have rejoiced. | Down from the heavens the Falcon brought thee hitherward, even thee, O Indu, thee whom all our hymns adorn. || 25. Seven Milch-kine glorify the Tawny-coloured One while with his wave in wool he purifies himself. | The living men, the mighty, have impelled the Sage into the waters' lap, the place of sacrifice. || 26. Indu, attaining purity, plunges through the foe, making his ways all easy for the pious man. | Making the kine his mantle, he, the lovely Sage, runs like a sporting courser onward through the fleece. || 27. The ceaseless watery fountains with their hundred streams sing, as they hasten near, to him the Golden-hued | Him, clad in robes of milk, swift fingers beautify on the third height and in the luminous realm of heaven. || 28. These are thy generations of celestial seed thou art the Sovereign Lord of all the world of life. | This universe, O Pavamāna, owns thy sway; thou, Indu, art the first establisher of Law. || 29. Thou art the sea, O Sage who bringest all to light: under thy Law are these five regions of the world. | Thou reachest out beyond the earth, beyond the heavens: thine are the lights, O Pavamāna, thine the Sun. || 30. Thou in the filter, Soma Pavamāna, art purified to support the region for the Gods. | The chief, the longing ones have sought to hold thee fast, and all these living creatures have been turned to thee. || 31. Onward the Singer travels o'er the fleecy sieve. the Tawny Steer hath bellowed in the wooden vats. | Hymns have been sung aloud in resonant harmony, and holy songs kiss him, the Child who claims our praise. || 32. He hath assumed the rays of Sūrya for his robe, spinning, as he knows bow, the triply-twisted thread. | He, guiding to the newest rules of Holy Law, comes as the Women's Consort to the special place. || 33. On flows the King of rivers and the Lord of heaven: he follows with a shout the paths of Holy Law. | The Golden-hued is poured forth, with his hundred streams, Wealth-bringer, lifting up his voice while purified. || 34. Fain to be cleansed, thou, Pavamāna, pourest out, like wondrous Sūrya, through the fleece, an ample sea. | Purified with the hands, pressed by the men with stones, thou speedest on to mighty booty-bringing war. || 35. Thou, Pavamāna, sendest food and power in streams. thou sittest in the beakers as a hawk on trees, | For Indra poured as cheering juice to make him glad, as nearest and farseeing bearer-up of heaven. || 36. The Sisters Seven, the Mothers, stand around the Babe, the noble, new-born Infant, skilled in holy song, | Gandharva of the floods, divine, beholding men, Soma, that he may reign as King of all the world. || 37. As Sovereign Lord thereof thou Passest through these worlds, O Indu, harnessing thy tawny well-winged Mares. | May they pour forth for thee milk and oil rich in sweets: O Soma, let the folk abide in thy decree. || 38. O Soma, thou beholdest men from every side: O Pavamāna, Steer, thou wanderest through these. | Pour out upon us wealth in treasure and in gold: may we have strength to live among the things that be. || 39. Winner of gold and goods and cattle flow thou on, set as impregner, Indu, mid the worlds of life. | Rich in brave men art thou, Soma, who winnest all: these holy singers wait upon thee with the song. || 40. The wave of flowing meath hath wakened up desires: the Steer enrobed in milk plunges into the streams. | Borne on his chariot-sieve the King hath risen to war, and with a thousand rays hath won him high renown. || 41. Dear to all life, he sends triumphant praises forth, abundant, bringing offspring, each succeeding day. | From Indra crave for us, Indu, when thou art quaffed, the blessing that gives children, wealth that harbours steeds. || 42. When days begin, the strong juice, lovely, golden-hued, is recognized by wisdom more and more each day, | He, stirring both the Races, goes between the two, the bearer of the word of men and word of Gods. || 43. They balm him, balm him over balm him thoroughly, caress the mighty strength and balm it with the meath. | They seize the flying Steer at the stream's breathing-place: cleansing with gold they grasp the Animal herein. || 44. Sing forth to Pavamāna skilled in holy song: the juice is flowing onward like a mighty stream. | He glideth like a serpent from his ancient skin, and like a playful horse the Tawny Steer hath run. || 45. Dweller in floods, King, foremost, he displays his might, set among living things as measurer of days. | Distilling oil he flows, fair, billowy, golden-hued, borne on a car of light, sharing one home with wealth. || 46. Loosed is the heavens! support, the uplifted cheering juice: the triply-mingled draught flows round into the worlds. | The holy hymns caress the stalk that claims our praise, when singers have approached his beauteous robe with song. || 47. Thy streams that flow forth rapidly collected run over the fine fleece of the sheep as thou art cleansed. | When, Indu, thou art. balmed with milk within the bowl, thou sinkest in the jars, O Soma, when expressed. || 48. Winner of power, flow, Soma, worthy of our laud: run onward to the fleece as well-beloved meath. | Destroy, O Indu, all voracious Rākṣhasas. With brave sons in the assembly let our speech be bold.

Hymn 9:87. Soma Pavamāna.

1. Run onward to the reservoir and seat thee: cleansed by the men speed forward to the battle. | Making thee beauteous like an able courser, forth to the sacred grass with reins they lead thee. || 2. Indu, the well-armed God, is flowing onward, who quells the curse and guards from treacherous onslaught, | Father, begetter of the Gods, most skilful, the buttress of the heavens and earth's supporter. | 3. Ṛiṣhi and Sage, the Champion of the people, cleft and sagacious, Uśanā in wisdom, | He hath discovered even their hidden nature, the Cows' concealed and most mysterious title. || 4. This thine own Soma rich in meath, O Indra, Steer for the Steer, hath flowed into the filter. | The strong Free-giver, winning hundreds, thousands, hath reached the holy grass that never fails him. || 5. These Somas are for wealth of countless cattle, renown therefore, and mighty strength immortal. | These have been sent forth, purified by strainers, like steeds who rush to battle fain for glory. || 6. He, while he cleanses him, invoked of many, hath flowed to give the people all enjoyment. | Thou whom the Falcon brought, bring, dainty viands, bestir thyself and send us wealth and booty. || 7. This Soma, pressed into the cleansing filter, hath run as 'twere a host let loose, the Courser; | Like a strong bull who whets his horns keen-pointed, like a brave warrior in the fray for cattle. || 8. He issued forth from out the loftiest mountain, and found kine hidden somewhere in a stable. | Soma's stream clears itself for thee, O Indra, like lightning thundering through the clouds of heaven, || 9. Cleansing thyself, and borne along with Indra, Soma, thou goest round the herd of cattle. | May

thy praise help us, Mighty One, prompt Giver, to the full ample food which thou bestowest.

Hymn 9:88. Soma Pavamāna.

1. For thee this Soma is effused, O Indra: drink of this juice; for thee the stream is flowing— | Soma, which thou thyself hast made and chosen, even Indu, for thy special drink to cheer thee. ‖ 2. Like a capacious car hath it been harnessed, the Mighty; to acquire abundant treasures. | Then in the sacrifice they celebrated all triumphs won by Nahus in the battle. ‖ 3. Like Vāyu with his team, moving at pleasure, most gracious when invoked like both Nāsatyas, | Thou art thyself like the Wealth-Giver, Soma! who grants all boons, like song-inspiring Pūṣhan. ‖ 4. Like Indra who hath done great deeds, thou, Soma, art slayer of the Vṛitras, Fort-destroyer. | Like Pedu's horse who killed the brood of serpents, thus thou, O Soma, slayest every Dasyu. ‖ 5. Like Agni loosed amid the forest, fiercely he winneth splendour in the running waters. | Like one who fights, the roaring of the mighty, thus Soma Pavamāna sends his current. ‖ 6. These Somas passing through the fleecy filter, like rain descending from the clouds of heaven, | Have been effused and poured into the beakers, swiftly like rivers running lowly seaward. ‖ 7. Flow onward like the potent band of Marutas, like that Celestial Host whom none revileth. | Quickly be gracious unto us like waters, like sacrifice victorious, thousand-fashioned. ‖ 8. Thine are King Varuṇa's eternal statutes, lofty and deep, O Soma, is thy glory. | All-pure art thou like Mitra the beloved, adorable, like Aryaman, O Soma.

Hymn 9:89. Soma Pavamāna.

1. This chariot-horse hath moved along the pathways, and Pavamāna flowed like rain from heaven. | With us hath Soma with a thousand currents sunk in the wood, upon his Mother's bosom. | 2. King, he hath clothed him in the robe of rivers, mounted the straightest-going ship of Order. | Sped by the Hawk the drop hath waxed in waters: the father drains it, drains the Father's offspring. ‖ 3. They come to him, red, tawny, Lord of Heaven, the watchful Guardian of the meath, the Lion. | First, Hero in the fight, he seeks the cattle, and with his eye the Steer is our protector. ‖ 4. They harness to the broad-wheeled car the mighty Courser whose back bears meath, unwearied, awful. | The twins, the sisters brighten him, and strengthen these children of one dame the vigorous Racer. ‖ 5. Four pouring out the holy oil attend him, sitting together in the same container. | To him they flow, when purified, with homage, and still, from every side, are first about him. ‖ 6. He is the buttress of the heavens, supporter of earth, and in his hand are all the people. | Be the team's Lord a well to thee the singer: cleansed is the sweet plant's stalk for deed of glory. ‖ 7. Fighting, uninjured come where Gods are feasted; Soma, as Vṛitra-slayer flow for Indra. | Vouchsafe us ample riches very splendid may we be masters of heroic vigour.

Hymn 9:90. Soma Pavamāna,

1. Urged on, the Father of the Earth and Heaven hath gone forth like a car to gather booty, | Going to Indra, sharpening his weapons, and in his hand containing every treasure. ‖ 2. To him the tones of sacred song have sounded, Steer of the triple height, the Life-bestower. | Dwelling in wood as Varuṇa in rivers, lavishing treasure he distributes blessings ‖ 3. Great Conqueror, warrior-girt, Lord of all heroes, flow on thy way as he who winneth riches; | With sharpened. arms, with swift bow, never vanquished in battle, vanquishing in fight the foemen. ‖ 4. Giving security, Lord of wide dominion, send us both earth and heaven with all their fullness. | Striving to win the Dawns, the light, the waters, and cattle, call to us abundant vigour. ‖ 5. O Soma, gladden Varuṇa and Mitra; cheer, Indu Pavamāna! Indra, Vishṇu. | Cheer thou the Gods, the Company of Marutas: Indu, cheer mighty Indra to rejoicing. ‖ 6. Thus like a wise and potent King flow onward, destroying with thy vigour all misfortunes. | For our well-spoken hymn give life, O Indu. Do ye preserve us evermore with blessings.

Hymn 9:91. Soma Pavamāna.

1. As for a chariot-race, the skilful Speaker, Chief, Sage, Inventor, hath, with song, been started. | The sisters ten upon the fleecy summit drive on the Car-horse to the resting places. ‖ 2. The drop of Soma, pressed by wise Nahuṣhas, becomes the banquet of the Heavenly People— | Indu, by hands of mortal men made beauteous, immortal, with the sheep and cows and waters. ‖ 3. Steer roaring unto Steer, this Pavamāna, this juice runs to the white milk of the milch-cow. | Through thousand fine hairs goes the tuneful Singer, like Sūra by his fair and open pathways. ‖ 4. Break down the, strong seats even of the demons: cleansing thee, Indu, rob'd thyself in vigour. | Rend with thy swift bolt, coming from above them, those who are near and those who yet are distant. ‖ 5. Prepare the forward paths in ancient manner for the new hymn, thou Giver of all bounties. | Those which are high and hard for foes to conquer may we gain from thee, Active! Food-bestower! ‖ 6. So purifying thee vouchsafe us waters, heaven's light, and cows, offspring and many children. | Give us health, ample land, and lights, O Soma, and grant us long to look upon the sunshine.

Hymn 9:92. Soma Pavamāna.

1. The gold-hued juice, poured out upon the filter, is started like a car sent forth to conquer. | He hath gained song and vigour while they cleansed him, and hath rejoiced the Gods with entertainments. ‖ 2. He who beholdeth man hath reached the filter: bearing his name, the Sage hath sought his dwelling. | The Ṛishis came to him, seven holy singers, when in the bowls he settled as Invoker. ‖ 3. Shared by all Gods, most wise, propitious, Soma goes, while they cleanse him, to his constant station. | Let him rejoice in all his lofty wisdom to the Five Tribes the Sage attains with labour. ‖ 4. In thy mysterious place, O Pavamāna Soma, are all the Gods, the Thrice-Eleven. | Ten on the fleecy height, themselves, self-prompted, and seven fresh rivers, brighten and adorn thee. ‖ 5. Now let this be the truth of Pavamāna, there where all singers gather them together, | That he hath given us room and made the daylight, hath holpen Manu and repelled the Dasyu. ‖ 6. As the priest seeks the station rich in cattle, like a true King who goes to great assemblies, | Soma hath sought the beakers while they cleansed him, and like a wild bull, in the wood hath settled.

Hymn 9:93. Soma Pavamāna.

1. Ten sisters, pouring out the rain together, swift-moving thinkers of the sage, adorn him. | Hither hath run the gold-hued Child of Sūrya and reached the vat like a fleet vigorous courser. ‖ 2. Even as a youngling crying to his mothers, the bounteous Steer hath flowed along to waters. | As youth to damsel, so with milk he hastens on to the. chose meeting-place, the beaker. ‖ 3. Yea, swollen is the udder of the milch-cow: thither in streams goes very sapient Indu. | The kine make ready, as with new-washed treasures, the Head and Chief with milk within the vessels. ‖ 4. With all the Gods, O Indu Pavamāna, while thou art roaring send us wealth in horses. | Hither upon her car come willing Plenty, inclined to us, to give us of her treasures. ‖ 5. Now unto us mete riches, while they cleanse thee, all-glorious, swelling wealth, with store of heroes. | Long be his life who worships, thee, O Indu. May he, enriched with prayer, come soon and early.

Hymn 9:94. Soma Pavamāna.

1. When beauties strive for him as for a charger, then strive the songs like soldiers for the sunlight. | Acting the Sage, he flows enrobed in waters and song as 'twere a stall that kine may prosper. ‖ 2. The worlds expand to him who from aforetime found light to spread the law of life eternal. | The swelling songs, like kine within the stable, in deep devotion call aloud on Indu. ‖ 3. When the sage bears his holy wisdom round him, like a car visiting all worlds, the Hero, | Becoming fame, mid Gods, unto the mortal, wealth to the skilled, worth praise mid the Ever-present, ‖ 4. For glory born be hath come forth to glory: he giveth life and glory to the singers. | They, clothed in glory, have become immortal. He, measured in his course, makes frays successful. ‖ 5. Stream to us food and vigour, kine and horses: give us broad lights and fill the Gods with rapture. | All these are easy things for thee to master thou, Pavamāna Soma, quellest foemen.

Hymn 9:95. Soma Pavamāna.

1. Loud neighs the Tawny Steed when started, settling deep in the wooden vessel while they cleanse him. | Led by the men he takes the milk for raiment: then shall he, through his powers, engender praise-songs. ‖ 2. As one who rows drives on his boat, he, Gold-hued, sends forth his voice, loosed on the path of Order. | As God, the secret names of Gods he utters, to be declared on sacred grass more widely. ‖ 3. Hastening onward like the waves of waters, our holy hymns are pressing nigh to Soma. | To him they come with lowly adoration, and, longing, enter him who longs to meet them. ‖ 4. They drain the stalk, the Steer who dwells on mountains, even as a Bull who decks him on the upland. | Hymns follow and attend him as he

bellows: Trita bears Varuṇa aloft in ocean. || 5. Sending thy voice out as Director, loosen the Invoker's thought, O Indu, as they cleanse thee. | While thou and Indra rule for our advantage, may we be masters of heroic vigour.

Hymn 9:96. Soma Pavamāna

1. In forefront of the cars forth goes the Hero, the Leader, winning spoil: his host rejoices. | Soma endues his robes of lasting colours, and blesses, for his friends, their calls on Indra. || 2. Men decked with gold adorn his golden tendril, incessantly with steed-impelling homage. | The Friend of Indra mounts his car well-knowing, he comes thereon to meet the prayer we offer. || 3. O God, for service of the Gods flow onward, for food sublime, as Indra's drink, O Soma. | Making the floods, bedewing earth and heaven, come from the vast, comfort us while we cleanse thee || 4. Flow for prosperity and constant Vigour, flow on for happiness and high perfection. | This is the wish of these friends assembled: this is my wish, O Soma Pavamāna. || 5. Father of holy hymns, Soma flows onward the Father of the earth, Father of heaven: | Father of Agni, Sūrya's generator, the Father who begat Indra and Vishṇu. || 6. Brahman of Gods, the Leader of the poets, Ṛishi of sages, Bull of savage creatures, | Falcon amid the vultures, Axe of forests, over the cleansing sieve goes Soma singing. || 7. He, Soma Pavamāna, like a river, hath stirred the wave of voice, our songs and praises. | Beholding these inferior powers in cattle, he rests among them as a Steer well-knowing. || 8. As Gladdener, Warrior never harmed in battle, with thousand genial streams, pour strength and vigour. | As thoughtful Pavamāna, urge O Indu, speeding the kine, the plant's wave on to Indra. || 9. Dear, grateful to the Gods, on to the beaker moves Soma, sweet to Indra, to delight him. | With hundred powers, with thousand currents, Indu, like a strong car-horse, goes to the assembly. || 10. Born in old time as finder-out of treasures, drained with the stone, decking himself in waters, | Warding off curses, King of all existence, he shall find way for prayer the while they cleanse him. || 11. For our sage fathers, Soma Pavamāna, of old performed, by thee, their sacred duties. | Fighting unvanquished, open the enclosures: enrich us with large gifts of steeds and heroes. || 12. As thou didst flow for Manu Life-bestowing, Foe-queller, Comforter, rich in oblations, | Even thus flow onward now conferring riches: combine with Indra, and bring forth thy weapons. || 13. Flow onward, Soma, rich in sweets and holy, enrobed in waters on the fleecy summit. | Settle in vessels that are full of fatness, as cheering and most gladdening drink for Indra. || 14. Pour, hundred-streamed, winner of thousands, mighty at the Gods' banquet, Pour the rain of heaven, | While thou with rivers roarest in the beaker, and blent with milk prolongest our existence. || 15. Purified with our holy hymns, this Soma o'ertakes malignities like some strong charger, | Like fresh milk poured by Aditi, like passage in ample room, or like a docile car-horse. || 16. Cleansed by the pressers, armed with noble weapons, stream to us the fair secret name thou bearest. | Pour booty, like a horse, for love of glory God, Soma, send us kine, and send us Vāyu. || 17. They deck him at his birth, the lovely Infant, the Marutas with their troop adorn the Car-horse. | By songs a Poet and a Sage by wisdom, Soma goes singing through the cleansing filter. || 18. Light-winner, Ṛishi-minded, Ṛishi-maker, hymned in a thousand hymns, Leader of sages, | A Steer who strives to gain his third form, Soma is, like Virāj, resplendent as a Singer. || 19. Hawk seated in the bowls, Bird wide-extended, the Banner seeking kine and wielding weapons, | Following close the sea, the wave of waters, the great Bull tells his fourth form and declares it. || 20. Like a fair youth who decorates his body, a courser rushing to the gain of riches, | A steer to herds, so, flowing to the pitcher, he with a roar hath passed into the beakers. || 21. Flow on with might as Pavamāna, Indu flow loudly roaring through the fleecy filter. | Enter the beakers sporting, as they cleanse thee, and let thy gladdening juice make Indra joyful. || 22. His streams have been effused in all their fullness, and he hath entered, balmed with milk, the goblets. | Singing his psalm, well-skilled in song, a Chanter, be comes as 'twere to his friend's sister roaring. || 23. Chasing our foes thou comest, Pavamāna Indu, besting, as lover to his darling. | As a bird flies and settles in the forest, thus Soma settles, purified, in goblets. || 24. With full stream and abundant milk, O Soma, thy beams come, like a woman, as they cleanse thee. | He, gold-hued, rich in boons, brought to the waters, hath roared within the goblet of the pious.

Hymn 9:97. Soma Pavamāna

1. Made pure by this man's urgent zeal and impulse the God hath to the Gods his juice imparted. | He goes, effused and singing, to the filter, like priest to measured seats supplied with cattle. || 2. Robed in fair raiment meet to wear in battle, a mighty Sage pronouncing invocations. | Roll onward to the beakers as they cleanse thee, far-seeing at the feast of Gods, and watchful. || 3. Dear, he is brightened on the fleecy summit, a Prince among us, nobler than the noble. | Roar out as thou art purified, run forward. Do ye preserve us evermore with blessings. || 4. Let us sing praises to the Gods: sing loudly, send ye the Soma forth for mighty riches. | Let him flow, sweetly-flavoured, through the filter, and let our pious one rest in the pitcher. || 5. Winning the friendship of the Deities, Indu flows in a thousand streams to make them joyful. | Praised by the men after the ancient statute, he hath come nigh, for our great bliss, to Indra. || 6. Flow, Gold-hued, cleansing thee, to enrich the singer: let thy juice go to Indra to support him. | Come nigh, together with the Gods, for bounty. Do ye preserve us evermore with blessings. || 7. The God declares the Deities' generations, like Uśanā, proclaiming lofty wisdom. | With brilliant kin, far-ruling, sanctifying, the Boar advances, singing, to the places. || 8. The Swans, the Vrishagaṇas from anear us have brought their restless spirit to our dwelling. | Friends come to Pavamāna meet for praises, and sound in concert their resistless music. || 9. He follows the Wide-strider's rapid movement: cows low, as 'twere, to him who sports at pleasure. | He with the sharpened horns brings forth abundance: the Silvery shines by night, by day the Golden. || 10. Strong Indu, bathed in milk, flows on for Indra, Soma exciting strength, to make him joyful. | He quells malignities and slays the demons, the King of mighty power who brings us comfort. || 11. Then in a stream he flows, milked out with press-stones, mingled with sweetness, through the fleecy filter— | Indu rejoicing in the love of Indra, the God who gladdens, for the God's enjoyment. || 12. As he is purified he pours out treasures, a God bedewing Gods with his own juices. | Indu hath, wearing qualities by seasons, on the raised fleece engaged, the ten swift fingers. || 13. The Red Bull bellowing to the kine advances, causing the heavens and earth to roar and thunder. | Well is he beard like Indra's shout in battle: letting this voice be known he hastens hither. || 14. Swelling with milk, abounding in sweet flavours, urging the meath-rich plant thou goest onward. | Raising a shout thou flowest as they cleanse thee, when thou, O Soma, art effused for Indra. || 15. So flow thou on inspiriting, for rapture, aiming death-shafts at him who stays the waters, | Flow to us wearing thy resplendent colour, effused and eager for the kine, O Soma. || 16. Pleased with us, Indu, send us as thou flowest good easy paths in ample space and comforts. | Dispelling, as 'twere with a club, misfortunes, run o'er the height, run o'er the fleecy summit. || 17. Pour on us rain celestial, quickly streaming, refreshing, fraught with health and ready bounty. | Flow, Indu, send these Winds thy lower kinsmen, setting them free like locks of hair unbraided. || 18. Part, like a knotted tangle, while they cleanse thee, O Soma, righteous and unrighteous conduct. | Neigh like a tawny courser who is loosened, come like a youth, O God, a house-possessor. || 19. For the God's service, for delight, O Indu, run o'er the height, run o'er the fleecy summit. | With thousand streams, inviolate, sweet-scented, flow on for gain of strength that conquers heroes. || 20. Without a car, without a rein to guide them, unyoked, like coursers started in the contest, | These brilliant drops of Soma juice run forward. Do ye, O Deities, come nigh to drink them. || 21. So for our banquet of the Gods, O Indu, pour down the rain of heaven into the vessels. | May Soma grant us riches sought with longing, mighty, exceeding strong, with store of heroes. || 22. What time the loving spirit's word had formed him Chief of all food, by statute of the Highest, | Then loudly lowing came the cows to Indu, the chosen, well-loved Master in the beaker. || 23. The Sage, Celestial, liberal, raining bounties, pours as he flows the Genuine for the Truthful. | The King shall be effectual strength's upholder: he by the ten bright reins is mostly guided. || 24. He who beholds mankind, made pure with filters, the King supreme of Deities and mortals, | From days of old is Treasure-Lord of riches: he, Indu, cherishes fair well-kept Order. || 25. Haste, like a steed, to victory for glory, to Indra's and to Vāyu's entertainment. | Give us food ample, thousandfold: be, Soma, the finder-out of riches when they cleanse thee. || 26. Effused by us let God-delighting Somas bring as they flow a

home with noble heroes. | Rich in all boons like priests acquiring favour, the worshippers of heaven, the best of Cheerers. || 27. So, God, for service of the Gods flow onward, flow, drink of Gods, for ample food, O Soma. | For we go forth to war against the mighty make heaven and earth well established by thy cleansing. || 28. Thou, yoked by strong men, neighest like a courser, swifter than thought is, like an awful lion. | By paths directed hitherward, the straightest, send thou us happiness, Indu, while they cleanse thee. || 29. Sprung from the Gods, a hundred streams, a thousand, have been effused: sages prepare and purge them. | Bring us from heaven the means of winning, Indu; thou art-forerunner of abundant riches. || 30. The streams of days, were poured as 'twere from heaven: the wise King doth not treat his friend unkindly. | Like a son following his father's wishes, grant to this family success and safety. || 31. Now are thy streams poured forth with all their sweetness, when, purified, thou goest through the filter. | The race of kine is thy gift, Pavamāna: when born thou madest Sūrya rich with brightness. || 32. Bright, bellowing along the path of Order, thou shinest as the form of life eternal. | Thou flowest on as gladdening drink for Indra, sending thy voice out with the hymns of sages. || 33. Pouring out streams at the Gods' feast with service, thou, Soma, lookest down, a heavenly Eagle. | Enter the Soma-holding beaker, Indu, and with a roar approach the ray of Sūrya. || 34. Three are the voices that the Courser utters: he speaks the thought of prayer, the law of Order. | To the Cow's Master come the Cows inquiring: the hymns with eager longing come to Soma. || 35. To Soma come the Cows, the Milch-kine longing, to Soma sages with their hymns inquiring. | Soma, effused, is purified and blended our hymns and Trishṭubh songs unite in Soma. || 36. Thus, Soma, as we pour thee into vessels, while thou art purified flow for our welfare. | Pass into Indra with a mighty roaring make the voice swell, and generate abundance. || 37. Singer of true songs, ever-watchful, Soma hath settled in the ladles when they cleanse him. | Him the Adhvaryus, paired and eager, follow, leaders of sacrifice and skilful-handed. || 38. Cleansed near the Sun as 'twere he as Creator hath filled full heaven and earth, and hath disclosed them. | He by whose dear help men gain all their wishes shall yield the precious meed as to a victor. || 39. He, being cleansed, the Strengthener and Increaser, Soma the Bounteous, helped us with his lustre, | Wherewith our sires of old who knew the footsteps found light and stole the cattle from the mountain. || 40. In the first vault of heaven loud roared the Ocean, King of all being, generating creatures. | Steer, in the filter, on the fleecy summit, Soma, the Drop effused, hath waxen mighty. || 41. Soma the Steer, in that as Child of Waters he chose the Gods, performed that great achievement. | He, Pavamāna, granted strength to Indra; he, Indu, generated light in Sūrya. || 42. Make Vāyu glad,, for furtherance and bounty: cheer Varuṇa and Mitra, as they cleanse thee. | Gladden the Gods, gladden the host of Marutas: make Heaven and Earth rejoice, O God, O Soma. || 43. Flow onward righteous slayer of the wicked, driving away our enemies and sickness, | Blending thy milk with milk which cows afford us. We are thy friends, thou art the Friend of Indra. || 44. Pour us a fount of meath, a spring of treasure; send us a hero son and happy fortune. | Be sweet to India when they cleanse thee, Indu, and pour down riches on us from the ocean. || 45. Strong Soma, pressed, like an impetuous courser, hath flowed in stream as a flood speeding downward. | Cleansed, he hath settled in his wooden dwelling: Indu hath flowed with milk and with the waters. || 46. Strong, wise, for thee who longest for his coming this Soma here flows to the bowls, O Indra. | He, chariot-borne, sun-bright, and truly potent, was poured forth like the longing of the pious. || 47. He, purified with ancient vital vigour, pervading all his Daughter's forms and figures, | Finding his threefold refuge in the waters, goes singing, as a priest, to the assemblies. || 48. Now, chariot-borne, flow unto us, God Soma, as thou art purified flow to the saucers, | Sweetest in waters, rich in meath, and holy, as Savitar the God is, truthful-minded. || 49. To feast him, flow mid song and hymn, to Vāyu, flow purified to Varuṇa and Mitra. | Flow to the song-inspiring car-borne Hero, to mighty Indra, him who wields the thunder. || 50. Pour on us garments that shall clothe us meetly, send, purified, milch-kine, abundant yielders. | God Soma, send us chariot-drawing horses that they may bring us treasures bright and golden. || 51. Send to us in a stream celestial riches, send us, when thou art cleansed, what earth containeth, | So that thereby we may acquire possessions and Ṛishihood in Jamadagni's manner. || 52. Pour forth this wealth with this purification: flow onward to the yellow lake, O Indu. | Here, too, the Ruddy, wind-swift, full of wisdom, Shall give a son to him who cometh quickly. || 53. Flow on for us with this purification to the famed ford of thee whose due is glory. | May the Foe-queller shake us down, for triumph, like a tree's ripe fruit, sixty thousand treasures. || 54. Eagerly do we pray for those two exploits, at the blue lake and Pṛiśana, wrought in battle. | He sent our enemies to sleep and slew them, and turned away the foolish and unfriendly. || 55. Thou comest unto three extended filters, and hastenest through each one as they cleanse thee. | Thou art the giver of the gift, a Bhaga, a Maghavan for liberal lords, O Indu. || 56. This Soma here, the Wise, the All-obtainer, flows on his way as King of all existence. | Driving the drops at our assemblies, Indu completely traverses the fleecy filter. || 57. The Great Inviolate are kissing Indu, and singing in his place like eager sages. | The wise men send him forth with ten swift fingers, and balm his form with essence of the waters. || 58. Soma, may we, with thee as Pavamāna, pile up together all our spoil in battle. | This boon vouchsafe us Varuṇa and Mitra, and Aditi and Sindhu, Earth and Heaven.

Hymn 9:98. Soma Pavamāna

1. Stream on us riches that are sought by many, best at winning strength | Riches, O Indu, thousandfold, glorious, conquering the great. || 2. Effused, he hath, as on a car, invested him in fleecy mail: | Onward hath Indu flowed in streams, impelled, surrounded by the wood. || 3. Effused, this Indu hath flowed on, distilling rapture, to the fleece: | He goes erect, as seeking kine in stream, with light, to sacrifice. || 4. For thou thyself, O Indu, God, to every mortal worshipper | Attractest riches thousandfold, made manifest in hundred forms. || 5. Good Vṛitra-slayer, may we be still nearest to this wealth of thine | Which many crave, nearest to food and happiness, Resistless One! || 6. Whom, bright with native splendour, crushed between the pair of pressing-stones— | The wavy Friend whom Indra loves-the twice-five sisters dip and bathe, || 7. Him with the fleece they purify, brown, golden-hued, beloved of all, | Who with exhilarating juice goes forth to all the Deities. || 8. Through longing for this sap of yours ye drink what brings ability, | Even him who, dear as heaven's own light, gives to our princes high renown. || 9. Indu at holy rites produced you, Heaven and Earth, the Friends of men, | Hill-haunting God the Goddesses. They bruised him where the roar was loud. || 10. For Vṛitra-slaying Indra, thou, Soma, art poured that he may drink, | Poured for the guerdon-giving man, poured for the God who sitteth there. || 11. These ancient Somas, at the break of day, have flowed into the sieve, | Snorting away at early morn these foolish evil-hearted ones. || 12. Friends, may the princes, ye and we, obtain this Most Resplendent One. | Gain him who hath the smell of strength, win him whose home is very strength.

Hymn 9:99. Soma Pavamāna.

1. They for the Bold and Lovely One ply manly vigour like a bow: | joyous, in front of songs they weave bright raiment for the Lord Divine. || 2. And he, made beautiful by night, dips forward into strengthening food, | What time the sacrificer's thoughts speed on his way the Golden-hued. || 3. We cleanse this gladdening drink of his the juice which Indra chiefly drinks— | That which kine took into their mouths, of old, and princes take it now. || 4. To him, while purifying, they have raised the ancient psalm of praise: | And sacred songs which bear the names of Gods have supplicated him. || 5. They purify him as he drops, courageous, in the fleecy sieve. | Him they instruct as messenger to bear the sage's morning prayer. || 6. Soma, best Cheerer, takes his seat, the while they cleanse him in the bowls. | He as it were impregns the cow, and babbles on, the Lord of Song. || 7. He is effused and beautified, a God for Gods, by skilful men. | He penetrates the mighty floods collecting all he knows therein. || 8. Pressed, Indu, guided by the men, thou art led to the cleaning sieve. | Thou, yielding Indra highest joy, takest thy seat within the bowls.

Hymn 9:100. Soma Pavamāna.

1. The Guileless Ones are singing praise to Indra's well beloved Friend, | As, in the morning of its life, the mothers lick the new-born calf. || 2. O Indu, while they cleanse thee bring, O Soma, doubly-waxing wealth | Thou in the worshipper's abode causest all treasures to increase. || 3. Set free the. song which mind hath yoked, even as thunder frees the rain: | All treasures of the earth and heaven, O Soma, thou dost multiply. || 4. Thy stream when

thou art pressed runs on like some victorious warrior's steed | Hastening onward through the fleece like a fierce horse who wins the prize. || 5. Flow on, Sage Soma, with thy stream to give us mental power and strength, | Effused for Indra, for his drink, for Mitra and for Varuṇa. || 6. Flow to the filter with thy stream, effused, best winner, thou, of spoil, | O Soma, as most rich in sweets for Indra, Vishṇu, and the Gods. || 7. The mothers, void of guiles, caress thee Golden-coloured, in the sieve, | As cows, O Pavamāna, lick the new-born calf, as Law commands. || 8. Thou, Pavamāna, movest on with wondrous rays to great renown. | Striving within the votary's house thou drivest all the glooms away. || 9. Lord of great sway, thou liftest thee above the heavens, above the earth. | Thou, Pavamāna hast assumed thy coat of mail in majesty.

Hymn 9:101. Soma Pavamāna

1. For first possession of your juice, for the exhilarating drink, | Drive ye away the dog, my friends, drive ye the long-tongued dog away. || 2. He who with purifying stream, effused, comes flowing hitherward, | Indu, is like an able steed. || 3. The men with all-pervading song send unassailable Soma forth, | By pressing-stones, to sacrifice. || 4. The Somas, very rich in sweets, for which the sieve is destined, flow, | Effused, the source of Indra's joy: may your strong juices reach the Gods. || 5. Indu flows on for Indra's sake: thus have the Deities declared. | The Lord of Speech exerts himself, Ruler of all, because of might. || 6. Inciter of the voice of song, with thousand streams the ocean flows, | Even Soma, Lord of opulence, the Friend of Indra, day by day. || 7. As Pūshan, Fortune, Bhaga, comes this Soma while they make him pure. | He, Lord of the multitude, hath looked upon the earth and heaven. || 8. The dear cows lowed in joyful mood together to the gladdening drink. | The drops as they were purified, the Soma juices, made then paths. || 9. O Pavamāna, bring the juice, the mightiest, worthy to be famed, | Which the Five Tribes have over them, whereby we may win opulence. || 10. For us the Soma juices flow, the drops best furtherers of our weal, | Effused as friends without a spot, benevolent, finders of the light. || 11. Effused by means of pressing-stones, upon the ox-hide visible, | They, treasure-finders, have announced food unto us from every side. || 12. These Soma juices, skilled in song, purified, blent with milk and curd, | When moving and when firmly laid in oil, resemble lovely Suns. || 13. Let not the power of men restrain the voice of the outpouring juice: | As Bhṛigu's sons chased Makha, so drive ye the greedy hound away. || 14. The Friend hath wrapped him in his robe, as in his parents arms, a son. | He went, as lover to a dame, to take his station suitor-like. || 15. That Hero who produces strength, he who hath propped both worlds apart, | Gold-hued, hath wrapped him in the sieve, to settle, priest-like, in his place. || 16. Soma upon the ox's skin through the sheep's wool flows purified. | Bellowing out, the Tawny Steer goes on to Indra's special place.

Hymn 9:102. Soma Pavamāna.

1. The Child, when blended with the streams, speeding the plan of sacrifice, | Surpasses all things that are dear, yea, from of old. || 2. The place, near the two pressing-stones of Trita, hath he occupied, | Secret and dear through seven lights of sacrifice. || 3. Urge to three courses, on the heights of Trita, riches in a stream. | He who is passing wise measures his courses out. || 4. Even at his birth the Mothers Seven taught him, for glory, like a sage, | So that he, firm and sure, hath set his mind on wealth. || 5. Under his sway, of one accord, are all the guileless Deities: | Warriors to be envied, they, when they are pleased. || 6. The Babe whom they who strengthen Law have generated fair to see, | Much longed for at the sacrifice, most liberal Sage, — || 7. To him, united, of themselves, come the young Parents of the rite, | When they adorn him, duly weaving sacrifice. || 8. With wisdom and with radiant eyes unbar to us the stall of heaven, | Speeding at solemn rite the plan of Holy Law.

Hymn 9:103. Soma Pavamāna.

1. To Soma who is purified as ordering Priest the song is raised: | Bring meed, as 'twere, to one who makes thee glad with hymns. || 2. Blended with milk and curds he flows on through the long wool of the sheep. | The Gold-hued, purified, makes him three seats for rest. || 3. On through the long wool of the sheep to the meath-dropping vat he flows: | The Ṛishis' sevenfold quire hath sung aloud to him. || 4. Shared by all Gods, Infallible, the Leader of our holy hymns, | Golden-hued Soma, being cleansed, hath reached the bowls. || 5. After thy Godlike qualities, associate with Indra, go, | As a Priest purified by priests, Immortal One. || 6. Like a car-horse who shows his strength, a God effused for Deities. | The penetrating Pavamāna flows along.

Hymn 9:104. Soma Pavamāna.

1. Sit down, O friends, and sing aloud to him who purifies himself: | Deck him for glory, like a child, with holy rites. || 2. Unite him bringing household wealth, even as a calf, with mother kine, | Him who hath double strength, the God, delighting juice. || 3. Purify him who gives us power, that he, most Blessed One, may be | A banquet for the Troop, Mitra, and Varuṇa. || 4. Voices have sung aloud to thee as finder-out of wealth for us: | We clothe the hue thou wearest with a robe of milk. || 5. Thou, Indu, art the food of Gods, O Sovereign of all gladdening drinks: | As Friend for friend, be thou best finder of success. || 6. Drive utterly away from us each demon, each voracious fiend, | The godless and the false: keep sorrow far away.

Hymn 9:105. Soma Pavamāna

1. Sing; ye aloud, O friends, to him who makes him pure for gladdening drink: | They shall make sweet the Child with sacrifice and laud. || 2. Like as a calf with mother cows, so Indu is urged forth and sent, | Glorified by our hymns, the God-delighting juice. || 3. Effectual means of power is he, he is a banquet for the Troop, | He who hath been effused, most rich in meath, for Gods. || 4. Flow to us, Indu, passing, strong, effused, with wealth of kine and steeds: | I will spread forth above the milk thy radiant hue. || 5. Lord of the tawny, Indu thou who art the God's most special food, | As Friend to friend, for splendour be thou good to men. || 6. Drive utterly, far away from us each godless, each voracious foe. | O Indu, overcome and drive the false afar.

Hymn 9:106. Soma Pavamāna.

1. To Indra, to the Mighty Steer, may these gold-coloured juices go, | Drops rapidly produced, that find the light of heaven. || 2. Effused, this juice victorious flows for Indra, for his maintenance. | Soma bethinks him of the Conqueror, as he knows. || 3. May Indra in his raptures gain from him the grasp that gathers spoil, | And, winning waters, wield the steer-strong thunderbolt. || 4. Flow vigilant for Indra, thou Soma, yea, Indu, run thou on: | Bring hither splendid strength that finds the light of heaven. || 5. Do thou, all-beautiful, purify for Indra's sake the mighty juice, | Path-maker thou, far seeing, with a thousand ways. || 6. Best finder of prosperity for us, most rich in sweets for Gods, | Proceed thou loudly roaring on a thousand paths. || 7. O Indu, with thy streams, in might, flow for the banquet of the Gods: | Rich in meath, Soma, in our beaker take thy place. || 8. Thy drops that swim in water have exalted Indra to delight: | The Gods have drunk thee up for immortality. || 9. Stream opulence to us, ye drops of Soma, pressed and purified, | Pouring down rain from heaven in floods, and finding light. || 10. Soma, while filtered, with his wave flows through the long wool of the sheep, | Shouting while purified before the voice of song. || 11. With songs they send the Mighty forth, sporting in wood, above the fleece: | Our psalms have glorified him of the triple height. || 12. Into the jars hath he been loosed, like an impetuous steed for war, | And lifting up his voice, while filtered, glided on. || 13. Gold-hued and lovely in his course, through tangles of the wool he flows, | And pours heroic fame upon the worshippers. || 14. Flow thus, a faithful votary: the streams of meath have been effused. | Thou comest to the filter, singing, from each side.

Hymn 9:107. Soma Pavamāna.

1. Hence sprinkle forth the juice effused, Soma, the best of sacred gifts, | Who, friend of man, hath run amid the water-streams. He hath pressed Soma out with stones. || 2. Now, being purified, flow hither through the fleece inviolate and most odorous. | We ladden thee in waters when thou art effused, blending thee still with juice and milk. || 3. Pressed out for all to see, delighting Gods, Indu, Far-sighted One, is mental power. || 4. Cleansing thee, Soma, in thy stream, thou flowest in a watery robe: | Giver of wealth, thou sittest in the place of Law, O God, a fountain made of gold. || 5. Milking the heavenly udder for dear meath, he hath sat in the ancient gathering-place. | Washed by the men, the Strong Farseeing One streams forth nutritious food that all desire. || 6. O Soma, while they cleanse thee, dear and watchful in the sheep's long wool, | Thou hast become a Singer most like Aṅgiras: thou madest Sūrya mount to heaven. ||

7. Bountiful, best of furtherers, Soma floweth on, Ṛishi and Singer, keen of sight. | Thou hast become a Sage most welcome to the Gods: thou madest Sūrya mount to heaven. || 8. Pressed out by pressers, Soma goes over the fleecy backs of sheep, | Goes, even as with a mare, in tawny-coloured stream, goes in exhilarating stream. || 9. Down to the water-Soma, rich in kine hath flowed with cows, with cows that have been milked. | They have approached the mixing-vessel as a sea: the cheerer streams for the carouse. || 10. Effused by stones, O Soma, and urged through the long wool of the sheep, | Thou, entering the saucers as a man the fort, gold-hued hast settled in the wood. || 11. He beautifies himself through the sheep's long fine wool, like an impetuous steed in war, | Even Soma Pavamāna who shall be the joy of sages and of holy bards. || 12. O Soma,—for the feast of Gods, river-like he hath swelled with surge, | With the stalk's juice, exhilarating, resting not, into the vat that drops with meath. || 13. Like a dear son who must be decked, the Lovely One hath clad him in a shining robe. | Men skilful at their work drive him forth, like a car, into the rivers from their bands. || 14. The living drops of Soma juice pour, as they flow, the gladdening drink, | Intelligent drops above the basin of the sea, exhilarating, finding light. || 15. May Pavamāna, King and God, speed with his wave over the sea the lofty rite: | May he by Mitra's and by Varuṇa's decree flow furthering the lofty rite. || 16. Far-seeing, lovely, guided by the men, the God whose home is in the sea— || 17. Soma, the gladdening juice, flows pressed for Indra with his Marut host: | He hastens o'er the fleece with all his thousand streams: men make him bright and beautiful. || 18. Purified in the bowl and gendering the hymn, wise Soma joys among the Gods. | Robed in the flood, the Mighty One hath clad himself with milk and settled in the vats. || 19. O Soma, Indu, every day thy friendship hath been my delight. | Many fiends follow me; help me, thou Tawny-hued; pass on beyond these barriers. || 20. Close to thy bosom am I, Soma, day and night. O Tawny-hued, for friendship sake. | Sūrya himself refulgent with his glow have we o'ertaken in his course like birds. || 21. Deft-handed! thou when purified liftest thy voice amid the sea. | Thou, Pavamāna, makest riches flow to us, yellow, abundant, much-desired. || 22. Making thee pure and bright in the sheep's long wool, thou hast bellowed, steer-like, in the wood. | Thou flowest, Soma Pavamāna, balmed with milk unto the special place of Gods. || 23. Flow on to win us strength, flow on to lofty lore of every kind. | Thou, Soma, as Exhilarator wast the first to spread the sea abroad for Gods. || 24. Flow to the realm of earth, flow to the realm of heaven, O Soma, in thy righteous ways. | Fair art thou whom the sages, O Far-seeing One, urge onward with their songs and hymns. || 25. Over the cleansing sieve have flowed the Pavamānas in a stream, | Girt by the Marutas, gladdening, Steeds with Indra's strength, for wisdom and for dainty food. || 26. Urged onward by the pressers, clad in watery robes, Indu is speeding to the vat. | He gendering light, hath made the glad Cows low, while he takes them as his garb of state.

Hymn 9:108. Soma Pavamāna.

1. For Indra, flow thou Soma on, as gladdening juice most sweet, intelligent, | Great, cheering, dwelling most in heaven. || 2. Thou, of whom having drunk the Steer acts like a steer. drinking of this that finds the light, | He, Excellently Wise, is come to strengthening food, to spoil and wealth like Etaśa. || 3. For, verily, Pavamāna, thou bast, splendidest, called all the generations of | The Gods to immortality. || 4. By whom Dadhyach Navagva opens fastened doors, by whom the sages gained their wish, | By whom they won the fame of lovely Amṛita in the felicity of Gods. || 5. Effused, he floweth in a stream, best rapture-giver, in the long wool of the sheep, | Sporting, as 'twere the waters' wave. || 6. He who from out the rocky cavern took with might the red-refulgent watery Cows, | Thou masterest the stable full of kine and steeds: burst it, brave Lord, like one in mail. || 7. Press ye and pour him, like a steed, laud-worthy, speeding through the region and the flood, | Who swims in water, roan in wood; || 8. Increaser of the water, Steer with thousand streams, dear to the race of Deities; | Who born in Law hath waxen mighty by the Law, King, God, and lofty Ordinance. || 9. Make splendid glory shine on us, thou Lord of strengthening food, God, as the Friend of Gods: | Unclose the fount of middle air. || 10. Roll onward to the bowls, O Mighty One, effused, as Prince supporter of the tribes. | Pour on us rain from heaven, send us the waters' flow: incite our thoughts to win the spoil. || 11. They have drained him the Steer of heaven, him with a thousand streams, distilling rapturous joy, | Him who brings all things excellent. || 12. The Mighty One was born Immortal, giving life, lightening darkness with his shine. | Well-praised by. sages he hath. by his wondrous power assumed the Threefold as his robe. || 13. Effused is he who brings good things, who brings us bounteous gifts and sweet refreshing food, | Soma who brings us quiet homes: || 14. He whom our Indra and the Marut host shall drink, Bhaga shall drink with Aryaman, | By whom we bring to us Mitra and Varuṇa and Indra for our great defence. || 15. Soma, for Indra's drink do thou, led by the men, well-weaponed and most gladdening, | Flow on with greatest store of sweets. || 16. Enter the Soma-holder, even Indra's heart, as rivers pass into the sea, | Acceptable to Mitra, Vāyu, Varuṇa, the noblest Pillar of the heavens.

Hymn 9:109. Soma Pavamāna.

1. Pleasant to Indra's Mitra's, Pūṣhan's Bhaga's taste, sped onward, Soma, with thy flowing stream. || 2. Let Indra drink, O Soma, of thy juice for wisdom, and all Deities for strength. || 3. So flow thou on as bright celestial juice, flow to the vast, immortal dwelling-place. || 4. Flow onward, Soma, as a mighty sea, as Father of the Gods to every form. || 5. Flow on, O Soma, radiant for the Gods and Heaven and Earth and bless our progeny. || 6. Thou, bright Juice, art Sustainer of the sky: flow, mighty, in accordance with true Law. || 7. Soma, flow splendid with thy copious stream through the great fleece as in the olden time. || 8. Born, led by men, joyous, and purified, let the Light-finder make all blessings flow: || 9. Indu, while cleansed, keeping the people safe, shall give us all possessions for our own. || 10. Flow on for wisdom, Soma, and for power, as a strong courser bathed, to win the prize. || 11. The pressers purify this juice of thine, the Soma, for delight, and lofty fame || 12. They deck the Gold-hued Infant, newly-born, even Soma, Indu, in the sieve for Gods. || 13. Fair Indu hath flowed on for rapturous joy, Sage for good fortune in the waters' lap. || 14. He bears the beauteous name of Indra, that wherewith he overcame all demon foes. || 15. All Deities are wont to drink of him, pressed by the men and blent with milk and curds. || 16. He hath flowed forth with thousand streams effused, flowed through the filter and the sheep's long wool. || 17. With endless genial flow the Strong hath run, purified by the waters, blent with milk. || 18. Pressed out with stones, directed by the men, go forth, O Soma, into Indra's throat. || 19. The mighty Soma with a thousand streams is poured to Indra through the cleansing sieve. || 20. Indu they balm with pleasant milky juice for Indra, for the Steer, for his delight. || 21. Lightly, for sheen, they cleanse thee for the Gods, gold-coloured, wearing water as thy robe. || 22. Indu to Indra streams, yea, downward streams, Strong, flowing to the floods, and mingling there.

Hymn 9:110. Soma Pavamāna.

1. O'er powering Vṛitras, forward run to win great strength: | Thou speedest to subdue like one exacting debts. || 2. In thee, effused, O Soma, we rejoice ourselves for great supremacy in fight. | Thou, Pavamāna, enterest into mighty deeds, || 3. O Pavamāna, thou didst generate the Sun, and spread the moisture out with power, | Hasting to us with plenty vivified with milk. || 4. Thou didst produce him, Deathless God mid mortal men for maintenance of Law and lovely Amṛita: | Thou evermore hast moved making strength flow to us. || 5. All round about hast thou with glory pierced for us as 'twere a never-failing well for men to drink, | Borne on thy way in fragments from the presser's arms. || 6. Then, beautifully radiant, certain Heavenly Ones, have sung to him their kinship as they looked thereon, | And Savitar the God opens as 'twere a stall. || 7. Soma, the men of old whose grass was trimmed addressed the hymn to thee for mighty strength and for renown: | So, Hero, urge us onward to heroic power. || 8. They have drained forth from out the great depth of the sky the old primeval milk of heaven that claims the laud: | They lifted up their voice to Indra at his birth. || 9. As long as thou, O Pavamāna, art above this earth and heaven and all existence in thy might, | Thou standest like a Bull the chief amid the herd. || 10. In the sheep's wool hath Soma Pavamāna flowed, while they cleanse him, like a playful infant, | Indu with hundred powers and hundred currents. || 11. Holy and sweet, while purified, this Indu flows on, a wave of pleasant taste, to Indra,— | Strength-winner, Treasure-finder, Life bestower. || 12. So flow thou on, subduing our assailants, chasing the demons hard to be encountered, | Well-armed and conquering our foes, O Soma.

Hymn 9:111. Soma Pavamāna.

1. With this his golden splendour purifying him, he with his own allies subdues all enemies, as Śara with his own allies. | Cleansing himself with stream of juice he shines forth yellow-hued and red, when with the praisers he encompasses all forms, with praisers having seven mouths. || 2. That treasure of the Paṇis thou discoveredst; thou with thy mothers deckest thee in thine abode, with songs of worship in thine home. | As 'twere from far, the hymn is heard, where holy songs resound in joy. He with the ruddy-hued, threefold hath won life-power, he, glittering, hath won life-power. || 3. He moves intelligent, directed to the East. The very beauteous car rivals the beams of light, the beautiful celestial car. | Hymns, lauding manly valour, came, inciting Indra to success, that ye may be unconquered, both thy bolt and thou, both be unconquered in the war.

Hymn 9:112. Soma Pavamāna.

1. We all have various thoughts and plans, and diverse are the ways of men. | The Brahman seeks the worshipper, wright seeks the cracked, and leech the maimed. Flow, Indu, flow for Indra's sake. || 2. The smith with ripe and seasoned plants, with feathers of the birds of air, | With stones, and with enkindled flames, seeks him who hath a store of gold. Flow, Indu, flow for Indra's sake. || 3. A bard am I, my dad's a leech, mammy lays corn upon the stones. | Striving for wealth, with varied plans, we follow our desires like kine. Flow, Indu, flow for Indra's sake. || 4. The horse would draw an easy car, gay hosts attract the laugh and jest. | The male desires his mate's approach, the frog is eager for the flood, Flow, Indu, flow for Indra's sake.

Hymn 9:113. Soma Pavamāna.

1. Let Vṛitra-slaying Indra drink Soma by Śaryaṇāvat's side, | Storing up vigour in his heart, prepared to do heroic deeds. Flow, Indu, flow for Indra's sake. || 2. Lord of the Quarters, flow thou on, boon Soma, from Ārjīka land, | Effused with ardour and with faith, and the true hymn of sacrifice. Flow, Indu, flow for Indra's sake. || 3. Hither hath Sūrya's Daughter brought the wild Steer whom Parjanya nursed. | Gandharvas have seized bold of him, and in the Soma laid the juice. Flow, Indu, flow for Indra's sake. || 4. Splendid by Law! declaring Law, truth-speaking, truthful in thy works, | Enouncing faith, King Soma! thou, O Soma, whom thy maker decks. Flow, Indu, flow for Indra's sake. || 5. Together flow the meeting streams of him the Great and truly Strong. | The juices of the juicy meet. Made pure by prayer, O Golden-hued, flow, Indu, flow for Indra's sake. || 6. O Pavamāna, where the priest, as he recites the rhythmic prayer, | Lords it o'er Soma with the stone, with Soma bringing forth delight, flow, Indu, flow for Indra's sake. || 7. O Pavamāna, place me in that deathless, undecaying world | Wherein the light of heaven is set, and everlasting lustre shines. Flow, Indu, flow for Indra's sake. || 8. Make me immortal in that realm where dwells the King, Vivasvat's Son, | Where is the secret shrine of heaven, where are those waters young and fresh. Flow, Indu, flow for Indra's sake. || 9. Make me immortal in that realm where they move even as they list, | In the third sphere of inmost heaven where lucid worlds are full of light. Flow, Indu, flow for Indra's sake. || 10. Make me immortal in that realm of eager wish and strong desire, | The region of the radiant Moon, where food and full delight are found. Flow, Indu, flow for Indra's sake: || 11. Make me immortal in that realm where happiness and transports, where | Joys and felicities combine, and longing wishes are fulfilled. Flow, Indu, flow for Indra's sake.

Hymn 9:114. Soma Pavamāna.

1. The man who walketh as the Laws of Indu Pavamāna bid,— | Men call him rich in children, him, O Soma, who hath met thy thought. Flow, Indu, flow for Indra's sake. || 2. Kaśyapa, Ṛishi, lifting up thy voice with hymn-composers' lauds, | Pay reverence to King Soma born the Sovereign Ruler of the plants. Flow, Indu, flow for Indra's sake. || 3. Seven regions have their several Suns; the ministering priests are seven; | Seven are the Āditya Deities,—with these, O Soma, guard thou us. Flow, Indu, flow for Indra's sake. || 4. Guard us with this oblation which, King Soma, hath been dressed for thee. | Let not malignity conquer us, let nothing evil do us harm. Flow, Indu, flow for Indra's sake.

Maṇḍala 10

Hymn 10:1. Agni.

1. High hath the Mighty risen before the dawning, and come to us with light from out the darkness. | Fair-shapen Agni with white-shining splendour hath filled at birth all human habitations. || 2. Thou, being born, art Child of Earth and Heaven, parted among the plants in beauty, Agni! | The glooms of night thou, Brilliant Babe, subduest, and art come forth, loud roaring, from thy Mothers. || 3. Here, being manifested, lofty Vishṇu, full wise, protects his own supremest station. | When they have offered in his mouth their sweet milk, to him with one accord they sing forth praises. || 4. Thence bearing food the Mothers come to meet thee, with food for thee who givest food its increase. | These in their altered form again thou meetest. Thou art Invoking Priest in homes of mortals. || 5. Priest of the holy rite, with car that glitters, refulgent Banner of each act of worship, | Sharing in every God through might and glory, even Agni Guest of men I summon hither. || 6. So Agni stands on earth's most central station, invested in well-decorated garments. | Born, red of hue, where men pour out libations, O King, as great High Priest bring the Gods hither. || 7. Over the earth and over heaven, O Agni, thou, Son, hast ever spread above thy Parents. | Come, Youthfullest! to those who long to meet thee, and hither bring the Gods, O Mighty Victor.

Hymn 10:2. Agni.

1. Gladden the yearning Gods, O thou Most Youthful: bring them, O Lord of Seasons, knowing seasons, | With all the Priests Celestial, O Agni. Best worshipper art thou of all Invokers. || 2. Thine is the Herald's, thine the Cleanser's office, thinker art thou, wealth-giver, true to Order. | Let us with Svāhā offer up oblations, and Agni, worthy God, pay the Gods worship. || 3. To the Gods' pathway have we travelled, ready to execute what work we may accomplish. | Let Agni, for he knows, complete the worship. He is the Priest: let him fix rites and seasons. || 4. When we most ignorant neglect the statutes of you, O Deities with whom is knowledge, | Wise Agni shall correct our faults and failings, skilled to assign each God his fitting season. || 5. When, weak in mind, of feeble understanding, mortals bethink them not of sacrificing, | Then shall the prudent and discerning Agni worship the Gods, best worshipper, in season. || 6. Because the Father hath produced thee, Leader of all our solemn rites, their brilliant Banner: | So win by worship pleasant homes abounding in heroes, and rich food to nourish all men. || 7. Thou whom the Heaven and Earth, thou whom the Waters, and Tvashṭar, maker of fair things, created, | Well knowing, all along the Fathers' pathway, shine with resplendent light, enkindled, Agni.

Hymn 10:3. Agni.

1. O King, the potent and terrific envoy, kindled for strength, is manifest in beauty. | He shines, all-knowing, with his lofty splendour: chasing black Night he comes with white-rayed Morning. || 2. Having o'ercome the glimmering Black with beauty, and bringing forth the dame the Great Sire's Daughter, | Holding aloft the radiant light of Sūrya, as messenger of heaven he shines with treasures. || 3. Attendant on the Blessed Dame the Blessed hath come: the Lover followeth his Sister. | Agni, far-spreading with conspicuous lustre, hath compassed Night with whitely shining garments. || 4. His goings-forth kindle as 'twere high voices the goings of the auspicious Friend of Agni. | The rays, the bright beams of the strong-jawed, mighty, adorable Steer are visible as he cometh. || 5. Whose radiant splendours flow, like sounds, about us, his who is lofty, brilliant, and effulgent, | Who reaches heaven with best and brightest lustres, sportive and piercing even to the summit. || 6. His powers, whose chariot fellies gleam and glitter have loudly roared while, as with teams, he hasted. | He, the most Godlike, far-extending envoy, shines with flames ancient, resonant, whitely-shining. || 7. So bring us ample wealth: seat thee as envoy of the two youthful Matrons, Earth and Heaven. | Let Agni rapid with his rapid, horses, impetuous with impetuous Steeds, come hither.

Hymn 10:4. Agni.

1. To thee will send praise and bring oblation, as thou hast merited lauds when we invoked thee. | A fountain in the desert art thou, Agni, O Ancient King, to man who fain would worship, || 2. Thou unto whom resort the gathered people, as the kine seek the warm stall, O Most Youthful. | Thou art the messenger of Gods and mortals, and goest

glorious with thy light between them. ‖ 3. Making thee grow as 'twere some noble infant, thy Mother nurtures thee with sweet affection. | Over the desert slopes thou passest longing, and seekest, like some beast set free, thy fodder. ‖ 4. Foolish are we, O Wise and free from error: verily, Agni, thou dost know thy grandeur. | There lies the form: he moves and licks, and swallows, and, as House-Lord, kisses the Youthful Maiden. ‖ 5. He rises ever fresh in ancient fuel: smoke-bannered, gray, he makes the wood his dwelling. | No swimmer, Steer, he presses through the waters, and to his place accordant mortals bear him. ‖ 6. Like thieves who risk their lives and haunt the forest, the twain with their ten girdles have secured him. | This is a new hymn meant for thee, O Agni: yoke as it were thy car with parts that glitter. ‖ 7. Homage and prayer are thine, O Jātavedas, and this my song shall evermore exalt thee. | Agni, protect our children and descendants, and guard with ever-watchful care our bodies.

Hymn 10:5. Agni.

1. He only is the Sea, holder of treasures: born many a time he views the hearts within us. | He hides him in the secret couple's bosom. The Bird dwells in the middle of the fountain. ‖ 2. Inhabiting one dwelling-place in common, strong Stallions and the Mares have come together. | The sages guard the seat of Holy Order, and keep the highest names concealed within them. ‖ 3. The Holy Pair, of wondrous power, have coupled: they formed the Infant, they who bred produced him. | The central point of all that moves and moves not, the while they wove the Sage's thread with insight ‖ 4. For tracks of Order and refreshing viands attend from ancient times the goodly Infant. | Wearing him as a mantle, Earth and Heaven grow strong by food of pleasant drink and fatness. ‖ 5. He, calling loudly to the Seven red Sisters, hath, skilled in sweet drink, brought them to be looked on. | He, born of old, in middle air hath halted, and sought and found the covering robe of Pūṣhan. ‖ 6. Seven are the pathways which the wise have fashioned; to one of these may come the troubled mortal. | He standeth in the dwelling of the Highest, a Pillar, on sure ground where paths are parted. ‖ 7. Not Being, Being in the highest heaven, in Aditi's bosom and in Dakṣha's birthplace, | Is Agni, our first-born of Holy Order, the Milch-cow and the Bull in life's beginning.

Hymn 10:6. Agni

1. This is that Agni, he by whose protection, favour, and help. the singer is successful; | Who with the noblest flames of glowing fuel comes forth encompassed with far-spreading lustre. ‖ 2. Agni, the Holy One, the everlasting, who shines far beaming with celestial splendours; | He who hath come unto his friends with friendship, like a fleet steed who never trips or stumbles. ‖ 3. He who is Lord of all divine oblation, shared by all living men at break of morning, | Agni to whom our offerings are devoted, in whom rests he whose car, through might, is scatheless. ‖ 4. Increasing by his strength. while lauds content him, with easy flight unto the Gods he travels. | Agni the cheerful Priest, best Sacrificer, balms with his tongue the Gods with whom he mingles. ‖ 5. With songs and adorations bring ye hither Agni who stirs himself at dawn like Indra, | Whom sages laud with hymns as Jātavedas of those who wield the sacrificial ladle. ‖ 6. In whom all goodly treasures meet together, even as steeds and riders for the booty. | Inclining hither bring us help, O Agni, even assistance most desired by Indra. ‖ 7. Yea, at thy birth, when thou hadst sat in glory, thou, Agni, wast the aim of invocations. | The Gods came near, obedient to thy summons, and thus attained their rank as chief Protectors.

Hymn 10:7. Agni.

1. O Agni, shared by all men living bring us good luck for sacrifice from earth and heaven. | With us be thine intelligence, Wonder-worker! Protect us, God, with thy far-reaching blessings. ‖ 2. These hymns brought forth for thee, O Agni, laud thee for bounteous gifts, with cattle and with horses. | Good Lord, when man from thee hath gained enjoyment, by hymns, O nobly-born, hath he obtained it. ‖ 3. Agni I deem my Kinsman and my Father, count him my Brother and my Friend for ever. | I honour as the face of lofty Agni in heaven the bright and holy light of Sūrya. ‖ 4. Effectual, Agni, are our prayers for profit. He whom, at home thou, Priest for ever, guardest | Is rich in food, drawn by red steeds, and holy: by day and night to him shall all be pleasant. ‖ 5. Men with their arms have generated Agni, helpful as some kind friend, adorned with splendours, | And established as Invoker mid the people the ancient Priest the sacrifice's lover. ‖ 6. Worship, thyself, O God, the Gods in heaven: what, void of knowledge, shall the fool avail thee? | As thou, O God, hast worshipped Gods by seasons, so, nobly-born! to thine own self pay worship. ‖ 7. Agni, be thou our Guardian and Protector bestow upon us life and vital vigour. | Accept, O Mighty One, the gifts we offer, and with unceasing care protect our bodies.

Hymn 10:8. Agni.

1. Agni advances with his lofty banner: the Bull is bellowing to the earth and heavens. | He hath attained the sky's supremest limits. the Steer hath waxen in the lap of waters. ‖ 2. The Bull, the youngling with the hump, hath frolicked, the strong and never-ceasing Calf hath bellowed. | Bringing our offerings to the God's assembly, he moves as Chief in his own dwelling-places. ‖ 3. Him who hath grasped his Parents' head, they established at sacrifice a wave of heavenly lustre. | In his swift flight the red Dawns borne by horses refresh their bodies in the home of Order. ‖ 4. For, Vasu thou precedest every Morning, and still hast been the Twins' illuminator. | For sacrifice, seven places thou retainest while for thine own self thou engenderest Mitra. ‖ 5. Thou art the Eye and Guard of mighty Order, and Varuṇa when to sacrifice thou comest. | Thou art the Waters' Child O Jātavedas, envoy of him whose offering thou acceptest. ‖ 6. Thou art the Leader of the rite and region, to which with thine auspicious teams thou tendest, | Thy light-bestowing head to heaven thou liftest, making thy tongue the oblation-bearer, Agni. ‖ 7. Through his wise insight Trita in the cavern, seeking as ever the Chief Sire's intention, | Carefully tended in his Parents' bosom, calling the weapons kin, goes forth to combat. ‖ 8. Well-skilled to use the weapons of his Father, Āptya, urged on by Indra, fought the battle. | Then Trita slew the foe seven-rayed, three-headed, and freed the cattle of the Son of Tvaṣhṭar. ‖ 9. Lord of the brave, Indra cleft him in pieces who sought to gain much strength and deemed him mighty. | He smote his three heads from his body, seizing the cattle of the omniform Son of Tvaṣhṭar.

Hymn 10:9. Waters.

1. Ye, Waters, are beneficent: so help ye us to energy | That we may look on great delight. ‖ 2. Give us a portion of the sap, the most auspicious that ye have, | Like mothers in their longing love. ‖ 3. To you we gladly come for him to whose abode ye send us on; | And, Waters, give us procreant strength. ‖ 4. The Waters. be to us for drink, Goddesses for our aid and bliss: | Let them stream to us health and strength. ‖ 5. I beg the Floods to give us balm, these Queens who rule o'er precious things, | And have supreme control of men. ‖ 6. Within the Waters-Soma thus hath told me-dwell all balms that heal, | And Agni, he who blesseth all. ‖ 7. O Waters, teem with medicine to keep my body safe from harm, | So that I long may see the Sun. ‖ 8. Whatever sin is found in me, whatever evil I have wrought, | If I have lied or falsely sworn, Waters, remove it far from me. ‖ 9. The Waters I this day have sought, and to their moisture have we come: | O Agni, rich in milk, come thou, and with thy splendour cover me.

Hymn 10:10. Yama, Yamī.

1. Fain would I win my friend to kindly friendship. So may the Sage, come through the air's wide ocean, | Remembering the earth and days to follow, obtain a son, the issue of his father. ‖ 2. Thy friend loves not the friendship which considers her who is near in kindred as stranger. | Sons of the mighty Asura, the Heroes, supporters of the heavens, see far around them. ‖ 3. Yea, this the Immortals seek of thee with longing, progeny of the sole existing mortal. | Then let thy soul and mine be knit together, and as a loving husband take thy consort. ‖ 4. Shall we do now what we ne'er did aforetime? we who spake righteously now talk impurely? | Gandharva in the floods, the Dame of Waters-such is our bond, such our most lofty kinship. ‖ 5. Even in the womb God Tvaṣhṭar, Vivifier, shaping all forms, Creator, made us consorts. | None violates his holy ordinances: that we are his the heavens and earth acknowledge. ‖ 6. Who knows that earliest day whereof thou speakest? Who hath beheld it? Who can here declare it? | Great is the Law of Varuṇa and Mitra. What, wanton! wilt thou say to men to tempt them? ‖ 7. I, Yamī, am possessed by love of Yama, that I may rest on the same couch beside him. | I as a wife would yield me to my husband. Like car-wheels let us speed to meet each other. ‖ 8. They stand not still, they never close their eyelids, those sentinels of Gods who wander

round us. | Not me-go quickly, wanton, with another, and hasten like a chariot wheel to meet him. || 9. May Sūrya's eye with days and nights endow him, and ever may his light spread out before him. | In heaven and earth the kindred Pair commingle. On Yamī be the unbrotherly act of Yama. || 10. Sure there will come succeeding times when brothers and sisters will do acts unmeet for kinsfolk. | Not me, O fair one,—seek another husband, and make thine arm a pillow for thy consort. || 11. Is he a brother when no lord is left her? Is she a sister when Destruction cometh? | Forced by my love these many words I utter. Come near, and hold me in thy close embraces. || 12. I will not fold mine arms about thy body: they call it sin when one comes near his sister. | Not me,—prepare thy pleasures with another: thy brother seeks not this from thee, O fair one. || 13. Alas! thou art indeed a weakling, Yama we find in thee no trace of heart or spirit. | As round the tree the woodbine clings, another will cling about thee girt as with a girdle. || 14. Embrace another, Yamī; let another, even as the woodbine rings the tree, enfold thee. | Win thou his heart and let him win thy fancy, and he shall form with thee a blest alliance.

Hymn 10:11. Agni

1. The Bull hath yielded for the Bull the milk of heaven: the Son of Aditi can never be deceived. | According to his wisdom Varuṇa knoweth all: may he, the Holy, hallow times for sacrifice. || 2. Gandharvī spake: may she, the Lady of the flood, amid the river's roaring leave my heart untouched. | May Aditi accomplish all that we desire, and may our eldest Brother tell us this as Chief. || 3. Yea, even this blessed Morning, rich in store of food, splendid, with heavenly lustre, hath shone out for man, | Since they, as was the wish of yearning Gods, brought forth that yearning Agni for the assembly as the Priest. || 4. And the fleet Falcon brought for sacrifice from afar this flowing Drop most excellent and keen of sight, | Then when the Ārya tribes chose as Invoking Priest Agni the Wonder-Worker, and the hymn rose up. || 5. Still art thou kind to him who feeds thee as with grass, and, skilled in sacrifice, offers thee holy gifts. | When thou, having received the sage's strengthening food with lauds, after long toil, comest with many more. || 6. Urge thou thy Parents, as a lover to delight: the Lovely One desires and craves it from his heart. | The priest calls out, the sacrificer shows his skill, the Asura tries his strength, and with the hymn is stirred. || 7. Far-famed is he, the mortal man, O Agni, thou Son of Strength, who hath obtained thy favour. | He, gathering power, borne onward by his horses, makes his days lovely in his might and splendour. || 8. When, Holy Agni, the divine assembly, the sacred synod mid the Gods, is gathered, | And when thou, Godlike One, dealest forth treasures, vouchsafe us, too, our portion of the riches. || 9. Hear us, O Agni, in your common dwelling: harness thy rapid car of Amṛita. | Bring Heaven and Earth, the Deities' Parents, hither: stay with us here, nor from the Gods be distant.

Hymn 10:12. Agni

1. Heaven and Earth, first by everlasting Order, speakers of truth, are near enough to hear us, | When the God, urging men to worship. sitteth as Priest, assuming all his vital vigour. || 2. As God comprising Gods by Law Eternal, bear, as the Chief who knoweth, our oblation, | Smoke-bannered with the fuel, radiant, joyous, better to praise and worship, Priest for ever. || 3. When the cow's nectar wins the God completely, men here below are heaven's sustainers. | All the Gods came to this thy heavenly Yajus which from the motley Pair milked oil and water. || 4. I praise your work that ye may make me prosper: hear, Heaven and Earth, Twain Worlds that drop with fatness. | While days and nights go to the world of spirits, here let the Parents with sweet meath refresh us || 5. Hath the King seized us? How have we offended against his holy ordinance? Who knoweth? | For even Mitra mid the Gods is angry there are both song and strength for those who come not. || 6. 'tis hard to understand the Immortal's nature, where she who is akin becomes a stranger. | Guard ceaselessly, great Agni, him who ponders Yama's name, easy to be comprehended. || 7. They in the synod where the Gods rejoice them, where they are seated in Vivasvat's dwelling, | Have given the Moon his beams, the Sun his splendour-the Two unweariedly maintain their brightness. || 8. The counsel which the Gods meet to consider, their secret plan,—of that we have no knowledge. | There let God Savitar, Aditi, and Mitra proclaim to Varuṇa that we are sinless. || 9. Hear us, O Agni, in your common dwelling: harness thy rapid car, the car of Amṛita. | Bring Heaven and Earth, the Deities' Parents, hither: stay with us here, nor from the Gods be distant.

Hymn 10:13. Havirdhānas.

1. I yoke with prayer your ancient inspiration: may the laud rise as on the prince's pathway. | All Sons of Immortality shall hear it, all the possessors of celestial natures. || 2. When speeding ye came nigh us like twin sisters, religious-hearted votaries brought you forward. | Take your place, ye who know your proper station: be near, be very near unto our Soma. || 3. Five paces have I risen from Earth. I follow her who hath four feet with devout observance. | This by the Sacred Syllable have I measured: I purify in the central place of Order, || 4. He, for God's sake, chose death to be his portion. He chose not, for men's good, a life eternal | They sacrificed Bṛihaspati the Ṛishi. Yama delivered up his own dear body. || 5. The Seven flow to the Youth on whom the Marutas wait: the Sons unto the Father brought the sacrifice. | Both these are his, as his they are the Lords of both: both toil; belonging unto both they prosper well.

Hymn 10:14. Yama.

1. Honour the King with thine oblations, Yama, Vivasvat's Son, who gathers men together, | Who travelled to the lofty heights above us, who searches out and shows the path to many. || 2. Yama first found for us a place to dwell in: this pasture never can be taken from | Us. | Men born on earth tread their own paths that lead them whither our ancient Fathers have departed. || 3. Mātalī prospers there with Kavyas, Yama with Aṅgiras' sons, Bṛihaspati with Ṛikvans: | Exalters of the Gods, by Gods exalted, some joy in praise and some in our oblation. || 4. Come, seat thee on this bed of grass, O Yama, in company with Aṅgirasas and Fathers. | Let texts recited by the sages bring thee O King, let this oblation make thee joyful. || 5. Come, Yama, with the Aṅgirasas the Holy, rejoice thee here with children of Virūpa. | To sit on sacred grass at this our worship, I call Vivasvat, too, thy Father hither. || 6. Our Fathers are Aṅgirasas, Navagvas, Atharvans, Bhṛigus who deserve the Soma. | May these, the Holy, look on us with favour, may we enjoy their gracious loving-kindness. || 7. Go forth, go forth upon the ancient pathways whereon our sires of old have gone before us. | 'Mere shalt thou look on both the Kings enjoying their sacred food, God Varuṇa and Yama. || 8. Meet Yama, meet the Fathers, meet the merit of free or ordered acts, in highest heaven. | Leave sin and evil, seek anew thy dwelling, and bright with glory wear another body. || 9. Go hence, depart ye, fly in all directions: this place for him the Fathers have provided. | Yama bestows on him a place to rest in adorned with days and beams of light and waters. || 10. Run and outspeed the two dogs, Saramā's offspring, brindled, four-eyed, upon thy happy pathway. | Draw nigh then to the gracious-minded Fathers where they rejoice in company with Yama. || 11. And those two dogs of thine, Yama, the watchers, four-eyed, who look on men and guard the pathway,— | Entrust this man, O King, to their protection, and with prosperity and health endow him. || 12. Dark-hued, insatiate, with distended nostrils, Yama's two envoys roam among the People; | May they restore to us a fair existence here and today, that we may see the sunlight. || 13. To Yama pour the Soma, bring to Yama consecrated gifts: | To Yama sacrifice prepared and heralded by Agni goes. || 14. Offer to Yama holy gifts enriched with butter, and draw near: | So may he grant that we may live long days of life among the Gods. || 15. Offer to Yama, to the King, oblation very rich in meath: | Bow down before the Ṛishis of the ancient times, who made this path in days of old. || 16. Into the six Expanses flies the Great One in Trikadrukas. | The Gāyatrī, the Trishṭubh, all metres in Yama are contained.

Hymn 10:15. Fathers.

1. May they ascend, the lowest, highest, midmost, the Fathers who deserve a share of Soma— | May they who have attained the life of spirits, gentle and righteous, aid us when we call them. || 2. Now let us pay this homage to the Fathers, to those who passed of old and those who followed, | Those who have rested in the earthly region, and those who dwell among the Mighty Races. || 3. I have attained the gracious-minded Fathers, I have gained son and progeny from Vishṇu. | They who enjoy pressed juices with oblation seated on sacred grass, come oftenest hither. || 4. Fathers who sit on sacred grass, come, help us: these offerings have we made for you; accept them. | So come to us with most auspicious favour, and give us health and strength without a trouble. || 5. May they, the Fathers, worthy of the Soma, invited to their favourite oblations. | Laid on the sacred grass, come nigh

and listen: may they be gracious unto us and bless us. ‖ 6. Bowing your bended knees and seated southward, accept this sacrifice of ours with favour. | Punish us not for any sin, O Fathers, which we through human frailty have committed. ‖ 7. Lapped in the bosom of the purple Mornings, give riches to the man who brings oblations. | Grant to your sons a portion of that treasure, and, present, give them energy, ye Fathers. ‖ 8. Our ancient Fathers who deserve the Soma, who came, most noble, to our Soma banquet,— | With these let Yama, yearning with the yearning, rejoicing eat our offerings at his pleasure. ‖ 9. Come to us, Agni, with the gracious Fathers who dwell in glowing light, the very Kavyas, | Who thirsted mid the Gods, who hasten hither, oblation winners, theme of singers' praises. ‖ 10. Come, Agni, come with countless ancient Fathers, dwellers in light, primeval, God-adorers, | Eaters and drinkers of oblations, truthful, who travel with the Deities and Indra. ‖ 11. Fathers whom Agni's flames have tasted, come ye nigh: ye kindly leaders, take ye each your proper place. | Eat sacrificial food presented on the grass: grant riches with a multitude of hero sons. ‖ 12. Thou, Agni Jātavedas, when entreated, didst bear the offerings which thou madest fragrant, | And give them to the Fathers who did eat them with Svadhā. Eat, thou God, the gifts we bring thee. ‖ 13. Thou, Jātavedas, knowest well the number of Fathers who are here and who are absent, | Of Fathers whom we know and whom we know not: accept the sacrifice well-prepared with portions. ‖ 14. They who, consumed by fire or not cremated, joy in their offering in the midst of heaven,— | Grant them, O Sovereign Lord, the world of spirits and their own body, as thy pleasure wills it.

Hymn 10:16. Agni.

1. Burn him not up, nor quite consume him, Agni: let not his body or his skin be scattered. | O Jātavedas, when thou hast matured him, then send him on his way unto the Fathers. ‖ 2. When thou hast made him ready, Jātavedas, then do thou give him over to the Fathers. | When he attains unto the life that waits him, he shall become the Deities' controller. ‖ 3. The Sun receive thine eye, the Wind thy spirit; go, as thy merit is, to earth or heaven. | Go, if it be thy lot, unto the waters; go, make thine home in plants with all thy members. ‖ 4. Thy portion is the goat: with heat consume him: let thy fierce flame, thy glowing splendour, burn him | With thine auspicious forms, o Jātavedas, bear this man to the region of the pious. ‖ 5. Again, O Agni, to the Fathers send him who, offered in thee, goes with our oblations. | Wearing new life let him increase his offspring: let him rejoin a body, Jātavedas. ‖ 6. What wound soe'er the dark bird hath inflicted, the emmet, or the serpent, or the jackal, | May Agni who devoureth all things heal it and Soma who hath passed into the Brahmans. ‖ 7. Shield thee with flesh against the flames of Agni, encompass thee about with fat and marrow, | So will the Bold One, eager to attack thee with fierce glow fail to girdle and consume thee. ‖ 8. Forbear, O Agni, to upset this ladle: the Gods and they who merit Soma love it. | This ladle, this which serves the Gods to drink from, in this the Immortal Deities rejoice them. ‖ 9. I send afar flesh eating Agni, bearing off stains may he depart to Yama's subjects. | But let this other Jātavedas carry oblation to the Gods, for he is skilful. ‖ 10. I choose as God for Father-worship Agni, flesh-eater, who hath past within your dwelling, | While looking on this other Jātavedas. Let him light flames in the supreme assembly. ‖ 11. With offerings meet let Agni bring the Fathers who support the Law. | Let him announce oblations paid to Fathers and to Deities. ‖ 12. Right gladly would we set thee down, right gladly make thee burn and glow. | Gladly bring yearning Fathers nigh to cat the food of sacrifice. ‖ 13. Cool, Agni, and again refresh the spot which thou hast scorched and burnt. | Here let the water-lily grow, and tender grass and leafy herb. ‖ 14. O full of coolness, thou cool Plant, full of fresh moisture, freshening Herb, | Come hither with the female frog: fill with delight this Agni here.

Hymn 10:17. Various Deities.

1. Tvaṣhṭar prepares the bridal of his Daughter: all the world hears the tidings and assembles. | But Yama's Mother, Spouse of great Vivasvat, vanished as she was carried to her dwelling. ‖ 2. From mortal men they hid the Immortal Lady, made one like her and gave her to Vivasvat. | Saraṇyū brought to him the Aśvin brothers, and then deserted both twinned pairs of children. ‖ 3. Guard of the world, whose cattle ne'er are injured, may Pūṣhan bear thee hence, for he hath knowledge. | May he consign thee to these Fathers' keeping, and to the gracious Gods let Agni give thee. ‖ 4. May Āyu, giver of all life, protect thee, and bear thee forward on the distant pathway. | Thither let Savitar the God transport thee, where dwell the pious who have passed-before thee. ‖ 5. Pūṣhan knows all these realms: may he conduct us by ways that are most free from fear and danger. | Giver of blessings, glowing, all-heroic, may he, the wise and watchful, go before us. ‖ 6. Pūṣhan was born to move on distant pathways, on the road far from earth and far from heaven. | To both most wonted places of assembly he travels and returns with perfect knowledge. ‖ 7. The pious call Sarasvatī, they worship Sarasvatī while sacrifice proceedeth. | The pious called Sarasvatī aforetime. Sarasvatī send bliss to him who giveth. ‖ 8. Sarasvatī, who camest with the Fathers, with them rejoicing thee in our oblations, | Seated upon this sacred grass be joyful, and give us strengthening food that brings no sickness. ‖ 9. Thou, called on as Sarasvatī by Fathers who come right forward to our solemn service, | Give food and wealth to present sacrificers, a portion, worth a thousand, of refreshment. ‖ 10. The Mother Floods shall make us bright and shining, cleansers of holy oil, with oil shall cleanse us: | For, Goddesses, they bear off all defilement: I, rise up from them purified and brightened. ‖ 11. Through days of earliest date the Drop descended on this place and on that which was before it. | I offer up, throughout the seven oblations, the Drop which still to one same place is moving. ‖ 12. The Drop that falls, thy stalk which arms have shaken, which from the bosom of the press hath fallen, | Or from the Adhvaryu's purifying filter, I offer thee with heart and cry of Vaṣhaṭ! ‖ 13. That fallen Drop of thine, the stalk which from the ladle fell away, | This present God Bṛihaspati shall pour it forth to make us rich. ‖ 14. The plants of earth are rich in milk, and rich in milk is this my speech; | And rich in milk the essence of the Waters: make me pure therewith.

Hymn 10:18. Various Deities.

1. Go hence, O Death, pursue thy special pathway apart from that which Gods are wont to travel. | To thee I say it who hast eyes and hearest: Touch not our offspring, injure not our heroes. ‖ 2. As ye have come effacing Mṛityu's footstep, to further times prolonging your existence, | May ye be rich in children and possessions. cleansed, purified, and meet for sacrificing. ‖ 3. Divided from the dead are these, the living: now be our calling on the Gods successful. | We have gone forth for dancing and for laughter, to further times prolonging our existence. ‖ 4. Here I erect this rampart for the living; let none of these, none other, reach this limit. | May they survive a hundred lengthened autumns, and may they bury Death beneath this mountain. ‖ 5. As the days follow days in close succession, as with the seasons duly come the seasons, | As each successor fails not his foregoer, so form the lives of these, O great Ordainer. ‖ 6. Live your full lives up! find old age delightful, all of you striving one behind the other. | May Tvaṣhṭar, maker of fair things, be gracious and lengthen out the days of your existence. ‖ 7. Let these unwidowed dames with noble husbands adorn themselves with fragrant balm and unguent. | Decked with fair jewels, tearless, free from sorrow, first let the dames go up to where he lieth. ‖ 8. Rise, come unto the world of life, O woman: come, he is lifeless by whose side thou liest. | Wifehood with this thy husband was thy portion, who took thy hand and wooed thee as a lover. ‖ 9. From his dead hand I take the bow be carried, that it may be our power and might and glory. | There art thou, there; and here with noble heroes may we o'ercome all hosts that fight against us. ‖ 10. Betake thee to the lap of Earth the Mother, of Earth far-spreading, very kind and gracious. | Young Dame, wool-soft unto the guerdon-giver, may she preserve thee from Destruction's bosom. ‖ 11. Heave thyself, Earth, nor press thee downward heavily: afford him easy access, gently tending him. | Cover him, as a mother wraps her skirt about her child, O Earth. ‖ 12. Now let the heaving earth be free from motion: yea,—let a thousand clods remain above him. | Be they to him a home distilling fatness, here let them ever be his place of refuge. ‖ 13. I stay the earth from thee, while over thee I place this piece of earth. May I be free from injury. | Here let the Fathers keep this pillar firm for thee, and there let Yama make thee an abiding-place. ‖ 14. Even as an arrow's feathers, they have set me on a fitting day. | The fit word have I caught and held as 'twere a courser with the rein.

Hymn 10:19. Waters or Cows.

1. Turn, go not farther on your way: visit us, O ye Wealthy Ones. | Agni and

Soma, ye who bring riches again, secure us wealth. || 2. Make these return to us again, bring them beside us once again. | May. Indra give them back to us, and Agni drive them hither-ward. || 3. Let them return to us again: under this herdsman let them feed. | Do thou, O Agni, keep them here, and let the wealth we have remain. || 4. I call upon their herdsman, him who knoweth well their coming nigh, | Their parting and their home-return, and watcheth their approach and rest. || 5. Yea, let the herdsman, too, return, who marketh well their driving-forth; | Marketh their wandering away, their turning back and coming home. || 6. Home-leader, lead them home to us; Indra, restore to us our kine: | We will rejoice in them alive. || 7. I offer you on every side butter and milk and strengthening food. | May all the Holy Deities pour down on us a flood of wealth. || 8. O thou Home-leader, lead them home, restore them thou who bringest home. | Four are the quarters of the earth; from these bring back to us our kine,

Hymn 10:20. Agni.

1. Send unto us a good and happy mind. || 2. I worship Agni, Youthfullest of Gods, resistless, Friend of laws; | Under whose guard and heavenly light the Spotted seek the Mother's breast: || 3. Whom with their mouth they magnify, bannered with flame and homed in light. | He glitters with his row of teeth. || 4. Kind, Furtherer of men, he comes, when he hath reached the ends of heaven, | Sage, giving splendour to the clouds. || 5. To taste man's offerings, he, the Strong, hath risen erect at sacrifice: | Fixing his dwelling he proceeds. || 6. Here are oblation, worship, rest: rapidly comes his furtherance. | To sword-armed Agni come the Gods. || 7. With service for chief bliss I seek the Lord of Sacrifice, Agni, whom | They call the Living, Son of Cloud. || 8. Blest evermore be all the men who come from us, who magnify | Agni with sacrificial gifts. || 9. The path he treads is black and white and red, and striped, and brown, crimson, and glorious. | His sire begat him bright with hues of gold. || 10. Thus with his thoughts, O Son of Strength, O Agni, hath Vimada, accordant with the Immortals, | Offered thee hymns, soliciting thy favour. Thou hast brought all food, strength, a prosperous dwelling.

Hymn 10:21. Agni.

1. With offerings of our own we choose thee, Agni, as Invoking Priest, | For sacrifice with trimmed grass,—at your glad carouse—piercing and brightly shining. Thou art waxing great. || 2. The wealthy ones adorn thee, they who bring us horses as their gift: | The sprinkling ladle, Agni,—at your glad carouse—and glowing offering taste thee. Thou art waxing great. || 3. The holy statutes rest by thee, as 'twere with ladles that o'erflow. | Black and white-gleaming colours,—at your glad carouse—all glories thou assumest. Thou art waxing great. || 4. O Agni, what thou deemest wealth, Victorious and Immortal One! | Bring thou to give us vigour,—at your glad carouse—splendid at sacrifices. Thou art waxing great. || 5. Skilled in all lore is Agni, he whom erst Atharvan brought to life. | He was Vivasvat's envoy, at your glad carouse—the well-loved friend of Yama, Thou art waxing great. || 6. At sacrifices they adore thee, Agni, when the rite proceeds. | All fair and lovely treasures—at your glad carouse—thou givest him who offers. Thou art waxing great. || 7. Men, Agni, have established thee as welcome Priest at holy rites, | Thee whose face shines with butter,—at your glad carouse—bright, with eyes most observant. Thou art waxing great. || 8. Wide and aloft thou spreadest thee, O Agni, with thy brilliant flame. | A Bull art thou when bellowing,—at your glad carouse—thou dost impregn the Sisters. Thou art waxing great.

Hymn 10:22. Indra.

1. Where is famed Indra heard of? With what folk is he renowned today as Mitra is,— | Who in the home of Ṛishis and in secret is extolled with song? || 2. Even here is Indra famed, and among us this day the glorious Thunderer is praised, | He who like Mitra mid the folk hath won complete and full renown. || 3. He who is Sovereign Lord of great and perfect strength, exerter of heroic might, | Who bears the fearless thunder as a father bears his darling son. || 4. Harnessing to thy car, as God, two blustering Steeds of the Wind-God, O Thunderer, | That speed along the shining path, thou making ways art glorified. || 5. Even to these dark Steeds of Wind thou of thyself hast come to ride, | Of which no driver may be found, none, be he God or mortal man. || 6. When ye approach, men ask you, thee and Uśanā: Why come ye to our dwelling-place? | Why are ye come to mortal man from distant realms of earth and heaven? || 7. O Indra, thou shalt speak us fair: our holy prayer is offered up. | We pray to thee for help as thou didst strike the monster Śuṣhṇa dead. || 8. Around us is the Dasyu, riteless, void of sense, inhuman, keeping alien laws. | Baffle, thou Slayer of the foe, the weapon which this Dāsa wields. || 9. Hero with Heroes, thou art ours: yea, strong are they whom thou dost help. | In many a place are thy full gifts, and men, like vassals, sing thy praise. || 10. Urge thou these heroes on to slay the enemy, brave Thunderer! in the fight with swords. | Even when hid among the tribes of Sages numerous as stars. || 11. Swift come those gifts of thine whose hand is prompt to rend and burn, O Hero Thunder-armed: | As thou with thy Companions didst destroy the whole of Śuṣhṇa's brood. || 12. Let not thine excellent assistance come to us, O Hero Indra, profitless. | May we, may we enjoy the bliss of these thy favours, Thunderer! || 13. May those soft impulses of thine, O Indra, be fruitful and innocent to us. | May we know these whose treasures are like those of milch-kine, Thunderer! || 14. That Earth, through power of knowing things that may be known, handless and footless yet might thrive, | Thou slewest, turning to the right, Śuṣhṇa for every living man. || 15. Drink, drink the Soma, Hero Indra; be not withheld as thou art good, O Treasure-giver. | Preserve the singers and our liberal princes, and make us wealthy with abundant riches.

Hymn 10:23. Indra.

1. Indra, whose right hand wields the bolt, we worship, driver of Bay Steeds seeking sundered courses. | Shaking his beard with might he hath arisen, casting his weapons forth and dealing bounties. || 2. The treasure which his Bay Steeds found at sacrifice,—this wealth made opulent Indra slayer of the foe. | Ṛibhu, Ṛibhukṣhan, Vāja—he is Lord of Might. The Dāsa's very name I utterly destroy. || 3. When, with the Princes, Maghavan, famed of old, comes nigh the thunderbolt of gold, and the Controller's car | Which his two Tawny Coursers draw, then Indra is the Sovereign Lord of power whose glory spreads afar. || 4. With him too is this rain of his that comes like herds: Indra throws drops of moisture on his yellow beard. | When the sweet juice is shed he seeks the pleasant place, and stirs the worshipper as wind disturbs the wood. || 5. We laud and praise his several deeds of valour who, father-like, with power hath made us stronger; | Who with his voice slew many thousand wicked ones who spake in varied manners with contemptuous cries. || 6. Indra, the Vimadas have formed for thee a laud, copious, unparalleled, for thee Most Bountiful. | We know the good we gain from him the Mighty One when we attract him as a herdsman calls the kine. || 7. Ne'er may this bond of friendship be dissevered, the Ṛishi Vimada's and thine, O Indra. | We know thou carest for us as a brother with us, O God, be thine auspicious friendship.

Hymn 10:24. Indra. Aśvins.

1. O Indra, drink this Soma, pressed out in the mortar, full of sweets. | Send down to us great riches,—at your glad carouse—in thousands, O Most healthy. Thou art waxing great. || 2. To thee with sacrifices, with oblations, and with lauds we come. | Lord of all strength and power, grant—at your glad carouse—the best choice-worthy treasure. Thou art waxing great. || 3. Thou who art Lord of precious boons, inciter even of the churl. | Guardian of singers, Indra,—at your glad carouse—save us from woe and hatred. Thou art waxing great. || 4. Strong, Lords of Magic power, ye Twain churned the united worlds apart, | When ye, implored by Vimada, Nāsatyas, forced apart the pair. || 5. When the united pair were rent asunder all the Gods complained. | The Gods to the Nāsatyas cried, Bring these together once again. || 6. Sweet be my going forth, and rich in sweets be my approach to home. | So, through your Deity, both Gods, enrich us with all pleasantness.

Hymn 10:25. Soma.

1. Send us a good and happy mind, send energy and mental power. | Then —at your glad carouse—let men joy in thy love, Sweet juice! as kine in pasture. Thou art waxing great. || 2. In all thy forms, O Soma, rest thy powers that influence the heart. | So also these my longings—at your glad carouse—spread themselves seeking riches. Thou art waxing great. || 3. Even if, O Soma, I neglect thy laws through my simplicity, | Be gracious—at your glad carouse—as sire to son. Preserve us even from slaughter. Thou. art waxing great. || 4. Our songs in concert go to thee as streams of water to the wells. | Soma, that we may live, grant—at your glad carouse—full

powers of mind, like beakers. Thou art waxing great. || 5. O Soma, through thy might who art skilful and strong, these longing men, | These sages, have thrown open—at your glad carouse—the stall of kine and horses. Thou art waxing great || 6. Our herds thou guardest, Soma, and the moving world spread far and wide. | Thou fittest them for living,—at your glad carouse—looking upon all beings. Thou art waxing great. || 7. On all sides, Soma, be to us a Guardian ne'er to be deceived. | King, drive away our foemen—at your glad carouse:—let not the wicked rule us. Thou art waxing great. || 8. Be watchful, Soma, passing wise, to give us store of vital strength. | More skilled than man to guide us,—at your glad carouse—save us from harm and sorrow. Thou art waxing great. || 9. Chief slayer of our foemen, thou, Indu, art Indra's gracious Friend, | When warriors invoke him—at your glad carouse—in fight, to win them offspring. Thou art waxing great. || 10. Victorious is this gladdening drink: to Indra dear it grows in strength. | This—at your glad carouse—enhanced the mighty hymn of the great sage Kakṣhīvant. Thou art waxing great. || 11. This to the sage who offers gifts brings power that comes from wealth in kine. | This, better than the seven, hath—at your glad carouse—furthered the blind, the cripple. Thou art waxing great.

Hymn 10:26. Pūṣhan.

1. Forward upon their way proceed the ready teams, the lovely songs. | Further them glorious Pūṣhan with yoked chariot, and the Mighty Twain! || 2. With sacred hymns let this man here, this singer, win the God to whom | Belong this majesty and might. He hath observed our eulogies. || 3. Pūṣhan the Strong hath knowledge of sweet praises even as Indu hath. | He dews our corn with moisture, he bedews the pasture of our kine. || 4. We will bethink ourselves of thee, O Pūṣhan, O thou God, as One. | Who brings fulfilment of our hymns, and stirs the singer and the sage. || 5. joint-sharer of each sacrifice, the driver of the chariot steeds; | The Ṛiṣhi who is good to man, the singer's Friend and faithful Guard. || 6. One who is Lord of Śucha, Lord of Śucha caring for herself: | Weaving the raiment of the sheep and making raiment beautiful. || 7. The mighty Lord of spoil and wealth, Strong Friend of all prosperity; | He with light movement shakes his beard, lovely and ne'er to be deceived. || 8. O Pūṣhan, may those goats of thine turn hitherward thy chariot-pole. | Friend of all suppliants; art thou, born in old time, and arm and sure. || 9. May the majestic Pūṣhan speed our chariot with his power and might. | May he increase our store of wealth and listen to this call of ours.

Hymn 10:27. Indra.

1. This, singer, is my firm determination, to aid the worshipper who pours the Soma. | I slay the man who brings no milk oblation, unrighteous, powerful, the truth's perverter. || 2. Then Will I, when I lead my friends to battle against the radiant persons of the godless, | Prepare for thee at home a vigorous bullock, and pour for thee the fifteen-fold strong juices. || 3. I know not him who sayeth and declareth that he hath slain the godless in the battle. | Soon as they see the furious combat raging, men speak forth praises of my vigorous horses. || 4. While yet my deeds of might were unrecorded, all passed for Maghavans though I existed. | The potent one who dwelt in peace I conquered, grasped by the foot and slew him on the mountain. || 5. None hinder me in mine heroic exploits, no, not the mountains when I will and purpose. | Even the deaf will tremble at my roaring, and every day will dust be agitated. || 6. To see the Indraless oblation-drinkers, mean offerers, o'ertaken by destruction! | Then shall the fellies of my car pass over those who have blamed my joyous Friend and scorned him. || 7. Thou wast, thou grewest to full vital vigour: an earlier saw, a later one shall see thee. | Two canopies, as 'twere, are round about him who reacheth to the limit of this region. || 8. The freed kine eat the barley of the pious. I saw them as they wandered with the herdsman. | The calling of the pious rang around them. What portion will these kine afford their owner? || 9. When we who cat the grass of men are gathered I am with barley-eaters in the corn-land. | There shall the captor yoke the yokeless bullock, and he who hath been yoked seek one to loose him. || 10. There wilt thou hold as true my spoken purpose, to bring together quadrupeds. and bipeds. | I will divide, without a fight, his riches who warreth here, against the Bull, with women. || 11. When a man's daughter hath been ever eyeless, who, knowing, will be wroth with her for blindness? | Which of the two will loose on him his anger-the man who leads her home or he who woos her? || 12. How many a maid is pleasing to the suitor who fain would marry for her splendid riches? | If the girl be both good and fair of feature, she finds, herself, a friend among the people. || 13. His feet have grasped: he eats the man who meets him. Around his head he sets the head for shelter. | Sitting anear and right above he smites us, and follows earth that lies spread out beneath him. || 14. High, leafless, shadowless, and swift is Heaven: the Mother stands, the Youngling, loosed, is feeding. | Loud hath she lowed, licking Another's offspring. In what world hath the Cow laid down her udder? || 15. Seven heroes from the nether part ascended, and from the upper part came eight together. | Nine from behind came armed with winnowing-baskets: ten from the front pressed o'er the rock's high ridges. || 16. One of the ten, the tawny, shared in common, they send to execute their final purpose. | The Mother carries on her breast the Infant of noble form and soothes it while it knows not. || 17. The Heroes dressed with fire the fatted wether: the dice were thrown by way of sport and gaming. | Two reach the plain amid the heavenly waters, hallowing and with means of purifying. || 18. Crying aloud they ran in all directions: One half of them will cook, and not the other. | To me hath Savitar, this God, declared it: He will perform, whose food is wood and butter. || 19. I saw a troop advancing from the distance moved, not by wheels but their own God-like nature. | The Friendly One seeks human generations, destroying, still new bands of evil beings. || 20. These my two Bulls, even Pramara's, are harnessed: drive them not far; here let them often linger. | The waters even shall aid him to his object, and the all-cleansing Sun who is above us. || 21. This is the thunderbolt which often whirleth down from the lofty misty realm of Sūrya. | Beyond this realm there is another glory so through old age they pass and feel no sorrow. || 22. Bound fast to every tree the cow is lowing, and thence the man-consuming birds are flying, | Then all this world, though pressing juice for Indra and strengthening the Ṛiṣhi, is affrighted. || 23. In the Gods' mansion stood the first-created, and from their separation came the later. | Three warm the Earth while holding stores of water, and Two of these convey the murmuring moisture. || 24. This is thy life: and do thou mark and know it. As such, hide not thyself in time of battle. | He manifests the light and hides the vapour: his foot is never free from robes that veil it.

Hymn 10:28. Indra. Vasukra.

1. Now all my other friends are here assembled: my Sire-in-law alone hath not come hither. | So might he eat the grain and drink the Soma, and, satisfied, return unto; his dwelling. || 2. Loud belloweth the Bull whose horns are sharpened: upon the height above earth's breadth he standeth. | That man I guard and save in all his troubles who fills my flanks when he hath shed the Soma. || 3. Men with the stone press out for thee, O Indra, strong, gladdening Soma, and thereof thou drinkest. | Bulls they dress for thee, and of these thou eatest when, Maghavan, with food thou art invited. || 4. Resolve for me, O singer, this my riddle: The rivers send their swelling water backward: | The fox steals up to the approaching lion: the jackal drives the wild-boar from the brushwood. || 5. How shall I solve this riddle, I, the simple, declare the thought of thee the Wise and Mighty? | Tell us, well knowing, as befits the season: Whitherward is thy prosperous car advancing? || 6. Thus do they magnify me, me the mighty higher than even high heaven is my car-pole. | I all at once demolish many thousands: my Sire begot me with no foe to match me. || 7. Yea, and the Gods have known me also, Indra, as mighty, fierce and strong in every exploit. | Exulting with the bolt I slaughtered Vṛitra, and for the offerer opened with might the cow-stall. || 8. The Deities approached, they carried axes; splitting the wood they came with their attendants. | They laid good timber in the fire-receivers, and burnt the grass up where they found it growing. || 9. The hare hath swallowed up the opposing razor: I sundered with a clod the distant mountain. | The great will I make subject to the little: the calf shall wax in strength and cat the bullock. || 10. There hath the strong-winged eagle left his talon, as a snared lion leaves the trap that caught him. | Even the wild steer in his thirst is captured: the leather strap still holds his foot entangled. || 11. So may the leather strap their foot entangle who fatten on the viands of the Brahman. | They all devour the bulls set free to wander, while they themselves destroy their bodies' vigour. || 12. They were well occupied with holy duties who sped in person with their lauds to Soma. | Speaking like man, mete to us wealth and booty: in

heaven thou hast the name and fame of Hero.

Hymn 10:29. Indra.

1. As sits the young bird on the tree rejoicing, ye, swift Pair, have been roused by clear laudation, | Whose Herald-Priest through many days is Indra, earth's Guardian, Friend of men, the best of Heroes. || 2. May we, when this Dawn and the next dance hither, be thy best servants, most heroic Hero! | Let the victorious car with triple splendour bring hitherward the hundred chiefs with Kutsa. || 3. What was the gladdening draught that pleased thee, Indra? Speed through our doors to songs, for thou art mighty. | Why comest thou to me, what gift attracts thee? Fain would I bring thee food most meet to offer. || 4. Indra, what fame hath one like thee mid heroes? With what plan wilt thou act? Why hast thou sought us? | As a true Friend, Wide-Strider! to sustain us, since food absorbs the thought of each among us. || 5. Speed happily those, as Sūrya ends his journey, who meet his wish as bridegrooms meet their spouses; | Men who present, O Indra strong by nature, with food the many songs that tell thy praises. || 6. Thine are two measures, Indra, wide-well-meted, heaven for thy majesty, earth for thy wisdom. | Here for thy choice are Somas mixed with butter: may the sweet meath be pleasant for thy drinking. || 7. They have poured out a bowl to him, to Indra, full of sweet juice, for faithful is his bounty. | O'er earth's expanse hath he grown great by wisdom, the Friend of man, and by heroic exploits. || 8. Indra hath conquered in his wars, the Mighty: men strive in multitudes to win his friendship. | Ascend thy chariot as it were in battle, which thou shalt drive to us with gracious favour.

Hymn 10:30. Waters.

1. As 'twere with swift exertion of the spirit, let the priest speed to the celestial Waters, | The glorious food of Varuṇa and Mitra. To him who spreadeth far this laud I offer. || 2. Adhvaryus, he ye ready with oblations,, and come with longing to the longing Waters, | Down on which looks the purple-tinted Eagle. Pour ye that flowing wave this day, deft-handed. || 3. Go to the reservoir, O ye Adhvaryus worship the Waters' Child with your oblations. | A consecrated wave he now will give you, so press for him the Soma rich in sweetness. || 4. He who shines bright in floods, unfed with fuel, whom sages worship at their sacrifices: | Give waters rich in sweets, Child of the Waters, even those which gave heroic might to Indra: || 5. Those in which Soma joys and is delighted, as a young man with fair and pleasant damsels. | Go thou unto those Waters, O Adhvaryu, and purify with herbs what thou infusest. || 6. So maidens bow before the youthful gallant who comes with love to them who yearn to meet him. | In heart accordant and in wish one-minded are the Adhvaryus and the heavenly Waters. || 7. He who made room for you when fast imprisoned, who freed you from the mighty imprecation,— | Even to that Indra send the meath-rich current, the wave that gratifies the Gods, O Waters. || 8. Send forth to him the meath-rich wave, O Rivers, which is your offspring and a well of sweetness, | Oil-balmed, to be implored at sacrifices. Ye wealthy Waters, hear mine invocation. || 9. Send forth the rapture-giving wave, O Rivers, which Indra drinks, which sets the Twain in motion; | The well that springeth from the clouds, desirous, that wandereth triple-formed, distilling transport. || 10. These winding Streams which with their double current, like cattle-raiders, seek the lower pastures,— | Waters which dwell together, thrive together, Queens, Mothers of the world, these, Ṛishi, honour. || 11. Send forth our sacrifice with holy worship send forth the hymn and prayer for gain of riches. | For need of sacrifice disclose the udder. Give gracious hearing to our call, O Waters. || 12. For, wealthy Waters, ye control all treasures: ye bring auspicious intellect and Amṛita. | Ye are the Queens of independent riches Sarasvatī give full life to the singer! || 13. When I behold the Waters coming hither, carrying with them milk and meath and butter, | Bearing the well-pressed Soma juice to Indra, they harmonize in spirit with Adhvaryus. || 14. Rich, they are come with wealth for living beings, O friends, Adhvaryus, seat them in their places. | Seat them on holy grass, ye Soma-bringers in harmony with the Offspring of the Waters. || 15. Now to this grass are come the longing Waters: the Pious Ones are seated at our worship. | Adhvaryus, press the Soma juice for Indra so will the service of the Gods be easy.

Hymn 10:31. Viśvedevas.

1. May benediction of the Gods approach us, holy, to aid us with all rapid succours. | Therewith may we be happily befriended, and pass triumphant over all our troubles. || 2. A man should think on wealth and strive to win it by adoration on the path of Order, | Counsel himself with his own mental insight, and grasp still nobler vigour with his spirit. || 3. The hymn is formed, poured are the allotted portions: as to a ford friends come unto the Wondrous. | We have obtained the power of case and comfort, we have become acquainted, with Immortals. || 4. Pleased be the Eternal Lord who loves the household with this man whom God Savitar created. | May Bhaga Aryaman grace him with cattle: may he appear to him, and be, delightful. || 5. Like the Dawns' dwelling-place be this assembly, where in their might men rich in food have gathered. | Striving to share the praises of this singer. To us come strengthening and effectual riches! || 6. This Bull's most gracious far-extended favour existed first of all in full abundance. | By his support they are maintained in common who in the Asura's mansion dwell together. || 7. What was the tree, what wood, in sooth, produced it, from which they fashioned forth the Earth and Heaven? | These Twain stand fast and wax not old for ever: these have sung praise to many a day and morning. || 8. Not only here is this: more is beyond us. He is the Bull, the Heaven's and Earth's supporter. | With power divine he makes his skin a filter, when the Bay Coursers bear him on as Sūrya. || 9. He passes o'er the broad earth like a Stega: he penetrates the world as Wind the mist-cloud. | He, balmed with oil, near Varuṇa and Mitra, like Agni in the wood, hath shot forth splendour. || 10. When suddenly called the cow that erst was barren, she, self-protected, ended all her troubles. | Earth, when the first son sprang from sire and mother, cast up the Śamī, that which men were seeking. || 11. To Nṛishad's son they gave the name of Kaṇva, and he the brown-hued courser won the treasure. | For him dark-coloured streamed the shining udder: none made it swell for him. Thus Order willed it.

Hymn 10:32. Indra.

1. Forth speed the Pair to bring the meditating God, benevolent with boons sent in return for boons. | May Indra graciously accept both gifts from us, when he hath knowledge of the flowing Soma juice. || 2. Thou wanderest far, O Indra, through the spheres of light and realms of earth, the region, thou whom many praise! | Let those who often bring their solemn rites conquer the noisy babblers who present no gifts. || 3. More beautiful than beauty must this seem to me, when the son duly careth for his parents' line. | The wife attracts the husband: with a shout of joy the man's auspicious marriage is performed aright. || 4. This beauteous place of meeting have I looked upon, where, like milch-cows, the kine order the marriage train; | Where the Herd's Mother counts as first and best of all, and round her are the seven-toned people of the choir. || 5. The Pious One hath reached your place before the rest: One only moves victorious with the Rudras' band. | To these your helpers pour our meath, Immortal Gods, with whom your song of praise hath power to win their gifts. || 6. He who maintains the Laws of God informed me that thou wast lying hidden in the waters. | Indra, who knoweth well, beheld and showed thee. By him instructed am I come, O Agni. || 7. The stranger asks the way of him who knows it: taught by the skilful guide he travels onward. | This is, in truth, the blessing of instruction: he finds the path that leads directly forward. || 8. Even now he breathed: these days hath he remembered. Concealed, he sucked the bosom of his Mother. | Yet in his youth old age hath come upon him: he hath grown gracious, good, and free from anger. || 9. O Kalaśa, all these blessings will we bring them, O Kuruśravaṇa, who give rich presents. | May he, O wealthy princes, and this Soma which I am bearing in my heart, reward you.

Hymn 10:33. Various Deities.

1. The urgings of the people have impelled me, and by,the nearest way I bring you Pūshan. | The Universal Gods have brought me safely. The cry was heard, Behold, Duḥśāsu cometh! || 2. The ribs that compass me give pain and trouble me like rival wives. | Indigence, nakedness, exhaustion press me sore: my mind is fluttering like a bird's. || 3. As rats eat weavers' threads, cares are consuming me, thy singer, Śatakratu, me. | Have mercy on us once, O Indra, Bounteous Lord: be thou a Father unto us. || 4. I the priests' Ṛishi chose as prince most liberal Kuruśravaṇa, | The son of Trasadasyu's son, || 5. Whose three bays harnessed to the car bear me straight onward: I will laud | The giver of a thousand meeds, || 6. The sire of Upamaśravas, even him whose words were passing sweet, | As a fair field is to its lord. || 7. Mark, Upamaśravas, his son, mark, grandson of Mitrātithi: |

I am thy father's eulogist. ‖ 8. If I controlled Immortal Gods, yea, even were I Lord of men, | My liberal prince were living still. ‖ 9. None lives, even had he hundred lives, beyond the statute of the Gods | So am I parted from my friend.

Hymn 10:34. Dice, etc.

1. Sprung from tall trees on windy heights, these rollers transport me as they turn upon the table. | Dearer to me the die that never slumbers than the deep draught of Mūjavant's own Soma. ‖ 2. She never vexed me nor was angry with me, but to my friends and me was ever gracious. | For the die's sake, whose single point is final, mine own devoted wife I alienated. ‖ 3. My wife holds me aloof, her mother hates me: the wretched man finds none to give him comfort. | As of a costly horse grown old and feeble, I find not any profit of the gamester. ‖ 4. Others caress the wife of him whose riches the die hath coveted, that rapid courser: | Of him speak father, mother, brothers saying, We know him not: bind him and take him with you. ‖ 5. When I resolve to play with these no longer, my friends depart from me and leave me lonely. | When the brown dice, thrown on the board, have rattled, like a fond girl I seek the place of meeting. ‖ 6. The gamester seeks the gambling-house, and wonders, his body all afire, Shall I be lucky? | Still do the dice extend his eager longing, staking his gains against his adversary. ‖ 7. Dice, verily, are armed with goads and driving-hooks, deceiving and tormenting, causing grievous woe. | They give frail gifts and then destroy the man who wins, thickly anointed with the player's fairest good. ‖ 8. Merrily sports their troop, the three-and-fifty, like Savitar the God whose ways are faithful. | They bend not even to the mighty's anger: the King himself pays homage and reveres them. ‖ 9. Downward they roll, and then spring quickly upward, and, handless, force the man with hands to serve them. | Cast on the board, like lumps of magic charcoal, though cold themselves they bum the heart to ashes. ‖ 10. The gambler's wife is left forlorn and wretched: the mother mourns the son who wanders homeless. | In constant fear, in debt, and seeking riches, he goes by night unto the home of others. ‖ 11. Sad is the gambler when he sees a matron, another's wife, and his well-ordered dwelling. | He yokes the brown steeds in the early morning, and when the fire is cold sinks down an outcast. ‖ 12. To the great captain of your mighty army, who hath become the host's imperial leader, | To him I show my ten extended fingers: I speak the truth. No wealth am I withholding. ‖ 13. Play not with dice: no, cultivate thy corn-land. Enjoy the gain, and deem that wealth sufficient. | There are thy cattle there thy wife, O gambler. So this good Savitar himself hath told me. ‖ 14. Make me your friend: show us some little mercy. Assail us not with your terrific fierceness. | Appeased be your malignity and anger, and let the brown dice snare some other captive.

Hymn 10:35. Viśvedevas.

1. These fires associate with Indra are awake, bringing their light when first the Dawn begins to shine. | May Heaven and Earth, great Pair, observe our holy work. We claim for us this day the favour of the Gods. ‖ 2. Yea, for ourselves we claim the grace of Heaven and Earth, of Śaryaṇāvat, of the Hills and Mother Streams. | For innocence we pray to Sūrya and to Dawn. So may the flowing Soma bring us bliss today. ‖ 3. May the great Twain, the Mothers, Heaven and Earth, this day preserve us free from sin for peace and happiness. | May Morning sending forth her light drive sin afar. We pray to kindled Agni for felicity. ‖ 4. May this first Dawn bring us the host of gracious Gods: rich, may it richly shine for us who strive for wealth. | The wrath of the malignant may we keep afar. We pray to kindled Agni for felicity. ‖ 5. Dawns, who come forward with the bright beams of the Sun, and at your earliest flushing bring to us the light, | Shine ye on us today auspicious, for renown. We pray to kindled Agni for felicity. ‖ 6. Free from all sickness may the Mornings come to us, and let our fires mount upward with a lofty blaze. | The Aśvin Pair have harnessed their swift-moving car. We pray to kindled Agni for felicity. ‖ 7. Send us today a portion choice and excellent, O Savitar, for thou art he who dealeth wealth. | I cry to Dhiṣhaṇā, Mother of opulence. We pray to kindled Agni for felicity. ‖ 8. Further me this declaring of Eternal Law, the Law of Gods, as we mortals acknowledge it! | The Sun goes up beholding all the rays of morn. We pray to kindled Agni for felicity. ‖ 9. This day we pray with innocence in strewing grass, adjusting pressing-stones, and perfecting the hymn. | Thou in the Ādityas' keeping movest restlessly. We pray to kindled Agni for felicity. ‖ 10. To our great holy grass I bid the Gods at morn to banquet, and will seat them as the seven priests,— | Varuṇa, Indra, Mitra, Bhaga for our gain. We pray to kindled Agni for felicity. ‖ 11. Come hither, O Ādityas, for our perfect weal: accordant help our sacrifice that we may thrive. | Pūṣhan, Bṛihaspati, Bhaga, both Aśvins, and enkindled Agni we implore for happiness. ‖ 12. Ādityas, Gods, vouchsafe that this our home may be praise-worthy, prosperous, our heroes' sure defence, | For cattle, for our sons, for progeny, for life. We pray to kindled Agni for felicity. ‖ 13. This day may all the Marutas, all he near us with aid: may all our fires be well enkindled. | May all Gods come to us with gracious favour. May spoil and wealth he ours, and all possessions. ‖ 14. He whom ye aid, O Deities, in battle, whom ye protect and rescue from affliction, | Who fears no danger at your milk-libation, -such may we be to feast the Gods, ye Mighty.

Hymn 10:36. Viśvedevas.

1. There are the Dawn and Night, the grand and beauteous Pair, Earth, Heaven, and Varuṇa, Mitra, and Aryaman. | Indra I call, the Marutas, Mountains, and the Floods, Ādityas, Heaven and Earth, the Waters, and the Sky. ‖ 2. May Dyaus and Pṛithivī, wise, true to Holy Law, keep us in safety from distress and injury. | Let not malignant Nirṛiti rule over us. We crave today this gracious favour of the Gods. ‖ 3. Mother of Mitra and of opulent Varuṇa, may Aditi preserve us safe from all distress. | May we obtain the light of heaven without a foe. We crave this gracious favour of the Gods today. ‖ 4. May ringing press-stones keep the Rākṣhasas afar, ill dream, and Nirṛiti, and each voracious fiend. | May the Ādityas and the Marutas shelter us. We crave this gracious favour of the Gods today. ‖ 5. Full flow libations; on our grass let Indra sit; Bṛihaspati the singer laud with Sāman hymns! | Wise be our hearts' imaginings that we may live. We crave this gracious favour of the Gods today. ‖ 6. Ye Aśvins, make our sacrifice ascend to heaven, and animate the rite that it may send us bliss, | Offered with holy oil, with forward-speeding rein. We crave the gracious favour of the Gods today. ‖ 7. Hither I call the band of Marutas, swift to hear, great, purifying, bringing bliss, to he our Friends. | May we increase our wealth to glorify our name. We crave this gracious favour of the Gods today. ‖ 8. We bring the Stay of Life, who makes the waters swell, swift-hearing, Friend of Gods, who waits on sacrifice. | May we control that Power, Soma whose rays are bright. We crave this gracious favour of the Gods today. ‖ 9. Alive ourselves, with living sons, devoid of guilt, may we win this with winners by fair means to win. | Let the prayer-haters bear our sin to every side. We crave this gracious favour of the Gods today. ‖ 10. Hear us, O ye who claim the worship of mankind, and give us, O ye Gods, the gift for which we pray, | Victorious wisdom, fame with heroes and with wealth. We crave today this gracious favour of the Gods. ‖ 11. We crave the gracious favour of the Gods today, great favour of great Gods, sublime and free from foes, | That we may gain rich treasure sprung from hero sons. We crave this gracious favour of the Gods today. ‖ 12. In great enkindled Agni's keeping, and, for bliss, free from all sin before Mitra and Varuṇa. | May we share Savitar's best animating help. We crave this gracious favour of the Gods today. ‖ 13. All ye, the Gods whom Savitar the Father of truth, and Varuṇa and Mitra govern, | Give us prosperity with hero children, and opulence in kine and various treasure. ‖ 14. Savitar, Savitar from cast and westward, Savitar, Savitar from north and southward, | Savitar send us perfect health and comfort, Savitar let our days of life be lengthened!

Hymn 10:37. Sūrya.

1. Do homage unto Varuṇa's and Mitra's Eye: offer this solemn worship to the Mighty God, | Who seeth far away, the Ensign, born of Gods. Sing praises unto Sūrya, to the Son of Dyaus. ‖ 2. May this my truthful speech guard me on every side wherever heaven and earth and days are spread abroad. | All else that is in motion finds a place of rest: the waters ever flow and ever mounts the Sun. ‖ 3. No godless man from time remotest draws thee down when thou art driving forth with winged dappled Steeds. | One lustre waits upon thee moving to the cast, and, Sūrya, thou arisest with a different light. ‖ 4. O Sūrya, with the light whereby thou scatterest gloom, and with thy ray impellest every moving thing, | Keep far from us all feeble, worthless sacrifice, and drive away disease and every evil dream. ‖ 5. Sent forth thou guardest well the Universe's law, and in thy wonted way arisest free from wrath. | When Sūrya, we address our prayers to thee today, may the Gods favour this our purpose and desire. ‖ 6. This invocation, these

our words may Heaven and Earth, and Indra and the Waters and the Marutas hear. | Ne'er may we suffer want in presence of the Sun, and, living happy lives, may we attain old age. || 7. Cheerful in spirit, evermore, and keen of sight, with store of children, free from sickness and from sin, | Long-living, may we look, O Sūrya, upon thee uprising day by day, thou great as Mitra is! || 8. Sūrya, may we live long and look upon thee still, thee, O Far-seeing One, bringing the glorious light, | The radiant God, the spring of joy to every eye, as thou art mounting up o'er the high shining flood. || 9. Thou by whose lustre all the world of life comes forth, and by thy beams again returns unto its rest, | O Sūrya with the golden hair, ascend for us day after day, still bringing purer innocence. || 10. Bless us with shine, bless us with perfect daylight, bless us with cold, with fervent heat and lustre. | Bestow on us, O Sūrya, varied riches, to bless us in our home and when we travel. || 11. Gods, to our living creatures of both kinds vouchsafe protection, both to bipeds and to quadrupeds, | That they may drink and eat invigorating food. So grant us health and strength and perfect innocence. || 12. If by some grievous sin we have provoked the Gods, O Deities, with the tongue or thoughtlessness of heart, | That guilt, O Vasus, lay upon the Evil One, on him who ever leads us into deep distress.

Hymn 10:38. Indra.

1. O Indra, in this battle great and glorious, in this loud din of war help us to victory, | Where in the strife for kine among bold ring-decked men arrows fly all around and heroes are subdued. || 2. At home disclose to us opulence rich in food, streaming with milk, O Indra, meet to be renowned. | Śakra, may we be thine, the friendly Conqueror's: even as we desire, O Vasu, so do thou. || 3. The godless man, much-lauded Indra, whether he be Dāsa or be Ārya, who would war with us,— | Easy to conquer he for thee, with us, these foes: with thee may we subdue them in the clash of fight. || 4. Him who must be invoked by many and by few, who standeth nigh with comfort in the war of men, | Indra, famed Hero, winner in the deadly strife, let us bring hitherward today to favour us. || 5. For, Indra, I have heard thee called Self. capturer, One, Steer! who never yields, who urges even the churl. | Release thyself from Kutsa and come hither. How shall one like thee sit still bound that he may not move?

Hymn 10:39. Aśvins.

1. As 'twere the name of father, easy to invoke, we all assembled here invoke this Car of yours, | Aśvins, your swiftly-rolling circumambient Car which he who worships must invoke at eve and dawn. || 2. Awake all pleasant strains and let the hymns flow forth: raise up abundant fullness: this is our desire. | Aśvins, bestow on us a glorious heritage, and give our princes treasure fair as Soma is. || 3. Ye are the bliss of her who groweth old at home, and helpers of the slow although he linger last. | Men call you too, Nāsatyas, healers of the blind, the thin and feeble, and the man with broken bones. || 4. Ye made Chyavāna, weak and worn with length of days, young again, like a car, that he had power to move. | Ye lifted up the son of Tugra from the floods. At our libations must all these your acts be praised. || 5. We will declare among the folk your ancient deeds heroic; yea, ye were Physicians bringing health. | You, you who must be lauded, will we bring for aid, so that this foe of ours, O Aśvins, may believe. || 6. Listen to me, O Aśvins; I have cried to you. Give me-your aid as sire and mother aid their son. | Poor, without kin or friend or ties of blood am I. Save me before it be too late, from this my curse. || 7. Ye, mounted on your chariot brought to Vimada the comely maid of Purumitra as a bride. | Ye, came unto the calling of the weakling's dame, and granted noble offspring to the happy wife. || 8. Ye gave again the vigour of his youthful life to the sage Kali when old age was coming nigh. | Ye rescued Vandana and raised him from the pit, and in a moment gave Viśpalā power to move. || 9. Ye Aśvins Twain, endowed with manly strength, brought forth Ṛibīsa when hidden in the cave and well-nigh dead, | Freed Saptavadhri, and for Atri caused the pit heated with fire to be a pleasant resting-place. || 10. On Pedu ye bestowed, Aśvins, a courser white, mighty with nine-and-ninety varied gifts of strength, | A horse to be renowned, who bore his friend at speed, joy-giving, Bhaga-like to be invoked of men. || 11. From no side, ye Two Kings whom none may check or stay, doth grief, distress, or danger come upon the man | Whom, Aśvins swift to hear, borne on your glowing path, ye with your Consort make the foremost in the race. || 12. Come on that Chariot which the Ṛibhus wrought for you, the Chariot, Aśvins, that is speedier than thought, | At harnessing whereof Heaven's Daughter springs to birth, and from Vivasvat come auspicious Night and Day. || 13. Come, Conquerors of the sundered mountain, to our home, Aśvins who made the cow stream milk for Śayu's sake, | Ye who delivered even from the wolf's deep throat and set again at liberty the swallowed quail. || 14. We have prepared this laud for you, O Aśvins, and, like the Bhṛigus, as a car have framed it, | Have decked it as a maid to meet the bridegroom, and brought it as a son, our stay for ever.

Hymn 10:40. Aśvins.

1. Your radiant Chariot-whither goes it on its way?-who decks it for you, Heroes, for its happy course, | Starting at daybreak, visiting each morning every house, borne hitherward through prayer unto the sacrifice? || 2. Where are ye, Aśvins, in the evening, where at morn? Where is your halting-place, where rest ye for the night? | Who brings you homeward, as the widow bedward draws her husband's brother, as the bride attracts the groom? || 3. Early ye sing forth praise as with a herald's voice, and, meet for worship, go each morning to the house. | Whom do ye ever bring to ruin? Unto whose libations come ye, Heroes, like two Sons of Kings? || 4. Even as hunters follow two wild elephants, we with oblations call you down at morn and eve. | To folk who pay you offerings at appointed times, Chiefs, Lords of splendour, ye bring food to strengthen them. || 5. To you, O Aśvins, came the daughter of a King, Ghoṣhā, and said, O Heroes, this I beg of you: | Be near me in the day, he near me in the night: help me to gain a car-borne chieftain rich in steeds. || 6. O Aśvins, ye are wise: as Kutsa comes to men, bring your car nigh the folk of him who sings your praise. | The bee, O Aśvins, bears your honey in her mouth, as the maid carries it purified in her hand. || 7. To Bhujyu and to Vaśa ye come near with help, O Aśvins, to Śiñjāra and to Uśanā. | Your worshipper secures your friendship for himself. Through your protection I desire felicity. || 8. Kṛiśa and Śayu ye protect, ye Aśvins Twain: ye Two assist the widow and the worshipper; | And ye throw open, Aśvins, unto those who win the cattle-stall that thunders with its sevenfold mouth. || 9. The Woman hath brought forth, the Infant hath appeared, the plants of wondrous beauty straightway have sprung up. | To him the rivers run as down a deep descent, and he this day becomes their master and their lord. || 10. They mourn the living, cry aloud, at sacrifice: the men have set their thoughts upon a distant cast. | A lovely thing for fathers who have gathered here,—a joy to husbands,—are the wives their arms shall clasp || 11. Of this we have no knowledge. Tall it forth to us, now the youth rests within the chambers of the bride. | Fain would we reach the dwelling of the vigorous Steer who loves the kine, O Aśvins: this is our desire. || 12. Your favouring grace hath come, ye Lords of ample wealth: Aśvins, our longings are stored up within your hearts. | Ye, Lords of splendour, have become our twofold guard: may we as welcome friends reach Aryaman's abode. || 13. Even so, rejoicing in the dwelling-place of man, give hero sons and riches to the eloquent. | Make a ford, Lords of splendour, where men well may drink: remove the spiteful tree-stump standing in the path. || 14. O Aśvins, Wonder-Workers, Lords of lustre, where and with what folk do ye delight yourselves today? | Who hath detained them with him? Whither are they gone? Unto what sage's or what worshipper's abode?

Hymn 10:41. Aśvins.

1. That general Car of yours, invoked by many a man, that comes to our libations, three-wheeled, meet for lauds, | That circumambient Car, worthy of sacrifice, we call with our pure hymns at earliest flush of dawn. || 2. Ye, O Nāsatyas, mount that early-harnessed Car, that travels early, laden with its freight of balm, | Wherewith ye, Heroes, visit clans who sacrifice, even the poor man's worship where the priest attends. || 3. If to the deft Adhvaryu with the meath in hand, or to the Kindler firm in strength, the household friend, | Or to the sage's poured libations ye approach, come thence, O Aśvins, now to drink the offered meath.

Hymn 10:42. Indra.

1. Even as an archer shoots afar his arrow, offer the laud to him with meet adornment. | Quell with your voice the wicked's voice, O sages. Singer, make Indra rest beside the Soma. || 2. Draw thy Friend to thee like a cow at milking: O Singer, wake up Indra as a lover. | Make thou the Hero haste to give us riches even as a vessel filled brimful with treasure. || 3. Why, Maghavan, do they call thee Bounteous; Giver? Quicken me: thou, I hear,

art he who quickens. | Śakra, let my intelligence be active, and bring us luck that finds great wealth, O Indra. || 4. Standing, in battle for their rights, together, the people, Indra, in the fray invoke thee. | Him who brings gifts the Hero makes his comrade: with him who pours no juice he seeks not friendship. || 5. Whoso with plenteous food for him expresses strong Somas as much quickly-coming treasure, | For him he overthrows in early morning his swift well-weaponed foes, and slays the tyrant. || 6. He unto whom we offer praises, Indra, Maghavan, who hath joined to ours his wishes,— | Before him even afar the foe must tremble: low before him must bow all human glories. || 7. With thy fierce bolt, O God invoked of many, drive to a distance from afar the foeman. | O Indra, give us wealth in corn and cattle, and make thy singer's prayer gain strength and riches. || 8. Indra, the swallower of strong libations rich in the boons they bring, the potent Somas, | He, Maghavan, will not restrict his bounty he brings much wealth unto the Soma-presser. || 9. Yea, by superior play he wins advantage, when he, a gambler, piles his gains in season. | Celestial-natured, he o'erwhelms with riches the devotee who keeps not back his treasure. || 10. O Much-invoked, may we subdue all famine and evil want with store of grain and cattle. | May we allied, as first in rank, with princes obtain possessions by our own exertion. || 11. Bṛihaspati protect us from the rearward, and from above, and from below, from sinners! | May Indra from the front, and from the centre, as Friend to friends, vouchsafe us room and freedom.

Hymn 10:43. Indra.

1. In perfect unison all yearning hymns of mine that find the light of heaven have sung forth Indra's praise. | As wives embrace their lord, the comely bridegroom, so they compass Maghavan about that he may help. || 2. Directed unto thee my spirit never strays, for I have set my hopes on thee, O Much-invoked! | Sit, Wonderful! as King upon the sacred grass, and let thy drinking-place be by the Soma juice. || 3. From indigence and hunger Indra turns away: Maghavan hath dominion over precious wealth. | These the Seven Rivers flowing on their downward path increase the vital vigour of the potent Steer. || 4. As on the fair-leafed tree rest birds, to Indra flow the gladdening Soma juices that the bowls contain. | Their face that glows with splendour through their mighty power hath found the shine of heaven for man, the Āryas' light. || 5. As in the game a gambler piles his winnings, so Maghavan, sweeping all together, gained the Sun | This mighty deed of thine none other could achieve, none, Maghavan, before thee, none in recent time. || 6. Maghavan came by turns to all the tribes of men: the Steer took notice of the people's songs of praise. | The man in whose libations Śakra hath delight by means of potent Somas vanquisheth his foes. || 7. When Soma streams together unto Indra flow like waters to the river, rivulets to the lake, | In place of sacrifice sages exalt his might, as the rain swells the corn by moisture sent from heaven. || 8. He rushes through the region like a furious Bull, he who hath made these floods the dames of worthy lords. | This Maghavan hath found light for the man who brings oblation, sheds the juice, and promptly pours his gifts. || 9. Let the keen axe come forth together with the light: here be, as erst, the teeming cow of sacrifice. | Let the Red God shine bright with his refulgent ray, and let the Lord of heroes glow like heaven's clear sheen. || 10. O Much-invoked, may we subdue all famine and evil want with store of grain and cattle. | May we allied, as first in rank, with princes obtain possessions by our own exertion. || 11. Bṛihaspati protect us from the rearward, and from above, and from below, from sinners. | May Indra from the front, and from the centre, as Friend to friends, vouchsafe us room and freedom.

Hymn 10:44. Indra.

1. May Sovereign Indra come to the carousal, he who by Holy Law is strong and active, | The overcomer of all conquering forces with his great steer-like power that hath no limit. || 2. Firm-seated is thy car, thy Steeds are docile; thy hand, O King, holds, firmly grasped, the thunder. | On thy fair path, O Lord of men, come quickly: we will increase thy powers when thou hast drunken. || 3. Let strong and mighty Steeds who bear this Mighty Indra, the Lord of men, whose arm wields thunder, | Bring unto us, as sharers of our banquet, the Steer of conquering might, of real vigour. || 4. So like a Bull thou rushest to the Lord who loves the trough, the Sage, the prop of vigour, in the vat, | Prepare thine energies, collect them in thyself: be for our profit as the Master of the wise. || 5. May precious treasures come to us-so will I pray. Come to the votary's gift offered with beauteous laud. | Thou art the Lord, as such sit on this holy grass: thy vessels are inviolate as Law commands. || 6. Far went our earliest invocation of the Gods, and won us glories that can never be surpassed. | They who could not ascend the ship of sacrifice, sink down in desolation, trembling with alarm. || 7. So be the others, evil-hearted, far away, whose horses, difficult to harness, have been yoked. | Here in advance men stand anear to offer gifts, by whom full many a work that brings reward is done. || 8. He firmly fixed the plains and mountains as they shook. Dyaus thundered forth and made the air's mid-region quake. | He stays apart the two confronting bowls; he sings lauds in the potent Soma's joy when he hath drunk. || 9. I bear this deftly-fashioned goad of thine, wherewith thou, Maghavan, shalt break the strikers with the hoof. | At this libation mayst thou be well satisfied. Partake the juice, partake the worship, Maghavan. || 10. O Much-invoked, may we subdue all famine and evil want with store of grain and cattle. | May we allied, as first in rank, with princes obtain possessions by our own exertion. || 11. Bṛihaspati protect us from the rearward, and from above, and from below, from sinners. | May Indra from the front and from the centre, as Friend to friends, vouchsafe us room and freedom.

Hymn 10:45. Agni.

1. First Agni sprang to life from out of Heaven: the second time from us came Jātavedas. | Thirdly the Manly-souled was in the waters. The pious lauds and kindles him the Eternal. || 2. Agni, we know thy three powers in three stations, we know thy forms in many a place divided. | We know what name supreme thou hast in secret: we know the source from which thou hast proceeded. || 3. The Manly-souled lit thee in sea and waters, man's Viewer lit thee in the breast of heaven, | There as thou stoodest in the third high region the Steers increased thee in the water's bosom. || 4. Agni roared out, like Dyaus what time he thunders: he licked the ground about the plants he flickered. | At once, when born, he looked around enkindled, and lightened heaven and earth within with splendour. || 5. The spring of glories and support of riches, rouser of thoughts and guardian of the Soma, | Good Son of Strength, a King amid the waters, in forefront of the Dawns he shines enkindled. || 6. Germ of the world, ensign of all creation, be sprang to life and filled the earth and heavens. | Even the firm rock he cleft when passing over, when the Five Tribes brought sacrifice to Agni. || 7. So among mortals was Immortal Agni established as holy wise and willing envoy. | He waves the red smoke that he lifts above him, striving to reach the heavens with radiant lustre. || 8. Like gold to look on, far he shone refulgent, beaming imperishable life for glory, | Agni by vital powers became immortal when his prolific Father Dyaus begat him. || 9. Whoso this day, O God whose flames are lovely, prepares a cake, O Agni, mixed with butter, | Lead thou and further him to higher fortune, to bliss bestowed by Gods, O thou Most Youthful. || 10. Endow him, Agni, with a share of glory, at every song of praise sung forth enrich him. | Dear let him be to Sūrya, dear to Agni, preeminent with son and children's children. || 11. While, Agni, day by day men pay thee worship they win themselves all treasures worth the wishing. | Allied with thee, eager and craving riches, they have disclosed the stable filled with cattle. || 12. Agni, the Friend of men, the Soma's keeper, Vaiśvānara, hath been lauded by the Ṛishis. | We will invoke benignant Earth and Heaven: ye Deities, give us wealth with hero children.

Hymn 10:46. Agni.

1. Established for thee, to lend thee vital forces, Giver of wealth, Guard of his servant's body. | The Great Priest, born, who knows the clouds, Abider with men, is seated in the lap of waters. || 2. Worshipping, seeking him with adoration like some lost creature followed by its footprints, | Wise Bhṛigus, yearning in their hearts, pursued him, and found him lurking where the floods are gathered. || 3. On the Cow's forehead, with laborious searching, Trita, the offspring of Vibhūvas, found him. | Born in our houses, Youthful, joy-bestower, he now becomes the central point of brightness. || 4. Yearning, with homage, they have set and made him blithe Priest among mankind, oblation-bearer, | Leader of rites and Purifier, envoy of men, as sacrifice that still advances. || 5. The foolish brought the ne'er-bewildered forward, great, Victor, Song-inspirer, Fort-destroyer. | Leading the Youth gold-bearded, like a courser gleaming with wealth,

they turned their hymn to profit. || 6. Holding his station firmly in the houses, Trita sat down within his home surrounded | Thence, as Law bids, departs the Tribes' Companion having collected men with no compulsion. || 7. His are the fires, eternal, purifying, that make the houses move, whose smoke is shining, | White, waxing in their strength, for ever stirring, and sitting in the wood; like winds are Somas. || 8. The tongue of Agni bears away the praise-song, and, through his care for Earth, her operations. | Him, bright and radiant, living men have established as their blithe Priest, the Chief of Sacrificers. || 9. That Agni, him whom Heaven and Earth engendered, the Waters. Tvaṣhṭar, and with might, the Bhṛigus, | Him Mātariśvan and the Gods have fashioned holy for man and first to be entreated. || 10. Agni, whom Gods have made oblation-bearer, and much-desiring men regard as holy, | Give life to him who lauds thee when he worships, and then shall glorious men in troops adore thee.

Hymn 10:47. Indra Vaikuṇṭha.

1. Thy right hand have we grasped in ours, O Indra, longing for treasure, Treasure-Lord of treasures! | Because we know thee, Hero, Lord of cattle: vouchsafe us mighty and resplendent riches. || 2. Wealth, fully armed, good guard and kind protector, sprung from four seas, the prop and stay of treasures, | Fraught with great bounties, meet for praise and glory; vouchsafe us mighty and resplendent riches. || 3. Wealth, with good Brahmans, Indra! God-attended, high, wide, and deep, arid based on broad foundations, | Strong, with famed Ṛishis, conquering our foemen: vouchsafe us mighty and resplendent riches. || 4. Victorious, winning strength, with hero sages, confirmed in power, most useful, wealth-attracting, | True, Indra! crushing forts and slaying Dasyus: vouchsafe us mighty and resplendent riches. || 5. Wealthy in heroes and in cars and horses, strength hundredfold and thousandfold, O Indra, | With manly sages, happy troops, light-winning: vouchsafe us mighty and resplentdent riches. || 6. To Saptagu the sage, the holy-minded, to him, Bṛihaspati, the song approaches, | Aṅgiras' Son who must be met with homage: vouchsafe us mighty and resplendent riches. || 7. My lauds, like envoys, craving loving-kindness, go forth to Indra with their strong entreaty, | Moving his heart and uttered by my spirit: vouchsafe us mighty and resplendent riches. || 8. Grant us the boon for which I pray, O Indra, a spacious home unmatched among the people. | To this may Heaven and Earth accord approval: vouchsafe us mighty and resplendent riches.

Hymn 10:48. Indra Vaikuṇṭha.

1. I was the first possessor of all precious gear: the wealth of every man I win and gather up. | On me as on a Father living creatures call; I deal enjoyment to the man who offers gifts. || 2. I, Indra, am Atharvan's stay and firm support: I brought forth kine to Trita from the Dragon's grasp. | I stripped the Dasyus of their manly might, and gave the cattle-stalls to Mātariśvan and Dadhyach. || 3. For me hath Tvaṣhṭar forged the iron thunderbolt: in me the Gods have centred intellectual power. | My sheen is like the Sun's insufferably bright: men honour me as Lord for past and future deeds. || 4. I won myself these herds of cattle, steeds and kine, and gold in ample store, with my destructive bolt. | I give full many a thousand to the worshipper, what time the Somas and the lauds have made me glad. || 5. Indra am I none ever wins my wealth from me never at any time am I a thrall to death. | Pressing the Soma, ask riches from me alone: ye, Pūrus, in my friendship shall not suffer harm. || 6. These, breathing loud in fury, two and two, who caused Indra to bring his bolt of thunder to the fray, | The challengers, I struck with deadly weapon down: firm stand what words the God speaks to his worshippers. | This One by stronger might I conquered singly; yea, also two: shall three prevail against me? | Like many sheaves upon the floor I thrash them. How can my foes, the Indraless, revile me? || 8. Against the Gungus I made Atithigva strong, and kept him mid the folk like Vṛitra-conquering strength, | When I won glory in the great foe-slaying fight, in battle where Karañja fell, and Parṇaya. || 9. With food for mine enjoyment Sāpya Namī came: he joined me as a friend of old in search of kine. | As I bestowed on him an arrow for the fight I made him worthy of the song and hymn of praise. || 10. One of the two hath Soma, seen within it; the Herdsman with the bone shows forth the other. | He, fain to fight the Bull whose horns were sharpened, stood fettered in the demon's ample region. || 11. I, as a God, ne'er violate the statutes of Gods, of Vasus, Rudriyas, Ādityas. | These Gods have formed me for auspicious vigour, unconquered and invincible for ever.

Hymn 10:49. Indra Vaikuṇṭha.

1. I have enriched the singer with surpassing wealth; I have allowed the holy hymn to strengthen me. | I, furtherer of him who offers sacrifice, have conquered in each fight the men who worship not. || 2. The People of the heavens, the waters, and the earth have established me among the Gods with Indra's name. | I took unto myself the two swift vigorous Bays that speed on divers paths, and the fierce bolt for strength. || 3. With deadly blows I smote Atka for Kavi's sake; I guarded Kutsa well with these saving helps. | As Śuṣhṇa's slayer I brandished the dart of death: I gave not up the Ārya name to Dasyu foes. || 4. Smadibha, Tugra, and the Vetasus I gave as prey to Kutsa, father-like, to succour him. | I was a worthy King to rule the worshipper, when I gave Tuji dear inviolable gifts. || 5. I gave up Mṛigaya to Śrutarvan as his prey because he ever followed me and kept my laws. | For Āyu's sake I caused Veśa to bend and bow, and into Savya's hand delivered Paḍgṛibhi. || 6. I crushed Navavāstva of the lofty car, the Dāsa, as the Vṛitra-slayer kills the fiends; | When straightway on the region's farthest edge I brought the God who makes the lights to broaden and increase. || 7. I travel round about borne onward in my might by the fleet-footed dappled Horses of the Sun. | When man's libation calls me to the robe of state I soon repel the powerful Dasyu with my blows. || 8. Stronger am I than Nahus, I who slew the seven: I glorified with might Yadu and Turvaśa. | I brought another low, with strength I bent his strength: I let the mighty nine-and-ninety wax in power. || 9. Bull over all the streams that flow along the earth, I took the Seven Rivers as mine own domain. | I, gifted with great wisdom, spread the floods abroad: by war I found for man the way to high success. || 10. I set within these cows the white milk which no God, not even Tvaṣhṭar's self, had there deposited,— | Much-longed-for, in the breasts, the udders of the kine, the savoury sweets of meath, the milk and Soma juice. || 11. Even thus hath Indra Maghavan, truly bounteous, sped Gods and men with mighty operation. | The pious glorify all these thine exploits, Lord of Bay Coursers, Strong, and Self-resplendent.

Hymn 10:50. Indra Vaikuṇṭha.

1. I laud your Mighty One who joyeth in the juice, him who is shared by all men, who created all; | Indra, whose conquering strength is powerful in war, whose fame and manly vigour Heaven and Earth revere. || 2. He with his friend is active, lauded, good to man, Indra who must be glorified by one like me. | Hero, Lord of the brave, all cars are thy delight, warring with Vṛitra, or for waters, or for spoil. || 3. Who are the men whom thou wilt further, Indra, who strive to win thy bliss allied with riches? | Who urged thee forward to exert thy power divine, to valour, in the war for waters on their fields? || 4. Thou, Indra, through the holy prayer art mighty, worthy of sacrifice at all libations. | In every fight thou castest heroes on the ground: thou art the noblest song, O Lord of all the folk. || 5. Help now, as Highest, those who toil at sacrifice: well do the people know thy great protecting might. | Thou shalt be Everlasting, Giver of success yea, on all these libations thou bestowest strength. || 6. All these libations thou makest effectual, of which thou art thyself supporter, Son of Power. | Therefore thy vessel is to be esteemed the best, sacrifice, holy text, prayer, and exalted speech. || 7. They who with flowing Soma pray to thee, O Sage, to pour on them thy gifts of opulence and wealth, | May they come forward, through their spirit, on the path of bliss, in the wild joy of Soma juice effused.

Hymn 10:51. Agni. Gods.

1. Large was that covering, and firm of texture, folded wherein thou enteredst the waters. | One Deity alone, O Jātavedas Agni, saw all thy forms in sundry places. || 2. What God hath seen me? Who of all their number clearly beheld my forms in many places? | Where lie, then, all the sacred logs of Agni that lead him God-ward, Varuṇa and Mitra? || 3. In many places, Agni Jātavedas, we sought thee hidden in the plants and waters. | Then Yama marked thee, God of wondrous splendour! effulgent from thy tenfold secret dwelling, || 4. I fled in fear from sacrificial worship, Varuṇa, lest the Gods should thus engage me. | Thus were my forms laid down in many places. This, as my goal, I Agni saw before me. || 5. Come; man is pious and would fain do worship, he waits prepared: in gloom thou, Agni, dwellest. | Make pathways leading God-ward clear and easy, and bear

oblations with a kindly spirit. ‖ 6. This goal mine elder brothers erst selected, as he who drives a car the way to travel. | So, Varuṇa, I fled afar through terror, as flies the wild-bull from an archer's bowstring. ‖ 7. We give thee life unwasting, Jātavedas, so that, employed, thou never shalt be injured. | So, nobly born! shalt thou with kindly spirit bear to the Gods their share of men's oblations. ‖ 8. Grant me the first oblations and the latter, entire, my forceful shares of holy presents, | The soul of plants, the fatness of the waters, and let there be long life, ye Gods, to Agni. ‖ 9. Thine be the first oblations and the latter, entire, thy forceful shares of holy presents. | Let all this sacrifice be thine, O Agni, and let the world's four regions how before thee.

Hymn 10:52. Gods.

1. Instruct me, all ye Gods, how I, elected your Priest, must seat me here, and how address you. | Instruct me how to deal to each his portion, and by what path to bring you man's oblation. ‖ 2. I sit as Priest most skilled in sacrificing: the Marutas and all Deities impel me. | Aśvins, each day yours is the Adhvaryu's duty: Brahman and wood are here: 'tis yours to offer. ‖ 3. Who is the Priest? Is he the Priest of Yama? On whom is thrust this God-appointed honour? | He springs to life each month, each day that passes; so Gods have made him their oblation-bearer. ‖ 4. The Gods have made me bearer of oblations, who slipped away and passed through many troubles. | Wise Agni shall ordain for us the worship, whether five-wayed, threefold, or seven-threaded. ‖ 5. So will I win you strength and life for ever. O Gods, that I may give you room and freedom. | To Indra's arms would I consign the thunder; in all these battles shall he then be victor. ‖ 6. The Deities three hundred and thirty-nine, have served and honoured Agni, | Strewn sacred grass, anointed him with butter, and seated him as Priest, the Gods' Invoker.

Hymn 10:53. Agni Sauchika. Gods.

1. He hath arrived, he whom we sought with longing, who skilled in sacrifice well knows its courses. | Let him discharge his sacrificial duties: let him sit down as Friend who was before | Us. ‖ 2. Best Priest, he hath been won by being seated, for he hath looked on the well-ordered viands. | Come, let us worship Gods who must be worshipped, and pouring oil, laud those who should be lauded. ‖ 3. Now hath he made the feast of Gods effective: now have we found the secret tongue of worship. | Now hath he come, sweet, robed in vital vigour, and made our calling on the Gods effective. ‖ 4. This prelude of my speech I now will utter, whereby we Gods may quell our Asura foemen. | Eaters of strengthening food who merit worship, O ye Five Tribes, be pleased with mine oblation. ‖ 5. May the Five Tribes be pleased with mine oblation, and the Cow's Sons and all who merit worship. | From earthly trouble may the earth protect us, and air's mid realm from woe that comes from heaven. ‖ 6. Spinning the thread, follow the region's splendid light: guard thou the path ways well which wisdom hath prepared. | Weave ye the knotless labour of the bards who sing: be Manu thou, and bring the Heavenly People forth. ‖ 7. Lovers of Soma, bind the chariot traces fast: set ye the reins in order and embellish them. | Bring hitherward the car with seats where eight may sit, whereon the Gods have brought the treasure that we love. ‖ 8. Here flows Aśmanvatī: hold fast each other, keep yourselves up, and pass, my friends, the river. | There let us leave the Powers that brought no profit, and cross the flood to Powers that are auspicious. ‖ 9. Tvaṣhṭar, most deft of workmen, knew each magic art, bringing most blessed bowls that hold the drink of Gods. | His axe, wrought of good metal, he is sharpening now, wherewith the radiant Brahmaṇaspati will cut. ‖ 10. Now, O ye Sapient Ones, make ye the axes sharp wherewith ye fashion bowls to hold the Amṛita. | Knowing the secret places make ye ready that whereby the Gods have gotten immortality. ‖ 11. Ye with a secret tongue and dark intention laid the maiden deep within, the calf within the mouth. | They evermore are near us with their gracious help: successful is the song that strives for victory.

Hymn 10:54. Indra.

1. I sing thy fame that, Maghavan, through thy Greatness the heavens and earth invoked thee in their terror, | Thou, aiding Gods, didst quell the power of Dāsas, what time thou holpest many a race, O Indra. ‖ 2. When thou wast roaming, waxen strong in body, telling thy might, Indra, among the people, | All that men called thy battles was illusion: no foe hast thou today, nor erst hast found one. ‖ 3. Who are the Ṛishis, then, who comprehended before our time the bounds of all thy greatness? | For from thy body thou hast generated at the same time the Mother and the Father. ‖ 4. Thou, Mighty Steer, hast four supremest natures, Asura natures that may ne'er be injured. | All these, O Maghavan, thou surely knowest, wherewith thou hast performed thy great achievements. ‖ 5. Thou hast all treasures in thy sole possession, treasures made manifest and treasures hidden. | Defer not thou, O Maghavan, my longing: thou, art Director, Indra, thou art Giver. ‖ 6. To him who set the light in things of splendour, and with all sweetness blent essential sweetness, | To Indra hath this welcome hymn that strengthens been uttered by the votary Bṛihaduktha.

Hymn 10:55. Indra.

1. Far is that secret name by which, in terror, the worlds invoked thee and thou gavest vigour | The earth and heaven thou settest near each other, and Maghavan, madest bright thy Brother's Children. ‖ 2. Great is that secret name and far-extending, whereby thou madest all that is and shall be. | The Five Tribes whom he loveth well have entered the light he loveth that was made aforetime. ‖ 3. He filled the heaven and earth and all between them, Gods five times sevenfold in their proper seasons. | With four-and-thirty lights he looks around him, lights of one colour though their ways are divers. ‖ 4. As first among the lights, O Dawn, thou shonest, whereby thou broughtest forth the Stay of Increase, | Great art thou, matchless is thine Asura nature, who, high above, art kin to those beneath thee. ‖ 5. The old hath waked the young Moon from his slumber who runs his circling course with many round him. | Behold the Gods' high wisdom in its greatness: he who died yesterday today is living. ‖ 6. Strong is the Red Bird in his strength, great Hero, who from of old hath had no nest to dwell in. | That which he knows is truth and never idle: he wins and gives the wealth desired of many. ‖ 7. Through these the Thunderer gained strong manly vigour, through whom he waxed in power to smite down Vṛitra,— | Who through the might of Indra's operation came forth as Gods in course of Law and Order. ‖ 8. All-strong, performing works with his companion, All-marking, rapid Victor, Curse-averter, | The Hero, waxing, after draughts of Soma, blew far from heaven the Dasyus with his weapon.

Hymn 10:56. Viśvedevas.

1. Here is one light for thee, another yonder: enter the third and he therewith united. | Uniting with a body be thou welcome, dear to the Gods in their sublimest birthplace. ‖ 2. Bearing thy body, Vājin, may thy body afford us blessing and thyself protection. | Unswerving, establish as it were in heaven thine own light as the mighty God's supporter. ‖ 3. Strong Steed art thou: go to the yearning Maidens with vigour, happily go to heaven and praises: | Fly happily to the Gods with easy passage, according to the first and faithful statutes. ‖ 4. Part of their grandeur have the Fathers also gained: the Gods have seated mental power in them as Gods. | They have embraced within themselves all energies, which, issuing forth, again into their bodies pass. ‖ 5. They strode through all the region with victorious might, establishing the old immeasurable laws. | They compassed in their bodies all existing things, and streamed forth offspring in many successive forms. ‖ 6. In two ways have the sons established in his place the Asura who finds the light, by the third act, | As fathers, they have set their heritage on earth, their offspring, as a thread continuously spun out. ‖ 7. As in a ship through billows, so through regions of air, with blessings, through toils and troubles | Hath Bṛihaduktha brought his seed with glory, and placed it here and in the realms beyond us.

Hymn 10:57. Viśvedevas.

1. Let us not, Indra, leave the path, the Soma-presser's sacrifice: | Let no malignity dwell with us. ‖ 2. May we obtain, completely wrought, the thread spun out to reach the Gods, | That perfecteth the sacrifice. ‖ 3. We call the spirit hither with the Soma of our parted sires, | Yea, with the Fathers' holy hymns. ‖ 4. Thy spirit come to thee again for wisdom, energy, and life, | That thou mayst long behold the sun! ‖ 5. O Fathers, may the Heavenly Folk give us our spirit once again, | That we may be with those who live. ‖ 6. O Soma with the spirit still within us, blest with progeny, | May we be busied in the law.

Hymn 10:58. Mānas or Spirit.

1. Thy spirit, that went far away to Yama to Vivasvat's Son, | We cause to

come to thee again that thou mayst live and sojourn here. || 2. Thy spirit, that went far away, that passed away to earth and heaven, | We cause to come to thee again that thou mayst live and sojourn here. || 3. Thy spirit, that went far away, away to the four-cornered earth, | We cause to come to thee again that thou mayst live and sojourn here. || 4. Thy spirit, that went far away to the four quarters of the world, | We cause to come to thee again that thou mayst live and sojourn here. || 5. Thy spirit, that went far away, away unto the billowy sea, | We cause to come to thee again that thou mayst live and sojourn here. || 6. Thy spirit, that went far away to beams of light that flash and flow, | We cause to come to thee again that thou mayst live and sojourn here. || 7. Thy spirit, that went far away, went to the waters and the plants, | We cause to come to thee again that thou mayst live and sojourn here. || 8. Thy spirit, that went far away, that visited the Sun and Dawn. | We cause to come to thee again that thou mayst live and sojourn here. || 9. Thy spirit, that went far away, away to lofty mountain heights, | We cause to come to thee again that thou mayst live and sojourn here. || 10. Thy spirit, that went far away into this All, that lives and moves, | We cause to come to thee again that thou mayst live and sojourn here. || 11. Thy spirit, that went far away to distant realms beyond our ken, | We cause to come to thee again that thou mayst live and sojourn here. || 12. Thy spirit, that went far away to all that is and is to be, | We cause to come to thee again that thou mayst live and sojourn here.

Hymn 10:59. Nirṛiti and Others.

1. His life hath been renewed and carried forward as two men, car-borne, by the skilful driver. | One falls, then seeks the goal with quickened vigour. Let Nirṛiti depart to distant places. || 2. Here is the psalm for wealth, and food, in plenty: let us do many deeds to bring us glory. | All these our doings shall delight the singer. Let Nirṛiti depart to distant places. || 3. May we o'ercome our foes with acts of valour, as heaven is over earth, hills over lowlands. | All these our deeds the singer hath considered. Let Nirṛiti depart to distant places. || 4. Give us not up as prey to death, O Soma still let us look upon the Sun arising. | Let our old age with passing days be kindly. Let Nirṛiti depart to distant places. || 5. O Asunīti, keep the soul within us, and make the days we have to live yet longer. | Grant that we still may look upon the sunlight: strengthen thy body with the oil we bring thee. || 6. Give us our sight again, O Asunīti, give us again our breath and our enjoyment. | Long may we look upon the Sun uprising; O Anumati, favour thou and bless us. || 7. May Earth restore to us our vital spirit, may Heaven the Goddess and mid-air restore it. | May Soma give us once again our body, and Pūshan show the Path of peace and comfort. || 8. May both Worlds bless Subandhu, young Mothers of everlasting Law. | May Heaven and Earth uproot and sweep iniquity and shame away: nor sin nor sorrow trouble thee. || 9. Health-giving medicines descend sent down from heaven in twos and threes, | Or wandering singly on the earth. May Heaven and Earth uproot and sweep iniquity and shame away: nor sin nor sorrow trouble thee. || 10. Drive forward thou the wagon-ox, O Indra, which brought Uśīnarāṇī's wagon hither. | May Heaven and Earth uproot and sweep iniquity and shame away: nor sin nor sorrow trouble thee.

Hymn 10:60. Asamāti and Others.

1. Bringing our homage we have come to one magnificent in look. | Glorified of the mighty Gods || 2. To Asamāti, spring of gifts, lord of the brave, a radiant car, | The conqueror of Bhajeratha || 3. Who, when the spear hath armed his hand, or even weaponless o'erthrows | Men strong as buffaloes in fight; || 4. Him in whose service flourishes Ikṣhvāku, rich and dazzling-bright. | As the Five Tribes that are in heaven. || 5. Indra, support the princely power of Rathaproṣhṭhas matched by none, | Even as the Sun for all to see. || 6. Thou for Agastya's sister's sons yokest thy pair of ruddy steeds. | Thou troddest niggards under foot, all those, O King, who brought no gifts. || 7. This is the mother, this the sire, this one hath come to be thy life. | What brings thee forth is even this. Now come, Subandhu, get thee forth. || 8. As with the leather thong they bind the chariot yoke to hold it fast, | So have I held thy spirit fast, held it for life and not for death, held it for thy security. || 9. Even as this earth, the mighty earth, holds fast the monarchs of the wood. | So have I held thy spirit fast, held it for life and not for death, held it for thy security. || 10. Subandhu's spirit I have brought from Yama, from Vivasvat's Son, | Brought it for life and not for death, yea, brought it for security. || 11. The wind blows downward from on

high, downward the Sun-God sends his heat, | Downward the milch-cow pours her milk: so downward go thy pain and grief. || 12. Felicitous is this mine hand, yet more felicitous is this. | This hand contains all healing balms, and this makes whole with gentle touch.

Hymn 10:61. Viśvedevas.

1. The welcome speaker in the storm of battle uttered with might this prayer to win the Aśvins, | When the most liberal God, for Paktha, rescued his parents, and assailed the seven Hotras. || 2. Chyavāna, purposing deceptive presents, with all ingredients, made the altar ready. | Most sweet-voiced Tūrvayāṇa poured oblations like floods of widely fertilizing water. || 3. To his oblations, swift as thought, ye hurried, and welcomed eagerly the prayers he offered. | With arrows in his hand the Very Mighty forced from him all obedience of a servant. || 4. I call on you the Sons of Dyaus, the Aśvins, that a dark cow to my red kine be added. | Enjoy my sacrifice, come to my viands contented, not deceiving expectation. || 5. Membrum suum virile, quod vrotentum fuerat, mas ille retraxit. Rursus illud quod in juvenem filiam sublatum fuerat, non aggressurus, ad se rerahit. || 6. Quum jam in medio connessu, semiperfecto opere, amorem in puellam pater impleverat, ambo discedentes seminis paulum in terrae superficiem sacrorum sede effusum emiserunt. || 7. Quum pater suam nilam adiverat, cum ed congressus suum semen supra wrrarn effudit. Tum Dii benigni precem (brahma) prgeduerunt, et Vastoshpatim, legum sacrarum custodem, formaverunt. || 8. Ille tauro similis spumam in certamine jactavit, tunc discedens pusillaximis huc profectus est. Quasi dextro pede claudus processit, 'inutiles fuerunt illi mei complexus,' ita locutus. || 9. 'The fire, burning the people, does not approach quickly (by day): the naked (Rakashas approach) not Agni by night; the giver of fuel, and the giver of food, he, the upholder (of the rite), is born, overcoming enemies by his might.' || 10. Uttering praise to suit the rite Navagvas came speedily to win the damsel's friendship. | They who approached the twice-strong stable's keeper, meedless would milk the rocks that naught had shaken. || 11. Swift was new friendship with the maid they quickly accepted it as genuine seed and bounty. | Milk which the cow Sabardughā had yielded was the bright heritage which to thee they offered. || 12. When afterwards they woke— and missed the cattle, the speaker thus in joyful mood addressed them: | Matchless are singers through the Vasu's nature; he bringeth them all food and all possessions. || 13. His followers then who dwelt in sundry places came and desired too slay the son of Nṛishad. | Resistless foe, be found the hidden treasure of Śuṣhṇa multiplied in numerous offspring. || 14. Thou, called Effulgence, in whose threefold dwelling, as in the light of heaven, the Gods are sitting, | Thou who art called Agni or Jātavedas, Priest, hear us, guileless Priest of holy worship. || 15. And, Indra, bring, that I may laud and serve them, those Two resplendent glorious Nāsatyas, | Blithe, bounteous, man-like, to the sacrificer, honoured among our men with offered viands. || 16. This King is praised and honoured as Ordainer: himself the bridge, the Sage speeds o'er the waters. | He hath stirred up Kakṣhīvant, stirred up Agni, as the steed's swift wheel drives the felly onward. || 17. Vaitaraṇa, doubly kinsman, sacrificer, shall milk the cow who ne'er hath calved, Sabardhu, | When I encompass Varuṇa and Mitra with lauds, and Aryaman in safest shelter. || 18. Their kin, the Prince in heaven, thy nearest kinsman, turning his thought to thee thus speaks in kindness: | This is our highest bond: I am his offspring. How many others came ere I succeeded? || 19. Here is my kinship, here the place I dwell in: these are my Gods; I in full strength am present. | Twice-born am I, the first-born Son of Order: the Cow milked this when first she had her being. || 20. So mid these tribes he rests, the friendly envoy, borne on two paths, refulgent Lord of fuel. | When, like a line, the Babe springs up erectly, his Mother straight hath borne him strong to bless us. || 21. Then went the milch-kine forth to please the damsel, and for the good of every man that liveth. | Hear us, O wealthy Lord; begin our worship. Thou hast grown mighty through Āśvaghna's virtues. || 22. And take thou notice of us also, Indra, for ample riches, King whose arm wields thunder! | Protect our wealthy nobles, guard our princes unmenaced near thee, Lord of Tawny Coursers. || 23. When he goes forth, ye Pair of Kings, for booty, speeding to war and praise to please the singer,— | I was the dearest sage of those about him,—let him lead these away and bring them safely. || 24. Now for this noble man's support and comfort, singing with easy voice we thus implore thee: | Impetuous be

his son and fleet his courser: and may I be his priest to win him glory. ‖ 25. If, for our strength, the priest with adoration to win your friendship made the laud accepted, | That laud shall be a branching road to virtue for every one to whom the songs are suited. ‖ 26. Glorified thus, with holy hymns and homage: Of noble race, with Waters, God-attended | May he enrich us for our prayers and praises: now can the cow be milked; the path is open. ‖ 27. Be to us, then, ye Gods who merit worship, be ye of one accord our strong protection, | Who went on various ways and brought us vigour, ye who are undeceivable explorers.

Hymn 10:62. Viśvedevas, etc.

1. Ye, who, adorned with guerdon through the sacrifice, have won you Indra's friendship and eternal life, | Even to you be happiness, Aṅgirasas. Welcome the son of Manu, ye who are most wise. ‖ 2. The Fathers, who drave forth the wealth in cattle, have in the year's courses cleft Vala by Eternal Law: | A lengthened life be yours, O ye Aṅgirasas. Welcome the son of Manu, ye who are most wise. ‖ 3. Ye raised the Sun to heaven by everlasting Law, and spread broad earth, the Mother, out on every side. | Fair wealth of progeny be yours, Aṅgirasas. Welcome the son of Manu, ye who are most wise. ‖ 4. This kinsman in your dwelling-place speaks pleasant words: give car to this, ye Ṛishis, children of the Gods. | High Brahman dignity be yours, Aṅgirasas. Welcome the son of Manu, ye who are most wise. ‖ 5. Distinguished by their varied form, these Ṛishis have been deeply moved. | These are the sons of Aṅgirasas: from Agni have they sprung to life. ‖ 6. Distinguished by their varied form, they sprang from Agni, from the sky. | Navagva and Daśagva, noblest Aṅgiras, he giveth bounty with the Gods. ‖ 7. With Indra for associate the priests have cleared the stable full of steeds and kine, | Giving to me a thousand with their eight marked cars, they gained renown among the Gods. ‖ 8. May this man's sons be multiplied; like springing corn may Manu grow, | Who gives at once in bounteous gift a thousand kine, a hundred steeds. ‖ 9. No one attains to him, as though a man would grasp the heights of heaven. | Sāvarṇya's sacrificial meed hath broadened like an ample flood. ‖ 10. Yadu and Turva, too, have given two Dāsas, well-disposed, to serve, | Together with great store of kine. ‖ 11. Blest be the hamlet's chief, most liberal Manu, and may his bounty rival that of Sūrya. | May the God let Sāvarṇi's life be lengthened, with whom, unwearied, we have lived and prospered.

Hymn 10:63. Viśvedevas.

1. May they who would assume kinship from far away, Vivasvat's generations, dearly loved of men, | Even the Gods who sit upon the sacred grass of Nahusha's son Yayāti, bless and comfort us. ‖ 2. For worthy of obeisance, Gods, are all your names, worthy of adoration and of sacrifice. | Ye who were born from waters, and from Aditi, and from the earth, do ye here listen to my call. ‖ 3. I will rejoice in these Ādityas for my weal, for whom the Mother pours forth water rich in balm, | And Dyaus the Infinite, firm as a rock, sweet milk,—Gods active, strong through lauds, whose might the Bull upholds. ‖ 4. Looking on men, ne'er slumbering, they by their deserts attained as Gods to lofty immortality. | Borne on refulgent cars, sinless, with serpents' powers, they robe them, for our welfare, in the height of heaven. ‖ 5. Great Kings who bless us, who have come to sacrifice, who, ne'er assailed, have set their mansion in the sky,— | These I invite with adoration and with hymns, mighty Ādityas, Aditi, for happiness. ‖ 6. Who offereth to you the laud that ye accept, O ye All-Gods of Manu, many as ye are? | Who, Mighty Ones, will prepare for you the sacrifice to bear us over trouble to felicity? ‖ 7. Ye to whom Manu, by seven priests, with kindled fire, offered the first oblation with his heart and soul, | Vouchsafe us, ye Ādityas, shelter free from fear, and make us good and easy paths to happiness. ‖ 8. Wise Deities, who have dominion o'er the world, ye thinkers over all that moves not and that moves, | Save us from uncommitted and committed sin, preserve us from all sin today for happiness. ‖ 9. In battles we invoke Indra still swift to hear, and all the holy Host of Heaven who banish grief, | Agni, Mitra, and Varuṇa that we may gain, Dyaus, Bhaga, Marutas, Pṛithivī for happiness: ‖ 10. Mightily-saving Earth, incomparable Heaven the good guide Aditi who gives secure defence | The well-oared heavenly Ship that lets no waters in, free from defect, will we ascend for happiness. ‖ 11. Bless us, all Holy Ones, that we may have your help, guard and protect us from malignant injury. | With fruitful invocation may we call on you, Gods, who give ear to us for grace, for happiness. ‖ 12. Keep all disease afar and sordid sacrifice, keep off the wicked man's malicious enmity. | Keep far away from us all hatred, O ye Gods, and give us ample shelter for our happiness. ‖ 13. Untouched by any evil, every mortal thrives, and, following the Law, spreads in his progeny. | Whom ye with your good guidance, O Ādityas, lead safely through all his pain and grief to happiness. ‖ 14. That which ye guard and grace in battle, O ye Gods, ye Marutas, where the prize is wealth, where heroes win, | That conquering Car, O Indra, that sets forth at dawn, that never breaks, may we ascend for happiness. ‖ 15. Vouchsafe us blessing in our paths and desert tracts, blessing in waters and in battle, for the light; | Blessing upon the wombs that bring male children forth, and blessing, O ye Marutas, for the gain of wealth. ‖ 16. The noblest Svasti with abundant riches, who comes to what is good by distant pathway,— | May she at home and far away preserve us, and dwell with us under the Gods' protection ‖ 17. Thus hath the thoughtful sage, the son of Plati, praised you, O Aditi and all Ādityas, | Men are made rich by those who are Immortal: the Heavenly Folk have been extolled by Gaya.

Hymn 10:64. Viśvedevas.

1. What God, of those who hear, is he whose well-praised name we may record in this our sacrifice; and how? | Who will be gracious? Who of many give us bliss? Who out of all the Host will come to lend us aid? ‖ 2. The will and thoughts within my breast exert their power: they yearn with love, and fly to all the regions round. | None other comforter is found save only these: my longings and my hopes are fixt upon the Gods. ‖ 3. To Narāśaṃsa and to Pūṣhan I sing forth, unconcealable Agni kindled by the Gods. | To Sun and Moon, two Moons, to Yama in the heaven, to Trita, Vāta, Dawn, Night, and the Aśvins Twain. ‖ 4. How is the Sage extolled whom the loud singers praise? What voice, what hymn is used to laud Bṛihaspati? | May Aja-Ekapāda with Ṛikvans swift to hear, and Ahi of the Deep listen unto our call. ‖ 5. Aditi, to the birth of Dakṣha and the vow thou summonest the Kings Mitra and Varuṇa. | With course unchecked, with many chariots Aryaman comes with the seven priests to tribes of varied sort. ‖ 6. May all those vigorous Coursers listen to our cry, hearers of invocation, speeding on their way; | Winners of thousands where the priestly meed is won, who gather of themselves great wealth in every race. ‖ 7. Bring ye Purandhi, bring Vāyu who yokes his steeds, for friendship bring ye Pūṣhan with your songs of praise: | They with one mind, one thought attend the sacrifice, urged by the favouring aid of Savitar the God. ‖ 8. The thrice-seven wandering Rivers, yea, the mighty floods, the forest trees, the mountains, Agni to our aid, | Kṛiśānu, Tiṣhya, archers to our gathering-place, and Rudra strong amid the Rudras we invoke. ‖ 9. Let the great Streams come hither with their mighty help, Sindhu, Sarasvatī, and Sarayu with waves. | Ye Goddess Floods, ye Mothers, animating all, promise us water rich in fatness and in balm. ‖ 10. And let Bṛihaddiva, the Mother, hear our call, and Tvaṣhṭar, Father, with the Goddesses and Dames. | Ṛibhukṣhan, Vāja, Bhaga, and Rathaspati, and the sweet speech of him who labours guard us well! ‖ 11. Pleasant to look on as a dwelling rich in food is the blest favour of the Marutas, Rudra's Sons. | May we be famed among the folk for wealth in kine. and ever come to you, ye Gods, with sacred food. ‖ 12. The thought which ye, O Marutas, Indra and ye Gods have given to me, and ye, Mitra and Varuṇa,— | Cause this to grow and swell like a milch-cow with milk. Will ye not bear away my songs upon your car? ‖ 13. O Marutas, do ye never, never recollect and call again to mind this our relationship? | When next we meet together at the central point, even there shall Aditi confirm our brotherhood. ‖ 14. The Mothers, Heaven and Earth, those mighty Goddesses, worthy of sacrifice, come with the race of Gods. | These Two with their support uphold both Gods and men, and with the Fathers pour the copious genial stream. ‖ 15. This invocation wins all good that we desire Bṛihaspati, highly-praised Aramati, are here, | Even where the stone that presses meath rings loudly out, and where the sages make their voices heard with hymns. ‖ 16. Thus hath the sage, skilled in loud singers' duties, desiring riches, yearning after treasure, | Gaya, the priestly singer, with his praises and hymns contented the Celestial people. ‖ 17. Thus hath the thoughtful sage the son of Plati, praised you, O Aditi and all Ādityas. | Men are made rich by those who are Immortal: the Heavenly Folk have been extolled by Gaya.

Hymn 10:65. Viśvedevas.

1. May Agni, Indra, Mitra, Varuṇa consent, Aryaman, Vāyu, Pūṣhan, and Sarasvatī, | Ādityas, Maruts, Viṣhṇu, Soma, lofty Sky, Rudra and Aditi, and Brahmaṇaspati. || 2. Indra and Agni, Hero-lords when Vṛitra fell, dwelling together, speeding emulously on, | And Soma blent with oil, putting his greatness forth, have with their power filled full the mighty firmament. || 3. Skilled in the Law I lift the hymn of praise to these, Law-strengtheners, unassailed, and great in majesty. | These in their wondrous bounty send the watery sea: may they as kindly Friends send gifts to make us great. || 4. They with their might have stayed Heaven, Earth, and Pṛithivī, the Lord of Light, the firmament, -the lustrous spheres. | Even as fleet-foot steeds who make their masters glad, the princely Gods are praised, most bountiful to man. || 5. Bring gifts to Mitra and to Varuṇa who, Lords of all, in spirit never fail the worshipper, | Whose statute shines on high through everlasting Law, whose places of sure refuge are the heavens and earth. || 6. The cow who yielding milk goes her appointed way hither to us as leader of holy rites, | Speaking aloud to Varuṇa and the worshipper, shall with oblation serve Vivasvat and the Gods. || 7. The Gods whose tongue is Agni dwell in heaven, and sit, aiders of Law, reflecting, in the seat of Law. | They propped up heaven and then brought waters with their might, got sacrifice and in a body made it fair. || 8. Born in the oldest time, the Parents dwelling round are sharers of one mansion in the home of Law. | Bound by their common vow Dyaus, Pṛithivī stream forth the moisture rich in oil to Varuṇa the Steer. || 9. Parjanya, Vāta, mighty, senders of the rain, Indra and Vāyu, Varuṇa, Mitra, Aryaman: | We call on Aditi, Ādityas, and the Gods, those who are on the earth, in waters, and in heaven. || 10. Tvaṣhṭar and Vāyu, those who count as Ṛibhus, both celestial Hotar-priests, and Dawn for happiness, | Winners of wealth, we call, and wise Bṛihaspati, destroyer of our foes, and Soma Indra's Friend. || 11. They generated prayer, the cow, the horse, the plants, the forest trees, the earth, the waters, and the hills. | These very bounteous Gods made the Sun mount to heaven, and spread the righteous laws of Āryas o'er the land. || 12. O Aśvins, ye delivered Bhujyu from distress, ye animated Śyāva, Vadhrimatī's son. | To Vimada ye brought his consort Kamadyū, and gave his lost Viṣhṇāpū back to Viśvaka. || 13. Thunder, the lightning's daughter, Aja-Ekapāda, heaven's bearer, Sindhu, and the waters of the sea: | Hear all the Gods my words, Sarasvatī give ear together with Purandhi and with Holy Thoughts. || 14. With Holy Thoughts and with Purandhi may all Gods, knowing the Law immortal, Manu's Holy Ones, | Boon-givers, favourers, finders of light, and Heaven, with gracious love accept my songs, my prayer, my hymn. || 15. Immortal Gods have I, Vasiṣhṭha, lauded, Gods set on high above all other beings. | May they this day grant us wide space and freedom: ye Gods, preserve us evermore with blessings.

Hymn 10:66. Viśvedevas.

1. I call the Gods of lofty glory for our weal, the makers of the light, well-skilled in sacrifice; | Those who have waxen mightily, Masters of all wealth, Immortal, strengthening Law, the Gods whom Indra leads. || 2. For the strong band of Marutas will we frame a hymn: the chiefs shall bring forth sacrifice for Indra's troop, | Who, sent by Indra and advised by Varuṇa, have gotten for themselves a share of Sūrya's light || 3. May Indra with the Vasus keep our dwelling safe, and Aditi with Ādityas lend us sure defence. | May the God Rudra with the Rudras favour us, and Tvaṣhṭar with the Dames further us to success. || 4. Aditi, Heaven and Earth, the great eternal Law, Indra, Viṣhṇu, the Marutas, and the lofty Sky. | We call upon Ādityas, on the Gods, for help, on Vasus, Rudras, Savitar of wondrous deeds. || 5. With Holy Thoughts Sarasvat, firm-lawed Varuṇa, great Vāyu, Pūṣhan, Viṣhṇu, and the Aśvins Twain, | Lords of all wealth, Immortal, furtherers of prayer, grant us a triply-guarding refuge from distress. || 6. Strong be the sacrifice, strong be the Holy Ones, strong the preparers of oblation, strong the Gods. | Mighty be Heaven and Earth, true to eternal Law, strong be Parjanya, strong be they who laud the Strong. || 7. To win us strength I glorify the Mighty Twain, Agni and Soma, Mighty Ones whom many laud. | May these vouchsafe us shelter with a triple guard, these whom the strong have served in worship of the Gods. || 8. Potent, with firm-fixt laws, arranging sacrifice, visiting solemn rites in splendour of the day, | Obeying Order, these whose priest is Agni, free from falsehood, poured the waters out when Vṛitra died. || 9. The Holy Ones engendered,

for their several laws, the heavens and earth, the waters, and the plants and trees. | They filled the firmament with heavenly light for help: the Gods embodied Wish and made it beautiful. || 10. May they who bear up heaven, the Ṛibhus deft of hand, and Vāta and Parjanya of the thundering Bull, | The waters and the plants, promote the songs we sing: come Bhaga, Rāti, and the Vājins to my call. || 11. Sindhu, the sea, the region, and the firmament, the thunder, and the ocean, Aja-Ekapāda, | The Dragon of the Deep, shall listen to my words, and all the Deities and Princes shall give ear. || 12. May we, be yours, we men, to entertain the Gods: further our sacrifice and give it full success. | Ādityas, Rudras, Vasus, givers of good gifts, quicken the holy hymns which we are singing now || 13. I follow with success upon the path of Law the two celestial Hotars, Priests of oldest time. | We pray to him who dwelleth near, Guard of the Field, to all Immortal Gods who never are remiss. || 14. Vasiṣhṭha's sons have raised their voices, like their sire. Ṛiṣhi-like praying to the Gods for happiness. | Like friendly-minded kinsmen, come at our desire, O Gods, and shake down treasures on us from above. || 15. Immortal Gods have I, Vasiṣhṭha, lauded, Gods set on high above all other beings. | May they this day grant us wide space and freedom: ye Gods, preserve us evermore with blessings.

Hymn 10:67. Bṛihaspati.

1. This holy hymn, sublime and seven-headed, sprung from eternal Law, our sire discovered. | Ayāsya, friend of all men, hath engendered the fourth hymn as he sang his laud to Indra. || 2. Thinking aright, praising eternal Order, the sons of Dyaus the Asura, those heroes, | Aṅgirasas, holding the rank of sages, first honoured sacrifice's holy statute. || 3. Girt by his friends who cried with swanlike voices, bursting the stony barriers of the prison, | Bṛihaspati spake in thunder to the cattle, and uttered praise and song when he had found them. || 4. Apart from one, away from two above him, he drave the kine that stood in bonds of falsehood. | Bṛihaspati, seeking light amid the darkness, drave forth the bright cows: three he made apparent. || 5. When he had cleft the lairs and western castle, he cut off three from him who held the waters. | Bṛihaspati discovered, while he thundered like Dyaus, the dawn, the Sun, the cow, the lightning. || 6. As with a hand, so with his roaring Indra cleft Vala through, the guardian of the cattle. | Seeking the milk-draught with sweat-shining comrades he stole the Paṇi's kine and left him weeping. || 7. He with bright faithful Friends, winners of booty, hath rent the milker of the cows asunder. | Bṛihaspati with wild boars strong and mighty, sweating with heat, hath gained a rich possession. || 8. They, longing for the kine, with faithful spirit incited with their hymns the Lord of cattle. | Bṛihaspati freed the radiant cows with comrades self-yoked, averting shame from one another. || 9. In our assembly with auspicious praises exalting him who roareth like a lion, | May we, in every fight where heroes conquer, rejoice in strong Bṛihaspati the Victor. || 10. When he had won him every sort of booty and gone to heaven and its most lofty mansions, | Men praised Bṛihaspati the Mighty, bringing the light within their mouths from sundry places. || 11. Fulfil the prayer that begs for vital vigour: aid in your wonted manner even the humble. | Let all our foes be turned and driven backward. Hear this, O Heaven and Earth, ye All-producers. || 12. Indra with mighty strength cleft asunder the head of Arbuda the watery monster, | Slain Ahi, and set free the Seven Rivers. O Heaven and Earth, with all the Gods protect us.

Hymn 10:68. Bṛihaspati.

1. Like birds who keep their watch, plashing in water, like the loud voices of the thundering rain-cloud, | Like merry streamlets bursting from the mountain, thus to Bṛihaspati our hymns have sounded. || 2. The Son of Aṅgirasas, meeting the cattle, as Bhaga, brought in Aryaman among us. | As Friend of men he decks the wife and husband: as for the race, Bṛihaspati, nerve our coursers. || 3. Bṛihaspati, having won them from the mountains, strewed down, like barley out of winnowing—baskets, | The vigorous, wandering cows who aid the pious, desired of all, of blameless form, well-coloured. || 4. As the Sun dews with meath the seat of Order, and casts a flaming meteor down from heaven. | So from the rock Bṛihaspati forced the cattle, and cleft the earth's skin as it were with water. || 5. Forth from mid air with light he drave the darkness, as the gale blows a lily from the fiver. | Like the wind grasping at the cloud of Vala, Bṛihaspati gathered to himself the cattle, || 6. Bṛihaspati, when he with fiery lightnings cleft through the weapon of reviling Vala, | Consumed him as

tongues cat what teeth have compassed: he threw the prisons of the red cows open. || 7. That secret name borne by the lowing cattle within the cave Bṛihaspati discovered, | And drave, himself, the bright kine from the mountain, like a bird's young after the egg's disclosure. || 8. He looked around on rock-imprisoned sweetness as one who eyes a fish in scanty water. | Bṛihaspati, cleaving through with varied clamour, brought it forth like a bowl from out the timber. || 9. He found the light of heaven, and fire, and Morning: with lucid rays he forced apart the darkness. | As from a joint, Bṛihaspati took the marrow of Vala as he gloried in his cattle. || 10. As trees for foliage robbed by winter, Vala mourned for the cows Bṛihaspati had taken. | He did a deed ne'er done, ne'er to be equalled, whereby the Sun and Moon ascend alternate. || 11. Like a dark steed adorned with pearl, the Fathers have decorated heaven With constellations. | They set the light in day, in night the darkness. Bṛihaspati cleft the rock and found the cattle. || 12. This homage have we offered to the Cloud God who thunders out to many in succession. | May this Bṛihaspati vouchsafe us fullness of life with kine and horses, men, and heroes.

Hymn 10:69. Agni.

1. Auspicious is the aspect of Vadhryaśva's fire good is its guidance, pleasant are its visitings. | When first the people of Sumitra kindle it, with butter poured thereon it crackles and shines bright. || 2. Butter is that which makes Vadhryaśva's fire grow strong: the butter is its food, the butter makes it fat. | It spreads abroad when butter hath been offered it, and balmed with streams of butter shines forth like the Sun. || 3. Still newest is this face of thine, O Agni, which Manu and Sumitra have enkindled. | So richly shine, accept our songs with favour, so give us strengthening food, so send us glory. || 4. Accept this offering, Agni, whom aforetime Vadhryaśva, hath entreated and enkindled. | Guard well our homes and people, guard our bodies, protect thy girt to us which thou hast granted. || 5. Be splendid, guard us Kinsman of Vadhryaśva: let not the enmity of men o'ercome thee, | Like the bold hero Chyavāna, I Sumitra tell forth the title of Vadhryaśva's Kinsman. || 6. All treasures hast thou won, of plains and mountains, and quelled the Dāsas' and Āryas' hatred. | Like the bold hero Chyavāna, O Agni, mayst thou subdue the men who long for battle. || 7. Deft Agni hath a lengthened thread, tall oxen, a thousand heifers, numberless devices. | Decked by the men, splendid among the splendid, shine brightly forth amid devout Sumitras. || 8. Thine is the teeming cow, O Jātavedas, who pours at once her ceaseless flow, Sabardhuk, | Thou. art lit up by men enriched with guerdon, O Agni, by the pious-souled Sumitras. || 9. Even Immortal Gods, O Jātavedas, Vadhryaśva's Kinsman, have declared thy grandeur. | When human tribes drew near with supplication thou conqueredst with men whom thou hadst strengthened. || 10. Like as a father bears his son, O Agni, Vadhryaśva bare thee in his lap and served thee. | Thou, Youngest God, having enjoyed his fuel, didst vanquish those of old though they were mighty. || 11. Vadhryaśva's Agni evermore hath vanquished his foes with heroes who had pressed the Soma. | Lord of bright rays, thou burntest up the battle, subduing, as our help, e'en mighty foemen. || 12. This Agni of Vadhryaśva, Vṛitra-slayer, lit from of old, must be invoked with homage. | As such assail our enemies, Vadhryaśva, whether the foes be strangers or be kinsmen.

Hymn 10:70. Āprīs.

1. Enjoy, O Agni, this my Fuel, welcome the oil-filled ladle where we pour libation. | Rise up for worship of the Gods, wise Agni, on the earth's height, while days are bright with beauty. || 2. May he who goes before the Gods come hither with steeds whose shapes are varied, Narāśaṃsa. | May he, most Godlike, speed our offered viands with homage God-ward on the path of Order. || 3. Men with oblations laud most constant Agni, and pray him to perform an envoy's duty. | With lightly-rolling car and best draught-horses, bring the Gods hither and sit down as Hotar. || 4. May the delight of Gods spread out transversely: may it be with us long in length and fragrant. | O Holy Grass divine, with friendly spirit bring thou the willing Gods whose Chief is Indra. || 5. Touch ye the far-extending height of heaven or spring apart to suit the wide earth's measure. | Yearning, ye Doors, with those sublime in greatness, seize eagerly the heavenly Car that cometh. || 6. Here in this shrine may Dawn and Night, the Daughters of Heaven, the skilful Goddesses, be seated. | In your wide lap, auspicious, willing Ladies may the Gods seat them with a willing spirit. || 7. Up stands the stone, high burns the fire enkindled: Aditi's lap contains the Friendly Natures | Ye Two Chief Priests who serve at this our worship, may ye, more skilled, win for us rich possessions. || 8. On our wide grass, Three Goddesses be seated: for you have we prepared and made it pleasant. | May Iḷā, she whose foot drops oil, the Goddess, taste, man-like, sacrifice and well-set presents. || 9. Since thou, God Tvaṣhṭar, hast made beauty perfect, since thou hast been the Aṅgirasas' Companion, | Willing, most wealthy, Giver of possessions, grant us the Gods' assembly, thou who knowest. || 10. Well-knowing, binding with thy cord, bring hither, Lord of the Wood, the Deities' assembly. | The God prepare and season our oblations may Heaven and Earth be gracious to my calling. || 11. Agni, bring hither Varuṇa to help us, Indra from heaven, from air's mid-realm the Marutas. | On sacred grass all Holy ones be seated and let the Immortal Gods rejoice in Svāhā.

Hymn 10:71. Jñānam.

1. When men, Bṛihaspati, giving names to objects, sent out Vāk's first and earliest utterances, | All that was excellent and spotless, treasured within them, was disclosed through their affection. || 2. Where, like men cleansing corn-flour in a cribble, the wise in spirit have created language, | Friends see and recognize the marks of friendship: their speech retains the blessed sign imprinted. || 3. With sacrifice the trace of Vāk they followed, and found her harbouring within the Ṛishis. | They brought her, dealt her forth in many places: seven singers make her tones resound in concert. || 4. One man hath ne'er seen Vāk, and yet he seeth: one man hath hearing but hath never heard her. | But to another hath she shown her beauty as a fond well-dressed woman to her husband. || 5. One man they call a laggard, dull in friendship: they never urge him on to deeds of valour. | He wanders on in profitless illusion: the Voice he heard yields neither fruit,nor blossom. || 6. No part in Vāk hath he who hath abandoned his own dear friend who knows the truth of friendship. | Even if he hears her still in vain he listens: naught knows he of the path of righteous action. || 7. Unequal in the quickness of their spirit are friends endowed alike with eyes and hearing. | Some look like tanks that reach the mouth or shoulder, others like pools of water fit to bathe in. || 8. When friendly Brahmans sacrifice together with mental impulse which the heart hath fashioned, | They leave one far behind through their attainments, and some who count as Brahmans wander elsewhere. || 9. Those men who step not back and move not forward, nor Brahmans nor preparers of libations, | Having attained to Vāk in sinful fashion spin out their thread in ignorance like spinsters. || 10. All friends are joyful in the friend who cometh in triumph, having conquered in assembly. | He is their blame-averter, food-provider prepared is he and fit for deed of vigour. || 11. One plies his constant task reciting verses. one sings the holy psalm in Śakvarī measures. | One more, the Brahman, tells the lore of being, and one lays down the rules of sacrificing.

Hymn 10:72. The Gods.

1. Let us with tuneful skill proclaim these generations of the Gods, | That one may see them when these hymns are chanted in a future age. || 2. These Brahmaṇaspati produced with blast and smelting, like a Smith, | Existence, in an earlier age of Gods, from Non-existence sprang. || 3. Existence, in the earliest age of Gods, from Non-existence sprang. | Thereafter were the regions born. This sprang from the Productive Power. || 4. Earth sprang from the Productive Power the regions from the earth were born. | Dakṣha was born of Aditi, and Aditi was Dakṣha's Child. || 5. For Aditi, O Dakṣha, she who is thy Daughter, was brought forth. | After her were the blessed Gods born sharers of immortal life. || 6. When ye, O Gods, in yonder deep close-clasping one another stood, | Thence, as of dancers, from your feet a thickening cloud of dust arose. || 7. When, O ye Gods, like Yatis, ye caused all existing things to grow, | Then ye brought Sūrya forward who was lying hidden in the sea. || 8. Eight are the Sons of Aditi who from her body sprang to life. | With seven she went to meet the Gods she cast Mārtāṇḍa far away. || 9. So with her Seven Sons Aditi went forth to meet the earlier age. | She brought Mārtāṇḍa thitherward to spring to life and die again.

Hymn 10:73. Indra.

1. Thou wast born mighty for victorious valour, exulting, strongest, full of pride and courage. | There, even there, the Marutas strengthened Indra when. his most rapid Mother stirred the Hero. || 2. There with fiend's ways e'en Pṛiśni was seated: with much laudation they exalted Indra. | As if encompassed by the Mighty-footed, from darkness, near at hand, forth

came the Children. ‖ 3. High are thy feet when on thy way thou goest: the strength thou foundest here hath lent thee vigour. | Thousand hyenas in thy mouth thou holdest. O Indra, mayst thou turn the Aśvins hither. ‖ 4. Speeding at once to sacrifice thou comest for friendship thou art bringing both Nāsatyas. | Thou hadst a thousand treasures in possession. The Aśvins, O thou Hero, gave thee riches. ‖ 5. Glad, for the race that rests on holy Order, with friends who hasten to their goal, hath Indra | With these his magic powers assailed the Dasyu: he cast away the gloomy mists, the darkness. ‖ 6. Two of like name for him didst thou demolish, as Indra striking down the car of Ushas. | With thy beloved lofty Friends thou camest, and with the assurance of thine heart thou slewest. ‖ 7. War-loving Namuchi thou smotest, robbing the Dāsa of his magic for the Rishi. | For man thou madest ready pleasant pathways, paths leading as it were directly God-ward. ‖ 8. These names of thine thou hast fulfilled completely: as Lord, thou boldest in thine arm, O Indra. | In thee, through thy great might, the Gods are joyful: the roots of trees hast thou directed upward. ‖ 9. May the sweet Soma juices make him happy to cast his quoit that lies in depth of waters. | Thou from the udder which o'er earth is fastened hast poured the milk into the kine and herbage. ‖ 10. When others call him offspring of the Courser, my meaning is that Mighty Power produced him. | He came from Manyu and remained in houses: whence he hath sprung is known to Indra only. ‖ 11. Like birds of beauteous wing the Priyamedhas, Rishis, imploring, have come nigh to Indra: | Dispel the darkness and fill full our vision deliver us as men whom snares entangle.

Hymn 10:74. Indra.

1. I am prepared to laud with song or worship the Noble Ones who are in earth and heaven, | Or Coursers who have triumphed in, the contest, or those who famed, have won the prize with glory. ‖ 2. Their call, the call of Gods, went up to heaven: they kissed the ground with glory-seeking spirit, | There where the Gods look on for happy fortune, and like the kindly heavens bestow their bounties. ‖ 3. This is the song of those Immortal Beings who long for treasures in their full perfection. | May these, completing prayers and sacrifices, bestow upon us wealth where naught is wanting. ‖ 4. Those living men extolled thy deed, O Indra, those who would fain burst through the stall of cattle, | Fain to milk her who bare but once, great, lofty, whose Sons are many and her streams past number. ‖ 5. Śachīvan, win to your assistance Indra who never bends, who overcomes his foemen. | Ribhukshan, Maghavan, the hymn's upholder, who, rich in food, bears man's kind friend, the thunder. ‖ 6. Since he who won of old anew hath triumphed, Indra hath earned his name of Vritra-slayer. | He hath appeared, the mighty Lord of Conquest. What we would have him do let him accomplish.

Hymn 10:75. The Rivers.

1. The singer, O ye Waters in Vivasvat's place, shall tell your grandeur forth that is beyond compare. | The Rivers have come forward triply, seven and seven. Sindhu in might surpasses all the streams that flow. ‖ 2. Varuṇa cut the channels for thy forward course, O Sindhu, when thou rannest on to win the race. | Thou speedest o'er precipitous ridges of the earth, when thou art Lord and Leader of these moving floods. ‖ 3. His roar is lifted up to heaven above the earth: he puts forth endless vigour with a flash of light. | Like floods of rain that fall—in thunder from the cloud, so Sindhu rushes on bellowing like a bull. ‖ 4. Like mothers to their calves, like milch kine with their milk, so, Sindhu, unto thee the roaring rivers run. | Thou leadest as a warrior king thine army's wings what time thou comest in the van of these swift streams. ‖ 5. Favour ye this my laud, O Gaṅgā, Yamunā, O Śutudrī, Parushṇī and Sarasvatī: | With Asiknī, Vitastā, O Marudvṛidha, O Ārjīkīya with Sushoma hear my call. ‖ 6. First with Trishṭāmā thou art eager to flow forth, with Rasā, and Susartu, and with Śvetyā here, | With Kubhā; and with these, Sindhu and Mehatnu, thou seekest in thy course Krumu and Gomatī. ‖ 7. Flashing and whitely-gleaming in her mightiness, she moves along her ample volumes through the realms, | Most active of the active, Sindhu unrestrained, like to a dappled mare, beautiful, fair to see. ‖ 8. Rich in good steeds is Sindhu, rich in cars and robes, rich in gold, nobly-fashioned, rich in ample wealth. | Blest Sīlamāvatī and young Ūrṇāvatī invest themselves with raiment rich in store of sweets. ‖ 9. Sindhu hath yoked her car, light-rolling, drawn by steeds, and with that car shall she win booty in this fight. | So have I praised its power, mighty and unrestrained, of independent glory, roaring as it runs.

Hymn 10:76. Press-stones.

1. I grasp at you when power and strength begin to dawn: bedew ye, Indra and the Marutas, Heaven and Earth, | That Day and Night, in every hall of sacrifice, may wait on us and bless us when they first spring forth. ‖ 2. Press the libation out, most excellent of all: the Pressing-stone is grasped like a hand-guided steed. | So let it win the valour that subdues the foe, and the fleet courser's might that speeds to ample wealth. ‖ 3. Juice that this Stone pours out removes defect of ours, as in old time it brought prosperity to man. | At sacrifices they established holy rites on Tvashṭar's milk-blent juice bright with the hue of steeds. ‖ 4. Drive ye the treacherous demons far away from us: keep Nirṛiti afar and banish Penury. | Pour riches forth for us with troops of hero sons, and bear ye up, O Stones, the song that visits Gods. ‖ 5. To you who are more mighty than the heavens themselves, who, finishing your task with more than Vibhvan's speed, | More rapidly than Vāyu seize the Soma juice, better than Agni give us food, to you I sing. ‖ 6. Stirred be the glorious Stones: let it press out the juice, the Stone with heavenly song that reaches up to heaven, | There where the men draw forth the meath for which they long, sending their voice around in rivalry of speed. ‖ 7. The Stones press out the Soma, swift as car-borne men, and, eager for the spoil, drain forth the sap thereof | To fill the beaker, they exhaust the udder's store, as the men purify oblations with their lips. ‖ 8. Ye, present men, have been most skilful in your work, even ye, O Stones who pressed Soma for Indra's drink. | May all ye have of fair go to the Heavenly Race, and all your treasure to the earthly worshipper.

Hymn 10:77. Marutas.

1. As with their voice from cloud they sprinkle treasure so are the wise man's liberal sacrifices. | I praise their Company that merits worship as the good Marutas' priest to pay them honour. ‖ 2. The youths have wrought their ornaments for glory through many nights,—this noble band of Marutas. | Like stags the Sons of Dyaus have striven onward, the Sons of Aditi grown strong like pillars. ‖ 3. They who extend beyond the earth and heaven, by their own mass, as from the cloud spreads Sūrya; | Like mighty Heroes covetous of glory, like heavenly gallants who destroy the wicked. ‖ 4. When ye come nigh, as in the depth of waters, the earth is loosened, as it were, and shaken. | This your self-feeding sacrifice approaches: come all united, fraught, as 'twere with viands. ‖ 5. Ye are like horses fastened to the chariot poles, luminous with your beams, with splendour as at dawn; | Like self-bright falcons, punishers of wicked men, like hovering birds urged forward, scattering rain around. ‖ 6. When ye come forth, O Marutas, from the distance, from the great treasury of rich possessions, | Knowing, O Vasus, boons that should be granted, even from afar drive back the men who hate us. ‖ 7. He who, engaged in the rite's final duty brings, as a man, oblation to the Marutas, | Wins him life's wealthy fullness, blest with heroes: he shall be present, too, where Gods drink Soma. ‖ 8. For these are helps adored at sacrifices, bringing good fortune by their name Ādityas. | Speeding on cars let them protect our praises, delighting in our sacrifice and worship.

Hymn 10:78. Marutas.

1. Ye by your hymns are like high-thoughted singers, skilful, inviting Gods with sacrifices; | Fair to behold, like Kings, with bright adornment, like spotless gallants, leaders of the people: ‖ 2. Like fire with flashing flame, breast-bound with chains of gold, like tempest-blasts, self-moving, swift to lend your aid; | As best of all foreknowers, excellent to guide, like Somas, good to guard the man who follows Law. ‖ 3. Shakers of all, like gales of wind they travel, like tongues of burning fires in their effulgence. | Mighty are they as warriors clad in armour, and, like the Fathers' prayers, Most Bounteous Givers. ‖ 4. Like spokes of car-wheels in one nave united, ever victorious like heavenly Heroes, | Shedding their precious balm like youthful suitors, they raise their voice and chant their psalm as singers. ‖ 5. They who are fleet to travel like the noblest steeds, long to obtain the prize like bounteous charioteers, | Like waters speeding on with their precipitous floods, like omniform Aṅgirasas with Sāman-hymns. ‖ 6. Born from the stream, like press-stones are the Princes, for ever like the stones that crush in pieces; | Sons of a beauteous Dame, like playful children, like a great host upon the march with splendour. ‖ 7. Like rays of Dawn, the visitors of

sacrifice, they shine with ornaments as eager to be bright. | Like rivers hasting on, glittering with their spears, from far away they measure out the distances. || 8. Gods, send us happiness and make us wealthy, letting us singers prosper, O ye Marutas. | Bethink you of our praise and of our friendship: ye from of old have riches to vouchsafe us.

Hymn 10:79. Agni.

1. I have beheld the might of this Great Being. Immortal in the midst of tribes of mortals. | His jaws now open and now shut together: much they devour, insatiately chewing. || 2. His eyes are turned away, his head is hidden: unsated with his tongue he eats the fuel. | With hands upraised, with reverence in the houses, for him they quickly bring his food together. || 3. Seeking, as 'twere, his Mother's secret bosom, he, like a child, creeps on through wide-spread bushes. | One he finds glowing like hot food made ready, and kissing deep within the earth's recesses. || 4. This holy Law I tell you, Earth and Heaven: the Infant at his birth devours his Parents. | No knowledge of the God have I, a mortal. Yea, Agni knoweth best, for he hath wisdom. || 5. This man who quickly gives him food, who offers his gifts of oil and butter and supports him,— | Him with his thousand eyes he closely looks on: thou showest him thy face from all sides, Agni. || 6. Agni, hast thou committed sin or treason among the Gods? In ignorance I ask thee. | Playing, not playing, he gold-hued and toothless, hath cut his food up as the knife a victim. || 7. He born in wood hath yoked his horses rushing in all directions, held with reins that glitter. | The well-born friend hath carved his food with Vasus: in all his limbs he hath increased and prospered.

Hymn 10:80. Agni.

1. Agni bestows the fleet prize-winning courser: Agni, the hero famed and firm in duty. | Agni pervades and decks the earth and heaven, and fills the fruitful dame who teems with heroes. || 2. Blest be the wood that feeds the active Agni: within the two great worlds hath Agni entered. | Agni impels a single man to battle, and with him rends in pieces many a foeman. || 3. Agni rejoiced the car of him who praised him, and from the waters burnt away Jarūtha. | Agni saved Atri in the fiery cavern, and made Nṛimedha rich with troops of children. || 4. Agni hath granted wealth that decks the hero, and sent the sage who wins a thousand cattle. | Agni hath made oblations rise to heaven: to every place are Agni's laws extended. || 5. With songs of praise the Ṛishis call on Agni; on Agni, heroes worsted in the foray. | Birds flying in the region call on Agni around a thousand cattle Agni wanders. || 6. Races of human birth pay Agni worship, men who have sprung from Nahus' line adore him. | Established in holy oil is Agni's pasture, on the Gandharva path of Law and Order. || 7. The Ṛibhus fabricated prayer for Agni, and we with mighty hymns have called on Agni. | Agni, Most Youthful God, protect the singer: win us by worship, Agni, great possessions.

Hymn 10:81. Viśvakarman.

1. He who sate down as Hotar-priest, the Ṛishi, our Father, offering up all things existing,— | He, seeking through his wish a great possession, came among men on earth as archetypal. || 2. What was the place whereon he took his station? What was it that supported him? How was it? | Whence Viśvakarman, seeing all, producing the earth, with mighty power disclosed the heavens. || 3. He who hath eyes on all sides round about him, a mouth on all sides, arms and feet on all sides, | He, the Sole God, producing earth and heaven, weldeth them, with his arms as wings, together. || 4. What was the tree, what wood in sooth produced it, from which they fashioned out the earth and heaven? | Ye thoughtful men inquire within your spirit whereon he stood when he established all things. || 5. Nine highest, lowest, sacrificial natures, and these thy mid-most here, O Viśvakarman, | Teach thou thy friends at sacrifice, O Blessed, and come thyself, exalted, to our worship. || 6. Bring thou thyself, exalted with oblation, O Viśvakarman, Earth and Heaven to worship. | Let other men around us live in folly here let us have a rich and liberal patron. || 7. Let us invoke today, to aid our labour, the Lord of Speech, the thought-swift Viśvakarman. | May he hear kindly all our invocations who gives all bliss for aid, whose works are righteous.

Hymn 10:82. Viśvakarman.

1. The Father of the eye, the Wise in spirit, created both these worlds submerged in fatness. | Then when the eastern ends were firmly fastened, the heavens and the earth were far extended. || 2. Mighty in mind and power is Viśvakarman, Maker, Disposer, and most lofty Presence. | Their offerings joy in rich juice where they value One, only One, beyond the Seven Ṛishis. || 3. Father who made us, he who, as Disposer, knoweth all races and all things existing, | Even he alone, the Deities' name-giver, him other beings seek for information. || 4. To him in sacrifice they offered treasures,—Ṛishis of old, in numerous troops, as singers, | Who, in the distant, near, and lower region, made ready all these things that have existence. || 5. That which is earlier than this earth and heaven, before the Asuras and Gods had being,— | What was the germ primeval which the waters received where all the Gods were seen together? || 6. The waters, they received that germ primeval wherein the Gods were gathered all together. | It rested set upon the Unborn's navel, that One wherein abide all things existing. || 7. Ye will not find him who produced these creatures: another thing hath risen up among you. | Enwrapt in misty cloud, with lips that stammer, hymn-chanters wander and are discontented.

Hymn 10:83. Manyu.

1. He who hath reverenced thee, Manyu, destructive bolt, breeds for himself forthwith all conquering energy. | Ārya and Dāsa will we conquer with thine aid, with thee the Conqueror, with conquest conquest-sped. || 2. Manyu was Indra, yea, the God, was Manyu, Manyu was Hotar, Varuṇa, Jātavedas. | The tribes of human lineage worship Manyu. Accordant with thy fervour, Manyu, guard us. || 3. Come hither, Manyu, mightier than the mighty; chase, with thy fervour for ally, our foemen. | Slayer of foes, of Vṛitra, and of Dasyu, bring thou to us all kinds of wealth and treasure. || 4. For thou art, Manyu, of surpassing vigour, fierce, queller of the foe, and self-existent, | Shared by all men, victorious, subduer: vouchsafe to us superior strength in battles. || 5. I have departed, still without a portion, wise God! according to thy will, the Mighty. | I, feeble man, was wroth thee, O Manyu I am myself; come thou to give me vigour. || 6. Come hither. I am all thine own; advancing turn thou to me, Victorious, All-supporter! | Come to me, Manyu, Wielder of the Thunder: bethink thee of thy friend, and slay the Dasyus. || 7. Approach, and on my right hand hold thy station: so shall we slay a multitude of foemen. | The best of meath I offer to support thee: may we be first to drink thereof in quiet.

Hymn 10:84. Manyu.

1. Borne on with thee, O Manyu girt by Marutas, let our brave men, impetuous, bursting forward, | March on, like flames of fire in form, exulting, with pointed arrows, sharpening their weapons. || 2. Flashing like fire, be thou, O conquering Manyu, invoked, O Victor, as our army's leader. | Slay thou our foes, distribute their possessions: show forth thy vigour, scatter those who hate us. || 3. O Manyu, overcome thou our assailant on! breaking, slaying, crushing down the foemen. | They have not hindered thine impetuous vigour: Mighty, Sole born! thou makest them thy subjects. || 4. Alone or many thou art worshipped, Manyu: sharpen the spirit of each clan for battle. | With thee to aid, O thou of perfect splendour, we will uplift the glorious shout for conquest. || 5. Unyielding bringing victory like Indra, O Manyu, be thou here our Sovereign Ruler. | To thy dear name, O Victor, we sing praises: we know the spring from which thou art come hither. || 6. Twin-born with power, destructive bolt of thunder, the highest conquering might is thine, Subduer! | Be friendly to its in thy spirit, Manyu, O Much-invoked, in shock of mighty battle. || 7. For spoil let Varuṇa and Manyu give us the wealth of both sides gathered and collected; | And let our enemies with stricken spirits, o'erwhelmed with terror, slink away defeated.

Hymn 10:85. Sūrya's Bridal.

1. Truth is the base that bears the earth; by Sūrya are the heavens sustained. | By Law the Ādityas stand secure, and Soma holds his place in heaven. || 2. By Soma are the Ādityas strong, by Soma mighty is the earth. | Thus Soma in the midst of all these constellations hath his place. || 3. One thinks, when they have brayed the plant, that he hath drunk the Soma's juice; | Of him whom Brahmans truly know as Soma no one ever tastes. || 4. Soma, secured by sheltering rules, guarded by hymns in Bṛihatī, | Thou standest listening to the stones none tastes of thee who dwells on earth. || 5. When they begin to drink thee then, O God, thou swellest out again. | Vāyu is Soma's guardian God. The Moon is that which shapes the years. || 6. Raibhī was her dear bridal friend, and Nārāśaṃsī led her home. | Lovely was Sūrya's

robe: she came to that which Gātha had adorned. || 7. Thought was the pillow of her couch, sight was the unguent for her eyes: | Her treasury was earth and heaven, when Sūrya went unto her Lord. || 8. Hymns were the cross-bars of the pole, Kurīra-metre decked the car: | The bridesmen were the Aśvin Pair Agni was leader of the train. || 9. Soma was he who wooed the maid: the groomsmen were both Aśvins, when | The Sun-God Savitar bestowed his willing Sūrya on her Lord. || 10. Her spirit was the bridal car; the covering thereof was heaven: | Bright were both Steers that drew it when Sūrya approached her husband's, home. || 11. Thy Steers were steady, kept in place by holy verse and Sāman-hymn: | All car were thy two chariot wheels: thy path was tremulous in the sky, || 12. Clean, as thou wentest, were thy wheels wind, was the axle fastened there. | Sūrya, proceeding to her Lord, mounted a spirit-fashioned car. || 13. The bridal pomp of Sūrya, which Savitar started, moved along. | In Maghā days are oxen slain, in Arjunīs they wed the bride. || 14. When on your three-wheeled chariot, O Aśvins, ye came as wooers unto Sūrya's bridal, | Then all the Gods agreed to your proposal Pūṣhan as Son elected you as Fathers. || 15. O ye Two Lords of lustre, then when ye to Sūrya's wooing came, | Where was one chariot wheel of yours? Where stood ye for die Sire's command? || 16. The Brahmans, by their seasons, know, O Sūrya, those two wheels of thine: | One kept concealed, those only who are skilled in highest truths have learned. || 17. To Sūrya and the Deities, to Mitra and to Varuṇa. | Who know aright the thing that is, this adoration have I paid. || 18. By their own power these Twain in close succession move; | They go as playing children round the sacrifice. | One of the Pair beholdeth all existing things; the other ordereth seasons and is born again. || 19. He, born afresh, is new and new for ever ensign of days he goes before the Mornings | Coming, he orders for the Gods their portion. The Moon prolongs the days of our existence. || 20. Mount this, all-shaped, gold-hued, with strong wheels, fashioned of Kiṃśuka and Śalmali, light-rolling, | Bound for the world of life immortal, Sūrya: make for thy lord a happy bridal journey. || 21. Rise up from hence: this maiden hath a husband. I laud Viśvāvasu with hymns and homage. | Seek in her father's home another fair one, and find the portion from of old assigned thee. || 22. Rise up from hence, Viśvāvasu: with reverence we worship thee. | Seek thou another willing maid, and with her husband leave the bride. || 23. Straight in direction be the path:s, and thornless, whereon our fellows travel to the wooing. | Let Aryaman and Bhaga lead us: perfect, O Gods, the union of the wife and husband. || 24. Now from the noose of Varuṇa I free thee, wherewith Most Blessed Savitar hath bound thee. | In Law's seat, to the world of virtuous action, I give thee up uninjured with thy consort. || 25. Hence, and not thence, I send these free. I make thee softly fettered there. | That, Bounteous Indra, she may live blest in her fortune and her sons. || 26. Let Pūṣhan take thy hand and hence conduct thee; may the two Aśvins on their car transport thee. | Go to the house to be the household's mistress and speak as lady to thy gathered people. || 27. Happy be thou and prosper with thy children here: be vigilant to rule thy household in this home. | Closely unite thy body with this; man, thy lord. So shall ye, full of years, address your company. || 28. Her hue is blue and red: the fiend who clingeth close is driven off. | Well thrive the kinsmen of this bride the husband is bound fast in bonds. || 29. Give thou the woollen robe away: deal treasure to the Brahman priests. | This female fiend hath got her feet, and as a wife attends her lord. || 30. Unlovely is his body when it glistens with this wicked fiend, | What time the husband wraps about his limbs the garment of his wife. || 31. Consumptions, from her people, which follow the bride's resplendent train,— | These let the Holy Gods again bear to the place from which they came. || 32. Let not the highway thieves who lie in ambush find the wedded pair. | By pleasant ways let them escape the danger, and let foes depart. || 33. Signs of good fortune mark the bride come all of you and look at her. | Wish her prosperity, and then return unto your homes again. || 34. Pungent is this, and bitter this, filled, as it were, with arrow-barbs, Empoisoned and not fit for use. | The Brahman who knows Sūrya well deserves the garment of the bride. || 35. The fringe, the cloth that decks her head, and then the triply parted robe, — | Behold the hues which Sūrya wears these doth the Brahman purify. || 36. I take thy hand in mine for happy fortune that thou mayst reach old age with me thy husband. | Gods, Aryaman, Bhaga, Savitar, Purandhi, have given thee to be my household's mistress. || 37. O Pūṣhan, send her on as most auspicious, her who shall be the sharer of my pleasures; | Her who shall twine her loving arms about me, and welcome all my love and mine embraces. || 38. For thee, with bridal train, they, first, escorted Sūrya to her home. | Give to the husband in return, Agni, the wife with progeny. || 39. Agni hath given the bride again with splendour and with ample life. | Long lived be he who is her lord; a hundred autumns let him live. || 40. Soma obtained her first of all; next the Gandharva was her lord. | Agni was thy third husband: now one born of woman is thy fourth. || 41. Soma to the Gandharva, and to Agni the Gandharva gave: | And Agni hath bestowed on me riches and sons and this my spouse. || 42. Be ye not parted; dwell ye here reach the full time of human life. | With sons and grandsons sport and play, rejoicing in your own abode. || 43. So may Prajāpati bring children forth to us; may Aryaman adorn us till old age come nigh. | Not inauspicious enter thou thy husband's house: bring blessing to our bipeds and our quadrupeds. || 44. Not evil-eyed, no slayer of thy husband, bring weal to cattle, radiant, gentle hearted; | Loving the Gods, delightful, bearing heroes, bring blessing to our quadrupeds and bipeds. || 45. O Bounteous Indra, make this bride blest in her sons and fortunate. | Vouchsafe to her ten sons, and make her husband the eleventh man. || 46. Over thy husband's father and thy husband's mother bear full sway. | Over the sister of thy lord, over his brothers rule supreme. || 47. So may the Universal Gods, so may the Waters join our hearts. | May Mātariśvan, Dhātar, and Deṣhṭrī together bind us close.

Hymn 10:86. Indra.

1. Men have abstained from pouring juice they count not Indra as a God. | Where at the votary's store my friend Vṛiṣhākapi hath drunk his fill. Supreme is Indra over all. || 2. Thou, Indra, heedless passest by the ill Vṛiṣhākapi hath wrought; | Yet nowhere else thou findest place wherein to drink the Soma juice. Supreme is Indra over all. || 3. What hath he done to injure thee, this tawny beast Vṛiṣhākapi, | With whom thou art so angry now? What is the votary's foodful store? Supreme is Indra over all. || 4. Soon may the hound who hunts the boar seize him and bite him in the car, | O Indra, that Vṛiṣhākapi whom thou protectest as a friend, Supreme is Indra over all. || 5. Kapi hath marred the beauteous things, all deftly wrought, that were my joy. | In pieces will I rend his head; the sinner's portion shall be woo. Supreme is Indra over all. || 6. No Dame hath ampler charms than I, or greater wealth of love's delights. | None with more ardour offers all her beauty to her lord's embrace. Supreme is Indra over all. || 7. Mother whose love is quickly won, I say what verily will be. | My breast, O Mother, and my head and both my hips seem quivering. Supreme is Indra over all. || 8. Dame with the lovely hands and arms, with broad hair-plaits add ample hips, | Why, O thou Hero's wife, art thou angry with our Vṛiṣhākapi? Supreme is Indra over all. || 9. This noxious creature looks on me as one bereft of hero's love, | Yet Heroes for my sons have I, the Marutas' Friend and Indra's Queen. Supreme is Indra over all. || 10. From olden time the matron goes to feast and general sacrifice. | Mother of Heroes, Indra's Queen, the rite's ordainer is extolled. Supreme is Indra over all. || 11. So have I heard Indrāṇī called most fortunate among these Dames, | For never shall her Consort die in future time through length of days. Supreme is Indra overall. || 12. Never, Indrāṇī, have I joyed without my friend Vṛiṣhākapi, | Whose welcome offering here, made pure with water, goeth to the Gods. Supreme is Indra over all. || 13. Wealthy Vṛiṣhākapāyi, blest with sons and consorts of thy sons, | Indra will eat thy bulls, thy dear oblation that effecteth much. Supreme is Indra over all. || 14. Fifteen in number, then, for me a score of bullocks they prepare, | And I devour the fat thereof: they fill my belly full with food. Supreme is Indra over all. || 15. Like as a bull with pointed horn, loud bellowing amid the herds, | Sweet to thine heart, O Indra, is the brew which she who tends thee pours. Supreme is Indra over all.[1] || 18. O Indra this Vṛiṣhākapi hath found a slain wild animal, | Dresser, and new-made pan, and knife, and wagon with a load of wood. Supreme is Indra over all. || 19. Distinguishing the Dāsa and the Ārya, viewing all, I go. | I look upon the wise, and drink the simple votary's Soma juice. Supreme is Indra over all. || 20. The desert plains and steep descents, how many leagues in length they spread! | Go to the nearest

1. Griffith omitted verses 16-17 with the following note: "I pass over stanzas 16 and 17, which I cannot translate into decent English."

houses, go unto thine home, Vṛishākapi. Supreme is Indra over all. ‖ 21. Turn thee again Vṛishākapi: we twain will bring thee happiness. | Thou goest homeward on thy way along this path which leads to sleep. Supreme is Indra over all. ‖ 22. When, Indra and Vṛishākapi, ye travelled upward to your home, | Where was that noisome beast, to whom went it, the beast that troubles man? Supreme is Indra over all. ‖ 23. Daughter of Manu, Parśu bare a score of children at a birth. | Her portion verily was bliss although her burthen caused her grief.

Hymn 10:87. Agni.

1. I balm with oil the mighty Rakṣhas-slayer; to the most famous Friend I come for shelter | Enkindled, sharpened by our rites, may Agni protect us in the day and night from evil. ‖ 2. O Jātavedas with the teeth of iron, enkindled with thy flame attack the demons. | Seize with thy tongue the foolish Gods' adorers: rend, put within thy mouth the raw-flesh eaters. ‖ 3. Apply thy teeth, the upper and the lower, thou who hast both, enkindled and destroying. | Roam also in the air, O King, around us, and with thy jaws assail the wicked spirits. ‖ 4. Bending thy shafts through sacrifices, Agni, whetting their points with song as if with whetstones, | Pierce to the heart therewith the Yātudhānas, and break their arms uplifted to attack thee. ‖ 5. Pierce through the Yātudhāna's skin, O Agni; let the destroying dart with fire consume him. | Rend his joints, Jātavedas, let the eater of flesh, flesh-seeking, track his mangled body. ‖ 6. Where now thou seest Agni Jātavedas, one of these demons standing still or roaming, | Or flying on those paths in air's mid-region, sharpen the shaft and as an archer pierce him. ‖ 7. Tear from the evil spirit, Jātavedas, what he hath seized and with his spears hath captured. | Blazing before him strike him down, O Agni; let spotted carrion-eating kites devour him. ‖ 8. Here tell this forth, O Agni: whosoever is, he himself, or acteth as, a demon, | Him grasp, O thou Most Youthful, with thy fuel to the Mati-seer's eye give him as booty. ‖ 9. With keen glance guard the sacrifice, O Agni: thou Sage, conduct it onward to the Vasus. | Let not the fiends, O Man-beholder, harm thee burning against the Rākṣhasas to slay them. ‖ 10. Look on the fiend mid men, as Man-beholder: rend thou his three extremities in pieces. | Demolish with thy flame his ribs, O Agni, the Yātudhāna's root destroy thou triply. ‖ 11. Thrice, Agni, let thy noose surround the demon who with his falsehood injures Holy Order. | Loud roaring with thy flame, O Jātavedas, crush him and cast him down before the singer. ‖ 12. Lead thou the worshipper that eye, O Agni, wherewith thou lookest on the hoof-armed demon. | With light celestial in Atharvan's manner burn up the foot who ruins truth with falsehood. ‖ 13. Agni, what curse the pair this day have uttered, what heated word the worshippers have spoken, | Each arrowy taunt sped from the angry spirit,—pierce to the heart therewith the Yātudhānas. ‖ 14. With fervent heat exterminate the demons; destroy the fiends with burning flame, O Agni. | Destroy with fire the foolish Gods' adorers; blaze and destroy the insatiable monsters. ‖ 15. May Gods destroy this day the evil-doer may each hot curse of his return and blast him. | Let arrows pierce the liar in his vitals, and Viśva's net enclose the Yātudhāna. ‖ 16. The fiend who smears himself with flesh of cattle, with flesh of horses and of human bodies, | Who steals the milch-cow's milk away, O Agni,—tear off the heads of such with fiery fury. ‖ 17. The cow gives milk each year, O Man-regarder: let not the Yātudhāna ever taste it. | If one would glut him with the biestings, Agni, pierce with thy flame his vitals as he meets thee. ‖ 18. Let the fiends drink the poison of the cattle; may Aditi cast off the evildoers. | May the God Savitar give them up to ruin, and be their share of plants and herbs denied them. ‖ 19. Agni, from days of old thou slayest demons: never shall Rākṣhasas in fight o'ercome thee. | Burn up the foolish ones, the flesh-devourers: let none of them escape thine heavenly arrow. ‖ 20. Guard us, O Agni, from above and under, protect us from behind us and before us; | And may thy flames, most fierce and never wasting, glowing with fervent heat, consume the sinner. ‖ 21. From rear, from front, from under, from above us, O King, protect us as a Sage with wisdom. | Guard to old age thy friend, O Friend, Eternal: O Agni, as Immortal, guard us mortals. ‖ 22. We set thee round us as a fort, victorious Agni, thee a Sage, | Of hero lineage, day by day, destroyer of our treacherous foes. ‖ 23. Burn with thy poison turned against the treacherous brood of Rākṣhasas, | O Agni, with thy sharpened glow, with lances armed with points of flame. ‖ 24. Burn thou the paired Kimīdins, burn, Agni, the Yātudhāna pairs. | I sharpen thee, Infallible, with hymns. O Sage, be vigilant. ‖ 25. Shoot forth, O Agni, with thy flame demolish them on every side. | Break thou the Yātudhāna's strength, the vigour of the Rākṣhasa.

Hymn 10:88. Agni.

1. Dear, ageless sacrificial drink is offered in light-discovering, heaven-pervading Agni. | The Gods spread forth through his Celestial Nature, that he might bear the world up and sustain it. ‖ 2. The world was swallowed and concealed in darkness: Agni was born, and light became apparent. | The Deities, the broad earth, and the heavens, and plants, and waters gloried in his friendship. ‖ 3. Inspired by Gods who claim our adoration, I now will laud Eternal Lofty Agni, | Him who hath spread abroad the earth with lustre, this heaven, and both the worlds, and air's mid-region. ‖ 4. Earliest Priest whom all the Gods accepted, and chose him, and anointed him with butter, | He swiftly made all things that fly, stand, travel, all that hath motion, Agni Jātavedas. ‖ 5. Because thou, Agni, Jātavedas, stoodest at the world's head with thy refulgent splendour, | We sent thee forth with hymns and songs and praises: thou filledst heaven and earth, God meet for worship. ‖ 6. Head of the world is Agni in the night-time; then, as the Sun, at morn springs up and rises. | Then to his task goes the prompt Priest foreknowing the wondrous power of Gods who must be honoured. ‖ 7. Lovely is he who, kindled in his greatness, hath shone forth, seated in the heavens, refulgent. | With resonant hymns all Gods who guard our bodies have offered up oblation in this Agni. ‖ 8. First the Gods brought the hymnal into being; then they engendered Agni, then oblation. | He was their sacrifice that guards our bodies: him the heavens know, the earth, the waters know him. ‖ 9. He, Agni, whom the Gods have generated, in whom they offered up all worlds and creatures, | He with his bright glow heated earth and heaven, urging himself right onward in his grandeur. ‖ 10. Then by the laud the Gods engendered Agni in heaven, who fills both worlds through strength and vigour. | They made him to appear in threefold essence: he ripens plants of every form and nature. ‖ 11. What time the Gods, whose due is worship, set him as Sūrya, Son of Aditi, in heaven, | When the Pair, ever wandering, sprang to being, all creatures that existed looked upon them. ‖ 12. For all the world of life the Gods made Agni Vaiśvānara to be the days' bright Banner,— | Him who hath spread abroad the radiant Mornings, and, coming with his light, unveils the darkness. ‖ 13. The wise and holy Deities engendered Agni Vaiśvānara whom age ne'er touches. | The Ancient Star that wanders on for ever, lofty and. strong, Lord of the Living Being. ‖ 14. We call upon the Sage with holy verses, Agni Vaiśvānara the ever-beaming, | Who hath surpassed both heaven and earth in greatness: lie is a God below, a God above us. ‖ 15. I have heard mention of two several pathways, ways of the Fathers and of Gods and mortals. | On these two paths each moving creature travels, each thing between the Father and the Mother. ‖ 16. These two united paths bear him who journeys born from the head and pondered with the spirit | He stands directed to all things existing, hasting, unresting in his fiery splendour. ‖ 17. Which of us twain knows where they speak together, upper and lower of the two rite-leaders? | Our friends have helped to gather our assembly. They came to sacrifice; who will announce it? ‖ 18. How many are the Fires and Suns in number? What is the number of the Dawns and Waters? | Not jestingly I speak to you, O Fathers. Sages, I ask you this for information. ‖ 19. As great as is the fair-winged Morning's presence to him who dwells beside us, Mātariśvan! | Is what the Brahman does when he approaches to sacrifice and sits below the Hotar.

Hymn 10:89. Indra.

1. I will extol the most heroic Indra who with his might forced earth and sky asunder; | Who hath filled all with width as man's Upholder, surpassing floods and rivers in his greatness. ‖ 2. Sūrya is he: throughout the wide expanses shall Indra turn him, swift as car-wheels, hither, | Like a stream resting not but ever active he hath destroyed, with light, the black-hued darkness. ‖ 3. To him I sing a holy prayer, incessant new, matchless, common to the earth and heaven, | Who marks, as they were backs, all living creatures: ne'er doth he fail a friend, the noble Indra. ‖ 4. I will send forth my songs in flow unceasing, like water from the ocean's depth, to Indra. | Who to his car on both its sides securely hath fixed the earth and heaven as with an axle. ‖ 5. Rousing with draughts, the Shaker, rushing

onward, impetuous, very strong, armed as with arrows | Is Soma; forest trees and all the bushes deceive not Indra with their offered likeness. || 6. Soma hath flowed to him whom naught can equal, the earth, the heavens, the firmament, the mountains,— | When heightened in his ire his indignation shatters the firm and breaks the strong in pieces. || 7. As an axe fells the tree so be slew Vṛitra, brake down the strongholds and dug out the rivers. | He cleft the mountain like a new-made pitcher. Indra brought forth the kine with his Companions. || 8. Wise art thou, Punisher of guilt, O Indra. The sword lops limbs, thou smitest down the sinner, | The men who injure, as it were a comrade, the lofty Law of Varuṇa and Mitra. || 9. Men who lead evil lives, who break agreements, and injure Varuṇa, Aryaman and Mitra,— | Against these foes, O Mighty Indra, sharpen, as furious death, thy Bull of fiery colour. || 10. Indra is Sovereign Lord of Earth and Heaven, Indra is Lord of waters and of mountains. | Indra is Lord of prosperers and sages Indra must be invoked in rest and effort. || 11. Vaster than days and nights, Giver of increase, vaster than firmament and flood of ocean, | Vaster than bounds of earth and wind's extension, vaster than rivers and our lands is Indra. || 12. Forward, as herald of refulgent Morning, let thine insatiate arrow fly, O Indra. | And pierce, as 'twere a stone launched forth from heaven, with hottest blaze the men who love deception. || 13. Him, verily, the moons, the mountains followed, the tall trees followed and the plants and herbage. | Yearning with love both Worlds approached, the Waters waited on Indra when he first had being. || 14. Where was the vengeful dart when thou, O Indra, clavest the demon ever beat on outrage? | When fiends lay there upon the ground extended like cattle in the place of immolation? || 15. Those who are set in enmity against us, the Ogaṇas, O Indra, waxen mighty,— | Let blinding darkness follow those our foemen, while these shall have bright shining nights to light them. || 16. May plentiful libations of the people, and singing Ṛishis' holy prayers rejoice thee. | Hearing with love this common invocation, come unto us, pass by all those who praise thee. || 17. O Indra, thus may we be made partakers of thy new favours that shall bring us profit. | Singing with love, may we the Viśvāmitras win daylight even now through thee, O Indra. || 18. Call we on Maghavan, auspicious Indra, best hero in the fight where spoil is gathered, | The Strong who listens, who gives aid in battles, who slays the Vṛitras, wins and gathers riches.

Hymn 10:90. Purusha.

1. A thousand heads hath Puruṣha, a thousand eyes, a thousand feet. | On every side pervading earth he fills a space ten fingers wide. || 2. This Puruṣha is all that yet hath been and all that is to be; | The Lord of Immortality which waxes greater still by food. || 3. So mighty is his greatness; yea, greater than this is Puruṣha. | All creatures are one-fourth of him, three-fourths eternal life in heaven. || 4. With three-fourths Puruṣha went up: one fourth of him again was here. | Thence he strode out to every side over what eats not and what eats. || 5. From him Virāj was born; again Puruṣha from Virāj was born. | As soon as he was born he spread eastward and westward o'er the earth. || 6. When Gods prepared the sacrifice with Puruṣha as their offering, | Its oil was spring, the holy gift was autumn; summer was the wood. || 7. They balmed as victim on the grass Puruṣha born in earliest time. | With him the Deities and all Sādhyas and Ṛishis sacrificed. || 8. From that great general sacrifice the dripping fat was gathered up. | He formed the creatures of the air, and animals both wild and tame. || 9. From that great general sacrifice Ṛichas and Sāman-hymns were born: | Therefrom were spells and charms produced; the Yajus had its birth from it. || 10. From it were horses born, from it all cattle with two rows of teeth: | From it were generated kine, from it the goats and sheep were born. || 11. When they divided Puruṣha how many portions did they make? | What do they call his mouth, his arms? What do they call his thighs and feet? || 12. The Brahman was his mouth, of both his arms was the Rājanya made. | His thighs became the Vaiśya, from his feet the Śūdra was produced. || 13. The Moon was gendered from his mind, and from his eye the Sun had birth; | Indra and Agni from his mouth were born, and Vāyu from his breath. || 14. Forth from his navel came mid-air; the sky was fashioned from his head | Earth from his feet, and from his ear the regions. Thus they formed the worlds. || 15. Seven fencing-sticks had he, thrice seven layers of fuel were prepared, | When the Gods, offering sacrifice, bound, as their victim, Puruṣha. || 16. Gods, sacrificing, sacrificed the victim: these were the earliest

holy ordinances. | The Mighty Ones attained the height of heaven, there where the Sādhyas, Gods of old, are dwelling.

Hymn 10:91. Agni.

1. Brisk, at the place of Ilā, hymned by men who wake, our own familiar Friend is kindled in the house; | Hotar of all oblation, worthy of our choice, Lord, beaming, trusty friend to one who loveth him. || 2. He, excellent in glory, guest in every house, finds like a swift-winged bird a home in every tree. | Benevolent to men, he scorns no living man: Friend to the tribes of men he dwells with every tribe. || 3. Most sage with insight, passing skilful with thy powers art thou, O Agni, wise with wisdom, knowing all. | As Vasu, thou alone art Lord of all good things, of all the treasures that the heavens and earth produce. || 4. Foreknowing well, O Agni, thou in Ilā's place hast occupied thy regular station balmed with oil. | Marked are thy comings like the comings of the Dawns, the rays of him who shineth spotless as the Sun. || 5. Thy glories are, as lightnings from the rainy cloud, marked, many-hued, like heralds of the Dawns' approach, | When, loosed to wander over plants and forest trees, thou crammest by thyself thy food into thy mouth. || 6. Him, duly coming as their germ, have plants received: this Agni have maternal Waters brought to life. | So in like manner do the forest trees and plants bear him within them and produce him evermore. || 7. When, sped and urged by wind, thou spreadest thee abroad, swift piercing through thy food according to thy will, | Thy never-ceasing blazes, longing to consume, like men on chariots, Agni, strive on every side. || 8. Agni, the Hotar-priest who fills the assembly full, Waker of knowledge, chief Controller of the thought,— | Him, yea, none other than thyself, doth man elect at sacrificial offerings great and small alike. || 9. Here, Apī, the arrangers, those attached to thee, elect thee as their Priest in sacred gatherings, | When men with strewn clipt grass and sacrificial gifts offer thee entertainment, piously inclined. || 10. Thine is the Herald's task and Cleanser's duly timed; Leader art thou, and Kindler for the pious man. | Thou art Director, thou the ministering Priest: thou art the Brahman, Lord and Master in our home. || 11. When mortal man presents to thee Immortal God, Agni, his fuel or his sacrificial gift, | Then thou art his Adhvaryu, Hotar, messenger, callest the Gods and orderest the sacrifice. || 12. From us these hymns in concert have gone forth to him, these holy words, these Ṛichas, songs and eulogies, | Eager for wealth, to Jātavedas fain for wealth: when they have waxen strong they please their Strengthener. || 13. This newest eulogy will I speak forth to him, the Ancient One who loves it. May he hear our voice. | May it come near his heart and make it stir with love, as a fond well-dressed matron clings about her lord. || 14. He in whom horses, bulls, oxen, and barren cows, and rams, when duly set apart, are offered up,— | To Agni, Soma-sprinkled, drinker of sweet juice, Disposer, with my heart I bring a fair hymn forth. || 15. Into thy mouth is poured the offering, Agni, as Soma into cup, oil into ladle. | Vouchsafe us wealth. strength-winning, blest with heroes, wealth lofty, praised by men, and full of splendour.

Hymn 10:92. Viśvedevas.

1. I praise your Charioteer of sacrifice, the Lord of men, Priest of the tribes, refulgent, Guest of night. | Blazing amid dry plants, snatching amid the green, the Strong, the Holy Herald hath attained to heaven. || 2. Him, Agni, Gods and men have made their chief support, who drinks the fatness and completes the sacrifice. | With kisses they caress the Grandson of the Red, like the swift ray of light, the Household Priest of Dawn. || 3. Yea, we discriminate his and the niggard's ways: his branches evermore are sent forth to consume. | When his terrific flames have reached the Immortal's world, then men remember and extol the Heavenly Folk. || 4. For then the net of Law, Dyaus, and the wide expanse, Earth, Worship, and Devotion meet for highest praise, | Varuṇa, Indra, Mitra were of one accord, and Savitar and Bhaga, Lords of holy might. || 5. Onward, with ever-roaming Rudra, speed the floods: over Aramati the Mighty have they run. | With them Parijman, moving round his vast domain, loud bellowing, bedews all things that are within. || 6. Straightway the Rudras, Marutas visiting all men, Falcons of Dyaus, home-dwellers with the Asura, — | Varuṇa, Mitra, Aryaman look on with these, and the swift-moving Indra with swift-moving Gods. || 7. With Indra have they found enjoyment, they who toil, in the light's beauty, in the very Strong One's strength; | The singers who in men's assemblies forged for him, according

to his due, his friend the thunderbolt. ‖ 8. Even the Sun's Bay Coursers hath lie held in check: each one fears Indra as the mightiest of all. | Unhindered, from the air's vault thunders day by day the loud triumphant breathing of the fearful Bull. ‖ 9. With humble adoration show this day your song of praise to mighty Rudra, Ruler of the brave: | With whom, the Eager Ones, going their ordered course, he comes from heaven Self-bright, auspicious, strong to guard. ‖ 10. For these have spread abroad the fame of human kind, the Bull Bṛihaspati and Soma's brotherhood. | Atharvan first by sacrifices made men sure: through skill the Bhṛigus were esteemed of all as Gods. ‖ 11. For these, the Earth and Heaven with their abundant seed, four-bodied Narāśaṃsa, Yama, Aditi, | God Tvashṭar Wealth-bestower, the Ṛibhukshans, Rodasī, Marutas, Vishṇu, claim and merit praise. ‖ 12. And may he too give car, the Sage, from far away, the Dragon of the Deep, to this our yearning call. | Ye Sun and Moon who dwell in heaven and move in turn, and with your thought, O Earth and Sky, observe this well. ‖ 13. Dear to all Gods, may Pūshan guard the ways we go, the Waters' child and Vāyu help us to success. | Sing lauds for your great bliss to Wind, the breath of all: ye Aśvins prompt to hear, hear this upon your way. ‖ 14. With hymns of praise we sing him who is throned as Lord over these fearless tribes, the Self-resplendent One. | We praise Night's youthful Lord benevolent to men, the foeless One, the free, with all celestial Dames. ‖ 15. By reason of his birth here Aṅgiras first sang: the pressing-stones upraised beheld the sacrifice— | The stones through which the Sage became exceeding vast, and the sharp axe obtains in fight the beauteous place.

Hymn 10:93. Viśvedevas.

1. Mighty are ye, and far-extended, Heaven and Earth: both Worlds are evermore to us like two young Dames. | Guard us thereby from stronger foe; guard us hereby to give us strength. ‖ 2. In each succeeding sacrifice that mortal honoureth the Gods, | He who, most widely known and famed for happiness, inviteth them. ‖ 3. Ye who are Rulers over all, great is your sovereign power as Gods. | Ye all possess all majesty: all must be served in sacrifice. ‖ 4. These are the joyous Kings of Immortality, Parijman, Mitra, Aryaman, and Varuṇa. | What else is Rudra, praised of men? the Marutas, Bhaga, Pūshaṇa? ‖ 5. Come also to our dwelling, Lords of ample wealth, common partakers of our waters, Sun and Moon, | When the great Dragon of the Deep hath settled down upon their floors. ‖ 6. And let the Aśvins, Lords of splendour, set us free,—both Gods, and, with their Laws, Mitra and Varuṇa. | Through woes, as over desert lands, he speeds to ample opulence. ‖ 7. Yea, let the Aśvins Twain he gracious unto us, even Rudras, and all Gods, Bhaga, Rathaspati; | Parijman, Ṛibhu, Vāja, O Lords of all wealth Ṛibhukshans. ‖ 8. Prompt is Ṛibhukshan, prompt the worshipper's strong drink: may thy fleet Bay Steeds, thine who speedest on, approach. | Not man's but God's is sacrifice whose psalm is unassailable. ‖ 9. O God Savitar, harmed by none, lauded, give us a place among wealthy princes. | With his Car-steeds at once 'hath our Indra guided the reins and the car of these men. ‖ 10. To these men present here, O Heaven and Earth, to us grant lofty fame extending over all mankind. | Give us a steed to win us strength, a steed with wealth for victory. ‖ 11. This speaker, Indra—for thou art our Friend—wherever he may be, guard thou, Victor! for help, ever for help | Thy wisdom, Vasu! prosper him. ‖ 12. So have they strengthened this mine hymn which seems to take its bright path to the Sun, and reconciles the men: | Thus forms a carpenter the yoke of horses, not to be displaced. ‖ 13. Whose chariot-seat hath come again laden with wealth and bright with gold, | Lightly, with piercing ends, as 'twere two ranks of heroes ranged for fight. ‖ 14. This to Duḥśīma Pṛithavāna have I sung, to Vena, Rāma, to the nobles, and the King. | They yoked five hundred, and their love of us was famed upon their way. ‖ 15. Besides, they showed us seven -and-seventy horses here. | Tānva at once displayed his gift, Pārthya at once displayed his gift; and straightway Māyava showed his.

Hymn 10:94. Press-stones.

1. Let these speak loudly forth; let us speak out aloud: to the loud speaking Pressing-stones address the speech; | When, rich with Soma juice, Stones of the mountain, ye, united, swift to Indra bring the sound of praise. ‖ 2. They speak out like a hundred, like a thousand men: they cry aloud to us with their green-tinted mouths, | While, pious Stones, they ply their task with piety, and, even before the Hotar, taste the offered food. ‖ 3. Loudly they speak, for they have found the savoury meath: they make a humming sound over the meat prepared. | As they devour the branch of the Red-coloured Tree, these, the well-pastured Bulls, have uttered bellowings. ‖ 4. They cry aloud, with strong exhilarating drink, calling on Indra now, for they have found the meath. | Bold, with the sisters they have danced, embraced by them, making the earth re-echo with their ringing sound. ‖ 5. The Eagles have sent forth their cry aloft in heaven; in the sky's vault the dark impetuous ones have danced. | Then downward to the nether stone's fixt place they sink, and, splendid as the Sun, effuse their copious stream. ‖ 6. Like strong ones drawing, they have put forth all their strength: the Bulls, harnessed together, bear the chariot-poles. | When they have bellowed, panting, swallowing their food, the sound of their loud snorting is like that of steeds. ‖ 7. To these who have ten workers and a tenfold girth, to these who have ten yoke-straps and ten binding thongs, | To these who bear ten reins, the eternal, sing ye praise, to these who bear ten car-poles, ten when they are yoked. ‖ 8. These Stones with ten conductors, rapid in their course, with lovely revolution travel round and round. | They have been first to drink the flowing Soma juice, first to enjoy the milky fluid of the stalk. ‖ 9. These Soma-eaters kiss Indra's Bay-coloured Steeds: draining. the stalk they sit upon the ox's hide. | Indra, when he hath drunk Soma-meath drawn by them, waxes in strength, is famed, is mighty as a Bull. ‖ 10. Strong is your stalk; ye, verily, never shall be harmed; ye have refreshment, ye are ever satisfied. | Fair are ye, as it were, through splendour of his wealth, his in whose sacrifice, O Stones, ye find delight. ‖ 11. Bored deep, but not pierced through with holes, are ye, O Stones, not loosened, never weary, and exempt from death, | Eternal, undiseased, moving in sundry ways, unthirsting, full of fatness, void of all desire. ‖ 12. Your fathers, verily, stand firm from age to age: they, loving rest, are not dissevered from their seat. | Untouched by time, ne'er lacking green plants and green trees, they with their voice have caused the heavens and earth to hear. ‖ 13. This, this the Stones proclaim, what time they are disjoined, and when with ringing sounds they move and drink the balm. | Like tillers of the ground when they are sowing seed, they mix the Soma, nor, devouring, minish it. ‖ 14. They have raised high their voice for juice, for sacrifice, striking the Mother earth as though they danced thereon. | So loose thou too his thought who hath effused the sap, and let the Stones which we are honouring be disjoined.

Hymn 10:95. Urvaśī. Purūravas.

1. Ho there, my consort! Stay, thou fierce-souled lady, and let us reason for a while together. | Such thoughts as these of ours, while yet unspoken in days gone by have never brought us comfort. ‖ 2. What am I now to do with this thy saying? I have gone from thee like the first of Mornings. | Purūravas, return thou to thy dwelling: I, like the wind, am difficult to capture. ‖ 3. Like a shaft sent for glory from the quiver, or swift-steed winning cattle winning hundreds. | The lightning seemed to flash, as cowards planned it. The minstrels bleated like a lamb in trouble. ‖ 4. Giving her husband's father life and riches, from the near dwelling, when her lover craved her, | She sought the home wherein she found her pleasure, accepting day and night her lord's embraces. ‖ 5. Thrice in the day didst thou embrace thy consort, though coldly she received thy fond caresses. | To thy desires, Purūravas, I yielded: so wast thou king, O hero, of my body. ‖ 6. The maids Sujūrṇi, Śreṇi, Sumne-āpi, Charaṇyu, Granthinī, and Hradechakshus,— | These like red kine have hastened forth, the bright ones, and like milch-cows have lowed in emulation. ‖ 7. While he was born the Dames sate down together, the Rivers with free kindness gave him nurture; | And then, Purūravas, the Gods increased thee for mighty battle, to destroy the Dasyus. ‖ 8. When I, a mortal, wooed to mine embraces these heavenly nymphs who laid aside their raiment, | Like a scared snake they fled from me in terror, like chariot horses when the car has touched them. ‖ 9. When, loving these Immortal Ones, the mortal hath converse with the nymphs as they allow him. | Like swans they show the beauty of their bodies, like horses in their play they bite and nibble. ‖ 10. She who flashed brilliant as the falling lightning brought me delicious presents from the waters. | Now from the flood be born a strong young hero May Urvaśī prolong her life for ever ‖ 11. Thy birth hath made me drink from earthly milch-kine: this power, Purūravas, hast thou vouchsafed me. | I knew, and, warned thee, on that day. Thou wouldst not hear me. What sayest thou, when naught avails thee? ‖ 12. When will the

son be born and seek his father? Mourner-like, will he weep when first he knows him? | Who shall divide the accordant wife and husband, while fire is shining with thy consort's parents? || 13. I will console him when his tears are falling: he shall not weep and cry for care that blesses. | That which is thine, between us, will I send thee. Go home again, thou fool;.thou hast not won me. || 14. Thy lover shall flee forth this day for ever, to seek, without return, the farthest distance. | Then let his bed be in Destruction's bosom, and there let fierce rapacious wolves devour him. || 15. Nay, do not die, Purūravas, nor vanish: let not the evil-omened wolves devour thee. | With women there can be no lasting friendship: hearts of hyenas are the hearts of women. || 16. When amid men in altered shape I sojourned, and through four autumns spent the nights among them, | I tasted once a day a drop of butter; and even now with that am I am contented. || 17. I, her best love, call Urvaśī to meet me, her who fills air and measures out the region. | Let the gift brought by piety approach thee. Turn thou to me again: my heart is troubled. || 18. Thus speak these Gods to thee, O son of Ilā: As death hath verily got thee for his subject, | Thy sons shall serve the Gods with their oblation, and thou, moreover, shalt rejoice in Svarga.

Hymn 10:96. Indra.

1. In the great synod will I laud thy two Bay Steeds: I prize the sweet strong drink of thee the Warrior-God, | His who pours lovely oil as 'twere with yellow drops. Let my songs enter thee whose form hath golden tints. || 2. Ye who in concert sing unto the gold-hued place, like Bay Steeds driving onward to the heavenly seat, | For Indra laud ye strength allied with Tawny Steeds, laud him whom cows content as 'twere with yellow drops. || 3. His is that thunderbolt, of iron, golden-hued, gold-coloured, very dear, and yellow in his arms; | Bright with strong teeth, destroying with its tawny rage. In Indra are set fast all forms of golden hue. || 4. As if a lovely ray were laid upon the sky, the golden thunderbolt spread out as in a race. | That iron bolt with yellow jaw smote Ahi down. A thousand flames had he who bore the tawny-hued. || 5. Thou, thou, when praised by men who sacrificed of old. hadst pleasure in their lauds, O Indra golden-haired. | All that befits thy song of praise thou welcomest, the perfect pleasant gift, O Golden-hued from birth. || 6. These two dear Bays bring hither Indra on his car, Thunder-armed, joyous, meet for laud, to drink his fill. | Many libations flow for him who loveth them: to Indra have the gold-hued Soma juices run. || 7. The gold-hued drops have flowed to gratify his wish: the yellow drops have urged the swift Bays to the Strong. | He who speeds on with Bay Steeds even as he lists hath satisfied his longing for the golden drops. || 8. At the swift draught the Soma-drinker waxed in might, the Iron One with yellow beard and yellow hair. | He, Lord of Tawny Coursers, Lord of fleet-foot Mares, will bear his Bay Steeds safely over all distress. || 9. His yellow-coloured jaws, like ladles move apart, what time, for strength, he makes the yellow-tinted stir, | When, while the bowl stands there, he grooms his Tawny Steeds, when he hath drunk strong drink, the sweet juice that he loves. || 10. Yea, to the Dear One's seat in homes of heaven and earth the Bay Steeds' Lord hath whinnied like a horse for food. | Then the great wish hath seized upon him mightily, and the Beloved One hath gained high power of life, || 11. Thou, comprehending with thy might the earth and heaven, acceptest the dear hymn for ever new and new. | O Asura, disclose thou and make visible the Cow's beloved home to the bright golden Sun. || 12. O Indra, let the eager wishes of the folk bring thee, delightful, golden-visored, on thy car, | That, pleased with sacrifice wherein ten fingers toil, thou mayest, at the feast, drink of our offered meath. || 13. Juices aforetime, Lord of Bays, thou drankest; and thine especially is this libation. | Gladden thee, Indra, with the meath-rich Soma: pour it down ever, Mighty One! within thee.

Hymn 10:97. Praise of Herbs.

1. Herbs that sprang up in time of old, three ages earlier than the Gods,— | Of these, whose hue is brown, will I declare the hundred powers and seven. || 2. Ye, Mothers, have a hundred homes, yea, and a thousand are your growths. | Do ye who have a thousand powers free this my patient from disease. || 3. Be glad and joyful in the Plants, both blossoming and bearing fruit, | Plants that will lead us to success like mares who conquer in the race. || 4. Plants, by this name I speak to you, Mothers, to you the Goddesses: | Steed, cow, and garment may I win, win back thy very self, O man. || 5. The Holy Fig tree is your home, your mansion is the Parṇa tree: | Winners of cattle shall ye be if ye regain for me this man. || 6. He who hath store of Herbs at hand like Kings amid a crowd of men,— | Physician is that sage's name, fiend-slayer, chaser of disease. || 7. Herbs rich in Soma, rich in steeds, in nourishments, in strengthening power,— | All these have I provided here, that this man may be whole again. || 8. The healing virtues of the Plants stream forth like cattle from the stall,— | Plants that shall win me store of wealth, and save thy vital breath, O man. || 9. Reliever is your mother's name, and hence Restorers are ye called. | Rivers are ye with wings that fly: keep far whatever brings disease. || 10. Over all fences have they passed, as steals a thief into the fold. | The Plants have driven from the frame whatever malady was there. || 11. When, bringing back the vanished strength, I hold these herbs within my hand, | The spirit of disease departs ere he can seize upon the life. || 12. He through whose frame, O Plants, ye creep member by member, joint by joint,— | From him ye drive away disease like some strong arbiter of strife. || 13. Fly, Spirit of Disease, begone, with the blue jay and kingfisher. | Fly with the wind's impetuous speed, vanish together with the storm. || 14. Help every one the other, lend assistance each of you to each, | All of you be accordant, give furtherance to this speech of mine. || 15. Let fruitful Plants, and fruitless, those that blossom, and the blossomless, | Urged onward by Bṛihaspati, release us from our pain and grief; || 16. Release me from the curse's plague and woe that comes from Varuṇa; | Free me from Yama's fetter, from sin and offence against the Gods. || 17. What time, descending from the sky, the Plants flew earthward, thus they spake: | No evil shall befall the man whom while he liveth we pervade, || 18. Of all the many Plants whose King is, Soma, Plants of hundred forms, | Thou art the Plant most excellent, prompt to the wish, sweet to the heart. || 19. O all ye various Herbs whose King is Soma, that o'erspread the earth, | Urged onward by Bṛihaspati, combine your virtue in this Plant. || 20. Unharmed be he who digs you up, unharmed the man for whom I dig: | And let no malady attack biped or quadruped of ours. || 21. All Plants that hear this speech, and those that have departed far away, | Come all assembled and confer your healing power upon this Herb. || 22. With Soma as their Sovereign Lord the Plants hold colloquy and say: | O King, we save from death the man whose cure a Brahman undertakes. || 23. Most excellent of all art thou, O Plant thy vassals are the trees. | Let him be subject to our power, the man who seeks to injure us.

Hymn 10:98. The Gods.

1. Come, be thou Mitra, Varuṇa, or Pūshan, come, O Bṛihaspati, to mine oblation: | With Marutas, Vasus, or Ādityas, make thou Parjanya pour for Śantanu his rain-drops. || 2. The God, intelligent, the speedy envoy whom thou hast sent hath come to me, Devāpi: | Address thyself to me and turn thee hither within thy lips will I put brilliant language. || 3. Within my mouth, Bṛihaspati, deposit speech lucid, vigorous, and free from weakness, | Thereby to win for Śantanu the rain-fall. The meath-rich drop from heaven hath passed within it. || 4. Let the sweet drops descend on us, O Indra: give us enough to lade a thousand wagons. | Sit to thy Hotar task; pay worship duly, and serve the Gods, Devāpi, with oblation. || 5. Knowing the God's good-will, Devāpi Ṛishi, the son of Ṛishṭishena, sate as Hotar. | He hath brought down from heaven's most lofty summit the ocean of the rain, celestial waters. || 6. Gathered together in that highest ocean, the waters stood by deities obstructed. | They hurried down set free by Ārishṭishena, in gaping clefts, urged onward by Devāpi. || 7. When as chief priest for Śantanu, Devāpi, chosen for Hotar's duty, prayed beseeching, | Graciously pleased Bṛihaspati vouchsafed him a voice that reached the Gods and won the waters. || 8. O Agni whom Devāpi Ārishṭishena, the mortal man, hath kindled in his glory, | Joying in him with all the Gods together, urge on the sender of the rain, Parjanya. || 9. All ancient Ṛishis with their songs approached thee, even thee, O Much-invoked, at sacrifices. | We have provided wagon-loads in thousands: come to the solemn rite, Lord of Red Horses. || 10. The wagon-loads, the nine-and-ninety thousand, these have been offered up to thee, O Agni. | Hero, with these increase thy many bodies, and, stimulated, send us rain from heaven. || 11. Give thou these ninety thousand loads, O Agni, to Indra, to the Bull, to be his portion. | Knowing the paths which Deities duly travel, set mid the Gods in heaven Aulāna also. || 12. O Agni, drive afar our foes, our troubles chase malady away and wicked demons. | From this air-ocean,

from the lofty heavens, send down on us a mighty flood of waters.

Hymn 10:99. Indra.

1. What Splendid One, Loud-voiced, Far-striding, dost thou, well knowing, urge us to exalt with praises? | What give we him? When his might dawned, he fashioned the Vṛitra-slaying bolt, and sent us waters. ‖ 2. He goes to end his work with lightning flashes: wide is the seat his Asura glory gives him. | With his Companions, not without his Brother, he quells Saptatha's magic devices. ‖ 3. On most auspicious path he goes to battle he toiled to win heaven's light, full fain to gain it; | He seized the hundred-gated castle's treasure by craft, unchecked, and slew the lustful demons. ‖ 4. Fighting for kine, the prize of war, and I roaming among the herd be brings the young streams hither, | Where, footless, joined, without a car to bear them, with jars for steeds, they pour their flood like butter. ‖ 5. Bold, unsolicited for wealth, with Rudras he came, the Blameless, having left his dwelling, | Came, seized the food of Vamra and his consort, and left the couple weeping and unsheltered. ‖ 6. Lord of the dwelling, he subdued the demon who roared aloud, six-eyed and triple-headed. | Trita, made stronger by the might he lent him, struck down the boar with shaft whose point was iron. ‖ 7. He raised himself on high and shot his arrow against the guileful and oppressive foeman. | Strong, glorious, manliest, for us he shattered the forts of Nahus when he slew the Dasyus. ‖ 8. He, like a cloud that rains upon the pasture, hath found for us the way to dwell in safety. | When the Hawk comes in body to the Soma, armed with his iron claws he slays the Dasyus. ‖ 9. He with his potent Friends gave up the mighty, gave Śushṇa up to Kutsa for affliction. | He led the lauded Kavi, he delivered Atka as prey to him and to his heroes. ‖ 10. He, with his Gods who love mankind, the Wondrous, giving like Varuṇa who works with magic, | Was known, yet young as guardian of the seasons; and he quelled Ararat, four-footed demon. ‖ 11. Through lauds of him hath Auśija Ṛijiśvan burst, with the Mighty's aid, the stall of Pipru. | When the saint pressed the juice and shone as singer, he seized the forts and with his craft subdued them. ‖ 12. So, swiftly Asura, for exaltation, hath the great Vamraka come nigh to Indra. | He will, when supplicated, bring him blessing: he hath brought all, food, strength, a happy dwelling.

Hymn 10:100. Viśvedevas.

1. Be, like thyself, O Indra, strong for our delight: here lauded, aid us, Maghavan, drinker of the juice. | Savitar with the Gods protect us: hear ye Twain. We ask for freedom and complete felicity. ‖ 2. Bring swift, for offering, the snare that suits the time, to the pure-drinker Vāyu, roaring as he goes, | To him who hath approached the draught of shining milk. We ask for freedom and complete felicity. ‖ 3. May Savitar the God send us full life, to each who sacrifices, lives aright and pours the juice | That we with simple hearts may wait upon the Gods. We ask for freedom and complete felicity. ‖ 4. May Indra evermore be gracious unto us, and may King Soma meditate our happiness, | Even as men secure the comfort of a friend. We ask for freedom and complete felicity. ‖ 5. Indra hath given the body with its song and strength: Bṛihaspati, thou art the lengthener of life. | The sacrifice is Manu, Providence, our Sire. We ask for freedom and complete felicity. ‖ 6. Indra possesseth might celestial nobly formed: the singer in the house is Agni, prudent Sage. | lie is the sacrifice in synod, fair, most near. We ask for freedom and complete felicity, ‖ 7. Not often have we sinned against you secretly, nor, Vasus, have we openly provoked the Gods. | Not one of its, ye Gods, hath worn an alien shape. We ask for freedom and complete felicity. ‖ 8. May Savitar remove from us our malady, and may the Mountains keep it far away from where | The press-stone as it sheds the meath rings loudly forth. We ask for freedom and complete felicity. ‖ 9. Ye Vasus, let the stone, the presser stand erect: avert all enmities and keep them far remote. | Our guard to be adored is Savitar this God. We ask for freedom and complete felicity. ‖ 10. Eat strength and fatness in the pasture, kine, who are balmed at the reservoir and at the seat of Law. | So let your body be our body's medicine. We ask for freedom and complete felicity. ‖ 11. The singer fills the spirit: all mens, love hath he. Indra takes kindly care of those who pour the juice. | For his libation is the heavenly udder full. We ask for freedom and complete felicity. ‖ 12. Wondrous thy spirit-filling light, triumphant; thy hosts save from decay and are resistless. | The pious votary by straightest pathway speeds to possess the best of all the cattle.

Hymn 10:101. Viśvedevas.

1. Wake with one mind, my friends, and kindle Agni, ye who are many and who dwell together. | Agni and Dadhikrās and Dawn the Goddess, you, Gods with Indra, I call down to help us. ‖ 2. Make pleasant hymns, spin out your songs and praises: build ye a ship equipped with oars for transport. | Prepare the implements, make all things ready, and let the sacrifice, my friends, go forward. ‖ 3. Lay on the yokes, and fasten well the traces: formed is the furrow, sow the seed within it. | Through song may we find bearing fraught with plenty: near to the ripened grain approach the sickle. ‖ 4. Wise, through desire of bliss from Gods, the skilful bind the traces fast, And lay the yokes on either side. ‖ 5. Arrange the buckets in their place securely fasten on the straps. | We will pour forth the well that hath a copious stream, fair-flowing well that never fails. ‖ 6. I pour the water from the well with pails prepared and goodly straps, | Unfailing, full, with plenteous stream. ‖ 7. Refresh the horses, win the prize before you: equip a chariot fraught with happy fortune. | Pour forth the well with stone wheel, wooden buckets, the drink of heroes, with the trough for armour. ‖ 8. Prepare the cow-stall, for there drink your heroes: stitch ye the coats of armour, wide and many. | Make iron forts, secure from all assailants let not your pitcher leak: stay it securely. ‖ 9. Hither, for help, I turn the holy heavenly mind of you the Holy Gods, that longs for sacrifice. | May it pour milk for us, even as a stately cow who, having sought the pasture, yields a thousand streams. ‖ 10. Pour golden juice within the wooden vessel: with stone-made axes fashion ye and form it. | Embrace and compass it with tenfold girdle, and to both chariot-poles attach the car-horse. ‖ 11. Between both poles the car-horse goes pressed closely, as in his dwelling moves the doubly-wedded. | Lay in the wood the Sovereign of the Forest, and sink the well although ye do not dig it. ‖ 12. Indra is he, O men, who gives us happiness: sport, urge the giver of delight to win us strength | Bring quickly down, O priests, hither to give us aid, to drink the Soma, Indra Son of Nishṭigrī.

Hymn 10:102. Indra.

1. For thee may Indra boldly speed the car that works on either side. | Favour us, Much-invoked! in this most glorious fight against the raiders of our wealth. ‖ 2. Loose in the wind the woman's robe was streaming what time she won a car-load worth a thousand. | The charioteer in fight was Mudgalānī: she Indra's dart, heaped up the prize of battle. ‖ 3. O Indra, cast thy bolt among assailants who would slaughter us: | The weapon both of Dāsa and of Ārya foe keep far away, O Maghavan. ‖ 4. The bull in joy had drunk a lake of water. His shattering horn encountered an opponent. | Swiftly, in vigorous strength, eager for glory, he stretched his forefeet, fain to win and triumph. ‖ 5. They came anear the bull; they made him thunder, made him pour rain down ere the fight was ended. | And Mudgala thereby won in the contest well-pastured kine in hundreds and in thousands. ‖ 6. In hope of victory that bull was harnessed: Keśī the driver urged him on with shouting. | As he ran swiftly with the car behind him his lifted heels pressed close on Mudgalānī. ‖ 7. Deftly for him he stretched the car-pole forward, guided the bull thereto and firmly yoked him. | Indra vouchsafed the lord of cows his favour: with mighty steps the buffalo ran onward. ‖ 8. Touched by the goad the shaggy beast went nobly, bound to the pole by the yoke's thong of leather. | Performing deeds of might for many people, he, looking on the cows, gained strength and vigour. ‖ 9. Here look upon this mace, this bull's companion, now lying midway on the field of battle. | Therewith hath Mudgala in ordered contest won for cattle for himself, a hundred thousand. ‖ 10. Far is the evil: who hath here beheld it? Hither they bring the bull whom they are yoking. | To this they give not either food or water. Reaching beyond the pole it gives directions. ‖ 11. Like one forsaken, she hath found a husband, and teemed as if her breast were full and flowing. | With swiftly-racing chariot may we conquer, and rich and blessed be our gains in battle. ‖ 12. Thou, Indra, art the mark whereon the eyes of all life rest, when thou, | A Bull who drivest with thy bull, wilt win the race together with thy weakling friend.

Hymn 10:103. Indra.

1. Swift, rapidly striking, like a bull who sharpens his horns, terrific, stirring up the people, | With eyes that close not, bellowing, Sole Hero, Indra. subdued at once a hundred armies. ‖ 2. With him loud-roaring, ever watchful, Victor, bold, hard to overthrow, Rouser of battle, | Indra. the

Strong, whose hand bears arrows, conquer, ye warriors, now, now vanquish in the combat. || 3. He rules with those who carry shafts and quivers, Indra who with his band rings hosts together, | Foe-conquering, strong of arm, the Soma-drinker, with mighty bow, shooting with well-laid arrows. || 4. Bṛihaspati, fly with thy chariot hither, slayer of demons, driving off our foemen. | Be thou protector of our cars, destroyer, victor in battle, breaker-up of armies. || 5. Conspicuous by thy strength, firm, foremost fighter, mighty and fierce, victorious, all-subduing, | The Son of Conquest, passing men and heroes, kine-winner, mount thy conquering car, O Indra. || 6. Cleaver of stalls, kine-winner, armed with thunder, who quells an army and with might destroys it. | Follow him, brothers! quit yourselves like heroes, and like this Indra show your zeal and courage. || 7. Piercing the cow-stalls with surpassing vigour, Indra, the pitiless Hero, wild with anger, | Victor in fight, unshaken and resistless,may he protect our armies in our battles. || 8. Indra guide these: Bṛihaspati precede them, the guerdon, and the sacrifice, and Soma; | And let the banded Marutas march in forefront of heavenly hosts that conquer and demolish. || 9. Ours be the potent host of mighty Indra, King Varuṇa, and Marutas, and Ādityas. | Uplifted is the shout of Gods who conquer high-minded Gods who cause the worlds to tremble. || 10. Bristle thou up, O Maghavan, our weapons: excite the spirits of my warring heroes. | Urge on the strong steeds' might, O Vṛitra-slayer, and let the din of conquering cars go upward. || 11. May Indra aid us when our flags are gathered: victorious be the arrows of our army. | May our brave men of war prevail in battle. Ye Gods, protect us in the shout of onset. || 12. Bewildering the senses of our foemen, seize thou their bodies and depart, O Apvā. | Attack them, set their hearts on fire and burn them: so let our foes abide in utter darkness. || 13. Advance, O heroes, win the day. May Indra be your sure defence. | Exceeding mighty be your arms, that none may wound or injure you.

Hymn 10:104. Indra.

1. Soma hath flowed for thee, Invoked of mat Speed to our sacrifice with both thy Coursers. | To thee have streamed the songs or mighty singers, imploring, Indra, drink of our libation. || 2. Drink of the juice which men have washed in waters, and fill thee full, O Lord of Tawny Horses. | O Indra, hearer of the laud, with Soma which stones have mixed for thee enhance thy rapture. || 3. To make thee start, a strong true draught I offer to thee, the Bull, O thou whom Bay Steeds carry. | Here take delight, O Indra, in our voices while thou art hymned with power and all our spirit. || 4. O Mighty Indra, through thine aid, thy prowess, obtaining life, zealous, and skilled in Order, | Men in the house who share the sacred banquet stand singing praise that brings them store of children. || 5. Through thy directions, Lord of Tawny Coursers, thine who art firm, splendid, and blest, the people | Obtain most liberal aid for their salvation, and praise thee, Indra, through thine excellencies. || 6. Lord of the Bays, come with thy two Bay Horses, come to our prayers, to drink the juice of Soma. | To thee comes sacrifice which thou acceptest: thou, skilled in holy rites, art he who giveth. || 7. Him of a thousand powers, subduing foemen, Maghavan praised with hymns and pleased with Soma,— | Even him our songs approach, resistless Indra: the adorations of the singer laud him. || 8. The way to bliss for Gods and man thou foundest, Indra, seven lovely floods, divine, untroubled, | Wherewith thou, rending forts, didst move the ocean, and nine-and-ninety flowing streams of water. || 9. Thou from the curse didst free the mighty Waters, and as their only God didst watch and guard them. | O Indra, cherish evermore thy body with those which thou hast won in quelling Vṛitra. || 10. Heroic power and noble praise is Indra yea, the song worships him invoked of many. | Vṛitra he quelled, and gave men room and freedom: Śakra, victorious, hath conquered armies. || 11. Call we on Maghavan, auspicious Indra. best Hero in this fight where spoil is gathered, | The Strong, who listens, who gives aid in battles, who slays the Vṛitras, wins and gathers riches.

Hymn 10:105. Indra.

1. When, Vasu, wilt thou love the laud? Now let the channel bring the stream. | The juice is ready to ferment. || 2. He whose two Bay Steeds harnessed well, swerving, pursue the Bird's tail-plumes, | With Rowing manes, like heaven and earth, he is the Lord with power to give. || 3. Bereft of skill is Indra, if, like some outwearied man he fears | The sinner, when the Mighty hath prepared himself for victory. || 4. Indra with these drives round, until he meets with one to worship him: | Indra is Master of the pair who snort and swerve upon their way. || 5. Borne onward by the long-maned Steeds who stretch themselves as 'twere for food, | The God who wears the helm defends them with his jaws. || 6. The Mighty sang with Lofty Ones: the Hero fashioned with his strength, | Like skilful Mātariśvan with his power and might, || 7. The bolt, which pierced at once the vitals of the Dasyu easy to be slain, | With jaw uninjured like the wondrous firmament. || 8. Grind off our sins: with song will we conquer the men who sing no hymns: | Not easily art thou pleased with prayerless sacrifice. || 9. When threefold flame burns high for thee, to rest on poles of sacrifice, | Thou with the living joyest in the self-bright Ship. || 10. Thy glory was the speckled cup, thy glory was the flawless scoop. | Wherewith thou pourest into thy receptacle. || 11. As hundreds, O Immortal God, have sung to thee, so hath Sumitra, yea, Durmitra praised thee here, | What time thou holpest Kutsa's son, when Dasyus fell, yea, holpest Kutsa's darling when the Dasyus died.

Hymn 10:106. Aśvins.

[stanzas 5-11 here are borrowed from Wilson's translation]

1. This very thing ye Twain hold as your object: ye weave your songs as skilful men weave garments. | That ye may come united have I waked you: ye spread out food like days of lovely weather. || 2. Like two plough-bulls ye move along in traces, and seek like eager guests your bidder's banquet. | Ye are like glorious envoys mid the people: like bulls, approach the place where ye are watered. || 3. Like the two pinions of a bird, connected, like two choice animals, ye have sought our worship. | Bright as the fire the votary hath kindled, ye sacrifice in many a spot as roamers. || 4. Ye are our kinsmen, like two sons, two fathers, strong in your splendour and like kings for conquest; | Like rays for our enjoyment, Lords to feed us, ye, like quick bearers, have obeyed our calling. || 5. You are like two pleasantly moving well-fed (hills) like Mitra and Varuṇa, the two bestowers of felicity, veracious, possessors of infinite wealth, happy, like two horses plump with fodder, abiding in the firmament, like two rams (are you) to be nourished with sacrificial food, to be cherished (with oblations). || 6. You are like two mad elephants bending their forequarters and smiting the foe, like the two sons of Nitośa destroying (foes), and cherishing (friends); you are bright as two water-born (jewels), do you, who are victorious, (render) my decaying mortal body free from decay. || 7. Fierce (Aśvins), like two powerful (heroes), you enable this moving, perishable mortal (frame) to cross over to the objects (of its destination) as over water; extremely strong, like the Ṛibhus, your chariot, attained its destination swift as the wind, it pervaded (everywhere), it dispensed riches. || 8. With your bellies full of the Soma, like two saucepans, preservers of wealth, destroyers of enemies. (you are) armed with hatchets, moving like two flying (birds) with forms like the moon, attaining success through the mind, like two laudable beings, (you are) approaching (the sacrifice). || 9. Like giants, ye will find firm ground to stand on in depths, like feet for one who fords a shallow. | Like cars ye will attend to him who orders: ye Two enjoy our wondrous work as sharers. || 10. Like toiling bees ye bring to us your honey, as bees into the hide that opens downward. || 11. May we increase the laud and gain us vigour: come to our song, ye whom one chariot carries. | Filled be our kine with ripened meath like glory: Bhūtāṃśa hath fulfilled the Aśvins' longing.

Hymn 10:107. Dakṣhiṇā.

1. These men's great bounty hath been manifested, and the whole world of life set free from darkness. | Great light hath come, vouchsafed us by the Fathers: apparent is the spacious path of Guerdon. || 2. High up in heaven abide the Guerdon-givers: they who give steeds dwell with the Sun for ever. | They who give gold are blest with life eternal. they who give robes prolong their lives, O Soma. || 3. Not from the niggards—for they give not freely—comes Meed at sacrifice, Gods' satisfaction: | Yea, many men with hands stretched out with Guerdon present their gifts because they dread dishonour. || 4. These who observe mankind regard oblation as streamy Vāyu and light-finding Arka. | They satisfy and give their gifts in synod, and pour in streams the seven-mothered Guerdon. || 5. He who brings Guerdon comes as first invited: chief of the hamlet comes the Guerdon-bearer. | Him I account the ruler of the people who was the first to introduce the Guerdon. || 6. They call him Ṛishi, Brahman, Sāman-

chanter, reciter of the laud, leader of worship. | The brightly-shining God's three forms he knoweth who first bestowed the sacrificial Guerdon. || 7. Guerdon bestows the horse, bestows the bullock, Guerdon bestows, moreover, gold that glisters. | Guerdon gives food which is our life and spirit. He who is wise takes Guerdon for his armour. || 8. The liberal die not, never are they ruined: the liberal suffer neither harm nor trouble. | The light of heaven, the universe about us,—all this doth sacrificial Guerdon give them. || 9. First have the liberal gained a fragrant dwelling, and got themselves a bride in fair apparel. | The liberal have obtained their draught of liquor, and conquered those who, unprovoked, assailed them. || 10. They deck the fleet steed for the bounteous giver: the maid adorns herself and waits to meet him. | His home is like a lake with lotus blossoms, like the Gods' palaces adorned and splendid. || 11. Steeds good at draught convey the liberal giver, and lightly rolling moves the car of Guerdon. | Assist, ye Gods, the liberal man in battles: the liberal giver conquers foes in combat.

Hymn 10:108. Saramā. Paṇis.

1. What wish of Saramā hath brought her hither? The path leads far away to distant places. | What charge hast thou for us? Where turns thy journey? How hast thou made thy way o'er Rasā's waters. || 2. I come appointed messenger of Indra, seeking your ample stores of wealth, O Paṇis. | This hath preserved me from the fear of crossing: thus have I made my way o'er Rasā's waters. || 3. What is that Indra like, what is his aspect whose envoy, Saramā, from afar thou comest? | Let him approach, and we will show him friendship: he shall be made the herdsman of our cattle. || 4. I know him safe from harm: but he can punish who sent me hither from afar as envoy. | Him rivers flowing with deep waters bide not. Low will ye be, O Paṇis, slain by Indra. || 5. These are the kine which, Saramā, thou seekest, flying, O Blest One, to the ends of heaven. | Who will loose these for thee without a battle? Yea, and sharp-pointed are our warlike weapons. || 6. Even if your wicked bodies, O ye Paṇis, were arrow-proof, your words are weak for wounding; | And were the path to you as yet unmastered, Bṛihaspati in neither case will spare you. || 7. Paved with the rock is this our treasure-chamber; filled full of precious things, of kine, and horses. | These Paṇis who are watchful keepers guard it. In vain hast thou approached this lonely station. || 8. Ṛishis will come inspirited with Soma, Aṅgirasas unwearied, and Navagvas. | This stall of cattle will they part among them: then will the Paṇis wish these words unspoken. || 9. Even thus, O Saramā, hast thou come hither, forced by celestial might to make the journey. | Turn thee not back, for thou shalt be our sister: O Blest One, we will give thee of the cattle. || 10. Brotherhood, sisterhood, I know not either: the dread Aṅgirasas and Indra know them. | They seemed to long for kine when I departed. Hence, into distance, be ye gone, O Paṇis. || 11. Hence, far away, ye Paṇis! Let the cattle lowing come forth as holy Law commandeth, | Kine which Bṛihaspati, and Soma, Ṛishis, sages, and pressing-stones have found when hidden.

Hymn 10:109. Viśvedevas.

1. These first, the boundless Sea, and Mātariśvan, fierce-glowing Fire, the Strong, the Bliss-bestower. | And heavenly Floods, first-born by holy Order, exclaimed against the outrage on a Brahman. || 2. King Soma first of all, without reluctance, made restitution of the Brahman's consort. | Mitra and Varuṇa were the inviters: Agni as Hotar took her hand and led her. || 3. The man, her pledge, must by her hand be taken when they have cried, She is a Brahman's consort. | She stayed not for a herald to conduct her: thus is the kingdom of a ruler guarded. || 4. Thus spake of her those Gods of old, Seven Ṛishis who sate them down to their austere devotion: | Dire is a Brahman's wife led home by others: in the supremest heaven she plants confusion. || 5. The Brahmachārī goes engaged in duty: he is a member of the Gods' own body. | Through him Bṛihaspati obtained his consort, as the Gods gained the ladle brought by Soma. || 6. So then the Gods restored her, so men gave the woman back again. | The Kings who kept their promises restored the Brahman's wedded wife, || 7. Having restored the Brahman's wife, and freed them, with Gods' aid, from sin, | They shared the fullness of the earth, and won themselves extended sway.

Hymn 10:110. Āprīs.

1. Thou in the house of man this day enkindled worshippest Gods as God, O Jātavedas. | Observant, bright as Mitra, bring them hither: thou art a sapient and foreknowing envoy. || 2. Tanūnapāt, fair-tongued, with sweet meath balming the paths and ways of Order, make them pleasant. | Convey our sacrifice to heaven, exalting with holy thoughts our hymns of praise and worship. || 3. Invoked, deserving prayer and adoration, O Agni, come accordant with the Vasus. | Thou art, O Youthful Lord, the Gods' Invoker, so, best of Sacrificers, bring them quickly. || 4. By rule the Sacred Grass is scattered eastward, a robe to clothe this earth when dawns are breaking. | Widely it spreads around and far-extended, fair for the Gods and bringing peace and freedom. || 5. Let the expansive Doors be widely opened, like wives who deck their beauty for their husbands. | Lofty, celestial, all-impelling Portals, admit the Gods and give them easy entrance. || 6. Pouring sweet dews let holy Night and Morning, each close to each, he seated at their station, | Lofty, celestial Dames with gold to deck them. assuming all their fair and radiant beauty. || 7. Come the two first celestial sweet-voiced Hotars, arranging sacrifice for man to worship | As singers who inspire us in assemblies, showing the eastward light with their direction. || 8. Let Bhāratī come quickly to our worship, and Iḷā showing like a human being. | So let Sarasvatī and both her fellows, deft Goddesses, on this fair grass be seated. || 9. Hotar more skilled in sacrifice, bring hither with speed today God Tvashṭar, thou who knowest. | Even him who formed these two, the Earth and Heaven the Parents, with their forms, and every creature. || 10. Send to our offerings which thyself thou balmest the Companies of Gods in ordered season. | Agni, Vanaspati the Immolator sweeten our offered gift with meath and butter. || 11. Agni, as soon as he was born, made ready the sacrifice, and was the Gods' preceder. | May the Gods cat our offering consecrated according to this true Priest's voice and guidance.

Hymn 10:111. Indra.

1. Bring forth your sacred song ye prudent singers, even as are the thoughts of human beings. | Let us draw Indra with true deeds anear us: he loves our songs, the Hero, and is potent. || 2. The hymn shone brightly from the seat of worship: to the kine came the Bull, the Heifer's Offspring | With mighty bellowing hath he arisen, and hath pervaded even the spacious regions. || 3. Indra knows, verily, how to hear our singing, for he, victorious, made a path for Sūrya. | He made the Cow, and be became the Sovereign of Heaven, primeval, matchless, and unshaken. || 4. Praised by Aṅgirasas, Indra demolished with might the works of the great watery monster | Full many regions, too, hath he pervaded, and by his truth supported earth's foundation. || 5. The counterpart of heaven and earth is Indra: he knoweth all libations, slayeth Śushṇa. | The vast sky with the Sun hath he extended, and, best of pillars, stayed it with a pillar. || 6. The Vṛitra-slayer with his bolt felled Vṛitra: the magic of the godless, waxen mighty, | Here hast thou, Bold Assailant, boldly conquered. Yea, then thine arms, O Maghavan, were potent. || 7. When the Dawns come attendant upon Sūrya their rays discover wealth of divers colours. | The Star of heaven is seen as 'twere approaching: none knoweth aught of it as it departeth. || 8. Far have they gone, the first of all these waters, the waters that flowed forth when Indra sent them. | Where is their spring, and where is their foundation? Where now, ye Waters, is your inmost centre? || 9. Thou didst free rivers swallowed by the Dragon; and rapidly they set themselves in motion, | Those that were loosed and those that longed for freedom. Excited now to speed they run unresting. || 10. Yearning together they have sped to Sindhu: the Fort-destroyer, praised, of old, hath loved them. | Indra, may thy terrestrial treasures reach us, and our full songs of joy approach thy dwelling.

Hymn 10:112. Indra.

1. Drink of the juice, O Indra, at thy plea. sure, for thy first draught is early morn's libation. | Rejoice, that thou mayst slay our foes, O Hero, and we with lauds will tell thy mighty exploits. || 2. Thou hast a car more swift than thought, O Indra; thereon come hither, come to drink the Soma. | Let thy Bay Steeds, thy Stallions, hasten hither, with whom thou comest nigh and art delighted. || 3. Deck out thy body with the fairest colours, with golden splendour of the Sun adorn it. | O Indra, turn thee hitherward invited by us thy friends; be seated and be joyful. || 4. O thou whose grandeur in thy festive transports not even these two great worlds have comprehended. | Come, Indra, with thy dear Bay Horses harnessed, come to our dwelling and the food thou lovest. || 5. Pressed for thy joyous banquet is the Soma, Soma whereof thou, Indra, ever drinking, | Hast waged unequalled battles with thy foemen, which prompts the mighty flow of thine abundance. || 6.

Found from of old is this thy cup, O Indra: Śatakratu, drink therefrom the Soma. | Filled is the beaker with the meath that gladdens, the beaker which all Deities delight in. || 7. From many a side with proffered entertainment the folk are calling thee, O Mighty Indra. | These our libations shall for thee be richest in sweet meath: drink thereof and find them pleasant. || 8. I will declare thy deeds of old, O Indra, the mighty acts which thou hast first accomplished. | In genuine wrath thou loosenedst the mountain so that the Brahman easily found the cattle. || 9. Lord of the hosts, amid our bands be seated: they call thee greatest Sage among the sages. | Nothing is done, even far away, without thee: great, wondrous, Maghavan, is the hymn I sing thee. || 10. Aim of our eyes be thou, for we implore thee, O Maghavan, Friend of friends and Lord of treasures. | Fight, Warrior strong in truth, fight thou the battle: give us our share of undivided riches.

Hymn 10:113. Indra.

1. The Heavens and the Earth accordant with all Gods encouraged graciously that vigorous might of his. | When he came showing forth his majesty and power, he drank of Soma juice and waxed exceeding strong. || 2. This majesty of his Vishṇu extols and lauds, making the stalk that gives the meath flow forth with might. | When Indra Maghavan with those who followed him had smitten Vṛitra he deserved the choice of Gods. || 3. When, bearing warlike weapons, fain to win thee praise, thou mettest Vṛitra, yea, the Dragon, for the fight, | Then all the Marutas who were gathered with dice there extolled, O Mighty One, thy powerful majesty. || 4. Soon as he sprang to life he forced asunder hosts: forward the Hero looked to manly deed and war. | He cleft the rock, he let concurrent streams flow forth, and with his skilful art established the heavens' wide vault. || 5. Indra hath evermore possessed surpassing power: he forced, far from each other, heaven and earth apart. | He hurled impetuous down his iron thunderbolt, a joy to Varuṇa's and Mitra's worshipper. || 6. Then to the mighty powers of Indra, to his wrath, his the fierce Stormer, loud of voice, they came with speed; | What time the Potent One rent Vṛitra with his strength, who held the waters back, whom darkness compassed round. || 7. Even in the first of those heroic acts which they who strove together came with might to execute, | Deep darkness fell upon the slain, and Indra won by victory the right of being first invoked. || 8. Then all the Gods extolled, with eloquence inspired by draughts of Soma juice, thy deeds of manly might. | As Agni eats the dry food with his teeth, he ate Vṛitra, the Dragon, maimed by Indra's deadly dart. || 9. Proclaim his many friendships, met with friendship, made with singers, with the skilful and the eloquent. | Indra, when he subdues Dhuni and Chumuri, lists to Dabhīti for his faithful spirit's sake. || 10. Give riches manifold with noble horses, to be remembered while my songs address thee. | May we by easy paths pass all our troubles: find us this day a ford wide and extensive.

Hymn 10:114. Viśvedevas.

1. Two perfect springs of heat pervade the Threefold, and come for their delight is Mātariśvan. | Craving the milk of heaven the Gods are present: well do they know the praise song and the Sāman. || 2. The priests beard far away, as they are ordered, serve the three Nirṛitis, for well they know them. | Sages have traced the cause that first produced them, dwelling in distant and mysterious chambers. || 3. The Youthful One, well-shaped, with four locks braided, brightened with oil, puts on the ordinances. | Two Birds of mighty power are seated near her, there where the Deities receive their portion. || 4. One of these Birds hath passed into the sea of air: thence he looks round and views this universal world. | With simple heart I have beheld him from anear: his Mother kisses him and he returns her kiss. || 5. Him with fair wings though only One in nature, wise singers shape, with songs, in many figures. | While they at sacrifices fix the metres, they measure out twelve chalices of Soma. || 6. While they arrange the four and six-and-thirty, and duly order, up to twelve, the measures, | Having disposed the sacrifice thoughtful sages send the Car forward with the Ṛich and Sāman. || 7. The Chariot's majesties are fourteen others: seven sages lead it onward with their Voices. | Who will declare to us the ford Āpnāna, the path whereby they drink first draughts of Soma? || 8. The fifteen lauds are in a thousand places that is as vast as heaven and earth in measure. | A thousand spots contain the mighty thousand. Vāk spreadeth forth as far as Prayer extendeth. || 9. What sage hath learned the metres' application? Who hath gained Vāk, the spirit's aim and object? | Which ministering priest is called eighth Hero? Who then hath tracked the two Bay Steeds of Indra? || 10. Yoked to his chariot-pole there stood the Coursers: they only travel round earth's farthest limits. | These, when their driver in his home is settled, receive the allotted meed of their exertion.

Hymn 10:115. Agni.

1. Verily wondrous is the tender Youngling's growth who never draweth nigh to drink his Mothers' milk. | As soon as she who hath no udder bore him, he, faring on his great errand, suddenly grew strong. || 2. Then Agni was his name, most active to bestow, gathering up the trees with his consuming tooth; | Skilled in fair sacrifice, armed with destroying tongue, impetuous as a bull that snorteth in the mead. || 3. Praise him, your God who, bird-like, rests upon a tree, scattering drops of juice and pouring forth his flood, | Speaking aloud with flame as with his lips a priest, and broadening his paths like one of high command. || 4. Thou Everlasting, whom, far-striding fain to burn, the winds, uninterrupted, never overcome, | They have approached, as warriors eager for the fight, heroic Trita, guiding him to gain his wish. || 5. This Agni is the best of Kaṇvas, Kaṇvas' Friend, Conqueror of the foe whether afar or near. | May Agni guard the singers, guard the princes well: may Agni grant to us our princes' gracious help. || 6. Do thou, Supitrya, swiftly following, make thyself the lord of Jātavedas, mightiest of all, | Who surely gives a boon even in thirsty land most powerful, prepared to aid us in the wilds. || 7. Thus noble Agni with princes and mortal men is lauded, excellent for conquering strength with chiefs, | Men who are well-disposed as friends and true to Law, even as the heavens in majesty surpass mankind. || 8. O Son of Strength, Victorious, with this title Upastuta's most potent voice reveres thee. | Blest with brave sons by thee we will extol thee, and lengthen out the days of our existence. || 9. Thus, Agni, have the sons of Vṛishṭihavya, the Ṛishis, the Upastutas invoked thee. | Protect them, guard the singers and the princes. With Vashaṭ! have they come, with hands uplifted, with their uplifted hands and cries of Glory!

Hymn 10:116. Indra.

1. Drink Soma juice for mighty power and vigour, drink, Strongest One, that thou mayst smite down Vṛitra. | Drink thou, invoked, for strength, and riches: drink thou thy fill of meath and pour it down, O Indra. || 2. Drink of the foodful juice stirred into motion, drink what thou choosest of the flowing Soma. | Giver of weal, be joyful in thy spirit, and turn thee hitherward to bless and prosper. || 3. Let heavenly Soma gladden thee, O Indra, let that effused among mankind delight thee. | Rejoice in that whereby thou gavest freedom, and that whereby thou conquerest thy foemen. || 4. Let Indra come, impetuous, doubly mighty, to the poured juice, the Bull, with two Bay Coursers. | With juices pressed in milk, with meath presented, glut evermore thy bolt, O Foe-destroyer. || 5. Dash down, out-flaming their sharp flaming weapons, the strong-holds of the men urged on by demons. | I give thee, Mighty One, great strength and conquest: go, meet thy foes and rend them in the battle. || 6. Extend afar the votary's fame and glory, as the firm archer's strength drives off the foeman. | Ranged on our side, grown strong in might that conquers, never defeated, still increase thy body. || 7. To thee have we presented this oblation: accept it, Sovereign Ruler, free from anger. | Juice, Maghavan, for thee is pressed and ripened: eat, Indra, drink of that which stirs to meet thee. || 8. Eat, Indra, these oblations which approach thee: be pleased with food made ready and with Soma. | With entertainment we receive thee friendly: effectual be the sacrificer's wishes. || 9. I send sweet speech to Indra and to Agni: with hymns I speed it like a boat through waters. | Even thus, the Gods seem moving round about me, the fountains and bestowers of our riches.

Hymn 10:117. Liberality.

1. The Gods have not ordained hunger to be our death: even to the well-fed man comes death in varied shape. | The riches of the liberal never waste away, while he who will not give finds none to comfort him. || 2. The man with food in store who, when the needy comes in miserable case begging for bread to eat, | Hardens his heart against him—even when of old he did him service—finds not one to comfort him. || 3. Bounteous is he who gives unto the beggar who comes to him in want of food and feeble. | Success attends him in the shout of battle. He makes a friend of him in future

troubles. ‖ 4. No friend is he who to his friend and comrade who comes imploring food, will offer nothing. | Let him depart—no home is that to rest in—and rather seek a stranger to support him. ‖ 5. Let the rich satisfy the poor implorer, and bend his eye upon a longer pathway. | Riches come now to one, now to another, and like the wheels of cars are ever rolling. ‖ 6. The foolish man wins food with fruitless labour: that food—I speak the truth—shall be his ruin. | He feeds no trusty friend, no man to love him. All guilt is he who eats with no partaker. ‖ 7. The ploughshare ploughing makes the food that feeds us, and with its feet cuts through the path it follows. | Better the speaking than the silent Brahman: the liberal friend out-values him who gives not. ‖ 8. He with one foot hath far outrun the biped, and the two-footed catches the three-footed. | Four-footed creatures come when bipeds call them, and stand and look where five are met together. ‖ 9. The hands are both alike: their labour differs. The yield of sister milch-kine is unequal. | Twins even differ in their strength and vigour: two, even kinsmen, differ in their bounty.

Hymn 10:118. Agni.

1. Agni, refulgent among men thou slayest the devouring fiend, | Bright Ruler in thine own abode. ‖ 2. Thou springest up when worshipped well the drops of butter are thy joy | When ladies are brought near to thee. ‖ 3. Honoured with gifts he shines afar, Agni adorable with song: | The dripping ladle balms his face. ‖ 4. Agni with honey in his mouth, honoured with gifts, is balmed with oil, | Refulgent in his wealth of light. ‖ 5. Praised by our hymns thou kindlest thee, Oblation-bearer, for the Gods | As such do mortals call on thee. ‖ 6. To that Immortal Agni pay worship with oil, ye mortal men,— | Lord of the house, whom none deceives. ‖ 7. O Agni, burn the Rākṣhasas with thine unconquerable flame | Shine guardian of Eternal Law. ‖ 8. So, Agni, with thy glowing face burn fierce against the female fiends, | Shining among Urukṣhayas. ‖ 9. Urukṣhayas have kindled thee, Oblation-bearer, thee, with hymns. | Best Worshipper among mankind.

Hymn 10:119. Indra.

1. This, even this was my resolve, to win a cow, to win a steed: | Have I not drunk of Soma juice? ‖ 2. Like violent gusts of wind the draughts that I have drunk have lifted me | Have I not drunk of Soma juice? ‖ 3. The draughts I drank have borne me up, as fleet-foot horses draw a car: | Have I not drunk of Soma juice? ‖ 4. The hymn hath reached me, like a cow who lows to meet her darling calf: | Have I not drunk of Soma juice? ‖ 5. As a wright bends a chariot-seat so round my heart I bend the hymn: | Have I not drunk of Soma juice? ‖ 6. Not as a mote within the eye count the Five Tribes of men with me: | Have I not drunk of Soma juice? ‖ 7. The heavens and earth themselves have not grown equal to one half of me | Have I not drunk of Soma juice? ‖ 8. I in my grandeur have surpassed the heavens and all this spacious earth | Have I not drunk of Soma juice? ‖ 9. Aha! this spacious earth will I deposit either here or there | Have I not drunk of Soma juice? ‖ 10. In one short moment will I smite the earth in fury here or there: | Have I not drunk of Soma juice? ‖ 11. One of my flanks is in the sky; I let the other trail below: | Have I not drunk of Soma juice? ‖ 12. I, greatest of the Mighty Ones, am lifted to the firmament: | Have I not drunk of Soma juice? ‖ 13. I seek the worshipper's abode; oblation-bearer to the Gods: | Have I not drunk of Soma juice?

Hymn 10:120. Indra.

1. In all the worlds That was the Best and Highest whence sprang the Mighty Gods, of splendid valour. | As soon as born he overcomes his foemen, be in whom all who lend him aid are joyful. ‖ 2. Grown mighty in his strength, with ample vigour, he as a foe strikes fear into the Dāsa, | Eager to win the breathing and the breathless. All sang thy praise at banquet and oblation. ‖ 3. All concentrate on thee their mental vigour, what time these, twice or thrice, are thine assistants. | Blend what is sweeter than the sweet with sweetness: win. quickly with our meath that meath in battle. ‖ 4. Therefore in thee too, thou who winnest riches, at every banquet are the sages joyful. | With mightier power, Bold God, extend thy firmness: let not malignant Yātudhānas harm thee. ‖ 5. Proudly we put our trust in thee in battles, when we behold great wealth the prize of combat. | I with my words impel thy weapons onward, and sharpen with my prayer thy vital vigour. ‖ 6. Worthy of praises, many-shaped, most skilful, most energetic, Āptya of the Āptyas: | He with his might destroys the seven Dānus, subduing many who were deemed his equals. ‖ 7. Thou in that house which thy protection guardeth bestowest wealth, the higher and the lower. | Thou establishest the two much-wandering Mothers, and bringest many deeds to their completion. ‖ 8. Bṛihaddiva, the foremost of light-winners, repeats these holy prayers, this strength of Indra. | He rules the great self-luminous fold of cattle, and all the doors of light hath he thrown open. ‖ 9. Thus hath Bṛihaddiva, the great Atharvan, spoken to Indra as himself in person. | The spotless Sisters, they who are his Mothers, with power exalt him and impel him onward.

Hymn 10:121. Ka.

1. In the beginning rose Hiraṇyagarbha, born Only Lord of all created beings. | He fixed and holdeth up this earth and heaven. What God shall we adore with our oblation? ‖ 2. Giver of vital breath, of power and vigour, he whose commandments all the Gods acknowledge. | The Lord of death, whose shade is life immortal. What God shall we adore with our oblation? ‖ 3. Who by his grandeur hath become Sole Ruler of all the moving world that breathes and slumbers; | He who is Lord of men and Lord of cattle. What God shall we adore with our oblation? ‖ 4. His, through his might, are these snow-covered mountains, and men call sea and Rasā his possession: | His arms are these, his are these heavenly regions. What God shall we adore with our oblation? ‖ 5. By him the heavens are strong and earth is steadfast, by him light's realm and sky-vault are supported: | By him the regions in mid-air were measured. What God shall we adore with our oblation? ‖ 6. To him, supported by his help, two armies embattled look while trembling in their spirit, | When over them the risen Sun is shining. What God shall we adore with our oblation? ‖ 7. What time the mighty waters came, containing the universal germ, producing Agni, | Thence sprang the Gods' one spirit into being. What God shall we adore with our oblation? ‖ 8. He in his might surveyed the floods containing productive force and generating Worship. | He is the God of Gods, and none beside him. What God shall we adore with our oblation? ‖ 9. Ne'er may he harm us who is earth's Begetter, nor he whose laws are sure, the heavens' Creator, | He who brought forth the great and lucid waters. What God shall we adore with our oblation? ‖ 10. Prajāpati! thou only comprehendest all these created things, and none beside thee. | Grant us our hearts' desire when we invoke thee: may we have store of riches in possession.

Hymn 10:122. Agni.

1. I praise the God of wondrous might like Indra, the lovely pleasant Guest whom all must welcome. | May Agni, Priest and Master of the household, give hero strength and all-sustaining riches. ‖ 2. O Agni, graciously accept this song of mine, thou passing-wise who knowest every ordinance. | Enwrapped in holy oil further the course of prayer: the Gods bestow according to thy holy law. ‖ 3. Immortal, wandering round the seven stations, give, a liberal Giver, to the pious worshipper, | Wealth, Agni, with brave sons and ready for his use: welcome the man who comes with fuel unto thee. ‖ 4. The seven who bring oblations worship thee, the Strong, the first, the Great Chief Priest, Ensign of sacrifice, | The oil-anointed Bull, Agni who hears, who sends as God full hero strength to him who freely gives. ‖ 5. First messenger art thou, meet for election: drink thou thy fill invited to the Amṛita, | The Marutas in the votary's house adorned thee; with lauds the Bhṛigus gave thee light and glory. ‖ 6. Milking the teeming Cow for all-sustaining food. O Wise One, for the worship-loving worshipper, | Thou, Agni, dropping oil, thrice lighting works of Law, showest thy wisdom circling home and sacrifice. ‖ 7. They who at flushing of this dawn appointed thee their messenger, these men have paid thee reverence. | Gods strengthened thee for work that must be glorified, Agni, while they made butter pure for sacrifice. ‖ 8. Arrangers in our synods, Agni, while they sang Vasiṣhṭha's sons have called thee down, the Potent One. | Maintain the growth of wealth with men who sacrifice. Ye Gods, preserve us with your blessings evermore.

Hymn 10:123. Vena.

1. See, Vena, born in light, hath driven hither, on chariot of the air, the Calves of Pṛiśni. | Singers with hymns caress him as an infant there where the waters and the sunlight mingle. ‖ 2. Vena draws up his wave from out the ocean. mist-born, the fair one's back is made apparent, | Brightly he shone aloft on Order's summit: the hosts sang glory to their common

birthplace. ‖ 3. Full many, lowing to their joint-possession, dwelling together stood the Darling's Mothers. | Ascending to the lofty height of Order, the bands of singers 'sip the sweets of Amṛita. ‖ 4. Knowing his form, the sages yearned to meet him: they have come nigh to hear the wild Bull's bellow. | Performing sacrifice they reached the river: for the Gandharva found the immortal waters. ‖ 5. The Apsaras, the Lady, sweetly smiling, supports her Lover in sublimest heaven. | In his Friend's dwelling as a Friend he wanders: he, Vena, rests him on his golden pinion. ‖ 6. They gaze on thee with longing in their spirit, as on a strong-winged bird that mounteth sky-ward; | On thee with wings of gold, Varuṇa's envoy, the Bird that hasteneth to the home of Yama. ‖ 7. Erect, to heaven hath the Gandharva mounted, pointing at us his many-coloured weapons; | Clad in sweet raiment beautiful to look on, for he, as light, produceth forms that please us. ‖ 8. When as a spark he cometh near the ocean, still looking with a vulture's eye to heaven, | His lustre, joying in its own bright splendour, maketh dear glories in the lowest region.

Hymn 10:124. Agni, etc.

1. Come to this sacrifice of ours, O Agni, threefold, with seven threads and five divisions. | Be our oblation-bearer and preceder: thou hast lain long enough in during darkness. ‖ 2. I come a God foreseeing from the godless to immortality by secret pathways, | While I, ungracious one, desert the gracious, leave mine own friends and seek the kin of strangers. ‖ 3. I, looking to the guest of other lineage, have founded many a rule of Law and Order. | I bid farewell to the Great God, the Father, and, for neglect, obtain my share of worship. ‖ 4. I tarried many a year within this altar: I leave the Father, for my choice is Indra. | Away pass Agni, Varuṇa and Soma. Rule ever changes: this I come to favour. ‖ 5. These Asuras have lost their powers of magic. But thou, O Varuṇa, if thou dost love me, | O King, discerning truth and right from falsehood, come and be Lord and Ruler of my kingdom. ‖ 6. Here is the light of heaven, here all is lovely; here there is radiance, here is air's wide region. | Let us two slaughter Vṛitra. Forth, O Soma! Thou art oblation: we therewith will serve thee. ‖ 7. The Sage hath fixed his form by wisdom in the heavens: Varuṇa with no violence let the waters flow. | Like women-folk, the floods that bring prosperity have caught his hue and colour as they gleamed and shone. ‖ 8. These wait upon his loftiest power and vigour: he dwells in these who triumph in their Godhead; | And they, like people who elect their ruler, have in abhorrence turned away from Vṛitra. ‖ 9. They call him Swan, the abhorrent floods' Companion, moving in friendship with celestial Waters. | The poets in their thought have looked on Indra swiftly approaching when Anushṭubh calls him.

Hymn 10:125. Vāk.

1. I travel with the Rudras and the Vasus, with the Ādityas and All-Gods I wander. | I hold aloft both Varuṇa and Mitra, Indra and Agni, and the Pair of Aśvins. ‖ 2. I cherish and sustain high-swelling Soma, and Tvashṭar I support, Pūshan, and Bhaga. | I load with wealth the zealous sacrificer who pours the juice and offers his oblation ‖ 3. I am the Queen, the gatherer-up of treasures, most thoughtful, first of those who merit worship. | Thus Gods have established me in many places with many homes to enter and abide in. ‖ 4. Through me alone all eat the food that feeds them,—each man who sees, breathes, hears the word outspoken | They know it not, but yet they dwell beside me. Hear, one and all, the truth as I declare it. ‖ 5. I, verily, myself announce and utter the word that Gods and men alike shall welcome. | I make the man I love exceeding mighty, make him a sage, a Ṛishi, and a Brahman. ‖ 6. I bend the bow for Rudra that his arrow may strike and slay the hater of devotion. | I rouse and order battle for the people, and I have penetrated Earth and Heaven. ‖ 7. On the world's summit I bring forth the Father: my home is in the waters, in the ocean. | Thence I extend o'er all existing creatures, and touch even yonder heaven with my forehead. ‖ 8. I breathe a strong breath like the wind and tempest, the while I hold together all existence. | Beyond this wide earth and beyond the heavens I have become so mighty in my grandeur.

Hymn 10:126. Viśvedevas.

1. No peril, no severe distress, ye Gods, affects the mortal man, | Whom Aryaman and Mitra lead, and Varuṇa, of one accord, beyond his foes. ‖ 2. This very thing do we desire, Varuṇa, Mitra, Aryaman, | Whereby ye guard the mortal man from sore distress, and lead him safe beyond his foes. ‖ 3. These are, each one, our present helps, Varuṇa, Mitra, Aryaman. | Best leaders, best deliverers to lead us on and bear as safe beyond our foes. ‖ 4. Ye compass round and guard each man, Varuṇa, Mitra, Aryaman: | In your dear keeping may we be, ye who are excellent as guides beyond our foes. ‖ 5. Ādityas are beyond all foes,—Varuṇa, Mitra, Aryaman: | Strong Rudra with the Marut host, Indra, Agni let us call for weal beyond our foes. ‖ 6. These lead us safely over all, Varuṇa, Mitra, Aryaman, | These who are Kings of living men, over all troubles far away beyond our foes. ‖ 7. May they give bliss to aid us well, Varuṇa, Mitra, Aryaman: | May the Ādityas, when we pray, grant us wide shelter and defence beyond our foes. ‖ 8. As in this place, O Holy Ones, ye Vasus freed even the Gaurī when her feet were fettered. | So free us now from trouble and affliction: and let our life be lengthened still, O Apī.

Hymn 10:127. Night.

1. With all her eyes the Goddess Night looks forth approaching many a spot: | She hath put all her glories on. ‖ 2. Immortal. she hath filled the waste, the Goddess hath filled height and depth: | She conquers darkness with her light. ‖ 3. The Goddess as she comes hath set the Dawn her Sister in her place: | And then the darkness vanishes. ‖ 4. So favour us this night, O thou whose pathways we have visited | As birds their nest upon the tree. ‖ 5. The villagers have sought their homes, and all that walks and all that flies, | Even the falcons fain for prey. ‖ 6. Keep off the she-wolf and the wolf, O Ūrmyā, keep the thief away; | Easy be thou for us to pass. ‖ 7. Clearly hath she come nigh to me who decks the dark with richest hues: | O Morning, cancel it like debts. ‖ 8. These have I brought to thee like kine. O Night, thou Child of Heaven, accept | This laud as for a conqueror.

Hymn 10:128. Viśvedevas.

1. Let me win glory, Agni, in our battles: enkindling thee, may we support our bodies. | May the four regions bend and bow before me: with thee for guardian may we win in combat. ‖ 2. May all the Gods be on my side in battle, the Marutas led by Indra, Vishṇu, Agni. | Mine be the middle air's extended region, and may the wind blow favouring these my wishes. ‖ 3. May the Gods grant me riches; may the blessing and invocation of the Gods assist me. | Foremost in fight be the divine Invokers: may we, unwounded, have brave heroes round us. ‖ 4. For me let them present all mine oblations, and let my mind's intention be accomplished. | May I he guiltless of the least transgression: and, all ye Go-is, do ye combine to bless us. ‖ 5. Ye six divine Expanses, grant us freedom: here, all ye Gods, acquit yourselves like heroes. | Let us not lose our children or our bodies: let us not benefit the foe, King Soma! ‖ 6. Baffling the wrath of our opponents, Agni, guard us as our infallible Protector. | Let these thy foes turn back and seek their houses, and let their thought who watch at home be ruined. ‖ 7. Lord of the world, Creator of creators the saviour God who overcomes the foeman. | May Gods, Bṛihaspati, both Aśvins shelter from ill this sacrifice and sacrificer. ‖ 8. Foodful, and much-invoked, at this our calling may the great Bull vouchsafe us wide protection. | Lord of Bay Coursers, Indra, blew our children: harm us not, give us riot as prey to others. ‖ 9. Let those who are our foemen stay afar from us: with Indra and with Agni we will drive them off. | Vasus, Ādityas, Rudras have exalted me, made me far-reaching, mighty, thinker, sovereign lord.

Hymn 10:129. Creation.

1. Then was not non-existent nor existent: there was no realm of air, no sky beyond it. | What covered in, and where? and what gave shelter? Was water there, unfathomed depth of water? ‖ 2. Death was not then, nor was there aught immortal: no sign was there, the day's and night's divider. | That One Thing, breathless, breathed by its own nature: apart from it was nothing whatsoever. ‖ 3. Darkness there was: at first concealed in darkness this All was indiscriminated chaos. | All that existed then was void and form less: by the great power of Warmth was born that Unit. ‖ 4. Thereafter rose Desire in the beginning, Desire, the primal seed and germ of Spirit. | Sages who searched with their heart's thought discovered the existent's kinship in the non-existent. ‖ 5. Transversely was their severing line extended: what was above it then, and what below it? | There were begetters, there were mighty forces, free action here and energy up yonder ‖ 6. Who verily knows and who can here declare it, whence it was born and whence comes this creation? | The Gods are later than this world's

production. Who knows then whence it first came into being? || 7. He, the first origin of this creation, whether he formed it all or did not form it, | Whose eye controls this world in highest heaven, he verily knows it, or perhaps he knows not.

Hymn 10:130. Creation.

1. The sacrifice drawn out with threads on every side, stretched by a hundred sacred ministers and one,— | This do these Fathers weave who hitherward are come: they sit beside the warp and cry, Weave forth, weave back. || 2. The Man extends it and the Man unbinds it: even to this vault of heaven hath he outspun, it. | These pegs are fastened to the seat of worship: they made the Sāman-hymns their weaving shuttles. || 3. What were the rule, the order and the model? What were the wooden fender and the butter? | What were the hymn, the chant, the recitation, when to the God all Deities paid worship? || 4. Closely was Gāyatrī conjoined with Agni, and closely Savitar combined with Uṣhṇih. | Brilliant with Ukthas, Soma joined Anuṣhṭubh: Bṛihaspati's voice by Bṛihatī was aided. || 5. Virāj adhered to Varuṇa and Mitra: here Triṣhṭubh day by day was Indra's portion. | Jagatī entered all the Gods together: so by this knowledge men were raised to Ṛiṣhis. || 6. So by this knowledge men were raised to Ṛiṣhis, when ancient sacrifice sprang up, our Fathers. | With the mind's eye I think that I behold them who first performed this sacrificial worship. || 7. They who were versed in ritual and metre, in hymns and rules, were the Seven Godlike Ṛiṣhis. | Viewing the path of those of old, the sages have taken up the reins like chariot-drivers.

Hymn 10:131. Indra.

1. Drive all our enemies away, O Indra, the western, mighty Conqueror, and the eastern. | Hero, drive off our northern foes and southern, that we in thy wide shelter may be joyful. || 2. What then? As men whose fields are full of barley reap the ripe corn removing it in order, | So bring the food of those men, bring it hither, who went not to prepare the grass for worship. || 3. Men come not with one horse at sacred seasons; thus they obtain no honour in assemblies. | Sages desiring herds of kine and horses strengthen the mighty Indra for his friendship. || 4. Ye, Aśvins, Lords of Splendour, drank full draughts of grateful Soma juice, | And aided Indra in his work with Namuchi of Asura birth. || 5. As parents aid a son, both Aśvins, Indra, aided thee with their wondrous Powers and wisdom. | When thou, with might. hadst drunk the draught that gladdens, Sarasvatī, O Maghavan, refreshed thee. || 6. Indra is strong to save, rich in assistance may he, possessing all, be kind and gracious. | May he disperse our foes and give us safety, and may we be the lords of hero vigour. || 7. May we enjoy his favour, his the Holy may we enjoy his blessed loving kindness. | May this rich Indra, as our good Protector, drive off and keep afar all those who hate us.

Hymn 10:132. Mitra. Varuṇa.

1. May Dyaus the Lord of lauded wealth, and Earth stand by the man who offers sacrifice, | And may the Aśvins, both the Gods, strengthen the worshipper with bliss. || 2. As such we honour you, Mitra and Varuṇa, with hasty zeal, most blest, you who sustain the folk. | So may we, through your friendship for the worshipper, subdue the fiends. || 3. And when we seek to win your love and friendship, we who have precious wealth in our possession, | Or when the worshipper augments his riches let not his treasures be shut up || 4. That other, Asura! too was born of Heaven thou art, O Varuṇa, the King of all men. | The chariot's Lord was well content, forbearing to anger Death by sin so great. || 5. This sin hath Śakapūta here committed. Heroes who fled to their dear friend he slayeth, | When the Steed bringeth down your grace and favour in bodies dear and worshipful. || 6. Your Mother Aditi, ye wise, was purified with water even as earth is purified from heaven. | Show love and kindness here below: wash her in rays of heavenly light. || 7. Ye Twain have seated you as Lords of Wealth, as one who mounts a car to him who sits upon the pole, upon the wood. | These our disheartened tribes Nṛimedhas saved from woe, Sumedhas saved from Woe.

Hymn 10:133. Indra.

1. Sing strength to Indra that shall set his chariot in the foremost place. | Giver of room in closest fight, slayer of foes in shock of war, be thou our great encourager. Let the weak bowstrings break upon the bows of feeble enemies. || 2. Thou didst destroy the Dragon: thou sentest the rivers down to earth. | Foeless, O Indra, wast thou born. Thou tendest well each choicest thing. Therefore we draw us close to thee. Let the weak bowstrings break upon the bows of feeble enemies. || 3. Destroyed be all malignities and all our enemy's designs. | Thy bolt thou castest, at the foe, O Indra, who would smite us dead: thy liberal bounty gives us wealth. || 4. The robber people round about, Indra, who watch and aim at us,— | Trample them down beneath thy foot; a conquering scatterer art thou. || 5. Whoso assails us, Indra, be the man a stranger or akin, | Bring down, thyself, his strength although it be as vast as are the heavens. || 6. Close to thy friendship do we cling, O Indra, and depend, or, thee. | Lead us beyond all pain and grief along the path of holy Law. || 7. Do thou bestow upon us her, O Indra, who yields according to the singer's longing, | That the great Cow may, with exhaustless udder, pouring a thousand streams, give milk to feed us.

Hymn 10:134. Indra.

1. As, like the Morning, thou hast filled, O Indra, both the earth and heaven. | So as the Mighty One, great King of all the mighty world of men, the Goddess Mother brought thee forth, the Blessed Mother gave thee life. || 2. Relax that mortal's stubborn strength whose heart is bent on wickedness. | Trample him down beneath thy feet who watches for and aims at us. The Goddess Mother brought thee forth, the Blessed Mother gave thee life. || 3. Shake down, O Slayer of the foe, those great all splendid enemies. | With all thy powers, O Śakra, all thine helps, O Indra, shake them down: || 4. As thou, O Śatakratu, thou, O Indra, shakest all things down | As wealth for him who sheds the juice, with thine assistance thousandfold. || 5. Around, on every side like drops of sweat let lightning-flashes fall. | Let all malevolence pass away from us like threads of Dūrvā grass. || 6. Thou bearest in thine hand a lance like a long hook, great Counsellor! | As with his foremost foot a goat, draw down the branch, O Maghavan. || 7. Never, O Gods, do we offend, nor are we ever obstinate: we walk as holy texts command. | Closely we clasp and cling to you, cling to your sides, beneath your arms.

Hymn 10:135. Yama.

1. In the Tree clothed with goodly leaves where Yama drinketh with the Gods, | The Father, Master of the house, tendeth with love our ancient Sires. || 2. I looked reluctantly on him who cherishes those men of old, | On him who treads that evil path, and then I yearned for this again. || 3. Thou mountest, though thou dost not see, O Child, the new and wheel-less car | Which thou hast fashioned mentally, one-poled but turning every way. || 4. The car which thou hast made to roll hitherward from the Sages, Child! | This hath the Sāman followed close, hence, laid together on a ship. || 5. Who was the father of the child? Who made the chariot roll away? | Who will this day declare to us how the funeral gift was made? || 6. When the funeral gift was placed, straightway the point of flame appeared. | A depth extended in the front: a passage out was made behind. || 7. Here is the seat where Yama dwells, that which is called the Home of Gods: | Here minstrels blow the flute for him here he is glorified with songs.

Hymn 10:136. Keśins.

1. He with the long loose locks supports Agni, and moisture, heaven, and earth: | He is all sky to look upon: he with long hair is called this light. || 2. The Munis, girdled with the wind, wear garments soiled of yellow hue. | They, following the wind's swift course go where the Gods have gone before. || 3. Transported with our Munihood we have pressed on into the winds: | You therefore, mortal men. behold our natural bodies and no more. || 4. The Muni, made associate in the holy work of every God, | Looking upon all varied forms flies through the region of the air. || 5. The Steed of Vāta, Vāyu's friend, the Muni, by the Gods impelled, | In both the oceans hath his home, in eastern and in western sea. || 6. Treading the path of sylvan beasts, Gandharvas, and Apsarases, | He with long locks, who knows the wish, is a sweet most delightful friend || 7. Vāyu hath churned for him: for him he poundeth things most hard to bend, | When he with long loose locks hath drunk, with Rudra, water from the cup.

Hymn 10:137. Viśvedevas.

1. Ye Gods, raise up once more the man whom ye have humbled and brought low. | O Gods, restore to life again the man who hath committed sin. || 2. Two several winds are blowing here, from Sindhu, from a distant land. | May one breathe energy to thee, the other blow disease away. || 3. Hither, O Wind, blow healing balm, blow all disease away, thou Wind; |

For thou who hast all medicine comest as envoy of the Gods. || 4. I am come nigh to thee with balms to give thee rest and keep thee safe. | I bring thee blessed strength, I drive thy weakening malady away. || 5. Here let the Gods deliver him, the Marutas' band deliver him: | All things that be deliver him that he be freed from his disease. || 6. The Waters have their healing power, the Waters drive disease away. | The Waters have a balm for all: let them make medicine for thee. || 7. The tongue that leads the voice precedes. Then with our ten-fold branching hands, | With these two chasers of disease we stroke thee with a gentle touch.

Hymn 10:138. Indra.

1. Allied with thee in friendship, Indra, these, thy priests, remembering Holy Law, rent Vṛitra limb from limb, | When they bestowed the Dawns and let the waters flow, and when thou didst chastise dragons at Kutsa's call. || 2. Thou sentest forth productive powers, clavest the hills, thou dravest forth the kine, thou drankest pleasant meath. | Thou gavest increase through this Tree's surpassing might. The Sun shone by the hymn that sprang from Holy Law. || 3. In the mid-way of heaven the Sun unyoked his car: the Ārya found a match to meet his Dam foe. | Associate with Ṛijiśvan Indra overthrew the solid forts of Pipru, conjuring Asura. || 4. He boldly cast down forts which none had e'er assailed: unwearied he destroyed the godless treasure-stores. | Like Sun and Moon he took the stronghold's wealth away, and, praised in song, demolished foes with flashing dart. || 5. Armed with resistless weapons, with vast power to cleave, the Vṛitra-slayer whets his darts and deals forth wounds. | Bright Ushas was afraid of Indra's slaughtering bolt: she went upon her way and left her chariot there. || 6. These are thy famous exploits, only thine, when thou alone hast left the other reft of sacrifice. | Thou in the heavens hast set the ordering of the Moons: the Father bears the felly portioned out by thee.

Hymn 10:139. Savitar.

1. Savitar, golden-haired, hath lifted eastward, bright With the sunbeams, his eternal lustre; | He in whose energy wise Pūshan marches, surveying all existence like a herdsman. || 2. Beholding men he sits amid the heaven filling the two world-halves and air's wide region. | He looks upon the rich far-spreading pastures between the eastern and the western limit. || 3. He, root of wealth, the gatherer-up of treasures, looks with his might on every form and figure. | Savitar, like a God whose Law is constant, stands in the battle for the spoil like Indra. || 4. Waters from sacrifice came to the Gandharva Viśvāvasu, O Soma, when they saw him. | Indra, approaching quickly, marked their going, and looked around upon the Sun's enclosures. || 5. This song Viśvāvasu shall sing us, meter of air's mid-realm celestial Gandharva, | That we may know aright both truth and falsehood: may he inspire our thoughts and help our praises. || 6. In the floods' track he found the booty-seeker: the rocky cow-pen's doors he threw wide open. | These, the Gandharva told him, Rowed with Amṛita. Indra knew well the puissance of the dragons.

Hymn 10:140. Agni.

1. Agni, life-power and fame are thine: thy fires blaze mightily, thou rich in wealth of beams! | Sage, passing bright, thou givest to the worshipper, with strength, the food that merits laud. || 2. With brilliant, purifying sheen, with perfect sheen thou liftest up thyself in light. | Thou, visiting both thy Mothers, aidest them as Son: thou joinest close the earth and heaven. || 3. O Jātavedas, Son of Strength, rejoice thyself, gracious, in our fair hymns and songs. | In thee are treasured various forms of strengthening food, born nobly and of wondrous help. || 4. Agni, spread forth, as Ruler, over living things: give wealth to us, Immortal God. | Thou shinest out from beauty fair to look upon: thou leadest us to conquering power. || 5. To him, the wise, who orders sacrifice, who hath great riches under his control, | Thou givest blest award of good, and plenteous food, givest him wealth that conquers all. || 6. The men have set before them them for their welfare Agni, strong, visible to all, the Holy. | Thee, Godlike One, with ears to hear, most famous, men's generations magnify with praise-songs.

Hymn 10:141. Viśvedevas.

1. Turn hither, Agni, speak to us: come to us with a gracious mind. | Enrich us, Master of the house: thou art the Giver of our wealth. || 2. Let Aryaman vouchsafe us wealth, and Bhaga, and Bṛihaspati. | Let the Gods give their gifts, and let Sūnṛitā, Goddess, grant us wealth. || 3. We call King Soma to our aid, and Agni with our songs and hymns, | Ādityas, Vishṇu, Sūrya, and the Brahman Priest Bṛihaspati. || 4. Indra, Vāyu, Bṛihaspati, Gods swift to listen, we invoke, | That in the synod all the folk may be benevolent to us. || 5. Urge Aryaman to send us gifts, and Indra, and Bṛihaspati, | Vāta, Vishṇu, Sarasvatī and the Strong Courser Savitar. || 6. Do thou, O Agni, with thy fires strengthen our prayer and sacrifice: | Urge givers to bestow their wealth to aid our service of the Gods.

Hymn 10:142. Agni.

1. With thee, O Agni, was this singer of the laud: he hath no other kinship, O thou Son of Strength. | Thou givest blessed shelter with a triple guard. Keep the destructive lightning far away from us. || 2. Thy birth who seekest food is in the falling flood, Agni: as Comrade thou winnest all living things. | Our coursers and our songs shall be victorious: they of themselves advance like one who guards the herd. || 3. And thou, O Agni, thou of Godlike nature, sparest the stones, while caring up the brushwood. | Then are thy tracks like deserts in the corn-lands. Let us not stir to wrath thy mighty arrow. || 4. O'er hills through vales devouring as thou goest, thou partest like an army fain for booty | As when a barber shaves a beard, thou shavest earth when the wind blows on thy flame and fans it. || 5. Apparent are his lines as he approaches the course is single, but the cars are many, | When, Agni, thou, making thine arms resplendent, advancest o'er the land spread out beneath thee. || 6. Now let thy strength, thy burning flames fly upward, thine energies, O Agni, as thou toilest. | Gape widely, bend thee, waxing in thy vigour: let all the Vasus sit this day beside thee. || 7. This is the waters' reservoir, the great abode of gathered streams. | Take thou another path than this, and as thou listest walk thereon. || 8. On thy way hitherward and hence let flowery Dūrvā grass spring up | Let there be lakes with lotus blooms. These are the mansions of the flood.

Hymn 10:143. Aśvins.

1. Ye made that Atri, worn with eld, free as a horse to win the goal. | When ye restored to youth and strength Kakshīvant like a car renewed, || 2. Ye freed that Atri like a horse, and brought him newly-born to earth. | Ye loosed him like a firm-tied knot which Gods unsoiled by dust had bound. || 3. Heroes who showed most wondrous power to Atri, strive to win fair songs; | For then, O Heroes of the sky, your hymn of praise shall cease no more. || 4. This claims your notice, Bounteous Gods!—oblation, Aśvins! and our love, | That ye, O Heroes, in the fight may bring us safe to ample room. || 5. Ye Twain to Bhujyu tossed about in ocean at the region's end, | Nāsatyas, with your winged steeds came nigh, and gave him strength to win. || 6. Come with your joys, most liberal Gods, Lords of all treasures, bringing weal. | Like fresh full waters to a well, so, Heroes come and be with us.

Hymn 10:144. Indra.

1. This deathless Indu, like a steed, strong and of full vitality, | Belongs to thee, the Orderer. || 2. Here, by us, for the worshipper, is the wise bolt that works with skill. | It brings the bubbling beverage as a dexterous man brings the effectual strong drink. || 3. Impetuous Ahīśuva, a bull among cows of his, | looked down upon the restless Hawk. || 4. That the strong-pinioned Bird hath brought, Child of the Falcon, from afar, | What moves upon a hundred wheels along the female Dragon's path. || 5. Which, fair, unrobbed, the Falcon brought thee in his foot, the red-hued dwelling of the juice; | Through this came vital power which lengthens out our days, and kinship through its help awoke. || 6. So Indra is by Indu's power; e'en among Gods will it repel great treachery. | Wisdom, Most Sapient One, brings force that lengthens life. May wisdom bring the juice to us.

Hymn 10:145. Sapatnībādhanam.

1. From out the earth I dig this plant, a herb of most effectual power, | Wherewith one quells the rival wife and gains the husband for oneself. || 2. Auspicious, with expanded leaves, sent by the Gods, victorious plant, | Blow thou the rival wife away, and make my husband only mine. || 3. Stronger am I, O Stronger One, yea, mightier than the mightier; | And she who is my rival wife is lower than the lowest dames. || 4. Her very name I utter not: she takes no pleasure in this man. | Far into distance most remote drive we the rival wife away. || 5. I am the conqueror, and thou, thou also act victorious: | As victory attends us both we will subdue my fellow-wife. || 6. I have gained thee for vanquisher, have grasped thee with a stronger spell. |

As a cow hastens to her calf, so let thy spirit speed to me, hasten like water on its way.

Hymn 10:146. Araṇyānī.

1. Goddess of wild and forest who seemest to vanish from the sight. | How is it that thou seekest not the village? Art thou not afraid? || 2. What time the grasshopper replies and swells the shrill cicala's voice, | Seeming to sound with tinkling bells, the Lady of the Wood exults. || 3. And, yonder, cattle seem to graze, what seems a dwelling-place appears: | Or else at eve the Lady of the Forest seems to free the wains. || 4. Here one is calling to his cow, another there hath felled a tree: | At eve the dweller in the wood fancies that somebody hath screamed. || 5. The Goddess never slays, unless some murderous enemy approach. | Man eats of savoury fruit and then takes, even as he wills, his rest. || 6. Now have I praised the Forest Queen, sweet-scented, redolent of balm, | The Mother of all sylvan things, who tills not but hath stores of food.

Hymn 10:147. Indra.

1. I trust in thy first wrathful deed, O Indra, when thou slewest Vṛitra and didst work to profit man; | What time the two world-halves fell short of thee in might, and the earth trembled at thy force, O Thunder-armed. || 2. Thou with thy magic powers didst rend the conjurer Vṛitra, O Blameless One, with heart that longed for fame. | Heroes elect thee when they battle for the prey, thee in all sacrifices worthy of renown. || 3. God Much-invoked, take pleasure in these princes here, who, thine exalters, Maghavan, have come to wealth. | In synods, when the rite succeeds, they hymn the Strong for sons and progeny and riches undisturbed. || 4. That man shall find delight in well-protected wealth whose care provides for him the quick-sought joyous draught. | Bringing oblations, strengthened Maghavan, by thee, he swiftly wins the spoil with heroes in the fight. || 5. Now for our band, O Maghavan, when lauded, make ample room with might, and grant us riches. | Magician thou, our Varuṇa and Mitra, deal food to us, O Wondrous, as Dispenser.

Hymn 10:148. Indra.

1. When we have pressed the juice we laud thee, Indra, and when, Most Valorous we have won the booty. | Bring us prosperity, as each desires it under thine own protection may we conquer. || 2. Sublime from birth, mayst thou O Indra, Hero, with Sūrya overcome the Dāsa races. | As by a fountain's side, we bring the Soma that lay concealed, close-hidden in the waters. || 3. Answer the votary's hymns, for these thou knowest, craving the Ṛishis' prayer, thyself a Singer | May we be they who take delight in Somas: these with sweet food for thee, O Chariot-rider. || 4. These holy prayers, O Indra, have I sung thee: grant to the men the strength of men, thou Hero. | Be of one mind with those in whom thou joyest: keep thou the singers safe and their companions. || 5. Listen to Pṛithi's call, heroic Indra, and be thou lauded by the hymns of Venya, | Him who hath sung thee to thine oil-rich dwelling, whose rolling songs have sped thee like a torrent.

Hymn 10:149. Savitar.

1. Savitar fixed the earth with bands to bind it, and made heaven steadfast where no prop supported. | Savitar milked, as 'twere a restless courser, air, sea bound fast to what no foot had trodden. || 2. Well knoweth Savitar, O Child of Waters, where ocean, firmly fixt, o'erflowed its limit. | Thence sprang the world, from that uprose the region: thence heaven spread out and the wide earth expanded. || 3. Then, with a full crowd of Immortal Beings, this other realm came later, high and holy. | First, verily, Savitar's strong-pinioned Eagle was born: and he obeys his law for ever. || 4. As warriors to their steeds, kine to their village, as fond milk giving cows approach their youngling, | As man to wife, let Savitar come downward to us, heaven's bearer, Lord of every blessing. || 5. Like the Aṅgirasa Hiraṇvastūpa, I call thee, Savitar, to this achievement: | So worshipping and lauding thee for favour I watch for thee as for the stalk of Soma.

Hymn 10:150. Agni.

1. Thou, bearer of oblations, though kindled, art kindled for the Gods. | With the Ādityas, Rudras, Vasus, come to us: to show us favour come to us. || 2. Come hither and accept with joy this sacrifice and hymn of ours. | O kindled God, we mortals are invoking thee, calling on thee to show us grace. || 3. I laud thee Jātavedas, thee Lord of all blessings, with my song. | Agni, bring hitherward the Gods whose Laws we love, whose laws we love, to show us grace. || 4. Agni the God was made the great High-Priest of Gods, Ṛishis have kindled Agni, men of mortal mould. | Agni I invocate for winning ample wealth. kindly disposed for winning wealth. || 5. Atri and Bharadvāja and Gavishṭhira, Kaṇva and Trasadasyu, in our fight he helped. | On Agni calls Vasishṭha, even the household priest, the household priest to win his grace.

Hymn 10:151. Faith.

1. By Faith is Agni kindled, through Faith is oblation offered up. | We celebrate with praises Faith upon the height of happiness. || 2. Bless thou the man who gives, O Faith; Faith, bless the man who fain would give. | Bless thou the liberal worshippers: bless thou the word that I have said. || 3. Even as the Deities maintained Faith in the mighty Asuras, | So make this uttered wish of mine true for the liberal worshippers. || 4. Guarded by Vāyu, Gods and men who sacrifice draw near to Faith. | Man winneth Faith by yearnings of the heart, and opulence by Faith. || 5. Faith in the early morning, Faith at noonday will we invocate, | Faith at the setting of the Sun. O Faith, endow us with belief.

Hymn 10:152. Indra.

1. A mighty Governor art thou, Wondrous, Destroyer of the foe, | Whose friend is never done to death, and never, never overcome. || 2. Lord of the clan, who brings us bliss, Strong, Warrior, Slayer of the fiend, | May India, Soma-drinker, go before us, Bull who gives us peace. || 3. Drive Rākshasas and foes away, break thou in pieces Vṛitra's jaws: | O Vṛitra-slaying Indra, quell the foeman's wrath who threatens us. || 4. O Indra, beat our foes away, humble the men who challenge us: | Send down to nether darkness him who seeks to do us injury. || 5. Baffle the foeman's plan, ward off his weapon who would conquer us. | Give shelter from his furious wrath, and keep his murdering dart afar.

Hymn 10:153. Indra.

1. Swaying about, the Active Ones came nigh to Indra at his birth, | And shared his great heroic might. || 2. Based upon strength and victory and power, O Indra is thy birth: | Thou, Mighty One, art strong indeed. || 3. Thou art the Vṛitra-slayer, thou, Indra, hast spread the firmament: | Thou hast with might upheld the heavens. || 4. Thou, Indra, bearest in thine arms the lightning that accords with thee, | Whetting thy thunderbolt with might. || 5. Thou, Indra, art preeminent over all creatures in thy might: | Thou hast pervaded every place.

Hymn 10:154. New Life.

1. For some is Soma purified, some sit by sacrificial oil: | To those for whom the meath flows forth, even to those let him depart. || 2. Invincible through Fervour, those whom Fervour hath advanced to heaven, | Who showed great Fervour in their lives,—even to those let him depart. || 3. The heroes who contend in war and boldly cast their lives away, | Or who give guerdon thousandfold, even to those let him depart. || 4. Yea, the first followers of Law, Law's pure and holy strengtheners, | The Fathers, Yama! Fervour-moved,even to those let him depart. || 5. Skilled in a thousand ways and means, the sages who protect the Sun, | The Ṛishis, Yama! Fervour-moved, —even to those let him depart.

Hymn 10:155. Various.

1. Arāyī, one-eyed limping hag, fly, ever-screeching, to the hill. | We frighten thee away with these, the heroes of Śirimbiṭha. || 2. Scared from this place and that is she, destroyer of each germ unborn. | Go, sharp-horned Brahmaṇaspati and drive Arāyī far away. || 3. Yon log that floats without a man to guide it on the river's edge,— | Seize it, thou thing with hideous jaws, and go thou far away thereon. || 4. When, foul with secret stain and spot, ye hastened onward to the breast, | All Indra's enemies were slain and passed away like froth and foam. || 5. These men have led about the cow, have duly carried Agni round, | And raised their glory to the Gods. Who will attack them with success?

Hymn 10:156. Agni.

1. Let songs of ours speed Agni forth like a fleet courser in the race, | And we will win each prize through him. || 2. Agni the dart whereby we gain kine for ourselves with help from thee,— | That send us for the gain of wealth. || 3. O Agni, bring us wealth secure, vast wealth in horses and in kine: | Oil thou the socket, turn the wheel. || 4. O Agni, thou hast made the Sun, Eternal Star, to mount the sky, | Bestowing light on living men. || 5.

Thou, Agni, art the people's light, best, dearest, seated in thy shrine: | Watch for the singer, give him life.

Hymn 10:157. Viśvedevas.

1. We will, with Indra and all Gods to aid us, bring these existing worlds into subjection. || 2. Our sacrifice, our bodies, and our offspring, let Indra form together with Ādityas. || 3. With the Ādityas, with the band of Marutas, may Indra be Protector of our bodies. || 4. As when the Gods came, after they had slaughtered the Asuras, keeping safe their Godlike nature, || 5. Brought the Sun hitherward with mighty powers, and looked about them on their vigorous Godhead.

Hymn 10:158. Sūrya.

1. May Sūrya guard us out of heaven, and Vāta from the firmament, | And Agni from terrestrial spots. || 2. Thou Savitar whose flame deserves hundred libations, be thou pleased: | From failing lightning keep us safe. || 3. May Savitar the God, and may Parvata also give us sight; | May the Creator give us sight. || 4. Give sight unto our eye, give thou our bodies sight that they may see: | May we survey, discern this world. || 5. Thus, Sūrya, may we look on thee, on thee most lovely to behold, | See clearly with the eyes of men.

Hymn 10:159. Śachī Paulomī.

1. Yon Sun hath mounted up, and this my happy fate hate mounted high. | I knowing this, as conqueror have won my husband for mine own. || 2. I am the banner and the head, a mighty arbitress am I: | I am victorious, and my Lord shall be submissive to my will. || 3. My Sons are slayers of the foe, my Daughter is a ruling Queen: | I am victorious: o'er my Lord my song of triumph is supreme. || 4. Oblation, that which Indra gave and thus grew glorious and most high,— | This have I offered, O ye Gods, and rid me of each rival wife. || 5. Destroyer of the rival wife, Sole Spouse, victorious, conqueror, | The others' glory have I seized as 'twere the wealth of weaker Dames. || 6. I have subdued as conqueror these rivals, these my fellow-wives, | That I may hold imperial sway over this Hero and the folk.

Hymn 10:160. Indra.

1. Taste this strong draught enriched with offered viands: with all thy chariot here unyoke thy Coursers. | Let not those other sacrificers stay thee, Indra: these juices shed for thee are ready. || 2. Thine is the juice effused, thine are the juices yet to be pressed: our resonant songs invite thee. | O Indra, pleased today with this libation, come, thou who knowest all and drink the Soma. || 3. Whoso, devoted to the God, effuses Soma for him with yearning heart and spirit,— | Never doth Indra give away his cattle: for him he makes the lovely Soma famous. || 4. He looks with loving favour on the mortal who, like a rich man, pours for him the Soma. | Maghavan in his bended arm supports him: he slays, unasked, the men who hate devotion. || 5. We call on thee to come to us, desirous of goods and spoil, of cattle, and of horses. | For thy new love and favour are we present: let us invoke thee, Indra, as our welfare.

Hymn 10:161. Indra.

1. For life I set thee free by this oblation from the unknown decline and from Consumption; | Or, if the grasping demon have possessed him, free him from her, O Indra, thou and Agni. || 2. Be his days ended, be he now departed, be he brought very near to death already, | Out of Destruction's lap again I bring him, save him for life to last a hundred autumns. || 3. With hundred-eyed oblation, hundred-autumned, bringing a hundred lives, have I restored him, | That Indra for a hundred years may lead him safe to the farther shore of all misfortune. || 4. Live, waxing in thy strength, a hundred autumns, live through a hundred springs, a hundred winters. | Through hundred-lived oblation Indra, Agni, Bṛihaspati, Savitar yield him for a hundred! || 5. So have I found and rescued thee thou hast returned with youth renewed. | Whole in thy members! I have found thy sight and all thy life for thee.

Hymn 10:162. Agni

1. May Agni, yielding to our prayer, the Rakṣhas-slayer, drive away | The malady of evil name that hath beset thy labouring womb. || 2. Agni, concurring in the prayer, drive off the eater of the flesh, | The malady of evil name that hath attacked thy babe and womb. || 3. That which destroys the sinking germ, the settled, moving embryo, | That which will kill the babe at birth,even this will we drive far away. || 4. That which divides thy legs that it may lie between the married pair, | That penetrates and licks thy side,—even this will we exterminate. || 5. What rests by thee in borrowed form of brother, lover, or of lord, | And would destroy thy Progeny,—even this will we exterminate. || 6. That which through sleep or darkness hath deceived thee and lies down by thee, | And will destroy thy progeny,—even this will we exterminate.

Hymn 10:163.

1. From both thy nostrils, from thine eyes, from both thine ears and from thy chin, | Forth from thy head and brain and tongue I drive thy malady away. || 2. From the neck-tendons and the neck, from the breast-bones and from the spine, | From shoulders, upper, lower arms, I drive thy malady away. || 3. From viscera and all within, forth from the rectum, from the heart, | From kidneys, liver, and from spleen, I drive thy malady away. || 4. From thighs, from knee-caps, and from heels, and from the forepart of the feet, | From hips from stomach, and from groin I drive thy malady away. || 5. From what is voided from within, and from thy hair, and from they nails, | From all thyself from top to toe, I drive thy malady away. || 6. From every member, every hair, disease that comes in every joint, | From all thyself, from top to toe, I drive thy malady away.

Hymn 10:164. Dream-charm.

1. Avaunt, thou Master of the mind Depart, and vanish far away. | Look on Destruction far from hence. The live man's mind is manifold. || 2. A happy boon do men elect, a mighty blessing they obtain. | Bliss with Vaivasvata they see. The live man's mind seeks many a place. || 3. If by address, by blame, by imprecation we have committed sin, awake or sleeping, | All hateful acts of ours, all evil doings may Agni bear away to distant places. || 4. When, Indra, Brahmaṇaspati, our deeds are wrongful and unjust, | May provident Aṅgirasa prevent our foes from troubling, us. || 5. We have prevailed this day and won: we are made free from sin and guilt. | Ill thoughts, that visit us awake or sleeping, seize the man we hate, yea, seize the man who hateth us.

Hymn 10:165. Viśvedevas.

1. Gods, whatsoe'er the Dove came hither seeking, sent to us as the envoy of Destruction, | For that let us sing hymns and make atonement. Well be it with our quadrupeds and bipeds. || 2. Auspicious be the Dove that hath been sent us, a harmless bird, ye Gods, within our dwelling. | May Agni, Sage, be pleased with our oblation, and may the Missile borne on wings avoid us. || 3. Let not the Arrow that hath wings distract us: beside the fire-place, on the hearth it settles. | May, it bring welfare to our men and cattle: here let the Dove, ye Gods, forbear to harm us. || 4. The screeching of the owl is ineffective and when beside the fire the Dove hath settled, | To him who sent it hither as an envoy, to him be reverence paid, to Death, to Yama. || 5. Drive forth the Dove, chase it with holy verses: rejoicing, bring ye hither food and cattle, | Barring the way against all grief and trouble. Let the swift bird fly forth and leave us vigour.

Hymn 10:166. Sapatnanāśanam.

1. Make me a bull among my peers, make me my rivals, conqueror: | Make me the slayer of my foes, a sovereign ruler, lord of kine || 2. I am my rivals' slayer, like Indra unwounded and unhurt, | And all these enemies of mine are vanquished and beneath my feet. || 3. Here, verily, I bind you fast, as the two bow-ends with the string. | Press down these men, O Lord of Speech, that they may humbly speak to me. || 4. Hither I came as conqueror with mighty all-effecting power, | And I have mastered all your thought, your synod, and your holy work. || 5. May I be highest, having gained your strength in war, your skill in peace | my feet have trodden on your heads. | Speak to me from beneath my feet, as frogs from out the water croak, as frogs from out the water croak.

Hymn 10:167. Indra.

1. This pleasant meath, O Indra, is effused for thee: thou art the ruling Lord of beaker and of juice. | Bestow upon us wealth with many hero sons: thou, having glowed with Fervour, wonnest heavenly light. || 2. Let us call Śakra to libations here effused, winner of light who joyeth in the potent juice. | Mark well this sacrifice of ours and come to us: we pray to Maghavan the Vanquisher of hosts. || 3. By royal Soma's and by Varuṇa's decree, under Bṛihaspati's and Anumati's guard, | This day by thine authority, O Maghavan, Maker, Disposer thou! have I enjoyed the jars. || 4. I, too, urged on, have had my portion, in the bowl, and as first Prince I drew forth this

my hymn of praise, | When with the prize I came unto the flowing juice, O Viśvāmitra, Jamadagni, to your home.

Hymn 10:168. Vāyu.

1. O the Wind's chariot, O its power and glory! Crashing it goes and hath a voice of thunder. | It makes the regions red and touches heaven, and as it moves the dust of earth is scattered. || 2. Along the traces of the Wind they hurry, they come to him as dames to an assembly. | Borne on his car with these for his attendants, the God speeds forth, the universe's Monarch. || 3. Travelling on the paths of air's mid-region, no single day doth he take rest or slumber. | Holy and earliest-born, Friend of he waters, where did he spring and from what region came he? || 4. Germ of the world, the Deities' vital spirit, this God moves ever as his will inclines him. | His voice is heard, his shape is ever viewless. Let us adore this Wind with our oblation.

Hymn 10:169. Cows.

1. May the wind blow upon our Cows with healing: may they eat herbage full of vigorous juices. | May they drink waters rich in life and fatness: to food that moves on feet be gracious, Rudra. || 2. Like-coloured, various-hued, or single-coloured, whose names through sacrifice are known to Agni, | Whom the Aṅgirasas produced by Fervour, vouchsafe to these, Parjanya, great protection. || 3. Those who have offered to the Gods their bodies, whose varied forms are all well known to Soma,— | Those grant us in our cattle-pen, O Indra, with their full streams of milk and plenteous offspring. || 4. Prajāpati, bestowing these upon me, one-minded with all Gods and with the Fathers, | Hath to our cow-pen brought auspicious cattle: so may we own the offspring they will bear us.

Hymn 10:170. Sūrya.

1. May the Bright God drink glorious Soma-mingled meath, giving the sacrifice's lord uninjured life; | He who, wind-urged, in person guards our offspring well, hath nourished them with food and shines o'er many a land. || 2. Radiant, as high Truth, cherished, best at winning strength, Truth based upon the statute that supports the heavens, | He rose, a light, that kills Vṛitras and enemies, best slayer of the Dasyus, Asuras, and foes. || 3. This light, the best of lights, supreme, all-conquering, winner of riches, is exalted with high laud. | All-lighting, radiant, mighty as the Sun to see, he spreadeth wide unfailing victory and strength. || 4. Beaming forth splendour with thy light, thou hast attained heaven's lustrous realm. | By thee were brought together all existing things, possessor of all Godhead, All-effecting God.

Hymn 10:171. Indra.

1. For Iṭa's sake who pressed the juice, thou, Indra, didst protect his car, | And hear the Soma-giver's call. || 2. Thou from his skin hast borne the head of the swift-moving combatant, | And sought the Soma-pourer's home. || 3. Venya, that mortal man, hast thou, for Āstrabudhna the devout, | O Indra, many a time set free. || 4. Bring, Indra, to the east again that Sun who now is in the west, | Even against the will of Gods.

Hymn 10:172. Dawn.

1. With all thy beauty come: the kine approaching with full udders follow on thy path. || 2. Come with kind thoughts, most liberal, rousing the warrior's hymn of praise, with bounteous ones, || 3. As nourishers we tie the thread, and, liberal with our bounty, offer sacrifice. || 4. Dawn drives away her Sister's gloom, and, through her excellence, makes her retrace her path.

Hymn 10:173. The King.

1. Be with us; I have chosen thee: stand steadfast and immovable. | Let all the people wish for thee let not thy kingship fall away. || 2. Be even here; fall not away be like a mountain unremoved. | Stand steadfast here like Indra's self, and hold the kingship in the grasp. || 3. This man hath Indra established, made secure by strong oblation's power. | May Soma speak a benison, and Brahmaṇaspati, on him. || 4. Firm is the sky and firm the earth, and steadfast also are these hills. | Steadfast is all this living world, and steadfast is this King of men. || 5. Steadfast, may Varuṇa the King, steadfast, the God Bṛihaspati, | Steadfast, may Indra, steadfast too, may Agni keep thy steadfast reign. || 6. On constant Soma let us think with constant sacrificial gift | And then may Indra make the clans bring tribute unto thee alone.

Hymn 10:174. The King.

1. With offering for success in fight whence Indra was victorious. | With this, O Brahmaṇaspati, let us attain to royal sway. || 2. Subduing those who rival us, subduing all malignities, | Withstand the man who menaces, withstand the man who angers us. || 3. Soma and Savitar the God have made thee a victorious King | All elements have aided thee, to make thee general conqueror. || 4. Oblation, that which Indra. gave and thus grew glorious and most high,— | This have I offered, Gods! and hence now, verily, am rival-less. || 5. Slayer of rivals, rival-less, victorious, with royal sway, | Over these beings may I rule, may I be Sovereign of the folk.

Hymn 10:175. Press-stones.

1. May Savitar the God, O Stones, stir you according to the Law: | Be harnessed to the shafts, and press. || 2. Stones, drive calamity away, drive ye away malevolence: | Make ye the Cows our medicine. || 3. Of one accord the upper Stones, giving the Bull his bull-like strength, | Look down with pride on those below. || 4. May Savitar the God, O Stones, stir you as Law commands for him | Who sacrifices, pouring juice.

Hymn 10:176. Agni.

1. With hymns of praise their sons have told aloud the Ṛibhus' mighty deeds. | Who, all-supporting, have enjoyed the earth as, twere a mother cow. || 2. Bring forth the God with song divine, being Jātavedas hitherward, | To bear our gifts at once to heaven. || 3. He here, a God-devoted Priest, led forward comes to sacrifice. | Like a car covered for the road, he, glowing, knows, himself, the way. || 4. This Agni rescues from distress, as 'twere from the Immortal Race, | A God yet mightier than strength, a God who hath been made for life.

Hymn 10:177. Māyābheda.

1. The sapient with their spirit and their mind behold the Bird adorned with all an Asura's magic might. | Sages observe him in the ocean's inmost depth: the wise disposers seek the station of his rays. || 2. The flying Bird bears Speech within his spirit: erst the Gandharva in the womb pronounced it: | And at the seat of sacrifice the sages cherish this radiant, heavenly-bright invention. || 3. I saw the Herdsman, him who never resteth, approaching and departing on his pathways. | He, clothed in gathered and diffusive splendour, within the worlds continually travels.

Hymn 10:178. Tārkṣhya.

1. This very mighty one whom Gods commission, the Conqueror of cars, ever triumphant, | Swift, fleet to battle, with uninjured fellies, even Tārkṣhya for our weal will we call hither. || 2. As though we offered up our gifts to Indra, may we ascend him as a ship for safety. | Like the two wide worlds, broad, deep far-extended, may we be safe both when he comes and leaves you. || 3. He who with might the Five Lands hath pervaded, like Sūrya with his lustre, and the waters— | His strength wins hundreds, thousands none avert it, as—the young maid repelleth not her lover.

Hymn 10:179. Indra.

1. Now lift ye up yourselves and look on Indra's seasonable share. | If it be ready, offer it; unready, ye have been remiss. || 2. Oblation is prepared: come to us, Indra; the Sun hath travelled over half his journey. | Friends with their stores are sitting round thee waiting like lords of clans for the tribe's wandering chieftain. || 3. Dressed in the udder and on fire, I fancy; well-dressed, I fancy, is this recent present. | Drink, Indra, of the curd of noon's libation with favour, Thunderer, thou whose deeds are mighty.

Hymn 10:180. Indra.

1. O much-invoked, thou hast subdued thy foemen: thy might is loftiest; here display thy bounty. | In thy right hand, O Indra, bring us treasures: thou art the Lord of rivers filled with riches. || 2. Like a dread wild beast roaming on the mountain thou hast approached us from the farthest distance. | Whetting thy bold and thy sharp blade, O Indra, crush thou the foe and scatter those who hate us. || 3. Thou, mighty Indra, sprangest into being as strength for lovely lordship o'er the people. | Thou drovest off the folk who were unfriendly, and to the Gods thou gavest room and freedom.

Hymn 10:181. Viśvedevas.

1. Vasiṣhṭha mastered the Rathantara, took it from radiant Dhātar, Savitar, and Viṣhṇu, | Oblation, portion of fourfold oblation, known by the names of Saprathas and Prathas. | 2. These sages found what lay remote and hidden, the sacrifice's loftiest secret essence. | From radiant Dhātar,

Savitar, and Vishṇu, from Agni, Bharadvāja brought the Bṛihat. ‖ 3. They found with mental eyes the earliest Yajus, a pathway to the Gods, that had descended. | From radiant Dhātar, Savitar, and Vishṇu, from Sūrya did these sages bring the Gharma.

Hymn 10:182. Bṛihaspati.

1. Bṛihaspati lead us safely over troubles and turn his evil thought against the sinner; | Repel the curse, and drive away ill-feeling, and give the sacrificer peace and comfort! ‖ 2. May Narāśaṃsa aid us at Prayāja: blest be our Anuyāja at invokings. | May he repel the curse, and chase ill-feeling, and give the sacrificer peace and comfort. ‖ 3. May he whose head is flaming burn the demons, haters of prayer, so that the arrow slay them. | May he repel the curse and chase ill-feeling, and give the sacrificer peace and comfort.

Hymn 10:183. The Sacrificer, etc.

1. I saw thee meditating in thy spirit what sprang from Fervour and hath thence developed. | Bestowing offspring here, bestowing riches, spread in thine offspring, thou who cravest children. ‖ 2. I saw thee pondering in thine heart, and praying that in due time thy body might be fruitful. | Come as a youthful woman, rise to meet me: spread in thine offspring, thou who cravest children. ‖ 3. In plants and herbs, in all existent beings I have deposited the germ of increase. | All progeny on earth have I engendered, and sons in women who will be hereafter.

Hymn 10:184.

1. May Vishṇu form and mould the womb, may Tvashṭar duly shape the forms, | Prajāpati infuse the stream, and Dhātar lay the germ for thee. ‖ 2. O Sinīvālī, set the germ, set thou the germ, Sarasvatī: | May the Twain Gods bestow the germ, the Aśvins crowned with lotuses. ‖ 3. That which the Aśvins Twain rub forth with the attrition-sticks of gold,— | That germ of thine we invocate, that in the tenth month thou mayst bear.

Hymn 10:185. Aditi.

1. Great, unassailable must he the heavenly favour of' Three Gods, | Varuṇa, Mitra, Aryaman. ‖ 2. O'er these, neither at home nor yet abroad or pathways that are Strange, | The evil-minded foe hath power ‖ 3. Nor over him, the man on whom the Sons of Aditi bestow Eternal light that he may live.

Hymn 10:186. Vāyu.

1. Filling our hearts with health and joy, may Vāta breathe his balm on us | May he prolong our days of life. ‖ 2. Thou art our Father, Vāta, yea, thou art a Brother and a friend, | So give us strength that we may live. ‖ 3. The store of Amṛita laid away yonder, O Vāta, in thine home,— | Give us thereof that we may live.

Hymn 10:187. Agni.

1. To Agni send I forth my song, to him the Bull of all the folk: | So may he bear us past our foes. ‖ 2. Who from the distance far away shines brilliantly across the wastes: | So may he bear us past our foes. ‖ 3. The Bull with brightly-gleaming flame who utterly consumes the fiends | So may he bear us past our foes. ‖ 4. Who looks on all existing things and comprehends them with his view: | So may he bear us past our foes. ‖ 5. Resplendent Agni, who was born in farthest region of the air: | So may he bear us past our foes.

Hymn 10:188. Agni.

1. Now send ye Jātavedas forth, send hitherward the vigorous Steed | To seat him on our sacred grass. | 2. I raise the lofty eulogy of Jātavedas, raining boons, | With sages for his hero band. ‖ 3. With flames of Jātavedas which carry oblation to the Gods, | May he promote our sacrifice.

Hymn 10:189. Sūrya.

1. This spotted Bull hath come, and sat before the Mother in the east, | Advancing to his Father heaven. ‖ 2. Expiring when he draws his breath, she moves along the lucid spheres: | The Bull shines out through all the sky. ‖ 3. Song is bestowed upon the Bird: it rules supreme through thirty realms | Throughout the days at break of morn.

Hymn 10:190. Creation.

1. From Fervour kindled to its height Eternal Law and Truth were born: | Thence was the Night produced, and thence the billowy flood of sea arose. ‖ 2. From that same billowy flood of sea the Year was afterwards produced, | Ordainer of the days nights, Lord over all who close the eye. ‖ 3. Dhātar, the great Creator, then formed in due order Sun and Moon. | He formed in order Heaven and Earth, the regions of the air, and light.

Hymn 10:191. Agni.

1. Thou, mighty Agni, gatherest up all that is precious for thy friend. | Bring us all treasures as thou art enkindled in libation's place ‖ 2. Assemble, speak together: let your minds be all of one accord, | As ancient Gods unanimous sit down to their appointed share. ‖ 3. The place is common, common the assembly, common the mind, so be their thought united. | A common purpose do I lay before you, and worship with your general oblation. ‖ 4. One and the same by your resolve, and be your minds of one accord. | United be the thoughts of all that all may happily agree.

Texts of the White Yajurveda

[Vājasaneya-Saṃhitā]

Translated by Ralph T.H. Griffith, 1899

Preface

The Yajurveda—derived from the roots *yaj*, to sacrifice or, worship, and *vid*, to know—is the Knowledge of Sacrifice or Sacrificial Texts and Formulas as distinguished from the Ṛigveda or Knowledge of Recited Praise, the Sāmaveda or Knowledge of Chanted Hymns, and the Atharva or Brahmaveda which is the Knowledge of Prayer, Charm, and Spells. Though ranking second in the Indian enumeration of the Vedas and containing much that is of very ancient origin, its compilation in its present form, exhibiting as it does the almost complete development of castes and mixt castes and considerable advance in arts and sciences, trades, handicrafts and occupations, is evidently of later date than that even of the Atharva. The Saṃhitā or Collection of its hymns, texts, and formulas, constituting the hymn-book and prayer-book of the Adhvaryu priests as distinguished from the Hotar, the Udgātar, and the Brahman, the special priests, respectively, of the three other Vedas, owes its origin to the increasing multiformity and complication of the Indian ritual and the recognized insufficiency of the simple and unsystematically arranged Collection of Ṛigveda Hymns to meet the requirements of the performers of various essentially important rites and ceremonies.

The Yajurveda, owing to a schism among its earliest teachers and their followers, was divided into two distinct Saṃhitās or Collections called—probably from the names of the Ṛishis or inspired Seers who are respectively their reputed compilers—the Taittirīya and the Vājasaneya or Vājasaneyi; the former and older being known also by the title Kṛishṇa or Black—probably from its dark or obscure appearance, the collection of sacrificial texts and formulas being perplexingly intermingled with the Brāhmaṇa or exegetical portion which explains them and teaches their ritual application—and the latter being called Śukla or White, the revised, systematic and clear collection, containing the texts and formulas by themselves with a totally distinct Brāhmaṇa, the Śatapatha, as an appendix. In the two divisions, besides these essential points of difference, are found occasional verbal and orthoepic variations which are generally of little importance. The order of rites and ceremonies is substantially identical, but the White contains a few more texts than the Black.

The Saṃhitā of the White Yajurveda consists of forty Adhyāyas or Books containing, with frequent repetitions of the same text, about two thousand verses. A large portion of these are Ṛichas or Strophes borrowed—frequently with variations—from the Ṛigveda, and sometimes from the Atharva these, of course, are metrical. Nearly equal in quantity are the Yajus texts or sacrificial formulas—the most characteristic portion, from which the Veda derives its name—composed in measured prose "which rises now and then," as Professor Weber observes, "to a true rhythmical swing," and long passages, such as the lists of victims to be tied up and dedicated at the Aśvamedha and the Puruṣhamedha, which are necessarily in the simplest prose.

For further information with regard to this Veda the reader should consult Professor Weber's *History of Indian Literature* (English Translation by John Mann and Theodor Zachariae: Trübner's Oriental Series); Professor Max Müller's *History of Ancient Sanskrit Literature;* Professor J. Eggeling's Introduction, Vol. XII. of the *Sacred Books of the East*, or, for a briefer account, Mrs. Manning's *Ancient and Mediaeval India*, Vol. I. pp. 107-109.

My translation follows the fine edition of the White Yajurveda or Vājasaneyi-Saṃhitā, in the two recensions—the Mādhyandina and the Kāṇva—with Mahīdhara's Commentary, the Vedadīpa, or Lamp of Knowledge, written towards the close of the sixteenth century, published under the patronage of the Honourable Court of Directors of the East India Company in 1849 at Berlin by Dr. Albrecht Weber, at that time Docent of the Sanskrit language at that University. This excellent edition consisting of three Parts the latter two of which contain the Śatapatha-Brāhmaṇa in the Mādhyandina recension with extracts from the Commentaries of Sāyaṇa, Harisvāmin, and Dvivedaganga, and the Śrauta-Sūtra of Kātyāyana with extracts from the Commentaries of Karka and Yājñikadeva, has not been reprinted and is now practically unobtainable. In India the text of the Mādhyandina recension with Mahīdhara's Commentary has been issued in a cheap form at Calcutta by Pandit Jībānanda Vidyāsāgara, B. A., Superintendent of the Free Sanskrit College, of which a second edition appeared in 1892; and a lithographed edition of the text with a Hindi translation of Mahīdhara's Commentary was published in 1874, at Besma in the North-Western Provinces, by Rājā Giriprasādavarman of that place. A cheap edition of the text, in unbound MS. form, has been published at Bombay.

No separate translation of the whole Saṃhitā or Collection of Texts and Formulas has appeared in any European language. It was Professor Weber's intention, as signified in his History of Indian Literature, to bring out a translation giving the ceremonial belonging to each verse, together with a full glossary, but "this promise has not been fulfilled, owing to the pressure of other labours." This scholar had previously published a Latin translation, with annotations in the same language, of Adhyāyas 9 and 10 in his Vājasaneya-Sanhitae Specimen (Breslau, 1846), and more recently a German version of Adhyāya 16 in Indische Studien II. pp. 14 ff., and of the list of men and women to be dedicated at the Puruṣhamedha in his treatise on Human Sacrifice among Indians of the Vedic Age reprinted in his Indische Streifen I. pp. 76-84. Of Adhyāya 40 as an Upaniṣhad there are several translations into English.

Moreover, nearly the whole of the first eighteen Adhyāyas has been incorporated—dissected and explained clause by clause—in the first nine Books of the Śatapatha-Brāhmaṇa; and an admirable translation of this vast work by Professor Julius Eggeling is now nearly completed in the *Sacred Books of the East*, four volumes (XII., XXVI., XLI., XLIII. of that series) having already appeared, and the concluding volume (XLV) being in the press. From this translation—which, but for its bulk and costliness would make half of my work superfluous—and from Professor Eggeling's annotations, I have derived the greatest assistance, and most gratefully record my obligations.

All that I have attempted to do is to give a faithful translation, to the best of my ability, of the texts and sacrificial formulas of the Veda, with just sufficient commentary, chiefly from Mahīdhara, to make them intelligible. Much additional information way be found in Professor A.

Hillebrandt's Ritual-Litteratur, Vedische Opfer and Zauber (Grundriss der Indo-Arischen Philologie and Altertumskunde), Strassburg: 1897; and further minute details of the various sacrifices, rites and ceremonies are given in the Śatapatha-Brāhmaṇa as already mentioned, and in various articles, referred to in my notes, by Professor A. Weber, the great authority on the Yajurveda and all that is connected with it.

R. T. H. Griffith.

Kotagiri, Nilgiris, May, 1899.

Adhyāya 1.

1. Thee for food. Thee for vigour. Ye are breezes. | To noblest work God Savitar impel you. Inviolable! swell his share for Indra. | No thief, no evil-minded man shall master you rich in off-spring, free from pain and sickness. | Be constant, numerous to this lord of cattle. Guard thou the cattle of the Sacrificer. || 2. Strainer of Vasu art thou. Thou art heaven. Earth art thou. Thou art Mātariśvan's cauldron. | Thou art the All-container. Stand thou firmly, secure by Law Supreme, and do not totter. Nor be thy Lord of Sacrifice unsteady. || 3. Thou art the strainer, hundred-streamed, of Vasu. Thou art the strainer, thousand-streamed, of Vasu. | May Savitar the God with Vasu's strainer, thousand-streamed, rightly cleansing, purify thee. || 4. Which didst thou milk? This is the cow Vishvāyu. This Viśvakarman This is Vishvadhāyas. | Thee, Indra's share, with Soma do I curdle. Be thou protector of the oblation, Vishṇu. || 5. I will observe the vow, Lord of Vows, Agni! May I have strength therefore. Success attend me. | Now into truth from untruth do I enter. || 6. Who is it that unites thee? He unites thee. For what doth he yoke thee? For that he yokes thee. | You two for work, you two for its completion. || 7. Scorched are the fiends, scorched the malignant beings. Burnt out are fiends, burnt out malignant beings. | Throughout the spacious middle air I travel. || 8. Thou art the yoke. Injure thou him who injures. Harm him who harm us. Harm the man we injure. | Thou art the Gods' best carrier, bound most firmly, filled fullest, welcomest, Gods' best invoker. || 9. Thou art unbent, receiver of oblations. Stand firmly in thy place and do not totter. | Nor be thy Lord of sacrifice unsteady. | Let Vishṇu mount thee. To the wind lie open. The demons are expelled. Let the five grasp it. || 10. By impulse of God Savitar I take thee with arms of Aśvins, with the hands of Pūshan, | Thee dear to Agni, dear to Agni-Soma. || 11. Thee for abundance, not for evil spirit. May mine eye look upon the light of heaven. | May those with doors stand on the earth securely. Throughout the spacious middle air I travel. | Upon the navel of the earth I place thee, on Aditi's lap. Protect the oblation, Agni! || 12. Ye two are strainers that belong to Vishṇu. By Savitar's impulse, with this flawless strainer I purify you with the rays of Sūrya. | Bright Waters, flowing forward, foremost drinkers, lead forward now this sacrifice, lead forward the Sacrifice's Lord, the God-devoted Lord of the Sacrifice, the liberal giver. || 13. Indra elected you in fight with Vṛitra: in fight with Vṛitra you elected Indra. | By over-sprinkling are ye consecrated. I sprinkle thee agreeable to Agni. I sprinkle thee welcome to Agni-Soma. | Pure for the work divine be ye, and holy, pure for the sacrifice to Gods. Whatever of yours the impure have by their touch polluted, hereby I cleanse for you from all defilement. || 14. Giver art thou of happiness. Rejected are fiends, rejected are malignant beings. | Aditi's akin art thou. May Aditi receive thee. A wooden stone art thou. Thou art a broad-based stone. May the skin of Aditi receive thee. || 15. Body of Agni art thou, the releaser of speech. I seize thee for the Gods' enjoyment. | A mighty stone art thou, formed out of timber. | Make ready for the Deities this oblation: with careful preparation make it ready. | Havishkṛit, come! Havishkṛit, come! Havishkṛit, come! || 16. Thou art a cock whose tongue is sweet with honey. Call to us hither sap and manly vigour. | May we with thee in every fight be victors. Rain-grown art thou. May the rain-grown receive thee. | Cleared off are fiends, cleared off are evil beings. Expelled are fiends. May Vāyu separate you. May Savitar the God, the golden-handed, with flawless hand unto himself receive you. || 17. Bold art thou. Cast away the Corpse-consumer. Drive off the fire that eats raw flesh, O Agni. | That which makes offerings to the Gods bring hither. | Firm art thou. Make earth firm. For the foe's slaughter I set thee on, devoted to the priesthood, devoted to the nobles and the kinsmen. || 18. Agni, do thou accept our holy service. | Keeper art thou: make firm the Air's mid-region. For the foe's death I set thee on, devoted to priesthood and nobility and kinsmen. | Thou art a stay: uphold the sky securely. For the foe's death, etc. | I set thee on for sake of all the regions. Formers of layers are ye, and heap-formers, With Bhṛigus' and Aṅgirasas' heat be heated. || 19. Giver of happiness art thou. Rejected are fiends, rejected are malignant beings. Aditi's skin art thou, May Aditi receive thee. | Bowl, rock art thou. May Aditi's skin receive thee. | Thou art the sky's supporting pillar. | Bowl from the rock art thou. The rock receive thee. || 20. Grain art thou. Please the Gods. Thee for in-breathing. For out-breath thee. Thee for diffusive breathing. May I impart to life a long extension. | May Savitar the God, the golden-handed, with flawless hand unto himself receive you. | Thee for the eye. Juice art thou of the Great Ones. || 21. By impulse of God Savitar I strew thee, with arms of Aśvins, with the hands of Pūshan. | With plants let waters, plants with sap he mingled. United be the rich ones with the moving. The sweet ones and the sweet be joined together. || 22. For generation's sake I join thee. This is Agni's. This Agni-Soma's. Thee for food. | Thou art the cauldron, life of all that liveth. Spread thyself widely forth, thou, widely spreading. So may thy Lord of sacrifice spread widely. | Thy skin let Agni harm not. In highest heaven let the God Savitar hake thee. || 23. Fear not. Shrink not. Let not the sacrifice be languid, not languid he the Sacrificer's offspring. | For Trita thee. For Dvita thee. For Ekata thee. || 24. By impulse of God Savitar I take thee, with arms of Aśvins, with the hands of Pūshan, thee who for Gods performest sacred service. | Indra's right arm art thou: sharp with a thousand spikes, a hundred edges. The keen-edged Wind art thou, the foeman's slayer. || 25. O Earth, whereon men serve the Gods with worship, let me not do thy plant's root any damage. | Go to the pen, the cow-stall Heaven rain for thee. | On this earth's farthest end, God Savitar, bind him, with hundred fetters bind the man who hates us and whom we hate. Thence do not thou release him. || 26. May I drive Araru away from Earth, the seat of men's oblations to the Gods. Go to the pen . . . . . release him (as in verse 25). | O Araru, thou shalt not soar to heaven. Let not thy drop mount upward to the sky. | Go to the pen . . . . . release him (as in verse 25). || 27. I with the metre Gāyatrī enclose thee. I lay the Trishṭubh metre round about thee. With Jagatī metre I confine and gird thee. | Sprung from good soil art thou, and bliss-bestowing. Pleasant art thou, and a fair seat to rest on. Thou hast both strengthening food and drink in plenty. || 28. Before the cruel foe's secret departure, Mighty One, raising high earth, life-bestower, which to the Moon they lifted by oblations, that earth the sages still point out and worship. | Deposit in its place the sprinkling-water, Thou art the slayer of the man who hates us. || 29. Scorched are the demons, scorched the evil beings. Burnt out are fiends, burnt out malignant creatures. | Unsharpened, thou art slayer of the foemen. Thee, rich in food, I cleanse for the food's kindling. | Scorched . . . . . creatures (as above). | Thee rich in food, I cleanse for the food's kindling. || 30. A zone for Aditi art thou. Pervader of Vishṇu art thou. For great strength I take thee. I look upon thee with an eye uninjured. | Thou art the tongue of Agni. Good invoker of Gods be thou at every holy station, at every sacrificial text I utter. || 31. By Savitar's impulsion do I cleanse thee, with flawless strainer, with the rays of Sūrya. | By Savitar's impulsion do I cleanse you, with flawless strainer, with the rays of Sūrya. | Light art thou; thou art splendid; thou art Amṛita. Thou, truly, art the Gods' beloved station, inviolable means of holy worship.

Adhyāya 2.

1. Thou art a black-buck dwelling in the covert. I sprinkle thee agreeable to Agni. | Thou art the altar. Thee welcome to the sacred grass I sprinkle. | Thou art the sacred covering-grass. I sprinkle thee grateful to the sacrificial ladles. || 2. Thou art what giveth Aditi her moisture. Thou art the hair-tuft on the head of Vishṇu. I spread thee, wool-soft, good for Gods to sit on. | Hail to the Earth's Lord! To the World's Lord Hail! Hail to the Lord of Beings! || 3. For safety of this all let the Gandharva Viśvāvasu lay thee round as a protection. Thou art the Sacrificer's guard, thou, Agni, lauded and worthy to receive laudation. | Indra's right arm art thou. For safety . . . . . laudation. | For safety of This All, with firm law, northward let Mitra. Varuṇa lay thee round as keeper. Thou art the Sacrificer's guard . . . . . laudation. || 4. Thee, Sage, who offerest to Gods their banquet, we will enkindle till thou shinest brightly, thee mighty in the sacrifice, O Agni. || 5. Thou art a kindler. From the east let Sūrya keep thee secure from every imprecation. | You are the arms of Savitar. I spread thee as soft as wool, good for the Gods to sit on. On thee sit Vasus, Rudras, and Ādityas! || 6. Thou who art called Juhū art rich in fatness. On this dear seat, with the

dear home, be seated. | Thou, Upabhṛit by name, art rich in fatness. On this . . . . . be seated. | Thou who art called Dhruvā, art rich in fatness. On this, etc. | In the Law's lap they have sat down in safety | Guard these. Guard thou the Sacrifice, O Vishṇu. Keep thou the Sacrifice's Lord in safety. || 7. O Agni, Winner of the Spoil, I cleanse thee, thee who wilt hasten to the spoil, Spoil-winner. | Obeisance to the Gods! Svadhā to Fathers! Be both of you easy for me to handle. || 8. May I today offer Gods unspilt butter. Let me not with my foot offend thee, Vishṇu. | Agni, may I approach thy shade abounding in store of riches. Thou art Vishṇu's mansion, | Hence Indra wrought his deed of manly vigour. The sacrifice stood firmly elevated. || 9. O Agni, undertake the Hotar's office, take on thyself the duty of an envoy. | Heaven and Earth guard thee! Guard thou Earth and Heaven. | May Indra be, by this presented butter, maker to Gods of fair oblation. Svāhā! Let light combine with light. || 10. Indra bestow on me that Indra-power! May wealth in full abundance gather round us. Let blessings wait on us, yea, real blessings. | Our Mother, Earth, hath been invited hither. May Earth, our Mother, in return invite us. I, through my Kindler-ship, am Agni. Svāhā! || 11. The Father Heaven hath been invited hither. May Heaven the Father in return invite us. | By impulse of God Savitar I receive thee with arms of Aśvins, with the hands of Pūshan I feed upon thee with the mouth of Agni. || 12. God Savitar, this sacrifice of thine have they proclaimed unto Bṛihaspati the Brahman Priest. | Therefore protect the sacrifice, protect the sacrifice's lord, protect thou me. || 13. The butter's rapid flow delight his spirit! Bṛihaspati extend this act of worship. May he restore the sacrifice uninjured. | Here let all Gods rejoice. Om! Step thou forward. || 14. This is the stick for kindling thee, O Agni. By means of this grow strong and swell to greatness. May we too grow in strength and swell to greatness. | O Agni, thou who winnest food, I cleanse thee, thee who hast hastened to the food, Food-winner. || 15. After the victory of Agni Soma may I obtain the victory. By impulse of sacrificial food I speed me onward. | May Agni-Soma drive off him who hates us, drive off the man whom we detest. By impulse of sacrificial food away I drive him. | After the victory of Indra-Agni may I obtain the victory. By impulse of sacrificial food I speed me forward. | May Indra-Agni . . . . . I drive him. || 16. For Vasus thee. For Rudras thee. Thee for Ādityas | Be, Heaven and Earth, accordant with each other. With rain may Mitra-Varuṇa assist thee. | May the birds go, licking what is anointed. | Go to the Marutas' speckled mares. Go, having become a speckled cow thyself, to heaven, and from that place bring the rain for us hither. | Thou art the eye's guard: guard mine eye, O Agni. || 17. The stick which thou, God Agni, laidest round thee, what time thou wast kept hidden by the Paṇis, this do I bring to thee for thine enjoyment. May it remain with thee and ne'er be fruitless. | Approach, ye two, the place which Agni loveth. || 18. The residue ye have to be your portion, mighty by food, ye Gods, ye who are stationed on the grass-bunch, and to be laid as fences. | All ye, applauding this my speech, be seated on this grass-bunch and there be joyful. Svāhā! Vāṭ! || 19. Rich in oil are ye. Guard the two yoke-fellows. Ye two are full of grace, to grace conduct me. | Glory to thee, O Sacrifice, and increase! Stand firm in my auspicious, righteous worship. || 20. O Agni of unweakened strength, far-reaching, protect me from the lightning-flash, protect me from bondage. from defect in sacrificing, from food injurious to health protect me. | Make thou the food that feeds us free from poison in the home good to sit in. Svāhā! Vāṭ! | Hail to the Lord of close embracements, Agni! Hail to Sarasvatī enriched with glory! || 21. Veda art thou, whereby, O godlike Veda, thou hast become for Deities their Veda: thereby mayst thou become for me a Veda. | O Deities, ye knowers of the Pathway, walk on the pathway having known the Pathway. | God, Lord of Spirit, hail! bestow upon the Wind this sacrifice. || 22. Blest be the Grass with sacred food and butter. Let Indra be united with the Ādityas, the Vasus, Marutas, and the Viśvedevas Let Svāhā-offerings rise to heavenly ether. || 23. Who liberates thee from the yoke? He frees thee. For whom? For him he looses thee. For plenty. | Thou art the Rākshasas' allotted portion. || 24. We have combined with lustre, vigour, bodies; we have united with the blessed spirit. May Tvashṭar, bounteous giver, grant us riches, and clear each fault and blemish from the body. || 25. By Jagatī metre in the sky strode Vishṇu. Therefrom excluded is the man who hates us and whom we detest. | By Trishṭubh metre in the air strode Vishṇu. Therefrom, etc. | By Gāyatrī upon the earth strode Vishṇu. Therefrom, etc. | From this food From this resting-place excluded. | We have reached heaven. We have combined with lustre. || 26. Thou, noblest ray of light, art Self-existent. Giver art thou of splendour. Give me splendour. | I move along the path that Sūrya travels. || 27. Agni, may I become a good householder, through thee, Home-master, O Householder Agni. Mayst thou become an excellent Householder through me the master of the house, O Agni. | Through hundred winters may our household matters—not like a one-ox car—be smoothly managed. | I move along the path that Sūrya travels. || 28. I have performed the vow, Lord of Vows, Agni! Full power was mine, and it has proved successful. | Now am I he I truly am, no other. || 29. To Agni Hail! who bears gifts due to Sages. To Soma Hail! accompanied by Fathers. | Expelled are Asuras and fiends who sate upon the covering grass. || 30. The Asuras, attracted by oblation, who roam at will assuming varied figures, from this our world may Agni drive them, whether they clothe themselves in large or little bodies. || 31. O Fathers, here enjoy yourselves. Come hither, like bulls, come each to his allotted portion. | The Fathers have enjoyed themselves, and hither, like bulls, come each to his allotted portion. || 32. Obeisance to your genial sap, O Fathers! Fathers, obeisance unto you for Ardour! Fathers, obeisance unto you for Svadhā! Obeisance unto you for Life, O Fathers! | Fathers, to you obeisance for the Awful! Fathers, obeisance unto you for Passion! O Fathers, unto you be adoration. | Bestow upon us houses, O ye Fathers, what is ours, O Fathers, will we give you. With this your raiment clothe yourselves, O Fathers. || 33. Fathers, bestow on me a babe, a boy enwreathed with lotuses, so that there may be here a man. || 34. Bearers of vigour and immortal fatness, milk and sweet beverage and foaming liquor, ye are a freshening draught. Delight my Fathers.

Adhyāya 3.

1. Serve Agni with the kindling-brand, with drops of butter wake the Guest. | In him pay offerings to the Gods. || 2. To Agni Jātavedas, to the flame, the well-enkindled God, Offer thick sacrificial oil. || 3. Thee, such, O Aṅgiras, with brands and sacred oil we magnify, O very brilliant, Youthfullest. || 4. Rich in oblations, dropping oil, to thee, sweet Agni, let them go. | Accept with favour these my brands. || 5. Earth! Ether! Sky! | Like heaven in plenty and like earth in compass! Upon thy back, Earth, place of sacrificing to Gods, for gain of food I lay food-eating Agni. || 6. This spotted Bull hath come and sat before the Mother and before | The Father, mounting up to heaven. || 7. As expiration from his breath his radiance penetrates within: | The Bull shines out through all the sky. || 8. He rules supreme through thirty realms. Song is bestowed upon the Bird | Throughout the days at break of morn. || 9. Agni is light, and light is Agni. Hail! | Sūrya is light, and light is Sūrya. Hail! | Agni is splendour, light is splendour. Hail! | Sūrya is splendour, light is splendour. Hail! | Light is Sūrya, Sūrya is light. Hail! || 10. Accordant with bright Savitar and Night with Indra at her side, | May Agni, being pleased, enjoy. All-hail! || 11. Approaching sacrifice, may we pronounce a text to Agni who | Heareth us even when afar. || 12. Agni is head and height of heaven, the Master of the earth is he: | He quickeneth the waters' seed. || 13. You two will I invoke, O Indra-Agni, will please you both together with oblation. | Givers, you twain, of vigorous strength and riches, you twain do I invoke for gain of vigour. || 14. This is thine ordered place of birth whence, sprung to life, thou shonest forth. | Knowing this, Agni, rise thou up and cause our riches to increase. || 15. Here by ordainers was this God appointed first Invoker, best at worship, to be praised at rites, | Whom Apnavāna and the Bhṛigus caused to shine, bright-coloured in the wood, spreading to every house. || 16. After his ancient splendour they, the bold, have drawn the bright milk from | The Sage who wins a thousand gifts. || 17. Thou, Agni, art our bodies' guard. Guard thou my body. | Giver of life art thou, O Agni. Give me life. | Giver of splendour art thou, Agni. Give me splendour. | All that is wanting in my body, Agni, supply for me. || 18. Enkindled we enkindle thee through hundred winters, thee the bright; | We, healthy, thee who givest health; we strong, thee author of our strength; | We, never injured, Agni, thee uninjured injurer of foes. | O rich in shining lights, may I in safety rich the end of thee. || 19. Thou hast attained, O Agni, to the splendour of Sūrya, to the eulogy of Ṛishis, and to the habitation which thou lovest. | May I attain to lengthened life, to splendour, to offspring and abundant store of riches. || 20. Ye are food, may I enjoy your food. Ye are might, may I

enjoy your might. Ye are energy, may I enjoy your energy. Ye are abundant riches, may I enjoy your abundant riches. || 21. Sport, wealthy ones, in this abode, this fold, this spot, this dwelling-place. | Remain just here, and go not hence. || 22. Composed art thou of every form and colour. With sap and ownership of kine approach me. | To thee, dispeller of the night, O Agni, day by day with prayer, | Bringing thee reverence, we come; || 23. Ruler of sacrifices, guard of Law eternal, radiant One, | Increasing in thine own abode. || 24. Be to us easy of approach, even as a father to his son: | Agni, be with us for our weal. || 25. O Agni, be our nearest Friend; be thou a kind deliverer and gracious Friend. | Excellent Agni, come thou nigh to us, and give us wealth most splendidly renowned. || 26. To thee then, O most bright, O radiant God, we come with prayer for happiness for our friends. | So hear us, listen to this call of ours, and keep us far from every evil man. || 27. O Iḍā, come, O Aditi, come hither. Come hither, much-desired! From you may I obtain my heart's desire. || 28. O Brahmaṇaspati, make him who presses Soma glorious, Even Kakshīvant Auśija || 29. The rich, the healer of disease, who findeth wealth, increaseth store, | The prompt,—may he be with us still. || 30. Let not the foeman's curse, let not a mortal's treachery fall on us: | Preserve us, Brahmaṇaspati! || 31. Great, heavenly, unassailable, ours be the favour of the Three, Aryaman, Mitra, Varuṇa || 32. For over them, neither at home nor upon pathways perilous, | The evil-minded foe hath power. || 33. For they, the Sons of Aditi, bestow eternal light upon | A mortal man that he may live. || 34. Ne'er art thou fruitless, Indra, ne'er dost thou forsake thy worshipper. | But now, O Liberal Lord, thy bounty as a God is ever poured forth more and more. || 35. May we attain that excellent glory of Savitar the God: | So may he stimulate our prayers. || 36. May thine inviolable car wherewith thou guardest worshippers | Come near to us from every side. || 37. Earth! Ether! Sky! May I be rich in offspring, well-manned with men and opulent with riches. Friendly to men! do thou protect my offspring. Worthy of praise! do thou protect my cattle. | O pointed One, protect the food that feeds me. || 38. We have approached the Omniscient, best finder-out of wealth for us. Splendour and strength bestow on us, O Agni, thou Imperial Lord. || 39. Lord of the Home, this Agni Gārhapatya is best at finding riches for our children. | Splendour and strength bestow on us, O Agni, Master of the Home. || 40. Rich, furtherer of plenty is this Agni, Master-of the Herd. | Splendour and strength bestow on us, O Agni, Master of the Herd. || 41. Fear not, nor tremble thou, O House. To thee who bearest strength we come. | I, bearing strength, intelligent and happy, come to thee, House, rejoicing in my spirit. || 42. The home on which the wanderer thinks, where cheerfulness and joy abound— | We call the Home to welcome us. May it know us who know it well. || 43. Here have the cows been called to us, the goats and sheep have been called near, | And in our home we have addressed the meath that sweeteneth our food. | I come to thee for safety and for quiet. May joy be ours, felicity, and blessing. || 44. We invocate the Marutas, the voracious, eaters of their foes, | Delighting in their mess of meal. || 45. We expiate by sacrifice each sinful act that we have done, | Whether in village or the wild, in company or corporeal sense. Svāhā! || 46. Let us not here contend with Gods, O Indra, for, Fierce One! here is thine own sacred portion, | Thine, Mighty One, whose friends, the bounteous Marutas, his song who pours oblation, stream-like, honours. || 47. The skilful workers have performed their work with voice that gives delight. | Having performed the work for Gods, go, ye companions, to your home. || 48. O ever-moving Cleansing Bath, thou movest gliding on thy way. | With Gods may I wash out the sin that I have sinned against the Gods, with men the sin against mankind. | Preserve me safe from injury, O God, from him who loudly roars. || 49. Full, fly away, O spoon, and filled completely fly thou back to us. | O Śatakratu, let us twain barter, like goods, our food and strength. || 50. Give me, I give thee gifts: bestow on me, and I bestow on thee. | To me present thy merchandise, and I to thee will give my wares. || 51. Well have they eaten and regaled: the friends have risen and passed away. | The sages, luminous in themselves, have praised thee with their latest hymn. | Now, Indra, yoke thy two Bay Steeds. || 52. Thee will we reverence, thee, O Lord of Bounty, who art fair to see. | Thus praised, according to our wish come now with richly-laden car. Now, Indra, yoke thy two Bay Steeds. || 53. We call the spirit hither with a hero-celebrating strain, | Yea, with the Fathers' holy hymns. || 54. The spirit comes to us again for wisdom, energy, and life, | That we may long behold the Sun. || 55. O Fathers, may the Heavenly Folk give us the spirit once again, | That we may be with those who live. || 56. O Soma, with the spirit still within us, blest with progeny, | May we be busied in thy law. || 57. O Rudra, this is thine allotted portion. With Ambikā thy sister kindly take it. This, Rudra, is thy share, the rat thy victim. || 58. We have contented Rudra, yea, put off Tryambaka the God, | That he may make us wealthier, may make us yet more prosperous, may make us vigorous to act. || 59. Thou art a healing medicine, a balm for cow and horse and man, a happiness to ram and ewe. || 60. Tryambaka we worship, sweet augmenter of prosperity. | As from its stem a cucumber, may I be freed from bonds of death, not reft of immortality. | We worship him, Tryambaka, the husband-finder, sweet to smell. | As from its stem a cucumber, hence and not thence may I be loosed. || 61. This, Rudra, is thy food: with this depart beyond the Mūjavants. | With bow unstrung, with muffled staff, clothed in a garment made of skin, gracious, not harming us, depart. || 62. May Jamadagni's triple life, the triple life of Kaśyapa, | The triple life of Deities—may that same triple life be ours. || 63. Gracious, thy name; the thunder is thy father. Obeisance be to thee: forbear to harm me. | I shave thee for long life, for food to feed thee, for progeny, for riches in abundance, for noble children, for heroic vigour.

Adhyāya 4.

1. We have reached this earth's place of sacrificing, the place wherein all Deities delighted. | Crossing by Ṛich, by Sāman, and by Yajus, may we rejoice in food and growth of riches. | Gracious to me be these Celestial Waters! | Protect me, Plant. O Knife, forbear to harm him. || 2. The Mother Floods shall make us bright and shining, cleansers of holy oil, with oil shall cleanse us. | For, Goddesses, they bear off all defilement. I rise up from them purified and brightened. | The form of Consecration and of Fervour art thou. I put thee on, the kind and blissful, maintaining an agreeable appearance. || 3. The Great Ones' milk art thou. Giver of splendour art thou: bestow on me the gift of splendour. | Pupil art thou of Vṛitra's eye. The giver of eyes art thou. Give me the gift of vision. || 4. Purify me the Lord of Thought! Purify me the Lord of Speech! Purify me God Savitar with perfect strainer, with the beams of Sūrya! | Of thee, Lord of the Strainer! who art by the strainer purified, | With what desire I purify myself, may I accomplish it. || 5. We come to you for precious wealth, O Gods, as sacrifice proceeds. | O Gods, we call on you to give blessings that wait on sacrifice. || 6. Svāhā! from mind the sacrifice. Svāhā! from spacious firmament. | Svāhā! from Dyaus and Pṛithivī Svāhā! from Wind I seize. Svāhā! || 7. To Resolution, Motive, Agni, Svāhā! All-hail to Wisdom, and to Mind, and Agni! | All-hail to Consecration, Fervour, Agni! Hail to Sarasvatī, Pūṣhan, and Agni! | Ye vast, divine, all-beneficial Waters, ye Heaven and Earth and spacious Air between them, | Let us adore Bṛihaspati with oblation. All-hail! || 8. May every mortal man elect the friendship of the guiding God. | Each one solicits him for wealth: let him seek fame to prosper him. || 9. Ṛich's, Sāman's counterparts are ye. I touch you. Protect me till the sacrifice be ended. | Thou art a place of refuge. Give me refuge. Obeisance unto thee! Forbear to harm me. || 10. Strength of Aṅgirasas art thou. Wool-soft, bestow thou strength on me. | Thou art the garment-knot of Soma. Vishṇu's refuge art thou, the Sacrificer's refuge. | Thou art the womb of Indra. Make the crops produce abundant grain. | Stand up erect, O Tree. Protect me from harm until this sacrifice be ended. || 11. Prepare ye vow-food. Agni is the Brahman, Agni is sacrifice, the tree is holy. | For aid we meditate divine Intelligence, most merciful, | Free-giver, bringing worship May it guide us gently, as we would. | Favour us Gods, mind-horn, endowed with mind and intellectual might! All-hail to them! May they be our protectors. || 12. Waters that we have drunk! become refreshing, become auspicious draughts within our belly. | Free from all sin and malady and sickness, may they be pleasant to our taste, divine Ones, immortal, strengtheners of eternal Order. || 13. This is thy sacrificial form. | Not offspring, waters I discharge. Freeing from sin and consecrate by Svāhā enter ye the earth. Be thou united with the earth. || 14. O Agni, watch thou well. May we take joy in most refreshing sleep. | Protect us with unceasing care. From slumber waken us again. || 15. Thought hath returned to me, and life; my breath and soul have come again. | Our bodies' guard, unscathed, Vaiśvānara Agni preserve us from misfortune and dishonour. ||

16. Thou, Agni, art the guardian God of sacred vows among mankind, thou meet for praise at holy rites. | Grant this much, Soma! bring yet more. God Savitar who giveth wealth hath given treasure unto us. || 17. This is thy form, O Bright One, this thy lustre. Combine with this thy form and go to splendour. | Impetuous art thou, upheld by mind, and Vishṇu loveth thee. || 18. Moved by thine impulse who hast true impulsion, may I obtain a prop to stay my body. | Pure art thou, glistering art thou, immortal, dear to all the Gods. || 19. Thought art thou, mind, intelligence, the Guerdon, royal, worshipful, Aditi with a double head. Succeed for us in going forth, succeed for us in thy return. May Mitra bind thee by the foot. May Pūshan guard thy pathways for Indra whose eye is over all. || 20. Thy mother give thee leave to go, thy father, thine own brother, and thy friend of the same herd with thee! | Go thou, O Goddess, to the God. To Soma go for Indra's sake. | May Rudra turn thee back. Return safely with Soma as thy friend. || 21. Thou art a Vasvī, thou art Aditi, thou art an Āditya, thou art a Rudrā, thou art a Chandrā. | Bṛihaspati vouchsafe thee rest and comfort! Rudra with Vasus looks on thee with favour. || 22. On Aditi's head I sprinkle thee, on the earth's place of sacrifice. | Footstep of Iḍā art thou, filled with fatness. Hail! | Rejoice in us. Thy kinship is in us. In thee are riches. Mine be riches! Let us not be deprived of abundant riches. Thine, thine are riches. || 23. I with my thought have commerced with divine far-sighted Dakshiṇā. | Steal not my life. I will not thine. May I, O Goddess, in thy sight find for myself a hero son. || 24. Tell Soma this for me: This is thy share allied with Gāyatrī. | For me say this to Soma: This is thine allotted Trishṭubh share. | Tell Soma this for me: This is thy share allied with Jagatī. | Tell Soma this for me: Win thou sole lordship of the metres' names. | Ours art thou: pure thy juice for draught. Let separators pick thee out. || 25. I sing my song of praise to him, Savitar, God between the Bowls, strong with the wisdom of the wise, of true impulsion, wealth-giver, the well-beloved thoughtful Sage. | To him at whose impulsion shone aloft in heaven the splendid light. | Most wise, the Golden-handed hath measured the sky with skilled design. | For living creatures, thee. Let living creatures breathe after thee. Breathe after living creatures. || 26. Thee who art pure, with what is pure I purchase, the bright with bright, immortal with immortal. | The Sacrificer keep thy cow. Let thy gold pieces be with us. | Fervour's form art thou, and Prajāpati's nature. With the most noble animal art thou purchased. May I increase with thousandfold abundance. || 27. As friend, the giver of good friends, approach us! | Take thou thy seat on the right thigh of Indra, yearning on yearning, pleasing on the pleasing. | Aṅghāri, Svāna, Bhrāja, and Bambhāri, O Hasta, and Suhasta and Kṛiśānu, | These are your prices for the Soma purchase. Keep them securely, let them never fail you. || 28. Keep me, O Agni, from unrighteous conduct: make me a sharer in the path of goodness. | I, following Immortals, have arisen with longer life, with a good life before me. || 29. Now have we entered on the path that leads to bliss without a foe, | The path whereon a man escapes all enemies and gathers wealth. || 30. The skin of Aditi art thou. Sit on the lap of Aditi. | The Bull hath propped the sky and air's mid-region, the compass of the broad earth hath he measured. | He, King Supreme, approached all living creatures. Truly all these are Varuṇa's ordinances. || 31. Over the woods the air hath he extended, put milk in kine and vigorous speed in horses, | Set intellect in hearts and fire in houses, Sūrya in heaven and Soma on the mountain. || 32. Ascend the eye of Sūrya, mount the pupil set in Agni's eye | Where, radiant through the Wise One, thou speedest along with dappled steeds. || 33. Approach, ye oxen, fit to bear the yoke; be yoked without a tear. | Slaying no man, urging the Brahman forward, go happily to the Sacrificer's dwelling. || 34. Lord of the World, thou art my gracious helper: move forward on thy way to all the stations. | Let not opponents, let not robbers find thee, let not malignant wolves await thy coming. | Fly thou away having become a falcon. Go to the dwelling of the Sacrificer. That is the special place for us to rest in. || 35. Do homage unto Varuṇa's and Mitra's eye: offer this solemn worship to the Mighty God, | Who seeth far away, the Ensign born of Gods. Sing praises unto Sūrya, to the Son of Dyaus. || 36. Thou art a prop for Varuṇa to rest on. Ye are the pins that strengthen Varuṇa's pillar. | Thou art the lawful seat where Varuṇa sitteth. Sit on the lawful seat where Varuṇa sitteth. || 37. Such of thy glories as with poured oblations men honour, may they all invest our worship. | Wealth-giver, furtherer with troops of heroes, sparing the brave, come, Soma, to our houses.

Adhyāya 5.

1. Body of Agni art thou. Thee for Vishṇu. Body of Soma art thou. Thee for Vishṇu. Thou art the Guest's Reception. Thee for Vishṇu. Thee for the Soma-bringing Falcon. Thee for Vishṇu. Thee for the giver of abundance, Agni. Thee for Vishṇu. || 2. Birth-place art thou of Agni. Ye are sprinklers. Thou art Urvaśī. Thou art Āyu. Thou art Purūravas. | I rub and churn thee with Gāyatrī metre. I rub and churn thee with the Trishṭubh metre. I rub and churn thee with the Jagatī metre. || 3. Be ye for us one-minded, be one-thoughted, free from spot and stain. | Harm not the sacrifice, harm not the sacrifice's lord. Be kind to us this day, Omniscient Ones! || 4. Preserver from the curse, Son of the Ṛishis, Agni is active having entered Agni. | Here for us kindly with fair worship offer oblation to the Gods with care unceasing. Svāhā! || 5. For him who flies around and rushes onward I take thee, for Tanūnapāt the mighty, the very strong, of all-surpassing vigour. | Strength of the Gods, inviolate, inviolable still art thou, the strength that turns the curse away, uncursed and never to be cursed. | May I go straight to truth. Place me in comfort. || 6. O Agni, Guardian of the Vow, O Guardian of the Vow, in thee | Whatever form there is of thine, may that same form be here on me: on thee be every form of mine. | O Lord of Vows, let our vows be united. May Dīkshā's Lord allow my Consecration, may holy Fervour's Lord approve my Fervour. || 7. May every stalk of thine wax full and strengthen for Indra Ekadhanavid, God Soma! | May Indra grow in strength for thee: for Indra mayest thou grow strong. | Increase us friends with strength and mental vigour. May all prosperity be thine, God Soma. May I attain the solemn Soma-pressing. | May longed-for wealth come forth for strength and fortune. Let there be truth for those whose speech is truthful. To Heaven and Earth be adoration offered. || 8. That noblest body which is thine, O Agni, laid in the lowest deep, encased in iron, hath chased the awful word, the word of terror. Svāhā! | That noblest .... encased in silver, etc. Svāhā | That noblest ..... with gold around it, etc. Svāhā! || 9. For me thou art the home of the afflicted. For me thou art the gathering-place of riches. Protect me from the, woe of destitution. | Protect me from the state of perturbation. | May Agni know thee, he whose name is Nabhas. Go, Agni, Aṅgiras, with the name of Āyu | Thou whom this earth containeth, down I lay thee with each inviolate holy name thou bearest. | Thou whom the second earth, etc. Thou whom the third earth, etc. | Thee, further, for the Gods' delight. || 10. A foe-subduing lioness art thou: be fitted for the Gods. | A foe-subduing lioness art thou: be purified for Gods. | A foe-subduing lioness art thou: adorn thyself for Gods. || 11. Indra's shout guard thee in the front with Vasus. The Wise One guard thee from the rear with Rudras. The Thought-swift guard thee on the right with Fathers. The Omnific guard thee, leftward, with Ādityas. | This heated water I eject and banish from the sacrifice. || 12. Thou art a lioness. All-hail! Thou art a lioness winning Ādityas All-hail! | Thou art a lioness winning Brahmans and Nobles. All-hail! | Thou art a lioness that wins fair offspring, win abundant wealth. All-hail! | A lioness art thou. Bring the Gods hither for him who offers sacrifice. All-hail! | To living creatures; thee. || 13. Firm art thou, steady thou the earth. Firm-seated art thou, steady thou the air. | Movelessly set art thou, steady the sky. Agni's completion art thou. || 14. The priests of him the lofty Priest well-skilled in hymns harness their spirits, yea harness their holy thoughts. | He only knowing works assigns their priestly tasks. Yea, lofty is the praise of Savitar the God. All-hail! || 15. Forth through This All strode Vishṇu: thrice his foot he planted, and the whole was gathered in his footstep's dust. All-hail! || 16. Rich in sweet food be ye, and rich in milch-kine, with fertile pastures, fair to do men service. | Both these worlds, Vishṇu, hast thou stayed asunder, and firmly fixed the earth with pegs around it. || 17. Heard by the Gods, ye twain, to Gods proclaim it. | Go eastward, O ye twain, proclaiming worship. Swerve ye not: bear the sacrifice straight upward. | To your own cow-pen speak, ye godlike dwellings. | Speak not away my life, speak not away my children. | On the earth's summit here may ye be joyful. || 18. Now will I tell the mighty deeds of Vishṇu, of him who measured out the earthly regions. | Who propped the highest place of congregation, thrice setting down his foot and widely striding. | For Vishṇu thee. || 19. Either from heaven or from the earth, O Vishṇu, or, Vishṇu, from the vast wide

air's mid-region, | Fill both thy hands full with abundant riches, and from the right and from the left bestow them. | For Viṣṇu thee. ‖ 20. For this his mighty deed is Viṣṇu lauded, like some wild beast, dread, prowling, mountain-roaming, | He within whose three wide-extended paces all living creatures have their habitation, ‖ 21. Thou art the frontlet for the brow of Viṣṇu. Ye are the corners of the mouth of Viṣṇu. Thou art the needle for the work of Viṣṇu. Thou art the firmly-fastened knot of Viṣṇu. To Viṣṇu thou belongest. Thee for Viṣṇu. ‖ 22. By impulse of God Savitar I take thee with arms of Aśvins and with hands of Pūṣhan | Thou art a woman. Here I cut the necks of Rākṣhasas away. | Mighty art thou, mighty the sound thou makest. Utter thy mighty-sounding voice to Indra: ‖ 23. Fiend-killing, charm-destroying voice of Viṣṇu. | Here I cast out that charm of magic power which stranger or house-mate for me hath buried. | Here I cast out the charm of magic power buried for me by equal or unequal. | Here I cast out the charm that hath been buried for me by non-relation or relation. | I cast the charm of magic out. ‖ 24. Self-ruler art thou, conquering foes. Ruler for ever art thou, killing enemies. | Men's ruler art thou, slaying fiends. All ruler, killing foes, art thou. ‖ 25. I sprinkle you whom Viṣṇu owns, killers of fiends and evil charms. | I lay down you whom Viṣṇu loves, killers of fiends and wicked charms. | I scatter you whom Viṣṇu loves, killers of fiends and wicked charms. | You two whom Viṣṇu loves, who kill fiends and ill charms do I lay down. | You two whom Viṣṇu loves, who kill fiends and ill charms I compass round. | To Viṣṇu thou belongest. Ye are Viṣṇu's. ‖ 26. By impulse of God Savitar I take thee with arms of Aśvins, with the hands of Pūṣhan. | Thou art a woman. Here I cut the necks of Rākṣhasas away. | Barley art thou. Bar off from us our haters, bar our enemies. | Thee for heaven, thee for earth, thee for air's region. | Pure be the worlds, the Fathers' dwelling-places. Thou art the habitation of the Fathers. ‖ 27. Prop heaven, fill full the air, on earth stand firmly. Dyutāna, offspring of the Marutas, plant thee!, Mitra and Varuṇa with firm upholding. | I close thee in, thou winner of the Brahmans, winner of Nobles and abundant riches. | Strengthen the Brahmans, strengthen thou the Nobles, strengthen our vital power, strengthen our offspring. ‖ 28. Firm-set art thou. Firm be this Sacrificer within this home with offspring and with cattle. | O Heaven and Earth, be ye filled full of fatness. | Indra's mat art thou, shelter of all people. ‖ 29. Lover of song, may these our songs encompass thee on every side; | Strengthening thee of lengthened life, may they be dear delights to thee ‖ 30. Thou art the needle for the work of Indra. Thou art the firmly fastened knot of Indra. Indra's art thou. Thou art the Viśvedevas'. ‖ 31. All-present art thou, carrying off. Oblation-bearing priest art thou. | Thou art the Swift, the Very Wise. Tutha art thou, who knoweth all. ‖ 32. Thou art the yearning one, the sage. Aṅghāri, Bambhāri art thou. | Aid-seeker art thou, worshipping. Cleanser art thou, the cleansing-place. Kriśānu, Sovereign Lord, art thou. | Thou art the Pavamāna of the assembly. Thou art the welkin ever moving forward. Swept clean art thou, preparer of oblations. Thou art the seat of Law, heaven's light and lustre. ‖ 33. A sea art thou of all-embracing compass. Aja art thou, who hath one foot to bear him. Thou art the Dragon of the Depths of ocean. Speech art thou, thou the Sadas, thou art Indra's. Doors of the sacrifice, do not distress me! | Lord, Ruler of the pathways, lead me onward. In this God-reaching path may I be happy. ‖ 34. Look ye upon me with the eye of Mitra. | O Agnis, ye, receivers of oblations, are by a lauded name lauded together. Protect me, Agnis! with your glittering army. Fill me with riches, Agnis! be my keepers. To you be adoration. Do not harm me. ‖ 35. Thou art a light that wears all forms and figures, serving the general host of Gods as Kindler. | Thou, Soma, wilt withhold thy wide protection from body-wounding hatreds shown by others. All-hail! | Let the Swift graciously enjoy the butter. All-hail! ‖ 36. By goodly paths lead us to riches, Agni, thou God who knowest every sacred duty. | Remove the sin that makes us stray and wander: most ample adoration will we bring thee. ‖ 37. Wide room and comfort may this Agni give us, and go before us cleaving down our foemen. | May he win booty in the fight for booty: May he quell foes in his triumphant onset. ‖ 38. O Viṣṇu, stride thou widely forth, give ample room for our abode. | Drink butter, homed in butter! Still speed on the sacrifice's lord. All-hail! ‖ 39. To thee, God Savitar, belongs this Soma. Guard him securely: let not demons harm thee. | Now hast thou joined the

Gods as God, God Soma: men have I joined here through abundant riches. | All-hail! from Varuṇa's noose am I delivered. ‖ 40. O Agni, Guardian of the Vow, O Guardian of the Vow, on me whatever form of thine path been, may that same form be upon thee. Whatever form of mine hath been on thee, may that he here on me. | O Lord of Vows, our vows have been accomplished. Dīkṣhā's | Lord hath approved my Consecration, and holy Fervour's | Lord allowed my Fervour. ‖ 41. O Viṣṇu, stride thou widely forth, make ample room for our abode. | Drink butter, homed in butter! Still speed on the sacrifice's lord. All Hail! ‖ 42. I have passed others, not approached to others. On the near side of those that were more distant, and farther than the nearer have I found thee. | So, for the worship of the Gods, with gladness we welcome thee God, Sovereign of the Forest! Let the Gods welcome thee for the Gods' service. For Viṣṇu thee. Plant, guard! | Axe, do not harm it! ‖ 43. Graze not the sky. Harm not mid-air. Be in accordance with the earth. | For this well-sharpened axe hath led thee forth to great felicity. | Hence, with a hundred branches, God, Lord of the Forest, grow thou up. | May we grow spreading with a hundred branches.

Adhyāya 6.

1. By impulse of God Savitar I take thee with arms of Aśvins, with the hands of Pūṣhan Thou art a woman. Here I cut the necks of Rākṣhasas away. Barley art thou. Bar off from us our haters, bar our enemies. | Thee for heaven, thee for earth, thee for the welkin. Pure be the worlds, the Fathers' dwelling-places. Thou art the habitation of the Fathers. ‖ 2. Thou art a leader, easy, to Unnetars, of access. Know this. It will stand upon thee. | Savitar, God, anoint thee with sweet butter. Thee for the plants laden with goodly fruitage! | Thou with thy top hast touched the sky, hast with thy middle filled the air, and steadied with thy base the earth. ‖ 3. Those seats of thine which we desire to visit, where there are many-horned and nimble. oxen, | There, of a truth, was mightily imprinted the loftiest step of widely-striding Viṣṇu. | I close thee in, the winner of the Brahmans, winner of Nobles and abundant riches. | Strengthen the Brahmans, strengthen thou the Nobles, strengthen our vital power, strengthen our offspring. ‖ 4. Look ye on Viṣṇu's works, whereby the Friend of Indra, close-allied, | Hath let his holy ways be seen. ‖ 5. The princes evermore behold that loftiest place where Viṣṇu is, | Laid as it were an eye in heaven. ‖ 6. Thou art invested. Heavenly hosts invest thee! Riches of men invest this Sacrificer! | Heaven's son art thou. This is thine earthly station. Thine is the beast whose home is in the forest. ‖ 7. Encourager art thou. The hosts of heaven have come to yearning Gods, the best conductors. | God Tvaṣhṭar, make the wealth of cattle quiet. Delightful to the taste be thine oblations. ‖ 8. Joy, wealthy ones! Brihaspati, save our riches. | I bind thee with the noose of holy Order, thou offering to the Gods. Bold be the Slayer. ‖ 9. By impulse of God Savitar I bind thee, with arms of Aśvins and with hands of Pūṣhan, thee welcome unto Agni and to Soma. | Thee for the waters, thee for plants. Thy mother grant thee permission, and thy father, brother born of one dam, thy friend, thy herd-companion. I sprinkle thee welcome to Agni-Soma. ‖ 10. Drinker art thou of water. May the Waters, the Goddesses, add sweetness to the oblation prepared for Gods, even though already sweetened. | Thy breath join wind, thy limbs those meet for worship, the sacrifice's lord the boon he prays for. ‖ 11. Balmed, both of you, with butter, guard the cattle. Grant, Rich! the Sacrificer's prayer. Approach thou. | Meeting with heavenly Wind, from air's mid-region. Be thou united with this offering's body. | O Great One, lead the sacrifice's master on to a sacrifice of loftier order. All-hail to Gods! To Gods All-hail! ‖ 12. Become no serpent, thou, become no viper. To thee, O widely-spread, be adoration. | Advance, unhindered, on thy way. To rivers of butter move along the paths of Order. ‖ 13. Bear the oblation to the Gods, ye Waters celestial and pure and well-provided. May we become providers well-provided. ‖ 14. I cleanse thy voice, thy breath, thine eye, thine ear, thy navel, and thy feet, thy sexual organ, and thy rump. ‖ 15. Let thy mind, voice, and breath increase in fullness, thine eye be fuller, and thine ear grow stronger. | Whatever there is in thee sore or wounded, may that be filled for thee, cleansed and united. | Blest be the days. Plant, guard! Axe, do not harm him. ‖ 16. Thou art the demons' share. Expelled are demons. Here I tread down; here I repel the demons; here lead the demons into lowest darkness. | Invest, ye two, the heaven and earth with fatness. | O Vāyu, eagerly enjoy the droppings. Let

Agni eagerly enjoy the butter. All-hail! | Go, both of you, by Svāhā consecrated, to Ūrdhvanabhas, offspring of the Marutas. || 17. Ye Waters, wash away this stain and whatsoever taint be here, | Each sinful act that I have done, and every harmless curse of mine. | May Waters rid me of that guilt, and Pavamāna set me free. || 18. Be they united, with the Mind thy mind, and with the Breath thy breath. | Thou quiverest. Let Agni make thee ready. Waters have washed together all thy juices. | Thee for the Wind's rush, for the speed of Pūshan. From heated vapour may it reel and totter,—the disconcerted hatred of our foemen. || 19. Ye drinkers-up of fatness, drink the fatness; drink up the gravy, drinkers of the gravy! Thou art the oblation of the air's mid-region. All-hail! | The regions, the fore-regions, the by-regions, the intermediate and the upper regions,—to all the regions Hail! || 20. In every limb is Indra's out-breath seated, in every limb is Indra's in-breath settled. | God Tvashṭar, let thine ample forms be blended, that what wears different shapes may be one-fashioned. | To please thee let thy friends, mother and father, joy over thee as to the Gods thou goest. || 21. Go to the sea. All-hail! Go to the air. All-hail! Go to God Savitar. All hail! | Go thou to Mitra-Varuṇa All-hail! Go thou to Day and Night. All-hail! Go to the Metres. till-hail! Go to Heaven and Earth. All-hail! Go to the sacrifice. All-hail! Go to Soma. All-hail! Go to the heavenly ether. All-hail! Go to Vaiśvānara Agni. All hail! Bestow upon me mind and heart. | Thy smoke mount to the sky, to heaven thy lustre. Fill thou the spacious earth full with thine ashes. || 22. Harm not the Waters, do the Plants no damage. From every place, King Varuṇa, thence save us. | Their saying that we swear our oath by sacred cows, by Varuṇa, | O Varuṇa, save us therefrom. | To us let Waters and let Plants be friendly; to him who hates us, whom we hate, unfriendly. || 23. These waters teem with sacred food: rich in that food, one longs for them. | Rich be the holy rite therein. In sacred food be Sūrya rich. || 24. I set you down in Agni's seat whose home is indestructible. | Indra-and-Agni's share are ye, Mitra-and-Varuṇa's share are ye. | The share of all the Gods are ye. | May waters gathered near the Sun, and those wherewith the Sun is joined, | Speed on this sacred rite of ours. || 23. Thee for the heart, thee for the mind, thee for the heaven, thee for the Sun. | Bear up erect to heaven, to Gods, this rite these sacrificial calls. || 26. Descend, O Soma, King, to all thy people. Down, unto thee, go, one and all, thy people! | May Agni with his fuel hear my calling. Hear it the Waters and the Bowls, Divine Ones! Hear, Stones, as knowing sacrifice, my calling. May the God Savitar hear mine invocation. All hail! || 27. Waters Divine, your wave, the Waters' offspring, fit for oblation, potent, most delightful— | Upon those Gods among the Gods bestow it, who drink the pure, of whom ye are the portion. All-hail! || 28. Drawing art thou: I draw thee up that Ocean ne'er may waste or wane. | Let waters with the waters, and the plants commingle with the plants. || 29. That man is lord of endless strength whom thou protectest in the fight, | Agni, or urgest to the fray. || 30. By impulse of God Savitar I take thee with arms of Aśvins, with the hands of Pūshan | Free with thy gifts art thou. Perform for Indra this deep, most excellently ordered worship. | With the most noble bolt I pay the worship enriched with strengthening food and milk and sweetness. | Ye are Nigrābhya waters. heard by Deities: make me content. || 31. Content my mind, content my speech, content my breath, content mine eye, content mine ear, content my soul, content my progeny, content my herds, content the troops of men about me: never may the bands of men about me suffer thirst. || 32. For Indra girt by Vasus and accompanied by Rudras, thee. | For Indra with Ādityas, thee. For Indra foe-destroyer, thee. Thee for the Soma-bringing Hawk. For plenty-giving Agni, thee. || 33. Soma, what light there is of thine in heaven, what on the earth, what in mid-air's wide region, | Therewith give broad space to the Sacrificer for his enrichment: Comfort thou the giver. || 34. Auspicious are ye, conquerors of Vṛitra, formed for bestowing wealth, the Immortal's Consorts. | Lead to the Gods this sacrifice, Divine Ones! and at our invitation drink of Soma. || 35. Be not afraid; shake not with terror. Take thou strength. | Ye two Bowls, being firm, stay firm, and take ye strength. | Mishap—not Soma—hath been killed. || 36. East, west, north, south, from every side to meet thee let the regions run. | Fill him, O Mother, let the noble meet together. || 37. Thou, verily, O Mightiest, as God shalt gladden mortal man. | O Bounteous Lord, there is no comforter but thou. Indra, I speak my words to thee.

Adhyāya 7.

1. Flow for Vāchaspati, cleansed by hands from the two off-shoots of the Bull. | Flow pure, a Deity thyself, for Deities whose share thou art. || 2. Sweeten the freshening draughts we drink. | Soma, whatever name thou hast, unconquerable, giving life, | To that thy Soma, Soma! Hail! || 3. Self-made art thou from all the Powers that are in heaven and on the earth. | May the Mind win thee, thee, All-hail! for Sūrya, O thou nobly-born. | Thee for the Deities who sip light-atoms. | Truly fulfilled, O Plant divine, be that for which I pray to thee. | With ruin falling from above may So-and-So be smitten, crash! | Thee for out-breathing, thee for breath diffused! || 4. Taken upon a base art thou. Hold in, Rich Lord! be Soma's guard. | Be thou protector of our wealth: win strengthening food by sacrifice. || 5. The heaven and spacious earth I lay within thee, I lay within thee middle air's wide region. | Accordant with the Gods lower and higher, Rich Lord, rejoice thee in the Antaryāma. | O Self-made art thou ..... light-atoms (verse 3. repeated). | Thee for the upward breath. || 7. O Vāyu, drinker of the pure, be near us: a thousand teams are thine, All-bounteous Giver. | To thee the rapture-giving juice is offered, whose first draught, God, thou takest as thy portion. || 8. These, Indra-Vāyu! have been shed; come for our offered dainties' sake: | The drops are yearning for you both. | Taken upon a base art thou. For Vāyu, Indra-Vāyu, thee. | This is thy home. Thee for the close-knit friends. || 9. This Soma hath been shed for you, Law-strengtheners, Mitra-Varuṇa! | Here listen ye to this my call. | Taken upon a base art thou. For Mitra thee, for Varuṇa || 10. May we, possessing much, delight in riches, Gods in oblation, and the kine in pasture; | And that Milch-cow who shrinks not from the milking, O Indra-Varuṇa, give to us daily. | This is thy home. Thee for the righteous Twain. || 11. Distilling honey is your whip, Aśvins, and full of pleasantness: | Sprinkle therewith the sacrifice. | Taken upon a base art thou. Thee for the Aśvins This is thy home. Thee for the Honey-lovers. || 12. Thou in the first old time, as all were wont, so now drawest from him, light-finder, throned on sacred grass, | Pre-eminence and strength, from him turned hither, swift, roaring, who winneth those whereby thou waxest strong. | Taken upon a base art thou. Thee for Śaṇḍa. | This is thy home. Protect thou manly power. | Śaṇḍa hath been removed, may Deities who drink the pure libation lead thee forward. Invincible art thou. || 13. Well stored with heroes and begetting heroes, with growth of wealth surround the Sacrificer. | The Bright, conjoined with Heaven and with Earth, with the brightly-shining one. | Expelled is Śaṇḍa. Thou art Śukra's dwelling. || 14. May we, O radiant Soma, be the keepers of thine uninjured strength and growth of riches. | This is the first all-bounteous Consecration: he the first, Varuṇa, Mitra, and Agni. || 15. He is the first Bṛihaspati, the Prudent. Offer ye juice with Svāhā! to that Indra. | Content be priestly offices, those with good sacrifice of meath, those that are pleased when they have gained fair offerings with the solemn Hail! | The Kindler of the Fire hath sacrificed. || 16. See, Vena, born in light hath driven hither on chariot of the air the calves of Pṛiśni. | Singers with hymns caress him as an infant there where the waters and the sunlight mingle. | Taken upon a base art thou. Thee for Marka. || 17. To his oblation, swift as thought ye hurried and welcomed eagerly the prayers he offered. | With arrows in his hand the Very Mighty forced from him all obedience of a servant. | This is thy dwelling-place. Protect the people. Marka hath been removed. | Gods, drinkers of the Manthin, lead thee forward! Invincible art thou. || 18. Well stored with people and begetting people, with growth of wealth surround the Sacrificer. | The Manthin joined with Heaven and Earth and with the Manthin-shining one. | Expelled is Marka. Thou art Manthin's dwelling. || 19. O ye eleven Gods whose home is heaven, O ye eleven who make earth your dwelling. | Ye who with might, eleven, live in waters, accept this sacrifice, Ye Gods, with pleasure. || 20. Taken upon a base art thou. Thou art Āgrayaṇa, good first libation. | Be thou the guard of sacrifice: protect the sacrifice's lord. | Vishṇu with might protect thee. Guard thou Vishṇu. Guard on all sides the Soma sacrifices. || 21. Soma flows pure, Soma flows pure for this Priesthood, for the Nobility, pure for the worshipper who presses out the juice, flows pure for food and energy, for waters and for plants; flows pure for general prosperity. Thee for the Universal Gods. This is thy home. Thee for the Universal Gods. || 22. Taken upon a base art thou. For Indra Lord of the Bṛihat, strong with vital vigour, I take thee lover of

the invocation. | Indra, what mighty vigour thou possessest, for that do I take thee, take thee for Vishṇu | This is thy home. Thee for the recitations. | For the Gods take I thee, the Gods' protector; yea, for the sacrifice's life I take thee. || 23. For Mitra-Varuṇa thee, the Gods protector, yea, for the sacrifice's life I take thee. | For Indra, thee, etc. For Indra-Agni, thee, etc. For Indra-Varuṇa, thee, etc. For Indra-Bṛihaspati thee, etc. For Indra-Vishṇu thee, etc. || 24. Him, messenger of earth and head of heaven, Agni Vaiśvānara, born in holy Order, | The Sage, the King, the Guest of men, a vessel fit for their mouths, the Gods have generated. || 25. Taken upon a base art thou. Firm, firmly resting, the firmest of the firm, the most securely grounded of those who never have been shaken. | This is thy home. Thee for Vaiśvānara | I pour forth with firm mind, with voice, firm Soma. So now may Indra verily make our people all of. One heart and mind and free from foemen. || 26. Whatever drop of thine leaps forth, whatever stalk from the bowls' lap, shaken by the press-stone, | From the Adhvaryu's hand or from the filter, that, consecrated in my mind with Vashaṭ I offer unto thee with cry of Svāhā! | Thou art the way by which the Gods ascended. || 27. Giver of splendour, grow thou pure for splendour for my outward breath. | Giver of splendour, grow thou pure for splendour for my spreading breath. | Giver, etc. . . . . . for my upward breath. | Giver, etc. . . . . . for my power of speech. | Giver, etc. . . . . . for my sense and will. | Giver, etc. . . . . . for my hearing power. | Givers of splendor, grow ye pure for splendour for my orbs of sight. || 28. Giver of splendour, grow thou pure for splendour for my living self. | Giver, etc. . . . . . for my energy. | Giver, etc. . . . . . for my vital power. | Givers of splendour, grow ye pure for splendour for all sprung from me. || 29. Who art thou? Which of all art thou? Whose art thou? Who art thou by name? | Even thou on whose name we have meditated, then whom we have delighted with our Soma. || 30. Taken upon a base art thou. For Madhu thee: Taken upon a base art thou. For Mādhava thee. | Taken, etc. For Śukra thee. Taken, etc. For Śuchi thee. Taken, etc. For Nabhas thee. Taken, etc. For Nabhasya thee. Taken, etc. For Food thee. Taken, etc. For Energy thee. Taken, etc. For Sahas thee. Taken, etc. For Sahasya thee. Taken, etc. For Tapas thee. Taken, etc. For Tapasya thee. Taken, etc. For Aṃhasaspati thee. || 31. Moved, Indra-Agni, by our hymns, come to the juice, the precious dew. | Drink ye thereof, impelled by song. | Taken upon a base art thou. For Indra-Agni thee. This is thy dwelling. Thee for Indra-Agni. || 32. Hitherward! they who light the flame and straightway strew the sacred grass, | Whose Friend is Indra ever young. | Taken upon a base art thou. For Indra-Agni thee. This is thy dwelling. Thee for Indra-Agni. || 33. Ye Viśvedevas who protect, reward, and cherish men, approach Your worshipper's drink-offering. | Taken upon a base art thou. Thee for the Universal Gods. | This is thy home. Thee for the Viśvedevas || 34. O ye All-Gods, come hitherward: hear this my invocation seat | Yourselves upon this sacred grass. | Taken upon a base art thou. Thee for the Universal Gods. | This is thy home. Thee for the Viśvedevas || 35. Here drink the Soma, Indra girt by Marutas! as thou didst drink the juice beside Śāryāta | Under thy guidance, in thy keeping, Hero! the singers serve, skilled in fair sacrifices. | Taken upon a base art thou. For Indra girt by Marutas thee. | This is thy home. For Indra girt by Marutas thee. || 36. The Bull whose strength hath waxed, whom Marutas follow, free-giving Indra, the Celestial Ruler, | Mighty, all-conquering, the victory-giver, him we invoke to give us new protection. | Taken upon a base art thou. For Indra girt by Marutas thee. | This is thy home. For Indra girt by Marutas thee. | Taken upon a base art thou. Thee for the Marutas' energy. || 37. Indra, accordant with the banded Marutas, drink Soma, Hero! as wise Vṛitra-slayer | Slay thou our foemen, drive away assailants, and make us safe on every side from danger. | Taken, etc. For Indra girt by Marutas thee. This is thy home. For Indra girt by Marutas thee. || 38. Drink, Indra Marut-girt, as Bull, the Soma: for joy, for rapture even as thou pleasest. | Pour down the wave of meath within thy belly thou art | the King of juices shed fortnightly. | Taken, etc. . . . . . Marutas thee (as above). || 39. Great, hero-like, controlling men is Indra, unwasting in his powers, doubled in vastness. | He, turned to us, hath grown to hero vigour: broad, wide, he hath been decked by those who serve him. | Taken upon a base art thou. Thee for Mahendra. | This is thy dwelling-place. Thee for Mahendra. || 40. Indra, great in his power and might, and like Parjanya rich in rain, | Is magnified by Vatsa's lauds. | Taken, etc. (as in 39). || 41. His bright rays bear him up aloft, the God who knoweth all that lives, | Sūrya, that all may look on him. All-hail! || 42. The brilliant presence of the Gods hath risen, the eye of Mitra, Varuṇa, and Agni. | Soul of all moving, soul of all that moves not, the Sun hath filled the air and earth and heaven. || 43. By goodly paths lead us to riches, Agni, thou God who knowest every sacred duty. | Remove the sin that makes us stray and wander: most ample adoration will we bring thee. || 44. Wide room and comfort may this Agni give us, and go before us cleaving down our foemen. | May he win booty in the fight for booty: may he quell foes in his triumphant onset. || 45. I through your beauty have attained to beauty. The Tutha, the omniscient, allot you! | Go forth, bright-gifted! on the path of Order. Look thou upon the heaven and air's mid-region. Unite thee with the priests who keep the Sadas. || 46. This day may it he mine to find a Brahman sprung from a lauded father and grandfather, | Offspring of Ṛishis and himself a Ṛishi, the fit recipient of priestly guerdon. | Go to the Gods, bestowed by me, and enter into him who gives. || 47. To Agni, yea, to me let Varuṇa give thee. May I gain life that shall endure for ever. | Be thou strong vital power to him who gives thee, and comfort unto me the gift's receiver. | To Rudra, yea, to me let Varuṇa . . . . . for ever. | Be thou the breath of life to him who gives thee, and vigour unto me the gift's receiver. | To me Bṛihaspati let Varuṇa . . . . . for ever. | Be thou a covering skin to him who gives thee, and comfort unto me the gift's receiver. | To Yama, yea, to me let Varuṇa . . . . . for ever. | Be thou a steed to him who gives the guerdon, and vital power to me the gift's receiver. || 48. Who hath bestowed it? Upon whom bestowed it? | Desire bestowed it, for Desire he gave it. Desire is giver and Desire receiver. This, O Desire, to thee is dedicated.

Adhyāya 8.

1. Taken upon a base art thou. Thee for the Ādityas | Here, O Far-striding Vishṇu, is thy Soma. Guard it from injury. Let them not harm thee. || 2. Ne'er art thou fruitless, Indra; ne'er dost thou desert thy worshipper. | But now, O Liberal Lord, thy bounty as a God is poured forth ever more and more. Thee for the Ādityas || 3. Never art thou neglectful: thou guardest both races with thy care. | The Soma feast, O Fourth Āditya, is thy strength. Amṛita is established in the heavens. Thee for the Ādityas || 4. The sacrifice obtains the Gods' acceptance. Be graciously inclined to us, Ādityas | Hitherward let your favour be directed and be our best deliverer from trouble. Thee for the Ādityas || 5. This is thy Soma draught, O bright Āditya: take delight therein. | To this mine utterance, O ye men, give credence, what good the man and wife obtain by praying: | A manly son is burn and gathers riches, and thrives for ever sinless in the dwelling. || 6. Fair wealth, O Savitar, today, tomorrow, fair wealth produce for us each day that passes. | May we, through this our song, be happy gainers, God! of a fair and spacious habitation. || 7. Taken upon a base art thou. | Savitar's giver of delight art thou. Giver of joy art thou: vouchsafe me joy. | Speed thou the sacrifice, speed thou the sacrifice's lord to win his share. Thee for the God, for Savitar. || 8. Taken upon a base art thou. | Thou art a good protector, firmly established To the Great Bull be reverential homage. Thee for the Viśvedevas | This is thy home: Thee for the Viśvedevas || 9. Taken upon a base art thou. | May it be mine to prosper the libations of thee Bṛihaspati's son, O radiant Soma, of thee, strong Indu, mated with thy Consorts. | I am in heaven above, on earth beneath it. The intermediate region was my father. | I saw the Sun both from above and under. I am what Gods in secret hold the highest. || 10. Agni, associate with the Dames, accordant with the God | Tvashṭar, drink. All-hail! | Thou art Prajāpati, strong male, impregner: may I obtain from thee, strong male, impregner, a son who shall himself become a father. || 11. Taken upon a base art thou. | Thou art bay-coloured, yoker of Bay Coursers. Thee for the pair of tawny-coloured horses. | United with the Soma, ye, for Indra, are corn for his two tawny steeds to feed on. || 12. That draught of thine which winneth cows or horses, offered with sacrificial text and lauded | With chanted hymns and songs of adoration—of that permitted do I take permitted. || 13. Of sin against the Gods thou art atonement. Of sin against mankind thou art atonement. | For sin against the Fathers thou atonest. Of sin against oneself thou art atonement. | Of every sort of sin thou art atonement. The sin that I have knowingly committed, the sin that unawares I have committed, of all that wickedness thou art the atonement. || 14. We with our bodies have again

united, with lustre, vital sap, and happy spirit. | Giver of boons, may Tvashṭar grant us riches and smooth whate'er was injured in our body. || 15. Lead us with thought to wealth in kine, O Indra, to princes, Lord of Bounty! and to welfare. | Lead thou us on to God-inspired devotion, to favour of the Gods who merit worship. All-hail! || 16. Verse 14. repeated. || 17. May this please Savitar and liberal Dhātar, Prajāpati the Treasure-Guard, bright Agni, | Tvashṭar, and Vishṇu: blessing him with children, grant store of riches to the Sacrificer. || 18. Gods, we have made your seats easy of access, who, pleased with us, have come to this libation. | Bearing and bringing hitherward your treasures, grant to this man, good Lords, abundant riches. All-hail! || 19. The willing Gods whom, God, thou hast brought hither, send them to their own dwelling-place, O Agni. | As all of you have eaten and have drunken, approach the air, the heat, the light of heaven. || 20. Here, Agni, as this sacrifice proceedeth, have we elected thee to be our Hotar. | Special have been thine offerings and thy labour. Well knowing sacrifice, as sage, come near us. || 21. Do ye, O Gods, discoverers of the Pathway, go forward on the path when ye have found it. | O God, thou Lord and Master of the Spirit, bestow—All-hail!—this sacrifice on Vāta. || 22. Go, Sacrifice, to the sacrifice: seek thou the sacrifice's lord, seek thine own home. All-hail! | Lord of the sacrifice, this is thy sacrifice, followed by many heroes, loud with hymns of praise. Accept it thou. All-hail! || 23. Become no serpent thou, become no viper. | King Varuṇa hath made a spacious pathway, a pathway for the Sun wherein to travel. | Where no way was he made him set his footstep, and warned afar whate'er afflicts the spirit. | To Varuṇa be reverential homage! Varuṇa's noose beneath our feet is trampled. || 24. The waters, face of Agni, have I entered, O Waters' Child, repelling evil spirits. | Offer the fuel in each home, O Agni. Let thy tongue dart—All-hail!—to meet the butter. || 25. Thy heart is in the flood, within the waters. With thee let plants and waters be commingled, | That, Lard of Sacrifice, we may adore thee with singing praise and telling forth our homage. All-hail! || 26. This, O celestial Waters, is your offspring. Support him dearly loved and gently nurtured. | This is thy station, O celestial Soma; therein bring happiness and ward off evil. || 27. O restless Purifying Bath, thou glidest onward restlessly. | May I with aid of Gods remove the stain of sin against the Gods, and wash away with mortals' help the wrong that hath been done to men. Preserve me, God, from injury, from the loud-roaring demon foe. Thou art the fuel of the Gods. || 28. Let, still unborn, the ten-month calf move with the following after-birth. | Even as the-wind is moving, as the gathered flood of ocean moves, | So may this ten-month calf come forth together with the after-birth. || 29. O thou who hast a womb of gold and offspring meet for sacrifice, | Him with all limbs unbroken have I brought together with his dam. All-hail! || 30. Multiform, rich in wondrous operation, the strong juice hath enrobed itself with greatness. | Let the worlds praise her uniped and biped, three-footed and four-footed and eight-footed. All-hail! || 31. Verily, best of guardians hath he in whose dwelling-place ye drink, | O Marutas, giants of the sky. || 32. May Heaven and Earth, the Mighty Pair, besprinkle this our sacrifice, | And feed us full with nourishments. || 33. Slayer of Vṛitra, mount thy car: thy Bay Steeds have been yoked by prayer. | May, with its voice, the pressing-stone draw thine attention hither ward. | Taken upon a base art thou. For Indra thee, for Shoḍaśin. This is a dwelling-place for thee. For Indra thee, for | Shoḍaśin. || 34. Harness thy pair of strong Bay Steeds, long-maned, whose bodies fill the girths, | And, Indra, Soma-drinker, come to listen to our songs of praise. | Taken upon a base, etc., as in 33. || 35. His pair of tawny Coursers bring Indra of unresisted might Hither to Ṛishis' songs of praise and sacrifice performed by men. | Taken upon a base, etc., as in 33. || 36. Than whom there is none other born more mighty, who hath pervaded all existing creatures— | Prajāpati, rejoicing in his offspring, he, Shoḍaśin, maintains the three great lustres. || 37. Indra chief Lord and Varuṇa the Sovereign have made this draught of thine the first and foremost. | I, after, drink their draught. May she, the Goddess of Speech, rejoicing, sate herself with Soma—All-hail!—with Prāṇa as her feast-companion. || 38. Skilled in thy task, O Agni, pour lustre and hero strength on us, | Granting me wealth and affluence. | Taken upon a base art thou. For Agni thee, for splendour | This is thy home. For Agni thee, for splendour. | Thou, lustrous Agni, mid the Gods art splendid. May I among mankind be bright with lustre. || 39. Arising in thy might thy jaws thou shookest, Indra, having drunk | The Soma which the mortar pressed. | Taken upon a base art thou. For Indra thee, for mighty strength. | This is thy home. For Indra thee, for might. | Among the Gods thou art the mightiest, Indra. Among mankind I fain would be most mighty. || 40. His herald rays are seen afar refulgent o'er the world of men, | Like flames of fire that burn and blaze. | Taken upon a base art thou. For Sūrya, for the Bright One, thee. | This is thy home. For Sūrya, for the Bright One, thee. | Thou among Gods art brightest, brightest Sūrya. Among mankind I fain would be the brightest. || 41. His herald rays bear him aloft, the God who knoweth all that lives, Sūrya, that all may look at him. | Taken upon a base, etc., as in 40. || 42. Smell thou the vat. Let Soma drops pass into thee, O Mighty One. | Return again with store of sap. Pour for us wealth in thousands thou with full broad streams and floods of milk. Let riches come again to me. || 43. Iḍā, delightful, worshipful, loveable, splendid, shining One, | Inviolable, full of sap, the Mighty One, most glorious, | These are thy names, O Cow: tell thou the Gods that I act righteously. || 44. O Indra, beat our foes away, humble the men who challenge us: | Send down to nether darkness him who seeks to do us injury. | Taken upon a base art thou. For Indra, foe-dispeller, thee. | This is thy home. For Indra, foe-dispeller, thee. || 45. Let us invoke today, to aid our labour, the Lord of Speech, the thought-swift Viśvakarman | May he hear kindly all our invocations, who gives all bliss for aid, whose works are righteous. | Taken upon a base art thou. For Indra Viśvakarman thee. | This is thy home. For Indra Viśvakarman thee. || 46. With strengthening libation, Viśvakarman, thou madest Indra an undying guardian. | The people of old time bowed down before him because the Mighty One was meet for worship. | Taken upon a base, etc., as in 45. || 47. Taken upon a base art thou. | I take thee lord of Gāyatrī for Agni. For Indra take I thee the lord of Trishṭubh | I take thee lord of Jagatī for All-Gods. Anushṭubh is the song that sings thy praises. || 48. I stir thee for the fall of cloud-borne waters. I stir thee for the fall of streams that gurgle. I stir thee for the fall of those that gladden. I stir thee for their fall who are most lovely. I stir thee for their fall that are the sweetest. I stir thee for the waters' fall, I stir thee, pure one, in the pure, in the day's form, in Sūrya's beams. || 49. The Bull's majestic form is shining brightly, the pure the pure's preceder, Soma Soma's. | Whatever name invincible, stimulating, is thine, O Soma, for that name I take thee. | All-hail to Soma, unto thee, O Soma. || 50. O radiant Soma, eagerly draw nigh to Agni's well-loved food. | O radiant Soma, willingly go to the food that Indra loves. | Go, radiant Soma, as our friend, to the All-Gods' beloved food. || 51. Here is delight: enjoy yourselves; here surety, surety of your own. All-hail! | Loosing the suckling to his dam, the suckling as he milks his dam— | May he maintain the growth of wealth among us. All-hail! || 52. Thou art the Session's happy termination. | We have attained the light and grown immortal. | We have gone up from earth to sky, have found the Gods and heaven and light. || 53. Indra and Parvata, our champions in the fight, drive ye away the man who fain would war with us, drive him far from us with the bolt. | Welcome to him concealed afar shall be the lair that he hath found. | So may the Render rend our foes on every side, rend them. | O Hero, everywhere. | Earth! Ether! Sky! May we be rich in offspring, rich in brave sons and rich in food to feed us. || 54. Parameshṭhin when contemplated. Prajāpati in uttered speech. | Food when approached. Savitar in the partition. Viśvakarman in Consecration. Pūshan in the Soma-purchasing cow. || 55. As Indra and the Marutas he is stationed ready for the sale: Asura, being bought and sold. Mitra when purchased; Vishṇu Śipivishṭa when on the Sacrificer's thigh he resteth; Vishṇu Narandhisha brought on the barrow; || 56. Soma when come: when seated on the platform, Varuṇa; Agni in the sacred fire-place; | Indra upon the sacrificial barrow; Atharvan when deposited for pounding; || 57. All-Gods when offered in the scattered fragments; Vishṇu, the guard of those who soothe his anger, when he is filled and swelling in the waters; Yama in pressing; Vishṇu in collection; | Vāyu what time they cleanse and purify him; the Bright when cleansed; the Bright with milk about him; Manthin commingled with the meal of barley; || 58. All-Gods when he is drawn away in beakers; Life when uplifted for the fire-oblation; Rudra when offered; Vāta when reverted; Man-viewer when beheld; drink when they drink him; deposited, the Nārāśaṃsa Fathers; || 59. Sindhu when ready for the bath that cleanses the sea when he is carried to the waters; Water is he when he is plunged beneath it. | To those most mighty hath it gone, most manly in vigour, by whose strength the worlds were established, | Who rule as Lords resistless in their grandeur, Viṣṇu and Varuṇa, at the prayer of morning. ‖ 60. To Gods, to sky the sacrifice hath gone: come riches thence to me! | To men, to air the sacrifice hath gone: come riches thence to me! | To Fathers, earth, the sacrifice hath gone: come riches thence to me! | Whatever sphere the sacrifice hath reached, may wealth come thence to me ‖ 61. The threads that have been spun, the four-and-thirty, which establish this our sacrifice with Svadhā, | Of these I join together what is broken. All-hail! to Gods go the warm milk oblation! ‖ 62. Spread far and wide is sacrifice's milking: eightfold along the heaven hath it extended. | Pour, Sacrifice! in plenty on mine offspring: may I obtain prosperity for ever. All-hail! ‖ 63. Soma, send wealth in gold and steeds and heroes. All-hail! bring hitherward booty in cattle.

Adhyāya 9.

1. Our sacrifice, God Savitar, speed onward: speed to his share the sacrifice's patron. | May the celestial Gandharva, cleanser of thought and will, make clean our thought and purpose: the Lord of Speech sweeten the food we offer. ‖ 2. Thee, firmly set, settled in man, in spirit. | Taken upon a base art thou. I take thee, draught acceptable to Indra. This is thy home. Thee, welcomest to Indra. | Thee Set in waters, butter, realm of ether. Taken upon . . . . . Indra. | Thee seated in the sky, earth, air's mid-region, among the Gods and in the vault of heaven. Taken, etc. as above. ‖ 3. The strength-arousing essence of the waters, gathered in the Sun, Essence of waters' essence, that, most excellent, | I take for you. | Taken, etc., as above. ‖ 4. Cups of strength-giving sacrifice, inspirers of the sage's hymn | Of you, the handleless, have I collected all the sap and strength. | Taken, etc., as above. | United are ye twain: with bliss unite me. Parted are ye: keep me apart from evil. ‖ 5. Thou art the thunderbolt of Indra, winner of wealth: with thee may this man win him riches. | In gain of wealth we celebrate with praises her, Aditi by name, the Mighty Mother, | On whom this Universe of life hath settled. Thereon God Savitar promote our dwelling! ‖ 6. Amṛita is in the Waters, in the Waters healing medicine. Yea, Horses! at our praises of the Waters grow ye fleet and strong. | Whatever wave, O ye celestial Waters, wealth-giving, towering high, and swiftly rushing, is yours, therewith may this man win him riches. ‖ 7. It was the wind, or it was thought, or the Gandharvas twenty-seven— | These at the first harnessed the horse: they set the power of speed in him. ‖ 8. Steed, being yoked grow wind-swift: be beauteous as Indra's right-hand steed. | Omniscient Marutas harness thee! Tvaṣṭar put swiftness in thy feet! ‖ 9. What speed, O Horse, was laid in thee in secret, what passed in wind, bestowed upon the falcon, | With that same strength be strong for us, O Courser, wealth-winning and victorious in battle. | Starting to run your course, winners of riches, smell ye Bṛihaspati's portion, O ye Horses. ‖ 10. By impulse of God Savitar, true Impeller, may ascend Bṛihaspati's highest heaven. | By impulse of God Savitar, true Impeller, may I ascend the highest heaven of Indra. | By impulse of God Savitar, true Impeller, Bṛihaspati's highest heaven have I ascended. | By impulse of God Savitar, true Impeller, I have ascended Indra's loftiest heaven. ‖ 11. Bṛihaspati, win the prize. Lift up your voices to Bṛihaspati Make ye Bṛihaspati win the prize. | Do thou, O Indra, win the prize. To Indra lift your voices up. Make Indra winner of the prize. ‖ 12. True hath been this your league whereby ye made Bṛihaspati win the prize. | Bṛihaspati have ye caused to win the prize. Be freed, ye Forest-lords. | Faithful was this your league whereby ye have made Indra win the prize. | Ye have made Indra win the prize. Be ye set free, ye Forest-lords. ‖ 13. Through impulse of God Savitar, true Impeller, mine be Bṛihaspati's prize who winneth prizes. | On to the goal, ye Steeds, winners of prizes, blocking the ways and meting out the courses! ‖ 14. Bound by the neck and at the flanks and in the mouth, that vigorous Courser lends new swiftness to his sped. | Drawing himself together as his strength allows, Dadhikrās speeds along the windings of the paths. All-hail! ‖ 15. His pinion, rapid runner, fans him on his way, as of a bird that hastens onward to its aim, | And, as it were a falcon's gliding through the air, strikes Dadhikrāvan's side as he speeds on with might. All-hail! ‖ 16. Bless us the Coursers when we call, while slowly they move, strong singers, to the Gods' assembly. | Crushing the wolf, the serpent, and the demons, may they completely banish all affliction. All-hail! ‖ 17. May all those vigorous Coursers listen to our cry, hearers of invocation, speeders on their way; | Winners of thousands, fain to win where meed is won, who gather of themselves great wealth in every race. ‖ 18. Deep-skilled in Law Eternal, wise, immortal, O Coursers, help us in each fray for booty. | Drink of this meath, be satisfied, be joyful: then go on paths which Gods are wont to travel. ‖ 19. To me come plenteous growth of wealth! Approach me these, Heaven and Earth, who wear each form and figure! | Hither may Father come to me, and Mother. Soma with immortality approach me! ‖ 20. To the Friend, Hail! To the Good Fiend, Hail! To the Later-born, Hail! To Resolution, Hail! To the Vasu, Hail! To the Lord of Days, Hail! To the Failing Day, Hail! To the Failing sprung from the Transitory, Hail! To the Transitory sprung from the Final, Hal! To the Final Mundane, Hail! To the Lord of the World, Hail! To the Sovereign Lord, Hail! ‖ 21. May life succeed through sacrifice. May life-breath thrive by sacrifice. May the eye thrive by sacrifice. May the ear thrive by sacrifice. May the back thrive by sacrifice. May sacrifice thrive by sacrifice. | We have become the children of Prajāpati. Gods, we have gone to heaven. We have become immortal. ‖ 22. In us be your great might and manly vigour, in us be your intelligence and splendour. | Obeisance to our Mother Earth! Obeisance to our Mother Earth! | This is thy Sovereignty. Thou art the ruler, thou art controller, thou art firm and steadfast | Thee for land-culture, thee for peace and quiet, thee for wealth, thee for increase of our substance. ‖ 23. Of old the furtherance of strength urged onward this Sovereign Soma in the plants and waters. | For us may they be stored with honey: stationed in front may we be watchful in the kingdom. All-hail! ‖ 24. The furtherance of strength extended over this heaven and all the worlds as sovereign ruler. | He, knowing, makes the churl a bounteous giver: wealth may he grant us with full store of heroes. All-hail ‖ 25. Surely the furtherance of strength pervaded all these existing worlds in all directions. | From olden time the King moves round, well knowing, strengthening all the people and our welfare. ‖ 26. As suppliants, for aid we grasp Soma the King, and Agni, the Ādityas, Viṣṇu, Sūrya, and the Brahman-priest Bṛihaspati ‖ 27. Urge Aryaman to send us gifts, and Indra and Bṛihaspati, | Vāk, Viṣṇu, and Sarasvatī, and the strong Courser Savitar. ‖ 28. Agni, speak kindly to us here, be graciously inclined to us. | Winner of thousands, grant us boons, for thou art he who giveth wealth. ‖ 29. Let Aryaman vouchsafe us wealth, and Pūṣhan, and Bṛihaspati | May Vāk the Goddess give to us. All-hail! ‖ 30. Thee by the radiant Savitar's impulsion, with arms of Aśvins, with the hands of Pūṣhan | To Vāk Sarasvatī's controlling guidance, hers the controlling leader, I consign thee. | I with Bṛihaspati's supreme dominion endow thee by the balm of consecration ‖ 31. With the monosyllable Agni won vital breath: may I win that. With the dissyllable the Aśvins won bipeds: may I win those. With the trisyllable | Viṣṇu won the three worlds: may I win those. With quadrisyllabic metre | Soma won four-footed cattle: may I win those. ‖ 32. With five-syllable metre Pūṣhan won the five regions: may I win them. | With six-syllable metre Savitar won the six seasons: may I win them. | With seven-syllable metre the Marutas won the seven domestic animals: | May I win them. With octosyllabic metre Bṛihaspati won the Gāyatrī: may I win that. ‖ 33. With nine-syllable metre Mitra won the Trivṛit Stoma: may I win that. With decasyllabic metre Varuṇa won Virāj: may I win that. | With hendecasyllabic metre Indra won Triṣhṭubh: may I win that. | With dodecasyllabic metre the All-Gods won Jagatī: may I win that. ‖ 34. The Vasus by thirteen-syllable metre won the Thirteenfold Stoma: may I win that. The Rudras by fourteen-syllable metre won the fourteenfold Stoma: may I win that. The Ādityas with fifteen-syllable metre won the Fifteenfold Stoma: may I win that. Aditi with sixteen-syllable metre won the Sixteenfold Stoma: may I win that. Prajāpati with seventeenfold metre won the Seventeenfold Stoma: may I win that. ‖ 35. This is thy portion, Nirṛiti! Accept it graciously. All-hail! | To Gods whose guide is Agni, to the eastward-seated Gods, All-hail! | To Gods whose guide is Yama, to the southward-seated Gods, All-hail! | To Gods whose guides are the All-Gods, those who are seated westward, Hail! | Hail to the northward-seated Gods, to those whose guides are Mitra and Varuṇa or the Marut host! | To Gods whose guide is Soma, who, worshipful, sit on high, All-hail! ‖ 36. Gods who have Agni as their guide, whose seat is eastward, Hail to them! | Gods who have Yama as their guide, whose seat is southward, Hail to them! | Gods

who have All-Gods as their guides, whose seat is westward, Hail to them! | Gods who have Mitra-Varuṇa for guides, north-seated, Hail to them! | Gods who have Soma as their guide, high-seated, worshipful, Hail to them! || 37. Agni, subdue opposing bands and drive our enemies away. | Invincible, slay godless foes: give splendour to the worshipper. || 38. Thee at the radiant Savitar's impulsion, with Aśvins' arms and with the hands of Pūṣhan, | I offer with the strength of the Upāṃśu. Slain is the demon brood. All-hail! | Thee for the slaughter of the brood of demons. The demons have we slain, have slain. So-and-So, So-and-So is slain. || 39. Savitar quicken thee for sway of rulers, Agni of householders, of the trees Soma, | Bṛihaspati of Speech, for lordship Indra, Rudra for cattle, Mitra for true-speaking, Varuṇa for the sway of Law's protectors. || 40. Gods, quicken him that none may be his rival, for mighty domination, mighty lordship, | Him, son of Such-a-man and Such-a-woman, of Such-a-tribe. This is your King, ye Tribesmen. Soma is Lord and King of us the Brahmans.

Adhyāya 10.

1. The Gods drew waters with their store of sweetness, succulent and observant, king-creating, | Wherewith they sprinkled Varuṇa and Mitra, wherewith they guided Indra past his foemen. || 2. Wave of the male art thou, giver of kingship. Do thou—All-hail!—bestow on me the kingdom. | Wave of the male art thou, giver of kingship. Do thou on So-and-So bestow the kingdom. | Thou hast a host of males, giver of kingship. Do thou—All-hail!—bestow on me the kingdom. | A host of males hast thou, giver of kingship. Do thou on So-and-So bestow the kingdom. || 3. Swift at your work are ye, givers of kingship. Do ye—All-hail!—bestow on me the kingdom. | Swift at your work are ye, givers of kingship. Do ye on So-and-So bestow the kingdom. | Endowed with strength are ye, givers of kingship, etc. | O'erflowing floods are ye, etc. | The Waters' Lord art thou, giver of kingship. Do thou, etc. | The Waters' Child art thou, etc. || 4. With sun-bright skins are ye, givers, etc. | Brilliant as Suns are ye, etc. | Bringers of joy are ye, etc. | Dwellers in cloud are ye, etc. | Desirable are ye, etc. | Most powerful are ye, etc. | Endowed with might are ye, etc. | Man-nourishing are ye, etc. | All-nourishing are ye, etc. | Self-ruling Waters are ye, giving kingship. On So-and-So do ye bestow the kingdom. | Together with the sweet let sweet ones mingle, obtaining for the Kṣhatriya mighty power. | Rest in your place inviolate and potent, bestowing on the Kṣhatriya mighty power. || 5. Brilliance of Soma art thou: may my brilliance grow like thine. | To Agni Hail! To Soma Hail! To Savitar Hail! To Sarasvatī Hail! To Pūṣhan Hail! To Bṛihaspati Hail! To Indra Hail! To the Noise Hail! To Fame Hail To Aṃśa Hail! To Bhaga Hail! To Aryaman Hail! || 6. Ye are two strainers, Varuṇa's own possession. I make you pure at Savitar's impulsion, with flawless strainer, with the beams of Sūrya. | Thou, friend of speech, heat-born, art undefeated. Soma's share art thou. Hail, ye king producers! || 7. Sharers in joy are these majestic Waters, inviolate, industrious, investing. | In these as homes hath Varuṇa made his dwelling, he, Child of Waters, in the best of mothers. || 8. Thou art the inner caul of princely power, Thou art the outer caul of princely power. Of princely power thou art the womb, the navel. | Thou art the Vṛitra-slaying arm of Indra. Mitra's art thou, thou Varuṇa's possession. With thee to aid may this man slaughter Vṛitra. | Cleaver art thou; thou Render; thou art Shaker. Protect him ye in front, protect him rearwards; protect him sidewards; from all quarters guard him. || 9. Visible, O ye men, Informed is Agni, Master of the House. hold. Informed is Indra of exalted glory. Informed are Mitra-Varuṇa, Law-Maintainers. Informed is Pūṣhan, Lord of all Possessions. Informed are Heaven and Earth, the All-propitious. Informed is Aditi who gives wide shelter. || 10. Appeased by sacrifice are biting creatures, Ascend the East. May Gāyatrī protect thee, the psalm Rathantara, the triple praise-song, the season Spring, and the rich treasure, Priesthood. || 11. Ascend the South. Be thy protectors Triṣhṭubh, the Bṛihat Sāman, the fifteenfold praise-song, the Reason Summer, and the treasure Kingship. || 12. Ascend the West. May Jagatī protect thee, the psalm Vairūpa, the seventeenfold praise-song, the Rain-time, and that store of wealth, the People. || 13. Ascend the North. Thy guardians be Anuṣhṭubh, Vairāja psalm, the twenty-onefold praise-song, the season Autumn, that rich treasure Fruitage. || 14. Ascend the Zenith. Paṅkti be thy keeper, Śākvara, Raivata the pair of Sāmans, | Praise-songs the thirty-threefold and thrice-ninefold, both seasons, Winter, Dews, that treasure lustre. | The head of Namuchi hath been cast from me. || 15. Brilliance of Soma art thou, may my brilliance grow like thine. | Save me from death. Vigour art thou, victory, everlasting life. || 16. With golden bodies, at the flush of morning, ye rise on high, two Sovereign Lords, and Sūrya. | Ascend your car, O Varuṇa and Mitra: thence view infinity and limitation. | Thou art Mitra, thou art Varuṇa || 17. Thee with the strength of Soma, Agni's lustre, with Sūrya's splendour, Indra's might I sprinkle. | Be Lord of princes: safe past arrows guard him. || 18. = 9:40. || 19. Forth from the summit of the bull, the mountain, pouring spontaneously, the ships keep moving. | They, lifted up, have turned them back and downward, still flowing onward, after Ahirbudhnya. | Thou art the stepping-forth of Viṣhṇu: thou art Viṣhṇu's outstep; Viṣhṇu's step art thou. || 20. Prajāpati, thou only comprehendest all these created forms, and none beside thee. | Give us our heart's desire when we invoke thee. So-and-So's father is this man. Sire of this man is So-and-So. | May we—All-hail!—be lords of rich possessions. | What active highest name thou hast, O Rudra, therein thou art an offering, art an offering at home. All-hail! || 21. Indra's bolt art thou. I by the direction of Mitra-Varuṇa, Directors, yoke thee. | I, the uninjured Arjuna, mount thee for firmness, thee for food. | By quickening of the Marutas be thou victor. May we obtain by mind: with power united. || 22. Let us not, Indra, conqueror of the mighty, unfit through lack of prayer fail to obtain thee. | Ascend the car which thou whose hand bears thunder controllest, and the reins with noble horses. || 23. All hail to Agni, Master of the Household! All-hail to Soma, Sovereign of the Forest! | All-hail to the great vigour of the Marutas! All-hail to the effectual might of Indra! | Injure me not, O Mother Earth, and may I never injure thee. || 24. The Haṃsa throned in light, the Vasu in mid-air, the Priest beside the altar, Guest within the house, | Dwelling in noblest place, mid men, in truth, in sky, born of flood, kine, truth, mountain, be is mighty Law. || 25. So great art thou: life art thou; give me life, | Mate art thou: thou art splendour; give me splendour. | Strength art thou: give me strength. I draw you downward, two arms of Indra mighty in achievement. || 26. Fair art thou, good to sit on, womb of kingship. | Sit on the fair one, sit on that which offers a pleasant seat: sit in the womb of kingship. || 27. Varuṇa, Law's maintainer, hath sat down among his people, he | Most wise, for universal sway. || 28. Supreme Lord art thou. May these five regions of thine be prosperous. Brahman! Thou art Brahman, Savitar art thou, faithful in impulsion, Varuṇa art thou, he whose power is real. Indra art thou, whose strength is of the people. Rudra art thou, the very kind and gracious. | Doer of much, Improver, Wealth-increaser! | Indra's bolt art thou. Be therewith my vassal. || 29. May spacious Agni, Lord of Duty, gladly, vast Agni, Duty's Lord, accept the butter. All-hail! | Hallowed by Svāhā, with the beams of Sūrya, strive for his central place among the kinsmen. || 30. I creep forth urged onward by Savitar the Impeller; by Sarasvatī, Speech; by Tvaṣhṭar, created forms; by Pūṣhan, cattle; by this Indra; by Bṛihaspati, Devotion; by Varuṇa, Power; by Agni, Brilliance; by Soma, the King; by Viṣhṇu the tenth Deity. || 31. Get dressed for the Aśvins Get dressed for Sarasvatī: Get dressed for Indra the Good Deliverer: | Soma the Wind, purified by the strainer, Indra's meet friend, hath gone o'erflowing backward. || 32. What then? As men whose fields are full of barley reap the ripe corn, removing it in order, | So bring the food of these men, bring it hither, who pay the Sacred Grass their spoken homage. | Taken upon a base art thou. Thee for the Aśvins. | Thee for Sarasvatī, and thee for Indra, for the Excellent Protector. || 33. Ye Aśvins, Lords of Splendour, drank full draughts of grateful Soma juice, | And aided Indra in his deeds with Namuchi of Asura birth. || 34. As parents aid a son, both Aśvins aided thee, Indra, with their wondrous powers and wisdom. | When thou with might hadst drunk the draught that gladdens, Sarasvatī, O Bounteous Lord, refreshed thee.

Adhyāya 11.

1. Harnessing, first of all, the mind, Savitar having stretched the thought | With reverent look upon the light of Agni bore them up from earth. || 2. By impulse of God Savitar we with our spirit harnessed strive | With might to win the heavenly. || 3. Savitar, having harnessed Gods who go to light and heavenly thought, | Who will create the lofty light—Savitar urge

them on their way! || 4. The priests of him the lofty priest well skilled in hymns, harness their spirit, yea, harness their holy thoughts. | He only, skilled in rules, assigns their priestly tasks. Yea, lofty is the praise of Savitar the God. || 5. I yoke with prayer your ancient inspiration: may the laud rise as on the prince's pathway. | All Sons of the Immortal One shall hear it, who have resorted to celestial dwellings. || 6. Even he, the God whose going forth and majesty the other Deities have followed with their might, | He who hath measured the celestial regions out by his great power, he is the Courser Savitar. || 7. Our sacrifice, God Savitar! speed forward: speed to his share the sacrifice's patron. | May the celestial Gandharva, Cleanser of thought and will, make clean our thoughts and wishes. | The Lord of Speech sweeten the words we utter! || 8. God Savitar, speed this God-loved sacrifice of ours, friend-finding, ever-conquering, winning wealth and heaven. | Speed praise-song with the sacred verse, Rathantara with Gāyatra, Bṛihat that runs in Gāyatra. All-hail! || 9. By impulse of God Savitar I take thee, with arms of Aśvins, with the hands of Pūṣhan, in Aṅgiras' manner, with Gāyatrī metre. | From the earth's seat bring thou Purīṣhya Agni, as Aṅgiras was wont, with Triṣhṭubh metre. || 10. Spade art thou; woman art thou. Ours be power with thee to dig out Agni in his dwelling, as Aṅgiras was wont, with Jagatī metre. || 11. Savitar, bearing in his hand the gold spade which he took therewith, | Looking with reverence on the light of Agni, raised it from the earth, | With the Anuṣhṭubh metre and as Aṅgiras was wont to do. || 12. Run hither, urged to speed, O Horse, along the most extended space. | Thy loftiest birthplace is in heaven. thy navel is in air's mid-realm, the womb that bare thee is on earth. || 13. Upon this course, O lords of wealth, harness; ye twain, the Ass who bears | Agni, and kindly favours us. || 14. In every need, in every race we call, as friends, to succour us, | Indra, the mightiest of all. || 15. Come speeding on and trampling imprecations; come gladdening to the chieftainship of Rudra. | Speed through the wide air thou whose paths are pleasant, with Pūṣhan for thy mate, providing safety. || 16. From the Earth's seat, like Anginas, bring thou Purīṣhya Agni forth. | After the wont of Aṅgiras we to Purīṣhya Agni go. | Agni Purīṣhya we will bear after the went of Aṅgiras || 17. Agni hath looked along the van of Mornings, looked on the days, the earliest Jātavedas, | And many a time along the beams of Sūrya: along the heaven and earth hast thou extended. || 18. The Courser, started on his way, shakes from him all hostilities. | He longs to look with reverent eye on Agni is the mighty seat. || 19. O Courser, having come to earth, seek Agni with a longing wish. | Tell us by trampling on the ground where we may dig him from the earth. || 20. Heaven is thy back, the earth thy seat, the air thy soul, the sea thy womb. | Looking around thee with thine eye trample the adversaries down. || 21. Wealth-giver, Courser, from this place step forth to great felicity. | May we enjoy Earth's favour while we dig forth Agni from her || 22. Down hath he stepped, wealth-giver, racer, courser. Good and auspicious room on earth thou madest. | Thence let us dig forth Agni, fair to look on, while to the loftiest vault we mount, to heaven. || 23. I thoughtfully besprinkle thee with butter, thee dwelling near to all existing creatures. | Broad, vast through vital power that moves transversely, conspicuous, strong with all the food that feeds thee. || 24. I sprinkle him who moves in all directions: may he accept it with a friendly spirit. | Agni with bridegroom's face and lovely colour may not be touched when all his form is fury. || 25. Round the oblation bath he paced, Agni the wise, the Lord of Strength, | Giving the offerer precious boons. || 26. We set thee round us as a fort, victorious Agni, thee a Sage, | Of hero lineage, day by day destroyer of our treacherous foes. || 27. Thou, Agni, with the days, fain to shine hitherward, art brought to life from out the waters, from the stone, | From out the forest trees and herbs that grow on ground. thou, Sovereign Lord of men, art generated pure. || 28. At Savitar's, the Shining One's, impulsion, with arms of Aśvins and with hands of Pūṣhan, | As Aṅgiras was wont to do, I dig thee forth from the seat of Earth, Agni Purīṣhya. | Thee, Agni, luminous and fair of aspect, resplendent with imperishable lustre, gracious to living creatures, never harming, | As Aṅgiras was wont to do, we dig thee forth from the seat of Earth, Agni Purīṣhya || 29. Thou art the Waters' back, the womb of Agni, around the ocean as it swells and surges. | Waxing to greatness, resting on the lotus, spread thou in amplitude with heaven's own measure. || 30. Yea are a shelter and a shield, uninjured both, and widely spread. | Do ye; expansive, cover him: bear ye Purīṣhya Agni up. || 31. Cover him, finders of the light, united both with breast and self, | Bearing between you Agni, the refulgent, everlasting One. || 32. Thou art Purīṣhya, thou support of all. Atharvan was the first, Agni, who rubbed thee into life. | Agni, Atharvan brought thee forth by rubbing from the lotus, from | The head of Viśva, of the Priest. || 33. Thee too as Vṛitra-slayer, thee breaker of forts, the Sage Dadhyach, | Son of Atharvan, lighted up. || 34. Pāthya the Bull, too, kindled thee the Dasyus' most destructive foe, | Winner of spoil in every fight. || 35. Sit, Hotar, in the Hotar's place, observant: lay down the sacrifice in the place of worship. | Thou, dear to Go is, shalt serve them with oblation. Agni, give long life to the Sacrificer. || 36. Accustomed to the Hotar's place, the Hotar hath seated him, bright, splendid, passing mighty, | Whose foresight keeps the Law from violation, excellent, pure-tongued, bringing thousands, Agni. || 37. Seat thee, for thou art mighty: shine, best entertainer of the Gods. | Worthy of sacred food, praised Agni! loose the smoke, ruddy and beautiful to see. || 38. Pour heavenly Waters honey-sweet here for our health, for progeny. | Forth from the place whereon they fall let plants with goodly berries spring. || 39. May Vāyu Mātariśvan heal and comfort thy broken heart as there supine thou liest. | Thou unto whom the breath of Gods gives motion, to Ka, yea, unto thee, O God, be Vaṣhaṭ! || 40. He, nobly born with lustre, shield and refuge, hath sat down in light. | O Agni, Rich in Splendour, robe thyself in many-hued attire. || 41. Lord of fair sacrifice; arise! With Godlike thought protect us well. | With great light splendid to behold come, Agni, through sweet hymns of praise. || 42. Rise up erect to give us aid, stand up like Savitar the God; | Erect as strength-bestower when we call aloud, with unguents and with priests on thee. || 43. Thou, being horn, art Child of Earth and Heaven, parted, fair Babe, among the plants, O Agni. | The glooms of night thou, brilliant child, subduest, and art come forth, loud roaring, from the Mothers. || 44. Steady be thou, and firm of limb. Steed, be a racer fleet of foot. | Broad be thou, pleasant as a seat, bearing the store which Agni needs. || 45. Be thou propitious, Aṅgiras, to creatures of the human race. | Set not on fire the heaven and earth, nor air's mid-region, nor the trees. || 46. Forth with loud neighing go the Steed, the Ass that shouteth as he runs. | Bearing Purīṣhya Agni on, let him not perish ere his time, | Male bearer of male Agni, Child of Waters, Offspring of the Sea. Agni, come hither to the feast. || 47. The Law the Truth, the Law the Truth. As Aṅgiras was wont to do, we bear Purīṣhya Agni on. | Ye Plants, with joyous welcome greet this Agni, auspicious One who cometh on to meet you. | Removing all distresses and afflictions, here settle down and banish evil purpose. || 48. Welcome him joyfully, ye Plants, laden with bloom and goodly fruit. | This seasonable Child of yours hath settled in his ancient seat. || 49. Resplendent with thy wide-extending lustre dispel the terrors of the fiends who hate us. | May lofty Agni be my guide and shelter, ready to hear our call, the good Protector. || 50. Ye, Waters, are beneficent, so help ye us to energy | That we may look on great delight. || 51. Give us a portion of the sap, the most propitious that ye have. | Like mothers in their longing love. || 52. To you we gladly come for him to whose abode ye lead us on: | And, Waters, give us procreant strength. || 53. Mitra, having commingled earth and ground together with the light— | For health to creatures mix I thee Omniscient and nobly born. || 54. The Rudras, having mixed the earth, set all aglow the lofty light. | Bright and perpetual their light verily shines among the Gods. || 55. The lump of clay that hath been mixed by Vasus, Rudras, by the wise, | May Sinīvālī with her hands soften and fit it for the work. || 56. May Sinīvālī with fair braids, with beauteous crest, with lovely locks, | May she, O mighty Aditi, bestow the Fire-pan in thy hands. || 57. Aditi shape the Fire-pan with her power, her arms, her intellect, | And in her womb bear Agni as a mother, in her lap, her son. || 58. With Gāyatrī, like Aṅgiras the Vasus form and fashion thee! | Steadfast art thou, thou art the Earth. Establish in me progeny, command of cattle, growth of wealth, kinsmen for me the worshipper. | With Triṣhṭubh may the Rudras, like Aṅgiras, form and fashion thee. | Steadfast art thou, thou art the Air. Establish in me, etc., as above. | With Jagatī, like Aṅgiras, Ādityas form and fashion thee! | Steadfast art thou, thou art the Sky. Establish in me, etc. | Friends of all men, the All-Gods with Anuṣhṭubh form thee Aṅgiras-like. | Steadfast art thou, thou art the Quarters. Establish in me, etc. || 59. The zone of Aditi art thou. Aditi seize thy hollow space. | She, having made the great Fire-pan, a womb for Agni, formed of clay, | Aditi, gave it to her Sons and, Let them bake it, were her words. || 60. The Vasus make thee fragrant, as Aṅgiras did, with Gāyatrī! | The Rudras make thee fragrant with the Triṣhṭubh, as did Aṅgiras! | With Gāyatrī, like Aṅgiras, may the Ādityas perfume thee. | Dear to all men, may the All-Gods with the Anuṣhṭubh sweeten thee, as Aṅgiras was wont to do. | May Indra make thee odorous. May Varuṇa make thee odorous. May Viṣhṇu make thee odorous. || 61. Pit! Aṅgiras-like may Aditi the Goddess, beloved by all Gods, dig thee in Earth's bosom. | Pan! Aṅgiras-like may the Gods' heavenly Consorts, dear to all Gads, in the Earth's bosom place thee. | Pan! Aṅgiras-like may Dhishaṇās, Divine Ones, dear to all Gods, in the Earth's bosom light thee. | Pan! Aṅgiras-like may the divine Varūtrīs, dear to all Gods, in the earth's bosom heat thee, | Pan! Aṅgiras-like may the celestial Ladies, dear to all Gods, in the earth's bosom bake thee. | Aṅgiras-like may the celestial Matrons, beloved by all the Gods, with unclipped pinions, within the lap of Earth, O Fire pan, bake thee. || 62. The gainful grace of Mitra, God, supporter of the race of man, | Is glorious, of most wondrous fame. || 63. With lovely arms, with lovely hands, with lovely fingers may the God Savitar make thee clean, yea, by the power be hath. | Not trembling on the earth fill thou the regions, fill the Quarters full. || 64. Having arisen wax thou great, yea, stand thou up immovable. | To thee, O Mitra, I entrust this Fire-pan for security. May it remain without a break. || 65. Thee may the Vasus, Aṅgiras-like, fill with the metre Gāyatrī. | Thee may the Rudras, Aṅgiras-like, fill with the Triṣhṭubh metre full. | Thee may Ādityas, Aṅgiras-like, fill with the metre Jagatī. | With the Anuṣhṭubh metre may the All-Gods, dear to all men, fill thee full, as Aṅgiras was wont. || 66. Intention, Agni. Motive, Hail! Mind, Wisdom, Agni, Motive, Hail! | Thought, Knowledge, Agni, Motive, Hail! Rule of Speech, Agni, Motive, Hail! | To Manu Lord of creatures, Hail! To Agni dear to all men, Hail! || 67. May every mortal man elect the friendship of the guiding God. | Each one solicits him for wealth: let him seek fame to prosper him. All-hail! || 68. Break not, nor suffer any harm. Endure, O Mother, and be brave; | This work will thou and Agni do. || 69. Be firm for weal, O Goddess Earth. Made in the wonted manner thou | Art a celestial design. | Acceptable to Gods be this oblation. Arise thou in this sacrifice uninjured. || 70. Wood-fed, bedewed with sacred oil, ancient, Invoker, excellent, | The Son of Strength, the Wonderful. || 71. Abandoning the foeman's host, pass hither to this company: | Assist the men with whom I stand. || 72. From the remotest distance come, Lord of the Red Steeds, hitherward. | Do thou Purīṣhya, Agni, loved of many, overcome our foes. || 73. O Agni, whatsoever be the fuel that we lay on thee, | May that he butter unto thee. Be pleased therewith, Most Youthful God. || 74. That which the termite eats away, that over which the emmet crawls— | Butter be all of this to thee. Be pleased therewith, Most Youthful God. || 75. Bringing to him, with care unceasing, fodder day after day as to a stabled courser, | Joying in food and in the growth of riches, may we thy neighbours, Agni, ne'er be injured. || 76. While on earth's navel Agni is enkindled, we call, for ample increase of our riches, | On Agni joying in the draught, much-lauded, worshipful; victor conquering in battle. || 77. Whatever hosts there are, fiercely assailant, charging in lengthened lines, drawn up in order, | Whatever thieves there are, whatever robbers, all these I cast into thy mouth, O Agni. || 78. Devour the burglars with both tusks, destroy the robbers with thy teeth. | With both thy jaws, thou Holy One, eat up those thieves well champed and chewed. || 79. The burglars living among men, the thieves and robbers in the wood, | Criminals lurking in their lairs, these do I lay between thy jaws. || 80. Him who would seek to injure us, the man who looks oh us with hate | Turn thou to ashes, and the man who slanders and would injure us. || 81. Quickened is this my priestly rank, quickened is manly strength and force, | Quickened is his victorious power of whom I am the Household priest. || 82. The arms of these men have I raised, have raised their lustre and their strength | With priestly power I ruin foes and lift my friends to high estate. || 83. A share of food, O Lord of Food, vouchsafe us, invigorating food that brings no sickness. | Onward, still onward lead the giver. Grant us maintenance both for quadruped and biped.

Adhyāya 12.

1. Far hath he shone abroad like gold to look on, beaming imperishable life for glory. | Agni by vital powers became immortal when his prolific Father Dyaus begat him. || 2. Night and Dawn, different in hue, accordant, meeting together, suckle one same infant. | Golden between the heaven and earth he shineth. The wealth-possessing Gods supported Agni. || 3. The Sapient One arrays himself in every form: for quadruped and biped he hath brought forth good. | Excellent Savitar hath looked on heaven's high vault: he shineth after the outgoings of the Dawn. || 4. Thou art the goodly-pinioned Bird: thou hast the Trivṛit for thy head. | Gāyatra is thine eye, thy wings are Bṛihat and Rathantara. | The hymn is self, the metres are his limbs, the formulas his name. | The Vāmadevya Sāman is thy form, the Yajñāyajñiya thy tail, the fire-hearths are thy hooves. | Thou art the goodly-pinioned Bird: go skyward, soar to heavenly light. || 5. Thou art the riyal-slaying stride of Viṣhṇu. Mount the Gāyatra metre: stride along the earth. | Thou art the foe-destroying stride of Viṣhṇu. Mount the Triṣhṭubh metre: stride along mid-air. | Thou art the traitor-slaying stride of Viṣhṇu. Mount the Jagatī metre: stride along the sky. | Thou art the foeman-slaying stride of Viṣhṇu. Mount Anuṣhṭubh metre: stride along the Quarters. || 6. Agni roared out like Dyaus what time he thunders: licking full oft the earth round plants he flickered. | At once, when born, he looked about, enkindled: he shineth forth between the earth and heaven. || 7. Return to me, thou still-returning Agni, with life, with lustre, progeny, and treasure, | With profit, wisdom, riches, and abundance. || 8. A hundred, Agni Aṅgiras! be thy ways, a thousand thy returns. | With increment of increase bring thou back to us what we have lost. Again bring hitherward our wealth. || 9. Return again with nourishment; Agni, again with food and life. Again preserve us from distress. || 10. Agni, return with store of wealth. Swell with thine overflowing stream that feedeth all on every side. || 11. I brought thee: thou hast entered in. Stand steadfast and immovable. | Let all the people long for thee. Let not thy kingship fall away. || 12. Varuṇa, from the upmost bond release us, let down the lowest and remove the midmost. | So in thy holy law may we made sinless belong to Aditi, O thou Āditya || 13. High hath the Mighty risen before the Mornings, and come to us with light from out the darkness. | Fair-shapen Agni with white-shining splendour hath filled at birth all human habitations. || 14. The Haṃsa homed in light, the Vasu in mid-air, the Priest beside the altar, Guest within the house, | Dweller in noblest place, mid men, in truth, in sky, born of flood, kine, truth, mountain, he is holy Law. The Great. || 15. Knowing all holy ordinances, Agni, be seated in the lap of this thy mother. | Do not with heat or glowing flame consume her: shine thou within her with refulgent lustre. || 16. Within this Fire-pan with thy light, O Agni, in thy proper seat, | Glowing with warmth, be gracious thou, O Jātavedas, unto her. || 17. Being propitious unto me, O Agni, sit propitiously. | Having made all the regions blest, in thine own dwelling seat thyself. || 18. First Agni sprang to life from out of heaven, the second time from us came Jātavedas. | Thirdly the Manly-souled was in the waters. The pious lauds and kindles him Eternal. || 19. Agni, we know thy three powers in three stations, we know thy forms in many a place divided. | We know what name supreme thou hast in secret: we know the source from which thou hast proceeded. || 20. The Manly-souled lit thee in sea and waters, Man's Viewer lit thee in the breast of heaven. | There as thou stoodest in the third high region the Bulls increased thee in the waters' bosom. || 21. Agni roared out, etc. (verse 6. repeated). || 22. The spring of glories and support of riches, rouser of thoughts and guardian of the Soma, | Good Son of Strength, a King amid the waters, in forefront of the Dawns he shines enkindled. || 23. Germ of the world, ensign of all creation, he sprang to life and filled the earth and heaven. | Even the firm rock he cleft when passing over, when the Five Tribes brought sacrifice to Agni. || 24. So among mortals was immortal Agni established as cleansing, wise, and eager envoy. | He waves the red smoke that he lifts above him, striving to reach the heaven with radiant lustre. || 25. Far hath he shone, etc. (verse 1. repeated). || 26. Whoso this day, O God whose flames are lovely, makes thee a cake, O Agni, mixed with butter, | Lead thou and further him to higher fortune, to bliss bestowed by Gods, O thou Most Youthful. || 27. Endow him, Agni, with a share of glory, at every, song of praise sung forth enrich him. | Dear let him be to Sūrya, dear to Agni, pre-eminent with son and

children's children. ‖ 28. While, Agni, day by day men pay thee worship they win themselves all treasures worth the wishing. | Allied with thee, eager and craving riches, they have disclosed the stable filled with cattle. ‖ 29. Agni, man's gracious Friend, the Soma's keeper, Vaiśvānara, hath been lauded by the Ṛishis | We will invoke benignant Earth and Heaven: ye Deities, give us wealth with hero children. ‖ 30. Pay service unto Agni with your fuel, rouse your Guest with oil: | In him present your offerings. ‖ 31. May all the Gods, O Agni, bear thee upward with their earnest thoughts: | Not to be looked on, rich in light, be thou propitious unto us, ‖ 32. Agni, go forth resplendent, thou with thine auspicious flames of fire. | Shining with mighty beams of light harm not my people with thy form. ‖ 33. Agni roared out, etc. (verse 21. repeated.) ‖ 34. Far famed is this the Bhārata's own Agni: he shineth like the Sun with lofty splendour. | He who hath vanquished Pūru in the battle, the heavenly Guest hath shone for us benignly. ‖ 35. Receive these ashes, ye celestial Waters, and lay them in a fair place full of fragrance. | To him bow down the nobly-wedded Matrons! Bear this on waters as her son a mother. ‖ 36. Agni, thy home is in the floods: into the plants thou forcest way, | And as their child art born anew. ‖ 37. Thou art the offspring of the plants, thou art the offspring of the trees: | The offspring thou of all that is, thou, Agni, art the Waters' Child, ‖ 38. With ashes having reached the womb, the waters, Agni and the earth, | United with the mothers, thou blazing hast seated thee again. ‖ 39. Seated again upon thy seat, the waters, Agni! and the earth, | In her, thou, most auspicious One, liest as in a mother's lap ‖ 40, 41. Return again, etc. Agni, return, etc. (verses 9. and 10. repeated). ‖ 42. Mark this my speech, Divine One, thou Most Youthful, offered to thee by him who gives most freely: | One hates thee, and another sings thy praises. I thine adorer laud thy form, O Agni. ‖ 43. Be thou for us a liberal Prince, Giver and Lord of precious things. | Drive those who hate us far away. | To the Omnific One All-hail! ‖ 44. Again let the Ādityas, Rudras, Vasus, and Brahmans with their rites light thee, Wealth-bringer! | Increase thy body with presented butter: effectual be the Sacrificer's wishes. ‖ 45. Go hence, depart, creep off in all directions, both ancient visitors and recent comers: | Yama hath given a place on earth to rest in. This place for him the Fathers have provided. ‖ 46. Knowledge art thou: accomplishment of wishes. In me be the fulfilment of thy wishes. | Thou art the ashes, thou the mould of Agni. Rankers are ye, rankers around. Rankers right upward, be ye fixed. ‖ 47. This is that Agni where the longing Indra took the pressed Soma deep within his body. | Winner of spoils in thousands like a courser, with prayer art thou exalted, Jātavedas. ‖ 48. The splendour which is thine in heaven, O Agni, in earth, O Holy One, in plants, in waters, | Wherewith thou hast o'erspread mid-air's broad region, that light is brilliant, billowy, man-surveying. ‖ 49. O Agni, to the flood of heaven thou mountest, thou tallest hither Gods, the thought-inspirers. | The waters, those beyond the light of Sūrya, and those that are beneath it here, approach thee. ‖ 50. May the Purīṣhya Agnis in accord with those that spring from floods, | May they, benevolent, accept the sacrifice, full, wholesome draughts. ‖ 51. As holy food, Agni, to thine invoker give wealth in cattle, lasting, rich in marvels. | To us be born a son and spreading offspring. Agni, be this thy gracious will to us-ward. ‖ 52. This is thine ordered place of birth whence, sprung to life, thou shonest forth. | Knowing this, Agni, mount on high and cause our riches to increase. ‖ 53. Ranker art thou: Aṅgiras-like sit steady with that Deity. | Ranker-round art thou: Aṅgiras-like sit steady with that Deity. ‖ 54. Fill up the room, supply the void, then settle steady in thy place. | Indra-Agni and Bṛihaspati have set thee down in this abode. ‖ 55. The dappled kine who stream with milk prepare his draught of Soma juice— | Clans in the birthplace of the Gods, in the three luminous realms of heaven. ‖ 56. All sacred songs have magnified Indra expansive as the sea, | The best of warriors borne on cars, the Lord, the very Lord of Strength. ‖ 57. Combine ye two and harmonize together, dear to each other, brilliant, friendly-minded, | Abiding in one place for food and vigour. ‖ 58. Together have I brought your minds, your ordinances, and your thoughts. | Be thou our Sovereign Lord, Agni Purīṣhya; give food and vigour to the Sacrificer. ‖ 59. Thou art Purīṣhya Agni, thou art wealthy, thou art prosperous. | Having made all the regions blest, here seat thee in thine own abode. ‖ 60. Be ye one-minded unto us, both of one thought, free from deceit. | Harm not the sacrifice, harm not the Patron of the sacrifice. Be gracious unto us today, ye knowers of all things that be. ‖ 61. Even as a mother bears her son, Earth, Ukhā hath borne within her womb Purīṣhya Agni. | Maker of all, accordant with the All-Gods and Seasons, may Prajāpati release her. ‖ 62. Seek him who pours not, offers not oblation; follow the going of the thief and robber. | This is thy way; leave us and seek some other. To thee, O Goddess Nirṛiti, be homage. ‖ 63. To thee, sharp-pointed Nirṛiti, full homage! Loose and detach this iron bond that binds him. | Unanimous with Yama and with Yamī to the sublimest vault of heaven uplift him. ‖ 64. Thou, Awful One, thou in whose mouth I offer for the unloosing of these binding fetters, | Whom people hail as Earth with their glad voices, as Nirṛiti in every place I know thee. ‖ 65. The binding noose which Nirṛiti the Goddess hath fastened on thy neck that none may loose it, | I loose for thee as from the midst of Āyus. Sped forward now, eat thou the food we offer: | To Fortune, her who hath done this, be homage. ‖ 66. Establisher, the gatherer of treasures, he looks with might on every form and figure. | Like Savitar the God whose laws are constant, like Indra, he hath stood where meet the pathways. ‖ 67. Wise, through desire of bliss with Gods, the skilful bind the traces fast, and lay the yokes on either side. ‖ 68. Lay on the yokes and fasten well the traces; formed is the furrow sow the seed within it. | Through song may we find hearing fraught with plenty: near to the ripened grain approach the sickle. ‖ 69. Happily let the shares turn up the ploughland, happily go the ploughers with the oxen! | Śuna and Sīra, pleased with our oblation, cause ye our plants to bear abundant fruitage. ‖ 70. Approved by Viśvedevas and by Marutas, balmed be the furrow with sweet-flavoured fatness. | Succulent, teeming with thy milky treasure, turn hitherward to us with milk, O Furrow. ‖ 71. The keen-shared plough that bringeth bliss, good for the Soma-drinker's need, | Shear out for me a cow, a sheep, a rapid drawer of the car, a blooming woman, plump and strong! ‖ 72. Milk out their wish, O Wishing-Cow, to Mitra and to Varuṇa, | To Indra, to the Aśvins, to Pūṣhan, to people and to plants. ‖ 73. Be loosed, inviolable, Godward-farers! We have attained the limit of this darkness: we have won the light. ‖ 71. The year together with the darksome fortnights; Dawn with the ruddy-coloured cows about her; the Aśvins with their wonderful achievements; the Sun together with his dappled Courser; Vaiśvānara with Iḍā and with butter. Svāhā! ‖ 75. Herbs that sprang up in time of old, three ages earlier than the Gods,— | Of these, whose hue is brown, will I declare the hundred powers and seven. ‖ 76. Ye, Mothers, have a hundred homes, yea, and a thousand are your growths. | Do ye who have a thousand powers free this my patient from disease. ‖ 77. Be glad and joyful in the Plants, both blossoming and bearing fruit, | Plants that will lead us to success like mares who conquer in the race. ‖ 78. Plants, by this name I speak to you, Mothers, to you the Goddesses: | Steed, cow, and garment may I win, win back thy very self, O man. ‖ 79. The Holy Fig tree is your home, your mansion is the Parṇa tree: | Winners of cattle shall ye be if ye regain for me this man. ‖ 80. He who hath store of Herbs at hand like Kings amid a crowd of men,— | Physician is that sage's name, fiend-slayer, chaser of disease. ‖ 81. Herbs rich in Soma, rich in steeds, in nourishment in strengthening power, | All these have I provided here, that this man may be whole again. ‖ 82. The healing virtues of the Plants stream forth like cattle from the stall,— | Plants that shall win me store of wealth, and save thy vital breath, O man. ‖ 83. Reliever is your mother's name, and hence Restorers are ye called. | Rivers are ye with wings that fly: keep far whatever brings disease. ‖ 84. Over all fences have they passed, as steals a thief into the fold. | The Plants have driven from the frame whatever malady was there. ‖ 85. When, bringing back the vanished strength, I hold these herbs within my hand, | The spirit of disease departs ere he can seize upon the life. ‖ 86. He through whose frame, O Plants, ye creep member by member, joint by joint, | From him ye drive away disease like some strong arbiter of strife. ‖ 87. Fly, Spirit of Disease, begone, with the blue jay and kingfisher. | Fly, with the wind's impetuous speed, vanish together with the storm. ‖ 88. Help every one the other, lend assistance each of you to each, | All of you be accordant, give furtherance to this speech of mine. ‖ 89. Let fruitful Plants, and fruitless, those that blossom, and the blossomless, | Urged onward by Bṛihaspati, release us from our pain and grief; ‖ 90. Release me from the curse's plague and woe that comes from Varuṇa; | Free me from Yama's fetter, from sin and offence against the Gods. ‖ 91. What time, descending from the sky, the Plants flew earthward, thus they spake: | No evil shall befall the man whom while he liveth we pervade. || 92. Of all the many Plants whose King is Soma, Plants of hundred forms, | Thou art the Plant most excellent, prompt to the wish, sweet to the heart. || 93. O all ye various Herbs whose King is Soma, that o'erspread the earth, | Urged onward by Bṛihaspati, combine your virtue in this Plant. || 94. All Plants that hear this speech, and those that have departed far away, | Come all assembled and confer your healing power upon this Herb. || 95. Unharmed be he who digs you up, unharmed the man for whom I dig: | And let no malady attack biped or quadruped of ours. || 96. With Soma as their Sovereign Lord the Plants hold colloquy and say: | O King, we save from death the man whose cure a Brahman undertakes. || 97. Most excellent of all art thou, O Plant: thy vassals are the trees. | Let him be subject to our power, the man who seeks to injure us. || 98. Banisher of catarrh art thou, of tumours and of hemorrhoids; | Thou banished Pākāru and Consumption in a hundred forms. || 99. Thee did Gandharvas dig from earth, thee Indra and Bṛihaspati | King Soma, knowing thee, O Plant, from his Consumption was made free. || 100. Conquer mine enemies, the men who challenge me do thou subdue. | Conquer thou all unhappiness: victorious art thou, O Plant. || 101. Long-lived be he who digs thee, Plant, and he for whom I dig thee up. | So mayst thou also, grown long-lived, rise upward with a hundred shoots. || 102. Most excellent of all art thou, O Plant; thy vassals are the trees. | Let him be subject to our power, the man who seeks to injure us. || 103. May he not harm me who is earth's begetter, nor he whose laws are faithful, sky's pervades; | Nor he who first begot the lucid waters. To Ka the God let us present oblation. || 104. Turn thyself hitherward, O Earth, to us with sacrifice and milk. | Thy covering skin Agni, urged forth, hath mounted. || 105. All, Agni, that in thee is bright, pure, cleansed, and meet for sacrifice, | That do we bring unto the Gods. || 106. I from this place have fed on strength and vigour, the womb of holy Law, stream of the mighty. | In cows let it possess me and in bodies. I quit decline and lack of food, and sickness. || 107. Agni, life-power and fame are thine: thy fires blaze mightily, thou rich in wealth of beams! | Sage, passing bright, thou givest to the worshipper, with strength, the food that merits laud. || 108. With brilliant, purifying sheen, with perfect sheen thou liftest up thyself in light. | Thou, visiting both thy Mothers, aidest them as Son: thou joinest close the earth and heaven. || 109. O Jātavedas, Son of Strength, rejoice thyself, gracious, in our fair hymns and songs. | In thee are treasured various forms of strengthening food, born nobly and of wondrous help. || 110. Agni, spread forth, as Ruler, over living things: give wealth to us, Immortal God. | Thou shinest out from beauty fair to look upon: thou leadest us to conquering power. || 111. To him, the wise, who orders sacrifice, who hath great riches under his control, | Thou givest blest award of good, and plenteous food, givest him wealth that conquers all. || 112. The men have set before them for their welfare Agni, strong, visible to all, the Holy. | Thee, Godlike One, with ears to hear, most famous, men's generations magnify with praise-songs. || 113. Soma, wax great. From every side may vigorous powers unite in thee. | Be in the gathering-place of strength. || 114. In thee be juicy nutriments united, and power and mighty foe-subduing vigour. | Waxing to immortality, O Soma, win highest glory for thyself in heaven. || 115. Wax, O most gladdening Soma, great through all thy filaments, and be | A friend of most illustrious fame to prosper us. || 116. May Vatsa draw thy mind away, even from thy loftiest dwelling-place, | Agni, with song that yearns for thee. || 117. Agni, best Aṅgiras, to thee all people who have pleasant homes | Apart have turned to gain their wish. || 118. In dear homes, Agni, the desire of all that is and is to be, | Shines forth the One Imperial Lord.

Adhyāya 13.

1. I take within me Agni first, for increase of my wealth, good offspring, manly strength: | So may the Deities wait on me. || 2. Thou art the waters' back, the womb of Agni, around the ocean as it swells and surges. | Waxing to greatness, resting on the lotus, spread forth in amplitude with heaven's own measure. || 3. Eastward at first was Brahma generated. Vena o'erspread the bright Ones from the summit, | Disclosed his deepest nearest revelations, womb of existent and of non-existent. || 4. In the beginning rose Hiraṇyagarbha, born Only Lord of all created being. | He fixed and holdeth up this earth and heaven. Worship we Ka the God with our oblation. || 5. The Drop leaped onward through the earth and heaven, along this place and that which was before it. | I offer up, throughout the seven oblations, the Drop still moving to the common dwelling. || 6. Homage be paid to Serpents unto all of them that are on earth, | To those that dwell in air, to those that dwell in sky be homage paid. || 7. To those that are the demons' darts, to those that live upon the trees, | To all the Serpents that lie low in holes be adoration paid. || 8. Or those that are in heaven's bright sphere, or those that dwell in the Sun's beams: | Serpents, whose home has been prepared in waters, homage unto them! || 9. Put forth like a wide-spreading net thy vigour: go like a mighty King with his attendants. | Thou, following thy swift net, shootest arrows: transfix the fiends with darts that burn most fiercely. || 10. Forth go in rapid flight thy whirling weapons: follow them closely glowing in thy fury. | Spread with thy tongue the winged flames, O Agni: unfettered cast thy firebrands all around thee. || 11. Send thy spies forward, fleetest in thy motion: be, ne'er deceived, the guardian of this people | From him who, near or far, is bent on evil, and let no trouble sent from thee o'ercome us. || 12. Rise up, O Agni, spread thee out before us, burn down our foes, thou who hast sharpened arrows. | Him, blazing Agni! who hath worked us mischief, consume thou utterly like dried-up stubble. || 13. Rise, Agni, drive off those who fight against us: make manifest thine own celestial vigour. | Slacken the strong bows of the demon-driven: destroy our foemen whether kin or stranger. | I settle thee with Agni's fiery ardour. || 14. Agni is head and height of heaven, the Master of the earth is he: | He quickeneth the waters' seed. | I settle thee with the great strength of Indra. || 15. Thou art the leader of the rite and region to which with thine auspicious teams thou tendest. | Thy light-bestowing head to heaven thou liftest, making thy tongue the oblation-bearer, Agni! || 16. Steady art thou, sustainer, laid by Viśvakarman in thy place. | Let not the ocean nor the bird harm thee: unshaking, steady earth. || 17. Thee let Prajāpati settle on the waters' back, in Ocean's course, | Thee the capacious, widely spread. Thou art the Wide One: spread thee wide || 18. Thou art the earth, the ground, thou art the all-sustaining Aditi, she who supporteth all the world. | Control the earth, steady the earth, do thou the earth no injury. || 19. For all breath, out-breath; through-breath, upward-breathing, for high position, for prescribed observance, | May Agni keep thee safe with great well-being, with the securest shelter. As aforetime with Aṅgiras, with that Deity lie steady. || 20. Upspringing from thine every joint, upspringing from each knot of thine, | Thus with a thousand, Dūrvā! with a hundred do thou stretch us out. || 21. Thou spreading with a hundred, thou that branched with a thousand shoots, | Thee, such, with our oblation will we worship, O celestial Brick. || 22. Thy lights, O Agni, in the Sun that with their beams o'erspread the sky,— | With all of those assist thou us today to light and progeny. || 23. Lights of yours in the Sun, O Gods, or lights that are in kine and steeds, | O Indra-Agni, with all those vouchsafe us light, Bṛihaspati! || 24. The Far-Refulgent held the light. The Self-Refulgent held the light. | Thee, luminous, may Prajāpati settle upon the back of Earth. | Give, to all breathing, all the light, to out-breath, to diffusive breath. | Thy Sovereign Lord is Agni. With that Deity, as with Aṅgiras, lie firmly settled in thy place. || 25. Madhu and Mādhava, the two Spring seasons—thou art the innermost cement of Agni. | May Heaven and Earth, may Waters, Plants and Agnis help, separate, accordant, my precedence. | May all the Fires 'twixt heaven and earth, one-minded, well-fitted, gather round these two Spring seasons, | As the Gods gathering encompass Indra: firm with that Deity, Aṅgiras-like, be seated. || 26. Thou art Aṣhāḍhā, Conquering One. Conquer our foemen, conquer thou the men who fain would-fight with us. | A thousand manly powers hast thou: so do thou aid and quicken me. || 27. The winds waft sweets, the rivers pour sweets for the man who keeps the Law: | So may the plants be sweet for us. || 28. Sweet be the night and sweet the dawns, sweet the terrestrial atmosphere: | Sweet be our Father Heaven to us. || 29. May the tall tree be full of sweets for us and, and full of sweets the Sun: | May our milch-kine be sweet for us. || 30. Seat thyself in the deepness of the waters, lest Sūrya, lest Vaiśvānara Agni scorch thee. | With wing unclipped, survey created beings: may rain that cometh down from heaven attend thee. || 31. He crept across the three heaven-reaching oceans, the Bull of Bricks, the Master of the Waters. | Clad in the world with his, the Well-

made's, vesture, go whither those before thee have departed. || 32. May Heaven and Earth, the Mighty Pair, besprinkle this our sacrifice, | And feed us full with nourishments. || 33. Look ye on Vishṇu's works whereby the Friend of Indra, close allied, | Hath let his holy ways be seen. || 34. Firm art thou, a sustainer. Hence engendered, forth from these wombs at first came Jātavedas. | By Gāyatrī, by Trishṭubh, by Anushṭubh, may he who knows bear to the Gods oblation. || 35. Take thou thine ease for food, for store of riches, for might in splendour, and for strength and offspring. | Thou art all-ruling, independent Ruler: both fountains of Sarasvatī protect thee! || 36. O radiant Agni, harness thou thy steeds which are most excellent! | They bear thee as thy spirit wills. || 37. Yoke, Agni, as a charioteer, thy steeds who best invoke the Gods: | As ancient Hotar take thy seat. || 38. Like rivers our libations flow together, cleansing themselves in inmost heart and spirit. | I look upon the flowing streams of butter: the golden reed is in the midst of Agni. || 39. Thee for the praise-verse, thee for sheen, thee for bright splendour, thee for light. | This hath become the energetic spirit of all the world and of Vaiśvānara Agni. || 40. Agni, all-luminous with light, splendid with splendour, golden One. | Giver of thousands art thou: for a thousand thee. || 41. Balm thou with milk the unborn babe Āditya, wearing all forms, creator of a thousand. | Spare, him with heat, nor plot against him: give him a hundred years of life while thou art building. || 42. The wind's impetuous rush, Varuṇa's navel! the horse that springs to life amid the waters! | The rivers' tawny child, based on the mountain, harm not, O Agni, in the loftiest region. || 43. Unwasting Drop, red, eager, pressing forward, Agni I worship with repeated homage. | Forming thyself with joints in proper order, harm not the Cow, Aditi widely ruling! || 44. Her who is Tvashṭar's guardian, Varuṇa's navel, the Ewe brought forth from out the loftiest region, | The Asura's mighty thousandfold contrivance, injure not in the highest sphere, O Agni. || 45. The Agni who from Agni had his being, from heat of Earth or also heat of Heaven, | Whereby the Omnific One engendered creatures, him may thy fierce displeasure spare, O Agni. || 46. The brilliant presence of the Gods hath risen, the eye of Mitra, Varuṇa, and Agni. | The soul of all that moveth not or moveth, the Sun hath filled the air, and earth and heaven. || 47. Injure not, thousand-eyed, while thou art building for sacrifice, this animal, the biped. | Accept as pith man's counterfeit the victim, Agni: therewith building thy forms, be settled. | Let thy flame reach man's counterfeit: let thy flame reach the man we hate. || 48. Harm not this animal whose hooves are solid, the courser neighing in the midst of coursers. | I dedicate to thee the forest Gaura: building thy bodies up with him be settled. | Let thy flame reach the Gaura, let thy flame reach him whom we detest. || 49. Thousandfold, with a hundred streams, this fountain, expanded in the middle of the waters, | Infinite, yielding butter for the people, harm not, O Agni, in the highest region. | This wild bull of the forest I assign thee: building thy bodies up therewith be settled. | Let thy flame reach the wild hull, etc. (as in 48). || 50. This creature clothed in wool, Varuṇa's navel, the skin of animals quadruped and biped, | The first that was produced of Tvashṭar's creatures, O Agni, harm not in the highest region. | The forest buffalo do I assign thee: building, etc., as above *mutato mutando*. || 51. From Agni's warmth the he-goat had his being: he looked at first upon his generator. | Thereby the Gods at first attained to Godhead: those meet for worship to the height ascended. | The forest Śarabha do I assign thee: building, etc. || 52. Do thou, Most Youthful God, protect the men who offer, hear their songs, | Protect his offspring and himself. || 53. I set thee in the passage of the waters. I set thee in the swelling of the waters. I set thee in the ashes of the waters. I set thee in the lustre of the waters. I set thee in the way which waters travel. I set thee in the flood, the place to test in. I set thee in the sea, the place to rest in. I set thee in the stream, the place to rest in. I set thee in the water's habitation. I set thee in the resting-place of waters. I set thee in the station of the waters. I set thee in the meeting-place of waters. I set thee in the birthplace of the waters. I set thee in the refuse of the waters. I set thee in the residence of waters. I settle thee with the Gāyatrī metre. I settle thee with the Trishṭubh metre. I settle thee with the Jagatī metre. I settle thee with the Anushṭubh metre. I settle thee with the Paṅkti metre. || 54. This, in front, is Bhuvar. His offspring, Breath, is Bhauvāyana. Spring is Prāṇāyana. The Gāyatrī is the daughter of Spring. From the Gāyatrī comes the Gāyatra tune. From the Gāyatra the Upāṃśu. From the Upāṃśu the Trivṛit From the Trivṛit the Rathantara. The Ṛishi Vasishṭha. By thee, taken by Prajāpati, I take vital breath for creatures. || 55. This on the right, the Omnific. His, the Omnific's offspring, Mind. Summer sprang from Mind. The Trishṭubh is the daughter of Summer. From the Trishṭubh came the Svāra song. From the Svāra the Antaryāma. From the Antaryāma the Pañchadaśa. From the Pañchadaśa the Bṛihat The Ṛishi Bharadvāja. By thee, taken by Prajāpati, I take Mind for creatures. || 56. This on the western side, the All-Embracer. His, the All-Embracer's offspring, the Eye. The Rains sprang from the Eye. The Jagatī is the daughter of the Rains. From the Jagatī came the Ṛikshama. From the Ṛikshama the Śukra From the Śukra the Saptadaśa. From the Saptadaśa the Vairūpa. The Ṛishi Jamadagni. By thee, taken by Prajāpati, I take the Eye for creatures. || 57. This on the north side, heaven. This, heaven's offspring, the Ear. Autumn, the daughter of the Ear. The Anushṭubh sprang from Autumn. From the Anushṭubh came the Aiḍa. From the Aiḍa the Manthin. From the Manthin the Ekaviṃśa. From the Ekaviṃśa the Vairāja. The Ṛishi Viśvāmitra By thee, taken by Prajāpati, I take the Ear for creatures. || 58. This above, Intellect. Its, Intellect's offspring, Speech. Winter the offspring of Speech. Paṅkti sprang from Winter. From Paṅkti the Nidhanavat. From the Nidhanavat came the Āgrayaṇa. From the Āgrayaṇa the Triṇava and the Trayastriṃśa. From the Triṇava and the Trayastriṃśa the Śākvara and the Raivata. The Ṛishi Viśvakarman. By thee, taken by Viśvakarman, I take Speech for people. | Fill up the room, etc. The dappled kine, etc. All sacred songs, etc., three texts repeated from 12:54-56.

Adhyāya 14.

1. With steadfast site and birthplace thou art steadfast: settle thou duly in thy steadfast birthplace, rejoicing in the Ukhya's first appearance. | Here let the Aśvins, the Adhvaryus, seat thee. || 2. Nesting, intelligent, dripping with butter, in the auspicious seat of earth be seated. | Let Rudras, Vasus welcome thee with praises: fill full these prayers for our propitious fortune. | Here let the Aśvins, the Adhvaryus, seat thee. || 3. Here, Guard of Strength, with thine own powers be seated for the Gods' happiness and great enjoyment. | Even as a father to his son, be friendly: with easy entrance enter with thy body. Here let the Aśvins, the Adhvaryus seat thee: || 4. Thou art the filling-stuff of earth called Apsas. May all the Gods celebrate thee with praises. | Enriched with songs of praise, Pṛishṭhas and butter, sit here and give us wealth with store of children. | Here let the Aśvins, etc. || 5. Upon the back of Aditi I lay thee the sky's supporter, pillar of the Quarters, | Queen over creatures. Wave and drop of waters art thou; and Viśvakarman is thy Ṛishi || 6. Śukra and Śuchi, seasons, both, of summer—thou art the innermost cement of Agni. | May Heaven and Earth, may Waters, Plants and Agnis help, separate, accordant, my precedence. | Let all the Agnis 'twixt the earth and heaven gather together round these summer seasons, as the Gods gather in their hosts round Indra, | Firm, with that Deity, Aṅgiras-like, be seated. || 7. Associate with the Seasons, with the Modes with the Gods, with the health-establishing Gods—may the Aśvins the Adhvaryus settle thee here for Agni Vaiśvānara. | Associate . . . . . with the Vasus, etc. | Associate . . . . . with the Rudras, etc. | Associate . . . . . with the Ādityas, etc. | Associate . . . . . with the Viśvedevas, etc. || 8. Guard thou my breath. Guard my out-breathing. Guard my through-breathing. Illume mine eye with far-reaching vision. Give power of hearing to mine ear. Pour forth waters. Quicken plants. Protect bipeds. Protect quadrupeds. Send rain from heaven. || 9. The head is vital vigour. Prajāpati became the metre. Royalty is vital vigour, health-giving metre. The Supporter is vital vigour, the Sovereign Lord the metre. Viśvakarman is vital vigour, Parameshṭhin the metre. The he-goat is vital vigour, excellent the metre. The bull is vital vigour, extensive the metre. Man is vital vigour, languid the metre. The tiger is vital vigour, invincible the metre. The lion is vital vigour, covering the metre. The four-year bull is vital vigour, Bṛihatī the metre. The ox is vital vigour, Kakubh the metre. The steer is vital vigour, Satobṛihatī the metre. || 10. The bullock is vital vigour, Paṅkti the metre. The milch-cow is vital vigour, Jagatī the metre. The eighteen-month calf is vital vigour, Trishṭubh the metre. The two year old steer is vital vigour, Virāj the metre. The thirty-month old ewe is vital vigour, Gāyatrī the metre. The three year old steer is vital vigour, Ushṇih the metre. The four

year old ox is vital vigour, Anushṭubh the metre. Fill up the room, etc. The dappled kine, etc. All sacred songs, etc. are three texts repeated from 12:54-56. See also 13:58. || 11. Indra and Agni, in its place securely set the unshaking brick. | Thou with thy back sunderest heaven and the broad earth and firmament. || 12. On the air's back let Viśvakarman set thee, thee the capacious, thee the far-extended. | Control the air, fix firm the air, do thou the air no injury. | For all breath, out-breath, through-breath, upward breathing, for high position, for prescribed observance, | May Vāyu keep thee safe with great well-being, with securest shelter. In the manner of Aṅgiras, with that Deity lie steady. || 13. Queen art thou, Quarter of the East. Wide-ruler, Quarter of the South. West Quarter, thou art Sovereign. Thou Autocrat, Quarter of the North. | Queen Paramount art thou, the Lofty Point. || 14. On the air's back may Viśvakarman set thee luminous. | Control all light for all breath, for out-breath, up-breath, through-breath. | Thy Lord is Vāyu, with that Deity, Aṅgiras-like, lie firm. || 15. Two Rainy Seasons, Nabhas and Nabhasya—thou art the innermost cement of Agni, etc. (as in 13:25). || 16. Isha and Ūrja, two Autumnal Seasons—thou art the innermost cement of Agni, etc. || 17. Preserve my life. Preserve my breath. Guard mine out-breath. Preserve mine eyes. Preserve mine ears. Strengthen my voice. Quicken my mind. Preserve my self. Vouchsafe me light. || 18. Mā metre. Pramā metre. Pratimā metre. Asrīvayas metre. Paṅkti metre. Ushṇih metre. Bṛihatī metre. Anushṭubh metre. Virāj metre. Gāyatrī metre, Trishṭubh metre. Jagatī metre. || 19. Earth metre. Sky metre. Heaven metre. Years metre. Nakshatras metre. Vāk metre. Mind metre. Husbandry metre. Gold metre. Cow metre. She-goat metre. Horse metre. || 20. The Deity Agni. The Deity Vāta. The Deity Sūrya. The Deity Moon. The Deity Vasus. The Deity Rudras. The Deity Ādityas The Deity Marutas. The Deity Viśvedevas The Deity Bṛihaspati The Deity Indra. The Deity Varuṇa || 21. Chief art thou, bright, supporting, firm, thou art the great sustainer, Earth. | Thee for life, thee for lustre, thee for tillage, thee for peace and rest. || 22. Controller, brilliant art thou, managing controller, firm sustainer. For strength, for energy thee, for riches thee, for prosperity thee. | Fill up the room, etc. The dappled kine, etc. All sacred songs, etc. (as in 10). || 23. This Swift, the triple praise-song. The Shining, the Pañchadaśa hymn. Heaven, the Saptadaśa The Supporter, the Ekaviṃśa Speed, the Ashṭādaśa. Ardour, the Navadaśa. Triumphant Onset, Saviṃśa, Vigour, Dvāviṃśa. Maintenance, Trayoviṃśa. Womb, Chaturviṃśa. Embryos, Pañchaviṃśa. Energy, the Triṇava Intention, the Ekatriṃśa. The Basis, the Trayastriṃśa The Bright One's Station, the Chatustriṃśa. The Vault of Heaven, the Shaṭtriṃśa. The Revolving One, the Ashṭāchatvāriṃśa. The Support, the Four-divisioned praise-song. || 24. Thou art the portion of Agni, chief control of Consecration. The Priesthood is saved; the Trivṛit Stoma. | Thou art the portion of Indra, the sovereignty of Vishṇu. The Nobility is saved; the Pañchadaśa Stoma. | Thou art the share of the Man-beholders; the supremacy of the Creator; the birthplace is saved; the Saptadaśa Stoma. | Thou art the share of Mitra, the sovereignty of Varuṇa Rain of heaven and wind are saved; the Ekaviṃśa Stoma. || 25. Thou art the share of the Vasus, the sovereignty of the Rudras. Quadrupeds are saved; the Chaturviṃśa Stoma. | Thou art the share of the Ādityas; the sovereignty of the Marutas. The Embryos are saved; the Pañchaviṃśa Stoma. | Thou art the share of Aditi; the sovereignty of Pūshan Strength is saved; the Triṇava Stoma. | Thou art the share of God Savitar; the sovereignty of Bṛihaspati The universal Quarters are saved; the Chatushṭoma Stoma. || 26. Thou art the share of the Yavas; the sovereignty of the Ayavas. Creatures are saved; the Chatuśchatvāriṃśa Stoma. | Thou art the share of the Ṛibhus; the sovereignty of the Viśvedevas The Being is saved; the Trayastriṃśa Stoma. || 27. Sahas, Sahasya, the two Winter Seasons—thou art the innermost cement of Agni, etc. (as in 13:25). || 28. With one they praised; creatures were produced. Prajāpati was over-lord. | With three they praised; the Priesthood was created. Bṛihaspati was over-lord. | With five they praised; beings were created. The Lord of Beings was over-lord. | With seven they praised; the Seven Ṛishis were created. Dhātar was over-lord. || 29. With nine they praised; the Fathers were created. Aditi was Sovereign Lady. | With eleven they praised; the Seasons were created. The Season-Lords were over-lords. | With thirteen they praised; the Months were created. The Year was over-lord. | With fifteen they praised; the Nobility was created. Indra was over-lord. | With seventeen they praised; domestic animals were created. Bṛihaspati was over-lord. || 30. With nineteen they praised; Śūdra and Ārya were created. Day and Night were Sovereign Ladies. | With twenty-one they praised; solid-hoofed animals were created. Varuṇa was over-lord. | With twenty-three they praised; small animals were created. Pūshan was over-lord. | With twenty-five they praised; forest animals were created. Vāyu was over-lord. | With twenty-seven they praised; earth and heaven came apart. Vasus, Rudras, Ādityas followed separately, so they were over-lords. || 31. With twenty-nine they praised; Trees were created. Soma was over-lord. | With thirty-one they praised; creatures were created. The Yavas and the Ayavas were over-lords. | With thirty-three they praised; living beings. were happy. Prajāpati, the Supreme in Place, was over-lord. | Fill up the room, etc. The dappled kine, etc. All sacred songs, etc. Repeated from 12:14-16.

Adhyāya 15.

1. Drive our born enemies away, O Agni; drive from us foes unborn, O Jātavedas. | Graciously-minded, free from anger, bless us: may we enjoy my firm thrice-guarding shelter. | Drive off with might our foemen born and living: keep off these yet unborn, O Jātavedas. | Benevolent in thought and spirit bless us. May we remain alive: drive off our foemen. || 3. The Sixteenfold Stoma, strength and wealth. The Forty-fourth Stoma, splendour and wealth. | Apsas art thou, the complement of Agni. As such may all the Gods greet thee with praises. | Enriched with songs of praise, Pṛishṭhas, and butter, sit here and give us wealth with store of children. || 4. Course metre. Space metre. Happy metre, Encompassing metre. Covering metre. Mind metre. Expanse metre. River metre. Sea metre. Water metre. Kakubh metre. Trikakubh metre. Kāvya metre. Aṅkupa metre Aksharapaṅkti metre. Padapaṅkti metre. Vishṭārapaṅkti metre. Kshurabhrāja metre. || 5. Covering metre. Clothing metre. Collecting metre. Parting metre. Bṛihat metre. Rathantara metre, Group metre. Vivadha metre. Swallower metre. Bright metre. Saṃstup metre. Anushṭubh metre. Course metre. Space metre. Vigour metre. Vigour-giving metre. Emulating metre. Spacious metre, Inaccessible metre. Slow metre. Aṅkāṅka metre. || 6. With the ray for truth quicken thou truth. With advance by duty quicken duty. With following by heaven quicken heaven. With union by middle air quicken middle air. With Pratidhi by Earth quicken Earth. With support by rain quicken rain. With blowing away by day quicken day. With following by eight quicken night. With clarified butter by the Vasus quicken the Vasus. With perception by the Ādityas quicken the Ādityas || 7. With the thread by prosperity quicken prosperity. With the creeper by revelation quicken revelation. With refreshment by plants quicken plants. With the best by bodies quicken bodies. With the invigorating by religious study quicken religious study. With the victorious by brilliance quicken brilliance. || 8. Thou art Pratipad, for Pratipad thee. Thou art Anupad, for Anupad thee. Thou art Sampad, for Sampad thee. Thou art brilliance, for brilliance thee. || 9. Trivṛit (triple) art thou, thee for Trivṛit. Pravṛit art thou, thee for Pravṛit. Vivṛit art thou, thee for Vivṛit. Savṛit art thou, thee for Savṛit. Thou art attack, thee for attack. Thou art concurrence, thee for concurrence. Thou art ascent, thee for ascent. Thou art upstriding, thee for upstriding. With Energy as over-lord quicken food-essence. || 10. Thou art the Queen, the Eastern region. The bright Vasus are thine overlords. Agni is thy warder-off of hostile weapons. May the Trivṛit Stoma assist thee on earth. The Ājya Uktha fix thee firmly against slipping. The Rathantara Sāman establish thee in the sky for secure station. May the first-born Ṛishis extend thee among the Gods by the measure and amplitude of heaven. May this Disposer and the Over-Lord extend thee. May all, concordant, settle thee on the ridge of heaven in the world of Svarga. || 11. Thou art Far-ruling, the Southern region. The bright Rudras are thine over-lords. Indra is thy warder-off of arrows. May the Pañchadaśa Stoma support thee on earth. The Prauga Uktha fix thee firmly against slipping. The Bṛihat Sāman establish thee in the sky, etc. (the rest as in 10). || 12. Thou art Universal Ruler, the Western region. The Ādityas are thine over-lords. Varuṇa is thy warder-off of missiles. The Saptadaśa Stoma support thee on earth. The Marutvatīya Uktha fix thee firmly against slipping. The Vairūpa Sāman establish thee, etc. (as above). || 13. Thou art Independent Ruler, the Northern region. (The

rest is identical with 12, with the substitution of Marutas ... Soma .... Viṃśa Stoma ... Niṣhkevalya Uktha.... Vairāja Sāman for the corresponding names). || 14. Thou art Lady-Paramount, the Lofty region. (The rest as above, Viśvedevas .. Brihaspati ...Triṇava and Trayastriṃśa Stomas ... Vaiśvadeva and Māruta Ukthas ... Śākvara and Raivata Sāmans being substituted for the corresponding names. || 15. This one in front, golden-tressed, with sunbeams; the leader of his host and his chieftain are Rathagritsa and Rathaujas, and Puñjikasthalā: and Kratusthalā his Apsarases. Biting animals are his weapon, homicide his missile weapon; to them be homage: may they protect us, may they have mercy upon us. In their jaws we place the man whom we hate and who hates us. || 16. This one on the right, the Omnific; the leader of his host and his chieftain are Rathasvana and Rathechitra, and Menakā and Sahajanyā his Apsarases. Yātudhānas are his weapon, Rākṣhasas his missile weapon; to them be homage, etc. (as in 15). || 17. This one behind, the All-comprising; the leader of his host and his chieftain are Rathaprota and Asamaratha, and Pramlochantī and Anumlochantī are his Apsarases. Tigers are his weapon, Serpents his missile weapon; to them be homage, etc. || 18. This one on the left, Lord of uninterrupted riches; the leader of his host and his chieftain are Tārkṣhya and Ariṣhtanemi, and Viśvāchī and Ghritāchī his Apsarases. Water is his weapon, wind his missile weapon; to them be homage, etc. || 19. This one above, Wealth-giver; the leader of his host and his chieftain are Senajit and Suṣhena, and Urvaśī and Pūrvachitti his Apsarases. Thundering is his weapon and lightning his missile weapon; to them be homage, etc. || 20. Agni is head and height of heaven, the Master of the earth is he. He quickeneth the waters' seed. || 21. This Agni is the Master of spoil thousandfold and hundredfold, the sapient one, the head of wealth. || 22. Agni, Atharvan brought thee forth by rubbing from the lotus-leaf, the head of Viśva, of the Priest. || 23. Guide of the rite art thou and of the region to which with thine auspicious teams thou tendest. | Thy light-bestowing head to heaven thou liftest, making thy tongue oblation-bearer, Agni. || 24. Agni is wakened by the people's fuel to meet the Dawn who cometh like a milch-cow. | Like young trees shooting up on high their branches his flames are rising to the vault of heaven. || 25. To him adorable, sage, strong and mighty we have sung forth our song of praise and homage. | Gaviṣhṭhira hath raised with prayer to Agni this laud far-reaching as the gold in heaven. || 26. Here by ordainers was this God appointed first Invoker, best at worship, to be praised at rites; | Whom Apnavāna and the Bhṛigus caused to shine bright-coloured in the wood, spreading to every house. || 27. The watchful Guardian of the people hath been born, Agni the very strong, for fresh prosperity. | With oil upon his face, with high heaven-touching flame, he shineth splendidly, pure for the Bhāratas. || 28. Agni, Aṅgirasas discovered thee what time thou layest hidden, fleeing back from wood to wood. | Thou by attrition art produced as conquering, might, and men, O Aṅgiras, call thee the Son of Strength. || 29. Offer to Agni, O my friends, your seemly food, your seemly praise; | To him supremest o'er the folk, the Son of Strength, the Mighty Lord. || 30. Thou, mighty Agni, gatherest up all that is precious for thy friend: | Bring us all treasure as thou art enkindled in libation's place. || 31. O Agni, loved of many, thou of fame most wondrous, in their homes | Men call on thee whose hair is flame to be the bearer of their gifts. || 32. With this my reverent hymn I call Agni for you, the Son of Strength, | Dear, wisest envoy, served with noble sacrifice, immortal messenger of all. || 33. Immortal messenger of all, immortal messenger of all, | His two red steeds, all-cherishing; he harnesseth: let him, well-worshipped, urge them fast. || 34. Let him well-worshipped urge them fast, let him well-worshipped urge them fast. | Then hath the sacrifice good prayer and happy end, and heavenly gift of wealth to men. || 35. O Agni, thou who art the Lord of wealth in kine, the Son of Strength, | Vouchsafe to us, O Jātavedas, high renown. || 36. He, Agni, kindled, good and wise, must be exalted in our song: | Shine, thou of many forms, shine radiantly on us. || 37. O Agni, shining of thyself by night and when the morning breaks, | Burn, thou whose teeth are sharp, against the Rākṣhasas || 38. May Agni, worshipped, bring us bliss, may the gift, Blessed One! and sacrifice bring bliss, | Yea, may our praises bring us bliss. || 39. Yea, may our praises bring us bliss. Show forth the mind that brings success in war with fiends, wherewith thou conquerest in fights: || 40. Wherewith thou conquerest in fights. Bring

down the many firm hopes of our enemies, and let us vanquish with thine aid. || 41. I value Agni, that good Lord, the home to which the kind return; | Whom fleet-foot coursers seek as home, and strong enduring steeds as home. Bring food to those who sing thy praise. || 42. 'Tis Agni whom we laud as good, to whom the milch-kine come in herds, | To whom the coursers swift of foot, to whom our well-born princes come. Bring food to those who sing thy praise. || 43. Thou, brilliant God, within thy mouth warmest both ladles of the oil. | So fill us also in our hymns abundantly, O Lord of Strength. Bring food to those who sing thy praise. || 44. Agni, with lauds this day may we bring thee that which thou lovest, | Right judgment, like a horse, with our devotions. || 45. For thou hast ever been the car-driver, Agni, of noble | Strength, lofty sacrifice, and rightful judgment. || 46. Through these our praises come thou to meet us, bright as the sunlight, | O Agni, well-disposed, with all thine aspects. || 47. Agni I hold as Herald, the munificent, the gracious Son of Strength who knoweth all that live, as holy singer knowing all; | Lord of fair rites, a God with form erected, turning to the Gods, | He, when the flame hath sprung forth from the sacred oil, the offered fatness, longeth for it with his glow. || 48. O Agni, be our nearest Friend, be thou a kind deliverer and a gracious Friend. | Come as good Agni, come as excellent and give us wealth most splendidly renowned. | To thee then, O most bright, O radiant God, we come with prayer for happiness for our friends. || 49. With what devotion, winning light, the Ṛiṣhis came, kindling Agni, to the Holy session, | Even with that in heaven I establish Agni whom men call him whose sacred grass is scattered. || 50. Gods, let us follow him with wives beside us, with sons, with brothers, with our gold adornments, | Grasping the sky up in the world of virtue, on the third height, the luminous realm of heaven. || 51. This Agni mounted up to Speech's Centre, Lord of the Brave, observant, ever-active. | Laid on the back of Earth, may he, resplendent, cast under foot those who would fight against us. || 52. May this most manly Agni, strength-bestower, giver of thousands, shine with care that fails not. | Resplendent in the middle of the water, make thine approach to the celestial mansions. || 53. Make him go forth from all sides: meet, Approach ye. O Agni, make the paths for Godward travel. | Making the Parents young with life's renewal, the out spun thread in thee have they extended. || 54. Wake up, O Agni, thou, and keep him watchful. Wish and fruition, meet, and he, together. | In this and in the loftier habitation be seated, All-Gods! and the Sacrificer. || 55. Convey our sacrifice to heaven that it may reach the God with that | Whereby thou, Agni, bearest wealth in thousands and all precious things. || 56. This is thine ordered place of birth whence sprung to life thou shonest forth. | Knowing this, Agni, rise thou up and cause our riches to increase. || 57. Tapa, Tapasya, pair of Dewy Seasons: thou art, etc. (as in 13:25). || 58. On the sky's back may Parameṣhṭhin lay thee, etc. (as in 14:14). | Thy Lord is Sūrya, etc. (as in 14:14). || 59. Repeated from 12:54. || 60. Repeated from 12:55. || 61. Repeated from 12:56. || 62. Like a horse neighing, eager for the pasture, when he hath stepped forth from the great enclosure: | Then the wind following blows upon his splendour, and, straight, the path is black which thou hast travelled. || 63. In Āyu's seat I set thee, in the shadow of the protector in the heart of Ocean, | Thee luminous, bright with eyes, thee who illumest the sky, the earth, and air's broad realm between them. || 64. On the sky's back may Parameṣhṭhin set thee, etc. (as in 14:12, substituting sky for air and Sūrya for Vāyu). || 65. Thou art the measure of a thousand. Thou art the representative of a thousand. Thou art the equivalent of a thousand. Thou art worth a thousand. Thee for a thousand.

Adhyāya 16.

1. Homage be paid unto thy wrath, O Rudra, homage to thy shaft: to thy two arms be homage paid. || 2. With that auspicious form of thine, mild, Rudra! pleasant to behold, | Even with that most blessed form, look, Mountain-haunter! here on us. || 3. The shaft which, Mountain-haunter, thou art holding in thy hand to shoot, | Make that auspicious, Mountain-Lord! Injure not man nor moving thing. || 4. O Dweller on the Mountain, we salute thee with auspicious hymn; | That all, yea, all our people may be healthy and well-satisfied. || 5. The Advocate, the first divine Physician, hath defended us. | Crushing all serpents, drive away all Yātudhānīs down below. || 6. That most auspicious One whose hue is coppery and red and

brown, | And those, the Rudras who maintain their station in the regions, who surround him in a thousand bands, of these we deprecate the wrath. || 7. May he who glides away, whose neck is azure, and whose hue is red, | He whom the herdsmen, whom the girls who carry water have beheld, may he when seen be kind to us. || 8. Homage to him the Azure-nested, the thousand-eyed, the bountiful, | Yea, and his spirit ministers—to them I offer reverence. || 9. Loosen thy bowstring, loosen it from thy bow's two extremities, | And cast away, O Lord Divine, the arrows that are in thy hand. || 10. Now stringless be Kapardin's bow, his quiver hold no pointed shaft. | The shafts he had have perished and the sheath that held his sword is bare. || 11. Thy weapon, O Most Bountiful, the bow that resteth in thy hand,— | With that, deprived of power to harm, protect thou us on every side. || 12. So may the arrow of thy bow, in all directions, pass us by, | And in a place remote from us lay thou the quiver that thou hast. || 13. Having unbent thy how O thou hundred-eyed, hundred-quivered One! | And dulled thy pointed arrows' heads, be kind and gracious unto us. || 14. To thy fierce weapon, now unstrung, be reverent obeisance paid. | Homage be paid to both thine arms, and to thy bow be reverence! || 15. Do thou no injury to great or small of us, harm not the growing boy, harm not the full grown man. | Slay not a sire among us, slay no mother here, and to our own dear bodies, Rudra! do no harm. || 16. Harm us not in our seed or in our progeny, harm us not in our life or in our cows or steeds. | Slay not our heroes in the fury of their wrath. We with oblations ever call on only thee. || 17. Homage to the golden-armed leader of hosts, lord of the regions, to the trees with their green tresses, to the Lord of beasts be homage; homage to him whose sheen is like green grass, homage to the radiant Lord of paths, homage to the golden-haired wearer of the sacrificial cord, homage to the Lord of the well-endowed. || 18. Homage to the brown-hued piercer, to the Lord of food be homage. Homage to Bhava's weapon, homage to the Lord of moving things! homage to Rudra whose bow is bent to slay, to the Lord of fields homage, homage to the charioteer who injures, none, to the Lord of forests be homage. || 19. Homage to the red architect, to the Lord of trees homage! Homage to him who stretched out the earth, to him who gives relief be homage. Homage to the Lord of Plants, homage to the prudent merchant! Homage to the Lord of bushes, to the shouting Lord of foot-soldiers who makes foes weep be homage. || 20. Homage to the runner at full stretch, to the Lord of ministering spirits, homage! Homage to the conquering, piercing Lord of assailing bands, homage to the towering sword-bearer, to the Lord of thieves homage! Homage to the gliding robber, to the roamer, to the Lord of forests homage! || 21. Homage to the cheat, to the arch-deceiver, to the Lord of stealers homage! Homage to the wearer of sword and quiver, to the Lord of robbers homage! Homage to the bolt-armed homicides, to the Lord of pilferers homage! Homage to the sword-bearers, to those who roam at night, to the Lord of plunderers homage! || 22. To the turban-wearing haunter of mountains, Lord of land-grabbers homage! Homage to you who bear arrows and to you who carry bows. Homage to you with bent bows, and to you who adjust your arrows, to you who draw the bow and to you who shoot be homage! || 23. Homage to you who let fly and to you who pierce, homage to you who sleep and to you who wake, homage to you who lie and to you who sit, homage to you who stand and to you who run. || 24. Homage to assemblies and to you lords of assemblies, homage to horses and to you masters of horses, homage to you hosts that wound and pierce, to you destructive armies with excellent bands be homage. || 25. Homage to the troops and to you lords of troops be homage. | Homage to the companies and to you lords of companies, homage. | Homage to sharpers and to you lords of sharpers, homage. | Homage to you the deformed, and to you who wear all forms, homage! || 26. Homage to armies and to you the leaders of armies, homage. | Homage to you car-borne and to you who are carless, homage. | Homage to the charioteers and to you drivers of horses, homage. | Homage to you the great and to you the small, homage. || 27. Homage to you carpenters, and to you chariot-makers homage. | Homage to you potters and to you blacksmiths, homage. | Homage to you Nishādas and to you Puñjishṭhas, homage. | Homage to you dog-leaders, and to you hunters, homage. || 28. Homage to dogs, and to you masters of dogs, homage. | Homage to Bhava, and to Rudra homage, homage to Śarva and to Paśupati, and to Nīlagrīva and Śitikaṇṭha, homage. || 29. Homage to him with braided hair and to him with shaven hair, homage! homage to the thousand-eyed and to him with a hundred bows, homage! | To the mountain-haunter and to Śipivishṭa, homage! | To the most bountiful, armed with arrows, homage! || 30. Homage to the short, and to the dwarf, homage, homage to the great and to the adult, homage! Homage to the full-grown and to the growing, to the foremost and to the first be homage. || 31. Homage to the swift, and to the active be homage, and to the hasty and to the rapid mover be homage! Homage to him who dwells in waves, and in still waters, to him who dwells in rivers and on islands. || 32. Homage to the eldest and to the youngest, to the first-born and to the last-born, homage! Homage to the middle-most and to the immature, to the lowest and to him who is in the depth, be homage! || 33. Homage to Sobhya and to the dweller in the magic amulet, homage! Homage to him who is allied to Yama, to him who prospers be homage! Homage to the famous and to the endmost, to him of the sown corn-land and to him of the threshing-floor be homage. || 31. Homage to him in woods and to him in bushes, homage! Homage to him as sound and to him as echo, homage! Homage to him with swift armies and to him with swift chariots, homage! Homage to the hero, and to him who rends asunder be homage. || 35. Homage to him who wears a helmet, and to him who wears a cuirass, homage! To him who wears mail and defensive armour, homage! To the renowned one and to him whose army is renowned be homage, to him who is in drums and to him who makes himself known by beating them. || 36. Homage to the bold one and to the prudent, homage to him who carries sword and quiver, homage to him who hath keen arrows and is armed with weapons, homage to him who hath good weapons and a good bow. || 37. Homage to him who dwells on paths and roads, homage to him who dwells in rugged spots and on the skirts of mountains, homage to him who dwells in water courses and lakes, homage to him who dwells in rivers and mores. || 38. Homage to him who dwells in wells and pits, homage to him who dwells in bright sky and sunlight. Homage to him who dwells in cloud and lightning, homage to him who dwells in rain and to him who dwells in fair weather. || 39. Homage to him who dwells in wind and to him who dwells in tempest, homage to the dweller in houses and to the house-protector. Homage to Soma and to Rudra, homage to the copper-coloured and to the ruddy One. || 40. Homage to the giver of weal, and to Paśupati, homage to the fierce and to the terrific. Homage to him who slays in front and to him who slays at a distance, homage to the slayer and to the frequent slayer, homage to the green-tressed trees, homage to the deliverer. || 41. Homage to the source of happiness and to the source of delight, homage to the causer of happiness and to the causer of delight, homage to the auspicious, homage to the most auspicious. || 42. Homage to him who is beyond and to him who is on this side, homage to him who crosses over and to him who crosses back. Homage to him who is in fords and on river banks, homage to him who is in tender grass and in foam. || 43. Homage to him who is in sand and to him who is in running water, homage to him who is on pebbly ground and to him who is where still water stands. Homage to him who wears braided hair and to him whose hair is smooth. Homage to him who is in deserts and to him who is on broad roads. || 44. Homage to him who is in herds of cattle and to him who is in cow-pens, homage to him who is on beds and to him who is in houses. Homage to him who is in hearts, and to him who is in whirlpools, homage to him who is in wells and to him who is in abysses. || 45. Homage to him who is in dry things and to him who is in green things. Homage to him who is in dust and to him who is in vapour. Homage to him who is in inaccessible places, homage to him who is in creeping plants, homage to him who is in the earth and to him who is in good soil. || 46. Homage to him who is in leaves and to him who is in the falling of leaves. Homage to him with the threatening voice and to him who slays, homage to him who troubles and to him who afflicts. Homage to you arrow-makers and to you bow-makers, homage to you sprinklers, to the hearts of the Gods. Homage to the discerners, homage to the destroyers; homage to the indestructible. || 47. Pursuer, Lord of Soma juice, thou cleaver, coloured blue and red, | Cleave not, destroy not one of these our children, nor of these our beasts, let nothing that is ours be sick. || 48. To the strong Rudra bring we these our songs of praise, to him the Lord of Heroes, with the braided hair, | That it be well with all our cattle and our men, that in this village all be healthy and well-fed. ‖ 49. Rudra, with that auspicious form of thine which healeth every day, | Auspicious, healer of disease, be kind to us that we may live. ‖ 50. May Rudra's missile turn aside and spare us, the great wrath of the impetuous One avoid us. | Turn, Bounteous God, thy strong bow from our princes, and be thou gracious to our seed and offspring. ‖ 51. Most bounteous, most auspicious, be auspicious, well inclined to us. | On some remotest tree lay down thy weapon. and clad in robe of skin approach, bearing thy bow come hitherward. ‖ 52. O Wound averter, purple-hued, to thee be homage, holy Lord! | May all those thousand darts of thine strike dead another one than us. ‖ 53. Thousands of thousands are the shafts, the missiles ready in thy hands: | Thou holy Lord, who hast the power, turn thou their points away from us. ‖ 54. Innumerable thousands are the Rudras on the face of earth: | Of all these Rudras we unbend the bows a thousand leagues away. ‖ 55. Bhavas there are above us in this mighty billowy sea of air, | Of all of these do we unbend, etc. ‖ 56. Rudras are dwelling in the sky, whose necks are blue, whose throats are white: | Of these do we unbend the bows a thousand leagues away from us. ‖ 57. Śarvas haunt realms beneath the earth—their necks are blue, their throats are white: | Of these, etc. ‖ 58. These, green like young grass, in the trees, with azure necks and purple hue, | Of those, etc. ‖ 59. Those, ministering spirits' lords, with no hair-tufts, with braided locks, | Of these, etc. ‖ 60. Those, the protectors of the paths, bringers of food, who fight for life. | Of these, etc. ‖ 61. Those who with arrows in their hand, and armed with words, frequent the fords, | Of these, etc. ‖ 62. Those who, inhabiting the food, vex men while drinking from their cups, etc. ‖ 63. Rudras so many and still more, lodged in the quarters of the sky, etc. ‖ 64. Homage to Rudras, those whose home is sky, whose arrows floods of rain. | To them ten eastward, southward ten, ten to the south, ten to the north, ten to the region uppermost! | To them be homage! May they spare and guard us. Within their jaws we lay the man who hates us and whom we abhor. ‖ 65. Homage to Rudras, those whose home is air, whose arrows is the rain. To them, etc. ‖ 66. Homage to Rudras, those whose home is earth, whose arrows is men's food. | To them be homage, etc.

Adhyāya 17.

1. The food and strength contained in stone and mountain, drink gathered from the plants and trees and waters, | That food and strength, Marutas! free-givers, grant us. | In the stone is thy hunger. In me is thy food. Let thy pain reach the man we hate. ‖ 2. O Agni, may these bricks be mine own milch kine: one, and ten, and ten tens, a hundred, and ten hundreds, a thousand, and ten thousand a myriad, and a hundred thousand, and a million, and a hundred millions, and an ocean middle and end, and a hundred thousand millions, and a billion. | May these bricks be mine own milch-kine in yonder world and in this world. ‖ 3. Ye are the Seasons, strengthening Law, fixed in due season, strengthening Law, | Called Splendid, dropping butter down and honey, yielders of every wish, imperishable. ‖ 4. With the lake's mantling need we robe thee, Agni: to us he purifying and auspicious. ‖ 5. With cold's investing garb we gird thee, Agni: to us be purifying and auspicious. ‖ 6. Descend upon the earth, the reed, the rivers: thou art the gall, O Agni, of the waters. | With them come hither, female Frog, and render this sacrifice of ours bright-hued, successful. ‖ 7. This is the place where waters meet; here is the gathering of the flood. | Let thy shaft burn others than us: be thou cleanser, propitious unto us. ‖ 8. O Agni, purifier, God, with splendour and thy pleasant tongue | Bring hither, and adore, the Gods. ‖ 9. So, Agni, purifying, bright, bring hither to our sacrifice, | To our oblation bring the Gods. ‖ 10. He who with purifying, eye-attracting form hath shone upon the earth as with the light of Dawn; | Who speeding on, as in the fleet steed's race, in fight, cometh untouched by age, as one athirst in heat. ‖ 11. Obeisance to thy wrath and glow! Obeisance to thy fiery flame! | Let thy shot missiles burn others than us: be thou cleanser, propitious unto us. ‖ 12. To him who dwells in man, Hail! To him who dwells in waters, Hail! | To him who dwells in sacred grass, Hail! To him who dwells in the wood, Hail! To him who finds the light, Hail! ‖ 13. Worshipful Gods of Gods who merit worship, those who sit down beside their yearly portion, | Let them who eat not sacrificial presents drink in this rite of honey and of butter. ‖ 14. Those Gods who have attained to Godhead over Gods, they who have led the way in this our holy work, | Without whose aid no body whatsoever moves, not on heaven's heights are they, nor on the face of earth. ‖ 15. Giver of breath, of out-breath, breath diffusive, giver of lustre, giving room and freedom, | Let thy shot missiles burn others than us: be thou cleanser, propitious unto us. ‖ 16. May Agni with his sharpened blaze cast down each fierce devouring fiend. | May Agni win us wealth by war. ‖ 17. He who sate down as Hotar priest, the Ṛishi, our Father offering, up all things existent | He, seeking with his wish a great possession, came among men on earth as archetypal. ‖ 18. What was the place whereon he took his station? What was it that upheld him? What the manner, | Whence Viśvakarman, seeing all, producing the earth, with mighty power disclosed the heavens? ‖ 19. He who hath eyes on all sides round about him, a mouth on all sides, arms and feet on all sides, | He the sole God, producing earth and heaven, weldeth them with his arms as wings together. ‖ 20. What was the tree, what wood in sooth produced it, from which they fashioned out the earth and heaven? | Ye thoughtful men, inquire within your spirit whereon he stood when he established all things. ‖ 21. Thine highest, lowest sacrificial natures, and these thy midmost here, O Viśvakarman, | Teach thou thy friends at sacrifice, O Blessed, and come thyself, exalted, to our worship. ‖ 22. Bring those, thyself exalted with oblation, O Viśvakarman, Earth and Heaven to worship. | Let enemies around us live in folly: here let us have a rich and liberal patron. | 23, 24. = 8:45, 46. ‖ 25. The Father of the eye, the Wise in spirit, created both these worlds submerged in fatness. | Then when the eastern ends were firmly fastened, the heavens and the earth were far extended. ‖ 26. Mighty in mind and power is Viśvakarman, Maker, Disposer, and most lofty Presence. | Their offerings joy in rich juice where they value One, only One beyond the Seven Ṛishis ‖ 27. Father who made us, he who, as Disposer, knoweth all races and all things existing, | Even he alone, the Deities' name-giver,—him other beings seek for information. ‖ 28. To him in sacrifice they offered treasures,—Ṛishis of old, in numerous troops, as singers, | Who, in the distant, near, and lower region, made ready all these things that have existence. ‖ 29. That which is earlier than this earth and heaven, before the Asuras and Gods had being, | What was the germ primeval which the waters received where the first Gods beheld each other? ‖ 30. The waters, they received that germ primeval wherein the Gods were gathered all together. | It rested set upon the Unborn's navel, that One wherein abide all things existing. ‖ 31. Ye will not find him who produced these creatures: another thing hath risen up among you. | Enwrapt in misty cloud, with lips that stammer, hymn-chanters wander and are discontented. ‖ 32. First was the God engendered, Viśvakarman: then the Gandharva sprang to life as second. | Third in succession was the plants' begetter: he laid the waters' germ in many places. ‖ 33. Swift, rapidly striking, like a bull who sharpens his horns, terrific, stirring up the people, | With eyes that close not, bellowing, Sole Hero, Indra subdued at once a hundred armies. ‖ 34. With him loud-roaring, ever watchful, Victor, bold, hard to overthrow, Rouser of battle, | Indra the Strong, whose hand bears arrows, conquer, ye warriors, now, now vanquish in the combat. ‖ 35. He rules with those who carry shafts and quivers, Indra who with his band brings hosts together, | Foe-conquering, strong of arm, the Soma-drinker, with mighty bow, shooting with well-laid arrows. ‖ 36. Bṛihaspati, fly with thy chariot hither, slayer of demons, driving off our foemen. | Be thou protector of our cars, destroyer, victor in battle, breaker-up of armies. ‖ 37. Conspicuous by thy strength, firm, foremost fighter, mighty and fierce, victorious, all-subduing, | The Son of Conquest, passing men and heroes, kine-winner, mount thy conquering car, O Indra. ‖ 38. Cleaver of stalls, kine-winner, armed with thunder, who quells an army and with might destroys it, | Follow him, brothers! quit yourselves like heroes, and like this Indra show your zeal and courage. ‖ 39. Piercing the cow-stalls with surpassing vigour, Indra, the pitiless Hero, wild with anger, | Victor in fight, unshaken and resistless,—may he protect our armies in our battles. ‖ 40. Indra guide these: Bṛihaspati precede them, the guerdon, and the sacrifice, and Soma; | And let the banded Marutas march in forefront of heavenly hosts that conquer and demolish. ‖ 41. Ours be the potent host of mighty Indra, King Varuṇa, and Marutas, and Ādityas | Uplifted is the shout of Gods who conquer, high-minded Gods who cause the worlds to tremble. ‖ 42. Bristle thou up, O Bounteous Lord, our weapons: excite the spirits of my warring heroes. | Urge on the strong steeds' might, O Vṛitra-

slayer, and let the din of conquering cars go upward. ‖ 43. May Indra aid us when our flags are gathered: victorious be the arrows of our army. | May our brave men of war prevail in battle. Ye Gods protect us in the shout of onset. ‖ 44. Bewildering the senses of our foemen, seize thou their bodies and depart, O Apvā. | Attack them, set their hearts on fire and burn them: so let our foes abide in utter darkness. ‖ 45. Loosed from the bowstring fly awry, O Arrow, sharpened by our prayer. | Go to the foemen, strike them home, and let not one of them escape. ‖ 46. Advance, O heroes, win the day. May Indra be your sure defence. | Exceeding mighty be your arms, that none may wound or injure you. ‖ 47. That army of our enemies, O Marutas, that comes against us with its might, contending, | Meet ye and wrap it in unwelcome darkness so that not one of them may know another. ‖ 48. There where the flights of arrows fall like boys whose locks are yet unshorn, | May Indra, may Bṛihaspati, may Aditi protect us well, protect us well through all our days. ‖ 49. Thy vital parts I cover with thine armour: with immortality King Soma clothe thee. | Varuṇa give thee what is more than ample, and in thy triumph may the Gods be joyful. ‖ 50. Worshipped with butter, Agni, lead this man to high preeminence. | Vouchsafe him growth of riches and multiply him with progeny. ‖ 51. Indra, lead him to eminence: controller of his foes be he. | Vouchsafe him lustre: let him give their sacred portions to the Gods. ‖ 52. The man within whose house we pay oblation, Indra, prosper him. | May the Gods bless and comfort him, they and this Brahmaṇaspati ‖ 53. May the All-Gods, O Agni, bear and lift thee upward with their thoughts. | Fair to be looked on, rich in light, he thou propitious unto us. ‖ 54. May the Five Regions guard, divine, our worship, Goddesses chasing lack of thought and hatred, | Giving the Sacrificer growth of riches. Let sacrifice be based on growth of riches. ‖ 55. Inspirited above enkindled Agni, adorable, winged with hymns, was it accepted, | When the Gods offered sacrifice with viands, circling the heated cauldron, paving worship. ‖ 56. Lord of a hundred draughts. benign, God-serving—to him divine, establisher, protector, | The Gods approached the sacrifice, encircling. Gods for the Gods stood fain for sacred service. ‖ 57. When the fourth sacrifice reaches the oblation, accepted offering which hath been made ready, fit for the Immolator's sacrificing, | Thence bless us prayers and holy recitations! ‖ 58. Savitar, golden-hued, hath lifted eastward, bright with the sunbeams, his eternal lustre, | He at whose furtherance wise Pūṣhan marches surveying all existence like a herdsman. ‖ 59. He sits, the measurer, in the midst of heaven, filling the two world-halves and air's mid-region. | He looks upon the rich far-spreading pastures between the eastern and the western limit. ‖ 60. Steer, Sea, Red Bird with strong wings, he hath entered the dwelling-place of the Primeval Father. | A gay-hued Stone set in the midst of heaven, he hath gone forth and guards the air's two limits. ‖ 61. All sacred songs have glorified Indra expansive as the sea, | The best of warriors borne on cars, the Lord, the Very Lord of strength. ‖ 62. May God-invoking sacrifice bring the Gods hitherward to us. | May bless-invoking sacrifice bring the Gods hitherward to us. | May Agni, God, make offering and hither bring the Gods to us. ‖ 63. May the abundant growth of wealth with elevation lift me up, | And with his subjugating power may Indra keep my foemen down. ‖ 64. Upraising and depression and devotion may the Gods increase. | May Indra, too, and Agni drive my foes away to every side. ‖ 65. Go ye by Agni to the sky bearing the Ukhya in your hands. | Reaching the heights of sky and heaven stay intermingled with the Gods. ‖ 66. Agni, go forward to the eastern region, well-skilled, be here the fire in front of Agni. | Illuming all the quarters, shine with splendour: supply with food our quadrupeds and bipeds. ‖ 67. From earth to air's mid-region have I mounted, and from mid-air ascended up to heaven. | From the high pitch of heaven's cope I came into the world of light. ‖ 68. Mounting the sky they look not round: they rise to heaven through both the worlds— | Sages who span the sacrifice that pours its stream on every side. ‖ 69. Foremost of those who seek the Gods come forward, thou who art eye of Gods and men, O Agni. | Accordant with the Bhṛigus, fain to worship, to heaven in safety go the Sacrificers. ‖ 70. Night and Dawn, different in hue, accordant, etc., as in 12:2. ‖ 71. O Agni, thousand-eyed and hundred-headed, thy breaths are hundred, thy through-breaths a thousand. | Thou art the Lord of thousandfold possessions. To thee; for strength, may we present oblation. ‖ 72. Thou art the Bird of goodly wing: be seated on the ridge of earth. | Fill air's mid-region with thy glow, supporting with thy light the sky, confirm the quarters with thy sheen. ‖ 73. Receiving offerings, fair of aspect, eastward be duly seated in thy place, O Agni. | In this the more exalted habitation be seated All-Gods and the Sacrificer. ‖ 74. That wondrous all-mankind-embracing favour of Savitar, choice-worthy, I solicit, | Even his which Kaṇva wont to milk, the mighty, the teeming Cow who yields a thousand milk-streams. ‖ 75. May we adore thee in thy loftiest birth place, Agni! with praise-songs in thy lower station. | The place whence those hast issued forth I worship. In thee, well kindled, have they paid oblations ‖ 76. Shine thou before us, Agni, well enkindled, with flame, most youthful God, that never fadeth. | Unceasing unto thee come sacred viands. ‖ 77. Agni, this day with lands, etc., as in 15:44. ‖ 78. I dedicate the thought with mind and butter so that the Gods may come who love oblation, strengthening Law, | To Viśvakarman, Lord of all the earth, I offer up day after day the inviolable sacrifice. ‖ 79. Seven fuel logs hast thou, seven tongues, O Agni, seven Ṛishis hast thou, seven beloved mansions. | Seven-priests in sevenfold manner pay thee worship. Fill full—All-hail to thee!—seven wombs with butter. ‖ 80. Purely-Bright, Wonderfully-Bright, Really-Bright, All-Luminous, | Bright, Law's-Protector, Safe-from-Ill; ‖ 81. Such, Other-Looking, Equal, Similar, Measured, Commensurate, Jointly-Bearing-up. ‖ 82. Right, Real, Firm, Strong-to-Support, Bearer, Disposer, Manager. ‖ 83. Winner-of-Right, Winner-of-Truth, Host-Conquering, Lord-of-Goodly-Host, | Whose-Friends-are-Near-at-Hand, Whose-Banded-Enemies-are-Far-Away: ‖ 84. To day in this our sacrifice be present, Such, Looking-Thus, Same, Similar-in-appearance, | Measured, Commensurate, Joint-Bearers, Marutas! ‖ 85. Self-Powerful, Voracious-One, Kin-to-the-Sun, The House-holder, | Play-Lover, Mighty, Conqueror. | Fierce, Terrible, The Resonant, The Roaring. Victorious, Assailant, and Dispeller, All-Hail! ‖ 86. The Marutas, clans divine, became the followers of Indra; as | The Marutas, clans divine, became the followers of Indra, so | May clans divine and human he the Sacrificer's followers. ‖ 87. Drink in the middle of the flood, O Agni, this breast stored full of sap, teeming with water. | Welcome this fountain redolent of sweetness. O Courser, enter those thy watery dwelling. ‖ 88. Oil hath been mixed: oil is his habitation. In oil he rests: oil is his proper province. | Come as thy wont is. O thou Steer, rejoice thee. Bear off the oblation duly consecrated. ‖ 89. Forth from the ocean sprang the wave of sweetness: together with the stalk it turned to Amṛita, | That which is holy oil's mysterious title: but the Gods' tongue is truly Amities centre. ‖ 90. Let us Declare aloud the name of Ghṛita, and at this sacrifice held it up with homage. | So let the Brahman hear the praise we utter. This hath the four-horned Buffalo emitted. ‖ 91. Four are his horns, three are the feet that bear him: his heads are two, his hands are seven in number. | Bound with a triple bond the Bull roars loudly: the mighty God hath entered into mortals. ‖ 92. That oil in triple shape the Gods discovered laid down within the Cow, concealed by Paṇis. | Indra produced one shape, Sūrya another: by their own power they formed the third from Vena. ‖ 93. From inmost reservoir in countless channels flow down these rivers which the foe beholds not. | I look upon the streams of oil descending, and lo! the Golden Reed is there among them. ‖ 94. Like rivers our libations flow together, cleansing themselves in inmost heart and spirit. | The streams of holy oil pour swiftly downward like the wild beasts that fly before the bowman. ‖ 95. As rushing down the rapids of a river, flow swifter than the wind the vigorous currents, | The streams of oil in swelling fluctuation like a red courser bursting through the fences. ‖ 96. Like women at a gathering fair to look on and gently smiling, they incline to Agni. | The streams of holy oil attain the fuel, and Jātavedas joyfully receives them. ‖ 97. As maidens deck themselves with gay adornment to join the bridal feast, I now behold them. | Where Soma flows and sacrifice is ready, thither the streams of holy oil are running. ‖ 98. Send to our eulogy a herd of cattle: bestow upon us excellent possessions. | Bear to the Gods the sacrifice we offers the streams of oil flow pure and full of sweetness. ‖ 99. The universe depends upon thy power and might within the sea, within the heart, within all life. | May we attain that sweetly-flavoured wave of thine, brought, at this gathering, o'er the surface of the floods.

Adhyāya 18.

1. May my strength and my gain, and my inclination and my influence, and my thought and my mental power, and my praise and my fame, and my renown and my light, and my heaven prosper by sacrifice. ‖ 2. May my breathing and my out-breathing, and my through-breathing and my vital spirit, and my thought and my reflection, and my voice and my mind, and my eye and my ear, and my ability and my strength prosper by sacrifice. ‖ 3. May my energy and my force, and my self and my body, and my shelter and my shield, and my limbs and my bones, and my joints and my members, and my life and my old age prosper by sacrifice. ‖ 4. May my pre-eminence and my overlordship, and my wrath and my angry passion, and my violence and my impetuosity, and my victorious power and my greatness, and my breadth and my width, and my height and my length, and my increase and my improvement prosper by sacrifice. ‖ 5. May my truth and my faith, and my cattle and my wealth, and my goods and my pleasure, and my play and my enjoyment, and my children and my future children, and my hymn and my pious act prosper by sacrifice. ‖ 6. May my religious rite and my immortality, and my freedom from consumption and my freedom from disease, and my life and my longevity, and my freedom from enemies and my freedom from danger, and my happiness and my lying down, and my fair dawn and my fair day prosper by sacrifice. ‖ 7. May my controller and my supporter, and my security and my firmness, and my goods and my pleasure, and my knowledge and my understanding, and my begetting and my propagation, and my plough and my harrow prosper by sacrifice. ‖ 8. May my welfare and my comfort, and what I hold dear and what I desire, and my love and my gratification, and my enjoyment and my substance, and my happiness and my felicity, and my higher bliss and my fame prosper by sacrifice. ‖ 9. May my vigour and my pleasantness, and my milk and my sap, and my butter and my honey, and my meal in company and my drinking in company, and my ploughing and my husbandry, and my superiority and my pre-eminence prosper by sacrifice. ‖ 10. May my wealth and my property, and my prosperity and my growth, and my pervading power and my lordship, and my abundance and my greater abundance, and my bad harvest and my unwasted crop, and my food and my satiety prosper by sacrifice. ‖ 11. May my gain and my future gain, and what I have and what I shall have, and my good road and my good path, and my success and my succeeding, and my achievement and my contrivance, and my thought and my good counsel prosper by sacrifice. ‖ 12. May my rice-plants and my barley, and my beans and my sesamum, and my kidney-beans and my vetches, and my millet and my Panicum Milliaceum, and my Panicum Frumentaceum and my wild rice, and my wheat and my lentils prosper by sacrifice. ‖ 13. May my stone and my clay, and my hills and my mountains, and my pebbles and my trees, and my gold and my bronze, and my copper and my iron, and my lead and my tin prosper by sacrifice. ‖ 14. May my fire and my water, and my creepers and my plants, and lily plants with culture-ripened fruit and my plants with fruit ripened without culture, and my domestic animals and my wild animals, and my substance and my future substance, and my belongings and my power be produced by sacrifice. ‖ 15. May my treasure and my dwelling, and my religious service and my ability to perform it, and my object and my course, and my way and my going prosper by sacrifice. ‖ 16. May my Agni and my Indra, and my Soma and my Indra, and my Savitar and my Indra, and my Sarasvatī and my Indra, and my Pūṣhan and my Indra prosper by sacrifice. ‖ 17. May my Mitra and my Indra, and my Varuṇa and my Indra, and my Dhātar and my Indra, and my Marutas and my Indra, and my All-Gods and my Indra prosper by sacrifice. ‖ 18. May my earth and my Indra, and my Air and my Indra, and my Sky and my Indra, and my Half-months and my Indra, and my Lunar Mansions and my Indra, and my Sky-regions and my Indra prosper by sacrifice. ‖ 19. May my Aṃśu and my Raśmi, and my Adhipati and my Upāṃśu, and my Antaryāma and my Aindra-Vāyava, and my Maitrāvaruṇa, and my Āśvina and my Pratiprasthāna, and my Śukra and my Manthin proper by sacrifice. ‖ 20. May my Āgrayaṇa and my Vaiśvadeva, and my Dhruvā and my Vaiśvānara, and my Aindrāgna and my Mahāvaiśvadeva, and my Marutvatīya and my Niṣhkevalya, and my Sāvitra and my Sārasvata, and my Pātnīvata and my Hāriyojana prosper by sacrifice. ‖ 21. May my ladles and my cups, and my Vāyu, vessels and my Soma reservoirs, and my pressing-stones and my two press-boards, and my Pūtabhṛit and my Ādhavanīya, and my altar and altar-grass, and my Avabhṛitha and my cries of Good-speed prosper by sacrifice. ‖ 22. May my Agni and my charms, and my Arka and my Sūrya, and my Prāṇa and my Aśvamedha, and my Pṛithivī and my Aditi, and my Diti and my Sky, and my fingers, powers, and sky-regions prosper by sacrifice. ‖ 23. May my vow and my seasons, and my austere devotion, and my day and night, thighs and knees, and two Great Rathantaras prosper by sacrifice. ‖ 24. May me One and my Three, and my Three and my Five, and my Five and my Seven (and similarly up to thirty-three) prosper by sacrifice. ‖ 25. May my Four and my Eight and my Twelve (and similarly up to forty-eight) prosper by sacrifice ‖ 26. May my eighteen-months steer and my eighteen-months heifer, and my two-year bull and cow (and similarly up to four-year) prosper by sacrifice. ‖ 27. May my six-year bull and my six-year cow, and my bull and my barren cow, and my young bull and my calf-slipping cow, and my ox and my milch-cow prosper by sacrifice. ‖ 28. To strength, Hail! To Gain, Hail! To After-born, Hail! To Power, Hail! To Vasu, Hail! To the Lord of Days, Hail! To the Failing Day, Hail! To the Failing Sprung from the Transitory, Hail! To the Transitory sprung from the Final, Hail! To the Final Mundane, Hail! To the Lord of the World, Hail! To the Sovereign Lord, Hail! To Prajāpati, Hail! This is thy kingdom. Thou art a guiding controller for the friend. Thee for vigour, thee for rain, thee for the sovereign lordship of creatures. ‖ 29. May life succeed through sacrifice. May life-breath thrive by sacrifice. May the eye thrive by sacrifice. May the ear thrive by sacrifice. May the voice thrive by sacrifice. May the mind thrive by sacrifice. May the self thrive by sacrifice. May Brahma thrive by sacrifice. May light succeed by sacrifice. May heaven succeed by sacrifice. May the hymn thrive by sacrifice. May sacrifice thrive by sacrifice; And laud and sacrificial text, and verse of praise and Sāman chant, The Bṛihat and Rathantara. | Gods, we have gone to light. We have become the children of Prajāpati. We have become immortal. ‖ 30. In gain of wealth we celebrate, etc.: = 9:5. ‖ 31. This day come all the Marutas, all to aid us! Let all the fires be thoroughly enkindled. | May the All-Gods come hither with protection. May we possess all property and riches. ‖ 32. May our strength fill the regions seven, fill the four distant places full. | Here may our riches guard us with the All-Gods in the gain of wealth. ‖ 33. May strength today procure for us donations strength range the Gods together with the Seasons. | Yea, strength hath made me rich in store of heroes. As lord of strength may I gain all the regions. ‖ 34. Strength be before us, in the midst among us. May strength exalt the Gods with our oblation. | Yea, strength hath made me rich in store of heroes. As lord of strength may I gain all the regions. ‖ 35. With milk of Pṛithivī do I unite me, unite myself with waters and with plants. | As such may I gain strength, O Agni. ‖ 36. Store milk in earth and milk in plants, milk in the sky and milk in air. | Teeming with milk for me he all the regions. ‖ 37. Thee by the radiant Savitar's impulsion, with arms of Aśvins, with the hands of Pūṣhan, | Controlled by Vāk Sarasvatī's Controller, with Agni's sole dominion I besprinkle. ‖ 38. Maintainer of Law, true by nature, Agni is the Gandharva. | The plants are his Apsarases, namely Delights. May he protect this our Priesthood and Nobility. To him All-hail! Ave! To those All-hail! ‖ 39. The Conjoined, Viśvasāman, Sūrya is the Gandharva. His motes are his Apsarases, Swift-moving. May he protect, etc., as in 38. ‖ 40. The Highly-Blessed, the Moon whose rays are like the Sun's, is the Gandharva. The Asterisms are his Apsarases, Luminous. May he protect, etc. ‖ 41. The Quick, All-reaching, Wind is the Gandharva. The Waters are his Apsarases, named Energies. May he protect, etc. ‖ 42. The Protecting, Strong-winged, Sacrifice is the Gandharva. Guerdons are his Apsarases, called Praisers. May he protect, etc. ‖ 43. The Lord of Creatures, Omnific, Mind is the Gandharva. Ṛichas and Sāmans are his Apsarases, called Wishings. May he protect, etc. ‖ 44. Lord of the World, Prajāpati, whose are the homes above and here, | Give great protection unto these, the Priesthood and Nobility. ‖ 45. Thou art the vapoury sea that giveth moisture. Blow on me, thou, healthful and blessing-laden. | Thou art the Marutas' own, the band of Marutas. Blow on me, etc. | Seeker of aid art thou, receiving worship. Blow on me, etc. ‖ 46. Thy lights, O Agni, in the Sun, etc., as in 13:22. ‖ 47. Lights of yours in the Sun, O Gods, etc., as in 13:23. ‖ 48. Give lustre to our holy priests, set lustre in our ruling chiefs | Lustre to Vaiśyas, Śūdras: give, through lustre; lustre unto

me. ‖ 49. I ask this of thee with my prayer, adoring: thy worshipper asks this with his oblations. | Varuṇa, stay thou here and be not angry: steal not our life from us, O thou Wide-Ruler. ‖ 50. Heaven-like is Warmth, Hail! Heaven-like is Arka, Hail! Heaven-like is the Bright One, Hail! Heaven-like is Light, Hail! Heaven-like is Sūrya, Hail! ‖ 51. I yoke with power and flowing butter Agni, divine, strong-pinioned, great with vital vigour. | Through him may we approach the Bright One's station, ascending to the loftiest sky, to heaven. ‖ 52. With these thy two ne'er-wasting feathered pinions wherewith thou drivest fiends away, O Agni, | Let us fly to the regions of the pious whither have gone the first-born ancient Ṛiṣhis ‖ 53. The Drop, the powerful, the falcon, righteous, impetuous bird borne on his golden pinions, | Great, steadfast, settled in the habitation—to thee be reverence! Forbear to harm thee! ‖ 54. Centre of earth, heaven's head art thou, essence of waters and of plants. | Eternal, far spread refuge. Homage to the Path! ‖ 55. Attached thou standest at the head of all the world. Thy heart is in the sea, thy life is in the floods. Give water: cleave the reservoir. | Help us with rain sent from the sky, Parjanya, firmament, or earth. ‖ 56. By Bhṛigus and by Vasus hath prayer-granting sacrifice been paid. | Come, Wealth, into the house of him our dear, our well-beloved one. ‖ 57. May Agni, served with sacrifice and gifts, protect our offered food: | This homage be Good-speed to Gods! ‖ 58. That which hath flowed from purpose or from judgment, or gathered from the wind or from the vision, | Follow ye to the region of the pious whither have gone the first-born ancient Ṛiṣhis ‖ 59. To thee I trust this man. Celestial Dwelling! treasure which Jātavedas shall bring hither. | After you will the Sacrificer follow. Here recognize him in the highest heaven. ‖ 60. Acknowledge him, ye Gods, in highest heaven. Ye who are present, know the shape he weareth. | When he approacheth by the God-ward pathways, reveal to him the meed of pious actions. ‖ 61. Wake up, O Agni, etc., as in 15:54. ‖ 62. Convey our sacrifice to heaven, etc., as in 15:55, ‖ 63. With Darbha-bunch, with fencing-wood, with spoon, with altar, holy grass, | With laud, lead this our sacrifice to go to heaven among the Gods. ‖ 64. Our gifts, our charitable grants, our pious works, our fees to priests, | May the Omnific's Agni set all this among the Gods in heaven. ‖ 65. There where all never-failing streams of honey and of butter flow, | May Agni, Viśvakarman's own, place us in heaven among the Gods. ‖ 66. Agni am who know by birth all creatures. Mine eye is butter, in my mouth is nectar. | I am the triple light, the region's meter: exhaustless heat am I, named burnt oblation. ‖ 67. Praise-verses, sacrificial texts, and chanted hymns am I in name. | Thou art the best of all the Fires among the fivefold race of man | That burn upon this earth of ours. Speed thou us on to lengthened life. ‖ 68. O Indra, for the strength that slays Vṛitra and conquers in the fight | We turn thee hitherward to us. ‖ 69. Thou, Indra, much-invoked, didst crush to pieces, Kunāru, handless fiend who dwelt with Dānus. | Thou with might, Indra, smotest dead the scorner, the footless Vṛitra as he waxed in vigour. ‖ 70. O Indra, beat our foes away, etc. as in 8:44. ‖ 71. Like some dread wild beast roaming on the mountain thou hast approached us from the farthest distance. | Whetting thy bolt and thy sharp blade, O Indra, crush thou the foes and scatter those who hate us. ‖ 72. To aid us let Vaiśvānara come from the distance far away: | Come Agni, to our eulogies! ‖ 73. Sought in the sky, sought on the earth, sought after, all plants that grow on ground hath Agni entered. | May Agni, may Vaiśvānara with vigour, sought for, by day and night from harm preserve us. ‖ 74. Help its that we may gain this wish, O Agni, gain riches, Wealthy One! with store of heroes. | Desiring strength from thee may we be strengthened, and win, Eternal! thine eternal glory. ‖ 75. Approaching with raised hands and adoration, we have this day fulfilled for thee thy longing. | Worship the Gods with most devoted spirit as Priest with no unfriendly thought. O Agni. ‖ 76. Home-hider Agni, Indra, and Brahma, and bright Bṛihaspati— | May the All Gods, one-minded, guard our sacrifice in happy place. ‖ 77. Guard thou the Sacrificer's men, O Youthfullest, etc., as in 13:52.

Adhyāya 19.

1. Sweet with the sweet, I sprinkle thee with Soma, strong with the strong, the nectar with the nectar, | The honey-sweet with what is sweet as honey. | Soma art thou. Get dressed for the Aśvins Get dressed for Sarasvatī. Get dressed for Indra the Good Deliverer. ‖ 2. Hence pour ye forth the flowing juice, Soma, best Sacrificial food. | He who, man's friend, hath run within the waters hath with the pressing-stones poured out the Soma. ‖ 3. Purified by Vāyu's strainer, Soma that has passed away forward is Indra's proper friend. | Purified by Vāyu's strainer, Soma that has passed away backward is Indra's proper friend. ‖ 4. By means of this eternal sieve may Sūrya's Daughter purify | The Soma that flows forth from thee. ‖ 5. Soma with Wine, pressed; filtered for the banquet, cleanses priest, noble, brilliancy and vigour. | God, with the Bright give Deities enjoyment: give food with flavour to the Sacrificer. ‖ 6. What then? As men whose fields are full of barley, etc., as in 10:32. | Taken upon a base art thou. I take thee for the Aśvin Pair. Thee for Sarasvatī. Thee for Indra the Good Deliverer. | This is thy home. For splendour thee. Thee for man's vigour. Thee for strength. ‖ 7. For each of you is made a God-appointed place: so grant to me a portion in the highest sphere. | Surā the strong art thou. This here is Soma. Entering thine own place do me no mischief. ‖ 8. Taken upon a base art thou. Splendour of Aśvins, Sarasvatī's manly vigour, might of Indra. | This is thy home. I take thee for enjoyment. I take thee for delight, take thee for greatness. ‖ 9. Thou art lustre: give me lustre, Thou art manly vigour: give me manly vigour. | Thou art strength: give me strength. Thou art energy: give me energy. | Thou art passion: Give me passion. Thou art conquering might: give me conquering might. ‖ 10. My she, Viṣhūchikā, who guards these two, the tiger and the wolf, | The lion and the winged hawk, may she guard this man from distress. ‖ 11. When, a delighted boy, I bruised my mother as I sucked her breast, | Free from my debt, O Agni, I become thereby. My parents are by me unharmed. | United are ye all: with bliss unite me. Parted are ye, keep me apart from evil. ‖ 12. The Aśvins, the Physicians, Gods, stretched out the healing sacrifice, | Sarasvatī with speech was a Physician, all with heroic powers investing Indra. ‖ 13. Symbols of Dīkṣhā are grass buds, of Prāyaṇīya sprouts of corn, | Of Soma-purchasing fried grains are symbols, Soma-shoots and meath. ‖ 14. Ātithya's sign is Māsara, the Gharma's symbol Nagnahu. | Three nights with Surā poured, this is the symbol of the | Upasads. ‖ 15. Emblem of purchased Soma is Parisrut, foaming drink effused: | Indra's balm milked for Indra by the Aśvins and Sarasvatī. ‖ 16. The Sacrificer's seat is the throne's symbol, the jar containing Surā of the Altar. | The mid-space is the northern Altar's symbol: the cloth for filtering is the physician. ‖ 17. Altar by Altar is produced, power, holy grass by holy grass. | The stake is by the stake obtained, by Agni Agni carried forth. ‖ 18. The Aśvins are the Soma store, Sarasvatī the sacred hearth. | For Indra formed is Indra s seat, the Matrons' Hall, the house-lord's fire. ‖ 19. Orders he gains by orders, by Āprīs Āprīs of sacrifice, | Post-offerings by fore-offerings, and by calls of Vaṣhaṭ Āhutis. ‖ 20. By victims he gains victims, by ground rice-cakes sacrificial food, | By metres kindling-verses, and Vaṣhaṭ-calls by Inviting prayers. ‖ 21. Grain roasted, gruel, barley-meal, grains of rice roasted, milk and curd | Are types of Soma: mingled milk, sweet whey, of sacrificial food. ‖ 22. Type of parched corn is jujube-fruit; wheat of the roasted grains of rice; Jujube the type of barley-meal, and Indra-grains of gruel-groats. ‖ 23. Symbol of milk are barley-grains, symbol of curd are jujube-fruits. | Whey is the type of Soma, and milk-mixture type of Soma's pap. ‖ 24. The Strophe is the cry, Bid hear? the answer is the antistrophe. | Sacrifice! is the Dhāyyā's form, Pragāthas' the Yajāmahas. ‖ 25. By verse-halves comes the Ukthas' type, Nivids by Padas he obtains. | The type of Śastras is obtained by Praṇavas, Soma by milk. ‖ 26. Gained by the Aśvins is the morn's libation, Indra's libation of mid-day by Indra. | Sarasvatī obtains the third outpouring, the offering sacred to the Viśvedevas. ‖ 27. By Vāyu cups he gains the cups of Vāyu, and by the basket gains the vat for Soma. | By the two jars he gains two cleansing-vessels, and by the cooking-pot the pot for cooking. ‖ 23. By sacrificial texts are gained the Grahas, and by the Grahas lauds and laud-arrangements. | By metres are obtained Ukthas and praise-songs, and by the Sāman-chant the Avabhṛitha ‖ 29. Draughts he obtains by pouring out libations, and wishes by the utterance of praises, | By Śamyu he obtains Patnīsaṃyājas, and Consummation by Samiṣhṭayajus. ‖ 30. He gains by vow of fasting Consecration, by Consecration gains the priestly guerdon. | He gains by priestly guerdon faith: by faith comes knowledge of the truth. ‖ 31. So far the type of sacrifice was formed by Brahma, and the Gods. | All this he gains, when juice is shed, in the Sautrāmaṇī sacrifice. ‖ 32. The rite with sacred grass, wine, store of heroes, the mighty ones speed on with

adorations. | May we, sweet-singing sacrificers, setting Soma mid Gods in heaven, give joy to Indra. || 33. All essence of thine own in plants collected, all strength of Soma when poured out with Surā— | Therewith impel with joy the sacrifice, Sarasvatī, the Aśvins, Indra, Agni. || 34. That which Sarasvatī poured out for Indra, by Aśvins brought from Namuchi the demon, | This flowing drop, brilliant and full of sweetness, I drink and feed on here, the King, the Soma. || 35. Whatever portion of the savoury fluid is clinging here, what Indra drank with powers, | That drop thereof with pure and holy spirit I drink and feed upon, the King, the Soma. || 36. To Fathers who claim Svadhā be Svadhā and homage! | To Grandfathers who claim Svadhā be Svadhā and homage! | To Great-grandfathers who claim Svadhā be Svadhā and homage! | The Fathers have eaten. The Fathers have rejoiced. The Fathers have been satisfied, Fathers, be ye purified. || 37. Cleanse me the Fathers who enjoy Soma! Grandfathers make me clean! | May Great-grandfathers cleanse me with a sieve that brings a century. | May my Grandfathers cleanse me, may my Great-grand-fathers make me clean. | With sieve that brings a century may I obtain full length of life. || 33. Agni, thou poorest life: send down upon us food and vigorous strength. | Drive thou misfortune far away. || 39. Cleanse me the companies of Gods! May thoughts with spirit make me clean. | Cleanse me all things that be! Do thou, O Jātavedas, make me clean. || 40. Purify me, O Agni, God, refulgent with thy pure bright sieve, | With powers according to thine own. || 41. O Agni, may the cleansing sieve, diffused through all thy fiery glow, | Holy devotion, make me clean. || 42. May Pavamāna with his sieve, Guest of all tribes, cleanse us today, | He who is Cleanser make us clean. || 43. Savitar, God, by both of these, libation, purifying power, | Purify me on every side. || 44. Dear to all Gods hath come the cleansing Goddess, she who contains these many smooth-backed figures. | Through her may we in sacrificial banquets taking our pleasure be the lords of riches. || 45. The Fathers who in Yama's realm are equal and unanimous— | Their world is Svadhā, reverence. To Gods let sacrifice be paid. || 46. Equals, unanimous, my folk yet living among those who live— | On me be set their glory through a hundred years in this our world. || 47. I have heard mention of two several pathways, way of the Fathers, way of Gods and mortals. | On these two roads each moving creature travels, each thing between the Father and the Mother. || 48. May this my sacrifice bring store of children, with ten brave sons, full-companied, for welfare— | Life-winning, winning offspring, winning cattle, winning this world of ours and peace and safety. | May Agni make nay progeny abundant. Do ye confer food, milk, and wanly vigour. || 49. May they ascend, the lowest, highest, midmost, the Fathers who deserve a share of Soma. | May Fathers who have gained the world of spirits, gentle and righteous, aid us when we call them. || 50. Our Fathers are Aṅgirasas, Navagvas, Atharvans, Bhṛigus, who deserve the Soma. | May these the holy look on us with favour: may we enjoy their gracious loving-kindness. || 51. Our ancient Fathers who deserve the Soma, who came, most noble, to our Soma banquet— | With these let Yama, yearning with the yearning, rejoicing eat our offerings at his pleasure. || 52. Thou, Soma, art preeminent for wisdom: along the straightest path thou art our leader. | Our prudent Fathers by thy wisdom, Soma, dealt out among the Gods their share of treasure. || 53. For our sage Fathers, Soma Pavamāna, of old performed by thee their sacred duties. | Fighting unvanquished, open the enclosures: enrich us with large gifts of steeds and heroes. || 54. Associate with the Fathers thou, O Soma, hast spread thyself abroad through earth and heaven. | So with oblation let us serve thee, Indu, and so let us become the lords of riches. || 55. Fathers who sit on sacred grass, come help us: these offerings we have made for you; accept them. | So come to us with most auspicious favour, and give us health and strength without a trouble. || 56. I have attained the gracious-minded Fathers, have gained a son and progeny from Vishṇu. | They who enjoy pressed juices with oblation, seated on sacred grass, come oftenest hither. || 57. May they, the Fathers, worthy of the Soma, invited to their favourite oblations | Laid on the sacred grass, come nigh and listen: may they be gracious unto us and bless us. || 58. May they our Fathers whom the flames have tasted, worthy of Soma, come on God-ward pathways. | Enjoying at this sacrifice their portion, may they be gracious unto us and bless us. || 59. Fathers whom Agni's flames have tasted, come ye nigh: ye kindly leaders, take ye each your proper place. | Eat sacrificial food presented on the grass: grant riches with a multitude of hero sons. || 60. For those who, burnt with fire or not cremated, joy in their portion in the midst of heaven, | May the Self-Ruler form the world of spirits and this their body as his pleasure wills it. || 61. We call the Agnishvāttas, true to seasons, those who drank Soma in the Nārāśaṃsa. | Prompt to give ear to us be they, the sages, and then let us be lords of wealth and treasure. || 62. Bowing the bended knee and seated southward, accept ye, all, this sacrifice with favour. | Injure us not for any sin, O Fathers, which we through human frailty have committed. || 63. Lapped in the bosom of the purple Mornings give riches to the man who brings oblation. | Grant to his sons a portion of your treasure, and, present, give us energy, ye Fathers. || 64. O Agni Kavyavāhana, cause us to praise before the Gods, | As our associate meet for lauds, wealth which e'en thou reputest wealth. || 65. May Agni, Kavya-bearer, who hath worshipped Fathers true to Law. | Announce to Gods and Fathers these our sacrificial offerings. || 66. Thou. Agni Kavya-bearer, when entreated, didst bear the offerings which thou madest fragrant, | And gavest to the Fathers who did eat them with Svadhā. Eat, thou God, the gifts we bring thee. || 67. Thou, Jātavedas, knowest well the number of Fathers who are here and who are absent, | Of Fathers whom we know and whom we know not. Accept the sacrifice arranged with portions. || 68. Now let us pay this homage to the Fathers, to those who passed of old and those who followed, | Those who have rested in the earthly region and those who dwell among the Mighty Races. || 69. As in the days of old our ancient Fathers speeding the work of holy worship, Agni! | Sought pure light and devotion, singing praises, they cleft the ground and made red Dawns apparent. || 70. Right gladly do we set thee down, right gladly make thee burn and glow. | Gladly bring yearning Fathers nigh to eat the food of sacrifice. || 71. Indra, with waters' foam didst thou wrench off the head of Namuchi, | Subduing all contending hosts. || 72. King Soma, pressed, the Drink of Life, left Death behind with Soma-dregs. | By Law came truth and Indra-power, the pure bright drinking-off of juice. The power of Indra was this sweet immortal milk. || 73. The Snipe of Aṅgiras by thought from out the waters drank up milk. | By Law came truth, etc., as in 72. || 74. The Haṃsa throned in light drank up by metre Soma from the floods. | By Law, etc. || 75. Prajāpati by Brahma drank the essence from the foaming food, the princely power, milk, Soma juice. | By Law, etc. || 76. The generative part enters the *yoni:* it leaves aside the *retas* and the *mūtra*. | The caul-invested embryo leaves by its birth the covering folds. | By Law, etc. || 77. Viewing both forms Prajāpati gave truth and falsehood different shapes. | Prajāpati assigned the lack of faith to falsehood, faith to truth. | By Law, etc. || 78. By holy lore Prajāpati drank up both forms, pressed and unpressed. | By Law, etc. || 79. Seeing the farming liquor's sap, Prajāpati with the bright drank nut the bright the milk, the Soma juice. By Law, etc. || 80. Wise, with mind, lead, and thread of wool the sages twine an amulet. | Sarasvatī, Savitar, Varuṇa, the Aśvins span sacrifice and healed his form for Indra. || 81. This his immortal shape with mighty powers three Deities bestowing gifts compounded. | His hair they made with sprouts of grass and barley, and roasted grain with skin and flesh supplied him. || 82. His inner shape Sarasvatī arranges and, borne on bright paths, the Physician Aśvins: | With Māsaras and sieve his bone and marrow, as on the Oxen's hide they lay the liquor. || 83. By thought Sarasvatī with both Nāsatyas forms lovely treasure and a beauteous body. | Like shuttle through the loom the steady ferment mixes the red juice with the foaming spirit. || 84. By milk they generated bright immortal, productive seed, by Surā seed from urine, | Chasing afar folly and ill intention, crude food and wind and meat that loads the stomach. || 85. Heart with his heart Indra Good Guardian gendered: with rice-cake Savitar gave truth its being. | Varuṇa, doctoring the lungs and liver, forms, as with Vāyu cups, the gall and kidneys. || 86. Cooking-pots pouring honey were the entrails: like a well-milking cow the pans were bowels. | A hawk's wing was the spleen: through mighty powers the stool as mother was navel and belly. || 87. The pitcher was the father of the rectum by powers, the womb which first contained the infant. | Plain was the hundred-streaming fount as penis: the jar poured forth libations to the Father. || 88. His face the basket, thence his head; the strainer his tongue, his mouth Sarasvatī and Aśvins | The Chapya was his rump, his leech the filter, the bladder was his penis keen with ardour. || 89. Aśvins with both cups made his eye immortal, the goat and cooked oblation gave it keenness. | With wheat eyelashes and with jujube eyebrows they clothe as 'twere a black and brilliant figure. || 90. The sheep, the ram to give his nostril vigour. the immortal path of breath by both libations. | By Indra-grains and sacrificial jujubes Sarasvatī produced through-breath and nose hairs. || 91. The hull for strength made Indra's form: the immortal bearing for both his ears by two libations. | Barley and sacred grass composed his eyebrows: from his mouth came the jujube and sweet honey. || 92. Hair of the wolf was on his waist and body: the beard upon his face was hair of tigers. | Lions hair were his locks, for fame and beauty, worn on his head, his crest and sheen and vigour. || 93. The Aśvins, Leeches, joined his limbs and body, Sarasvatī put limbs and frame together, | Giving the form and vital power of Indra, hundredfold, deathless and delightful lustre. || 94. Sarasvatī, as Consort of the Aśvins, bears in her womb the nobly fashioned Infant. | King Varuṇa with waters' wealthy essence begetting Indra in the floods for glory. || 95. Splendour of victims, powerful oblation, honey and meath with milk and foaming liquor, | Healing Sarasvatī effused, and Aśvins; from pressed and unpressed Soma, deathless Indu.

Adhyāya 20.

1. Birth-place of princely power art thou: centre art thou of princely power. | Harm not thyself: do me no harm. || 2. Varuṇa, Law's maintainer, hath sat down, etc., as in 10:27. | Save me from death. Save me from lightning. || 3. Thee, by the radiant Savitar's impulsion, with arms of Aśvins, with the hands of Pūṣhan, | With leech-craft of the Aśvins, I besprinkle for splendour, for the lustre of a Brahman; | With leech-craft of Sarasvatī, besprinkle for manly vigour and for food to feed thee; | Besprinkle thee, by special power of Indra, for strength of body and for fame and glory. || 4. Thou art Ka. Noblest Ka art thou. Thee for the state and rank of Ka. | Sumaṅgala! Suśloka! Satyarājan! || 5. My head be grace, my mouth be fame, my hair and beard be brilliant sheen! | My breath be King and deathlessness, mine eye Sole Lord, mine ear the Prince! || 6. My tongue be bliss, my voice be might, my mind be wrath, my rage self-lord! | Joys be my fingers, and delight my members, conquering strength my friend! || 7. Let my two arms be Indra's power, my hands be deed of manly might, my soul and breast be princely rule! neck || 8. My ribs be royal government, my belly, shoulders, neck, and hips, | Thighs, elbows, knees, the people, yea, my members universally! || 9. My navel intellect, etc., etc. . . . . . | Duty am I in legs and feet, established King among the folk. || 10. I take my stand on princely power and Kingship, on cows am I dependent, and on horses. on vital breath. | On members I depend, and on the body, dependent and on welfare, on heaven and earth and sacrifice dependent. || 11. May Deities, eleven threes, the three and thirty bounteous Ones | Whose House-Priest is Bṛihaspati, by impulse of bright Savitar, the Gods protect me with the Gods. || 12. May the first Gods with the second, the second with the third, the third with Truth, Truth with Sacrifice, Sacrifice with sacrificial texts, sacrificial texts with Sāmans, Sāmans with praise-verses, praise-verses with fore and after-sentences. fore-sentences with inviting-texts, inviting-texts with Vaṣhaṭ-calls, Vaṣhaṭ calls with oblations, and oblations, fulfil my desires, Earth! All-hail! || 13. My hair is effort and attempt, my skin is reverence and approach. My flesh is inclination, wealth my bone, my marrow reverence. || 14. Gods, Deities, whatever fault of ours have stirred the wrath of Gods, | May Agni set me free from that iniquity and all distress. || 15. If in the day-time or at night we have committed acts of sin, | May Vāyu set me free from that iniquity and all distress. || 16. If when awake or in our sleep we have committed acts of sin, | May Sūrya set me free from that iniquity and all distress. || 17. Each fault in village or in wild, company or corporeal sense, | Each sinful act that we have done to Śūdra or Ārya, or to either's disadvantage, e'en of that sin thou art the expiation. || 18. Waters, Inviolable ones, etc. Said to be repeated from 6:22. | O ever-moving Cleansing Bath, etc. Repeated from 3:48. || 19. Thy heart is in the flood, etc. Repeated from 8:25. | To us let Waters, etc. Repeated from 6:22. || 20. As one unfastened from a stake, or cleansed by bathing after toil, | As butter which the sieve hath purged, let water clean me from my sin. || 21. Looking upon the loftier light above the darkness we have come | To Sūrya, God among the Gods, the light that is most excellent. || 22. The waters I this day have sought, and to their essence have we come. | Agni, come hither rich in milk, splendour and brilliancy bestow on me, and progeny and wealth. || 23. A brand art thou: fain would we thrive. Fuel art thou and splendour: give me splendour. | Earth comes again, the Dawn, the Sun. This Universe all comes again. | May I possess Vaiśvānara's light, may I attain my vast desires. Earth! All-hail! || 24. O Agni, Master of the Vow, on thee I lay the kindling-stick. | To the fast-vow and faith I come. I, consecrated, kindle thee. || 25. Fain would I know that holy world where Deities with Agni dwell, | Where priestly rank and princely power together in accordance move. || 26. Fain would I know that holy world where want and languor are unknown, | Where in complete accordance move Indra and Vāyu side by side || 27. Let thy shoot be united with his tendril, joint combine with joint. | Imperishable sap for joy, thine odour be the Soma's guard! || 28. They pour it out, they sprinkle it, they scatter it, they make it pure. | In the brown Surā's ecstasy he says What art thou? What art thou? || 29. Indra, at morn accept our cake accompanied with grain and groats, with wheaten bread and hymns of praise. || 30. To Indra sing the lofty hymn, Marutas? that slayeth Vṛitra best, | Whereby the Holy Ones created for the God the radiant light that never dies. || 31. Adhvaryu, on the straining cloth pour thou the Soma pressed with stones: | Purify it for Indra's drink. || 32. The Sovereign Lord of living things, he upon whom the worlds depend, | Mighty, the mighty's King—by him I take thee, take thee on myself. || 33. Taken upon a base art thou. Thee for the Aśvins This is thy home, etc. || 34. Guard of my breath and outward breath, the guardian of mine eye and ear, | All-healer of my voice, thou art the mollifier of my mind. || 35. Invited I feed upon thee invited, | Whom Aśvins, whom Sarasvatī, whom Indra, Good Protector, made. || 36. Kindred in forefront of the Mornings, Indra with forward light, long-active, waxing mighty, | With three-and thirty Gods, the Thunder-wielder, smote Vṛitra dead and threw the portals open. || 37. Son of Himself, the Praise of Men, the hero, measuring out the sacrificial stations, | Rich in bulls' fat, anointing with sweet butter, wise, bright with gauds of gold, he sacrificeth. || 38. Lauded by Gods, Lord of Bay Steeds, the Helper, showing his greatness. worshipped with oblations. | Fort-render, Cowpen-cleaver, Thunder-wielder, may he approach our sacrifice rejoicing || 39. May Indra, Lord of Bays, sit by direction eastward on earth, accepting our oblation, | And sacred grass, fair, far-spread, widely-stretching, anointed by Ādityas and by Vasus. || 40. To the strong Indra go the sounding Portals, dames with a goodly husband, swiftly moving! | Well-manned, divine, wide be the Doors thrown open, expanding in their greatness fir the Hero! || 41. Dawn and Night, lofty, sapful, richly-yielding, fair-showing, as they weave with varied colour | The long-extended thread in concert, worship the God of Gods, the lofty Hero Indra. || 42. The two first pleasant-voiced celestial Hotars, arranging rites for man in sundry places, | At head of sacrifice establishing Indra, increase the eastern light with sweet oblation. || 43. Thriving by sacrifice may the three Bright Ones, taking delight like wedded dames in Indra, | Sarasvatī, Iḍā, Bhāratī all-surpassing, with milk preserve our sacred thread unbroken. || 44. May Tvaṣhṭar coming frail afar, the active, give strength and plenty to strong glorious Indra, | And strong, prolific, worshipping, the Mighty at sacrifice's head give the Gods honour. || 45. Let the divine Stake, like an Immolator, bind, as one ordered, to himself the victim, | And, filling Indra's belly with ablations, season the sacrifice with sweets and butter. || 46. Indra the Bull, swift conqueror, wildly rushing bull-like to meet the Indu of the droppings— | Delighting in a mind that scatters fatness, let the immortal Gods rejoice in Svāhā. || 47. May Indra come to us for our protection, here, lauded Hero, be our feast-companion. | May he whose powers are many, waxen mighty, cherish, like Dyaus, the sovereign sway of princes. || 48. From near or far away may mighty Indra, giver of succour, come for our protection, | Lord of men, armed with thunder, with the Strongest, slaying his foes in conflict, in the battles. || 49. May Indra come to us with Tawny Coursers, inclined to us, to favour and enrich us. | May Maghavan, loud-voiced and wielding thunder, stand by us at this sacrifice, in combat. || 50. Indra the Rescuer, Indra the Helper, Hero who listens at each invocation, | Śakra I call, Indra invoked of many. May Indra, Bounteous Lord, prosper and bless us. || 51. May helpful Indra as our Good Protector, Lord of all treasures, favour us with succour, | Baffle our foes and give us rest and safety, and may we be the lords of hero vigour. || 52. May we enjoy the grace of him the Holy, yea, may we dwell in his auspicious

favour. | May helpful Indra as our Good Preserver drive from us even from afar, our foemen. || 53. Come hither, Indra, with Bay Steeds, joyous, with tails like peacock plumes, | Let no men check thy course as fowlers stay the bird: pass o'er them as o'er desert lands. || 54. Verily the Vasiṣhṭhas hymn with praises Indra the mighty One whose arm wields thunder. | Praised, may he guard our wealth in men and cattle. Ye Gods, preserve us evermore with blessings. || 55. Fire hath been kindled, Aśvins Twain! the Gharma warmed, the Radiant pressed, | Here the Milch-Cow Sarasvatī hath poured bright Soma, Indra's own. || 56. When Soma flows Sarasvatī and both the Aśvins, Leeches and | Body-guards, bear to Indra strength by passage through the realms of air. || 57. When Soma flowed the Aśvins Twain, the Leeches, brought sweet medicine, | With Men's Desire Sarasvatī for Indra, Soma, Nagnahu. || 58. Worshipped, Sarasvatī bestowed on Indra, senses, manly power. | The Aśvins, through oblations paid, combined food, energy, and wealth. || 59. The Aśvins brought from Namuchi pressed Soma bright with foaming juice. | Sarasvatī with sacred grass brought that to Indra for his drink. || 60. Sarasvatī and Indra with the Aśvins Twain milked out desires | From heaven and earth, the regions, the resounding and expansive doors. || 61. Ye Aśvins, Dawn and Night, by day and in the evening, fair of hue, | Accordant, with Sarasvatī, deck Indra with surpassing powers. || 62. Guard us, O Aśvins, through the day, guards us by night, Sarasvatī. | Celestial Hotars, Leeches! both guard Indra when the juice is pressed. || 63. The Aśvins, and the Three, apart, Sarasvatī, Iḍā, Bhāratī, | As drink to gladden Indra, poured strong Soma with the foaming juice. || 64. The Aśvins, our Sarasvatī, and Tvaṣhṭar, when the juice was shed, | Gave Indra balm, yea, mead as balm, glory and fame and many a shape. || 65. Praising with foaming liquor at due times, Indra, Vanaspati, | Sarasvatī as cow gave forth sweet beverage with the Aśvins Twain. || 66. Aśvins, to Indra ye with cows, with Māsara and foaming drink | Gave, with Sarasvatī—All hail!—the pressed-out Soma juice and mead. || 67. The Aśvins and Sarasvatī by wit from fiendish Namuchi | Brought unto Indra sacred food, strength, brilliant treasure, ample wealth. || 68. That Indra, strong through sacrifice by Aśvins and Sarasvatī, | Cleft Vala through to win him wealth, with Namuchi of Asura birth. || 69. Supporting him in sacrifice with sacred food and mighty powers, | Sarasvatī, both Aśvins and the cattle hymned that Indra's praise. || 70. Indra whom Bhaga, Savitar, and Varuṇa supplied with power, | Lord of the sacrifice, may he, Good Guardian, love the worshipper. || 71. Savitar, Varuṇa bestow gifts on the liberal offerer, | Strength, power and treasure which the Good Protector took from Namuchi! || 72. Varuṇa giving sway and power, Savitar grace with happiness, | The Good Protector giving strength with fame, obtained the sacrifice. || 73. With cows the Aśvins, mighty power, with horses manly vigour, strength, | With sacred food Sarasvatī, made Indra, Sacrificer, strong. || 74. May those Nāsatyas, fair of form, the Men who ride on paths of gold, | Oblation-rich Sarasvatī, thou, Indra! help us in our rites. || 75. Those Leeches righteous in their deeds, She, rich in milk, Sarasvatī, | That Vṛitra-slayer hundred-powered, invested Indra with his might. || 76. Ye Aśvins and Sarasvatī, joint drinkers of the Śara draught, | In Namuchi of Asura birth, give aid to Indra in his deeds. || 77. As parents aid a son, etc., as in 10:34. || 78. He in whom horses, bulls, oxen, and barren cows, and rams, when duly set apart, are offered up, | To Agni, Soma-sprinkled, drinker of sweet juice, Disposer, with thy heart bring forth a pleasant hymn. || 79. Within thy mouth is poured the offering, Agni, as Soma into cup, oil into ladle. | Vouchsafe us wealth, strength-winning, blest with heroes, wealth lofty, praised by men, and full of splendour. || 80. The Aśvins gave, with lustre, sight, Sarasvatī manly strength with breath. | Indra with voice and might gave Indra vigorous power. || 81. With kine, Nāsatyas! and with steeds, come, Aśvins, Rudras! to the house, the sure protector of its men; || 82. Such, wealthy Gods! as none afar or standing near to us may harm, yea, no malicious mortal foe. || 83. Do ye, O longed-for Aśvins, lead us on to wealth of varied form, wealth that shall bring us room and rest. || 84. Wealthy in spoil, enriched with hymns, may pure Sarasvatī desire with eager love our sacrifice. || 85. She who awakens sounds of joy, inspires our hymns, Sarasvatī, she hath allowed our sacrifice. || 86. Sarasvatī, the mighty flood, she with her light illuminates, she brightens every pious thought. || 87. O Indra, marvellously bright, come, these libations long for thee, thus by fine fingers purified. || 88. Urged by the holy singer, sped by song, come, Indra, to the prayers of the libation-pouring priest. || 89. Approach, O Indra, hasting thee, Lord of Bay Horses, to the prayer: in our libations take delight. || 90. Accordant with Sarasvatī let the two Aśvins drink the meath, | May Indra, Vṛitra-slayer, Good Guardian, accept the Soma meath.

Adhyāya 21.

1. Varuṇa, hear this call of mine: be gracious unto us this day. | Longing for help I yearn for thee. || 2. I ask this of thee with my prayer, etc., as in 18:49. || 3. Do thou who knowest Varuṇa, O Agni, put far away from us the God's displeasure. | Best Sacrificer, brightest One, refulgent, remove thou far from us all those who hate us. || 4. Be thou the nearest unto us, O Agni, our closest Friend while now this Morn is breaking. | Reconcile Varuṇa to us, be bounteous: show thy compassion and be swift to hear us. || 5. We call to succour us the mighty Mother of those whose sway is just, the Queen of Order, | Strong-ruler, far-expanding, ne'er decaying, Aditi gracious guide and good protectress. || 6. Sinless may we ascend, for weal, this vessel rowed with good oars, divine, that never leaketh, | Earth our strong guard, incomparable Heaven. Aditi gracious guide and good protectress. || 7. May I ascend the goodly ship, free from defect, that leaketh not, | Moved by a hundred oars, for weal. || 8. O Mitra-Varuṇa, gracious Pair, with fatness dew our pasturage, | With mead the regions of the air. || 9. Stretch forth your arms and let our lives be lengthened: with fatness dew the pastures of our cattle. | Ye Youthful, make us famed among the people: hear, Mitra-Varuṇa, these mine invocations. || 10. Bless us the Coursers when we call, etc., as in 9:16. || 11. Deep-skilled in Law, etc., as in 9:18. || 12. Kindled is Agni with the brand, yea, kindled well, the excellent. | The metre Gāyatrī, the steer of eighteen months, give power and life! || 13. Tanūnapāt whose acts are pure, our bodies' guard Sarasvatī, | Uṣhṇihā metre and the steer of two years' age give power and life! || 14. Agni with offerings, meet for praise, and Soma the immortal God, | Anuṣhṭubh metre and the steer of thirty months give power and life! || 15. Agni with goodly grass spread out, deathless with Pūṣhan at his side, | Bṛihatī metre and a steer of three years' age give power and life! || 16. The Doors divine, the mighty Regions, Brahma, God Bṛihaspati, | The metre Paṅkti, here a bull in his fourth year, give power and life || 17. The two young Darns of lovely form, the deathless Universal Gods, | The Triṣhṭubh metre, here, a bull in his sixth year, give power and life! || 18. The two celestial Hotars, both Physicians, Indra's close-knit friends, | The metre Jagatī, an ox who draws the wain, give power and life! || 19. The Three, Iḍā, Sarasvatī, and Bhāratī, the Marut folk, | Virāj the metre, here, a cow in milk, a bull, give power and life! || 20. Tvaṣhṭar the wondrous, full of seed, Indrāgnī furtherers of weal, | Dvipadā metre, and a cow and vigorous bull give power and life! || 21. Our slaughterer, Vanaspati, Savitar who promoteth wealth, | The metre Kakubh, here, a cow who casts her calf, give power and life! || 22. With Svāhā mighty Varuṇa give healing power to Sacrifice! | The Atichandas, Bṛihat, and a steer and bull give power and life! || 23. With the Spring Season may the Gods the Vasus praised with triple hymn | And with Rathantara, give life to Indra, splendour, sacrifice. || 24. With Summer may the Rudras, Gods, praised in the Pañchadaśa hymn | With Bṛihat, give to Indra strength; with fame, and sacrifice and life. || 25. May the Ādityas with the Rains, lauded in Saptadaśa hymn | And with Vairūpa, with folk, strength, give Indra sacrifice and life. || 26. With Autumn may the Ṛibhus, Gods, praised in the Ekaviṃśa hymn | And with Vairāja, give with grace to Indra grace, life, sacrifice. || 27. With Winter may the Marutas, Gods, praised in the laud of thrice nine parts, | The Śakvarīs, with strength give might to Indra, sacrifice and life. || 28. With Dew-time may the deathless Gods praised in the Thirty-three-part laud, | The Revatīs, with truth give sway to Indra, sacrifice and life. || 29. Let the Hotar sacrifice with fuel to Agni in the place of libation, to the Aśvins, Indra, Sarasvatī. A grey-coloured he-goat with wheat, jujube-fruit and sprouts of rice becomes a sweet salutary remedy, splendour, might, milk, Soma. Let them enjoy sweet butter with foaming liquor. Hotar, present offerings of butter. || 30. Let the Hotar, Tanūnapāt, worship Sarasvatī. A sheep, a ram, a salutary remedy on the honey-sweet path, bearing to the Aśvins and Indra heroic strength, with jujube-fruit, Indra-grains, sprouts of rice, becomes a salutary remedy, milk, Soma. Let them enjoy, etc., as in verse 29. || 31. Let the Hotar worship

Narāśamsa and the Lord Nagnahu. A ram with Surā a salutary remedy, Sarasvatī the Physician, the golden car of the Aśvins, the victim's omentum, with jujube-fruit, Indra-grains, and rice-sprouts, become a salutary remedy, the manly strength of Indra, milk, Soma. Let them, etc. ‖ 32. Let the Hotar, magnified with oblations, offering sacrifice, worship Sarasvatī and Indra, increasing them with strength, with a bull and a cow. Strength and medicine to the Aśvins and Indra are meath with jujube-fruit, Māsara with parched grain, milk, Soma. Let them, etc. ‖ 33. Let the Hotar worship the wool-soft Altar-grass, the Physicians Nāsatyas, the Physicians Aśvins. A mare with a foal, a milch-cow is a physician. Sarasvatī the Physician yields medicine to Indra, milk, Soma. Let them enjoy, etc. ‖ 34. Let the Hotar worship the Doors, the Regions, the resounding, expansive Doors, the Regions, with the Aśvins Indra milks the two milky worlds. The Mulch-cow Sarasvatī yields medicine for the Aśvins and Indra, pure light and strength. Milk, Soma. Let them, etc. ‖ 35. Let the Hotar worship the two fair-formed Dawns. At night and by day the Aśvins with Sarasvatī compose impetuous power, like healing balm, in Indra, like a falcon, Māsara with light, thought, and grace. Milk, Soma. Let them enjoy, etc. ‖ 36. Let the Hotar worship the two divine Hotars, the Physician Aśvins, and Indra. Watchfully by day and night Sarasvatī as Physician, with balms, with lead, yields strength and power. Milk, Soma. Let them enjoy, etc. ‖ 37. Let the Hotar worship the three Goddesses. The three active ones, with three sacrificial elements, lay balm and golden hue on Indra. The Aśvins, Iḍā, Bhāratī—Sarasvatī with Speech yields might and power to Indra. Milk, Soma. Let them enjoy, etc. ‖ 38. Let the Hotar worship Tvaṣṭar full of good seed, the Bull active for men, Indra, the Aśvins, Sarasvatī the Physician. Vigour, speed, power, a fierce wolf as physician, fame with Surā is a medicine, Māsara with grace. Milk, Soma. Let them enjoy, etc. ‖ 39. Let the Hotar worship Vanaspati the Immolator, the Lord of Hundred Powers, and awful Passion, the King, the Tiger, and the Aśvins, with reverence. Sarasvatī the Physician yields wrath and power to Indra. Milk, Soma. Let them enjoy, etc. ‖ 40. Let the Hotar worship Agni. Of the drops of clarified butter, Svāhā! Of the fat, omentum, etc., severally, Svāhā! Svāhā! the goat for the Aśvins Svāhā! the ram for Sarasvatī. Svāhā! the bull for Indra. To the Lion, to his might, power. Svāhā! Agni the salutary remedy. Svāhā! Soma, the power. Svāhā! Indra the Good Deliverer. Savitar, Varuṇa Lord of Physicians. Svāhā! Vanaspati, beloved, food and medicine. Svāhā! Gods who drink clarified butter. Agni accepting the medicine. Milk, Soma. Let them enjoy, etc. ‖ 41. Let the Hotar worship the Aśvins with the omentum of a he-goat. Let them enjoy the fat. Hotar, offer the sacrificial oblation. ǀ Let the Hotar worship Sarasvatī with the omentum of a ram. Let her enjoy the fat. Hotar offer the sacrificial oblation. ǀ Let the Hotar worship Indra with the omentum of a bull. Let him, etc. ‖ 42. Let the Hotar worship the Aśvins, Sarasvatī, Indra the Good Deliverer. These your Somas, pressed, rejoicing with goats, rams, bulls, giving pleasure with rice-shoots, young blades of corn, parched grain, joy-givers adorned with Māsara, bright, milky, immortal, presented, dropping honey. these let the Aśvins, Sarasvatī, Indra the Good Deliverer, Vṛitra-slayer, accept. Let them drink, rejoice in, enjoy the Soma meath. Hotar, sacrifice. ‖ 43. Let the Hotar worship the Aśvins Let them eat of the he-goat, the sacrifice. Let them today eat the fat, taken from the middle, before those who hate us, before human handling. Yea, let them eat amid the fodder of fields fresh with moisture, with their expanse of barley, limbs of those tasted by Agni, belonging to the Hundred Rudras, portions covered with fat, from the sides, from the thighs, from the fore-feet from the chine. From every member of the divided victims these two make their repast. Thus let the Aśvins accept. Hotar, offer the sacrificial oblation. ‖ 44. Let the Hotar worship Sarasvatī. Let her approach the ram, the sacrifice. ǀ Today let her eat, etc., the rest of verse 43. repeated *mutatis mutandis.* ‖ 45. Let the Hotar worship Indra, etc., as in 44. *mutatis mutandis.* ‖ 46. Let the Hotar worship Vanaspati. He has held with a very well formed and very strong rope. There where the favourite stations of the Aśvins are, of the he-goat the sacrifice; of Sarasvatī, of the ram the sacrifice; of Indra, of the bull the sacrifice; there where the favourite stations of Agni are, of Soma, of Indra the Good Deliverer, of Savitar, of Varuṇa, the favourite places of Vanaspati, the favourite stations of Gods who drink clarified butter, and of Agni the Hotar, there let him arrange these victims when he has praised

and lauded them, and perform when he has made them very strong. Let divine Vanaspati accept. Hotar, offer oblation. ‖ 47. Let the Hotar worship Agni Sviṣṭakṛit. Let Agni worship the favourite stations of the Aśvins, of the he-goat the sacrifice; of Sarasvatī, of the ram the sacrifice; of Indra, of the bull the sacrifice; there, etc., to 'butter' as in 46. Let him worship the favourite stations of Agni the Hotar. Let him worship his own majesty. Let him win for himself by sacrifice food worthy of sacrifice. Let him, Knower of Beings, perform the sacred rites. Let him accept the sacrificial food. Hotar, offer oblation. ‖ 48. The Grass divine, for the right Gods, Sarasvatī, the Aśvins Twain, ǀ Give Indra splendour, with the Grass, sight of his eyes and mighty strength! For gain of wealth let them enjoy. Thou, Hotar, offer sacrifice. ‖ 49. The Doors, the Doors divine, the Two Aśvins, Leeches, Sarasvatī— ǀ May they give breath to Indra in his nostrils, and heroic strength. ǀ For gain of wealth, etc., as in verse 48. ‖ 50. May Dawn and Night, the Goddesses, both Aśvins, and Sarasvatī ǀ Lay, with both Dawns, strength, voice within Indra the Good Deliverer's mouth. ǀ For gain of wealth, etc. ‖ 51. Both nursing Goddesses, the Pair of Aśvins, and Sarasvatī ǀ Have with both nurses given strength to Indra, fame, and power to hear. ǀ For gain of wealth, etc. ‖ 52. Bringers of strengthening sacrifice, both Goddesses, well-yielding cows, ǀ Sarasvatī, both Aśvins, the Physicians, these are Indra's guards. ǀ Forth from their breasts by sacrifice they give him brilliant light and power. ǀ For gain of wealth, etc. ‖ 53. Both Gods, the Hotars of the Gods, the Aśvins the Physicians and ǀ Sarasvatī with Vaṣhaṭ-calls, with the two Hotars have bestowed on Indra brilliant light and power, and planted wisdom in his heart. ǀ For gain of wealth, etc. ‖ 54. Goddesses three, three Goddesses—Aśvins, Iḍā, Sarasvatī ǀ In Indra's midmost navel have laid store of energy and power. ǀ For gain of wealth, etc. ‖ 55. God Narāśaṃsa, Indra thrice-protecting, whose car moves by Sarasvatī and Aśvins ǀ May Tvaṣhṭar lay seed, deathless form in Indra, a fitting place of birth and mighty powers. ǀ For gain of wealth, etc. ‖ 56. God with the Gods, Vanaspati of golden leaves and goodly fruit ǀ Ripens till Indra finds it sweet, with Aśvins and Sarasvatī. ‖ 57. Strewn, soft as wool, in sacrifice, with Aśvins and Sarasvatī, ǀ The sacred robe of water-plants be, Indra, a fair seat for thee! ǀ Together with the sacred grass limy they, for sovereignty, bestow King Passion and great power on thee. ǀ For gain of wealth, etc. ‖ 58. Let the God Agni Sviṣṭakṛit worship the Gods as is meet and right for each, the two Hotars, Indra, the Aśvins, Vāk with speech, Sarasvatī, Agni, Soma. Sviṣṭakṛit has been well worshipped, Indra Good Deliverer, Savitar, Varuṇa the Physician have been worshipped. The God Vanaspati, the Gods who drink clarified butter have been well worshipped, Agni by Agni. Let the Hotar Sviṣṭakṛit give the Hotar fame, great power, energy, honour, Ancestral libation. ‖ 59. Today this Sacrificer cooking viands, cooking sacrificial rice-cakes, binding a goat for the Aśvins, a ram for Sarasvatī, a hull for Indra, pressing Surā and Soma juices for the Aśvins, Sarasvatī, and Indra the Good Deliverer, has chosen Agni as Hotar. ‖ 60. Today the divine Vanaspati has done good service to the Aśvins with a goat, to Sarasvatī with a ram, to Indra with a bull. They have eaten these from the marrow onwards, they have accepted the cooked viands, they have waxed strong with the rice-cakes. The Agnis, Sarasvatī, and Indra have drunk the Surā and Soma draughts. ‖ 61. Thee, today, O Ṛiṣhi, Ṛiṣhi's son, descendant of Ṛiṣhis, hath this Sacrificer chosen for many collected, saying: This (Agni) shall win by sacrifice for me choice-worthy treasures among the Gods. O God, what gifts the Gods have given, these do thou desire and approve. And thou art a commissioned Hotar, a human Hotar sent forward for benediction, for good speech, Speak thou good words.

Adhyāya 22.

1. Splendour art thou, bright, deathless, life-protector. Protector of my life be thou. ǀ By impulse of God Savitar I take thee with arms of Aśvins, with the hands of Pūṣhan ‖ 2. This girdle, which in their religious meetings sages assumed in earlier time of worship, ǀ Is present with us here at this libation, in the Law's hymn, proclaiming rich abundance. ‖ 3. Famous art thou, thou art the world, controller and upholder thou. ǀ Go, consecrate by Svāhā to Agni Vaiśvānara widely-famed. ‖ 4. For Gods and for Prajāpati I fit thee. For Gods and for Prajāpati, O Brahman, ǀ Will I tie up the horse. Thence may I prosper! Binding him for Prajāpati and Gods be thou successful. ‖ 5. Thee welcome to Prajāpati I sprinkle. I sprinkle thee

welcome to Indra-Agni. I sprinkle thee acceptable to Vāyu. Thee welcome to the All-Gods I besprinkle. Thee welcome to all Deities I sprinkle. | With fury Varuṇa attacks the man who fain would slay the steed. | Avaunt the man! Avaunt the dog! || 6. To Agni Hail! To Soma Hail! Hail to the Waters' Joy! Hail to Savitar! Hail to Vāyu! Hail to Vishṇu! Hail to Indra! Hail to Bṛihaspati! Hail to Mitra! Hail to Varuṇa! || 7. Hail to the sound *hiṅ!* Hail to the uttered *hiṅ!* Hail to the neigh! Hail to the down-neigh! Hail to the snort! Hail to the roar! Hail to his smell! Hail to him smelt at! Hail to him seated! Hail to him seated down! Hail to him weary! Hail to him going! Hail to him sitting! Hail to him lying! Hail to him sleeping! Hail to him waking! Hail to him whinnying! Hail to him wakened! Hail to him yawning! Hail to him outstretched! Hail to him drawn together! Hail to him risen! Hail to his going! Hail to his good going! Hail! || 8. Hail to him as he goes! Hail to him running! Hail to him running away! Hail to him when he has run away! Hail to the cry Shoo! Hail to him scared with Shoo! Hail to him seated! Hail to him risen! Hail to his speed! Hail to his strength! Hail to him rolling! Hail to him when he has rolled! Hail to him tossing about! Hail to him when he has tossed about! Hail to him listening! Hail to him hearing. Hail to him looking! Hail to him looked at! Hail to him closely looked at! Hail to his closing his eye! Hail to his food! Hail to his drink! Hail to his stale! Hail to him in action! Hail to what he has done! || 9. May we attain that excellent glory of Savitar the God: | So may he stimulate our prayers. || 10. For our protection I invoke the golden-handed Savitar: | He knoweth, as a God, the place. || 11. We specially invoke the grace of Savitar, observant God, | The great good-will that gives true boons. || 12. We seek the eulogy and gift of Savitar who strengthens grace, | Yea, of the God who knows our thoughts. || 13. I invocate the heroes' Lord, free-giving Savitar, and call | The Cheerer to the feast of Gods. || 14. The judgment of bright Savitar, that cheers the All-Gods' company, | With prayer we estimate as bliss. || 15. Wake Agni with thy laud and set the Immortal One aflame, let him | Bestow our offerings on the Gods. || 16. Oblation-bearer, well-inclined, immortal, eager Messenger, | Agni comes near us with the thought. || 17. Agni, Envoy, I place in front, the oblation-bearer I address: | Here let him seat the Deities. || 18. Yea, Pavamāna, thou didst generate the Sun and spread the moisture out with power, | Hasting to us with plenty vivified with milk. || 19. Mighty through thy dam, eminent through thy sire, thou art a horse, thou art a steed, thou art a courser, thou art a comfort, thou art a racer, thou art a yoke-horse, thou art a strong steed, thou art a stallion, thou art manly-minded. Thou art called Yayu, thou art called Śiśu. Follow thou the flight of the Ādityas | Gods, Warders of the Regions, protect for the Gods this horse besprinkled for sacrifice. | Here is delight. Here take thy pleasure. Here is content. Here is self-content. || 20. Hail to Ka! Hail to Who?! Hail to Which?! Hail to him who has experienced pain! Hail to Prajāpati who knows the mind! Hail to him who discerns the thought! Hail to Aditi! Hail to good Aditi! Hail to gracious Aditi! Hail to Sarasvatī! Hail to purifying Sarasvatī! Hail to great Sarasvatī! Hail to Pūshan! Hail to Pūshan of the highways! Hail to Pūshan observer of men! Hail to Tvashṭar! Hail to swift Tvashṭar! Hail to Tvashṭar of many forms! Hail to Vishṇu! Hail to Vishṇu Nibhūyapa! Hail to Vishṇu Śipivishṭa! || 21. Let every mortal man elect, etc., repeated from 4:8. || 22. O Brahman, let there be born in the kingdom the Brahman illustrious for religious knowledge; let there be born the Rājanya, heroic, skilled archer, piercing with shafts, mighty warrior; the cow giving abundant milk; the ox good at carrying; the swift courser; the industrious woman. May Parjanya send rain according to our desire; may our fruit-bearing plants ripen; may acquisition and preservation of property be secured to us. || 23. Hail to vital breath! Hail to out-breathing! Hail to diffusive breath! Hail to the eye! Hail to the ear! Hail to Speech! Hail to Mind! || 24. Hail to the Eastern Region! Hail to the hitherward Region! Hail to the Southern Region! Hail to the hitherward Region! Hail to the Western Region! Hail to the hitherward Region! Hail to the Northern Region! Hail to the hitherward Region! Hail to the Upward Region! Hail to the hitherward Region! Hail to the Downward Region! Hail to the hitherward Region! || 25. Hail to waters! Hail to floods! Hail to water! Hail to standing waters! flail to flowing waters! Hail to trickling waters! Hail to well waters! Hail to spring waters! Hail to the foaming sea! Hail to the ocean! Hail to the deep! || 26. Hail to wind! Hail to mist! Hail to vapour! Hail to cloud! Hail to cloud lightening! Hail to cloud thundering! Hail to it bursting! Hail to it raining! Hail to it pouring! Hail to it violently raining! Hail to it swiftly raining! Hail to it holding up! Hail to it when it has held up! Hail to it sprinkling! Hail to it drizzling! Hail to its drops! Hail to thunderbolts! Hail to hoar frosts! || 27. Hail to Agni! Hail to Soma! Hail to Indra! Hail to Earth! Hail to Firmament! Hail to Sky! Hail to Regions? Hail to Quarters! Hail to the Upward Region! Hail to the Downward Region! || 23. Hail to the lunar asterisms! Hail to those connected with the lunar asterisms! Hail to Day and Night! Hail to the half-months! Hail to the mouths! Hail to the Seasons! Hail to the Season-groups! Hail to the Year! Hail to Heaven and Earth! Hail to the Moon! Hail to the Sun! Hail to his rays! Hail to the Vasus! Hail to the Rudras! Hail to the Ādityas! Hail to the Marutas! Hail to the All-Gods! Hail to roots! Hail to branches! Hail to forest trees! Hail to flowers! Hail to fruits! Hail to herbs! || 29. Hail to Earth! Hail to Firmament t Hail to Sky! Hail to Sun! Hail to Moon! Hail to lunar asterisms! Hail to waters! Hail to herbs! Hail to forest trees! Hail to creatures that swim! Hail to things moving and stationary! Hail to things that creep and crawl! || 30. Hail to breath! Hail to the Vasu! Hail to the Mighty! Hail to Vivasvat! Hail to the trooping one! Hail to the Troop's Lord! Hail to the Superior! Hail to the Overlord! Hail to Strength! Hail to Saṃsarpa! Hail to the Moon! Hail to light! Hail to Malimlucha! Hail to him who flies by day! || 31. Hail to Madhu! Hail to Mādhava! Hail to Śukra! Hail to Śuchi! Hail to Nabhas! Hail to Nabhasya! Hail to Isha! Hail to Ūrja! Hail to Sahas! Hail to Sahasya! Hail to Tapas! Hail to Tapasya! Hail to Aṃhasaspati! || 32. Hail to Strength! Hail to impulse! Hail to After-born! Hail to will! Heaven, Hail? Hail to the head! Hail to Vyaśnuvin! To the final, Hail! Hail to the mundane final! Hail to the Lord of the world! Hail to the Overlord! Hail to the Lord of Creatures! || 33. May life succeed by sacrifice, Hail! May breath succeed by sacrifice, Hail! May downward breath, diffusive. breath, upward breath, digestive breath, vision, hearing, speech, mind, self, devotion, light, heaven, hymn-arrangement, sacrifice succeed by sacrifice. All-hail! || 34. Hail to One! Hail to Two! Hail to Hundred! Hail to Hundred-and-One! Hail to Daybreak! Hail to Heaven!

Adhyāya 23.

1. In the beginning rose Hiraṇyagarbha, etc.: || 2. Taken upon a base art thou. I take thee welcome to Prajāpati. | This is thy place: Sūrya thy majesty. | The majesty that has accrued to thee in the day, in a year, that majesty which has accrued in the wind, in the firmament, to that majesty of thine, to Prajāpati, to the Gods, All-hail! || 3. Who, by his, grandeur hath become sole Ruler of all the. moving world that breathes and slumbers; | He who is Sovereign of these men and cattle—what God shall we adore with our oblation? || 4. Taken upon a base art thou. I take thee welcome to Prajāpati, | This is thy place: the Moon thy majesty. | Thy majesty that has accrued to thee by night, in a year, thy majesty that has accrued in the earth, in Agni, in the stars and in the Moon, to that majesty of thine, to Prajāpati and to the Gods, All-hail! || 5. They who stand round hills as he moves harness the bright, the ruddy Steed: | The lights are shining in the sky. || 6. On both sides to the car they yoke the two. Bay Coursers dear to him, | Bold; tawny, bearers of the Chief. || 7. When, swift as wind, the Horse has reached the form that Indra loves, the flood, | Again, O singer, by this path bring thou our Courser hitherward. || 8. Let the Vasus anoint thee with Gāyatrī metre. Let the Rudras anoint thee with Trishṭubh metre. Let the Ādityas anoint thee with Jagatī metre. Earth! Ether! Heaven! O Gods, eat this food, parched grains and groats in the product of barley and in the product of cows: eat this food, Prajāpati. || 9. Who moveth single and alone? Who is brought forth to life again? | What is the remedy of cold, or what the great receptacle? || 10. The Sun moves single and alone. The Moon is brought to life again, | Fire is the remedy of cold; Earth is the great receptacle. || 11. What was the antecedent thought? What was the bird of mighty size? | The slippery matron, who was she? Who was the reddish-coloured one? || 12. Heaven was the antecedent thought. The Courser was the mighty bird. | The slippery matron was the earth, Night was the reddish-coloured one. || 13. Vāyu help thee with cooked viands! Blackneck with goats; Nyagrodha with cups; Śalmali with increase; this Stallion here, good for the chariot—let him verily come with his four feet. Brahmākṛishṇa help us! Obeisance to Agni! || 14. The car is fitted with the rein, the steed is fitted with the rein.

| Fitted in waters, water-born, is Brahmā following Soma's lead. || 15. Steed, from thy body, of thyself, sacrifice and accept thyself. | Thy greatness can be gained by none but thee. || 16. No, here thou diest not, thou art not injured: only by fair paths to the Gods thou guest, | May Savitar the God in that world place thee where dwell the pious, whether they have journeyed. || 17. Agni was the victim. With him they sacrificed. He won this world in which Agni is. This shall become thy world. This shalt thou win. Drink these waters. Vāyu was the victim. With him they sacrificed. He won this world in which Vāyu is. This shall become, etc., as above. Sūrya was the victim, etc., He won the world in which Sūrya is. This shall become, etc. || 18. To vital breath, Hail! To out-breathing, Hail! To diffusive breath, Hail! | Ambā! Ambikā! Ambālikā! No one is taking me away. | The sorry horse will lie beside another, as Subhadrā, the dweller in Kāmpīla. || 19. Thee we invoke, troop-lord of troops, Thee we invoke, the loved ones' lord. | Thee, lord of treasures, we invoke. My precious wealth![1] || 32. Now have I glorified with praise strong Dadhikrāvan, conquering steed, | Sweet may he make our mouths: may he prolong the days we have to live. || 33. Gāyatrī, Trishṭubh, Jagatī, and Paṅkti with Anushṭubh joined, | Bṛihatī, Kakubh, Ushṇihā pacify thee with needle-points! || 34. Two-footed, those that have four feet, those with three feet and those with five, | Metreless, with one metre; these pacify thee with needle-points! || 35. May Mahānāmnīs, Revatīs, all far-spread Regions of the sky, | Voices, and lightnings from the cloud pacify thee with needle-points! || 36. May married dames of human birth skilfully separate thy hair: | The Regions, Consorts of the Gods, pacify thee with needle-points! || 37. They, made of silver, gold, and lead, are used as helpers in the work. | As lines on the strong Courser's skin may they console and give thee rest. || 38. What then? As men whose fields are full of barley, etc., as in 10:32. || 39. Who flays thee? Who dissects thee? Who prepares thy limbs for sacrifice? | Who is the Sage that slaughters thee? || 40. In due time let the seasons as thy Slaughterers divide thy joints, | And with the splendour of the Year sacrifice thee with holy rites. || 41. Let the Half-months and let the Months, while sacrificing, flay thy limbs: | Let Day and Night and Marutas mend each fault in sacrificing thee. || 42. Let the divine Adhvaryus flay thy body and dissect thy frame, | And let the sacrificing lines prepare thy members joint by joint, || 43. May Sky, Earth, Air, and Wind supply each failing and defect of thine: | May Sūrya with the Stars of heaven duly prepare a world for thee. || 44. Well be it with thine upper parts, well be it with the parts below! | Well be it with thy bones and with thy marrow and with all thy frame! || 45. Who moveth singly? etc., as in verse 9. || 46. The Sun moves singly, etc., as in verse 10. || 47. What lustre is like Sūrya's light? What lake is equal to the Sea? | What is more spacious than the Earth? What thing is that which naught can mete? || 48. Brahma is lustre like the Sea. Heaven is a flood to match the Sea. | Indra is vaster than the Earth. Beyond all measure is the Cow. || 49. Friend of the Gods, I ask, for information, if thou in spirit hast obtained the knowledge, | Hath Vishṇu this whole Universe pervaded in the three steps wherein the God is worshipped? || 50. I also am in those three steps of Vishṇu wherewith this Universe he permeated. | The earth and heaven I circle in a moment and this heaven's summit with a single organ. || 51. What are the things which Purusha hath entered? What things hath Purusha contained within him? | This riddle we propound to thee, O Brahman. Why dost thou give no answer to my question? || 52. Within five things hath Purusha found entrance; these Purusha hath within himself connected. | This is the thought which I return in answer. Thou art not my superior in wisdom. || 53. What was the antecedent thought? etc., as in verse 11. || 54. Heaven was the antecedent thought, etc., as in 12. || 55. Who, tell me, is the yellowish she? Who is the darkly-yellowish? | Who moves with rapid spring and bound? Who glides and winds along the path? || 56. The she-goat, Sir, is yellowish, dark-yellowish is the porcupine. | The hare moves swift with leap and bound: the snake creeps winding on the path. || 57. How many different forms hath this, how many syllables, burnt-oblations, brands for kindling? | Here, of the rites of sacrifice I ask thee. How many Hotars in due season worship? || 68. Sixfold its form, its syllables a hundred, eighty burnt-offerings, just three brands for kindling. | To thee I tell the rites of sacrificing. Seven Hotars worship in appointed season. || 59. Who knoweth this world's central point? Who knoweth the heaven, the earth, and the wide air between them? | Who knows the birthplace of the mighty Sūrya? Who knows the Moon, whence he was generated? || 60. I know the centre of the world about us. I know heaven, earth, and the wide air between them. | I know the birthplace of the mighty Sūrya. I know the Moon, whence he was generated. || 61. I ask thee of the earth's extremest limit, where is the centre of the world, I ask thee. | I ask thee of the Stallion's genial humour, I ask of highest heaven where Speech abideth. || 62. This altar is the earth's extremest limit; this sacrifice of ours is the world's centre. | This Soma is the Stallion's genial humour, this Brahman highest heaven where Speech abideth. || 63. The Strong, the Self-existent One, the First, within the mighty flood | Laid down the timely embryo from which Prajāpati was born. || 64. Let the Hotar sacrifice to Prajāpati from the Mahiman-Soma. Let him accept. Let him drink the Soma. Hotar, sacrifice. || 65. Prajāpati, thou only, etc., as in 10:20.

Adhyāya 24.

1. Horse, hornless goat, Gomṛiga, these belong to Prajāpati. A black-necked goat, devoted to Agni, (is to be bound) in front to the forehead (of the horse); Sarasvatī's ewe below his jaws; two goats belonging to the Aśvins, with marks on the lower parts of the body, to his fore-legs; a dark-coloured goat, Soma's and Pūshan's, to his navel; a white and a black, sacred to Soma and Yama, to his sides; Tvashṭar's two, with bushy tails, to his hind feet; Vāyu's white goat to his tail; for Indra the Good Worker a cow who slips her calf; a dwarf belonging to Vishṇu. || 2. The red goat, the smoky-red, the jujube-red, these belong to Soma. The brown, the ruddy-brown, the parrot-brown, these are Varuṇa's One with white ear holes, one with partly white, one with wholly white, belong to Savitar. One with fore feet white, partly white, wholly white, belongs to Bṛihaspati She goats speckled, with small spots, with big spots, these belong to Mitra-Varuṇa || 3. The bright-tailed, the wholly bright-tailed, the jewel-tailed, these belong to the Aśvins The white, the white-eyed, the reddish, these are for Rudra Lord of Beasts. Long-eared goats are for Yama; proud ones for Rudra; cloud-coloured ones for Parjanya. || 4. Goats speckled, transversely speckled, upward speckled are for the Marutas. The reddish she-goat, the red-haired, the white, these belong to Sarasvatī. The goat with diseased ears, the short-eared, the red eared are Tvashṭar's The black-necked, the white-flanked, one with bright-coloured thighs belong to Indra and Agni. Those with black marks, small marks, large marks belong to Dawn. || 5. Parti-coloured female victims belong to the All-Gods; red-coloured, eighteen mouths old to Vāk; victims without distinguishing marks to Aditi; those of one same colour to Dhātar; weaned kids sacred to the Consorts of the Gods. || 6. Black-necked victims for Agni; white browed for the Vasus; red for Rudra; bright ones for the Ādityas; cloud-coloured for Parjanya. || 7. The tall goat, the sturdy, the dwarf, these are Indra-Vishṇu's; the tall, the white fore-footed, the black-backed, Indra-Bṛihaspati's; parrot-coloured the Vājins'; speckled Agni-Marutas'; dark-coloured Pūshan's || 8. Variegated, Indra-Agni's; two-coloured, Agni-Soma's; dwarf oxen, Agni-Vishṇu's; barren cows, Mitra-Varuṇa's; partly variegated, Mitra's. || 9. Black-necked ones, Agni's; brown, Soma's; white, Vāyu's; undistinguished, Aditi's; self-coloured, Dhātar's; weanlings, the Gods' Consorts'. || 10. Black ones for Earth; smoke-coloured for Firmament; tall ones for Sky; brindled ones for Lightning; blotched ones for Stars. || 11. Smoke-coloured ones he sacrifices to Spring; white to Summer; black to the Rains; red ones to Autumn; speckled to Winter; reddish-yellow to the Dewy Season. || 12. Calves eighteen months old to Gāyatrī; steers of two and a half years to Trishṭubh; two year old steers to Jagatī; three year olds to Anushṭubh; four year olds to Ushṇih. || 13. Four year old steers to Virāj; full grown bulls to Bṛihatī; strong bulls to Kakubh; draught oxen to Paṅkti; milch-cows to Atichandas. || 14. Black-necked victims sacred to Agni; brown to Soma; spotted to Savitar; weaned she-kids to Sarasvatī; dark-coloured goats to Pūshan; speckled victims to the Marutas; many-coloured to the All-Gods; barren cows to Heaven and Earth. || 15. Called contemporary, the dappled belong to Indra-Agni; black ones to Varuṇa; speckled to the Marutas; hornless he-goats to Ka. || 16. To

1. Verses 20-31 were omitted by Griffith, with the following note: "... the following nine stanzas are not reproducible even in the semi-obscurity of a learned European language; and stanzas 30, 31 would be unintelligible without them."

Agni foremost in place he sacrifices firstling goats; to the consuming Marutas those born of one mother; to the Marutas who perform domestic rites those born after a long time; to the sportive Marutas those born together; to the self-strong Marutas those born in succession. ‖ 17. Called contemporaneous, the dappled belonging to Indra-Agni; those with projecting horns to Mahendra; the many-coloured to Viśvakarman ‖ 18. Smoke-coloured, those of brownish hue, to be offered to the Soma-possessing Fathers; the brown and the smoky-looking to the Fathers who sit on sacred grass; the black and the brownish-looking to the Fathers who have been tasted by Agni; the black and the spotted belong to Tryambaka. ‖ 19. Called contemporaneous, the dappled belong to Śuna and Sīra; white ones to Vāyu; white ones to Sūrya. ‖ 20. To Spring he offers Kapiñjalas; to Summer sparrows; to the Rains partridges; to Autumn quails; to Winter. Kakaras; to the Dewy Season Vikakaras. ‖ 21. To the Sea he sacrifices porpoises; to Parjanya frogs; to the Waters fishes; to Mitra Kulīpayas; to Varuṇa crocodiles. ‖ 22. To Soma he sacrifices wild geese; to Vāyu female cranes; to Indra-Agni curlews; to Mitra divers; to Varuṇa Chakravākas. ‖ 23. To Agni he sacrifices cocks; to Vanaspatis owls; to Agni-Soma blue jays; to the Aśvins peacocks; to Mitra-Varuṇa pigeons. ‖ 24. To Soma he sacrifices quails; to Tvaṣhṭar Kaulīkas; Mainas to the Gods' Consorts; Kulīkas to the Gods' Sisters; Pārushṇas to Agni Lord of the Homestead. ‖ 25. To Day he sacrifices doves; to Night Sīchāpūs; to the Joints of Day and Night bats; to the Months gallinules; to the Year great eagles. ‖ 26. To Ground he sacrifices rats; to Firmament field-rats; to Day voles; to the Quarters mungooses; to the Intermediate Spaces brownish ichneumons. ‖ 27. To the Vasus he sacrifices black-bucks; to the Rudras stags; to the Ādityas Nyanku deer; to the All-Gods spotted deer; to the Sādhyas Kulinga antelopes, ‖ 28. To Īśāna he sacrifices wild asses; to Mitra Gauras; to Varuṇa buffaloes; to Bṛihaspati Gayals; to Tvaṣhṭar camels. ‖ 29. To Prajāpati he sacrifices men elephants; to Vāk white ants; to Sight flies; to Hearing black bees. ‖ 30. To Prajāpati and to Vāyu a Gayal is to be offered; to Varuṇa a wild ram; to Yama a black ram; to a human king a monkey; to the Tiger a red doe; to the Bull a female Gayal, to the Kṣhipraśyena a quail; to the Nīlaṅgu a worm; to the Sea a porpoise; to the Snowy Mountain an elephant. ‖ 31. The Kinnara belongs to Prajāpati; the Ula, the Halikṣhṇa, the cat belong to Dhātar; the heron belongs to the Quarters; the Dhuṅkṣhā to Agni; sparrow, red snake, Sāras, these are Tvaṣhṭar's; the curlew belongs to Vāk. ‖ 32. To Soma an antelope is to be offered; wild goat, mungoose, Śakā. these are Pūṣhan's; the jackal is the Māyu's; the Gaura Indra's; Pidva, antelope, cock, these are Anumati's; the Chakravāka is for Echo. ‖ 33. The female crane is Sūrya's; Śārga, Sṛijaya, Śayāṇḍaka, these are Mitra's; to Sarasvatī belongs the human-voiced Maina; to Ground the porcupine; tiger, wolf, viper belong to Passion; to Sarasvat the human-voiced parrot. ‖ 34. The eagle is Parjanya's; the Āṭi, the Vāhasa, the wood-pecker, these are for Vāyu; for Bṛihaspati Lord of Speech is the Paiṅgarāja; the Alaja belongs to Firmament; pelican, cormorant, fish, these belong to the Lord of Rivers; the tortoise belongs to Heaven and Earth. ‖ 35. The book belongs to the Moon; iguana, Kālakā, woodpecker, these belong to the Vanaspatis; the cock belongs to Savitar; the swan is Vāta's; crocodile, dolphin, Kulīpaya, these belong to the Sea; the porcupine to Modesty. ‖ 36. The Black-doe belongs to Day; frog, female rat, partridge, these belong to the Serpents; the jackal belongs to the Aśvins; the Black-buck to Night; bear, bat, Suṣhilīkā, these belong to the Other Folk; the polecat belongs to Viṣhṇu. ‖ 37. The cuckoo belongs to the Half Months; antelope, peacock, eagle, these are the Gandharvas'; the otter belongs to the Months; tortoise, doe-antelope, iguana, Golathikā belong to the Apsarases; the black snake belongs to Death. ‖ 38. The frog belongs to the Seasons; the vole, the rat, the mouse, these are the Fathers'; the Python, the Balāya belong to the Vasus; Kapiñjala, pigeons owl, hare belong to Nirṛiti; the wild ram to Varuṇa ‖ 39. The white animal belongs to the Ādityas; the camel, the Ghṛiṇīvān, the rhinoceros to Mati; the Sṛimara belong to the Forest-God; the Ruru buck is Rudra's; Kvayi, cock, gallinule, these are the Vājins'; the cuckoo belongs to Kāma. ‖ 40. The Khaṅga is the All-Gods'; the black dog, the long eared, the ass, the hyena, these are the Rākṣhasas; the boar is for Indra; the lion is for the Marutas; the chameleon, the Pippakā, the vulture, these belong to Śaravyā; the spotted antelope belongs to the All-Gods.

Adhyāya 25.

1. I gratify Fresh Grass with his teeth, Avakā with his gums, Clay with his tooth-sockets, Tegas with his fangs. The tongue-tip for Sarasvatī; I gratify the root of the tongue and the palate with his neigh, Vāja with his jaws, the Waters with his mouth, the Stallion with his testicles, the Ādityas with the beard, Path with his eyebrows, Heaven and Earth with his eyelashes, Lightning with the pupils of his eyes. Hail to the white! Hail to the black! Effectual are his eyelashes, irresistible are his lower eyelashes; irresistible are his eyelashes, effectual are his lower eyelashes. ‖ 2. With his breath I gratify Vāta; with his outbreath the two Nostrils; with his lower lip the Upayāma; with his upper lip Existence. With his bright look I please Antara, with his reflection Bāhya; the Whirlpool with his head; Thunder with his frontal bone; the Lightning-flash with his brain; Lightning with the pupils of his eyes; Hearing with his external ears; Ears with his internal ears; Blood with his lower neck; Waters with the fleshless part of his neck; Thought with the back neck-tendons; Aditi with his head; Nirṛiti with his ragged head; Vital Breathings with his roars; Tempest with his crest. ‖ 3. I gratify Flies with his hair; Indra with his active shoulder; Bṛihaspati with his quick spring; Tortoises with his hoofs; Approach with his fetlocks; Kapiñjalas with his heel-ropes; Speed with his two thighs; the Way with his two fore-legs; the Forest-God with a knee-pan; Agni with his two knees; Pūṣhan with his two fore-feet; the Aśvins with his shoulders; Rudra with his shoulder-joints, ‖ 4. The first rib is Agni's; the second Vāyu's; the third Indra's; the fourth Soma's; the fifth Aditi's; the sixth Indrāṇī's; the seventh the Marutas'; the eighth Bṛihaspati's; the ninth Aryaman's; the tenth Dhātar's; the eleventh Indra's; the twelfth Varuṇa's; the thirteenth Yama's. ‖ 5. (On the left side) the first rib belongs to Indra-Agni; the second to Sarasvatī; the third to Mitra; the fourth to the Waters; the fifth to Nirṛiti; the sixth to Agni-Soma; the seventh to the Serpents; the eighth to Viṣhṇu; the ninth to Pūṣhan; the tenth to Tvaṣhṭar; the eleventh to Indra; the twelfth to Varuṇa; the thirteenth to Yama. The right flank belongs to Heaven and Earth, the left to the All-Gods. ‖ 6. The shoulders belong to the Marutas; the first rib-cartilages to the All-Gods; the second to the Rudras; the third to the Ādityas; the tail belongs to Vāyu; the hind-quarters to Agni-Soma. I gratify the two Curlews with the hips; Indra-Bṛihaspati with the thighs; Mitra-Varuṇa with the groins; Approach with the buttocks; Strength with the two cavities of the loins. ‖ 7. I gratify Pūṣhan with the rectum; Blind-worms with the large intestines; Serpents with the entrails; Worms with the guts; the Waters with the bladder; Scrotum with the testicles; the Vājins with his penis; Offspring with his seed; Blue jays with his bile; Fissures with his arms; Kūśmas with his lumps of dung. ‖ 8. His chest belongs to Indra; his belly to Aditi; his clavicles to the Quarters; his nether hind-part to Aditi. I gratify Clouds with his aorta; Firmament with his pericardium; Mist with his belly; the two Chakravākas with his cardiac bones; Sky with his kidneys; Mountains with his ducts; hocks with his spleen; Ant-hills with his lungs; Shrubs with his heart-vessels; Streams with his veins; Lakes with his flanks; Sea with his belly; Vaiśvānara with his ashes. ‖ 9. I gratify Separation with his navel; Butter with his flavour; the Waters with his broth; Sunbeams with his drops of fat; Hoar-frost with his heat; Ice with his marrow; Hailstones with his tears; Thunderbolts with the rheum of his eyes; Rākṣhasas with his blood; Bright things with his limbs; Stars with his beauty; Earth with his skin. All-hail to Jumbaka! ‖ 10. In the beginning rose Hiraṇyagarbha, etc., as in 13:4; 23:1. ‖ 11. Who by his grandeur, etc., as in 23:3. ‖ 12. Whose, by his might, are these snow-covered mountains, and men call sea and Rasā his possession: | Whose are these arms, whose are these heavenly regions. What God shall we adore with our oblation? ‖ 13. Giver of vital breath, of power and vigour, he whose commandment all the Gods acknowledge: | The Lord of death, whose shade is life immortal. What God shall we adore with our oblation? ‖ 14. May powers auspicious come to us from every side, never deceived, unhindered and victorious, | That the Gods ever may be with us for our gain, our guardians day by day, unceasing in their care. ‖ 15. May the auspicious favour of the Gods be ours, on us descend the bounty of the righteous Gods. | The friendship of the Gods have we devoutly sought: so may the Gods extend our life that we may live. ‖ 16. We call them hither with a hymn of olden time, Bhaga, the friendly Dakṣha, Mitra, Aditi, | Aryaman, Varuṇa, Soma, the Aśvins May Sarasvatī, auspicious, grant

felicity. || 17. May the Wind waft to us that pleasant medicine, may Earth our Mother give it, and our Father Heaven, | And the joy-giving stones that press the Soma's juice. Aśvins, may ye, for whom our spirits long, hear this. || 18. Him we invoke for aid who reigns supreme, the Lord of all that stands or moves, inspirer of the soul, | That Pūṣhan may promote the increase of our wealth, our keeper and our guard infallible for our good. || 19. Illustrious far and wide, may Indra prosper us: may Pūṣhan prosper us, the Master of all wealth. | May Tārkṣhya with uninjured fellies prosper us: Bṛihaspati vouchsafe to us prosperity. || 20. The Marutas, Sons of Pṛiśni, borne by spotted steeds, moving in glory, oft visiting holy rites, | Sages whose tongue is Agni and their eyes the Sun,—hither let all the Gods for our protection come. || 21. Gods, may we with our ears listen to what is good, and with our eyes see what is good, ye Holy Ones. | With limbs and bodies firm may we extolling you attain the term of life appointed by the Gods. || 22. A hundred autumns stand before us, O ye Gods, within whose space ye bring our bodies to decay; | Within whose space our sons become fathers in turn. Break ye not in the midst our course of fleeting life. || 23. Aditi is the heaven, Aditi is mid-air, Aditi is the Mother and the Sire and Son. | Aditi is all Gods, Aditi five-classed men, Aditi all that hath been born and shall be born. || 24. Slight us not Varuṇa, Aryaman, or Mitra, Ṛibhukṣhan, Indra, Āyu, or the Marutas, | When we declare amid the congregation the virtues of the Strong Steed, God-descended. || 25. What time they bear before the Courser, covered with trappings and with wealth, the grasped oblation, | The dappled goat goeth straightforward, bleating, to the place dear to Indra and to Pūṣhan || 26. Dear to all Gods, this goat, the share of Pūṣhan, is first led forward with the vigorous Courser, | While Tvaṣhṭar sends him forward with the Charger, acceptable for sacrifice, to glory. || 27. When thrice the men lead round the Steed, in order, who goeth to the Gods as meet oblation, | The goat precedeth him, the share of Pūṣhan, and to the Gods the sacrifice announceth. || 28. Invoker, ministering priest, stoner, fire-kindler, Soma-presser, sage, reciter, | With this well ordered sacrifice, well finished, do ye fill full the channels of the rivers. || 29. The hewers of the post and those who carry it, and those who carve the knob to deck the Horse's stake; | Those who prepare the cooking-vessels for the Steed,—may the approving help of these promote our work. || 30. Forth, for the regions of the Gods, the Charger with his smooth back is come; my prayer attends him. | In him rejoice the singer and the sages. A good friend have we won for the Gods' banquet. || 31. May the fleet Courser's halter and his heel-ropes, the headstall and the girths and cords about him, | And the grass put within his mouth to bait him,—among the Gods, too, let all these be with thee. || 32. What part of the Steed's flesh the fly hath eaten, or is left sticking to the post or hatchet, | Or to the slayer's hands and nails adhereth,—among the Gods, tog, may all this he with thee. || 33. Food undigested steaming from his belly, and any odour of raw flesh remaining, | This let the immolators set in order and dress the sacrifice with perfect cooking. || 34. What from thy body which with fire is roasted, when thou art set upon the spit, distilleth,— | Let not that lie on earth or grass neglected, but to the longing Gods let all be offered. || 35. They who, observing that the Horse is ready, call out and say, The smell is good; remove it; | And, craving meat, await the distribution,—may their approving help promote our labour. || 36. The trial-fork of the flesh cooking cauldron, the vessels out of which the broth is sprinkled, | The warming-pots, the covers of the dishes, hooks, carving-boards,—all these attend the Charger. || 37. Let not the fire, smoke-scented, make thee crackle, nor glowing cauldron smell and break to pieces. | Offered, beloved, approved, and consecrated,—such Charger do the Gods accept with favour. || 38. The starting-place, his place of rest and rolling, the ropes wherewith the Charger's feet were fastened, | The water that he drank, the food he tasted,—among the Gods, too, may all these attend thee. || 39. The robe they spread upon the Horse to clothe him, the upper covering and the golden trappings, | The halters which restrain the Steed, the heel-ropes,—all these, as grateful to the Gods, they offer. || 40. If one, when seated, with excessive urging hath with his heel or with his whip distressed thee, | All these thy woes, as with oblation's ladle at sacrifices, with my prayer I banish. || 41. The four-and-thirty ribs of the swift Courser, kin to the Gods, the slayer's hatchet pierces. | Cut ye with skill so that the parts be flawless, and piece by piece declaring them dissect them. || 42. Of Tvaṣhṭar's Courser there is one dissector: this is the custom: two there are who guide him. | Such of his limbs as I divide in order, all these, amid the lumps, in fire I offer. || 43. Let not thy dear soul burn thee as thou comest, let not the hatchet linger in thy body. | Let not a greedy clumsy immolator, missing the joints, mangle thy limbs unduly. || 44. No, here thou diest not, thou art not injured: only by easy paths to Gods thou goest. | Both Bays, both Spotted Mares are now thy fellows, and to the Ass's pole is yoked the Courser. || 45. May this Steed bring us all-sustaining riches, wealth in good kine, good horses, manly offspring. | Freedom from sin may Aditi vouchsafe us; the Steed with our oblations gain us lordship! || 46. We will, with Indra and all Gods to help us, bring these existing worlds into subjection. | With the Ādityas, with the band of Marutas, may Indra give us medicine to heal us. | Our sacrifice, our bodies, and our offspring may Indra regulate with the Ādityas || 47. O Agni, be our nearest Friend, etc., as in 3:25. | To thee then, O Most Bright, etc., as in 3:26.

Adhyāya 26.

1. Agni and Pṛithivī, closely connected, may they bring low for me the boon I mention. | Vāyu and Firmament, closely connected, may they, etc. | Closely connected Dyaus and the Āditya, may they, etc. | Closely connected Varuṇa and Waters, may they, etc. | Lord of the seven communities and her who forms all beings, eighth, | Make our ways full of pleasantness: may So-and-So and I agree. || 2. That I to all the people may address this salutary speech, | To priest and nobleman, Śūdra and Ārya, to one of our own kin and to the stranger. | Dear may I be to Gods and guerdon-giver. Fulfilled be this my hope: be that my portion! || 3. Give us, Bṛihaspati, that wondrous treasure, that which exceeds the merit of the foeman, | Which shines among the folk effectual, splendid, that, Son of Law, which is with might refulgent. | Taken upon a base art thou. Thee for Bṛihaspati This is thy home. Thee for Bṛihaspati, || 4. Come hither, Indra, rich in kine! Drink Soma, Lord of Hundred Powers, | Effused by braying pressing-stones. | Taken upon a base art thou. Thee for Indra, rich in kine. This is thy home. Thee for Indra, rich in kine. || 5. O Indra, Vṛitra-slayer, come. Drink Soma, Lord of | Hundred Powers, | Expressed with stones whose wealth is kine. | Taken upon a base art thou, etc., as in verse 4. || 6. Vaiśvānara the righteous One, the Lord of sacrifice and light, | The heat that wasteth not, we seek. | Taken upon a base art thou. Thee for Vaiśvānara | This is thy home: thee for Vaiśvānara || 7. Still in Vaiśvānara's grace may we continue: yea, he is King Supreme o'er all things living. | Sprung hence to life upon this All he looketh. Vaiśvānara hath rivalry with Sūrya. | Taken upon a base art thou, etc., as in verse 6. || 8. Hitherward come Vaiśvānara to succour us from far away, | Agni through laud that brings him near! | Taken upon a base, etc., as in verse 6. || 9. Agni is Pavamāna, Sage, the Tribe-Priest of the Races Five: | To him of mighty wealth we pray. | Taken upon a base art thou. Thee for lustre. This is thy home. Thee for lustre. || 10. May mighty Indra, thunder-armed, may Ṣhoḍaśin protect us well, and slay the wicked man who hateth us. | Taken upon a base art thou. Thee for Mahendra. This is thy home. Thee for Mahendra. || 11. As cows low to their calves in stalls so with our songs we glorify | This Indra, e'en your wondrous God who checks assault, who joys in the delicious juice. || 12. Agni's is the most fetching song. Shine mightily, thou rich in light! | Like the Chief Consort of a King, riches and strength proceed from thee. || 13. Come, here, O Agni, will I sing verily other songs to thee, | And with these drops shalt thou grow strong. || 14. The Seasons spread thy sacrifice! the Mouths protect thine offering! | May the Year guard our sacrifice for thee and keep our children safe. || 15. There where the mountains downward slope, there by the meeting of the streams | The sage was manifest with song. || 16. High is thy juice's birth: though sat in heaven, on earth it hath obtained | Strong sheltering power and great renown. || 17. Finder of room and freedom, flow for Indra, meet for worship, flow | For Varuṇa and the Marut host. || 18. Striving to win, with him we gain all wealth of the ungodly one, | Yea, all the glories of mankind. || 19. May we be prosperous with brave sons, cattle, horses, each wish of ours, and varied blessings, | With quadrupeds, and with the men about us. May the Gods guide our sacrifice in season. || 20. O Agni, bring thou hitherward the yearning Consorts of the Gods | Bring Tvaṣhṭar to the Soma-draught. || 21. O Neṣhṭar girt by Dames, accept our sacrifice: with Ṛitu drink, | For thou art

he who giveth wealth. || 22. He with the Ṛitus fain would drink, Wealth-river, from the Neṣhṭar's bowl. | Begin, pay offerings: hasten ye. || 28. Thine is this Soma: come thou near, approach it. Drink thou thereof, benevolent, and cease not. | Sit on the sacred grass at this our worship, and take these drops into thy belly, Indra. || 24. Come unto us, ye swift to listen! as at home, upon the sacred grass sit and enjoy yourselves. | And, Tvaṣhṭar, well content be joyful in the juice with Gods and Goddesses in gladsome company. || 25. In sweetest and most gladdening stream flow pure, O Soma, on thy way, | Pressed out for Indra, for his drink. || 26. Fiend-queller, Friend of all men, he hath in the vat attained unto | His place, his iron-fashioned home.

Adhyāya 27.

1. Half-Years and Seasons strengthen thee, O Agni, the Years and all the Verities and Ṛiṣhis! | Flash forth with thy celestial effulgence: illumine all four regions of the heaven. || 2. Kindle thee, Agni, rake this man to knowledge: rise up erect for great and happy fortune. | Agni, be those uninjured who adore thee, thy priests be glorious and none beside them! || 3. The Brahmans present here elect thee, Agni: be thou propitious in our sanctuary. | Slayer of rivals, Agni, quell our foemen: watch in thy house with care that never ceases. || 4. Even here do thou, O Agni, establish wealth: let not oppressors injure thee by thinking of thee first. | Light be thy task of ruling, Agni, with thy power: may he who worships thee wax strong, invincible. || 5. Kind to the people, grasp thy power, O Agni: contend thou with the Friend by way of friendship. | Placed, Agni, in the centre of our kinsmen, flash forth to be invoked by Kings around thee. || 6. Past those who slay, past enemies, past thoughtless men, past those who hate,— | Yes, Agni, drive away all woe and trouble: vouchsafe us opulence with men about us. || 7. Holder of sway, shine here refulgent, Agni! invincible, unconquered Jātavedas. | Light all the regions, chasing human terrors: with happy helps guard us today for increase. || 8. Bṛihaspati, Savitar, give this man knowledge: sharpen him thoroughly though already sharpened. | To great and high felicity exalt him: in him let all the Gods rejoice and triumph. || 9. As thou, Bṛihaspati, from curse hast freed us, from dwelling yonder in the realm of Yama, | The Aśvins, Leeches of the Gods, O Agni, have chased Death far from us with mighty powers. || 10. Looking upon the loftier light, etc., as in 20:21. || 11. Uplifted are the brands that are his fuel: lofty and brilliant are the flames of Agni, | Splendidly bright of the Son fair of aspect. || 13. Tanūnapāt the Asura, all-possessing, God among Gods, the God with mead and butter shall bedew the paths. || 13. With mead to sacrifice thou comest, Agni, earnest as friendly-minded Narāśaṃsa, and Savitar righteous God who brings all blessings. || 14. He cometh hitherward with power and fatness, the luminous, implored with adoration. | While rites proceed the ladles move to Agni. || 15. Let him pay worship to this Agni's greatness, daintily fed: he verily gives enjoyments: | The wisest Vasu he, and best wealth giver. || 16. Widely expansive, ruling by foundation, the Doors divine— and, after, all— | Preserve this Agni's holy works. || 17. May Dawn and Night protect—his heavenly Consorts—in a his home this our sacrificial worship. || 18. Ye two celestial Hotars, greet with praises this lofty rite of ours, the tongue of Agni. | Cause that our sacrifice be well conducted. || 19. Upon this grass three Goddesses be seated, Iḍā, Sarasvatī, Bhāratī the Mighty glorified with song. || 20. This our productive wondrous flow may Tvaṣhṭar pour down on this man's kin, and wealth and heroes. || 21. Vanaspati, presenting of thyself, send God-ward! Let Agni, Immolator, season our oblation. || 22. Pay sacrifice to Indra, Jātavedas Agni! with Hail! All Gods accept the gift we offer! || 23. Wise, bright, arranger of his teams, he seeketh men with rich food whose treasures are abundant. | They have stood firm of one accord with Vāyu: yea, the men wrought all noble operations. || 24. The God whom both these worlds brought forth for riches, whom heavenly Dhiṣhaṇā for our wealth appointeth— | His team of harnessed horses waits on Vāyu and, foremost, on the radiant treasure-holder. || 26. What time the mighty waters came containing the universal germ, producing Agni, | Thence sprang the Gods' one spirit into being. What God shall we adore with our oblation? || 26. Who in his might surveyed the floods enclosing productive force and generating Worship, | He who is God mid Gods, and none beside him—What God shall we adore with our oblation? || 27. The teams wherewith thou seekest him who offers, within his house, O Vāyu, to direct him, | Therewith send wealth to us with full enjoyment, a hero son and gifts of kine and horses. || 28. With thy yoked teams in hundreds and in thousands come to our sacrifice and solemn worship. | O Vāyu, make thee glad at this libation. Preserve us evermore, ye Gods, with blessings. || 29. Drawn by thy team, O Vāyu, come: to thee is offered this, the pure. | Thou visitest the presser's house. || 30. Vāyu, the bright is offered thee, best of the meath at holy rites. | Come thou to drink the Soma juice, God longed-for, on thy team-drawn car. || 31. Lover of worship, leader, come Vāyu with thought, to sacrifice, | Propitious with propitious teams! || 32. With all the thousand chariots that are thine, O Vāyu, come to us, | Team-drawn, to drink the Soma juice. || 33. Come thou with one, and ten, O Self-Existent! with two unto the sacrifice, and twenty. | Three are the teams and thirty which convey thee. O Vāyu, in this place unyoke thy coursers. || 34. Wonderful Vāyu, Lord of Truth, thou who art Tvaṣhṭar's Son in-law, | Thy saving succour we elect. || 35. Like kine unmilked we call aloud, Hero, to thee and sing thy praise, | Looker on heavenly light, Lord of this moving world, Lord, Indra! of what moveth not. || 36. None other like to thee, of earth or of the heavens, hath been or ever will be born. | Desiring horses, Indra, Bounteous Lord! and kine, as men of might we call on thee. || 37. That we may win us wealth and power, we poets call on only thee. | In war men call on thee, Indra! the hero's Lord, in the steed's race-course call on thee. || 38. As such, O Wonderful, whose hand holds thunder, praised as mighty, Caster of the Stone! | Pour on us boldly, Indra, kine and chariot-steeds ever to be the conqueror's strength. || 39. What succour will he bring to us, wonderful, ever-prospering Friend? | With what most mighty company? || 40. What, genuine and most liberal draught will spirit thee with juice to burst | Open e'en strongly-guarded wealth || 41. Do thou who art protector of us thy friends who praise thee | With hundred aids approach us. || 42. Sing to your Agni with each song, at every sacrifice, for strength. | Come, let us praise the Wise and Everlasting God even as a well-beloved Friend. || 43. Protect us, Agni, through the first, protect us through the second hymn. | Protect us through three hymns, O Lord of Power and Might; through four hymns, Vasu! guard thou us. || 44. The Son of Strength; for is he not our Friend? Let us serve him for offering our gifts. | In battles may he be our help and strengthener, yea, be the saviour of our lives. || 45. Thou art Saṃvatsara; thou art Parivatsara; thou art Idāvatsara; thou art Idvatsara; thou art Vatsara. | Prosper thy Dawns! Prosper thy Day-and-Nights! Prosper thy Half-months, Months, Seasons, and Years! | Combine them for their going and their coming, and send then forward on their ordered courses. | In eagle's shape thou art piled up and layered. With that divinity, Aṅgiras-like, lie steady.

Adhyāya 28.

1. On the earth's centre, at libation's place let the Priest worship Indra with the kindling-stick. | The mightiest of the lords of men is kindled on the height of heaven. | Let him enjoy the butter. Hotar, worship. || 2. Him let the Hotar worship, him Tanūnapāt with ready aids; the conqueror never overcome, | Indra, the God who finds heaven's light on paths most rich in pleasant sweets, with Narāśaṃsa all aglow. Let him enjoy, etc., as in verse 1. || 3. With viands let the Hotar worship Indra immortal, praised, receiver of oblations. | The God, the equal of the Gods in vigour, the thunder-wielder, breaker-down of castles. Let him enjoy, etc. || 4. Let the Priest worship Indra, Bull who sitteth on sacred grass, doer of manly actions. | Let him be seated on the grass with Vasus and Rudras and Ādityas for companions. Let him enjoy, etc. || 5. Let the Priest sacrifice. The Doors have strengthened Indra, his force and conquering might and vigour. | At this our worship let the Doors be opened, easy to pass, the strengtheners of Order: wide let them open out for bounteous Indra. Let them enjoy, etc. || 6. Let the Priest sacrifice to Night and Morning, the teeming Cows of Indra, Mighty Mothers. | Indra their calf with lustre have they strengthened, even as two mothers of a calf in common. Let them enjoy, etc. || 7. Let the Priest worship both the heavenly Hotars, Friends, Leeches, healing Indra with oblation. | The sages, Gods pre-eminent for wisdom bestow on Indra his surpassing power. Let them enjoy, etc. || 8. Let the Priest offer sacrifice to the three Goddesses and balm. | Let the three triple active Ones, let Iḍā and Sarasvatī and Bhāratī the mighty Dames, Consorts

of Indra, who receive our sacrificial offerings, enjoy the butter, etc. ‖ 9. Let the Priest worship Tvaṣhṭar radiant Indra, Physician good at sacrifice, graced with butter, | Multiform and prolific, rich and bounteous. Let Tvaṣhṭar, giving wondrous powers to Indra, enjoy, etc. ‖ 10. Let the Priest worship him, the Forest-Sovereign, the Immolator, Lord of Hundred Powers, the lover of the prayer, the friend of Indra. | Balming with mead, may he on easy pathways sweeten our sacrifice with savoury butter. Let him enjoy, etc. ‖ 11. Let the Priest offer sacrifice to Indra: with Hail! to Gods of butter; with Hail! to Gods of marrow; with Hail! to Gods of drops; with Hail! to Gods of offerings paid with Svāhā; with Hail! to Gods of sacrificial hymns. | All hail! May butter-drinking Gods and Indra rejoicing taste the butter. Hotar, worship. ‖ 12. Vigorous, strewn by Gods upon the altar the right Gods' sacred Grass hath strengthened Indra. | Cut in the day, cherished by night it hath surpassed those who have sacrificial Grass with wealth. For gain of riches let him taste. Pay sacrifice. ‖ 13. Firm, closely joined, the Doors divine have strengthened Indra in the rite. | Pressed by a calf or tender boy may they drive off the courser as he tosses up the sand. For gain of wealth let then enjoy. Pay sacrifice. ‖ 14. Morning and Night, the Goddesses, have called on Indra as the rite advanced. | May they well-pleased and ordered well make the Celestial Tribes come forth. For gain of wealth let them enjoy. Pay sacrifice. ‖ 15. Two Goddesses, wealth-givers, kind, have heightened radiant Indra's strength. | One drives away hatreds and sins; the other shall bring the Sacrificer boons and treasure. | Instructed, let them both enjoy, for gain of wealth. Pay sacrifice. ‖ 16. Bringers of strengthening sacrifice, the Goddesses, the teeming Cows, have prospered Indra with their milk. | Let one bring food and energy, the other feast and banqueting. | Bringers of strengthening sacrifice, allotting the several portions they have put together old energy with new and new with olden, strengthening boons and treasures for the Sacrificer. Instructed, let them, etc., as in verse 15. ‖ 17. The two Celestial Hotars, Gods, have heightened radiant Indra's might. | Freed from slain sinners these have brought the Sacrificer wealth and boons. Instructed, let them, etc. ‖ 18. Goddesses three, three Goddesses have heightened their Lord Indra's strength. | One, Bhāratī, hath touched the sky, Sarasvatī the sacrifice with Rudras, and, enriched with wealth, Iḍā the homesteads of the folk. For gain of wealth let them enjoy. Pay sacrifice. ‖ 19. The radiant Indra, Praise of Men, thrice-shielding, borne on three car-seats, hath heightened radiant Indra's strength. | Set on a hundred white-backed cows, yea, on a thousand forth he goes. Mitra and Varuṇa alone deserve to be his Hotar-priests, Bṛihaspati his Chanter, and the Aśvins his Adhvaryus. For gain of wealth let him enjoy. Pay sacrifice. ‖ 20. Vanaspati, a God with Gods, with golden leaves, sweet boughs, fair fruit, hath heightened radiant Indra's strength. | Sky with his summit hath he touched, and firmament, and established earth. For gain of wealth let him enjoy. Pay sacrifice. ‖ 21. The grassy robe of water-plants, divine, hath heightened Indra's strength. | This, the fair seat where Indra sits, hath topped all other sacred grass. For gain of wealth let it enjoy. Pay sacrifice. ‖ 22. Agni, Fair-offering-maker, bright, hath heightened radiant Indra's strength. | Today may Sviṣhṭakṛit, Fair-offering-maker, paying good sacrifice, for us perform it. For gain of wealth let him enjoy. Pay sacrifice. ‖ 23. Today the Sacrificer hath elected—dressing messes of cooked food and a rice-cake, binding a goat for Indra—Agni as his Hotar. | Today divine Vanaspati hath with a goat served Indra well. | He hath eaten from the fat, he hath accepted the cooked food, he hath waxed strong with the rice-cake. | Thee, today, O Ṛishi, etc., as in 21:61. ‖ 21. Let the Priest worship Agni, Indra, kindled, splendidly kindled, excellent strength-giver, | Lending him mighty power, Gāyatrī metre, a cow aged eighteen months, and vital vigour. Let him enjoy the butter. Hotar, worship. ‖ 25. Let the Priest serve with sacrifice him who breaks forth, Tanūnapāt, the germ which Aditi conceived, pure Indra who bestoweth strength, | Bringing him mighty power, the Uṣhṇih metre, an ox of two years old, and vital vigour. Let him enjoy; etc. ‖ 26. Let the Priest sacrifice to Soma, Indra, adorable, adored, best Vṛitra-slayer, strength-giver, might, to be adored with viands, | Bringing him mighty power, Anuṣhṭubh metre, a cow of thirty months, and vital vigour. Let him enjoy, etc. ‖ 27. Let the Priest worship Indra, strength-bestower, immortal, with fair grass, allied with Pūṣhan, seated on sacred grass, dear, everlasting, | Bringing him mighty power, Bṛihatī metre, a steer of three years' age and

vital vigour. Let him enjoy, etc. ‖ 28. Let the Priest worship the wide-opening Portals, easy to pass, divine, Law-strengthening, golden, Indra, the Brahman Priest, the strength-bestower, | Bringing him mighty power, the Paṅkti metre, a bullock four years old, and vital vigour. Let them enjoy the butter. Hotar, worship. ‖ 29. Let the Priest worship lofty Night and Morning, well-decked, of varied hue, lovely to look on, Indra the Universal, strength-bestower, | Bringing him mighty power, the Triṣhṭubh metre, a bullock four years old, and vital vigour. Let them enjoy the butter. Hotar, worship. ‖ 30. Let the Priest worship both celestial Hotars, the Gods' best glory, sages famed for wisdom, the two companions, Indra strength-bestower, | Bringing him mighty power, Jagatī metre, an ox that draws the wain, and vital vigour. Let them enjoy the butter. Hotar, worship. ‖ 31. Let the Priest sacrifice to three well-decorated Goddesses, gold-decked, great, lofty, Bhāratīs, Indra their Lord who giveth strength, | Bringing him mighty power, Virāj the metre, and a cow in milk. Let him enjoy the butter. Hotar, worship. ‖ 32. Let the Priest worship Tvaṣhṭar the prolific, strengthener of growth, maintaining varied growth and form, Indra who giveth vital force, | Bringing him Dvipadā metre, mighty power, and an ox full-grown. Let him enjoy the butter. Hotar, sacrifice. ‖ 33. Let the Priest serve with sacrifice the Forest Lord Vanaspati, the Immolator, hundred-powered, praise-worthy, golden-leafed, who wears the girdle, loved, the gracious Lord, Indra who gives the strength of life, | Giving him Kakubh metre, mighty power, a barren, a calf-slipping cow, and vital vigour. Let him enjoy the butter. Hotar, sacrifice. ‖ 34. Let the Priest offer worship to the Svāhākṛiti Goddesses, to Agni Household Lord apart, to Varuṇa the Leech and Sage, might, Indra who bestoweth strength, | Bringing him Atichandas metre, great and mighty power, a strong bull, his prime, and vital vigour. Let them enjoy the butter. Hotar, sacrifice. ‖ 35. The Grass divine hath added might to radiant Indra strength-giver, | Laying in Indra wondrous power and sight and strength by Gāyatrī. For gain of wealth let him enjoy the butter. Offer sacrifice. ‖ 36. The Doors divine have magnified bright Indra, who bestoweth strength. | With Uṣhṇih laying mighty power in Indra, vital breath and force. For gain of wealth let them enjoy the butter. Offer sacrifice. ‖ 37. Morning and Night, divine Ones, have strengthened bright Indra, strength-giver, the Goddesses advanced the God, | With the Anuṣhṭubh laying power in Indra, strength and vital force. For gain of wealth let them enjoy. Pay sacrifice. ‖ 38. Kind, bounteous, and divine, they have strengthened bright Indra, force-giver, the Goddesses advanced the God, | Laying in Indra power and force and hearing with the Bṛihatī For gain of wealth let them enjoy. Pay sacrifice. ‖ 39. Bringers of strengthening sacrifice, the Goddesses, two teeming cows, have heightened Indra's power with milk, | Laying bright power in Indra with Paṅkti, and vital energy. For gain of wealth let them enjoy. Pay sacrifice. ‖ 40. The Gods, two heavenly Hotars, have strengthened bright Indra, force-giver, those Gods have magnified the God, | With Triṣhṭubh giving Indra power, impetuous might, and vital strength. For gain of wealth let them enjoy. Pay sacrifice. ‖ 41. Goddesses three, three Goddesses have heightened their Lord Indra's strength, his who bestoweth vital force, | Laying in Indra power and might and vital strength with Jagatī. For gain of wealth let them enjoy. Pay sacrifice. ‖ 42. The God, the Praise of all men, hath strengthened bright Indra force-giver, the God hath magnified the God, | Laying in Indra with Virāj beauty and power and vital force. For gain of wealth let him enjoy. Pay sacrifice. ‖ 43. The God the Forest Sovereign hath strengthened bright Indra, force-giver, the God hath magnified the God, | With Dvipadā storing Indra with fortune and power and vital strength. For gain of wealth let him enjoy. Pay sacrifice. ‖ 44. The Grass divine of water-plants hath helped bright Indra force-giver, the God hath magnified the God, | Laying in Indra mighty power with Kakubh, fame and vital strength. For gain of wealth let it enjoy. Pay sacrifice. ‖ 45. Agni, the God who makes fair rites, hath strengthened Indra force-giver, the God hath magnified the God, | Laying with Atichandas power in Indra, sway, and vital strength. For gain of wealth let him enjoy. Pay sacrifice. ‖ 46. Today the Sacrificer hath elected, etc., as in verse 23. | Today divine Vanaspati, etc. . . . . . | Thee, today, O Ṛishi, etc. . . . . .

Adhyāya 29.

1. Decking the treasure-house of prayers, O Agni, enkindled, pouring forth sweet-tasted butter, | Swift-moving, bearing curd, O Jātavedas, bear what they love to the Gods' habitation. || 2. Balming the paths that lead to heaven with fatness, let the Steed go unto the Gods well-knowing. | Courser, the Quarters of the sky attend thee! Bestow thou food upon this Sacrificer. || 3. Thou, Steed, art meet for laud and veneration; swift, fit for sacrifice art thou, O Courser. | In concert with the Gods and Vasus Agni Omniscient waft thee a contented bearer! || 4. Pleased with much Sacred Grass which we have scattered wide spread upon the earth, a pleasant carpet, | Joined with the Gods may Aditi, accordant, bestowing bliss award it happy fortune. || 5. May these your Doors divine that wear all colours, auspicious, with uplifted leaves unfolding, | Lofty and closely fitted and sonorous, rich in adornment, offer easy passage. || 6. Your two Dawns rich in gold and varied colour, travelling on 'twixt Varuṇa and Mitra, | Acquainted with the face of sacrifices, I settle here within the home of Order. || 7. Your two chief Hotars have I pleased, bright-coloured, borne on one car, Gods who behold all creatures, | Those who prepare your rules and ordinances and make you see the light by their direction. || 8. Bhāratī with Ādityas love our worship! Sarasvatī with Rudras be our helper, | And Iḍā in accord, invoked with Vasus! Goddesses, place our rite among the Immortals. || 9. The God-devoted son Tvaṣhṭar produces: from Tvaṣhṭar springs to life your fleet-foot Courser. | Tvaṣhṭar gave being to this All about us. Priest, worship here the mighty work's achiever. || 10. Let the Steed seek his home, and balmed with butter go of himself unto the Gods in season. | To the Gods' world Vanaspati, well-knowing, bear our oblations which the fire has tasted! || 11. Thou, waxing by Prajāpati's strong fervour, born quickly, guardest sacrifice, O Agni. | With consecrated offering go, preceding, and let the Sādhyas, Gods, eat our oblation. || 12. What time, first springing into life, thou neighedst, proceeding from the sea or cloudy vapour, | Limbs of the deer hadst thou, and eagle pinions. O Steed, thy birth is high and must be lauded. || 13. This Steed, bestowed by Yama, Trita harnessed, and Indra was the first to mount and ride him. | His bridle the Gandharva grasped. O Vasus, from out the Sun ye fashioned forth the Courser. || 14. Yama art thou, O Horse; thou art Āditya; Trita art thou by secret operation. | From Soma thou art thoroughly divided. They say there are three bonds in heaven that hold thee. || 15. Three bonds, they say, thou hast in heaven to bind thee, three in the waters, three within the ocean. | To me thou seemest Varuṇa, O Courser, there where they say is thy sublimest birthplace. || 16. Here, Courser, are the places where they groomed thee; here are the traces of thy hooves as winner. | Here have I seen the auspicious reins that guide thee, which those who guard the holy Law keep safely. || 17. Thyself from far I recognized in spirit, a Bird that from below flew through the heaven. | I saw thy head still soaring, striving upward by paths unsoiled by dust, pleasant to travel. || 18. Here I beheld thy form matchless in beauty, eager to win thee food at the Cow's station. | Whene'er a man brings thee to thine enjoyment, thou swallowest the herbs, most greedy eater. || 19. After thee, Courser, come the car, the bridegroom, the kine come after, and the charm of maidens. | Full companies have followed for thy friendship: the pattern of thy vigour Gods have followed. || 20. His horns are golden and his feet are iron. Less fleet than he, though swift as thought, was Indra. | The Gods came only to the oblation-banquet of him who mounted first of all the Courser. || 21. Symmetrical in flank, with rounded haunches, mettled like heroes, the celestial Coursers | Put forth their strength like swans in lengthened order when they, the Steeds, have reached the heavenly causeway. || 22. A body formed for flight hast thou, O Charger; swift as the wind in motion is thy spirit. | Thy horns are spread abroad in all directions; they move with restless beat in wildernesses. || 23. The strong Steed hath come forward to the slaughter, pondering with a mind directed God-ward. | The goat who is his kin is led before him: the sages and the singers follow after. || 21. The Steed is come unto the noblest mansion, is come unto his Father and his Mother. | This day shall he approach the Gods, most welcome: then he declares good gifts to him who worships. || 25. Thou in the house of man this day enkindled worshippest Gods, a God, O Jātavedas. | Wealthy in friends! observant, bring them hither. Thou art a sapient envoy, full of wisdom. || 26. Tanūnapāt, fair-tongued, with sweet mead balming the paths and ways of Order, make them pleasant. | Convey our sacrifice to heaven, exalting with holy thoughts our hymns of praise and worship. || 27. With sacrifice to these we with laudations will honour holy Narāśaṃsa's greatness— | To these the pure, most wise, the thought-inspirers, Gods who enjoy both sorts of our oblations. || 28. Invoked, deserving laud and adoration, O Agni, come accordant with the Vasus. | Thou art, O vigorous One, the Gods' Invoker, so, best of Sacrificers, bring them quickly. || 29. By rule the Sacred Grass is scattered eastward, a robe to clothe the earth when dawns are breaking. | Widely it spreads around and far extended, fair for the Gods and bringing peace and freedom. || 30. Let the expansive Doors be widely opened, like wives who deck their beauty for their husbands. | Lofty, celestial, all-impelling Portals, admit the Gods and give them easy access. || 31. Pouring sweet dews, let holy Night and Morning, each close to each, be seated at their station— | Lofty, celestial Dames, with gold to deck them, assuming all their fair and radiant beauty. || 32. Come the two chief celestial sweet-voiced Hotars, arranging sacrifice for man to worship, | As singers who inspire us in assemblies, showing the eastward light with their direction! || 33. Let Bhāratī come quickly to our worship, and Iḍā showing like a human being. | So let Sarasvatī and both her fellows, deft Goddesses, on this fair grass be seated. || 34. Hotar more skilled in sacrifice, bring hither with speed today God Tvaṣhṭar, thou who knowest, | Even him who framed these two, the Earth and Heaven, the Parents, with their forms, and every creature. || 35. Send to our offerings which thyself thou balmest the Companies of Gods in ordered season. | Agni, Vanaspati, the Immolator sweeten our offered gift with mead and butter. || 36. Agni as soon as he was born made ready the sacrifice and was the Gods' preceder. | May the Gods eat our offering consecrated according to the true Priest's voice and guidance. || 37. Thou, making light where no light was, and form, O men! where form was not, | Wast born together with the Dawns. || 38. The warrior's look is like a thunderous rain-cloud's when, armed with mail, he seeks the lap of battle. | Be thou victorious with unwounded body: so let the thickness of thine armour save thee. || 39. With Bow let us win kine, with Bow the battle, with Bow be victors in our hot encounters. | The Bow brings grief and sorrow to the foeman: armed with the Bow may we subdue all regions. || 40. Close to his ear, as fain to speak, She presses, holding her well-loved Friend in her embraces. | Strained on the Bow, She whispers like a woman—this Bow-string that preserves us in the combat. || 41. These, meeting like a woman and her lover, bear, mother-like, their child upon their bosom. | May the two Bow-ends, starting swift asunder scatter, in unison, the foes who hate us. || 42. With many a son, father of many daughters, He clangs and clashes as he goes to battle. | Slung on the back, pouring his brood, the Quiver vanquishes all opposing bands and armies. || 43. Upstanding in the Car the skilful Charioteer guides his strong Horses on whithersoe'er he will. | See and admire the strength of those controlling Reins which from behind declare the will of him who drives || 44. Horses whose hoofs rain dust are neighing loudly, yoked to the Chariots, showing forth their vigour. | With their forefeet descending on the foemen, they, never flinching, trample and destroy them. || 45. Car-bearer is the name of his oblation, whereon are laid his Weapons and his Armour. | So let us here, each day that passes, honour the helpful Car with hearts exceeding joyful. || 46. In sweet association lived the fathers who gave us life, profound and strong in trouble, | Unwearied, armed with shafts and wondrous weapons, free, real heroes, conquerors of armies. || 47. The Brahmans, and the Fathers meet for Soma draughts, and, graciously inclined, unequalled Heaven and Earth. | Guard us from evil, Pūṣhan! guard us strengtheners of Law! let not the evil-wisher master us. || 48. Her tooth a deer, dressed in an eagle's feathers, bound with cow-hide, launched forth, She flieth onward. | There where the heroes speed hither and thither, there may the arrows shelter and protect us. || 49. Avoid as thou whose flight is straight, and let our bodies be as stone. | May Soma kindly speak to us, and Aditi protect us well. || 59. He lays his blows upon their backs, He deals his strokes upon their thighs. | Thou Whip who urgest horses, drive sagacious chargers in the fray. || 51. It compasses the arm with serpent windings, fending away the friction of the bowstring: | So may the Brace, well skilled in all its duties, guard manfully the man from every quarter. || 52. Lord of the Wood, be firm and strong in body: be, bearing us, a brave victorious hero. | Show forth thy strength, compact with straps of leather,

and let thy rider win all spoils of battle. || 53. Its mighty strength was borrowed from the heaven and earth its conquering force was brought from sovereigns of the wood. | Honour with holy gifts the Car like Indra's bolt, the Car bound round with straps, the vigour of the floods. || 54. Thou bolt of Indra, Vanguard of the Marutas, close knit to Varuṇa and Child of Mitra,— | As such, accepting gifts which here we offer, receive, O Godlike Chariot, these oblations. || 55. Send forth thy voice aloud through earth and heaven, and let the world in all its breadth regard thee; | O Drum, accordant with the Gods and Indra, drive thou afar, yea, very far, our foemen. || 56. Thunder out strength and fill us fall of vigour: yea, thunder forth and drive away all dangers. | Drive hence, O War-drum, drive away misfortune: thou art the Fist of Indra: show thy firmness. || 57. Drive hither those, and these again bring hither: the War-drum speaks aloud as battle's signal. | Our heroes, winged with horses, come together. Let our car-warriors, Indra, be triumphant. || 58. The black-necked victim belongs to Agni; the ewe to Sarasvatī; the brown victim is Soma's; the dusky Pūṣhan's; the white-backed is Bṛihaspati's; the dappled belongs to the All-Gods; the red to Indra; the spotted to the Marutas; the strong-bodied to Indra-Agni; one with white marks below to Savitar; to Varuṇa a black ram with one white foot || 59. To Agni Anīkavat is sacrificed a red-marked ox; two with white spots below are for Savitar; two with silvery navels for Pūṣhan; two yellow hornless he-goats for the All-Gods; a spotted one for the Marutas; the black-faced he-goat is Agni's; the ewe is Sarasvatī's; the ram is Varuṇa's || 60. To Agni of the Gāyatrī, of the Trivṛit hymn and of the Rathantara Sāman is to be offered a rice-cake on eight potsherds; to Indra of the Triṣhṭubh, the Pañchadaśa hymn and the Bṛihat Sāman one on eleven potsherds; to the All-Gods of the Jagatī, the Seventeenfold hymn and the Vairūpa Sāman, one on twelve potsherds; to Mitra-Varuṇa of the Anuṣhṭubh, the Ekaviṃśa hymn, and the Vairāja Sāman, a mess of curdled milk; to Bṛihaspati of the Paṅkti metre, the Triṇava hymn, and the Śākvara Sāman, an oblation of rice boded in milk; to Savitar of the Uṣhṇih, the Thirty-threefold hymn, and the Raivata Sāman, a rice-cake on eight potsherds; a mess of boiled rice is to be made for Prajāpati; the same for Viṣhṇu's Consort Aditi; to Agni Vaiśvānara is to be offered a rice-cake on twelve potsherds, and to Anumati one on eight.

Adhyāya 30.

1. Our sacrifice, God Savitar! speed onward: speed to his share the sacrifice's patron. | May the Celestial Gandharva, cleanser of thought and will, make clean our thoughts and wishes. | The Lord of Speech sweeten the words we utter! || 2. May we attain that excellent glory of Savitar the God: | So may he stimulate our prayers. || 3. Savitar, God, send far away all troubles and calamities, | And send us only what is good. || 4. We call on him distributor of wondrous bounty and of wealth, | On Savitar who looks on men. || 5. For Brahman (Priesthood) he binds a Brahman to the stake; for Kṣhatra (Royalty) a Rājanya; for the Marutas a Vaiśya; for Penance a Śūdra; for Darkness a robber; for Hell a homicide or a man who has lost his consecrated fire; for Misfortune a eunuch; for Venality an Ayogū; for Kāma a harlot; for Excessive Noise a Māgadha; || 6. For Dance a stable-master; for Song a public dancer; for Duty one who attends court; for Pastime a timid man; for Sport a chatterer; for Laughter an artist; for Pleasure a woman-lover; for Desire a damsel's son; for Dexterity a car-builder; for Firmness a carpenter; || 7. For Trouble a potter's son; for Device an artificer; for Beauty a jeweller; for Welfare a sower; for the Arrow-deity a maker of shafts; for Injury a bowyer; for Action a bowstring-maker; for Fate a rope-maker; for Death a hunter; for the Finisher a dog-leader; || 8. For Rivers a fisherman; for Ṛikṣhīkās a Niṣhāda's son; for the Man-tiger a madman; for the Gandharvas and Apsarases a Vrātya; for Motives one demented; for Serpents and Genii an untrustworthy man; for Dice a gambler; for Excitement a non-gambler; for Piśāchas a woman who splits cane; for Yātudhānas a woman who works in thorns; || 9. For Rendezvous a lover; for Homestead a paramour; for Trouble an unmarried elder brother; for Nirṛiti a younger brother who has married before his elder; for Misfortune the husband of a younger sister whose elder sister has not been married; for Representation a woman who embroiders; for Agreement a woman who deals in love-charms; for Garrulity a by-sitter; for Colour an obstinate man; for Strength a yielding man; || 10. For Interruptions a hunch-back; for Delight a dwarf, for Doors a blear-eyed man; for Sleep a blind man; for Unrighteousness a deaf man; for Purifying Medium a physician; for Insight an astrologer; for Craving for Knowledge an inquisitive man; for Desire of extra Knowledge an extra-inquisitive man; for Moral Law a question solver; || 11. For Eye-diseases an elephant-keeper; for Speed a horse-keeper; for Nourishment a cowherd; for Manliness a shepherd; for Keenness a goatherd; for Refreshment a ploughman; for Sweet Beverage a preparer of Surā; for Weal a house-guard; for Well-being a possessor of wealth; for Supervision a doorkeeper's attendant; || 12. For Light a wood-bringer; for Brightness a fire-kindler; for the Sun's Station a besprinkler; for Highest Heaven a high steward; for the World of Gods a carver; for the World of Men a distributor; for All-Worlds a pourer-out: for Poverty, Affliction a stirrer-up of strife; for Sacrifice a washerwoman; for Delight a female dyer; || 13. For Assault a thievish-hearted man; for Homicide a slanderer; for Discrimination a door-keeper; for Inspection a door-keeper's attendant; for Strength a servant; for Plenty a running footman; for the Beloved a sweet speaker; for Safety the rider of a horse; for the World of Svarga a dealer-out of portions; for Highest Heaven a high steward; || 14. For Passion an iron-smelter; for Anger a remover; for Yoking a yoker; for Pain an assailant; for Quiet an unyoker; for Up-hill and Down-hill one who stands on three legs; for Form a conceited man; for Virtue a female ointment-maker; for Nirṛiti a female scabbard-maker; for Yama a barren woman; || 15. For Yama a mother of twins; for the Atharvans a woman who has miscarried; for the First Year a gad-about; for the Parivatsara one who has not borne a child; for the Idāvatsara one who exceeds; for the Idvatsara one who transgresses; for the Vatsara one who is worn out; for the Saṃvatsara one with grey hair; for the Ṛibhus a hide-dresser; for the Sādhyas a currier; || 16. For Lakes a fisherman; for Standing Waters a fisher; for Tank-waters a Niṣhāda; for Reed-beds a fish-vender; for the Opposite Bank one who gropes for fish; for This Bank a fish-catcher; for Fords an Ānda; for shallows a Maināla; for Sounds a Bhilla; for Caverns a Kirāta; for Mountain-heights a destructive savage; for Mountains a wild man; || 17. For Abhorrence a Paulkasa; for Colour a goldsmith; for Balance a merchant; for Repentance a sluggard; for All Spirits a leper; for Prosperity a watchful man; for Failure a sleepy man; for Mischief a chatterer; for Misfortune a shameless man; for Undoing one who cuts up into small pieces; || 18. For the Dice-king a gambler; for the die Kṛita one who contemplates his adversary's ill luck, for the Tretā a gamble-manager; for the Dvāpara a chief manager; for Āskanda one who will not leave the gambling-hall; for Mṛityu one who approaches cows; for Antaka a Cow-killer; for Hunger one who goes begging to a man who is cutting up a cow; for Misdeed a leader of the Charakas; for Misery a robber; || 19. For Echo a reviler; for Noise a snarler; for End a very talkative man; for Endless a mute; for Sound a drummer; for Might a lute-player; for Cry a flute-blower; for Confused Tone a Conch-blower; for the Wood a wood-ranger; for Partly-wooded Land a forest fire guard; || 20. For Pastime a harlot; for Laughter a jester; for Lust a woman with spotty skin; for Might these, the head-man of a village, an astrologer, and a watchman; a lute-player; a hand-clapper, a flutist, these for Dance; for Pleasure a musician; || 21. For Fire a fat man; for Earth a cripple; for Wind a Chāṇḍāla; for Mid-Air a pole-dancer; for Sky a bald-head; for the Sun a green-eyed man; for Stars a spotty man; for the Moon a leper; for Day a white yellow-eyed man; for Night a black man with yellow eyes. || 22. Now he ties up the eight following variform men: one too tall, one too short, one too stout, one too thin, one too white, one too black, one too bald, one too airy. These must be neither Śūdras nor Brahmans, and must be dedicated to Prajāpati. A minstrel, a harlot, a gambler, and a eunuch—neither of Śūdra nor Brahman caste—are to be dedicated to Prajāpati.

Adhyāya 31.

1. Puruṣha hath a thousand heads, a thousand eyes, a thousand feet. | Pervading earth on every side he fills a space ten fingers broad. || 2. Puruṣha is in truth this All, what hath been and what yet shall be; | Lord, too, of immortality which waxes greater still by food. || 3. So mighty in his grandeur; yea, greater than this is Puruṣha | All creatures are one fourth of him, three fourths eternal life in heaven. || 4. With three fourths Puruṣha rose up: one fourth of him again was here. | Thence he moved forth to

every side over what eats not and what eats. ‖ 5. From him Virāj was born; again Puruṣha from Virāj was born. | When born, he spread to west and east beyond the boundaries of earth. ‖ 6. From that great General Sacrifice the dripping fat was gathered up. | He formed the creatures of the air and animals both wild and tame. ‖ 7. From that great General Sacrifice Richas and Sāman hymns were born: | Therefrom were spells and charms produced; the Yajus had its birth from it. ‖ 8. From it were horses born, from it all cattle with two rows of teeth | From it were generated kine, from it were goats and sheep produced. ‖ 9. They balmed as victim on the grass Puruṣha born in earliest time. | With him the Deities and all Sādhyas and Riṣhis sacrificed. ‖ 10. When they divided Puruṣha how many portions did they make? | What was his mouth? what were his arms? what are the names of thighs and feet? ‖ 11. The Brahman was his mouth, of both his arms was the Rājanya made. | His thighs became the Vaiśya, from his feet the Śūdra was produced. ‖ 12. The Moon was gendered from his mind, and from his eye the Sun had birth; | Vāyu and Prāṇa from his ear, and from his mouth was Agni born. ‖ 13. Forth from his navel came mid-air; the sky was fashioned from his head; | Earth from his feet, and from his ear the Quarters. Thus they formed the worlds. ‖ 14. When Gods performed the sacrifice with Puruṣha as offering | Spring was the butter, Autumn the oblation, Summer was the wood. ‖ 15. Then seven were his enclosing-sticks, his kindling-brands were three times seven, | When Gods, performing sacrifice, bound as their victim Puruṣha ‖ 16. Gods, sacrificing, sacrificed the victim: these were the earliest holy ordinances. | The Mighty Ones attained the height of heaven, there where the Sādhyas, Gods of old, are dwelling. ‖ 17. In the beginning he was formed, collected from waters, earth, and Viśvakarman's essence. | Fixing the form thereof Tvaṣhṭar proceedeth. This was at first the mortal's birth and godhead. ‖ 18. I know this mighty Puruṣha whose colour is like the Sun, beyond the reach of darkness. | He only who knows him leaves Death behind him. There is no path save this alone to travel. ‖ 19. In the womb moves Prajāpati: he, never becoming born, is born in sundry figures. | The wise discern the womb from which he springeth. In him alone stand all existing creatures. ‖ 20. He who gives light and heat to Gods, first, foremost Agent of the Gods, | Born ere the Gods—to him the bright, the holy One, be reverence! ‖ 21. Thus spake the Gods at first, as they begat the bright and holy One: | The Brahman who may know thee thus shall have the Gods in his control. ‖ 22. Beauty and Fortune are thy wives: each side of thee are Day and Night. | The constellations are thy form: the Aśvins are thine open jaws. | Wishing, wish yonder world for me, wish that the Universe be mine.

Adhyāya 32.

1. Agni is That; the Sun is That; Vāyu and Chandramās are That. | The Bright is That; Brahma is That, those Waters, that Prajāpati. ‖ 2. All twinklings of the eyelid sprang from Puruṣha, resplendent One. | No one hath comprehended him above, across, or in the midst. ‖ 3. There is no counterpart of him whose glory verily is great. | In the beginning rose Hiraṇyagarbha, etc. Let not him harm me, etc. Than whom there is no other born, etc. ‖ 4. This very God pervadeth all the regions; yea, born aforetime, in the womb he dwelleth. | He verily born and to be born hereafter meeteth his offspring, facing all directions. ‖ 5. Before whom naught whatever sprang to being; who with his presence aids all living creatures, | Prajāpati, rejoicing in his offspring, he, Ṣhodaśin, maintains the Three great Lustres. ‖ 6. By whom the heavens are strong and earth stands firmly, by whom light's realm and sky-vault are supported; | By whom the regions in mid-air were measured. What God shall we adore with our oblation? ‖ 7. To whom, supported by his help, two armies embattled look while trembling in their spirit, | Where over them the risen Sun is shining. What God shall we adore with our oblation? | What time the mighty waters, etc. He in his might surveyed, etc. ‖ 8. The Sage beholdeth That mysterious Being wherein this All hath found one only dwelling. | Therein unites the Whole, and thence it issues: far-spread it is the warp and woof in creatures. ‖ 9. Knowing Eternity, may the Gandharva declare that station, parted, kept in secret. | Three steps thereof in mystery are hidden: he who knows these shall be the father's father. ‖ 10. He is our kin, our Father and Begetter: he knows all beings and all Ordinances, | In whom the Gods obtaining life eternal have risen upward to the third high

station. ‖ 11. Having encompassed round existing creatures, the world; and all the Quarters and Mid-quarters, | Having approached the first-born Child of Order he with his Self into The Self hath entered. ‖ 12. Having gone swiftly round the earth and heaven, around the worlds, around the sky, the Quarters, | Having spread out the lengthened thread of Order, he views, and he becomes and is That Being. ‖ 13. To the Assembly's wondrous Lord, to Indra's lovely Friend who gives | Wisdom. have I drawn near in prayer. ‖ 14. That wisdom which the Companies of Gods, and Fathers, recognize, | Even with that intelligence, O Agni, make me wise today. All-hail! ‖ 15. Varuṇa grant me wisdom! grant it Agni and Prajāpati! | Wisdom may Indra, Vāyu grant. May the Creator grant it me. All-hail! ‖ 16. Let these the Priests and Nobles both enjoy the splendour that is mine. | Best splendour may the Gods bestow on me. To thee, that splendour, hail!

Adhyāya 33.

1. His be the fires, eternal, purifying, protectors of our homes, whose smoke is shining, | White, waxing in their strength, for ever stirring, and seated in the wood: like winds are Somas. ‖ 2. Gold-coloured, bannered with the smoke, urged by the wind, aloft to heaven | Rise, lightly borne, the flames of fire. ‖ 3. Bring to us Mitra-Varuṇa, bring the Gods to the great sacrifice; | Bring them, O Agni, to thine home. ‖ 4. Yoke, Agni, as a charioteer, thy steeds who best invoke the Gods: | As ancient Hotar take thy seat. ‖ 5. To fair goals travel Two unlike in semblance: each in succession nourishes an infant. | One bears a Godlike Babe of golden colour: bright and fair-shining is be with the other. ‖ 6. Here by ordainers was this God appointed first Invoker, best at worship, to be praised at rites, | Whom Apnavāna and the Bhṛigus caused to shine, bright-coloured in the wood, spreading to every house. ‖ 7. Three times a hundred Gods, and thrice a thousand, and three times ten, and nine have worshipped Agni, | For him spread sacred grass, balmed him with butter, and established him as Priest and Sacrificer. ‖ 8. Him, messenger of earth and head of heaven, Agni Vaiśvānara, born in holy Order, | The Sage, the King, the Guest of men, a vessel fit for their mouths, the Gods have generated. ‖ 9. May Agni slay the foemen,—fain for riches, through the love of song | Kindled, bright, served with sacrifice. ‖ 10. With the All-Gods, with Indra and with Vāyu drink the Soma mead, | O Agni, after Mitra's laws. ‖ 11. When splendour reached the Lord of men to speed him, down from the heaven was shed the brilliant moisture. | Agni brought forth to light and filled with spirit the youthful host benevolent and blameless. ‖ 12. Show thyself strong for mighty bliss, O Agni; most excellent be thine effulgent splendours. | Make easy to maintain our household lordship and trample down the might of those who hate us. ‖ 13. We have elected thee as most delightful for thy beams' glow: hear our great laud, O Agni. | The best men praise thee as the peer of Indra in strength, mid Gods, like Vāyu in thy bounty. ‖ 14. O Agni who art worshipped well, dear let our princes be to thee, | Our wealthy patrons who are governors of men, who part in gifts their stalls of kine. ‖ 15. Hear, Agni who hast ears to hear, with all thy train of escort Gods. | Let Mitra, Aryaman, seeking betimes our rite, seat them upon the sacred grass. ‖ 16. The Freedom of all Gods who merit worship, freely received as Guest in all men's houses, | Agni who hath secured the Gods' high favour, may he be gracious to us, Jātavedas. ‖ 17. In great enkindled Agni's keeping and, for bliss, free from all sin before Mitra and Varuṇa, | May we share Savitar's best animating help. We crave this gracious favour of the Gods today. ‖ 18. Like barren cows, moreover, swelled the waters: singers approached thy holy cult, O Indra. | Come thou to us as to his team comes Vāyu. Thou through our solemn hymns bestowest bounty. ‖ 19. Ye Cows, protect the fount. The two mighty Ones bless the sacrifice. | The handles twain are wrought of gold. ‖ 20. Now when the Sun hath risen today may sinless Mitra, Aryaman, | Bhaga, and Savitar speed us forth. ‖ 21. Pour on the juice the ornament which reaches both the heaven and earth; | Supply the liquid to the Bull. | Thou in the first old time. See, Vena. ‖ 22. As he was rising up they all revered him: self-luminous he travels, clothed in splendour. | That is the Bull's, the Asura's lofty nature: he, Omniform, hath reached the eternal waters. ‖ 23. I laud your Mighty One who joyeth in the juice, him who is good to all men, who pervadeth all; | Indra whose conquering strength is powerful in war, whose fame and manly vigour Heaven and Earth revere. ‖ 24. Great is their fuel, strung their laud, wide is their

sacrificial post | Whose Friend is Indra, ever young. || 25. Come, Indra, and delight thee with the juice at all the Soma feasts, | Conqueror, mighty in thy strength. || 26. Leading his band, Indra encompassed Vṛitra; weak grew the wily leader of enchanters. | He who burns fierce in forests slaughtered Vyaṃsa, and made the milch-kine of the nights apparent. || 27. Whence comest thou alone, thou who art mighty, Indra, Lord of the Brave? What is thy purpose? | Thou greetest us, encountering us the Bright Ones. Lord of Bay Steeds, say what thou hast against us. | Indra, great in his power and might. Ne'er art thou fruitless. Never art thou neglectful. || 28. Those men extolled that deed of thine, O Indra, those who would fain burst through the stall of cattle, | Fain to milk her who bare but once, great, lofty, whose sons are many and her streams a thousand. || 29. To thee the Mighty One I bring this mighty hymn, for thy desire hath been gratified by my laud. | In Indra, yea, in him victorious through his might, the Gods have joyed at feast and when the Soma flowed. || 30. May the Bright God drink glorious Soma-mingled mead, giving the sacrifice's lord uninjured life; | He who, wind-urged, in person guard our offspring well, hath nourished them with food and shone o'er many a land. || 31. His bright rays bear him up aloft, the God who knoweth all that lives, | Sūrya, that all may look on him. || 32. Pure Varuṇa, with that same eye wherewith thou lookest upon one | Actively stirring mid the folk— || 33. Ye two divine Adhvaryus, come hither upon a sun-bright car: | Bedew our sacrifice with stead. | Thou in the first old time. See, Vena. The brilliant presence. || 34. Loved of all men, may Savitar through praises offered as sacred food come to our synod, | That ye too, through our hymns, ye ever youthful, may gladden at your visit all our people. || 35. Whatever, Vṛitra-slayer! thou Sūrya hast risen on today, | That, Indra, all is in thy power. || 36. Swift, visible to all art thou, O Sūrya, maker of the light, | Illuming all the radiant realm. || 37. This is the Godhead, this the might of Sūrya: he hath withdrawn what spread o'er work unfinished. | When he hath loosed his horses from their station, straight over all Night spreadeth out her garment. || 38. In the sky's lap the Sun this form assumeth that Varuṇa and Mitra may behold it. | His Bay Steeds well maintain their power eternal, at one time bright, and darksome at another. || 39. Verily, Sūrya, thou art great; truly, Āditya, thou art great. | As thou art great indeed thy greatness is admired: yea, verily thou, God, art great. || 40. Yea, Sūrya, thou art great in fame: thou, evermore, O God, art great. | Thou by thy greatness art the Gods' Home-Priest, divine, far-spread, unconquerable light. || 41. Turning, as 'twere, to meet the Sun, enjoy from Indra all good things. | When he who will be horn is born with power we look to treasures as our heritage. || 42. Today, ye Gods, when Sūrya hath ascended, deliver us front trouble and dishonour. | This boon may Varuṇa and Mitra grant us, and Aditi and Sindhu, Earth and Heaven. || 43. Throughout the dusky firmament advancing, laying to rest the immortal and the mortal, | Borne on his golden chariot he cometh, Savitar, God, beholding living creatures. || 44. Soft to the tread the sacred grass is scattered: these go like Kings amid the band around them, | At the folk's early call on Night and Morning,—Vāyu, and Pūṣhan with his team to bless us. || 45. Indra, Vāyu, Bṛihaspati, Mitra, Agni, Pūṣhan, Bhaga, | Ādityas, and the Marut host. || 46. Be Varuṇa our chief defence, let Mitra guard us with all aids: | Both make us rich exceedingly! || 47. Regard us, Indra, Viṣhṇu, here, ye Aśvins, and the Marut host, us who are kith and kin to you. | Thou in the first old time. See, Vena. O ye eleven Gods. Loved of all men, may Savitar. With the All-Gods. Ye Viśvedevas who protect. || 48. O Agni, Indra, Varuṇa, and Mitra, give, O ye Gods, and Marut host, and Viṣhṇu. | May both Nāsatyas, Rudra, heavenly Matrons, Pūṣhan, Sarasvatī, Bhaga accept us. || 49. Indra, Agni, Mitra, Varuṇa, Aditi, the Waters, Mountains, Marutas, Sky, and Earth and Heaven, | Viṣhṇu I call, Pūṣhan and Brahmaṇaspati, and Bhaga, Śaṃsa, | Savitar that they may help. || 50. With us are raining Rudras, clouds accordant in call to battle at the death of Vṛitra, | The strong, assigned to him who sings and praises. May Gods with Indra as their chief protect us. || 51. Turn yourselves hitherward this day, ye Holy, that fearing in my heart I may approach you. | Protect us, Gods, let not the wolf destroy us. Save us, ye Holy, from the pit and falling. || 52. This day come all the Marutas, etc., as in 18:31. || 53. Listen, All-Gods, to this mine invocation, ye who inhabit heaven and air's mid-region. | All ye; O Holy Ones, whose tongue is Agni, seated upon this sacred grass be joyful. || 54. For thou at first producest for the holy Gods the noblest of all portions, immortality. | Thereafter as a gift to men, O Savitar, thou openest existence, life succeeding life. || 55. I with a lofty song call hither Vāyu all-bounteous, filler of his car, most wealthy. | Thou, Sage, with bright path, Lord of harnessed horses, impetuous, promptly honourest the prudent. || 56. These, Indra-Vāyu, have been shed, etc., as in 7:8. || 57. Mitra of holy strength I call, and foe-destroying Varuṇa, | Who make the oil-fed rite complete. || 58. Nāsatyas, Wonder-workers, yours are these libations with clipt grass. | Come ye whose paths are bright with glow. || 59. When Saramā had, found the mountain's fissure, that vast and ancient place she plundered thoroughly. | In the floods' van she led them forth, light-footed: she who well knew came first unto their lowing. || 60. For nowhere did they find another envoy to lead the way than this Vaiśvānara Agni. | The Gods immortal strengthened the immortal Vaiśvānara to win the land in battle. || 61. The strong, dispellers of the foe, Indra and Agni, we invoke: | May they be kind to one like me. || 62. Sing forth to Indu, O ye men, to him as he is purified, | Fain to pay worship to the Gods. || 63. Drink Soma, Indra, handed with the Marutas who, Boon Lord! strengthened thee at Ahi's slaughter, | 'Gainst Śambara, Lord of Bays! in winning cattle, and now rejoice in thee, the holy singers. || 64. Thou vast born mighty for victorious valour, exulting, strongest, full of pride and courage. | There, even there the Marutas strengthened Indra when his most rapid Mother stirred the Hero. || 65. O thou who slewest Vṛitra, come, O Indra, hither to our side, | Mighty One with thy mighty aids. || 66. Thou in thy battles, Indra, art subduer of all hostile bands. | Father art thou, all-conquering, cancelling the curse: vanquish the men who fight with us. || 67. Heaven and Earth cling close to thy victorious might | As sire and mother to their child. || 68. The sacrifice obtains the Gods' acceptance, etc., as in 8:4. || 69. Protect our habitation, Savitar, this day with guardian aids around, propitious, ne'er beguiled. | God of the golden tongue, keep us for newest bliss: let not the evil-wisher have us in his power. || 70. For you have flowed, through noble ministration, pressed by Adhvaryus, bright sweet-flavoured juices. | Drive on thy team and come thou hither, Vāyu: drink for thy rapture of the sap of Soma. || 71. Ye Cows, protect, etc., as in verse 14. || 72. Come ye foe-slayers to the place of meeting, to the birth-places of the two great Sages, | With force of intellect unto the dwelling. || 73. Ye two divine Adhvaryus, etc., as in verse 33. Thou in the time of old. See, Vena. || 74. Transversely was the severing line extended: was it above, or was it, haply, under? | There were begetters, there were mighty forces, free action here and energy up yonder. || 75. He hath filled heaven and earth and the great realm of light, when at his birth the skilful held him in their hold. | He like a steed is led forth to the sacrifice, Sage, graciously inclined, that he may win us wealth. || 76. Call hither with the song and lauds the two best slayers of the foe, | Delighting even in our hymn. || 77. All Sons of Immortality shall listen to the songs we sing, | And be exceeding good to us. || 78. Mine are devotions, hymns, sweet are libations. Strength stirs, and hurled forth is my rocky weapon. | They call for me, for me their lauds are longing. To their libations these my Bay Steeds bear me. || 79. Nothing, O Bounteous Lord, stands firm before thee: among the Gods not one is found thine equal. | None born or springinge into life comes near thee. Do what thou hast to do, exceeding mighty! || 80. In all the worlds That was the Best and Highest whence sprang the mighty God of splendid valour. | Quickly when born he overcomes his foemen, he in whom all who lend him aid are joyful. || 81. May these my songs of praise exalt thee, Lord, who hast abundant wealth. | Men skilled in holy hymns, pure, with the hues of fire, have sung them with their lauds to thee. || 82. Good Lord of wealth is he to whom all Āryas, Dāsas here belong. | E'en over unto thee, the pious Ruśama Pavīru, is that wealth brought nigh. || 83. He, with his might advanced by Ṛiṣhis thousandfold, hath like an ocean spread himself. | His majesty is praised as true at solemn rites, his power where holy singers rule. || 84. Protect our habitation, Savitar, etc., as in verse 69. || 85. Come, Vāyu, drawn by fair hymns, to our sacrifice that reaches heaven. | Poured on the middle of the straining-cloth and dressed, this bright drink hath been offered thee. || 86. Indra and Vāyu, fair to see and swift to hear, we call to us, | That in assembly all, yea, all the folk may be benevolent to us and free from malady. || 87. Yea, specially that mortal man hath toiled for service of the Gods, | Who quickly hath brought near Mitra and Varuṇa to share his sacrificial gifts. || 38. Approach ye, and be near to us.

Drink, O ye Aśvins, of the mead. | Draw forth the milk, ye mighty, rich in genuine wealth! Injure us not, and come to us. || 89. May Brahmaṇaspati draw nigh, may Sūnṛitā the Goddess come, | And Gods bring to our rite which gives the fivefold gift the Hero, lover of mankind. || 90. Within the Waters runs the Moon, he with the beauteous wings, in heaven. | To yellow-hued abundant wealth, object of many a man's desire, loud-neighing goes the tawny Steed. || 91. Singing their praise with godlike hymn let us invoke each God for grace, | Each God to bring you help, each God to strengthen you. || 92. Agni Vaiśvānara, set in heaven, with mighty splendour hath shone forth. | Increasing in his power on earth, benevolent, he quells the darkness with his light. || 93. First, Indra-Agni! hath this Maid come footless unto those with feet. | Stretching her head and speaking loudly with her tongue, she hath gone downward thirty steps. || 94. For of one spirit are the Gods with mortal man, co-sharers all of gracious gifts. | May they increase our strength hereafter and today, providing ease and ample room. || 95. Indra who quells the curse blew curses far away, and then in splendour came to us. | Indra, refulgent with the Marut host! the Gods eagerly strove to win thy love. || 96. To Indra, to your mighty Chief, Marutas, sing forth a mighty prayer. | Let Śatakratu, Vṛitra-slayer, kill the fiend with hundred-knotted thunderbolt. || 97. Indra increased his manly strength at sacrifice, in the wild rapture of this juice; | And living men today, even as of old, sing forth their praises to his majesty. | May these. Good Lord of wealth. He with his might. Stand up erect.

Adhyāya 34.

1. That which, divine, mounts far when man is waking, that which returns to him when he is sleeping, | The lights' one light that goeth to a distance, may that, my mind, be moved by right intention. || 2. Whereby the wise and thoughtful in assemblies, active in sacrifice, perform their duties, | The peerless spirit stored in living creatures, may that, my mind, be moved by right intention. || 3. That which is wisdom, intellect, and firmness, immortal light which creatures have within them, | That without which men do no single action, may that, my mind, be moved by right intention. || 4. Whereby, immortal, all is comprehended, the world which is, and what shall be hereafter, | Whereby spreads sacrifice with seven Hotars, may that, my mind, be moved by right intention. || 5. Wherein the Ṛichas, Sāmans, Yajus-verses, like spokes within a car's nave, are included, | And all the thought of creatures is inwoven, may that, my mind, be moved by right intention. || 6. Controlling men, as, with the reins that guide them, a skilful charioteer drives fleet-foot horses, | Which dwells within the heart, agile, most rapid, may that, my mind, be moved by right intention. || 7. Now will I glorify great strength's upholder, Food, | By whose invigorating might Trita rent Vṛitra limb from limb. || 8. Do thou, in truth, Anumati, assent and grant us happiness. | Urge us to strength and energy: prolong the days we have to live. || 9. Anumati this day approve our sacrifice among the Gods! | Oblation-bearing Agni be, and thou, bliss to the worshipper! || 10. O broad-tressed Sinīvālī, thou who art the sister of the Gods, | Accept the offered sacrifice, and, Goddess, grant us progeny. || 11. Five rivers flowing on their way speed onward to Sarasvatī, | But then became Sarasvatī a fivefold river in the land. || 12. O Agni, thou the earliest Aṅgiras, the Seer, hast, God thyself, become the Gods' auspicious Friend. | After thy holy ordinance the Marutas, sage, active through wisdom, with their glittering spears, were born. || 13. Worthy to be revered, O Agni, God, preserve our wealthy patrons with thy succours, and ourselves. | Guard art thou of our seed and progeny and cows, incessantly protecting in thy holy law. || 14. Lay this with care on her who lies extended: straight, when impregned, hath she brought forth the Hero. | With his bright pillar—radiant is his lustre—in our skilled task is born the Son of Iḍā || 15. In Iḍā's place, the centre of the earth, will we deposit thee, | That, Agni Jātavedas, thou mayst bear our offerings to the Gods. || 16. Like Aṅgiras a gladdening laud we ponder to him who loveth song, exceeding mighty. | Let us sing glory to the far-famed Hero who must be praised with fair hymns by the singer. || 17. Unto the Great One bring great adoration, a chant of praise to him the very potent, | Through whom our sires, Aṅgirasas, singing praises, and knowing well the places, found the cattle. || 18. The friends who offer Soma long to find thee: they pour forth Soma and present their viands. | They bear, Unmoved, the cursing of the people, for all our wisdom comes from thee, O Indra. || 19. Not far for thee are mid-air's loftiest regions: start hither, Lord of Bays, with both Bay Horses. | Pressed for the Firm and Strong are these libations. The pressing-stones are set, the fire is kindled. || 20. Invincible in fight, saviour in battles, guard of our camp, winner of light and water, | Born amid hymns, well-housed, exceeding famous, victor, in thee may we rejoice, O Soma. || 21. To him who worships Soma gives a milch cow, a fleet steed, and a man of active knowledge, | Skilled in home duties, competent in council, meet for the court, the glory of his father. || 22. These herbs, these milch-kine, and these running waters, all these, O Soma, thou hast generated. | The spacious firmament hast thou expanded, and with the light thou hast dispelled the darkness. || 23. Do thou, God Soma, with thy God-like spirit, victorious, win for us a share of riches. | Let none prevent thee: thou art Lord of valour. Provide for these and those in fight for cattle. || 24. The earth's eight points his brightness hath illumined, three desert regions, and the Seven Rivers. | God Savitar the gold-eyed hath come hither, giving choice treasures to the man who worships. || 25. Savitar, golden-handed, swiftly moving, goes on his way between the earth and heaven, | Drives away sickness, bids the Sun approach us, and spreads the bright sky through the darksome region. || 26. May, he, gold-handed Asura, kind leader, come hitherward to us with help and favour. | Driving off Rākṣhasas and Yātudhānas, the God is present, praised in hymns at evening. || 27. O Savitar, thine ancient dustless pathways are well established in the air's mid-region. | O God, come by those paths so fair to travel: preserve thou us from harm this day and bless us. || 28. Drink our libations, Aśvins twain, grant us protection, both of you, | With aids which none may interrupt. || 29. Make ye our speech effectual, O Aśvins, and this our hymn, ye mighty Wonder-workers. | In luckless game I call on you for succour: strengthen us also on the field of battle. || 30. With undiminished blessings, O ye Aśvins, through days and nights on every side protect us. | This prayer of ours may Varuṇa grant, and Mitra, and Aditi and Sindhu, Earth and Heaven. || 31. Throughout the dusky firmament, etc., as in 33:43. || 32. Night! the terrestrial realm hath been filled with the Father's power and might. | Thou spreadest thee on high unto the seats of heaven: terrific darkness cometh nigh. || 33. O Dawn enriched with ample wealth, bestow on us that wondrous gift | Wherewith we may support children and children's sons. || 34. Agni at dawn, and Indra we invoke at dawn, and Varuṇa and Mitra and the Aśvins twain, | Bhaga at dawn, Pūṣhan and Brahmaṇaspati, Soma at dawn, Rudra may we invoke at dawn. || 35. May we invoke strong early-conquering Bhaga, the Son of Aditi, the great Arranger, | Thinking of whom the poor, yea, even the mighty, even the King says, Let me share in Bhaga. || 36. Bhaga our guide, Bhaga whose gifts are faithful, favour this prayer and give us wealth, O Bhaga. | Bhaga, increase our store of kine and horses: Bhaga, may we be rich in men and heroes. || 37. So may felicity be ours at present, and when the day approaches, and at noontide; | And may we still, O Bounteous One, at sunset be happy in the Deities' loving-kindness. || 38. May Bhaga verily he Bliss-bestower, and through him, Gods! may happiness attend us. | As such, O Bhaga, all with might invoke thee: as such be thou our Champion here, O Bhaga. || 39. To this our worship may the Dawns incline them, and come to the pure place like Dadhikrāvan. | As strong steeds draw a chariot may they bring us hitherward Bhaga who discovers treasure. || 40. May friendly Mornings dawn on us for ever, with wealth of kine, of horses, and of heroes, | Streaming with all abundance, pouring fatness. Preserve us evermore, ye Gods, with blessings. || 41. Secure in thy protecting care, O Pūṣhan, never may we fail: | We here are singers of thy praise. || 42. I praise with eloquence hire who guards all pathways. He, when his love impelled him, went to Arka. | May he vouchsafe us gear with gold to grace it: may Pūṣhan make each prayer of ours effective. || 43. Viṣhṇu the undeceivable Protector strode three steps, thenceforth | Establishing his high decrees. || 44. This, Viṣhṇu's station most sublime, the singers ever vigilant. | Lovers of holy song, light up. || 45. Filled full of fatness, compassing all things that be, wide, spacious, dropping meath, beautiful in their form, | The Heaven and the Earth by Varuṇa's decree, unwasting, rich in seed, stand parted each from each. || 46. Let those who are our foemen stand afar from us: with Indra and with Agni we will drive them off. | Vasus, Ādityas, Rudras have exalted me, made me pre-eminent, mighty, thinker, sovereign lord. || 47. Come, O Nāsatyas, with the thrice eleven Gods: come, O ye Aśvins, to

the drinking of the meath. | Prolong our days of life, and wipe out all our sins: ward off our enemies; be with us evermore. || 48. May this your praise, may this your song, O Marutas, sung by the poet, Māna's son, Māndārya, | Bring offspring for ourselves with food to feed us. May we find strengthening food in full abundance. || 49. They who were versed in ritual and metre, in hymns and rules, were the Seven godlike Ṛishis. | Viewing the path of those of old, the sages have taken up the reins like chariot-drivers. || 50. Bestowing splendour, length of life, increase of wealth, and conquering power, | This brightly shining gold shall be attached to me for victory. || 51. This gold no demons injure, no Piśāchas; for this is might of Gods, their primal offspring. | Whoever wears the gold of Dakṣha's children lives a long life among the Gods, lives a long life among mankind. || 52. This ornament of gold which Dakṣha's children bound, with benevolent thoughts, on Śatānīka, | I bind on me for life through hundred autumns, that I may live till ripe old age o'ertakes me. || 53. Let Ahirbudhnya also hear our calling, and Aja-Ekapāda and Earth and Ocean. | All Gods Law-strengtheners, invoked and lauded, and Texts recited by the sages, help us! || 54. These hymns that drop down fatness, with the ladle I ever offer to the Kings Ādityas. | May Mitra, Aryaman, and Bhaga hear us, the mighty Varuṇa, | Dakṣha, and Aṃśa. || 55. Seven Ṛiṣhis are established in the body: seven guard it evermore with care unceasing. | Seven waters seek the world of him who lies asleep: two sleepless Gods are feast-fellows of him who wakes. || 56. O Brahmaṇaspati, arise. God-fearing men, we pray to thee. | May they who give good gifts, the Marutas, come to us. Indra, be thou most swift with them. || 57. Now Brahmaṇaspati speaks forth aloud the solemn hymn of praise. | Wherein Indra and Varuṇa, Mitra, Aryaman, the Gods have made their dwelling-place. || 58. O Brahmaṇaspati, be thou controller of this our hymn, and prosper thou our children. | All that the Gods regard with love is blessed. Loud may we speak, with brave sons, in assembly. | He who sate down. Mighty in mind. Father who made us. A share of good, O Lord of Food.

Adhyāya 35.

1. Begone the Paṇis, hence away, rebellious, scorners of the Gods! | The place is his who poured the juice. || 2. Let Savitar approve a spot upon the earth for thy remains: | And let the bulls be yoked for it. || 3. Let Vāyu purify. Let Savitar purify. With Agni's glitter. With Savitar's lustre. Let the bulls be unyoked. || 4. The Holy Fig Tree is your home, your mansion is the Parṇa Tree: | Winners of cattle shall ye be if ye regain for me this man. || 5. Let Savitar lay down thy bones committed to the Mother's lap. | Be pleasant to this man, O Earth. || 6. Here in the God Prajāpati, near water, Man, I lay thee down: | May his light drive mishap from us. || 7. Go hence, O Death, pursue thy special pathway apart from that which Gods are wont to travel. | To thee I say it who hast eyes and hearest: Touch not our offspring, injure not our heroes. || 8. Pleasant to thee be wind and sun, and pleasant be the bricks to thee. | Pleasant to thee be the terrestrial fires: let them not scorch thee in their flames. || 9. Prosper for thee the regions and the waters, and let the seas for thee be most propitious. | Auspicious unto thee be Air. Prosper all Quarters well for thee! || 10. On flows the stony flood: hold fast each other, keep yourselves up, my friends, and pass the river. | Here let us leave the powers that brought no profit, and cross the flood to Powers that are auspicious. || 11. Drive away evil, drive away fault, sorcery, and guiltiness. | Do thou, O Apāmārga, drive the evil dream away from us. || 12. To us let waters and the plants be friendly, to him who hates us, whom we hate, unfriendly. || 13. For our prosperity we touch the ox the son of Surabhi. | Be bearer and deliverer to us as Indra to the Gods. || 14. Looking upon the loftiest light, etc., as in 20:21. || 15. Here I erect this rampart for the living: let none of these, none other, reach this limit. | May they survive a hundred lengthened autumns, and may they bury Death beneath this mountain. || 16. Agni, thou pourest life, etc., as in 19:38. || 17. Waxing with sacrifice live long, O Agni, with butter on thy face and homed in fatness. | When thou hast drunk the cows' fair savoury butter, guard, as a father guards his son, these people. || 18. These men have led about the ox, have duly carried Agni round, | And raised their glory to the Gods. Who will attack them with success? || 19. I drive Corpse-eating Agni to a distance: sin-laden let him go to Yama's kingdom. | Here let this other, Jātavedas, carry oblation to the Deities, foreknowing. || 20. Carry the fat to Fathers, Jātavedas, where, far away, thou knowest, them established. | Let rivulets of marrow flow to meet them, and let their truthful wishes be accomplished. All-hail! || 21. Pleasant be thou to us, O Earth, without a thorn, our resting-place. | Vouchsafe us shelter reaching far. May thy light drive mishap from us. || 22. Born art thou, Agni, from this man: let him again be born from thee, | For Svarga's world, the man I name. All-hail!

Adhyāya 36.

1. Refuge I take in Speech as Ṛich: refuge in Mind as Yajus-text; refuge in Breath as Sāman-chant; refuge in Hearing and in Sight. | Speech-energy endowed with strength, inbreath and outbreath are in me. || 2. Whatever deeply-sunk defect I have of eye, or mind, or heart, that way Bṛihaspati amend! | Gracious to us be he, Protector of the world. || 3. Earth! Ether! Heaven! May we attain that excellent, etc., as in 3:33. | 4.| With what help will he come to us etc., as in 27:39. || 5. What genuine, etc., as in 27:40. || 6. Do thou who art, etc., as in 27:41. || 7. O Hero, with what aid dost thou delight us, with what succour bring | Riches to those who worship thee? || 8. Indra is king of all that is: may weal attend our bipeds and our quadrupeds. || 9. Gracious he Mitra unto us, and Varuṇa and Aryaman; | Indra, Bṛihaspati be kind, and Viṣhṇu of the mighty stride. || 10. Pleasantly blow the wind for us, may Sūrya warm us pleasantly. | Pleasantly, with a roar, the God Parjanya send the rain on us. || 11. May days pass pleasantly for us, may nights draw near delightfully. | Befriend us with their aids Indra and Agni, Indra and Varuṇa who taste oblations. | Indra and Pūṣhan be our help in battle, Indra and Soma give health, strength, and comfort. || 12. May the celestial Waters, our helpers, be sweet for us to drink, | And flow with health and strength to us. || 13. Pleasant be thou to us, O Earth, etc., as in 35:21. || 14. Ye, Waters, are, etc., as in 11:50. || 15. Give us a portion, etc., as in 11:51. || 16. To you we gladly come, etc., as in 11:52, || 17. Sky alleviation, Air alleviation, Earth alleviation, Plants alleviation, | Trees alleviation, All-Gods alleviation, Brahma alleviation, Universe alleviation, just Alleviation alleviation—may that alleviation come to me! || 18. Cauldron, strengthen me. May all beings regard me with the eye of a friend. May I regard all beings with the eye of a friend. | With the eye of a friend do we regard one another. || 19. Do thou, O Cauldron, strengthen me. Long may I live to look on thee. Long may I live to look on thee. || 20. Obeisance to thy wrath and glow, etc., as in 22:11. || 21. Homage to thee the lightning flash, homage to thee the thunder's roar! | Homage, O Bounteous Lord, to thee whereas thou fain wouldst win to heaven! || 22. From whatsoever trouble thou desirest, give us safety thence. | Give to our children happiness and to our beasts security. || 23. To us let Waters and let Plants be friendly, etc., as in 6:23. || 21. Through hundred autumns may we see that bright Eye, God-appointed, rise, | A hundred autumns may we live. | Through hundred autumns may we hear; through hundred autumns clearly speak: through hundred autumns live content; a hundred autumns, yea, beyond a hundred autumns may we see.

Adhyāya 37.

1. By impulse of God Savitar I take thee, etc. Spade art thou. Woman art thou, etc., as in 11:9, 10. || 2. The priests of him the lofty Priest, etc., as in 5:14. || 3. O Heaven and Earth divine, may I duly prepare for you this day the head of Makha on the place of earth where the Gods sacrificed. | For Makha thee, thee for the head of Makha! || 4. Ye who were born the earliest of creation, Ants divine, may I duly prepare for you this day the head of Makha on the place of earth where the Gods sacrificed. | For Makha thee, thee for the head of Makha! || 5. Only so large was it at first. Duly may I prepare for you this day the head of Makha on earth's place where the Gods sacrificed. | For Makha thee, thee for the head of Makha! || 6. Indra's effective might are ye. Duly may I prepare for you this day the head of Makha on earth's place where the Gods sacrificed. | For Makha thee, thee for the head of Makha! For Makha thee, thee for the head of Makha! For Makha thee, thee for the head of Makha! || 7. May Brahmaṇaspati draw nigh, etc., as in 33:89. | For Makha thee, thee for the head of Makha, etc., as in verse 6. || 8. Thou art the head of Makha. Thee for Makha, thee for Makha's head! Thou art the head of Makha. Thee for Makha, thee for Makha's head! Thou art the head of Makha, thee for Makha, thee for

Makha's head! | For Makha thee, thee for the head of Makha, etc., as in verse 6. || 9. Thee on Gods' sacrificial ground with stallion's dung I fumigate. | For Makha thee, thee for the head of Makha! | For Makha thee, thee for the head of Makha! For Makha thee, thee for the head of Makha! For Makha thee, thee for the head of Makha! || 10. Thee for the True. Thee for the Good. Thee for the place of happy rest. | For Makha thee, thee for the head of Makha! For Makha thee, thee for the head of Makha! For Makha thee, thee for the head of Makha! || 11. For Yama thee. For Makha thee. For Sūrya's fervent ardour thee. | May Savitar the God with balm anoint thee. Guard thou the touches of the earth. | Flame art thou; thou art radiance; thou art heat. || 12. Unconquerable, eastward, in Agni's overlordship, give me life. | Rich in sons, southward, in Indra's overlordship give me offspring. | Fair-seated, westward, in God. Savitar's overlordship, give me sight. | Range of hearing, northward, in Dhātar's overlordship, give me increase of wealth. | Arrangement, upward, in Bṛihaspati's overlordship, give me energy. | From all destructive spirits guard us. Thou art Manu's mare. || 13. All-hail! By Marutas be thou compassed round. | Guard the sky's touches. Mead, mead, mead. || 14. Germ of the Gods, Father of hymns, all living creatures' guardian Lord, | Radiant, with radiant Savitar united, with the Sun he shines. || 15. Agni combined with flaming fire, combined with Savitar divine, hath shone together with the Sun. || 16. He shines on earth upholder of the sky and heat, the Gods upholder, God, immortal, born of heat. | To him address a speech devoted to the Gods. || 17. I saw the Herdsman, him who never stumbles, approaching by his pathways and departing. | He, clothed with gathered and diffusive splendour, within the worlds continually travels. || 18. Lord of all earths, Lord of all mind, Lord of all speech, thou Lord of speech entire. | Heard by the Gods, Cauldron divine, do thou, a God, protect the Gods. | Here, after, let it speed you twain on to the banquet of the Gods. | Sweetness for both the sweetness-lovers! Sweetness for those the twain who take delight in sweetness! || 19. Thee for the heart, thee for the mind, thee for the sky, for Sūrya thee. | Standing erect lay thou the sacrifice in heaven among the Gods. || 20. Thou art our Father, father-like regard us. Obeisance be to thee. Do not thou harm us. | May we, accompanied by Tvashṭar, win thee. Vouchsafe me sons and cattle. Grant us offspring. Safe may I be together with my husband. || 21. May Day together with his sheen, pair-lighted with his light, accept. All-hail! | May Night together with her sheen, fair lighted with her. light, accept. All-hail!

Adhyāya 38.

1. By impulse of God Savitar I take thee with arms of Aśvins, with the Hands of Pūṣhan | A zone for Aditi art thou. || 2. Iḍā, come hither. Aditi, come hither. Sarasvatī, come hither. | Come hither, So-and-So. Come hither, So-and-So. Come hither, So-and-So. || 3. Thou art a zone for Aditi, a diadem for Indrāṇī Pūṣhan art thou. Spare some for the Gharma. || 4. Overflow for the Aśvins Overflow for Sarasvatī. Overflow for Indra | All-hail, what belongs to Indra! All-hail, what belongs to Indra! All-hail, what belongs to Indra! || 5. That breast of thine, exhaustless, fount of pleasure, wealth-giver, treasure-finder, free-bestower, | Wherewith thou rearest all things that are choicest,—bring that, Sarasvatī, that we may drain it. | Throughout the spacious middle air I travel. || 6. Thou art Gāyatra metre. Thou art Trishṭubh metre. With Heaven and Earth I grasp thee. With the Firmament I raise thee up. | Indra and Aśvins, drink ye the hot draught of sweet honey: sacrifice, ye Vasus. Vāṭ! All-hail to the rain-winning beam of the Sun! || 7. Thee with Svāhā to Vāta the sea. Thee with Svāhā to Vāta the flood. | Thee with Svāhā to Vāta the unconquerable. Thee with Svāhā to Vāta the irresistible. | Thee with Svāhā to Vāta the protection-seeker. Thee with Svāhā to Vāta the non-destructive. || 8. Thee with Svāhā to Indra Lord of Vasus. Thee with Svāhā to Indra Lord of Rudras. | Thee with Svāhā to Indra killer of foes. Thee with Svāhā to Savitar attended by Ṛibhu, Vibhu, and Vāja. Thee with Svāhā to Bṛihaspati beloved of all the Gods. || 9. Svāhā to Yama attended by the Aṅgirasas, attended by the Fathers! | Svāhā to the Gharma! The Gharma for the Father! || 10. Here hath he worshipped, seated south, all the sky-regions, all the Gods. | Drink, Aśvins, of the heated draught, the Svāhā-consecrated mead. || 11. In heaven lay thou this sacrifice; lay thou this sacrifice in heaven. | To sacrificial Agni hail! May bliss be ours from Yajus texts. || 12. Drink, Aśvins, with your daily helps, the Gharma, strengthener of hearts. | To him who draweth out the thread be homage, and to Heaven and Earth. || 13. The Gharma have the Aśvins drunk: with Heaven and Earth have they agreed. | Here, verily, be their boons bestowed. || 14. Overflow for food. Overflow for energy. Overflow for the Priesthood. Overflow for the Nobility. Overflow for Heaven and Earth. Thou, O duteous one, art Duty. Innocent one, in us establish manly powers; establish the People. || 15. All-hail to Pūṣhan, to the milk's skin! All-hail to the press-stones! | All-hail to their echoes! All-hail to the Fathers who are above the grass, who drink the Gharma! All-hail to Heaven and Earth! All-hail to the All-Gods! || 16. All-hail to Rudra invoked by worshippers! All-hail! Let light combine with light. | May Day together with his sheen, fair-lighted with his light, accept. All hail! | May Night together with her sheen, fair-lighted with her light, accept. All-hail! | May we enjoy the mead offered in most Indra-like Agni. Homage to thee, divine Gharma! Do not thou injure me. || 17. Thy far-spread majesty, instinct with wisdom, hath surpassed this heaven, | And, with its glorious fame, the earth. | Seat thee, for thou art mighty: shine, best entertainer of the Gods. | Worthy of sacred food, praised Agni! loose the smoke ruddy and beautiful to see. || 18. Gharma, that heavenly light of thine in Gāyatrī, in the Soma-store,— | May it increase and be confirmed for thee, that light. | Gharma, that light of thine in air, in Trishṭubh, in the sacred hearth,— | May it increase and be confirmed for thee, that light. | Gharma, that light of thine on earth, in Jagatī, of the priest's shed,— | May that increase and be confirmed for thee, that light. || 19. Thee for the sure protection of the Nobles. Guard thou from injury the Brahman's body. | We follow thee in interest of the People, for the renewal of our peace and comfort. || 20. Square, far-spread is the sacrifice's navel: it spreads for us wide, full of all existence, spreads wide for us full of complete existence. | We turn against the hate and guiles of him who keeps an alien law. || 21. This, Gharma! is thy liquid store. Swell out and wax in strength thereby. | May we too grow in strength and wax to greatness. || 22. Loudly the tawny Stallion neighed, mighty, like Mitra fair to see. | Together with the Sun the sea, the store shone out with flashing light. || 23. To us let Waters and let Plants be friendly; to him who hates us, whom we hate, unfriendly. || 24. Looking upon the loftier light above the darkness we have come | To Sūrya, God among the Gods, the light that is most excellent. || 25. A brand art thou, fain would we thrive, Fuel art thou, and splendour: Give me splendour, || 26. Far as the heaven and earth are spread in compass, far as the Seven Rivers are extended, | So vast thy cup which I with strength am taking, Indra, unharmed in me, uninjured ever. || 27. In me be that great hero power, in me be strength and mental force: | The Gharma shines with triple light, with lustre fulgent far away, with holy lore, with brilliancy. || 28. Brought hither is the seed of milk. Through each succeeding year may we enjoy the bliss of draining it. | Invited, I enjoy a share of that which hath been offered me, the savoury draught by Indra drunk and tasted by Prajāpati.

Adhyāya 39.

1, Svāhā to the Vital Breathings with their Controlling Lord! To Earth Svāhā! To Agni Svāhā! To Firmament, Svāhā! To Vāyu Svāhā! To Sky Svāhā! To Sūrya Svāhā! || 2. To the Quarters Svāhā! To the Moon Svāhā! To the Stars Svāhā! To the Waters Svāhā! To Varuṇa Svāhā! To the Navel Svāhā! To the Purified Svāhā! || 3. To Speech Svāhā! To Breath Svāhā! To Breath Svāhā! To Sight Svāhā! To Sight Svāhā! To Hearing Svāhā! To Hearing Svāhā! || 4. The wish and purpose of the mind and truth of speech may I obtain. | Bestowed on me be cattle's form, swept taste of food, and fame and grace. Svāhā! || 5. Prajāpati while in preparation; Samrāj when prepared; All-Gods' when seated; Gharma when heated with fire; Splendour when lifted up; the Aśvins' while milk is poured in; Pūṣhan's when the butter trickles down it; the Marutas' when the milk is clotting; Mitra's when the milk's skin is spreading; Vāyu's when it is carried off; Agni's while offered as oblation; Vāk when it has been offered. || 6. Savitar on the first day; Agni on the second; Vāyu on the third; Āditya (the Sun) on the fourth; Chandramās (the Moon) on the fifth; Ṛitu on the sixth; the Marutas on the seventh; Bṛihaspati on the eighth; Mitra on the ninth; Varuṇa on the tenth; Indra on the eleventh; the All-Gods on the twelfth. || 7. Fierce; Terrible; The Resonant; The Roarer; Victorious; Assailant; and

Dispeller. Svāhā. || 8. Agni with the heart; Lightning with the heart's point; Paśupati with the whole heart; Bhava with the liver. | Śarva with the two cardiac bones; Īśāna with Passion; Mahādeva with the intercostal flesh; the Fierce God with the rectum; Vasishṭha-hanuḥ, Śiṅgis with two lumps of flesh near the heart. || 9. The Fierce with blood; Mitra with obedience, Rudra with disobedience; Indra with pastime; the Marutas with strength; the Sādhyas with enjoyment. | Bhava's is what is on the throat; Rudra's what is between the ribs; Mahādeva's is the liver; Śarva's the rectum; Paśupati's the pericardium. || 10. To the hair Svāhā! To the hair Svāhā! To the skin Svāhā! To the skin Svāhā! To the blood Svāhā! To the blood Svāhā! To the fats Svāhā! To the fats Svāhā! To the fleshy parts Svāhā! To the fleshy parts Svāhā! To the sinews Svāhā! To the sinews Svāhā! Svāhā to the bones! Svāhā to the bones! To the marrows Svāhā! To the marrows Svāhā! To the seed Svāhā! To the anus Svāhā! || 11. To Effort Svāhā! To Exertion Svāhā! To Endeavour Svāhā! To Viyāsa Svāhā! To Attempt Svāhā! || 12. To Grief Svāhā! To the Grieving Svāhā! To the Sorrowing Svāhā! To Sorrow Svāhā! | To Heat Svāhā! To him who grows hot Svāhā! To him who is being heated Svāhā! To him who has been heated Svāhā! To Gharma Svāhā! | To Atonement Svāhā! To Expiation Svāhā! To Remedy Svāhā! || 13. To Yama Svāhā! To the Finisher Svāhā! To Death Svāhā! To the Priesthood Svāhā! To Brahmanicide Svāhā! To the All-Gods Svāhā! To Heaven and Earth Svāhā!

Adhyāya 40.

1. Enveloped by the Lord must be This All—each thing that moves on earth. | With that renounced enjoy thyself. Covet no wealth of any man. || 2. One, only doing Karma here, should wish to live a hundred years. | No way is there for thee but this. So Karma cleaveth not to man. || 3. Aye, to the Asuras belong those worlds enwrapt in blinding gloom. | To them, when life on earth is done, depart the men who kill the Self. || 4. Motionless, one, swifter than Mind—the Devas failed to o'ertake it speeding on before them. | It, standing still, outstrips the others running. Herein Both Mātariśvan establish Action. || 5. It moveth; it is motionless. It is far distant; it is near. | It is within This All; and it surrounds This All externally. || 6. The man who in his Self beholds all creatures and all things that be, | And in all beings sees his Self, thence doubts no longer, ponders not. || 7. When, in the man who clearly knows, Self hath become all things that are, | What wilderment, what grief is there in him who sees the One alone? || 8. He hath attained unto the Bright, Bodiless, Woundless, Sinewless, the Pure which evil hath not pierced. | Far-sighted, wise, encompassing, he self-existent hath prescribed aims, as propriety demands, unto the everlasting Years. || 9. Deep into shade of blinding gloom fall Asaṃbhūti's worshippers. | They sink to darkness deeper yet who on Sambhūti are intent. || 10. One fruit, they say, from Sambhava, another from Asaṃbhava. | Thus from the sages have we heard who have declared this lore to us. || 11. The man who knows Sambhūti and Vināśa simultaneously, | He, by Vināśa passing death, gains by Sambhūti endless life. || 12. To blinding darkness go the men who make a cult of Nescience. | The devotees of Science enter darkness that is darker still. || 13. Different is the fruit, they say, of Science and of Nescience. | Thus from the sages have we heard who have declared this lore to us. || 14. The man who knoweth well these two, Science and Nescience combined, | O'ercoming death by Nescience by Science gaineth endless life. || 15. My breath reach everlasting Air! In ashes let my body end. | Om! Mind, remember thou; remember thou my sphere; remember thou my deeds. || 16. By goodly path lead us to riches, Agni, thou God who knowest all our works and wisdom. | Remove the sin that makes us stray and wander: most ample adoration will we bring thee. || 17. The Real's face is hidden by a vessel formed of golden light. | The Spirit yonder in the Sun, the Spirit dwelling there am I. | Om! Heaven! Brahma!

Texts of the Black Yajurveda

[Taittiriya Saṃhitā]

Translated by Arthur Berriedale Keith, 1914

Preface

We omit the full text of Keith's extensive introduction to the Black Yajurveda, which can be read in the original publication (Harvard Oriental Series, vol. 18, 1914). Griffith's preface to the White Yajurveda sufficiently introduces the text of both the black and white.

Note: in the following translation the reader will come across the abbreviation "N. N." on several occasions. This evidently stands for the Latin term *nomen nescio*, which indicates an anonymous or unnamed person or subject.

Kāṇḍa I.

Prapāṭhaka 1.

The New and Full Moon Sacrifices

Mantra 1:1:1.

a. For food thee, for strength thee! ‖ *b.* Ye are winds, ye are approachers. ‖ *c.* Let the God Savitar impel you to the most excellent offering. ‖ *d.* O invincible ones, swell with the share for the Gods, | Full of strength, of milk, rich in offspring, free from sickness, from disease. ‖ *e.* Let no thief, no evil worker, have control over you. ‖ *f.* Let Rudra's dart avoid you. ‖ *g.* Abide ye, numerous, with this lord of cattle. ‖ *h.* Do thou protect the cattle of the sacrificer.

Mantra 1:1:2.

a. Thou art the substance of the sacrifice. ‖ *b.* The Rakṣhas is burned up, the evil spirits are burned up. ‖ *c.* The Vedi hath come to the sacrificial straw, | Made by Manu, fashioned with the Svadhā call. | The sages fetch it from in front, | The delightful straw for the Gods to sit on here. ‖ *d.* Thou art impelled by the Gods. ‖ *e.* Thou art made to grow by the rains. ‖ *f.* O divine straw, lot me not hit thee either across or along, ‖ *g.* Let me hit thy joints, ‖ *h.* Let me come to no harm in cutting thee. ‖ *i.* O divine straw, rise with a hundred shoots, | Let us rise with a thousand shoots. ‖ *k.* Guard from the contact of earth. ‖ *l.* I gather thee with good gathering. ‖ *m.* Thou art the girdle of Aditi, the cord of Indrāṇī. ‖ *n.* Let Pūṣhan tie a knot for thee, that knot shall mount me. ‖ *o.* I hold thee up with the arms of Indra, I seize thee with the head of Bṛihaspati. ‖ *p.* Fare along the wide atmosphere. ‖ *q.* Thou art going to the Gods.

Mantra 1:1:3.

a. Be ye pure for the divine rite, the sacrifice to the Gods. ‖ *b.* Thou art the cauldron of Mātariśvan ‖ *c.* Thou art the heaven, thou art the earth. ‖ *d.* Thou art the all-supporting with the highest support. ‖ *e.* Be firm, waver not. ‖ *f.* Thou art the strainer of the Vasus, of a hundred streams, thou art that of the Vasus, of a thousand streams. ‖ *g.* The spot (*stoka*) has been offered, the drop has been offered. ‖ *h.* To Agni, to the mighty firmament! ‖ *i.* Hail to sky and earth! ‖ *k.* This is she of all life, this is the all-encompassing, this is the all-doing. ‖ *l.* Be ye united, that follow holy orders, | Ye that wave and are fullest of sweetness, | Delightful for the gaining of wealth. ‖ *m.* With Soma I curdle thee, curds for Indra. ‖ *n.* O Viṣhṇu, guard the offering.

Mantra 1:1:4.

a. For the rite you two, for the Gods may I be strong. ‖ *b.* Thee for accomplishment! ‖ *c.* The Rakṣhas is burnt up, the evil spirits are burnt up. ‖ *d.* Thou art the yoke. ‖ *e.* Injure him who injures us, injure him whom we injure. ‖ *f.* Thou art of Gods the most firmly jointed, the most richly filled, | the most agreeable, the best of carriers, the best caller of the Gods. ‖ *g.* Thou art the oblation-holder that wavers not. ‖ *h.* Be firm, waver not. ‖ *i.* I gaze on thee with the eye of Mitra. ‖ *k.* Be not afraid, be not troubled, let me harm thee not. ‖ *l.* (Be thou) wide open to the wind. ‖ *m.* On the impulse of the God Savitar, with the arms of the Aśvins, | with the hands of Pūṣhan, I offer thee dear to Agni, to Agni and Soma. ‖ *n.* This of the Gods, this of us too. ‖ *o.* For prosperity thee, not for misfortune. ‖ *p.* May I behold the light, the radiance for all men. ‖ *q.* May they that have doors stand firm in heaven and earth. ‖ *r.* Fare along the wide atmosphere. ‖ *s.* I place thee in the lap of Aditi. ‖ *t.* O Agni, guard the offering.

Mantra 1:1:5.

a. Let the God Savitar purify you, with a filter that has no flaw, | with the rays of the bright sun. ‖ *b.* Ye divine waters, that go in front and first purify, forward lead | this sacrifice, place in front the lord of the sacrifice. ‖ *c.* You Indra chose for the contest with Vṛitra, ye chose Indra for | the contest with Vṛitra ‖ *d.* Ye are sprinkled. ‖ *e.* I sprinkle you agreeable to Agni, to Agni and Soma. ‖ *f.* Be ye pure for the divine rite, for the sacrifice to the Gods. ‖ *g.* The Rakṣhas is shaken off, the evil spirits are shaken off. ‖ *h.* Thou art the skin of Aditi, may the earth recognize thee. ‖ *i.* Thou art the plank of wood, may the skin of Aditi recognize thee. ‖ *k.* Thou art the body of Agni, loostener of speech. ‖ *l.* I grasp thee for the joy of the Gods. ‖ *m.* Thou art the stone of wood. ‖ *n.* Do thou with good labour elaborate this offering for the Gods. ‖ *o.* Utter food, utter strength; ‖ *p.* Make ye glorious sounds. ‖ *q.* May we be victorious in contest. ‖ *r.* Thou art increased by the rain. ‖ *s.* May that which is increased by the rain recognize thee. ‖ *t.* The Rakṣhas is cleared away, the evil spirits are cleared away. ‖ *u.* Thou art the share of the Rākṣhasas. ‖ *v.* Let the wind separate you. ‖ *w.* Let the God Savitar of golden hands, seize you.

Mantra 1:1:6.

a. The Rakṣhas is shaken off, the evil spirits are shaken off. ‖ *b.* Thou art the skin of Aditi, may the earth recognize thee. ‖ *c.* Thou art the supporter of the sky, may the skin of Aditi recognize thee. ‖ *d.* Thou art a bowl of rock, may the supporter of the sky recognize thee. ‖ *e.* Thou art a bowl made of the rock, may the rock recognize thee. ‖ *f.* On the impulse of the God Cavity, with the arms of the Aśvins, with the hands of Pūṣhan, I pour thee out. ‖ *g.* Thou art stimulating, stimulate the Gods. ‖ *h.* For expiration thee, for inspiration thee, for through-breathing thee (I pound). ‖ *i.* May I extend for long the life (of the sacrificer). ‖ *k.* Let the God Savitar, of golden hands, seize you.

Mantra 1. 1. 7.

a. Bold art thou, support our prayer. ‖ *b.* O Agni, drive off the fire that eats raw flesh, send away the corpse-eating one, bring hither the fire that sacrifices to the Gods. ‖ *c.* The Rakṣhas is burnt, the evil spirits are burnt. ‖ *d.* Thou art firm; make firm the earth, make life firm, make offspring firm, make his follows subordinate to this sacrificer. ‖ *e.* Thou art a supporter, make firm the atmosphere, make expiration firm, make inspiration firm, make his fellows subordinate to this sacrificer. ‖ *f.* Thou are supporting, make the heaven firm, make the eye firm, make the ear firm, make his fellows, etc. ‖ *g.* Thou art a support, make the quarters firm, make the organ firm, make offspring firm, make his fellows, etc. ‖ *h.* Ye are gatherers, bring offspring to this sacrificer, wealth to him, make his fellows, etc. ‖ *i.* Be ye heated with the heat of the Bhṛigus and the Aṅgirasas ‖ *k.* The potsherds which wise men collect for the cauldron, these are in Pūṣhan's guardianship. Lot Indra and Vāyu set them free.

Mantra 1:1:8.

a. I pour together. ‖ *b.* The waters have joined with the waters, the plants with sap. ‖ *c.* Join ye rich ones with the moving ones, sweet ones with the sweet. ‖ *d.* From the waters ye are born, be united with the waters. ‖ *e.* For generation I unite thee. ‖ *f.* For Agni thee, for Agni and Soma. ‖ *g.* Thou art the head of Makha. ‖ *h.* Thou art the cauldron that contains all life. ‖ *i.* Be extended wide, let the lord of the sacrifice be extended wide. ‖ *k.* Grasp the skin. ‖ *l.* The Rakṣhas is obstructed, the evil spirits are obstructed. ‖ *m.*

Let the God Savitar make thee ready on the highest firmament. ‖ *n.* May Agni burn not too much thy body. ‖ *o.* O Agni, guard the offering. ‖ *p.* Be united with our prayer. ‖ *q.* Hail to Ekata, hail to Dvita, hail to Trita.

Mantra 1:1:9.

a. I grasp (thee). ‖ *b.* Thou art Indra's right arm with a thousand spikes, a hundred edges. ‖ *c.* Thou art the wind of sharp edge. ‖ *d.* O earth whereon sacrifice is offered to the Gods, let me harm not the root of thy plant. ‖ *e.* Araru is smitten away from the earth. ‖ *f.* Go to the fold where the cattle are. ‖ *g.* May heaven rain for thee. ‖ *h.* O God Savitar, bind thou in the furthest distance with a hundred fetters him who hateth us and whom we hate, thence let him not free. ‖ *i.* Araru is smitten away from the earth, the place of sacrifice. ‖ *k.* Go to the fold where the cattle are. ‖ *l.* May heaven rain for thee. ‖ *m.* O God Savitar etc. ‖ *n.* Araru is smitten away from the earth, he that sacrifices not to the Gods. ‖ *o.* Go to the fold where the cattle are. ‖ *p.* May heaven rain for thee. ‖ *q.* O God Savitar, etc. ‖ *r.* Let not Araru mount the sky for thee. ‖ *s.* Let the Vasus grasp thee with the Gāyatrī metre, let the Rudras grasp thee with the Trishṭubh metre, let the Ādityas grasp thee with the Jagatī metre. ‖ *t.* On the impulse of the God Savitar wise ones perform the rite. ‖ *u.* Thou art the right, thou art the seat of right, thou art the glory of right. ‖ *v.* Thou art the holder, thou art the self-holder. ‖ *w.* Thou art broad, and wealthy art thou. ‖ *x.* Before the cruel foe slips away, O glorious one, | Taking up the earth, with plenteous drops, | The earth which they place in the moon by their offerings, | Which wise men use to guide them in the sacrifice.

Mantra 1:1:10.

a. The Rakṣhas is burnt up, the evil spirits are burnt up. ‖ *b.* With Agni's keenest flame I burn you. ‖ *c.* May I not brush the place of the cattle, I brush thee that art strong and overcomest foes. ‖ *d.* Speech, breath, eye, ear, offspring, the organ of generation may I not brush, I brush thee that art strong and overcomest foes. ‖ *e.* Beseeching favour, offspring, prosperity, in devotion to Agni, | I gird my body for good action. ‖ *f.* With fair offspring, with noble husbands, | We are come to thee, | O Agni, to thee that deceivest the foe, | The undeceivable, we that are not deceived. ‖ *g.* I loosen this bond of Varuṇa, | Which Savitar the kindly hath bound, | And in the birthplace of the creator, in the place of good action, | I make it pleasant for me with my husband. ‖ *h.* With life, with offspring, | O Agni, with splendour again, | As wife with my husband I am united. | United be my spirit with my body. ‖ *i.* Of the great ones thou art the milk, of plants the sap. Of thee that art the imperishable I make the offering. ‖ *k.* Thou art the milk of the great ones, of plants the sap; with undeceived eye I gaze on thee for fair offspring. ‖ *l.* Thou art brilliance; follow thou brilliance; may Agni not take away the brilliance. ‖ *m.* Thou art the tongue of Agni, the good one of the Gods. ‖ *n.* Be thou (good) for every sacrifice, for the Gods, for every prayer. ‖ *o.* Thou art the shining, the radiance, the brilliance. ‖ *p.* May the God Savitar purify you | With a flawless strainer, | With the rays of the bright sun. ‖ *q.* I grasp thee shining in the shining, for every sacrifice, for the Gods, for every prayer. ‖ *r.* I grasp thee radiance in the radiance, thee resplendent in the resplendence for every sacrifice, for the Gods, for every prayer.

Mantra 1:1:11

a. Thou I art a black deer, living in the lair, to Agni thee, hail! ‖ *b.* Thou art the altar, to the strew thee, hail! ‖ *c.* Thou art the strew, to the ladles thee, hail ‖ *d.* To the sky thee, to the atmosphere thee, to the earth thee! ‖ *e.* Be thou refreshment to the fathers, strength to those that sit on | the strew. ‖ *f.* With strength go ye to the earth. ‖ *g.* Thou art the hair-knot of Viṣhṇu. ‖ *h.* Soft as wool I strew thee, offering a good seat to the Gods. ‖ *i.* Thou art the Gandharva, Vivacious (possessing all wealth), the fence of the sacrificer from every attacker, praised and to be praised. ‖ *k.* Thou art the right arm of Indra, the fence of the sacrificer, praised and to be praised. ‖ *l.* May Mitra and Varuṇa lay thee around in the north with firm law, thou art the fence of the sacrificer, praised and to be praised. ‖ *m.* May the sun in the east protect thee from all evil. ‖ *n.* May we kindle thee, O wise one, | That dost invite to the sacrifice, the radiant one, | O Agni, thee that art mighty at the sacrifice. ‖ *o.* Ye two are the props of the people. ‖ *p.* Sit on the seat of the Vasus, Rudras, Ādityas ‖ *q.* Thou art named *Juhū, Upabhṛit, Dhruvā*, loving the ghee, sit on thy dear seat with thy dear name. ‖ *r.* These have sat down in the world of good action. ‖ *s.* Protect them, O

Viṣhṇu. ‖ *t.* Protect the sacrifice, protect the lord of the sacrifice, protect me that conduct the sacrifice.

Mantra 1:1:12

a. Thou art the world, be extended. ‖ *b.* O Agni, sacrificer, this reverence. ‖ *c.* O *Juhū*, come hither, Agni summons thee for the sacrifice to the Gods. ‖ *d.* O *Upabhṛit*, come hither, the God Savitar summons thee for the sacrifice | to the Gods. ‖ *e.* O Agni and Viṣhṇu, let me not step down upon you. ‖ *f.* Be ye parted, consume me not. ‖ *g.* Make ye a place for me, ye place-makers. ‖ *h.* Thou art the abode of Viṣhṇu. ‖ *i.* Hence Indra wrought mighty deeds. ‖ *k.* Great, grasping the sky, imperishable. | l. The sacrifice of the lord of the sacrifice is undisturbed. ‖ *m.* Offered to Indra, hail! ‖ *n.* Great light. ‖ *o.* Guard me, O Agni, from misfortune, place me in good fortune. ‖ *p.* Thou art the head of Makha, be light united with light.

Mantra 1:1:13

a. With the impulse of strength, | With elevation he hath lifted me up; | Then Indra hath made my enemies | Humble by depression. ‖ *b.* The Gods have increased my prayer. | What is elevation and depression; | Then do ye, O Indra and Agni, | Scatter my foes on every side. ‖ *c.* To the Vasus thee, to the Rudras thee, to the Ādityas thee! ‖ *d.* Licking the anointed lot the birds go asunder. ‖ *e.* May I not brush offspring and the organ. ‖ *f.* Swell, ye waters and plants. ‖ *g.* Ye are the spotted steeds of the Marutas. ‖ *h.* Fare to the sky, thence bring us rain. ‖ *i.* Guardian of life art thou, O Agni, guard my life. ‖ *k.* Guardian of the eye art thou, O Agni, guard my eye. ‖ *l.* Thou art the secure one. ‖ *m.* The fence which thou didst put round thee | When thou wast beset by the Panis, O God Agni, | That do I bring here to thee that thou mayst rejoice in it, | That it be not removed from thee. ‖ *n.* Go ye two to the place of the Gods. ‖ *o.* Ye are sharers in the remains (of the oblation), well nourished, mighty | Ye Gods that are on the *Prastara* and sit on the strew. | Accepting this supplication, do ye all, | Seated on this strew enjoy yourselves. ‖ *p.* I set thee in the seat of Agni whose abode is secure. ‖ *q.* For goodwill, O ye two with goodwill, place me in goodwill. ‖ *r.* Guard ye the yoke-horses at the yoke. ‖ *s.* O Agni, with life unhurt, with not-cool body, guard me this day from the sky, guard from bondage, guard from error in sacrifice, guard from evil food, guard from ill deed. ‖ *t.* Make our food free from poison, the lap pleasant to sit in; hail! ‖ *u.* O ye Gods that know the way, knowing the way, go ye the way. ‖ *v.* O lord of mind, this sacrifice for us place among the Gods, O God, hail! in speech, hail! in the wind, hail!

Mantra 1:1:14

a. Ye twain shall be summoned, O Indra and Agni. | Ye twain shall rejoice together in the offering. | You both givers of food and riches, | You both I summon for the winning of strength. ‖ *b.* For I have heard that ye both are more generous | Than a worthless son-in-law or a wife's brother. | So with the offering of Soma I make for you, | O Indra and Agni, a new hymn of praise; ‖ *c.* O Indra and Agni, ninety forts | Of which the Dāsas were lords ye overthrew | Together in one deed. ‖ *d.* This pure new-born hymn of praise this day, | O Indra and Agni, slayers of Vṛitra, accept with joy. | For on you both I call that are ready to listen, | You that are ever readiest to give strength to the eager. ‖ *e.* We thee, O lord of the path, | As a chariot to win the prize, | Have yoked for our prayer, O Pūshan. ‖ *f.* Lord of each way with eloquence; | Driven by love he went to Arka; | May he give us the comfort of gold, | May Pūshan further our every prayer. ‖ *g.* By the lord of the field | As by a friend may we win | What nourishes our kine and horses; | May he be favourable to such as we are. ‖ *h.* O lord of the field, the honey-bearing wave, | As a cow milk, so for us milk; | May the lords of right graciously accord us | That which drops honey and is well purified like ghee. ‖ *i.* O Agni, lead us by a fair path to wealth, | O God, knowing all the ways; | Keep away from us the sin that makes us wander; | We will accord to thee most abundant honour. ‖ *k.* We have come to the path of the Gods | To accomplish that which we have power to do; | Let wise Agni sacrifice, let him be Hotar | Let him arrange the offerings him the seasons. ‖ *l.* What carrieth best is for Agni; | Sing aloud, O thou of brilliant radiance. | From thee wealth, like a cow, | From thee strength riseth forth. ‖ *m.* O Agni, once more lead us | With thy favour over every trouble. | Be a broad, thick, wide fortress for us, | Health and wealth for our children and descendants. | Thou, O Agni, art the guardian of law, | Among the Gods and mortals; | Thou art to be invoked at the sacrifices. ‖ *o.* If laws of you wise ones, O

Gods, | In our ignorance we transgress, | May Agni make good all that, | He that knoweth the seasons wherein he may satisfy the Gods.

Prapāṭhaka 2.

The Soma Sacrifice

Mantra 1:2:1

a. May I the waters wet (thee) for life, | For length of days, for glory. || *b.* O plant, protect him. || *c.* Axe, hurt him not. || *d.* Obedient to the Gods I shear these. || *e.* With success may I reach further days. || *f.* Let the waters, the mothers, purify us, | With ghee let those that purify our ghee purify us, | Let them bear from us all pollution, | Forth from these waters do I come bright, in purity. || *g.* Thou art the body of Soma, guard my body. || *h.* Thou art the milk of the great ones, thou art the giver of splendour; splendour place in me. || *i.* Thou art the pupil of Vṛitra's eye, thou art the guardian of the eye, guard my eye. || *k.* Let the lord of thought purify thee, let the lord of speech purify thee, let the God Savitar purify thee | With the flawless purifier, | With the rays of the bright sun. || *l.* O lord of the purifier, with thy purifier for whatsoever I purify myself, that may I have strength to accomplish. || *m.* We approach you, O Gods, | Ye that have true ordinances at the sacrifice | What O Gods ye can assent to, | For that we ask you, O holy ones. || *n.* Indra and Agni, heaven and earth, waters, plants. || *o.* Thou art the lord of consecrations, guard me that am here.

Mantra 1:2:2

a. To the purpose, to the impulse, to Agni, hail! To wisdom, to thought, to Agni, hail! To consecration, to penance, to Agni, hail! To Sarasvatī, to Pūṣhan, to Agni, hail! || *b.* O ye divine, vast, all-soothing waters! | Heaven and earth, wide atmosphere! May Bṛihaspati rejoice in our oblation, hail! || *c.* Let every man choose the companionship | Of the God who leadeth. | Every man prayeth for wealth; | Let him choose glory that he may prosper, hail! || *d.* Ye are images of the Ṛich and the Sāman I grasp you two; do ye two protect me until the completion of this sacrifice. || *e.* O God,Varuṇa, do thou sharpen this prayer of him who implores thee, | Sharpen his strength, his insight; | May we mount that safe ship | Whereby we may pass over all our difficulties. || *f.* Thou art the strength of the Aṅgirasas, soft as wool; grant me strength, guard me, harm me not. || *g.* Thou art the protection of Viṣhṇu, the protection of the sacrificer, grant me protection. || *h.* Guard me from the lustre of the Nakṣhatras. || *i.* Thou art the birthplace of Indra; harm me not. || *k.* For ploughing thee, for good crops, || *l.* For the plants with good berries thee! || *m.* Thou art of easy access, divine tree. Being erect, guard me until the completion (of the sacrifice). || *n.* Hail! with my mind the sacrifice (I grasp); hail! from heaven and earth, bail! from the broad atmosphere, hail! from the wind the sacrifice I grasp.

Mantra 1:2:3

a. The thought divine we meditate, | Merciful, for our help, | That giveth glory, and carrieth the sacrifice. | May it guide us safely according as we will. || *b.* The Gods, mind-born, mind-using, | The wise, the sons of wisdom, | May they guard us, may they protect us, | To them honour! to them hail! || *c.* O Agni, be thou wakeful; | Let us be glad; | Guard us to prosperity; | Grant to us to wake again. || *d.* Thou, O Agni, art the guardian of vows, | Among the Gods and men. | Thou art to be invoked at our sacrifices. || *e.* All the Gods have surrounded me, | Pūṣhan with gain, Soma with a gift, | The God Savitar the giver of brightness. || *f.* O Soma, give so much, and bear more hither. || *g.* May he that filleth never miss of fullness. Let me not be parted with life. || *h.* Thou art gold; be for my enjoyment. Thou art raiment; be for my enjoyment. Thou art a cow; be for my enjoyment. Thou art a horse; be for my enjoyment. Thou art a goat; be for my enjoyment. Thou art a ram; be for my enjoyment. || *i.* To Vāyu thee; to Varuṇa thee; to Nirṛiti thee; to Rudra thee! || *k.* O divine waters, son of the waters, the stream | Fit for oblation, mighty, most exhilarating, | That stream of yours may I not step upon. || *l.* Along an unbroken web of earth may I go. || *m.* From good to better do thou advance. || *n.* May Bṛihaspati be thy leader; | Then set him free, on the chosen spot of earth; | Drive afar the foes with all thy strength. || *o.* We have come to the place on earth for sacrifice to the Gods, | Wherein aforetime all the Gods rejoiced. | Accomplishing (the rite) with Ṛich, Sāman, and Yajus, | Let us rejoice in fullness of wealth, in sustenance.

Mantra 1:2:4

a. This is thy body, O pure one. This is thy splendour. With it be united. Win brightness. || *b.* Thou art the strong, grasped by mind, acceptable to Viṣhṇu. || *c.* In the impulse of thee, of true impulse, may I win a support for my speech. Hail! || *d.* Thou art pure, thou art nectar, thou art the sacrifice for all the Gods. || *e.* I have mounted the eye of the sun. | The pupil of the eye of Agni, | When thou goest with thy steeds, | Blazing with the wise. || *f.* Thou art thought, thou art mind, thou art meditation, thou art the gift (to the priests), thou art of the sacrifice, thou art of kingly power, thou art Aditi, double-headed. || *g.* Be thou successful for us in going, successful in returning. || *h.* May Mitra bind thee by the foot. || *i.* May Pūṣhan guard the ways, || *k.* For Indra, the overseer! || *l.* May thy mother approve thee, thy father, thy brother sprung of the same womb, thy friend in the herd. || *m.* Go, Goddess, to the God, to Soma for Indra's sake. || *n.* May Rudra guide thee hither in the path of Mitra. || *o.* Hail! Return with Soma as thy comrade, with wealth.

Mantra 1:2:5

a. Thou art a Vasvī, thou art a Rudra, thou art Aditi, thou art an Āditya, thou art Śukra, thou art Chandrā. || *b.* May Bṛihaspati make thee rejoice in happiness. May Rudra with the Vasus be favourable to thee. || *c.* I pour thee on the head of the earth, on the place of sacrifice, | on the abode of the offering, rich in ghee; hail! || *d.* The Rakṣhas is enclosed, the evil spirits are enclosed. Thus I cut the neck of the Rakṣhas || *e.* Thus I cut the neck of him who hates us and whom we hate. || *f.* With us be wealth, with thee be wealth, thine be wealth. || *g.* Gaze, O Goddess, together with the Goddess Urvaśī || *h.* Let me attend on thee, with Tvaṣhṭar's aid; rich in seed, bearing seed, may I find a hero in thy presence. || *i.* May I not be separated from abundance of wealth.

Mantra 1:2:6

a. Let thy shoot be joined with shoot, joint with joint, let thy scent further desire, let thy savour which falls not cause rejoicing. Thou art a home dweller, thy libation is bright. || *b.* Unto that God, Savitar, within the two bowls, | The sage, I sing, him of true impulse, | The bestower of treasures, unto tile wise friend; | He at whose impulse the resplendent light shone high, | The golden-banded sage hath measured the heaven with his form. || *c.* For offspring thee! For expiration thee! For cross-breathing thee! Breathe thou after offspring. Let offspring breathe after thee.

Mantra 1:2:7

a. I buy Soma from thee, strong, rich in sap, full of force, overcoming the foe, the pure with the pure I buy, the bright with the bright, the immortal with the immortal, to match thy cow. || *b.* With us be the gold. || *c.* Thou art the bodily form of penance, Prajāpati's kind, I buy (Soma) with the last offspring of thee that bast a thousandfold prosperity. || *d.* With us be union with thee; with me let thy wealth abide. || *e.* With us be light, darkness be on the Soma-seller. || *f.* Come as a friend to us, creating firm friendships. || *g.* Enter the right thigh of Indra, glad the glad, tender the tender. || *h.* O Svāna, Bhrāja, Aṅghāri, Bambhāri, Hasta, Suhasta, and Kṛiśānu, here are your wages for Soma; guard them, let them not fail you.

Mantra 1:2:8

a. Up with life, with fair life, | Up with the sap of plants, | Up with the force of Parjanya, | Up have I arisen along with the immortals. || *b.* Fare along the wide atmosphere. || *c.* Thou art the seat of Aditi. || *d.* Sit on the seat of Aditi. || *e.* The bull hath established the sky, the atmosphere; | Hath meted the breadth of the earth; | Hath set him in all worlds as king. | All these are Varuṇa's ordinances. || *f.* He hath stretched out the sky over the woods; | He hath placed strength in horses, milk in kine; | Varuṇa hath set skill in the heart, Agni in dwellings, | The sun in the sky, the Soma on the hill. || *g.* Thee, all-knowing God, | Thy rays bear upwards, | The sun for all to see. || *h.* Come hither, ye oxen, strong to bear the yoke, | Tearless, slaying not man, furthering the prayer. || *i.* Thou art the pillar of Varuṇa || *k.* Thou art the prop of Varuṇa's pillar. || *l.* Varuṇa's noose is tied.

Mantra 1:2:9

a. Move I forward, O lord of the world, | To all thy stations. | Let no opponent find thee, | Let not robbers find thee; | Let not the evil-working wolves (find) thee; | Nor the Gandharva, Viśvāvasu, injure thee. || *b.* Become an eagle and fly away to the place in the house of the sacrificer which we have prepared with the Gods (for thee). Thou art the good luck of the sacrificer. ‖ *c*. We have reached the path | Which leadeth to bliss, without a foe, | Whereby a man defeateth all his foes and winneth wealth. ‖ *d*. Honour to the radiance of Mitra and Varuṇa | This worship, this reverence offer to the God; | To the far seeing, God-born, the banner, | The son of the sky, the sun, do ye sing. ‖ *e*. Thou art the pillar of Varuṇa ‖ *f*. Thou art the prop of Varuṇa's pillar. ‖ *g*. Varuṇa's noose is loosened.

Mantra 1:2:10.

a. Thou art the hospitality of Agni. For Viṣṇu thee! Thou art the hospitality of Soma. For Viṣṇu thee! Thou art the hospitality of the stranger. For Viṣṇu thee! For Agni thee, giver of wealth, for Viṣṇu thee; for the eagle, bringer of the Soma, thee, for Viṣṇu thee! ‖ *b*. Thy powers which they honour with oblation, | May they all envelop the sacrifice! | Giver of wealth, impeller, rich in heroes, | Slaying not heroes, O Soma, enter the dwellings. ‖ *c*. Thou art the seat of Aditi; sit on the seat of Aditi. ‖ *d*. Thou art Varuṇa who guardeth law; thou art of Varuṇa ‖ *e*. Be prosperity ours from our friendship with the Gods. May we be not severed from our service of the Gods. ‖ *f*. For him who rushes on I seize thee; for him who rushes around I seize thee; for Tanūnapāt I seize thee; for the mighty I seize thee; for the mightiest in strength I seize thee. ‖ *g*. Thou art unapproached, the unapproachable might of the Gods, guarding from imprecations, impervious to imprecations. ‖ *h*. May the lord of consecration approve my consecration, the lord of penance my penance. Speedily may I attain truth. Place me in good fortune.

Mantra 1:2:11

a. May thy every shoot, O God Soma, swell, | For Indra who gaineth the chiefest wealth; | May Indra swell for thee; | Do thou swell for Indra. ‖ *b*. Make thy comrades to swell with wealth and skill; with good fortune | may I accomplish thy pressing, O God Soma. ‖ *c*. Desired are riches exceedingly for food, for prosperity. Be right to the proclaimers of right. Honour to the sky, honour to the earth! ‖ *d*. Agni, lord of vows, thou art the vow-lord of vows; this body of mine be in thee, that body of thine be in me. Together, O lord of vows, be the vows of us two that keep vows. ‖ *e*. Thy dread form, O Agni, with that protect us; hail to that form of thine! ‖ *f*. That form of thine, O Agni, which rests in iron, which rests in silver, which rests in gold, the highest, that dwells in the cleft, ‖ *g*. (By it) I have driven away harsh speech, (by it) I have driven away angry speech. Hail!

Mantra 1:2:12

a. Thou I art the abode of riches for me; thou art the resort of the afflicted for me; protect me when in want; protect me when afflicted. ‖ *b*. May Agni, named Nabhas, know (thee). ‖ *c*. Agni Aṅgiras, thou who art in this earth, come with the name of Āyus Whatsoever unapproached, holy name is thine, therewith I take thee up. ‖ *d*. Agni Aṅgiras, thou who art in the second (the third) earth, come with the name of Āyus Whatever inviolate, holy name is thine, therewith I take thee up. ‖ *e*. Thou art a lioness; thou art a buffalo. ‖ *f*. Extend wide; let the lord of the sacrifice extend wide for thee. ‖ *g*. Thou art firm. ‖ *h*. Be pure for the Gods; be bright for the Gods. ‖ *i*. May the cry of Indra guard thee in front with the Vasus; may the swift of mind guard thee on the right with the Pitṛis; may the wise one guard thee behind with the Rudras; may Viśvakarman guard thee on the left with the Ādityas ‖ *k*. Thou art a lioness, overcoming rivals; hail! Thou art a lioness, bestowing fair offspring; hail! Thou art a lioness, bestowing increase of wealth; hail! Thou art a lioness, winning (the favour of) the Ādityas hail! Thou art a lioness; bring the Gods to the pious sacrificer; hail! ‖ *l*. To beings thee! ‖ *m*. Thou containest all life, strengthen the earth; thou restest firm, strengthen the atmosphere; thou restest inviolable, strengthen the heaven. ‖ *n*. Thou art the ashes of Agni; thou art the rubble of Agni.

Mantra 1:2:13

a. They yoke their minds, and yoke their thoughts, | The priests of the mighty wise priest; | He alone, who knows the way, ordains their priestly functions; | Great is the praise of the God Savitar ‖ *b*. With fair voice, O God, do thou address the dwelling. ‖ *c*. Ye two, famed among the Gods, make proclamation among the Gods. ‖ *d*. For us be born a hero of great deeds, | On whom we may all depend, | Who shall be ruler over many. ‖ *e*. Over this Viṣṇu strode; | Thrice did he set down his foot; | (All) is gathered in its dust. ‖ *f*. So then be ye two rich in food, in cows, | In good grass, ye that are famous, for man | These two firmaments Viṣṇu held asunder; |

He holdeth the earth on all sides with pegs. ‖ *g*. Come ye two then forward, ordaining the offering; bring upward the sacrifice; do not falter; there rest on the height of the earth. ‖ *h*. From the sky, O Viṣṇu, or from the earth, | Or from the great (sky), or from the atmosphere, | Fill thy hands with many good things, | Give to us from right and from left. ‖ *i*. I shall proclaim the mighty deeds of Viṣṇu | Who meted out the spaces of the earth, | Who established the highest abode, | Stepping thrice, the far-goer. ‖ *k*. Thou art the forehead of Viṣṇu; thou art the back of Viṣṇu. ‖ *l*. Ye two are the corners' of Viṣṇu's mouth. ‖ *m*. Thou art the thread of Viṣṇu. ‖ *n*. Thou art the fixed point of Viṣṇu. ‖ *o*. Thou art of Viṣṇu; to Viṣṇu thee!

Mantra 1:2:14

a. Put forth thy strength like a spreading net; | Come like a mighty king with thy retainers; | Hurling thy swift net thou shootest arrows; | Pierce the Rākṣhasas with thy keenest (darts). ‖ *b*. Swiftly thy whirling flames descend; | bring upward Follow them, glowing in thy fury; | Thy heat, O Agni, thy winged (flames) with thy tongue, | Unfettered, on all sides spread thy firebrands. ‖ *c*. Send forth thy spies, swiftest in thy motion; | Be an unfailing guardian to this folk, | From him who afar plans evil, from him who near; | O Agni let no trouble from thee overwhelm us. ‖ *d*. Arise, O Agni; spread thyself out; | Burn up our foes, O thou of keen dart; | Him who hath wrought evil for us, O blazing one, | Do thou consume utterly like dry stubble. ‖ *e*. Arise; drive from us (our foes); | Reveal thy heavenly strength, O Agni, | Slacken the strung (weapon) of the demon-driven; | Crush our foes, kin or not kin. ‖ *f*. He knows thy loving kindliness, O most youthful one, | Who hath given furtherance to this devotion; | All happy days for him, glory, and wealth |—Opening the doors of the miser —he hath revealed. ‖ *g*. Let him, O Agni, be fortunate and munificent, | Who with constant oblation, who with praise, | Seeks to delight thee in his life in his house; | May all days be happy for him; be that the will. ‖ *h*. I praise thy loving kindness; loud sounding (thou singest) a reply; | Let this song of mine, beloved of thee, sing with thee | With good steeds and fair chariots may we adorn thee; | Maintain for us the lordly power as the days go by. ‖ *i*. Here let each serve thee readily, | That shinest in the darkness, as the days go by; | Happy and joyous may we attend thee | That dost surpass the glories of men. ‖ *k*. He who with good steeds and rich in gold | Approacheth thee, O Agni, with a rich chariot, | His protector thou art, the comrade of him | Who duly offereth thee glad reception. ‖ *l*. The great I overcome through kinship and my songs; | That hath descended to me from Gotama, my sire; | Pay heed to this song of ours, | O Hotar, most youthful, skilful, friend of the house. ‖ *m*. Sleepless, speedy, propitious, | Unwearied, never hostile, unexhausted, | May thy guardians, O Agni, taking their places here united, | Protect us, O wise one. ‖ *n*. Thy guardians, O Agni, who seeing, | Guarded from ill the blind Māmateya, | He of all wisdom guarded these kindly ones; | The foes that were fain to deceive could not deceive. ‖ *o*. In unison with thee, aided by thee, | Under thy leadership, let us gain strength; | Fulfil both our desires, O truthful one; | Perform it forthwith, O fearless one. ‖ *p*. With this fuel, O Agni, will we serve thee; | Accept the song of praise recited for thee; | Burn those that revile, the Rākṣhasas; guard us, | From the foe, the reviler, O rich in friends, from blame. ‖ *q*. I touch the steed that slayeth the Rākṣhasas; | I go for shelter to the friend most spreading; | May Agni, enkindled with our offerings, sharpening (his dart) | Guard us by day, from harm and by night. ‖ *r*. With great radiance Agni shineth; | All things doth he reveal by his might; | He overcometh godless and malign enchantments | He sharpeneth his horns to pierce the Rakṣhas ‖ *s*. Let the roarings of Agni rise to the heaven, | Sharp weapons to slay the Rakṣhas; | In the carouse his radiance bursteth forth | The godless assailers cannot restrain him.

Prapāṭhaka 3.

The Victim for Agni and Soma

Mantra 1:3:1

a. On the impulse of the God Savitar, with the arms of the Aśvins, with the hands of Pūṣhan, I take thee; thou art the spade, thou art the | woman. ‖ *b*. The Rakṣhas is encompassed, the evil spirits are encompassed, here do I cut off the neck of the Rakṣhas ‖ *c*. He who hates us and whom we hate, here do I cut off his neck. ‖ *d*. To sky thee, to atmosphere thee, to earth thee! ‖ *e.* Pure be the world where the Pitṛis sit. ‖ *f.* Thou art barley (*yava*); bar (*yavaya*) from us foes, bar evil spirits. ‖ *g.* Thou art the seat of the Pitṛis ‖ *h.* Support the sky, fill the atmosphere, make firm the earth. ‖ *i.* May Dyutāna Māruta set thee up according to the established law of Mitra and Varuṇa ‖ *k.* Thee that art winner of Brahmans, winner of nobles, winner of fair offspring, winner of increase of wealth, I close in. ‖ *l.* Strengthen the Brahmans, strengthen the nobles, strengthen offspring, strengthen increase of wealth. ‖ *m.* With ghee, O sky and earth, be filled. ‖ *n.* Thou art the seat of Indra, the shade of all folk. ‖ *o.* May these our songs, O lover of song, | Encompass thee on all sides, | Strengthening thee whose life is strong; | May they be dear delights. ‖ *p.* Thou art the string of Indra; thou art the fixed point of Indra. ‖ *q.* Thou art of Indra. ‖ *r.* To Indra thee!

Mantra 1:3:2

a. I dig those which slay the Rakṣhas, which slay the spell, which | are of Viṣhṇu. ‖ *b.* Here do I cast out the spell which an equal or an unequal hath | buried against us. ‖ *c.* Here do I overthrow him who equal or unequal is ill-disposed to us. ‖ *d.* The spell is overcome by the Gāyatrī metre. ‖ *e.* What is here? Good. Let it be ours. ‖ *f.* Thou art Virāj, slaying our rivals; thou art Samrāj, slaying our foes; thou art Svarāj, slaying the enemy; thou art Viśvarāj, slayer of all destructive things. ‖ *g.* I sprinkle those which slay the Rakṣhas, which slay the spell, and which are of Viṣhṇu. ‖ *h.* I pour down those which slay the Rakṣhas, which slay the spell, and which are of Viṣhṇu. ‖ *i.* Thou art barley (*yava*); bar (*yavaya*) from us foes, bar evil spirits. ‖ *k.* I bestrew those which slay the Rakṣhas, which slay the spell, and which are of Viṣhṇu. ‖ *l.* I pour the libation over those which slay the Rakṣhas, which slay the spell, and which are of Viṣhṇu. ‖ *m.* I lay down the two Which slay the Rakṣhas, which slay the spell, and which are of Viṣhṇu. ‖ *n.* I surround the two which slay the Rakṣhas, which slay the spell, and which are of Viṣhṇu. ‖ *o.* I bestrew the two which slay the Rakṣhas, which slay the spell, and which are of Viṣhṇu. ‖ *p.* The two which slay the Rakṣhas, which slay the spell, and which are of Viṣhṇu. ‖ *q.* Thou art great, with a great pressing stone; call forth to Indra with a great voice.

Mantra 1:3:3

a. Thou I art the expanding, the carrier. ‖ *b.* Thou art the bearer which carrieth the offering. ‖ *c.* Thou art the savoury, the wise. ‖ *d.* Thou art Tutha, the all-knower. ‖ *e.* Thou art Uśij, the wise. ‖ *f.* Thou art Aṅghāri, Bambhāri. ‖ *g.* Thou art the seeker of aid, the worshipper. ‖ *h.* Thou art the bright, the Mārjālīya. ‖ *i.* Thou art the king, Kṛiśānu. ‖ *k.* Thou art the purifying, around which men must sit. | 1. Thou art the impetuous, the cloudy. ‖ *m.* Thou art the untouched, the preparer of the offering. ‖ *n.* Thou art be whose home is right, whose light is the heaven. ‖ *o.* Thou art be whose light is the Brahman, whose home is the heaven. ‖ *p.* Thou art the goat with one foot. ‖ *q.* Thou art the dragon of the deep. ‖ *r.* With thy dread countenance guard me, Agni; content me; hurt me not.

Mantra 1:3:4

a. Thou, O Soma, art the giver of wide protection from hostility, brought about by ourselves or by others; hail! ‖ *b.* May the active one gladly partake of the ghee. ‖ *c.* May Agni here make room for us; | May he go before us cleaving the foe; | Joyously may he conquer our foes; | May he win booty in the contest for booty. ‖ *d.* Step widely, O Viṣhṇu; | Give us broad space for dwelling in; | Drink the ghee, thou whose birthplace is in the ghee; | Lengthen (the years) of the lord of the sacrifice. ‖ *e.* Soma goeth, who knoweth the way; | He approacheth the place of the Gods, | To sit on the birthplace of Order. ‖ *f.* Thou art the seat of Aditi. ‖ *g.* Do thou sit on the seat of Aditi. ‖ *h.* This, God Savitar, is the Soma of you (Gods); guard it; let it escape you not. ‖ *i.* So, O Soma, God to the Gods, hast thou gone, and I here man to man, with offspring, with increase of wealth. ‖ *k.* Honour to the Gods I Homage to the Pitṛis! | 1. Here (may) I (be free) from Varuṇa's noose; may I gaze on the heaven, on the light that is for all men, ‖ *m.* Agni, lord of vows, thou art the vow-lord of vows. ‖ *n.* May my body that bath been in thee be here in me; may thy body that hath been in me be there in thee. ‖ *o.* Be aright the vows, O vow-lord, of both of us votaries.

Mantra 1:3:5

a. I have passed by some, I have not approached others. ‖ *b.* I have found thee nearer than the farther, farther than the near. ‖ *c.* So I welcome thee, that art of Viṣhṇu, for the sacrifice to the Gods. ‖ *d.* Let the God Savitar anoint thee with honey. ‖ *e.* O plant, guard it. ‖ *f.* O axe, harm it not. ‖ *g.* With thy top graze not the sky, with thy middle harm not the atmosphere, with earth be united. ‖ *h.* O tree, grow with a hundred shoots; may we grow with a thousand shoots. ‖ *i.* Thou, whom this sharp axe hath brought forward for great good | fortune, uncut, with wealth of heroes, (give us) riches.

Mantra 1:3:6

a. To I earth thee! To atmosphere thee! To sky thee! ‖ *b.* Pure be the world where the Pitṛis sit. ‖ *c.* Thou art barley (yava); bar (yavaya) from us foes, bar evil spirits. ‖ *d.* Thou art the seat of the Pitṛis ‖ *e.* Thou art easy of approach, first among leaders; the tree will mount thee, be aware of it. ‖ *f.* Let the God Savitar anoint thee with honey. ‖ *g.* For the plants with good berries thee! ‖ *h.* Support the sky, fill the atmosphere, with thy base make firm the earth. ‖ *i.* To these dwellings of thine are we fain to go, | Where are the many-horned active kine; | There is resplendent the highest step | Of the wide-stepping Viṣhṇu, the mighty! ‖ *k.* Behold the deeds of Viṣhṇu | Wherein he displayed his laws, | Indra's true friend. ‖ *l.* That highest step of Viṣhṇu | The singers ever gaze upon | Like an eye stretched in the sky. ‖ *m.* Thee that art winner of Brahmans, winner of nobles, winner of fair | offspring, winner of increase of wealth, I close in. ‖ *n.* Strengthen the Brahmans, strengthen the nobles, strengthen offspring, | strengthen increase of wealth, ‖ *o.* Thou art invested; lot the clans of the Gods invest thee; let increase | of wealth, let (the clans) of men invest the sacrificer here. ‖ *p.* On the slope of the atmosphere I conceal thee.

Mantra 1:3:7

a. For striving thee! ‖ *b.* Thou art the impeller. ‖ *c.* To the Gods the servants of the Gods have come, the priests, the eager | ones. ‖ *d.* O Bṛihaspati, guard wealth. ‖ *e.* Let thy oblations taste sweet. ‖ *f.* O God Tvaṣhṭar make pleasant our possessions. ‖ *g.* Stay, ye wealthy ones, ‖ *h.* Thou art the birthplace of Agni. ‖ *i.* Ye are the two male ones. ‖ *k.* Thou art Urvaśī, thou art Āyu, thou art Purūravas ‖ *l.* Anointed with ghee, do ye produce a male. ‖ *m.* Be born with the Gāyatrī metre, with the Triṣhṭubh metre, be born with the Jagatī metre. ‖ *n.* Be ye of one mind for us, one dwelling, spotless. ‖ *o.* Harm not the sacrifice nor the lord of the sacrifice, O all-knowing; | be ye two auspicious today with us. ‖ *p.* The fire moveth entering into the fire, | The son of the Ṛishis, the overlord he; | With the cry of Hail! I offer to thee with devotion; | Do thou not spoil the share of the Gods.

Mantra 1:3:8

a. I grasp thee. ‖ *b.* Offering to the Gods, I seize thee with the noose of sacred order. ‖ *c.* Fear not men. ‖ *d.* For the waters thee, for the plants thee, I sprinkle. ‖ *e.* Thou art a drinker of the waters. ‖ *f.* Ye divine waters, make it palatable, a very palatable offering for the Gods. ‖ *g.* Let thy breath be united with the wind, thy limbs with the sacrificial, the lord of the sacrifice with his prayer. ‖ *h.* Anointed with ghee, do ye guard the beast. ‖ *i.* Ye wealthy ones, do ye kindly I resort to the lord of the sacrifice. ‖ *k.* O broad atmosphere, in unison with the God wind, sacrifice with the life of this offering; be united with its body; extending more broadly, make the sacrifice of the lord of the sacrifice most successful. ‖ *l.* Guard from contact with earth. ‖ *m.* Homage to thee, O extended one. ‖ *n.* Come forward, irresistible, along the stream of ghee, with offspring, with increase of wealth. ‖ *o.* O ye waters, Goddesses, purifying and pure, do ye bring the Gods; may we, pure and served (by you), be servers upon you.

Mantra 1:3:9

a. Let thy speech swell, let thy breath swell, let thine eye swell, let | thine ear swell. ‖ *b.* The pain that hath reached thy vital airs, that (hath reached) thine eye, that (hath reached) thine ear, what is harsh in thee, what is in its place,—let that swell, let that hereby be pure. ‖ *c.* Lot thy navel swell, let thine anus swell. ‖ *d.* Be thy feet pure. ‖ *e.* Hail to the waters! Hail to the plants! Hail to earth! Hail to night and day! ‖ *f.* O plant, protect him. ‖ *g.* O axe, harm him not. ‖ *h.* Thou art the share of the Rākṣhasas ‖ *i.* This Rakṣhas here I lead to the lowest darkness. ‖ *k.* Him who hateth us and whom we hate, here him I lead to the lowest darkness. ‖ *l.* For food thee! ‖ *m.* In ghee, O sky and earth, be covered. ‖ *n.* Uncut, with wealth of heroes, (give us) riches. ‖ *o.* Fare along the broad atmosphere. ‖ *p.* O Vāyu, taste the drops. ‖ *q.* Hail! go to Ūrdhvanabhas, offspring of the Marutas.

Mantra 1:3:10.

a. Let thy mind with the mind, let thy breath with the breath (of the

Gods be united). ‖ *b.* Be this offering rich in ghee pleasing to the Gods; hail! ‖ *c.* May Indra's expiration be set in every limb; | May Indra's inspiration be in every limb. ‖ *d.* O God Tvaṣhṭar, let mind be united for thee, | When ye that are various become of one form; | Over thee as thou goest among the Gods for help let thy comrades | And thy father and mother rejoice. ‖ *e.* Thou art fortune (*śri*). ‖ *f.* Let Agni cook (*śrinatu*) thee. ‖ *g.* The waters are come together. ‖ *h.* For the whirl of the wind thee, for the rush of Pūṣhan, for the growth of the waters, of the plants. ‖ *i.* Drink ghee, ye drinkers of ghee; drink fat, ye drinkers of fat. ‖ *k.* Thou art the oblation of the atmosphere. ‖ *l.* Hail! thee to the atmosphere! ‖ *m.* The quarters, the Pradiśes, the Ādiśes, the Vidiśes, the Uddiśes. ‖ *n.* Hail to the quarters! ‖ *o.* Homage to the quarters.

Mantra 1:3:11

a. Go to the ocean, hail! Go to the atmosphere, hail! Go to God Savitar, hail! Go to day and night, hail! Go to Mitra and Varuṇa, hail! Go to Soma, hail! Go to the sacrifice, hail! Go to the metes, hail! Go to the sky and the earth, hail! Go to the clouds of the sky, hail! Go to Agni Vaiśvānara, hail! ‖ *b.* To the waters thee! To the plants thee! ‖ *c.* Give me mind and heart! ‖ *d.* May I acquire body, skin, son, and grandson. ‖ *e.* Thou art pain; pain him who hateth us and whom we hate. ‖ *f.* From every rule of thine, O King Varuṇa, set us free; | From whatever oath by the waters, by the kine, by Varuṇa, we have sworn, | From that, O Varuṇa, set us free.

Mantra 1:3:12

a. These waters are rich in oblation, | Rich in oblation is the divine sacrifice, | Rich in oblation he seeks to win (the Gods?), | Rich in oblation be the sun. ‖ *b.* In the seat of Agni whose home is abiding I set you down, kindly | for kindness, accord to me kindness. ‖ *c.* Ye are the share of Indra and Agni; ye are the share of Mitra and | Varuṇa; ye are the share of the all-Gods. ‖ *d.* Be watchful over the sacrifice.

Mantra 1:3:13

a. To the heart thee! To mind thee! To the sky thee! To the sun thee! ‖ *b.* Raise aloft the sacrifice; in the sky guide to the Gods the prayers. ‖ *c.* O King Soma, come hither, descend. ‖ *d.* Fear not, tremble not. ‖ *e.* Lot me not harm thee. ‖ *f.* Do thou descend to creatures; let creatures descend to thee. ‖ *g.* Let Agni (kindled) with the kindling-stick hear my appeal, | Let the waters hear, and the divine Dhiṣhaṇās; | Hearken, ye pressing stones, to the sacrifice of me the wise one, | Let the God Savitar hearken to my appeal. ‖ *h.* Ye divine waters, child of the waters, that wave, | Which is rich in oblation, powerful and sweetest, | Give to the Gods among the Gods, | Pure to the drinkers of the pure, (to them) whose share ye are; hail ‖ *i.* Thou art the dragger; do thou (drag) away the foe of the waters. ‖ *k.* I draw you for the sustenance of the waters. ‖ *l.* That mortal, O Agni, whom thou hast helped in the battles, | Whom thou hast strengthened in the contest for booty, | He winneth I abiding strength.

Mantra 1:3:14

a. Thou, O Agni, art Rudra, the Asura of the mighty sky, | Thou art the host of the Marutas, thou art lord of food; | Thou farest with ruddy winds, blessing the household; | Thou, as Pūṣhan dost, protectest thy worshippers with thyself. ‖ *b.* Rudra, king of the sacrifice, | True offerer, priest of both worlds, | Agni before the dreadful thunder, | Of golden colour, win ye for help. ‖ *c.* Agni hath set him down as priest, good sacrificer, | On the lap of his mother, in the fragrant place, | The youthful, the wise, pre-eminent among men, righteous, | Supporter of the folk in whose midst he is kindled. ‖ *d.* Good hath he made our sacrifice this day; | The hidden tongue of the sacrifice have we found | He hath come, fragrant, clothed in life; | He hath made our sacrifice this day to prosper. ‖ *e.* Agni hath cried like Dyaus thundering, | Licking the earth, devouring the plants; | Straightway on birth he shone aflame; | He blazeth with his light within the firmaments. | In thee, O many-faced sacrificer, | Morning and evening, the sacrificers place their treasures, | In whom, purifying, good things are placed, even as the heaven and earth (support) all beings. ‖ *q.* To thee, best of Aṅgirasas, | All folk with fair dwellings severally, | O Agni, have turned to gain their wish. ‖ *h.* May we win by thy help, O Agni, our wish, | Wealth with fair offspring, O wealthy one: | May we win booty, seeking for booty; | May we win, O deathless, undying glory. ‖ *i.* O Agni, of the Bhāratas, youngest, | Bear to us excellent, glorious wealth, | O bright one, wealth which many desire. ‖ *k.* White robed is he, thundering, standing in the firmament. | Youngest, with loud-sounding immortal ones, | Who, purifying, most manifold, | Agni, marcheth devouring many broad (forests). ‖ *l.* May he give thee life on every side, | Agni here, the desirable. | Let thy breath come back to thee; | I drive away the disease from thee. ‖ *m.* Giving life, O Agni, rejoicing in the oblation | Be thou faced with ghee, and with birthplace of ghee | Having drunk the ghee, the sweet, the delightful product of the cow, | As a father his son, do thou protect him. ‖ *n.* To thee, the eager one, | O knower of all, O active one, | Agni, I offer this fair praise. ‖ *o.* From the sky was Agni first born, | From us secondly he who knoweth all, | In the waters thirdly the manly; | The pious man singeth of him, the undying, as he kindleth him. ‖ *p.* Pure, O purifying one, to be lauded, | O Agni, mightily thou shinest, | To whom offering is made with ghee. ‖ *q.* Shining like gold, he hath become widely resplendent, | For glory shining with immortal life; | Agni became immortal in his strength, | What time prolific Dyaus begat him. ‖ *r.* What time his glory urged the lord to strength, | Then (did) Dyaus (let) the pure seed be sprinkled openly; | Agni begot the host, the blameless, the youthful, | The worshipping, and gave it impulse. ‖ *s.* He (flourishes) with keener mind, aided by thee. | O giver! give (us wealth) in good offspring; | O Agni, may we enjoy wealth richest in heroes; | (Wealth) that is excellent, uttering praises to thee. ‖ *t.* O Agni, bring us strong wealth, | By the force of thy glory, | That is above all men | And openly prevaileth in contests for booty. ‖ *u.* O Agni, mighty one, bring to us | That wealth which prevaileth in contests; | For thou art true, wondrous, | The giver of booty of kine. ‖ *v.* To Agni let us make service with hymns, | Who feedeth on bull and cow, | The disposer, backed with Soma. ‖ *w.* For thou art, O son, a singer, seated at the feast; | Agni made at birth a path and food; | Do thou, O giver of strength, bestow strength upon us; | Be victorious like a king; thou rulest within without a foe. ‖ *x.* O Agni, thou purifiest life; | Do thou give food and strength to us; | Far away drive ill-fortune. ‖ *y.* O Agni, good worker, purify for us | Glory in good heroes; | Giving increase and wealth to me. ‖ *z.* O Agni the purifying, with thy light, | O God, with thy pleasant tongue, | Bring hither the Gods and sacrifice. ‖ *aa.* Do thou, O shining and purifying one, | O Agni, bring hither the Gods | To our sacrifice and our oblation. ‖ *bb.* Agni, of purest vows, | Pure sage, pure poet, | Shineth in purity, when offering is made. ‖ *cc.* O Agni, thy pure, | Bright, flaming (rays) arise, | Thy lights, thy flames.

Prapāṭhaka 4.

The Soma Cups

Mantra 1:4:1

a. I take thee. Thou art the stone which maketh the sacrifice for the Gods; make this sacrifice deep, with thy highest edge, (make) the Soma well pressed for Indra, rich in sweetness, in milk, bringing rain. ‖ *b.* To Indra, slayer of Vṛitra, thee! To Indra, conqueror of Vṛitra, thee! To Indra, slayer of foes, thee! To Indra with the Ādityas, thee! To Indra with the all-Gods, thee! ‖ *c.* Ye are savoury, conquerors of Vṛitra, delightful through your gifts, spouses of immortality, | Do ye, O Goddesses, place this sacrifice among the Gods | Do ye, invoked, drink the Soma; | Invoked by you let Soma drink. ‖ *d.* With thy light which is in the sky, on the earth, in the broad atmosphere, do thou for this sacrificer spread wealth broadly; be favour able to the giver. ‖ *c.* Ye Dhiṣhaṇās, that are strong, be strengthened; gather strength, and give me strength; let me not harm you, harm me not. ‖ *f.* Forward, backward, upward, downward, let these quarters speed to you; O mother, come forth. ‖ *g.* Thy unerring, watchful name, O Soma, to that of thee, O Soma, to Soma, hail!

Mantra 1:4:2

a. Be pure for the lord of speech, O strong one; male, purified by the arms with the shoots of the male; thou art the God purifier of Gods; to those thee whose portion thou art! ‖ *b.* Thou art he who is appropriated; make our food full of sweetness for us; to all the powers of sky and earth thee! ‖ *c.* May mind enter thee. ‖ *d.* Fare along the broad atmosphere. ‖ *e.* Hail! Thee, of kindly nature, to the sun! ‖ *f.* To the Gods that drink the rays thee f ‖ *g.* This is thy birthplace; to expiration thee!

Mantra 1:4:3

a. Thou art taken with a support. ‖ *b.* O bounteous one, restrain (it), protect Soma, guard wealth, win food by sacrifice, I place within thee sky and earth, within thee the broad atmosphere; in unison with the Gods, the lower and the higher, O bounteous one, do thou rejoice in the Antaryāma (cup). ‖ *e.* Thou art he who is appropriated; make our food full of sweetness for us; to all the powers of sky and earth thee! ‖ *d.* May mind enter thee. ‖ *e.* Fare along the broad atmosphere. ‖ *f.* Hail! Thee, of kindly nature, to the sun! ‖ *g.* To the Gods that drink the rays thee! ‖ *h.* This is thy birthplace; to inspiration thee!

Mantra 1:4:4

a. O Vāyu, drinker of the pure, come to us; | A thousand are thy teams, O thou that hast all choice boons. | For thee this sweet drink hath been drawn, | Whereof, O God, thou hast the first drink. ‖ *b.* Thou art taken with a support; to Vāyu thee! ‖ *c.* O Indra and Vāyu, these draughts are ready; | Come ye for the libations, | For the drops desire you. ‖ *d.* Thou art taken with a support; to Indra and Vāyu thee! This is thy birthplace; to the comrades thee!

Mantra 1:4:5

a. This Soma is pressed for you, O Mitra and Varuṇa, | Who prosper holy order; | Hearken ye now to my supplication. ‖ *b.* Thou art taken with a support; to Mitra and Varuṇa thee! This is | thy birthplace; to the righteous thee!

Mantra 1:4:6

a. That I whip of yours which is rich in sweetness | And full of mercy, O Aśvins, | With that touch the sacrifice. ‖ *b.* Thou art taken with a support; to the Aśvins thee! This is thy birthplace; to the sweet thee!

Mantra 1:4:7

a. Ye that yoke early be unloosed | O Aśvins, come ye hither, | To drink this Soma. ‖ *b.* Thou art taken with a support; to the Aśvins thee! This is thy birthplace; to the Aśvins thee!

Mantra 1:4:8

a. Vena hath stirred those born of Pṛiśni, | He enveloped in light, in the expanse of the welkin; | Him in the meeting-place of the waters, of the sun, | Like a child, the priests tend with their songs. ‖ *b.* Thou art taken with a support; to Śaṇḍa thee! This is thy birthplace; guard the folk.

Mantra 1:4:9

a. Him, as aforetime, as of old, as always, as now, | The prince, who hath his seat on the strew and knoweth the heaven, | The favouring, the strong, thou milkest with thy speech, | The swift who is victor in those among whom thou dost wax. ‖ *b.* Thou art taken with a support; to Marka thee! This is thy birth-place; guard offspring.

Mantra 1:4:10.

a. Ye Gods that are eleven in the sky, | Eleven on the earth, | Who sit mightily in the waters, eleven in number, | Do ye accept this sacrifice. ‖ *b.* Thou art taken with a support; thou art the leader, thou art the good leader; quicken the sacrifice, quicken the lord of the sacrifice; guard the pressings; let Vishṇu guard thee, do thou guard the folk with thy power; this is thy birthplace; to the All-Gods thee!

Mantra 1:4:11

a. Three and thirty in troops the Rudras | Frequent the sky and earth, the destructive ones, | Eleven seated on the waters; | May all of them accept the Soma pressed for the pressing. ‖ *b.* Thou art taken with a support; thou art the leader, thou art the good leader; quicken the sacrifice, quicken the lord of the sacrifice; guard the pressings; let Vishṇu guard thee, do thou guard the folk with thy power; this is thy birthplace; to the all-Gods thee!

Mantra 1:4:12

a. Thou art taken with a support. | To Indra thee, to him of the Bṛihat (Sāman), | The strong, eager for praise. | Thy great strength, O Indra, | To that thee! | To Vishṇu thee! This is thy birthplace; to Indra, eager for praise, thee!

Mantra 1:4:13

a. The head of the sky, the messenger of earth, | Vaiśvānara, born for holy order, Agni, | The sage, the king, the guest of men, | The Gods have produced as a cup for their mouths. ‖ *b.* Thou art taken with a support; to Agni Vaiśvānara thee! Thou art secure, of secure foundation, most secure of the secure, with securest foundation of those which are secure. This is thy birthplace; to Agni | Vaiśvānara thee!

Mantra 1:4:14

a. Thou art Madhu and Mādhava; thou art Śukra and Śuchi; thou art Nabha and Nabhasya; thou art Isha and Ūrja; thou art Saha and Sahasya; thou art Tapa and Tapasya. ‖ *b.* Thou art taken with a support. ‖ *c.* Thou art Saṃsarpa ‖ *d.* To Aṃhaspatya thee!

Mantra 1:4:15

a. O Indra and Agni, come | For our prayers to the pressed drink, the delightful fumes | Drink ye of it, impelled by our prayer. ‖ *b.* Thou art taken with a support; to Indra and Agni thee! This is thy birthplace; to Indra and Agni thee!

Mantra 1:4:16

a. Ye dread ones, guardians of men, | O All-Gods, come ye, | Generous, to the pressed drink of the generous one. ‖ *b.* Thou art taken with a support; to the All-Gods thee! This is thy birthplace; to the All-Gods thee!

Mantra 1:4:17

a. Him with the Marutas, the mighty bull, | The bountiful, the divine ruler, Indra, | All-powerful, the dread, giver of strength, | For present aid let us invoke. ‖ *b.* Thou art taken with a support; to Indra with the Marutas thee! This is thy birthplace; to Indra with the Marutas thee!

Mantra 1:4:18

a. O Indra with the Marutas drink here the Soma, | As thou didst drink the pressed drink with Śāryāta | Under thy guidance, in thy protection, O hero, | The singers skilled in sacrifice are fain to serve. ‖ *b.* Thou art taken with a support; to Indra with the Marutas thee! This is thy birthplace; to Indra with the Marutas thee!

Mantra 1:4:19

a. Indra with the Marutas, the bull, for gladness, | Drink the Soma, for joy, to thy content; | Pour within thy belly the wave of sweetness; | Thou art from of old the king of the pressed drinks. ‖ *b.* Thou art taken with a support; to Indra with the Marutas thee, This is thy birthplace; to Indra with the Marutas thee!

Mantra 1:4:20.

a. Great is Indra who through his might | Is like Parjanya with the rain; | He waxeth with the praises of Vatsa. ‖ *b.* Thou art taken with a foundation; to Mahendra thee! This is thy birthplace; to Mahendra thee!

Mantra 1:4:21

a. Great is Indra, manfully controlling men, | Unfailing in strength, of double force; | Towards us for strength doth he wax; | Broad and wide hath he been adorned by the offerers. ‖ *b.* Thou art taken with a foundation; to Mahendra thee! This is thy birthplace; to Mahendra thee!

Mantra 1:4:22

a. Never art thou barren, O Indra, | Never dost thou fail thy worshipper; | Now more and more is thy divine gift increased, | O bountiful one. ‖ *b.* Thou art taken with a support; to the Ādityas thee! ‖ *c.* At no time art thou heedless, | But dost guard the two generations; | The pressing is thy strength, O fourth Āditya | The ambrosia is ready in the sky. ‖ *d.* The sacrificer seeketh the favour of the Gods; | Be ye kindly, O Ādityas; | May thy loving kindness come hither, | That it may the more free us from affliction. ‖ *e.* O bright Āditya, this is thy Soma drink, | Delight in it, have gladness in it; may we that gladden thee have gladness; | With the rain of the sky I mix thee.

Mantra 1:4:23

a. Prosperity today, O Savitar, prosperity tomorrow, | Day by day prosperity mayst thou procure for us; | Through this prayer may be won the prosperity | Of many a prosperous dwelling, O God. ‖ *b.* Thou art taken with a foundation; to the God Savitar thee!

Mantra 1:4:24

a. O Savitar with unfailing guardians, | Propitious, do thou today guard our house; | Golden-tongued do thou protect us for new prosperity; | May no plotter of evil overpower us. ‖ *b.* Thou art taken with a support; to the God Savitar thee

Mantra 1:4:25

a. To help us I summon | The golden-handed Savitar | He as a God knoweth the place. ‖ *b.* Thou art taken with a support; to the God Savitar thee!

Mantra 1:4:26

a. Thou givest good protection, and art well established. ‖ *b.* Homage to the great bull! ‖ *c.* This is thy birthplace; to the All-Gods thee!

Mantra 1:4:27

a. Of thee, O drop, pressed by Bṛihaspati, and possessing power, I draw | the cup connected with the wives. ‖ *b.* O Agni, with the wives, in unison with the God Tvaṣṭar, drink the Soma, hail.

Mantra 1:4:28

a. Thou art a bay, yoker of bays, mounter on the bays, bearer of the bolt, lover of Pṛiśni; to thee, O God Soma, for whom the formula of sacrifice is uttered, the song sung, the hymn recited, I draw the cup connected with the bays. ‖ *b.* Ye two are bays; ye are the grains for the bays, mixed with Soma. ‖ *c.* To Indra hail!

Mantra 1:4:29

a. O Agni, thou purifiest life; | Do thou give food and strength to us; | Far away drive ill fortune. ‖ *b.* Thou art taken with a support; to Agni the radiant thee! This is thy birthplace; to Agni the radiant thee!

Mantra 1:4:30.

a. Arising in might, | Thou didst move thy jaws, O Indra, | When thou hadst drunk the cup-pressed Soma. ‖ *b.* Thou art taken with a support; to Indra the mighty thee! This is thy birthplace; to Indra the mighty thee!

Mantra 1:4:31

a. Overcoming, seen of all, | Light-making art thou, Sūrya; | Thou dost illumine all the firmament. ‖ *b.* Thou art taken with a support; to Sūrya the radiant thee! This is thy birthplace; to Sūrya the radiant thee!

Mantra 1:4:32

a. Swell, O sweetest Soma, | With all thy aids, | Be fullest of help for us.

Mantra 1:4:33

a. Departed are those mortals who in days gone by behold | An earlier dawn of morning; | Dawn now hath become visible to us; | They come who shall behold her in days to come.

Mantra 1:4:34

a. I place thee that hast light. ‖ *b.* I place thee that makest light. ‖ *c.* I place thee that findest light. ‖ *d.* I place thee that shinest. ‖ *e.* I place thee that burnest. ‖ *f.* I place thee that flashest. ‖ *g.* I place thee that art aflame. ‖ *h.* I place thee that blazest. ‖ *i.* I place thee that art immortal. ‖ *k.* I place thee that hast great light. ‖ *l.* I place thee that awakenest. ‖ *m.* I place thee that art awake.

Mantra 1:4:35

a. To energy hail! To effort hail! To distraction hail! To attempt hail! To endeavour hail! To striving hail! To heat hail! To burning hail! To heating hail! To the hot hail! To the slaying of a Brahman hail! To all hail!

Mantra 1:4:36

a. Chitta with the sinew, Bhava with the liver, Rudra with the *taniman*, Paśupati with the thick heart, Agni with the heart, Rudra with the blood, Śarva with the kidneys, Mahādeva with the intestinal flesh, him that slayest most quickly with the entrails.

Mantra 1:4:37

a. Mount thy car, O slayer of Vṛitra; | Thy steeds are yoked by our prayer; | May the pressing-stone with its voice | Incline thy mind towards us. ‖ *b.* Thou art taken with a support; to Indra of the Ṣhoḍaśin thee! This is thy birthplace; to Indra of the Ṣhoḍaśin thee!

Mantra 1:4:38

a. Indra his two steeds bear, | Him of unequalled strength, | To the praises of the Ṛiṣhis and the sacrifice of men. ‖ *b.* Thou art taken with a support; to Indra of the Ṣhoḍaśin thee! This is thy birthplace; to Indra of the Ṣhoḍaśin thee!

Mantra 1:4:39

a. The Soma hath been pressed for thee O Indra; | O most strong, O impetuous one, come hither; | Let power encompass thee, | Even as the sun encompasses the atmosphere with its rays. ‖ *b.* Thou art taken with a support; to Indra of the Ṣhoḍaśin thee! This is thy birthplace; to Indra of the Ṣhoḍaśin thee!

Mantra 1:4:40.

a. Earth, covering all, | Hath placed thee in her lap; | Be gentle and rest kindly on him | Grant him protection, extending wide. ‖ *b.* Thou art taken with a support; to Indra of the Ṣhoḍaśin thee! This is thy birthplace; to Indra of the Ṣhoḍaśin thee!

Mantra 1:4:41

a. Great is Indra of the Ṣhoḍaśin, | With the bolt in his arm, may he grant protection; | May the bountiful give us prosperity, | May he smite him who hateth us. ‖ *b.* Thou art taken with a support; to Indra of the Ṣhoḍaśin thee! This is thy birthplace; to Indra of the Ṣhoḍaśin thee!

Mantra 1:4:42

a. In unison and in fellowship with the Marutas, Indra, | Drink the Soma, O slayer of Vṛitra, O hero, O wise one; | Slay our foes, drive away the enemies, | And thus make for us on all sides security. ‖ *b.* Thou art taken with a support; to Indra of the Ṣhoḍaśin thee! This is thy birthplace; to Indra of the Ṣhoḍaśin thee!

The Dakṣhiṇā Offerings

Mantra 1:4:43

a. His rays bear up the God | Who knoweth all, | The sun for all to see. ‖ *b.* The radiant countenance of the Gods hath risen, | The eye of Mitra, Varuṇa, Agni; | He hath filled the sky and earth and atmosphere; | The sun is the self of all that moveth and standeth. ‖ *c.* O Agni, lead us by a fair path to wealth, | O God, knowing all the ways; | Drive from us the sin that maketh us wander; | We will accord to thee most abundant honour. ‖ *d.* Go to the sky, fly to heaven. ‖ *e.* With my form I approach your form; with my age your age. ‖ *f.* May Tutha, all knowing, allot to you in the highest firmament. ‖ *g.* This gift of thine, Agni, cometh, impelled by the Soma. ‖ *h.* Lead it by the path of Mitra. ‖ *i.* Go ye on by the path of holy order, of brilliant gifts, | Leading prosperity by the path of the sacrifice. ‖ *k.* May I win a Brahman today, a seer and sprung from seers, of (famous) father and grandfather, fit for the sacrificial gift. ‖ *l.* Gaze on the heaven, gaze on the atmosphere. ‖ *m.* Join those in the seat. ‖ *n.* Given by us, go to the Gods, full of sweetness; enter the giver; without leaving us fare by the path leading to the Gods; sit in the world of the righteous. ‖ *o.* Be this complete for us.

Mantra 1:4:44

a. May Dhātar the giver, may Savitar, rejoice in this, | Prajāpati, the lord of treasures, and Agni, for our sake; | May Tvaṣhṭar, Viṣhṇu, accord generously | Wealth with offspring to the sacrificer. ‖ *b.* O Indra, unite us in heart, with cattle, | O bountiful one, with generous ones, with prosperity; | With the holy power that is made by the Gods, | With loving kindness of the Gods to whom sacrifice is made. ‖ *c.* With glory, with milk, with ourselves, | Are we united, with auspicious hearts; | May Tvaṣhṭar make fortune for us; | May he set right whatever is amiss in our bodies. ‖ *d.* In that today, O Agni, we choose thee | As Hotar as our sacrifice proceeded, | Prosperously hast thou sacrificed, | Prosperously hast thou laboured; | Come wise and foreseeing one to the sacrifice. ‖ *e.* With Hail! to you, O Gods, have we made this seat, | Ye who have come hither rejoicing in this as the pressing; | When ye have eaten and drunken, | Ye all, give to us, wealthy ones, wealth. ‖ *f.* The Gods whom eager thou didst bring hither, O God, | Them, O Agni, do thou incite in their own abode; | Bearing and bringing oblations, | The rich draught, do ye mount the sky. ‖ *g.* O sacrifice, go to the sacrifice; go to the lord of the sacrifice; go to thine own birthplace; hail! ‖ *h.* This is thy sacrifice, O lord of the sacrifice, with its utterance of hymns and producing noble heroes; hail! ‖ *i.* Ye Gods that find the way, finding the way, go on the way. ‖ *k.* O lord of mind, place this sacrifice, O God, for us among the Gods, hail! or speech, hail! or the wind, hail!

Mantra 1:4:45

a. King Varuṇa hath made a broad path | For the sun to travel; | He hath made him set his feet in the pathless way; | He driveth away whatever woundeth the heart. ‖ *b.* A hundred remedies are thine, O king, a thousand; | Broad and deep be thy loving kindness. | Overcome the enmity, the hostility; | Remove from us whatever sin hath been committed. ‖ *c.* The noose of Varuṇa is overcome. ‖ *d.* The face of Agni hath entered the waters, | The child of the waters guarding against the demons' power, | In each home do thou offer the kindling-stick, O Agni; | Let thy tongue seek the ghee. ‖ *e*. In the sea is thy heart, within the waters; | Let the plants and the waters enter thee; | With the offerings of the sacrifice, O lord of the sacrifice, | Let us worship at the utterance of the hymn, at the utterance of homage. ‖ *f*. O bath, O flood, thou glidest, O flood; thou hast removed by sacrifice the sin committed by the Gods, through the Gods, the sin committed by mortals, through mortals; guard us, O God, from wide hostility. ‖ *g*. Be the water and plants friendly to us; be they hostile to him who hateth us and whom we hate. ‖ *h*. Ye divine waters, this is thy foetus, glad and well tended have we made it for you; proclaim us as doers of good deeds among the Gods. ‖ *i*. The noose of Varuṇa is tied, the noose of Varuṇa is loosed. ‖ *k*. Thou art fuel; may we prosper; thou art kindling; thou art brilliance, grant me brilliance. ‖ *l*. I have penetrated to the waters; | We are united with the sap; | have come rich in milk, O Agni; | Do thou unite me with radiance.

Mantra 1:4:46

a. I who deeming thee immortal, | Mortal myself, call on thee with prayerful heart. | Upon us, O wise one, bestow glory; | O Agni, through offspring may I attain immortality. ‖ *b*. He, for whom, O Agni, thou dost make, O wise one, | For his good deeds a kindly world, | Shall win prosperity and wealth, | Rich in sons, in heroes, in kine. ‖ *c*. To thee, O son of strength, they turn | Who have desires to be fulfilled; | None excelleth thee, O Indra. ‖ *d*. At each hymn the Soma delighteth Indra, | The pressed (juices), the bountiful one, | What time in unison with equal effort | They call him to aid, like sons a father. ‖ *e*. O Agni, O wise one, with sap, | With brilliance thou shinest, | Slayer of Rākṣhasas, suppressor of demons. ‖ *f*. I have penetrated to the waters | We are united with the sap; | I have come rich in milk, O Agni; | Do thou unite me with radiance. ‖ *g*. Rich art thou, lord of riches, | O Agni, rich in radiance; | May we enjoy thy loving kindness. ‖ *h*. Thou, O Agni, riches-lord of riches, | I hail, O lord in the sacrifices; | Through thee in strife may we be victorious; | May we overcome the hostilities of mortal men. ‖ *i*. Thee, O Agni, best gainer of booty, | The sages nourish, well lauded; | Do thou give us wealth of heroes. ‖ *k*. May Agni here make room for us; | May he go before us cleaving the foe | Joyfully may he conquer our foes; | May he win booty in the contest for booty. ‖ *l*. By Agni is Agni kindled, | The wise, the young, the lord of the house, | The bearer of the oblation, with ladle in his mouth. ‖ *m*. Thou, O Agni, by Agni, | The sage by the sage, the good by the good, | The comrade by the comrade, art kindled. ‖ *n*. O Agni, thy pure. ‖ *o*. With radiance.

Prapāṭhaka 5.

The Rekindling of the Fire

Mantra 1:5:1

The Gods and the Asuras were in conflict; the Gods, in anticipation of the contest, deposited in Agni their desirable riches (thinking), 'This will still be ours, if they defeat us.' Agni desired it and went away with it. The Gods having defeated (the Asuras) pursued (Agni) desirous of recovering it. They sought violently to take it from him. He wept; in that he wept (*arodit*), that is why Rudra has his name. The tear that was shed became silver; therefore silver is not a suitable gift, for it is born of tears. He who gives on the strew, in his house before the year is out they weep; therefore one should not give on the strew. Agni said, 'Let me have a share; then this will be yours.' They replied, 'The re-establishing shall be thine alone.' 'He shall prosper,' he said, who shall establish the fire with me as its divinity.' Pūṣhan established it; therefore did Pūṣhan prosper; therefore cattle are said to be Pūṣhan's. Tvaṣhṭar established it; therefore did Tvaṣhṭar prosper; therefore cattle are said to be Tvaṣhṭar's. Manu established it; therefore did Manu prosper; therefore offspring are said to be Manu's. Dhātar established it; therefore Dhātar prospered; Dhātar is the year; therefore offspring and cattle are born in the course of the year. He who knows thus the prosperity of the re-establishing prospers. He who knows his connexions becomes possessed of connexions himself. Agni desiring a share after being established assailed the offspring and cattle of the sacrifice. Having removed it, one should re-establish it; thus he unites him with his own portion; verily he is appeased. He should establish under Punarvasu; Punarvasu is the Nakṣhatra for the re-establishing; verily by establishing it under its own deity he becomes resplendent. He establishes with Darbha grass, for variety. He establishes with Darbha; verily winning it from the waters and the plants he establishes it. The sacrificial cake is offered on five potsherds; the seasons are five; verily he wins it from the seasons and establishes it.

Mantra 1:5:2

He who removes the fire casts away the sacrifice and cattle. The sacrificial cake is offered on five potsherds; the sacrifice is fivefold, cattle are fivefold; verily he wins the sacrifice and cattle. Now he who removes the fire is the slayer of the hero among the Gods; Brahmans desirous of holiness did not aforetime eat his food; the Yājyās and Anuvākyās are in the Paṅkti metre; the sacrifice is fivefold, man is fivefold; verily making recompense to the Gods for the hero he re-establishes the fire. They are of a hundred syllables; man lives a hundred years and has a hundred powers; verily he rests on life and power. In that Agni when established does not prosper, (it is that he is) desiring a greater portion; in that it is all Agni's, that is his prosperity. Speech is uttered together in the house of him who removes the fire; the sacrificer is liable to perish on account of the uttering together of speech. There are discriminations, to sever speech and preserve the sacrificer. He makes a discrimination; verily he makes the holy power (Brahman). He speaks the Yajus, muttering; it is as if one who has found a rich treasure hides it. To Agni Sviṣhṭakṛit he speaks aloud; it is as if one who has found a rich treasure is fain to go openly. Uttering the discrimination he makes the Vaṣhaṭ cry with the fore-sacrifice; verily he leaves not his abode. The sacrificial cake is the sacrificer, the oblations are cattle; in that he offers these libations on either side of the cake, he thus surrounds the sacrificer on either side with cattle. 'After performing the Yajus and collecting the apparatus,' they say: 'the apparatus should not be collected, the Yajus should not be performed,' they say: the apparatus should be collected and the Yajus performed, for the prosperity of the sacrifice. The sacrificial fee is a renovated chariot, a newly-sewn garment, a draught ox let loose again, for the prosperity of the re-establishing. 'Seven are thy kindling-sticks, O Agni, seven thy tongues'; (with these words) he offers the Agnihotra. Wherever there is anything of his nature, thence does he win him. Now he who removes the fire is the slayer of the hero among the Gods, Varuṇa is the exactor of the recompense; he should make an offering on eleven potsherds to Agni and Varuṇa; him whom he slays and him who exacts the recompense he delights with their own portion; the sacrificer is not ruined.

Mantra 1:5:3

a. (Thou I art) earth in depth, sky in breadth, atmosphere in greatness; | In thy lap, O Goddess Aditi, Agni | I place, food-eater for the eating of food. ‖ *b*. The spotted bull hath come | And reached again the mother | And the father, faring to the heaven. ‖ *c*. Thirty places be ruleth; | Speech resorteth to the bird | Bear it with the days. ‖ *d*. With her inspiration from his expiration, | She wandereth between the worlds; | The bull discerneth the heaven. ‖ *e*. If thee in anger I have scattered, | In rage or through misfortune, | That of thee, O Agni, be in good order, | Again thee we relight. ‖ *f*. Whatever of thee scattered in rage | Was spread over the earth, | That the Ādityas, the All-Gods | And the Vasus gathered together. ‖ *g*. Mind, light, rejoice in the oblation. | May be unite this scattered sacrifice; | May Bṛihaspati extend it; | May the All-Gods rejoice herein. ‖ *h*. Seven are thy kindling-sticks, O Agni, seven thy tongues; | Seven seers, seven dear abodes, | Seven priesthoods sevenfold sacrifice to thee; | Seven birthplaces with ghee do thou fill. ‖ *i*. Return with strength, return, | O Agni, with food and life; | Again guard us on all sides. ‖ *k*. Return with wealth, O Agni, | Fatten with the stream, | All gaining on every side. ‖ *l*. Leka, Saleka, Suleka, may these Ādityas rejoicing partake of our oblation; Keta, Saketa, Suketa, may these Ādityas rejoicing partake of our oblation; Vivasvat, Aditi, Devajūti, may these Ādityas rejoicing partake of our oblation.

Mantra 1:5:4

'Earth in depth, sky in breadth,' he says; with this benediction he establishes it. The serpents thought that they were growing worn out; Kasarṇīra Kādraveya beheld this Mantra; then did they strike off their worn-out skins. With the verses of the queen of serpents he establishes the Gārhapatya, and so renewing it he establishes it as immortal. Pure food did not come to the earth; she beheld this Mantra; then food came to her. In that he establishes the Gārhapatya with the verses of the serpent queen (it serves) for the winning of food; verily he establishes it firm in the (earth).

'If thee in anger I have scattered,' he says; verily he conceals it from him. 'Again thee we relight,' he says; verily he kindles him all together. 'Whatever of thee scattered in rage,' he says; verily by means of the deities he unites him. The sacrifice of him who removes the fire is split; he pays reverence with a verse containing the word Bṛihaspati; Bṛihaspati is the holy power (Brahman) of the Gods; verily by holy power (Brahman) he unites the sacrifice. 'May he unite this scattered sacrifice,' he says, for continuity, 'May the All-Gods rejoice herein,' he says; verily continuing the sacrifice he points it out to the Gods. 'Seven are thy kindling-sticks, O Agni, seven thy tongues,' he says, for sevenfold in seven-wise are the dear forms of Agni; verily he wins them. 'Return with strength,' 'Return with wealth,' (with these words) he offers oblations on either side of the sacrificial cake; verily with strength and with wealth he surrounds on either side the sacrificer. The Ādityas went from this world to yonder world, they were thirsty in yonder world, having returned to this world and having established the fire, they offered these oblations; they prospered, they went to the world of heaven. He, who establishes a fire after the second establishment, should offer these oblations; be prospers with the prosperity where with the Ādityas prospered.

The Reverence of the Fire

Mantra 1:5:5

a. As we approach the sacrifice, | Let us utter a hymn to Agni, | Who heareth us, even from afar. ‖ *b.* After his ancient splendour, | The bold ones have drawn the white milk | From the seer who winneth a thousand. ‖ *c.* Agni is the head of the sky, the height, | Lord of the earth here, | He quickeneth the seed of the waters. ‖ *d.* Here hath he first been established by the establishers, | Youngest Hotar to be invoked at the sacrifices, | Whom Apnavāna and the Bhṛigus caused to shine, | Bright in the woods, spreading from house to house. ‖ *e.* Ye twain shall be summoned, O Indra and Agni, | Ye twain shall rejoice together in the offering | You both, givers of food and riches, | You both I summon for the winning of strength. ‖ *f.* This is thy due place of birth, | Whence born thou didst shine; | Mount it, O Agni, knowing it, | And make our wealth increase. ‖ *g.* O Agni, thou purifiest life; | Do thou give food and strength to us; | Far away drive ill-fortune. ‖ *h.* O Agni, good worker, purify for us | Glory in good heroes, | Giving increase of wealth to me. ‖ *i.* O Agni, the purifying, with thy light, | O God, with thy pleasant tongue, | Bring hither the Gods and sacrifice. ‖ *k.* Do thou, O shining and purifying one, | O Agni, bring hither the Gods | To our sacrifice and our oblation. ‖ *l.* Agni, of purest vows, | Pure sage, pure poet, | Shineth in purity when offering is made. ‖ *m.* O Agni, thy pure, | Bright, flaming (rays) arise, | Thy lights, thy flames. ‖ *n.* Thou art giver of life, O Agni; give me life. Thou art giver of radiance, O Agni; give me radiance. Thou art guardian of the body, O Agni; guard my body. ‖ *o.* O Agni, whatever is deficient in my body, do thou make that good for me. ‖ *p.* O thou of various splendour, in safety may I reach the end of thee. ‖ *q.* Kindling thee may we kindle thee for a hundred winters, in radiance, strong the giver of strength, famous the giver of fame, with good heroes, the undeceived, O Agni, the deceiver of foes in the highest firmament. ‖ *r.* Thou, O Agni, hast attained the radiance of the sun, the praises of the Ṛishis, thy beloved abode. ‖ *s.* Thou, O Agni, hast the radiance of the sun; grant me life, radiance, and offspring.

Mantra 1:5:6

a. I gaze on offspring, | Offspring of Iḍā, connected with Manu; | May they all be in our house. ‖ *b.* Ye are water; may I share your water. Ye are greatness, may I share your greatness; ye are might, may I share your might; ye are strength, may I share your strength. ‖ *c.* Ye wealthy ones, stay in this place, this fold, this dwelling, this birthplace; be ye here; go not hence; be many for me. ‖ *d.* Thou art composed of every form; enter me with strength, with lordship of kine, with increase of wealth. ‖ *e.* May I prosper with your thousandfold prosperity; may your wealth rest in me. ‖ *f.* To thee, O Agni, day by day, | That shinest in the darkness, with our devotion, | We come bearing honour. ‖ *g.* Lord of the sacrifices, | Guardian of holy order, shining, | Waxing in his own home. ‖ *h.* O Agni, be of easy access to us, | As a father to his son; | Befriend us for prosperity. ‖ *i.* O Agni be thou our nearest, | Our protector, kindly, a shield; | Thee, O shining and most radiant one, | We implore for favour, for our friends; | Agni, bright, of bright fame, | Come hither in thy greatest splendour and give us wealth. ‖ *k.* With strength I gaze on you; gaze on me with strength. With increase of wealth I gaze on you; gaze on me with increase of wealth. ‖ *l.* Ye are food, making sweetness; kindly enter me, nourishment and drink; may I prosper with your thousandfold prosperity, may your wealth rest on me, ‖ *m.* That excellent glory of Savitar | The God we meditate, | That be may stimulate our prayers.' ‖ *n.* Make famous the Soma-presser, | O lord of prayer, | Even as (thou did make famous) Kakṣhīvant Auśija. ‖ *o.* Never art thou barren, O Indra, | Never dost thou fail thy worshipper; | Now more and more is thy divine gift increased, | O bountiful one. ‖ *p.* May we set thee around us, O Agni, | The sage, the strong, as a fort, | Of daring hue, day by day | Destroyer of that which may be broken. ‖ *q.* O Agni, lord of the house, through thee as lord of the house, may I be a good lord of the house; through me as lord of the house, mayst thou be a good lord of the house; for a hundred winters, this blessing I invoke, bringing light for the race; this blessing I invoke, bringing light for N. N.

Mantra 1:5:7

There is no sacrifice without a Sāman 'As we approach the sacrifice,' he says; verily he yokes a Stoma with it. 'Approach,' he says; offspring and cattle approach the world; verily he approaches cattle and offspring and this world. 'After his ancient splendour,' he says; the ancient is the world of heaven; verily he mounts upon the world of heaven. 'Agni is the head of the sky, the height,' he says; verily he makes him the head of his equals, and verily from the world of the Gods he rests in the world of men. 'Here hath he first been established by the establishers,' he says; verily he makes him the principal. 'Ye twain shall be summoned, O Indra and Agni,' he says; verily he wins might and force. 'This is thy due place of birth,' he says; wealth is cattle; verily he wins cattle. With six (verses) he pays reverence; the seasons are six; verily he rests on the seasons. With six subsequent (verses) he pays reverence; they make up twelve; the year has twelve months; verily he rests on the year. Just as a man, a horse, a cow, are worn out, so the fire when established wears out; at the end of the year he pays reverence with (verses) containing the words Agni and *pū;* verily he renews it and makes it unageing, and also purifies it. He pays reverence; that is his union. He pays reverence; that is his bond. He pays reverence; that is his appeal. He pays reverence; that is as if an inferior brings (something) to a superior and pays him honour. 'Thou art giver of life, O Agni; give me life,' he says, for he is a giver of life. 'Thou art giver of radiance, O Agni; give me radiance,' he says, for he is a giver of radiance. I Thou art guardian of the body, O Agni; guard my body,' he says, for he is a guardian of the body. 'O Agni, whatever is deficient in my body, do thou make that good for me,' he says; 'whatever is deficient in my offspring and cattle, do thou make that good for me,' be says in effect. 'O thou of various splendour, in safety may I reach the end of thee,' he says; that of various splendour is the night. The Brahmans aforetime feared its not dawning; verily he wins the dawn. 'Kindling thee for a hundred winters,' he says; man lives a hundred years and has a hundred powers; verily he rests on life and power. This is a pipe with projections; by it the Gods made piercings of hundreds of the Asuras; in that he takes up the kindling-stick with this verse, the sacrificer hurls the hundred-slaying (verse) as a bolt against his enemy to lay (him) low without fail. 'Thou, O Agni, hast attained the radiance of the sun,' he says; 'that thou art, thus may I be,' he says in effect. 'Thou, O Agni, hast the radiance of the sun,' he says; verily he invokes this blessing.

Mantra 1:5:8

'I gaze on offspring,' he says; verily he wins all the domesticated animals. 'Ye are water; may I share your water,' he says, for they are water. 'Ye are greatness; may I share your greatness,' he says, for they are greatness. 'Ye are might; may I share your might,' he says, for they are might. 'Ye are strength; may I share your strength,' he says, for they are strength. 'Ye wealthy ones, stay,' he says; the wealthy ones are cattle; verily he makes cattle stay with himself. 'Be ye here; go not hence,' he says; verily he makes them constant, departing not. Now one fire is piled with bricks, one with cattle. 'Thou art composed Of every form,' (with these words) he strokes the calf; verily he piles it up and makes it piled with cattle. He falls away from this world who pays reverence to the Āhavanīya; he pays reverence to the Gārhapatya; verily he rests on this world, and also he makes amends to the Gārhapatya He pays reverence with Gāyatrī verses; the Gāyatrī is brilliance; verily he confers brilliance upon himself; moreover in that he repeats the triad (of verses), (it serves) for continuity. Because of the Gārhapatya men are born with two feet; to him who knowing thus pays reverence to the Gārhapatya with (verses) of two feet, a hero son is born. 'With strength I gaze upon you; gaze on me with strength,' he says; verily he invokes this blessing. 'That excellent glory of Savitar,' he says, for instigation. 'Famous the Soma-presser,' he says; verily he wins the Soma draught. 'Make, O lord of prayer,' he says; verily he wins splendour. 'Never art thou barren,' be says; no barren night does he pass, who knowing thus pays reverence to the fire. May we (set) thee around, O Agni, as a fort,' he says; verily he sets around a barrier, that nothing be spilt. 'O Agni, lord of the house,' he says; that is according to the text. 'For a hundred winters,' he says; 'for a hundred winters may I kindle thee,' he says in effect. He utters the name of his son; verily he makes him an eater of food. 'This blessing I invoke bringing light for the race,' he should say, who has no son born; verily is born to him a son brilliant and resplendent. 'This blessing I invoke bringing light for N. N.,' he should say who has a son born; verily he confers upon him brilliance and splendour.

Mantra 1:5:9

He offers the Agnihotra; whatever there is of the Sacrificer's own, that is (still) his. In the generative organ he pours seed, for Agni is the generative organ. Then he burns at the end the plants; they then grow more numerous. In that he offers in the evening, he thus pours seed, and makes it productive by the morning (offering). Seed when poured does not prove fruitful unless modified by Tvaṣhṭar; as many modifications of seed when poured as Tvaṣhṭar makes, in so many shapes does it become fruitful; the sacrificer is the divine Tvaṣhṭar. He pays reverence with many (verses); verily he makes many modifications of the seed when poured. He is fruitful and day by day becomes greater, who knowing thus pays reverence to the fire. The day was the Gods,' the night the Asuras'. The Asuras entered night with all the precious wealth of the Gods; the Gods thought that they were abandoned; they perceived, 'The night is Agni's, cattle are Agni's; verily let us praise Agni here; he being praised by us will restore our cattle.' They praised Agni; be praised by them delivered their cattle from night to day; the Gods having gained their cattle per formed their desires. He who knowing thus pays reverence to the fire becomes possessed of cattle. The sun went from this world to yonder world; he having gone to yonder world bethought him again of this world; having returned to this world he had fear of death, for this world is, as it were, yoked with death. He reflected, 'Let me praise Agni here; he, praised, will make me go to the world of heaven.' He praised Agni; he, praised, made him go to the world of heaven. He who knowing thus pays reverence to the fire, goes to the world of heaven and lives all his days. He mounts these two fires who pays reverence to them; he acts according to the desires of one who has attained a higher place. He pays reverence at night, not in the morning, for vows are mingled at night, the bad and the good are on the same level, the fire is the light, the evening is the darkness; in that he pays reverence by night, he overcomes the darkness by light. 'Should reverence be paid to the fire or not?' they say; 'he who day by day makes a present to a man and then begs of him assuredly molests him; and who then will day by day beg of the Gods?' Then they say, 'The sacrificer sacrifices for the sake of the benediction.' The reverence of the fire is the benediction of him who has established a fire; therefore reverence should be paid to the fire. Prajāpati created cattle; being created they entered day and night; he recovered them by means of the metres. In that he pays reverence with the metres, he seeks to recover his own. 'There is not monotony then,' they say, 'if one pays reverence day by day.' If a man pays reverence to the fire facing it, it burns him; if with averted (face), he is deprived of offspring and cattle; he should pay reverence with (face) somewhat to the side, then (the fire) does not burn him, he is not deprived of offspring or cattle.

Mantra 1:5:10.

a. The name that first, O all-knower, | My father and my mother bestowed upon me aforetime, | Do thou bear it until I return; | O Agni, may I bear thy name. || *b.* My name and thine, O all-knower, | Which like men changing garments we bear, | Let us exchange again, | Thou for life, and we to live. || *c.* Homage to Agni, the unpierced, | Homage to the unapproachable, homage to the king! | Irresistible is Agni, the very vigorous, all-conquering, | Powerful, the best, the Gandharva. || *d.* O Agni, the Gods have thee for father, | Offer to thee oblations, and have thee as an umpire | With life, with lordship of cattle (endow) me | And bestow on me good fortune. || *e.* Agni here is of all the best, | He is most adorable, | Must ready to win (us) a thousand; | To him be all good strength. || *f.* Mind, light, rejoice in the oblation | May he unite the scattered sacrifice; | The offerings at dawn and evening | I unite with oblation and ghee. || *g.* Rich in milk are the plants, | The milk of the shoot is rich in milk, | With the milk of the milk of the waters, | O Indra, do thou unite me. || *h.* O Agni, lord of vows, I shall perform this vow; may I accomplish it; may it be successful for me. || *i.* Agni, the priest, I summon hither; | The Gods worthy of sacrifice whom we invoke, | Let these Gods come in kindly mind; | Let the Gods enjoy this oblation of me. || *k.* Who yoketh thee? Let him yoke thee. || *l.* The potsherds for the cauldron, | Which wise men collect, | These are in Pūṣhan's guardianship; | Indra and Vāyu set them free. || *m.* Unbroken is the cauldron, sprinkling abundantly, | It hath returned to that whence it came; | The kindling-wood, the Vedi, and all the enclosing-sticks | Attend the life of the sacrifice. || *n.* The three and thirty threads that stretch, | That maintain in security the sacrifice, | Of these the broken one I restore; hail! | Let the cauldron go to the Gods.

Mantra 1:5:11

a. Let Vaiśvānara with succour for us | Come from afar, | Agni through the hymn which brings (him). || *b.* The righteous Vaiśvānara, | Lord of right and of light, | The immortal cauldron we seek.' || *c.* A greater than the marvels of Vaiśvānara | By his craftsmanship the sage hath performed alone; | Magnifying both parents, sky and earth, | Rich in seed, was Agni born. || *d.* Desired in the sky, Agni, desired on earth, | Desired he entereth all the plants; | Agni Vaiśvānara eagerly desired, | May he by day and night protect us from the foe. || *e.* In that, when born, O Agni, thou didst survey the worlds, | Like a busy herd that goeth around his flock, | Do thou, O Vaiśvānara, find a way for the Brahman; | Do ye protect us ever with your blessings. || *f.* Thou, O Agni, blazing with light, | Didst fill the firmament at thy birth; | Thou, O Vaiśvānara, wise one, by thy might | Didst free the Gods from misfortune.' || *g.* O Agni, among our bountiful lords, preserve | The lordship, uninjured, unageing, rich in heroes; | May we win booty a hundred, a thousandfold, | O Vaiśvānara, O Agni, through thy help. || *h.* May we enjoy the loving kindness of Vaiśvānara, | For he is the king, the orderer of the worlds | Hence born be discerneth all the (earth), | Vaiśvānara vieth with the sun. || *i.* Thine anger, O Varuṇa, would we avert with reverence, | With sacrifices, with oblations | Ruling, O wise Asura, O king, | Do thou unloose the sins we have committed. || *k.* Unloose from us, O Varuṇa, the highest, | The lowest, the midmost knot; | Then may we, O Āditya, in thy rule, | Be guiltless before Aditi. || *l.* Of Dadhikrāvan have I sung, | The swift strong horse; | May he make our mouths fragrant; | May he lengthen our days. || *m.* Dadhikrā with his glory hath overspread the five peoples, | As the sun with his light the waters; | May the strong steed, winning a hundred, a thousand, | Fill with honey these words of ours. || *n.* Agni, the head. || *o.* Thou art. || *p.* O Marutas, what time seeking your favour | We call on you from the sky, | Do ye come unto us. || *q.* The protections which ye have for the earnest worshipper, | Threefold do ye grant them to the generous giver, | To us, O Marutas, do ye accord them; | O strong ones, give us wealth rich in heroes: || *r.* Let Aditi save us, | Let Aditi give us protection, | Let Aditi guard us from tribulation. || *s.* The mighty mother of the righteous, | The spouse of holy order, let us invoke to aid us, | The powerful, the unageing, the wide | Aditi, who giveth good protection and good guidance. || *t.* Earth strong to save, sky unrivalled, | Aditi who giveth good protection and good guidance, | The divine ship with good oars, the blameless, | Which leaketh not, let us mount for prosperity. || *u.* Happily have I mounted this ship | With a hundred oars and a hundred spars, | Without leak, able to convey across.

Prapāṭhaka 6.

The Part of the Sacrificer in the New and Full Moon Sacrifices.

Mantra 1:6:1

a. By the Yajus I pour on thee | Offspring, life, and wealth. | Instigated by Bṛihaspati may the sacrificer here come to no harm. || *b.* Thou art butter, thou art truth, thou art the overseer of truth, thou art the oblation of

Vaiśvānara, of the All-Gods, with pure strength, of true might; thou art power, overpowering; overpower hostility, overpower those who practise hostility; overpower enmity, overpower those who practise enmity; thou art of a thousandfold strength; do thou quicken me; thou art of butter the butter; thou art of truth the truth; thou hast true life; thou hast true strength; with truth I besprinkle thee; may I share thee that art such. ‖ *c.* For a prop, a support, of the five winds I take thee. ‖ *d.* For a prop, a support, of the five seasons I take thee. ‖ *e.* For a prop, a support, of the five quarters I take thee. ‖ *f.* For a prop, a support, of the five five-peoples I take thee. ‖ *g.* For a prop, a support, of the pot with five holes I take thee. ‖ *h.* For the brilliance of the Brahman, for a prop, a support, I take thee. ‖ *i.* For the might of the ruling class, for a prop, a support, I take thee. ‖ *k.* For the people, for a prop, a support I take thee. ‖ *l.* For excellence of strength I take thee. ‖ *m.* For wealth of offspring I take thee. ‖ *n.* For increase of wealth I take thee. ‖ *o.* For splendour I take thee. ‖ *p.* The earth ours, the oblation the Gods, the benedictions the sacrificers'; for the divinities of the Gods I take thee. ‖ *q.* For desire I take thee.

Mantra 1:6:2

a. Thou art secure; may I be secure among my equals, wise, a guardian, a granter of wealth. ‖ *b.* Thou art dread; may I be dread among my equals, dread, a guardian, a granter of wealth. ‖ *c.* Thou art overcoming; may I be overcoming among my equals, overcoming, a guardian, a granter of wealth. ‖ *d.* I yoke thee with the divine Brahman, | To bear this oblation, O wise one; | Kindling thee, may we live long with good children, | With good heroes, bearing thee tribute. ‖ *e.* Whatever, O Agni, in this sacrifice of mine may be spoiled, | Whatever of the butter, O Viṣhṇu, may be spilt, | Therewith do I smite the rival who is hard to slay; | I place him on the lap of destruction. ‖ *f.* Bhūr, Bhuvar, Svar! ‖ *g.* O Agni, do thou strengthen the sacrificer; weaken him who plotteth evil. ‖ *h.* O Agni, kindled by the Gods, kindled by Manu, with sweet tongue, | I touch the head of thee, the immortal, O Hotar, for increase of wealth, good offspring, strength. ‖ *i.* Thou art mind, derived from Prajāpati; with mind in true existence do thou enter me. ‖ *k.* Thou art speech, derived from Indra, destroying the foe; do thou enter me with speech, with power (*indriyeṇa*). ‖ *l.* Of the seasons spring I delight; delighted may it delight me. ‖ *m.* Of the seasons summer I delight; delighted may it delight me. ‖ *n.* Of the seasons the rains I delight; delighted may they delight me. ‖ *o.* Of the seasons the autumn I delight; delighted may it delight me. ‖ *p.* Of the seasons the winter and the cool I delight; delighted may they two delight me. ‖ *q.* By sacrifice to the Gods, Agni and Soma, may I be possessed of sight. ‖ *r.* By sacrifice to the God Agni, may I be an eater of food. ‖ *s.* Thou art a deceiver; may I be undeceived, may I deceive N. N. ‖ *t.* By sacrifice to the Gods, Agni and Soma, may I be a slayer of foes. ‖ *u.* By sacrifice to the Gods, Indra and Agni, may I be powerful and an eater of food. ‖ *v.* By sacrifice to the God Indra, may I be powerful. ‖ *w.* By sacrifice to the God Mahendra, may I attain superiority and greatness. ‖ *x.* By sacrifice to the God Agni Sviṣhṭakṛit, may I attain security through the sacrifice, enjoying long life.

Mantra 1:6:3

a. May I Agni protect me from evil sacrifice, Savitar from evil report. ‖ *b.* Him who near or afar plots evil against me, with this may I conquer. ‖ *c.* O thou of fair rain colour, come | To this blessed home, | Approach me in devotion. ‖ *d.* Touch the heads. ‖ *e.* O Iḍā, come hither; O Aditi, come hither; O Sarasvatī, come hither. ‖ *f.* Thou art delight, thou art delighting, thou art fair. ‖ *g.* O thou in whom joy is taken, may I attain joy from thee; O thou who art invoked, may I obtain invocation from thee. ‖ *h.* May the prayer of the sacrificer be fulfilled for me. ‖ *i.* With untroubled mind may I have strength for this. ‖ *k.* May the sacrifice mount the sky, may the sacrifice reach the sky. ‖ *l.* The path that leadeth to the Gods, along it may the sacrifice go to the Gods. ‖ *m.* On us may Indra bestow power; | Us may wealth and sacrifices attend | Ours be blessings; | To us be she dear, victorious, bountiful. ‖ *n.* Thou art joy, give joy to us; thou art enjoyed by us, may I attain joy from thee. ‖ *o.* Mind, light, rejoice in the sacrifice | May he unite this scattered sacrifice; | May Bṛihaspati extend this for us. | May the All-Gods rejoice here. ‖ *p.* Swell, O ruddy one. ‖ *q.* May (my act) as I give be not destroyed; may (my act) as I work not perish. ‖ *r.* Thou art the portion of Prajāpati, full of strength and milk. ‖ *s.* Protect my expiration and inspiration; protect my breathing together | and cross-breathing; protect my out-breathing and cross-breathing. ‖ *t.* Thou art imperishable, for imperishableness thee; mayst thou not perish for me, yonder, in yonder world.

Mantra 1:6:4

a. By sacrifice to the divine straw, may I be possessed of children. ‖ *b.* By sacrifice to the God Narāśaṃsa, may I be possessed of cattle. ‖ *c.* By sacrifice to the God Agni Sviṣhṭakṛit, may I attain security through the sacrifice, having long life. ‖ *d.* May I be victorious through the victory of Agni. ‖ *e.* May I be victorious through the victory of Soma. ‖ *f.* May I be victorious through the victory of Agni. ‖ *g.* May I be victorious through the victory of Agni and Soma. ‖ *h.* May I be victorious through the victory of Indra and Agni. ‖ *i.* May I be victorious through the victory of Indra. ‖ *k.* May I be victorious through the victory of Mahendra. ‖ *l.* May I be victorious through the victory of Agni Sviṣhṭakṛit. ‖ *m.* With the impulse of strength, | With elevation he hath seized me; then Indra hath made my enemies | Humble with depression. ‖ *n.* The Gods have increased my prayer | Which is elevation and depression; | Then do ye, O Indra and Agni, | Scatter my foes on every side. ‖ *o.* Hither these blessings have come, fain for milking, | Possessing Indra, may we win, | May we milk offspring and food. ‖ *p.* With the red steed may Agni convey thee to the God; with the tawny ones may Indra convey thee to the God; with Etaśa may Sūrya convey thee to the God. ‖ *q.* I unyoke thy head ropes, thy reins, | Thy yokings, thy harness; | Bestow upon us wealth and what is good; | Proclaim us sharers among the Gods. ‖ *r.* By sacrifice to the God Viṣhṇu, by the sacrifice, may I attain health and wealth, and security. ‖ *s.* By sacrifice to the God Soma, possessing good seed, may I impregnate seed. ‖ *t.* By sacrifice to the God Tvaṣhṭar, may I prosper the form of cattle. ‖ *u.* The wives of the Gods, Agni lord of the house, are the pair of the sacrifice; by sacrifice to these deities, may I be propagated with a pair. ‖ *v.* Thou art the bundle, thou art gain, may I gain. ‖ *w.* Thou art action, thou art making, may I make. ‖ *x.* Thou art winning, thou art the winner, may I win. ‖ *y.* May the bundle bestow increase of wealth, | Rich in ghee, rich in houses, | A thousandfold, strong.

Mantra 1:6:5

a. Let the Dhruvā swell with ghee, | For each sacrifice for the worshippers; | In the udder of the sun maiden, in the lap of Aditi, | Broad streamed be the earth at this sacrifice. ‖ *b.* Prajāpati's is the world called Vibhān. In it I place thee along with the sacrificer. ‖ *c.* Thou art real, be real for me; thou art all, be all for me; thou art full, be full for me; thou art imperishable, perish not for me. ‖ *d.* In the eastern quarter may the Gods, the priests, make (me) bright; in the southern quarter may the months, the fathers, make (me) bright; in the western quarter may the houses, the cattle, make (me) bright; in the northern quarter may the waters, the plants, the trees make (me) bright; in the zenith may the sacrifice, the year, the lord of the sacrifice make (me) bright. ‖ *e.* Thou art the step of Viṣhṇu, smiting enmity; with the Gāyatrī metre I step across the earth; excluded is he whom we hate. ‖ *f.* Thou art the step of Viṣhṇu, smiting imprecations; with the Triṣhṭubh metre I step across the atmosphere; excluded is he whom we hate. ‖ *g.* Thou art the step of Viṣhṇu, smiter of him who practiseth evil; with the Jagatī metre I step across the sky; excluded is he whom we hate. ‖ *h.* Thou art the step of Viṣhṇu, smiter of the hostile one; with the Anuṣhṭubh metre I stop across the quarters; excluded is he whom we hate.

Mantra 1:6:6

a. We have come to the heaven; to the heaven we have come. ‖ *b.* May I not be cut off from seeing thee; what heat is thine, to that of thee may I not be brought low. ‖ *c.* Thou art good, the best of rays, thou art life-bestowing, bestow life | upon me; thou art radiance-bestowing, bestow radiance upon me. ‖ *d.* Here do I exclude my enemy, N. N., from these quarters, this sky, this atmosphere, this earth, this food. Excluded is he whom we hate. ‖ *e.* I have been united with the light. ‖ *f.* I turn the turning of Indra. ‖ *g.* May I be united with offspring, offspring with me. ‖ *h.* May I be united with increase of wealth, increase of wealth with me. ‖ *i.* Kindled, O Agni, shine for me; kindling thee, O Agni, may I shine. ‖ *k.* Be rich the sacrifice; may I be rich. | ɪɪ. O Agni, thou purifiest life; | Do thou give food and strength to us; | Far away drive ill-fortune. ‖ *m.* O Agni, good worker, purify for us | Glory in good heroes, | Giving increase and wealth to me. || *n*. O Agni, lord of the house, through thee as lord of the house, may I be a good lord of the house; through me as lord of the house, mayst thou be a good lord of the house; for a hundred winters; this blessing I invoke bringing light for the race; this blessing I invoke bringing light for N. N. || *o*. Who yoketh thee? Let him set thee free. || *p*. O Agni, lord of vows, I have performed my vow; for that I have had strength; that hath been accomplished by me. || *q*. The sacrifice hath become, it hath come into being, | It hath been born, it hath waxed great; | It hath become the overlord of the Gods, | May it make us overlords, | May we be lords of wealth. || *r*. Rich in cattle, in sheep, O Agni, in horses, is the sacrifice, | With manly companions, ever unalterable; | Rich in food is this, O Asura, rich in offspring, | Enduring wealth, deep based and rich in houses.

Mantra 1:6:7

Even as the Soma (sacrifices) come together in competition, so the new and full moon (sacrifices) are sacrifices which come together in competition. Whose sacrifice then do the Gods approach and whose not? He, who among many sacrificers first appropriates the Gods, sacrifices to them when the next day comes. The Āhavanīya is the abode of the Gods, between the fires of cattle, the Gārhapatya of men, the Anvāhāryapachana of the fathers. He takes the fire; verily he appropriates the Gods in their own abode; to them he sacrifices when the next day comes. By means of a vow is Agni, lord of vows, pure, the Brahman is a supporter of vows. When about to undertake a vow he should say, 'O Agni, lord of vows, I shall perform the vow.' Agni is the lord of vows among the Gods; verily after announcement to him he undertakes the vow. At the full moon be undertakes his vow with the (strewing of the) straw, with the (driving away of the) calves at new moon; for that is their abode. 'The fires, both in the front and at the back, must be bestrewed,' they say; men indeed desire what is bestrewed, and, how much more the Gods whose is a new dwelling. With him, when sacrifice is to be made on the next day, do the Gods dwell, who knowing this bestrews the fire. 'The sacrificer should win both beasts of the wild and of the village,' they say; in that he refrains from those of the village, thereby be wins them; in that he eats of the wild, thereby he wins them of the wild. If be were to fast without eating, the Pitṛis would be his divinity; he eats of the wild, the wild is power, and so he bestows power upon himself. If he were to fast without eating, he would be hungry; if he were to eat, Rudra would plan evil against his cattle; he partakes of water; that is neither eaten nor not eaten; he is not hungry and Rudra does not plot evil against his cattle. The sacrificer is a bolt, the enemy of man is hunger; in that he fasts without eating, he straightway smites with the bolt the enemy, hunger.

Mantra 1:6:8

He who offers sacrifice without faith, they place not faith in his sacrifice. He brings waters forward, the waters are faith; verily with faith he offers sacrifice, and both Gods and men place faith in his sacrifice. They say, 'They foam over the barrier, they foam over speech, but over mind they do not foam.' He brings them forward with mind; mind is this (earth); verily with this (earth) he brings them forward. The sacrifice of him who knows thus does not spill. He collects the weapons of the sacrifice; the weapons of the sacrifice are the sacrifice; verily he collects the sacrifice. If he were to collect them one by one, they would have the Pitṛis as their divinity; if all together, (they would have) men as their divinity. He collects them in pairs, and so he makes the form of the Yājyā and the Anuvākyā, and thus there is a pair. If a man knows the ten weapons of the sacrifice, his sacrifice is in order at the beginning. The wooden sword, the potsherds, the offering-spoon, the basket, the black antelope skin, the pin, the mortar and pestle, the lower and upper millstones, these are the ten weapons of the sacrifice; the sacrifice of him who knows thus is in order at the beginning. If a man sacrifices after announcing the sacrifice to the Gods, they delight in his sacrifice. He should as the oblation is being offered recite (the words), 'Agni, the priest, him I summon hither.' Thus he announces the sacrifice to the Gods and sacrifices, and the Gods delight in his sacrifice. This is the taking of the sacrifice and so after taking the sacrifice he sacrifices. After speaking he remains silent, to support the sacrifice. Now Prajāpati performed the sacrifice with mind; verily he performs the sacrifice with mind to prevent the Rākṣhasas following. He who yokes the sacrifice when the yoking (time) arrives yokes it indeed among the yokers. 'Who (*ka*) yoketh thee? Let him yoke thee,' he says. *Ka* is Prajāpati—verily by Prajāpati he yokes it; he yokes indeed among the yokers.

Mantra 1:6:9

Prajāpati created the sacrifices, the Agnihotra, the Agniṣhṭoma, the full moon sacrifice, the Ukthya, the new moon sacrifice and the Atirātra These he meted out; the Agniṣhṭoma was the size of the Agnihotra, the Ukthya that of the full moon sacrifice, the Atirātra that of the new moon sacrifice. He who knowing thus offers the Agnihotra obtains as much as by offering the Agniṣhṭoma; he who knowing thus offers the full moon sacrifice obtains as much as by offering the Ukthya; he who knowing thus offers the new moon sacrifice obtains as much as by offering the Atirātra This sacrifice was in the beginning Parameṣhṭhin's, and by means of it he reached the supreme goal. He furnished Prajāpati with it, and by means of it Prajāpati reached the supreme goal. He furnished Indra with it, and by means of it Indra reached the supreme goal. He furnished Agni and Soma with it, and by means of it Agni and Soma reached the supreme goal. He who knowing thus offers the new and full moon sacrifices reaches the supreme goal. He who sacrifices with an abundant offering is multiplied with offspring, with cattle, with pairings. 'The year has twelve months, there are twelve pairs of new and full moon sacrifices; these are to be produced,' they say. He lets the calf go free and puts the pot on the fire: he puts down (the rice), and beats the millstones together; he scatters (the grains) and collects the potsherds; the cake he puts on the fire and the melted butter; he throws the clump of grass, and gathers it in; he surrounds the Vedi and he girds the wife (of the sacrificer); he puts in place the anointing waters and the melted butter. These are the twelve pairs in the new and full moon sacrifices. He, who thus sacrifices with these, sacrifices with an abundant offering and is multiplied with offspring, with cattle, with pairings.

Mantra 1:6:10.

'Thou I art secure; may I be secure among my equals,' he says; verily he makes them secure.' 'Thou art dread; may I be dread among my equals'; verily he makes them harmonious. 'Thou art overcoming; may I be overcoming among my equals,' he says; verily he overthrows him who rises against him. 'I yoke thee with the divine Brahman,' he says; this is the yoking of the fire; verily with it he yokes it. With the prosperous part of the sacrifice the Gods went to the world of heaven, with the unsuccessful part they overcame the Asuras. 'Whatever, O Agni, in this sacrifice of mine may be spoiled,' he says; verily with the prosperous part of the sacrifice the sacrificer goes to the world of heaven, with the unsuccessful part he overcomes the foes. With these Vyāhṛitis he should set down the Agnihotra. The Agnihotra is the beginning of the sacrifice, these Vyāhṛitis are the Brahman; verily at the beginning of the sacrifice he makes the Brahman. When the year is completed he should thus with these (Vyāhṛitis) perform the setting down; verily with the Brahman he surrounds the year on both sides. He who is undertaking the new and full moon and the four monthly offerings should set in place the oblations with these Vyāhṛitis. The new and full moon and the four monthly sacrifices are the beginning of the sacrifice, these Vyāhṛitis are the Brahman; verily at the beginning of the sacrifice he makes the Brahman. When the year is completed, he should thus with them (Vyāhṛitis) set down (the oblations), and so with the Brahman he surrounds the year on both sides. To the kingly class falls the blessing of the part of the sacrifice which is performed with the Sāman; to the people (falls) the blessing of what (is performed) with the Ṛich; now the Brahman sacrifices with an offering without a blessing; when he is about to recite the kindling-verses he should first insert the Vyāhṛitis; verily he makes the Brahman the commencement, and thus the Brahman sacrifices with an offering which has a blessing. If he desire of a sacrificer, 'May the blessing of his sacrifice fall to his foe,' he should insert for him those Vyāhṛitis in the Puronuvākyā (verse); the Puronuvākyā has the foe for its divinity; verily the blessing of his sacrifice falls to his foe. If he desire of sacrificers, 'May the blessing of the sacrifice fall to them equally,' he should place for them one of the Vyāhṛitis at the half-verse of the Puronuvākyā, one before the Yājyā, and one at the half-verse of the Yājyā, and thus the blessing of the sacrifice falls to them equally. Even as Parjanya rains down good rain, so the sacrifice rains for the sacrificer; they surround the water with a mound, the sacrificer surrounds the sacrifice with a blessing. 'Thou art mind derived from Prajāpati, with mind and true existence do thou enter me,' he says; mind is derived from Prajāpati, the sacrifice is derived from Prajāpati; verily he confers upon himself mind and the sacrifice. 'Thou art speech, derived from Indra, destroying the foe; do thou enter me with speech, with power,' he says; speech is derived from Indra; verily he confers upon himself speech as connected with Indra.

Mantra 1:6:11

He who knows the seventeenfold Prajāpati as connected with the sacrifice rests secure through the sacrifice, and falls not away from the sacrifice. 'Do thou proclaim' has four syllables; 'Be it proclaimed' has four syllables; 'Utter' has two syllables; 'We that do utter' has five syllables; the Vaṣhaṭ has two syllables; this is the seventeenfold Prajāpati as connected with the sacrifice; he who knows thus rests secure through the sacrifice and does not fall away from the sacrifice. He who knows the beginning, the support, the end of the sacrifice reaches the end with a secure and uninjured sacrifice. 'Do thou proclaim'; 'Be it proclaimed'; 'Utter'; 'We that do utter'; the Vaṣhaṭ call, these are the beginning, the support, the end of the sacrifice; he who knows thus reaches the end with a secure and uninjured sacrifice. He who knows the milking of the generous one milks her indeed. The generous one is the sacrifice; (with the words) 'Do thou proclaim,' he calls her; with 'Be it proclaimed,' he lets (the calf) go up to her; with 'Utter,' he raises (the pail); with 'We that do utter,' he sits down beside her, and with the Vaṣhaṭ call he milks. This is the milking of the generous one; he who knows thus milks her indeed. The Gods performed a sacrificial session; the quarters were dried up; they discerned this moist set of five; (with the words) 'Do thou proclaim,' they produced the east wind; with 'Be it proclaimed,' they caused the clouds to mass together; with 'Utter' they begat the lightning; with 'We that do sacrifice' they made rain to fall, and with the Vaṣhaṭ call they caused the thunder to roll. Then for them the quarters were made to swell; for him who knows thus the quarters are made to swell. One knows Prajāpati, Prajāpati knows one; whom Prajāpati knows, he becomes pure. This is the Prajāpati of the texts, 'Do thou proclaim,' 'Be it proclaimed,' 'Utter,' 'We that do utter,' the Vaṣhaṭ call; he who knows thus becomes pure. 'Of the seasons spring I delight,' he says; the fore-sacrifices are the seasons; verily he delights the seasons; they delighted place themselves in order for him; the seasons are in order for him who knows thus. 'By sacrifice to the Gods, Agni and Soma, may I be possessed of sight,' he says; the sacrifice is possessed of sight through Agni and Soma; verily by means of them he confers sight upon himself. 'By sacrifice to the God Agni, may I be an eater of food,' he says; Agni is among the Gods the eater of food; verily by means of him he confers the eating of food upon himself. 'Thou art a deceiver; may I be undeceived; may I deceive N. N.,' he says; by that deceit the Gods deceived the Asuras; verily by this he deceives his foe. 'By sacrifice to the Gods, Agni and Soma, may I be a slayer of foes,' he says; by means of Agni and Soma Indra slew Vṛitra; verily by means of them he lays low his foe. 'By sacrifice to the Gods, Indra and Agni, may I be powerful and an eater of food,' he says; verily he becomes powerful and an eater of food. 'By sacrifice to the God Indra, may I be powerful,' he says; verily he becomes powerful. 'By sacrifice to the God Mahendra, may I attain superiority and greatness,' he says; verily he attains superiority and greatness. 'By sacrifice to the God Agni Sviṣhṭakṛit, may I attain security through the sacrifice, enjoying long life,' he says; verily he confers long life upon himself and attains security through the sacrifice.

Mantra 1:6:12.

a. Indra for you we invoke | On all sides from other men; | Be he ours only. | a Indra men call in reverence | That he may cause their prayers to be accomplished; | Hero, men overpowering, delighting in strength, | Do thou confer upon us a stall full of kine. ‖ *c.* O Śatakratu, the strength of thine | That is in the five folks, | That do I choose of thee. ‖ *d.* To thee hath been assigned for mighty power, | For ever, in the slaying of Vṛitra, | All lordship, and all strength, O thou that art worthy of sacrifice | In the overcoming of man, by the Gods, O Indra. ‖ *c.* In whom the seven Vāsavas rest | As it were firm rooted, | The Ṛiṣhi of farthest hearing, | The glowing pot is the guest of Indra. ‖ *f.* In the raw thou didst produce the cooked, | And madest the sun to mount in the sky; | Like the glowing pot heat ye the Sāman | With good prayers, delightful to the lover of song. ‖ *g.* Indra the singers aloud, | Indra with praises the praisers, | Indra the songs have praised. ‖ *h.* The singers sing thee; | The praisers hymn thy praise; | The Brahmans raise thee, | O Śatakratu, like a pole. ‖ *i.* Let us offer our praise to him who delivereth from trouble, | Swiftest to give, celebrating his loving kindness; | O Indra, accept this oblation; | May the desires of the sacrificer be fulfilled. ‖ *k.* That to which Dhiṣhaṇā impelled me have I produced; | I shall praise Indra before the decisive day; | Him that goeth as with a ship | Both parties invoke that there he may rescue us. ‖ *l.* First lord of sacrifices, | Freeing from trouble, the best of those worthy of offering, | Son of the waters, the impeller, O ye Aśvins; | Do ye confer power and strength on this one. ‖ *m.* Smite away our foes, O Indra; | Cast down the warriors; | Make him low | Who is hostile to us. ‖ *n.* O Indra, thou wast born for rule, for prosperous strength | Of the people, O strong one; | Thou didst smite away the unfriendly folk, | And madest wide room for the Gods. ‖ *o.* Like a dread beast, evil, roaming the mountains, | He hath come from the furthest place; | Sharpening thy lance, thy sharp edge, O Indra, | Smite the foes, drive away the enemy. ‖ *p.* Drive away the foe, the enemy, | Smash the jaws of Vṛitra; | In rage do thou avert the anger | Of him who is hostile to us. ‖ *q.* The guardian Indra, the helper Indra, | The hero ready to hear at every call, Indra, | I invoke the strong one, invoked of many, Indra; | May Indra in his bounty bestow on us prosperity. ‖ *r.* May we not, O strong one, in this distress, | Be handed over to evil, O lord of the ways; | Guard us with true protection; | May we be dear to you among the princes. ‖ *s.* The Anus have wrought a chariot for thy steed; | Tvaṣhṭar a glorious bolt, O thou invoked of many; | The Brahmans magnifying Indra with their praises | Have strengthened him for the slaying of the serpent. ‖ *t.* What time the strong sang praise to the strong, | O Indra, the stones and Aditi in unison, | Without steeds or chariots were the fellies | Which, sped by Indra, rolled against the Dasyus.

Prapāṭhaka 7.

The Part of the Sacrificer in the New and Full Moon Sacrifices

Mantra 1:7:1

a. Cattle attend the cooked offerings of him who has established a fire. The cooked offering is the Iḍā; it is placed in the world of the sacrifice between the fore- and the after-offerings. Over it as it is brought up he should say, 'O thou of fair rain colour, come hither'; the cattle are the Iḍā; verily he summons cattle. The Gods milked the sacrifice, the sacrifice milked the Asuras; the Asuras, being milked by the sacrifice, were defeated; he, who knowing the milking of the sacrifice sacrifices, milks another sacrificer. 'May the blessing of this sacrifice be fulfilled for me,' he says; this is the milking of the sacrifice; verily with it he milks it. The cow is milked willingly, and willingly the Iḍā is milked for the sacrificer; these are the teats of Iḍā, 'Iḍā is invoked'. Vāyu is the calf. When the Hotar summons the Iḍā, then the sacrificer looking at the Hotar should in mind reflect on Vāyu; verily he lets the calf go to the mother. By the whole sacrifice the Gods went to the world of heaven; Manu laboured with the cooked offering; the Iḍā went to Manu; the Gods and the Asuras called severally upon her, the Gods directly, the Asuras indirectly; she went to the Gods; the cattle choose the Gods, cattle deserted the Asuras. If he desire of a man, 'May he be without cattle,' he should invoke the Iḍā indirectly for him; verily he becomes without cattle. If he desire of a man, 'May he be rich in cattle,' he should invoke the Iḍā directly for him; verily he becomes rich in cattle. The theologians say, 'He would invoke the Iḍā indeed who in invoking the Iḍā should invoke himself in the Iḍā.' 'To us be she dear, victorious, bountiful,' he says; verily in invoking the Iḍā he invokes himself in the Iḍā. The Iḍā is as it were a breach in the sacrifice; half they eat, half they wipe; in this regard the sacrifice of the Asuras was broken; the Gods united it by the holy power (Brahman). 'May Bṛihaspati extend this for us,' he says; Bṛihaspati is the holy power (Brahman) of the Gods; verily by the holy power (Brahman) he unites the sacrifice. 'May he unite this scattered sacrifice,' he says, for continuity. 'May the All-Gods rejoice here,' he says; verily continuing the sacrifice he indicates it to the Gods. The sacrificial fee which he gives at the sacrifice his cattle accompany; he having sacrificed is like to become without cattle; 'the sacrificer must so arrange,' they say, 'that he may place among the Gods what is given, but keep his cattle with himself.' 'Swell, O ruddy one,' he says; the ruddy one is the sacrifice; verily he magnifies the sacrifice; thus he places among the Gods what is given, but keeps his cattle with himself. 'May (my act) as I give be not destroyed,' he says; verily he avoids destruction; 'May (my act) as I work not perish,' he says; verily he attains prosperity.

Mantra 1:7:2

Saṃśravas Sauvarchanasa said to Tumiñja Aupoditi: 'When thou hast been a Hotar of Sattrins, what Iḍā hast thou invoked?' 'Her I have invoked,' he said, 'who supports the Gods by her expiration, men by her cross-breathing, and the Pitṛis by her inspiration.' 'Does she divide, or does she not divide' (he asked). 'She divides,' he replied. 'Her body then hast thou invoked,' he said. Her body is the cow; of the cow were they two talking. She who is given in the sacrifice supports the Gods with her expiration; she by whom men live (supports) men by her cross-breathing; she whom they slay for the Fathers (supports) the Fathers by her inspiration; he who knows thus becomes rich in cattle. 'Her too I have invoked,' he said, 'who is available to people as they increase.' 'Her food then hast thou invoked,' he replied. This food is plants, plants are available to people as they increase; he who knows thus becomes an eater of food. 'Her too I have invoked,' he said, who supports people in distress and succours them as they improve.' Her support then hast thou invoked,' he replied. Her support is this (earth), this (earth) supports people in distress and succours them as they improve; he who knows thus finds support. 'Her too I have invoked,' he said, 'in whose step people drink the ghee they live upon.' 'Does she divide, or does she not divide?' (he asked). 'She does not divide,' he said, 'but she propagates.' 'Indeed hast thou invoked the Iḍā herself', he replied. The Iḍā is rain; in the step of rain people drink the ghee they live upon; he who knows thus is propagated with offspring; he becomes an eater of food.

Mantra 1:7:3

Secretly offering is made to one set of Gods, openly to another. The Gods who receive offering secretly, he thus offers to them in sacrifice; in that he brings the Anvāhārya mess—the Brahmans are the Gods openly—them he verily delights. This is his sacrificial fee: verily he mends the rent in the sacrifice; whatever in the sacrifice is harsh or is injured, that he makes good (*anvāharati*) with the Anvāhārya mess, and that is why it has its name. Now the priests are the messengers of the Gods; in that he brings the Anvāhārya mess, he delights the messengers of the Gods. Prajāpati distributed the sacrifice to the Gods; he reflected that he was empty; he perceived this Anvāhārya mess unallotted; he conferred it upon himself. The Anvāhārya is connected with Prajāpati; he, who knowing thus brings the Anvāhārya, assuredly enjoys Prajāpati An unlimited amount should be poured out, Prajāpati is unlimited; (verily it serves) to win Prajāpati. Whatever the Gods did in the sacrifice, the Asuras did; the Gods perceived the Anvāhārya connected with Prajāpati; they seized it then the Gods prospered, the Asuras were defeated; he who knowing thus brings the Anvāhārya prospers himself, his foe is defeated. By the sacrifice there is offering, by the cooked food satisfying. He who knowing thus brings the Anvāhārya, accomplishes at once sacrifice and satisfaction. 'Thou art the portion of Prajāpati,' he says; verily he unites Prajāpati with his own portion. 'Full of strength and milk,' he says; verily he confers upon him strength and milk. 'Protect my expiration and inspiration; protect my breathing together and cross-breathing,' he says; verily he invokes this blessing. 'Thou art imperishable, for imperishableness thee; mayst thou not perish for me, yonder, in yonder world,' he says. Food perishes in yonder world, for given hence in yonder world people live upon it; in that he touches thus, he makes it imperishable; his food perishes not in yonder world.

Mantra 1:7:4

'By I sacrifice to the divine strew, may I be possessed of children,' he says; by the strew Prajāpati created offspring, verily he creates offspring. 'By sacrifice to the God Narāśaṃsa, may I be possessed of cattle,' he says; by Narāśaṃsa Prajāpati created cattle; verily he creates cattle. 'By sacrifice to the God, Agni Sviṣhṭakṛit, may I attain security through the sacrifice, having long life,' he says; verily he confers life on himself, and finds support through the sacrifice. With the victory of the new and full moon sacrifices the Gods conquered, and by means of the new and full moon sacrifices they drove away the Asuras. 'May I be victorious through the victory of Agni,' he says; verily through the victory of the deities in the new and full moon sacrifices the sacrificer is victorious, and by means of the new and full moon offerings drives away his enemies. With two verses containing the word 'strength,' he accompanies the separation (of the ladles) strength is food verily he wins food; (he uses) two, for support. He who sacrifices knowing the two milkings of the sacrifice milks thus the sacrifice on both sides, in front and behind; this is one milking of the sacrifice, another is in the Iḍā. When the Hotar utters the name of the sacrificer, then he should say, 'Hither these blessings have come, fain for milking'; verily he milks the deities which he praises together; verily he milks the sacrifice on both sides, in front and behind. 'With the red steed may Agni convey thee to the God,' he says; these are the steeds of the Gods, the straw is the sacrificer; in that he casts forward the straw with them, he makes the sacrificers to go by the steeds of the Gods to the world of heaven. 'I unyoke thy head ropes, thy reins,' he says; that is the unyoking of Agni; verily thereby he unyokes him. 'By sacrifice to the God Viṣhṇu, by the sacrifice may I attain health and wealth and security,' he says; Viṣhṇu is the sacrifice; verily the sacrifice finds support at the end. 'By sacrifice to the God Soma, possessing good seed, may I impregnate seed,' he says; Soma is the impregnator of seed; verily he confers seed upon himself. 'By sacrifice to the God Tvaṣhṭar, may I prosper the form of cattle'; Tvaṣhṭar is the form-maker of the pairings of cattle, and thereby he confers upon himself the form of cattle. 'The wives of the Gods, Agni, the lord of the house, are the pair of the sacrifice; by sacrifice to these deities may I be propagated with a pair.' 'Thou art the bundle, thou art gain, may I gain,' he says; by the bundle (*vedena*) the Gods won (*avindanta*) the desirable wealth of the Asuras, and that is why the bundle has its name. Whatever of his foe's he may covet, the name of that he should utter; verily he wing it all from him. 'May the bundle bestow increase of wealth, rich in ghee, rich in houses, a thousandfold, strong,' he says; he obtains a thousand cattle. In his offspring a strong one is born who knows thus.

Mantra 1:7:5

Through the emptying of the Dhruvā the sacrifice is emptied, through the sacrifice the sacrificer, through the sacrificer offspring. Through the swelling of the Dhruvā, the sacrifice is made to swell, through the sacrifice the sacrificer, through the sacrificer offspring. 'Let the Dhruvā swell with ghee,' he says; verily he makes the Dhruvā to swell; through its swelling the sacrifice is made to swell, through the sacrifice the sacrificer, through the sacrificer offspring. 'Prajāpati's is the world called Vibhān In it I place thee along with the sacrificer,' he says; the world of Prajāpati, named Vibhān, is this (world); verily he places it in it along with the sacrificer. In that he sacrifices he is as it were emptied; in that he eats the sacrificer's portion, he fills himself. The sacrifice is the size of the sacrificer's portion, the sacrificer is the sacrifice; in that he eats the sacrificer's portion, he places the sacrifice in the sacrifice. There is good grass and good water where the strew and the waters are; the Vedi is the abode of the sacrificer; in that he places the full bowl within the Vedi, he establishes good grass and good water in his own abode. 'Thou art real, be real for me,' he says; the sacrifice is the waters, ambrosia is the water; verily he bestows upon himself the sacrifice and the waters. All creatures attend him who is performing the vow. 'In the eastern quarter may the Gods, the priests, make (me) bright,' he says; this is the concluding bath of the new and full moon sacrifices. He goes to the bath along with the creatures which attend him as he performs the vow. Headed by Viṣhṇu the Gods won these worlds by the metres so as to be irrecoverable; in that he takes the steps of Viṣhṇu the sacrificer becoming Viṣhṇu wins these worlds by the metres so as to be irrecoverable. 'Thou art the step of Viṣhṇu, smiting imprecations,' he says; the earth is the Gāyatrī, the atmosphere is connected with the Triṣhṭubh, the sky is the Jagatī, the quarters are connected with the Anuṣhṭubh; verily by the metres he wins these worlds in order.

Mantra 1:7:6

'We have come to the heaven: to the heaven we have come,' he says; verily he goes to the world of heaven. 'May I not be cut off from seeing thee; what heat is thine, to that of thee may I not be brought low,' he says; that is according to the text. 'Thou art good, the best of rays; thou art life-bestowing, bestow life upon me,' he says; verily he invokes this blessing. He falls away from this world, who takes the steps of Vishṇu, for from the world of heaven the steps of Vishṇu are taken. The theologians say, 'He indeed would take the steps of Vishṇu who after acquiring these worlds of his foe should descend again to this world.' This is his return descent to this world, in that he says, 'Here do I exclude my enemy N. N. from these quarters, from this sky'; verily having acquired these worlds of his foe he descends again to this world. 'I have been united with the light,' he says; verily he rests on this world. 'I turn the turning of Indra,' he says; Indra is yonder sun; verily he turns his turning. He turns to the right; verily he revolves round his own strength; therefore the right side of a man is the stronger; verily also he turns the turning of the sun. 'May I be united with offspring, offspring with me,' he says; verily he invokes this blessing. 'Kindled, O Agni, shine for me; kindling thee, O Agni, may I shine,' he says; that is according to the text. 'Be rich the sacrifice; may I be rich,' he says; verily he invokes this blessing. Within the Gārhapatya much variegated work is performed; with two verses to Agni, the purifier, he pays reverence to the Gārhapatya; verily he purifies the fire, he purifies himself; (he uses) two for support. 'O Agni, lord of the house,' he says; that is according to the text. 'For a hundred winters,' he says; 'for a hundred winters may I kindle thee,' he says in effect. He utters the name of his son; verily he makes him an eater of food. 'This prayer I utter, bringing light for the race,' he should say who has no son born to him, verily is born to him a brilliant and resplendent son. 'This prayer I utter, bringing light to N. N.,' he should say who has a son born; verily he bestows upon him brilliance and splendour. He who having yoked the sacrifice does not let it free becomes without a support. 'Who yoketh thee? Let him set thee free,' he says; Who (*ka*) is Prajāpati; verily by Prajāpati he yokes him, by Prajāpati he lets him free, for support. The vow if not released is liable to consume (the sacrificer); 'O Agni, lord of vows, I have performed my vow,' he says; verily he releases his vow, for atonement, to prevent burning. The sacrifice goes away, and turns not back; to him who sacrifices knowing the restoration of the sacrifice it does turn back; 'The sacrifice hath become, it hath come into being,' he says; this is the restoration of the sacrifice, and thereby he restores it. Excellence has not been obtained by him who having established a fire has no retinue; cattle indeed are the retinue of a Brahman. Having sacrificed, he should step forward to the east and say, 'Rich in cattle, in sheep, O Agni, in horses is the sacrificer'; he wins his retinue, he obtains a thousand cattle, in his offspring a strong one is born.

The Vājapeya

Mantra 1:7:7

a. O God Savitar, instigate the sacrifice, instigate the lord of the sacrifice for good luck; may the divine Gandharva who purifieth thoughts purify our thought; may the lord of speech today make sweet our utterance. || *b.* Thou art the thunderbolt of Indra, slaying obstructions, with thee may this one smite Vṛitra || *c.* On the instigation of strength, the mother, the mighty one, | We shall proclaim with our speech, Aditi, by name, | Into whom all this world hath entered; | In her may the God Savitar instigate right for us. || *d.* In the waters is ambrosia, in the waters is medicine; | Through the guidance of the waters | Be ye steeds, O ye that are strong. || *e.* Or Vāyu thee, or Manu thee, | The seven and twenty Gandharvas; | They first yoked the steed; | They placed swiftness in it. || *f.* Child of the waters, swift one, the towering onrushing wave most fain to win the prize, with it may he win the prize. || *g.* Thou art the stepping of Vishṇu, thou art the step of Vishṇu, thou art the stride of Vishṇu. || *h.* May the two Aṅkas, the two Nyaṅkas, which are on either side of the chariot, | Speeding on with the rushing wind, | The far-darting, powerful one, the winged one, | The fires which are furtherers, further us.

Mantra 1:7:8

a. On the instigation of the God Savitar, through Bṛihaspati, winner of the prize, may I win the prize. || *b.* On the instigation of the God Savitar, through Bṛihaspati, winner of the prize, may I mount the highest vault. || *c.* To Indra utter your voices, make Indra win the prize, Indra hath won the prize. || *d.* O whip, strong, having strength for the prizes, | Do thou in the contests strengthen the steeds. || *e.* The swift art thou, the runner, the strong. || *f.* O steeds, hasten for the prize; conquer on the instigation of the Marutas: measure ye the leagues; establish the ways; attain the goal. || *g.* For each prize aid us, O ye steeds, | For the rewards, O ye wise, immortal, righteous ones; | Drink of this mead, rejoice in it; | Delighted go by paths on which the Gods go. || *h.* May the swift coursers, who hear the call, | All hearken to our cry. || *i.* Strong limbed, winning a thousand, | Eager to gain in the gaining of praise, | The steeds, which have won in the contests great prizes, | May they be propitious to us when we call. || *k.* Among the Gods, strong limbed, good praisers, | Destroying the serpent, the wolf, the Rākṣhasas, | For ever may they remove from us evil. | 1. This steed speedeth his swift course, | Bound at the neck, the shoulder, and the mouth; | Displaying his strength Dadhikrā | springeth along the bends of the ways. || *m.* After him as he hasteneth in triumphant speed | Bloweth the wind as after the wing of the bird, | Of the impetuous eagle, (after him) Dadhikrāvan, | As in his might he crosseth the winding ways. || *n.* May there come to me the instigation of strength; | May there come sky and earth with all healing; | Come to me father and mother; | May Soma come to me for immortality. || *o.* O ye steeds, prize winning, about to run for the prize, about to win the prize, do ye touch Bṛihaspati's portion. || *p.* O ye steeds, prize winning, that have run for the prize, that have won the prize, do ye be pure in Bṛihaspati's portion. || *q.* True hath been the compact | That ye did make with Indra. || *r.* Ye have made Indra win the prize, O trees; now be ye loosed.

Mantra 1:7:9

a. Thou art the caul of the kingly class, thou art the womb of the kingly class. || *b.* O wife, come hither to the heaven; let us two mount! Yes, let us two mount the heaven; I will mount the heaven for us both. || *c.* Strength, instigation, the later born, inspiration, heaven, the head, the Vyaśniya, the offspring of the last, the last, the offspring of being, being, the overlord. || *d.* May life accord with the sacrifice, may expiration accord with the sacrifice, may inspiration accord with the sacrifice, may cross-breathing accord with the sacrifice, may eye accord with the sacrifice, may ear accord with the sacrifice, may mind accord with the sacrifice, may the body accord with the sacrifice, may the sacrifice accord with the sacrifice. || *e.* We have come to the heaven, to the Gods; we have become immortal; we have become the offspring of Prajāpati || *f.* May I be united with offspring, offspring with me; may I be united with increase of wealth, increase of wealth with me. || *g.* For food thee! For proper food thee! For strength thee! For the conquering of strength thee! || *h.* Thou art ambrosia, thou art prospering, thou art begetting.

Mantra 1:7:10.

a. The instigation of strength pressed in aforetime | This Soma, the lord in the plants, in the waters; | Be they full of sweetness for us; | May we as Purohitas watch over the kingship. || *b.* The instigation of strength hath pervaded | This (world) and all these worlds on every side; | He goeth around knowing pre-eminence, | Increasing offspring and prosperity for us. || *c.* The instigation of strength rested on this sky | And all these worlds as king; | May the wise one make the niggard to be generous, | And may he accord us wealth with all heroes. || *d.* O Agni, speak to us; | To us be thou kindly disposed; | Further us, O lord of the world | Thou art the giver of wealth to us. || *e.* May Aryaman further us, | May Bhaga, may Bṛihaspati, | May the Gods, and the bounteous one; | May the Goddess speech be bountiful to us. || *f.* Aryaman, Bṛihaspati, Indra, | Impel to give us gifts, | Speech, Vishṇu, Sarasvatī, | And Savitar the strong. || *g.* Soma the king, Varuṇa, | Agni, we grasp, | The Ādityas, Vishṇu, Sūrya | And Bṛihaspati, the Brahman (priest). || *h.* On the instigation of the God Savitar with the arms of the Aśvins, with the hands of Pūshan, with the bond of Sarasvatī, of speech, the binder, I anoint thee with the lordship of Agni, with the lordship of Indra of Bṛihaspati I anoint thee.

Mantra 1:7:11

Agni with one syllable won speech; the Aśvins with two syllables won expiration and inspiration; Vishṇu with three syllables won the three worlds; Soma with four syllables won four-footed cattle; Pūshan with five syllables won the Paṅkti; Dhātar with six syllables won the six seasons; the Marutas with seven syllables won the seven-footed Śakvarī; Bṛihaspati with eight syllables won the Gāyatrī; Mitra with nine syllables won the threefold Stoma; Varuṇa with ten syllables won the Virāj; Indra with eleven syllables won the Trishṭubh; the All-Gods with twelve syllables won the Jagatī; the Vasus with thirteen syllables won the thirteenfold Stoma; the Rudras with fourteen syllables won the fourteenfold Stoma; the Ādityas with fifteen syllables won the fifteenfold Stoma; Aditi with sixteen syllables won the sixteen fold Stoma; Prajāpati with seventeen syllables won the seventeenfold Stoma.

Mantra 1:7:12

a. Thou art taken with a support; thee that sittest among men, that sittest in the wood, that sittest in the world, I take acceptable to Indra this is thy birthplace; to Indra thee! ‖ *b.* Thou art taken with a support; thee that sittest in the waters, that sittest in the ghee, that sittest in the sky, I take acceptable to Indra; this is thy birthplace; to Indra thee! ‖ *c.* Thou art taken with a support; thee that sittest on the earth, that sittest on the atmosphere, that sittest on the vault, I take acceptable to Indra; this is thy birthplace; to Indra thee! ‖ *d.* The cups of the five folk, | Of which three are of highest birth, | (And for which) the divine cask has been forced out | Of these that have no handles | The food and strength have I seized; | This is thy birthplace; to Indra thee! ‖ *e.* The sap of the waters, the vigorous, | The ray of the sun that has been gathered, | The sap of the sap of the waters, | That of you I take which is the best; | This is thy birthplace; to Indra thee! ‖ *f.* By this shape producing mighty deeds, | He is dread, a broad way for gain, | He hath come to the top, bearing sweetness, | What time he moved a body in his own body. ‖ *g.* Thou art taken with a support; agreeable to Prajāpati I take thee | this is thy birthplace; to Prajāpati thee!

Mantra 1:7:13

a. The months, the woods, | The plants, the mountains, | The earth and sky in longing, | The waters, followed Indra on his birth. ‖ *b.* To thee hath been assigned for mighty power, | For ever, in the slaying of Vṛitra, | All lordship, and all strength, O thou that art worthy of sacrifice | In the overcoming of man by the Gods, O Indra, ‖ *c.* Indrāṇī beyond other women | I have heard to be favoured with a spouse, | For never at any time | Shall her husband die of old age. ‖ *d.* I have not joyed, O Indrāṇī, | Without my friend Vṛishākapi, | Whose oblation rich in water | Goeth dear to the Gods. ‖ *e.* He who first born in his wisdom | A God, surpassed the Gods in insight, | From whose breath the sky and earth recoiled, | In the greatness of his manhood, he, O ye men, is Indra. ‖ *f.* Hitherward be thy might with aid, O dread Indra, | What time the armies meet in combat, | And the arrow flieth from the arms of the strong men; | Let not thine anger spread on every side. ‖ *g.* Destroy us not; bring and give to us | That plenteous bounty which thou hast to give to the pious man, | For this new gift, this song we have sung to thee; | Let us speak forth in praise of Indra. ‖ *h.* Bring it to us, let none intercept it; | For we know thee as wealth lord of riches; | That mighty gift of thine, O Indra, | Vouchsafe it us, O lord of the bay steeds. ‖ *i.* With our oblation we summon | Indra, the giver; | Fill both thy hands with bounty; | Give to us from the left and the right. ‖ *k.* The giver, the bolt-bearer, the bull, the overpowering, | The impetuous, the king, slayer of Vṛitra, drinker of the Soma, | Seated at this sacrifice on the strew, | Be thou health and wealth to the sacrificer. ‖ *l.* Indra, the protector, the granter of aid with his aids; | All knowing, be kindly to us; | Let him restrain the enemy, let him make security, | May we be lords of strength. ‖ *m.* May we enjoy the favour of him the worshipful, | And also his loving kindness; | May the protector Indra, the granter of aid, | For ever fend far from us the enemy. ‖ *n.* Rich banquets be ours with Indra, | With mighty strength, | Wherewith fed we may be glad. ‖ *o.* To Indra, here sing strength | To place his chariot in the front; | Even in conflict in battle he maketh wide room; | Slayer of foes in the contests | Be thou our comforter; | Let the feeble bowstrings | Of the others break on their bows.

Prapāṭhaka 8.

The Rājasūya

Mantra 1:8:1

a. Anumati he offers a cake on eight potsherds; the sacrificial fee is a cow. The (grains) which are thrown down to the west of the support he (offers) on one potsherd to Nirṛiti; the sacrificial fee is a black garment with a black fringe. ‖ Go away, hail! rejoicing in the oblation. | This is thy share, O Nirṛiti; | O thou who hast prospered, thou art rich in oblation; | Free him from evil. Hail! | Honour to him who hath done this. ‖ He offers an oblation to Āditya; the sacrificial fee is a choice (ox). (He offers) to Agni and Vishṇu on eleven potsherds; the sacrificial fee is a dwarf beast of burden. (He offers) to Agni and Soma on eleven potsherds; the sacrificial fee is gold. (He offers) to Indra on eleven potsherds; the sacrificial fee is a bull as a beast of burden. (He offers) to Agni on eight potsherds, and curds to Indra; the sacrificial fee is a bull as a beast of burden. (He offers) to Indra and Agni on twelve potsherds, and an oblation (*caru*) to the All-Gods; the sacrificial fee is a first-born calf. (He offers) an oblation of millet to Soma; the sacrificial fee is a garment. (He offers) an oblation to Sarasvatī, and an oblation to Sarasvat; the sacrificial fee is a pair of oxen.

Mantra 1:8:2

He offers to Agni on eight potsherds, an oblation to Soma, to Savitar on twelve potsherds, an oblation to Sarasvatī, an oblation to Pūshan, to the Marutas on seven potsherds, clotted curds to the All-Gods, and on eleven potsherds to sky and earth.

Mantra 1:8:3

a. He offers on eleven potsherds to Indra and Agni, clotted curds to the Marutas, clotted curds to Varuṇa, and on one potsherd to Ka. ‖ *b.* The voracious we invoke, | The Marutas who bear the sacrifice, | Rejoicing in the mush. ‖ *c.* Be not against us in battles, O God Indra | Let there be expiation to satisfy thee, O impetuous one; | For great is the barley heap of this bountiful one; | Rich in oblation are the Marutas whom our song praises. ‖ *d.* The wrong we have done in village or wild, | In the assembly, in our members, | The wrong to Śūdra or Ārya, | The wrong contrary to the law of either, | Of that thou art the expiation; hail! ‖ *e.* The doers of the deed have performed the deed, | With wondrous speech; | Having done the deed to the Gods go ye | To your home, ye bounteous ones.

Mantra 1:8:4

a. To Agni Anīkavat he offers a cake on eight potsherds as the sun rises, an oblation to the Marutas as the heaters at midday, and to the Marutas as lords of the house he milks at evening an oblation of all (the cows). ‖ *b.* O ladle, fly away filled, | And well filled do thou fly back; | Like wares, O Śatakratu, | Let us barter food and strength. ‖ *c.* Give thou to me; I shall give to thee; | Bestow upon me; I shall bestow upon thee; | Accept my offering; | I shall accept thy offering. ‖ *d.* To the Marutas, the playful, he offers a cake on seven potsherds at the rising of the sun; he offers to Agni on eight potsherds, an oblation to Soma, to Savitar on twelve potsherds, to Sarasvatī an oblation, to Pūshan an oblation, to Indra and Agni on eleven potsherds, to Indra an oblation, to Viśvakarman on eleven potsherds.

Mantra 1:8:5

a. He offers to Soma with the Pitṛis a cake on six potsherds, to the Pitṛis who sit on the straw fried grains, for the Pitṛis prepared by Agni he milks a beverage from a cow which has to be won over (to another calf). ‖ *b.* This for thee, O father, and for thy line; | This for thee, O grandfather, great-grandfather, and for thy line | Do ye Pitṛis rejoice in your portions. ‖ *c.* May we gladden thee, | O bountiful one, fair to see; | Forth now with full chariot seat | Being praised, dost thou fare according to our will; | Yoke, O Indra, thy two bay steeds. ‖ *d.* They have eaten, they have rejoiced, | The dear ones have dispelled (evil), | The radiant sages have been praised with newest hymn; | Yoke, O Indra, thy two bay steeds. ‖ *e.* The Pitṛis have eaten, the Pitṛis have rejoiced, the Pitṛis have been glad, the Pitṛis have purified themselves. ‖ *f.* Go away, O ye Pitṛis, Soma loving, | With your majestic ancient paths; | Then reach ye the kindly Pitṛis | Who carouse in company with Yama. ‖ *h.* Mind let us summon hither | With the praise of Narāśaṃsa | And the reverence of the Pitṛis ‖ *h.* Let mind return to us | For vigour, for insight, for life, | And that long we may see the sun. ‖ *i.* May the Pitṛis restore mind to us, | May the host of the Gods; | May we belong to the band of the living. ‖ *k.* Whatever hurt we have done to atmosphere, to earth, to sky, | To mother or to father, | May Agni of the house free me from this sin; | May he make me blameless | In respect of all the ill we have wrought.

Mantra 1:8:6

a. For each he offers on one potsherd, and one over. ‖ *b.* As many as we are of the house, to them have I made prosperity. ‖ *c.* Thou art the protection of cattle, the protection of the sacrifice; give | me protection. ‖ *d.* Rudra alone yieldeth to no second. ‖ *e.* The mole is thy beast, O Rudra; rejoice in it. ‖ *f.* This is thy portion, O Rudra, with thy sister Ambikā; rejoice in it. ‖ *g.* (Give) medicine for ox, for horse, for man, | And medicine for us, medicine | That it be rich in healing, | Good for ram and sheep. || *h.* We have appeased, O lady, Rudra, | The God Tryambaka; | That he may make us prosperous, | That he may increase our wealth, | That he may make us rich in cattle, | That he may embolden us. || *i.* To Tryambaka we make offering, | The fragrant, increaser of prosperity; | Like a cucumber from its stem, | From death may I be loosened, not from immortality. || *k.* This is thy portion, O Rudra; rejoice in it; with it for food, do thou go away beyond the Mūjavants. || *l.* With unstrung bow, thy club in thy hand, clad in skins.

Mantra 1:8:7

a. (He I offers) to Indra and Agni on twelve potsherds, an oblation to the All-Gods, a cake on twelve potsherds to Indra Śunāsīra, milk to Vāyu, to Sūrya on one potsherd; the sacrificial fee is a plough for twelve oxen. || *b.* To Agni he offers on eight potsherds, to Rudra an oblation of Gavīdhukā, to Indra curds, to Varuṇa an oblation made of barley; the sacrificial fee is a cow for draught purposes. || *c.* The Gods that sit in the east, led by Agni; that sit in the south, led by Yama; that sit in the west, led by Savitar; that sit in the north, led by Varuṇa; that sit above, led by Bṛihaspati; that slay the Rākṣhasas; may they protect us, may they help us; to them homage; to them hail! || *d.* The Rākṣhasas are collected, the Rākṣhasas are burnt up; here do I burn up the Rākṣhasas || *e.* To Agni, slayer of Rākṣhasas, hail! To Yama, Savitar, Varuṇa, Bṛihaspati, the worshipful, the slayer of Rākṣhasas, hail! || *f.* The sacrificial fee is a chariot with three horses. || *g.* On the instigation of the God Savitar, with the arms of the Aśvins, with the hands of Pūṣhan, I offer (for) the death of the Rākṣhasas; the Rākṣhasas are slain; we have killed the Rākṣhasas || *h.* The sacrificial fee is what he wears.

Mantra 1:8:8

He offers a cake on twelve potsherds to Dhātar, to Anumati an oblation, to Rākā an oblation, to Sinīvālī an oblation, to Kuhū an oblation; the sacrificial fee is a pair of cattle. To Agni and Viṣhṇu he offers on eleven potsherds, to Indra and Viṣhṇu on eleven potsherds, to Viṣhṇu on three potsherds; the sacrificial fee is a dwarf beast of burden. To Agni and Soma he offers on eleven potsherds, to Indra and Soma on eleven potsherds, to Soma an oblation; the sacrificial fee is a brown (animal). To Soma and Pūṣhan he offers an oblation, to Indra and Pūṣhan an oblation, to Pūṣhan an oblation; the sacrificial fee is a dark (animal). To (Agni) Vaiśvānara he offers on twelve potsherds; the sacrificial fee is gold. To Varuṇa (he offers) an oblation made of barley; the sacrificial fee is a horse.

Mantra 1:8:9

To Bṛihaspati he offers an oblation in the house of the Brahman (priest); the sacrificial fee is a white-backed (animal). (He offers) to Indra on eleven potsherds in the house of a Rājanya; the sacrificial fee is a bull. To Āditya (he offers) an oblation in the house of the chief wife; the sacrificial fee is a cow. To Nirṛiti (he offers) an oblation in the house of the neglected wife, made up of rice broken by the nails; the sacrificial fee is a black hornless (cow). To Agni (he offers) on eight potsherds in the house of the leader of the host; the sacrificial fee is gold. To Varuṇa (he offers) on ten potsherds in the house of the minstrel; the sacrificial fee is a great castrated (ox). To the Marutas (he offers) on seven potsherds in the house of the village headman; the sacrificial fee is a dappled (cow). To Savitar (he offers) on twelve potsherds in the house of the carver; the sacrificial fee is a speckled (ox). To the Aśvins (he offers) on two potsherds in the house of the charioteer; the sacrificial fee is two born of one mother. To Pūṣhan (he offers) an oblation in the house of the divider; the sacrificial fee is a black (ox). To Rudra (he offers) an oblation of Gavīdhukā in the house of the thrower of the dice; the sacrificial fee is a speckled (ox) with raised tail. To Indra, the good protector, he offers a cake on eleven potsherds and to Indra, who frees from distress, (with the words), || May the king, the slayer of Vṛitra, | Be our king and slay the foe. || There is (an offering) to Mitra and Bṛihaspati; in the milk of a white (cow) with a white calf which has curdled itself, and in butter which has churned itself, in a dish of Aśvattha wood with four corners (made) of a branch which has fallen of itself, he should scatter husked and unhusked rice grains; the husked ones in the milk are Bṛihaspati's, the unhusked in the butter are Mitra's; the Vedi must be self-made, the strew self-cut, the kindling-stick self-made; the sacrificial fee is the white (cow) with a white calf.

Mantra 1:8:10.

a. To Agni, lord of the house, he offers a cake of black rice on eight potsherds; to Soma, lord of the forest, an oblation of millet; to Savitar, of true instigation, a cake of swift-growing rice on twelve potsherds; to Rudra, lord of cattle, an oblation of Gavīdhukā; to Bṛihaspati, lord of speech, an oblation of wild rice; to Indra, the noblest, a cake of large rice on eleven potsherds; to Mitra, the true, an oblation of Ambā grain, and to Varuṇa, lord of right, an oblation made of barley. || *b.* May Savitar of instigations instigate thee, Agni of lords of the house, Soma of lords of the forest, Rudra of cattle, Bṛihaspati of speech, Indra of nobles, Mitra of truth, Varuṇa of lords of right. || *c.* O ye Gods that instigate the Gods, do ye instigate him, descendant of N. N., to freedom from foes, to great lordship, to great overlordship, to great rule over the people. || *d.* This is your king, O Bhāratas; Soma is the king of us Brahmans. || *e.* This kingdom hath verily been conferred, | Varuṇa hath diffused his own body; | We have become obedient to pure Mitra; | We have magnified the name of the great holy order. || *f.* These have become all the hosts of Varuṇa, | Mitra in his course hath overcome hostility; | The worshipful ones have taken order according to sacred law: | Trita hath taken possession of our old age. || *g.* Thou art the stepping of Viṣhṇu, thou art the step of Viṣhṇu, thou art the stride of Viṣhṇu.

Mantra 1:8:11

a. Ye are active, thou art the lord of the waters, thou art the male wave, thou art the male host, ye are the pen-dwellers, ye are the strength of the Marutas, ye have the radiance of the sun, ye have the brightness of the sun, ye are delightful, ye are obedient, ye are powerful, ye are all supporters, ye are supporters of men, ye have the brilliance of Agni, ye are the sap of the waters, of the plants. || *b.* They have taken the waters, divine, | Rich in sweetness, full of strength, caring for the royal consecration; | Whereby they anointed Mitra and Varuṇa, | Whereby they led Indra beyond his foes. || *c.* Ye are givers of the kingdom; give ye the kingdom, hail! Ye are givers of the kingdom; give N. N. the kingdom.

Mantra 1:8:12

a. O ye divine waters, be ye united | Full of sweetness with the sweet, | Winning great radiance for the Kṣhatriya. || *b.* Unsurpassed, sit ye down, full of strength, | Bestowing great radiance upon the Kṣhatriya. || *c.* Friend of speech, born of heat, thou art undefeated; thou art the share of Soma. || *d.* The pure I purify you with the pure, the bright with the bright, the immortal with ambrosia, hail! caring for the royal consecration. || *e.* Clothed in these (waters), sharing joy, glorious in strength, | Undefeated and busy, | In the waters hath Varuṇa made his abode, | The child of the waters in those most motherly. || *f.* Thou art the caul of kingly power, thou art the womb of kingly power. || *g.* Notified is Agni, lord of the house; notified is Indra, of ancient fame; notified is Pūṣhan, all-knower; notified are Mitra and Varuṇa, increasing holy order; notified are sky and earth, of sure vows; notified is the Goddess Aditi, of all forms; notified is he, N. N., descendant of N. N., in this folk, this kingdom, for great lordship, for great overlordship, for great rule over the people. || *h.* This is your king, O Bhāratas; Soma is the king of us Brahmans. || *i.* Thou art the bolt of Indra slaying foes; with thee may he slay his foe. || *k.* Ye are overcomers of foes. || *l.* Protect me in front, protect me at the side, protect me from behind; from the quarters protect me; from all deadly things protect me. || *m.* Gold hued in the glowing of the dawns, | Bronze pillared at the rising of the sun, | O Varuṇa, O Mitra, mount your chariot seat, | And thence behold ye Aditi and Diti.

Mantra 1:8:13

a. Do I thou mount the kindling (quarter); let the Gāyatrī of metres help thee; the Trivṛit Stoma, the Rathantara Sāman, the deity Agni, the treasure the Brahman class. || *b.* Do thou mount the dread (quarter); let the Triṣhṭubh of metres help thee, the Pañchadaśa Stoma, the Bṛihat Sāman, the deity Indra, the treasure the ruling class. || *c.* Do thou mount the shining (quarter); let the Jagatī of metres help thee, the Saptadaśa Stoma, the Vairūpa Sāman, the deity the Marutas, the treasure the peasant class. || *d.* Do thou mount the northern (quarter); let the Anuṣhṭubh of metres help thee, the Ekaviṃśa Stoma, the Vairāja Sāman, the deity Mitra and Varuṇa, the treasure the host. || *e.* Do thou mount the zenith; let the

Paṅkti of metres help thee, the Triṇava, and Trayastriṃśa Stomas, the Śākvara and Raivata Sāmans, the deity Bṛihaspati, the treasure radiance. || *f.* Such like, other like, thus like, similar, the measured, commensurate, harmonious, || *g.* Of pure radiance, of varied radiance, of true radiance, the radiant, true, protector of holy order, beyond distress. || *h.* To Agni hail! To Soma hail! To Savitar hail! To Sarasvatī hail! | To Pūṣhan hail! To Bṛihaspati hail! To Indra hail! To sound hail! | To verse hail! To Aṃśa hail! To Bhaga hail! To the lord of the field hail! || *i.* To earth hail! To atmosphere hail! To sky hail! To the sun hail! To the moon hail! To the Nakṣhatras hail! To the waters hail! To plants hail! To trees hail! To moving creatures hail! To swimming creatures hail! To creeping creatures hail!

Mantra 1:8:14

a. Thou art the glittering of Soma; as thine may my glittering be. || *b.* Thou art ambrosia; from death protect me. || *c.* From the thunderbolt protect me. || *d.* Propitiated are biting flies. || *e.* Cast away is Namuchi's head. || *f.* Soma, king Varuṇa, and the Gods which instigate righteousness, may they instigate thy speech, may they instigate thy breath, may they instigate thy sight, may they instigate thine ear. || *g.* With the glory of Soma I besprinkle thee, with the brilliance of Agni, with the radiance of the sun, with the power of Indra, with the strength of Mitra and Varuṇa, with the force of the Marutas. || *h.* Thou art the lord of kingly powers. || *i.* Protect from the sky. || *k.* Out from below have they come, | Following the serpent of the deep; | On the back of the mountain, the hill, | The ships that pour spontaneously go ever. || *l.* O Rudra, that highest active name of thee, to that thou art offered, thou art offered to Yama. || *m.* O Prajāpati, none other than thou | Hath encompassed all these beings; | Be that ours for which we sacrifice to thee | May we be lords of wealth.

Mantra 1:8:15

a. Thou art the bolt of Indra, slaying foes; with thee may he slay his foe. || *b.* By the precept of Mitra and Varuṇa, the directors, I yoke thee with the yoking of the sacrifice. || *c.* Thou art the stepping of Viṣhṇu, thou art the step of Viṣhṇu, thou art the stride of Viṣhṇu || *d.* On the instigation of the Marutas may I conquer. || *e.* Be mind ready. || *f.* May I be united with power and strength. || *g.* Thou art the spirit of cattle; like them may my spirit be. || *h.* Homage to mother earth; may I not harm mother earth; may mother earth harm me not. || *i.* So great art thou, thou art life, bestow life upon me; thou art strength, bestow strength upon me; thou art the yoker; thou art radiance, bestow radiance upon me. || *k.* To Agni, lord of the house, hail! To Soma, lord of the forest, hail! To Indra's strength hail! To the Marutas' force hail! || *l.* The gander seated in purity, the bright one seated in the atmosphere, | The Hotar seated at the altar, the guest seated in the house, | Seated among men, seated in the highest, seated in holy order, seated in the firmament, | Born of the waters, born of the cows, born of holy order, born of the mountain, the great holy order.

Mantra 1:8:16

a. Thou art Mitra, thou art Varuṇa || *b.* May I be united with the All-Gods. || *c.* Thou art the navel of kingly power, thou are the womb of kingly power. || *d.* Sit thou on the smooth, sit thou on the pleasant seat. || *e.* May she hurt thee not; may she hurt me not. || *f.* Varuṇa, of sure vows, hath set him down | In the waters, with keen insight, for lordship. || *g.* O Brahman! Thou, O king, art the Brahman priest, thou art Savitar of true instigation. O Brahman! Thou, O king, art the Brahman priest, thou art Indra of true force. O Brahman! Thou, O king, art the Brahman priest; thou art Indra, the kindly. O Brahman! Thou, O king, art the Brahman priest; thou art Varuṇa, of true rule. || *h.* Thou art the bolt of Indra, slaying foes; with this subject to me. || *i.* This king hath surmounted the quarters. || *k.* O thou of good fame! O thou of prosperity! O thou of true rule! || *l.* To the son of the waters hail! To the son of strength hail! To Agni, lord of the house, hail!

Mantra 1:8:17

He offers to Agni on eight potsherds; the sacrificial fee is gold. (He offers) to Sarasvatī an oblation; the sacrificial fee is a calf. To Savitar (he offers) on twelve potsherds; the sacrificial fee is a speckled (ox). To Pūṣhan (he offers) an oblation; the sacrificial fee is a dark (ox), To Bṛihaspati (he offers) an oblation; the sacrificial fee is a white-backed (ox). To Indra (he offers) on eleven potsherds; the sacrificial fee is a bull. To Varuṇa (he offers) on ten potsherds; the sacrificial fee is a great castrated (ox). To Soma (he offers) an oblation; the sacrificial fee is a brown (ox). To Tvaṣhṭar (he offers) on eight potsherds; the sacrificial fee is a white (ox) To Viṣhṇu (he offers) on three potsherds; the sacrificial fee is a dwarf (ox).

Mantra 1:8:18

On the same day they consecrate, on the same day they buy the Soma. He presents a lotus wreath. He buys the Soma with calves. There is a drink for ten. A hundred Brahmans drink. The Stotra is the Saptadaśa. The two ornaments he gives to the Adhvaryu, the garland to the Udgātar, the round ornament to the Hotar, a horse to the Prastotar and Pratihartar, twelve heifers to the Brahman, a cow to the Maitrāvaruṇa, a bull to the Brāhmaṇācchaṃsin, garments to the Neṣhṭar and Potar, a wagon drawn by one ox laden with barley to the Achāvāka, a draught ox to the Agnīdh. The Hotar is a Bhārgava; the Sāman of the Brahman is the Śrāyantīya; the Agniṣhṭoma Sāman is the Vāravantīya. He takes water of the Sarasvatī.

Mantra 1:8:19

To Agni he offers on eight potsherds; the sacrificial fee is gold. To Indra (he offers) on eleven potsherds; the sacrificial fee is a bull. To the All-Gods (he offers) an oblation; the sacrificial fee is a tawny heifer. To Mitra and Varuṇa (he offers) clotted curds; the sacrificial fee is a cow. To Bṛihaspati (he offers) an oblation; the sacrificial fee is a white-backed (ox). To the Ādityas he sacrifices a sheep in young, to the Marutas a dappled heifer. To the Aśvins and Pūṣhan he offers a cake on twelve potsherds; to Sarasvatī of true speech an oblation; to Savitar of true instigation a cake on twelve potsherds; the sacrificial fee is a dry skin bag and a bow with three arrows.

Mantra 1:8:20.

To Agni he offers on eight potsherds; to Soma, an oblation; to Savitar on twelve potsherds; to Bṛihaspati an oblation; to Tvaṣhṭar on eight potsherds; to (Agni) Vaiśvānara on twelve potsherds; the sacrificial fee is the southern drawer of the chariot stand. To Sarasvatī he offers an oblation; to Pūṣhan an oblation; to Mitra an oblation; to Varuṇa an oblation; to the lord of the fields an oblation; to the Ādityas an oblation; the sacrificial fee is the northern drawer of the chariot stand.

Mantra 1:8:21

a. The sweet with the sweet, bitter with the bitter, immortal with the immortal, with the Soma I unite thee; thou art Soma; be ready for the Aśvins, be ready for Sarasvatī, be ready for Indra, the good protector. || *b.* Let the daughter of the Sun | Purify for thee the flowing Soma | With the eternal sieve. || *c.* Vāyu purified by the strainer, | Soma hath sped away, | Indra's dear friend. || *d.* What then? As men who have barley | Reap the barley in order, removing it, | Hither bring the food of those | Who have not gone to the reverential cutting of the straw. || *e.* To the Aśvins he sacrifices a dusky (ox), to Sarasvatī a ram, to Indra a bull. || *f.* To Indra he offers on eleven potsherds, to Savitar on twelve potsherds, to Varuṇa on ten potsherds. || *g.* O Pitṛis, beaded by Soma, rejoice. || *h.* The sacrificial fee is a mare.

Mantra 1:8:22

a. O Agni and Viṣhṇu, great is your greatness; | Rejoice ye in the secret names of the ghee; | Placing in every house seven treasures, | May your tongue move forth to the ghee. || *b.* O Agni and Viṣhṇu, great is your dear abode; | Ye taste the ghee, rejoicing in its secrets; | In every home increasing lauds, | May your tongue move forth to the ghee. || *c.* May the Goddess Sarasvatī | With strength, rich in mares, | Further us, she that aideth prayer. || *d.* To us from the sky, from the great mountain; | May Sarasvatī, the worshipful, come to the sacrifice | May the Goddess rejoicing in our supplication, rich in ghee, | May she hearken gladly to our effectual speech. || *e.* O Bṛihaspati, with the All-Gods, | Do thou rejoice in our oblations; | Grant riches to the generous giver. || *f.* Then to the father, with the All-Gods, to the strong one, | Let us pay honour with sacrifices, with reverence, with oblations; | O Bṛihaspati, with good offspring, with heroes, | May we be lords of wealth. || *g.* That various wealth bestow upon us, | O Bṛihaspati, that shall surpass the enemy, | That shall shine glorious, with insight among men, | That shall be resplendent in glory, O thou who art born of holy order. || *h.* O Mitra and Varuṇa, | Bedew our pasturage with ghee | With mead the regions, O ye wise ones. || *i.* Do ye unloose your arms for us to live; | Do ye bedew our pasturage with ghee; | Make us famous among the folk, O ye young ones; | Hearken, O Mitra and Varuṇa, to these my supplications. ‖ *k.* Agni for you I honour in song, | The God first of the bright ones; | Honouring him who prospereth the fields | Like a much loved friend. ‖ *l.* Swiftly (goeth) the chariot of the worshipper | Like a hero in every contest; | He who by sacrifice is fain to win the mind of the Gods | Shall prevail over those who sacrifice not. ‖ *m.* Thou art not harmed, O sacrificer, | Nor thou, O pourer, nor thou, O pious one; | There shall be wealth of heroes, | And plenteousness of swift steeds; | No one shall in act approach him, | No one shall anticipate him nor stay him. ‖ *n.* Streams, health-bringing, like milch cows, | Pour up to the man who hath sacrificed and shall sacrifice; | Him who filleth and satiateth, bringing fame, | Streams of ghee approach on all sides. ‖ *o.* O Soma and Rudra, do ye drive away | The evil spirit that hath entered our abode; | Far away from us smite misfortune; | Whatever sin we have done remove from us. ‖ *p.* O Soma and Rudra, do ye give to us, | In our bodies, all these medicines; | Loosen and remove the evil we have done | That is bound within our bodies. ‖ *q.* O Soma and Pūṣhan, begetters of wealth, | Begetters, of sky, begetters of earth, | Born as protectors of the whole world, | The Gods have made (you) the navel of immortality. ‖ *r.* In the birth of these Gods they rejoiced; | They concealed the hateful darkness; | Through these two, Soma and Pūṣhan, | The Indra made the cooked (milk) among the raw cows.

Kāṇḍa 2.

Prapāṭhaka 1.

The Special Animal Sacrifices

Mantra 2:1:1

He who desires prosperity should offer a white (beast) to Vāyu; Vāyu is the swiftest deity; verily he has recourse to him with his own share; verily he makes him attain prosperity; he prospers. 'He is an overswift deity,' they say, 'he has power to burn him up.' This (beast) he should offer to Vāyu of the team; the team is his support; verily, being supported he attains prosperity to avoid being burnt; he prospers. He who desires a village should offer to Vāyu of the team; Vāyu leads these creatures tied by the nose; verily he has recourse to Vāyu of the team with his own share; verily he assigns him creatures led by the nose; he becomes possessed of a village. It is offered to (Vāyu) of the team; verily he makes creatures abide steadfast with him. He who desires offspring should offer to Vāyu of the team; Vāyu is expiration, the team is inspiration; expiration and inspiration depart from the offspring of him who being fit for offspring yet obtains not offspring. Verily he has recourse to Vāyu of the team with his own share; verily he for him begets offspring by means of expiration and inspiration; he obtains offspring. He who has long been ill should offer to Vāyu of the team; Vāyu is expiration, the team is inspiration, expiration and inspiration depart from him whose illness is long. Verily he has recourse to Vāyu of the team with his own share, he bestows on him expiration and inspiration; even if his life be gone, he yet lives. Prajāpati was here alone; he desired, 'May I create offspring and cattle'; he took out from his body the omentum, and placed it in the fire. The hornless goat then came to life; he offered it to its own deity; then did he create offspring and cattle. He who desires offspring and cattle should offer to Prajāpati a hornless goat. Verily he has recourse to Prajāpati with his own share; verily he begets for him offspring and cattle. The beard is the characteristic of man, the lack of horns of the horse, having incisors on one side only that of cattle, having sheep-like hooves that of sheep, the goat-nature that of goats; so many are the domesticated animals; verily by their characteristics he wins them. He who desires cattle should offer one of a triplet to Soma and Pūṣhan; the she-goat has two teats, two are born separately, the third for strength and growth. Verily he has recourse to Soma and Pūṣhan with their own share; verily they produce cattle for him; Soma is the depositor of seed, Pūṣhan the producer of cattle; Soma deposits seeds for him, Pūṣhan produces cattle. The sacrificial post is of Udumbara; the Udumbara is strength, cattle are strength; verily by strength he wins for him strength and cattle.

Mantra 2:1:2

Prajāpati created offspring; they being created went away from him; they went to Varuṇa; he pursued them and asked them back; he would not give them back to him; he said, 'Choose a boon, and then give them back to me.' He chose a boon from them, it was the black (beast) with one white foot. He who is seized by Varuṇa should offer this black (beast) with one white foot to Varuṇa Verily he has recourse to Varuṇa with his own share; verily he sets him free from Varuṇa's noose. It is a black (beast) with one white hoof, for it has Varuṇa for its deity (and serves) for prosperity. Svarbhānu, the Asura, pierced the sun with darkness; the Gods desired an atonement for him; the first darkness of his they struck off became a black sheep; the second a bright-coloured one; the third a white one; what they cut from the upper part of the bone became a barren ewe. The Gods said, 'Here has come into being a divine beast; to whom shall we offer him?' Now then the earth was small, plants were not born, they offered the barren ewe to the Ādityas as desire.' Then the earth became broad, the plants grew. He who desires, 'May I be extended with cattle, with offspring be propagated' should offer this barren ewe to the Ādityas as desire. Verily he has recourse to the Ādityas as desire with their own share; verily they extend him with cattle and propagate him with offspring. Yonder sun did not shine; the Gods desired an atonement for him; for him they offered these dew-lapped (beasts), to Agni one with a black neck, to Indra one of different colours, to Bṛihaspati a white one; verily by means of them they restored his brilliance, For him who desires splendour he should offer dew-lapped (beasts), to Agni one with a black neck, to Indra one of different colours, to Bṛihaspati a white one. Verily he has recourse to these deities with their own share; verily they bestow splendour upon him; he becomes resplendent. In the spring in the morning should he offer (the beast) with a black neck to Agni; in the summer at midday (the beast) of different colours to Indra; in the autumn in the after noon the white (beast) to Bṛihaspati These are the brilliances of the sun, in the spring in the morning, in the summer at midday, in the autumn in the afternoon; verily he wins whatever brilliances there are. They are offered in the course of the year; the year is the giver of splendour; verily the year gives him splendour; he becomes resplendent. They are (beasts) with young; the foetus is power; verily he bestows power upon him. He who being master of uttering speech cannot speak properly should offer a ewe to Sarasvatī; Sarasvatī is speech; verily he has recourse to Sarasvatī with her own share, she bestows on him speech, and he becomes an utterer of speech. Its teeth are complete; therefore men utter speech whole. He who is long ill should offer to Agni (a beast) with black neck, and a brown (beast) to Soma; the body of him whose illness is long goes to Agni, the sap to Soma; verily he ransoms from Agni his body, from Soma his sap, and even if his life is gone, yet he lives. He who desires offspring should offer to Soma a brown (beast), and to Agni one with a black neck; Soma is the depositor of seed, Agni the producer of offspring; verily Soma deposits seed for him, Agni produces offspring; he obtains offspring. The Brahman who despite study does not win fame should offer to Agni (a beast) with a black neck, and to Soma a brown (one); in that (the beast) is offered to Agni, thereby he places brilliance in him; in that (the beast) is offered to Soma, thereby (be places) splendour. The one with a black neck is for Agni; verily he drives away the darkness from him: it is white; verily he bestows brilliance on him. There is a brown one for Soma; verily he bestows splendour and radiance on him. He who has a dispute for a Purohitaship should offer (a beast) with a black neck to Agni, a brown one to Soma, and one with a black neck to Agni; the Brahman is connected with Agni, the prince with Soma; on either side of (the beast) for Soma there is one for Agni; verily with brilliance, with the Brahman, he seizes on either side the kingdom, and forthwith appropriates it; they choose him as Purohita.

Mantra 2:1:3

The Gods and the Asuras strove for these worlds; Viṣhṇu saw this dwarf, he offered it to its own deity; then he conquered these worlds. One who is engaged in a struggle should offer a dwarf (beast) to Viṣhṇu; then he becomes Viṣhṇu and conquers these worlds. He should offer on an uneven (place), for these worlds are uneven as it were; (verily it serves) for prosperity. He who is engaged in a contest should offer (a beast) with a spot on its forehead and horns bent forward to Indra, the angry, the wise. By power (*indriyā*), by anger, by wisdom, one wins a contest. Verily he has recourse to Indra, the angry, the wise, with his own share; verily he bestows on him power, anger, wisdom; he wins that contest. He who desires a village should offer (a beast) with dappled thighs to Indra with the

Marutas. Verily he has recourse to Indra with the Marutas with his own share; verily he subdues his relatives to him; he becomes possessed of a village. In that it is an ox, it is Indra's; in that it is dappled, it is of the Marutas, for prosperity. It has dappled thighs behind; verily he makes the folk dependent on him. He who desires food should offer a brown (beast) to Soma; food is connected with Soma; verily he has recourse to Soma with his own share; he bestows food on him; verily he becomes an eater of food. It is brown; that is the colour of food; (verily it serves) for prosperity. He who being meet for kingship obtains not a kingdom should offer a brown (beast) to Soma; the kingdom is connected with Soma; verily he has recourse to Soma with his own share; Soma bestows on him a kingdom; the kingdom comes to him. It is brown, that is the colour of Soma; (verily it serves) for prosperity. He whose prosperity is gone and who desires support should offer (a beast) with a spot on the forehead and horns bent forward to Indra, the conqueror of Vṛitra; verily he overcomes the evil foe and attains support. 'He who is seized by evil should offer (a beast) with a spot on the forehead and horns bent forward to Indra, the overcomer of enemies; the enemy is the evil; verily he has recourse to Indra, the overcomer of enemies with his own share, and he drives away from him the enemy, the evil. He who being meet for kingship obtains not a kingdom should offer (a beast) with a spot on the forehead and horns bent forward to Indra of the thunderbolt. Verily he has recourse to Indra of the thunderbolt with his own share; he bestows his thunderbolt on him, the bolt kindles him for prosperity, the kingdom comes to him. It has a spot on its forehead and horns bent for ward, that is the shape of the bolt, (and so it serves) for prosperity.

Mantra 2:1:4

Yonder sun did not shine; the Gods desired an atonement for him; for him they offered this offering of ten bulls; verily thereby they restored his brilliance. For him who desires splendour he should offer this offering of ten bulls; verily he has recourse to yonder sun with his own share; verily he bestows on him splendour; he becomes resplendent. He should offer in the spring in the morning three with spots on the forehead; in the summer at midday three with white backs; in the autumn in the afternoon three with white tails. Three are the brilliances of the sun, in the spring in the morning; in the summer at midday; in the autumn in the afternoon; verily he wins whatever brilliances there are. They are offered in sets of three; verily in order he bestows brilliance on him. They are offered in the course of the year; the year is the giver of splendour; verily the year gives him splendour; he becomes resplendent. At the end of the year he should offer a reddish brown one to Prajāpati all the Gods are Prajāpati; verily he rests on all the Gods. If he fears, 'I shall become diseased in the skin,' he should offer a dark (beast) to Soma and Pūshan; man has Soma as his deity, cattle have Pūshan; verily by his own deity, by cattle, he makes a skin for him; be does not become diseased in the skin. The Gods and Yama were at strife over this world; Yama appropriated (*ayuvata*) the power and strength of the Gods; therefore Yama has his name. The Gods reflected, 'Yama here has become what we are.' They had recourse to Prajāpati Prajāpati from his body fashioned out the bull and the cow; the Gods offered a cow to Vishṇu and to Varuṇa, a bull to Indra; they caused him to be seized by Varuṇa and by Vishṇu, the sacrifice, they drove him away; his power they appropriated by means of that for Indra. He who has foes should in strife offer to Vishṇu and Varuṇa a cow, to Indra a bull; verily causing his foe to be seized by Varuṇa, by Vishṇu, the sacrifice, he drives him away, he appropriates his power by means of that for Indra, he prospers, his foe is defeated. Indra slew Vṛitra; him Vṛitra slain bound with sixteen coils; from the head of Vṛitra came out cows, they were (cows) of Videha; behind them came the bull. It Indra perceived; he reflected, 'He who shall offer him shall be freed from this evil'; he offered to Agni one with a black neck, to Indra a bull. Agni, being approached with his own share, burned into sixteen pieces the coils of Vṛitra, and by (the offering) to Indra he bestowed power on himself. He who is seized by evil should offer (a beast) with a black neck to Agni, and a bull to Indra; verily Agni, being approached with his own share, burns away his evil, and by (the offering) to Indra he bestows power on himself, he is freed from the evil, he prospers. He who is long in exile should offer a cow to sky and earth; for he is not established in them; verily also he who is long in exile has recourse to sky and earth with their own share; verily they establish them; he is established. It is one which is long in labour, for long in labour as it were is the kingdom of him who is long in exile; (verily it serves) for prosperity. To Vāyu he should offer a calf; Vāyu is their calf; these worlds are barren for him, the people are barren; verily also he who is long in exile has recourse to Vāyu with his own share; verily Vāyu causes these worlds and the people to give to him; these worlds drop milk for him; the people wait upon him in service.

Mantra 2:1:5

Indra opened the hole of Vṛitra; the topmost cattle he grasped by the back and pulled out; a thousand cattle followed it, it became hump backed. He who desires cattle should offer this humpbacked (one) to Indra; verily he has recourse to Indra with his own share; verily he bestows cattle upon him; he becomes possessed of cattle. It is humpbacked; the hump backed is fortune a thousandfold; verily by fortune he wins cattle. When he obtains a thousand cattle, he should offer a dwarf (beast) to Vishṇu; upon it the thousand rested; therefore the dwarf, stretched out, affords support to cattle when born. 'Who can obtain a thousand cattle?' they say; verily he should make up a thousand days and nights and sacrifice. The days and nights are cattle; verily he gives support to cattle when born. He who desires offspring should offer a barren cow to the plants, the plants hinder him from offspring who being fit for offspring does not obtain offspring; the plants indeed destroy the pregnancy of that one which becomes barren, verily he has recourse to the plants with their own share; verily they from his own self beget him offspring; he obtains offspring. The plants are the waters, man is what is not; verily the waters give him being from non-existence; therefore they say, both he who knows thus and who (knows) not, 'The waters verily give being from non-existence.' He who desires prosperity should offer to Indra (a cow) which is barren after one birth; he is unborn who being fit for prosperity obtains it not; the (cow) became barren after bearing Indra,; verily he has recourse to Indra with his own share; verily he causes him to attain prosperity; he prospers. He should offer to Indra (the calf) through bearing which (the cow) became barren; that indeed is power (*indriyā*); verily straightway he obtains power. He whose ancestors and himself for three generations have not drunk Soma should offer (a bull) which has again been let loose to Indra and Agni; the Soma drinking of a Brahman is interrupted if his ancestors and himself for three generations have not drunk Soma; verily he has recourse to Indra and Agni with their own share; verily they bestow on him the drinking of Soma, the drinking of Soma comes to him. In that it is offered to Indra, the Soma drink is power; verily he wins power, the Soma-drink. In that it is offered to Agni, the Brahman is connected with Agni, verily he continues his own deity. It is let loose again, for his drinking of Soma is as it were let loose again; (verily it serves) for prosperity. When practising witchcraft, he should offer a hornless (beast) to Brahmaṇaspati; verily he has recourse to Brahmaṇaspati with his own share; verily he cuts him down to him; swiftly he reaches destruction. It is a hornless one; prosperity is razor-edged; in that it is hornless, (it serves) for prosperity. The sacrificial post is shaped like a wooden sword; the wooden sword is a thunderbolt; verily he hurls a thunderbolt against him; the strew is made of Śara grass; verily he crushes him; the kindling-wood is of Vibhīdaka; verily he splits him.

Mantra 2:1:6

He who desiring a village desires, 'May I be the back of my equals,' should offer to Bṛihaspati (a beast) with a white back; verily he has recourse to Bṛihaspati with his own share; verily he makes him to be the back of his peers; he becomes possessed of a village. It is with a white back, for it has Bṛihaspati as its deity; (verily it serves) for prosperity. He who desires food should offer a dark (beast) to Pūshan; Pūshan is food; verily he has recourse to Pūshan with his own share; verily he gives him food; he becomes an eater of food. It is dark, that is the form of food; (verily it serves) for prosperity. He who desires food should offer a dappled (beast) to the Marutas; the Marutas are food; verily he has recourse to the Marutas with their own share; verily they give him food; he becomes an eater of food. It is dappled; that is the form of food; (verily it serves) for prosperity. He who desires power should offer a ruddy (beast) to Indra; verily he has recourse to Indra with his own; verily he bestows power on him; he becomes possessed of power. It is ruddy and has eyebrows; that is the form of Indra; (verily it serves) for prosperity. He who desires gain should offer to Savitar a spotted (beast); Savitar is lord of production; verily he has recourse to Savitar with his own share; verily he produces gain for him, his offspring desire gifts. It is spotted, for it has Savitar as its deity; (verily it serves) for prosperity. He who desires food should offer to the All-Gods (a beast) of many forms; food is connected with the All-Gods; verily he has recourse to the All-Gods with their own share; verily they give him food; he becomes an eater of food. It is of many forms; food is of many forms; (verily it serves) for prosperity. He who desires a village should offer to the All-Gods (a beast) of many forms; his relatives are connected with the All-Gods; verily he has recourse to the All-Gods with their own share; verily they subdue his relations to him; he becomes possessed of a village. It is of many forms, for it is connected with many deities; (verily it serves) for prosperity. He who is long ill from an unknown cause should offer to Prajāpati (a beast) without horns; man is connected with Prajāpati; Prajāpati verily knows of him who is long ill from an unknown cause; verily he has recourse to Prajāpati with his own share; verily he releases him from this weariness. It is without horns, for it has Prajāpati as its deity; (verily it serves) for prosperity.

Mantra 2:1:7

The Vaṣhaṭ cry cleft the head of the Gāyatrī; the sap thereof fell away. Bṛihaspati seized it; it became a cow with a white back. The second (sap) which fell Mitra and Varuṇa seized; it became a cow of two forms. The third (sap) which fell the All-Gods seized; it became a cow of many forms. The fourth (sap) which fell entered the earth; Bṛihaspati seized it, (saying), 'Be this (mine) for enjoyment'; it became a bull and a cow. The blood which fell Rudra seized; it became a fierce red cow. He who desires splendour should offer to Bṛihaspati (a beast) with white back; verily he has recourse to Bṛihaspati with his own share; verily he bestows splendour upon him; he becomes resplendent. The cow is the sap of the metres; splendour is as it were sap; verily with the sap of the metres he wins the sap which is splendour. He who desires rain should offer to Mitra and Varuṇa (a cow) of two forms; the day is connected with Mitra, the night with Varuṇa; by day and night Parjanya rains; verily he has recourse to Mitra and Varuṇa with their own share; verily they by day and night make Parjanya rain for him. The cow is the sap of the metres, the rain indeed is as it were sap; verily by the sap of the metres he wins the sap which is rain. He who desires offspring should offer to Mitra and Varuṇa (a cow) of two forms; the day is connected with Mitra, the night with Varuṇa; by day and night indeed offspring are born; verily he has recourse to Mitra and Varuṇa with their own share; verily they by day and night beget offspring for him. The cow is the sap of the metres, offspring indeed are as it were sap; verily with the sap of the metres he wins the sap which is offspring. He who desires food should offer to the All-Gods (a cow) of many forms; food is connected with the All-Gods; verily he has recourse to the All-Gods with their own share; verily they give him food; he becomes an eater of food. The cow is the sap of the metres, food indeed is as it were sap; verily by the sap of the metres he wins the sap that is food. He who desires a village should offer to the All-Gods (a cow) of many forms; his relatives are connected with the All-Gods; verily he has recourse to the All-Gods with their own share; verily they subject his relatives to him; he becomes possessed of a village. The cow is the sap of the metres, relatives indeed are as it were sap; verily with the sap of the metres he wins the sap which is relatives. He who desires splendour should offer to Bṛihaspati a bull and a cow; verily he has recourse to Bṛihaspati with his own share; verily he bestows splendour on him; he becomes resplendent. The bull grazes at will, splendour indeed is as it were will; verily by will he wins will which is splendour. He who practises witchcraft should offer a red (cow) to Rudra; verily he has recourse to Rudra with his own share; verily he cuts him down to him; swiftly he reaches destruction; it is red, for it has Rudra as its deity; (verily it serves) for prosperity. The sacrificial post is shaped like the wooden sword, the wooden sword is a thunderbolt; verily he hurls a thunderbolt against him; the strew is made of Śara grass; verily he crushes him; the kindling-wood is of Vibhīdaka; verily he splits him.

Mantra 2:1:8

Yonder sun did not shine; the Gods desired an atonement for him; for him they offered a white cow to Sūrya; verily thereby they restored his brilliance. For him who desires splendour, he should offer this white cow to Sūrya; verily he has recourse to yonder sun with his own share; verily he bestows splendour upon him; he becomes resplendent. The sacrificial post is of Bilva wood. Whence yonder sun was born, thence the Bilva arose; verily he wins splendour with its place of origin. He who practises witchcraft should offer to Brahmaṇaspati (a cow) with brown ears; first he should make to Varuṇa an offering on ten potsherds; verily he causes Varuṇa to seize his foe and lays him low with the Brahman. It has brown ears; that is the symbol of the Brahman; (verily it serves) for prosperity. The sacrificial post is shaped like the wooden sword; the wooden sword is a thunderbolt; verily he hurls a thunderbolt against him; the strew is made of Śara grass; verily he crushes him; the kindling-wood is of Vibhīdaka; verily he splits him. He to whom the sacrifice does not come should offer a dwarf (beast) to Viṣhṇu; the sacrifice is Viṣhṇu; verily he has recourse to Viṣhṇu with his own share; verily he gives him the sacrifice, the sacrifice comes to him. It is a dwarf (beast), for it has Viṣhṇu for its deity; (verily it serves) for prosperity. He who desires cattle should offer to Tvaṣhṭar a horse; Tvaṣhṭar is the producer of pairings of animals; verily he has recourse to Tvaṣhṭar with his own share; verily he produces animals in pairs for him, for in him offspring and cattle have entered; verily also the male horse straightway wins offspring and cattle. He who when a contest is joined desires an agreement should offer to Mitra a white (beast); verily he has recourse to Mitra with his own share; verily he brings him into harmony with his friend. It is spacious; verily he encourages him. He who desires rain should offer to Prajāpati a black (beast), Prajāpati is the lord of rain; verily he has recourse to Prajāpati with his own share; verily he makes Parjanya rain for him. It is black, that is the form of rain; verily by its form he wins rain. It is spotted; verily he produces the lightning and makes rain for him. It has low horns; verily he brings down the rain for him.

Mantra 2:1:9

Food came not to Varuṇa when he had pressed. He beheld this black cow which is Varuṇa's; it he offered to its own deity; then food came to him. He to whom being fit for food food does not come should offer to Varuṇa this black cow; verily he has recourse to Varuṇa with his own form; verily he gives him food; he becomes an eater of food. It is black, for it has Varuṇa as its deity; (verily it serves) for prosperity. He who desires food should offer a white (beast) to Mitra and a black to Varuṇa at the union of the waters and the plants; the plants are connected with Mitra, and the waters with Varuṇa; on the sap of the water and of the plants do we live; verily lie has recourse to Mitra and Varuṇa with their own share; verily they give him food; he becomes an eater of food. He should offer at the union of the waters and of the plants, to attain both. The sacrificial post is bifurcate, for there are two deities; (verily it serves) for prosperity. He who is long ill should offer a white (beast) to Mitra, and a black to Varuṇa; in that one is offered to Mitra, by means of Mitra he appeases Varuṇa for him; in that one is offered to Varuṇa, straightway he sets him free from Varuṇa's noose; even if his life be gone, he yet lives. The Gods could not find prosperity; they saw it in the pair; they could not agree about it; the Aśvins said, 'Ours is it; do not claim it.' It became the Aśvins' only. He who desires prosperity should offer to the Aśvins a twin cow; verily he has recourse to the Aśvins with their own share; verily they bestow prosperity upon him; he prospers in offspring and cattle.

Mantra 2:1:10.

He who being a bad Brahman desires to drink Soma should offer to the Aśvins a dusky (beast) with spots on the forehead; the Aśvins were among the Gods those who did not drink Soma; they later acquired the drinking of Soma; the Aśvins are the Gods of the bad Brahman who desires to drink Soma; verily he has recourse to the Aśvins with their own share; verily they give to him the drinking of Soma; the drinking of Soma comes to him. In that it is dusky, verily he drives away the darkness from him. In that it has spots on the forehead, verily at the beginning he bestows brilliance on him. He whom men calumniate though he has slain no one should offer a Gayal to Vāyu; impure speech comes to him whom men calumniate though he has slain no one; the Gayal is neither a domestic nor a wild animal; he is neither in the village nor the forest whom men calumniate though he has slain no one; Vāyu is the purifier of the Gods; verily he has recourse to Vāyu with his own share; verily he purifies him. The dawn shines away from him and he enters the darkness, the evil, to whom when the litany to the Aśvins is being recited the sun becomes not visible; he should offer to Sūrya (a beast) of many forms; verily he has resort to yonder sun with its own share; verily it drives away the darkness, the evil, from him, the dawn shines upon him, he strikes away the darkness, the evil.

Mantra 2:1:11

a. Indra on all sides. ‖ *b.* On Indra men. ‖ *c.* O Marutas, what time from the sky. ‖ *d.* The protection which ye. ‖ *e.* In contests we invoke Indra, swift to hear, | The divine folk working good, freeing from distress, | Agni, Mitra, Varuṇa, for gain, Bhaga, | Sky and earth, the Marutas for welfare. ‖ *f.* May the moving one who strikes at morning delight us; | May Vāta delight us, pourer of waters; | Indra and Parvata quicken us; | May the All-Gods vouchsafe us this. ‖ *g.* I hail the dear names of yon impetuous ones, | That, O Marutas, calling they may rejoice. ‖ *h.* For glory they are wreathed in flames, | In the rays (of the sun), adorned with rings they (are accompanied) with singers; | They wearing daggers, impetuous, fearless, | Here found the dear home of the Marutas. ‖ *i.* First let Agni with the Vasus aid us; | Let Soma with the Rudras protect (us); | Let Indra with the Marutas act in due course; | Let Varuṇa with the Ādityas quicken us.' ‖ *k.* God Agni with the Vasus, | Soma with the dread forms, | Indra with the Marutas, worthy of sacrifice, | Varuṇa with the Ādityas hath been in harmony with us. ‖ *l.* As the Ādityas are united with the Vasus, | The Rudras with the Marutas, | So, O thou of three names, | May the All-Gods without anger be of one mind. ‖ *m.* He in whose presence wheresoever | Men rejoice in the dwellings of men, | Whom in honour they kindle, | Whom together they produce. ‖ *n.* When we offer food, | The oblations of men, | He by the might of his glory, | Graspeth the reins of sacred law. ‖ *o.* The sacrifice seeketh the goodwill of the Gods; | Be kindly, O ye Ādityas; | Make your loving kindness turn (to us), | Which shall more plenteously deliver us from distress. ‖ *p.* Pure he dwelleth, undeceived, | Among waters rich in grass, waxing old with noble sons; | None slayeth him from near or from afar, | Who is in the guidance of the Ādityas ‖ *q.* Ye Ādityas support the world, | Gods, guardians of all the universe, | Far-seeing, guarding the holy, | Righteous, enacting debts. ‖ *r.* Three earths they support, and three skies; | Three rules are in their ordinance; | Through sacred law great is your mightiness, O Ādityas; | Sweet is that, O Aryaman, O Mitra, O Varuṇa ‖ *s.* Let us make supplication | To those heroes, the Ādityas, | The tender, for help. ‖ *t.* Nor right is visible, nor left; | Nor the east, O Ādityas, nor the west; | Despite my feeble mind, O Vasus, | Led by you, may I attain the light without fear. ‖ *u.* With the most recent help of the Ādityas, | With their most present succour, may we be united; | May the mighty ones, hearkening, establish this sacrifice | For release from sin, for freedom. ‖ *v.* Hear my cry, O Varuṇa, | And be merciful this day; | Seeking for help I call on thee. ‖ *w.* I implore this of thee, praising thee with my hymn; | The sacrificer seeketh this with his offerings; | Be here, not angry, O Varuṇa; | O wide ruler, strike not away our life.

Prapāṭhaka 2.

The Special Sacrifices

Mantra 2:2:1

Prajāpati created offspring. On their creation Indra and Agni hid them away. Prajāpati reflected, 'Indra and Agni have hidden away from me offspring.' He then perceived this offering to Indra and Agni on eleven potsherds, and offered it, and the two (Gods) restored offspring to him. Indra and Agni indeed conceal his offspring, who being fit for offspring, yet obtains not offspring; so let a man who desires offspring offer a sacrifice to Indra, and Agni on eleven potsherds. Verily Indra and Agni he has recourse to with their own share; verily they make manifest offspring to him, he obtains offspring. | He should make an offering to Indra and Agni on eleven potsherds who has a dispute about a field or with his neighbours. Verily Indra and Agni he has recourse to with their own share, by means of them he over powers the power and strength of his rival, he overcomes the evil foe. Now power and strength depart from him who advances to battle; let him who is about to advance to battle offer to Indra and Agni an offering on eleven potsherds. Verily Indra and Agni he has recourse to with their own share; verily they two place power and strength in him; with power and strength he approaches the battle and conquers in it. Now power and strength is he bereft of who wins a battle; let him who has won a battle make an offering to Indra and Agni on eleven potsherds. Verily Indra and Agni he has recourse to with their own share; verily they two place power and strength in him, he is not bereft of power and strength. Now power and strength depart from him who goes to the assembly; let him who is about to go to the assembly make an offering to Indra and Agni on eleven potsherds. Verily Indra and Agni he has recourse to with their own share; verily they two place power and strength in him, with power and strength he goes to the assembly. Let him next offer an oblation to Pūṣhan. Pūṣhan is the giver of power and strength, verily Pūṣhan he has recourse to with his own share; verily he gives to him power and strength. When he has gone to the assembly he should offer an oblation to Kṣhetrapati; Kṣhetrapati is this (earth); verily on this earth he takes firm root. Thereafter let him make the offering to Indra and Agni on eleven potsherds; verily taking stand on this earth he next places power and strength in his body.

Mantra 2:2:2

To Agni, maker of paths, he should offer a cake on eight potsherds who being a sacrificer at full and new moon passes over the offering either at the new or the full moon; he wanders from the path on a trackless way who being a sacrificer at new and full moon passes over the offering either at the new or the full moon; verily he has recourse to Agni with his own share; verily he leads him to the path from the trackless way. A draught ox is the sacrificial fee, for it is the drawer; (verily it serves) for prosperity. To Agni, lord of vows he should offer a cake on eight potsherds, who having established a sacred firebreaks his vow as it were; verily he has recourse to Agni, lord of vows, with his own share; verily he makes good his vow for him; he becomes a keeper of vows. To Agni, slayer of Rākṣhasas, he should offer a cake on eight potsherds, whom Rākṣhasas infest; verily he has recourse to Agni, slayer of Rākṣhasas, with his own share; verily he smites away the Rākṣhasas from him. He should offer at night, for at night the Rākṣhasas are active; verily he smites them when active; he should offer in (a place) which is closed in, to prevent the Rākṣhasas entering; the Yājyā, and the Anuvākyā are Rakṣhas-slaying, to lay low the Rākṣhasas To Agni with the Rudras he should offer a cake on eight potsherds when he practises witchcraft; Rudra is his dread form; verily he cuts him down to him; swiftly he reaches misfortune. He whose cows or men perish or who is afraid should offer to Agni, the fragrant, a cake on eight potsherds; the fragrant is his healing form; verily by it he applies healing to him; it is offered to the fragrant, to smite away the fetid odour. When a battle is joined he should offer a cake on eight potsherds to Agni, the burnt; verily by his own share he pacifies him and indicates his foes; whomsoever of those near (him) they pierce, he lives; whomsoever of the foe, he dies; he wins that battle. He loves to frequent those whose oldest and youngest die continuously, for the human sacrifice is dearest to him, lie should offer to Agni, the burnt, a cake on eight potsherds; verily with his own share he pacifies him, and none other of them dies before his day. He loves to frequent the house of him whose house he burns; he should offer a cake on eight potsherds to Agni, the burnt; verily he pacifies him with his own share, and he burns not his house again.

Mantra 2:2:3

He who does not attain his desires should offer a cake on eight potsherds to Agni as desire; verily he has recourse to Agni as desire with his own share; verily he unites him with his desire; his desire comes to him. He who has a dispute over a field or with his relatives should offer a cake on eight potsherds to Agni, the youngest; verily he has recourse to Agni, the youngest, with his own share; verily thereby he appropriates the power and strength of his foe; he overcomes the evil foe. He against whom witchcraft is practised should offer a cake on eight potsherds to Agni, the youngest; verily he has recourse to Agni, the youngest, with his own share; verily he drives away the Rākṣhasas from him; he who practises witchcraft does not lay him low. He who desires, 'May I live all my days,' should offer a cake on eight potsherds to Agni of life; verily he has recourse to Agni of life with his own share; verily he bestows life upon him; he lives all his days. He who desires prosperity should offer a cake on eight potsherds to Agni, the all-knower; verily he has recourse to Agni, the all-knower, with his own share; verily he makes him attain prosperity; he prospers. He who desires radiance should offer a cake on eight potsherds to Agni, the radiant; verily he has recourse to Agni, the radiant, with his own share; verily he bestows radiance on him; he is radiant. He who desires brilliance should offer a cake on eight potsherds to Agni, the brilliant; verily he has recourse to Agni, the brilliant, with his own share; verily he bestows brilliance upon him; he becomes brilliant. He who seeks to be strong should offer a cake on eight potsherds to Agni, the strong; verily he has recourse to Agni, the strong, with his own share; verily thereby he is strong who seeks to be strong.

Mantra 2:2:4

He who desires, 'May I possess food,' should offer to Agni, possessor of food, a cake on eight potsherds; verily he has recourse to Agni, possessor of food, with his own share; verily he makes him to possess food; he becomes a possessor of food. He who desires, 'May I be an eater of food,' should offer a cake on eight potsherds to Agni, eater of food; verily he has recourse to Agni, eater of food, with his own share; verily he makes him an eater of food; he becomes an eater of food. He who desires, 'May I be a lord of food,' should offer to Agni, lord of food, a cake on eight potsherds; verily he has recourse to Agni, lord of food, with his own share; verily he makes him a lord of food; he becomes a lord of food. He who is long ill should offer a cake on eight potsherds to Agni, the purifying, to Agni, the purifier, to Agni, the pure; in that he offers to Agni, the purifying, thereby he bestows health upon him; in that (he offers) to Agni, the purifier, thereby he bestows speech upon him; in that (he offers) to Agni, the pure, thereby he bestows life upon him; even if his life is gone, he yet lives. He who desires sight should make the same offering; in that he offers to Agni, the purifying, he thereby bestows breath upon him; in that (he offers) to Agni, the purifier, thereby he bestows speech upon him; in that (he offers) to Agni, the pure, thereby he bestows sight upon him; even if he is blind, he yet sees. He who desires offspring should offer a cake on eight potsherds to Agni with sons, and a cake on eleven potsherds to Indra, who has sons; verily Agni begets offspring for him and Indra makes it grow. He who desires, 'May I be possessed of sap,' should offer an oblation cooked in goat's milk to Agni, full of sap; verily he has recourse to Agni, full of sap, with his own share; verily he makes him possessed of sap; he becomes possessed of sap. It is cooked in goat's milk; the she-goat is connected with Agni; verily straightway he wins sap. He who desires, 'May I be possessed of wealth,' should offer a cake on eight potsherds to Agni, possessed of wealth; verily he has recourse to Agni, possessed of wealth, with his own share, and he makes him possessed of wealth; he becomes possessed of wealth. When battle is joined, he should offer a cake on eight potsherds to Agni, the racer, for a race he desires to run, who is fain to conquer in battle; Agni of the Gods is the racer; verily he has recourse to Agni with his own share; he runs the race, he slays the foe, he conquers in the battle, and like Agni he is not to be overcome. He for whom fire they take out again (from the Gārhapatya fire) to place on the Āhavanīya should offer a cake on eight potsherds to Agni with Agni; one of these (fires) has a portion assigned, one has not a portion assigned; they uniting overpower the sacrificer, and he is liable to suffer ruin; in that he offers to Agni with Agni, he appeases him with his own share; the sacrificer does not suffer ruin. He whose fire goes out after it has been taken out (from the Gārhapatya) before the Agnihotra has been offered should offer a cake on eight potsherds to Agni with light; (they say), 'Should another be taken out, after lighting up (from the Gārhapatya)'? That should not be done. Since the former is taken out for a definite share, how should another be taken out for (it)? He should deposit the extinguished embers and produce fire by friction, (with the words), 'Hence first was Agni born, from his own womb, the all-knower; he with Gāyatrī, Trishṭubh, Jagatī shall bear the oblation to the Gods, the wise ones'; with the metres he begets him from his own womb; 'this is the fire,' they say, 'what falls from it is light'; in that he offers to Agni with light, he wins the light which has fallen from it.

Mantra 2:2:5

He who is calumniated should offer on twelve potsherds to Vaiśvānara, an oblation to Varuṇa, and an oblation to Dadhikrāvan; in that there is (an offering) on twelve potsherds to Vaiśvānara, and Agni Vaiśvānara is the year; verily he satisfies him with the year, he smites off the evil hue; by (the offering) to Varuṇa he frees him from the noose of Varuṇa; by Dadhikrāvan he purifies him. The sacrificial fee is gold; gold is a purifier; verily he purifies him; his food becomes fit to eat. The same (offering) he should make who desires offspring; the year unpropitiated burns up the womb of offspring, of cattle, for him who being fit for offspring does not obtain offspring; in that there is (an offering) on twelve potsherds for Vaiśvānara, and Agni Vaiśvānara is the year; verily he propitiates the year with its own share; it propitiated begets offspring for him from his own womb; by (the offering) to Varuṇa he frees him from the noose of Varuṇa; by Dadhikrāvan he purifies him. The sacrificial fee is gold; gold is a purifier; verily he purifies him; he obtains offspring. When a son is born he should offer on twelve potsherds to Vaiśvānara; in that there is (an offering) on eight potsherds, he purifies him with the Gāyatrī, with splendour; in that there is (an offering) on nine potsherds, he bestows brilliance upon him with the Trivṛit (Stoma); in that there is (an offering) on ten potsherds, he bestows proper food upon him with the Virāj; in that there is (an offering) on eleven potsherds, he bestows power upon him with the Trishṭubh; in that there is (an offering) on twelve potsherds, he bestows cattle upon him with the Jagatī; he upon whose birth he offers this sacrifice becomes pure, brilliant, an eater of food, powerful, possessed of cattle. He is cut off from the world of heaven who, being a sacrificer at new and full moon, the sacrifice either at the new or the full moon omits, for the new and full moon offerings are made for the world of heaven; if he has omitted the sacrifice either at the new or the full moon, he should offer to Vaiśvānara on twelve potsherds; Agni Vaiśvānara is the year; verily he delights the year; verily also he brings up the year for him for the winning of the world of heaven; verily also grasping the deities he goes to the world of heaven. He who removes the fire is the slayer of the hero among the Gods; formerly righteous Brahmans did not eat his food; he should offer to Agni on eight potsherds, to Vaiśvānara on twelve potsherds, when he is about to remove the fire; in that there is (an offering) on eight potsherds, the Gāyatrī has eight syllables, Agni is connected with the Gāyatrī; to Agni in his full extent he shows hospitality; verily also that is as when one makes preparation for a man about to go to (another) people. (The offering) to Vaiśvānara is on twelve potsherds; the year has twelve months; the birthplace of Agni is the year; verily he makes him go to his own birth place; his food becomes fit to eat. He who desires a village should offer on twelve potsherds to Vaiśvānara, and to the Marutas on seven potsherds. (the offering) to Vaiśvānara he places on the Āhavanīya, that to the Marutas on the Gārhapatya, for the avoidance of confusion. (The offering) to Vaiśvānara is on twelve potsherds; the year has twelve months; verily by the year he removes his rivals for him; there is one to the Marutas; the Marutas are the subject class among the Gods; verily by the subjects among the Gods he wins for him the subjects among men; (the offering) is on seven potsherds; the Marutas are in seven troops; verily in troops he wins his rivals for him; he deposits (the offering) when (the verses) are being repeated; verily he makes the people follow him.

Mantra 2:2:6

He who is about to engage in a conflict should offer an oblation to Aditi; Aditi is this (earth); verily in time gone by they were used to rest upon it. He who has come to the place should offer to Vaiśvānara on twelve potsherds; Agni Vaiśvānara is the year, the place of the Gods is the year; from that place the Gods drove the Asuras in defeat; in that he offers to Vaiśvānara on twelve potsherds, he strives for the abode of the Gods; he wins this conflict. Those two wipe (their sin) off upon him who eats the food of two enemies; he who has eaten the food of two enemies should offer to Vaiśvānara on twelve potsherds; Agni Vaiśvānara is the year; verily he eats what the year has made sweet; those two do not wipe (their sin) off upon him. For the year these two make compact who make compact; him of them who first acts with treachery Varuṇa seizes; he who of two who have made compact first shows treachery should offer on twelve potsherds to Vaiśvānara; Agni Vaiśvānara is the year; verily having obtained the year thereafter he acts with treachery against one who has lost Varuṇa's protection; Varuṇa does not seize him. The nature of the sheep he accepts who accepts a sheep; having accepted a sheep he should offer to Vaiśvānara, Agni Vaiśvānara is the year; verily he accepts (the ewe) made suitable by the year; he does not accept the nature of the sheep. A measure of himself he obtains who accepts (an animal) with teeth in both jaws, whether horse or man; he who has accepted (an animal) with teeth in both jaws should offer on twelve potsherds to Vaiśvānara; Agni Vaiśvānara is the year; verily he accepts it made suitable by the year; he does not obtain a measure of himself. He who is eager to win wealth should offer to Vaiśvānara on twelve potsherds; Agni Vaiśvānara is the year; when a man for a year goes about among folk he becomes worthy of wealth. In that he offers to Vaiśvānara on twelve potsherds, he moves towards wealth gained by the year: people are fain to give him gifts. He, who having yoked the year, does not let it go, becomes without support; after his return he should offer the same sacrifice to Vaiśvānara; (the year) which he yokes he lets go with its own share, for support; the rope with which he drives the last of his cows he should cast against his foe; verily he casts misfortune upon him.

Mantra 2:2:7

He who desires cattle should offer an oblation to Indra; cattle are connected with Indra; verily he has recourse to Indra with his own share; verily he gives him cattle; verily he becomes possessed of cattle; it is an oblation; verily for him from his own place of birth he produces cattle. He who desires cattle should offer a cake on eleven potsherds to Indra, the powerful; cattle are power; verily he has recourse to Indra, the powerful, with his own share; he gives him power and cattle; verily he becomes possessed of cattle. He who desires splendour should offer a cake on eleven potsherds to Indra, possessed of heat; heat is splendour; verily he has recourse to Indra with his own share; he bestows upon him splendour, verily he becomes resplendent. He who desires food should offer a cake on eleven potsherds to Indra of the hymn; the hymn is the food of the Gods; verily he has recourse to Indra of the hymn with his own share; he gives him food; verily he becomes an eater of food. He who desires prosperity should offer a cake on eleven potsherds to Indra, possessed of heat, and to Indra, the powerful, and to Indra of the hymn; in that he offers to Indra, possessed of heat, he thereby makes his head; in that (he offers) to Indra, the powerful, he thereby makes his body; in that (he offers) to Indra of the hymn, he becoming prosperous finds support in food; verily he prospers. He who is seized by misfortune should offer a cake on eleven potsherds to Indra, deliverer from tribulation, tribulation is misfortune; verily he has recourse to Indra, deliverer from tribulation, with his own share; verily he delivers him from the misfortune, from tribulation. He whom enemies menace or invade his realms should offer a cake on eleven potsherds to Indra, repeller of foes; verily he has recourse to Indra, repeller of foes, with his own share; verily he repels foes from him. He who is bound or beset should offer a cake on eleven potsherds to Indra, the protector; verily he has recourse to Indra, the protector, with his own share; verily he protects him. He to whom the great sacrifice does not resort should offer a cake on eleven potsherds to Indra, of the Arka and the Aśvamedha; the Arka and the Aśvamedha are the two end bodies of the great sacrifice; verily he has recourse to Indra, of the Arka and the Aśvamedha, with his own share; verily he moves for him the great sacrifice from the ends, and the great sacrifice resorts to him.

Mantra 2:2:8

He who desires a village should offer a cake on eleven potsherds to Indra, who goes straight forward; verily he has recourse to Indra, who goes straight forward, with his own share; verily he makes his followers obedient to him; he becomes possessed of a village. He whose dart is not as it were sharp should offer an oblation to Indrāṇī; the deity of the arrow is Indrāṇī; verily he has recourse to Indrāṇī with her own share; she sharpens his arrow. Balbaja grass he should fasten to the kindling-stick; where the cow being covered made water, thence grew the Balbaja; verily making him follow the way of the cows he causes him to obtain cows. To Indra, the angry, the wise, he should offer a cake on eleven potsherds when battle is joined; with power, with anger, and with wisdom one wins the battle; verily he has recourse to Indra, the angry, the wise, with his own share; verily he bestows upon him power, anger, and mind; he wins the battle. The same offering should he make whose mind is affected and who as it were injures himself, for these are departed from him; verily he whose mind is affected and who injures himself has recourse to Indra, the angry, the wise, with his own share; verily he bestows upon him power, anger, and wisdom; his mind is not affected and he does not injure himself. He who desires, 'May people be fain to give to me,' should offer a cake on eleven potsherds to Indra, the giver; verily he has recourse to Indra, the giver, with his own share; verily he makes people fain to give to him; people become fain to give to him. He upon whom what is as it were ready to be given is not bestowed should offer a cake on eleven potsherds to Indra, the bestower; verily he has recourse to Indra, the bestower, with his own share; verily he makes (men) bestow upon him. He who has been expelled or is being expelled should offer a cake on eleven potsherds to Indra, the good protector; verily he has recourse to Indra, the good protector, with his own share; verily he protects him; he becomes unexpellable. Indra was equal with the Gods, he did not attain distinction, he had recourse to Prajāpati, for him, he offered this (offering) to Indra on eleven potsherds, and thereby he bestowed power upon him; he makes the Yājyā and the Puronuvākyā of the Śakvarī (metre); the Śakvarī is the thunderbolt, the thunderbolt kindled him for prosperity, he became prosperous; having become prosperous, be became afraid, (thinking) 'It shall burn me'; he had recourse again to Prajāpati; Prajāpati from the Śakvarī fashioned the (verse containing the word) 'rich,' for atonement, to prevent burning. For him who being fit for prosperity is equal with his fellows he should offer this (offering) for Indra on eleven potsherds; verily he has recourse to Indra with his own share; verily he bestows power upon him. The (verse containing the word) 'rich' is the Puronuvākyā, for atonement, to prevent burning; the Yājyā is in the Śakvarī (metre), the Śakvarī is the thunderbolt, the thunderbolt kindles him for prosperity, he becomes prosperous.

Mantra 2:2:9

He who practises witchcraft should offer to Agni and Vishṇu on eleven potsherds; Sarasvatī should have a portion of the butter, and to Bṛihaspati an oblation (be offered); in that there is (an offering) on eleven potsherds to Agni and Vishṇu, and all the Gods are Agni and the sacrifice is Vishṇu, with all the Gods and the sacrifice be practises witchcraft against him; Sarasvatī has a portion of the butter; Sarasvatī is speech; verily with speech he practises against him; the oblation is Bṛihaspati's, Bṛihaspati is the holy power (Brahman) of the Gods; verily with the holy power (Brahman) he practises against him. Him who practises witchcraft they practise then against; he should double each of the Puronuvākyās, for special employment. With the same (offering) should he sacrifice who is practised against; verily he sets Gods against Gods, the sacrifice against the sacrifice, speech against speech, the Brahman against the Brahman; between the Gods and the sacrifice he creeps along; from no quarter is be injured; he who practises against him does not lay him low. He to whom the sacrifice does not resort should offer on eleven potsherds to Agni and Vishṇu; all the Gods are Agni, the sacrifice is Vishṇu; verily he has recourse to Agni and Vishṇu with their own share; verily they give him the sacrifice; the sacrifice resorts to him. He who desires sight should offer an oblation in ghee to Agni and Vishṇu by the eye of Agni men see, (by the eye) of the sacrifice the Gods (see) verily he has recourse to Agni and Vishṇu with their own share; verily they bestow sight upon him; he becomes possessed of sight. The butter is the seed of the cow, the rice grain of the ox; verily from the pair he produces for him sight. The oblation is (made) in ghee, ghee is brilliance, sight is brilliance; verily by brilliance he wins for him brilliance and sight. His foe in sacrificing gains the power and strength of him who sacrifices not; when his foe is sacrificing he should offer against him a sort of sacrifice; he does not then gain his power and strength. He should offer before speech is uttered; all the speech of his foe he thus gains unuttered, and his speech as uttered other speeches follow after; they bestow upon the sacrificer power and strength. Just at the time of the morning pressing he should offer on eight potsherds to Agni and Vishṇu; Sarasvatī should have a share of the butter, and to Bṛihaspati an oblation (be offered); in that it is (offered) on eight potsherds, and the Gāyatrī has eight syllables, and the morning pressing is connected with the Gāyatrī, he obtains thereby the morning pressing. Just at the time of the midday pressing he should offer on eleven potsherds to Agni and Vishṇu; Sarasvatī should have a portion of the butter and to Bṛihaspati an oblation (be offered); in that (the offering) is on eleven potsherds, and the Trishṭubh has eleven syllables, and the midday pressing is connected with the Trishṭubh, he obtains thereby the midday pressing. Just at the time of the third pressing he should offer to Agni and Vishṇu on twelve potsherds; Sarasvatī should have a share of the butter, and to Bṛihaspati the oblation (be offered); in that (the offering) is on twelve potsherds, and the Jagatī has twelve syllables, and the third pressing is connected with the Jagatī, he obtains thereby the third pressing. Verily he sets Gods against Gods, the sacrifice against the sacrifice, speech against speech, the Brahman against the Brahman; verily by means of the potsherds he makes up the metres, by means of the cakes the pressings. At the time of the (offering of the) cow, he should offer on one potsherd to Mitra and Varuṇa, this (offering) corresponds to his foe's cow which is to be slaughtered; his (offering) is on one potsherd, for he cannot obtain the animal (offering) by means of (many) potsherds.

Mantra 2:2:10.

Yonder sun did not shine, the Gods sought an atonement for him, for him they offered this oblation to Soma and Rudra: verily thereby they bestowed brightness upon him. If he desires to become resplendent, he should offer for him this oblation to Soma and Rudra; verily he has recourse to Soma and Rudra with their own portion; verily they bestow upon him splendour; he becomes resplendent. He should offer on the full moon day of the month Tishya; Tishya is Rudra, the full moon is Soma; verily straightway he wins splendour. He makes him sacrifice on an enclosed (altar), to acquire splendour. The butter is churned from milk of a white (cow) with a white calf; butter is used for the sprinkling, and they purify themselves with butter; verily he produces whatever splendour exists. 'Too much splendour is produced,' they say, 'he is liable to become a leper'; he should insert the verses of Manu's; whatever Manu said is medicine; verily he makes medicine for him. If he fear, 'I shall become a leper,' he should offer an oblation to Soma and Pūshan; man has Soma as his deity, cattle are connected with Pūshan; verily he makes him a skin by means of his own deity and cattle; he does not become a leper. He who desires offspring should offer an oblation to Soma and Rudra; Soma is the bestower of seed, Agni is the begetter of offspring; verily Soma bestows on him seed, Agni begets offspring; he obtains offspring. He who practises witchcraft should offer an oblation to Soma and Rudra; man has Soma as his deity, Agni is this Rudra; verily ransoming him from his own deity he entrusts him to Rudra; swiftly he attains ruin. He who is long ill should offer an oblation to Soma and Rudra; the sap of him who is long ill goes to Soma, the body to Agni; verily from Soma he ransoms his sap, from Agni his body; even if his life be gone, he yet lives. The Hotar loosens him that is swallowed by Soma and Rudra and he is liable to be ruined; an ox must be given by the Hotar; the ox is a carrier, the Hotar is a carrier; verily he saves himself as a carrier by means of a carrier. He who desires, 'In his own abode may I produce a foe for him,' should offer an oblation to Soma and Rudra; selecting an altar he should dig up half, and half not, spread half the strew, and half not, pile on half the kindling-wood and half not; verily in his own abode he produces a foe for him.

Mantra 2:2:11

He who desires a village should offer on eleven potsherds to Indra, on seven potsherds to the Marutas; verily he has recourse to Indra and the Marutas with their own share; verily they make his fellows subject to him; he becomes possessed of a village. He places (the offering) for Indra on the Āhavanīya, that for the Marutas on the Gārhapatya, for the prevention of confusion. (The offering) for the Marutas is on seven potsherds; the Marutas are in seven troops; verily by troops he wins his fellows for him. He places (it) down when the recitation is proceeding; verily he makes the people obedient to him. The same offering should he make who desires, 'May I cause strife between the ruling class and the people.' As he cuts off from Indra's (cake), he should say, 'Do thou recite for Indra'; having directed (the Agnīdh) to utter the Śraushaṭ call, he should say, 'Utter the Yājyā, for the Marutas'; as he cuts off from the Marutas' cake, he should say, 'Do thou recite for the Marutas'; having directed (the Agnīdh), he should say, 'Utter the Yājyā for Indra'; verily he produces strife between them for their shares, and they keep piercing each other. The same offering should he make who desires, 'May they be at unity.' According to each deity should he cut off and according to each utter the Yājyā; verily he arranges them in due order with their portions; they are at unity. He who desires a village should offer on eleven potsherds to Indra, and on twelve potsherds to the All-Gods; verily he has recourse to Indra and the All-Gods with their own share; verily they subject his fellows to him; he becomes possessed of a village. Having cut off from Indra's (cake) he should cut off from the All-Gods, and then from Indra's; verily with power (*indriyena*) he surrounds his fellows on both sides. The sacrificial fee is a garment with a fringe, for the delectation of his fellows. He who desires a village should offer to the Marutas an oblation of panic seed in the milk of a speckled (cow); from the milk of a speckled (cow) were the Marutas born, of the speckled (cow) panic seed; his fellows have the Marutas for their deity; verily he has recourse to the Marutas with their own share; verily they subject his fellows to him; he becomes possessed of a village. The Yājyā and the Anuvākyā contain the word 'dear'; verily he makes him dear to his fellows; the Puronuvākyā, has two feet; verily he wins bipeds; the Yājyā has four feet; verily he wins quadrupeds. The Gods and the Asuras were in conflict; the Gods were mutually at variance; unwilling to accept the pre-eminence of another they went apart in four bodies, Agni with the Vasus, Soma with the Rudras, Indra with the Marutas, Varuṇa with the Ādityas Indra had recourse to Prajāpati; he made him sacrifice with the verse for harmony; to Agni with the Vasus he offered a cake on eight potsherds, to Soma with the Rudras an oblation, to Indra with the Marutas a cake on eleven potsherds, to Varuṇa with the Ādityas an oblation; then indeed the Gods agreed to recognize Indra's pre-eminence. Him who is mutually at variance with his fellows he should cause to offer with the verse for harmony; he should offer to Agni with the Vasus a cake on eight potsherds, to Soma with the Rudras an oblation, to Indra with the Marutas a cake on eleven potsherds, to Varuṇa with the Ādityas an oblation; so him becoming Indra his fellows recognize as superior; he becomes the best of his fellows.

Mantra 2:2:12

a. The golden germ. ‖ *b.* When the waters. ‖ *c.* O Prajāpati ‖ *d.* He as a son knoweth the father, he the mother, | He is a son, he is of generous returns; | He hath enveloped the sky, the atmosphere, he the heaven; | He hath become all the worlds, he hath come to be. ‖ *e.* Up that. ‖ *f.* The radiant. ‖ *g.* Thou from of old with thy new glory, | O Agni, with thy companion light, | Hast mightily outstretched. ‖ *h.* He doth put down the wise contrivings of every worshipper; | Bearing in his arm many a manly deed; | Agni hath become the lord of riches, | Making ever all immortal things. ‖ *i.* To help us I summon | The golden-handed Savitar; | He as a God knoweth the place. ‖ *k.* Prosperity today, O Savitar prosperity tomorrow, | Day by day prosperity mayst thou procure for us; | Through this prayer may we win the prosperity | Of many a prosperous dwelling, O God. ‖ *l.* O earth, thou bearest | The weight of the mountains, | Thou that dost, O great earth, | With thy hills, quicken with thy might. ‖ *m.* The songs salute thee, | Thee that extendest far, each day, | Thee that, O bright one, dost shoot forward | The seed like great riches. ‖ *n.* May I be in companionship with the friend pleasant within, | Who being drunk shall not harm me, O thou of the tawny steeds; | This Soma that hath been deposited within us, | For that I go to Indra to prolong (my life). ‖ *o.* Giving spirit when drunken, with swift onset, | Impetuous, strong, bearing arrows, with the residue is Soma; | All plants and trees deceived not aforetime | As substitutes Indra. ‖ *p.* Soma the righteous as pressed becometh visible, | Jamadagni singing the hymn to Indra; | Thou art the mighty restrainer of impetuous might; | Ward it off and strengthen the support for the singer. ‖ *q.* In unison men that make prayers offer to thee this prayer | That giveth delight and invigoration; | When the hymn with the radiance of Soma shall speed forth, | Then shall Indra show his might in the contests. ‖ *r.* From the mouth to thee, O Vishṇu, do I utter the Vashaṭ call; | Do thou accept my oblation, O Śipivishṭa; | Let my fair hymns of praise cause thee to wax great; | Do ye protect us ever with blessings. ‖ *s.* That name of thee, the noble, today I celebrate, | O Śipivishṭa, knowing the ways; | I, the weaker, sing thee the strong, | That rulest beyond this region.' ‖ *t.* What was there to be disclosed in thee, O Vishṇu, | What time thou didst declare, 'I am Śipivishṭa'? | Conceal not from us that form of thine | What time thou dost change thy shape in battle. ‖ *u.* O Agni, give to the giver | Wealth of heroes in abundance; | Quicken us to richness in sons. ‖ *v.* Give to us, O Agni, a hundred, give a thousandfold; | Like doors disclose for us booty for renown; | Make with the prayer sky and earth propitious; | Like bright heaven the dawns have shone forth. ‖ *w*. Agni give wealth that decketh the hero; | Agni the Ṛishi who winneth thousands; | Agni hath placed the oblation in the sky; | In many a place are the abodes of Agni. ‖ *x*. Destroy us not. ‖ *y*. Bring to us. ‖ *z*. Thy body is faultless, | Like ghee purified, like pure gold | That of thine shineth like an ornament, O thou powerful one. ‖ *aa*. O bright one, in thy mouth thou cookest | Both ladles (full) of butter; | Do thou make us full | For our hymns, O lord of strength; | Do thou bear food to the praisers. ‖ *bb*. O Vāyu, a hundred of bay (steeds) | Worthy of nourishment do thou yoke; | Or let the chariot of thee that hast a thousand (steeds) | Come with might. ‖ *cc*. The teams wherewith thou comest to the giver, | O Vāyu, for seeking in the house, | Grant us wealth rich in enjoyment, | And a treasure of heroes, of horses, of cows. ‖ *dd*. Rich banquets be ours with Indra, | With mighty strength, | Wherewith fed we may rejoice. ‖ *ee*. Rich should he be, the praiser | Of a generous and wealthy one like thee; | (Famed) be (the praiser) of thee that art famed, O thou with the bays.

Prapāṭhaka 3.

The Special Sacrifices (continued)

Mantra 2:3:1

He who desires prosperity should offer to the Ādityas, giving prosperity; it is the Ādityas who repel from prosperity him who being fit for prosperity does not obtain prosperity; verily he has recourse to the Ādityas, giving prosperity, with their own share; verily they make him attain prosperity; he becomes prosperous. He who has been expelled or is being expelled should offer an oblation to the Ādityas, the sustainers; the Ādityas are the expellers, the Ādityas are the procurers; verily he has recourse to the Ādityas, the sustainers with their own share; verily they support him in the people; he is unexpellable. 'O Aditi, do thou confirm,' (with these words) be who is being expelled should take the foot (dust) of him (who is expelling him); Aditi is this (earth); verily she confirms the kingdom for him; 'Be the blessing fulfilled,' he says; verily he makes the blessing come true; 'Mind here,' he says; verily he makes the people of one mind with him; 'Come hither, O ye Marutas rich in dew, with this lord of the people against yon king,' he says; the people are connected with the Marutas, the lord of the people is the highest; verily he unites him with the people and the realm. From the house of a village judge further on he should take rice; he should separate out the white and the black; of the white he should offer an oblation to the Ādityas; the people have the Ādityas for their deity; verily he attains the people; 'The people he has attained, the realm he has not attained,' they say; of the dark ones he should offer an oblation to Varuṇa; the realm is connected with Varuṇa; verily he attains both the people and the realm. Should he not attain (them), he should offer (saying), 'To the Ādityas this portion I offer to attain the people N. N. for N. N.'; verily the Ādityas desiring the portion make him attain the people. Should he not attain (them), he should knock in seven pegs of Aśvattha wood in the middle shaft, (saying), 'Here do I bind the Ādityas to attain the people N. N. from N. N.'; verily the Ādityas, their heroes bound, make him attain the people. Should he not attain (them), he should offer this oblation to the Ādityas and attach pegs to the kindling-wood; verily he attains what cannot be taken away. (The pegs) are of Aśvattha wood; the Aśvattha is the might of the Marutas; verily with might he attains the people; seven are they, the Marutas are in seven troops; verily in troops he attains the people.

Mantra 2:3:2

The Gods were afraid of death; they had recourse to Prajāpati for them he offered this (offering) to Prajāpati of a hundred Kṛishṇalas in weight verily by it he bestowed upon them immortality; for him who fears death he should offer to Prajāpati this (offering) of a hundred Kṛishṇalas: verily he has recourse to Prajāpati with his own share; verily he bestows life upon him; he lives all his days. It is of a hundred Kṛishṇalas in weight; man has a hundred (years of) life, and a hundred powers; verily in life, in power he finds support. (The offering) is in ghee; ghee is life, gold is immortality; verily he unites him with life and immortality; four Kṛishṇalas weight on each occasion he cuts off to obtain the four cuttings-off; one by one he brings to the Brahman priest, and one by one he bestows life upon the sacrificer. Yonder sun did not shine, the Gods sought an atonement for it, for it they offered this oblation to Sūrya; verily thereby they bestowed upon it radiance. For him who desires splendour he should offer this oblation to Sūrya; verily he has recourse to yonder sun with his own share; verily he bestows upon him splendour; he becomes resplendent. On both sides are ornaments (of gold); verily on both sides he bestows radiance upon him. At each fore-offering he offers a Kṛishṇala weight; verily from the quarters he wins splendour for him, He should offer on eight potsherds to Agni, on twelve potsherds to Savitar, and an oblation to earth who desires, 'May I gain gold; may gold resort to me.' In that it is (offered) to Agni, gold is connected with Agni; verily by him whose is gold he gains it; it is (offered) to Savitar; verily instigated by Savitar he gains it; to earth an oblation is offered; verily on it he gains it; gold resorts to him. He who gains gold is deprived of power and strength; the same offering should he make who gains gold; he is not deprived of power and strength. The same offering he should make whose gold is lost; in that it is (offered) to Agni, and gold is connected with Agni, by him whose is gold he gains it; it is (offered) to Savitar; verily instigated by Savitar he gains it; to earth an oblation is offered; in this what is lost is lost; verily in it he gains it. Indra by force drunk the Soma of Tvashṭar, he went apart on all sides, he was deprived of power, of Soma drinking; what he vomited up, that became panic seeds; he had recourse to Prajāpati; for him he offered this oblation of panic seeds to Soma and Indra; verily thereby he bestowed upon him power and Soma drinking; he who vomits Soma is deprived of power, of Soma drinking; for him who vomits Soma, he should offer this oblation of panic seeds; verily he has recourse to Soma and Indra; verily they bestow upon him power and Soma drinking; he is not deprived of power and of Soma drinking. In that it is (offered) to Soma, he wins Soma drinking; in that it is (offered) to Indra, and Soma drinking is power, verily he wins power and Soma drinking; it is of panic seeds, Soma is it; verily straightway he wins Soma drinking. He who desires cattle should offer a cake on eight potsherds to Agni, the giver, and a cake on eleven potsherds to Indra, the bestower; verily Agni produces cattle for him, Indra makes them grow up. These are curds, honey, ghee, waters, and parched grain; that is the form of cattle; verily by their form he wins cattle; there are five takings, for cattle are fivefold; I it is of many forms, for cattle are of many forms, (verily it serves) for completion; it is offered to Prajāpati; cattle are connected with Prajāpati; verily Prajāpati produces cattle for him; honey is the body of man; in that he offers honey on the fire, verily thus the sacrificer places his body in the fire; the Yājyā and the Anuvākyā are in the Paṅkti metre, man is fivefold, cattle are fivefold; verily ransoming his body from death he wins cattle.

Mantra 2:3:3

The Gods desiring glory performed a sacrificial session bounded by success; to Soma the king among them glory came, he went to the hill, Agni followed him; Agni and Soma, those two, united; Indra, being parted from the sacrifice followed after them; to them be said, 'Make me to sacrifice.' For him they offered this sacrifice, to Agni on eight potsherds, to Indra on eleven potsherds, to Soma an oblation; verily thereby they conferred upon him brilliance, power, and splendour. For him who is parted from the sacrifice he should offer this sacrifice, to Agni on eight potsherds, to Indra on eleven potsherds, to Soma an oblation; in that it is (offered) to Agni, thereby he bestows brilliance upon him; in that it is (offered) to Indra, thereby (he bestows) power upon him; in that it is (offered) to Soma, thereby (he bestows) splendour; part of the offerings to Agni and Soma he should unite with that to Indra; verily he unites him with brilliance and splendour. He whose desire is not fulfilled should offer on eleven potsherds to Agni and Soma; the Brahman is connected with Agni, he drinks Soma; verily he has recourse to his own deity with his own share; verily he unites him with his desire; his desire is fulfilled. He who desires splendour should offer on eight potsherds to Agni and Soma; verily he has recourse to Agni and Soma with their own share; verily they bestow upon him splendour; he becomes resplendent. In that it is on eight potsherds, it is connected with Agni; in that it is of panic seeds, it is connected with Soma; (verily it serves) for prosperity. He who is afraid of impotence should offer,an oblation of panic seeds to Soma, the strong. For the seed, the strength, departs from him, then he fears impotence; verily he has recourse to Soma, the strong; verily he bestows upon him seed and strength; he does not become impotent. He who desires a village should offer on eleven potsherds to Brahmaṇaspati; verily he has recourse to Brahmaṇaspati with his own share; verily he subjects his fellows to him; he becomes possessed of a village. The Yājyā and the Anuvākyā have the word 'troop'; verily he makes him possess troops of his fellows. The same sacrifice should he offer who desires, 'May I bring the people to ruin with respect to the Brahman'; he should use as the Yājyā and the Anuvākyā verses referring to the Marutas; verily he brings the people to ruin with respect to the Brahman.

Mantra 2:3:4

He who desires the heaven should offer an oblation to Aryaman; Aryaman is yonder sun; verily he has recourse to Aryaman with his own share; he makes him attain the world of heaven. He should offer an oblation to Aryaman who desires, 'May people be fain to give to me'; Aryaman is yonder sun, Aryaman is he who gives; verily he has recourse to Aryaman with his own share; he makes people fain to give to him; people are fain to give to him. He should offer an oblation to Aryaman who desires, 'May I go prosperously among men'; Aryaman is yonder sun; verily he has recourse to Aryaman with his own share; verily be makes him go whither he is fain to go. Indra was the lowest in rank of the Gods, he had recourse to Prajāpati; for him he offered this (offering) of the after-shoots of rice to Indra on eleven potsherds; verily he led him to the top of the Gods; he made as the Yājyā and the Anuvākyā (verses) containing the words 'depth' and 'top'; verily from the depths he led him to the top; for the prince who is low in rank he should offer to Indra on eleven potsherds this (offering) of the after-shoots of rice; verily he has recourse to Indra with his own share; verily he leads him to the top of his fellows; the Yājyā, and the Anuvākyā contain the words 'depth' and 'top'; verily from the depth he leads him to the top; it is of the after-shoots of rice, for it is the deity of him who is low in rank; (verily it serves) for prosperity. For the Brahman who is low in rank he should offer to Bṛihaspati this oblation of the after-shoots of rice; verily he has recourse to Bṛihaspati with his own share; verily he leads him to the top of his equals; the Yājyā and the Anuvākyā contain the words 'depth' and 'top'; verily he leads from the depth to the top; it is of the after-shoots of rice, for it is the deity of him who is low in rank; (verily it serves) for prosperity.

Mantra 2:3:5

Prajāpati had thirty-three daughters; he gave them to Soma, the king; of them he associated with Rohiṇī; they returned in anger; then he followed and asked for them back; them he would not return; he said, 'Swear on oath that thou wilt equally associate (with them): then will I return them to you.' He took the oath, and he returned them. He associated with Rohiṇī alone. Illness seized him; 'Illness has seized the king,' that (saying) is the origin of the 'king's evil'; in that he became worse, that is (the origin) of the 'bad illness'; because he got it from his wives, that is (the origin) of the 'wife's disease' (Jāyenya); him who knows thus the origin of these illnesses, these illnesses do not visit. He approached them respectfully; they said, 'Let us choose a boon; do thou associate equally with us.' For him they offered this oblation to the Ādityas; they freed him from his evil case. For him who is seized by the bad illness he should offer this oblation to the Ādityas; verily he has recourse to the Ādityas with their own share; verily they free him from his evil case. He should offer at the new moon; verily with its waxing he makes him wax. The Puronuvākyā is, 'He is born ever new'; verily thereby he bestows life upon him. The Yājyā is, 'The shoot which the Ādityas make to wax'; verily thereby he makes him wax.

Mantra 2:3:6

Prajāpati assigned food to the Gods; he said, 'Whatever shall be left over these worlds, be that mine.' That was left over these worlds, Indra, the king, Indra, the overlord, Indra, the sovereign; thence he milked these worlds threefold; that is the cause of its having three elements. For him of whom he desires, 'May he be an eater of food,' let him offer this (offering) of three elements, to Indra, the king, a cake on eleven potsherds, to Indra, the overlord, to Indra, the sovereign. Indra, the king, is this (world of earth), Indra, the overlord, is this (atmosphere), Indra, the sovereign, is yonder (world of heaven); verily he has recourse to these worlds with their own share; verily they bestow food on him; he becomes an eater of food. Even as one milks a cow ready to give milk by reason of its calf, so he milks these worlds, made ready, for desire, for food; he places (the cake) on potsherds face upwards, for variety. There are three cakes, these worlds are three; (verily they serve) to obtain these worlds; each one above the other is larger, for so as it were are these worlds; (verily they serve) for prosperity; he cuts off from all (the cakes) as he sets them up without making a failure; be recites (the verses) alternating, to prevent burning.

Mantra 2:3:7

The Gods and the Asuras were in conflict: the Asuras conquered the Gods, the Gods being defeated became the servants of the Asuras; from them power and strength departed; Indra perceived this; he departed in pursuit of it; he could not win it. Then he departed from it, he had recourse to Prajāpati; he made him sacrifice with this (offering) with all the Pṛishṭha (Stotras); verily with it he bestowed upon him power and strength. Him who desires power, desires strength, he should make him sacrifice with this (offering) with all the Pṛishṭhas; verily he has recourse to these deities with their own share; verily they bestow upon him power and strength. In that he offers to Indra of the Rathantara, verily he wins the brilliance of Agni; in that (he offers) to Indra of the Bṛihat, verily he wins the brilliance of Indra; in that (he offers) to Indra of the Vairūpa, verily he wins the brilliance of Savitar; in that (he offers) to Indra of the Vairāja, verily he wins the brilliance of the creator; in that (he offers) to Indra of the Śākvara, verily he wins the brilliance of the Marutas; in that (he offers) to Indra of the Raivata, verily he wins the brilliance of Bṛihaspati So many are the brilliances, verily he wins them; he places (the cakes) on potsherds face upwards, for variety; the cake is on twelve potsherds, to secure the All-Gods. He cuts off all around; verily all around he bestows on the sacrificer power and strength; he recites (the verses) alternating, to prevent burning. A horse, a bull, a ram, a goat, these are the sacrificial fee; for manliness. With this he should sacrifice who is being practised against; if these deities eat his food, men eat his also.

Mantra 2:3:8

Rajana Kauṇeya went to Kratujit Jānaki for a cure for eyesight; for him he offered this sacrifice, to Agni, the blazing, a cake on eight potsherds, to Sūrya an oblation, to Agni, the blazing, a cake on eight potsherds; verily thereby he bestowed sight upon him. For him who desires sight he should offer this sacrifice, to Agni, the blazing, a cake on eight potsherds; to Sūrya an oblation, to Agni, the blazing, a cake on eight potsherds; by the eye of Agni men see, (by the eye) of the sun the Gods; verily he has recourse to Agni and Sūrya with their own share; verily they bestow sight upon him; he becomes possessed of sight. In that there are two for Agni, he restores his eyes for him; in that there is (an oblation) for Sūrya, (he restores) his nose; the two for Agni are on either side of that for Sūrya; therefore the two eyes are on either side of the nose, therefore by the nose the eyes are separated. The Yājyā, and the Anuvākyā, are alike, for the eye is alike; (verily it serves) for prosperity. 'Up that God that knoweth all,' 'Seven bays in thy chariot,' 'The radiant countenance of the Gods hath arisen,' (with these words) he offers lumps; verily he gives sight to him; what was his, that (is his again).

Mantra 2:3:9

a. Thou art secure; may I be secure among my equals, wise, a guardian, a gainer of wealth; thou art secure; may I be secure among my equals, dread, a guardian, a gainer of wealth; thou art secure; may I be secure among my equals, dread, a guardian, a gainer of wealth. ‖ *b*. Thou art affection; O ye Gods of affection, those equals, youths, of one mind, them I love with my heart; may they love me with their hearts; make them of one mind with me; hail! Thou art affection; O ye Gods of affection, the women of one mind, them I love with my heart; may they love me with their hearts; make them of one mind with me; hail! ‖ He who desires a village should offer to the All-Gods (the sacrifice) for taking possession; his equals are connected with the All-Gods; verily he has recourse to the All-Gods with their own share; verily they subject his equals to him; he becomes possessed of a village. It is (the offering) for taking possession; taking possession is grasping the mind; verily he grasps the mind of his equals. 'Thou art secure; may I be secure among my equals,' (with these words) he puts the enclosing-sticks round; verily he invokes this blessing. Then all this comes to pass with regard to the equals of him for whom knowing thus these enclosing-sticks are put around. 'Thou art affection; O ye Gods of affection,' (with these words) he offers three oblations; so many are his equals, great, small, and women, them he wins, they being won wait on him.

Mantra 2:3:10.

a. What went new that became fresh butter; what crept that became clarified butter; that which became firm became ghee. ‖ *b.* Thou art the breath of the Aśvins; of that to thee let the two give whose breath thou art; hail! Thou art the breath of Indra; of that to thee let him give whose breath thou art; hail! Thou art the breath of Mitra and Varuṇa; of that to thee let them give whose' breath thou art; hail! Thou art the breath of the All-Gods; of that to thee let them give whose breath thou art; hail! ‖ *c.* Stream of ghee, path of ambrosia, | Given by Indra, presented by the Marutas, | Thee Vishṇu perceived, | Then Iḍā moved thee in the cow. ‖ *d.* Let the God Savitar set thee free for life, for living, with the Pavamāna Stoma, with the path of the Gateway (Sāman), with the strength of | the Upāṃśu (Graha); let the God Savitar set thee free for life, for living, | with the Bṛihat and Rathantara's Stoma with the path of the Trishṭubh, | with the strength of the Śukra (Graha); let the God Savitar set thee free | with the measure of Agni, with the path of the Jagatī, With the strength | of the Āgrayaṇa (Graha). ‖ *e.* Him quicken, O Agni, for life, for radiance, | Make dear his seed, O Varuṇa, O Soma, O king; | Like a mother, O Aditi, give him protection, | O ye All-Gods, that he may win old age. ‖ *f.* Agni is full of life; he is full of life through the trees; with this life I make thee full of life. Soma is full of life; he is (full) through the plants; the sacrifice is full of life; it is (full) through the sacrificial fees; the Brahman is full of life; that is full of life through the Brahmans; the Gods are full of life; they are (full of life) through the ambrosia; the Pitṛis are full of life; they are full of life through the Svadhā-call with this life I make thee full of life.

Mantra 2:3:11

To Agni his body goes, to Soma his sap,—Varuṇa grasps him with Varuṇa's noose—to Sarasvatī the speech, to Agni and Vishṇu the body Of him who long is ill. For him who is long ill or who desires, 'May I live all my days,' he should offer this sacrifice, to Agni on eight potsherds, to Soma an oblation, to Varuṇa on ten potsherds, to Sarasvatī an oblation, to Agni and Vishṇu on eleven potsherds; verily he ransoms his body from Agni, his sap from Soma; by the offering to Varuṇa he frees him from Varuṇa's noose; by the offering to Sarasvatī he bestows speech; all the Gods are Agni, the sacrifice is Vishṇu; verily by the Gods and the sacrifice he heals him; even if his life is gone, he yet lives. 'What went new, that became fresh butter,' (with these words) he looks upon the butter; verily he describes its form and greatness. 'Thou art the breath of the Aśvins,' he says; the Aśvins are the physicians of the Gods; verily by them he makes healing for him. 'Thou art the breath of Indra,' he says; verily thereby he bestows power upon him. 'Thou art the breath of Mitra and Varuṇa,' he says; verily thereby he bestows expiration and inspiration upon him. 'Thou art the breath of the All-Gods,' be says; verily thereby he bestows strength on him. 'Stream of ghee, path of ambrosia,' he says; that is according to the text. 'With the Pavamāna Stoma thee,' he says; verily thereby he bestows breath upon him. 'By the Bṛihat and Rathantara's Stoma thee,' he says; verily thereby he bestows force upon him. 'With the measure of Agni thee,' he says; verily thereby he bestows body upon him. The priests speak (these words) around; as many as are the priests, they heal him. Grasping the hand of the Brahman (priest) they speak around (him); separately they bestow life on the sacrificer; what was his that (is his again). From the gold he drinks away the ghee; ghee is life, gold is ambrosia; verily from the ambrosia he drinks away life; it is a hundred (Kṛishṇalas) in weight; man has a hundred (years) of life, a hundred powers; verily he finds support in life, in power. Or as many seasons as he deems that he will live, so many be the number, for prosperity. 'Him quicken, O Agni, for life, for radiance,' he says; verily he bestows life and radiance upon him. 'O ye All-Gods, that he may win old age,' he says; verily he makes him win old age. 'Agni is full of life,' (with these words) he takes his hand; these Gods are full of life, they bestow life upon him, he lives all his life.

Mantra 2:3:12

Prajāpati led the horse to Varuṇa, it went to its own deity, he was afflicted; he saw this (offering) to Varuṇa on four potsherds, he offered it; then indeed was he set free from Varuṇa's noose. Varuṇa seizes him who accepts the horse. As many horses as he accepts, so many (offerings) to Varuṇa should he offer; verily he has recourse to Varuṇa with his own share; verily he frees him from Varuṇa's noose. (The offerings) are on four potsherds, for the horse has four feet; (verily they serve) for prosperity. He should offer an extra one; whatever (horse) he is going to accept or whatever (horse) he has overlooked, from that noose of Varuṇa is he set free. If he is going to accept another, he should offer in supplement an offering to Sūrya, on one potsherd; verily he makes yonder sun to rise. He goes to the waters as the final bath, Varuṇa is in the waters; verily straightway he appeases Varuṇa After his return he should offer an oblation to Aponaptrīya; the horse has its birthplace in the waters; verily he makes him go to his own birthplace; appeased he attends on him.

Mantra 2:3:13

a. That body of yours, to be striven for, 'O Indra and Varuṇa, with that do ye free this one from tribulation; that strong, protecting, brilliant body of yours, with that do ye free him from tribulation. ‖ *b.* That disease of yours, O Indra and Varuṇa, that is in the fire, that of yours I appease hereby; that disease of yours, O Indra and Varuṇa, that is in the two-footed cattle, the four-footed, the cattle-yard, the houses, the waters, the plants, the trees, that of yours I appease hereby. ‖ Indra departs with his power, Varuṇa seizes him with Varuṇa's noose, who is seized by evil; for him who is seized by evil, he should offer this (offering of) clotted milk to Indra and Varuṇa; verily Indra bestows power upon him, Varuṇa frees him from Varuṇa's noose. (The offering) is of clotted milk, for milk departs from him; verily he is seized with evil; in that it is of clotted milk, thereby he bestows milk upon him. In the clotted milk he puts down the cake; verily he makes him possessed of a body, and also possessed of an abode. He separates it into four pieces; verily he finds supports in the quarters; he unites (the fires) again; verily he procures healing for him from the quarters; having united (them) he cuts off (portions); that is as when one cuts up what has been pierced. (That disease of yours, O Indra and Varuṇa, that is in the fire, that of yours I appease hereby,' he says; verily he protects him from error in sacrifice. 'That disease of yours, O Indra and Varuṇa, that is in the two footed cattle, that of yours I appease hereby,' he says; so many are the waters, the plants, the trees, offspring and cattle on whom to live; verily does he free them for him from Varuṇa's noose.

Mantra 2:3:14

a. Thou from of old. ‖ *b.* The wise contrivings. ‖ *c.* Indra on all sides. ‖ *d.* Indra men. ‖ *e.* Do thou guard us, O Soma, on all sides, | O king, from him who plots evil; | Lot not the friend of such as thou come to harm. ‖ *f.* Thy places in the sky, in the earth, | In the mountains, in the plants, in the waters, | With all of these, kindly and without anger, | Do thou, O king Soma, accept our oblations. ‖ *g.* O Agni and Soma, united, | With common offering, accept our prayers, | Ye were born together among the Gods. ‖ *h.* Ye, O Agni and Soma, with common inspiration, | Placed these lights in the sky; | Ye freed the streams from the dread imprecation | When they were held fast. ‖ *i.* O Agni and Soma, hearken kindly, | O ye strong ones, to my invocation; | Accept gladly our songs, | Be a refreshment to the giver. ‖ *k.* One from the sky Mātariśvan bore, | The falcon churned another from the rock; | Agni and Soma, waxing great through prayer, | Ye made broad room for the sacrifice. ‖ *l.* O Agni and Soma, the oblation which is set forth, | Do ye taste, accept it, rejoice in it, O ye strong ones | Of good protection, of good help be ye, | And give to the sacrificer health and wealth. ‖ *m.* Swell. ‖ *n.* Together thee. ‖ *o.* Troop lord of troops we invoke thee, | Sage of sages, most famous; | Highest king of Brahmans, O lord of prayer, | Hearkening to us with help do thou sit on thy place. ‖ *p.* He shall win booty and prizes with tribe, | With clan, with family, with sons, with men, | Who shall seek to win the father of the Gods, | Pious with oblations, the lord of prayer. ‖ *q.* He with his fair singing, harmonious troop, | Crushed Vala and Phaliga with his cry; | Bṛihaspati drove out the cows, which mix the offerings, | Thundering as they lowed. ‖ *r.* O Marutas, what time from the sky. ‖ *s.* The protections that ye. ‖ *t.* Aryaman goeth, the mighty bull, | The giver of wealth, much invoked, deserving; | With a thousand eyes, opening the cow-pens, with the thunderbolt in his arm, | May the God bestow upon us wealth. ‖ *u.* Thy many paths, O Aryaman, on which the Gods go, | O king, which come from the sky, | With these, O God, grant us great protection; | Be auspicious to our bipeds, to our quadrupeds. ‖ *v*. From the depth to the top, sung by the Aṅgirasas, | He moved asunder the firm places of the mountains; | He burst their cunningly-made obstructions; | These things did Indra in the joy of the Soma. ‖ *w*. From the depth with the top he meted with measures, | With the thunderbolt he crushed the hollows of the streams; | Lightly he freed them with paths of long wanderings; | These things did Indra in the joy of the Soma. ‖ *x*. Who was born knowing his connexion, | The God declareth all births, | From the middle of holy power he bore out holy power, | From low on high he arose at his will. ‖ *y*. Born in greatness, he established apart the great ones, | The sky as a seat and the atmosphere of earth; | From the depth be hath won to the top with his race, | Whose deity is Bṛihaspati, the sovereign. ‖ *z*. Him who with might riseth from the depth to the top, | Bṛihaspati the Gods desire to win; | He broke Vala, he rendeth the forts, | Thundering he won the heaven and the waters.

Prapāṭhaka 4.

The Special Sacrifices (continued)

Mantra 2:4:1

The Gods, men, and the Pitṛis were on one side, the Asuras, Rākṣhasas, and Piśāchas on the other. Of the Gods the little blood they drew the Rākṣhasas smothered by the nights and dawn dawned on them smothered and dead. The Gods understood, 'Him who of us dies, it is the Rākṣhasas who kill.' They invited the Rākṣhasas; they said, 'Let us choose a boon; what we win from the Asuras, let that be shared between us.' Then indeed did the Gods conquer the Asuras, and having conquered the Asuras, they drove away the Rākṣhasas The Rākṣhasas (saying), 'Ye have done falsely,' surrounded the Gods on all sides. The Gods found a protector in Agni; they offered to Agni, the forward, a cake on eight potsherds, to Agni, the overcomer, to Agni with the face. In that they offered to Agni, the forward, the Rākṣhasas in front they repelled thereby; in that (they offered) to Agni, the overcomer, the Rākṣhasas that were around they repelled thereby; in that (they offered) to Agni with the face, the Rākṣhasas behind were repelled thereby. That the Gods prospered, the Rākṣhasas were defeated. He who has foes should in conflict sacrifice with this offering; he should offer to Agni, the forward, a cake on eight potsherds, to Agni, the overcomer, to Agni with the face. In that he offers to Agni, the forward, he repels thereby the foe who is superior to him; in that (he offers) to Agni, the overcomer, he repels thereby (the foe) who is equal to him; in that (he offers) to Agni with the face, he repels thereby the foe which is inferior to him. He repels the foe who is superior, he surpasses him who is like, the inferior does not equal him who knowing thus sacrifices with this offering.

Mantra 2:4:2

The Gods and the Asuras were in conflict; the Gods said, 'Let us hold on to the strongest of us'; they said to Indra, 'Thou art the strongest of us; let us hold on to thee.' He said, 'Three are these forms of my own that have strength; satiate them, and then shall ye overcome the Asuras.' They said, 'Name (them).' He said, 'This is that which frees from tribulation; this is that which drives away the foe; this is that which has power.' They offered to Indra, the freer from tribulation, a cake on eleven potsherds, to Indra, the driver away of the foe, to Indra, the powerful. In that they offered to Indra, the freer from tribulation, thereby they were freed from tribulation; in that they offered to Indra, the driver away of foes, thereby they drove away foes; in that they offered to Indra, the powerful, thereby they bestowed power upon themselves. They offered a cake on thirty-three potsherds; the Gods are thirty-three; verily Indra takes hold of them in himself, for prosperity. That was the highest victory that the Gods won over the Asuras. He who has foes should in conflict sacrifice with this offering; to Indra, the freer from tribulation, he should offer a cake on eleven potsherds, to Indra, the driver away of the foe, to Indra, the powerful; by tribulation is he seized whose foe is superior to him; in that he offers to Indra, the freer from tribulation, he is freed thereby from tribulation; by foes is he beset, to whom one of his equals is superior, even if no foe; in that (he offers) to Indra, the driver away of the foe, he smites away thereby his foes; in that (he offers) to Indra, the powerful, he bestows thereby power upon himself; he offers a cake on thirty-three potsherds; the Gods are thirty-three; verily the sacrificer takes hold of them in himself, for prosperity, Thus is the sacrifice called 'the victorious'; he who knowing thus sacrifices with this offering wins thus the highest victory over his foe.

Mantra 2:4:3

The Gods and the Asuras were in conflict; the Gāyatrī, grasping and taking their force, might, power, strength, offspring, and cattle, remained away; they reflected, I Whomsoever of us she shall resort to, they shall become this (world)'; they hailed her in rivalry, 'O All worker,' said the Gods; 'O Deceiver,' said the Asuras; neither did she resort to. The Gods saw this formula, 'Thou art force, thou art strength, thou art might, thou are blazing, thou art by name the home of the Gods, thou art all, of all life thou art everything, thou art of every life, the overcoming.' (So saying) the Gods appropriated the force, might, power, strength, offspring, and cattle of the Asuras. Because the Gāyatrī remained away, therefore they style this offering the Gāyatrī; the Gāyatrī is the year, so the year remained away; because the Gods thereby appropriated the force, might, power, strength, offspring, and cattle of the Asuras, therefore they style this offering the gatherer. He who has foes should in conflict sacrifice with this offering. To Agni, the gatherer, he should offer a cake on eight potsherds; this when cooked and put in place he should stroke with this formula; verily he appropriates the force, might, power, strength, offspring, and cattle of his foe; he prospers with himself, his foe is defeated.

Mantra 2:4:4

Prajāpati created offspring; they created went away from him; where they stayed, thence sprung the bean. Those he followed with Bṛihaspati; Bṛihaspati said, 'With this will I go before thee, then shall offspring have resort to thee.' He went before him; then indeed did offspring resort to Prajāpati For him who desires offspring he should offer this oblation of beans to Prajāpati verily he has recourse to Prajāpati with his own share; verily he produces offspring for him. Prajāpati created cattle; they created went away from him; where they stayed, thence sprung the bean; those he followed with Pūṣhan; Pūṣhan said, 'With this do thou go before me; then shall cattle resort to thee.' 'Do thou go before me,' said Soma, 'mine is what grows on untilled (land).' 'Both of you shall I go before,' he said; he went before them both; then indeed did cattle resort to Prajāpati For him who desires cattle should he offer this oblation of beans to Soma and Pūṣhan; verily he has recourse to Soma and Pūṣhan with their own share; verily they produce cattle for him. Soma is the impregnator of seed, Pūṣhan the producer of cattle; verily Soma bestows seed upon him, Pūṣhan produces cattle.

Mantra 2:4:5

a. O Agni come to us with kine; | O drop, delight us with increase; | Indra is the supporter in our homes. ‖ *b*. Savitar, the thousandfold, | May he delight us in our homes; | May Pūṣhan come, may wealth (be ours). ‖ *c*. May Dhātar give us wealth, | The lord, the ruler of the world; | May he favour us with a full (gift). ‖ *d*. Tvaṣhṭar the bull, the strong, | May he delight us in our homes, | With a thousand, with ten thousand. ‖ *e*. Thou whereby the Gods moved immortality, | Enduring fame, in the sky, | O increase of wealth, vouchsafe us | A herd of kine for life. ‖ *f*. Agni, lord of the house, Soma, all-winning, Savitar the wise; hail! ‖ *g*. O Agni, lord of the house, with thy ghee portion do thou vouchsafe strength and force to him who advanceth; may I not wander from the highest of the path; may I become the head; hail!

Mantra 2:4:6

He who desires cattle should sacrifice with the Chitrā (offering); Chitrā is this (earth); in that in this (earth) all things are produced, thereby is this (earth) variegated (*chitrā*); he who knowing thus sacrifices with the Chitrā desirous of cattle is propagated with offspring, with cattle, with pairings. With the offering to Agni he strews, with that to Soma he impregnates seed, the seed impregnated Tvaṣhṭar develops into forms; there are (offerings) to Sarasvat and Sarasvatī; that is the divine pair; verily in the midst he bestows upon him a divine pair, for growth, for propagation. There is an oblation to Sinīvālī; Sinīvālī is speech, speech is growth; verily he approaches speech and growth. The last is to Indra, and thereby there is a pair. Seven are these offerings, the tame animals are seven, the wild seven; the metres are seven, for the winning of both. Then he offers these oblations; these Gods are the lords of growth; verily they bestow growth upon him, he grows with offspring and cattle; moreover in that he offers these oblations, (they serve) for support.

Mantra 2:4:7

a. Thou I art connected with the Marutas, thou art the force of the Marutas, cleave the stream of the waters. || *b.* Stay, O Marutas, the speeding falcon, | Swift as mind, the strong, the glorious; | That whereby the dread host goeth set loose, | Do ye, O Aśvins, put around; hail! || *c.* East wind, raining, quicken; Rāvat! Hail! Storming, raining, dread; Rāvat! Hail! Thundering, raining, formidable; Rāvat! Hail! Thundering without lightning, lightning, raining, resplendent; Rāvat! Hail! Raining over night, satisfying; Rāvat! Hail! Famed as having rained I much; Rāvat! Hail! Raining while the sun shines, radiant; Rāvat! Hail! Thundering, lightning, raining, waxing great; Rāvat! Hail! || *d.* Gladdening, obedient, purifying, agile, | Full of light, full of darkness, flooding, with fair foam, | Supporting friends, supporting the warrior caste, | With fair realms, do ye help me. || *e.* Thou art the fetter of the strong steed; for rain I yoke thee.

Mantra 2:4:8

a. O Gods granting protection, O Mitra and Varuṇa, Aryaman; | O Gods who drink together, O son of the waters, with swift onset, | Give of the water, cleave the holder of the waters; from the sky, from Parjanya, from the atmosphere, from the earth, thence do ye help us with rain. || *b.* Even by day they make the darkness, | With Parjanya, water bearer; | What time they inundate the earth. || *c.* The treasure-house of sky which the heroes rich in dew | Make to shake for the generous giver, | The Parjanyas set thee free from along the firmaments; | The rains pour over the desert. || *d.* From the ocean, O Marutas, ye make (the rain) to start, | Ye make the rain to fall, O ye that are rich in moisture; | Your cows, O ye wondrous, fail not; | As ye fly swiftly your chariots turned. || *e.* Set free the rain from heaven; | With waters fill the ocean; | Thou art born of waters, first-born; | Thou art the might of the ocean. || *f.* Flood the earth, | Break this divine cloud; | Give to us of the divine water, | Ruling loosen the water bag. || *g.* The Gods whose portion is in the sky, the Gods whose portion is in the atmosphere, the Gods whose portion is on earth, may they aid this sacrifice, may they enter this place, may they inhabit this place.

Mantra 2:4:9

'Thou art connected with the Marutas, thou art the force of the Marutas,' (with these words) he puts on a black garment with a black fringe; that is the hue of rain; verily becoming of like hue he causes Parjanya to rain. 'Stay, O Marutas, the speeding falcon,' (with these words) he pushes back the west wind; verily he produces the east wind, to win the rains. He makes offering to the names of the wind; the wind rules the rain; verily he has recourse to the wind with its own share; verily it makes Parjanya rain for him. Eight offerings he makes; the quarters are four, the intermediate quarters are four; verily from the quarters he makes the rain to move. He unites (them) on a black antelope skin; verily he makes the offering; he unites within the Vedi, for accomplishment. When the Yatis were being eaten, their heads fell away; they became Kharjūras; their sap rose upwards, they became Karīras; the Karīras are connected with Soma; the offering connected with Soma makes rain to move from the sky; in that there are Karīras (in the sacrifice), by means of an offering which is connected with Soma he wins the rain from the sky. With honey he unites (them); honey is the sap of the waters and the plants; verily it rains from the waters and the plants; verily also he brings down rain from the waters and the plants. 'Gladdening, obedient,' (with these words) he unites (them); verily he approaches them by their names; just as one may say, 'Come hither, N. N.,' so by their names he makes them move forward. Thou art the fetter of the strong horse; for rain I yoke thee,' he says the horse is strong, Parjanya is strong; becoming black as it were he rains; verily he unites him with his hue, to win the rains.

Mantra 2:4:10.

'O Gods having wealth, O Gods granting protection, O Gods drinking together,' (with these words) he ties on; verily by means of the Gods he daily seeks rain. If it should rain, so much only should be offered; if it should not rain, on the next day he should offer an oblation. Mitra and Varuṇa are day and night, by day and night Parjanya rains, for by night or by day he rains; verily he has recourse to Mitra and Varuṇa with their own share; verily they make Parjanya rain for him by day and night. To Agni, hiding his abode, he should offer a cake on eight potsherds, to the Marutas on seven potsherds, to Sūrya on one potsherd; Agni thence causes the rain to arise, the Marutas lead it out when produced; when yonder Sun Moves low with his rays, then he rains; becoming a hider of his abode, as it were, he rains; these deities are the lords of rain; them he has recourse to with their own share; they make Parjanya rain for him; even if he is not minded to rain yet he rains. 'Let free the rain from heaven; with waters fill the ocean,' he says; verily these and yonder waters he unites; then with these he approaches yonder (waters). 'Thou art born of waters, first-born; thou art the might of the ocean,' he says; that is according to the text. 'Flood the earth,' (with these words) he offers in a *Boerhavia procumbens*; this of plants is that which wins rain, and thereby he causes rain to fall. 'The Gods whose portion is in the sky,' (with these words) he shakes the black antelope skin; verily to him these worlds become dear and desired.

Mantra 2:4:11

'All' the metres are to be recited in this sacrifice,' they say; the Kakubh is the strength of the Trishṭubh, the Ushṇih of the Jagatī; in that he repeats the Ushṇih and the Kakubh, thereby he wins all the metres. The Ushṇih is the Gāyatrī; the four syllables over are four-footed cattle; just as cake is over cake, so it is with the syllables which are over the verse; if he were to close with a Jagatī, he would end the sacrifice; he closes with a Trishṭubh, the Trishṭubh is power and strength; verily he establishes the sacrifice on power and strength, he does not end it. 'O Agni, three are thy strengths, three thy abodes,' with this (verse) containing the word 'three' he closes, for similarity of form: that which has three constituents is the whole of the sacrifice; for every desire it is employed, for the sacrifice is employed for all desires. He who is practising witchcraft should sacrifice with that of three constituents; that which has three constituents is the whole of the sacrifice; verily with the whole of the sacrifice he bewitches him, and lays him low. With the same (offering) should he sacrifice who is practised against, that which has three constituents is the whole of the sacrifice; verily he sacrifices with the whole of the sacrifice, and he who practises witchcraft does not lay him low. With the same (offering) should he sacrifice who is going to sacrifice with a thousand; verily he produces and gives (it). He who has sacrificed with a thousand should sacrifice with the same (offering) he goes to the end of cattle who sacrifices with a thousand; Prajāpati created cattle; he created them with (the offering) of three constituents; he who knowing thus sacrifices, desirous of cattle, with (the offering) of three constituents, creates cattle from the very source whence Prajāpati created them; and the thousand resorts to him. He becomes a prey to the Gods who having said, 'I shall sacrifice,' does not sacrifice; he should sacrifice with (the offering) of three constituents; (the offering) of three constituents is the whole of the sacrifice; verily he sacrifices with the whole of the sacrifice, and does not become a prey to the Gods. The cake is on twelve potsherds; these are three (sets of) four potsherds, to bring about the three. There are three cakes, these worlds are three; (verily they serve) to win these worlds. Each one above the other is larger, for so as it were are these worlds. The middle one is made of barley, that is the form of the atmosphere; (verily it serves) for prosperity. He cuts off from all (the cakes) as he sets them up without making a failure. He gives gold; verily he wins brilliance; he gives the silken garment; verily he wins cattle; he gives a cow; verily he wins his prayers; gold is the colour of the Sāman, the silken garment of the formulae, the cow of the praises and rejoicings; verily he wins all these colours.

Mantra 2:4:12

Tvashṭar, his son slain, offered Soma excluding Indra. Indra desired an invitation to the rite, but he did not invite him, (saying), 'Thou hast slain my son.' He made a disturbance of the sacrifice, and forcibly drank the Soma. The remains of it Tvashṭar cast upon the Āhavanīya (fire), saying, 'Hail! wax great, Indra's foe. While (the fire) was flaming upwards to strike, just then of itself it stayed; whether so much was before, or so much was over the fire, be sprang up alive and came into union with Agni and Soma. He grew on all sides an arrow(shot), he enveloped these worlds. Because he enveloped these worlds, therefore is Vṛitra, Vṛitra Indra feared him, and Tvashṭar too; Tvashṭar dipped his bolt for him; the bolt was fervour; he could not restrain it. Vishṇu was another God; he said, 'Vishṇu, come hither; we will grasp that by which he is this world. Vishṇu deposited himself in three places, a third on the earth, a third in the atmosphere, a third in the sky, for he was afraid of his growth. By means of the third on earth Indra raised his bolt, aided by Vishṇu. He said, 'Hurl it not at me; there is this strength in me; I will give it to you.' He gave it to him, he accepted it, and (saying), 'Thou didst further me,' gave it to Vishṇu. Vishṇu accepted it (saying), 'Let Indra place power (*indriyā*) in us.' By means of the third in the atmosphere Indra raised his bolt, aided by Vishṇu. He said, 'Hurl it not at me; there is this strength in me; I will give it to you.' He gave it to him; he accepted it, and (saying), 'Twice hast thou furthered me,' gave it to Vishṇu. Vishṇu accepted it (saying), 'Let Indra place power in us.' By means of the third in the sky Indra raised his bolt, aided by Vishṇu. He said, 'Hurl it not at me; I will give to thee that by which I am this world! He said, 'Yes.' (He replied), 'Let us make a compact; let me enter thee.' 'If thou dost enter me, in what way wilt thou enjoy me?' 'I will kindle thee; I will enter thee for thine enjoyment,' he answered. Vṛitra entered him. Vṛitra is the belly; hunger is man's enemy; he who knows this slays the enemy hunger. He gave it to him; he accepted it, and (saying), 'Thrice hast thou furthered me,' gave it to Vishṇu. Vishṇu accepted it (saying), 'Let Indra place power in us.' In that thrice he gave and thrice he accepted, that is the reason of the threefold character of the threefold. In that Vishṇu aided him and he gave (it) to Vishṇu, therefore the offering belongs to Indra and Vishṇu. Whatever there is here he gave to him, the Ṛichas, the Sāmans, the Yajusas. A thousand he gave to him; therefore there are a thousand gifts.

Mantra 2:4:13

The Gods were afraid of the warrior on his birth. While still within (the womb) they fettered him with a bond. The warrior thus is born fettered; if he were born not fettered he would continually slay his foes. If one desire of a warrior, 'May he be born not fettered, may he continually slay his foes,' one should offer for him the offering for Indra and Bṛihaspati, for the warrior is connected with Indra, Bṛihaspati is the holy power (Brahman); verily by the holy power (Brahman) he frees him from the bond that fetters him. The sacrificial present is a golden bond; verily manifestly he frees him from the bond that fetters him.

Mantra 2:4:14

a. He is born ever new; | The banner of the days goeth before the dawns. | He appointeth their portion to the Gods as he advanceth | The moon extendeth length of days. ‖ *b*. The drop which the Ādityas make to swell, | The imperishable which the imperishable drink, | With that may king Varuṇa, Bṛihaspati, | The guardians of the world make us to swell. ‖ *c*. In the eastern quarter thou art king, O Indra | In the northern, O slayer of Vṛitra, thou art slayer of foes | Where the streams go, thou hast conquered; | On the south be the bull whom we invoke. ‖ *d*. Indra shall conquer, he shall not be conquered; | Over-lord among kings shall he rule; | In all conflicts shall he be a protector, | That he may be reverenced and honoured. ‖ *e*. His greatness surpasseth | Sky or earth or heaven; | Indra sole lord, hailed by all, in his home | Boisterous and brave, waxeth great for the conflict. ‖ *f*. We call on thee, O hero, in praise, | Like kine unmilked, | Lord of this moving world, seeing the heavenly light, | Lord, O Indra, of what standeth. ‖ *g*. We call on thee, | We poets, to gain the prize; | Men call on thee, lord of heroes, O Indra, amongst foes, | On thee in the racing of the horse. ‖ *h*. If, O Indra, a hundred skies, | A hundred earths were thine, | Not a thousand suns could match thee at birth, | Nor the two worlds. ‖ *i*. Drink the Soma, O Indra; let it gladden thee, | (The Soma) which for thee, O lord of bays, the stone | Through the arms of the presser, like a horse well guided hath expressed. ‖ *k*. With Indra may splendid feasts be ours, | Rich in strength, | Wherewith we may rejoice in food. ‖ *l*. O Agni, thy pure. ‖ *m*. With the light. ‖ *n*. Thee, Jātavedas ‖ *o*. Seven bays in thy chariot | Bear thee, O God Sūrya, | With hair of light, O wise one. ‖ *p*. The radiant countenance of the Gods hath arisen, | The eye of Mitra, Varuṇa, and Agni; | He hath filled the sky, the earth, and the atmosphere; | Sūrya is the soul of that which moveth and standeth. ‖ *q*. May the All-Gods who further right, | Who hearken to the call in due season, | Find pleasure in this proper drink. ‖ *r*. O ye All-Gods, hear my invocation, | Ye that are in the atmosphere, ye that are in the sky; | Ye with Agni as your tongue, worthy of sacrifice, | Sit on this strew and rejoice.

Prapāṭhaka 5.

The New and Full Moon Sacrifices

Mantra 2:5:1

a. Viśvarūpa, son of Tvashṭar, was the domestic priest of the Gods, and the sister's son of the Asuras. He had three heads, one which drank Soma, one Sūra, and one which ate food. He promised openly the share to the Gods, secretly to the Asuras. Men promise openly the share to every one; if they promise any one secretly, his share is indeed promised. Therefore Indra was afraid (thinking), 'Such an one is diverting the sovereignty (from me).' He took his bolt and smote off his heads. (The head) which drank Soma became a hazelcock; (the head) which drank Sūra a sparrow; (the head) which ate food a partridge. He seized with his hand the guilt of slaying him, and bore it for a year. Creatures called out upon him, 'Thou art a Brahman slayer.' He appealed to the earth, 'Take a third part of my guilt.' She said, 'Let me choose a boon. I deem that I shall be overcome through digging. Let me not be overcome by that.' He replied, 'Before a year is out it will grow up for thee.' Therefore before the year is out the dug-out portion of earth grows up again, for that was what she chose as a boon. She took a third of his guilt. That became a natural fissure; therefore one who has piled up a fire-altar and whose deity is faith should not choose a natural fissure, for that is the colour of guilt. He appealed to the trees, 'Take a third part of my guilt.' They said, 'Let us choose a boon. We deem that we shall be overcome through pruning. Let us not be overcome by that.' He replied, 'From pruning shall more (shoots) spring up for you.' Therefore from the pruning of trees more (shoots) spring up, for that was what they chose as a boon. They took a third part of his guilt, it became sap; therefore one should not partake of sap, for it is the colour of guilt. Or rather of the sap which is red or which comes from the pruning one should not partake, but of other sap at will. He appealed to a concourse of women, 'Take the third of my guilt.' They said, 'Let us choose a boon; let us obtain offspring from after the menses; let us enjoy intercourse at will up to birth.' Therefore women obtain offspring from after the menses, and enjoy intercourse at will up to birth, for that was what they chose as a boon. They took a third of his guilt, it became (a woman) with stained garments; therefore one should not converse with (a woman) with stained garments, one should not sit with her, nor eat her food, for she keeps emitting the colour of guilt. Or rather they say, 'Woman's food is unguent, and there fore one should not accept (from her) unguent, but anything else (can be accepted) at will.' The son born of intercourse with (a woman) with stained garments is accursed; (the son born) of intercourse in the forest is a thief; (the son born) of intercourse with a (woman) who turns away is shamefaced and retiring; (the son born) of intercourse with a woman bathing is fated to drown; (the son born) of one who anoints herself has a skin disease; (the son born) of one who combs her hair is bald and feeble; (the son born) of one who anoints (her eyes) is blind; (the son born) of one who cleans her teeth has dirty teeth; (the son born) of one who cuts her nails has bad nails; (the son born) of one who spins is a eunuch; (the son born) of one who weaves ropes is unrestrained; (the son born) of one who drinks from a leaf is drunken; (the son born) of one who drinks from a mutilated (vessel) is mutilated. For three nights he should keep a vow and should drink from his hand or from a perfect vessel, to guard his offspring.

Mantra 2:5:2

Tvashṭar, his son being slain, offered Soma excluding Indra. Indra desired an invitation to the rite, but he did not invite him; (saying) 'Thou hast slain my son.' He made a disturbance of the sacrifice, and forcibly drank the Soma. The remains of it Tvashṭar cast upon the Āhavanīya (fire), (saying), 'Hail! wax great, Indra's foe.' In that he cast it (*avartayat*), Vṛitra is Vṛitra; in that he said, 'Hail! wax great, Indra's foe,' therefore Indra became his foe. He sprang into life and came into union with Agni and Soma. He grew on all sides an arrow(shot), he enveloped these worlds. Because he enveloped these worlds, therefore is Vṛitra, Vṛitra Indra feared him. He ran up to Prajāpati, (saying), 'A foe has sprung up for me.' He dipped his bolt and gave it to him, (saying), 'Slay with it.' He went against (him) with it. Agni and Soma said, 'Hurl it not; we are within.' 'Ye are mine,' he replied, 'come to me.' They asked for a share; he gave them at the full moon this offering for Agni and Soma on eleven potsherds. They said, 'We are bitten all round, and cannot come.' Indra produced from himself cold and fever heat; that was the origin of cold and fever heat. Him who knows thus the origin of cold and fever heat neither cold nor fever heat slays. By them he led him on, and as he gaped Agni and Soma went forth from him. Then expiration and inspiration deserted him; skill is expiration, intelligence is inspiration; therefore one who gapes should say, 'Skill and intelligence (remain) in me'; verily he places expiration and inspiration in himself and lives all his days. He, having called off the Gods from. Vṛitra offered at the full moon the oblation to the Vṛitra slayer; they slay him at the full moon, but make him swell at the new moon; therefore verses are uttered at the full moon referring to the slaying of Vṛitra, at the new moon referring to his increase. Having performed the oblation to the Vṛitra slayer, he took his bolt and again went against (him). Sky and earth said, 'Hurl it not; he rests in us two.' They said, 'Let us choose a boon.' 'May I be adorned with the Nakṣhatras,' said yonder (sky); I May I be adorned with variegated things,' said this (earth). Therefore yonder (sky) is adorned with the Nakṣhatras, this (earth) with variegated things. He who knows thus the boon of sky and earth attains a boon. Indra thus impelled by these two slew Vṛitra The Gods having slain Vṛitra said to Agni and Soma, 'Bear the offering for us.' They said, 'We two have lost our brilliance, our brilliance is in Vṛitra.' They said, 'Who is there to go for it?' 'The cow,' they said, 'The cow is the friend of all.' She said, 'Let me choose a boon; ye shall feed off both when they are in me.' The cow brought the (brilliance); therefore they feed off both things that are in the cow; ghee indeed is the brilliance of Agni, milk the brilliance of Soma. He who knows thus the brilliance of Agni and Soma becomes brilliant. The theologians say, 'What is the deity of the full moon (rite)?' He should reply, 'Prajāpati; by means of it he established his eldest son, Indra.' Therefore they establish their eldest sons with wealth.

Mantra 2:5:3

When Indra had slain Vṛitra, his enemies threatened him. He saw this enemy-dispelling (oblation) to be offered subsequently at the full moon. He offered it, and with it drove away his enemies. In that the enemy-dispelling (oblation) is to be offered subsequently at the full moon, the sacrificer by it drives away his enemies. Indra, having slain Vṛitra, lost the Gods and his power. He saw the (offering) to Agni on eight potsherds at the new moon, and the curds for Indra. He offered it, and by it he won the Gods and his power. In that at the new moon there is (an offering) to Agni on eight potsherds, and curds for Indra, the sacrificer wins by it the Gods and power. When Indra had slain Vṛitra, his power and strength went into the earth; then the plants and roots were born. He ran up to Prajāpati, (saying), 'Now that I have slain Vṛitra, my power and strength have gone into the earth; then the plants and roots have been born.' Prajāpati said to cattle, 'Collect it for him.' The cattle collected it from the plants in themselves; they milked it. In that they collected it, has the collected oblation (*sāṃnāyya*) its name; in that they milked it, has fresh milk its name (*pratidhuk*). 'They have collected it; they have milked it; but it rests not in me,' he said. 'Make it ready for him,' he replied. They made it ready for him; they made power and strength rest in him; verily the ready (milk) has its name (*śṛita*). 'They have collected it; they have milked it; they have made it ready; but it does not impel me,' he said. 'Make it curds for him,' he replied. They made it curds for him; that impelled (*ahinot*) him; verily curds (*dadhi*) has its name. The theologians say, 'One should offer curds first, for curds is made first'. One should disregard that and offer ready (milk) first; verily one places power and strength in him and later impels him by curds; and he proceeds in order (of production). If he curdles it with Pūtīka plants or with bark, that is fit for Soma; if with jujubes, that is for the Rākṣhasas; if with rice grains, for the All-Gods; if with rennet, for men; if with curds, that has Indra. He curdles it with curds that it may have Indra. He curdles the remains of the Agnihotra, for the continuity of the sacrifice. Indra having slain Vṛitra went to a great distance, thinking, 'I have sinned.' The Gods sought to start him. Prajāpati said, I He who first finds him will have the first share.' The Pitṛis found him; therefore an offering is made to the Pitṛis on the day before. He approached the new moon night; the Gods met him, (saying), 'Our treasure today at home dwells,' for Indra is the treasure of the Gods, and that is why the new moon night has its name (*amā-vāsya*), 'home dwelling'). The theologians say, What is the deity of the Sāṃnāyya?' 'The All-Gods,' he should reply, for so the All-Gods won that as their share.' Or rather he should reply, 'Indra, for it was in healing Indra that they won it.'

Mantra 2:5:4

a. The theologians say, 'He would indeed offer the new and full moon (sacrifices) who should offer them with Indra.' At the full moon there is the subsequent offering of the enemy-dispelling (oblation), and by it the full moon has Indra. There are curds for Indra at the new moon; verily the new moon has Indra. He who knowing thus offers,' the new and full moon sacrifices, offers them with Indra, and day after day it becomes better for him who has so sacrificed. What the Gods did at the sacrifice, the Asuras did. The Gods saw this offering, one on eleven potsherds for Agni and Viṣhṇu, an oblation for Sarasvatī, an oblation for Sarasvat; after performing the full moon (sacrifice) they offered this. Then the Gods prospered, the Asuras were defeated. He who has enemies should offer this offering after performing the full moon (sacrifice). With the full moon (sacrifice) he hurls the bolt at his enemy, with (the offering) to Agni and Viṣhṇu he appropriates the Gods and the sacrifice of his enemy, his pairing cattle with (the offerings) to Sarasvatī and Sarasvat. Whatever he has, all that he appropriates. One should sacrifice at the full moon, if one has enemies, not at the new moon; having slain one's enemy one does not cause him to grow again. He who desires cattle should sacrifice with the Sākamprasthāyīya. The man to whom they bring (any thing) in small measure is not himself pleased, and does not give to another. But he, to whom they bring in large measure, is himself pleased, and gives to another. One should offer in full and large measure; Indra then being pleased delights him with offspring and cattle. He offers with a wooden vessel, for an earthenware one does not hold the offering. It is of Udumbara wood; the Udumbara is strength, cattle are strength; verily by strength he wins for him strength and cattle. One should not sacrifice to, Mahendra, if one is not prosperous. The prosperous are three; a learned (Brahman), a village headman, and a warrior. Their deity is Mahendra. He who sacrifices beyond his own deity loses his own deity, and does not obtain another, and becomes worse. For a year one should sacrifice to Indra, for the vow extends not beyond the year; verily his own deity, being sacrificed to, kindles him with prosperity and he becomes richer. After the year he should offer a cake on eight potsherds to Agni, lord of vows; verily for a year Agni, lord of vows, causes him to take up the vow who has slain his foe (*vṛitra*). Thereafter he may sacrifice at will.

Mantra 2:5:5

No one who is not a Soma sacrificer should offer the Sāṃnāyya. For the milk of him who is not a Soma sacrificer is imperfect, and if one who is not a Soma sacrificer offers the Sāṃnāyya he is a thief and does wrong, and (his milk) is poured forth in vain. A Soma sacrificer only should offer the Sāṃnāyya Soma is milk, the Sāṃnāyya is milk; verily with milk he places milk in himself. The moon deprives him of offspring and cattle, and makes his enemy wax great on whose sacrifice when offered it rises in the east. He should divide the rice grains into three parts; the mean size he should make into a cake on eight potsherds for Agni, the giver, the largest lie should give as a mess to Indra, the bestower, the smallest (he should give) as a mess in boiled (milk) to Viṣhṇu Śipiviṣhṭa. Agni thus generates offspring for him; Indra gives it in crease; Viṣhṇu is the sacrifice, and Śipi cattle; verily on the sacrifice and cattle he rests. He should not offer twice. If he were to offer now with the first he would make a failure with the second; if with the second now, he would make a failure with the first; there is no offering at all and no sacrifice, for that cause a son is born shamefaced and retiring. One offering only should one make; a valiant son is born to him. One should disregard this and offer twice. With the first (offering) one grasps the mouth of the sacrifice, and sacrifices with the second. Verily one wins the Gods with the first, power with the second; verily one conquers the world of the Gods with the first; the world of men with the second; he performs several forms of sacrifice. This offering is called 'the friendly'; for him there is in this world prosperity on whom the moon rises in the west after he hag sacrificed on that day. He who desires heaven should sacrifice with the Dākṣhāyaṇa sacrifice. On the full moon he should offer the Sāṃnāyya; on the new moon he should sacrifice with clotted curds for Mitra and Varuṇa On the full moon (the Soma) is pressed for the Gods; during this half-month it is pressed forth for them, and a cow for Mitra and Varuṇa is to be slaughtered for them at the new moon. In that he sacrifices on the day before, he makes the sacrificial enclosure. In that he drives away the calves, he metes out the seat and the oblation holder. In that he sacrifices, he produces with the Gods the pressing day. He drinks for the half-month Soma in carouse with the Gods. In that he sacrifices at the new moon with clotted curds for Mitra and Varuṇa, the cow which is slaughtered for the Gods becomes his also. He mounts upon the Gods in truth who mounts upon their sacrifice. Just as a great man who has attained (fortune) desires (and does), so he does. If he misses the mark he becomes worse; if he does not, he remains the same. One who desires distinction should sacrifice with it, for this sacrifice has a razor edge, and swiftly he becomes holy or perishes. His vow is: he shall not speak untruth; be shall not eat meat; he shall not approach for all a woman; they shall not clean his raiment with cleansing stuff; for all these things the Gods do not do.

Mantra 2:5:6

The new and the full moon (sacrifices) are the chariot of the Gods. He, who having offered the new and the full moon (sacrifices) Sacrifices with Soma, rests in the chosen resting-place of the Gods which is conspicuous for its chariot (tracks). The new and the full moons are the limbs and joints of the year; he who knowing thus offers the new and the full moon (sacrifices) thus unites the limbs and joints of the year. The new and the full moon are the eyes of the year; he who knowing thus offers the new and the full moon (sacrifices) thus sees with them along the world of heaven. The new and the full moon are the striding of the Gods; he who knowing thus offers the new and the full moon (sacrifices) steps in the striding of the Gods. The new and the full moon are the path on which the Gods fare; he who knowing thus offers the new and the full moon (sacrifices) mounts the path on which the Gods fare. The new and the full moons are the bay steeds of the Gods; he who knowing thus offers the new and the full moon (sacrifices) carries to the Gods with their two bay steeds the offering. The new and the full moon (sacrifices) are the mouth of the Gods; he who knowing thus offers the new and the full moon (sacrifices) manifestly sacrifices in the mouth of the Gods. He who offers the new and the full moon sacrifices possesses an oblation holder. He offers the Agnihotra morn and evening, he offers the new and the full moon (sacrifices); on every day (the Soma) of those who have oblation holders is pressed. By him who knowing thus offers the new and the full moon (sacrifices) regarding himself as possessing an oblation holder, everything is given as on the strew. The Gods could not find the suitable day for the sacrifice. They purified the new and full moons; the new and the full moon (sacrifices) are these pure and sacrificial (days). He who knowing thus offers the new and the full moon (sacrifices) offers them as pure and sacrificial. One should not approach a woman on the new moon or the full moon night; if one were to do so, one would be impotent. The nights of the half-month were the wives of King Soma; of these be did not approach the new moon night and the full moon night. They grasped him about, and illness seized him. 'Illness has seized the king'; that (saying) is the origin of the 'king's evil.' In that he became worse, that is (the origin) of the 'bad illness'; because he got it from his wives, that is (the origin) of the 'wife's disease' (Jāyenya), him who knows thus the origin of these illnesses, these illnesses do not visit. He ran up to these two in reverence; they said, 'Let us choose a boon; let us be the appointers of portions for the Gods; from us let the Gods be sacrificed to.' Therefore of the series of nights it is on the new and the full moon night that the Gods are sacrificed to; for they are the appointers of portions for the Gods. Men appoint portions to him who knows thus. Creatures slew hunger, man at once, the Gods at the half-month, the Pitṛis in a month, trees in a year. Therefore day by day men desire food, at the half-month the Gods are sacrificed to, every month offering is made to the Pitṛis, in a year trees produce fruit. He who knows thus slays the enemy, hunger.

The Part of the Hotar at the New and Full Moon Sacrifices

Mantra 2:5:7

The Gods could not rest on the Ṛich or the Yajus. On the Sāman only could they rest. He makes the noise 'Him'; verily he makes the Sāman He makes the noise 'Him'; where the Gods rested, there he sets them in motion. He makes the noise 'Him'; this is the yoking of speech. He makes the noise 'Him'; thus the sacrificers produce offspring. He repeats the first (verse) thrice, the last thrice; verily he ties the end of the sacrifice so that it may not slip. He repeats (it) continuously, for the continuity of the breaths and of food, and for the smiting away of the Rākṣhasas The first he repeats is connected with the Rathantara (Sāman), this world is connected with the Rathantara; verily he conquers this world. He divides it thrice; these worlds are three; verily he conquers these worlds. The last he repeats is connected with the Bṛihat (Sāman); yonder world is connected with the Bṛihat; verily he conquers yonder world. 'Forward your viands,' he repeats, a verse which has not any indication (of its deity) and (therefore) is addressed to Prajāpati Prajāpati is the sacrifice; verily he grasps the sacrifice as Prajāpati 'Forward your viands,' he repeats; viands are food; verily he wins food. 'Forward your viands,' he repeats; therefore seed is deposited in front. 'O Agni, come hither for the feast,' he repeats; therefore offspring are born at the back. 'Forward your viands,' he repeats; 'viands' are the months, 'heavenwards' are the half-months, 'rich in the oblation' are the Gods, 'full of butter' is the cow, 'he goes to the Gods' (that is) the sacrifice, 'desirous of favour ' is the sacrificer. 'Thou art this, thou art this,' (with these words) he wins the dear abode of the sacrifice. If he desire for a man, 'May he live all his days,' he should repeat for him 'Forward your viands,' and then continuously the next half-verse of 'Agni, come hither to the feast'. Verily by expiration does he make steadfast his inspiration, and he lives all his days. He, who knows the elbow of the Sāmidhenīs, puts his enemy in his elbow. He joins the half-verses; this is the elbow of the Sāmidhenīs; he who knows thus puts his foe in his elbow. The Sāmidhenīs were brought out by Ṛiṣhi after Ṛiṣhi; if they were not connected together, they would go away from the sacrificer's offspring and cattle. He unites the half-verses; verily he connects them together, and being so connected and secured they yield him all his desires.

Mantra 2:5:8

Without a Sāman there is no sacrifice. 'O Agni, come hither for the feast,' he says; this is the character of the Rathantara. 'Thee with the kindling-sticks, O Aṅgiras,' he says; this is the character of the Vāmadevya 'The great and powerful one, O Agni,' he says. This is the character of the Bṛihat In that he repeats this Ṭṛicha, he makes the sacrifice have Sāmans Agni was in yonder world, the sun in this; these worlds were disturbed. The Gods said, 'Let us change them about.' (Saying), 'O Agni, come hither for the feast,' they placed Agni in this world, and (saying), 'The great and powerful one, O Agni,' they placed the sun in yonder world. Then indeed these worlds became calm. In that he repeats (it) thus, (it serves) for the calming of these worlds; these worlds become calm for him who knows thus. He repeats fifteen Sāmidhenīs. The nights of the half-month are fifteen; the year is made up of half-months. There are three hundred and sixty syllables in the Sāmidhenīs; there are as many nights in the year; verily by syllables he obtains the year. Nṛimedha and Parucchepa had a theological dispute (and said), 'Let us generate fire in the dry wood (to see) which of us two is the more of a theologian.' Nṛimedha spoke; he generated smoke. Parucchepa spoke; he generated fire. 'O Ṛiṣhi,' he said,, 'seeing that our knowledge is equal, how didst thou generate fire and not I?' 'I know the character of the Sāmidhenīs,' he replied. The character of the Sāmidhenīs is the quarter-verse which is repeated with the word 'ghee' in it. 'Thee with the kindling-sticks, Aṅgiras,' he says; verily he generates light in the Sāmidhenīs They are feminine in that they are Ṛich (verses), they are feminine in that they are Gāyatrī (verses), they are feminine in that they are Sāmidhenīs He repeats a verse with the word 'Male' in it. By it he gives them a husband, makes them possess Indra, and mates them. Agni was the messenger of the Gods, Uśanas Kāvya of the Asuras. They went to question Prajāpati; he turned away (from Uśanas) (with the words). 'Agni as messenger we choose.' Then the Gods prospered, the Asuras were defeated. The man for whom, knowing thus, he repeats, 'Agni as messenger we choose, prospers himself, his enemy is defeated. He repeats a verse with the word 'imperishable'; verily by it he causes his enemy to perish. 'The flaming locked, him we adore,' he says; that is purifying; verily with it he makes pure the sacrificer. 'Thou art lit, O Agni, worshipped,' he says; verily he places around a barrier that may not be climbed. If he were to add anything further, it would be just as when (a libation) falls outside the barriers. There are three Agnis, the oblation bearer of the Gods, the bearer of the offering of the Pitṛis, the guardian of the Asuras. They repeat, 'Me will he choose, me.' 'Choose ye the bearer of the oblation,' he says; 'let him choose him who is of the Gods. He chooses one of a Ṛishi's family; verily he departs not from the connexion, (and so it serves) for continuity. He chooses, beginning at the further end, in order of descent; therefore the Pitṛis drink after men in order of descent, beginning at the further end.

Mantra 2:5:9

'O Agni, thou art great,' he says, for Agni is great. 'O Brahman,' he says, for he is a Brahman. 'O Bhārata,' he says, for he bears the sacrifice to the Gods. 'Kindled by the Gods,' he says, for the Gods kindled him. 'Kindled by Manu,' he says, for Manu kindled him after the Gods. 'Praised by the Ṛishis,' he says, for the Ṛishis praised him. 'Rejoiced in by sages,' he says, for learned people are sages. 'Celebrated by the poets,' he says, for learned people are the poets. 'Quickened by the holy power (Brahman),' he says, for he is quickened by the holy power (Brahman). 'With ghee offering,' he says, for ghee is his dearest offering. 'Leader of the sacrifices,' he says, for he is the leader of the sacrifices. 'Charioteer of the rites,' he says, for he is the chariot of the Gods. 'The Hotar unsurpassed,' he says, for no one surpasses him. 'Surpassing, bearing the oblation,' he says, for he surpasses all. 'The mouth dish, the ladle of the Gods,' he says, for he is the ladle of the Gods. 'The bowl from which the Gods drink,' he says, for he is the bowl from which the Gods drink. 'O Agni, like a felly the spokes, thou dost surround the Gods,' he says, for he surrounds the Gods. If he were to say, 'Bring hither the Gods to the pious sacrificer,' he would produce an enemy for him. 'Bring hither the Gods to the sacrificer,' he says; verily with that be makes the sacrificer to grow great. 'O Agni, bring Agni hither, bring Soma hither,' he says; verily he summons the Gods in order. 'Bring hither the Gods, O Agni; and sacrifice to them with a fair sacrifice, O Jātavedas,' he says; verily he quickens Agni, and quickened by him he bears the oblation to the Gods. 'Agni the Hotar,' he says; Agni is the Hotar of the Gods; him he chooses who is the Hotar of the Gods. 'We are,' he says; verily he makes himself attain reality. 'Fair be to thee the deity, O sacrificer,' he says; verily he invokes this blessing (on him). If he were to say 'Who hast chosen Agni as Hotar,' he would surround the sacrificer with Agni on both sides, and he would be liable to perish. The ladle has the sacrificer for its deity, the Upabhṛit the enemy as its deity. If he were to say two as it were, he would produce an enemy for him. 'Take, Adhvaryu, the spoon (*sruch*) with ghee,' he says; verily by it he causes the sacrificer to wax great. 'Pious,' he says, for he aids the Gods, 'With all boons,' he says, for he aids all. 'Let us praise the Gods worthy of praise; let us honour those worthy of honour; let us sacrifice to those worthy of sacrifice,' he says. Those worthy of praise are men; those worthy of honour are the Pitṛis; those worthy of sacrifice are the Gods; verily he sacrifices to the deities according to their portions.

Mantra 2:5:10.

In the case of a Rājanya let him repeat the Tṛichas thrice three other sorts of men are there besides the warrior, the Brahman, Vaiśya and Śūdra; verily he makes them obedient to him. He should repeat fifteen (Sāmidhenīs) in the case of a Rājanya; the Rājanya is fifteenfold; verily he makes him find support in his own Stoma. Let him surround it with a Trishṭubh; the Trishṭubh is power, the Rājanya sacrifices in desire of power; verily by the Trishṭubh he secures power for him. If he desires, 'May there be splendour,' he should surround it with a Gāyatrī, the Gāyatrī is splendour; verily there is splendour. He should repeat seventeen for a Vaiśya; the Vaiśya is seventeenfold; verily he makes him find support in his own Stoma. He should surround it with a Jagatī; cattle are connected with the Jagatī, the Vaiśya sacrifices in desire of cattle; verily by the Jagatī he secures cattle for him. He should repeat twenty one for one who desires support; the Ekaviṃśa is the support of the Stomas; (verily twenty-one serve) for support. He should repeat twenty-four for one who desires splendour: the Gāyatrī has twenty-four syllables, splendour is the Gāyatrī; verily by the Gāyatrī he secures splendour for him. He should repeat thirty for one who desires food; the Virāj has thirty syllables, the Virāj is food; verily by the Virāj he secures food for him. He should repeat thirty-two, for one who desires support; the Anushṭubh has thirty-two syllables, the Anushṭubh is the support of the metres; (verily thirty-two serve) for support. He should repeat thirty-six for one who desires cattle; the Bṛihatī has thirty-six syllables, cattle are connected with the Bṛihatī; verily by the Bṛihatī he secures cattle for him. He should repeat forty-four for one who desires power, the Trishṭubh has forty-four syllables, the Trishṭubh is power; verily by the Trishṭubh he secures power for him. He should repeat forty-eight for one who desires cattle; the Jagatī has forty-eight syllables, cattle are connected with the Jagatī; verily with the Jagatī he secures cattle for him. He should repeat all the metres for one who makes many sacrifices, for all the metres are won by him who makes many sacrifices. He should repeat indefinitely to win that which is not definite.

Mantra 2:5:11

The thread is worn around the neck for men, over the right shoulder for the Pitṛis, over the left for the Gods. He puts it over the left shoulder; verily he makes the mark of the Gods. He repeats standing, for standing he speaks more audibly. He repeats standing, to conquer the world of heaven. He sacrifices sitting; verily he finds support in this world. In that he repeats in the Krauñcha note, that is connected with the Asuras, in the low note, that is connected with men, in the intermediate note, that is connected with the Gods. One should repeat in the intermediate note, to secure the Gods. Clever indeed were the Hotars of old; there fore the ways were held apart, and the paths did not conflict. One foot should be within the sacrificial altar, the other outside; then he repeats, to hold the ways apart and to avoid conflict of the paths. Then does he win the past and the future, the measured and the unmeasured does he win, domestic and wild cattle both does he win; verily also the world of the Gods and the world of men he conquers. ‖ The Gods having repeated the Sāmidhenīs could not see the sacrifice. Prajāpati in silence performed the sprinkling of the butter. Then indeed did the Gods see the sacrifice. In that he silently sprinkles, (it serves) to light up the sacrifice. Verily also he anoints the kindling-sticks. He who knows thus becomes soft. Verily also he delights them. He delights in offspring and cattle who knows thus. If he were to sprinkle with one (verse), he would delight one; if with two, (he would delight) two; if with three, he would make (the offering) go beyond (all others). He sprinkles (repeating the verse) in the mind, for what is imperfect is made perfect by mind. He sprinkles across so as not to make a failure. Speech and mind disputed; 'I will bear the offering to the Gods,' speech said; 'I to the Gods,' mind said. They went to question Prajāpati; he said, Prajāpati, 'Thou art the messenger of mind, for what one thinks of in the mind, one utters in speech.' 'Then assuredly they will not sacrifice to you with speech,' said (speech). Therefore in the mind they offer to Prajāpati, for Prajāpati is, as it were, the mind; (verily it serves) to obtain Prajāpati He rubs the enclosing-sticks; verily he purifies them. (He rubs) the middle one thrice; the breaths are three; verily he conquers the breaths. (He rubs) the southern one thrice; these worlds are three; verily he conquers these worlds. (He rubs) the northern one thrice; three are the paths leading to the Gods; verily he conquers them. Thrice he fans (the fire); the worlds of the Gods are three; verily he conquers the worlds of the Gods. They make twelve; the year has twelve months; verily he delights the year; verily also he brings up the year for him, to gain the world of heaven. He sprinkles; the world of heaven is as it were secret; verily he makes the world of heaven resplendent for him. He sprinkles straight, for the breath is as it were straight. He sprinkles continuously, for the continuity of the breaths and of food and for the smiting away of the Rākṣhasas If he desire of a man, 'May he be likely to perish,' he should sprinkle crookedly for him; verily he leads his breath crookedly from him, and swiftly he perishes. The sprinkling is the head of the sacrifice, the ladle is the body. Having sprinkled, he anoints the ladle; verily he places the head of the sacrifice on its body. Agni was the messenger of the Gods, Daivya of the Asuras; they went to question Prajāpati Prajāpati spake to a Brahman (saying), 'Explain the phrase, "Make announcement",' 'Hearken to this, O ye Gods,' he said; 'Agni the God is the Hotar,' (he said). He chose him of the Gods. Then the Gods prospered, the Asuras were defeated. The man, who knows thus and for whom they chose his list of ancestors, prospers himself, his enemy is defeated. If a Brahman and a non-Brahman have a litigation, one should support the Brahman; if one supports the Brahman, one supports oneself; if one opposes the Brahman, one opposes oneself therefore one should not oppose a Brahman.

Mantra 2:5:12

a. Life to thee. || *b.* Life-giving, O Agni, || *c.* Swell up. || *d.* Together thee. || *e.* Thy wrath. || *f.* The uppermost. || *g.* Forward, O Goddess. || *h.* From the sky to us. || *i.* O Agni and Vishṇu. || *k.* O Agni and Vishṇu. || *l.* This for me, O Varuṇa || *m.* To thee for that I go. || *n.* Upwards that. || *o.* The radiant. || *p.* The child of the waters hath mounted the lap | Of the devious ones, rising up and clothed in the lightning; | Bearing his highest greatness | The golden-coloured young ones go about. || *q.* Some meet, some go up, | The streams fill their common stall; | Round the pure shining son of the waters | The pure waters stand. || *r.* The austere maidens, go around the youth; | The waters, making him clean; | Agni shineth forth with pure radiance with wealth, | Unkindled, butter-clad in the waters. || *s.* I seek the help | Of Mitra and Varuṇa, joint kings; | May they be gracious to such as I. || *t.* O Indra and Varuṇa, grant ye great protection | To our tribe, our people, for the sacrifice | May we conquer in battle the evil-minded, | Him who is fain to overpower the man who long sacrificeth. || *u.* To us, O Mitra and Varuṇa || *v.* Forth your arms. || *w.* O Agni, do thou, wise one, | Appease by sacrifice for us the wrath of Varuṇa; | Best sacrificer, best of bearers, radiant, | Free us from every foe. || *x.* Do thou, O Agni, be nearest to us, | Closest to help, at the dawning of this dawn; | Appease for us by sacrifice Varuṇa, bestowing (on him); | Show thy mercy and be ready to hear our call. || *y.* Far-famed is this Agni of Bhārata, | Since his great light shineth like the sun; | He who overcame Pūru in battle, | Hath shone forth, the heavenly guest, propitious for us. || *z.* I sacrifice to thee, I cast forward my prayer to thee, | That thou mayst be invoked at our invocation; | Thou art like a well in the desert, | Thou, O Agni, to the man eager to worship, O ancient king. || *aa.* With his lustre. || *bb.* With light. || *cc.* Agni, with thy front, | Burn the sorceresses, | Shining in the broad dwellings. || *dd.* Thee of fair face, of fair look, the rapid one, | The wiser, let us ignorant people follow; | Let him sacrifice who knoweth all the ways, | Let him proclaim the oblation among the immortals. || *ee.* To the freer from trouble. || *ff.* Which hath entered me. || *gg.* Away for us, O Indra. || *hh.* O Indra, might. || *ii.* Powers, O Śatakratu. || *kk.* To thee hath been given.

Prapāṭhaka 6.

The New and Full Moon Sacrifices

Mantra 2:6:1

He offers to the kindling-sticks; verily he wins spring among the seasons. He offers to Tanūnapāt; verily he wins the hot season. He offers to the oblations; verily he wins the rains. He offers to the sacrificial strew, verily lie wins autumn. He offers with the cry of 'Hail!'; verily he wins the winter. Therefore in winter animals over which the cry of 'Hail!' is raised perish. He offers to the kindling-sticks; verily he wins the dawns of the Goddesses. He offers to Tanūnapāt; verily he wins the sacrifice. He offers to the oblations; verily he wins cattle. He offers to the sacrificial strew; verily he wins offspring. He takes (the oblation) from the Upabhṛit The oblation is brilliance, the sacrificial strew off spring; verily he places brilliance in offspring. He offers with the cry of 'Hail!'; verily he wins speech. They make up ten, the Virāj has ten syllables, the Virāj is food; verily he wins food by the Virāj He offers to the kindling-sticks; verily he finds support in this world. He offers to Tanūnapāt; verily in the sacrifice and in the atmosphere he finds support. He offers to the oblations; verily in cattle he finds support. He offers to the sacrificial strew; verily he finds support in the paths that lead to the Gods. He offers with the cry of 'Hail!'; verily he finds support in the world of heaven. So many are the worlds of the Gods; verily in them in order he finds support. The Gods and the Asuras contended as to these worlds. The Gods by the fore-sacrifices drove the Asuras away from these worlds; that is why the fore-sacrifices are so called. He for whom knowing thus are offered the fore-sacrifices, drives his enemy away from these worlds. He offers stepping near, for conquest. He who knows the pairing of the fore sacrifices is propagated with offspring, with cattle, with pairings. He offers to the kindling-sticks as many, to Tanūnapāt as one, and that makes a pair. He offers to the kindling-sticks as many, to the sacrificial strew as one, and that makes a pair. That is the pairing of the fore-sacrifices. He who knows thus is propagated with offspring, with cattle, with pairings. These deities were not sacrificed to by the Gods; then the Asuras were fain to harm the sacrifice. The Gods divided the Gāyatrī, five syllables in front and three behind. Then the sacrifice was protected, and the sacrificer. In that the fore- and after-sacrifices are offered, protection is afforded to the sacrifice and to the sacrificer, for the overcoming of the enemy. Therefore a covering is larger in front and smaller behind. The Gods thought that the sacrifice must be completed (in the fore-sacrifice) before the Rākṣhasas with the cry of 'Hail!' They completed it with the cry of 'Hail!' in the fore-sacrifices. They split the sacrifice who complete it with the cry of 'Hail!' in the fore-sacrifices. Having offered the fore sacrifices he sprinkles the oblations, for the continuity of the sacrifice; then verily he makes the oblation, and then he proceeds in order. The fore-sacrifices are the father, the after-sacrifices the son; in that having offered the fore-sacrifices he sprinkles the oblations, the father makes common property with the son. Therefore they say, who know it or who know not, 'How is it the son's only, how is the father's common?' That which spills when the fore-sacrifices are offered is not really spilt. The Gāyatrī conceives through it, and produces offspring and cattle for the sacrificer.

Mantra 2:6:2

The two portions of the oblation are the eyes of the sacrifice. In that he offers the two portions of the oblation, he inserts the two eyes of the sacrifice. He offers in the front place; therefore the eyes are in front. He offers evenly; therefore the eyes are even. By Agni the sacrificer discerns the world of the Gods, by Soma the world of the Pitṛis; in the north part he offers to Agni, in the south to Soma, for these worlds are thus, as it were, to illumine these worlds. Agni and Soma are the kings of the Gods. They are sacrificed to between the Gods, to separate the Gods. Therefore men are separated by the king. The theologians say, 'What is it that the sacrificer does in the sacrifice to support both those animals which have incisors on one side only and those which have incisors on both?' When he has repeated a Ṛich, he makes an offering of the portion of the oblation with the *juṣhāṇā* formula; by that means he supports those with incisors on one side only. When he has repeated a Ṛich, he makes an offering of the sacrificial food (*havis*) with a Ṛich; by that means he supports those with incisors on both sides. The Puronuvākyā contains the word 'head'; verily he makes him head of his peers. He offers with averse containing the word 'team' (*niyut*); verily he appropriates (*ni-yu*) the cattle of his enemy. Keśin Sātyakāmi said to Keśin Dārbhya, 'The seven-footed Śakvarī I shall use for thee at the sacrifice tomorrow, by whose strength one defeats the enemies that have arisen and those that shall be, by the first half of whose strength the ox feeds, by the second half the cow.' The Puronuvākyā is marked in front; verily he defeats the enemies that have arisen; the Yājyā is marked behind; verily he defeats the enemies that shall be. The Puronuvākyā is marked in front; verily he places light in this world; the Yājyā is marked behind; verily he places light in yonder world. Full of light become these worlds to him who knows thus. The Puronuvākyā, is marked in front; therefore the ox feeds with the first half. The Yājyā is marked behind; therefore the cow feeds with the second half. Him who knows thus these two enjoy. The oblation is a bolt, the portions of the oblation are a bolt, the Vaṣhaṭ call is a bolt; thus forges be a threefold bolt and hurls it at his foe, so as not to make a failure. He utters the Vaṣhaṭ call in anger, to lay low his foe. The Puronuvākyā is the Gāyatrī, the Yājyā the Trishṭubh; verily he makes the ruling class dependent on the priestly class; therefore the Brahman is the chief. The chief he becomes who knows thus. He proclaims him with the Puronuvākyā, leads him forward with the Yājyā, and makes him go with the Vaṣhaṭ call. He takes him with the Puronuvākyā, he gives him with the Yājyā, and establishes him with the Vaṣhaṭ call. The Puronuvākyā has three feet; these worlds are three; verily he finds support in these worlds. The Yājyā has four feet; verily he wins four footed cattle. The Vaṣhaṭ call has two syllables, the sacrificer has two feet; verily afterwards he finds support in cattle. The Puronuvākyā is the Gāyatrī, the Yājyā, the Trishṭubh, and this is the seven-footed Śakvarī Whatever the Gods were fain to do by it, that they were able to do; he who knows thus can do whatever he is fain to do.

Mantra 2:6:3

Prajāpati assigned the sacrifices to the Gods. He placed in himself the oblation. The Gods said to him, 'The oblation is the sacrifice; let us have a share in it.' He said, 'Lot them offer to you the portions of the oblation, let them pour out (a layer), let them sprinkle (it).' Therefore they offer the portions of the oblation, they pour out (a layer), and sprinkle (it). The theologians say, 'For what reason are the other offerings worn out, but the oblation fresh?' He should reply, 'Because it is Prajāpati's, for Prajāpati is of the Gods the fresh one.' The metres ran away from the Gods (saying), 'We will not bear the offering, if we have no share.' They kept for them (the offering) divided into four parts, for the Puronuvākyā, the Yājyā, the deity, the Vaṣhaṭ call. In that he offers (the offering) in four parts, he delights the metres, and they delighted by him carry the offering to the Gods. The Aṅgirasas were the last to go hence to the world of heaven. The Ṛishis came to the place of sacrifice; they saw the sacrificial cake creeping about, having become a tortoise. They said to it, 'Be firm for Indra; be firm for Bṛihaspati: be firm for the All-Gods.' It did not become firm. They said to it, 'Be firm for Agni.' It became firm for Agni. In that (the cake) for Agni on eight potsherds is unmoved at the full and at the new moon, (it serves) to conquer the world of heaven. They said to it, 'How hast thou been left?' 'I have not been anointed,' he said, 'just as an axle not anointed goes wrong, so I have gone wrong.' After anointing it above, he anoints it below, to gain the world of heaven. He spreads (the cake) on all the fragments; so many cakes does he conquer in yonder world. That which is burnt belongs to Nirṛiti, that which is not cooked to Rudra, that which is cooked to the Gods. Therefore one should cook it, without burning it, for the Gods. He covers it with ashes; therefore the bones are clothed with flesh. He covers it with the bunch of grass; therefore the head is covered with hair. The offering which is cooked without being sprinkled has fallen from this world, but has not reached the world of the Gods. He sprinkles it before covering it; verily he makes it go among the Gods. If one fragment were lost, one month of the year would be omitted, and the sacrificer would perish. If two were lost, two months of the year would be omitted, and the sacrificer would perish. He counts before covering, to guard the sacrificer. If it be lost, be should make an offering on two potsherds to the Aśvins, and on one potsherd to sky and earth. The Aśvins are the physicians of the Gods; verily by them he heals it. Then is offered an offering on one potsherd to sky and earth; in them is lost what is lost; verily in them he finds it, (and it serves) for support.

Mantra 2:6:4

(Saying) 'On the impulse of the God Savitar thee,' he takes the sword, for impelling. 'With the arms of the Aśvins,' he says, for the Aśvins were the Adhvaryus of the Gods. 'With the hands of Pūṣhan,' he says, for restraint. 'Thou art a hundred-edged, of the tree, slayer of the foe,' he says; verily he sharpens the bolt, being about to hurl it at his enemy. He throws away the grass with a Yajus. The earth is the size of the altar; verily he deprives his enemy of so much of that. Therefore they do not deprive one who has no share. He throws it away thrice; these worlds are three; verily he excludes him from these worlds. He throws it silently a fourth time; verily he excludes him from the unmeasured. He uproots it; verily what of it is impure he cuts off. He uproots it; therefore the plants perish. He cuts the root; verily he cuts the root of the enemy. If dug too deep, it has the Pitṛis for its deity; so much does he dig as is measured by Prajāpati as the mouth of the sacrifice. He digs until (he reaches) support; verily he causes the sacrificer to reach support. He makes it higher on the south; verily he makes it the form of the sacrificial ground. He makes it full of loose earth; loose earth is offspring and cattle; verily he makes him full of offspring and cattle. He performs the second drawing of a boundary. The earth is the size of the altar; verily having excluded his enemy from so much of it, he performs the second drawing of a boundary for himself. Cruelly he acts in making an altar. (With the words) 'Thou art the holder, thou art the self holder,' it is made smooth, for healing. He places the sprinkling waters; the waters are Rakṣhas-slaying; (verily they serve) for slaying the Rākṣhasas He places them in the path made by the sword, for the continuity of the sacrifice. He should think of any one whom he hates; verily does he inflict trouble upon him.

Mantra 2:6:5

The theologians say, 'Thou hast sprinkled the offerings with water; but the waters with what?' 'With the holy power (Brahman),' he should say, for verily he sprinkles the offerings with water, and the waters with the holy power (Brahman). He sprinkles the kindling-wood and the sacrificial strew; verily he makes it pure. He sprinkles the altar, the altar was rough, hairless, and impure; verily he makes it pure. 'To the sky thee, to the atmosphere thee, to earth thee,' (with these words) he places the sacrificial strew and sprinkles it; verily he sprinkles it for these worlds. Cruelly indeed does he act in that he digs. He pours down the waters, for healing. He takes the bunch in front; verily he makes it the chief. He takes so much as is measured by Prajāpati as the mouth of the sacrifice. He spreads the sacrificial strew, the sacrificial strew is offspring, the altar is the earth; verily he places offspring on the earth. He strews it so as not to be very discernible; verily he makes him not very discernible by offspring and cattle. He puts the bundle over the sacrificial strew, the strew is offspring, the bundle the sacrificer; verily he makes the sacrificer superior to the non-sacrificer. Therefore the sacrificer is superior to the non-sacrificer. He puts (grass) between, for separation. He anoints it; verily he makes it into an offering and causes it to go to the world of heaven. He anoints it in three places; these worlds are three; verily he anoints it for these worlds. He does not break off (its edges); if he were to break them off, it would not go aloft for the sacrificer. He pushes it upwards as it were, for the world of heaven is upwards as it were. He depresses it; verily he brings down rain for him. He should not put forward the points too much; if he were to do so, there would be a violent torrent to destroy the Adhvaryu. He should not throw it (so that the roots are) in front. If he were to do this, he would thrust the sacrificer from the world of heaven. He puts it forward (with its points) to the east; verily he makes the sacrificer go to the world of heaven. He should not spread (the bunch) in all directions. If he were to spread (it) in all directions, a daughter would be born to him. He strews it upwards, for upwards is as it were connected with a man; verily a male child is born to him. If he were to smooth it with the sword or the poking-stick, that would be his ruin. He smooths it with his hand, for the protection of the sacrificer. The theologians say, 'What in the sacrifice is the sacrificer' 'The bundle' (is the reply). 'Where in it is the world of heaven?' 'The Āhavanīya (fire)' he should reply. In that he puts the bundle on the Āhavanīya, he makes the sacrificer go to the world of heaven. The sacrificer is rent in that they smooth the bundle; he throws the strew along after it, for calming. The Adhvaryu has no support, and he is liable to be seized by shivering. (With the words), 'Thou art firm (*dhruvā*),' he strokes it; the Dhruvā is this (earth); verily he finds support in it, and shivers not. 'Has he gone, O Agnīdh? he says. If (the Agnīdh) were to say, 'Agni has gone?' he would make Agni go into the fire, and exclude the sacrificer from the world of heaven. So he should say only 'Has he gone?' Verily he makes the sacrificer go to the world of heaven.

Mantra 2:6:6

Agni had three elder brothers; they perished while carrying the offering to the Gods. Agni was afraid, 'Thus indeed will this one fall on misfortune.' He ran away, and entered the waters. The Gods sought to start him up. The fish proclaimed him, and he cursed it, 'At Pleasure may they slay thee, since thou hast proclaimed me.' So they slay the fish at pleasure, for he is cursed. They found him; they said, 'Come to us, and carry the offering for us.' He said, 'Let me choose a boon; whatever of the offering when it is taken (in the ladle) falls outside the enclosing-sticks, let that be the share of my brothers.' There fore whatever of the offering when it is taken falls outside the enclosing sticks is their share; verily by it he delights them. He puts the enclosing sticks around, to smite away the Rākṣhasas He makes them touch, so that the Rākṣhasas may not creep through. He puts none in front, for the sun rises in front and smites away the Rākṣhasas He places the two kindling-sticks upright, for upwards they smite away the Rākṣhasas (He places) one with a Yajus, the other in silence, to make a pair. He places two, the sacrificer has two feet, for support. The theologians say, 'He indeed would be a sacrificer who should be the stronger for a failure in the sacrifice.' (The words), 'To the lord of earth hail! To the lord of the world, hail! To the lord of creatures hail! ' he should pronounce over the spilt (offering). Thus by a failure in the sacrifice he becomes stronger, for he delights more Gods (than usual). There is sameness in the sacrifice, in that there are two sacrificial cakes (offered) in order. Between them he offers the silent sacrifice, to break the sameness and to make a pair. Agni was in yonder world, Yama in this. The Gods said, 'Come, let us interchange them'; with food the Gods invited Agni, with the kingdom the Pitṛis Yama; therefore is Agni the food-eater of the Gods, Yama the king of the Pitṛis; he who knows thus obtains the kingdom and food. To him they gave that share which they cut off for Agni Sviṣhṭakṛit. In that he cuts off a share for Agni Sviṣhṭakṛit, he gives Rudra a share. He cuts off one in each case, for Rudra is one as it were. He cuts off from the north part, for this is Rudra's quarter; verily he appeases Rudra in his own quarter. He sprinkles it twice, to make it divided into four. The former offerings are cattle, Agni is Rudra here; if he were to pour over the former offerings, he would give Rudra cattle, and the sacrificer would be without cattle. He offers leaving the former oblations aside, to protect the cattle.

The Part of the Hotar in the New and Full Moon Sacrifice

Mantra 2:6:7

Manu desired what of earth was sacrificial. He found the poured out ghee. He said, 'Who is able to produce this also at the sacrifice?' Mitra and Varuṇa said, 'We are able to produce the cow.' Then they set the cow in motion. Wherever she stepped, there ghee was pressed out; therefore she is called ghee-footed; that is her origin. 'The Rathantara is invoked with the earth,' he says. The Rathantara is this (earth); verily he invokes her with food. 'The Vāmadevya is invoked with the atmosphere,' he says. The Vāmadevya, is cattle; verily he invokes cattle with the atmosphere. 'The Bṛihat is invoked with the sky,' he says. The Bṛihat is connected with food; verily he invokes food with the sky. ' The seven Hotras are invoked,' he says; verily he invokes the Hotras. 'The cow is invoked with the bull,' he says; verily he invokes a pair. 'The friend food is invoked,' he says; verily he invokes the Soma drink. 'It is invoked; ho!' he says; verily he invokes the self, for the self is the best of those invoked. He invokes food, food is cattle; verily he invokes cattle. He invokes four, for cattle are four-footed. 'Offspring of Manu,' he says, for Manu first saw her. 'Ghee-footed,' he says. Because ghee was pressed out of her foot, therefore be says thus. 'Of Mitra and Varuṇa,' he says, for Mitra and Varuṇa set her in motion. 'The Brahman, God made, is invoked,' he says; verily he invokes the Brahman. 'The divine Adhvaryus are invoked, the human are invoked,' he says; verily he invokes the Gods and men. 'Who shall help this sacrifice and make the lord of the sacrifice prosper,' he says; verily he invokes a blessing for the sacrifice and the sacrificer. 'Sky and earth are invoked,' he says; verily he invokes sky and earth. 'Born of yore, the righteous,' he says, for they were born of yore and are righteous. 'Divine, with Gods for children,' he says, for they are divine and have Gods for children. 'Invoked is this sacrificer,' he says; verily he invokes the sacrificer. 'Invoked in the highest sacrifice, invoked in the greater offering, invoked in the divine abode,' he says. The highest sacrifice is offspring, the greater offering is cattle, the divine abode is the world of heaven. (With the words), 'Thou art this; thou art this,' he invokes the dear abode of the sacrifice. 'All that is dear to it is invoked,' he says; verily not vainly does he invoke.

Mantra 2:6:8

Food is cattle, he takes it himself; verily by himself he fills his desires of cattle, for no one else can grant him his desire of cattle. 'Thee offered to the lord of speech I eat,' he says; verily he delights speech with a share. 'Thee offered to the lord of the Sadas I eat,' he says, for completion.' (The food) is divided. in four; what is divided in four is the offering, what is divided in four is cattle; if the Hotar were to eat it, the Hotar would experience misfortune; if he were to offer it in the fire, he would give the cattle to Rudra, and the sacrificer would be without cattle. 'Thee offered to the lord of speech I eat,' he says; verily secretly does he offer it. 'Thee offered to the lord of the Sadas,' he says, for completion. They eat; they eat at a suitable moment; he gives a sacrificial gift; at a suitable moment be gives a gift. They cleave the sacrifice, if they eat in the middle. They purify it with water; all the Gods are the waters; verily they connect the sacrifice with the Gods. The Gods excluded Rudra from the sacrifice; he pierced the sacrifice, the Gods gathered round it (saying), 'May it be right for us.' They said, 'Well offered will this be for us, if we propitiate him.' That is why Agni is called the 'well offerer' (*sviṣhṭakrit*). When it was pierced (by him) they cut off (a piece) of the size of a barleycorn; therefore one should cut off (a piece) the size of a barleycorn. If one were to cut off more, he would confuse that part of the sacrifice. If he were to make a layer and then to sprinkle, lie would make it swell on both sides. He cuts it off and sprinkles it; there are two operations; the sacrificer has two feet, for support. If he were to transfer it (to the Brahman) crosswise, he would pierce the unwounded part of the sacrifice; lie transfers it in front; verily he transfers it in the proper way. They transferred it for Pūṣhan. Pūṣhan having eaten it lost his teeth; therefore Pūṣhan has pounded food for his share, for he has no teeth. The Gods said of him, 'He has lost (his teeth), he is not fit for the offering.' They transferred it to Bṛihaspati Bṛihaspati was afraid, 'Thus indeed will this one fall on misfortune.' He saw this Mantra; 'With the eye of the sun I gaze on thee,' he said, for the eye of the sun harms no one. He was afraid, 'It will harm me as I take it.' 'On the impulse of the God Savitar, with the arms of the Aśvins, with the hands of Pūṣhan I take thee,' he says; verily, impelled by Savitar, he took it with the holy power (Brahman) and with the Gods. He was afraid, 'It will harm me as I eat.' 'Thee with the mouth of Agni I eat,' he said, for nothing harms the mouth of Agni. He was afraid, 'It will harm me when I have eaten.' 'With the belly of the Brahman,' he said, for nothing harms the belly of the Brahman. 'With the holy power (Brahman) of Bṛihaspati,' (he said), for he is fullest of the holy power (Brahman). The breaths indeed depart from him who eats this offering; by purifying it with water he grasps the breaths; the breaths are ambrosia, the waters ambrosia; verily he summons the breaths according to their places.

Mantra 2:6:9

He takes a portion for the Agnīdh; verily he delights the seasons whose mouth is Agni. He takes a kindling-stick, for the support of the subsequent offerings; verily he pours on that which has a kindling stick. He rubs the enclosing-sticks; verily he purifies them. He rubs each once, for the sacrifice there is as it were turned away. It makes up four, cattle are four-footed; verily he wins cattle. 'O Brahman, will we set out?' he says; there indeed is the sacrifice placed, where the Brahman is; where the sacrifice is placed, thence does he commence it. If he were to instigate him with his hand, he would shiver; if with his head, he would have a headache; if he were to sit in silence, the sacrifice would not proceed; he should say, 'Set out! In speech the sacrifice is placed; where the sacrifice is placed, thence does he bestow it. 'O God Savitar, that he hath proclaimed to thee,' he says, for impelling. 'Bṛihaspati is the (priest) Brahman,' he says, for he is fullest of the holy power (Brahman). 'Do thou guard the sacrifice, guard the lord of the sacrifice, guard me,' he says; for the sacrifice, the sacrificer, and himself, for these he thus invokes a blessing, to prevent misfortune, Having caused (him) to call out, he says, 'Utter the verse for sacrifice to the Gods.' The theologians say, 'The Gods have been sacrificed to; what Gods are they?' 'The metres,' he should reply, 'Gāyatrī Triṣhṭubh, and Jagatī' Then they say, 'The metres are the Brahmans'; verily he sacrifices to them. The deities were sacrificed to by the Gods; then Agni did not burn forth; the Gods found him by the offerings in the after-sacrifices; in that he offers the after-sacrifices verily thus one kindles Agni. There was an Asura, named Etadu. He then appropriated the blessing of the sacrifice. If one were to say, 'That indeed (etād *u*) hath been glorious, O sky and earth,' one would cause Etadu to attain the blessing of the sacrifice. 'This (*idām*) has been glorious, sky and earth,' he should say; verily he makes the sacrificer attain the blessing of the sacrifice. 'We have won the utterance of prayer and homage,' he says; 'we have won this,' he says in effect. 'It resteth on sky and earth,' he says, for the sacrifice rests on the sky and earth. 'Helpful for thee in this sacrifice, O sacrificer, be sky and earth,' he says; verily he invokes this blessing. If he were to say, 'easy of access and easy to dwell on,' the sacrificer would be likely to perish, for when he perishes he has recourse to this (earth). 'Easy of approach, and easy to move on,' he should say; verily he invokes for him a wider sphere, and he is not likely to perish. 'In the knowledge of these two Agni hath rejoiced in this offering,' he says; 'the Gods we have sacrificed to, we have made them to prosper,' he says in effect. If he were not to indicate (the sacrificer), the blessing of the sacrifice would go to his neighbour. 'This sacrificer imploreth (a blessing) N. N.,' he says; verily by indicating him he makes him attain the world of heaven. 'He imploreth length of days, he imploreth a noble offspring, he says; verily he invokes this blessing. 'He imploreth superiority over his equals,' he says; his equals are the breaths; verily he does not obstruct his breaths.

'Agni shall win, God, from the Gods, we men from Agni,' he says, 'Agni wins from the Gods, we from men,' he says in effect. 'Here is the path of favour, and this our homage to the Gods,' he says; to both the Gods whom he sacrifices to and those to whom he does not sacrifice, he pays homage, for his own security.

Mantra 2:6:10.

The Gods could not find any one to utter the call Svagā at the sacrifice. They spoke to Śamyu Bārhaspatya, 'Perform the Svagā call at this sacrifice for us.' He said, 'Let me choose a boon; if a faithless man sacrifice, or a man sacrifices without prescription, let the blessing of such a sacrificer be mine.' Therefore if a faithless man sacrifices, or a man sacrifices without prescription, the blessing of such a sacrifice goes to Śamyu Bārhaspatya 'That is mine,' he said, 'What is to belong to my offspring?.' 'Him, who reviles him, he shall fine with a hundred; him, who strikes him, he shall fine with a thousand; he, who draws blood from him, shall not behold the world of the Pitṛis for as many years as are the grains of dust which the blood in its fall seizes upon,' (they replied). Therefore one should not revile a Brahman, nor strike him, nor draw blood from him; for so great is his sin. 'That health and wealth we choose,' he says; verily he utters the call Svagā, over the sacrifice. 'That health and wealth we choose,' he says; verily he gives Śamyu Bārhaspatya his portion. 'Success to the sacrifice, success to the sacrificer,' he says; verily he invokes this blessing. He sacrifices to Soma; verily he places seed; he sacrifices to Tvaṣhṭar; seed is placed and Tvaṣhṭar moulds forms; he sacrifices to the wives of the Gods, to make a pair; he sacrifices to Agni, lord of the house, for support. There is sameness in the sacrifice in that the fore-sacrifices are offered with butter, and the sacrifices to the wives (are offered) with butter. Having repeated the Ṛich, of the sacrifices to the wives he offers with a Ṛich, to prevent sameness, and to make a pairing. The sacrifice has a fivefold prelude and a fivefold end; there are offered five fore-sacrifices; there are four sacrifices to the wives, the fifth is the Samiṣhṭayajus by they make up five as a prelude, and five as an end.

Mantra 2:6:11

a. Yoke like a charioteer, Agni, | The steeds that best invite the Gods | Set down as ancient Hotar ‖ *b.* And, O God, for us do thou the Gods, | Most wise one, call hither; | Make all our wishes true; ‖ *c.* Since thou, O most young, | O son of strength, who art sacrificed to, | Art righteous and worthy of sacrifice. ‖ *d.* This Agni is lord of a thousandfold, | A hundredfold, strength; | The sage, the head of wealth. ‖ *e.* Bring him hither with common call | Lower to our sacrifice, O Aṅgiras | As the Ṛibhus bend the felly (of the chariot) ‖ *f.* To him, the heavenly, | Now with constant voice, O Virupa, | To the strong one urge the hymn of praise. ‖ *g.* What Paṇi shall we lay low among the kine | With the missile of this Agni | Who seeth from afar? ‖ *h.* May not the clans of the Gods forsake us, | Like the dawns entering the waters, | As cows a poor man. ‖ *i.* Let not the assault | Of any ill-minded foe smite us, | As a wave a ship. ‖ *k.* Homage to thee, O Agni, for might, | The people sing, O God; | With strength trouble thou the foe. ‖ *l.* Wilt thou not, O Agni, | Bring us wealth for our quest for cattle? | O room maker, make room for us. ‖ *m.* Cast us not aside in this great contest, | Like a bearer his burden; | Gather wealth and conquer it. ‖ *n.* May this terror, this misfortune, | O Agni, fasten on another than us; | Increase our impetuous strength. ‖ *o.* The reverent or generous man | In whose offering he hath delighted, | Agni aideth indeed with furtherance. ‖ *p.* From a far region | Come hither to these lower ones, | Favour those in the region where I am. ‖ *q.* Since we have known of old | Of thy help, O Agni, as a father's, | Now we seek thy favour. ‖ *r.* Thou, who art like a mighty man who slayeth with the dart | Or a sharp-horned bull, | O Agni, hast rent the forts. ‖ *s.* O friends, together (offer) fit | Food and praise to Agni, | Highest over the folk, | The son of strength, the mighty. ‖ *t.* Thou gatherest, O strong one, | All that belongeth, O Agni, to the niggard; | Thou art kindled in the place of offering; | Do thou bear us good things. ‖ *u.* O Prajāpati ‖ *v.* He knoweth. ‖ *w.* O Soma and Pūṣhan. ‖ *x.* These Gods.

Mantra 2:6:12

a. Eagerly we hail thee, | Eagerly would we kindle thee; | Eager bring the eager, | The fathers, to eat the offering. ‖ *b.* Thou, O Soma, art pre-eminent in wisdom; | Thou movest along the straightest path; | Through thy guidance, O drop, our fathers wisely divided | The treasure among the Gods. | By thee, O Soma Pavamāna, our ancient fathers | Wisely ordained the offerings; | Conquering, untroubled, do thou open the barriers; | Be generous to us in heroes and horses. ‖ *d.* Thou, O Soma, in accord with the fathers, | Hast stretched over sky and earth; | To thee, O drop, let us make sacrifice with offering; | Let us be lords of wealth. ‖ *e.* O fathers, made ready by Agni, come hither; | With good leadership sit ye on each seat; | Eat ye the offerings set out on the strew; | And give us wealth with many heroes. ‖ *f.* O fathers that sit on the sacrificial strew, come hither with your aid; | We have made these offerings for you; accept them, | And then come to us with your most healing aid, | Give us health, wealth, and safety! ‖ *g.* I have found the kindly fathers, | The scion and the step of Viṣhṇu; | They that sit on the sacrificial strew and enjoy the drink | That is pressed for them with the Svadhā call are most eager to come hither. ‖ *h.* Invoked are the fathers who love the Soma | To their dear homes on the sacrificial strew; | May they come hither; may they hear us here | May they speak for us; and may they aid us. ‖ *i.* Let them arise, the lower and the higher | And the middle fathers who love the Soma; | They who lived their lives in goodness and without sin; | May these fathers help us when we call. ‖ *k.* Be this homage today to the fathers, | Who went before and who went after; | Who are seated in the earthly region | Or who are now in abodes with fair dwellings. ‖ *l.* As our fathers before, | Of old, O Agni, furthering right, | Sought the pure, the devotion, singing hymns | Cleaving the earth they disclosed the red ones. ‖ *m.* When, O Agni, bearer of oblations, | Thou sacrificest to the righteous fathers, | Thou shalt bear the oblations | To the Gods and to the fathers. ‖ *n.* Thou, O Agni, praised, all-knower, | Didst carry the offerings making them fragrant; | Thou didst give them to the fathers who ate them at the Svadhā call; | Eat thou, O God, the offerings set before thee. ‖ *o.* Mātalī with the Kavyas, Yama with the Aṅgirasas, | Bṛihaspati rejoicing with the Ṛikvans, | Those whom the Gods magnified and those who magnified the Gods; | Some in the Svāhā call, some in the Svadhā rejoice. ‖ *p.* Sit on this strew, O Yama, | In accordance with the Aṅgirasas, the fathers | Let the verses made by the poets bring thee hither | Rejoice, O king, in this offering. | Come with the Aṅgirasas who deserve the sacrifice | Yama, rejoice here with the Vairūpas; | I summon Vivasvat who is thy father, | Sitting down on the strew at this sacrifice. ‖ *r.* The Aṅgirasas, our fathers, the Navagvas, | Atharvans, Bhṛigus, who love the Soma; | May we be in the favour of those ones worthy of sacrifice, | May we have their kindly good will.

Kāṇḍa 3.

Prapāṭhaka 1

The Supplement to the Soma Sacrifice

Mantra 3:1:1

Prajāpati desired, 'May I create offspring.' He did penance, he created serpents. He desired, 'May I create offspring.' He did penance a second time, he created birds. He desired, 'May I create offspring.' He did penance a third time, he saw this speech of the consecrated, he spoke it. Then indeed did he create offspring. In that after undergoing penance he speaks the speech of the consecrated, the sacrificer thus creates offspring. If one who is consecrated sees anything impure, the consecration departs from him; his dark colour, his beauty goes away. 'Mind unbound; eye weak; sun best of lights; O consecration, forsake me not,' he says, and consecration departs not from him, his dark colour and his beauty go not away. If rain falls on one who is consecrated, the heavenly waters if unappeased destroy his force, might, consecration, and penance. 'Do ye flowing waters place might (in me), place force, place might; do not destroy my consecration, nor my penance,' he says; verily he places all that in himself; they do not destroy his force, might, consecration, or penance. Agni is the divinity of the consecrated man, and he is concealed as it were from him, when he goes (out), and the Rākṣhasas are able to hurt him. 'From good to better do thou advance; may Bṛihaspati be thy forerunner,' he says. Bṛihaspati is the holy power (Brahman) of the Gods; verily he grasps hold of him, and he brings him safely through. 'Here we have come (*a-idam*) to the place on earth for sacrifice to the Gods,' he says, for he comes to the place on earth for sacrifice, who sacrifices. 'Wherein aforetime all the Gods rejoiced,' he says, for all the Gods delight in it, in that the Brahmans so do. 'Accomplishing (the rite) with Ṛich, Sāman, and Yajus,' he says, for he who sacrifices accomplishes (the rite) with Ṛich, Sāman, and Yajus. 'Let us rejoice in fullness of wealth, in sustenance,' he says; verily he invokes this blessing.

Mantra 3:1:2

'This is thy Gāyatrī part,' say for me to Soma. | 'This is thy Trishṭubh, Jagatī, part,' say for me to Soma. | 'Become lord of the Chandomas,' say for me to Soma. | He who purchases King Soma after making it go to the world of lordship, becomes lord of his own (people). The world of lordship of King Soma is the metres; he should utter these verses before the purchase of Soma. It is to the world of lordship that he makes it go when he buys (Soma), and he becomes lord of his own. He, who knows the support of the Tānūnaptra finds support. The theologians say, 'They do not eat, nor offer; then where does the Tānūnaptra find support?' 'In Prajāpati, in the mind, he should reply. He should smell at it thrice, (saying), 'In Prajāpati thee, in the mind I offer'; this indeed is the support of the Tānūnaptra; he who knows thus finds support. He who knows the support of the Adhvaryu finds support. He should call (on the Āgnīdhra) standing in the place without moving whence he is minded to sacrifice. This is the support of the Adhvaryu; he who knows thus finds support. If he were to sacrifice moving about, he would lose his support; therefore he should sacrifice standing in the same place, for support. He who knows the possession of the Adhvaryu, becomes possessed (of what he needs). His possession is the offering-spoon, his possession is the Vāyu cup, his possession is the beaker. If he were to call without holding the Vāyu cup or the beaker, he would lose his own; therefore he must hold it when he calls; verily he loses not his own. If he begins the litany without placing the Soma, the Soma is not supported, the Stoma is not supported, the hymns are not supported, the sacrificer is not supported, the Adhvaryu is not supported. The support of the Soma is the Vāyu cup, the support of it is the beaker, (the support) of the Stoma is Soma, (the support) of the hymns is the Stoma. He should grasp the cup or fill up the beaker, and then begin the litany; a support to the Soma he verily (*eva*) gives, to the Stoma, to the hymns; the sacrificer finds support, the Adhvaryu finds support.

Mantra 3:1:3

They gather together the sacrifice when (they gather the dust of) the footprint of the Soma cow; the oblation-holders are the mouth of the sacrifice; when they move forward the oblation-holders, then he should oil the axle with it; verily he extends the sacrifice in the mouth of the sacrifice. They lead Agni forward, they take the wife forward, and they make the carts follow after. Now the altar of him (Agni) is deserted; he broods on it, and is liable to become terrible (rudrā), and lay to rest the offspring and cattle of the sacrificer. When they are leading northward the sacrificial animal over which the Āprīs have been said, he should take (from the altar the fire) for cooking it; verily he makes him share in it. The Āhavanīya is the sacrificer; if they take (the fire) for cooking the victim from the Āhavanīya, they tear the sacrificer asunder; the fire should therefore be thus, or he should make it by friction, so that the sacrificer's body may remain together. If a portion of the victim be lost, he should cut off an equivalent portion of the butter; that is then the atonement. If men disturb his victim and he wish of them, 'May they come to ruin,' he should make an offering in the Agnīdh's altar with the Ṛich containing the word 'paying of homage' (and beginning), 'What then?' Verily he appropriates their paying of homage and speedily do they go to ruin.

Mantra 3:1:4

a. The offspring, being born of Prajāpati | And those that have been born, | To him declare them; | Lot the wise one reflect thereon. || *b.* This victim, O lord of cattle, for thee today, | I bind, O Agni, in the midst of righteous action; | Approve it, and let us sacrifice with a good offering | May this offering be welcome to the Gods. || *c.* The ancient wise ones grasp | The breath as it speedeth from the limbs; | Go to heaven by the paths which lead to the Gods; | Be among the plants with thy members. || *d.* What cattle the lord of cattle ruleth, | Both the four-footed and the two-footed, | May he, bought off, go to his sacrificial share; | May abundances of wealth fall to the sacrificer. || *e.* Those, who being bound, contemplated | With mind and with eye him who was being bound | Let the God Agni first release them, | Lord of offspring, in harmony with offspring. || *f.* The cattle of the forest, of all forms, | Of various forms, many of one form. | Let the God Vāyu first release them, | Lord of offspring, in harmony with offspring. || *g.* Releasing the seed of being, | Do ye further the sacrificer, O Gods; | May that which hath stood ready and strenuous, | Go alive to the place of the Gods. || *h.* The breath of the sacrificer is apart from the victim; | The sacrifice goeth to the Gods with the Gods; | Let it go alive to the place of the Gods; | Fulfilled may the desires of the sacrificer be. || *i.* If the victim has uttered a cry, | Or striketh its breast with its feet, | May Agni release me from that sin, | From all misfortune. || *k.* O ye slayers, come | To the sacrifice sped by the Gods; | Free the victim from the noose, | The lord of the sacrifice from the bond. || *l.* May Aditi loosen this noose; | Homage to the cattle, to the lord of cattle, I pay; | I cast down the enemy; | On him whom we hate I fasten the noose. || *m.* Thee they keep to carry the offering, | To cook (the victim) and as worthy of sacrifice; | O Agni, with thy strength and thy body, be present | And accept our offerings, O Jātavedas || *n.* O Jātavedas, go with the caul to the Gods, | For thou art the first Hotar; | With ghee do thou strengthen their bodies; | May the Gods eat the offering made with the cry of 'hail!' || *o.* Hail to the Gods; to the Gods hail!

Mantra 3:1:5

Cattle belong to Prajāpati; their overlord is Rudra. In that he prepares (them) with these two (verses), verily by addressing him with them he secures him, so that his self is not injured. He prepares (them) with two; the sacrificer has two feet; (verily it serves) for support. Having prepared them, he offers five libations; cattle are fivefold; I verily he wins cattle. Now the victim is led to death, and if he should lay hold on it, the sacrificer would be likely to die. ' The breath of the sacrifice is apart from the victim,' he says, for distinction. 'If the victim has uttered a cry'—(with these words) he offers a libation, for calming. 'O ye slayers, come to the sacrifices,' he says; that is according to the text. When the omentum. is being taken, the strength goes away from Agni. 'Thee they keep to carry the offering'—(with these words) he pours a libation over the omentum; verily he wins the strength of Agni; (it serves) also for making (the victim) ready. In the case of some Gods the cry of 'hail!' is uttered before (an offering), in the case of others the cry of 'hail!' is uttered after. 'Hail to the Gods, to the Gods hail!'—(with these words) he pours a libation on either side of the omentum; verily he delights both (sets of Gods).

Mantra 3:1:6

a. 'He who performs the sacrifice not according to the deities falls a victim to the deities, he becomes worse. He who (performs) in accordance with the deities does not fall a victim to the deities, he becomes better. He should rub the Agnīdh's place with a verse addressed to Agni, the oblation-holder with one addressed to Vishṇu, the offering-spoons with one addressed to Agni, the Vāyu cups with one addressed to Vāyu, the Sadas with one addressed to Indra. Thus he forms the sacrifice in accordance with the deities, he does not fall a victim to the deities, he becomes better. || *b.* I yoke earth for thee with light, I yoke wind for thee with the atmosphere, I yoke speech for thee with the sun, I yoke the three spaces of the sun for thee. || *c.* Agni is the deity, Gāyatrī the metre, thou art the vessel of the silent offering. Soma is the deity, Trishṭubh the metre, thou art the vessel of the restrained offering. Indra is the deity, Jagatī the metre, thou art the vessel of Indra and Vāyu Bṛihaspati is the deity, Anushṭubh the metre, thou art the vessel of Mitra and Varuṇa The Aśvins are the deity, Paṅkti the metre, thou art the vessel of the Aśvins. Sūrya is the deity, Bṛihatī the metre, thou art the vessel of the pure (Soma). Chandramās is the deity, Satobṛihatī the metre, thou art the vessel of the mixed (Soma). The All-Gods are the deity, Ushṇih the metre, thou art the vessel of the opening offering. Indra is the deity, Kakubh the metre, thou art the vessel of the hymns. Earth is the deity, Virāj the metre, thou art the vessel of the reserved (offering).

Mantra 3:1:7

The Adhvaryu is he that brings trouble on the sacrificer, and he that brings trouble himself is ruined before the trouble. 'From the formula spoken, guard me, from every execration'—(with these words) he should pour a libation before the morning litany (of the Hotar). So the Adhvaryu girds himself in front with a protection, to avert trouble. || For entry thee, for rest thee, for the overcoming of the Gāyatrī, of the Trishṭubh, of the

Jagatī, hail! O expiration and inspiration, protect me from death, O expiration and inspiration forsake me not. ‖ They contend as to the deities and to expiration and inspiration, whose Soma (offerings) compete. 'For entry thee, for rest thee,' he says; entry and rest are the metres; verily by the metres he appropriates his metres. The Ājya (Stotras) have the word 'forward' in them, for conquest. The beginning verses are addressed to the Marutas, for victory. Both the Bṛihat and the Rathantara (Sāmans) are used. The Rathantara is this (earth), the What yonder (sky); verily he cuts him off from these two. The Rathantara is today, the Bṛihat tomorrow; verily he cuts him off from today and tomorrow. The Rathantara is the past, the Bṛihat the future; verily he cuts him off from the past and the future. The Rathantara is the measured, the Bṛihat the unmeasured; verily he cuts him off from the measured and the unmeasured. Viśvāmitra and Jamadagni had a quarrel with Vasiṣhṭha. Jamadagni saw this Vihavyā (hymn), and by means of it he appropriated the power and strength of Vasiṣhṭha. In that the Vihavyā is recited, the sacrificer appropriates the power and strength of his enemy. 'He who performs more rites of sacrifice,' they say, 'appropriates the Gods.' If the Soma (sacrifice) on the other side is an Agniṣhṭoma, he should perform an Ukthya; if it is an Ukthya, he should perform an Atirātra; verily by means of rites of sacrifice he appropriates his deities; he becomes better.

Mantra 3:1:8

a. Ye are the Nigrābhyas, heard by the Gods. Delight my life, delight my expiration, delight my inspiration, delight my cross-breathing, delight my eye, delight my ear, delight my mind, delight my speech, delight my trunk, delight my limbs, delight my offspring, delight my cattle, delight my house, delight my troops, delight me with all my troops, delight me; may my troops not go thirsty. ‖ *b.* The plants are the subjects of Soma; the subjects indeed are able to give up the king; Soma is connected with Indra. 'I have made you grow in my mind, O ye well born; O ye born of right, may we enjoy your favour; may the divine plants in accord with Indra grant us the Soma for the pressing,' he says verily having begged him from the plants, his subjects, and his deity he presses him. ‖ *c.* When the Soma is pressed the first drop which falls has potency to destroy the power, strength, offspring, and cattle of the sacrificer; he should pronounce over it the formula, 'Thou hast fallen to me with offspring, with abundance of wealth; destroy not my power and strength'; verily he invokes this blessing to prevent the destruction of his power, strength, offering, and cattle. ‖ *d.* The drop hath fallen on the earth, the sky, | On this seat and on the one which was aforetime | The drop that wandereth over the third seat | offer in the seven Hotras.'

Mantra 3:1:9

a. He who bestows upon the Gods the glory of the Gods, and on men the glory of men, has the divine glory among the Gods, the human glory among men. The libations which he draws off before the Āgrayaṇa libation, he should draw off silently; those after with noise; verily he bestows upon the Gods the glory of the Gods, and on men the glory of men; verily he has the divine glory among the Gods, the human glory among men. ‖ *b.* May Agni protect us at the morning pressing, | He that belongeth to all men, all-wealful in his might; | May he, the purifier, grant us wealth; | May we that share the draught be long-lived ‖ *c.* May the All-Gods, the Marutas, Indra, | Not leave us at the second pressing; | Long-lived, speaking what is pleasing to them, | May we enjoy the favour of the Gods. ‖ *d.* This third libation belongeth to the sages | Who righteously set the beaker in motion; | May these Saudhanvanas, who have attained heaven, | Bear our good offering to what is better. ‖ *e.* Some libations have bases, some have not. Those which have a sprinkling have bases, those of Soma have not bases. Taking (the cup) for Indra and Vāyu he should sprinkle it (saying), 'May the sacrifice be harmless for plants, for our cattle, for our folk; for all creatures harmless thou art; swell like ghee, O God Soma.' Verily so he makes the libations of Soma to have a base. He becomes possessed of a base who knows thus. Verily also he wets with ghee the sky and earth: they being wet are to be lived upon; he is to be lived upon who knows thus. ‖ *f.* This is thy share, O Rudra, for which thou didst ask; rejoice in it, find (for us) the lordship of cows, abundance of wealth, with good heroes and a year's prosperity.' ‖ *g.* Manu divided his property among his sons. He deprived Nābhānediṣhṭha, who was a student, of any portion. He went to him, and said, 'How hast thou deprived me of a portion?' He replied, 'I have not deprived you of a portion; the Aṅgirasas here are performing a Sattra; they cannot discern the world of heaven; declare this Brāhmaṇa to them; when they go to the, world of heaven they will give thee their cattle.' He told them it, and they when going to the world of heaven gave him their cattle. Rudra approached him as he went about with his cattle in the place of sacrifice, and said, 'These are my cattle.' He replied, 'They have given them to me.' They have not the power to do that,' he replied, (whatever is left on the place of sacrifice is mine.' Then one should not resort to a place of sacrifice. He said, 'Give me a share in the sacrifice, and I will not have designs against your cattle. He poured out for him the remnants of the mixed (Soma). Then indeed had Rudra no designs against his cattle. When one who knows thus offers the remnants of the mixed (Soma), Rudra has no designs against his cattle.

Mantra 3:1:10.

a. May I be pleasing to speech; pleasing to the lord of speech, O divine speech. The sweetness of speech place in me; hail to Sarasvatī ‖ *b.* By the Ṛich make the Soma to prosper, | By the Gateway the Rathantara, | The Bṛihat with the Gāyatrī for its metre. ‖ *c.* The drop that falleth of them, that shoot, | Shaken by the arms, from the womb of the pressing-planks, | Or from the filter of the Adhvaryu, | Over it I say Hail! and offer it to Indra. ‖ *d.* The drop, the shoot, that hath fallen on the ground, | From the rice grains, the cake, the mush, | From the Soma with grain, from the mixed, O Indra, from the pure, | Over it I say Hail! and offer it to Indra. ‖ *e.* Thy sweet drop, powerful, | Over which Hail! is said and which goeth back to the Gods | From the sky, the earth, the atmosphere | Over it I say Hail! and offer it to Indra. ‖ *f.* The Adhvaryu is the first of the priests to start work, verily they say the Stoma should be started by him. ‖ *g.* 'May speech that goes in front go in front, going straight to the Gods, placing glory in me, breath in cattle, offspring in me and in the sacrificer,' he says; verily he yokes speech at the beginning of the sacrifice. The place of the sacrifice is made when having drawn off the libations they creep to the Bahiṣhpavamāna; for they go away, and they praise with verses which go away; he returns, and with a verse addressed to Viṣhṇu reverences (the Soma); Viṣhṇu is the sacrifice; verily he makes the sacrifice. 'O Viṣhṇu, as our nearest, O mighty one, grant us protection; the streams dripping honey milk for thee the unfailing source,' he says; verily he makes to swell by it whatever of the Soma has dried up through lying (in the barrels).

Mantra 3:1:11

a. By Agni may one win wealth | And abundance day by day, | Glory, full of heroes. ‖ *b.* Rich in cattle, in sheep, O Agni, in horses is the sacrifice; | With manly companions, ever unalterable; | Rich in food is this, O Asura, in offspring, | Enduring, wealth, deep based and rich in houses. ‖ *c.* Swell up. ‖ *d.* Together for thee. ‖ *e.* Here Tvaṣhṭar the first, | Of all forms, I call. | May he be ours only. ‖ *f.* That procreant strength for us do thou, | O God Tvaṣhṭar, graciously lot loose, | Whence is born a hero of great deeds, of skill, | Who wieldeth the pressing-stone and loveth the Gods. ‖ *g.* Come hither, O Tvaṣhṭar, propitious, | Pervasive for abundance, and of thy own will, | Aid us in every sacrifice. ‖ *h.* The hero is born, loving the Gods, | Of brilliant hue, strong, and full of vigour; | Tvaṣhṭar accord us offspring and descendants; | May he go to the place of the Gods. ‖ *i.* Forth for us, O Goddess. ‖ *k.* From the sky. ‖ *l.* May we milk offspring and food | From Sarasvat's breast, | Swelling for all to see. ‖ *m.* May we enjoy the favour | Of thy waves, O Sarasvat, | Which are full of honey and drip ghee. ‖ *n.* Let us call for aid on this Sarasvat, | Whose ordinance all cattle follow, | Whose ordinance the waters obey, | And in whose ordinance the lord of increase doth rest. ‖ *o.* The divine, well-feathered bird, the great one, | Germ of the waters, male of the plants, | Who delighteth with rain from near, | This Sarasvat let us call on for aid. ‖ *p.* O Sinīvālī, with broad braids, | Who art the sister of the Gods, | Accept the offering which is made; | Reveal, O Goddess, offspring unto us. ‖ *q.* To her that hath fair hands, fair fingers, | Prolific, and mother of many, | To her the queen Sinīvālī, | Pour the offering. ‖ *r.* Indra from all sides. ‖ *s.* Indra men. ‖ *t.* The dark-coloured steeds with fair feathers, | Clad in the mist, spring up to the sky; | They turn hitherward having established their abodes; | Then the earth is wet with ghee. ‖ *u.* He hath golden tresses in the expanse of the air, | A raging serpent like the rushing wind, | With pure radiance, knowing the dawn, |

Like true, glorious and toiling (women). ‖ *v.* Thy winged (steeds) have charged them as they are wont; | The dark bull hath roared when this was; | He hath come hither with (lightnings) that smile like kindly (women); | The rains fall, the clouds thunder. ‖ *w.* Like a cow the lightning loweth; | It tendeth its young like a mother, | When their rain hath been let loose. ‖ *x.* The mountain that hath waxed great is afraid | Even the ridge of heaven trembleth at your roaring; | When ye sport, O Marutas, with your spears, | Ye speed along together like the waters. ‖ *y.* Roar and thunder, deposit a germ, | Fly around with thy chariot water-laden; | Draw downward thy opened water-skin, | And let the heights and the depths be level. ‖ *z.* Even these immovable things (dost thou eat), | O Agni, like a beast at grass; | What time, O immortal, the hosts of thee, | The strong, rend the woods. ‖ *aa.* O Agni, many are the hosts of the immortal all-knower, | O God, powerful; and (many) the wiles of the wily | Which of yore they deposited in thee, | O thou that impellest all, O seeker of friends. ‖ *bb.* From the sky grant us rain, O ye Marutas; | Make ye to swell the streams of the strong steed | Come hither with this thunder, | Pouring the waters, the Asura our father. ‖ *cc.* The bounteous Marutas make to swell the waters | Which yield milk with ghee for the sacrifices; | The strong steer they lead about as it were for rain; | They milk the thundering and never-failing spring. ‖ *dd.* O ye Marutas, swimming in water, send forth | The rain, which all the Marutas strengthen; | May it call aloud like a maiden, | Like a wife with her husband in union. ‖ *ee.* With ghee anoint sky and earth, with honey; | Make the plants rich in milk, the waters; | Make to swell strength and goodwill, | When, O hero Marutas, ye pour the honey, ‖ *ff.* Upwards that. ‖ *gg.* The radiant. ‖ *hh.* Like Aurva, like Bhṛigu, like Apnavāna, | I summon the pure | Agni who is clothed with the sea. ‖ *ii.* As the impulse of Savitar, | The favour of Bhaga, I call | Agni who is clothed with the sea. ‖ *kk.* I call the wise one, who soundeth like the wind, | The might that roareth like Parjanya, | Agni who is clothed with the sea.

Prapāṭhaka 2.

The Supplement to the Soma Sacrifice (continued)

Mantra 3:2:1

a. He who sacrifices knowing the 'ascent' verses of the Pavamāna (Stotras) mounts on the Pavamānas and is not cut off from the Pavamānas 'Thou art the hawk, with the Gāyatrī for thy metre; I grasp thee; bring me over in safety. Thou art the eagle, with the Trishṭubh for thy metre; I grasp thee; bring me over in safety. Thou art the vulture, with the Jagatī for thy metre; I grasp thee; bring me over in safety,' he says. These are the ascents of the Pavamānas; he who knowing thus these sacrifices mounts on the Pavamānas, and is not cut off from the Pavamānas He who knows the continuity of the Pavamāna lives all his days; he does not die before his time; be becomes rich in cattle; he obtains offspring. The Pavamāna cups are drawn off, but these are not drawn off by him, the wooden vessel, the stirring-vessel, and the vessel which holds the purified Soma. If he were to begin (the Stotra) without drawing them off, he would split the Pavamāna, and with its being split the breath of the Adhvaryu would be split. 'Thou art taken with a support; to Prajāpati thee!,' (with these words) he should rub the wooden vessel; 'to Indra thee!,' (with these words) the stirring-vessel; 'to the All-Gods thee!,' (with these words) the vessel which holds the purified Soma verily he renders continuous the Pavamāna, he lives all his days; he does not die before his time; he becomes rich in cattle; he obtains offspring.

Mantra 3:2:2

There are three pressings. Now they spoil the third pressing if there are no stalks of the Soma in it. Having offered the silent cup, he puts a shoot in the vessel which holds it, and placing it with the third pressing he should press it out. In that he makes it swell, it has a stalk (of the Soma); in that he presses it out, it has the lees (of the Soma); verily he makes all the pressings have stalks and pure Soma, and be of equal strength. ‖ Two oceans are there extended, unperishing; | They revolve in turns like the waves in the bosom of the sea; | Seeing they pass over one of them, | Seeing not they pass over the other with a bridge. | Two garments continuous one weareth; | With locks, knowing all the worlds; | He goeth in secret clad in the dark; | He putteth on his bright robe abandoning that of the worn-out one. ‖ Whatever the Gods did at the sacrifice the Asuras did. The Gods saw this great sacrifice, they extended it, they performed the Agnihotra as the vow; therefore one should perform the vow twice, for twice they offer the Agnihotra. They performed the full moon rite, as the animal sacrifice to Agni and Soma. They performed the new moon rite, as the animal sacrifice to Agni. They performed the sacrifice to the All-Gods as the morning pressing. They performed the Varuṇapraghāsas, as the midday pressing. They performed the Sākamedhas, the sacrifice to the fathers, and the offering to Tryambaka, as the third pressing. The Asuras sought to follow their sacrifice, but could not get on its tracks. They said, 'These Gods have become inviolable (*adhvartavyāḥ*). That is why the sacrifice (*adhvara*) is inviolable. Then the Gods prospered, the Asuras were defeated. He who knowing thus offers the Soma, prospers himself, the enemy is defeated.

Mantra 3:2:3

a. Surrounding Agni, surrounding Indra, surrounding the All-Gods, surrounding me with splendour, be purified for us, with healing for cattle, healing for men, healing for the horses, healing, O king, for the plants; may we possess the abundance of wealth that is thine who art unbroken and of heroic power, O lord of wealth; of that give me, of that may I share, of that that is thine I procure this. ‖ *b.* For my expiration, be purified, giving splendour, for splendour; ‖ *c.* For my inspiration; ‖ *d.* For my cross-breathing; ‖ *e.* For my speech; ‖ *f.* For my skill and strength; ‖ *g.* For my two eyes do ye be purified, giving splendour, for splendour; ‖ *h.* For my ear; ‖ *i.* For my trunk; ‖ *k.* For my members; ‖ *l.* For my life; ‖ *m.* For my strength ‖ *n.* Of Vishṇu, ‖ *o.* Of Indra, ‖ *p.* Of the All-Gods thou art the belly, giving splendour to me, be purified for splendour. ‖ *q.* Who art thou? (Thou art) who by name. To who (*kāsmai*) thee, to who (*kāya*) thee, thee whom I have delighted with Soma, thee whom I have gladdened with Soma. May I be possessed of fair offspring with offspring, of noble heroes with heroes, of excellent splendour with splendour, of great abundance with abundances. ‖ *r.* To all my forms giving splendour, be purified for splendour; of that give me; of that may I share, of that that is thine I procure this. ‖ He who desires to be great should look (on the offerings); Prajāpati is here in the vessels, Prajāpati is the sacrifice; verily he delights him, and he being delighted is purified for him with prosperity. He who desires splendour should look (on the offerings); Prajāpati is here in the vessels, Prajāpati is the sacrifice; verily he delights him, and he being delighted is purified for him with splendour. He who is ill should look (on the offerings); Prajāpati is here in the vessels, Prajāpati is the sacrifice; verily he delights him, and he being delighted is purified for him with life. He who practises witchcraft should look (on the offerings); Prajāpati is here in the vessels, Prajāpati is the sacrifice; verily he delights him, and he being delighted cuts off him (the enemy) from expiration and inspiration, from speech, from skill and strength, from his eyes, from his ears, from his trunk, from the members, from life; swiftly he comes to ruin.

Mantra 3:2:4

a. The wooden sword is safety, the hammer is safety, the knife, the sacrificial enclosure, the axe is safety; sacrificial ye art, makers of the sacrifice; do ye invite me to this sacrifice. ‖ *b.* May sky and earth invite me; | (May) the place of singing, the bowl, Soma, the fire (invite me); | (May) the Gods, the sacrifice, | The Hotras call upon me in invitation. ‖ *c.* 'Homage to Agni, slayer of Makha; may the glory of Makha impel me'—(with these words) he reverences the Āhavanīya Makha is the sacrifice; verily he slays the sacrifice; verily paying homage to him he creeps to the Sadas, for his own safety. ‖ *d.* 'Homage to Rudra, slayer of Makha; for this homage guard me' (with these words he reverences) the place of the Agnīdh; verily paying homage to him he creeps to the Sadas, for his own safety. ‖ *e.* 'Homage to Indra, slayer of Makha; injure not my power and strength'—(with these words he reverences) the place of the Hotar; verily he invokes this blessing, for the preserving of his power and strength. ‖ *f.* He who creeps forward knowing the Gods who cause ruin at the Sadas is not ruined at the Sadas. 'Homage to Agni, slayer of Makha,' he says. These Gods cause ruin at the Sadas. He, who knowing them thus creeps forward, is not ruined at the Sadas. ‖ *g.* Ye two are firm, loose; united guard me from trouble. ‖ *h.* May the sun, the God, guard me from trouble from the sky, Vāyu from the atmosphere, Agni from earth, Yama from the fathers, Sarasvatī from men. ‖ *i.* O ye divine doors, oppress me not. ‖ *k.* Homage to the Sadas, homage to the lord of the Sadas, homage to the eye of the friends who go before, homage to sky, homage to earth. ‖ *l.* Ho! son of a second marriage, get thee hence; sit on the seat of another more foolish than we are. ‖ *m.* From the low, from the high may I go. ‖ *n.* O sky and earth protect me from this day today. | When he creeps forward to the seat, the fathers creep along after him; they have power to injure him; having crept to the seat he should look along the south side (saying), 'Come, O ye fathers; through you may I possess the fathers; may ye have good offspring in me'; verily paying reverence to them he creeps to the Sadas, for his own safety.

Mantra 3:2:5

a. Food come hither, enter me for long life, for health, for increase of wealth, for splendour, for good offspring. Come hither, O Vasu, preceded by wealth; thou art dear to my heart. ‖ *b.* May I grasp thee with the arms of the Aśvins. ‖ *c.* With clear sight may I gaze' upon thee, O God Soma, who regardest men. ‖ *d.* Gentle control, banner of the sacrifices, may speech accept and delight in the Soma; I may Aditi, gentle, propitious, with head inviolable, as speech, accept and delight in the Soma. ‖ *e.* Come hither, O thou who art of all men, with healing and favour; with safety come to me, O tawny-coloured, for skill, for strength, for increase of wealth, for good heroes. ‖ *f.* Terrify me not, O king, pierce not my heart with thy radiance, for manly strength, for life, for splendour. ‖ *g.* Of thee, O God Soma, who hast the Vasus for thy troop, who knowest the mind, who belongest to the first pressing, who hast the Gāyatrī as thy metre, who art drunk by Indra, who art drunk by Narāśaṃsa, who art drunk by the fathers, who hast sweetness, and who art invited, I invited eat. ‖ *h.* Of thee, O God Soma, who hast the Rudras for thy troop, who knowest the mind, who belongest to the midday pressing, who hast the Trishṭubh for thy metre, who art drunk by Indra, who art drunk by Narāśaṃsa, who art drunk by the fathers, who hast sweetness, and who art invited, I invited eat. ‖ *i.* Of thee, O God Soma, who hast the Ādityas for thy troop, who knowest the heart, who belongest to the third pressing, who hast the Jagatī for thy metre, who art drunk by Indra, who art drunk by Narāśaṃsa, who art drunk by the fathers, who hast sweetness, and who art invited, I invited eat. ‖ *k.* Swell up, lot thy strength be gathered | From all sides, O Soma; | Be strong in the gathering of might. ‖ *l.* Impel my limbs, O thou with tawny steeds, | Do not distress my troops; | Propitious do thou honour for me the seven sages; | Do not go below my navel. ‖ *m.* We have drunk the Soma, we have become immortal, | We have seen the light, we have found the Gods; | What can the enmity, what the treachery, | Of mortal man do to us, O immortal? ‖ *n.* Whatever fault has been mine, | Agni hath put that right, all-knower, he who belongeth to all men; | Agni hath given back the eye, | Indra and Bṛihaspati have given it back; | Do ye two, O Aśvins, | Replace my eye within its sockets. ‖ *o.* Of thee, O God Soma, over whom the Yajus is spoken, the Stoma sung, the Uktha recited, who hast tawny steeds, who art drunk by Indra, who hast sweetness, and who art invited, I invited eat. ‖ *p.* Ye are to be filled; fill me | With offspring and wealth. ‖ *q.* That is thine, O father, and those that are after thee. That is thine, O grandfather, O great-grandfather, and those that are after thee. ‖ *r.* Rejoice therein, O fathers, according to your shares. ‖ *s.* Homage to your taste, O fathers; homage to your birth, O fathers; homage to your life, O fathers; homage to your custom, O fathers; homage to your anger, O fathers; homage to your terrors, O fathers; O fathers, homage to you. ‖ *t.* Ye that are in that world, may they follow you; ye that are in this world, may they follow me. ‖ *u.* Ye that are in that world, of them be ye the most fortunate; ye that are in this world, of these may I be the most fortunate. ‖ *v.* O Prajāpati, none other than thou | Comprehendeth all these creatures. | What we seek when we sacrifice to thee, let that be ours; | May we be lords of riches. ‖ *w.* Thou art the expiation of sin committed by the Gods, thou art the expiation of sin committed by men, thou art the expiation of sin committed by the fathers. ‖ *x.* Of thee, O God Soma, that art purified in the waters, that art pressed by men, over whom the Yajus is spoken, the Stoma sung, the Śastra recited, who art made by the fathers into food to win horses and cows, and who art invited, I invited eat.

Mantra 3:2:6

a. Thou art the milk of the great ones, the body of the All-Gods; may I today accomplish the cup of the speckled ones; thou art the cup of the speckled ones; thou art the heart of Vishṇu, once hath Vishṇu stepped apart along thee, O vigorous one; with curds and ghee may prosperity be increased; may wealth come to me from this which is offered and enjoyed thou art the light for all men, milked from the dappled one. ‖ *b.* As great as are sky and earth in mightiness, | As great as the expense of the seven rivers, | So great is the cup of thee, O Indra, | Which unvanquished I draw off with strength. ‖ If a black bird touch the speckled butter, his slaves would be likely to die; if a dog touch it, his four-footed cattle would be likely to die; if it were to be spilt, the sacrificer would be likely to die. The speckled butter is the cattle; his cattle fall, if his speckled butter falls; in that he takes again the speckled butter, he takes again cattle for him. The speckled butter is the breath; his breath falls, if his speckled butter falls; in that he takes again the speckled butter, he takes again breath for him. He takes it after placing gold (in the ladle), gold is immortality, the speckled butter is the breath; verily he places immortality in his breath. It is of a hundred measures, man has a hundred years of life, a hundred powers; verily on life and power he rests. He makes a horse sniff it, the horse is connected with Prajāpati; verily from his own place of origin he fashions offspring for him. His sacrifice is broken whose speckled butter is spilt. He takes it again with a Ṛich addressed to Vishṇu; Vishṇu is the sacrifice; verily he unites the sacrifice by the sacrifice.

Mantra 3:2:7

a. O God Savitar, he hath declared that to thee; that do thou impel and offer. ‖ *b.* The Brahman is Bṛihaspati ‖ *c.* Depart not from the life-giving Ṛich, from the Sāman which protecteth the body. ‖ *d.* Let your wishes be accomplished, let your purposes (be accomplished). ‖ *e.* Speak right and truth. ‖ *f.* Praise ye on the impulse of the God Savitar ‖ *g.* The praised of the praised art thou, may the praised milk strength for me, may the praised of the praised come to me. ‖ *h.* Thou art the Śastra of the Śastra, may the Śastra milk strength for me, may the Śastra of the Śastra come to me. ‖ *i.* With power may we conquer, | May we milk offspring and food. ‖ *k.* May my wish be accomplished among the Gods. ‖ *l.* May splendour come to me. ‖ *m.* The sacrifice hath become, it hath come into being, | It hath been born, it hath waxed great; | It hath become the overlord of the Gods, | May it make us overlords, | May we be lords of wealth. ‖ *n.* Either the sacrifice milks the lord of the sacrifice, or the lord of the sacrifice milks the sacrifice. Him, who sacrifices not knowing the milking of the Stotra and the Śastra, the sacrifice milks, he after sacrificing becomes worse; he, who knowing the milking of these two sacrifices, milks the sacrifice; he after sacrificing becomes better. 'The praised of the praised art thou, may the praised milk strength for me, may the praised of the praised come to me. The Śastra, of the Śastra thou art, may the Śastra milk strength for me, may the Śastra of the Śastra come to me,' he says; this is the milking of the Stotra and the Śastra; he who sacrifices knowing thus milks the sacrifice, and by sacrificing becomes better.

Mantra 3:2:8

a. To the flying eagle hail! Vat! To him who approveth himself homage. To the support, the law, hail! Vat! To him who approveth himself homage. To the enclosing-stick which extendeth men hail! Vat! To him who approveth himself homage. To the strength of the Hotras hail! Vat! To him who approveth himself homage. To the milk of the Hotras hail! Vat! To him who approveth himself homage. To Prajāpati, to Manu, hail! Vat! To him who approveth himself homage. Right, guardian of right, heaven-bearing, hail! Vat! To him who approveth himself homage. ‖ *b.* Let the Hotras delight in the sweet ghee. ‖ *c.* To the lord of the sacrifice the Ṛishis said, | 'By thy sin creatures are famishing and troubled'; | He did not secure the two drops of honey; | May Viśvakarman unite us with them. ‖ *d.* Dread are the Ṛishis; homage be to them, | In the union with their eye and mind; | To Bṛihaspati great, real, and glorious reverence; | Homage to Viśvakarman; may he guard us. ‖ *e.* Deeming that the Soma-drinkers are his own, | Knowing the breath like a valiant man in battle,— | He hath committed a great sin and is bound by them— | Him set free, O Viśvakarman, for safety. ‖ *f.* Those who eating deserved not riches, | Whom the fires of the hearths did trouble, | That is their offering to expiate the ill sacrifice | A good sacrifice for us may Viśvakarman make it. ‖ *g.* Homage to the Pitṛis, who have watched around us, | Making the sacrifice, loving the sacrifice, the benignant deities; | We have not brought you the offering without desires; | Trouble us not for this sin. || *h*. All those who are in the Sadas must have presents; he who did not give them a present would fall a victim to them; in that he offers the libations to Viśvakarman, he thus delights those who are in the Sadas. || *i*. Ye Gods, have regard to this wonder, | The good thing which the husband and wife win with the milk admixture; | A male child is born, be findeth riches, | And all the house prospereth unhurt. || *k*. May the husband and wife who give the milk admixture win good; | May wealth unharmed attend them dwelling in harmony; | May he, who poureth that which hath been milked together with the pot (of Soma), | By the sacrifice leave misfortune on his way. || *l*. Butter-necked, fat is his wife; | Fat his sons and not meagre, | Who with his wife eager to offer a good sacrifice | Hath given to Indra the milk admixture together with the pot (of Soma). || *m*. May the milk admixture place in me strength and good offspring | And food, wealth and fair fame, | (Me that am) conquering the fields with might, O Indra, | And casting down my rivals. || *n*. Thou art being, place me in being; thou art the mouth, may I be | the mouth. || *o*. From sky and earth I take thee. || *p*. May the All-Gods, belonging to all men, move thee forward. || *q*. In the sky make firm the Gods, in the atmosphere the birds, on earth the creatures of earth. || *r*. With the firm offering the firm | Soma, we transfer, | That the whole world may be for us | Free of sickness and of kindly intent; || *s*. That Indra may make | All the clans for us of one mind, | That all the quarters | May be ours alone.

Mantra 3:2:9

In that the Hotar addresses the Adhvaryu, he makes the thunder bolt advance towards him; 'O reciter of hymns,' he says in response at the morning pressing; the syllables herein are three, the Gāyatrī has three Padas, the morning pressing is connected with the Gāyatrī; verily with the Gāyatrī he places the thunderbolt within the morning pressing. 'The hymn hath been uttered,' he says in response at the midday pressing; the syllables herein are four, the Trishṭubh has four Padas, the midday pressing is connected with the Trishṭubh; verily with the Trishṭubh he places the thunderbolt within the midday pressing. 'The hymn hath been uttered to Indra,' he says in response at the third pressing; the syllables herein are seven, the Śakvarī has seven Padas, the thunder bolt is connected with the Śakvarī; verily with the thunderbolt he places the thunderbolt within the third pressing. The theologians say, 'He indeed would be an Adhvaryu who should produce the metres in the responses according to the pressings; he would bestow brilliance upon himself at the morning pressing, power at the midday pressing, and cattle at the third pressing.' 'O reciter of hymns,' he says in response at the morning pressing; the syllables herein are three,, the Gāyatrī has three Padas, the morning pressing is connected with the Gāyatrī; verily at the morning pressing he produces the metres in the response; now the Gāyatrī is brilliance, the morning pressing is brilliance; verily at the morning pressing he bestows brilliance upon himself. 'The hymn hath been uttered,' he says in response at the midday pressing; the syllables herein are four, the Trishṭubh has four Padas, the midday pressing is connected with the Trishṭubh; verily at the midday pressing he produces the metres in the response; now the Trishṭubh is power, the midday pressing is power; verily at the midday pressing he bestows power upon himself. 'The hymn hath been uttered to Indra,' he says in response at the third pressing; the syllables herein are seven, the Śakvarī has seven Padas, cattle are connected with the Śakvarī, the third pressing is connected with the Jagatī; verily at the third pressing he produces the metres in the response; now the Jagatī is cattle, the third pressing is cattle; verily at the third pressing he bestows cattle upon himself that the Hotar addresses the Adhvaryu, he puts fear in him; if be were not to smite it off, they would have fear in his house before the year (was over). 'Recite, let us two rejoice,' he responds, and thereby he smites it off. Just as one looks for the exact interval, so the Adhvaryu looks for the response. If he were to respond in advance, that would be as when one goes to meets the exact interval. If the (response) were to be omitted after the half-verse, that would be as when one is left behind those that are running. The Udgīthas are similar for the priests, the Udgītha for the Udgātars, the Ṛichas and the Praṇavas for the singers of hymns, the response for the Adhvaryus. He, who knowing thus responds, becomes an eater of food, a strong one is born among his offspring. The Hotar is this (earth), the Adhvaryu yonder (sky); in that he recites sitting, so the Hotar goes not away from the (earth), for this (earth) is seated as it were; verily thereby the sacrifice milks this (earth). In that he responds standing, so the Adhvaryu goes not away from yonder (sky), for yonder (sky) stands as it were; verily thereby the sacrificer milks yonder (sky). In that he recites sitting, therefore the Gods live on that which is given hence; in that he responds standing, therefore men live on what is given thence. In that he recites seated towards the east, and he responds standing towards the west, therefore seed is impregnated in front, offspring are born behind. In that the Hotar addresses the Adhvaryu, he makes the thunderbolt advance towards him; he turns towards the West; verily he overcomes the thunderbolt.

Mantra 3:2:10.

a. Thou art taken with a support; thou art seated in speech for the guardians of speech, for the guardians of insight, for the overseers of this established sacrifice do I take thee. || *b*. Thou art taken with a support; thou art seated in holy order; for the guardians of sight, etc., do I take thee. || *c*. Thou art taken with a support; thou art seated in holy lore; for the guardians of the ear, etc., do I take thee. || *d*. For the Gods thee! || *e*. For the All-Gods thee! || *f*. For all the Gods thee! || *g*. O Vishṇu, wide striding, this is thy Soma; guard it let not the evil-eyed one espy this of thine. || *h*. In me is the Vasu, whom wealth precedeth, who guardeth the voice; guard my voice. || *i*. In me is the Vasu, who winneth wealth, who guardeth the eye; guard my eye. || *k*. In me is the Vasu, who keepeth wealth together, who guardeth the ear; guard my ear. || *l*. Thou art Bhūr, best of rays, guardian of expiration; guard my expiration. || *m*. Thou art Dhūr, best of rays, guardian of inspiration; guard my inspiration. || *n*. The foe who, O Indra and Vāyu, is hostile to us, | Who seeketh to assail us, O lords of splendour, | May I here burl him below my feet, | So that, O Indra, I may shine as the highest. || *o*. (The foe who), O Mitra and Varuṇa, etc. || *p*. (The foe who), O Aśvins, etc.

Mantra 3:2:11

a. He by thy help, O Agni, | With good heroes, making strength, is victorious, | Whose companionship thou dost favour. || *b*. Your ancient lofty praise bear | To Agni, the Hotar | The creator who beareth as it were the light of songs. || *c*. O Agni, three are thy powers, three thy stations, | Three are thine ancient tongues, O born of holy order; | Three are thy bodies in which the Gods find pleasure, | With them guard thou our songs unfailing. || *d*. With the rite, with food I impel you, | O Indra and Vishṇu, to the end of this work; | Rejoice in the sacrifice and bestow wealth, | Furthering us with safe ways. || *e*. Both are victorious, they are not defeated | Neither of them at any time hath been defeated; | When, with Indra, O Vishṇu, ye did strive, | Then did ye in three divide the thousand. || *f*. Three ages are thine, O All-knower, | Three births in the dawns, O Agni; | With them, knowing, do thou propitiate the Gods, | And be for the sacrificer health and wealth. || *g*. Agni abideth in three abodes | Of three foundations, the sage; | May he offer and may he satisfy for us, | The three sets of eleven (Gods); | The wise envoy made ready, | Let the others all be rent asunder. || *h*. O Indra and Vishṇu, ye overthrew | The nine and ninety strong forts of Śambara; | Of Varchin, the Asura, a hundred and a thousand heroes | Do ye slay irresistibly. || *i*. Then did his mother seek to persuade him, | 'O son, these Gods are abandoning thee.' | Then said Indra, about to slay Vṛitra, | 'O friend Vishṇu, step thou more widely.'

Prapāṭhaka 3.

The Supplement to the Soma Sacrifice (continued).

Mantra 3:3:1

a. O Agni, brilliant, be thou brilliant among the Gods; make me brilliant, of long life, radiant among men; for the brilliance of consecration and of penance do I offer to thee. || *b*. Thou dost win brilliance; may brilliance forsake me not, may I forsake not brilliance, may brilliance forsake me not. || *c*. O Indra, full of force, be thou full of force among the Gods, make me full of force, of long life, radiant among men; for the force of the Brahmanhood and royalty do I offer to thee. || *d*. Thou dost win force; may force forsake me not, may I forsake not force, may force forsake me not. || *e*. O sun, blazing, be thou blazing among the Gods; make me blazing, of long life, radiant among men; for the blazing of the wind and of the waters do I offer to thee. ‖ *f.* Thou dost win the light; may the light forsake me not, may I not forsake the light, may the light forsake me not. ‖ *g.* On me wisdom, on me offspring, on me brilliance may Agni bestow; on me wisdom, on me offspring, on me power may Indra bestow; on me wisdom, on me offspring, on me blazing may Sūrya bestow.

Mantra 3:3:2

a. The maker of the sound 'Him' is Vāyu, the Prastotar is Agni, the Sāman is Prajāpati, the Udgātar is Bṛihaspati, the subordinate singers are the All-Gods, the Pratihartṛis are the Marutas, the finale is Indra; may these Gods who support breath bestow breath upon me. ‖ *b.* All this the Adhvaryu, as he begins, begins for the Udgātars; 'May these Gods who support breath bestow breath upon me,' he says; verily he bestows all this on himself. ‖ *c.* May Iḍā who summoneth the Gods, Manu who leadeth the sacrifice, ‖ *d.* May Bṛihaspati recite the hymns and acclamations. ‖ *e.* The All-Gods are reciters of the hymns. ‖ *f.* O earth mother, do not harm me. ‖ *g.* Of honey shall I think, honey shall I produce, honey shall I proclaim, honey shall I speak, may I utter speech full of honey for the Gods, and acceptable to men. ‖ *h.* May the Gods aid me to radiance, may the Pitṛis rejoice in me.

Mantra 3:3:3

a. Let the Vasus press thee with the Gāyatrī metre; go thou to the dear place of Agni. ‖ *b.* Lot the Rudras press thee with the Trishṭubh metre; go thou to the dear place of Indra. ‖ *c.* Let the Ādityas press thee with the Jagatī metre; go thou to the dear place of the All-Gods. ‖ *d.* The pure for thee, O pure one, I stir in the gladdening (water); ‖ *e.* In the joyous (ones); ‖ *f.* In the Kotanās; ‖ *g.* In the new (ones); ‖ *h.* In the Reśīs; ‖ *i.* In the Meṣhīs; ‖ *k.* In the roaring (ones); ‖ *l.* In the all-supporting (ones); ‖ *m.* In the sweet (ones); ‖ *n.* In the lofty (ones); ‖ *o.* In the strong (ones); ‖ *p.* In the pure ones, I stir the pure for thee, O pure. ‖ *q.* The pure for thee I take with the pure form of day, with the rays of the sun. ‖ *r.* Herein the dread (ones) have moved themselves, | The streams of the sky have consorted. ‖ *s.* The lofty form of the bull shineth on high; | Soma precedeth Soma, | The pure precedeth the pure. ‖ *t.* That undeceived, watchful, name of thine, O Soma, to that of thine, O Soma, to Soma hail! ‖ *u.* Gladly do thou, O God Soma, go to the dear place of Agni with the Gāyatrī metre. ‖ *v.* Willingly do thou, O God Soma, go to the dear place of Indra with the Trishṭubh metre. | W Our friend, do thou, O God Soma, go to the dear place of the All-Gods with the Jagatī metre. ‖ *x.* Come breath to us from afar, | From the atmosphere, from the sky, | Life from the earth; | Thou art ambrosia; for breath thee! ‖ *y.* May Indra and Agni confer radiance upon me, | Radiance (may) Soma and Bṛihaspati (confer); | Radiance on me the All-Gods, | Radiance confer on me, O ye Aśvins. ‖ *z.* When one doth hasten after him, | Or uttereth prayers, he doth accept it | All knowledge doth he embrace, | Even as the felly the wheel.

Mantra 3:3:4

The stirrings are the secret name of the waters; 'The pure for thee, O pure one, I stir in the gladdening (waters),' he says; verily with the secret name of the waters he wins the rain from the sky. 'The pure for thee I take with the pure,' he says; the night is of the form of the day, the rays of the sun, he makes the rain to fall from the sky. 'Herein the dread (ones) have moved themselves,' he says; that is as in the text. 'The lofty form of the bull shineth on high,' he says; the rain is in its lofty form; verily by the form he wins the rain. 'That undeceived, watchful, name of thine, O Soma,' he says; he indeed offers an oblation with an oblation who drawing the Adābhya (cup) offers it to Soma. The life and breath him who draws the Aṃśu depart; 'Come breath to us from afar,' he says; verily he bestows life and breath upon himself. 'Thou art ambrosia; for breath thee!' (with these words) he breathes over the gold; the gold is ambrosia, breath is life; verily with ambrosia he bestows life upon him self. It is of a hundred (Kṛishṇalas) in weight; man has a hundred years of life, a hundred powers; verily he finds support in life and power. He touches the waters; the waters are medicine; verily he makes medicine.

Mantra 3:3:5

a. Thou art the wind, expiration by name, in the lordship of Savitar give me expiration. ‖ *b.* Thou art the eye, the ear by name, in the lordship of Dhātar give me life. ‖ *c.* Thou art the form, colour by name, in the lordship of Bṛihaspati, give me offspring. ‖ *d.* Thou art holy order, truth by name, in the lordship of Indra, give me lordly power. ‖ *e.* Thou art the past, the future by name, in the lordship of the Pitṛis, expugnate the waters and the plants. ‖ *f.* Thee for the realm of holy order! ‖ *g.* Thee for the might of holy order! ‖ *h.* Thee for the circumference of holy order! ‖ *i.* Thee for the truth of holy order! ‖ *k.* Thee for the light of holy order! ‖ Prajāpati saw the Virāj; by it he created the past and the future; he concealed it from the Ṛishis; by penance Jamadagni beheld it, and by it he created various delights; that is why the various (cups) have their name. In that the various (cups) are drawn, so the sacrificer wins various delights. 'Thou art the wind, expiration by name,' he says; verily he wins expiration and inspiration.' 'Thou art the eye, the ear by name,' he says; verily he wins life. 'Thou art the form, colour by name,' he says; verily he wins offspring. 'Thou art holy order, truth by name,' he says; verily he wins lordly power. 'Thou art the past, the future by name,' he says; the foetus of the waters and the plants is cattle; verily he wins cattle. So much as is around a man, that does he thus win. 'Thee for the realm of holy order,' he says; the realm of holy order is this (earth); verily he conquers this (earth). 'Thee for the might of holy order,' he says; the might of holy order is the atmosphere; verily he conquers the atmosphere. 'Thee for the circumference of holy order,' he says; the circumference of holy order is the sky; verily he conquers the sky. 'Thee for the truth of holy order,' he says; the truth of holy order is the quarters; verily he conquers the quarters. 'Thee for the light of holy order,' he says; the light of holy order is the world of heaven; verily he conquers the world of heaven. So many are the worlds of the Gods; verily he conquers them. They make up ten; the Virāj has ten syllables, the Virāj is food; verily he finds support in the Virāj, the eating of food.

Mantra 3:3:6

What the Gods could not win by the sacrifice, that they won by the Para (Grahas), and that is why the Paras have their name. In that the Paras are drawn, (it serves) to win that which one does not win by the sacrifice. The first he draws, by this he conquers the world; the second (he draws), by this he conquers the atmosphere; the third (he draws), by this he conquers yonder world. In that they are drawn, (they serve) to conquer these worlds. In the latter days they are drawn hitherward from yonder, verily having conquered these worlds they descend again towards this world. In that in the former days they are drawn thitherward from hence, therefore these worlds are thitherward from hence; in that in the latter days they are drawn hitherward from thence, therefore these worlds are hitherward from thence; therefore men depend on the worlds in variation. The theologians say, 'For what reason do plants spring from the waters, the food of man is plants, and offspring are born through Prajāpati?' 'Through the Paras,' he should reply. In that he draws (saying), 'For the waters thee, for the plants I take,' therefore from the waters plants spring; in that he draws (saying), 'For the plants thee, for offspring I take,' therefore the food of man is the plants; in that he draws (saying), 'For offspring thee, for Prajāpati I take,' therefore through Prajāpati offspring are born.

Mantra 3:3:7

Prajāpati created the Gods and the Asuras; thereafter the sacrifice was created, after the sacrifice the metres; they went away in all directions, the sacrifice went after the Asuras, the metres after the sacrifice; the Gods reflected, 'These have become what we are'; they had recourse to Prajāpati; Prajāpati said, 'Taking the strength of the metres I shall bestow it upon you.' He took the strength of the metres and bestowed it upon them. Then the metres ran away, and the sacrifice followed the metres. Then the Gods prospered, the Asuras were defeated. He who knows the strength of the metres—'Do thou proclaim,' 'Be it proclaimed,' 'Utter,' 'We that utter,' the Vaṣhaṭ call—prospers himself, his foe is defeated. The theologians say, 'For whose gain does the Adhvaryu cause (him) to proclaim?' 'For the strength of the metres,' he should reply; 'Do thou proclaim,' 'Be it proclaimed,' 'Utter,' 'We that utter,' the Vaṣhaṭ call, that is the strength of the metres; he who knows thus sings what ever he sings with the metres in full strength. 'In that Indra, slew Vṛitra, there is impurity, in that he destroyed the Yatis, there is impurity; then why is the sacrifice Indra's up to the completion?' they say. The sacrifice is the sacrificial body of Indra, and it is this they sacrifice. To him who knows thus the sacrifice resorts.

Mantra 3:3:8

a. Giving life, O Agni, rejoicing in the oblation, | Be thou faced with ghee and with thy birthplace of ghee; | Having drunk the ghee, the sweet, the delightful product of the cow, | As a father his son, do thou protect him. || The sacrificer falls a victim to the two fires in that having made (the offering) ready in them he goes elsewhere to the final bath; 'Giving life, O Agni, rejoicing in the oblation,' (with these words) should he offer when about to go to the final bath; verily by the offering he appeases the two (fires); the sacrificer does not go to destruction. || *b.* That loan which I have not yet paid back, | The tribute that I still owe to Yama, | Here do I make requital for it; | Here, O Agni, may I be freed from that debt. || *c.* O Viśvalopa, I offer thee in the mouth of the burner of all; | One is an eater of the uneaten, one an eater of the unoffered, one an eater of that which is gathered; | May they make for us medicine, | An abode, delightful strength.' || *d.* May he that fatteneth protect us | From in front with the cloud | Many be our houses, | That houses fail us not. || *e.* Do thou, O lord of cloud, | Bestow on us strength with kindliness; | Return to us what is lost, | Return wealth to us. || *f.* O God that dost fatten, thou art a lord of a thousandfold prosperity; do thou give us increase of wealth unfailing, rich in heroes, prosperity abiding through the year. || Yama is Agni, Yama is this (earth); the sacrificer becomes under a debt to Yama in that he strews the altar with plants; if he were to go away with out burning (them), they would drag him about bound by the neck in yonder world. In that he burns, (saying) 'The loan which I have not yet paid,' being here, having made requital of the loan to Yama, he goes freed from the debt to the world of heaven. If he does manifold things as it were, he should offer in the forest (fire) groats with his hand; the forest (fire) is Agni Vaiśvānara; verily he appeases him. On the Ekāṣhṭakā the divider of the days, he should cook a cake of four Śarāvas in size, and early with it should fire the thicket; if it burns, it becomes a good season, if it does not burn, a bad season. By this mode of prognostication the seers of old used to undertake a long Sattra. He who knowing the seer, the hearer, the reciter, sacrifices, is united in yonder world with what he has sacrificed and bestowed. The seer is Agni, the hearer is Vāyu, the reciter Āditya; he, who offers knowing thus to them, in yonder world is united with what be has sacrificed and bestowed. 'May he from in front with the cloud,' he says; (he that is) from in front with the cloud is Agni; verily he says to Agni, 'Guard this for me.' 'Do thou, O lord of cloud,' he says; the lord of cloud is Vāyu; verily he says to Vāyu, 'Guard this for me.' 'O God, that dost fatten,' he says; the God that fattens is yonder Āditya; verily he says to Āditya, 'Guard this for me.'

The Special Animal Offerings

Mantra 3:3:9

a. This young one I put around you, | Playing with him that is dear do ye move; | Afflict us not in birth, O ye prosperous ones; | May we rejoice in increase of wealth, in food. || *b.* Homage to thy greatness, to thine eye, | O father of the Marutas, that do I sing; | Be propitious, with a fair sacrifice may we offer; | Be this oblation acceptable to the Gods. || *c.* This was the bundle of the Gods, | The germ of the waters smeared upon the plants; | Pūṣhan chose a drop of Soma; | A great stone was there then for them. || *d.* Father of calves, husband of cows, | And father too of great gulfs, | Calf, afterbirth, fresh milk, bee-stings, | Clotted milk, curd, ghee is his seed. || *e.* Thee the cows chose for lordship, | Thee the Marutas, sweet singers, bailed; | Resting on the summit, the pinnacle, of lordly power, | Then O dread one to us assign wealth. || Unsuccessful is his animal offering for whom these (rites) are not performed; successful is the offering of him for whom they are performed.

Mantra 3:3:10.

a. Sūrya, the God, for those that sit in the sky, Dhātar for lordly power, Vāyu for offspring, Bṛihaspati for Prajāpati offer thee radiant. || *b.* Thee have I united with the Gods, | Who hast a tawny embryo | And a womb of gold, | Whose limbs are uninjured. || *c.* Bring near, O bringer, | Remove away, O remover, | O Indra Nardabuda, | With the four quarters of the earth | Do thou bring near. || *d.* I split apart thy urinator, | Thy womb, the two groins, | The mother and the child, | The embryo and the after-birth. || *e.* Apart from thee let it be. So! || *f.* The drop, far extending, of all forms, | Purified, wise, hath anointed the embryo. || *g.* With one foot, two feet, three feet, four feet, five feet, six feet, seven feet, eight feet may she extend over the worlds; hail! || *h.* Nay the two great ones, sky and earth, | Mingle for us this sacrifice, | May they sustain us with support.

Mantra 3:3:11

a. This oblation is dear in your mouth, | O Indra and Bṛihaspati, | The hymn and acclamation is recited. || *b.* This Soma is poured for you, | O Indra and Bṛihaspati, | Dear for delight, for drinking. || *c.* To us, O Indra and Bṛihaspati, | Grant wealth of a hundred kine, | Of horses a thousandfold. || *d.* From behind may Bṛihaspati guard us, | From above, from below, from the plotter of evil; | May Indra from the front, from the middle, | Friend to friend, grant us wide room. || *e.* Sped by the winds on all sides, O Agni, | Thy flames, O pure one, pure are diffused | Mightily destroying, the divine ones, the Navagvas | Assail the forests, rudely crushing (them). || *f.* Thee, O Agni, the tribes of men praise, | Who knowest the Hotar's duty, discerning, best bestower of jewels, | Who art in secret yet, O happy one, seen by all, | Of impetuous spirit, a good sacrificer, brilliant with ghee. || *g.* May Dhātar give us wealth, | The lord the ruler of the world, | May he favour us with a full (gift). || *h.* Dhātar is lord of offspring and of wealth, | Dhātar created all this world. | Dhātar giveth a son to the sacrificer | To him let us offer the oblation rich in ghee. || *i.* may Dhātar give us wealth, | Life in days to come and unfailing; | May we obtain the favour | Of the God whose gifts are true. || *k.* May Dhātar give wealth to the giver, | Desiring offspring, generous in his home; | Let all the immortal Gods roll themselves up for him, | The All-Gods and Aditi in unison. || *l.* For us today may Anumati | Among the Gods favour our sacrifice, | And be she and Agni, bearer of the oblation, | A joy to the giver. || *m.* Accord thy favour, O Anumati, | And grant us wealth; | For inspiration, for insight impel us, | Lengthen our days for us. || *n.* May she favouring, favour (us) | With wealth, undecaying, rich in offspring; | In her disfavour may we not fall; | May the Goddess easy to invoke grant us protection. || *o.* Anumati men reverence in the quarter | Wherein is that which shineth; | May she in whose lap is the broad atmosphere, | The Goddess, easy to invoke, grant us protection. || *p.* Rākā, easy to invoke, I invoke with fair praise; | May the fortunate one hear us and be aware of us | With needle that breaks not may she sew her task; | May she give a hero, whose wergild is a hundred, worthy of song. || *q.* The fair thoughts of thine, O Rākā, | Whereby thou art wont to give wealth to the giver, | With them today come to us in kindliness, | Granting, O fortunate one, a thousandfold prosperity. || *r.* O Sinīvālī, || *s.* The fair-handed || *t.* I invoke at the sacrifice Kuhū the fortunate, | Who accomplisheth her work, the easy to invoke; | May she give us the fame of our fathers; | To thee, O Goddess, let us offer with oblation. || *u.* Kuhū, lady of the Gods and of immortality, | Worthy of invocation, may she be aware of the oblation | To the giver may she assign much good fortune, | To the wise may she grant increase of wealth.

Prapāṭhaka 4.

The Optional and Occasional Offerings

Mantra 3:4:1

The sacrifice of him whose offering is too large is unsuccessful; 'Sūrya, the God, for those that sit in the sky,' he says; verily with the aid of Bṛihaspati and Prajāpati he makes good the deficiency in the sacrifice. Now the Rākṣhasas infest the victim if it being offered to one deity is greater (than normal); 'Thou who hast a tawny embryo,' he says; verily he sends it to the Gods, to smite away the Rākṣhasas 'Bring near, O bringer,' he says; verily with the holy power he brings it. 'I split apart thy urinator,' he says; that is according to the text. 'The drop, far extending, of all forms,' he says; the drop is offspring and cattle; verily with offspring and cattle he unites him. To the sky the deficiency of the sacrifice goes, to the earth the redundancy; if he were not to appease it, the sacrificer would be ruined; 'May the two great ones, sky and earth, for us,' he says; verily by means of sky and earth he appeases both the deficiency and the redundancy of the sacrifice; the sacrificer is not ruined. He covers (the offering) with ashes for the call of 'Godspeed'; now this is the embryo of these two; verily in these two he deposits it. If he were to cut off, he would make it redundant; if he were not to cut off, he would fail to cut off from the victim which has been offered; one portion he should cut off from in front of the navel, another behind it; the expiration is in front of the navel, the inspiration behind;

verily he cuts off from the whole extent of the victim. He offers to Vishṇu Śipivishṭa; Vishṇu Śipivishṭa is the redundancy of the sacrifice, the greatness of the victim, the prosperity thereof; verily in the redundant he deposits the redundant, to appease the redundant. The sacrificial fee is gold of eight measures, for the (victim) has eight feet; the self is the ninth; (verily it serves) to win the victim. It is enveloped in a turban in an inner box, for so as it were is the victim, the omentum, the skin, the flesh, the bone; verily he obtains and wins the whole extent of the victim. He, for whom in the sacrifice this expiration is offered, by his sacrificing becomes richer.

Mantra 3:4:2

a. O Vāyu, drinker of the pure, come to us; | A thousand are thy teams, O thou that hast all choice boons; | For thee the sweet drink bath been drawn, | Whereof, O God, thou hast the first drink. ‖ *b.* For intent thee, for desire thee, for prosperity thee; Kikkiṭā thy mind! to Prajāpati hail! Kikkiṭā thy breath, to Vāyu hail! Kikkiṭā thy eye, to Sūrya hail! Kikkiṭā thy ear, to sky and earth hail! Kikkiṭā, thy speech, to Sarasvatī hail! ‖ *c.* Thou, the fourth, art the barren, the eager one, | Since once in thought the embryo hath entered thy womb; | Do thou, the barren, go eagerly to the Gods, | Be the desires of the sacrificer fulfilled. ‖ *d.* Thou art the goat, resting on wealth, sit on the earth, mount aloft on the atmosphere, in the sky be thy great radiance. ‖ *e.* Stretching the thread of the atmosphere do thou pursue the light; | Guard the paths of light made by prayer. ‖ *f.* Weave ye without a flaw the work of the singers; | Become Manu; produce thou. the host divine. ‖ *g.* Thou art the offering of mind, the colour of Prajāpati, may we share thy limbs.

Mantra 3:4:3

These two were together, Vāyu blew them apart; they conceived a child, Soma generated it, Agni swallowed it. Prajāpati saw this (offering) to Agni on eight potsherds, he offered it, and thereby he redeemed this (victim) from Agni. Therefore though sacrificing it to another God, still one should first offer on eight potsherds to Agni; verily redeeming it from Agni he offers it. Because Vāyu blew (them apart), therefore is it connected with Vāyu; because these two conceived, therefore is it connected with sky and earth; because Soma generated, and Agni swallowed, there fore is it connected with Agni and Soma; because when the two parted speech was uttered, therefore is it connected with Sarasvatī; because Prajāpati redeemed it from Agni, therefore is it connected with Prajāpati; the barren goat is connected with all the Gods. To Vāyu should he offer it who desires wealth. the swiftest deity is Vāyu; verily he has recourse to Vāyu with his own share, and he causes him to attain wealth. To sky and earth should he offer it who in ploughing desires support; verily from the sky Parjanya rains for him, plants spring up in this (earth), his corn prospers. To Agni and Soma should he offer it who desires, 'May I be possessed of food, an eater of food'; by Agni he wins food, by Soma the eating of food; verily he becomes possessed of food, an eater of food. To Sarasvatī should he offer it who, being able to utter speech, cannot utter speech; Sarasvatī is speech; verily he has recourse to Sarasvatī with her own share, and she bestows speech upon him. To Prajāpati should he offer it who desires, 'May I gain that which has not been gained'; all the deities are Prajāpati; verily by the deities he gains what has not been gained. He brings (the victims) up with a verse ad dressed to Vāyu; verily winning it from Vāyu he offers it. 'For intent thee, for desire thee!' he says; that is according to the text. He offers with the sound *kikkiṭā*; at the sound *kikkiṭā* the domestic animals stop, the wild run away. In that he offers with the sound *kikkiṭā*, (it serves) to support domestic animals. He offers while the circumambulation by fire is taking place; verily alive he sends it to the world of heaven. 'Thou, the fourth, art the barren, the eager one,' he says; verily he sends it to the Gods. 'Be the desires of the sacrificer fulfilled,' he says; this is the desire of the sacrificer that (the sacrifice) should proceed to its conclusion without injury. 'Thou art the goat, resting in wealth,' he says; verily in these worlds he makes it find support. 'In the sky be thy great radiance,' he says; verily in the world of heaven he bestows light upon him. 'Stretching the thread of the atmosphere do thou pursue the light,' he says; verily he makes these worlds full of light for him. 'Weave ye without a flaw the work of the singers,, he says; whatever flaw is committed in the sacrifice, this serves to atone for it. 'Become Manu; produce thou the host divine,' he says; offspring are connected with Manu; verily he makes them fit for food. 'Thou art the offering of mind,' he says, to make 'Godspeed'. 'May we share thy limbs,' he says; verily he invokes this blessing. Of this (victim) there is one time unpropitious for sacrifice to the Gods, when a cloud appears when it has been offered; if a cloud should appear when it has been offered, he should either cast it into the waters or eat it whole; if he were to cast it into the waters, he would con fuse the sacrifice; he should eat it whole; verily he bestows power upon himself. By three people is this to be performed, him who performs a year-long Sattra, him who offers with a thousand (gifts), and him who is a domestic sacrificer; with it let them sacrifice, for them is it fit.

The Jaya, Abhyātāna, and Rāshṭrabhṛit Offerings

Mantra 3:4:4

a. Thought and thinking, intent and intention, known and knowledge, mind and power, the new and the full moon, the Bṛihat and the Rathantara. ‖ *b.* Prajāpati bestowed victories on Indra | The strong, he who is dread in battle contest, | To him all the people bowed in reverence, | For he waxed dread, worthy of offering. ‖ The Gods and the Asuras were in conflict. Indra had recourse to Prajāpati, to him he gave these victories (offerings); he offered them; then indeed were the Gods victorious over the Asuras; in that they were victorious, that is why (the offerings) are called 'victorious'. They should be offered by one engaged in conflict; verily does he win in the conflict.

Mantra 3:4:5

a. Agni overlord of creatures, may he help me; Indra of powers, Yama of earth, Vāyu of the atmosphere, Sūrya of the sky, Chandramās of Nakshatras, Bṛihaspati of holy power, Mitra of truths, Varuṇa of waters, the ocean of streams, food of lordships overlord, may it help me; Soma of plants, Savitar of instigations, Rudra of cattle, Tvashṭar of forms, Vishṇu of mountains, the Marutas of troops overlords, may they help me. ‖ *b.* O ye fathers, ye grandfathers, ye further, ye nearer, ye dadas, ye granddadas, do ye here help me. ‖ *c.* In this holy power, this worldly power, this prayer, this Purohitaship, this rite, this invocation of the Gods.

Mantra 3:4:6

What the Gods did at the sacrifice, the Asuras did. The Gods saw these overpowering (Homas), they performed them; the rite of the Gods succeeded, that of the Asuras did not succeed. If he is desirous of prospering in a rite, then should he offer them, and in that rite he prospers. In that the All-Gods brought together (the materials), the Abhyātānas are connected with the All-Gods; in that Prajāpati bestowed the victories (Jayas), therefore the Jayas are connected with Prajāpati; in that they won the kingdom by the Rāshṭrabhṛits, that is why the Rāshṭrabhṛits (supporters of the kingdom) have their name. The Gods overpowered the Asuras with the Abhyātānas, conquered them with the Jayas, and won the kingdom with the Rāshṭrabhṛits; in that the Gods overpowered (*abhyātānvata*) the Asuras with the Abhyātānas, that is why the Abhyātānas have their name; in that they conquered (*ājayan*) them with the Jayas, that is why the Jayas have their name; in that they won the kingdom with the Rāshṭrabhṛits, that is why the Rāshṭrabhṛits have their name. Then the Gods prospered, the Asuras were defeated. He who has foes should offer these (offerings); verily by the Abhyātānas he overpowers his foes, by the Jayas he conquers them, by the Rāshṭrabhṛits he wins the kingdom; he prospers himself, his foe is defeated.

Mantra 3:4:7

a. Supporting holy order, abounding in truth, Agni is the Gandharva; his Apsarases are the plants, called strength; may he protect this holy power, this lordly power; may they protect this holy power, this lordly power; to him hail! To them hail! ‖ *b.* The compact, possessing all the Sāmans, the sun is the Gandharva, his Apsarases are the rays (called) active, etc. ‖ *c.* The all-blessed, sun-rayed Chandramās is the Gandharva; his Apsarases are the Nakshatras, (called) the bright, etc. ‖ *d.* The active, the winged sacrifice is the Gandharva, his Apsarases are the sacrificial fees, (called) praises, etc. ‖ *e.* Prajāpati, all-creator, the mind, is the Gandharva; his Apsarases are the Ṛich and Sāman verses, (called) hymns, etc. ‖ *f.* The swift, all-pervading wind is the Gandharva; his Apsarases are the waters, (called) delights, etc. ‖ *g.* O lord of the world, thou who hast houses above and here, do thou give us increase of wealth, unfailing, rich in heroes, prosperity abiding through the year. || *h.* The supreme ruler, the overlord, death is the Gandharva; his Apsarases are the whole (world), (called) the worlds. etc. || *i.* With fair abode, fair wealth, doer of good deeds, holding the light, Parjanya. is the Gandharva; his Apsarases are the lightnings, (called) the radiant, etc. || *k.* Whose dart speeds afar, the pitiless, death is the Gandharva; the Apsarases are his offspring, (called) the timid, etc. || *l.* The dear one, looking with desire, love is the Gandharva; his Apsarases are thoughts, (called) the burning; may he protect this our holy power, our lordly power; may they protect this our holy power, our lordly power; to him hail! To them hail! || *m.* O lord of the world, thou who hast houses above and here, do thou accord wide, great, protection to this holy power, this holy work.

Mantra 3:4:8

They should be offered for one who desires the kingdom; the Rāṣhṭrabhṛits are the kingdom; verily with the kingdom he wins the kingdom for him; he becomes the kingdom. They should be offered for oneself; the Rāṣhṭrabhṛits are the kingdom, the people are the kingdom, cattle are the kingdom, in that he becomes the highest he is the kingdom; verily with the kingdom he wins the kingdom, he becomes the richest of his equals. They should be offered for one who desires a village; the Rāṣhṭrabhṛits are the kingdom, his fellows are the kingdom; verily with the kingdom he wins for him his fellows and the kingdom; he becomes possessed of a village. He offers on the dicing-place; verily on the dicing-place he wins his fellows for him, and being won they wait upon him. They should be offered on the mouth of the chariot for him who desires force; the Rāṣhṭrabhṛits are force, the chariot is force; verily by force he wins force for him; he becomes possessed of force. They should be offered for him who is expelled from his kingdom; to all his chariots he should say, 'Be yoked'; verily he yokes the kingdom for him. The oblations of him whose realm is not in order are disordered; he should take off the right wheel of his chariot and offer in the box; so he puts in order his oblation, and the kingdom comes into order in accord with their coming into order. They should be offered when battle is joined; the Rāṣhṭrabhṛits are the kingdom, and for the kingdom do they strive who go to battle together; he for whom first they offer prospers, and wins this battle. The kindling-wood is from the Madhuka tree; the coals shrinking back make the host of his foe to shrink back. They should be offered for one who is mad; for it is the Gandharva and the Apsarases who madden him who is mad; the Rāṣhṭrabhṛits are the Gandharva and the Apsarases. 'To him hail! To them hail!' (with these words) he offers, and thereby he appeases them. Of Nyagrodha, Udumbara, Aśvattha, or Plakṣha (wood) is the kindling-wood; these are the homes of the Gandharva and the Apsarases; verily he appeases them in their own abode. They should be offered in inverse order by one who is practising witchcraft; so he fastens on his breaths from in front, and then at pleasure lays him low. He offers in a natural cleft or hollow; that of this (earth) is seized by misfortune; verily on (a place) seized by misfortune he makes misfortune seize upon him. With what is harsh in speech he utters the Vaṣhaṭ call; verily with the harshness of speech he cuts him down; swiftly he is ruined. If he desire of a man, 'Let me take his eating of food,' he should fall at length in his hall and (with the words), 'O lord of the world,' gather blades of grass; the lord of the world is Prajāpati; verily by Prajāpati he takes his eating of food. 'Here do I take the eating of food of N. N., descendant of N. N.,' he says; verily he takes his eating of food. With six (verses) he takes, the seasons are six; verily the seasons having taken by Prajāpati his eating of food bestow it on him. If the head of a family is expelled, they should be offered for him, placing him on a mound and cooking a Brahman's mess of four Śarāvas in size; the Rāṣhṭrabhṛits are pre-eminence, the mound is pre-eminence; verily by pre-eminence he makes him pre-eminent among his equals. (The offering) is of four Śarāvas in size; verily he finds support in the quarters; it is made in milk; verily he bestows brilliance upon him; he takes it out, to make it cooked; it is full of butter, for purity; four descended from Ṛiṣhis partake of it; verily he offers in the light of the quarters.

Mantra 3:4:9

He who desires offspring should offer (the oblations to) the minor deities; the minor deities are the metres, offspring are as it were the metres; verily by the metres he produces offspring for him. He makes Dhātar first; verily he produces pairing with him, Anumati gives approval to him, Rākā gives, Sinīvālī produces, and in offspring when produced by Kuhū he places speech. These (offerings) also should he make who desires cattle; the minor deities are the metres, cattle are as it were the metres; verily by the metres he produces offspring for him. He makes Dhātar first; by him he scatters, Anumati gives approval to him, Rākā gives, Sinīvālī produces, and by Kuhū he establishes offspring when produced. These (offerings) also should he make who desires a village; the minor deities are the metres, a village is as it were the metres; verily by the metres he wins a village for him. He puts Dhātar in the middle; verily he places him in the middle of a village. These (offerings) also should he offer who is long ill; the minor deities are the metres, the metres are unfavourable to him whose illness is long; verily by the metres he makes him well. He puts Dhātar in the middle, it is not in order in the middle of him whose illness is long; verily thereby in the middle he puts (things) in order for him. These (offerings) also should he offer to whom the sacrifice does not resort; the minor deities are the metres, the metres do not resort to him to whom the sacrifice does not resort. He puts Dhātar first; verily in his mouth he places the metres; the sacrifice resorts to him. These (offerings) also should he make who has sacrificed; the minor deities are the metres, the metres of him who has sacrificed are worn out as it were. He puts Dhātar last; verily afterwards he wins for him metres unwearied; the next sacrifice resorts to him. These (offerings) should he make to whom wisdom does not resort; the minor deities are the metres, the metres do not resort to him to whom wisdom does not resort. He puts Dhātar first; verily in his mouth he places the metres; wisdom resorts to him. These (offerings) also should he make who desires brilliance; the minor deities are the metres, brilliance is as it were the metres; verily by the metres he bestows brilliance upon him. They are made in milk; verily he bestows brilliance upon him. He puts Dhātar in the middle; verily he places him in the middle of brilliance. Anumati is the Gāyatrī, Rākā the Triṣhṭubh, Sinīvālī the Jagatī, Kuhū the Anuṣhṭubh, Dhātar the Vaṣhaṭ call. Rākā is the first fortnight, Kuhū the second, Sinīvālī the new moon (night), Anumati the full moon (night), Dhātar the moon. The Vasus are eight, the Gāyatrī has eight syllables; the Rudras are eleven, the Triṣhṭubh has eleven syllables; the Ādityas are twelve, the Jagatī has twelve syllables, the Anuṣhṭubh is Prajāpati, the Vaṣhaṭ call Dhātar. Thus indeed the minor deities are all the metres and all the Gods and the Vaṣhaṭ call. If he were to offer them all at once, they would be likely to burn him up; he should offer first two, and a third for Dhātar, and then offer likewise the last two; thus they do not burn him up, and for whatever desire they are offered that he obtains by them.

Mantra 3:4:10.

a. O Vāstoṣhpati, accept us; | Be of kind entrance for us and free from ill; | That which we seek from thee, do thou accord us, | And health be thou for our bipeds, health for our quadrupeds. || *b.* O Vāstoṣhpati, may we be comrades of thee | In a friendship, effectual, joyful, and proceeding well; | Aid our wishes in peace, in action; | Do ye guard us ever with blessings. || In that evening and morning he offers the Agnihotra the sacrificer thus piles up the oblation bricks; the bricks of him who has established a sacred fire are the days and nights; in that he offers evening and morning, verily he obtains the days and nights, and making them into bricks piles them up. He offers ten in the same place; the Virāj has ten syllables; verily having obtained the Virāj, he makes it into a brick and piles it up; verily in the Virāj he obtains the sacrifice; the piling up must be repeated by him. Therefore that is the place of sacrifice where he advances having spent ten (nights); not suitable is the place where (he spends) less time than that Now Vāstoṣhpati is Rudra. If he were to go on without offering to Vāstoṣhpati, the fire becoming Rudra would leap after him and slay him; he offers to Vāstoṣhpati; verily with his own share he appeases him; the sacrificer does not come to ruin. If he were to offer with the chariot yoked, that would be as when one offers an oblation on a place he has left; if he were to offer without the chariot being yoked, that would be as when one offers an oblation at rest; verily no offering would be made to Vāstoṣhpati. The right (animal) is yoked, the left not yoked, and thus he offers to Vāstoṣhpati; verily he does both, and appeases him completely. If he were to offer with one (verse) he would make (it) a ladle offering; having pronounced the Puronuvākyā he offers with the Yājyā, to win the Gods. If he were to load (his cart) after the offering, he would make Rudra enter his house. If he were to set out without extinguishing the smouldering embers, it would be like a con fusion of the sacrifice or a burning. 'This is thy birthplace in season,' (with these words) he places (the embers) on the kindling-sticks; this is the birthplace of Agni; verily he mounts it on its own birthplace. Now they say, 'If being placed on the kindling-sticks it should be lost, his fire would be dispersed, it would have to be piled up again. 'With thy body, O Agni, worthy of sacrifice, come hither and mount,' (with these words) he makes it mount on himself; the birthplace of fire is the sacrificer; verily on its own birthplace he causes it to mount.

Mantra 3:4:11

a. Long life thou givest, O Agni, | O God, to the giver, | Sage, lord of the house, the youthful. || *b.* Bearing the oblations, Agni, immortal, our father, | Wide extending, widely refulgent, fair to see for us, | With good household fire, do thou shine forth food, | Mete out to uswards renown. || *c.* O do thou, O Soma, will life for us, | That we may not die, | Thou that lovest praise, lord of the forest. || *d.* Brahman of the Gods, leader of poets, | Sage of seers, bull of wild beasts, | Eagle of vultures, axe of the forests, | Soma goeth over the sieve singing. || *e.* With our hymns today we choose | The God of all, the lord of the true, | Savitar of true instigation. || *f.* Coming with true light, | Placing the mortal and the immortal, | With golden car Savitar | The God advanceth gazing on the worlds. || *g.* That Aditi may accord | To our cattle, our men, our kine, | To our offspring, Rudra's grace. || *h.* Harm us not in our children, our descendants, nor in our life, | Harm us not in our cattle, in our horses | Smite not in anger our heroes, O Rudra, | With oblations let us serve thee with honour. || *i.* Like watchful birds swimming in water, | Like the noises of the loud thundercloud, | Like joyous waves breaking forth from the mountains, | The praises have lauded Bṛihaspati || *k.* With comrades shouting like swans, | Casting aside his stone-made fetters, | Bṛihaspati thundered towards the cows, | And praised and sang in celebration perceiving them. || *l.* Hither, O Indra, enduring wealth, | Victorious, bearing all, | Highest for help, do thou bring. || *m.* O thou much invoked, thou dost endure the foes; | Best be thy strength, thy gift here; | Bring riches with thy right (hand), O Indra, | Thou art the lord of rich rivers. || *n.* Thou were born, in full size at once, | For the drinking of (Soma) when pressed, | O Indra, O wise one, for pre-eminence. || *o.* Thou art mighty, O Indra, with holy power, | To be adored at every pressing; | Thou art an overthrower of men in every conflict, | And highest song, O lord of all the people. || *p.* The fame of Mitra, supporter of the people, | Of the God is eternal, | True, and most varied in fame. || *q.* Mitra stirreth men, the wise one, | Mitra supporteth earth and sky; | Mitra regardeth men with unwinking (eye); | To the true one, let us offer an oblation rich in ghee. || *r.* Rich in food be that mortal, O Mitra, | Who, O Āditya, seeks to follow thy law; | Aided by thee he is not slain nor oppressed; | Affliction cometh to him neither from near nor from afar. || *s.* Whatever law of thine, as men, | O God Varuṇa, | Day by day we transgress. || *t.* Whatever wrong we mortals here do | Against the host divine, | Whatever breach of thy laws we make through lack of thought, | For that sin, O God, harm us not. || *u.* As gamesters cheat in dicing, | What we know in truth or what we know not, | All that do thou, O God, loosen as it were, | And may we be dear to thee, O Varuṇa

Prapāṭhaka 5.

Miscellaneous Supplements

Mantra 3:5:1

a. Full behind, and full in front, | In the middle hath she of the full moon been victorious; | In her let the Gods dwelling together | Rejoice here in the highest firmament. || *b.* The share that the Gods dwelling together | In greatness bestowed on thee, O new moon, | (Therewith) do thou fill our sacrifice, O thou of every boon | Grant us wealth of good heroes, O fortunate one. || *c.* Holder and gatherer of riches, | Clad in all rich forms, | Granting a thousandfold prosperity, | The fortunate one hath come to us with radiance accordant. || *d.* O Agni and Soma, the first in strength, | Do ye quicken the Vasus, the Rudras, the Ādityas here; | Rejoice in him of the full moon in the midst, | Ye that are made to grow by holy power, won by good deeds, | And allot to us wealth with heroes. || The Ādityas and the Aṅgirasas piled up the fires, they desired to obtain the new and the full moon (offerings); the Aṅgirasas offered the oblation, then the Ādityas saw these two offerings, and offered them; then they first grasped the new and full moon (offerings). He who is commencing the new and full moon (sacrifices) should first offer these two (offerings); verily straightway he commences the new and full moon (sacrifices). The theologians say, 'He indeed would begin the new and full moon (sacrifices) who should know the normal and reversed order'. What follows on the new moon is the normal, what is after the full moon is the reversed order; if he were to begin the full moon (offering) first, he would offer these two (libations) in reverse order; he would waste away as the moon waned; he should offer these libations to Sarasvat and Sarasvatī in front; Sarasvatī is the new moon; verily he commences them in normal order; he waxes as the moon waxes. He should offer first on eleven potsherds to Agni and Vishṇu, to Sarasvatī an oblation, to Sarasvat on twelve potsherds. In that it is (offered) to Agni, and the mouth of the sacrifice is Agni, verily he places in front prosperity and the mouth of the sacrifice; in that it is (offered) to Vishṇu, and Vishṇu is the sacrifice, verily commencing the sacrifice he continues it. There is an oblation for Sarasvatī, and (an offering) on twelve potsherds for Sarasvat; Sarasvatī is the new moon, Sarasvat is the full moon; verily straightway he commences these (offerings), he prospers by them. That to Sarasvat is on twelve potsherds, for pairing, for generation. The sacrificial fee is a pair of kine, for prosperity.

Mantra 3:5:2

The Ṛishis could not see Indra face to face; Vasishṭha saw him face to face; he said, 'Holy lore shall I proclaim to you so that people will be propagated with thee as Purohita; therefore do thou proclaim me to the other Ṛishis.' To him he proclaimed these shares in the Stoma, therefore people were propagated with Vasishṭha as their Purohita; therefore a Vasishṭha should be chosen as the Brahman priest; verily he is propagated. 'Thou art the ray; for dwelling thee! Quicken the dwelling,' he says; the dwelling is the Gods; verily to the Gods he announces the sacrifice. 'Thou art advance; for right thee! Quicken right,' he says; right is men; verily to men he announces the sacrifice. 'Thou art following; for sky thee! Quicken the sky,' he says; verily to these worlds he announces the sacrifice. 'Thou art a prop; for rain thee! Quicken rain,' he says; verily he wins rain. 'Thou art blowing forward; thou art blowing after,' he says, for pairing. 'Thou art the eager; for the Vasus thee! Quicken the Vasus,' he says; the Vasus are eight, the Rudras eleven, the Ādityas twelve; so many are the Gods; verily to them he announces the sacrifice. 'Thou art force; to the Pitṛis thee! Quicken the Pitṛis,' he says; verily the Gods and the Pitṛis he connects. 'Thou art the thread; for offspring thee! Quicken offspring,' he says; verily the Pitṛis and offspring he connects. 'Thou dost endure the battle; for cattle thee! Quicken cattle,' he says; verily offspring and cattle he connects. 'Thou art wealthy; for the plants thee! Quicken the plants,' he says; verily in the plants he makes cattle find support. 'Thou art the victorious, with ready stone; for Indra thee! Quicken Indra,' he says, for victory. 'Thou art the overlord; for breath thee! Quicken breath,' he says; verily upon offspring he bestows breath. 'Thou art the Trivṛit, thou art the Pravṛit,' he says, for pairing. 'Thou art the mounter, thou art the descender,' he says, for propagating. 'Thou art the wealthy, thou art the brilliant, thou art the gainer of good,' he says, for support.

Mantra 3:5:3

a. By Agni, the God, I win battles, with the Gāyatrī metre, the Trivṛit Stoma, the Rathantara Sāman, the Vashaṭ call, the thunderbolt, I trample under foot my foes born before me, I depress them, I repel them, in this home, in this world of earth; him who hateth us and him whom we hate I step over him with the stride of Vishṇu. || *b.* By Indra, the God, I win battles, with the Trishṭubh metre, the Pañchadaśa Stoma the Bṛihat Sāman, the Vashaṭ call, the thunderbolt, (I trample under foot my foes) born along (with me), etc. || *c.* By the All-Gods I win battles, with the Jagatī metre, the Saptadaśa Stoma, the Vāmadevya Sāman, the Vashaṭ call, the thunderbolt, (I trample under foot my foes) born after (me), etc. || *d.* In unison with Indra, may we | Withstand our foes, | Smiting the enemy irresistibly. || *e.* With the brilliance that is thine, O Agni, may I become brilliant; with the radiance that is thine, O Agni, may I become radiant; with the splendour that is thine, O Agni, may I become resplendent.

Mantra 3:5:4

a. The Gods, destroying the sacrifice, stealing the sacrifice, | That are seated on earth, | May Agni protect me from them; | May we go to those that do good deeds. || *b*. We have come, O noble ones, Mitra and Varuṇa, | To the share of the nights that is yours, | Grasping the firmament, in the place of good deeds, | On the third ridge above the light of the sky. || *c*. The Gods, destroyers of the sacrifice, stealers of the sacrifice, | That sit in the atmosphere, | From them may Vāyu guard me; | May we go to those that do good deeds. || *d*. The nights of thine, O Savitar, that go, traversed by Gods, | Between sky and earth, | With all your houses and offspring, | Do ye first mounting the light traverse the regions. || *e*. The Gods, destroyers of the sacrifice, stealers of the sacrifice, | That sit in the sky, | From them may Sūrya guard me; | May we go to those that do good deeds. || *f*. That highest oblation wherewith, O All-knower, | Thou didst collect milk for Indra, | Therewith, O Agni, do thou make him grow; | Bestow on him lordship over his fellows. || The Gods are destroyers of the sacrifice, stealers of the sacrifice; they sit these worlds taking and destroying from him who gives and sacrifices. 'The Gods, destroyers of the sacrifice, that sit on the earth, that (sit) in the atmosphere, that sit in the sky,' he says; verily traversing the worlds, he goes to the world of heaven with his household, with his cattle. From him who has sacrificed with the Soma (sacrifice), the deities and the sacrifice depart; he should offer to Agni on five potsherds as the final act; all the deities are Agni, the sacrifice is fivefold; verily he wins the deities and the sacrifice. Now Agni is connected with the Gāyatrī and has the Gāyatrī as his metre; he severs him from his metre, if he offers on five potsherds; it should be made on eight potsherds; the Gāyatrī has eight syllables, Agni is connected with the Gāyatrī and has the Gāyatrī for his metre; verily he unites him with his own metre. The Yājyā and the Anuvākyā are in the Paṅkti metre the sacrifice is fivefold; verily thereby he does not depart from the sacrifice.

Mantra 3:5:5

a. May Sūrya, the God, protect me from the Gods, Vāyu from the atmosphere; may Agni, the sacrificer, protect me from the (evil) eye; O strong one, O impetuous one, O instigator, O thou of all men, with these names, O Soma, we will worship thee; with these names, O Soma, we will worship thee. || *b*. I from above, I from below, | I revealed the darkness with the light; | The atmosphere hath become my father; | On both sides have I seen the sun; | May I become highest of my equals. || *c*. To the ocean, to the atmosphere, Prajāpati makes the cloud to fall; may Indra distil (it), may the Marutas cause (it) to rain. || *d*. Flood the earth, | Break this divine cloud; | Give to us of the divine water; | Ruling loosen the water bag. || *e*. The Āditya (cup) is these cattle, Agni is Rudra here, having cast plants in the fire he offers the Āditya (cup); verily he hides the cattle from Rudra, and causes the cattle to find support in the plants. || *f*. The sage stretcheth the path of the sacrifice, | On the back of the vault, above the light of the sky, | Whereby thou carriest the offering, thou goest as messenger, | Hence wisely, thence with more gain. || *g*. All the fire-sticks that are thine, O Agni, | Or on earth, on the strew, or in the sun, | Lot these of thine approach the oblation of ghee, | A protection to the pious sacrificer. || *h*. Invoking increase of wealth, | Rich in heroes and rich in steeds, | Bidden 'Godspeed' by Bṛihaspati, with wealth | Abide thou for me, the sacrificer.

Mantra 3:5:6

a. I yoke thee with milk, with ghee; | I yoke thee with water, and plants; | I yoke thee with offspring; | Today being consecrated do thou win strength for us. || *b*. Let the lady of holy power advance, | Let her sit on the altar with fair colour; || *c*. Then may I, full of desire, | Enter my own place, here. || *d*. With fair offspring, with noble husbands, | We are come to thee, | O Agni, to thee that deceivest the foe, | The undeceivable, we that are not deceived. || *e*. I loosen this bond of Varuṇa, | Which Savitar, the kindly, hath bound, | And in the birthplace of the creator, in the place of good action, | I make it pleasant for me with my husband. || *f*. Go forth, go up, to the lovers of holy order; may Agni lead thy head, Aditi give (thee) a middle, thou art that let loose by Rudra, Yuvā by name; harm me not. || *g*. For the Vasus, the Rudras, the Ādityas, for the All-Gods, I take you, foot-washing (waters); || *h*. For the sacrifice I place you, foot-washing (waters). || *i*. In the sight of thee that art all, that hast all, that hast manly power, O Agni, in the lovers, may I deposit all seed. || *k*. The sacrifice hath come to the Gods, the Goddesses have left the sacrifice for the Gods, to the sacrificer that poureth blessings, accompanied by the cry 'Hail!,' standing in the waters, do ye follow the Gandharva, in the rush of the wind, food that is praised.

Mantra 3:5:7

The Vaṣhaṭ call cleft the head of the Gāyatrī; its sap fell away, it entered the earth, it became the Khadira; he, whose dipping-spoon is make of Khadira wood, cuts off with the sap of the metres; his oblations are full of sap. Soma was in the third sky from hence; the Gāyatrī fetched it, a leaf of it was cut off, that became the Parṇa, that is why the Parṇa is so called. He whose ladle is made of Parṇa wood has his oblations acceptable; the Gods rejoice in his oblation. The Gods discussed regarding holy power; the Parṇa overheard it; he whose ladle is made of Parṇa wood is styled famous; he hears no evil bruit. The Parṇa is holy power, the Marutas are the people, the people are food, the Aśvattha is connected with the Marutas; he whose ladle is made of Parṇa wood, and his spoon (*upabhṛit*) is of Aśvattha, by holy power wins food, and the holy class puts over the people. The Parṇa is the royalty, the Aśvattha is the people; in that the ladle is made of Parṇa wood and the spoon of Aśvattha, verily he puts the royalty over the people. Prajāpati sacrificed; where the oblation found support, thence sprung the Vikaṅkata; there he created offspring; the oblation of him whose Dhruvā, is made of Vikaṅkata, wood finds rest; verily he is propagated. That is the form of the offering-spoons; on him whose spoons are so formed all forms of cattle attend, nothing unshapely is born in him.

Mantra 3:6:8

a. Thou art taken with a support; for Prajāpati thee, for him full of light, thee full of light I take; for Dakṣha who increases cleverness, (thee) that are acceptable to the Gods, thee for those whose tongue is Agni, who are righteous, whose highest is Indra, whose king is Varuṇa, whose friend is Vāta, whose breath is Parjanya, for sky thee, for atmosphere thee, for earth thee! || *b*. Smite away, O Indra, the mind of him who hateth us, | Who desireth to oppress us, | Smite him away who practiseth evil against us. || *c*. For expiration thee, for inspiration thee, for cross-breathing thee for | being thee, for not being thee; for the waters thee, for the plants for | all beings thee; whence offspring arose unhurt, for that thee, for Prajāpati, of bounteous gifts, full of light, (thee) full of light I offer.

Mantra 3:5:9

To that deity whom the Adhvaryu and the sacrificer overlook do they fall victims; he should draw the cup of curd for Prajāpati, all the Gods are Prajāpati; verily they make reparation to the Gods. This is the foremost of cups; verily he for whom it is drawn attains a foremost place. This cup is the form of all the deities; on him for whom it is drawn all forms of cattle attend. 'Thou are taken with a support; for Prajāpati thee, for him full of light, (thee) full of light I take,' he says; verily he makes him a light of his equals. 'For those whose tongue is Agni, who are righteous,' he says; so many are the deities; verily for all of them he draws it. 'Smite away, O Indra, the mind of him who hateth us,' he says, for the smiting away of foes. 'For expiration thee, for inspiration thee,' he says; verily he bestows the breaths on the sacrificer. 'For that thee, for Prajāpati, of bounteous gifts, full of light, (thee) full of light I offer,' he says; all the deities are Prajāpati; verily for all the deities he offers it. He should draw the cup of butter for one who desires brilliance; butter is brilliance; verily he becomes brilliant; he should draw the cup of Soma for one who desires splendour; Soma is splendour; verily he becomes resplendent; he should draw the cup of curd for one who desires cattle; curd is strength, cattle are strength; verily by strength he wins him strength and cattle.

Mantra 3:5:10.

a. All turn their minds towards thee | When these twice or thrice become helpers; | Mix with the sweet what is sweeter than sweet, | I have won with the mead the mead. || *b*. Thou art taken with a support; to Prajāpati I take thee acceptably; this is thy birthplace; for Prajāpati thee! || He draws the Prāṇa, cups; so much is there as are these cups, these Stomas, these metres, these Pṛiṣhṭha (Stotras), these quarters; whatever there is that he wins. The highest Brahmans have proclaimed these before; they have therefore won all the quarters. He for whom these are drawn attains supremacy, he conquers the quarters. Five are drawn, the quarters are five; verily they prosper in all the quarters. Nine each are drawn; nine are the vital airs in man; verily upon the sacrificers he bestows the vital airs. At the beginning and at the end they are drawn; the Prāṇa cups are the vital airs; verily they begin with the vital airs, and end with the vital airs. Now offspring leave their vital airs in that the Vāmadevya (Sāman) departs from its norm; on the tenth day the Vāmadevya departs from its norm; in that they are drawn on the tenth day, offspring leave not their vital airs.

Mantra 3:5:11

a. Bring onward with meditation divine | The God, who knoweth all; | May he duly bear our sacrifices. ‖ *b.* He, the Hotar is led forward for the sacrifice, | The servant of the Gods; | Like a covered chariot glowing | He himself knoweth health. ‖ *c.* This Agni rescueth | Us from the immortal race, | He that is stronger than strength, | The God made for life. ‖ *d.* In the place of Iḍā we set thee down, | On the navel of the earth, | O Agni, all-knower, | To bear the oblation. ‖ *e.* O Agni of kindly aspect, do thou with the All-Gods | Sit first on the birthplace made of wool, | Nest-like, rich in ghee, for Savitar | Do thou lead well the sacrifice, for the sacrificer. ‖ *f.* Sit thou, O Hotar, in thine own world, wise, | Place thou the sacrifice in the birthplace of good deeds | Eager for the Gods, do thou sacrifice to them with oblation; | O Agni, bestow great strength on the sacrificer. ‖ *g.* The Hotar hath sat him down in the place of the Hotar wise, | Glittering, shining, skilful, | With vows and foresight undeceived, most wealthy, | Bearing a thousand, pure-tongued Agni. ‖ *h.* Thou art the envoy, thou our guardian, | Thou, O bull, leadest us to better fortune; | O Agni, be thou the guardian of our offspring, our descendants | In their bodies, unfailing and radiant. ‖ *i.* To thee, O God Savitar, | Lord of things delightful, | We come for fortune, O thou of constant help. ‖ *k.* May the great ones, sky and earth, | Mingle for us this sacrifice, | May they sustain us with support. ‖ *l.* Thee, O Agni, from the lotus | Atharvan passed out, | From the head of every priest. ‖ *m.* Thee the sage, Dadhyach, | Son of Atharvan, doth kindle, | Slayer of Vṛitra, destroyer of forts. ‖ *n.* Thee Pāthya Vṛishan doth kindle, | Best slayer of foes, | Winner of booty in every conflict. ‖ *o.* Let men say too, | 'Agni hath been born, slayer of Vṛitra, | Winning booty in every conflict.' ‖ *p.* Whom, like a quoit in their bands, | Like a child at birth, they bear, | Agni, fair sacrificer of the folk. ‖ *q.* Bring forward the God, best finder of riches, | For offering to the Gods; | May he sit down in his own birthplace. ‖ *r.* In the all-knower cause to rest | The dear guest on birth, | In a pleasant place, the lord of the house. ‖ *s.* By Agni is Agni kindled, | The wise, the young, the lord of the house, | The bearer of the oblation, with ladle in his mouth. ‖ *t.* Thou, O Agni, by Agni, | The sage by the sage, the good by the good, | The comrade by the comrade, art kindled. ‖ *u.* Him they make bright, the wise, | Victorious in the contests, | Strong in his abodes. ‖ *v.* By the sacrifice the Gods sacrificed the sacrifice; | These were the first ordinances; | These mighty powers frequent the vault | Where are the ancient Sādhya Gods.

Kāṇḍa 4.

The Piling of the Fire Altar

Prapāṭhaka 1

The Placing of the Fire in the Fire-pan

Mantra 4:1:1

a. Yoking mind first, | Extending his thoughts, Savitar | Discerning the light, | Hath brought Agni from the earth. ‖ *b.* Yoking with mind the Gods, | Going to the heaven, the sky, with thought, | Those that are to make great light, | Savitar instigates. ‖ *c.* With mind well yoked are we | In the instigation of God Savitar, | For strength to go to the heaven. ‖ *d.* They yoke their minds, they yoke their thoughts, | The priests of the mighty wise priest, | He alone, who knoweth the way, appointeth their functions | Great is the praise of the God Savitar ‖ *e.* I yoke with honour your ancient prayer; | The praises go like Sūras on their way; | All the sons of immortality hear (it), | Who have achieved dwellings divine. ‖ *f.* He whose advance others followed, | Gods, of the God praising might, | He who meted out the regions of earth, | He is the brilliant God Savitar in greatness. ‖ *g.* O God Savitar, instigate the sacrifice, instigate the lord of the sacrifice to good luck; may the divine Gandharva, who purifieth thoughts purify our thought; may the lord of speech today make sweet our utterance. ‖ *h.* This sacrifice for us, O God Savitar | Do thou instigate, serving the Gods, | Finding comrades, ever victorious, | Winning booty, winning heaven. ‖ *i.* By the Ṛich make the Stoma to prosper, | By the Gateway the Rathantara, | The Bṛihat with the Gāyatrī for its metre. ‖ *k.* On the impulse of the God Savitar, with the arms of the Aśvins, with the hands of Pūṣhan, with the Gāyatrī metre, I take thee, in the manner of Aṅgiras ‖ *l.* Thou art the spade, thou art the woman, from the abode of the earth I bear Agni of the dust in the manner of Aṅgiras; with the Trishṭubh metre I grasp thee in the manner of Aṅgiras ‖ *m.* Thou art the bearer, thou art the woman; through thee may we be strong to dig Agni of the dust in his place; with the Jagatī metre I grasp thee in the manner of Aṅgiras ‖ *n.* Grasping in thy hand, Savitar, | Bearing the spade of gold, | Therewith digging Agni | Do thou bring for us light unperishing. | With the Anuṣhṭubh metre I grasp thee in the manner of Aṅgiras

Mantra 4:1:2

a. This bond of order they grasped | At their assemblies in ages gone by, the sages; | Therewith the Gods mastered the pressed (juice)— | In the Sāman of order proclaiming the stream. ‖ *b.* Swiftly run hither, O steed, | Along the most extended space; | In the sky is thy highest birth, | In the atmosphere thy navel, on the earth thy birthplace. ‖ *c.* Yoke ye two the ass, | In this course, O ye of mighty wealth, | Which beareth Agni, serving us. ‖ *d.* In each need more strong, | In each contest, we invoke, | As friends, Indra to aid us. ‖ *e.* Hastening come hither, trampling the enemy, | Come with wondrous skill from the leadership of Rudra; | Fare along the broad atmosphere, | With happy pastures, bestowing security. ‖ *f.* With Pūṣhan as fellow, from the abode of the earth do thou approach | Agni of the dust in the manner of Aṅgiras ‖ *g.* We approach Agni of the dust in the manner of Aṅgiras ‖ *h.* We will bear Agni of the dust in the manner of Aṅgiras ‖ *i.* We bear Agni of the dust in the manner of Aṅgiras ‖ *k.* Agni gazed along the forefront of the dawns, | Along the days first, the all-knower, | And in many ways along the rays of the sun, | He hath extended along sky and earth. ‖ *l.* The steed coming from the way | Driveth every foe; | He is fain to gaze with his eye | On Agni in his great abode. ‖ *m.* Coming to earth, O steed, | Do thou seek Agni with thy radiance; | Turning from earth I tell us | Whence we shall dig him up. ‖ *n.* Thy back is the sky, thy abode earth, | Thy breath the atmosphere, thy birthplace the ocean; | Discerning with thine eye, | Do thou overcome the enemy. ‖ *o.* Arise for great prosperity | From this abode, giving wealth, O steed; | May we enjoy the loving favour of earth, | That are about to dig fire in her lap. ‖ *p.* The strong steed hath stepped forward, giving wealth; | He hath made the place of earth well wrought; | Thence let us dig Agni of fair aspect, | Mounting the heaven on the top of the vault. ‖ *q.* The water divine do thou pour, full of sweetness | To avert diseases for men, | From their place let arise | Plants with fair leaves. ‖ *r.* I touch Agni with mind, with ghee, | Who lordeth it over all the worlds, | Broad, vast, with pervading vital power, | Most extensive, impetuous, winning, food. ‖ *s.* I touch thee with speech, with ghee, | With friendly mind accept it; | With mortal glory, with engaging colour, | Agni, with body full of life may not be touched. ‖ *t.* Round the offerings hath Agni gone, | The sage, the lord of strength, | Bestowing jewels on the donor. ‖ *u.* May we set thee around us, O Agni, | The sage, O strong one, as a fort, | Of daring due, day by day, | Destroyer of that which may be broken. ‖ *v.* Thou, O Agni, with days, fain to shine towards us, | Thou from the waters, thou from the rock, | Thou from the woods, thou from the plants, | Thou, O lord of men, art born pure.

Mantra 4:1:3

a. On the impulse of the God Savitar, with the arms of the Aśvins, with the hands of Pūṣhan, in the abode of earth, I dig Agni of the dust in the manner of Aṅgiras ‖ *b.* Full of light, thou, O Agni; of fair aspect, | Shining with unaging radiance, | Auspicious and harmless to offspring, | In the abode of earth, I dig Agni of the dust in the manner of Aṅgiras ‖ *c.* Thou art the back of the waters, expansive, wide, | About to bear Agni, least to be laid aside; | Growing to might as the lotus-flower, | Do thou extend in width with the measure of heaven. ‖ *d.* Ye two are protectors and a help, | Unbroken, both expansive; | Do ye expanding be united; | Bear Agni of the dust. ‖ *e.* Be ye united, that win the heaven, | In union of heart and self; | Who shall bear within Agni | Full of light and unaging. ‖ *f.* Thou art of the dust, all-supporting; Atharvan first pressed out thee, O Agni. ‖ *g.* Thee, O Agni, from the lotus | Atharvan pressed out, | From the head of every priest. ‖ *h.* Thee the sage, Dadhyach, | Son of Atharvan, doth kindle, | Slayer of Vṛitra, destroyer of foes. ‖ *i.* Thee Pāthya Vṛishan doth kindle, | Best slayer of foes, | Winner of booty in every conflict. ‖ *k.* Sit thou, O Hotar, in thine own world, wise, | Place thou the sacrifice in the birthplace of good deeds, | Eager for the Gods, do thou sacrifice to them with oblation; | O Agni, bestow great strength on the sacrificer. ‖ *l.* The Hotar hath sat him down in the place of the Hotar, wise, | Glittering, shining, skilful, | With vows and foresight undeceived, most wealthy, | Bearing a thousand, pure-tongued Agni. ‖ *m.* Sit thou down, thou art great, | Burn best servant of the Gods; | O Agni, pure one, send forth the ruddy smoke, | O famous one, that can be seen afar. ‖ *n.* Be born noble in the forefront of the days, | Kind to the kindly, red in the woods; | Bestowing seven jewels in every home | Hath Agni sat him down as Hotar.

Mantra 4:1:4

a. May I Vāyu, Mātariśvan, unite | The broken heart of thee that art outstretched | To him who moveth with the expiration of the Gods, | With thee, O Goddess, be Vaṣhaṭ ‖ *b.* Well-born, with light, | Guard and protector, thou hast sat on the heaven; | O Agni, thy garment of many hues, | Put on, O thou that dost abound in light. ‖ *c.* Arise, thou of fair sacrifice, | Aid us with thy divine radiance; | Brilliant to behold, with mighty blaze, | Do thou come hither, O Agni, in response to our prayers. ‖ *d.* Arise erect to aid us, | Like Savitar, the God; | Erect to win the booty, | When in contest we call on thee with the shining praisers. ‖ *e.* Born, thou art the child of the two worlds, | O Agni; a brilliant child distributed among the plants; | A beauteous babe beyond the darkness outspread, | Thou didst come thundering from thy mothers. ‖ *f.* Be firm, of strong limbs, | Swift, a mighty steed; | Be broad, of kindly seat, | Thou art the carrier of dust for Agni. ‖ *g.* Be auspicious, for offspring | Of men, O Aṅgiras; | Scorch not sky and earth, | Nor the atmosphere, nor the trees. ‖ *h.* Let the steed advance, thundering | And resounding, the ass, the flier; | Bearing Agni of the dust | May he fall not before his day. ‖ *i.* The ass, well yoked to your chariot, | O ye strong ones, that thundereth, | May he as swift envoy | Bear hence Agni of the dust. ‖ *k.* The strong, bearing the strong Agni, | Germ of the waters, him of the ocean, | O Agni, come hither, for enjoyment, | As holy order and truth. ‖ *l.* O plants, do ye accept Agni here | Who cometh auspicious towards you; | Casting aside all hostilities, all evil imaginings, | Sitting down, may he smite away from us misfortune. ‖ *m.* O plants, do ye rejoice in him, | O ye that are rich in flowers, and have fair berries; | This germ of yours, of due season, | Hath sat him in his ancient seat.

Mantra 4:1:5

a. Radiant with extending blaze, | Do thou repel the enemy, the Rakṣhas's hostility; | May I enjoy the protection of the great protector, | May I enjoy the leadership of Agni, easy to invoke. ‖ *b.* Ye, waters, are healing; | Further us to strength, | To see great joy. ‖ *c.* The most auspicious flavour that is yours, | Accord to us here, | Like eager mothers. ‖ *d.* To him may we come with satisfaction, | To whose dwelling ye quicken us, | O waters, and propagate us. ‖ *e.* Mitra, having united the earth | And the ground with light, | Agni well-born, all-knower, | Common to all men, the wide extending. ‖ *f.* For health I unite thee, for offspring; may the All-Gods, common to all men, unite thee with the Anuṣhṭubh metre, in the manner of Aṅgiras ‖ *g.* The Rudras, having gathered together the earth, | Kindled a great light; | Their ray undying | Shineth clear among the Gods. ‖ *h.* United by the Vasus, the cunning Rudras, | The mud fit for the rite, | Making it smooth with her hands, | May Sinīvālī fashion this (pan). ‖ *i.* Sinīvālī, of fair braids, | Of fair head-dress, with fair locks, | May she, O Aditi, O great one, | Place within thy hands the pan. ‖ *k.* Let Aditi fashion the pan with might, | With her arms, with wisdom, | Let her bear Agni in her womb | As a mother a child in her lap. ‖ *l.* Thou art the head of Makha. ‖ *m.* Ye are the two feet of the sacrifice. ‖ *n.* May the Vasus fashion thee with the Gāyatrī metre, in the manner of Aṅgiras Thou art the earth; may the Rudras fashion thee with the Triṣhṭubh metre, in the manner of Aṅgiras Thou art the atmosphere; may the Ādityas fashion thee with the Jagatī metre in the manner of Aṅgiras Thou art the sky; may the All-Gods, common to all men, fashion thee with the Anuṣhṭubh metre, in the manner of Aṅgiras Thou art the quarters; thou art the fixed (quarter); fix in me offspring, increase of wealth, richness in cattle, richness in heroes, (subject) his fellows to the sacrificer. ‖ *o.* Thou art the girdle of Aditi. ‖ *p.* Let Aditi seize thy hole with the Paṅkti metre, in the manner of Aṅgiras ‖ *q.* Having made the great pan, | Wrought of clay, as a birthplace for Agni, | Aditi gave it to her sons, | (Saying), 'Let them cook it.'

Mantra 4:1:6

a. May the Vasus fumigate thee with the Gāyatrī metre, in the manner of Aṅgiras; may the Rudras fumigate thee with the Triṣhṭubh metre, in the manner of Aṅgiras; may the Ādityas fumigate thee with the Jagatī metre, in the manner of Aṅgiras; may the All-Gods, common to all men, fumigate thee with the Anuṣhṭubh metre, in the manner of Aṅgiras; may Indra fumigate thee in the manner of Aṅgiras; may Viṣhṇu fumigate thee in the manner of Aṅgiras; may Varuṇa fumigate thee in the manner of Aṅgiras ‖ *b.* May Aditi, connected with the All-Gods, the Goddess, dig thee on the abode of earth, in the manner of Aṅgiras, O trench. ‖ *c.* May the wives of the Gods, the Goddesses, connected with the All-Gods, place thee on the abode of earth, in the manner of Aṅgiras, O pan. ‖ *d.* May the Dhiṣhaṇās, the Goddesses connected with the All-Gods, kindle thee on the abode of earth, in the manner of Aṅgiras, O pan; may the wives, the Goddesses, connected with the All-Gods, prepare thee on the abode of earth, in the manner of Aṅgiras, O pan; may the protectors, the women, the Goddesses, connected with the All-Gods, cook thee on the abode of earth, in the manner of Aṅgiras, O pan. ‖ *e.* O Mitra, cook this pan; may it not break. ‖ *f.* This I place around thee, to prevent breaking. ‖ *g.* Mitra, extending, compasseth | This sky in greatness, | And the earth with his fame. ‖ *h.* The fame of Mitra, supporter of the people, | Of the God is eternal, | True, and most varied in fame. ‖ *i.* May the God Savitar dig thee out, | With fair hands, fair fingers, | Fair arms, with his might. ‖ *k.* Breaking not, O earth, | Do thou fill the regions, the quarters; | Arise, become great, | Stand upright, be thou firm. ‖ *l.* May the Vasus fill thee with the Gāyatrī metre, in the manner of Aṅgiras: may the Rudras fill thee with the Triṣhṭubh metre, in the manner of Aṅgiras; may the Ādityas fill thee with the Jagatī metre, in the manner of Aṅgiras; may the All-Gods, common to all men, fill thee with the Anuṣhṭubh metre, in the manner of Aṅgiras

Mantra 4:1:7

a. Let the half-years, the seasons, increase thee, O Agni, | The years, the Ṛishis, and what truths there are; | Shine with thy heavenly lustre, | Illuminate all the quarters of the earth. ‖ *b.* Be kindled, O Agni, and awake him; | Arise for great good fortune; | May he that waiteth on thee, O Agni, be not harmed; | May thy priests be famous, not the others. ‖ *c.* These Brahmans, O Agni, choose thee; | Be thou propitious, O Agni, to us in the sanctuary; | Slaying our rivals, conquering the foes, | Do thou watch unfailing in thine own home. ‖ *d.* Here, O Agni, do thou grant wealth; | May not the overcomers, anticipating (us); overcome thee; | May the lordly power be easily wielded by thee, O Agni | Let him who waiteth on thee prosper, unassailed. ‖ *e.* With good life, O Agni, unite thee with the lordly power; | O Agni, vie with Mitra in friendlihood; | Be thou the midmost of thine equals; | O Agni, shine forth here to be invoked by kings. ‖ *f.* (Be thou) over the enemy, the obstructor, | Unwisdom, niggardliness, O Agni, | All obstacles do thou overcome, | And bestow upon us wealth with heroes. ‖ *g.* Unassailable, all-knower, unoverpowered, | Ruling, O Agni, supporting the lordly power, do thou shine here; | Through all the regions, freeing men from fear, | Do thou this day guard us for increase with kindliness. ‖ *h.* O Bṛihaspati, instigator, awake him; | The sharp do thou more thoroughly sharpen; | Increase him to great prosperity | Let the All-Gods rejoice in him. ‖ *i.* What time, O Bṛihaspati, thou didst free | From life yonder, from Yama's enmity, | The Aśvins removed death from him, | O Agni, the physicians of the Gods with their powers. ‖ *k.* We from the darkness, | Gazing on the higher light, | Sūrya a God among the Gods, | Have come to the highest light.

Mantra 4:1:8

a. Uplifted are his kindling-sticks, | Uplifted and pure are the rays of Agni, | Most brilliant (are they) of the son of fair countenance. ‖ *b.* The son of self, the Asura, all-knower, | God, God among Gods, | Anointeth the ways with mead and ghee. ‖ *c.* With mead thou attainest the sacrifice, | Delighting, as Narāśaṃsa, O Agni, | The kindly God Savitar, with every boon. ‖ *d.* Hither he cometh, with might, with ghee, | The priest implored with adoration; | To Agni the ladles (move) when the rites proceed. || *e.* Worship let him pay to the greatness of him, of Agni; | He indeed is pre-eminent among the delightful, | The wealthy, the wisest, best bestower of wealth. || *f.* The divine doors—all—preserve | The rules of him, of Agni, | Of wide expanse, lording it with dominion. || *g.* May day and night | Like heavenly maidens in his birthplace | Protect this our sacrifice and offering. || *h.* O ye divine Hotars, sing ye | To our uplifted sacrifice, to Agni's tongue, | Make for us good offering. || *i.* May the three Goddesses sit on this strew, | Iḍā, Sarasvatī, Bhāratī, the great, being sung. || *k.* That seminal fluid of ours, wondrous, | Abundant, may Tvashṭar release | As increase of wealth with good heroes, as offspring to us. || *l.* O tree, let free, | Bestowing with thyself among the Gods; | Let Agni as queller make ready the oblation. || *m.* O Agni, utter 'Hail!' O all-knower, over the oblation for Indra; | May all the Gods rejoice in this offering. || *n.* The golden germ first arose; | Born he was the only lord of creation; | He supporteth the earth and the sky | To what God shall we offer with oblation? || *o.* He that alone by his might is king | Of the breathing, the winking world, | Who is lord of these bipeds and quadrupeds; | To what God shall we offer with oblation? || *p.* He who is giver of breath, giver of strength, | Upon whose bidding all, even the Gods, wait, | Whose shadow is immortality and death; | To what God shall we offer with oblation? | He whose are these snowy mountains through his might, | Whose they call the ocean with the Rasā, | Whose two arms are these quarters; | To what God shall we offer with oblation? || *r.* To whom the armies established | Through his aid gazed with minds disturbed, | Over whom on the rising of the sun it goeth; | To what God shall we offer with oblation? || *s.* He by whom the dread earth and the sky were made firm, | By whom the heaven was established, by whom the vault, | Who is the measure of the region in the atmosphere; | To what God shall we offer with oblation? || *t.* When the waters, the great ones, went | Bearing all strength, begetting Agni, | Then one breath of the Gods arose; | To what God shall we offer with oblation? || *u.* He who in his might beheld the waters | Bearing strength, begetting Agni, | Who was the God alone over the Gods; | To what God shall we offer with oblation?

Mantra 4:1:9

a. Purpose, Agni, impulse, hail! Mind, intellect, Agni, impulse, hail! Thought, knowledge, Agni, impulse, hail! Discrimination of speech, Agni, impulse, hail! To Manu, lord of creatures, hail! To Agni Vaiśvānara hail! || *b.* Let every man choose the companionship | Of the God who leadeth; | Every man prayeth for wealth; | Let him choose glory that he may prosper; hail! || *e.* Be not broken, nor come to harm; | Be firm and enduring; | O mother, daringly show thy heroism; | With Agni wilt thou do this deed. || *d.* Be firm, O Goddess earth, for prosperity; | Thou art the wile of the Asura, made with power; | Let this oblation be pleasing to the Gods; | Do thou emerge uninjured at this our sacrifice. || *e.* O Mitra, heat this pan; may it not break. || *f.* This I place around thee, to prevent breaking. || *g.* Feeding on wood, sipping clarified butter, | The ancient desirable Hotar, | Son of strength, the wondrous. || *h.* From a far region | Come hither to these lower ones | Favour those in the region where I am. || *i.* From a far distance | Do thou of ruddy steeds come hither; | Of the dust, dear to many, | O Agni, do thou overcome obstructions. || *k.* Do thou sit down in the lap of this mother, | O Agni, knowing all the ways; | Consume her not with light nor with heat, | Within her shine with pure radiance. || *l.* O Agni, with glow | Within thine own seat of the pan, | Heating with her blaze, | Be thou, O all-knower, auspicious. || *m.* Becoming auspicious to me, O Agni, | Do thou sit down auspicious; | Having made all the quarters auspicious | Sit here on thine own birthplace.

Mantra 4:1:10.

a. Whatever logs we place | In thee, O Agni, | Be that ghee for thee; | Accept it, O youngest one. || *b.* What the insect eateth, | What the ant climbeth over, | All that be ghee for thee; | Accept it, O youngest one. || *c.* Mighty by night, unfailingly bearing (food) | For him as fodder to a stalled horse, | May we, O Agni, thy neighbours, be not harmed, | Rejoicing in increase of wealth, in food. || *d.* Kindled on earth's navel, Agni | We invoke for great increase of wealth, | Delighting in drink, recipient of great praise, worthy of offering, | The victor, Agni, sustainer in battles. || *e.* The hosts that attack, | That pierce, the trooping, | The thieves and the robbers, | Them, O Agni, do I place in thy mouth. || *f.* With thy tusks the burglars, | With thy teeth the robbers, | With thy jaws the thieves, O blessed one, | Do thou chew, well chewed. || *g.* The burglars among men, | The thieves and robbers in the forest, | The mischief-workers in the thickets, | Them I place within thy jaws. || *h.* The man who is hostile to us, | And him who hateth us, | Him who revileth us, and him who seeketh to hurt, | Every one of them do thou crush to atoms. || *i.* Sharpened is my holy power, | Sharpened the strength and might, | Sharpened the conquering lordly power of him | Whose domestic priest I am. || *k.* Their arms have I uplifted, | Their radiance, their might; | With holy power I waste the foes, | I support my own. || *l.* Shining like gold, he hath become widely resplendent, | For glory shining with immortal life; | Agni became immortal in his strength | What time prolific Dyaus begat him. || *m.* The sage showeth all forms; | He hath produced bliss for biped and quadruped; | Savitar, the desirable, hath discerned the vault; | After the moving forward of the dawn he shineth. || *n.* Night and the dawn, one-minded but of various form, | United suckle one child; | The radiant one shineth between sky and earth | The Gods, granters of wealth, support Agni. || *o.* Thou art the bird of fair feathers; thy head the Trivṛit (Stoma), thy eye the Gateway, thy breath the Stoma, thy body the Vāmadevya Sāman, thy wings the Bṛihat and the Rathantara, thy tail the Yajñāyajñiya, thy limbs the metres, thy hoofs the altars, thy name the Yajus formulae. || *p.* Thou art the bird of fair feathers; go to the sky, fly to the heaven.

Mantra 4:1:11

a. O Agni, that sacrifice, that offering, | Which on all sides thou dost encircle, | It of a truth goeth to the Gods. || *b.* O Soma, the wondrous aids | That there are of thine for the generous man, | With these be thou our helper. || *c.* Agni the, head. || *d.* Be. || *e.* Thou, O Soma. || *f.* These abodes of thine. || *g.* That excellent glory of Savitar, | The God, we meditate, | That he may stimulate our prayers. || *h.* What we have done in thoughtlessness against the host divine, | With feeble insight, with violence as is man's way, | Among Gods and men, do thou, O Savitar, | There instigate us to sinlessness. || *i.* Impeller of righteousness, | Instigator of devotions, | Sarasvatī hath established the sacrifice. || *k.* May the maiden of the lightning, the one of varied life, | Sarasvatī, wife of a hero, inspire our devotion; | In accord with the ladies, may she accord to the singer | Protection uninjured, and guardianship unsurpassable. || *l.* May Pūshan follow the cows for us, | May he guard our horses; | May Pūshan win booty for us. || *m.* Bright is part of thee, worthy of offering another, | Like day and night of various hue, like the sky art thou; | All magic thou dost further, O powerful one; | Propitious here, O Pūshan, be thy bounty. || *n.* They grew in might with their own power; | They mounted the vault, they made a broad seat; | When Vishṇu helped the strong one who causeth gladness, | Like birds they sat on the dear strew. || *o.* Bear ye variegated praise to the strong singer, | The host of the Marutas, which hath strength; | Who with might endure might, | For the jocund ones, O Agni, the earth shakes. || *p.* The All-Gods. || *q.* O All-Gods. || *r.* May sky and earth this day | Place among the Gods this sacrifice, | Successful, touching the sky. || *s.* Bring forward the parents born of old with now songs, | In the seat of holy order, | Come to us, O sky and earth, with the host divine; | Great is your protection. || *t.* Awaken Agni with the praise, | Kindling the immortal; | May he place our oblations among the Gods. || *u.* Bearing the oblation, immortal, | The eager messenger, well-inclined, | Agni uniteth with our prayer. || *v.* Health be they. || *w.* For each prize.

Prapāṭhaka 2.

The Preparation of the Ground for the Fire

Mantra 4:2:1

a. Thou art the step of Vishṇu, overcoming hostility, mount the Gāyatrī metre, step along the earth, excluded is he whom we hate. Thou art the step of Vishṇu, overcoming imprecations, mount the Trishṭubh metre, step along the atmosphere, excluded is he whom we hate. Thou art the step of Vishṇu, overcomer of the enemy, mount the Jagatī metre, step along the sky, excluded is he whom we hate. Thou art the stop of Vishṇu, overcomer of the foe, mount the Anushṭubh metre, step along the quarters, excluded is he whom we hate. || *b.* Agni hath cried, like Dyaus thundering, | Licking the earth, devouring the plants | Straightway on birth he shone aflame, | He blazeth with his light within the firmaments. ‖ *c.* O Agni, returner, to us return | With life, with radiance, with gain, with wisdom, with offspring, with wealth. ‖ *d.* O Agni, O Aṅgiras, a hundred be thy returns, | A thousand thy movements; | With the increase of their increase | Do thou bring back for us what is lost, | Bring back to us wealth. ‖ *e.* Return with strength, | Return, O Agni, with food and life; | Again guard us on all sides. ‖ *f.* Return with wealth, | O Agni, fatten with the stream, | All-gaining on every side. ‖ *g.* Unloose from us, O Varuṇa, the highest, | The lowest, the midmost knot; | Then may we, O Āditya, in thy rule, | Be guiltless before Aditi. ‖ *h.* I have drawn thee, thou hast become within, | Be thou firm and motionless, | Lot all the folk desire thee; | In him establish the kingship. ‖ *i.* In greatness hath he arisen erect in the van of the dawns; | Emerging from the darkness, he hath come with the light; | Agni, with radiant brilliance, fair limbed, | On birth hath filled every seat. ‖ *k.* Do thou sit down in the lap of this mother, | O Agni, knowing all the ways; | Consume her not with light nor with heat, | Within her shine with pure radiance. | 1. O Agni, with glow | Within thine own seat of the pan, | Heating with her blaze, | Be thou, O all-knower, auspicious. ‖ *m.* Becoming auspicious to me, O Agni, | Do thou sit down auspicious; | Having made all the quarters auspicious, | Sit here on thine own birthplace. ‖ *n.* The gander seated in purity, the bright one seated in the atmosphere, | The Hotar seated at the altar, the guest seated in the house, | Seated among men, seated in the highest, seated in holy order, seated in the firmament, | Born of the waters, born of the cows, born of holy order, born of the mountain, the great holy order.

Mantra 4:2:2

a. From the sky was Agni first born, | From us secondly he who knoweth all, | In the waters thirdly the manly, | The pious man singeth of him, the undying, as he kindleth him. ‖ *b.* We know thy three places threefold, O Agni, | We know thy seat that is established in many places; | We know thy highest name in secret; | We know the spring whence thou hast come. ‖ *c.* The manly souled kindleth thee in the ocean, in the waters, | In the breast of the sky, O Agni, he who gazeth on men; | Thee standing in the third region, | In the birthplace of holy order, the steers inspirited. ‖ *d.* Agni hath cried, like Dyaus thundering, | Licking the earth, devouring the plants; | Straightway on birth he shone aflame, | He blazeth with his light within the firmaments. ‖ *e.* Eager, purifying, the envoy, the wise one, | Agni, the immortal, hath been established among men; | He beareth and darteth forward his ruddy smoke; | The sky he attaineth with his pure radiance. ‖ *f.* The banner of the whole world, the germ, | Filled on birth the firmaments; | Even the firm mountain he cleft passing over, | When the five peoples sacrificed to Agni. ‖ *g.* Receptacle of prosperity, supporter of riches, | Granter of thoughts, guardian of the Soma, | Son of the bright one, of strength, the king | Is resplendent within the waters, kindled before the dawns. ‖ *h.* He who first maketh for thee today, O thou of wondrous radiance, | A cake rich in ghee, O God Agni; | Do thou bear him ever on to the better, | To glory allotted by the Gods, O youngest one. ‖ *i.* Give him portion, O Agni, in praises; | Give him portion in every hymn that is sung, | Dear shall he be before Sūrya, dear before Agni | With what is born, what is to be born shall he be victorious. ‖ *k.* Thee, O Agni, the sacrificers through the days | Bear as many riches desirable; | With thee desiring wealth, | Eagerly they revealed the stall rich in kine. ‖ *l.* Shining like gold, he hath become widely resplendent, | For glory shining with immortal life; | Agni became immortal in his strength, | What time prolific Dyaus begat him.

Mantra 4:2:3

a. O Lord of food, accord us food, | Uninjurious, impetuous; | Do thou further the donor, | Bestow strength on our bipeds, our quadrupeds. ‖ *b.* May the All-Gods thee, | O Agni, bear up with their thoughts; | Be thou to us most propitious, | With kindly face, abounding in light, ‖ *c.* Come forward, O Agni, rich in light, | With auspicious rays; | Shining with great radiance, | Harm not our offspring with thy body. ‖ *d.* With kindling-wood serve Agni, | Awaken the guest with ghee; | In him offer oblations. ‖ *e.* Far-famed is this Agni of Bhārata, | Since his great light shineth like the sun; | He who overcame Pūru in battle | Hath shone forth, the heavenly guest, propitious for us. ‖ *f.* O ye waters divine, accept these ashes; | Place them on a resting-place, in the fragrant region | To him may the ladies with noble spouses bow; | Like a mother her son, do ye kindly bear him. ‖ *g.* In the waters, O Agni, is thy seat, | Thou enterest the plants; | Being in the germ thou art born again. ‖ *h.* Thou art the germ of plants, | The germ of trees, | The germ of all things, | O Agni, thou art the germ of the waters. ‖ *i.* With ashes having satisfied thy birthplace | And the waters, on the earth, O Agni, | In unison with thy mothers, | Full of light hast thou again taken thy seat. ‖ *k.* Having again come to thy seat, | And to the waters, to the earth, O Agni, | Within her thou liest, most auspicious, | As on the lap of a mother. ‖ *l.* Return with strength, | Return, O Agni, with food and life; | Again guard us on all sides. ‖ *m.* Return with wealth, | O Agni, fatten with the stream, | All-gaining on every side. ‖ *n.* May the Ādityas, the Rudras, the Vasus, kindle thee again; | The Brahmans again with offerings, O bringer of wealth; | With ghee do thou increase our bodies; | May the wishes of the sacrificer become true. ‖ *o.* Hearken to this our call, that is offered, O youngest one, | Of the most generous one, O thou that hast power; | One hateth, one praiseth. | As praiser I praise thy body, O Agni. ‖ *p.* Be thou a bounteous patron, | Giver of riches, lord of riches; | Repel from us the foes.

Mantra 4:2:4

a. Go hence depart, creep away, hence, | Ye that are here of old and ye that are new, | Yama hath given this resting-place of earth, | The Pitṛis have made this world for him. ‖ *b.* Thou art the ash of Agni, thou art the dust of Agni. ‖ *c.* Thou art accord, fulfilling love; in me be the fulfilling of thy love. ‖ *d.* Be united your dear bodies, | Be united your dear hearts, | Be your breath united, | United my body. ‖ *e.* This is that Agni in whom as a belly | Indra placed the pressed Soma eagerly; | Thou art praised, O all-knower, for winning | Booty a thousandfold, like a swift steed. ‖ *f.* O Agni, thou comest to the wave of the sky, | To the Gods thou speakest, those of the altar; | The waters above in the realm of the sun, | And those below wait (on thee). ‖ *g.* O Agni, thy radiance in the sky, the earth, | The plants, or the waters, O holy one, | That whereby thou didst outspread the broad atmosphere, | Glittering is thy gleam, moving and men espying. ‖ *h.* May the Agnis of the dust | In unison with those of the floods | Accept the oblation offered, | The rich healthful viands. ‖ *i.* As food, O Agni, accord to the sacrificer | The gain of a cow, wondrous enduring; | Be to us a son, a scion, full of life; | This, O Agni, be thy loving kindness towards us. ‖ *k.* This is thy due place of birth, | Whence born thou didst shine, | Mount it, O Agni, knowing it, | And make our wealth increase. ‖ *l.* Thou art a piler; in the manner of Aṅgiras be firm with that deity. ‖ *m.* Thou art a piler round; in the manner of Aṅgiras be firm with that deity. ‖ *n.* Fill the world, fill the hole, do thou sit down auspicious; | Indra and Agni and Bṛihaspati | Have placed thee on this birthplace ‖ *o.* The dappled kine, streaming with milk, | Mix the Soma, | Clans in the birthplace of the Gods, | In the three realms of sky.

Mantra 4:2:5

a. Be united, be in harmony, in affection, | Radiant, with kindly thought, | Clothed in food and strength, | United have I made your minds, your ordinances, your hearts. ‖ *b.* O Agni of the dust be overlord for us; | Bestow food and strength on the sacrificer. ‖ *c.* Thou, O Agni, art of the dust, | Rich, full of increase, | Making all the regions propitious | Thou hast sat down on thine own birthplace. ‖ *d.* Be ye of one mind for us, | One dwelling, spotless; | Harm not the sacrifice, nor the lord of the sacrifice, O all-knowers; | Be ye two auspicious today unto us. ‖ *e.* As a mother her son, the earth, | The pan, hath borne Agni of the dust in his own birthplace | In unison with the All-Gods, the seasons, | Let Prajāpati, all-worker, release it. ‖ *f.* The bright light | Born beyond this firmament, | May that convey us beyond our foes, | O Agni Vaiśvānara, hail! ‖ *g.* Homage to thee, O Nirṛiti of every form, | Loosen ye this bond made of iron; | Do thou in accord with Yama and Yamī | Mount this highest vault. ‖ *h.* The bond that Nirṛiti, the Goddess, | Bound on thy neck, not to be loosened, | This I loosen for thee as from the middle of life; | Then living, let loose, do thou eat the food. ‖ *i.* Thee in whose cruel mouth here I make offering, | For the loosening of these bonds, | As 'earth' men know thee, | As 'Nirṛiti,' I know thee on every side. ‖ *k.* Seek the man who poureth not offering nor sacrifices; | The road of the thief and robber thou followest; | Seek another than us, that is thy road; | Homage be to thee, O Nirṛiti, O Goddess. ‖ *l.* Praising Nirṛiti, the Goddess, | Like a father his son, I weary her with my words; | She who knoweth all that is born, | Discerneth, the lady, every head. ‖ *m.* Abode and collector of riches, | Every form she discerneth with might, | Like the God Savitar of true laws, | Like Indra, she standeth at the meeting of the ways. ‖ *n.* Make firm the straps, | Fasten the buckets; | We shall drain the well full of water, | That never is exhausted, never faileth. ‖ *o.* The well with buckets fastened, | With strong straps, that yieldeth abundantly, | Full of water, unexhausted, I drain. ‖ *p.* The sages yoke the ploughs; | They stretch apart the yokes, | Wise with goodwill among the Gods. ‖ *q.* Yoke the ploughs, stretch apart the yokes, | Here sow in the womb made ready the seed | Through our song be there audience with profit for us; | May the ripe (grain) be brought low by the sickle. ‖ *r.* The plough, of keen share, | Propitious, with well-polished handle, | Plougheth up a cow, a sheep, | And a fat blooming maid, | A chariot support with a platform. ‖ *s.* With prosperity may our ploughs cleave the ground, | With prosperity may the ploughers go round the yokes; | Prosperity (may) Parjanya (give) with honey and milk, | And do ye, O Śuna and Sīra, accord prosperity to us. ‖ *t.* Wishes, O milker of wishes, do thou milk | To Mitra and Varuṇa; | To Indra, to Agni, to Pūṣhan, | To the plants, and to offspring. ‖ *u.* The furrow anointed with ghee, with honey, | Approved by the All-Gods, the Marutas, | Full of strength, swelling with milk, | Do thou, O furrow, turn towards us with milk.

Mantra 4:2:6

a. The plants born | Three generations before the Gods, | Of the brown ones I celebrate | The seven and a hundred abodes. ‖ *b.* A hundred, O mother, are your abodes, | A thousand too your shoots, | Therefore do ye, with a hundred powers, | Make him whole for me. ‖ *c.* With flowers, with shoots, | Fruit-bearing and without fruit, | Like steeds victorious | The plants are strong to help. ‖ *d.* 'Plants,' O ye mothers, | I hail you, O Goddesses; | Go bearing away defilement, | Defilement destroying. ‖ *e.* In the Aśvattha is your seat, | In the Parṇa is your dwelling made; | Cows shall in truth be your share | If ye shall gain this man. ‖ *f.* In that in strength I seize | These plants in my hand, | The soul of the disease perisheth, | As before one that taketh alive. ‖ *g.* When the plants come together | Like princes at the assembly, | Sage is the physician called, | Slayer of Rākṣhasas, overpowerer of diseases. ‖ *h.* Remover is your mother by name, | And ye are helpers; | Ye are winged streams; | Remove whatever is unwell. ‖ *i.* Let one of you aid another, | Let one be of assistance to another; | All the plants in unison | Do ye further this speech of mine. ‖ *k.* The strength of the plants hath arisen | Like cows from the pasturage, | Of them that are fain to win gain, | To the self of thee, O man. ‖ *l.* Beyond all obstacles, | Like the thief the pen, they have strode, | The plants have shaken away | Every defilement in the body. ‖ *m.* Those that have mounted thy self, | That have entered every limb, | May they repel thy disease, | Like a dread intercessor. ‖ *n.* O disease, do thou fly forth | With the eagle, the blue jay (*kikidivi*) | With the rush of the wind, | With the whirlwind do thou disappear. ‖ *o.* Rich in steeds, rich in Soma, | Full of strength, full of power, | I have found all the plants | For his safety. ‖ *p.* The fruitful, the fruitless, | The flowering, the flowerless, | Impelled by Bṛihaspati, | May they free us from tribulation. ‖ *q.* The plants whose king is Soma, | And which have entered the earth, | Of them thou art the highest, | Impel us to long life. ‖ *r.* Falling from the sky | The plants said, | 'He, whom we reach while in life, | Shall not come to ill.' ‖ *s.* Those that hear now | And those that are gone far away, | Coming all together here | Give ye him healing. ‖ *t.* May the digger of you come to no ill, | Nor he for whom I dig you; | May all our bipeds and quadrupeds | Be free from disease. ‖ *u.* The plants hold converse | With Soma, the king, | 'The man for whom the Brahman prepares (us), | We, O king, bring to safety.'

Mantra 4:2:7

a. May I be harm us not who is father of earth | Or who, of true law, created the sky, | And he who created the great bright waters; | To what God shall we offer with oblation? ‖ *b.* Turn towards (us), O earth, | With the sacrifice, with milk; | Over thy caul let Agni, aroused, creep. ‖ *c.* O Agni, that of thee which is pure, which is bright, | Which is cleansed, which is fit for offering, | That we bear to the Gods. ‖ *d.* Food and strength do I take hence, | From the abode of holy order, from the birthplace of immortality. | May it enter us, in cattle and in plants; | I abandon decline, lack of food, and ill-health. ‖ *e.* O Agni, strength and fame are thine, | Thy rays shine mightily, O rich in light; | O thou of broad radiance, with thy might, strength worthy of laud, | Thou bestowest on the worshipper, O sage. ‖ *f.* Do thou extend over men, O Agni, | Ruling over wealth for us, O immortal one; | Thou art the master of a glorious form, | Thou fillest glorious wealth. ‖ *g.* O son of strength, O all-knower, | Rejoice in our fair praises, being adored in our prayers; | In thee have they placed food, rich in seed, | Of wondrous aid, of prosperous birth. ‖ *h.* With pure radiance, with bright radiance, | With undiminished radiance, thou comest forth with thy light; | Visiting thy parents thou aidest them; | Thou fillest both worlds. ‖ *i.* The righteous, the bull, common to all men, | Agni, men place before them for favour, | Thee with their speech, that art ready to hear and most extending, | The divine, the generations of men. ‖ *k.* Preparer of the sacrifice, the wise, | Who ruleth for great gain, | The giver of the Bhṛigus, the eager, skilled in the sacrifice | Thou fillest glorious wealth. ‖ *l.* Ye are pilers, ye are pilers around, do ye pile upwards as a support, | with that deity, sit ye firm in the manner of Aṅgiras ‖ *m.* Swell up, let thy strength be gathered | From all sides, O Soma. | Be strong in the gathering of might. ‖ *n.* Let thy milk draughts, thy strength be united, | The mightinesses of him who overcometh the foe; | Swelling for immortality, O Soma, | Place in the sky the highest glories,

Mantra 4:2:8

a. He hath overcome every foe, every enemy; | That Agni saith, that saith Soma too; | Bṛihaspati, Savitar, say this of me, | Pūṣhan hath placed me in the world of good action. ‖ *b.* When first thou didst cry on birth, | Arising from the ocean or the dust, | The wings of the eagle, the limbs of the gazelle, | That is thy famed birth, O steed. ‖ *c.* Thou art the back of the waters, the birthplace of Agni, | The ocean swelling on either side; | Growing to might as the lotus flower, | Do thou extend in width with the measure of heaven. ‖ *d.* The holy power born first in the east | Vena hath disclosed from the shining boundary, | He hath revealed its fundamental nearest forms, | The womb of being and of not being. ‖ *e.* The golden germ first rose; | Born he was the only lord of creation; | He supporteth the earth and the sky; | To what God shall we offer with oblation. ‖ *f.* The drop hath fallen on the earth, the sky, | On this seat, and on the one which was aforetime; | The drop that wandereth over the third seat ‖ I offer in the seven Hotras. ‖ *g.* Homage to the serpents | Which are on the earth, | The serpents in the atmosphere, in the sky, | To those serpents homage. ‖ *h.* Those that are there in the vault of the sky, | Or those who are in the rays of the sun, | Those whose seat is made in the waters, | To those serpents honour. ‖ *i.* Those that are the missiles of sorcerers, | Or those that are among the trees, | Or those that lie in the wells, | To those serpents honour.

Mantra 4:2:9

a. Thou art firm, supporting, unoverpowered, | Well wrought by Viśvakarman; | Let not the ocean smite thee, nor the eagle; | Unshaking do thou make firm the earth. ‖ *b.* May Prajāpati seat thee on the back of earth, capacious, extending; thou art extent, thou art earth, thou art the world, thou art the earth, thou art Aditi all-sustaining, sustainer of all the world; sustain the earth, make firm the earth, harm not the earth, for all expiration, cross-breathing, up-breathing, for support, for motion; may Agni protect thee with great prosperity, with most auspicious covering; with that deity, in the manner of Aṅgiras, do thou sit firm. ‖ *c.* Arising from every stem, | From every joint, | Do thou, O Dūrvā, extend us | With a thousand, a hundred. ‖ *d.* Thou that extendest with a hundred, | That arisest with a thousand, | To thee, O Goddess, O brick, | Let us sacrifice with oblation. ‖ *e.* Unovercomable art thou, overcoming, overcome our enemies, over come those that practise enmity. ‖ *f.* Overcome the foe, overcome the foemen of a thousandfold strength art thou; do thou inspirit me. ‖ *g.* To the pious the winds pour honey, | The streams honey; | Be sweet to us the plants. ‖ *h.* Sweet is the night, and sweet | At dawn the air of earth, | Sweet be the sky, our father. ‖ *i.* Sweet to us be the lord of the forest, | Sweet the sun, | Sweet be the cows to us. ‖ *k.* May the two great ones, sky and earth, | Mingle for us this sacrifice; | May they sustain us with support. ‖ *l.* That highest step of Viṣhṇu | The singers ever gaze upon | Like an eye stretched in the sky. ‖ *m.* Thou art firm, O earth, | Overcome the foemen; | Fashioned by the Gods hast thou come with ambrosia. ‖ *n.* Those beams of thine, O Agni, which rising | In the sun with rays envelop the sky, | With all of them bring us to brilliance, to men. ‖ *o.* Those flames of yours in the sun, | O Gods, in cattle, in horses, | O Indra and Agni, O Bṛihaspati, | With all of these grant us brilliance. || *p.* The brilliant bore the light, the shining bore the light, the self-resplendent bore the light. || *q.* O Agni, yoke, | O God, thy good steeds, | The swift that readily bear. || *r.* Yoke, like a charioteer, O Agni, | The steeds that best invite the Gods | Sit down as ancient Hotar || *s.* The drop hath fallen on the earth, the sky, | On this seat and on the one which was aforetime | The drop that wandereth over the third seat || I offer in the seven Hotras. || *t.* There hath come into being this might of all the world, | And of Agni Vaiśvānara, | Agni full of light with light, | The disk radiant with radiance. || *u.* For the verse thee, for brilliance thee || *v.* Like streams the offerings flow together, | Purified within with heart and mind; || I behold the streams of ghee; | A golden reed is there in the midst of them. || *w.* In it sitteth an eagle, honey-making, nested, | Assigning honey to the deities, | On its brink sit seven tawny ones, | Milking at will the stream of ambrosia.

Mantra 4:2:10.

a. Anointing with milk Āditya, the embryo, | Counterpart of a thousand, of every form, | Spare him, injure him not with thy heat; | Make him of a hundred (years of) life, as thou art piled. || *b.* Injure not this biped of animals, | O hundred-eyed one, being piled for the sacrifice; | I appoint for thee the wailer in the forest; | Therewith piling thy forms, be seated. || *c.* The rush of the wind, the navel of Varuṇa, | Born as a steed in the midst of the waters, | The child of the streams, the tawny one, rooted in the mountain, | O Agni, harm him not in the highest heaven. || *d.* Harm not this one-hooved of cattle, | The thundering, the courser among the contests; | I appoint for thee the Gayal of the forest; | Therewith piling thy forms, be seated. || *e.* The undying drop, the ruddy, the active, | Agni I hymn with praises with first inspiration; | Do thou forming thyself with joints in due order, | Harm not the cow, Aditi, the resplendent. || *f.* This ocean, the spring of a hundred streams, | Expanded in the middle of the world, | Aditi milking ghee for men, | O Agni, harm not in the highest heaven; | I appoint for thee the Gayal of the forest; | Therewith piling thy forms, be seated. || *g.* Guard of Tvaṣhṭar, navel of Varuṇa, | Born as the sheep from the furthest region, | The great thousandfold wile of the Asura, | O Agni, harm not in the highest heaven. || *h.* This woolly wile of Varuṇa, | The skin of cattle, biped and quadruped, | The first birthplace of the offspring of Tvaṣhṭar, | O Agni, harm not in the highest heaven; | I appoint for thee the buffalo of the forest; | Therewith piling thy forms, be seated. || *i.* The Agni born of the heat of Agni, | From the burning of the earth or of the sky, | That whereby Viśvakarman attained creatures, | Him, O Agni, let thy wrath spare. || *k.* The goat was born from Agni as an embryo; | She beheld her begetter before; | Thereby those worthy of sacrifice attained pre-eminence, | Thereby first the Gods attained godhead; | I appoint for thee the Śarabha of the forest; | Therewith piling thy forms, be seated.

Mantra 4:2:11

a. O Indra and Agni, the realms of the sky | Ye adorn in your strength; | That might of yours is dear. || *b.* The foe shall he pierce and wealth he doth gain | Who worshippeth Indra and Agni, the strong ones, | Who rule over much wealth, | The most strong who with strength show their power. || *c.* Men ye surpass in the battle call, | Earth ye surpass, and sky, | The mountains and the streams (ye surpass) in greatness, | And, O Indra and Agni, all other worlds. || *d.* In whose house, O Marutas, | Ye drink, O joyous ones of the sky | That man hath the best of guardians. || *e.* Either through sacrifices receiving worship, | Or from the prayers of the singer, | Do ye, O Marutas, hearken to our call. || *f.* For glory they are wreathed in flames, | In the rays (of the sun), adorned with rings they (are accompanied) with singers; | They wearing daggers, impetuous, fearless, | Have found the dear home of the Marutas. || *g.* Thy wrath. || *h.* The highest. || *i.* With what aid will he come to us, | Our wondrous, ever-waxing, friend? | With what most potent aid? || *k.* Who today yoketh to the pole of holy order | The oxen, eager, of keen spirits, the furious, | With darts in their mouths, heart-piercing, healthful? | He who attaineth their service shall live. || *l.* O Agni, lead. || *m.* Of the Gods. || *n.* May they be prosperous for us || *o.* In every contest. | In the waters, O Agni, is thy seat, | Thou enterest the plants; | Being in the germ thou art born again. || *q.* Thou art strong, O Soma, and bright; | Thou art strong, O God, and strong thy rule; | Strong laws dost thou establish. || *r.* This for me, O Varuṇa || *s.* That of thine I approach. || *t.* Thou, O Agni. || *u.* Do thou to us, O Agni.

Prapāṭhaka 3.

The Five Layers of Bricks

Mantra 4:3:1

a. I place thee in the going of the waters; I place thee in the rising of the waters; I place thee in the ashes of the waters; I place thee in the light of the waters; I place thee in the movement of the waters. || *b.* Sit on the billows as thy place of rest; sit on the ocean as thy place of rest; sit on the stream as thy place of rest; sit in the abode of the waters; sit on the seat of the waters. || *c.* I place thee in the seat of the waters; I place thee in the dwelling of the waters; I place thee in the dust of the waters; I place thee in the womb of the waters; I place thee in the stronghold of the waters. || *d.* The metro the Gāyatrī; the metre the Trishṭubh; the metro the Jagatī; the metre the Anushṭubh; the metre the Paṅkti

Mantra 4:3:2

a. This one in front the existent; his, the existent's breath; spring born of the breath; the Gāyatrī born of the spring; from the Gāyatrī the Gāyatrī (Sāman); from the Gateway the Upāṃśu (cup); from the Upāṃśu the Trivṛit (Stoma); from the Trivṛit the Rathantara; from the Rathantara Vasishṭha, the Ṛishi; with thee taken by Prajāpati, I take breath for offspring. || *b.* This one on the right, the all-worker; his, the all-worker's, mind; summer born of mind; the Trishṭubh born of summer; from the Trishṭubh the Aiḍa (Sāman); from the Aiḍa the Antaryāma (cup); from the Antaryāma the fifteenfold (Stoma); from the fifteenfold the Bṛihat; from the Bṛihat Bharadvāja, the Ṛishi; with thee taken by Prajāpati, I take mind for offspring. || *c.* This one behind, the all-extending; his, the all-extending's eye; the rains born of the eye; the Jagatī born of the rains; from the Jagatī the Ṛikshama (Sāman); from the Ṛikshama the Śukra (cup); from the Śukra the seventeenfold (Stoma); from the seventeenfold the Vairūpa; from the Vairūpa Viśvāmitra, the Ṛishi; with thee taken by Prajāpati, I take the eye for my offspring. || *d.* This one on the left, the light; his, the light's, ear; the autumn born of the ear; the Anushṭubh connected with the autumn; from the Anushṭubh the Svāra (Sāman); from the Svāra the Manthin (cup); from the Manthin the twenty-onefold (Stoma); from the twenty-onefold the Vairāja; from the Vairāja Jamadagni, the Ṛishi; with thee taken by Prajāpati, I take the ear for offspring. || *e.* This one above, thought; his, thought's, speech; the winter born of speech; the Paṅkti born of winter; from the Paṅkti that which has finales; from that which has finales the Āgrayaṇa (cup); from the Āgrayaṇa the twenty-sevenfold and the thirty-threefold (Stomas); from the twenty-sevenfold and the thirty-threefold the Śākvara and Raivata; from the Śākvara and Raivata Viśvakarman, the Ṛishi; with thee taken by Prajāpati, I take speech for offspring.

Mantra 4:3:3

a. The east of the quarters; the spring of the seasons; Agni the deity; holy power the wealth; the Trivṛit the Stoma, and it forming the path of the fifteenfold (Stoma); the eighteen-month-old calf the strength; the Kṛita of throws of dice; the east wind the wind; Sānaga the Ṛishi. || *b.* The south of the quarters; the summer of the seasons; Indra the deity; the kingly power the wealth; the fifteenfold the Stoma, and it forming the path of the seventeenfold (Stoma); the two-year-old the strength; the Tretā of throws; the south wind the wind; Sanātana, the Ṛishi. || *c.* The west of the quarters; the rains of the seasons; the All-Gods the deity; the peasants the wealth; the seventeenfold the Stoma, and it forming the path of the twenty-onefold (Stoma); the three-year-old the strength; the Dvāpara of throws; the west wind the wind; Ahabhūna the Ṛishi. || *d.* The north of the quarters; the autumn of the seasons; Mitra and Varuṇa the deity; prosperity the wealth; the twenty-onefold the Stoma; and it forming a path of the twenty-sevenfold (Stoma); the four-year-old the strength; the Āskanda of throws; the north wind the wind; Pratna the Ṛishi. || *e.* The zenith of the quarters; the winter and the cool season of the seasons; Bṛihaspati the deity; radiance the wealth; the twenty-sevenfold the Stoma, and it forming a path of the thirty-threefold; the draught ox the strength; the Abhibhū of throws; the wind all through the wind; Suparṇa the Ṛishi. || *f.* Fathers, grandfathers, near and far, may they protect us, may they help us, in this holy power, this lordly power, this prayer, this Purohitaship, this rite, this invocation of the Gods.

Mantra 4:3:4

a. Firm is thy dwelling, thy place of birth, firm art thou | Settle thou duly in thy firm place of birth; | Banner of the fire in the pan, | May the two Aśvins, the leeches, set thee here first in the east. || *b.* In thine own skill sit thou whose sire is skill, | As the great earth bountiful among the Gods, | Be of kindly approach and come with thy body, | Kindly as a father to his son; | May the two Aśvins, the leeches, set thee here. || *c.* Nesting, rich in wealth, strength bestowing, | Increase for us wealth, abundant, rich in heroes, | Driving away hostility and enmity, | Granting the lord of the sacrifice a share in increase of wealth, | Do thou bestow the heaven as increase to the sacrificer; | May the two Aśvins, the leeches, set thee here. || *d.* Thou art the dust of Agni, the leader of the Gods; | May the All-Gods favour thee as such; | With Stomas for thy back, rich in ghee, sit thou here, | And win to us by sacrifice riches with offspring. | May the two Aśvins, the leeches, set thee here! || *e.* Thou art the head of sky, the navel of earth, the holder apart of the quarters, the lady paramount of the worlds, the wave, the drop of the waters thou art; Viśvakarman is thy seer; may the two Aśvins, the leeches, set thee here. || *f.* In unison with the seasons, in unison with the ordainers, in unison with the Vasus, in unison with the Rudras, in unison with the Ādityas, in unison with the All-Gods, in unison with the Gods, in unison with the Gods establishing strength, to Agni Vaiśvānara, thee; may the two Aśvins, the leeches, set thee here. || *g.* Protect my expiration; protect my inspiration; protect my cross breathing; make my eye to shine widely; make my ear to hear. || *h.* Make thick the waters; quicken the plants; protect bipeds; help quadrupeds; from the sky make rain to start.

Mantra 4:3:5

a. (Thou art) the calf of eighteen months in strength, the Trishṭubh metre; the two-year-old in strength, the Virāj metre; the two-and-a-half year-old in strength, the Gāyatrī metre; the three-year-old in strength, the Ushṇih metre; the four-year-old in strength, the Anushṭubh metre; the draught ox in strength, the Bṛihatī metre; the bull in strength, the Satobṛihatī metre; the bullock in strength, the Kakubh metre; the milch cow in strength, the Jagatī metre; the beast of burden in strength, the Paṅkti metre; the goat in strength, the spacious metre; the ram in strength, the slow metre; the tiger in strength, the unassailable metre; the lion in strength, the covering metre; the support in strength, the overlord metre; the lordly power in strength, the delight-giving metre; the all-creating in strength, the supreme lord metro; the head in strength, the Prajāpati metre.

Mantra 4:3:6

a. O Indra and Agni, do ye two make firm | The brick that quaketh not; | And let it with its back repel | The sky and earth and atmosphere. || *b.* Let Viśvakarman place thee in the ridge of the atmosphere, encompassing, expanding, resplendent, possessing the sun, thee that dost illumine the sky, the earth, the broad atmosphere, support the atmosphere, make firm the atmosphere, harm not the atmosphere; for every expiration, inspiration, cross-breathing, out-breathing, support, movement; let Vāyu protect thee with great prosperity, with a covering most healing; with that deity do thou sit firm in the manner of Aṅgiras || *c.* Thou art the queen, the eastern quarter; thou art the ruling, the southern quarter; thou art the sovereign, the western quarter; thou art the self-ruling, the northern quarter; thou art the lady paramount, the great quarter. || *d.* Protect my life; protect my expiration; protect my inspiration; protect my cross-breathing; protect my eye; protect my ear; quicken my mind; strengthen my voice; protect my breath; accord me light.

Mantra 4:3:7

a. (Thou art) Ma metre, Pramā metre, Pratimā metre, Asrīvis metre, Paṅkti metre, Ushṇih metre, Bṛihatī metre, Anushṭubh metre, Virāj metre, Gāyatrī metre, Trishṭubh metre, Jagatī metre. (Thou art) earth metre, atmosphere metro, sky metre, seasons metre, Nakshatras metre, mind metre, speech metre, ploughing metre, gold metre, cow metre, female goat metre, horse metre. (Thou art) Agni, the deity, Vāta, the deity, Sūrya, the deity, Chandramās, the deity, the Vasus, the deity, the Rudras, the deity, the Ādityas, the deity, the All-Gods, the deity, the Marutas, the deity, Bṛihaspati, the deity, Indra, the deity, Varuṇa, the deity. || *b.* The head thou art, ruling; thou art the firm, the supporting; thou art the prop, the restrainer; for food thee; for strength thee; for ploughing thee: for safety thee! (Thou art) the prop, ruling; thou art the firm, the supporting; thou art the holder, the sustainer; for life thee; for radiance thee; for force thee; for might thee!

Mantra 4:3:8

(Thou art) the swift, the triple (Stoma); the shining, the fifteenfold; the sky, the seventeenfold; speed, the eighteenfold; fervour, the nineteen. fold; attack, the twentyfold; support, the twenty-onefold; radiance, the twenty-twofold; maintenance, the twenty-threefold; the womb, the twenty-fourfold; the embryo, the twenty-fivefold; might, the twenty sevenfold; inspiration, the thirty-onefold; support, the thirty-threefold; the surface of the tawny one, the thirty-fourfold; the vault, the thirty-six fold; the revolving, the forty-eightfold; the support, the fourfold Stoma.

Mantra 4:3:9

a. Thou art the portion of Agni, the overlordship of consecration, the holy power saved, the threefold Stoma. || *b.* Thou art the portion of Indra, the overlordship of Vishṇu, the lordly power saved, the fifteenfold Stoma. || *c.* Thou art the portion of them that gaze on men, the overlordship of Dhātar, the birthplace saved, the seventeenfold Stoma. || *d.* Thou art the portion of Mitra, the overlordship of Varuṇa, the rain from the sky, the winds saved, the twenty-onefold Stoma. || *e.* Thou art the portion of Aditi, the overlordship of Pūshan, force saved, the twenty-sevenfold Stoma. || *f.* Thou art the portion of the Vasus, the overlordship of the Rudras, the quadruped saved, the twenty-fourfold Stoma. || *g.* Thou art the portion of the Ādityas, the overlordship of the Marutas, offspring saved, the twenty-fivefold Stoma. || *h.* Thou art the portion of the God Savitar, the overlordship of Bṛihaspati, all the quarters saved, the fourfold Stoma. || *i.* Thou art the portion of the Yavas, the overlordship of the Ayavas, offspring saved, the forty-fourfold Stoma. || *k.* Thou art the portion of the Ṛibhus, the overlordship, of the All-Gods, being calmed and saved, the thirty-threefold Stoma.

Mantra 4:3:10.

They praised with one, creatures were established, Prajāpati was overlord. They praised with three, the holy power: was created, the lord of holy power was overlord. They praised with fire, beings were created, the lord of beings was the overlord. They praised with seven, the seven seers were created, Dhātar was the overlord. They praised with nine, the fathers were created, Aditi was the overlady. They praised with eleven, the seasons were created, the seasonal one was the overlord. They praised with thirteen, the months were created, the year was the overlord. They praised with fifteen, the lordly class was created, Indra was the overlord. They praised with seventeen, cattle were created, Bṛihaspati was the overlord. They praised with nineteen, the Śūdra and the Ārya were created, day and night were the overlords. They praised with twenty-one, the whole-hooved cattle were created, Varuṇa was the overlord. They praised with twenty-three, small cattle were created, Pūshan was the overlord. They praised with twenty-five, wild cattle were created, Vāyu was the overlord. They praised with twenty-seven, sky and earth went apart, the Vasus, Rudras, and Ādityas followed their example, theirs was the overlordship. They praised with twenty-nine, trees were created, Soma was the overlord. They praised with thirty-one, creatures were created, the Yavas and the Ayavas had the overlordship. They praised with thirty-three, creatures came to rest, Prajāpati was the overlord and chief.

Mantra 4:3:11

a. This is she that first dawned; | Within this (earth) she hath entered and moveth; | The new-made bride as mother beareth the mothers; | Three greatnesses attend her. || *b.* Charming, the dawns, adorned, | Moving along a common birthplace, | Wives of the sun, they move, wise ones, | Making a banner of light, unaging, rich in seed. || *c.* Three have followed the path of holy order, | Three cauldrons have come with the light, | Offspring one guardeth, strength one, | Another the law of the pious guardeth. || *d.* The fourth hath become that of four Stomas, | Becoming the two wings of the sacrifice, O Ṛishis; | Yoking the Gāyatrī, Trishṭubh, Jagatī, and Anushṭubh, the Bṛihat, | The hymn, they have borne forward this heaven. || *e.* By five the creator disposed this (world), | What time he produced sisters of them, five by five, | By their mingling go five strengths | Clad in various forms. ‖ *f.* Thirty sisters go to the appointed place, | Putting on the same badge, | The sages spread out the seasons, the knowing ones | With the metres in their midst, go about in brilliance. ‖ *g.* The shining one putteth on clouds, | The ways of the sun, the night divine; | The beasts of many forms that are born | Look around on the lap of their mother. ‖ *h.* The Ekāṣhṭakā, undergoing penance, | Hath borne a child, the great Indra; | Therewith the Gods overpowered the Asuras; | Slayer of Asuras he became in his might. ‖ *i.* Ye have made me, who am not younger, the younger; | Speaking the truth I desire this; | May I enjoy his loving kindness as do ye; | May not one of you supplant another. ‖ *k.* He hath enjoyed my loving kindness, the all-knower; | He hath found a support, for he hath won the shallow; | May I enjoy his loving kindness as do ye | May not one of you supplant another. ‖ *l.* On the five dawns follow the five milkings, | On the cow with five names the five seasons; | The five quarters are established by the fifteenfold (Stoma), | With equal heads over the one world. ‖ *m.* She who first shone forth is the child of holy order; | One supporteth the might of the waters; | One moveth in the places of the sun, | And one in those of the heat; Savitar governeth one. ‖ *n.* She who first shone forth | Hath become a cow with Yams; | Do thou, rich in milk, milk for us | Season after season. | O She of bright bulls hath come with the cloud, the light, | She of all forms, the motley, whose banner is fire; | Accomplishing thy common task, | Bringing old age, thou hast come, O unaging dawn. | P Lady, of seasons the first, she hath come hither, | Leading the days, and bearer of offspring; | Though one, O Uṣhas, in many places dost thou shine forth | Unaging thou dost make to age all else.

Mantra 4. 3.12.

a. O Agni, drive away those foes of ours that are born; | Drive away those too that are unborn, O all-knower; | Shine out for us in kindliness and without anger, | In thy protection may I be with threefold protection and victorious. ‖ *b.* O Agni, drive away those foes of ours that are born with force; | Drive away those that are unborn, O all-knower; | Favour us in kindliness, | May we (enjoy thy protection); drive away our foes. ‖ *c.* (Thou art) the forty-fourfold Stoma, radiance the wealth. ‖ *d.* (Thou art) the sixteenfold Stoma, force the wealth. ‖ *e.* Thou art the dust of earth, called Apsas. ‖ *f.* (Thou art) the course metre; the space metre; the health-bringing metre; the overpowering metre; the covering metre; the mind metre; the expanse metre; the river metre; the sea metro; the water metre; the uniting metro; the separating metre; the Bṛihat metro; the Rathantara metre; the collecting metre; the parting metre; the voices metre; the radiant metro; the Saṣhṭubh metre; the Anuṣhṭubh metre; the Kakubh metre; the Trikakubh metre; the poetic metre; the water metre; the Padapaṅkti metre, the Akṣharapaṅkti metre, the Viṣhṭārapaṅkti metre: the razor-with-strop metre; the enveloping metre; the side metre; the course metre; the space metre; the strength metre; the maker of strength metre; the expansive metre; the conflict metre; the covering metre; the difficult of access metre; the slow metre; the Aṅkāṅka metre.

Mantra 4:3:13

a. May Agni slay the foe, | Eager for wealth, joyfully, | Kindled, pure as offered. ‖ *b.* Thou Soma art very lord, | Thou art king, and slayer of foes; | Thou art favouring strength. ‖ *c.* Favouring is thy look, O fair-faced Agni, | That art dread and extending, pleasant (is it); | Thy radiance they cover not with the darkness; | The defiling leave no stain in thy body. ‖ *d.* Favouring is thy face, O mighty Agni; | Even by the side of the sun it is bright, | Radiant to behold it is seen even by night, | Pleasant to the sight is food in thy form. ‖ *e.* With his countenance the kindly one | Will sacrifice to the Gods for us, most skilled to win prosperity by sacrifice; | Guardian undeceived and protector of us, | O Agni, shine forth with radiance and with wealth. ‖ *f.* Prosperity for us from sky, O Agni, from earth, | With full life do thou procure, O God, for worship; | That splendid thing, O sky-born, which we ask, | Do thou bestow upon us that radiant wealth. ‖ *g.* As thou, O Hotar, in man's worship, | O son of strength, shalt sacrifice with offerings, | Verily do thou today, gladly, offer sacrifice | To the glad Gods together assembled. ‖ *h.* I praise Agni, domestic priest, | God of the sacrifice and priest, | The Hotar, best bestower of jewels. ‖ *i.* Thou art strong, O Soma, and bright, | Thou art strong, O God, and strong thy rule, | Strong laws dost thou establish. ‖ *k.* O Marutas, that burn, this offering (is yours) | Do ye rejoice in it, | For your aid, ye destroyers of the foe. ‖ *l.* The man of evil heart, O bright ones, O Marutas, | Who is fain to smite us contrary to right, | In the noose of destruction may he be caught, | Slay him with your most burning heat. ‖ *m.* The Marutas, of the year, fair singers, | With wide abodes, in troops among men, | May they from us unloosen the bonds of tribulation, | Those that burn, delighting, granting delight, ‖ *n.* Delight the eager Gods, O thou most young, | Knowing the seasons, O lord of the season, do thou sacrifice here; | With the priests divine, O Agni, | Thou art the best sacrificer of Hotars ‖ *o.* O Agni, whatever today, O offering Hotar of the people, | O pure and radiant one, thou dost enjoy, for thou art the sacrificer, | Rightly shalt thou sacrifice, since thou hast grown in might, | Carry the oblations that are thine today, O thou most young. ‖ *p.* By Agni may one win wealth | And abundance, day by day, | Glory full of heroes. ‖ *q.* Enricher, slayer of disease, | Wealth-finder, prospering prosperity, | O Soma, be a good friend to us. ‖ *r.* Come hither, O ye that tend the house, | Depart not, O Marutas, | Freeing us from tribulation. ‖ *s.* For in autumns gone by | We have paid worship, O Marutas, | With the means of mortal men. ‖ *t.* Your greatness surgeth forth from the depths, | Make known your names, O active ones; | O Marutas, accept the thousandth share of the house, | Of the householder's offering. ‖ *u.* Him to whom, the strong, the youthful maiden, | Rich in oblation, bearing ghee, approacheth night and morning, | To him his own devotion (approacheth) seeking wealth. ‖ *v.* O Agni, these most acceptable oblations, | Immortal one, bear for the divine worship; | Let them accept our fragrant (offerings). ‖ *w.* The playful horde of the Marutas, | Sporting, resplendent on the chariot, | O Kaṇvas, do ye celebrate. ‖ *x.* The Marutas, speeding like steeds, | Disport themselves like youths gazing at a spectacle, | Standing in the home like beauteous younglings, | Bestowing milk, like playful calves. ‖ *y.* At their advance the earth moves as if trembling, | When they yoke (their teams) for their journeys, for brilliance; | Playing, resounding, with flaming weapons, | They display their own greatness, the shakers. ‖ *z.* What time on the steeps ye pile the moving one, | Like birds, O Marutas, on whatever path, | The clouds spill their water on your chariots; | Do ye sprinkle for the praiser ghee of honey hue. ‖ *aa.* Agni with invocations | They ever invoke, lord of the people, | Bearer of the oblation, dear to many. ‖ *bb.* For him they ever praise, | The God with ladle dripping ghee, | Agni to bear the oblation. ‖ *cc.* O Indra and Agni, the spaces of sky. ‖ *dd.* Pierce Vṛitra ‖ *ee.* Indra from all sides. ‖ *ff.* Indra men. ‖ *gg.* O Viśvakarman, waxing great with the oblation. ‖ *hh.* O Viśvakarman, with the oblation as strengthening.

Prapāṭhaka 4.

The Fifth Layer of Bricks (continued)

Mantra 4:4:1

a. Thou art the ray; for dwelling thee! Quicken the dwelling. Thou art advance; for right thee! Quicken right. Thou art following; for sky thee! Quicken the sky. Thou art union; for atmosphere thee! Quicken the atmosphere. Thou art propping; for earth thee! Quicken earth. Thou art a prop; for rain thee! Quicken rain. Thou art blowing forward; for day thee! Quicken day. ‖ *b.* Thou art blowing after; for night thee! Quicken night. Thou art eager; for the Vasus thee! Quicken the Vasus. Thou art intelligence; for the Rudras thee! Quicken the Rudras. Thou art the brilliant; for the Ādityas thee! Quicken the Ādityas Thou art force; for the Pitṛis thee! Quicken the Pitṛis Thou art the thread; for offspring thee! Quicken offspring. Thou dost endure the battle; for cattle thee! Quicken cattle. ‖ *c.* Thou art wealthy; for plants thee! Quicken plants. Thou art the victorious with ready stone; for Indra thee! Quicken Indra. Thou art the overlord; for expiration thee! Quicken expiration. Thou art the restrainer; for inspiration thee! Quicken inspiration. Thou art the glider; for the eye thee! Quicken the eye. Thou art the bestower of strength; for the ear thee! Quicken the ear. Thou art threefold. ‖ *d.* Thou art Pravṛit, thou art Samvṛit, thou art Vivṛit. Thou art the mounter, thou art the descender, thou art the fore mounter, thou art the after mounter. ‖ *e.* Thou art the wealthy, thou art the brilliant, thou art the gainer of good.

Mantra 4:4:2

a. Thou art the queen, the eastern quarter; the Vasus, the deities, are thine overlords, Agni stayeth missiles from thee; may the threefold Stoma support thee on earth, may the Ājya hymn establish thee in firmness, the Rathantara Sāman be thy support. ‖ *b.* Thou art the ruling, the southern quarter; the Rudras, the deities, are thine overlords, Indra stayeth missiles from thee; may the fifteenfold Stoma support thee on earth, may the Prauga hymn establish thee, in firmness, the Bṛihat Sāman be thy support. ‖ *c.* Thou art the sovereign, the western quarter; the Ādityas, the deities, are thine overlords, Soma stayeth missiles from thee; may the seventeenfold Stoma support thee on earth, the Marutvatīya hymn establish thee in firmness, the Vairūpa Sāman be thy support. ‖ *d.* Thou art the self-ruling, the northern quarter; the All-Gods are thine overlords, Varuṇa stayeth missiles from thee; may the twenty-onefold Stoma support thee on earth, the Nishkevalya Uktha establish thee, in firmness, the Vairāja Sāman be thy support. ‖ *e.* Thou art the lady paramount, the great quarter; the Marutas, the deities, are thine overlords, Bṛihaspati stayeth missiles from thee; may the twenty-sevenfold and the-thirty-threefold Stomas secure thee on earth, the Vaiśvadeva and the Āgnimāruta hymns establish thee in firmness, the Śākvara and Raivata Sāmans be thy support. ‖ *f.* For the atmosphere may the Ṛishis firstborn among the Gods extend thee with the measure, the breadth, of the sky, and be that is disposer and overlord; let all of them in unison establish thee and the sacrificer on the ridge of the vault, on the world of heaven.

Mantra 4:4:3

a. This in the front, with tawny hair, with the sun's rays; the leaders of his host and bands are Rathagritsa and Rathaujas, and Puñjikasthalā and Kṛitasthalā his Apsarases, his missile wizards, his weapon the Rākshasas ‖ *b.* This on the right, all worker; the leaders of his host and bands are Rathasvana and Rathechitra, and Menakā and Sahajanyā his Apsarases, his missile biting beasts, his weapon the death of men. ‖ *c.* This behind, all extending; the leaders of his host and bands are Rathaprota and Asamaratha, and Pramlochantī and Anumlochantī his Apsarases, his missile the serpents, his weapon tigers. ‖ *d.* This on the left, collecting riches; the leaders of his host and bands are Senajit and Sushena, and Viśvāchī and Ghṛitāchī his Apsarases, his missile the waters, his weapon the wind. ‖ *e.* This above, bringing riches; the leaders of his host and bands Tārkshya and Arishṭanemi, and Urvaśī and Pūrvachitti his Apsarases, his missile the lightning, his weapon the thunder. ‖ *f.* To them homage; be they gracious to us; him whom we hate and who hateth us I place in your jaws. ‖ *g.* I place thee in the seat of the living, in the shadow of the helper; homage to the ocean, homage to the splendour of the ocean. ‖ *h.* May the supreme lord place thee on the ridge of the vault, encompassing, expanding, mighty, powerful, overcoming; support the sky, make firm the sky, harm not the sky; for every expiration, inspiration, cross-breathing, out-breathing, support, movement; let Sūrya protect thee with great prosperity, with a covering most healing; with that deity do thou sit firm in the manner of Aṅgiras ‖ *i.* Like a horse neighing eager for the pasture, | When he hath wandered from the great enclosure, | Then the wind bloweth after his splendour, | And then thy path becometh black.

Mantra 4:4:4

a. Agni is the head of the sky, the height, | Lord of the earth here, | He quickeneth the seed of the waters. ‖ *b.* Thee, O Agni, from the lotus | Atharvan pressed out | From the head of every priest. ‖ *c.* This Agni is lord of a thousandfold, | A hundredfold, strength; | The sage, the head of wealth. ‖ *d.* Leader of the sacrifice and the region art thou, | Where with steeds auspicious thou dost resort; | Thou placest in the sky thy head winning light, | Thou makest, O Agni, thy tongue to bear the oblation. ‖ *e.* Agni hath been awakened by the kindling-stick of men | To meet the dawn that cometh on like a cow; | Like young ones rising up to a branch, | The rays rise towards the vault. ‖ *f.* We have uttered to the sage, the worshipful, | Our voice of praise, to the strong bull; | Gavishṭhira with his homage hath raised to Agni this laud, | Wide extending like brilliance in the sky. ‖ *g.* He hath been born as guardian of men, wakeful, | Agni, skilful, for fresh prosperity; | Ghee-faced, with mighty sky-reaching (blaze) | He shineth gloriously, pure for the Bhāratas. ‖ *h.* Thee, O Agni, the Aṅgirasas found | When hidden in secret, resting in every wood; | Thou when rubbed art born as mighty strength; | Son of strength they call thee, O Aṅgiras ‖ *i.* Banner of the sacrifice, first domestic priest, | Agni men kindle in the three stations; | With Indra and the Gods conjoined on the strew | Let him sit, as Hotar, well skilled for sacrificing. ‖ *k.* Thee of most resplendent fame | Men invoke in their dwellings, | With flaming hair, O dear to many, | O Agni, to bear the oblation. | *ɪɪ.* O friends, together (offer) fit | Food and praise to Agni, | Highest over the folk, | The son of strength, the mighty. ‖ *m.* Thou gatherest, O strong one, | O Agni, all that belongeth to the niggard; | Thou art kindled in the place of offering; | Do thou bear us good things. ‖ *n.* With this homage Agni, | Son of strength, I invoke, | Dear, most effectual messenger, the good sacrificer, | The envoy of all, immortal. ‖ *o.* He, the ruddy, shall yoke (his steeds) all cherishing, | He shall hasten when well adored; | The sacrifice hath good prayer and strong effort, | Of the Vasus, the divine gift of men. ‖ *p.* The radiance of the bounteous offerer | Hath mounted on high, | The ruddy smoke (riseth) touching the sky; | Men in unison kindle Agni. ‖ *q.* O Agni, lording it over strength rich in kine, | Youthful son of strength, | Bestow upon us, O all-knower, great fame. ‖ *r.* Being kindled, bright, sage, | Agni, to be praised with song, | Do thou shine with wealth for us, O thou of many faces. ‖ *s.* O Agni, lord of the night, | And of the morning, and of the dawn, | Do thou burn against the Rākshasas with sharp jaws. ‖ *t.* May we kindle thee, O Agni, | Radiant, O God, and unaging; | When this most desirable | Kindling-stick maketh radiance for thee in the sky, | Do thou bear food to thy praisers. ‖ *u.* With the song, O Agni, the oblation, | O lord of brilliant light, | Bright shining, wonder-worker, lord of the people, | O bearer of the oblation, is offered to thee; | Do thou bear food to thy praisers. ‖ *v.* O bright one, in thy mouth thou cookest | Both ladles (full) of butter; | Do thou make us full, | For our hymns, O lord of strength; | Do thou bear food to thy praisers. ‖ *w.* O Agni today, let us make to prosper by praises, | By devotions, for thee this (sacrifice) like a (good) steed, | Like a noble resolve which toucheth the heart. ‖ *x.* O Agni, thou hast become master | Of noble resolve, of true inspiration, | Of mighty holy order. ‖ *y.* With these songs singing to thee, O Agni, | This day let us pay worship; | Thy strengths thunder forth as from the sky. ‖ *z.* At these our hymns of praise do thou be propitious, | Like the light of heaven, | O Agni, propitious with all thy faces. ‖ *aa.* Agni I deem the Hotar, the generous wealth-giver, | The son of strength, the all-knower, | Who knoweth all as a sage, ‖ *bb.* Who offereth sacrifice well, | With beauty soaring aloft towards the Gods, the God, | Following the flames of the ghee, | Of the butter of brilliant radiance when offered up. ‖ *cc.* O Agni, be thou our nearest, | Our protector, kindly, a shield; ‖ *dd.* Thee, O shining and most radiant one, | We implore for favour, for our friends. ‖ *ee.* Agni, bright, of bright fame, | Come hither in thy greatest splendour and give us wealth.

Mantra 4:4:5

a. I yoke thee in bonds of fellowship with Indra and Agni, with the ghee sprinklings, with brilliance, with radiance, with the hymns, with the Stomas, with the metres, for the increase of wealth, for pro-eminence among thy fellows; I yoke thee in bonds of fellowship with me. ‖ *b.* Ambā, Dulā, Nitatnī, Abhrayantī, Meghayantī, Varshayantī, Chupuṇīkā, art thou by name, with Prajāpati, with our every prayer, I deposit thee. ‖ *c.* The earth penetrated by food, a reservoir of water (thou art), men are thy guardians, Agni is placed in this (brick), to it I resort, and may it be my protection and my refuge. ‖ *d.* The over-sky penetrated by holy power, the atmosphere (thou art); the Marutas are thy guardians, Vāyu is placed in this (brick), to it I resort, and may it be my protection and my refuge. ‖ *e.* The sky, penetrated by ambrosia, the unconquered (thou art); the Ādityas are thy guardians, the sun is deposited in this (brick), to it I resort, and may it be my protection and my refuge.

Mantra 4:4:6

a. Let Bṛihaspati place thee on the ridge of earth, full of light, for every expiration, inspiration; support all the light, Agni is thine overlord. ‖ *b.* Let Viśvakarman place thee on the ridge of the atmosphere, full of light, for every expiration, inspiration; support all the light, Vāyu is thine overlord. ‖ *c.* Let Prajāpati place thee on the ridge of the sky, full of light, for every expiration, inspiration; support all the light, the supreme lord is thine overlord. ‖ *d.* Thou art the bringer of the east wind; thou art the winner of rain; thou art the winner of lightning; thou art the winner of thunder; thou art the winner of rain. ‖ *e.* Thou art the path of Agni; thou art the Gods' path of Agni. ‖ *f.* Thou art the path of Vāyu; thou art the Gods' path of Vāyu ‖ *g.* Thou art the path of the atmosphere; thou art the Gods' path of the atmosphere. ‖ *h.* Thou art the atmosphere; to the atmosphere thee! ‖ *i.* To the ocean thee, to water thee, to the watery thee, to impulse thee, to the wise thee, to the radiant thee, to the light of the sky thee, to the Ādityas thee! || *k.* To the Ṛich thee, to radiance thee, to the shining thee, to the blaze thee, to the light thee! || *l.* Thee, giving glory, in glory; thee, giving brilliance, in brilliance; thee, giving milk, in milk; thee, giving radiance, in radiance; thee giving wealth, in wealth I place; with this seer, the holy power, this deity, sit firm in the manner of Aṅgiras

Mantra 4:4:7

a. Thou art the furtherer; thou art the maker of wide room; thou art the eastern; thou art the zenith; thou art the sitter in the atmosphere, sit on the atmosphere. || *b.* Thou art the sitter on the waters; thou art the sitter on the hawk thou art the sitter on the vulture; thou art the sitter on the eagle; thou art the sitter on the vault. || *c.* In the wealth of earth I place thee; in the wealth of the atmosphere I place thee; in the wealth of the sky I place thee; in the wealth of the quarters I place thee; giver of wealth I place thee in wealth. || *d.* Protect my expiration; protect my inspiration; protect my cross-breathing; protect my life; protect all my life; protect the whole of my life. || *e.* O Agni, thy highest name, the heart, | Come let us join together, | Be thou, O Agni, among those of the five races. || *f.* (Thou art) the Yavas, the Ayavas, the courses, the helpers, the Sabda, the ocean, the firm one.

Mantra 4:4:8

(Thou I art) all overcoming through Agni; self-ruling through the sun; lord of strength through might; creator with the bull; bountiful through the sacrifice; heavenly through the sacrificial fee; slayer of enemies through rage; supporter of the body through kindliness; wealth through food; through the earth he hath won; (thou art) eater of food with verses; increased by the Vaṣhaṭ cry; protector of the body through the Sāman; full of light with the Virāj; drinker of Soma through the holy power; with cows he supporteth the sacrifice; with lordly power men; with horse and car bearer of the bolt; lord with the seasons; enclosing with the year; unassailable through penance; the sun with bodies.

Mantra 4:4:9

(Thou art) Prajāpati in mind, when come to the Soma; the creator in the consecration; Savitar in the bearing; Pūṣhan in the cow for the purchase of the Soma; Varuṇa when bound (in the cloth); Asura in the being bought; Mitra when purchased; Śipiviṣhṭa when put in place; delighter of men when being drawn forward; the overlord on arrival; Prajāpati being led on; Agni at the Agnīdh's altar; Bṛihaspati on being led from the Agnīdh's altar; Indra at the oblation-holder; Aditi when put in place; Viṣhṇu when being taken down; Atharvan when made wet; Yama when pressed out; drinker of unpurified (Soma) when being cleansed; Vāyu when purifying; Mitra as mixed with milk; the Manthin when mixed with groats; that of the All-Gods when taken out; Rudra when offered; Vāyu when covered up; the gazer on men when revealed; the food when it comes; the famed of the fathers; life when taken; the river when going to the final bath; the ocean when gone; the water when dipped; the heaven when arrived at completion.

Mantra 4:4:10.

a. (Thou art) Kṛittikās, the Nakṣhatra, Agni, the deity; ye are the radiances of Agni, of Prajāpati, of the creator, of Soma; to the Re thee, to radiance thee, to the shining thee, to the blaze thee, to the light thee || *b.* (Thou art) Rohiṇī the Nakṣhatra, Prajāpati the deity; Mṛigaśīrsha the Nakṣhatra, Soma the deity; Ārdrā the Nakṣhatra, Rudra the deity; the two Punarvasus the Nakṣhatra, Aditi the deity; Tiṣhya the Nakṣhatra, Bṛihaspati the deity; the Aśleṣhā the Nakṣhatra, the serpents the deity; the Maghā the Nakṣhatra, the fathers the deity; the two Phalgunīs the Nakṣhatra, Aryaman the deity; the two Phalgunīs the Nakṣhatra, Bhaga the deity; Hasta the Nakṣhatra, Savitar the deity; Chitrā the Nakṣhatra, Indra the deity; Svātī the Nakṣhatra, Vāyu the deity; the two Viśākhās the Nakṣhatra, Indra and Agni the deity; Anūrādhā the Nakṣhatra, Mitra the deity; Rohiṇī the Nakṣhatra, Indra the deity; the two Vichṛits the Nakṣhatra; the fathers the deity; the Aṣhāḍhās the Nakṣhatra, the waters the deity; the Aṣhāḍhās the Nakṣhatra, the All-Gods the deity; Śroṇā the Nakṣhatra, Viṣhṇu the deity; Śraviṣhṭhā the Nakṣhatra, the Vasus the, deity; Śatabhiṣha the Nakṣhatra, Indra the deity; Proṣhṭhapadas the Nakṣhatra, the goat of one foot the deity; the Proṣhṭhapadas the Nakṣhatra, the serpent of the deep the deity; Revatī the Nakṣhatra, Pūṣhan the deity; the two Aśvayujas the Nakṣhatra, the Aśvins the deity; the Apabharaṇīs the Nakṣhatra, Yama the deity. || *c.* Full on the west; what the Gods placed.

Mantra 4:4:11

a. (Ye are) Madha and Mādhava, the months of spring. || *b.* (Ye are) Śukra and Śuchi, the months of summer. || *c.* (Ye are) Nabha and Nabhasya, the months of rain. || *d.* (Ye are) Iṣha and Ūrja, the months of autumn. || *e.* (Ye are) Saha and Sahasya, the months of winter. || *f.* (Ye are) Tapa and Tapasya, the months of the cool season. || *g.* Thou art the internal bond of the fire, | Be sky and earth in place, | Be waters and plants in place, | Be the fires severally in place | In unison for my greatness | May the fires which of one mind | Are between sky and earth, | Taking place according to the months of the cool season, | Attend (on them), as the Gods on Indra. || *h.* (Thou art) the uniter and forethinker of Agni, Soma, Sūrya. || *i.* Thou art the dread, the terrible, of the fathers, of Yama, of Indra. || *k.* Thou art the firm (quarter) and the earth of the God Savitar, the Marutas, Varuṇa || *l.* Thou art the support, the upholder, of Mitra and Varuṇa, Mitra, Dhātar, || *m.* Thou art the eastern, the western (quarter) of the Vasus, the Rudras, the Ādityas || *n.* These are thine overlords, to them honour, be they gracious to us, him whom we hate and who hateth us I place in your jaws. || *o.* Thou art the measure of a thousand, thou art the image of a thousand, thou art the size of a thousand, thou art the replica of a thousand, thou art of a thousand, for a thousand thee! || *p.* May these bricks, O Agni, be milch cows for me, one, and a hundred, and a thousand, and ten thousand, and a hundred thousand, and a million, and ten million, and a hundred million, and a thousand million, and ten thousand million, and a hundred thousand million, and ten hundred thousand million, and a hundred hundred thousand million; may these bricks, O Agni, be for me milch cows, sixty, a thousand, ten thousand unperishing; ye are standing on holy order, increasing holy order, dripping ghee, dripping honey, full of strength, full of power; may these bricks, O Agni, be for me milkers of desires named the glorious yonder in yon world.

The Horse Sacrifice

Mantra 4:4:12

a. May the kindling-stick of the quarters, that winneth the heaven, (Guard us) according to our hopes; from Madhu may Mādhava protect us; | Agni, the God, hard to overcome, the undeceivable, | May he guard our kingly power, may he protect us. || *b.* May the Rathantara with the Sāmans protect us, | The Gāyatrī with every form of metres, | The Trivṛit Stoma with the order of the days, | The ocean, the wind, make full this strength. || *c.* (May) the dread among the quarters, the overpowering, giver of strength, | Pure, full of might on a bright day (protect us); | O Indra, as overlord, make full, | And for us on all sides do thou preserve this great kingly power. || *d.* (May) the Bṛihat Sāman, which supporteth kingly power, with vast strength, | The force made beautiful by the Triṣhṭubh, that of fierce strength (protect us); | O Indra, with the fifteenfold Stoma | Do thou guard this in the midst with the wind, with the ocean. || *e.* (May) the eastern among the quarters, famous and renowned, | O ye All-Gods, heavenly with the rain of the days (protect us); | Let this kingly power be unassailable, | Force unoverpowerable, a thousandfold and mighty. || *f.* Here in the Vairūpa Sāman may we have strength for this; | With the Jagatī we place him in the people; | O ye All-Gods through the seventeenfold (Stoma) this radiance, | This kingly power with the ocean wind (be) dread. || *g.* The supporter among the quarters doth support this lordly power, | The stay of the regions; may force rich in friends be ours; | O Mitra and Varuṇa, ye wise ones with the autumn of the days, | Do ye accord great protection to this kingdom. || *h.* In the Vairāja Sāman is my devotion; | By the Anuṣhṭubh (be) manly strength collected; | This kingly power rich in friends, with dripping wet, | Do ye, O Mitra and Varuṇa, guard through your overlordship. || *i.* May the victorious among quarters, with the Sāman, the strong one, | The season winter in order make us full; | May the great ones, the Śakvarī (verses), with favouring winds | Aid this sacrifice, full of ghee. || *k.* May the heavenly of the quarters, the easily milked, the rich in milk, | The Goddess aid us, full of ghee; | Thou art the protector, who goest in front and behind; | O Bṛihaspati, yoke a voice in the south. | *l.* (May) the upright of the quarters, the bounteous region of the plants, | And Savitar with the year of the days (aid us); | The Revat Sāman, and the Atichandas metre; | Without a foe, be kindly to us. ‖ *m.* O thou of the three-and-thirtyfold Stoma, lady of the world, | Breathed on by Vivasvat, do thou be gracious to us; | Rich in ghee, O Savitar, through thy overlordship, | Be the bounteous region rich in milk, for us. | The firm among the quarters, lady of Vishṇu, the mild, | Ruling over this strength, the desirable, | Bṛihaspati, Mātariśvan, Vāyu, | The winds blowing together be gracious to us. ‖ *o.* Prop of the sky, supporter of the earth, | Ruling this world, lady of Vishṇu, | All-extending, seeking food, with prosperity, | May Aditi be auspicious to us in her life. ‖ *p.* Vaiśvānara to our help. ‖ *q.* Present in the sky. ‖ *r.* Us today Anumati. ‖ *s.* O Anumati, thou. ‖ *t.* With what to us radiant shall he be? ‖ *u.* Who today yoketh?

Prapāṭhaka 5.

The Offerings to Rudra

Mantra 4:5:1

a. Homage to thy wrath, O Rudra, | To thine arrow homage also; | Homage to thy bow, | And homage to thine arms. ‖ *b.* With thy most kindly arrow, | And kindly bow, | With thy kindly missile, | Be gentle to us, O Rudra. ‖ *c.* That body of thine, O Rudra, which is kindly, | Not dread, with auspicious look, | With that body, most potent to heal, | O haunter of the mountains, do thou look on us. ‖ *d.* The arrow which, O haunter of mountains, | In thy hand thou bearest to shoot, | That make thou kindly, O guardian of mountains; | Harm not the world of men. ‖ *e.* With kindly utterance thee | We address, O liver on the mountains, | That all our folk | Be free from sickness and of good cheer. ‖ *f.* The advocate hath spoken in advocacy, | The first divine leech, | Confounding all the serpents | And all sorceries. ‖ *g.* The dusky, the ruddy, | The brown, the auspicious, | And the Rudras which in thousands | Lie around this (earth) in the quarters, | Their wrath do we deprecate. ‖ *h.* He who creepeth away, | Blue-necked and ruddy, | Him the cowherds have seen, | Have seen the bearers of water | And him all creatures; | May be, seen, be gentle unto us. ‖ *i.* Homage to the blue-necked, | Thousand-eyed one, the bountiful | And to those that are his warriors | I have paid my homage. ‖ *k.* Unfasten from the two notches | Of thy bow the bowstring, | And cast thou down | The arrows in thy hand. ‖ *l.* Unstringing thy bow, | Do thou of a thousand eyes and a hundred quivers, | Destroying the points of thine arrows, | Be gentle and kindly to us. ‖ *m.* Unstrung is the bow of him of the braided hair | And arrowless his quiver; | His arrows have departed, | Empty is his quiver. ‖ *n.* O most bountiful one, the missile | That is in thy hand, thy bow, | With it on all sides do thou guard us, | Free from sickness. ‖ *o.* Homage to thy weapon, | Unstrung, dread; | And homage to thy two hands, | To thy bow. ‖ *p.* May the missile from thy bow | Avoid us on every side, | And do thou lay far from us | This quiver that is thine.

Mantra 4:5:2

a. Homage to the golden-armed leader of hosts, and to the lord of the quarters homage! ‖ *b.* Homage to the trees with green tresses, to the lord of cattle homage! ‖ *c.* Homage to the one who is yellowish-red like young grass, to the radiant, to the lord of paths homage! ‖ *d.* Homage to the brown one, to the piercer, to the lord of food homage! ‖ *e.* Homage to the green-haired, wearer of the cord, to the lord of prosperity homage! ‖ *f.* Homage to the dart of Bhava, to the lord of the moving world homage! ‖ *g.* Homage to Rudra, with bent bow, to the lord of fields homage! ‖ *h.* Homage to the minstrel, the inviolate, to the lord of the woods homage! ‖ *i.* Homage to the ruddy one, the ruler, to the lord of woods homage! ‖ *k.* Homage to the minister, the trader, to the lord of thickets homage! ‖ *l.* Homage to the extender of the world, the offspring of the maker of room, to the lord of plants homage! ‖ *m.* Homage to the loud calling, the screaming, to the lord of footmen homage! ‖ *n.* Homage to the wholly covered, to the running, to the lord of warriors homage!

Mantra 4:5:3

a. Homage to the strong, the piercing, to the lord of assailers homage! ‖ *b.* Homage to the leader, the holder of the quiver, to the lord of thieves homage! ‖ *c.* Homage to the holder of the quiver, to the owner of the quiver, to the lord of robbers homage! ‖ *d.* Homage to the cheater, the swindler, to the lord of burglars homage! ‖ *c.* Homage to the glider, to the wanderer around, to the lord of the forests homage! ‖ *f.* Homage to the bolt-armed destructive ones, to the lord of pilferers homage! ‖ *g.* Homage to the bearers of the sword, the night wanderers, to the lord of cut-purses homage! ‖ *h.* Homage to the turbaned wanderer on the mountains, to the lord of pluckers homage! ‖ *i.* Homage to you, bearers of arrows, and to you, bowmen, homage! ‖ *k.* Homage to you that string (the bow), and to you that place (on the arrow), homage! ‖ *l.* Homage to you that bend (the bow), and to you that let go the arrow) homage! ‖ *m.* Homage to you that hurl, and to you that pierce homage! ‖ *n.* Homage to you that art seated, and to you that lie homage! ‖ *o.* Homage to you that sleep, and to you that wake homage! ‖ *p.* Homage to you that stand, and to you that run homage! ‖ *q.* Homage to you assemblies, and to you, lords of assemblies, homage! ‖ *r.* Homage to you horses, and to you, lords of horses, homage!

Mantra 4:5:4

a. Homage to you that wound, and to you that pierce homage! ‖ *b.* Homage to you that are in bands, and to you that are destructive homage! ‖ *c.* Homage to you sharpers, and to you, lords of sharpers, homage! ‖ *d.* Homage to you hosts, and to you, lord of hosts, homage! ‖ *e.* Homage to you troops, and to you, lords of troops, homage ‖ *f.* Homage to you of misshapen form, and to you of all forms homage! ‖ *g.* Homage to you that are great, and to you that are small homage! ‖ *h.* Homage to you that have chariots, and to you that are chariotless homage! ‖ *i.* Homage to you chariots, and to you, lords of chariots, homage! ‖ *k.* Homage to you hosts, and to you, lords of hosts, homage! ‖ *l.* Homage to you, doorkeepers, and to you, charioteers, homage! ‖ *m.* Homage to you, carpenters, and to you, makers of chariots, homage! ‖ *n.* Homage to you, potters, and to you, smiths, homage! ‖ *o.* Homage to you, Puñjishṭas, and to you, Nishādas, homage! ‖ *p.* Homage to you, makers of arrows, and to you, makers of bows, homage! ‖ *q.* Homage to you, hunters, and to you, dog-leaders, homage! ‖ *r.* Homage to you dogs, and to you, lords of dogs, homage!

Mantra 4:5:5

a. Homage to Bhava and to Rudra. ‖ *b.* Homage to Śarva and to the lord of cattle. ‖ *c.* Homage to the blue-necked one, and to the white-throated. ‖ *d.* Homage to the wearer of braids, and to him of shaven hair. ‖ *e.* Homage to him of a thousand eyes, and to him of a hundred bows. ‖ *f.* Homage to him who haunteth the mountains, and to Śipivishṭa. ‖ *g.* Homage to the most bountiful, and to the bearer of the arrow. ‖ *h.* Homage to the short, and to the dwarf. ‖ *i.* Homage to the great, and to the stronger. ‖ *k.* Homage to him who hath waxed, and to the waxing. ‖ *l.* Homage to the chief, and to the first. ‖ *m.* Homage to the swift, and to the active. ‖ *n.* Homage to the rapid, and to the hasty. ‖ *o.* Homage to him of the wave, and to the roaring. ‖ *p.* Homage to him of the stream, and to him of the island.

Mantra 4:5:6

a. Homage to the oldest, and to the youngest. ‖ *b.* Homage to the first born, and to the later born. ‖ *c.* Homage to the midmost, and to the immature. ‖ *d.* Homage to the hindmost, and to him in the depth. ‖ *e.* Homage to Sobhya, and to him of the amulet. ‖ *f.* Homage to him who dwelleth with Yama, and to him at peace. ‖ *g.* Homage to him of the ploughed field, and to him of the threshing-floor. ‖ *h.* Homage to him of fame, and to him at his end. ‖ *i.* Homage to him of the wood, and to him of the thicket. ‖ *k.* Homage to sound, and to echo. ‖ *l.* Homage to him of the swift host, and to him of the swift car. ‖ *m.* Homage to the hero, and the destroyer. ‖ *n.* Homage to the armoured, and to the corsleted. ‖ *o.* Homage to the mailed, and to the cuirassed. ‖ *p.* Homage to the famous, and to him of a famous host.

Mantra 4:5:7

a. Homage to him of the drum, and to him of the drumstick. ‖ *b.* Homage to the bold, and to the cautious. ‖ *c.* Homage to the messenger, and to the servant. ‖ *d.* Homage to the quiver-bearer, and to the owner of the quiver. ‖ *e.* Homage to him of the sharp arrow, and to him of the weapon. ‖ *f.* Homage to him of the good weapon, and to him of the good bow. ‖ *g.* Homage to him of the stream, and to him of the way. ‖ *h.* Homage to him of the hole, and to him of the pool. ‖ *i.* Homage to him of the ditch, and to him of the lake. ‖ *k.* Homage to him of the stream, and to him of the tank | *l.* Homage to him of the cistern, and to him of the well. ‖ *m.* Homage to him of the rain, and to him not of the rain. ‖ *n.* Homage to him of the cloud, and to him of the lightning. ‖ *o.* Homage to him of the cloudy sky, and to him of the heat. ‖ *p*. Homage to him of the wind, and to him of the storm. ‖ *q*. Homage to him of the dwelling, and to him who guardeth the dwelling.

Mantra 4:5:8

a. Homage to Soma, and to Rudra. ‖ *b*. Homage to the dusky one, and to the ruddy one. ‖ *c*. Homage to the giver of weal, and to the lord of cattle. ‖ *d*. Homage to the dread, and to the terrible. ‖ *e*. Homage to him who slayeth in front, and to him who slayeth at a distance. ‖ *f*. Homage to the slayer, and to the special slayer. ‖ *g*. Homage to the trees with green tresses. ‖ *h*. Homage to the deliverer. ‖ *i*. Homage to the source of health, and to the source of delight. ‖ *k*. Homage to the maker of health, and to the maker of delight. ‖ *l*. Homage to the auspicious, and to the more auspicious. ‖ *m*. Homage to him of the ford, and to him of the bank. ‖ *n*. Homage to him beyond, and to him on this side. ‖ *o*. Homage to him who crosseth over, and to him who crosseth back. ‖ *p*. Homage to him of the crossing, and to him of the ocean. ‖ *q*. Homage to him in the tender grass, and to him in foam. ‖ *r*. Homage to him in the sand, and to him in the stream.

Mantra 4:5:9

a. Homage to him in the cleft, and to him in the distance. ‖ *b*. Homage to him dwelling in the stony and to him in habitable places. ‖ *c*. Homage to him of braided hair, and to him of plain hair. ‖ *d*. Homage to him who dwelleth in the cowshed, and to him of the house. ‖ *e*. Homage to him of the bed, and to him of the dwelling. ‖ *f*. Homage to him of the hole, and to him of the abyss. ‖ *g*. Homage to him of the lake, and to him of the whirlpool. ‖ *h*. Homage to him of the dust, and to him of the mist. ‖ *i*. Homage to him of the dry, and to him of the green. ‖ *k*. Homage to him of the copse, and to him of the grass. ‖ *l*. Homage to him in the earth, and to him in the gully. ‖ *m*. Homage to him of the leaf, and to him of the leaf-fall. ‖ *n*. Homage to him who growleth, and to him who smiteth away. ‖ *o*. Homage to him who draggeth, and to him who repelleth. ‖ *p*. Homage to you, sparkling hearts of the Gods. ‖ *q*. Homage to the destroyed. ‖ *r*. Homage to the intelligent. ‖ *s*. Homage to the unconquerable. ‖ *t*. Homage to the destroyers.

Mantra 4:5:10.

a. O chaser, lord of the Soma plants, | O waster, red and blue, | Frighten not nor injure | (Any) of these people, of these cattle; | Be not one of these injured. ‖ *b*. That auspicious form of thine, O Rudra, | Auspicious and ever healing, | Auspicious and healing (form of) Rudra, | With that show mercy on us for life. ‖ *c*. This prayer we offer up to the impetuous Rudra, | With plaited hair, destroyer of men, | That health be for our bipeds and quadrupeds, | And that all in this village be prosperous and free from ill. ‖ *d*. Be merciful to us, O Rudra, and give us delight; | With honour let us worship thee, destroyer of men; | The health and wealth which father Manu won by sacrifice, | May we attain that, O Rudra, under thy leadership. ‖ *e*. Neither our great, nor our small, | Our waxing or what has waxed, | Do thou slay, nor father nor mother; | Injure not, O Rudra, our dear bodies. ‖ *f*. Harm us not in our children, our descendants, our life; | Harm us not in our cattle, in our horses; | Smite not in anger our heroes, O Rudra; | With oblations lot us serve thee with honour. ‖ *g*. From afar to thee, slayer of cows, and slayer of men, | Destroyer of heroes, be goodwill for us; | Guard us and accord us aid | And grant us protection in abundance. ‖ *h*. Praise the famous youth, mounted on the chariot seat, | Dread and destructive like a fierce wild beast; | Being praised, O Rudra, be merciful to the singer; | Let thy missiles smite down another than us. ‖ *i*. May the missile of Rudra spare us, | May the wrath of the brilliant evil worker (pass over us); | Unstring for the generous donors (thy) strong (bows); | O bounteous one, be merciful to our children and descendants. ‖ *k*. O most bounteous, most auspicious, | Be auspicious and favourably inclined to us; | Placing down thy weapon on the highest tree, | Clad in thy skin, come, | And approach us bearing the spear. ‖ *l*. O blood-red scatterer, | Homage to thee, O adorable one; | May thy thousand missiles | Smite down another than us. ‖ *m*. A thousandfold in thousands | Are the missiles in thine arms; | O adorable one, do thou turn away | The points of those which thou dost rule.

Mantra 4:5:11

a. The Rudras that are over the earth | In thousands by thousands, | Their bows we unstring | At a thousand leagues. ‖ *b*. The Bhavas in this great ocean, | The atmosphere— ‖ *c*. The Śarvas of black necks, and white throats, | Who wander below on the earth— ‖ *d*. The Rudras who abide in the sky, | Of black necks and white throats— ‖ *e*. Those who of black necks and ruddy, | Grass green, are in the trees— ‖ *f*. The overlords of creatures, | Without top-knot, with braided hair— ‖ *g*. Those that assault men in their food | And in their cups as they drink— ‖ *h*. Those that guard the paths, | Bearing food, warriors— ‖ *i*. Those that resort to fords, | With spears and quivers— ‖ *k*. The Rudras that so many and yet more | Occupy the quarters, their bows we unstring | At a thousand leagues. ‖ *l, m, n*. Homage to the Rudras on the earth, in the atmosphere, in the sky, whose arrows are food, wind, and rain, to them ten eastwards, ten to the south, ten to the west, ten to the north, ten upwards; to them homage, be they merciful to us, him whom we hate and him who hateth us, I place him within your jaws.

Prapāṭhaka 6.

The Preparation of the Fire

Mantra 4:6:1

a. The strength resting on the stone, the bill, | On the wind, on Parjanya, on the breath of Varuṇa, | Brought together from the waters, from the plants, from the trees; | That food and strength do ye, O Marutas, bounteously bestow upon us. ‖ *b*. In the stone is thy hunger; let thy pain reach N. N., whom we hate. ‖ *c*. With the wind of the ocean | We envelop thee, O Agni; | Be thou purifying and auspicious to us. ‖ *d*. With the caul of winter | We envelop thee, O Agni; | Be thou purifying and auspicious to us. ‖ *e*. Down upon earth, upon the reed, | Upon the waters lower (do thou descend); | Thou, O Agni, art the bile of the waters, ‖ *f*. O female frog, with these come hither; | Do thou make this sacrifice of ours | Pure in hue and auspicious. ‖ *g*. Pure, with radiance wonderful, | On earth he hath shone as with the light of dawn. ‖ *h*. Who (cometh) to battle, | Moving with strength as on Etaśa's course, | In the heat unathirst, immortal. ‖ *i*. O Agni, the purifying, with thy light, | O God, with thy pleasant tongue, | Bring hither the Gods, and sacrifice. ‖ *k*. Do thou, O shining and purifying one, | O Agni, bring hither the Gods | To our sacrifice and our oblation. | I. This is the meeting of the waters, | The abode of the ocean; | May thy bolts afflict another than us; | Be thou purifying and auspicious to us. ‖ *m*. Homage to thy heat, thy blaze | Homage be to thy light; | May thy bolts afflict another than us; | Be thou purifying and auspicious to us. ‖ *n*. To him that sitteth in man, hail! To him that sitteth in the waters, hail! To him that sitteth in the wood, hail! To him that sitteth on the strew, hail! To him that findeth the heaven, hail! ‖ *o*. Those Gods among Gods, worshipful among the worshipful, | Who await their yearly portion, | Who eat not oblations, in this sacrifice | Do ye delight yourselves with honey and ghee. ‖ *p*. The Gods who above the Gods attained godhead, | Who lead the way to this holy power, | Without whom no place whatever is pure, | Neither on the heights of sky or earth are they. ‖ *q*. Giver of expiration art thou, of inspiration, of cross-breathing, | Giver of eyesight, giver of splendour, giver of wide room; | May thy bolts afflict another than us; | Be thou purifying and auspicious to us. ‖ *r*. May Agni with his piercing blaze | Cast down every foe; | May Agni win for us wealth. ‖ *s*. With his countenance the kindly one | Will sacrifice to the Gods for us, most skilled to win prosperity by sacrifice; | Guardian undeceived and protector of us, | O Agni, shine forth with radiance and with wealth.

Mantra 4:6:2

a. He who sat down, offering all these beings, | As Hotar, the seer, our father, | He seeking wealth with prayer, | Hath entered into the boon of the first of coverers. ‖ *b*. Since Viśvakarman is mighty in mind, | Disposer, ordainer, and highest seer, | Their offerings rejoice in food, | Where say they is one beyond the seven Ṛishis. ‖ *c*. He who is our father, our begetter, the ordainer, | Who begot us from being unto being, | Who alone assigneth their names to the Gods, | Him other beings approach for knowledge. ‖ *d*. Wealth they won by offering to him | The seers of old like singers in abundance, | They who fashioned these beings illumined and unillumined | In the expanse of space. ‖ *e*. Ye shall not find him who produced this world; | Another thing shall be betwixt you; | Enveloped in mist and with stammering | The singers of hymns move enjoying life. ‖ *f*.

Beyond the sky, beyond this earth, | Beyond the Gods, what is secret from the Asuras, | What germ first did the waters bear, | When all the Gods came together? ‖ *g.* This germ the waters first bore, | When all the Gods came together; | On the navel of the unborn is set the one | On which doth rest all this world. ‖ *h.* Viśvakarman, the God, was born; | Then second the Gandharva; | Third the father, begetter of plants. | In many a place did he deposit the germ of the waters. ‖ *i.* Father of the eye, the sage with his mind, | Produced these two worlds rich in ghee, | When the fore ends were made firm, | Then did sky and earth extend. ‖ *k.* With eyes on every side, with a face on every side, | With hands on every side, with feet on every side, | The one God producing sky and earth | Welds them together with arms, with wings. ‖ *l.* What was the basis? | Which and what his support? | When producing earth Viśvakarman, all-seeing, | Disclosed the sky with his might. ‖ *m.* What was the wood, and what the tree, | Whence they formed sky and earth? | O ye wise ones, inquire with your minds | On what he stood as he supported the worlds. ‖ *n.* Thy highest, lowest, | Midmost abodes here, O Viśvakarman, | In the offering do thou teach thy comrades, O faithful one; | Do thou thyself sacrifice to thyself, rejoicing. ‖ *o.* The lord of speech, Viśvakarman, | Let us invoke this day to aid us, thought yoked for strength, | May he delight in our nearest offerings, | He with all healing, to aid (us), the doer of good deeds. ‖ *p.* O Viśvakarman, waxing great with the oblation, | Do thou thyself sacrifice to thyself rejoicing; | May the others around, our foes, be confused; | May our patrons here be rich. ‖ *q.* O Viśvakarman, with the oblation as strengthening, | Thou didst make Indra, the protector, free from scathe, | To him the clans of old bowed in homage, | That he might be dread, to be severally invoked. ‖ *r.* To the ocean, the moving, | The lord of streams, homage! | To the lord of all the streams | Do ye offer, to Viśvakarman, | Through all the days the immortal offering.

Mantra 4:6:3

a. O Agni, to whom ghee is offered, | Do thou lead him forward; | Unite him with increase of wealth, | With offspring and with wealth. ‖ *b.* O Indra, bring him to the fore, | That he may be lord over his fellows; | Unite him with splendour, | That he may assign their shares to the Gods. ‖ *c.* Him, O Agni, do thou exalt | In whose house we make the offering; | To him may the Gods lend aid, | And he the lord of holy power. ‖ *d.* May the All-Gods thee, | O Agni, bear up with their thoughts; | Be thou to us most propitious, | With kindly face, abounding in light. ‖ *e.* May the five regions divine aid the sacrifice, | The Goddesses driving away poverty and hostility, | And giving to the lord of the sacrifice increase of wealth. | In increase of wealth the sacrifice hath been established, | Waxing great on the kindled fire, | Grasped with hymns as wings, to be adored; | They sacrificed embracing the heated cauldron. ‖ *g.* When with strength the Gods laboured at the sacrifice | For the divine supporter, the enjoyer, | Serving the Gods, benign, with a hundred drinks (was it); | The Gods kept embracing the sacrifice. ‖ *h.* With the rays of the sun, with tawny hair, | Savitar hath raised before (us) his unending light; | On his instigation fareth Pūṣhan the God, | The guardian, gazing on all things. ‖ *i.* The Gods stand serving as priests for the Gods; | Ready (is it) for the immolator, let the immolator sacrifice; | Where the fourth offering goeth to the oblation, | Thence let our pure invocations be accepted. ‖ *k.* As measurer he standeth in the midst of the sky, | Filling the two worlds and the atmosphere; | The all-reaching, the butter-reaching, he discerneth, | Between the eastern and the western mark. ‖ *l.* Bull, ocean, ruddy bird, | He hath entered the birthplace of his ancient sire; | In the middle of the sky is the dappled stone set down | He hath stepped apart, he guardeth the two ends of space. ‖ *m.* All songs have caused Indra to wax | To encompass the ocean, | Best charioteer of charioteers, | True lord and lord of strength. ‖ *n.* Let the sacrifice invite favour, and bring (to us) the Gods; let the God, Agni, offer and bring (to us) the Gods. ‖ *o.* With the impulse of strength, | With elevation he hath seized me; | Then Indra hath made my enemies | Humble by depression. ‖ *p.* The Gods have increased my prayer, | Which is elevation and depression; | Then do ye, O Indra and Agni, | Scatter my foes on every side.

Mantra 4:6:4

a. Swift, like a bull sharpening his horns, the warrior | Fond of slaughter, disturber of the people, | Bellowing, unwinking, sole hero, | Indra at once conquered a hundred hosts. ‖ *b.* With the bellowing, unwinking, conquering, | Fighter, hard to overthrow, and daring Indra, | With Indra do ye conquer, do ye withstand | The foe, O heroes, with the strong one who holdeth the arrow in his hands. ‖ *c.* He is mighty with those who have arrows in their hands and quivers, | Indra who joineth hosts with his band, | Conquering in combat, drinker of Soma, with many a band, | With bow uplifted, and shooter with well-drawn arrows. ‖ *d.* O Bṛihaspati, fly round with thy chariot, | Slaying the foe, driving away the enemy; | Defeating hosts, destroyer, victor in battle, | Be thou protector of our chariots. ‖ *e.* The cleaver of the cow-stalls, finder of the cows, with the thunderbolt on his arm, | Victorious, crushing in might a host, | Be heroes, O my fellows, like him; | O comrades, follow in Indra's footsteps. ‖ *f.* Conspicuous by might, strong, heroic, | Enduring, mighty, steadfast, dread, | Surpassing heroes and warriors born of strength, | Do thou, winning kine, mount, O Indra, thy victorious car. ‖ *g.* In might penetrating the cow-stalls, | Impetuous, the hero, Indra, with wrath a hundredfold, | Hard to resist, enduring in battle, unovercomable, | May he aid our armies in the battles. ‖ *h.* Indra (be) their leader, and let Bṛihaspati, | The sacrificial fee, the sacrifice and Soma go before; | Let the Marutas precede the hosts divine, | That overthrow and conquer. ‖ *i.* Of Indra, the strong, of Varuṇa, the king, | Of the Ādityas, of the Marutas the mighty host— | The voice hath ascended of the Gods | Great-hearted that shake the worlds as they conquer. ‖ *k.* Ours (be) Indra, when the standards meet; | Ours be the arrows that conquer; | Ours be the heroes who are victors, | And us do ye aid, O Gods, at our invocations. ‖ *l.* Exalt our weapons, O bounteous one, | Exalt the might of my warriors; | Exalt the strength of the steed, O slayer of Vṛitra, | Let the sound of the conquering chariots arise. ‖ *m.* Go ye forward, O heroes; conquer; | Be your arms strong; | May Indra accord you protection | That ye may be unassailable. ‖ *n.* Let loose, fly forward, | O arrow, expelled with holy power; | Go to our foes, and enter them; | Not one of them do thou spare. ‖ *o.* Thy vital parts I clothe with armour; | May Soma, the king, cover thee with immortality, | Space broader than broad be thine; | May the Gods take delight in thy victory. ‖ *p.* When the arrows fly together | Like boys unshorn, | Then may Indra, slayer of foes, | Accord us protection for ever.

Mantra 4:6:5

a. Along the eastern quarter do thou advance, wise one; | Be thou, O Agni, of Agni the harbinger here; | Illumine with thy radiance all the regions; | Confer strength on our bipeds and quadrupeds. ‖ *b.* Mount ye, with Agni, to the vault, | Bearing him of the pan in your hands; | Having gone to the ridge of the sky, to the heaven, | Do ye eat, mingled with the Gods. ‖ *c.* From earth have I mounted to the atmosphere; | From the atmosphere have I mounted to the sky; | From the ridge of the vault of the sky | Have I attained the heaven, the light. ‖ *d.* Going to the heaven, they look not away; | They mount the sky, the two worlds, | They who extended, wisely, | The sacrifice, streaming on every side. ‖ *e.* O Agni, advance, first of worshippers, | Eye of Gods and mortals; | Pressing on in unison with the Bhṛigus, | Let the sacrificers go to heaven, to prosperity. ‖ *f.* Night and the dawn, one-minded, but of various form, | United suckle one child; | The radiant one shineth between sky and earth; | The Gods, granters of wealth, support Agni. ‖ *g.* O Agni, of a thousand eyes, of a hundred heads, | A hundred are thy expirations, a thousand thine inspirations; | Thou art lord of wealth a thousandfold; | To thee as such let us pay homage for strength, hail! ‖ *h.* Thou art the winged bird, sit on the earth; sit on the ridge of earth; with thy blaze fill the atmosphere, with thy light establish the sky, with thy brilliance make firm the quarters. ‖ *i.* Receiving offering, fair of face, O Agni; | Sit down in front in thine own birthplace, in due order; | In this higher place, | O All-Gods, do ye sit with the sacrificer. ‖ *k.* Enkindled, O Agni, shine before us, | O most youthful, with unfailing beam; | Ever upon thee strength awaiteth. ‖ *l.* Let us pay homage to thee in thy highest birth, O Agni; | Let us pay homage with praises in thy lower abode; | The place of birth whence thou didst come, to that I offer; | In thee when kindled they offered the oblations. ‖ *m.* That various loving kindness given to all men, | Of Savitar the adorable, I choose, | That mighty fat cow of his which Kaṇva milked, | Streaming with a thousand (draughts) of milk. ‖ *n.* Seven are thy kindling-sticks, O Agni, seven thy tongues, | Seven seers, seven dear abodes; | Seven Hotras sevenfold sacrifice to thee | Seven birthplaces with ghee do thou fill. ‖ *o.* Such like, other like, thus like, similar, measured, commensurate, harmonious; ‖ *p.* Of pure radiance, of varied radiance, of true radiance, the radiant, true, protector of holy order, beyond distress; ‖ *q.* Winning holy order, winning truth, host-conquering, having a good host, with foes within, with foes afar, the troop; ‖ *r.* Holy order, true, secure, supporting, supporter, upholder, upholding; ‖ *s.* Such like, thus like, do ye come to us, similar and equal. ‖ *t.* Measured and commensurate, to aid us, harmonious, at this sacrifice, O Marutas. ‖ *u.* On Indra attend the divine folk, the Marutas; even as the divine folk, the Marutas, attend on Indra, so may the folk divine and human, attend on this sacrificer.

The Horse Sacrifice

Mantra 4:6:6

a. As of a thunder-cloud is the face of the warrior | As he advanceth to the lap of the battles; | Be victorious with unpierced body; | Let the might of thine armour protect thee. ‖ *b.* By the bow cows, by the bow the contest may we win, | By the bow dread battles may we win; | The bow doth work displeasure to the foe; | By the bow let us win in all the quarters. ‖ *c.* As if about to speak it approacheth the ear, | Embracing its dear comrade, | Like a woman this bowstring twangeth stretched over the bow, | Saving in the battle. ‖ *d.* They coming together as a maiden to the assembly, | As a mother her child, shall bear (the arrow) in their lap; | In unison shall they pierce the foes, | These two ends springing asunder, the enemies. ‖ *e.* Father of many (daughters), many his sons, | He whizzeth as he goeth to battle, | The quiver, slung on the back, yielding its content, | Doth conquer every band and army. ‖ *f.* Standing on the chariot be guideth his steeds before him | Wheresoever he desireth, good charioteer; | The might of the reins do ye admire; | The reins behind obey the mind (of the driver). ‖ *g.* Shrilly the strong-hooved horses neigh, | As with the cars they show their strength; | Trampling with their forefeet the enemy | They unflinchingly destroy the foe. ‖ *h.* The chariot-bearer is his oblation by name, | Where is deposited his armour and his weapon; | Then may we sit on the strong car, | All the days, with friendly hearts. ‖ *i.* The fathers with pleasant seats, granting strength, | A support in trouble mighty and profound, | With varied hosts, with arrows to strengthen them, free, | With real heroes, broad conquerors of hosts. ‖ *k.* The Brahmans, the fathers worthy of the Soma, | And sky and earth, unequalled be propitious to us; | May Pūṣhan guard us from misfortune, us that prosper holy order | Do thou guard; may no foe overpower us. ‖ *l.* A feather her garment, a deer her tooth, | Tied with cowhide she flieth shot forth; | Where men run together and apart, | There may the arrows accord us protection. ‖ *m.* O thou of straight path, avoid us; | Be our body as of stone | May Soma favour us, | And Aditi grant protection! ‖ *n.* Their backs it smites, | Their thighs it belabours; | O horse-whip, do ye stimulate | The skilled horses in the battles. ‖ *o.* Like a snake with its coils it encircleth his arm, | Fending off the friction of the bowstring, | Let the hand-guard, knowing all cunning, | Manfully guard the man on all sides. ‖ *p.* O lord of the forest, be strong of limb, | Our comrade, efficacious, of great strength; | Thou art tied with cowhide, be thou strong; | Let him that mounteth thee conquer what is to be conquered. ‖ *q.* From sky, from earth is might collected, | From trees is strength gathered; | The might of the waters surrounded with the kine, | Indra's thunderbolt, the chariot, do thou adore with oblation. ‖ *r.* The thunderbolt of Indra, the face of the Marutas, | The embryo of Mitra, the navel of Varuṇa, | Do thou, accepting this our sacrifice, | O chariot divine, take to thyself the oblations. ‖ *s.* Roar to earth and sky; | Let the scattered world be ware of thee in many places; | Do thou, O drum, in unison with Indra and the Gods, | Drive away the foe further than far. ‖ *t.* Roar thou! Grant us force and might. | Thunder, overthrowing obstacles; | Snort away, O drum, misfortune hence; | Indra's fist art thou; show thy strength. ‖ *u.* Drive to us those, and these make to come to us; | The drum speaketh aloud for a signal (of battle) | Our heroes winged with steeds meet together; | Be our chariotmen victorious, O Indra.

Mantra 4:6:7

a. When first thou didst cry on birth, | Arising from the ocean or the dust, | The wings of the eagle, the limbs of the gazelle, | That is thy famed birth, O steed. ‖ *b.* The steed given by Yama hath Trita yoked, | It Indra first mounted, | The bridle of it the Gandharva grasped; | O Vasus, from the sun ye fashioned the steed. ‖ *c.* Thou art Yama, O steed, thou art Āditya; | Thou art Trita by secret ordinance; | Thou art entirely separated from Soma; | Three, they say, are thy bonds in the sky. ‖ *d.* Three, they say, are thy bonds in the sky, | Three in the waters, three within the ocean | And like Varuṇa to me thou appearest, O steed, | Where, say they, is thy highest birthplace. ‖ *e.* These, O swift one, are thy cleansings, | These the placings down of thy hooves in victory; | Here I have seen thy fair ropes, | Which the guards of holy order guard. ‖ *f.* The self of thee with my mind I perceived from afar, | Flying with wings from below through the sky; | Thy head I saw speeding with wings | On paths fair and dustless. ‖ *g.* Here I saw thy highest form, | Eager to win food in the footstep of the cow; | When a mortal man pleaseth thy taste, | Then most greedily dost thou consume the plants. ‖ *h.* Thee follows the chariot, thee the lover, O steed, | Thee the kine, thee the portion of maidens; | Thy friendship the companies have sought; | The Gods have imitated thy strength. ‖ *i.* Golden his horns, iron his feet; | Swift as thought, Indra was his inferior; | The Gods came to eat his oblation | Who first did master the steed. ‖ *k.* Full haunched, of slender middle, | The heroic divine steeds, | Vie together like cranes in rows, | When the horses reach the divine coursing-place | II. Thy body is fain to fly, O steed; | Thy thought is like the blowing wind; | Thy horns are scattered in many places, | They wander busy in the woods. ‖ *m.* To the slaughter the swift steed hath come, | Pondering with pious mind; | The goat, his kin, is led before, | Behind him come the sages to sing. ‖ *n.* To his highest abode hath the steed come, | To his father and his mother; | Today do thou go, most welcome, to the Gods; | Then boons shall he assign to the generous.

Mantra 4:6:8

a. Let not Mitra, Varuṇa, Aryaman, Āyu, | Indra, Ṛibhukṣhan, the Marutas disregard us, | When we shall proclaim before the assembly | The might of the strong God-born steed. ‖ *b.* When they bear before him, covered with a garment and with wealth | The gift they have seized, | The goat, all-formed, bleating, | Goeth straight to the dear stronghold of Indra and Pūṣhan. ‖ *c.* This goat is led before the strong steed | As share of Pūṣhan, connected with the All-Gods, | When Tvaṣhṭar impels him as an acceptable sacrifice | Together with the steed for fair renown. ‖ *d.* When men thrice lead round in due season | The steed going to the Gods as an acceptable offering | Then first goeth Pūṣhan's share, | The goat announcing the sacrifice to the Gods. ‖ *e.* Hotar Adhvaryu, atoner, fire kindler, | Holder of the stone, and skilled reciter, | With this well-prepared sacrifice | Well offered do ye fill the channels. ‖ *f.* The cutters of the stake, the bearers of the stake, | And they that fashion the top piece for the stake for the horse, | And they that collect the cooking-pot for the steed, | May their approval quicken us. ‖ *g.* He hath come forth—efficacious hath been my prayer— | To the regions of the Gods, straight backed; | In him the sages, the seers, rejoice, | For the prosperity of the Gods a good friend have we made. ‖ *h.* The bond of the strong one, the tie of the steed, | The head stall, the rope of him, | And the grass placed in his mouth, | May all these of thine be with the Gods. ‖ *i.* Whatever of the horse's raw flesh the fly eateth, | Whatever on the chip or the axe hath stuck, | Whatever is on the hands, the nails of the slayer, | May all these of thine be with the Gods. ‖ *k.* The refuse that bloweth forth from the belly, | The smell of raw flesh, | Let the slayers see that in order | Let them cook the fat to a turn. ‖ *l.* Whatever flieth away from thy limb | As it is cooked by the fire when thou art spitted, | Let it fall not on earth, nor on the grass; | Be that given to the eager Gods.

Mantra 4:6:9

a. Those who watch for the cooking of the strong one, | And call out, 'It is fragrant; take it out,' | And who wait to beg for the meat of the steed, | May their approval quicken us. ‖ *b.* The trial spoon of the meat-cooking pot, | The vessels to hold the juice, | The coverings of the dishes for warming, | The hooks, the crates, attend the steed. ‖ *c.* The starting-place, the sitting down, the turning, | The hobbles of the steed, | What it hath drunk, what it hath eaten as fodder, | May all these of thine be with the Gods. ‖ *d.* May Agni, smoke smelling, not make thee crackle; | May not the radiant pot be broken, smelling; | Offered, delighted in, approved, offered with the Vaṣhaṭ cry, | The Gods accept the horse. ‖ *e.* The garment they spread for the horse, | The upper garment, the golden (trappings), | The bond of the steed, the hobble, | As dear to the Gods they offer. ‖ *f.* If one hath smitten thee, riding thee driven with force, | With heel or with whip, | As with the ladle the parts of the oblation in the sacrifice, | So with holy power all these of thine I put in order. ‖ *g.* The four and thirty ribs of the strong steed, | Kin of the Gods, the axe meeteth; | Skilfully do ye make the joints faultless; | Declaring each part, do ye cut it asunder. ‖ *h.* One carver is there of the steed of Tvashṭar | Two restrainers are there, so is the use; | Those parts of thy limbs that I place in order, | Those in balls I offer in the fire. ‖ *i.* Let not thy dear self distress thee as thou comest; | Let not the axe stay in thy body; | May no greedy skilless carver, | Missing the joints, mangle thy limbs with the knife. ‖ *k.* Thou dost not die, indeed, thou art not injured, | On easy paths thou goest to the Gods; | The bays, the dappled ones, have become thy yoke-fellows; | The steed bath stood under the yoke of the ass. ‖ *l.* Wealth of kine for us, may the strong one (grant), wealth in horses, | Men and sons, and every form of prosperity; | May Aditi confer on us sinlessness; | Kingship for us may the horse rich in offering gain.

Prapāṭhaka 7.

The Piling of the Fire Altar (Continued)

Mantra 4:7:1

a. O Agni and Vishṇu, may these songs gladden you in unison; come ye with radiance and strength. ‖ *b.* May for me strength, instigation, influence, inclination, thought, inspiration, speech, fame, renown, reputation, light, heaven, expiration, inspiration, cross-breathing, breath, mind, learning, voice, mind, eye, ear, skill, might, force, strength, life, old age, breath, body, protection, guard, limbs, bones, joints, bodies (prosper through the sacrifice).

Mantra 4:7:2

May for me pre-eminence, overlordship, spirit, anger, violence, impetuosity, victorious power, greatness, breadth, extent, greatness, length, growth, growing, truth, faith, world, wealth, power, radiance, play, delight, what is born, what is to be born, good words, good deeds, finding, what there is to find, what has been, what will be, easy road, good way, prosperity, prospering, agreement, agreeing, thought, good thought (prosper through the sacrifice).

Mantra 4:7:3

May for me prosperity, comfort, desire, wish, longing, kindliness, good, better, superior, fame, good luck, riches, restrainer, supporter, peace, firmness, all, greatness, discovery, knowledge, begetting, procreation, plough, harrow, holy order, immortality, freeness from disease, freedom from illness, life, longevity, freedom from foes, fearlessness, ease of going, lying, fair dawning, and fair day (prosper through the sacrifice).

Mantra 4:7:4

May for me strength, righteousness, milk, sap, ghee, honey, eating and drinking in company, ploughing, rain, conquest, victory, wealth, riches, prosperity, prospering, plenteousness, lordship, much, more, fun, fuller, imperishableness, bad crops, food, freedom from hunger, rice, barley, beans, sesame, kidney beans, vetches, wheat, lentils, Millet, *Panicum miliaceum*, *Panicum frumentaceum*, and wild rice (prosper through the sacrifice).

Mantra 4:7:5

May I for me the stone, clay, hills, mountains, sand, trees, gold, bronze, lead, tin, iron, copper, fire, water, roots, plants, what grows on ploughed land, what grows on unploughed land, tame and wild cattle prosper through the sacrifice; may for me wealth and gaining wealth, attainment and attaining, riches, dwelling, act, power, aim, strength, moving and going (prosper through the sacrifice).

Mantra 4:7:6

May Agni for me and Indra, may Soma and Indra, may Savitar and Indra, may Sarasvatī and Indra, may Pūshan and Indra, may Bṛihaspati and Indra, may Mitra and Indra, may Varuṇa and Indra, may Tvashṭar and Indra, may Dhātar and Indra, may Vishṇu and Indra, may the Aśvins and Indra, may the Marutas and Indra, may the All-Gods and Indra, may earth and Indra, may the atmosphere and Indra, may sky and Indra, may the quarters and Indra, may the head and Indra, may Prajāpati and Indra (be auspicious for me through the sacrifice).

Mantra 4:7:7

May the Aṃśu cup for me, the Raśmi, the Adābhya, the overlord (cup), the Upāṃśu, the Antaryāma, the (cup) for Indra and Vāyu, the (cup) for Mitra and Varuṇa, the (cup) for the Aśvins, the Pratiprasthāna (cup) the Śukra, the Manthin, the Āgrayaṇa, the (cup) for the All-Gods, the Dhruvā, the (cup) for Vaiśvānara, the season cups, the Atigrāhyas, the (cup) for Indra and Agni, the (cup) for the All-Gods, the (cups) for the Marutas, the (cup) for Mahendra, the (cup) for Āditya, the (cup) for Savitar the (cup) for Sarasvatī, the (cup) for Pūshan, the (cup) for (Tvashṭar) with the wives (of the Gods), the Hāriyojana (cup) (prosper for me through the sacrifice).

Mantra 4:7:8

May the kindling-wood for me, the strew, the altar, the lesser altars, the offering-spoons, the cups, the pressing-stones, the chips (of the post), the sounding-holes, the two pressing-boards, the wooden tub, the Vāyu cups, the (bowl) for the purified Soma, the mixing (bowl), the Agnīdh's altar, the oblation-holder, the house, the Sadas, the cakes, the cooked (offerings), the final bath, the cry of 'Godspeed' (prosper for me through the sacrifice).

Mantra 4:7:9

May the fire for me, the cauldron, the beam, the sun, breath, the horse sacrifice, earth, Aditi, Diti, sky, the Śakvarī verses, the fingers, the quarters prosper through the sacrifice; may the Re, the Sāman, the hymn tune, the Yajus, consecration, penance, the season, the vow (prosper) through the rain of day and night, the Bṛihat and Rathantara prosper for me through the sacrifice.

Mantra 4:7:10.

May the embryo for me, the calves, the one-and-a-half-year-old male and female, the two-year-old male and female, the two-and-a-half-year-old male and female, the three-year-old male and female, the four-year-old male and female, the draught ox and the draught cow, the bull and the cow that is barren, the steer and the cow that miscarries, the bullock and the cow (prosper through the sacrifice); may life prosper through the sacrifice, may expiration prosper through the sacrifice, may inspiration prosper through the sacrifice, may cross-breathing prosper through the sacrifice, may the eye prosper through the sacrifice, may the ear prosper through the sacrifice, may mind prosper through the sacrifice, may speech prosper through the sacrifice, may the self prosper through the sacrifice, may the sacrifice prosper through the sacrifice.

Mantra 4:7:11

a. May one for me, three, five, seven, nine, eleven, thirteen, fifteen, seventeen, nineteen, twenty-one, twenty-three, twenty-five, twenty-seven, twenty-nine, thirty-one, thirty-three; ‖ *b.* four, eight, twelve, sixteen, twenty, twenty-four, twenty-eight, thirty-two, thirty-six, forty, forty-four, forty-eight; ‖ *c.* strength, instigation, the later born, inspiration, heaven, the head, the Vyaśniya, the offspring of the last, the last, the offspring of being, being, the overlord (prosper with the sacrifice).

Mantra 4:7:12

a. May strength aid us through the seven quarters, | The four distances, | Strength aid us here with the All-Gods | For the gaining of wealth. ‖ *b.* May all the Marutas today be present, all, to aid us, | Be the fires all enkindled present; | May the All-Gods come to us with aid; | All wealth, and strength, be ours. ‖ *c.* O Gods, come in your cars of gold | For the instigation of strength, | Agni, Indra, Bṛihaspati | And the Marutas to drink the Soma. ‖ *d.* For each prize, aid us, O ye steeds, | For the rewards, O ye wise, immortal, righteous ones; | Drink of this mead, rejoice in it; | Delighted go by paths on which the Gods go. ‖ *e.* Strength is in front, in the midst of us; | Strength shall assort the Gods in due season | The instigation of strength is propitious; | In all the quarters may I become a lord of strength. ‖ *f.* Milk may I place on earth, milk on the plants, | Milk in the sky, in the atmosphere milk, | Be the quarters rich in milk for me. ‖ *g.* I unite myself with milk, with ghee, | I united myself. with waters and plants; | Strength may I win, O Agni. ‖ *h.* Night and the dawn, one-minded, but of various form | United suckle one child; | The radiant one shineth between sky and earth; | The Gods, granters of wealth, support Agni. ‖ *i.* Thou art the ocean, full of mist, granting moisture, blow over me with healing, with wonder-working; hail! Thou art of the Marutas, the horde of the Marutas, blow over me with healing, with wonder-working; hail! Thou art the helper, the worshipper, blow over me with healing, with wonder-working; hail!

Mantra 4. 7.13.

a. Agni I yoke with glory, with ghee, | The bird divine mighty in strength; | Therewith may we fly to the expanse of the ruddy one, | Mounting the heaven above the highest vault. || *b.* These are wings unaging of thee, the winged, | Wherewith thou dost smite away the Rākṣhasas, O Agni; | With these may we fly to the world of good men, | Where are the seers, the first-born, those of yore. || *c.* Thou art piling, born of the ocean, the drop, | The skilled one, the eagle, the righteous, | The golden-winged busy bird, mighty, | That hath sat down firmly in its place. || *d.* Homage be to thee; harm me not, | Thou dost stand resting on the head of all; | Within the ocean is thy heart, thy life; | Sky and earth are placed on the worlds. || *e.* Give of the water, cleave the holder of the water; from the sky, from Parjanya, from the atmosphere, from the earth, thence do ye help us with rain; thou art the head of the sky, the navel of earth, the strength of waters and plants, protection of all life, extending; homage to the way! || *f.* With that devotion wherewith the seers performed the session of sacrifice, | Kindling Agni, bearing aloft the heaven, | I set on this vault that Agni | Whom men call him for whom the spread is strewed. || *g.* Him with our wives let us pursue, O Gods, | With our sons, our brothers, or by gold, | Seizing the vault in the world of good action, | Above the third firmament, in the light of the sky. || *h.* To the middle of speech hath the busy one arisen, | Agni here, lord of the good, the wise; | Established on the back of the earth, the radiant one, | He casteth beneath his feet the combatants. || *i.* Let Agni here, the most manly, strength-bestowing, | Of a thousand shapes, shine unwearying, | Radiant in the midst of the ocean; | Do ye approach the abodes divine. || *k.* Move ye forward, go ye long together; | Make ye the paths Gods travelled, O Agni; | In this highest abode | O All-Gods, sit ye with the sacrificer. || *l.* That by which thou bearest a thousand, | Thou, O Agni, all wealth, | With that highest (path) for the Gods to travel, | Do thou bear this sacrifice for us. || *m.* Awake, O Agni; be roused for him; | With this one do thou create sacrifice and donation; | Making thee, his father, young again | He hath stretched over thee this covering. || *n.* This is thy due place of birth, | Whence born thou didst shine, | Mount it, O Agni, knowing it, | And make our wealth increase.

Mantra 4:7:14

a. May radiance be mine, O Agni, in rival invocations, | May we, kindling thee, make ourselves to prosper; | To me let the four quarters bow; | With thee as overseer may we conquer the fighters. || *b.* Let all the Gods be at my invocation, | The Marutas with Indra, Viṣhṇu, Agni; | May the broad atmosphere be my guardian; | May the wind blow for me unto this desire. || *c.* May the Gods bestow wealth upon me through sacrifice; | May blessing be mine, and mine divine invocation; | The divine sacrificers of old shall win for us; | Unharmed may we be in ourselves, rich in heroes. || *d.* For me let them sacrifice whatever sacrifices are mine | Fulfilled be the intent of my mind; | No sin whatever may I commit; | May the All-Gods befriend me. || *e.* O ye six spaces divine, for us make broad room; | O ye All-Gods, here show your prowess; | May we not lose offspring nor ourselves; | May we not fall victims to our foe, O king Soma. || *f.* Agni, driving away wrath in front, | As guardian unfailing, do thou guard us on all sides; | Let thy foes turn away again | And be their plotting at home ruined through thy foresight. || *g.* The creator of creators, lord of the world, | The God Savitar overcoming enmity, | This sacrifice may the two Aśvins and Bṛihaspati, | The Gods (guard) and protect the sacrificer from misfortune. || *h.* May the bull, wide extending, afford us protection rich in food, | He much invoked in this invocation; | O thou of the bay steeds, be gracious unto our progeny; | Harm us not, abandon not us. || *i.* May our rivals depart; | With Indra and Agni we overthrow them; | The Vasus, the Rudras, the Ādityas have made me | A dread corrector and overlord, sky reaching. || *k.* Hitherward do we summon Indra from thence, | Him who is winner of cows, of booty, and winner too of horses; | Do thou accept this sacrifice at our invocation; | Ally of it we make thee, O lord of the bays.

The Horse Sacrifice

Mantra 4:7:15

a. Of Agni first I reckon, the wise ones, | Him of the five folk whom many kindle; | Him who hath entered into every concourse do we implore, | May he relieve us from tribulation. || *b.* Him whose is that which breatheth, which winketh, which moveth, | Whose alone is that which has been born and is being born, | Agni I praise; I invoke seeking aid, | May he relieve us from tribulation. || *c.* Of Indra first I reckon, the wise one; | Praise of the slayer of Vṛitra hath come to me, | He who cometh at the call of the generous doer of good deeds, | May he relieve us from tribulation. || *d.* Him who in might leadeth forth the host for battle, | Who commingleth the three possessions; | Indra I praise; I invoke seeking aid, | May he relieve us from tribulation. || *e.* Of you, O Mitra and Varuṇa, I reckon | Take heed of him, O ye of true strength, strong ones, whom ye afflict; | Ye who go in might against the king in his chariot, | May ye relieve us from sin. || *f.* You whose chariot with straight reins, of true path, | Approacheth to spoil him who acteth falsely, | Mitra and Varuṇa I praise; I invoke seeking aid, | May ye relieve us from sin. || *g.* We venerate the ordinances of Vāyu and of Savitar, | Who support that which hath life and guard it, | Who surround all things; | May ye relieve us from sin. || *h.* The best blessings have come to us | In the realm of the two Gods; || I praise Vāyu and Savitar; I invoke seeking aid, | May ye relieve us from sin. || *i.* Best charioteers of carmen, I hail for aid, | That go most smoothly with well-guided steeds; | Ye whose might among the Gods, O Gods, is unextinguished, | May ye relieve us from sin. || *k.* What time ye came to the wedding of Sūrya, | Choosing a seat together on the three-wheeled (chariot), || I praise you, Aśvins, Gods, invoke seeking aid, | May ye relieve us from sin. || *l.* Of the Marutas I reckon; may they aid us; | May they all help this every prayer (of ours); | The swift, easily controlled (ones) I call to help, | May they relieve us from evil. || *m.* The sharp weapon, strong and mighty, | The divine host keen in the battles, || I praise the Gods, the Marutas; I invoke seeking aid, | May they relieve us from evil. || *n.* Of the Gods I reckon; may they aid us; | May they all help this every prayer; | The swift, easily controlled (ones) I call to help, | That they may relieve us from evil. || *o.* That which now consumeth me | From deed of men or Gods, || I praise the All-Gods; I invoke seeking aid, | May they free us from evil. || *p.* Us today Anumati. || *q.* O Anumati, thou. || *r.* Vaiśvānara for aid to us. || *s.* Present in sky. || *t.* Those that expanded with unmeasured might, | Those that became the supports of wealth, || I praise sky and earth; I invoke seeking aid, | May ye relieve us from tribulation. || *u.* O ye broad firmaments, make room for us; | O rulers of the field, aid us; || I praise sky and earth; I invoke seeking aid, | May ye relieve us from tribulation. || *v.* Whatever sin we commit against thee, | As men are wont in ignorance, O most young, | Make us blameless before Aditi, | Remove our evil deeds on all sides, O Agni. || *w.* Even as ye did set free, O bright ones, | O ye that are worthy of offering, the buffalo cow bound by the foot, | So do thou remove from us tribulation; | Be our life prolonged further, O Agni.

Kāṇḍa 5.

The Explanation of the Piling of the Fire Altar

Prapāṭhaka 1

The Placing of the Fire in the Fire-pan

Mantra 5:1:1

He offers the Savitar offerings, for instigation. He offers with (an oblation) ladled up four times, cattle have four feet; verily he wins cattle; the quarters are four; verily he finds support in the quarters. The metres departed from the Gods (saying), 'We will not carry your oblation without sharing (in it)'; for them they kept this (oblation) ladled up four times, for the Puronuvākyā the Yājyā, the deity, the Vaṣhaṭ call; in that he offers what has been ladled up four times, he delights the metres, and they delighted carry to the Gods his oblation. If he desire of a man, 'May he become worse,' he should offer each separately for him; verily he makes him severed from the libations; he becomes worse. If he desire of a man, 'May he become better,' he should offer all for him continuously; verily he makes him master of the libation; he becomes better. This is the mastering of the sacrifice. He abandons prosperity in the beginning of the sacrifice who departs from Agni as the deity; these offerings to Savitar number eight, the Gāyatrī has eight syllables, Agni is connected with the

Gāyatrī; verily he does not abandon prosperity at the beginning of the sacrifice, nor Agni as the deity. The offerings to Savitar number eight, the libation (as a whole) is the ninth; verily he extends the threefold (Stoma) at the beginning of the sacrifice. If he desire, 'May I confer on the metres the glory of the sacrifice,' he should make a Ṛich verse last; verily he confers on the metres the glory of the sacrifice. If he desire, 'May I confer on the sacrificer the glory of the sacrifice,' he should make a Yajus formula last; verily he confers on the sacrificer the glory of the sacrifice. 'By the Ṛich make the Stoma to flourish,' he says, for prosperity. With four (verses) he takes up the spade; the metres are four; verily (he takes it up) with the metres. 'On the instigation of God Savitar,' he says, for instigation. Agni went away from the Gods, he entered the reed; he resorted to the hole which is formed by the perforation of the reed; the spade is perforated to make it his birthplace; wherever he lived, that became black; (the spade) is stained, for perfection of form; it is pointed at both ends, for the winning of light both hence and from yonder world; it is a fathom long; so much is the strength in man; (verily it is) commensurate with his strength; it is unlimited in girth, to win what is unlimited; that tree which has fruit is strong among trees, the reed bears fruit, (the spade) is of reed, to win strength.

Mantra 5:1:2

That part of the sacrifice is unsuccessful which is performed with no Yajus. 'This bond of order they grasped,' (with these words) he takes up the horse's halter, to make a Yajus and to make successful the sacrifice. 'Swiftly run hither, O steed,' (with these words) he halters the horse; verily he proclaims its greatness in this form. 'Yoke ye the ass,' (with these words) (he halters) the ass; verily he establishes the ass on the non-existent; therefore the ass is less real than the horse. 'In each need more strong,' he says; verily in each need he yokes him; 'in each contest we invoke,' he says; the contest is food; verily he wins food. 'As friends, Indra to aid us,' he says; verily he wins power. Agni went away from the Gods, him Prajāpati found; the horse is connected with Prajāpati, with the horse he collects (it), for the finding (of Agni). Now confusion occurs in that they perform the same thing with a better and worse (instrument), for the ass is worse than the horse; they lead the horse in front to avoid confusion; therefore the worse follows after the better. Many are the foes of the man who waxes great, he waxes great as it were who piles the fire, the steed has a thunderbolt; 'hastening come hither, trampling the enemy,' he says; verily he tramples with the thunderbolt on the evil foe; 'from the lordship of Rudra,' he says; cattle are connected with Rudra; verily having begged from Rudra cattle he acts for his own interest. 'With Pūṣhan as fellow,' he says; Pūṣhan is the leader together of roads; (verily it serves) for attainment. The fire has dust for its abode; the Aṅgirasas brought it together before the deities; 'from the abode of earth do thou approach Agni of the dust in the mode of Aṅgiras,' he says; verily he brings it together in one abode with the deities. 'We approach Agni of the dust in the manner of Aṅgiras,' he says; verily he appropriates the strength of him whom he meets. 'The fire should be brought together after announcing it to Prajāpati,' they say; Prajāpati is this earth, the ant-heap is its ear; 'we will bear Agni of the dust in the manner of Aṅgiras,' (with these words) he pays reverence to the mound of an ant-heap; verily after announcing it to Prajāpati face to face, he brings together the fire. 'We bear Agni of the dust in the manner of Aṅgiras,' he says; verily he appropriates the strength of him whom he meets. 'Agni hath gazed along the forefront of the dawns,' he says, to light up (the heaven). 'The steed coming, from the way,' 'Coming to earth, O steed,' he says; verily he wishes for it with the first and obtains it with the second; with two (verses) he makes it come, for support; (with two) of the same form, therefore cattle are born of the same form. 'Thy back is the sky, thy abode earth,' he says; Prajāpati quickened him from these worlds; verily he proclaims its greatness in this form. The steed is possessed of the thunderbolt, by its incisors it is more puissant than those with one row of incisors, by its hair than those with two rows; him whom he hates he should conceive as beneath its feet; verily with the thunderbolt he lays him low.

Mantra 5:1:3

'The strong steed hath stepped forth,' with these two (verses) he makes it step forth; (with two) of the same form, therefore cattle are born of the same form. He pours water down; where there are waters, there Plants take root, and where plants take root cattle find support through them, the sacrifice (finds support) in cattle, the sacrificer in the sacrifice, offspring in the sacrificer; therefore he pours water down, for support. If the Adhvaryu were to pour the libation on that which is without fire, the Adhvaryu would be blind, the Rākṣhasas would destroy the sacrifice; he puts gold down and offers; verily he pours on what has fire, the Adhvaryu does not become blind, the Rākṣhasas do not destroy the sacrifice. 'I touch Agni with mind, with ghee,' he says, for with mind man approaches the sacrifice; 'who lordeth it over all the worlds,' he says, for he lords it over all; 'broad, vast, with pervading vital power,' he says, for he born small becomes great; 'most extensive, impetuous, winning food,' he says; verily he makes pleasant food for him; all is pleasant for him who knows thus. 'I touch thee with speech, with ghee,' he says; therefore what a man conceives with mind he utters with speech; 'with friendly (mind) he says, to smite away the Rākṣhasas; 'with mortal glory, with engaging colour, Agni,' he says; verily he bestows beauty upon him; he is possessed of beauty who knows thus. By mind must he obtain that libation which the Adhvaryu offers in that which is without fire; he offers with two verses containing the word 'mind,' to obtain the two libations; with two (he offers), for support. As the beginning of the sacrifice is performed the Rākṣhasas are fain to destroy the sacrifice; now then is this (place) the beginning of the sacrifice when the libation comes upon it; he draws a line around, to smite away the Rākṣhasas; with three (verses) he draws a line around, Agni is threefold; verily from the whole extent of Agni he smites away the Rākṣhasas; with a Gāyatrī verse he draws a line around, the Gāyatrī is brilliance; verily with brilliance, he encircles him; with a Triṣhṭubh verse he draws a line around, the Triṣhṭubh is power; verily he encircles him with power; with an Anuṣhṭubh verse he draws a line around, the Anuṣhṭubh, envelops all the metres, (verily it serves) for complete attainment; with the Anuṣhṭubh in the middle (he draws), the Anuṣhṭubh is speech, therefore from the middle we speak with speech; with the Gāyatrī first he draws, then with the Anuṣhṭubh, then with the Triṣhṭubh; the Gāyatrī is brilliance, the Anuṣhṭubh the sacrifice, the Triṣhṭubh power; verily he encircles the sacrifice, with brilliance and power, on both sides.

Mantra 5:1:4

'On the instigation of the God Savitar thee,' (with these words) he digs, for instigation. Then with it he produces smoke; 'Full of light, thee, O Agni, of fair aspect,' he says, and thereby he produces light. Agni on birth afflicted creatures with pain, him the Gods appeased by the half-verse; 'auspicious and harmless to offspring,' he says; verily he makes him appeased for offspring. He digs with two (verses), for support. 'Thou art the back of the waters,' (with these words) he takes the lotus leaf; the lotus leaf is the back of the waters; verily with its own form he takes it. He gathers with a lotus leaf; the lotus leaf is the birthplace of Agni; verily he gathers Agni with his own birthplace. He gathers with a black antelope skin; the black antelope skin is the sacrifice; verily he gathers the sacrifice with the sacrifice. If he were to gather with the skin of tame animals he would afflict with pain tame animals; he gathers with a black antelope skin; verily he afflicts with pain wild animals; therefore of animals of even birth the wild animals are the smaller, for they are afflicted with pain. He gathers on the hairy side, for on that side is it pure. He strews the lotus leaf and the black antelope skin together; the black antelope skin is this (earth), the lotus leaf yonder (sky); verily on both sides he encircles him with these two. Agni departed from the Gods, Atharvan perceived him; 'Atharvan first pressed thee out, O Agni,' he says; verily he gathers him with him who perceived him. 'Thee, O Agni, from the lotus,' he says, for in the lotus leaf he found him reposing. 'Thee the sage, Dadhyach,' he says; Dadhyach, son of Atharvan, was full of brilliance; verily he bestows brilliance upon him. 'Thee Pāthya Vṛishan,' he says; verily with the latter (verse) he hails him whom he has previously addressed. He gathers with four (verses), the metres are four; verily (he gathers) with the metres. (He gathers) with Gāyatrī verses for a Brahman, for the Brahman is connected with the Gāyatrī; with Triṣhṭubh verses for a Rājanya, for the Rājanya is connected with the Triṣhṭubh; if he desire of a man, 'May he be richer,' he should gather for him with both sets; verily upon him he bestows brilliance and power together. With eight (verses) he gathers; the Gāyatrī has eight syllables, Agni is connected with the Gāyatrī; verily he gathers all the extent of Agni. 'Sit thou, O Hotar,' he says; verily he makes the deities sit down for him; 'The Hotar down,' (with these words he makes) men (sit down); 'Sit thou down,' (with these words he makes) birds (sit down); 'Be born noble in the forefront of the days,' he says; verily he produces for him the common session of Gods and men.

Mantra 5:1:5

In that he digs he acts as it were harshly to this (earth); he pours water down, the waters are appeased; verily with the waters appeased he calms her pain. 'May for thee Vāyu, Mātariśvan unite,' he says; Vāyu is breath; verily with breath he unites her breath; 'may for thee Vāyu,' he says; therefore the rain speeds from the sky, made to fall by Vāyu 'To him, O Goddess, be Vaṣhaṭ with thee,' he says; the seasons are six; verily upon the seasons he bestows rain; therefore in all the seasons it rains. If he were to utter the Vaṣhaṭ cry, his Vaṣhaṭ cry would be exhausted; if he were not to utter the Vaṣhaṭ cry, the Rākṣhasas would destroy the sacrifice; 'Vaṭ,' he says; verily, mysteriously he utters the Vaṣhaṭ cry; his Vaṣhaṭ cry is not exhausted, the Rākṣhasas do not destroy the sacrifice. 'Well born with light,' (with these words) he ties up with an Anuṣhṭubh verse; all the metres are the Anuṣhṭubh, Agni's dear body is the metres; verily he encircles him with his dear body; likely to win a garment is he who knows thus. Agni when tied up is connected with Varuṇa; 'Arise, thou of fair sacrifice,' 'Arise, erect, to aid us,' with two (verses) addressed to Savitar he rises up; verily, instigated by Savitar, he sends aloft the wrath of Varuṇa that is in him; with two (verses) (he arises), for support. 'Born, thou art the child of the two worlds, he says; the two worlds are these two (sky and earth), Agni is the child of the two; therefore he says thus. 'O Agni, brilliant, distributed among the plants,' he says, for when they distribute him, then he becomes more brilliant. 'Thou didst come thundering from thy mothers,' he says; his mothers are the plants; verily from them he makes him to fall. 'Be firm, of strong limbs,' (with these words) he places (Agni) on the ass; verily thereby he yokes it for strength. He gathers with the ass; therefore the ass is the best burden-gatherer of animals. He gathers with the ass; therefore the ass, even when grazing is bad, becomes fat beyond other animals, for by it they gather food and light. He gathers with the ass; therefore the ass, being of double seed, is born as the least of animals, for Agni burns his place of birth. Now he is mounted upon offspring, and is strong to burn with pain offspring. 'Be auspicious, for offspring,' he says; verily he makes him calm for offspring. '(For offspring) of man, O Aṅgiras,' he says, for offspring are of men. 'Scorch not sky and earth, nor the atmosphere, nor the trees,' he says; verily he makes him calm for these worlds. 'Let the steed advance, thundering,' he says, for he is a steed. 'The sounding, the donkey, the flier,' he says, for the seers called him the 'donkey'. 'Bearing Agni of the dust,' he says, for he bears Agni. 'May he fall not before his day,' he says; verily he bestows life upon him; therefore an ass lives all its days; therefore are men afraid when an ass perishes before its day. 'The strong, bearing the strong Agni,' he says, for he is strong, and Agni is strong. 'Germ of the waters, him of the ocean,' he says, for Agni is the germ of the waters. 'O Agni, come hither for enjoyment,' (at these words) the two worlds burst apart; in that he says, 'O Agni, come hither for enjoyment,' it is for the separation (*vityai*) of these worlds. He, having left his place and not having reached a support, then thinks of the Adhvaryu and the sacrificer; 'holy order and truth,' he says; holy order is this (earth), truth is yonder (sky); verily in these two he establishes him, and neither the Adhvaryu nor the sacrificer is ruined. Agni when tied up, as Varuṇa, attacks the sacrificer; 'O plants, do ye accept Agni here,' he says, for atonement. 'Casting aside all hostilities, all evil imaginings,' he says, to smite away the Rākṣhasas 'Sitting down, may he smite away from us misfortune,' he says, for support. 'O plants, do ye rejoice in him,' he says; Agni's portion is the plants; verily he unites him with them. 'Rich in flowers and having fair leaves,' he says; therefore plants produce fruit. 'This germ of yours, of due season, hath sat him in his ancient seat,' he says; verily in those he establishes them from whom he makes him to fall. With two verses he deposits (it), for support.

Mantra 5:1:6

Agni when tied up is connected with Varuṇa; 'With extending blaze,' (with these words) he unloosens (him); verily, instigated by Savitar, he lets loose on all sides the wrath of Varuṇa that is in him. He pours water down; the waters are appeased; verily by the waters appeased he calms his pain; with three (verses) he pours (it) down, Agni is three fold; verily he calms Agni's pain throughout his whole extent. 'Mitra having united the earth,' he says; Mitra is the auspicious one of the Gods; verily with him he unites him, for atonement. If he were to unite him with sherds of domestic pots, he would afflict domestic pots with pain; he unites (him) with fragments of broken pots; these are not used for life; verily he afflicts them with pain. He unites (him) with sand, for support, and for healing. He unites (him) with goat-hair; the female goat is Agni's dear form; verily he unites him with his dear form, and thus with brilliance. He unites him with the hairs of a black antelope skin; the black antelope skin is the sacrifice; verily he unites the sacrifice with the sacrifice. 'The Rudras, having gathered together the earth,' he says; these deities first gathered him together; verily with them he gathers him together. 'Thou art the head of Makha,' he says; Makha is the sacrifice, the fire-pan is his head; therefore he says thus. 'Ye are the two feet of the sacrifice,' he says, for these are the two feet of the sacrifice; and also (it serves) for support. He hands (the pan) over with one set (of verses), and addresses it with another, to make a pairing. He makes it with a triple stand; these worlds are three; (verily it serves) to obtain these worlds. He makes (it) with the metres; the metres are strength; verily he makes it with strength. He makes a hole with a Yajus, for discrimination. He makes it so great, of equal girth with Prajāpati, the beginning of the sacrifice. He makes it with two breasts, for the milking of sky and earth; he makes it of four breasts, for the milking of cattle; he makes it of eight breasts, for the milking of the metres. For him who practises witchcraft he should make it nine cornered; verily gathering together the threefold thunderbolt he hurls it at his foe, to lay him low. 'Having made the great pan,' (with these words) he deposits (it); verily he establishes it among the deities.

Mantra 5:1:7

With seven (verses) he fumigates; the breaths in the head are seven, the pan is the head of the sacrifice; verily he places the breaths in the head of the sacrifice; therefore seven are the breaths in the head. He fumigates with horse-dung; the horse is connected with Prajāpati; (verily it serves) to connect it with its place of birth. 'May Aditi thee,' he says; Aditi is this (earth); verily with Aditi in Aditi he digs, to avoid injury to it, for one hurts not oneself. 'May the wives of the Gods thee,' he says; the wives of the Gods made it first; verily with them he places it. 'May the Dhiṣhaṇās thee,' he says; the Dhiṣhaṇās are the sciences; verily he enkindles it with the sciences. 'May the wives thee,' he says; the wives are the metres; verily with the wives he makes it cooked. 'May the protectors, he says; the protectors are the Hotar's offices; verily with the Hotar's offices he cooks it. 'May the women thee,' he says; the women are the wives of the Gods; verily with them he cooks it. With six (verses) he cooks; the seasons are six; verily with the seasons he cooks it. 'May they cook,' he says twice; therefore twice in the year does the corn ripen. The pan when enkindled is connected with Varuṇa; he approaches it with (a verse) addressed to Mitra, for atonement. 'May the God Savitar dig thee out,' he says; verily, instigated by Savitar, he digs it out with holy power and with the deities. 'Breaking not, O earth, fill the regions, the quarters,' he says; therefore Agni shines along all the quarters. 'Arise, become great, stand upright, be thou firm,' he says, for support. A bowl that is not poured upon is connected with the Asuras; he pours upon it; verily he makes it to be with the Gods; with goats' milk he pours upon it; the milk of the goat is the highest form of draught; verily he pours upon it with the highest draught; (he pours) with a Yajus, for discrimination. He pours with the metres; with the metres it is made; verily with the metres he pours upon the metres.

Mantra 5:1:8

With twenty-one beans he approaches the head of the man; beans are impure, the man's head is impure; verily by the impure he redeems its impurity and making it pure takes it. There are twenty-one; man is composed of twenty-one parts; (verily they serve) to obtain man. The man's head is impure as bereft of the breaths; he deposits (it near) an ant-heap pierced in seven places; the breaths in the head are seven; verily he unites it with the breaths, to make it pure. Of all those that were comrades of death Yama holds the overlordship; he sings the verses of Yama; verily from Yama he redeems it; with three he sings; three are these worlds; verily from these worlds he redeems it; therefore one should not give to one who sings, for the Gāthā appropriates it. To the fires he offers animals; the fires are desires; verily he wins his desires. If he were not to offer the animals, then he would not obtain animals; if he were to let them go after circumambulation with fire, he would disturb the sacrifice; if he were to keep them until the conclusion, the heads would be exhausted; in that he offers the animals, he wins thereby animals; in that he lets them go after circumambulation with fire, (it serves) to prevent the exhaustion of the heads; he concludes (the rite) with (an animal) for Prajāpati; Prajāpati is the sacrifice; verily he concludes the sacrifice in the sacrifice. Prajāpati created offspring, he thought himself empty, he saw these April (verses), with them from the head he satisfied himself. In that there are these April verses, and Prajāpati is the sacrifice, he satisfies the sacrifice from the beginning with them. They are of unlimited metres; Prajāpati is unlimited; (verily they serve) to obtain Prajāpati The pairs are deficient and redundant, for propagation; hairy by name is that metre of Prajāpati, animals are hairy; verily he wins animals. There are all forms in these; all forms are made when Agni has to be piled up, therefore these appertain to Agni, to be piled. Twenty-one kindling-(verses) be repeats; the twenty-onefold (Stoma) is light; verily he attains light, and a support besides, for the twenty-one fold (Stoma) is support. Twenty-four (verses) he recites; the year has twenty-four half-months, Agni Vaiśvānara is the year; verily straightway he wins Vaiśvānara He recites them straight on, for the world of heaven is as it were going straight away. 'Let the half-years, the seasons, increase thee, O Agni ', he says; verily with the half-years he causes Agni to increase, with the seasons the year. 'Illuminate all the quarters of the earth,' he says; therefore Agni illuminates all the quarters. 'The Aśvins removed death from him,' he says; verily from him he repels death. 'We from the darkness,' he says; the darkness is the evil one; verily from him he smites away the evil one. 'We have come to the highest light,' he says; the highest light is yonder sun; verily he attains unity with the sun. The year lags not, his future fails not, for whom these are performed. The last he recites with the word 'light' in it; verily he bestows on him light above, to reveal the world of heaven.

Mantra 5:1:9

With six (verses) he consecrates; the seasons are six; verily he consecrates him with the seasons. With seven he consecrates; the metres are seven; verily he consecrates him with the metres. 'Let every man of the God that leads,' with the final Anuṣhṭubh he offers; the Anuṣhṭubh is speech; therefore speech is the highest of the breaths. The first quarter foot is deficient by one syllable; therefore men live upon the incomplete part of speech. He offers with a full (one), for Prajāpati is full as it were; (verily it serves) to obtain Prajāpati; he offers with one that is deficient, for from the deficient Prajāpati created offspring; (verily it serves) for the creation of offspring. If he were to heat it on the flame, he would win what has been, if on the embers, what is to be; he heats it on the embers; verily he wins what is to be, for what is to be is greater than what has been. With two verses he heats (it); the sacrificer has two feet; (verily it serves) for support. The pan is gathered together with holy power and the Yajus; if it should break, the sacrificer would be ruined, and his sacrifice destroyed. 'O Mitra, do thou heat this pan,' he says; Mitra is holy power; verily on holy power he establishes it; the sacrificer is not ruined, nor is his sacrifice destroyed. If it should break, he should unite it with the selfsame potsherds; that is the atonement for it. If a man has attained prosperity, he should for him deposit (the fire) after producing it by friction; this is one that has succeeded; verily he approaches his own deity. For him who desires prosperity should be used (the fire) which comes to life from the pan, for from it is it produced, it is self-produced by name; verily he becomes prosperous. If he desire of a man, 'May I produce a foe for him,' he should take for him (fire) from elsewhere, and deposit it; verily straightway he produces a foe for him. From a frying-pan he should (take fire) and deposit (it) for one who desires food; in a frying-pan food is kept; verily he wins food with its birth place. He deposits Muñja-grass; Muñja is strength; verily he bestows upon him strength. Agni departed from the Gods, he entered the Krumuka wood; he deposits Krumuka; verily he wins what of Agni is there imbued. With butter he joins (it); butter is the dear home of Agni; verily he unites him with his dear abode, and with brilliance also. He puts on (a stick) of Vikaṅkata wood; verily he wins radiance; he puts on one of Śamī, for atonement. 'Do thou sit down in the lap of this mother,' with three (verses) he adores (the fire) when born; three are these worlds; verily he attains reputation in these worlds; verily also he bestows breaths on himself.

Mantra 5:1:10.

Formerly Agni would not burn what was not cut by the axe, but Prayoga, the seer, made that acceptable to him. 'Whatever logs we place on thee,' (with these words) he puts on a kindling-stick; verily he makes what is not cut by the axe acceptable to him; all is acceptable to him who knows thus. He puts on one of Udumbara wood; the Udumbara is strength; verily he confers strength upon him. Prajāpati created Agni; him on creation the Rākṣhasas were fain to destroy; he saw that (hymn) of the Rakṣhas-slaying (one); therewith he smote away the Rākṣhasas; in that it is (the hymn) of the Rakṣhas-slaying one, thereby he drives away the Rākṣhasas from Agni when born. He puts on one of Aśvattha wood; of trees the Aśvattha is the overcomer of foes; (verily it serves) for victory. He puts on one of Vikaṅkata; verily he wins light. He puts on one of Śamī wood, for atonement. 'Sharpened is my holy power,' 'Their arms have I uplifted,' (with these words) he makes him speak over the last two Udumbara (sticks); verily by means of the holy power he quickens the kingly power, and by the kingly power the holy power; therefore a Brahman who has a princely person is superior to another Brahman; therefore a prince who has a Brahman is superior to another prince. Now Agni is death, gold is immortality; he puts a gold plate within; verily he severs immortality from death; it has twenty-one projections, the worlds of the Gods are twenty-one, the twelve months, the four seasons, these three worlds, and as twenty-first yonder sun; so many are the worlds of the Gods; verily from them he severs his foe. By means of the projections the Gods reduced the Asuras to straits (*nirbāde*); that is the reason why projections (*nirbādhāḥ*) have their names; it is covered with projections; verily he reduces his foes to straits. He puts (it) on with a verse addressed to Savitar, for instigation. 'Night and the dawn,' with (this as) second; verily he raises him with day and night. 'The Gods, granters of wealth, support Agni,' be says; the Gods, granters of wealth, are the breaths; verily having raised him with day and night he supports him with the breaths. Sitting he puts (it) on; therefore offspring are born sitting; the black antelope skin is above; gold is brilliance, the black antelope skin is holy power; verily on both sides he encircles him, with brilliance and with holy power. The sling is of six fathoms in extent; the seasons are six; verily he raises him with the seasons; if it is of twelve fathoms, (he raises him) with the year. It is of Muñja-grass; the Muñja is strength; verily he unites him with strength. 'Thou art the bird of fair feathers,' (with these words) he gazes; verily he declares his greatness in that form. 'Go to the sky, fly to the heaven,' he says; verily he makes him to go to the world of heaven.

The Āprī Hymn for the Horse Sacrifice

Mantra 5:1:11

a. Enkindled, decking the store-room of prayers, | Swelling with sweet butter, O Agni, | Steed bearing the strong drink, O all-knower, | Carry it to the dear place of the Gods. ‖ *b.* With ghee adorning the paths leading to the Gods, | Let the strong one, wise, go to the Gods; | May thee, O courser, the regions attend, | Bestow strength on this sacrificer. ‖ *c.* To be praised thou art, and to be celebrated, O steed; | Swift and pure art thou, O courser; | May Agni in unison with the Gods, the Vasus, | Bear thee, a glad messenger, he the all-knower. ‖ *d.* Rejoicing in the strewn grass, well strewed, | That doth extend wide and broad on the earth, | Joined with the Gods, may Aditi in unison, | Bestowing pleasantness, cause it to prosper. ‖ *c.* These happy (doors), all formed, | Opening with their sides, with the centre, | Lofty and sounding, adorning themselves, | The doors divine, may they be of pleasant entrance. ‖ *f.* Moving between Mitra and Varuṇa, | Well knowing the beginning of sacrifices, | The two dawns for you, rich in gold, rich in adornment, ‖ I settle here in the birthplace of holy order. ‖ *g.* First for you have I made glad the two, who share one car, fair of hue, | The Gods that gaze on all the worlds, | Those that ordain your ordinances, | The two Hotars, that indicate the light in its place. ‖ *h.* May Bhāratī with the Ādityas love our sacrifice; | Sarasvatī with the Rudras hath holpen us, | And Iḍā invoked with the Vasus in unison; | Our sacrifice, O Goddesses, place ye with the immortals. ‖ *i.* Tvashṭar begot the hero with love for the Gods; | From Tvashṭar is born the courser, the swift steed; | Tvashṭar produced all this world; | The maker of much do thou offer to, as Hotar ‖ *k.* May the steed, anointed with glee, of his own impulse | Go to the Gods in due season to their abode; | May the forest lord knowing the world of the Gods, | Bear the oblations made ready by Agni. ‖ *l.* Waxing with the fervour of Prajāpati, | Immediately on birth, O Agni, thou didst support the sacrifice | As harbinger with the oblation offered with Hail! | Do thou go; let the Gods eat the oblation duly.

Prapāṭhaka 2.

The Preparation of the Ground for the Fire

Mantra 5:2:1

Headed by Vishṇu the Gods won finally these worlds by the metres; in that he strides the strides of Vishṇu, the sacrificer becoming Vishṇu wins finally these worlds. 'Thou art the step of Vishṇu, overcoming hostility,' he says; the earth is connected with the Gāyatrī, the atmosphere with the Trishṭubh, the sky with the Jagatī, the quarters with the Anushṭubh; verily he wins in order these worlds with the metres. Prajāpati created Agni; he being created went away from him; he followed him with this (verse), 'He hath cried'; with it he won the home dear to Agni; in that he repeats this (verse), he wins thereby the home dear to Agni. Now he who steps the strides of Vishṇu is apt as he goes away to be burnt up; he turns with four (verses); the. metres are four, Agni's dear body is the metres; verily he turns round on his dear body; he turns round from left to right; verily he turns round on his own strength; therefore the right side of the body is the stronger; verily also does he turn with the turning of the sun. Varuṇa seized Śunaḥśepa Ājīgarti, he saw this verse addressed to Varuṇa, by it he freed himself from the noose of Varuṇa; Varuṇa seizes him who takes the fire-pan; 'From us the highest knot, O Varuṇa,' he says; verily thereby he frees himself from Varuṇa's noose. 'I have drawn thee,' he says, for he draws him. 'Be thou firm and motionless,' he says, for support. 'Let all the folk desire thee,' he says; verily with the folk he unites him. 'In him establish the kingdom,' he says; verily in him he makes the kingdom to abide. If he desire of a man, 'May he be a ruler,' he should think of him with his mind; verily he becomes a ruler. 'In greatness he hath risen erect in the van of the dawns,' he says; verily he makes him the first of his peers. 'Emerging from the darkness,' he says; verily he smites away darkness from him. 'He hath come with the light,' he says; verily he bestows light upon him. He places him with four (verses); the metres are four; verily with the metres (he places him); with an Atichandas as the last; the Atichandas is the highest of metres; verily he makes him the highest of his peers; it contains the word 'sit' (*sad*); verily he makes him attain reality (*sat-tvām*). With (the hymn) of Vatsaprī he reverences (him); by that did Vatsaprī Bhālandana win the home dear to Agni; verily by it he wins the home dear to Agni. It has eleven (verses); verily in eleven places he bestows strength on the sacrificer. By the Stoma the Gods prospered in this world, by the metres in yonder world; the hymn of Vatsaprī is the type of the Stoma; in that he pays reverence with (the hymn) of Vatsaprī, he wins with it this world; in that he strides the steps of Vishṇu, he wins by them yonder world. On the first day he strides forth, on the next day he pays reverence; therefore the minds of some creatures are set on energy, those of others on rest; therefore the active lords it over him who takes his ease therefore the active fixes upon a man who takes his ease. He clenches his fist, he restrains his speech, for support.

Mantra 5:2:2

'O lord of food, accord us food,' he says; the lord of food is Agni; verily he grants him food. 'Uninjurious, impetuous,' he says; he means in fact 'free from disease'. 'Do thou further the donor, bestow strength on our bipeds, our quadrupeds,' he says; verily he invokes this blessing. 'May the All-Gods bear thee up,' he says; the All-Gods are the breaths; verily with the breaths he raises him. 'O Agni, with their thoughts,' he says; with the purpose for which he raises him, he verily unites him. He places (him) with four (verses); the metres are four; verily with the metres (he places him); with an Atichandas as the last; the Atichandas is the highest of the metres; verily he makes him the highest of his peers; it contains the word 'sit' (sad); verily he makes him attain reality (*sat-tvām*). 'Come forward, O Agni, rich in light,' he says; verily he bestows light upon him. With his body he injures him whom he injures; 'Harm not our offspring with thy body,' he says; verily for his offspring he makes him gentle. The Rākshasas infest that sacrifice where the axle creaks; 'He hath cried,' he repeats, to smite away the Rākshasas They bear (him) with a cart; verily he confers honour upon him; therefore he that has a cart and he that has a chariot are of guests the most honoured: honour is his who knows thus. 'With kindling-wood serve Agni,' (with these words) he puts a kindling-stick, made wet with ghee, upon him when put in place; that is as when hospitality with melted butter is offered to a guest on arrival; (he puts it on) with a Gāyatrī for a Brahman, for the Brahman is connected with the Gāyatrī, with a Trishṭubh for a Rājanya, for the Rājanya is connected with the Trishṭubh. He casts the ash into the waters; Agni's place of birth is in the waters; verily he makes him attain his own place of birth; with three (verses) he casts (it); Agni is threefold; verily he makes Agni attain support through all his extent. Now he casts away Agni who puts the ash into the waters; he places it (in the pan) with (verses) containing the word 'light'; verily he bestows light upon him; with two (he places it), for support. He throws away offspring and cattle who puts the ash in the waters; 'Return with strength,' 'With wealth,' (with these words) he comes back; verily he bestows upon himself offspring and cattle. 'May the Ādityas, the Rudras, the Vasus kindle thee again,' he says; these deities first kindled him; verily by them he kindles him. 'Hearken,' 'Be thou,' (with these words) he pays reverence; verily he awakens him; therefore after sleeping creatures awake. In his place he pays reverence, and therefore cattle returning go to their place.

Mantra 5:2:3

Yama holds the overlordship of the whole extent of earth; he who without asking from Yama a place of it for divine sacrifice piles up the fire is piling it for Yama. 'Go hence,' (with these words) he makes him fix (on the place); verily having asked from Yama a place of it for divine sacrifice, he piles the fire for himself. Seeking they could not find so much as an arrow point of it which was not covered with death; the Gods saw this Yajus, 'Go hence'; in that he makes him fix with this, he piles the fire on a place freed from death. He throws up (the earth); verily he smites away any impurity in it; he sprinkles water on, for atonement. He puts down sand; that is the form of Agni Vaiśvānara; verily by his form he wins Vaiśvānara He puts down salt; salt is the nourishment and the propagating; verily he piles the fire in nourishment, in propagation, and also in concord; for the salt is the concord of cattle. Sky and earth were together; separating they said, 'Let us share together what is worthy of sacrifice'. What of yonder (sky) was worthy of sacrifice, it placed in this (earth), that became salt; what of this (earth) was worthy of sacrifice, it placed in yonder (sky) and that is yonder black in the moon; when he puts down the salt he should think of yonder (black); verily he piles the fire in that of sky and earth which is worthy of sacrifice. 'This is that Agni' is Viśvāmitra's hymn; by that Viśvāmitra won the abode dear to Agni; verily by it he wins the abode dear to Agni. By the metres the Gods went to the world of heaven; he places four (bricks) pointing east the metres are four; verily by the metres the sacrificer goes to the world of heaven. As they went to the world of heaven, the quarters were confused; they put down two in front, facing the same way, and two behind, facing the same way; by them they made firm the quarters. In that he places two in front, facing the same way, and two behind, facing the same way, (it serves) to make firm the quarters; again, the metres are cattle; verily he makes cattle available for him. He places eight (bricks); the Gāyatrī has eight syllables, Agni is connected with the Gāyatrī; verily he piles Agni in his full extent. He places eight; the Gāyatrī has eight syllables; the Gāyatrī knows in truth the world of heaven; (verily it serves) to reveal the world of heaven. He places thirteen world-fillers; they make twenty-one, the twenty-onefold Stoma is a support, the Gārhapatya is a support, verily he finds support in the support of the twenty-onefold (Stoma), the Gārhapatya; he who knows thus finds support in the fire which he has piled. He who first piles (the fire) should pile in five layers; the sacrifice is fivefold, cattle are fivefold; verily he wins the sacrifice and cattle. He who piles for a second time should pile in three layers; these worlds are three; verily he finds support in these worlds. He who piles for a third time should pile in one layer; the world of heaven is in one place; verily he goes to the world of heaven by the single (layer). He makes (them) firm with mortar; therefore the bone is covered with meat; he who knows thus does not become diseased of skin. There are five layers, he makes firm with five (sets of) dust; they make up ten, the Virāj has ten syllables, the Virāj is food; verily he finds support in the Virāj, in proper food.

Mantra 5:2:4

The Agni that was before and the one in the fire-pan are at variance; 'Be united,' with four (verses) he unites them together; the metres are four, Agni's dear body is the metres; verily with his dear body he puts them in order. 'Be united, he says; therefore the kingly power unites with the holy power; in that after uniting (them) he separates (them), therefore the holy power separates from the kingly power. With the seasons they consecrate him; with the seasons likewise he must be set free; 'As a mother her son, the earth Agni of the dust,' he says; verily having consecrated him with the seasons, with the season he sets him free. With (a verse) addressed to Vaiśvānara, he takes the sling; verily he makes it ready. For Nirṛiti there are three (bricks) black, dried by a chaff fire; chaff is the portion of Nirṛiti, black is the form of Nirṛiti; verily by her own form he propitiates Nirṛiti They go to this quarter; this is the quarter of Nirṛiti; verily in her own quarter he propitiates Nirṛiti He places (it) in a self-made hole or a cleft; that is the abode of Nirṛiti; verily he propitiates Nirṛiti in her own abode. He places (them) over against the sling, the noose is connected with Nirṛiti; verily he frees him straightway from the noose of Nirṛiti He places three, man is threefold in arrangement; verily he removes by sacrifice Nirṛiti from the whole extent of man. He places them going away (from the place of sacrifice); verily he drives away Nirṛiti from him. They return without looking round, to conceal Nirṛiti Having purified, they pay reverence, for purity. To the Gārhapatya they pay reverence; verily having wandered in the world of Nirṛiti, they return, purified, to the world of the Gods. They pay reverence with one (verse); verily in one place they bestow strength on the sacrificer. 'Abode and collector of riches,' he says; rich are offspring and cattle; verily he unites him with offspring and cattle.

Mantra 5:2:5

With man's measure he metes out; man is commensurate with the sacrifice; verily he metes him with a member of the sacrifice; so great is he as a man with arms extended; so much strength is there in man; verily with strength he metes him. Winged is he, for wingless he could not fly; these wings are longer by an ell; therefore birds have strength by their wings. The wings and the tail are a fathom in breadth; so much is the strength in man, he is commensurate in strength. He metes with a bamboo; the bamboo is connected with Agni; (verily it serves) to unite him with his birthplace. With a Yajus he yokes (the team), with a Yajus he ploughs, for discrimination. He ploughs with a (team) of six oxen; the seasons are six; verily with the seasons he ploughs him. In that (he ploughs) with (a team) of twelve oxen, (he ploughs) with the year. This (earth) was afraid of excessive burning by Agni; she saw this of two sorts, ploughed and unploughed, then indeed he did not burn her excessively; in that there is ploughed and unploughed, (it serves to prevent) her being excessively burned. 'He should restrain Agni when twofold,' they say; in that there is ploughed and unploughed (it serves) to restrain Agni. So many are animals, bipeds and quadrupeds; if he were to let them loose to the east, he would give them over to Rudra; if to the south, he would deliver them to the Pitṛis; if to the west, the Rākṣhasas would destroy them; to the north he let them loose; this is the auspicious quarter of Gods and men (3); verily he lets them loose in that direction. Again he lets them loose to this quarter, the breath is yonder sun: verily he lets them loose following the breath. From left to right they turn, around their own strength they turn; therefore the right side of the body is the stronger; verily they turn with the turning of the sun. Therefore cattle depart from (us), and come back towards (us). Three by three he ploughs the furrows; verily he extends the threefold (Stoma) in the beginning of the sacrifice. He scatters plants, by holy power he wins food, in the Arka the Arka is piled. With fourteen verses he scatters; the domesticated plants are seven, the wild are seven; (verily they serve) to win both sets. He scatters (seeds) of diverse kinds of food, to win diverse foods. He scatters on the ploughed (ground), for in the ploughed plants find support. He scatters along the furrows, for propagation. In twelve furrows he scatters; the year has twelve months; verily with the year he cooks food for him. If he who piles the fire should eat of what has not been obtained, he would be separated from what has been obtained. Those trees which bear fruit he should sprinkle in the kindling-wood, to obtain what has not been obtained. From the quarters he gathers clods; verily winning the strength of the quarters, he piles the fire in the strength of the quarters; he should take a clod from the quarter where is he whom he hates, (saying), 'Food and strength do I take hence,' verily he wins from that quarter food and strength, and hungry is he who is in that quarter. He scatters over the high altar, for on the high altar is the fire piled; the high altar is cattle; verily he wins cattle; (verily it serves) for the avoidance of passing over a limb of the sacrifice.

Mantra 5:2:6

'O Agni, strength and fame are thine,' (with these words) he scatters sand; that is the hymn of Agni Vaiśvānara; verily with the hymn he wins (Agni) Vaiśvānara With six (verses) he scatters; the year has six seasons, Agni Vaiśvānara is the year; verily straightway he wins Vaiśvānara This metre is called the ocean; offspring are born like the ocean; in that he scatters sand with this (hymn), (it is) for the propagation of offspring. Indra hurled his bolt at Vṛitra; it parted into three, one third the wooden sword, one-third the chariot, one-third the sacrificial post; the interior reeds which were crushed became gravel; that is the explanation of gravel; gravel is a thunderbolt, the fire is an animal; in that he supports the fire with gravel, he encircles with the bolt cattle for him; therefore cattle are encircled with the bolt; therefore the stronger does not receive the weaker. He should support (the fire) with twenty-one (pieces of gravel) for one who desires cattle; there are seven breaths in the head, cattle are the breaths; verily he wins cattle for him by the breaths. With twenty-seven (should he support it) for one who has foes; thus making the threefold bolt he hurls it at his foe, to lay him low. He should support (it) with unnumbered ones, to win what is unnumbered. If he desire of a man, 'May he be without cattle,' then without piling the gravel in support, he should separate the sand; verily he pours forth for him the seed on all sides in (a place) not encircled; verily he becomes without cattle. If he desire of a man, 'May he be rich in cattle,' he should separate the sand, after piling the gravel; verily he pours forth for him the seed in one direction in an encircled (place), and he becomes rich in cattle. With (a verse) addressed to Soma he separates (the sand); Soma is impregnator of seed; verily he impregnates seed; with a Gāyatrī for a Brahman, for the Brahman is connected with the Gāyatrī, with a Triṣhṭubh for a Rājanya, for the Rājanya is connected with the Triṣhṭubh. To Śamyu, son of Bṛihaspati, the sacrifice did not resort; it entered the fire; it departed from the fire in the form of a black antelope, it entered the horse, it became the intermediate hoof of the horse; in that he makes the horse advance, he wins the sacrifice which has entered the horse. 'By Prajāpati must the fire be piled,' they say; the horse is connected with Prajāpati; in that he makes the horse advance, by Prajāpati he piles the fire. He puts down a lotus leaf; the lotus leaf is the birthplace of the fire; verily he piles the fire with its own birthplace. 'Thou art the back of the waters,' (with these words) he puts (it) down; the lotus leaf is the back of the waters; verily with its form he puts it down.

Mantra 5:2:7

'The holy power born,' (with these words) he puts down the gold disk. Prajāpati created creatures with the Brahman class as first; verily the sacrificer creates offspring with the Brahman as first; 'the holy power born,' he says; therefore the Brahman is the first; the first he becomes who knows thus. The theologians say, 'Nor on earth, nor in the atmosphere, nor on sky should the fire be piled'; if he were to pile (it) on earth, he would afflict the earth with pain; nor trees, nor plants would be born; if he should pile (it) in the atmosphere, he would afflict the atmosphere with pain, the birds would not be born; if he should pile (it) in the sky, he would afflict the sky with pain, Parjanya would not rain. He puts down a gold disk; gold is immortality; verily in immortality he piles the fire, for propagation. He puts down a golden man, to support the world of the sacrificer; if he were to put it over the perforation in the brick, he would obstruct the breath of cattle and of the sacrificer; he puts it down on the south side with head to the east: he supports the world of the sacrificer; he does not obstruct the breath of cattle and the sacrificer. Or rather he does place it over the perforation of the brick, to allow the breath to pass out. 'The drop hath fallen,' (with these words) he touches it; verily he establishes it in the Hotar's offices. He puts down two ladles, one made of Kārṣhmarya and full of butter, one of Udumbara and full of curds; that made of Kārṣhmarya is this (earth), that of Udumbara is yonder (sky); verily he deposits these two (earth and sky). In silence he puts (them) down, for he should not obtain them with a Yajus; the Kārṣhmarya on the south, the Udumbara on the north; therefore is yonder (sky) higher than this (earth); the Kārṣhmarya filled with butter, the butter is a thunderbolt, the Kārṣhmarya is a thunderbolt; verily by the thunderbolt he smites away the Rākṣhasas from the south of the sacrifice; the Udumbara filled with curds, curds are cattle, the Udumbara is strength; verily he confers strength upon cattle. He puts (them) down filled; verily filled they wait on him in yonder world. 'In the Virāj should the fire be piled,' they say; the Virāj is the ladle; in that he puts down two ladles, he piles Agni in the Virāj As each beginning of the sacrifice is being performed, the Rākṣhasas seek to destroy the sacrifice; the golden disk is a beginning of the sacrifice; in that he pours butter over the gold disk, he smites away the Rākṣhasas from the beginning of the sacrifice. With five (verses) he pours butter; the sacrifice is fivefold; verily he smites away the Rākṣhasas from the whole extent of the sacrifice; he pours butter transversely; therefore animals move their limbs transversely, for support.

Mantra 5:2:8

He puts down the naturally perforated brick; the naturally perforated brick is this (earth); verily he puts down the (earth). He makes the horse sniff it; verily he bestows breath upon it; now the horse is connected with Prajāpati; verily he piles the fire with Prajāpati The first brick that is put down obstructs the breath of cattle and of the sacrificer; it is a naturally perforated one, to permit the breath to pass, and also to reveal the world of heaven. 'In the fire must the fire be piled,' they say; the Brahman is Agni Vaiśvānara, and to him should he hand over the first brick over which a Yajus has been recited; with the Brahman he should deposit it; verily in the fire he piles the fire. Now he who ignorantly puts down a brick is liable to experience misfortune. Three boons should he give, the breaths are three; (verily they serve) to guard the breaths; two only should be given, for the breaths are two; one only should be given, for the breath is one. The fire is an animal here; animals do not find pleasure in want of grass; a brick of Dūrvā grass he puts down, to support animals; with two (verses), for support. 'Arising from every stem,' he says, for it finds support with every stem; 'do thou, O Dūrvā, extend us with a thousand, a hundred,' he says; Prajāpati is connected with a thousand; (verily it serves) to obtain Prajāpati The fact that it has three lines on it is a mark of the Gods; the Gods put it down with the mark uppermost, the Asuras with the mark undermost; if he desire of a man, 'May he become richer,' he should put it down for him mark uppermost; verily he becomes richer; if he desire of a man, 'May he become worse off,' he should put his down mark undermost; verily he makes him depressed in accordance with its birthplace among the Asuras, and he becomes worse off. (The brick) has three lines on it; that with three lines is these worlds; verily he excludes its foe from these worlds. When the Aṅgirasas went to the world of heaven, the sacrificial cake becoming a tortoise crawled after them; in that he puts down a tortoise, just as one who knows a place leads straight (to it), so the tortoise leads him straight to the world of heaven. The tortoise is the intelligence of animals; in that he puts down the tortoise, animals resort there, seeing their own intelligence; in that the heads of the dead animals are deposited, a burial-ground is made; in that he puts down the living tortoise, he is no maker of a burial-ground, the tortoise is suitable for a dwelling. 'To the pious the winds honey,' (with these words) he anoints with curds, mixed with honey; verily he makes him ready; curds is a food of the village, honey of the wild; in that he anoints with curds mixed with honey, (it serves) to win both. 'May the two great ones, heaven and earth,' he says; verily with them he encircles him on both sides. He puts it down to the east, to attain the world of heaven; he puts it down to the east facing west; therefore to the east facing west the animals attend the sacrifice. If he piles the fire without a navel, (the fire) enters the navel of the sacrificer, and is liable to injure him. He puts down the mortar; this is the navel of the fire; verily he piles the fire with its navel, to avoid injury. (The mortar) is of Udumbara wood; the Udumbara is strength; verily he wins strength; in the middle he puts it down; verily in the middle he bestows strength upon him; therefore in the middle men enjoy strength. So large is it, commensurate with Prajāpati, the mouth of the sacrifice. He pounds; verily he makes food; he puts (it) down with (a verse) addressed to Viṣhṇu; the sacrifice is Viṣhṇu, the trees are connected with Viṣhṇu; verily in the sacrifice he establishes the sacrifice.

Mantra 5:2:9

The pan is the concentrated light of these lights; in that he puts down the pan, verily he wins the light from these worlds; in the middle he puts (it) down; verily he bestows upon it light; therefore in the middle we reverence the light; with sand he fills (it); that is the form of Agni Vaiśvānara; verily by his form he wins Vaiśvānara If he desire of a man, 'May he become hungry,' he should put down for one (a pan) deficient in size; if he desire of a man, 'May he eat food that fails not,' he should put it down full; verily he eats food that fails not. The man accords a thousand of cattle, the other animals a thousand; in the middle he puts down the head of the man, to give it strength. In the pan he puts (it) down; verily he makes it attain support; the head of the man is impure as devoid of breaths; the breaths are immortality, gold is immortality; on the (organs of the) breaths he hurls chips of gold; verily he makes it attain support, and unites it with the breaths. He fills (it) with curds mixed with honey, (saying) 'May I be fit to drink honey'; (he fills with curds) to be curdled with hot milk, for purity. The curds are the food of the village, honey of the wild; in that he fills (it) with curds mixed with honey, (it serves) to win both. He puts down the heads of the animals; the heads of the animals are cattle; verily he wins cattle. If he desire of a man, 'May he have no cattle,' he should put them down, looking away, for him; verily he makes cattle look away from him; he becomes without cattle. If he desire of a man, 'May he be rich in cattle,' he should put (them) down looking with (the man's head); verily he makes the cattle look with him; he becomes rich in cattle. He puts (the head) of the horse in the east looking west, that of the bull in the west looking east; the beasts other than the oxen and the horses are not beasts at all; verily he makes the oxen and the horses look with him. So many are the animals, bipeds and quadrupeds; them indeed he puts down in the fire, in that he puts down the heads of the animals. 'I appoint for thee N.N. of the forest,' he says; verily from the cattle of the village he sends pain to those of the wild; therefore of animals born at one time the animals of the wild are the smaller, for they are afflicted with pain. He puts down the head of a snake; verily he wins the brilliance that is in the snake. If he were to put it down looking with the heads of the animals, (the snakes) would bite the animals of the village; if turned away, those of the wild; he should speak a Yajus, he wins the brilliance that is in the snake, he injures not the animals of the village, nor those of the wild. Or rather should it be put down; in that he puts down, thereby he wins the brilliance that is in the serpent; in that he utters a Yajus, thereby is it appeased.

The First Layer of Bricks

Mantra 5:2:10.

The fire is an animal, now the birthplace of the animal is changed in that before the putting up of the bricks the Yajus is performed. The water bricks are seed; be puts down the water bricks; verily he places seed in the womb. Five he puts down (on the east) cattle are fivefold; verily he produces cattle for him; five on the south, the water bricks are the thunderbolt; verily with the thunderbolt he smites away the Rākṣhasas from the south of the sacrifice; five he puts down on the west, pointing east; seed is impregnated in front from behind; verily from behind he deposits seed for him in front. Five he puts down on the east, pointing west; five on the west pointing east; therefore seed is impregnated in front, offspring are born at the back. On the north he puts down five metre bricks; the metre bricks are cattle; verily he brings cattle on birth to his own dwelling. This (earth) was afraid of excessive burning by the fire; she saw these water bricks, she put them down, then (the fire) did not burn her excessively; in that he puts down the water bricks, (it is) to avoid excessive burning. She said, 'He shall eat food with holy power, for whom these shall be put down, and he who shall know them thus.' He puts down the breath-supporting (bricks); verily he places the breaths in the seed; therefore an animal is born with speech, breath, sight, and bearing. 'This one in front, the existent'; (with these words) he puts down on the east; verily with these he supports breath. 'This one on the right, the all-worker,' (with these words he puts down) on the south; verily with these he supports mind. 'This one behind, the all-extending,' (with these words he puts down) on the west; verily with these he supports sight. 'This one on the left, the light,' (with these words he puts down) on the north; verily with these he supports hearing. 'This one above, thought,' (with these words he puts down) above; verily with these he supports speech. Ten by ten he puts (them) down, to give strength. Transversely he puts (them) down; therefore transversely do animals move their limbs, for support. With those (put down) on the east Vasiṣhṭha prospered, with those on the south Bharadvāja, with those on the west Viśvāmitra, with those on the north Jamadagni, with those above Viśvakarman. He who knows thus the prosperity in these (bricks) prospers; he who knows thus their relationship becomes rich in relations; he who knows thus their ordering, (things) go orderly for him; he who knows thus their abode becomes possessed of an abode; he who knows thus their support becomes possessed of support. Having put down the breath-supporters he puts down the unifying (bricks); verily having deposited in him the breaths he unifies them with the unifying (bricks); that is why the unifying have their name. Then too he puts inspiration upon expiration; therefore expiration and inspiration move together. He puts (them) down pointing in different directions; therefore expiration and inspiration go in different directions. The ununified part of the fire is not worthy of heaven; the fire is worthy of heaven; in that he puts down the unifying (bricks), he unifies it; verily he makes it worthy of heaven. 'The eighteen-month-old calf the strength, the Kṛita of throws at dice,' he says; verily by the strengths he wins the throws, and by the throws the strengths. On all sides (these verses) have the word wind,' and therefore the (wind) blows on all sides.

The Horse Sacrifice (continued)

Mantra 5:2:11

a. May the Gāyatrī, the Triṣhṭubh, the Jagatī, | The Anuṣhṭubh, with the Paṅkti, | The Bṛihatī, the Uṣhṇih, and the Kakubh, | Pierce thee with needles. ‖ *b.* May the two-footed, the four-footed, | The three-footed, the six-footed, | The metrical, the unmetrical, | Pierce thee with needles. ‖ *c.* May the Mahānāmnīs, the Revatīs, | All the regions that are rich in fruits, | The lightnings of the clouds, the voices. | Pierce thee with needles. ‖ *d.* The silver, the gold, the leaden, | Are yoked as workers with the works, | On the skin of the strong horse, | May they pierce thee with needles. ‖ *e.* May the ladies, the wives, | With skill separate thy hair, | The wives of the Gods, the quarters, | Pierce thee with needles. ‖ *f.* What then? As men who have barley | Reap the barley in order, removing it, | Hither bring the food of those | Who have not gone to the reverential cutting of the strew.

Mantra 5:2:12

a. Who cutteth thee? Who doth divide thee | Who doth pierce thy limbs? | Who, too, is thy wise dissector? ‖ *b.* May the seasons in due season, | The dissectors, divide thy joints, | And with the splendour of the year | May they pierce thee with needles. ‖ *c.* May the divine Adhvaryus cut thee, | And divide thee; | May the piercers piercing | Joint thy limbs. ‖ *d.* May the half-months, the months, | Cut thy joints, piercing, | May the days and nights, the Marutas, | Make whole thine injuries. ‖ *e.* May the earth with the atmosphere, | May Vāyu heal thy rent, | May the sky with the Nakṣhatras | Arrange thy form aright. ‖ *f.* Healing to thy higher limbs, | Healing to thy lower; | Healing to bones, marrow, | Healing too to thy body!

Prapāṭhaka 3.

The Second and Later Layers of Bricks

Mantra 5:3:1

Now this fire (ritual) is an extensive sacrifice; what part of it is performed or what not? The part of the sacrifice which is performed that is omitted becomes rotten; be puts down the Aśvin (bricks); the Aśvins are the physicians of the Gods; verily by them be produces medicine for it. Five he puts down; the sacrifice is fivefold; verily he produces medicine for the whole extent of the sacrifice. He puts down the seasonal (bricks), to arrange the seasons. Five he puts down; the seasons are five; verily he arranges the seasons in their whole number. They begin and end alike; therefore the seasons are alike; they differ in one foot; therefore the seasons differ likewise. He puts down the breath-supporters; verily he places the breaths in the months; therefore being alike the seasons do not grow old; moreover he generates them. The breath is the wind; in that having put down the seasonal (bricks) he puts down the breath-sup porters, therefore the wind accompanies all the seasons. He puts down the rain-winners; verily he wins rain. If he were to put them down in one place, then would fall rain in one season only; he puts them down after carrying them round in order; therefore it rains in all the seasons. Since having put down the breath-supporters he puts down the rain-winners, therefore the rain starts from the sky, impelled downwards by the wind. The strengthening (bricks) are cattle; cattle have various purposes and various customs, but only as regards water are they of one purpose; if he desire of a man, 'May he be without cattle,' he should put down for him the strengthening (bricks) and then put down the water (bricks); verily he makes discord for him with cattle; verily he becomes without cattle. If he desire of a man, 'May he possess cattle,' he should put down for him the water (bricks) and then put down the strengthening (bricks); verily he makes concord for him with cattle and he becomes possessed of cattle. He puts down four in front; therefore the eye has four forms, two white, two black. The (verses) contain the word 'head'; therefore the head (of the fire) is in front. Five he puts down in the right hip, five in the left; therefore the animal is broader behind and receding in front; 'The goat in strength,' (with these words he puts down) on the right shoulder; (with) 'The ram in strength,' on the left; verily he puts together the shoulders (of the fire). 'The tiger in strength,' (with these words) he puts down in the right wing, (with) 'The lion in strength' on the left; verily he gives strength to the wings. (With) 'The man in strength' (he puts down) in the middle; therefore man is overlord of animals.

Mantra 5:3:2

'O Indra and Agni, (the brick) that quaketh not,' (with these words) he puts down the naturally perforated (brick); these worlds are separated by Indra and Agni; (verily it serves) to separate these worlds. Now the middle layer is, as it were, insecure, it is as it were the atmosphere; 'Indra and Agni,' he says; Indra and Agni are the supporters of force among the Gods; verily he piles it with force in the atmosphere, for support. He puts down the naturally perforated (brick); the naturally perforated (brick) is the atmosphere; verily he puts down the atmosphere. He makes the horse sniff it; verily he puts breath in it; now the horse is connected with Prajāpati; verily by Prajāpati he piles the fire. It is a naturally perforated (brick), to allow the passage of the breaths, and also for the lighting up of the world of heaven. When the Gods went to the world of heaven, the quarters were in confusion; they saw these regional (bricks), they put them down, and by them they made firm the quarters; in that he put down the regional bricks, (it is) to support the quarters. Ten breath supporters he places in the east; the breaths in man are nine, the navel is the tenth; verily he places the breaths in front; therefore the breaths are in front. He puts down the last with the word 'light'; there fore speech, which is the last, is the light of the breaths. He put down ten; the Virāj has ten syllables, the light of the metres is the Virāj; verily he puts the light in the east; therefore we revere the light in the east. The metres ran a race for the cattle; the Bṛihatī won them; there fore cattle are called connected with the Bṛihatī. 'Ma metre,' (with these words) he puts down on the south; therefore the months turn south wards; (with) 'Earth metre' (he puts down) on the west, for support; (with) 'Agni, the deity' (he puts down) on the north; Agni is might; verily on the north he places might; therefore he that advances to the north is victorious. They make up thirty-six; the Bṛihatī has thirty-six syllables, cattle are connected with the Bṛihatī; verily by the Bṛihatī he wins cattle for him. The Bṛihatī holds the sovereignty of the metres; he for whom these are put down attains sovereignty. He puts down seven Vālakhilyā, (bricks) in the east, seven in the west; in the head there are seven breaths, two below; (verily they serve) to give the breaths strength. 'The head thou art, ruling,' (with these words) he puts down on the east; 'Thou art the prop ruling,' (with these words) he puts down on the west; verily he makes the breaths accordant for him.

Mantra 5:3:3

Whatever the Gods did at the sacrifice the Asuras did. The Gods saw these

Akṣhṇayāstomīyā (bricks), they put them down on one place after reciting in another; the Asuras could not follow it; then the Gods prospered, the Asuras were defeated. In that he puts down the Akṣhṇayāstomīyās in one place after reciting in another, (it is) to overcome foes: he prospers himself, his foe is defeated. 'The swift, the triple,' (with these words) he puts down on the east; the triple is the beginning of the sacrifice; verily in the east he establishes the beginning of the sacrifice. 'The sky, the seventeenfold ', (with these words be puts down) on the south; the sky is food, the seventeenfold is food; verily on the south he places food; therefore with the right (hand) is food eaten. 'Support, the twenty-onefold,' (with these words he puts down) on the west; the twenty-onefold is support; (verily it serves) for support. 'The shining, the fifteenfold,' (with these words he puts down) on the north; the shining is force; verily he places force on the north; therefore he that advances to the north is victorious. 'Speed, the eighteenfold,' (with these words) he puts down on the east; two threefold ones he establishes in the beginning of the sacrifice in order. 'Attack, the twentyfold,' (with these words he puts down) on the south; Attack is food, the twentyfold is food; verily he places food on the south therefore with the right is food eaten. 'Radiance, the twenty-twofold,' (with these words he puts down) on the west; in that there are twenty, thereby there are two Virāj verses; in that there are two there is support; verily in order he finds support in the Virāj verses and in the eating of food. 'Fervour, the nineteenfold,' (with these words he puts down) on the north; therefore the left hand has the greater fervour. 'The womb, the twenty-fourfold,' (with these words) he puts down on the east; the Gāyatrī has twenty-four syllables, the beginning of the sacrifice is the Gāyatrī; verily on the east he establishes the beginning of the sacrifice. 'The embryo, the twenty-fivefold,' (with these words he puts down) on the south; embryos are food, the twenty-fivefold is food; verily he places food on the south; therefore with the right is food eaten. 'Force the twenty sevenfold,' (with these words he puts down) on the west; the twenty-seven fold is these worlds; verily he finds support in these worlds. 'Maintenance, the twenty-fourfold,' (with these words he puts down) on the north; therefore the left hand is most to be maintained. 'Inspiration, the thirty-onefold,' (with these words) he puts down on the east; inspiration is speech, speech is the beginning of the sacrifice; verily he establishes the beginning of the sacrifice on the east. 'The surface of the tawny one, the thirty fourfold,' (with these words he puts down) on the south; the surface of the tawny one is yonder sun; verily he places splendour on the south; therefore the right side is the more resplendent. 'Support, the thirty threefold,' (with these words he puts down) on the west, for support. 'The vault, the thirty-sixfold,' (with these words he puts down) on the north'; the vault is the world of heaven; (verily it serves) to attain the world of heaven.

Mantra 5:3:4

'Thou art the portion of Agni,' (with these words he puts down) on the east; Agni is the beginning of the sacrifice, consecration is the beginning of the sacrifice, holy power is the beginning of the sacrifice, the threefold is the beginning of the sacrifice; verily on the east he establishes the beginning of the sacrifice. 'Thou art the portion of them that gaze on men,' (with these words he puts down) on the south; those that gaze on men are the learned, Dhātar is food; verily on birth he gives him food; therefore on birth he eats food. 'The birthplace saved, the seventeenfold Stoma,' he says; the birthplace is food, the seventeen fold is food; verily he places food on the south; therefore with the right food is eaten. 'Thou art the portion of Mitra,' (with these words he puts down) on the west; Mitra is expiration, Varuṇa inspiration; verily he confers on him expiration and inspiration. 'The rain from the sky, the winds saved, the twenty-onefold Stoma,' he says; the twenty-onefold is support, (verily it serves) for support. 'Thou art the portion of Indra,' (with these words he puts down) on the north; Indra is force, Viṣhṇu, is force, the lordly power is force, the fifteenfold is force; verily on the north he places force; therefore he that advances to the north is victorious. 'Thou art the portion of the Vasus,' (with these words) he put down on the east; the Vasus are the beginning of the sacrifice, the Rudras are the beginning of the sacrifice, the twenty-fourfold is the beginning of the sacrifice; verily on the east he establishes the beginning of the sacrifice. 'Thou art the portion of the Ādityas,' (with these words he puts down) on the south; the Ādityas are food, the Marutas are food, embryos are food, the twenty-fivefold is food; verily be places food on the south; therefore with the right food is eaten. 'Thou art the portion of Aditi,' (with these words he puts down) on the west; Aditi is support, Pūṣhan is support, the twenty-sevenfold is support; (verily it serves) for support. 'Thou art the portion of the God Savitar,' (with these words he puts down) on the north; the God Savitar is holy power, Bṛihaspati is holy power, the fourfold Stoma is holy power; verily he places splendour on the north; therefore the northern half is more resplendent. (The verse) contains a word connected with Savitar; (verily it serves) for instigation; therefore is their gain produced in the north for Brahmans. 'The support, the fourfold Stoma,' (with these words) he puts down on the east; the support is the beginning of the sacrifice, the fourfold Stoma is the beginning of the sacrifice; verily he establishes on the east the beginning of the sacrifice. 'Thou art the portion of the Yavas,' (with these words he puts down) on the south; the Yavas' are the months, the Ayavas are the half-months; therefore the months turn to the south; the Yavas are food, offspring is food; verily he places food on the south; therefore with the right food is eaten. 'Thou art the portion of the Ṛibhus,' (with these words he puts down) on the west, for support. 'The revolving, the forty-eightfold,' (with these words he puts down) on the north, to confer strength on these two worlds; therefore these two worlds are of even strength. He becomes first for whom these are placed on the east as the beginning (of the sacrifice), and his son is born to be first; he eats food for whom on the south these (are placed) rich in food, and a son is born to him to eat food; he finds support for whom these (are placed) on the west, full of support; he becomes forcible for whom these (are placed) on the north, full of force, and a forcible son is born to him. The fire is a hymn; I verily in that this arrangement is made are its Stotra and Śastra produced; verily in the hymn the Arkya (Sāman and Śastra) is produced; he eats food, and his son is born to eat food, for whom this arrangement is made, and he too who knows it thus. He puts down the creating (bricks); verily he wins things as created. Now there was neither day nor night in the world, but it was undiscriminated; the Gods saw these dawn (bricks), they put them down; then did this shine forth; for him for whom these are put down the dawn breaks; verily he smites away the dark.

Mantra 5:3:5

'O Agni, drive away those foes of ours that are born,' (with these words) he puts down on the east; verily he drives away his foes on birth. 'That are born with force,' (with these words he puts down) on the west; verily he repels those that are to be born. 'The forty-fourfold Stoma,' (with these words he puts down) on the south; the forty-fourfold is splendour; verily he places splendour on the south; therefore the right side is the more resplendent. 'The sixteenfold Stoma,' (with these words he puts down) on the north; the sixteenfold is force; verily he places force on the north; therefore he that advances to the north is victorious. The forty-fourfold is a thunderbolt, the sixteenfold is a thunder bolt; in that he puts down these two bricks, he hurls the bolt after the foe born and to be born whom he has repelled, to lay them low. He puts down in the middle (a brick) full of dust, the middle of the body is faeces (*pūrīṣha*); verily he piles the fire with its own body, and with his own body he is in yonder world who knows thus. These bricks are called the unrivalled; no rival is his for whom they are put down. The fire is an animal; he puts down the Virāj (bricks) in the highest layer; verily be confers upon cattle the highest Virāj; therefore he that is possessed of cattle speaks the highest speech. Ten by ten he puts (them) down, to confer power on them. Transversely he puts (them) down; therefore cattle move their limbs transversely, for support. By those metres which were heavenly, the Gods went to the world of heaven; for that the seers toiled; they practised fervour, these they saw by fervour, and from them they fashioned these bricks. 'The course metre; the space metre,' (with these words) they put them down; with these they went to the world of heaven; in that he puts down these bricks, the sacrifice goes to the world of heaven with the metres that are heavenly. By the sacrifice Prajāpati created creatures; he created them by the Stomabhāgas; in that he puts down the Stomabhāgas, the sacrificer creates offspring. In the Stomabhāgas Bṛihaspati collected the brilliance of the sacrifice; in that he puts down the Stomabhāga (bricks) he piles the fire with its brilliance. In the Stomabhāgas Bṛihaspati saw the support of the sacrifice; in that he puts down the Stomabhāgas, (it is) for the support of the sacrifice. Seven by seven he puts down, to confer strength, three in the middle, for support.

Mantra 5:3:6

(With the words) 'ray,' he created Āditya; with 'advance,' right; with 'following,' the sky; with 'union,' the atmosphere; with 'propping,' the earth; with 'prop,' the rain; with blowing forward,' the day; with 'blowing after,' the night; with eager,' the Vasus; with 'intelligence,' the Rudras; with 'brilliant,' the Ādityas; with 'force,' the Pitṛis; with 'thread,' offspring; with 'enduring the battle,' cattle; with 'wealthy,' plants. 'Thou art the victorious, with ready stone; for Indra thee Quicken Indra,' (with these words) he fastened the thunderbolt on his right side, for victory. He created offspring without expiration; on them he bestowed expiration (with the words) 'Thou art the overlord'; inspiration (with the word) 'Restrainer'; the eye (with) 'the gliding'; the ear (with) 'the bestower of strength'. Now these offspring, though having expiration and inspiration, hearing and seeing, did not couple; upon them he bestowed copulation (with the words) 'Thou art the Trivṛit.' These offspring though coupling were not propagated; he made them propagate (with the words) 'Thou art the mounter, thou art the descender'. These offspring being propagated did not find support; he made them find support in these worlds (with the words) 'Thou art the wealthy, thou art the brilliant, thou art the gainer of good,' verily he makes offspring when propagated find support in these worlds, he with his body mounts the atmosphere, with his expiration he finds support in yonder world, of expiration and inspiration he is not liable to be deprived who knows thus.

Mantra 5:3:7

By the 'sitters on the vault' the Gods went to the world of heaven; that is why the 'sitters on the vault' have their name. In that he puts down the 'sitters on the vault,' the sacrificer thus goes by the 'sitters on the vault' to the world of heaven; the vault is the world of heaven; for him for whom these are put down there is no misfortune (*nā-ākam*); the 'sitters on the vault' are the home of the sacrificer; in that he puts down the 'sitters on the vault,' the sacrificer thus makes himself a home. The 'sitters on the vault' are the collected brilliance of the Pṛishṭha (Stotras); in that he puts down the 'sitters on the vault,' verily he wins the brilliance of the Pṛishṭhas. He puts down the five crested; verily becoming Apsarases they wait on him in yonder world; verily also they are the bodyguards of the sacrificer. He should think of whomever he hates as he puts (them) down; verily he cuts him off for these deities; swiftly he goes to ruin. He puts (them) above the 'sitters on the vault'; that is as when having taken a wife one seats her in the house; he puts the highest on the west, pointing east; therefore the wife attends on the west, facing east. He puts as the highest the naturally perforated and the earless (bricks); the naturally perforated is breath, the earless is life; verily he places breath and life as the highest of the breaths; therefore are breath and life the highest of the breaths. No brick higher (than these) should he put down; if he were to put another brick higher, he would obstruct the breath and life of cattle and of the sacrificer; there fore no other brick should be put down higher. He puts down the naturally perforated brick; the naturally perforated brick is yonder (sky); verily he puts down yonder (sky). He makes the horse sniff it; verily be places breath in it; again the horse is connected with Prajāpati; verily by Prajāpati he piles the fire. It is naturally perforated, to let out the breaths, and also to light up the world of heaven. The earless is the triumph of the Gods; in that he puts down the earless, he triumphs with the triumph of the Gods; to the north he puts it down; therefore to the north of the fire is action carried on; (the verse) has the word 'wind,' for kindling.

Mantra 5:3:8

He puts down the metre bricks; the metres are cattle; verily he wins cattle; the good thing of the Gods, cattle, are the metres; verily he wins the good thing, cattle. Yajñasena Chaitriyāyaṇa taught this layer; by this he won cattle; in that he puts it down, he wins cattle. He puts down the Gāyatrīs on the east; the Gāyatrī is brilliance; verily at the beginning he places brilliance; they contain the word 'head'; verily he makes him the head of his equals. He puts down the Trishṭubhs; the Trishṭubh is power; verily he places power in the middle He puts down the Jagatīs; cattle are connected with the Jagatī; verily he wins cattle. He puts down the Anushṭubhs; the Anushṭubh is breath; (verily it serves) to let the breaths out. Bṛihatīs, Ushṇihs, Paṅktis, Aksharapaṅktis, these various metres he puts down; cattle are various, the metres are cattle; verily he wins various cattle; variety is seen in his house for whom these are put down, and who knows them thus. He puts down an Atichandas; all the metres are the Atichandas; verily he piles it with all the metres. The Atichandas is the highest of the metres; in that he puts down an Atichandas, be makes him the highest of his equals. He puts down two-footed (bricks); the sacrificer has two feet; (verily they serve) for support.

Mantra 5:3:9

For all the Gods is the fire piled up; if he were not to put (them) down in unison, the Gods would divert his fire; in that he puts (them) down in unison, verily he piles them in unison with himself; he is not deprived of his fire; moreover, just as man is held together by his sinews, so is the fire held together by these (bricks). By the fire the Gods went to the world of heaven; they became yonder Kṛittikās; he for whom these are put down goes to the world of heaven, attains brilliance, and becomes a resplendent thing. He puts down the circular bricks; the circular bricks are these worlds; the citadels of the Gods are these worlds; verily he enters the citadels of the Gods; he is not ruined who has piled up the fire. He puts down the all-light (bricks); verily by them he makes these worlds full of light; verily also they support the breaths of the sacrificer; they are the deities of heaven; verily grasping them he goes to the world of heaven.

Mantra 5:3:10.

He puts down the rain-winning (bricks); verily he wins the rain. If he were to put (them) down in one place, it would rain for one season; he puts down after carrying them round in order; therefore it rains all the seasons. 'Thou art the bringer of the east wind,' he says; that is the form of rain; verily by its form he wins rain. With the Saṃyānīs the Gods went (sām *ayus*) to these worlds; that is why the Saṃyānīs have their name; in that he puts down the Saṃyānīs, just as one goes in the waters with a ship, so the sacrificer with them goes to these worlds. The Saṃyānīs are the ship of the fire; in that he puts down the Saṃyānīs, verily he puts down a boat for the fire; moreover, when these have been put down, if the waters strive to drag away his fire, verily it remains unmoved. He puts down the Āditya bricks; it is the Ādityas who repel from prosperity him who being fit for prosperity does not obtain prosperity; verily the Ādityas make him attain prosperity. It is yonder Āditya who takes away the brilliance of him who having piled up a fire does not display splendour; in that he puts down the Āditya bricks, yonder sun confers radiance upon him; just as yonder sun is radiant, so he is radiant among men. He puts down ghee bricks; the ghee is the home dear to Agni; verily he unites him with his dear home, and also with brilliance. He places (them) after carrying (them) round; verily he confers upon him brilliance not to be removed. Prajāpati piled up the fire, he lost his glory, he saw these bestowers of glory, he put them down; verily with them he conferred glory upon himself; five he puts down; man is fivefold; verily he confers glory on the whole extent of man.

Mantra 5:3:11

The Gods and the Asuras were in conflict; the Gods were the fewer, the Asuras the more; the Gods saw these bricks, they put them down; 'Thou art the furtherer,' (with these words) they became multiplied with the trees, the plants; (with) 'Thou art the maker of wide room,' they conquered this (earth); (with) 'Thou art the eastern,' they conquered the eastern quarter; (with) 'Thou art the zenith,' they conquered yonder (sky); (with) 'Thou art the sitter on the atmosphere; sit on the atmosphere,' they conquered the atmosphere; then the Gods prospered, the Asuras were defeated. He for whom those are put down becomes greater, conquers these worlds, and prospers himself; his foe is defeated. 'Thou art the sitter on the waters; thou art the sitter on the hawk,' he says; that is the form of Agni; verily by his form he wins Agni. 'In the wealth of earth I place thee,' he says; verily with these (bricks) he makes these worlds wealthy. He puts down the life-giving (bricks); verily he bestows life upon him. 'O Agni, thy highest name, the heart,' he says; that is the home dear to Agni; verily he obtains his dear home. 'Come, let us join together,' he says; verily with him to aid he encircles him. 'Be thou, O Agni, among those of the five races.' The fire of the five layers is the fire of the five races; therefore he speaks thus. He puts down the seasonal (bricks); the seasonal (bricks) are the abode dear to the seasons; verily he wins the abode dear to the seasons.

'The firm one,' he says; the firm one is the year; verily he obtains the abode dear to the year.

The Horse Sacrifice (continued)

Mantra 5:3:12

The eye of Prajāpati swelled, that fell away, that became a horse; because it swelled (*āśvayat*), that is the reason why the horse (*āśva*) has its name. By the horse sacrifice the Gods replaced it. He who sacrifices with the horse sacrifice makes Prajāpati whole; verily he becomes whole; this is the atonement for everything, and the cure for everything. All evil by it the Gods overcame; by it also the Gods overcame (the sins of) Brahman-slaying; all evil he overcomes, he overcomes Brahman-slaying who sacrifices with the horse sacrifice, and he who knows it thus. It was the left eye of Prajāpati that swelled; therefore they cut off from the horse on the left side, on the right from other animals. The mat is of reeds; the horse has its birthplace in the waters, the reed is born in the waters; verily he establishes it in its own birthplace. The Stoma is the fourfold one; the bee tore the thigh of the horse, the Gods made it whole with the fourfold Stoma; in that there is the fourfold Stoma, (it is) to make whole the horse.

Prapāṭhaka 4.

The Piling of the Fire Altar (continued)

Mantra 5:4:1

The Gods and the Asuras were in conflict, they could not decide the issue; Indra saw these bodies, he put them down; with them he conferred upon himself power, strength, and body; then the Gods prospered, the Asuras were defeated. In that he puts down Indra's bodies, the sacrificer with them bestows on himself power, strength, and body; verily also he piles up the fire with Indra and with a body; be prospers himself, his foe is defeated. The sacrifice departed from the Gods; they could not recover it; they saw these bodies of the sacrifice, they put them down, and by them they recovered the sacrifice. In that he puts down the bodies of the sacrifice, the sacrificer by them wins the sacrifice. Three and thirty he puts down; the Gods are three and thirty; verily he wins the Gods; verily also he piles up the fire with itself and with a body; he becomes with his body in yonder world, who knows thus. He puts down the lighted (bricks); verily he confers light upon it; the fire blazes piled up with these (bricks); verily with them he kindles it; in both worlds is there light for him. He puts down the constellation bricks; these are the lights of the sky; verily he wins them; the Nakṣhatras are the lights of the doers of good deeds; verily he wins them; verily also he makes these lights into a reflection to light up the world of heaven. If he were to place them in contact, he would obstruct the world of rain, Parjanya would not rain; he puts them down without touching; verily he produces the world of rain, Parjanya is likely to rain; on the east he puts down some pointing west, on the west some pointing east; therefore the constellations move both west and east.

Mantra 5:4:2

He puts down the seasonal (bricks), to arrange the seasons. He puts down a pair; therefore the seasons are in pairs. This middle layer is as it were unsupported; it is as it were the atmosphere; he puts down a pair on the other layers, but four in the middle one, for support. The seasonal (bricks) are the internal cement of the layers; in that he puts down the seasonal (bricks), (it is) to keep apart the layers. He puts down next an Avakā plant; this is the birthplace of Agni; verily he piles up the fire with its birthplace. Viśvāmitra says, 'He shall eat food with holy power, for whom these shall be put down, and he who shall know them thus'. It is the year which repels from support him who having piled up the fire does not find support; there are five layers preceding, and then he piles up the sixth; the year has six seasons; verily in the seasons the year finds support. These are the bricks, called the over-ladies; he for whom they are put down becomes the overlord of his equals; he should think of him whom he hates as he puts (them down); verily he cuts him off for those deities; swiftly he goes to ruin. The Aṅgirasas, going to the world of heaven, made over to the seers the accomplishment of the sacrifice; it became gold; in that he anoints with fragments of gold, (it is) for the completion of the sacrifice; verily also he makes healing for it; moreover he unites it with its form, and with golden light he goes to the world of heaven. He anoints with that which contains the word 'of a thousand'; Prajāpati is of a thousand; (verily it serves) to win Prajāpati 'May these bricks, O Agni, be for me milch cows,' he says; verily he makes them milch cows; they, milking desires, wait upon him yonder in yonder world.

Mantra 5:4:3

The fire is Rudra; he is born then when he is completely piled up; just as a calf on birth desires the teat, so he here seeks his portion; if he were not to offer a libation to him, he would suck the Adhvaryu and the sacrificer. He offers the Śatarudrīya (oblation); verily he appeases him with his own portion; neither Adhvaryu nor sacrificer goes to ruin. If he were to offer with the milk of domesticated animals, he would afflict domestic animals with pain; if (with that) of wild (animals), wild (animals); he should offer with groats of wild sesame or with groats of Gavīdhukā grass; he harms neither domesticated nor wild animals. Then they say, 'Wild sesame and Gavīdhukā grass are not a proper offering'; he offers with goat's milk, the female goat is connected with Agni; verily he offers with a proper offering; he harms neither domesticated nor wild animals. The Aṅgirasas going to the world of heaven spilled the cauldron on the goat; she in pain dropped a feather (like hair), it became the Arka (plant); that is why the Arka has its name. He offers with a leaf of the Arka, to unite it with its birthplace. He offers standing facing north; this is the quarter of Rudra; verily he propitiates him in his own quarter. He offers on the last brick; verily at the end he propitiates Rudra. He offers dividing it into three; these worlds are three; verily he makes these worlds of even strength; at this height he offers, then at this, then at this; these worlds are three; verily he appeases him for these worlds. Three further libations he offers; they make up six, the seasons are six; verily with the seasons he appeases him. If he were to offer while wandering round, he would make Rudra come within (the sacrifice). Or rather they say, 'In what quarter is Rudra or in what?' He should offer them while wandering round; verily he appeases him completely. The highest (bricks) are the heavenly deities; over them he makes the sacrificer speak; verily by them he makes him attain the world of heaven; he should throw (the leaf) down in the path of the cattle of him whom he hates; the first beast that steps upon it goes to ruin.

Mantra 5:4:4

'The strength on the stone,' (with these words) he moistens (the fire), and so purifies it; verily also he delights it; it delighted attends him, causing him neither hunger nor pain in yonder world; he rejoices in offspring, in cattle who knows thus. 'That food and strength, do ye, O Marutas, bounteously bestow on us,' he says; strength is food, the Marutas are food; verily he wins food. 'In the stone is thy hunger; let thy pain reach N.N., whom we hate,' he says; verily he afflicts him whom he hates with its hunger and pain. He goes round thrice, moistening; the fire is threefold; verily he calms the pain of the whole extent of the fire. Thrice again he goes round; they make up six, the seasons are six; verily with the seasons he calms its pain. The reed is the flower of the waters, the Avakā is the cream of the waters; he draws over (it) with a branch of reeds and with Avakā plants; the waters are appeased; verily with them appeased he calms his pain. The beast that first steps over the fire when piled, it is liable to burn it up with its heat. He draws over (it) with a frog; this of animals is the one on which one does not subsist, for neither among the domesticated nor the wild beasts has it a place; verily he afflicts it with pain. With eight (verses) he draws across; the Gāyatrī has eight syllables, the fire is connected with the Gāyatrī; verily he calms the pain of the whole extent of the fire. (He draws) with (verses) containing (the word) 'purifying,' the purifying (one) is food; verily by food he calms its pain. The fire is death; the black antelope skin is the form of holy power; he puts on a pair of black sandals; verily by the holy power he shuts himself away from death. 'He shuts himself away from death, and away from eating food,' they say; one he puts on, the other not; verily he shuts himself away from death and wins the eating of food. 'Honour to thy heat, thy blaze,' he says, for paying honour they wait on a richer man; 'may thy bolts afflict another than us,' he says; verily him whom he hates he afflicts with its pain; 'be thou purifying and auspicious to us,' he says; the purifying (one) is food; verily he wins food. With two (verses) he strides over (it), for support; (with two) containing (the word) 'water,' for soothing.

Mantra 5:4:5

'To him that sits in man hail!' (with these words) he pours butter on; verily with the Paṅkti and the offering he takes hold of the beginning of the sacrifice. He pours on butter transversely; therefore animals move their limbs transversely, for support. If he were to utter the Vaṣhaṭ cry, his Vaṣhaṭ cry would be exhausted; if he were not to utter the Vaṣhaṭ cry, the Rākṣhasas would destroy the sacrifice; Vat he says; verily, mysteriously he utters the Vaṣhaṭ cry; his Vaṣhaṭ, cry is not exhausted, the Rākṣhasas do not destroy the sacrifice. Some of the Gods eat the offerings, others do not; verily he delights both sets by piling up the fire. 'Those Gods among Gods,' (with these words) he anoints (it) with curds mixed with honey; verily the sacrificer delights the Gods who eat and those who do not eat the offerings; they delight the sacrificer. He delights those who eat the offerings with curds, and those who do not with honey; curds is a food of the village, honey of the wild; in that he anoints with curds mixed with honey, (it serves) to win both. He anoints with a large handful (of grass); the large handful is connected with Prajāpati; (verily it serves) to unite it with its birthplace; with two (verses) he anoints, for support. He anoints going round in order; verily he delights them completely. Now he is deprived of the breaths, of offspring, of cattle who piling the fire steps upon it. 'Giver of expiration art thou, of inspiration,' he says; verily he bestows on himself the breaths; 'giver of splendour, giver of wide room,' he says; splendour is offspring; wide room is cattle; verily he bestows on himself offspring and cattle. Indra slew Vṛitra; him Vṛitra slain grasped with sixteen coils; he saw this libation to Agni of the front; he offered it, and Agni of the front, being delighted with his own portion, burnt in sixteen places the coils of Vṛitra; by the offspring to Viśvakarman he was set free from evil; in that he offers a libation to Agni of the front, Agni of the front, delighted with his own portion, burns away his evil, and he is set free from his evil by the offering to Viśvakarman. If he desire of a man, 'May he be set free slowly from evil,' he should offer one by one for him; verily, slowly he is set free from evil; if he desire of a man, 'Swiftly may he be set free from evil,' he should run over all of them for him and make one offering; swiftly is he set free from evil. Or rather he sacrifices separately with each hymn; verily severally he places strength in the two hymns; (verily they serve) for support.

Mantra 5:4:6

'Do thou lead him forward,' (with these words) he puts on the kindling-sticks; that is as when one provides hospitality for one who has come on a visit. He puts down three; the fire is threefold; verily he provides his portion for the whole extent of the fire. They are of Udumbara wood, the Udumbara is strength; verily he gives him strength. 'May the All-Gods thee,' he says; the All-Gods are the breaths; verily with the breaths he raises him up; I bear up with their thoughts, O Agni,' he says; verily he unites him with the thought for which he lifts him up. 'May the five regions divine aid the sacrifice, the Goddesses,' he says, for he moves forward along the quarters. 'Driving away poverty and hostility,' he says, for smiting away the Rākṣhasas 'Giving to the lord of the sacrifice increase of wealth,' he says; increase of wealth is cattle; verily he wins cattle. He takes (him) with six (verses); the seasons are six; verily with the seasons he takes him; two have (the word) 'embracing,' for the smiting away of the Rākṣhasas 'With the rays of the sun, with tawny hair, before us,' he says, for instigation. 'Then let our pure invocations be accepted,' he says; the pure (one) is food; verily he wins food. The Gods and the Asuras were in conflict; the Gods saw the unassailable (hymn) and with it they conquered the Asuras; that is why the unassailable (hymn) has its name. In that the second Hotar recites the unassailable (hymn) the sacrificer conquers his foes therewith unassailably; verily also he conquers what has not been conquered. (The hymn) has ten verses; the Virāj has ten syllables, by the Virāj are kept apart these two worlds; (verily it serves) to keep apart these two worlds. Again the Virāj has ten syllables, the Virāj is food; verily he finds support in the Virāj, in eating food. The atmosphere is as it were unreal; the Agnīdh's altar is as it were the atmosphere; on the Agnīdh's altar he puts down a stone, for reality; with two (verses), for support. 'As measurer, he standeth in the midst of the sky,' he says; verily with this he measures; 'in the middle of the sky is the dappled stone set down,' he says; the dappled is food; verily he wins food. With four (verses) he goes up to the tail; the metres are four; verily (he goes) with the metres. 'All have caused Indra to wax,' he says; verily he attains increase. 'True lord and lord of strength,' he says; strength is food; verily he wins food. 'Let the sacrifice invoke favour, and bring the Gods,' he says; favour is offspring and cattle; verily be bestows on himself offspring and cattle. 'Let the God, Agni, offer and bring to us the Gods,' he says, to make the cry, Godspeed! 'He hath seized me with the impulse of strength, with 'elevation,' he says; elevation is yonder sun in rising; depression is it when setting; verily with holy power he elevates himself, with holy power he depresses his foe.

Mantra 5:4:7

'Along the eastern quarter do thou advance, wise one,' he says; verily with this (verse) he moves to the world of heaven. 'Mount ye, with Agni, to the vault,' he says; verily with this he mounts these worlds. 'From earth have I mounted to the atmosphere,' he says; verily with it he mounts these worlds. 'Going to the heaven they look not away,' he says; verily he goes to the world of heaven. 'O Agni, advance first of worshippers,' he says; verily with it he bestows eyesight upon both Gods and men. He steps upon (the altar) with five (verses); the sacrifice is fivefold; verily he goes to the world of heaven with the full extent of the sacrifice. 'Night and dawn,' he recites as the Puronuvākyā, for preparation. O Agni, of a thousand eyes,' he says; Prajāpati is of a thousand; (verily it serves) to obtain Prajāpati 'To thee as such let us pay honour; to strength hail!' he says; strength is food; verily he wins food. He offers on the naturally perforated brick (a ladle) of Udumbara wood filled with curds; curds are strength, the Udumbara is strength, the naturally perforated is yonder (sky); verily he places strength in yonder (sky); therefore we live on strength coming hitherward from yonder. He puts (it) in place with three (verses); the fire is threefold; verily be makes the whole extent of the fire attain support. 'Enkindled, O Agni, shine before us,' (with these words) he takes (the kindling-stick) of Udumbara wood; this is a pipe with projections; by it the Gods made piercings of hundreds of the Asuras; in that he takes up the kindling-stick with this (verse), the sacrificer hurls the hundred-slaying (verse) as a bolt at his enemy, to lay him low without fail. 'Let us pay homage to thee in thy highest birth, O Agni ', (with these words) he takes up (the kindling-stick) of Vikaṅkata wood; verily he wins radiance. 'That various of Savitar, the adorable,' (with these words) be takes up (the kindling-stick) of Śamī wood, for soothing. The fire milks the piler-up of the fire; the piler-up, milks the fire; 'that various of Savitar, the adorable,' he says; this is the milking of the fire. This of it Kaṇva Śrāyasa knew, and with it he was wont to milk it; in that be takes up the kindling-stick with the verse, the piler-up of the fire milks the fire. 'Seven are thy kindling-sticks, O Agni, seven tongues'; verily he delights seven sevens of his. With a full (ladle) he offers, for Prajāpati is as it were full, to obtain Prajāpati. He offers with a half-filled (ladle), for from the half-filled Prajāpati created creatures, for the creation of offspring. Agni departed from the Gods; he entered the quarters; he who sacrifices should think in his mind of the quarters; verily from the quarters he wins him; with curds he offers at first, with butter afterwards; verily he bestows upon him brilliance and power in accord. There is (an offering) to Vaiśvānara on twelve potsherds; the year has twelve months, Agni Vaiśvānara is the year; verily straightway he wins Vaiśvānara If he were to offer the fore- and after-sacrifices, there would be a bursting of the sacrifice; he offers an oblation with a ladle, for the support of the sacrifice. Vaiśvānara is the kingly power, the Marutas the people; having offered the offering to Vaiśvānara, he offers those to the Marutas; verily he attaches the people to the kingly power. He utters aloud (the direction to the Agnīdh) for Vaiśvānara, he offers the offerings of the Marutas muttering; therefore the kingly power speaks above the people. (The offerings) are for the Marutas; the people of the Gods are the Marutas; verily he wins for him by the people of the Gods the people among men. There are seven; the Marutas are in seven troops; verily in troops he wins the people for him; running over troop by troop he offers; verily he makes the people obedient to him.

Mantra 5:4:8

He offers the stream of wealth; 'May a stream of wealth be mine,' (with this hope) is the offering made; this stream of ghee waits upon him in yonder world, swelling up. He offers with butter; butter is brilliance, the stream of wealth is brilliance; verily by brilliance he wins brilliance for him. Again the stream of wealth is desires; verily he wins desires. If he desire of a man, 'May I separate his breaths and his eating of food,' he should offer separately for him; verily he separates his breaths and his eating of food; if he desire of a man, 'May I continue his breaths and his eating of food,' he should offer for him in a continuous stream; verily he continues his breaths and his eating of food. Twelve sets of twelve he offers; the year has twelve months; verily by the year he wins food for him. 'May for me food, for me freedom from hunger,' he says; that is the form of food; verily he wins food. 'May for me fire, for me the waters,' be says; this is the birthplace of food; verily he wins food with its birthplace. He offers those where Indra, is half; verily he wins the deities; since Indra is half of all and a match, therefore Indra is the most appropriating of Gods; he says Indra later; verily he places strength in him at the top. He offers the weapons of the sacrifice; the weapons of the sacrifice are the sacrifice; verily he wins the sacrifice. Again this is the form of the sacrifice; verily he wins the sacrifice by its form. 'May for me the final bath and the cry of Godspeed!' he says, to utter Godspeed! 'May the fire for me, the cauldron,' he says; that is the form of splendour; verily by the form he wins splendour. 'May the Ṛich for me, the Sāman,' he says; that is the form of the metres; verily by the form he wins the metres. 'May the embryo for me, the calves,' he says; that is the form of cattle; verily by the form he wins cattle. He offers the orderers, to order the disordered. He offers the even and the odd, for pairing; they are in ascending ratio, for ascent. 'May one for me, three,' he says; one and three are the metres of the Gods, four and eight the metres of men; verily he wins both the metres of Gods and men. Up to thirty-three he offers; the Gods are three and thirty; verily he wins the Gods; up to forty-eight he offers, the Jagatī has forty eight syllables, cattle are connected with the Jagatī: verily by the Jagatī he wins cattle for him. 'Strength, instigation,' (with these words) he offers a set of twelve; the year has twelve months; verily he finds support in the year.

Mantra 5:4:9

Agni departed from the Gods, desiring a portion; the Gods said to him, 'come back to us, carry the oblation for us.' He said, 'Let me choose a born; let them offer to me the Vājaprasavīya'; therefore to Agni they offer the Vājaprasavīya. In that he offers the Vājaprasavīya, he unites Agni with his own portion; verily also this is his consecration. He offers with fourteen (verses); there are seven domesticated, seven wild [1] animals; (verily it serves) to win both sets. He offers of every kind of food, to win every kind of food. He offers with an offering-spoon of Udumbara wood; the Udumbara is strength, food is strength; verily by strength he wins for him strength and food. Agni is the consecrated of Gods, the piler of the fire of men; therefore when it rains a piler of the fire should not run, for he has thus obtained food; rain is as it were food; if he were to run he would be running from food. He should go up to it; verily be goes up to food. 'Night and dawn,' (with these words) he offers with the milk of a black cow with a white calf; verily by the day he bestows night upon him, by night day; verily day and night being bestowed upon him milk his desire and the eating of food. He offers the supporters of the kingly power; verily he wins the kingdom. He offers with six (verses); the seasons are six; verily he finds support in the seasons. 'O lord of the world,' (with these words) he offers five libations at the chariot mouth; the chariot is a thunderbolt; verily with the thunderbolt he conquers the quarters. In yonder world the wind blows over the piler of the fire; he offers the names of the winds; verily over him in yonder world the wind blows; three he offers, these worlds are three; verily from these worlds he wins the wind. 'Thou art the ocean, full of mist,' he says; that is the form of the wind; verily by the form he wins the wind. He offers with his clasped hands, for not other wise can the oblation of these be accomplished.

Mantra 5:4:10.

The chariot of the Gods is yoked for the world of heaven, the chariot of man for wherever his intention is fixed; the fire is the chariot of the Gods. 'Agni I yoke with glory, with ghee,' he says; verily he yokes him; he, yoked, carries him to the world of heaven. If he were to yoke with all five together, his fire yoked would fall away, the libations would be without support, the Stomas without support, the hymns without support. He strokes (the fire) with three (verses) at the morning pressing; the fire is threefold; verily he yokes the full extent of the fire; that is as when something is placed on a yoked cart; the oblations find support, the Stomas find support, the hymns find support. He strokes with two (verses) in the Stotra of the Yajñāyajñiya; the sacrifice is as great as is the Agnishṭoma; a further extension is performed over and above it; verily he mounts at the end the whole extent of the sacrifice. (He strokes) with two (verses), for support; when it is not completed by one (verse), then does he stroke; the rest of the sacrifice resorts to him; (verily it serves) for continuity. He who piles up the fire falls away from this world; his libation cannot be performed in a place without bricks; whatever libation he offers in a place without bricks, it runs away, and with its running away the sacrifice is ruined, with the sacrifice the sacrificer; in that he piles up a second piling, (it is) to support the libations; the libations find support, the sacrifice is not ruined, nor the sacrificer. He puts down eight; the Gāyatrī has eight syllables; verily he piles it with the Gāyatrī metre; if eleven, with the Trishṭubh, if twelve with the Jagatī verily he piles it with the metres. The fire that is re-piled is called the descendant; he who knowing thus re-piles the fire eats food up to the third generation. The re-piling is like the re-establishment of the fire; he who does not succeed through the establishment of the fire re-establishes it; he who does not succeed by the piling up of the fire re-piles it. In that he piles up the fire, (it is) for prosperity. Or rather they say, 'one should not pile it up.' The fire is Rudra, and it is as if one stirs up a sleeping lion. But again they say, 'One should pile it up.' It is as if one awakens a richer man with his due portion. Manu piled the fire; with it he did not prosper; he saw this re-piling, he piled it, with it he prospered; in that he piles the re-piling, (it is) for prosperity.

Mantra 5:4:11

He who desires cattle should pile a piling with the metres; the metres are cattle; verily he becomes rich in cattle. He should pile in hawk shape who desires the sky; the hawk is the best flier among birds; verily becoming a hawk he flies to the world of heaven. He should pile in heron form who desires, 'May I be possessed of a head in yonder world'; verily he becomes possessed of a head in yonder world. He should pile in the form of an Alaja bird, with four furrows, who desires support; there are four quarters; verily he finds support in the quarters. He should pile in the form of a triangle, who has foes; verily he repels his foes. He should pile in triangle form on both sides, who desires, 'May I repel the foes I have and those I shall have'; verily he repels the foes he has and those he will have. He should pile in the form of a chariot wheel, who has foes; the chariot is a thunderbolt; verily he hurls the thunderbolt at his foes. He should pile in the form of a wooden trough who desires food; in a wooden trough food is kept; verily he wins food together with its place of birth. He should pile one that has to be collected together, who desires cattle; verily he becomes rich in cattle. He should pile one in a circle, who desires a village; verily he becomes possessed of a village. He should pile in the form of a cemetery, who desires, 'May I be successful in the world of the fathers'; verily he is successful in the world of the fathers. Viśvāmitra and Jamadagni had a feud with Vasiṣhtha; Jamadagni saw these Vihavyā (bricks); he put them down, and with them he appropriated the power and strength of Vasiṣhtha; in that he puts down the Vihavyās, the sacrificer with them appropriates the power and strength of his foe. He puts down on the altar of the Hotar; the Hotar is the abode of the sacrificer; verily in his abode he wins for him power and strength. Twelve he puts down; the Jagatī has twelve syllables, cattle are connected with the Jagatī; verily with the Jagatī he wins cattle for him. Eight each he puts down in the other altars; cattle have eight half-hooves; verily he wins cattle. (He puts down) six on the Mārjālīya; the seasons are six, the Gods, the fathers, are the seasons; verily he delights the seasons, the Gods, the fathers.

The Horse Sacrifice (continued)

Mantra 5:4:12

'Be 'pure for the winning of strength,' this is the Anuṣhṭubh strophe; three Anuṣhṭubhs make four Gāyatrīs; in that there are three Anuṣhṭubhs, therefore the horse when standing stands on three feet; in that there are four Gāyatrī is, therefore he goes putting down all four feet. The Anuṣhṭubh is the highest of metres, the fourfold Stoma is the highest of Stomas, the three-night sacrifice the highest of sacrifices, the horse the highest of animals; verily by the highest he makes him go to the highest state. It is the twenty-onefold day, on which the horse is slain, there are twelve months, five seasons; these worlds are three; the twenty-onefold (Stoma) is yonder sun; this is Prajāpati, the horse is connected with Prajāpati; verily he wins it straightway. The Pṛishṭha (Stotra) is of Śakvarī verses to make the horse complete, there are various metres, different sets of animals are offered, both domesticated and wild; in that the Pṛishṭha is of Śakvarī verses, (it is) to complete the horse. The Sāman of the Brahman is that of Pṛithuraśmi; by the rein the horse is restrained, a horse unrestrained and unsupported is liable to go to the furthest distance; (verily it serves) to restrain and support the horse. The Achāvāka's Sāman is the Saṃkṛiti; the horse sacrifice is an extensive sacrifice; 'who knows,' they say, 'if all of it is done or not?' In that the Achāvāka's Sāman is the Saṃkṛiti, (it serves) to make the horse whole, to win it entirely, to prevent interference. The last day is an Atirātra with all the Stomas, to obtain all, to conquer all; verily he obtains all, he conquers all with it.

Prapāṭhaka 5.

The Piling of the Fire Altar (continued)

Mantra 5:5:1

In that he completes (the sacrifice) with one animal, (it is) for the continuity of the sacrifice and to avoid cutting it in two. The male animals belong to Indra; in that being Indra's they are offered to the fires, he causes strife among the deities. He should use Trishṭubh verses, appertaining to Agni, for the Yājyās and Anuvākyās; in that they appertain to Agni, (the verses) are Agni's, in that they are Trishṭubhs (they are) Indra's; (verily they serve) for prosperity; he does not cause strife among the deities. To Vāyu of the team he offers a hornless (animal); Vāyu is the brilliance of Agni; it is offered to brilliance; therefore wheresoever the wind blows, the fire burns; verily it follows its own brilliance. If he were not to offer to him of the team, the sacrificer would go mad; (an offering) is made to him of the team, to prevent the sacrificer going mad. The Yājyā and the Anuvākyā, contain (the words) 'wind' and 'white,' to secure brilliance. 'The golden germ first arose,' (with these words) he pours out the butter portion; the golden germ is Prajāpati; (verily it serves) for likeness to Prajāpati This (animal) is slain to make up all forms of animals; its hairs are the form of man, its lack of horns that of horses, the possession of one set of incisors only that of cows, the sheep-like hooves that of sheep, that it is a goat, that is the form of goats. The wind is the abode dear to cattle; in that it is offered to Vāyu, in accord cattle wait upon him. 'Should an animal be offered to Vāyu, or to Prajāpati?' they say; if he were to offer it to Vāyu, he would depart from Prajāpati; if he were to offer it to Prajāpati, he would depart from Vāyu; in that the animal is offered to Vāyu, therefore he does not depart; in that a cake is offered to Prajāpati, therefore he does not depart from Prajāpati; in that it is offered on twelve potsherds, therefore he does not depart from Vaiśvānara When about to consecrate himself, he offers to Agni and Vishṇu on eleven potsherds; all the deities are Agni; the sacrifice is Vishṇu; verily he lays hold of the deities and the sacrifice; Agni is the lowest of the deities, Vishṇu the highest; in that he offers to Agni and Vishṇu on eleven potsherds, the sacrificer envelops the Gods on both sides and wins them. By the cake the Gods prospered in yonder world, by the oblation in this; he who desires, 'May I prosper in yonder world,' should offer a cake; verily he prospers in yonder world. In that it is offered on eight pot sherds, it is connected with Agni, in that it is offered on three potsherds, it is connected with Vishṇu; (verily it serves) for prosperity. He who desires, 'May I prosper in the world,' should offer an oblation; the ghee belongs to Agni, the rice grains to Vishṇu, therefore an oblation should be offered; verily he prospers in this world. It is (an offering) to Aditi; Aditi is this (earth); verily he finds support in this (earth); verily also be extends the sacrifice over this. He who piles the fire without keeping it in the pan for a year-(it is with him) as when an embryo is dropped prematurely would go to ruin; he should offer before (the others) on twelve potsherds to Vaiśvānara; Agni Vaiśvānara is the year; even as (an embryo) attaining a year's growth, is born when the due season is come, so he having obtained the year when the due season is come, piles the fire; he goes not to ruin. Vaiśvānara is the form dear to Agni; verily he wins the form dear to him. These offerings are three; these worlds are three; (verily they serve) for the mounting of these worlds.

Mantra 5:5:2

Prajāpati after creating creatures in affection entered into them; from them he could not emerge; he said, 'He shall prosper who shall pile me again hence.' The Gods piled him; then they prospered; in that they piled him, that is why the piling has its name. He who knowing thus piles the fire is prosperous. 'For what good is the fire piled?' they say. 'May I be possessed of the fire,' (with this aim) is the fire piled; verily be becomes possessed of the fire. 'For what good is the fire piled?' they say. 'May the Gods know me,' (with this hope) is the fire piled; the Gods know him. 'For what good is the fire piled?' they say. 'May I have a house,' (with this hope) is the fire piled; verily he becomes possessed of a house. 'For what good is the fire piled?' they say. 'May I be rich in cattle,' (with this hope) is the fire piled; verily he becomes rich in cattle. 'For what good is the fire piled?' they say. 'May the seven men live upon me,' (with this hope) is the fire piled; three before, three behind, the self the seventh; so many live upon him in yonder world. Prajāpati desired to pile the fire; to him spake earth; 'Thou shalt not pile the fire on me; thou wilt burn me excessively, and I being burned excessively will shake you apart; thou wilt fall into a sorry state.' He replied, 'So shall I act that it will not burn thee excessively.' He stroked it, (saying), 'May Prajāpati seat thee; with that deity, in the manner of Aṅgiras, do thou sit firm'; verily making this a brick he put it down, to prevent excessive burning. That on which he is to pile the fire he should stroke, (saying), 'May Prajāpati seat thee; with that deity in the manner of Aṅgiras, do thou sit firm'; verily making this a brick he sets it down to prevent excessive burning. Prajāpati desired, 'Let me be propagated,' he saw this (fire) in the pan, he bore it for a year, then was he propagated. Therefore for a year must it be borne, then is he propagated. To him the Vasus said, 'Thou hast been propagated; let us be propagated.' He gave it to the Vasus, they bore it for three days, thereby they created three hundred, three and thirty; therefore should it be borne for three days; verily is he propagated. To them the Rudras said, 'Ye have been propagated, let us be propagated.' They gave it to the Rudras; they bore it for six days, thereby they created three hundred, three and thirty; therefore should it be borne for six days; verily is he propagated. To them the Ādityas said, 'Ye have been propagated; let us be propagated'. They gave it to the Ādityas, they bore it for twelve days, thereby they created three hundred, three and thirty; therefore should it be borne for twelve days; verily is he propagated. Thereby they created a thousand, the pan being the thousandth; he who knows thus the pan as the thousandth obtains a thousand cattle.

Mantra 5:5:3

'With a Yajus it is made, with a Yajus it is cooked, with a Yajus it is set loose, this pan; it is therefore exhausted, it cannot be used again,' they say. 'O Agni, yoke thy (steeds),' 'Yoke them that best invoke the Gods,' (with these words) he offers in the pan; verily he yokes it again and thereby is it not exhausted. He, who yokes Agni where the yoking is to be performed, yokes him (best) among those who are yoking. 'O Agni, yoke thy (steeds),' 'Yoke them that best invoke the Gods,' he says; this is the yoking of Agni; verily he yokes him, and yokes him (best) among those who are yoking. The theologians say, 'Should the fire be piled up with face down, or face upwards?' Now the fire is piled in the likeness of birds; if he were to pile it face downward, the libations would reach it behind; if upwards, it could not fly, it would not be heavenly for him; he puts down the human head towards the east, face upwards; verily the libations reach it in the mouth; he does not pile it face upwards; verily it is heavenly for him. He offers with (a verse) addressed to Sūrya; verily he bestows sight upon it; twice he offers, for there are two eyes; he offers with the same verse, for sight is the same, for prosperity. The Gods and the Asuras were in conflict, they deposited their desirable wealth; the Gods appropriated it by means of the Vāmabhṛit (brick); that is why the Vāmabhṛit (supporting the desirable) has its name. In that he puts down the Vāmabhṛit, the sacrificer by it appropriates the desirable wealth of his foe. It has a head of gold; gold is light, the desirable is light; verily by light he appropriates the desirable which is light; there are two Yajusas, for support.

Mantra 5:5:4

The waters were the wives of Varuṇa; Agni longed for them, he had union with them; his seed fell away, it became this (earth); what second fell away became yonder (sky); this is the Virāj, yonder the Svarāj; in that he puts down two Virāj (bricks) he puts down these two (worlds). Now the seed which yonder (sky) impregnates, finds support in this (earth), it is propagated, it becomes plants and shoots; them the fire eats. He who knows thus is propagated, and becomes an eater of food. If a man be full of seed, one should put both down in the first layer for him; verily these in accord pour seed for him; if a man have poured his seed, he should put one in the first layer for him and one in the last; verily he encloses by the two (worlds) the seed he has impregnated. For a year to no man should he descend in honour; for these two (worlds) descend in honour for no man; that is their rule. He who piles the fire without a head, becomes headless in yonder world, he who piles it with a head becomes possessed of a head in yonder world. 'To thought I offer with mind, with ghee, that the Gods may come hither, delighting in the offerings, increasing holy order; on the path of the moving ocean I offer all the days to Viśvakarman the undying oblation,' (with these words) he puts down the naturally perforated brick and offers; that is the head of the fire; verily he piles the fire with its head. He becomes possessed of a head in yonder world who know thus. The fire is piled for the world of heaven; whatever is done out of order, that is not heavenly; the fire is heavenly; having put down the layer he should stroke it, (saying), 'May the wise discern wisdom and folly, like backs straight and crooked, like men; for wealth and good offspring, O God, grant us freedom, and keep bondage from us.' Verily he puts it down in order. He piles (the fire) facing east; it becomes heavenly for him.

Mantra 5:5:5

Viśvakarman, lord of the quarters, may he protect our cattle, may he protect us, to him homage! Prajāpati; Rudra; Varuṇa; Agni; lord of the quarters; may he protect our cattle, may he protect us, to him homage! | These are the deities, overlords of these animals; to them he is cut off who puts down the heads of the animals. He puts down the gold bricks; verily he pays honour to these deities. The theologians say, 'In the fire he places the domesticated animals, with pain he afflicts the wild animals; what then does he leave?' In that he puts down the golden bricks, and gold is immortality, by immortality he makes healing for the domesticated animals, he hurts them not. The first naturally perforated brick is expiration, the second cross -breathing, the third inspiration. Having put down the first naturally perforated brick he should breathe out along it; verily he unites expiration with expiration; having put down the second he should breathe across; verily he unites cross-breathing with cross-breathing; having put down the third, he should breathe in; verily he unites inspiration with inspiration; verily he kindles him with the breaths. 'Bhūr, Bhuvar, Svar,' (with these words) he puts down the naturally perforated bricks; the naturally perforated bricks are these worlds; with these exclamations Prajāpati was propagated; in that he puts down the naturally perforated bricks with these exclamations, he puts down these worlds, and over these worlds he is propagated. | For expiration, for cross-breathing, for inspiration; for speech thee; for sight thee; with that deity, in the manner of Aṅgiras, do thou sit firm. By Agni the Gods sought to go to the world of heaven, with him they could not fly; they saw these four naturally perforated bricks, they put them down in the quarters, with him with eyes on all sides they went to the world of heaven. In that he puts down four naturally perforated bricks in the quarters, the sacrificer with Agni with eyes on all sides goes to the world of heaven.

Mantra 5:5:6

a. 'O Agni, come to enjoy,' he says; verily he summons him. || *b.* 'Agni we choose as envoy,' he says; verily having called he chooses him. || *c.* 'By Agni Agni is kindled,' he says; verily he kindles him. || *d.* 'May Agni slay the foes,' he says; verily he confers power on him when kindled. || *e.* 'O Agni, we exalt the praise,' he says; verily he exalts him. | These are the forms of the days; verily each day he piles him, and wins the forms of the days. The theologians say, 'For what reason are other bricks exhausted, the space-filler not?' 'Because it is connected with Indra and Agni and with Bṛihaspati,' he should say, for Indra and Agni and Bṛihaspati are those among the Gods who are not exhausted. It has a follower to avoid monotony. He follows it with an Anuṣhṭubh; the space filler is the body, the Anuṣhṭubh the breath; therefore breath comes through all the limbs. 'They of him, streaming with milk,' he says; therefore there is sap in every joint; 'the dappled mix the Soma,' he says; the dappled (cow) is food; verily he wins food; Agni is praise, food is praise; verily he wins food; 'the clans in the birthplace of the Gods, in the three realms of sky,' he says; verily he makes these worlds full of light for him. He who knows the support of the bricks finds support. 'With that deity, in the manner of Aṅgiras, do thou sit firm,' he says; this is the support of the bricks; he who knows thus finds support.

Mantra 5:5:7

The fire is piled up for the world of heaven; the set of eleven stakes is a thunderbolt; if he were to set up eleven stakes in the fire, he would shut it off from the world of heaven with the thunderbolt; if he were not to set it up, he would sever the animals from the chips; one stake he sets up; verily he does not shut it off from the world of heaven, nor sever the animals from the chips. He who piling the fire steps down on it is deprived of power and strength; he should, with a verse addressed to Indra, put down a brick opposite his step; verily he is not deprived of power and strength. The fire is Rudra, his are three missiles, one that comes straight on, one that strikes transversely, and one that follows up. To them he is cut off who piles the fire; having piled the fire he should give (a bow) with three arrows to a Brahman, unasked; verily to them he pays homage, and also he ransoms himself from them. || The bow of thine, O Rudra, in the east, may the wind blow after it for thee, to thee, O Rudra, with the year I pay homage. | The bow of thine, O Rudra, on the south, may the wind blow after it for thee, to thee, O Rudra, with the full year I pay homage. | The bow of thine, O Rudra, on the west, may the wind blow after it for thee, to thee, O Rudra, with the Iḍā year I pay homage. | The bow of thine, O Rudra, on the north, may the wind blow after it for thee, to thee, O Rudra, with the Idu year I pay homage. | The bow of thine, O Rudra, above, may the wind blow after it for thee, to thee, O Rudra, with the year I pay homage. || Agni is Rudra; just as a tiger stands in anger, so he also (stands); when piled with these he reverences him; verily with homage he soothes him. || The fires of the dust | That have entered within the earth, | Of them thou art the highest; | Do thou instigate us to life. || 'Thee, O Agni, with the mind have I obtained; thee, O Agni, with the fervour have I obtained; thee, O Agni, with the consecration have I obtained; thee, O Agni, with the observances have I obtained; thee, O Agni, with the pressing-day have I obtained; thee, O Agni, with the sacrificial fees have I obtained; thee, O Agni, with the concluding bath have I obtained; thee, O Agni, with the barren cow have I obtained; thee, O Agni, with the cry of Godspeed I have I obtained,' he says; I this is the obtaining of Agni verily therewith he obtains him.

Mantra 5:5:8

He pays reverence in front with the Gateway (Sāman); verily he confers breath upon him. (He reverences) the wings with the Bṛihat and the Rathantara; verily he confers might upon him. (He reverences) the tail with the seasonal Yajñāyajñiya; verily he finds support in the seasons. He pays reverence with the Pṛiṣhṭha (Stotras); the Pṛiṣhṭhas are brilliance; verily he confers brilliance upon him. Prajāpati created Agni; he, created, went away from him; him he checked (*avārayata*) by the Vāravantīya, and that is why the Vāravantīya has it name. By the Śyaita he congealed him, and that is why the Śyaita has its name. In that he reverences, with the Vāravantīya, he restrains him, and by the Śyaita he congeals him. At the joinings of the wings he reverences with the heart of Prajāpati; verily he attains his affection. || With the eastern quarter I place thee, with the Gāyatrī metre, with Agni as the deity; with the head of Agni I put down the head of Agni. | With the southern quarter I place thee, with the Trishṭubh metre, with Indra as the deity; with the wing of Agni I put down the wing of Agni. | With the western quarter I place thee, with the Jagatī metre, with Savitar as the deity; with the tail of Agni I put down the tail of Agni. | With the northern quarter I place thee, with the Anuṣhṭubh metre, with Mitra and Varuṇa as the deity; with the wing of Agni I put down the wing of Agni. | With the upright quarter I place thee, with the Paṅkti metre, with Bṛihaspati as the deity, with the back of Agni I put down the back of Agni. || He who piles the fire without its body is without a body in yonder world; he who piles it with its body is with his body in yonder world. He puts down the body bricks; this is the body of the fire; verily he piles the fire with its body; he has his body in yonder world who knows thus.

Mantra 5:5:9

a. O Agni, the ocean, thy arrow called the young, with it be gentle | to us; homage to this of thine; may we prosper, living on this of thine. || *b.* O Agni, the boisterous; || *c.* the abysmal; || *d.* the strong; e the desirable; thy arrow called young, with it be gentle to us; homage to this of thine; may we prosper, living on this of thine. || *e.* The layers are the five Agnis, the first is the ocean by name, the second the boisterous, the third the abysmal, the fourth the strong, the fifth the desirable; if he were not to offer libations to them they would burn the Adhvaryu and the sacrificer; in that he offers these libations, verily he soothes them with their proper portion; neither Adhvaryu nor sacrificer goes to ruin. || *f.* May speech be mine in the mouth, breath in the nostrils, sight in the eyes, hearing in the ears, might in the arms, force in the thighs, may all my members be uninjured; may thy body be with my body; homage to thee; harm me not. || *g.* The breaths depart from him who piling the fire steps down on it; 'May speech be mine in the mouth, breath in the nostrils,' he says; verily he bestows the breaths on himself. || *h.* The Rudra in the fire, in the waters, in the plants, the Rudra that hath entered all beings, to that Rudra be homage. || *i.* Some Rudras have shares in the libations (*āhuti*), others have shares in the oblations (*havis*); having offered the Śatarudrīya, he should put down on the last brick an oblation of Gavīdhukā; verily he soothes him with his portion. 'For him indeed is the Śatarudrīya offered in truth,' they say, 'for whom this (oblation) is made on the fire.' || *k.* May the Vasus, with the Rudras, protect thee on the east; may the Pitṛis whose lord is Yama, with the Pitṛis, protect thee on the south; may the Ādityas, with the All-Gods, protect thee on the west; may Dyutāna Māruta, with the Marutas, protect thee on the north; may the Gods, whose chief is Indra, protect thee from below and from above. || *l.* It is not purified, nor made worthy of sacrifice, nor really anointed, if it is anointed before this point; in that he anoints it with ghee after it has been piled, thereby is it purified, made worthy of sacrifice and really anointed.

Mantra 5:5:10.

a. Thou art the eastern quarter, the favourable by name; of thee as such Agni is the overlord, the black (snake) the guardian; the overlord and the guardian, to them homage; may they be gentle to us; him whom we hate and who hateth us I place within the jaws of you two. | Thou art the southern quarter, the mighty by name; of thee as such Indra is the overlord, the scorpion, etc. | Thou art the western quarter, the forward by name; of thee as such Soma is the overlord, the viper, etc. | Thou art the northern quarter, the stable by name; of thee as such Varuṇa is overlord, the striped snake, etc. | Thou art the great quarter, the lady paramount by name; of thee as such Bṛihaspati is overlord, the white, etc. | Thou art this quarter, the powerful by name; of thee as such Yama is the overlord, the spotted necked (snake) the guardian; the overlord and the guardian, to them homage; may they be gentle to us; him whom we hate and who hateth us I place within the jaws of you two. || *b.* These deities guard the fire when kindled; if he were not to offer libations to them, they would suck the Adhvaryu and the sacrificer; in that he offers these libations he soothes them with their proper portion; neither Adhvaryu nor sacrificer goes to ruin. || *c.* Ye are missiles by name; your houses are in the east; your arrows are Agni; the water, etc. | Ye are smearers by name; your houses are in the south, your arrows are the fathers; the ocean, etc. | Ye are the bearers of the bolt by name; your houses are in the west, your arrows are sleep; the cleft, etc. | Ye are the stable by name; your houses are in the north; your arrows are the waters; the sea, etc. | Ye are overlords by name; your houses are above; your arrows are the rain; the helper, etc. | Ye are the raw-flesh eaters by name, of the earth; your houses are bore; your arrows are food; winking is the name of the wind; to you homage; be ye gentle to us; him whom we hate and who hateth us I put in your jaws. || *d.* Some Gods eat the offerings, others do not; verily the piler of the fire delights both sets. He offers these libations with curds mixed with honey; verily he delights them with their proper portion. Or rather they say, 'The Gods who eat not the oblations are the bricks'. He offers going round in order; verily he delights them completely. || *e.* Suck this mighty breast of the waters, | Filled in the midst of the flood, O Agni; | Rejoice in the spring of sweetness, O ocean, | Enter thy seat of the sea. || *f.* If one having yoked the fire does not set it free, then just as a horse yoked and not set free in hunger is overcome, so his fire is overcome, and with it being overcome the sacrificer is overcome; he having piled the fire becomes aheat; 'Suck this mighty breast of the waters,' (with these words) he offers a ladle full of butter; this is the freeing of the fire; verily setting it free he gives it food. Therefore they say, both he who knows and he who knows not. 'A horse well loaded carries well'; the horse is Agni; verily he delights him, he delighted delights him; he becomes richer.

The Horse Sacrifice (continued)

Mantra 5:5:11

To Indra, the king, a boar; to Varuṇa, the king, a black (antelope); to Yama, the king, a deer; to the bull, the king, a Gayal; to the tiger, the king, a Bos Gavaeus; to the king of men a monkey; for the swift falcon a quail; for the Nīlaṅgu (snake) a worm; for Soma, the king, a gazelle; for the ocean a crocodile; for the snowy mountain an elephant.

Mantra 5:5:12

The ape is for Prajāpati; the owl, the Halīkṣhṇa the cat, are for Dhātar; to Sarasvatī the white starling, of human speech; the wild goat, the ichneumon, the Śakā, these are for Pūṣhan; the curlew to speech.

Mantra 5:5:13

To the offspring of waters a fish; the crocodile, the dolphin, the Kulīkaya are for the ocean; to speech the Paiṅgarāja; to Bhaga the sea-crow; the swan, the Vāhasa, the woodpecker, these are for Vāyu; to the quarters the Chakravāka.

Mantra 5:5:14

To might, a boa-constrictor; the mole, the Sṛijaya, the lizard, these are for Mitra; to death the dark (serpent); to wrath the viper; the pot-nosed, the lotus-sitter, the copper snake, these are for Tvaṣhṭar; to the echo the Vāhasa

Mantra 5:5:15

The human beast to the moon; the lizard, the Kālakā, the woodpecker, these are for the trees; the dappled (deer) to day; the black (antelope) to night; the cuckoo, the Kṣhviṅkā, the black-headed, these are (to be offered) to Aryaman; the crab for Dhātar

Mantra 5:5:16

For the sun the crane; the deer, the peacock, the hawk, these are for the Gandharvas; for the Vasus the francolin partridge; for the Rudras the partridge; the red doe, the Kuṇḍṛiṇāchī, the Golathikā, these are for the Apsarases; to the wood the Sṛimara.

Mantra 5:5:17

The dappled (deer) is for the All-Gods; the Pitva, Nyaṅku, the Kaśa, these are (to be offered) to Anumati; the cuckoo is for the half months; the tortoise for the months; the Kvayi, the Kuṭaru, the gallinule, these are (to be offered) to Sinīvālī; to Bṛihaspati the cat.

Mantra 5:5:18

The Śakā, is for earth; the field-rat, the Kaśa, the flying fox, these are for the fathers; the pole-cat for the seasons; the quail to the year; the pigeon, the owl, the hare, these are for Nirṛiti; the cock for Savitar

Mantra 5:5:19

The deer for Rudra; the chameleon, the bird, the Pippakā, these are (to be offered) to the arrow shot; the gazelle for the Marutas; the Śārga to the Brahman; the hyena, the black (deer), the dog of four eyes, the ass, these are for other men; to Agni the crow.

Mantra 5:5:20.

The Alaja is for the atmosphere; the otter, the diver, the swimmer, these for the waters; to Aditi the Haṃsasāchi; to Indrāṇī the Kīrśā; the vulture, the white-breasted, the Vārdhrāṇasa, these are for the sky; the hedgehog is for sky and earth.

Mantra 5:5:21

The eagle for Parjanya; the swan, the wolf, the cat, these are for Indra; the otter for the waters; the jackal is (to be offered) to Aryaman; the lion, the ichneumon, the tiger, these are (to be offered) to great Indra; the rhinoceros to desire.

Mantra 5:5:22

For Agni the black-necked; for Sarasvatī the ewe; the brown one for

Soma; the dark for Pūshan; the white-backed for Bṛihaspati; the variegated for the All-Gods; the ruddy one for Indra; the speckled one for the Marutas; the mixed one for Indra and Agni; the one spotted below for Savitar; the ram for Varuṇa

Mantra 5:5:23

The horse, the hornless one, the Gayal, these are for Prajāpati; for Agni the two with black necks; for Tvashṭar the two with hairy thighs; the two white-backed for Bṛihaspati; to Dhātar the speckled bellied one; for the sun the white ram.

Mantra 5:5:24

To Agni of the front the red-limbed ox; the two spotted below for Savitar; the two red-navelled for Pūshan; the two hornless tawny ones for the All-Gods; the speckled for the Marutas; the black goat for Agni the ewe for Sarasvatī; the black ram with one white foot for Varuṇa

Prapāṭhaka 6.

The Piling of the Fire Altar (continued)

Mantra 5:6:1

a. Golden of colour, pure, purifying, | In which was born Kaśyapa, in which Indra, | They have conceived Agni as a germ, of varied forms; | May these waters be gentle and kindly to us. || *b.* Those in whose midst Varuṇa doth go, | Gazing on the truth and falsehood of men, | Dripping honey, pure, purifying; | May these waters be gentle and kindly to us. || *c.* Those of which in the sky the Gods make their food, | Those that are in many places in the sky, | Those that inundate the earth with their sap, the pure ones | May these waters be gentle and kindly to us. || *d.* With auspicious eye gaze on me, O waters; | With auspicious body, do ye touch my skin; || I invoke all you Agnis that sit in the waters; | Do ye confer upon me radiance and might and force. || *e.* When as ye went below | Ye cried (*ānadata*) on the slaying of the serpent, | Therefore are yo criers (*nadyāḥ*) by name; | These are your names, O streams. || *f.* When instigated by Varuṇa | Ye wallowed speedily, | Then Indra obtained (*apnot*) you as ye went | Therefore ye are waters (*āpaḥ*). || *g.* As ye glided against his will, | He stayed (*āvīvarata*) your courses, | Indra with his might, O Goddesses; | Therefore your name is water (*vāḥ*). || *h.* One God stepped upon them, | As they glided, according to his will, | (Saying) 'The great ones have breathed forth (*ūd*) | Therefore they are called water. || *i.* The waters are kindly, the waters were ghee; | These waters bear Agni and Soma; | The bitter sap of those dispensing sweetness, the satisfying, | Hath come to me with breath, with radiance. || *k.* I behold, or I hear; | The cry cometh to me, the voice of them to us; | I consider that I have enjoyed the ambrosia then, | When I delighted you, O ye of golden hue. || *l.* Ye, waters, are healing; | Further us to strength, | To see great joy. || *m.* The most auspicious flavour that is yours, | Accord to us here, | Like eager mothers. || *n.* To him may we come with satisfaction, | To whose dwelling ye quicken us, | O waters, and propagate us. || *o.* Arise to the sky, aim at the atmosphere, be united with the earth; | thou art splendour; for splendour thee!

Mantra 5:6:2

He draws cups of water; the cups are the royal consecration; the fire is the consecration; the royal consecration is the consecration of Varuṇa; (the fire) to be piled is Agni's consecration; verily by them is he consecrated; verily also he conquers both the worlds, that of him who has offered the royal consecration and that of the piler of the fire. There are waters; the waters are foes of Agni; in that he puts the waters down below the fire, (they serve) to overcome his foe; he prospers himself, his foe is defeated. The waters are ambrosia; therefore they sprinkle with water him who is faint; he does not go to ruin, he lives all his life, for whom these are put down, and who knows them thus. The waters are food, the waters are cattle, cattle are food; an eater of food and rich in cattle he becomes, for whom these are put down, and who knows them thus. They are twelve; the year has twelve months; verily by the year he wins food for him; there are vessels used; in a vessel is food eaten; verily he wins food with its birthplace; up to the twelfth generation he eats food; moreover, he is not cut off from his vessel for whom these are put down, nor he who knows them thus. The pots and the pans make pairs, for the propagation of pairing; with offspring, with cattle, with pairings is he propagated for whom these are put down and he who knows them thus. Agni is pain; he afflicts the Adhvaryu, the sacrificer, and offspring with pain; in that he puts down water, he soothes his pain; neither Adhvaryu nor sacrificer goes to ruin; offspring are soothed where these are put down. The waters are the hearts of the waters; in that he puts these down, he unites these with (the waters) of the sky; Parjanya becomes likely to rain. He who knows their home and their arrangement becomes possessed of a home, things go in order for him. Along the furrows he puts (them) down; this is their home, their arrangements; he who knows thus becomes possessed of a home, and things go in order for him. The others he puts down in pairs, but four in the middle, for support. The bricks are food, this oblation is food in very presence; in that he puts down this oblation, verily straightway he wins food for him; in the middle he puts (them) down; verily he bestows food on him in the middle; therefore in the middle is food eaten. It is offered to Bṛihaspati; Bṛihaspati is the holy power of the Gods: verily by holy power he wins food for him. 'Thou art splendour; for splendour thee!' he says; brilliant and resplendent does he become, for whom these are put down, and he who knows it thus.

Mantra 5:6:3

He puts down the bricks of being; in every place is death born; wherever death is born, thence he removes it by sacrifice; therefore the piler of the fire lives all his life, for all deaths are removed by him; therefore the piler of the fire is not to be practised against; his witchcraft turns upon him (who does so) and lays him low. He who piles the fire is consecrated; these are the offerings of the divine consecrators; so many are the consecrations of the Gods, and they confer consecrations upon him; they consecrate him, the fire is consecration; the royal consecration is the consecration of Varuṇa; (the fire) to be piled is the consecration of holy power. 'On the instigation of the God Savitar, thee,' he says; verily instigated by Savitar he consecrates him with holy power, with the deities. He pours down every sort of food, to win every sort of food. He pours down over him from the front face to face; for from the front face to face is food eaten. He pours down from the head, for from the head is food eaten; he causes (the water) to flow over up to the mouth; verily on the mouth he bestows food-eating upon him. 'With the lordship of Agni I consecrate thee,' he says; this is the consecration of Agni; verily he consecrates him with it. 'With the lordship of Bṛihaspati I consecrate thee,' he says; Bṛihaspati is the holy power of the Gods; verily with holy power he consecrates him. 'With the lordship of Indra I consecrate thee,' he says; verily he confers power from above upon him. That is the form of the royal consecration. He who knowing thus piles the fire conquers both the worlds, that of him who has offered the royal consecration and that of the piler of the fire. When Indra had been consecrated, his power and strength fell away in ten places; the Gods brought it together with the Sautrāmaṇī; he who piles the fire is consecrated; having piled the fire he should sacrifice with the Sautrāmaṇī; verily collecting power and strength he places them in himself.

Mantra 5:6:4

The year in unison with the Ayāvans the dawn in unison with the | ruddy (cows); Sūrya in unison with the steed; the Aśvins in unison with the wondrous works. Agni Vaiśvānara in unison with the food | offerings; with ghee; hail! || The year is the year, the Ayavas are the months, the red one the dawn, the steed Sūrya, the Aśvins these two (worlds), Agni Vaiśvānara the year, the food offerings cattle, ghee cattle. With the year cattle are born; verily with the year he produces cattle for him. He offers on a blade of Darbha grass; the Darbhas are the ambrosia, the strength of the (earth); he offers on it; verily he is propagated. An eater of food he becomes for whom they offer thus. These deities are the foremost portions of Agni; verily he delights them; verily too he places the eye of Agni in front; he becomes not blind who knows thus. Waters were the world at first, the Moving ocean; Prajāpati, becoming wind, rocked about on a lotus leaf; he could find no support; he saw that nest of the waters, on it he piled the fire, that became this (earth), then indeed did he find support. (The brick) which he put down in front became the head, that is the eastern quarter; (the brick) which he put down on the right became the right side, that is the southern quarter; (the brick) which he put down behind became the tail, that is the western quarter; (the brick) which he put down on the left became the left side, that is the northern quarter; (the brick) which he put down above became the back, that is the zenith. Agni of the five bricks is this (earth); therefore when they dig in it they knock up against the brick, against gravel. Now all this (earth) in the eyes of the birds shines at night, therefore birds do not at night rest upon it. He who knowing this piles a fire finds support, and conquers all the quarters. The Brahman is connected with Agni, therefore the Brahman finds prosperity in all the quarters; verily every quarter he goes to is his own. The fire is the nest of the waters; therefore waters draw the fire; verily they enter their own birthplace.

Mantra 5:6:5

Having kept the fire in the pan for a year in the second year he should offer on eight potsherds to Agni, to Indra on eleven potsherds, to the All-Gods on twelve potsherds, to Bṛihaspati an oblation, to Viṣhṇu on three potsherds; in the third year he should sacrifice with the Abhijit (offering). In that there is (an offering) on eight potsherds, the Gāyatrī has eight syllables, and the morning pressing is connected with Agni and the Gāyatrī, verily he supports by it the morning pressing and the Gāyatrī metre. In that there is (an offering) on eleven potsherds, the Triṣṭubh has eleven syllables, and the midday pressing is connected with Indra and the Triṣṭubh, verily he supports by it the midday pressing and the Triṣṭubh metre. In that there is (an offering) on twelve potsherds, the Jagatī has twelve syllables, and the third pressing is connected with the All-Gods and the Jagatī, verily he supports by it the third pressing and the Jagatī metre. In that there is an oblation to Bṛihaspati, and Bṛihaspati is the holy power of the Gods, verily he supports by it holy power. In that there is (an offering) to Viṣhṇu on three potsherds, and Viṣhṇu is the sacrifice, verily he supports by it the sacrifice. In that he sacrifices with the Abhijit in the third year, (it serves) for conquest. In that he keeps the fire in the pan for a year, he saves this world by it; in that he piles the fire in the second year, he saves the atmosphere by it; in that he sacrifices in the third year, he saves yonder world by it. This (fire) Para Āṭnāra, Kakṣhīvant Auśija, Vītahavya Śrāyasa, and Trasadasyu Paurukutsya piled, being desirous of offspring; then indeed did they win thousands each of children; he is extended with offspring, with cattle, that measure he attains which they attained, who knowing thus piles the fire.

Mantra 5:6:6

a. Prajāpati piled the fire; it kept being razor-edged; the Gods in terror did not approach it; they, clothing themselves in the metres, approached it, and that is why the metres have their name. The metres are holy power; the black antelope skin is the form of holy power; he puts on a pair of black antelope skin shoes; verily clothing himself with the metres he approaches the fire, to prevent injury to himself. ‖ *b.* The fire is put down as a treasure of the Gods. Now a treasure unguarded others find, or he cannot recollect where it is; he steps on the fire-pan; verily he makes himself its overlord, for guardianship. Or rather they say, ‘It should not be stepped on’; the pan is connected with Nirṛiti; if he were to step on it, he would hand himself over to Nirṛiti; therefore it should not be stepped on. He puts down the human head, for guardianship; and moreover this is just as if one should say, ‘Guard that for me’. ‖ *c.* Atharvan is Prajāpati; Dadhyach Ātharvaṇa is the fire, his bones are the bricks; as to that the seer says, ‘Indra with the bones of Dadhyach.’ In that he piles the fire with the bricks, he piles up the fire with itself; he has his own self in yonder world who knows thus. ‖ *d.* (The fire) to be piled is the body of Agni, Vaiśvānara is the self; in that he offers to Vaiśvānara after the piling, he prepares its body and mounts it; the sacrificer thus prepares his body, in that he piles the fire; in that he offers to Vaiśvānara after the piling, verily having prepared his body he mounts it with the self; therefore they do not cut off from it; verily living he goes to the Gods. ‖ *e.* He puts on dust with a verse addressed to Vaiśvānara; Agni Vaiśvānara is this (earth), the dust is its piling; verily he piles Agni Vaiśvānara; Vaiśvānara is the form dear to Agni; verily he wins the form dear to him.

Mantra 5:6:7

The Gods obtained the brilliance (*virājam*) of Agni by means of the consecration; for three nights should he be consecrated; the Virāj has three feet, he obtains the Virāj For six nights should he b consecrated; the year consists of six seasons; the Virāj is the year, he obtains the Virāj For ten nights should he be consecrated; the Virāj has ten syllables; he obtains the Virāj For twelve nights should he be consecrated; the year has twelve months; the Virāj is the year; he obtains the Virāj He should be consecrated for thirteen nights; the year has thirteen months; the Virāj is the year; he obtains the Virāj For fifteen nights should he be consecrated; the nights of the half-month are fifteen; the year is made up by the half-months; the Virāj is the year; he obtains the Virāj For seventeen nights should he be consecrated; the year has twelve months and seven seasons; the Virāj is the year; he obtains the Virāj For twenty-four nights should he be consecrated; the year has twenty-four half-months; the Virāj is the year; he obtains the Virāj For thirty nights should he be consecrated; the Virāj has thirty syllables; he obtains the Virāj For a month should he be consecrated; the year is the month; the Virāj is the year; he obtains the Virāj For four months should he be consecrated; for four months the Vasus bore him, they conquered the earth, the Gāyatrī metre; for eight the Rudras, they conquered the atmosphere, the Triṣṭubh metre; for twelve the Ādityas, they conquered the sky, the Jagatī metre; then they attained distinction, supremacy over the Gods. Therefore after keeping the fire for twelve months, should one pile it up; the year has twelve months, the fire to be piled is the year, the bricks are days and nights; he piles him with the bricks obtained; verily also he attains distinction, supremacy over his equals.

Mantra 5:6:8

a. Agni is piled for the world of heaven; if he were not to mount after him the sacrificer would be excluded from the world of heaven. ‘I have mounted on the earth; let not breath forsake me’; ‘I have mounted on the atmosphere; let not offspring forsake me’; ‘I have mounted on the sky, we have attained the light,’ he says; this is the mounting after Agni verily by it he mounts after him, to attain the world of heaven. ‖ *b.* If he were to set up (the eleven posts) commensurate with the wings, he would make the sacrificial rite too small, his offspring would be worse off than himself. He sets (it) up commensurate with the altar; verily he makes the sacrificial rite larger, his offspring does not become worse than himself. ‖ *c.* He should pile (the fire) of a thousand (bricks) when first piling (it); this world is commensurate with a thousand; verily he conquers this world. He should pile (it) of two thousand when piling a second time; the atmosphere is commensurate with two thousand; verily be conquers the atmosphere. He should pile (it) of three thousand when piling for the third time; yonder world is commensurate with three thousand; verily he conquers yonder world. ‖ *d.* Knee deep should he pile (it), when piling for the first time; verily with the Gāyatrī he mounts this world; navel deep should he pile (it) when piling for the second time; verily with the Triṣṭubh he mounts the atmosphere; neck deep should he pile (it) when piling for the third time; verily with the Jagatī he mounts yonder world. ‖ *e.* After piling the fire he should not have intercourse with a woman of pleasure, thinking, ‘I shall deposit seed in that which is no womb’; nor after piling for the second time should he have intercourse with the wife of another, nor after piling for a third time should he have intercourse with any woman whatever. In that he piles the fire, he deposits seed; if he were to have intercourse. he would be deprived of seed. Or rather they say, ‘If he were not to have intercourse, there would be no offspring.’ In that he puts down the two Retaḥsich (bricks), they support the seed of the sacrificer; therefore he should have intercourse, for the non-spilling of seed.’ ‖ *f.* Three seeds are there, father, son, grandson; if he were to put down two Retaḥsich (bricks), he would cleave his seed; three he puts down, for the continuity of seed; the first Retaḥsich is this (earth), this (earth) is speech, therefore they see this (earth), they see speech speaking; the second is the atmosphere, the atmosphere is breath, therefore they see not the atmosphere, nor breath; the third is yonder (sky), yonder (sky) is the eye, therefore they see yonder (sky), they see the eye. With a Yajus he sets down this one and yonder one, but with mind only the middle, to arrange these worlds, and also the breaths. ‖ *g.* ‘The sacrifice offered by the Bhṛigus, the Vasus, accord our desires; of thee thus offered, enjoyed, may I here enjoy wealth,’ he says; verily he milks thereby the song and the recitation. ‖ *h.* ‘Father Mātariśvan, bestow flawless abodes; the flawless abodes the Uśijs have made; let Soma, all knowing, the leader, be leader; let Bṛihaspati recite hymns and rejoicing,’ he says; that is Agni’s hymn, and with it he recites after him.

Mantra 5:6:9

a. That fire which is kept in the pan is consecrated of fires; if he were to put it down their embryos would be liable to abortion, and that would be like descending after consecration. He sets it on a throne, to support and prevent the falling of embryos, and he makes thus a consecration. ‖ *b.* (The fire) in the pan is an embryo, the sling is the womb; if he were to remove the pan from the sling, he would strike the embryo from the womb; the sling has six ropes; man is sixfold, the body, the head, four limbs; verily in himself he bears it. ‖ *c.* The fire is Prajāpati, his breasts are the pan and the mortar; his offspring live on them; in that he puts down the pan and the mortar, with them the sacrificer milks the fire in yonder world. ‖ *d.* The fire is the year, its bricks are arranged threefold, those of Prajāpati, of Vishṇu, of Viśvakarman; the Prajāpati (bricks) are the days and nights; in that he keeps (the fire) in the pan, he puts down the Prajāpati (bricks); in that he takes up the kindling-sticks, and the trees are Vishṇu's, verily he puts down the Vishṇu (bricks); in that he piles the fire with bricks, and Viśvakarman is this (earth), verily he puts down the Viśvakarman (bricks). Therefore they say, 'Threefold is Agni.' ‖ *e.* This thus should the sacrificer himself pile; if another pile his fire, if he should not prosper him with sacrificial gifts, he would appropriate his fire; him who piles his fire he should prosper with sacrificial gifts; verily thus he preserves his fire.

Mantra 5:6:10.

Prajāpati piled the fire as the year by the seasons; by the spring he piled its front half, by the summer its right wing, by the rains its tail, by the autumn its left wing, by the winter its middle. By the Brahman class he piled its front half, by the lordly class its right wing, by cattle its tail, by the people its left wing, by hope its middle. He who knowing thus piles the fire piles it with the seasons; verily he wins all; they hearken to him who has piled the fire, he eats food, he is resplendent. The first layer is this (earth), the mortar the plants and trees; the second is the atmosphere, the mortar the birds; the third is yonder (sky), the mortar the Nakshatras; the fourth the sacrifice, the mortar the sacrificial fee; the fifth the sacrificer, the mortar offspring; if he were to pile it with three layers, he would obstruct the sacrifice, the fee, the self, offspring; therefore should it be piled with five layers; verily he preserves all. In that there are three layers, (it is) since Agni is threefold; in that there are two (more), the sacrificer has two feet, (it is) for support; there are five layers, man is five fold; verily he preserves himself. There are five layers, he covers (them) with five (sets of) mortar, these make up ten, man has ten elements; he preserves man in his full extent. Again the Virāj has ten elements, the Virāj is food; verily he finds support in the Virāj and the eating of food. The sixth layer is the year, mortar is the seasons; there are six layers, six (sets of) mortar, they make up twelve, the year has twelve months; verily he finds support in the year.

The Horse Sacrifice (continued)

Mantra 5:6:11

The red, the dark red, the jujube red, these are for Prajāpati; the brown, the reddish-brown, the parrot brown, these are for Rudra. The white, the white-eyed, the white-necked, these have the fathers as their deities. Three black barren cows are for Varuṇa, three white barren cows for the Sun; the dusky-spotted hornless ones are for Mitra and Bṛihaspati

Mantra 5:6:12

The dappled, the one with cross-lines dappled, the one with dappled marks running up, these are for the Marutas; the bright, the ruddy woolled, the white, are for Sarasvatī; the piebald, the grey piebald, the slightly piebald, these are for the All-Gods; three dark barren cows are for Pūshan, three ruddy barren cows for Mitra; the red-spotted hornless ones are for Indra and Bṛihaspati

Mantra 5:6:13

The white limbed, the one with white limbs on one side the one with white limbs on both sides, these are for Indra and Vāyu; the one with white ear-holes, that with one white ear-hole, the one with both white ear-holes, they are for Mitra and Varuṇa; the one with a pure tail, the one with a completely pure tail, the one with a tail in lumps, these are for the Aśvins; three barren cows of varied colours are for the All-Gods, three white for the supreme lord; the white-spotted hornless ones are for Soma and Pūshan.

Mantra 5:6:14

The humped, the bull, the dwarf (animal), these are for Indra and Varuṇa; the one with white hump, the white-backed, the white-rumped, these are for Indra and Bṛihaspati; the white-footed, the white-lipped, the white-browed, these are for Indra and Vishṇu; the three white-flecked barren cows are for Viśvakarman; the three with piebald bellies are (to be offered) to Dhātar; the white-spotted hornless ones are for Indra and Pūshan.

Mantra 5:6:15

Three long-eared ones are for Yama; three white-footed for Soma; three ichneumons are (to be offered) to Agni, the youngest; three ruddy eighteen-month-old (sheep), these are for the Vasus; three red gallinules, these are for the Rudras; the brown-spotted hornless ones are for Soma and Indra.

Mantra 5:6:16

Three small-eared are for Vishṇu; three with red-tipped ears are (to be offered) to Vishṇu, the wide strider; three with dewlaps are (to be offered) to Vishṇu, the wide goer; three of two and a half years old are for the Ādityas; three of three years old are for the Aṅgirasas; the yellow spotted hornless ones are for Indra and Vishṇu.

Mantra 5. 6.17.

To Indra, the king, are (to be offered) three white-backed; to Indra, the overlord, three with white humps; to Indra, the self-ruler, three with white buttocks; three four-year-old (cows) are for the Sādhyas; three draught cows are for the All-Gods; the black-spotted hornless ones are for Agni and Indra.

Mantra 5:6:18

To Aditi are (to be offered) three ruddy-spotted; to Indrāṇī three black-spotted; to Kuhū three red-spotted; three calves to Rākā; three heifers to Sinīvālī; the red-spotted hornless ones are for Agni and Vishṇu.

Mantra 5:6:19

Three reddish-brown ones are for Soma; to Soma, the king, are (to be offered) three dappled ones; the cloud-formed are for Parjanya; three goats with dewlaps are (to be offered) to Indrāṇī; three ewes are for Aditi; those of auspicious mark and hornless are for sky and earth.

Mantra 5:6:20.

There are three black-spotted for Varuṇa; to Varuṇa, the king, are (to be offered) three red-spotted; to Varuṇa, destroyer of foes, three ruddy-spotted; three of varied colours are for the All-Gods; three dappled for all the deities; the white-spotted hornless ones are for Indra and Sūrya.

Mantra 5:6:21

To Soma, self-ruler, there are (to be offered) two oxen which drag the cart; to Indra and Agni, the givers of force, two camels; to Indra and Agni, givers of might, two sheep that drag the plough; two heifers are for earth; to the quarters are (to be offered) two mares; two heifers are for earth; two females are for the Virāj two heifers are for earth; two oxen that drag the carriage are (to be offered) to Vāyu; two black, barren cows are for Varuṇa; two bulls with high horns, destructive, are for the sky.

Mantra 5:6:22

In the morning eleven beasts of the ox kind are offered; the goat with spots, the blue jay, the Vidīgaya, these are for Tvashṭar. For Sūrya there are nine white barren cows to be offered; those for Agni, Indra and Agni, and the Aśvins are offered at the great stake.

Mantra 5:6:23

There are three reddish-brown ones for spring; three dappled ones for summer; three piebald (deer) for the rains; three dappled for autumn; three with dappled thighs for winter; three smeared over for the cool season; to the year are (offered) those with hanging bellies.

Prapāṭhaka 7.

The Piling of the Fire Altar (continued)

Mantra 5:7:1

a. 'He who piles the fire without regard to the deity falls a victim to the deities; he becomes poorer; he who (piles it) according to the deity does not fall a victim to the deities; he becomes richer. With a Gāyatrī (verse) addressed to Agni should he stroke the first layer; with a Trishṭubh the second; with a Jagatī the third; with an Anushṭubh the fourth; with a

Paṅkti the fifth; verily he piles the fire according to the deity. He falls not a victim to the deities; he becomes richer. This is the dividing of the sacrificial food; the food is cattle, and he piles it with cattle. ‖ *b.* He who piles the fire after announcing to Prajāpati does not go to ruin. The horses should stand on either side, on the left the black, on the right the white; having offered them he should put down the bricks; that is the form of Prajāpati, the horse is connected with Prajāpati; verily having announced to Prajāpati in real presence he piles the fire, he does not go to ruin; the white horse is the form of day, the black of night; the bricks are the form of day, the mortar of night; when about to put down the bricks he should stroke the white horse, when about to put down the mortar he should stroke the black; verily with the days and nights he piles it. ‖ *c.* A golden vessel full of honey he gives, (saying), 'May I be possessed of honey'; with (a verse) addressed to Sūrya, containing the word 'brilliant,' he should gaze (on it); verily it becomes brilliant in the midday; he causes the horse to sniff it; Indra is yonder sun, Prajāpati is he; the horse is connected with Prajāpati; verily he wins him straightway.

Mantra 5:7:2

a. To thee, O Agni, the bull, the wise, | I have come, generating thee ever new; | Be our household rites not halting; | With thy keen holy power sharpen us. | The bricks are cattle, in each layer he puts down a bull (brick); verily in his sacrifice he makes a pairing for propagation; therefore in every herd there is a bull. ‖ *b.* The image of the year | Which men revere in thee, O night, | Making his offspring rich in heroes, | May he obtain all life. | He puts down this Prajāpati (brick); the sole eighth day is this (earth); in that food is made on the sole eighth day, he wins it thereby; this is the wish cow of Prajāpati; verily by it the sacrificer in yonder world milks the fire. ‖ *c.* With the light wherewith the Gods went upward, | Wherewith the Ādityas, the Vasus, the Rudras, | Wherewith the Aṅgirasas attained greatness, | With that let the sacrificer go in prosperity. | The fire is piled for the world of heaven; (with the words) With the light wherewith the Gods went upwards,' he lights the fire in the pan; verily he puts down the bricks connected with the trees, to win the world of heaven. ‖ *d.* (Homage) to the hundred-weaponed, him of a hundred powers, | Him of a hundred aids, the overcomer of hostility, | To Indra who shall lead us over all obstacles | Through autumns without fail. ‖ *e.* The four paths going to the Gods | Which stretch between sky and earth, | To him, O Gods, do ye all accord us | Who brought to them unfailing power and untirelessness. ‖ *f.* Summer, winter, and spring for us, | Autumn, the rains be favourable for us; | May we enjoy the favour and protection | Of these seasons through a hundred autumns. ‖ *g.* To the Idu year, the complete year, the year | Pay ye honour great; | In their loving kindness that are worthy of sacrifice | May we long be unfailing, unsmitten. ‖ *h.* Better than good have the Gods brought together; | With thee as aid may we win thee; | Do thou, wonder-working, O drop, enter us, | Be propitious and kindly to our children, our descendants. ‖ *i.* He puts down these unfailing (bricks), they are the Gods unconquered; verily he enters them; he is not conquered. ‖ *k.* The theologians say, 'Since the months, the half-months, the seasons, the years cook the plants, then why is the offering of first-fruits made to other deities?' The Gods conquered these (plants); if he were to offer to the seasons, he would cause strife with the Gods; having offered the offering of first-fruits, he offers these libations; verily he delights the half-months, the months, the seasons, the year; he does not cause strife with the Gods. 'Better than good have the Gods brought together,' he says, for the eating of the offering, to prevent the defeat of the sacrificer.

Mantra 5:7:3

a. Thou art the thunderbolt of Indra, slaying foes; | Guarding our bodies, lying in wait; | He who in east, south, west, | In the north, as a foe plots against us, | May he strike on this rock. | The Gods and the Asuras were in conflict; the Asuras sought to force them from the quarters; the Gods repelled them with arrow and thunder bolt; in that he puts down the thunderbolt (bricks), he repels his foes with arrow and thunderbolt; in the quarters he puts down; verily he puts round him those citadels of the Gods, which guard the body. ‖ *b.* O Agni and Viṣhṇu, | May these songs gladden you in unison; | Come ye with radiance and strength. | The theologians say, 'Since they do not offer to any deity, then what deity has the stream of wealth?' Wealth is Agni, this stream is his; wealth is Viṣhṇu, this stream is his; with a verse addressed to Agni and Viṣhṇu he offers the stream of wealth; verily he unites them with their proper portions; verily also he makes this libation to have an abode; he wins that for desire of which he makes this offering. The fire is Rudra; now two are his bodies, the dread the one, the auspicious the other; in that he offers the Śatarudrīya, he soothes with it his dread form; in that he offers the stream of wealth, he delights with it his auspicious form. He, who knows the support of the stream of wealth, finds support. If there is any butter left over, in it he should cook a mess for the Brahmans, four Brahmans should eat it; the Brahman is Agni Vaiśvānara, Vaiśvānara, is the form dear to Agni; verily he establishes it in his dear form. He should give four cows; verily with them the sacrificer in yonder world milks the fire.

Mantra 5:7:4

a. 'To thought I offer with mind, with ghee,' he says; the oblation to Viśvakarman is called the undeceivable; the foe cannot deceive him who has piled; verily also he wins the Gods. ‖ *b.* 'O Agni, today,' (with these words) he offers with a Paṅkti verse, and by the Paṅkti and the libation he grasps the beginning of the sacrifice. ‖ *c.* 'Seven are thy kindling-sticks, O Agni; seven thy tongues,' he says; verily he wins the Hotar's offices. Agni went away from the Gods, desiring a portion; to him they assigned this as a portion; that is the Agnihotra, of Agni; then is he born indeed when he is completely piled. Verily to him on birth he gives food; he delighted delights him, he becomes richer. ‖ *d.* The theologians say, 'Since it is as the Gārhapatya that (the fire) is piled, then where is its Āhavanīya?' 'Yonder sun,' he should reply, for in it they offer to all the Gods. He who knowing thus piles the fire straightway makes pleased the Gods. ‖ *e.* O Agni, the glorious, lead him to glory; | Bring hither the fame that is Indra's; | May he be head, overlord, resplendent, | Most famed of his equals. | With look auspicious first they underwent | Fervour and consecration, the seers who found the heavenly light; | Thence was born the kingly power, might and force; | May the Gods in unison accord that to us. | Disposer, ordainer, and highest onlooker, | Prajāpati, supreme lord, the ruler; | The Stomas, the metres, the Nivids, mine they call; | To him may we secure the kingdom. | Turn towards me, come to me; | May he be your ruler, your overlord; | On his discernment do ye depend; | Upon him henceforth do ye all serve. ‖ He puts down these supporters of the realm; this is the realm supporting piling of the fire; verily with it he bestows on him the kingly power, he becomes the kingly power, the kingly power does not fall away from him.

Mantra 5:7:5

a. Just as a son born dies, so dies he whose fire in the pan is extinguished. If he were to make it by friction, he would divide (the fire), he would produce a foe for him. It must again be kindled (with wood) around; verily he produces it from its own birthplace, he does not produce a foe for him. Darkness seizes on him whose fire in the pan is extinguished, darkness is death; a black garment, a black heifer are the sacrificial fees; verily with darkness he smites away the darkness which is death. Gold he gives, gold is light; verily with the light he smites away the darkness; moreover gold is brilliance; verily he confers brilliance upon himself. ‖ *b.* Like heavenly light, the heat; hail! Like heavenly light, the Arka hail! Like heavenly light, the bright; hail! Like heavenly light, the light; hail! Like heavenly light, the sun; hail!' | The fire is Arka, the horse sacrifice is yonder sun; in that he offers these libations he unites the lights of the Arka and the horse sacrifice; he indeed is an offerer of the Arka and the horse sacrifice, for whom this is done in the fire. ‖ *c.* The waters were first this world, the moving; Prajāpati saw this first layer, it he put down, it became this (earth). To him Viśvakarman said, 'Let me come to thee'; 'There is no space here,' he answered. He saw this second layer, he put it down, it became the atmosphere. The sacrifice said to Prajāpati, 'Let me come to thee'; 'There is no space here,' he answered. He said to Viśvakarman, 'Let me come to thee.' 'In what way wilt thou come to me? ' 'By the regional (bricks),' he replied. He came with the regional (bricks), he put them down, they became the regions. The supreme lord said to Prajāpati, 'Let me come to thee'; 'There is no space here,' he answered. He said to Viśvakarman and the sacrifice, 'Let me come to you two'; 'There is no space here,' they answered. He saw this third layer, he put it down, it became yonder (world). Āditya said to Prajāpati, 'Let me come to thee'; 'There is no space here,' he answered. He said to Viśvakarman and the sacrifice, 'Let me come to you two'; 'There is no space here,' they answered. He said to the supreme lord, 'Let me come to thee.' 'In what way wilt thou come to me?' 'By the space-filler,' he replied. He came to him by the space filler; therefore the space-filler is unexhausted, for yonder Āditya is unexhausted. To them the seers said, 'Let us come to you.' 'In what way will ye come?' 'By greatness,' they replied. To them they came with two (more) layers; (the fire) became one of five layers. He who knowing thus piles the fire becomes greater, he conquers these worlds, the Gods know him; moreover he attains community with these deities.

Mantra 5:7:6

a. The fire is a bird; if the piler of the fire were to eat of a bird, he would be eating the fire, he would go to ruin. For a year should he observe the vow, for a vow goes not beyond a year. ‖ *b.* The fire is an animal; now an animal destroys him who moves up to it face to face; therefore he should go up to it from behind while it is looking towards the front, to prevent injury to himself. ‖ *c.* 'Brilliance art thou, grant me brilliance, restrain earth, guard me from the earth. Light art thou, grant me light, restrain the atmosphere, guard me from the atmosphere. Heavenly light art thou, grant me heavenly light, restrain the heavenly light, guard me from the sky,' he says; by these are these worlds supported; in that he puts them down, (it is) for the support of these worlds. Having put down the naturally perforated (bricks) he puts down the gold bricks; the naturally perforated are these worlds, gold is light; in that having put down the naturally perforated he puts down the gold bricks; verily he makes these worlds full of light by means of them; verily also by them these worlds shine forth for him. ‖ *d.* Those flames of thine, O Agni, which rising in the sun, | With rays envelop the sky, | With all of them bring us to brilliance, to man. | Those flames of yours in the sun, O Gods, | Those flames in cattle, in horses, | O Indra and Agni, with all of these | Grant us brilliance, O Bṛihaspati | Grant us brilliance in our Brahmans, | Place brilliance in our princes, | Brilliance in Viśyas and Śūdras; | With thy flame grant me brilliance. | The glory and power of him who has piled the fire go apart twofold, or to the fire which he has piled or to the man who has sacrificed. In that he offers these libations, he places in himself power and fame. ‖ *e.* He who having piled the fire steps on it is liable to go to ruin. 'To thee I come praising with holy power'; with this verse addressed to Varuṇa should he offer; that is the soothing of the fire and the protection of himself. ‖ *f.* He who piles the fire is made into an offering; just as an offering spills, so he spills who having piled the fire approaches a woman; with clotted curds for Mitra and Varuṇa he should sacrifice; verily he approaches unity with Mitra and Varuṇa, to avoid his spilling. ‖ *g.* He who knows the fire to rest on the seasons, for him the seasons go in order; he finds support. The fire resting on the seasons is the year; the head is the spring, the right side summer, the tail the rains, the left side autumn, the middle winter, the layers the first half-months, the mortar the second half-months, the bricks the days and nights; this is the fire resting on the seasons; he who knows thus, for him the seasons go in order; he finds support. ‖ *h.* Prajāpati, desirous of supremacy, put down the fire; then did he attain supremacy; he who knowing thus piles the fire attains thus supremacy.

Mantra 5:7:7

a. What has flowed from purpose, or heart, | Or what is gathered from mind or sight, | Follow to the world of good deed, | Where are the seers, the first-born, the ancient ones. ‖ *b.* This I place around thee, O abode, the treasure | Whom the all-knower hath brought here; | After you the lord of the sacrifice will follow; | Know ye him in the highest firmament. ‖ *c.* Know ye him in the highest firmament, | O Gods associates, ye know his form; | When he shall come by the paths, God-travelled, | Do ye reveal to him what is sacrificed and bestowed. ‖ *d.* Move ye forward; go ye along together, | Make ye the paths, God-travelled, O Agni | In this highest abode, | O All-Gods, sit ye with the sacrificer. ‖ *e.* With the strew, the encircling-stick, | The offering-ladle, the altar, the grass (*barhis*), | With the Ṛich, bear this sacrifice for us | To go to the heaven to the Gods. ‖ *f.* What is offered, what is handed over, | What is given, the sacrificial fee, | That may Agni Vaiśvānara | Place in the sky among the Gods for us. ‖ *g.* That by which thou bearest a thousand, | Thou, O Agni, all wealth, | By that (path) do thou bear the sacrifice of ours, | To go to the Gods in heaven. ‖ *h.* By that (path) by which, O Agni, the priests, busy, | Bear the fees, the sacrifice, | By that do thou bear this sacrifice of ours, | To go to the Gods in heaven. ‖ *i.* By that (path) by which, O Agni, the doers of good deeds, | Obtain the streams of honey, | By that do thou bear this sacrifice of ours, | To go to the Gods in heaven. ‖ *k.* Where are the streams that fail not | Of honey and of ghee, | May Agni Vaiśvānara place us | In heaven among the Gods.

Mantra 5:7:8

a. Thy kindling-sticks, O Agni, thine abodes, | Thy tongues, O all-knower, thy light, | Thy cracklings, thy drops, | With these pile thyself, well knowing. | The fire is an extended sacrifice; what of it is performed, what not? What the Adhvaryu in piling the fire omits, that of himself he omits. 'Thy kindling-sticks, O Agni, thine abodes,' he says; this is the self piling of the fire; verily the fire piles the fire, the Adhvaryu omits nothing from himself. ‖ *b.* To the four quarters let the fires advance; | May he bear this sacrifice for us, well knowing; | Making rich the ghee, immortal, full of heroes, | The holy power is the kindling-stick of the libations. | The tortoise is put down for the world of heaven; 'To the four quarters let the fires advance,' he says; verily by it he recognizes the quarters; 'May he bear this sacrifice for us, well knowing,' he says, for guidance to the world of heaven; 'The holy power is the kindling-stick of the libations,' he says. By means of the holy power the Gods went to the world of heaven; in that he puts down (the tortoise) with (a verse) containing the word 'holy power,' by the holy power the sacrificer goes to the world of heaven. ‖ *c.* The fire is Prajāpati here; cattle are the offspring; the form the metres; all colours of bricks should he make; verily by the form he wins offspring, cattle, the metres; verily also he piles it winning it for offspring, cattle, the metres.

Mantra 5:7:9

a. In me I take first Agni, | For increase of wealth, for good offspring with noble heroes; | In me offspring, in me radiance I place; | May we be unharmed in our body with good heroes. | The immortal Agni who hath entered | Into us mortals within the heart, O fathers, | May we enclose him in ourselves; | May he not abandon us and go afar. | If the Adhvaryu without taking the fire in himself were to pile it, he would pile his own fire also for the sacrificer. Now cattle depend upon the fire; cattle would be likely to depart from him. 'In me I take first Agni,' he says; verily in himself he supports his own fire, cattle depart not from him. ‖ *b.* The theologians say, 'Since clay and water are not food for Agni, then why is he piled with clay and water?' In that he joins with water and all the deities are the waters, verily he unites him with the waters. In that he piles with clay and Agni Vaiśvānara is this earth, verily he piles Agni with Agni. ‖ *c.* The theologians say, 'Since the fire is piled with clay and water, then why is it called the fire?' In that he piles with the metres and the metres are fires, therefore is it called fire. Moreover Agni Vaiśvānara is this (earth); in that he piles with clay, therefore is it called the fire. ‖ *d.* He puts down golden bricks; gold is light; verily be confers light upon him; again gold is brilliance; verily he confers radiance upon himself. He, who piles (the fire) with faces on all sides, eats food in all his offspring, conquers all the quarters. In the east he puts down a Gāyatrī, a Trishṭubh on the south, a Jagatī on the west, an Anushṭubh on the north, a Paṅkti in the middle; this is the fire with faces on all sides: he, who knowing thus piles it, eats food in all his offspring, conquers all the quarters; verily also he weaves quarter in quarter; therefore quarter is woven in quarter.

Mantra 5:7:10.

Prajāpati created the fire; it created ran away east from him; he cast the horse at it, it turned to the south; he cast the ram at it, it turned to the west; he cast the bull at it, it turned to the north; he cast the goat at it, it ran upwards. He cast the man at it. In that he puts down the heads of animals, he piles it, winning it on every side. The heads of animals are bricks, breath supporting, full of sight; in that he puts down the heads of animals, the sacrificer breathes with them in yonder world; verily also these worlds shine forth for him by them. He puts them down after smearing with mud, for purity. The fire is an animal, animals are food, the heads of animals are this fire; if he desire of a man, 'May his food be less,' he should put down for him the heads of animals more closely together; his food becomes less; if he desire of a man, 'May his food be similar (to what he has now),' he should put them down for him at a mean distance; verily his food becomes the same; if he desire of a man, 'May his food become more,' he should put them down separating them at the ends of the pile; verily at the ends also he wins food for him; his food becomes more.

The Horse Sacrifice (continued)

Mantra 5:7:11

Flies with the teeth, frogs with the grinders; the cater with the gnawer; strength with the digester; the wild with the knee-cap; clay with the gums; Avakā grass with pieces of gravel; with the Avakās gravel; with the hump the tongue; with the shouter the palate, Sarasvatī with the tongue tip.

Mantra 5:7:12

Strength with the jaws; the waters with the mouth; the Ādityas with the hair; support with the lower lip; the existent with the upper; the clearness with what is between; by the gloss the external (radiance); by the knob the thundering; by the eyes Sūrya and Agni; by the two pupils the two lightnings; the lightning-stroke by the brain; might by the marrow parts.

Mantra 5:7:13

Tortoises with the hooves; with the flesh of the hooves francolin | partridges; the Sāman with the dewclaws; speed with the legs; health | with the two knees; strength with the two Kuhās; fear with the two | movers; the secret with the two sides; the Aśvins with the two shoulders | Aditi with the head; Nirṛiti with the bald head.

Mantra 5:7:14

The yoke-thong with the pits of the legs; the yoke with the | bent part; thought with the neck; sounds with the breaths; with the | gloss skin; with the Parākāśa the interior; with hair the flies; Indra with | the hard-working bearing part; Bṛihaspati with the seat of the birds; | the chariot with the cervical vertebrae.

Mantra 5:7:15

Indra and Varuṇa with the two buttocks; Indra and Agni with the flesh below the buttocks; Indra and Bṛihaspati with the two thighs; Indra and Vishṇu with the knees; Savitar with the tail; the Gandharvas with the penis; the Apsarases with the testicles; the purifying with the anus; the strainer with the two Potras; the going with the two Sthūras; the going to with the two centres of the loins.

Mantra 5:7:16

For Indra the breast, for Aditi the flanks, for the quarters the cervical cartilages; the clouds with the heart and its covering; atmosphere with the pericardium; the mist with the flesh of the stomach; Indrāṇī with the lungs; ants with the liver, the hills with the intestines; the ocean with the stomach; Vaiśvānara with the fundament.

Mantra 5:7:17

For Pūshan the rectum; for the blind serpent the large entrails; serpents with the entrails; seasons with the transverse processes; sky with the back; for the Vasus the first vertebra; for the Rudras the second; for the Ādityas the third; for the Aṅgirasas the fourth; for the Sādhyas the fifth; for the All-Gods the sixth.

Mantra 5:7:18

Force with the neck; Nirṛiti with the bones; Indra with the hard-working bearing part; for Rudra the moving shoulder; for day and night the second (part); for the half-months the third; for the months the fourth; for the seasons the fifth; for the year the sixth.

Mantra 5:7:19

Joy with the delighter; love with the two Pratyāsas; fear with the two Śitīmas; command with the two Praśāsas; sun and moon with the two kidney parts; the dark and the light with the two kidneys; the dawning with the form; the setting with the formless.

Mantra 5:7:20.

Day with the flesh; night with the fat; the waters with the juice; ghee with the sap; ice with the fat (*vāsā*); hail with the rheum of the eyes; with tears hoar-frost; sky with the form; the Nakṣhatras with the shadow; earth with the hide; the skin with the skin; to it brought up hail! To it slaughtered hail! To it offered hail!

Mantra 5:7:21

For Agni the first rib; for Sarasvatī the second; for Soma the third; for the waters the fourth; for the plants the fifth; for the year the sixth; for the Marutas the seventh; for Bṛihaspati the eighth; for Mitra the ninth; for Varuṇa the tenth; for Indra the eleventh for the All-Gods the twelfth; for sky and earth the side; for Yama the side bone.

Mantra 5:7:22

For Vāyu the first rib; for Sarasvat the second; for the moon the third; for the Nakṣhatras the fourth; for Savitar the fifth; for Rudra the sixth for the serpents the seventh; for Aryaman the eighth; for Tvaṣhṭar the ninth for Dhātar the tenth; for Indrāṇī the eleventh; for Aditi the twelfth; for sky and earth the side; for Yama the side bone.

Mantra 5:7:23

The path with the two parts near the kidneys; continuance with the two sinew parts; parrots with bile; jaundice with the liver; the Halīkṣhṇas with the evil wind; Kūśmas with dung; the worms with the contents of the intestines; dogs with the cutting up; serpents with the smell of the blood, birds with the smell of the cooking; ants with the fragments.

Mantra 5:7:24

With strides the courser hath strode out, | In unison with the All-Gods worthy of sacrifice;. | Do thou bear us to the world of good deeds; | May we rejoice in thy strength.

Mantra 5:7:25

a. Thy back is the sky; thy place earth; thy breath the atmosphere; thy birthplace the ocean. || *b.* Thine eye the sun; thy breath the wind; thine ear the moon; thy joints the months and the half-months; thy limbs the seasons; thy greatness the year.

Mantra 5:7:26

Agni was the animal; with it they sacrificed; it won this world where Agni is; this is thy world, thou wilt win it, and so snuff (it). | Vāyu was the animal; with it they sacrificed; it won this world where Vāyu is; this is thy world, therefrom will I obstruct thee if thou dost not snuff (it). | Āditya was the animal; with it they sacrificed; it won this world where Āditya is; this is thy world, thou wilt win it if thou dost snuff it.

Kāṇḍa 6.

The Explanation of the Soma Sacrifice

Prapāṭhaka 1

The Exposition of the Soma Sacrifice

Mantra 6:1:1

He makes a hall with beams pointing east. The Gods and men divided the quarters, the Gods (obtained) the eastern, the Pitṛis the southern, men the western, the Rudras the northern. In that he makes a hall with beams pointing east, the sacrificer approaches the world of the Gods. He covers it over, for the world of the Gods is hidden from the world of men. 'It is not easy,' they say, 'to go from this world; for who knows if he is in yonder world or not.' He makes at the corners apertures, for the winning of both worlds. He shaves his hair and beard, he trims his nails. The hair and the beard are dead and impure skin, and by thus destroying the dead and impure skin he becomes fit for the sacrifice and approaches the sacrifice. The Aṅgirasas going to the world of heaven placed in the waters consecration and penance. He bathes in the waters; verily visibly he secures consecration and penance. He bathes at a ford, for at a ford did they place (consecration and penance); he bathes at a ford; verily he becomes a ford for his fellows. He sips water; verily he becomes pure within. He consecrates him with a garment; the linen garment has Soma for its deity. He who consecrates himself approaches Soma as his deity. He says, 'Thou art the body of Soma; guard my body.' He approaches his own deity; verily also he invokes this blessing. (Of the garment) the place where the border is belongs to Agni, the wind-guard to Vāyu, the fringe to the Pitṛis, the fore-edge to the plants, the warp to the Ādityas, the woof to the All-Gods, the meshes to the Nakṣhatras The garment is thus connected with all the Gods; in that he consecrates him with the garment, verily with all the Gods he consecrates him. Man has breath without; his eating is his breath, he eats; verily he consecrates himself with breath. He becomes satiated. As great as is his breath, with it he approaches the sacrifice. Ghee pertains to the Gods, sour cream to the Pitṛis, well-seasoned butter to men, fresh butter is connected with all the Gods; verily in anointing with fresh butter he satisfies all the Gods. The man who is consecrated has fallen from this world and yet not gone to the world of the Gods; fresh butter is as it were midway; therefore he anoints with fresh butter, along the hair, with a Yajus, for destruction. Indra slew Vṛitra; his eyeball fell away; it became collyrium. When he anoints, verily he takes away the eye of his enemy. He anoints his right eye first, for men anoint the left first. He does not rub (the ointment) on, for men rub (the ointment) on. Five times he anoints; the Paṅkti has five syllables, the sacrifice is fivefold; verily he obtains the sacrifice. He anoints a limited number of times, for men anoint an unlimited number of times. He anoints with (a stalk) which has a tuft, for men anoint with (a stalk) which has no tuft; (verily he anoints them) for discrimination. If he were to anoint with (a stalk) having no tuft, he would be as it were a thunder bolt. He anoints with one which has a tuft, for friendship. Indra slew Vṛitra, he died upon the waters. Of the waters what was fit for sacrifice, pure, and divine, that went out of the waters, and became Darbha grass. In that he purifies (the sacrificer) with bunches of Darbha grass, verily he purifies him with the waters which are fit for sacrifice, pure, and divine. He purifies (him) with two (stalks); verily he purifies him by days and nights. He purifies (him) with three (stalks); three are these worlds; verily he purifies him by these worlds. He purifies (him) with five stalks; the Paṅkti has five syllables, the sacrifice is fivefold; verily he purifies him by the sacrifice. He purifies (him) with six (stalks); six are the seasons; verily he purifies him by the seasons. He purifies (him) with seven (stalks); seven are the metres; verily he purifies him by the metres. He purifies (him) with nine (stalks); nine are the breaths in man; verily he purifies him along with his breaths. He purifies (him) with twenty-one (stalks); there are ten fingers and ten toes, and the body is the twenty first; he thus completely purifies the man. He says, 'Let the lord of thought purify thee'; the mind is the lord of thought; verily by the mind he purifies him. He says, 'Let the lord of speech purify thee'; verily by speech he purifies him. He says, 'Let the God Savitar purify thee'; verily being instigated by Savitar, he purifies him. He says, 'O lord of the purifier, with thy purifier, for whatsoever I purify myself, that may I have strength to accomplish.' Verily does he invoke this blessing.

Mantra 6:1:2

All the Gods who purified themselves for the sacrifice waxed great. He who knowing thus purifies himself for the sacrifice waxes great. Having purified him without he makes him go within. Verily having purified him in the world of men, he leads him forward purified to the world of the Gods. 'He is not consecrated by one oblation ', they say; verily he offers four with the dipping-ladle for consecration; the fifth he offers with the offering-ladle; the Paṅkti has five syllables, the sacrifice is fivefold; verily he wins the sacrifice. 'To the purpose, to the impulse, to Agni, hail!' he says, for with purpose does a man employ the sacrifice, planning to sacrifice. 'To wisdom, to thought, to Agni, hail!' he says, for by wisdom and thought man approaches the sacrifice. 'To Sarasvatī, to Pūshan, to Agni, hail! 'he says. Sarasvatī is speech, Pūshan the earth;. verily with speech and the earth he performs the sacrifice. 'O ye divine, vast, all-soothing waters,' he says. The waters of the rain are the divine, vast, all-soothing waters; if he said not that praise, the divine waters would descend in anger on this world. He says, 'O ye divine, vast, all-soothing waters.' Verily he makes them soothing for this world; accordingly being soothed they approach this world. 'Heaven and earth,' he says, for the sacrifice is in heaven and earth. 'Wide atmosphere,' he says, for the sacrifice is in the atmosphere. 'May Bṛihaspati rejoice in our oblation,' he says. Bṛihaspati is the holy power (Brahman) of the Gods; verily by the holy power he wins this sacrifice for him. If he were to say *vidheḥ* then he would stumble on the sacrificial post; he says *vṛidhātu*; verily he avoids the sacrificial post. Prajāpati created the sacrifice. Being created it went away. It crushed the Yajus, it crushed the Sāman; the Ṛich raised it; in that the Ṛich raised (it), hence the elevating offering has the name. With a Ṛich he sacrifices, to support the sacrifice. 'It was the Anushṭubh among the metres which supported it,' they say. Therefore he sacrifices with an Anushṭubh, to support the sacrifice. 'It was the twelve "calf-binders" which supported it,' they say. Therefore with twelve those who know the 'calf-binders,' consecrate. This Ṛich is an Anushṭubh; the Anushṭubh is speech; in that he consecrates him with this Ṛich, he consecrates him with the whole of speech. 'Let every (man) of the God who leads ', he says. By that (the Ṛich) is connected with Savitar '(Let every) man choose the companionship,' he says. By that (the Ṛich) has the Pitṛis for its deity.' 'Every man prayeth for wealth,' he says. By that (the Ṛich) is connected with the All-Gods. 'Let him choose glory that he may prosper,' he says. By that (the Ṛich) is connected with Pūshan. This Ṛich indeed is connected with all the Gods. In that he consecrates with this Ṛich, he consecrates him with all the Gods. The first quarter-verse is of seven syllables; the other three are of eight syllables. The three approach the eight; the four the eight. Because it has eight syllables it is a Gāyatrī Because it has eleven syllables it is a Trishṭubh. Because it has twelve syllables, it is a Jagatī This Ṛich indeed is all the metres. In that he consecrates him with this Ṛich, he consecrates him with all the metres. The first quarter verse is of seven syllables; the Śakvarī is of seven syllables, the Śakvarī is cattle; verily he wins cattle. The first quarter-verse is defective by one syllable. Therefore men live on what of speech is defective. He offers with a full (verse) to win Prajāpati; full as it were is Prajāpati He offers with a defective (verse), for the creation of offspring, for from what is defective Prajāpati created offspring.

Mantra 6:1:3

The Ṛich and the Sāman, unwilling to remain with the Gods for the sacrifice, taking the form of a black antelope departed and remained away. The (Gods) reflected, 'He whom they shall resort to will become all this world.' They called to them, and they depositing their might in day and night came up to them. This is the colour of the Ṛich, the white of the skin of the black antelope; the black is the colour of the Sāman 'Ye are images of the Ṛich and Sāman,' he says; verily he wins the Ṛich and the Sāman. The white of the black antelope skin is the colour of the day, the black of the night. Whatever is imbued in those two, he wins. He consecrates (him) with a black antelope skin. The black antelope skin is the form of the holy power; verily he consecrates him with the holy power. 'O God, this prayer of him who imploreth,' he says. That is according to the text. The man who is consecrated is a foetus; the clothing is the caul; be covers. Therefore foetuses are born covered (with the caul). He should not uncover before the purchasing of the Soma. If he were to uncover before the purchasing of the Soma, the foetuses of offspring would be liable to miscarriage. He uncovers when the Soma has been purchased; verily he is born. It is also as when one uncovers to a superior. The Aṅgirasas going to the world of heaven divided their strength. What was left over became Śara grass; Śara grass is strength. In that the girdle is of Śara grass, he wins strength. He girds it in the middle; verily he gives him strength in the middle. Therefore in the middle men enjoy strength. The part of man above the navel is pure, that below is impure. In that he girds him in the middle he discriminates between the pure and impure parts. Indra hurled his thunderbolt against Vṛitra; it divided into three parts; one-third the wooden sword, one-third the chariot, and one-third the sacrificial post. The internal arrows which were split (*aśīryanta*) became Śara grass, and that is why Śara grass is so called. The thunderbolt is Śara grass; hunger indeed is the foe of man. In that the girdle is of Śara grass, he clearly drives away the enemy hunger from the middle (of man's body). It is threefold. The breath is threefold; verily he places the threefold breath in the middle of the sacrificer. It is broad, for the discrimination of the strands. He consecrates the sacrificer with a girdle, with a yoke his wife, for the sake of offspring. The sacrifice reflected on the gift (to the priests). He had intercourse with her. Indra perceived this and reflected, 'He who will be born from this union will be this world.' He entered her; from her verily was Indra born; he reflected, 'He who hence other than I will be born will be this world'. Stroking her womb he split it, she became barren after birth, and that is the origin of the (cow) which is barren after birth. He wrapped it (the *yoni*) in his hand, he deposited it among the wild beasts, it became the horn of the black antelope. 'Thou art the birthplace of Indra; harm me not,' (with these words) he hands the horn of the black antelope. Verily he makes the sacrifice united with the womb, the gift with the womb, Indra with the womb, for union with the womb. 'For ploughing thee, for good crops,' he says. Therefore plants grow up without ploughing. 'For those of good fruits thee, for the plants,' he says. Therefore plants bear fruit. If he were to scratch himself with his hand his offspring would be liable to the itch; if he were to smile, they would become naked. He scratches himself with the horn of the black antelope and smiles, holding it for the protection of his offspring. He should not let go the horn of the black antelope before the bringing of the gifts (to the priests). If he were to let go the horn of the black antelope before the bringing of the gifts, the womb of his offspring will be liable to miscarriage. When the gifts have been brought, he casts away the horn of the black antelope in the pit. The pit is the womb of the sacrificer; the horn of the black antelope is the womb; verily he places womb in womb, that the sacrificer may have a womb.

Mantra 6:1:4

Speech went away from the Gods, not being willing to serve for the sacrifice. She entered the trees. It is the voice of the trees, the voice that is heard in the drum, the lute, and the flute. In that he offers the staff of the initiated, he wins speech. The (staff) is of Udumbara wood; the, Udumbara is strength; verily he wins strength. It is level with his mouth; verily from the mouth (downwards) he wins strength for him. Therefore from the mouth they enjoy strength. After the buying of the Soma he hands the staff to the Maitrāvaruṇa (priest). For the Maitrāvaruṇa first assigns to the priests their utterance, and the priests plant it in the sacrificer. 'Hail! with my mind the sacrifice,' he says; for man approaches the sacrifice with his mind. 'Hail! from heaven and earth,' he says; for the sacrifice is in heaven and earth. 'Hail! from the broad atmosphere,' he says; for the sacrifice is in the atmosphere. 'Hail! from the wind the sacrifice I grasp,' he says. The sacrifice is he who blows here; verily he clearly wins him. He clenches his fist; he restrains his speech, for the support of the sacrifice. 'This Brahman has consecrated himself,' he says thrice in a whisper; verily he proclaims him to the Gods. Thrice aloud (he says it); verily he proclaims him to both Gods and men. He should not utter speech until the Nakṣhatras appear. If he were to utter speech before the Nakṣhatras appear, he would divide the sacrifice. When the Nakṣhatras have arisen, be utters speech, 'Prepare the fast food.' The consecrated is bound by a vow of sacrifice; verily with regard to the sacrifice does he utter speech. Should he utter speech, he should then repeat a Ṛich addressed to Viṣhṇu. Viṣhṇu is the sacrifice; verily he unites the sacrifice with the sacrifice. 'The thought divine we meditate,' he says. Thus he makes smooth the sacrifice. 'May it guide us safely according as we will,' he says. Verily he wins the dawn. The theologians say, 'Should an offering be made in the house of one who is consecrated, or should an offering not be made?' The man who is consecrated is the oblation, and if he were to sacrifice he would offer a part of the sacrificer; if he were not to sacrifice, then he would omit a joint of the sacrifice. 'The Gods, mind born, mind using,' he says. The Gods, mind born, mind using, are the breaths; verily in them he sacrifices secretly, and the sacrifice is both offered as it were and yet not offered. Now the Rākṣhasas are fain to hurt him who is consecrated while he sleeps. Agni indeed is the slayer of the Rākṣhasas 'O Agni, be thou wakeful. Let us be glad,' he says; verily having made Agni his guardian, for the smiting away of the Rākṣhasas, he sleeps. Now, if a man who is consecrated sleeps, he does something that as it were is contrary to his vow. I Thou, O Agni, art the guardian of vows,' he says. Agni indeed is among the Gods the guardian of vows; verily he causes him to take up his vow again. 'Among the Gods and men,' he says for he, being a God, is (guardian of vows) among men. 'Thou art to be invoked at our sacrifices,' he says; for him they invoke at the sacrifices. Now power and the Gods depart from the man who is consecrated when he is asleep. 'All the Gods have surrounded me,' he says; verily he unites him with both power and the Gods. If he were not to utter that formula (Yajus), so many cattle would be as he might consecrate himself for. 'O Soma, give so much and bear more hither,' he says; verily he obtains innumerable cattle. 'Thou art gold; be for my enjoyment,' he says; verily he takes each according to its deity. He says, 'To Vāyu thee, to Varuṇa thee!' If he did not so specify them, he would put the gifts out of correspondence with the deities, and would be brought low to the deities. Because he thus specifies them, he puts the gifts in correspondence with the deities, and is not brought low to the deities. 'O divine waters, son of the waters,' he says. 'That divine part of yours, which is pure and fit for the sacrifice, may I not step upon,' that he says in effect. 'The unbroken web of earth may I follow,' he says; verily making a bridge he crosses over.

Mantra 6:1:5

The Gods, having fixed up a place of sacrifice, could not distinguish the quarters. They ran up to one another, (saying) 'By thee shall we distinguish them, by thee.' They fixed upon Aditi, (saying, 'By thee shall we distinguish them.' She said, 'Let me choose a guerdon. Let the opening oblation in the sacrifice be mine, and the concluding oblation be mine.' Therefore the opening oblation of the sacrifice belongs to Aditi, and the concluding oblation belongs to Aditi. He offers to five Gods; there are five quarters, (and so it serves) for the distinction of the quarters. Now the Paṅkti is of five elements, the sacrifice is fivefold; verily he wins the sacrifice. They made sacrifice to Pāthya Svasti. The eastern quarter they distinguished by her, by Agni the southern, by Soma the western, by Savitar the northern, by Aditi the zenith. He offers to Pāthya Svasti; verily he distinguishes the eastern quarter. Having offered to Pāthya Svasti, he offers to Agni and Soma. Agni and Soma indeed are the eyes of the sacrificer; verily he sees with them. Having offered to Agni and Soma, he offers to Savitar; verily on the instigation of Savitar he sees. Having offered to Savitar, he offers to Aditi; Aditi indeed is this (earth); verily taking his stand on it he sees. Having offered to Aditi, he repeats the verse to the Marutas. The Marutas are the subjects of the Gods. As the subjects of the Gods are in harmony, so he brings the human subjects into harmony.' In that he repeats the verse to the Marutas, it is to bring subjects into harmony. The theologians say, 'The opening oblation should be performed with a fore-offering, but without an after-offering; the concluding oblation should be performed with all after-offering, but without a fore-offering.' These are the fore-offerings, and these the after-offerings, and this is the course of the sacrifice. This is not to be followed. The fore-offerings are the self; the after-offerings the offspring. If he were to omit the fore-offerings, he would omit the self; if he were to omits the after-offerings, he would omit offspring. In so far as the whole of the sacrifice is not performed, in so far does the sacrifice come to ruin, and the sacrificer comes to ruin along with the sacrifice. Verily the opening oblation should be performed with both fore- and after-offerings, and the concluding oblation should be performed both with fore- and after offerings. He does not omit the self, nor offspring; the sacrifice does not come to ruin, nor the sacrificer. He offers the concluding oblation in the scrapings of the opening oblation; this is the course of the sacrifice. Now if he were to make the Yājyā verses of the opening libation the Yājyā verses of the concluding libation, he would mount to the other world away from this, and would be liable to die. The Puronuvākyā verses of the opening libation should be made the Yājyā verses of the concluding libation; verily he finds support in this world.

Mantra 6:1:6

Kadrū and Suparṇī had a dispute (for the stake of) each other's form. Kadrū defeated Suparṇī. She said, 'In the third heaven from here is the Soma; fetch it, and by it buy your release.' Kadrū is this (earth), Suparṇī yonder (heaven), the descendants of Suparṇī the metres. She said, 'For this do parents rear children; "in the third heaven from here is the Soma; fetch it, and by it buy your release," so has Kadrū said to me.' The Jagatī flew up, of fourteen syllables, but returned without obtaining it; it lost two syllables, but returned with the (sacrificial) animals and consecration. Therefore the Jagatī is the richest in cattle of the metres, and consecration waits upon a man who is rich in cattle. The Triṣhṭubh flew up, of thirteen syllables, but returned without obtaining it; it lost two syllables, but returned with the (sacrificial) gifts and penance. Therefore in the world of the Triṣhṭubh, the midday oblation, the gifts are brought. 'That in truth is penance,' they say, 'if a man gives his wealth.' The Gāyatrī flew up, of four syllables, together with a female goat with light. Then the goat won (Soma) for her, and so the goat has the name. The Gāyatrī brought back the Soma and the four syllables, and so became of eight syllables. The theologians say, 'For what reason is it that the Gāyatrī, the smallest of the metres, holds the forefront of the sacrifice?' Because it brought down the Soma, it held the forefront of the sacrifice; therefore it is the most glorious (of the metres). By the feet it grasped two of the oblations, and by the mouth one. The one it grasped by the mouth it sucked; therefore two oblations are made of the pure Soma, the morning and midday oblations;

therefore at the third oblation they pour out the dregs of the Soma; for they regard it as sucked as it were. He removes any admixture so that it may be pure; verily also he makes ready it (the *ṛijīṣha*). When the Soma was being borne away, the Gandharva Viśvāvasu stole it. It was for three nights stolen; therefore after purchase the Soma is kept for three nights. The Gods said, 'The Gandharvas love women; let us redeem it with a woman.' They made speech unto a woman of one year old, and with her redeemed it. She adopted the form of a deer and ran away from the Gandharvas that was the origin of the deer. The Gods said, 'She has run from you; she comes not to us; let us both summon her.' The Gandharvas uttered a spell, the Gods sang, she went to the Gods as they sang. Therefore women love one who sings; enamoured are women of him who thus knows. So if there is in a family one person who knows thus, men give their daughters in wedlock to that family, even if there be other (wooers) in plenty. He buys Soma with a (cow) one year old; verily he buys it with the whole of speech. Therefore men utter speech when one year old. He buys with a cow which has no horns, small ears, is not one-eyed or lame, and has not seven hooves; verily he buys it with all. If he were to buy it with a white cow, the sacrificer would become leprous. If he were to buy with a black one, it would be a funeral cow, and the sacrificer would be likely to die. If with one of both colours, it would be one sacred to Vṛitrahan, and he would either overcome his foe or his foe him. He buys with a ruddy, yellow-eyed one. This is the form of Soma; verily he buys it with its own deity.

Mantra 6:1:7

That became gold. Therefore they purify gold forth from the waters. The theologians say, 'How is it that offspring are produced through that which is boneless, and yet are born with bones?' Because he offers the gold, placing it in the ghee, therefore are offspring produced, through that which is boneless, and yet are born with bones. The ghee is Agni's loved abode, the gold, is radiance. 'This is thy body, O pure one. This is thy splendour,' he says; verily he unites Agni with his radiance and his body; verily also he makes him ready. If he were to deposit (the gold) without fastening it on, then the foetuses of offspring would be liable to miscarriage. He deposits it fastening it on, to secure the foetuses. He fastens it so that it cannot be untied, for the production of offspring. The cow with which the Soma is bought is speech. 'Thou art the strong,' he says; for what he strengthens in his mind, that he expresses in speech. 'Grasped by mind,' he says; for by mind is speech grasped. 'Acceptable to Vishṇu he says. Vishṇu is the sacrifice; verily be makes her accept able to the sacrifice. 'Through the impulse of thee, of true impulse,' he says; verily he wins speech which is impelled by Savitar As each part is performed, the Rākṣhasas are fain to injure the sacrifice; the path of Agni and Sūrya is one which the Rākṣhasas cannot injure. 'I have mounted the eye of the sun, the pupil of the eye of Agni,' he says. He mounts the path which is not injured by the Rākṣhasas. The cow with which the Soma is bought is speech. 'Thou art thought, thou art mind,' he says; verily he instructs her. Therefore children are born instructed. 'Thou art thought,' he says, for what one thinks in the mind one expresses in speech. 'Thou art mind,' he says; for what one grasps by the mind one performs. 'Thou art meditation,' he says; for what one meditates with the mind one expresses in speech. 'Thou art the gift (to the priests),' he says; for (the cow) is the gift. 'Thou art of the sacrifice,' he says; verily he makes her fit for the sacrifice. 'Thou art of kingly power,' he says, for she is of kingly power. 'Thou art Aditi, double-headed,' he says. In that to Aditi belong the opening and the concluding oblations of the sacrifices, therefore does he say that. If (the cow) were not bound, she would be unrestrained; if she were bound by the foot, she would be the funeral cow, and the sacrificer would be likely to perish. If she were held by the ears, she would belong to Vṛitrahan, and the sacrificer would oppress another, or another would oppress him. 'May Mitra bind thee by the foot,' he says. Mitra is the auspicious one of the Gods; verily with his help he binds her by the foot. 'May Pūṣhan guard the ways,' he says. Pūṣhan is this (earth); verily he makes her lady of this (earth), for the gaining thereof. 'For Indra the guardian!' he says; verily he makes Indra her guardian. 'May thy mother approve, thy father,' he says; verily he buys with her approved. 'Go, O Goddess, to the God,' he says; for she is a Goddess, and Soma is a God. 'To Indra Soma,' he says; for the Soma is borne to Indra. If he were not to say that text, the cow with which the Soma is bought would go away. 'May Rudra guide thee hither,' he says. Rudra is the harsh one of the Gods; verily he places him below her, for guiding hither. He does as it were a harsh thing when he recites that (text) of Rudra's. 'In the path of Mitra,' he says, for soothing. He buys indeed by speech when he buys by the cow with which the Soma is bought. Hail! Return with Soma as thy comrade, with wealth,' he says, verily having purchased by means of speech, he restores speech to himself. The speech of him who knows thus is not likely to fail.

Mantra 6:1:8

He follows six steps. Speech does not speak beyond the sixth day. He wins speech in the size in which she is found in the path of the year. He offers in the seventh footprint. The Śakvarī has seven feet, the Śakvarī is cattle; verily he wins cattle. There are seven domesticated animals, and seven wild; there are seven metres to win both sets of animals. 'Thou art a Vasvī, thou art a Rudra,' he says; verily thus by her form he expounds her greatness. 'May Bṛihaspati make thee rejoice in happiness,' he says. Bṛihaspati is the holy power of the Gods; verily by means of the holy power be wins cattle for him. 'May Rudra with the Vasus be favourable to thee,' he says, for the sake of protection. 'I pour thee on the head of the earth, on the place of sacrifice,' he says; for the place of sacrifice is the head of the earth. 'On the abode of the offering,' he says; for the foot of the cow by which the Soma is bought is the abode of the offering. 'Rich in ghee; hail!,' he says. Because it was from her foot that ghee was pressed out, he says thus. If the Adhvaryu were to offer a libation where there were no fire, the Adhvaryu would become blind, and the Rākṣhasas would destroy the sacrifice. He offers after putting down the gold; verily he offers in that which has fire, the Adhvaryu does not become blind, and the Rākṣhasas do not destroy the sacrifice. As each part is performed, the Rākṣhasas are fain to injure the sacrifice. 'The Rakṣhas is enclosed, the evil spirits are enclosed,' he says, for the smiting away of the Rākṣhasas. 'Thus I cut the necks of the Rakṣhas'; 'Who hateth us and whom we hate,' he says. There are two persons, one whom he hates and one who hates him; verily successively he cuts their necks. The foot of the cow with which the Soma is bought is cattle; he pours (the dust of the footprint) so far as it is mixed with the ghee; verily he wins cattle. (Saying) 'Ours be wealth,' he pours it; verily the Adhvaryu does not deprive himself of cattle. Saying 'Thine be wealth,' he hands it to the sacrificer, and so bestows wealth on the sacrificer. Saying 'Thine be wealth,' (the sacrificer hands it) to his wife. For a wife is the half of oneself, and to do so is as it were to deposit it in one's house. 'Let me attend on thee with Tvaṣhṭar's aid,' he says. Tvaṣhṭar is the maker of the forms of offspring, of pairings; verily he places form in cattle. For this world the Gārhapatya fire is piled up; for yonder world the Āhavanīya If he were to cast it on-the Gārhapatya fire, he would be rich in cattle in this world; if on the Āhavanīya, he would be rich in cattle in yonder world he casts it on both; verily he makes him rich in cattle in both worlds.

Mantra 6:1:9

The theologians say, 'Should the Soma be clarified or not?' Soma indeed is the king of plants; whatever falls upon it is swallowed by it. If be were to clarify it, it would be as when one expels from the mouth what has been swallowed; if he were not to clarify it, it would be as when something falls upon the eye and moves to and fro; the Adhvaryu would be hungry, the sacrificer would be hungry. 'O Soma-seller, purify the Soma,' he should say; so whether it be the one or the other'. he involves the Soma-seller in both (faults), and therefore the Soma-seller is hungry. Aruṇa Aupaveśi said, 'At the buying of the Soma I win the third pressing.' He measures (the Soma) on the skin of beasts verily he wins cattle, for cattle are the third pressing. If he desire of a man, 'May he be without cattle,' he should measure it for him on the rough side. The rough side indeed is not connected with cattle; verily he becomes without cattle. If he desire of a man, 'May he be rich in cattle,' he should measure for him on the hairy side. That indeed is the form of cattle; verily by the form he obtains cattle for him; verily he becomes rich in cattle. He buys it at the end of the waters; verily he buys it with its sap. 'Thou art a home dweller,' he says; verily he makes it at home. 'Thy libation is bright,' he says; for bright is its libation. He advances (for it) with a cart; verily he advances to its mightiness. He advances with a cart, therefore what lives on the level is to be borne by a cart. Where, however, they bear it on their heads, therefore what lives on the hill is to be borne on the head. With a verse, 'That God, Savitar,' in the Atichandas metre he measures. The Atichandas is all the metres; verily with all the metres he measures it. The Atichandas is the highest of the metres. In that he measures with a verse in the Atichandas metre, he makes it the highest of its peers. With each (finger) separately he measures; verily he measures it with each fresh in turn; therefore the fingers have various strengths. He presses down the thumb on them all; therefore it has equal strength with the other fingers; therefore all it accompanies. If he were to measure with all (the fingers), the fingers would grow united; with each separately he measures; therefore they grow separate. He measures five times with the Yajus. The Paṅkti has five syllables, the sacrifice is fivefold; verily he wins the sacrifice. (He measures) five times in silence. They make up ten. The Virāj has ten syllables, the Virāj is food; verily by the Virāj he wins proper food. In that he measures with the Yajus, he wins the past; in that he measures in silence, the future. Now if there were only so much Soma as that which he measures, there would be enough for the sacrificer only, and not also for the priests in the Sadas. With the words, 'For offspring thee!' he draws (the cloth for the Soma) together; verily he makes the priests in the Sadas share in it; with a garment he ties it up; the garment is connected with all the Gods; verily he unites it with all the Gods, the Soma is cattle; (with the words) 'For expiration thee,' he ties it; verily he confers expiration upon cattle. (With the words) 'For cross-breathing thee,' he looses it; verily he confers cross-breathing upon cattle; therefore the vital breaths do not desert a sleeper.

Mantra 6:1:10.

If he were to barter (it) in response (to the words), 'Let me buy with one-sixteenth (of the cow) from thee, with one-eighth,' he would make the Soma not worth a cow, the sacrificer not worth a cow, the Adhvaryu not, worth a cow, but he would not depreciate the mightiness of the cow. 'With a cow let me buy from thee,' verily he should say; verily he makes the Soma worth a cow, the sacrificer worth a cow, the Adhvaryu worth a cow, yet still he does not depreciate the mightiness of the cow. He buys (it) with a she-goat; verily he buys it full of fervour; he buys (it) with gold; verily he buys it bright; he buys (it) with a milch cow; verily he buys it with milk for the mixing: he buys (it) with a bull; verily he buys it with Indra; he buys (it) with a draught ox, the draught ox is the bearer; verily by the bearer he buys the bearer of the sacrifice; he buys with two as a pair, to win a pair; he buys with a garment, the garment is connected with all the Gods; verily he buys it for all the Gods. These,, make up ten. The Virāj has ten syllables, the Virāj is food; verily by the Virāj he wins proper food. 'Thou art the bodily form of penance, Prajāpati's kind,' he says, verily the Adhvaryu makes atonement to the cattle, that he may not be cut off. He attains prosperity, be obtains cattle who knows thus. 'The bright with the bright for thee I buy,' he says that is according to the text. The Gods retook by force the gold where with they purchased the Soma, saying, 'Who shall barter brilliance?' The gold by which he buys the Soma he should retake by force; verily he bestows brilliance upon himself. 'Ours be light, darkness be on the Soma seller,' he says; verily he places light in the sacrificer, and bestows darkness on the Soma-seller. If he were to strike (the Soma-seller) without inter twining (the flock of wool), then the serpents would bite during that year. 'Thus do I intertwine the necks of the biting serpents,' he says; the serpents do not bite that year, he pierces the Soma-seller with darkness. 'O Svāna, Bhrāja,' he says; they indeed in yonder world guarded the Soma; from them they grasped the Soma; if he were not to indicate to them those that serve as the price of Soma, he would not have purchased the Soma, and they would not guard the Soma for him in yonder world. In that he indicates to them those that serve as the price of Soma, he really purchases the Soma, and they guard the Soma for him in yonder world.

Mantra 6:1:11

The Soma when bought and tied up is connected with Varuṇa Come as a friend to us, creating firm friendships,' he says, for atonement. Enter the right thigh of Indra,' he says; the Gods placed the Soma which they purchased in the right thigh of Indra; now the sacrificer is Indra; therefore he says thus. 'With life, with fair life,' he says; verily seizing the Gods he rises up. 'Fare along the wide atmosphere,' he says; for Soma has the atmosphere for its deity. 'Thou art the seat of Aditi. Sit on the seat of Aditi,' he says; that is according to the text. He severs it indeed when he makes what is connected with Varuṇa connected with Mitra; he sets it down with a verse addressed to Varuṇa; verily he unites it with its own deity. He covers it round with a garment, the garment is connected with all the Gods; verily with all the Gods he unites it, and thus (it serves) for the smiting away of the Rākṣhasas 'He hath stretched the atmosphere within the woods,' he says; for within the woods he stretched the atmosphere. 'Strength in horses,' he says; for (he placed) strength in horses. 'Milk in kine,' he says; for (he placed) milk in kine. 'Skill in the heart,' he says; for (he placed) skill in the heart. 'Varuṇa, Agni in dwellings,' he says; for Varuṇa (placed) Agni in dwellings. 'The sun in the sky,' he says; for (he placed) the sun in the sky. 'The Soma in the hill,' he says; the hills are the pressing-stones; he places the Soma in them, who sacrifices; therefore he says thus. 'Thee, all-knowing God' with this verse addressed to Sūrya he fastens the black antelope skin, to smite away the Rākṣhasas 'Come hither, O ye oxen, strong to bear the yoke,' he says; that is according to the text. 'Move forward, O lord of the world,' he says; for he is the lord of creatures; 'to all thy stations,' be says; for he moves forward to all his stations. 'Let no opponent find thee,' he says; since the Gandharva Viśvāvasu stole the Soma when it was being carried below, he says that, to prevent its being stolen. 'Thou art the good luck of the sacrificer,' he says; verily thus the sacrificer grasps the sacrifice, that it be not interrupted. The Soma when bought and tied up indeed approaches the sacrificer in the shape of Varuṇa. 'Honour to the radiance of Mitra and Varuṇa,' he says, for atonement. They bring forward this Soma, it rests with Agni, they in uniting overpower the sacrificer. Now the consecrated person has for long been holding himself ready for the sacrifice. In that he offers an animal to Agni and Soma, that is a buying-off of himself; therefore of it he should not eat; for as it were it is a buying-off of a man. Or rather they say, 'By Agni and Soma Indra slew Vṛitra.' In that he offers an animal to Agni and Soma, it slays hostile things for him; therefore he should eat of it. He honours it with a verse addressed to Varuṇa; verily he honours it with its own deity.

Prapāṭhaka 2.

The Exposition of the Soma Sacrifice (continued)

Mantra 6:2:1

If he should offer hospitality after unyoking both (the oxen), he would break up the sacrifice. If (he should offer) before he has unyoked both, it would be as when hospitality is offered to one who has not yet arrived. One ox is unyoked, one ox is not unyoked; then he offers hospitality, for the continuance of the sacrifice. The wife (of the sacrificer) holds on (to the cart); for the wife is mistress of the household gear; verily he offers what is approved by the wife. The share of the wife in the sacrifice makes a pair; so the wife also grasps the sacrifice that it may not be interrupted. With whatever retinue the king comes, to all of them hospitality is offered; the metres are the retinue of King Soma. 'Thou art the hospitality of Agni. For Viṣhṇu thee!' he says; thus he offers (hospitality) to the Gāyatrī 'Thou art the hospitality of Soma. 'For Viṣhṇu thee!' he says; thus he offers (hospitality) to the Triṣhṭubh. 'Thou art the hospitality of the stranger. For Viṣhṇu thee!' he says; thus he offers (hospitality) to the Jagatī. 'For Agni thee, giver of wealth, for Viṣhṇu thee!' he says; thus he offers (hospitality) to the Anuṣhṭubh. 'For the eagle, bringer of the Soma, thee, for Viṣhṇu thee!' he says; thus he offers (hospitality) to the Gāyatrī He offers five times. The Paṅkti has five syllables, the sacrifice is fivefold; verily he wins the sacrifice. The theologians say, 'For what reason is the Gāyatrī offered to on either side of the offering of hospitality?' Because the Gāyatrī brought the Soma down; therefore is it offered to on both sides of hospitality, before and after. Hospitality is the head of the sacrifice, the sacrificial cake is offered on nine potsherds, therefore the head has nine apertures. The sacrificial cake is offered on nine potsherds. The three sets of three potsherds are commensurate with the Trivṛit Stoma, the Trivṛit is brilliance; verily he places brilliance in the head of the sacrifice. The sacrificial cake is offered on nine potsherds. The three sets of three potsherds are commensurate with the threefold breath, the breath is threefold; verily in order he places the threefold breath in the head of the sacrifice. Now the *Saccharum spontaneum* shoots are the eyelashes of Prajāpati, and his lids are pieces of sugar-cane. In that the strew is of *Saccharum spontaneum* and the dividing-stakes of sugar-cane, verily he brings together the eye of Prajāpati Now the libations made by the Gods the Asuras tore and ate. The Gods saw the *Gmelina arborea* tree. (Thinking) 'It is fit for work; by it one can perform work,' they made the enclosing sticks of *Gmelina arborea* wood, and by them they smote away the Rākṣhasas In that the enclosing-sticks are made of *Gmelina arborea* wood, it is for the smiting away of the Rākṣhasas He makes them touch, that the Rākṣhasas may not go through them. He does not place one in front, for the sun which rises in front smites away the Rākṣhasas He places the kindling-sticks erect; verily from above he smites away the Rākṣhasas; (he places one) with a Yajus, the other in silence, to make a pair. He places two; the sacrifice has two feet; (verily they serve) for support. The theologians say, 'There are both Agni and Soma here; why is hospitality offered to Soma and not to Agni?' In that having kindled fire he places it on the fire, by that verily is hospitality offered to Agni. Or rather they say, 'Agni is all the Gods.' In that he kindles fire after placing the oblation, he thus produces all the Gods for the oblation when it has been placed.

Mantra 6:2:2

The Gods and the Asuras were in conflict. The Gods fell out among themselves. Being unwilling to accept one another's pre-eminence, they separated in five bodies, Agni with the Vasus, Soma with the Rudras, Indra with the Marutas, Varuṇa with the Ādityas, Bṛihaspati with the All-Gods. They reflected, 'Our foes, the Asuras, we are profiting in that we are falling out among ourselves; let us remove (from us) and deposit together those bodies which are dear to us; from these shall he depart who first of us is hostile to another.' Therefore of those who perform the Tānūnaptra rite he who first is hostile goes to destruction. In that he divides up the Tānūnaptra, (it serves) for the overcoming of the foe; he himself prospers, his foe is defeated. He divides five times; for five times did they divide. Then again the Paṅkti has five syllables, the sacrifice is fivefold; verily he wins the sacrifice. 'For him who rusheth on I seize thee,' he says; he who rushes on is the breath; verily he delights the breath. 'For him who rusheth around,' he says; he who rushes around is the mind; verily he delights the mind. 'For Tānūnaptra,' he says; for they divided up these bodies. 'For the mighty,' he says; for they divided them up for strength. 'For the greatest in strength,' he says; for they divided up the greatest part of themselves. 'Thou art unsurmounted, the unsurmountable,' he says; for that is unsurmounted and unsurmountable. 'The force of the Gods,' be says; for that is the force of the Gods. 'Guarding from imprecations, impervious to imprecations,' he says; for that guards from imprecations and is impervious to imprecations. 'May the lord of consecration approve my consecration,' he says; that is according to the text. The Gods making the ghee a weapon smote Soma; now they come near the Soma as it were, when they perform the Tānūnaptra 'May thy every shoot, O God Soma, swell,' be says. Whatever of it becomes spoiled' or is lost, that he purifies by it. 'May Indra swell for thee; do thou swell for Indra,' he says; verily he makes to swell both Indra and Soma. 'Make thy comrades to swell with wealth and skill,' he says. The priests are his comrades; verily he makes them to swell. 'With good fortune may I accomplish thy pressing, O God Soma,' he says; verily he invokes this blessing (on himself). Those who make the Soma to swell fall away from this world, for the Soma when made to swell has the atmosphere as its deity. 'Desired are riches exceedingly, for food, for prosperity,' he says; verily by paying homage to heaven and earth they find support in this world. The Gods and the Asuras were in conflict. The Gods in fear entered Agni; therefore they say, 'Agni is all the Gods'. They, making Agni their protection, overcame the Asuras. Now he as it were enters Agni who undergoes the intermediate consecration, (and it serves) for the overcoming of his foes; he prospers himself, his foe is overcome. He protects himself by the consecration, his offspring by the intermediate consecration. The girdle he makes tighter; for his offspring are closer to him than himself. He drinks warm milk, and rubs himself with bubbling water; for fire is extinguished by cold, (and these serve) for kindling. 'Thy dread form, O Agni,' he says; verily with its own deity he consumes the hot milk, for unity, for atonement.

Mantra 6:2:3

The Asuras had three citadels; the lowest was of iron, then there was one of silver, then one of gold. The Gods could not conquer them; they sought to conquer them by siege; therefore they say—both those who know thus and those who do not—'By siege they conquer great citadels.' They made ready an arrow, Agni as the point, Soma as the socket, Viṣhṇu as the shaft. They said, 'Who shall shoot it?' 'Rudra,' they said, 'Rudra is cruel, let him shoot it.' He said, 'Let me choose a boon; let me be overlord of animals.' Therefore is Rudra overlord of animals. Rudra let it go; it cleft the three citadels and drove the Asuras away from these worlds. The observance of the Upasads is for the driving away of foes. One should not offer another libation in front; if be were to offer another libation in front, he would make something else the beginning. He sprinkles clarified butter with the dipping-ladle to proclaim the sacrifice. He makes the offering after crossing over without coming back; verily he drives away his foes from these worlds so that they come not back. Then returning he offers the Upasad libation; verily having driven away his foes from these worlds and having conquered he mounts upon the world of his foes. Now the Gods by the Upasads which they performed in the morning drove away the Asuras from the day, by the Upasads (performed) in the evening (they drove away the Asuras) from the night. In that both morning and evening Upasads are performed, the sacrificer drives away his foes from day and night. The Yājyās used in the morning should be made Puronuvākyās at night, for variety. He performs three Upasads, these worlds are three; verily he delights these worlds; they together make six, the seasons are six; verily he delights the seasons. He performs twelve at an Ahīna Soma sacrifice, the year consists of twelve months; verily he de lights the year. They make twenty-four, the half-months number twenty four; verily he delights the half-months. He should perform an awl-shaped intermediate consecration who wishes, 'May there be prosperity for me in this world,' (that is) one to begin with, then two, then three, then four; this indeed is the awl-shaped intermediate consecration; verily there is prosperity for him in this world. He should perform an intermediate consecration broader at the top than below who wishes, 'May there be prosperity for me in yonder world,' (that is) four to begin with, then three, then two, then one; this indeed is the intermediate consecration broader at the top than below; verily there is prosperity for him in yonder world.

Mantra 6:2:4

They go to the world of heaven who perform the Upasads. Of them he who takes out (a little food) is left behind; one must take out carefully, (thinking) 'I have not taken out anything.' He who is left behind wearied among those who go on their own mission sticks behind and lives at (home). Therefore after once taking out, one should not take out a second time. One should take out of curd, that is the symbol of cattle; verily by the symbol he wins cattle. The sacrifice went away from the Gods in the form of Viṣhṇu, and entered the earth. The Gods sought him grasping hands. Indra passed over him. He said, 'Who has passed over me?' 'I am he who smites in the stronghold; who art thou?' 'I am he who brings from the stronghold.' He said, 'Thou art called he who smites in the stronghold. Now a boar, stealer of the good, keeps the wealth of the Asuras which is to be won beyond the seven hills. Him smite, if thou art he who smites in the stronghold.' He plucked out a bunch of Darbha grass, pierced the seven hills, and smote him. He said, 'Thou art called he who brings from the stronghold; bring him.' So the sacrifice bore off the sacrifice for them; in that they won the wealth of the Asuras which was to be won (*vedyam*), that alone is the reason why the Vedi is so called. The Asuras indeed at first owned the earth, the Gods had so much as one seated can espy. The Gods said, 'May we also have a share in the earth?' 'How much shall we give you?' 'Give us as much as this Salāvṛikī can thrice run round.' Indra taking the form of a Salāvṛikī thrice ran round on all sides the earth. So they won the earth, and in that they won it therefore is the Vedi so called. All this earth is the Vedi, but they measure off and sacrifice on so much as they deem they can use. The back cross-line is thirty feet, the eastern line is thirty-six feet, the front cross-line is twenty-four feet. These make up tens; the Virāj has ten syllables; the Virāj is food; verily by the Virāj he wins food. He digs up (the earth); verily he digs away whatever in it is impure. He digs up; therefore the plants perish. He spreads the sacrificial strew; therefore the plants again revive. He spreads over the strew the upper strew. The strew is the people; the upper strew is the sacrificer; verily he makes the sacrificer higher than the man who does not sacrifice; therefore the sacrificer is higher than the man who does not sacrifice.

Mantra 6:2:5

If a weak man take up a burden, he breaks up into pieces. If there were twelve Upasads in the one-day rite, and three in the Ahīna, the sacrifice would be upset. There are three Upasads in the one-day rite, twelve in the Ahīna, to preserve the strength of the sacrifice; thus it is in order. One teat (of the cow) is used for a child, for that is fortunate. So he takes one teat for his milk drink, then two, then three, then four. That is the razor-edged drink by which he drives away his foes when born and repels them when about to be born; verily also with the smaller he approaches the greater. He takes the four teats first for his drink, then three, then two, then one. That is the drink called 'of a beatific back,' full of fervour, and of heavenly character; verily also is he propagated with children and cattle. Gruel is the drink of the Rājanya; gruel is as it were harsh; the Rājanya is as it were harsh, it is the symbol of the thunderbolt, (and serves) for success. Curds (is the drink) of the Vaiśya, it is the symbol of the sacrifice of cooked food, (and serves) for prosperity. Milk (is the drink) of the Brahman, the Brahman is brilliance, milk is brilliance; verily by brilliance he endows himself with brilliance and milk. Again by milk foetuses grow; the man who is consecrated is as it were a foetus; in that milk is his drink, verily thus he causes himself to grow. Manu was wont thrice to take drink, the Asuras twice, the Gods once. Morning, midday, evening, were the times of Manu's drinking, the symbol of the sacrifice of cooked food, (serving) for prosperity. Morning and evening were those of the Asuras, without a middle, a symbol of hunger; thence were they overcome. Midday and midnight were those of the Gods; thence they prospered and went to the world of heaven. Now with regard to his drinking at midday and at midnight, it is in the middle that people feed themselves; verily he places strength in the middle of himself, for the overcoming of his foes. He prospers himself, his foe is overcome. Now the man who is consecrated is a foetus, the consecration-shed is the womb (in which he is). If the man who is consecrated were to leave the consecration-shed, it would be as when a foetus falls from the womb. He must not leave, to guard himself. The fire here is a tiger to guard the house. Therefore if the man who is consecrated were to leave (the shed), he would be likely to spring up and slay him. He must not leave, to protect himself. He lies on the right side; that is the abode of the sacrifice; verily he lies in his own abode. He lies turned towards the fire; verily he lies turned towards the Gods and the sacrifice.

Mantra 6:2:6

On a place of sacrifice where the sacrifice faces the east should he make him to sacrifice for whom he wishes, 'May the higher sacrifice condescend to him, may he gain the world of heaven.' That is the place of sacrifice where the sacrifice faces the east, where the Hotar as be recites the Prātaranuvāka gazes upon the fire, water, and the sun. To him the higher sacrifice condescends, he gains the world of heaven. On a contiguous (*aptā*) place of sacrifice should he make him to sacrifice who has foes. He should make it touch the road or a pit so that neither a wagon nor a chariot can go between. That is a contiguous place of sacrifice. He conquers (*āpnoti*) his foe, his foe conquers him not. On a place of sacrifice which is elevated in one place he should make him to sacrifice who desires cattle. The Aṅgirasas produced cattle from a place of sacrifice elevated in one place. It should be elevated between the seat and the oblation-holders. That is a place of sacrifice elevated in one place; verily he becomes possessed of cattle. On a place of sacrifice which is elevated in three places should he make him to sacrifice who desires heaven. The Aṅgirasas went to the world of heaven from a place of sacrifice elevated in three places. It should be elevated between the Āhavanīya fire and the oblation holder, between the oblation-holder and the seat, and between the seat and the Gārhapatya fire. That is a place of sacrifice elevated in three places; verily he goes to the world of heaven. On a place of sacrifice which is firm should he make him to sacrifice who desires support. That is a place of sacrifice which is firm, which is level on all sides; verily he finds, support. Where diverse plants are intertwined, there should he make him sacrifice who desires cattle. That is the form of cattle; verily by the form he wins cattle for him; verily be becomes possessed of cattle. On a place of sacrifice seized by destruction should he make him to sacrifice for whom he desires, 'May I cause his sacrifice to be seized by destruction.' That is a place of sacrifice seized by destruction where there is a bare patch of level ground; verily he causes his sacrifice to be seized by destruction. On a place of sacrifice which is distinctly marked should he cause him to sacrifice regarding whom they have doubts as to (admitting him to) common meals or to marriage. It should be sloping east of the Āhavanīya and west of the Gārhapatya That is a place of sacrifice which is distinctly marked, be is distinguished from his evil foe, they doubt not of him for common meal or wedding. On a place of sacrifice which is artificial should he make him sacrifice who desires wealth. Man must be made; verily he prospers.

Mantra 6:2:7

The high altar taking the form of a lioness went away and remained between the two parties. The Gods reflected, 'Whichever of the two she joins, they will become this.' They called to her; she said, 'Let me choose a boon; through me shall ye obtain all your desires, but the oblation shall come to me before (it comes to) the fire.' Therefore do they besprinkle the high altar before (they sprinkle) the fire, for that was its chosen boon. He measures (it) round with the yoke-pin, that is its measure; verily also by what is fitting he wins what is fitting. 'Thou art the abode of riches (vittā) for me,' he says, for being found (vittā) she helped them; thou art the resort of the afflicted for me,' he says, for she helped them in affliction; 'protect me when in want,' he says, for she protected them when in want; 'protect me when afflicted,' he says, for she protected them when afflicted. 'May Agni, named Nabhas, know (thee), O Agni Aṅgiras,' (with these words) he thrice strokes with (the wooden sword); verily he wins the fires that are in these worlds. He strokes in silence for the fourth time, verily he wins that which is not indicated. 'Thou art a lioness; thou art a buffalo,' he says, for it (the high altar) taking the form of a lioness went away and remained between the two parties. 'Extend wide; let the lord of the sacrifice extend wide for thee,' he says; verily he enriches the sacrificer with offspring and cattle. 'Thou art firm,' (with these words) he strikes (the earth) together, for firmness. 'Be pure for the Gods; be bright for the Gods,' (with these words) he moistens it and scatters (sand) on it, for purity. 'May the cry of Indra guard thee in front with the Vasus,' be says; verily be sprinkles it from the quarters. 'Since the high altar has gone to the Gods, here must we conquer' (thought) the Asuras, and with bolts ready they advanced on the Gods. Them the cry of Indra with the Vasus repelled in front; the swift of mind with the Pitṛis on the right, the wise one with the Rudras behind, and Viśvakarman with the Ādityas on the left. In that he sprinkles the high altar, verily thus does the sacrificer repel his foes from the quarters. Indra gave the Yatis to the Sālāvṛikas; them they ate on the right of the high altar. Whatever is left of the sprinkling waters he should pour on the right of the high altar; whatever cruel is there that he appeases thereby. He should think of whomever he hates; verily he brings affliction upon him.

Mantra 6:2:8

The high altar said, 'Through me ye shall obtain all your desires.' The Gods desired, 'Let us overcome the Asuras our foes.' They sacrificed (with the words), 'Thou art a lioness, overcoming rivals; hail!' They over came the Asuras, their foes. Having overcome the Asuras, their foes, they felt desire, 'May we obtain offspring.' They sacrificed (with the words), 'Thou art a lioness, bestowing fair offspring, hail!' They obtained offspring. They having obtained offspring felt desire, 'May we obtain cattle.' They sacrificed (with the words), 'Thou art a lioness, bestowing increase of wealth; hail!' They obtained cattle. Having obtained cattle, they felt desire, 'May we obtain support.' They sacrificed (with the words), 'Thou art a lioness, winning (the favour of) the Ādityas; hail!' They found support here. Having found support here, they felt desire, 'May we approach the deities for blessings.' They sacrificed (with the words), 'Thou art a lioness; bring the Gods to the pious sacrificer; hail!' They approached the deities for blessings. He sprinkles five times; the Paṅkti has five syllables, the sacrifice is fivefold; verily he wins the sacrifice. He sprinkles transversely; therefore cattle move their limbs transversely, for support. 'For beings thee!' (with these words) he takes up the ladle; of the Gods that are that is the share; verily he therewith delights them. He puts round the enclosing-sticks of *Butea frondosa*, for the holding apart of these worlds. Agni had three elder brothers. They perished when carrying the offering to the Gods. Agni was afraid, 'This one here will come to ruin.' He went away. The (night) he spent among the trees was with the *Butea frondosa*: the (night) among the plants was with the *Sugandhitejana*; the (night) among the cattle was between the horns of a ram. The Gods sought to start him forth. They found him, and said to him, 'Return to us; bear the offering for us.' He said, 'Let me choose a boon. Whatever of the offering when taken up falls outside the enclosing sticks, let that be the portion of my brothers.' Therefore whatever of the offering when taken up falls outside the enclosing-sticks, that is their portion; verily therewith be delights them. He reflected, 'My brothers of old perished because they had bones. I will shatter bones.' The bones he shattered became the *Butea frondosa*, the flesh which died on them bdellium. In that he brings together these paraphernalia, verily thus be brings Agni together. 'Thou art the rubble of Agni,' he says, for the paraphernalia are the rubble of Agni. Or rather they say, 'These enclosing-sticks of *Butea frondosa* which lie around are in truth his brothers.'

Mantra 6. 2.9.

He loosens the knot; verily he sets them free from the noose of Varuṇa; verily he makes them fit for the sacrifice. Having sacrificed with a verse to Savitar, he brings forward the oblation-holders; verily on the instigation of Savitar he brings them forward. The axle which is tied on both sides is Varuṇa of evil speech; if it were to creak, it would creak against the house of the sacrificer. 'With fair voice, O God, do thou address the dwelling,' he says; the dwelling is the house; (verily it serves) for atonement. The wife (of the sacrificer) anoints (them), for the wife is every one's friend, for friendship. The share of the wife in the sacrifice makes a pair; verily also the wife grasps the sacrifice that it may not be interrupted. Now the Rākṣhasas following in its track seek to injure the sacrifice; he makes a libation in the two tracks with Ṛich verses addressed to Viṣhṇu. The sacrifice is Viṣhṇu; verily he drives away the Rākṣhasas from the sacrifice. If the Adhvaryu were to pour the libation in (a place) without fire, the Adhvaryu would become blind, the Rākṣhasas would injure the sacrifice. He puts gold down on it before making the libation; verily he makes the libation in that which has fire; the Adhvaryu does not become blind, the Rākṣhasas do not injure the sacrifice. 'Come ye two forward, ordaining the offering,' he says; verily he makes them go to the world of heaven. 'There rejoice on the height of the earth,' he says, for the place of sacrifice is the height of the earth. Now the oblation-holder is the head of the sacrifice. 'From the sky, O Viṣhṇu, or from the earth,' with this Ṛich verse which contains a blessing he strikes in the prop of the southern oblation-holder; verily the sacrificer at the beginning of the sacrifice wins blessings. Now Daṇḍa Aupara split by the Vaṣhaṭ call the axle of the third oblation-holder; the third cover put on the oblation-holder (serves) to make up the third oblation-holder, The oblation-holder is the head of the sacrifice. 'Thou art the forehead of Viṣhṇu: thou art the back of Viṣhṇu,' he says. Therefore so often is the head divided. 'Thou art the string of Viṣhṇu; thou art the fixed point of Viṣhṇu,' he says, for the oblation-holder is connected with Viṣhṇu as its deity. Now the knot which he first ties, if he were not to unloose it, the Adhvaryu would perish from suppression of urine; therefore it must be unloosed.

Mantra 6:2:10.

'On the impulse of the God Savitar,' (with these words) he takes up the spade, for impelling. 'With the arms of the Aśvins he says, for the Aśvins were the priests of the Gods. 'With the hands of Pūṣhan,' be for restraint. Now the spade is as it were a bolt; 'Thou art the spade; thou art the, woman,' he says, to appease it. Now, as each part is performed, the Rākṣhasas seek to injure the sacrifice; 'The Rakṣhas is encompassed, the evil spirits are encompassed,' he says, to smite away the Rākṣhasas. 'Here do I cut off the neck of the Rakṣhas, who hateth us, and whom we hate,' he says; there are two people, he whom he hates and he who hates him; verily straightway he cuts their necks. 'To sky thee, to atmosphere thee, to earth thee!' he says; verily he anoints it for these worlds. He anoints from the top downwards; therefore men live on strength from the top downwards. Now he does a cruel deed in that he digs; he pours down water, for atonement. He pours down (water) mixed with barley; barley is strength, the Udumbara is strength; verily he unites strength with strength. (The post) is of Udumbara wood of the height of the sacrificer. As great as is the sacrificer, so much strength does he put in it. 'Thou art the seat of the Pitṛis,' (with these words) he spreads the strew, for what is dug in has the Pitṛis for its deity. If he were to set it up without strewing, it would be dug in and have the Pitṛis for its deity; he sets it up after strewing; verily he sets it up in this (earth), and makes it firm-rooted.' 'Support the sky, fill the atmosphere,' he says, for the distinction of these worlds. 'May Dyutāna Māruta set thee up,' he says; Dyutāna Māruta was wont to set up the Udumbara (post) of the Gods; verily by him he sets this (post) up. 'Thee that art winner of Brahmans, winner of nobles,' he says; that is according to the text. 'With ghee, O sky and earth, be filled,' (with these words) he sacrifices on the Udumbara (post); verily with moisture he anoints sky and earth. He makes it run right to the end; verily completely does he anoint the sacrificer with brilliance. 'Thou art of Indra,' (with these words) he puts down the covering, for the seat has Indra as its deity. 'The shade of all folk,' he says, for the seat is the shade of all folk. (A roof of) nine coverings should he fix for one who desires brilliance, commensurate with the Trivṛit Stoma; the Trivṛit is brilliance; verily he becomes brilliant; one of eleven coverings (he should fix) for one who desires power; the Triṣhṭubh has eleven syllables, the Triṣhṭubh is power; verily he becomes powerful. (A roof of) fifteen coverings (he should fix) for one who has foes; the thunderbolt is fifteenfold; (verily it serves) for the overcoming of foes. (A roof of) seventeen coverings (he should fix) for one who desires offspring; Prajāpati is sixteenfold. (verily it serves) to gain Prajāpati (A roof of) twenty-one coverings (he should fix) for one who desires support; the Ekaviṃśa is the support of the Stomas; (verily it serves) for support. The Sadas is the stomach, the Udumbara is strength, in the middle he fixes (the post) of Udumbara wood; verily he places strength in the midst of offspring; therefore in the middle they enjoy strength. In the world of the sacrificer are the southern coverings, in that of his foe are the northern; he makes the southern the higher; verily he makes the sacrificer higher than the man who does not sacrifice; therefore the sacrificer is higher than the man who does not sacrifice. He fills up the crevices, for distinction; therefore people depend on the forest. 'May our songs, O lover of song,' he says; that is according to the text. 'Thou art the string of Indra;. thou art the fixed point of Indra,' he says; for the Sadas has Indra for its deity. Now the knot which he first ties, if he were not to unloose it, the Adhvaryu would perish through suppression of urine; therefore it must be unloosed.

Mantra 6:2:11

The oblation-holder is the head of the sacrifice, the sounding holes are the vital airs. They are dug in the oblation-holder; therefore. the vital airs are in the head. They are dug below; therefore the vital airs are below the head. 'I dig those which slay the Rakṣhas, which slay the spell, and which are of Viṣhṇu,' he says, for the sounding-holes have Viṣhṇu for their deity. The Asuras in retreat dug in spells against the vital airs of the Gods; they found them at the distance of an arm; therefore they are dug an arm's length deep. 'Here do I cast out the spell which an equal or an unequal hath buried,' he says; there are two sorts of men, the equal and the unequal; verily whatever spell they dig against him he thus casts out. He unites them; therefore the vital airs are united within. He does not combine them; therefore the vital airs are not combined. He pours water over; therefore the vital airs are moist within. (The water) he pours is mixed with barley; barley is strength, the sounding-holes are the vital airs; verily he places strength in the vital airs. He spreads over the strew; therefore the vital airs are hairy within. He besprinkles (the holes) with butter; butter is brilliance, the sounding-holes are the vital airs; verily he places brilliance in the vital airs. The pressing-boards are the jaws of the sacrifice; he does not join them, for the jaws are not joined; or rather at a long Soma sacrifice they should be joined, for firmness. The oblation-holder is the head of the sacrifice, the sounding-holes are the vital airs, the pressing-boards the jaws, the skin the tongue, the pressing-stones the teeth the Āhavanīya the mouth, the high altar the nose, the Sadas the stomach. When he eats with his tongue on his teeth, (the food) goes to the mouth; when it goes to the mouth, then it goes to the stomach, therefore they press (the juice) with the pressing-stones on the oblation-holder over the skin, sacrifice in the Āhavanīya, retire towards the west, and consume (the Soma) in the Sadas. He who knows the milking of the Virāj in the mouth of the sacrifice milks her; the Virāj is this (cow), the skin is its hide, the pressing-boards its udder, the sounding-holes its teats, the pressing-stones its calves, the priests the milkers, Soma the milk. He, who knows thus, milks her.

Prapāṭhaka 3.

The Exposition of the Soma Sacrifice (continued)

Mantra 6:3:1

From the pit he scatters (earth) on the altars; the pit is the birthplace of the sacrifice; (verily it serves) to unite the sacrifice with its birthplace. The Gods lost by conquest the sacrifice; they won it again from the Agnīdh's altar; the Agnīdh's altar is the invincible part of the sacrifice. In that he draws off the altar fires from that of the Agnīdh, he renews the sacrifice from the invincible part of it. Conquered as it were they go who creep to the Bahiṣhpavamāna (Stotra) when the Bahiṣhpavamāna has been sung, he says, 'Agnīdh, draw off the fires, spread the strew, make ready the sacrificial cake.' Verily having re-won the sacrifice they keep renewing it. At two pressings he draws off by means of embers, at the third with (flaming) splinters, to give it glory verily he completes it. The altars guarded the Soma in yonder world they took away the Soma from them; they followed it and surrounded it. He who knows thus wins an attendant. They were deprived of the Soma drink; they besought the Gods for the Soma drink; the Gods said to them, 'Take two names each; then shall ye gain it, or not.' Then the altars became fires (also); therefore a Brahman who has two names is likely to prosper. Those which came nearest gained the Soma drink viz. the Āhavanīya, the Agnīdh's altar, the Hotar's, and the Mārjālīya; therefore they sacrifice on them. He leaves them out in uttering the cry for sacrifice, for they were deprived of the Soma drink. The Gods drove away the Asuras who were in front by the sacrifices which they offered on the eastern side, and the Asuras who were behind by those which they offered on the western side. Soma libations are offered in the east, seated to the west he besprinkles the altars; verily from behind and from in front the sacrificer smites away his enemies; therefore offspring are engendered behind, and are brought forth in front. The altars are the breaths; if the Adhvaryu were to go past the altars to the west, he would mingle the breaths, he would be liable to die. The Hotar is the navel of the sacrifice; the expiration is above the navel, the inspiration is below; if the Adhvaryu were to go past the Hotar to the west, he would place the expiration in the inspiration, he would be liable to die. The Adhvaryu should not accompany the song; the Adhvaryu's strength is his voice; if the Adhvaryu were to accompany the song, he would confer his voice on the Udgātar, and his voice would fail. The theologians say, 'The Adhvaryu should not go beyond the Sadas to the west before the Soma offering is completed. Then how is he to go to offer the sacrifices in the southern fire? Because that is the end of the fires. But how are the Gods to know whether it is the end or not?' He goes round the Agnīdh's altar to the north and offers the sacrifices in the southern fire; verily he does not mingle the breaths. Some of the altars are besprinkled, some not; those which he besprinkles he delights; those which he does not besprinkle he delights by indicating them.

Mantra 6:3:2

The Vaisarjana offerings are made for the world of heaven. He offers in the Gārhapatya with two verses; the sacrificer has two feet; (verily it serves) for support. He offers in the Agnīdh's fire; verily he approaches the atmosphere; he offers in the Āhavanīya; verily he makes him go to the world of heaven. The Rākṣhasas sought to harm the Gods as they were going to the world of heaven; they smote away the Rākṣhasas through Soma, the king, and making themselves active went to the world of heaven, to prevent the Rākṣhasas seizing them. The Soma is ready at hand; so he offers the Vaisarjanas, to smite away the Rākṣhasas 'Thou, O Soma, brought about by ourselves,' he says, for he is the one who brings about by himself; 'from hostility brought about by others,' he says, for the Rākṣhasas are brought about by others; 'thou art the giver of wide protection,' he says; in effect he says, 'give us wide (protection).' 'May the active one gladly partake of the ghee,' he says; verily he makes the sacrificer active and causes him to go to the world of heaven, to prevent the Rākṣhasas seizing him. They take up the Soma, the pressing-stones, the cups for Vāyu, the wooden trough; they lead forth the wife (of the sacrificer), they make the carts move along with them; verily whatever is his he goes with it to the world of heaven. He offers in the Agnīdh's fire with a verse containing the word 'lead,' for leading to the world of heaven. He places on the Agnīdh's altar the pressing-stones, the cups for Vāyu, and the wooden trough, for they take it away from them; if he were to put it with them, it would become spoiled. He makes it go forward with a verse addressed to Soma; verily by means of its own divinity he makes it go forward. 'Thou art the seat of Aditi; do thou sit on the seat of Aditi,' he says; that is according to the text. Hitherto the sacrificer has guarded the Soma. 'This, O God Savitar, is the Soma of you (Gods),' he says; verily instigated by Savitar, he hands it over to the Gods. 'Thou, O Soma, God to the Gods, hast thou gone,' he says, for it being a God goes to the Gods. 'I here, man to men,' he says, for he being a man goes to men. If he were not to say that formula, the sacrificer would be without offspring or cattle. 'With offspring, with increase of wealth,' he says; verily he abides in this world with offspring and with cattle. 'Homage to the Gods,' he says, for homage is the due of the Gods; 'Svadhā to the Pitṛis,' he says, for the Svadhā call is the due of the Pitṛis. 'Here (may) I (be free) from Varuṇa's noose,' he says; verily he is freed from Varuṇa's noose. 'O Agni, lord of vows,' (he says). 'One should recover one's former body,' they say, 'for who knows if the richer, when his will is accomplished will restore it or not.' The pressing-stones are the troop of thieves of King Soma; him, who knowing thus, places the pressing-stones on the Agnīdh's altar, the troop of thieves finds not.

Mantra 6:3:3

Having sacrificed with a verse addressed to Viṣhṇu, he approaches the post. The post has Viṣhṇu for its deity; verily he approaches it with its own deity. 'I have passed by others, I have not approached others,' he says, for he passes by others, and does not approach others. I have found thee nearer than the farther, farther than the near,' he says, for he finds it nearer than the farther, farther than the near. 'I welcome thee that art of Viṣhṇu, for the sacrifice to the Gods,' he says, for he welcomes it for the sacrifice to the Gods. 'Let the God Savitar anoint thee with honey,' he says; verily he anoints it with glory. 'O plant, guard it; O axe, harm it not,' he says; the axe is the thunderbolt; (verily it serves) for atonement. The brilliance of the tree which fears the axe falls away with the first chip; the first chip which falls he should take up; verily he takes it up with its brilliance. These worlds are afraid of the falling forward of the tree. 'With thy top graze not the sky, with thy middle harm not the atmosphere,' he says; verily he makes it tender for these worlds. 'O tree, grow with a hundred shoots,' (with these words) he sacrifices on the stump; therefore many (shoots) spring up from the stump of trees. 'May we grow with a thousand shoots,' he says; verily he invokes this blessing. He should cut it so that it will not touch the axle. If he were to cut it so that it would touch the axle, the cattle of the sacrificer would be liable to perish. If he desire of any one, 'May he be without support,' he should cut for him a branch; this among trees is not supported; verily he is without support. If he desire of any one, 'May he be without cattle,' he should cut for him (a post) without leaves and with a withered top; this among trees is without cattle; verily he becomes without cattle. If he desire of any one, 'May he be rich in cattle,' he should cut for him one with many leaves and many branches; this among trees is rich in cattle; verily he becomes rich in cattle. He should cut one that is supported for one who desires support; this among trees is supported which grows from its own birthplace on level ground and is firm. He should cut one which leans towards the west, for it is leaning over for the sacrifice. He should cut one of five cubits for him of whom he desires, 'May the higher sacrifice condescend to him'; the Paṅkti has five syllables, the sacrifice is fivefold, the higher sacrifice condescends to him. (He should cut one) of six cubits for one who desires support; the seasons are six; verily he finds support in the seasons. (He should cut one) of seven cubits for one who desires cattle; the Śakvarī has seven feet, the Śakvarī is cattle; verily he wins cattle. (He should cut one) of nine cubits for one who desires brilliance, commensurate with the Trivṛit Stoma; the Trivṛit is brilliance; verily he becomes brilliant. (He should cut one) of eleven cubits for one who desires power; the Triṣhṭubh has eleven syllables, the Triṣhṭubh is power; verily he becomes powerful. (He should cut one) of fifteen cubits for one who has foes; the thunderbolt is fifteenfold; (verily it serves) for the overcoming of foes. (He should cut one) Of seventeen cubits for one who desires offspring;

Prajāpati is seventeenfold; (verily it serves) to gain Prajāpati (He should cut one) of twenty-one cubits for one who desires support; the Ekaviṃśa is the support of the Stomas; (verily it serves) for support. It has eight corners; the Gāyatrī has eight syllables, the Gāyatrī is brilliance, the Gāyatrī is the beginning of the sacrifice; verily it is commensurate with brilliance, the Gāyatrī, the beginning of the sacrifice.

Mantra 6:3:4

'To earth thee! To atmosphere thee! To sky thee!' he says; verily for these worlds he anoints it. He anoints from the foot upwards, for upwards as it were is the world of heaven. Cruel as it were is that which he does when he digs; he pours water over, for expiation he pours (water) mixed with barley; barley is strength. The post is of the height of the sacrificer. As great as is the sacrificer, so much strength does he put in it. 'Thou art the seat of the Pitṛis,' (with these words) he spreads the strew, for what is dug in has the Pitṛis for its deity.' If he were to set it up without strewing, it would be dug in and have the Pitṛis for its deity; he sets it up after strewing; verily he sets it up in this (earth). He throws down the splinter of the post; verily he sets it up with its glory. 'Thee to the plants with fair berries,' (with these words) he fixes on the top therefore at the top plants bear fruit. He anoints it, butter is glory. The corner near the fire is of the same height as the sacrificer; in that he anoints the corner near the fire, he anoints with brilliance the sacrificer. He anoints it to the end; verily completely does he anoint the sacrificer with brilliance. He rubs it all around; verily he places brilliance in him completely. 'Support the sky, fill the atmosphere, with thy base make firm the earth,' he says, for the separation of these worlds. With a verse addressed to Vishṇu he arranges it; the post has Vishṇu for its deity; verily he arranges it with its own deity. He arranges it with two (verses); the sacrificer has two feet; (verily it serves) for support. If he desire of a man, 'May I deprive him of brilliance, of the deities, of power,' he should move the corner near the fire to one side or the other of the Āhavanīya; verily he deprives him of brilliance, of the deities, of power. If he desire of a man, 'May I unite him with brilliance, with the deities, with power,' he should set up for him the corner (of the post) near the fire in a line with the Āhavanīya; verily he unites him with brilliance, with the deities, with power. Thee that art winner of Brahmans, winner of nobles,' he says that is according to the text. He winds round (the grass); the girdle is strength, the post is of the same height as the sacrificer; verily he unites the sacrificer with strength. He winds (it) round at the level of the navel; verily at the level of the navel he bestows upon him strength; therefore at the level of the navel men enjoy strength. If he desire of a man, 'May I deprive him of strength,' he should put (it) on either upwards or downwards; verily he deprives him of strength. If he desire, 'May Parjanya rain,' he should put it on downwards, verily he brings down rain; if he desire, 'May Parjanya not rain,' he should put it on upwards; verily he holds up rain. What is dug in belongs to the Pitṛis, what is above the part dug in up to the girdle belongs to men, the girdle belongs to the plants, what is above the girdle up to the top to the All-Gods, the top to Indra, the rest to the Sādhyas The post is connected with all the Gods; verily in setting up the post he delights all the Gods. By means of the sacrifice the Gods went to the world of heaven; they reflected, 'Men will equal us'; they blocked the way by the post and went to the world of heaven; the Ṛishis discerned that (world) by means of the post, and that is why it is called post. In that be sets up the post, (it is) to discern the world of heaven. He puts (it) up to the east (of the fire), for before the sacrifice it is proclaimed, for what is not proclaimed is that of which when it is passed men say, 'This should have been done.' The Sādhya Gods despised the sacrifice; the sacrifice touched them not; what was superabundant in the sacrifice touched them. The superabundant part of the sacrifice is the producing of fire and casting it on the fire; the superabundant part of the post is the part above the top; that is their share; verily by it he delights them. The Gods when the Soma sacrifice was complete cast the offering-spoons (into the fire) and the post; they reflected, 'Here we are making a disturbance of the sacrifice,' they saw a ransom in the bunch of grass for the offering-spoons, in the chip for the post. When the Soma sacrifice is complete he casts (in the fire) the bunch of grass, he offers the chip, to avoid disturbing the sacrifice.

Mantra 6:3:5

The Sādhya Gods were in this world and nothing else living. They offered Agni as a sacrifice to Agni, for they found nothing else to offer; thence indeed these creatures were born; in that he casts the fire on the fire after producing it, (it serves for) the propagation of offspring. Now the fire is Rudra, the beast the sacrificer; if he were to produce the fire after offering the beast, he would place the sacrificer in the power of Rudra, and he would be liable to die. Or rather they say, 'All the Gods are the fire, the beast the offering'. In that he produces the fire after offering the beast, he brings forth all the Gods for the offering which is made ready. The fire should be produced, after bringing up (the beast). The offering is then neither finished nor not begun. 'Thou art the birthplace of Agni,' he says, for that is the birthplace of Agni. 'Ye are the two male ones,' he says, for they are the two male ones. 'Thou art Urvaśī, thou art Āyu,' he says, to make a pair. 'Anointed with ghee do ye produce a male,' he says, for they produce a male who (produce) Agni. 'Be born with the Gāyatrī metre,' he says; verily he produces him with the metres. 'Recite for Agni as he is being produced,' he says; he recites a verse to Savitar; verily, instigated by Savitar he produces him. 'Recite for him who is born,' 'For him who is being cast forward recite,' he says; verily as each part is performed he completes him. He recites all Gāyatrī verses; Agni has the Gāyatrī as his metre; verily he unites him with his own metre. The fire is in front; having produced fire he casts it forward; the two uniting overpower the sacrificer; 'Be of one mind with us,' he says, to appease (them). He offers after casting (the fire) forward; verily he gives him food on birth; he offers with melted butter; the melted butter is the dear home of Agni; verily he unites him with his dear home, and also with brilliance.

Mantra 6:3:6

'For food thee!' (with these words) he takes up the strew, for he who sacrifices strives (*ichāte*) as it were. 'Thou art the impeller,' he says, for he brings them up. 'To the Gods the servants of the Gods have come,' he says, for being the servants of the Gods they go to the Gods. 'The priests, the eager ones,' he says; the priests are the priests, the eager ones, therefore he says thus. 'O Bṛihaspati, guard wealth,' he says; Bṛihaspati is the holy power (Brahman) of the Gods; verily by the holy power he wins cattle for him. 'Let thy oblations taste sweet,' be says; verily he makes them sweet. 'O God Tvashṭar, make pleasant our possessions,' he says; Tvashṭar is the form-maker of the pairings of cattle; verily he places form in cattle. 'Stay, ye wealthy ones,' he says; the wealthy ones are cattle; verily he makes cattle abide for him. 'On the impulse of God Savitar,' (with these words) he takes up the rope, for instigation. 'With the arms of the Aśvins,' he says, for the Aśvins were the Adhvaryus of the Gods. 'With the hands of Pūshan,' he says, for restraining. 'O offering to the Gods, I seize thee with the noose of sacred order,' he says; sacred order is truth; verily with truth which is sacred order he seizes it. He winds (the rope) round transversely, for they fasten a (beast) for killing in front; (verily it serves) for distinction. 'Fear not men,' (with these words) he fastens it, for security. 'For the waters thee, for the plants thee I sprinkle,' be says, for from the waters, from the plants, the beast is born. 'Thou art a drinker of the waters,' he says, for he is a drinker of the waters who is offered in sacrifice. 'O ye divine waters, make it palatable, a very palatable offering for the Gods,' he says; verily he makes it palatable. From above he sprinkles (it); verily he makes it pure from above; he makes it drink; verily within he makes it pure; from below he besprinkles (it); verily all over he makes it pure.

Mantra 6:3:7

By means of Agni as Hotar the Gods defeated the Asuras. Recite for Agni as he is kindled,' he says, for the overcoming of foes. He recites seventeen kindling-verses; Prajāpati is seventeenfold; (verily it serves) to win Prajāpati He recites seventeen; there are twelve months and seven seasons, that is the year; offspring are born in the course of the year; (verily it serves) for the propagation of offspring. The Gods, after reciting the kindling-verses, could not discern the sacrifice; Prajāpati silently performed the libation of ghee; then did the Gods discern the sacrifice; in that silently he performs the libation of ghee, (it serves) for the revelation of the sacrifice. The sacrifice was with the Asuras; the Gods took it by the silent offering; in that silently he performs the libation of ghee, he takes away the sacrifice of his foe. He rubs the enclosing-sticks; verily he purifies them. Thrice each he rubs them, for the sacrifice is thrice repeated; also (it serves) to smite away the Rākshasas They make up twelve; the year has twelve months;

verily he delights the year, verily also he endows him with the year, for the gaining of the world of heaven. The libation of ghee is the head of the sacrifice, the fire is all the Gods; in that he performs the libation of ghee, verily the sacrificer at the beginning of the sacrifice wins all the Gods. The libation of ghee is the head of the sacrifice, the beast is the body; having performed the libation of ghee he anoints the beast; verily on the body of the sacrifice he places the head. 'Let thy breath be united with the wind,' he says; the breath has the wind for its deity; verily he offers its breath in the wind. 'Thy limbs with the sacrificers, the lord of the sacrifice with his prayer,' he says; verily he causes the lord of the sacrifice to obtain its blessing. Viśvarūpa, Tvaṣhṭar's son, vomited over the beast from above; therefore they do not cut off (portions) from the beast above; in that he anoints the beast from above, verily he makes it pure. He chooses the priests, verily he chooses the metres, he chooses seven; there are seven tame animals, seven wild; there are seven metres, (and so it serves) to win both. He offers eleven fore-sacrifices; ten are the vital airs of the beast, the body is the eleventh; verily his fore-offerings are of the same size as the beast. One (of them) lies around the omentum; verily the body lies around the body. The axe is a thunderbolt, the splinter of the sacrificial post is a thunderbolt, the Gods by making a thunderbolt of the ghee smote Soma. 'Anointed with ghee, do ye guard the beast,' he says; verily, overpowering it by means of the thunderbolt, he offers it.

Mantra 6:3:8

He encircles (it) with fire; verily he makes it completely offered, that nothing may be lost, for that which falls of the oblation is (thus) not lost. He encircles (it) with fire thrice, for the sacrifice is thrice repeated; also (it serves) to smite away the Rākṣhasas The theologians say, 'Should the beast be grasped hold of, or not?' Now the beast is led to death; if he were to grasp hold of it, the sacrificer would be likely to die. Or rather they say, 'The beast is led to the world of heaven'; if he were not to grasp hold of it, the sacrificer would be bereft of the world of heaven. He grasps hold (of it) by means of the omentum-forks; that is as it were neither grasped nor yet not grasped. 'Give directions, O Hotar, for making ready the oblations to the Gods,' he says, for an act that is directed is carried out. 'Ye wealthy ones, do ye kindly resort to the lord of the sacrifice,' he says; that is according to the text. With the fire he goes in front, to smite away the Rākṣhasas 'Guard from contact with earth,' (with these words) he casts down the strew, that nothing may be lost, for that which falls on the strew is not lost; verily also he places it on the strew. The Adhvaryu turns away from the beast as it is slaughtered; verily he conceals himself from cattle, that he may not be cut off. He attains fortune, and obtains cattle who knows thus. The wife is led forward from the back place; 'Homage to thee, O extended one,' he says; the extended are the rays of the sun; verily he pays homage to them. 'Come forward, irresistible,' he says; the resisting is the foe; (verily it serves) to beat away the foe. 'Along the stream of ghee, with offspring, with increase of wealth,' he says; verily he invokes this blessing. 'O ye waters, Goddesses, purifying,' he says; that is according to the text.

Mantra 6:3:9

When the beast is offered in sacrifice, pain seizes its vital airs. 'Let thy speech swell, let thy breath swell' he says; verily he removes the pain from the vital airs. From the vital airs the pain enters the earth; (with the words) 'Hail to the and night!' he pours it down; verily he removes the pain of the earth by day and night. 'O plant, protect him,' 'O axe, harm him not,' he says; the axe is a thunderbolt; (verily it serves) for atonement. He cuts from the sides, for men cut from the middle; be cuts crossways, for men cut along; for distinction. 'Thou art the share of the Rākṣhasas ', (with these words) he casts the strew, having anointed it on the thick part; verily with the blood he propitiates the Rākṣhasas 'This Rakṣhas here I lead to the lowest darkness, who hateth us and whom we hate,' he says; there are two (kinds of) persons, he whom he hates and he who hates him; both these he leads to the lowest darkness.' 'For food (*iṣhe*) thee!' (with these words) he draws out the omentum, for he who sacrifices strives as it were. If he were to pierce (it), Rudra would be likely to slay his cattle; if he were not to pierce (it), it would not be fixed; with one he pierces, with the other not, for support. 'In ghee, O sky and earth, be covered,' he says; verily with fat he anoints sky and earth. 'Uncut with wealth of heroes (give us) riches,' he says; that is according to the text. Now cruel as it were is what he does when he draws out the omentum. 'Fare along the broad atmosphere,' he says, for atonement. Now he who grasps hold of the beast as it is led to death falls away from this world; he takes again hold of the omentum-forks; verily he finds support in this world. With the fire he goes in front, to smite away the Rākṣhasas; verily also with the oblation he follows the deities. He should not pass over the last of the embers; if he were to pass over the last of the embers, he would despise the deities. 'O Vāyu, taste the drops,' he says; therefore the drops are produced separately. The omentum is the chief part of cattle, the strew the chief of plants; verily he unites the chief with the chief; verily also in the plants he establishes cattle. 'Give directions for the Svāhā cries,' he says, for the completion of the sacrifice. The speckled butter is the expiration and inspiration of cattle, the omentum is the body; having poured butter on the speckled ghee, he pours on the omentum; verily in the body of cattle he deposits expiration and inspiration. 'Hail! Go to Ūrdhvanabhas, the offspring of the Marutas,' he says; Ūrdhvanabhas, the offspring of the Marutas, used to cast forward the omentum-forks of the Gods; verily through him he casts them forward. He casts them forward in opposite directions; therefore expiration and inspiration are in opposite directions.

Mantra 6:3:10.

Having offered in sacrifice the beast, he strews over (it) a cake, verily he sacrifices it with its sap. Having performed the rite with the omentum, he performs with the cake; the cake is strength; verily he places strength in the midst of cattle; verily also he closes the cut in the beast. Having made offering of the speckled ghee, he thrice asks, 'Is the oblation cooked, Śamitṛi?' for the Gods found truth in three (cookings). He who says what is not cooked is cooked (is burdened) with sin. The speckled butter is the expiration and the inspiration of cattle; when the beast is offered the body comes into the heart; in that he sprinkles the heart with speckled ghee, he thus places expiration and inspiration in the body of cattle. By means of the beast the Gods went to the world of heaven. They reflected, 'Men will mount after us.' They cut off its head and made its sap stream forth; it became the Prakṣha (tree); that is the nature of the Prakṣha. In that there is a branch of the Prakṣha above the strew, so he cuts off from the victim when it has its sap. As the beast is borne along the Rākṣhasas follow after it; he takes it between the sacrificial post and the Āhavanīya, to smite away the Rākṣhasas When the beast is offered its mind departs. 'Recite to Manotā, for the oblation which is being divided,' he says verily he secures its mind. He cuts off eleven portions; ten are the vital airs of the beast, the body is the eleventh, he cuts off as much as is the size of the beast. First he makes a portion of the heart, then of the tongue, then of the breast: what he conceives with the heart, that he says with the tongue; what he says with the tongue, that he utters from the breast. That is the order in the case of the beast. If he cuts off thus and then cuts from the rest at will, still the cutting off from that animal has been made in order. In the middle he makes a portion of the intestines, for breath is in the middle; he makes a portion of the upper part, for breath is in the upper part; whether he does one, or the other, there is variation in both cases. A Brahman on birth is born with a threefold debt, of pupilship to the Ṛiṣhis, of sacrifice to the Gods, of offspring to the Pitṛis He is freed from his debt who has a son, is a sacrificer, and who has lived as a pupil: this (debt) he performs (*āvadayate*) by these cuttings off,' and that is why the cuttings-off (*avadāna*) have their name. The Gods and the Asuras were in conflict. The Gods said to Agni, 'With thee as our hero let us overcome the Asuras.' He said, 'Let me choose a boon; let me have a choice part of the beast.' He chose that choice part (of the beast), the shoulder from the fore part, the intestines from the middle, the hip from the hind part. Then the Gods prospered, the Asuras were defeated; in that he makes portions of three members it is for the overcoming of his foe; he prospers himself, his foe is defeated. He cuts off transversely; therefore cattle move forward their limbs transversely, for support.

Mantra 6:3:11

He covers the dipping-spoons with fat; cattle are distinguished by fat; verily he bestows on cattle their distinguishing mark. He covers (them) after putting (the fat) on the soup; the soup is the sap of cattle; verily he bestows sap upon cattle. He stirs the oblation of fat with the rib; the rib is the middle of cattle, the fat is the sap of cattle; in that he stirs the oblation of fat with the rib, he places sap in the middle of cattle. Now they kill the beast when they dispose of it; the expiration has Indra for its deity, the inspiration has Indra also. 'May Indra's expiration be set in every limb,' he says; verily he bestows expiration and inspiration upon cattle. 'O God Tvaṣhṭar, let much be united for thee,' he says; for cattle have Tvaṣhṭar as their deity. 'When ye that are various become of one form,' he says; for they being various become then of one form. 'Over thee as thou goest among the Gods for help let thy comrades and thy father and mother rejoice,' he says; verily he makes him, approved by his mother and his father, go to the world of heaven. With a half-verse he offers the oblation of fat; the half-verse is yonder (sky) and the half-verse is this (earth); verily with sap he adorns both. He offers to the quarters; verily with sap he adorns the quarters; verily from the quarters he wins strength and sap. The speckled butter is the expiration and the inspiration of cattle; cattle have the lord of the forest for their deity; in that having made offering of the speckled butter he says, 'Recite for the lord of the forest, give directions for the lord of the forest,' he bestows expiration and inspiration upon cattle. Of each he divides the divided pieces; there fore cattle have various forms. He moistens (it) with soup; soup is the sap of cattle; verily he bestows sap upon cattle. He invokes the Iḍā; the Iḍā is cattle; verily he invokes cattle. Four times he invokes, for cattle have four feet. If he desire of a man, 'May he have no cattle,' he should take for him (a piece) without fat; cattle are distinguished by fat; verily by means of their distinctive mark he deprives him of cattle, and he has no cattle. If he desire of a man, 'May he have cattle,' he should take for him (a piece) with fat; cattle are distinguished by fat; verily by means of their distinctive mark he wins cattle for him, and he has cattle. Prajāpati created the sacrifice; he first created the butter, in the middle the beast, last the speckled butter; therefore the fore-sacrifices are performed with butter, the beast (is offered) in the middle, and the after-sacrifices with speckled butter. Therefore that is mixed as it were, for it was created last. He offers eleven after-sacrifices; ten are the vital airs of the beast, the body is the eleventh; he offers as many after-sacrifices as is the size of the beast. Now they kill the beast when they dispose of it; the speckled butter is the expiration and the inspiration of cattle; in that he per forms the after-sacrifices with speckled butter, verily he bestows expiration and inspiration upon cattle.

Prapāṭhaka 4.

The Exposition Of the Soma Sacrifice (continued)

Mantra 6:4:1

By means of the sacrifice Prajāpati created offspring; verily he created them by the subsidiary sacrifices; in that he offers the subsidiary sacrifices, verily thus the sacrificer creates offspring. He cuts off from the hind portion, for from the hind portion offspring are born; he cuts off from the thick side, for offspring are born from the thick side; he cuts off without confusion, to prevent confusion of the vital airs. He does not turn (it) round; if he were to turn (it) round, disease would be likely to seize his offspring. 'Go to the ocean, hail!' he says verily thus he produces seed. 'Go to the atmosphere, hail!' he says; verily by means of the atmosphere he begets offspring for him, for in accord with the atmosphere offspring are born. 'Go to God Savitar, hail!' he says; verily, instigated by Savitar, he begets offspring for him. 'Go to day and night, hail!' he says; verily by means of day and night he begets offspring for him, for in accord with day and night offspring are born. 'Go to Mitra and Varuṇa, hail!' he says; verily he bestows expiration and inspiration on offspring when born. 'Go to Soma, hail!' he says, for offspring have Soma for their deity. 'Go to the sacrifice, hail!' he says; verily he makes offspring fit for the sacrifice. 'Go to the metres, hail!' he says; the metres are cattle; verily he wins cattle. 'Go to the sky and the earth, hail!' he says; verily on either side he supports offspring when born with the sky and the earth. 'Go to the clouds of the sky, hail!' he says; verily he procures rain for offspring when born; 'Go to Agni Vaiśvānara, hail!' he says; verily he establishes in this (world) offspring when born. He makes a portion of the vital airs, who makes a portion of the intestines; 'Give me mind and heart,' he says; verily he summons the vital airs according to their places. When the beast is offered, pain reaches its heart; it gathers round the heart-spit. If he were to place the heart-spit on the earth, he would cause pain to the earth; if on the waters, he would

cause pain to the waters; he places it in the meeting-place of dry and wet, to appease both. He should think of whomsoever he hates; verily he causes him pain.

Mantra 6:4:2

The Gods divided the sacrifice on the Agnīdh's altar: of what was left over they said, 'Let this remain here.' That is why the Vasatīvarī (waters) have their name. But in the morning they could not arrange (to divide it); they placed it in the waters, they became the Vasatīvarīs. He takes the Vasatīvarīs; the Vasatīvarīs are the sacrifice; verily having taken from the beginning the sacrifice he stays (with it). If the sun set, on one who has not taken (the waters), his sacrifice would not be begun, and he would split the sacrifice. He should either take waters with radiance in them, or having deposited gold he takes them with light in them, or he should take them from the tank of a Brahman who performs many sacrifices, for he is one who has taken the Vasatīvarīs He takes the Vasatīvarīs; the Vasatīvarīs are cattle; verily having taken cattle from the beginning he stays (with them). If he were to take them along the stream, his cattle would be likely to wander from him; he takes them standing against the stream; verily he obstructs cattle and seizes them for him. Indra slew Vṛtra; he died upon the waters; of them what was pure, fit for sacrifice, and divine, that was set free. They became the Vahantīs. He takes of the Vahantīs; verily he takes those of waters which are pure, fit for sacrifice, and divine. He should not pass over the nearest Vahantīs; if he were to pass over the nearest Vahantīs, he would despise the sacrifice. He should not take of stagnant (waters); the stagnant (waters) are seized by Varuṇa; if he were to take of stagnant (waters), be would cause Varuṇa to seize his sacrifice. If it is done by day, the night enters the waters; therefore the waters appear dusky by day; if it is done by night, the day enters the waters; therefore the waters appear shining by night; he takes (them) at the union of shade and light; verily for him he secures the colour of day and night. 'These waters are rich in oblation,' he says; verily he takes them made into an oblation. 'Rich in oblation be the sun,' be says; verily he takes them with light in them. He takes with an Anuṣhṭubh; the Anuṣhṭubh is speech; verily with the whole of speech he takes them. He takes with a verse of four feet, he places them thrice, they make up seven, the Śakvarī has seven feet, the Śakvarī is cattle; verily he wins cattle. For this world the Gārhapatya is established, for yonder the Āhavanīya; if he were to place (them) on the Gārhapatya, he would have cattle in this world, if on the Āhavanīya, in yonder world he would have cattle. He places (them) on both; verily he makes him have cattle in both worlds. He carries (them) round everywhere, to smite away the Rākṣhasas 'Ye are the share of Indra and Agni,' he says; that is according to the text. He places (them) on the Agnīdh's altar; the Agnīdh's altar is the invincible part of the sacrifice; verily he places (them) on the invincible part of the sacrifice. Wherever in the performance of a sacrifice nothing is done, in that (place) the Rākṣhasas infest the sacrifice. In that he takes of the Vahantīs, that part of the sacrifices lies being performed, to prevent the infestation of the Rākṣhasas, for they do not move them, but they lie around until the third pressing, for the continuity of the sacrifice.

Mantra 6. 4.3.

The theologians say, 'He indeed would be an Adhvaryu who in making Soma descend should make it descend for all the Gods.' 'To the heart thee!' he says; verily he makes it for men; 'To mind thee!' he says; verily he makes it for the Pitṛis; 'To the sky thee! To the sun thee!' he says; verily he makes it for the Gods; so many are the Gods; verily he makes it descend for them all. Before the utterance of speech he begins the morning litany; verily he wins all that there is of speech. 'The waters' is the first thing he utters; the waters are the sacrifice verily over the sacrifice he utters speech. He recites all (kinds of) metres the metres are cattle; verily he wins cattle. For one who desires brilliance he should conclude with a Gāyatrī verse, for one who desires power with a Triṣhṭubh verse, for one who desires cattle with a Jagatī verse, for one who desires support with an Anuṣhṭubh verse, for one who desires the sacrifice with a Paṅkti verse, for one who desires food with a Virāj verse. 'Let Agni (kindled) with the kindling-stick hear my appeal,' he says; verily, instigated by Savitar, having made proclamation to the Gods, he goes for the waters. 'O Hotar, give directions for the waters,' he says; for an action which is directed is done. 'O bowl priest of the

Maitrāvaruṇa, run hither'. he says; Mitra and Varuṇa are the leaders of the waters; verily with them he goes for them. 'O ye divine waters, child of the water,' he says; verily by the oblation requiting them he seizes them: then he takes of them made into an oblation and covered with ghee. 'Thou art the dragger,' he says; verily he removes dirt from them. 'I draw you for the sustenance of the ocean,' he says; therefore the waters though eaten and drunk do not waste away. The pit is the birthplace of the sacrifice, the Vasatīvarīs are the sacrifice; bringing the bowls of the Hotar and the Maitrāvaruṇa into contact he pours in the Vasatīvarīs reciprocally, so that the sacrifice may have its birthplace; verily he produces it from its own birthplace. 'O Adhvaryu, didst thou seek the waters?' he says; 'they came to me; look upon them,' in effect he says. If it is an Agnishṭoma, he makes a libation; if an Ukthya, he rubs (butter) on the enclosing-sticks; if it is an Atirātra, he goes forward uttering a text, to distinguish the sacrifices.

Mantra 6:4:4

'On the instigation of God Savitar (with these words) he takes up the pressing-stone, for instigation, 'with the arms of the Aśvins,' he says; for the Aśvins were the Adhvaryus of the Gods; 'with the hands of Pūshan,' he says, for support. The Soma is cattle, the Upāṃśu pressing-(stone) is cross breathing; in that he measures round the Upāṃśu pressing-(stone), he confers cross-breathing upon cattle. 'To Indra thee! To Indra thee!' (with these words) he measures, for the Soma is taken for Indra. Five times he measures with the text; the Paṅkti has five syllables, the sacrifice is fivefold, verily he wins the sacrifice. Five times (he measures) in silence; these make up ten; the Virāj has ten syllables, the Virāj is food; verily he wins food by the Virāj 'Ye are savoury, conquerors of Vṛitra,' he says; this is the Soma-drinking of the waters; he who knows thus reaches not destruction in the waters. 'With thy light which is in the sky,' he says; verily from these worlds he gathers him. Soma, the king, reflected on the quarters, he entered the quarters; 'forward, behind, upward, downward,' he says, verily from the quarters he gathers him; verily also he wins the quarters for him. 'O mother, come forth,' he says; women are likely to desire him who knows thus. 'Thy unerring, watchful name, O Soma,' he says; this is Soma's Soma-drinking; he who knows thus reaches not destruction from Soma. When they press Soma they kill him; he keeps back shoots; verily he protects him. The shoots are the vital airs, Soma is cattle; he later lets go the shoots; verily he bestows vital airs upon cattle; two by two he lets them go; therefore the vital airs are in pairs.

Mantra 6:4:5

The Upāṃśu Cup is breath; in that the cups are drawn beginning with the Upāṃśu, they follow on breath. Aruṇa Aupaveśi used to say, 'At the morning pressing I establish the sacrifice and then I proceed with it when it has been established.' He first presses eight times; the Gāyatrī has eight syllables, the morning pressing is connected with the Gāyatrī; verily thereby he obtains the morning pressing. (He presses) eleven times on the second occasion; the Trishṭubh has eleven syllables, the midday pressing is connected with the Trishṭubh; verily thereby he obtains the midday pressing. (He presses) twelve times on the third occasion; the Jagatī has twelve syllables, the third pressing is connected with the Jagatī; verily thereby he obtains the third pressing. This is what he calls the establishment of the sacrifice, to prevent loss; for what falls when the sacrifice is established is not lost. Or rather they say, 'The Gāyatrī is not open to question at the morning pressing'; he who knows thus is not liable to question from his foe; therefore eight times in each case should press. The theologians say, 'Other cups are drawn with a strainer; what strainer has the Upāṃśu?' 'Speech is the strainer,' he should reply. 'Be pure for the lord of speech, O strong one,' he says; verily by speech he purifies him. 'With the shoots of the male,' he says, for the shoots of the Soma are the shoots of the male; 'purified by the arms,' he says, for by the arms he purifies him; 'thou art the God, purifier of Gods,' he says, for he being a God is the purifier of Gods; 'to those thee whose portion thou art,' he says, for he draws him for those whose portion he is. 'Thou art he who is appropriated,' he says; verily he makes breath his own; 'make our food full of sweetness for us,' he says; verily he makes all food sweet for him; 'to all the powers of sky and earth thee!' he says; verily upon both Gods and men he bestows the vital airs. 'May mind enter thee!' he says; verily he attains mind. 'Fare along the broad atmosphere,' he says, for the breath has the atmosphere as its deity. 'Hail! Thee, of kindly nature, to the sun!' he says; the Gods of kindly nature are the breaths; verily in them he secretly offers. 'To the Gods that drink the rays thee!' he says; the Gods that drink the rays are the rays of the sun; that is their share; verily thereby he delights them. If he desire, 'May Parjanya rain,' he should rub (the cup) with the (palm of) the hand downwards; verily he brings down the rain. If he desire, 'May it not rain,' he should rub with the hand upwards; verily he keeps up the rain. If he practise witchcraft, 'Slay N.N.; then will I sacrifice to thee,' he should say; verily desiring the libation he slays him. If he be far away, he should stand until he is weary; verily he follows his breath and slays him. If he practise witchcraft, he should put (it) down (with the words), 'I set thee down on the breath of N.N.'; the breath is restless; verily he brings his breath to rest. He purifies by means of six shoots; the seasons are six; verily he purifies him by means of the seasons; thrice he purifies these worlds are three; verily he purifies him by means of these worlds. The theologians say, 'For what reason is it that three animals take by the hand?' In that thrice he draws separately the Upāṃśu with his hand, therefore there are three animals which take by the hand, man, the elephant, and the ape.

Mantra 6:4:6

Whatever the Gods did as the sacrifice, that the Asuras did. The Gods saw that the sacrifice must be established in the Upāṃśu (cup), and they established it in the Upāṃśu The Asuras grasping the thunderbolt attacked the Gods; the Gods in fear ran up to Indra, Indra obstructed them by means of the Antaryāma (cup), and that is why the Antaryāma has its name, 'the obstructor'. In that the Antaryāma cup is drawn, verily thus the sacrificer obstructs his foes. 'Through thee I interpose sky and earth, I interpose the broad atmosphere,' he says; verily with these worlds the sacrificer obstructs his foes. The Gods reflected, 'Indra hath now become what we are'; they said, 'O bounteous one, give us a share'; 'In unison with the Gods, the lower and the higher,' he replied; to both (the sets of) Gods, the lower and the higher, he gave a share. 'In unison with the Gods, the lower and the higher,' he says; to both (the sets of) Gods, the lower and the higher, he gives a share. 'O bounteous one, do thou rejoice in the Antaryāma,' he says; verily he does not cut off the sacrificer from the sacrifice. 'Thou art taken with a support,' he says, for the support of inspiration. If both (cups) were drawn without a filter, inspiration would follow expiration, he would be likely to die. The Antaryāma is drawn with a filter, to separate expiration and inspiration. The Upāṃśu and the Antaryāma (cups) are expiration and inspiration, the Upāṃśu pressing-(stone) is cross-breathing. If he desire of a man, 'May he be likely to die,' he should set them down for him without being in contact; verily he severs his expiration and inspiration from cross-breathing; swiftly he dies. If he desire of a man, 'May he live all his days,' he should set them down for him in contact; verily he connects his expiration and inspiration with cross-breathing; he lives all his days.

Mantra 6:4:7

The cup for Indra and Vāyu is speech; in that the cups are drawn beginning with that to Indra and Vāyu, verily they follow speech. The Gods said to Vāyu, 'Let us slay Soma, the king'; he replied, 'Let me choose a boon; let your cups be drawn with mine first.' Therefore the cups are drawn with those for Indra and Vāyu first. They slew him; he became putrid; the Gods could not endure him, they said to Vāyu, 'Make him sweet for us'; he replied, 'Let me choose a boon; let your vessels, be said to have me as their deity.' Therefore, being of various deities, they are said to have Vāyu as their deity. Verily did Vāyu make him sweet for him; therefore what becomes putrid they hang out in a windy place, for Vāyu is its purifier, its sweetener. They could not find its distribution; Aditi said, 'Let me choose a boon; then shall ye distribute through me, verily with me as deity may your Soma (draughts) be set down'. 'Thou art taken with a support,' he says, and thereby have they Aditi for their deity, for those vessels that are made of wood are born from her womb, those that are made of clay are clearly hers; therefore he says thus. Speech aforetime spoke without discrimination; the Gods said to Indra, 'Do thou discriminate this speech for us'; he replied, 'Let me choose a boon; let this (cup) be drawn for me and for Vāyu together.' Therefore the cup is drawn together for Indra and Vāyu Indra approaching it in the midst discriminated it; therefore is speech spoken distinctly. Therefore is it drawn once, in the middle, for

Indra, and twice for Vāyu, for he chose two boons.

Mantra 6:4:8

The Gods said to Mitra, 'Let us slay Soma, the king'; he replied, 'Not I; for I am the friend of all'; they answered, 'Still we will slay him'; he replied, 'Let me choose a boon; let them mix the Soma for me with milk.' Therefore they mix with milk (the Soma) for Mitra and Varuṇa From him cattle departed (saying), 'He that was a friend hath done a cruel deed'; a cruel deed as it were does he do who sacrifices with Soma; from him cattle depart. In that he mixes with milk (the Soma) for Mitra and Varuṇa, he unites Mitra with cattle, and the sacrificer with cattle. Aforetime indeed was Mitra thus aware,' When I have done this cruel deed, cattle will depart from me'; therefore he chose thus. The Gods said to Varuṇa, 'With thee as helper we will slay Soma, the king'; he replied, 'Let me choose a boon, for me and Mitra together let this (cup) be drawn.' Therefore it is drawn for Mitra and Varuṇa together; therefore with a king as helper they slay a king, with a Vaiśya a Vaiśya, with a Śūdra a Śūdra This was not day or night, but undiscriminated; the Gods said to Mitra and Varuṇa, 'Make this to shine forth for us'; they replied, 'Let us choose a boon; let one cup only be drawn before ours.' Therefore the cup for Indra and Vāyu is drawn before that for Mitra and Varuṇa, for the Upāṃśu and the Antaryāma (cups) are expiration and inspiration. Mitra produced the day, Varuṇa the night; then indeed did this shine forth; in that (a cup) is drawn for Mitra and Varuṇa, (it is) for shining forth.

Mantra 6:4:9

The head of the sacrifice was cut; the Gods said to the Aśvins, Ye are physicians; do ye replace the head of the sacrifice,' they replied. Let us choose a boon; let there be drawn a cup for us also herein.' For them they drew this cup for the Aśvins; then indeed did they replace the head of the sacrifice; in that (the cup) for the Aśvins is drawn, (it is) to restore the sacrifice. The Gods said of these two, 'Impure are they, wandering among men and physicians.' Therefore a Brahman should not practise medicine, for the physician is impure, unfit for the sacrifice. Having purified them by the Bahiṣhpavamāna (Stotra) they drew for them this cup for the Aśvins; therefore (the cup) for the Aśvins is drawn when the Bahiṣhpavamāna has been sung. Therefore by one who knows thus the Bahiṣhpavamāna should be performed; verily he purifies himself. Their skill as physicians they deposited in three places, in Agni a third, in the waters a third, in the Brahman a third. Therefore one should put beside him a pot of water and sit on the right hand of a Brahman when practising medicine; all medicine he performs thereby, his remedy becomes effective. The theologians say, 'For what reason are cups for two deities drawn in one vessel, but offered in two?' In that (the cups) are drawn in one vessel, therefore there is one breath within; they are offered in two vessels, therefore the breaths outside are in pairs. Those that are for two deities are the breaths, the Iḍā is cattle; if he should summon the Iḍā before those that are for two deities, he would obstruct his breaths by cattle, he would be likely to perish. Having eaten those for two deities, he summons the Iḍā; verily having placed the breaths in himself he summons the Iḍā. (The cup) for Indra and Vāyu is speech, that for Mitra and Varuṇa is the eye, that for the Aśvins is the ear; he eats in front that for Indra and Vāyu, therefore in front he speaks with speech; in front that for Mitra and Varuṇa, therefore in front he sees with the eye; moving all round, that for the Aśvins; therefore on all sides he hears with the ear. Those for two deities are the breaths, he sets down full vessels; therefore the breaths are full within; wherever in the performance of the sacrifice nothing is done, in that place the Rākṣhasas attack the sacrifice; in that he sets down full vessels the part of the sacrifice being performed is deposited to prevent the entry of the Rākṣhasas He sets down in the north track of the southern oblation-cart; verily he places speech in speech. They lie (there) until the third pressing, for the continuity of the sacrifice.

Mantra 6:4:10.

Bṛihaspati was the Purohita of the Gods, Śaṇḍa and Marka of the Asuras; the Gods had the holy power (Brahman), the Asuras had the holy power (Brahman); they could not overcome one another; the Gods invited Śaṇḍa and Marka; they replied, 'Let us choose a boon; let cups be drawn for us also herein.' For them they drew these cups for Śukra and Manthin; then did the Gods prosper, the Asuras were defeated. He for whom knowing thus these Śukra and Manthin (cups) are drawn, prospers himself, his foe is defeated. Having driven away these two, the Gods offered to themselves,' to Indra. 'Driven away are Śaṇḍa and Marka together with N.N.,' he should say of whom he hates; with him whom he hates he thus drives them away. 'This is the first preparer, all maker,' (with these words) they offered to themselves, to Indra, these (cups), for Indra kept making these forms. The Śukra is yonder sun, the Manthin is the moon; they depart towards the east, closing their eyes; therefore men do not see them as they go east. Turning back towards the west they sacrifice, therefore men see them going west. The Śukra and the Manthin are the eyes of the sacrifice, the high altar is the nose. They offer having gone round (the altar) on both sides; therefore the eyes are on either side of the nose; therefore the eyes are held apart by the nose; they walk round on all sides, to smite away the Rākṣhasas Now the offerings the Gods made on the east, with them they drove away the Asuras who were in front; with those on the west they drove away the Asuras who were behind; other sacrifices are made in the east, the Śukra and Manthin on the west; verily behind and in front the sacrificer drives away his foes; therefore offspring are engendered behind and are brought forth in front. In accordance with the Śukra and Manthin are offspring born, the eaters and the eaten. 'Engendering heroic off spring), come forth, Śukra, with pure radiance,' 'Engendering prolific offspring, come forth, Manthin, with mixed radiance,' he says; 'the eaters are those who are heroic, the eaten those that are prolific. The offspring of him who knows thus becomes an eater, not eaten. The eye of Prajāpati swelled; it fell away, it entered the Vikaṅkata, it did not stay in the Vikaṅkata; it entered barley, it stayed in barley; that is why barley has its name. In that the Manthin vessel is of Vikaṅkata and he mixes with groats, verily thus he gathers together the eye of Prajāpati The theologians say, 'For what reason does the Manthin vessel not go to the Sadas?' 'It is the vessel of misfortune,' he should say; if it were to go there, the Adhvaryu would be blind, he would be ruined; therefore it does not go there.

Mantra 6:4:11

Whatever the Gods did at the sacrifice the Asuras did. The Gods saw the cups with the Āgrayaṇa at their head; they drew them; then indeed did they reach the top; he for whom knowing thus the cups are drawn with the Āgrayaṇa at their head reaches the top of his equals. With a verse containing the word 'destructive' he should draw for him who has a rival; verily having destroyed his rival he reaches the top of his equals. 'Ye Gods that are eleven in the sky,' he says; so many are the deities; verily he draws it for all of them. 'This is thy birthplace; to the All-Gods thee!' he says, for it has the All-Gods for its deity. Speech departed from the Gods, not being willing to remain for the sacrifice; when speech had departed the Gods silently drew the cups; speech reflected, 'They are excluding me'; it went into the Āgrayaṇa; that is why the Āgrayaṇa has its name. Therefore in the Āgrayaṇa speech is uttered. In that the former cups are drawn in silence, that is as when the hunter lets go (his arrow), (thinking), 'So far off is my mark at so far I shall not miss.' The Adhvaryu taking the Āgrayaṇa, commencing the sacrifice, utters his speech; thrice he utters 'Him'; verily thus he chooses the Udgātars; the Āgrayaṇa is Prajāpati; in that he utters 'Him' after taking the Āgrayaṇa, verily thus Prajāpati sniffs offspring; therefore the cow sniffs the calf on birth. The Āgrayaṇa is the self of the sacrifice; at each pressing he draws it; verily he continues the sacrifice in itself. He brings (it) up from above verily thus he impregnates seed; he takes (it) from below verily he generates it. The theologians say, 'For what reason does the Gāyatrī, the least of the metres, support the pressings?' 'The Āgrayaṇa is the calf of the Gāyatrī; verily turning back towards it it supports all the pressings. Therefore a cow turns back towards the calf which is taken away.

Prapāṭhaka 5.

The Exposition of the Soma Sacrifice (continued)

Mantra 6:5:1

Indra raised his bolt to hurl at Vṛitra; Vṛitra was afraid of the bolt when raised to be hurled; he said, 'Hurl it not at me; there is this strength in me, that will I bestow on thee'; on him he bestowed the Ukthya. At him he raised (the bolt) to hurl a second time; he said, 'Hurl it not at me; there is this strength in me, that will I bestow on thee'; on him he bestowed again the Ukthya. At him he raised (the bolt) to hurl a third time; Vishṇu supported him (saying), 'Smite'; he said, 'Hurl it not at me; there is this strength in me, that will I bestow on thee'; he bestowed on him again the Ukthya. Him when he had lost his magic power he slew, for the sacrifice was his magic power. In that the Ukthya is drawn, verily the sacrificer thus appropriates the power and strength of his foe. 'To Indra thee, to him of the Bṛihat, the strong,' he says, for to Indra he gave it; 'to him thee! To Vishṇu thee!' he says; in that Vishṇu supported him (saying), 'Strike,' he gives Vishṇu a share therein. Thrice he draws, for thrice he gave to him. This is thy birthplace; thou art the renewed offering,' he says, for repeatedly he draws from it. The Ukthya is the eye of the sacrifice; therefore the Somas follow the Ukthya when offered; therefore the body follows the eye; therefore as one goes many follow; therefore one becomes superior among many; therefore one wins many wives. If the Adhvaryu desire, 'May I bestow upon myself the glory of the sacrifice,' standing between the Āhavanīya and the oblation-holder he should pour (it) down; verily he bestows upon himself the glory of the sacrifice. If he desire, 'May I bestow upon the sacrificer the glory of the sacrifice,' he should pour (it) down standing between the Sadas and the oblation-holder; verily he bestows upon the sacrificer the glory of the sacrifice. If he desire, 'May I bestow upon the Sadasyas the glory of the sacrifice,' he should pour (it) down, grasping the Sadas; verily he bestows upon the Sadasyas the glory of the sacrifice.

Mantra 6:5:2

The Dhruvā (cup) is the life of the sacrifice; it is drawn the last of the cups; therefore life is the last of the breaths. 'The head of the sky, the messenger of earth,' he says; verily he makes him the head of his equals. 'Vaiśvānara, born for holy order,' he says, for life has Vaiśvānara as its deity. It is drawn with Vaiśvānara on both sides; therefore there are breaths on both sides, below and above. The other cups that are drawn make a half, the Dhruvā makes a half; therefore the breath below is a half of the other breaths. The other cups are deposited on strewn (ground), the Dhruvā on unstrewn; therefore in bone some creatures find support, in flesh others. The Asuras from above desired to turn round the earth; the Gods made it firm (*adṛinhan*) with the Dhruvā; that is why the Dhruvā has its name; in that the Dhruvā is set down from above, (it serves) for firmness. The Dhruvā is the life of the sacrifice, the Hotar is the body; in that he pours the Dhruvā down into the goblet of the Hotar, so he places life in the body of the sacrifice. 'Before the Uktha it should be poured down,' they say, for in front one enjoys life; 'In the middle it should be poured down,' they say, for the middle one enjoys life; 'In the latter part it should be poured down,' they say, for with the last one enjoys life. He pours (it) down while the verse to the All-Gods is being recited; offspring are connected with the All-Gods; verily he confers life upon offspring.

Mantra 6:5:3

By means of the sacrifice the Gods went to the world of heaven; they reflected, 'Men will follow after us here'; they blocked (the way) by the year and went to the world of heaven. It the Ṛishis discerned by means of the season-cups; in that the season-cups are drawn, (they serve) to reveal, the world of heaven. Twelve are drawn; the year consists of twelve months; (verily they serve) to reveal the year. The first two are drawn together, the last two together; therefore the seasons are in pairs. The season-vessel has mouths on both sides, for who knows where is the mouth of the seasons? 'Give directions for the season,' six times he says, the seasons are six; verily he delights the seasons; 'For the seasons,' four times; verily he delights four-footed cattle; twice again he says, 'For the season'; verily he delights two-footed (cattle). 'Give directions for the season,' six times he says; 'For the seasons,' four times; therefore four-footed cattle depend upon the seasons; twice again, 'For the season,' he says; therefore bipeds live upon quadrupeds. 'Give directions for the season,' six times he says; 'For the seasons,' four times; twice again, 'For the season'; verily the sacrificer makes himself a ladder and bridge to attain the world of heaven. One should not follow the other; if one were to follow the other, season would follow season, the seasons would be confused; therefore in order the Adhvaryu sets out by the southern (door), the Pratiprasthātṛi by the northern; therefore the sun goes south for six months, north for six months.' 'Thou art taken with a support; thou art Saṃsarpa; to Aṃhaspatya thee!' he says; 'There is a thirteenth month,' they say; verily he delights it.

Mantra 6:5:4

The season-cups are drawn for the world of heaven; Indra and Agni are the light; in that he draws the cup for Indra and Agni with the season-vessel, verily he places light above it, to light up the world of heaven. Indra and Agni are the bearers of force among the Gods; in that (the cup) for Indra and Agni is drawn, verily he wins force. He draws (the cup) for the All-Gods with the Śukra-vessel; people are connected with the All-Gods, the Śukra is yonder sun, in that he draws (the cup) for the All-Gods with the Śukra-vessel, yonder sun rises turned to all people; therefore each one thinks, 'Towards me hath it arisen.' He draws (the cup) for the All-Gods with the Śukra-vessel; people are connected with the All-Gods, the Śukra is brilliance; in that he draws (the cup) for the All-Gods with the Śukra vessel, verily he bestows brilliance upon people.

Mantra 6:5:5

Indra in league with the Marutas slew Vṛitra at the midday pressing; in that (the cups) for the Marutas are drawn at the midday pressing, they are drawn for the sacrificer as slaying the foe. Of him, when he had slain Vṛitra, the seasons were confused; with the season vessel he drew (the cups) for the Marutas; then indeed did he discern the seasons; in that (the cups) for the Marutas are drawn with the season-vessel, (they serve) to reveal the seasons. (The cups) for the Marutas are a weapon which the sacrificer hurls at his foe; with the first he raises it aloft, with the second he hurls it; with the third he lays (him) low. (The cups) for the Marutas are a weapon which the sacrificer makes ready; the first is a bow, the second a bowstring, the third an arrow; with the first he fits the arrow, with the second he lets it go, with the third he pierces. Indra having slain Vṛitra went to the furthest distance, thinking, 'I have done amiss'; he became of bay colour, he saw these (cups) for the Marutas, to save himself; he drew them; verily with the first he won expiration, with the second inspiration, himself with the third, (the cups) for the Marutas are drawn to save the self of the sacrificer; verily he wins expiration with the first, inspiration by the second, and himself with the third. Indra slew Vṛitra; the Gods said of him, 'Great hath he become who hath slain Vṛitra'; that is why Mahendra (great Indra) has his name. He drew this libation for Mahendra, having slain Vṛitra and being above the other deities; in that (the cup) for Mahendra is drawn, so the sacrificer draws this libation, being above other people. He draws with the Śukra vessel; (the cup) for Mahendra has the sacrificer as its deity, the Śukra is brilliance; in that he draws (the cup) for Mahendra in the Śukra-vessel, verily he bestows brilliance on the sacrificer.

Mantra 6:5:6

Aditi, desirous of offspring, cooked a Brahman's mess for the Sādhya Gods; to her the gave the remains, she ate it, she became pregnant; of her the four Ādityas were born. A second (mess) she cooked; she reflected, 'They have been born for me from the remains; if I eat first, then stronger ones will be born from me'; she ate first, she became pregnant, from her was born an egg which miscarried. She cooked a third (mess) for the Ādityas, (saying) 'Let this labour be for enjoyment to me'; they said, 'Let us choose a boon; let him who shall be born hence be one of us; let him who shall be prosperous among his offspring be for our enjoyment'; then was born the Āditya Vivasvat, men are his offspring here, among them he alone is successful who sacrifices, he serves for enjoyment of the Gods. The Gods kept Rudra away from the sacrifice, he followed the Ādityas; they took refuge in (the cups) for two deities, them they did not give up; therefore men do not give up even one worthy of death who has come for help. Therefore (the cup) for the Ādityas is drawn from those for two deities, in that they were born from the remnant, therefore it is drawn from the remnant. He draws with three verses; mother, father, son, verily that is this pairing; the amnion, embryo, the chorion, verily that is this pairing. The Āditya (cup) is cattle; curds are strength; he mixes with curds in the middle; verily he places strength in the middle of cattle; (with curds) to be coagulated with boiled milk, for purity. Therefore the raw milks the cooked. The Āditya (cup) is cattle; he-draws after covering (the cup); verily he draws securing cattle for him. The Āditya (cup) is those cattle; Agni is Rudra here; he draws after covering; verily he shuts off cattle from Rudra. (The stone) for pressing out the Upāṃśu (cup) is this Āditya Vivasvat; it lies round this Soma drink until the third pressing. 'O bright Āditya, this is thy Soma drink,' he says; verily he unites the Āditya Vivasvat with the Soma drink. 'With the rain of the sky I mix thee,' (with these words) he should mix for one who desires rain; verily he wins rain. If it should fall quickly, Parjanya would be likely to rain; if long, (he would) not (be likely). He does not place (the cup) down, for from that which is not depressed offspring are produced. He should not utter the secondary Vaṣhaṭ; if he were to do so, he would let Rudra go after his offspring; after sacrificing he should not look after (it); if he were to look after (it) his eye would be likely to be destroyed; therefore he should not look after (it).

Mantra 6:5:7

He draws (the cup) for Savitar from the Āgrayaṇa with the Antaryāma-vessel; the Āgrayaṇa is Prajāpati; (verily it serves) for the begetting of offspring. He does not place (the cup) down, for from that which is not depressed offspring are produced. He does not utter the secondary Vaṣhaṭ; if he were to do so, he would let Rudra go after his offspring. Savitar is among the Gods he who is connected with the Gāyatrī; in that the Āgrayaṇa (is drawn), it is drawn in the world of the Gāyatrī; in that he draws (the cup) for Savitar from the Āgrayaṇa with the Antaryāma vessel, verily he draws it off from its own birthplace. The All-Gods could not perform the third pressing; they led Savitar who shares in the first pressing to the third pressing; then indeed they performed the third pressing. In that (the cup) for Savitar is drawn at the third pressing, (it serves) for performing the third pressing. He draws (the cup) for the All-Gods from the tub with the Savitar-vessel; people are connected with the All-Gods, the tub is connected with the All-Gods, Savitar rules instigations; in that he draws (the cup) for the All-Gods from the tub with the Savitar vessel, verily instigated by Savitar he produces offspring for him. He draws Soma in Soma; verily thus he impregnates seed. 'Thou givest good protection, and art well established,' he says, for he draws Soma in Soma, for support. In this same cup (offering) is made for men, Gods, and Pitṛis; 'Thou givest good protection, and art well established,' he says; verily thereby he makes (it) for men; 'The great,' he says; verily thereby he makes (it) for the Gods; 'Homage,' he says; verily thereby he makes (it) for the Pitṛis; so many are the Gods; verily he draws it for them all. 'This is thy birthplace; to the All-Gods thee!' he says, for it is connected with the All-Gods.

Mantra 6:5:8

The Upāṃśu is the breath; in that the first and the, last cups are drawn with the Upāṃśu-vessel, verily they follow forward the breath, they follow back the breath. The Āgrayaṇa is Prajāpati, the Upāṃśu is the breath, the wives produce offspring; in that he draws (the cup) for (Tvaṣhṭar) with the wives from the Āgrayaṇa with the Upāṃśu-vessel, (it serves) for the production of offspring. Therefore offspring are born in accordance with the breath. The Gods desired that the wives should go to the world of heaven; they could not discern the world of heaven, they saw this (cup) for the wives, they drew it; then indeed did they discern the world of heaven; in that (the cup) for the wives is drawn, (it serves) to reveal the world of heaven. Soma could not bear being drawn for women; making the ghee a bolt they beat it, they drew it when it had lost its power; therefore women are powerless, have no inheritance, and speak more humbly than even a bad man. In that he mixes (the cup) for (Tvaṣhṭar) with the wives with ghee, he overpowers it with a bolt and draws it. 'Thou art taken with a support,' he says; the support is this (earth); therefore offspring are born on this (earth). 'Of thee, pressed by Bṛihaspati,' he says; Bṛihaspati is the holy power of the Gods; verily by the holy power he produces offspring for him. 'O drop,' he says; the drop is seed; verily thus he impregnates seed. 'Possessing power,' he says; power is offspring; verily he produces offspring for him. 'O Agni,' he says; the impregnator of seed is Agni; 'With the wives,' he says, for pairing; 'in unison with the God Tvaṣhṭar drink the Soma,' he says; Tvaṣhṭar is the maker of the forms of pairings of animals; verily he places form in animals. The Gods sought to slay Tvaṣhṭar; he went to the wives, they would not give him up; therefore men do not give up even one worthy of death who has come for help. Therefore in (the cup) for the wives for Tvaṣhṭar also a drawing is made. He does not put (the cup) down, for from what is not depressed offspring are produced. He does not utter the secondary Vaṣhaṭ; if he were to do so, he would let Rudra go after his offspring; if he were not to do so, the Agnīdh would consume the Soma before it had been appeased; he says the secondary Vaṣhaṭ muttering, he does not let Rudra go after his offspring, the Agnīdh consumes the Soma after it has been appeased. 'O Agnīdh, sit on the lap of the Neṣhṭar; O Neṣhṭar, lead up the wife,' he says verily the Agnīdh impregnates the Neṣhṭar, the Neṣhṭar the wife. He causes the Udgātar to look (at the wife); the Udgātar is Prajāpati; (verily it serves) for the production of offspring. He causes water to follow along; verily thus he pours seed; along the thigh he causes it to flow, for along the thigh is seed poured; baring the thigh he causes it to flow, for when the thigh is bared, they pair, then seed is poured, then offspring are born.

Mantra 6:5:9

Indra slew Vṛitra; he forced out his skull-bone, it became the wooden tub, from it the Soma flowed, it became (the cup) for the yoker of bays; he reflected regarding it, 'Shall I offer, or shall I not offer?' He reflected, 'If I shall offer, I shall offer what is raw; if I shall not offer, I shall make confusion in the sacrifice.' He decided to offer; Agni said, 'Thou shalt not offer what is raw in me'; he mixed it with fried grains, and when it had become cooked he offered it. In that he mixes (the cup) for the yoker of bays with fried grains, (it serves) to make it cooked; verily he offers it when it has become cooked. He mixes with many; so many are his (cows) yielding his wishes in yonder world. Or rather they say, '(The fried grains) for the yoker of bays are the dappled (cows) of Indra yielding wishes'; therefore he should mix with many. The bays of Indra, which drink the Soma, are the Ṛich and the Sāman, the enclosing-sticks are their bridles; if he should offer without removing the enclosing-sticks, he would offer fodder to them still bridled; he offers after removing the enclosing-sticks; verily he offers fodder to them with their bridles removed. It is the Unnetar who offers; the Adhvaryu when he has uttered 'Godspeed!' is as one who has finished his journey; if the Adhvaryu were to offer, it would be as when one yokes again (a horse) unyoked. He offers after putting it on his head, for from the head it sprung; he offers after striding, for Indra slew Vṛitra after striding; (verily it serves) for attainment. (The grains) for the yoker of bays are cattle; if he were to crush (them), few cattle would attend and wait on him; if he were not to crush them, many cattle would attend, but not wait on him; in his mind he crushes them together, and effects both; many cattle attend and wait on him. They await the invitation from the Unnetar; verily they win the Soma-drinking that is here. He throws down (the remnants) on the high altar; the high altar is cattle, (the grains) for the yoker of bays are cattle verily they make cattle find support in cattle.

Mantra 6:5:10.

Offspring and cattle are born through the cups, goats and sheep through the Upāṃśu and Antaryāma, men through the Śukra and Manthin, whole-hooved animals through the season-cups, kine through the Āditya cup. The Āditya cup is drawn with the largest number of Ṛichas; therefore kine axe the most numerous of cattle; in that he thrice draws apart with his hand the Upāṃśu (cup), therefore the female goat gives birth to two or three, but sheep are more numerous. The Āgrayaṇa is the father, the tub is the son; if the Āgrayaṇa is exhausted, he should draw from the tub; that is as when a father in destitution has recourse to his son. If the tub is exhausted, he should draw from the Āgrayaṇa; that is as when a son in destitution has recourse to his father. The Āgrayaṇa is the self of the sacrifice; if the cup or the tub should be exhausted, he should draw from the Āgrayaṇa; verily from the self he develops the sacrifice. The Āgrayaṇa is drawn (with a verse) in which there is no discriminating mark; he draws with a pot, he offers with (the vessel) for Vāyu; therefore (a man) is a slayer of a Brahman (through slaying) an embryo which has not been discriminated. They go to the final bath; they deposit the pots, but lift up (the vessels) for Vāyu; therefore they deposit a daughter on birth, a son they lift up. In that be utters the Puroruch, it is as when one brings (something) to a superior; in that he draws the cup, it is as when having brought (something) to a superior one proclaims (it); in that he puts it down, it is as when having deposited something with a superior one goes away. Whatever of the sacrifice is accompanied by a Sāman or Yajus, is loose; whatever by a Ṛich is firm; they are drawn with a support in front to the accompaniment of a Yajus, (they are drawn) with a support behind to the accompaniment of a Ṛich, for the support of the sacrifice.

Mantra 6:5:11

Some vessels are used (repeatedly), others not. With those that are employed once only (*parāchīnāni*) he conquers yonder world, for yonder world is as it were turned away (*parān*). With those which are used again he conquers this world, for this world is repeated as it were again and again. Some vessels are used (repeatedly), and others not. Through those that are used once only the plants fade; through those which are used again the plants revive again. Some vessels are used repeatedly, others not. Through those which are used once only the wild animals go to the forest; through those which are used again the domestic animals come back again to the village. He who knows the foundation of the cups becomes possessed of a (sure) foundation. The hymn called the Ājya (Śastra), that is the foundation of the cups; in that he recites muttering, that is (the foundation) of the Upāṃśu and the Antaryāma (cups); in that (he recites) aloud, that is (the foundation) of the other cups; he who knows thus becomes possessed of a foundation. He who knows the pairing of the cups is propagated with offspring, with cattle, with pairings. Some cups are drawn with pots, some with (vessels) for Vāyu; that is the pairing of the cups. He who knows thus is propagated with offspring, with cattle, with pairings. Indra forcibly drank the Soma of Tvaṣhṭar; he went to pieces on all sides; he found no stay in himself; he saw these cakes,as an addition to the pressing, them he offered, and with them he made a stay in himself; therefore as additional to the pressing the cakes are offered; therefore as additional to the pressing he should partake of the cakes; verily he makes a stay in himself, and the Soma does not flow through him. The theologians say, 'Neither by Ṛich nor by Sāman is the five made up; what then is the fivefold character of the sacrifice?' Fried grains, mush, rice grains, the cake, clotted milk, thereby the five is made up; that is the fivefold character of the sacrifice.

Prapāṭhaka 6.

The Exposition of the Dakṣhiṇā and other Offerings

Mantra 6:6:1

The sacrifices with the gifts are offered for the world of heaven. He offers with two (verses) on the Gārhapatya; the sacrificer has two feet; (verily it serves) for support. He offers in the Agnīdh's altar; verily he ascends the atmosphere. He approaches the Sadas; verily he makes him go to the world of heaven. He offers in the Gārhapatya with verses addressed to Sūrya; verily he makes him mount yonder world. He offers in the Agnīdh's altar with a verse containing the word 'Lead,' for leading to the world of heaven. 'Go to the sky, fly to heaven,' (with these words) he takes out the gold after the offering; verily he makes him go to the world of heaven. 'With my form I approach your form,' he says; for by his form he approaches their form, in that (he approaches) with gold. 'May Tutha, all knowing, allot to you,' he says; Tutha, all knowing, was wont to allot the gifts of the Gods; verily thereby he divides them. 'This gift of thine, O Agni, cometh, impelled by the Soma,' he says, for his gift comes impelled by the Soma. 'Lead it by the path of Mitra,' he says, for atonement. 'Go ye on by the path of holy order, of brilliant gifts,' he says; holy order is truth; verily with truth, with holy order, he divides them. 'Leading prosperity by the path of the sacrifice,' he says, for the gifts go by the path of the sacrifice. 'May I win a Brahman today, a seer and sprung from seers,' he says; the learned man is a Brahman, a seer and sprung from seers; therefore he says thus. 'Gaze on the heaven, gaze on the atmosphere,' he says; verily he makes him go to the world of heaven. 'Join those in the seat,' he says, for friendship. 'Given by us, go to the Gods, full of sweetness; enter the giver,' he says; 'we here are givers; do ye there enter us, full of sweetness,' he says in effect. He gives gold; gold is light; verily he places light before, to light up the world of heaven. He gives to the Agnīdh; verily he delights the seasons headed by Agni; he gives to the Brahman priest, for instigation; he gives to the Hotar; the Hotar is the self of the sacrifice; verily he unites the self of the sacrifice with the gifts.

Mantra 6:6:2

He offers the Samiṣhṭayajusas, for the completion of the sacrifice. Whatever is harsh or injured in the sacrifice, what he passes over, what he does not pass over, what he does redundantly, what he does not do, all that he propitiates with them. He offers nine; nine are the breaths in man, the sacrifice is commensurate with man; all the sacrifice he delights thus. He offers six with Ṛichas; the seasons are six; verily he delights the seasons; he offers three with Yajusas; these worlds are three; verily he delights these worlds. 'O sacrifice, go to the sacrifice; go to the lord of the sacrifice,' he says; verily he makes it go to the lord of the sacrifice. 'Go to thine own birthplace,' he says; verily be makes it go to his own birthplace. 'This is thy sacrifice, O lord of the sacrifice, with its, utterance of hymns and producing noble heroes,' he says; verily he confers strength upon the sacrificer. Vasiṣhṭha Sātyahavya asked Devabhāga, 'When thou didst cause to sacrifice the Sṛiñjayas, with many sacrificers, didst thou cause the sacrifice to rest upon the sacrifice or on the lord of the sacrifice? He replied, 'On the lord of the sacrifice.' 'But in truth Sṛiñjayas have been defeated,' he said, 'the sacrifice should have been made to rest on the sacrifice, to prevent the defeat of the sacrificer.' 'Ye Gods, that find the way, finding the way, go on the way,' he says; verily he makes the sacrifice to rest upon the sacrifice, to prevent the defeat of the sacrificer.

Mantra 6:6:3

He offers the Avabhṛithayajusas; whatever sin he has committed in the year before, verily that thereby he propitiates. He goes to the waters for the final bath; Varuṇa is in the waters; verily straightway he propitiates Varuṇa The Rākṣhasas, following along by the path, seek to injure the sacrifice; the Prastotar follows along with the Sāman, the slayer of Rākṣhasas, is the Sāman; (verily it serves) for the smiting away of the Rākṣhasas Thrice he performs the finale; these worlds are three; verily from these worlds he smites away the Rākṣhasas Each one performs the finale; for each one is infested by the Rākṣhasas, for the smiting away of the Rākṣhasas 'King Varuṇa hath made a broad (path),' he says, for support. 'A hundred remedies are thine, O king, a thousand,' he says; verily he makes medicine for him. 'The noose of Varuṇa is overcome,' he says verily he overcomes the noose of Varuṇa He makes offering over the strew, for the support of the oblations; verily also he offers in what has fire. He offers the fore-offerings omitting that to the strew; the strew is offspring; verily he frees offspring from Varuṇa's noose. He offers the two portions of butter; verily he does not obstruct the two eyes of the sacrifice. He sacrifices to Varuṇa; verily he frees him from Varuṇa's noose. He sacrifices to Agni and Varuṇa; verily straightway he frees him from Varuṇa's noose. He offers two after-offerings, omitting that to the strew; the strew is offspring; verily he frees offspring from Varuṇa's noose. He offers four fore-offerings and two after-offerings; they make up six, the seasons are six; verily he finds support in the seasons. 'O bath, O flood,' he says; verily he propitiates by this utterance Varuṇa In the sea is thy heart, within the waters,' he says, for Varuṇa is in the sea. 'Let the plants and the waters enter thee,' he says; verily he unites him with the waters and the plants. 'Ye divine waters, this is thy foetus,' he says; that is according to the text. The Soma is cattle; if he were to partake of the drops, he would be possessed of cattle, but Varuṇa would seize him; if he were not to partake, he would have no cattle, but Varuṇa would not seize him; he should touch them only, he becomes possessed of cattle, Varuṇa seizes him not. 'The noose of Varuṇa is loosed,' he says; verily is he freed from Varuṇa's noose. They advance without looking round, for concealment from Varuṇa 'Thou art fuel may we prosper,' he says; verily with the kindling-stick they approach the fire in reverence. 'Thou art brilliance; grant me brilliance,' he says; verily he bestows brilliance upon himself.

Mantra 6:6:4

With the wooden sword he digs up the altar, with the axle of a chariot he measures. He sets up the sacrificial post; verily gathering together a threefold bolt he hurls it at his foe, to lay him low. If he were to set it up within the altar, he would win the world of the Gods; if outside the altar, the world of men; he sets it up in the place where the altar and the edge (outside) meet, for the winning of both worlds. He should set (the set) up with the lower parts alike for one who desires the world of the Pitṛis, with the girdle part alike for one who desires the world of men, with the top pieces alike for one who desires power, and all alike for one who desires support; the three in the middle alike for one who desires cattle; for through them cattle attend (on him); verily he becomes possessed of cattle. He should interlock the others; verily he interlocks him with offspring and cattle. If he desire of a man, 'May he be liable to die,' he should set it up for him in grave fashion, the northern half the higher, then (the southern) the lower; this is the grave fashion; he for whom he sets it up thus swiftly dies. For him who desires the heaven he should set it up with the southern half the higher, then the (northern) half the lower; verily the sacrificer makes it a ladder and a bridge to attain the world of heaven. In that on one post he twines round two girdles, therefore one man wins two wives; in that he does not wind one girdle round two posts, therefore one wife does not find two husbands. If he desire of a man, 'Be a girl born to him,' he should intertwine (the girdles) near the ends; verily a girl is born to him; if he desire of a man, 'Be a son born to him,' he should cover it round right up to the end; verily a son is born to him. The Asuras drove the Gods to the south, the Gods repelled them by the Upaśaya (post); that is why the Upaśaya has its name. In that the Upaśaya lies near (*upaśāye*) on the south, (it serves) to drive away the foe. All the other posts have victims (attached), the Upaśaya has none, its victim is the sacrificer; if he were not to indicate (a victim), the sacrificer would be ruined. 'N.N. is thy victim,' (with these words) he should indicate whomsoever he hates; whom he hates, him he indicates as a victim to it. If he hates not, 'The mole is thy victim,' he should say; he harms not domestic nor wild animals. Prajāpati created offspring; he was destitute of proper food, he saw this set of eleven, and therewith he won proper food. In that there are ten posts, the Virāj has ten syllables, and the Virāj is food, he wins proper food by the Virāj; thereby he milks the eleventh breast of her. In that the set of eleven (is set up), a thunderbolt is set up; it is liable to crush the sacrifice face to face; in that he sets up (the stake) (for Tvashṭar) with the wives, (it serves) to establish the sacrifice and to bind.

Mantra 6:6:5

Prajāpati created offspring; he thought himself emptied, he saw this set of eleven (victims), with it he bestowed life, power, and strength upon himself; he who sacrifices creates as it were offspring; then he is as it were emptied; in that this set of eleven is (offered), with it the sacrificer bestows life, power, and strength upon himself. With (the victim) for Agni he scatters, with that for Sarasvatī he makes a pairing, with that for Soma he impregnates seed, with that for Pūshan he propagates. There is one for Bṛihaspati; Bṛihaspati is the holy power (Brahman) of the Gods; verily with the holy power (Brahman) he produces offspring for him. There is one for the All-Gods; offspring are connected with the All-Gods; verily he produces offspring, for him. By that for Indra he wins power, by that for the Marutas the people, by that for Indra and Agni force and might. That for Savitar is for instigation, that for Varuṇa to free oneself from Varuṇa's (noose). In the middle he offers that for Indra; verily in the middle he bestows power on the sacrificer. In front of that for Indra he offers that for the All-Gods; food is connected with the All-Gods; verily he puts food in front; therefore food is eaten in front. Having offered that for Indra he offers that for the Marutas; the Marutas are the people; verily he fastens the people to him. If he desire, 'May he who has attained (power) be banished; may he who is banished return (to power),' in the place of that for Indra he should offer that for Varuṇa, in the place of that for Varuṇa that for Indra. He who has attained (power) is banished, he who is banished returns (to power). If he desire, 'May the people fall into confusion,' he should interchange the animals; verily he causes the people to fall into confusion. If he should offer that to Varuṇa along the stream of the waters, Varuṇa would seize his offspring; he offers (the victim) facing north on the south side against the stream of the waters, to prevent Varuṇa seizing his offspring.

Mantra 6:6:6

Indra caused Manu to sacrifice with his wife; after she had been encircled with fire he let her go; therewith Manu prospered; in that he lets go (the victim), (for Tvashṭar with the wives, the sacrificer prospers with the prosperity with which Manu prospered. From what is unsupported in the sacrifice the sacrifice comes to ruin; as the sacrifice comes to ruin the sacrificer comes to ruin along with it; in that he completes (the offering) (for Tvashṭar) with the wives with butter, (it serves) to support the sacrifice, and as the sacrifice finds support, the sacrificer finds support along with it. The offering of the caul has been performed, the offering of the cow is not yet over, then he performs (the offering) (for Tvashṭar) with the wives; verily he performs it at the right moment; then indeed comes the conclusion. It is for Tvashṭar; Tvashṭar of the seed that is spilt moulds forms, him he sets loose as a male among wives; he for him moulds forms.

Mantra 6:6:7

They kill the Soma in that they press it; in that there is (an oblation) of Soma, that is as when they slay for the dead a barren cow. If he were to offer in the northern half or the middle, he would cause conflict with the Gods; he offers on the southern half; this is the quarter of the Pitṛis; verily in their own quarter he propitiates the Pitṛis They give to the Udgātars, (the oblation) of Soma has the Sāman for its deity; whatever of the Sāman they do amiss, that is the atonement for it. They look at (the victim) for Soma is a purifier; verily they purify themselves. He who cannot see himself would be dead. Having made it full all round, he should look at (it), for in it he sees himself; verily also he purifies himself. He whose mind is gone should look at (it), (saying), 'That mind of mine which hath gone away, or which hath gone elsewhere, by means of King Soma, we keep within us'; verily he keeps his mind in himself, his mind is not gone. At the third pressing the sacrifice departs from him who has sacrificed to him who has not sacrificed; he offers ghee with a verse to Agni and Vishṇu; all the deities are Agni, the sacrifice is Vishṇu; verily he supports the deities and the sacrifice. He sacrifices muttering, for pairing. The theologians say, 'Mitra appropriates the well-performed part of the sacrifice, Varuṇa the ill-performed; where then is the sacrifice, and where the sacrificer?; In that he offers a cow to Mitra and Varuṇa, by Mitra he propitiates the well-performed part of the sacrifice, by Varuṇa the ill-performed; the sacrificer is not ruined. Even as men plough the field with the plough, so do the Ṛich and the Sāman plough the sacrifice; in that he offers a cow to Mitra and Varuṇa, verily he rolls a roller over the ploughed-up sacrifice, for atonement. The metres of him who has sacrificed are worn out, the cow is the sap of the metres; in that he offers the cow to Mitra and Varuṇa, he again delights the metres, to drive away weariness; verily also he bestows sap upon the metres.

Mantra 6:6:8

The Gods divided up power and strength; what there was left over became the Atigrāhya cups, and that is why the Atigrāhyas have their name. In that the Atigrāhyas are drawn, verily thus the sacrificer bestows. upon himself power and strength, brilliance by that for Agni, power by that for Indra, splendour by that for Sūrya. The Atigrāhyas are the support of the sacrifice, the Pṛishṭhas are the two wheels, if he were not to draw them in the Pṛishṭhya (rite), the Pṛishṭhas would destroy the sacrifice in front; if he were to draw them in the Ukthya, the Atigrāhyas would destroy the sacrifice behind; but they should be drawn in the Viśvajit with all the Pṛishṭhas, so that the sacrifice may have all its strength. Prajāpati indicated the sacrifices to the Gods, he put away their dear forms, they became the Atigrāhya; 'Bodiless is his sacrifice,' they say, 'for whom the Atigrāhyas are not drawn.' They should be drawn also in the Agnishṭoma, so that the sacrifice may have its body. All the deities were alike, and were not discriminated; these Gods saw these cups and drew them, Agni that for Agni, Indra that for Indra, Sūrya that for Sūrya; then indeed were they discriminated from the other Gods; he, for whom knowing thus these cups are drawn, is discriminated from his evil foe. 'These worlds must be made full of light, with like strength,' they say; verily with that for Agni he bestows light on this world, with that for Indra on the atmosphere, for Indra and Vāyu are yoke-fellows; with that for Sūrya on yonder world he bestows light; full of light these worlds become for him; he makes them of like strength. Bamba and Viśvavayasa found these cups, and to them these worlds, the distant and the near, became revealed; to him, for whom knowing thus these cups are drawn, these worlds, the distant and the near, become revealed.

Mantra 6:6:9

Whatever the Gods did at the sacrifice the Asuras did. The Gods caused the metres and the pressings to find support in the Adābhya; then the Gods prospered, the Asuras were defeated; he, for whom knowing thus the Adābhya is drawn, prospers himself, his foe is defeated. Because the Gods deceived the Asuras with the Adābhya (undeceivable), that is why the Adābhya has its name. He who knows thus deceives his foe; his foe deceives him not. The Adābhya is the form of Prajāpati, called the freer; he draws from (the Soma) which is tied up, for freedom; he who knows thus is set free from his evil foe. They kill the Soma in that they press it; in the slaying of the Soma the sacrifice is slain, with the sacrifice the sacrificer. The theologians say, 'What is it that the sacrificer does in the sacrifice whereby he goes alive to the world of heaven?' The Adābhya is the taking alive; he draws from (the Soma) before pressing; verily he makes him go alive to the world of heaven. Now they break the sacrifice asunder when they make it find support in the Adābhya; he lets go the shoots, for the continuance of the sacrifice.

Mantra 6:6:10.

The Gods drew the cups in a line; Prajāpati saw this Aṃśu, drew it, and therewith prospered. Verily he, for whom knowing thus the Aṃśu is drawn, prospers. He draws from (the Soma) when it has been once pressed, for once he prospered thereby. He draws with the mind, for Prajāpati is mind as it were; (verily it serves) to obtain Prajāpati He draws with (a vessel) of Udumbara; the Udumbara is strength; verily he wins strength; it has four corners; verily he finds support in the quarters. He who knows the foundation of the Aṃśu becomes possessed of a foundation. The Sāman is that called the Vāmadevya; singing in his mind that foundation he draws; verily he becomes possessed of a foundation. If the Adhvaryu were not to make a success of drawing the Aṃśu, for both the Adhvaryu and the sacrificer would it go ill; if he were to make a success, for both would it go well; he draws without breathing; this is its success. He breathes over gold; gold is immortality, breath is life; verily with life he quickens immortality; it is of a hundred (Kṛishṇalas) in weight, man has a hundred (years of) life, a hundred powers; verily in life, in power he finds support.

Mantra 6:6:11

Prajāpati assigned the sacrifices to the Gods; he thought himself emptied; he pressed over himself the power and strength of the sacrifice in sixteen ways; that became the Ṣhoḍaśin; there is no sacrifice called Ṣhoḍaśin; in that there is a sixteenth Stotra and a sixteenth Śastra, therefore is it the Ṣhoḍaśin, and that is why the Ṣhoḍaśin has its name. In that the Ṣhoḍaśin is drawn, so the sacrificer bestows power and strength upon himself. To the Gods the world of heaven did not become manifest; they saw this Ṣhoḍaśin, and drew it; then did the world of heaven become manifest to them; in that the Ṣhoḍaśin is drawn, (it serves) for the conquest of the world of heaven. Indra was the youngest of the Gods, he had recourse to Prajāpati, he bestowed on him the Ṣhoḍaśin, he drew it; then indeed did he attain the summit of the Gods; he for whom knowing thus the Ṣhoḍaśin is drawn attains the summit of his equals. He draws at the morning pressing; the Ṣhoḍaśin is the thunderbolt, the morning pressing is the thunderbolt; verily he draws it from its own birthplace. At each pressing he draws; verily from each pressing he produces it. At the third pressing he should draw (it) for one who desires cattle; the Ṣhoḍaśin is the thunderbolt, the third pressing is cattle; verily by means of the thunderbolt he wins for him cattle from the third pressing. He should not draw (it) in the Ukthya; the Ukthas are offspring and cattle; if he were to draw (it) in the Ukthya, he would consume his offspring and cattle. He should draw (it) for one who desires cattle in the Atirātra; the Ṣhoḍaśin is the thunderbolt; verily having won cattle for him by the thunderbolt, he calms them later with (the Śastras of) the night. He should also draw (it) in the Agniṣhṭoma for a Rājanya, for a Rājanya sacrifices desiring distinction; verily in the day rite he grasps a bolt for him, and the bolt kindles him to prosperity, or it burns him; the twenty-onefold is the Stotra used, for support; what is recited has the word 'bay' in it; he obtains the dear abode of Indra. The smaller metres were among the Gods, the larger among the Asuras; the Gods recited the larger metre with the smaller on either side; then indeed did they appropriate the world of the Asuras. In that he recites the larger metre with a smaller metre on either side, verily thus he appropriates the world of his foe. They make six syllables redundant; the seasons are six; verily he delights the seasons. They place four in front; verily he wins four-footed cattle; two last; verily he wins two-footed (cattle); they make up an Anuṣhṭubh; the Anuṣhṭubh is speech, therefore speech is the highest of the breaths. When the sun is half-set, he sets about the Stotra of the Ṣhoḍaśin; in this world Indra slew Vṛitra; verily straightway be hurls the bolt against his foe. The sacrificial fee is a reddish-brown horse; that is the form of the bolt; (verily it serves) for success.

Kāṇḍa 7.

The Explanation of the Soma Sacrifice (continued).

Prapāṭhaka 1

The One Day Sacrifices

Mantra 7:1:1

Production of offspring is light. Agni is the light of the Gods; the Virāj is the light of the metres. The Virāj of speech ends in Agni; it is produced according to the Virāj Therefore it is called light. Two Stomas bear the morning pressing, like expiration and inspiration; two the midday pressing, like eye and ear; two the third pressing, like speech and support. This sacrifice is commensurate with man, and is perfect. Whatever desire a man has, he wins by it, for one wins all by that which is perfect. By means of the Agniṣhṭoma Prajāpati created off spring; by means of the Agniṣhṭoma he grasped them. When he grasped them the mule escaped. Following it he took its seed, and placed it in the ass. Therefore the ass has double seed. They also say, 'He placed it in the mare.' Therefore the mare has double seed. They also say, 'In the plants he placed it.' Therefore plants, though not anointed, glisten.' They also say, 'He placed it in offspring.' Therefore twins are born. Therefore the mule has no offspring, for his seed has been taken from him. Therefore he is not suitable for the sacrifice, but is suitable if there is a sacrifice when one gives (to the priests) all one's goods or a thousand, for he escaped. He who knowing thus sacrifices with the Agniṣhṭoma begets unborn offspring and grasps those that are born. Therefore they say, 'It is the best of sacrifices.' Prajāpati indeed is the best, for he sacrificed with it first. Prajāpati desired, 'May I have offspring.' He meted out the Trivṛit from his mouth. After it the God Agni was created, the Gāyatrī metre, the Rathantara Sāman, of men the Brahman, of cattle the goat; therefore are they the chief, for they were produced from the mouth. From the breast and arms he meted out the Pañchadaśa Stoma. After it the God Indra was created, the Triṣhṭubh metre, the Bṛihat Sāman, of men the Rājanya, of cattle the sheep. There fore they are strong, for they were created from strength. From the middle he meted out the Saptadaśa Stoma. After it the All-Gods as deities were created, the Jagatī metre, the Vairūpa Sāman, of men the Vaiśya, of cattle cows. Therefore are they to be eaten, for they were created from the receptacle of food. Therefore are they more numerous than others, for they were created after the most numerous of the Gods. From his feet he meted out the Ekaviṃśa Stoma. After it the Anuṣhṭubh metre was created, the Vairāja Sāman, of men the Śūdra, of cattle the horse. Therefore the two, the horse and the Śūdra, are dependent on others. Therefore the Śūdra is not fit for the sacrifice, for he was not created after any Gods. Therefore they depend on their feet, for they were created from the feet. The Trivṛit is the breaths; the Pañchadaśa the half-months; the Saptadaśa Prajāpati; these worlds are three; the Ekaviṃśa is the sun yonder. In this they rest, in this they find support. He who knows thus rests on this, finds, support in this.

Mantra 7:1:2

At the morning pressing he keeps glorifying the Trivṛit Stoma by the Gāyatrī metre; the Pañchadaśa Stoma by the Trivṛit, which is splendour; the Saptadaśa by the Pañchadaśa which is force and strength; the Ekaviṃśa by the Saptadaśa which is connected with Prajāpati and causes begetting. Verily thus Stoma glorifies Stoma; verily also Stoma leads Stoma forth. As many as are the Stomas, so many are desires, so many the worlds, so many the lights; verily so many Stomas, so many desires, so many worlds, so many lights does he win.

Mantra 7:1:3

The theologians say, 'He indeed would really sacrifice, who having sacrificed with the Agniṣhṭoma should also sacrifice with the Śarvaṣhṭoma.' If they omit the Trivṛit Stoma, then his vital airs are omitted, but he who offers the sacrifice does so with the wish, 'May it be in my vital airs. If they omit the Pañchadaśa Stoma, his strength is omitted, but he who offers the sacrifice does so with the wish, 'May it be in my strength.' If they omit the Saptadaśa Stoma, his offspring is omitted, but he who offers the sacrifice does so with the wish, 'May it be in my offspring.' If they omit the Ekaviṃśa Stoma, his support is omitted, but he who offers the sacrifice does so with the wish, 'May it be in my support.' If they omit the Triṇava Stoma, his seasons and the strength of the Nakṣhatras are omitted, but he who offers the sacrifice does so with the wish, 'May it be in my seasons and the strength of the Nakṣhatras.' If they omit the Trayastriṃśa Stoma, his deities are omitted, and he who offers the sacrifice does so with the wish, 'May it be in my deities.' He who knows the lowest of the Stomas attaining the first place, obtains him self the first place. The Trivṛit is the lowest of Stomas, the Trivṛit occupies the first place. He who know thus obtains the first place.

THE EXPOSITION OF THE SATTRAS

The Ahīna Sacrifices

Mantra 7:1:4

The Aṅgirasas performed a sacrificial session. They went to the world of heaven. Of them Haviṣhmant and Haviṣhkṛit were left behind. They desired, 'May we two go to the world of heaven.' They two saw this two-night rite, they grasped it, and sacrificed with it. Then they went to the world of heaven. He, who knowing thus offers the two-night sacrifice, goes to the world of heaven. They went with the first day and arrived with the second. The first day is the Abhiplava, the second the complete (*gati*). The first day is the Jyotiṣhṭoma form of the Agniṣhṭoma; with it he wins splendour. The second day is an Atirātra with all the Stomas, that he may obtain all and win all. On the first day the Sāman is in the Gāyatrī (metre). The Gāyatrī is brilliance and splendour; verily he bestows brilliance and splendour on himself. On the second day (the Sāman) is in the Triṣhṭubh metre. The Trishṭubh is force and strength; verily he bestows force and strength on himself. The Sāman on the first day is the Rathantara. The Rathantara is this (earth); verily he stands firm on this (earth). (The Sāman) on the second is the Bṛihat The Bṛihat is yonder (sky); verily he stands firm on yonder (sky). They say, 'Where are the Jagatī and the Anuṣhṭubh?' On the first day the Sāman is that of Vikhānas; verily he does not leave the Jagatī On the second it is the Ṣhoḍaśin; verily he does not leave the Anuṣhṭubh. Then they say, 'If the days fall in the same half month, then the strength of one day only will belong to the rite.' The first day takes place on the night of new moon; the second on the next day, verily the days fall on separate half-months, and have the several strengths. The first day has Haviṣhmant, the second Haviṣhkṛit in the finale, for support.

Mantra 7:1:5

This was in the beginning the waters, the ocean. In it Prajāpati becoming the wind moved. He saw her, and becoming a boar he seized her. Her, becoming Viśvakarman, he wiped. She extended, she became the earth, and hence the earth is called the earth (lit. 'the extended'). In her Prajāpati made effort. He produced the Gods, Vasus, Rudras, and Ādityas The Gods said to Prajāpati, 'Let us have offspring.' He said, 'As I have created you by penance, so seek ye offspring in penance.' He gave to them Agni as a support, saying, 'Strive with that support.' They strove with Agni as a support. After a year they produced one cow. They gave it to the Vasus, Rudras, and Ādityas, saying 'Guard it.' The Vasus, Rudras, and Ādityas guarded it. It produced for the Vasus, Rudras, and Ādityas (each) three hundred and thirty-three. Thus she became the thousandth. The Gods said to Prajāpati, 'Cause sacrifice to be made to us with a thousand.' He caused sacrifice to be made by the Vasus with the Agniṣhṭoma. They won this world and gave (the thousandth). He caused sacrifice to be made by the Rudras with the Ukthya. They won the atmosphere and gave (the thousand). He caused sacrifice to be made by the Ādityas with the Atirātra They won yonder world, and gave (the thousand). Now the atmosphere was broken. Therefore the Rudras are murderous, for they have no support. Therefore they say, 'The midmost day of the three-day night is not fixed; for it was moved.' The Ājya (Śastra) of the midmost day is in the Triṣhṭubh metre. He recites the Saṃyāna hymns, then recites the Ṣhoḍaśin, that the day may be made firm and be not loose. Therefore in the three-night rite, the first day should be an Agniṣhṭoma, then an Ukthya, then an Atirātra, for the separation of these worlds. On each day in succession he gives three hundred continuously, for the continuance of these worlds. He should not break the decades lest he should thus destroy the Virāj Now for the thousandth Indra and Viṣhṇu strove. Indra reflects, 'By this Viṣhṇu will appropriate all the thousand.' They made arrangement as to it, Indra got two-thirds, Viṣhṇu the remaining third; verily the fact is recorded in the verse, 'Ye twain have conquered.' It is the Achāvāka who recites this verse. Now (some say), 'The thousandth is to be given to the Hotar'; what is left over, is left over for the Hotar; the Hotar is the receiver of what has not been taken. Then others say, 'It is to be given to the Unnetar' This is left over of the thousand, and the Unnetar is the one of the priests who is left over. Then some say, 'It is to be given to all those who have a place in the Sadas.' Then some say, 'It should be driven away and allowed to wander at will.' Then some say, 'It is to be given to the Brahman and the Agnīdh, two shares to the Brahman and the third to the Agnīdh For the Brahman is connected with Indra, the Agnīdh with Viṣhṇu; (verily the division is) just as they two agreed upon. Then some say, 'The one which is beautiful and of varied colour is the one to be given.' Then others say, 'The one which has two colours and on either side is spotted is the one to be given,' for the gaining of a thousand. That indeed is the march of the thousand (*sahāsrasyāyana*). There are a thousand Stotrīyas, a thousand gifts (to the priests); the world of heaven is measured by a thousand; (verily it serves) for the winning of the heavenly world.

Mantra 7:1:6

Soma found a thousand; Indra discovered it after him. Yama approached them and said to them, 'May I have a share too in it.' They said to him, 'Be it so.' Yama saw in one of the (cows) strength. He said to them, 'This one has the strength of the thousand, this be mine, the rest yours.' They said, 'We all see that in this one is strength. Let us each have a portion.' So they took shares in the one. They put her into the waters, saying, 'Come out for Soma.' She came out in the shape of a red brown cow of one year old, together with three hundred and thirty three. Therefore let one buy the Soma with a red brown cow one year old. He, who knowing thus buys the Soma with a red brown cow one year old, buys the Soma with three hundred and thirty-three and sacrifices with Soma for which he has paid a good price. They put her into the waters, saying, 'Come out for Indra.' She came out in the shape of a red draught animal with good characteristics, destroying foes, together with three hundred and thirty-three. Therefore one should give a red draught animal with good characteristics, destroying foes. He who knowing thus gives a red draught animal with good characteristics, destroying foes, gives her as three hundred and thirty-three. They put her into the waters' saying, 'Come out for Yama.' She came out in the shape of an aged, stupid, utterly bad animal, together with three hundred and thirty-three. Therefore one should offer as the funeral cow one that is aged, stupid, utterly bad. If a man knowing thus offers a cow that is aged, stupid, utterly bad, as the funeral cow, she becomes for him in yonder world three hundred and thirty-three. Speech is the thousandth. Therefore a boon must be given; for she is a boon, and when she is given she is a thousand. Therefore one must not accept a boon; for she is a boon; verily he would be accepting a thousand. Let him say, 'She is a boon,' and of another, 'Let this be mine'; verily he avoids accepting a thousand. She should be spotted on either side. They say, 'Let her be spotted on one side only; spotted is the thousand on the other side.' The one for a boon should be beautiful, perfect in form; for she is a boon; (verily it serves for) prosperity. Leading her round to the north of the Agnīdh's place he makes her smell the wooden tub near the Āhavanīya fire, saying, || 'Smell the tub, O great one, with broad stream rich in milk; | Let the drops enter thee as the streams the ocean; | Give me a share in a thousand, with offspring, with cattle; | Let wealth again visit me.' || Verily he unites him with offspring, with cattle, with wealth. He becomes rich in offspring, in cattle, in wealth, who knows thus. Having gone round the Agnīdh's place with her, he should offer in front, while the cow stands facing (him), Saying, || Ye twain have conquered; ye are not conquered; | Neither of the two of them hath been defeated; | Indra and Viṣhṇu when ye contended, | Ye did divide the thousand into three.' || The thousand is divided into three parts at the three-night festival; verily he makes her possessed of a thousand, he makes her the measure of a thousand. He offers to her forms; verily he unites her with her forms. Rising up he mutters in her ear, || 'O Iḍā, Ranti, Aditi, Sarasvatī, Priyā, Preyasī, Mahī, Viśrutī, | These, O inviolable one, are thy names; | Proclaim me among the Gods as a doer of good deeds.' || Verily she proclaims him among the Gods, and the Gods take note of him.

Mantra 7:1:7

By the thousandth the sacrifice goes to the world of heaven. She makes him go to the world of heaven. 'Do thou make me go to the world of heaven,' he says; verily she makes him go to the world of heaven. 'Do thou make me go to the world of light,' he says; verily she makes him go to the world of light. 'Do thou make me go to all holy worlds,' he says; verily she makes him go to all holy worlds. 'Do thou make me go to a secure place, with offspring and cattle, let wealth again visit me,' (he says); verily she establishes him with offspring and cattle in wealth. Rich in offspring, cattle, and wealth he becomes who knows thus. He should give her to the Agnīdh, or the Brahman, or the Hotar or the Udgātar, or the Adhvaryu. In giving her, he gives a thousand. A thousand he accepts who not knowing accepts her. He should accept her, (saying), 'Thou art one, not a thousand. Thee as one I accept, not a thousand; come to me as one, not as a thousand'; verily he who knows thus accepts her as one, not as a thousand. 'Thou art gentle, resting well, auspicious; come to me as gentle, well resting, auspicious,' he says; verily she becoming gentle, well resting, auspicious, comes to him, and harms him not. The theologians say, 'Does the thousandth follow the thousand? or the thou sand the thousandth?' If he were to let her go to the east, the thousandth would follow the thousand; now the thousand has no understanding, and would not recognize the world of heaven. He lets her go to the west; the thousand follow after her. She knowing goes to the world of heaven. He lets her go towards the sacrificer. Quickly a thousand springs up. The (thousandth) is the last to be taken, but the first to go to the Gods.

Mantra 7:1:8

Atri gave offspring to Aurva who was desirous of children. She deemed herself empty, without strength, weak, worn out. He saw the four night rite; he grasped it, and sacrificed with it. Then indeed were four sons born for him, a good Hotar, a good Udgātar, a good Adhvaryu, a good councillor. He, who knowing thus offers the four-night rite, has four sons born for him, a good Hotar, a good Udgātar, a good Adhvaryu, a good councillor. The Pavamāna (Stomas) which are twenty-fourfold are splendour; the increasing Stomas are prosperity. Atri who had faith as his deity and offered sacrifices was not visited by the four strengths, brilliance, power, splendour, food. He saw these four Soma libations with the four Stomas; he grasped them and sacrificed with them. He won brilliance with the first, power with the second, splendour with the third, food with the fourth. He, who knowing thus, grasps the four Soma libations with the four Stomas and sacrifices with them, wins brilliance with the first, power with the second, splendour with the third, food with the fourth. With the success which Atri had, the sacrificer prospers.

Mantra 7:1:9

Jamadagni desiring prosperity, sacrificed with the four-night rite. He prospered therein, and accordingly the two descendants of Jamadagni are not seen as grey-haired. That prosperity is his who knowing thus offers the four-night rite. On the Upasads offerings of the sacrificial cake are made. The sacrificial cake is cattle; verily he wins cattle. The sacrificial cake is food; verily he wins food. An eater of food and owner of cattle he becomes who knowing thus offers the four-day rite.

Mantra 7:1:10.

The year was alone in the world. He desired, 'May I create the seasons.' He saw this five-night rite; he grasped it and sacrificed with it. Then indeed he created the seasons. He who knowing thus offers the five-night rite gains offspring. The seasons being created were not distinguished. They saw this five-night rite. They grasped it and sacrificed with it. Then they were distinguished. He who knowing thus offers the five-night rite is distinguished from the enemy that hates him. Sārvaseni Śauceya desired, 'May I be rich in cattle.' He grasped this five-night rite and sacrificed with it. Then indeed he obtained a thousand cattle. He who knowing thus offers the five-night rite obtains a thousand cattle. Babara Prāvāhaṇi desired, 'May I be a speaker of speech.' He grasped the five-night rite and sacrificed with it. Then indeed he became a speaker of speech. He, who knowing thus offers the five-night rite, becomes a speaker of speech, and men call him 'lord of speech'. The four-night rite is incomplete; the six-night rite is redundant, the correct sacrifice is the five-night rite. He who knowing thus sacrifices with the five-night rite sacrifices with the correct sacrifice. The (sacrifices) last five nights; the year consists of five seasons; verily he stands firm in the year with its five seasons. Again the Paṅkti has five elements, the sacrifice is fivefold; verily he wins the sacrifice. There is an Agniṣhṭoma characterized by the Trivṛit (Stoma); verily he wins brilliance. There is a Pañchadaśa (Stoma); verily he wins power. There is a Saptadaśa (Stoma), for the obtainment of food; verily also he gains offspring by reason of it. There is an Agniṣhṭoma with the Pañchadaśa (Stoma), for the gaining of Prajāpati; (it has) the characteristics of the Mahāvrata, for the gaining of food. There is a Viśvajit Atirātra, with all the Pṛiṣhṭha (Stotras), for the winning of all.

The Horse Sacrifice (continued)

Mantra 7:1:11

a. On the instigation of God Savitar, I take thee with the arms of the Aśvins, with the hands of Pūṣhan. ‖ *b.* This bond of order they grasped | At their assemblies in ages gone by, the sages; | Therewith the Gods mastered the pressed (juice), | In the Sāman of order declaring the stream. ‖ *c.* Thou art surrounding; thou art the world; thou art the restrainer; thou art the supporter; do thou go, with the cry of 'Hail!' to Agni Vaiśvānara, the extending. ‖ *d.* Thou art the restrainer, the ruler on earth; thou art the restrainer who dost restrain; thou art the supporter who dost support. ‖ *c.* For ploughing thee! For comfort thee! For wealth thee! For increase thee! ‖ *f.* For earth thee! For the atmosphere thee! For sky thee! ‖ *g.* For being thee! For not being thee! For the waters thee! For the plants thee! For all creatures thee!

Mantra 7:1:12

a. Many through thy dam, powerful through thy sire, thou art a horse, thou art a steed, thou art a runner, thou art a male, thou art a strong horse, thou art a racer, thou art powerful, thou art a stallion, thou art heroic hearted; 'goer' is thy name; do thou follow the course of the Ādityas ‖ *b.* To Agni hail! Hail to Indra and Agni! Hail to Prajāpati! Hail to the All-Gods! Hail to all the deities! ‖ *c.* Here is support, hail! Here is keeping apart, hail! Here is joy, hail! Here is delight, hail! ‖ *d.* Thou art becoming; to being thee, to what is becoming thee, to what shall be thee! To all beings thee! ‖ *e.* O Gods that guard the quarters, do ye guard for the Gods for sacrifice this horse duly besprinkled.

Mantra 7:1:13

To the going hail! | To the advancing hail! | To the running hail! | To him after be hath run hail! | To the crying of 'shoo' hail! | To him over whom is cried 'shoo' hail! | To him who hath moved hail! | To him who hath moved forward hail! | To him springing forward hail! | To him jumping away hail! | To him who advanceth hail! | To him who advanceth forward hail! | To all hail!

Mantra 7:1:14

To Agni hail! | To Soma hail! | To Vāyu hail! | To the joy of the waters hail! | To Savitar hail! | To Sarasvatī hail! | To Indra hail! | To Bṛihaspati hail! | To Mitra hail! | To Varuṇa hail! | To all hail!

Mantra 7:1:15

To earth hail! | To atmosphere hail! | To sky hail! | To the sun hail! | To the moon hail! | To the Nakṣhatras hail! | To the eastern quarter hail! | To the southern quarter hail! | To the western quarter hail! | To the northern quarter hail! | To the zenith hail! | To the quarters hail! | To the intermediate quarters hail! | To the half-years hail! | To the autumns hail! | To the days and nights hail! | To the half-months hail! | To the months hail! | To the seasons hail! | To the year hail! | To all hail!

Mantra 7:1:16

To Agni hail! | To Soma hail! | To Savitar hail! | To Sarasvatī hail! | To Pūṣhan hail! | To Bṛihaspati hail! | To the joy of the waters hail! | To Vāyu hail! | To Mitra hail! | To Varuṇa hail! | To all hail!

Mantra 7:1:17

To earth hail! | To atmosphere hail! | To sky hail! | To Agni hail! | To Soma hail! | To the sun hail! | To the moon hail! | To the day hail! | To the night hail! | To the straight hail! | To the good hail! | To fair dwelling hail! | To hunger hail! | To satisfaction hail! | To disease hail! | To snow hail! | To ice hail! | To heat hail! | To the wild hail! | To heaven hail! | To the world hail! | To all hail!

Mantra 7:1:18

a. Thou hast come into being by the toil; the work of the Gods thou art the way of holy order. With the Vasus, the Gods, as deity, with the Gāyatrī metre I yoke thee, with the spring season as oblation I consecrate thee. ‖ *b.* With the Rudras, the Gods, as deity, with the Trishṭubh metro, I yoke thee; with the summer season as oblation I consecrate thee. ‖ *c.* With the Ādityas, the Gods, as deity, with the Jagatī metre, I yoke thee; with the rainy season as oblation I consecrate thee. ‖ *d.* With the All-Gods as deity, with the Anushṭubh metro, I yoke thee; with the autumn season as oblation I consecrate thee. ‖ *e.* With the Aṅgirasas, the Gods, as deity, with the Paṅkti metre, I yoke thee; with the winter and cool seasons as oblation I consecrate thee. ‖ *f.* I have mounted upon consecration, the wife of holy order, with the Gāyatrī metro and holy power; holy order have I placed upon truth; truth have I placed upon holy order. ‖ *g.* The great. ‖ *h.* The protecting. ‖ *i.* Here is support, hail! ‖ *k.* Here is keeping apart, hail! ‖ *l.* Here is joy, hail! ‖ *m.* Here is delight, hail!

Mantra 7:1:19

To the sounding of 'Īm' hail! | To him over whom 'Īm' is sounded hail! | To him neighing hail! | To him neighing down hail! | To him snorting hail! | To him snorting forth hail! | To the smell hail! | To what is smelt hail! | To expiration hail! | To cross-breathing hail! | To inspiration hail! | To him being bound hail! | To him after being bound hail! | To him being untied hail! | To him untied hail! | To him about to run hail! | To him having run hail! | To him about to rest hail! | To him having rested hail! | To him about to go to rest hail! | To him going to rest hail! | To him having gone to rest hail! | To him about to sit down hail! | To him sitting down hail! | To him having sat down hail! | To him about to stand hail! | To him who is standing hail! | To him who hath stood hail! | To him about to go down hail! | To him going down hail! | To him having gone down hail! | To him about to lie hail! | To him lying hail! | To him who hath lain hail! | To him about to close the eyes hail! | To him closing the eyes hail! | To him having closed the eyes hail! | To him about to sleep hail! | To him who hath slept hail! | To him about to wake hail! | To him awakening hail! | To him who hath awakened hail! | To him about to become awake hail! | To him becoming awake hail! | To him who hath become awake hail! | To him about to hear hail! | To him hearing hail! | To him who hath heard hail! | To him about to look hail! | To him who is looking hail! | To him who hath looked hail! | To him who is about to go out hail! | To him going out hail! | To him who hath gone out hail! | To him about to roll about hail! | To him rolling about hail! | To him who hath rolled about hail! | To him about to get up hail! | To him getting up hail! | To him who hath got up hail! | To him about to shake himself hail! | To him shaking himself hail! | To him who hath shaken himself hail! | To him about to step out hail! | To him stepping out hail! | To him who hath stopped out hail! | To him who is about to rush hail! | To him who is rushing hail! | To him who hath rushed hail! | To him about to scratch hail! | To him scratching hail! | To him having scratched hail! | To him about to rub hail! | To him rubbing hail! | To him who hath rubbed hail! | What he eateth, to that hail! | What he drinketh, to that hail! | To what he evacuateth, to that hail! | To the dung he maketh hail! | To seed hail! | To offspring hail! | To begetting hail! | To all hail!

Mantra 7:1:20.

a. To Agni hail! To Vāyu hail! To Sūrya hail! ‖ *b.* Thou art holy order, thou art the holy order of holy order; thou art truth, thou art the truth of truth! ‖ *c.* Thou art the path of holy order, the shadow of the Gods, the name of immortality; thou art truth, thou art Prajāpati ‖ *d.* When on him as on a steed in swift movements, | The folk of the sky vie with the sun; | Choosing the waters the sage becometh pure, | Like a beast the busy guardian that goeth around.

Prapāṭhaka 2.

The Ahīna Sacrifices (continued)

Mantra 7:2:1

The Sādhya Gods, desirous of heaven, saw this (rite) of six nights. They grasped it, and sacrificed with it. Then indeed did they go to the world of heaven. Those, who knowing thus perform (the rite) of six nights, go to the world of heaven. (The rite) of six nights is a Sattra of the Gods, for these Pṛishṭhas are obvious. Those, who knowing thus perform (the rite) of six nights, mount evidently upon the Gods. (The rite) is of six nights; the seasons are six, the Pṛishṭhas are six; verily by the Pṛishṭhas they mount the seasons, by the seasons the year; verily in the year they find support. They proceed with the Bṛihat and the Rathantara, (Sāmans). The Rathantara, is this (earth), the Bṛihat is yonder (sky); verily with them do they proceed; verily also in them do they find support. These indeed are the quick paths of the sacrifice; verily by them do they proceed to the world of heaven. There is an Agnishṭoma with the Trivṛit (Stoma); verily they win brilliance. There is a Pañchadaśa (Stoma); verily they win power. There is a Saptadaśa (Stoma), for the winning of food; verily also by it they are propagated. There is an Ekaviṃśa (Stoma), for support; verily also they place radiance in themselves. There is a Triṇava (Stoma), for con quest. There is a Trayastriṃśa (Stoma), for support. They should sacrifice with this (rite) of six nights with both Sadas and oblation-holder. The oblation-holder and the Agnīdh's seat should be of Aśvattha wood, for that is heavenly. They should have wheels, for gaining the world of heaven. The sacrificial post is mortar-based, for support. They go forward, for forward as it were is the world of heaven. They go with the Sarasvatī This is the path that goes to the Gods; verily they mount upon it. They go calling aloud; verily fastening misfortune on another they attain support. When ten (cows) make a hundred, then is one time to stop. Man is of a hundred (years of) life and of a hundred powers; verily in life and power do they find support. When a hundred make a thousand, then is one time to stop. Yonder world is measured by a thousand; verily they conquer yonder world. If one of them perish or they be oppressed, then is one time to stop, for that is a suitable opportunity.

Mantra 7:2:2

Kusurubinda Auddālaki desired, 'May I be rich in cattle.' He grasped this (rite) of seven nights, and sacrificed with it. Then indeed did be win all the domestic animals. He, who knowing thus sacrifices with (the rite) of seven nights, wins all domestic animals. (The rite) is of seven nights; the domesticated animals are seven, the wild seven, the metres seven, for winning both. There is an Agnishṭoma with the Trivṛit (Stoma); verily he wins brilliance. There is a Pañchadaśa (Stoma); verily he wins power. There is a Saptadaśa (Stoma), for the winning of food; verily also by it he is propagated. There is an Ekaviṃśa (Stoma), for support; verily he places radiance in himself. There is a Triṇava (Stoma), for conquest. There is an Agnishṭoma with the Pañchadaśa (Stoma) to obtain Prajāpati; it has (the characteristics of) the Mahāvrata, to win food. There is a Viśvajit Atirātra with all the Pṛishṭhas, to conquer all. If they were in the preceding days to perform the Pṛishṭhas in the obvious way, and similarly in the Viśvajit, the last day would be as when one sits down to a cow which has already been milked; it would not be good enough for even a single night (rite). In the preceding days they perform the Bṛihat and the Rathantara. The Rathantara is this (earth), the Bṛihat yonder (sky); verily they depart not from them; verily also in them do they find support. In that they perform the Pṛishṭhas in the Viśvajit in the obvious manner, it is as when one milks a cow which is ready to give.

Mantra 7:2:3

Bṛihaspati desired, 'May I be resplendent.' He saw this rite of eight nights, he grasped it, and sacrificed with it. Then indeed did he become resplendent. He, who knowing thus sacrifices with (the rite) of eight nights, becomes resplendent. (The rite) is of eight nights; the quarters are four, the intermediate quarters four; verily from the quarters he wins splendour. There is an Agnishṭoma with the Trivṛit (Stoma); verily he wins brilliance. There is a Pañchadaśa (Stoma); verily he wins power. There is a Saptadaśa (Stoma), for the winning of food; verily also by it he is propagated. There is an Ekaviṃśa (Stoma), for support verily he places radiance in himself. There is a Triṇava (Stoma), for conquest. There is a Trayastriṃśa (Stoma), for support. There is an Agnishṭoma with the Pañchadaśa (Stoma), to obtain Prajāpati; it has (the characteristics of) the Mahāvrata, to win food. There is a Viśvajit Atirātra with all the Pṛishṭhas, to conquer all.

Mantra 7:2:4

Prajāpati created offspring. They being created were ahungered. He saw this (rite) of nine nights, he grasped it, and sacrificed with it. Then indeed was he able to help offspring, When offspring are ahungered, one should sacrifice with (the rite) of nine nights, for these worlds are not fitted for them, and thus they are ahungered; verily he makes these worlds fitted for them, and as they become fitted he becomes fit for offspring along with them; these worlds become fit for him, and strength he places in offspring. By means of three nights he makes fit this world, by means of three nights the atmosphere, by means of three nights yonder world. As a man casts thread on thread, so he casts world on world, for firmness, and to avoid looseness. The Stomas are known as Jyotis, Go, and Āyus The Jyotis is this (earth), the Go the atmosphere, the Āyus yonder (sky); verily they find support in these worlds, and he becomes famous among people. (The rite) is of nine nights; verily in order he places brilliance on him. If a man be a long time ill, he should sacrifice with (the rite) of nine nights; for his breaths are loosened, and thus is he ill long; verily he supports his breaths in him, and even if his life be gone, yet he lives.

Mantra 7:2:5

Prajāpati desired, 'May I be propagated.' He saw this Daśahotṛi, and offered it. By this he created (the rite) of ten nights, and by this (rite) often nights he was propagated. If one is about to consecrate oneself for (the rite) of ten nights one should offer the Daśahotṛi; verily he creates by the Daśahotṛi (the rite) of ten nights, and by (the rite) of ten nights he is propagated. The sacrifice of ten nights is connected with the Virāj He, who knowing thus sacrifices with (the rite) of ten nights, attains the Virāj The sacrifice of ten nights is connected with Prajāpati. He, who knowing thus sacrifices with (the rite) of ten nights, is propagated. Indra was on a level with the Gods, he was not separated from them. He ran up to Prajāpati; he gave him this (rite) of ten nights. He grasped it, and sacrificed with it. Then indeed he became separated from the other Gods. He, who knowing thus sacrifices with (the rite) of ten nights, attains separation from the evil enemy. The sacrifice of ten nights has three eminences; the Pañchadaśa (Stoma) is one eminence; the Ekaviṃśa one eminence, the Trayastriṃśa one eminence. He, who knowing thus sacrifices with (the rite) of ten nights, becomes thrice eminent among his peers. The sacrificer is the Pañchadaśa; the sacrificer the Ekaviṃśa, the sacrificer the Trayastriṃśa, and the others are the citadels. If a man have witchcraft practised against him, he should sacrifice with (the rite) of ten nights; verily he surrounds himself with the divine citadels; no harm whatever can befall him, the practiser of witchcraft overcomes him not. The Gods and the Asuras were in conflict. The Gods saw in (the rite) of ten nights the divine citadels. They surrounded themselves with them; no harm whatever befell them; then the Gods prospered, the Asuras were defeated. He who has enemies should sacrifice with (the rite) of ten nights; verily he surrounds himself with the divine citadels; no harm whatever befalls him; he prospers and his enemy is defeated. Stoma serves Stoma; verily he makes his enemy his servant. In that they perform the lesser Stoma after per forming the greater there is uniformity; to break the uniformity the Agniṣhṭoma Sāmans are before and after (the greater Stoma). There is an Agniṣhṭoma, with the Trivṛit (Stoma), in praise of Agni, with verses addressed to Agni; verily he wins brilliance. There is an Ukthya, with the Pañchadaśa (Stoma), and verses addressed to Indra; verily he wins power. There is an Agniṣhṭoma, with the Trivṛit (Stoma), and verses addressed to the All-Gods; verily he wins prosperity. There is an Agni stoma, with the Saptadaśa (Stoma), and verses addressed to Prajāpati, in which the Soma offering is bitter, to win food; verily also by it he is propagated. There is an Ukthya with the Ekaviṃśa (Stoma), and verses addressed to the sun, for support; verily he places radiance in himself. There is an Agniṣhṭoma, with the Saptadaśa (Stoma), and verses addressed to Prajāpati, (called) the added oblation; verily he is invited by all. There are two Agniṣhṭomas, with the Triṇava (Stoma) on either side (of the Ukthya), with verses addressed to Indra, for conquest. There is an Ukthya, with the Trayastriṃśa (Stoma) with verses addressed to the All-Gods, for rest. There is an Atirātra Viśvajit with all the Pṛiṣhṭhas, for supremacy.

Mantra 7:2:6

The seasons, desirous of offspring, could not procure offspring. They desired, 'May we create offspring, may we win offspring, may we procure offspring, may we possess offspring.' They saw this (rite) of eleven nights; they grasped it, and sacrificed with it. Then indeed did they create offspring, win offspring, procure offspring, and possess offspring. They became the seasons, and that is why the seasonal periods are seasonal periods. They are the children of the seasons, and therefore they are said to be connected with the seasons. Those, who knowing thus perform (the rite) of eleven nights, create offspring, win offspring, procure offspring, and possess offspring. There is an Atirātra with the form of light; verily they place light before them, to reveal the world of heaven. There is a Pṛiṣhṭhya Ṣhaḍaha; the seasons are six, the Pṛiṣhṭhas are six; verily by the Pṛiṣhṭhas they mount upon the seasons, by the seasons upon the year; verily in the year they find support. There is a Chaturviṃśa; the Gāyatrī has twenty-four syllables, splendour is connected with the Gāyatrī; verily in the Gāyatrī and in splendour they find support. There is a Chatuśchatvāriṃśa; the Triṣhṭubh has forty-four syllables, the Triṣhṭubh is power; verily in the Triṣhṭubh and in power they find support. There is an Aṣhṭāchatvāriṃśa; the Jagatī has forty-eight syllables, cattle are connected with the Jagatī; verily in the Jagatī and in cattle they find support. (The rite) is of eleven nights, the seasons are five, the seasonal periods are five; verily in the seasons, in the seasonal periods, and in the year they find support and win offspring. There are Atirātras on either side, to secure offspring.

Mantra 7:2:7

He should draw the cup for Indra and Vāyu first if he desire, 'May my offspring accord in order of seniority.' Offspring are in accord according to the arrangement of the sacrifice, and if the sacrifice is disarranged, they are at discord. Verily he makes his offspring in accord in order of seniority; the younger does not overstep the older. He should draw the cup for Indra and Vāyu first for one who is ill. For he who is ill is separated from breath, the cup for Indra and Vāyu is breath; verily he unites him with breath. They should draw the cup for Mitra and Varuṇa first if when they are consecrated one die. From expiration and inspiration are they separated of whom when consecrated one dies, Mitra and Varuṇa are expiration and inspiration; verily at the commencement they grasp expiration and inspiration. He should draw the Āśvina cup first who is infirm. The Aśvins are of the Gods those who are infirm, late as it were came they to the front. The Aśvins are the Gods of him who is infirm; they lead him to the front. He who desires support having attained prosperity should draw the Śukra Cup first. The Śukra is yonder sun, this is the end; a man when he has reached the end of prosperity stops; verily from the end he grasps the end, and becomes not worse. He who practises witchcraft should draw the Manthin cup first. The Manthin vessel is a vessel of misfortune; verily he causes death to seize on him; swiftly does he reach misfortune. He should draw the Āgrayaṇa cup first whose father and grandfather are holy, and who yet does not possess holiness. From speech and power is he separated whose father and grandfather are holy, and who yet does not possess holiness. The Āgrayaṇa (cup) is the breast as it were and the speech as it were of the sacrifice; verily with speech and with power he unites him, then he becomes not worse. He against whom witchcraft is practised should draw the Ukthya cup first. The Ukthya vessel is the power of all vessels; verily he yokes him with all power. He should take as Puroruch (the verse) 'O Sarasvatī, lead us to prosperity.' Sarasvatī is speech; verily with speech he yokes him. 'May we go not through thee to joyless fields,' he says. The joyless fields are those of death; verily he goes not to the fields of death. He should draw full cups for one who is ill. Pain afflicts the breaths of him who is ill, the cups are breaths; verily he frees his breaths from pain, and even if his life is gone, yet he lives. He should draw full cups if rain does not fall. Pain afflicts the breaths of the people if rain does not fall, the cups are breaths; verily he frees the breaths of the people from pain, and rain soon falls.

Mantra 7:2:8

(The cup) for Indra and Vāyu is connected with the Gāyatrī, the opening day is connected with the Gāyatrī, and therefore on the opening day (the cup) for Indra and Vāyu is drawn; verily he draws it in its own abode. The Śukra is connected with the Triṣhṭubh, the second day is connected with the Triṣhṭubh, and therefore on the second day the Śukra is drawn; verily he draws it in its own abode. The Āgrayaṇa is connected with the Jagatī, the third day is connected with the Jagatī, and therefore on the third day the Āgrayaṇa is drawn; verily he draws it in its own abode. In that it completes the metres, it completes the sacrifice; in that the Āgrayaṇa is drawn on the next day, where they have seen the sacrifice, thence does he again employ it. The second three nights begin with the Jagatī, the Āgrayaṇa is connected with the Jagatī; in that the Āgrayaṇa is drawn on the fourth day, he draws it in its own abode; verily also they revolve round their own metre. (The cup) for Indra and Vāyu is connected with the Rathantara (Sāman), the fifth day is connected with the Rathantara, and therefore on the fifth day (the cup) for Indra and Vāyu is drawn; verily he draws it in its own abode. The Śukra is connected with the Bṛihatī, the sixth day is connected with the Bṛihatī, and therefore on the sixth day the Śukra is drawn; verily he draws it in its own abode. In that it completes the metres, it completes for the second time the sacrifice; in that the Śukra is drawn on the next day, where they have seen the sacrifice, thence does he again employ it. The third three nights begin with the Trishṭubh, the Śukra is connected with the Trishṭubh; in that the Śukra is drawn on its seventh day, he draws it in its own abode, and they revolve round their own metre. The Āgrayaṇa, is speech, the eighth day is speech, and therefore on the eighth day the Āgrayaṇa is drawn; verily he draws it in its own abode. (The cup) for Indra and Vāyu is breath, the ninth day is breath, and therefore on the ninth day (the cup) for Indra and Vāyu is drawn; verily he draws it in its own abode. In that it completes the metres, it completes for the third time the sacrifice; in that (the cup) for Indra and Vāyu is drawn on the next day, where they have seen the sacrifice, thence does he again employ it, and they revolve round their own metre. They go by a trackless way leaving the path who start with anything except (the cup) for Indra and Vāyu The tenth day is the end of the sacrifice, (the cup) for Indra and Vāyu is drawn on the tenth day; verily having reached the end of the sacrifice, they proceed from the trackless way to the path, and it is as when men go pushing on with a strong (team). The metres set their wishes on one another's world, and the Gods then interchanged them. The fourth day is the abode of (the cup) for Indra and Vāyu, the Āgrayaṇa is drawn on this (day); therefore (the cup) for Indra and Vāyu is drawn on the ninth day, the abode of the Āgrayaṇa The fifth day is the abode of the Śukra, (the cup) for Indra and Vāyu is drawn on this (day); therefore the Śukra is drawn on the seventh day, the abode of (the cup) for Indra and Vāyu The sixth day is the abode of the Āgrayaṇa, the Śukra is drawn on this (day); therefore the Āgrayaṇa is drawn on the eighth day, the abode of the Śukra. Verily thus does he exchange the metres, and he who knows thus obtains interchange with the richer; verily also he causes concord in the sacrifice for the Gods. Therefore one gives this to another.

Mantra 7:2:9

Prajāpati desired, 'May I be propagated.' He saw this (rite) of twelve nights; he grasped it, and sacrificed with it. Then indeed was he propagated. He who desires, 'May I be propagated,' should sacrifice with (the rite) of twelve nights; verily he is propagated. The theologians say, 'The sacrifices have Agnishṭomas at the beginning; why then is Atirātra first employed?' The two Atirātras are the eyes of the sacrifice, the two Agnishṭomas the pupils; if they were to employ the Agnishṭoma first, they would put the pupils outside; therefore the Atirātra is employed first; verily having inserted the eyes of the sacrifice they put the pupils in them. He, who knows the Gāyatrī to have sides of light, goes to the world of heaven with light and radiance. The sides are the Agnishṭomas, the eight Ukthyas in between are the body; verily the Gāyatrī has sides of light. He who knows thus goes to the world of heaven with light and radiance. The twelve nights' (rite) is Prajāpati in twelve divisions. The two sides are the Atirātras, the eight Ukthyas within are the body; Prajāpati in such guise touches truth with the Sattra, truth is the breaths; verily he touches the breaths. Those who perform the Sattra perform it with the breath of all people, and therefore they ask, 'Are these performers of a Sattra?' Dear to people and noble is he who knows thus.

Mantra 7:2:10.

This (rite) with a Vaiśvānara on one side (only) was not able to win the world of heaven; it was stretched upwards and the Gods piled round this Vaiśvānara, to overcome the world of heaven. The seasons made Prajāpati sacrifice with it, and in them because of it he prospered. He prospers among the priests who knowing thus sacrifices with (the rite) of twelve days. They were desirous of obtaining (their desires) from him. He gave to the spring the sap, to the hot season barley, to the rains plants, to autumn rice, beans and sesamum to winter and the cool season. Prajāpati made Indra sacrifice with it. Then indeed did Indra become Indra; therefore they say, 'It is the sacrifice of the inferior,' for he by it first sacrificed. He eats a corpse who accepts a present at a Sattra; a human corpse or the corpse of a horse. Food is the cow; in that he does not purify the vessel in which they carry food, filth is produced from it. One should sacrifice by oneself, for Prajāpati prospered by himself. One should be consecrated for twelve nights; the year consists of twelve months, Prajāpati is the year, he is Prajāpati, he is born indeed who is born from fervour. The twelve Upasads are these four sets of three nights; with the first three he prepares the sacrifice, with the second three he grasps the sacrifice, with the third three he cleanses the vessels, and with the fourth three he purifies himself within. He who eats his victim, eats his flesh, who eats his sacrificial cake, eats his brains, who eats his fried grain, eats his excrement, who eats his ghee, eats his marrow, who eats his Soma, eats his sweat, and also he eats the excrements from his head, who accepts (a present) at the twelve-day (rite). Therefore one should not cause one to sacrifice with the twelve-day (rite), to avert evil.

The Horse Sacrifice (continued)

Mantra 7:2:11

To one hail! | To two hail! | To three hail! | To four hail! | To five hail! | To six hail! | To seven hail! | To eight hail! | To nine hail! | To ten hail! | To eleven hail! | To twelve hail! | To thirteen hail! | To fourteen hail! | To fifteen hail! | To sixteen hail! | To seventeen hail! | To eighteen hail! | To nineteen hail! | To twenty-nine hail! | To thirty-nine hail! | To forty-nine hail! | To fifty-nine hail! | To sixty-nine hail! | To seventy-nine hail! | To eighty-nine hail! | To ninety-nine hail! | To a hundred hail! | To two hundred hail! | To all hail!

Mantra 7:2:12

To one hail! | To three hail! | To five hail! | To seven hail! | To nine hail! | To eleven hail! | To thirteen hail! | To fifteen hail! | To seventeen hail! | To nineteen hail! | To twenty-nine hail! | To thirty-nine hail! | To forty-nine hail! | To fifty-nine hail! | To sixty-nine hail! | To seventy-nine hail! | To eighty-nine hail! | To ninety-nine hail! | To a hundred hail! | To all hail!

Mantra 7:2:13

To two hail! | To four hail! | To six hail! | To eight hail! | To ton hail! | To twelve hail! | To fourteen hail! | To sixteen hail! | To eighteen hail! | To twenty hail! | To ninety-eight hail! | To a hundred hail! | To all hail!

Mantra 7:2:14

To three hail! | To five hail! | To seven hail! | (Then as in 12. down to) To all hail!

Mantra 7:2:15

To four hail! | To eight hail! | To twelve hail! | To sixteen hail! | To twenty hail! | To ninety-six hail! | To a hundred hail! | To all hail!

Mantra 7:2:16

To five hail! | To ten hail! | To fifteen hail! | To twenty hail! | To ninety-five hail! | To a hundred hail! | To all hail!

Mantra 7:2:17

To ten hail! | To twenty hail! | To thirty hail! | To forty hail! | To fifty hail! | To sixty hail! | To seventy hail! | To eighty hail! | To ninety hail! | To a hundred hail! | To all hail!

Mantra 7:2:18

To twenty hail! | To forty hail! | To sixty hail! | To eighty hail! | To a hundred hail! | To all hail!

Mantra 7:2:19

To fifty hail! | To a hundred hail! | To two hundred hail! | To three hundred hail! | To four hundred hail! | To five hundred hail! | To six hundred hail! | To seven hundred hail! | To eight hundred hail! | To nine hundred hail! | To a thousand hail! | To all hail!

Mantra 7:2:20.

To a hundred hail! | To a thousand hail! | To ten thousand hail! | To a hundred thousand hail! | To ten hundred thousand hail! | To ten million hail! | To a hundred million hail! | To a thousand million hail! | To ten thousand million hail! | To a hundred thousand million hail! | To ten hundred thousand million hail! | To dawn hail! | To the dawning hail! | To him that will rise hail! | To the rising hail! | To the risen hail! | To heaven hail! | To the world hail! | To all hail!

Prapāṭhaka 3.

The Sattras

Mantra 7:3:1

They go swiftly in that it is the tenth day. In that it is the tenth day they loosen their sins. He who among men going swiftly falls in with a trackless way, he who strikes a post, and he who stumbles, are left out. So he, who on this tenth day, the Avivākya, comes to grief, is left out. If one points out (an error) to one who comes to grief, he seizes hold of him and comes out successfully, and then the one who pointed out (his error) is left out. Therefore on the tenth day, the Avivākya, one should not point out (errors) to one who comes to grief. Or rather they say, 'By that which was successful in the sacrifice the Gods went to the world of heaven, and overcame the Asuras by what was unsuccessful.' What is successful in the sacrifice belongs to the sacrificer, what is unsuccessful to his enemy. Now he, who comes to grief on the tenth day, the Avivākya, produces overmuch. Those who are outside as spectators should point out (his error). If there be none there, then (the error) should be pointed out from within the Sadas. If there be none there, then it should be pointed out by the Gṛihapati. At any rate it should be pointed out. They sing the verses of the serpent queen on that day. The queen of what creeps is this (earth). Whatever on this (earth) they praise, whatever they have praised, through that is this (earth) the serpent queen. Now whatever they have praised with speech and what they will praise thereafter, (it is done thinking), 'Having won both and obtained them, let us stop.' They sing these (verses) with the mind. Neither a horse chariot nor a mule chariot can in one moment encompass this (earth), but mind can in one moment encompass it, mind can overcome it. Then they repeat the Brahman. The Ṛich verses are limited, the Sāmans are limited, and the Yajusas are limited, but of the Brahman there is no end, and that he should declare to the one who responds. That is the response.

Mantra 7:3:2

The theologians say, 'By the first day of the twelve-day rite what is it that the sacrificer takes from the priests?' 'Brilliance and power' is (the answer). 'What by the second?' 'The breaths and food.' 'What by the third?' 'These three worlds.' 'What by the fourth?' 'Four-footed cattle.' 'What by the fifth?' 'The Paṅkti with its elements.' 'What by the sixth?' 'The six seasons.' 'What by the seventh?' 'The Śakvarī with its seven feet.' 'What by the eighth?' 'The Gāyatrī with its eight syllables.' 'What by the ninth?' 'The Trivṛit Stoma.' 'What by the tenth?' 'The Virāj with its ten syllables.' 'What by the eleventh?' 'The Trishṭubh with its eleven syllables.' 'What by the twelfth?' 'The Jagatī with its twelve syllables.' So much is there as that. So much as that he takes from them.

Mantra 7:3:3

(The rite) of thirteen nights is a complete (rite of) twelve days, for the opening and concluding days are the same. There are three Atirātras, three are these worlds, for the obtaining of these worlds. The first Atirātra is the expiration, the second cross-breathing, the third inspiration; verily they find support in expiration, inspiration, out-breathing, and food, and reach their full life, who knowing thus perform (the rite) of thirteen nights. They say, '(The rite) of twelve days is the sequence of speech. They would cleave it if they put an Atirātra in the middle, and the speech of the householder would be liable to fail.' They perform the Mahāvrata after the Chandomas; verily they maintain the sequence of speech, and the speech of the householder is not likely to fail. The Chandomas are cattle, the Mahāvrata food; in that they perform the Mahāvrata after the Chandomas, they find support in cattle and in food.

Mantra 7:3:4

The Ādityas desired, 'May we be prosperous in both worlds.' They saw this (rite) of fourteen nights; they grasped it, and sacrificed with it. Then indeed they prospered in both worlds, this and yonder. Those, who knowing thus perform (the rite) of fourteen nights, prosper in both worlds, this and yonder. (The rite) is of fourteen nights, there are seven domesticated plants and seven wild; (verily it serves) to win both. In that the Pṛishṭhas are performed in succession, they conquer by them yonder world. In that the Pṛishṭhas are reversed, they conquer by them this world. There are two Trayastriṃśa Stomas in the middle; verily they attain sovereignty. (These two) are overlords; verily they become overlords of their peers. There are Atirātras on either side, for security.

Mantra 7:3:5

Prajāpati went to the world of heaven. The Gods followed him, and the Ādityas and the cattle followed them. The Gods said, 'The cattle on which we have lived have followed us.' They arranged this (rite) of fourteen nights away for them. The Ādityas mounted the world of heaven with the Pṛishṭhas; they arranged the cattle in this world with the two Tryahas. By means of the Pṛishṭhas the Ādityas prospered in yonder world, the cattle in this world by the Tryahas. Those who, knowing thus, perform (the rite of) fourteen nights, prosper in both worlds, in this and in yonder; by the Pṛishṭhas they prosper in yonder world and by the Tryahas in this world. The three days are the Jyotis, Go, and Āyus The Jyotis is this (earth), the Go the atmosphere, the Āyus yonder (sky); verily they mount upon these worlds. If the Pṛishṭhas were on one side, there would be a lack of balance; the Pṛishṭhas are in the middle, for balance. The Pṛishṭhas are force and strength; verily they place force and strength in the middle. They proceed with the Bṛihat and the Rathantara (Sāmans). The Rathantara is this (earth), the Bṛihat yonder (sky); verily with them do they proceed; verily also in them they find support. These indeed are the quick paths of the sacrifice; verily by them do they proceed to the world of heaven. They mount the world of heaven turning away (from earth), who perform the Pṛishṭhas in succession. The Tryaha is reversed, for the return (from heaven), and for support. Having prospered in either world they cease (the rite). The (nights) are fourteen. As for ten of them, the Virāj is ten-syllabled, the Virāj is food; verily by the Virāj they win food. As for four, the quarters are four; verily they find support in the quarters. There are Atirātras on either side, for security.

Mantra 7:3:6

Indra was on a level with the Gods, he was not distinguished from them. He ran up to Prajāpati; he gave him this (rite) of fifteen nights. He grasped it, and sacrificed with it. Then indeed he became distinguished from the other Gods. Those who knowing thus perform (the rite) of fifteen nights attain distinction from the evil enemy. The three days are Jyotis, Go, and Āyus The Jyotis is this (earth), the Go the atmosphere, the Āyus yonder (sky); verily they find support in these worlds. There can be no Sattra where there is no Chandoma; in that there axe Chandomas, there is the Sattra. The Gods they win by the Pṛishṭhas, the cattle by the Chandomas. The Pṛishṭhas are force and strength, the strength, and in cattle, they Chandomas cattle; verily in force and find support. (The rite) is of fifteen nights; the bolt is fifteenfold; verily they hurl the bolt at their enemies. There are Atirātras on either side, for securing power.

Mantra 7:3:7

Indra was as it were loose and unfixed. He was afraid of the Asuras. He ran up to Prajāpati; he gave him this (rite) of fifteen nights as a bolt. With it he overcame and conquered the Asuras and attained prosperity. By the Agnishṭut he burned away the evil, by (the rite) of fifteen nights he placed force, might, power, and strength in himself. Those, who knowing thus perform (the rite) of fifteen nights overcome and conquer their enemies and attain prosperity. By the Agnishṭut they burn away the evil, by (the rite) of fifteen nights they place force, might, power, and strength in themselves. These (nights) are full of cattle. Fifteen indeed are the nights of the half-month, the year is made up of half-months, cattle are born throughout the year; therefore (these nights) are full of cattle. These (nights) are heavenly. Fifteen indeed are the nights of the half-month, the year is made up of half-months, the world of heaven is the year; verily (these nights) are heavenly. There are the three days, Jyotis, Āyus, and Go. The Jyotis is this (earth), the Go the atmosphere, the Āyus yonder (sky); verily they mount upon these worlds. If the Pṛishṭhas were on one side, there would be a lack of balance; the Pṛishṭhas are in the middle, for balance. The Pṛishṭhas are force and strength; verily they place force and strength in the middle. They proceed with the Bṛihat and the Rathantara (Sāmans). The Rathantara is this (earth), the Bṛihat yonder (sky); verily with them do they proceed; verily also in them they find support. These indeed are the quick paths of the sacrifice; verily by them do they proceed to the world of heaven. They mount the world of heaven turning away (from earth), who perform the Pṛishṭhas in succession. The Tryaha is reversed, for the return (from heaven), and for support. Having prospered in either world they cease (the rite). These (nights) are fifteen. As for ten of them, the Virāj is ten-syllabled, the Virāj is food; verily by the Virāj they win food. As for five, the quarters are five; verily they find support in the quarters. There are Atirātras on either side, for securing power, strength, offspring, and cattle.

Mantra 7:3:8

Prajāpati desired, 'May I be an eater of food.' He saw this (rite of) seventeen nights; he grasped it, and sacrificed with it. Then indeed he became an eater of food. Those, who knowing thus perform (the rite) of seventeen nights, become eaters of food. There is a period of five days; the seasons are five in the year; verily in the seasons and the year they find sup port. Again the Paṅkti is of five elements, the sacrifice is fivefold; verily they win the sacrifice. There can be no Sattra where there is no Chandoma; in that there are Chandomas, there is the sacrifice. The Gods they win by the Pṛishṭhas, the cattle by the Chandomas. The Pṛishṭhas are force and strength, the Chandomas cattle; verily in force and strength, and in cattle, they find support. (The rite is) of seventeen nights; Prajāpati is seventeenfold; (verily it serves) to obtain Prajāpati There are Atirātras on either side, for securing food.

Mantra 7:3:9

The Virāj dividing itself stayed among the Gods with the holy power (Brahman), among the Asuras with food. The Gods desired, 'May we acquire both the holy power (Brahman) and food! They saw (the rite of) these twenty nights. Then indeed they acquired both the holy power (Brahman) and food, and became resplendent and eaters of food. Those, who knowing thus perform (the rite of) these nights, acquire both the holy power (Brahman) and food, and become resplendent and eaters of food. They (make up) two Virājs; verily separately in them they find support. Man is twentyfold, ten fingers and ten toes; verily obtaining the greatness of man they cease (the rite). There are Tryahas consisting of Jyotis, Go, and Āyus The Jyotis is this (earth), the Go the atmosphere, the Āyus yonder (sky); verily they mount upon these worlds. The Tryahas go in order; verily in order they mount the world of heaven. If the Pṛishṭhas were on one side there would be a lack of balance; the Pṛishṭhas are in the middle, for balance. The Pṛishṭhas are force and strength; verily they place force and strength in the middle. They proceed with the Bṛihat and the Rathantara (Sāmans). The Rathantara is this (earth), the Bṛihat yonder (sky); verily with them do they proceed, verily also in them they find support. These indeed are the quick paths of the sacrifice; verily by them do they proceed to the world of heaven. They mount the world of heaven turning away (from earth), who perform the Pṛishṭhas in succession. The Tryaha is re versed, for the return (from heaven), and for support. Having prospered in either world they cease (the rite). There are Atirātras on either side, for securing splendour and food.

Mantra 7:3:10.

Yonder sun was in this world. The Gods surrounded it with the Pṛishṭhas and removed it to the world of heaven. They surrounded it from below with the Para (Sāmans), and placed it with the Divākīrtya (Sāman) in the world of heaven. They surrounded it from above with the Para (Sāmans), and with the Pṛishṭhas they descended (from heaven). Yonder sun indeed in yonder world is surrounded by the Para (Sāmans) on both sides. In that there are Pṛishṭhas the sacrificers go by them to the world of heaven; they surround it from below with the Para (Sāmans), and by the Divākīrtya (Sāman) find support in the world of heaven. They surround it from above with the Para (Sāmans), and descend with the Pṛishṭhas. If there were not Paras above, they would depart away from the world of heaven; if there were none below, they would. burn creatures. There are Paraḥsāmans on both sides of the Divākīrtya; verily they surround them on both sides in the world of heaven. The Divākīrtya is the sacrificers, the Paraḥsāmans the year; the Paraḥsāmans are on both sides of the Divākīrtya; verily on both sides they find support in the year. The Divākīrtya is the back, the Paraḥsāmans the two sides; the Paraḥsāmans are on both sides of the Divākīrtya; therefore the sides are on both sides of the back. (In the rite) the greatest number of libations are made, the greatest number of Śastras recited; verily in the middle of the sacrifice they tie a knot not to slip. There are seven libations; seven are the breaths in the head; verily they place breaths in the sacrificers. In that the Pṛishṭhas are in succession, they mount upon yonder world with them. If they were not to descend to this world, the sacrificers would either go mad or perish. In that the Pṛishṭhas are reversed they descend to this world with them; verily also they find support in this world, for sanity. Indra was unsettled. He ran up to Prajāpati; he gave him this (rite) of twenty-one nights; he grasped it, and sacrificed with it. Then indeed he became settled. Those, who sacrifice much and are unsettled [41, should perform (the rite) of twenty-one nights. There are twelve months, five seasons, three worlds here, and yonder sun as the twenty-first. So many are the worlds of the Gods; verily in them in order they find support. Yonder sun did not shine. He ran up to Prajāpati; he gave him this (rite) of twenty-one nights; he grasped it, and sacrificed with it. Then in deed did he shine. Those, who knowing thus perform (the rite) of twenty one nights, shine also. (The rite) is of twenty-one nights, the Ekaviṃśa (Stoma) is radiance; verily they attain radiance, and support also, for the Ekaviṃśa is support. There are Atirātras on either side, for securing splendour.

The Horse Sacrifice (continued)

Mantra 7:3:11

a. Let the sacrifice come forward | From yonder over to me, | The sacrifice which the Ṛishis have brought forward. ‖ *b.* May the fault in the sacrifice settle on him who hateth us, | Making his body godless, strengthless, | Distorted and inert; | May it rest with him who hateth us. ‖ *c.* O sacrifice, come to me | With the brilliance of the sacrifice. | I summon the Brahmans, the priests, the Gods, | With the brilliance of thee, the sacrifice, O offering. ‖ *d.* With the sacrifice I summon the cooked food to thee, O offering. | I gather for thee good deeds, offspring, and cattle. ‖ *e.* The Praiṣhas, the kindling-(verses), the butter sprinklings, the shares of the ghee, | The call, the reply, I prepare for thee, | The fore- and after-sacrifices, the Sviṣhṭakṛit, the Iḍā. | The prayers, I win, the light. ‖ *f.* By Agni, by Indra, by Soma, | By Sarasvatī, by Viṣhṇu, by the Gods, | By the Yājyā and the Anuvākyā, I summon for thee, O offering. | I take for thee the sacrifice with the Vaṣhaṭ cry. ‖ *g.* The chant, the Śastra, the response, | The libation, the Iḍā, the prayers, I win, the light. | I summon for thee the sacrifices of the wives, O offering, | I take thy I offering and sacrificial utterance. ‖ *h.* Cattle, the pressed (Soma), the sacrificial cakes, | The pressings, the sacrifice, | The Gods with Indra, I summon for thee, O offering, | Lead by Agni, with Soma, and them all.

Mantra 7:3:12

The past, the present, the future, Vaṣhaṭ, hail, reverence! | The Ṛich, the Sāman, the Yajus, Vaṣhaṭ, hail, reverence! | The Gāyatrī, the Triṣhṭubh, the Jagatī, Vaṣhaṭ, hail, reverence! | The earth, the atmosphere, the sky, Vaṣhaṭ, hail, reverence! | Agni, Vāyu, Sūrya, Vaṣhaṭ, hail, reverence! | Expiration, cross-breathing, inspiration, Vaṣhaṭ, hail, reverence! | Food, ploughing, rain, Vaṣhaṭ, hail, reverence! | Father, son, grandson, Vaṣhaṭ, hail, reverence! | Bhūr, Bhuvar, Svar, Vaṣhaṭ, hail, reverence!

Mantra 7:3:13

a. May a house be mine, may offspring be mine; | May the strong sacrifice come to me. | May the divine and holy waters come to me; | May the abundance of a thousandfold (wealth) fail me not. ‖ *b.* May the cup be mine; may the Puroruch be mine; | May the chant and the Śastra come to me in union. | May the Ādityas, the Rudras, the Vasus, be present at the rite; | May the abundance of a thousandfold (wealth) fail me not. ‖ *c.* May the Agniṣhṭoma, come to me, and the Ukthya; | May the nocturnal Atirātra come to me. | May the (draughts) which have stood over night, well offered, come to me; | May the abundance of a thousandfold (wealth) fail me not.

Mantra 7:3:14

By fire he surmounted fervour, by speech holy power, by a gem forms, by Indra the Gods, by the wind the breaths, by the sun the sky, by the moon the Nakṣhatras, by Yama the Pitṛis, by the king men, by fruit the flavours, by the boa constrictor serpents, by the tiger wild beasts, by the eagle birds, by the stallion horses, by the bull kine, by the he-goat goats, by the ram sheep, by rice food, by barley plants, by the banyan trees, by the Udumbara strength, by the Gāyatrī the metres, by the Trivṛit the Stomas, by the Brāhmaṇa speech.

Mantra 7:3:15

Hail! (To) meditation (I offer). | To that meditated upon hail! | Hail! (To) that which we meditate on (I offer). | To mind hail! Hail! (To) mind (I offer). | To Prajāpati hail! To Ka hail! To Who hail!' To Whoever (*katamāsmai*) hail! | To Aditi hail! To Aditi the great hail! To Aditi the gentle hail! | To Sarasvatī hail! To Sarasvatī the mighty hail! To Sarasvatī, the purifying hail! | To Pūṣhan hail! To Pūṣhan guardian of travellers hail! To Pūṣhan watcher of men hail! | To Tvaṣhṭar hail! To Tvaṣhṭar the seminal hail! To Tvaṣhṭar the multiform hail! | To Viṣhṇu hail! To Viṣhṇu the Nikhuryapa hail! To Viṣhṇu the Nibhūyapa hail!

Mantra 7:3:16

To the teeth hail! | To the jaws hail! | To the lips hail! | To the mouth hail! | To the nostrils hail! | To the eyes hail! | To the ears hail! | The eyelashes above the lower eyelashes-(to them) hail! | The eyelashes below the upper eyelashes-(to them) hail!, | To the head hail! | To the brows hail! | To the forehead hail! | To the (upper part of the) head hail! | To the brain hail! | To the hairs hail! | To the part that bears (the yoke) hail! | To the cervical vertebrae hail! | To the neck bones hail! | To the spinal column hail! | To the vertical column hail! | To the flank hail! | To the sides hail! | To the shoulders hail! | To the upper forefeet hail! | To the lower forefeet hail! | To the legs hail! | To the hips hail! | To the thighs hail! | To the knees hail! | To the legs hail! | To the buttocks hail! | To the mane hail! | To the tail hail! | To the testicles hail | To the member hail! | To the seed hail! | To offspring hail! | To begetting hail! | To the feet hail! | To the hoofs hail! | To the hairs (of the body) hail! | To the skin hail! | To the blood hail! | To the flesh hail! | To the sinews hail! | To the bones hail! | To the marrow hail! | To the limbs hail! | To the trunk hail! | To all hail!

Mantra 7:3:17

To the glossy and variegated one hail! | To the glossy-thighed one hail! | To the white-footed hail! | To the white-humped one hail! | To the one with white openings hail! | To the white-backed one hail! | To the white-shouldered one hail! | To the flower-cared one hail! | To the white-lipped one hail! | To the white-browed one hail! | To the one with white buttocks hail! | To the white shining one hail! | To the glossy hail! | To the marked one hail! | To the black-kneed hail! | To the black-speckled hail! | To the red-speckled hail! | To the ruddy-speckled hail! | To such hail! | To what sort hail! | To one like this hail! | To a like one hail! | To a different one hail! | To a fair-like one hail! | To form hail! | To all hail!

Mantra 7:3:18

To the black hail! | To the white hail! | To the tawny hail! | To the spotted hail! | To the ruddy hail! | To the yellow hail! | To the brown hail! | To the ichneumon(-coloured) hail! | To the red hail! | To the purple hail! | To the dark brown hail! | To the dark blue hail; | To the dead black hail! | To the fair-shaped hail! | To the one of like form hail! | To the one of different form hail! | To the one of the same form hail! | To the one of matching form hail! | To the tawny hail! | To the pale red hail! | To the speckled hail! | To the speckled-thighed hail! | To all hail!

Mantra 7:3:19

To the plants hail! | To the roots hail! | To the panicles hail! | To the joints hail! | To the twigs hail! | To the flowers hail! | To the fruits hail! | To those that are used hail! | To those that are not used hail! | To those that have fallen off hail! | To those that are lying (on the ground) hail! | To all hail!

Mantra 7:3:20.

To the trees hail! | To the roots hail! | To the panicles hail! | To the corona hail! | To the branches hail! | To the leaves hail! | To the flowers hail! | To the fruits hail! | To those that are used hail! | To those that are not used hail! | To those that have fallen off hail! | To those that are lying (on the ground) hail! | To the one that is left hail! | To the one that is left over hail! | To the one that is left around hail! | To the one that is left along hail! | To the one left out hail! | To the one deprived (of leaves) hail! | To the one not deprived hail! | To the one deprived around hail! | To the one deprived along hail! | To the one deprived altogether hail | To all hail!

Prapāṭhaka 4.

The Sattras (continued)

Mantra 7:4:1

Bṛihaspati desired, 'May the Gods have faith in me, and may I become their Purohita.' He saw this (rite) of twenty-four nights; he grasped it, and sacrificed with it. Then the Gods had faith in him, and he became their Purohita. In those who knowing thus perform the twenty four night (rite) men have faith, and they become their Purohitas. There are the three days Jyotis, Go, and Āyus The Jyotis is this (earth), the Go the atmosphere, and the Āyus yonder (sky); verily they mount upon these worlds. The three days occur in order; verily in order do they mount upon the world of heaven. There can be no Sattra where there is no Chandoma; in that there are Chandomas, there is the Sattra. The Gods they win by the Pṛiṣhṭhas, the cattle by the Chandomas. The Pṛiṣhṭhas are force and strength, the Chandomas cattle; verily in force and strength, and in cattle they find support. They proceed with the Bṛihat and the Rathantara (Sāmans). The Rathantara, is this (earth), the Bṛihat yonder (sky); verily with them do they proceed; verily also in them they find support. These indeed are the quick paths of the sacrifice; verily by them do they proceed to the world of heaven. (The rite is one) of twenty-four nights. Twenty four half-months make up the year; the year is the world of heaven; verily they find support in the year, the world of heaven. Now the Gāyatrī is of twenty-four syllables; the Gāyatrī is splendour; verily by the Gāyatrī they win splendour. There are Atirātras on either side, to secure splendour.

Mantra 7:4:2

As are men, so were the Gods in the beginning. They desired, 'Let us strike off the misfortune, the evil of death, and reach the conclave of the Gods.' They saw this twenty-four night (rite); they grasped it, and sacrificed with it. Then they struck off the misfortune, the evil of death, and reached the conclave of the Gods. Those who knowing thus perform the twenty-four night (rite) strike off the misfortune, the evil, and win prosperity, for the conclave of the Gods is in the case of man prosperity. The Atirātra is light, for the lighting up of the world of heaven. There is a Pṛiṣhṭhya Ṣhaḍaha. The year consists of six seasons, and, entering it, the months, the half-months and the seasons reached the conclave of the Gods. Those who knowing thus perform the twenty-four night rite, entering the year, reach a better station. There are three Trayastriṃśas before, and three Trayastriṃśas behind; verily with Trayastriṃśas on either hand they strike off the evil of misfortune and in the middle reach the conclave of the Gods, for the conclave of the Gods is the Pṛiṣhṭhas. There is uniformity in that there are three Trayastriṃśas in succession, and a break in the uniformity in that there is in the middle one which is not defined. The Pṛiṣhṭhas go onwards, the Chandomas go onwards; with both forms they go to the world of heaven. There can be no Sattra where there is no Chandoma; in that there are Chandomas, there is the Sattra. The Gods they win by the Pṛiṣhṭhas, the cattle by the Chandomas. The Pṛiṣhṭhas are force and strength, the Chandomas cattle; verily in force and strength and in cattle they find support. There are three Trayastriṃśas before, and three Trayastriṃśas behind; in the middle there are the Pṛiṣhṭhas. The Trayastriṃśas are the breast, the Pṛiṣhṭhas the breath; verily thus the sacrificers don a protection for the breath, to avoid injury. They proceed with the Bṛihat and the Rathantara. The Rathantara is this (world), the Bṛihat yonder (world); verily they proceed with them; verily also in them they find support. These indeed are the quick paths of the sacrifice; verily by them do they proceed to the world of heaven. They mount the world of heaven turning away (from earth) who perform the Pṛiṣhṭhas in succession. The six-day (rite) is reversed for the return (from the heaven), and for support. Having prospered in either world they cease (the rite). They go from a Trivṛit to a Trivṛit, for the attainment of the Stomas, for pre eminence. There is an Agniṣhṭoma in the Jyotis form. This dwelling is this (world); verily by reason thereof they depart not from this dwelling. (The rite is one) of twenty-four nights. Twenty-four half-months make up the year, the year is the world of heaven; verily they find support in the year, the world of heaven. Now the Gāyatrī is of twenty-four syllables; the Gāyatrī is splendour; verily by the Gāyatrī they win splendour. There are Atirātras on either side, to secure splendour.

Mantra 7:4:3

This (earth) was bare and hairless. It desired, 'Let me be propagated with plants and trees.' It saw these thirty nights. Then indeed it was propagated with plants and trees. Those who desire offspring and cattle should perform (the rite of) these (nights); they are propagated with offspring and cattle. This (earth) was hungry. It saw this Virāj, and placing it within itself it won food, plants, trees, offspring, cattle. Thereby it grew, it attained victoriousness and greatness. Those, who knowing thus perform (the rite of) these (nights), placing the Virāj in themselves, win food, grow great with offspring and cattle, and attain victoriousness and might. There is a Jyotiṣhṭoma Atirātra, for the revealing of the world of heaven. There is a Pṛiṣhṭhya Ṣhaḍaha. The seasons are six, the Pṛiṣhṭhas are six; verily by the Pṛiṣhṭhas they reach the seasons, with the seasons the year; verily; the year they find support. From the Trayastriṃśas they go to the Trayastriṃśa, for the continuity of the sacrifice. Now the Trayastriṃśa is Prajāpati; verily they seize hold of Prajāpati, for support. There is a Triṇava, for victory. There is an Ekaviṃśa, for support; verily they place radiance in themselves. There is a praise of Agni with the Trivṛit; verily they bum away evil with it. Now the Trivṛit is brilliance; verily they place brilliance in themselves. There is a praise of Indra with the Pañchadaśa; verily they win power (*indriyā*). There is a Saptadaśa, for the winning of food; verily by it they are propagated. There is an Ekaviṃśa, for support; verily they place radiance in themselves. There is a Chaturviṃśa Twenty-four half-months make up the year, the year is the world of heaven; verily they find support in the year, the world of heaven. Now there is the chief (day), and those who knowing thus perform (the rite of) these (nights) become the chief. From the Chaturviṃśa they go to the Pṛiṣhṭhas. Verily having found support in the year they attain the Gods. From the Trayastriṃśa they go to the Trayastriṃśa The Gods are three and thirty; verily in the Gods they find support. There is a Triṇava The Triṇava is these worlds; verily in these worlds they find support. There are two Ekaviṃśas, for support; verily they place radiance in themselves. There are many Sodaśins, and therefore there are many males among offspring. In that these Stomas are intermingled, therefore this (earth) is covered with mingled plants and trees. Those who knowing thus perform (the rite of) these (nights) have both offspring and cattle. These go imperfect to the world of heaven, for they resort to various Stomas; in that the Stomas are arranged in order, they go in order to the world of heaven, and there is order in both these worlds. These (nights) are thirty in number, the Virāj has thirty syllables; verily by the Virāj they win food. There are Atirātras on either hand, to secure food.

Mantra 7:4:4

Prajāpati went to the world of heaven. But with whatever metre the Gods yoked him, they achieved not him. They saw (the rite of) these thirty-two nights. The Anuṣhṭubh has thirty-two syllables, Prajāpati is connected with the Anuṣhṭubh; verily having gained Prajāpati by his own metre they mounted on him and went to the world of heaven. Those who knowing thus perform (the rite of) these thirty-two (nights)—the Anuṣhṭubh has thirty-two syllables, Prajāpati is connected with the Anuṣhṭubh-gaining Prajāpati by his own metre, go to prosperity, for the world of heaven for man is prosperity. These (nights) are thirty-two, the Anuṣhṭubh has thirty-two syllables, the Anuṣhṭubh is speech; verily they gain all speech; all become speakers of speech, for all attain prosperity. There are the three days, Jyotis, Go, and Āyus The Jyotis is this (earth), the Go the atmosphere, and the Āyus yonder (sky); verily they mount upon these worlds. The three days occur in order; verily in order do they mount upon the world of heaven. They proceed with the Bṛihat and Rathantara (Sāmans). The Rathantara is this (earth), the Bṛihat yonder (sky); verily with them do they proceed; verily also in them they find support. These indeed are the quick paths of the sacrifice; verily by them do they proceed to the world of heaven. Those who perform the three days in succession mount upon the world of heaven turning away (from earth). There is a three day period reversed, for returning (from heaven), and also for support. Having prospered in both worlds they cease (the rite). These (nights) are thirty-two. As for thirty of them, the Virāj has thirty syllables, the Virāj is food; verily by the Virāj they win food. As for the (remaining) two, they are days and nights, and by both forms they go to the world of heaven. There are Atirātras on either side, for security.

Mantra 7:4:5

There are two Sattras of the Gods, that of twelve days and that of thirty-three days. Those, who knowing thus perform (the rite of) thirty-three days, mount openly upon the deities. As a great man who has reached (the goal) seeks (more), so he does. If he fail he becomes worse; if he fail not, he remains the same. Those, who knowing thus perform (the rite of) thirty-three days, are distinguished from the evil enemy. The Gods in the beginning seized these (nights), sharing the days. One took one day, one another, and with them all equally prospered. Those, who knowing thus perform (the rite) of thirty-three days, all equally prosper, all gain the rank of village chief. There are five day periods; the year has five seasons; verily they rest on the seasons, the year. Again the Paṅkti has five syllables, the sacrifice is fivefold; verily they win the sacrifice. There are three (days with the) Āśvina (Śastra); three are these worlds; verily in these worlds they find support. Again three are the powers of the sacrifice; verily they win them. There is a Viśvajit (day), for the winning of food. It has all the Pṛiṣhṭhas, for the conquest of all. The twelve-day (rite) is speech. If they were to perform the twelve-day (rite) before (what has already gone), they would perform speech imperfectly, and their speech would be likely to fail. They perform the twelve-day (rite) afterwards; verily they perform speech perfectly, and therefore we utter speech from above. Intermediately indeed by means of a ten-nights' (rite) did Prajāpati create offspring. In that there is a ten-nights' (rite), the sacrificers create offspring. Udaṅka Śaulbāyana has declared the ten-night rite to be the prosperity of the Sattra. In that there is a ten-nights' rite, (it serves) for the prosperity of the Sattra. Verily also whatever is wrongly done in the former days, it serves to atone. These nights form two rows, the sacrificers are the Viśvajit, the first are sixteen with the Atirātra, the second are sixteen with the Atirātra To those, who knowing thus perform (the rite) of thirty-three days, are born children in two rows. There are Atirātras on either side, for security.

Mantra 7:4:6

The Ādityas desired, 'Let us go to the world of heaven.' They discerned not the world of heaven, they went not to the world of heaven. They saw this (rite) of thirty-six nights; they grasped it, and sacrificed with it. Then indeed did they discern the world of heaven, and went to the world of heaven. Those, who knowing thus perform (the rite) of thirty six nights, discern the world of heaven, and go to the world of heaven. The Atirātra is light; verily they put light before them, to reveal the world of heaven. There are Ṣhaḍahas; six are the seasons; verily in the seasons they find support. There are four (Ṣhaḍahas); four are the quarters; verily in the quarters they find support. There can be no Sattra where there is no Chandoma; in that there are Chandomas, there is the Sattra. The Gods they win by the Pṛiṣhṭhas, the cattle by the Chandomas. The Pṛiṣhṭhas are force and strength, the Chandomas cattle; verily in force and strength they find support. (The rite has) thirty-six nights; the Bṛihatī has thirty-six syllables, cattle are connected with the Bṛihatī; verily by the Bṛihatī they win cattle. The Bṛihatī obtained the sovereignty over the metres. They obtain sovereignty who knowing thus perform (the rite) of thirty-six nights; verily they go to the world of heaven. There are Atirātras on either side, for the securing of the world of heaven.

Mantra 7:4:7

Vasiṣhṭha, his sons slain, desired, 'May I win offspring, and defeat the Saudāsas.' He saw this (rite)Ekāṣhṭakā.-nine nights; he grasped it, and sacrificed with it. Then indeed did he win offspring and defeated the Saudāsas. Those, who knowing thus perform (the rite) of forty-nine nights, win offspring and defeat their enemies. There are three Agniṣhṭomas with the Trivṛit; verily they sharpen the point of the bolt. There are ten Pañchadaśas; the bolt is fifteenfold; verily they take away the bolt from their rivals. The tenth day has a Ṣhoḍaśin; verily they place strength in the bolt. There axe twelve Saptadaśas, to win food; verily also they are propagated by them. There is a Pṛiṣhṭhya Ṣhaḍaha. Six are the seasons, six the Pṛiṣhṭhas; verily by the Pṛiṣhṭhas they mount upon the seasons, by the seasons upon the year; verily in the year they find support. There are twelve Ekaviṃśas, for support; verily they place radiance in themselves. There are many Ṣhoḍaśins, for conquest. There are six (days) with the Āśvina (Śastra), six are the seasons; verily they rest on the seasons. These nights are deficient and redundant. They are deficient in that they are fifty less one, redundant in that they are (one) more than forty-eight. Both from the deficient, indeed, and from the redundant Prajāpati was propagated. Those who desire offspring and cattle should perform (the rite of) these nights; verily are they propagated with offspring and cattle. This sacrifice is connected with the Virāj because it is one of forty-nine (nights). Those, who knowing thus perform (the rite) of forty-nine nights, attain the Virāj, and become eaters of food. There are Atirātras on either side, for the securing of food.

Mantra 7:4:8

Those who are about to consecrate themselves for the year (rite) should consecrate themselves on the Ekāṣṭakā. The Ekāṣṭakā is the wife of the year; on that night he dwells with her; verily they consecrate themselves grasping openly the year. Those who consecrate themselves on the Ekāṣṭakā consecrate themselves in the troubled part of the year, for then are the two months called the end. Those who consecrate themselves on the Ekāṣṭakā consecrate themselves on the torn part of the year, for them are the two seasons called the end. They should consecrate themselves on the full moon in Phalgunī. The full moon in Phalgunī is the beginning of the year; verily they consecrate them selves grasping the year at its beginning. To that there is this one objection that the Viṣhūvant day falls in the cloudy season. They should consecrate themselves on the full moon in Chitra. The full moon in Chitra, is the beginning of the year; verily they consecrate themselves grasping the year at the beginning. In that there is no objection at all. They should consecrate themselves on the fourth day before the full moon. Then the buying (of the Soma) falls for them on the Ekāṣṭakā; verily they do not waste the Ekāṣṭakā. In their case the pressing-(day) falls on the first half (of the month), the months end in the first half, they complete (the rite) in the first half, and when they complete the rite the plants and trees come out after them. And after them follows the fair report, 'These sacrificers have succeeded,' and therefore all succeed.

Mantra 7:4:9

They go to the world of heaven who perform the Sattra. They kindle themselves with the Dīkṣhās, and cook themselves with the Upasads. With two they cut off their hair, with two their skin, with two their blood, with two their flesh, with two their bones, with two their marrow. In the Sattra the self is the sacrificial gift; verily taking the self as the gift they go to the world of heaven. They cut off the top-knot, for prosperity, (thinking), 'More swiftly may we attain the world of heaven.'

Mantra 7:4:10.

The theologians say, 'The Atirātra is the highest of the forms of sacrifice. Why do they perform it first?' Now in doing so they really perform in order first the Agniṣhṭoma, then the Ukthya, then the Ṣhoḍaśin, then the Atirātra, all the forms of sacrifice, and seizing and holding them, they keep drinking the Soma. They perform the Jyotiṣhṭoma first; the Jyotiṣhṭoma is the beginning of the Stomas; verily they commence the Stomas from the beginning. The Stomas being sung together make up the Virāj, and two verses are redundant; the Goṣhṭoma has one too many, and the Āyuṣhṭoma one too few. The Jyotiṣhṭoma is the world of heaven, the Virāj is strength; verily by it they go to the world of heaven. 'The Rathantara is used in the day, the Rathantara at night,' say the theologians, 'what is used to avoid repetition?' The great Sāman of Sobhari is used as the Brahmasāman at the third pressing; it they place in the middle, to separate them; verily there is no repetition.

Mantra 7:4:11

They first perform the Jyotiṣhṭoma; verily by it they find support in this world. They perform secondly the Goṣhṭoma; verily by it they find support in the atmosphere. They perform thirdly the Āyuṣhṭoma; verily by it they find support in yonder world. The Jyotis is this (earth), the Go the atmosphere, and the Āyus yonder (sky). In that they perform these Stomas, the performers of the Sattra keep finding support in these worlds. These, (Stomas) being sung together make up the Virāj, and two verses are redundant; the Goṣhṭoma has one too many, and the Āyuṣhṭoma one too few. The Jyotiṣhṭoma is the world of heaven, the Virāj is strength; verily they win strength. They experience not misery through hunger, and are not hungry, for the performers of Sattras are as it were afflicted with hunger. The two Agniṣhṭomas on either side are the rims, the Ukthyas in

the middle the nave, and that is the circling wheel of the Gods. In that they go by that Ṣhaḍaha, they mount the wheel of the Gods, for safety. They obtain prosperity. They go with the Ṣhaḍaha; there are six seasons; verily in the seasons they find support. The go with a Jyotiṣhṭoma on either hand; verily on either hand they find support in the world of heaven. There are two Ṣhaḍahas, they make up twelve days. Man is of twelve parts, two thighs, two arms, the trunk and the head, four members, and the breasts as the eleventh and twelfth. Therefore (the days) follow man. There are three Ṣhaḍahas, they make up eighteen days, nine and nine. Nine are the breaths in man; verily they follow the breaths. There are four Ṣhaḍahas, they make up twenty-four days. The year consists of twenty-four half-months; verily they follow the year. 'The year is not fixed,' they say. 'It is greater than a support.' The Brāhmaṇa of the month is that of the year also verily they go finding support in each month.

The Horse Sacrifice (continued)
Mantra 7:4:12

a. Let the ram aid thee with cooked food, the dark-necked with goats, the cotton-tree with increase, the Parṇa-tree with the holy power (Brahman), the fig-tree with the sacrifice, the banyan with the beakers, the Udumbara with strength, the Gāyatrī with the metres, the Trivṛit with the Stomas. ‖ *b.* Ye are helpers; let the helpers help thee. Deal among dear things, best among things to be sought, treasure lord of treasures, thee we hail, O my radiant one.

Mantra 7:4:13

To (the waters of) wells hail! | To those of the pools hail! | To those of the clefts hail! | To those of holes hail! | To those which are dug for hail! | To those of lakes hail! | To those of morasses hail! | To those of ponds hail! | To those of tanks hail! | To those of marshes hail! | To those of rain hail! | To those without rain hail! | To those of hail hail! | To those of rime hail! | To those which glide hail! | To those which are stagnant hail! | To those of the streams hail! | To those of the rivers hail! | To those of the ocean hail! | To all hail!

Mantra 7:4:14

To waters hail! | To those that flow hail! | To those that flow around hail | To those that flow all about hail! | To those that flow swiftly hail! | To those that flow quickly hail! | To those that flow wildly hail! | To those that flow terribly hail! | To the waters of earth hail! | To those of the atmosphere hail! | To those of the sky hail! | To all hail!

Mantra 7:4:15

a. Him who is fain to injure the steed | Varuṇa punisheth. | Away the man, away the dog! ‖ *b.* I and thou, Vṛitra-slayer, | Have been united to win spoils; | Even the foe, O hero with the bolt, | Must think of us; | Good are Indra's gifts. ‖ *c.* Thou hast surpassed in might, O Indra, on the earth | The regions comprehend not thy greatness; | For with thine own strength thou didst slay Vṛitra; | No foe hath found the end of thee in fight.

Mantra 7:4:16

Homage to the king! | Homage to Varuṇa! | Homage to the horse! | Homage to Prajāpati! | Homage to the overlord! | Thou art an overlord; make me an overlord; may I be overlord of creatures. | Place me, place in me. | To him that is driven near hail! | To him that is taken hold of hail! | To him that is sacrificed hail!

Mantra 7:4:17

a. Let the healing wind blow upon our cows, | Let them feed on strengthening herbs; | Let them drink waters full of life and fatness; | Rudra, be gracious to the food that hath feet. ‖ *b.* Those which are of one, of various hues, or of like hue | Those whose names Agni knoweth by sacrifice; | Those which the Aṅgirasas made here by devotion, | To those, O Parjanya, grant abundant protection. ‖ *c.* Those who offered to the Gods their bodies; | Those whose every form Soma knoweth; | O Indra, place them in our pastures, | Swelling with milk and rich in offspring. ‖ *d.* Prajāpati, bestowing these on me, | In harmony with all the Gods and Pitṛis, | Hath brought them, auspicious, to our pastures. | May we possess their offspring. ‖ *e.* Here is support, hail! ‖ *f.* Here is keeping apart, hail! ‖ *g.* Here is joy, hail! ‖ *h.* Here is delight, hail! ‖ *i.* The great. ‖ *k.* The protecting.

Mantra 7:4:18

a. What was the first conception? | What was the great age? | What was the tawny one? | What was the smooth one? ‖ *b.* The sky was the first conception. | The horse was the great age. | The night was the tawny one. | The sheep was the smooth one. ‖ *c.* Who moveth alone? | Who too is born again? | What is a remedy for the cold? | What is the great enveloper? ‖ *d.* The sun moveth alone. | The moon is born again. | Fire is the remedy for the cold. | Earth is the great enveloper. ‖ *e.* I ask thee of the furthest end of the earth. | I ask thee of the navel of the world. | I ask thee of the seed of the strong horse. | I ask thee of speech's highest realm. ‖ *f.* They call the altar-ground the furthest end of the earth. | They call the sacrifice the navel of the world. | They call Soma the seed of the strong horse. | (They call) the Brahman the highest realm of speech.

Mantra 7:4:19

a. O Ambā! O Ambālī! O Ambikā! ‖ *b.* No one leadest me. | The wicked horse is sleeping. ‖ *c.* O fair one, clad in fair raiment in the world of heaven be ye two covered. . . .[1] ‖ *l.* When the deer eateth grain, | He deemeth not his flock fat. | When the Śūdra woman is the loved of the Ārya, | She seeketh not wealth for prosperity. . . .[2] ‖ *q.* Dadhikrāvan have I sung, | The swift strong horse. | May he make our mouths fragrant; | May he lengthen our days. ‖ *r.* Ye waters are healing; | Further us to strength, | To see great joy. ‖ *s.* The most auspicious flavour that is yours | Accord to us here | Like eager mothers. ‖ *t.* To him may we come with satisfaction, | To whose dwelling ye quicken us, | O waters, and propagate us.

Mantra 7:4:20.

a. Bhūr! Bhuvar! Svar! ‖ *b.* Let the Vasus anoint thee with the Gāyatrī metre. Let the Rudras anoint thee with the Trishṭubh metre. Let the Ādityas anoint thee with the Jagatī metre. ‖ *c.* As the wind hath gone to the waters, | Indra's dear body, | By that path, O praiser, | Bring back to us the horse. ‖ *d.* O thou that hast barley, that hast grain, (bring) renown for me; ‖ *e.* For barley, for milk, this food eat, O ye Gods; this food eat, O Prajāpati ‖ *f.* They yoke the tawny ruddy one, | Which goeth round them that stand; | The lights shine in the sky. ‖ *g.* They yoke his dear steeds | On either side of the chariot, | Dark, strong, bearing heroes. | A Making a banner for that which hath none, | Form for the formless, O ye men, | Thou wert born with the dawns.

Mantra 7:4:21

To expiration hail! | To cross-breathing hail! | To inspiration hail! | To sinews hail! | To ligatures hail! | To surrounding ligatures hail! | To joints hail! | To joinings hail! | To bodies hail! | To the sacrifice hail! | To the sacrificial gifts hail! | To heaven hail! | To the world hail! | To all hail!

Mantra 7:4:22

To the bound hail! | To the unbound hail! | To the fastened hail! | To the unfastened hail! | To the yoked hail! | To the unyoked hail! | To the well-yoked hail! | To the unyoked hail! | To the one set free hail! | To the one lot go hail! | To that which moveth crookedly hail! | To that which moveth around hail! | To that which moveth together hail! | To that which moveth along hail! | To that which goeth hail! | To that which riseth hail! | To that which standeth hail! | To all hail!

Prapāṭhaka 5.

The Gavām Ayana

Mantra 7:5:1

The cows performed that Sattra, being hornless, with the desire, 'May horns be born to us.' For ten months they performed it, and then horns were born, and they ceased (the rite), (saying), 'We have obtained (our desire).' Then those whose horns were not born ceased (the rite) after making up the year, (saying), 'We have obtained (our desire).' Both those which obtained horns and those which did not ceased, (saying), 'We have obtained (our desire).' The year is the cows' Sattra, and those who knowing thus perform the year (sacrifice) are prosperous. Therefore a hornless cow has pleasure during the two months of the rainy season, for that is won for it by the Sattra. Therefore whatever is done in the house of one who performs for a year (a Sattra), that is done completely, successfully, and adequately. Those who perform the year (Sattra) are swimming on the ocean. He who does not see the further bank of the ocean cannot get out from it. The ocean is the year. Its further banks are the two Atirātras Those who knowing thus perform the year (Sattra) reach the end without injury. The former Atirātra is this (earth), the latter is yonder (sky); the former is mind, the latter speech; the former expiration, the latter inspiration; the former the commencement, the latter the end. The Atirātra is a Jyotishṭoma, of Vaiśvānara; verily they put light before them, to reveal the world of heaven. There is a fore offering, accompanied by the Chaturviṃśa Stoma. The year has twenty-four half-months; verily as they go on they find support in the year. There are three hundred and sixty Stotrīyas; so many are the nights of the year; verily they attain both forms of the year. | They perform (the rites of) the next days for rest, for safety. There are six-day periods. The year has six seasons; verily they find support in the seasons, the year. The Go and the Āyus (Stomas) are the Stomas in the middle; verily they place a pair in the middle of the year for procreation. On either side there is the Jyotishṭoma. It is the releasing; verily the metres are released; verily also they go to the world of heaven with the six-day (rite) which has a Jyotishṭoma on either side. The theologians say, 'They sit; by what path do they go?' One should reply, 'By the path that leads to the Gods. The path that leads to the Gods is the metres, the Gāyatrī, Trishṭubh, and Jagatī The Gāyatrī is the Jyotishṭoma, the Trishṭubh, the Goshṭoma, the Jagatī the Āyushṭoma. In that there are these Stomas, so do they go by the path that leads to the Gods. There is used the same Sāman The Sāman is the world of the Gods; verily they leave not the world of the Gods. There are used various verses. The verses are the world of man; verily they keep mounting one world of Gods after another from the world of men. There is the Brahman's Sāman as the Abhivarta to win the world of heaven. There is the Abhijit (day) for the gaining of the world of heaven. There is the Viśvajit (day) for the gaining of all. Month by month they perform the Pṛishṭhas, month by month the Atigrāhyas are drawn; verily in each month they place strength, for the support of the months. They perform the Pṛishṭhas in the latter part of the month. Therefore it is on the top that the plants bear fruit.

Mantra 7:5:2

The cows performed that Sattra, being hornless and desiring to obtain horns. For ten months they performed it, and then horns appeared. They said, 'We have gained (them), let us cease (the rite), for we have attained the desire for the sake of which we began (the rite).' But others said, either half of them or as many as might be the case, 'Let us perform (the rite) for these months, the eleventh and the twelfth, and when we have made up the year, let us cease'. In their case their horns grew in the twelfth month. Whether by faith, or by lack of faith—that is, those which have no horns-both indeed were prosperous, those which gained horns and those which won strength. He who ceases after ten months is prosperous, and he who ceases after twelve also, if he knows thus. They go by their feet, and he who goes by his foot attains (what he seeks). The Ayana is successful, and therefore is it productive of cows.

Mantra 7:5:3

They perform the Pṛishṭhas in the first month, they perform them in the middle month, they perform them in the last month. They say, 'In the case of a cow which they milk thrice a day, she yields sparingly at the latter two milkings; how then can she be milked who is twelve times milked?' Having made up the year, they should perform the Pṛishṭhas once in the last month; verily the sacrificers win the sacrifice and cattle. It is an ocean without a near or a further shore that they enter upon who perform the year (rite). If they employ the Bṛihat and the Rathantara Sāmans, it would be as if they were to provide a boat in the middle of the ocean. Going continuously with the Bṛihat and the Rathantara they obtain support. The union is milked for all desires; thus the sacrificers obtain all desires.

Mantra 7:5:4

The Ṛichas are the same. The Ṛichas are the world of men; verily they leave not the world of man. There are different Sāmans; the Sāman is the world of the Gods; verily they descend from the world of the Gods to one world after another of men. They first use the Jagatī, and the metres descend from the Jagatī, the cups from the Āgrayaṇa, the Pṛishṭhas from

1. Several verses were omitted here by Keith, with the note that "the next verses are hardly translatable." (Ed.)

2. Several more verses were omitted here by Keith, with a note explaining some of the difficulties in translating them. (Ed.)

the Bṛihat, the Stomas from the Trayastriṃśa Therefore the younger descends before an elder. The Viśvakarman cup is drawn; verily by it the sacrificers win all rites. The cup for Aditi is drawn. Aditi is this (earth); verily they rest on this (earth). The one and the other are drawn, for pairing, for propagation. Of old Prajāpati created offspring by means of the ten-night (rite); in that the ten-night rite is performed, the sacrificers create offspring. Udaṅka Śaulbāyana has declared the ten-night rite to be the prosperity of the Sattra, and the ten-night rite serves for the prosperity of the Sattra. Verily also whatever is done wrongly in the earlier days, this serves to atone for it.

Mantra 7:5:5

If two libations are offered simultaneously, then one should perform the early litany in the advanced part of the night. He who does it first wins the speech, the Gods, and the metres (of the others). The strophe should contain the word 'strong (*vṛiṣhan*)'; verily he takes Indra away from their morning pressing. Or rather they say, 'The strophe at the beginning of each pressing should be of this kind'; verily he takes Indra away from each of their pressings. | For entry, for rest, for the overcoming, of the Gāyatrī, of the Triṣhṭubh, of the Jagatī, of the Anuṣhṭubh, of the Paṅkti, hail! | Entry and rest are the metres; verily by the metres, he takes away their metres. One should recite the Janissary hymn; one should recite the Vihavyā hymn; one should recite the Kayāśubhīya hymn of Agastya. This indeed is so much as that, verily he takes away so much as is theirs. If at the early pressing the bowl is broken, they should sing verses addressed to Viṣhṇu and containing the epithet Śipiviṣhṭa. Whatever in the sacrifice is redundant, is redundant with regard to Viṣhṇu Śipiviṣhṭa; verily Viṣhṇu Śipiviṣhṭa places the redundant in the redundant. Verily having obtained the redundant by the redundant, they win it. If it is broken at the midday pressing, they should make the Sāman have the Vaṣhaṭkāra as its finale. The support of the sacrifice is the Vaṣhaṭkāra; verily they make the Sāman obtain support. If it breaks at the third pressing, the same thing (should be done).

Mantra 7:5:6

Having made up the month with the six-day periods they leave out a day, for they behold the months by the six-day periods. Having made up the months with the half-months, they leave out a day, for they behold the months by the half-months. Having made up the months by the new moon night, they leave out a day, for they behold the months by the new moon night. Having made up the months by the full moon night, they leave out a day, for they behold the month by the full moon night. He who pours (liquid) into a full (vessel) wastes the liquid; he who pours out from a full (vessel) places breath in it. In that, having made up the months with the full moon night, they leave out a day, they place breath in the year, and the performers of the Sattra breathe along it. If they did not leave out a day, then the year would fall asunder, as falls asunder a skin bag tied tight, and they would be ruined. In that, having made up the months with the full moon night, they leave out a day, they place out-breathing in the year, and the performers of the Sattra breathe out along it, and are not ruined. At the full moon (the Soma) of the Gods is pressed. In that, having made up the months with the full moon night, they leave out a day, with the sacrifice to the Gods they go to another sacrifice. They cleave asunder the sacrifice, in that (after performing it) as a series of six-day rites they leave out a day. They offer an animal for Prajāpati Prajāpati is all the Gods; verily with the Gods do they offer the sacrifice. They leave the pressing, who leave out the day. The Sāṃnāyya is the fourth pressing. Because there is the Sāṃnāyya, they do not leave the pressing. They partake of it after uttering the invocation, for they have this then as their Soma drink. The deities who share in the pressings of those who leave out the day go to their places; they offer the sacrificial cakes in each of the pressings; verily they win the deities who share in the pressing from their several places. (They offer the cakes) on eight potsherds at the early pressing, on eleven potsherds at the midday pressing, and on twelve potsherds at the third pressing; verily they obtain and win the metres. They offer an oblation to the All-Gods at the third pressing. The third pressing belongs to the All-Gods; verily they leave not the third pressing.

Mantra 7:5:7

The theologians consider, 'Should (a day) be left out, or should it not be left out?' They say, 'It should be left out.' They say, 'It should be left out at the new moon and at the full moon, for these two guide the sacrifice.' 'These two must not be left out,' they say, 'for these two determine the dependent sacrifice.' '(The day) should be left out on the first Vyaṣhṭakā,' they say, 'for this is what rends the month.' They should not leave out a day which is appointed. If they should leave out one which is appointed, they should leave it out on the seventh day after making up the months with six-day periods, whatever be the recur rent position which it occupies in the course of the six-day period. They should then offer to Agni, with the Vasus, a cake on eight potsherds, to Indra curds, to Indra with the Marutas a cake on eleven potsherds, to the All-Gods a cake on twelve potsherds. The early pressing belongs to Agni with the Vasus; in that they offer to Agni with the Vasus a cake on eight potsherds, they make the God share in it, and they approach the pressing with eight. In that the curds belong to Indra, they do not shut out Indra from a share. The midday pressing belongs to Indra with the Marutas. In that they offer to Indra with the Marutas a cake on eleven potsherds, they make the God share in it, and they approach the pressing with eleven. The third pressing belongs to the All-Gods with the Ṛibhus In that they offer to the All-Gods a cake on twelve pot sherds, they make the Gods share in it, and they approach the pressing with twelve. They offer a beast to Prajāpati—Prajāpati is the sacrifice that the sacrifice may not be abandoned. For six months (as they go) hence the Brahman's Sāman should be the 'victorious'. The 'victorious' is the holy power (Brahman); verily they go winning the world of heaven by the holy power (Brahman); for the world of heaven is as it were opposite from hence. When they come thence the Brahman's Sāman for six months should be 'O Indra, bear us strength, as a father to his sons. Guide us, O thou that art much invoked, on our path. Living, may we attain the light.' The light is this world, the light is offspring; verily they come, gazing on this world by repeating the verse.

Mantra 7:5:8

When the Gods had come to the end, their power and strength departed. They won them again by the Krośa (Sāman), and that is why the Krośa has the name. In that they sing the Krośa at the end of the pit, they win power and strength at the end of the sacrifice. They sing the Sattra syarddhi (Sāman) at the end of the Āhavanīya; verily, making Agni a witness, they advance to prosperity. They sing the Prajāpater Hṛidaya within the shed; verily they win his favour. They sing the Śloka (Sāman) in front of the Sadas, the Anuśloka (Sāman) behind; verily fame is their portion at the end of the sacrifice. The Adhvaryu sings nine (verses). Nine are the breaths in man; verily he places breaths in the sacrificers. All of them are addressed to Indra; verily he places power (indriyā) in the breaths. He sings without the Pratihāra. Therefore a man can contract all the other members (of the body) except the head, but the bead not. The Rathantara (Sāman) has the Pañchadaśa (Stoma); verily they win power. The Bṛihat has the Saptadaśa, for the winning of food; verily also they are propagated by it. The Bhadra (Sāman) has the Ekaviṃśa (Stoma) with Dvipadā verses, for support. The wives (of the sacrificers) sing, for offspring, for propagation. Prajāpati created offspring; he desired, 'May I gain the kingship over them.' He obtained the kingship over them by the Rājana (Sāman), and that is why the Rājana has the name. In that there is the Rājana, the sacrificers obtain the kingship over offspring. It has the Pañchaviṃśa (Stoma), to win Prajāpati. They sing five (verses) standing; verily they win the world of the Gods; five sitting; verily they win the world of men. These come to ten; the Virāj is of ten syllables, the Virāj is food; verily they win food by the Virāj In five places they sing sitting down; there are five quarters; verily they rest on the quarters. They come up each before one verse has been sung; verily they bear food from the quarters. The Udgātar sings these (verses); verily having borne food from the quarters they place glory in themselves. Therefore one breath protects all the limbs. Therefore, just as a bird about to fly upwards raises its head aloft, so the sacrificers are highest among people. The Udgātar mounts a throne; verily they attain rule. The Hotar (mounts) a swing; verily they mount the back of the firmament. The Adhvaryu (mounts) two mats; verily they reach the surface of the ruddy one. So many indeed are the worlds, and in them in order they find support. Then the sacrificers make thus a bridge to mount, for the gaining of the world of heaven.

Mantra 7:5:9

By means of the Arkya (Sāman) Prajāpati created offspring in thousands. From them by means of the Ilāṃda (Sāman) he took away the food they had gathered. In that there is the Arkya, the sacrificers create offspring; in that there is the Ilāṃda, they take away from the offspring which has been created the food they have gathered. Therefore, in whatever year the Sattra is performed, the offspring are hungry in that year, for they take their food and strength; in whatever year the Sattra is imperfect, the offspring are not hungry in that year; for they take not their food and strength. They raise a loud noise. As men being freed from bonds cry aloud, so the sacrificers freed from the bonds of the Gods cry aloud, placing food and strength in themselves. The lute has a hundred strings. Man is of a hundred (years) of age, and of a hundredfold strength; verily they find support in age and strength. They run a race, to win what has not yet been won. They beat drums; the voice of the drum is the highest (form of) speech; verily they win the highest (form of) speech. They beat the earth-drum; verily they win that speech which has entered this (earth); verily also they conquer the earth. All (forms of) speech they utter, to gain all (forms of speech). Two strive on a dry hide, to gain strength. One reviles, another extols. He who reviles purifies them, he who extols places food in them after they are purified. They win by the first months what is done by the Ṛishis and by the Gods; in that the Bhūtechad Sāmans are used, both are gained. Those who perform the year rite lose their virility. There are a pair united within the sacrificial ground; verily they lose not virility.

Mantra 7:5:10.

They pierce the hide; verily they remove the sin of the (sacrificers). 'Do not miss, do not pierce through,' he says; verily they now remove their sin. Slave girls dance round the Mārjālīya fire with water-pots on their heads, beating the ground with their feet, and singing 'This is honey.' Honey indeed is the chiefest food of the Gods; verily they win the chiefest food. They beat the ground with their feet; verily they endow the (sacrificers) with might.

The Horse Sacrifice (continued)

Mantra 7:5:11

To earth hail! | To the atmosphere hail! | To the sky hail! | To that which will stream together hail! | To that which is streaming together hail! | To that which hath streamed together hail! | To that which will cloud hail! | To that which cloudeth hail! | To that which hath been clouded hail! | To cloud hail! | To mist hail! | To storm hail! | To freezing hail! | To springing hail! | To that which will lighten hail! | To that which lighteneth hail! | To that which lighteneth together hail! | To that which will thunder hail! | To that which thundereth hail! | To that which thundereth terribly hail! | To that which will rain hail! | To that which raineth hail! | To that which raineth around hail! | To that which raineth about hail! | To that which raineth together hail! | To that which raineth along hail! | To that which will sprinkle hail! | To that which sprinkleth hail! | To that which is sprinkled hail! | To that which will warm hail! | To that which warmeth hail! | To that which warmeth around hail! | To that which will cease hail! | To that which ceaseth hail! | To that which hath ceased hail! | To that which will stream away hail! | To that which streameth away hail! | To that which hath streamed away hail! | To that which will burn hail! | To that which burneth hail! | To that which burneth terribly hail! | To the Ṛich verses hail! | To the Yajus verses hail! | To the Sāmans hail! | To the Aṅgirasas hail! | To the Vedas hail! | To the Gāthās hail! | To the Nārāśaṃsīs hail! | To the Raibhīs hail! | To all hail!

Mantra 7:5:12

To the toothed hail! | To the toothless hail! | To the breathing hail! | To that which hath not breath hail! | To that which hath a face hail! | To the faceless hail! | To that which hath a nose hail! | To the noseless hail! | To that which hath eyes hail! | To the eyeless hail! | To that which hath ears hail! | To the earless hail! | To that which hath a head hail! | To the headless hail! | To that which hath feet hail! | To the footless hail! | To that which breatheth hail! | To that which breatheth not hail! | To that which speaketh hail! | To the speechless hail! | To that which seeth hail! | To that which seeth not hail! | To that which heareth hail! | To that which heareth not hail! | To that which hath a mind hail! | To the mindless hail! | To that which hath seed hail! | To the seedless hail! | To offspring hail! | To begetting hail! | To that which hath hair hail! | To the hairless hail! | To skin hail! | To the skinless hail! | To that which hath a hide hail! | To the hideless hail! | To that which hath blood hail! | To the bloodless hail! | To that which hath flesh hail! | To the fleshless hail! | To sinews hail! | To that which hath no sinews hail! | To that which hath bones hail | To the boneless hail! | To that which hath marrow hail! | To the marrowless hail! | To that which hath limbs hail! | To the limbless hail! | To the trunk hail! | To the trunkless hail!

Mantra 7:5:13

Who yoketh thee? Let him yoke thee. Let Vishṇu yoke thee, for the prosperity of this sacrifice, for my pre-eminence, for N.N.'s pleasure; for life thee, for expiration thee, for inspiration thee, for cross-breathing thee, for dawning thee, for wealth thee, for prosperity thee, for sound thee, for nourishing thee, for calling from afar thee, for falling thee (I yoke).

Mantra 7:5:14

To Agni, of the Gāyatrī (metre), the Trivṛit (Stoma), the Rathantara (Sāman), the spring (season), (offering is made) on eight potsherds. To Indra, of the Trishṭubh (metre), the Pañchadaśa, (Stoma), the Bṛihat (Sāman), the summer (season), (offering is made) on eleven potsherds. To the All-Gods of the Jagatī (metre), the Saptadaśa (Stoma), the Vairūpa (Sāman), the rainy (season), (offering is made) on twelve potsherds. To Mitra and Varuṇa, of the Anushṭubh (metre), the Ekaviṃśa (Stoma), the Vairāja (Sāman), the autumn (season), curds. To Bṛihaspati, of the Paṅkti (metre), the Triṇava (Stoma), the Śākvara (Sāman), the winter (season), an oblation (is made). To Savitar, of the Atichandas (metre), the Trayastriṃśa (Stoma), the Raivata (Sāman), the cool (season), (offering is made) on twelve potsherds. To Aditi, as Vishṇu's consort, an oblation (is made). To Agni Vaiśvānara (offering is made) on twelve potsherds. To Anumati an oblation (is made). To Ka (offering is made) on one potsherd.

Mantra 7:5:15

Now for the fire which is produced on the fire-altar and for Soma, the king, the beast for Agni and Soma is the guest-offering. Again the fire which is piled up is cruel, and if one were not to cast upon the fire which has been piled up these oblations, the cruel fire would spring up in wrath, and injure the offspring and cattle of the sacrificer. In that he casts the oblations on the fire which has been piled up, he appeases it with its own portion, and the cruel fire does not spring up in wrath and injure his offspring and cattle. There are ten oblations. Nine are the breaths in man, and the navel is the tenth; verily he places breaths in the sacrificer. Again the Virāj is of ten syllables; the Virāj is food; verily he finds support in the Virāj as food. 'It must be piled with the seasons, the metres, the Stomas, and the Pṛishṭhas,' they say. In that he casts these oblations, he piles it with the seasons, the metres, the Stomas, and the Pṛishṭhas. 'The quarters can be won by one who has pressed the Soma' they say. In that he casts these oblations, (it is) for the winning of the quarters. The Gods made Indra sacrifice with it, and therefore is it Indra's pressing; men made Manu sacrifice with it, and therefore is it Manu's pressing. As Indra among the Gods, as Manu among men, becomes he who knowing thus sacrifices with this sacrifice. The Puronuvākyās contain the word 'quarter,' for the conquest of the quarters.

Mantra 7:6:16

a. Who is the sole lord of the world, | Which breatheth and winketh, through his greatness, | Who is the lord of biped and of quadruped here, | Who is the God whom we are to worship with oblation? ‖ *b.* Thou art taken with a foundation. I take thee dear to Prajāpati Of thee the sky is the greatness, the Nakshatras the form, the sun the splendour; to his greatness, to Prajāpati, thee (I offer). Hail!

Mantra 7:5:17

a. He who is the giver of soul, the giver of strength, | On whose instruction all, on whose (instruction) the Gods depend. | Whose shadow is immortality, whose shadow is death; | Who is the God whom we are to worship with oblation? ‖ *b.* Thou art taken with a foundation. I take thee dear to Prajāpati Of thee the earth is the greatness, the plants and trees the form, the fire the splendour; to his greatness, to Prajāpati, thee (I offer). Hail!

Mantra 7:5:18

In the priesthood may a Brāhmaṇa be born of spiritual glory. In this kingdom may a prince be born, an archer, a hero, and a great car fighter; a milk cow; a draught ox; a swift racer; a prolific woman; a victorious warrior; a youth fit for the assembly. To this sacrificer be a hero born. May Parjanya rain for us whensoever we desire. May our plants ripen with fruit. May union and peace be ours.

Mantra 7:5:19

a. The steed hath come to the earth; the strong steed hath made Agni his yoke-fellow. | The steed hath come to the atmosphere; the strong steed hath made Vāyu his yoke-follow. | The steed hath come to the sky; the strong steed hath made Sūrya his yoke-fellow. ‖ *b.* Agni is thy yoke-fellow, O steed; I grasp thee; bear me prosperously. | Vāyu is thy yoke-fellow, O steed; I grasp thee; bear me prosperously. | The Āditya is thy yoke-fellow, O steed; I grasp thee; bear me prosperously. | Thou art the supporter of expiration; support my expiration. | Thou art the supporter of cross-breathing; support my cross-breathing. | Thou art the supporter of inspiration; support my inspiration. | Thou art the eye; place the eye in me. | Thou art the ear; place the ear in me. | Thou art life; place life in me.

Mantra 7:5:20.

May the seed be living, Parjanya rain, the corn be ripened, the plants rich in leaves, this (earth) easy to walk on, the fire easy of approach, the atmosphere easy to see through, the wind purifying, the sky easy of access, he that burns yonder kindly, the day and night as of old, the half months of fifteen days, the months of thirty days, the seasons in due order, and the year auspicious.

Mantra 7:5:21

To) Agni (offering is made) on eight potsherds; to Soma an oblation; to Savitar (offering) on eight potsherds; to Pūṣhan an oblation; to Rudra an oblation; to Agni Vaiśvānara (offering) on eight potsherds; if he should not go to the wild beast's lair; to Agni, saviour from distress, (offering is made) on eight potsherds; to Sūrya milk (is offered); Vāyu receives a share in the butter offering.

Mantra 7:5:22

To Agni, saviour from distress, (offering is made) on eight potsherds; to Indra, saviour from distress, on eleven potsherds; to Mitra and Varuṇa, saviours from sin, a milk offering; to Vāyu and Savitar saviours from sin, an oblation; to the Aśvins, saviours from sin, grain; to the Marutas, saviours from evil, on seven potsherds; to the All-Gods, saviours from evil, on twelve potsherds; to Anumati an oblation; to Agni, Vaiśvānara on twelve potsherds; to heaven and earth, saviours from evil, on two potsherds.

Mantra 7:5:23

To Agni he made obeisance; to the earth he made obeisance; as Agni with the earth made harmony, so for me may favourable harmonies be made. | To Vāyu he made obeisance, to the atmosphere he made obeisance; as Vāyu with the atmosphere (made harmony, so etc.). | To Sūrya he made obeisance, to the sky he made obeisance; as Sūrya with the sky (made harmony, so etc.). | To the moon he made obeisance, to the Nakṣhatras he made obeisance; as the moon with the Nakṣhatras (made harmony, so etc.). | To Varuṇa he made obeisance, to the waters he made obeisance; as Varuṇa with the waters (made harmony, so etc.). | To the Sāman he made obeisance, to the Ṛich he made obeisance; as the Sāman with the Ṛich (made harmony, so etc.). | To the Brahman (caste) he made obeisance, to the Kṣhatriya (caste) he made obeisance; as the Brahman with the Kṣhatriya (made harmony, so etc.). | To the king he made obeisance, to the people he made obeisance; as the king with the people (made harmony, so etc.). | To the chariot he made obeisance, to the horses he made obeisance; as the chariot with the horses (made harmony, so etc.). | To Prajāpati he made obeisance, to creatures he made obeisance; as Prajāpati with creatures made harmony, so for me may favourable harmonies be made.

Mantra 7:5:24

a. Thine ancient paths, O Savitar, | That are extended dustless through the atmosphere, | With these today, with thy paths easy to travel, | Guard us, and, O God, speak for us. ‖ *b.* Reverence to Agni, dweller on earth, maker of room; grant room to this thy sacrificer. Reverence to Vāyu, dweller in the atmosphere, maker of room; grant room to this thy sacrificer. Reverence to Sūrya, dweller in the sky, maker of room; grant room to this thy sacrificer.

Mantra 7:5:25

He who knows the head of the sacrificial horse becomes possessed of a head and fit for sacrifice. The head of the sacrificial horse is the dawn, the eye the sun, the breath the wind, the ear the moon, the feet the quarters, the ribs the intermediate quarters, the winking the day and night, the joints the half-months, the joinings the months, the limbs the seasons, the trunk the year, the hair the rays (of the gun), the form the Nakṣhatras, the bones the stars, the flesh the mist, the hair the plants, the tail hairs the trees, the mouth Agni, the open (mouth) Vaiśvānara, the belly the sea, the anus the atmosphere, the testicles the sky and the earth, the *membrum virile*, the pressing-stone, the seed the Soma. When it chews, there is lightning; when it moves about, there is thundering; when it makes water, there is rain; its speech is speech. The Mahiman (cup) indeed is born before the birth of the horse as the day. The Mahiman (cup) is born after it as the night. These two Mahiman (cups) surround on either side the horse. As Haya (steed) it carried the Gods, as Arvan (courser) the Asuras, as Vājin (racer) the Gandharvas, as Aśva (horse) men. The birthplace of the horse, indeed, is the sea, its kindred is the sea.

Hymns of the Sāmaveda

Translated by Ralph T.H. Griffith, 1895

Preface

The *Sāmaveda*, or Veda of Holy Songs, third in the usual order of enumeration of the three Vedas, ranks next in sanctity and liturgical importance to the *Ṛigveda* or Veda of Recited praise. Its Saṃhitā, or metrical portion, consists chiefly of hymns to be chanted by the Udgātar priests at the performance of those important sacrifices in which the juice of the Soma plant, clarified and mixed with milk and other ingredients, was offered in libation to various deities. The Collection is made up of hymns, portions of hymns, and detached verses, taken mainly from the *Ṛigveda*, transposed and re-arranged, without reference to their original order, to suit the religious ceremonies in which they were to be employed. In these compiled hymns there are frequent variations, of more or less importance, from the text of the *Ṛigveda* as we now possess it, which variations, although in some cases they are apparently explanatory, seem in others to be older and more original than the readings of the Ṛigveda. In singing, the verses are still further altered by prolongation, repetition and insertion of syllables, and various modulations, rests, and other modifications prescribed, for the guidance of the officiating priests, in the Gaṇas or Song-books. Two of these manuals, the Grāmageyagāna, or Congregational, and the Āraṇyagāna or Forest Song-Book, follow the order of the verses of Part I of the Saṃhitā, and two others, the Ūhagāna, the Ūhyagāna, of Part 2. This Part is less disjointed than Part 1, and is generally arranged in triplets whose first verse is often the repetition of a verse that has occurred in Part 1.

There is no clue to the date of the compilation of the *Sāmaveda Hymns*, nor has the compiler's name been handed down to us. There are three recensions of the text of the *Sāmaveda Saṃhitā*, the Kauthuma Śākhā or recension is current in Guzerat, the Jaiminīya in the Carnatic, and the Rānāyanīya in the Mahratta country. A translation, by Dr. Stevenson, of the Rānāyanīya recension—or, rather, a free version of Sāyaṇa's paraphrase—was edited by Professor Wilson, in 1842; in 1848, Professor Benfey of Göttingen brought out an excellent edition of the same text with a metrical translation, a complete glossary, and explanatory notes; and in 1874-78, Pandit Satyavrata Sāmaśrami of Calcutta published in the *Bibliotheca Indica* a most meritorious edition of the Saṃhitā according to the same recension, with Sāyaṇa's commentary, portions of the Song-books, and other illustrative matter. I have followed Benfey's text, and have, made much use of his glossary and notes. Pandit Satyavrata Sāmaśrami's edition also has been of the greatest service to me. To Mr. Venis, Principal of the Benares Sanskrit College, I am indebted for, the loan of the College manuscripts of the text and commentary.

I repeat the expression of my obligations to those scholars whose works assisted me in my translation of the *Hymns of the Ṛigveda*. For help in translating the non-Ṛigvedic Hymns of the *Sāmaveda*, I am additionally indebted to the late Professor Benfey and to Professor Ludwig whose version will be found in his *Der Rgveda*, vol. III, pp. 19-25.

For further information regarding the *Sāmaveda,* Weber's *History of Indian Literature*, and Max Müller's *History of Ancient Sanskrit Literature*, or the article on the Veda in *Chamber's Encyclopedia* should be consulted.

R. T. H. Griffith, Kotagiri, Nilgiri, 25th May,1893.

Part 1. Pūrva Ārchika.

Prapāṭhaka 1.

Āgneyaṃ Kāṇḍa.

Ardha 1.

Om. Glory to the Sāmaveda! To Lord Gaṇeśa glory! Om.[1]

Daśati 1:1:1:1. Agni.

1. Come, Agni, praised with song, to feast and sacrificial offering: sit | As Hotar on the holy grass! || 2. O Agni, thou hast been ordained Hotar of every sacrifice, | By Gods, among the race of men. || 3. Agni we choose as envoy, skilled performer of this holy rite, | Hotar, possessor of all wealth. || 4. Served with oblation, kindled, bright, through love of song may Agni, bent | On riches, smite the Vṛitras dead! || 5. I laud your most beloved guest like a dear friend, O Agni, him | Who, like a chariot, wins us wealth. || 6. Do thou, O Agni, with great might guard us from all malignity, | Yea, from the hate of mortal man! || 7. O Agni, come; far other songs of praise will I sing forth to thee. | Wax mighty with these Soma-drops! || 8. May Vatsa draw thy mind away even from thy loftiest dwelling place! | Agni, I yearn for thee with song. || 9. Agni, Atharvan brought thee forth by rubbing from the sky, the head | Of all who offer sacrifice. || 10. O Agni, bring us radiant light to be our mighty succour, for | Thou art our visible deity!

Daśati 1:1:1:2. Agni.

1. O Agni, God, the people sing reverent praise to thee for strength: | With terrors trouble thou the foe || 2. I seek with song your messenger, oblation-bearer, lord of wealth, | Immortal, best at sacrifice. || 3. Still turning to their aim in thee the sacrificer's sister hymns | Have come to thee before the wind. || 4. To thee, illuminer of night, O Agni, day by day with prayer, | Bringing thee reverence, we come. || 5. Help, thou who knowest lauds, this work, a lovely hymn in Rudra's praise, | Adorable in every house! || 6. To this fair sacrifice to drink the milky draught art thou called forth: | O Agni, with the Marutas come! || 7. With homage will I reverence thee, Agni, like a long-tailed steed, | Imperial lord of holy rites. || 8. As Aurva and as Bhṛigu called, as Apnavāna called, I call | The radiant Agni robed with sea. || 9. When he enkindles Agni, man should with his heart attend the song: | I kindle Agni till he glows. || 10. Then, verily, they see the light refulgent of primeval seed, | Kindled on yonder side of heaven.

Daśati 1:1:1:3. Agni.

1. Hither, for powerful kinship, I call Agni, him who prospers you, | Most frequent at our solemn rites. || 2. May Agni with his pointed blaze cast down each fierce devouring fiend: | May Agni win us wealth by war! || 3. Agni, be gracious; thou art great: thou hast approached the pious man, | Hast come to sit on sacred grass. || 4. Agni, preserve us,from distress consume our enemies, O God, | Eternal, with thy hottest flames || 5. Harness, O Agni, O thou God, thy steeds which are most excellent! | The fleet ones bring thee rapidly. || 6. Lord of the tribes, whom all must seek, we worshipped Agni set thee down, | Refulgent, rich in valiant men. || 7. Agni is head and height of heaven, the master of the earth is he | He quickeneth the waters' seed. || 8. O Agni, graciously announce this our good fortune of the Gods, | And this our newest hymn of praise! || 9, By song, O Agni, Aṅgiras! Gopavana hath brought thee forth | Hear thou my call, refulgent one! || 10. Agni, the Sage, the Lord of Strength, hath moved around the sacred gifts, | Giving the offerer precious things. || 11. His heralds bear him up aloft, the God who knoweth all that lives, | The Sun, that all may look on him. | 12, Praise Agni in the sacrifice, the Sage whose holy laws are true | The God who driveth grief away. || 13. Kind be the Goddesses to lend us help, and kind that we may drink: | May their streams bring us health and wealth || 14. Lord of the brave, whose songs dost thou in thine abundance now inspire, | Thou whose hymns help to win the kine?

Daśati 1:1:1:4. Agni.

1. Sing to your Agni with each song, at every sacrifice for strength. | Come, let us praise the wise and, everlasting God even as a well-beloved friend, || 2. Agni, protect thou us by one, protect us by the second song, | Protect us by three hymns, O Lord of power and might, bright God, by four hymns guard us well! || 3. O Agni, with thy lofty beams, with thy pure brilliancy, O God, | Kindled, most youthful one! by Bharadvāja's hand, shine on us richly, holy Lord! || 4. O Agni who art worshipped well, dear let our princes be to thee, | Our wealthy patrons who are governors of men, who part, as gifts, the stall of kine! || 5. Agni, praise-singer! Lord of men, God! burning up the Rākṣhasas, | Mighty art thou, the ever-present, household-lord! home-friend and guardian from the sky. || 6. Immortal Jātavedas, thou bright-hued refulgent gift of Dawn, | Agni, this day to him who pays oblations bring the Gods who waken with the morn! || 7. Wonderful, with thy favouring help, send us thy bounties, gracious Lord. | Thou art the charioteer, Agni, of earthly wealth: find rest and safety for our seed! || 8. Famed art thou, Agni, far and wide, preserver, righteous, and a Sage. | The holy singers, O enkindled radiant one, ordainers, call on thee to come. || 9. O holy Agni, give us wealth famed among men and strengthening life! | Bestow on us, O helper, that which many crave, more glorious still through righteousness! || 10. To him, who dealeth out all wealth, the sweet-toned Hotar-priest of men, | To him like the first vessels filled with savoury juice, to Agni let the lauds go forth.

Daśati 1:1:1:5. Agni.

1. With this mine homage I invoke Agni for you, the Son of Strength, | Dear, wisest envoy, skilled in noble sacrifice, immortal messenger of all. || 2. Thou liest in the logs that are thy mothers: mortals kindle thee. | Alert thou bearest off the sacrificer's gift, and then thou shinest to the Gods. || 3. He hath appeared, best prosperer, in whom men lay their holy acts: | So may our songs of praise come nigh to Agni who was born to give the Ārya strength! || 4. Chief Priest is Agni at the laud, as stones and grass at sacrifice. | Gods! Marutas! Brahmaṇaspati! I crave with song the help that is most excellent. || 5. Pray Agni of the piercing flame, with sacred songs, to be our help; | For wealth, famed Agni, Purumīḷha and ye men! He is Sudīti's sure defence. || 6. Hear, Agni who hast ears to hear, with all thy train of escort Gods! | With those who come at dawn let Mitra, Aryaman sit on the grass at sacrifice. || 7. Agni of Divodāsa, God, comes forth like Indra in his might. | Rapidly hath he moved along his mother earth: he stands in high heaven's dwelling-place. || 8. Whether thou come from earth or from the lofty lucid realm of heaven, | Wax stronger in thy body through my song of praise: fill full all creatures, O most wise! || 9. If, loving well the forests, thou wentest to thy maternal floods, | Not to be scorned, Agni, is that return of thine when, from afar, thou now art here. || 10. O Agni, Manu established thee a light for all the race of men: | With Kaṇva hast thou blazed, Law-born and waxen strong, thou whom the people reverence.

Ardha 2.

Daśati 1:1:2:1. Agni.

1. The God who giveth wealth accept your full libation poured to, him! | Pour ye it out, then fill the vessel full again, for so the God regardeth you. || 2. Let Brahmaṇaspati come forth, let Sūnṛitā the Goddess come, | And Gods bring to our rite which yields a fivefold gift the hero, lover of mankind! || 3. Stand up erect to lend us aid, stand up like Savitar the God, | Erect as strength-bestower when we call on thee with priests who balm our offerings! || 4. The man who bringeth gifts to thee, bright God who fain wouldst lead to wealth, | Winneth himself a brave son, Agni! skilled in lauds, one prospering in a thousand ways. || 5. With hymns and holy eulogies we supplicate your Agni, Lord | Of many families who duly serve the Gods, yea, him whom others too inflame. || 6. This Agni is the Lord of great prosperity and hero, strength, | Of wealth with noble offspring and with store of kine, the Lord of battles with the foe. || 7. Thou, Agni, art the

1. The benedictory line is a modern addition. Om is a sacred exclamation that may be uttered inaudibly to profane ears at the beginning and end of a reading of the Vedas or before a prayer. *Gaṇeśa*, Lord of the Gaṇas or troops of inferior deities, is a post-Vedic God, regarded as the remover of obstacles and hence propitiated at the beginning of important undertakings and invoked at the commencement of books.

homestead's Lord, our Hotar-priest at sacrifice. | Lord of all boons, thou art the Potar, passing wise. Pay worship, and enjoy the good! || 8. We as thy friends have chosen thee, mortals a God, to be our help. | The Waters' Child, the blessed, the most mighty one, swift conqueror, and without a peer.

Daśati 1:1:2:2. Agni.

1. Present oblations, make him splendid: set ye as Hotar in his place the Home's Lord, worshipped | With gifts and homage where they pour libations! Honour him meet for reverence in our houses. || 2. Verily wondrous is the tender youngling's growth who never draweth nigh to drink his mother's milk. | As soon as she who hath no udder bore him, he, faring on his great errand, suddenly grew strong. || 3. Here is one light for thee, another yonder: enter the third and, be therewith united. | Beautiful be thy union with the body, beloved in the Gods' sublimest birthplace! || 4. For Jātavedas, worthy of our praise, will we frame with our mind this eulogy as 'twere a car; | For good, in his assembly, is this care of ours. Let us not, in thy friendship, Agni, suffer harm! || 5. Agni Vaiśvānara, born in course of Order, the messenger of earth, the head of heaven, | The Sage, the sovereign, guest of men, our vessel fit for their mouth, the Gods have generated. || 6. Even as the waters from the mountain ridges, so sprang the; Gods, through lauds, from thee, O Agni. | To thee speed hymns and eulogies, as horses haste, bearing him who loves the song, to battle. || 7. Win to protect you, Rudra, lord of worship, priest of both worlds, effectual sacrificer, | Agni, invested with his golden colours, before the thunder strike and lay you senseless! || 8. The King whose face is decked with oil is kindled with homage offered by his faithful servant. | The men, the priests adore him with oblations. Agni hath shone forth at the flush of morning. || 9. Agni advanceth with his lofty banner: through earth and heaven the Bull hath loudly bellowed | He hath come nigh from the sky's farthest limit: the Steer hath waxen in the waters' bosom. || 10. From the two fire-sticks have the men engendered with thoughts, urged by the hand, the glorious Agni, | Far-seen, with pointed flame, Lord of the Homestead.

Daśati 1:1:2:3. Agni.

1. Agni is wakened by the people's fuel to meet the Dawn who cometh like a milch-cow. | Like young trees shooting up on high their branches, his flames. are mounting to the vault of heaven. || 2. Set forth the gleaming one, the song-inspirer, not foolish with. the foolish, fort-destroyer, | Who leadeth with his hymns to thought of conquest, gold-bearded, richly splendid with his armour || 3. Thou art like heaven: one form is bright, one holy, like Day and Night dissimilar in colour. | All magic powers thou aidest, self-dependent! Auspicious be thy bounty here, O Pūshan! || 4. As holy food, Agni, to thine invoker give wealth in cattle, lasting, rich in marvels! | To us be born a son and spreading offspring. Agni, be this thy gracious will to us-ward! || 5. Established to fill the juice with vital vigour, giver of wealth, guard of his servant's body, | The great Priest, born, who knows the clouds, abider with men, is seated in the waters' eddy. || 6. Let the song, honouring the best, with longing honour the Asura's most famous sovereign, | The deeds of him the mighty, deeds like Indra's, the manly one in whom the folk must triumph! || 7. In the two kindling-blocks lies Jātavedas like the well-cherished germ in pregnant women,— | Agni who day by day must be entreated by men who watch provided with oblations. || 8. Agni, from days of old thou slayest demons: never shall Rākṣhasas in fight o'ercome thee. | Burn up the foolish ones, raw flesh devourers: let none of them escape thine heavenly arrow!

Daśati 1:1:2:4. Agni.

1. Bring us most mighty splendour thou, Agni, resistless on thy way: | Prepare for us the path that leads to glorious opulence and strength! || 2. May the brave man, if full of zeal he serve and kindle Agni's flame, | Duly presenting sacred gifts, enjoy the Gods' protecting help. || 3. Thy bright smoke lifts itself aloft, and far-extended shines in heaven, | For, Purifier! like the Sun thou beamest with thy radiant glow. || 4. Thou, Agni, even as Mitra, hast a princely glory of thine own. | Bright, active God, thou makest fame increase like means of nourishment. || 5. At dawn let Agni, much-beloved, guest of the house, be glorified, | In whom, the everlasting one, all mortals make their offerings blaze. || 6. Most moving song be Agni's: shine on high, O rich in radiant light! | Like the chief consort of a King riches and strength proceed from thee. || 7. Exerting all our strength with thoughts of power we glorify in speech | Agni your dear familiar friend, the darling guest in every house. || 8. His beam hath lofty power of life: sing praise to Agni, to the God | Whom men have set in foremost place, like Mitra for their eulogy! || 9. To noblest Agni, friend of man, chief Vṛitra-slayer, have we come— | Who with Śrutarvan, Ṛikṣha's son, in lofty presence is inflamed. || 10. Born as the loftiest Law commands, comrade of those who grew with him. | Agni, the sire of Kaśyapa by faith, the mother, Manu, Sage.

Daśati 1:1:2:5. Agni.

1. We in King Soma place our trust, in Agni, and in Varuṇa, | The Āditya, Vishṇu, Sūrya, and the Brahman-priest Bṛihaspati || 2. Hence have these men gone up on high and mounted to the heights of heaven: | On! conquer on the path by which Aṅgirasas travelled to the skies! || 3. That thou mayst send us ample wealth, O Agni, we will kindler thee: | So, for the great oblation, Steer, pray Heaven and Earth to come to us! || 4. He runs when one calls after him, This is the prayer of him who prays. | He holds all knowledge in his grasp even as the felly rounds the wheel. || 5. Shoot forth, O Agni, with thy flame: demolish them on every side! | Break down the Yātudhāna's strength, the vigour of the Rākshasa! || 6. Worship the Vasus, Agni! here, the Rudras and Ādityas, all | Who know fair sacrifices, sprung from Mann, scattering blessings down!

Prapāṭhaka 2.

Ardha 1.

Daśati 1:2:1:1. Agni.

1. Agni, thy faithful servant I call upon thee with many a gift, | As in the keeping of the great inciting God. || 2. To Agni, to the Hotar-priest offer your best, your lofty speech, | To him ordainer-like who bears the light of songs. || 3. O Agni, thou who art the lord of wealth in kine, thou Son of Strength, | Bestow on us, O Jātavedas, high renown || 4. Most skilled in sacrifice, bring the Gods, O Agni, to the pious, man: | A joyful Priest, thy splendour drives our foes afar || 5. Taught by seven mothers at his birth was he, for glory of the wise. | He, firm and sure, hath set his mind on glorious wealth || 6. And in the day our prayer is this: May Aditi come nigh to help, | With loving-kindness bring us weal and chase our foes || 7. Worship thou Jātavedas, pray to him who willingly accepts, | Whose smoke wanders at will, and none may grasp his flame || 8. No mortal man can e'er prevail by arts of magic over him | Who hath served Agni well, the oblation-giving God. || 9. Agni, drive thou the wicked foe, the evil-hearted thief away, | Far, far, Lord of the brave! and give us easy paths! || 10. O hero Agni, Lord of men, on hearing this new laud of mine | Burn down the Rākṣhasas, enchanters, with thy flame!

Daśati 1:2:1:2. Agni.

1. Sing forth to him the holy, most munificent, sublime with his refulgent glow, | To Agni, ye Upastutas || 2. Agni, he conquers by thine aid that brings him store of valiant sons and does great deeds, | Whose bond of friendship is thy choice || 3. Sing praise to him the Lord of light! The Gods have made the God to be their messenger, | To bear oblation to the Gods. || 4. Anger not him who is our guest! He is the bright God Agni, praised by many a man, | God Hotar, skilled in sacrifice. || 5. May Agni, worshipped, bring us bliss: may the gift, blessed one! and sacrifice bring bliss. | Yea, may our eulogies bring bliss. || 6. Thee have we chosen skilfullest in sacrifice, immortal Priest among the Gods, | Wise finisher of this holy rite. || 7. Bring us that splendour, Agni, which may overcome each greedy fiend in our abode, | And the malicious wrath of men! || 8. Soon as the eager Lord of men is friendly unto Manu's race | Agni averteth from us all the Rākṣhasas!

Indra Kāṇḍa.

Daśati 1:2:1:3. Indra.

1. Sing this, beside the flowing juice, to him your hero, much-invoked, | To please him as a mighty Bull || 2. O Śatakratu Indra, now rejoice with that carouse of thine | Which is most glorious of all! || 3. Ye cows, protect the fount: the two mighty ones bless the sacrifice. | The handles twain are wrought of gold. || 4. Sing praises that the horse may come; sing, Śrutakakṣha, that the cow | May come, that Indra's might may come || 5. We make this Indra very strong to strike, the mighty Vṛitra dead: | A vigorous hero shall he be. || 6. Based upon strength and victory and power,

O Indra, is thy birth: | Thou, mighty one! art strong indeed, || 7. The sacrifice made Indra great when he unrolled the earth, and made | Himself a diadem in heaven. || 8. If I, O Indra, were, like thee, the single ruler over wealth | My worshipper should be rich in kine. || 9. Pressers, blend Soma juice for him, each draught most excellent, for him | The brave, the hero, for his joy. || 10. Here is the Soma juice expressed. O Vasu, drink till thou art full: | Undaunted God, we give it thee.

Daśati 1:2:1:4. Indra.

1. Sūrya, thou mountest up to meet the hero famous for his wealth, | Who hurls the bolt and works for man. || 2. Whatever, Vṛitra-slayer! thou, Sūrya hast risen upon today, | That, Indra, all is in thy power. || 3. That Indra is our youthful friend, who with his trusty guidance led | Turvaśa, Yadu from afar. || 4. O Indra, let not ill designs surround us in the sunbeams' light | This may we gain with thee for friend! || 5. Indra, bring wealth that gives delight, the victor's ever-conquering wealth, | Most excellent, to be our aid || 6. In mighty battle we invoke Indra, Indra is lesser fight, | The friend who bends his bolt at fiends. || 7. In battle of a thousand arms Indra drank Kadrū's Soma juice | There he displayed his manly might. || 8. Faithful to thee, we sing aloud, heroic Indra, songs to thee | Mark, O good Lord, this act of ours! || 9. Hitherward! they who light the flame and straightway trim the sacred grass, | Whose friend is Indra ever young. || 10. Drive all our enemies away, smite down the foes who press around, | And bring the wealth for which we long!

Daśati 1:2:1:5. Indra and others.

1. I Hear, as though 'twere close at hand, the cracking of the whips they hold: | They gather splendour on their way. || 2. Indra, these friends of ours, supplied with Soma, wait and look to thee | As men with fodder to the herd. || 3. Before his hot displeasure all the peoples, all the men bow down, | As rivers bow them to the sea. || 4. We choose unto ourselves that high protection of the mighty Gods, | That it may help and succour us. || 5. O Brahmaṇaspati, make thou Kakshīvant Auśija a loud | Chanter of flowing Soma juice! || 6. Much honoured with libations may the Vṛitra-slayer watch for us: | May Śakra listen to our prayer || 7. Send us this day, God Savitar, prosperity with progeny | Drive thou the evil dream away! || 8. Where is that ever-youthful Steer, strong-necked and never yet bent down? | What Brahman ministers to him? || 9. There where the mountains downward slope, there at the meeting of the streams | The Sage was manifest by song. || 10. Praise Indra whom our songs must laud, sole sovereign of mankind, the chief | Most liberal who controlleth men.

Ardha 2.

Daśati 1:2:2:1. Indra and others.

1. Indra whose jaws are strong hath drunk of worshipping Sudakṣha's draught, | The Soma juice with barley brew. || 2. O Lord of ample wealth, these songs of praise have called aloud to thee, | Like milch-kine lowing to their calves! || 3. Then straight they recognized the mystic name of the creative Steer, | There in the mansion of the Moon. || 4. When Indra, strongest hero, brought the streams, the mighty waters down, | Pūṣhan was standing by his side. || 5. The Cow, the streaming mother of the liberal Marutas, pours her milk, | Harnessed to draw their chariots on. || 6. Come, Lord of rapturous joys, to our libation with thy bay steeds, come | With bay steeds to the flowing juice || 7. Presented strengthening gifts have sent Indra away at sacrifice, | With night, unto the cleansing bath. || 8. I from my Father have received deep knowledge of eternal Law: | I was born like unto the Sun. || 9. With Indra splendid feasts be ours, rich in all strengthening things, wherewith, | Wealthy in food, we may rejoice || 10. Soma and Pūṣhan, kind to him who travels to the Gods, provide | Dwellings all happy and secure.

Daśati 1:2:2:2. Indra.

1. Invite ye Indra with a song to drink your draught of Soma steeds, juice, | All-conquering Śatakratu, most munificent of all who live || 2. Sing ye a song, to make him glad, to Indra, Lord of tawny | The Soma-drinker, O my friends! || 3. This, even this, O Indra, we implore: as thy devoted friends | The Kaṇvas praise thee with their hymns! || 4. For Indra, lover of carouse, loud be our songs about the juice | Let poets sing the song of praise. || 5. Here, Indra, is thy Soma draught, made pure upon the sacred grass: | Run hither, come and drink thereof || 6. As a good cow to him who milks, we call the doer of good deeds | To our assistance day by day. || 7. Hero, the Soma being shed, I pour the juice for thee to drink | Sate thee and finish thy carouse! || 8. The Soma, Indra, which is shed in saucers and in cups for thee, | Drink thou, for thou art lord thereof! || 9. In every need, in every fray we call, as friends, to succour us, | Indra, the mightiest of all. || 10. O come ye hither, sit ye down: to Indra sing ye forth your song, | Companions, bringing hymns of praise.

Daśati 1:2:2:3. Indra.

1. So, Lord of affluent gifts, this juice hath been expressed for thee with strength: | Drink of it, thou who lovest song! || 2. Great is our Indra from of old; greatness be his, the Thunderer | Wide as the heaven extends his might. || 3. Indra, as one with mighty arm, gather for us with thy right hand | Manifold and nutritious spoil! || 4. Praise, even as he is known, with song Indra the guardian of the kine, | The Son of Truth, Lord of the brave. || 5. With what help will he come to us, wonderful, ever-waxing friend? | With what most mighty company? || 6. Thou speedest down to succour us this ever-conquering God of yours | Him who is drawn to all our songs. || 7. To the assembly's wondrous Lord, the lovely friend of Indra, I | Had prayed for wisdom and success. || 8. May all thy paths beneath the sky whereby thou speddest Vyaśva on, | Yea, let all spaces hear our voice || 9. Bring to us all things excellent, O Śatakratu, food and strength, | For, Indra, thou art kind to us! || 10. Here is the Soma ready pressed: of this the Marutas, yea, of this, | Self-luminous the Aśvins drink.

Daśati 1:2:2:4. Indra and others.

1. Tossing about, the active ones came nigh to Indra at his birth, | Winning themselves heroic might. || 2. Never, O Gods, do we offend, nor are we ever obstinate | We walk as holy texts command. || 3. Evening is come: sing loudly thou Atharvan's nobly singing son: | Give praise to Savitar the God! || 4. Now Morning with her earliest light shines forth, dear daughter of the Sky: | High, Aśvins, I extol your praise. || 5. Armed with the bones of dead Dadhyach, Indra, with unresisted might | The nine-and-ninety Vṛitras slew. || 6. Come, Indra, and delight thee with the juice at all our Soma feasts, | Protector, mighty in thy strength || 7. O thou who slayest Vṛitras, come, O Indra, hither to our side, | Mighty one, with thy mighty aids! || 8. That might of his shone brightly forth when Indra brought together, like | A skin, the worlds of heaven and earth, || 9. This is thine own Thou drawest near, as turns a pigeon to his mate: | Thou carest, too, for this our prayer. || 10. May Vāta breathe his balm on us, healthful, delightful to our heart: | May he prolong our days of life.

Daśati 1:2:2:5. Indra and others.

1. Ne'er is he injured whom the Gods Varuṇa, Mitra, Aryaman. | The excellently wise, protect. || 2. According to our wish for kine, for steeds and chariots, as of old, | Be gracious to our wealthy chiefs || 3. Indra, these spotted cows yield thee their butter and the milky draught, | Aiders, thereby, of sacrifice. || 4. That thou much-lauded! many-named! mayst, with this thought, that longs for milk, | Come to each Soma sacrifice. || 5. May bright Sarasvatī, endowed with plenteous wealth and spoil, enriched | With prayer, desire the sacrifice. || 6. Why amid the Nahuṣha tribes shall sate this Indra with his Soma juice? | He shall bring precious things to us. || 7. Come, we have pressed the juice for thee; O Indra, drink this Soma here: | Sit thou on this my sacred grass || 8. Great, unassailable must be the heavenly favour of the Three, | Varuṇa, Mitra, Aryaman. || 9. We, Indra, Lord of ample wealth, our guide, depend on one like thee, | Thou driver of the tawny steeds!

Prapāṭhaka 3.

Ardha 1.

Daśati 1:3:1:1. Indra.

1. Let Soma juices make thee glad! Display thy bounty, Thunderer: | Drive off the enemies of prayer! || 2. Drink our libation, Lord of hymns! with streams of meath thou art bedewed: | Yea, Indra, glory is thy gift. || 3. Indra hath ever thought of you and tended you with care. The God, | Heroic Indra, is not checked. || 4. Let the drops pass within thee as the rivers flow into the sea | O Indra, naught excelleth thee! || 5. Indra, the singers with high praise, Indra reciters with their lauds, | Indra the choirs have glorified. || 6. May Indra give, to aid us wealth handy that rules the skilful ones! | Yea, may the Strong give potent wealth || 7. Verily Indra, conquering

all, drives even mighty fear away, | For firm is he and swift to act. || 8. These songs with every draught we pour come, lover of the song, to thee | As milch-kine hasten to their calves. || 9. Indra and Pūshan will we call for friendship and prosperity, | And for the winning of the spoil. || 10. O Indra, Vṛitra-slayer, naught is better, mightier than thou | Verily there is none like thee!

Daśati 1:3:1:2. Indra.

1. Him have I magnified, our Lord in common, guardian of your folk, | Discloser of great wealth in kine. || 2. Songs have outpoured themselves to thee, Indra, the strong, the guardian Lord, | And with one will have risen to thee! || 3. Good guidance hath the mortal man whom Aryaman, the Marut host, | And Mitras, void of guile, protect. || 4. Bring us the wealth for which we long, O Indra, that which is concealed | In strong firm place precipitous. || 5. Him your best Vṛitra-slayer, him the famous champion of mankind | I urge to great munificence. || 6. Indra, may we adorn thy fame, fame of one like thee, hero! deck, | Śakra! thy fame at highest feast! || 7. Indra, accept at break of day our Soma mixt with roasted corn, | With groats, with cake, with eulogies! || 8. With waters' foam thou torest off, Indra, the head of Namuchi, | When thou o'ercamest all the foes. || 9. Thine are these Soma juices, thine, Indra, those still to be expressed: | Enjoy them, Lord of princely wealth! || 10. For thee, O Indra, Lord of light, Somas are pressed and grass is strewn: | Be gracious to thy worshippers!

Daśati 1:3:1:3. Indra and others.

1. We seeking strength, with Soma drops fill full your Indra like a well, | Most liberal, Lord of boundless might. || 2. O Indra, even from that place come unto us with food that gives | A hundred, yea, a thousand powers! || 3. The new-born Vṛitra-slayer asked his mother, as he seized his shaft, | Who are the, fierce and famous ones? || 4. Let us call him to aid whose hands stretch far, the highly-lauded, who | Fulfils the work to favour us || 5. Mitra who knoweth leadeth us, and Varuṇa who guideth straight, | And Aryaman in accord with Gods. || 6. When, even as she were present here, red Dawn hath shone from far away, | She spreadeth light on every side. || 7. Varuṇa, Mitra, sapient pair, pour fatness on our pastures, pour | Meath on the regions of the air! || 8. And, at our sacrifices, these, sons, singers, have enlarged their bounds, | So that the cows must walk knee-deep. || 9. Through all this world strode Vishṇu: thrice his foot he planted, and the whole | Was gathered in his footstep's dust.

Daśati 1:3:1:4. Indra.

1. Pass by the wrathful offerer; speed the man who pours libation, drink | The juice which he presents to thee! || 2. What is the word addressed to him, God great and excellently wise? | For this is what exalteth him. || 3, His wealth who hath no store of kine hath ne'er found out recited laud, | Nor song of praises that is sung. || 4. Lord of each thing that giveth strength, Indra delighteth most in lauds, | Borne by bay steeds, libations' friend. || 5. With wealth to our libation come, be not thou angry with us, like | A great man with a youthful bride. || 6. When, Vasu, wilt thou love the laud? Now let the Channel bring the stream. | The juice is ready to ferment. || 7. After the Seasons. Indra, drink the Soma from the Brahman's gift: | Thy friendship is invincible! | S. O Indra, lover of the song, we are the singers of thy praise | O Soma-drinker, quicken us! || 9. O Indra, in each fight and fray give to our bodies manly strength: | Strong Lord, grant ever-conquering might! || 10. For so thou art the brave man's friend; a hero, too, art thou, and strong: | So may thine heart be won to us!

Daśati 1:3:1:5. Indra.

1. Like kine unmilked we call aloud, hero, to thee, and sing thy praise, | Looker on heavenly light, Lord of this moving world, Lord, Indra, of what moveth not! || 2. That we may win us wealth and power we poets, verily, call on thee: | In war men call on thee, Indra, the hero's Lord, in the steed's race-course call on thee: || 3. To you will I sing Indra's praise who gives good gifts as well we know; | The praise of Maghavan who, rich in treasure, aids his singers with wealth thousandfold. || 4. As cows low to their calves in stalls, so with our songs we glorify | This Indra, even your wondrous God who checks attack, who takes delight in precious juice. || 5. Loud singing at the sacred rite where Soma flows we priests invoke | With haste, that he may help, as the bard's cherisher, Indra who findeth wealth for you || 6. With Plenty for his true ally the active man will gain the spoil. | Your Indra, much-invoked, I bend with song, as bends a wright his wheel of solid wood. || 7. Drink, Indra, of the savoury juice, and cheer thee with our milky draught! | Be, for our weal, our friend and sharer of the feast, and let thy wisdom guard us well! || 8. For thou—come to the worshipper!—wilt find great wealth to make us rich. | Fill thyself full, O Maghavan, for gain of kine, full, Indra, for the gain of steeds! || 9. Vasishṭha will not overlook the lowliest one among you all | Beside our Soma juice effused today let all the Marutas drink with eager haste! || 10. Glorify naught besides, O friends; so shall no sorrow trouble you! | Praise only mighty Indra when the juice is shed, and say your lauds repeatedly!

Ardha 2.

Daśati 1:3:2:1. Indra.

1. No one by deed attains to him who works and strengthens evermore: | No, not by sacrifice, to Indra praised of all, resistless, daring, bold in might. || 2. He without ligature, before making incision in the neck, | Closed up the wound again, most wealthy Maghavan, who healeth the dissevered parts. || 3. A thousand and a hundred steeds are harnessed to thy golden car: | Yoked by devotion, Indra, let the long-maned bays bring thee to drink the Soma juice! || 4. Come hither, Indra, with bay steeds, joyous, with tails like peacock's plumes! | Let no men check thy course as fowlers stay the bird: pass o'er them as o'er desert lands! || 5. Thou as a God, O mightiest, verily blessest mortal man. | O Maghavan, there is no comforter but thou: Indra, I speak my words to thee. || 6. O Indra, thou art far-renowned, impetuous Lord of power and might. | Alone, the never-conquered guardian of mankind, thou smitest | down resistless foes. || 7. Indra for worship of the Gods, Indra while sacrifice proceeds, | Indra, as warriors in the battle-shock, we call, Indra that we may win the spoil. || 8. May these my songs of praise exalt thee, Lord, who hast abundant wealth! | Men skilled in holy hymns, pure, with the hues of fire, have sung them with their lauds to thee. || 9. These songs of ours exceeding sweet, these hymns of praise ascend to thee, | Like ever-conquering chariots that display their strength gain wealth and give unfailing help. || 10. Even as the wild-bull, when he thirsts, goes to the desert's watery pool, | Come to us quickly both at morning and at eve, and with the Kaṇvas drink thy fill!

Daśati 1:3:2:2. Indra and others.

1. Indra, with all thy saving helps assist us, Lord of power and might! | For after thee we follow even as glorious bliss, thee, hero, finder-out of wealth. || 2. O Indra, Lord of light, what joys thou broughtest from the Asuras, | Prosper therewith, O Maghavan, him who lauds that deed, and those whose grass is trimmed for thee! || 3. To Aryaman and Mitra sing a reverent song, O pious one, | A pleasant hymn to Varuṇa who shelters us: sing ye a laud unto the Kings! || 4. Men with their lauds are urging thee, Indra, to drink the Soma first. | The Ṛibhus in accord have lifted up their voice, and Rudras sung thee as the first. || 5. Sing to your lofty Indra, sing, Marutas, a holy hymn of praise | Let Śatakratu, Vṛitra-slayer, slay the foe with hundred-knotted thunderbolt! || 6. To Indra sing the lofty hymn, Marutas! that slays the Vṛitras best, | Whereby the holy ones created for the God the light divine that ever wakes. || 7. O Indra, give us wisdom as a sire gives wisdom to his sons | Guide us, O much-invoked, in this our way: may we still live and look upon the light! || 8. O Indra, turn us not away: be present with us at our feast | For thou art our protection, yea, thou art our kin: O Indra, turn us not away! || 9. We compass these like waters, we whose grass is trimmed and Soma pressed. | Here where the filter pours its stream, thy worshippers round | thee, O Vṛitra-slayer, sit. || 10. All strength and valour that is found, Indra, in tribes of Nahushas, | And all the splendid fame that the Five Tribes enjoy, bring, yea, all manly powers at once!

Daśati 1:3:2:3. Indra.

1. Yea, verily thou art a Bull, our guardian, rushing like a bull: | Thou, mighty one, art celebrated as a Bull, famed as a Bull both near and far. || 2. Whether, O Śakra, thou be far, or, Vṛitra-slayer, near at hand, | Thence by heaven-reaching songs he who bath pressed the juice invites thee with thy long-maned steeds. || 3. In the wild raptures of the juice sing to your hero with high laud, to him the wise, | To Indra glorious in his name, the mighty one, even as the hymn alloweth it! || 4. O Indra, give us for our weal a triple refuge, triply strong! | Bestow a dwelling-place on our rich lords and me, and keep thy dart afar from these! || 5. Turning, as 'twere, to meet the Sun enjoy from Indra all good things! | When he who will be born is born with power we look to treasures as our heritage. || 6. The godless mortal

gaineth not this food, O thou whose life is long! | But one who yokes the bright-hued horses, Etaśas; then Indra yokes his tawny steeds. || 7. Draw near unto our Indra who must be invoked in every fight! | Come, thou most mighty Vṛitra-slayer, meet for praise, come to, libations and to hymns! || 8. Thine, Indra, is the lowest wealth, thou cherishest the midmost wealth, | Thou ever rulest all the highest: in the fray for cattle none resisteth thee. || 9. Where art thou? Whither art thou gone? For many a place attracts thy mind. | Haste, warrior, fort-destroyer, Lord of battle's din! haste, holy songs have sounded forth! || 10. Here, verily, yesterday we let the thunder-wielder drink his fill. | Bring him the juice poured forth in sacrifice today. Now range you by the glorious one!

Daśati 1:3:2:4. Indra.

1. He who as sovereign Lord of men moves with his chariots unrestrained, | The Vṛitra-slayer, vanquisher of fighting hosts, pre-eminent, is praised in song. || 2. Indra, give us security from that whereof we are afraid | Help us, O Maghavan, let thy favour aid us thus; drive away foes and enemies! || 3. Strong pillar thou, Lord of the home! armour of Soma-offerers! | The drop of Soma breaketh all the strongholds down, and Indra is the Ṛishis' friend. || 4. Verily, Sūrya, thou art great; truly, Āditya, thou art great! | O most admired for greatness of thy majesty, God, by thy greatness thou art great! || 5. Indra! thy friend, when fair of form and rich in chariots, steeds, and kine, | Hath ever vital power that gives him strength, and joins the company with radiant men. || 6. O Indra, if a hundred heavens and if a hundred earths were thine,— | No, not a hundred suns could match thee at thy birth, not both the worlds, O Thunderer! || 7. Though, Indra, thou art called by men eastward and west ward, north and south, | Thou chiefly art with Anava and Turvaśa, brave champion urged by men to come. || 8. Indra whose wealth is in thyself, what mortal will attack this man? | The strong will win the spoil on the decisive day through faith in thee, O Maghavan! || 9. First, Indra! Agni! hath this Maid come footless unto those with feet. | Stretching her head and speaking loudly with her tongue, she hath gone downward thirty steps. || 10. Come, Indra, very near to us with aids of firmly-based resolve | Come, most auspicious, with thy most auspicious help; good kinsman, with good kinsmen come!

Daśati 1:3:2:5. Indra.

1. Call to your aid the eternal one who shoots and none may shoot at him, | Inciter, swift, victorious, best of charioteers, unconquered, Tugriya's strengthener! || 2. Let none, no, not thy worshippers, delay thee far away from us | Even from faraway come thou unto our feast, or listen if already here! || 3. For Indra Soma-drinker, armed with thunder, press the Soma juice; | Make ready your dressed meats: cause him to favour us! The giver blesses him who gives. || 4. We call upon that Indra who, most active, ever slays the foe | With boundless spirit, Lord of heroes, manliest one, help thou and prosper us in fight! || 5. Ye rich in strength, through your great power vouchsafe us blessings day and night! | The offerings which we bring to you shall never fail gifts brought by us shall never fail. || 6. Whenever mortal worshipper will sing a bounteous giver's praise, | Let him with song inspired laud Varuṇa who supports the folk who follow varied rites. || 7. Drink milk to Indra in the joy of Soma juice, Medhātithi! | To golden Indra ever close to his bay steeds, the thunder-armed, the golden one! || 8. Both boons,—may Indra, hitherward turned listen to this prayer of ours, | And mightiest Maghavan, with thought inclined to us come near to drink the Soma juice! || 9. Not for an ample price dost thou, Stone-caster! give thyself away, | Not for a thousand, Thunderer! nor ten thousand, nor a hundred, Lord of countless wealth! || 10. O Indra, thou art more to me than sire or niggard brother is. | Thou and my mother, O good Lord, appear alike, to give me wealth abundantly.

Prapāṭhaka 4.

Ardha 1.

Daśati 1:4:1:1. Indra and others.

1. These Soma juice mixt with curd have been expressed for Indra here: | Come with thy bay steeds, Thunder-wielder, to our home, to drink them till they make thee glad! || 2. Indra, these Somas with their lauds have been prepared for thy delight. | Drink of the pleasant juice and listen to our songs; lover of song, reward the hymn! || 3. I call on thee, Sabardughā, this day, inspirer of the psalm. | Indra, the richly-yielding milch-cow who provides unfailing food in ample stream. || 4. Indra, the strong and lofty hills are powerless to bar thy way | None stays that act of thine when thou wouldst fain give wealth to one like me who sings thy praise. || 5. Who knows what vital power he wins, drinking beside the flowing juice? | This is the fair-cheeked. God who, joying in the draught, breaks down the castles in his strength. || 6. What time thou castest from his seat and punishest the riteless man, | Strengthen for opulence, O Indra Maghavan, our plant desired by many a one! || 7. Let Tvaṣhṭar, Brahmaṇaspati, Parjanya guard our heavenly word, | Aditi with her sons, the brothers, guard for us the invincible, the saving word! || 8. Ne'er art thou fruitless, Indra, ne'er dost thou desert the worshipper: | But now, O Maghavan, thy bounty as a God is poured forth ever more and more. || 9. Best slayer of the Vṛitras, yoke thy bay steeds, Indra, far away | Come with the high ones hither, Maghavan, to us, mighty, to, drink the Soma juice! || 10. O Thunderer, zealous worshippers gave thee drink this time yesterday: | So, Indra, listen here to him who offers lauds: come near unto, our dwelling-place!

Daśati 1:4:1:2. Indra and others.

1. Advancing, sending forth her rays, the daughter of the Sky is seen. | The mighty one lays bare the darkness with her eye, the friendly Lady makes the light. || 2. These morning sacrifices call you, Aśvins, at the break of day. | For help have I invoked you rich in power and might: for, house by house, ye visit all. || 3. Where are ye, Gods? What mortal man, O Aśvins, glows with zeal for you, | Urging you with the crushing stone and with the stalk of Soma thus or otherwise? || 4. This sweetest Soma juice hath been expressed for you at morning rites. | Aśvins, drink this prepared ere yesterday and give treasures to him who offers it! || 5. Let me not, still beseeching thee with might and sound of Soma drops, | Anger at sacrifice a fierce wild creature! Who would not beseech the almighty one! || 6. Adhvaryu, let the Soma flow, for Indra longs to drink thereof. | He even now hath yoked his vigorous bay steeds: the Vṛitra-slayer hath come nigh. || 7. Bring thou all this unto the good, O Indra, to the old and young! | For, Maghavan, thou art rich in treasures from of old, to be invoked in every fight. || 8. If I, O Indra, were the lord of riches ample as thine own, | I would support the singer, God who scatterest wealth! and not abandon him to woe. || 9. Thou in thy battles, Indra, art subduer of all hostile bands. | Father art thou, all-conquering, cancelling the curse, thou victor of the vanquisher! || 10. For in thy might thou stretchest out beyond the mansions of the sky. | The earthly region, Indra, comprehends thee not. Thou hast waxed mighty over all.

Daśati 1:4:1:3. Indra.

1. Pressed is the juice divine with milk commingled: thereto hath Indra ever been accustomed. | We wake thee, Lord of bays, with sacrifices: mark this our laud in the wild joys of Soma! || 2. A home is made for thee to dwell in, Indra: O much-invoked one, with the men go thither! | Thou, that thou mayest guard us and increase us, givest us wealth and joyest in the Somas. || 3. The well thou clavest, settest free the fountains, and gavest rest to floods that were obstructed. | Thou, Indra, laying the great mountain open, slaying the Dānava, didst loose the torrents. || 4. When we have pressed the juice we laud thee, Indra, most valorous! even about to win the booty. | Bring us prosperity, and by thy great wisdom, under thine own protection, may we conquer! || 5. Thy right hand have we grasped in ours, O Indra, longing, thou very Lord of wealth, for treasures. | Because we know thee, hero, Lord of cattle: vouchsafe us mighty and resplendent riches! || 6. Men call on Indra in the armed encounter that he may make the hymns they sing decisive. | Hero in combat and in love of glory, give us a portion of the stall of cattle! || 7. Like birds of beauteous wing the Priyamedhas, Ṛishis, imploring, have come nigh to Indra. | Dispel the darkness and fill full our vision: deliver us as men whom snares entangle! || 8. They gaze on thee with longing in their spirit, as on a strong-winged bird that mounteth sky-ward; | On thee with wings of gold, Varuṇa's envoy, the Bird that hasteneth to the home of Yama. || 9. First in the ancient time was Prayer engendered: Vena disclosed the bright ones from the summit, | Laid bare this world's lowest and highest regions, womb of the existent and the non-existent. || 10. They have prepared and fashioned for this hero words never matched, most plentiful, most auspicious, | For him the ancient, great, strong, energetic, the very mighty wielder of the thunder.

Daśati 1:4:1:4. Indra.

1. The black drop sank in Aṃśumatī's bosom, advancing with ten thousand round about it. | Indra with might longed for it as it panted: the hero-hearted King laid down his weapons. || 2. Flying in terror from the snort of Vṛitra all deities who were thy friends forsook thee. | So, Indra, with the Marutas be thy friendship: in all these battles thou shalt be the victor. || 3. The old hath waked the young Moon from his slumber who runs his circling course with many round him. | Behold the God's high wisdom in its greatness: he who died yesterday today is living. || 4. Then, at thy birth, thou wast the foeman, Indra, of those the seven who ne'er had met a rival. | The hidden pair, heaven and the earth, thou foundest, and to the mighty worlds thou gavest pleasure. || 5. A friend we count thee, sharp-edged, thunder-wielder, Steer strong of body, overthrowing many. | Thou, helping, causest pious tribes to conquer: Indra, I laud the, heavenly Vṛitra-slayer || 6. Bring to the wise, the great, who waxeth mighty your offerings, and make ready your devotion! | Go forth to many tribes as man's controller! || 7. Call we on Maghavan, auspicious Indra, best hero in this fight where spoil is gathered, | Strong, listening to give us aid in battles, who slays the Vṛitras, wins and gathers riches! || 8. Prayers have been offered up-through love of glory: Vasiṣhṭha, honour Indra in the battle! | He who with fame extends through all existence hears words which I, his faithful servant, utter. || 9. May the sweet Soma juices make him happy to cast his quoit that lies in depth of waters! | Thou from the udder which o'er earth is fastened hast poured the milk into the kine and herbage.

Daśati 1:4:1:5. Indra and others.

1. This vigorous one whom deities commission, the conqueror of cars, the strong and mighty, | Swift, fleet to battle, with uninjured fellies, even Tārkṣhya for our weal will we call hither. || 2. Indra the rescuer, Indra the helper, hero who listens at each invocation, | Śakra I call, Indra invoked of many. May Indra Maghavan accept our presents! || 3. Indra whose right hand wields the bolt we worship, driver of bay steeds seeking sundered courses. | Shaking his beard with might he hath arisen, terrible with his weapons, with his bounty. || 4. The ever-slaying, bold and furious Indra, the bright bolt's Lord, the strong, the great, the boundless, | Who slayeth Vṛitra and acquireth booty, giver of blessings, Maghavan the bounteous. || 5. The man who lies in wait and fights against us, deeming himself a giant or a hero,— | By battle or with strength destroy him, Indra! With thy help, manly-souled! may we be victors! || 6. He whom men call when striving with their foemen, or speeding onward in array of battle, | Whom bards incite where heroes win the booty, or in the way to waters, He is Indra. || 7. On a high car, O Parvata and Indra, bring pleasant viands, with brave heroes, hither! | Enjoy our presents, Gods, at sacrifices: wax strong by hymns, rejoice in our oblation! || 8. In ceaseless flow hath he poured forth his praises, as waters from the ocean's depth, to Indra, | Who to his car on both its sides securely hath fixed the earth and heaven as with an axle. || 9. May our friends turn thee hitherward to friendship! Mayst thou approach us even o'er many rivers! | May the Disposer, radiant in this mansion with special lustre, bring the father's offspring! || 10. Who yokes today unto the pole of Order the strong and passionate steers of checkless spirit, | Health-bringing, bearing in their mouths no fodder? Long shall he live who richly pays their service.

Ardha 2.

Daśati 1:4:2:1. Indra.

1. The singers hymn thee, they who chant the psalm of praise are lauding thee. | The Brahmans have exalted thee, O Śatakratu, like a pole. || 2. All sacred-songs have magnified Indra expansive as the sea, | Best of all warriors borne on cars, the Lord of heroes, Lord of strength. || 3. This poured libation, Indra, drink, immortal, gladdening, excellent: | Streams of the bright have flowed to thee here at the seat of holy Law. || 4. Stone-darting Indra, wondrous God, what wealth thou hast not given me here, | That bounty, treasure-finder! bring, filling full both thy hands, to us! || 5. O Indra, hear Tiraśchi's call, the call of him who serveth thee! | Satisfy him with wealth of kine and valiant offspring! Great art thou. || 6. This Soma hath been pressed for thee, O Indra: bold one, mightiest, come! | May Indra-vigour fill thee full, as Sūrya fills mid-air with rays || 7. Come hither, Indra, with thy bays, come thou to Kaṇva's eulogy! | Ye by command of yonder Dyaus, God bright by day! have gone to heaven. || 8. Song-lover! like a charioteer come songs to thee when Soma flows. | Together, they have called to thee as mother-kine unto their calves. || 9. Come now and let us glorify pure Indra with pure Sāman hymn! | Let milk-blent juice delight him made stronger with pure, pure songs of praise! || 10. That which, most wealthy, makes you rich, in splendours most illustrious, | Soma is pressed: thy gladdening drink, Indra libation's Lord! is this.

Daśati 1:4:2:2. Indra Dadhikrāvan.

1. Bring forth oblations to the God who knoweth all who fain would drink, | The wanderer, lagging not behind the hero, coming nigh with speed! || 2. To us the mighty, lying in all vital power, who resteth in the deep, who standeth in the east. | Drive thou the awful word away. || 3. Even as a car to give us aid, we draw thee nigh to favour us, | Strong in thy deeds, quelling attack, Indra, Lord, mightiest! of the brave. || 4. With powers of mighty ones hath he, the friend, the ancient, been equipped, | Through whom our father Manu made prayers efficacious with the Gods. || 5. What time the swift and shining steeds, yoked to the chariots, draw them on, | Drinking the sweet delightful juice, there men perform their glorious acts. || 6. Him for your sake I glorify as Lord of Strength who wrongeth none, | Indra the hero, mightiest, all-conquering and omniscient. || 7. I with my praise have glorified strong Dadhikrāvan, conquering steed | Sweet may he make our mouths: may he prolong the days we have to live! || 8. Render of forts, the young, the wise, of strength unmeasured, was he born, | Sustainer of each sacred rite, Indra, the Thunderer, much-extolled.

Daśati 1:4:2:3. Indra and others.

1. Offer the triple sacred draught to Indu hero-worshipper! | With hymn and plenty he invites you to complete the sacrifice. || 2. Those whom they call the attendant pair of Kaśyapa who knows the light, | Lords of each holy duty when the wise have honoured sacrifice. || 3. Sing, sing ye forth your songs of praise, men, Priyamedhas, sing your songs: | Yea, let young children sing their lauds: yea, glorify our firm stronghold! || 4. To Indra must a laud be said, a joy to him who freely gives, | That Śakra may be joyful in our friendship and the juice we pour. || 5. Your Lord of might that ne'er hath bent, that ruleth over all mankind, | I call, that he, as he is wont, may aid the chariots and the men. || 6. Even he who is thine own, through thought of Heaven, of mortal man who toils, | He with the help of lofty Dyaus comes safe through straits of enmity. || 7. Wide, Indra Śatakratu, spreads the bounty of thine ample grace: | So, good and liberal giver, known to all men, send us splendid wealth! || 8. Bright Uṣhas, when thy times return, all quadrupeds and bipeds stir, | And round about flock winged birds from all the boundaries of heaven. || 9. Ye Gods who yonder have your home amid the luminous realm of heaven, | What count ye right? what endless life? What is the ancient call on you? || 10. We offer laud and psalm wherewith men celebrate their holy rites. | They govern at the sacred place and bear the sacrifice to Gods.

Daśati 1:4:2:4. Indra.

1. Heroes of one accord brought forth and formed for kingship Indra who wins the victory in all encounters, | For power, in firmness, in the field, the great destroyer, fierce and exceeding strong,stalwart and full of vigour. || 2. I trust in thy first wrathful deed, O Indra, when thou slewest Vṛitra and didst work to profit man; | When the two world-halves fled for refuge unto thee, and earth even trembled at thy strength, O Thunder-armed! || 3. Come all with might together to the Lord of heaven, the only one who is indeed the guest of men. | He is the first: to him who fain would come to us all pathways turn; he is in truth the only one. || 4. Thine, Indra, praised of many, excellently rich, are we who trusting in thy help draw near to thee. | For none but thou, song-lover, shall receive our lauds: as Earth loves all her creatures, welcome this our hymn! || 5. High hymns have sounded forth the praise of Maghavan, supporter of mankind, of Indra meet for lauds; | Him who hath waxen mighty, much-invoked with prayers, immortal one whose praise each day is sung aloud. || 6. In perfect unison have all your longing hymns that find the light of heaven sounded forth Indra's praise. | As wives embrace their lord, the comely bridegroom, so they compass Maghavan about that he may help. || 7. Make glad with songs that Ram whom many men invoke, worthy hymns of praise, Indra the sea of wealth; | Whose boons spread like the heavens, the lover of mankind: sing praise to him the Sage, most liberal for our good! || 8. I glorify that Ram who finds the light of heaven, whose hundred strong and mighty ones go

forth with him. | With prayers may I turn hither Indra to mine aid;-the car which like a swift steed hasteth to the call! || 9. Filled full of fatness, compassing all things that be, wide, spacious, dropping meath, beautiful in their form, | The heaven and the earth by Varuṇa's decree, unwasting, rich in germs, stand parted each from each. || 10. As like the Morning, thou hast filled, O Indra, both the earth. and heaven, | So as the mighty one, great King of all the mighty race of men, the Goddess mother brought thee forth, the blessed mother gave thee life. || 11. Sing, with oblation, praise to him who maketh glad, who with. Ṛijiśvan drove the dusky brood away! | Let us, desiring help, call him for friendship, him the strong, the Marut-girt, whose right hand wields the bolt!

Daśati 1:4:2:5. Indra.

1. When Somas flow thou makest pure, Indra, thy mind that merits laud | For gain of strength that ever grows: for great is he. || 2. Sing forth to him whom many men invoke, to him whom many laud: | Invite the potent Indra with your songs of praise || 3. We sing this strong and wild delight of thine which conquer; in the fray, | Which, Caster of the Stone! gives room and shines like gold, || 4. Whether thou drink the Soma by Vishṇu's or Trita Āptya's side, | Or with the Marutas, Indra! quaff the following drops. || 5. Come, priest, and of the savoury juice pour forth a yet more gladdening draught: | So is the hero praised who ever prospers us. || 6. Pour out the drops for Indra; let him drink the meath of Soma juice! | He through his majesty sends forth his bounteous gifts. || 7. Come, sing we praise to Indra, friends! the hero who deserves the laud, | Him who with none to aid o'ercomes all tribes of men. || 8. Sing ye a psalm to Indra, sing a great song to the lofty Sage, | To him who maketh prayer, inspired who loveth laud! || 9. He who alone bestoweth wealth on mortal man who offereth gifts | Is Indra only, potent Lord whom none resist. || 10. Companions, let us learn a prayer to Indra, to the Thunderer, | To glorify your bold and most heroic friend!

Prapāṭhaka 5.

Ardha 1.

Daśati 1:5:1:1. Indra Ādityas.

1. Indra, this might of thine I praise most highly for the sacrifice | That thou, O Lord of Power, dost slay Vṛitra with might || 2. For thee this Soma hath been pressed, in whose wild joy thou madest once | Śambara Divodāsa's prey: O Indra, drink! || 3. Come unto us, O Indra, dear, still conquering, unconcealable! | Wide as a mountain spread on all sides, Lord of heaven! || 4. Joy, mightiest Indra, that perceives, sprung from deep Soma draughts, whereby | Thou smitest down the greedy fiend,—that joy we crave! || 5. Ādityas, very mighty ones, grant to our children and our seed | This lengthened term of life that they may live long days! || 6. Though knowest, Indra, Thunder-armed! how to avoid destructive powers, | As one secure from pitfalls each returning day. || 7. Drive ye disease and strife away, drive ye away malignity: | Ādityas, keep us far removed from sore distress! || 8. Drive Soma, Indra, Lord of bays! and let it cheer thee: the stone, like a well-guided courser.

Daśati 1:5:1:2. Indra.

1. Still, Indra, from all ancient time rivalless ever and companionless art thou: | Thou seekest friendship but in war. || 2. Him who of old hath brought to us this and that blessing, him I magnify for you, | Even Indra, O my friends, for help. || 3. Fail not when marching onward: come hither, like-spirited, stay not far away | Ye who can tame even what is firm! || 4. Come hither to the dropping juice, O Lord of corn-land Lord of horses, Lord of kine: | Drink thou the Soma, Soma's Lord! || 5. Hero, may we, with thee for friend, withstand the man who pants against us in his wrath, | In fight with people rich in kine! || 6. Yea, kin by common ancestry, the Marutas, even the oxen, close united friends! | Are licking one another's back. || 7. O Indra, bring great strength to us, bring valour, Śatakratu, thou most active, bring | A hero conquering in war! || 8. So, Indra, friend of song, do we draw nigh to thee with longing; we have streamed to thee | Coming like floods that follow floods || 9. Sitting like birds beside thy meath, mingled with milk, which gladdeneth and exalteth thee, | Indra, to thee we sing aloud. || 10. We call on thee, O matchless one! We, seeking help, possessing nothing firm ourselves, | Call on thee, wondrous, Thunder-armed.

Daśati 1:5:1:3. Indra.

1. The juice of Soma thus diffused, sweet to the taste the bright cows drink, | Who travelling in splendour close to mighty Indra's side rejoice, good in their own supremacy. || 2. Thus hath the Soma, gladdening draught, produced the prayer that giveth joy: | Thou, mightiest, Thunder-armed, hast driven by force the Dragon from the earth, lauding thine own supremacy. || 3. By men hath Indra been advanced, the Vṛitra-slayer, to joy and strength. | Him only we invoke for help in battles whether great or small: be he our aid in deeds of might! || 4. Unconquered strength is only thine, Indra, Stone-caster, Thunder-armed! | When thou with thy surpassing power smotest to death that guileful beast, lauding thine own supremacy. || 5. Go forward, meet the foe, be bold; thy bolt of thunder is not checked! | Manliness, Indra, is thy strength. Slay Vṛitra, make the waters thine, lauding thine own supremacy! || 6. When war and battles are on foot, booty is offered to the bold. | Yoke thou thy wildly-rushing bays. Whom wilt thou slay, and whom enrich? Do thou, O Indra, make us rich! || 7. Well have they eaten and rejoiced; the friends have risen and passed away: | The sages luminous in themselves have praised thee with their latest hymn. Now, Indra, yoke thy two bay steeds! || 8. Graciously listen to our songs. Maghavan, be not negligent! | When wilt thou make us glorious? Make this, only this thine end and aim. Now, Indra! yoke thy two bay steeds. || 9. Within the waters runs the Moon, he with the beauteous wings in heaven. | Ye lightnings with your golden wheels, men find not your abiding-place. Mark this my woe, ye Earth and Sky! || 10. To meet your treasure-bringing car, the mighty car most dear to us. | Aśvins, the Ṛishi is prepared, your worshipper, with songs of praise. Lovers of sweetness, hear my call!

Daśati 1:5:1:4. Agni and others.

1. O Agni, God, we kindle thee, refulgent, wasting not away, | That this more glorious fuel may send forth for thee its shine to heaven. Bring food to those who sing thy praise! || 2. With offerings of our own we choose thee, Agni, as our Hotar priest, | Piercing and brightly shining-at your glad carouse-served with trimmed grass at sacrifice. Thou waxest great. || 3. O heavenly Dawn, awaken us to ample opulence today, | Even as thou didst waken us with Satyaśravas, Vayya's son, high born! delightful with thy steeds! || 4. Send us a mind that brings delight, send energy and mental power. | Then-at your glad carouse-let men joy in thy love, sweet juice! as kine in pasturage. Thou waxest great, || 5. Great, as his nature is, through power, terrible, he hath waxed in strength, | Lord of bay steeds, strong-jawed, sublime, he in joined hands for glory's sake hath grasped his iron thunderbolt. || 6. He, Indra, verily will mount the powerful car that finds the kine, | Who thinks upon the well-filled bowl, the tawny coursers' harnesser. Now, Indra, yoke thy two bay steeds! || 7. I think of Agni who is kind, whom, as their home, the milch-kine seek: | Whom fleet-foot coursers seek as home, and strong enduring steeds as home. Bring food to those who sing thy praise! || 8. No peril, no severe distress, ye Gods, affects the mortal man | Whom Aryaman and Mitra lead, and Varuṇa, of one accord, beyond his foes.

Daśati 1:5:1:5. Soma Pavamāna.

1. Flow forth, O Soma, flow thou onward, sweet to Indra's Mitra's, Pūshan's, Bhaga's taste. || 2. Run forth to battle, conquering the Vṛitras; thou speedest to quell the foes like one exacting debts. || 3. Flow onward, Soma, as a mighty sea, as Father of the Gods, to every form. || 4. Flow onward, Soma, flow for mighty strength, as a strong courser, bathed, to win the prize. || 5. Fair Indu hath flowed on for rapturous joy, sage, for good fortune, in the waters' lap. || 6. In thee, effused. O Soma, we rejoice ourselves for great supremacy in fight: | Thou, Pavamāna, enterest into mighty deeds. || 7. Who are these radiant men in serried rank, Rudra's young heroes, too, with noble steeds? || 8. Agni, with hymns may we now accomplish that which thou lovest, | Strength, like a horse, auspicious strength with service. || 9. The strong youths have come forth to view, to show their strength, God Savitar's quickening energy: | Ye warrior horsemen, win the heavens. || 10. Soma, flow splendid with thy copious stream in due succession through the ample fleece.

Ardha 2.

Daśati 1:5:2:1. Indra.

1. Giver from all sides, bring to us from every side, thou whom as strongest

we entreat! ‖ 2. This Brahman, comer at due time, named Indra, is renowned and praised. ‖ 3. The Brahmans with their hymns exalting Indra increased his strength that he might slaughter Ahi. ‖ 4. Anavas wrought a chariot for thy courser, and Tvashṭar, much-invoked! the bolt that glitters: ‖ 5. Rest, wealth to him who longs for wealth! the riteless stirs not his love nor wins his way to riches. ‖ 6. The cows are ever pure and all-supporting, the Gods are ever free from stain and blemish. ‖ 7. With all thy beauty come! The kine approaching with full udders follow on thy path. ‖ 8. May we, inhabiting a meath-rich dwelling, increase our wealth, and think of thee, O Indra! ‖ 9. The Marutas with fair hymns chant out their praise-song: this Indra, famed and youthful, shouts accordant. ‖ 10. Sing to your Indra, mightiest Vṛitra-slayer, sing to the Sage the song that he accepteth!

Daśati 1:5:2:2. Agni Indra.

1. Observant Agni hath appeared, oblation-bearer with his car. ‖ 2. O Agni, be our nearest friend, yea, our protector and our kind deliverer! ‖ 3. Like wondrous Bhaga, Agni deals treasure among the mighty. ‖ 4. Far off or present even now, send forth thy shouting first of all! ‖ 5. Dawn drives away her sister's gloom, and through her excellence makes her retrace her path. ‖ 6. May we, with Indra and the Gods to aid us, bring these existing worlds to full completion! ‖ 7. Like streams of water on their way, let bounties, Indra, flow from thee! ‖ 8. With this may we obtain strength God-appointed, happy with brave sons through a hundred winters! ‖ 9. With strength let Mitra, Varuṇa swell oblations; do thou prepare for us rich food, O Indra! ‖ 10. Indra is King of all the world.

Daśati 1:5:2:3. Indra and others.

1. At the Trikadrukas the great and strong enjoyed the barley-brew. With Vishṇu did he drink the pressed-out Soma juice, even as he would. | That hath so heightened him the great, the wide to do his mighty work. So did the God attend the God, true Indu Indra who is true. ‖ 2. This God who sees for thousands of mankind, the light, the thought of poets, and the Law, | The brilliant one, hath sent forth hither all the Dawns: spotless, one-minded, zealous in their home they dwell, with thought upon the Steer. ‖ 3. Come to us, Indra, from afar, conducting us, as, to the gatherings, a Lord of heroes, as an archer King, the heroes' Lord! | We come with gifts of pleasant food, with flowing juice, invoking thee, as sons invite a sire, that we may win the spoil, thee, bounteousest, for gain of spoil. ‖ 4. Loudly I call that Indra Maghavan, the mighty, resistless, evermore possessing many glories. | Holy, most liberal, may he lead us on to riches, through songs, and, thunder-armed make all our pathways pleasant! ‖ 5. Heard be our prayer! In thought I honour Agni first: now straightway we elect this heavenly company, Indra and Vāyu we elect. | For when our latest thought is raised and on Vivasvat centred well, then do our holy songs go forward on their way, our songs as 'twere unto the Gods. ‖ 6. To Vishṇu, to the mighty whom the Marutas follow, let your hymns born in song go forth, Evayāmarut! | To the strong, very holy band adorned with bracelets, that rushes on in joy and ever roars for vigour! ‖ 7. With this his golden splendour purifying him, be with his own allies subdues all enemies, as Sūra with his own allies. | Cleansing himself with stream of juice he shines forth yellow-hued and red, when with the praisers he encompasses all, forms, with praisers having seven mouths. ‖ 8. I praise this God, parent of heaven and earth, exceeding wise, possessed of real energy, giver of treasure, thinker dear to all, | Whose splendour is sublime, whose light shone brilliant in, creation, who, wise and golden-handed, in his beauty made the sky. ‖ 9. Agni I deem our Hotar-priest, munificent wealth-giver, Son of Strength, who, knoweth all that is, even as the Sage who, knoweth all. | Lord of fair rites, a God with form erected turning to the Gods, he, when the flame hath sprung forth from the holy oil, the offered fatness, longs for it as it glows bright. ‖ 10. This, Indra! dancer! was thy hero deed, thy first and ancient work, worthy to be told forth in heaven, | Even thine who furtheredst life with a God's own power, freeing the floods. All that is godless may he conquer with his might, and, Lord of Hundred Powers, find for us strength and food!

Pāvamāna Kāṇḍa.

Daśati 1:5:2:4. Soma Pavamāna.

1. High is thy juice's birth: though set it heaven, on earth it hath obtained dread sheltering power and great renown. ‖ 2. In sweetest and most gladdening stream flow pure, O Soma, on thy way, pressed out for Indra, for his drink! ‖ 3. Flow onward mighty with thy stream, inspiriting the Marutas' Lord, winning all riches with thy power! ‖ 4. Flow onward with that juice of thine most excellent, that brings delight, slaying the wicked, dear to Gods! ‖ 5. Three several words are uttered: kine are lowing, cows who give the milk; the tawny-hued goes bellowing on. ‖ 6. For Indra girt by Marutas, flow, thou Indu, very rich in meath, to seat thee in the place of song! ‖ 7. Strong, mountain-born, the stalk hath been pressed in the streams for rapturous joy. Hawk-like he settles in his home. ‖ 8. Gold-hued! as one who giveth strength flow on for Gods to drink, a draught for Vāyu and the Marut host! ‖ 9. Soma, the dweller on the hills, effused, hath flowed into the sieve. All-bounteous art thou in carouse. ‖ 10. The Sage of heaven whose heart is wise, when laid between both hands, with roars, gives us delightful powers of life.

Daśati 1:5:2:5. Soma Pavamāna.

1. The rapture-shedding Somas have flowed forth in our assembly, pressed to glorify our liberal lords. ‖ 2. The Somas, skilled in song, the waves, have led the water forward, like buffaloes speeding to the woods. ‖ 3. Indu flow on, a mighty juice; glorify us among the folk: drive all our enemies away! ‖ 4. For thou art strong by splendour: we, O Pavamāna, call on thee, the brilliant looker on the light. ‖ 5. Indu, enlightener, dear, the thought of poets, hath flowed clearly, like a charioteer who starts the steed. ‖ 6. Through our desire of heroes, kine, and horses, potent Soma drops, brilliant and swift, have been effused. | God, working with mankind, flow on; to Indra go thy gladdening juice: to Vāyu mount as Law commands! | From heaven hath Pavamāna made, as 'twere, the marvellous thunder, and the lofty light of all mankind. ‖ 9. Pressed for the gladdening draught the drops flow forth abundantly with song, flow onward with the stream of meath. ‖ 10. Reposing on the river's wave, the Sage hath widely flowed around, bearing the bard whom many love.

Prapāṭhaka 6.

Ardha 1.

Daśati 1:6:1:1. Soma Pavamāna.

1. The Gods have come to Indu well-descended, beautified with milk, the active crusher of the foe. ‖ 2. Active, while being purified, he hath assailed all enemies: they deck the Sage with holy hymns. ‖ 3. Pouring all glories hither, he, effused, hath passed within the jar: Indu on Indra is bestowed. ‖ 4. From the two press-boards is the juice sent, like a car-horse, to the sieve: the steed steps forward to the goal. ‖ 5. Impetuous, bright, have they come forth, unwearied in their speed, like bulls, driving the black skin far away. ‖ 6. Soma, thou flowest chasing foes, finder of wisdom and delight: drive thou the godless folk afar! | Flow onward with that stream wherewith thou gavest splendour to the Sun, speeding the waters kind to man! ‖ 8. Flow onward thou who strengthenedst Indra to slaughter Vṛitra who compassed and stayed the mighty floods! ‖ 9. Flow onward, Indu, with this food for him who in thy wild delights battered the nine-and-ninety down! ‖ 10. Flow, pressed, into the filter, speed the heavenly one who winneth wealth, who bringeth booty through our juice!

Daśati 1:6:1:2. Soma Pavamāna.

1. The tawny Bull hath bellowed, fair as mighty Mitra to behold: he gleams and flashes with the Sun. ‖ 2. We choose today that chariot-steed of thine, the strong, that brings us bliss, the guardian, the desire of all. ‖ 3. Adhvaryu, to the filter lead the Soma juice expressed with stones: make thou it pure for Indra's drink. ‖ 4. Swift runs this giver of delight, even the stream of flowing juice: Swift runs this giver of delight. ‖ 5. Pour hitherward, O Soma, wealth in thousands and heroic strength, and keep renown secure for us! | -6. The ancient living ones have come unto a newer resting-place. They made the Sun that he might shine. ‖ 7. Soma, flow on exceeding bright with loud roar to the reservoirs, resting in wooden vats, thy home! ‖ 8. O Soma, thou, art strong and bright, potent, O God, with potent sway: thou, mighty one, ordainest laws. ‖ 9. For food, flow onward with thy stream, cleansed and made bright by sapient men: Indu. with sheen approach the milk! ‖ 10. Soma, flow on with pleasant stream, strong and devoted to the Gods, our friend, unto the woollen sieve. ‖ 11. By this solemnity, Soma, thou, though great, hast been increased: in joy thou,

verily actest like a bull! || 12. Most active and benevolent, this Pavamāna sent to us for lofty friendship meditates. || 13. Indu, to us for this great rite, bearing as 'twere thy wave to Gods, unwearied, thou art flowing on. || 14. Chasing our foemen, driving off the godless, Soma floweth on, going to Indra's settled place.

Daśati 1:6:1:3. Soma Pavamāna.

1. Cleansing thee, Soma, in thy stream, thou flowest in a watery robe: giver of wealth, thou sittest in the place of Law, O God, a fountain made of gold. || 2. Hence sprinkle forth the juice effused, Soma, the best of sacred gifts, who, friend of man, hath run amid the water-streams! He hath pressed Soma out with stones. || 3. Expressed by stones, O Soma, and urged through the long wool of the sheep, thou, entering the press-boards even as men a fort, gold-hued hast settled in the vats. || 4. O Soma,—for the feast of Gods, river-like he hath swelled with surge, sweet with the liquor of the stalk, as one who wakes, into the vat that drops with meath. || 5. Pressed out by pressers, Soma goes over the fleecy backs of sheep, goes, even as with a mare, in tawny-coloured stream, goes in a sweetly-sounding stream. || 6. O Soma, Indu, every day thy friendship hath been my delight. Many fiends follow me help me, thou tawny-hued: pass on beyond these barriers! || 7. Deft-handed! thou when purified liftest thy voice amid the sea. Thou, Pavamāna, makest riches flow to us, yellow, abundant, much desired. || 8. The living drops of Soma juice pour, as they flow, the gladdening drink, intelligent drops above the station of the sea, exhilarating, dropping meath. || 9. Soma, while thou art cleansed, most dear and watchful in the sheep's long wool, most like to Aṅgiras! thou hast become a sage. Sprinkle our sacrifice with mead! || 10. Soma, the gladdening juice, flows pressed for Indra with his Marut host: he hastens o'er the fleece with all his thousand streams: him, him the men make pure and bright. || 11. Flow on, best winner of the spoil, to precious gifts of every sort! Thou art a sea according to the highest law, joy-giver, Soma! to the Gods || 12. Over the cleansing sieve have flowed the Pavamānas in a stream, girt by the Marutas, gladdening, steeds with Indra's strength, for wisdom and for dainty food.

Daśati 1:6:1:4. Soma Pavamāna.

1. Run onward to the reservoir and seat thee: cleansed by the men speed forward to the battle! | Making thee glossy like an able courser, forth to the sacred grass with reins they lead thee. || 2. The God declares the deities' generations, like Uśanā, proclaiming lofty wisdom. | With brilliant kin, far-ruling, sanctifying, the wild boar, singing with his foot, advances. || 3. Three are the voices that the car-steed utters: he speaks the lore of prayer, the thought of Order. | To the cows' master come the cows inquiring: the hymns with eager longing come to Soma. || 4. Made pure by this man's urgent zeal and impulse, the God hath with his juice the Gods pervaded. | Pressed, singing, to the sieve he goes, as passes the Hotar to enclosures holding cattle. || 5. Father of holy hymns Soma flows onward, the father of the earth, father of heaven; | Father of Agni, Sūrya's generator, the father who begat Indra and Vishṇu || 6. To him, praiseworthy, sacred tones have sounded, Steer of the triple height, the life-bestower. | Dwelling in wood, like Varuṇa, a river, lavishing treasure, he distributes blessings. || 7. Guard of all being, generating creatures, loud roared the sea as highest law commanded. | Strong, in the filter, on the fleecy summit, pressed from the stone, Soma hath waxen mighty. || 8. Loud neighs the tawny steed when started, settling deep in the wooden vessel while they cleanse him. | Led by the men he makes the milk his raiment; then shall he, of himself, engender worship. || 9. This thine own Soma, rich in meath, O Indra, the Strong, hath flowed into the Strong One's filter. | The swift steed, bounteous, giving hundreds, thousands, hath reached the sacred grass which never fails him. || 10. Flow onward, Soma, rich in meath, and holy, enrobed in waters, on the fleecy summit! | Settle in vessels that are full of fatness, as cheering and most gladdening drink for Indra!

Daśati 1:6:1:5. Soma Pavamāna.

1. In forefront of the cars forth goes the hero, the leader, seeking spoil: his host rejoices. | Soma endues his robe of lasting colours, and blesses, for his friends, their calls on Indra. || 2. Thy streams have been poured forth with all their sweetness, when, cleansed thou passest through the woollen filter. | The race of kine thou cleansest, Pavamāna! Thou didst beget: and speed the Sun with splendours. || 3. Let us sing praises to the Gods: sing loudly, send ye the Soma forth for mighty riches! | Let him flow, sweetly-flavoured, through the filter: let the God Indu settle in the beaker! || 4. Urged on, the father of the earth and heaven hath gone forth like a car to gather booty. | Going to Indra, sharpening his weapons, and in his hands containing every treasure. || 5. When, by the law of the Most High, in presence of heaven and earth, the fond mind's utterance formed him. | Then, loudly lowing, came the cows to Indu, the chosen, well-loved master in the beaker. || 6. Ten sisters, pouring out the rain together, the sage's quickly-moving thoughts, adorn him. | Hither hath run the gold-hued child of Sūrya, and reached the vat like a fleet vigorous courser. || 7. When beauties strive for him as for a charger, then strive the songs as people for the sunlight. | A mighty Sage, he flows enrobed in waters and hymns as 'twere a stall that kine may prosper. || 8. Strong Indu, bathed in milk, flows on for Indra, Soma exciting, strength, for his carousal. | He quells malignity and slays the demons, King of the homestead, he who gives us comfort. || 9. Pour forth this wealth with this purification: flow onward to the yellow lake, O Indu! | Here, too, the bright one, wind-swift, full of wisdom, shall give a son to him who cometh quickly. || 10. Soma, the mighty, when, the waters' offspring, he chose the Gods, performed that great achievement. | He, Pavamāna, granted strength to Indra: he, Indu, generated light in Sūrya. || 11. As for a chariot-race, the skilful speaker, first hymn, inventor, hath with song been started. | The sisters ten upon the fleecy summit adorn the car-horse in the resting-places. || 12. Hastening onward like the waves of waters our holy hymns are coming forth to Soma. | To him they go with lowly adoration, and, longing, enter him who longs to meet them.

Ardha 2.

Daśati 1:6:2:1. Soma Pavamāna.

1. For first possession of your juice. for the exhilarating drink, | Drive ye away the dog, my friends, drive ye the long-tongued dog away! || 2. As Pūshan Fortune, Bhaga, comes this Soma while they make him pure. | He, Lord of all the multitude, hath looked upon the earth and heaven. || 3. The Somas, very rich in sweets, for which the sieve is destined, flow | Effused, the source of Indra's joy: may your strong juices reach the Gods! || 4. For us the Soma juices flow, the drops best furtherers of weal, | Effused as friends, without a spot, benevolent, finders of the. light. || 5. Stream on us riches that are craved by hundreds, best at winning spoil, | Riches, O Indu, thousandfold, most splendid, that surpass the light! || 6. The guileless ones are singing praise to Indra's well-beloved friend, | As, in the morning of its life, the mothers lick the new-born calf. || 7. They for the bold and lovely one ply manly vigour like a bow; | Bright, glad, in front of songs they spread to form a vesture for the Lord. || 8. Him with the fleece they purify, brown, golden-hued, beloved of all, | Who with exhilarating juice goes forth to all the deities. || 9. Let him, as mortal, crave this speech, for him who presses, of the juice, | As Bhṛigu's sons chased Makha, so drive ye the niggard hound away!

Daśati 1:6:2:2. Soma Pavamāna.

1. Graciously-minded he is flowing on his way to win dear names o'er which the youthful one grows great. | The mighty and far-seeing one hath mounted now the mighty Sūrya's car which moves to every side. || 2. Spontaneous let our drops of Soma juice flow on, pressed out and tawny-coloured, mightily, to the Gods! | Still let our enemies, the godless, be in want, though filled with food; and let our prayers obtain success! || 3. Most beauteous of the beauteous, Indra's thunderbolt, this Soma, rich in sweets, hath clamoured in the vat. | Dropping with oil, abundant, streams of sacrifice flow unto him, and milch-kine, lowing, with their milk. || 4. Indu hath started forth for Indra's settled place, and slights not, as a friend, the promise of his friend. | Soma comes onward like a youth with youthful maids, and gains the beaker by a course of hundred paths. || 5. On flows the potent juice, sustainer of the heavens; the strength of Gods, whom men must hail with shouts of joy. | Thou, gold-hued, started like a courser by brave men, art lightly showing forth thy splendour in the streams. || 6. Far-seeing Soma flows, the Steer, the Lord of hymns, the furtherer of days, of mornings, and of heaven. | Breath of the rivers, he hath roared into the jars, and with the help of sages entered Indra's heart. || 7. The three-times seven milch-kine in the loftiest heaven have for this Soma poured the genuine milky draught. | Four other beauteous creatures

hath he made for his adornment when he waxed in strength through holy rites. ‖ 8. Flow on to Indra, Soma, carefully effused: let sickness stay afar together with the fiend! | Let not the double-tongued delight them with thy juice: here be thy flowing drops laden with opulence! ‖ 9. Even as a King hath Soma, red and tawny Bull, been pressed: the wondrous one hath bellowed to the kine. | While purified thou passest through the filtering fleece to seat thee hawk-like on the place that drops with oil. ‖ 10. The drops of Soma juice, like cows who yield their milk, have flowed forth, rich in meath, unto the deity, | And, seated on the grass, raising their voice, assumed the milk, the covering robe wherewith the address stream. ‖ 11. They balm him, balm him over, balm him thoroughly, caress the mighty strength and balm it with the meath. | They seize the flying Steer at the stream's breathing-place: cleansing with gold they grasp the animal herein. ‖ 12. Spread is thy cleansing filter, Brahmaṇaspati: as prince thou enterest its limbs from every side. | The raw, whose mass hath not been heated, gains not this: they only which are dressed, which bear, attain to it.

Daśati 1:6:2:3. Soma Pavamāna.

1. To Indra, to the mighty one, let these gold-coloured juices go, | Drops born as Law prescribes, that find the light of heaven. ‖ 2. Flow vigilant for Indra, thou Soma, yea, Indu, run thou forth; | Bring hither splendid strength that finds the light of heaven! ‖ 3. Sit down, O friends, and sing aloud to him who purifies himself. | Deck him for glory, like a child, with holy rites! ‖ 4. Friends, hymn your Lord who makes him pure for rapturous | carouse: let them | Sweeten him, as a child, with lauds and sacred gifts! ‖ 5. Breath of the mighty Dames, the Child, speeding the plan of sacrifice, | Surpasses all things that are dear, yea, from of old! ‖ 6. In might, O Indu, with thy streams flow for the banquet of the Gods: | Rich in meath, Soma, in our beaker take thy seat! ‖ 7. Soma, while filtered, with his wave flows through the long wool of the sheep, | Roaring, while purified, before the voice of song. ‖ 8. The speech is uttered for the Sage, for Soma being purified: | Bring meed as 'twere to one who makes thee glad with hymns! ‖ 9. Flow to us, Indu, very strong, effused, with wealth of kine and, steeds, | And do thou lay above the milk thy radiant hue! ‖ 10. Voices have sung aloud to thee as finder-out of wealth for us: | We clothe the hue thou wearest with a robe of milk. ‖ 11. Gold-hued and lovely in his course through tangles of the wool he flows: | Stream forth heroic fame upon the worshippers! ‖ 12. On through the long wool of the sheep to the meath-dropping vat he flows: | The Ṛishis' sevenfold quire hath sung aloud to him.

Daśati 1:6:2:4. Soma Pavamāna.

1. For Indra flow, thou Soma, on, as most inspiring drink, exceeding rich in sweets. | Great, most celestial, gladdening drink! ‖ 2. Make high and splendid glory shine hitherward, Lord of food, God, on the friend of Gods: | Unclose the cask of middle air! ‖ 3. Press ye and pour him, like a steed, laud-worthy, speeding through the region and the flood, | Who swims in water, dwells in wood! ‖ 4. Him, even this Steer who milks the heavens, him with a thousand streams, distilling rapturous joy, | Him who brings all things excellent. ‖ 5. Effused is he who brings good things, who brings us store of wealth and sweet refreshing food, | Soma who brings us quiet homes. ‖ 6. For, verily, Pavamāna, thou, divine! endued with brightest splendour calling all | Creatures to immortality. ‖ 7. Effused, he floweth in a stream, best rapture-giver, in the long wool of the sheep, | Sporting, as 'twere the waters' wave. ‖ 8. He who from out the rocky cavern with his might took forth the red-refulgent cows— | Thou drewest to thyself the stall of kine and steeds: burst it, | brave Lord, like one in mail; yea, burst it, O brave Lord, like one in mail!

Note: the Āraṇya Ārchika and the Mahānāmnya Ārchika are omitted in Griffith's translation, as they were not present in the Sanskrit edition (Benfey, 1848) which was utilized for this translation.—Ed.

Part 2. Uttara Ārchika.

Prapāṭhaka 1.

Ardha 1.

Om. Glory to the Sāmaveda! to Lord Gaṇeśa glory! Om.

Daśati 4:1:1:1. Soma Pavamāna.

1. Sing forth to Indu, O ye men, to him who now is purified, | Fain to pay worship to the Gods! ‖ 2, Together with thy pleasant juice the Atharvans have commingled. milk. | Divine, God-loving, for the God. ‖ 3. Bring health to cattle with thy flow, health to the people, health, to steeds, | Health, O thou King, to growing plants!

Daśati 4:1:1:2. Soma Pavamāna.

1. Bright are these Somas blent with milk, with light that flashes brilliantly, | And form that shouteth all around. ‖ 2. Roused by his drivers and sent forth, the strong Steed hath come: nigh for spoil, | As warriors when they stand arrayed. ‖ 3. Specially, Soma, Sage, by day, coming together for our weal, | Like Sūrya, flow for us to see!

Daśati 4:1:1:3. Soma Pavamāna.

1. The streams of Pavamāna, thine, Sage, mighty one, have poured them forth, | Like coursers eager for renown. ‖ 2. They have been poured upon the Reece towards the meath-distilling vat: | The holy songs have rung aloud. ‖ 3. Like milch-kine coming home, the drops of Soma juice have reached the lake, | Have reached the shrine of sacrifice.

Daśati 4:1:1:4. Agni.

1. Come, Agni, praised with song to feast and sacrificial offerings: sit | As Hotar on the holy grass! ‖ 2. So, Aṅgiras, we make thee strong with fuel and with holy oil. | Blaze high, thou youngest of the Gods! ‖ 3. For us thou winnest, Agni, God, heroic strength exceeding great, Far-spreading and of high renown.

Daśati 4:1:1:5. Mitra Varuṇa.

1. Varuṇa, Mitra, sapient pair, pour fatness on our pastures, pour | Meath on the regions of the air! ‖ 2, Gladdened by homage, ruling far, ye reign by majesty of might, | Pure in your ways, for evermore. ‖ 3. Lauded by Jamadagni's song, sit in the shrine of sacrifice: | Drink Soma, ye who strengthen Law!

Daśati 4:1:1:6. Indra.

1. Come, we have pressed the Juice for thee; O Indra, drink this Soma here: | Sit thou on this my sacred grass! ‖ 2. O Indra, let thy long-maned bays, yoked by prayer, bring thee hitherward! | Give ear and listen to our prayers! ‖ 3. We Soma-bearing Brahmans call thee Soma-drinker with thy friend, | We, Indra, bringing Soma juice.

Daśati 4:1:1:7. Indra Agni.

1. Indra and Agni, moved by songs, come to the juice, the precious dew: | Drink ye thereof, impelled by prayer! ‖ 2. Indra and Agni, with the man who lauds comes visible sacrifice: | So drink ye both this flowing juice! ‖ 3. With force of sacrifice I seek Indra, Agni who love the wise: | With Soma let them sate them here!

Daśati 4:1:1:8. Soma Pavamāna.

1. High is thy juice's birth: though set in heaven, on earth it hath obtained | Dread sheltering power and great renown. ‖ 2. Finder of room and freedom, flow for Indra whom we must adore, | For Varuṇa and the Marut host! ‖ 3. Striving to win, with him we gain all riches from the enemy, | Yea, all the glories of mankind.

Daśati 4:1:1:9. Soma Pavamāna.

1. Cleansing thee, Soma, in thy stream, thou flowest in watery robe. | Giver of wealth, thou sittest in the place of Law, O God, a fountain made of gold. ‖ 2. He, milking for dear meath the heavenly udder, hath sat in the ancient gathering-place. | Washed by the men, far-sighted, strong, thou streamest to the honourable reservoir.

Daśati 4:1:1:10. Soma Pavamāna.

1. Run onward to the reservoir and seat thee: cleansed by the men speed forward to the battle. | Making thee glossy like an able courser, forth to the sacred grass with reins they lead thee. ‖ 2. Indu, the well-armed God is flowing onward, he who averts the curse and guards the homesteads. |

Father, begetter of the Gods, most skilful, the buttress of the heavens and earth's supporter.

Daśati 4:1:1:11. Indra.

1. Like kine unmilked we call aloud, hero, to thee, and sing thy | praise, | Looker on heavenly light, Lord of this moving world, Lord, Indra! of what moveth not. || 2. None other like to thee, of earth or of the heavens, hath been or ever will be born. | Desiring horses, Indra Maghavan! and kine, as men of might we call on thee.

Daśati 4:1:1:12. Indra.

1. With what help will he come to us, wonderful, ever-waxing friend? | With what most mighty company? || 2. What genuine and most liberal draught will spirit thee with juice to burst | Open e'en strongly-guarded wealth? || 3. Do thou who art protector of us thy friends who praise thee | With hundred aids approach us!

Daśati 4:1:1:13. Indra.

1. As cows low to their calves in stalls, so with our songs we glorify | This Indra, even your wondrous God who checks attack, who takes delight in precious juice. || 2. Celestial, bounteous giver, girt about with might, rich, mountain-like, in pleasant things,— | Him swift we seek for foodful booty rich in kine, brought hundredfold and thousandfold.

Daśati 4:1:1:14. Indra.

1. Loud-singing at the sacred rite where Soma flows, we priests invoke. | With haste, that he may help, as the bard's cherisher. Indra who findeth wealth for you. || 2. Whom, fair of cheek, in rapture of the juice, the firm resistless slayers hinder not: | Giver of glorious wealth to him who sings his praise, honouring him who toils and pours.

Daśati 4:1:1:15. Soma Pavamāna.

1. In sweetest and most gladdening stream flow pure, O Soma, on thy way, | Pressed out for Indra, for his drink! || 2. Fiend-queller, friend of all men, he hath reached his shrine, his dwelling-place. | Within the iron-hammered vat. || 3. Be thou best Vṛitra-slayer, best granter of room, most liberal: | Promote our wealthy princes' gifts!

Daśati 4:1:1:16. Soma Pavamāna.

1. For Indra flow, thou Soma, on, as most inspiring drink, most rich in sweets, | Great, most Celestial, gladdening drink! || 2. Thou of whom having drunk the Steer acts like a steer: having drunk this that finds the light, | He, excellently wise, hath come anear to food and booty, even as Etaśa.

Daśati 4:1:1:17. Indra.

1. To Indra, to the mighty let these golden-coloured juices go, | Drops born as Law prescribes, that find the light of heaven! || 2. This juice that gathers spoil flows, pressed, for Indra, for his maintenance. | Soma bethinks him of the conqueror, as he knows. || 3. Yea, Indra in the joys of this obtains the grasp that gathers spoil, | And, winning waters, wields the mighty thunderbolt.

Daśati 4:1:1:18. Soma Pavamāna.

1. For first possession of your juice, for the exhilarating drink, | Drive ye away the dog, my friends, drive ye the long-tongued dog away! || 2. He who with purifying stream, effused, comes flowing hitherward, | Indu, is like an able steed. || 3. With prayer all-reaching let the men tend unassailable Soma: be | The stones prepared for sacrifice!

Daśati 4:1:1:19. Soma Pavamāna.

1. Graciously-minded he is flowing on his way to win dear names o'er which the youthful one grows great. | The mighty and far-seeing one hath mounted now the mighty | Sūrya's car which moves to every side. || 2. The speaker, unassailable master of this prayer, the tongue of sacrifice, pours forth the pleasant meath. | As son be sets the name of mother and of sire in the far distance, in the third bright realm of heaven. || 3. Sending forth flashes he hath bellowed to the jars, led by the men into the golden reservoir. | The milkers of the sacrifice have sung to him: Lord of three heights, thou shinest brightly o'er the Dawns.

Daśati 4:1:1:20. Agni.

1. Sing to your Agni with each song, at every sacrifice for strength! | Come, let us praise the wise and everlasting God, even as a well-beloved friend: || 2. The Son of Strength; for is be not our gracious Lord? Let us serve him who bears our gifts! | In battles may he be our help and strengthener, yea, be the saviour of our lives!

Daśati 4:1:1:21. Agni.

1. O Agni, come; far other songs of praise will I sing forth to thee. | Wax mighty with these Soma drops! || 2. Where'er thy mind applies itself, vigour preeminent hast thou: | There wilt thou gain a dwelling-place. || 3. Not for a moment only lasts thy bounty, Lord of many men: | Our service therefore shalt thou gain.

Daśati 4:1:1:22. Indra.

1. We call on thee, O matchless one. We, seeking help, possessing nothing firm ourselves. | Call on thee, wondrous, thunder-armed: || 2. On thee for aid in sacrifice, This youth of ours, the bold, the terrible, bath gone forth. | We therefore, we thy friends, Indra, have chosen thee, spoil winner, as our succourer.

Daśati 4:1:1:23. Indra.

1. So, Indra, friend of song, do we draw near to thee with longing; we have streamed to thee | Coming like floods that follow floods. || 2. As rivers swell the ocean, so, hero, our prayers increase thy might, | Though of thyself, O Thunderer, waxing day by day. || 3. With holy song they bind to the broad wide-yoked car the bay steeds of the quickening God, | Bearers of Indra, yoked by word.

Ardha 2.

Daśati 4:1:2:1. Indra.

1. Invite ye Indra with a song to drink your draught of Soma juice. | All-conquering Śatakratu, most munificent of all who live! || 2. Lauded by many, much-invoked, leader of song renowned of old: | His name is Indra, tell it forth! || 3. Indra, the dancer, be to us the giver of abundant wealth: | The mighty bring it us knee-deep!

Daśati 4:1:2:2. Indra.

1. Sing ye a song, to make him glad, to Indra, Lord of tawny steeds, | The Soma-drinker, O my friends! || 2. To him, the bounteous, say the laud, and let us glorify, as men | May do, the giver of true gifts! || 3. O Indra, Lord of boundless might, for us thou seekest spoil and kine, | Thou seekest gold for us, good Lord!

Daśati 4:1:2:3. Indra.

1. This, even this, O Indra, we implore: as thy devoted friends, | The Kaṇvas praise thee with their hymns. || 2. Naught else, O Thunderer, have I praised in the skilled singer's eulogy; | On thy laud only have I thought. || 3. The Gods seek him who presses out the Soma; they desire not sleep: | They punish sloth unweariedly.

Daśati 4:1:2:4. Indra.

1. For Indra, lover of carouse, loud be our songs about the juice: | Let poets sing the song of praise || 2. We summon Indra to the draught, in whom all glories rest, in whom | The seven communities rejoice. || 3. At the Trikadrukas the Gods span sacrifice that stirs the mind: | Let our songs aid and prosper it!

Daśati 4:1:2:5. Indra.

1. Here, Indra, is thy Soma draught, made pure upon the sacred grass: | Run hither, come and drink thereof! || 2. Strong-rayed! adored with earnest hymns! this juice is shed for thy delight: | Thou art invoked, Ākhaṇḍala! || 3. To Kuṇḍapāyya, grandson's son, grandson of Śṛiṅgavṛiṣh! to thee, | To him have I addressed my thought.

Daśati 4:1:2:6. Indra.

1. Indra, as one with mighty arm, gather for us with thy right hand, | Manifold and nutritious spoil! || 2. We know thee mighty in thy deeds, of mighty bounty, mighty wealth. | Mighty in measure, prompt to aid. || 3. Hero when thou wouldst give thy gifts, neither the Gods nor mortal men | Restrain thee like a fearful bull.

Daśati 4:1:2:7. Indra.

1. Hero, the Soma being shed, I pour the juice for thee to drink: | Sate thee and finish thy carouse! || 2. Let not the fools, or those who mock, beguile thee when they seek thine aid: | Love not the enemy of prayer! || 3. Here let them cheer thee well supplied with milk to great munificence: | Drink as the wild bull drinks the lake!

Daśati 4:1:2:8. Indra.

1. Here is the Soma juice expressed: O Vasu, drink till thou art full! | Undaunted God, we give it thee! || 2. Washed by the men, pressed out with stones, strained through the filter made of wool, | 'Tis like a courser bathed in streams. || 3. This juice have we made sweet for thee like barley, blending it with milk. | Indra, I call thee to our feast.

Daśati 4:1:2:9. Indra.

1. So, Lord of affluent gifts, this juice hath been expressed for thee with strength: | Drink of it, thou who lovest song! || 2. Incline thy body to the juice which suits thy godlike nature well: | Thee, Soma-lover! let it cheer! || 3. O Indra, let it enter both thy flanks, enter thy head with prayer, | With bounty, hero! both thine arms!

Daśati 4:1:2:10. Indra.

1. O Come ye hither, sit ye down; to Indra sing ye forth your song, | Companions, bringing hymns of praise, || 2. Laud Indra, richest of the rich, who ruleth over noblest wealth, | Beside the flowing Soma juice! || 3. May he stand near us in our need with all abundance, for our wealth: | With strength may he come nigh to us!

Daśati 4:1:2:11. Indra.

1. In every need, in every fray we call, as friends to succour us, | Indra, the mightiest of all. || 2. I call him, mighty to resist, the hero of our ancient home, | Thee whom my sire invoked of old. || 3. If he will hear us, let him come with succour of a thousand kinds, | With strength and riches, to our call!

Daśati 4:1:2:12. Indra.

1. When Somas flow thou makest pure, Indra, thy mind that merits laud, | For gain of strength that ever grows: for great is he. || 2. In heaven's first region, in the seat of Gods, is he who brings success, | Most glorious, prompt to save, who wins the water-floods || 3. Him I invoke, to win the spoil, even mighty Indra for the fray. | Be thou most near to us for bliss, a friend to aid!

Daśati 4:1:2:13. Agni.

1. With this mine homage I invoke Agni for you, the Son of Strength. | Dear, wisest envoy, skilled in noble sacrifice, immortal, messenger of all. || 2. His two red horses, all-supporting, let him yoke: let him, well-worshipped, urge them fast! | Then hath the sacrifice good prayers and happy end, the heavenly gift of wealth to men.

Daśati 4:1:2:14. Dawn.

1. Advancing, sending forth her rays, the daughter of the Sky is seen. | The mighty one lays bare the darkness with her eye, the friendly Lady makes the light. || 2. The Sun ascending, the refulgent star, pours down his beams. together with the Dawn. | O Dawn, at thine arising, and, the Sun's, may we attain the share allotted us!

Daśati 4:1:2:15. Aśvins.

1. These morning sacrifices call you, Aśvins, at the break of day. | For help have I invoked you rich in power and might: for, house by house, ye visit all. || 2. Ye, heroes, have bestowed wonderful nourishment: send it to him whose songs are sweet. | One-minded, both of you, drive your car down to us: drink ye the savoury Soma juice!

Daśati 4:1:2:16. Soma Pavamāna.

1. After his ancient splendour, they, the bold, have drawn the bright milk from | The Sage who wins a thousand spoils. || 2. In aspect he is like the Sun: he runneth forward to the lakes: Seven currents flowing to the sky. || 3. He, while they purify him, stands high over all things that exist Soma, a God as Sūrya is.

Daśati 4:1:2:17. Soma Pavamāna.

1. By generation long ago this God, engendered for the Gods, | Flows tawny to the straining cloth. || 2. According to primeval plan this poet hath been strengthened by, | The sage as God for all the Gods. || 3. Shedding the ancient fluid thou art poured into the cleansing sieve: | Roaring, thou hast produced the Gods.

Daśati 4:1:2:18. Soma Pavamāna.

1. Bring near us those who stand aloof: strike fear into our enemy: | O Pavamāna, find us wealth! || 2. To him the active, nobly born. || 3. Sing ye your songs to him, O men!

Daśati 4:1:2:19. Soma Pavamāna.

1. The Somas skilled in song, the waves have led the water forward, like | Buffaloes speeding to the woods. || 2. With stream of sacrifice the brown bright drops have flowed with strength in store | Of kine into the wooden vats. || 3. To Indra, Vāyu Varuṇa to Vishṇu and the Marutas let | The Soma juices flow expressed.

Daśati 4:1:2:20. Soma Pavamāna.

1. O Soma, for the feast of Gods, river-like he hath swelled with surge, | Sweet with the liquor of the stalk, as one who wakes, into the vat that drops with meath. || 2. Like a dear son how must be decked, the bright and shining one hath clad him in his robe. | Men skilful at their work drive him forth, like a car, into the rivers from their hands.

Daśati 4:1:2:21. Soma Pavamāna.

1. The rapture-shedding Somas have flowed forth in our assembly, pressed. | To glorify our liberal lords. || 2. Now like a swan he maketh all the company sing each his hymn | He like steed is bathed in milk. || 3. And Trita's maidens onward urge the tawny-coloured with the stones, | Indu for Indra, for his drink.

Daśati 4:1:2:22. Soma Pavamāna.

1. Herewith flow on, thou friend of Gods! Singing, thou runnest round the sieve on every side. | The streams of meath have been effused. || 2. Lovely, gold-coloured, on he flows. || 3. For him who presses, of the juice.

Prapāṭhaka 2.

Ardha 1.

Daśati 4:2:1:1. Soma Pavamāna.

1. Soma, as leader of the song, flow onward with thy wondrous aid. | For holy lore of every sort! || 2. Do thou as leader of the song, stirring the waters of the sea, | Flow onward, known to all mankind!1. O Soma, O thou Sage, these worlds stand ready to enhance thy might: | The milch-kine run for thy behoof.

Daśati 4:2:1:2. Soma Pavamāna.

1. Indu, flow on, a mighty juice; glorify us among the folk: | Drive all our enemies away! || 2. And in thy friendship, Indu, most sublime and glorious, may we | Subdue all those who war with us! || 3. Those awful weapons which thou hast, sharpened at point to strike men down— | Guard us therewith from every foe!

Daśati 4:2:1:3. Soma Pavamāna.

1. O Soma, thou art strong and bright, potent, O God, with potent sway, || 2. Steer-strong thy might is like a steer's, steer-strong the wood, steer-strong the juice: | A steer indeed, O Steer, art thou. || 3. Thou, Indu, as a vigorous horse, hast neighed together steeds and kine: | Unbar for us the doors to wealth!

Daśati 4:2:1:4. Soma Pavamāna.

1. For thou art strong by splendour: we, O Pavamāna call on thee, | The brilliant looker on the light. || 2. When thou art sprinkled with the streams, thou reachest, purified by men, | Thy dwelling in the wooden vat. || 3. Do thou, rejoicing, nobly-armed! pour upon us heroic strength. | O Indu, come thou hitherward!

Daśati 4:2:1:5. Soma Pavamāna.

1. We seek to win thy friendly love, even Pavamāna's flowing o'er | The limit of the cleansing sieve. || 2. With those same waves which in their stream o'erflow the purifying sieve, | Soma, be gracious unto us! || 3. O Soma, being purified, bring us from all sides—for thou canst— | Riches and food with hero sons!

Daśati 4:2:1:6. Agni.

1. Agni we choose as envoy, skilled performer of this holy rite, | Hotar, possessor of all wealth. || 2. With constant calls they invocate Agni, Agni, Lord of the house, | Oblation-bearer, much-beloved || 3. Bring the Gods hither, Agni, born for him who trims the Sacred grass: | Thou art our Hotar, meet for praise!

Daśati 4:2:1:7. Mitra Varuṇa.

1. Mitra and Varuṇa we call to drink the draught of Soma juice, | Those born endowed with holy strength. || 2. Those who by Law uphold the Law, Lords of the shining light of Law, | Mitra I call, and Varuṇa || 3. Let Varuṇa

be our chief defence, let Mitra guard us with all aids, | Both make us rich exceedingly!

Daśati 4:2:1:8. Indra.

1. Indra the singers with high praise, Indra reciters with their lauds, | Indra the choirs have glorified. || 2. Indra is close to his two bays, with chariot ready at his word, | Indra the golden, thunder-armed. || 3. Help us in battles Indra, in battles where thousand spoils are gained, | With awful aids, O awful one! || 4. Indra raised up the son aloft in heaven, that he may see afar: | He burst the mountain for the kine.

Daśati 4:2:1:9. Indra-Agni.

1. To Indra and to Agni we bring reverence high and holy hymn, | And, craving help, soft words with prayer. || 2. For all these holy singers thus implore these twain to succour them, | And priests that they may win them strength. || 3. Eager to laud you, we with songs invoke you, bearing sacred food, | Fain for success in sacrifice.

Daśati 4:2:1:10. Soma Pavamāna.

1. Flow onward, mighty with thy stream, inspiriting the Marut's Lord, | Winning all riches with thy power! || 2. I send thee forth to battle from the press, O Pavamāna, strong, | Sustainer, looker on the light! || 3. Acknowledged by this song of mine, flow, tawny-coloured, with thy stream: | Incite to battle thine ally!

Daśati 4:2:1:11. Soma Pavamāna.

1. A Red Bull bellowing to the kine, thou goest, causing the heavens and earth to roar and thunder. | A shout is heard like Indra's in the battle: thou flowest on, sending this voice before thee. || 2. Swelling with milk, abounding in sweet juices, urging the meath-rich plant thou goest onward. | Making loud clamour, Soma Pavamāna, thou flowest when thou art effused for Indra. || 3. So flow thou on inspiriting, for rapture, turning the weapon of the water's holder! | Flow to us wearing thy resplendent colour, effused and eager for the kine. O Soma!

Daśati 4:2:1:12. Indra.

1. That we may win us wealth and power we poets verily, call on thee: | In war men call on thee, Indra, the hero's Lord, in the steed's race-course call on thee || 2. As such, O wonderful, whose hand holds thunder, praised as mighty, Caster of the Stone! | Pour on us boldly, Indra, kine and chariot-steeds, ever to be the conqueror's strength!

Daśati 4:2:1:13. Indra.

1. To you will I sing Indra's praise who gives good gifts, as we I we know; | The praise of Maghavan who, rich in treasure, aids his singers with wealth thousandfold. || 2. As with a hundred hosts, he rushes boldly on, and for the offerer slays his foes. | As from a mountain flow the water-brooks, thus flow his gifts who feedeth many a one.

Daśati 4:2:1:14. Indra.

1. O Thunderer, zealous worshippers gave thee drink this time yesterday: | So, Indra, listen here to him who offers lauds: come near unto our dwelling-place! || 2. Lord of bay steeds, fair-helmed, rejoice thee: thee we seek. Here the disposers wait on thee. | Thy glories, meet for praise! are highest by the juice, O Indra, lover of the song.

Daśati 4:2:1:15. Soma Pavamāna.

1. Flow onward with that juice of thine most excellent, that brings delight, | Slaying the wicked, dear to Gods! || 2. Killing the foeman and his hate, and daily winning spoil and strength, | Gainer art thou of steeds and kine. || 3. Red-hued, be blended with the milk that seems to yield its lovely breast, | Falcon-like resting in thine home!

Daśati 4:2:1:16. Soma Pavamāna.

1. As Pūṣhan, Fortune, Bhaga, comes this Soma while they make him pure. | He, Lord of all the multitude, hath looked upon the earth and heaven. || 2. The dear cows sang in joyful mood together to the gladdening drink. | The drops as they are purified, the Soma juices, make the paths. || 3. O Pavamāna, bring the juice, the mightiest, worthy to be famed, | Which the Five Tribes have over them, whereby we may win opulence!

Daśati 4:2:1:17. Soma Pavamāna.

1. Far-seeing Soma flows, the Steer, the Lord of hymns, the furtherer of days, of mornings, and of heaven. | Breath of the rivers, he hath roared into the jars, and with the help of sages entered Indra's heart. || 2. On, with the sages, flows the poet on his way, and guided by the men, hath streamed into the vats. | He, showing Trita's name, hath caused the meath to flow, increasing Vāyu's strength to make him Indra's friend. || 3. He, being purified, hath made the mornings shine, and it is he who gave the rivers room to flow. | Making the three-times seven pour out the milky stream, Soma, the cheerer, yields whate'er the heart finds sweet.

Daśati 4:2:1:18. Indra.

1. For so thou art the brave man's friend; a hero, too, art thou, and strong: | So may thy heart be won us! || 2. So hath the offering. wealthiest Lord, been paid by all the worshippers. | So dwell thou, Indra, even with us! || 3. Be not thou like a slothful priest, O Lord of spoil and strength: rejoice | In the pressed Soma blent with milk!

Daśati 4:2:1:19. Indra.

1. All sacred songs have magnified Indra expansive as the sea. | Best of all warriors borne on cars, the Lord of heroes, Lord of strength. || 2. Lord of might, Indra, may we ne'er, strong in thy friendship, be afraid! | We glorify with praises thee, the never conquered conqueror. || 3. The gifts of Indra from of old, his saving succours never fail, | When to his worshippers he gives the boon of booty rich in kine.

Ardha 2.

Daśati 4:2:2:1. Soma Pavamāna.

1. These rapid Soma-drops have been poured through the purifying sieve. | To bring us all felicities. || 2. Dispelling manifold mishap, giving the courser's progeny, | Yea, and the warrior steed's, success. || 3. Bringing prosperity to kine, they pour perpetual strengthening food | On us for noble eulogy.

Daśati 4:2:2:2. Soma Pavamāna.

1. King Pavamāna is implored with holy songs, on man's behalf, | To travel through, the realm of air. || 2. Pressed for the banquet of the Gods, O Soma, bring us might, and speed, | Like beauty for a brilliant show! || 3. Bring us, O Indu, hundredfold increase of kine, and noble steeds. | The gift of fortune for our help!

Daśati 4:2:2:3. Soma Pavamāna.

1. With sacrifice we seek to thee fair cherisher of manly might | In mansions of the lofty heavens. || 2. Drink gladdening, crusher of the bold, praiseworthy, with most mighty sway, | Destroyer of a hundred forts. || 3. Hence riches came to thee, the King, O sapient one: the strong-winged bird, | Unwearied, brought thee from the sky. || 4. And now, sent forth, he hath attained to mighty power and majesty, | Active and ready to assist. || 5. That each may see the light, the bird brought us the guard of Law, the friend | O fall, the speeder through the air.

Daśati 4:2:2:4. Soma Pavamāna.

1. For food, flow onward with thy stream, cleansed and made bright by sapient men: | Indu, with sheen approach the milk! || 2. While thou art cleansed, song-lover. bring comfort and vigour to the folk, | Poured, tawny one! on milk and curds! || 3. Purified for feast of Gods, go thou to Indra's resting-place, | Resplendent, furthered by the strong!

Daśati 4:2:2:5. Agni.

1. By Agni Agni is inflamed, Lord of the house, wise, young, who bears | Our gifts: the ladle is his mouth. || 2. God, Agni, be his sure defence who, lord of sacrificial gifts. | Worshippeth thee the messenger. || 3. Be gracious, brilliant God, to him who, rich in sacred gifts,would fain | Call Agni to the feast of Gods!

Daśati 4:2:2:6. Mitra Varuṇa.

1. Mitra of holy strength I call, and foe-destroying Varuṇa, | Who perfect prayer with offered oil. || 2. By Law, O Mitra, Varuṇa, Law-strengtheners who cleave to Law, | Have ye obtained your lofty power. || 3. The Sages, Mitra, Varuṇa, of wide dominion, mighty ones, | Bestow on us effectual strength.

Daśati 4:2:2:7. Marutas.

1. So mayst thou verily be seen coming with fearless Indra: both | Of equal splendour, bringing bliss! || 2. Thereafter they, as is their wont, resumed the state of new-born babes, | Taking their sacrificial name. || 3. Thou, Indra, with the rapid Gods who shatter even what is firm, | Even in the cave didst find the cows.

Daśati 4:2:2:8. Indra-Agni.

1. I call the twain whose deed wrought here hath all been famed in ancient time: | Indra and Agni harm us not! || 2. The strong, the scatterers of the foe, Indra and Agni we invoke: | May they be kind to one like me: || 3. Ye slay our Ārya foes, O Lords of heroes, slay our Dāsa foes: | Ye drive all enemies away.

Daśati 4:2:2:9. Soma Pavamāna.

1. The living drops of Soma juice pour, as they flow the gladdening drink, | Intelligent drops above the station of the sea, exhilarating, dropping meath. || 2. May Pavamāna, King and God, speed with his wave over the sea the lofty rite! | Do thou by Mitra's and by Varuṇa's decree flow furthering the lofty rite: || 3. Far-seeing, lovely, guided by the men, the God whose habitation is the sea!

Daśati 4:2:2:10. Soma Pavamāna.

1. Three are the voices that the car-steed utters: he speaks the lore of prayer, the thought of Order. | To the cows' master come the cows inquiring: the hymns with eager longing come to Soma. || 2. To Soma come the cows, the milch-kine longing, to Soma sages with their hymns inquiring. | Soma, effused, is purified and lauded: our hymns and Trishṭubh songs unite in Soma. || 3. Thus, Soma, as we pour thee into vessels, while thou art purified, flow for our welfare! | Pass into Indra. with great joy and rapture: make the voice swell, and generate abundance!

Daśati 4:2:2:11. Indra.

1. O Indra, if a hundred heavens and if a hundred earths were thine,— | No, not a hundred suns could match thee at thy birth, not both the worlds, O Thunderer. || 2. Thou, hero, hast performed thy hero deeds with might, yea, all with strength, O strongest one. | Maghavan, help us to a stable full of kine, O Thunderer, with wondrous aids!

Daśati 4:2:2:12. Indra.

1. We compass thee like water, we whose grass is trimmed and Soma pressed. | Here where the filter pours its stream, thy worshippers round thee, O Vṛitra-slayer, sit. || 2. Men, Vasu! by the Soma with lauds call thee to the foremost place. | When cometh he athirst unto the juice as home, O Indra, like a bellowing bull? || 3. O valiant hero, boldly win thousandfold spoil with Kaṇva's sons! | O active Maghavan, with eager prayer we crave the yellow-hued with store of kine.

Daśati 4:2:2:13. Indra.

1. With Plenty for his true ally the active man will gain the spoil. | Your Indra, much-invoked, I bend with song, as bends a wright his wheel of solid wood. || 2. They who bestow great riches love not paltry praise: wealth comes not to the niggard churl. | Light is the task to give, O Maghavan, to one like me on the decisive day.

Daśati 4:2:2:14. Soma Pavamāna.

1. Three several words are uttered: kine are lowing cows. who give the milk: | The tawny-hued goes bellowing on. || 2. The young and sacred mothers of the holy rite have uttered praise, | Embellishing the Child of Heaven. || 3. From every side, O Soma, for our profit, pour thou forth four seas. | Filled full of riches thousandfold!

Daśati 4:2:2:15. Soma Pavamāna.

1. The Somas, very rich in sweets, for which the sieve is destined, | flow Effused, the source of Indra's joy: may you strong juices reach the Gods! || 2. Indu flows on for Indra's sake,—thus have the deities declared. | The Lord of Speech exerts himself, controller of all power and might. || 3. Inciter of the voice of song, with thousand streams the ocean flows. | Even Soma, Lord of opulence, the friend of Indra, day by day.

Daśati 4:2:2:16. Soma Pavamāna.

1. Spread is thy cleansing filter, Brahmaṇaspati: as prince thou enterest its limbs from every side. | The raw; whose mass bath not been heated. gains not this: they only which are dressed, which bear, attain to it. || 2. High in the seat of heaven is placed the scorcher's sieve: its, threads are standing separate, glittering with light. | The swift ones favour him who purifieth this: with brilliancy they mount up to the height of heaven. || 3. The foremost spotted Steer bath made the Mornings shine: he bellows, fain for war, among created things. | By his high wisdom have the mighty Sages wrought: the Fathers who behold mankind laid down the germ.

Daśati 4:2:2:17. Agni.

1. Sing forth to him, the holy, most munificent, sublime with his refulgent glow, | To Agni, ye Upastutas || 2. Worshipped with gifts, enkindled, splendid, Maghavan shall win | himself heroic fame: | And will not his more plentiful benevolence come to us with abundant strength?

Daśati 4:2:2:18. Indra.

1. We sing this strong and wild delight of thine which conquers in the fray, | Which, Caster of the Stone! gives room and shines like gold. || 2. Wherewith thou foundest shining lights for Āyu and for Manu's sake: | Now joying in this sacred grass thou beamest forth. || 3. This day too singers of the hymn praise, as of old, this might of thine: | Win thou the waters every day, thralls of the strong!

Daśati 4:2:2:19. Indra.

1. O Indra, hear Tiraśchi's call, the call of him who serveth thee. | Satisfy him with wealth of kine and valiant offspring! Great art thou. || 2. For he, O Indra, hath produced for thee the newest gladdening song, | A hymn that springs from careful drop thought, ancient and full of sacred truth. || 3. That Indra will we laud whom songs and hymns of praise have magnified. | Striving to win, we celebrate his many deeds of hero might.

Prapāṭhaka 3.

Ardha 1.

Daśati 4:3:1:1. Soma Pavamāna.

1. Fleet as swift steeds thy cows celestial have been poured, O Pavamāna, with the milk into the vat. | Sages who make thee bright, O friend whom Ṛishis love, have shed continuous streams from out the realm of air. || 2. The beams of Pavamāna, sent from earth and heaven his ensigns who is ever steadfast, travel round. | When on the sieve the golden-hued is cleansed he rests within the jars as one who seats him in his place. || 3. O thou who seest all things, sovereign as thou art and passing strong, thy rays encompass every form. | Pervading with thy natural powers thou flowest on, and as the whole world's Lord, O Soma, thou art King.

Daśati 4:3:1:2. Soma Pavamāna.

1. From heaven hath Pavamāna, made, as 'twere, the marvellous thunder, and | The lofty light of all mankind. || 2. The gladdening and auspicious juice of thee, O Pavamāna, King! | Flows o'er the woollen straining-cloth. || 3. Thy juice, O Pavamāna, sends its rays abroad like splendid skill, | Like lustre, all heaven's light, to see.

Daśati 4:3:1:3. Soma Pavamāna.

1. Impetuous, bright, have they come forth, unwearied in their speed, like bulls, | Driving the black skin far away. || 2. May we attain the bridge of bliss, leaving the bridge of woe behind: | The riteless Dāsa may we quell! || 3. The mighty Pavamāna's roar is heard as 'twere the rush of rain | The lightning-Rashes move in heaven. || 4. Indu, pour out abundant food with store of cattle and of gold, | Of heroes, Soma! and of steeds! || 5. Flow onward, dear to all mankind! fill full the mighty heaven and earth, | As Dawn, as Sūrya with his beams || 6. On every side, O Soma, flow round us with thy protecting stream, | As Rasā flows around the world!

Daśati 4:3:1:4. Soma Pavamāna.

1. Flow on, O thou of lofty thought, flow swift in thy beloved form, | Saying, I go where dwell the Gods. || 2. Preparing what is unprepared, and bringing store of food to man, | Make thou the rain descend from heaven || 3. Even here is he who, swift of course, hath with the river's wave Rowed down. | From heaven upon the straining cloth. || 4. With might. producing glare, the juice enters the purifying sieve, | Far-seeing, sending forth its light. || 5. Inviting him from far away, and even from near at hand, the juice | For Indra is poured forth as meath. || 6. In union they have sung the hymn: with stones they urge the golden-hued, | Indu for Indra, for his drink.

Daśati 4:3:1:5. Soma Pavamāna.

1. The glittering maids send Sūra forth, the glorious sisters, close allied, | Send Indu forth, their mighty Lord. || 2. Pervade, O Pavamāna, all our treasures with repeated light, | Pressed out, O God thyself, for Gods! || 3. Pour on us, Pavamāna! rain, as service and fair praise for Gods: | Pour forth unceasingly for food!

Daśati 4:3:1:6. Agni.

1. The watchful guardian of the people hath been born, Agni, the very strong, for fresh prosperity. | With oil upon his face. with high heaven-touching flame, he shineth splendidly, pure, for the Bhāratas. || 2. O Agni, the Aṅgirasas discovered thee what time thou layest hidden, fleeing back from wood to wood. | Thou by attrition art produced as conquering might, and men, O Aṅgiras, call thee the Son of Strength. || 3. The men enkindle Agni in his threefold seat, ensign of sacrifice, the earliest household-priest. | With Indra and the Gods together on the grass let the wise priest sit to complete the sacrifice!

Daśati 4:3:1:7. Mitra-Varuṇa.

1. This Soma hath been pressed for you, Low-strengtheners, Mitra, Varuṇa! | List, list ye here to this may call! || 2. Both Kings who never injure aught have come to their sublimest home, | The thousand-pillared, firmly based. || 3. Worshipped with fat libation. Lords of gifts, Ādityas, sovereign Kings, | They wait on him whose life is true.

Daśati 4:3:1:8. Indra.

1. Armed with the bones of dead Dadhyach, Indra with unresisted. might | The nine-and-ninety Vṛitras slew. || 2. He, searching for the horse's head that in the mountains lay concealed, | Found it in Śaryaṇāvat lake. || 3. Then straight they recognized the mystic name of the creative Steer. | There in the mansion of the Moon.

Daśati 4:3:1:9. Indra Agni.

1. As rain from out the cloud, for you, Indra and Agni, from my thought | This noblest praise hath been produced. || 2. Indra and Agni, listen to the singer's call: accept his songs. | Fulfil, ye mighty Lords, his prayers! || 3. Give us not up to indigence, ye heroes, Indra, Agni, nor | To Slander and reproach of men!

Daśati 4:3:1:10. Soma Pavamāna.

1. Gold-Hued! as one who giveth strength flow on for Gods to drink, a draught | For Vāyu and the Marut host! || 2. The Steer shines brightly with the Gods, dear Sage in his appointed home. | Even Pavamāna unbeguiled. || 3. O Pavamāna, sent by prayer, roaring about thy dwelling-place, | Ascend to Vāyu as Law bids!

Daśati 4:3:1:11. Soma Pavamāna.

1. O Soma, Indu, every day thy friendship hath been my delight. | Many fiends follow me; help me, thou tawny-hued: pass on beyond these barriers! || 2. Close to thy bosom am I. Soma, day and night draining the milk, O golden hued. | Sūrya himself refulgent with his glow have we, as birds, o'ertaken in his course.

Daśati 4:3:1:12. Soma Pavamāna.

1. Active, while being purified, he hath assailed all enemies: They deck the Sage with holy hymns. || 2. The Red hath mounted to his shrine; strong Indra hath approached the juice: | In his firm dwelling let him rest! || 3. O Indu, Soma, send us now great opulence from every side: | Pour on us treasures thousandfold!

Daśati 4:3:1:13. Indra.

1. Drink Soma, Indra Lord of bays! and let it cheer thee: the stone, like a well-guided courser, | Directed by the presser's arms bath pressed it. || 2. So let the draught of joy, thy dear companion, by which, O Lord of bays, thou slayest Vṛitras, | Delight thee, Indra, Lord of princely treasures! || 3. Mark closely, Maghavan, the word I utter, this eulogy recited by Vasiṣhṭha: | Accept the prayers I offer at thy banquet!

Daśati 4:3:1:14. Indra.

1. Heroes of one accord brought forth and formed for kingship | Indra who wins the victory in all encounters, | For power, in firmness, in the field, the great destroyer, fierce and exceeding strong, stalwart and full of vigour. || 2. The holy sages form a ring, to view and sing unto the Ram. | Inciters, very brilliant, from all deceit, are with your chanters nigh to hear. || 3. Bards joined in song to Indra so that he might drink the Soma juice. | The Lord of light, that he whose laws stand fast might aid with power and with the help he gives.

Daśati 4:3:1:15. Indra.

1. He who as sovereign Lord of men moves with his chariots unrestrained, | The Vṛitra-slayer, conqueror of all fighting hosts, pre-eminent, is praised in song. || 2. Honour that Indra, Puruhanman! for his aid, him in whose hand of old the fair | Sustaining bolt of thunder, mighty like the God, like Sūrya, was deposited!

Daśati 4:3:1:16. Soma Pavamāna.

1. The Sage of heaven whose heart is wise, when laid between both hands, with roars, | Gives us delightful powers of life. || 2. He, the bright son, when born, illumed his parents who had sprung to life, | Great Son, great strengtheners of Law. || 3. On, onward to a glorious home, free from all guile and dear to. men, | Flow with enjoyment to our praise!

Daśati 4:3:1:17. Soma Pavamāna.

1. For, verily, Pavamāna, thou, divine! endued with brightest splendour, calling all | Creatures to immortality. || 4. With whom Dadhyach Navagva opened fastened doors, by whom the sages gained their wish, | By whom they won the fame of lovely Amṛita in the felicity of Gods.

Daśati 4:3:1:18. Soma Pavamāna.

1. Soma, while filtered, with his wave flows through the long wool of the sheep, | Roaring, while purified, before the voice of song. || 2. With prayers they cleanse the mighty steed, sporting in wood, above the fleece: | Our hymns, intoned, have praised him of the triple height. || 3. He hath been hastened to the jars, bountiful, like an eager horse, | And, lifting up his voice, while filtered, glided on.

Daśati 4:3:1:19. Soma Pavamāna.

1. Father of holy hymns, Soma flows onward, the father of the earth, father of heaven. | Father of Agni, Sūrya's generator, the father who begat Indra and Viṣhṇu. || 2. Brahman of Gods, the leader of the poets, Ṛiṣhi of sages, chief of savage creatures, | Falcon amid the vultures, axe of forests, over the cleansing sieve goes Soma singing. || 3. He, Soma Pavamāna, like a river, hath stirred the wave of voice, our songs and praises | Beholding these inferior powers, the hero, well knowing, takes his stand among the cattle.

Daśati 4:3:1:20. Agni.

1. Hither, for powerful kinship, I call Agni, him who prospers you, | Most frequent at our solemn rites. || 2. That through this famed one's power he may stand by us, even as Tvaṣhṭar comes | Unto the forms that must be shaped. || 3. This Agni is the Lord supreme above all glories' mid the Gods: | May he come nigh to us with strength.

Daśati 4:3:1:21. Indra.

1. This poured libation, Indra drink, immortal, gladdening, excellent! | Streams of the bright have flowed to thee here at the seat of holy Law. || 2. When, Indra, thou dost guide thy bays, there is no better charioteer: | None hath surpassed thee in thy might, none with good steeds o'ertaken thee. || 3. Sing glory now to Indra, say to him your solemn eulogies! | The drops poured forth have made him glad: pay reverence to his noblest might!

Daśati 4:3:1:22. Indra.

1. Indra, be pleased: drive forward, hero, striker of thy bays! | Fair, like a sage, delighting in the meath, drink of the juice for rapturous joy. || 2. O Indra, fill thy belly anew with meath that seems to flow from heaven. | The sweet-voiced raptures of this juice have come, as 'twere to heaven. to thee. || 3. Indra, victorious, Mitra-like, smote, like a Yati, Vṛitra dead. | As Bhṛigu quelled his foes, he cleft Vala in Soma's rapturous joy.

Ardha 2.

Daśati 4:3:2:1. Soma Pavamāna.

1. Winner of gold and gear and cattle flow thou on, set as impregner, Indu! amid the worlds of life! | Rich in brave men art thou, Soma, who winnest all: these holy singers wait upon thee with song. || 2. O Soma, thou beholdest men from every side: O Pavamāna, Steer, thou wanderest through these. | Pour out upon us wealth in treasure and in gold: may we have strength to live among the things that be! || 3. Thou passest to these worlds as sovereign Lord thereof, O Indu, harnessing thy tawny well-winged mares. | May they pour forth for thee milk and oil rich in sweets: | O Soma, let the folk abide in thy decree!

Daśati 4:3:2:2. Soma Pavamāna.

1. The streams of Pavamāna, thine, finder of all I have been effused, | Even as Sūrya's rays of light. || 2. Making the light that shines from heaven thou flowest on to every form, | Soma, thou swellest like a sea. || 3. Shown forth

thou sendest out thy voice, O Pavamāna, with a roar. | Like Sūrya, God, as Law commands.

Daśati 4:3:2:3. Soma Pavamāna.

1. Hitherward have the Somas streamed, the drops while they are purified: | When blent, in waters they are raised. || 2. The milk hath run to meet them like floods rushing down a precipice: | They come to Indra, being cleansed. || 3. O Soma Pavamāna, thou flowest as Indra's gladdener: The men have seized and lead thee forth. || 4. Thou, Indu, when, expressed by stones, thou runnest to the filter, art | Ready for Indra's high decree. || 5. Victorious, to be hailed with joy, O Soma, flow delighting men, | As the supporter of mankind! || 6. Flow on, best Vṛitra-slayer; flow meet to be hailed with joyful lauds, | pure, purifying, wonderful || 7. Pure, purifying, is he called, Soma effused and full of sweets, | Slayer of sinners, dear to Gods.

Daśati 4:3:2:4. Soma Pavamāna.

1. The Sage hath robed him in the sheep's wool for the banquet of the Gods, | Subduing all our enemies. || 2. For he, as Pavamāna, sends thousandfold riches in the shape | Of cattle to the worshippers. || 3. Thou graspest all things with thy mind, and purifiest thee with thoughts: | As such, O Soma, find us fame! || 4. Pour on us lofty glory, send sure riches to our liberal lords: | Bring food to those who sing thy praise! || 5. As thou art cleansed, O wondrous steed, O Soma, thou hast entered, like | A pious king, into the songs, || 6. He, Soma, like a courser in the floods invincible, made bright | With hands, is resting in the press. || 7. Disporting, like a liberal chief, thou goest. Soma to the sieve, | Lending the laud heroic strength.

Daśati 4:3:2:5. Soma Pavamāna.

1. Pour on us with thy juice all kinds of corn, each sort of nourishment! | And, Soma, all felicities! || 2. As thine, O Indu, is the praise, and thine what springeth from, the juice, | Seat thee on the dear sacred grass! || 3. And, finding for us steeds and kine, O Soma, with thy juice flow on | Through days that fly most rapidly! || 4. As one who conquers, ne'er subdued, attacks and slays the enemy, | Thus, vanquisher of thousands! flow!

Daśati 4:3:2:6. Soma Pavamāna.

1. Thou, Indu, with thy streams that drop sweet juices, which were poured for help, | Hast settled in the cleansing sieve. || 2. So flow thou onward through the fleece, for Indra flow to be his drink, | Seating thee in the shrine of Law! || 3. As giving room and freedom, as most sweet, pour butter forth and milk, | O Soma, for the Aṅgirasas!

Daśati 4:3:2:7. Agni.

1. Thy glories are, like lightnings from the rainy cloud, visible, Agni, like the comings of the Dawns, | When, loosed to wander over plants and forest trees, thou crammest by thyself thy food into thy mouth. || 2. When, sped and urged by wind, thou spreadest thee abroad, soon piercing through thy food according to thy will, | The hosts, who ne'er decayest, eager to consume, like men on chariots, Agni! strive on every side. || 3. Agni, the Hotar-priest who fills the assembly full, waker of wisdom, chief controller of the thought— | Thee, yea, none other than thyself, doth man elect priest of the holy offering, great and small, alike.

Daśati 4:3:2:8. Mitra-Varuṇa.

1. Even far and wide, O Varuṇa and Mitra, doth your help extend: | May I obtain your kind good-will! || 2. True Gods, may we completely gain food and a dwelling place from you: | Ye Mitras, may we be your own! || 3. Guard us, ye Mitras, with your guards, save us, ye skilled to save: may we | Subdue the Dasyus by ourselves!

Daśati 4:3:2:9. Indra.

1. Arising in thy might, thy jaws thou shookest Indra, having drunk | The Soma which the press had shed. || 2. Indra, both world gave place to thee as thou wast fighting, when thou wast | The slayer of the Dasyu hosts. || 3. From Indra, have I measured out a song eight-footed with nine parts, | Delicate, strengthening the Law.

Daśati 4:3:2:10. Indra-Agni.

1. Indra and Agni, these our songs of praise have sounded forth to you: | Ye who bring blessings! drink the juice || 2. Come, Indra, Agni, with those teams, desired of many, which ye have, | O heroes, for the worshipper || 3. With those to his libation poured, ye heroes, Indra, Agni, come: | Come ye to drink the Soma-juice!

Daśati 4:3:2:11. Soma Pavamāna.

1. Soma, flow on exceeding bright with loud roar to the reservoirs, | Resting in wooden vats thy home! || 2. Let water winning Somas flow to Indra, Vāyu, Varuṇa, | To Vishṇu and Marut host! || 3. Soma, bestowing food upon our progeny, from every side | Pour on us riches thousandfold.

Daśati 4:3:2:12. Soma Pavamāna.

1. Pressed out by pressers Soma goes over the fleecy backs of sheep, | Goes even as with a mare in tawny-coloured stream, goes in a sweetly-sounding stream. || 2. Down to the water Soma, rich in kine, bath flowed with cows, with cows that have been milked. | They have approached the mixing-vessels as a sea: the cheerer streams for the carouse.

Daśati 4:3:2:13. Soma Pavamāna.

1. O Purifying Soma, bring to us the wondrous treasure, meet. | For lauds, that is in earth and heaven! || 2. Cleansing the lives of men, thou, Steer, bellowing on the sacred grass, | Gold-hued, hast settled in thy home. || 3. For ye twain, Indra, Soma, are Lords of heaven's light, Lords of the kine: | Prosper, as mighty ones, our prayers

Daśati 4:3:2:14. Indra.

1. By men hath Indra been advanced, the Vṛitra-slayer, to joy and strength. | Him only we invoke for help in battles whether great or small be he our aid in deeds or might! || 2. For, hero, thou art like a host, art giver of abundant spoil. | Strengthening e'en the feeble, thou aidest the sacrificer, thou givest great wealth to him who pours. || 3. When war and battles are on foot, booty is offered to the bold. | Yoke thou thy wildly-rushing bays! Whom wilt thou slay, and whom enrich? Do thou, O Indra, make us rich!

Daśati 4:3:2:15. Indra.

1. The juice of Soma thus diffused, sweet to the taste, the bright cows drink, | Who travelling in splendour close to mighty Indra's side rejoice, good in their own supremacy. || 2. Craving his touch the dappled kine mingle the Soma with their milk. | The milch-kine dear to Indra send forth his death dealing thunder-bolt, good in their own supremacy. || 3. With veneration, passing wise, they honour his victorious might. | They follow close his many laws to win them due preeminence, good in their own supremacy.

Daśati 4:3:2:16. Soma Pavamāna.

1. Strong, mountain-born, the stalk hath been pressed in the streams for rapturous joy. | Hawk-like he settles in his home. || 2. Fair is the juice beloved of Gods, washed in the waters, pressed by men: | The milch kine sweeten it with milk || 3. Then, like a steed, have they adorned the inciter for eternal life, | The meath's juice at the festival.

Daśati 4:3:2:17. Soma Pavamāna.

1. Make high and splendid glory shine hitherward, Lord of food, God, on the friend of Gods | Unclose the cask of middle air || 2. Roll onward from the press, O mighty one, effused, as kings, supporter of the tribes | Pour on us rain from heaven, send us the water's flow, urging our thoughts to win the spoil!

Daśati 4:3:2:18. Soma Pavamāna.

1. Breath of the mighty Dames, the Child, speeding the plan of sacrifice, | Surpasses all things that are dear, yea, from of old. || 2. The place that is concealed hath gained a share of Trita's pressing-stones, | By the seven laws of sacrifice, even that dear place. || 3. He hath sent forth unto the heights the three, in stream, as Trita's wealth: | He who is passing wise measures his pathways out.

Daśati 4:3:2:19. Soma Pavamāna.

1. Flow to the filter with thy stream, effused, to win us spoil and wealth, | Soma exceeding rich in meath for Indra, Vishṇu, and the Gods || 2. The hymns that know not guile, caress thee, golden-coloured, in the sieve. | As mothers, Pavamāna, lick the new-born calf, as Law commands. || 3. Lord of great sway, thou liftest thee above the heavens, above the earth. | Thou, of Pavamāna, hast assumed thy coat of mail with majesty.

Daśati 4:3:2:20. Soma Pavamāna.

1. Strong Indu, bathed in milk, flows on for Indra, Soma exciting strength, for his carousal. | He quells malignity and slays the demons, King of the homestead, he who gives us comfort. || 2. Then in a stream he flows, milked out with press-stones, mingled with sweetness, through the fleecy filter— | Indu rejoicing in the love of Indra, the God who gladdens for the God's enjoyment. || 3. He flows, as he is cleansed, to sacred duties, a God

bedewing Gods with his own juices. | Indu hath, clothed in powers that suit the season, on the raised fleece engaged the ten swift fingers.

Daśati 4:3:2:21. Agni.

1. O Agni, God, we kindle thee, refulgent, wasting not away, | That this more glorious fuel may send forth for thee its shine to heaven. Bring food to those who sing thy praise! || 2. To thee the splendid, Lord of light! bright! wondrous! prince of men! is brought. | Oblation with the holy verse, O Agni, bearer of our gifts! Bring food to those who sing thy praise! || 3. Thou heatest both the ladles in thy mouth, O brilliant prince of men! | So fill us also in our hymns abundantly, thou Lord of Strength. Bring food to those who sing thy praise!

Daśati 4:3:2:22. Indra.

1. Sing ye a psalm to Indra; sing a great song to the lofty Sage, | To him who maketh prayer, inspired, who loveth laud. || 2. Thou, Indra, art the conqueror: thou gavest splendour to the Sun. | Maker of all things, thou art mighty and All-God. || 3. Radiant with light thou wentest to the sky, the luminous realm of -heaven. | The Gods, O Indra, strove to win thy friendly love.

Daśati 4:3:2:23. Indra.

1. This Soma hath been pressed for thee, O Indra, bold one, mightiest, come! | May Indra vigour fill thee full, as Sūrya fills mid-air with rays || 2. Slayer of Vṛitra, mount thy car! The bay steeds have been yoked by prayer. | May, with its voice, the pressing-stone draw thine attention hitherward! || 3. His pair of tawny coursers bring Indra, resistless in his might. | Hither to Ṛishis' songs of praise and sacrifice performed by men.

Prapāṭhaka 4.

Ardha 1.

Daśati 4:4:1:1. Soma Pavamāna.

1. Light of the sacrifice, be pours delicious meath most wealthy, father and begetter of the Gods. | He, gladdening, best of cheerers, juice that Indra loves, enriches with mysterious treasure earth and heaven. || 2. The Lord of heaven, the vigorous and far-seeing one, flows shouting to the beaker with his thousand streams. | Coloured like gold he rests in seats where Mitra dwells, the Steer made beautiful by rivers and by sheep. || 3. As Pavamāna thou flowest before the streams: thou goest on, before the hymn, before the kine. | Thou sharest mighty booty in the van of war Soma, well-armed, thou art pressed out by men who press.

Daśati 4:4:1:2. Soma Pavamāna.

1. Through our desire of heroes, kine, and horses, vigorous Soma-drops, | Brilliant and swift, have been effused. || 2. They, beautified by holy men and purified in both the hands, | Are flowing through the fleecy cloth. || 3. These Soma juices shall pour forth all treasures for the worshipper, | From heaven and earth and firmament.

Daśati 4:4:1:3. Soma Pavamāna.

1. Flow, Soma, Indu, dear to Gods, swift through the purifying sieve, | And enter Indra in thy strength || 2. As mighty food speed hitherward, Indu, as a most splendid steer: | Sit in thy place as one with power || 3. The well-loved meath was made to flow, the stream of the creative juice: | The Sage drew waters to himself. || 4. The mighty waters, yea, the floods accompany thee mighty one, | When thou wilt clothe thee with the milk. || 5. The lake is brightened in the floods. Soma, our friend, heaven's prop and stay, | Falls on the purifying cloth. || 6. The tawny Bull hath bellowed. fair as mighty Mitra to behold | He gleams and flashes with the Sun. || 7. Songs, Indra, active in their might, are beautified for thee, wherewith | Thou deckest thee for rapturous joy. || 8. To thee who givest ample room we pray, to win the wild delight, | That Thou mayst have exalted praise, || 9. Winner of kine Indu, art thou, winner of heroes, steeds, and spoil: | Primeval soul of sacrifice. || 10. Pour on us, Indu! Indra-strength with a full stream of sweetness, like | Parjanya, sender of the rain!

Daśati 4:4:1:4. Soma Pavamāna.

1. O Soma Pavamāna, be victorious, win us high renown; And make us better than we are! || 2. Win thou the light, win heavenly light, and, Soma, all felicities; | And make us better than we are! || 3. Win skilful strength and mental power! O Soma, drive away our foes; | And make us better than we are! || 4. Ye purifiers, purify Soma for Indra, for his drink; | Make thou us better than we are! || 5. Give us our portion in the Sun through thine own mental power and aids; | And make us better than we are! || 6. Through thine own mental power and aids long may we look upon the Sun: | Make thou us better than we are! || 7. Well-weaponed Soma, pour to us a stream of riches doubly great; | And make us better than we are! || 8. As one victorious unsubdued in battle, pour forth wealth to us: | And make us better than we are! || 9. With offerings, Pavamāna! men have strengthened thee as Law commands: | Make thou us better than we are! || 10. O Indu, bring us wealth in steeds brilliant and quickening all life; | And make us better than we are!

Daśati 4:4:1:5. Soma Pavamāna.

1. Swift runs this giver of delight, even the stream of flowing juice: | Swift runs this giver of delight. || 2. The Morning knows all precious things, the Goddess knows her grace to man: | Swift runs this giver of delight. || 3. We have accepted thousands from Dhvasra's and Purushanti's hands: | Swift runs this giver of delight. || 4. From whom we have accepted thus thousands and three-times ten besides: | Swift runs this giver of delight.

Daśati 4:4:1:6. Soma Pavamāna.

1. Forth with his stream who gladdens best these Soma juices have been poured, | Lauded with songs for mighty strength. || 2. Thou flowest to enjoy the milk, and bringest valour, being, cleansed: | Winning the spoil flow hitherward || 3. And, hymned by Jamadagni, let all nourishment that kine supply, | And general praises, flow to us!

Daśati 4:4:1:7. Agni.

1. For Jātavedas, worthy of our praise, will we frame with our mind this eulogy as 'twere a car. | For good, in his assembly, is this care of ours. Let us not, in thy friendship, Agni, suffer harm! || 2. We will bring fuel and prepare our sacred gifts, reminding thee at each successive holy time. | Fulfil our thoughts that we may lengthen out our lives | Let us not, in thy friendship, Agni, suffer harm! || 3. May we have power to kindle thee! Fulfil our prayers in thee the Gods eat the presented sacrifice. | Bring hither the Ādityas, for we long for them! Let us not, in thy friendship, Agni, suffer harm!

Daśati 4:4:1:8. Mitra, Varuṇa, Aryaman.

1. Soon as the Sun hath risen I sing to you, to Mitra, Varuṇa, | And Aryaman who slays the foe. || 2. With wealth of gold may this my song bring unmolested might; may this, | Sages! obtain the sacrifice! || 3. May we be thine, God Varuṇa, and with our princes, Mitra, thine: | May we gain food and heavenly light!

Daśati 4:4:1:9. Indra.

1. Drive all our enemies away, smite down the foes who press around, | And bring the wealth for which we long: || 2. Of which the world shall know forthwith as given by thee abundantly: | Bring us the wealth for which we long: || 3. O Indra, that which is concealed in strong firm place precipitous: | Bring us the wealth for which we long!

Daśati 4:4:1:10. Indra-Agni.

1. Yea, ye are priests of sacrifice, winners in war and holy works | Indra and Agni, mark this well! || 2. Bountiful, riders on the car, slayers of Vṛitra unsubdued, Indra and Agni, mark this well! || 3. The men with pressing-stones have pressed this meath of yours which gives delight: | Indra and Agni, mark this well!

Daśati 4:4:1:11. Soma Pavamāna.

1. For Indra girt by Marutas, flow, thou Indu, very rich in meath, | To seat thee in the place of song! || 2. Sage: who know the lore of speech deck thee, the strong sustainer, well: | Men make thee bright and beautiful. || 3. Let Mitra, Varuṇa, Aryaman drink Pavamāna's juice, yea, thine. | Sage! let the Marutas drink thereof.

Daśati 4:4:1:12. Soma Pavamāna.

1. Deft-handed! thou when purified liftest thy voice amid the sea. | Thou, Pavamāna makest riches flow to us, yellow, abundant, much-desired. || 2. Made pure, as Pavamāna, in the sheep's long wool, the Steer bath bellowed in the vat. | Thou flowest, Soma Pavamāna! balmed with milk unto the meeting-place of Gods.

Daśati 4:4:1:13. Soma Pavamāna.

1. Him here, the offspring of the sea, the ten swift fingers beautify: | With the Ādityas is he seen. || 2. With Indra and with Vāyu he, effused, flows

onward with the beams | Of Sūrya to the cleansing sieve. || 3. Flow rich in sweets and lovely for our Bhaga, Vāyu, Pūṣhan, fair | For Mitra and for Varuṇa!

Daśati 4:4:1:14. Indra.

1. With Indra splendid feasts be ours, rich in all strengthening things, wherewith, | Wealthy in food, we may rejoice! || 2. Like thee, thyself, for singers yoked, thou movest, as it were besought, | Bold one, the axle of the car, || 3. That, Śatakratu, thou, to serve and please thy praisers, as it were, | Stirrest the axle with thy strength.

Daśati 4:4:1:15. Indra.

1. As a good cow to him who milks, we call the doer of good deeds, | To our assistance day by day. || 2. Come thou to our libations, drink of Soma, Soma-drinker! yea, | The rich one's rapture giveth kine. || 3. So may we be acquainted with thine innermost benevolence: | Neglect us not; come hitherward!

Daśati 4:4:1:16. Indra.

1. As, like the Morning, thou has filled, O Indra, both the earth and heaven, | So as the mighty one, great King of all the mighty race of men, the Goddess mother brought thee forth, the blessed mother gave thee life. || 2. Thou bearest in thine hand a lance like a long hook, great counsellor. | As with his foremost foot a goat, draw down the branch O Maghavan. The Goddess mother brought thee forth, the blessed mother gave thee life. || 3. Relax that mortal's stubborn strength whose heart is bent on wickedness. | Trample him down beneath thy feet who watches for and aims at us. The Goddess mother brought thee forth, the blessed mother gave thee life.

Daśati 4:4:1:17. Soma Pavamāna.

1. Soma, the dweller on the hills, effused, hath flowed into the sieve. | All-bounteous art thou in carouse. || 2. Thou art a holy bard, a Sage; the meath offspring of thy sap: | All bounteous art thou in carouse. || 3. All-deities of one accord have come that they may drink of thee: | All-bounteous art thou in carouse.

Daśati 4:4:1:18. Soma Pavamāna.

1. Effused is he who brings good things, who brings us store of wealth, and sweet refreshing food, | Soma who brings us quiet homes: || 2. He whom our Indra and the Marut host shall drink, Bhaga shall drink with Aryaman, | By whom we bring to us Mitra and Varuṇa, and Indra for our great defence.

Daśati 4:4:1:19. Soma Pavamāna.

1. Friends, hymn your Lord who makes him pure for rapturous carouse: let them | Sweeten him, as a child, with lauds and sacred gifts || 2. Like as a calf with mother cows, so Indu is urged forth and sent, | Glorified by our hymns;, the God-delighting juice. || 3. Effectual help to power is he. he is a banquet for the troop, | He who hath been effused, more rich in meath, for Gods.

Daśati 4:4:1:20. Soma Pavamāna.

1. For us the Soma juices flow, the drops best furtherers of weal, | Effused as friends, without a spot, benevolent, finders of the light. || 2. These Soma juices, skilled in song, purified, blent with milk and curd, | Hastening on and firmly set in oil resemble beauteous suns. || 3. Effused by means of pressing-stones, upon the ox-hide visible, | They, treasure-finders, have announced food unto us from every side.

Daśati 4:4:1:21. Soma Pavamāna.

1. Pour forth this wealth with this purification: flow onward to the yellow lake, O Indu! | Here, too, the bright one, wind-swift, full of wisdom, shall give a son to him who cometh quickly. || 2. Flow on for us with this purification to the famed ford of thee whose due is glory! | May the foe-queller shake us down, for triumph, like a tree's ripe fruit, sixty thousand treasures! || 3. Eagerly do we pray for those two exploits, at the blue lake and Pṛiśana, wrought in battle. | He sent our enemies to sleep and slew them, and turned away the foolish and unfriendly.

Daśati 4:4:1:22. Agni.

1. O Agni, be our nearest friend, yea, our protector and our kind deliverer! || 2. As gracious Agni, famed for treasures, come, and, most resplendent, give us store of wealth! || 3. To thee then, O most bright, O radiant God, we come with prayer for happiness for our friends.

Daśati 4:4:1:23. Indra.

1. May we, with Indra and the Gods to aid us, bring these existing worlds to full completion! || 2. Our sacrifice, our bodies, and our offspring, let Indra with the Ādityas—form and finish! || 3. With the Ādityas, with the band of Marutas, let Indra send us medicines to heal us!

Daśati 4:4:1:24. Indra.

1. Sing to your Indra, mightiest Vṛitra-slayer, sing to the Sage the song that he accepteth!

Ardha 2.

Daśati 4:4:2:1. Soma Pavamāna.

1. The God declares the deities' generations, like Uśanā, proclaiming lofty wisdom. | With brilliant kin far-ruling, sanctifying, the wild boar, singing with his foot, advances. || 2. The swans, the Vṛiṣhagaṇas from anear us, restless, have brought their clamour to our dwelling— | Friends come to Pavamāna, meet for praises-and sound in concert their resistless music. || 3. He takes the swiftness of the great Far strider: cows low as, 'twere to him who sports at pleasure. | He with the sharpened horns brings forth abundance: the silvery shines by night, by day the golden. || 4. Like cars that thunder on their way, like coursers eager for renown, | Have Soma drops flowed forth for wealth. || 5. Forth have they rushed from holding hands, like chariots that are urged to speed, | Like joyful songs of singing-men. || 6. The Somas deck themselves with milk as kings are graced with eulogies, | And, with seven priests, the sacrifice. || 7. Pressed for the gladdening draught the drops flow forth abundantly with song, | Flow with the stream of savoury juice. || 8. Winning Vivasvat's glory and speeding the light of Dawn, the suns, | Pass through the openings of the cloth. || 9. The singing-men of ancient time open the doors of sacred songs— | The men who bring the mighty One. || 10. In close society have come the priests, the sevenfold brotherhood, | Filling the station of the One. || 11. He makes us kin with Gods, he joins the Sun, for seeing, with mine eye; | I milk the Sage's offspring forth. || 12. The Sun beholdeth with his eye the heaven's dear quarter which the priests | Have set within the sacred cell.

Daśati 4:4:2:2. Soma Pavamāna.

1. Forth on their way the glorious drops have flowed for maintenance of Law, | Knowing what suits this worshipper. || 2. Down in the mighty waters sinks the stream of Meath, most excellent, | Oblation best of all in worth. || 3. About the holy place the Steer, true, guileless, noblest, hath sent forth, | Continuous voices in the wood. || 4. When the Sage, purging manly deeds and lofty wisdom flows, around, || 5. When purified, he sits enthroned as King over the warring clans. | What time the sages speed him on. || 6. Most dear, gold-coloured, in the fleece he sinks, and settles in the wood: | The singer is besieged with song. || 7. He goes to Indra, Vāyu, and the Aśvins with the rapturous joy, | To whomsoe'er his power delights. || 8. The waves of pleasant Soma flow to Bhaga, Mitra, Varuṇa, | Well knowing, through his mighty powers. || 9. Gain for us, O ye Heaven and Earth, riches of Meath to win us strength: | Gain for us treasures and renown. || 10. We choose today that chariot-steed of thine, the strong, that brings us bliss, | The guardian, the desire of all; || 11. The excellent, the gladdener, the Sage with heart that understands. | The guardian, the desire of all; || 12. Who for ourselves, O thou most wise, is wealth and fair intelligence, | The guardian, the desire of all.

Daśati 4:4:2:3. Agni.

1. Agni Vaiśvānara, born in course of Order, the messenger of earth, the head of heaven, | The Sage, the Sovereign, guest of men, our vessel fit for their mouth, the Gods have generated. || 2. To thee, immortal! when to life thou springest all the Gods sing for joy as to their infant. | They by thy mental powers were made immortal, Vaiśvānara when thou shonest from thy parents. || 3. Him have they praised, mid-point of sacrifices, great cistern of libations, seat of riches. | Vaiśvānara, conveyer of oblations, ensign of worship, have the Gods engendered.

Daśati 4:4:2:4. Mitra-Varuṇa.

1. Sing forth unto your Varuṇa and Mitra with a song inspired: | They, mighty Lords, are lofty law. || 2. Full springs of fatness, sovereign Kings, Mitra and Varuṇa, the twain, | Gods glorified among the Gods, || 3. So help ye us to riches, great celestial and terrestrial wealth! | Vast is your sway among the Gods.

Daśati 4:4:2:5. Indra.

1. O Indra marvellously bright, come, these libations long for thee, | Thus by fine fingers purified! || 2. Urged by the holy singer, sped by song, come nigh, O Indra, to | The sacrificing suppliant's prayers! || 3. Approach, O Indra, basting thee, Lord of bay horses, to our prayers: | In our libation take delight!

Daśati 4:4:2:6. Indra-Agni.

1. Glorify him who compasses all forests with his glowing Dame, | And leaves them blackened by his tongue. || 2. He who gains Indra's grace by fire enkindled, finds as easy way | Over the floods to splendid wealth. || 3. Give us, ye twain, swift steeds to bring Indra and Agni, and bestow | Abundant food with wealth on us.

Daśati 4:4:2:7. Soma Pavamāna.

1. Indu hath started forth for Indra's settled place, and slights not, as a friend, the promise of his friend. | Soma comes onward like a youth with youthful maids, and gains the beaker by a course of hundred paths. || 2. Your hymns of pleasant sound, praiseworthy, fond of lauds, have come into the hall enclosed for sacrifice. | Singers have hymned the golden-coloured as he sports, and milch-kine have come near to meet him with their milk, || 3. O Soma, Indu, while they cleanse thee, with thy wave pour orb us plentiful accumulated food, | Which, ceaseless, thrice a day shall yield us hero power enriched. with store of nourishment, and strength, and meath.

Daśati 4:4:2:8. Indra.

1. No one by deed attains to him who works and strengthens evermore: | No, not by sacrifice, to Indra praised of all, resistless, daring, bold in might; || 2. The powerful conqueror, invincible in war, him at whose birth the mighty ones, | The kine who spread afar, sent their loud voices out, heavens, earths sent their loud voices out.

Daśati 4:4:2:9. Soma Vaiśvānara.

1. Sit down, O friends, and sing aloud to him who purifies himself: | Deck him for glory, like a child, with holy rites || 2. Loose him who bringeth household wealth, even as a calf with. mother kine, | Him who bath double strength, strong, God-delighting juice! || 3. Purify him who gives us power, most blissful one, that he may be | A banquet for the troop, Mitra, and Varuṇa!

Daśati 4:4:2:10. Soma Pavamāna.

1. The Strong hath flowed forth in a thousand streams, flowed through the filter and the sheep's long wool. || 2. With ceaseless genial flow the Strong hath run, purified by the waters, blent with milk. || 3. Pressed out with stones, directed by the men, go forth, O Soma, into Indra's throat!

Daśati 4:4:2:11. Soma Pavamāna.

1. The Soma juices which have been expressed afar or near at hand, | Or there on Śaryaṇāvat's bank, || 2. Those pressed among Ārjīkas, pressed among the active, in, men's homes, | Or pressed among the Fivefold Tribes — || 3. May these celestial drops, expressed, pour forth upon us, as they flow, | Rain from the heavens and hero strength!

Daśati 4:4:2:12. Agni.

1. May Vatsa draw thy mind away even from thy loftiest dwelling-place! | Agni, I yearn for thee with song. || 2. Thou art alike in many a place: through all the regions thou art Lord. | In fray and fight we call on thee. || 3. When we are seeking spoil we call Agni to help us in the strife, | Giver of wondrous gifts in war.

Daśati 4:4:2:13. Indra.

1. O Indra, bring great strength to us, bring valour, Śatakratu, thou most active, bring | A hero conquering in war! || 2. For, gracious Śatakratu, thou hast ever been a mother and a sire to us, | So now for bliss we pray to thee. || 3. To thee, strong! much-invoked! who showest forth thy strength, made very mighty! do I speak: | So grant thou us heroic power!

Daśati 4:4:2:14. Indra.

1. Stone-Darting Indra, wondrous God, what wealth thou hast not given me here, | That bounty, treasure-finder! bring, filling full both thy hands, to us! || 2. Bring what thou deemest worth the wish, O Indra that which is in heaven! | So may we know thee as thou art a giver boundless in thy gifts! || 3. Thy lofty spirit famed in all the regions as appeasable,— | With this thou rendest even things firm, Stone-darter! so to win thee strength.

Prapāṭhaka 5.

Ardha 1.

Daśati 4:5:1:1. Soma Pavamāna.

1. The Marutas with their troop adorn and brighten, even at his birth, the Sage, the lovely infant. | By songs a poet, and a Sage by wisdom, Soma goes singing through the cleansing filter. || 2. Light-winner, Ṛishi-minded, Ṛishi-maker, hymned in a thousand hymns, leader of sages, | Eager to gain his third form, mighty, Soma is, like Virāj, resplendent as a singer. || 3. Hawk seated in the press, bird wide-extended, the banner seeking kine and wielding weapons, | Uniting with the sea, the wave of waters, the mighty tells his fourth form and declares it.

Daśati 4:5:1:2. Soma Pavamāna.

1. Obeying Indra's dear desire these Soma juices have flowed forth | Increasing his heroic might. || 2. Laid in the press and flowing pure to Vāyu and the Aśvins, may | These give us great heroic strength. || 3. Soma, as thou art purified, incite to bounty Indra's heart, | To seat him in the shrine of Gods! || 4. The ten swift fingers deck thee forth seven ministers impel thee on, | The sages have rejoiced in thee. || 5. When through the filter thou art poured we clothe thee with a robe of milk, | To be a rapturous feast for Gods. || 6. When purified within the jars, Soma bright-red and golden-hued, | Hath veiled him in a milky dress. || 7. Flow onward to our wealthy lords. Drive all our enemies away: | O Indu, pass into thy friend! || 8. May we obtain thee, Indra's drink, who viewest men and findest light, | Gain thee and progeny and food! || 9. Send down the rain from heaven and make splendour upon the earth! Give us, | O Soma, victory in war!

Daśati 4:5:1:3. Soma Pavamāna.

1. Poured through the fleece in thousand streams purified Soma floweth to, | Indra's and Vāyu's meeting-place. || 2. Sing forth, ye men who long for help, to Pavamāna, to the Sage, | Effused to entertain the Gods! || 3. The Soma drops with thousand powers are purified to win us strength, | Hymned to become the feast of Gods. || 4. Yea, as thou flowest bring great store of food that we may win us strength: | Indu, bring splendid manly might || 5. Like coursers by their drivers urged, they were poured forth, to win us strength, | Swift through the woollen straining-cloth. || 6. May they in flowing give us wealth in thousands, and heroic power,— | These godlike Soma drops effused! || 7. The roaring Soma drops flow on, like milch-kine lowing to, their calves: | They have run forth from both the hands. || 8. Beloved by Indra, bringing joy, roaring as thou art purified, | Drive all our enemies away. || 9. As Pavamānas, driving off the godless, looking on the light, | Sit in the place of sacrifice.

Daśati 4:5:1:4. Soma Pavamāna.

1. The Soma drops, exceeding rich in sweets, to Indra have been poured, | Shed with the stream of sacrifice. || 2. Sages have called to Indra, like cows, milch-kine, lowing to their calves, | Called him to drink the Soma juice. || 3. In the stream's wave wise Soma dwells, distilling rapture, in his. seat, | Resting upon a wild cow's hide. || 4. Far-sighted Soma, Sage and bard, is worshipped in the central point, | Of heaven, the straining-cloth of wool. || 5. In close embracement Indu holds Soma when poured within the: jars. | And on the purifying sieve. || 6. Indu sends forth a voice on high, up in the region of the sea. | Stirring the cask that drops with meath. || 7. The tree whose praises never fail dwells in the stream of holy milk, | Urged onward by its human friend. || 8. O Pavamāna bring us wealth bright with a thousand splendours; yea, | O Indu, give us ready help! || 9. Sage, poet, poured with all his stream, Soma is driven, far away, | To the dear places of the sky.

Daśati 4:5:1:5. Soma Pavamāna.

1. Loud as a river's roaring wave thy powers have lifted up themselves: | Urge on thine arrow's sharpened point! || 2. At thine effusion upward rise three voices fresh and strong, when thou. | Flowest upon the fleecy ridge. || 3. On to the fleece they urge with stones the dear, the golden-coloured one, | Even Pavamāna dropping meath. || 4. Flow with thy current to the sieve, O Sage, best giver of delight, | To seat these in the shrine of song! || 5. Best giver of delight, flow on anointed with the milk for balm, | And enter into Indra's throat!

Daśati 4:5:1:6. Soma Pavamāna.

1. Flow onward, Indu, with this food for him who in thy wild delights, | Battered the nine-and-ninety down. || 2. Smote swiftly forts, and Śambara, then Yadu and that Turvaśa, | For pious Divodāsa's sake! || 3. Finder of horses, pour on us horses and wealth in kine and gold, | And Indu, food in boundless store!

Daśati 4:5:1:7. Soma Pavamāna.

1. Chasing our foemen, driving off the godless, Soma floweth on, | Going to Indra's settled place. || 2. O Pavamāna, hither bring great riches, and destroy our foes: | O Indu, grant heroic fame! || 3. A hundred obstacles have ne'er checked thee when rain to give thy boons, | When, being cleansed, thou combatest.

Daśati 4:5:1:8. Soma Pavamāna.

1. Flow onward with that stream wherewith thou gavest splendour to the sun, | Speeding the waters kind to man! || 2. He, Pavamāna, high o'er man, yoked the Sun's courser Etaśa, | To travel through the realm of air. || 3. Yea, those bay steeds he harnessed to the chariot that the Sun might come: | Indu, he said, is Indra's self.

Daśati 4:5:1:9. Agni.

1. Associate with fires, make your God Agni envoy at sacrifice, best skilled in worship, | Established firm among mankind, the holy flame-crowned and fed with oil, the purifier! || 2. Like a steed neighing eager for the pasture, when he hath stepped forth from the great enclosure: | Then the wind following blows upon his splendour, and, straight, the path is black which thou hast travelled. || 3. From thee, a bull but newly born, O Agni, the kindled everlasting flames rise upward. | Aloft to heaven as ruddy smoke thou mountest: Agni, thou speedest to the Gods as envoy.

Daśati 4:5:1:10. Indra.

1. We make this Indra very strong to strike the mighty Vṛitra dead: | A vigorous hero shall he be. || 2. This Indra, made for giving gifts, is established, mightiest, in strength, | Bright, meet for Soma, famed in song. || 3. By song, as 'twere the powerful bolt which none may parry, was prepared: | Strong and invincible he grew.

Daśati 4:5:1:11. Soma Pavamāna.

1. Adhvaryu, to the filter lead the Soma-juice expressed with stones: | Make thou it pure for Indra's drink! || 2. These Gods and all the Marut host, Indu! enjoy this juice of thine, | This Pavamāna's flowing meath. || 3. Pour out for Indra, Thunder-armed, the milk of heaven, the Soma's juice, | Most excellent, most rich in sweets!

Daśati 4:5:1:12. Soma Pavamāna.

1. On flows the potent juice, sustainer of the heavens, the strength of Gods, whom men must hail with shouts of joy, | Thou, gold-hued, started like a courser by brave men, art lightly showing forth thy splendour in the streams. || 2. He takes his weapons, like a hero, in his hands, fain to win light, car-borne, in forays for the kine. | Indu, while stimulating Indra's might, is urged forward and balmed by sages skilful in their task. || 3. Soma, as thou art purified with flowing wave, exhibiting thy strength enter thou Indra's throat. | Make both worlds stream for us, as lightning doth the clouds: mete out exhaustless powers for us through this our prayer!

Daśati 4:5:1:13. Indra.

1. Though, Indra, thou art called by men eastward and westward, north and south, | Thou chiefly art with Anava and Turvaśa, brave champion! urged by men to come. || 2. Or, Indra, when with Ruma, Ruśama, Śyāvaka, and Kṛipa thou rejoicest thee, | Still do the Kaṇvas, bringing prayer, with hymns of praise O Indra, draw thee hither: come!

Daśati 4:5:1:14. Indra.

1. Both boons,—may, Indra, hitherward turned, listen to this prayer of ours. | And mightiest Maghavan with thought inclined to us come near to drink to Soma juice! || 2. For him, strong, independent ruler, Heaven and Earth have fashioned forth with power and might. | Thou seatest thee as first among thy peers in place, for thy soul longs for Soma juice.

Daśati 4:5:1:15. Soma Pavamāna.

1. God, working with mankind flow on; to Indra go thy gladdening juice: | To Vāyu mount as Law commands! || 2. O Soma Pavamāna, thou pourest out wealth that may be famed: | O Indu, pass into the lake! || 3. Soma, thou flowest chasing foes, finder of wisdom and delight: | Drive thou the godless folk afar!

Daśati 4:5:1:16. Soma Pavamāna.

1. Stream on us riches that are craved by hundreds, best at winning spoil, | Riches, O Indu, thousandfold, most splendid, that surpass the light! || 2. May we, O Vasu, be most near to this thy bounty, food, and wealth! | Desired by many men, and in thy favour, O resistless one! || 3. Effused, this Indu hath flowed on, distilling rapture, to the fleece. | He streams erect to sacrifice, as 'twere with splendour, seeking kine.

Daśati 4:5:1:17. Soma Pavamāna.

1. Flow onward, Soma, as a mighty sea, as Father of the Gods, to every form! || 2. Flow on, O Soma, radiant for the Gods, blissful to heaven and earth and living things! || 3. Thou art, bright juice, sustainer of the sky: flow, mighty, in accordance with true law!

Daśati 4:5:1:18. Agni.

1. I laud your most beloved guest, like a dear friend, | O Agni, him! | Who, like a chariot, wins us wealth. || 2. Whom as a Sage who merits praise the Gods have, from the olden time, | Established among mortal men. || 3. Do thou, most youthful God, protect the men who offer, hear their songs, | And of thyself preserve their seed!

Daśati 4:5:1:19. Indra.

1. Come unto us, O Indra, dear, still conquering, unconcealable | Wide as a mountain spread on all sides, Lord of heaven. || 2. O truthful Soma-drinker, thou art mightier than both the worlds. | Thou strengthenest him who pours libation, Lord of heaven. || 3. For thou art he, O Indra, who upholdeth all our fortresses, | The Dasyu's slayer, man's sustainer, Lord of heaven.

Daśati 4:5:1:20. Indra.

1. Render of forts, the young, the wise, of strength unmeasured, was he born, | Sustainer of each sacred rite, Indra, the Thunderer, much extolled, || 2. Thou wielder of the stone, didst burst the cave of Vala rich in kine. | The Gods came pressing to thy side, and free from terror aided thee. || 3. They glorified with hymns of praise Indra who reigneth by his might, | Whose bounteous gifts in thousands come, yea, even more abundantly.

Ardha 2.

Daśati 4:5:2:1. Soma Pavamāna.

1. Guard of all being, generating creatures, loud roared the sea as highest law commanded. | Strong in the filter, on the fleecy summit, pressed from the stone, Soma hath waxen mighty. || 2. Make Vāyu glad, for furtherance and bounty: cheer Varuṇa and Mitra, as they cleanse thee! | Gladden the Gods, gladden the host of Marutas: make Heaven and Earth rejoice, O God, O Soma! || 3. Soma, the mighty, when, the water's offspring, he chose the Gods, performed that great achievement. | He, Pavamāna, granted strength to Indra: he, Indu, generated strength in Sūrya.

Daśati 4:5:2:2. Soma Pavamāna.

1. Here present this immortal God flies, like a bird upon her wings, | To settle in the vats of wood. || 2. Praised by the sacred bards, this God dives into waters, and bestows | Rich gifts upon the worshipper. || 3. He. like a warrior going forth with heroes, as he flows along. | Is fain to win all precious boons. || 4. This God as he is flowing on speeds like a car and gives his aid: | He lets his voice be heard of all. || 5. This God, while flowing, is adorned, gold-coloured, for the spoil, by men | Devout and skilled in holy songs. || 6. This God, made ready with the hymn runs swiftly through the winding ways, | Inviolable as he flows. || 7. A way he rushes with his stream, across the regions, into heaven, | And roars as he is flowing on. || 8. While flowing, meet for sacrifice, he hath gone up to heaven, across | The regions, never overthrown. || 9. By generation long ago, this God, engendered for the Gods, | Flows tawny to the straining-cloth. || 10. This Lord of many holy laws, even at his birth engendering strength, | Effused, flows onward in a stream.

Daśati 4:5:2:3. Soma Pavamāna.

1. Through the fine fingers, with the song, this hero comes with rapid cars, | Going to Indra's settled place. || 2. In holy thought he ponders much for the great service of the Gods, | Where the immortals have their seat. || 3. Men beautify him in the vats, him worthy to be beautified, | Him who brings forth abundant food. || 4. He is deposited and led along the

consecrated path | When zealous men are urging him, || 5. He moves, a vigorous steed, adorned with beauteous rays of shining gold, | He who is Sovereign of the streams. || 6. He brandishes his horns on high, and whets them, bull who leads the herd, | Doing with might heroic deeds. || 7. He, over places rough to pass bringing rich treasures, closely pressed. | Descends into the reservoirs. || 8. Him, even him the golden-hued, well armed, best giver of delight, | Ten fingers urge to run his course.

Daśati 4:5:2:4. Soma Pavamāna.

1. This Bull, this chariot robes him in the sheep's long wool as he proceeds. | To war that wins a thousand spoils. || 2. The dames of Trita with the stones urge forth this golden-coloured one, | Indu to Indra for his drink. || 3. He like a falcon settles down amid the families of men, | Like lover speeding to his love. || 4. This young exhilarating juice looks downward from its place in heaven, | This Soma drop that pierced the sieve. || 5. Pressed for the draught, this tawny juice flows forth intelligent, calling out, | Unto the well-beloved place. || 6. Him, here, the gold-decked skilful ten cleanse carefully, who make him bright. | And beauteous for the gladdening draught.

Daśati 4:5:2:5. Soma Pavamāna.

1. Urged by the men, this vigorous steed, Lord of the mind omniscient, | Flies to the long wool of the sheep. || 2. Within the filter hath he flowed, this Soma for the Gods effused. | Entering all their essences. || 3. He shines in beauty there, this God, immortal, in his dwelling-place, | Foe-slayer, dearest to the Gods. || 4. Directed by the sisters ten, bellowing on his way this Steer | Runs onward to the wooden vats. || 5. This Pavamāna, gladdening drink within the purifying sieve, | Gave splendour to the Sun in heaven. || 6. Unconquerable Lord of speech, dwelling beside Vivasvat, he | Mounts up together with the Sun.

Daśati 4:5:2:6. Soma Pavamāna.

1. This Sage, exalted by our lands, flows to the purifying sieve, | Scattering foes as he is cleansed. || 2. Giver of strength, winner of light, for Indra and for Vāyu he | Is poured upon the filtering-cloth. || 3. The men conduct him, Soma, Steer, omniscient the head of heaven. | Effused into the vats of wood. || 4. Longing for kine, longing for gold hath Indu Pavamāna roared, | Still conqueror, never overcome. || 5. To Indra in the firmament this mighty tawny Steer hath flowed | This Indu, being purified. || 6. This Soma being purified flows mighty and invincible, Slayer of sinners, dear to Gods.

Daśati 4:5:2:7. Soma Pavamāna.

1. This Soma, strong effused for draught, flows to the purifying sieve, | Slaying the fiends, loving the Gods. || 2. Far sighted, tawny-coloured, he flows to the sieve intelligent, | Bellowing to his place of rest. || 3. This vigorous Pavamāna runs forth to the luminous realm of heaven, | Fiend-slayer, through the sheep's long wool. || 4. This Pavamāna, up above on Trita's ridge, hath made the Sun, | Together with the Sisters, shine. || 5. Effused, this Soma, Steer, who slays Vṛitra, room-giver, unbeguiled, | Hath gone as 'twere to win the spoil. || 6. Urged by the sage upon his way, this God speeds forward to the: vats, | Indu to Indra, giving boons.

Daśati 4:5:2:8. Soma Pavamāna.

1. The man who reads the essence stored by saints, the Pavamāna hymns, | Tastes food completely purified, made sweet by Mātariśvan's touch. || 2. Whoever reads the essence stored by saints, the Pavamāna hymns, | For him Sarasvatī pours forth water and butter, milk and meath. || 3. Yea, for the Pavamānas flow richly, drop fatness, bring us weal,— | Amṛita deposited among the Brahmans, essence stored by saints. || 4. So may the Pavamāna hymns bestow on us this world and that, | And gratify our hearts' desires—the Goddesses combined with Gods! || 5. The purifying flood wherewith Gods ever purify themselves,— | With that, in thousand currents, may the Pavamānas make us clean! || 6. The Pavamāna hymns bring weal: by these man goes to Paradise, | And, eating pure and holy food, attains to immortality.

Daśati 4:5:2:9. Agni.

1. We with great reverence have approached the Youngest, who hath shone forth well kindled in his dwelling, | Wondrously bright between wide earth and heaven, well worshipped, looking forth in all directions. || 2. Through his great might o'ercoming all misfortunes, praised in the house is Agni Jātavedas | May he preserve us from disgrace and trouble, both us who laud him and our wealthy princes! || 3. O Agni, thou art Varuṇa and Mitra: Vasiṣhṭhas! with their holy hymns exalt thee. | With thee be most abundant gain of treasure! | Do ye preserve us evermore with blessing!

Daśati 4:5:2:10. Indra.

1. Indra, great in his power and might, and like Parjanya rich in rain. | Hath been increased by Vatsa's lauds. || 2. Since Kaṇvas have with lauds made him completer of the sacrifice, | Words are their own appropriate arms. || 3. When priests who magnify the Son of holy law present their gifts, | Sages with Order's hymn of praise.

Daśati 4:5:2:11. Soma Pavamāna.

1. Of gold-hued Pavamāna, great destroyer, radiant streams have flowed, | Swift streams of him whose gleams are swift. || 2. Best rider of the chariot, praised with fairest praise amid beauteous ones, | Gold gleaming with the Marut host, || 3. Penetrate, Pavamāna, best at winning booty, with thy rays, | Giving the Singer hero strength!

Daśati 4:5:2:12. Soma Pavamāna.

1. Hence sprinkle forth the juice effused, Soma, the best of sacred gifts, | Who, friend of man, hath run among the water-streams He hath pressed Soma out with stones. || 2. Now, being purified, flow hither through the fleece, invincible and more odorous! | We joy in thee in waters when thou art effused, blending thee still with juice and milk. || 3. Pressed out for all to see, delighting Gods, Indu, far-seeing one, is mental power.

Daśati 4:5:2:13. Soma Pavamāna.

1. Even as a King hath Soma, red and tawny Bull, been pressed the wondrous one hath bellowed to the kine. | While purified thou passest through the filtering fleece to seat thee hawk-like in the place that drops with oil. || 2. Parjanya is the sire of the leaf-bearing Bull: on mountains, in earth's centre hath he made his home. | The waters have flowed forth, the Sisters, to the kine: he meets the pressing-stones at the beloved rite. || 3. To glory goest thou, a Sage with ordering skill, like a groomed steed thou rushest forward to the prize. | Be gracious to us, Soma, driving off distress! Thou goest, clothed in butter, to a robe of state.

Daśati 4:5:2:14. Indra.

1. Turning as 'twere to meet the Sun, enjoy from Indra all good things! | When he who will be born is born with power we look to treasures as our heritage. || 2. Praise him who sends us wealth, prompt with his liberal boons Good are the gifts that Indra gives. | He is not wroth with one who satisfies his wish: he instigates, his mind to give.

Daśati 4:5:2:15. Indra.

1. Indra, give us security from that whereof we are afraid | Help us, O Maghavan, let thy favour aid us thus drive away foes and enemies! || 2. For thou, O liberal Lord of ample bounty, art the ruler of our house and home. | So, Indra Maghavan, thou lover of the song, we with pressed Soma call on thee.

Daśati 4:5:2:16. Soma Pavamāna.

1. Thou, Soma, hast a running stream, sweet-toned most strong at sacrifice: | Flow bounteously bestowing wealth || 2. Thou most delightful, when effused, running, the best of gladdeners, art | Indu, still conquering, ne'er subdued. || 3. Do thou, poured forth by pressing-stones, flow hither uttering a roar, | And bring us brightly-glorious strength!

Daśati 4:5:2:17. Soma Pavamāna.

1. In might, O Indu, with thy streams flow for the banquet of the Gods: | Rich in meath, Soma, in our beaker take thy seat! || 2. Thy drops that swim in water have exalted Indra to delight | The Gods have drunk thee up for immortality. || 3. Stream opulence to us, ye drops of Soma, pressed and purified | Pouring down rain from heaven in floods, and finding light!

Daśati 4:5:2:18. Soma Pavamāna.

1. Him with the fleece they purify, brown, golden-hued beloved of all, | Who with exhilarating juice goes forth to all the deities || 2. Whom, bright with native splendour, crushed between the pressing-stones, a friend. | Whom Indra dearly loves, the waves and ten companions dip and bathe || 3. For Vṛitra-slaying Indra, thou, Soma, art poured that he may drink, | And for the guerdon-giving man, the hero sitting in his seat.

Daśati 4:5:2:19. Soma Pavamāna.

1. Flow onward Soma, flow for mighty strength, as a strong courser, bathed, to win the prize. ‖ 2. The pressers clarify this juice of thine, the Soma for delight and lofty fame. ‖ 3. They deck the gold-hued infant, newly-born, even Soma, Indu, in the sieve, for Gods.

Daśati 4:5:2:20. Soma Pavamāna.

1. The Gods have come to Indu well-descended, beautified with milk, | The active crusher of the foe. ‖ 2. Even as mother cows their calf, so let our praise-songs strengthen him, | Yea, him who winneth Indra's heart! ‖ 3. Soma, pour blessings on our kine, pour forth the food that streams with milk: | Increase the sea, praiseworthy one!

Daśati 4:5:2:21. Indra.

1. Hitherward! they who light the flame and straightway trim the sacred grass, | Whose friend is Indra ever young. ‖ 2. Large is their fuel, much their laud, wide is their splinter from the stake, | Whose friend is Indra ever young. ‖ 3. Unquelled in fight the hero leads his army with the warrior chiefs, | Whose friend is Indra ever young.

Daśati 4:5:2:22. Indra.

1. He who alone bestoweth wealth on mortal man who offereth gifts, | Is Indra only, potent Lord whom none resist. ‖ 2. Whoever with the Soma pressed draws thee away from many men,— | Verily Indra gains thereby tremendous power. ‖ 3. When will he trample, like a weed, the man who hath no gift for him? | When, verily, will Indra hear our songs of praise?

Daśati 4:5:2:23. Indra.

1. The singers hymn thee, they who chant the psalm of praise are lauding thee. | The Brahmans have exalted thee, O Śatakratu, like a pole. ‖ 2, When thou wast climbing ridge from ridge, he looked upon the toilsome task: | Indra takes notice of that wish, and the Ram hastens with his troop. ‖ 3. Harness thy pair of strong bay steeds, long-maned, whose bodies fill the girths. | And, Indra, Soma drinker, come to listen to our songs Of praise!

Prapāṭhaka 6.

Ardha 1.

Daśati 4:6:1:1. Agni.

1. Agni,well kindled bring the Gods for him who offers holy gifts; | And worship them, pure Hotar-priest! ‖ 2. O Sage, Tanūnapāt, present our sacrifice to Gods today, | Sweet to the taste, that they may help! ‖ 3. Dear Narāśaṃsa, sweet of tongue, presenter of oblations, I | Invoke to this our sacrifice. ‖ 4. Agni, on thy most easy car, entreated, hither bring the Gods! | Manus' appointed Priest art thou.

Daśati 4:6:1:2. Ādityas.

1. So when the Sun hath risen today may sinless Mitra, Aryaman, Bhaga, and Savitar send us forth! ‖ 2. May this our home be guarded well: forward, ye bounteous, on the way, Who bear us safely o'er distress! ‖ 3. Yea, Aditi, and those great Kings whose statute is inviolate, Are sovereigns of a vast domain.

Daśati 4:6:1:3. Indra.

1. Let Soma juices make thee glad! Display thy bounty, Thunderer: | Drive off the enemies of prayer! ‖ 2. Crush with thy foot the niggard churls who bring no gifts! mighty art thou: | There is not one to equal thee. ‖ 3. Thou art the Lord of Somas pressed, Somas unpressed are also thine: | Thou art the Sovereign of the folk.

Daśati 4:6:1:4. Soma Pavamāna.

1. True object of our hymns, Sage, watchful Soma hath settled in the press as they refine him. | Him the Adhvaryus, paired and eager, follow, leaders of sacrifice and skilful-handed. ‖ 2. He, purified and bringing gifts to Sūrya, hath filled full heaven and earth, and hath disclosed them. | He by whose dear help heroes gain their wishes will yield the precious meed as to a victor. ‖ 3. He, being cleansed, the strengthener and increaser, bountiful Soma helped us his lustre, | Wherein our sires of old who knew the footsteps found light and sought the kine within the mountain.

Daśati 4:6:1:5. Indra.

1. Glorify naught besides, O friends, so shall no sorrow trouble you! | Praise only mighty Indra, when the juice is shed, and say your lauds repeatedly! ‖ 2. Even him, the swift one, like a bull who rushes down men's conqueror, bounteous like a cow; | Him who is cause of both, of enmity and peace, to both sides most munificent.

Daśati 4:6:1:6. Indra.

1. These songs of our exceeding sweet, these hymns of praise ascend to thee, | Like ever-conquering chariots that display their strength, gain wealth and give unfailing help. ‖ 2. The Bhṛigus are like suns, like Kaṇvas, and have gained each thing whereon their thought was bent. | The living men of Priyamedha's race have sun g exalting Indra with their lauds.

Daśati 4:6:1:7. Soma Pavamāna.

1. Run forth to battle conquering the Vṛitras! thou Speedest to quell the foe like one exacting debts. ‖ 2. Thou Pavamāna, didst beget the Sun with might, and rain in the supporting sky, | Hasting to us with plenty vivified with milk. ‖ 3. For, Soma, we rejoice ourselves in thee effused for great supremacy in fight; | Thou, Pavamāna, enterest into mighty deeds.

Daśati 4:6:1:8. Soma Pavamāna.

1. Flow forth, O Soma, flow thou onward, sweet to Indra's, | Mitra's, Pūṣhan's, Bhaga's taste! ‖ 2. So flow thou on as bright celestial juice, flow to the vast immortal dwelling-place! ‖ 3. Let Indra drink, O Soma, of thy juice for wisdom, and all deities for strength!

Daśati 4:6:1:9. Soma Pavamāna.

1. Even as the beams of Sūrya, urging men to speed, they issue forth together, gladdening as they flow, | These swift outpourings in long course of holy rites: no form save only Indra shows itself so pure. ‖ 2. The thought is deeply fixed, the savoury juice is shed; the tongue with joyous sound is stirring in the mouth: | And Pavamāna, like the shout of those who press, the drop, rich in sweet juice, is flowing through the fleece. ‖ 3. The bull is bellowing; the cows are coming nigh: the Goddesses approach the God's own resting-place. | Onward hath Soma pressed through the sheep's fair bright fleece, and hath, as 'twere, endued a garment newly washed.

Daśati 4:6:1:10. Agni.

1. From the two fire-sticks have the men engendered, with thought, urged by the hand, the glorious Agni, | Far-seen, with pointed flame, Lord of the Homestead. ‖ 2. The Vasus set that Agni in the dwelling, fair to behold, for help, from every quarter: | Who, in the house for ever, must be honoured. ‖ 3. Shine thou before us, Agni, well-enkindled, with flame, most youthful God, that never fadeth! | To thee come goods and treasures all together.

Daśati 4:6:1:11. Sūrya.

1. This spotted Bull hath come and sat before the mother in the east, | Advancing to his father heaven. ‖ 2. As expiration from his breath, his radiance penetrates within | The Bull shines out through all the sky. ‖ 3. Song is bestowed upon the Bird: it reigns supreme through thirty realms. | Throughout the days at break of morn.

Ardha 2.

Daśati 4:6:2:1. Agni.

1. Chant we a hymn to Agni while we go to sacrifice, to him | Who hears us even from afar! ‖ 2. Who from of old, in carnage, when the folk were gathered, hath preserved. | His household for the worshipper. ‖ 3. May that most blissful Agni guard our wealth and all our family. | And keep us safe from pain and grief ‖ 4. Yea, let men say, Agni is born, even he who slayeth Vṛitra, he, | Who winneth wealth in every fight!

Daśati 4:6:2:2. Agni.

1. Harness, O Agni, O thou God, thy steeds which are most excellent! | The fleet ones bring the rapidly. ‖ 2. Come hither, bring the Gods to us to taste the sacrificial feast, | To drink the draught of Soma juice! ‖ 3. O Agni of the Bhāratas, flame splendid with unfading might | Shine forth and gleam, eternal one!

Daśati 4:6:2:3. Soma Pavamāna.

1. Let him, as mortal, crave this speech for him who presses of the juice! | As Bhṛigu's sons chased Makha, so drive ye the niggard hound away. ‖ 2. The kinsman hath endued his robe even as a son is clasped in arms. | He went, as lover to a dame, to take his station suitor-like. ‖ 3. That hero who produces strength, he who hath propped both worlds apart, | Gold-hued, hath wrapped him in the sieve to settle, priest-like, in his place.

Daśati 4:6:2:4. Indra.

1. Still, Indra, from all ancient time rivalless ever and companionless art

thou: | Thou seekest friendship but in war. || 2. Thou findest not the wealthy man to be thy friend: those scorn thee who are flown with wine. | What time thou thunderest and gatherest, then thou, even as a father, art invoked.

Daśati 4:6:2:5. Indra.

1. A thousand and a hundred steeds are harnessed to thy golden car: | Yoked by devotion, Indra, let the long-maned bays bring thee to drink the Soma juice! || 2. Yoked to thy chariot wrought of gold, may thy two bays with, peacock tails. | Convey thee hither, steeds with their white backs, to quaff sweet juice that makes us eloquent! || 3. So drink, thou lover of the song, as the first drinker, of this juice. | This the outpouring of the savoury sap prepared is good and meet to gladden thee.

Daśati 4:6:2:6. Soma Pavamāna.

1. Press ye and pour him, like a steed, laud-worthy, speeding through the region and the flood, | Who swims in water, dwells in wood || 2. The Steer with thousand streams who poureth out the rain, dear to the race of deities; | Who, born in Law, hath waxen mighty by the Law, King, God, and lofty ordinance.

Daśati 4:6:2:7. Agni.

1. Served with oblation, kindled, bright, through love of song, may Agni, bent | On riches, smite the Vṛitras dead || 2. His father's father, shining in his mother's ever-lasting side, | Set on the seat of sacrifice! || 3. O active Jātavedas, bring devotion that wins progeny, Agni, that it may shine to heaven!

Daśati 4:6:2:8. Soma Pavamāna.

1. Made pure by this man's urgent zeal and impulse, the God hath with his juice the Gods pervaded. | Pressed, singing, to the sieve he goes, as passes the Hotar to enclosures holding cattle. || 2. Robed in fair raiment meet to wear in combat, a mighty Sage pronouncing invocations, | Roll onward to the press-boards as they cleanse thee, far-seeing at the feast of Gods and watchful! || 3. Dear, he is brightened on the fleecy summit, a prince among us, nobler than the noble. | Roar out as thou art purified, run forward! Do ye preserve us evermore with blessings!

Daśati 4:6:2:9. Indra.

1. Come now and let us glorify pure Indra with pure Sāman hymn! | Let milk-blent juice delight him made stronger with pure, pure songs of praise! || 2. O Indra, come thou pure to us, with pure assistance pure thyself! | Pure, send thou riches down to us, and, meet for Soma! pure, rejoice! || 3. O Indra, pure, vouchsafe us wealth, and, pure enrich the worshipper! | Pure, thou dost strike the Vṛitras dead, and strivest pure, to win the spoil.

Daśati 4:6:2:10. Agni.

1. Eager for wealth we meditate Agni's effectual laud today, | Laud of the God who touches heaven. || 2. May Agni who is Hotar-priest among mankind accept our songs, | And worship the celestial folk! || 3. Thou, Agni, art spread widely forth, Priest dear and excellent through thee | Men make the sacrifice complete.

Daśati 4:6:2:11. Soma Pavamāna.

1. To him, praiseworthy, sacred tones have sounded, Steer of the triple height, the life-bestower. | Dwelling in wood, like Varuṇa, a river, lavishing treasure, he distributes blessings. || 2. Great conqueror, warrior girt, Lord of all heroes, flow on thy way as he who winneth riches: | With sharpened arms, with swift bow, never vanquished in battle, vanquishing in fight the foemen! || 3. Giving security, Lord of wide dominion, send us both heaven and earth with all their fullness! | Striving to win the Dawns, the light, the waters, and cattle, call to us abundant booty!

Daśati 4:6:2:12. Indra.

1. O Indra, thou art far-renowned, impetuous Lord of power and might. | Alone, the never-conquered guardian of mankind, thou smitest down resistless foes. || 2. As such we seek thee now, O Asura, the most wise, craving thy bounty as our share | Thy sheltering defence is like an ample cloak. So may thy favours reach to us.

Daśati 4:6:2:13. Agni.

1. Thee have we chosen, skilfullest in sacrifice, immortal, Priest, among the Gods, | Best finisher of this holy rite: || 2. The Waters' Child, the blessed brightly-shining one, Agni whose, light is excellent. | May he by sacrifice win us in heaven the grace of Mitra, Varuṇa, and the Floods!

Daśati 4:6:2:14. Agni.

1. Lord of all food is he, the man whom thou protectest in the fight, | Agni, and urgest to the fray. || 2. Him, whosoever he may be, no one may vanquish, mighty one! | Nay, very glorious wealth is his. || 3. May he who dwells with all mankind conquer in fight with steeds of war, | With sages may he win the spoil.

Daśati 4:6:2:15. Soma Pavamāna.

1. Ten sisters, pouring out the rain together, the sage's quickly | moving thoughts, adorn him. | Hither hath run the gold-hued Child of Sūrya, and reached the vat like a fleet vigorous courser. || 2. Even as a youngling shouting with his mothers, the bounteous Steer hath flowed along with waters. | As youth to damsel, so with milk he hastens on to the settled meeting-place, the beaker. || 3. Yea, swollen is the udder of the milch-cow; thither in streams. comes very sapient Indu. | The kine make ready, as with new-washed treasures, the head and chief with milk within the vessels.

Daśati 4:6:2:16. Indra.

1. Drink, Indra, of the savoury juice, and cheer thee, with our milky draught! | Be, for our weal, our friend and sharer of the feast, and let thy wisdom guard us well! || 2. In thy kind grace and favour may we still be strong: cast us not down before the foe! | With manifold assistance guard and succour us, and establish us in thy good-will!

Daśati 4:6:2:17. Soma Pavamāna.

1. The three-times seven milch-kine in the loftiest heaven have for this Soma poured the genuine milky draught. | Four other beauteous creatures hath he made for his adornment when he waxed in strength through holy rites. || 2. Enjoying lovely Amṛita by his wisdom he divided, each apart from other, earth and heaven. | He gladly wrapped himself in the most lucid floods, when through their glory they-found the God's resting-place. || 3. May those his brilliant rays be ever free from death, inviolate for both classes of created things— | Rays wherewith powers of men and Gods are purified! Yea, even for this have sages welcomed him as King.

Daśati 4:6:2:18. Soma Pavamāna.

1. Lauded with song, to feast him, flow to Vāyu, flow purified to Varuṇa and Mitra! | Flow to the song inspiring car-borne hero, to mighty Indra, him who wields the thunder! || 2. Pour on us garments that shall clothe us meetly, send, purified, milch-kine, abundant yielders! | God Soma, send us chariot-drawing horses that they may bring us treasures bright and golden! || 3. Send to us in a stream celestial riches, send us when thou art cleansed, what earth containeth, | So that thereby we may acquire possessions and Ṛishihood in Jamadagni's manner!

Daśati 4:6:2:19. Indra.

1. When thou, unequalled Maghavan, wast born to smite the Vṛitras dead, | Thou spreadest out the spacious earth and didst support and prop the heavens. || 2. Then was the sacrifice produced for thee, the laud, and song of joy. | In might thou art above this All, all that now is and yet shall be. || 3. Raw kine thou filledst with ripe milk. Thou madest Sūrya rise to heaven. | Heat him as milk is heated with pure Sāman hymns, great joy to him who loves the song!

Daśati 4:6:2:20. Indra.

1. Rejoice: thy glory hath been quaffed, Lord of bay steeds! as 'twere the bowl's enlivening mead. | Thine, Steer, is Indu, Steer, the Strong, best winner of a thousand spoils. || 2. Let our strong drink, most excellent, exhilarating, come to thee, | Victorious, Indra! bringing gain, immortal conquering in fight! || 3. Thou, hero, winner of the spoil, urgest to speed the car of man. | Burn, like a vessel with the flame, the riteless Dasyu, conqueror!

Ardha 3.

Daśati 4:6:3:1. Soma Pavamāna.

1. Pour down the rain upon us, pour a wave of waters from the sky. | And plenteous store of wholesome food! || 2. Flow onward with that stream of thine, whereby the cows have come to us. | The kine of strangers to our home. || 3. Dearest to Gods in sacred rites, pour on us fatness with thy stream, | Pour down on us a flood of rain! || 4. To give as vigour, with thy stream run through the fleecy straining-cloth! | For verily the Gods will hear. || 5. Onward hath Pavamāna flowed and beaten off the Rākṣhasas | Flashing out splendour as of old.

Daśati 4:6:3:2. Indra.

1. Bring forth oblations to the God who knoweth all, who fain would drink. | The wanderer, lagging not behind the hero, coming nigh with, speed! || 2. With Somas go ye nigh to him chief drinker of the Soma's juice: | With beakers to the impetuous God, to Indra with the flowing, drops! || 3. What time with Somas, with the drops effused,, ye come before the God, | Full wise, he knows the hope of each, and, bold one strikes this. foe and that. || 4. To him, Adhvaryu! yea, to him give offerings of the juice expressed! | Will he not keep us safely from the spiteful curse of each, presumptuous high-born foe?

Daśati 4:6:3:3. Soma Pavamāna.

1. Sing ye a song to Soma brown of hue, of independent might, | The Red, who reaches up to heaven! || 2. Purify Soma when effused with stones which hands move rapidly, | And pour the sweet milk in the meath. || 3. With humble homage draw ye nigh; blend the libation with the curds: | To Indra offer Indu up || 4. Soma, foe-queller, strong and swift, doing the will of Gods, pour forth, | Prosperity upon our kine || 5. Heart-knower, Sovereign of the heart, thou art effused, O Soma, that, | Indra may drink thee and rejoice. || 6. O Soma Pavamāna, give us riches and heroic strength, Indu, with Indra. our ally!

Daśati 4:6:3:4. Indra.

1. Sūrya, thou mountest up to meet the hero famous for his wealth, | Who hurls the bolt and works for men; || 2. Him who with might of both his arms broke nine-and-ninety castles down, | Slew Vṛitra and smote Ahi dead. || 3. This Indra is our gracious friend. He sends, like a full-streaming cow, | Riches in horses, kine, and corn.

Daśati 4:6:3:5. Sūrya.

1. May the bright God drink glorious Soma-mingled meath, giving | the sacrifices lord unbroken life | He who, wind-urged, in person guards our offspring well, nourishes them with food and shines o'er many a land. || 2. Radiant, as high Truth, cherished, best at winning strength, Truth based upon the statute that supports the heavens, | He rose, a light that kills Vṛitras and enemies, best slayer of the Dasyus, Asuras, and foes. || 3. This light, the best of lights, supreme, all conquering, winner of riches, is exalted with high laud. | All-lighting, radiant, mighty as the Sun to see, he spreadeth wide unshaken victory and strength.

Daśati 4:6:3:6. Indra.

1. O Indra, give us wisdom as a sire gives wisdom to his sons, | Guide us, O much-invoked, in this our way: may we still live and look upon the light! || 2. Grant that no mighty foes, unknown, malevolent unhallowed, tread us to the ground! | With thine assistance, hero, may we pass through all the waters that are rushing down!

Daśati 4:6:3:7. Indra.

1. Protect us, Indra, each today, each to morrow, and each following day! | Through all the days shalt thou, Lord of the brave, preserve our singers both by day and night! || 2. A crushing warrior, passing rich, is Maghavan, endowed with all heroic strength. | Thine arms, O Śatakratu, are exceeding strong, those arms, | which grasp the thunderbolt.

Daśati 4:6:3:8. Sarasvat.

1. We call upon Sarasvat as unmarried men who long for wives, | As bounteous men who yearn for sons.

Daśati 4:6:3:9. Sarasvatī.

1. Yea, she most dear amid dear streams, seven-sistered, loved with foundest love. | Sarasvatī, hath earned our praise.

Daśati 4:6:3:10. Savitar. Brahmaṇaspati Agni.

1. May we attain that excellent glory of Savitar the God: So may he stimulate our prayers! || 2. O Brahmaṇaspati, make thou Kakṣhīvant Auśija a loud Chanter of flowing Soma juice! || 3. Agni, thou pourest life: send down upon us food and vigorous strength; | Drive thou misfortune far away!

Daśati 4:6:3:11. Mitra-Varuṇa.

1. So help ye us to riches, great celestial and terrestrial wealth | Vast is your sway among the Gods! || 2. Carefully tending Law with law they have attained their vigorous might: | Both Gods, devoid of guile, wax strong. || 3. With rainy skies and streaming floods, Lords of the food that falls in dew, | A lofty seat have they attained.

Daśati 4:6:3:12. Indra.

1. They who stand round him as he moves harness the bright, the ruddy steed: | The lights shining in the sky. || 2. On both sides to the car they yoke the two bay coursers dear to him, | Brown, bold, who bear the hero on. || 3. Thou, making light where no light was, and form, O men where form was not, | Wast born together with the Dawns.

Daśati 4:6:3:13. Soma Pavamāna.

1. For thee this Soma is effused. O Indra: drink of this juice; for thee the stream is flowing— | Soma, which thou thyself hast made and chosen, even Indu for thy special drink to cheer thee! || 2. Like a capacious car hath it been harnessed, the mighty, to acquire abundant treasures. | Then in the sacrifice they shouted lauding all triumphs won by Nahus in the battle. || 3. Flow onward like the potent band of Marutas, like that celestial host which none revileth! | Quickly be gracious unto us like waters, like sacrifice victorious, thousand-fashioned!

Daśati 4:6:3:14. Agni.

1. O Agni, thou hast been ordained Hotar of every sacrifice, By Gods, among the race of men. | So with sweet-sounding tongues for us sacrifice nobly in this rite: | Bring thou the Gods and worship them || 3. For, as disposer, Agni, God, most wise in sacrifices, thou knowest straightway the roads and paths.

Daśati 4:6:3:15. Agni.

1. Immortal, Hotar-priest, and God, with wondrous power he leads the way, | Urging the congregations on. || 2. Strong, he is set on deeds of strength. He is led forth in holy rites, | Sage who completes the sacrifice. || 3. Excellent, he was made by thought. The germ of beings have gained. | Yea, and the Sire of active power.

Daśati 4:6:3:16. Agni.

1. Pour on the juice the heated milk which hasteneth to heaven and. earth; | Bestow the liquid on the Bull! || 2. These know their own abiding-place: like calves beside the mother cows, | They come together with their kin. || 3. Devouring in their greedy jaws, they make sustaining food in heaven, | For Indra, Agni, homage, light.

Daśati 4:6:3:17. Indra.

1. In all the worlds That was the best and highest whence sprang the mighty one, of splendid valour, | As soon as he is born he smites his foemen, he in whom all | who lend him aid are joyful foe || 2. Grown mighty in his strength, of ample vigour, he as a strikes fear into the Dāsa, | Eager to win the breathing and the breathless. All sang thy praise at banquet and oblation. || 3. All concentrate on thee their mental vigour, what time these, once or twice, are thine assistants. | Blend what is sweeter than the sweet with sweetness: win quickly with our meath that meath in battle.

Daśati 4:6:3:18. Indra.

1. At the Trikadrukas the great and strong enjoyed the barley-brew. With Viṣhṇu did he drink the pressed-out Soma juice, even as he would. | That hath so heightened him the great, the wide, to do his mighty work. So may the God attend the God, true Indu Indra who is true! || 2. Brought forth together with wisdom and potent strength thou grewest great: with hero deeds subduing the malevolent, most swift in act; | Giving prosperity and lovely wealth to him who praiseth thee. | So may the God attend the God, true Indu Indra who is true! || 3. So he resplendent in the battle overcame Krivi by might. He with his majesty bath filled the earth and heaven, and waxen strong. | One share of the libation bath he swallowed down: one share he left. Enlighten us! So may the God attend the God, true Indu Indra who is true!

Prapāṭhaka 7.

Ardha 1.

Daśati 4:7:1:1. Indra.

1. Praise, even as he is known, with song Indra the guardian of the kine, | The Son of Truth, Lord of the brave, || 2. Hither have his bay steeds been sent, red steeds are on the sacred grass | Where we in concert sing our songs. || 3. For Indra, thunder-armed, the kine have yielded mingled milk and meath, | What time he found them in the vault.

Daśati 4:7:1:2. Indra.

1. Draw near unto our Indra who must be invoked in every fight! | Come, thou most mighty Vṛitra-slayer, meet for praise come to | libations and to hymns. || 2. Thou art the best of all in sending bounteous gifts, true art thou,, lordly in thine act. | We claim alliance with the very glorious one, yea, with the | mighty Son of Strength.

Daśati 4:7:1:3. Soma Pavamāna.

1. They have drained forth from out the great depth of the sky the old divine primeval milk that claims the laud: | They lifted up their voice to Indra at his birth. || 2. Then, beautifully radiant, certain heavenly ones proclaimed their kinship with him as they looked thereon: | Savitar opens, as it were, the fold of heaven. || 3. And now that thou, O Pavamāna, art above this earth and heaven and all existence in thy might, | Thou shinest like a bull supreme among the herd.

Daśati 4:7:1:4. Agni.

1. O Agni, graciously announce this our good fortune to the Gods, | And this our newest hymn of praise! || 2. Thou dealest gifts, resplendent one! nigh, as with wave of Sindhu, thou | Swift streamest to the worshipper. || 3. Give us a share of wealth most high, a share of wealth most near to us, | A share of wealth that is between.

Daśati 4:7:1:5. Indra.

1. I from my Father have obtained deep knowledge of eternal Law; | I was born like unto the Sun. || 2. After the ancient manner I, like Kaṇva, beautify my songs, | And Indra's self gains power thereby. || 3. Whatever Ṛishis have not praised thee, Indra, or have praised thee, wax | Mighty indeed when praised by me!

Daśati 4:7:1:6. Agni.

1. Agni, produced by strength, do thou with all thy fires accept our prayer: | With those that are with Gods, with those that are with men exalt our songs! || 2. Forth come to us with all his fires that Agni, whose the mighty are, | Come, fully girt about with wealth for us and for our kith and kin! || 3. Do thou, O Agni, with thy fires strengthen our prayer and sacrifices: | Incite them to bestow their wealth to aid our service of the Gods!

Daśati 4:7:1:7. Soma Pavamāna.

1. Some, the men of old whose grass was trimmed addressed the hymn to thee for mighty strength and for renown: | So, hero, urge us onward to heroic power. || 2. All round about hast thou with glory pierced for us as 'twere a never-failing well for men to drink, | Borne on thy way as 'twere in fragments from both arms. || 3. Thou didst produce him, deathless one! for mortal man, for maintenance of Law and lovely Amṛita: | Thou evermore hast moved making wealth flow to us.

Daśati 4:7:1:8. Indra.

1. Pour out the drops f or Indra; let him drink the meath of Soma Juice! | He through his majesty sends forth his bounteous gifts. || 2. I spake to the bay coursers' Lord, to him who grants the boon. of wealth: | Now hear the son of Aśva as he praises thee? || 3. Never was any hero born before thee mightier than thou: | None certainly like thee in riches and in praise.

Daśati 4:7:1:9. Indra.

1. Thou wishest for thy kine a bull, lord of thy cows whom none may kill, | For those who long for his approach, for those who turn away from him.

Daśati 4:7:1:10. Agni.

1. The God who giveth wealth accept the full libation poured to him! | Pour ye it out, then fill the vessel full again, for so the God regardeth you! || 2. The Gods made him the Hotar-priest of sacrifice, oblation-bearer, passing wise. | Agni gives wealth and valour to the worshipper, to man who offers up his gifts.

Daśati 4:7:1:11. Agni.

1. He hath appeared, best prosperer, in whom men lay their holy acts: | So may our songs of praise come nigh to Agni who was born to give the Ārya strength. || 2. Him before whom the people shrink when he performs his glorious deeds, | Him who wins thousands at the sacrifice, himself, that Agni, reverence with songs! || 3. Agni of Divodāsa, God, comes forth like Indra in his might. | Rapidly hath he moved along his mother earth; he stands in high heaven's dwelling-place.

Daśati 4:7:1:12. Agni.

1. Agni, thou pourest life: send down upon us food and vigorous strength: | Drive thou misfortune far away! || 2. Agni is Pavamāna, Sage, Chief Priest of all the fivefold tribes; To him whose wealth is great we pray. || 3. Skilled in thy task, O Agni, pour splendour with hero strength on us, Granting me wealth that nourishes!

Daśati 4:7:1:13. Agni.

1. O Agni, holy and divine with splendour and thy pleasant tongue. Bring thou the Gods and worship them! || 2. We pray thee bathed in butter, O bright-rayed! who lookest on the sun, Bring the Gods hither to the feast! || 3. Sage, we have kindled thee, the bright, the feaster on oblation, thee, O Agni, great in sacrifice!

Daśati 4:7:1:14. Agni.

1. Adorable in all our prayers, favour us, Agni, with thine aid. | What time the psalm is chanted forth! || 2. Bring to us ever-conquering wealth, wealth, Agni, worthy of our choice, | Invincible in all our frays! || 3. Grant us, O Agni, through thy grace wealth to support us evermore, | Thy favour so that we may live!

Daśati 4:7:1:15. Agni.

1. Let songs of ours speed Agni forth like a fleet courser in the race, | And we will win each prize through him || 2. Agni! the host whereby we gain kine for ourselves with help from thee,— | That send us for the gain of wealth! || 3. O Agni, bring us wealth secure, vast wealth in horses and in kine: | Oil thou the socket, turn the wheel! || 4. O Agni, thou hast made the Sun, the eternal star, to mount the sky, | Giving the boon of light to men. || 5. Thou, Agni, art the people's light, best, dearest, seated in thy shrine | Watch for the singer, give him life!

Daśati 4:7:1:16. Agni.

1. Agni is head and height of heaven, the master of the earth is he: | He quickeneth the waters' seed. || 2. Yea, Agni, thou as Lord of light rulest o'er choicest gifts may I, | Thy singer, find defence in thee || 3. Upward, O Agni, rise thy flames, pure and resplendent, blazing high, | Thy lustres, fair effulgences.

Ardha 2.

Daśati 4:7:2:1. Agni.

1. Who, Agni, is thy kin, of men? who honours thee with sacrifice? | On whom dependent? who art thou? || 2. The kinsman, Agni! of mankind, their well-beloved friend art thou, | A friend whom friends may supplicate. || 3. Bring Mitra, Varuṇa, bring the Gods hither to. our great sacrifice: | Bring them, O Agni, to thine home

Daśati 4:7:2:2. Agni.

1. Meet to be worshipped and implored, showing in beauty through the gloom, | Agni, the strong, is kindled well. || 2. Strong Agni is enkindled well, even as the horse that brings the Gods: | Men with oblations pray to him. || 3. We will enkindle thee, the strong, we, hero! who axe strong ourselves,

Daśati 4:7:2:3. Agni.

1. Thy mighty flames, O Agni, when thou art enkindled, rise on high, | Thy bright flames, thou refulgent one || 2. Beloved! let my ladies full of sacred oil come nigh to thee. | Agni, accept our offerings! || 3. I pray to Agni —may he hear!—the Hotar with sweet tones, the Priest, | Wondrously splendid, rich in light.

Daśati 4:7:2:4. Agni.

1. Agni, protect them us with one, protect us by the second song, | Protect us by three hymns, Lord of power and might, bright God, by four hymns guard us well! || 2. Preserve us from each demon who bestows no gift, in battles succour us and save! | For we obtain in thee the nearest friend of all, for the Gods' service and our weal.

Daśati 4:7:2:5. Agni.

1. O King, the potent and terrific envoy, kindled for strength, is | manifest in beauty. | He shines, observant, with his lofty splendour; chasing black night he comes with white-rayed morning. || 2. Having o'ercome the glimmering Black with beauty, and bringing forth the Dame, the great Sire's daughter, | Holding aloft the radiant lights of Sūrya, as messenger of heaven he shines with treasures. || 3. Attendant on the blessed Dame the

blessed hath come: the lover followeth his sister. | Agni, far-spreading with conspicuous lustre, hath covered night with whitely-shining garments.

Daśati 4:7:2:6. Agni.

1. What is the praise wherewith, O God, Aṅgiras, Agni, Son of Strength, | We, after thine own wish and thought, || 2. May serve thee, O thou Child of Power, and with what sacrifice's plan? | What reverent word shall I speak here?

Daśati 4:7:2:7. Agni.

1. Agni, come hither with thy fires; we choose thee as our Hotar; let | The proffered ladle filled with offerings balm thee, best of priests, to sit on sacred grass! || 2. For unto thee, O Aṅgiras, O Son of Strength, move ladles in the sacrifice. | We pray to Agni, Child of Force, whose locks drop oil, foremost in sacrificial rites.

Daśati 4:7:2:8. Agni.

1. Let our songs come anear to him beauteous and bright with piercing flame, | Our sacrifices with our homage unto him much-lauded, very rich, for help: || 2. To Agni Jātavedas, to the Son of Strength, that he may give us precious gifts, || 3. Immortal, from of old Priest among mortal men, whose tones are sweetest in the house!

Daśati 4:7:2:9. Agni.

1. Invincible is Agni, he who goes before the tribes of men, | A chariot swift and ever new. || 2. By bringing offerings unto him the mortal worshipper obtains | A home from him whose light is pure. || 3. Inviolable power of Gods, subduing all his enemies, Agni is mightiest in fame.

Daśati 4:7:2:10. Agni.

1. May Agni, worshipped, bring us bliss: may the gift, blessed one! and sacrifice bring bliss, | Yea, may our eulogies bring bliss || 2. Show forth the mind that brings success in war with fiends, wherewith thou conquerest in fight! | Bring down the many firm hopes of our enemies, and for thy victory let us win!

Daśati 4:7:2:11. Agni.

1. O Agni thou who art the Lord of wealth in kine, thou Son of Strength, | Bestow on us, O Jātavedas, high renown || 2. He, Agni, kindled, good and wise, must be entreated with a. song; | Shine, thou of many forms, shine thou with wealth on us || 3. And, Agni, shining of thyself by night and when the morning breaks, | Burn, thou whose teeth are sharp, against the Rākṣhasas

Daśati 4:7:2:12. Agni.

1. Exerting all our strength with thoughts of power we glorify in speech, | Agni, your dear familiar friend, the darling guest of every house: || 2. Whom, served with sacrificial oil, like Mitra, men presenting gifts, | Glorify with their songs of praise || 3. Much-lauded Jātavedas, him who sends oblations up to heaven, | Prepared in service of the Gods.

Daśati 4:7:2:13. Agni.

1. Agni, inflamed with fuel, in my song I sing, pure bright, and steadfast set in front at sacrifice. | Wise Jātavedas we implore with prayers for grace, the Sage, the Hotar-priest, bounteous, and void of guile. || 2. Men, Agni, in each age, have made thee, deathless one, their envoy, offering-bearer, guard adorable. | With reverence Gods and mortals have established thee as ever-watchful and almighty household Lord. || 3. Though, Agni ordering the works and ways of both, as envoy of the Gods traversest both the realms. | When we lay claim to thy regard and gracious care, be thou to us a thrice-protecting friendly guard?

Daśati 4:7:2:14. Agni.

1. Still turning to their aim in thee the sacrificer's sister hymns | Have come to thee before the wind. || 2. Even the waters find their place in him whose three fold sacred grass | Is spread unbound, unlimited. || 3. The station of the bounteous God, by his unconquerable aid, | Hath a fair aspect like the Sun.

Ardha 3.

Daśati 4:7:3:1. Indra.

1. Men with their lauds are urging thee, Indra, to drink the Soma first. | The Ṛibhus in accord have lifted up their voice, and Rudras sung thee as the first. || 2. Indra, at sacrifice, increased his manly strength, in the wild rapture of this juice: | And living men today, even as of old, sing forth their praises to his majesty.

Daśati 4:7:3:2. Indra-Agni.

1. Indra and Agni! singers skilled in melody, with lauds, hymn you: | I choose you both to bring me food. || 2. Indra and Agni! ye shook down, together, with one mighty deed, The ninety forts which Dāsas held. || 3. To Indra and to Agni prayers go forward from the holy task, Along the path of sacred Law. || 4. Indra and Agni, powers are yours, yours are oblations and abodes: Good is your zealous energy.

Daśati 4:7:3:3. Indra.

1. Indra, with all thy saving helps assist us, Lord of power and might! | For after thee we follow even as glorious bliss, thee, hero, finder-out of wealth! || 2. Increaser of our steeds and multiplying kine, a golden well, G God, art thou, | For no one may impair the gift laid up in thee. Bring me whatever thing I ask!

Daśati 4:7:3:4. Indra.

1. For thou—come to the worshipper!—wilt find great wealth to make us rich. | Fill thyself full, O Maghavan, for gain of kine, full, Indra, for the gain of steeds! || 2. Thou as thy gift bestowest many hundred herds, yea, many thou-sands dost thou give. | With singers' hymns have we brought the fort-render near, singing to Indra for his grace.

Daśati 4:7:3:5. Agni.

1. To him who dealeth out all wealth, the sweet-toned Hotar-priest of men, | To him, like the first vessels filled with savoury juice, to Agni let the lauds go forth! || 2. Votaries, bounteous givers, deck him with their songs, even as the steed who draws the car. | To both, strong Lord of men! to kith and kin convey the bounties of our wealthy lords!

Daśati 4:7:3:6. Varuṇa.

1. Hear this my call, O Varuṇa, and show thy gracious love today: | Desiring help I long for thee!

Daśati 4:7:3:7. Indra.

1. O Hero, with what aid dost thou delight us, with what succour bring, | Riches to those who worship thee?

Daśati 4:7:3:8. Indra.

1. Indra, for service of the Gods, Indra while sacrifice proceeds, | Indra, as worshippers, in battle-shock we call, Indra that we may win the spoil. || 2. With might hath Indra spread out heaven and earth, with power hath Indra lighten up the Sun. In Indra are all creatures closely held; in him meet the distilling Soma-drops.

Daśati 4:7:3:9. Viśvakarman.

1. Bring, Viśvakarman strengthened by oblation, thyself, thy body-'tis thine own-for worship | Let other men around us live in folly here let us have, a rich and liberal patron!

Daśati 4:7:3:10. Soma Pavamāna.

1. With this his golden splendour purifying him, he with his own allies subdues all enemies. as Sūra with his own allies. | Cleansing himself with stream of juice he shines forth yellow-hued and red, when with his praisers he encompasses all forms, with praisers having seven mouths. || 2. He moves intelligent directed to the east. The every beauteous car rivals the beams of light, the beautiful celestial car. | Hymns, lauding manly valour, came inciting Indra to success, that ye may be unconquered, both thy bolt and thou, both be unconquered in the war. || 3. That treasure of the Paṇis thou discoveredst. Thou with the Mothers deckest thee in thine abode, with, songs of worship in thine home. | As 'twere from far away is heard the psalm where hymns resound in joy. He, with the triple Dames red-hued, hath won life-power, he, gleaming, hath won vital strength.

Daśati 4:7:3:11. Pūṣhan.

1. Yea, cause our hymn to gain for us cattle and steeds and store of wealth, | That it may help us manfully!

Daśati 4:7:3:12. Marutas.

1. Heroes of real strength, ye mark either the sweat of him who toils, | Or his desire who supplicates.

Daśati 4:7:3:13. Viśvedevas.

1. The Sons of immortality shall listen to our songs of praise, | And be exceeding kind to us.

Daśati 4:7:3:14. Heaven and Earth.

1. To both of you, O Heaven and Earth, we bring our lofty song of praise, |

Pure pair! to glorify you both. || 2. Ye sanctify each other's form by your own proper strength ye rule: | Further the sacrifice evermore! || 3. Promoting and fulfilling, ye, mighty ones, perfect Mitra's law: | Ye sit around our sacrifice.

Daśati 4:7:3:15. Indra.

1. This is thine own. Thou drawest near, as turns a pigeon to his mate: | Thou carest, too, for this our prayer. || 2. O hero, Lord of bounties, praised in hymns, may glorious fame and might | Be his who sings the laud to thee || 3. Lord of a Hundred Powers, rise up to be our succour in this fight: | In other fights let us agree

Daśati 4:7:3:16. Oblations.

1. Ye cows, protect the fount: the two mighty ones bless the sacrifice. | The handles twain are wrought of gold. || 2. The pressing-stones are set at work: the meath is poured into the tank | At the out-shedding of the fount. || 3. With reverence they drain the fount that circles with its wheel above. | Exhaustless, with the mouth below.

Daśati 4:7:3:17. Indra.

1. Let us not tire or be afraid with thee, the mighty, for our friend! | May we see Turvaśa and Yadu! thy great deed, O hero, must be glorified. || 2. On his left hip the hero hath reclined himself: the proffered feast offends him not. | The milk is blended with the honey of the bee: quickly come hither, haste, and drink!

Daśati 4:7:3:18. Indra.

1. May these my songs of praise exalt thee, Lord, who hast abundant wealth! | Men skilled in holy hymns, pure, with the hues of fire, have | sung them with their lauds to thee. || 2. He, when a thousand Ṛishis have enhanced his might, hath like an ocean spread himself. | His majesty is praised as true at solemn rites, his power where holy singers rule.

Daśati 4:7:3:19. Indra.

1. Good Lord of wealth is he to whom all Āryas, Dāsas here belong. | Directly unto thee, the pious Ruśama Pavīru, is that wealth brought nigh. || 2. In zealous haste the singers have sung forth a song distilling | fatness, rich in sweets. | Riches have spread among us and heroic strength, with us are flowing Soma-drops.

Daśati 4:7:3:20. Soma Pavamāna.

1. Flow to us, Indu, very strong, effused, with wealth of kine and steeds, | And do thou lay above the milk thy radiant hue || 2. Lord of the tawny, Indu, thou who art the Gods' most special food, | As friend to friend, for splendour be thou good to men! || 3. Drive utterly, far away from us each godless, each voracious; foe; | O Indu, overcome and drive the false afar!

Daśati 4:7:3:21. Soma Pavamāna.

1. They balm him, balm him over, balm him thoroughly, caress. the mighty strength and balm it with the meath. | They seize the flying Steer at the stream's breathing place cleansing with gold they grasp the animal herein. || 2. Sing forth to Pavamāna skilled in holy song! the juice is flowing onward like a mighty stream. | He glideth like a serpent from his ancient skin, and like a. playful horse the tawny Steer hath run. || 3. Dweller in floods, King, foremost, he displays his might, set among living things as measure of days. | Distilling oil he flows, fair, billowy, golden-hued, borne on car of light, sharing on home with wealth.

Prapāṭhaka 8.

Ardha 1.

Daśati 4:8:1:1. Agni.

1. With all thy fires, O Agni, find pleasure in this our sacrifice, | And this our speech, O son of Strength! || 2. Whate'er, in this perpetual course, we sacrifice to God and God, | That gift is offered but in thee. || 3. May he be our beloved King and excellent sweet-toned Hotar may | We with bright fires be dear to him

Daśati 4:8:1:2. Indra.

1. For you from every side we call Indra away from other men | Ours, and none others, may he be! || 2. Unclose, our manly hero! thou for ever bounteous, yonder cloud | For us, thou irresistible || 3. As the strong bull leads on the herds, he stirs the people with his might, | The ruler irresistible.

Daśati 4:8:1:3. Agni.

1. Wonderful, with thy saving help, send us thy bounties, gracious Lord! | Thou art the charioteer, Agni, of earthly wealth: find rest and safety for our seed! || 2. Prosper our kith and kin with thy protecting powers inviolate, never negligent! | Keep far from us, O Agni, all celestial wrath. and wickedness of godless men!

Daśati 4:8:1:4. Vishṇu.

1. What, Vishṇu, is the name that thou proclaimest when thou declaredst, I am Śipivishṭa? | Hide not this form from us, nor keep it secret, since thou didst wear another shape in battle. || 2. This offering today, O Śipivishṭa, I, skilled in rules, extol, to thee the noble. | Yea, I, the poor and weak, praise thee, the mighty, who dwellest in the realm beyond this region. || 3. O Vishṇu, unto thee my lips cry Vashaṭ! Let this mine offering, Śipivishṭa, please thee! | May these my songs of eulogy exalt thee! Do ye preserve us evermore with blessings!

Daśati 4:8:1:5. Vāyu, Indra and Vāyu.

1. Vāyu, the bright is offered thee, best of the meath, at morning rites. | Come thou to drink the Soma juice, God, longed for on thy team-drawn car! || 2. O Vāyu, thou and Indra are meet drinkers of these Soma draughts, | For unto you the drops proceed like waters gathering to the vale. || 3. Vāyu and Indra, mighty twain, borne on one chariot, Lords of strength, | Come to our succour with your steeds, that ye may drink the | Soma juice!

Daśati 4:8:1:6. Soma Pavamāna.

1. Then thou, made beautiful by night, enterest into mighty deeds, | When prayers impel the golden-hued to hasten from Vivasvat's place. || 2. We cleanse this gladdening drink of his, the juice which Indra chiefly drinks, | That which kine took into their mouths, of old, and princes take it now. || 3. Thy with the ancient psalm have sung to him as he is purified, | And sacred songs which bear the Dames of Gods have supplicated him.

Daśati 4:8:1:7. Agni.

1. With homage will I reverence thee, Agni, like a long-tailed steed, | Imperial Lord of holy rites. || 2. May the far-striding Son of Strength, our friend who brings felicity, | Who pours his gifts like rain, be ours || 3. From near and far away do thou, the everlasting, evermore | Protect us from the sinful man!

Daśati 4:8:1:8. Indra.

1. Thou in thy battles, Indra, art subduer of all hostile bands. | Father art thou, all-conquering, cancelling the curse, thou victor of the vanquisher! || 2. The earth and heaven cling close to thy victorious might, as sire and mother to their child. | When thou attackest Vṛitra, all the hostile bands shrink and faint, Indra, at thy wrath.

Daśati 4:8:1:9. Indra.

1. The sacrifice made Indra great when he unrolled the earth, and made | Himself a diadem in heaven. || 2. In Soma's ecstasy Indra spread the firmament and realms of light, | When he cleft Vala limb from limb. || 3. Showing the hidden, he drave forth the cows for the Aṅgirasas, | And Vala he cast headlong down.

Daśati 4:8:1:10. Indra.

1. Thou speedest down to succour us this-ever-conquering God of yours, | Him who is drawn to all our songs; || 2, The warrior whom none may wound, the Soma-drinker ne'er o'erthrown, | The chieftain of resistless might. || 3. O Indra, send us riches, thou omniscient, worthy of our hymns: | Help us in the decisive fray!

Daśati 4:8:1:11. Indra.

1. That lofty power and might of thine, thy strength and thine intelligence, | And thy surpassing thunderbolt, the wish makes keen. || 2. O Indra, heaven and earth augment thy manly force and thy renown: | The waters and the mountains stir and urge thee on: || 3. Vishṇu in the lofty ruling power, Varuṇa, Mitra sing thy praise: | In thee the Marutas' company have great delight.

Daśati 4:8:1:12. Agni.

1. O Agni, God, the people sing reverent praise to thee for strength: | With terrors trouble thou the foe || 2. Wilt thou not, Agni, lend us aid to win the cattle, win the wealth? | Maker of room, make room for us || 3. In the great fight cast us not off, Agni, as one who bears a load: | Snatch up the wealth and win it all!

Daśati 4:8:1:13. Indra.

1. Before his hot displeasure all the peoples, all the men bow down, | As rivers bow them to the sea. || 2. Even fiercely-moving Vṛitra's head he served with his thunderbolt, | His mighty hundred-knotted bolt. || 3. That might of his shone brightly forth when Indra brought together, like | A skin, the worlds of heaven and earth.

Daśati 4:8:1:14. Indra.

1. Kind-thoughted is the noble, gladdening, friendly one. || 2. Approach, O beauteous hero, this auspicious pair that draws the car! | These two are coming near to us. || 3. Bend lowly down, as 'twere, your beads: be stands amid the water-flood, | Pointing with his ten horns the way.

Ardha 2.

Daśati 4:8:2:1. Indra.

1. Pressers, blend Soma juice for him, each draught most excellent, for him | The brave, the: hero, for his joy! || 2. The two strong bay steeds, yoked by prayer, hither shall bring to us our friend, | Indra, song-lover, through our songs. || 3. The Vṛitra-slayer drinks the juice. May he who gives a hundred | aids | Approach, nor stay afar from us!

Daśati 4:8:2:2. Indra.

1. Let the drops pass within thee as the rivers flow into the sea | O Indra, naught excelleth thee. || 2. 'Thou' wakeful hero, by thy might hast taken food of Soma juice, | Which, Indra, is within thee now. || 3. O Indra, Vṛitra-slayer, let Soma be ready for thy maw, The drops be ready for thy forms!

Daśati 4:8:2:3. Agni.

1. Help, thou who knowest lauds, this work, a lovely hymn in Rudra's praise, | Adorable in every house || 2. May this our God, great, limitless, smoke-bannered, excellently bright, | Urge us to holy thought and wealth || 3. Like soma rich lord of men, may he, Agni, the banner of the Gods, | Refulgent, hear us through our lauds!

Daśati 4:8:2:4. Indra.

1. Sing this, beside the flowing juice, to him, your hero, much invoked, | To please him as a mighty Bull! || 2. He, excellent, withholdeth not his bounteous gift of wealth in kine. | When lie bath listened to our songs. || 3. May he with might unclose for us the cow's stall, whosesoe'er it be, | To which the Dasyu-slayer goes!

Daśati 4:8:2:5. Vishṇu.

1. Through all this world strode Vishṇu: thrice his foot he planted, and the whole | Was gathered in his footstep's dust. || 2. Vishṇu, the guardian, he whom none deceiveth, made three steps, thenceforth | Establishing his high decrees. || 3. Look ye on Vishṇu's works whereby the friend of Indra, close allied, | Hath let his holy ways be seen || 4. The princes evermore behold that loftiest place of Vishṇu, like | An eye extended through the heavens. || 5. This, Vishṇu's station most sublime, the sages, ever-vigilant, | Lovers of holy song, light up. || 6. May the Gods help and favour us out of the place whence Vishṇu strode | Over the back and ridge of earth.

Daśati 4:8:2:6. Indra.

1. Let none, no, not thy worshippers, delay thee far away from us! | Even from far away come thou unto our feast, or listen it already here! || 2. For here, like rites on honey, those who pray to thee sit by the juice that they have poured. | Wealth-craving singers have on Indra set their hope, as men set foot upon a car.

Daśati 4:8:2:7. Indra.

1. Sung is the song of ancient time: to Indra have ye said the prayer. | They have sung many a Bṛihatī of sacrifice, poured forth the worshipper's many thoughts. || 2. Indra hath tossed together mighty stores of wealth, and both the worlds, yea, and the sun. | Pure, brightly-shining, mingled with the milk, the draughts of Soma have made Indra glad.

Daśati 4:8:2:8. Soma Pavamāna.

1. For Vṛitra-slaying Indra, thou, Soma, art poured that he may drink, | And for the guerdon-giving man, the hero sitting in his seat. || 2. Friends, may the princes, ye and we, obtain this most resplendent one, | Gain him who hath the smell of strength, win him whose home is very strength! || 3. Him with the fleece they purify, brown, golden-hued, beloved of all. | Who with exhilarating juice flows forth to all the deities.

Daśati 4:8:2:9. Indra.

1. Indra whose wealth is in thyself, what mortal will attack this man? | The strong will win the spoil on the decisive day through faith in thee, O Maghavan! || 2. In battles with the foe urge on our mighty ones who give the treasures dear to thee | And may we with our princes, Lord of tawny steeds! pass through all peril, led by thee!

Daśati 4:8:2:10. Indra.

1. Come, priest, and of the savoury juice pour forth a yet more gladdening draught! | So is the hero praised who ever prospers us. || 3. Indra, whom tawny coursers bear, praise such as thine, preeminent, | None by his power or by his goodness hath attained. || 3. We, seeking glory, have invoked this God of yours, the Lord of wealth, | Who must be magnified by constant sacrifice.

Daśati 4:8:2:11. Agni.

1. Sing praise to him, the Lord of light. The Gods have made the God to be their messenger, | To bear oblation to the Gods. || 2. Agni, the bounteous giver, bright with varied flames, laud thou, O singer Sobhari, | Him who controls this sacred food with Soma blent, who hath first claim to sacrifice!

Daśati 4:8:2:12. Soma Pavamāna.

1. Expressed by stones, O Soma, and urged through the long wool of the sheep, | Thou, entering the press-boards, even as men a fort, gold-hued, hast settled in the vats. || 2. He beautifies himself through the sheep's long fine wool, the bounteous, like the racing steed, | Even Soma Pavamāna who shall be the joy of sages and of holy bards.

Daśati 4:8:2:13. Indra.

1. Here, verily, yesterday we let the Thunder-wielder drink his fill. | Bring him the juice poured forth in sacrifice today! Now range you by the glorious one! || 2. Even the wolf, the savage beast that rends the sheep, follows the path of his decrees. | So graciously accepting, Indra, this our praise, with wondrous thought come forth to us!

Daśati 4:8:2:14. Indra-Agni.

1. Indra and Agni, in your deeds of might ye deck heaven's lucid realms: | Famed is that hero strength of yours. || 2. To Indra and to Agni prayers go forward from the holy task. | Along the path of sacred Law. || 3. Indra and Agni, powers are yours, yours are oblations and abodes: | Good is your zealous energy.

Daśati 4:8:2:15. Indra.

1. Who knows what vital power he wins, drinking beside the flowing juice? | This is the fair-cheeked God who, joying in the draught, breaks down the castles in his strength. || 2. As a wild elephant rushes on, this way and that way mad with | heat, | None may restrain thee, yet come hither to the draught! Thou, movest mighty in thy power. || 3. When he, the terrible, ne'er o'erthrown, steadfast, made ready for the fight— | When Indra Maghavan lists to his praiser's call, he will not stand aloof, but come.

Daśati 4:8:2:16. Soma Pavamāna.

1. The Pavamānas have been poured, the brilliant drops of Soma juice, | For holy lore of every kind. || 2. From heaven, from out the firmament hath Pavamāna been effused | Upon the back and ridge of earth. || 3. The Pavamānas have been shed, the beautified swift Soma-drops, | Driving all enemies afar.

Daśati 4:8:2:17. Indra-Agni.

1. Indra and Agni I invoke, joint-victors, bounteous, unsubdued, | Foe-slayers, best to win the spoil. || 2. Indra and Agni, singers skilled in melody hymn you bringing lauds: | I choose you both to bring me food. || 3. Together, with one mighty deed, Indra and Agni, ye shook down. | The ninety forts which Dāsas held.

Daśati 4:8:2:18. Agni.

1. O Child of Strength, to thee whose look is lovely, with oblations we, | O Agni, have poured forth our songs. || 2. To thee for shelter are we come, as to the shade from fervent heat, | Agni, who glitterest like gold || 3. Mighty as one who slays with shafts, or like a bull with sharpened horn, | Agni, thou brakest down the forts.

Daśati 4:8:2:19. Agni.

1. To give eternal glow, we pray Vaiśvānara the holy one, Lord of the light

of sacrifice. || 2. Who, furthering the light of Law, hath spread himself to meet this work: | He sends the seasons, mighty one. || 3. Love of what is and what shall be, Agni, in his beloved forms, | Shines forth alone as sovereign Lord.

Ardha 3.

Daśati 4:8:3:1. Agni.

1.Wise Agni, in the ancient way, making his body beautiful, | Hath been exalted by the sage. || 2. I invocate the Child of Strength, Agni whose glow is bright and pure, | In this well-ordered sacrifice. || 3. So, Agni, rich in many friends, with fiery splendour seat thyself. | With Gods upon our sacred grass!

Daśati 4:8:3:2. Soma Pavamāna.

1. O thou with stones for arms, thy powers, rending the fiends, have raised themselves: | Drive off the foes who compass us || 2. Hence conquering with might when car meets car, and when the prize is staked, | With fearless heart will I sing praise. || 3. None, evil-minded, may assail this Pavamāna's holy laws | Crush him who fain would fight with thee! || 4. For Indra to the streams they urge the tawny rapture-dropping steed, | Indu, the bringer of delight.

Daśati 4:8:3:3. Indra.

1. Come hither, Indra, with bay steeds, joyous, with tails like peacocks' plumes! | Let no men check thy course as fowlers stay the bird: pass o'er them as o'er desert lands! || 2. Vṛitra's devourer, he who burst the cloud, brake forts, and drave the floods, | Indra, who mounts his chariot at his bay steeds' cry, shatters e'en things that stand most firm. || 3. Like pools of water deep and full, like kine thou cherishest thy might; | Like the milch-cows that go well-guarded to the mead, like water-brooks that reach the lake.

Daśati 4:8:3:4. Indra.

1. Even as the wild bull, when he thirsts, goes to the desert's watery pool, | Come hither quickly both at morning and at eve, and with the Kaṇvas drink thy fill! || 2. May the drops gladden thee, Lord Indra, and obtain bounty for him who pours the juice! | Soma, shed in the press, thou stolest and didst drink, and hence hast won surpassing might.

Daśati 4:8:3:5. Indra.

1. Thou as a God. O mightiest, verily blessest mortal man. | O Maghavan, there is no comforter but thou: Indra, I speak my words to thee. || 2. Let not thy bounteous gifts, let not thy saving help all fail us good Lord, at any time! | And measure out to us, thou lover of man-kind, all riches hitherward from men

Daśati 4:8:3:6. Dawn.

1. This Lady, excellent and kind, after her sister shining forth, Daughter of Heaven, hath shown herself. || 2. Red, like a mare, and beautiful, holy, the mother of the kine, The Dawn became the Aśvins' friend. || 3. Yea, and thou art the Aśvins', friend the mother of the cows art thou: O Dawn, thou rules over wealth

Daśati 4:8:3:7. Aśvins.

1. Now Morning with her earliest light shines forth, dear daughter of the Sky: | High, Aśvins, I extol your praise || 2. Children of Ocean, mighty ones, discoverers of riches, Gods, | Finders of treasure through our prayer! || 3. Your lofty coursers hasten over the everlasting realm, when your car flies with winged steeds.

Daśati 4:8:3:8. Dawn.

1. O Dawn who hast a store of wealth, bring unto us that splendid gift | Wherewith we may support children and children's sons || 2. Thou radiant Lady of sweet strains, with wealth of horses and of kine | Shine thou on us this day, O Dawn, auspiciously || 3. O Dawn who hast a store of wealth, yoke red steeds to thy car today. | Then bring us all delight and all felicities

Daśati 4:8:3:9. Aśvins.

1. O Aśvins, wonderful in act, do ye unanimous direct | Your chariot to our home wealthy in kine and gold! || 2. Hither may they who wake at dawn bring, to drink Soma, both the Gods, | Health-givers, wonder-workers, borne on paths of gold! || 3. Ye who brought down the hymn from heaven, a light that giveth light to men, | Do ye, O Aśvins, bring strength hither unto us!

Daśati 4:8:3:10. Agni.

1. I think of Agni who is kind, whom, as their home, the milch-kine seek; | Whom fleet-foot coursers seek as home, and strong enduring, steeds as home. | Bring food to those who sing thy praise! || 2. For Agni, God of all mankind, gives the strong courser to the man. | Agni gives ready gear for wealth, he gives the best when he ix pleased. | Bring food to those who sing thy praise! || 3. The Agni who is praised as kind, to whom the milch-kine come. in herds, | To whom the racers, swift of foot, to whom our well-born princes come. Bring food to those who sing thy praise!

Daśati 4:8:3:11. Dawn.

1. O heavenly Dawn, awaken us to ample opulence today, | Even as thou didst waken us with Satyaśravas, Vayya's, Son, high-born! delightful with thy steeds! || 2. Daughter of heaven, thou dawnedst of Sunītha, Śuchadratha's son; | So dawn thou on one mightier still, on Satyaśravas, Vayya's son, high-born! delightful with thy steeds! || 3. So bringing treasure, shine today on us, thou daughter, of the Sky, | As on one mightier thou hast dawned, on Satyaśravas, Vayya's son, high-born! delightful with thy steeds!

Daśati 4:8:3:12. Aśvins.

1. To meet your treasure-bringing car, the car that is most dear to us, | Aśvins the Ṛishi is prepared, your worshipper with, songs of praise. Lovers of sweetness, hear my call || 2. Pass, Aśvins, over all away. May I obtain you for myself, | Wonderful, with your golden paths, most gracious, bringers of the flood! Lovers of sweetness, hear my call! || 3. Come to us, O ye Aśvins twain, bringing your precious treasures, come | Ye Rudras, on your paths of gold, rejoicing, with your store of wealth! Lovers of sweetness, hear my call!

Daśati 4:8:3:13. Agni.

1. Agni is wakened by the people's fuel to meet the Dawn who cometh like a milch-cow. | Like young trees shooting up on high their branches, his flames mounting to the vault of heaven. || 2. For the Gods' worship hath the priest been wakened: kind Agni hath arisen erect at morning. | Kindled, his radiant might is made apparent, and the great God hath been set free from darkness. || 3. When he hath roused the line of his attendants, with the bright milk bright Agni is anointed. | Then is prepared the effectual oblation, which spread in front, with tongues, erect, he drinketh,

Daśati 4:8:3:14. Dawn.

1. This light is come, amid all lights the fairest: born is the brilliant, far-extending brightness. | Night, sent away for Savitar's uprising, hath yielded up a birthplace for the morning. || 2. The fair, the bright is come with her white offspring to her the Dark one hath resigned her dwelling. | Akin, immortal, following each other, changing their colours both the heavens move onward. || 3. Common, unending is the sisters' pathway: taught by the Gods alternately they travel, | Fair-formed, of different hues and yet one-minded, Night and Dawn clash not, neither do they tarry.

Daśati 4:8:3:15. Aśvins.

1. Agni, the bright face of the Dawns, is shining: the singers' pious voices have ascended. | Borne on your chariot, Aśvins, turn you hither, and come unto our brimming warm libation! || 2. Most frequent guests, they scorn not what is ready: even now the lauded Aśvins are beside us. | With promptest aid they come at morn and evening, the worshipper's most healthful guards from trouble. || 3. Yea, come at milking-time, at early morning, at noon of day, and when the Sun is setting, | By day, at night, with most auspicious favour! Not only now the draught hath drawn the Aśvins

Daśati 4:8:3:16. Dawn.

1. These Dawns have raised their banner: in the eastern half of middle air they spread abroad their shining light. | Like heroes who prepare their weapons for the fray, the cows are coming on, the mothers, red of hue. || 2. Rapidly have the ruddy beams of light shot up: the red cows have they harnessed, easy to be yoked. | The Dawns have made their pathways as in former times: red-hued, they have attained refulgent brilliancy. || 3. They sing their song like women active in their tasks, along their common path hither from far away, | Bringing refreshment to the liberal devotee, yea, all things to the worshipper who pours the juice.

Daśati 4:8:3:17. Aśvins.

1. Agni is wakened: Sūrya riseth from the earth. Bright Dawn hath opened

out the mighty twain with light. | The Aśvins have equipped their chariot for the course. God Savitar hath roused the world in sundry ways. || 2. When, O ye Aśvins, ye equip your mighty car, with fatness and with honey balm, ye twain, our power! | To our devotion give victorious strength in war: may we win riches in the heroes' strife for spoil! || 3. Nigh to us come the Aśvins' lauded three wheeled car, the car laden with meath and drawn by fleet-foot steeds, | Three-seated, opulent, bestowing all delight: may it bring weal to us, to cattle and to men!

Daśati 4:8:3:18. Soma Pavamāna.

1. Thy streams that never fail or waste flow forth like showers of rain from heaven, | To bring a thousand stores of wealth. || 2. He, flows beholding on his way all well-beloved sacred lore, | Green-tinted, brandishing his arms. || 3. He, when the people deck him like a docile king of elephants, | Sits as a falcon in the wood. || 4. So bring thou hitherward to us, Indu, while thou art purified. | All treasures both of heaven and earth!

Prapāṭhaka 9.

Ardha 1.

Daśati 4:9:1:1. Soma Pavamāna.

1. Forward have flowed the streams of power, of this the mighty one effused, | Of him who waits upon the Gods. || 2. The singers praise him with their song, and learned priests adorn the steed | Born as the light that merits laud. || 3. These things thou winnest quickly, while men cleanse thee, Soma, nobly rich!

Daśati 4:9:1:2. Indra.

1. This Brahman, comer at the due time, named Indra, is renowned and praised. || 2. To thee alone, O Lord of Strength, go, as it were, all songs of praise. || 3. Like streams of water on their way, let bounties, Indra, flow from thee!

Daśati 4:9:1:3. Indra.

1. Even as a car to give us aid, we draw thee nigh to favour us, | Strong in thy deeds, quelling attack, Indra, Lord, mightiest! of the brave. || 2. Great in thou power and wisdom, strong, with thought that comprehendeth all! | Wide hast thou spread in majesty. || 3. Thou very mighty one, whose hands by virtue of thy greatness wield | The golden bolt that beaks its way!

Daśati 4:9:1:4. Agni.

1. He who hath lighted up the joyous castle, wise courser like the steed of cloudy heaven, | Bright like the Sun with hundredfold existence || 2. He, doubly born, hath spread in his effulgence through the three luminous realms, through all the regions, | Best sacrificing Priest where waters gather. || 3. Priest doubly born, he through his love of glory hath in his keeping all things worth the choosing. | The man who brings him gifts hath noble offspring.

Daśati 4:9:1:5. Agni.

1. Agni, with hymns may we now accomplish that which thou lovest, | Strength, like a horse auspicious, with service! || 2. For, Agni, thou art now the promoter of strength auspicious, | Lofty sacrifice, power effective. || 3. Through these our praises, come thou to meet us, bright as the sunlight, | Agni, kindly with all thy faces!

Daśati 4:9:1:6. Agni.

1. Immortal Jātavedas, thou bright-hued refulgent gift of Dawn. | Agni, this day to him who pays oblations bring the Gods who waken with the morn! || 2. For thou art offering-bearer, well-loved messenger, and charioteer of holy rites. | Accordant with the Aśvins and with Dawn grant us heroic strength and lofty fame!

Daśati 4:9:1:7. Indra.

1. The old hath waked the young Moon from his slumber who runs his circling course with many round him | Behold the God's high wisdom in its greatness: he who died yesterday today is living. || 2. Strong is the red Bird in his strength, great hero, who from of old bath had no nest to dwell in. | That which he knows is truth and never idle: he wins and gives the wealth desired of many. || 3. Through these Thunderer gained strong manly vigour, through whom he waxed in strength to slaughter Vṛitra; | These who through might of actual operation sprang forth as Gods in course of Law and Order.

Daśati 4:9:1:8. Marutas.

1. Here is the Soma ready pressed: of this the Marutas, yea, of this | Self-luminous, the Aśvins, drink. || 2. Of this, moreover, purified, set in three places, procreant, | Drink Varuṇa, Mitra, Aryaman. || 3. Yea, Indra, like the Hotar-priest, will in the early morning | drink, | At pleasure, of the milky juice:

Daśati 4:9:1:9. Sūrya.

1. Verily, Sūrya, thou art great; truly, Āditya, thou art great. | O most admired for greatness of thy majesty, God, by thy greatness thou art great. || 2. Yea, Sūrya, thou art great in fame: thou evermore, O God, art great. | Thou by thy greatness art the Gods' High-Priest, divine, far spread unconquerable light.

Daśati 4:9:1:10. Indra.

1. Come, Lord of rapturous joys, to our libations with thy bay steeds, come | With bay steeds to our flowing juice! || 2. Known as best Vṛitra-slayer erst, as Indra Śatakratu, come | With bay steeds to our flowing juice! || 3. For, Vṛitra-slayer, thou art he who drinks these drops of Soma come | With bay steeds to our flowing juice!

Daśati 4:9:1:11. Indra.

1. Bring to the wise, the great, who waxeth mighty your offerings and make ready your devotion. | Go forth to many tribes as man's controller! || 2. For Indra the sublime, the far-pervading, have singers generated prayer and praises; | The sages never violate his statutes. || 3. The choirs have established Indra King for ever for victory him, whose anger is resistless: | And for the bays' Lord strengthened those he loveth.

Daśati 4:9:1:12. Indra.

1. If I, O Indra, were the lord of riches ample as thine own, | I would support the singer, God who scatterest wealth! and, not abandon him to woe. || 2. Each day would I enrich the man who sang my praise, in whatsoever place he were. | No kinship is there better, Maghavan, than thine: a father even, is no more.

Daśati 4:9:1:13. Indra.

1. Here thou the call of the juice-drinking press-stone: mark thou the sage's hymn who sings and lauds thee! | Take to thine inmost self these adorations! || 2. I know and ne'er forget the hymns and praises of thee, the conqueror, of thy power immortal. | Thy name I ever utter, self-refulgent! || 3. Among mankind many are thy libations, and many a time the pious sage invokes thee. | O Maghavan, be not long distant from us!

Daśati 4:9:1:14. Indra.

1. Sing strength to Indra that shall. set his chariot in the foremost | place! | Giver of room in closest fight, slayer of foes in shock of war, be thou our great encourager! Let the weak bowstrings break upon the bows of our weak enemies! || 2. Thou didst destroy the Dragon: thou sentest the rivers down to Earth. | Foeless, O Indra, wast thou born. Thou tendest well each choicest thing. Therefore we draw us close to thee. Let the weak bowstrings break upon the bows of our weak enemies! | Destroyed be all malignities and all our enemy's designs! || 3. Thy bolt thou castest at the foe, O Indra, who would smite us dead: thy liberal bounty gives us wealth. Let the weak bowstrings break upon the bows of our weak enemies!

Daśati 4:9:1:15. Indra.

1. Rich be the praiser of one rich and liberal, Lord of days! like thee: | High rank be his who lauds the juice! || 2. His wealth who hath no store of kine hath ne'er found out recited laud, | Nor song of praises that is sung. || 3. Give us not, Indra, as a prey unto the scornful or the proud: | Help, mighty one, with power and might!

Daśati 4:9:1:16. Indra.

1. Come hither, Indra, with thy bays, come thou to Kaṇva's eulogy! | Ye by command of yonder Dyaus, God bright by day! have gone to heaven. || 2. The stones' rim shakes the Soma here like a wolf worrying a sheep. | Ye by command of yonder Dyaus, God bright by day I have gone to heaven. || 3. May the stone bring thee as it speaks, the Soma-stone with ringing voice! | Ye by command of yonder Dyaus, God bright by day! have gone to heaven.

Daśati 4:9:1:17. Soma Pavamāna.

1. For Indra flow most rich in sweets, O Soma, bringing him delight! || 2.

Bright, meditating sacred song, these juices have sent Vāyu forth. || 3. They were sent forth to feast the Gods, like chariots speeding in the race.

Daśati 4:9:1:18. Agni.

1. Agni I deem our Hotar priest, munificent wealth-giver, Son of Strength, who knoweth all that is even as the Sage who knoweth all. | Lord of fair rites, a God with form erected turning to the Gods, he when the flame hath sprung forth from the holy oil, the offered fatness, longs for it as it grows bright. || 2. We, sacrificing, call on the best worshipper thee eldest of Aṅgirasas, singer! with hymns, thee, brilliant one! with singers' hymn; | Thee, wandering round, as 'twere the sky, thee who art Hotar-priest of men, whom, Bull with hair of flame, the people must observe, tile people that he speed them on. || 3. He with his blazing Power refulgent far and wide, he verily it is who conquers demon foes, conquers the demons like an axe: | At whose close touch things solid part, and what is stable yields he keeps his ground and flinches not,like trees. Subduing all from the skilled archer flinches not.

Ardha 2.

Daśati 4:9:2:1. Agni.

1. O Agni, strength and fame are thine: thy fires blaze forth on high, O thou refulgent God! | Sage, passing bright, thou givest to the worshipper with power, the wealth that merits laud. || 2. With brilliant, purifying sheen, with perfect sheen thou liftest up thyself in light. | Thou, visiting both thy mothers, aidest them as son; thou joinest close the earth and heaven. || 3. O Jātavedas, Son of Strength, rejoice thyself, gracious, in our fair hymns and songs! | In thee have they heaped viands various, many formed; wealth-born, of wondrous help are they. || 4. Agni, spread forth, as ruler, over living things: give wealth, to | us, immortal God! | Thou shinest out from beauty fair to look upon: thou leadest | us to beauteous Power. || 5. I laud the Sage, who orders sacrifice, who hath great riches under his control. | Thou givest blest award of good, and plenteous food, thou givest wealth that wins success. || 6. The men have set before them, for his favour, Agni, strong, visible to all, the holy. | Thee, Lord divine, with ears to hear, most famous, mens' generations magnify with praise-songs.

Daśati 4:9:2:2. Agni.

1. Agni, he conquers by thine aid that brings him store of valiant sons and does great deeds, | Whose bond of friendship is thy choice. || 2. Thy spark is black and crackling; kindled in due time, O bounteous, it is taken up. | Thou art the dear friend of the mighty Mornings: thou shinest in glimmerings of the night.

Daśati 4:9:2:3. Agni.

1. Him, duly coming, as their germ have plants received: this Agni have maternal Waters brought to life. | So, in like manner, do the forest trees and plants bear him within them and produce him evermore.

Daśati 4:9:2:4. Agni.

1. Agni grows bright for Indra: he shines far resplendent in the sky: | He sends forth offspring like a queen.

Daśati 4:9:2:5. Agni.

1. The sacred hymns love him who wakes and watches: to him who watches the holy verses. | This Soma saith to him Who wake my dwelling in thy friendship.

Daśati 4:9:2:6. Agni.

1. Agni is watchful, and the Ṛichas love him: Agni is watchful, Sāman hymns approach him. | Agni is watchful, to him saith this Soma, I rest and have my dwelling in thy friendship.

Daśati 4:9:2:7. Gods.

1. Praise to the friends who sit in front! to those seated together,praise | I use the hundred-footed speech speech. || 2. I use the hundred-footed speech, I sing what hath a thousand paths, | Gāyatra, Trishṭubh, Jagat hymn. || 3. Gāyatra, Trishṭubh, Jagat hymn,the forms united and complete, | Have the Gods made familiar friends.

Daśati 4:9:2:8. Agni.

1. Agni, is light, light is Agni, Indra is light, light is Indra | Sūrya is light, light is Sūrya. || 2. O Agni, turn again with strength, turn thou again with food and life: | Save us again from grief and woe! || 3. O Agni, turn again with wealth sprinkle thou us from every side. | With thine own all-supporting stream!

Daśati 4:9:2:9. Indra.

1. If I, O Indra, were like thee, the single ruler over wealth. | My worshipper should be rich in kine. || 2. I should be fain, O Lord of power, to strengthen and enrich the sage, | Where I the ford of herds of kine. || 3. Thy goodness, Indra, is a cow yielding in plenty kine and steeds. | To worshippers who press the juice.

Daśati 4:9:2:10. The Waters.

1. Yea, Waters, ye bring health and bliss: so help ye us to energy. | That we may look on great delight! || 2. Give us a portion of the dew, the most auspicious that ye have, | Like mothers in their longing love! || 3. For you we gladly go to him to whose abode ye speed us on, | And, Waters, give us procreant strength!

Daśati 4:9:2:11. Vāta.

1. May Vāta breathe his balm on us, healthful, delightful to our heart: | May he prolong our days of life! || 2. Thou art our father, Vāta, yea, thou art our brother and our friend: | So give us strength that we may live! || 3. The store of Amṛita that laid away yonder, O Vāta, in thine home— | Give us strength that we may live!

Daśati 4:9:2:12. Agni.

1. The fleet steed wearing divers forms, the eagle bearing his golden raiment to his birthplace, | Clothed in due season with the light of Sūrya, red, hath begot the sacrifice in person. || 2. Multiform seed he laid in waters, lustre which gathered on the earth and there developed. | In the mid-air establishing his greatness, he cries aloud, seed of the vigorous courser. || 3. He hath, enduing thousand robes that suit him, as sacrifice upheld the light of Sūrya, | Giver of ample gifts in hundreds, thousands, supporter of the heavens, earth's Lord and ruler.

Daśati 4:9:2:13. Vena.

1. They gaze on thee with longing in their spirit, as on a strong-winged bird that mounteth sky-ward; | On thee with wings of gold, Varuṇa's envoy, the Bird that hasteneth to the home of Yama. || 2. Erect, to heaven hath the Gandharva mounted, pointing at us his many-coloured weapons: | Clad in sweet raiment beautiful to look on, for he, as light, produceth forms that please us. || 3. When as a spark he cometh near the ocean, looking with vulture's eye as Law commandeth, | His lustre, joying in its own bright splendour, maketh dear glories in the loftiest region.

Ardha 3.

Daśati 4:9:3:1. Indra.

1. Swift, rapidly striking, like a bull who sharpens his horns, terrific, stirring up the people. | With eyes that close not, bellowing, sole hero, Indra subdued at once a hundred armies. || 2. With him loud-roaring, ever watchful victor, bold, hard to overthrow, rouser of battle, | Indra. the strong, whose hand bears arrows, conquer, ye heroes, now, now vanquish in the combat! || 3. He rules with those who carry shafts and quivers, Indra who with his band brings hosts together, | Foe-conquering strong of arm the Soma-drinker, with mighty bow, shooting with well-laid arrows.

Daśati 4:9:3:2. Bṛihaspati Indra.

1. Bṛihaspati, fly with thy chariot hither, slayer of demons, driving off our foemen! | Be thou protector of our cars, destroyer, victor in battle, breaker-up of armies! || 2, Conspicuous. by thy strength, firm, foremost fighter, mighty and | fierce, victorious, all-subduing, | The Son of Conquest, passing men and heroes, kine-winner, mount thy conquering car, O Indra! || 3. Cleaver of stalls, kine-winner, armed with thunder, who quells an army and with might destroys it— | Follow him, brothers! quit yourselves like heroes, and like this Indra show your zeal and courage!

Daśati 4:9:3:3. Indra. Bṛihaspati.

1. Piercing with conquering strength the cow-stalls, Indra, pitiless hero with unbounded anger, | Victor in fight, unshaken and resistless—may he protect our armies in our battles! || 2. Indra guide these! Bṛihaspati, and Soma, the guerdon and the sacrifice precede them; | And let the banded Marutas march in forefront of heavenly hosts that conquer and demolish! || 3. Ours be the potent host of mighty Indra, King Varuṇa the Marutas, and Ādityas! | Uplifted is the shout of Gods who conquer, high-minded Gods who cause the worlds to tremble.

Daśati 4:9:3:4. Indra. Marutas.

1. Bristle thou up, O Maghavan, our weapons: excite the spirits, of my warring heroes! | Urge on the strong steed's might, O Vṛitra-slayer, and let the din of conquering cars go upward || 2. May Indra aid us when our flags are gathered: victorious be the arrows of our army! | May our brave men of war prevail in battle. Ye Gods, protect us in the shout of onset! || 3. That army of the foemen, O ye Marutas, which, striving in its. mighty strength, approaches, | Hide ye and bury it in pathless darkness that not a man of them may know the other!

Daśati 4:9:3:5. Aghā.

1. Bewildering the senses of our foemen, seize thou their bodies, and depart, O Aghā! | Attack them, set their hearts on fare with sorrows; so let our foes abide in utter darkness! || 2. Advance, O heroes, win the day, May Indra be your sure defence! | Mighty and awful be your arms, that none may wound or injure you! || 3. Loosed from the bowstring fly away, thou arrows sharpened by | our prayer! | Go to the foemen, strike them home, and let not one be left alive!

Daśati 4:9:3:6. Indra and others.

1. Let ravens and strong-pinioned birds pursue them: yea, let that army be the food of vultures! | Indra, let none escape, no sin-remover: behind them all let following birds be gathered! || 2. This host of foemen Maghavan! that cometh on in warlike show— | Meet it, O Vṛitra-slayer, thou, Indra, and Agni, with your flames! || 3. There where the flights of arrows fall like boys whose locks are yet unshorn. | Even there may Brahmaṇaspati, may Aditi protect us well, protect us well through all our days!

Daśati 4:9:3:7. Indra.

1. Drive Rākṣhasas and foes away, break thou in pieces Vṛitra's jaws: | O Vṛitra-slaying Indra, quell the foeman's wrath who threatens us! || 2. O Indra, beat our foes away, humble the men who challenge us: | Send down to nether darkness him who seeks to do us injury! || 3. Strong, ever-youthful are the arms of Indra, fair unassailable, never to be vanquished: | These first let him employ when need hath come on us, wherewith the Asuras' great might was overthrown.

Daśati 4:9:3:8. Soma, Varuṇa.

1. Thy vital parts I cover with thine armour: with immortality King Soma clothe thee! | Varuṇa give thee what is more than ample, and in thy victory may Gods be joyful! || 2. Blind, O my foemen, shall ye be, even as headless serpents are | May Indra slay each best of you when Agni's flame hath struck you down! || 3. Whoso would kill us, whether he be a stranger foe or one of us, | May all the Gods discomfit him! My nearest, closest mail is prayer, my closest armour and defence.

Daśati 4:9:3:9. Indra. All-Gods.

1. Like a dread wild beast roaming on the mountain thou hast approached us from the farthest distance. | Whetting thy bolt and thy sharp blade, O Indra, crush thou the foe and scatter those who hate us! || 2. Gods, may our ears hear that which is auspicious, may our eyes see that which is good, ye holy! | Extolling you with still strong limbs and bodies, may we attain the age by Gods appointed! || 3. Illustrious far and wide, may Indra bless us, may Pūṣhan bless us, master of all riches! | May Tārkṣhya with uninjured fellies bless us! Bṛihaspati bestow on us his favour! Bṛihaspati bestow on us his favour!

Hymns of the Atharvaveda

Translated by Ralph T.H. Griffith, 1895

Preface

The Atharvaveda is a comparatively late addition to the three ancient Vedas, the Ṛik, Yajus, and Sāman—the Vedas respectively of recited praise, sacrifice, and song or chanted hymn—which formed the foundation of the early religious belief and worship of the Hindus. Unlike these three Vedas, the Atharvaveda derives the name by which it is generally known, not from the nature of its contents but from a personage of indefinitely remote antiquity named Atharvan, who is spoken of in the Ṛigveda as the first priest who "rubbed Agni forth," or produced fire by attrition, who "first by sacrifices made the paths," or established ways of communication between men and Gods, and overcame hostile demons by means of the miraculous powers which he had received from heaven. To the descendants of this Atharvan, associated with the Aṅgirasas and the Bhṛigus, members of other ancient priestly families often mentioned in the Ṛigveda, the collected hymns—called also the Atharvāngirasas and the Bhṛigvangirasas, that is the Songs of the Atharvans and Aṅgirasas and the Songs of the Bhṛigus and Aṅgirasas, and, in the Gopatha-Brāhmaṇa, the Ātharvaṇa-veda and the Āngirasa-veda—were, it is said, originally revealed.

Yet another name of the collection of hymns is Brahmaveda, which is variously explained as (1) the Veda of the Brahman or chief sacrificial priest whose duty it was to supervise and direct the whole sacrifice and to remedy all faults of omission and commission in its performance, while the other Vedas are respectively those of the Hotar, the Adhvaryu, and the Udgātar who are regarded as the assistants and inferiors of the Brahman; (2) as the Knowledge of Prayers (*brahmāṇi*), including benediction, imprecation, spells and charms—the Veda which teaches to appease the Gods and secure their protecting favour, to bless friends, and to curse and destroy human and ghostly enemies, and all noxious creatures; (3) as the Knowledge or Doctrine of Brahma, the Supreme Self, Soul, or Spirit with which the soul of man is finally reintegrated; the followers of this Veda asserting its superiority to the three more ancient Vedas on the ground that, while they teach men to fulfil the *dharma* or religious law, the Brahmaveda imparts the sublime and mysterious doctrine which enables those who study it to attain *moksha*, deliverance from further transmigration, and, in the end, complete absorption into the Absolute. The second of these explanations seems, from our point of view, to be the correct one, and the Atharva or Brahmaveda may be regarded as the Veda of Prayers, Charms, and Spells.

I have called the Atharvaveda a comparatively late addition to the three ancient Vedas, of which, it may be observed, one only, the Ṛigveda, is original and historical, the other two being merely liturgical compilations. The Atharva is, like the Ṛik, in the main historical and original, but its contents cannot, as a whole, lay claim to equal antiquity. Professor Whitney says:

> "The greater portion of the hymns are plainly shown, both by their language and internal character, to be of much later date than the general contents of the other historic Veda, and even than its tenth book with which they stand nearly connected in import and origin.... This, however, would not imply that the main body of the Atharva hymns were not already in existence when the compilation of the Ṛik took place. Their character would be ground enough for their rejection and exclusion from the canon until other hands were found to undertake their separate gathering into an independent collection."

Professor Weber also observes:

> "The origin of the Atharva-Saṃhitā dates from the period when Brahmanism had become dominant. It is in other respects perfectly analogous to the Ṛik-Saṃhitā, and contains the store of song of this Brahmanical epoch. Many of these songs are to be found also in the last, that is the least ancient book of the Ṛik-Saṃhitā. In the latter they are the latest additions made at the time of its compilation; in the Atharvan they are the proper and natural utterance of the present. The spirit of the two collections is indeed widely different. In the Ṛik there breathes a lively natural feeling, a warm love for nature; while in the Atharvan there prevails, on the contrary, only an anxious dread of her evil spirits and their magical powers. In the Ṛik we find the people in a state of free activity and independence; in the Atharvan we see it bound in the fetters of the hierarchy and superstition. But the Atharva-Saṃhitā likewise contains pieces of great antiquity, which may perhaps have belonged more to the people proper, to its lower grades; whereas the songs of the Ṛik appear rather to have been the property of the higher families. It was not without a long struggle that the songs of the Atharvan were permitted to take their place as a fourth Veda. There is no mention made of them in the more ancient portions of the Brāhmaṇas of the Ṛik, Sāman, and Yajus."

Still as Professor Max Müller says:

> "The songs known under the name of the Atharvāngirasas formed probably an additional part of the sacrifice from a very early time. They were chiefly intended to counteract the influence of any untoward event that might happen during the sacrifice. They also contained imprecations and blessings, and various formulas such as popular superstition would be sure to sanction at all times and in all countries. If once sanctioned, however, these magic verses would grow in importance, nay, the knowledge of the other Vedas would necessarily become useless without the power of remedying accidents, such as could hardly be avoided in so complicated a ceremonial as that of the Brahmans. As that power was believed to reside in the songs of the Atharvāngirasas, a knowledge of these songs became necessarily an essential part of the theological knowledge of Ancient India,"

The Atharvaveda Saṃhitā or Collection is divided into twenty *Kāṇḍas*, Books or Sections, containing some seven hundred and sixty hymns and about six thousand verses. In Kāṇḍas 1-7 the hymns or pieces are arranged according to the number of their verses, without any reference to their subjects or the nature of their contents. The hymns of Kāṇḍa 1 contain on an average four verses each; those of Kāṇḍa 2, five; those of 3, six; those of 4, seven; those of 5, from eight to eighteen; those of 6, three; those of 7, many single verses, and upwards to eleven. Kāṇḍas 8-20 contain longer pieces, some of which extend to fifty, sixty, seventy, and even eighty verses. In Kāṇḍas 1-13, the contents are of the most heterogeneous description with no attempt at any kind of systematic arrangement of subjects. They consist principally of prayers, formulas, and charms for protection against evil spirits of all sorts and kinds, against sorcerers and sorceresses, diseases, snakes, and other noxious creatures, of benedictions and imprecations, invocations of magical herbs, prayers for children and long life, for general and special protection and prosperity, success in love, trade, and gambling, together with formulas to be employed in all kinds of domestic occurrences. In Kāṇḍas 14-18, the subjects are systematically arranged; 14 treating of marriage ceremonies; 15 of the glorification of the Vrātya or religious wandering mendicant; 16 and 17 of certain conjurations; 18 of funeral rites and the offering of obsequial cakes to the Manes or spirits of departed ancestors. Kāṇḍa 19 contains a somewhat miscellaneous collection of supplementary hymns. Kāṇḍa 20 consists—with the exception of what is called the Kuntāpa Section, comprising hymns 127-136—of pieces addressed to Indra and taken entirely from the Ṛigveda. These two Kāṇḍas, which are not noticed in the Atharvaveda Prātiśākhya—a grammatical treatise on the phonetic changes of words in the text—are manifestly a later addition to the Collection. Many of the Atharva hymns reappear in the Ṛigveda, about one-seventh of the Collection, sometimes unchanged and sometimes with important variations, being found in the older compilation. Interspersed in several of the Kāṇḍas are pieces of varying length consisting of curious cosmogonical and mystico-theological speculations which are not without interest as containing the germs of religious and philosophical doctrines afterwards fully developed in the Brāhmaṇas and Upanishads.

In this strange collection of heterogeneous material there is much that is obscure, much that is unintelligible, much that is intolerably tedious, and not a little that is offensive and disgusting to European taste. Yet the spiritual portions of the work have sometimes a strange beauty and grandeur of their own which attracts and fascinates the orthodox Hindu, while the occasional glimpses of light which it throws upon the daily life, the toils and pleasures, the hopes and fears, the joy sand sorrows of the average man invests it, I think, for the European reader with greater and more human interest than is possessed by the more ancient Veda. Setting aside the rivalries, wars, and conquests of kings and princes, and the lofty claims and powers of the hierarchy, we may follow the course of the middle-class Ārya's life from the cradle to the funeral pile, and even accompany him to his final home in the world of the Departed. We hear the benedictive charm pronounced over the expectant mother before her child is born, the blessing on the new-born infant, and in due time on the darling's first two teeth. We attend the solemn ceremony in which the youth is invested with his *toga virilis*, the new garment whose assumption signifies his recognition as an adult member of the family with new responsibilities and new duties to perform. As his fancy turns to thoughts of love, we hear him murmuring the charm which shall win him the maiden of his choice, and the lullaby which shall seal every eye but hers in his beloved's house and enable him to visit her without detection or suspicion. We follow him in his formal and somewhat unromantic wooing of a bride through a friend who acts as match-maker; we see the nuptial procession and the bride's introduction to her new home; we hear her benediction on the bridegroom, and the epithalamium pronounced over the wedded pair. The young husband is an agriculturist, and we see him in his field superintending the ploughmen and praying to Indra and Pūshan and the Genii of agriculture to bless their labours, Anon, with propitiatory prayer, he is cutting a new channel to bring the water of the brook to the land which is ready for irrigation; or he is praying for rain and an abundant crop. Again, when the corn is ripe he is busy among the men who gather in the harvest, invoking the aid of the good-natured goblins—the counterparts of our Robin Goodfellows—and leaving on the ground some sheaves to remunerate their toil. At sunset he superintends the return of the cows who have been grazing under the protection of the Wind-God in the breezy pastures, and their return under divine guidance, and the re-union of all the members of the household, are celebrated with symbolical mixt oblation, with milk and a brew of grain.

His wealth and family increase in answer to his repeated prayer for children and riches, and a new house must be built on a larger scale. The building is erected under the careful eye of the master and blessed and consecrated with prayers to the Gods and to the Queen of the Home. The mistress of the house brings forth the well-filled pitcher, all present are regaled with "the stream of molten butter blent with nectar"—which seems to be a euphemistic name for some sort of good liquor—and the householder enters and takes formal possession of his new dwelling with fire and water, the two most important necessaries of human life. The house, moreover—a wooden building with a thatched roof—has been specially assured against fire by a prayer to Agni the God of that element with the additional security offered by the immediate neighbourhood of a good stream or pool of water.

Such, or something like this, was the ordinary life of the average middle-class agriculturist. A devout believer in the Gods, he did not spend his substance on the performance of costly sacrifices, but was content with simple ceremonies and such humble offerings as he could well afford, His chief care was for the health and well-being of himself, his wife, children, and dependents, for plentiful harvests, and for thriving and multiplying cattle; and these were the blessings for which he most frequently prayed. His chief troubles were an occasional touch of malarial fever or rheumatism, a late or scanty rain-fall, a storm that lodged his ripe barley, lightning that struck his cattle, and similar mischances caused by the anger of the Gods or the malevolence of demons; and he was always armed with prayers and spells against the recurrence of such disasters. He was a man of importance in his village, and when he attended the Assembly—which may have been a kind of Municipal Committee or Parish Council —his great ambition was to command respect and attention as a speaker, and with this view he fortified himself with charm and magic herb that inspired eloquence and enabled him to overpower his opponents in debate. His life, on the whole, was somewhat monotonous and dull, but it seems to have suited him as he was continually praying that it might be extended to its full natural duration of a hundred years. At the end of that time, with his sons and his sons' children around him, he was ready to pass away to the felicity that awaited him in the world of the Fathers.

The small merchant or trader lived a less settled life and saw more of the world than the agriculturist. We see him on the point of starting on a journey for business purposes with his little stock of goods. He first propitiates Indra who is a merchant also, the God who trades and traffics with his worshippers, requiring and receiving prayer and oblations in exchange for the blessings which he sends, and who will now free the travelling merchant's path from wild beasts, robbers, and enemies of every kind. He prays also to many other deities that he may make rich profit and gain a hundred treasures, and commits the care of his children and cattle in his absence to Agni the God of all Ārya men. His ritual is an extensive one as he may be about to journey to all points of the compass, and he must accordingly conciliate all the divine Warders of the heavenly regions. He has to recite some ten hymns of Kāṇḍa 6, invoking the aid of all protecting deities, not forgetting to consult the Weather-Prophet and to obtain from him the promise of auspicious mornings, noons, and nights. He bids an affectionate farewell to the houses of his village, and departs on his way encouraged by the hymn which ensures him a safe and successful journey. In due time he returns having bartered his wares for the treasures of distant places, for bdellium and other fragrant gums and unguents, for Kushṭha and other foreign plants and drugs of healing virtue, for mother-of-pearl, ornaments for the women, and perhaps cloth of finer wool.

The merchant's object in life is gain, and he is not always very scrupulous in his dealings. If he is in debt he would prefer to be freed by the intervention of a God, and not by hie own exertions; and he is bold enough even to pray for release from debts which he has incurred without intending to pay them. He is probably the gambler who prays for success in play, and for pardon when he has been guilty of cheating.

We naturally see much less of the life of women in the Atharvaveda, but a fair proportion of the hymns is devoted to them and their interests. We find interspersed among them the love-charms of enamoured maidens, the Bride Oracle or ceremony of finding a husband, the nuptial procession, and the bride's entry into her husband's house as its honoured mistress, the epithalamian benediction, and many spells and charms to ensure her safety and well-being. The mistress of the household had her share of duties, cares, and troubles as well as her quiet joys and pleasures, and she sometimes launches a furious and revengeful imprecation against her unfaithful husband, and with a solemn incantation invokes death and destruction upon her successful rivals.

The text of the Atharvaveda, with "some amendment of the numerous and obvious false readings of the manuscripts, and some attempts to bring sense out of the utter nonsense which constitutes part of the last two books," was published at Berlin, in 1856, by Professors Rudolf von Roth and W. D. Whitney. The intention of these distinguished scholars was to prepare and publish a second volume containing complete indexes, notes, and translation. Circumstances have, unfortunately prevented the full execution of this project; but a most valuable portion of the intended work, Professor Whitney's Index Verborum to the Published Text, appeared in 1881 as Vol. XII. of the *Journal of the American Oriental Society*. The Śaunakīyā Chaturādhyāyikā, or the Atharvaveda Prātiśākhya, text, translation, and notes, was published by Professor Whitney, in 1862, in Vol. VII. of the same Society. Of the two existing ritual Sūtras of this Veda, an excellent edition of the Kauśika, with extracts from the commentaries of Dārila and Keśava, has been brought out, as Vol. XIV. of the *Journal of the American Oriental Society*, by Professor Maurice Bloomfield; and Dr. Richard Garbe has published a careful edition of the text of the Vaitāna, with critical notes and indexes, followed by a commented translation of the work. An Anukramaṇī or Index to the Atharvaveda is extant. I am indebted to Mr. W. H. Wright, Principal of Queen's College, Benares, and to the Librarian of the Sanskrit College, for the loan of a copy of this work borrowed from a gentleman of Benares.

Portions of a Commentary ascribed—but without sufficient authority—to Sāyaṇa, were discovered, some fourteen years ago, by Rāo Bahādur Shankar Pandurang Pandit, of Bombay, and have been printed, but not published, in their incomplete state. The Pandit is still waiting hopelessly, I fear, for the missing portions, of which no trace has as yet been found. I have not succeeded in obtaining the printed sheets, but Professor Whitney who has seen them says (Festgruss an Rudolf von Roth zum Doktor-Jubilaum, 1893, p, 96): "What there is that is valuable in the Atharvaveda commentary, apart from the various readings, is, on the whole, only what it derives and reports from the auxiliary literature to which we also have access. Independently, and as commentary, I have not found that it anywhere makes important contribution to the understanding of the text." One Brāhmaṇa, the Gopatha (published in the *Bibliotheca Indica*, 1870-72), belongs to the Atharvaveda, and its Upanishads, many of which are of comparatively recent date, are said to number one hundred and forty-five.

There is no complete or nearly complete translation of the Atharvaveda in any European language. Professor von Roth has published versions of a few hymns in his History and Literature of the Veda, and elsewhere. Professor Weber has published in *Indische Studien*, Vols. IV., XIII., and XVII., an excellent translation, with exhaustive notes, of Kāṇḍas 1-3, and in Vol. V. the nuptial formulas contained in Kāṇḍa 14, with a great variety of love-charms and similar formulas from other Kāṇḍas. Mr. Muir has translated some entire hymns and many fragments and detached verses and lines in his *Original Sanskrit Texts*, especially in the fifth volume of that excellent work. Professor Ludwig has translated—unfortunately without a commentary—about two hundred and thirty of the most important hymns. Dr. Grill in his *Hundert Lieder des Atharvaveda* has translated and annotated one hundred. M. Victor Henry has published a translation and commentary of Kāṇḍas 7 and 13. Herr Florenz has published a version of about half of Kāṇḍa 6. Dr. Lucian Scherman has translated and elucidated thirteen of the philosophical hymns, chiefly from Kāṇḍas 10, 11, 13, and 19, and Professor Maurice Bloomfield has thoroughly discussed and partly translated seven hymns of Kāṇḍas 1, 2, and 6 in the *American Journal of Philology*, vol. VII. 4.

I have not been able to obtain a copy of Herr Florenz's work, but with this exception I have derived the greatest possible benefit and assistance from all the translations and commentaries that I have mentioned, and I readily and thankfully acknowledge my general indebtedness to their authors independently of, and in addition to, special references in my notes and Index of Names, etc. I need hardly say that the great St. Petersburg Lexicon has been constantly referred to, as well as the dictionaries of Sir M. Monier-Williams and Professor Macdonell, von Roth's edition of the Nirukta, Th. Zachariae's edition of the Anekārthasamgraha, Delbrück's *Das Altindische Verbum*, and the *Vedische Studien* of Professors Pischel and Geldner. The Index Verborum edited by Professor Whitney I have found of the very greatest service. Professor Zimmer's *Altindisches Leben* has also greatly assisted me, and much light has been thrown upon obscure passages by Professor Bloomfield's edition of the Kauśika-Sūtra and Dr. Garbe's Vaitāna-Sūtra.

My plan of translation is that previously adopted in my versions of the Hymns of the Ṛigveda and Sāmaveda. While aiming especially at close fidelity to the letter and spirit of the original I have endeavoured to make my translation as readable and intelligible as the nature of subjects and other circumstances permit. I have also attempted to preserve something of the external form of the original hymns by rendering them in general, so far as I found it possible or expedient in syllabically commensurate hemistichs and verses. The prevailing metres of the original hymns are Gāyatrī, Anushṭubh, Paṅkti, Trishṭubh, and Jagatī, consisting, the first three of three, four, and five octosyllabic Pādas or divisions, and the last two of four hendecasyllabic and dodecasyllabic Pādas respectively. In translating the first set I have employed corresponding numbers of the common octosyllabic or dimeter iambic line, and in the second of the ordinary hypercatalectic blank verse line and the Alexandrine. I have not attempted to reproduce the rhythm or tonic metre of the original: such a task, supposing its satisfactory execution to be possible, would require more skill than I possess, and more time and labour than I could spare for the purpose. Moreover, I have found it impossible to carry out universally my general plan of translation. Parts of the Atharvaveda, for instance Kāṇḍa 15 and the greater portion of 16, are entirely in prose, and hymns, verses, and parts of verses in prose are found in other Books also. "It is not possible," as Professor Whitney observes, "to draw everywhere a sharp line between metrical and non-metrical matter; prose and loose verse slide into one another sometimes in a perplexing manner, or are mixed up in the same stanza."

T. H. Griffith.
Kotagibi, Nilgiri Hills, 1st November, 1894.

Kāṇḍa 1.

Hymn 1:1.

1. Now may Vāchaspati assign to me the strength and powers of Those | who, wearing every shape and form, the triple seven, are wandering round. || 2. Come thou again, Vāchaspati, come with divine intelligence. | Vasoṣhpati, repose thou here. In me be Knowledge, yea, in me. || 3. Here, even here, spread sheltering arms like the two bow-ends strained with cord. | This let Vāchaspati confirm. In me be Knowledge, yea, in me. || 4. Vāchaspati hath been invoked: may he invite us in reply. | May we adhere to Sacred Lore. Never may I be reft thereof.

Hymn 1:2.

1. We know the father of the shaft, Parjanya, liberal nourisher, | Know well his mother: Pṛithivī, Earth with her manifold designs. || 2. Do thou, O Bowstring, bend thyself around us: make my body stone. | Firm in thy strength drive far away malignities and hateful things. || 3. When, closely clinging round the wood, the bowstring sings triumph to the swift and whizzing arrow, | Indra, ward off from us the shaft, the missile. || 4. As in its flight the arrow's point hangs between earth and firmament, | So stand this Muñja-grass between ailment and dysenteric ill!

Hymn 1:3.

1. We know the father of the shaft, Parjanya strong with hundred powers: | By this may I bring health unto thy body: let the channels pour their burthen freely as of old. || 2. We know the father of the shaft, Mitra, the Lord of hundred powers: | By this, etc. || 3. We know the father of the shaft, Varuṇa, strong with hundred powers: | By this, etc. || 4. We know the father of the shaft, the Moon endowed with hundred powers: | By this, etc. || 5. We know the father of the shaft, the Sun endowed with hundred powers: | By this may I bring health unto thy body: let the channels pour their burthen freely as of old. || 6. Whate'er hath gathered, as it flowed, in bowels, bladder, or in groins, | Thus let the conduit, free from check, pour all its burthen as of old. || 7. I lay the passage open as one cleaves the dam that bars the lake: | Thus let, etc. || 8. Now hath the portal been unclosed as, of the sea that holds the flood: | Thus let, etc. || 9. Even as the arrow flies away when loosened from the archer's bow, | Thus let the burthen be discharged from channels that are checked no more.

Hymn 1:4.

1. Along their paths the Mothers go, sisters of priestly ministrants, | Blending their water with the mead. || 2. May yonder Waters near the Sun, or those wherewith the Sun is joined, | Send forth this sacrifice of ours. || 3. I call the Waters, Goddesses, hitherward where our cattle drink: | The streams must share the sacrifice. || 4. Amṛita is in the Waters, in the Waters balm. | Yea, through our praises of the Floods, O horses, be ye fleet and strong, and, O ye kine, be full of strength.

Hymn 1:5.

1. Ye, Waters, truly bring us bliss: so help ye us to strength and power | That we may look on great delight. || 2. Here grant to us a share of dew, that most auspicious dew of yours, | Like mothers in their longing love. || 3. For you we fain would go to him to whose abode ye send us forth, | And, Waters, give us procreant strength. || 4. I pray the Floods to send us balm, those who bear rule o'er precious things, | And have supreme control of men.

Hymn 1:6.

1. The Waters be to us for drink, Goddesses, for our aid and bliss: | Let them stream health and wealth to us. || 2. Within the Waters—Soma thus hath told me—dwell all balms that heal, | And Agni, he who blesseth all. || 3. O Waters, teem with medicine to keep my body safe from harm, | So that I long may see the Sun. || 4. The Waters bless us, all that rise in desert lands or marshy pools! | Bless us the Waters dug from earth, bless us the Waters brought in jars, bless us the Waters of the Rains!

Hymn 1:7.

1. Bring the Kimīdin hither, bring the Yātudhāna self-declared | For Agni, God, thou, lauded, hast become the Dasyu's slaughterer. || 2. O Jātavedas, Lord Supreme, controller of our bodies, taste | The butter, Agni, taste the oil: make thou the Yātudhānas mourn. || 3. Let Yātudhānas mourn, let all greedy Kimīdins weep and wail: | And, Agni, Indra, may ye both accept this sacrifice of ours. || 4. May Agni seize upon them first, may strong-armed Indra drive them forth: | Let every wicked sorcerer come hither and say, Here am I. || 5. Let us behold thy strength, O Jātavedas. Viewer of men, tell us the Yātudhānas. | Burnt by thy heat and making declaration let all approach this sacrifice before thee. || 6. O Jātavedas, seize, on them: for our advantage art thou born: | Agni, be thou our messenger and make the Yātudhānas wail. || 7. O Agni, bring thou hitherward the Yātudhānas bound and chained. | And afterward let Indra tear their heads off with his thunder-bolt.

Hymn 1:8.

1. This sacrifice shall bring the Yātudhānas as the flood brings foam: | Here let the doer of this deed woman or man, acknowledge it. || 2. This one hath come confessing all: do ye receive him eagerly. | Master him thou, Bṛihaspati; Agni and Soma, pierce him through. || 3. O Soma-drinker, strike and bring the Yātudhāna's progeny: | Make the confessing sinner's eyes fall from his head, both right and left. || 4. As thou, O Agni Jātavedas, knowest the races of these secret greedy beings, | So strengthened by the power of prayer, O Agni, crushing them down a hundred times destroy them.

Hymn 1:9.

1. May Indra, Pūṣhan, Varuṇa, Mitra, Agni, benignant Gods, maintain this man in riches. | May the Ādityas and the Viśvedevas set and support him in supremest lustre. || 2. May light, O Gods, be under his dominion, Agni, the Sun, all; that is bright and golden. | Prostrate beneath our feet his foes and rivals. Uplift him to the loftiest cope of heaven. || 3. Through that most mighty prayer, O Jātavedas, wherewith thou. broughtest milk to strengthen Indra, | Even therewith exalt this man, O Agni, and give him highest rank among his kinsmen. || 4. I have assumed their sacrifice, O Agni, their hopes, their glory, and their riches' fullness | Prostrate beneath our feet his foes and rivals. Uplift him to the-loftiest cope of heaven.

Hymn 1:10.

1. This Lord is the Gods' ruler; for the wishes of Varuṇa the King must be accomplished. | Therefore, triumphant with the prayer I utter, I rescue this man from the Fierce One's anger. || 2. Homage be paid, King Varuṇa, to thine anger; for thou, dread God, detectest every falsehood. | I send a thousand others forth together: let this thy servant live a hundred autumns. || 3. Whatever falsehood thou hast told, much evil spoken with the tongue, | I liberate thee from the noose of Varuṇa the righteous King. || 4. I free thee from Vaiśvānara, from the great surging flood of sin. | Call thou thy brothers, Awful One! and pay attention to our prayer.

Hymn 1:11.

1. Vaṣhaṭ to thee. O Pūṣhan At this birth let Aryaman the Sage perform as Hotar-priest, | As one who bears in season let this dame be ready to bring forth her child. || 2. Four are the regions of the sky, and four the regions of the earth: | The Gods have brought the babe; let them prepare the woman for the birth. || 3. Puerpera (infatem) detegat: nos uterum aperimus. Lexa teipsam, puerpera. Tu, parturiens! emitte eum non carni, non adipi, non medullae adhäerntem. || 4. Descendat viscosa placenta, cani, comedenda placenta; decidat placenta. || 5. Diffindo tuum urinae ductum, diffindo vaginam, diffindo inguina. | Matrem natumque divido, puerum a placenta divido: decidat placenta. || 6. Sicut ventus, sicut mens, sicut alites volant, sic, decem mensium puer, cum placenta descende: descendat placenta.[1]

Hymn 1:12.

1. Born from the womb, brought forth from wind and from the cloud, the first red bull comes onward thundering with the rain. | Our bodies may he spare who, cleaving, goes straight on; he who, a single force, divides himself in three. || 2. Bending to thee who clingest to each limb with heat,

1. As in other places, Griffith gave these verses in Latin, in the present case with the note: "the details given in stanzas 3-6 are strictly obstetric and not presentable in English. The text appears to be mutilated in some places, and the metre is irregular." (Ed.)

fain would we worship thee with offered sacrifice, | Worship with sacrifice the bends and curves of thee who with a vigorous grasp hast seized on this one's limbs. || 3. Do thou release this man from headache, free him from cough which has entered into all his limbs and joints. | May he, the child of cloud, the offspring of the wind, the whiz-zing lighting, strike the mountains and the trees. || 4. Well be it with my upper frame, well be it with my lower parts. | With my four limbs let it be well. Let all my body be in health.

Hymn 1:13.

1. Homage to thee, the Lightning's flash, homage to thee, the Thunder's roar! | Homage to thee, the Stone which thou hurlest against the undevout! || 2. Homage to thee, Child of the Flood whence thou collectest fer-vent heat! | Be gracious to our bodies, give our children happiness and joy. || 3. Yea, homage be to thee, O Offspring of the Flood! Homage we pay to thee, the dart and fiery flame: | For well we know thy secret and sublimest home, where thou as central point art buried in the sea. || 4. Thou, Arrow, which the host of Gods created, making it strong and mighty for the shooting, | Be gracious, lauded thus, to our assembly. To thee, that Arrow, be our homage, Goddess!

Hymn 1:14.

1. As from the tree a wreath, have I assumed her fortune and her fame: | Among her kinsfolk long may she dwell, like a mountain broadly-based. || 2. King Yama, let this maiden be surrendered as a wife to thee: | Bound let her be meanwhile within, her mother's, brother's, father's house. || 3. Queen of thy race is she, O King: to thee do we deliver her. | Long with her kinsfolk may she sit, until her hair be white with age. || 4. With Asita's and Kaśyapa's and Gaya's incantation, thus | As sisters pack within a chest, I bind and tie thy fortune up.

Hymn 1:15.

1. Let the streams, flow together, let the winds and birds assembled come. | Let this my sacrifice delight them always. I offer it with duly mixt oblation. || 2. Come to my call, Blent Offerings, come ye very nigh. And, singers, do ye strengthen and increase this man. | Hither come every animal: with this man let all wealth abide. || 3. All river founts that blend their streams for ever inexhaustible— | With all these confluent streams of mine we make abundant riches flow. || 4. All streams of melted butter, and all streams of water and of milk | With all these confluent streams of mine we make abundant riches flow.

Hymn 1:16.

1. May potent Agni who destroys the demons bless and shelter us. | From greedy fiends who rise in troops at night-time when the moon is dark. || 2. Varuṇa's benison hath blessed the lead, and Agni strengthens it. | Indra hath given me the lead: this verily repels the fiends. || 3. This overcomes Vishkandha, this drives the voracious fiends away: | By means of this have I, o'erthrown all the Piśāchī's demon brood. || 4. If thou destroy a cow of ours, a human being, or a steed, | We pierce thee with this piece of lead so that thou mayst not slay our men.

Hymn 1:17.

1. Those maidens there, the veins, who run their course in robes of ruddy hue, | Must now stand quiet, reft of power, like sisters who are brother-less. || 2. Stay still, thou upper vein, stay still, thou lower, stay, thou midmost one, | The smallest one of all stands still: let the great vessel e'en be still. || 3. Among a thousand vessels charged with blood, among a thousand veins, | Even these the middle-most stand still and their extremities have rest. || 4. A mighty rampart built of sand hath circled and encompassed you: | Be still, and quietly take rest.

Hymn 1:18.

1. We drive away the Spotted Hag, Misfortune, and Malignity: | All blessings to our children then! We chase Malignity away. || 2. Let Savitar, Mitra, Varuṇa, and Aryaman drive away Stinginess from both the hands and feet: | May Favour, granting us her bounties, drive her off. The Gods created Favour for our happiness. || 3. Each fearful sign upon thy body, in thyself, each inauspicious mark seen in thy hair, thy face, | All this we drive away and banish with our speech. May Savitar the God graciously further thee. || 4. Antelope-foot, and Bullock-tooth, Cow-terrifier, Vapour-form, | The Licker, and the Spotted Hag, all these we drive away from us.

Hymn 1:19.

1. Let not the piercers find us, nor let those who wound discover us. | O Indra, make the arrows fall, turned, far from us, to every side. || 2. Turned from us let the arrows fall, those shot and those that will be shot. | Shafts of the Gods and shafts of men, strike and transfix mine enemies: || 3. Whoever treateth us as foes, be he our own or strange to us, a kinsman or a foreigner, | May Rudra with his arrows pierce and slay these enemies of mine. || 4. The rival and non-rival, he who in his hatred curses us | May all the deities injure him! My nearest, closest mail is prayer.

Hymn 1:20.

1. May it glide harmless by in this our sacrifice, O Soma, God! Marutas, be gracious unto us. | Let not disaster, let not malison find us out; let not abominable guiles discover us. || 2. Mitra and Varuṇa, ye twain, turn carefully away from us | The deadly dart that flies today, the missile of the wicked ones. || 3. Ward off from this side and from that, O Varuṇa, the deadly dart: | Give us thy great protection, turn the lethal weapon far away. || 4. A mighty Ruler thus art thou, unconquered, vanquisher of foes, | Even thou whose friend is never slain, whose friend is never over-come.

Hymn 1:21.

1. Lord of the clans, giver of bliss, fiend-slayer, mighty o'er the foe, | May Indra, Soma-drinker, go before us, Bull, who brings us peace. || 2. Indra, subdue our enemies, lay low the men who fight with us: | Down into nether darkness send the man who shows us enmity: || 3. Strike down the fiend, strike down the foes, break thou asunder | Vṛitra's jaws. O Indra, Vṛitra-slayer, quell the wrath of the assailing foe. || 4. Turn thou the foeman's thought away, his dart who fain would conquer us: | Grant us thy great protection; keep his deadly weapon far away.

Hymn 1:22.

1. As the Sun rises, let thy sore disease and yellowness depart. | We compass and surround thee with the colour of a ruddy ox. || 2. With ruddy hues we compass thee that thou mayst live a lengthened life: | So that this man be free from harm, and cast his yellow tint away. || 3. Devatyās that are red of hue, yea, and the ruddy-coloured kine, | Each several form, each several force—with these we compass thee about. || 4. To parrots and to starlings we transfer thy sickly yellowness: | Now in the yellow-coloured birds we lay this yellowness of thine.

Hymn 1:23.

1. O Plant, thou sprangest up at night, dusky, dark-coloured, black in hue! | So, Rajanī, re-colour thou these ashy spots, this leprosy. || 2. Expel the leprosy, remove from him the spots and ashy hue: | Let thine own colour come to thee; drive far away the specks of white. || 3. Dark is the place of thy repose, dark is the place thou dwellest in: | Dusky and dark, O Plant, art thou: remove from him each speck and spot. || 4. I with my spell have chased away the pallid sign of leprosy, | Caused by infection, on the skin, sprung from the body, from the bones.

Hymn 1:24.

1. First, before all, the strong-winged Bird was born; thou wast the gall thereof. | Conquered in fight, the Āsurī took then the shape and form of plants. || 2. The Āsurī made, first of all, this medicine for leprosy, this banisher of leprosy. | She banished leprosy, and gave one general colour to the skin. || 3. One-coloured, is thy mother's name, One-coloured is thy father called: | One-colour-maker, Plant! art thou: give thou one colour to this man. || 4. Śyāmā who gives one general hue was formed and fashioned from the earth: | Further this work efficiently. Restore the colours that were his.

Hymn 1:25.

1. When Agni blazed when he had pierced the Waters, whereat the Law-observers paid him homage, | There, men assever, was thy loftiest birthplace: O Fever, yielding to our prayer avoid us. || 2. If thou be fiery glow, or inflammation, or if thy birthplace call for chips of fuel, | Rack is thy name, God of the sickly yellow! O Fever, yielding to our prayer avoid us. || 3. Be thou distress, or agonizing torment, be thou the son King Varuṇa hath begotten, | Rack is thy name, God of the sickly yellow! O Fever, yielding to our prayer avoid us. || 4. I offer homage to the chilly Fever, to his fierce burning glow I offer homage. | Be adoration paid to Fever coming each other day, the third, of two days running.

Hymn 1:26.

1. Let that Destructive Weapon be far distant from us, O ye Gods; far be the Stone ye wont to hurl. || 2. Our friend be that Celestial Grace, Indra and Bhaga be our friends, and Savitar with splendid Wealth. || 3. Thou, Offspring of the water-flood, ye Marutas, with your sun-bright skins, give us protection reaching far. || 4. Further us rightly, favour ye our bodies with your gracious love. | Give thou our children happiness.

Hymn 1:27.

1. There on the bank those Vipers lie, thrice-seven, having cast their skins: | Now we with their discarded sloughs bind close and cover up the eyes of the malicious highway thief. || 2. Far let her go, cutting her way, brandishing, as it were, a club: | Diverted be the new-born's mind: ne'er are the wicked prosperous. || 3. Not many have had power enough; the feeble ones have not prevailed, | Like scattered fragments of a reed: ne'er are the wicked prosperous. || 4. Go forward, feet, press quickly on, bring to the house of him who pays. | Unconquered and unplundered, let Indrāṇī, foremost, lead the way.

Hymn 1:28.

1. God Agni hath come forth to us, fiend-slayer, chaser of disease, | Burning the Yātudhānas up, Kimīdins, and deceitful ones. || 2. Consume the Yātudhānas, God! meet the Kimīdins with thy flame: | Burn up the Yātudhānīs as they face thee, thou whose path is black! || 3. She who hath cursed us with a curse, or hath conceived a murderous sin; | Or seized our son to take his blood, let her devour the child she bare. || 4. Let her, the Yātudhānī eat son, sister, and her daughter's. child. | Now let the twain by turns destroy the wild-haired Yātudhānīs and crush down Arāyīs to the earth!

Hymn 1:29.

1. With that victorious Amulet which strengthened Indra's power-and might | Do thou, O Brahmaṇaspati, increase our strength for kingly sway. || 2. Subduing those who rival us, subduing all malignities, | Withstand the man who menaces, and him who seeks to injure-us. || 3. Soma and Savitar the God have strengthened and exalted thee: | All elements have aided thee, to make thee general conqueror. || 4. Slayer of rivals, vanquisher, may that victorious Amulet | Be bound on me for regal sway and conquest of mine enemies. || 5. Yon Sun hath mounted up on high, and this my word hath mounted up | That I may smite my foes and be slayer of rivals, rivalless. || 6. Destroyer of my rivals, strong, victorious, with royal sway, | May I be ruler of these men, and King and sovereign of the folk.

Hymn 1:30.

1. Guard and protect this man, all Gods and Vasus. Over him keep-ye watch and ward, Ādityas. | Let not death reach him from the hands of brothers from hands of aliens, or of human beings. || 2. Listen, one-minded, to the word I, utter, the sons, O Gods, among you, and the fathers! | I trust this man to all of you: preserve him happily, and to length of days conduct him. || 3. All Gods who dwell on earth or in the heavens, in air, within. the plants, the beasts, the waters, | Grant this man life to full old age, and let him escape the hundred other ways of dying. || 4. You, claiming Anuyājas or Prayājas, sharers, or not consumers, of oblation, | You, to whom heaven's five regions are apportioned, I make companions at his sacred sessions.

Hymn 1:31.

1. Here will we serve with sacrifice the great Controllers of the world, | The four immortal Warders who protect the regions of the sky. || 2. Ye, Guardians of the regions, Gods who keep the quarters of the heavens, | Rescue and free us from the bonds of Nirṛiti, from grief and woe! || 3. I, free from stiffness, serve thee with oblation, not lame I sacrifice with oil and fatness. | Let the strong Warder God, who keeps the regions bring to us hither safety and well-being. || 4. Well be it with our mother and our father, well be it with our cows, and beasts, and people. | Ours be all happy fortune, grace, and favour. Long, very long may we behold the sunlight.

Hymn 1:32.

1. Ye people, hear and mark this well: he will pronounce a mighty prayer: | That which gives breathing to the Plants is not on earth nor in, the heaven. || 2. Their station, as of those who rest when weary, is in midmost air: | The base whereon this world is built, the sages know or know it not. || 3. What the two trembling hemispheres and ground produced and fashioned forth. | This All, is ever fresh today, even as the currents of the sea. || 4. This All hath compassed round the one, and on the other lies at rest. | To Earth and all-possessing Heaven mine adoration have I paid.

Hymn 1:33.

1. May they, the golden-hued, the bright, the splendid, they wherein Savitar was born and Agni, | They who took Agni as a germ, fair-coloured, the Waters, bring felicity and bless us! || 2. They in the midst whereof King Varuṇa moveth, viewing men's righteous and unrighteous dealing. | They who took Agni as a germ, fair-coloured,—those Waters bring felicity and bless us! || 3. Whom the Gods make their beverage in heaven, they who wax manifold in air's mid-region, | They who took Agni as a germ, fair-coloured,—those Waters bring felicity and bless us! || 4. Ye Waters, with auspicious eye behold me: touch ye my skin with your auspicious body. | May they, the bright and pure, distilling fatness, those Waters, bring felicity and bless us.

Hymn 1:34.

1. From honey sprang this Plant to life; with honey now we dig thee up. | Make us as sweet as honey, for from honey hast thou been produced. || 2. My tongue hath honey at the tip, and sweetest honey at the root: | Thou yieldest to my wish and will, and shalt be mine and only mine. || 3. My coming in is honey-sweet and honey-sweet, my going forth: | My voice and words are sweet: I fain would be like honey in my look. || 4. Sweeter am I than honey, yet more full of sweets than licorice: | So mayst thou love me as a branch full of all sweets, and only me. || 5. Around thee have I girt a zone of sugar-cane to banish hate. | That thou mayst be in love with me, my darling never to depart.

Hymn 1:35.

1. This Ornament of Gold which Dakṣha's children bound, with benevolent thoughts, on Śatānīka, | This do I bind on thee for life, for glory, for long life lasting through a hundred autumns. || 2. This man no fiends may conquer, no Piśāchas, for this is might of Gods, their primal offspring. | Whoever wears the Gold of Dakṣha's children hath a long lengthened life among the living. || 3. The light, the power, the lustre of the Waters, the strength of Trees, and all their forceful vigour, | We lay on him as powers abide in Indra: so let him wear this Gold and show his valour. || 4. With monthly and six-monthly times and seasons, with the full year's sweet essence do we fill thee, | May Indra, Agni, and all Gods together, showing no anger, grant thee what thou wishest.

Kāṇḍa 2.

Hymn 2:1

1. Vena beholds That Highest which lies hidden, wherein this All resumes one form and fashion. | Thence Pṛiśni milked all life that had existence: the hosts that know the light with songs extolled her. || 2. Knowing Eternity, may the Gandharva declare to us that highest secret station. | Three steps thereof lie hidden in the darkness: he who knows these shall be the father's father. || 3. He is our kinsman, father, and begetter: he knows all beings and all Ordinances. | He only gave the Gods their appellations: all creatures go to him to ask direction. || 4. I have gone forth around the earth and heaven, I have approached the first-born Son of Order. | He, putting voice, as 'twere, within the speaker, stands in the world, he, verily is Agni. || 5. I round the circumjacent worlds have travelled to see the far-extended thread of Order. | Wherein the Gods, obtaining life eternal, have risen upward to one common birthplace.

Hymn 2:2.

1. Lord of the World, divine Gandharva, only he should be honoured in the Tribes and worshipped. | Fast with my spell, celestial God, I hold thee. Homage to thee! | Thy home is in the heavens. || 2. Sky-reaching, like the Sun in brightness, holy, he who averts from us the Gods' displeasure. | Lord of the World, may the Gandharva bless us, the friendly God who only must be worshipped. || 3. I came, I met these faultless, blameless beings: among the Apsarases was the Gandharva. | Their home is in the sea—so men have told me,—whence they come quickly hitherward and vanish. || 4. Thou, Cloudy! ye who follow the Gandharva Viśvāvasu, ye, Starry!

Lightning-Flasher! | You, O ye Goddesses, I truly worship. || 5. Haunters of darkness, shrill in voice, dice-lovers, maddeners of the mind | To these have I paid homage, the Gandharva's wives, Apsarases.

Hymn 2:3.

1. That little spring of water which is running downward from the hill | I turn to healing balm for thee that thou mayst be good medicine. || 2. Hither and onward! Well! Come on! Among thy hundred remedies | Most excellent of all art thou, curing disease and morbid flow. || 3. The Asuras bury deep in earth this mighty thing that healeth wounds. | This is the cure for morbid flow, this driveth malady away. || 4. The emmets from the water-flood produce this healing medicine: | This is the cure for morbid flow, this driveth malady away. || 5. Mighty is this wound-healing balm: from out the earth was it produced. | This is the cure for morbid flow, this driveth malady away. || 6. Bless us the Waters! be the Plants auspicious! | May Indra's thunderbolt drive off the demons. Far from us fall the shafts they shoot against us!

Hymn 2:4.

1. For length of life, for mighty joy, uninjured, ever showing strength. | We wear Vishkandha's antidote, the Amulet of Jaṅgiḍa. || 2. Amulet of a thousand powers, Jaṅgiḍa save us, all around. | From Jambha, and from Viśara, Vishkandha, and tormenting pain. || 3. This overcomes Vishkandha, this chases the greedy fiends away: | May this our panacea, may Jaṅgiḍa save us from distress. || 4. With Jaṅgiḍa that brings delight, Amulet given by the Gods, | We in the conflict overcome Vishkandha and all Rākshasas || 5. May Cannabis and Jaṅgiḍa preserve me from Vishkandha,—that | Brought to us from the forest, this sprung from the saps of husbandry. || 6. This Amulet destroys the might of magic and malignity: | So may victorious Jaṅgiḍa prolong the years we have to live.

Hymn 2:5.

1. Indra, be gracious, drive thou forth, come, Hero, with thy two bay steeds. | Taste the libation, hither, enjoying meath and the hymn, come, fair, to the banquet. || 2. O Indra, even as one athirst, fill thee with meath as 'twere from heaven. | Sweet-toned, the raptures of this juice have come to thee as to the light. || 3. Swift-conquering Indra, Mitra like, smote, as a Yati, Vṛitra dead. | Like Bhṛigu he cleft Vala through, and quelled his foes in Soma's rapturous joy. || 4. O Indra, let the juices enter thee. Fill full thy belly, sate thee, mighty one! Let the hymn bring thee. | Hear thou my call, accept the song I sing, here, Indra, with thy friends enjoy thyself, to height of rapture. || 5. Now will I tell the manly deeds of Indra, the first that he achieved, the thunder-wielder. | He slew the Dragon, then disclosed the waters, and cleft the channels of the mountain torrents. || 6. He slew the Dragon lying on the mountain: his heavenly bolt of thunder Tvashṭar fashioned. | Like lowing kine in rapid flow descending the waters glided downward to the ocean. || 7. Impetuous as a bull he chose the Soma, and quaffed the juices in three sacred beakers. | Maghavan grasped the thunder for his weapon, and smote to death this first-born of the dragons.

Hymn 2:6.

1. Half-years and seasons strengthen thee, O Agni, the years, and all the Verities, and Ṛishis! | Flash forth with thy celestial effulgence: illumine all four regions of the heavens. || 2. Kindle thee, Agni, and make this man prosper: rise up erect for high and happy fortune. | Agni, be those uninjured who adore thee, and may thy priests be glorious and no others. || 3. These Brahmans have elected thee, O Agni: be thou propitious in our sacred chamber. | Slayer of rivals, Agni, quell our foemen: watch in our house with care that never ceases. || 4. Seize, Agni, on thy power and firmly hold it: contend thou with the Friend by way of friendship. | Placed in the centre of our fellows, Agni, flash forth to be invoked by kings around thee. || 5. Past those who slay, past enemies, past thoughtless men, past those who hate, | Yea, Agni, hear us safe past all distresses: give thou us opulence with men about us.

Hymn 2:7.

1. Hated by sinners, sprung from Gods, this Plant that turns the curse away | Hath washed from me all curses, as water makes clean from spot and stain. || 2. All curses of a rival, each curse of a female relative, Curse uttered by an augry priest, all these we tread beneath our feet. || 3. Spread on the surface of the earth, downward from heaven thy root depends: | With this that hath a thousand joints keep thou us safe on every side. || 4. Guard on all sides this woman, guard my children, us, and all our wealth! | Let not malignity o'ercome, nor adversaries conquer us. || 5. Upon the curser fall his curse! Dwell we with him whose heart is true! | We split the cruel villain's ribs whose evil eye bewitches us.

Hymn 2:8.

1. Twin Stars of happy omen, named Releasers, have gone up. May they | Loose, of inherited disease, the uppermost and lowest bond. || 2. Vanish this Night, extinct in Dawn! Let those who weave their spells depart. | So let the plague-destroying Plant remove inherited disease. || 3. With straw of barley tawny-brown in colour with its silvery ears, with stalk and stem of Sesamum— | So let the plague-destroying Plant remove inherited disease. || 4. Let homage to thy ploughs be paid, our homage to the pole and yokes. | So let the plague-destroying Plant remove inherited disease. || 5. Homage to men with blinking eyes, homage to those who hear and act! To the Field's Lord be homage paid. | So let the plague-destroying Plant remove inherited disease.

Hymn 2:9.

1. Free this man, Daśavṛiksha! from the demon, from Grāhi who hath seized his joints and members, | And raise him up again, O Tree, into the world of living men. || 2. He hath arisen and come once more, rejoined the band of those who live. | May he become the sire of sons, and of all men most fortunate. || 3. He hath returned to consciousness, rejoined the living's firm abodes, | For hundred leeches are in this, yea, and a thousand healing herbs. || 4. The Gods, the Brahman-priests, and plants observed the way to gather thee: | All deities described the way men gather thee upon the earth. || 5. Let him who made it also heal: he, truly, is the deftest leech. | Pure, with a leech he verily shall give thee medicines that heal.

Hymn 2:10.

1. From family sickness, kinsmen's curse, Destruction, from Druh, from Varuṇa's noose I free and save thee. | With spell and prayer I make thee pure and sinless: to thee be both, the Earth and Heaven, auspicious! || 2. Gracious to thee be Agni with the Waters, let Soma with the Plants be kind and bless thee. | From family sickness, kinsmen's curse, Destruction, from Druh, from Varuṇa's noose I thus release thee. || 3. May kind Wind strengthen thee in air's mid-region, to thee may heaven's four quarters be auspicious. | From family sickness, kinsmen's curse, Destruction, from Druh, from Varuṇa's curse I thus release thee. || 4. These Goddesses, four regions of the heavens, on whom the Sun looks kindly, wives of Vāta— | From family sickness, kinsmen's curse, Destruction, from Druh, from Varuṇa's noose I thus release thee. || 5. For long life, in the midst of these I set thee. Away pass Nirṛiti, away Consumption! | From family sickness, kinsmen's curse, Destruction, from Druh, from Varuṇa's noose I thus release thee. || 6. Thou hast been freed from Phthisis and from trouble, from shame, and from the snare of Druh and Grain. | From family sickness, kinsmen's curse, Destruction, from Druh, from Varuṇa's noose I thus release thee. || 7. Joy hast thou found, and left ill-will behind thee: thou hast attained the happy world of virtue. | From family sickness, kinsmen's curse, Destruction, from Druh, from Varuṇa's noose I thus release thee. || 8. The Gods have freed from, sinfulness, redeeming the Sun, the Law from darkness and from Grāhi. | From family sickness, kinsmen's curse, Destruction, from Druh, from Varuṇa's noose I thus release thee. | With spell and prayer I make thee pure and sinless: to thee be both, the Earth and Heaven, auspicious!

Hymn 2:11.

1. Dart against dart, destroyer of destruction, thou art the missile sent to meet the missile. | Reach thy superior, thou; surpass thine equal. || 2. Sraktya art thou, an Amulet art thou, a counter-charm of spells, | Reach thy superior, thou; surpass thine equal. || 3. Use spells against the man we hate, against the man who hateth us. | Reach thy superior, thou; surpass thine equal. || 4. A prince art thou, giver of speech, thou art our bodies' strong defence. | Reach thy superior, thou; surpass thine equal. || 5. Fulgent art thou, and splendid, thou art heavenly lustre, thou art light. | Reach thy superior, thou; surpass thine equal.

Hymn 2:12.

1. The spacious Firmament, and Earth and Heaven, the Field's Queen, and

the wonderful Wide-Strider, | Yea, the broad middle air which Vāta guardeth, may these now burn with heat while I am burning. || 2. Listen to this, ye Gods who merit worship. Hymns here are sung for me by Bharadvāja. | Bound in the noose may he be doomed to trouble whoever mars this that our mind hath purposed. || 3. Hear this my call, O Indra, Soma-drinker, as with a burning heart I oft invoke thee. | I smite, as 'twere a tree felled with a hatchet, the man who marreth this my plan and purpose. || 4. Together with thrice-eighty Sāman-singers, Aṅgirasas, and Vasus, and Ādityas, | May the felicity of the Fathers guard us. I seize that man with fire that Gods have kindled. || 5. O Heaven and Earth, regard me with your favour, and, all ye Gods, stand on my side and help me. | Aṅgirasas, Fathers worthy of the Soma! woe fall on him who, caused the hateful outrage! || 6. Whoever either scorns us, O ye Marutas, or blames devotion which we now are paying. | Let his own wicked deeds be fires to burn him. May Heaven consume the man who hates devotion. || 7. Thy sevenfold vital breath, thine eight marrows I rend away with prayer. | With Agni as thine envoy, go, prepared, to Yama's dwelling place. || 8. In Jātavedas kindled flame I set the place assigned to thee. | Let fire consume thy body, and thy voice go to the general breath.

Hymn 2:13.

1. Strength-giver, winning lengthened life, O Agni, with face and back shining with molten butter, | Drink thou the butter and fair milk and honey, and, as a sire his sons, keep this man safely. | 2. For us surround him, cover him with splendour, give him long life, and death when age removes him. | The garment hath Bṛihaspati presented to Soma, to the King, to w rap about him. || 3. Thou for our weal hast clothed thee in the mantle: thou hast become our heifers' guard from witchcraft. | Live thou a hundred full and plenteous autumns, and wrap thee in prosperity of riches. || 4. Come hither, stand upon the stone: thy body shall become a stone. | The Universal Gods shall make thy life a hundred autumns long. || 5. So may the Universal Gods protect thee, whom we divest of raiment worn aforetime. | So after thee, well-formed and growing stronger, be born a multitude of thriving brothers.

Hymn 2:14.

1. Forth from the hall the bold, the sharp, the greedy one, the single-voiced, | Sadānvās, and all progeny of Chaṇḍa we exterminate. || 2. We drive you forth from cattle-shed, from axle, from within the wain, | Ye daughters of Magundī, we frighten and chase you from out homes. || 3. Yonder let the Arāyīs dwell, there where that house is down below. | Let utter indigence and all the Yātudhānīs settle there. || 4. May Bhūtapati drive away, and Indra, the Sadānvās hence. | Let Indra with his bolt quell those who sit upon our dwelling's floor. || 5. Whether ye be of farm and field, or whether ye be sent by men, | Or be ye sprung from Dasyu race, vanish, Sadānvās, and begone. || 6. I have gone round their homes as runs a fleet-foot racer round the post, | And in all races conquered you. Vanish, Sadānvās, and begone.

Hymn 2:15.

1. As Heaven and Earth are not afraid, and never suffer loss or harm, | Even so, my spirit, fear not thou. || 2. As Day and Night are not afraid, nor ever suffer loss or harm, | Even so, my spirit, fear not thou. || 3. As Sun and Moon are not afraid, nor ever suffer loss or harm. | Even so, my spirit, fear not thou. || 4. As Brahmanhood and Princely Power fear not, nor suffer loss, or harm, | Even so, my spirit, fear not thou. || 5. As Truth and Falsehood have no fear, nor ever suffer loss or harm, | Even so, my spirit, fear not thou. || 6. As What Hath Been and What Shall Be fear not, nor suffer loss or harm, | Even so, my spirit, fear not thou.

Hymn 2:16.

1. Guard me from death, Inhaling and Exhaling! All bliss to you! || 2. Guard me from overhearing, Earth and Heaven! All hail to you! || 3. Do thou, O Sūrya, with thine eye protect me! All hail to thee! || 4. Agni Vaiśvānara, with all Gods preserve me! All hail to thee! || 5. Preserve me with all care. O All-Sustainer! All hail to thee!

Hymn 2:17.

1. Power art thou, give me power. All hail! || 2. Might art thou, give me might. All hail! || 3. Strength art thou, give me strength. All hail! || 4. Life art thou, give me life. All hail! || 5. Ear art thou, give me hearing! Hail! || 6. Eye art thou, give me eyes. All hail! || 7. Shield art thou, shield me well. All hail!

Hymn 2:18.

1. Destruction of the foe art thou, give me the scaring of my foes. All hail! || 2. The rival's ruiner art thou, give me to drive my rivals off. All hail! || 3. Arāyīs' ruiner art thou, give me to drive Arāyīs off. All hail! || 4. Piśāchas' ruiner art thou, give me to drive Piśāchas off. All hail! || 5. Sadānvās' ruiner art thou, give me to drive Sadānvās off. All hail!

Hymn 2:19.

1. Burn thou, O Agni, with that heat of thine against the man who hates us, whom we hate. || 2. Flame thou, O Agni, with that flame of thine against the man who hates us, whom we hate. || 3. Shine out, O Agni, with that sheen of thine against the man who hates us, whom we hate. || 4. Blaze thou, O Agni, with that blaze of thine against the man who hates us, whom we hate. || 5. O Agni, with the splendour that is thine darken the man who hates us, whom we hate.

Hymn 2:20.

1. Burn thou, O Vāyu, with that heat of thine against the man who hates us, whom we hate. || 2. Flame thou, O Vāyu, with that flame of thine against the man who hates us, whom we hate. || 3. Shine out, O Vāyu, with that sheen of thine against the man who hates us, whom we hate. || 4. Blaze thou, O Vāyu, with that blaze of thine against the man who hates us, whom we hate. || 5. O Vāyu, with the splendour that is thine darken the man who hates us, whom we hate.

Hymn 2:21.

1. Burn thou, O Sūrya, with that heat of thine against the man who hates us, whom we hate. || 2. Flame thou, O Sūrya, with that flame of thine against the man who hates us, whom we hate. || 3. Shine out, O Sūrya, with that sheen of thine against the man who hates us, whom we hate. || 4. Blaze thou, O Sūrya, with that blaze of thine against the man who hates us, whom we hate. || 5. O Sūrya, with the splendour that is thine darken the man who hates us, whom we hate.

Hymn 2:22.

1. Burn thou, O Moon, with that heat of thine against the man who hates us, whom we hate. || 2. Flame thou, O Moon, with that flame of thine against the man who hates us, whom we hate. || 3. Shine out, O Moon, with that sheen of thine against the man who hates us, whom we hate. || 4. Blaze thou, O Moon, with that blaze of thine against the man who hates us, whom we hate. || 5. O Moon, with the splendour that is thine darken the man who hates us, whom we hate.

Hymn 2:23.

1. Burn thou, O Waters, with that heat of thine against the man who hates us, whom we hate. || 2. Flame thou, O Waters, with that flame of thine against the man who hates us, whom we hate. || 3. Shine out, O Waters, with that sheen of thine against the man who hates us, whom we hate. || 4. Blaze thou, O Waters, with that blaze of thine against the man who hates us, whom we hate. || 5. O Waters, with the splendour that is thine darken the man who hates us, whom we hate.

Hymn 2:24.

1. O Śerabhaka, Śerabha, back fall your arts of witchery! Back, | Kimīdins! let your weapon fall. | Eat your possessor; eat ye him who sent you forth; || 2. Śevṛidhaka, O Śevṛidha, back fall your arts of witchery! Back, | Kimīdins! let your weapon fall, etc. || 3. O Mroka, Anumroka, back return your arts of witchery! Back, | Kimīdins! let your weapon fall, etc. || 4. O Sarpa, Anusarpa, back return your arts of witchery! Back, Kimīdins! let your weapon fall, etc. || 5. Back fall your witcheries, Jūrṇi! back your weapon, ye Kimīdins, etc. || 6. Back fall your spells, Upabdi! back your weapon, ye Kimīdins, etc. || 7. Back fall your witchcrafts, Arjuni! your weapon, ye Kimīdins, etc., || 8. Back, O, Bharūji! fall your charms, your weapon, ye Kimīdins | Eat your possessor; eat ye him who sent you forth; eat your own flesh.

Hymn 2:25.

1. The Goddess Pṛiśniparṇī hath blest us, and troubled Nirṛiti | Fierce crusher of the Kaṇvas she: her have I gained, the mighty one. || 2. Victorious in the olden time this Pṛiśniparṇī was brought forth: | With her

I cleave, as 'twere a bird's, the head of the Detestables.[1] || 4. The hateful fiend who drinks the blood, and him who take away the growth, | The Kaṇva who devours the germ, quell, Pṛiśniparṇī! and! destroy. || 5. Drive and imprison in a hill these Kaṇvas harassers of life: | Follow them Pṛiśniparṇī, thou Goddess, like fire consuming. them. || 6. Drive thou away these Kaṇvas, drive the harassers of life afar. | Whither the shades of darkness go, I send the fiends who feed on flesh.

Hymn 2:26.

1. Let them come home, the cattle that have wandered, whom Vāyu hath delighted to attend on, | Whose forms and figures are well known to Tvashṭar These cows let Savitar drive within this stable. || 2. Let the beasts stream together to this cow-pen. Bṛihaspati who knoweth lead them hither! | Let Sinīvālī guide the foremost homeward. When they have come, Anumati! enclose them. || 3. Together stream the cattle! stream together horses and the men! | Hitherward press all growth of grain! I offer sacrifice with mixt oblation. || 4. I pour together milk of kine, with butter blending strength and juice. | Well sprinkled be our men, as true to me as cows are to their herd! || 5. Hither I bring the milk of cows, hither have brought the juice of corn. | Hitherward have our men been brought, hitherward to this house our wives.

Hymn 2:27.

1. Let not the enemy win the cause! Strong and predominant art thou. | Refute mine adversary's speech. Render them dull and flat, O Plant. || 2. The strong-winged bird discovered thee, the boar unearthed thee with his snout. | Refute mine adversary's speech. Render them dull and flat, O Plant. || 3. Yea, Indra laid thee on his arm, to cast the Asuras to the ground. | Refute mine adversary's speech. Render them dull and flat, O Plant. || 4. Indra devoured the Pāṭā plant that he might lay the Asuras low. | Refute mine adversary's speech! Render them dull and flat, O Plant. || 5. With this I overcome my foes as Indra overcame the wolves. | Refute mine adversary's speech! Render them dull and flat, O Plant. || 6. O Rudra, Lord of Healing Balms, dark-crested, skilful in thy work!— | Refute mine adversary's speech. Render them dull and flat, O Plant. || 7. Indra, defeat the speech of him who meets us with hostility. | Comfort us with thy power and might. Make me superior in debate.

Hymn 2:28.

1. This Child, Old Age! shall grow to meet thee only: none of the hundred other deaths shall harm him. | From trouble caused by friends let Mitra guard him, as a kind mother guards the son she nurses. || 2. Mitra or Varuṇa the foe-destroyer, accordant, grant him death in course of nature! | Thus Agni, Hotar-priest, skilled in high statutes, declareth all the deities' generations. || 3. Thou art the Lord of all terrestrial cattle, of cattle born and to be born hereafter. | Let not breath drawn or breath emitted fail him. Let not his friends, let not his foemen slay him. || 4. Let Heaven thy father and let Earth thy mother, accordant, give thee death in course of nature, | That thou mayst live on Aditi's bosom, guarded, a hundred winters, through thy respirations. || 5. Lead him to life, O Agni, and to splendour, this dear child, Varuṇa! and thou King Mitra! | Give him protection, Aditi! as a mother; All Gods, that his be life of long duration;

Hymn 2:29.

1. Gods, give him all that earth hath best with bodily strength and happy fate. | Agni and Sūrya grant him life, Bṛihaspati give him eminence! || 2. Bestow thou life on him, O Jātavedas. Store him with future progeny, O Tvashṭar | Send him, O Savitar, full growth of riches. Let this thy servant live a hundred autumns. || 3. May this our prayer bring strength and goodly offspring. Give, both of you one-minded, strength and riches. | Let him with might win fields and victory, Indra! setting beneath his feet the rest, his rivals. || 4. As Indra's gift, by Varuṇa instructed the fierce one came to us sent by the Marutas. | Let him, O Heaven and Earth, rest in your bosom. Let him not hunger, let him not be thirsty. || 5. Ye twain endowed with vigour, grant him vigour. Ye who are rich in milk, give milk to feed him. | These twain have given him vigour, Earth and Heaven, and all the Gods, the Marutas, and the Waters. || 6. With health-bestowing drops thine heart I comfort: all-bright again, and undiseased, enjoy them. | Dressed in like robes let these two drink the mixture, wearing the Aśvins' form as an illusion. || 7. Erst Indra, wounded, made this strengthening portion, eternal food: thine is it, here presented. | With this live full of vigour through the autumns. Let not thy strength be drained. Leeches have helped thee.

Hymn 2:30.

1. As the wind shake this Tuft of Grass hither and thither on the ground. | So do I stir and shake thy mind, that thou mayst be in love with me, my darling, never to depart. || 2. Ye, Aśvins, lead together, ye unite and bring the loving pair. | Now have the fortunes of you twain, now have your vows and spirits met. || 3. When eagles, calling out aloud, are screaming in the joy of health, | Then to my calling let her come, as to the arrow's neck the shaft. || 4. Let what is inward turn outside, let what is outward be within: | Seize and possess, O Plant, the mind of maidens rich in every charm. || 5. Seeking a husband she hath come! and I came longing for a wife: | Even as a loudly-neighing steed may fate and fortune have I met.

Hymn 2:31.

1. With Indra's mighty millstone, that which crushes worms of every sort, | I bray and bruise the worms to bits like vetches on the grinding stone. || 2. The Seen and the Invisible, and the Kurūru have I crushed: | Alāṇḍus, and all Chhalunas, we bruise to pieces with our spell. || 3. I kill Alāṇḍus with a mighty weapon: burnt or not burnt they now have lost their vigour. | Left or not left, I with the spell subdue them: let not a single worm remain uninjured. || 4. The worm that lives within the ribs, within the bowels, in the head. | Avaskava and Borer, these we bruise to pieces with the spell. || 5. Worms that are found on mountains, in the forests, that live in plants, in cattle, in the waters, | Those that have made their way within our bodies,— these I destroy, the worms' whole generation.

Hymn 2:32.

1. Uprising let the Sun destroy, and when he sinketh, with his beams. | The Worms that live within the cow. || 2. The four-eyed worm, of every shape, the variegated, and the white | I break and crush the creature's ribs, and tear away its head besides. || 3. Like Atri I destroy you, Worms! in Kaṇva's, Jamadagni's way: | I bray and bruise the creeping things to pieces with Agastya's spell. || 4. Slain is the sovereign of these Worms, yea, their controlling lord is slain: | Slain is the Worm, his mother slain, brother and sister both are slain. || 5. Slain are his ministers, and slain his followers and retinue: | Yes, those that seemed the tiniest things, the Worms have all been put to death. || 6. I break in pieces both thy horns wherewith thou pushest here and there: | I cleave and rend the bag which holds the venom which is stored in thee.

Hymn 2:33.

1. From both thy nostrils, from both eyes, from both thine ears, and from thy chin, | Forth from thy brain and tongue I root Consumption seated in thy head. || 2. Forth from the neck and from the nape, from dorsal vertebrae and spine. | From arms and shoulder-blades I root Consumption seated in thine arms. || 3. Forth from thy heart and from thy lungs, from thy gall-bladder and thy sides, | From kidneys, spleen and liver thy Consumption we eradicate. || 4. From bowels and intestines, from the rectum and the belly, | I Extirpate thy Consumption, from flanks, navel and mesentery. || 5. Forth from thy thighs and from thy knees, heels and the fore-parts of thy feet. | Forth from thy loins and hips I draw Consumption setted in thy loins. || 6. Forth from thy marrows and thy bones, forth from thy tendons and thy veins | I banish thy Consumption, from thy hands, thy fingers, and thy nails. || 7. In every member, every hair, in every joint wherein it lies, | We with the exorcising spell of Kaśyapa drive far away Consumption settled in thy skin.

Hymn 2:34.

1. May this, of all the beasts that Paśupati rules, Lord of animals, quadruped and biped, | Come, purchased, to the sacrificial portion. May growth of wealth attend the sacrificer. || 2. Loosing the seed of future-time existence, give good success, O Gods, to him who worships. | May what is present, duly brought, the victim, go to the deities' beloved region. || 3. Those who are looking, deep in meditation, on the bound animal with eye and spirit | To them, the first, may Agni, God, give freedom, rejoicing in his creatures, Viśvakarman || 4. Tame animals of every shape, though varied in

1. Verse 3 was omitted in Griffith's translation, with no explanation given. (Ed.)

colour, manifold alike in nature | To them, the first, may Vāyu, God, give freedom, Prajāpati. rejoicing in his creatures. || 5. Let those who know receive before all others the vital breath proceeding from the body. | Go to the sky. Stay there with all thy members. By paths which Gods have travelled go to Svarga.

Hymn 2:35.

1. We who enjoying it have grown no richer, for whom the sacred altar-fires have sorrowed, | We who compounded with deficient worship,—may Viśvakarman make our service prosper. || 2. Ṛishis have called the sacrifice's patron amerced through sin, sorrowing for his offspring. | Those drops of meath whereof the missed enjoyment,—may Viśvakarman with those drops unite us. || 3. Regarding niggard churls as Soma-drinkers, skilful in sacrifice, weak at the meeting, | Whatever sin the captive hath committed, do thou for weal release him, Viśvakarman! || 4. Awful are Ṛishis: unto them be homage, and to their eye and truthfulness of spirit! | Loud homage to Bṛihaspati, O mighty! Homage to thee, O Viśvakarman! Guard us. || 5. The eye of sacrifice, source, and beginning—with voice, ear, spirit unto him I offer. | To this our sacrifice wrought by Viśvakarman may the Gods come gracious and kindly-hearted.

Hymn 2:36.

1. To please us may the suitor come, O Agni, seeking this maid and bringing us good fortune. | Approved by wooers, lovely in assemblies, may she be soon made happy with a husband. || 2. As bliss beloved by Soma, dear to Prayer, and stored by Aryaman, | With the God Dhātar's truthfulness I work the bridal oracle. || 3. O Agni, may this woman find a husband. Then verily King Soma makes her happy. | May she bear sons, chief lady of the household, blessed and bearing rule beside her consort. || 4. As this lair, Maghavan! that is fair to look on was dear to wild things as a pleasant dwelling, | So may this woman here be Bhaga's darling. Loved by her lord and prizing his affection. || 5. Mount up, embark on Bhaga's ship, the full, the inexhaustible, | Thereon bring hitherward to us the lover whom thou fain wouldst wed. || 6. Call out to him, O Lord of Wealth! Make thou the lover well-inclined. | Set each on thy right hand who is a lover worthy of her choice. || 7. Here is the bdellium and the gold, the Aukṣha and the bliss are here: | These bring thee to the husbands, so to find the man whom thou. wouldst have. || 8. May Savitar lead and bring to thee the husband whom thy heart desires. | O Plant, be this thy gift to her!

Kāṇḍa 3.

Hymn 3:1.

1. Let the wise Agni go against our foemen, burning against ill-will and imprecation | Let him bewilder our opponents' army, Let Jātavedas smite and make them handless. || 2. Mighty are ye for such a deed, O Marutas. Go forward, overcome them and destroy them. | The Vasus slew, and these were left imploring. Wise Agni as our messenger assail them! || 3. O Maghavan, O Indra, thou who slayest fiends, and, Agni, thou, | Burn, both of you, against these men, the foeman's host that threatens us. || 4. Shot down the slope, with thy two tawny coursers, forth go thy bolt, destroying foes, O Indra! | Slay those who fly, slay those who stand and follow. | On every side fulfil these men's intention. || 5. Indra, bewilder thou the foemen's army. | With Agni's, Vāta's furious rush drive them away to every side. || 6. Let Indra daze their army. Let the Marutas slay it with their might. | Let Agni take their eyes away, and let the conquered host retreat.

Hymn 3:2.

1. May Agni, he who knows, our envoy, meet them, burning against ill-will and imprecation. | May he bewilder our opponent's senses. May Jātavedas smite and make them handless. || 2. This Agni hath bewildered all the senses that were in your hearts: | Now let him blast you from your home, blast you away from every side. || 3. Dazing their senses, Indra, come hitherward with the wish and will. | With Agni's, Vāta's furious rush drive them to every side away. || 4. Vanish, ye hopes and plans of theirs, be ye confounded, all their thoughts! | Whatever wish is in their heart, do thou expel it utterly. || 5. Bewildering the senses of our foemen, seize on their bodies and depart, O Apvā! | Go meet them, flame within their hearts and burn them. Smite thou the foes with darkness and amazement. || 6. That army of our enemies, O Marutas, that comes against us with its might, contending— | Meet ye and strike it with unwelcome darkness so that not one. of them may know another.

Hymn 3:3.

1. Loudly he roared. Here let him labour deftly. Spread, Agni, over spacious earth and heaven. | Let Marutas who possesses all treasures yoke thee. Bring him who reverently paid oblations. || 2. Though he be far away, let the red horses bring Indra, bring the sage to us and friendship, | Since with Sautrāmaṇī Gods for him o'er-power Gāyatrī, Bṛihatī, and hymn of praises. || 3. King Varuṇa call thee hither from the waters! From hills and mountains Soma call thee hither! | Let Indra call thee hither to these people. Fly hither to these people as a falcon. || 4. May the hawk bring the man who must be summoned, from far away, in alien land, an exile. | May both the Aśvins make thy pathway easy. Come, and unite yourselves with him, ye Kinsmen. || 5. Let thine opponents call thee back. Thy friends have chosen, thee again. | Indra and Agni, all the Gods have kept thy home amid the tribe. || 6. He who disputes our calling thee, be he a stranger or akin. | Drive him, O Indra, far away, and do thou bring this man to us.

Hymn 3:4.

1. To thee hath come the kingship with its splendour: On! shine as lord, sole ruler of the people. | King! let all regions of the heavens invite thee. Here let men wait on thee and bow before thee. || 2. The tribesmen shall elect thee for the Kingship, these five celestial regions shall elect thee. | Rest on the height and top of kingly power: thence as a mighty man award us treasures. || 3. Kinsmen, inviting thee, shall go to meet thee, with thee go Agni as an active herald. | Let women and their sons be friendly-minded. Thou mighty one, shalt see abundant tribute. || 4. First shall the Aśvins, Varuṇa and Mitra, the Universal Gods, and Marutas call thee. | Then turn thy mind to giving gifts of treasures, thence, mighty one, distribute wealth among us. || 5. Speed to us hither from the farthest distance. Propitious unto thee be Earth and Heaven. | Even so hath Varuṇa this King asserted, he who himself hath called thee: come thou hither. || 6. Pass to the tribes of men. O Indra, Indra. Thou the Varuṇas hast been found accordant. | To his own place this one hath called thee, saying, Let him adore the Gods and guide the clansmen. || 7. The Bounteous Paths in sundry forms and places, all in accord, have given thee room and comfort. | Let all of these in concert call thee hither. Live thy tenth decade here, a strong kind ruler.

Hymn 3:5.

1. This Parṇa-Amulet hath come, strong and destroying with its strength my rivals. | The power of the Gods, the plants' sweet essence, may it incite me ceaselessly with vigour. || 2. O Parṇa-Amulet, in me set firmly might and opulence. | Within the compass of my rule may I be rooted and supreme. || 3. That dear mysterious Amulet which Gods have set within the tree, | May the Gods grant to me to wear together with extended life. || 4. As Indra's gift, by Varuṇa instructed, Parṇa hath come, the mighty strength of Soma: | This would I, brightly shining, love and cherish for long life lasting through a hundred autumns. || 5. The Parṇa-Charm hath come to me for great security from ill. | That I may be exalted, yea, above the wealth of Aryaman. || 6. Sagacious builders of the car, cleaver and skilful artisans,— | Make all the men on every side, Parṇa, obedient to my will || 7. The kings and makers of the kings, troop-leaders, masters of the horse, | Make all the men on every side, Parṇa, obedient to my will. || 8. Thou, Parṇa, art my body's guard, man kin my birth to me a man. | With splendour of the circling year I bind thee on me, Amulet!

Hymn 3:6.

1. Masculine springs from masculine, Aśvattha grows from Khadira, | May it destroy mine enemies, who hate me and whom I detest. || 2. Crush down my foes, Aśvattha! Rend, O Burster, those who storm and rage, | With Indra, slayer of the fiends, with Mitra and with Varuṇa || 3. As thou hast rent and torn apart, Aśvattha! in the mighty sea, | So rend asunder all those men who hate me and whom I detest. || 4. Thou who like some victorious bull displayest thy surpassing might, | With thee, with thee, Aśvattha! we would overcome our enemies. || 5. Nirṛiti bind them with the bonds of Death which never may be loosed. | Mine enemies, Aśvattha! those who hate me and whom I detest. || 6. As thou, Aśvattha!, mountest on the trees and overthrowest them, | So do thou break my foeman's head asunder and o'er-power him. || 7. Let them drift downward like a boat torn from the rope that fastened it. | There is no turning back for those whom He who

Cleaves hath driven away. || 8. With mental power I drive them forth, drive them with intellect and charm. | We banish and expel them with the branch of an Aśvattha tree.

Hymn 3:7.

1. The fleet-foot Roebuck wears upon his head a healing remedy. | Innate disease he drives away to all directions with his horn. || 2. With his four feet the vigorous Buck hath bounded in pursuit of thee. | Unbind the chronic sickness, Horn! deeply inwoven in the heart. || 3. That which shines yonder, like a roof resting on four walls, down on us,— | Therewith from out thy body we drive all the chronic malady, || 4. May those twin stars, auspicious, named Releasers, up in yonder sky. | Loose of the chronic malady the uppermost and lowest bond. || 5. Water, indeed, hath power to heal, Water drives malady away. | May water—for it healeth all—free thee from permanent disease. || 6. Hath some prepared decoction brought inveterate disease on thee, | I know the balm that healeth it: we drive the malady away. || 7. What time the starlight disappears, what time the gleams of Dawn depart, | May evil fortune pass from us, the chronic sickness disappear.

Hymn 3:8.

1. Let Mitra come, arranging, with the Seasons, lulling the Earth to rest with gleams of splendour. | And so let Agni, Varuṇa, and Vāyu make our dominion tranquil and exalted. || 2. May Indra, Tvaṣhṭar hear my word with favour, may Dhātar, Rāti, Savitar accept it. | I call the Goddess Aditi, heroes' mother, that I may be the centre of my kinsmen. || 3. Soma I call, and Savitar with homage, and all the Ādityas in the time of contest. | Long may this fire send forth its splendour, lighted by kinsmen uttering no word against me. || 4. Here, verily, may you stay: go ye no farther. The strong Herd, Lord of Increase, drive you hither! | To please this man may all the Gods together come unto you and be as dames who love him. || 5. We bend together all your minds, your vows and purposes we bend. | We bend together you who stand apart with hopes opposed to ours. || 6. I with my spirit seize and hold your spirits. Follow with thought and wish my thoughts and wishes. | I make your hearts the thralls of my dominion; on me attendant come thy way I guide you.

Hymn 3:9.

1. Heaven is the sire, the mother Earth, of Karśapha and Viśapha. | As ye have brought them hither, Gods! so do ye move therm hence away. || 2. The bands hold fast without a knot: this is the way that Manu used. | I make Viṣhkandha impotent as one emasculateth bulls. || 3. Then to a tawny-coloured string the wise and skilful bind a brush. | Let bandages make impotent the strong and active Kābava. || 4. Ye who move active in your strength like Gods with Asuras' magic powers, | Even as the monkey scorns the dogs, Bandages! scorn the Kābava. || 5. Yea, I will chide thee to thy shame, I will disgrace the Kābava. | Under our imprecations ye, like rapid cars, shall pass away. || 6. One and one hundred over earth are the Viṣhkandhas spread abroad. | Before these have they fetched thee forth. Viṣhkandha quelling Amulet.

Hymn 3:10.

1. The First hath dawned. With Yama may it be a cow to pour forth milk. | May she be rich in milk and stream for us through many a coming year. || 2. May she whom Gods accept with joy, Night who approacheth. as a cow, | She who is Consort of the Year, bring us abundant happiness || 3. Thou whom with reverence we approach, O Night, as model of the Year, | Vouchsafe. us children long to live; bless us with increase of our wealth. || 4. This same is she whose light first dawned upon us: she moves established in the midst of others: | Great powers and glories are contained within her: a first-born bride, she conquers and bears children. || 5. Loud was the wooden pass-gear's ring and rattle, as it made annual oblation ready. | First Aṣhṭakā! may we be lords of riches, with goodly children and good men about us. || 6. The shrine of Iḍā flows with oil and fatness: accept, O Jātavedas, our oblations. | Tame animals of varied form and colour—may all the seven abide with me contented. || 7. Come thou to nourish me and make me prosper. Night! may the favour of the Gods attend us. | Filled full, O Ladle, fly thou forth. Completely filled fly back again. | Serving at every sacrifice bring to us food and energy. || 8. This Year hath come to us, thy lord and consort, O Ekāṣhṭakā. | Vouchsafe us children long to live, bless us with increase of our wealth. || 9. The Seasons, and the Seasons' Lords I worship, annual parts and groups. | Half years, Years, Months, I offer to the Lord of all existing things. || 10. I offer to the Seasons, to their several groups, to Months, to Years. | Dhātar, Vidhātar, Fortune, to the lord of all existing things. || 11. With fatness and libation we sacrifice and adore the Gods. | Wealthy in kine may we retire to rest us in our modest homes. || 12. Ekāṣhṭakā, burning with zealous fervour, brought forth her babe the great and glorious Indra. | With him the Gods subdued their adversaries: the Lord of Might became the Dasyus' slayer. || 13. Indra's and Soma's mother! thou art daughter of Prajāpati. | Satisfy thou our hearts' desires. Gladly accept our sacrifice.

Hymn 3:11.

1. For life I set thee free by this oblation both from unmarked decline and from consumption: | Or if the grasping demon have possessed him, free him from her, O Indra, thou and Agni! || 2. Be his days ended, be he now departed, be he brought very near to death already, | Out of Destruction's lap again I bring him, save him for life to last a hundred autumns. || 3. With sacrifice thousand-eyed and hundred-powered, bringing a hundred lives, have I restored him, | That Indra through the autumns may conduct him safe to the farther shore of all misfortune. || 4. Live, waxing in thy strength a hundred autumns, live through a hundred springs, a hundred winters! | Indra, Agni, Savitar, Bṛihaspati give thee a hundred! With hundred-lived oblation have I saved him, || 5. Breath, Respiration, come to him, as two car-oxen to their stall! | Let all the other deaths, whereof men count a hundred, pass away. || 6. Breath, Respiration, stay ye here. Go ye not hence away from him, | Bring, so that he may reach old age, body and members back again. || 7. I give thee over to old age, make thee the subject of old age. | Let kindly old age lead thee on. Let all the other deaths, whereof men count a hundred, pass away! || 8. Old age hath girt thee with its bonds even as they bind a bull with rope. | The death held thee at thy birth bound with a firmly-knotted noose, | Therefrom, with both the hands of Truth, Bṛihaspati hath loosened thee.

Hymn 3:12.

1. Here, even here I fix my firm-set dwelling; flowing with fatness may it stand in safety. | May we approach thee, House! with all our people, uncharmed and goodly men, and dwell within thee, || 2. Even here, O House, stand thou on firm foundation, wealthy in horses, rich in kine and gladness. | Wealthy in nourishment. in milk and fatness, rise up for great felicity and fortune. || 3. A spacious store, O House, art thou, full of clean corn and lofty-roofed. | Let the young calf and little boy approach thee, and milch-kine streaming homeward in the evening. || 4. This House may Savitar and Vāyu establish, Bṛihaspati who knows the way, and Indra. | May the moist Marutas sprinkle it with fatness, and may King Bhaga make our corn-land fruitful. || 5. Queen of the home! thou, sheltering, kindly Goddess, wast established by the Gods in the beginning. | Clad in thy robe of grass be friendly-minded, and give us wealth with goodly men about us. || 6. Thou Pole, in ordered fashion mount the pillar. Strong, shining forth afar, keep off our foemen. | House! let not those who dwell within thee suffer. Live we with all our men, a hundred autumns. || 7. To this the tender boy hath come, to this the calf with all the beasts, | To this crock of foaming drink, hither with jars of curdled milk. || 8. Bring hitherward, O dame, the well-filled pitcher, the stream of molten butter blent with nectar. | Bedew these drinkers with a draught of Amṛita. May all our hopes' fulfilment guard this dwelling. || 9. Water that kills Consumption, free from all Consumption, here I bring. | With Agni, the immortal one, I enter and possess the house.

Hymn 3:13.

1. As ye, when Ahi had been slain, flowed forth together with a roar, | So are ye called the Roaring Ones: this, O ye Rivers, is your name. || 2. As driven forth by Varuṇa ye swiftly urged your rolling waves, | There Indra reached you as you flowed; hence ye are still the Water-floods. || 3. Indra restrained you with his might. Goddesses, as ye glided on | Not in accordance with his will: hence have ye got the name of Streams. || 4. One only God set foot on you flowing according to your will, | The mighty ones breathed upward fast: hence; Water is the name they bear. || 5. Water is good, water indeed is fatness. Agni and Soma, truly, both bring water. | May the strong rain of those who scatter sweetness come helpful unto me with breath and vigour. || 6. Then verily, I see, yea, also hear them: their

sound approaches me, their voice comes hither. | Even then I think I am enjoying Amṛita, what time I drink my fill of you, gold coloured! || 7. Here, O ye Waters, is your heart. Here is your calf, ye holy ones. | Flow here, just here, O mighty Streams, whither I now am leading you.

Hymn 3:14.

1. A Pen wherein to dwell at ease, abundance and prosperity, | Whate'er is called the birth of day, all this do we bestow on you. || 2. May Aryaman pour gifts on you, and Pūṣhan, land Bṛihaspati, | And Indra, winner of the prize. Make ye my riches grow with me. || 3. Moving together, free from fear, with plenteous droppings in this pen, | Bearing sweet milk-like Soma-juice, come hither free from all disease. || 4. Come hither, to this place, O Cows: here thrive as though ye were manured. | Even here increase and multiply; let us be friendly, you and me. || 5. Auspicious be this stall to you. Prosper like cultivated rice. | Even here increase and multiply. Myself do we bestow on you. || 6. Follow me, Cows, as master of the cattle. Here may this Cow-pen make you grow and prosper, | Still while we live may we approach you living, ever increasing with the growth of riches.

Hymn 3:15.

1. I stir and animate the merchant Indra; may he approach and be our guide and leader. | Chasing ill-will, wild beast, and highway robber, may he who hath the power give me riches. || 2. The many paths which Gods are wont to travel, the paths which go between the earth and heaven, | May they rejoice with me in milk and fatness that I may make rich profit by my purchase. || 3. With fuel. Agni! and with butter, longing, mine offering I present for strength and conquest; | With prayer, so far as I have strength, adoring—this holy hymn to gain a hundred treasures. || 4. Pardon this stubbornness of ours. O Agni, the distant pathway which our feet have trodden. | Propitious unto us be sale and barter, may interchange of merchandise enrich me. | Accept, ye twain, accordant, this libation! Prosperous be our ventures and incomings. || 5. The wealth wherewith I carry on my traffic, seeking, ye Gods! wealth with the wealth I offer, | May this grow more for me, not less: O Agni, through sacrifice chase those who hinder profit! || 6. The wealth wherewith I carry on my traffic, seeking, ye Gods! wealth with the wealth I offer, | Herein may Indra, Savitar, and Soma, Prajāpati, and Agni give me splendour. || 7. With reverence we sign thy praise, O Hotar-priest Vaiśvānara | Over our children keep thou watch, over our bodies, kine, and lives. || 8. Still to thee ever will we bring oblation, as to a stabled horse, O Jātavedas. | Joying in food and in the growth of riches may we thy servants, Agni, never suffer.

Hymn 3:16.

1. Agni at dawn, and Indra we invoke at dawn, and Varuṇa and Mitra, and the Aśvins twain: | Bhaga at dawn, Pūṣhan and Brahmaṇaspati, Soma at dawn, and Rudra we invoke at dawn. || 2. We all strong Bhaga, conqueror in the morning, the son of Aditi, the great Disposer, | Whom each who deems himself poor, strong and mighty, a king, addresses thus, Grant thou my portion! || 3. Bhaga, our guide, Bhaga whose gifts are faithful, favour this hymn and give us wealth, O Bhaga. | Bhaga, augment our store of kine and horses. Bhaga, may we be rich in men and heroes. || 4. So may felicity be ours at present, and when the Sun advances, and at noontide; | And may we still, O Bounteous One, at sunset be happy in the Gods' protecting favour. || 5. May Bhaga verily be bliss-bestower, and through him, Gods! may happiness attend us. | As such with all my might I call and call thee: as such be thou our leader here, O Bhaga. || 6. To this our sacrifice may the Dawns incline them, and come to the pure place like Dadhikrāvan. | As strong steeds draw a chariot may they bring me hitherward Bhaga who discovers treasure. || 7. May the kind Mornings dawn on us for ever with, wealth of kine, of horses, and of heroes. | Streaming with all abundance, pouring fatness, Do ye preserve us evermore with blessings!

Hymn 3:17.

1. Wise and devoted to the Gods the skilful men bind plough-ropes fast, | And lay the yokes on either side. || 2. Lay on the yokes and fasten well the traces: formed is the furrow, sow the seed within it. | Virāj vouchsafe us hearing fraught with plenty! | Let the ripe grain come near and near the sickle. || 3. The keen-shared plough that bringeth bliss, furnished with traces and with stilts, | Shear out for me a cow, a sheep, a rapid drawer of the car, a blooming woman, plump and strong! || 4. May Indra press the furrow down, may Pūṣhan guard and cherish her. | May she, well stored with milk yield milk for us through each succeeding year. || 5. Happily let the shares turn up the ploughland, the ploughers happily follow the oxen. | Pleased with our sacrifice, Śuna and Sīra! make the plants bring this man abundant produce. || 6. Happily work our steers and men! May the plough furrow happily, | Happily be the traces bound. Happily ply the driving-goad. || 7. Śuna and Sīra, welcome ye this laud, and with the milk that ye have made in heaven, | Bedew ye both this earth of ours. || 8. Auspicious Sītā, come thou near: we venerate and worship thee. | That thou mayst bless and prosper us and bring us fruits abundantly. || 9. Loved by the Viśvedevas and the Marutas, let Sītā be bedewed. with oil and honey. | Turn thou to us with wealth of milk, O Sītā, in vigorous strength and pouring streams of fatness.

Hymn 3:18.

1. From out the earth I dig this Plant, and herb of most effectual power, | Wherewith one quells the rival wife and gains the husband for one's self. || 2. Auspicious, with expanded leaves, sent by the Gods, victorious Plant, | Drive thou, the rival wife away, and make my husband only mine. || 3. Indeed he hath not named her name: thou with this husband dalliest not, | Far into distance most remote we drive the rival wife away. || 4. Stronger am I, O stronger one, yea, mightier than the mightier; | Beneath me be my rival wife, down, lower than the lowest dames! || 5. I am the conqueror, and thou, thou also art victorious: | As victory attends us both we will subdue my fellow wife. || 6. I've girt thee with the conquering Plant, beneath thee laid the mightiest one. | As a cow hastens to her calf, so let thy spirit speed to me, hasten like water on its way.

Hymn 3:19.

1. Quickened is this my priest rank, quickened is manly strength and force, | Quickened be changeless power, whereof I am the conquering President! || 2. I quicken these men's princely sway, the might, the manly strength and force; | I rend away the foemen's arms with this presented sacrifice. || 3. Down fall the men, low let them lie, who fight against our mighty prince, | I ruin foemen with my spell, and raise my friends to high estate. || 4. Keener than is the axe's edge, keener than Agni's self are they, | Keener than Indra's bolt are they whose Priest and President am I. || 5. The weapons of these men I whet and sharpen, with valiant heroes I increase their kingdom. | Victorious be their power and ever ageless! May all the Gods promote their thoughts and wishes. || 6. Let their fierce powers, O Maghavan, be heightened, and upward go the shout of conquering heroes. | Apart and clear, let shout and roar and shriek and lamentation rise! | Let the Gods led by Indra, let the Marutas with our army go. || 7. Advance and be victorious, men I Exceeding mighty be your arms! | Smite with sharp-pointed arrows those whose bows are weak. | With your strong arms and weapons smite the feeble foe. || 8. Loosed from the bowstring fly away, thou Arrow, sharpened by our prayer. | Assail the foemen, vanquish them, conquer each bravest man of theirs, and let not one of them escape.

Hymn 3:20.

1. This is thine ordered place of birth whence sprung to life thou shinest forth. | Knowing this, Agni, mount on high and cause our riches to increase. || 2. Turn hither, Agni, speak to us, come to us with a friendly mind. | Enrich us, Sovereign of the Tribes! Thou art the giver of our wealth. || 3. Let Aryaman vouchsafe us, wealth, and Bhaga, and Bṛihaspati, | The Goddesses grant wealth to us, Sūnṛitā, Goddess, give me wealth! || 4. We call King Soma to our aid, and Agni with our songs and. hymn, | The Ādityas, Viṣhṇu, Sūrya, and the Brahman-priest Bṛihaspati || 5. Do thou, O Agni, with thy fires strengthen our prayer and. sacrifice. | Incite thou us, O God, to give, and send us riches to bestow. || 6. Both Indra here and Vāyu we invoke with an auspicious call, | That in assembly all the folk may be benevolent to us, and be inclined to give us gifts. || 7. Urge Aryaman to send us gifts, and Indra, and Bṛihaspati, | Vāta, Viṣhṇu, Sarasvatī, and the strong courser Savitar. || 8. Now have we reached the ordering of power, and all these worlds of life are held within it. | Let him who knows urge e'en the churl to bounty Give wealth. to us with all good men about us. || 9. May heaven's five spacious regions pour their milk for me with all their might. | May I obtain each wish and hope formed by my spirit and my heart. || 10. May speech that winneth cows be mine. With splendour mount thou over me. | May Vāyu

hedge me round about May Pūṣhan make me prosperous.

Hymn 3:21.

1. All Fires that are in water and in Vṛitra, all those that man and stones contain within them, | That which hath entered herbs and trees and bushes—to all these Fires be this oblation offered. || 2. That which abides in Soma and in cattle, that which lies deep in birds and sylvan creatures, | That which hath entered quadrupeds and bipeds—to all these Fires be this oblation offered. || 3. The Fire that rideth by the side of Indra, the God Vaiśvānara, yea all-consuming, | Whom, as the victor, I invoke in battles —to all these Fires be this oblation offered. || 4. The all-devouring God whom men call Kāma, he whom they call the Giver and Receiver, | Invincible, pervading, wise, and mighty—to all these Fires be this oblation offered. || 5. To thee, strength-giver, glorious, rich in pleasant strains, whom. in their minds the thirteen creatures of the world, | And the five sons of man regard as Hotar-priest—to all these-Fires be this oblation offered. || 6. To him who feeds on ox and cow, sage, bearing Soma on his back, | To all Vaiśvānara's followers—to these be this oblation paid. || 7. All fiery flames that follow after lightning, flashing o'er earth, through firmament and heaven, | All that are in the wind and skyey regions—to all these Fires be this oblation offered. || 8. The golden-handed Savitar and Indra, Bṛihaspati, Varuṇa, Mitra, and Agni, | The Aṅgirasas we call, the Viśvedevas: let them appease this Agni, Flesh-devourer. || 9. Flesh-eating Agni is appeased, appeased is he who hurteth men. | Now him who burneth every thing, the Flesh-consumer, have I stilled. || 10. The mountains where the Soma grows, the waters lying calm and still, | Vāta, Parjanya, Agni's self have made the Flesh-consumer rest.

Hymn 3:22.

1. Famed be the Elephant's strength, the lofty glory, which out of Aditi's body took existence! | They all have given me this for my possession, even all the Gods and Aditi accordant. || 2. On this have Mitra, Varuṇa, Indra, and Rudra fixed their thought. | May those all-fostering deities anoint and balm me with his strength. || 3. The strength wherewith the Elephant was dowered, that decks a | King among the men, in waters, O Agni, even with that strength make thou me vigorous today. || 4. The lofty strength which sacrifice brings, Jātavedas! unto thee, | What strength the Sun possesses, all strength of the royal Elephant—such strength vouchsafe to me the pair of Aśvins lotus-garlanded! || 5. Far as the heaven's four regions spread, far as the eye's most distant ken. | So wide, so vast let power be mine, this vigour of the Elephant. || 6. Now hath the Elephant become chief of all pleasant beasts to ride. | With his high fortune and his strength I grace and consecrate myself.

Hymn 3:23.

1. From thee we banish and expel the cause of thy sterility. | This in another place we lay apart from thee and far removed. || 2. As arrow to the quiver, so let a male embryo enter thee. | Then from thy side be born a babe, a ten-month child, thy hero son. || 3. Bring forth a male, bring forth a son. Another male shall follow him. | The mother shalt thou be of sons born and hereafter to be born. || 4. With that auspicious general flow wherewith steers propagate their kind, | Do thou obtain thyself a son: be thou a fruitful mother-cow. || 5. I give thee power to bear a child: within, thee pass the germ of life! | Obtain a son, O woman, who shall be a blessing unto thee. Be thou a blessing unto him. || 6. May those celestial herbs whose sire was Heaven, the Earth their mother, and their root the ocean. | May those celestial healing Plants assist thee to obtain a son.

Hymn 3:24.

1. The plants of earth are rich in milk, and rich in milk is this my word, | So from the rich in milk I bring thousandfold profit hitherward. || 2. Him who is rich in milk I know. Abundant hath he made our corn. | The God whose name is Gatherer, him we invoke who dwelleth in his house who sacrifices not. || 3. All the five regions of the heavens, all the five races of man-kind, | As after rain the stream brings drift, let them bring increase hitherward. || 4. Open the well with hundred streams, exhaustless, with a thousand streams. | So cause this corn of ours to be exhaustless, with a thousand streams. || 5. O Hundred-handed, gather up. O Thousand-handed, pour thou forth. | Bring hither increase of the corn prepared and yet to be pre-pared. || 6. Three sheaves are the Gandharvas' claim, the lady of the house hath four. | We touch thee with the sheaf that is the most abundant of them all. || 7. Adding and Gathering are thy two attendants, O Prajāpati. | May they bring hither increase, wealth abundant, inexhaustible.

Hymn 3:25.

1. Let the Impeller goad thee on. Rest not in peace upon thy bed. | Terrible is the shaft of Love: therewith I pierce thee to the heart. || 2. That arrow winged with longing thought, its stem Desire, its neck, Resolve, | Let Kāma, having truly aimed, shoot forth and pierce thee in the heart. || 3. The shaft of Kāma, pointed well, that withers and consumes the spleen. | With hasty feathers, all aglow, therewith I pierce thee to the heart. || 4. Pierced through with fiercely-burning heat, steal to me with thy parching lips, | Gentle and humble, all mine own, devoted, with sweet words of love. || 5. Away from mother and from sire I drive thee hither with a whip, | That thou mayst be at my command and yield to every wish of mine. || 6. Mitra and Varuṇa, expel all thought and purpose from her heart. | Deprive her of her own free will and make her subject unto me.

Hymn 3:26.

1. Ye Gods who dwell within this eastward region, entitled Weapons, Agni forms your arrows. | Be kind and gracious unto us and bless us. To you be reverence, to you be welcome! || 2. Ye Gods who dwell within this southward region, entitled Eager, Kāma forms your arrows. | Be kind, etc. || 3. Ye Gods who dwell within this westward region, whose name is Radiant, Water forms your arrows. | Be kind, etc. || 4. Ye Gods who dwell within this northward region, whose name is Piercers, Vāta forms your arrows. | Be kind, etc. || 5. Ye Gods whose home is in this firm-set region—Nilimpas is your name—Plants are your arrow. | Be kind, etc. || 6. Ye Gods whose home is in this upmost region, Yearners by name, Bṛihaspati forms your arrows. | Be kind and gracious unto us and bless us. To you be reverence, to you be welcome!

Hymn 3:27.

1. Agni is regent of the East, its warder is Asita, the Ādityas are the arrows. | Worship to these the regents, these the warders, and to the arrows, yea, to these be worship! | Within your jaws we lay the man who hateth us and whom we hate. || 2. Indra is regent of the South, its warder Tiraśchirājī, and the shafts the Fathers. | Worship to these the regents, these the warders, and to the arrows, yea, to these be worship! | Within your jaws we lay the man who hateth us and whom we hate. || 3. Of the West region Varuṇa is ruler, Pṛidākū warder, Nourishment the arrows. | Worship, etc. || 4. Soma is ruler of the Northern region, Svaja the warder, lightning's flash the arrows. | Worship, etc. || 5. Vishṇu is ruler of the firm-set region, Kalmāṣhagrīva warder, Plants the arrows. | Worship, etc. || 6. Bṛihaspati controls the topmost region, Śvitra is warder, and the Rain the arrows. | Worship to these the regents, these the warders, and to the arrows, yea, to these be worship! | Within your jaws we lay the man who hateth us and whom we hate.

Hymn 3:28.

1. This cow was born to bring forth offspring singly, though they created kine of every colour. | When she produces twins in spite of Order, sullen, with groan and grudge she harms the cattle. || 2. She brings destruction on the beasts, turned to a flesh-devouring worm. | Yes, give her to the Brahman that she may bring luck and happiness. || 3. Be thou auspicious to our folk, bring luck to horses and to kine. | Auspicious unto all this farm, bring luck and happiness to us. || 4. Let there be rain and increase here, here be thou most munificent. | Mother of twins, prosper our herd. || 5. Where, having left all sickness of their bodies, the pious lead, as friends, their lives of gladness | Nigh to that world approached the twin calves' mother. Let her not harm our people and our cattle. || 6. Where lies the world of those dear friends, the pious, those who have brought due sacrifice to Agni | Nigh to that world approached the twins calves' mother. Let her not harm our people and our cattle.

Hymn 3:29.

1. When yonder kings who sit beside Yama divide among themselves the sixteenth part of hopes fulfilled, | A ram bestowed as sacrifice, white-footed, frees us from the tax. || 2. He satisfies each hope and want, prevailing, present and pre-pared. | The wish-fulfilling ram, bestowed, white-footed is exhaustless still. || 3. He who bestows a white-hooved ram,

adequate to the place he holds. | Ascends to the celestial height, the heaven where tribute is not paid to one more mighty by the weak. || 4. He who bestows a white-hooved ram, adequate to the place he holds. | Offered with five cakes, lives on that, unwasting, in the Fathers' world. || 5. He who bestows a white-hooved ram, adequate to the place he holds, | Offered with five cakes, lives on that, wasteless, while Sun and Moon endure. || 6. Like a refreshing draught, like sea, the mighty flood, he faileth not. | Like the two Gods whose home is one, the ram white-footed, faileth not. || 7. Whose gift was this, and given to whom? Kāma to Kāma gave the gift. | Kāma is giver, Kāma is receiver. Kāma has passed into the sea. | Through Kāma do I take thee to myself. O Kāma, this is thine. || 8. May Earth receive thee as her own, and this great interspace of air. | Neither in breath and body nor in progeny may this acceptance do me harm.

Hymn 3:30.

1. Freedom from hate I bring to you, concord and unanimity. | Love one another as the cow loveth the calf that she hath borne. || 2. One-minded with his mother let the son be loyal to his sire. | Let the wife, calm and gentle, speak words sweet as honey to her lord. || 3. No brother hate his brother, no sister to sister be unkind. | Unanimous, with one intent, speak ye your speech in friendliness. || 4. That spell through which Gods sever not, nor ever bear each other hate, | That spell we lay upon your home, a bond of union for the men. || 5. Intelligent, submissive, rest united, friendly and kind, bearing the yoke together. | Come, speaking sweetly each one to the other. I make you one-intentioned and one-minded. || 6. Let what you drink, your share of food be common together, with one common bond I bid you. | Serve Agni, gathered round him like the spokes about the chariot nave. || 7. With binding charm I make you all united, obeying one sole leader and one-minded. | Even as the Gods who watch and guard the Amṛita, at morn and eve may ye be kindly-hearted.

Hymn 3:31.

1. May Gods release from failing strength, thou Agni, from malignity! | I free from every evil, from decline: I compass round with life. || 2. May Pavamāna free from harm, and Śakra from unrighteous deed. | I free from every evil, from decline: I compass round with life. || 3. Tame beasts have parted from wild beasts, water and thirst have gone apart | I free, etc. || 4. Parted are heaven and earth, and paths turned to each quarter of the sky. | I free, etc. || 5. Tvashṭar prepares the bridal of his daughter; then all this world of life departs and leaves him. | I free, etc. || 6. Agni combines the vital airs. The moon is closely joined with breath. | I free. etc. || 7. The Gods have lifted up with breath the Sun whose might is everywhere. | I free, etc. || 8. Die not. Live with the breath of those who make and who enjoy long life. | I free, etc. || 9. Die not. Stay here. Breathe with the breath of those who draw the vital air. | I free, etc. || 10. Rise up with life, conjoined with life. Up, with the sap of growing plants! | I free, etc. || 11. We as immortal beings have arisen with Parjanya's rain, | I free from every evil, from decline: I compass round with life.

Kāṇḍa 4.

Hymn 4:1.

1. Eastward at first the prayer was generated: Vena disclosed bright flashes from the summit, | Disclosed his deepest, nearest revelations, womb of the non-existent and existent. || 2. Let this Queen come in front, her Father's daughter, found in the worlds for earliest generation. | For him they set this radiant vault in motion. Let them prepare warm milk for him who first would drink. || 3. He who was born as his all-knowing kinsman declareth all the deities' generations. | He from the midst of prayer his prayer hath taken. On high, below, spread forth his godlike nature. || 4. For he, true to the law of Earth and Heaven, established both the mighty worlds securely. | Mighty when born, he propped apart the mighty, the sky, our earthly home, and air's mid-region. || 5. He from the depth hath been reborn for ever, Bṛihaspati the world's sole Lord and Ruler. | From light was born the Day with all its lustre: through this let sages live endowed with splendour. || 6. The sage and poet verily advanceth the statute of that mighty God primeval. | He was born here with many more beside him: they slumbered when the foremost side was opened. || 7. The man who seeks the friend of Gods, Atharvan the father, and Bṛihaspati, with worship, | Crying to him, Be thou all things' creator! the wise God, self-dependent, never injures.

Hymn 4:2

1. Giver of breath, giver of strength and vigour, he whose commandment all the Gods acknowledge, | He who is Lord of this, or man and cattle:—What God shall we adore with our oblation? || 2. Who by his grandeur hath become sole ruler of all the moving world that breathes and slumbers, | Whose shade is death, whose lustre makes immortal:—What God shall we adore with our oblation? || 3. To whom both hosts embattled, look with longing, and Heaven and Earth invoke him in their terror; | Whose is this path that measures oat the region:—What God shall we adore with our oblation? || 4. Whose is the mighty earth and spacious heaven, and yonder ample firmament between them, | Whose is yon Sun extended in his grandeur:—What God shall we adore with our oblation? || 5. Whose, through his might, are all the Snowy Mountains, and whose, they say is Rasā in the ocean, | The arms of whom are these celestial quarters:—What God shall we adore with our oblation? || 6. The deathless Waters, born in Law, receiving, protected all the germ in the beginning, | Waters divine who had the God above them:—What God shall we adore with our oblation? || 7. In the beginning rose Hiraṇyagarbha, even at his birth sole Lord of all creation. | He fixt and firmly established earth and heaven:—What God shall we adore with our oblation? || 8. In the beginning, generating offspring, the Waters brought an embryo into being; | And even as it sprang to life it had a covering of gold.

Hymn 4:3.

1. Three have gone hence and passed away, the man, the tiger, and the wolf. | Down, verily, the rivers flow, down goeth the celestial Tree, down let our foemen bend and bow. || 2. On distant pathway go the wolf, on pathway most remote the thief! | On a far road speed forth the rope with teeth, and the malicious man! || 3. We crush and rend to pieces both thine eyes, O Tiger, and thy jaws and all the twenty claws we break. || 4. We break and rend the tiger first of creatures that are armed. with teeth; | The robber then, and then the snake, the sorcerer, and then the wolf. || 5. The thief who cometh near today departeth bruised and crushed to bits. | By nearest way let him be gone. Let Indra slay him with his bolt. || 6. Let the beast's teeth be broken off, shivered and shattered be his ribs! | Slack be thy bowstring: downward go the wild beast that pursues the hare! || 7. Open not what thou hast compressed, close not what thou hast not compressed. | Indra's and Soma's child, thou art Atharvan's tiger-crushing charm.

Hymn 4:4.

1. We dig thee from the earth, the Plant which strengthens and exalts the nerves, | The Plant which the Gandharva dug for Varuṇa whose power was lost. || 2. Let Us has and let Sūrya rise, let this the speech I utter rise. | Let the strong male Prajāpati arise with manly energy. || 3. Sicut tui surgentis (membrum virile) tanquam inflammatum palpitat, hoc illud tui ardentius haec herba faciat. || 4. Sursum (estote) herbarum vires, taurorum vigor. Tu, Indra, corporis potens, virorum masculum robur in hoc homine depone. || 5. Ros aquarum primigenitus atque arborum, Somae etiam frater es, vatum sacrorum masculus vigor es. || 6. Hodie, Agnis! hodie Savitar! hodie dea Sarasvatīs! hodie Brahmaṇaspatis! hujus fascinum velut arcum extende. || 7. Velut nervum in arcu ego tuum fascinum extendo. Aggredere (mulierem) semper indefessus velut cervus damam. || 8. Quae sunt equi vires, muli, capri, arietis, atque tauri, illas, corporis potens! in hoc homine depone.

Hymn 4:5.

1. The Bull who hath a thousand horns, who rises up from out the sea, | By him the strong and mighty one we lull the folk to rest and. sleep. || 2. Over the surface of the earth there breathes no wind, there looks. no eye. | Lull all the women, lull the dogs to sleep, with Indra as thy friend! || 3. The woman sleeping in the court, lying without, or stretched on beds, | The matrons with their odorous sweets—these, one and all, we lull to sleep. || 4. Each moving thing have I secured, have held and held the eye and breath. | Each limb and member have I seized in the deep darkness of the night. || 5. The man who sits, the man who walks, whoever stands and clearly sees | Of these we closely shut the eyes, even as we closely shut this house. || 6. Sleep mother, let the father sleep, sleep dog, and master of the home. | Let all her kinsmen sleep, sleep all the people who are round about. || 7. With soporific charm, O Sleep, lull thou to slumber all the folk. | Let the rest sleep till

break of day, I will remain awake till dawn, like Indra free from scathe and harm.

Hymn 4:6.

1. The Brahman first was brought to life ten-headed and with faces ten. | First drinker of the Soma, he made poison ineffectual. || 2. Far as the heavens and earth are spread in compass, far as the Seven Rivers are extended, | So far my spell, the antidote of poison, have I spoken hence, || 3. The strong-winged Bird Garutmān first of all, O Poison fed on thee: | Thou didst not gripe or make him drunk: aye, thou becamest food for him. || 4. Whoever with five fingers hath discharged thee from the crooked bow, | I from the shaft have charmed away the poison of the fastening band. || 5. The poison have I charmed away from shaft, cement, and feathered end; | Yea, from the barb, the neck, the horn, the poison have I charmed away. || 6. Feeble, O Arrow, is thy shaft, thy poison, too, hath lost its strength. | Made of a worthless tree, thy bow, O feeble one, is impotent. || 7. The men who brayed it, smeared it on, they who discharged it, sent it forth, | All these are made emasculate, emasculate the poison-hill. || 8. Thy diggers are emasculate, emasculate, O, Plant art thou. | The rugged mountain that produced this poison is emasculate.

Hymn 4:7.

1. So may this water guard us on the bank of Varaṇāvatī. | Therein hath Amṛita been infused: with that I ward thy poison off. || 2. Weak is the poison of the East, weak is the poison of the North, | So too this poison of the South counts as a cake of curds and meal. || 3. When he hath made of thee a cake, broad, steaming, swelling up with fat, | And even in hunger eaten thee, then gripe him not, thou hideous one! || 4. Intoxicater! like a shaft we make thy spirit fly away, Like a pot boiling on the fire, we with our word remove thee hence. || 5. We set around thee with the spell as 'twere a gathered armament. | Stay quiet like a rooted tree. Dug up with mattocks, gripe not thou. || 6. For coverings men have bartered thee, for skins of deer and woven cloths. | Thou art a thing of sale, O Plant. Dug up with mattocks, gripe not thou! || 7. None have attained to those of old, those who wrought holy acts for you. | Let them not harm our heroes here. Therefore I set before you this.

Hymn 4:8.

1. The Being lays the sap of life in beings: he hath become the sovereign Lord of creatures. | Death comes to this man's royal consecration: let him as King own and allow this kingdom. || 2. Come forward, turn not back in scorn, strong guardian, slayer of the foes. | Approach, O gladdener of thy friends. The Gods have blessed and strengthened thee. || 3. All waited on him as he came to meet them. He self-resplendent moves endued with glory. | That is the royal hero's lofty nature: he, manifold, hath gained immortal powers. || 4. Stride forth to heaven's broad regions, thou, a tiger on a tiger's skin. | Let all the people long for thee. Let heavenly floods be rich in milk. || 5. Heaven's waters joyous in their milk, the waters of middle air, and those that earth containeth. I with the gathered power and might of all these waters sprinkle thee, || 6. The heavenly waters rich in milk have sprinkled thee with power and might. | To be the gladdener of thy friends. May Savitar so fashion thee. || 7. These, compassing the tiger, rouse the lion to great joy and bliss. | As strong floods purify the standing ocean, so men adorn the leopard in the waters.

Hymn 4:9.

1. Approach! thou art the mountain's eye, the living thing that saveth us; | A gift bestowed by all the Gods, yea, the defence that guardeth life. || 2. Thou art the safeguard of the men, thou art the safeguard of the kine, | Thou standest ready to protect the horses that are fleet of foot. || 3. Thou, also, Salve! art a defence that rends and crushes sorcerers. | Thou knowest, too, of Amṛita, thou art the delight of all who live, a jaundice-curing balm art thou. || 4. Whomso thou creepest over, Salve! member by member, joint by joint, | From him, like some strong arbiter of strife, thou banishest decline. || 5. No imprecation reaches him, no magic, no tormenting fiend, | O Salve, Vishkandha seizes not the man who carries thee about. || 6. From lying speech, from evil dream, from wicked act and sinfulness, | From hostile and malignant eye,—from these, O Salve, protect us well. || 7. I, knowing this, O Salve, will speak the very truth and not a lie: | May I obtain both horse and ox, may I obtain thy life, O man. || 8. Three are the slaves that serve the Salve, Fever, Consumption, and the Snake. | Thy father is the loftiest of mountains, named the Triple-peaked. || 9. Sprung from the Snowy Mountain's side, this Ointment of the Three-peaked hill. | Crushes and rends all sorcerers and every witch and sorceress. || 10. If thou art from the Three-peaked hill or hast thy name from Yamunā, | These names are both auspicious: by these two protect thou us, O Salve!

Hymn 4:10.

1. Child of the wind firmament, sprung from the lightning and the light, | May this the gold-born Shell that bears the pearl preserve us from distress. || 2. Shell that wast born from out the sea, set at the head of things that shine! | With thee we slay the Rākṣhasas and overcome voracious fiends. || 3. We stay disease and indigence, and chase Sadānvās with the Shell. | May the all-healing Shell that bears the pearl preserve us from distress. || 4. Born in the heaven, sprung from the sea, brought to us hither from the flood. | This gold-born Shell shall be to us an amulet to lengthen life. || 5. From ocean sprang the Amulet, from Vṛitra sprang the Lord of Day: | May this protect us round about from shaft of God and Asura. || 6. Peerless amid golden ornaments art thou: from Soma wast thou born. | Thou gleamest on the quiver, thou art beautiful upon the car: may it prolong our days of life! || 7. Bone of the Good became the pearl's shell-mother endowed with soul it moveth in the waters. | I bind this on thee for life, strength, and vigour, for long life lasting through a hundred autumns. | May the pearl's mother keep and guard thee safely!

Hymn 4:11.

1. The Bull supports the wide-spread earth and heaven, the Bull supports the spacious air between them. | The Bull supports the sky's six spacious regions: the universal world hath he pervaded. || 2. The Bull is Indra o'er the beasts he watches. He, Śakra measures out three several pathways. | He, milking out the worlds, the past, the future, discharges all the Gods' eternal duties. || 3. Being produced among mankind as Indra, the Cauldron works heated and brightly glowing. | Let him not, with good sons, pass off in vapour who hath not eaten of the Ox with knowledge. || 4. The Ox pours milk out in the world of virtue: in earliest time, he, Pavamāna, swells it. | Parjanya is the stream, Marutas his udder, sacrifice is the milk, the meed his milking. || 5. That which not sacrifice nor sacrificer, not giver nor receiver rules and governs, | All-winning, all-supporting, all-effecting,—which of all quadrupeds, tell us! is the Cauldron? || 6. May we, fame-seekers, reach the world of virtue by service of the Gharma and through fervour, | Whereby the Gods went up to heaven, the centre of life eternal, having left the body. || 7. Prajāpati, supreme and sovereign ruler, Indra by form and by his shoulder Agni, | Came to Viśvānara, came to all men's Bullock: he firmly fortified and held securely. || 8. The middle of the Bullock's neck, there where the shoulder-bar is placed, | Extends as far to east of him as that is settled to the west. || 9. He whosoever knows the seven exhaustless pourings of the Ox, | Wins himself offspring and the world: the great Seven Ṛishis know this well. || 10. With feet subduing weariness, with legs extracting freshening draughts, | Through toil the plougher and the Ox approach the honeyed beverage. || 11. Assigned are these twelve nights, they say, as holy to Prajāpati: | Whoever knows their proper prayer performs the service of the Ox. || 12. At evening he is milked, is milked at early morn, is milked at noon. | We know that streams of milk that flow from him are in-exhaustible.

Hymn 4:12.

1. Thou art the healer, making whole, the healer of the broken bone: | Make thou this whole, Arundhatī! || 2. Whatever bone of thine within thy body hath been wrenched or cracked, | May Dhātar set it properly and join together limb by limb. || 3. With marrow be the marrow joined, thy limb united with the limb. | Let what hath fallen of thy flesh, and the bone also grow again. || 4. Let marrow close with marrow, let skin grow united with the skin. | Let blood and bone grow strong in thee, flesh grow together with the flesh. || 5. Join thou together hair with hair, join thou together skin with skin. | Let blood and bone grow strong in thee. Unite the broken part, O Plant. || 6. Arise, advance, speed forth; the car hath goodly fellies, naves, and wheels! | Stand up erect upon thy feet. || 7. If he be torn and shattered, having fallen into a pit, or a cast stone have struck him, | Let the skilled leech join limb with limb, as 'twere the portions of a car.

Hymn 4:13.

1. Gods, raise again the man whom ye, O Gods, have humbled and brought low. | Ye Gods, restore to life again, him, Gods! who hath committed sin. || 2. Here these two winds are blowing far as Sindhu from a distant land. | May one breathe energy to thee, the other blow thy fault away. || 3. Hither, O Wind, blow healing balm, blow every fault away, thou Wind! | For thou who hast all medicine comest as envoy of the Gods. || 4. May the Gods keep and save this man, the Marutas' host deliver him. | All things that be deliver him that he be freed from his offence. || 5. I am come nigh to thee with balms to give thee rest and keep thee safe. | I bring thee mighty strength, I drive thy wasting malady away. || 6. Felicitous is this my hand, yet more felicitous is this. | This hand contains all healing balms, and this makes whole with gentle touch. || 7. The tongue that leads the voice precedes. Then with our tenfold-branching hands. | With these two healers of disease, we stroke thee with a soft caress.

Hymn 4:14.

1. The Goat was verily produced from Agni. Through sorrow he beheld, at first, his father. | Through him at first the Gods attained to godhead, and, meet for sacrifices, were exalted. || 2. Bearing in hands seethed viands, go with Agni to the cope of heaven. | Reaching the sky that touches heaven, mix with the company of Gods. || 3. From earth's high ridge to middle air I mounted, and from mid-air ascended up to heaven. | From the high pitch of heaven's cope I came into the world of light. || 4. Mounting the sky they look not round; they rise to heaven through both the worlds, | Sages who paid the sacrifice that pours its streams on every side. || 5. First among all the deities, come forward, thou who art eye of Gods and men, O Agni. | Imploring, and accordant with the Bhṛigus, to heaven in safety go the sacrificers! || 6. With milk and butter I anoint the mighty, celestial Goat, strong-winged, and full of juices. | Through him will we attain the world of virtue, ascending to the loftiest cope, to heaven. || 7. Set the Goat's head toward the eastern region, and turn his right side to the southern quarter. | His hinder part turn to the western quarter, and set his left side to the northern region. || 8. Set the Goat's backbone upmost in the zenith, and lay his belly downward in the nadir; set his mid-portion in mid-air between them. || 9. O'er the dressed Goat lay a dressed skin to robe him prepared, in perfect form, with all his members. | Rise upward to the loftiest vault of heaven: with thy four feet stand firmly in the regions.

Hymn 4:15.

1. Let all the misty regions fly together, let all the rain-clouds sped by wind, assemble. | Let waters satisfy the earth, the voices of the great mist-enveloped Bull who roareth. || 2. Let them show forth, the strong, the bounteous Marutas: let plants and shrubs be hung with drops of moisture. | Let floods of rain refresh the ground with gladness and herbs spring various with each form and colour. || 3. Cause us who sing to see the gathering vapours: out burst in many a place the rush of waters! | Let floods of rain refresh the ground with gladness; and herbs spring various with each form and colour. || 4. Apart, Parjanya! let the troops of Marutas, roaring, swell the song. | Let pouring torrents of the rain that raineth rain upon the earth. || 5. Up from the sea lift your dread might, ye Marutas: as light and splendour, send the vapour upward! | Let waters satisfy the earth, the voices of the great mist-enveloped Bull who roareth. || 6. Roar, thunder, set the sea in agitation, bedew the ground with thy sweet rain, Parjanya! | Send plenteous showers on him who seeketh shelter, and let the owner of lean kine go homeward. || 7. Let the boon Marutas, let the springs and coiling serpents tend! you well. | Urged by the Marutas let the clouds pour down their rain upon. the earth. || 8. Let lightning flash on every side: from all the regions blow the winds! | Urged by the Marutas let the clouds pour down their rain upon the earth. || 9. May waters, lightning, cloud, and rain, boon springs and serpents tend you well. | Urged by the Marutas let the clouds pour down their rain upon the earth. || 10. May he who hath become the plants' high regent, suiting our bodies, Agni of the Waters, | May Jātavedas send us rain from heaven, Amṛita and vital breath to earthly creatures. || 11. Sending up waters from the flood and ocean Prajāpati move the sea to agitation! | Forth flow the moisture of the vigorous stallion! | With this thy roar of thunder come thou hither, || 12. Our father, Lord divine pouring the torrents. Let the streams breathe, O Varuṇa, of the waters. | Pour the floods down: along the brooks and channels let frogs with speckled arms send out their voices. || 13. They who lay quiet for a year, the Brahmans who fulfil their vows. | The frogs, have lifted up their voice, the voice Parjanya hath. Inspired. || 14. Speak forth a welcome, female frog! Do thou O frog, accost the rain. | Stretch thy four feet apart, and swim in the middle of the lake. || 15. Khaṇvakhā, ho! Khaimakhā, ho! thou in the middle, Taduri! | Fathers, enjoy the rain from one who strives to win the Marutas heart. || 16. Lift up the mighty cask and pour down water; let the wind blow, and lightnings flash around us. | Let sacrifice be paid, and, widely scattered, let herbs and plants be full of joy and gladness.

Hymn 4:16.

1. The mighty Ruler of these worlds beholds as though from close at hand, | The man who thinks he acts by stealth: all this the Gods perceive and know. || 2. If a man stands or walks or moves in secret, goes to his lying-down or his uprising, | What two men whisper as they sit together, King Varuṇa knows: he as the third is present. || 3. This earth, too, is King Varuṇa's possession, and the high heaven whose ends are far asunder. | The loins of Varuṇa are both the oceans, and this small drop of water, too, contains him. || 4. If one should flee afar beyond the heaven, King Varuṇa would still be round about him. | Proceeding hither from the sky his envoys look, thousand-eyed, over the earth beneath them. || 5. All this the royal Varuṇa beholdeth, all between heaven and earth and all beyond them. | The twinklings of men's eyelids hath he counted. As one who plays throws dice he settles all things. || 6. Those fatal snares of thine which stand extended, threefold, O Varuṇa, seven by seven, | May they all catch the man who tells a falsehood, and pass unharmed the man whose words are truthful. || 7. Varuṇa, snare him with a hundred nooses! Man's watcher! let not him who lies escape thee. | There let the villain sit with hanging belly and bandaged like a cask whose hoops are broken. || 8. Varuṇa sends, and drives away, diseases: Varuṇa is both native and a stranger, | Varuṇa is celestial and is human. || 9. I bind and hold thee fast with all these nooses, thou son of such a man and such a mother. | All these do I assign thee as thy portion.

Hymn 4:17.

1. We seize and hold thee, Conquering One! the queen of medicines that heal. | O Plant, I have endowed thee with a hundred powers for every man, || 2. Still conquering, banishing the curse, mighty, with thy reverted. bloom. | Thee and all Plants have I invoked: Hence let it save us! was my prayer. || 3. She who hath cursed us with a curse, or hath conceived a murderous sin, | Or seized our son to take his blood, may she devour the child she bare. || 4. What magic they have wrought for thee in dish unbaked or burnt dark-red, | What they have wrought in flesh undressed,—conquer the sorcerers therewith. || 5. Ill dream and wretchedness of life, Rākṣhasa, monster, stingy hags, | All the she-fiends of evil name and voice, we drive away from us. || 6. Death caused by famine, caused by thirst, failure of children, loss of kine, | With thee, O Apāmārga, all this ill we cleanse and wipe away. || 7. Death caused by thirst, death caused by stress of hunger, loss at play with dice, | All this, O Apāmārga with thine aid we cleanse and wipe away. || 8. The Apāmārga is alone the sovereign of all Plants that grow. | With this we wipe away whate'er hath fallen on thee: go in health!

Hymn 4:18.

1. The moonlight equalleth the sun, night is the rival of the day. | I make effectual power my help: let magic arts be impotent. || 2. Gods! if one make and bring a spell on some man's house who knows it not, | Close as the calf that sucks the cow may it revert and cling to him. || 3. When one puts poison in a dish of unbaked clay to kill a man, | It cracks when set upon the fire with the sharp sound of many stones. || 4. Endowed with thousand powers! adjure the bald and those with necks awry. | Back to its author turn the spell like a dear damsel to her friend! || 5. I with this Plant have ruined all malignant powers of witchery. | The spell which they have laid upon thy field, thy cattle, or thy men. || 6. No power had he who wrought the spell: he hurt his foot, he broke his toe. | His act hath brought us happiness and pain and sorrow to him-self. || 7. Let Apāmārga sweep away chronic disease and every curse, | Sweep sorceresses clean away, and all malignant stingy hags. || 8. Sweep thou away the sorcerers, all stingy fiendish hags away. | All this, O Apāmārga, with thine aid we wipe away from us.

Hymn 4:19.

1. Thou breakest ties of kith and kin, thou causest, too, relation-ship: | So bruise the sorcerer's offspring, like a reed that groweth in the Rains. || 2. Thou hast been blessed with blessing by the Brahman, Kaṇva Nārṣhada. | Thou fliest like a flashing dart: there is no fear or danger, Plant! within the limit of thy range. || 3. Illumining, as 'twere, with light, thou movest at the head of plants. | The saviour of the simple man art thou, and slayer of the fiends. || 4. As once when time began the Gods with thee expelled the Asuras, | Even thence, O Plant, wast thou produced as one who wipes and sweeps away. || 5. Thy father's name was Cleaver. Thou with thousand branches cleavest all. | Do thou, turned backward, cleave and rend the man who treateth us as foes. || 6. The evil sprang from earth; it mounts to heaven and spreads to vast extent. | Reverted, shaking him with might, thence on its maker let it fall. || 7. For thou hast grown reverted, and turned backward also is thy fruit. | Remove all curses far from me, keep most remote the stroke of death. || 8. Preserve me with a hundred, yea, protect me with a thousand aids. | May mighty Indra, Lord of Plants! give store of strength and. power to thee.

Hymn 4:20.

1. It sees in front, it sees behind, it sees afar away, it sees | The sky, the firmament, and earth: all this, O Goddess, it beholds. || 2. Through thee, O godlike Plant, may I behold all creatures that exist, | Three several heavens, three several earths, and these six regions one by one. || 3. The pupil, verily, art thou of that celestial Eagle's eye. | On earth hast thou alighted as a weary woman seeks her couch. || 4. The God who hath a thousand eyes give me this Plant in my right hand! | I look on every one therewith, each Śūdra and each Ārya man. || 5. Make manifest the forms of things; hide not their essences from sight. | And, thou who hast a thousand eyes, look the Kimīdins in the face. || 6. Make me see Yātudhānas, make thou Yātudhānīs visible. | Make me see all Piśāchas With this prayer, O Plant, I hold thee fast. || 7. Thou art the sight of Kaśyapa and of the hound who hath four eyes. | Make the Piśācha manifest as Sūrya when he rides at noon. || 8. Kimīdin, Yātudhāna from their hiding-places have I dragged. | I look on every one with this, Śūdra and Ārya man alike. || 9. Make that Piśācha visible, the fiend who flies in middle air, | The fiend who glides across the sky, and him who deems the earth his help.

Hymn 4:21.

1. The kine have come and brought good fortune: let them rest in the cow-pen and be happy near us. | Here let them stay prolific, many-coloured, and yield through many morns their milk for Indra. || 2. Indra aids him who offers sacrifice and praise: he takes not what is his, and gives him more thereto. | Increasing ever more and ever more his wealth, he makes the pious dwell within unbroken bounds. || 3. These are ne'er lost, no robber ever injures them: no evil-minded foe attempts to harass them. | The master of the kine lives a long life with these, the Cows whereby he pours his gifts and serves the Gods. || 4. The charger with his dusty brow o'ertakes them not, and never to the shambles do they take their way. | These Cows, the cattle of the pious worshipper, roam over wide-spread pasture where no danger is. || 5. To me the Cows seem Bhaga, they seem Indra, they seem a portion of the first poured Soma. | These present Cows, they, O ye men, are Indra. I long for Indra with my heart and spirit. || 6. O Cows, ye fatten e'en the worn and wasted, and make the unlovely beautiful to look on. | Prosper my home, ye with auspicious voices! Your power is magnified in our assemblies. || 7. In goodly pasturage, bright-hued, prolific, drinking pure water at fair drinking-places, | Never be thief or sinful man your master, and may the dart of Rudra still avoid you!

Hymn 4:22.

1. Exalt and strengthen this my Prince, O Indra, Make him sole lord and leader of the people. | Scatter his foes, deliver all his rivals into his hand in struggles for precedence. || 2. Give him a share in village, kine, and horses, and leave his enemy without a portion. | Let him as King be head and chief of Princes, Give up to him, O Indra, every foeman. || 3. Let him be treasure-lord of goodly treasures, let him as King be master of the people. | Grant unto him great power and might, O Indra, and strip his enemy of strength and vigour. || 4. Like milch-kine yielding milk for warm libations, pour, Heaven and Earth! on him full many a blessing. | May he as King be Indra's well-beloved, the darling of the kine, the plants, the cattle. || 5. I join in league with thee victorious Indra, with whom men conquer and are ne'er defeated. | He shall make thee the folk's sole lord and leader, shall make thee highest of all human rulers. || 6. Supreme art thou, beneath thee are thy rivals, and all, O King, who were thine adversaries. | Sole lord and leader and allied with Indra, bring, conqueror, thy foremen's goods and treasures. || 7. Consume, with lion aspect, all their hamlets, with tiger aspect, drive away thy foemen. | Sole lord and leader and allied with Indra, seize, conqueror, thine enemies' possessions.

Hymn 4:23.

1. I fix my heart on wise and ancient Agni, the Five Tribes' Lord, in many a place enkindled. | We seek him who hath entered all our houses. May he deliver us from grief and trouble. || 2. As thou conveyest offerings, Jātavedas! and fashionest the sacrifice with knowledge, | So bear thou to the Gods the prayer we utter. May he deliver us from grief and trouble. || 3. I pray to Agni in each act successful, employed in every sacrifice, the strongest, | Fiend-slayer, served with fatness, strengthening worship. May he deliver us from grief and trouble. || 4. We invoke the oblation-bearer, well-born Agni Jātavedas, | Him, Vaiśvānara, almighty. May he set us free from trouble. || 5. With whom as friend the Ṛishis gave their power new splendour, with whom they kept aloof the Asuras' devices, | Agni, with whom Indra subdued the Paṇis. May he deliver us. from grief and trouble. || 6. Through whom the Gods discovered life eternal, through whom they stored the plants with pleasant juices, | Through whom they brought to men the light of heaven. May he deliver us from grief and trouble. || 7. I, suppliant, praise and ever call on Agni, sole Lord of all this world, of all that shineth, | Of what exists and shall exist hereafter. May he deliver us from grief and trouble.

Hymn 4:24.

1. I think of Indra, only him for ever, fiend-slayer, May these lauds of mine come near him. | He cometh to the pious offerer's calling. May he deliver us from grief and trouble. || 2. Who with strong arms o'ercame his strong opponents, who broke and crushed the power of the demons, | Who won the rivers and the kine in battle. May he deliver us from grief and trouble. || 3. Ruler of men, finder of light, the hero: the pressing-stones declare his valour, master. | Of sweetest sacrifice with seven Hotars. May he deliver us from grief and trouble. || 4. The lord of barren cows and bulls and oxen, finder of light for whom the posts are planted, | For whom the bright juice flows cleansed by devotion. May he deliver us from grief and trouble. || 5. Whose favour those desire who offer Soma, whom, arrow-bearer, men invoke in battle, | On whom the hymn depends, in whom is power, May he deliver us from grief and trouble. || 6. Why was born, first, for active operation, whose valour as the first hath been awakened, | Who raised his bolt when he encountered Ahi. May he deliver us from grief and trouble. || 7. Strong Lord, who leadeth hosts to meet for battle, who sendeth riches both of earth and heaven, | I, suppliant, praise and ever call on Indra. May he deliver us from grief and trouble.

Hymn 4:25.

1. I think on Vāyu's and Savitar's holy rites, ye twain who penetrate and guard the living world: | Ye who have come to be this All's pervaders, deliver us, ye two from grief and trouble. || 2. Ye who have counted up the earth's expanses, and in the sky smoothed out the air's mid-region, | Whose going-forth hath ne'er been reached by any, deliver us, ye two, from grief and trouble. || 3. Beauteously bright! men rest in thy dominion when thou hast risen up and hastened onward. | Ye, Vāyu, Savitar, preserve all creatures. Deliver us, ye, twain, from grief and trouble. || 4. Hence, Vāyu, Savitar drive evil action, chase Śimidā away, drive off the demons. | Ye give us store of energy and power. Deliver us, ye twain, from grief and trouble. || 5. Of their own selves let Savitar and Vāyu send favourable strength and wealth and plenty. | Here give us perfect freedom from consumption. Deliver us, ye twain, from grief and trouble. || 6. Ye, Savitar and Vāyu, to assist us, enjoy the hymn and the delightful cheerer. | Come hither downward from the stream of blessing. Deliver us, ye twain, from grief and trouble. || 7. Like noblest benisons they have stayed in the God loving man's abode. | I glorify bright Savitar and Vāyu. Deliver us, ye twain, from grief and trouble.

Hymn 4:26.

1. O Heaven and Earth, I think on you, wise, givers of abundant gifts, ye

who through measureless expanses have spread forth. | For ye are seats and homes of goodly treasures. Deliver us, ye twain from grief and trouble. || 2. Yea, seats and homes are ye of goodly treasures, grown strong, divine, blessed, and far-extending, | To me, O Heaven and Earth, be ye auspicious. Deliver us, ye twain, from grief and trouble. || 3. I call on you who warm and cause no sorrow, deep, spacious, meet to be adored by poets. | To me, O Heaven and Earth, be ye auspicious. Deliver us, ye twain, from grief and trouble. || 4. Ye who maintain Amṛita and sacrifices, ye who support rivers and human beings, | To me, O Heaven and Earth, be ye auspicious, Deliver us, ye twain, from grief and trouble. || 5. Ye by whom cows and forest trees are cherished within whose range all creatures are included, | To me, O Heaven and Earth, be ye auspicious. Deliver us, ye twain, from grief and trouble. || 6. Ye who delight in nectar and in fatness, ye without whom men have no strength or power, | To me, O Heaven and Earth, be ye auspicious. Deliver us, ye twain, from grief and trouble. || 7. The grief that pains me here, whoever caused it, not sent by fate, hath sprung from human action. | I, suppliant, praise Heaven, Earth, and oft invoke them. Deliver us, ye twain, from grief and trouble.

Hymn 4:27.

1. I think upon the Marutas: may they bless me, may they assist me to this wealth in battle. | I call them like swift well-trained steeds to help us. May they deliver us from grief and trouble. || 2. Those who surround the never-failing fountain for ever, and bedew the plants with moisture, | The Marutas, Pṛiśni's sons, I chiefly honour. May they deliver us from grief and trouble. || 3. Bards, who invigorate the milk of milch-kine, the sap of growing plants, the speed of coursers | To us may the strong Marutas be auspicious. May they deliver us from grief and trouble. || 4. They who raised water from the sea to heaven and send it from the sky to earth in showers, | The Marutas who move mighty with their waters, may they deliver us from grief and trouble. || 5. They who delight in nectar and in fatness, they who bestow upon us health and vigour. | The Marutas who rain mighty with their waters, may they deliver us from grief and trouble. || 6. Whether with stormy might the Marutas established this All, or Gods with their celestial power, | Ye, kindly Gods, are able to restore it. May they deliver us from grief and trouble. || 7. Potent in battles is the Marutas' army, impetuous train, well-known, exceeding mighty. | I, suppliant, praise and oft invoke the Marutas. May they deliver us from grief and trouble.

Hymn 4:28.

1. I Reverence you—mark this—Bhava and Śarva, ye under whose control is this that shineth. | Lords of this world both quadruped and biped. Deliver us, ye twain, from grief and trouble. || 2. Lords of all near and even of what is distant, famed as the best and skilfullest of archers, | Lords of this world both quadruped and biped, Deliver us, ye twain, from grief and trouble. || 3. Thousand-eyed foe-destroyers, I invoke you, still praising you the strong, of wide dominion: | Lords of this world both quadruped and biped, Deliver us, ye twain, from grief and trouble. || 4. Ye who of old wrought many a deed in concert, and showed among mankind unhappy omens; | Lords of this world both quadruped and biped, Deliver us, ye twain, from grief and trouble. || 5. Ye from the stroke of whose destroying weapon not one among the Gods or men escapeth, | Lords of this world both quadruped and biped, Deliver us, ye twain, from grief and trouble. || 6. Hurl your bolt, strong Gods, at the Yātudhāna, him who makes ready roots and deals in magic: | Lords of this world both quadruped and biped, Deliver us, ye twain, from grief and trouble. || 7. Comfort and aid us, ye strong Gods, in battles, at each Kimīdin send your bolt of thunder. | I, suppliant, praise and ever call on Bhava and Śarva. Set us free from grief and trouble.

Hymn 4:29.

1. You twain, O Mitra, Varuṇa, I honour, Law-strengtheners, wise, who drive away oppressors. | Ye who protect the truthful in his battles, deliver us, ye twain, from grief and trouble. || 2. Ye the wise Gods who drive away oppressors, ye who protect the truthful in his battles, | Who come, men's guards, to juice pressed forth by Babhru, deliver us, ye twain, from grief and trouble. || 3. Mitra and Varuṇa who help Agasti, Atri, and Aṅgiras, and Jamadagni, | Ye who help Kaśyapa, who help Vasiṣhṭha, deliver us, ye twain, from grief and trouble. || 4. Mitra and Varuṇa, who help Śyāvāśva, Atri, and Purumīḷha, and Vadhryaśva, | Ye who help Vimada and Saptavadhri, deliver us, ye twain, from grief and trouble. || 5. Ye, Varuṇa, Mitra, who give aid to Kutsa, Gaviṣhṭhira, Bharadvāja, Viśvāmitra, | Who help Kakṣhīvant and give aid to Kaṇva, deliver us, ye twain, from grief and trouble. || 6. Ye, Mitra, Varuṇa, who help Triśoka, Medhātithi, and Uśanā son of Kavi, | Ye, Gotama's and Mudgala's protectors, deliver us, ye twain, from grief and trouble. || 7. Whose straight-reined car that keeps the track of goodness assails and ruins him who walks perversely | I, suppliant, praise with constant invocation Mitra and Varuṇa Save us from affliction.

Hymn 4:30.

1. I travel with the Rudras and the Vasus, with the Ādityas and All-Gods I wander. | I hold aloft both Varuṇa and Mitra, I hold aloft Indra and both the Aśvins || 2. I am the Queen, the gatherer-up of treasures, most thoughtful, first of those who merit worship. | The Gods, making me enter many places, in diverse spots have set mine habitation. || 3. I, verily, myself announce and utter the word that Gods, and men alike shall welcome. | I make the man I love exceeding mighty, make him a sage, a Ṛiṣhi, and a Brahman. || 4. Through me alone all eat the food that feeds them, each man who sees, breathes, hears, the word out-spoken. | They know it not, but yet they dwell beside me. Hear, one and all, the truth as I declare it. || 5. I bend the bow for Rudra that his arrow may strike and slay the hater of devotion. | I rouse and order battle for the people, and I have penetrated Earth and Heaven. || 6. I cherish and sustain high-swelling Soma, and Tvaṣhṭar I support, Pūṣhan, and Bhaga. | I load with wealth the zealous sacrificer who pours the juice and offers his oblation. || 7. On the world's summit I bring forth the Father: my home is in the waters, in the ocean. | Thence I extend o'er all existing creatures, and touch even yonder heaven with my forehead. || 8. I breathe a strong breath like the wind and tempest, the while I hold together all existence. | Beyond this wide earth and beyond the heavens I have become so mighty in my grandeur.

Hymn 4:31.

1. Borne on with thee, O Manyu girt by Marutas, let our brave men, impetuous, bursting forward, | March on, like flames of fire in form, exulting, with pointed arrows, sharpening their weapons. || 2. Flashing like fire, be thou, O conquering Manyu, invoked, O victor, as our army's leader. | Slay thou our foes, distribute their possession: show forth thy vigour, scatter those who hate us. || 3. O Manyu, overcome those who assail us. On! breaking, slaying, crushing down the foemen. | They have not hindered thine impetuous vigour: mighty! sole born! reduce them to subjection. || 4. Alone of many thou art worshipped, Manyu: sharpen the spirit of each clan for combat. | With thee to aid, O thou of perfect splendour, we raise the glorious battle-shout for conquest. || 5. Unyielding, bringing victory like Indra, O Manyu be thou here our sovereign ruler. | To thy dear name. O victor, we sing praises: we know the spring from which thou art come hither. || 6. Twin-borne with power, destructive bolt of thunder the highest conquering might is thine, subduer! | Be friendly to us in thy spirit, Manyu! O much-invoked, in shock of mighty battle! || 7. For spoil let Varuṇa and Manyu give us the wealth of both sides gathered and collected; | And let our enemies with stricken spirits, o'er-whelmed with. terror, sling away defeated.

Hymn 4:32.

1. He who hath reverenced thee, Manyu, destructive bolt! breeds. for himself forthwith all conquering energy. | Ārya and Dāsa will we conquer with thine aid, with thee the conqueror, with conquest conquest-sped. || 2. Manyu was Indra, yea, the God was Manyu; Manyu was Hotar, Varuṇa, Jātavedas. | The tribes of human lineage worship Manyu. Accordant, with thy fervour, Manyu! guard us. || 3. Come hither, Manyu, mightier than the mighty: smite, with thy fervour, for ally, our foemen. | Slayer of foes, of Vṛitra, and of Dasyu, bring thou to us all kinds of wealth and treasure. || 4. For thou art, Manyu, of surpassing vigour, fierce, queller of the foe, and self-existent, | Shared by all men, victorious, subduer: vouchsafe to us superior strength in battles. || 5. I have departed still without a portion, wise God! according to thy will, the mighty. | I, feeble man, was wroth with thee, O Manyu. Come in thy proper form and give us vigour. || 6. Come hither, I am all thine own: advancing, turn thou to me, victorious, all-bestowing. | Come to me, Manyu, wielder of the thunder: bethink thee of thy friend, and slay the Dasyus. || 7. Approach, and on our right hand hold thy station, then let us slay a multitude of foemen. | The best of meath I

offer to support thee: may we be first to drink thereof in quiet.

Hymn 4:33.

1. Chasing our pain with splendid light, O Agni, shine thou wealth on us. | His lustre flash our pain away. || 2. For goodly fields, for pleasant homes, for wealth we sacrifice to thee. | His lustre flash our pain away! || 3. Best praiser of all these be he, and foremost be our noble chiefs. | His lustre flash our pain away! || 4. So that thy worshipper and we, thine, Agni! in our sons may live. | His lustre flash our pain away! || 5. As ever conquering Agni's beams of splendour go to every side, | His lustre flash our pain away. || 6. To every side thy face is turned, thou art triumphant everywhere. | His lustre flash our pain away! || 7. O thou whose face looks every way, bear off our foes as in a ship. | His lustre flash our pain away! || 8. As in a ship across the flood, transport us to felicity. His lustre flash our pain away.

Hymn 4:34.

1. The head of this is prayer, its back the Bṛihat, Odanas's belly is the Vāmadevya; | Its face reality, its sides the metre, Vishṭāri sacrifice produced from fervour. || 2. Boneless, cleansed, purified by him who cleanseth, they go resplendent to the world of splendour. | Fire burneth not their organ of enjoyment: much pleasure have they in the world of Svarga. || 3. Never doth want or evil fortune visit those who prepare oblation called Vishṭāri. | He goes unto the Gods, he dwells with Yama, he joys among Gandharvas meet for Soma. || 4. Yama robs not of generative vigour the men who dress oblation called Vishṭāri. | Borne on his car, a charioteer, he travels: endowed with wings he soars beyond the heavens. || 5. Strongest is this, performed, of sacrifices: he hath reached heaven who hath prepared Vishṭāri. | The oval-fruited lotus spreads his fibre: there bloom the nenuphar and water-lilies. | Abundant with their overflow of sweetness, these streams shall reach thee in the world of Svarga, whole lakes with lotus-blossom shall approach thee. || 6. Full lakes of butter with their banks of honey, flowing with wine, and milk and curds and water | Abundant with their overflow of sweetness, these streams shall reach thee in the world of Svarga, whole lakes with lotus-blossom shall approach thee. || 7. I give four pitchers, in four several places, filled to the brim with milk and curds and water. | Abundant with their overflow of sweetness, these streams shall reach thee in the world of Svarga, whole lakes with lotus-blossom shall approach thee. || 8. I part this Odana among the Brahmans, Vishṭāri, conquering worlds and reaching heaven. | Let me not lose it: swelling by its nature, be it my perfect Cow to grant all wishes!

Hymn 4:35.

1. Odana which Prajāpati, the firstborn of Order, dressed with fervour for the Brahman, which guards the worlds from breaking at the centre,—I with this | Odana will conquer Mṛityu || 2. Whereby the World-Creators vanquished Mṛityu, that which they found by fervour, toil and trouble, | That which prayer first made ready for the Brahman,—I with this Odana will conquer Mṛityu || 3. That which upholds the Earth, the all-sustainer, that which hath filled air's middle realm with moisture, | Which, raised on high in grandeur, established heaven,—I with this Odana will conquer Mṛityu || 4. From which the months with thirty spokes were moulded, from which the twelve-spoked year was formed and fashioned. | Which circling day and night have ne'er o'ertaken,—I with this Odana will conquer Mṛityu || 5. Which hath become breath-giver, life-bestower; to which the worlds flow full of oil and fatness, | To whom belong all the refulgent regions,—I with this Odana will conquer Mṛityu || 6. From which, matured, sprang Amṛita into being, which hath become Gāyatrīs lord and ruler, | In which the perfect Vedas have been treasured,—I with this Odana will conquer Mṛityu, || 7. I drive away the hostile God-despiser: far off be those who are mine adversaries, | I dress Brahmaudana that winneth all things. May the Gods hear me who believe and trust them.

Hymn 4:36.

1. Endowed with true strength, let the Bull, Agni Vaiśvānara, burn them up. | Him who would pain and injure us, him who would treat us as a foe. || 2. Him who, unharmed, would injure us, and him who, harmed, would do us harm, | I lay between the doubled fangs of Agni, of Vaiśvānara || 3. Those who, what time the moon is dark, hunt with loud cry and answering shout, | Flesh-eaters, others who would harm,—all these I overcome with might. || 4. I conquer the Piśāchas with my power, and take their wealth away. | All who would injure us I slay. Let mine intention have success. || 5. With Gods who flee with him, and match their rapid motion with the Sun, | I with those animals who dwell in rivers and on hills am found. || 6. I trouble the Piśāchas as the tiger plagues men rich in kine. | They, even as dogs when they have seen a lion, find no hiding-place. || 7. Naught with Piśāchas can I do, with thieves, with roamers of the wood. | Piśāchas flee and vanish from each village as I enter it. || 8. Into whatever village this mine awful power penetrates, | Thence the Piśāchas flee away, and plot no further mischief there. || 9. Those who enrage me with their prate, as flies torment an elephant, | I deem unhappy creatures, like small insects troublesome to man. || 10. Destruction seize upon the man, as with a cord they hold a horse, | The fool who is enraged with me! He is not rescued from the noose.

Hymn 4:37.

1. With thee, O Plant, in olden time Atharvans smote and slew the fiends. | Kaśyapa smote with thee, with thee did Kaṇva and Agastya smite. || 2. With thee we scare and drive away Gandharvas and Apsarases. | O Ajaśṛiṅgī, chase the fiends. Cause all to vanish with thy smell. || 3. Let the Apsarases, puffed away, go to the river, to the ford,— | Guggulū, Pīlā, Naladī, Aukshagandhi, Pramandanī. | Ye have become attentive since the Apsarases have past away. || 4. Where great trees are, Aśvatthas and Nyagrodhas with their leafy crests, | There where your swings are green and bright, and lutes and cymbals sound in tune, 'Ye have become attentive since the Apsarases have past away. || 5. Hither hath come this one, the most effectual of herbs and plants. || 6. Let Ajaśṛiṅgī penetrate, Arāṭakī with sharpened horn. || 7. From the Gandharva, dancing near, the lord of the Apsarases, | Wearing the tuft of hair, I take all manhood and virility. || 8. With those dread hundred iron spears, the darts of Indra, let it pierce. | The Blyxa-fed Gandharvas, those who bring no sacrificial gift. || 9. With those dread hundred golden spears, the darts of Indra, let it pierce. | The Blyxa-fed Gandharvas, those who bring no sacrificial gift. || 10. O Plant, be thou victorious, crush the Piśāchas, one and all, | Blyxa-fed, shining in the floods, illumining the selfish ones. || 11. Youthful, completely decked with hair, one monkey-like, one like a dog,— | So the Gandharva, putting on a lovely look, pursues a dame. | Him with an efficacious charm we scare and cause to vanish hence. || 12. Your wives are the Apsarases, and ye, Gandharvas, are their lords. | Run ye, immortal ones, away: forbear to interfere with men!

Hymn 4:38.

1. Hither I call the Apsaras, victorious, who plays with skill, | Her who comes freely fort to view, who wins the stakes in games of dice. || 2. Hither I call that Apsaras who scatters and who gathers up. | The Apsaras who plays with skill and takes her winnings in the game. || 3. Dancing around us with the dice, winning the wager by her play. | May she obtain the stake for us and gain the victory with skill. | May she approach us full of strength: let them not win this wealth of ours. || 4. Hither I call that Apsaras, the joyous, the delightful one— | Those nymphs who revel in the dice, who suffer grief and yield to wrath. || 5. Who follow in their course the rays of Sūrya, or as a particle of light attend him. | Whose leader from afar, with store of riches, compasses quickly all the worlds and guards them. | Pleased, may he come to this our burnt oblation, together with the Air, enriched with treasure. || 6. Together with the Air, O rich in treasure, guard here the white cow and the calf, O mighty! | Here are abundant drops for thee, come hither! Here is thy white calf, let thy mind be with us. || 7. Together with the Air, O rich in treasure, keep the white calf in safety here, O mighty! | Here is the grass, here is the stall, here do we bind the calf. We are your masters, name by name. All Hail!

Hymn 4:39.

1. Agni no earth hath had mine homage. May he bless me. | As I have bowed me down to Agni on the earth, so let the Favouring Graces bow them down to me. || 2. Earth is the Cow, her calf is Agni. May she with her calf Agni yield me food, strength, all my wish, life first of all, and off-spring, plenty, wealth. All Hail! || 3. Vāyu in air hath had mine homage. May he bless me. | As I have bowed me down to Vāyu in the air, so let the Favouring Graces bow them down to me. || 4. Air is the Cow, her calf is Vāyu. May she with her calf Vāyu yield me food, strength, all my wish, life first of all, and off-spring, plenty, wealth. All Hail! || 5. The Sun in heaven hath had my homage. May he bless me. | As I have bowed me down unto

the Sun in heaven, so let the Favouring Graces bow them down to me. || 6. Heaven is the Cow, her calf Āditya. May she yield with her calf the Sun food, strength, and all my wish, life first of all, and offspring, plenty, wealth. All Hail! || 7. To Chandrā in the quarters have I bowed me. May he bless me. | As unto Chandrā in the quarters I have bent, so let the Favouring Graces bow them down to me. || 8. The quarters are the Cows, their calf is Chandrā May they yield with their calf the Moon food, strength and all my wish, life first of all, and offspring, plenty, wealth. All Hail! || 9. Agni moves having entered into Agni, the Ṛishis' son, who guards from imprecations, | I offer unto thee with reverent worship. Let me not mar the Gods' appointed service. || 10. Skilled in all ways, O God, O Jātavedas, I offer what is cleansed by heart and spirit. | To all thy seven mouths, O Jātavedas. Do thou accept with pleasure my libation.

Hymn 4:40.

1. O Jātavedas, eastward sacrificers, as foes assail us from the eastern quarter. | May they, turned back, be pained for harming Agni. I drive them backward with mine incantation. || 2. O Jātavedas, southward sacrificers as foes assail us from the southern quarter. | May they, turned back, be pained for harming Yama. I smite them backward with mine incantation. || 3. O Jātavedas, westward sacrificers as foes assail us from the western quarter. | For harming Varuṇa be they turned and troubled! I smite them backward with mine incantation. || 4. Jātavedas, northward sacrificers as foes assail us from the northern quarter. | For harming Soma be they turned and troubled! I smite them backward with mine incantation. || 5. O Jātavedas, nether sacrificers, as foes assail us from the stead-fast quarter. | For harming Earth let them be turned and troubled. I smite them backward with mine incantation. || 6. Those who pay sacrifice, O Jātavedas, from air assail us from the midway quarter. | For harming Vāyu be they turned and troubled! I smite them backward with mine incantation. || 7. The sacrificers from above assail us, O Jātavedas, from the lofty quarter. | For wronging Sūrya be they turned and troubled! I smite them backward with mine incantation. || 8. Those from all points assail us, Jātavedas, who sacrifice from intermediate regions. | For wronging Prayer let them be turned and troubled, I smite them backward with mine incantation.

Kāṇḍa 5.

Hymn 5:1.

1. He who with special plans and deathless spirit, waxing, well-born, hath come unto his birth-place, | As he who shines upholds the days, thus Trita, of pure life, bears the Three as their supporter. || 2. He who, the first, approached the holy statutes makes, after, many beauteous forms and figures. | Eager to drink, his birth-place first he entered who understands the word when yet unspoken. || 3. He who—the fluid gold, with radiant kinsmen—to fervent glow delivered up thy body, | On him both set names, that shall live for ever: to him the regions shall send robes to clothe him, || 4. As these have gone to their primeval station, each gaining an imperishable dwelling, | May kissing mothers of the bards' beloved bring the pole-drawing husband to the sister. || 5. By holy wisdom I a sage, Far-Strider! offer to thee this lofty adoration. | This worship both the mighty eddying rivers, coming together to this station, heighten. || 6. Seven are the pathways which the wise have fashioned: to one of these may come the troubled mortal. | On sure ground where the ways are parted standeth Life's Pillar in the dwelling of the Highest. || 7. Working, I go my way with deathless spirit: life, spirit, bodies have gone gladly thither. | Aye, Śakra also gives his gift of treasure as when the sacrificer meets with power. || 8. Yea, the son asks dominion of his father: this they declared the noblest path to welfare. | Varuṇa, let them see thy revelations: display the wondrous shapes of times to follow. || 9. Halt with the milk, its other half, thou minglest and with that half, strong! unbeguiled! increasest. | Let us exalt the gracious friend, the mighty, Varuṇa son of Aditi, strength-giver. | We have told him the marvels sung by poets. The utterance of Heaven and Earth is truthful.

Hymn 5:2.

1. In all the worlds That was the best and highest whence sprang the Mighty One of splendid valour. | As soon as born he overcomes his foemen, when those rejoice in him who bring him succour. || 2. Grown mighty in his strength, with ample vigour, he as a foe strikes fear into the Dāsa, | Eager to win the breathing and the breathless: All sang thy praise at banquet and oblation. || 3. All concentrate on thee their mental vigour what time these, twice or thrice, are thine assistants, | Blend what is sweeter than the sweet with sweetness win quickly with our meath that meath in battle. || 4. If verily in every war the sages joy and exult in thee who winnest treasures, | With mightier power, strong God, extend thy firmness: let not malevolent Kaśokas harm thee. || 5. Proudly we put our trust in thee in battles, when we behold great wealth the prize of combat. | I with my words impel thy weapons onward, and sharpen with my prayer thy vital vigour. || 6. Thou in that house, the highest or the lowest, which thy protection guards, bestowest riches. | Establish ye the ever-wandering mother, and bring full many deeds to their completion. || 7. Praise in the height Him who hath many pathways, courageous, strongest, Āptya of the Āptyas | Through strength he shows himself of ample power: pattern of Pṛithivī, he fights and conquers. || 8. Bṛihaddiva, the foremost of light-winners, hath made these holy prayers, this strength for Indra. | Free Lord, he rules the mighty fold of cattle, winning, aglow, even all the billowy waters. || 9. Thus hath Bṛihaddiva, the great Atharvan, spoken to Indra as himself in person. | Two sisters free from stain, the Mātariśvans, with power impel him onward and exalt him.

Hymn 5:3.

1. Let strength be mine while I invoke thee, Agni! enkindling thee may we support our bodies. | May the four regions bend and bow before me: with thee for guardian may we win the combat. || 2. Baffling the range of our opponents, Agni! guard us as our protector round about us. | Down the steep slope go they who hate us, backward, and let their thought who watch at home be ruined. || 3. May all the Gods be on my side in battle, the Marutas led by Indra, Vishṇu, Agni. | Mine be the middle air's extended region, and may the Wind blow favouring these my wishes. || 4. For me let them present all mine oblations, and let my mind's intention be accomplished. | May I be guiltless of the least transgression: may all the Gods come hither and protect me. || 5. May the Gods grant me riches, may the blessing and invocation of the Gods assist me. | This boon shall the celestial Hotars win us: may we, unwounded, have brave heroes round us. || 6. Ye six divine Expanses, give us freedom. Here, all ye Gods, acquit yourselves like heroes. | Let not calamity or curse o'ertake us, nor deeds of wickedness that merit hatred. || 7. Do ye three Goddesses give ample shelter and all success to us ourselves and children. | Let us not lose our children or our bodies: let us not benefit the foe, King Soma! || 8. Foodful and much-invoked, at this our calling may the far-reaching Bull grant us wide shelter. | Lord of bay coursers, Indra, bless our children: harm us not, give us not as prey to others. || 9. Lord of the world, Creator and Disposer, may the God Savitar who quells assailants, | May the Ādityas, Rudras, both the Aśvins, Gods, guard the sacrificer from destruction. || 10. Let those who are our foemen stay afar from us: with Indra and with Agni we will drive them off. | The Ādityas and the Rudras, over us on high, have made me strong, a thinker, and a sovereign lord. || 11. Yea, we call Indra hitherward, the winner of wealth in battle and of kine and horses. | May he mark this our worship when we call him, Lord of bay steeds, thou art our friend and comrade.

Hymn 5:4.

1. Thou who wast born on mountains, thou most mighty of all plants that grow. | Thou Banisher of Fever, come, Kushṭha! make Fever pass away. || 2. Brought from the Snowy Mountain, born on the high hill where eagles breed, | Men seek to buy thee when they hear: for Fever's Banisher they know. || 3. In the third heaven above us stands the Aśvattha tree, the seat of Gods. | There the Gods sought the Kushṭha Plant, embodiment of end-less life. || 4. There moved through heaven a golden ship, a ship with cordage wrought of Gold. | There the Gods won the Kushṭha Plant, the blossom of eternal life. || 5. They sailed on pathways paved with gold, the oars they piled were wrought of gold: | All golden were the ships wherein they carried Kushṭha down to earth. || 6. O Kushṭha, bring thou hitherward this man of mine, restore his health, | Yes, free him from disease for me. || 7. Thou art descended from thee Gods, Soma's benignant friend art thou, | Befriend my breath and vital air be gracious unto this mine eye. || 8. Sprung, northward, from the Snowy Hill thou art conveyed to eastern men. | There

they deal out among themselves Kuṣhṭha's most noble qualities. || 9. Most excellent, indeed, art thou, Kuṣhṭha! most noble is thy sire. | Make all Consumption pass away and render Fever powerless. || 10. Malady that affects the head, eye-weakness, bodily defect— | All this let Kuṣhṭha heal and cure: aye, godlike is the vigorous power.

Hymn 5:5.

1. Aryaman is thy grandsire, Night thy mother, and the Cloud thy sire. | Thy name is called Silāchī. Thou, thyself, art sister of the Gods. || 2. Whoever drinketh thee hath life: thou savest and protectest man. | As nursing mother of mankind, thou takest all upon thy lap. || 3. Thou clingest close to every tree, as a fond damsel clasps her love. | Thy name is called The Conqueror, She who Stands Fast, The Rescuer. || 4. Whatever wound the arrow, or the staff, or violence inflicts, | Thereof thou art the remedy: as such restore this man to health. || 5. Thou springest from blest Plakṣha, or Aśvattha, Dhava, Khadira, | Parṇa, or blest Nyagrodha, so come thou to use, Arundhatī! || 6. Gold-coloured, bringing happy fate, most lovely, brilliant as the Sun, | Mayst thou, O Healing! come unto the fracture: Healing is thy name. || 7. Gold-coloured, bringing happy fate, odorous, hairy-bodied one, | The sister of the Waters art thou, Lākṣhā! and thy soul is Wind. || 8. Silāchī is thy name: thy sire, O goat-brown! is a damsel's son. | Thou hast been sprinkled by the mouth of Yama's tawny-coloured horse. || 9. Issuing from the horse's blood away she glided to the trees. | Become a winged water-brook, and come to us, Arundhatī!

Hymn 5:6.

1. Eastward at first the prayer was generated: Vena disclosed bright flashes from the summit, | Disclosed his deepest nearest revelations, womb of the non-existent and existent. || 2. None have attained to those of old, those who wrought holy acts for you, | Let them not harm our heroes here. Therefore I set before you this. || 3. Sweet-tongued, exhaustless, they have sent their voices down together in heaven's vault that pours a thousand streams. | His wildly-restless warders never close an eye: in every place the snarers stand to bind men fast. || 4. Speed forward, conquering all foes, to win the spoil, | Thou comest on thy haters with a surging sea. Thy name is Fragile. The thirteenth month is Indra's home. || 5. Through this now hast thou sent thy gifts. All hail! | With sharpened arms and missiles, kind and friendly, be gracious unto us, Soma and Rudra! || 6. Through this hast thou been left in want. All hail! | With sharpened arms and missiles, kind and friendly, be gracious unto us, Soma and Rudra! || 7. Through this hast thou committed faults. All hail! | With sharpened arms and missiles, kind and friendly, be gracious unto us, Soma and Rudra! || 8. Free us from trouble, free us from dishonour, accept our worship, give us life immortal. || 9. O missile of the eye, missile of spirit, thou missile of devotion and of fervour! | Thou art the weapon shot against the weapon. Let those be weaponless who sin against us. || 10. Make with thy weapon weaponless, O Agni, all wicked men who deal with us as foemen with eye, with thought, with spirit, or intention. || 11. Thou art the house of Indra. I betake me to thee, I enter thee with all my cattle, | With all my people and with all my body, with all my soul, with mine entire possessions. || 12. Thou art the guard of Indra. I betake me to thee, etc. || 13. Thou art the shield of Indra. I betake me to thee, etc. || 14. Indra's protection art thou. I betake me to thee, I enter thee with all my cattle. | With all my people and with all my body, with all my soul, with mine entire possessions.

Hymn 5:7.

1. Bring thou to us, bar not the way, Arāti! Stay not the guerdon that is being brought us. | Homage be paid to Failure, to Misfortune, and Malignity. || 2. The man whom thou preferrest, O Arāti, he who prates to us— | This man of thine, we reverence. Baffle not thou my heart's desire, || 3. May our desire which Gods have roused fulfil itself by day and night. | We seek to win Arāti: to Arāti be our homage paid. || 4. We, suppliant, call on Bhaga, on Sarasvatī, Anumati, | Pleasant words have I spoken, sweet as honey is, at invocations of the Gods. || 5. The portion that I crave with speech intelligent and full of power, | May faith, presented with the gift of tawny Soma, find today. || 6. Do not thou make our words or wishes fruitless. Let the twain Indra Agni, bring us treasures. | All, fain today to give us gifts, welcome Arāti with your love. || 7. Misfortune! go thou far away: we turn thy harmful dart aside. | I know thee well, Arāti! as oppressor, one who penetrates. || 8. Oft, coming as a naked girl thou hauntest people in their sleep, | Baffling the thought, Arāti! and the firm intention of a man. || 9. To her the mighty vast in size, who penetrates all points of space, | To her mine homage have I paid, Nirṛiti with her golden hair. || 10. Auspicious, with her golden hue, pillowed on gold, the mighty one | To this Arāti clad in robes of gold mine homage have I paid.

Hymn 5:8.

1. With fuel of Vikaṅkata bring molten butter to the Gods. | O Agni, make them joyful here: let them all come unto my call. || 2. O Indra, come unto my call, This will I do. So hear it thou. | Let these exertions for the sake of Indra guide my wish aright. | Therewith, O Jātavedas, Lord of Bodies! may we win us strength. || 3. Whatever plot from yonder, O ye Gods, that godless man would frame, | Let not the Gods come to his call, nor Agni bear his offering up. | Come, ye, come hither to my call. || 4. Run, ye Exertions, farther on By Indra's order smite and slay. | As a wolf worrieth a sheep, so let not him escape from you while life remains. Stop fast his breath. || 5. The Brahman whom those yonder have appointed priest, for injury, | He, Indra! is beneath thy feet. I cast him to the God of Death. || 6. If they have issued forth, strongholds of Gods, and made their shield of prayer, | Gaining protection for their lives, protection round about, make all their instigation powerless. || 7. Exertions which that man hath made, Exertions which he yet will make | Turn them, O Indra, back again, O Vṛitra-slayer, back again on him that they may kill that man. || 8. As Indra, having seized him, set his foot upon Udvāchana, | Even so for all the coming years I cast those men beneath my feet. || 9. Here, Indra Vṛitra-slayer, in thy strength pierce thou their vital. parts. | Here, even here, attack them, O Indra. Thine own dear friend am I. | Indra, we closely cling to thee. May we be in thy favouring grace.

Hymn 5:9.

1. All hail to Heaven! || 2. All hail to Earth! || 3. All hail to Air! || 4. All hail to Air! || 5. All hail to Heaven! || 6. All hail to Earth! || 7. Mine eye is Sūrya and my breath is Vāta, Air is my soul and Pṛithivī my body. | I verily who never have been conquered give up my life to Heaven and Earth for keeping. || 8. Exalt my life, my strength, my deed and action; increase my understanding and my vigour. | Be ye my powerful keepers, watch and guard me, ye mistresses of life and life's creators! Dwell ye within me, and forbear to harm me.

Hymn 5:10.

1. Thou art my wall of stone against the sinner who fights against me from the eastern quarter. | May he encounter it! || 2. Thou art my wall of stone against the sinner who fights against me from the southern quarter. | May he encounter it! || 3. Thou art my wall of stone against the sinner who fights against me from the western quarter. | May he encounter it! || 4. Thou art my wall of stone against the sinner who fights against me from northern quarter. | May he encounter it! || 5. Thou art my wall of stone against the sinner who fights against me from the steadfast region. | May he encounter it! || 6.Thou art my wall of stone against the sinner who fights against me from the lofty region! | May he encounter it! || 7. Thou art my wall of stone against the sinner who from points intermediate fights against me. | May he encounter it! || 8. With Bṛihat I invoke the mind, with Mātariśvan both the breaths, | The eye from Sūrya, and the ear from Air, the body from the Earth. | We, with Sarasvatī who suits the mind, call Speech to come to us.

Hymn 5:11.

1. How, terrible in might, hast thou here spoken to the great God, how to the gold-hued Father! | Thy mind watched, greedy Varuṇa! to recover the brindled cow thou hadst bestowed as guerdon. || 2. Not through desire do I revoke my present: I bring this brindled cow to contemplate her. | Now by what lore, by what inherent nature, knowest thou all things that exist, Atharvan? || 3. Truly I am profound in wisdom, truly I know by nature all existing creatures. | No Dāsa by his greatness, not an Ārya, may violate the law that I will establish. || 4. None, self-dependent Varuṇa! existeth wiser than thou or sager by his wisdom. | Thou knowest well all these created beings: even the man of wondrous powers fears thee. || 5. O self-dependent Varuṇa, wise director, thou knowest verily all generations. | What is, unerring one! beyond this region? What more remote than that which is most distant? || 6. One thing there is beyond this air, and something beyond that one, most hard to reach, remotest. | I, Varuṇa, who know, to thee declare it. Let churls be mighty in the lower regions. Let Dāsas sink

into the earth beneath them. || 7. Many reproaches, Varuṇa, dost thou utter against the misers. who revoke their presents. | Be not thou added to that crowd of niggards: let not men call thee an illiberal giver. || 8. Let not men call me an illiberal giver. I give thee back the brindled cow, O singer. | Attend in every place where men inhabit, with all thy powers, the hymn that tells my praises. || 9. Let hymns of praise ascend to thee, uplifted in every place of human habitation. | But give me now the gift thou hast not given. Thou art my friend for ever firm and faithful. || 10. One origin, Varuṇa! one bond unites us I know the nature of that common kinship. | I give thee now the gift that I retracted. I am thy friend for ever firm and faithful. || 11. God, giving life unto the God who lauds me, Sage strengthener of the sage who sings my praises. | Thou, self-dependent Varuṇa! hast begotten the kinsman of the Gods, our sire Atharvan. | On him bestow most highly-lauded riches. Thou art our friend, high over all, our kinsman.

Hymn 5:12.

1. Thou in the house of man this day enkindled worshippest Gods as God, O Jātavedas. | Observant, bright as Mitra, bring them hither. Thou art a sapient and foreknowing envoy. || 2. Tanūnapāt, fair-tongued! with sweet meath balming the baths and ways of Order, make them pleasant. | Bear to the Gods our sacrifice, exalting with holy thoughts our hymns of praise and worship. || 3. Invoked, deserving prayer and adoration, O Agni, come accordant with the Vasus. | Thou art, O youthful Lord, the Gods' Invoker, so, best of sacrificers, bring them quickly. || 4. By rule the Sacred Grass is scattered eastward, a robe to clothe this earth when dawns are breaking. | Widely it spreads around and far extended, fair for the Gods and bringing peace and freedom, || 5. Let the expansive Doors be widely opened, like wives who deck their beauty for their husbands. | Lofty, celestial, all-impelling Portals, admit the Gods and give them easy entrance! || 6. Pouring sweet dews let holy Night and Morning, each close to each, be seated at their station,— | Lofty, celestial Dames with gold to deck them, assuming all their fair and radiant beauty. || 7. Come the first two celestial sweet-voiced Hotars, arranging sacrifice for man to worship, | As singers who inspire us in assemblies, showing the eastern light with their direction! || 8. Let Bhāratī come quickly to our worship and Ilā showing like a human being. | So let Sarasvatī and both her fellows, deft Goddesses, on this fair grass be seated. || 9. Hotar more skilled in sacrifice, bring hither with speed today God Tvaṣhṭar, thou who knowest, | Even him who formed these two, the Earth and Heaven, the Parents, with their forms, and every creature. || 10. Bring thou to our oblations which thou balmest the companies of Gods in ordered season. | Agni, Vanaspati, the Immolator sweeten our offered gifts with meath and butter! || 11. Agni as soon as he was born made ready the sacrifice and was the Gods' preceder. | May the Gods eat our offering consecrated according to this true Priest's voice and guidance.

Hymn 5:13.

1. Varuṇa, Sage of heaven, hath given me the gift: with spells of mighty power I draw thy poison out. | Dug up, not dug, adherent, I have seized it fast: low hath thy venom sunk like water in the sands. || 2. All the non-fluid portion of thy venom, I receive in these. | I take thy middle-most, thy highest, lowest juice: may it be spent and lest by reason of thy fear. || 3. Strong is my cry like thunder with the rainy cloud: with powerful incantation let thy strength be stayed. | I, with the men to aid, have seized that juice of his; as light from out the gloom, let Sūrya rise on high || 4. I with this eye destroy thine eye, and with this poison conquer thine. | Live not, O Snake, but die the death: back go thy venom on thyself. || 5. Listen to me, Black Snakes and hateful creatures, Lurker-in-Grass, Karait, and Brown, and Spotty, | Approach not near the house my friend inhabits: give warning, and rest quiet with your poison. || 6. Even as the cord that strings the bow, I slacken, as it were, the cars. | Of the All-conquering serpent's wrath, of the fierce rage of Black, and Brown, Taimāta, and Apodaka. || 7. And Āligī and Viligī, their father and the mother too,— | What will ye do? Your venomed sap, we know, is utterly powerless. || 8. Daughter of Urugūlā, she-fiend whom the black, skinned mother bare— | All female serpents poison who crept swiftly near is impotent. || 9. Dwelling beside the mountain's slope, the quick-eared porcupine exclaimed: | Of all these she-snakes homed in earth the poison is most powerless. || 10. Tābuva or not Tābuva, thou verily art not Tābuva: poison is killed by Tābuva. | Tastuva or not Tastuva, thou verily art not Tastuva: poison is killed by Tastuva.

Hymn 5:14.

1. An eagle found thee: with his snout a wild boar dug thee from the earth. | Harm thou, O Plant, the mischievous, and drive the sorcerer away. || 2. Beat thou the Yātudhānas back, drive thou away the sorcerer; | And chase afar, O Plant, the man who fain would do us injury. || 3. As 'twere a strip cut round from skin of a white-footed antelope, | Bind, like a golden chain, O God, his witchcraft on the sorcerer. || 4. Take thou his sorcery by the hand, and to the sorcerer lead it back. | Lay it before him, face to face, that it may kill the sorcerer. || 5. Back on the wizard fall his craft, upon the curser light his curse! | Let witchcraft, like a well-naved car, roll back upon the sorcerer. || 6. Whoso, for other's harm hath dealt-woman or man-in magic arts, | To him we lead the sorcery back, even as a courser with a rope. || 7. Now whether thou hast been prepared by Gods or been pre-pared by men, | We, with our Indra at our side to aid us, lead thee back again. || 8. Agni, victorious in fight, subdue the armies of our foes! | Back on the sorcerer we cast his sorcery, and beat it home. || 9. Thou who hast piercing weapons, pierce him who hath wrought it; conquer him. | We do not sharpen thee to slay the man who hath not practised it. || 10. Go as a son goes to his sire: bite as a trampled viper bites. | As one who flies from bonds, go back, O Witchcraft, to the sorcerer. || 11. Even as the timid antelope or hind from her assailant flees, | So swiftly let the sorcery o'ertake and reach the sorcerer. || 12. Straighter than any arrow let it fly against him, Heaven and Earth. | So let that witchcraft seize again the wizard like a beast of chase. || 13. Let it go contrary like flame, like water following its course. | Let witchcraft, like a well-naved car, roll back upon the sorcerer.

Hymn 5:15.

1. Plant! I have those who shall avert the threatened danger, ten and one. | O sacred Plant, produced aright! make sweetness, sweet thy self, for me. || 2. Twenty and two, O Plant, have I who shall avert the threatened ill. | O sacred Plant, produced aright! make sweetness, sweet thyself, for me.[1]

Hymn 5:16.

1. Bull! if thou art the single bull, beget. Thou hast no vital sap.[2]

Hymn 5:17.

1. These first, the boundless Sea, and Mātariśvan, fierce glowing Fire, the Strong, the Bliss-bestower, | And heavenly Floods, first-born by holy Order, exclaimed against the outrage on a Brahman. || 2. King Soma first of all, without reluctance, made restitution of the Brahman's consort. | Mitra and Varuṇa were the inviters: Agni as Hotar took her hand and led her. || 3. The man, her pledge, must by the hand be taken when he hath cried, She is a Brahman's consort. | She stayed not for a herald to conduct her: thus is the kingdom of a ruler guarded. || 4. She whom they call the star with loosened tresses, descending as. misfortune on the village, | The Brahman's consort, she disturbs the kingdom where hath appeared the hare with fiery flashing. || 5. Active in duty serves the Brahmachārī: he is a member of the Gods' own body. | Through him Bṛihaspati obtained his consort, as the Gods gained the ladle brought by Soma. || 6. Thus spake of her those Gods of old, Seven Ṛishis, who sate them down to their austere devotion: | Dire is a Brahman's wife led home by others: in the supremest heaven she plants confusion. || 7. When infants die, untimely born, when herds of cattle waste away, | When heroes strike each other dead, the Brahman's wife destroyeth them. || 8. Even if ten former husbands—none

1. The remainder of this Hymn was omitted by Griffith, with the following note: "Stanzas 3-11 of the hymn . . . are exactly the same with the exception of the numbers which increase by eleven in each stanza (thirty and three, forty and four, and so on) up to one hundred and ten in stanza 10, stanza 11 concluding with one thousand and one hundred." (Ed.)

2. The remainder of this Hymn was omitted by Griffith, with the following note: "The hymn . . . contains ten other similar lines, the only difference being that in the place of *ekavṛiṣhaḥ*, single bull, *dvivṛiṣhaḥ*, double bull, or, two bulls, *trivṛiṣhaḥ*, triple bull, or, worth three bulls, and so on follow in regular order up to *ekādaśaḥ*, eleven-fold, in stanza 11, in which *apodakaḥ*, waterless, stands instead of the *arasaḥ* sapless, of the preceding lines." (Ed.)

a Brahman—had espoused a dame, | And then a Brahman took her hand, he is her husband, only he, || 9. Not Vaiśya, not Rājanya, no, the Brahman is indeed her lord: | This Sūrya in his course proclaims to the Five Races of man-kind. || 10. So then the Gods restored her, so men gave the woman back again. | Princes who kept their promises restored the Brahman's wedded wife. || 11. Having restored the Brahman's wife, and freed them, with Gods' aid, from sin, | They shared the fullness of the earth and worn themselves ex-tended sway. || 12. No lovely wife who brings her dower in hundreds rests upon his bed, | Within whose kingdom is detained, through want of sense, a Brahman's dame. || 13. No broad-browed calf with wide-set ears is ever in his homestead born. | Within whose kingdom is detained, through want of sense, a Brahman's dame. || 14. No steward, golden-necklaced, goes before the meat-trays of the man. | Within whose kingdom is detained, through want of sense, a Brahman's dame. || 15. No black-eared courser, white of hue, moves proudly, harnessed to his car, | In whose dominion is detained, through want of sense, a Brahman's dame. || 16. No lily grows with oval bulbs, no lotus-pool is in his field, | In whose dominion is detained, through senseless love, a Brahman's dame. || 17. The men whose task it is to milk drain not the brindled cow for him, | In whose dominion is detained, through senseless love, a Brahman's dame. || 18. His milch-cow doth not profit one, his draught-ox masters not the yoke, | Wherever, severed from his wife, a Brahman spends the mournful night.

Hymn 5:18.

1. The Gods, O Prince, have not bestowed this cow on thee to eat thereof. | Seek not, Rājanya, to devour the Brahman's cow which none may eat. || 2. A base Rājanya, spoiled at dice, and ruined by himself, may eat. | The Brahman's cow and think, Today and not tomorrow, let me live! || 3. The Brahman's cow is like a snake, charged with due poison, clothed with skin. | Rājanya! bitter to the taste is she, and none may eat of her. || 4. She takes away his strength, she mars his splendour, she ruins everything like fire enkindled. | That man drinks poison of the deadly serpent who counts the Brahman as mere food to feed him. || 5. Whoever smites him, deeming him a weakling-blasphemer, coveting his wealth through folly | Indra sets fire alight within his bosom. He who acts thus is loathed by Earth and Heaven. || 6. No Brahman must be injured, safe as fire from him who loves himself. | For Soma is akin to him and Indra guards him from the curse. || 7. The fool who eats the Brahmans' food and thinks it pleasant to the taste, | Eats, but can ne'er digest, the cow that bristles with a hundred barbs, || 8. His voice an arrow's neck, his tongue a bowstring, his windpipes fire-enveloped heads of arrows, | With these the Brahman pierces through blasphemers, with God-sped bows that quell the hearts within them. || 9. Keen arrows have the Brahmans, armed with missiles: the shaft, when they discharge it, never faileth. | Pursuing him with fiery zeal and anger, they pierce the foeman even from a distance. || 10. They who, themselves ten hundred, were the rulers of a thousand men, | The Vaitahavyas, were destroyed for that they ate a Brahman's cow. || 11. The cow, indeed, when she was slain o'erthrew those Vaitahavyas, who | Cooked the last she-goat that remained of Kesaraprābandhā's flock. || 12. One and a hundred were the folk, those whom the earth shook off from her: | When they had wronged the Brahman race they perished inconceivably. || 13. Among mankind the Gods' despiser moveth: he hath drunk poison, naught but bone is left him. | Who wrongs the kinsman of the Gods, the Brahman, gains not the sphere to which the Fathers travelled. || 14. Agni, in sooth, is called our guide, Soma is called our next of kin. | Indra quells him who curses us. Sages know well that this is so. || 15. Prince! like a poisoned arrow, like a deadly snake, O lord of kine! | Dire is the Brahman's arrow: he pierces his enemies therewith.

Hymn 5:19.

1. The sons of Vītahavya, the Sṛiñjayas, waxed exceeding strong. | They well-nigh touched the heavens, but they wronged Bhṛigu and were overthrown. || 2. When men pierced Bṛihatsāman through, the Brahman, son of Aṅgiras, | The ram with teeth in both his jaws, the sheep, devoured their progeny. || 3. If men have spat upon, or shot their rheum upon a Brahman, they. | Sit in the middle of a stream running with blood, devouring hair. || 4. While yet the Brahman's cow which men are dressing quivers in her throe: | She mars the kingdom's splendour: there no vigorous hero springs to life. || 5. Terrible is her cutting-up: her bitter flesh is cast away, | And it is counted sin among the Fathers if her milk is drunk. || 6. If any King who deems himself mighty would eat a Brahman up, | Rent and disrupted is that realm wherein a Brahman is oppressed. || 7. She grows eight-footed, and four-eyed, four-eared, four-jawed, two-faced, two-tongued, | And shatters down the kingdom of the man who doth the Brahman wrong. || 8. As water swamps a leaky ship so ruin overflows that realm. | Misfortune smites the realm wherein a Brahman suffers scathe and harm. || 9. The very trees repel the man, and drive him from their sheltering shade, | Whoever claims, O Nārada, the treasure that a Brahman owns. || 10. That wealth, King Varuṇa hath said, is poison by the Gods prepared. | None hath kept watch to guard his realm who hath devoured a Brahman's cow. || 11. Those nine-and-ninety people whom Earth shook and cast away from her, | When they had wronged the Brahman race were ruined inconceivably || 12. Oppressor of the Brahmans! thus the Gods have spoken and declared, | The step-effacing wisp they bind upon the dead shall be thy couch. || 13. Oppressor of the Brahmans! tears wept by the man who suffers wrong, | These are the share of water which the Gods have destined to be thine. || 14. The share of water which the Gods have destined to be thine, is that, | Oppressor of the priest! wherewith men lave the corpse and wet the beard. || 15. The rain of Mitra-Varuṇa falls not on him who wrongs the priest. | To him no counsel brings success: he wins, no friend to do his will.

Hymn 5:20.

1. Formed out of wood, compact with straps of leather, loud is the: War-drum as he plays the hero. | Whetting thy voice and vanquishing opponents, roar at them like a lion fain to conquer! || 2. The fastened frame hath roared as 'twere a lion, like a bull bellowing to meet the heifer. | Thou art a bull, thine enemies are weaklings: thine is the foe-subduing strength of Indra. || 3. Like a bull marked by strength among the cattle, roar seeking kine and gathering up the booty. | Pierce through our adversaries' heart with sorrow, and let our routed foes desert their hamlets. || 4. Victorious in the battle, loudly roaring, seizing what may be seized, look all around thee. | Utter, O Drum, thy heavenly voice with triumph. Bring, as a priest, our enemies' possessions. || 5. Hearing the Drum's far-reaching voice resounding, let the foe's dame, waked by the roar, afflicted, | Grasping her son, run forward in her terror amid the conflict of the deadly weapons. || 6. Thou, first of all, O Drum, thy voice shalt utter: over the ridge of earth speak forth exultant. | Crunching with might the army of the foemen, declare thy message pleasantly and clearly. || 7. Loud be thy roar between the earth and heaven. Swift let thy sounds go forth in all directions. | Neigh at them, thunder, set in opposition, song-maker, good ally that friends may conquer. || 8. He shall send forth his voice whom art hath fashioned. Make thou the weapons of our warriors bristle. | With Indra for ally call out our heroes, and with thy friends scatter and chase the foemen || 9. Resonant, roaring, with thy powerful weapons, warning, and heard by troops in many places, | Knowing all rules and winning us advantage, deal fame to many where two kings are fighting. || 10. Bent on advantage, mightier, gaining treasures, victor in war, the spell hath made thee keener. | As, in the press, the stone to stalks of Soma, thus, Drum! go dancing to our foes' possessions. || 11. Foe-conqueror, victor, vanquishing opponents, seeker of booty, mastering, destroying. | Speak out as a skilled speaker tells his counsel, speak strength to us that we may win the battle. || 12. Shaker of things unshaken, readiest corner to battles; conquering foes, resistless leader, | Guarded by Indra, watching our assemblies, go quickly, breaker of their hearts who hate us.

Hymn 5:21.

1. Speak to our enemies, O Drum, discouragement and wild dismay. | We bring upon our foemen fear and discord and discomfiture. Drum! drive these enemies away. || 2. When sacrificial butter hath been offered, let our foemen flee. | Through consternation, terrified, trembling in mind and eye and heart. || 3. Wrought out of wood, compact with straps of leather, dear to all the clan, | Bedewed with sacrificial oil, speak terror to our enemies. || 4. As the wild creatures of the wood flee in their terror from a man, | Even so do thou, O Drum, roar out against our foes to frighten them, and then bewilder thou their thoughts. || 5. As, when the wolf approaches, goats and sheep run sorely terrified, | Even so do thou, O

Drum, roar out against our foes to frighten them, and then bewilder thou their thoughts. || 6. As birds of air, day after day, fly in wild terror from the hawk, as from a roaring lion's voice, | Even so do thou, O Drum, roar out against our foes to frighten them, and then bewilder thou their thoughts. || 7. May all the deities whose might controls the fortune of the fray | Frighten away our enemies with Drum and skin of antelope. || 8. Let those our enemies who go yonder in their battalions shake. | In fear at shadows and the sounds of feet which Indra sporteth with. || 9. To all the quarters of the sky let clang of bowstrings and our Drums. | Cry out to hosts of foes that go discomfited in serried ranks. || 10. Āditya, take their sight away! Follow them close, ye motes of light. | Let them cleave fast to foot-bound hosts when strength of arm hath past away. || 11. Do ye, O mighty Marutas, sons of Pṛiśni, crush down, with Indra for ally, our foemen. | King Soma. Varuṇa, great God and sovereign, Indra too, aye, Death,— || 12. May these embattled Gods, brilliant as Sūrya—All hail!—one-minded conquer those who hate us.

Hymn 5:22.

1. Hence, filled with holy strength let Agni, Soma, and Varuṇa, the Press-stone, and the Altar. | And Grass, and glowing Fuel banish Fever. Let hateful things stay at a distance yonder. || 2. And thou thyself who makest all men yellow, consuming them with burning heat like Agni, | Thou, Fever! then be weak and ineffective. Pass hence into the realms below or vanish. || 3. Endowed with universal power! send Fever down-ward, far away, | The spotty, like red-coloured dust, sprung from a spotty ancestor. || 4. When I have paid obeisance to Fever I send him downward forth. | So let Śakambhara's boxer go again to the Mahāvṛishas. || 5. His mansions are the Mūjavants, and the Mahāvṛishas his home, | Thou, Fever, ever since thy birth hast lived among the Bahlikas. || 6. Fever, snake, limbless one, speak out! Keep thyself far away from us. | Seek thou a wanton Dāsī girl and strike her with thy thunder-bolt. || 7. Go, Fever, to the Mūjavants, or, farther, to the Bahlikas. | Seek a lascivious Śara girl and seem to shake her through and through. || 8. Go hence and eat thy kinsmen the Mahāvṛishas and Mūjavants | These or those foreign regions we proclaim to Fever for his home. || 9. In a strange land thou joyest not; subdued, thou wilt be kind to us. | Fever is eager to depart, and to the Bahlikas will go, || 10. Since thou now cold, now burning hot, with cough besides, hast made us shake, | Terrible, Fever, are thy darts: forbear to injure us with these. || 11. Take none of these to be thy friends, Cough, or Consumption or Decline: | Never come thence again to us! O Fever, thus I counsel thee. || 12. Go, Fever, with Consumption, thy brother, and with thy sister, Cough. | And with thy nephew Herpes, go away unto that alien folk. || 13. Chase Fever whether cold or hot, brought by the summer or the rains, | Tertian, intermittent, or autumnal, or continual. || 14. We to Gandhāris, Mūjavants, to Aṅgas and to Magadhas. | Hand over Fever as it were a servant and a thing of price.

Hymn 5:23.

1. I have called Heaven and Earth to aid, have called divine Sarasvatī, | Indra and Agni have I called: Let these destroy the worm, I prayed. || 2. O Indra, Lord of Treasures, kill the worms that prey upon this boy. | All the malignant spirits have been smitten by my potent spell. || 3. We utterly destroy the worm, the worm that creeps around the eyes. | The worm that crawls about the nose, the worm that gets between the teeth. || 4. Two of like colour, two unlike, two coloured black, two coloured red. | The tawny and the tawny-eared, Vulture and Wolf, all these are killed. || 5. Worms that are white about the sides, those that are black with black-hued arms, | All that show various tints and hues, these worms we utterly destroy. || 6. Eastward the Sun is mounting, seen of all, destroying thing unseen, | Crushing and killing all the worms invisible and visible. || 7. Let the Yevāshas, Kashkashas, Ejatkas, Śipavitnukas, | Let both the worm that we can see, and that we see not, be destroyed. || 8. Slain the Yevāsha of the worms, slain too is the Nadaniman. | I have reduced them all to dust like vetches with the pounding-stone. || 9. The worm Sāraṅga, white of hue, three-headed, with a triple hump, | I split and tear his ribs away, I wrench off every head he has. || 10. I kill you, worms, as Atri, as Kaṇva and Jamadagni killed. | I crush the worms to pieces with a spell that erst Agastya used. || 11. The King of worms hath been destroyed, he who was lord of these is slain. | Slain is the worm whose mother, whose brother and sister have been slain. || 12. Destroyed are his dependants, who those dwell around him are destroyed, | And all the worms that seem to be the little ones are done to death || 13. Of every worm and insect, of the female and the male alike, | I crush the head to pieces with a stone and burn the face with fire.

Hymn 5:24.

1. Savitar, Lord of furthering aids, protect me, in this my prayer, in this mine act, in this my sacerdotal charge, in this performance, in this thought, in this my plan and wish, in this my calling on the Gods! All hail! || 2. May Agni, Lord of forest trees, protect, me, in, etc. || 3. May Heaven and Earth, the Queens of bounties, save me. || 4. May Varuṇa, the Lord of waters, save me. || 5. May Mitra-Varuṇa, Lords of rain, preserve me. || 6. Lords of the mountains, may the Marutas save me. || 7. May, Soma, Lord of plants and herbs, protect me. || 8. May Vāyu, Lord of middle air, protect me. || 9. May Sūrya, sovereign Lord of eyes, protect me. || 10. May the Moon, Lord of constellations, save me. || 11. May Indra who is Lord of heaven protect me. || 12. The Marutas' father, Lord of cattle, save me. || 13. May Mṛityu, Lord of living creatures, save me. || 14. May Yama, Regent of the Fathers, save me. || 15. May the Forefathers of old time protect me. || 16. May Fathers of succeeding ages save me. || 17. Next may the Fathers of our fathers save me, in this my prayer, in this mine act, in this my sacerdotal charge, in this performance, in this thought, in this my plan and wish, in this my calling on the Gods! All hail!

Hymn 5:25.

1. Let the man, sower of the germ, lay, as a feather on a shaft. | Limb drawn from limb, whate'er is culled from cloud and from the womb of heaven. || 2. Even as this broad earth received the germ of all the things that be, | Thus within thee I lay the germ. I call thee, Earth, to strengthen it. || 3. O Sinīvālī, set the germ, set thou the germ, Sarasvatī! In thee let both the Aśvins, crowned with lotuses, bestow the germ. || 4. Let Mitra-Varuṇa and God Bṛihaspati lay the germ in thee. | Indra and Agni lay the germ, Dhātar bestow the germ in thee. || 5. Let Vishṇu form and mould the womb, let Tvashṭar duly shape the forms, | Prajāpati infuse the stream, and Dhātar lay for thee the germ. || 6. Drink thou the procreative draught well-known to Varuṇa the King, | Known to divine Sarasvatī, and Indra slayer of the foe. || 7. Thou art the germ of plants and herbs, thou art the germ of forest trees, | The germ of each existing thing, so here, O Agni, lay the germ. || 8. Rise up, put forth thy manly strength, and lay thy germ within the womb. | A bull art thou with vigorous strength: for progeny we bring thee near. || 9. Prepare thee, Bārhatsāmā, let the germ be laid within thy side. | The Soma-drinking Gods have given a son to thee, thy son and mine. || 10. O Dhātar, thou Disposer, lay within the body of this dame. | A male germ with the noblest form, for her, in the tenth month, to bear. || 11. Tvashṭar, celestial artist, lay within the body of this dame. | A male germ with the noblest form for her in the tenth month to bear. || 12. Savitar, vivifier, lay within the body of this dame A male germ with the noblest form for her in the tenth month to bear. || 13. O Lord of Life, Prajāpati, within this woman's body lay | A male germ with the noblest form for her in the tenth month to bear.

Hymn 5:26.

1. In sacrifice for you may sapient Agni—All hail!—use Yajus texts and fuel. || 2. May Savitar the God—All hail!—foreknowing, chief in this sacrifice, employ them. || 3. In this great rite—All hail!—may sapient Indra use lauds, rejoicings, well-yoked coursers. || 4. Bring Praishas in the rite—All hail!—and Nivids, learned, connected, with the Consorts. || 5. As a dame brings her son—All hail!—O Marutas, connected, in the rite bring measures. || 6. Here Aditi is come—All hail!—preparing the rite with grass and lustral waters. || 7. Let Vishṇu in this rite in varied manner—All hail! —use well-yoked steeds, his fervours. || 8. Let Tvashṭar in this rite in varied manner—All hail!—use forms, his well-yoked coursers. || 9. Let Bhaga in this rite use prayers, foreknowing—All hail! for this use well-yoked coursers. || 10. Let Soma in this rite in varied manner—All hail!—use milk-streams, well-yoked coursers. || 11. Let Indra in this rite in varied manner—All hail!—use powers, his well-yoked coursers. || 12. Hitherward come ye with the prayer, O Aśvins, exalting sacrifice with cry of Vashaṭ! | Bṛihaspati!—All hail!—with prayer come hither. Here is the rite, here heaven for him who worships.

Hymn 5:27.

1. Uplifted be this sacrificer's fuel: lofty and brilliant be the flames of Agni! | Splendidly bright, fair-faced, with all his offspring, Tanūnapāt the Asura, many-handed. || 2. God among Gods, the God bedews the paths with fatness and with mead. || 3. With store of mead to sacrifice comes Agni, comes Narāśaṃsa Agni, friendly-minded, comes Savitar, righteous God who brings all blessings. || 4. Hither he comes with power and fatness also, the luminous, implored with adoration. || 5. At holy rites and offerings Agni loveth the scoops: let this man worship Agni's greatness. || 6. He is the furtherer at glad oblations: there stood the Vasus and the treasure-givers. || 7. Ever the Doors divine, and all protect this worshipper's holy work. || 8. Far-reaching, ruling by the Law of Agni, May Dawn and Night, the holy, speeding near us, aid this our sacrificial ceremony. || 9. Celestial Hotars, with the tongues of Agni praise and extol our lofty ceremony, so that our sacrifice be well conducted! || 10. Three Goddesses upon this grass, be seated, Iḍā, Sarasvatī, Mahī, and Bhāratī adored with praise. || 11. This our nutritious genial flow, God Tvaṣhṭar! and growth of wealth, pour down on this man's kindred. || 12. Vanaspati, rejoicing, of thyself send God-ward! Let Agni, Immolator, sweeten our libation. || 13. Pay sacrifice to Indra, Jātavedas Agni, with Hail! Let all the Gods accept the gifts we offer.

Hymn 5:28.

1. For lengthened life, to last through hundred autumns, they equalize with nine the nine aspirations. | Three in gold, three in silver, three in iron by heat are established in their several places. || 2. May Agni, Sun, and Moon, and Earth, and Waters, Sky, Air, the Quarters and the Points between them, | And Parts of Years accordant with the Seasons by this three-threaded Amulet preserve me. || 3. In three-threaded Charm rest triple fullness! Let Pūṣhan cover it with milk and butter. | Here rest abundant store of food and people, may ample store of cattle rest within it. || 4. Enrich this charm, Ādityas, with your treasure; magnify this, when magnified, O Agni. | Endow it with heroic strength, O Indra: therein be lodged a triple power of increase. || 5. With gold let Earth protect thee, and with iron, accordant, all-sustaining Agni save thee! | And in accordance with the plants may silver, regarding thee with favour, grant thee vigour. || 6. This gold, born threefold at its first production, grew the one thing that Agni loved most dearly: it fell away, one part of injured Soma. | One part they call seed of the sapient Waters. This gold bring thee long life when triply threaded! || 7. Three lives of Jamadagni, thrice the vital force of Kaśyapa, | Three sights of immortality, three lives have I prepared for thee. || 8. When with the three-stringed charm came three strong eagles, sharing the Sacred Syllable and mighty, | With immortality they drove off Mṛityu, obscuring and concealing all distresses. || 9. The golden guard thee from the sky, the silver guard thee from the air, | The iron guard thee from the earth! This man hath reached the forts of Gods. || 10. May these three castles of the Gods keep thee secure on every side. | Endowed with strength, possessing these, be thou the master of thy foes, || 11. The God who first bound on in the beginning the deities' immortal golden castle,— | Him I salute with ten extended fingers. Blest be the three-stringed charm I bind upon thee. || 12. Aryaman be thy binder-on, and Pūṣhan and Bṛihaspati: | Whatever name the brood of day possess, therewith we fasten thee. || 13. With Seasons and with Lengths of Time, for vigour and extended life, | With all the splendour of the Sun we fasten thee about the neck. || 14. Drawn forth from butter and with meath besprinkled, firm as the earth, unshakable, triumphant. | Breaking down foes and casting them beneath me, be fastened on me for exalted fortune!

Hymn 5:29.

1. Made ready in the east drive forth, take notice of what is happening here, omniscient Agni! | Thou bringest medicine and healest sickness: through thee may we win horses, kine, and people. || 2. Accordant with all Gods, O Jātavedas Agni, perform this work as we beseech thee, | That this defence of his may fall, whoever hath caused us pain, whoever hath consumed us. || 3. Unanimous, with all the Gods together, so do this thing O Agni | Jātavedas, that this defence of his may fall and fail him. || 4. Pierce both his eyes, pierce thou the heart within him, crush thou his teeth and cleave his tongue asunder. | Rend thou, most youthful Agni, that Piśācha whoso amid them all of this hath eaten. || 5. Whatever of his body hath been taken, plundered, borne off, or eaten by Piśāchas, | This, Agni, knowing it, again bring hither! We give back flesh and spirit to his body. || 6. If some Piśācha in my food raw, ready, thoroughly cooked, or, spotty, hath deceived me, | Let the Piśāchas with their lives and offspring atone for this, and let this man be healthy. || 7. If one hath cheated me in milk or porridge, in food from grain or plants that need no culture. | Let the Piśāchas, etc. || 8. If one, flesh eater, in a draught of water have wronged me lying in the bed of goblins, | Let the Piśāchas, etc. || 9. If one, flesh-eater, in the day or night-time have wronged me lying in the bed of goblins, | Let the Piśāchas, etc. || 10. O Agni Jātavedas, slay the bloody Piśācha, flesh-devourer, mind-destroyer, | Strong Indra strike him with his bolt of thunder, courageous Soma cut his head to pieces! || 11. Thou, Agni, ever slayest Yātudhānas, the fiends have never conquered thee in battles. | Consume thou from the root the flesh-devourers, let none of them escape thy heavenly weapon || 12. Collect, O Jātavedas, what hath been removed and borne away. | Let this man's members grow, let him swell like the tendril of a plant. || 13. Like as the Soma's tendril, thus, O Jātavedas let him swell, | Let him live, Agni I Make him fat, free from consumption, full of sap. || 14. Here, Agni, is the fuel, here are logs that crush Piśāchas down. | O Jātavedas, willingly accept them and be pleased therewith. || 15. Accept, O Agni, with thy flame the billets of Tārṣhṭāgha wood. | Let the flesh-eater who would take the flesh of this man lose his form.

Hymn 5:30.

1. From thy vicinity I call, from near, from far, from night at hand. | Stay here: depart not: follow not the Fathers of the olden time. I bind thy vital spirit fast. || 2. If any man, a stranger or akin, hath cast a spell on thee, | I with my voice to thee declare thy freedom and release there-from. || 3. If in thy folly thou hast lied or cursed a woman or a man, | I with my voice declare to thee thy freedom and release there-from. || 4. If thou art lying there because of mother's or of father's sin, | I with my voice declare to thee thy freedom and release there-from. || 5. Accept the healing medicine, the balm thy mother and thy sire, | Thy sister and thy brother bring. I make thee live through lengthened years. || 6. O man, stay here among us; stay with all thy spirit: follow not | Yama's two messengers. Approach the castles where the living dwell. || 7. Come back as thou art called to come, knowing the outlet of the path, | And the Approach and its ascent, the way of every living man. || 8. Be not alarmed: thou wilt not die. I give thee lengthened years of life. | Forth from thy members have I charmed Decline that caused the fever there. || 9. Gone is the pain that racked thee, gone thy fever, gone thy heart's disease. | Consumption, conquered by my voice, hath, like a hawk, fled far away. || 10. Two sages, Sense and Vigilance, the sleepless and the watchful one, | These, the protectors of thy life, shall be awake both day and night. || 11. This Agni must be waited on. Here let the Sun mount up for thee. | Rise from deep death and come away, yea, from black darkness rise thou up! || 12. Homage be paid to Yama, to Mṛityu, and to the Fathers, and to those who guide us! | I honour first, for this man's preservation, that Agni who well knoweth how to save him. || 13. Let breath and mind return to him, let sight and vigour come again | Let all his body be restored and firmly stand upon its feet. || 14. Provide this man with breath and sight, O Agni, and with his body and his strength unite him. | Thou knowest Amṛita: let him not go hence, nor dwell in house of clay. || 15. Let not thine inward breathing fail, let not thine outward breath be lost. | Let Sūrya who is Lord Supreme raise thee from death with beams of light. || 16. Tied, tremulously moving, here the tongue is speaking in the mouth. | With thee I charmed Decline away and Fever's hundred agonies. || 17. This living world, unconquered of the Gods, is most beloved of all. | To whatsoever death thou wast destined when thou wast born, O man, | This death and we call after thee. Die not before decrepit age!

Hymn 5:31.

1. The spell that they have cast for thee on unbaked dish or mingled meal, | The witchcraft wrought on undressed meat, this I strike back again on them. || 2. The spell that they have cast for thee on jungle-cock, goat, horned ram, | The witchcraft wrought upon thy ewe, this I strike back again on them. || 3. The spell that they have cast upon thy beast that hath uncloven hooves, | The ass with teeth in both his jaws, this I strike back again on them. || 4. The secret spell upon thy plants Amūlā or Narāchī, spell | That they have cast upon thy field, this I strike back again on them. ||

5. The spell that wicked men have cast on thine original household-fire, | And on thy sacrificial hall, this I strike back again on them. || 6. The spell that they have cast upon thy public room thy gambling-board, | Spell they have cast upon thy dice, this I strike back again on them. || 7. The spell that they have cast upon thine army or thy shafts and arms, | Spell they have cast upon the drum, this I throw back again on them. || 8. Charm they have laid within thy well or buried in the burning-ground, | Charm they have laid within thy home, this I throw back again on them. || 9. The spell that they have wrought for thee in flickering fire of human bones,— | Mroka, consuming, cannibal, this I throw back again on them. || 10. He brought this by no proper path, by the right path we drive it back. | The fool in folly brought it to those who observe established bounds. || 11. No power had he who wrought the spell: he hurt his foot, he broke his toe. | Unlucky for his wealthy lords, he hath wrought happiness for us. || 12. May Indra slay with mighty bolt, may Agni with his missile pierce. | The sorcerer who brings the curse, who deals with roots and secret spells.

Kāṇḍa 6.

Hymn 6:1.

1. Sing, Ātharvaṇa, at eve, sing loudly, bring a splendid present: hymn God Savitar with praises. || 2. Yea, praise him whose home is in the river, Son of Truth, the youthful, gracious friend whose word is guileless. || 3. Savitar our God shall send us many everlasting treasures, that both paths may well be travelled.

Hymn 6:2.

1. For Indra, ministering priests! run ye and press the Soma juice, | That he may hear his praiser's word, and this my call. || 2. Thou into whom the drops find way as sap pours life into a tree, | Drive off in thine abundant might our demon foes. || 3. For Indra, thunder-armed, who drinks the Soma press the Sôma out: | He, youthful, conqueror, and Lord is praised by all.

Hymn 6:3.

1. Guard us the Marutas! Guard us well, O Indra, Pūṣhan, Aditi. | Guard us, O Waters' Child, and Rivers Seven. May Viṣhṇu guard us, and the Sky. || 2. May Heaven and Earth take care of us for victory, may Pressing-Stone and Soma save us from distress. | Sarasvatī, auspicious Goddess, guard us well: preserve us Agni and his kind protecting powers. || 3. Preserve us both the Aśvins, Gods and Lords of Light, and let the Dawns and Night bring us deliverance. | The Waters' Child protect our house from every harm. Do thou, God Tvaṣhṭar, make us strong for health and wealth.

Hymn 6:4.

1. May Tvaṣhṭar, Brahmaṇaspati, Parjanya hear my holy prayer. | May Aditi with all her sons, the brothers, guard us, invincible, protecting power. || 2. May Aṃśa, Bhaga, Varuṇa, and Mitra, Aryaman, Aditi, and Marutas guard us. | May we be freed from that oppressor's hatred. May he keep off that foeman who is near us. || 3. May both the Aśvins further our devotion. With ceaseless care deliver us, Wide-Ranger! O Father Heaven, keep from us all misfortunes.

Hymn 6:5.

1. Agni, adored with sacred oil, lift up this man to high estate. | Endow him with full store of strength and make him rich in progeny. || 2. Advance him, Indra! Let him be ruler of all akin to him. | Grant him sufficiency of wealth: guide him to life and length of days. || 3. Prosper this man, O Agni, in whose house we offer sacrifice. | May Soma bless him, and the God here present, Brahmaṇaspati.

Hymn 6:6.

1. The godless man whoever plots against us, Brahmaṇaspati, | Thou shalt give up as prey to me the worshipper who pour the juice. || 2. If, Soma, any spiteful man hath aimed at us whose thoughts are kind, | Smite with thy bolt upon his face: he, crushed to pieces, vanisheth. || 3. Soma, whoever troubleth us, be he a stranger or akin, | Deprive him of the strength he hath: slay him thy-self like mighty Dyaus!

Hymn 6:7.

Soma! what pathway Aditi and the three guileless Mitras use, come thou with help to us thereby. || 2. Thereby thou, conquering Soma, wilt give Asuras to be our prey, thereby be ye our advocates.|| 3. Whereby ye Gods repelled and stayed the powers of the Asuras, thereby give shelter unto us.

Hymn 6:8.

1. Like as the creeper throws, her arms on every side around the tree, | So hold thou me in thine embrace that thou mayst be in love with me, my darling, never to depart. || 2. As, when he mounts, the eagle strikes his pinions downward on the earth, | So do I strike thy spirit down that thou mayst be in love with me, my darling, never to depart. || 3. As in his rapid course the Sun encompasses the heaven and: earth, | So do I compass round thy mind that thou mayst be in love with. me, my darling, never to depart.

Hymn 6:9.

1. Desire my body, love my feet, love thou mine eyes, and love my legs. | Let both thine eyes and hair, fond girl! be dried and parched. through love of me. || 2. I make thee hang upon mine arm, I make thee lie upon my heart. | Thou yieldest to my wish, that thou mayst be submissive to my will. || 3. May they whose kisses are a bond, a love-charm laid within the heart, | Mothers of butter, may the cows incline that maid to love of me.

Hymn 6:10.

1. All hail for hearing to the Earth, to Trees, to Agni, sovereign Lord! || 2. All hail for breath to Air, for power to life to Vāyu, sovereign Lord! || 3. All hail for vision to the Stars, to Heaven, to Sūrya, sovereign Lord!

Hymn 6:11.

1. Aśvattha on the Śamī-tree. There a male birth is certified. | There is the finding of a son: this bring we to the women-folk. || 2. The father sows the genial seed, the woman tends and fosters it. | This is the finding of a son: thus hath Prajāpati declared. || 3. Prajāpati, Anumati, Sinīvālī have ordered it. | Elsewhere may he effect the birth of maids, but here prepare a boy.

Hymn 6:12.

1. I, As the Sun goes round the heaven, have travelled round the Serpents' race. | I ward thy poison off, as Night parts all else living from the Sun. || 2. With this, discovered in the days of old by Brahmans, Ṛiṣhis, Gods, | With this I ward thy poison off, thou Biter! formed and forming now. || 3. With mead I mingle flowing streams: the hills and mountains shall be mead. | Paruṣhṇī and Śipālā mead. May it be well with mouth and heart.

Hymn 6:13.

1. Worship to weapons of the Gods! worship to weapons of the Kings! | Then worship to the people's arms! worship, O Death, be paid to thee! || 2. Let worship be to thy defence and to thine accusation paid. | Death! be this worship paid to thy good-will and thy malevolence! || 3. Worship to thy physicians, to thy sorcerers be worship paid! | Death! let this reverence be done unto thy Brahmans and thy roots.

Hymn 6:14.

1. Remove thou all Decline that lurks within the members and the joints, | The firmly-settled heart-disease that racks the bones and rends the limbs. || 2. From the consumptive man I pluck Decline as 'twere a severed part. | I cut the bond that fetters him, even as a root of cucumber. || 3. Begone, Consumption, hence away, like a young foal that runs at speed. | Then, not pernicious to our men, flee, yearly visitant like grass!

Hymn 6:15.

1. Most excellent of all the plants art thou: thy vassals are the trees. | Let him be subject to our power, the man who seeks to injure us. || 2. Whoever seeks to injure us, with kinsmen or no kin to aid, | May I be uppermost of all, even as this Plant is queen of trees. || 3. As Soma hath been made the best of all oblations amid the plants, | So, as Talāśā is the queen of trees, may I be chief of all.

Hymn 6:16.

1. O Ābayu, non-Ābayu, dire is thy juice, O Ābayu; we eat the gruel made of thee. || 2. Vihalha is thy father's name, thy mother's is Madāvatī. Yea, verily thou art not he, thou who hast well protected life. || 3. Go thou to rest, Tauvilikā! This noisy cry hath sunk to rest. Go hence, depart, Nirāla, thou! the tawny and the tawny-eared.

Hymn 6:17.

1. Even as this mighty Earth conceived the germ of all the things that be, | So may the germ of life be laid in thee that thou mayst bear a son. || 2. Even as this mighty Earth hath borne and bears the stately forest trees, | So may

the germ of life be borne in thee that thou mayst bear a son. ‖ 3. Even as this mighty Earth hath borne and bears the mountains and the hills, | So may the germ of life be borne in thee that thou mayst bear a son. ‖ 4. Even as this mighty Earth supports the moving world that dwells thereon, | So may the germ of life be borne in thee that thou mayst bear a son.

Hymn 6:18.

1. The first approach of Jealousy, and that which followeth the first, | The pain, the fire that burns within thy heart we quench and drive away. ‖ 2. Even as the earth is dead to sense, yea, more unconscious than the dead, | Even as a corpse's spirit is the spirit of the jealous man. ‖ 3. The thought that harbours in thy heart, the fluttering doubt that dwells therein. | Yea, all thy jealousy, like heat born of the dance, I banish thence.

Hymn 6:19.

1. Let the Gods purify me, let men purify me with a prayer. | Cleanse me all creatures that exist! may Pavamāna make me pure. ‖ 2. May Pavamāna make me pure for wisdom and for power and life, and unassailed security. ‖ 3. God Savitar, by both of these, filter and pressing out this juice, purify us that we may see.

Hymn 6:20.

1. He goes away as 'twere from this fierce burning fire, inebriated and lamenting he departs. | Let him, the lawless, seek another and not us. Worship be paid to Fever armed with fiery heat. ‖ 2. To Rudra and to Fever be our worship paid: worship be paid to Varuṇa the splendid King! | Worship to Dyaus, to Earth, worship be paid to Plants! ‖ 3. Thou who, aglow with heat, makest all bodies green, to thee, red, brown, I bow, the Fever of the wood.

Hymn 6:21.

1. Of all the three terrestrial realms the ground is verily the best. | I from the skin that covers these gather a healing medicine. ‖ 2. Thou art the best of medicines, most excellent of Plants art thou, | As Soma amid the wandering stars, as Varuṇa among the Gods. ‖ 3. Endowed with wealth, denying not, give freely fain to give your gifts! | Ye stay the hair from falling off: ye strengthen and increase its growth.

Hymn 6:22.

1. Dark the descent; the strong-winged birds are golden: they fly aloft to heaven, enrobed in waters. | They have come hither from the seat of Order, and inundated earth with streams of fatness. ‖ 2. Ye make floods rich in milk, make plants propitious, what time ye stir, O golden-breasted Marutas! | Pour down your showers of vigorous strength and favour there where ye sprinkle mead, O Marutas, heroes! ‖ 3. O Marutas, send ye down, streaming with water rain which, may, filling all the sloping valleys, | Leap like a bold girl in a man's embraces, or like a matron tumbled by her husband.

Hymn 6:23.

1. Here flow the restless ones, they flow unceasing through the day and night, | Most excellently wise I call the Goddess Waters hitherward. ‖ 2. Let the deft Waters, summoned, give permission that we bear them off, | And quickly set us on our way. ‖ 3. Let all the people celebrate the rite of Savitar the God. | Sweet unto us be Waters, Plants propitious!

Hymn 6:24.

1. Forth from the Hills of Snow they stream, and meet in Sindhu here or there. | To me the sacred Waters gave the balm that heals the heart's disease. ‖ 2. Whatever rupture I have had that injured eyes or heels or toes. | All this the Waters, skilfullest physicians, shall make well again, ‖ 3. All Rivers who have Sindhu for your Lady, Sindhu for your Queen, | Give us the balm that heals this ill: this boon let us enjoy from you.

Hymn 6:25.

1. May all the five-and-fifty which meet round the tendons of the neck. | Depart and vanish hence away like plaguing insects buzz and hum! ‖ 2. Those seventy-and-seven which meet round the upper vertebrae, | Let them all vanish hence away like plaguing insects' buzz and hum! ‖ 3. Those nine-and-ninety which, combined, attack the shoulder round about, | Let them all vanish hence away like plaguing insects' buzz and hum!

Hymn 6:26.

1. Let me go free, O Misery: do thou, the mighty, pity us. | Set me uninjured in the world of happiness, O Misery. ‖ 2. From thee, from thee who fliest not from us, O Misery, we fly. | Then at the turning of the paths let Misery fall on someone else. ‖ 3. May the immortal, thousand eyed, dwell otherwhere apart from us. | Let him afflict the man we hate: smite only him who is our foe.

Hymn 6:27.

1. Gods! whatsoe'er the Dove came hither seeking, sent to us as the envoy of Destruction, | For that let us sing hymns and make atonement, Well be it with our quadrupeds and bipeds! ‖ 2. Auspicious be the Dove that hath been sent us, a harmless bird, O Gods, that seeks our dwelling! | May Agni, Sage, be pleased with our oblation, and may the missile borne on wings avoid us. ‖ 3. Let not the arrow that hath wings distract us. Beside the fireplace, on the hearth it settles. | May it bring welfare to our men and cattle: here let the Dove, ye Gods, forbear to harm us.

Hymn 6:28.

1. Drive forth the Dove, chase it with holy verses: rejoicing bring we hither food and cattle, | Obliterating traces of misfortune. Most fleet may it fly forth and leave us vigour. ‖ 2. These men have strengthened Agni's might, these men have brought the kine to us. | They have sung glory to the Gods. Who is the man that conquers them? ‖ 3. Be reverence paid to him who, while exploring the path for many, first approached the river, | Lord of this world of quadrupeds and bipeds; to him be reverence paid, to Death, to Yama!

Hymn 6:29.

1. On these men yonder fall the winged missile: the screeching of the Owl is ineffective, | And that the Dove beside the fire hath settled. ‖ 2. Thine envoys who came hither, O Destruction, sent or not sent by thee unto our dwelling, | The Dove and Owl, effectless be their visit! ‖ 3. Oft may it fly to us to save our heroes from slaughter, oft perch here to bring fair offspring, | Turn thee and send thy voice afar: cry to the region far away; | That I may see thee in the home of Yama reft of all thy power, that I may see thee impotent.

Hymn 6:30.

1. Over a magic stone, beside Sarasvatī, the Gods Ploughed in this barley that was blent with mead. | Lord of the plough was Indra, strong with hundred powers: the ploughers were the Marutas they who give rich gifts. ‖ 2. Thy joy in hair that falleth or is scattered, wherewith thou subjectest a man to laughter— | To other trees, far from thee will I drive it. Grow up, thou Śamī, with a hundred branches. ‖ 3. Auspicious, bearing mighty leaves, holy one, nurtured by the rain, | Even as a mother to her sons, be gracious, Śamī to our hair.

Hymn 6:31.

1. This spotted Bull hath come and sat before his mother in the east. | Advancing to his father Heaven. ‖ 2. As expiration from his breath his radiance penetrates within. The Bull shines out through all the sky. ‖ 3. He rules supreme through thirty realms—One winged with song hath made him mount | Throughout the days at break of morn.

Hymn 6:32.

1. With butter, in his hall where fire is burning, perform that sacrifice which quells the goblins. | Burn from afar against the demons Agni! Afflict not in thy fury us who praise thee. ‖ 2. Let Rudra break your necks, O ye Piśāchas, and split your ribs asunder, Yātudhānas! Your herb of universal power with Yama hath allied itself. ‖ 3. Here, Mitra-Varuṇa! may we dwell safely: with splendour drive the greedy demons backward, Let them not find a surety or a refuge, but torn away go down to Death together.

Hymn 6:33.

1. He who controls this air and men who aid his strength, and wood, and heaven, the lofty seat which Indra loves. ‖ 2. The bold whose overpowering might the boldest never hath defied,— | As erst still, unassailable is Indra's wrath, and fame, and force. ‖ 3. May he bestow on us that wealth, far-spreading, bright with yellow hue. | Indra is mightiest Lord among the folk.

Hymn 6:34.

1. Send forth thy voice to Agni, to the manly hero of our homes, | So may he bear us past our foes. ‖ 2. That Agni who with sharpened flame of fire consumes the Rākṣhasas, | So may he bear us past our foes. ‖ 3. He who from distance far remote shineth across the tracts of land, | May he transport us

past our foes. ‖ 4. He who beholds all creatures, who observes them with a careful eye, | May he transport us past our foes. ‖ 5. That brilliant Agni who was born beyond this region of the air, | May he transport us past our foes!

Hymn 6:35.

1. Forth from the distance far away Vaiśvānara come to succour us! Agni approach our eulogies! ‖ 2. Vaiśvānara with friendly thoughts hath come to this our sacrifice, Agni who saves from woe, to lauds. ‖ 3. Vaiśvānara hath formed the hymn and laud of the Aṅgirasas. To these may he bring glorious right.

Hymn 6:36.

1. Holy Vaiśvānara we seek, the Lord of light and endless life, the burning One who fadeth not. ‖ 2. He hath directed all things; he sends forth the Seasons in his might, furthering sacrifice's power. ‖ 3. Agni Kāma in other homes shines forth the sole imperial Lord of all that is and is to be.

Hymn 6:37.

1. Hitherward, having yoked his steeds, came Imprecation, thousand-eyed, | Seeking my curser, as a wolf the home of one who owneth sheep. ‖ 2. Avoid us, Imprecation! as consuming fire avoids the lake. | Smite thou the man who curses us, as the sky's lightning strikes the tree. ‖ 3. Who curses us, himself uncursed, or, cursed, who curses us again, | Him cast I as a sop to Death, as to a dog one throws a bone.

Hymn 6:38.

1. What energy the lion hath, the tiger, adder, and burning fire, Brahman, or Sūrya, | And the blest Goddess who gave birth to Indra, come unto us conjoined with strength and vigour! ‖ 2. All energy of elephant and panther, all energy of gold, men, kine, and waters, | And the blest Goddess who gave birth to Indra come unto us conjoined with strength and vigour. ‖ 3. Might in car, axles, in the strong bull's courage, in Varuṇa's breath, in Vāta, in Parjanya, | In Warrior, in the war-drum stretched for battle, in the man's roar and in the horse's mettle, | May the blest Goddess who gave birth to Indra come unto us conjoined with strength and vigour.

Hymn 6:39.

1. Let sacrifice, like fame, thrive sped by Indra, inspired, well-ordered, with a thousand powers. | To highest rank raise me who bring oblation, me who move forth to far-extended vision. ‖ 2. We will pay sacrifice and serve with worship our glorious Indra, famous for his glories. | Give thou us sway which Indra hath promoted, and in this boon of thine may we be famous. ‖ 3. Indra was glorious at his birth; Agni, Soma were born renowned. | And glorious am I, the most illustrious of all that is.

Hymn 6:40.

1. Here may we dwell, O Heaven and Earth, in safety. May Savitar and Soma send us safety. | Our safety be the wide air: ours be safety through the oblation of the Seven Ṛishis. ‖ 2. May the Four Quarters give this hamlet power: Savitar favour us and make us happy! | May Indra make us free from foes and danger: may wrath of Kings be turned to other places. ‖ 3. Make thou us free from enemies both from below and from above. | O Indra, give us perfect peace, peace from behind and from before.

Hymn 6:41.

1. For mind, for intellect, for thought, for purpose, for intelligence, | For sense, for hearing, and for sight, let us adore with sacrifice. ‖ 2. For expiration, vital air, and breath that amply nourishes, | Let us with sacrifice adore Sarasvatī whose reach is wide. ‖ 3. Let not the Ṛishis, the divine, forsake us, our own, our very selves, our lives' protectors. | Do ye, immortal, still attend us mortals, and give us vital power to live the longer.

Hymn 6:42.

1. I loose the anger from thy heart as 'twere the bowstring from a bow, | That we, one-minded now, may walk together as familiar friends. ‖ 2. Together let us walk as friends: thy wrathful feeling I remove. | Beneath a heavy stone we cast thy wrath away and bury it. ‖ 3. I trample on thine anger thus, I tread it down with heel and toe: | So dost thou yield thee to my will, to speak no more rebelliously.

Hymn 6:43.

1. For stranger and for friend alike this Darbha-grass removeth wrath. | Soother of Anger is it called because it calms the angry man. ‖ 2. This Plant that hath abundant roots spreads to the place where waters meet. | Soother of anger is the name Darbha-grass that springs from earth. ‖ 3. We draw thine obstinacy forth, set in thy mouth and in thy jaw: | So dost thou yield thee to my will. to speak no more rebelliously.

Hymn 6:44.

1. Firm stood the heaven, firm stood the earth, firm stood this universal world. | Firm stood the trees that sleep erect: let this thy malady be still. ‖ 2. Of all thy hundred remedies, a thousand remedies combined. | This is the surest cure for flux, most excellent to heal disease. ‖ 3. Thou art the stream that Rudra pours, the closest kin of Amṛita. | Thy name is called Vishāṇakā: thou sprangest from the Fathers' root, removing illness caused by wind.

Hymn 6:45.

1. Sin of the Mind, avaunt! begone! Why sayest thou what none should say? | Go hence away, I love thee not. Go to the forests and the trees. My heart is in our homes and cows. ‖ 2. Whatever wrong we have committed, sleeping or waking, by ill-wish, dislike, or slander, | All these offences, which deserve displeasure, may Agni take from us and keep them distant. ‖ 3. Indra and Brahmaṇaspati! whatever foolish deed we plan, | May provident Aṅgirasa preserve us from the sin and woe.

Hymn 6:46.

1. Thou, neither quick nor dead, O Sleep, art fraught with Amṛita of the Gods. | Thy name is Araru: thy sire is Yama; Varuṇānī bare thee. ‖ 2. We know thy birth, O Sleep, thou art son of the sisters of the Gods; the minister of Yama thou, thou art Antaka, thou art Death. | So well we know thee who thou art. Sleep, guard us from the evil dream. ‖ 3. As men discharge a debt, as they pay up an eighth and half-an-eighth, | So the whole evil dream do we pay and assign unto our foe.

Hymn 6:47.

1. Dear to all men, all-prosperer, all-creating, may Agni, guard us at the morn's libation. | May he, the brightly pure one, give us riches: may we have life enjoying food together. ‖ 2. At this our second offering may Indra, Marutas, and Viśvedevas never fail us. | Still may the favour of the Gods be with us, blest with long life and speaking words that please them. ‖ 3. We pour this third libation of the Sages who fashioned forth the cup in proper order. | Winners of heaven, may they, Sudhanvan's children, lead our fair sacrifice to happy fortune.

Hymn 6:48.

1. Thou art the Hawk, Gāyatrī's lord: I hold thee fast. Happily bear me to the goal of this my sacrifice. All hail! ‖ 2. Thou art the Ṛibhu, lord of Jagatī: I hold thee fast. Happily bear me to the goal of this my sacrifice. Al I hail! ‖ 3. Thou art the Bull, the Trishṭubh's lord: I hold thee fast. Happily bear me to the goal of this my sacrifice. All hail!

Hymn 6:49.

1. O Agni, in thy body man hath never found a wounded part. | The Ape devours the arrow's shaft as a cow eats her after-birth. ‖ 2. Thou like a fleece contractest and expandest thee what time the upper stone and that below devour. | Closely compressing head with head and breast with breast he crunches up the tendrils with his yellow jaws. ‖ 3. The Eagles have sent forth their voice aloud to heaven: in the sky's vault the dark impetuous ones have danced. | When they come downward to repair the lower stone, they, dwellers with the Sun, have gained abundant seed.

Hymn 6:50.

1. Destroy the rat, the mole, the boring beetle, cut off their heads and crush their ribs, O Aśvins. | Bind fast their mouths; let them not eat our barley: so guard, ye twain, our growing corn from danger. ‖ 2. Ho! boring beetle, ho! thou worm, ho! noxious grub and grasshopper! | As a priest leaves the unfinished sacrifice, go hence devouring not, injuring not this corn. ‖ 3. Hearken to me, lord of the female borer, lord of the female grub! ye rough-toothed vermin! | Whate'er ye be, dwelling in woods, and piercing, we crush and mangle all those piercing insects.

Hymn 6:51.

1. Cleansed by the filter of the Wind comes Soma past all our enemies, meet friend of Indra. ‖ 2. May the maternal Waters make us ready: cleanse us with fatness they who cleanse with fatness! | The Goddesses bear off each blot and tarnish: I come forth from the waters cleansed and stainless. ‖ 3. O Varuṇa, whatever the offence may be, the sin which men commit against the heavenly folk— | When, through our want of thought we violate thy

laws, punish us not, O God, for that iniquity.

Hymn 6:52.

1. Slaying the Rākṣhasas, the Sun mounts upward in the front of heaven, | Āditya, from the mountains, seen of all, destroying things unseen. || 2. The kine had settled in their pen, wild animals sought their lairs | The wavelets of the brooks had passed away, and were beheld no more. || 3. I have brought Kaṇva's famous Plant, life-giving, and itself inspired, | The medicine that healeth all: may it suppress my hidden foes.

Hymn 6:53.

1. May Heaven and Earth, wise pair, may lofty Śukra grant me this thing by reason of the guerdon. | May Agni, Soma mark through this libation: may Vāyu, Savitar, and Bhaga guard us. || 2. Again return to us our breath and spirit, again come back to us our life and vision! | Vaiśvānara, unscathed, our bodies' guardian, stand between us and every woe and danger! || 3. We are again united with our bodies, with happy mind, with spirit, strength, and splendour. | May Tvaṣhṭar here make room for us, and freedom and smooth whate'er is injured in our bodies.

Hymn 6:54.

1. Win the love of Indra that his friend may reach yet higher state. | Increase, as rain the grass, this man's dominion and his lofty fame. || 2. Confirm the princely power in him, Agni and Soma! grant him wealth. | In all the circuit of his rule make him yet higher for your friend. || 3. The man who shows us enmity, whether a stranger or akin, | Thou wilt give up entire to me who sacrifice and press the juice.

Hymn 6:55.

1. Of all the many God-frequented pathways that traverse realms between the earth and heaven, | Consign me, all ye Gods to that which leadeth to perfect and inviolable safety. || 2. Maintain us in well-being Summer, Winter Dew-time and Spring, Autumn, and Rainy Season. | Give us our share of cattle and of Children. May we enjoy your unassailed protection. || 3. Pay to the Year your lofty adoration, to the first Year, the second, and the present. | Many we abide in the auspicious favour and gracious love of these who claim our worship.

Hymn 6:56.

1. Let not the serpent slay us, O Gods, with our children and our folk. | Let it not close the opened mouth nor open that which now is closed. || 2. Be worship paid unto the black, worship to that with stripes across! | To the brown viper reverence, reverence to the demon brood! || 3. I close together fangs with fang, I close together jaws with jaw. | I close together tongue with tongue, I close together mouth with mouth.

Hymn 6:57.

1. This is a medicine indeed, Rudra's own medicine is this, | Wherewith he warns the arrow off one-shafted, with a hundred tips. || 2. Besprinkle it with anodyne, bedew it with relieving balm: | Strong, soothing is the medicine: bless us therewith that we may live. || 3. Let it be health and joy to us. Let nothing vex or injure us. | Down with the wound! Let all to us be balm, the whole be medicine.

Hymn 6:58.

1. May Indra Maghavan give me name and glory. May Heaven and Earth, this couple, make me famous. | May Savitar the deity make me honoured. Here may the man who gives the guerdon love me. || 2. Indra from Heaven and Earth receiveth glory among the plants the Waters have their glory; | Even so may we be glorious amid all the Universal Gods. || 3. Indra and Agni were renowned, famous was Soma at his birth; | So too am I illustrious, most glorious of all that is.

Hymn 6:59.

1. First, O Arundhatī, protect our oxen and milky kine: | Protect each one that is infirm, each quadruped that yields no milk. || 2. Let the Plant give us sheltering aid, Arundhatī allied with Gods; | Avert Consumption from our men and make our cow-pen rich in milk. || 3. I welcome the auspicious Plant, life-giving, wearing every hue. | Far from our cattle may it turn the deadly dart which Rudra casts.

Hymn 6:60.

1. With forelock loosened o'er his brow here comes the wooer of the bride, | Seeking a husband for this maid, a wife for this unmarried man. || 2. Wooer! this girl hath toiled in vain, going to others' marriages. | Now to her wedding, verily, wooer! another maid shall come. || 3. Dhātar upholds the spacious earth, upholds the sky, upholds the Sun. | Dhātar bestow upon this maid a husband suited to her wish!

Hymn 6:61.

1. The Waters send me what is sweet and pleasant, Sūra bring all I need for light and vision! | The deities, and all of pious nature, and Savitar the God afford me freedom! || 2. I set the heaven and the earth asunder, I brought all seven seasons into being. | My word is truth, what I deny is falsehood, above celestial Vāk, above the nations. || 3. I gave existence to the earth and heaven, I made the seasons and the seven rivers. | My word is truth; what I deny is falsehood, I who rejoice in Agni's, Soma's friendship.

Hymn 6:62.

1. Cleanse us Vaiśvānara with rays of splendour! With breath and clouds let quickening Vāyu cleanse us. | And, rich in milky rain, let Earth and Heaven, worshipful, holy, cleanse us with their water. || 2. Lay hold on Sūnṛitā whose forms and regions have fair smooth backs, her who is all men's treasure. | Through her may we, in sacrificial banquets singing her glory, be the lords of riches. || 3. For splendour, seize on her whom all men worship, becoming pure yourselves, and bright, and brilliant. | Here, through our prayer rejoicing in the banquet, long may we look upon the Sun ascending.

Hymn 6:63.

1. That collar round thy neck, not to be loosened, which Nirṛiti the Goddess bound and fastened, | I loose for thy long life and strength and vigour. Eat, liberated, food that brings no sorrow. || 2. To thee, sharp-pointed Nirṛiti, be homage! Loose thou the binding fetters wrought of iron. | To me, in truth, again doth Yama give thee. To him, to Yama, yea, to Death, be homage! || 3. Compassed by death which comes in thousand manners, here art thou fastened to the iron pillar. | Unanimous with Yama and the Fathers, make this man rise and reach the loftiest heaven. || 4. Thou, mighty Agni, good and true, gatherest up all precious things. | Bring us all treasures as thou art enkindled at libation's place.

Hymn 6:64.

1. Agree and be united: let your minds be all of one accord, | Even as the Gods of ancient days, unanimous, await their share. || 2. The rede is common, common the assembly, common the law, so be their thoughts united. | I offer up your general oblation: together entertain one common purpose. || 3. One and the same be your resolve, be all your hearts in harmony: | One and the same be all your minds that all may happily consent.

Hymn 6:65.

1. The angry spirit hath relaxed: loose are the arms that act with mind. | Do thou, destroyer, overcome and drive these foemen's might away, and then bring opulence to us. || 2. The shaft for handless fiends which, Gods! ye cast against the handless ones,— | With this, in shape of sacrifice, I rend the arms of enemies. || 3. Indra made first for Asuras the shaft designed for handless foes: | Victorious shall my heroes be with Indra as their constant friend.

Hymn 6:66.

1. Handless be every foeman who assaileth, they who with missiles come to fight against us! | Dash them together with great slaughter, Indra! and let their robber chief run pierced with arrows. || 2. Ye who run hither bending bows, brandishing swords and casting darts. | Handless be ye, O enemies! Let Indra mangle you to-day. || 3. Handless be these our enemies! We enervate their languid limbs. | So let us part among ourselves, in hundreds, Indra! all their wealth.

Hymn 6:67.

1. Indra and Pūṣhan have gone forth along the ways on every side. | Today those hosts of enemies must flee bewildered far away. || 2. Ye foes, come hitherward dismayed like serpents when their heads are gone. | Let Indra slay each bravest one of you whom Agni hath confused. || 3. Gird thou a bullock's hide on these, make those as timid as the deer. | Let the foe flee away, and let his kine come hitherward to us.

Hymn 6:68.

1. Savitar hath come hither with the razor: come thou, O Vāyu, with the heated water. | One-minded let Ādityas, Rudras, Vasus moisten the hair:

shave ye who know King Soma. || 2. Let Aditi shave the beard, and let the Waters bathe it with their strength: | Prajāpati restore his health for sight and days of lengthened life! || 3. The razor used by Savitar, for shaving, who knoweth Varuṇa and royal Soma,— | Even with this shave ye this man, O Brahman. Let him be rich in horses, kine, and children.

Hymn 6:69.

1. Mine be the glory in the hill, in vales, in cattle, and in gold, | Mine be the sweetness that is found in nectar and in flowing wine! || 2. With your delicious honey balm me, Aśvins, Lords of splendid light! | That clear and resonant may be the voice I utter to mankind. || 3. In me be strength, in me be fame, in me the power of sacrifice: | Prajāpati establish this in me as firm as light in heaven!

Hymn 6:70.

1. As wine associates with flesh, as dice attend the gaming-board, | As an enamoured man's desire is firmly set upon a dame, So let thy heart and soul, O Cow, be firmly set upon thy calf. || 2. As the male elephant pursues with eager step his female's track, | As an enamoured man's desire is firmly set upon a dame, So let thy heart and soul, O Cow, be firmly set upon the calf. || 3. Close as the felly and the spoke, fixt as the wheel-rim on the nave, | As an enamoured man's desire is firmly set upon a dame, | So let thy heart and soul, O Cow, be firmly set upon thy calf.

Hymn 6:71.

1. What food I eat of varied form and nature, food whether gold, or horse, sheep, goat, or bullock, | Whatever gift I have received, may Agni the Hotar make it sacrifice well-offered. || 2. Whatever, sacrificed or not, hath reached me, bestowed by men and sanctioned by the Fathers, | Whereby my heart seems to leap up, may Agni the Hotar make that sacrifice well-offered. || 3. What food I eat unjustly, Gods! or, doubtful between bestowing and refusing, swallow, | Through greatness of Vaiśvānara the mighty may that same food be sweet to me and blessed!

Hymn 6:72.

1. Sicut anguis niger ad voluntatem se extendit, Asurarum arte magica formas novas efficiens, sic fascinum tuum, partem cum parte, conjunctum, hic hymnus efficiat. || 2. Velut penis (tayadarus quem ventus permagnum fecit, quantus. est onagri penis, tantus penis tuus increscat. || 3. Quantum estonagri membrum masculinum, elephanti, asinique, quantum est fortis equi, tantus penis tuus increscat.

Hymn 6:73.

1. Let Varuṇa come hither, Soma, Agni, Bṛihaspati come hither with the Vasus! | Unanimous, ye kinsmen, come united, come to the glory of this mighty guardian. || 2. The inclination which your hearts have harboured, the purpose which hath occupied your spirits, | This I annul with sacrifice and butter. In me be your sweet resting-place, O kinsmen. || 3. Stand even here; forsake me not. Before us may Pūṣhan make your path unfit to travel. | Vāstoṣhpati incessantly recall you! In me be your sweet resting-place, O kinsmen!

Hymn 6:74.

1. Close gathered be your bodies: be your minds and vows in unison! | Here present Brahmaṇaspati and Bhaga have assembled you. || 2. Let there be union of your minds, let there be union of your hearts: | All that is troubled in your lot with this I mend and harmonize. || 3. As, free from jealousy, the strong Ādityas have been the Vasus' and the Rudras' fellows. | So free from jealousy, Lord of Three Titles! cause thou these people here to be one-minded.

Hymn 6:75.

1. Forth from his dwelling drive that man, the foeman who assaileth us: | Through the Expellent sacrifice hath Indra rent and mangled him. || 2. Indra, Foe-Slayer, drive him forth into the distance most remote, | Whence never more shall be return in all the years that are to come. || 3. To the three distances, beyond mankind's Five Races, let him go, | Beyond the three skies let him go, whence he shall never come again | In all the years that are to be, long as the Sun is in the heaven.

Hymn 6:76.

1. Those who are sitting round this babe prepare him to be looked upon. | Let Agni thoroughly inflamed with all his tongues rise from his heart. || 2. For length of life I use the name of Agni the Consuming God, | Whose smoke the sage who knows the truth beholds proceeding. from his mouth. || 3. The man who knows his fuel laid in order by the Kṣhatriya | Sets not his foot upon the steep declivity that leads to Death. || 4. Those who encompass slay him not: he goes not near his lurking foes— | The Kṣhatriya who, knowing well, takes Agni's name for length of life.

Hymn 6:77.

1. Firm stands the heaven, firm stands the earth, firm stands this universal world, | Firm stand the rooted mountains. I have put the horses in the stall. || 2. I call the Herdsman, him who knows the way to drive the cattle forth, | Who knows the way to drive them home, to drive them back and drive them in. || 3. O Jātavedas turn them back: a hundred homeward ways be thine! | Thou hast a thousand avenues: by these restore our kine to us.

Hymn 6:78.

1. Let this man be again bedewed with this presented sacrifice. | And comfort with the sap of life the bride whom they have brought to him. || 2. With life's sap let him comfort her, and raise her high with princely sway. | In wealth that hath a thousand powers, this pair be inexhaustible! || 3. Tvaṣhṭar formed her to be thy dame, Tvaṣhṭar made thee to be her lord. | Long life let Tvaṣhṭar give you both. Let Tvaṣhṭar give a thousand lives.

Hymn 6:79.

1. May this our Lord of Cloudy Sky, bedewed with liquid drops preserve unequalled riches in our homes. || 2. Lord of the Cloudy Sky, bestow vigour and strength on our abodes. Let wealth and treasure come to us. || 3. Thou, God bedewed with drops, art Lord of infinite prosperity. | Grant us thereof, give us thereof: may we enjoy this boon of thine.

Hymn 6:80.

1. He flieth in the firmament observing all the things that be: | We with this offering will adore the greatness of the Heavenly Hound. || 2. The three, the Kālakāñjas, set aloft in heaven as they were Gods— | All these I call to be our help and keep this man secure from harm. || 3. In waters is thy birth, in heaven thy station, thy majesty on earth and in the ocean. | We with this offering will adore the greatness of the Heavenly Hound.

Hymn 6:81.

1. Thou art a grasper, holding fast both hands: drivest fiends away. | A holder both of progeny and riches hath this Ring become. || 2. Prepare accordantly, O Ring, the mother for the infant's birth. | On the right way bring forth the boy. Make him come hither. I am here. || 3. The Amulet which Aditi wore when desirous of a son, | Tvaṣhṭar hath bound upon this dame and said, Be mother of a boy.

Hymn 6:82.

1. I call the name of him who comes, hath come, and still draws nigh to us. | Foe-slaying Indra's name I love, the Vasus' friend with hundred powers. || 2. Thus Bhaga spake to me: Let him bring thee a consort by the path. | Whereon the Aśvins brought the bride Sūryā the child of Savitar. || 3. Great, Indra. is that hook of thine, bestowing treasure, wrought of gold: | Therewith, O Lord of Might, bestow a wife on me who long to wed.

Hymn 6:83.

1. Hence, Sores and Pustules, fly away even as the eagle from his home. | Let Sūrya bring a remedy, the Moon shine forth and banish you. || 2. One bright with variegated tints, one white, one black, a couple red:— | The names of all have I declared. Begone, and injure not our men. || 3. Hence, childless, shall the Pustule flee, grand-daughter of the dusky one. | The Boil shall fly away from us, the morbid growth shall vanish hence. | Taste, happy in thy mind, thine own oblation, as I with Svāhā with my heart present it.

Hymn 6:84.

1. Thou in whose dread mouth I present oblation, that these bound victims may obtain their freedom, | The people deem that thou art Earth: I know thee thoroughly, and I say thou art Destruction. || 2. Be thou enriched, O Welfare, with oblations, here among us is thine allotted portion. | Free—Hail to thee!—from sin those here and yonder. || 3. Do thou, Destruction, thus, without a rival, release us from the iron bonds that hind us. | To me doth Yama verily restore thee. To him, to Yama, yea, to Death be worship! || 4. Thou hast been fastened to an iron pillar, here compassed with a thousand deaths around thee. | In full accord with Yama and the Fathers, send this man upward to the loftiest heaven.

Hymn 6:85.

1. Let Varaṇa the heavenly tree here present keep disease away. The Gods have driven off Decline that entered and possessed this man. || 2. We with the speech of Indra and of Mitra and of Varuṇa. | We with the speech of all the Gods will drive Decline away from thee. || 3. Even as Vṛitra checked and stayed these waters flowing every way, | With Agni, God of all mankind. I check and banish thy Decline.

Hymn 6:86.

1. This is the Lord of Indra, this the Lord of Heaven, the Lord of Earth, | The Lord of all existing things: the one and only Lord be thou, || 2. The Sea is regent of the floods, Agni is ruler of the land, | The Moon is regent of the stars: the one and only Lord be thou. || 3. Thou art the King of Asuras, the crown and summit of mankind: | Thou art the partner of the Gods: the one and only Lord be thou.

Hymn 6:87.

1. Here art thou: I have chosen thee. Stand steadfast and immovable. | Let all the clans desire thee: let not thy kingdom fall away. || 2. Be even here: fall not away: be like a mountain unremoved. | Stand steadfast here like Indra's self, and hold the kingship in the grasp. || 3. This man hath Indra established, made secure by constant sacrifice. Soma, and Brahmaṇaspati here present bless and comfort him!

Hymn 6:88.

1. Firm is the sky, firm is the earth, and firm is all this living world; | Firm are these mountains on their base, and steadfast is this King of men. || 2. Steadfast may Varuṇa the King, steadfast the God Bṛihaspati, | Steadfast may Indra steadfast, too, may Agni keep thy steadfast reign. || 3. Firm, never to be shaken, crush thy foemen, under thy feet lay those who strive against thee. | One-minded, true to thee be all the regions: faithful to thee, the firm, be this assembly!

Hymn 6:89.

1. This strength that Soma hath bestowed, the head of her who gladdeneth,— | With that which thence hath been produced we make thy spirit sorrowful. || 2. We make thy spirit sorrowful, we fill thy mind with pain and grief. | As smoke accompanies the wind, so let thy fancy follow me. || 3. May Varuṇa and Mitra, may Sarasvatī the Goddess, may | The centre of the earth, and both her limits bring thee close to me.

Hymn 6:90.

1. The shaft that Rudra hath shot forth against thy members and thy heart, | Here do we draw from thee to-day, and turn it hence to every side. || 2. From all the hundred vessels spread throughout the members of thy frame. | From all those vessels and canals we call the poisonous matter forth. || 3. Worship to thee, the archer, and O Rudra, to thy levelled shaft! | Yea, worship to thine arrow when it left the bow, and when it fell!

Hymn 6:91.

1. They made this barley ready with a team of eight, a team of six. | With this I drive to westward, far away, thy bodily disease. || 2. Vita breathes downward from above, and downward Sūrya sends his heat: | Downward is drawn the milch-cow's milk: so downward go thy malady! || 3. The Waters verily bring health, the Waters drive disease away. | The Waters cure all malady: may they bring medicine for thee.

Hymn 6:92.

1. Be fleet as wind, Strong Steed, when thou art harnessed; go forth as swift as thought at Indra's sending. | Let the possessors of all wealth, the Marutas, yoke thee, and Tvaṣhṭar in thy feet lay swiftness. || 2. That speed, that lies concealed in thee, O Charger, speed granted to the hawk or wind that wandered,— | Therewith, Strong Steed, saving in shock of battle endowed with might by might win thou the contest. || 3. Bearing thy body, Charger, may thy body run blessing us and winning thee protection. | May he, unswerving, to uphold the mighty, stablish his lustre as a God in heaven.

Hymn 6:93.

1. Yama, Death direly fatal, the Destroyer, with his black crest, Śarva the tawny archer, | And all the Gods uprisen with their army, may these on every side avoid our heroes. || 2. With mind, burnt offerings, butter, and libation, to royal Bhava and the archer Śarva, | To these the worshipful I pay my worship: may they turn elsewhere things with deadly venom. || 3. Save us, All-Gods and all-possessing Marutas, from murderous stroke and things that slay with poison. | Pure is the might of Varuṇa, Agni, Soma. May Vāta's and Parjanya's favour bless us.

Hymn 6:94.

1. We bend your minds in union, bend in harmony your hopes and plans: | You there, who turn to sundered ways, we bend and bow in unison. || 2. I with my spirit make your spirits captive: these with their thoughts follow my thought and wishes. | I make your hearts submissive to mine order closely attending go where I precede you. || 3. I have invoked both Heaven and Earth, invoked divine Sarasvatī, | Indra and Agni have I called: Sarasvatī, so may we thrive!

Hymn 6:95.

1. In the third heaven above us stands the Aśvattha tree, the seat of Gods. | There the Gods gained the Kuṣhṭha plant, embodiment of endless life. || 2. There moved through heaven a golden ship, a ship with cordage wrought of gold. | There Gods obtained the Kuṣhṭha plant, the flower of immortality. || 3. Thou art the infant of the plants, the infant of the Snowy Hills: | The germ of every thing that is: free this my friend from his disease.

Hymn 6:96.

1. The many plants of hundred shapes and forms that Soma rules as King, | Commanded by Bṛihaspati, deliver us from grief and woe! || 2. Let them release me from the curse and from the noose of Varuṇa, | Free me from Yama's fetter, and from every sin against the Gods! || 3. From every fault in look, in word, in spirit that we, awake or sleeping, have committed, | May Soma, with his godlike nature, cleanse us.

Hymn 6:97.

1. The sacrifice is victor, Agni victor, victorious is Soma, Indra conquers: | So will we bring oblation unto Agni, this sacrifice that I may win all battles. || 9. Praise to you, Mitra-Varuṇa, hymn-singers! Here swell with meath dominion blest with children. | Far into distant regions drive Destruction, and even from committed sin absolve us. || 3. In this strong hero be ye glad and joyful: cleave ye to him even as ye cleave to Indra. | Victorious, kine-winner, thunder-wielder, who quells a host and with his might destroys it.

Hymn 6:98.

1. Indra be victor, never to be vanquished, to reign among the Kings as sovereign ruler! | Here be thou meet for praise and supplication, to be revered and waited on and worshipped. || 2. Thou fain for glory, an imperial ruler, hast won dominion over men, O Indra, | Of these celestial tribes be thou the sovereign: long-lasting be thy sway and undecaying! || 3. Thou governest the north and eastern regions, Indra! fiendslayer! thou destroyest foemen. | Thou hast won all, far as the rivers wander. Bull, called to help, on our right hand thou goest.

Hymn 6:99.

1. Indra, before affliction comes, I call thee from the wide expanse. | The mighty guardian, born alone, wearer of many names, I call. || 2. Whatever deadly missile launched today flies forth to slaughter us. | We take both arms of Indra to encompass us on every side. || 3. We draw about us both the arms of Indra, our deliverer. May they protect us thoroughly. | O Savitar, thou God, O royal Soma, make thou me pious-minded for my welfare.

Hymn 6:100.

1. The Gods and Sūrya gave the gift, the Earth and Heaven bestowed the boon. | The three Sarasvatīs in full accord bestowed the antidote. || 2. That water, Upajīkās! which Gods poured for you on thirsty land, | With that same water sent by Gods, drive ye away this poison here. || 3. The daughter of the Asuras art thou, and sister of the Gods. | Thou who hast sprung from heaven and earth hast robbed the poison of its power.

Hymn 6:101.

1. Taurum age, palpita, incresce et teipsum extende: per totum membrum increscat penis: hoc tu caede feminam. || 2. Quo debilem stimulant, quo aegrum excitant (homines), hoc, O Brahmanaspatis, hujus penem in arcus modum extende. || 3. Velut nervum in arcu ego tuum fascinum extendo. Aggredere (mulierem) semper indefessus velut cervus damam.

Hymn 6:102.

1. Even as this ox, O Aśvins, steps and turns together with his mate, | So let thy fancy turn itself, come nearer, and unite with me. || 2. I, as the shaft-

horse draws the mare beside him, draw thee to myself. | Like grass that storm and wind have rent, so be thy mind attached to me! || 3. Swiftly from Bhaga's hands I bear away a love-compelling charm | Of ointment and of sugar-cane, of Spikenard and the Kuṣhṭha plant.

Hymn 6:103.

1. Bṛihaspati and Savitar prepare a rope to bind you fast! | Let Bhaga, Mitra, Aryaman, and both the Aśvins make the bond. || 2. I bind together all of them, the first, the last, the middlemost. | Indra hath girded these with cord: bind them together, Agni, thou! || 3. Those yonder who approach to fight, with banners raised along their ranks, | Indra hath girded these with cord: bind them together, Agni, thou!

Hymn 6:104.

1. We bind our foemen with a bond that binds them close and holds them fast. | Their breath and respiration I dissever, and their lives from life. || 2. This bond, made keen by Indra, I have formed with heat of holy zeal. | Securely bind our enemies, O Agni, who are standing here. || 3. Indra and Agni bind them fast, Soma the King, and both the Friends! | May Indra, girt by Marutas, make a bond to bind our enemies.

Hymn 6:105.

1. Rapidly as the fancy flies forth with conceptions of the mind. | So following the fancy's flight, O Cough, flee rapidly away. || 2. Rapidly as an arrow flies away with keenly-sharpened point, | So swiftly flee away, O Cough, over the region of the earth! || 3. Rapidly as the beams of light, the rays of Sūrya, fly away, | So, Cough! fly rapidly away over the current of the sea!

Hymn 6:106.

1. Let flowery Dūrvā grass grow up about thine exit and approach. | There let a spring of water rise, or lake with blooming lotuses. || 2. This is the place where waters meet, here is the gathering of the flood. | Our home is set amid the lake: turn thou thy jaws away from it. || 3. O House, we compass thee about with coolness to envelop thee. | Cool as a lake be thou to us. Let Agni bring us healing balm!

Hymn 6:107.

1. Entrust me, Viśvajit, to Trāyamāṇā. | Guard, Trāyamāṇā, all our men, guard all our wealth of quadrupeds. || 2. To Viśvajit entrust me, Trāyamāṇā. | O Viśvajit, guard all our men, etc. || 3. To Viśvajit entrust me, O Kalyāṇī. | Guard, O Kalyāṇī, all our men, etc. || 4. To Sarvavid entrust me, O Kalyāṇī. | O Sarvavid, guard all our men, guard all our wealth of quadrupeds.

Hymn 6:108.

1. Intelligence, come first to us with store of horses and of kine! | Thou with the rays of Sūrya art our worshipful and holy one. || 2. The first, devout Intelligence, lauded by sages, sped by prayer, | Trusted by Brahmachārīs, for the favour of the Gods I call. || 3. That excellent Intelligence which Ṛibhus know, and Asuras, | Intelligence which sages know, we cause to enter into me. || 4. Do thou, O Agni, make me wise this day with that Intelligence. | Which the creative Ṛishis, which the men endowed with wisdom knew. || 5. Intelligence at eve, at morn, Intelligence at noon of day, | With the Sun's beams, and by our speech we plant in us Intelligence.

Hymn 6:109.

1. The Berry heals the missile's rent, it heals the deeply-piercing wound. | The Gods prepared and fashioned it. This hath sufficient power for life. || 2. When from their origin they came, the Berries spake among themselves: | The man whom we shall find alive shall never suffer injury. || 3. Asuras buried thee in earth: the Gods again uplifted thee. | Healer of sickness caused by wounds and healer of the missile's rent.

Hymn 6:110.

1. Yea, ancient, meet for praise at sacrifices, ever and now thou sittest down as Hotar. | And now, O Agni, make thy person friendly, and win felicity for us by worship. || 2. Neath Jyeṣhṭhaghnī and Yama's Two Releasers this child was born: preserve him from uprooting. | He shall conduct him safe past all misfortunes to lengthened life that lasts a hundred autumns. || 3. Born on the Tiger's day was he, a hero, the Constellations' child, born brave and manly. | Let him not wound, when grown in strength, his father, nor disregard his mother, her who bare him.

Hymn 6:111.

1. Unbind and loose for me this man, O Agni, who bound and well restrained is chattering folly. | Afterward he will offer thee thy portion when he hath been delivered from his madness. || 2. Let Agni gently soothe thy mind when fierce excitement troubles it. | Well-skilled I make a medicine that thou no larger mayst be mad. || 3. Insane through sin against the Gods, or maddened by a demon's power— | Well-skilled I make a medicine to free thee from insanity. || 4. May the Apsarases release, Indra and Bhaga let thee go. May all the Gods deliver thee that thou no longer mayst be mad.

Hymn 6:112.

1. Let not this one, O Agni, wound the highest of these: preserve thou him from utter ruin. | Knowing the way do thou untie the nooses of the she-fiend: let all the Gods approve thee. || 2. Rend thou the; bonds of these asunder, Agni! the, threefold noose whereby the three were fastened. | Knowing the way untie the she-fiend's nooses: free all, the son, the father, and the mother. || 3. The elder brother's bonds, still left unwedded, fettered in every limb and bound securely, | Loose these, for they are bonds for loosing: Pūṣhan, turn woes away upon the babe-destroyer.

Hymn 6:113.

1. This sin the Gods wiped off and laid on Trita, and Trita wiped it off on human beings. | Thence if the female fiend hath made thee captive, the Gods by prayer shall banish her and free thee. || 2. Enter the particles of light and vapours, go to the rising fogs or mists, O Evil! | Hence! vanish in the foams of rivers. Pūṣhan, wipe woes away upon the babe-destroyer! || 3. Stored in twelve separate places lies what Trita hath wiped away, the sins of human beings. | Thence if the female fiend hath made thee captive, the Gods by prayer shall banish her and free thee.

Hymn 6:114.

1. Whatever God-provoking wrong we priests have done, O Deities. | Therefrom do ye deliver us, Ādityas! by the right of Law. || 2. Here set us free, O holy ones, Ādityas, by the right of Law. | When striving, bringing sacrifice, we failed to offer it aright. || 3. With ladle full of fatness we, worshippers, pouring holy oil, | Striving, have failed, O all ye Gods, against our will, to offer it.

Hymn 6:115.

1. Whatever wrong we wittingly or in our ignorance have done, | Do ye deliver us therefrom, O all ye Gods, of one accord. || 2. If I, a sinner, when awake or sleeping have committed sin, | Free me therefrom as from a stake, from present and from future guilt. || 3. As one unfastened from a stake, or cleansed by bathing after toil, | As butter which the sieve hath cleansed, so all shall purge me from the sin.

Hymn 6:116.

1. The wealth which husbandmen aforetime, digging, like men who find their food with knowledge, buried, | This to the King, Vivasvat's son, I offer, Sweet be our food and fit for sacrificing! || 2. May he, Vaivasvata, prepare our portion; May he whose share is mead with mead besprinkle. | Our sin in hasty mood against our mother, or guilt whereby a sire is wronged and angered. || 3. Whether this sin into our heart hath entered regarding mother, father, son or brother, | Auspicious be to us the zeal and spirit of all the fathers who are here among us.

Hymn 6:117.

1. That which I eat, a debt which still is owing, the tribute due to Yama, which supports me, | Thereby may I be free from debt, O Agni. Thou knowest how to rend all bonds asunder. || 2. Still dwelling here we give again this present; we send it forth, the living from the living. | Throwing away the grain whence I have eaten, thereby shall I be free from debt, O Agni. || 3. May we be free in this world and that yonder, in the third world may we be unindebted. | May we, debt-free, abide in all the pathways, in all the worlds which Gods and Fathers visit.

Hymn 6:118.

1. If we have sinned with both our hands, desiring to take the host of dice for our possession, | May both Apsarases today forgive us that debt, the fiercely-conquering, fiercely-looking. || 2. Stern viewers of their sins who rule the people, forgive us what hash happened as we gambled. | Not urging us to pay the debt we owed him, he with a cord hath gone to Yama's kingdom. || 3. My creditor, the man whose wife I visit, he, Gods! whom I approach with supplication, | Let not these men dominate me in speaking.

Mind this, ye two Apsarases, Gods' Consorts!

Hymn 6:119.

1. The debt which I incur, not gaming, Agni! and, not intending to repay, acknowledge, | That may Vaiśvānara, the best, our sovereign, carry away into the world of virtue. || 2. I cause Vaiśvānara to know, confessing the debt whose payment to the Gods is promised. | He knows to tear asunder all these nooses: so may we dwell with him the gentle-minded. || 3. Vaiśvānara the Purifier purge me when I oppose their hope and break my promise, | Unknowing in my heart. With supplication, whatever guilt there is in that, I banish.

Hymn 6:120.

1. If we have injured Air, or Earth, or Heaven, if we have wronged our Mother or our Father, | May Agni Gārhapatya here absolve us, and bear us up into the world of virtue. || 2. Earth is our Mother, Aditi our birth-place: our brother Air save us from imprecation! | Dyaus, Father, save us, from the world of Fathers! My world not lost, may I approach my kindred. || 3. There where our virtuous friends, who left behind them their bodily infirmities, are happy, | Free from distortion of the limbs and lameness, may we behold, in heaven, our sons and parents.

Hymn 6:121.

1. Spreading them out, untie the snares that hold us, Varuṇa's bonds, the upper and the lower. | Drive from us evil dream, drive off misfortune; then let us go into the world of virtue. || 2. If thou art bound with cord or tied to timber, fixt in the earth, or by a word imprisoned, | Our Agni Gārhapatya here shall free thee, and lead thee up into the world of virtue. || 3. The two auspicious stars whose name is called Releasers have gone up. Send Amṛita hither, let it come freeing the captive from his bonds! || 4. Open thyself, make room: from bonds thou shalt release the prisoner. | Freed, like an infant newly born, dwell in all pathways where thou wilt.

Hymn 6:122.

1. This portion I who understand deliver to Viśvakarman first-born son of Order. | So may we follow to the end, unbroken, beyond old age, the thread which we have given. || 2. This long-drawn thread some follow who have offered in ordered course oblation to the Fathers: | Some, offering and giving to the friendless, if they can give: herein they find their heaven. || 3., Stand on my side and range yourselves in order, ye two! The faithful reach this world of Svarga. | When your dressed food hath been bestowed on Agni, to guard it, wife and husband, come together! || 4. Dwelling with zeal I mount in spirit after the lofty sacrifice as it departeth. | Agni, may we, beyond decay, invited, in the third heaven, feast and enjoy the banquet. || 5. These women here, cleansed, purified, and holy, I place at rest singly, in hands of Brahmans. | May Indra, Marut-girt, grant me the blessing I long for as I pour you this libation.

Hymn 6:123.

1. Ye who are present, unto you I offer this treasure brought to us by Jātavedas. | Happily will the sacrificer follow: do ye acknowledge him in highest heaven. || 2. Do ye acknowledge him in highest heaven: ye know the world here present in assembly. | In peace will he who sacrifices follow: show him the joy which comes from pious actions. || 3. Gods are the Fathers, and the Fathers Gods. I am the very man I am. || 4. I cook, I give, I offer up oblation. From what I gave let me not be disparted. || 5. O King, take thou thy stand in heaven, there also let that gift be placed. | Recognize, King, the gift which we have given, and be gracious, God!

Hymn 6:124.

1. From the high firmament, yea, out of heaven a water-drop with dew on me hath fallen. | I, Agni! share the merit of the pious, with vigour, milk, and hymns and sacrifices. || 2. If from a tree that fruit hath fallen downward if, aught from air that is Vāyu. | Where it hath touched my body or my garment, thence may the Waters drive Destruction backward. || 3. It is a fragrant ointment, happy fortune, sheen all of gold, yea, purified from blemish. | Spread over us are all purifications. Death and Malignity shall not subdue us.

Hymn 6:125.

1. Mayst thou, O Tree, be firm indeed in body, our friend that furthers us, a goodly hero. | Put forth thy strength, compact with thongs of leather, and let thy rider win all spoils of battle. || 2. Its mighty strength was borrowed from the heaven and earth: its conquering force was brought from sovereigns of the wood. | Honour with sacrifice the Car like Indra's bolt, the Car girt round with straps, the vigour of the floods. || 3. Thou bolt of Indra, vanguard of the Marutas, close knit to Varuṇa and child of Mitra, | As such, accepting gifts which here we offer, receive, O godlike Chariot, these oblations.

Hymn 6:126.

1. Send forth thy voice aloud through earth and heaven, and let the world in all its breadth regard thee. | O Drum, accordant with the Gods and Indra, drive thou afar, yea, very far, our foemen. || 2. Thunder out strength and fill us full of vigour, yea, thunder forth and drive away misfortunes. | Drive hence, O Drum, drive thou away mischances. Thou art the fist of Indra, show thy firmness. || 3. Conquer those yonder and let these be victors. Let the Drum speak aloud as battle's signal. | Let our men, winged with horses, fly together. Let our car-warriors, Indra! be triumphant.

Hymn 6:127.

1. Of abscess, of decline, of inflammation of the eyes. O Plant, | Of penetrating pain, thou Herb, let not a particle remain. || 2. Those nerves of thine, Consumption! which stand closely hidden in thy groin— | I know the balm for that disease: the magic cure is Chīpudru. || 3. We draw from thee piercing pain that penetrates and racks thy limbs, | That pierces ears, that pierces eyes, the abscess, and the heart's disease. | Downward and far away from thee we banish that unknown. decline.

Hymn 6:128.

1. What time the heavenly bodies chose the Weather Prophet as their King, | They brought him favouring weather, and, Let this be his domain, they said. || 2. May we have weather fair at noon, May we have weather fair at eve, | Fair weather when the morning breaks, fair weather when the night is come. || 3. Fair weather to the day and night, and to the stars and sun and moon. | Give favourable weather thou, King, Weather Prophet, unto us. || 4. Be worship ever paid to thee, O Weather Prophet, King of Star s, | Who gavest us good weather in the evening and by night and day!

Hymn 6:129.

1. With fortune of the Sisu tree—with Indra as my friend to aid— | I give myself a happy fate. Fly and begone, Malignities! || 2. That splendour and felicity wherewith thou hast excelled the trees— | Give me therewith a happy fate. Fly and begone, Malignities || 3. Blind fortune, with reverted leaves that is deposited in trees— | Give me therewith a happy fate. Fly and begone, Malignities.

Hymn 6:130.

1. This is the Apsarases' love-spell, the conquering, resistless ones'. | Send the spell forth, ye Deities! Let him consume with love of me. || 2. I pray, may he remember me, think of me, loving and beloved. | Send forth the spell, ye Deities! Let him consume with love of me. || 3. That he may think of me, that I may never, never think of him, | Send forth the spell, ye Deities! Let him consume with love of me. || 4. Madden him, Marutas, madden him. Madden him, madden him, O Air. | Madden him, Agni, madden him. Let him consume with love of me.

Hymn 6:131.

1. Down upon thee, from head to foot, I draw the pangs of longing love. | Send forth the charm, ye Deities! Let him consume with love of me. || 2. Assent to this, O Heavenly Grace! Celestial Purpose, guide it well! | Send forth the charm, ye Deities! Let him consume with love of me. || 3. If thou shouldst run three leagues away, five leagues, a horse's daily stage, | Thence thou shalt come to me again and be the father of our sons.

Hymn 6:132.

1. The Philter, burning with the pangs of yearning love, which Gods have poured within the bosom of the floods, | That spell for thee I heat by Varuṇa's decree. || 2. The charm which, burning with the pangs of love, the General Gods have poured within the bosom of the floods, | That spell for thee I heat by Varuṇa's decree. || 3. The Philter, burning with the pangs of longing, which Indrāṇī hath effused within the waters' depth, That spell for thee I heat by Varuṇa's decree. || 4. The charm, aglow with longing, which Indra and Agni have effused within the bosom of the floods, | That spell for thee I heat by Varuṇa's decree. || 5. The charm aglow with longing which Mitra and Varuṇa have poured within the bosom of the floods, |

That spell for thee I heat by Varuṇa's decree.

Hymn 6:133.

1. By the direction of that God we journey, he will seek means to save and he will free us; | The God who hath engirt us with this Girdle, he who hath fastened it, and made us ready. || 2. Thou, weapon of the Ṛishis, art adored and served with sacrifice. | First tasting of the votive milk, Zone, be a hero-slayer thou! || 3. As I am now Death's Brahmachārī claiming out of the living world a man for Yama, | So with Austerity and Prayer and Fervour I bind this Girdle round the man before me. || 4. She hath become, Faith's daughter, sprung from Fervour, the sister of the world-creating Ṛishis; | As such, O Girdle, give us thought and wisdom, give us religious zeal and mental vigour. || 5. Thou whom primeval Ṛishis girt about them, they who made the world, | As such do thou encircle me, O Girdle, for long days of life.

Hymn 6:134.

1. This Thunderbolt shall take its fill of Order, scare life away and overthrow the kingdom. | Tear necks in pieces, rend napes asunder, even as the Lord of Might the neck of Vṛitra. || 2. Down, down beneath the conquerors, let him not rise, concealed in earth, but lie down-smitten with the bolt. || 3. Seek out the fierce oppressor, yea, strike only the oppressor dead. | Down on the fierce oppressor's head strike at full length, O Thunderbolt!

Hymn 6:135.

1. Whate'er I eat I turn to strength, and thus I grasp the Thunder-bolt, | Rending the shoulders of that man as Indra shattered Vṛitra's neck. || 2. I drink together what I drink, even as the sea that swallows all. | Drinking the life-breath of that man, we drink that man and swallow him. || 3. Whate'er I eat I swallow up, even as the sea that swallows all. | Swallowing that man's vital breath, we swallow him completely up.

Hymn 6:136.

1. Born from the bosom of wide Earth the Goddess, godlike Plant, art thou: | So we, Nitatnī! dig thee up to strengthen and fix fast the hair. || 2. Make the old firm, make new hair spring, lengthen what has already grown. || 3. Thy hair where it is falling off, and with the roots is torn away, | I wet and sprinkle with the Plant, the remedy for all disease.

Hymn 6:137.

1. The Plant which Jamadagni dug to make his daughter's locks. grow long, | This same hath Vītahavya brought to us from Asita's abode. || 2. They might be measured with a rein, meted with both extended arms. | Let the black locks spring thick and strong and grow like reeds upon thy head. || 3. Strengthen the roots, prolong the points, lengthen the middle part, O Plant. | Let the black locks spring thick and strong and grow like reeds upon thy head.

Hymn 6:138.

1. O Plant, thy fame is spread abroad as best of all the herbs that grow. | Unman for me to-day this man that he may wear the horn of hair. || 2. Make him a eunuch with a horn, set thou the crest upon his head. | Let Indra with two pressing-stones deprive him of his manly strength. || 3. I have unmanned thee, eunuch! yea, impotent! made thee impotent, and robbed thee, weakling! of thy strength. | Upon his head we set the horn, we set the branching ornament. || 4. Duas tuas venas, a Diis factas, in quibus stat vigor virilis, paxillo ligneo in testiculis ob istam mulierem tibi findo. || 5. Ut mulieres mattam (tegetem) facturae arundinem lapide findunt, sic fascinum tuum cum testiculis ob istam mulierem findo.

Hymn 6:139.

|| 1. Thou hast grown up, a source of joy to bless me with prosperity. | A hundred are thy tendrils, three-and-thirty thy descending shoots. | With this that bears a thousand leaves I dry thy heart and wither it. || 2. Let thy heart wither for my love and let thy month be dry for me. | Parch and dry up with longing, go with lips that love of me hath dried. || 3. Drive us together, tawny! fair! a go-between who wakens love. | Drive us together, him and me, and give us both one heart and mind. || 4. Even as his mouth is parched who finds no water for his burning thirst, | So parch and burn with longing, go with lips that love of me hath dried. || 5. Even as the Mungoose bites and rends and then restores the wounded snake, | So do thou, Mighty one, restore the fracture of our severed love.

Hymn 6:140.

1. Two tigers have grown up who long to eat the mother and the sire: | Soothe, Brahmaṇaspati, and thou, O Jātavedas, both these teeth. || 2. Let rice and barley be your food, eat also beans and sesamum. | This is the share allotted you, to be your portion, ye two Teeth. Harm not your mother and your sire. || 3. Both fellow teeth have been invoked, gentle and bringing happiness. | Else whither let the fierceness of your nature turn away, O Teeth! Harm not your mother or your sire.

Hymn 6:141.

1. Vāyu collected these: to find their sustenance be Tvaṣhṭar's care: | May Indra bless and comfort them, and Rudra look that they increase. || 2. Take thou the iron axe and make a pair by marks upon their ears. | This sign the Aśvins have impressed: let these increase and multiply. || 3. Even as Gods and Asuras, even as mortal men have done, | Do ye, that these may multiply in thousands, Aśvins! make the mark.

Hymn 6:142.

1. Spring high, O Barley, and become much through thine own magnificence: | Burst all the vessels; let the bolt from heaven forbear to strike thee down. || 2. As we invite and call to thee, Barley, a God who heareth us, | Raise thyself up like heaven on high and be exhaustless as the sea. || 3. Exhaustless let thine out-turns be, exhaustless be thy gathered heaps, | Exhaustless be thy givers, and exhaustless those who eat of thee.

Kāṇḍa 7

Hymn 7:1.

1. They who by thought have guided all that Speech hath best, or they who with their heart have uttered words of truth, | Made stronger by the strength which the third prayer bestows, have by the fourth prayer learned the nature of the Cow. || 2. Well knows this son his sire, he knows his mother well: he hath been son, and he hath been illiberal. | He hath encompassed heaven, and air's mid-realm, and sky; he hath become this All; he hath come nigh to us.

Hymn 7:2.

1. Invoke for us, proclaim in sundry places, the kinsman of the Gods, our sire Atharvan, | His mother's germ, his father's breath, the youthful, who with his mind hath noticed this oblation.

Hymn 7:3.

1. he, in this manner showing forth his exploits—for he, bright God, is our broad way for choosing— | Rose up to meet his stay, the mead's best position: of his own self he sent his body forward.

Hymn 7:4.

1. With thine eleven teams, to aid our wishes, yea, with thy two-and-twenty teams, O Vāyu, | With all thy three-and-thirty teams for drawing, here loose these teams, thou who art prompt to listen!

Hymn 7:5.

1. The Gods adored the Sacrifice with worship: these were the statutes of primeval ages. | Those mighty ones attained the cope of heaven, there where the Sādhyas, Gods of old, are dwelling. || 2. Sacrifice was, was manifest among us: it sprang to life and then in time grew stronger. | Then it became the deities' lord and ruler: may it bestow on us abundant riches. || 3. Where the Gods worshipped Gods with their oblation, worshipped immortals with immortal spirit, | There in the loftiest heaven may we be happy, and look upon that light when Sūrya rises. || 4. With their oblation, Puruṣha, the Gods performed a sacrifice. | A sacrifice more potent still they paid with the invoking hymn. || 5. With dog the Gods, perplexed, have paid oblation, and with cow's limbs in sundry sacrifices. | Invoke for us, in many a place declare him who with his mind. hath noticed this our worship.

Hymn 7:6.

1. Aditi is sky, and air's mid-region, Aditi is the father, son, and mother, | Aditi all the Gods and the Five Nations, Aditi what is now and what is future. || 2. We call for help the Queen of Law and Order, great mother of all those whose ways are righteous, | Far-spread, unwasting strong in her dominion, Aditi wisely leading, well protecting. || 3. Sinless may we ascend, for weal, the vessel, rowed with good oars, divine, that never leaketh, | Earth, our strong guard, incomparable Heaven, Aditi wisely leading, well protecting. || 4. Let us bring hither, in pursuit of riches, Aditi with our

word, the mighty mother, | Her in whose lap the spacious air is lying: may she afford us triply-guarding shelter!

Hymn 7:7.

1. I have sung praise to Diti's sons and Aditi's, those very lofty and invulnerable Gods. | For far within the depths of ocean is their home and in the worship paid them none excelleth these.

Hymn 7:8.

1. Go forward on thy way from good to better: Bṛihaspati pre-cede thy steps and guide thee! | Place this man here, within this earth's enclosure, afar from foes with all his men about him.

Hymn 7:9.

1. Pūṣhan was born to move on distant pathways, on roads remote from earth, remote from heaven. | To both most lovely places of assembly he travels and returns with perfect knowledge. || 2. Pūṣhan knows all these realms: may he conduct us by ways that are most free from fear and danger. | Giver of blessings, glowing, all heroic, may he the wise and watchful go before us. || 3. We are thy praisers here, O Pūṣhan: never let us be injured under thy protection. || 4. From out the distance, far and wide, may Pūṣhan stretch his right hand forth. | Let him drive back our lost to us, let us return with what is lost.

Hymn 7:10.

1. That breast of thine, exhaustless and delightful, good to invoke, beneficent, free giver. | Wherewith thou feedest all things that are choicest, bring that, Sarasvatī, that we may drain it.

Hymn 7:11.

1. That far-spread thunder, sent from thee, which cometh on all this world, a high celestial signal | Strike not, O God, our growing corn with lightning, not kill it with the burning rays of Sūrya.

Hymn 7:12.

1. In concord may Prajāpati's two daughters, Gathering and Assembly, both protect me. | May every man I meet respect and aid me. Fair be my words, O Fathers, at the meetings. || 2. We know thy name, O Conference: thy name is interchange of talk. | Let all the company who join the Conference agree with me. || 3. Of these men seated here I make the splendour and the lore mine own. | Indra, make me conspicuous in all this gathered company. || 4. Whether your thoughts are turned away, or bound and fastened here or there, | We draw them hitherward again: let your mind firmly rest on me.

Hymn 7:13.

1. As the Sun, rising, taketh to himself the brightness of the stars, | So I assume the glory of women and men mine enemies. | All ye among my rivals who behold me as I come to you, | I seize the glory of my foes as the Sun, rising, theirs who sleep.

Hymn 7:14.

1. I praise this God, parent of heaven and earth, exceeding wiser possessed of real energy, giver of treasure, thinker dear to all, || 2. Whose splendour is sublime, whose light shone brilliant in creation, who, wise, and golden-handed, in his beauty made the sky. || 3. As thou, God! quickening, for our ancient father, sentest him height above and room about him, | So unto us, O Savitar, send treasures, abundant, day by day, in shape of cattle. || 4. Savitar, God, our household friend, most precious, hath sent our fathers life and power and riches. | Let him drink Soma and rejoice when worshipped. Under his law even the Wanderer travels.

Hymn 7:15.

1. I choose, O Savitar, that glorious favour, with fruitful energy and every blessing, | Even this one's teeming cow, erst milked by Kaṇva, thousand-streamed, milked for happiness by the mighty.

Hymn 7:16.

1. Increase this man Bṛihaspati! Illume him, O Savitar, for high and happy fortune. | Sharpen him thoroughly though already sharpened: with glad acclaim let all the Gods receive him.

Hymn 7:17.

1. May the Ordainer give us wealth, Lord, ruler of the world of life: with full hand may he give to us. || 2. May Dhātar grant the worshipper henceforth imperishable life. | May we obtain the favour of the God who giveth every boon. || 3. To him may Dhātar grant all kinds of blessings who, craving children, serves him in his dwelling. | Him may the Gods invest with life eternal, yea, all the Gods and Aditi accordant. || 4. May this our gift please Savitar, Rāti, Dhātar, Prajāpati, and Agni Lord of Treasures. | May Tvaṣhṭar, Viṣhṇu, blessing him with children, give store of riches to the sacrificer.

Hymn 7:18.

1. Burst open, Pṛithivī, and cleave asunder this celestial cloud. | Untie, O Dhātar—for thou canst—the bottle of the breast of heaven. || 2. Let not the Sun's heat burn, nor cold destroy her. Let Earth with all her quickening drops burst open. | Even for her the waters flow, and fatness: where Soma is even there is bliss for ever.

Hymn 7:19.

1. Prajāpati engenders earthly creatures: may the benevolent Ordainer form them, | Having one common womb, and mind, and spirit. He who is Lord of Plenty give me plenty!

Hymn 7:20.

1. Anumati approve today our sacrifice among the Gods! | May Agni bear mine offerings away for me the worshipper. || 2. Do thou, Anumati! approve, and grant us health and happiness. | Accept the offered sacrifice, and, Goddess, give us progeny. || 3. May he approving in return accord us wealth inexhaustible with store of children. | Never may we be subject to his anger, but rest in his benevolence and mercy. || 4. Thy name is easy to invoke, good leader! approved, Anumati and rich in bounty. | Source of all bonds! fill up therewith our worship, and, Blest One! grant us wealth with goodly heroes. || 5. Anumati hath come to this our worship well-formed to give good lands and valiant heroes: | For her kind care hath blessed us. God-protected, may she assist the sacrifice we offer. || 6. Anumati became this All, whatever standeth or walketh, every-thing that moveth. | May we enjoy thy gracious love, O Goddess. Regard us, O Anumati, with favour.

Hymn 7:21.

1. With prayer come all together to the Lord of Heaven: he is the peerless one, far-reaching, guest of men. | He, God of ancient time, hath gained a recent thrall; to him alone is turned the path which all must tread.

Hymn 7:22.

1. Unto a thousand sages he hath given sight: thought, light is he in ranging all. || 2. The Bright One hath sent forth the Dawns, a closely gathered band, | Immaculate, unanimous, brightly refulgent in their homes.

Hymn 7:23.

1. The fearful dream, and indigence, the monster, the malignant hags. | All female fiends of evil name and wicked tongue we drive afar.

Hymn 7:24.

1. What treasure hath been dug for us by Indra, by Agni, Viśvedevas, tuneful Marutas, | On us may Savitar whose laws are faithful, Prajāpati, and Heavenly Grace bestow it.

Hymn 7:25.

1. The early morning prayer hath come to Viṣhṇu and Varuṇa, Lords through might, whom none hath equalled, | Gods by whose power the realms of air were established, strongest and most heroic in their vigour. || 2. The early prayer hath ever come to Viṣhṇu and Varuṇa by that God's high power and statute. | In whose control is all this world that shineth, all that hath powers to see and all that breatheth.

Hymn 7:26.

1. I will declare the mighty deeds of Viṣhṇu, of him who measured out the earthly regions, | Who propped the highest place of congregation, thrice setting down his footstep, widely striding. || 2. Loud boast doth Viṣhṇu make of this achievement, like some wild beast, dread, prowling, mountain-roaming. | May he approach us from the farthest distance. || 3. Thou within whose three wide-extended paces all worlds and creatures have their habitation, | Drink oil, thou homed in oil! promote the sacrificer more and more. || 4. Through all this world strode Viṣhṇu: thrice his foot he planted, and the whole | Was gathered in his footstep's dust. || 5. Viṣhṇu the guardian, he whom none deceiveth, made three steps, thenceforth. | Establishing these high decrees. || 6. Look ye on Viṣhṇu's works, whereby the friend of Indra, close-allied, | Hath let his holy ways be

seen. || 7. The princes evermore behold that loftiest place where Vishṇu is, | Like an extended eye in heaven, || 8. From heaven, O Vishṇu, or from earth, O Vishṇu, or from the great far-spreading air's mid-region, | Fill both thy hands full of abundant treasures, and from the right and left bestow them freely.

Hymn 7:27.

1. May Iḍā with her statute dwell beside us, she in whose place the pious purge and cleanse them. | She, mighty, Soma-decked, whose foot drops fatness, meet for All-Gods, hath come to aid our worship.

Hymn 7:28.

1. Blest be the Broom, may the Mace bring a blessing, and may the Altar and the Hatchet bless us. | Worshipful Gods, may they accept this worship, lovers of sacrifice, and sacrificers.

Hymn 7:29.

1. This is your glorious might, Agni and Vishṇu! Ye drink the essence of the mystic butter. | Placing in every home seven costly treasures. Let your tongue stretch to take the offered fatness. || 2. Ye love the great law, Agni Vishṇu! joying, ye feast on mystic essences of butter, | Exalted in each house with fair laudation. Let your tongue stretch to take the offered fatness.

Hymn 7:30.

1. Heaven, Earth, and Mitra here have caused mine eyes to be-anointed well, | Savitar, Brahmaṇaspati take care that they be duly balmed!

Hymn 7:31.

1. Rouse us today O Indra, Maghavan, hero, with thy best possible and varied succours, | May he who hateth us fall low beneath us, and him whom we detest let life abandon.

Hymn 7:32.

1. We bringing homage have approached the friend who seeks our wondering praise, | Young, strengthener of the sacrifice. May he bestow long life on me.

Hymn 7:33.

1. Let Pūshan, let the Marutas, let Bṛihaspati pour forth on me; | This present Agni pour on me children and riches in a stream! May he bestow long life on me.

Hymn 7:34.

1. Agni, drive off my rivals born and living, repel those yet unborn, O Jātavedas. | Cast down beneath my feet mine adversaries. In Aditi's regard may we be sinless.

Hymn 7:35.

1. Subdue with conquering might his other rivals, those yet unborn repel, O Jātavedas. | For great felicity protect this kingdom, and in this man let all the Gods be joyful. || 2. Hae quot tibi sunt venae atque arteriae harum omnium os tibi lapide occlusi. || 3. Uteri tui summam partem inferam facio: ne tibi soboles neque filius eveniat. Sterilem et infecundam te facio: lapidem tuum, operimentum facio.

Hymn 7:36.

1. Sweet are the glances of our eyes, our faces are as smooth as balm, | Within thy bosom harbour me; one spirit dwell in both of us!

Hymn 7:37.

1. With this my robe, inherited from Manu, I envelop thee, | So that thou mayst be all mine own and give no thought to other dames.

Hymn 7:38.

1. I dig this Healing Herb that makes my lover look on me and weep; | That bids the parting friend return and kindly greets him as he comes. || 2. This Herb wherewith the Āsurī drew Indra downward from the Gods, | With this same Herb I draw thee close that I may be most dear to thee. || 3. Thou art the peer of Soma, yea, thou art the equal of the Sun, | The peer of all the Gods art thou: therefore we call thee hither—ward. || 4. I am the speaker here, not thou: speak thou where the assembly meets. | Thou shalt be mine and only mine, and never mention other dames. || 5. If thou art far away beyond the rivers, far away from men, | This Herb shall seem to bind thee fast and bring thee back my prisoner.

Hymn 7:39.

1. May he establish in our home the master of riches, gladdening with rain in season, | Mighty, strong-winged, celestial, dropping moisture, Bull of the plants and embryo of waters.

Hymn 7:40.

1. We call Sarasvat, under whose protection all cattle wander, to preserve and aid us, | Him in whose ordinance abide the waters, to whose command the Lord of Plenty listens. || 2. Abiding here let us invoke Sarasvat, the seat of riches, glorious, wealth-increaser, | Him who inclines and gives to him who worships, the rich possessor and the Lord of Fullness

Hymn 7:41.

1. Observing men, and viewing home, the Falcon hath cleft his swift way over wastes and waters. | May he, with Indra for a friend, auspicious, traversing all air's lower realms, come hither. || 2. The heavenly Falcon, viewing men, well-pinioned, strength-giver, hundred-footed, hundred-nested, | Shall give us treasure which was taken from us. May it be rich in food among our Fathers.

Hymn 7:42.

1. Scatter and drive away, Soma and Rudra, the sickness that hath come within our dwelling, | Afar into the distance chase Destruction, and even from committed sin release us. || 2. Lay on our bodies, O ye twain, O Soma and Rudra, all those balms that heal diseases. | Set free and draw away the sin committed, which we have still inherent in our persons.

Hymn 7:43.

1. Some of thy words bode weal and some misfortune: thou scatterest them all with friendly feeling. | Deep within this three words are laid: among them one hath flown off even as the sound was uttered.

Hymn 7:44.

1. Ye twain have conquered, and have not been vanquished: not either of the pair hath been defeated. | Ye, Indra Vishṇu, when ye fought your battle; produced this infinite with three divisions.

Hymn 7:45.

1. Brought hitherward from Sindhu, from a folk of every mingled race, | Fetched from afar, thou art I deem, a balm that cureth. jealousy. || 2. As one with water quencheth fire, so calm this lover's jealousy, | Like heat of fire that burneth here, or flame that rageth through the wood.

Hymn 7:46.

1. O broad-tressed Sinīvālī, thou who art the sister of the Gods, | Accept the offered sacrifice, and, Goddess, grant us progeny. || 2. Present the sacrifice to her, to Sinīvālī, Queen of men, Beautiful-fingered, lovely-armed, prolific, bearing many a child. || 3. Thou who as Queen of men art Indra's equal, a Goddess coming with a thousand tresses, | To thee our sacrifices are performed, O Consort of Vishṇu: Goddess, urge thy Lord to bounty!

Hymn 7:47.

1. Oft in this sacrifice with favoured cry I call Kuhū, beneficent Goddess, skilled in all her works. | May she vouchsafe us wealth with every boon, and give a, hero meet for praise who gives a hundred gifts. || 2. Kuhū, the Queen of Gods and immortality, called to assist, enjoy this sacrifice of ours! | Let her, desirous of our worship, hear today: may she, intelligent, give increase of our wealth.

Hymn 7:48.

1. I call on Rākā with hair laud and reverent cry: may she, auspicious, hear us and herself observe. | With never-breaking needle may she sew her work, and send a glorious man who gives a hundred gifts. || 2. All thy kind favours, Rākā! lovely in their form, wherewith thou grantest treasures to the man who gives, | With these come thou to us this day benevolent, O blessed one, bestowing wealth of thousand sorts.

Hymn 7:49.

1. May the Gods' Consorts aid us of their own free will, help us to offspring and the winning of the spoil. | May Goddesses who quickly listen shelter us, both those on earth and they within the waters' realm. || 2. May the Dames, wives of Gods, enjoy our presents, Rāṭ, Aśvinī Indrāṇī and Agnāyī; | May Rodasī and Varuṇānī hear us, and Goddesses come at the matrons' season.

Hymn 7:50.

1. As evermore the lightning flash strikes, irresistible, the tree, | So, irresistible, may I conquer the gamblers with the dice. || 2. From every side, from hale and sick, impotent to defend them-selves, | May all the fortune

of the folk as winnings pass into my hands. || 3. I pray to Agni, him who guards his treasure: here, won by homage, may he pile our winnings. | As 'twere with racing cars I bring my presents: duly with reverence, let me laud the Marutas. || 4. With thee to aid us may we win the treasure: do thou assist our side in every battle. | Give us wide room and easy way, O Indra; break down, O Maghavan, the foemen's valour. || 5. I have completely cleaned thee out, won from thee what thou keptest back. | As a wolf tears and rends a sheep, so do I tear thy stake away. || 6. Yea, by superior play one gains advantage: in time he piles his spoil as doth a gambler. | He overwhelms with wealth's inherent powers the devotee who keeps not back his riches. || 7. May we all, much-invoked! repel with cattle want that brings sin, hunger with store of barley. | May we uninjured, first among the princes, obtain possessions by our own exertions. || 8. My right hand holds my winnings fast, and in my left is victory. | I would that I were winner of cattle and horses, wealth and gold. || 9. Dice, give me play that bringeth fruit as 'twere a cow with flowing milk! | And, as the bowstring binds, the bow, unite me with a stream of gains.

Hymn 7:51.

1. Bṛihaspati protect us from the sinner, from rearward, from above, and from below us! | May Indra from the front and from the centre, as friend to friends, vouchsafe us room and freedom.

Hymn 7:52.

1. Give us agreement with our own, with strangers give us unity: | Do ye, O Aśvins, in this place join us in sympathy and love. || 2. May we agree in mind, agree in purpose: let us not fight against the heavenly spirit. | Around us rise no din of frequent slaughter, nor Indra's arrow fly, for day is present!

Hymn 7:53.

1. As thou, Bṛihaspati, from the curse hast saved us, from dwelling yonder in the realm of Yama, | The Aśvins, leeches of the Gods, O Agni, have chased Death far from us with mighty powers. || 2. Move both together; do not leave the body. Let both the breathings stay for thee united. | Waxing in strength live thou a hundred autumns. Thy noblest guardian and thy lord is Agni. || 3. Return, thy life now vanished into distance! Return, the breath thou drawest and exhalest! | Agni hath snatched it from Destruction's bosom: into thyself again I introduce it. || 4. Let not the vital breath he draws forsake him, let not his expiration part and leave him. | I give him over to the Seven Ṛishis: let them conduct him to old age in safety. || 5. Enter him, both ye breaths, like two draught-oxen entering their stall. | Let him, the treasure of old age, still wax in strength, uninjured, here. || 6. I send thee back thy vital breath; I drive Consumption far from thee, | May Agni here, most excellent, sustain our life on every side. || 7. From out the depth of darkness, we, ascending to the highest heaven, | Have come to the sublimest light, to Sūrya, God among the Gods.

Hymn 7:54.

1. We worship holy Verse and Song, by which they carry out their acts, | Shining in order's seat these twain present the sacrifice to Gods. || 2. As I have asked about Verse, Song, Sacrifice, strength, force, Yajus-text, | So never let this lore that I have sought forsake me, Lord of Might!

Hymn 7:55.

1. Thy downward paths from heaven, whereby thou hast raised all the world to life, | Give us in gracious love, good Lord!

Hymn 7:56.

1. Whether it came from viper, from black snake or snake with transverse stripes, | Or Kaṅkaparvan's bite, this herb hath made the poison powerless. || 2. Honey-born, honey-dropping, rich in honey, honey-sweet, this herb, | Is medicine that heals the wound and kills the gnat that bites and stings. || 3. Whatever bit, or sucked thy blood, we summon thence away from thee | The ineffectual poison of the little sharply-stinging gnat. || 4. Thou here who crookest wicked jaws, thou tortuous, jointless, limbless thing, | These jaws thou, Brahmaṇaspati! shalt bend together like a reed. || 5. This scorpion here that creeps along, low on the ground and powerless— | I have removed his poison and then utterly demolished him. || 6. No strength in thy two arms hast thou, nor in thy head, nor in thy waist: | Then what is that small thing thou so viciously bearest in thy tail? || 7. The emmets make a meal of thee and peahens tear and mangle thee: | All ye are crying out, In sooth the scorpion's poison hath no strength. || 8. Thou creature who inflictest wounds both with thy mouth and with thy tail, | No poison in thy mouth hast thou: what at thy tail's root will there be?

Hymn 7:57.

1. Whatever trouble hath disturbed and shaken me—I speak with hope, I move, imploring, amid the folk | What harm my body in myself hath suffered, now let Sarasvatī relieve with fatness. || 2. Seven flow for him, the youth on whom the Marutas wait: the sons have taught the Father everlasting laws. | Both worlds are his: both shine belonging unto him. Both move together: both, as his possession thrive.

Hymn 7:58.

1. True to laws, Indra Varuṇa, drinkers of the juice, quaff this pressed Soma which shall give you rapturous joy! | Let sacrifice, your car, to entertain the Gods, approach its resting-place that they may drink thereof. || 2. O Indra Varuṇa, drink your fill, ye heroes, of this effectual and sweetest Soma. | This juice was shed by us that ye might quaff it. On this trimmed grass be seated and rejoice you.

Hymn 7:59.

1. Like a tree struck by lightning may the man be withered from the root. | Who curseth us who curse not him, or, when we curse him curseth us.

Hymn 7:60.

1. I, prudent, bringing power, a treasure-winner, with amicable eye that strikes no terror, | Come, praising and kind-thoughted, to these houses: be not afraid of me, be glad and joyful. || 2. Let these delightful Houses that are rich in power and store of milk, | Replete with wealth and standing firm, become aware of our approach. || 3. These Houses we invoke, whereon the distant exile sets his thought, | Wherein dwells many a friendly heart: let them beware of our approach. || 4. Thus greeted, ye of ample wealth, friends who enjoy delightful sweets. | Be ever free from hunger, free from thirst! Ye Houses, fear us not. || 5. Kind greeting to the cattle here, kind greeting to the goats and sheep! | Then, of the food within our homes, kind greeting to the pleasant drink! || 6. Full of refreshment, full of charms, of laughter and felicity, | Be ever free from hunger, free from thirst! Ye Houses, fear us not. | Stay here, and come not after me: prosper in every form and shape. | With happy fortune will I come! Grow more abundant still through me!

Hymn 7:61.

1. Since, Agni, with our fervent zeal we undergo austerity, | May we be dear to Sacred Lore, may we be wise and live long lives. || 2. Agni, we practise acts austere, we undergo austerity. | So listening to Holy Lore may we grow wise and full of days.

Hymn 7:62.

1. Like a car-warrior, Agni here, grown mighty, Lord of the brave, | Chief Priest, hath conquered footmen. | Laid on earth's centre he hath flashed and glittered. Low may he lay our enemies beneath us.

Hymn 7:63.

1. We call with lauds from his most lofty dwelling victorious Agni, conqueror in battles. | May he convey us over all distresses, may the God Agni bear us past our troubles.

Hymn 7:64.

1. From all that woe and trouble may the Waters save and rescue me, | Whate'er the Raven, black of hue, flying out hither ward, hath dropped. || 2. May Agni Gārhapatya save and set me free from all this guilt. | Which the black Raven with thy mouth, O Nirṛiti, hath wiped away.

Hymn 7:65.

1. With retroverted fruit hast thou, O Apāmārga, sprung and grown. | Hence into distance most remote drive every curse away from, me. || 2. Whatever evil we have done, whatever vile or sinful act, | With thee, O Apāmārga, who lookest all ways, we wipe it off. || 3. If with the cripple we have lived, whose teeth are black and nails deformed, | With thee, O Apāmārga, we wipe all that ill away from us.

Hymn 7:66.

1. If it was in the wind or air's mid-region, if it was in the trees or in the bushes, | To meet whose utterance forth streamed the cattle, may that

Celestial Power again approach us.

Hymn 7:67.

1. May sense return to me again, and spirit, return my Sacred Power and my possessions! | Again let fires, aflame on lesser altars, each duly stationed, here succeed and prosper.

Hymn 7:68.

1. Sarasvatī, in thy decrees, Goddess, in thy celestial laws, | Accept the offered sacrifice, and, Goddess, grant us progeny. || 2. Here is, Sarasvatī, thy fat libation, this sacrifice passing to the mouth of Fathers. | These most auspicious offerings have ascended to thee: through, these may we be full of sweetness. || 3. Be kind and most auspicious, be gracious to us, Sarasvatī, May we be ever in thy sight.

Hymn 7:69.

1. May the wind kindly breathe on us, may the Sun warm us. pleasantly. | May days pass happily for us, may night draw near delightfully, may dawn break joyfully for us!

Hymn 7:70.

1. Whatever sacrifice that man performeth with voice, mind, sacred formula, oblation, | May, in accord with Death, Destruction ruin his offering before it gain fulfilment. || 2. For him may sorcerers, Destruction, demons strike and prevent fulfilment through their falsehood. | Let Gods, by Indra sent, destroy his butter, and let his sacrifice be ineffective. || 3. Let the two Sovereigns, swift to come, like falcons swooping on their prey, | Destroy the butter of the foe whoever plots to injure us. || 4. I seize thine arms and draw them back, I bind a bandage on thy mouth. | I with the anger of the God Agni have killed thy sacrifice. || 5. Behind thy back I tie thine arms, I bind a bandage on thy mouth: | With the terrific Agni's wrath have I destroyed thy sacrifice.

Hymn 7:71.

1. We set thee round us as a fort, victorious Agni! thee a sage, | Bold in thy colour day by day, destroyer of the treacherous foe.

Hymn 7:72.

1. Rise up and look upon the share of Indra fixt by ritual use. | Whether ye poured libation dressed or took delight in it uncooked. || 2. Libation is prepared. Come to us, Indra: the Sun hath travelled over half his journey. | Friends with their treasures sit around thee, waiting like heads of houses for their wandering chieftain. || 3. Dressed in the udder and on fire, I fancy; well dressed, I fancy, is this new oblation. | Quaff thickened milk of noon's libation, Indra, well pleased, O Thunderer, famed for many an exploit!

Hymn 7:73.

1. Inflamed is Agni, Heroes! charioteer of heaven. The cauldron boils: the meath is drained to be your food. | For we, O Aśvins, singers sprung from many a house, invite you to be present at our banquetings. || 2. Aśvins, the fire is all aglow: your cauldron hath been heated;. come! | Here, even now, O Heroes, are the milch-kine milked. The priests, ye mighty ones! rejoice. || 3. Pure with the Gods is sacrifice with cry of Hail! That is the Aśvins' cup whence Gods are wont to drink. | Yea, the Immortal Ones accept it, one and all, and come to kiss that cup with the Gandharva's mouth. || 4. Milk, molten butter offered when the mornings break,—this is your portion, Aśvins! Come ye hitherward. | Lords of the brave, balm-lovers, guards of sacrifice, drink ye the warm libation in the light of heaven. || 5. Let the warm drink approach you with its Hotar-priest: let the Adhvaryu come to you with store of milk. | Come, O ye Aśvins, taste the meath that hath been drained, drink of the milk provided by this radiant cow. || 6. Come hither, quickly come, thou milker of the kine; into the cauldron pour milk of the radiant cow. | Most precious Savitar hath looked upon the heaven. After Dawn's going-forth he sends his light abroad. || 7. I invocate this milch-cow good for milking, so that the milker, deft of hand, may milk her. | May Savitar give goodliest stimulation. The cauldron hath been warmed. Let him proclaim it. || 8. She, sovereign of all treasures, is come hither yearning in spirit for her calf, and lowing. | May this cow yield her milk for both the Aśvins, and may she prosper to our great advantage. || 9. As dear house-friend, guest welcome in the dwelling, to this our sacrifice come thou who knowest. | And, Agni, having scattered all assailants, bring to us the possessions of our foemen. || 10. Show thyself strong for mighty bliss, O Agni! Most excellent be thine effulgent splendours! | Make easy to maintain our household lordship, and overcome the might of those who hate us. || 11. Fortunate mayst thou be with goodly pasture, and may we also be exceeding wealthy. | Feed on the grass, O Cow, at every season, and, coming hither, drink the limpid water.

Hymn 7:74.

1. Black is the mother, we have heard, from whom the red-hued Pustules sprang. | With the divine ascetic's root I pierce and penetrate them all. || 2. I pierce the foremost one of these, I perforate the middle-most, | And here I cut the hinder-most asunder like a lock of hair. || 3. With spell that Tvaṣhṭar sent to us I have dispelled thy jealousy. | We mitigate and pacify the anger that thou feltest, Lord! || 4. Lord of religious rites, by law, anointed, shine thou forth here for ever friendly-minded. | So may we all with children, Jātavedas! worship and humbly wait on thee enkindled.

Hymn 7:75.

1. Let not a thief or wicked man possess you: let not the dart of Rudra come anear you, | Prolific, shining in the goodly pasture, drinking at pleasant pools the limpid water. || 2. Ye know the place and rest content, close-gathered, called by many a name. Come to me, Goddesses, with Gods | Bedew with streams of fatness us, this cattle-pen, and all this place.

Hymn 7:76.

1. Rapidly dropping, quick to drop, more evil than the evil ones, | More sapless than a dried-up bone, swifter than salt to melt away. || 2. Pustules that rise upon the neck, Pustules upon the shoulder-joints, | Pustules that, falling of themselves, spring up on every twofold limb: || 3. I have expelled and banished all Scrofula harboured in the head, | And that which bores the breast-bone through, and that which settles in the sole. || 4. Scrofula flies borne on by wings: it penetrates and holds the man. | Here is the cure of either kind, the chronic and the transient. || 5. We know thine origin, Scrofula! know whence thou, Scrofula, art born. | How hast thou then struck this man here, him in whose house we sacrifice? || 6. Boldly drink Soma from the beaker, Indra! hero in war for treasure! Vṛitra-slayer | Fill thyself full at the mid-day libation: thyself possessing riches grant us riches.

Hymn 7:77.

1. Ye Marutas, full of fiery heat, accept this offering brought for you | To help us, ye who slay the foe. || 2. Marutas, the man who filled with rage against us beyond our thoughts would harm us, O ye Vasus, | May he be tangled in the toils of Mischief: smite ye him down with your most flaming weapon. || 3. Each year come, friends to man, the tuneful Marutas, dwelling in spacious mansions, trooped together. | Exhilarating, gladdening full of fiery heat, may they deliver us from binding bonds of sin.

Hymn 7:78.

1. I free thee from the cord, I loose the bond, I loose the fastening. | Even here, perpetual, Agni, wax thou strong. || 2. I with celestial prayer appoint thee, Agni, maintainer of this man in princely powers. | Here brightly shine for us with wealth: declare thou to Gods this favoured giver of oblations.

Hymn 7:79.

1. Night of the New-born Moon, whatever fortune the Gods who dwell with greatness have assigned thee, | Therewith fulfil our sacrifice, all-bounteous! Blessed One, grant us wealth with manly offspring. || 2. I am the New Moon's Night, the good and pious are my inhabitants, these dwell within me. | In me have Gods of both the spheres, and Sādhyas, with Indra as their chief, all met together. || 3. The Night hath come, the gatherer of treasures, bestowing strength, prosperity, and riches. | To New Moon's Night let us present oblation: pouring out strength, with milk hath she come hither. || 4. Night of New Moon! ne'er hath been born another than thou embracing all these forms and natures, | May we have what we longed for when we brought thee oblations: may we be the lords of riches.

Hymn 7:80.

1. Full in the front, full rearward, from the middle the Full Moon's Night hath conquered in the battle. | In her: may we, dwelling with Gods and greatness, feast in the height of heaven, on strengthening viands. || 2. To him, the Full Moon's mighty Bull, we pay our solemn sacrifice | May he bestow upon us wealth unwasting, inexhaustible. || 3. No one but thou, Prajāpati, none beside thee, pervading, gave to all these forms their being. |

Grant us our hearts' desire when we invoke thee: may we have store of riches in possession. ‖ 4. First was the Full Moon meet for adoration among the days and in the nights' deep darkness. | Into thy heaven, O Holy One, have entered those pious men who honour thee with worship.

Hymn 7:81.

1. Forward and backward by their wondrous power move these two youths, disporting, round the ocean. | One views all living things, and thou, the other, art born again arranging times and seasons. ‖ 2. Thou art re-born for ever new: thou marchest, ensign of days, in forefront of the mornings. | Marching thou dealest to the Gods their portion. Thou lengthenest, Moon! the days of man's existence. ‖ 3. O spray of Soma, Lord of Wars! all-perfect verily art thou. | Make me all-perfect, Beauteous One! in riches and in progeny. ‖ 4. Thou art the New Moon, fair to see, thou art complete in every part. | May I be perfect, fully blest in every way in steeds and kine, in children, cattle, home, and wealth. ‖ 5. Inflate thee with his vital breath who hates us and whom we detest. | May we grow rich in steeds and kine, in children, cattle, houses, wealth. ‖ 6. With that unwasting stalk which Gods, unwasting Gods, in-crease and eat, | May Varuṇa, Bṛihaspati, and Indra, the Lords and Guardians of the world, increase us.

Hymn 7:82.

1. Sing with fair laud the combat for the cattle. Bestow upon us excellent possessions. | Lead to the Gods the sacrifice we offer: let streams of oil flow pure and full of sweetness. ‖ 2. Agni I first appropriate with power, with splendour, and with might. | I give myself children and lengthened life, with Hail! take Agni to myself. ‖ 3. Even here do thou, O Agni, establish wealth: let not oppressors injure thee by thinking of thee first. | Light be thy task of ruling, Agni, with, thy power: may he who worships thee wax strong, invincible. ‖ 4. Agni hath looked upon the spring of Morning, looked on the days, the earliest Jātavedas. | So, following the gleams of Morning, Sūrya hath entered heaven and earth as his possession. ‖ 5. Agni hath looked upon the spring of Mornings, looked on the days, the earliest Jātavedas. | So he in countless places hath extended, full against heaven and earth, the beams of Sūrya. ‖ 6. Butter to thee in heaven thy home, O Agni! Manu this day hath kindled thee with butter. | Let the Celestial Daughters bring thee butter: Let cows pour butter forth for thee, O Agni.

Hymn 7:83.

1. Established amid the waters is, King Varuṇa, thy golden home. | Thence let the Sovereign who maintains the statutes loose all binding cords. ‖ 2. Hence free thou us, King Varuṇa, from each successive bond and tie. | As we have cried, O Varuṇa! have said, The Waters, they are kine, thence set us free, O Varuṇa ‖ 3. Loosen the bonds, O Varuṇa, that hold us, loosen the bond. above, between, and under. | So before Aditi may we be sinless under thy favouring auspices, Āditya! ‖ 4. Varuṇa, free us from all snares that bind us, Varuṇa's bonds, the upper and the lower. | Drive from us evil dream, drive off misfortune: then let us pass into the world of virtue.

Hymn 7:84.

1. Holder of sway, shine here refulgent, Agni! invincible immortal Jātavedas. | With succours friendly to mankind, auspicious, driving away all maladies, guard our dwelling. ‖ 2. Thou, Indra, lord and leader of the people, wast born for lovely strength and high dominion. | Thou dravest off the folk who were unfriendly, and madest for the Gods wide room and freedom. ‖ 3. Like a dread wild beast roaming on the mountain, may he. approach us from the farthest distance. | Whetting thy bolt and thy sharp blade, O Indra, crush down our foes and scatter those who hate us.

Hymn 7:85.

1. This very mighty one whom Gods urge onward, the conqueror of cars, ever triumphant, | Swift, fleet to battle, with uninjured fellies, even Tārkṣhya for our weal will we call hither.

Hymn 7:86.

1. Indra the rescuer, Indra the helper, Indra the brave who hears each invocation, | Śakra I call, Indra invoked of many. May Indra Maghavan prosper and bless us.

Hymn 7:87.

1. To Rudra in the fire, to him who dwells in floods, to Rudra who hath entered into herbs and plants, | To him who formed and fashioned all these worlds, to him this Rudra, yea, to Agni, reverence be paid!

Hymn 7:88.

1. Depart! thou art a foe, a foe. Poison with poison hast thou mixt, yea, verily poison hast thou mixt. | Go to the serpent: strike him dead.

Hymn 7:89.

1. The heavenly Waters have I ranged: we have been sated with their dew. | Here, Agni, bearing milk, am I. Endow me with the gift of strength. ‖ 2. Endow me with the gift of strength, with children, and a lengthened life. | May the Gods mark this prayer of mine, may Indra with the Ṛiṣhis mark. ‖ 3. Ye Waters, wash away this stain and whatsoever taint be here, | Each sinful wrong that I have done and every harmless curse of mine. ‖ 4. Thou art the wood, may I succeed! fuel, may I be glorified! splendour, give splendour unto me.

Hymn 7:90.

1. Tear thou asunder, as of old, like tangles of a creeping plant. | Demolish thou the Dāsa's might. ‖ 2. May we with Indra's help divide the gathered treasure of the foe. | I, by the law of Varuṇa, bring down thy pride and wantonness. ‖ 3. Ut virga abeat et feminis innocua fiat, (virga) membri humidi, membri quod verberat penetratque, id quod tentum est laxa, id quod sursum tentum est deorsum tende.

Hymn 7:91.

1. May Indra with his help, Lord of all treasures, be unto us a careful protector. | Drive off our foes and give us peace and safety. May we be lords of goodly store of heroes.

Hymn 7:92.

1. May this rich Indra as our good protector keep even far away the men who hate us. | May we enjoy his favour, his the holy: may we enjoy his blessed loving-kindness.

Hymn 7:93.

1. With Indra's and with Manyu's aid may we subdue our enemies, resistlessly destroying foes.

Hymn 7:94.

1. We lead the constant Soma on with constant sacrificial gift, | That Indra may make all the tribes unanimous and only ours.

Hymn 7:95.

1. To heaven, as 'twere, have soared this man's two vultures, staggering, dusky hued. | The Parcher and the Drier-up, the pair who parch and dry his heart. ‖ 2. I verily have stirred them up like oxen resting after toil. | Like two loud-snarling curs, or like two wolves who watch to make their spring: ‖ 3. Like two that thrust, like two that pierce, like two that strike with mutual blows. | I bind the conduit of the man or dame who hence hath taken aught.

Hymn 7:96.

1. The kine are resting in the stall, home to her nest hath flown the bird, | The hills are firmly rooted: I have fixed the kidneys in their place.

Hymn 7:97.

1. As we have here elected thee, skilled Hotar! today as this our sacrifice proceedeth, | Come to the firm place, mightiest! yea, come firmly. Knowing the sacrifice, approach the Soma. ‖ 2. With kine connect us, and with spirit, Indra! Lord of Bay Steeds, with princes and with favour, | With the God-destined portion of the Brahmans, and the good-will of Gods who merit worship. ‖ 3. The willing Gods whom, God, thou hast brought hither, send thou to their own dwelling-place, O Agni. | When ye have eaten and have drunk sweet juices, endow this man with precious wealth, ye Vasus. ‖ 4. Gods, we have made your seats of easy access, who, pleased with me, have come to my libation. | Bearing and bringing hitherward your treasures, after the rich warm beverage mount to heaven. ‖ 5. Go to the sacrifice, go to its master, Sacrifice! To thy birth-place go with Svāhā. ‖ 6. This is thy sacrifice with hole hymnal, Lord of the Rite, Svāhā! and fraught with vigour. ‖ 7. Vaṣhaṭ to paid and yet unpaid oblations! Ye Gods who know the way, find and pursue it! ‖ 8. Lord of the Mind, lay this our sacrifice in heaven among the Gods. Svāhā in heaven! Svāhā on earth! | Svāhā in air! In wind have I paid offerings. Hail!

Hymn 7:98.

1. Balmed is the Grass with butter and libation, with Indra. gracious Lord, and with the Marutas. | Hail! let the sacrifice go forth anointed to Indra

with the Gods and Viśvedevas.

Hymn 7:99.

1. Strew thou the Grass, and spread it on the Altar: rob not the sister who is lying yonder. | The Hotar's seat is green and golden: these are gold necklets, in the place of him who worships.

Hymn 7:100.

1. I turn away from evil dream, from dream of sin, from indigence. | I make the prayer mine inmost friend. Hence! torturing, dreamy phantasies!

Hymn 7:101.

1. The food that in a dream I eat is not perceived at early morn. | May all that food be blest to me because it is not seen by day.

Hymn 7:102.

1. When I have worshipped Heaven and Earth, reverenced Firmament and Death, | I will make water standing up. Let not the Sovereigns injure me.

Hymn 7:103.

1. What princely warrior, seeking higher fortune, will free us from this shameful fiend of mischief? | What friend of sacrifice? What guerdon-lover? Who winneth: amid the Gods a long existence?

Hymn 7:104.

1. Who will prepare the dappled Cow, good milker, ne'er without calf, whom Varuṇa gave Atharvan, | And, joying in Bṛihaspati's alliance, arrange according to his will her body?

Hymn 7:105.

1. Leaving humanity behind, making the heavenly word thy choice, | With all thy friends address thyself to furthering and guiding men.

Hymn 7:106.

1. Each thoughtless ill that we have done, O Agni, all error in our conduct, Jātavedas! | Therefrom do thou, O sapient God, preserve us. May we thy friends, for bliss, have life eternal.

Hymn 7:107.

1. The seven bright beams of Sūrya bring the waters downward from the sky, | The streams of ocean: these have made the sting that pained thee drop away.

Hymn 7:108.

1. Whoso by stealth or openly would harm us, a friend who knows us, or a stranger, Agni! | May the strange she-fiend armed with teeth attack them: O Agni, theirs be neither home nor children! || 2. Whoso oppresseth us O Jātavedas, asleep or waking, standing still or moving. | Accordant with Vaiśvānara thy comrade, O Jātavedas, meet them and consume them.

Hymn 7:109.

1. My homage to the strong, the brown, the sovereign lord among the dice! | Butter on Kali I bestow: may he be kind to one like me. || 2. Bear butter to the Apsarases, O Agni, and to the Dice bear dust and sand and water. | The Gods delight in both oblations, joying in sacrificial gifts apportioned duly. || 3. The Apsarases take pleasure in the banquet between the Sun and. the libation-holder. | With butter let them fill my hands, and give me, to be my prey, the man who plays against me. || 4. Evil be mine opponent's luck! Sprinkle thou butter over us. | Strike, as a tree with lightning flash, mine adversary in the game. || 5. The God who found for us this wealth for gambling, to cast the dice and count the winning number, | May he accept the sacrifice we offer, and with Gandharvas revel in the banquet. || 6. Fellow-inhabitants, such is your title, for Dice with looks of power support dominion. | As such with offerings may we serve you, Indus! May we have riches in our own possession. || 7. As I invoke the Gods at need, as I have lived in chastity, | May these, when I have grasped the Dice, the brown, be kind to one like me.

Hymn 7:110.

1. Resistless, Agni, Indra, smite his foemen for the worshipper, | For best foe-slayers are ye both. || 2. Agni I call, and Indra, foe-destroyers, swift moving, heroes, Gods who wield the thunder, | Through whom they won the light in the beginning, these who have made all worlds their habitation. || 3. The God Bṛihaspati hath won thy friendly favour with the cup. | With hymns, O Indra, enter us for the juice-pouring worshipper.

Hymn 7:111.

1. Belly of Indra art thou, Soma-holder! the very soul of Gods and human beings. | Here be the sire of offspring, thine here present! Here be they glad in thee who now are elsewhere.

Hymn 7:112.

1. Radiant with light are Heaven and Earth, whose grace is nigh, whose sway is vast. | Seven Goddesses have flowed to us: may they deliver us from woe; || 2. Release me from the curse's bond and plague that comes from Varuṇa; | Free me from Yama's fetter and from every sin against the Gods.

Hymn 7:113.

1. Rough Plant, thou rough rude parasite, cut thou that man, O Rough and Rude, | That thou mayst hinder from his act that man in all his manly strength. || 2. Thou, rugged Plant, art rude and rough, Vishā, Vishātakī art thou. | That thou mayest be cast off by him, as by a bull a barren cow.

Hymn 7:114.

1. I have extracted from thy sides, I have extracted from thy heart, | I have extracted from thy face the strength and splendour that were thine. || 2. Let pain and suffering pass away, let cares and curses vanish. hence. | Let Agni slay the fiendish hags, Soma kill bags who trouble us.

Hymn 7:115.

1. Hence. Evil Fortune! fly away, vanish from this place and from that. | We fix thee with an iron hook unto the man who hateth us. || 2. Granting us riches, Savitar! golden-banded, send thou away from us to other regions | That Fortune who, flying, abominable, hath, as a creeper climbs a tree, assailed me. || 3. One and a hundred Fortunes all together are at his birth born with a mortal's body. | Of these we send away the most unlucky: keep lucky ones for us, O Jātavedas. || 4. I have disparted these and those like cows who stray on common land. | Here let auspicious Fortunes stay: hence have I banished evil ones.

Hymn 7:116.

1. Homage to him the burning one, shaker, exciter, violent! | Homage to him the cold who acts according to his ancient will! || 2. May he, the lawless one, who comes alternate or two following days, pass over and possess the frog.

Hymn 7:117.

1. Come hither, Indra, with bay steeds, joyous, with tails like pea-cock plumes. | Let none impede thy way as fowlers stay the bird: pass o'er them as o'er desert lands.

Hymn 7:118.

1. Thy vital parts I cover with thine armour: with immortality King Soma clothe thee! | Varuṇa give thee what is more than ample, and in thy triumph let the Gods be joyful.

Kāṇḍa 8.

Hymn 8:1.

1. Homage to Death the Ender! May thy breathings, inward and outward, still remain within thee. | Here stay this man united with his spirit in the Sun's realm, the world of life eternal! || 2. Bhaga hath lifted up this man, and Soma with his filaments, | Indra and Agni, and the Gods the Marutas, raised him up to health. || 3. Here is thy spirit, here thy breath, here is thy life, here is thy soul: | By a celestial utterance we raise thee from Destruction's bonds. || 4. Up from this place, O man, rise! sink not downward, casting away the bonds of Death that hold thee. | Be not thou parted from this world, from sight of Agni and the Sun. || 5. Purely for thee breathe Wind and Mātariśvan, and let the | Waters rain on thee their nectar. | The Sun shall shine with healing on thy body; Death shall have mercy on thee: do not leave us! || 6. Upward must be thy way, O man, not downward: with life and mental vigour I endow thee. | Ascend this car eternal, lightly rolling; then full of years shalt thou address the meeting. || 7. Let not thy soul go thither, nor be lost to us: slight not the living, go not where the Fathers are. | Let all the Gods retain thee here in safety. || 8. Yearn not for the departed ones, for those who lead men far away. | Rise up from darkness into light: come, both thy hands we clasp in ours. || 9. Let not the black dog and the brindled seize thee, two warders of the way sent forth by Yama. | Come hither; do not hesitate: with mind averted stay not there. || 10. Forbear to tread this path, for it is awful: that path I speak of which thou hast not travelled. | Enter it not, O man; this way is darkness: forward is danger, hitherward is safety. || 11. Thy guardians be the Fires within the

Waters, thy guardian be the Fire which men enkindle. | Thy guardian be Vaiśvānara Jātavedas; let not celestial Fire with lightning burn thee. || 12. Let not the Flesh-Consumer plot against thee: depart thou far away from the Destroyer. | Be Heaven and Earth and Sun and Moon thy keepers, and from the dart of Gods may Air protect thee. || 13. May Vigilance and Watchfulness protect thee, Sleepless and Slumberless keep guard above thee! | Let Guardian and let Wakeful be thy warders. || 14. Let these be thy preservers, these thy keepers. All hail to these, to these be lowly worship! || 15. May saving Savitar, Vāyu, Indra, Dhātar restore thee to communion with the living. | Let not thy vigour or thy breath forsake thee: we recall thy life. || 16. Let not the fiend with snapping jaws, nor darkness find thee: tongue, holy grass: how shouldst thou perish? | May the Ādityas and the Vasus, Indra and Agni raise thee and to health restore thee. || 17. The Sky hath raised thee, and the Earth, Prajāpati hath raised thee up. | The Plants and Herbs with Soma as their King have rescued thee from Death. || 18. Here let this man, O Gods, remain: let him not go to yonder world. | We rescue him from Mṛityu with a charm that hath a thousand powers. || 19. I have delivered thee from Death. Strength-givers smelt and fashion thee! | Let not she-fiends with wild loose locks, or fearful howlers yell at thee. || 20. I have attained and captured thee: thou hast returned restored to youth. | Perfect in body: so have I found all thy sight and all thy life. || 21. Life hath breathed on thee; light hath come: darkness hath past away from thee. | Far from thee we have buried Death, buried Destruction and Decline.

Hymn 8:2.

1. Seize to thyself this trust of life for ever: thine be longevity which nothing shortens. | Thy spirit and thy life again I bring thee: die not, nor vanish into mist and darkness. || 2. Come to the light of living men, come hither: I draw thee to a life of hundred autumns. | Loosing the bonds of Death, the curse that holds thee, I give thee age of very long duration. || 3. Thy breath have I recovered from the Wind, thy vision from the Sun. | Thy mind I establish and secure within thee: feel in thy members, use thy tongue, conversing. || 4. I blow upon thee with the breath of bipeds and quadrupeds, as on a fire new-kindled. | To thee, O Death, and to thy sight and breath have I paid reverence. || 5. Let this man live, let him not die: we raise him, we recover him. | I make for him a healing balm. O Death, forbear to slay this man. || 6. Here for sound health I invocate a living animating plant, | Preserving, queller of disease, victorious, full of power and might. || 7. Seize him not, but encourage and release him: here let him stay, though thine, in all his vigour. | Bhava and Śarva, pity and protect him: give him full life and drive away misfortunes. || 8. Comfort him, Death, and pity him: let him arise and pass away, | Unharmed, with all his members, hearing well, with old, may he through hundred years win profit with his soul. || 9. May the Gods' missile pass thee by. I bring thee safe from the mist: from death have I preserved thee. | Far have I banished flesh-consuming Agni: I place a rampart for thy life's protection. || 10. Saving him from that misty path of thine which cannot be defined. | From that descent of thine, O Death, we make for him a shield of prayer. || 11. I give thee both the acts of breath, health, lengthened life, and death by age. | All Yama's messengers who roam around, sent by Vaivasvata, I chase away. || 12. Far off we drive Malignity, Destruction, Piśāchas banqueters on flesh, and Grāhi. | And all the demon kind, the brood of sin, like darkness, we dispel. || 13. I win thy life from Agni, from the living everlasting Jātavedas. | This I procure for thee, that thou, undying, mayst not suffer harm, that thou mayst be content, that all be well with thee. || 14. Gracious to thee be Heaven and Earth, bringing no grief, and drawing nigh! | Pleasantly shine the Sun for thee, the Wind blow sweetly to thy heart! | Let the celestial Waters full of milk flow happily for thee. || 15. Auspicious be the Plants to thee! I have upraised thee, borne thee from the lower to the upper earth: | Let the two Sons of Aditi, the Sun and Moon, protect thee there. || 16. Whatever robe to cover thee or zone thou makest for thyself, | We make it pleasant to thy frame: may it be soft and smooth to touch. || 17. When, with a very keen and cleansing razor, our hair and beards thou shavest as a barber, | Smoothing our face steal not our vital forces. || 18. Auspicious unto thee be rice and barley, causing no painful sickness or consumption, these deliver from calamity. || 19. Thy food, thy drink, whate'er they be corn grown by cultivation, milk, | Food eatable, uneatable, I make all poisonless for thee. || 20. We give thee over as a charge to Day and Night, in trust to both. | Keep him for me from stingy fiends, from those who fain would feed on him. || 21. A hundred, yea, ten thousand years we give thee, ages two, three, four. | May Indra, Agni, all the Gods, with willing favour look on thee. || 22. To Autumn we deliver thee, to Winter, Spring and Summer's care. | We trust thee with auspicious years wherein the plants and herbs grow up. || 23. Death is the lord of bipeds, Death is sovereign lord of quadrupeds. | Away I bear thee from that: Death the ruler: be not thou afraid. || 24. Thou, still uninjured, shalt not die: be not afraid; thou shalt not die. | Here where I am men do not die or go to lowest depths of gloom. || 25. Here verily all creatures live, the cow, the horse, the man, the beast, | Here where this holy prayer is used, a rampart that protecteth life. | Let it preserve thee from thy peers, from incantation, from thy friends. || 26. Live very long, be healthy, be immortal: let not the vital breath forsake thy body. || 27. One and a hundred modes of death, dangers that may be over-come, | May Gods deliver thee from this when Agni, dear to all men, bids. || 28. Body of Agni prompt to save, slayer of fiends and foes art thou, | Yea, banisher of malady, the healing balm called Pūtudru.

Hymn 8:3.

1. I balm with oil the mighty demon-slayer, to the most famous friend I come for shelter. | Enkindled, sharpened by our rites, may Agni protect us in the day and night from evil. || 2. O Jātavedas, armed with teeth of iron, enkindled with thy flame, attack the demons. | Seize with thy tongue the foolish Gods' adorers: rend, put within thy mouth the raw-flesh-eaters. || 3. Apply thy teeth, the upper and the lower, thou who hast both, enkindled and destroying. | Roam also in the air, O King, around us, and with thy jaws assail the wicked spirits. || 4. Pierce through the Yātudhāna's skin, O Agni; let the destroying dart with fire consume him. | Rend his joints, Jātavedas! let the eater of raw flesh, seeking flesh, tear and destroy him. || 5. Where now thou seest, Agni Jātavedas! a Yātudhāna, standing still or roaming. | Or one that flieth through the air's mid-region, kindled to fury as an archer pierce him. || 6. Bending thy shafts through sacrifices, Agni! dipping thine arrows in the hymn to point them, | Pierce to the heart therewith the Yātudhānas, and break their arms uplifted to attack thee. || 7. Rescue the captives also, Jātavedas! yea, those whom Yātudhānas' spears have captured. | Strike down that fiend, blazing before him, Agni! Let spotted carrion-eating kites devour him. || 8. Here tell this forth, O Agni: whosoever is, he himself, or acteth as, a demon, | Grasp him, O thou most youthful, with thy fuel: to the Man-Seer's eye give him as booty. || 9. With keen glance guard the sacrifice, O Agni: thou Sage, con-duct it onward to the Vasus. | Let not the fiends, O Man-Beholder, harm thee burning against the Rākṣhasas to slay them. || 10. Look on the fiend, amid men, as Man-Beholder: rend thou his three extremities in pieces. | Demolish with thy flame his ribs, O Agni: the Yātudhāna's root destroy thou triply. || 11. Thrice, Agni, let thy noose surround the demon who with his falsehood injures holy Order. | Loud roaring with thy flame, Jātavedas, fetter him in the pre-sense of the singer. || 12. Agni, what curse the pair this day may utter, what rude rough word the worshippers have spoken, | Each arrowy taunt sped from the angry spirit,—pierce to the heart therewith the Yātudhānas. || 13. With fervent heat exterminate the demons: destroy the fiends with glow and flame, O Agni. | Destroy with fire the foolish Gods' adorers: destroy the insatiate fiercely-burning creatures. || 14. May Gods destroy today the evil-doer: may uttered curses turn again and strike him. | Let arrows pierce the liar in his vitals, and Viśva's net enclose the Yātudhāna. || 15. The fiend who smears himself with flesh of cattle, with flesh of horses and of human bodies, | Who steals the milch-cow's milk away, O Agni,—tear off the heads of such with fiery fury. || 16. Let the fiends steal the poison of the cattle: may Aditi cast off the evil-doers. | May the God Savitar give them up to ruin, and be their share of herbs and plants denied them. || 17. The cow gives milk each year, O Man-Beholder: let not the Yātudhāna ever taste it. | Agni, if one should glut him with the biestings, pierce with thy flame his vitals as he meets thee. || 18. Agni, from days of old thou slayest demons: never have Rākṣhasas in fight o'ercome thee. | Burn up the foolish ones, the flesh-devourers: let none of them escape thy heavenly arrow. || 19. Guard us, O Agni, from above and under, protect us from behind and from before us; | And may thy flames, most fierce and never wasting, glowing with fervent heat, consume the sinner. ||

20. From rear, from front, from under, from above us, Agni, protect us as a sage with wisdom. | Guard to old age thy friend as friend eternal: O Agni, as immortal, guard us mortals. || 21. Lend thou the worshipper that eye, O Agni, where with thou lookest on the hoof-armed demons. | With light celestial in Atharvan's manner burn up the fool who ruins truth with falsehood. || 22. We set thee round us as a fort, victorious Agni! thee, a sage, | In conquering colour day by day, destroyer of the treacherous foe. || 23. With deadly poison strike thou back the treacherous brood of Rākṣhasas, | O Agni, with thy sharpened glow, with rays that flash with points of flame. || 24. Agni shines far and wide with lofty splendour, and by his greatness makes all things apparent. | He conquers godless and malign enchantments, and sharpens both his horns to gore the ogres. || 25. Thy two unwasting horns, O Jātavedas, keen-pointed weapons, sharpened by devotion | With these transfix the double-clicked Kimīdin, with fierce flame, Jātavedas! when he meets thee. || 26. Bright, radiant, meet to be adored, immortal with refulgent glow, | Agni drives Rākṣhasas away.

Hymn 8:4.

1. Indra and Soma, burn, destroy the demon foe! Send downward, O ye Bulls, those who add gloom to gloom. | Annihilate the fools, slay them and burn them up: chase them away from us, pierce the voracious fiends. || 2. Let sin, Indra and Soma! round the wicked boil, like as a cauldron set amid the flames of fire. | Against the foe of prayer, eater of gory flesh, the fearful-eyed Kimīdin, keep perpetual hate. || 3. Indra and Soma, plunge the wicked in the depth, yea, cast them into darkness that hath no support, | So that not one of them may ever thence return: so may your wrathful might prevail and conquer them. || 4. Indra and Soma, hurl your deadly crushing bolt down on the wicked fiend from heaven and from the earth. | Yea, fashion from the big clouds your celestial dart wherewith ye burn to death the waxing demon race. || 5. Indra and Soma, cast ye downward from the sky your deadly bolts of stone burning with fiery flame, | Eternal, scorching darts. Plunge the voracious fiends within the depth, and let them pass without a sound. || 6. Indra and Soma, let this hymn control you both, even as the girth encompasses two vigorous steeds | The song of praise which I with wisdom offer you. Do ye, as Lords of men, animate these my prayers. || 7. In your impetuous manner think ye both thereon: destroy those evil spirits, kill the treacherous fiends. | Indra and Soma, let the wicked have no bliss whoso at any time-attacks and injures us. || 8. Whoso accuses me with words of falsehood when I pursue my way with guileless spirit, | May he, the speaker of untruth, be, Indra! like water which the hollowed hand compresses. || 9. Those who destroy, as is their wont, the simple, and with their evil natures harm the righteous, | May Soma give them over to the serpent, or to the lap of Nirṛiti consign them. || 10. O Agni, whosoever seeks to injure the essence of our food, kine, steeds, or bodies, | May he, the adversary, thief, and robber, sink to destruction, both himself and offspring. || 11. May he be swept away, himself and children; may all the three earths press him down beneath them. | May his fair glory, O ye Gods, be blighted, who in the day or night would fain destroy us. || 12. The prudent finds it easy to distinguish the true and false: their words oppose each other. | Of these two that which is the true and honest Soma protects, and brings the false to nothing. || 13. Never doth Soma aid and guide the wicked or him who falsely claims the Warrior's title. | He slays the fiend and him who speaks untruly: both lie entangled in the noose of Indra. || 14. As if I worshipped deities of falsehood, or thought vain thoughts about the Gods, O Agni! | Why art thou angry with us, Jātavedas? Destruction fall on those who lie against thee! || 15. So may I die this day if I have harassed any man's life, or if I be a demon. | Yea, may he lose all his ten sons together who with false tongue hath called me Yātudhāna. || 16. May Indra slay him with a mighty weapon, and let the vilest of all creatures perish, | The fiend who says that he is pure, who calls me a demon though devoid of demon nature. || 17. She too who wanders like an owl at night-time, hiding her body in her guile and malice, | May she fall downward into endless caverns. May press-stones with loud ring destroy the demons. || 18. Spread out, ye Marutas, search among the people: seize ye and grind the Rākṣhasas to pieces, | Who fly abroad, transformed to birds, at night-time, and sully and pollute our holy worship. || 19. Hurl down from heaven thy bolt of stone, O Indra: sharpen it, Maghavan, made keen by Soma. | Forward, behind, and from above and under, smite down the demons with thy rocky weapon. || 20. They fly, the demon dogs, and, bent on mischief, fain would they harm indomitable Indra. | Śakra makes sharp his weapon for the wicked: now let him cast his bolt at fiendish wizards. || 21. Indra hath ever been the fiends' destroyer who spoil oblations of the Gods' invokers. | Yea, Śakra, like an axe that splits the timber, assails and smashes them like earthen vessels. || 22. Destroy the fiend shaped like an owl or owlet, destroy him in. the form of dog or cuckoo. | Destroy him shaped as eagle or as vulture: as with a stone, O Indra, crush the demon. || 23. Let not the fiend of witchcraft-workers reach us: may Dawn. drive off the couples of Kimīdins | Earth keep us safe from earthly woe and trouble! From grief that comes from heaven Mid-air preserve us! || 24. Indra destroy the demon, male and female, joying and triumphing in arts of magic! | Let the fools' Gods with bent necks fall and perish, and see no. more the Sun when he arises. || 25. Look, each one, hither, look around. Indra and Soma, watch ye well. | Cast forth your weapon at the fiends: against the sorcerers hurl your bolt.

Hymn 8:5.

1. Upon the strong is bound the strong, this magic cord, this Amulet, | Potent, foe-slayer, served by valiant heroes, happy and fortunate defence. || 2. This Charm, foe-slayer, served by many heroes, strong, powerful, victorious, and mighty, goes bravely forth to meet and ruin witchcraft. || 3. With this same Amulet wise Indra routed the Asuras, with this he slaughtered Vṛitra, | With this he won this pair, both Earth and Heaven, and made the sky's four regions his possession. || 4. May this encircling magic cord, this Amulet of Srāktya wood, | Mighty, subduing enemies, keep us secure on every side. || 5. This Agni hath declared, Soma declared it, Bṛihaspati, and Savitar, and Indra. | So may these Gods whom I have set before me oppose with saving charms and banish witchcraft. || 6. I have obscured the heaven and earth, yea, and the daylight and the sun. | So may these Gods whom I have set before me oppose with saving charms and banish witchcraft. || 7. Whoever for his armour takes an amulet of the Srāktya tree, | Like the Sun risen up to heaven, quells witchcraft with superior might. || 8. With Amulet of Srāktya wood, as with a thoughtful Ṛishi's aid, | In every fight have I prevailed; I smite the foes and Rākṣhasas || 9. All witchcraft of Aṅgirasas, all witchcraft wrought by Asuras, | All witchcraft self-originate, and all that others have prepared, | May these depart to both remotest spaces, past ninety ample water-floods. || 10. May the Gods bind the Charm on him for armour, Indra, and Vishṇu, Savitar Rudra, Agni, | Prajāpati, sublimest Parameṣhṭhin, Virāj, Vaiśvānara, and all the Ṛishis || 11. Thou art the chief of all the plants, even as a bull among the beasts. | A tiger of the beasts of prey. Him whom we sought for have we found, him lying near in wait for us. || 12. A tiger verily is he, he is a lion, and a bull, | Subduer of his foes is he, the man who wears this Amulet. || 13. No mortal beings slay him, no Gandharvas, no Apsarases; | O'er all the regions he is king, the man who wears this Amulet. || 14. Kaśyapa formed and fashioned thee, Kaśyapa raised and sent thee forth. | Indra wore thee, and, wearing thee, won in the wrestling-match with man. | The Amulet of boundless might the Gods have made a coat of mail. || 15. Whoever would destroy thee with Dīkṣhā-rites, sacrifices, spells, | Meet him and smite him, Indra! with thy hundred-knotted thunderbolt. || 16. Verily let this Amulet, circular, potent, conquering, | Happy and fortunate defence, preserve thy children and thy wealth. || 17. Brave Indra, set before us light, peace and security from below, | Peace and security from above, peace and security from behind. || 18. My coat of mail is Heaven and Earth, my coat of mail is Day and Sun: | A coat of mail may Indra and Agni and Dhātar grant to me. || 19. Not all the Gods may pierce, all leagued together, the vast strong shield which Indra gives, and Agni. | May that great shield on all sides guard my body, that to full old my life may be extended. || 20. Let the Gods' Charm be bound on me to keep me safe from every ill. | Come ye and enter all within this pillar, the safe-guard of the body, thrice-defended. || 21. In this let Indra lay a store of valour: approach ye Gods, and enter it together, | For his long life, to last a hundred autumns, that to full age his days may be extended. || 22. Lord of the clan who brings, us bliss, fiend-slayer, queller of the foe, | May he, the conqueror, ne'er subdued, may Indra bind the Charm on thee, | Bull, Soma-drinker, he who gives us peace. | May he protect thee round about, by night and day on every, side.

Hymn 8:6.

1. Let neither fiend of evil name, Alimṃśa, Vatsapa, desire | Thy pair of husband-wooers which thy mother cleansed when, thou wast born. || 2. Palāla, Anupalāla, Śarku, Koka, Malimlucha, Palījaka Vavrivāsas and Āśresha, Rikṣhagrīva and Pramīlin. || 3. Approach not, come not hitherward: creep not thou in-between her thighs. | I set, to guard her, Baja, that which chases him of evil name. || 4. Durṇāmā and Sunāmā both are eager to converse with her. | We drive away Arāyas: let Sunāmā seek the women-folk, || 5. The black and hairy Asura, and Stambaja and Tuṇḍika, | Arāyas from this girl we drive, from bosom, waist, and parts below. || 6. Sniffer, and Feeler, him who eats raw flesh, and him who licks his lips, | Arāyas with the tails of dogs, the yellow Baja hath destroyed. || 7. Whoever, in thy brother's shape or father's comes to thee in sleep, | Let Baja rout and chase them like eunuchs with woman's head-dress on. || 8. Whoever steals to thee asleep or thinks to harm thee when awake,— | These hath it banished, as the Sun travelling round drives shade away. || 9. Whoever causeth her to lose her child or bear untimely fruit,— | Destroy him, O thou Plant, destroy the slippery fiend who lusts for her. || 10. Those who at evening, with the bray of asses, dance around the house, Kukṣhilas, and Kusūlas, and Kakubhas, Srimas, Karumas, | These with thine odour, O thou Plant, drive far away to every side. || 11. Kukundhas and Kukūrabhas who dress themselves in hides and skins, | Who dance about like eunuchs, who raise a wild clamour in the wood, all these we banish far away. || 12. All those who cannot bear the Sun who warms us yonder from the sky, | Arāyas with the smell of goats, malodorous, with bloody mouths, the Makakas we drive afar. || 13. All those who on their shoulders bear a head of monstrous magnitude, | Who pierce the women's loins with pain,—those demons, Indra drive away! || 14. Those, bearing horns upon their hands, who first of all approach the brides; | Standing in ovens, laughing loud, those who in bushes flash forth light, all these we banish hence away. || 15. Those who have retroverted toes, and heels and faces in the front, | Khalajas, Śakadhūmajas, Uruṇḍas, all the Maṭmaṭas, impotent Kumbhamuṣhkas, these, | Drive thou, O Brahmaṇaspati, far from this girl with vigilance. || 16. Sightless and with distorted eyes, impotent. woman less be they. | O Healing Plant, cast each away who, not her husband, would approach this woman wedded to her lord. || 17. The Bristly-haired, the Maniac-haired, the Biter, and the Groper-fiend, | The Creeper-near, the Copper-hued, the Snouty, and the Śāluḍa, | With foot and heel kick over, as a hasty cow her milking-pan. || 18. If one should touch thy coming babe or kill thine infant newly born, | The yellow Plant with mighty bow shall pierce him even to the heart. || 19. Those who kill infants unawares, and near the new-made mothers lie, | Let Piṅga chase the amorous Gandharvas as wind chases cloud. || 20. Let it maintain the genial seed: let the laid embryo rest secure. | Let both strong Healers, to be worn within the girdle, guard the babe. || 21. From the Kimīdin, for thy lord and children, Piṅga shield thee well, | From Chāyaka, and Nagnaka, Taṅgalva, and Pavīnasa. || 22. From the five-footed, fingerless, from the four-eyed, the double-faced, | From the Close-creeper, from the Worm, from the Quick-roller guard her well. || 23. Those who eat flesh uncooked, and those who eat the bleeding flesh of men, | Feeders on babes unborn, long-haired, far from this place we banish these. || 24. Shy slinkers from the Sun, as slinks a woman from her husband's sire, | Deep down into the heart of these let Baja and let Piṅga pierce. || 25. Piṅga, preserve the babe at birth, make not the boy a female child. | Let not Egg-eaters mar the germs: drive the Kimīdins far away. || 26. Sterility, and infants' death, and weeping that announceth woe, | Dear! lay them on the fiend as thou wouldst pluck a garland from a tree.

Hymn 8:7.

1. The tawny-coloured, and the pale, the variegated and the red, | The dusky-tinted, and the black,—all Plants we summon hither-ward. || 2. This man let them deliver from Consumption which the Gods have sent. | The father of these Herbs was Heaven, their mother Earth, the Sea their root. || 3. The Waters are the best, and heavenly Plants. | From every limb of thine have they removed Consumption caused by sin. || 4. I speak to Healing Herbs spreading, and bushy, to creepers, and to those whose sheath is single, | I call for thee the fibrous and the reed-like, and branching. | Plants, dear to the Viśvedevas, powerful, giving life to men. || 5. The conquering strength, the power and might which ye, victorious Plants, possess, | Therewith deliver this man here from this Consumption, O ye Plants: so I prepare the remedy. || 6. The living Plant that giveth life, that driveth malady away, | Arundhatī, the rescuer, strengthening, rich a sweets I call, to free this man from scathe and harm. || 7. Hitherward let the sapient come, the friendly sharers o f my speech. | That we may give this man relief and raise him from his evil plight. || 8. Germ of the Waters, Agni's food, Plants ever growing fresh and new, | Sure, healing, bearing thousand names, let them be all collected here. || 9. Let Plants whose soul is water, girt with Avakās, piercing with their sharp horns expel the malady. || 10. Strong, antidotes of poison, those releasers, free from Varuṇa, | And those that drive away Catarrh, and those that frustrate magic arts, let all those Plants come hitherward. || 11. Let purchased Plants of mightier power, Plants that are praised for excellence. | Here in this village safely keep cattle and horses, man and beast. || 12. Sweet is their root, sweet are these Plants' top branches, sweet also is their intermediate portion; | Sweet is their foliage, and sweet their blossom, combined with sweetness is their taste of Amṛita: food, fatness let them yield, with kine preceding. || 13. These Plants that grow upon the earth, whate'er their number and their size, | Let these with all their thousand leaves free me from Death and misery. || 14. May the Plants' Tiger-amulet, protective, guardian from the curse, | Beat off the brood of demons, drive all maladies afar from us. || 15. Before the gathered Plants they fly and scatter, as though a lion's roar or fire dismayed them. | Expelled by Plants, let men's and kine's Consumption pass from us to the navigable rivers. || 16. Emancipated from the sway of Agni, of Vaiśvānara, go, covering the earth, ye Plants whose ruler is Vanaspati. || 17. May these be pleasant to our heart, auspicious, rich in store of milk, | These Plants of the Aṅgirasas which grow on mountains and on plains. || 18. The Plants I know myself, the plants that with mine eye I look upon, | Plants yet unknown, and those we know, wherein we find that power is stored, || 19. Let all the congregated Plants attend and mark mine utterance, | That we may rescue this man here and save him from severe distress. || 20. Aśvattha, Darbha, King of Plants, is Soma, deathless sacrifice | Barley and Rice are healing balms, the sons of Heaven who never die. || 21. Lift yourselves up, ye Healing Plants, loud is the thunder's crash and roar. | When with full flow Parjanya, ye Children of Pṛiśni! blesseth; you. || 22. We give the essence of that stream of nectar of this man to drink: | So I prepare a remedy that he may live a hundred years. || 23. Well doth the wild boar know a Plant, the mungoose knows the Healing Herb. | I call, to aid this man, the Plants which Serpents and Gandharvas know. || 24. Plants of Aṅgirasas which hawks, celestial Plants which eagles know; | Plants known to swans and lesser fowl, Plants known to all the birds that fly. | Plants that are known to sylvan beasts,—I call them all to aid this man. || 25. The multitude of herbs whereon the Cows whom none may slaughter feed, all that are food for goats and sheep, | So many Plants, brought hitherward, give shelter and defence to thee! || 26. Hitherward unto thee I bring the Plants that cure all maladies, | All Plants wherein physicians have discovered health-bestowing power. || 27. Let Plants with flower and Plants with bud, the fruitful and the fruitless, all, | Like children of one mother, yield their stores for this man's perfect health. || 28. From the Five-arrowed, from the Ten-arrowed have I delivered thee, | Freed thee from Yama's fetter and from all offence against the Gods.

Hymn 8:8.

1. Indra the Shaker shake them up, brave, hero, fort-demolisher, | That into thousand fragments we may strike the armies of our foes! || 2. Let Pūtirajju with her breath corrupt and putrefy that host, | And terror smite our foemen's heart when fire and smoke are seen afar. || 3. Aśvattha, rend those men; do thou devour them quickly, Khadira! | Like reeds let them be broken through, down-smitten by a lifted rush. || 4. Let Paruṣhāhva make them reeds, and let the bulrush strike them down: | Bound in a mighty net let them break quickly like an arrow's shaft. || 5. Air was the net; the poles thereof were the great quarters of the sky: | Śakra therewith enveloped and cast on the ground the Dasyus' host. || 6. Verily mighty is the net of mighty Śakra rich in wealth: | Therewith press all the foemen down so that not one of them escape! || 7. Great is thy net, brave Indra, thine the mighty match for a thousand, Lord of Hundred Powers! | Holding them, with his host, therewith hath Indra slaughtered Dasyus a hundred, thousand, myriad,

hundred millions. || 8. This world so mighty was the net of Śakra, of the Mighty One: | With this, the net of Indra, I envelop all those men with gloom. || 9. Great weakness and misfortune, pain which words can never charm away, | Languor, fatigue, bewilderment, with these I compass all the foes. || 10. I give those foemen up to Death: bound in the bonds of Death are they. | I bind and carry them away to meet Death's wicked messengers. || 11. Bear them away, Death's messengers! envoys of Yama! bind them fast. | More than a thousand be their slain: the club of Bhava pierce them through! || 12. Forth go the Sādhyas in their might bearing one net-pole raised aloft. | One pole the Rudras carry, one the Vasus, and the Ādityas one. || 13. The Viśvedevas from above shall come depressing it with might, | And in the midst the Aṅgirasas, slaying the mighty host, shall go. || 14. Trees of the forest, trees that bear flower and fruit, and herbs and plants, | Quadruped, biped send I forth that they may strike this army dead, || 15. Gandharvas, and Apsarases, Gods, Serpents, Fathers, Holy Men, | Seen and unseen, I send them forth that they may strike this army dead. || 16. Here spread are snares of Death wherefrom thou, once within them, ne'er art freed: | Full many a thousand of the host yonder this horn shall smite and slay. || 17. The Gharma hath been warmed with fire: this Homa slays a thousand men. | Let Bhava, Pṛiśnibāhu, and Śarva destroy that armament. || 18. Their portion be the fire of Death, hunger, exhaustion, slaughter, fear. | With your entangling snares and nets, Śarva and Indra! slay that host. || 19. Fly, conquered, in alarm, ye foes, run driven by the spell away! | Let not one man escape of those when routed by Bṛihaspati || 20. Down fall their weapons on the ground: no strength be theirs to point a shaft: | Then in their dreadful terror let their arrows wound their vital parts. || 21. Let Heaven and Earth roar out in wrath against them, and Air with all the Deities in concert, | Let them not find a surety or a refuge, but torn away go down to Death together. || 22. The mules of the Gods' car are heaven's four quarters; their hooves are sacred cakes, the air its body. | Its sides are Heaven and Earth, its reins the Seasons, Voice is its hood, its grooms are sky's mid-regions. || 23. Year is the car, Full Year the seat for driving, Virāj the pole, the chariot's front is Agni, Indra the warrior, and the Moon the driver. || 24. Hence conquer, conquer, Hail! be thou the victor! Let these be conquerors and those be conquered. | Good luck to these, ill luck to those men yonder! With the dark-blue-and-red our foes I cover.

Hymn 8:9.

1. Whence were these two produced? which was that region? | From what world, from which earth had they their being? | Calves of Virāj, these two arose from water. I ask thee of these twain, who was their milker. || 2. He who prepared a threefold home, and lying there made the water bellow through his greatness, | Calf of Virāj, giving each wish fulfilment, made bodies for him-self far off, in secret. || 3. Which are the three, the mighty three, whereof the fourth divides the voice, | This may the Brahman know by prayer and fervour, whereto belongs the one, whereto the other. || 4. Out of the Bṛihat as the sixth five Salmons have been fashioned forth: | From Bṛihatī was Bṛihat formed: whence was the Bṛihatī composed? || 5. On measure Bṛihatī is based, and measure on the measurer: | From magic might came magic might, from magic might came Mātalī || 6. Vaiśvānara's image is the sky above us, so far as Agni forced both spheres asunder. | Thence from that region as the sixth come praise-songs, and every sixth day hence again go upward. || 7. We, Kaśyapa! six present Ṛishis, ask thee—for thou hast proved things tried and meet for trial | They call Virāj the Father of Devotion: tell her to us thy friends in all her figures. || 8. She whom, advancing, sacrifices follow, and when she takes her station stand beside her, | By whose control and hest the spirit moveth, she is Virāj, in highest heaven, O Ṛishis || 9. Breathless, she moves by breath of living creatures, Svarāj pre-cedes, Virāj comes closely after. | Some men behold her not, and some behold her, Virāj meet-shaped, who thinks of all existence. || 10. Who hath perceived Virāj's duplication, perceived her seasons and her rule and practice? | Who knows her steps, how oft, how far extended, who knows her home and number of her dawnings? || 11. She here who first of all sent forth her lustre moves onward resting on these lower creatures. | Exalted power and might are stored within her: the woman hath prevailed, the new-come mother. || 12. Both Dawns on wings of song, with rich adornment, move on together to their common dwelling. | Sūrya's two wives, unwasting, most prolific, knowing their way, move, rich in light, together. || 13. The three have passed along the path of Order—three warm libations have regarded offspring | One quickens progeny, one strengthens vigour, and one protects the kingdom of the pious. || 14. She who was fourth was made by Agni, Soma, and Ṛishis as. they formed both halves of worship, | Gāyatrī, Trishṭubh, Jagatī, Anushṭubh, Bṛihadarkī lightening the sacrificer. || 15. Five milkings answer to the fivefold dawning, five seasons to the cow who bears five titles. | The five sky-regions made fifteen in number, one head have these to one sole world directed. || 16. Six Elements arose, first-born of Order: the six-day time is carried by six Sāmans. | Six-yoked the plough is, as each trace is numbered: they call both broad ones six; six, Earth and Heaven. || 17. They call the cold months six, and six the hot ones. Which, tell us, of the seasons is redundant? | Seven sages, eagles, have sat down together: seven metres match the seven Consecrations. || 18. Seven are the Homas, seven the logs for burning, seven are the streams of mead, and seven the seasons. | Into the world have come seven streams of butter; those we have heard of as the Seven Vultures. || 19. Seven metres, by four syllables increasing, each of the seven founded upon another | How are the hymns of praise on these supported, and how are these imposed upon the praise-songs? || 20. How hath the Gāyatrī filled out three triads? On the fifteen how is the Trishṭubh moulded, | Jagatī fashioned on the three-and-thirty? How is Anushṭubh formed? how Ekaviṃśa? || 21. Eight Elements sprang up, first born of Order: the Priests divine are eight in number, Indra! | Eight are the wombs of Aditi, eight her children; for the eighth night is the libation destined. || 22. So planning bliss for you have I come hither to win your friendship: kind am I, and gracious. | Born from one source, propitious is your wisdom: knowing full well to all of you it cometh. || 23. To Indra eight, to Yama six, seven to the Ṛishis, seven to each: | The number five accompanies waters and men and healing herbs. || 24. The Heifer, all his own, poured forth for Indra control and milk at her first time of milking; | And he then satisfied the four divisions, the Gods and men and Asuras and Ṛishis || 25. Who is the Cow? Who is the Single Ṛishi? What is the law, what are the benedictions? | What on the earth is the one only Spirit? Which of the number is the Single Season? || 26. One is the Cow, one is the Single Spirit, one is the law, single are benedictions. | The Spirit dwelling on the earth is single: the Single Season never is transcended.

Hymn 8:10.

1. Virāj at first was This. At birth all feared her; the thought, She will become this All, struck terror. || 2. She rose, the Gārhapatya fire she entered. He who knows this becomes lord of a household, performer of domestic sacrifices. || 3. She mounted up, the Eastward fire she entered. He who knows this becomes the Gods' beloved, and to his call they come when she invokes them. || 4. She mounted up, the Southward fire she entered. He who knows this becomes a fit performer of sacrifice, meet for honour, shelter-giver. || 5. She mounted up, she entered the Assembly. He who knows this becomes polite and courtly, and people come as guests to his assembly. || 6. She mounted up, she passed within the meeting. He who knows this becomes fit for the meeting, and to his hall of meeting come the people. || 7. She mounted up, she entered Consultation. Whoso knows this is fit to be consulted, and to his consultation come the people. || 8. She mounted up, and, into four divided, she took her station in the air's mid-region. || 9. Of her the Gods and men said, This she knoweth. That we may both have life let us invoke her. || 10. Thus did they cry to her: || 11. Come, Strength! come, Food! come, Charmer! come, Free-giver! || 12. Her calf, her well-beloved calf, was Indra: Gāyatrī was her rope, the cloud her udder. || 13. Two teats she had, Rathantara and Bṛihat, two, Yajñāyajñiya and Vāmadevya. || 14. With the Rathantara the Gods milked from her the Plants, and all the wide expanse with Bṛihat || 15. They drew the Waters forth with Vāmadevya, with Yajñāyajñiya they milked out worship. || 16. For him who knoweth this, Rathantara poureth out Plants, and Bṛihat yieldeth wide expansion. || 17. Waters from Vāmadevya come, from Yajñāyajñiya sacrifice. || 18. She rose, she came unto the tress: they killed her. A year went by and she again existed. | Hence in a year the wounds of trees heal over. He who knows this sees his loathed rival wounded. || 19. She mounted up, she came unto the Fathers: they killed her: in a month she re-existed. | Hence men give monthly offerings to the Fathers: who knows this, knows the path which they have trodden. || 20. She rose, she came

unto the Gods: they killed her: but in a fortnight she again was living. | Fortnightly, hence, men serve the Gods with Vashaṭ! Who knows this knows the way which Gods pass over. || 21. She mounted up, she came to men: they killed her Presently she regained her life and being. | Hence on both days to men they bring and offer—who knows this—near-seated in the dwelling. || 22. She rose, approached the Asuras: they called her: their cry was, Come, O Māyā, come thou hither. | Her dear calf was Virochana Prāhrādi: her milking vessel was a pan of iron. | Dvimūrdha Ārtvya milked her, yea, this Māyā, The Asuras depend for life on Māyā. He who knows this becomes a fit supporter. || 23. She mounted up, she came unto the Fathers. The Fathers called. to her, O Food, come hither. | King Yama was her calf, her pail was silvern. Antaka, Mṛityu's son, milked her, this Svadhā. | This Food the Fathers make their lives' sustainer. He who knows this becomes a meet supporter. || 24. She mounted up, she came to men. They called her, Come unto-us, come hither thou Free-giver! | Earth was her milking-pail, the calf beside her Manu Vaivasvata, Vivasvat's offspring. | Pṛithi the son of Vena was her milker: he milked forth husbandry and grain for sowing. | These men depend for life on corn and tillage. He who knows this becomes a meet supporter, successful in the culture of his cornland. || 25. She rose, she came unto the Seven Ṛishis They called her, | Come, Rich in Devotion! hither. | King Soma was her calf. the Moon her milk-pail. Bṛihaspati Aṅgirasa, her milker, | Drew from her udder Prayer and Holy Fervour. Fervour and Prayer maintain the Seven Ṛishis | He who knows this becomes a meet supporter, a priest illustrious for his sacred knowledge. || 26. She rose, she came unto the Gods. They called her, crying, O Vigour, come to us, come hither! | God Savitar milked her, he milked forth Vigour. The Gods depend for life upon that Vigour. He who knows this becomes a meet supporter. || 27. She rose approached the Apsarases and Gandharvas. They called her, Come to us, O Fragrant-scented! | The son of Sūryavarchas, Chitraratha, was her dear calf, her pail. a lotus-petal. | The son of Sūryavarchas, Vasuruchi, milked and drew from her most delightful fragrance. | That scent supports Apsarases and Gandharvas. He who knows this becomes a meet supporter, and round him ever breathes delicious odour. || 28. She mounted up, she came to Other People. They called her, crying, Come, Concealment! hither. | Her dear calf was Vaiśravaṇa Kubera, a vessel never tempered was her milk-pail. | Rajatanābhi, offspring of Kubera, milked her, and from her udder drew concealment. | By that concealment live the Other People. He who knows this becomes a meet supporter, and makes all evil disappear and vanish. || 29. She mounted up, she came unto the Serpents. The Serpents called her, Venomous! come hither. | Her calf was Takshaka, Vaiśala's offspring: a bottle-gourd supplied a milking-vessel. | Irāvat's offspring, Dhṛitarāshṭra milked her, and from her udder drew forth only poison. | That poison quickens and supports the Serpents: He who knows this becomes a meet supporter. || 30. One would ward off, for him who hath this knowledge, if with a bottle-gourd he sprinkled water. || 31. And did he not repel, if in his spirit he said, I drive thee back, he would repel it. || 32. The poison that it drives away, that poison verily repels. || 33. The man who hath this knowledge pours its venom on his hated foe.

Kāṇḍa 9.

Hymn 9:1.

1. The Aśvins' Honey-whip was born from heaven and earth, from middle air, and ocean, and from fire and wind. | All living creatures welcome it with joyful hearts, fraught with the store of Amṛita it hath gathered up. || 2. They call thee earth's great strength in every form, they call thee too the ocean's genial seed. | Whence comes the Honey-whip bestowing bounty, there Vital Spirit is, and Amṛita treasured. || 3. In sundry spots, repeatedly reflecting, men view upon the earth: her course and action; | For she, the first-born daughter of the Marutas, derives her origin from Wind and Agni. || 4. Daughter of Vasus, mother of Ādityas, centre of Amṛita breath of living creatures. | The Honey-whip, gold-coloured, dropping fatness, moves as a mighty embryo amid mortals. || 5. The deities begat the Whip of Honey: her embryo assumed all forms and fashions. | The mother nourishes that tender infant which at its birth looks on all worlds and beings. || 6. Who understandeth well, who hath perceived it, her heart's uninjured Soma-holding beaker? | Let the wise Brahman priest therein be joyful. || 7. He understandeth them, he hath perceived them, her breasts that pour a thousand streams, uninjured. | They unreluctantly yield strength and vigour. || 8. She who with voice upraised in constant clamour, mighty, life-giving, goes unto her function, | Bellowing to the heated three libations, suckles with streams of milk, and still is lowing. || 9. On whom, well-fed, the Waters wait in worship, and steers and self-refulgent bulls attend her. | For thee, for one like thee down pour the Waters, and cause desire and strength to rain upon thee. || 10. The thunder is thy voice, O Lord of Creatures: a Bull, thou castest on the earth thy vigour. | The Honey-whip, the Manus' first-born daughter, derives her origin from Wind and Agni. || 11. As at the morning sacrifice the Aśvins twain love Soma well, | Even so may both the Aśvins lay splendour and strength within my soul. || 12. As at the second sacrifice Indra and Agni love him well, | Let the pair, Indra Agni, lay splendour and strength within my soul. || 13. As at third sacrifice Soma is the Ṛibhus' well-beloved one, | Even so may they, the Ṛibhus, store splendour and strength within my soul. || 14. Fain would I bring forth sweetness, fain would make it mine. | Bringing milk, Agni! have I come: splendour and strength bestow on me! || 15. Grant me, O Agni, splendid strength, and progeny, and lengthened life. | May the Gods know me as I am, may Indra with the Ṛishis know. || 16. As honey-bees collect and add fresh honey to their honey store, | Even so may both the Aśvins lay splendour and strength within my soul. || 17. As over honey flies besmear this honey which the bees have made, | So may both Aśvins lay in me splendour and strength and power and might. || 18. May all the sweetness that is found in hills and mountains, steeds and kine, | And wine that floweth from the cup,—may all that sweetness be in me. || 19. May both the Aśvins, Lords of Light, balm me with honey of the bees, | That I may speak among the folk words full of splendour and of strength. || 20. The thunder is thy voice, O Lord of Creatures: a Bull, thou castest strength on earth and heaven. | To that all cattle look for their existence: with this she nourishes their force and vigour. || 21. The Whip itself is Heaven, Earth is the handle, the point of juncture is the Air's mid-region. | The lash is lightning, and the tip is golden. || 22. Whoever knows the Whip's seven kinds of honey, becomes himself a man endowed with sweetness. | Brahman and King, the draught-ox and the milch-cow, barley and rice, and honey is the seventh. || 23. Sweet is the man, sweet are his goods and chattels: he who knows this conquers the worlds of sweetness. || 24. The thundering of Prajāpati in heaven is verily manifest to living creatures. | Therefore I stand from right to left invested, and, O Prajāpati, I cry, regard me! | The man who hath this knowledge is regarded by living beings and the Lord of Creatures.

Hymn 9:2.

1. Kāma the Bull, slayer of foes, I worship with molten butter, sacrifice, oblation. | Beneath my feet cast down mine adversaries with thy great manly power, when I have praised thee. || 2. That which is hateful to mine eye and spirit, that harasses and robs me of enjoyment, | The evil dream I loose upon my foemen. May I rend him when I have lauded Kāma. || 3. Kāma, do thou, a mighty Lord and Ruler, let loose ill dream, misfortune, want of children, | Homelessness, Kāma! utter destitution, upon the sinner who designs my ruin. || 4. Drive them away, drive them afar, O Kāma; indigence fall on those who are my foemen! | When they have been cast down to deepest darkness, consume their dwellings with thy fire, O Agni. || 5. She, Kāma! she is called the Cow, thy daughter, she who is named Vāk and Virāj by sages. | By her drive thou my foemen to a distance. May cattle, vital breath, and life forsake them. || 6. By Kāma's might, King Varuṇa's and Indra's, by Vishṇu's strength, and Savitar's instigation, | I chase my foes with sacrifice to Agni, as a deft steersman drives his boat through waters. || 7. May Kāma, mighty one, my potent warder, give me full freedom from mine adversaries. | May all the Deities be my protection, all Gods come nigh to this mine invocation. || 8. Accepting this oblation rich with fatness, be joyful here, ye Gods whose chief is Kāma, | Giving me freedom from mine adversaries. || 9. Ye, Indra, Agni, Kāma! come together and cast mine adversaries down beneath me. | When they have sunk into the deepest darkness, O Agni, with thy fire consume their dwellings. || 10. Slay those who are mine enemies, O Kāma: headlong to depth of blinding darkness hurl them. | Reft be they all of manly strength and vigour! Let

them not have a single day's existence. || 11. Kāma hath slain those who were mine opponents, and given me ample room to grow and prosper. | Let the four regions bow them down before me, and let the six expanses bring me fatness. || 12. Let them drift downward like a boat torn from the rope that held it fast. | There is no turning back for those whom our keen arrows have repelled. || 13. Agni averts, Indra averts, and Soma: may the averting Gods avert this foeman. || 14. To be avoided by his friends, detested, repelled, with few men round him, let him wander. | Yea, on the earth descend the lightning-flashes: may the strong God destroy your adversaries. || 15. This potent lightning nourishes things shaken, and things unshaken yet, and all the thunders. | May the Sun, rising with his wealth and splendour, drive in victorious might my foemen downward. || 16. Thy firm and triply-barred protection, Kāma! thy spell, made weapon-proof extended armour | With that drive thou my foemen to a distance. May cattle, vital breath, and life forsake them. || 17. Far from the world wherein we live, O Kāma, drive thou my foemen with that selfsame weapon | Wherewith the Gods repelled the fiends, and Indra cast down the Dasyus into deepest darkness. || 18. As Gods repelled the Asuras, and Indra down to the lowest darkness drove the demons, | So, Kāma, from this world, to distant places, drive thou the men who are mine adversaries. || 19. First before all sprang Kāma into being. Gods, Fathers, mortal men have never matched him. | Stronger than these art thou, and great for ever. Kāma, to thee, to thee I offer worship. || 20. Wide as the space which heaven and earth encompass, far as the flow of waters, far as Agni, | Stronger than these art thou, and great for ever. Kāma, to thee, to thee I offer worship. || 21. Vast as the quarters of the sky and regions that lie between them spread in all directions, vast as celestial tracts and views of heaven, | Stronger than these art thou, and great for ever. Kāma, to thee, to thee I offer worship. || 22. Many as are the bees, and bats, and reptiles, and female serpents of the trees, and beetles, | Stronger art thou than these, and great for ever. Kāma, to thee, to thee I offer worship. || 23. Stronger art thou than aught that stands or twinkles, stronger art thou than ocean, Kāma! Manyu! | Stronger than these art thou, and great for ever. Kāma, to thee, to thee I offer worship. || 24. Not even Vāta is the peer of Kāma, not Agni, Chandramas the Moon, nor Sūrya. | Stronger than these art thou, and great for ever. Kāma, to thee, to thee I offer worship. || 25. Thy lovely and auspicious forms, O Kāma, whereby the thing thou wilt becometh real, | With these come thou and make thy home among us, and make malignant thoughts inhabit elsewhere.

Hymn 9:3.

1. We loose the ties and fastenings of the house that holds all precious things, | The bands of pillars and of stays, the ties of beams that form the roof. || 2. All-wealthy House! each knot and band, each cord that is attached to thee | I with my spell untie, as erst Bṛihaspati disclosed the cave. || 3. He drew them close, he pressed them fast, he made thy knotted. bands secure: | With Indra's help we loose them as a skilful Slaughterer severs joints. || 4. We loose the bands of thy bamboos, of bolts, of fastening, of thatch, | We loose the ties of thy side-posts, O House that holdest all we prize. || 5. We loosen here the ties and bands of straw in bundles, and of clamps, | Of all that compasses and binds the Lady Genius of the Home. || 6. We loose the loops which men have bound within thee, loops to tie and hold. | Be gracious, when erected, to our bodies, Lady of the Home. || 7. Store-house of Soma, Agni's hall, the ladies' bower, the residence, | The seat of Gods art thou, O Goddess House. || 8. We with our incantation loose the net that hath a thousand. eyes. | The diadem, securely tied and laid upon the central beam. || 9. The man who takes thee as his own, and he who was thy builder, House! | Both these, O Lady of the Home, shall live to long-extended years. || 10. There let her come to meet this man. Firm, strongly fastened, and prepared | Art thou whose several limbs and joints we part and loosen one by one. || 11. He who collected timber for the work and built thee up, O House, | Made thee for coming progeny, Prajāpati, the Lord Supreme. || 12. Homage to him! We worship too the giver and the Mansion's lord: | Homage to Agni! to the man who serves at holy rites for thee. || 13. Homage to kine and steeds! to all that shall be born within the house | We loose the bonds that fasten thee, mother of multitudes to come! || 14. Agni thou shelterest within, and people with domestic beasts. | We loose the bonds that fasten thee, mother of multitudes to come! || 15. All space that lies between the earth and heaven, therewith I take this house for thy possession, | And all that measures out the air's mid-region I make a hollow to contain thy treasures. Therewith I take the house for his possession. || 16. Rich in prosperity, rich in milk, founded and built upon the earth, | Injure not thy receivers, House who holdest food of every sort! || 17. Grass-covered, clad with straw, the house, like Night, gives rest to man and beast. | Thou standest, built upon the earth, like a she-elephant, borne on feet. || 18. I loosen and remove from thee thy covering formed by mats of reed. | What Varuṇa hath firmly closed Mitra shall open at early morn. || 19. May Indra, Agni, deathless Gods, protect the house where Soma dwells, | House that was founded with the prayer, built and erected by the wise. || 20. Nest upon nest hath been imposed, compartment on compartment laid: | There man shall propagate his kind, and there shall everything born. || 21. Within the house constructed with two side-posts, or with four, or six. | Built with eight side-posts, or with ten, lies Agni like a babe unborn. || 22. Turned to thee, House! I come to thee, innocent, turned to welcome me: | For Fire and Water are within, the first chief door of sacrifice. || 23. Water that kills Consumption, free from all Consumption, here I bring. | With Agni, the immortal one, I enter and possess the house. || 24. Lay thou no cord or noose on us: a weighty burthen, still be light! | Withersoever be our will, O House, we bear thee like a bride. || 25. Now from the east side of the house to the Great Power be homage paid! | Hail to the Gods whose due is Hail! || 26. Now from the south side of the house, etc. || 27. Now from the west side of the house, etc. || 28. Now from the north side of the house, etc. || 29. So from the mansion's every side to the Great Power be homage paid! | Hail to the Gods whose due is Hail!

Hymn 9:4.

1. The Bull, fierce, thousandfold, filled full of vigour, bearing within his flanks all forms and natures, | Bṛihaspati's Steer, hath stretched the thread, bestowing bliss on the worshipper, the liberal giver. || 2. He who at first became the Waters' model, a match for everyone, like Earth the Goddess; | The husband of the cows, the young calves' father, may be secure us thousandfold abundance. || 3. Masculine, pregnant, steadfast full of vigour, the Bull sustains a trunk of goodly treasure. | May Agni Jātavedas bear him offered, on pathways traversed by the Gods, to Indra. || 4. The husband of the cows, the young calves' father, father is he of mighty water-eddies. | Calf, after-birth, new milk drawn hot, and biestings, curds, butter, that is his best genial humour. || 5. He is the Gods' allotted share and bundle, essence of waters, and of plants, and butter. | Śakra elected him, the draught of Soma. What was his body was a lofty mountain. || 6. A beaker filled with Soma juice thou bearest. framer of forms, begetter of the cattle. | Kindly to us be these thy wombs here present, and stay for us, O Axe, those that are yonder. || 7. He bears oblation, and his seed is butter. Thousandfold plenty; sacrifice they call him. | May he, the Bull, wearing the shape of Indra, come unto us, O Gods, bestowed, with blessing. || 8. Both arms of Varuṇa, and Indra's vigour, the Marutas' hump is he, the Aśvins' shoulders. | They who are sages, bards endowed with wisdom, call him Bṛihaspati compact and heightened. || 9. Thou, vigorous, reachest to the tribes of heaven. Thee they call Indra, thee they call Sarasvat. | Turned to one aim, that Brahman gives a thousand who offers up the Bull as his oblation. || 10. Bṛihaspati, Savitar gave thee vital vigour: thy breath was brought from Tvaṣhṭar and from Vāyu. | In thought I offer thee in air's mid-region. Thy sacrificial grass be Earth and Heaven! || 11. Let the priest joyfully extol the limbs and members of the Bull | Who moved and roared among the kine as Indra moves among the Gods. || 12. The sides must be Anumati's, and both rib-pieces Bhaga's share, | Of the knee-bones hath Mitra said, Both these are mine, and only mine. || 13. The Ādityas claim the hinder parts, the loins must be Bṛihaspati's. | Vāta, the God, receives the tail: he stirs the plants and herbs therewith, || 14. To Sūrya they assigned the skin, to Sinīvālī inward parts. | The Slaughterer hath the feet, they said, when they distributed the Bull. || 15. They made a jest of kindred's curse: a jar of Soma juice was set, | What time the deities, convened, assigned the Bull's divided parts. || 16. They gave the hooves to tortoises, to Saramā scraps of the feet: | His undigested food they gave to worms and things that creep and crawl. || 17. That Bull, the husband of the kine, pierces the demons with his horns, | Banishes famine with his eye, and hears good tidings with his ears. || 18. With hundred sacrifices he worships: the fires consume him not: |

All Gods promote the Brahman who offers the Bull in sacrifice. || 19. He who hath given away the Bull to Brahmans frees and cheers his soul. | In his own cattle-pen he sees the growth and increase of his cows. || 20. Let there be cattle, let there be bodily strength and progeny: | All this may the Gods kindly grant to him who gives away the Bull. || 21. Indra here verily hath rejoiced: let him bestow conspicuous wealth. | May he draw forth at will from yonder side of heaven a deft cow, good to milk, whose calf is never wanting. || 22. With close connexion mingle with the cows in this our cattle-pen: | Mingle, the Bull's prolific flow, and, Indra! thine heroic strength! || 23. Here we restore this Bull, your youthful leader: sporting with him, go, wander at your pleasure. | Ne'er, wealthy ones! may he be reft of offspring; and do ye favour us with growth of riches.

Hymn 9:5.

1. Seize him and bring him hither. Let him travel. foreknowing, to the regions of the pious. | Crossing in many a place the mighty darkness, let the Goat mount to the third heaven above us. || 2. I bring thee hither as a share for Indra; prince, at this sacrifice, for him who worships. | Grasp firmly from behind all those who hate us: so let the sacrificer's men be sinless. || 3. Wash from his feet all trace of evil-doing: foreknowing, with cleansed hooves let him go upward. | Gazing on many a spot, crossing the darkness, let the Goat mount to the third heaven above us. || 4. Cut up this skin with the grey knife, Dissector! dividing joint from joint, and mangle nothing | Do him no injury: limb by limb arrange him, and send him up to the third cope of heaven. || 5. With verse upon the fire I set the cauldron: pour in the water; lay him down within it! | Encompass him with fire, ye Immolators. Cooked, let him reach the world where dwell the righteous. || 6. Hence come thou forth, vexed by no pain or torment. Mount to the third heaven from the heated vessel. | As fire out of the fire hast thou arisen. Conquer and win this lucid world of splendour. || 7. The Goat is Agni: light they call him, saying that living man must give him to the Brahman. | Given in this world by a devout believer, the Goat dispels and drives afar the darkness. || 8. Let the Pañchaudana Goat, about to visit the three lights, pass away in five divisions. | Go midst the pious who have paid their worship, and parted, dwell on the third cope of heaven. || 9. Rise to that world, O Goat, where dwell the righteous: pass, like a Śarabha veiled, all difficult places. | The Goat Pañchaudana, given to a Brahman, shall with all fullness satisfy the giver. || 10. The Goat Pañchaudana, given to a Brahman, sets the bestower on the pitch of heaven, | In the third vault, third sky, third ridge. One only Cow omni-form art thou, that yields all wishes. || 11. That is the third light that is yours, ye Fathers. He gives the Goat Pañchaudana to the Brahman. | Given in this world by the devout believer, the Goat dispels and drives afar the darkness. || 12. Seeking the world of good men who have worshipped, he gives the Goat Pañchaudana to the Brahman. | Win thou this world as thy complete possession. Auspicious unto us be he, accepted! || 13. Truly the Goat sprang from the glow of Agni, inspired as sage with all a sage's power. | Sacrifice, filled, filled full, offered with Vaṣhaṭ—this let the Gods arranged at proper seasons. || 14. Home-woven raiment let him give, and gold as guerdon to the priests. | So he obtains completely all celestial and terrestrial worlds. || 15. Near to thee, Goat! approach these streams of Soma, divine, distilling meath, bedecked with butter! | Stay thou the earth and sky and fix them firmly up on the seven-rayed pitch and height of heaven. || 16. Unborn art thou, O Goat: to heaven thou goest. Though thee Aṅgirasas knew that radiant region. | So may I know that holy world. || 17. Convey our sacrifice to heaven, that it may reach the Gods, with that | Whereby thou, Agni, bearest wealth in thousands, and all precious things. || 18. The Goat Pañchaudana, when cooked, transporteth, repelling Nirṛiti, to the world of Svarga. | By him may we win worlds which Sūrya brightens. || 19. The droppings of the Odanas attending the Goat which I have lodged with priest or people | May all this know us in the world of virtue, O Agni, at the meeting of the pathways. || 20. This Unborn cleft apart in the beginning: his breast became the earth, his back was heaven. | His middle was the air, his sides the regions; the hollows of his belly formed both oceans. || 21. His eyes were Truth and Right. The whole together was Truth: Virāj his head and Faith his breathing. | This Goat Pañchaudana was indeed a sacrifice unlimited. || 22. A boundless sacrifice he performs, he wins himself a boundless world: | Who gives the Goat Pañchaudana illumined with a priestly fee. || 23. Let him not break the victim's bones, let him not suck the marrow out. | Let the man, taking him entire, here, even here deposit him. || 24. This, even this is his true form: the man uniteth him therewith. | Food, greatness, strength he bringeth him who giveth the Goat Pañchaudana illumed with guerdon. || 25. The five gold pieces, and the five new garments, and the five milch-kine yield him all his wishes. | Who gives the Goat Pañchaudana illumined with a priestly fee. || 26. The five gold pieces, area light to light him, robes become armour to defend his body; | He winneth Svarga as his home who giveth the Goat Pañchaudana illumed with bounty. || 27. When she who hath been wedded finds a second husband after-ward, | The twain shall not be parted if they give the Goat Pañchaudana || 28. One world with the re-wedded wife becomes the second husband's home. | Who gives the Goat Pañchaudana illumined with the priestly fee. || 29. They who have given a cow who drops a calf each season, or an ox, | A coverlet, a robe, or gold, go to the loftiest sphere of heaven. || 30. Himself, the father and the son, the grandson, and the father's sire, | Mother, wife, her who bore his babes, all the beloved ones I call. || 31. The man who knows the season named the Scorching—the Goat Pañchaudana is this scorching season | He lives himself, he verily burns up his hated rival's fame, | Who gives the Goat Pañchaudana illumined with the priestly fee. || 32. The man who knows the season called the Working takes to himself the active fame, his hated rival's active fame. | The Goat Pañchaudana is this Working season. | He lives himself, etc. || 33. The man who knows the season called the Meeting takes to him-self the gathering fame, his hated rival's gathering fame. | The Goat Pañchaudana is this Meeting season. || 34. The man who knows the called the Swelling takes to himself the swelling fame, his hated rival's swelling fame. | The Goat Pañchaudana is this Swelling season. | He lives himself, etc. || 35. The man who knows the season called the Rising takes to him-self the rising fame, his hated rival's rising fame. | The Goat Pañchaudana in this Rising season. || 36. The man who knows the season called Surpassing takes to himself the conquering fame, his hated rival's conquering fame. | The Goat Pañchaudana is this Conquering season. | He lives himself, he verily burns up his hated rival's fame | Who gives the Goat Pañchaudana illumined with a priestly fee. || 37. He cooks the Goat and the five boiled rice messes. May the united Quarters, all accordant, and intermediate points, accept him from thee. || 38. May these preserve him for thee. Here I offer t o these the molten butter as oblation.

Hymn 9:6.

1. Whoso will know Prayer with immediate knowledge, whose members are the stuff, whose spine the verses: || 2. Whose hairs are psalms, whose heart is called the Yajus, whose coverlet is verily oblation— || 3. Verily when a host looks at his guests he looks at the place of sacrifice to the Gods. || 4. When he salutes them reverently he undergoes preparation for a religious ceremony: when he calls for water, he solemnly brings sacrificial water. || 5. The water that is solemnly brought at a sacrifice is this same water. || 6. The libation which they bring; the sacrificial victim dedicated to Agni and Soma which is tied to the post, that, verily, is this man. || 7. When they arrange dwelling-rooms they arrange the sacred chamber and the shed for housing the Soma cars. || 8. What they spread upon the floor is just Sacrificial Grass. || 9. With the couch that the men bring, he wins for himself the world of Svarga. || 10. The pillow-coverings that they bring are the green sticks that surround the sacrificial altar. || 11. The ointment that they bring for injunction is just clarified liquid butter. || 12. The food they bring before the general distribution represents the two sacrificial cakes of rice meal. || 13. When they call the man who prepares food they summon the preparer of oblation. || 14. The grains of rice and barley that are selected are just filaments of the Soma plant. || 15. The pestle and mortar are really the stones of the Soma press. || 16. The winnowing-basket is the filter, the chaff the Soma dregs, the water, the pressing-gear. || 17. Spoon, ladle, fork, stirring-prong are the wooden Soma tubs; the earthen cooking-pots are the mortar-shaped Soma vessels; this earth is just the black-antelope's skin. || 18. Or the host acts in this way to a Yajamāna's Brahman: when he looks at the furniture and utensils he says, More here t yet more here. || 19. When he says, Bring out more, he lengthens his life thereby. || 20. He brings oblations: he makes the men sit down. || 21. As the guest of the seated company he himself offers up sacrifice. || 22. With ladle, with hand, in life,

at the sacrificial post, with cry of Ladle! with exclamation of Vaṣhaṭ! || 23. Now these guests, as priests beloved or not beloved, bring one to the world of Svarga. || 24. He who hath this knowledge should not eat hating, should not eat the food of one who hates him, nor of one who is doubtful, nor of one who is undecided. || 25. This man whose food they eat hath all his wickedness blotted out. || 26. All that man's sin whose food they do not eat remains unblotted out. || 27. The man who supplies food hath always pressing stones adjusted, a wet Soma filter, well prepared religious rites, and mental power to complete the arranged sacrifice. || 28. The arranged sacrifice of the man who offers food is a sacrifice to Prajāpati. || 29. The man who offers food follows the steps of Prajāpati. || 30. The fire of the guests is the Āhavanīya, the fire in the dwelling is the Gārhapatya, that whereon they cook food is the Southern Sacrificial Fire. || 31. Now that man who eats before the guest eats up the sacrifice and the merit of the house. || 32. He devours the milk and the sap: || 33. And the vigour and prosperity. || 34. And the progeny and the cattle: || 35. And the fame and reputation. || 36. The man who eats before the guest eats up the glory and the understanding of the house. || 37. The man should not eat before the guest who is a Brahman versed in holy lore. || 38. When the guest hath eaten he should eat. This is the rule for the animation of the sacrifice and the preservation of its continuity. || 39. Now the sweetest portion, the produce of the cow, milk, or flesh, that verily he should not eat. || 40. The man who having this knowledge pours out milk and offers it wins for himself as much thereby as he gains by the performance of a very successful Agniṣhṭoma sacrifice. || 41. The man who having this knowledge pours out clarified butter and offers it wins for himself thereby as much as he gains by the performance of a very successful Atirātra sacrifice. || 42. He who pours out mead and offers it wins for himself thereby as much as he gains by the performance of a very successful Sattrasadya sacrifice. || 43. He who having this knowledge besprinkles flesh and offers it wins for himself thereby as much as he gains by the performance of a very successful Twelve-Day sacrifice. || 44. The man who having this knowledge pours out water and offers it obtains a resting-place for the procreation of living beings and becomes dear to living beings, even the man who having this knowledge pours out water and offers it. || 45. For him Dawn murmurs, and Savitar sings the prelude; Bṛihaspati chants with vigour, and Tvaṣhṭar joins in with increase; the Viśvedevas take up conclusion. He who hath this knowledge is the abiding-place of welfare, of progeny, and of cattle. || 46. For him the rising Sun murmurs, and Early Morning sings the prelude; Noon chants the psalm, Afternoon joins in; the setting Sun takes up the conclusion. He who hath this knowledge is the abiding place of welfare, of progeny, and of cattle. || 47. For him the Rain-cloud murmurs when present, sings the prelude when thundering, joins in when lightening, chants the psalm when raining, and takes up the conclusion when it stays the downpour. He who hath this knowledge is the abiding-place of welfare, of progeny, and of cattle. || 48. He looks at the guests, he utters a gentle sound; he speaks, he signs the prelude; he calls for water, he chants the psalm; he offers the residue of the sacrifice, he takes up the conclusion. || 49. When he summons the door-keeper he gives instruction. || 50. He (the door-keeper) pronounces the sacrificial formula in his answer to what he hears. || 51. When the attendants with vessels in their hands, foremost and hindmost, come in, they are just the priests who manage the Soma cups. || 52. Not one of them is incompetent to sacrifice. || 53. Or if the host, having offered food to his guest, goes up to the house, he virtually enters the bath of purification. || 54. When he distributes food he distributes priestly fees; what he performs he asks as favour. || 55. He having been invited on earth, regales, invited in that, which wears all various forms on earth. || 56. He, having been invited in air, regales, invited, in that which wears all various forms in air. || 57. He having been invited in the sky, regales, invited, in that which wears all various forms in the sky. || 58. He, having been invited among the Gods, regales, invited in that which wears all various forms among the Gods. || 59. He, having been invited in the worlds, regales, invited, in that which wears all various forms in the worlds. || 60. He, having been invited hath been invited. || 61. He gains this world and the world yonder. || 62. He who hath this knowledge wins the luminous spheres.

Hymn 9:7.

1. Prajāpati and Parameṣhṭhin are the two horns, Indra is the head, Agni the forehead, Yama the joint of the neck. || 2. King Soma is the brain, Sky is the upper jaw, Earth is the lower jaw. || 3. Lightning is the tongue, the Marutas are the teeth, Revatī is the neck, the Kṛittikās are the shoulders, the Gharma s the shoulder-bar. || 4. His universe is Vāyu, Svarga is his world, Kṛiṣhṇadram is the tendons and Vertebrae. || 5. The Śyena ceremony is the breast, Air is the region of the belly, Bṛihaspati is the hump, Bṛihatī the breast-bone and cartilages of the ribs. || 6. The consorts of the Gods are the ribs, the attendants are ribs. || 7. Mitra and Varuṇa are the shoulder-blades. Tvaṣhṭar and Aryaman the fore-arms, Mahādeva is the arms. || 8. Indrāṇī is the hinder parts, Vāyu the tail, Pavamāna the hair. || 9. Priestly rank and princely power are the hips, and strength is. the thigh. || 10. Dhātar and Savitar are the two knee-bones, the Gandharvas are the legs the Apsarases are bits of the feet, Aditi is the hooves. || 11. Thought is the heart, intelligence is the liver, law the pericardium. || 12. Hunger is the belly, refreshing drink is the rectum, mountains. are the inward parts. || 13. Wrath is the kidneys, anger the testes, offspring the generative organ. || 14. The river is the womb, the Lords of the Rain are the breasts, the thunder is the udder. || 15. The All-embracing (Aditi) is the hide, the herbs are her hair, and the Lunar Mansions her form. || 16. The hosts of Gods are her entrails, man are her bowels, and demons her abdomen. || 17. Rākṣhasas are the blood, the Other Folk are the contents of the Stomach. || 18. The rain-cloud is her fat, her resting-place her marrow. || 19. Sitting he is Agni, when he hath stood up he is the Aśvins || 20. Standing east-wards he is Indra, standing southwards, Yama. || 21. Standing westwards he is Dhātar, standing northwards Savitar. || 22. When he hath got his grass he is King Soma. || 23. He is Mitra when he looks about him, and when he hath turned round he is joy. || 24. When he is yoking he belongs to the All-Gods, when yoked he is Prajāpati, when unyoked he is All. || 25. This verily is omniform, wearing all forms, bovine-formed. || 26. Upon him wait omniform beasts, wearing every shape, each one who hath this knowledge.

Hymn 9:8.

1. Each pain and ache that racks the head, earache, and erysipelas, | All malady that wrings thy brow we charm away with this our spell. || 2. From both thine ears, from parts thereof, thine earache, and the throbbing pain, | All malady that wrings thy brow we charm away with this our spell. || 3. So that Consumption may depart forth from thine ears and from. thy mouth, | All malady that wrings thy brow we charm away with this our spell. || 4. The malady that makes one deaf, the malady that makes one blind, | All malady that wrings thy brow we charm away with this our spell. || 5. The throbbing pain in all thy limbs that rends thy frame with fever-throes, | All malady that wrings thy brow we charm away with this our spell. || 6. The malady whose awful look makes a man quiver with alarm, | Fever whom every Autumn brings we charm away with this our spell. || 7. Disease that creeps about the thighs and, after, reaches both the groins, | Consumption from thine inward parts we charm away with this our spell. || 8. If the disease originates from love, from hatred, from the heart, | Forth from the heart and from the limbs we charm the wasting malady. || 9. The yellow Jaundice from thy limbs, and Colic from the parts within, | And Phthisis from thine inward soul we charm away with this our spell. || 10. Let wasting malady turn to dust, become the water of disease. | I have evoked the poison-taint of all Consumptions out of thee. || 11. Forth from the hollow let it run, and rumbling sounds from thine inside. | I have evoked the poison-taint of all Consumptions out of thee. || 12. Forth from thy belly and thy lungs, forth from thy navel and thy heart. | I have evoked the poison taint of all Consumptions out of thee. || 13. The penetrating stabs of pain which rend asunder crown and head, | Let them depart and pass away, free from disease and harming not. || 14. The pangs that stab the heart and reach the breast-bone and connected parts, | Let them depart and pass away, free from disease and harming not. || 15. The stabs that penetrate the sides and pierce their way along the ribs, | Let them depart and pass away, free from disease and harming not. || 16. The penetrating pangs that pierce thy stomach as they shoot across, | Let them depart and pass away, free from disease and harming not. || 17. The pains that through the bowels creep, disordering the inward parts, | Let them depart and pass away, free from disease and harming not. || 18. The pains that suck the

marrow out, and rend and tear the bones apart, | May they speed forth and pass away, free from disease and harming not. || 19. Consumptions with their Colic pains which make thy limbs insensible | I have evoked the poison-taint of all Consumptions out of thee. || 20. Of piercing pain, of abscesses, rheumatic ache, ophthalmia— | I have evoked the poison-taint of all Consumptions out of thee. || 21. I have dispelled the piercing pains from feet, knees, hips, and hinder parts, | And spine, and from the neck and nape the malady that racked the head. || 22. Sound are the skull-bones of thy head and thy heart's beat is regular. | Thou, Sun, arising with thy beams hast chased away the head's disease, hast stilled the pain that racked the limbs.

Hymn 9:9.

1. The second brother of this lovely Hotar, hoary with eld, is the voracious Lightning. | The third is he whose back is balmed with butter. Here have I seen the King with seven male children. || 2. The seven make the one-wheeled chariot ready: bearing seven names the single Courser draws it. | The wheel, three-naved, is sound and undecaying: thereon these worlds of life are all dependent. || 3. The seven who on this seven-wheeled car are mounted have horses, seven in tale, who draw them onward. | Seven sisters utter songs of praise together, in whom the Cows' seven names are held and treasured. || 4. Who hath beheld at birth the Primal Being, when She who hath no bone supports the bony? | Where is the blood of earth, the life, the spirit? Who may approach the man who knows, to ask it? || 5. Let him who knoweth presently declare it, this lovely Bird's securely-founded station. | Forth from his head the Cows draw milk, and wearing his vesture with their foot have drunk the water. || 6. Unripe in mind, in spirit undiscerning, I ask of these the Gods' established places. | High up above the yearling Calf the sages, to form a web, their own seven threads have woven. || 7. Here, ignorant, I ask the wise who know it, as one who knows not, for the sake of knowledge, | What is That One, who in the Unborn's image hath established and fixed firm this world's six regions. || 8. The Mother gave the Sire his share of Order. With thought at first she wedded him in spirit. | She, coyly loth, was filled with dew prolific. With adoration men approached to praise her. || 9. Yoked was the Mother to the boon Cow's car-pole; in humid folds of cloud the infant rested. | Then the Calf lowed and looked upon the Mother, the Cow who wears all shapes in three directions. || 10. Bearing three mothers and three fathers, single he stood erect: they never made him weary. | On yonder heaven's high ridge they speak together in speech not known to all, themselves all-knowing. || 11. Upon the five-spoked wheel revolving ever, whereon all creatures rest and are dependent, | The axle, heavy-laden, is not heated: the nave from ancient time remains unheated. || 12. They call him in the farther half of heaven the Sire five-footed, of twelve forms, wealthy in watery store. | These others, later still, say that he takes his stand upon a seven-wheeled car, six-spoked, whose sight is clear. || 13. Formed with twelve spokes, too strong for age to weaken, this wheel of during Order rolls round heaven. | Herein established, joined in pairs together, seven hundred sons and twenty stand, O Agni. || 14. The wheel revolves, unwasting, with its felly: ten draw it, yoked to the far-stretching car-pole. | Girt by the region moves the eye of Sūrya, on whom dependent rest all living creatures. || 15. They told me these were males, though truly females. He who hath eyes sees this, the blind discerns not. | The son who is a sage hath comprehended: who knows this rightly is his father's father. || 16. Of the co-born they call the seventh single-born: the six twin, pairs are called the Ṛishis, sons of Gods. | Their good gifts sought of men are ranged in order due, and, various, form by form, move for their guiding Lord. || 17. Beneath the upper realm, above this lower, bearing her Calf at foot, the Cow hath risen. | Whitherward, to what place hath she departed? Where doth she calve? Not in this herd of cattle. || 18. Who, that the father of this Calf discerneth beneath the upper realm, above the lower, | Showing himself a sage, may here declare him? Whence hath the godlike spirit had its rising? || 19. Those that come hitherward they call departing, those that depart they call directed hither. | Whatever ye have made, Indra and Soma! steeds draw, as 'twere, yoked to the region's car-pole. || 20. Two Birds with fair wings, knit with bonds of friendship, in the same sheltering tree have found a refuge, | One of the twain eats the sweet Fig-tree's berry: the other, eating not, regardeth only. || 21. The tree whereon the fine Birds eat the sweetness, where they all rest and procreate their offspring | Upon the top, they say the fruit is luscious: none gaineth it who knoweth not the Father. || 22. Where the fine birds hymn ceaselessly their portion of life eternal, and the sacred synods. | There is the Universe's Guard and Keeper who, wise hath entered into me the simple.

Hymn 9:10.

1. How on the Gāyatrī the Gāyatrī was based; how from the Trishṭubh they fashioned the Trishṭubh forth: | How on the Jagatī was based the Jagatī—they who know this have won themselves immortal life. || 2. With Gāyatrī he measures out the praise-song, Sāman with praise-song, triplet with the Trishṭubh, | The triplet with the two or four-foot measure, and with the syllable they form seven metres. || 3. With Jagatī the flood in heaven he established, and saw the Sun in the Rathantara Sāman. | Gāyatrī hath, they say, three logs for burning: hence it excels in majesty and vigour. || 4. I invocate this Milch-cow good at milking, so that the Milker, deft of hand, may milk her. | May Savitar give goodliest stimulation. The cauldron is made hot: he will proclaim it. || 5. She, Lady of all treasures, hath come hither, yearning in spirit for her calf, and lowing. | May this Cow yield her milk for both the Aśvins, and may she prosper to our high advantage. || 6. The Cow hath lowed after her blinking youngling: she licks his forehead as she lows, to form it. | His mouth she fondly calls to her warm udder, and suckles him with milk while gently lowing. || 7. He also snorts, by whom encompassed round the Cow lows as she closely clings to him who sheds the rain. | She with her shrilling cries hath humbled mortal men, and turned to lightning, hath stripped off her covering robe. || 8. That which hath breath and life and speed and motion lies firmly established in the midst of houses. | The living moves by powers of the departed: the immortal is the brother of the mortal. || 9. The old hath waked the young Moon from his slumber, who runs his circling course with many round him. | Behold the God's high wisdom in its greatness: he who died yesterday today is living. || 10. He who hath made him doth not comprehend him: from him who saw him surely he is hidden. | He, yet enveloped in his mother's bosom, source of much life, hath sunk into destruction. || 11. I saw the Herdsman, him who never stumbles, approaching by his pathways and departing. | He clothed with gathered and diffusive splendours, within the worlds continually travels. || 12. Dyaus is our father, our begetter: kinship is here. This great Earth is our kin and mother. | Between the wide-spread world-halves is the birth-place. The Father laid the Daughter's germ within it. || 13. I bid thee tell me earth's extremest limit, about the Stallion's genial flow I ask thee; | I ask about the universe's centre, and touching highest heaven where Speech abideth. || 14. The earth's most distant limit is this altar: this Soma is the Stallion's genial humour; | This sacrifice the universe's centre: this Brahman highest heaven where Speech abideth. || 15. What thing I truly am I know not clearly: mysterious, fettered in my mind I wander. | When the first-born of holy Law approached me, then of this Speech I first obtain a portion. || 16. Back, forward goes he, grasped by power inherent, immortal born the brother of the mortal. | Ceaseless they move in opposite directions: men mark the one and fail to mark the other. || 17. Seven germs unripened yet are Heaven's prolific seed: their functions they maintain by Vishṇu's ordinance. | Endued with wisdom through intelligence and thought, present on every side they compass us about. || 18. Upon what syllable of holy praise-hymn, as 'twere their highest heaven, the Gods repose them | Who knows not this, what will he do with praise-hymn? But they who know it well sit here assembled. || 19. They, ordering the verse's foot by measure, with the half-verse arranged each thing that moveth. | Prayer was diffused in many forms three-footed thereby the world's four regions have their being || 20. Fortunate mayst thou be with goodly pasture, and may we also be exceeding wealthy. | Feed on the grass, O Cow, through all the seasons, and coming hitherward drink limpid water. || 21. Forming the water-floods the Cow herself hath lowed, one-footed or two-footed or four-footed, she, | Who hath become eight-footed or acquired nine feet, the uni-verse's thousand-syllabled Paṅkti From her descend in streams the seas of water. || 22. Dark the descent: the birds are golden-coloured. Robed in the floods they fly aloft to heaven. | Again from Order's seat have they descended, and inundated all the earth with fatness. || 23. The footless Maid precedeth footed creatures. Who marketh, Mitra Varuṇa! this your doing? | The Babe

unborn supporteth this world's burthen, supporteth Right and watcheth Wrong and Falsehood. ‖ 24. Virāj is Speech, and Earth, and Air's mid-region. He is Prajāpati, and he is Mṛityu | He is the Lord Imperial of the Sādhyas. He rules what is and what shall be hereafter. May he make me lord of what is and shall be. ‖ 25. I saw from far away the smoke of fuel with spires that rose on high o'er that beneath it. | The heroes cooked and dressed the spotted bullock. These were the customs in the days aforetime. ‖ 26. Three with long tresses show in ordered season. One of them sheareth when the year is ended. | One with his powers the universe regardeth. Of one the sweep is seen, but not the figure. ‖ 27. Speech hath been measured out in four divisions: the Brahmans who have wisdom comprehend them. | Three, kept in close concealment, cause no motion. Of Speech men speak the fourth division only. ‖ 28. They call him Indra, Mitra, Varuṇa, Agni; and he is heavenly nobly-winged Garutmān. | That which is One bards call by many a title: they call It Agni, Yama, Mātariśvan.

Kāṇḍa 10.

Hymn 10:1.

1. Afar let her depart: away we drive her whom, made with hands, all-beautiful, | Skilled men prepare and fashion like a bride amid her nuptial train. ‖ 2. Complete, with head and nose and ears, all-beauteous, wrought with magic skill | Afar let her depart: away we drive her. ‖ 3. Made by a Śūdra or a Prince, by priests or women let her go. | Back to her maker as her kin, like a dame banished by her lord. ‖ 4. I with this salutary herb have ruined all their magic arts, | The spell which they have cast upon thy field, thy cattle, or thy men. ‖ 5. Ill fall on him who doeth ill, on him who curseth fall the curse! | We drive her back that she may slay the man who wrought the witchery. ‖ 6. Against her comes the Aṅgirasa, the Priest whose eye is over us. | Turn back all witcheries and slay those practisers of magic arts. ‖ 7. Whoever said to thee, Go forth against the foeman up the stream, | To him, O Kṛityā, go thou back. Pursue not us, the sinless ones. ‖ 8. He who composed thy limbs with thought as a deft joiner builds a car, | Go to him: thither lies thy way. This man is all unknown to thee. ‖ 9. The cunning men, the sorcerers who fashioned thee and held thee fast,— | This cures and mars their witchery, this, repellent, drives it back the way it came. With this we make thee swim. ‖ 10. When we have found her ducked and drenched, a hapless cow whose calf hath died, | Let all my woe depart and let abundant riches come to me. ‖ 11. If, as they gave thy parents aught, they named thee, or at sacrifice, | From all their purposed evil let these healing herbs deliver thee. ‖ 12. From mention of thy name, from sin against the Fathers or the Gods, | These herbs of healing shall by prayer release thee, by power, by holy texts, the milk of Ṛishis ‖ 13. As the wind stirs the dust from earth and drives the rain cloud from the sky, | So, chased and banished by the spell, all misery departs from me. ‖ 14. Go with a resonant cry, depart, like a she-ass whose cords are loosed. | Go to thy makers: hence! away! Go driven by the potent spell. ‖ 15. This, Kṛityā, is thy path, we say, and guide thee. We drive thee back who hast been sent against us. | Go by this pathway, breaking loose for onslaught even as a host complete with cars and horses. ‖ 16. No path leads hitherward for thee to travel. Turn thee from us: far off, thy light is yonder. | Fly hence across the ninety floods, the rivers most hard to pass. | Begone, and be not wounded. ‖ 17. As wind the trees, so smite and overthrow them: leave not cow, horse, or man of them surviving | Return, O Kṛityā, unto those who made thee. Wake them from sleep to find that they are childless. ‖ 18. The charm or secret power which they have buried for thee in sacred grass, field, cemetery, | Or spell in household fire which men more cunning have wrought against thee innocent and simple,— ‖ 19. That tool of hatred, understood, made ready, stealthy and buried deep, have we discovered, | Let that go back to whence it came, turn thither like a horse and kill the children of the sorcerer. ‖ 20. Within our house are swords of goodly iron. Kṛityā, we know thy joints and all their places. | Arise this instant and begone! What, stranger! art thou seeking here? ‖ 21. O Kṛityā, I will cut thy throat and hew thy feet off. Run, be-gone! | Indra and Agni, Guardian Lords of living creatures, shield us well! ‖ 22. May Soma, gracious friend, imperial Sovereign, and the world's Masters look on us with favour. ‖ 23. Bhava and Śarva cast the flash of lightning, the weapon of the Gods, against the sinner who made the evil thing, who deals in witchcraft! ‖ 24. If thou hast come two-footed or four-footed, made by the sorcerer, wrought in perfect beauty, | Become eight-footed and go hence. Speed back again, thou evil one. ‖ 25. Anointed, balmed, and well adorned, bearing all trouble with thee, go. | Even as a daughter knows her sire, so know thy marker, Kṛityā, thou. ‖ 26. Kṛityā, begone, stay not. Pursue as 'twere the wounded creature's track. | He is the chase, the hunter thou he may not slight or humble thee. ‖ 27. He waits, and aiming with his shaft smites him who first would shoot at him, | And, when the foeman deals a blow before him, following strikes him down. ‖ 28. Hearken to this my word; then go thither away whence thou hast come; to him who made thee go thou back. ‖ 29. The slaughter of an innocent, O Kṛityā, is an awful deed. Slay not cow, horse, or man of ours. | In whatsoever place thou art concealed we rouse thee up there-from: become thou lighter than a leaf. ‖ 30. If ye be girt about with clouds of darkness, bound as with a net. | We rend and tear all witcheries hence and to their maker send them back. ‖ 31. The brood of wizard, sorcerer, the purposer of evil deed. | Crush thou, O Kṛityā spare not, kill those practisers of magic arts. ‖ 32. As Sūrya frees himself from depth of darkness, and casts away the night and rays of morning, | So I repel each baleful charm which an enchanter hath prepared; | And, as an elephant shakes off the dust, I cast the plague aside.

Hymn 10:2.

1. Who framed the heels of Purusha? Who fashioned the flesh of him? Who formed and fixed his ankles? | Who made the openings and well-moulded fingers? Who gave him foot-soles and a central station? ‖ 2. Whence did they make the ankles that are under, and the knee-bones of Purusha above them? | What led them onward to the legs' construction? Who planned and formed the knees' articulations? ‖ 3. A fourfold frame is fixt with ends connected, and up above the knees a yielding belly. | The hips and thighs, who was their generator, those props where-by the trunk grew firmly established? ‖ 4. Who and how many were those Gods who fastened the chest of Purusha and neck together? | How many fixed his breasts? Who formed his elbows? How many joined together ribs and shoulders? ‖ 5. Who put together both his arms and said, Let him show manly strength? | Who and what God was he who set the shoulder-blades upon the trunk? ‖ 6. Who pierced the seven openings in the head? Who made these ears, these nostrils, eyes, and mouth, | Through whose surpassing might in all directions bipeds and quadrupeds have power of motion? ‖ 7. He set within the jaws the tongue that reaches far, and thereon placed Speech the mighty Goddess. | He wanders to and fro mid living creatures, robed in the waters. Who hath understood it? ‖ 8. Who was he, first, of all the Gods who fashioned his skull and brain and occiput and forehead, | The pile that Purusha's two jaws supported? Who was that God who mounted up to heaven? ‖ 9. Whence bringeth mighty Purusha both pleasant and unpleasant things, | Of varied sort, sleep, and alarm, fatigue, enjoyments and de-lights? ‖ 10. Whence is there found in Purusha want, evil, suffering, distress? | Whence come success, prosperity opulence, thought, and utterance? ‖ 11. Who stored in him floods turned in all directions, moving diverse and formed to flow in rivers, | Hasty, red, copper-hued, and purple, running all ways in Purusha, upward and downward? ‖ 12. Who gave him visible form and shape? Who gave him magnitude and name? | Who gave him motion, consciousness? Who furnished Purusha with feet? ‖ 13. Who wove the vital air in him, who filled him with the down-ward breath? | What God bestowed on Purusha the general pervading air? ‖ 14. What God, what only Deity placed sacrifice in Purusha? | Who gave him truth and falsehood? Whence came Death and immortality? ‖ 15. Who wrapped a garment round him? Who arranged the life he hath to live? | Who granted him the boon of speech? Who gave this fleetness to his feet? ‖ 16. Through whom did he spread waters out, through whom did he make Day to shine? | Through whom did he enkindle Dawn and give the gift of even-tide? ‖ 17. Who set the seed in him and said, Still be the thread of life spun out? | Who gave him intellect besides? Who gave him voice and gestic power? ‖ 18. Through whom did he bedeck the earth, through whom did he encompass heaven? | Whose might made Purusha surpass the mountains and created things? ‖ 19. Through whom seeks he Parjanya out, and Soma of the piercing sight? | Through whom belief and sacrifice? Through whom was spirit laid in him? ‖ 20. What leads him to

the learned priest? What leads him to this Lord Supreme? | How doth he gain this Agni? By whom hath he measured out the year? || 21. He, Brahma gains the learned priest, he Brahma, gains this Lord Supreme. | As Brahma, Man wins Agni here Brahma hath measured out the year. || 22. Through whom doth he abide with Gods? Through whom with the Celestial Tribes? | Why is this other called a star? Why is this called the Real Power? || 23. Brahma inhabits with the Gods, Brahma among the Heavenly Tribes. | Brahma this other star is called. Brahma is called the Real Power. || 24. By whom was this our earth disposed? By whom was heaven placed over it? | By whom was this expanse of air raised up on high and stretched across? || 25. By Brahma was this earth disposed: Brahma is sky arranged above. | Brahma is this expanse of air lifted on high and stretched across. || 26. Together, with his needle hath Atharvan sewn his head and heart. | And Pavamāna hovered from his head on high above his brain. || 27. That is indeed Atharvan's head, the well-closed casket of the Gods. | Spirit and Food and Vital Air protect that head from injury. || 28. Stationed on high, Purușha hath pervaded all regions spread aloft and stretched transversely. | He who knows Brahma's cattle, yea, the fort whence Purușha is named, || 29. Yea, knows that fort of Brahma girt about with immortality, | Brahma and Brāhmas have bestowed sight, progeny, and life on him. || 30. Sight leaves him not, breath quits not him before life's natural decay, | Who knows the fort of Brahma, yea, the fort whence Purusha is named. || 31. The fort of Gods, impregnable, with circles eight and portals nine, | Contains a golden treasure-chest, celestial, begirt with light. || 32. Men deep in lore of Brahma know that Animated Being which | Dwells in the golden treasure-chest that hath three spokes and three supports. || 33. Brahma hath passed within the fort, the golden castle; ne'er subdued, | Bright with excessive brilliancy, compassed with glory round about.

Hymn 10:3.

1. Here is my charm the Varaṇa, slayer of rivals, strong in act. | With this grasp thou thine enemies, crush those who fain would injure thee. || 2. Break them in pieces; grasp them and destroy them. This Amulet shall go before and lead thee. | With Varaṇa the Gods, from morn to morning, have warded off the Asuras' enchantment. || 3. This charm, this Varaṇa healeth all diseases, bright with a thou-sand eyes and golden glister. | This charm shall conquer and cast down thy foemen. Be thou the first to slay the men who hate thee. || 4. This will stay witchcraft wrought for thee, will guard thee from the fear of man: | From all distress and misery this Varaṇa will shield thee well. || 5. Guard against ill of varied kind is Varaṇa this heavenly Plant. | The Gods have stayed and driven off Consumption which had seized this man. || 6. If in thy sleep thou see an evil vision, oft as the beast repeats his loathed approaches, | This Amulet, this Varaṇa will guard thee from sneeze, and from the bird's ill-omened message. || 7. From Mischief, from Malignity, from incantation, from alarm, | From death, from stronger foeman's stroke the Varaṇa will guard thee well. || 8. Each sinful act that we have done,—my mother, father, and my friends,— | From all the guilt this heavenly Plant will be our guard and sure defence. || 9. Affrighted by the Varaṇa let my rivals near akin to me | Pass to the region void of light: to deepest darkness let them go. || 10. Safe are my cattle, safe am I, long-lived with all my men around. | This Varaṇa, mine Amulet, shall guard me well on every side. || 11. This Varaṇa is on my breast, the sovereign, the celestial Plant. | Let it afflict my foemen as Indra quelled fiends and Asuras. || 12. Through hundred autumn seasons, long to live, I wear this Varaṇa | May it bestow on me great strength, cattle, and royalty and power. || 13. As with its might the wind breaks down the trees, the sovereigns of the wood, | So break and rend my rivals, born before me and born after. Let the Varaṇa protect thee well. || 14. As Agni and the wind devour the trees, the sovereigns of the wood, | Even so devour my rivals, born before me and born after. Let the Varaṇa protect thee well. || 15. As, shattered by the tempest, trees lie withering ruined on the ground. | Thus over throw my rivals thou, so crush them down and ruin. them, those born before and after. Let this Varaṇa protect thee well. || 16. Cut them in pieces, Varaṇa! before their destined term of life, | Those who would hurt his cattle, those who fain would harm. the realm he rules. || 17. As Sūrya shines with brightest sheen, as splendour hath been stored in him, | So may the Charm, the Varaṇa, give me prosperity and fame. | With lustre let it sprinkle me, and balm me with magnificence || 18. As glory dwelleth in the Moon and in the Sun who vieweth men, | So may the Charm, etc. || 19. As glory dwelleth in the Earth, and in this Jātavedas here, | So may the Charm etc. || 20. As glory dwelleth in a maid, and in this well-constructed car, | So may the Charm, etc. || 21. As glory dwelleth in the draught of Soma and the honeyed. drink, | So may the Charm, etc. || 22. As glory dwells in sacrifice to Agni, and the hallowing word, | So may the Charm, etc. || 23. As glory is bestowed upon the patron and this sacrifice, | So may the Charm, etc. || 24. As glory dwelleth in the Lord of Life and in this God Supreme, | So may the Charm, etc. || 25. As immortality and truth have been established in the Gods, | So may the Charm, the Varaṇa, give me prosperity and fame. With lustre let it sprinkle me, and balm me with magnificence.

Hymn 10:4.

1. The first of all is Indra's car, next is the chariot of the Gods the third is Varuṇa's alone. | The last, the Serpents' chariot, struck the pillar and then sped away. || 2. Their lustre is the Darbha-grass, its young shoots are their horse's tail: the reed's plume is their chariot seat. || 3. Strike out, white courser! with thy foot, strike both with fore and hinder foot, | Stay the dire poison of the Snakes, and make it weak as soaking wood. || 4. Loud neighing he hath dived below, and rising up again replied, | Stayed the dire poison of the Snakes, and made it weak as soaking wood. || 5. Paidva kills Kasarṇīla, kills both the white Serpent and the black, | Paidva hath struck and cleft in twain Ratharvī's and the Viper's head. || 6. Go onward, horse of Pedu! go thou first: we follow after thee. | Cast thou aside the Serpents from the pathway whereupon we tread. || 7. Here was the horse of Pedu born: this is the way that takes him hence. | These are the tracks the courser left, the mighty slayer of the Snakes. || 8. Let him not close the opened mouth, nor open that which now is closed. | Two snakes are in this field, and both, female and male, are powerless. || 9. Powerless are the serpents here, those that are near and those afar. | I kill the scorpion with a club, and with a staff the new-come snake. || 10. This is the remedy against Aghāśva and the adder, both: | Indra and Paidva have subdued and tamed the vicious snake for me. || 11. We fix our thoughts on Pedu's horse, strong, off-spring of a steadfast line. | Behind our backs the vipers here crouch down and lie in wait for us. || 12. Bereft of life and poison they lie slain by bolt-armed Indra's hand. Indra and we have slaughtered them. || 13. Tiraśchirājis have been slain, and vipers crushed and brayed to bits. | Slay Darvi in the Darbha-grass, Karikrata, and White and Black. || 14. The young maid of Kirāta race, a little damsel, digs the drug, | Digs it with shovels wrought of gold on the high ridges of the hills. || 15. Hither the young unconquered leech who slays the speckled snake hath come. | He verily demolishes adder and scorpion; both of them. || 16. Indra, Mitra and Varuṇa, and Vāta and Parjanya both have given the serpent up to me. || 17. Indra hath given him up to me, the female viper and the male, | The adder, him with stripes athwart. Kasarṇīla, Daśonasi. || 18. O Serpent, Indra hath destroyed the sire who first engendered thee: | And when these snakes are pierced and bored what sap and vigour will be theirs? || 19. Their heads have I seized firmly as a fisher grasps the spotted prey, | Waded half through the stream and washed the poison of the serpents off. || 20. Let the floods hurry on and bear the poison of all snakes afar. | Tiraśchirājis have been slain and vipers crushed and brayed to bits. || 21. As from the salutary plants I deftly pick the fibres out, And guide them skilfully like mares, so let thy venom, Snake! depart, || 22. All poison that the sun and fire, all that the earth and plants contain, | Poison of most effectual power—let all thy venom pass away. || 23. Serpents which fire or plants have generated, those which have sprung from waters or the lightning, | Whose mighty broods are found in many places, these serpents we will reverently worship. || 24. Thou art a maid called Taudī, or Ghṛitāchī is thy name. Thy place; | Is underneath my foot. I take the poison-killing remedy. || 25. From every member drive away the venom, and avoid the heart. | Then let the poison's burning heat pass downward and away-from thee. || 26. The bane hath fled afar. It wept, and asked the poison how it fared. || 27. Agni hath found the venom of the serpent, Soma drawn it out. | Back to the biter hath returned the poison, and the snake hath died.

Hymn 10:5.

1. Ye are the power of Indra, ye the force and strength of Indra, ye his hero might and manliness. | I join you with the bonds of Prayer to the

victorious enterprise. || 2. Ye are the power of Indra, ye the force and strength of Indra, ye his hero might and manliness. | I join you with the bonds of Sway to the victorious enterprise. || 3. Ye are the power of Indra, ye the force and strength of Indra, ye his hero might and manliness. | I join you with the bonds of Indra to the victorious enterprise. || 4. Ye are the power of Indra, ye the force and strength of Indra, ye his hero might and manliness. | I join you with the bonds of Soma to the victorious enterprise. || 5. Ye are the power of Indra, ye the force and strength of Indra, ye his hero might and manliness. | I join you with the bonds of the Waters to the victorious enterprise. || 6. For the victorious enterprise let all creation stand by me. For me ye, Waters, are prepared. || 7. Ye are the share of Agni. Grant, O heavenly Waters unto us the Waters' brilliant energy. | By statute of Prajāpati I set you down for this our world. || 8. Ye are the share of Indra. Grant, O heavenly Waters unto us the Waters' brilliant energy. | By statute of Prajāpati I set you down for this our world. || 9. Ye are the share of Soma. Grant, O heavenly Waters unto us the Waters' brilliant energy. | By statute of Prajāpati I set you down for this our world. || 10. Ye are the share of Varuṇa. Grant, O heavenly Waters unto us the Waters' brilliant energy. | By statute of Prajāpati I set you down for this our world. || 11. Ye are the share of Mitra-Varuṇa. Grant, O heavenly Waters unto us the Waters' brilliant energy. | By statute of Prajāpati I set you down for this our world. || 12. Ye are the share of Yama. Grant, O heavenly Waters unto us the Waters' brilliant energy. | By statute of Prajāpati I set you down for this our world. || 13. Ye are the share of the Fathers. Grant, O heavenly Waters unto us the Waters' brilliant energy. | By statute of Prajāpati I set you down for this our world. || 14. Ye are the share of God Savitar. Grant, O heavenly Waters unto us the Waters' brilliant energy. | By statute of Prajāpati I set you down for this our world. || 15. Waters, your ceremonial share (bhāga) of Waters which the waters hold, which aids our sacrifice to Gods, | This as a remnant here I leave. Do not thou wash it clean away. | With this we let the man go by who hates us and whom we abhor. | Him would I fain o'erthrow and slay with this our ceremonial act, with this our prayer, our thunder-bolt.[1] || 22. Whatever evil I have done within this last triennium, | From all that woe and misery let the waters shield and guard me well. || 23. Onward I urge your gathered floods: enter your own abiding-place, | Uninjured and with all your strength. Let nothing bend or bow us down. || 24. May the pure Waters cleanse us from defilement, | Fair to behold remove our sin and trouble, and bear away ill-dream and all pollution. || 25. Thou art the step of Vishṇu, rival-slayer, sharpened by earth, aglow with fire of Agni, | Earth have I ranged: from earth we bar him who hates us and whom we hate. || 26. Ours is superior place and ours is conquest: may I in all fights tread down spite and malice. | Let him not live, let vital breath desert him.[2] || 36. With this I here invest the power and splendour, the life of that man and his vital breathing, the son of such a sire and such a woman, here do I overthrow and cast him downward. || 37. I follow Sūrya's course in heaven, the course that takes him to the South. | May that bestow upon me wealth and glory of a Brahman's rank. || 38. I turn me to the regions bright with splendour. | May they bestow upon me wealth and glory of a Brahman's rank. || 39. I turn me to the Ṛishis Seven. | May they, etc. || 40. I turn me unto Prayer. | May that, etc. || 41. I turn me unto Brahmans. | May they etc. || 42. We hunt that man, we beat him down and slay him with our murderous blows. | We with the spell have hurried him to Parameshṭhin's opened jaws. || 43. Let the shot missile catch him with Vaiśvānara's two mighty fangs. | This offering, and the mightiest Goddess, the Fuel, eat him up! || 44. Thou art the bound of Varuṇa the King. | Bind, such an one, the son of such a woman, in vital breath and in the food that feeds him. || 45. All food of thine, O Lord of Life, that lies, upon the face of earth, | Thereof bestow thou upon us. O Lord of Life, Prajāpati! || 46. Celestial Waters have I sought: with juice have I besprinkled them. | With milk, O Agni, have I come; bestow upon me splendid strength. || 47. Give me the boon of splendid strength; give, Agni! progeny and life. | May the Gods know this prayer of mine, may Indra with the Ṛishis know. || 48. What curse soever couples launch against us, whatever bitter speech the chatterers utter, | With Manyu's arrow, offspring of the spirit, transfix thou to the heart the Yātudhānas, || 49. Destroy the Yātudhānas with thy fervour, consume the demons with thy wrath, O Agni. | Destroy the fool's Gods with thy fiery splendour, destroy the blazing ones, the insatiable. || 50. Well-skilled, against this man I hurl the Water's bolt with four spikes, to cleave his head asunder. | May it destroy all members of his body. Let the whole host of Gods approve my purpose.

1. Vers 15 is repeated in verses 16-21, wave, calf, bull, Hiraṇyagarbha (Germ of Golden Light) and the speckled heavenly stone (the thunderbolt) being substituted respectively, for "ceremonial share."

2. Verse 26 is repeated in verses 27-35, with the substitution, for Earth (thrice) and Agni, of Heaven (Dyaus) and Sūrya in 27; the Quarters and Mind (Manas) in 28; the Regions and Vāta in 29; the Ṛichas and Sāmans in 30; Sacrifice (Yajña) and Brahma or Prayer in 31; Plants and Soma (the Moon) in 32; Waters and Varuṇa in 33; Agriculture and Food in 34; Vital Breath (Prāṇa) and Man (Purusha) in 35.

Hymn 10:6.

1. With power I cut away the head of my malignant rival, of mine evil-hearted enemy. || 2. This Amulet of citron-wood shall make for me a trusty shield | Filled with the mingled beverage, with sap and vigour hath it come. || 3. What though the strong-armed carpenter have cleft thee with his hand and axe. | Pure animating waters shall cleanse thee and make thee bright again. || 4. This Amulet, decked with chain of gold, shall give faith, sacrifice, and might, and dwell as guest within our house. || 5. To this we give apportioned food, clarified butter, wine, and meath. | May it provide each boon for us as doth a father for his sons. | Again, again, from morn to morn, having approached the deities. || 6. The Charm Bṛihaspati hath bound, the fatness-dropping citron-wood, the potent Khadira for strength, | This Agni hath put on: it yields clarified butter for this man. | Again, again, from morn to morn. With this subdue thine enemies. || 7. The Charm Bṛihaspati hath bound, the fatness-dropping citron-wood, the potent Khadira, for strength, | This Charm hath Indra put on him for power and manly puissance. | It yieldeth strength to strengthen him, again, again, from morn to morn, having approached the deities. || 8. The Charm Bṛihaspati, etc. | This Charm hath Soma put on him for might, for hearing, and for sight. | This yields him energy indeed, again, again, etc. || 9. The Charm Bṛihaspati, etc. | This Sūrya put on him, with this conquered the regions of the sky. | This yieldeth him ability, again, etc. || 10. The Charm Bṛihaspati, etc. | This Charm did Chandrā wear, with this conquered the forts of Asuras, the golden forts of Navajos. | This yields him glory and renown, again, etc. || 11. The Amulet Bṛihaspati bound on the swiftly-moving Wind. | This yieldeth him a vigorous steed, again, etc. || 12. The Aśvins with this Amulet protect this culture of our fields. | This yields the two Physicians might, again, etc. || 13. Savitar wore this Amulet: herewith he won this lucid heaven. | This yields him glory and delight, again, etc. || 14. Wearing this Charm the Waters flow eternally inviolate. This yieldeth them ambrosia, again etc. || 15. King Varuṇa assumed and wore this salutary Amulet. | This yieldeth him his truthfulness, again, etc. || 16. Wearing this Amulet the Gods conquered in battle all the worlds. | This yieldeth victory for them, again, etc. || 17. The Amulet Bṛihaspati formed for the swiftly-moving Wind, | This salutary Amulet the Deities assumed and wore. | This yieldeth them the universe, again, again, from morn to morn. With this subdue thine enemies. || 18. The seasons formed that Amulet, the Groups of Seasons fashioned it. | The Year having constructed it preserveth everything that is. || 19. The regions of the heaven, the points that lie between them fashioned it. | Created by Prajāpati, may the Charm cast my foemen down. || 20. Atharvan made the Amulet, Atharvan's children fashioned it. | With them the sage Aṅgirasas broke through the Dasyus' fortresses. With this subdue thine enemies. || 21. Dhātar bound on this Amulet: he ranged and ordered all that is. With this do thou subdue thy foes. || 22. The Amulet Bṛihaspati formed for the Gods, that slew the fiends. | That Amulet here hath come to me combined with sap and energy. || 23. The Amulet, etc. | That Amulet here hath come to me, hath come with cows, and goats, and sheep, hath come with food and progeny. || 24. The Amulet, etc. | That Amulet here hath come to me with store of barley and of rice, with greatness and prosperity. || 25. The Amulet, etc. | That Amulet here hath come to me with streams of butter and of mead, with sweet delicious beverage. || 26. The Amulet, etc. | That Amulet here hath come to me with power and abundant strength, hath come with glory and with wealth. || 27. The Amulet, etc. | That Amulet here hath come to me with splendour and a blaze of light, with honour and

illustrious fame. || 28. The Amulet Bṛihaspati made for the Gods, that slew the fiends, | That Amulet here hath come to me combined with all prosperities. || 29. That Amulet may the Deities bestow on me to win success, | The conquering, strength-increasing Charm, the damager of enemies. || 30. I bind on me my happy fate with holy prayer and energy. | Foeless destroyer of the foe, it hath subdued mine enemies. || 31. May this Charm, offspring of the Gods, make me superior to my foe. | So may this charm whose milk expressed these three worlds longingly await, | Be fastened on me here, that it may crown me with surpassing power. || 32. The Charm to which men, Fathers, Gods look ever for their maintenance, | May this be fastened on me here, to crown me with surpassing power || 33. As, when the plough hath tilled the soil, the seed springs up in. fertile land, | Let cattle, progeny, and food of every kind spring up with me. || 34. Charm, forwarder of sacrifice, who hast a hundred priestly fees. | Speed to preeminence him to whom I have attached thy happy fate. || 35. Love thou, O Agni, pleased with burnt oblations, this sacred fuel that is ranged in order. | In him may we find grace and loving-kindness, happiness, progeny, and sight and cattle, in Jātavedas kindled with devotion.

Hymn 10:7.

1. Which of his members is the seat of Fervour: Which is the base of Ceremonial Order? | Where in him standeth Faith? Where Holy Duty? Where, in what part of him is truth implanted? || 2. Out of which member glows the light of Agni? Form which proceeds the breath of Mātariśvan? | From which doth Chandrā measure out his journey, travelling over Skambha's mighty body? || 3. Which of his members is the earth's upholder? Which gives the middle air a base to rest on? | Where, in which member is the sky established? Where hath the space above the sky its dwelling? || 4. Whitherward yearning blazeth Agni upward? Whitherward yearning bloweth Mātariśvan? | Who out of many, tell me, is that Skambha to whom with longing go the turning pathways? || 5. Whitherward go the half-months, and, accordant with the full year, the months in their procession? | Who out of many, tell me, is that Skambha to whom go seasons and the groups of seasons? || 6. Whitherward yearning speed the two young Damsels, accordant, Day and Night, of different colour? | Who out of many, tell me, is that Skambha to whom the Waters take their way with longing? || 7. Who out of many, tell me, is that Skambha, | On whom Prajāpati set up and firmly established all the worlds? || 8. That universe which Prajāpati created, wearing all forms,, the highest, midmost, lowest, | How far did Skambha penetrate within it? What portion did he leave unpenetrated? || 9. How far within the past hath Skambha entered? How much of him hath reached into the future? | That one part which he set in thousand places,—how far did Skambha penetrate within it? || 10. Who out of many, tell me, is that Skambha in whom men recognize the Waters, Brahma, | In whom they know the worlds and their enclosures, in whom are non-existence and existence? || 11. Declare that. Skambha, who is he of many, | In whom, exerting every power, Fervour maintains her loftiest vow; | In whom are comprehended Law, Waters, Devotion and Belief || 12. Who out of many, tell me, is that Skambha | On whom as their foundation earth and firmament and sky are set; | In whom as their appointed place rest Fire and Moon and Sun and Wind? || 13. Who out of many, tell me, is that Skambha | He in whose body are contained all three-and-thirty Deities? || 14. Who out of many, tell me, is that Skambha. | In whom the Sages earliest born, the Ṛichas, Sāman, Yajus, | Earth, and the one highest Sage abide? || 15. Who out of many, tell me, is the Skambha. | Who comprehendeth, for mankind, both immortality and death, | He who containeth for mankind the gathered waters as his veins? || 16. Who out of many, tell me, is that Skambha, | He whose chief arteries stand there, the sky's four regions, he irk whom Sacrifice putteth forth its might? || 17. They who in Purusha understand Brahma know Him who is Supreme. | He who knows Him who is Supreme, and he who knows the Lord of Life, | These know the loftiest Power Divine, and thence know Skambha thoroughly. || 18. Who out of many, tell me, is that Skambha | Of whom Vaiśvānara became the head, the Aṅgirasas his eye, and Yātus his corporeal parts? || 19. Who out of many, tell me, is that Skambha | Whose mouth they say is Holy Lore, his tongue the Honey-sweetened Whip, his udder is Virāj, they say? || 20. Who out of many, tell me, is that Skambha | From whom they hewed the Ṛichas off, from whom they chipped the Yajus, he | Whose hairs are Sāman-verses and his mouth the Atharvāṅgirasas? || 21. Men count as 'twere a thing supreme nonentity's conspicuous branch; | And lower man who serve thy branch regard it as an entity. || 22. Who out of many, tell me, is that Skambha | In whom Ādityas dwell, in whom Rudras and Vasus are contained, | In whom the future and the past and all the worlds are firmly set; || 23. Whose secret treasure evermore the three-and thirty Gods protect? | Who knoweth now the treasure which, O Deities ye watch and guard? || 24. Where the Gods, versed in Sacred Lore, worship the loftiest Power Divine | The priest who knows them face to face may be a sage who knows the truth. || 25. Great, verily, are those Gods who sprang from non-existence into life. | Further, men say that that one part of Skambha is nonentity. || 26. Where Skambha generating gave the Ancient World its shape and form, | They recognized that single part of Skambha as the Ancient World, || 27. The three-and-thirty Gods within his body were disposed as limbs: | Some, deeply versed in Holy Lore, some know those three-and-thirty Gods. || 28. Men know Hiraṇyagarbha as supreme and inexpressible: | In the beginning, in the midst of the world, Skambha poured that gold. || 29. On Skambha Fervour rests, the worlds and Holy Law repose on him. | Skambha, I clearly know that all of thee on Indra is imposed. || 30. On Indra Fervour rests, on him the worlds and Holy Law recline. | Indra, I clearly know that all of thee on Skambha findeth rest. || 31. Ere sun and dawn man calls and calls one Deity by the other's name. | When the Unborn first sprang into existence he reached that independent sovereign lordship; than which aught higher never hath arisen. || 32. Be reverence paid to him, that highest Brahma, whose base is Earth, his belly Air, who made the sky to be his head. || 33. Homage to highest Brahma, him whose eye is Sūrya and the Moon who groweth young and new again, him who made Agni for his mouth. || 34. Homage to highest Brahma, him whose two life-breathings were the Wind, | The Aṅgirasas his sight: who made the regions be his means of sense. || 35. Skambha set fast these two, the earth and heaven, Skambha maintained the ample air between them. | Skambha established the six spacious regions: this whole world Skambha entered and pervaded. || 36. Homage to highest Brahma, him who, sprung from Fervour and from toil, | Filled all the worlds completely, who made Soma for himself alone. || 37. Why doth the Wind move ceaselessly? Why doth the spirit take no rest? | Why do the Waters, seeking truth, never at any time repose? || 38. Absorbed in Fervour, is the mighty Being, in the world's centre, on the waters' surface. | To him the Deities, one and all betake them. So stand the tree-trunk with the branches round it. || 39. Who out of many, tell me, is that Skambha. | To whom the Deities with hands, with feet, and voice, and ear, and eye. | Present unmeasured tribute in the measured hall of sacrifice? || 40. Darkness is chased away from him: he is exempt from all distress. | In him are all the lights, the three abiding in Prajāpati. || 41. He verily who knows the Reed of Gold that stands amid the flood, is the mysterious Lord of Life. || 42. Singly the two young Maids of different colours approach the six-pegged warp in turns and weave it. | The one draws out the threads, the other lays them: they break them not, they reach no end of labour. || 43. Of these two, dancing round as 'twere, I cannot distinguish whether ranks before the other. | A Male in weaves this web, a Male divides it: a Male hath stretched it to the cope of heaven || 44. These pegs have buttressed up the sky. The Sāmans have turned them into shuttles for the weaving.

Hymn 10:8.

1. Worship to loftiest Brahma, Lord of what hath been and what shall be, | To him who rules the universe, and heavenly light is all his own! || 2. Upheld by Skambha's power these two, the heaven and the earth, stand fast. | Skambha is all this world of life, whatever breathes or shuts an. eye. || 3. Three generations have gone by and vanished and others near have entered into sunlight. | There stood on high he who metes out the region into green, plants hath passed the Golden-coloured. || 4. One is the wheel, the tires are twelve in number, the naves are three What man hath understood it? | Three hundred spokes have thereupon been hammered, and sixty pins set firmly in their places. || 5. Discern thou this, O Savitar. Six are the twins, one singly born. | They claim relationship in that among them which is born alone. || 6. Though manifest, it lies concealed in the

vast place they call the old: | Therein is firmly stationed all the moving, breathing universe. || 7. Up, eastward downward in the west, it rolleth, with countless elements, one-wheeled, single-fellied. | With half it hath begotten all creation. Where hath the other half become unnoticed? || 8. In front of these the five-horsed car moves onward: side-horses, harnessed with the others draw it. | No one hath seen its hither course untravelled; the height sees it more near, the depth more distant. || 9. The bowl with mouth inclined and bottom upward holds stored within it every form of glory. | Thereon together sit the Seven Ṛishis who have become this mighty One's protectors || 10. The Verse employed at opening and conclusion, the Verse employed in each and every portion; | That by which sacrifice proceedeth onward. I ask thee which is that of all the Verses. || 11. That which hath power of motion, that which flies, or stands, which breathes or breathes not, which, existing, shuts the eye | Wearing all forms that entity upholds the earth, and in its close consistence still is only one. || 12. The infinite to every side extended, the finite and the infinite around us, | These twain Heaven's Lord divides as he advances, knowing the past hereof and all the future || 13. Within the womb Prajāpati is moving: he, though unseen, is born in sundry places. | He with one half engendered all creation. What sign is there to tell us of the other? || 14. All men behold him with the eye, but with the mind they know not him. | Holding aloft the water as a water-bearer in her jar. || 15. With the full vase he dwells afar, is left far off what time it fails, | A mighty Being in creation's centre: to him the rulers of the realms bring tribute. || 16. That, whence the Sun arises, that whither he goes to take his rest, | That verily I hold supreme: naught in the world surpasses it. || 17. Those who in recent times, midmost, or ancient, on all sides. greet the sage who knows the Veda, | One and all, verily discuss Āditya, the second Agni, and the threefold Haṃsa || 18. This gold-hued Haṃsa's wings, flying to heaven, spread o'er a thousand days' continued journey. | Supporting all the Gods upon his bosom, he goes his way beholding every creature. || 19. By truth he blazes up aloft by Brahma, he looks down below: | He breathes obliquely with his breath, he on whom what is. highest rests. || 20. The sage who knows the kindling-sticks whence by attrition wealth is drawn, | Will comprehend what is most high, will know the mighty Brāhmaṇa || 21. Footless at first was he produced, footless he brought celestial light. | Four-footed grown, and meet for use, he seized each thing enjoyable. || 22. Useful will he become, and then will he consume great store of food | The man who humbly worshippeth the eternal and victorious God. || 23. Him too they call eternal; he may become new again today. | Day and Night reproduce themselves, each from the form the other wears. || 24. A hundred, thousand, myriad, yea a hundred million stores of wealth that passes count are laid in him. | This wealth they kill as he looks on, and now this God shines bright therefrom. || 25. One is yet finer than a hair, one is not even visible. And hence the Deity who grasps with firmer hold is dear to me. || 26. This fair one is untouched by age, immortal in a mortal's house. | He for whom she was made lies low, and he who formed her hath grown old. || 27. Thou art a woman, and a man; thou art a damsel and a boy. | Grown old thou totterest with a staff, new-born thou lookest every way. || 28. Either the sire or son of these, the eldest or the youngest child. | As sole God dwelling in the mind, first born, he still is in the womb. || 29. Forth from the full he lifts the full, the full he sprinkles with the full. | Now also may we know the source from which the stream is sprinkled round. || 30. Brought forth in olden time, the everlasting, high over all that is was she, the Ancient. | The mighty Goddess of the Morn, refulgent with one eye, looketh round with one that winketh, || 31. Known by the name of Guardian Grace the Deity sits girt by Right. | The trees have taken from her hue, green-garlanded, their robe of green. || 32. When he is near she leaves him not, she sees him not though he is near. | Behold the wisdom of the God; he hath not died, he grows not old. || 33. Voices that never were before emitted speak as fitteth them. | Whither they go and speak, they say there is the mighty Brāhmaṇa. || 34. I ask thee where the waters' flower by wondrous magic art was placed, | Thereon the Gods and men are set as spokes are fastened in the nave. || 35. Who gave command unto the wind that bloweth! | Who ranged the five united heavenly regions? | Who were the Gods who cared not for oblations! | Which of them brought the sacrificial waters? || 36. One God inhabiteth the earth we live on; another hath encompassed air's mid-region. | One, the Supporter, takes the heaven and bears it: some keeping watch guard all the quarters safely. || 37. The man who knows the drawn-out string on which these creatures all are strung, | The man who knows the thread's thread, he may know the mighty Brāhmaṇa || 38. I know the drawn-out string, the thread whereon these creatures all are strung. | I know the thread's thread also, thus I know the mighty Brāhmaṇa. || 39. When Agni passed between the earth and heaven devouring with his flame the all-consumer, | Where dwelt afar the spouses of one husband, where at that moment, where was Mātariśvan? || 40. Into the floods had Mātariśvan entered, the deities had past in-to the waters. | There stood the mighty measurer of the region: into the verdant plants went Pavamāna. || 41. Over the Gāyatrī, above the immortal world he strode away. | Those who by Song discovered Song—where did the Unborn see that thing? || 42. Luller to rest, and gatherer-up of treasures, Savitar like a God whose laws are constant, hath stood like Indra in the war for riches. || 43. Men versed in sacred knowledge know that living Being that abides. | In the nine-portalled Lotus Flower, enclosed with triple bands and bonds. || 44. Desireless, firm, immortal, self-existent, contented with the essence, lacking nothing, | Free from the fear of Death is he who knoweth that Soul courageous, youthful, undecaying.

Hymn 10:9.

1. Binding the mouths of those who threaten mischief, against my rivals cast this bolt of thunder, | Indra first gave the Hundredfold Oblation, welfare of him who worships, foe-destroying. || 2. Thy skin shall be the Altar; let thine hair become the Sacred Grass. | This cord hath held thee firmly: let this pressing-stone dance round on thee: || 3. The holy water be thy hair: let thy tongue make thee clean, O Cow. | Go, Hundredfold Oblation, made bright and adorable, to heaven. || 4. He who prepares the Hundredfold Oblation gains each wish thereby: | For all his ministering priests, contented, move as fitteth them. || 5. He rises up to heaven, ascends to yonder third celestial height. | Whoever gives the Hundredfold Oblation with the central cake. || 6. That man completely wins those worlds, both of the heavens and of the earth, | Whoever pays the Hundredfold. Oblation with its golden light. || 7. Thine Immolators, Goddess! and the men who dress thee for the feast, all these will guard thee, Hundredfold Oblation! | Have no fear of them. || 8. The Vasus from the South will be thy guards, the Marutas from the North, Ādityas from the West; o'ertake and pass the Agniṣhṭoma, thou! || 9. The Gods, the Fathers, mortal men, Gandharvas, and Apsarases, | All these will be the guards: o'ertake and pass the Atirātra, thou! || 10. The man who pays the Hundredfold Oblation winneth all the worlds, | Air, heaven, and earth, Ādityas, and Marutas, and regions of the sky. || 11. Sprinkling down fatness, to the Gods will the beneficent Goddess go. | Harm not thy dresser, Cow! To heaven, O Hundredfold Oblation, speed! || 12. From all the Gods enthroned in heaven, in air, from those who dwell on earth, | Draw forth for evermore a stream of milk, of butter, and of mead. || 13. Let thy head, let thy mouth, let both thine ears, and those two jaws of thine. | Pour for the giver mingled curd, and flowing butter, milk, and mead. || 14. Let both thy lips, thy nostrils, both thy horns, and these two eyes of thine. | Pour for the given, etc. || 15. Let heart and pericardium, let thy lungs with all the bronchial tubes, etc. || 16. Let liver, and let kidneys, let thine entrails, and the parts within, etc. || 17. Let rectum and omentum, let thy belly's hollows, and thy skin, etc. || 18. Let all thy marrow, every bone, let all thy flesh, and all thy blood, etc. || 19. Let both thy shoulders and thy hump, thy forelegs, and their lower parts, etc. || 20. Let neck and nape and shoulder-joints, thy ribs and intercostal parts, etc. || 21. So let thy thighs and thy knee-bones, thy hinder quarters, and thy hips, etc. || 22. So let thy tail and all the hairs thereof, thine udder, and thy teats, etc. || 23. Let all thy legs, the refuse of thy feet, thy heel-ropes, and thy hooves. | Pour for the giver mingled curd, and flowing butter milk, and mead. || 24. Let all thy skin, Śataudanā! let every hair thou hast, O Cow, | Pour for the giver mingled curd, and flowing butter, milk, and mead. || 25. Sprinkled with molten butter, let the two meal-cakes be sport for thee. | Make them thy wings, O Goddess, and bear him who dresses thee to heaven. || 26. Each grain of rice in mortar or on pestle, all on the skin or in the winnowing-basket, | Whatever purifying Mātariśvan, the Wind, hath sifted, let the Hotar Agni make of it an acceptable oblation. || 27. In the priest's hands I lay, in separate order,

the sweet celestial Waters, dropping fatness. | As here I sprinkle them may all my wishes be granted unto me in perfect fullness May we have ample wealth in our possession.

Hymn 10:10.

1. Worship to thee springing to life, and worship unto thee when born! | Worship, O Cow, to thy tail-hair, and to thy hooves, and to thy form! || 2. The man who knows the Seven Floods, who knows the seven distances, | Who knows the head of sacrifice, he may receive the holy Cow. || 3. I know the Seven Water-floods, I know the seven distances, | I know the head of sacrifice, and Soma shining bright in her. || 4. Hitherward we invite with prayer the Cow who pours a thou-sand streams, | By whom the heaven, by whom the earth, by whom these waters are preserved. || 5. Upon her back there are a hundred keepers, a hundred metal bowls, a hundred milkers. | The Deities who breathe in her all separately know the Cow. || 6. Her foot is sacrifice, her milk libation, Svadhā her breath, Mahīlukā the mighty: | To the God goes with prayer the Cow who hath Parjanya for her lord. || 7. Agni hath entered into thee; Soma, O Cow, hath entered thee. | Thine udder is Parjanya, O blest Cow; the lightnings are thy teats. || 8. Thou pourest out the Waters first, and corn-lands afterward, O Cow. | Thirdly thou pourest princely sway. O Cow, thou pourest food and milk. || 9. When, Holy One, thou camest nigh invited by the Ādityas' call, | Indra gave thee to drink, O cow, a thousand bowls of Soma juice. || 10. The Bull, what time thou followedst the way of Indra, summoned thee: | Thence the Fiend-slayer, angered, took thy water and thy milk away. || 11. O Cow, the milk which in his wrath the Lord of Riches took from thee, | That same the vault of heaven now preserveth in three reservoirs. || 12. The Cow Celestial received that Soma in three vessels, where | Atharvan, consecrated, sate upon the Sacred Grass of gold. || 13. Come hither with the Soma, come with every footed thing; the Cow | With Kalis and Gandharvas by her side hath stepped upon the sea. || 14. Come hither with the Wind, yea, come with every creature borne on wings. | Laden with holy verse and song the Cow hath leapt into the sea. || 15. Come with the Sun, come hitherward with every creature that hath eyes, | Bearing auspicious lights with her the Cow hath looked across the sea. || 16. When, covered round about with gold, thou stoodest there, O Holy One, | The ocean turned into a horse and mounted on thy back, O Cow, || 17. Then came and met the Blessed Ones, Deṣhṭri, the Cow, and Svadhā, where | Atharvan, consecrated sate upon the Sacred Grass of gold. || 18. The Kṣhatriya's mother is the Cow, thy mother, Svadhā! is the Cow. | Sacrifice is the weapon of the Cow: the thought arose from, her. || 19. From Brahma's summit there went forth a drop that mounted up on high: | From that wast thou produced, O Cow, from that the Hotar sprang to life. || 20. Forth from thy mouth the Gāthās came, from thy neck's nape sprang strength, O Cow. | Sacrifice from thy flanks was born, and rays of sunlight from. thy teats, || 21. From thy fore-quarters and thy thighs motion was generated, Cow! | Food from thine entrails was produced, and from thy belly came the plants. || 22. When into Varuṇa's belly thou hadst found a passage for thy-self, | The Brahman called thee thence, for he knew how to guide and lead thee forth. || 23. All trembled at the babe that came from him who brings not to the birth. | He hath produced her—thus they cried —He is a cow, and formed by spells, he hath become skin to her. || 24. He only joineth battle, yea, he who alone controlleth her. | Now sacrifices have become victories, and the Cow their eye. || 25. The Cow hath welcomed sacrifice: the Cow hath held the Sun in place. | Together with the prayer the mess of rice hath passed into the Cow. || 26. They call the Cow immortal life, pay homage to the Cow as Death. | She hath become this universe, Fathers, and Ṛiṣhis, hath become the Gods, and men, and Asuras. || 27. The man who hath this knowledge may receive the Cow with. welcoming. | So for the giver willingly doth perfect sacrifice pour milk. || 28. Within the mouth of Varuṇa three tongues are glittering with light. | That which shines midmost of them is this Cow most difficult to hold. || 29. Four-parted was the Cow's prolific humour. | One-fourth is Water, one-fourth life eternal, one-fourth is sacrifice, one-fourth are cattle. || 30. The Cow is Heaven, the Cow is Earth, the Cow is Viṣhṇu, Lord of Life. | The Sādhyas and the Vasus have drunk the out-pourings of the Cow. || 31. When these, Sādhyas and Vasus, have drunk the out-pourings of the Cow, | They in the Bright One's dwelling-place pay adoration to her milk. || 32. For Soma some have milked her: some worship the fatness she hath poured. | They who have given a cow to him who hath this knowledge have gone up to the third region of the sky. || 33. He who hath given a Cow unto the Brahmans winneth all the worlds. | For Right is firmly set in her devotion, and religious zeal. || 34. Both Gods and mortal men depend for life and being on the Cow. | She hath become this universe: all that the Sun surveys is she.

Kāṇḍa 11.

Hymn 11:1.

1. Agni, spring forth! Here Aditi, afflicted, cooks a Brahmaudana, yearning for children. | Let the Seven Ṛiṣhis, World-creators, rub thee into existence here with gift of offspring. || 2. Raise, as I bid, the smoke, my strong companions, lovers of freedom from deceit and malice! | Victor in fight heroic, here is Agni by whom the Gods subdued the hostile demons. || 3. Thou, Agni, wart produced for mighty valour, to cook Brahmaudana, O Jātavedas. | Seven Ṛiṣhis, makers of the world, begat thee, Grant to this woman wealth with store of heroes. || 4. Burn up, O Agni, kindled with the fuel. Knowing the Gods who merit worship, bring them. | Cooking, for these, oblation, Jātavedas! lift up this man to heaven's most lofty summit. || 5. Your portion from of old is triply parted, portion of Gods, of Fathers, and of mortals. | Know, all, your shares. I deal them out among you. The portion of the Gods shall save this woman. || 6. Strong art thou, Agni, conquering, all-surpassing. Crush down our foemen, ruin those who hate us. | So let this measure, measured, being measured, make all our kin thy tributary vassals. || 7. Increase with kinsmen and with all abundance: to mighty strength and power lift up this woman. | Erect, rise upward to the sky's high station, rise to the lofty world which men call Svarga. || 8. May this great Earth receive the skin, this Goddess Pṛithivī, showing us her love and favour. Then may we go unto the world of virtue. || 9. Fix on the skin these two joined press-stones, duly rending the fibres for the sacrificer. | Strike down and slay those who assail this woman, and elevating raise on high her offspring. || 10. Grasp with thy hand, O man, the well-formed press-stones: the holy Gods have come unto thy worship. | Three wishes of thy heart which thou electest, these happy gains for thee I here make ready. || 11. Here thy devotion is, here is thy birthplace. Aditi, Mother of brave sons, accept thee! | Wipe away those who fight against this woman with wealth and store of goodly sons endow her. || 12. Rest in the roaring frame of wood: be parted from husk and chaff, ye Sacrificial Fibres. | May we surpass in glory all our rivals. I cast beneath my feet the men who hate us. || 13. Go, Dame, and quickly come again: the waters, enclosed, have mounted thee that thou mayst bear them. | Take thou of these such as are fit for service: skilfully separating. leave the others. || 14. Hither these Dames have come in radiant beauty. Arise and seize upon thy strength, O woman. | To thee hath sacrifice come: take the pitcher, blest with a good lord, children, children's children. || 15. Instructed by the Ṛiṣhis, bring those waters, the share of strength which was of old assigned you. | Let this effectual sacrifice afford you protection, fortune, off-spring, men, and cattle. || 16. Agni, on thee the sacrificial cauldron hath mounted: shining, fiercely flaming, heat it. | May hottest flames, divine, sprung from the Ṛiṣhis, gathering, with the Seasons, heat this portion. || 17. Purified, bright, and holy, let these Women, these lucid waters glide into the cauldron | Cattle and many children may they give us. May he who cooks. the Odana go to heaven. || 18. Ye, Sacrificial Rice and Soma Fibres, cleansed and made pure by prayer and molten butter. | Enter the water: let the cauldron take you. May he who dresses this ascend to heaven. || 19. Expand thyself abroad in all thy greatness, with thousand Pṛiṣhṭhas, in the world of virtue. | Grandfathers, fathers, children, and descendants, fifteenth am I to thee when I have dressed it. || 20. With thousand streams and Pṛiṣhṭhas, undecaying, Brahmaudana is celestial, God-reaching. | Those I give up to thee with all their children. Force them to tribute, but to me be gracious. || 21. Rise to the altar: bless this dame with offspring. Promote this woman; drive away the demons. | May we surpass in glory all our rivals. I cast beneath my feet the men who hate us. || 22. Approach this woman here with store of cattle: together with the deities come to meet her. | Let not a curse or imprecation reach thee: in thine own seat shine forth exempt

from sickness. ‖ 23. Fashioned at first by Right, set by the spirit, this altar of Brahmaudana was appointed. | Place the pure boiler on it, woman! set thou therein the rice mess of Celestial Beings. ‖ 24. This second hand of Aditi, this ladle which the Seven Ṛiṣhis, world-creators, fashioned. | May this scoop deftly pile upon the altar, therein, the members of the rice-oblation. ‖ 25. Let the dressed offering and divine Ones serve thee: creep from. the fire again, own these as masters. | Made pure with Soma rest within the Brahmans: let not thine eaters, Ṛiṣhis' sons, be injured. ‖ 26. Give understanding unto these, King Soma! all the good Brahmans who attend and serve thee. | Oft, in Brahmaudana, and well I call on: Ṛiṣhis, their sons, and those who sprang from Fervour. ‖ 27. Here I set singly in the hands of Brahmans these cleansed and. purified and holy Women, | May Indra, Marut-girt, grant me the blessing which as I sprinkle you, my heart desireth. ‖ 28. Here is my gold, a light immortal: ripened grain from the field this Cow of Plenty give me! | This wealth I place among the Brahmans, making a path that leads to heaven among the Fathers. ‖ 29. Lay thou the chaff in Agni Jātavedas: remove the husks and drive them to a distance. | That, we have heard, that is the House-Lord's portion: we know the share allotted to Destruction. ‖ 30. Mark him who toils and cooks and pours oblation: make this man climb the path that leads to heaven, | That he may mount and reach life that is highest, ascending to the loftiest vault above us. ‖ 31. Adhvaryu, cleanse that face of the Supporter. Make room, well knowing, for the molten butter. | Purify duly all the limbs with fatness. I make a path to heaven amid the Fathers. ‖ 32. Supporter, send to those men fiends and battle, to all non-Brahmans who attend and serve thee. | Famous and foremost, with their great possessions, let not these here, the Ṛiṣhis sons, be injured. ‖ 33. I set thee, Odana, with Ṛiṣhis' children: naught here belongs to men not sprung from Ṛiṣhis | Let Agni my protector, all the Marutas, the Viśvedevas guard the cooked oblation. ‖ 34. May we adore thee, Sacrifice that yieldeth an everlasting son, cow, home of treasures, | Together with increasing store of riches, long life and immortality of children. ‖ 35. Thou art a Bull that mounts to heaven: to Ṛiṣhis and their off-spring go. | Rest in the world of pious men: there is the place prepared for us. ‖ 36. Level the ways: go thitherward, O Agni. Make ready thou the Godward-leading pathways. | By these our pious actions may we follow sacrifice dwelling in the seven-rayed heaven. ‖ 37. May we invested with that light go upward, ascending to the sky's most lofty summit. | Wherewith the Gods, what time they had made ready Brahmaudana, mounted to the world of virtue.

Hymn II:2.

1. Bhava and Śarva, spare us, be not hostile. Homage to you, twin Lords of beasts and spirits! | Shoot not the arrow aimed and drawn against us: forbear to harm our quadrupeds and bipeds. ‖ 2. Cast not our bodies to the dog or jackal, nor, Lord of Beasts! to carrion-kites or vultures. | Let not thy black voracious flies attack them; let not thy birds obtain them for their banquet. ‖ 3. We offer homage to thy shout, Bhava! thy breath, thy racking pains: | Homage, Immortal One! to thee, to Rudra of the thousand eyes. ‖ 4. We offer reverence to thee from eastward, and from north and south, | From all the compass of the sky, to thee and to the firmament. ‖ 5. Homage, O Bhava, Lord of Beasts, unto thy face and all thine eyes, | To skin, and hue, and aspect, and to thee when looked at from behind! ‖ 6. We offer homage to thy limbs, thy belly, and thy tongue, and mouth we offer homage to thy smell. ‖ 7. Never may we contend with him, the mighty archer, thousand-eyed. | Rudra who wears black tufts of hair, the slaughterer of Ardhaka. ‖ 8. May he, may Bhava from all sides avoid us, avoid us even as fire avoids the waters. Let him not threaten us. To him be homage! ‖ 9. Four times, eight times be homage paid to Bhava, yea, Lord of Beasts, ten times be reverence paid thee! | Thine are these animals, five several classes, oxen, and goats and sheep, and men, and horses ‖ 10. Thine the four regions, thine are earth and heaven, thine, Mighty One, this firmament between them; | Thine everything with soul and breath here on the surface of the land. ‖ 11. Thine is this ample wealth-containing storehouse that holds within it all these living creatures. | Favour us, Lord of Beasts, to thee be homage! Far from us go ill-omens, dogs, and jackals, and wild-haired women with their horrid shrieking! ‖ 12. A yellow bow of gold thou wieldest, slaying its hundred, tufted God! smiting its thousand. | Weapon of Gods, far flies the shaft of Rudra: wherever it may be, we pay it

homage. ‖ 13. Thou, Rudra, followest close the foe who lies in wait to conquer thee. | Even as a hunter who pursues the footsteps of the wounded game. ‖ 14. Accordant and allies, Bhava and Rudra, with mighty strength ye go to deeds of valour. Wherever they may be, we pay them homage. ‖ 15. Be homage, Rudra, unto thee approaching and departing hence! | Homage to thee when standing still, to thee when seated and at rest! ‖ 16. Homage at evening and at morn, homage at night, homage by day. | To Bhava and to Śarva, both, have I paid lowly reverence, ‖ 17. Let us not outrage with our tongue far-seeing Rudra, thousand-eyed, | Inspired with varied lore, who shoots his arrows forward, far away. ‖ 18. Foremost we go to meet his car, the chariot of the long-haired God, | Drawn by brown horses, dusky, black, o'erthrowing, slaying, terrible. Let reverence be paid to him. ‖ 19. Cast not thy club at us, thy heavenly weapon. Lord of Beasts, be not wroth with us. Let reverence be paid to thee. | Shake thy celestial branch above some others elsewhere, not o'er us. ‖ 20. Do us no harm, but comfort us: avoid thou us, and be not wroth. Never let us contend with thee. ‖ 21. Covet not thou our kine or men, covet not thou our goats or sheep. | Elsewhither, strong One! turn thine aim: destroy the mockers' family. ‖ 22. Homage to him whose weapon, Cough or Fever, assails one like the neighing of a stallion; to him who draws one forth and then another! ‖ 23. Homage be paid him with ten Śakvarī verses who stands established in the air's mid-region, slaying non-sacrificing God-despisers! ‖ 24. For thee were forest beasts and sylvan creatures placed in the wood, and small birds, swans, and eagles. | Floods, Lord of Beasts! contain thy living beings: to swell thy strength flow the celestial Waters. ‖ 25. Porpoises, serpents, strange aquatic monsters, fishes, and things unclean at which thou shootest. | Nothing is far for thee, naught checks thee, Bhava! The whole earth in a moment thou surveyest. From the east sea thou smitest in the northern. ‖ 26. o'erwhelm us not with Fever or with poison, nor, Rudra! with the fire that comes from heaven. Elsewhere, and not on us, cast down this lightning. ‖ 27. Ruler of heaven and Lord of earth is Bhava: Bhava hath filled the spacious air's mid-region. Where'er he be, to him be paid our homage! ‖ 28. King Bhava, favour him who offers worship, for thou art Paśupati, Lord of victims. | Be gracious to the quadruped and biped of the believer in the Gods' existence. ‖ 29. Harm thou among us neither great nor little, not one who bears us, not our future bearers. | Injure no sire among us, harm no mother. Forbear to injure our own bodies, Rudra. ‖ 30. This lowly reverence have I paid to Rudra's dogs with mighty mouths, | Hounds terrible with bark and howl, who gorge unmasticated food. ‖ 31. Homage to thy loud-shouting hosts and thy long-haired followers! | Homage to hosts that are adored, homage to armies that enjoy | Homage to all thy troops, O God. Security and bliss be ours!

Hymn II:3.

1. Of that Odana Bṛihaspati is the head, Brahma the mouth. ‖ 2. Heaven and Earth are the ears, the Sun and Moon are the eyes, the seven Ṛiṣhis are the vital airs inhaled and exhaled. ‖ 3. Vision is the pestle, Desire the mortar. 4. Diti is the winnowing basket, Aditi is she who holds it, Vāta is the sifter. ‖ 5. Horses are the grains, oxen the winnowed rice-grains, gnats the husks. ‖ 6. Kabru is the husked grain, the rain cloud is the reed. ‖ 7. Grey iron is its flesh, copper its blood. ‖ 8. Tin is its ashes, gold its colour, the blue lotus flower its scent. ‖ 9. The threshing-floor is its dish, the wooden swords its shoulders, the car-shafts its backbones. ‖ 10. Collar-bones are its entrails, straps its intestines. ‖ 11. This earth, verily becomes the jar, and heaven the cover of the Odana as it is cooking. ‖ 12. Furrows are its ribs, sandy soils the undigested contents of its stomach. ‖ 13. Law is its water for the hands and family custom its aspersion. ‖ 14. The jar covered with the Rich has been solemnly directed by the priestly office. ‖ 15. Received by the Brahman, it has been carried round. ‖ 16. The Bṛihat is, the stirring-spoon, the Rathantara the ladle. ‖ 17. The Seasons are the dressers, the Groups of Seasons kindle the fire. ‖ 18. The cauldron flames round the oblation (*charu*) whose mouth consists of five openings. ‖ 19. The sacrificial word, all worlds are to be won with Odana. ‖ 20. Whereon in order rest the three, the ocean, and the heaven, and earth. ‖ 21. Within the residue whereof the Gods arranged six eightieth parts— ‖ 22. I ask thee, of this Odana what is the mighty magnitude. ‖ 23. He who may know the magnitude of the Odana. ‖ 24. Would say, Not small, nor devoid of moistening sauce; not this, nor any-thing whatever. ‖ 25. He would not declare it to be greater

than the giver imagines it to be. || 26. The theologians say, Thou hast eaten the averted Odana and the Odana turned hither-ward. || 27. Thou hast eaten the Odana and the Odana will eat thee. || 28. Thou hast eaten this averted; thy inward breath will leave thee; so he said to this one. || 29. Thou hast eaten this turned hitherward; thy downward breath will leave thee; so he said to this one. || 30. I indeed have not eaten the Odana, nor has the Odana eaten me. || 31. The Odana has just eaten the Odana. || || 32. And thence he said to this one, Thou hast eaten this with a different head from that with which the ancient Ṛishis ate: thy offspring, reckoning from the eldest, will die. I have eaten it neither turned downward, nor turned away, nor turned hitherward. With Bṛihaspati as head: with him I have eaten, with him have I come to it. Now this Odana is complete with all members, joints, and body. Complete, verily, with all his members, joints, and body is he who possess this knowledge. || 33. And thence he said to him, Thou hast eaten this with other ears than those with which the ancient Ṛishis ate it. | Thou wilt be deaf. I have eaten it neither, etc. (as in verse 32.). With Heaven and Earth as ears, with these I have eaten it, with these I have come to it. Now this Odana, etc. (as in 32.). || 34. And thence he said to him. Thou hast eaten this with other eyes . . . thou wilt be blind. With Sun and Moon, etc. || 35. And thence, etc. . . with other month. Thy offspring will die, reckoning from the head . . . With Brahma as mouth. || 36. And thence, etc. . . . with other tongue . . . Thy tongue will die . . . With the tongue of Agni. || 37. And thence, etc. . .With other teeth . . . Thy teeth will fall out . . . With the Seasons as teeth. || 38. And thence, etc. . . . with other vital airs. . . . Thy vital airs will leave thee . . . With the Seven Ṛishis as the vital airs. || 39. And thence, etc. . . . with other expanse . . . Consumption will destroy thee . . . With the firmament as expanse. || 40. And thence, etc. . . . with other back. . . . Lightning will slay thee. . . With the heaven as back. || 41. And thence, etc. . . . with other breast . . . Thou wilt fail in agriculture. . . . With the earth as breast. || 42. And thence, etc. . . . with other belly . . . colic will destroy thee . . . With truth as belly. || 43. And thence, etc. . . . with other abdomen . . . Thou wilt die in the water . . . With the sea as abdomen. || 44. And thence, etc. . . . with other thighs . . . Thy thigh will perish . . . With Mitra-Varuṇa as thighs. || 45. And thence, etc. . . . with other knees . . . Thou wilt become a sick man . . . With the knees of Tvaṣhṭar || 46. And thence, etc. . . . with other feet . . . Thou wilt become a wanderer . . . With the feet of the Aśvins || 47. And thence, etc. . . with other fore-parts of the feet . . . A serpent will kill thee . . . With the fore-parts of Savitar's feet. || 48. And thence, etc. . . . with other hands . . . The Brāhmaṇa (divine power) will kill thee . . . With the hands of Right. || 49. And thence, etc. . . . with other basis . . . Without standing-ground and resting-place thou wilt die . . . Having taken my stand on truth. With this I ate it, with this I came to it. Now this Odana is complete with all members, joints, and body. Complete, verily, with all his members, joints, and body is he who possesses this knowledge.

Hymn 11:4.

1. Homage to Prāṇa, him who hath dominion o'er the universe, | Who hath become the Sovereign Lord of all, on whom the whole depends! || 2. Homage, O Prāṇa, to thy roar, to thunder-peal and lightning flash! | Homage, O Prāṇa, unto thee what time thou sendest down thy rain! || 3. When Prāṇa with a thunderous voice shouts his loud message to the plants, | They straightway are impregnate, they conceive, and bear abundantly. || 4. When the due season hath arrived and Prāṇa shouteth to herbs, | Then all is joyful, yea, each thing upon the surface of the earth. || 5. When Prāṇa hath poured down his flood of rain upon the mighty land. | Cattle and beasts rejoice thereat: Now great will he our strength, they cry. || 6. Watered by Prāṇa's rain the plants have raised their voices in accord: | Thou hast prolonged our life, they say, and given fragrance to us all. || 7. Homage to thee when coming nigh, homage to thee departing hence! | Homage, O Prāṇa, be to thee when standing and when sitting still. || 8. Homage to thee at every breath thou drawest in and sendest forth! | Homage to thee when turned away, homage to thee seen face to face! This reverence be to all of thee! || 9. Prāṇa, communicate to us thy dear, thy very dearest form. | Whatever healing balm thou hast, give us thereof that we may live. || 10. Prāṇa robes living creatures as a father his beloved son. Prāṇa is sovereign Lord of all, of all that breathes not, all that breathes || 11. Prāṇa is Fever, he is Death. Prāṇa is worshipped by the Gods. | Prāṇa sets in the loftiest sphere the man who speaks the words of truth. || 12. Prāṇa is Deshṭri, and Virāj Prāṇa is reverenced by all. He is the Sun, he is the Moon. Prāṇa is called Prajāpati. || 13. Both breaths are rice and barley, and Prāṇa is called the toiling ox: | In barley is the inbreath laid, and rice is named the outward breath. || 14. The human infant in the womb draws vital breath and sends it out: | When thou, O Prāṇa, quickenest the babe it springs anew to life. || 15. The name of Prāṇa is bestowed on Mātariśvan and on Wind. | On Prāṇa, past and future, yea, on Prāṇa everything depends. || 16. All herbs and plants spring forth and grow when thou, O Prāṇa quickenest, | Plants of Atharvan, Aṅgiras, plants of the deities and men. || 17. When Prāṇa hath poured down his flood of rain upon the mighty earth, | The plants are wakened into life, and every herd that grows on ground. || 18. The man who knows this truth of thee, O Prāṇa, and what bears thee up | To him will all present their gift of tribute in that loftiest will all present their gift of tribute in that loftiest world. || 19. As all these living creatures are thy tributaries, Prāṇa, so | Shall they bring tribute unto him who hears thee with attentive ears. || 20. Filled with a babe, mid deities he wanders: grown; near at hand, he springs again to being. | That Father, grown the present and the future, hath past into the son with mighty powers. || 21. Haṃsa, what time he rises up, leaves in the flood one foot unmoved. | If he withdrew it there would be no more tomorrow or today, | Never would there be night, no more would daylight shine or morning flush. || 22. It rolleth on, eight-wheeled and single-fellied, and with a thousand eyes, forward and backward. | With one half it engendered all creation. What sign is there to tell us of the other? || 23. Homage, O Prāṇa unto thee armed with swift bow among the rest, | In whose dominion is this All of varied sort that stirs and works! || 24. May he who rules this Universe of varied sort, that stirs and works, | Prāṇa, alert and resolute, assist me through the prayer I pray. || 25. Erect among the sleepers he wakes, and is never laid at length, | No one hath ever heard that he hath been asleep while others slept. || 26. Thou, Prāṇa, never shalt be hid, never shalt be estranged from me. | I bind thee on myself for life, O Prāṇa, like the Waters' germ.

Hymn 11:5.

1. Stirring both worlds the Brahmachārī moveth: in him the deities are all one-minded. | He hath established firmly earth and heaven: he satisfies his Master with his Fervour. || 2. After the Brahmachārī go the Fathers, the heavenly hosts, all Gods in separate order. | After him too have the Gandharvas followed, thirty and three, three hundred, and six thousand. He satisfies all Gods with his devotion. || 3. The Master, welcoming his new disciple, into his bowels takes the Brahmachārī | Three nights he holds and bears him in this belly. When he is born, the Gods convene to see him. || 4. This log is earth, the second log is heaven: he fills the air's mid region with the fuel. | With fuel, with his zone the Brahmachārī contents the worlds, with labour and with Fervour. || 5. The Brahmachārī, earlier born than Brahma, sprang up through Fervour, robed in hot libation. | From him sprang heavenly lore, the highest Brahma, and all the Gods, with life that lasts for ever. || 6. Lighted by fuel goes the Brahmachārī, clad in black-buck skin, consecrate, long-bearded. | Swiftly he goes from east to northern ocean, grasping the worlds, oft bringing them anear him. || 7. The Brahmachārī, fathering Prayer, world, Waters, Virāj, Prajāpati, and Parameṣhṭhin, | Lay as a germ within the Immortal's bosom, then became Indra and destroyed the demons. || 8. The Master fashioned both these cloudy regions, profound and spacious pair, the earth and heaven. | The Brahmachārī guards them with his Fervour. In him the deities are all one-minded. || 9. The Brahmachārī first of all brought hither this ample earth as alms, and heaven above it. | He makes these twain two fuel-logs, and worships, On these sup-ported rest all living creatures. || 10. Both treasuries of sacred lore lie hidden, one hitherward, beyond heaven's ridge the other. | The Brahmachārī with his Fervour guards them. He makes this all his own as knowing Brahma. || 11. Hitherward one, hence from the earth the other, two Agnis meet between these cloudy regions. | Close to these two firm rays of light are clinging. The Brahmachārī enters them through Fervour. || 12. Thundering, shouting, ruddy-hued, and pallid, he bears along the earth great manly vigour. | Down on the ridge of earth the Brahmachārī pours seed, and this gives life to heaven's four regions. || 13. The Brahmachārī stores with fuel Waters, and Fire, and Sun, and Moon,

and Mātariśvan | The Water's lights move separate in the rain-cloud, Man, rain, and water are their molten butter. || 14. The Master is Death, Varuṇa, Soma, the plants of earth, and milk. | The thunder-clouds were men of war. By these this heavenly light was brought. || 15. Varuṇa, made a Master, takes at home the butter to himself. | Whatever with Prajāpati he sought, the Brahmachārī gave like Mitra from his loftiest soul. || 16. The pupil is the Master, yea, the pupil is Prajāpati. | Prajāpati shines bright; the bright Virāj grew potent Indra's self. || 17. By Fervour and by self-restraint the King protects the realm he rules. | By self-restraint the Master seeks a Brahmachārī to instruct. || 18. By self-restraint a maiden finds a youth to be her wedded lord. | By self-restraint the ox and horse seek to win fodder for themselves. || 19. By Fervour and by self-restraint the Gods drave Death away from them, | And Indra brought by self-restraint heaven's lustre to the deities. || 20. The plants, what is and what shall be, day, night, the tall tree of the wood, | The year with seasons of the year, all from the Brahmachārī sprang. || 21. All creatures of the earth and heaven, tame animals and sylvan beasts, | Winged and wingless creatures, from the Brahmachārī sprang to life, || 22. All children of Prajāpati have breath distinctly in themselves. | The Brahma that is stored within the Brahmachārī guards them all. || 23. Piled up on high, but never yet ascended, that power of deities is brightly shining. | From that sprang heavenly lore, the loftiest Brahma, and all the Gods with, life that lasts for ever. || 24. The Brahmachārī wields the radiant Brahma wherein all Gods are woven close together; | Creating breath, inhaling and exhaling, voice, mind, and heart, Brahma and holy wisdom. || 25. Bestow on us the power of sight and hearing, glory and food and seed and blood and belly. || 26. These, standing on the flood, the Brahmachārī formed practising in sea his hot devotion. | When he hath bathed, brown, yellow-hued, he shines exceedingly on earth.

Hymn 11:6.

1. We call on Agni, on the trees lords of the forest, herbs and. plants, | Indra, Sūrya, Bṛihaspati: may they deliver us from woe. || 2. We call on Vishṇu, Bhaga, on Mitra and Varuṇa the King, | Aṃśa Vivasvat we address: may they deliver us from woe. || 3. We call on Savitar the God, on Pūshan the establisher, | Tvashṭar the foremost we address: may they deliver us from woe. || 4. Gandharvas and Apsarases; the Aśvins, Brahmaṇaspati, | Aryaman, God, by name we call: may they deliver us from woe. || 5. This word of ours to Day and Night, and to the Sun and Moon we speak, | All the Ādityas we address: may they deliver us from woe. || 6. Vāta, Parjanya we address, the Quarters, and the Firmament, | And all the Regions of the sky: may they deliver us from woe. || 7. From all that brings a curse may Day and Night and Dawn deliver me, | May Soma free me, God to whom they give the name of Chandramās. || 8. All creatures both of heaven and earth, wild beasts and sylvan animals, | And winged birds of air we call: may they deliver us from woe. || 9. Bhava and Śarva we address, and Rudra who is Lord of Beasts, | Their arrows which we feel and know: may they be ever kind to us. || 10. We speak to Constellations, Heaven, to Earth, to Genii, and to Hills, | To Seas, to Rivers, and to Lakes: may they deliver us from woe. || 11. Or the Seven Ṛishis we address, Waters divine, Prajāpati, | Fathers with Yama at their head: may they deliver us from woe. || 12. Gods whose abode is in the heaven and those who dwell in middle air, | And Mighty ones who rest on earth: may they deliver us from. woe. || 13. Ādityas, Rudra, Vasus, Gods aloft in heaven, Atharvan's sons, | The sages, sons of Aṅgiras: may they deliver us from woe. || 14. To sacrifice, to worshipper, hymns, songs, and healing charms, we speak, | To priestly acts and Yajus texts: may they deliver us from woe. || 15. To the five kingdoms of the plants which Soma rules as Lord we speak. | Darbha, hemp, barley, mighty power: may these deliver us from woe, || 16. To demons and fierce fiends we speak, to Holy Genii, Fathers, Snakes, | And to the hundred deaths and one: may these deliver us from woe. || 17. We speak to Seasons, Season-Lords, to years and sections of the year, | To Months, half-months, and years complete: may they deliver us from woe. || 18. Come hither from the south, ye Gods, rise and come forward from the west. | Gathered together, all ye Gods, ye mighty Ones, from east and and north: may they deliver us from woe. || 19. This we address to all the Gods, faithful, maintainers of the Right, | With all their Consorts by their side: may they deliver us from woe. || 20. We speak to the collected Gods, faithful, maintainers of the Right. | Present with their collective Dames: may these deliver us from woe. || 21. The spirit, yea, the spirits' Lord, ruler of spirits, we address. | Together let all spirits meet: may these deliver us from woe. || 22. The five Sky regions, Goddesses, and the twelve Seasons which are Gods. | The teeth of the completed year, may these deliver us from woe. || 23. The deathless balm that Mātalī knows, purchased at a chariot's price, | Indra effused into the floods. Waters, give us that healing balm!

Hymn 11:7.

1. The Residue of Sacrifice containeth name, and from, and world: | Indra and Agni and the whole universe are comprised therein. || 2. The Residue of Sacrifice holdeth Earth, Heaven, and all that is: | The Residue of Sacrifice holdeth sea, waters, Moon, and Wind. || 3. Real, non-real, both are there, Prajāpati, and Death, and strength: | Thereon depend the worldly ones: in me are glory Dra and Vra. || 4. The firm, the fast, the strong, the hard, Brahma, the All-creating Ten. | Gods, as a wheel about the nave, are fixed all round the Residue. || 5. Verse, Song, and Sacrificial Text, chanting, the prelude, and the laud, | The hum is in the Residue, the tone, the murmur of the psalm. || 6. Within the Residue, like babes unborn, the parts of sacrifice, | Aindrāgna Pavamāna lie. Mahānāmnī, Mahāvrata || 7. The Vājapeya, Royal Rite, the Agnishṭoma and its forms, | Hymns, joyfullest with living grass the Aśvamedha, are therein, || 8. Dīkshā and Agnyādheya rite that sates the wish, with magic-hymn, | Suspended rites, long sessions, are contained within the Residue. || 9. Faith fire-oblation, fervent zeal, service, and sacrificial cry, | Guerdon, good works and their reward, are stored within the Residue. || 10. Sacrifice of one night, or two, Sadyaḥkrī, Ukthya, and Prakrī, | Call, deep-toned summons are therein, fine parts, through lore, of sacrifice, || 11. Sacrifice of four nights, of five, of six nights, day and night conjoined, | Shoḍaśin, seven-night sacrifice, all these sprang from the Residue, these which the Immortal One contains. || 12. Pratihāra and Nidhanam, the Viśvajit, the Abhijit, | The two Sāhnātirātrās and Twelve-day rite are stored therein. || 13. Pleasantness, reverence, peace, and power, strength, vigour, immortality | All forward wishes are with love satisfied in the Residue. || 14. Nine several oceans, earths, and skies are set within, the Residue, | Bright shines the Sun therein, in me, the Residue, are Day and Night. || 15. The Residue the Father's sire, who bears this universe, supports | Vishūvant, Upahavya, and all worship offered secretly. || 16. The Father's sire, the Residue, grandson of Spirit, primal Sire, | Lord of the universe, the Bull, dwells on the earth victorious. || 17. Right, truth, dominion, fervent zeal, toil, duty, action, future, past, | Valour; prosperity, and strength dwell in the Residue in strength. || 18. Welfare, resolve and energy, the six expanses, kingship, sway, | Prayer, and direction, and the year, oblation, planets, are there-in; || 19. And the four Hotars, Āprī hymns, the Nivids, and Four-monthly rites, | Oblations, sacrifices, and animal offerings, and their forms. || 20. Months, half-months, sections of the year, seasons are in the Residue, | The waters resonant afar, the thunder, and the mighty noise. || 21. Pebbles, sand, stones, and herbs, and plants, and grass are in the Residue, | Closely embraced and laid therein are lightnings and the clouds and rain. || 22. Gain, acquisition, and success, fullness, complete prosperity. | Great gain and wealth, are laid, concealed and treasured, in the Residue. || 23. All things that breathe the breath of life, all creatures that have eyes to see, | All the celestial Gods whose home is heaven sprang from the Residue. || 24. Verses, and Songs, and magic hymns, Purāṇa, sacrificial text. | All the celestial Gods whose home is heaven sprang from the Residue. || 25. Inbreath and outbreath, eye and ear, decay and freedom from decay, | All the celestial Gods whose home is heaven sprang from the Residue. || 26. All pleasures and enjoyments, all delights and rapturous ecstasies, | All the celestial Gods whose home is heaven sprang from the Residue. || 27. The Deities, the Fathers, men, Gandharvas, and Apsarases. | All the celestial Gods whose home is heaven sprang from the Residue.

Hymn 11:8.

1. When Manyu brought his consort home forth from Saṃkalpa's dwelling-place, | Who were the wooers of the bride, who was the chief who courted her? || 2. Fervour and Action were the two, in depths of the great billowy sea? | These were the wooers of the bride; Brahma the chief who courted her. || 3. Ten Gods before the Gods were born together in the ancient time. | Whoso may know them face to face may now pronounce

the mighty word. || 4. Inbreath and outbreath, eye and ear, decay and freedom from. decay, | Spiration upward and diffused, voice, mind have brought us wish and plan. || 5. As yet the Seasons were unborn, and Dilator and Prajāpati, | Both Aśvins, Indra, Agni. Whom then did they worship as supreme? || 6. Fervour and Action were the two, in depths of the great billowy sea; | Fervour sprang up from Action: this they served and worshipped as supreme. || 7. He may account himself well versed in ancient time who knows by name. | The earth that was before this earth, which only wisest Sages know. || 8. From whom did Indra spring? from whom sprang Soma? whence was Agni born? | From whom did Tvaṣhṭar spring to life? and whence is Dilator's origin? || 9. Indra from Indra, Soma from Soma, Agni from Agni sprang | Tvaṣhṭar from Tvaṣhṭar was produced, Dilator was Dhātar's origin. || 10. Those Gods who were of old, the Ten begotten earlier than the Gods, | What world do they inhabit since they gave the world unto their sons? || 11. When he had brought together hair, sinew and bone, marrow and flesh. | And to the body added feet, then to what world did he depart? || 12. Whence, from what region did he bring the hair, the sinews, and the bones, | Marrow and limbs, and joints, and flesh? Who was the bringer, and from whence? || 13. Casters, those Gods were called who brought together all the elements: | When they had fused the mortal man complete, they entered into him. || 14. The thighs, the knee-bones, and the feet, the head, the face, Land both the hands, | The ribs, the nipples, and the sides—what Ṛishi hath constructed that? || 15. Head, both the hands, and face, and tongue, and neck, and inter-coastal parts, | All this, investing it with skins, Mahī conjoined with bond and tie. || 16. What time the might body lay firmly compact with tie and bond, | Who gave its colour to the form, the hue wherewith it shines today? || 17. All Deities had lent their aid: of this a noble Dame took note, | Īśā, the Consort of Command. She gave its colour to the form. || 18. When Tvaṣhṭar, Tvaṣhṭar's loftier Sire, had bored it out and hollowed it. | Gods made the mortal their abode, and entered and possessed the man. || 19. Sleep, specially, Sloth, Nirṛiti, and deities whose name is Sin, | Baldness, old age, and hoary hairs within the body found their way. || 20. Theft, evil-doing, and deceit, truth, sacrifice, exalted fame, | Strength, princely power, and energy entered the body as a home. || 21. Prosperity and poverty, kindnesses and malignities, | Hunger and thirst of every kind entered the body as a home. || 22. Reproaches, freedom from reproach, all blameable, all blameless deeds, | Bounty, belief, and unbelief entered the body as a home. || 23. All knowledge and all ignorance, each other thing that one may learn, | Entered the body, prayer, and hymns, and songs, and sacrificial texts. || 24. Enjoyments, pleasures, and delights, gladness, and rapturous ecstasies. | Laughter and merriment and dance entered the body as a home. || 25. Discourse and conversation, and the shrill-resounding cries of woe, | All entered in, the motives and the purposes combined there-with. || 26. Inbreath and outbreath, ear and eye, decay and freedom from decay. | Breath upward and diffused, voice, mind, these quickly with the body move, || 27. All earnest wishes, all commands, directions, and admonishments. | Reflections, all deliberate plans entered the body as a home. || 28. They laid in the abhorrent frame those waters hidden, bright, and thick, | Which in the bowels spring from blood, from mourning or from hasty toil. || 29. Fuel they turned to bone, and then they set light waters in the frame. | The molten butter they made seed: then the Gods entered into man. || 30. All Waters, all the Deities. Virāj with Brahma at her side: | Brahma into the body passed: Prajāpati is Lord thereof. || 31. The Sun and Wind formed, separate, the eye and vital breath of man. | His other person have the Gods bestowed on Agni as a gift. || 32. Therefore whoever knoweth man regardeth him as Brahman's self: | For all the Deities abide in him as cattle in their pen. || 33. At his first death he goeth hence, asunder, in three separate parts. | He goeth yonder with one part, with one he goeth yonder: here he sinketh downward with a third. || 34. In the primeval waters cold the body is deposited. | In this there is the power of growth: from this is power of growth declared.

Hymn 11:9.

1. All arms and every arrow, all the power and might that bows possess, | The warlike weapon, axes, swords, the plan and purpose in the heart, | All this, O Arbuda, make thou visible to our enemies, and let them look on mist and fog. || 2. Arise ye and prepare yourselves: ye, the celestial hosts, are friends. | Let your mysterious natures be seen by our friends O Arbuda || 3. Rise both of you: begin your work with fettering and binding fast, | Assail, both of you, Arbuda, the armies of our enemies. || 4. The God whose name is Arbuda, and Nyarbudi the Mighty One, | The two by whom the air and this great earth are compassed and possessed, | With these two friends of Indra I go forth to conquer with the host. || 5. Rise with our army stand thou up. O Godlike Being, Arbuda | Breaking the hosts of enemies, surround them with thy winding coils. || 6. Exhibiting, O Arbuda, seven children of the mist and fog, | When butter hath been offered, rise with all of these and with the host. || 7. Beating her breast, with tearful face, let the short-earned, the wild-haired hag. | Shriek loudly when a man is slain, pierced through by thee, O Arbuda; || 8. Snatching away the vertebra, while with her thought she seeks her son, | Her husband, brother, kin, when one, Arbuda! hath been pierced by thee. || 9. Let vultures, ravens, kites, and crows, and every carrion-eating bird. | Feast on our foes, and show where one, Arbuda! hath been pierced by thee. || 10. Then let each greedy beast of prey, and fly and worm regale itself | Upon the human corpse where one, Arbuda, hath been pierced by thee. || 11. Attack them, both of you; bear off their vital breath O Nyarbudi. | Let mingled shouts and echoing cries of woe amid our foemen show where thou, O Arbuda, hast pierced || 12. Shake them, and let them sink with fear: o'erwhelm our enemies with dread. | With widely-grasping bends of arm, O Arbuda, crush down our foes. || 13. Let those mens' arms grow faint and weak, dull be the purpose of their heart; | And let not aught of them be left when thou, O Arbuda, hast pierced. || 14. Self-smiting, beating breast and thigh, careless of unguent, with their hair dishevelled, weeping, hags shall run together, when a man is slain, when thou, O Arbuda, hast pierced. || 15. Apsarases with dog-like mates, and Rūpakās, O Arbuda, | And her who licks the cup inside, and seeks to wound in ill-kept place, | All these, O Arbuda, do thou make visible to our enemies and let them look on mists and fog. || 16. The fiend who creeps upon the sword, maimed, dwelling where the wounded lie, | The misty shapes that lurk concealed, Gandharvas and Apsarases, demons, and snakes and Other Folk; || 17. Armed with four fangs and yellow teeth, deformed, with faces smeared with blood, the terrible and fearless ones, || 18. Make thou, O Arbuda, those wings of hostile armies quake with dread. | Let Conqueror and Victor, friends of Indra, overcome our foes. || 19. Stifled and crushed, O Nyarbudi, low let the smitten foeman lie. | With tongue of fire and crest of smoke go conquering maidens with our host! || 20. May Indra, Lord of Might, strike down each bravest warrior of the foes, | Whom this our band hath put to flight: let not one man of those escape. || 21. Let their hearts burst asunder, let their breath fly up and pass away. | Let dryness of the mouth o'ertake our foemen, not the friendly ones. || 22. The clever and the foolish ones, those who are twisted round, the deaf, | The dusky-hued, the hornless goats and those whose voice is like the buck's, | All these, O Arbuda, do thou make visible to our enemies: cause them to look on mists and fog. || 23. Arbuda and Trishandhi fall upon our foes and scatter them, | So that, O Indra, Lord of Might, Slayer of Vṛitra, we may kill thousands of these our enemies! || 24. Tall trees, and those who live in woods, the herbs and creeping plants of Earth, Gandharvas, and Apsarases, Snakes, Beings, Fathers, Gods, | All these do thou, O Arbuda, make visible to our enemies: cause them to look on mists and fog. || 25. High sway have Marutas, and the God Āditya, Brahmaṇaspati, | High sway have Indra, Agni, and Dilator, Mitra, Prajāpati, | High sway have Ṛishis given to you, showing upon our enemies where thou, O Arbuda, hast pierced. || 26. With full dominion over these, rise, stand ye up, prepare your-selves, | Ye are our friends, celestial hosts. When ye have won this battle, go, each to his several sphere, apart.

Hymn 11:10.

1. Rise up, with all your banners rise; prepare your strength, ye vapoury Forms! | Serpents and fiends and Other Folk, charge and pursue our enemies! || 2. Let those who bear an evil name, in air, in heaven on earth, and men, | After Trishandhi's will, revere your power, the sway that Knowledge gives, together with your ruddy flags. || 3. Let those with iron faces, with faces like needles or like combs, | Flesh-eaters, rapid as the wind, cling closely to our foemen with Trishandhi for their thunderbolt. || 4. Omniscient Āditya, make full many a corpse to disappear. | Let this devoted army of Trishandhi be in my control. || 5. Rise up, O Godlike

Being, rise, Arbuda, with thine army: this, | Tribute is sacrificed to thee, Trishandhi's welcome offering ‖ 6. May this four-footed White-foot, may this arrow brace and bind thee fast: | Together with Trishandhi's host, be thou, O Witchcraft, meant for foes. ‖ 7. Down let the dim-eyed demon fly, and let her short-eared sister shriek: | Red be the banners when the host of Arbuda hath won the day. ‖ 8. Let all the birds that move on wings come downward, all fowls that roam the heavens and air's mid-region | Let beasts of prey and flies attacks, and vultures that eat raw flesh mangle and gnaw the carcase. ‖ 9. By that same binding treaty which thou madest, Bṛihaspati! with Indra! and with Brahma, | By Indra's pledge I bid the Gods come hither. Conquer on this side, not on their side yonder. ‖ 10. Bṛihaspati Aṅgirasa, Ṛishis made strong and keen by prayer, | Have set Trishandhi in the heaven, dire weapon that destroys the fiends. ‖ 11. The Gods enjoyed Trishandhi for the sake of energy and power, | Him under whose protection, both, Indra and yon Āditya stand. ‖ 12. The Gods, victorious, won themselves all worlds by this oblation, which | Bṛihaspati Aṅgirasa effused, a very thunderbolt, a weapon to destroy the friends. ‖ 13. That fiend-destroying weapon which Bṛihaspati Aṅgirasa poured out and made a thunderbolt, | Even therewith, Bṛihaspati, I brush that hostile armament, and strike the foemen down with might. ‖ 14. Over to us come all the Gods who eat the hallowed sacrifice | With this oblation be ye pleased: conquer on this side, not on that. ‖ 15. Over, to us let all Gods come: dear is Trishandhi's offering. | Keen the great pledge through which, of old, the Asuras were overthrown. ‖ 16. Let Vāyu bend the arrow-points of those who are our enemies. | Let Indra break their arms away: no power to lay the shaft be theirs! Āditya utterly destroy their missile! Chandramās bar the path of him who lingers! ‖ 17. If they have issued forth strongholds of Gods, and made their shields of prayer, | Gaining protection for their lives, protection round about, make all their instigation powerless ‖ 18. With the Flesh-eater and with Death, following the Purohita, | On! forward with Trishandhi's host! conquering enemies advance! ‖ 19. Do thou, Trishandhi, with the gloom of darkness compass round our foes; | Let none escape of them expelled with speckled butter mixt with curds. ‖ 20. Let White-foot fall upon those wings of our opponents' armament; | Mazed and bewildered be those hands of foes this day, O Nyarbudi. ‖ 21. Mazed are the foemen, Nyarbudi! Slay thou each bravest man of them: with this our army slaughter them. ‖ 22. Low lie the warrior, mailed, unmailed, each foeman in the rush of war. | Down-smitten with the strings of bows, the fastenings of mail, the charge! ‖ 23. The armour-clad, the armourless, enemies clothed with coats of mail, | All these struck down, O Arbuda, let dogs devour upon the earth. ‖ 24. Car-borne and carless fighting men, riders and those who go on foot, | All these, struck down, let vultures, kites, and all, the birds of air devour. ‖ 25. Low let the hostile army lie, thousands of corpses, on the ground, | Pierced through and rent to pieces where the deadly weapons clash in fight. ‖ 26. With eagles let them eat the evil-hearted, pierced in the vitals, lying crushed and howling. | The foe whoe'er will fight against this our protecting sacrifice. ‖ 27. With this which Gods attend, with this which never fails to gain its end, | Let Indra, Vṛitra-slayer, smite, and with Trishandhi as a bolt.

Kāṇḍa 12.

Hymn 12.1.

1. Truth, high and potent Law, the Consecrating Rite, Fervour, Brahma, and Sacrifice uphold the Earth. | May she, the Queen of all that is and is to be, may Pṛithivī make ample space and room for us. ‖ 2. Not overcrowded by the crowd of Manu's sons, she who hath many heights and floods and level plains; | She who bears plants endowed with many varied powers, may Pṛithivī for us spread wide and favour us. ‖ 3. In whom the sea, and Sindhu, and the waters, in whom our food and corn-lands had their being, | In whom this all that breathes and moves is active, this Earth assign us foremost rank and station! 4. She who is Lady of the earth's four regions, in whom our food and corn-lands had their being, | Nurse in each place of breathing, moving creatures, this Earth. vouchsafe us kine with milk that fails not! ‖ 5. On whom the men of old before us battled, on whom the Gods attacked the hostile demons, | The varied home of bird, and kine and horses, this Pṛithivī vouchsafe us luck and splendour! ‖ 6. Firm

standing-place, all-bearing, store of treasures, gold-breasted, harbourer of all that moveth. | May Earth who bears Agni Vaiśvānara, Consort of mighty Indra, give us great possessions ‖ 7. May Earth, may Pṛithivī, always protected with ceaseless care by Gods who never slumber, | May she pour out for us delicious nectar, may she bedew us with a flood of splendour. ‖ 8. She who at first was water in the ocean, whom with their wondrous powers the sages followed, | May she whose heart is in the highest heaven, compassed about wit h truth, and everlasting, | May she, this Earth, bestow upon us lustre, and grant us power in loftiest dominion. ‖ 9. On whom the running universal waters flow day and night with never-ceasing motion, | May she with many streams pour milk to feed us, may she bedew us with a flood of splendour. ‖ 10. She whom the Aśvins measured out, o'er whom the foot of Vishṇu strode, | Whom Indra, Lord of Power and Might, freed from all foemen for himself, | May Earth pour out her milk for us, a mother unto me her son. ‖ 11. O Pṛithivī, auspicious be thy woodlands, auspicious be thy hills and snow-clad mountains. | Unslain, unwounded, unsubdued, I have set foot upon the Earth, | On earth brown, black, ruddy and every-coloured, on the firm earth that Indra guards from danger. ‖ 12. O Pṛithivī, thy centre and thy navel, all forces that have issued from thy body | Set us amid those forces; breathe upon us. I am the son of Earth, Earth is my Mother. Parjanya is my Sire; may he promote me. ‖ 13. Earth on whose surface they enclose the altar, and all-performers spin the thread of worship; | In whom the stakes of sacrifice, resplendent, are fixed and raised on high before the oblation, may she, this Earth, prospering, make us prosper. ‖ 14. The man who hates us, Earth! who fights against us, who threaten us with thought or deadly weapon, make him our thrall as thou hast done aforetime. ‖ 15. Produced from thee, on thee move mortal creatures: thou bearest them, both quadruped and biped. | Thine, Pṛithivī, are these Five human Races, for whom, though mortal, Sūrya as he rises spreads with his rays the light that is immortal. ‖ 16. In concert may these creatures yield us blessings. With honey of discourse, O Earth, endow me. ‖ 17. Kind, ever gracious be the Earth we tread on, the firm Earth, | Pṛithivī, borne up by Order, mother of plants and herbs, the all-producer. ‖ 18. A vast abode hast thou become, the Mighty. Great stress is on thee, press and agitation, but with unceasing care great Indra guards thee. | So make us shine, O Earth, us with the splendour of gold. Let no man look on us with hatred. ‖ 19. Agni is in the earth, in plants; the waters hold Agni in them, in the stones is Agni. | Agni abideth deep in men: Agnis abide in cows and steeds. ‖ 20. Agni gives shine and heat in heaven: the spacious air is his, the God's. | Lover of fatness, bearer of oblation, men enkindle him. ‖ 21. Dark-kneed, invested with a fiery mantle, Pṛithivī sharpen me and give me splendour! ‖ 22. On earth they offer sacrifice and dressed oblation to the Gods. | Men, mortals, live upon the earth by food in their accustomed way. | May that Earth grant us breath and vital power. Pṛithivī give me life of long duration! ‖ 23. Scent that hath risen from thee, O Earth, the fragrance which. growing herbs and plants and waters carry, | Shared by Apsarases, shared by Gandharvas therewith make thou me sweet: let no man hate me. ‖ 24. Thy scent which entered and possessed the lotus, the scent which they prepared at Sūrya's bridal, | Scent which Immortals Earth! of old collected, therewith make thou me sweet: let no man hate me. ‖ 25. Thy scent in women and in men, the luck and light that is in. males, | That is in heroes and in steeds in sylvan beasts and elephants, | The splendid energy of maids, therewith do thou unite us, | Earth! Let no man look on us with hate. ‖ 26. Rock earth, and stone, and dust, this Earth is held together, firmly bound. | To this gold-breasted Pṛithivī mine adoration have I paid. ‖ 27. Hither we call the firmly held, the all-supporting Pṛithivī, | On whom the trees, lords of the wood, stand evermore immovable. ‖ 28. Sitting at ease or rising up, standing or going on our way. | With our right foot and with our left we will not reel upon the earth. ‖ 29. I speak to Pṛithivī the purifier, to patient Earth who groweth strong through Brahma. | O Earth, may we recline on thee who bearest strength, increase, portioned share of food, and fatness. ‖ 30. Purified for our bodies flow the waters: we bring distress on him who would attack us. | I cleanse myself, O Earth, with that which cleanseth. ‖ 31. Earth, be thine eastern and thy northern regions, those lying southward and those lying westward. | Propitious unto me in all my movements. Long as I tread the ground let me not stumble. ‖ 32. Drive us not from the west or east, drive us not from the north or south, |

Be gracious unto us, O Earth: let not the robbers find us; keep the deadly weapon far away. || 33. Long as, on thee, I look around, possessing Sūrya as a friend, | So long, through each succeeding year, let not my power of vision fail. || 34. When, as I lie, O Earth, I turn upon my right side and my left, | When stretched at all our length we lay our ribs on thee who meetest us. | Do us no injury there, O Earth who furnishest a bed for all. || 35. Let what I dig from thee, O Earth, rapidly spring and grow again. | O Purifier, let me not pierce through thy vitals or thy heart. || 36. Earth, may thy summer, and thy rains, and autumn, thy winter, and thy dewy frosts, and spring-time. | May thy years, Pṛithivī! and ordered seasons, and day and night pour out for us abundance. || 37. The purifier, shrinking from the Serpent, she who held fires that lie within the waters, | Who gives as prey the God-blaspheming Dasyus, Earth choosing | Indra for her Lord, not Vṛitra, hath clung to Śakra, to the Strong and Mighty. || 38. Base of the seat and sheds, on whom the sacrificial stake is reared, | On whom the Yajus-knowing priests recite their hymns and chant their psalms, | And ministers are busied that Indra may drink the Soma juice; || 39. On whom the ancient Ṛishis, they who made the world, sang forth the cows, | Seven worshippers, by session, with their fervent zeal and sacrifice; || 40. May she, the Earth, assign to us the opulence for which we yearn, | May Bhaga share and aid the task and Indra come to lead the way. || 41. May she, the Earth, whereon men sing and dance with varied shout and noise, | Whereon men meet in battle, and the war-cry and the drum resound, | May she drive off our foemen, may Pṛithivī rid me of my foes. || 42. On whom is food, barley and rice, to whom these Races Five belong, | Homage to her, Parjanya's wife, to her whose marrow is the rain! || 43. Whose castles are the work of Gods, and men wage war upon her plain | The Lord of Life make Pṛithivī, who beareth all things in her womb, pleasant to us on every side! || 44. May Earth the Goddess, she who bears her treasure stored up in many a place, gold, gems, and riches, | Giver of opulence, grant great possessions to us bestowing them with love and favour. || 45. Earth, bearing folk of many a varied language with divers rites as suits their dwelling-places, | Pour, like a constant cow that never faileth, a thousand streams of treasure to enrich me! || 46. Thy snake, thy sharply stinging scorpion, lying concealed, bewildered, chilled with cold of winter, | The worm, O Pṛithivī, each thing that in the Rains revives and stirs, | Creeping, forbear to creep on us! With all things gracious bless thou us. || 47. Thy many ways on which the people travel, the road for car and wain to journey over, | Thereon meet both the good and bad, that pathway may we attain without a foe or robber. With all things gracious bless thou us. || 48. Supporting both the foolish and the weighty she bears the death both of the good and evil. | In friendly concord with the boar, Earth opens herself for the wild swine that roams the forest. || 49. All sylvan beasts of thine that love the woodlands, man-eaters, forest-haunting, lions, tigers, | Hyena, wolf, Misfortune, evil spirit, drive from us, chase the demons to a distance. || 50. Gandharvas and Apsarases, Kimīdins, and malignant sprites, | Piśāchas all, and Rākṣhasas, these keep thou, Earth! afar from us. || 51. To whom the winged bipeds fly together, birds of each various kind, the swans, the eagles; | On whom the Wind comes rushing, Mātariśvan, rousing the dust and causing trees to tremble, and flame pursues the blast. hither and thither; || 52. Earth, upon whom are settled, joined together, the night and day, the dusky and the ruddy, Pṛithivī compassed by the rain about her, | Happily may she establish us in each delightful dwelling place. || 53. Heaven, Earth, the realm of Middle Air have granted me this ample room, | Agni, Sun, Waters, all the Gods have joined to give me mental power. || 54. I am victorious, I am called the lord superior on earth, | Triumphant, all-o'erpowering the conqueror on every side || 55. There, when the Gods, O Goddess, named thee, spreading thy wide expanse as thou wast broadening eastward, | Then into thee passed many a charm and glory: thou madest for thyself the world's four regions. || 56. In hamlets and in woodland, and in all assemblages on earth, | In gatherings, meeting of the folk, we will speak glorious things of thee. || 57. As the horse scattereth the dust, the people who dwelt upon the land, at birth, she scattered, | Leader and head of all the world, delightful, the trees' protectress and the plants' upholder. || 58. Whate'er I say I speak with honey-sweetness, whatever I behold for that they love me. | Dazzling, impetuous am I: others who fiercely stir I slay. || 59. Mild, gracious, sweetly odorous, milky, with nectar in her breast, | May Earth, may Pṛithivī bestow her benison, with milk, on me. || 60. Whom Viśvakarman with oblation followed, when she was set in mid-air's billowy ocean | A useful vessel, hid, when, for enjoyment, she was made manifest to those with mothers. || 61. Thou art the vessel that containeth people, Aditi, granter of the wish, far-spreading. | Prajāpati, the first-born Son of Order, supplieth thee with whatsoe'er thou lackest. || 62. Let thy breasts, free from sickness and Consumption, be Pṛithivī, produced for our advantage. | Through long-extended life wakeful and watching still may we be thy tributary servants. || 63. O Earth, my Mother, set thou me happily in a place secure. | Of one accord with Heaven, O Sage, set me in glory and in wealth.

Hymn 12:2.

1. This is no place to hold thee; mount the Naḍa: this lead is thine appointed share. Come hither. | Together with Consumption in the cattle, Consumption in our men, go hence, go southward. || 2. With this we chase and banish all consumptive malady and Death, | With sinner and malicious man, with helper and with minister, || 3. Death and Misfortune we expel, Malignity we drive away. | O Agni, thou who eatest not the corpse, eat him who hateth us: him whom we hate we send to thee. || 4. If the corpse-eating Agni, or a tiger leaving his lair, hath entered this our homestead, | With beans prepared in butter I expel him: far let him go to fires that lie in waters. || 5. When, angered that a man hath died, we in our wrath have banished thee, | That deed is easily set right through thee: we kindle thee again. || 6. Again have the Ādityas, Rudras, Vasus, the Brahman, bringer of good things, O Agni, | Again hath Brahmaṇaspati disposed thee for long life lasting through a hundred autumns. || 7. I sweep afar, for sacrifice to Fathers, corpse-eating Agni who hath come among us, | Although he saw this other, Jātavedas: in loftiest space let him inflame the cauldron || 8. I drive corpse-eating Agni to a distance: sin-laden let him go to Yama's vassals. | Here let this other, Jātavedas, carry oblation to the Deities, fore-knowing. || 9. I quickly sweep away corpse-eating Agni, Death, with his bolt depriving men of motion. | From household fire, well-knowing, I divide him: so in the world of Fathers be his portion. || 10. Corpse-eating Agni, toil-worn, meet for praises, I send away bypaths used by the Fathers. | Stay there; keep watch among the Fathers: come not again to us by ways whereon Gods travel. || 11. They being cleansed and bright, the purifiers, kindle Saṃkasuka for our well-being. | Impurity leaveth us and sin departeth: lighted by the good cleanser Agni cleanseth. || 12. Agni the God, the Breaker-up, hath mounted to the heights of heaven. | Released from all transgression, he hath from the curse delivered us. || 13. On Agni here, the Breaker-up, we wipe impurities away. | Cleansed, fit for sacrifice have we become: may he prolong our lives. || 14. The Breaker-up, the Burster, the Destroyer, and the Silent One, | These have expelled Consumption far, far off from thee and all thou hast, || 15. Corpse-eating Agni we expel, the Agni who bewilders men, | Him who is in our horses, in our heroes, cows, and goats, and sheep: || 16. We drive thee forth to other folk, to alien cattle, alien steeds, | Thee the corpse-eating Agni, thee the Agni who bewilders men, || 17. Whereon the Deities, whereon men too have purified themselves, | Exalting fatness, cleanse thyself, Agni, therein and mount to heaven. || 18. O Agni, kindled and adored, turn not away to visit us. | Shine brightly even there in heaven, so that we long may see the Sun. || 19. Wipe all away on lead and reed, on Agni, him who breaketh up, | Then on a black-hued sheep, and on a cushion pain that racks. the head, || 20. Wipe off pollution, lay it in the lead and in the black-hued sheep, | And headache in the cushion; then be cleansed and fit to sacrifice || 21. Go onward, Death, pursue thy special pathway apart from that which Gods are wont to travel. | To thee I say it who hast eyes and hearest: great grow the number of these men around us! || 22. Divided from the dead are these, the living: now is our calling on the Gods successful. | We have gone forth for dancing and for laughter: may we with brave sons speak to the assembly. || 23. Here I erect this rampart for the living: let none of these, none other, reach this limit. | May they survive a hundred lengthened autumns, and may they bury Death beneath this mountain. || 24. Live your full lives and find age delightful, all of you striving, one behind the other. | May Tvaṣhṭar, maker of fair things, be gracious, and lead your whole lives on to full existence. || 25. As the days follow days in close succession, as with the seasons duly come the seasons. | As each successor fails not his foregoer, so

constitute the lives of these, Ordainer! || 26. Gather your strength, my friends; the stream flows stony: acquit yourselves as men, and cross the river. | Abandon here the powers that were malignant, and let us cross to powers exempt from sickness. || 27. Rise up erect, cross over, my companions: the stream is stony that flows here before us. | Abandon here the powers that were ungracious, and let us cross to powers benign and friendly. || 28. Becoming pure and bright and purifying begin the Vaiśvadevī strain for splendour. | May we rejoice, o'erpassing troublous places, with all our heroes through a hundred winters. || 29. On pathways swept by wind, directed upward, passing beyond the lower, on the higher, | Thrice seven times have the Ṛishis, the Departed, forced Mṛityu backward with the fastened fetter. || 30. Effecting Mṛityu's footstep ye came hither, to further times pro-longing your existence, | Seated, drive Mṛityu to his proper dwelling: then may we, living, speak to the assembly. || 31. Let these unwidowed dames with goodly husbands adorn themselves with fragrant balm and unguent, | Decked with fair jewels, tearless, sound and healthy, first let the dames go up to where he lieth. || 32. I with oblation separate both classes, and with my prayer dis-part their several portions. | I offer food that wastes not to the Fathers, and to these men give life of long duration. || 33. That Agni, Fathers! who, himself immortal, hath entered and possessed our mortal bosoms, | Even him I grasp and hold the God with me, Let him not hate us, may we never hate him. || 34. When ye have left the household fire, with the Corpse-eater southward go. | Do that which is delightful to the Fathers, Brahmans, and your-selves. || 35. Agni, the banqueter on flesh, not banished, for the eldest son | Taketh a double share of wealth and spoileth it with poverty. || 36. What man acquires by plough, by war, all that he wins by toil of hand, | He loses all if Agni the Carnivorous be not set aside, || 37. Unholy, splendour-reft is he, his sacrifice unfit to eat. Kravyād deprives of tilth of cow, of riches him whom he pursues, || 38. Oft as a greedy beggar speaks the mortal who has brought distress, | Those whom Carnivorous Agni close at hand runs after and detects. || 39. When a dame's husband dies the house is tangled fast in Grāhi's net. | A learned Brahman must be sought to drive Carnivorous Agni, forth. || 40. From any evil we have done, act of impurity or sin, | Let waters purge me and from all that comes from Agni Breaker-up. || 41. By pathways travelled by the Gods these waters, well-knowing, from below have mounted upward. | High on the summit of the raining mountain the ancient rivers fresh and new are flowing. || 42. Drive off Carnivorous Agni, thou Agni who eatest not the flesh;. carry oblation paid to Gods. || 43. The Flesh-eater hath entered him: he hath pursued the Flesh-eater. | Making two tigers different-wise, I bear away the ungracious one. || 44. He who holds Gods within himself, the rampart and defence of men, | Agni, the sacred household fire, hath come and stands between them both. || 45. Prolong the lives of those who live, O Agni, Let the dead go unto world of Fathers. | As goodly household fire burn up Arāti; give this man dawn brighter than all the mornings. || 46. Subduing all our adversaries, Agni, give us their food, their strength and their possessions. || 47. Grasp ye this Indra, furtherer, satisfier: he will release you from disgrace and trouble. | With him drive back the shaft that flies against you, with him ward off the missile shot by Rudra. || 48. Seize with firm hold the Ox who boundeth forward: he will uplift you from disgrace and trouble. | Enter this ship of Savitar; let us flee from poverty over all the six expenses. || 49. Thou followest the day and night, supporting, standing, at peace, promoting, rich in heroes. | Long bearing undiseased and happy sleepers, be ours, O Bed, with smell of man about thee, || 50. They sever from the Gods, they live in sin and misery evermore, | Those whom from very near at hand Carnivorous Agni casteth down as a horse tramples down the reeds. || 51. The faithless, who from lust of wealth abide with him who feeds on flesh, | For ever set upon the fire an alien cauldron, not their own. || 52. Forward in spirit would he fly, and often turns he back again, | Whomso Carnivorous Agni from anear discovers and torments. || 53. Among tame beasts the black ewe is thy portion, and the bright lead is thine, they say, Flesh-eater! | Mashed beans have been assigned thee for oblation go seek the dark wood and the wildernesses. || 54. I sought the rustling sugar-cane, white sesamum, and cane and reed. | I made this Indra's fuel, and the Fire of Yama I removed. || 55. Against the sinking western Sun I set them; each sundered path, knowing my way, I entered. | I have warned off the ghosts of the Departed: to these I give the boon of long existence.

Hymn 12:3.

1. Mount, male from male, the skin. Go thither: summon those whom thou lovest, one and all, to meet thee, | Strong as ye were when first ye met each other, still be your strength the same in Yama's kingdom. || 2. So strong your sight, so many be your powers, so great your force, your energies so many, | When fire attends the body as its fuel, then may, ye gain full chargers, O ye couple. || 3. Together in this world, in God-ward pathway, together be ye in the realms of Yama. | Invite, made pure with means of purifying, whatever seed of yours hath been developed. || 4. Do ye, O sons, unite you with the waters, meeting this living man, ye life-sustainers, | Allot to them the Odana your mother is making ready, which they call immortal. || 5. That which your mother and your sire, to banish sin and uncleanness from their lips, are cooking. | That Odana with hundred streams, sky-reaching, hath in its might pervaded earth and heaven. || 6. Live with your sons, when life on earth is ended, live in the sphere most rich in light and sweetness. | In skies that have been won by sacrificers make both the worlds, earth, heaven, your habitation. || 7. Approach the eastern, yea: the eastern region, this is the sphere to which the faithful turn them, | Your cooked oblation that in fire was offered, together, wife and husband, meet to guard it. || 8. Now, as your steps approach the southern quarter, move in. your circling course about this vessel. | Herein, accordant with the Fathers, Yama shall mightily protect your cooked oblation. || 9. Best of the regions is indeed this western wherein the King and gracious Lord is Soma. | Thither resort for rest, follow the pious. Then gain the laden chargers, O ye couple. || 10. Ever victorious is the northern region: may the east quarter set us first and foremost. | The Man became the five-divisioned metre. May we abide with all our members perfect. || 11. This steadfast realm is Queen. To her be homage! To me and to my sons may she be gracious. | Guard thou, O Goddess Aditi, all-bounteous, our cooked oblation as an active warder. || 12. Embrace us as a father clasps his children. Here on the Earth let kindly breezes fan us. | Let the rice-mess these two cook here, O Goddess, know this our truthfulness and zealous fervour. || 13. If the dark bird hath come to us and, stealing the hanging morsel, settled in his dwelling, | Or if the slave-girl hath, wet-handed, smearing the pestle and the mortar, cleansed the waters, || 14. This pressing-stone, broad-based and strength-bestowing, made pure by cleansing means, shall chase the demon. | Mount on the skin: afford us great protection, Let not the sons' sin fall on wife and husband. || 15. Together with the Gods, banning Piśāchas and demons, hath Vanaspati come hither. | He shall rise up and send his voice out loudly. May we win all the worlds with him to help us. || 16. Seven victims held the sacrificial essence, the bright one and the one that hath grown feeble. | The three-and-thirty Deities attend them. As such, conduct us to the world of Svarga. || 17. Unto the world of Svarga shalt thou lead us: there may we dwell beside our wife and children. | I take thy hand Let not Destruction, let not Malignity come hither and subdue us. || 18. We have subdued that sinful-hearted Grāhi. Thou shalt speak sweetly having chased the darkness. | Let not the wooden gear made ready fail us, nor harm the grain of rice that pays due worship. || 19. Soon to be, decked with butter, all-embracing, come to this world wherewith birth unites thee. | Seize thou the winnowing-fan which rains have nourished, and let this separate the chaff and refuse. || 20. Three worlds hath Power Divine marked out and measured, heaven yonder, and the earth, and airs mid-region. | Grasp ye the stalks and in your hands retain them: let them be watered and again be winnowed. || 21. Manifold, various are the shapes of victims. Thou growest uniform by great abundance. | Push thou away this skin of ruddy colour: the stone will cleanse as one who cleanses raiment. || 22. Earth upon earth I set thee. This thy body is consubstantial, but in form it differs. | Whate'er hath been worn off or scratched in fixing, leak not thereat: I spread a charm to mend it. || 23. Thou for thy son shalt yearn as yearns a mother. I lay thee down and with the earth unite thee. | Conjoined with sacrificial gear and butter may pot and jar stand firmly on the altar. || 24. Eastward may Agni as he cooks preserve thee. Southward may Indra, grit by Marutas, guard thee, | Varuṇa strengthen and support thee westward, and Soma on the north hold thee together. || 25. Drops flow, made pure by filters, from the rain-cloud: to heaven and earth and to the worlds they

travel, | May Indra light them up, poured in the vessel, lively and steadfast, quickening living creatures. || 26. From heaven they come, they visit earth, and rising from earth unite themselves with air's mid-region, | Purified, excellent, they with shine in beauty. Thus may they lead us to the world of Svarga. || 27. Yea, and supreme, alike in conformation, and brilliant and refulgent and immortal, | As such, enjoined, well-guarding, water-givers, dress ye the Odana for wife and husband. || 28. Numbered, they visit earth, these drops of moisture, commensurate with plants and vital breathings, | Unnumbered, scattered, beautiful in colour, the bright, ones have pervaded all refulgence. || 29. Heated, they rage and boil in agitation, they cast about their foam and countless bubbles | Like a fond woman when she sees her husband—what time ye waters and these rice-grains mingle, || 30. Take up these rice-grains lying at the bottom: led them be blent and mingled with the waters. | This water I have measured in the vessel, if as mid-points the rice-grains have been meted. || 31. Present the sickle: quickly bring it hither. Let them out plants and joints with hands that harm not. | So may the plants be free from wrath against us, they o'er whose realm Soma hath won dominion. || 32. Strew ye fresh grass for the boiled rice to rest on: fair let it be, sweet to the eye and spirit. | Hither come Goddesses with Gods, and sitting here taste in proper season this oblation. || 33. On the strewn grass. Vanaspati, be seated; commensurate with Gods and Agnishṭomas. | Let thy fair form, wrought as by Tvashṭar's hatchet, mark these that yearn for thee within the vessel. || 34. In sixty autumns may the Treasure-Guardian seek to gain heavenly light by cooked oblation. | On this may sons and fathers live dependent. Send thou this mess to Fire that leads to heaven. || 35. On the earth's breast stand firmly as supporter: may Deities stir thee who ne'er hast shaken. | So living man and wife with living children remove thee from the hearth of circling Agni. || 36. All wishes that have blessed those with fulfilment, having won all the worlds have met together. | Let them plunge in both stirring-spoon and ladle: raise this and set it in a single vessel. || 37. Pour out the covering butter, spread it eastward: sprinkle this vessel over with the fatness. | Greet this, ye Deities, with gentle murmur, as lowing cows welcome their tender suckling. || 38. Thou hast poured oil and made the worlds: let heaven, unequalled, be spread out in wide extension. | Herein be cooked the buffalo, strong-pinioned: the Gods shall give the Deities this oblation. || 39. Whate'er thy wife, away from thee, makes ready, or what, O wife, apart from thee, thy husband, | Combine it all: let it be yours in common while ye produce one world with joint endeavour. || 40. All these now dwelling on the earth, mine offspring, these whom, this woman here, my wife, hath borne me, | Invite them all unto the vessel: knowing their kinship have the children met together. || 41. Swollen with savoury meath, the stream of treasures, sources of immortality blent with fatness | Soma retains all these; in sixty autumns the Guardian Lord of Treasures may desire them. || 42. The Lord of Treasures may desire this treasure: lordless on. every side be all the others. | Our mess, presented seeking heaven, hath mounted in three divisions all three realms of Svarga. || 43. May Agni burn the God-denying demon: let no carnivorous. Piśācha drink here. | We drive him off, we keep him at a distance. Ādityas and Aṅgirasas pursue him! || 44. This meath do I announce, mingled with butter, to the Aṅgirasas and the Ādityas. | With pure hands ne'er laid roughly on a Brahman go, pious couple, to the world of Svarga. || 45. Of this have I obtained the noblest portion from that same world whence Parameshṭhin gained it. | Pour forth, besprinkle butter rich in fatness: the share of Aṅgiras is here before us. || 46. To Deities, to Truth, to holy Fervour this treasure we consign, this rich deposit, | At play, in meeting led it not desert us, never give out to anyone besides me. || 47. I cook the offering, I present oblation: only my wife attends the holy service. | A youthful world, a son hath been begotten. Begin a life that brings success and triumph. || 48. There is no fault in this, no reservation, none when it goes with friends in close alliance. | We have laid down this vessel in perfection: the cooked mess shall re-enter him who cooked it. || 49. To those we love may we do acts that please them. Away to darkness go all those who hate us! | Cow, ox, and strength of every kind approach us! Thus let them banish death of human beings. || 50. Perfectly do the Agnis know each other, one visitor of plants and one of rivers, | And all the Gods who shine and glow in heaven. Gold is the light of him who cooks oblation. || 51. Man hath received this skin of his from nature: of other animals not one is naked. | Ye make him clothe himself with might for raiment. Odana's mouth is a home-woven vesture. || 52. Whatever thou may say at dice, in meeting, whatever falsehood through desire of riches, | Ye two, about one common warp uniting, deposit all impurity within it. || 53. Win thou the rain: approach the Gods. Around thee thou from the skin shalt make the smoke rise upward. | Soon to be, decked with butter, all-embracing, come to this world wherewith one birth unites thee. || 54. In many a shape hath heaven transformed its body, as in itself is known, of varied colour. | Cleansing the bright, the dark form hath it banished: the red form in the fire to thee I offer. || 55. To the eastern region, to Agni the Regent, to Asita the Protector, Āditya the Archer, we present thee, this offering of ours. Do ye preserve it from aggression | To full old age may Destiny conduct us; may full old age deliver us to Mṛityu Then may we be with our prepared oblation. || 56. To the southern region, to Indra the Regent, to Tiraśchirājī the Protector, to Yama the Archer, we present, etc. (as in stanza 55.) || 57. To the western region, to Varuṇa the Regent, to Pṛidākū the Protector, to Food the Archer, we present, etc. || 58. To the northern region, to Soma the Regent, to Svaja the Protector, to Thunderbolt the Archer, we present, etc. || 59. To the steadfast region, to Vishṇu the Regent, to Kalmāshagrīva the Protector, to Plants the Archers, we present, etc. || 60. To the upper region, to Bṛihaspati the Regent, to Śvitra the Protector, to Rain the Archer, we present thee, this offering of ours. Do ye preserve it from aggression. | To full old age may Destiny conduct us, may full old age deliver us to Mṛityu Then may we be with our prepared oblation.

Hymn 12:4.

1. Give the gift, shall be his word: and straightway they have bound the Cow | For Brahman priests who beg the boon. That bringeth sons and progeny. || 2. He trades and traffics with his sons, and in his cattle suffers loss. | Who will not give the Cow of Gods to Ṛishis children when they beg. || 3. They perish through a hornless cow, a lame cow sinks them in a pit. | Through a maimed cow his house is burnt: a one-eyed cow destroys his wealth. || 4. Fierce fever where her droppings fall attacks the master of the kine. | So have they named her Vaśa, for thou art called uncontrollable. || 5. The malady Vibhindu springs on him from ground whereon she stands, | And suddenly, from fell disease, perish the men on whom she sniffs. || 6. Whoever twitches up her ears is separated from the Gods. | He deems he makes a mark, but he diminishes his wealth thereby. || 7. If to his own advantage one applies the long hair of her tail, | His colts, in consequence thereof die, and the wolf destroys his calves. || 8. If, while her master owneth her, a carrion crow hath harmed her hair, | His young boys die thereof, Decline o'ertakes them after fell disease. || 9. What time the Dāsī woman throws lye on the droppings of the Cow, | Misshapen birth arises thence, inseparable from that sin. || 10. For Gods and Brahmans is the Cow produced when first she springs to life, | Hence to the priests must she be given: this they call guarding private wealth. || 11. The God-created Cow belongs to those who come to ask for her. | They call it outrage on the priests when one retains her as his own. || 12. He who withholds the Cow of Gods from Ṛishis' sons who ask the gift | Is made an alien to the Gods, and subject to the Brahmans' wrath: || 13. Then let him seek another Cow, whate'er his profit be in this. | The Cow, not given, harms a man when he denies her at their prayer. || 14. Like a rich treasure stored away in safety is the Brahmans' Cow. | Therefore men come to visit her, with whomsoever she is born. || 15. So when the Brahmans come unto the Cow they come unto their own. | For this is her withholding, to oppress these in another life. || 16. Thus after three years may she go, speaking what is not understood. | He, Nārada! would know the Cow, then Brahmans must be sought unto. || 17. Whoso calls her a worthless Cow, the stored-up treasure of the Gods, | Bhava and Śarva, both of them, move round and shoot a shaft at him. || 18. The man who hath no knowledge of her udder and the teats thereof, | She yields him milk with these, if he hath purposed to bestow the Cow. || 19. If he withholds the Cow they beg, she lies rebellious in his stall. | Vain are the wishes and the hopes which he, withholding her, would gain. || 20. The Deities have begged the Cow, using the Brahman as their mouth: | The man who gives her not incurs the enmity of all the Gods. || 21. Withholding her from Brahmans, he incurs the anger of the beasts, | When mortal man appropriates the destined portion of the Gods. || 22. If

hundred other Brahmans beg the Cow of him who owneth her, | The Gods have said, She, verily, belongs to him who knows the truth. || 23. Whoso to others, not to him who hath this knowledge, gives the Cow, | Earth, with the Deities, is hard for him to win and rest upon. || 24. The Deities begged the Cow from him with whom at first she was produced: | Her, this one, Nārada would know: with Deities he drove her forth. || 25. The Cow deprives of progeny and makes him poor in cattle who | Retains in his possession her whom Brahmans have solicited. || 26. For Agni and for Soma, for Kāma, Mitra and Varuṇa, | For these the Brahmans ask: from these is he who giveth not estranged. || 27. Long as her owner hath not heard, himself, the verses, let her move | Among his kine: when he hath heard, let her not make her home with him; || 28. He who hath heard her verses and still makes her roam among his kine. | The Gods in anger rend away his life and his prosperity || 29. Roaming in many a place the Cow is the stored treasure of the Gods, | Make manifest thy shape and form when she would seek her dwelling-place. || 30. Her shape and form she manifests when she would seek her dwelling-place; | Then verily the Cow attends to Brahman priests and their request. || 31. This thought he settles in his mind. This safely goeth to the Gods. | Then verily the Brahman priests approach that they may beg the Cow || 32. By Svadhā to the Fathers, by sacrifice to the Deities, | By giving them the Cow, the Prince doth not incur the mother's wrath. || 33. The Prince's mother is the Cow: so was it ordered from of old. | She, when bestowed upon the priests, cannot be given back, they say. || 34. As molten butter, held at length, drops down to Agni from the scoop, | So falls away from Agni he who gives no Cow to Brahman priests. || 35. Good milker, with rice-cake as calf, she in the world comes nigh to him, | To him who gave her as a gift the Cow grants every hope and. wish. || 36. In Yama's realm the Cow fulfils each wish for him who gave her up; | But hell, they say, is for the man who, when they beg, bestow her not. || 37. Enraged against her owner roams the Cow when she hath been impregned. | He deemed me fruitless is her thought; let him be bound in, snares of Death! || 38. Whoever looking on the Cow as fruitless, cooks her flesh at home, | Bṛihaspati compels his sons and children of his sons to beg. || 39. Downward she sends a mighty heat, though amid kine a Cow she roams. | Poison she yields for him who owns and hath not given her away. || 40. The animal is happy when it is bestowed upon the priests: | But happy is the Cow when she is made a sacrifice to Gods. || 41. Nārada chose the terrible Viliptī out of all the cows | Which the Gods formed and framed when they had risen up from sacrifice || 42. The Gods considered her in doubt whether she were a Cow or not. | Nārada spake of her and said, The veriest Cow of cows is she. || 43. How many cows, O Nārada, knowest thou, born among man-kind | I ask thee who dost know, of which must none who is no Brahman eat? || 44. Viliptī, cow, and she who drops no second calf, Bṛihaspati! | Of these none not a Brāhmaṇa should eat if he hope for eminence. || 45. Homage, O Nārada, to thee who hast quick knowledge of the cows. | Which of these is the direst, whose withholding bringeth death to man? || 46. Viliptī, O Bṛihaspati, cow, mother of no second calf— | Of these none not a Brahman should eat if he hope for eminence. || 47. Threefold are kine, Viliptī, cow, the mother of no second calf: | These one should give to priests, and he will not offend Prajāpati. || 48. This Brahmans! is your sacrifice: thus should one think when he is asked, | What time they beg from him the Cow fearful in the with-holder's house. || 49. He gave her not to us, so spake the Gods, in anger, of the Cow. | With these same verses they addressed Bheda: this brought him to his death. || 50. Solicited by Indra, still Bheda refused to give this Cow. | In strife for victory the Gods destroyed him for that sin of his. || 51. The men of evil counsel who advise refusal of the Cow, | Miscreants, through their foolishness, are subjected to Indra's wrath. || 52. They who seduce the owner of the Cow and say, Bestow her not. | Encounter through their want of sense the missile shot by Rudra's hand. || 53. If in his home one cooks the Cow, sacrificed or not sacrificed. | Wronger of Gods and Brahmans he departs, dishonest, from the world.

Hymn 12:5.

1. Created by toil and holy fervour, found by devotion, resting in right; || 2. Invested with truth, surrounded with honour, compassed about with glory; || 3. Girt round with inherent power, fortified with faith, protected, by consecration, installed at sacrifice, the world her resting-place; || 4. Brahma her guide, the Brahman her lord and ruler; || 5. Of the Kṣhatriya who taketh to himself this Brahman's cow and oppresseth the Brahman. || 6. The glory, the heroism, and the favouring fortune depart. || 7. The energy and vigour, the power and might the speech and mental strength, the glory and duty; || 8. Devotion and princely sway, kingship and people, brilliance and honour, and splendour and wealth; || 9. Long life and goodly form, and name and fame, inbreathing and expiration, and sight, and hearing; || 10. Milk and flavour, and food and nourishment, and right and truth, and action and fulfilment, and children and cattle; || 11. All these blessings of a Kṣhatriya depart from him when he oppresseth the Brahman and taketh to himself the Brahman's cow. || 12. Terrible is she this Brahman's cow, and fearfully venomous, visibly witchcraft. || 13. In her are all horrors and all death. || 14. In her are all dreadful, deeds, all slaughters of mankind. || 15. This, the Brahman's cow, being appropriated, holdeth bound in the fetter of Death the oppressor of the Brahman, the blasphemer of the Gods. || 16. A hundred-killing bolt is she: she slays the Brahman's injurer. || 17. Therefore the Brahmans' cow is held inviolable by the wise. || 18. Running she is a thunderbolt, when driven away she is Vaiśvānara; || 19. An arrow when she draweth up her hooves, and Mahādeva when she looketh around; || 20. Sharp as a razor when she beholdeth, she thundereth when she belloweth. || 21. Death is she when she loweth, and a fierce God when she whisketh her tail; || 22. Utter destruction when she moveth her ears this way and that, | Consumption when she droppeth water; || 23. A missile when milking, pain in the head when milked; || 24. The taking away of strength when she approacheth, a hand-to-hand fighter when roughly touched; || 25. Wounding like an arrow when she is fastened by her mouth, contention when she is beaten; || 26. Fearfully venomous when falling, darkness when she hath fallen down. || 27. Following him, the Brahman's cow extinguisheth the vital breath of the injurer of the Brahman. || 28. Hostility when being cut to pieces, woe to children when the portions are distributed, || 29. A destructive missile of Gods when she is being seized, misfortune when carried away; || 30. Misery while being additionally acquired, contumely and abuse while being put in the stall; || 31. Poison when in agitation, fever when seasoned with condiments; || 32. Sin while she is cooking, evil dream when she is cooked; || 33. Uprooting when she is being turned round, destruction when she hath been turned round; || 34. Discord by her smell, grief when she is being eviscerated: serpent with poison in its fang when drawn; || 35. Loss of power while sacrificially presented, humiliation when she hath been offered; || 36. Wrathful Śarva while being carved. Śimidā when cut up: || 37. Poverty while she is being eaten. Destruction when eaten. || 38. The Brahman's cow when eaten cuts off the injurer of Brahmans both from this world and from the world yonder. || 39. Her slaughter is the sin of witchcraft, her cutting-up is a thunder-bolt, her undigested grass is a secret spell. || 40. Homelessness is she when denied her rights. || 41. Having become Flesh-eating Agni the Brahman's cow entereth into and devoureth the oppressor of Brahmans. || 42. She sunders all his members, joints, and roots. || 43. She cuts off relationship on the father's side and destroys maternal kinship. || 44. The Brahman's cow, not restored by a Kṣhatriya, ruins the marriages and all the kinsmen of the Brahman's oppressor. || 45. She makes him houseless, homeless, childless: he is extinguished without posterity to succeed him. || 46. So shall it be with the Kṣhatriya who takes to himself the cow of the Brahman who hath this knowledge. || 47. Quickly, when he is smitten down by death, the clamorous vultures cry: || 48. Quickly around his funeral fire dance women with dishevelled locks, | Striking the hand upon the breast and uttering their evil shriek. || 49. Quickly the wolves are howling in the habitation where he lived: || 50. Quickly they ask about him, What is this? What thing hath happened here? || 51. Rend, rend to pieces, rend away, destroy, destroy him utterly. || 52. Destroy Āṅgirasī! the wretch who robs and wrongs the Brahmans, born. || 53. Of evil womb, thou witchcraft hid, for Vaiśvadevī is thy name, || 54. Consuming, burning all things up, the thunderbolt of spell and charm. || 55. Go thou, becoming Mṛityu sharp as razor's edge pursue thy course: || 56. Thou bearest off the tyrants' strength, their store of merit, and their prayers. || 57. Bearing off wrong, thou givest in that world to him who hath been wronged. || 58. O Cow, become a tracker through the curse the Brahman hath pronounced, || 59. Become a bolt, an arrow through his sin, be terribly venomous. || 60. O

Cow, break thou the head of him who wrongs the Brahmans, criminal, niggard, blasphemer of the Gods. || 61. Let Agni burn the spiteful wretch when crushed to death and slain by thee. || 62. Rend, rend to bits, rend through and through, scorch and consume and burn to dust, || 63. Consume thou, even from the root, the Brahmans' tyrant, God-like Cow! || 64. That he may go from Yama's home afar into the worlds of sin. its || 65. So, Goddess Cow, do thou from him, the Brahmans' tyrant, criminal, niggard, blasphemer of the Gods, || 66. With hundred-knotted thunderbolt, sharpened and edged with razor-blades, || 67. Strike off the shoulders and the head. || 68. Snatch thou the hair from off his head, and from his body strip the skin: || 69. Tear out his sinews, cause his flesh to fall in pieces from his frame. || 70. Crush thou his bones together, strike and beat the marrow out of him. || 71. Dislocate all his limbs and joints. || 72. From earth let the Carnivorous Agni drive him, let Vāyu burn. him from mid-air's broad region. || 73. From heaven let Sūrya drive him and consume him.

Kāṇḍa 13.

Hymn 13:1.

1. Rise, Mighty One, who liest in the waters, and enter this thy fair and glorious kingdom. | Let Rohita who made this All uphold thee carefully nurtured for supreme dominion. || 2. The strength that was in waters hath ascended. Mount o'er the tribes which thou hast generated. | Creating Soma, waters, plants and cattle, bring hitherward both quadrupeds and bipeds. || 3. Ye Marutas, strong and mighty, sons of Pṛiśni, with Indra for ally crush down our foemen. | Let Rohita, ye bounteous givers, hear you, thrice-seven Marutas who delight in sweetness! || 4. Up to the lap of births, to lofty places, hath Rohita, the germ of Dames, ascended. | Conjoined with these he found the six realms: seeing his way in front here he received the kingship. || 5. For thee hath Rohita obtained dominion, scattered thine enemies, become thy safeguard. | So by the potent Śakvarīs let Heaven and Earth be milked to-yield thee all thy wishes. || 6. Rohita gave the Earth and Heavens their being. There Parameṣhṭhin held the cord extended. | Thereon reposeth Aja-Ekapāda. He with his might hath established Earth and Heaven. || 7. Rohita firmly established Earth and Heaven: by him was ether fixt by him the welkin. | He measured out mid air and all the regions: by him the Gods found life that lasts for ever. || 8. Arranging shoots, springs, Rohita considered this Universe in all its forms and phases. | May he, gone up to heaven with mighty glory, anoint thy sovereignty with milk and fatness. || 9. Thy risings up, thy mountings and ascensions wherewith thou fillest heaven and air's mid-region— | By prayer for these, by milk of these, increasing, in Rohita's kingdom watch, among his people. || 10. The tribes thy heat produced have followed hither the Calf and Gāyatrī, the strain that lauds him. | With friendly heart let them approach to serve thee, and the Calf Rohita come with his mother. || 11. Erected, Rohita hath reached the welkin, wise, young, creating every form and figure. | Agni, refulgent with his heightened lustre, in the third realm hath brought us joy and gladness. || 12. Thousand-horned Bull, may Jātavedas, worshipped with butter, balmed with Soma, rich in heroes, | Besought, ne'er quit me; may I ne'er forsake thee. Give me abundant men and herds of cattle. || 13. Rohita is the sire and mouth of worship: to him with voice, ear, heart I pay oblation. | To Rohita come Gods with joyful spirit. May he by risings raise me till I join him. || 14. Rohita ordered sacrifice for Viśvakarman: thence have I obtained this strength and energy. | May I proclaim thee as my kin over the greatness of the world. || 15. On thee have mounted Bṛihatī and Paṅkti and Kakubh with great splendour, Jātavedas! | The cry of Vaṣhaṭ with the voice uplifted and Rohita with seed on thee have mounted. || 16. He goes into the womb of earth, he robes himself in heaven and air. | He on the Bright One's station hath reached heavenly light and all the worlds. || 17. To us, Vāchaspati, may Earth be pleasant, pleasant our dwelling, pleasant be our couches. | Even here may Prāṇa be our friend: may Agni, O Parameṣhṭhin give thee life and splendour. || 18. And those, Vāchaspati, our own five seasons, sacred to Viśvakarman their creator. | Even here our friend be Prāṇa: Parameṣhṭhin, may Rohita vouchsafe the life and splendour. || 19. Breed, O Vāchaspati, joy and understanding, kine in our stall and children in our consorts. | Even here may Prāṇa be our friend: may Agni, O Parameṣhṭhin, give thee life and splendour. || 20. With splendour let God Savitar, and Agni, with splendour Mitra, Varuṇa invest thee. | Treading down all Malignities, come hither. Pleasant and glorious hast thou made this kingdom. || 21. Rohita, carborne by a speckled leader, thou, pouring water, goest on in triumph. || 22. Golden, refulgent, lofty is the Lady, Rohiṇī, Rohita's devoted Consort. | Through her may we win various spoil and booty, through her be conquerors in every battle. || 23. Rohita's seat is Rohiṇī before us: that is the path the speckled Mare pursueth. | Kaśyapas and Gandharvas lead her upward, and heavenly sages ever watch and guard her, || 24. Sūrya's bay steeds refulgent and immortal draw the light-rolling chariot on for ever. | Drinker of fatness, Rohita, resplendent, hath entered into various-coloured heaven, || 25. Rohita, Bull whose horns are sharply pointed, superior of Agni and of Sūrya, | He who supports the sundered earth and heaven,—from him the Gods effect their own creations. || 26. Rohita rose to heaven from mighty ocean, Rohita rose and climbed all steeps and rises. || 27. Prepare the Milky One who teems with fatness: she is the Gods' never-reluctant milch-cow. | Indra drink Soma: ours be peace and safety. Let Agni lead the laud, and chase our foemen. || 28. Both kindling and inflamed, adored with butter and enhanced thereby. | May conquering Agni, conqueror of all, destroy mine enemies. || 29. Let him smite down in death and burn the foeman who attacketh me. | Our adversaries we consume through Agni the Carnivorous. || 30. Beat them down, Indra, with thy bolt, beat them down, mighty with thine arm. | I through the energy and force of Agni have secured my foes. || 31. Cast down our foes beneath our feet, O Agni. Bṛihaspati, oppress our rebel kinsman. | Low let them fall, O Indra-Agni. Mitra-Varuṇa, powerless to show their anger. || 32. Ascending up on high, O God. O Sūrya, drive my foes away. | Yea, beat them backward with the stone: to deepest darkness let them go. || 33. Calf of Virāj, the Bull of prayers and worship, white-backed, he hath gone up to air's mid-region. | Singing, they hymn the Calf, with gifts of butter: him who is Brahma they exalt with Brahma. || 34. Rise up to earth, rise up to heaven above it; rise up to opulence, rise up to kingship. | Rise up to offspring, rise to life immortal; rise, and with Rohita unite thy body. || 35. With all the Gods who circle round the Sun, upholding royal sway, | With all of these may Rohita accordant, give sovereignty to thee with friendly spirit. || 36. Cleansed by prayer, sacrifices bear thee upward: bay coursers, ever travelling, convey thee. Thy light shines over sea and billowy ocean. || 37. Rohita, conqueror of cows and riches and gathered spoil, is heaven's and earth's upholder. | Over earth's greatness would I tell my kinship with thee who hast a thousand births and seven. || 38. A glorious sight to beasts and men, thou goest glorious to the regions and mid-regions. | On earth's, on Aditi's bosom, bright with glory. Fain would I equal Savitar in beauty. || 39. Thou, yonder, knowest all things here, when here thou knowest what is there. | From here men see the sphere of light, Sūrya profoundly wise in heaven. || 40. A God, thou injurest the Gods: thou movest in the ocean's depth. | Men kindle common Agni: him only the higher sages know. || 41. Beneath the upper realm, above this lower, bearing her Calf at foot, the Cow hath risen | Whitherward, to what place hath she departed? Where doth she calve? Not in this herd of cattle. || 42. She hath become one-footed or two-footed, four-footed, or eight-footed or nine-footed, | This universe's thousand-syllabled Paṅkti Oceans flow forth from her in all directions. || 43. Rising to heaven, immortal, hear my calling. Cleansed by prayer, sacrifices bear thee upward. Bay coursers, ever on the road, convey thee. || 44. This, O Immortal One, I know of thee, thy progress to the sky thy dwelling-place in loftiest heaven. || 45. Beyond the sky, beyond the Earth looks Sūrya, and beyond the floods. | The single eye of all that is; to mighty heaven hath he arisen. || 46. The earth was made his altar, and the wide expanses were the fence. | There Rohita established both these Agnis, fervent heat and cold. || 47. He established heat and cold, he made the mountains sacrificial posts. | Then both the Agnis, Rohita's who found celestial light, with rain for molten butter, sacrificed. || 48. Rohita's Agni —his who found heaven's light—is kindled with the prayer. | From him the heat, from him the cold, from him the sacrifice was born. || 49. Both Agnis—Rohita's who found the light of heaven—made strong by prayer, | Waxing by prayer, adored with prayer, by prayer enkindled, sacrificed. || 50. One is deposited in Truth, one kindled in the waters: both | Agnis of Rohita who found the light are set aflame with prayer. || 51. That decked by

Wind, and that prepared by Indra Brahmaṇaspati, | Agnis of Rohita who found light, prayer-enkindled, sacrificed. || 52. Rohita made the earth to be his altar, heaven his Dakṣhiṇā. | Then heat he took for Agni, and with rain for molten butter he created every living thing. || 53. The earth became an altar, heat was Agni, and the butter rain. | There Agni made, by song and hymn, these mountains rise and stand erect. || 54. Then, having made the hills stand up, Rohita spake to Earth, and said: | In thee let every thing be born, what is and what is yet to be. || 55. This sacrifice, the first of all, the past, the present, had its birth. | From that arose this universe, yea, all this world of brightness, brought by Rohita the heavenly Sage. || 56. If thou should kick a cow, or by indecent act offend the Sun, | Thy root I sever; nevermore mayst thou cast shadow on the ground. || 57. Thou who, between the fire and me, passest across the line of shade. | Thy root I sever: nevermore mayst thou cast shadow on the ground. || 58. Whoe'er he be who, Sūrya, God! comes between thee and me today, | On him we wipe away ill-dream, and troubles, and impurity. || 59. Let us not, Indra, leave the path, the Soma-presser's sacrifice. | Let not malignities dwell with us. || 60. May we obtain, completely wrought, the thread spun out to reach the Gods, | That perfecteth our sacrifice.

Hymn 13:2.

1. Radiant, refulgent in the sky are reared the banners of his light, Āditya's, who beholdeth man, mighty in act and bountiful. || 2. Let us laud him, the whole world's Herdsman, Sūrya, who with his rays illumines all the regions, | Mark of the quarters, brightening them with lustre, swift, mighty-pinioned, flying in the ocean. || 3. From west to east thou speedest freely, making by magic day and night of diverse colours. | This is Āditya, thy transcendent glory, that thou alone art born through all creation. || 4. Victorious, inspired, and brightly shining, whom seven strong tawny-coloured coursers carry, | Whom Atri lifted from the flood to heaven, thus men behold thee as thy course thou runnest. || 5. Let them not snare thee speeding on thy journey: pass safely, swiftly places hard to traverse, | While measuring out the day and night thou movest—O Sūrya, even Heaven and Earth the Goddess. || 6. Hail to thy rapid car whereon, O Sūrya, thou circlest in a moment both the limits, | Whirled by thy bay steeds, best of all at drawing, thy hundred horses or seven goodly coursers! || 7. Mount thy strong car, O Sūrya, lightly rolling, drawn by good steeds, propitious, brightly gleaming, | Whirled by thy bays, most excellent at drawing, thy hundred horses or seven goodly coursers. || 8. Sūrya hath harnessed to his car to draw him seven stately bay steeds gay with wolden housings. | The Bright One started from the distant region: dispelling gloom the God hath climbed the heavens. || 9. With lofty banner hath the God gone upward, and introduced the light, expelling darkness. | He hath looked round on all the worlds, the Hero, the son of Aditi, Celestial Eagle. || 10. Rising, thou spreadest out thy rays, thou nourishest all shapes and forms. | Thou with thy power illumest both the oceans, encompassing all spheres with thy refulgence. || 11. Moving by magic power to east and westward, these two young creatures, sporting, circle ocean. | One of the pair beholds all living creatures: with wheels of gold the bay steeds bear the other. || 12. Atri established thee in heaven. O Sūrya, to create the month. | So on thou goest, firmly held, heating, beholding all that is. || 13. As the Calf both his parents so thou joinest both the distant bounds, | Surely the Gods up yonder knew this sacred mystery long ago. || 14. Sūrya is eager to obtain all wealth that lies along the sea, | Great is the course spread out for him, his eastward and his westward path. || 15. He finishes his race with speed and never turns his thought aside, | Thereby he keeps not from the Gods enjoyment of the Drink of Life. || 16. His heralds bear him up aloft, the God who knoweth all that live, | Sūrya, that all may look on him. || 17. The Constellations pass away, like thieves, departing in the night. | Before the all-beholding Sun. || 18. His herald rays are seen afar refulgent o'er the world of men, | Like flames of fire that burn and blaze. || 19. Swift and all-beautiful art thou, O Sūrya, maker of the light, | Illuming all the radiant realm. || 20. Thou goest to the hosts of Gods, thou comest hither to mankind, | Hither, all light to behold. || 21. With that same eye of thine wherewith thou seest, brilliant Varuṇa | The active one among mankind, || 22. Traversing sky and wide mid-air, thou metest with thy beams our days, | Sun, seeing all things that have life. || 23. Seven bay steeds harnessed to thy car bear thee, O thou far-seeing One, | God, Sūrya, with the radiant hair. || 24. Sūrya, hath yoked the pure bright seven, the daughters of the car, with these, | His own dear team, he travelleth. || 25. Devout, aflame with fervent heat, Rohita hath gone up to heaven. | He is re-born, returning to his birthplace, and hath become the Gods' imperial ruler. || 26. Dear unto all men, facing all directions, with hands and palms on every side extended, | He, the sole God, engendering earth and heaven, beareth them with his wings and arms together. || 27. The single-footed hath out-stepped the biped, the biped overtakes the triple-footed. | The biped hath out-stridden the six-footed: these sit around the single-footed's body. || 28. When he, unwearied, fain to go, hath mounted his bays, he makes two colours, brightly shining. | Rising with banners, conquering the regions, thou sendest light through all the floods, Āditya. || 29. Verily, Sūrya, thou art great: truly, Āditya, thou art great. | Great is thy grandeur, Mighty One: thou, O Āditya, thou art great. || 30. In heaven, O Bird, and in mid-air thou shinest: thou shinest on the earth and in the waters. | Thou hast pervaded both the seas with splendour: a God art thou, O God, light-winner, mighty. || 31. Soaring in mid-course hither from the distance, fleet and inspired, the Bird that flies above us, | With might advancing Viṣhṇu manifested, he conquers all that moves with radiant banner: || 32. Brilliant, observant, mighty Lord, an Eagle illuming both the spheres and air between them. | Day and the Night, clad in the robes of Sūrya, spread forth more widely all his hero powers. || 33. Flaming and radiant, strengthening his body, bestowing floods that promptly come to meet us, | He, luminous, winged, mighty, strength-bestower, hath mounted all the regions as he forms them. || 34. Bright presence of the Gods, the luminous herald Sūrya hath mounted the celestial regions. | Day's maker, he hath shone away the darkness, and radiant, passed o'er places hard to traverse. || 35. He hath gone up on high, the Gods' bright presence, the eye of Mitra, Varuṇa and Agni. | The soul of all that moveth not or moveth, Sūrya hath filled the earth and air and heaven, || 36. High in the midst of heaven may we behold thee whom men call Savitar, the bright red Eagle, | Soaring and speeding on thy way, refulgent, unwasting light which Atri erst discovered. || 37. Him, Son of Aditi, an Eagle hasting along heaven's height, I supplicate in terror, | As such prolong our lengthened life, O Sūrya: may we, unharmed, enjoy thy gracious favour. || 38. This gold-hued Haṃsa's wings, soaring to heaven, spread o'er a thousand days' continued journey | Supporting all the Gods upon his bosom, he goes his way beholding every creature. || 39. Rohita, in primeval days Prajāpati, was, after, Time, Mouth of all sacrifices, he, Rohita, brought celestial light. || 40. He, Rohita, became the world: Rohita gave the heaven its heat. | Rohita with his beams of light travelled along the earth and sea. || 41. To all the regions Rohita came, the imperial Lord of heaven. | He watches over ocean, heaven, and earth and all existing things. || 42. Mounting the lofty ones, he, bright, unwearied, splendidly shining, makes two separate colours, | While through all worlds that are he sends his lustre, radiant, observant, mighty, wind-approacher. || 43. One form comes on, the other is reverted: to day and night the Strong One shapes and fits him. | With humble prayer for aid we call on Sūrya, who knows the way, whose home is in the region. || 44. The suppliant's way, filling the earth, the Mighty circleth the world with eye that none deceiveth. | May he, all-seeing, well-disposed and holy, give ear and listen to the word I utter. || 45. Blazing with light his majesty hath compassed ocean and earth and heaven and air's mid-region. | May he, all-seeing, well-disposed and holy, give ear and listen to the word I utter. || 46. Agni is weakened by the people's fuel to meet the Dawn who cometh like a milch-cow, | Like young trees shooting up on high their branches, his flames are mounting to the vault of heaven.

Hymn 13:3.

1. He who engendered these, the earth and heaven, who made the worlds the mantle that he weareth, | In whom abide the six wide-spreading regions through which the Bird's keen vision penetrateth, | This God is wroth offended by the sinner who wrongs the Brahman who hath gained this knowledge | Agitate him, O Rohita; destroy him: entangle in thy snares the Brahman's tyrant. || 2. He from whom winds blow pure in ordered season, from whom the seas flow forth in all directions, | This God, etc. || 3. He who takes life away, he who bestows it; from whom comes breath to every living creature, | This God, etc. || 4. Who with the breath he draws sates earth and heaven, with expiration fills the ocean's belly, | This

God, etc. || 5. In whom Virāj, Prajāpati, Parameṣhṭhin, Agni Vaiśvānara abide with Paṅkti, | He who hath taken to himself the breathing of the Supreme, the vigour of the Highest, | This God, etc. || 6. On whom rest six expenses and five regions, four waters, and three syllables of worship, | He who hath looked between both spheres in anger, | This God, etc. || 7. He who, consuming food, became its master, the Lord of Prayer, the Regent of Devotion, | The world's Lord, present and to be hereafter, | This God, etc. || 8. He who metes out the thirteenth month, constructed with days and nights, containing thirty members, | This God, etc. || 9. Dark the descent; the strong-winged birds are golden: they fly aloft to heaven, enrobed in waters. | They have come hither from the seat of Order, | This God, etc. || 10. What silver. Kaśyapa, thou hast refulgent, what brightly-shining lotus-flower collected, | Wherein are gathered seven Suns together, | This God, etc. || 11. In front the Bṛihat-Sāman is his mantle, and from behind Rathantara enfolds him, | Ever with care robing themselves in splendour. | This God, etc. || 12. One of his wings was Bṛihat, and the other Rathantara, vigorous with one same purpose, | What time the Gods gave Rohita his being. | This God, etc. || 13. At evening he is Varuṇa and Agni, ascending in the morning he is Mitra. | As Savitar, he moves through air's mid region, as Indra warms-the heavens from the centre. | This God, etc. || 14. This gold-hued Haṃsa's wings, soaring to heaven spread o'er a thousand days' continued journey. | Supporting all the Gods upon his bosom, he goes his way beholding every creature. | This God, etc. || 15. This is the God who dwells-within the waters, the thousand-rooted, many-powered Atri, | He who brought all this world into existence. | This God; etc. || 16. With flying feet his tawny coursers carry the bright God through, the sky, aglow with splendour. | Whose limbs uplifted fire and heat the heavens: hither he shines-with beams of golden colour. | This God, etc. || 17. He beside whom his bay steeds bear the Ādityas, by whom as sacrifice go many knowing. | The sole light shining spread through various places. | This God, etc. || 18. This seven make the one-wheeled chariot ready: bearing seven names the single courser draws it. | The wheel, three-naved, is sound and undecaying: thereon these worlds of life are all dependent. | This God, etc. || 19. Eight times attached the potent Courser draws it, Sire of the Gods, father of hymns and praises. | So Mātariśvan, measuring in spirit the thread of Order, purifies all regions. | This God, etc. || 20. The thread that goes through all celestial quarters within the Gāyatrī, womb of life eternal. | This God, etc. || 21. There are the settings, three the upward risings, three are the-spaces, yea, and three the heavens. | We know thy triple place of birth, O Agni, we know the deities' triple generations. || 22. He who, as soon as born, laid broad earth open, and set the ocean in the air's mid-region, This God, etc. || 23. Thou, Agni, kind with lights and mental powers, hast up in heaven shone as the Sun, enkindled. | The Marutas, sons of Pṛiśni, sang his praises what time the Gods gave Rohita his being. This God, etc. || 24. Giver of breath, giver of strength and vigour, he whose commandment all the Gods acknowledge, | He who is Lord of this, of man and cattle, This God, etc. || 25. The single-footed hath out-stepped the biped, the biped overtakes the triple-footed. | The quadruped hath wrought when bipeds called him, standing and looking on the five collected. | This God is wroth offended by the sinner that wrongs the Brahman who hath gained this knowledge. | Agitate him, O Rohita; destroy him: entangle in thy snares the Brahman's tyrant. || 26. Born is the darksome Mother's Son, the whitely shining Calf of Night. | He, Rohita, ascendeth up to heaven, hath mounted to the heights.

Hymn 13:4.

1. Down looking, on the ridge of sky Savitar goes to highest heaven. || 2. To misty cloud filled with his rays Mahendra goes encompassed round. || 3. Creator and Ordainer, he is Vāyu, he is lifted cloud. || 4. Rudra, and Mahādeva, he is Aryaman and Varuṇa || 5. Agni is he, and Sūrya, he is verily Mahāyama. || 6. Calves, joined, stand close beside him, ten in number, with one single head. || 7. From west to east they bend their way: when he mounts up he shines afar. || 8. His are these banded Marutas: they move gathered close like porters' thongs. || 9. To misty cloud filled with his rays Mahendra goes encompassed round, || 10. His are the nine supports, the casks set in nine several places here. || 11. He keepeth watch o'er creatures, all that breatheth and that breatheth not. || 12. This conquering might hath entered him, He is the sole the simple One, the One alone. || 13. In him these Deities become simple and One || 14. Renown and glory, and force and cloud, the Brahman's splendour, and food, and nourishment, || 15. To him who knoweth this God as simple and one. || 16. Neither second, nor third, nor yet fourth is he called; || 17. He is called neither fifth, nor sixth, nor yet seventh || 18. He is called neither eighth, nor ninth, nor yet tenth. || 19. He watcheth over creatures, all that breatheth and that breatheth not. || 20. This conquering might hath entered him. He is the sole, the simple One, the One alone, || 21. In him these Deities become simple and One || 22. Devotion and Religious Fervour, and renown and glory, and force and cloud, the Brahman's splendour, and food and nourishment. || 23. And past and future, and Faith and lustre, and heaven and sweet oblation, || 24. To him who knoweth this God as simple and One. || 25. He, verily, is death, he is immortality, he is the monster, he is the fiend. || 26. He is Rudra, winner of wealth in the giving of wealth; in uttering homage he is the sacrificial exclamation Vaṣhaṭ duly employed. || 27. All sorcerers on earth obey with reverence his high behest. || 28. All constellations yonder, with the Moon, are subject to his will. || 29. He was brought forth from Day: and Day derives his origin. from him. || 30. He was brought forth from Night: and Night derives her origins from him. || 31. He was produced from Air: and Air derives its origin from him. || 32. He was produced from Wind: and Wind derives his origin from. him. || 33. From Heaven was he produced: and Heaven derives his origin from him. || 34. He sprang from regions of the sky: from him the heavenly regions sprang. || 35. He is the offspring of the Earth: Earth hath her origin from him. || 36. He was produced from fire: and fire derives its origin from him. || 37. He is the waters' offspring: and from him the waters were produced. || 38. From holy verses was he born: from him the holy verses sprang. || 39. He is the son of sacrifice: and sacrifice was born from him. || 40. Sacrifice, sacrifice's Lord, he was made head of sacrifice. || 41. He thundereth, he lighteneth, he casteth down the thunder-stone || 42. For misery or happiness, for mortal man or Asura. || 43. Whether thou formest growing plants, or sendest rain for happiness, or hast increased the race of man, || 44. Such is thy greatness, liberal Lord! A hundred bodily forms are thine. || 45. Millions are in thy million, or thou art a billion in thyself. || 46. Stronger than immortality is Indra: stronger thou than deaths; || 47. Yea, stronger than Malignity art thou, O Indra, Lord of Might. | Calling thee Master, Sovereign Chief, we pay our reverence to thee. || 48. Worship to thee whom all behold! Regard me, thou whom all regard, || 49. With food, and fame, and vigour, with the splendour of a Brahman's rank || 50. We pay thee reverence calling thee strength, power, and might, and conquering force. || 51. We pay thee reverence calling thee red power, the silvery expanse. || 52. We pay thee reverence calling thee vast, wide, the good, the universe. || 53. We pay thee reverence, calling thee extension, compass, width, and world. || 54. We pay thee reverence, calling thee rich, opulent in this and that, with wealth unceasing and secure || 55. Worship to thee whom all behold! Regard me, thou whom all regard. || 56. With food, and fame, and vigour, with the splendour of a Brahman's rank.

Kāṇḍa 14.

Hymn 14:1.

1. Truth is the base that bears the earth; by Sūrya are the heavens upheld. | By Law the Ādityas stand secure, and Soma holds his place in heaven. || 2. By Soma are the Ādityas strong, by Soma mighty is the earth: | Thus Soma in the lap of all these constellations hath his home. || 3. One thinks, when men have brayed the plant, that he hath drunk the Soma's juice. | Of him whom Brahmans truly know as Soma never mortal eats. || 4. When they begin to drink thee, then, O God, thou swellest out again. | Vāyu in Soma's sentinel. The month is that which shapes the years. || 5. Soma, preserved by covering rules, guarded by hymns in Bṛihatī, | Thou standest listening to the stones; none tastes of thee who dwells on earth. || 6. Thought was her coverlet, the power of sight was unguent for her eyes: | Her treasure-chest was earth and heaven, when Sūrya went unto her lord. || 7. Raibhī was her dear bridal friend, and Nārāśaṃsī led her home. | Lovely to see was Sūrya's robe: by Gāthā beautified she moves || 8. Songs were the cross-bars of the pole, Kurīra metre decked her head. | Both Aśvins were the paranymphs: Agni was leader of the train. || 9. Soma was he who wooed the maid: the

groomsmen were both Aśvins, when | The Sun-God Savitar bestowed his willing Sūrya on her lord. || 10. Her spirit was the bridal car, the canopy thereof was heaven: | Two radiant oxen formed the team when Sūrya came unto her lord. || 11. Steadily went the steers upheld by holy verse and song of praise, | The chariot-wheels were listening ears: thy path was tremulous in the sky. || 12. Pure, as thou wentest, were thy wheels, breath was the axle piercing them. | Sūrya advancing to her lord rode on the chariot of her heart. || 13. The bridal pomp of Sūrya, which Savitar started, moved along. | In Maghā days are oxen slain, in Phalgunīs they wed the bride. || 14. When on your three-wheeled chariot, O ye Aśvins, ye came as suitors unto Sūrya's bridal, | Where was one chariot-wheel of yours? Where stood ye for the sire's command? || 15. Twin Lords of Lustre, at the time when ye to Sūrya's wooing came, | Then all the Gods agreed to your proposal Pūṣhan as son elected you as father. || 16. Two wheels of thine the Brahmans know, Sūrya! according to their times. | That which is hidden only those who know the highest truths have learned. || 17. Worship we pay to Aryaman, finder of husbands, kindly friend. | As from its stalk a cucumber, from here I loose thee, not from there || 18. Hence and not thence I send her free. I make her softly fettered there. | That, bounteous Indra! she may live blest in her fortune and her sons. || 19. Now from the noose of Varuṇa I free thee, where with the blessed Savitar hath bound thee. | May bless be thine together with thy wooer in Order's dwelling, in the world of virtue. || 20. Let Bhaga take thy hand and hence conduct thee: let the two Aśvins on their car transport thee. | Go to the house to be the household's mistress, and speak as lady to thy gathered people. || 21. Happy be thou and prosper with thy children here: be vigilant to rule the household in this home. | Closely unite thy body with this man thy lord. So shalt thou, full of years, address thy company. || 22. Be not divided; dwell ye here; reach the full time of human life. | With sons and grandsons sport and play, rejoicing in your happy home. || 23. Moving by magic power from east to westward, these children twain go sporting round the ocean. | The one beholds all creatures: thou, the other, art born anew, duly arranging seasons. || 24. Thou, born afresh, art new and new for ever; ensign of days, before the Dawns thou goest. | Coming, thou orderest for Gods their portion. Thou lengthenest, Moon, the days of our existence. || 25. Give thou the woollen robe away: deal treasure to the Brahman-priests. | This Witchery hath got her feet: the wife attendeth on her lord. || 26. It turneth dusky-red: the witch who clingeth close is driven off. | Well thrive the kinsmen of this bride: the husband is bound fast in bonds. || 27. Unlovely is his body when it glistens with that wicked fiend, | What time the husband wraps about his limbs the garment of his wife. || 28. The butchering, the cutting-up, the severing of limb and joint— | Behold the forms which Sūrya wears: yet these the Brahman purifies, || 29. Pungent is this, bitter is this, filled as it were with arrow barbs, empoisoned and not fit for use. | The Brahman who knows Sūrya well deserves the garment of the bride. || 30. The Brahman takes away the robe as a fair thing that brings good luck. | He knows the expiating rite whereby the wife is kept unharmed. || 31. Prepare, ye twain, happy and prosperous fortune, speaking the truth in faithful utterances. | Dear unto her, Bṛihaspati, make the husband, and pleasant be these words the wooer speaketh. || 32. Remain ye even here and go no farther: strengthen this man, ye Cows, with plenteous offspring. | May Dawns that come for glory, bright with Soma, here may all Gods fix and enchant your spirits. || 33. Come, O ye Cows, with offspring dwell around him: he doth not stint the Gods' allotted portion. | To him, your friend, may Pūṣhan, all the Marutas, to him may Dhātar, Savitar send vigour. || 34. Straight in direction be the paths, and thornless, whereby our fellows travel to the wooing. | With Bhaga and with Aryaman Dhātar endue the pair with strength! || 35. Whatever lustre is in dice, whatever lustre is in wine, | Whatever lustre is in cows, Aśvins, endue this dame therewith. || 36. With all the sheen that balmeth wine, or thigh of female paramour, | With all the sheen that balmeth dice, even with this adorn the dame. || 37. He who in water shines unfed with fuel, whom sages worship in their sacrifices. | May he, the Waters' Child, send us sweet waters those that enhanced the power of mighty Indra. || 38. I cast away a handful here, hurtful, injurious to health. | I lift another handful up, sparkling and bringing happiness. || 39. Hither let Brahmans bring her bathing water; let them draw such as guards the lives of heroes. | Aryaman's fire let her encircle, Pūṣhan! Fathers-in-law stand, with their sons, expectant. || 40. Blest be the gold to thee, and blest the water, blest the yoke's opening, and blest the pillar. | Blest he the waters with their hundred cleansings: blest be thy body's union with thy husband. || 41. Cleansing Apālā, Indra! thrice, thou gavest sunbright skin to her | Drawn, Śatakratu! through the hole of car, of wagon, and of yoke. || 42. Saying thy prayer for cheerfulness, children, prosperity, and wealth, | Devoted to thy husband, gird thyself for immortality. || 43. As vigorous Sindhu won himself imperial lordship of the streams, | So be imperial queen when thou hast come within thy husband's home. || 44. Over thy husband's fathers and his brothers be imperial queen. | Over thy husband's sister and, his mother bear supreme control. || 45. They who have spun, and woven, and extended Goddesses who have drawn the ends together, | May they invest thee for full long existence. Heiress of lengthened life, endue this garment, || 46. They mourn the living, they arrange the sacred rite: the men have set their thoughts upon a distant cast: | They who have brought the Fathers this delightful gift, when wives allowed their lords the joy of their embrace. || 47. I place upon the lap of Earth the Goddess, a firm auspicious stone to bring thee children. | Stand on it, thou, greeted with joy, resplendent: a long long life may Savitar vouchsafe thee. || 48. As Agni in the olden time took the right hand of this our Earth. | Even so I take and hold thy hand: be not disquieted, with me, with children and with store of wealth. || 49. God Savitar shall take thy hand, and Soma the King shall make thee rich in goodly offspring, | Let Agni, Lord Omniscient, make thee happy, till old old age a wife unto thy husband. || 50. I take thy hand in mine for happy fortune that thou mayst reach old age with me thy consort, | Gods, Aryaman, Bhaga, Savitar, Purandhi, have given thee to be my household's mistress. || 51. Bhaga and Savitar the God have clasped that hand of thine in theirs, | By rule and law thou art my wife: the master of thy house am I. || 52. Be it my care to cherish her: Bṛihaspati hath made thee mine. | A hundred autumns live with me thy husband, mother of my sons! || 53. Tvaṣhṭar, by order of the holy sages, hath laid on her Bṛihaspati's robe for glory, | By means of this let Savitar and Bhaga surround this dame, like Sūrya, with her children. || 54. May Indra-Agni, Heaven-Earth, Mātariśvan, may Mitra-Varuṇa, Bhaga, both the Aśvins, | Bṛihaspati, the host of Marutas, Brahma, and Soma magnify this dame with offspring. || 55. It was Bṛihaspati who first arranged the hair on Sūrya's head, | And therefore, O ye Aśvins, we adorn this woman for her lord. || 56. This lovely form the maiden wears in spirit I long to look on as my wife approaching, | Her will I follow with my nine companions. Who is the sage that loosed the bonds that held her? || 57. I free her: he who sees, within my bosom, my heart's nest knows how her fair form hath struck me. | I taste no stolen food: myself untying Varuṇa's nooses I am freed in spirit. || 58. Now from the bond of Varuṇa I loose thee, wherein the blessed Savitar hath bound thee. | O bride, I give thee here beside thy husband fair space and room and pleasant paths to travel. || 59. Lift up your weapons. Drive away the demons. Transport this woman to the world of virtue. | Dilator, most wise, hath found for her a husband. Let him who knows, King Bhaga, go before her. || 60. Bhaga hath formed the four legs of the litter, wrought the four pieces that compose the frame-work. | Tvaṣhṭar hath decked the straps that go across it, May it be blest, and bring us happy fortune. || 61. Mount this, all-hued. gold tinted, strong wheeled, fashioned of Kiṃśuka, this chariot lightly rolling, | Bound for the world of life immortal, Sūrya! Made for thy lord a happy bride's procession. || 62. To us, O Varuṇa, bring her, kind to brothers; bring her, Bṛihaspati, gentle to the cattle. | Bring her, O Indra, gentle to her husband: bring her to us, O Savitar, blest with children. || 63. Hurt not the girl, ye Pillars twain upon the path which Gods have made. | The portal of the heavenly home we make the bride's auspicious road. || 64. Let prayer he offered up before and after, prayer in the middle, lastly, all around her. | Reaching the Gods' inviolable castle shine in thy lord's world gentle and auspicious.

Hymn 14:2.

1. For thee with bridal train they first escorted Sūrya to her home, | Give to the husband in return, Agni, the wife with future sons. || 2. Agni hath given the bride again with splendour and a lengthened. life. | Long-lived be he who is her lord: a hundred autumns let him live. || 3. She was the wife of Soma first: next the Gandharva was thy lord. | Agni was the third

husband: now one born of woman is thy fourth. || 4. Soma to the Gandharva, and to Agni the Gandharva gave. | Now, Agni hath bestowed on me riches and sons and this my bride. || 5. Your favouring grace hath come, ye who are rich in spoil! Aśvins, your longings are stored up within your hearts. | Ye, Lords of Splendour have become our twofold guard: may we as dear friends reach the dwelling of the friend. || 6. Thou, Dame, rejoicing, take with kindly spirit wealth worthy to be famed, with all thy heroes. | Give, Lords of Light a fair ford, good to drink at: remove the spiteful stump that blocks the pathway. || 7. May all the Rivers, all the Plants, may all the Forests, all the | Fields, O Bride, protect thee from the fiend, guard his sons' mother for her lord. || 8. Our feet are on this pleasant path, easy to travel, bringing bliss, | Whereon no hero suffers harm, which wins the wealth of other men. || 9. Here these my words, ye men, the benediction through which the wedded pair have found high fortune. | May the divine Apsarases, Gandharvas, all they who are these fruitful trees' protectors, | Regard this bride with their auspicious, favour, nor harm the nuptial pomp as it advances. || 10. Consumptions, which, through various folk, attack the bride's resplendent train, | These let the holy Gods again bear to the place from which they sprang. || 11. Let not the highway thieves who lie in ambush find the wedded pair. | Let wicked men's malignities go elsewhere by an easy path. || 12. I look upon the house and bride's procession with prayer and with the gentle eye of friendship. | All that is covered there in perfect beauty may Savitar make pleasant to the husband. || 13. She hath come home this dame come home to bless us: this her appointed world hath Dhātar shown her. | So may Prajāpati, and both the Aśvins, Aryaman, Bhaga gladden her with offspring. || 14. This dame hath come, an animated corn-field: there sow, thou man, the seed of future harvest. | She from her teeming side shall bear thee children, and feed them from the fountain of her bosom. || 15. Take thou thy stand, a Queen art thou, like Vishṇu here, | Sarasvatī! O Sinīvālī, let her bear children, and live in Bhaga's grace. || 16. So let your wave bear up the pins, and ye, O Waters, spare the thongs; | And never may the holy pair, sinless and innocent, suffer harm. || 17. Not evil-eyed no slayer of thy husband, be strong, mild, kind, and gentle to thy household. | Mother of heroes, love thy husband's father: be happy, and through thee may we too prosper. || 18. No slayer of thy husband or his father, gentle and bright, bring blessing on the cattle. | Loving thy husband's father, bring forth heroes. Tend well this household fire: be soft and pleasant. || 19. Up and begone! What wish hath brought thee hither from thine own house? Thy mightier, I conjure thee. | Vain is the hope, O Nirṛiti, that brought thee. Fly off, Malignity; stay here no longer. || 20. As first of all this woman hath adored the sacred household fire. | So do thou, Dame, pay homage to the Fathers and Sarasvatī || 21. Take thou this wrapper as a screen, to be a covering for the bride | O Sinīvālī, let her bear children, and live in Bhaga's grace. || 22. Let her who shall be blest with sons, the maid who finds a husband, step | Upon the rough grass that ye spread and on the skin ye lay beneath. || 23. Over the ruddy-coloured skin strew thou the grass, the Balbaja | Let her, the mother of good sons, sit there and serve this Agni here. || 24. Step on the skin and wait upon this Agni: he is the God who drives away all demons. | Here bear thou children to this man thy husband: let this thy boy be happy in his birthright. || 25. Let many babes of varied form and nature spring in succession from this fruitful mother. | Wait on this fire, thou bringer of good fortune. Here with thy husband serve the Gods with worship. || 26. Bliss-bringer, furthering thy household's welfare, dear gladdening thy husband and his father, enter this home, mild to thy husband's mother. || 27. Be pleasant to the husband's sire, sweet to thy household and thy lord, | To all this clan be gentle, and favour these men's prosperity. || 28. Signs of good fortune mark the bride. Come all of you and look at her. | Wish her prosperity: take on you her evil lucks and go your way. || 29. Ye youthful maidens, ill-disposed, and all ye ancient woman here, | Give all your brilliance to the bride, then to your several homes depart! || 30. Sūrya the child of Savitar mounted for high felicity | Her litter with its cloth of gold, wearing all forms of loveliness. || 31. Rise, mount the bridal bed with cheerful spirit. Here bring forth children to this man thy husband. | Watchful and understanding like Indrāṇī wake thou before the earliest light of Morning. || 32. The Gods at first lay down beside their consorts; body with body met in close embracement. | O Dame, like Sūrya perfect in her grandeur, here rich in future children, meet thy husband. || 33. Rise and go hence, Viśvāvasu: with reverence we worship thee. | Steal to her sister dwelling with her father: this is the share—mark this—of old assigned thee. || 34. Apsarases rejoice and feast together between the sun and place of sacrificing. | These are thy kith and kin: go thou and join them: I in due season worship thee Gandharva. || 35. Homage we pay to the Gandharva's favour, obeisance to his eye and fiery anger. | Viśvāvasu, with prayer we pay thee homage. Go hence to those Apsarases thy consorts. || 36. May we be happy with abundant riches. We from this place have banished the Gandharva. | The God is gone to the remotest region, and we have come where men prolong existence. || 37. In your due season, Parents! come together. Mother and sire be ye of future children. | Embrace this woman like a happy lover. Raise ye up offspring here: increase your riches. || 38. Send her most rich in every charm, O Pūshan, her who shall be the sharer of my pleasures; | Her who shall twine her eager arms about me, and welcome all my love and soft embraces. || 39. Up, happy bridegroom! with a joyous spirit caress thy wife and throw thine arm around her. | Here take your pleasure, procreate your offspring. May Savitar bestow long life upon you. || 40. So may the Lord of Life vouchsafe you children, Aryaman bind you, day and night, together. | Enter thy husband's house with happy omens, bring blessing to our quadrupeds and bipeds. || 41. Sent by the Gods associate with Manu, the vesture of the bride, the nuptial garment, | He who bestows this on a thoughtful Brahman, drives from the marriage-bed all evil demons. || 42. The priestly meed wherewith ye twain present me, the vesture of the bride, the nuptial garment, | This do ye both, Bṛihaspati and Indra, bestow with loving-kindness on the Brahman. || 43. On your soft couch awaking both together, revelling heartily with joy and laughter, | Rich with brave sons, good cattle, goodly homestead, live long to look on many radiant mornings. || 44. Clad in new garments, fragrant, well-apparelled, to meet refulgent Dawn have I arisen. | I, like a bird that quits the egg, am freed from sin and purified. || 45. Splendid are Heaven and Earth, still near to bless us, mighty in their power; | The seven streams have flowed: may they, Goddesses, free us from distress || 46. To Sūrya and the Deities, to Mitra and to Varuṇa, | Who know aright the thing that is, this adoration have I paid. || 47. He without ligature, before making incision in the neck. | Closed up the wound again, most wealthy Bounteous Lord who healeth the dissevered parts. || 48. Let him flash gloom away from us, the blue, the yellow and the red. | I fasten to this pillar here the burning pest Pṛishātakī. || 49. All witcheries that hang about this garment, all royal Varuṇa's entangling nooses. | All failure of success and all misfortunes here I deposit fastened to the pillar. || 50. My body that I hold most dear trembles in terror at this robe. | Tree, make an apron at the top. Let no misfortune fall on us. || 51. May all the hems and borders all the threads that form the web and woof. | The garment woven by the bride, be soft and pleasant to our touch. || 52. These maids who from their father's house have come with longing to their lord have let the preparation pass. All hail! || 53. Her whom Bṛihaspati hath loosed the Viśvedevas keep secure. | With all the splendour that is stored in cows do we enrich this. girl. || 54. Her whom Bṛihaspati hath loosed the Viśvedevas keep secure. | With all the vigour that is stored in cows do we enrich this girl. || 55. Her whom Bṛihaspati, etc. | With all good fortune, etc. || 56. Her whom Bṛihaspati, etc. | With all the glory, etc. || 57. Her whom Bṛihaspati, etc. | With all the milky store possessed by cows do we enrich this girl. || 58. Her whom Bṛihaspati hath freed the Viśvedevas keep secure. | With all the store of sap that cows contain do we enrich this. girl. || 59. If, wearing long loose hair, these men have danced together in thy house, committing sin with shout and cry, | May Agni free thee from that guilt, may Savitar deliver thee, || 60. If in thy house thy daughter here have wept, with wild dishevel-led locks, committing sin with her lament. | May Agni, etc. || 61. If the bride's sisters, if young maids have danced together in thy house, committing sin with shout and cry. | May Agni free thee from that guilt, may Savitar deliver thee. || 62. If any evil have been wrought by mischief-makers that affects thy cattle progeny or house, | May Agni free thee from the woe, may Savitar deliver thee. || 63. This woman utters wish and prayer, as down she casts the husks of corn: | Long live my lord and master! yea, a hundred autumns let him live! || 64. Join thou this couple, Indra! like the Chakravāka and his. mate: | May they attain to full old age with children in their happy home. || 65. Whatever magic hath been wrought on cushion, chair, or canopy. | Each spell to mar the wedding rites, all this we throw into the bath. || 66. Whatever fault or error was in marriage or in bridal pomp. | This woe we wipe away upon the cloak the interceder wears. || 67. We, having laid the stain and fault upon the interceder's cloak, | Are pure and meet for sacrifice. May he prolong our lives for us. || 68. Now let this artificial comb, wrought with a hundred teeth, remove | Aught of impurity that dims the hair upon this woman's head. || 69. We take away consumption from each limb and member of the bride. | Let not this reach Earth, nor the Gods in heaven, let it not reach the sky or air's wide region. | Let not this dust that sullies reach the Waters, nor Yama, Agni, nor the host of Fathers. || 70. With all the milk that is in Earth I gird thee, with all the milk that Plants contain I dress thee. | I gird thee round with children and with riches. Do thou, thus girt, receive the offered treasure. || 71. I am this man, that dame art thou I am the psalm and thou the verse. I am the heaven and thou the earth. | So will we dwell together here, parents of children yet to be. || 72. Unmarried men desire to wed; bountiful givers wish for sons. | Together may we dwell with strength unscathed for high prosperity. || 73. May they, the Fathers who, to view the bride, have joined this nuptial train, | Grant to this lady and her lord children and peaceful happiness. || 74. Her who first guided by a rein came hither, giving the bride, here offspring and possessions, | Let them convey along the future's pathway. Splendid, with noble children, she hath conquered. || 75. Wake to long life, watchful and understanding, yea, to a life shall last a hundred autumns | Enter the house to be the household's mistress. A long long life let Savitar vouchsafe thee.

Kāṇḍa 15.

Hymn 15:1.

1. There was a roaming Vrātya. He roused Prajāpati to action. || 2. Prajāpati beheld gold in himself and engendered it. || 3. That became unique, that became distinguished, that became great, that became excellent, that became Devotion, that be-came holy Fervour, that became Truth: through that he was born. || 4. He grew, he became great, he became Mahādeva. || 5. He gained the lordship of the Gods. He became Lord. || 6. He became Chief Vrātya. He held a bow, even that Bow of Indra. || 7. His belly is dark-blue, his back is red. || 8. With dark-blue he envelops a detested rival, with red he pierces the man who hates him: so the theologians say.

Hymn 15:2.

1. He arose and went his way to the eastern region. The Bṛihat, the Rathantara, the Ādityas and all the Gods followed him. That man is alienated from the Bṛihat, the Rathantara, the Ādityas, and all Gods who reviles the Vrātya who possesses this knowledge. He who hath this knowledge becomes the beloved home of the Bṛihat, the Rathantara the Ādityas, and all the Gods. In the eastern region Faith is his leman, the hymn his panegyrist, knowledge his vesture, day his turban, night his hair, Indra's two Bays his circular ornaments, the splendour of the stars his jewel. Present and Future are his running footmen, mind is his war-chariot, Mātariśvan and Pavamāna are they who draw it, Vita is his charioteer, Storm his goad, Fame and Glory are his harbingers. Fame and Glory come to him who hath this knowledge. || 2. He arose and went away to the southern region. Yajñāyajñiya and Vāmadevya and Sacrifice and Sacrificer and sacrificial victims followed him. The man who reviles the Vrātya possessing this knowledge is alienated from Yajñāyajñiya and Vāmadevya, Sacrifice, Sacrificer and sacrificial victims. He who hath this knowledge becomes the beloved home of Yajñāyajñiya,Vāmadevya, Sacrifice, Sacrificer, and sacrificial victims. In the southern region Dawn is his leman, Mitra his panegyrist, knowledge his vesture, day his turban, night his hair, Indra's two Bays are his circular ornaments, New Moon Night and Full Moon Night are his running attendants, Mind, etc. as in stanza 1. || 3. He arose and went away to the western region. Vairūpa and Vairāja, the Waters, and King Varuṇa followed him. He who reviles the Vrātya possessing this knowledge is alienated from Vairūpa and Vairāja, the Waters and Varuṇa the King. He who possesses this knowledge becomes the dear home of Vairūpa and Vairāja, the Waters and King Varuṇa In the western region Irā is his leman, Laughter his panegyrist, knowledge, etc., as above. Day and Night are his running attendants, Mind, etc., as above. || 4. He arose and went away to the northern region. Śyaita and Naudhasa, the Seven Ṛishis, and King Soma followed him. He who reviles the Vrātya possessing this knowledge is alienated from Śyaita, etc. He who hath this knowledge be-comes the dear home of Śyaita, etc. In the northern region Lightning is his leman, thunder his panegyrist, etc. as above. Revelation and Tradition are his running attendants, Mind, etc., as above.

Hymn 15:3.

1. For a whole year he stood erect. The Gods said unto him, Why standest thou, O Vrātya? He answered and said, Let them bring my couch. || 3. They brought the couch for that Vrātya. || 4. Two of its feet were Summer and Spring, and two were Autumn and the Rains. || 5. Bṛihat and Rathantara were the two long boards, Yajñāyajñiya and Vāmadevya the two cross-boards. || 6. Holy verses were the strings lengthwise, and Yajus formulas the cross-tapes. || 7. Sacred lore was the blanket, Devotion the coverlet. || 8. The Sāman was the Cushion, and chanting the bolster. || 9. The Vrātya ascended that couch. || 10. The hosts of Gods were his attendants, solemn vows his messengers, and all creatures his worshippers. || 11. All creatures become the worshippers of him who possesses this knowledge.

Hymn 15:4.

1. For him they made the two Spring months protectors from the eastern region, and Bṛihat and Rathantara superintendents. The two Spring months protect from the eastern region, and Bṛihat and Rathantara superintend, the man who possesses this knowledge. For him they made the two Summer months protectors from the southern region, and Yajñāyajñiya and Vāmadevya superintendents. The two Summer months, etc. as in Verse 1, *mutatis mutandis.* || 3. They made the two Rain months, his protectors from the western region, and Vairūpa and Vairāja superintendents. The two Rain months, etc. as above. || 4. They made the two Autumn months his protectors from the northern region, and Śyaita and Naudhasa superintendents. The two Autumn months. etc. as above. || 5. They made the two Winter months his protectors from the region of the nadir, and earth and Agni superintendents. The two Winter months, etc. || 6. They made the two Dewy months his protectors from the region of the zenith, and Heaven and the Ādityas superintendents. The two Dewy months, etc.

Hymn 15:5.

1. For him they made the Archer Bhava a deliverer from the inter-mediate space of the eastern region. Bhava the Archer, a deliverer, delivers him from the intermediate space of the eastern region. Neither Śarva nor Bhava nor Īśāna slays him who possesses this knowledge, or his cattle, or his kinsmen. || 2. They made Śarva the Archer his deliverer from the intermediate space of the southern region, etc., as in verse 1, *mutatis mutandis.* || 3. They made Paśupati the Archer his deliverer from the intermediate space of the western region, etc. || 4. They made the Awful God, the Archer, his deliverer from the intermediate space of the northern region, etc., as above. || 5. They made Rudra the Archer his deliverer from the intermediate space of the region of the nadir etc. || 6. They made Mahādeva his deliverer from the intermediate space of the region of the zenith, etc. || 7. They made Īśāna the Archer his deliverer from all the inter-mediate regions. Īśāna the Archer, a deliverer, delivers him from all the intermediate regions. Neither Śarva nor Bhava, nor Īśāna slays him who possesses this knowledge, or his cattle, or his kinsmen.

Hymn 15:6.

1. He went his way to the region of the nadir. Earth and Agni and herbs and trees and shrubs and plants followed him. He who possesses this knowledge becomes the dear home of Earth and Agni and herbs and trees and shrubs and plants. || 2. He went his way to the region of the zenith. Right and Truth and Sun and Moon and Stars followed him. He who possesses this knowledge becomes, etc., as in verse 1, *mutatis mutandis.* || 3. He went away to the last region. Ṛichas, Sāmans Yajus formulas and Devotion followed him. He who, etc., as above. || 4. He went away to the great region. Itihāsa and Purāṇa and Gāthās and Nārāśaṃsīs followed him. He who, etc. || 5. He went away to the supreme region. The Āhavanīya, Gārhapatya, and Southern Fires, and Sacrifice, and Sacrificer, and sacrificial victims followed him. He who, etc. || 6. He went away to the unindicated region. The Seasons, groups of seasons, the worlds and their

inhabitants, the months and half-months, and Day and Night followed him. He who, etc. || 7. He went away to the unfrequented region. Thence he thought that he should not return. Diti and Aditi and Iḍā and Indrāṇī followed him. He who, etc. || 8. He went away to the regions. Virāj and all the Gods and all the Deities followed him. He who, etc. || 9. He went away to all the intermediate spaces. Prajāpati and Parameṣhṭhin and the Father and the Great Father followed him. He who possesses this knowledge becomes the beloved home of Prajāpati and Parameṣhṭhin and the Father and the Great Father.

Hymn 15:7.

1. He, having become moving majesty, went to the ends of the earth. He became the sea. || 2. Prajāpati and Parameṣhṭhin and the Father and the Great Father and the Waters and Faith, turned into rain, followed him. || 3. The Waters, Faith, and rain approach him who possesses this knowledge. || 4. Faith, and Sacrifice and the world, having become food and nourishment, turned toward him. || 5. Faith Sacrifice, the world, food and nourishment approach him who possesses this knowledge.

Hymn 15:8.

1. He was filled with passion: from him sprang the Rājanya. || 2. He came to the people, to kinsmen, food and nourishment. || 3. He who possesses this knowledge becomes the dear home of the people, kinsmen, food and nourishment.

Hymn 15:9.

1. He went away to the people. || 2. Meeting and Assembly and Army and Wine followed him. || 3. He who hath this knowledge becomes the dear home of Meeting, Assembly, Army, and Wine.

Hymn 15:10.

1. So let the King, to whose house the Vrātya who possesses this knowledge comes as a guest. || 2. Honour him as superior to himself. So he Both not act against the interests of his princely rank or his kingdom. || 3. From him, verily, sprang Priesthood and Royalty. They said, Into whom shall we enter? || 4. Let Priesthood enter into Bṛihaspati, and Royalty into Indra, was the answer. || 5. Hence Priesthood entered into Bṛihaspati and Royalty into Indra. || 6. Now this Earth is Bṛihaspati, and Heaven is Indra. || 7. Now this Agni is Priesthood, and yonder Sun is Royalty. || 8. Priesthood comes to him, and he becomes endowed with priestly lustre. || 9. Who knows that Earth is Bṛihaspati and Agni Priesthood. || 10. Great power comes to him and he becomes endowed with great power. || 11. Who knows that Āditya is Royalty and that Heaven is Indra.

Hymn 15:11.

1. Let him to whose house the Vrātya who possesses this knowledge comes as a guest. || 2. Rise up of his own accord to meet him, and say, Vrātya, where didst thou pass the night? Vrātya, here is water, Let them refresh thee. Vrātya, let it be as thou pleasest. Vrātya, as thy wish is so let it be. Vrātya, as thy desire is so be it. || 3. When he says to his guest, Where didst thou pass the night? he reserves for himself thereby the paths that lead to the Gods. || 4. When he says to him, Here is water, he secures thereby water for himself. || 5. When he says to him, Let them refresh thee, he thereby wins vital breath to exceeding old age. || 6. When he says to him, Vrātya, let it be as thou pleasest, he secures to himself thereby what is pleasant. || 7. That which is pleasant comes to him, and he is the beloved of the beloved, who is possessed of this knowledge. || 8. When he says to him, Vrātya, as thy will is so let it be, he secures to himself thereby the fulfilment of his will. || 9. Authority comes to him who possesses this knowledge, and he becomes the controller of the powerful. || 10. When he says to him, Vrātya, as thy desire is so be it, he secures to himself thereby the attainment of his desire. || 11. His desire comes to him who possesses this knowledge and he gains the complete satisfaction of his wish.

Hymn 15:12.

1. The man, to whose house, when the fires have been taken up from the hearth and the oblation to Agni placed therein, the Vrātya possessing this knowledge comes as a guest. || 2. Should of his own accord rise to meet him and say, Vrātya, give me permission. I will sacrifice. || 3. And if he gives permission he should sacrifice, if he does not permit him he should not sacrifice. || 4. He who sacrifices when permitted by the Vrātya who possesses this knowledge. || 5. Well knows the path that leads to the Fathers and the way that. leads to the Gods. || 6. He does not act in opposition to the Gods. It becomes his sacrifice. || 7. The abode of the man who sacrifices when permitted by the Vrātya who possesses this knowledge is long left remaining in this world. || 8. But he who sacrifices without the permission of the Vrātya who-possesses this knowledge. || 9. Knows not the path that leads to the Fathers nor the way that leads to the Gods. || 10. He is at variance with the Gods. He hath offered no accepted. sacrifice. || 11. The abode of the man who sacrifices without the permission of the Vrātya who possesses this knowledge is not left remaining in this world.

Hymn 15:13.

1. He in whose house the Vrātya who possesses this knowledge abides one night secures for himself thereby the holy realms that are on earth. || 2. A second night . . . . the holy realms that are in the firmament (the rest as in verse 1). || 3. A third night . . . the holy realms that are in heaven. || 4. A fourth night . . . . the holy realms of the Holy. || 5. Unlimited nights . . . . unlimited holy realms. || 6. Now he to whose house a non-Vrātya, calling himself a Vrātya, and one in name only, comes as a guest. || 7. Should punish him and not punish him. || 8. He should serve him with food saying to himself, To this Deity I offer water: I lodge this Deity; I wait upon this, this Deity. || 9. To that Deity the sacrifice of him who has this knowledge is acceptable.

Hymn 15:14.

1. He when he went away to the eastern region, went away having become the Marut host, and having made Mind an eater of food. He who hath this knowledge eats food with Mind as food-eater. || 2. He, when he went away to the southern region, went away having become Indra, and having made Strength an eater of food. He who hath this knowledge eats food with strength as food-eater. || 3. He, when he went away to the western region, went away having become King Varuṇa, and having made the Waters eaters of food. He who hath this knowledge eats food with the Waters as food-eaters. || 4. He, when he went away to the northern region, went away having become King Soma and having made the Seven Ṛishis' oblation an eater of food. He who hath this knowledge eats food with oblation as food-eater. || 5. He, when he went away to the steadfast region, went away having become Vishṇu and having made Virāj an eater of food. He who hath this knowledge eats food with Virāj as food-eater. || 6. He, when he went away to animals, went away having become Rudra and having made herbs eaters of food. He who hath this knowledge eats food with herbs as food-eaters. || 7. He, when he went away to the Fathers, went away having become King Yama and having made the exclamation Svadhā an eater of food. He who hath this knowledge eats food with the exclamation Svadhā as food-eater. || 8. He, when he went away to men, went away having become Agni and having made the exclamation Svāhā an eater of food. He who hath this knowledge eats food with the exclamation Svāhā as food-eater. || 9. He, when he went away to the upper region, went away having become Bṛihaspati and having made the exclamation Vashaṭ an eater of food. He who hath this knowledge eats food with the exclamation Vashaṭ as food-eater. || 10. He, when he went away to the Gods, went away having become Īśāna and having made Passion an eater of food. He who hath this knowledge eats food with Passion as food-eater. || 11. He, when he went away to creatures, went away having become Prajāpati and having made vital breath an eater of food. He who hath this knowledge eats food with vital breath as food-eater || 12. He, when he went away to all the intermediate spaces, went away having become Parameṣhṭhin and having made Devotion an eater of food. He who hath this knowledge eats food with Devotion as food-eater.

Hymn 15:15.

1. Of that Vrātya. || 2. There are seven vital airs, seven downward breaths, seven diffused breaths. || 3. His first vital breath, called Upward, is this Agni. || 4. His second vital breath, called Mature, is that Āditya. || 5. His third vital breath, called Approached, is that Moon. || 6. His fourth vital breath, called Pervading is this Pavamāna. || 7. His fifth vital breath, called Source, are these Waters. || 8. His sixth vital breath, called Dear, are these domestic animals. || 9. His seventh vital breath, called Unlimited, are these creatures.

Hymn 15:16.

1. His first downward breath is the time of Full Moon. || 2. His second

downward breath is the eighth day after Full Moon. || 3. His third downward breath is the night of New Moon. || 4. His fourth downward breath is Faith. || 5. His fifth downward breath is Consecration. || 6. His sixth downward breath is Sacrifice. || 7. His seventh downward breath are these sacrificial fees.

Hymn 15:17.

1. His first diffused breath is this Earth. || 2. His second diffused breath is that Firmament. || 3. His third diffused breath is that Heaven. || 4. His fourth diffused breath are those Constellations. || 5. His fifth diffused breath are the Seasons. || 6. His sixth diffused breath are the Season-groups. || 7. His seventh diffused breath is the year. || 8. With one and the same object the Gods go round the Year and the Seasons follow round the Vrātya. || 9. When they surround the Sun on the day of New Moon, and that time of Full Moon. || 10. That one immortality of theirs is just an oblation.

Hymn 15:18.

1. Of that Vrātya. || 2. The right eye is the Sun and the left eye is the Moon. || 3. His right ear is Agni and his left ear is Pavamāna. || 4. Day and Night are his nostrils. Diti and Aditi are his head and skull. || 5. By day the Vrātya is turned westward, by night he is turned eastward. Worship to the Vrātya!

Kāṇḍa 16.

Hymn 16:1.

1. The Bull of the Waters hath been let go; the heavenly fires have been let go. || 2. Breaking, breaking down, crushing, crushing to pieces, || 3. Mroka, mind-destroying, rooting up, consuming, ruiner of the soul, ruiner of the body. || 4. Here I let him go: thou washest me clean of him. || 5. With this we let him loose who hates us and whom we hate. || 6. Thou art in front of the waters. I let loose your sea. || 7. I let loose the Agni who is within the waters, Mroka the up-rooter, the destroyer of the body. || 8. Your Agni who entered into the waters, even he here is that very dread of yours. || 9. May he anoint you with Indra's own mighty power! || 10. May stainless waters cleanse us from defilement. || 11. May they carry sin away from us, may they carry away from us the evil dream. || 12. Look on me with a friendly eye, O, Waters, and touch my skin with your auspicious body. || 13. We call the gracious Fires that dwell in waters. Goddesses, grant me princely power and splendour.

Hymn 16:2.

1. Away from distasteful food, strength and sweet speech, || 2. Are pleasant. May I obtain a pleasant voice. || 3. I have invoked the Protector; I have invoked his protection. || 4. Quick of hearing are mine ears; mine ears hear what is good. Fain would I hear a pleasant sound. || 5. Let not good hearing and overhearing fail the Eagle's eye, the undecaying light. || 6. Thou art the couch of the Ṛishis Let worship be paid to the divine couch.

Hymn 16:3.

1. I am the head of riches. Fain would I be the head of mine equals. || 2. Let not Ruja and Vena desert me. Let not the Head and the Preserver forsake me. || 3. Let not the Boiler and the Cup fail me: let not the Supporter and the Sustainer abandon me. || 4. Let not Unyoking and the Moist-fellied car desert me: let not the Sender of Moisture and Mātariśvan forsake me. || 5. Bṛihaspati is my soul, he who is called the Friend of man, dear to my heart. || 6. My heart is free from sorrow; spacious is my dwelling-place. I am the sea in capacity.

Hymn 16:4.

1. I am the centre of riches. Fain would I be the centre of mine equals. || 2. Pleasant art thou to sit by one, a mother: immortal among mortals. || 3. Let not inward breath desert me; let not outward breath depart and leave me. || 4. Let Sūrya protect me from Day, Agni from Earth, Vāyu from Firmament, Yama from men, Sarasvatī from dwellers on the earth. || 5. Let not outward and inward breath fail me. Be not thou destructive among the men. || 6. Propitious today be dawns and evenings. May I drink water with all my people safe around me. || 7. Mighty are ye, domestic creatures. May Mitra-Varuṇa stand beside me. May Agni give me inward and outward breath. May he give me ability.

Hymn 16:5.

1. We know thine origin, O Sleep. Thou art the son of Grāhi, the minister of Yama. Thou art the Ender, thou art Death. As such, O Sleep, we know thee well. As such preserve us from the evil dream. || 2. We know thine origin, O Sleep. Thou art the son of Destruction, the minister of Yama, etc. (as in verse 1). || 3. We know thine origin, O Sleep. Thou art the son of Misery, etc. || 4. We know thine origin, O Sleep. Thou art the son of Disappearance, etc. || 5. We know thine origin, O Sleep. Thou art the son of Defeat etc. || 6. We know thine origin, O Sleep. Thou art the son of the sisters of the Gods, the minister of Yama. Thou art the Ender, thou are Death. As such, O Sleep, we know thee well. As such, preserve us from the evil dream.

Hymn 16:6.

1. Now have we conquered and obtained: we have been freed from sin today. || 2. Let Morning with her light dispel that evil dream that frightened us. || 3. Bear that away to him who hates, away to him who curses us. || 4. To him whom we abhor, to him who hates us do we send it hence. || 5. May the Goddess Dawn in accord with Speech, and the Goddess Speech in accord with Dawn, || 6. The Lord of Dawn in accord with the Lord of Speech and the Lord of Speech in accord with the Lord of Dawn, || 7. Carry away to Such-an-one niggard fiends, hostile demons, and Sadānvās, || 8. Kumbhīkas, Dūṣhīkas, and Pīyakas, || 9. Evil day-dream, evil dream in sleep, || 10. Wishes for boons that will not come, thoughts of poverty, the snares of the Druh who never releases. || 11. This, O Agni, let the Gods bear off to Such-an-one that he may be a fragile good-for-nothing eunuch.

Hymn 16:7.

1. Herewith I pierce this man. With poverty I pierce him. With disappearance I pierce him. With defeat I pierce him. With Grāhi I pierce him. With darkness I pierce him. || 2. I summon him with the awful cruel orders of the Gods. || 3. I place him between Vaiśvānara's jaws. || 4. Thus or otherwise let her swallow him up. || 5. Him who hates us may his soul hate, and may he whom we hate hate himself. || 6. We scorch out of heaven and earth and firmament the man who hates us. || 7. Suyāman son of Chākṣhus. || 8. Here I wipe away the evil dream on the descendant of Such-an-one, son of Such-a-woman. || 9. Whatsoever I have met with, whether at dusk or during early night, || 10. Whether waking or sleeping, whether by day or by night. || 11. Whether I meet with it day by day, from that do I bribe him away. || 12. Slay him; rejoice in this; crush his ribs. || 13. Let him not live. Let the breath of life forsake him.

Hymn 16:8.

1. Whatever we have gained, whatever hath accrued to us, our Right, our energy, our Devotion, our heavenly light, our sacrifice, our domestic animals, our offspring, our men,—from all share herein we exclude Such-an-one, descendant of Such-an-one, son of Such-a-woman. Let him not be freed from the noose of Grāhi. Here I bind up his splendour, his energy, his vital breath, his life, and cast him down beneath me. || 2. Whatever we have gained, etc. (as in verse 1). Let him not be freed from the noose of Nirṛiti, etc. || 3. Whatever we have gained, etc. Let him not be freed from the noose of misery, etc. || 4. Whatever we have gained, etc. Let him not be freed from the noose of disappearance, etc. || 5. Whatever we have gained, etc. Let him not be freed from the noose of defeat, etc. || 6. Whatever we have gained, etc. Let him not be freed from the noose of the sisters of the Gods, etc. || 7. Whatever we have gained, etc. Let him not be freed from the noose of Bṛihaspati, etc. || 8. Whatever we have gained, etc. Let him not be freed from the noose of Prajāpati, etc. || 9. Whatever we have gained, etc. Let him not be freed from the noose of the Ṛishis, etc. || 10. Whatever we have gained, etc. Let him not be freed from the noose of the Ṛishis' children, etc. || 11. Whatever, etc. Let him not be freed from the noose of the Aṅgirasas, etc. || 12. Whatever, etc. Let him not be freed from the noose of the Aṅgirasas, etc. || 13. Whatever, etc. Let him not be freed from the noose of the Atharvans, etc. || 14. Whatever, etc. Let him not be freed from the noose of the Atharvans, etc. || 15. Whatever, etc. Let him not be freed from the noose of the Trees, etc. || 16. Whatever, etc. Let him not be freed from the noose of Shrubs, etc. || 17. Whatever, etc. Let him not be freed from the noose of the Seasons, etc. || 18. Whatever, etc. Let him not be freed from the noose of the Season-groups, etc. || 19. Whatever, etc. Let him not be freed from the noose of the Months, etc. || 20. Whatever, etc. Let him not be freed from the noose of the Half-months, etc. || 21. Whatever, etc.

Let him not be freed from the noose of Day and Night, etc. || 22. Whatever, etc. Let him not be freed from the noose of continued Day, etc. || 23. Whatever, etc. Let him not be freed from the noose of Heaven and Earth, etc. || 24. Whatever, etc. Let him not be freed from the noose of Indra-Agni, etc. || 25. Whatever, etc. Let him not be freed from the noose of Mitra-Varuṇa, etc. || 26. Whatever, etc. Let him not be freed from the noose of King Varuṇa, etc. || 27. Whatever we have gained, whatever hath accrued to us, our Right, our energy, our Devotion, our heavenly light, our sacrifice, our domestic animals, our offspring, our men,—from all share herein we exclude Such-as-one, descendant of Such-an-one, son of Such-a-woman. Let him not be freed from the fetter and noose of Death. Here I bind up his splendour, his energy, his vital breath, his life, and cast him down beneath me.

Hymn 16:9.

1. Ours is superior place and ours is conquest: may I in all fights tread down spite and malice. || 2. This word hath Agni, this hath Soma spoken. May Pūshan set me in the world of virtue. || 3. We have come to the light of heaven; to the light of heaven have we come: we have united with the light of Sūrya. || 4. Sacrifice is fraught with wealth for the increase of prosperity. I would win riches; fain would I be wealthy. Do thou bestow wealth upon me.

Kāṇḍa 17.

Hymn 17:1.

1. Vanquishing, overpowering, a conqueror, exceeding strong, | Victorious, winner of the light, winner of cattle and of spoil, | Indra by name, adorable, I call: a long, long life be mine! || 2. Vanquishing etc. | Indra by name, adorable I call: May I be dear to Gods. || 3. Vanquishing, etc. | Indra by name, adorable, I call: may creatures love me well. || 4. Vanquishing, etc. | Indra by name, adorable, I call: may cattle hold me dear. || 5. Vanquishing, etc. | Indra by name, adorable, I call: may equals love me well. || 6. Rise up, O Sūrya, rise thou up; with strength and splendour rise on me. | Let him who hates me be my thrall; let me not be a thrall to him. | Manifold are thy great deeds, thine, O Vishṇu. | Sate us with cattle of all forms and colours: set me in happiness, in loftiest heaven. || 7. Rise up, O Sūrya, rise thou up; with strength and splendour rise on me. | Make me the favourite of all, of those I see and do not see. | Manifold are thy great deeds, thine, O Vishṇu. || 8. Let not the fowlers who are standing ready injure thee in the flood, within the waters. | Ascend this heaven, leaving each curse behind thee, Favour us: let thy gracious love attend us. | Manifold are thy great deeds, thine, O Vishṇu. || 9. Do thou, O Indra, for our great good fortune, with thine in-violable rays protect us. | Manifold are thy great deeds, thine, O Vishṇu. || 10. Be thou most gracious unto us, Indra, with favourable aid, | Rising to heaven's third sphere, invoked with song to quaff the Soma juice, loving thy home to make us blest. | Manifold are thy great deeds, thine, O Vishṇu. || 11. Thou art the vanquisher of all, O Indra, omniscient Indra, and invoked of many. | Indra, send forth this hymn that fitly lauds thee. Favour us let thy gracious love attend us. | Manifold are thy great deeds, thine, O Vishṇu. || 12. In heaven and on the earth thou art uninjured, none reach thy greatness in the air's mid region. | Increasing by inviolate devotion as such in heaven grant us protection, Indra. | Manifold are thy great deeds, thine, O Vishṇu. || 13. Grant us protection, Indra, with that body of thine that is on earth, in fire, in waters, | That dwells within light-finding Pavamāna, wherewith thou hast pervaded air's mid region. | Manifold are thy great deeds, thine, O Vishṇu. || 14. Indra, exalting thee with prayer, imploring, Ṛishis have sat them down in holy Session. | Manifold are thy great deeds, thine, O Vishṇu, || 15. Round Trita, round the spring with thousand currents thou goest, round the light-finding assembly. | Manifold are thy great deeds, thine, O Vishṇu. || 16. Thou guardest well the four celestial regions, pervading heaven, and earth with light and splendour. | Thou givest help to all these living creatures, and, knowing, followest the path of Order. | Manifold are thy great deed, thine, O Vishṇu. || 17. With five thou sendest heat: with one removing the curse thou comest in bright sunshine hither. | Manifold are thy great deeds, thine, O Vishṇu. || 18. Indra art thou, Mahendra thou, thou art the world, the Lord of Life. | To thee is sacrifice performed: worshippers offer gifts to thee. | Manifold are thy great deeds, thine, O Vishṇu. || 19. What is based on what is not: the present lies on that which is. | Present on future is imposed and future on the present based. | Manifold are thy great deeds, thine, O Vishṇu. | Sate us with cattle of all varied colour. Set me in happiness, in loftiest heaven. || 20. Bright art thou, and refulgent: as thou shinest with splendour so I fain would shine with splendour. || 21. Lustre art thou, illuming: as thou glowest with lustre so I too would shine with cattle, with all the lustre of a Brahman's station. || 22. Glory to him when rising, when ascending! Glory to him when he hath reached the zenith! | To him far-shining, him the self-refulgent, to him the Sovereign Lord and King be glory! || 23. Worship to him when he is turning westward, to him when setting, and when set be worship! | To him far-shining, him the self-refulgent, to him the Sovereign Lord and King be glory! || 24. With all his fiery fervour this Āditya hath gone up on high, | Giving my foes into my hand. Let me not by my foeman's prey. | Manifold are thy great deeds, thine, O Vishṇu. | Sate us with cattle of all varied colours. Set me in happiness, in loftiest heaven. || 25. Thou for our weal, Āditya, hast mounted thy ship with hundred oars. | Thou hast transported me to day: so bear me evermore to night. || 26. Thou for our weal, O Sūrya, hast mounted thy ship with hundred oars. | Thou hast transported me to night: so bear me evermore to day. || 27. Encompassed by Prajāpati's devotion as shield, with Kaśyapa's bright light and splendour, | Reaching old age, may I made strong and mighty live through a thousand years with happy fortune. || 28. Compassed am I with prayer, my shield and armour; compassed with Kaśyapa's bright light and splendour. | Let not shafts reach me shot from heaven against me, nor those sent forth by men for my destruction. || 29. Guarded am I by Order and the Seasons, protected by the past and by the future. | Let not distress, yea, let not Death come nigh me: with water of my speech have I o'erwhelmed them. || 30. On every side let Agni guard and keep me; the rising Sun drive off the snares of Mṛityu! | Let brightly flushing Mornings, firm-set mountains, and lives a thousand be with me united.

Kāṇḍa 18.

Hymn 18:1.

1. Fain would I win my friend to kindly friendship. So may the Sage, come through the air's wide ocean, | Remembering the earth and days to follow, obtain a son the issue of his father. || 2. Thy friend loves not the friendship which considers her who is near in kindred as a stranger. | Sons of the mighty Asura, the heroes, supporters of the heaven, see far around them. || 3. Yea, this the Immortals seek of thee with longing, a scion of the only man existing. | Then let thy soul and mine be knit together. Embrace thy consort as her loving husband. || 4. Shall we do now what we ne'er did aforetime? we who spoke righteously now talk impurely? | Gandharva in the floods, the Dame of Waters—such is our bond, such our most lofty kinship. || 5. Even in the womb God Tvashṭar, vivifier, shaping all forms, Creator, made us consorts. | Ne'er are his holy statutes violated: that we are his the heaven and earth acknowledge. || 6. Who yokes today unto the pole of Order the strong and passionate steers of checkless spirit, | With shaft-armed mouths, heart-piercing, joy-bestowing? Long shall he live who duly pays them service. || 7. Who knows that earliest day whereof thou speakest, Who hath beheld it? Who can here declare it? | Great is the law of Varuṇa and Mitra. What, wanton, wilt thou say to men to tempt them? || 8. Yamī am possessed by love of Yama, that I may rest on the same couch beside him. | I as a wife would yield me to my husband. Like car-wheels let us speed to meet each other. || 9. They stand not still, they never close their eyelids, those sentinels of Gods who wander round us. | Not me—go quickly, wanton, with another, and hasten like a chariot-wheel to meet him. || 10. May Sūrya's eye with days and nights endow him, and ever may his light spread out before him. | In heaven and earth the kindred pair commingle. On Yamī be the unbrotherly act of Yama. || 11. Sure there will come succeeding times when brothers and sisters will do acts unmeet for kinsfolk. | Not me, O fair one—seek another husband, and make thine arm a pillow for thy consort. || 12. Is he a brother when no help is left her? Is she a sister when Destruction cometh? | Forced by my love these many words I utter. Come near, and hold me in thy close embraces, || 13. I am no help for thee, no refuge, Yamī, I will not clasp and press thee to my bosom. | This is abhorrent to my mind and spirit—a brother on the couch beside a

sister. || 14. I will not fold mine arms about thy body: they call it sin when one comes near a sister. | Not me—prepare thy pleasure with another. Thy brother seeks not this from thee, O fair one. || 15. Alas; thou art indeed a weakling Yama. We find in thee no trace o f heart or spirit. | As round a tree the woodbine clings, another will cling about thee girt as with a girdle. || 16. Embrace another, Yamī. Let some other, even as the woodbine rings a tree, enfold thee. | Win thou his heart and let him win thy fancy; so make with him a bond of blest alliance. || 17. Three hymns the Sages have disposed in order, the many-formed, the fair, the all-beholding. | These in one single world are placed and settled—the growing plants, the breezes, and the waters. || 18. The Bull hath yielded for the Bull the milk of heaven: inviolable is the Son of Aditi. | According to his wisdom Varuṇa knoweth all: he halloweth, the holy, times for sacrifice. || 19. Gandharvī spake. May she, the Lady of the Flood amid the river's roaring leave my heart untouched. | May Aditi accomplish all that we desire, and may our eldest Brother tell us this as chief. || 20. Yea, even this blessed Morning, rich in store of food, splendid, with heavenly lustre, hath shone out for man, | Since they as was the wish of yearning Gods, brought forth that yearning Agni for the assembly as the Priest. || 21. And the fleet Falcon brought for sacrifice from afar this flowing. drop most excellent and passing wise, | Then when the Ārya tribes chose as invoking Priest Agni the wonder-worker, and the hymn rose up. || 22. Still art thou kind to him who feeds thee as with grass, and. skilled in sacrifice offers thee holy gifts. | When thou having received the sage's strengthening food with lauds, after long toil comest with many more. || 23. Urge thou thy Parents, as a lover, to delight: the lovely One desires and craves it from his heart. | As Priest he calls aloud, as Warrior shows his skill, as Asura tries his strength, and with the hymn is stirred. || 24. Far famed is he, the mortal man, O Agni thou Son of strength, who hath obtained thy favour. | He, gathering power, borne onward by his horses, makes his, days lovely in his might and splendour. || 25. Hear us, O Agni, in the great assembly: harness thy rapid car, the car of Amṛita. | Bring Heaven and Earth, the Deities' Parents, hither: stay with us here, nor from the Gods be absent. || 26. When, holy Agni, the divine assembly, the holy synod mid the Gods, is gathered, | And when thou, godlike One, dealest forth treasures vouchsafe us too our portion of the riches. || 27. Agni hath looked upon the van of Mornings, and on the days the earliest Jātavedas. | After the Dawns, after their rays of brightness, Sūrya hath entered into earth and heaven. || 28. Agni hath looked against the van of Mornings, against the days the earliest Jātavedas; | In many a place against the beams of Sūrya, against the heavens and earth hath he extended. || 29. Heaven and Earth, first by everlasting Order, speakers of truth, are near enough to hear us, | When the God, urging men to worship, sitteth as Priest, assuming all his vital vigour. || 30. As God comprising Gods by Law eternal, bear, as the chief who knoweth, our oblation, | Smoke-bannered with the fuel, radiant, joyous, better to praise and worship, Priest for ever. || 31. I praise your work that ye may make me prosper: hear, Heaven and Earth, twain worlds that drop with fatness! | While days and Gods go to the world of spirits, have let the Parents with sweet mead refresh us. || 32. When the Cow's nectar wins the God completely, men here below are heaven's and earth's sustainers | All the Gods come to this thy heavenly Yajus which from the motley Pair milked oil and water || 33. Hath the King seized us? How have we offended against his holy Ordinance? Who knoweth? | For even Mitra mid the Gods is angry. There are both song and wealth for those who come not. || 34. 'Tis hard to understand the Immortal's nature, where she who is akin becomes a stranger. | Guard ceaselessly, great Agni, him who ponders Yama's name easy to be comprehended. || 35. They in the synod where the Gods rejoice them, where they are seated in Vivasvat's dwelling, | Have given the Moon his beams, the Sun his splendour: the two unweariedly maintain their brightness. || 36. The counsel which the Gods meet to consider, their secret plan, of that we have no knowledge. | There let God Savitar, Aditi, and Mitra proclaim to Varuṇa that we are sinless. || 37. Companions, let us learn a prayer to Indra whom the thunder arms, | To glorify your bold and most heroic Friend. || 38. For thou by slaying Vṛitra art the Vṛitra-slayer, famed for might. | Thou, Hero, in rich gifts surpassest wealthy chiefs. || 39. o'er the broad land thou goest like a Stega: here on vast earth let breezes blow upon us, | Here hath our dear Friend Varuṇa, united, like Agni in the wood, shot forth his splendour. || 40. Sing praise to him the chariot-borne, the famous, Sovereign of men, the dread and strong destroyer. | O Rudra, praised be gracious to the singer; let thy darts spare us and smite down another. || 41. The pious call Sarasvatī, they worship Sarasvatī while sacrifice proceedeth. | The virtuous call Sarasvatī to hear them. Sarasvatī send bliss to him who giveth! || 42. Sarasvatī is called on by the Fathers who come right forward to our solemn worship. | Seated upon this sacred grass rejoice you. Give thou us strengthening food that brings no sickness. || 43. Sarasvatī, who comest with the Fathers, joying in hymns, O Goddess, and oblations, | Give plenteous wealth to this the sacrificer, a portion, worth a thousand, of refreshment. || 44. May they ascend, the lowest, highest, midmost, the Fathers, who deserve a share of Soma. | May they who have attained to life, the Fathers, righteous and gentle, aid us when we call them. || 45. I have attained the gracious-minded Fathers, I have gained son and progeny from Vishṇu. | They who enjoy pressed juices with oblation, seated on sacred grass, come oftenest hither. || 46. Now be this homage offered to the Fathers, to those who passed of old and those who followed, | Those who have rested in the earthly region and those who dwell among the happy races. || 47. Mātalī prospers there with Kavyas, Yama with Aṅgiras' sons, Bṛihaspati with singers. | Exalters of the Gods, by Gods exalted, aid us those Fathers in our invocations? || 48. Yes, this is good to taste and full of sweetness, verily it is strong and rich in flavour. | No one may conquer Indra in the battle when he hath drunken of the draught we offer. || 49. Honour the King with your oblations, Yama, Vivasvat's son, who gathers men together. | Even him who travelled o'er the mighty rivers, who searches out and shows the path to many. || 50. Yama first found for us the road to travel: this pasture never can be taken from us. | Men born on earth tread their own paths that lead them whither our ancient Fathers have departed. || 51. Fathers who sit on sacred grass, come, help us: these offsprings have we made for you; accept them. | So come to us with most auspicious favour: bestow on us unfailing health and plenty. || 52. Bowing their bended knees and seated southward let all accept this sacrifice with favour. | Punish us not for any sin, O fathers which we through human frailty have committed. || 53. Tvashṭar prepares the bridal for his daughter: therefore the whole of this our world assembles. | But Yama's mother, spouse of great Vivasvat, vanished as she was carried to her dwelling. || 54. Go forth, go forth upon the homeward pathways whither our sires of old have gone before us. | Then shalt thou look on both the Kings enjoying their sacred food, God Varuṇa and Yama. || 55. Go hence, depart ye, fly in all directions. This world for him the Fathers have provided. | Yama bestow upon this man a dwelling adorned with days and beams of light and waters. || 56. We set thee down with yearning, and with yearning we enkindle thee, | Yearning, bring yearning Fathers nigh to eat the food of sacrifice. || 57. We, splendid men, deposit thee, we, splendid men, enkindle thee. | Splendid, bring splendid Fathers nigh to eat the sacrificial food. || 58. Our Fathers are Aṅgirasas, Navagvas, Atharvans, Bhṛigus, who deserve the Soma. | May these, the holy, look on us with favour; may we enjoy their gracious loving-kindness. || 59. Come, Yama, with Aṅgirasas, the holy; rejoice thee here with children of Virūpa. | Seated on sacred grass at this oblation: I call Vivasvat too, thy father, hither. || 60. Come, seat thee on this bed of grass. O Yama, accordant with Aṅgirasas and Fathers. | Let texts recited by the sages bring thee. O. King, let this oblation make thee joyful. || 61. He hath gone hence and risen on high mounting heaven's ridges by that path | Whereon the sons of Aṅgiras, the conquerors of earth, went up.

Hymn 18:2.

1. For Yama Soma juice flows clear, to Yama is oblation paid. | To Yama sacrifice prepared, and heralded by Agni, goes. || 2. Offer to Yama sacrifice most sweet in savour and draw near. | Bow down before the Ṛishis of the olden time, the ancient ones who made the path. || 3. Offer to Yama, to the King, butter and milk in sacrifice. | So may he grant that we may live long days of life mid living men, || 4. Burn him not up, nor quite consume him, Agni. Let not his body or his skin be scattered. | O Jātavedas, when thou hast matured him, then send him on his way unto the Fathers. || 5. When thou hast made him ready, Jātavedas, then do thou give him over to the Fathers. | When he attains unto the life that waits him he will obey the Deities' commandment. || 6. With the three jars Bṛihat alone makes pure the six wide-spreading realms. | The Gāyatrī, the Trishṭubh, all metres in

Yama are contained. || 7. The Sun receive thine eye, the wind thy spirit; go, as thy merit is, to earth or heaven. | Go, if it be thy lot, unto the waters: go, make thy home in plants with all thy members. || 8. Thy portion is the goat: with heat consume him: let thy fierce flame, thy glowing splendour, burn him. | With thine auspicious forms, O Jātavedas, bear this man to the region of the pious. || 9. Let all thy rapid flames, O Jātavedas, wherewith thou fillest heaven and earth's mid-region, | Follow the goat as he goes on, united: then with the others, most auspicious, aid us. || 10. Away O Agni, to the Fathers, send him who, offered in thee, goes with our oblations. | Wearing new life let him approach his offspring, and splendid, be invested with a body, || 11. Run and outspeed the two dogs, Saramā's offspring, brindled, four-eyed, upon thy happy pathway. | Draw nigh thou to the gracious-minded Fathers who take their pleasure in the feast with Yama. || 12. And those two dogs of thine, Yama, the watchers, four-eyed who look on men and guard the pathway | Entrust this man, O King, to their protection, and with prosperity and health endow him. || 13. Dark-hued, insatiate, with distended nostrils, Yama's two envoys roam among the people. | May they restore to us a fair existence here and today that we may see the sunlight. || 14. For some the Soma juice runs clear some sit by sacrificial oil. | To those for whom the meath flows forth, even to those let him depart. || 15. Let him, O Yama, go to those Ṛishis austere, of Fervour born, | First followers of Law, the sons of Law, upholders of the Law. || 16. Invincible through Fervour, they who by their Fervour went to heaven. | Who practised great austerity,—even to those let him depart. || 17. The heroes who contend in war and boldly cast their lives away. | Or who give guerdon thousandfold,—even to those let him depart. || 18. Let him, O Yama, go to those Ṛishis austere, of Fervour born, | Skilled in a thousand ways and means, the sages who protect the Sun. || 19. Be pleasant unto him, O Earth, thornless and lulling him to rest. | Vouchsafe him shelter broad and sure. || 20. In the free amplitude of earth take roomy space to lodge thee in. | Let all oblations which in life thou paidest drop thee honey now. || 21. Hither I call thy spirit with my spirit. Come thou; delighted, to these dwelling-places. | Unite thee with the Fathers and with Yama: strong and delicious be the winds that fan thee. || 22. Floating in water, bringing streams, let Marutas carry thee aloft, | And causing coolness by their rush sprinkle thee with their falling rain. || 23. I have recalled thy life to life, to being, power, and energy. | Let thy soul go unto its own: so to the Fathers hasten thou. || 24. Let not thy soul be left behind: here let not aught of thee remain, | Of spirit, body, members, sap. || 25. Let not a tree oppress thee, nor Earth the great Goddess weigh thee down. | Among the Fathers find thy home, and thrive mid those whom Yama rules. || 26. Each parted member, severed from thy body, thy vital breaths that in the wind have vanished, | With all of these, piece after piece, shall Fathers who dwell together meet and reunite thee. || 27. Him have the living banished from their houses: remove him to a distance from the hamlet. | Yama's observant messenger was Mṛityu he hath despatched men's lives unto the Fathers. || 28. Those Dasyus who, not eating our oblations, come with friends' faces mingled with the Fathers, | Those who wear gross those who wear subtle bodies,—from this. our sacrifice let Agni blast them. || 29. Bringing delight, prolonging our existence, here let our own, the Fathers, dwell together. | Coming with sacrifice may we assist them, living long lives through many autumn seasons. || 30. Now by this cow I bring thee, by the boiled rice set in milk for thee, | Be the supporter of the folk left here without a livelihood. || 31. Prolong the pleasant Dawn enriched with horses-or bearing us anew beyond the darkness. | Adjudged to die be he, the man who slew thee: this portion let him find, and not another. || 32. Yama is higher and Vivasvat lower: nothing whatever do I see above him. | This sacrifice of mine is based on Yama, Vivasvat spread the atmosphere about us. || 33. From mortal men they hid the immortal Lady, made one like her and gave her to Vivasvat. | Saraṇyū brought to him the Aśvin brothers, and then deserted both twinned pairs of children. || 34. Bring thou the Fathers one and all Agni, to eat the sacrifice. | The buried, and the cast away, those burnt with fire, and those exposed. || 35. Those, whether flames have burnt or not consumed them, who in the midst of heaven enjoy oblations— | Let them, when thou dost know them, Jātavedas, accept with sacred food the axe and worship. || 36. Burn gently, Agni, burn not up the body with too fervent heat. | Let all thy force and fury be expended on the woods and earth. || 37. I give this place to him who hath come hither and now is mine, to be a home to rest in: | This was the thought of Yama when he answered: This man is. mine. Let him come here to riches. || 38. This date we settle once for all, that it may ne'er be fixt again. A hundred autumns; not before. || 39. This date we order, etc. || 40. This date we limit, etc. || 41. This date we measure, etc. || 42. This date we mete out, etc. || 43. This date we establish, etc. || 44. This date we mete and measure out, that it may ne'er be fixt. again. A hundred autumns: not before. || 45. The period I have measured—come to heaven. I would my life were long | Not to be measured out again; a hundred autumns, not before. || 46. Inbreath and outbreath, breath diffused, life, sight to look upon the Sun | Seek by a straight unwinding path the Fathers whom King Yama rules, || 47. Unmarried men who toiled and have departed, the childless, having left their foes behind them, | Have found on high the world whereto they mounted, reflecting on the ridge of vaulted heaven. || 48. The lowest is the Watery heaven, Pīlumatī the middle-most; | The third and highest, that wherein the Fathers dwell, is called Pradyaus. || 49. The Fathers of our Father, his Grandfathers, those who have entered into air's wide region, | Those who inhabit earth or dwell in heaven, these Fathers will we worship with oblation. || 50. Thou seest now, and ne'er again shalt look upon, the Sun in heaven. | Cover him as a mother draws her skirt about her son, O Earth! || 51. This once,,and at no other time hereafter in a lengthened life: | Cover him, as a wife, O Earth, covers her husband with her robe! || 52. Round thee auspiciously I wrap the vesture of our Mother Earth: | Be bliss among the living mine, oblation mid the Fathers thine! || 53. Ye have prepared, path-makers, Agni-Soma, a fair world for the Gods to be the it treasure. | Go to that world and send us Pūṣhan hither to bear us on the paths the goat hath trodden. || 54. Guard of the world, whose cattle ne'er are injured, may Pūṣhan bear thee hence, for he hath knowledge. | May he consign thee to these Fathers' keeping, and to the gracious Gods let Agni give thee. || 55. Lord of all life, let Āyu guard thee, Pūṣhan convey thee forward on the distant pathway. | May Savitar the God conduct thee thither where dwell the pious who have gone before thee. || 56. For thee I yoke these carriers twain to bear thee to the spirit. world. | Hasten with them to Yama's home and join his gathered. companies. || 57. This is the robe that first was wrapped about thee: cast off the robe thou worest here among us. | Go, knowing, to the meed of virtuous action, thy many gifts. bestowed upon the friendless. || 58. Mail thee with flesh against the flames of Agni; encompass thee about with fat and marrow; | So will the bold One eager to attack thee with fierce glow fail to girdle and consume thee. || 59. From his dead hand I take the staff he carried, together with his lore and strength and splendour. | There art thou, there; and here with good men round us may we o'ercome all enemies and foemen. || 60. From his dead hand I take the bow he carried, together with his. power and strength and splendour. | Having collected wealth and ample treasure, come hither to the-world of living beings.

Hymn 18:3.

1. Choosing her husband's world, O man, this woman lays herself down beside thy lifeless body. | Preserving faithfully the ancient custom. Bestow upon here both wealth and offspring. || 2. Rise, come unto the world of life, O woman: come, he is lifeless by whose side thou liest. | Wifehood with this thy husband was thy portion who took thy hand and wooed thee as a lover. || 3. I looked and saw the youthful dame escorted, the living to the dead: I saw them, bear her. | When she with blinding darkness was enveloped, then did I turn her back and lead her homeward. || 4. Knowing the world of living beings, Aghnyā! treading the path. of Gods which lies before thee, | This is thy husband: joyfully receive him and let him mount into the world of Svarga. || 5. The speed of rivers craving heaven and cane, thou, Agni, art the waters' gall. || 6. Cool, Agni, and again refresh the spot which thou hast scorched and burnt. | Here let the water-lily grow, and tender grass and leafy plant. || 7. Here is one light for thee, another yonder: enter the third and be therewith united. | Uniting with a body be thou lovely, dear to the Gods in their sublimest mansion. || 8. Rise up, advance, run forward: make thy dwelling in water that shall be thy place to rest in | There dwelling in accordance with the Fathers delight thyself with Soma and libations. || 9. Prepare thy body: speed thou on thy journey: let not thy limbs, thy frame be left behind thee. | Follow to its repose thy resting spirit:

go to whatever spot of earth thou lovest. ‖ 10. With splendour may the Fathers, meet for Soma, with mead and. fatness may the Gods anoint me. | Lead me on farther to extended vision, and prosper me through life of long duration. ‖ 11. May Agni balm me thoroughly with splendour; may Vishṇu. touch my lips with understanding. | May all the Deities vouchsafe me riches, and pleasant Waters purify and cleanse me. ‖ 12. Mitra and Varuṇa have stood about me. Ādityas, Sacrificial Posts exalt me! | May Indra balm my hands with strength and splendour. A long, long life may Savitar vouchsafe me. ‖ 13. Worship with sacrificial gift King Yama, Vivasvat's son who gathers men together, | Yama who was the first to die of mortals, the first who travelled to the world before us. ‖ 14. Depart, O Fathers, and again come hither; this sacrifice of yours is balmed with sweetness. | Enrich us here with gift of great possessions; grant blessed wealth with ample store of heroes. ‖ 15. Kaṇva, Kakshīvant, Purumīḍha, Agastya, Śyāvāśva Sobhari, and Archanānas, | This Viśvāmitra, Jamadagni, Atri, Kaśyapa, Vāmadeva be our helpers! ‖ 16. Vasishṭha, Jamadagni, Viśvāmitra, Gotama, Vāmadeva, Bharadvāja! | Atri hath won your favour with homage. Gracious to us be ye praiseworthy Fathers. ‖ 17. They, making for themselves a new existence, wash off defilement in the brazen vessel. | May we be fragrant in our houses, ever increasing in our children and our riches. ‖ 18. They balm him, balm him over, balm him thoroughly, caress the mighty power and balm it with the mead, | They seize the flying steer at the stream's breathing-place: cleansing with gold they grasp the animal herein. ‖ 19. Fathers, be glorious in yourselves, and follow all that is glad in you and meet for Soma. | Give ear and listen, swiftly-moving Sages, benevolent, invoked in our assembly. ‖ 20. Atris, Aṅgirasas, Navagvas, givers of liberal gifts, continual sacrificers, | Devout and pious, granting guerdon freely, sit on this holy grass and be ye joyful. ‖ 21. As in the days of old our ancient Fathers, speeding the work of sacred worship, Agni! | Sought pure light and devotion, singing praises, they cleft the ground and made red Dawns apparent. ‖ 22. Gods, doing holy acts, devout, resplendent, smelting like ore their human generation, | Brightening Agni and exalting Indra, they came encompassing the stall of cattle. ‖ 23. Strong One! he marked them, and the Gods before them, like herds of cattle in a foodful pasture. | There man moaned forth their strong desires, to strengthen even the true; the nearest One, the living. ‖ 24. We have worked for thee, we have toiled and laboured: bright Dawns have shed their light upon our worship. | All that the Gods regard with love is blessed. Loud may we speak, with heroes, in assembly. ‖ 25. From eastward Indra, Lord or Marutas, guard me, as in her arms Earth guards the heaven above us! | Those who give room, who made the paths, we worship, you, mid the Gods, who share the gifts we offer. ‖ 26. Dhātar with Nirṛiti save me from southward, etc. (as in stanza 25). ‖ 27. From westward Aditi was Ādityas save me! etc. ‖ 28. From westward with the All-Gods save me Soma! etc. ‖ 29. May the strong firm Sustainer bear thee upright, as Savitar bears light above the heaven. | Those who give room, who made the paths, we worship, you mid the Gods, who share the gifts we offer. ‖ 30. Toward the eastward region I supply thee before thou goest homeward, with oblation, as in her arms, etc. (as in stanza 25). ‖ 31. Toward the southern region, etc. ‖ 32. Toward the western region, etc. ‖ 33. Toward the northern region, etc. ‖ 34. Toward the steadfast region, etc. ‖ 35. Toward the upmost region I supply thee, before thou goest homeward, with oblation, as in her arms Earth bears the heaven above us. | Those who give room, who made the paths, we worship, you, mid the Gods, who share the gifts we offer. ‖ 36. Thou art the Bull, Supporter, and Upholder, ‖ 37. Who purifiest wind and mead and water. ‖ 38. From this side and from that let both assist me. As, speeding, ye have come like two twin sisters, | Religious-hearted votaries brought you forward. Knowing your several places be ye seated. ‖ 39. Sit near, sit very near beside our Soma: for you I fit the ancient prayer with homage. | The praise-song, like a chieftain on his pathway, spreads far and wide. Let all Immortals hear it. ‖ 40. Three paces hath the stake gone up, and followed her, the four-footed, with devout observance. | He with the Syllable copies the praise-song; he thoroughly purifies at Order's centre. ‖ 41. Chose he then, death for Gods to be their portion? Why chose he not for men a life eternal? | Bṛihaspati span sacrifice, the Ṛishi; and Yama yielded up his own dear body. ‖ 42. Thou, Agni Jātavedas, when entreated, didst bear our offerings, having made them fragrant. | And give them to the Fathers who consumed them with Svadhā. Eat, thou God, the gifts we bring thee. ‖ 43. Lapped in the bosom of the purple Mornings, give riches to the man who brings oblations. | Grant to your sons a portion of that treasure, and, present, give them energy, O Fathers. ‖ 44. Fathers whom Agni's flames have tasted, come ye nigh: in perfect order take ye each your proper place. | Eat sacrificial food presented on the grass: grant riches with a multitude of hero sons. ‖ 45. May they, the Fathers who deserve the Soma, invited to their favourite oblations. | Laid on the sacred grass, come nigh and listen. May they be gracious unto us and bless us. ‖ 46. Our Father's Fathers and their sires before them who came, most noble, to the Soma banquet, | With these let Yama, yearning with the yearning, rejoicing eat our offerings at his pleasure. ‖ 47. Come to us, Agni, with the gracious Fathers who dwell in glowing light, the very Sages, | Who thirsted mid the Gods, who hasten hither, oblation-winners, theme of singers' praises. ‖ 48. Come, Agni, come with countless ancient Fathers, dwellers in light, primeval, God-adorers, | Eaters and drinkers of oblation, truthful, who travel with the Deities and Indra. ‖ 49. Betake thee to the lap of Earth, our mother, of Earth far-spreading, very kind and gracious. | May she, wool-soft unto the guerdon-giver, guard thee in front upon the distant pathway. ‖ 50. Heave thyself, Earth, nor press him downward heavily: afford him easy access pleasant to approach, | Cover him as a mother wraps her skirt about her child, O Earth! ‖ 51. Now let the heaving earth be free from motion: yea, let a thousand clods remain above him. | Be they to him a home distilling fatness: here let them ever be his place of refuge. ‖ 52. I stay the earth from thee, while over thee I place this piece of earth. May I be free from injury. | The Fathers firmly fix this pillar here for thee; and there let Yama make thee an abiding-place. ‖ 53. Forbear, O Agni, to upset this chalice: the Gods and they who merit Soma love it. | This cup, yea this which serves the Gods to drink from,—in this let the Immortals take their pleasure. ‖ 54. The chalice brimming o'er which erst Atharvan offered to Indra, Lord of wealth and treasure, | Indu therein sets draught of virtuous action, and ever purifies himself within it. ‖ 55. What wound soe'er the dark bird hath inflicted, the emmet, or the serpent, or the jackal, | May Agni who devoureth all things heal it, and Soma, who hath passed into the Brahmans. ‖ 56. The plants of earth are rich in milk, and rich in milk is this my milk. | With all the milky essence of the Waters let them make me clean. ‖ 57. Let these unwidowed dames with goodly husbands adorn themselves with fragrant balm and unguent. | Decked with fair jewels, tearless, free, from trouble, first let the dames go up to where he lieth. ‖ 58. Meet Yama, meet the Fathers, meet the merit of virtuous action in the loftiest heaven. | Leave sin and evil, seek anew thy dwelling: so bright with glory let him join his body. ‖ 59. Our Father's Fathers and their sires before them, they who have entered into air's wide region, | For them shall self-resplendent Asunīti form bodies now according to her pleasure. ‖ 60. Let the hoar-frost be sweet to thee. sweetly on thee the rain descend! | O full of coolness, thou cool Plant, full of fresh moisture, freshening Herb, | Bless us in waters, female Frog: calm and allay this Agni here. ‖ 61. Vivasvat make us free from fear and peril, good rescuer, quick-pouring, bounteous giver! | Many in number be these present heroes! Increase of wealth be mine in kine and horses! ‖ 62. In immortality Vivasvat set us! Go from us Death, come to us life eternal! | To good old age may he protect these people: let not their spirits pass away to Yama. ‖ 63. The Sage of Fathers, guardian of devotions who holds thee up with might in air's mid-region,— | Praise him ye Viśvāmitras, with oblation. To lengthened life shall be, this Yama, lead us. ‖ 64. Mount and ascend to highest heaven, O Ṛishis: be ye not afraid. | Soma-drinkers to you is paid this Soma-lover's sacrifice. We have attained the loftiest light. ‖ 65. Agni is shining forth with lofty banner: the Bull is bellowing to earth and heaven. | From the sky's limit even hath he stretched near us: the Steer hath waxen in the waters' bosom. ‖ 66. They gaze on thee with longing in their spirit, as on an eagle that is mounting skyward; | On thee with wings of gold, Varuṇa's envoy, the Bird that hasteth to the home of Yama. ‖ 67. O Indra, bring us wisdom as a sire gives wisdom to his sons. | Guide us, O much-invoked in this our way: may we still living look upon the Sun. ‖ 68. Let these which Gods have held for thee, the beakers covered o'er with cake, | Be full of sacred food for thee, distilling fatness, rich in mead. ‖ 69. Grains which for thee I scatter, mixt with sesamum, as holy food, | May they for thee be excellent and potent: King Yama look on them as thine with favour! || 70. O Tree, give back again this man who is deposited on thee. | That he may dwell in Yama's home addressing the assemblies there. || 71. Seize hold O Jātavedas; let thy flame be full of fervent heat. | Consume his body: to the world of pious ones transport this man. || 72. To these, thy Fathers who have passed away at first and after-ward, | Let the full brook of butter run, o'erflowing with a hundred streams. || 73. Mount to this life, removing all defilement: here thine own kindred shine with lofty splendour. | Depart thou; be not left behind: go forward, first of those here, unto the world of Fathers.

Hymn 18:4.

1. Rise to your mother, flames of Jātavedas! I send you up by paths which Fathers traverse. | With headlong speed the Oblation bearer bore our gifts: toil ye, and place the offerer where the righteous dwell. || 2. The Seasons, Deities, form and order Worship, butter, cake, ladles, sacrificial weapons. | Tread thou God-travelled paths whereby the righteous, payers of sacrifices, go to Svarga. || 3. Carefully look on Sacrifice's pathway whereon the Aṅgirasas, the righteous, travel. | By those same pathways go thou up to Svarga where the Ādityas take their fill of sweetness, There make thy home in the third vault of heaven, || 4. Three eagles in the region's roar are standing high on heaven's ridge in their appointed station. | The worlds of Svarga shall, filled full of Amṛita, yield food and power to him who sacrificeth. || 5. Upabhṛit established air, Juhū the heaven, Dhruvā supported earth securely founded. | As meed, the Svarga worlds, o'erspread with fatness shall yield the sacrificer all his wishes. || 6. Dhruvā, ascend thou earth the all sustainer: go thou, O Upabhṛit, to air's mid-region. | Juhū, go skyward with the sacrificer; go, and with Sruva be thy calf beside thee drain all the swelling unreluctant quarters. || 7. They ford the mighty rivers by the pathway which they who sacrifice, the righteous, travel. | There they gave room unto the sacrificer when they made regions and existing creatures. || 8. The Aṅgirasas' pathway is the eastern Agni, the Ādityas' path-way is the Gārhapatya: | The southward Agni is the way of Southerns. | To Agni's greatness whom the prayer divideth go powerful, unscathed with all thy members. || 9. Eastward let east fire happily consume thee, and westward happily the Gārhapatya. | Burn southern fire, thine armour and protection: from air's mid-region from the north and centre, on all sides, Agni, guard thou him from horror. || 10. Do ye, with your most kindly forms, O Agni, waft, turned to rapid steeds whose ribs bear burthens, | The sacrificer to the world of Svarga where with the Gods they banquet and are joyful. || 11. Happily from the rear burn this man, Agni, happily from before, above, and under. | One, triply parted, Jātavedas, place him happily in the world that holds the righteous. || 12. Happily lit, let fires, each Jātavedas, seize on Prajāpati's appointed victim. | Let them not cast it down while here they cook it. || 13. Sacrifice, duly offered, comes preparing the sacrificer for the. world of Svarga, | Let all the fires, each Jātavedas, welcome Prajāpati's completely offered victim. | Let them not cast it down while here they cook it. || 14. Fain to fly up from the sky's ridge to heaven, the worshipper hath mounted visible Agni. | Lucid from out the mist to him, the pious, gleams the God-travelled path that leads to Svarga. || 15. On thy right hand let Indra be thy Brahman, Bṛihaspati Adhvaryu Agni Hotar. | This ordered sacrifice goes offered thither whither presented gifts have gone aforetime. || 16. Enriched with cake and milk here let the Charu rest. | World-makers, makers of the path we worship you of the Gods who here partake oblations. || 17. Enriched with cake and curds, etc. (as in stanza 16). || 18. Enriched with cake and drops, etc. || 19. Enriched with cake and butter, etc. || 20. Enriched with cake and flesh, etc. || 21. Enriched with cake and food, etc. || 22. Enriched with cake and mead, etc. || 23. Enriched with cake and juice, etc. || 24. Here, mixt with cake and water rest the Charu! | World-makers, makers of the path, we worship those Gods of you who here partake oblations. || 25. Let these which Gods have held for thee, these beakers covered o'er with cake, | Be full of sacred food for thee, distilling fatness, rich in mead. || 26. Grains which for thee I scatter, mixt with sesamum, as holy food. | May they for thee be excellent and potent. King Yama look on, them as thine with favour! || 27. More immortality! || 28. On all the earth, to heaven, the drop descended, on this place and on that which was before it. | I offer up, throughout the seven oblations, the drop which still to one same place is moving. || 29. Those who observe men look on wealth as Vāyu with countless. streams, and as light-finding Arka; | Those drain out Guerdon sprung from seven mothers, who satisfy and evermore give presents. || 30. They for their weal drain out the cask, the beaker four-holed, the milch-cow Iḍā full of sweetness, | Injure not, Agni, in the loftiest heaven Aditi heightening strength among the people. || 31. On thee doth Savitar the God bestow this vesture for thy wear. | Clothe thee herein, and find meet robe in Yama's realm to cover thee. || 32. The grains of corn have now become a cow, the sesamum her calf. | He in the realm of Yama lives on her the inexhaustible. || 33. Let these become thy milch-kine, man! supplying all thy heart's desires. | There, speckled, white, like-hued and various-coloured, with calves of sesamum let them stand beside thee. || 34. Let the green grains become thy white, and speckled, The dusky corns become thy ruddy milch-kine. | Let those with calves of sesamum for ever yield strength to him and never flinch from milking. || 35. I offer in Vaiśvānara this oblation, thousandfold spring that pours a hundred steamlets. | This with a swelling flow supports the Father, supports grand-fathers and their sires before them. || 36. Beside the spring with hundred, thousand currents, expanding on the summit of the water, | Exhaustless, yielding strength, never reluctant, the Fathers with their sacred food are seated. || 37. This pile of wood, collected, heaped together, regard it, O ye, kinsmen, and come near it. | To immortality this mortal goeth: prepare a home for him, all ye his kindred. || 38. Be here, even here, acquiring wealth, here be thou thoughts here be thou strength. | Be stronger here in manly power, life-giver, never beaten back. || 39. Giving the son and grandson satisfaction, let these the present Waters full of sweetness, | Pouring forth food and Amṛita for the Fathers, refresh both these and those, the Goddess Waters. || 40. Waters, send Agni forward to the Fathers: let them accept the sacrifice I offer. | May they who follow Vigour that abideth there send us down wealth with full store of heroes. || 41. Lover of butter, deathless, him, Oblation-bearer, they inflame. | He knoweth well the treasured stores gone to the Fathers, far away. || 42. The mingled draught, the mess of rice, the flesh which I present to thee, | May these be full of food for thee, distilling fatness, rich in sweets. || 43. Grains which for thee I scatter, mixt with sesamum as sacred food, | May these for thee be excellent and potent. King Yama look on, them, as thine, with favour. || 44. This is the ancient, this the recent pathway, by which thy sires of olden time departed. | They who first travelled it, and they who followed, convey thee to the world where dwell the righteous. || 45. The pious call Sarasvatī: they worship Sarasvatī while sacrifice proceedeth. | The righteous doers of good deeds invoke her: Sarasvatī send bliss to him who giveth! || 46. Approaching on the south our solemn worship, the Fathers call Sarasvatī to hear them. | Sit on this holy grass and be ye joyful: give thou us strengthening food that brings no sickness. || 47. Sarasvatī, who tamest with them, joying in hymns and food, O Goddess, with the Fathers, | Here give the Sacrificer growth of riches, a portion, worth a thousand, of refreshment. || 48. As Pṛithivī rests on earth, so do I seat thee. May the God Dhātar lengthen our existence. | For you may he who parts in turn find treasures, but let the Dead among the Fathers. || 49. Depart ye two: wipe ye away whatever omens of evil fortune here have told you. | Go from this man, both Steers, to him who wills it: ye are my joys here by the giver's Fathers. || 50. From a good quarter have we gained this guerdon, gift of this man, strength giving, plenteous milker. | Bringing in youth old age unto the living, may she bear these together to the Fathers. || 51. I bring this clipped grass hither for the Fathers: grass living, higher, for the Gods I scatter. | Mount this, O man, as victim: let the Fathers recognize thee: when thou hast travelled yonder. || 52. Set on this grass thou hast become a victim. Fathers shall know thee yonder when they meet thee. | Gather thy body, limb by limb, together: I by the power of prayer arrange thy members. || 53. The royal Parṇa is the cauldrons' cover: strength have we gained, force, power, and might, and vigour. | Bestowing length of life upon the living, for long existence through a hundred autumns. || 54. The share of vigour which gave this man being, the stone won lordship over foods that nourish. | Hymn this with your oblations, Viśvāmitras: may he, may Yama, lengthen our existence. || 55. As the Five Races of mankind for Yama set apart a house. | Even so I set a house apart that greater numbers may be mine. || 56. Take thou and wear this piece of gold, the gold thy father used to wear. | Wipe tenderly the right hand of thy sire who goes

away to heaven. || 57. To all, the living and the dead, all that are born, the worshipful. | Let the full brook of fatness run, o'erflowing, with stream of mead. || 58. Far-seeing he flows on, the Bull, the Lord of hymns, promoter of the Sun, of Days, of Dawns, of Heaven. | Breath of the rivers he hath roared into the jars, and through his wisdom entered into Indra's heart. || 59. Let thy bright smoke envelop thee, spread forth, O Bright One, in the sky. | For, Purifier, like the Sun thou shinest with thy radiant glow. || 60. Indu is moving forth to Indra's destined place, and slights not as a friend the promise of his friend. | Thou, Soma, comest nigh as bridegroom meets the bride, reaching the beaker by a course of hundred paths. || 61. Well have they eaten and rejoiced: their dear ones have they shaken off. | Sages, self-luminous, have praised: we who are youngest supplicate. || 62. Come hither, Fathers, who deserve the Soma, by the deep path-ways which the Fathers travel. | Bestow upon us life and store of children, and favour us with increase of our riches. || 63. Depart, O Fathers, ye who merit Soma, by the deep pathways which the Fathers travel; | But in a month, rich in fair sons and heroes, come back into our homes to eat oblation. || 64. If Agni Jātavedas, as he bore you hence to the Fathers' world, hath left one single. | Limb of your bodies, here do I restore it. Fathers, rejoice in heaven with all your members! || 65. Meet for men's praises, Agni Jātavedas was sent as envoy when the day was closing. | Thou gavest to the Fathers with oblation. They ate; eat, God, our offered sacrifices. || 66. Here hast thou left thy heart; O man, as sisters leave their little pet. Do thou, O earth, envelop him. || 67. Bright be to thee those worlds where dwell the Fathers! I seat thee in that sphere which they inhabit. || 68. Thou art the grass whereon our Fathers seat them. || 69. Loosen, O Varuṇa, the bond that binds us; loosen the bond above, between, and under. | Then under thy protection, O Āditya, may we be sinless and restored to freedom. || 70. From all those bonds, O Varuṇa, release us, wherewith a man is bound at length and cross-wise. | Then may we live a hundred autumn seasons guarded by thee, O King, by thee protected. || 71. To Agni, bearer of oblation to the Manes, be Hail! and homage! || 72. To Soma connected with the Fathers Hail! and homage! || 73. To the Fathers connected with Soma Hail! and homage! || 74. To Yama connected with the Fathers Hail! and homage! || 75. To thee, O Great-grandfather, and those with thee be this cry of Hail || 76. To thee, Great-grandfather, and to those with thee be this cry of Hail! || 77. To thee, O Fathers, be this cry of Hail! || 78. Hail to the Fathers who inhabit earth! || 79. Hail to the Fathers who inhabit the firmament! || 80. Hail to the Fathers who dwell in heaven! || 81. Hail, Fathers, to your energy! Hail, Fathers, to your sap! || 82. Hail Father; to your wrath! Hail, Fathers, to your ardour! || 83. Hail, Fathers, to what is awful! Hail to what is terrible in you! || 84. Hail, Fathers, to all that is propitious! Hail to all that is pleasant in you! || 85. Homage to you Fathers! Hail to you, Fathers! || 86. All Fathers who are here, the Fathers here are you: let then-follow you. May ye be the most excellent of these. || 87. All living fathers who are here are we here: let them follow us. | May we be the most excellent of these. || 88. Bright Agni, we will kindle thee, rich in thy splendour, fading. not. | So that this glorious fuel may send forth to heaven its light for thee. Bring food to those who sing thy praise. || 89. Within the waters runs the Moon, the strong-winged Eagle soars. in heaven. | Ye Lightnings with your golden wheels, men find not your abiding-place. Hear this my call, O Heaven and Earth.

Kāṇḍa 19.

Hymn 19:1.

1. Let the streams flow together, let the winds and birds assembled come. | Strengthen this sacrifice of mine, ye singers. I offer up a duly mixt oblation. || 2. O Burnt Oblations, aid, and ye, Blent Offerings, this my sacrifice. | Strengthen this sacrifice of mine, ye singers. I offer up a duly mixt oblation. || 3. Each several form, each several force I seize, and compass round this man. | May the Four Quarters strengthen this my sacrifice. I offer up a duly mixt oblation.

Hymn 19:2.

1. Blest be the Streams from hills of snow, sweet be spring Waters unto thee. | Sweet be swift-running Waters, sweet to thee be Water of the Rains. || 2. Sweet unto thee be Waters of the waste and Waters of the pool. | Sweet be the Waters dug from earth, to thee, and Waters brought in jars. || 3. To those who delve without a tool to dig, the wise, the deeply moved, | To Waters better healers than physicians we address our prayer. || 4. Bathed in the Waters verily divine, in water of the streams, | Bathed in the Waters verily, O Horses, be ye fleet and strong. || 5. Blest be the Waters unto thee, suspicious Waters, bringing. health. | They cure the injured place for thee even as thy comfort craveth it.

Hymn 19:3.

1. Whithersoe'er, from sky, earth, air's mid-regions from plants and herbs, from tall trees, Jātavedas. | Is carried here and there to divers places, even thence come thou to us with loving-kindness. || 2. All majesty of thine in floods, in forest, in plants, in cattle, in the depths of waters | Closely uniting all thy forms, O Agni, come unto us wealth-giving, undecaying. || 3. Thy majesty among the Gods in Svarga, thy body which hath past into the Fathers. | Thy plenty far-diffused mid human beings, even with this, O Agni, give us riches. || 4. To him the wise, the famous, swift to listen, with words and verses I come nigh for bounty. | May we be safe from threatening danger. Soften by sacrifice the-wrath of Gods, O Agni.

Hymn 19:4.

1. The first oblation that Atharvan oared, earliest sacrifice paid by Jātavedas, | Even this I, foremost, with repeated worship, now offer unto thee. May Agni carry the sacrificer's present. Hail to Agni! || 2. In front I set Intention, blessed Goddess. Mother of thought, may she be prompt to hear us. | Mine, and mine only, be the hope I fashion! May I gain this that hath possessed my spirit. || 3. With Purpose, O Prajāpati, with Purpose come thou near to us. | Bestow on us a share of luck, and so be swift to hear our call. || 4. Prajāpati Aṅgirasa with favour regard this word and this my settled purpose! | May he, whence Gods and Deities had being Kāma attend us with his gentle guidance.

Hymn 19:5.

1. King of the living world and men is Indra, of all in varied form that earth containeth. | Thence to the worshipper he giveth riches: may he enrich even us when we have praised him.

Hymn 19:6.

1. Puruṣha hath a thousand arms, a thousand eyes, a thousand feet. | On every side pervading earth he fills a space ten fingers wide. || 2. He with three quarters rose to heaven here reappeared a fourth of him. | Thence he strode forth on every side to all that eats not and that eats. || 3. So mighty is his grandeur, yea, greater than this is Puruṣha. | All creatures are one-fourth of him, three-fourths what dieth not in heaven. || 4. Puruṣha is in truth this All, what hath been and what yet shall; be | Lord, too, of immortality—and what hath grown with some-what else. || 5. When they divided Puruṣha how many portions did they make? | What was his mouth? what were his arms? what are the names of thighs and feet? || 6. The Brahman was his mouth, of both his arms was the Rājanya made. | His waist became the Vaiśya, from his feet the Śūdra was produced. || 7. The Moon was gendered from his mind, and from his eye the Sun had birth. | Indra and Agni from his mouth were born and Vāyu from his breath. || 8. Forth from his navel come mid-air; the sky was fashioned from his head. | Earth from his feet, and from his ear the regions. Thus they formed the worlds. || 9. In the beginning rose Virāj: Puruṣha from Virāj was born. | As soon as he was born he spread westward and eastward o'er the earth. || 10. When Gods performed the sacrifice with Puruṣha as their offering. | Spring was the butter, summer was the fuel, autumn was the gift. || 11. That sacrifice, first-born Puruṣha, they hallowed with the sprinkled Rains. | The Deities, the Sādhyas, all the Vasus sacrificed with him. || 12. From it were horses born, from it all creatures with two rows of teeth. | From it were generated kine, from it were goats and sheep produced. || 13. From that great general sacrifice Ṛichas and Sāman hymns were born; | Therefrom the metres were produced: the Yajus had its birth from it. || 14. From that great general sacrifice the dripping fat was gathered up: | It formed the creatures fleet as wind, and animals both wild and tame. || 15. Seven fencing-logs had he, thrice seven layers of fuel were prepared. | When, offering sacrifice, the Gods bound as their victim Puruṣha || 16. Forth from head of the high God seven-and-seventy bright beams. | Sprang into being, of the King Soma produced from Puruṣha

Hymn 19:7.

1. The brilliant lights shining in heaven together, which through the world glide on with rapid motion. | And Days, and Firmament with songs I worship, seeking the Twenty-eight-fold for its favour. ‖ 2. Krittikās, Rohiṇī be swift to hear me! Let Mṛigaśiras bless me, help me Ārdrā! | Punarvasu and Sūnṛitā, fair Pushya, the Sun, Āśleshās, Maghā lead me onward! ‖ 3. My bliss be Svātī and benignant Chitrā, my right First Phalgunīs and present Hasta. | Rādhas, Viśākhās, gracious Anurādhā, Jyeshṭhā and happy-starred uninjured Mūla. ‖ 4. Food shall be earlier Ashāḍhās grant me; let those that follow bring me strength and vigour; | With virtuous merit Abhijit endow me! Śravaṇa and Śraviṣhṭhās make me prosper. ‖ 5. Śatabhiṣhā afford me ample freedom, and both the Proshṭhapadas guard me safely. | Revatī and the Aśvayujas bring me luck, and the Bharaṇis abundant riches!

Hymn 19:8.

1. Benign to me be all those Lunar Mansions to which the Moon as he moves on doth honour. | All that are in the sky, the air, the waters, on earth, on mountains, in the heavenly regions. ‖ 2. Propitious, mighty, let the eight-and-twenty together deal me out my share of profit. | Profit and wealth be mine, and wealth and profit! To Day and Night be adoration rendered! ‖ 3. Fair be my sunset, fair my morn and evening and day with. lucky chase and happy omens; | With blessing and success, immortal Agni, go to the mortal and. return rejoicing. ‖ 4. Excitement and invoking cry, ill-omened sneezing and reproof, | All sounds of empty pitchers send into the distance, Savitar! ‖ 5. May we escape an evil sneeze, enjoy the sneeze of happy luck, | And may our nostrils smelling what is pleasant pour forth fragrant scent. ‖ 6. These flames of Brahmaṇaspati borne to all quarters in the-wind, | Turn them all hither, Indra, and make them most gracious unto, me.

Hymn 19:9.

1. Gentle be heaven, gentle be earth, gentle this spacious, atmosphere. | Gentle be waters as they flow, gentle to us be plants and herbs! ‖ 2. Gentle be signs of coming change, and that which is and is not. done! | Gentle be past and future, yea, let all be gracious unto us. ‖ 3. Quickened by Prayer, this Goddess Vāk who standeth in the highest place, | By whom the awful spell was made, even through her to us be peace! ‖ 4. Or, made more keen by Prayer, this mind that standeth in the highest place, | Whereby the awful spell was made, even through this be peace to us! ‖ 5. These five sense-organs with the mind as sixth, sharpened by Prayer, abiding in my heart, | By which the awful spell was made, even by these be peace to us. ‖ 6. Favour us Mitra, Varuṇa, and Viṣhṇu, and Prajāpati! Gracious to us be Indra and Bṛihaspati and Aryaman. ‖ 7. Favour us Mitra, Varuṇa, Vivasvat, and the Finisher, | Portents on earth and in the air, and planets wandering in heaven! ‖ 8. Gracious to us be trembling earth, gracious the flaming meteor stroke! | Gracious be kine who yield red milk, gracious be earth when sinking down! ‖ 9. Gracious be meteor-stricken constellation, gracious to us be magic spells and witchcraft! | Gracious to us be buried charms, and gracious the meteors and the portents of the region! ‖ 10. Kind be the Powers who seize the Moon, with Rāhu be Ādityas kind! | Favour us Death and Cornet, and Rudras with penetrating might! ‖ 11. Rudras and Vasus favour us, Ādityas, Agnis favour us! | Favour us mighty Ṛishis, Gods, Goddesses, and Bṛihaspati! ‖ 12. Brahma, Dhātar, Prajāpati, Worlds, Vedas, Agnis, Ṛishis Seven. | All these have blessed my happy way. May Indra be my guardian, may Brahmā protect and shelter me. ‖ 13. May all the Gods protect me, may the Gods united shield me well. | May all alleviations in the world which the Seven Ṛishis know. | Be kind and gracious unto me. Bliss and security be mine! ‖ 14. Earth alleviation, air alleviation, heaven alleviation, waters alleviation, plants alleviation, trees alleviation, all Gods my alleviation, collective Gods my alleviation, alleviation by alleviations. By these alleviations, these universal alleviations, I allay all that is terrific here, all that is cruel, all that is wicked. This hath been calmed, this is now auspicious. | Let all be favourable to us.

Hymn 19:10.

1. Befriend us with their aids Indra and Agni, Indra and Varuṇa who receive oblations! | Indra and Soma give health, wealth and comfort, Indra and Pūshan be our strength in battle! ‖ 2. Auspicious friends to us be Bhaga. Śaṃsa, auspicious be Purandhi and all Riches, | The blessing of the true and well-conducted and Aryaman in many forms apparent. ‖ 3. Kind unto us be Maker and Sustainer and the far-reaching One with godlike nature. | Auspicious unto us be Earth and Heaven, the Mountain and the Gods' fair invocations. ‖ 4. Favour us Agni with his face of splendour, and Varuṇa and Mitra and the Aśvins | Favour us noble actions of the pious; impetuous Vāta blow on, us with favour! ‖ 5. Early invoked may Heaven and Earth be friendly, and Air's mid-region good for us to look on. | To us may herbs and forest trees be gracious, gracious the Lord victorious of the region. ‖ 6. Be the God Indra with the Vasus friendly, and with Ādityas Varuṇa who blesseth. | Kind with the Rudras be the healer Rudra, and with the Dames here Tvaṣhṭar kindly hear us. ‖ 7. Kind unto us be Soma and Devotions, kind be the sacrifice and Stones for pressing. | Kind be the fixing of the Sacred Pillars, kind be the tender Grass, and kind the Altar. ‖ 8. May the far-seeing Sun rise up to bless us: be the four quarters-of the heaven auspicious. | Auspicious be the firmly-seated Mountains, auspicious be the Rivers and the Waters. ‖ 9. May Aditi through holy works be gracious, and may the Marutas, loud in song, be friendly. | May Viṣhṇu give felicity, and, Pūshan, and Air that cherisheth. our lives, and Vāyu. ‖ 10. Prosper us Savitar, the God who rescues, and let the radiant. Mornings be propitious. | Propitious to our children be Parjanya, kind to us be the field's benign Protector!

Hymn 19:11.

1. May the great Lords of Truth protect and aid us: blest to us be our horses and our cattle. | Kind be the pious, skilful-handed Ṛibhus, kind be the Fathers at our invocations ‖ 2. Kind to us be the Gods and Viśvedevas, Sarasvatī with Holy Thoughts be gracious. | Friendly be they, the Liberal Ones, who seek us, yea, those who dwell in-heaven, on earth, in waters. ‖ 3. May Aja-Ekapāda the God be gracious, gracious the Dragon of the Deep, and Ocean. | Gracious be he, the swelling Child of Waters, gracious be Pṛiśni who hath Gods to guard her. ‖ 4. So may the Rudras, Vasus, and Ādityas accept the new hymn we now are making. | May all the Holy Ones of earth and heaven, and the Cow's off-spring hear our invocation. ‖ 5. Priests of the Gods, worthy of sacrifices, immortal, knowing Law, whom man must worship. | May these today give us broad paths to travel. Preserve us evermore, ye Gods, with blessings.

Hymn 19:12.

1. Dawn drives away her sister's gloom, and through her excellence makes her retrace her path. | Through her may we gain God-appointed treasure, and with brave sons be glad through hundred winters.

Hymn 19:13.

1. These the two sturdy, manly arms of Indra, these that are wondrous, mighty, and successful | First, when the need hath come will I employ them by which the heaven of Asuras was conquered. ‖ 2. Swift, like a dread bull sharpening his weapons, rapidly striking, stirring up the people, | Loud shouting, vigilant, the one sole Hero, Indra subdued a hundred hosts together. ‖ 3. With him loud-roaring, ever watchful, victor bold, hard to over-throw, whom none may vanquish, | Indra the strong whose hand bears arrows, conquer, ye heroes now, now vanquish in the combat. ‖ 4. He rules with those who carry shafts and quivers, Indra who with his hand brings hosts together, | Foe-conquering, strong of arm, the Soma-drinker, with mighty bow, shooting with well-laid arrows. ‖ 5. Conspicuous by thy strength, firm, foremost fighter, mighty and fierce, victorious, all-subduing, | O'ercoming might, excelling men and heroes, mount the kine-winning conquering car, O Indra. ‖ 6. Troop-vanquisher, kine-winner, armed with thunder, who quells an army and with might destroys it, | Follow him, comrades! quit yourselves like heroes, and like this Indra show your zeal and courage. ‖ 7. Piercing the cow-stalls with surpassing vigour, Indra the pitiless hero, wild with anger, | Victor in fight, unshaken and resistless,—may he protect our armies in our battles. ‖ 8. Bṛihaspati, fly with thy chariot hither, slayer of demons, driving. off our foemen. | Be thou protector of our bodies, crushing our enemies, destroying those who hate us. ‖ 9. Indra guide these! Bṛihaspati, the Guerdon, and Soma, and the Sacrifice precede them! | And let the banded Marutas march in forefront of heavenly hosts that conquer and demolish. ‖ 10. Ours be the potent host of mighty Indra, King Varuṇa, and Marutas and Ādityas. | Uplifted is the shout of Gods who conquer, high-minded God who cause the world to tremble. ‖ 11. May Indra aid us when our flags are gathered: victorious be

the arrows of our army. | May our brave men of war prevail in battle. Ye Gods, protect us in the shouts of onset.

Hymn 19:14.

1. I have attained this goodliest place to rest in. Both Heaven and, Earth have shown me grace and favour. | Without a foe for me be all the regions! We hate thee not. May we have peace and safety.

Hymn 19:15.

1. Indra, give us security from that whereof we are afraid. | Help us, O Maghavan, let thy succour grant us this: drive foes and enemies afar. || 2. We call on Indra, on the liberal giver: we will be prosperous in men and cattle. | Let not the hosts of cruel fiends approach us. Drive of the Druhs to every side, O Indra. || 3. Best, making household wealth increase. Indra our saviour, kills the foe. | May he from outmost point be our protector, and from the centre and from west and eastward. || 4. Lead us to ample room. O thou who knowest, to happiness security, and sunlight. | Strong, Indra, are the arms of thee the mighty: may we betake us to their lofty shelter. || 5. May air's mid-region give us peace and safety, safety may both these, Heaven and Earth, afford us. | Security be ours from west, from eastward, from north and south may we be free from danger. || 6. Safety be ours from friend and from the unfriendly, safety from what we know and what we know not. | Safety be ours by night and in the day-time! friendly to me be all my hopes and wishes!

Hymn 19:16.

1. Peace hath been given us from the east, and from the west security. | Savitar guard me from the south, and from the north the Lord of Might. || 2. May the Ādityas from the sky protect me, Agni from the earth. | May Indra-Agni guard me from the eastward, on all sides may the Aśvins give me shelter. | May Jātavedas guard, sidelong, our cattle. | Our shield on all sides be the World-Creators!

Hymn 19:17.

1. Agni from eastward guard me with the Vasus! To him I go, in him I rest: this fort I seek for refuge. | May he protect me, may he be my guardian. I give my soul—All hail! into his keeping. || 2. Vāyu with Air protect me from this region. To him I go, etc. || 3. May Soma from the south, with Rudras, guard me. To him, etc. || 4. Varuṇa with Ādityas guard me from this region! To him etc. || 5. Sūrya with Earth and Heaven from the western region guard me well. To him, etc. || 6. May Waters joined with Plants protect me from this region. To them I go, in them I rest: this fort I seek for refuge. | May they protect me, may they be my guardians. I give my soul—All hail!—into their keeping. || 7. May Viśvakarman with the Seven Ṛishis be my protector from the northern region. To him, etc. || 8. May Indra, Marut-girt, protect me from this region. To him, etc. || 9. Prajāpati, of generative power, with the Pratishṭhā save me from the nadir! To him, etc. || 10. Bṛihaspati, joined by the Viśvedevas, protect me from the region of the zenith! To him, I go, in him I rest; this fort I seek for refuge. | May he protect me, may he be my guardian. I give my soul—All hail!—into his keeping.

Hymn 19:18.

1. Let those who vex me from the eastern region, sinners, praise Agni followed by the Vasus. || 2. Let those who vex me from this quarter, sinners, praise Vāyu compassed by the Air's mid region. || 3. Let those who vex me from the southern quarter, sinners, sing praise to Soma with the Rudras. || 4. Let those who vex me from this quarter, sinners, praise Varuṇa connected with Ādityas. || 5. Let those who vex me from the western quarter, sinners, praise Sūrya linked with Earth and Heaven. || 6. Let those who vex me from this quarter, sinners give praise to plants' associates the Waters. || 7. Let those who from the north side vex me, sinners, praise Viśvakarman with the Seven Ṛishis || 8. Let those who vex me from this quarter, sinners, praise Indra with the Marut host about him. || 9. Let those who vex me from the nadir, sinners, extol Prajāpati of genial power. || 10. Let those who vex me from the zenith, sinners, extol Bṛihaspati with the Viśvedevas.

Hymn 19:19.

1. Mitra arose with Earth. To that fort I lead you: enter it, occupy it. Let it give you protection and defence. || 2. Vāyu arose with Air. To that fort, etc. || 3. Sūrya arose with Heaven. To that fort, etc. || 4. Chandramās arose with the Constellation. To that fort, etc. || 5. Sacrifice arose with Priestly Fees. To that fort, etc. || 6. Ocean arose with the Rivers. To that fort, etc. || 7. Brahma arose with the Brahmachārīs. To that fort, etc. || 8. Indra arose with Might. To that fort, etc. || 9. The Gods arose with Immortality. To that fort, etc. || 10. Prajāpati arose with Creatures. To that fort I lead you: enter it, occupy it give you protection and defence.

Hymn 19:20.

1. May Soma, Varuṇa the King, both Aśvins, Yama and Pūshan guard us well from Mṛityu— | Death caused by men, which Indra-Agni, Dhātar, Bṛihaspati and Savitar appointed. || 2. All that the World's Lord made, all that for creatures Prajāpati and Mātariśvan fashioned, | All things within the quarters and their spaces, let all these be my manifold defences. || 3. That which the Gods bound on them when they battled for their royal sway. | What Indra made his shield, may that protect us well on every side, || 4. My shield is Heaven and Earth, my shield is the bright Day, my shield the Sun. | The Viśva Devas made my shield. Let not misfortune fall on me.

Hymn 19:21.

1. Gāyatrī, Ushṇih, Anushṭubh, Bṛihatī, Trishṭubh, Jagatī.

Hymn 19:22.

1. With the first five chapters of the Aṅgirasas, Hail! || 2. To the sixth, Hail! || 3. To the seventh and eight, Hail! || 4. The black-clawed ones, Hail! || 5. To the golden-hued ones, Hail! || 6. To the small ones, Hail! || 7. To those composed in strophes, Hail! || 8. To the first shells, Hail! || 9. To the second shells, Hail! || 10. To the third shells, Hail! || 11. To the penultimates, Hail. || 12. To the last ones, Hail! || 13. To the latter ones, Hail! || 14. To the Ṛishis, Hail! || 15. To those with hair in tufts, Hail! || 16. To the Gaṇas, Hail! || 17. To the great Gaṇas, Hail! || 18. To all the Vidagaṇa Aṅgirasas, Hail! || 19. To those two with separate thousands, Hail! || 20. To Brahma, Hail! || 21. Collected manly powers are topped by Brahma. Brahma at first spread out the loftiest heaven. | Brahma was born first of all things existing. Who then is meet to be that Brahma's rival?

Hymn 19:23.

1. Hail to the four-verse strophes of the Ātharvaṇas! || 2. Hail to the five-versed! || 3. Hail to the six-versed! || 4. Hail to the seven-versed! || 5. Hail to the eight-versed! || 6. Hail to the nine-versed! || 7. Hail to the ten-versed! || 8. Hail to the eleven-versed! || 9. Hail to the twelve-versed! || 10. Hail to the thirteen-versed || 11. Hail to the fourteen-versed! || 12. Hail to the fifteen-versed! || 13. Hail to the sixteen-versed! || 14. Hail to the seventeen-versed! || 15. Hail to the eighteen-versed! || 16. Hail, nineteen! || 17. Hail, twenty! || 18. Hail to the Great Section! || 19. Hail to the triplets! || 20. Hail to the single-versed hymns! || 21. Hail to the little ones! || 22. Hail to the single non-Ṛich-versed ones! || 23. Hail to the Rohitas! || 24. Hail to the two Sūrya hymns! || 25. Hail to the two Vrātya hymns! || 26. Hail to the two Prajāpati hymns! || 27. Hail to the hymn of victory! || 28. Hail to the hymns for happiness! || 29. Hail to Brahma! || 30. Collected manly powers are topped by Brahma. Brahma at first spread out the loftiest heaven. | Brahma was born first of all things existing. Who then is fit to be this Brahma's rival?

Hymn 19:24.

1. Do ye, O Brahmaṇaspati, invest for the royal sway this man. | With that wherewith the Deities invested Savitar the God. || 2. Invest this Indra for long life, invest him for great princely power, | That I may lead him on to eld, that the man watch his princedom long. || 3. Invest this Soma for long life, invest him for great hearing power. | That I may lead him on to eld, that he may watch o'er hearing long. || 4. For us, surround him, cover him with splendour, give him long life, and death when age removes him. | This garment hath Bṛihaspati presented to Soma, to the King, to wrap about him. || 5. Advance to good old age: endue the mantle. Be thou our heifers' guard from imprecation. | Live thou a hundred full and plenteous autumns, and wrap thee in prosperity of riches. || 6. Thou for weal hast clothed thee in this garment: thou hast become our cows' sure guard from curses. | Live thou a hundred full and plenteous autumns: then living, fair thyself, shalt deal forth treasures. || 7. In every need, in every fray we call, as friends, to succour us, Indra the mightiest of all. || 8. Gold-coloured, undecaying, blest with heroes, dwell, dying in old age, with children round thee. | This is the spoken word of Agni, Soma, Bṛihaspati and Savitar, and Indra.

Hymn 19:25.

1. I yoke thee with the mind of one unwearied still and first of all. | Be thou a bearer up the hill: run hither bearing up thy load.

Hymn 19:26.

1. Gold that was born from Fire is immortal hath been deposited with mortal creatures. | He who knows this deserves to own this jewel, and in extreme old age dies he who wears it. || 2. The men of ancient time with children round them longed for this Gold, bright with the Sun's own colour, | This shall endow thee, as it shines, with splendour, and long shall be the life of him who wears it. || 3. Long life and splendour let it bring energy and strength to thee. | That thou mayst shine among the folk with all the brightness of the Gold. || 4. What Varuṇa the King knows well, and what the God Bṛihaspati, | And Indra, Slayer of the Foe, may that bestow long life on thee, may that increase thy splendid strength.

Hymn 19:27.

1. Let the Bull guard thee with the kine, the Stallion with the fleet-foot steeds. | Let Vāyu keep thee safe with prayer, and Indra with his mighty power. || 2. Let Soma guard thee with the plants, Sūrya protect thee with the stars; | With breath let Wind protect thee, and the Moon, foe-slayer, with the months. || 3. Three are the earths, they say, and three the heavens, three are the atmospheres, and four the oceans. | Threefold the hymn of praise, threefold the Waters. Let these with triple song and triplets guard thee. || 4. Three vaults of heaven, and three seas, three bright, three stationary ones, | Three Mātariśvans, and three suns, protectors, I arrange for thee. || 5. Increasing thee with butter I, Agni! with fatness sprinkle thee. | Let not magicians harm the life of Agni or of Moon or Sun. || 6. Let not magicians mar your heat, your vital or diffusive breath. | Brilliant and all-possessing Gods, run ye your course with God-like power. || 7. Fire they endow with vital breath, Wind is compact, with vital breath: | With vital breath the Gods produced the Sun whose face turn every way. || 8. Live with the Life-Creators' life. Die not, live on to lengthened age. | Live with the breath of men with souls. Submit not to the power of Death. || 9. The secret treasure of the Gods which Indra, by pathways travelled by the Gods, discovered, | That gold the Waters with the triplets guarded. May they keep thee with threefold hymn and triplets. || 10. With friendly thoughts the Deities, three-and thirty, and three great Powers preserved it in the Waters. | He made heroic powers with the gold that lies upon this Moon. || 11. O ye eleven Gods who are in heaven, accept this sacrifice. || 12. O ye eleven Gods who are in air, accept this sacrifice. || 13. O ye eleven Gods who are on earth, accept this sacrifice. || 14-15. repeated from 19:16. 1., 2.

Hymn 19:28.

1. On thee I bind this Amulet for lengthened life and brilliancy. | The rival-quelling Darbha grass that burns the spirit of a foe. || 2. Burning the spirit of the foe, vexing the heart of enemies. | Darbha, on every side, like heat, inflame all evil-hearted men. || 3. O Darbha, burning round like heat, consuming foes, O Amulet, | Like Indra rending Vala cleave mine adversaries' hearts in twain. || 4. Cleave through. O Darbha, Amulet, my foes,' mine adversaries' heart. | Rise thou and batter down their heads like growth that covereth the earth. || 5. Cleave thou my rivals, Darbha, cleave the men who fain would, fight with me. | Cleave all who wish me evil, cleave the men who hate me, Amulet! || 6. Wound thou, my rivals, Darbha, etc. (as in 5, substituting. 'wound' for cleave.) || 7. Tear thou my rivals, Darbha, etc. || 8. How thou my rivals, Darbha, etc. || 9. Carve thou my rivals, Darbha, etc. || 10. Pierce thou my rivals, Darbha, pierce the men who fain would fight with me. | Pierce those who wish me evil, pierce the men who hate me, Amulet!

Hymn 19:29.

1. Pierce thou my rivals, Darbha, pierce the men who fain would fight with me. | Pierce all who wish me evil, pierce the men who hate me, Amulet! || 2. Split thou my rivals, Darbha, etc. (as in 1, with 'split' for 'pierce' throughout). || 3. Check thou, etc. || 4. Crush thou, etc. || 5. Shake thou, etc. || 6. Bruise thou, etc. || 7. Burn thou, etc. || 8. Consume, etc. || 9. Slay thou my rivals. Darbha, slay the men who fain would fight with me. | Slay all who wish me evil, slay the men who hate me, Amulet.

Hymn 19:30.

1. Darbha, with that good shield of thine, of hundred guards tilt death in eld, | Arm thou this man, and with thy might strike thou his adversaries down. || 2. Darbha, thou hast a hundred shields, thou hast a thousand. manly powers. | All Gods have given thee to him to bear thee till extreme old age. || 3. They call thee, Darbha, shield of Gods, they call the Brahmaṇaspati. | They call thee shield of Indra: thou protectest kingdoms from attack. || 4. Darbha, destroyer of the foe, vexing the hearts of enemies, | An Amulet that strengthens rule I make thee, and the body's. guard. || 5. What time Parjanya roared to it with lightning flashes in the sea, | Thence came the drop, the golden drop, thence Darbha into being sprang.

Hymn 19:31.

1. Savitar make all cattle grow and prosper in my stable with. | Amulet of Udumbara, helper of him who longs for wealth! || 2. May he who was our Household Fire, the ruler of our cattle, strong. | Amulet of Udumbara endow us with prosperity. || 3. By power of the Udumbara Charm may Dhātar give me plenty, rich. | In the kine's droppings and in fruit, and, in our dwelling, food, and drink. || 4. I win great plenty, while I wear the Amulet of Udumbara. | Of quadrupeds and bipeds, of juices and food of every sort. || 5. I have obtained abundant wealth of cattle, bipeds and quadrupeds, and corn in plenty. | Savitar and Bṛihaspati vouchsafe me the milk of kine and herbs' refreshing juices! || 6. Fain would I be the lord of herds of cattle: may he who rules o'er riches send me riches! | May the Udumbara Amulet vouchsafe possessions unto me. || 7. To me with wealth and children come the Amulet of Udumbara. | With splendour come the Amulet hastened by Indra on its way! || 8. Divine, foe-quelling Amulet, wealth-winner for the gain of wealth— | May it give store of beasts and food and cause our kine to multiply. || 9. As thou, O Forest Tree, wast born with increase when thy life began, | So let Sarasvatī bestow abundant growth of wealth on me. || 10. Sarasvatī vouchsafe me wealth, household prosperity, and corn! | Let Sinīvālī bring them, and this Amulet of Udumbara. || 11. The Lord of amulets art thou, most mighty: in thee wealth's ruler hath engendered riches, | These gains are lodged in thee, and all great treasures. Amulet, conquer thou: far from us banish malignity and indigence, and hunger. || 12. Vigour art thou, in me do thou plant vigour: riches art thou, so do thou grant me riches. | Plenty art thou, so prosper me with plenty: House-holder, hear a householder's petition. || 13. Amulet of Udumbara, enrich us: vouchsafe us wealth with all good men about us. I bind thee on for increase of possessions. || 14. For hero is this hero bound, Amulet of Udumbara. | So may he make our offering sweetly-savoured, and grant us wealth with all good men about us.

Hymn 19:32.

1. For lengthened life I bind on thee the Darbha grass, the mighty plant. | Excellent, hard to overthrow, with hundred stems and thousand blades. || 2. They cut not off his hair, they strike blow upon the breast for him. | To whom one gives protection by Darbha that hath uninjured leaves. || 3. O Plant, thy root is in the sky, and thou art stationed on the earth: | With thee who hast a thousand stalks we strengthen all the powers of life. || 4. Through all three skies the plant hath pierced, and the three regions of the earth; | With thee I split in twain the tongue and words of the bad-hearted man. || 5. Thou art victorious in thy might I am endowed with conquering strength: | Possessed of overpowering force we two will quell our enemies. || 6. Subdue our foeman, overcome the men who fain would fight: with us. | Conquer all evil-hearted ones: make many well-disposed to me. || 7. With Darbha that hath sprung from Gods, stationed in heaven, full many a time. | With this have I won many men, have won and may I win them still. || 8. Do thou, O Darbha, make me dear to Brahman and Rājanya, dear to Śūdra, and to Ārya dear, | Yea, dear to every man we love, to every man with eyes to see. || 9. He who first born fixed earth in her position, he who established heaven and air's mid-region, | Whom sinner ne'er hath known as his supporter,—this Darbha be our shelter and protection! || 10. First of all plants it sprang into existence, victorious, hundred-stemmed, the foe-subduer, | So may this Darbha from all sides protect us: with this may I subdue our foes in battle.

Hymn 19:33.

1. Hundred stemmed, succulent, and worth a thousand, the Royal Rite of plants, the Water's Agni, | Let this same Darbha guard us from all quarters. This Godlike Amulet shall with life endow us. || 2. Drawn forth from

butter, juicy, sweetly-flavoured, firm as the earth, unshaken, overthrowing. | Driving off foes and casting them beneath me, mount with the strength of mighty Ones, O Darbha. || 3. Thou movest o'er the earth with vigour: lovely in sacrifice thou sittest on the altar. | The Ṛiṣhis bear thee as a purifier: cleanse thou us from all evil deeds' defilement. || 4. A stern and all-victorious king, foe-queller, dear to every man— | That energy of Gods and mighty power, I bind this on thee for long life and welfare. || 5. Achieve heroic deeds with Darbha, wearing this Darbha never let thy soul be troubled. | In splendour and precedence over others illumine like the Sun the heaven's four regions.

Hymn 19:34.

1. Jaṅgiḍa, thou art Aṅgiras: thou art a guardian, Jaṅgiḍa | Let Jaṅgiḍa, keep safely all our bipeds and our quadrupeds. || 2. Dice-witcheries, the fifty-threes, the hundred witchcraft-practisers, | All these may Jaṅgiḍa make weak, bereft of their effectual force. || 3. Baffle the loud factitious howl, make impotent the seven decays. | As when an archer speeds the shaft, drive away want, O Jaṅgiḍa, || 4. This counteracts the sorceress, this banishes malignity: | Then may victorious Jaṅgiḍa's prolong the days we have to live. || 5. Let Jaṅgiḍa's protecting might encompass us on every side. | Wherewith he quells Viṣhkandha and Saṃskandha, might by greater might. || 6. Three times the Gods engendered thee fixt on the surface of the earth; | The Brahmans of the olden time knew that thy name was Aṅgiras; || 7. The ancient plants surpass thee not, nor any herbs of recent days. | A potent charm is Jaṅgiḍa, a most felicitous defence. || 8. Then when thou sprangest into life, Jaṅgiḍa of unmeasured strength, | Indra, O mighty One, bestowed great power upon thee from the first. || 9. To thee in truth, O Forest Tree, Indra the mighty One gave strength. | Driving away all maladies, strike thou the demons down, O Plant. || 10. Lumbago and rheumatic pain, consumptive cough, and pleurisy, | And fever which each Autumn brings, may Jaṅgiḍa make powerless.

Hymn 19:35.

1. While their lips uttered Indra's name the Ṛiṣhis gave us Jaṅgiḍa. | Which in the earliest time Gods made a remedy, Viṣhkandha's cure. || 2. So may this Jaṅgiḍa guard us, even as a treasurer guards wealth, | Even this which Gods and Brahmans made a malice-quelling sure defence. || 3. Hard-hearted men, the cruel eye, the sinner who hath come to-us, | Destroy thou these with watchful care, O thou who hast a. thousand eyes. Thou, Jaṅgiḍa, art my defence. || 4. Guard me from earth and guard me from the heavens, guard me from middle air, from plants protect me. | Protect me from the present and the future. From every region Jaṅgiḍa preserve us! || 5. All sorcerers made by the Gods, all that arise from mortal men, | These, one and all, let Jaṅgiḍa, healer of all, make impotent.

Hymn 19:36.

1. The Hundred-haired hath banished hence fiends and Consumptions by its might. | With splendour hath the charm that scares demons of ill-name mounted up. || 2. It drives off demons with its horns and sorceresses with its root, | It stays Consumption with its waist: from this no wickedness escapes. || 3. Consumptions, light and serious, and those which sounds accompany, | All these the Amulet, Hundred-haired, scarer of fiends, hath banished hence. || 4. A hundred men hath it produced, hundred Consumptions chased away, | All fiends of evil-name it hath smitten, and shakes the Rākṣhasas || 5. The Bull that weareth horns of gold, this Amulet with hundred hairs, | Hath cleft the demons of ill-name and overcome the Rākṣhasas || 6. Hundred she-fiends, a hundred of Gandharvas and Apsarases, | A hundred of dog-mated nymphs, I keep away with Hundred-Hair

Hymn 19:37.

1. To me hath come this word given by Agni, fame, force and might, and strength, and life, and lustre. | May Agni too bestow on me three-times a hundred manly powers. || 2. For mighty strength, for action, I receive thee, for manly power, to last a hundred autumns. || 3. For conquering strength and energy and vigour | I fasten thee for chieftainship, for bearing royal dominion through a hundred autumns. || 4. With Seasons and with Season-groups, for vigour and extended life. | With splendour of the perfect year we fasten thee about the neck.

Hymn 19:38.

1. Never Consumption, never curse touches the man, Arundhatī! | Whom the delicious odour of the healing bdellium penetrates || 2. Consumptions flee apart from it as from a wild beast fly the deer. | If thou, O bdellium, art produced from Sindhu or hast come from sea, | The quality of both have I taken to keep this man unscathed.

Hymn 19:39.

1. Let Kuṣhṭha from the Hill of Snow come, a divine deliverer. | Banish thou all Consumption, drive all sorceresses far away. || 2. Kuṣhṭha, three several names hast thou, Naghamāra, Naghāriṣha: let not mishap befall this man, | For whom I make a charm of thee at eve, at morning, and by day. || 3. Jīvalā is thy mother's name, thy father's name is Jīvalā; let not mishap, etc. || 4. Thou art the best amid the plants, even as the ox is best of tame, the tiger of rapacious beasts: let not mishap, etc. || 5. Born thrice from the Ādityas, thrice from Bhṛigus, thrice from Aṅgiras' sons, born from the Viśvedevas thrice, | Healer of every malady, that Kuṣhṭha stands by Soma's side. | Banish thou all Consumption, drive all sorceresses far away. || 6. In the third heaven above us stands the Aśvattha tree, the seat of Gods: | There is embodiment of life that dies not: thence was Kuṣhṭha born. || 7. There moved through heaven a golden ship, a ship with cordage wrought of gold: | There is embodiment of life that dies not; thence was Kuṣhṭha born. || 8. Where is the Sinking of the Ship, the summit of the Hill of Snow, | There is embodiment of life that dies not: thence was Kuṣhṭha born. | Healer of every malady, that Kuṣhṭha stands by Soma's side. | Banish thou all Consumption, drive all sorceresses far away. || 9. Thou whom Ikṣhvāku's ancestor, whom he who well-loved Kuṣhṭha, knew, | Whom Vāyasa and Mātsya knew, hence healer of all ills art thou. || 10. O thou who hast all-reaching might drive away Fever, drive it down, | Head racking Fever, tertian, continual, lasting for a year.

Hymn 19:40.

1. For each defect of mine in voice and spirit I have approached One vehement and ardent. | With all the Deities, fully approving, Bṛihaspati supply the want! || 2. Disturb ye not our intellect, O Waters, nor the power of prayer. | Glide on your way, strength-giving, invocated: may I be vigorous and wise. || 3. Mar not our consecrating rite, our intellect, or fervent zeal. | Gracious to us for lengthened life, propitious let the Mothers be. || 4. Vouchsafe to us, ye Aśvins twain, such strength as, with attendant light, | May through the darkness carry us.

Hymn 19:41.

1. Desiring bliss, at first, light-finding Ṛiṣhis began religious rite and holy fervour. | Thence energy was born, and might, and kingship: so to this man let gathered Gods incline them.

Hymn 19:42.

1. Brahma is Hotar, sacrifice: with Brahma are the stakes set up. | From Brahma was the Adhvaryu born, from Brahma hidden offering. || 2. Brahma is fatness-dropping scoops: with Brahma was the altar reared. | Brahma is worship, lengthened rite, the Ṛiṣhis who pay sacrifice, the victim's Immolators. Hail! || 3. To him who frees from woe mine hymn I offer, to the Good Guardian, as I seek his favour. | Accept this offering of mine, O Indra. Fulfilled be all the sacrificer's wishes! || 4. With prayer I call on him who frees from trouble, Prince of Gods, Splendid, chief of sacrifices, | I call the Waters' Child and both the Aśvins, Vigour is mine, and strength bestowed by Indra.

Hymn 19:43.

1. Whither men versed in Brahma go, with fervour and the cleansing rite, | Thither let Agni lead me, let Agni give me intelligence, All hail to Agni! || 2. Whither etc. | Thither let Vāyu lead me, let Vāyu vouchsafe me vital breath. All hail to Vāyu! || 3. Whither, etc. | Thither let Sūrya lead me, let Sūrya vouchsafe me power of sight. All hail to Sūrya || 4. Whither, etc. | Thither let Chandrā lead me, let Chandrā vouchsafe me intellect. All hail to Chandrā! || 5. Whither, etc. | Thither let Soma lead me, let Soma vouchsafe me vital sap. All hail to Soma! || 6. Whither, etc. | Thither let Indra lead me, let Indra bestow upon me power. All hail to Indra! || 7. Whither, etc. | Thither, let Waters lead me, let the Waters give me deathless life. All hail to Waters! || 8. Whither, etc. | Thither let Brahma lead me, let Brahma give Brahma unto me. All hail to Brahma!

Hymn 19:44.

1. Thou art the lengthening of life, thy name is Universal Cure: | Then, Ointment! send felicity; Waters, send happiness and peace. || 2. The yellow hue, the feverish heat, the shooting pain that rends the limbs, | All the consumptive malady let the Ointment drive from out thy frame. || 3. Let the Salve born upon the earth, benignant, giving life to man. | Make the swift rider on the car sinless, exempt from sudden death. || 4. Preserve our breath, O Vital Breath, have mercy on our life, O Life. | From snares of Nirṛiti do thou, O Nirṛiti, deliver us. || 5. Thou art the babe of Sindhu, thou art lightnings' flower, wind, breath, and Sun: thou art the eye and milk of heaven. || 6. Gods' Ointment from the Three Peaked Hill, preserve thou me on every side. | No plants of earth surpass thee, none from mountain or from cultured ground. || 7. Now hath it gently crept within, fiend-slaying, chasing malady. | And driving all diseases hence, and evil omens, banished them. || 8. Full many a falsehood, O thou King Varuṇa, man hath uttered here: | Do thou who hast a thousand powers preserve us from that misery. || 9. If we have cried, O Waters! Cows! if we have cried, O Varuṇa! | For this endowed with thousand powers! deliver us from misery. || 10. Mitra and Varuṇa, O Salve have closely followed after thee | May they, when they have followed thee afar, restore thee for our use.

Hymn 19:45.

1. As debt from debt repay and send sorcery to the sorcerer's house. | Split, Salve! the cruel villain's ribs whose evil eye bewitches us. || 2. Whatever evil dream we have, what'er befall our kine or home, | Be this that is salubrity, the evil-hearted's foe applied. || 3. Increasing from the Waters' strength and vigour, sprung into life from Agni Jātavedas, | Strong as four heroes, mountain born, this Ointment make for thee quarters and mind-points auspicious! || 4. On thee is laid the Chaturvīra Ointment: let all the regions give thee peace and safety. | Secure like precious Savitar thou standest: to thee let all these regions bring their tribute. || 5. Make one thy salve, thine amulet another, drink one, and with another bathe thy body. | So let the Chaturvīra keep us guarded from the four bonds of Nirṛiti and Grāhi. || 6. May Agni protect me with fire for inspiration and expiration, for strength, for energy, for vigour, for weal and prosperity. All Hail! || 7. May Indra protect me with his Indra-power for inspiration, etc. || 8. May Soma protect me with Soma-power, etc. || 9. May Bhaga with good fortune protect me, etc. || 10. May the Marutas protect me with their troops for inspiration and expiration, for strength, for energy, for vigour, for weal and prosperity. All Hail!

Hymn 19:46.

1. For manly strength Prajāpati bound thee on first, invincible. | This for long life on thee I bind for splendour, strength, and energy. Invincible, let it guard thee well. || 2. Erect, invincible, be this man's watchful keeper: let not the Paṇis or the sorcerers harm thee. | Shake off thy foes as Indra scattered Dasyus: quell all enemies. Invincible, let it guard thee well. || 3. Indra hath lent the power of sight, and vital breath and strength to this. | Whom even a hundred combatants, striking, have failed to over-come. Invincible, let it guard thee well. || 4. Around thy limbs I place the mail of Indra who hath become the Gods' imperial Sovereign. | Again let all the Deities bring thee hither. Invincible let it guard thee well. || 5. One and a hundred manly powers, a thousand lives hath this Amulet, unconquered ever. | Go forth a tiger, strike down all thy foemen: let him who would oppose fall low beneath thee. Invincible, let it guard thee well. || 6. Drawn forth from butter, rich in milk and sweetness, hundred-lived, thousand-homed, bestowing vigour, | Kindly, delightsome, full of sap, and mighty, invincible let it guard thee well. || 7. That thou mayst be pre-eminent, slayer of rivals, rivalless, | May Savitar cause thee to be chief and controller of thy kin. Invincible, let it guard thee well.

Hymn 19:47.

1. Night! the terrestrial realm hath been filled with the Father's power and might. | Thou spreadest forth on high unto the seats of Heaven: darkness that strikes with awe comes near. || 2. Each moving thing finds rest in her whose yonder boundary is not seen, nor that which keeps her separate. | O spacious, darksome Night, may we uninjured reach the end of thee, reach, O thou blessed One, thine end. || 3. Thy ninety-nine examiners, O Night, who look upon mankind, | Eighty-and-eight in number, or seven-and-seventy are they. || 4. Sixty-and-six, O opulent, fifty-and-five, O happy One, | Forty-and-four and thirty-three are they, O thou enriched with spoil. || 5. Twenty-and-two hast thou, O Night, eleven, yea, and fewer still. | With these protectors guard us well. O Daughter of the Sky, today. || 6. Let not a fiends or spiteful man, let no ill-wisher master us. | Let not the robber seize our cows, nor the wolf take our sheep today. || 7. Let not the thief, O Blessed, seize our horses, nor she-fiends our men. | Let thief and robber run away on pathways most remote from us. || 8. Far from us let Rope with Fangs, far from us let the wicked flee. | Do thou make blind and headless. Night, the serpent with his pungent breath. || 9. Crush the wolf's jaws in pieces, strike the robber dead against a post. | In thee, O Night, do we abide: we here will sleep. Be watchful thou. || 10. Give thou protection to our kine; and to our horses, and our men.

Hymn 19:48.

1. Then all that we accumulate, all that the treasure-chest contains, | All this do we entrust to thee. || 2. Entrust thou us to Dawn, O Mother Night. | May Dawn entrust us to the Day, and Day to thee, O splendid One. || 3. Whatever flying thing be here, whatever thing that creeps and. crawls. | Whatever fastens on a joint, therefrom do thou protect us, Night. || 4. So guard thou us from west and east, protect us from the north and south. | O splendid One, preserve us: we, the singers of thy praise, are here. || 5. They who are followers of Night, and they who watch o'er living things. | They who protect all cattle, they keep watch and ward over our lives, over our herds keep watch and ward. || 6. Verily, Night, I know thy name, Dropper of Fatness art thou called. | Thee Bharadvāja knew as such: as such be watchful o'er our wealth.

Hymn 19:49.

1. Friend of the home, the strong and youthful maiden, Night, dear to Savitar the God, and Bhaga, | All-compassing, all-glorious, prompt to listen, hath with her greatness filled the earth and heaven. || 2. Over all depths hath she gone up, and mounted, most mighty One, the sky's exalted summit. | Over me now the loving Night is spreading with her auspicious. Godlike ways like Mitra. || 3. Excellent, high-born, blissful, meet for worship, Night, thou hast come: stay here with friendly spirit. | Guard us, the food for men that we have gotten, and all prosperity that comes of cattle. || 4. With eager haste hath Night assumed the vigour of leopard, tiger, or of tawny lion, | The horse's neighing and the wild-man's bellow, Thou takest many a form when thou appearest. || 5. Kind through the Night be absence of the sunshine: Mother of Frost, may she be swift to hear us. | Take notice of the hymn, thou highly favoured, wherewith I worship thee in all the regions. || 6. Even as a King, O splendid Night, thou takest pleasure in our hymn. | May we through Mornings as they flush have all our good men, round us, and become possessors of all wealth. || 7. Yes, Śamyā is the name thou hast assumed. The men who fain. would spoil. | My wealth do thou annoy, O Night, that not one robber may appear, none may a second time appear. || 8. Thou like a well-wrought cup, O Night, art lovely: thou, a young maid, art formed in perfect beauty. | Thou lovingly, for me with eyes to see them, hast bound on thee heaven's stars as thine adornment. || 9. Whatever robber comes today, mischievous mortal enemy. | Let Night go forth, encounter him, and smite away his neck and head; || 10. His feet that he may walk no more, his hands that he may do no harm. | The robber who comes hitherward goes crushed and mutilated hence, | Goes hence, goes far away from us, goes hence and bears no spoil away.

Hymn 19:50.

1. Blind him and make him headless, Night! the serpent with the pungent breath. | Strike from his head the wolf's two eyes, and dash the thief against a post. || 2. Those oxen that are thine, O Night, with sharpened horns and rapid pace, | With those transport us safe today o'er difficulties everywhere. || 3. Uninjured in our bodies may we pass through each succeeding night, | And let malignities fail to pass, as men without a boat the depth. || 4. As millet hurried through the air before us is beheld no more. | So cause the man to vanish, Night, who plans to do us injury. || 5. The thief hast thou kept far away, the robber driver of our kine. | Even him who having covered up the horse's head would lead him off. || 6. If dealing treasure thou hast come today, O highly favoured Night. | Cause thou us to enjoy it all so that this may not pass away. || 7. Do thou entrust us to the Dawn, all of us free from sin, O Night. | May Dawn deliver us to

Day, and Day to thee, O glorious One.

Hymn 19:51.

1. Undisturbed am I, undisturbed is my soul, undisturbed mine eye, undisturbed mine ear, undisturbed is mine in-breathing, undisturbed mine out-breathing, undisturbed my diffusive-breath, undisturbed the whole of me. || 2. Under the impulse of the God Savitar, sent forth from the arms-of the Aśvins and both hands of Pūṣhan I have taken thee.

Hymn 19:52.

1. Thereafter rose Desire in the beginning, Desire the primal seed and germ of Spirit. | O Kāma dwelling with the lofty Kāma, give growth of riches to the sacrificer. || 2. Thou, Kāma, art victorious, famous, potent, splendid, a friend. to him who seeks thy friendship. | Mighty and overpowering in battle, give strength and vigour to the sacrificer. || 3. They heard his prayers, and they begot, by Kāma, heavenly-light for him. | Who from a distance longed for it, a dealer ready to exchange. || 4. O Kāma, with whatever wish we make this offering to thee, | May it be all fulfilled to us. Then taste this sacrifice, All hail!

Hymn 19:53.

1. Prolific, thousand-eyed, and undecaying, a horse with seven reins Time bears us onward. | Sages inspired with holy knowledge mount him: his chariot wheels are all the worlds of creatures. || 2. This Time hath seven rolling wheels and seven naves immorality is the chariot's axle. | This Time brings hitherward all worlds about us: as primal Deity is he entreated. || 3. On Time is laid an overflowing beaker: this we behold in many a place appearing. | He carries from us all these worlds of creatures. They call him Kāla in the loftiest heaven. || 4. He only made the worlds of life, he only gathered the worlds of living things together. | Their son did he become who was their Father: no other higher power than he existeth. || 5. Kāla created yonder heaven, and Kāla made these realms of earth. | By Kāla, stirred to motion, both what is and what shall be expand. || 6. Kāla created land; the Sun in Kāla hath his light and heat. | In Kāla rest all things that be: in Kāla doth the eye discern. || 7. In Kāla mind, in Kāla breath, in Kāla name are fixt and joined. | These living creatures, one and all, rejoice when Kāla hath approached. || 8. Kāla embraces Holy Fire, the Highest, Brahma in himself. | Yea, Kāla, who was father of Prajāpati, is Lord of All. || 9. He made, he stirred this universe to motion, and on him it rests. | He, Kāla, having now become Brahma, holds Parameṣhṭhin up. || 10. Kāla created living things and, first of all, Prajāpati. | From Kāla self-made Kaśyapa, from Kāla Holy Fire was born.

Hymn 19:54.

1. From Kāla sprang the Waters, sprang the regions, Brahma, Holy Fire. | The Sun ascends by Kāla, and in Kāla sinks again to rest. || 2. By Kāla freshly blows the wind, mighty through Kāla is the Earth: on Kāla rests the mighty Sky. || 3. In Kāla erst the text produced what is and what is yet to be. | From Kāla sprang the Ṛichas, and from Kāla was the Yajus born. || 4. They formed in Kāla sacrifice, eternal portion for the Gods. | In Kāla the Gandharvas and Apsarases and worlds abide. || 5. Atharvan and this Aṅgiras in Kāla are supreme o'er heaven. | Both this world and the world that is most lofty, the pure worlds and pure intermediate spaces,— || 6. Yea, having conquered all the worlds by Brahma, Kāla as God Supreme is supplicated.

Hymn 19:55.

1. Bringing, as 'twere, with care unceasing fodder night after night to feed this stabled Courser, | Joying in food and in the growth of riches, may we thy neighbours, Agni, ne'er be injured. || 2. Here is thine own desire for wealth: through this be gracious unto us. | Joying in food and in the growth of riches, may we thy neighbours, Agni, ne'er be injured. || 3. Each eve that comes our household's Lord is Agni, showing his. loving-kindness every morning. | Bestow upon us treasure after treasure: enkindling thee may we increase thy body. || 4. Each morn that comes our household's Lord is Agni, showing. his loving-kindness every evening. | Vouchsafe us treasure after treasure: kindling thee may we prosper through a hundred winters. || 5. Never may I come short of food to feed me. | Glory to Agni, Rudra, the consumer and the Lord of food! || 6. Protect my company, protect its courteous members, courteous God! | Only through thee, O much-invoked, may I be ever rich in kine. || 7. Only to thee bringing our tribute, Agni, each day as fodder to a stabled courser, | Joying in food and in the growth of riches, may we the neighbours, Agni ne'er be injured.

Hymn 19:56.

1. Thou art come hither from the world of Yama: thou, resolute, affectest men with rapture. | Thou, Sleep, created in the Asura's dwelling, goest, well-knowing, with the solitary. || 2. At first the all-containing, depth beheld thee, ere Night was born, when only Day existed. | Thence hast thou come, thence, Sleep, hast thou come hither, concealing, deep within, all form and figure. || 3. Come from the Asuras in lofty, glory, he hath approached the Gods in search of greatness. | Winners of heavenly light, the Three-and-Thirty endowed this Sleep with his supreme dominion. || 4. Of him nor Fathers nor the Gods have knowledge, the Gods whose gentle talk is still about him. | Urged by command of Varuṇa the Ādityas, Heroes, transported Sleep to Trita Āptya. || 5. Thou whose severity hath reached ill-doers, and whose reward the good have gained in slumber, | Delightest heaven with thy most lofty kinship, born from his spirit who was worn and weary. || 6. Of old we know all places whence thou comest. O Sleep, we know him who is here thy ruler. | Protect us here illustrious with glory. Go, from afar, with poisons, into distance.

Hymn 19:57.

1. As men discharge the utmost debt, collect the eighth and sixteenth part, | So to the foeman we transfer together all the evil dream. || 2. Princes came together, debts came together, Kuṣhṭhas came together, | Sixteenths came together. The whole evil dream that hath visited us we send away as a bad dream to the man who hates us. || 3. Child of Gods' Consorts, minister of Yama is the good Dream: that which is my trouble we drive away to the enemy. || 4. Thou whose name is Rough art the mouth of the Black Bird. | As such we know thee, Dream, as such we know thee well. Like a horse art thou, O Dream. As they bind girth and surcingle on a horse, so bind the alien mischief-maker, the scorner of the Gods. || 5. The evil dream that threatens us, threatens our cattle or our home. | That let the scorner of the Gods, the alien mischief-maker bind as a gold jewel round his neck. || 6. Having measured off nine cubits' distance from us we give away the whole of the evil dream to the man who hates us.

Hymn 19:58.

1. Still equal be the flow of butter ever causing the Year to prosper with oblation. | Still be our hearing, sight, and breath uninjured: let us lose nothing of our life and vigour. || 2. Let lively breath invite us: we call vital breath to visit us. | Earth and air's middle realm have gathered, Soma, Bṛihaspati and Dhartar gathered vigour. || 3. The earth and heaven have come to be two gatherers up of vigorous might. | So let us gather vigour up and closely follow after Earth. | With glory come the cows and stand beside the master of the herd. Let us when we have gathered fame and glory closely follow Earth. || 4. Prepare the cow-stall, for there drink your heroes: stitch ye the coats of armour wide and many. | Make iron forts defying all assailants: let not your pitcher leak; stay it securely. || 5. The eye of sacrifice, source and beginning with voice, car, spirit unto him I offer. | To this our sacrifice, wrought by Viśvakarman, may the Gods come gracious and kindly-hearted. || 6. Let the Gods' Priests and those who merit worship, to whom oblation as their share is offered, | Come to this holy service with their Consorts, and all Gods revel in the food we bring them.

Hymn 19:59.

1. God among mortals, Agni, thou art guard of holy Law, thou art | To be adored in sacred rites. || 2. When, ignorant, we violate the statutes of you, O Deities, with whom is knowledge, | Wise Agni shall correct our faults and failings, and Soma who hath entered into Brahmans. || 3. To the Gods' pathway have we come desiring to execute what work we may accomplish. | Let Agni—for he knows—complete the worship. He is the Priest: let him fix rites and seasons.

Hymn 19:60.

1. May I have voice in my mouth, breath in my nostrils, sight in mine eyes, hearing in mine ears, hair that hath not turned gray, teeth free from yellowness, and much strength in mine arms. || 2. May I have power in my thighs, swiftness in my legs, stedfastness in my feet. May all my members be uninjured and my soul unimpaired.

Hymn 19:61.

1. May my self remain in my body: may I enjoy the full time of life, | Rest thee pleasantly: pour forth abundance, purifying thyself in Svarga.

Hymn 19:62.

1. Make me beloved among the Gods, beloved among the Princes, make | Me dear to everyone who sees, to Śūdra and to Ārya man.

Hymn 19:63.

1. Rise up, O Brahmaṇaspati; awake the Gods with sacrifice. | Strengthen the Sacrificer: aid life, breath, and off-spring, cattle, fame.

Hymn 19:64.

1. For lofty Jātavedas I have brought the fuel hither first. | May he who knoweth all bestow faith and intelligence on me. || 2. With fuel and with flaming wood we, Jātavedas, strengthen thee; | So do thou strengthen us in turn with children and with store of wealth. || 3. Whatever even be the logs which, Agni, we lay down for thee, propitious be it all to me: accept it, O most youthful God. || 4. Agni, these logs are thine: with these be, fain to burn! a flaming brand. | Vouchsafe us length of life and give us hope of immortality.

Hymn 19:65.

1. A Golden Eagle thou hast soared with light to heaven. Those who would harm thee as thou fliest skyward. | Beat down, O Jātavedas, with thy fury. The strong hath feared: to heaven mount up with light, O Sūrya.

Hymn 19:66.

1. The Asuras with iron nets, magicians, who roam about with hooks and bonds of iron, | With wrath I make thy thralls, O Jātavedas. Come as a bolt foe-quelling, thousand pointed.

Hymn 19:67.

1. A hundred autumns may we see. || 2. A hundred autumns may we live. || 3. A hundred autumns may we know. || 4. A hundred autumns may we grow. || 5. A hundred autumns may we thrive. || 6. A hundred autumns may we be. || 7. A hundred autumns may we bide. || 8. A hundred, yea, and even more.

Hymn 19:68.

1. Both of broad and narrow I with magic power unclose the mouth. | With these when we have raised the bunch of grass we pay the holy rites.

Hymn 19:69.

1. Ye are alive. I fain would live. I fain would live my complete term of life. || 2. Ye live dependent. I fain would live dependent. I fain would live my complete term of life. || 3. Ye remain alive. I fain would remain alive. I fain would live my complete term of life. || 4. Ye are life-givers. I fain would live. I fain would live my complete term of life.

Hymn 19:70.

1. Live, Indra. Live Sūrya. Live, ye Gods. I fain would live. Fain would I live my complete term of life.

Hymn 19:71.

1. Let my libations, giving boons, adoring, further the Twice-born's song that honours Soma. | Go ye to Brahma's world having enriched me with life and breath, with children and with cattle, with fame and wealth, and with a Brahman's lustre.

Hymn 19:72.

1. Within the chest whence we before extracted the bunch of grass, this do we now deposit. | Wrought is the sacrifice by power of Brahma. Through this assist me here, ye God, with Fervour.

Kāṇḍa 20.

Hymn 20:1.

1. Thee, Indra, we invoke, the Bull, what time the Soma hath been pressed. | Drink of the sweetly-flavoured juice. || 2. The best of guardian hath the man within whose dwelling-place ye drink, | O Marutas, giants of the sky. || 3. Let us serve Agni with our hymns, Sage who consumeth ox and cow, | Who beareth Soma on his back.

Hymn 20:2.

1. Let the Marutas drink Trishṭubhs from the Potar's cup, according to the season Soma from heaven. || 2. Let Agni from the Kindler's cup drink Trishṭubhs, according to the season Soma from heaven. || 3. Let Indra the Brahman from the Brahman's cup drink Trishṭubhs, according to the season Soma from heaven. || 4. Let the God, Granter of Wealth, from the Potar's cup drink | Trishṭubhs, according to the season Soma from heaven.

Hymn 20:3.

1. Come, we have pressed the juice for thee: O Indra, drink this Soma here. | Seat thee on this my sacred grass. || 2. Let both thy bay steeds, yoked by prayer long-maned, O Indra, bring thee nigh. || 3. We Soma-bearing Brahmans call thee Soma-drinker with thy friend, | We, Indra, who have pressed the juice.

Hymn 20:4.

1. Come unto us who poured the juice, come hither to our eulogies. | Drink of the juice, O fair of face. || 2. I pour it down within thee, so through all thy members let it run. | Take with thy tongue the pleasant drink. || 3. Sweet to thy body let it be, delicious be the savoury juice. | Sweet be the Soma to thy heart.

Hymn 20:5.

1. Like women, let this Soma juice invested with its raiment, glide. | Most active Indra, close to thee. || 2. Mighty in bulk, strong-necked, stout-armed in the wild rapture. of the juice | Doth Indra smite the foemen dead. || 3. Indra, advance, go forward thou who by thy might art Lord of all. | Slay, Vṛitra-slayer slay thy foes. || 4. Long be thy grasping-hook wherewith thou givest treasure unto him | Who pours the juice and worships thee. || 5. Here, Indra, is thy Soma draught, made pure upon the sacred. grass. | Run hither, come and drink thereof. || 6. Famed for thy radiance, worshipped well! this juice is shed for thy delight: | Thou art invoked, Ākhaṇḍala! || 7. To Kuṇḍapāyya, grandson's son, grandson of Śṛiṅgavṛiṣh, to thee, | To him have I addressed my thought.

Hymn 20:6.

1. Thee, Indra, we invoke, the Bull, what time the Soma is expressed. | So drink thou of the savoury juice. || 2. Indra, whom many laud, accept the strength-conferring Soma juice. | Quaff, pour down drink that satisfies. || 3. Indra, with all the Gods promote our wealth-bestowing sacrifice, | Thou highly-lauded Lord of men. || 4. Lord of the brave, to thee proceed these drops of Soma juice expressed, | The bright drops to thy dwelling-place. || 5. Within thy belly, Indra take Soma the juice most excellent: | The heavenly drops belong to thee. || 6. Drink our libation, Lord of hymns: with streams of meath thou art bedewed: | Our glory, Indra, is thy gift. || 7. To Indra go the treasures of the worshipper which never fail: | He drinks the Soma and is strong. || 8. From far away, from near at hand, O Vṛitra-slayer, come to us: | Accept the songs we sing to thee.

Hymn 20:7.

1. Sūrya, thou mountest up to meet the Hero famous for his wealth, | Who hurls the bolt and works for man: || 2. Him who with might of both his arms brake nine-and ninety castles down, | Slew Vṛitra and smote Ahi dead. || 3. This Indra is our gracious Friend. He sends us in a full broad stream | Riches in horses, kine, and corn. || 4. Indra, whom many laud, accept the strength-conferring Soma juice. | Quaff, pour down drink that satisfies.

Hymn 20:8.

1. Drink as of old, and let the draught delight thee: hear thou my prayer and let our songs exalt thee. | Make the Sun visible, make food abundant: slaughter the foes, pierce through and free the cattle. || 2. Come to us; they have called thee Soma-lover. Here is the pressed juice: drink thereof for rapture. | Widely-capacious, pour it down within thee, and invocated hear us like a father. || 3. Full is his chalice. Blessing! Like a pourer I have filled up the vessel for his drinking. | Presented on the right, dear Soma juices have brought us Indra, to rejoice him, hither.

Hymn 20:9.

1. As cows low to their calves in stalls, so with our songs we glorify | This Indra, even your wondrous God who checks attack, who joys in the delicious juice. || 2. Celestial, bounteous Giver, girt about with might, rich, mountain-like, in precious things | Him swift we seek for foodful booty rich in kine, brought hundredfold and thousandfold. || 3. I crave of thee that hero strength, that thou mayst first regard this prayer, | Wherewith thou helpest Bhrigu and the Yatis and Praskaṇva when the prize was staked. || 4. Wherewith thou sentest mighty waters to the sea, that, Indra,

is. thy hero strength. | For ever unattainable is this power of him to whom the worlds. have called aloud.

Hymn 20:10.

1. These songs of ours exceeding sweet, these hymns of praise ascend to thee, | Like ever-conquering chariots that display their strength, gain wealth and give unfailing aid. || 2. The Bhṛigus are like suns, like Kaṇvas, and have gained all that their thoughts were bent to win. | The living men of Priyamedha's race have sung exalting Indra with their lauds.

Hymn 20:11.

1. Fort-render, Lord of Wealth, dispelling foemen, Indra with lightnings hath o'ercome the Dāsa. | Impelled by prayer and waxen great in body, he hath filled earth and heaven, the bounteous Giver. || 2. I stimulate this zeal, the Strong, the Hero, decking my song of praise for thee Immortal. | O Indra, thou art equally the leader of heavenly hosts and human generations. || 3. Leading his band Indra encompassed Vṛitra; weak grew the wily leader enchanters. | He who burns fierce in forests slaughtered Vyaṃsa, and made the milch-kine of nights apparent. || 4. Indra, light-winner, days' creator, conquered, as guardian, hostile bands with those who loved him. | For man the days' bright ensign he illumined, and found the light for his great joy and gladness. || 5. Forward to fiercely falling blows pressed Indra, hero-like doing many hero exploits. | Those holy songs he taught the bard who praised him, and widely spread these Dawns' resplendent colour. || 6. They laud the mighty acts of him the mighty, the many glorious deeds performed by Indra. | He in his strength, with all-surpassing prowess, through wondrous arts crushed the malignant Dasyus. || 7. Lord of the brave, Indra who rules the people gave freedom to the Gods by might and battle. | Wise singers glorify with chanted praises these his achievements in Vivasvat's dwelling. || 8. Excellent, conqueror, the victory-giver, the winner of the light and godlike waters, | He who hath won this broad earth and this heaven,—in Indra they rejoice who love devotions. || 9. He gained possession of the Sun and horses; Indra obtained the cow who feedeth many. | Treasure of gold he won; he smote the Dasyus and gave protection to the race of Āryas || 10. He took the plants and days for his possession; he gained the forest trees and air's mid-region. | Vala he cleft, and chased away opponents: thus was he tamer of the overweening. || 11. Call we on Maghavan, auspicious Indra, best Hero in the fight where spoil is gathered, | The Strong, who listens, who gives aid in battles, who slays the Vṛitras, wins and gathers treasures.

Hymn 20:12.

1. Prayers have been offered up through love of glory: Vasiṣhṭha, honour Indra in the battle. | He who with might extends through all existence hears words which I, his faithful servant, utter. || 2. A cry was raised which reached the Gods, O Indra, a cry to them to send us strength in combat. | None among men knows his own life's duration: bear us in safety over these our troubles. || 3. The Bays, the booty-seeking car I harness: my prayers have reached him who accepts them gladly. | Indra, when he had slain resistless Vṛitras, forced with his might the two world-halves asunder. || 4. Like barren cows, moreover, swelled the waters: the singers sought thy holy rite, O Indra. | Come unto us as with his team comes Vāyu: thou, through our solemn hymns, bestowest booty. || 5. So may these gladdening draughts rejoice thee, Indra, the Mighty, very bounteous to the singer. | Alone among the Gods thou pitiest mortals: O Hero, make thee glad at this libation. || 6. Thus the Vasiṣhṭhas glorify with praises Indra, the Mighty One, whose arm wields thunder. | Praised, may he guard our wealth in kine and heroes. Ye Gods, preserve us evermore with blessings. || 7. Impetuous, Thunderer, strong, quelling the mighty, King, potent, Vṛitra-slayer, Soma-drinker, | May he come hither with his yoked bay horses. May Indra glad-den him at noon libation.

Hymn 20:13.

1. Lords of great wealth, Bṛihaspati and Indra, rejoicing at this sacrifice drink Soma. | Let the abundant drops sink deep within you: vouchsafe us riches with full store of heroes. || 2. Let your swift-gliding coursers bear you hitherward with their fleet pinions. Come ye forward with your arms. | Sit on the grass; a wide seat hath been made for you: delight yourselves, O Marutas, in the pleasant food. || 3. For Jātavedas, worthy of our praise, will we frame with our mind this eulogy as 'twere a car. | For good in his assembly is this care of ours. Let us not in thy friendship, Agni, suffer harm. || 4. With these, borne on one car, Agni, approach us; or borne on many, for thy steeds are able. | Bring, with their Dames, the Gods, the Three-and-Thirty, after thy Godlike nature, and he joyful.

Hymn 20:14.

1. We call on thee, O peerless One. We, seeking help, possessing nothing firm ourselves, | Call on thee wonderful in fight. || 2. On thee for aid in sacrifice. This youth of ours, the bold, the mighty, hath gone forth. | We, therefore, we thy friends, Indra, have chosen thee, free-giver, as our guardian God. || 3. Him who of old hath brought to us this and that blessing, him I magnify for you, | Even Indra, O my friends, for help: || 4. Borne by bay steeds, the Lord of heroes, ruling men, for it is he who takes delight. | The Bounteous Lord bestows on us his worshippers hundreds of cattle and of steeds.

Hymn 20:15.

1. To him most liberal, lofty Lord of lofty wealth, verily powerful and strong, I bring my hymn, | Whose checkless bounty, as of waters down a slope, is spread abroad for all that live, to give them strength. || 2. Now all this world, for worship, shall come after thee—the offerer's libations like descending floods, | When the well-loved one seems to rest upon the hill, the thunderbolt of Indra, shatterer wrought of gold. || 3. To him the terrible, most worthy of high praise, like radiant Dawn, bring gifts with reverence in this rite, | Whose being, for renown, yea, Indra-power and light, have been created, like bay steeds, to move with speed. || 4. Thine, Indra, praised by many excellently rich! are we who trusting in thy help draw near to thee. | Lover of praise, none else but thou receives our laud: as Earth loves all her creatures, love thou this our hymn. || 5. Great is thy power, O Indra, we are thine. Fulfil, O Maghavan, the wish of this thy worshipper. | After thee lofty heaven hath measured out its strength to thee and to thy power this earth hath bowed itself. || 6. Thou, who hast thunder for thy weapon, with thy bolt hast shattered into pieces this broad massive cloud. | Thou hast sent down obstructed floods that they may flow: thou hast, thine own for ever, all victorious might.

Hymn 20:16.

1. Like birds who keep their watch, plashing in water, like the loud voices of the thundering rain-cloud, | Like merry streamlets bursting from the mountain thus to Bṛihaspati our hymns have sounded. || 2. The son of Aṅgiras, meeting the cattle, as Bhaga, brought in Aryaman among us. | As Friend of men he decks the wife and husband. As for the race, Bṛihaspati, nerve our coursers. || 3. Bṛihaspati, having won them from the mountains, strewed down, like barley out of winnowing-baskets, | The vigorous, wandering cows who aid the pious, desired of all, of blameless form, well-coloured. || 4. As the Sun dews with meath the seat of Order, and casts a flaming meteor down from heaven, | So from the rock Bṛihaspati forced the cattle, and cleft the earth's skin as it were with water. || 5. Forth from mid-air with light he drave the darkness, as the gale blows a lily from the river. | Like the wind grasping at the cloud of Vala, Bṛihaspati gathered to himself the cattle. || 6. Bṛihaspati, when he with fiery lightnings cleft through the weapon of reviling Vala, | Consumed him as tongues eat what teeth have compassed: he threw the prisons of the red cows open. || 7. That secret name borne by the lowing cattle within the cave Bṛihaspati discovered, | And drave, himself, the bright kine from the mountain, like a bird's young after the eggs' disclosure. || 8. He looked around on rock-imprisoned sweetness as one who eyes a fish in scanty water. | Bṛihaspati, cleaving through with varied clamour, brought it forth like a bowl from out the timber. || 9. He found the light of heaven, and fire, and Morning: with lucid rays he forced apart the darkness. | As from a joint, Bṛihaspati took the marrow of Vala as he gloried in his cattle. || 10. As trees for foliage robbed by winter, Vala mourned for the cows Bṛihaspati had taken. | He did a deed ne'er done, ne'er to be equalled, whereby the sun and moon ascend alternate. || 11. Like a dark steed adorned with pearl, the Fathers have decorated heaven with constellations. | They set the light in day, in night the darkness, Bṛihaspati cleft the rock and found the cattle. || 12. This homage have we offered to the Cloud-God who thunders out to many in succession. | May this Bṛihaspati vouchsafe us fullness of life with kine and horses, men, and heroes.

Hymn 20:17.

1. In perfect unison all yearning hymns of mine that find the light of heaven have sung forth Indra's praise. | As wives embrace their lord, the comely bridegroom, so they compass Maghavan about that he may help. || 2. Directed unto thee my spirit never strays, for I have set my hopes on thee, O much-invoked! | Sit, wonderful! as King upon the sacred grass, and let thy drinking-place be by the Soma juice. || 3. From indigence and hunger Indra turns away: Maghavan hath dominion over precious wealth. | These the Seven Rivers flowing on their downward path increase the vital vigour of the Mighty Steer. || 4. As on the fair-leafed tree rest birds, to Indra flow the gladdening Soma juices that the bowls contain. | Their face that glows with splendour through their mighty power hath found the shine of heaven for man, the Āryas' light. || 5. As in the game a gambler piles his winnings, so Maghavan, sweeping all together, gained the Sun. | This mighty deed of thine none other could achieve, none, Maghavan, before thee, none in recent time. || 6. Maghavan came by turns to all the tribes of men: the Steer took notice of the people's songs of praise. | The man in whose libations Śakra hath delight by means of potent Somas vanquisheth his foes. || 7. As waters flow together to the river, thus Somas to Indra flow, as rivulets to the lake. | In place of sacrifice sages exalt his might, as the rain swells the corn by moisture sent from heaven. || 8. He rushes through the region like a furious bull, he who hath made these floods the dames of worthy lords. | This Maghavan hath found light for the man who brings oblation, sheds the juice, and promptly pours his gifts. || 9. Let the keen axe come forth together with the light: here be, as erst, the teeming cow of sacrifice. | Let the Red God shine pure with his refulgent ray, and let the Lord of heroes glow like heaven's clear sheen. || 10. O much-invoked, may we subdue all famine and evil want with store of grain and cattle. | May we allied, as first in rank, with princes, obtain possessions by our own exertion. || 11. Bṛihaspati protect us from the rearward, and from above, and from below, from sinners. | May Indra from the front, and from the centre, as friend to friends, vouchsafe us room and freedom. || 12. Ye twain are Lords of wealth in earth and heaven, thou, O Bṛihaspati, and thou, O Indra. | Mean though he be, give wealth to him who lauds you. Preserve us evermore, ye Gods, with blessings.

Hymn 20:18.

1. This, even this, O Indra, we implore: as thy devoted friends, | The Kaṇvas praise thee with their hymns. || 2. Naught else, O Thunderer, have I praised in the skilled singer's eulogy: | On thy laud only have I thought. || 3. The Gods seek him who presses out the Soma; they desire not sleep: | Incessantly they punish sloth. || 4. Faithful to thee we loudly sing, heroic Indra, songs to thee. | Mark, gracious Lord, this act of ours. || 5. Give us not up to man's reproach, to foeman's hateful calumny: | In thee alone is all my strength. || 6. Thou art mine ample coat of mail, my champion, Vṛitra-slayer, thou. | With thee for Friend I brave the foe.

Hymn 20:19.

1. O Indra, for the strength that slays the foe and conquers in the fight | We turn thee hitherward to us. || 2. O Indra, Lord of Hundred Powers, may those who praise thee hitherward. | Direct thy spirit and thine eye. || 3. O Indra, Lord of Hundred Powers, with all our songs we invocate. | Thy names for triumph over foes. || 4. We strive for glory through the powers immense of him whom many praise, | Of Indra who supports mankind. || 5. For the foe's slaughter I address Indra whom many invocate, | To win us booty in the wars. || 6. In battles be victorious. We seek thee, Lord of Hundred Powers, | O Indra, that the foe may fall. || 7. In splendid combats of the hosts, in glories where the fight is won, | Indra, be victor over foes.

Hymn 20:20.

1. Drink thou the Soma for our help, bright, vigilant, exceeding strong, | O Indra, Lord of Hundred Powers. || 2. O Śatakratu, powers which thou mid the Five Races hast dis-played | These, Indra, do I claim of thee. || 3. Indra, great glory hast thou gained. Win splendid fame which none may mar: | We make thy might perpetual. || 4. Come to us either from anear, or, Śakra, come from far away. | Indra, wherever be thy home, come to us thence, O Thunder-armed. || 5. Verily Indra, conquering all, driveth even mighty fear away; | For firm is he and swift to act. || 6. Indra be gracious unto us: sin shall not reach us afterward. | And good shall be before us still, || 7. From all the regions of the world let Indra send security. | The foe-subduer, swift to act.

Hymn 20:21.

1. We will present fair praise unto the Mighty One, our hymns to Indra in Vivasvat's dwelling-place; | For he hath ne'er found wealth in those who seem to sleep; those who give wealth to men accept no paltry praise. || 2. Giver of horses, Indra, giver, thou, of kine, giver of barley, thou art Lord and guard of wealth: | Man's helper from of old, not disappointing hope, Friend of our friends, to thee as such we sing this praise. || 3. Indra, most splendid, powerful, rich in mighty deeds, this treasure spread around is known to be thine own. | Gather therefrom. O Conqueror, and bring to us: fail not the hope of him who loves and sings to thee. || 4. Well-pleased with these bright flames and with these Soma drops, take thou away our poverty with steeds and kine. | With Indra scattering the Dasyu through these drops, freed from their hate may we obtain abundant food. || 5. Let us obtain, O Indra, plenteous wealth and food, with strength exceeding glorious, shining to the sky. | May we obtain the Goddess Providence, the strength of heroes, special source of cattle, rich in steeds. || 6. These our libations, strength inspiring Soma draughts, gladdened thee in the fight with Vṛitra, Hero-Lord, | What time thou slewest for the singer with trimmed grass ten thousand Vṛitras, thou resistless in thy might. || 7. Thou goest on from fight to fight intrepidly, destroying castle after castle here with strength; | Thou Indra, with thy friend who makes the foe bow down, slewest from far away the guileful Namuchi. || 8. Thou hast stuck down in death Karañja, Parṇaya, in Atithigva's very glorious going forth: | Unyielding, when Ṛijiśvan compassed them with siege, thou hast destroyed the hundred towns of Vaṅgṛida. || 9. With all-outstripping chariot wheel, O Indra, thou far-famed, hast overthrown the twice ten kings of men, | With sixty thousand nine-and-ninety followers, who came in arms to fight with friendless Suśravas || 10. Thou hast protected Suśravas with succour, and Tūrvayāṇa with thine aid, O Indra: | Thou madest Kutsa, Atithigva, Āyu subject unto this king, the young, the mighty. || 11. May we protected by the Gods hereafter remain thy very prosperous friends, O Indra. | Thee we extol, enjoying through thy favour life-long and joyful and with store of heroes.

Hymn 20:22.

1. Hero, the Soma being pressed I pour the juice for thee to drink | Sate thee and finish thy carouse. || 2. Let not the fools, or those who mock, beguile thee when they seek thine aid: | Love not the enemies of prayer. || 3. Here let them with rich milky draught cheer thee to great munificence: | Drink as the wild bull drinks the lake. || 4. Praise, even as he is known, with song Indra, the guardian of the kine, | The Son of Truth, Lord of the brave. || 5. Hither his bay steeds have been sent, red steeds are on the sacred grass. | Where we in concert sing our songs. || 6. For Indra, Thunder-armed, the kine have yielded mingled milk and meath, | What time he found them in the vault.

Hymn 20:23.

1. Invoked to drink the Soma juice come with thy bay steeds, Thunder-armed! | Come, Indra, hitherward, to me. || 2. Our priest is seated true to time; the grass is regularly strewn; | The pressing-stones were set at morn. || 3. These prayers, O thou who bearest prayer, are offered. Seat thee on the grass. | Hero, enjoy the offered cake. || 4. O Vṛitra-slayer, be thou pleased with these libations, with these hymns, | Song-loving Indra, with our lauds. || 5. Our hymns caress the Lord of Strength, vast, drinker of the Soma's juice, | Indra, as mother-cows their calf. || 6. Delight thee with the juice we pour for thine own great munificence: | Yield not thy singer to reproach. || 7. We, Indra, dearly loving thee, bearing oblation, sing thee hymns: | Thou, Vasu, nearly lovest us. || 8. O thou to whom thy Bays are dear, loose not thy horses far from us: | Here glad thee, Indra, Lord Divine. || 9. May long-maned courses, dropping oil, bring thee on swift car hitherward. | Indra, to seat thee on the grass.

Hymn 20:24.

1. Come to the juice that we have pressed, to Soma, Indra! blent with milk: | Come, favouring us, thy bay-drawn car! || 2. Come, Indra, to this gladdening drink, placed on the grass, pressed out with stones: | Wilt thou not drink thy fill thereof? || 3. To Indra have my songs of praise gone forth, thus rapidly sent hence, | To turn him to the Soma-draught. || 4. Hither with songs of praise we call Indra to drink the Soma. juice: | Will he not

come to us by lauds? || 5. Indra, these Somas are expressed, Take them within thy belly, | Lord Of Hundred Powers, thou Prince of wealth. || 6. We know thee winner of the spoil and resolute in battles, Sage! | Therefore thy blessing we implore. || 7. Borne hither by thy stallions, drink, Indra, this juice which we have pressed, | Mingled with barley and with milk. || 8. Indra, for thee in thine own place I urge the Soma for thy draught: | Deep in thy heart let it remain. || 9. We call on thee, the Ancient One, Indra, to drink the Soma juice, | We Kuśikas who seek thine aid.

Hymn 20:25.

1. Indra, the mortal man well guarded by thine aid goes foremost in the wealth of horses and of kine. | With amplest wealth thou fillest him, as round about the waters clearly seen afar fill Sindhu full. || 2. The heavenly waters come not nigh the priestly bowl: they but look down and see how far mid-air is spread: | The Deities conduct the pious man to them: like suitors they delight in him who loveth prayer. || 3. Praiseworthy blessing hast thou laid upon the pair who with uplifted ladle serve thee, man and wife. | Unchecked he dwells and prospers in thy law: thy power brings blessing to the sacrificer pouring gifts. || 4. First the Aṅgirasas won themselves vital power, whose fires were kindled through good deeds and sacrifice. | The men together found the Paṇi's hoarded wealth, the cattle, and the wealth in horses and in kine, || 5. Atharvan first by sacrifices laid the path; then, guardian of the Law, sprang up the loving Sun. | Uśanā Kāvya drove the kine hither with him: let us with offerings honour Yama's deathless birth. || 6. When sacred grass is trimmed to aid the auspicious work, or the hymn makes its voice of praise sound to the sky, | Where the stone rings as 'twere a singer skilled in laud,—Indra in truth delights when these come near to him. || 7. To make thee start, a strong true draught I offer to thee the Bull, O thou whom bay steeds carry. | Here take delight. O Indra, in our voices while thou art hymned with power and all our spirit.

Hymn 20:26.

1. In every need, in every fray we call, as friends, to succour us Indra the mightiest of all. || 2. If he will hear us let him come with succour of a thousand kinds, | And all that strengthens, to our call. || 3. I call him, mighty to resist, the Hero of our ancient home, | Thee whom my sire invoked of old. || 4. They who stand round him as he moves harness the bright, the ruddy steed: | The lights are shining in the sky. || 5. On both sides of the car they yoke the two bay coursers dear to him, | Bold, tawny, bearers of the thief. || 6. Thou, making light where no light was, and form, O Men! where form was not, | Wast born together with the Dawns.

Hymn 20:27.

1. If I, O Indra, were, like thee, the single sovereign of all wealth. | My worshipper should be rich in kine. || 2. I should be fain, O Lord of Might, to strengthen and enrich the sage, | Were I the lord of herds of kine, || 3. To worshippers who press the juice thy goodness, Indra, is a cow. | Yielding in plenty kine and steeds. || 4. None is there, Indra, God or man, to hinder thy munificence, | The wealth which, lauded, thou wilt give. || 5. The sacrifice made Indra strong when he unrolled the earth and made | Himself a diaden in heaven. || 6. Thine aid we claim, O Indra, thine who after thou hast waxen great. | Hast won all treasures for thine own.

Hymn 20:28.

1. In Soma's ecstasy Indra spread the firmament and realms of light. | When he cleft Vala limb from limb. || 2. Showing the hidden he drave forth the cows for the Aṅgirasas, | And Vala he cast headlong down. || 3. By Indra were the luminous realms of heaven established and secured. | Firm and immovable in their place. || 4. Indra, thy laud moves quickly like a joyous wave of water-floods. | Bright shine the drops that gladden thee.

Hymn 20:29.

1. For thou, O Indra, art the God whom hymns and praises magnify: | Thou blessest those who worship thee. || 2. Bay horses with their long manes bring Indra to drink the Soma juice, | The Bountiful to our sacrifice. || 3. With waters' foam thou torest off, Indra, the head of Namuchi, | Subduing all contending hosts. || 4. The Dasyus, when they fain would climb by magic arts and mount to heaven, | Thou, Indra, castest down to earth. || 5. As Soma-drinker conquering all, thou scatteredst to every side | Their band who poured no gifts to thee.

Hymn 20:30.

1. In the great synod will I laud thy two bay steeds: I prize the sweet strong drink of thee the Warrior-God, | His who pours lovely oil as 'twere with yellow drops. Let my songs enter thee whose form hath golden tints. || 2. Ye who—in concert sing unto the gold-hued place, like bay steeds driving onward to the heavenly seat, | For Indra laud ye strength allied with tawny steeds, laud him whom cows content as 'twere with yellow drops. || 3. His is that thunderbolt, of iron, golden-hued, gold-coloured, very dear, and yellow in his arms; | Bright with strong teeth, destroying with its tawny rage. In Indra are set fast all forms of golden hue. || 4. As if a lovely ray were laid upon the sky, the golden thunder-bolt spread out as in a race. | That iron bolt with yellow jaw smote Ahi down. A thousand flames had he who bore the tawny-hued. || 5. Thou, thou, when praised by men who sacrificed of old, hadst pleasure in their lauds, O Indra golden-haired. | All that befits thy song of praise thou welcomest, the perfect: pleasant gift, O golden-hued from birth.

Hymn 20:31.

1. These two dear Bays bring hither Indra on his car, thunder-armed, joyous, meet for laud, to drink his fill. | Many libations flow for him who loveth them: to Indra have: the gold-hued Soma juices run. || 2. The gold-hued drops have flowed to gratify his wish: the yellow. drops have urged the swift Bays to the Strong. | He who speeds on with bay steeds even as he lists hath satisfied his longing for the golden drops. || 3. At the swift draught the Soma-drinker waxed in might, the iron. One with yellow beard and golden hair, | He, Lord of tawny coursers. Lord of fleet-foot mares, will bear his bay steeds safely over all distress. || 4. His yellow-coloured jaws, like ladles, move apart, what time, for strength, he makes the yellow-tinted stir, | When, while the bowl stands there, he grooms his tawny steeds, when he hath drunk strong drink, the sweet juice that he loves. || 5. Yea, to the dear one's seat in homes of heaven and earth the-bay steeds' Lord hath whinnied like a horse for food. | Then the great wish hath seized upon him mightily, and the beloved One hath gained high power of life.

Hymn 20:32.

1. Thou, comprehending with thy might the earth and heaven, acceptest the dear hymn for ever new and new. | O Asura, disclose thou and make visible the Cow's beloved home to the bright golden Sun. || 2. O Indra, let the eager wishes of the folk bring thee the golden-jawed, delightful, on thy car. | That, pleased with sacrifice wherein ten fingers toil, thou mayest at the feast drink of our offered mead. || 3. Juices aforetime, Lord of Bays, thou drankest, and thine, and only thine, is this libation. | Gladden thee, Indra, with the mead-rich Soma: pour it down ever, Mighty One, within thee.

Hymn 20:33.

1. Drink of the juice which men have washed in waters and fill the-full, O Lord of tawny horses. | O Indra, hearer of the laud, with Soma which stones have mixed for thee enhance thy rapture. || 2. To make thee start, a strong true draught I offer to thee the Bull, O thou whom bay steeds carry. | Here take delight, O Indra, in our voices while thou art hymned with power and all our spirit. || 3. O mighty Indra, through thine aid, thy prowess, obtaining life, zealous, and skilled in worship. | Men in the house who share the sacred banquet stand singing praise that brings them store of children.

Hymn 20:34.

1. He who just born, chief God of lofty spirit, by power and might became the God's protector, | Before whose breath, through greatness of his valour, the two worlds trembled, He, O men, is Indra. || 2. He who fixed fast and firm the earth that staggered, and set at rest the agitated mountains, | Who measured out air's wider middle region and gave the heaven support, He, O men, is Indra. || 3. Who slew the Dragon, freed the Seven Rivers, and drave the kine forth from the cave of Vala, | Begat the fire between both stones, the spoiler in warrior's battle, He, O men, is Indra. || 4. By whom this universe was made to tremble, who chased away the humbled brood of demon, | Who, like a gambler gathering his winnings, seized the foe's riches, He, O men, is Indra. || 5. Of whom, the terrible, they ask, Where is He? or verily they say of him, He is not. | He wastes the foeman's wealth like stakes of gamblers. Have faith in him for He, O men, is Indra. || 6. Stirrer to action of the poor and lowly, of priest, of suppliant who sings his

praises | Who, fair-faced, favours him who presseth Soma with stones adjusted, He, O men, is Indra. || 7. He under whose supreme control are horses, all chariots, and the hamlets, and the cattle: | He who begat the Sun, begat the Morning, leader of waters. He, O men, is Indra. || 8. To whom both armies cry in close encounter, foe against foe, the stronger and the weaker; | Whom two invoke upon one chariot mounted, each for himself, He, O ye men, is Indra. || 9. He, without whom men conquer not in battle, whom, warring, they invoke for help and succour; | He, all this universe's type and image, who shakes what never shook, He, men, is Indra. || 10. He who hath smitten, ere they know their danger, with his hurled weapon many grievous sinners: | Who pardons not his boldness who provokes him, who slays the Dasyu, He, O men, is Indra. || 11. He who discovered in the fortieth autumn Śambara dwelling in the midst of mountains: | Who slew the Dragon putting forth his vigour, the demon lying there, He, men, is Indra. || 12. Who drank the juice poured at the seas of Order, subduing Śambara by superior prowess, | Who hoarded food within the mountain's hollow wherein he grew in strength, He, men, is Indra. || 13. Who, with seven guiding reins, the Bull, the mighty, set the Seven Rivers free to flow at pleasure; | Who, thunder-armed, rent Rauhiṇa in pieces when scaling heaven, He, O ye men, is Indra. || 14. Heaven, even, and the earth bow down before him, before his very breath the mountains tremble. | Known as the Soma-drinker, armed with thunder, the wielder of the bolt, He, men, is Indra. || 15. Who aids with favour him who pours the Soma, and him who brews it, sacrificer, singer; | Whose strength our prayer and offered Soma heighten, and this our gift, He, O ye men, is Indra. || 16. Born, manifested in his Parents' bosom, He knoweth as a son the Highest Father. | He who with vigorous energy assisted the companies of Gods. He, men, is Indra || 17. Lord of Bay steeds, who loves the flowing Soma, He before whom all living creatures tremble. | He who smote Śambara and slaughtered Śushṇa, He the Sole Hero, He, O men, is Indra. || 18. Thou verily art true strong God who sendest wealth to the man who brews and pours libation. | So may we evermore, thy friends, O Indra, address the synod with brave sons about us.

Hymn 20:35.

1. To him, to him swift, strong, and high-exalted, I bring my song of praise as dainty viands; | My thought to him resistless, meet for praises, prayers offered most devotedly to Indra. || 2. To him I offer praise as choice refreshment, bring forth my song, with seemly laud besiege him. | For Indra, Lord of olden time, the singers shall deck their hymns with heart and mind and spirit. || 3. To him then with my lips my song of praises, excellent, winning heavenly light, I offer, | To magnify with hymns of invocation and eulogies the Lord, most bounteous Giver. || 4. Even for him I frame a laud—so fashions the wright a chariot for the man who needs it | Songs for wise Indra hymned with invocation, a song composed with care and all-impelling. || 5. So with my tongue I deck, to please that Indra, my hymn as 'twere a horse, through love of glory, | To reverence the Hero, bounteous Giver, famed far and wide, destroyer of the castles. || 6. Even for him hath Tvashṭar forged the thunder, most deftly wrought, celestial, for the battle. | Wherewith he reached the vital parts of Vṛitra, striking—the vast, the mighty—with the striker, || 7. As soon as, at libations of his mother, great Vishṇu had drunk up the draught, he plundered. | The dainty cates, the cooked mess; but One stronger transfixed the wild boar, shooting through the mountain. || 8. To him, to Indra when he slew the Dragon, the Dames too, Consorts of the Gods, wove praises. | The mighty heaven and earth hath he encompassed: thy greatness heaven and earth, combined, exceed not. || 9. Yea, of a truth, his magnitude surpasseth the magnitude of earth, mid-air and heaven. | Indra whom all men praise, the Sovereign Ruler, waxed in his home loud-voiced and strong for battle. || 10. Through his own strength with bolt of thunder Indra smote piece-meal Vṛitra, drier up of waters. | He let the floods go free, like cows imprisoned, for glory, with a heart inclined to bounty. || 11. Through his resplendent power still stood the rivers when with his bolt on every side he stayed them. | With lordly might favouring him who worshipped, he made a ford, victorious, for Turvīti || 12. Vast, with thine ample power, with eager movement against this Vṛitra cast thy bolt of thunder. | Rend thou his joints, as of an ox dissevered, with bolt oblique that floods of rain may follow. || 13. Sing with new lauds his exploits wrought aforetime, the deeds of him, yea, him who moveth swiftly, | When, hurling forth his weapons in the battle, he with impetuous wrath lays low the foemen. || 14. When he, yea, he is born the firm-set mountains and the whole heaven and earth tremble in terror. | May Nodhas ever lauding the protection of this dear Friend win straightway strength heroic. || 15. Now unto him of these things hath been given what he, who rules alone o'er much, electeth. | Indra helped Etaśa, the Soma presser, contending in the chariot-race with Sūrya. || 16. Thus to thee, Indra, yoker of bay coursers, the Gotamas have brought their prayers and praises. | Bestow upon them thought, decked with all beauty. May he, enriched with prayer, come soon and early.

Hymn 20:36.

1. With these my hymns I glorify that Indra who is alone to be invoked by mortals. | The Lord, the Mighty One, of manly vigour, victorious, Hero, true, and full of wisdom. || 2. Our ancient sires, Navagvas, sages seven, while urging him to show his might, extolled him, | Dweller on heights, swift smiting down opponents, guileless in word, and in his thoughts most mighty. || 3. We seek that Indra to obtain his riches that yield much food, and men, and store of heroes. | O Lord of Bay Steeds, bring to make us joyful, celestial wealth abundant, undecaying. || 4. Declare to us—if at thy hand aforetime the earlier singers have obtained good fortune | What is thy share and portion, strong Subduer, Asura-slayer, rich, invoked of many? || 5. He who for car-borne, thunder-wielding Indra, hath a hymn, craving deeply-piercing, fluent, | Who sends a song effectual, firmly-grasping, and strength-bestowing, he comes near the mighty. || 6. Strong of thyself! thou with this art hast shattered with thought-swift Parvata, him who waxed against thee; | And, Mightiest! rager! boldly rent in pieces things that were firmly fixed and never shaken. || 7. Him will we fit for you with new devotion, the strongest, Ancient One, in ancient manner. | So way that Indra, boundless, faithful leader, conduct us o'er all places hard to traverse. || 8. Thou for the people who oppress hast kindled the earthly firmament and that of heaven. | With heat, O Bull, on every side consume them heat earth and flood for him who hates devotion: || 9. Of all the heavenly folk, of earthly creatures, thou art the King, O God of splendid aspect. | In thy right hand, O Indra, grasp the thunder: Eternal! thou destroyest all enchantments. || 10. Give us confirmed prosperity, O Indra, vast and exhaustless for the foes' subduing. | Strengthen therewith the Ārya's hate and Dāsa's; and let the arms of Nahushas be mighty. || 11. Come with thy teams which bring all blessings, hither, disposer, much-invoked, exceeding holy! | Come to me swiftly with these teams of coursers, these which no fiend, no God may stay or hinder.

Hymn 20:37.

1. He, like a bull with sharpened horns, terrific, singly excites and agitates all the people. | Then givest him who largely pours libation his wealth who pours not, for his own possession. || 2. Thou verily, Indra, gavest help to Kutsa, willingly lending ear to him in battle. | When, aiding Ārjuneya, thou subduedst to him both Kuyava and the Dāsa Śushṇa || 3. O Bold One, thou with all thine aids hast boldly helped Sudās whose offerings were accepted, | Pūru in winning land and slaying foemen, and Trasadasyu son of Purukutsa. || 4. At the Gods' banquet, Hero-souled! with heroes, Lord of Bay Steeds, thou slewest many Vṛitras. | Thou sentest in swift death to sleep the Dasyu, both Chumuri and Dhuni, for Dabhīti, || 5. These were thy mighty powers that, Thunder-wielder! then swiftly crushedst nine-and ninety castles. | Thou capturedst the hundredth in thine onslaught; thou slewest Namuchi, thou slewest Vṛitra || 6. Old are the blessings, Indra, which thou gavest Sudās the worshipper who brought oblations. | For thee, the strong I yoke thy strong bay horses: let them, approach our prayers and wealth, Most Mighty! || 7. Give us not up, Lord of Bay Horses, victor, in this our time of-trouble, to the wicked. | Deliver us with true and faithful succour: dear may we be to thee among the princes. || 8. May we men, Bounteous Lord, the friends thou lovest, near thee be joyful under thy protection. | Fain to fulfil the wish of Atithigva, bow Turvaśa, bow down, the son of Yadu. || 9. Swiftly, in truth, O Bounteous Lord, about thee men skilled in hymning sing their songs and praises. | Elect us shares of their love and friendship who by their calls on, thee despoiled the niggards. || 10. Thine are these Lauds, O manliest of heroes, Lauds which revert to us and give us riches. | Favour these, Indra, when they strike the foemen, as Friend

and Hero and the heroes' helper. || 11. Now, lauded for thine aid, heroic Indra, sped by our prayer,, wax mighty in thy body. | To us apportion wealth and habitations. Ye Gods, protect us-evermore with blessings.

Hymn 20:38.

1. Come, we have pressed the juice for thee. O Indra, drink the Soma here. | Sit thou on this my sacred grass. || 2. O Indra, let thy long-maned Bays, yoked by prayer, bring thee hitherward. | Give ear and listen to our prayers. || 3. We, Soma-bearing Brahmans, call thee, Soma-drinker, with thy friend, | We, Indra, bringing juice expressed. || 4. Indra the singers with high praise, Indra reciters with their lauds, | Indra the choirs have glorified. || 5. Indra hath ever close to him his two bay steeds and word-yoked: car, | Indra, the golden, Thunder-armed. || 6. Indra hath raised the Sun aloft in heaven that he may see afar. | He burst the mountain for the kine.

Hymn 20:39.

1. For you, from every side, we call Indra away from other men: | Ours, and none others', let him be. || 2. In Soma's ecstasy Indra spread the firmament and realms of light. | When he cleft Vala limb from limb. || 3. Showing the hidden cows he drave them forth for the Aṅgirasas, | And Vala he cast headlong down. || 4. By Indra were the luminous realms of heaven established and secured, | Firm and immovable from their place. || 5. Indra, thy laud moves quickly like a joyous wave of waters: bright. | Have shone the drops that gladden thee.

Hymn 20:40.

1. Mayest thou verily be seen coming by fearless Indra's side: | Both joyous: equal in your sheen. || 2. With Indra's well-beloved hosts, the blameless, hastening to heaven, | The sacrificer cries aloud. || 3. Thereafter they, as is their wont, threw off the state of babes unborn, | Assuming sacrificial name.

Hymn 20:41.

1. With bones of Dadhyach for his arms, Indra, resistless in attack, | Struck nine-and-ninety Vṛitras dead, || 2. He, searching for the horse's head, removed among the mountains, found | At Śaryaṇāvat what he sought. || 3. Then verily they recognized the essential form of Tvaṣhṭar's Bull. | Here in the mansion of the Moon.

Hymn 20:42.

1. From Indra have I measured an eight-footed and nine-cornered. song, | Delicate, faithful to the Law. || 2. Indra, both worlds complained to thee when uttering thy fearful roar, | What time thou smotest Dasyus dead. || 3. Arising in thy might thy jaws thou shookest, Indra, having quaffed | The Soma poured into the bowls.

Hymn 20:43.

1. Drive all our enemies away, smite down the foes who press around, | And bring the wealth for which we long; || 2. O Indra, that which is concealed in firm strong place precipitous: | Bring us the wealth for which we long: || 3. Great riches which the world of men shall recognize as sent by thee: | Bring us the wealth for which we long,

Hymn 20:44.

1. Praise Indra whom our songs must laud, great Sovereign of man-kind, the Chief, | Most liberal who controlleth men. || 2. In whom the hymns of praise delight, and all the glory-giving songs, | Like the flood's longing for the sea. || 3. Him I invite with eulogy, best King, effective in the fight, | Strong for the gain of mighty spoil.

Hymn 20:45.

1. This is thine own. Thou drawest near, as the dove turneth to his mate. | Thou carest too for this our prayer. || 2. O Hero, Lord of Bounties, praised in hymns, may power and pleasantness | Be his who signs the laud to thee. || 3. Lord of a Hundred Powers, stand up to lend us succour in this fight: | In others too let us agree.

Hymn 20:46.

1. Him who advances men to wealth, sends light to lead them in their wars, | And quells their foemen in the fray: || 2. May he, the saviour much-invoked, may Indra bear us in a ship | Safely beyond all enemies. || 3. As such, O Indra, honour us with wealth and treasure: further us, | And lead us to felicity.

Hymn 20:47.

1. We make this Indra show his strength, to strike the mighty Vṛitra dead: | A vigorous Hero shall he be. || 2. Indra was made for giving, most powerful, friendly in carouse, | Bright, meet for Soma, famed in song. || 3. By song, as 'twere, the mighty bolt, which none may parry, was prepared: | Lofty, invincible he grew. || 4. Indra the singers with high praise, Indra reciters with their lauds, | Indra the choirs have glorified. || 5. Indra hath ever close to him his two bay steeds and word-yoked: car, | Indra, the golden, Thunder-armed. || 6. Indra hath raised the Sun aloft in heaven that he may see afar. | He burst the mountain for the kine. || 7. Come, we have pressed the juice for thee. O Indra, drink the Soma here. | Sit thou on this my sacred grass. || 8. O Indra, let thy long-maned Bays, yoked by prayer, bring thee hitherward. | Give ear and listen to our prayers. || 9. We, Soma-bearing Brahmans, call thee, Soma-drinker, with thy friend, | We, Indra, bringing juice expressed. || 10. They who stand round him as he moves harness the bright, the ruddy Steed: | The lights are shining in the sky. || 11. They yoke on both sides to the car the two bay coursers dear to him, | Bold, tawny, bearers of the Chief. || 12. Thou, making light where no light was, and form, O Men! where no form was, | Wast born together with the Dawns. || 13. His bright rays bear him up aloft, the God who knoweth all that is, | Sūrya, that every one may see. || 14. The constellations pass away, like thieves, together with their-beams, | Before the all-beholding Sun. || 15. His herald rays are seen afar refulgent o'er the world of men, | Like fiery flames that burn and blaze. || 16. Swift and all-beautiful art thou, O Sūrya, maker of the light. | Illuming all the radiant realm. || 17. Thou guest to the troops of Gods, thou comest hither to man-kind, | Hither, all light for us to see. || 18. Thou with that eye of thine wherewith thou seest, brilliant Varuṇa, | The active one throughout mankind. || 19. Pervadest heaven and wide mid-air, melting the days out with. thy beams, | Sun, seeing all things that have birth. || 20. Seven bay steeds, harnessed to thy car, bear thee, O thou far-seeing One, | God, Sūrya, thee with radiant hair. || 21. Sūrya hath yoked the seven bright mares, the daughters of the car: With these, | His own dear team, he travelleth.

Hymn 20:48.

1. The swiftly-moving songs of praise pour on thee streams of vital strength | As mother cows refresh the calf. || 2. Swift move the bright ones while they blend the Milk with vital vigour, as | A dame her infant with her heart. || 3. Fair hymns bring glory to the Strong, and Indra-vigour; unto, me | Fatness and milk and length of days. || 4. This brindled Bull hath come and sat before the Mother in the east, | Advancing to the Father Heaven. || 5. As expiration from breath she moves along the lucid spheres: | The Bull shines forth through all the sky. || 6. Song is bestowed upon the Bird. It reigns supreme throughout thirty realms | Throughout the days at break of morn.

Hymn 20:49.

1. When voices, fain to win mid-air, ascended to the Mighty One, | The vigorous God was filled with joy. || 2. Praise with the voice the Mighty, praise the awful with the voice: in heaven | He, the most bounteous, hath been glad. || 3. Praise with the voice the Mighty: he rules in each realm. In transport he | Hath set upon the sacred grass. || 4. As cows low to their calf in stalls, so with our songs we glorify | This Indra, even your wondrous God who checks attack, who joys in the delightful juice. || 5. Celestial, bounteous Giver, God, with power and might, rich, mountain-like, in precious things. | Him soon we see for foodful booty rich in kine, brought hundredfold and thousandfold. || 6. I crave of thee that hero strength—that thou mayst first regard this prayer | Wherewith thou helpest Bhṛigu and the Yatis and Praskaṇva when the prize was staked. || 7. Wherewith thou sentest mighty waters to the sea—Indra, that manly strength of thine. | For ever unattainable is this power of him to whom the worlds have cried aloud.

Hymn 20:50.

1. What newest of imploring hymns shall, then, the zealous mortal sing? | For have not they who laud his might and Indra-power won for themselves the light of heaven? || 2. When shall they keep the Law and praise thee mid the Gods? Who counts as Ṛishi and as sage? | When wilt thou ever, Indra, Bounteous Lord, come nigh to presser's or to praiser's call?

Hymn 20:51.

1. For you will I sing Indra's praise who gives good gifts as well we know; | Praise of the Bounteous Lord who, rich in treasure, aids his singers with wealth thousandfold. ‖ 2. As with a hundred hosts he rushes boldly on, and for the offerer slays his foes. | As from a mountain flow the water-brooks, thus flow his gifts who feedeth many a one. ‖ 3. Śakra I praise, for victory, far-famed, exceeding bountiful. | Who gives, as 'twere in thousands, precious wealth to him who sheds the juice and worships him. ‖ 4. Arrows with hundred points, unconquerable, are this Indra's mighty arms in war. | He streams on liberal worshippers like a hill with springs, when juices poured have gladdened him.

Hymn 20:52.

1. We compass thee like waters, we whose grass is trimmed and Soma pressed. | Here where the filter pours its stream thy worshipper round thee, O Vṛitra-slayer, sit. ‖ 2. Men, Vasu! by the Soma, with lauds call thee to the foremost place. | When comest thou athirst unto the juice as home, O Indra, like a bellowing bull? ‖ 3. Boldly, bold Hero, bring us spoil in thousands for the Kaṇvas' sake. | O active Maghavan, with eager prayer we crave the yellow-hued with store of kine.

Hymn 20:53.

1. Who knows what vital power he wins, drinking beside the flowing juice? | This is the fair-cheeked God who, joying in the draught, breaks down the castles in his strength. ‖ 2. As a wild elephant rushes on, this way and that way, mad with heat. | None may restrain thee; yet come hither to the draught: thou movest mighty in thy power. ‖ 3. When he, the mighty, ne'er o'erthrown, steadfast, made ready for the fight. | When Indra, Bounteous Lord, lists to his praiser's call, he will not stand aloof, but come.

Hymn 20:54.

1. Of one accord they made and formed for kingship Indra, the Hero who in all encounters overcometh, | Most eminent for power, destroyer in the conflict, fierce and exceeding strong, stalwart and full of vigour. ‖ 2. Bards joined in song to Indra so that he might drink the Soma juice, | The Lord of Light, that he whose laws stand fast might aid with power and with help he gives. ‖ 3. The holy sages form a ring, looking and singing to the Ram. | Your very bright inciters, void of all deceit, are with the chanters nigh to hear.

Hymn 20:55.

1. Oft, oft I call that Indra, Maghavan the mighty, who evermore possesses power, ever resistless. | Holy, most liberal, may he lead us on to riches, and, thunder armed, make all our pathways pleasant for us. ‖ 2. Indra, what joys as Lord of Light thou broughtest from the Asuras, | Prosper therewith, O Maghavan, him who lauds that deed, and those whose grass is trimmed for thee. ‖ 3. The wasteless share of steeds and kine which, Indra, thou hast fast secured. | Grant to the worshipper who presses Soma and gives guerdon, not unto the churl.

Hymn 20:56.

1. Indra, foe-slayer, hath been raised to joy and power by the men. | Him, verily, we invocate in battles whether great or small: be he our aid in fights for spoil. ‖ 2. For, Hero, thou art like a host, art giver of abundant prey. | Strengthening even the feeble, thou aidest the sacrificer, thou givest the worshipper ample wealth. ‖ 3. When war and battles are on foot, booty is laid before the bold. | Yoke thou thy wildly rushing Bays. Whom wilt thou slay and whom enrich? Do thou, O Indra, make us rich, ‖ 4. He, righteous-hearted, at each time of rapture gives us herds of kine. | Gather in both thy hands for us treasures of many hundred sorts. Sharpen thou us, and bring us wealth. ‖ 5. Refresh thee, Hero, with the juice outpoured for bounty and for strength. | We know thee Lord of ample store, to thee have sent our heart's desires: be therefore our protector thou. ‖ 6. These people, Indra, keep for thee all that is worthy of thy choice. | Discover thou, as Lord, the wealth of men who offer up no gifts: bring thou to us this wealth of theirs.

Hymn 20:57.

1. As a good cow to him who milks, we call the doer of fair deeds. | To our assistance day by day. ‖ 2. Come thou to our libations, drink of Soma, Soma-drinker thou! | The rich One's rapture giveth kine. ‖ 3. So may we be acquainted with thine innermost benevolence: | Neglect us not, come hitherward. ‖ 4. Drink for our help the Soma bright, vigilant, and exceeding strong, | O Indra, Lord of Hundred Powers. ‖ 5. O Śatakratu, powers which thou mid the Five Races hast displayed, | These, Indra, do I claim of thee. ‖ 6. Indra, great glory hast thou gained. Win splendid fame which none may mar. | We make thy might perpetual. ‖ 7. Come to us either from anear, or, Śakra, come from far away. | Indra, wherever be thy home, come thence, O Caster of the Stone. ‖ 8. Verily Indra, conquering all, driveth even mighty fear away. | For firm is he and swift to act. ‖ 9. Indra be gracious unto us: sin shall not reach us afterward, | And good shall be before us still. ‖ 10. From all the regions of the world let Indra send security. | The foe-subduer, swift to act. 11. Who knows what vital power he wins, drinking beside the flowing juice? | This is the fair-cheeked God who, joying in the draught, breaks down the castles in his strength. ‖ 12. As a wild elephant rushes on, this way and that way, mad with heat. | None may restrain thee; yet come hither to the draught: thou movest mighty in thy power. ‖ 13. When he, the mighty, ne'er o'erthrown, steadfast, made ready for the fight. | When Indra, Bounteous Lord, lists to his praiser's call, he will not stand aloof, but come. ‖ 14. We compass thee like waters, we whose grass in trimmed and Soma pressed. | Here where the filter pours its stream thy worshippers round thee, O Vṛitra-slayer, sit. ‖ 15. Men, Vasu, by the Soma with lauds call thee to the foremost place. | When comest thou athirst unto the juice as home, O Indra, like a bellowing bull? ‖ 16. Boldly, bold Hero, bring us spoil in thousands for the Kaṇvas' sake. | O active Maghavan, with eager prayer we crave the yellow-hued with store of kine.

Hymn 20:58.

1. Turning, as 'twere, to meet the Sun, enjoy from Indra all good things. | When he who will be born is born with power we look to treasures as our heritage. ‖ 2. Praise him who sends us wealth, whose bounties injure none. Good are the gifts which Indra gives. | He is not wroth with one who satisfies his wish: he turns his mind to granting boons. ‖ 3. Verily, Sūrya, thou art great; truly, Āditya, thou art great. | As thou art great indeed thy greatness is admired: yea, verily, great art thou, O God. ‖ 4. Yea, Sūrya, thou art great in fame: thou evermore, O God, art great. | By greatness thou art President of Gods, divine, far-spread, inviolable light.

Hymn 20:59.

1. These songs of ours exceeding sweet, these hymns of praise ascend to thee, | Like ever-conquering chariots that display their strength, gain wealth and give unfailing aid. ‖ 2. The Bhṛigus are like suns, like Kaṇvas, and have gained all that their thoughts were bent to win. | The living men of Priyamedha's race have sung exalting Indra with their lauds. ‖ 3. His portion is exceeding great, like a victorious soldier's spoil. | Him who is Indra, Lord of Bays, no foes subdue. He gives the Soma-pourer strength. ‖ 4. Make for the holy Gods a hymn that is not mean, but well arranged and fair in form. | Full many snares and bonds subdue not him who dwells with Indra through his sacrifice.

Hymn 20:60.

1. For so thou art the hero's Friend, a Warrior too art thou, and strong: | So may thy heart be won to us. ‖ 2. So hath the offering; wealthiest Lord, been paid by all the worshippers: | So dwell thou, Indra, even with me. ‖ 3. Be not thou, like a slothful priest, O Lord of wealth and spoil: rejoice. | In the pressed Soma blent with milk. ‖ 4. So also is his excellence, great copious, rich in cattle, like | A ripe branch to the worshipper. ‖ 5. For verily thy mighty powers, Indra, are saving helps at once | Unto a worshipper like me. ‖ 6. So are his lovely gifts: let laud be said and praise to Indra sung. | That he may drink the Soma juice.

Hymn 20:61.

1. We sing this strong and wild delight of thine which conquers in the fray, | Which, Caster of the Stone, gives room and shine like gold. ‖ 2. Wherewith thou also foundest lights for Āyu and for Manu's sake: | Now joying in this sacred grass thou beamest forth. ‖ 3. This day to singers of the hymn praise, as of old, this, might of thine. | Win thou the waters, day by day, thralls of the strong. ‖ 4. Sing forth to him whom many men invoke, to him whom many laud: | Invite the potent Indra with your songs of praise; ‖ 5. Whose lofty might—for doubly strong is he—supports the heaven and earth. | And hills and plains and floods and light with manly power. ‖ 6. Such, praised by many! thou art King: alone thou smitest foe-men dead, | To gain, O Indra, spoils of war and high renown.

Hymn 20:62.

1. We call on thee, O peerless One. We, seeking help, possessing nothing firm ourselves, | Call on thee wonderful in fight. || 2. On thee for aid in sacrifice. This youth of ours, the bold, the mighty, hath gone forth. | We, therefore, we thy friends, Indra, have chosen thee, free-giver, as our guardian God. || 3. Him who of old hath brought to us this and that blessing, him I magnify for you, | Even Indra, O my friends, for help: || 4. Borne by bay steeds, the Lord of heroes, ruling men, for it is he who takes delight. | The Bounteous Lord bestows on us his worshippers hundreds of cattle and of steeds. || 5. To Indra sing a Sāman, sing to the high Sage a lofty song, | To him who keeps the Law, inspired and fain for praise. || 6. Thou, Indra, art preeminent: thou gavest splendour to the Sun. | Maker of all things, thou art mighty and All-God. || 7. Radiant with light thou wentest to the sky, the luminous realms: of heaven. | The Gods, O Indra, strove to win thee for their friend. || 8. Sing forth to him whom many men invoke, to him whom many laud: | Invite the potent Indra with your songs of praise; || 9. Whose lofty might—for doubly strong is he—supports the heaven and earth, | And hills and plains and floods and light with manly power. || 10. Such, praised by many! thou art King. Alone thou smitest foemen dead, | To gain, O Indra, spoils of war and high renown.

Hymn 20:63.

1. We will, with Indra, and all Gods to aid us, bring these existing. worlds into subjection. | Our sacrifice, our bodies, and our offspring, let Indra form together with the Ādityas. || 2. With the Ādityas with the band of Marutas, may Indra be protector of our bodies; | As when the Gods came, after they had slaughtered the Asuras, keeping safe their godlike nature, || 3. Brought the Sun hitherward with mighty powers, and looked! about them on their vigorous God-head. | With this may we obtain strength God-appointed, and brave sons gladden us through a hundred winters. || 4. He who alone bestoweth might on mortal man who offereth gifts, | The ruler of resistless power, is Indra, sure. || 5. When will he trample like a weed the man who hath no gift for him? | When verily will Indra hear our songs of praise? || 6. He who with Soma juice prepared among the many harbours. thee, | Verily Indra gains thereby tremendous might. || 7. Joy, mightiest Indra, known and marked, sprung most from Soma draughts, wherewith | Thou smitest down the greedy fiend, for that we pray. || 8. Wherewith thou helpest Adhrigu, the great Daśagva, and the God | Who stirs the sunlight, and Sea, for that we pray. || 9. Wherewith thou dravest forth like cars Sindhu and all the mighty floods. | To go the way ordained by Law, for that we pray.

Hymn 20:64.

1. Come unto us, O Indra, dear, still conquering, unconcealable, | Vast as a mountain spread on all sides, Lord of heaven. || 2. O truthful Soma-drinker, thou art mightier than both the worlds. | Thou strengthenest him who pours libation, Lord of heaven. || 3. For thou art, he, O Indra, who stormest all castles of the foe, | Slayer of Dasyus, man's supporter, Lord of heaven. || 4. O ministering priest, pour out of the sweet juice what gladdens most. | So is the Hero praised who ever prospers us. || 5. Indra whom tawny coursers bear, praise such a thine, preeminent, | None by his power or by his goodness hath attained || 6. We seeking glory, have invoked this Master of all power and might. | Who must be glorified by constant sacrifice.

Hymn 20:65.

1. Come, sing we praise to Indra, friends! the Hero who deserves the laud, | Him who with none to aid o'ercomes all tribes of men. || 2. To him who wins the kine, who keeps no cattle back, celestial God, | Speak wondrous speech more sweet than butter and than mead. || 3. Whose hero powers are measureless, whose bounty ne'er may be surpassed, | Whose liberality, like light, is over all.

Hymn 20:66.

1. As Vyaśva did, praise Indra, praise the strong unfluctuating guide. | Who gives the foe's possessions to the worshipper. || 2. Now, son of Vyaśva, praise thou him who to the tenth time still is new. | The very wise, whom living men must glorify. || 3. Thou knowest, Indra, thunder-armed, how to avoid destructive Powers, | As one secure from pitfalls each succeeding day.

Hymn 20:67.

1. The pourer of oblations gains the home of wealth pouring his gift conciliates hostilities, yea, the hostilities of Gods. | Pouring he strives, unchecked and strong, to win him riches thousandfold. | Indra gives lasting wealth to him who pours forth gifts; yea, wealth he gives that long shall last. || 2. Ne'er may those manly deeds of yours for us grow old, never may your bright glories fall into decay, never before your time decay. | What deed of yours, new every age, wondrous, surpassing man, rings forth, | Whatever, Marutas may be difficult to gain grant us whate'er is hard to win. || 3. I think on Agni, Hotar, the munificent, the gracious Son of strength, who knoweth all that live, as holy Sage who knoweth all. | Lord of fair rites, a God with form erected turning to the Gods. | He, when the flame hath sprung forth from the holy oil, the offered fatness, longeth for it with his glow. || 4. Busied with sacrifice, with spotted deer and spears, gleaming. upon your way with ornaments, yea, our friends, | Sitting on sacred grass, ye sons of Bhārata, drink Soma from the Potar's bowl, O Men of heaven. || 5. Bring the Gods hither, Sage, and offer sacrifice. At the three altars seat thee willingly O Priest. | Accept for thy delight the proffered Soma mead: drink from the Kindler's bowl and sate thee with thy share. || 6. This is the strengthener of thy body's manly might: strength, victory for all time are laid within thine arms. | Pressed for thee, Maghavan, it is offered unto thee: drink from the chalice of this Brahman, drink thy fill. || 7. Him whom of old I called on, him I call on now. He is to be invoked: his name is He who Gives. | Here brought by priests in Soma mead. Granter of Wealth, drink Soma with the Seasons from the Hotar's Cup.

Hymn 20:68.

1. As a good cow to him who milks, we call the doer of fair deeds. | To our assistance day by day. || 2. Come thou to our libations, drink of Soma, Soma-drinker thou! | The rich One's rapture giveth kine. || 3. So may we be acquainted with thine innermost benevolence: | Neglect us not, come hitherward. || 4. Go to the wise unconquered One, ask thou of Indra, skilled in song, | Him who is better than thy friends. || 5. Whether the men who mock us say, Depart unto another place, | Ye who serve Indra and none else; || 6. Or whether, God of wondrous deeds, all our true people call us blest, | Still may we dwell in Indra's care. || 7. Unto the swift One bring the swift, man-cheering, grace of sacrifice. | That to the Friend gives wings and joy. || 8. Thou, Śatakratu, drankest this and wast the Vṛitras' slayer; thou. | Helpest the warrior in the fray. || 9. We strengthen, Śatakratu, thee, yea, thee the powerful in fight, | That, Indra, we may win us wealth. || 10. To him the mighty stream of wealth, prompt Friend of him who pours the juice, | Yea, to this Indra sing your song. || 11. O come ye hither, sit ye down: to Indra sing ye forth your song, | Companions, bringing hymns of praise. || 12. To him the richest of the rich, the Lord of treasures excellent, | Indra, with Soma juice outpoured.

Hymn 20:69.

1. May he stand by us in our need and in abundance for our wealth: | With riches may he come to us; || 2. Whose pair of tawny horses yoked in battles foemen challenge not: | To him, to Indra, sing your song. || 3. Nigh to the Soma-drinker come, for his enjoyment, these bright drops, | The Somas mingled with the curd. || 4. Thou, grown at once to perfect strength, wast born to drink the Soma juice, strong Indra, for preeminence. || 5. O Indra, lover of the song, may these quick Somas enter thee: | May they bring bliss to thee the Sage. || 6. O Lord of Hundred Powers, our chants of praise and lauds have strengthened thee: | So strengthen thee the songs we sing! || 7. Indra, whose succour never fails, accept this treasure thousand-fold, | Wherein all manly powers abide. || 8. O Indra, thou who lovest song, let no man hurt our bodies, keep. | Slaughter far from us, for thou canst. || 9. They who stand round him as he moves harness the bright, the ruddy steed: | The lights are shining in the sky. || 10. On both sides of the car they yoke the two bay coursers dear to him, | Bold, tawny, bearers of the thief. || 11. Thou, making light where no light was, and form, O Men! where form was not, | Wast born together with the Dawns. || 12. Thereafter they, as is their wont, threw off the state of babes unborn, | Taking their sacrificial name.

Hymn 20:70.

1. Thou, Indra, with the Tempest-Gods, the breakers down of what is firm, | Foundest the kine even in the cave. || 2. Worshipping even as they list, singers laud him who findeth wealth, | The far-renowned, the mighty One. || 3. Then, faring on by Indra's side, the fearless, let thyself be seen, |

Both gracious and in splendour peers. || 4. With Indra's well-beloved hosts, the blameless, tending heaven-ward, | The sacrificer cries aloud. || 5. Come from this place, O wanderer, or downward from the light of heaven! | Our songs of praise all yearn for this. || 6. Or Indra we implore for help from here, from heaven above the earth, | Or from the spacious firmament. || 7. Indra the singers with high praise, Indra reciters with their lauds, | Indra the choirs have glorified. || 8. Indra hath ever close to him his two bay steeds and word-yoked car, | Indra the golden, Thunder-armed. || 9. Indra hath raised the Sun on high in heaven, that he may see afar: | He burst the mountain for the kine. || 10. Help us, O Indra, in the frays, yea, frays where thousand spoils are gained, | With awful aids, O awful One. || 11. In mighty battle we invoke, Indra, Indra in lesser fight, | The friend who bends his bolt at fiends. || 12. Unclose, our manly Hero, thou for ever bounteous, yonder cloud, | For us, thou irresistible. || 13. Still higher, at each strain of mine, thunder-armed Indra's, praises rise: | I find no laud worthy of him. || 14. Even as the bull drives on the herds, he drives the people with his might, | The ruler irresistible: || 15. Indra who rules with single sway men, riches, and the fivefold race. | Of those who dwell upon the earth. || 16. For your sake from each side we call Indra away from other men: | Ours, and none others', may he be. || 17. Indra, bring wealth that gives delight, the victor's ever-conquering wealth, | Most excellent, to be our aid; || 18. By means of which we may repel our foes in battle hand to hand. | By thee assisted with the car. || 19. Aided by thee, the Thunder-armed, Indra; may we lit up the bolt, | And conquer all our foes in fight. || 20. With thee, O Indra, for ally, with missile-darting heroes may | We conquer our embattled foes.

Hymn 20:71.

1. Mighty is Indra, yea, supreme; greatness becomes the Thunderer! | Wide as the heaven extends his power; || 2. Which aideth those to win them sons who come as heroes to the fight, | Or singers loving holy thoughts. || 3. His belly drinking deepest draughts of Soma like an ocean swells, | Like wide streams from the cope of heaven. || 4. So also is his excellence, great copious, rich in cattle, like | A ripe branch to the worshipper. || 5. For verily thy mighty powers, Indra, are saving helps at once | Unto a worshipper like me. || 6. So are his lovely gifts: let laud be said and praise to Indra sung. | That he may drink the Soma juice. || 7. Come, Indra, and delight thee with the juice at all the Soma feasts, | Protector, mighty in thy strength. || 8. To Indra pour ye forth the juice, the active gladdening juice, to him | The gladdening omnific God. || 9. O Lord of all men, fair of cheek, rejoice thee in the gladdening buds, | Present at these drink-offerings. || 10. Songs have outpoured themselves to thee, Indra, the strong, the guardian Lord. | And raised themselves unsatisfied. || 11. Send to us bounty manifold, O Indra, worthy of our wish, | For power supreme is only thine. || 12. O Indra, stimulate thereto us emulously fain for wealth. | And glorious, O most splendid One. || 13. Give, Indra, wide and lofty fame, wealthy in cattle and in strength, | Lasting our life-time, failing not. || 14. Grant us high fame, O Indra, grant riches bestowing thousands, those | Fair fruits of earth borne home in wains. || 15. Praising with songs the praise-worthy who cometh to our aid, we call Indra, the Treasure-Lord of wealth. || 16. To lofty Indra, dweller by each libation, the pious man Sings forth aloud a strengthening hymn.

Hymn 20:72.

1. In all libations men with hero spirit urge thee, Universal, One, each seeking several light, each fain to win the light apart. | Thee, furthering like a ship, will we set to the chariot pole of strength, | As men who win with sacrifices Indra's thought, men who win Indra with their lauds. || 2. Couples desirous of thine aid are storming thee, pouring their presents forth to win a stall of kine, pouring gifts, Indra, seeking thee. | When two men seeking spoil or heaven thou bringest face to face in war, | Thou showest Indra, then the bolt thy constant friend, the bull that ever waits on thee, || 3. Also this morn may he be well inclined to us, mark at our call our offerings and our song of praise, our call that we may win the light. | As thou, O Indra Thunder-armed, wilt, as the Strong One, slay the foe, | Listen, thou to the prayer of me a later sage, hear thou a later sage's prayer.

Hymn 20:73.

1. All these libations are for thee, O Hero: to thee I offer these my prayers that strengthen. | Ever, in every place, must men invoke thee. || 2. Never do men attain, O Wonder-worker, thy greatness, Mighty One who must be lauded, | Nor, Indra, thine heroic power and bounty. || 3. Bring to the Wise, the Great who waxeth mighty your offerings and make ready your devotion: | To many clans he goeth, man's Controller. || 4. When, with the Princes, Maghavan, famed of old, comes nigh the thunderbolt of gold and the Controller's car | Which his two tawny coursers draw, then Indra is the Sovereign Lord of power whose fame spreads far and wide. || 5. With him too is this rain of his that comes like herds: Indra throws drops of moisture on his yellow beard. | When the sweet juice is shed he seeks the pleasant place, and stirs the worshipper as the wind disturbs the wood. || 6. We laud and praise his several deeds of valour who, father-like, with power hath made us stronger; | Who with his voice slew many thousand wicked ones who spake in varied manner with contemptuous cries.

Hymn 20:74.

1. O Soma-drinker, ever true, utterly hopeless though we be, | Do thou, O Indra, give us hope of beauteous horses and of kine, | In thousands, O most wealthy One. || 2. O Lord of strength, whose jaws are strong, great deeds are thine, the powerful: | Do thou, O Indra, give us hope of beauteous horses and of kine, | In thousands, O most wealthy One. || 3. Lull thou asleep, to wake no more, the pair who on each other look: | Do thou, O Indra, give us hope of beauteous horses and of kine, | In thousands, O most wealthy One. || 4. Hero, let hostile spirits sleep, and every gentler Genius wake: | Do thou, O Indra, give us hope of beauteous horses and of kine, | In thousands, O most wealthy One. || 5. Destroy this ass, O Indra, who in tones discordant brays to thee: | Do thou, O Indra, give us hope of beauteous horses and of kine, | In thousands, O most wealthy One. || 6. Far distant on the forest fall the tempest in a circling course; | Do thou, O Indra, give us hope of beauteous horses and of kine, | In thousands, O most wealthy One. || 7. Slay each reviler and destroy him who in secret injures us: | Do thou, O Indra, give us hope of beauteous horses and of kine, | In thousands, O most wealthy One.

Hymn 20:75.

1. Couples desirous of thine aid are storming thee, pouring their presents forth to win a stall of king pouring gifts, Indra, seeking thee. | When two men seeking spoil or heaven thou bringest face to face in war, | Thou showest, Indra, then the bolt, thy constant friend, the bull that ever waits on thee. || 2. This thine heroic power full well the people knew, wherewith thou brakest down, Indra, autumnal forts, brakest them down with conquering might. | Thou hast chastised. O Indra, Lord of strength, the man who worships not, | And made thine own this great earth and these water-floods, with joyous heart these water-floods. || 3. And they have bruited far this hero might, when thou, O Strong One, in thy joy helpest thy suppliants who sought to win thee for their Friend. | Their battle-cry thou madest sound victorious in the shocks of war. | One stream after another have they gained from thee, eager for glory have they gained.

Hymn 20:76.

1. As sits the young bird on the tree rejoicing, ye, swift pair, have been roused by clear laudation, | Whose Hotar-priest through many days is Indra, earth's guardian, friend of men, the best of heroes. || 2. May we, when this Dawn and the next dance hither, be thy best servants, most heroic Hero! | Let the victorious car with triple splendour bring hitherward the hundred chiefs with Kutsa. || 3. What was the gladdening draught that pleased thee, Indra? | Speed to our doors, our songs, for thou art mighty. | Why comest thou to me, what gift attracts thee? | Fain would I bring thee food most meet to offer. || 4. Indra, what fame hath one like thee mid heroes? With what plan wilt thou act? Why hast thou sought us? | As a true friend, Wide-Strider! to sustain us, since food absorbs the thought of each among us. || 5. Speed happily those, as Sūrya ends his journey, who meet his wish as bridegrooms meet their spouses; | Men who support, O Indra strong by nature, with food the many songs that tell thy praises. || 6. Thine are two measures, Indra, wide, well-meted, heaven for thy majesty, earth for thy wisdom. | Here for thy choice are Somas mixed with butter: may the sweet meath be pleasant for thy drinking. || 7. They have poured out a bowl to him, to Indra, full of sweet juice, for faithful is his bounty. | o'er earth's expanse hath he grown great by wisdom, the friend of man, and by heroic exploits. || 8. Indra hath conquered in his wars the mighty: men strive in multitudes

to win his friendship. | Ascend thy chariot as it were in battle, which thou shalt drive to us with gracious favour.

Hymn 20:77.

1. Impetuous, true, let Maghavan come hither, and let his tawny coursers speed to reach us. | For him have we pressed juice exceeding potent: here, praised with song, let him effect his visit. || 2. Unyoke, as at thy journey's end, O Hero, to gladden thee today at this libation. | Like Uśanā, the priest a laud shall utter, a hymn to thee, the Lord Divine, who markest. || 3. When the Bull quaffing praises our libation, as a sage paying holy rites in secret, | Seven singers here from heaven hath he begotten, who e'en by day have wrought their works while singing. || 4. When heaven's fair light by hymns was made apparent. (they made great splendour shine at break of morning), | He with his succour, best of heroes, scattered the blinding darkness so that men saw clearly. || 5. Indra, impetuous One, hath waxed immensely: he with his vastness hath filled earth and heaven. | E'en beyond this his majesty extendeth who hath exceeded all the worlds in greatness, || 6. Śakra who knoweth well all human actions hath with his eager friends let loose the waters. | They with their songs cleft e'en the mountain open, and willingly disclosed the stall of cattle. || 7. He smote away the flood's obstructer Vṛitra: Earth conscious lent her aid to speed thy thunder. | Thou sentest forth the waters of the ocean as Lord through power and might, O daring Hero. || 8. When, Much-invoked! the waters' rock thou deftest, Saramā showed herself and went before thee. | Hymned by Aṅgirasas, bursting the cow-stalls, thou foundest ample strength for us as leader.

Hymn 20:78.

1. Sing this, what time the juice is pressed, to him your Hero much-invoked, | To please him as a mighty, Bull. || 2. He, excellent, withholdeth not his gift of power and wealth in kine, | When he hath listened to our songs. || 3. May he with might disclose for us the cows' stall, whosesoe'er it be, | To which the Dasyu-slayer goes.

Hymn 20:79.

1. O Indra, give us wisdom as a sire gives wisdom to his sons. | Guide us, O Much-invoked, on this our foray: may we, living, still enjoy the light. || 2. Grant that no mighty foes, unknown, malevolent, unhallowed, tread us to the ground. | With thine assistance, Hero! may we pass through all the waters that are rushing down.

Hymn 20:80.

1. Bring us, O Indra, name and fame, enriching, mightiest, excellent, | Wherewith, O wondrous God, fair-cheeked and thunder-armed, thou hast filled full this earth and heaven. || 2. We call on thee, O King, mighty among the Gods, ruler of men, to succour us, | All that is weak in us, excellent God, make firm: make our foes easy to subdue.

Hymn 20:81.

1. O Indra, if a hundred heavens and if a hundred earths were: thine | No, not a hundred suns could match thee at thy birth, not, both, the worlds, O Thunderer. || 2. Thou, Hero, hast performed thy hero needs with might, yea, all with strength, O Strongest One. | Maghavan, help us to a stable full of kine, O Thunderer, with) wondrous aids.

Hymn 20:82.

1. If I, O Indra, were the lord of riches ample as thine own, | I should support the singer, God who scatterest wealth! and! not abandon him to woe. || 2. Each day would I enrich the man who sang my praise, in whatsoever place he were. | No kinship is there better, Maghavan, than thine: a father even) is no more.

Hymn 20:83.

1. O Indra, grant a happy home, a triple refuge, triply strong. | Bestow a dwelling-place on the rich lords and me, and keep thy dart afar from these. || 2. They who with minds intent on spoil subdue the foe, boldly attack and smite him down. | From these, O Indra, Bounteous Lord who lovest song, be closest guardian of our lives.

Hymn 20:84.

1. O Indra marvellously bright, come, these libations long for thee, | Thus by fine fingers purified. || 2. Urged by the holy singer, sped by song, come, Indra, to the prayers. | Of the libation-pouring priest. || 3. Approach, O Indra, hasting thee, Lord of Bay Horses, to the prayers: | Take pleasure in the juice we pour.

Hymn 20:85.

1. Glorify naught besides, O friends; so shall no sorrow trouble you. | Praise only mighty Indra when the juice is shed, and say your lauds repeatedly: || 2. Even him, eternal, like a bull who rushes down, men's conqueror, bounteous like a cow; | Him who is cause of both, of enmity and peace, to both sides most munificent. || 3. Although these men in sundry ways invoke thee to obtain thine aid. | Be this our prayer, addressed, O Indra, unto thee, thine exaltation every day. || 4. Those skilled in song, O Maghavan, among these men o'ercome with might the foeman's songs, | Come hither, bring us strength in many a varied form most near that it may succour us.

Hymn 20:86.

1. Those who are yoked by prayer with prayer I harness, the two. fleet friendly Bays who joy together. | Mounting thy firm and easy car, O Indra, wise and all-knowing come thou to the Soma.

Hymn 20:87.

1. Priests, offer to the Lord of all the people the milked-out stalk of Soma, radiant-coloured. | No wild bull knows his drinking-place like Indra who ever seeks him who hath pressed the Soma. || 2. Thou dost desire to drink, each day that passes, the pleasant food which thou hast had aforetime. | O Indra, gratified in heart and spirit, drink eagerly the Soma set before thee. || 3. Thou, newly-born, for strength didst drink the Soma; thy mother told thee of thy future greatness. | O Indra, thou hast filled mid-air's wide region, and given the Gods by battle room and freedom. || 4. When thou hast urged the arrogant to combat, proud in their strength of arm, we will subdue them. | Or, Indra, when thou fightest girt by heroes, we in the glorious fray with thee will conquer. || 5. I will declare the earliest deeds of Indra, and recent acts which Maghavan hath accomplished. | When he had conquered godless wiles and magic, Soma became his own entire possession. || 6. Thine is this world of flocks and herds around thee, which with the eye of Sūrya thou beholdest. | Thou, Indra, art alone the Lord of cattle: may we enjoy the treasure which thou givest. || 7. Ye twain are Lords of wealth in earth and heaven, thou, O Bṛihaspati, and thou, O Indra. | Mean though he be, give wealth to him who lauds you. Preserve us evermore, ye Gods, with blessings.

Hymn 20:88.

1. Him who with might hath propped earth's ends, who sitteth in threefold seat, Bṛihaspati, with thunder, | Him of the pleasant tongue have ancient sages, deep thinking, holy singers, set before them. || 2. Wild in their course, in well-marked wise rejoicing were they, Bṛihaspati, who pressed around us | Preserve, Bṛihaspati, the stall uninjured, this company's raining ever-moving birth-place. || 3. Bṛihaspati, from thy remotest distance have they sat down who love the law eternal. | For thee were dug wells springing from the mountain, which murmuring round about pour streams of sweetness. || 4. Bṛihaspati, when first he had his being from mighty splendour in supremest heaven. | Strong, with his sevenfold mouth, with noise of thunder, with his seven rays blew and dispersed the darkness. || 5. With the loud-shouting band who sang his praises, with thunder, he destroyed malignant Vala. | Bṛihaspati thundering drave forth the cattle, the lowing cows who make oblations ready. || 6. Serve we with sacrifices, gifts, and homage even thus the Steer of all the Gods, the Father. | Bṛihaspati, may we be lords of riches, with noble progeny and, store of heroes.

Hymn 20:89.

1. Even as an archer shoots afar his arrow, offer the laud to him with meet adornment. | Quell with your voice the wicked's voice, O sages, Singer, make Indra rest beside the Soma. || 2. Draw thy Friend to thee like a cow at milking: O singer, wake up Indra as a lover. | Make thou the Hero haste to give us riches even as a vessel filled brimful with treasure. || 3. Why, Maghavan, do they call thee bounteous Giver? Quicken me: thou, I hear, art he who quickens. | Śakra, let my intelligence be active, and bring us luck that finds great wealth, O Indra. || 4. Standing, in battle for their rights, together, the people, Indra, in the fray invoke thee. | Him who brings gifts the Hero makes his comrade: with him who pours no juice he seeks not friendship. || 5. Whoso with plenteous juice for him expresses strong Somas as much quickly-coming treasure, | For him he overthrows in early morning his swift well-weaponed foes and slays the tyrant. || 6. He

unto whom we offer praises, Indra, Maghavan, who hath joined to ours his wishes | Before him even afar the foe must tremble: low before him must bow all human glories. || 7. With thy fierce bolt, O God invoked of many, drive to a distance from afar the foeman. | O Indra, give us wealth in corn and cattle, and make the singer's prayer gain strength and riches. || 8. Indra the swallower of strong libations with their thick residue, the potent Somas, | He, Maghavan, will not restrict his bounty: he brings much wealth unto the Soma-presser. || 9. Yea, by superior play he wins advantage when he, a gambler, piles his gains in season. | Celestial-natured, he o'erwhelms with riches the devotee who keeps not back his money. || 10. O much-invoked, may we subdue all famine and evil want with store of grain and cattle. | May we allied, as first in rank, with princes,;obtain possessions by our own exertion || 11. Bṛihaspati protect us from the rearward, and from above and from below, from sinners. | May Indra from the front and from the centre, as friend to friends, vouchsafe us room and freedom.

Hymn 20:90.

1. Served with oblations, first-born, mountain-render, Aṅgiras' Son, Bṛihaspati the holy. | With twice-firm path, dwelling in light, our Father, roars loudly, as a bull, to earth and heaven. || 2. Bṛihaspati who made for such a people wide room and verge when Gods were invocated— | Slaying his foe he breaketh down their castles, quelling his enemies and those who hate him. || 3. Bṛihaspati in war hath won rich treasures, hath won, this God, the great stalls filled with cattle. | Striving to win waters and light, resistless, Bṛihaspati with lightning smites the foeman.

Hymn 20:91.

1. This holy hymn sublime and seven-headed, sprung from eternal Law, our sire discovered. | Ayāsya, friend of all men, hath engendered the fourth hymn as he sang his laud to Indra. || 2. Thinking aright, praising eternal Order, the sons of Dyaus the Asura, those heroes, | Aṅgirasas, holding the rank of sages, first honoured sacrifice's holy statute. || 3. Girt by his friends who cried with swanlike voices, bursting the stoney barriers of the prison, | Bṛihaspati spake in thunder to the cattle, and uttered praise and. song when he had found them. || 4. Apart from one, away from two above him, he drave the kine that stood in bonds of falsehood. | Bṛihaspati, seeking light amid the darkness, drave forth the bright cows: three he made apparent. || 5. When he had cleft the lairs and western castle, he cut off three from him who held the waters. | Bṛihaspati discovered, while he thundered like Dyaus, the dawn, the sun, the cow, the lightning. || 6. As with a hand, so with his roaring Indra cleft Vala through, the guardian of the cattle. | Seeking the milk-draught with sweat-shining comrades he stole: the Paṇi's kine and left him weeping. || 7. He with bright faithful friends, winners of booty, hath rent the milker of the cows asunder. | Bṛihaspati with wild boars strong and mighty sweating with heat hath gained a rich possession. || 8. They, longing for the kine, with faithful spirit incited with their hymns the Lord of cattle. | Bṛihaspati freed the radiant cows with comrades self-yoked, averting shame from one another. || 9. In our assembly with auspicious praises exalting him who roareth. like a lion. | May we in every fight where heroes conquer rejoice in strong Bṛihaspati the victor. || 10. When he had won him strength of every nature and gone to heaven and its most lofty mansions, | Men praised Bṛihaspati the mighty, bringing the light within their mouths from sundry places. || 11. Fulfil the prayer that begs for vital vigour: aid in your wonted manner e'en the humble. | Let all our foes be turned and driven backward. Hear this, O Heaven and Earth, ye all-producers. || 12. Indra with mighty strength hath cleft asunder the head of Arbuda the watery monster, | Slain Ahi, and set free the Seven Rivers. O Heaven and Earth, with all the Gods, protect us.

Hymn 20:92.

1. Praise, even as he is known, with song Indra the guardian of the kine, | The Son of Truth, Lord of the brave. || 2. Hither his bay steeds have been sent, red steeds are on the sacred grass. | Where we in concert sing our songs. || 3. For Indra thunder-armed the kine have yielded mingled milk and meath. | What time he found them in the vault. || 4. When I and Indra amount on high up to the bright One's place and home, | We, having drunk of meath, will reach his seat whose Friends are three-times-seven. || 5. Sing, sing ye forth your songs of praise, ye Priyamedhas, sing your songs: | Yea, let young children sing their lauds: as a strong castle praise ye him. || 6. Now loudly let the viol sound, the lute send out its voice with might, | Shrill be the music of the string. To Indra is the hymn upraised. || 7. When hither speed the dappled cows, unflinching, easy to be milked, | Seize quickly, as it bursts away, the Soma juice for Indra's drink. || 8. Indra hath drunk; Agni hath drunk all Deities have drunk their fill. | Here Varuṇa shall have his home, to whom the floods have sung aloud as mother-kine unto their calves. || 9. Thou, Varuṇa, to whom belong the Seven Streams, art a glorious God. | The waters flow into thy throat as 'twere a pipe with ample mouth. || 10. He who hath made the fleet steeds spring, well-harnessed, to the worshipper, | He, the swift guide, is that fair form that loosed the horses near at hand. || 11. Indra, the very mighty, holds his enemies in utter scorn. | He, far away, and yet a child, cleft the cloud smitten by his voice. || 12. He, yet a boy exceeding small, mounted his newly-fashioned car. | He for his Mother and his Sire cooked the wild mighty buffalo. || 13. Lord of the Home, with beauteous cheeks, ascend thy chariot wrought of gold. | We will attend the heavenly One; the thousand-footed, red of hue, matchless, who blesses where he goes. || 14. With reverence they come hitherward to him as to a sovereign lord, | That they may bring him near for this man's good success, to prosper and bestow his gifts. || 15. The Priyamedhas have observed the offering of the men of old, | Of ancient custom, while they strewed the sacred grass and spread their sacrificial food. || 16. He who as sovereign Lord of men moves with his chariots unrestrained, | The Vṛitra-slayer, queller of all fighting hosts, preeminent, is praised in song. || 17. Honour that Indra, Puruhanman! for his aid, in whose sustaining hand of old. | The splendid bolt of thunder was deposited, as the great Sun was set in heaven. || 18. No one by deed attains to him who works and strengthens evermore: | No, not by sacrifice, to Indra praised of all, resistless, daring, bold in might; || 19. The potent Conqueror, invincible in war, him at whose birth the mighty ones, | The kine who spread afar, sent their loud voices out, heavens, earths sent their loud voices out. || 20. O Indra, if a hundred heavens and if a hundred earths were thine | No, not a thousand suns could match thee at thy birth, not both the worlds, O Thunderer. || 21. Thou, Hero, hast performed thy hero deeds with might, yea, all with strength, O Strongest One. | Maghavan, help us to a stable full of kine, O Thunderer, with wondrous aids.

Hymn 20:93.

1. May our hymns give thee great delight. Display thy bounty, Thunderer. | Drive off the enemies of prayer. || 2. Crush with thy foot the niggard churls who bring no gifts. | Might art thou: There is not one to equal thee. || 3. Thou art the Lord of Soma pressed, Soma unpressed is also thine, | Thou art the Sovereign of the folk. || 4. Swaying about the active Ones came nigh to Indra at his birth, | And shared his great heroic might. || 5. Based upon strength and victory and power, O Indra is thy birth. | Thou, Mighty One, art strong indeed. || 6. Thou art the Vṛitra-slayer, thou, Indra, hast spread the firmament: | Thou hast with might upheld the heavens. || 7. Thou, Indra, bearest in thine arms the lightning that accords with thee, | Whetting thy thunderbolt with might. || 8. Thou, Indra, art pre-eminent over all creatures in thy strength: | Thou hast pervaded every place.

Hymn 20:94.

1. May Sovereign Indra come to the carousal, he who by holy Law is strong and active. | The overcomer of all conquering forces with his great bull-like power that hath no limit. || 2. Firm-seated is thy car, thy steeds are docile: thy hand, O King, holds, firmly grasped, the thunder. | On thy fair path, O Lord of men, come quickly: we will increase thy power when thou hast drunken. || 3. Let strong and mighty steeds who bear this mighty Indra, the Lord of men, whose arm wields thunder, | Bring unto us, as shares of our banquet, the Bull of conquering might, of real vigour. || 4. So like a bull thou rushest to the Lord who loves the trough, the Sage, the prop of vigour, in the vat. | Prepare thine energies, collect them in thyself: be for our profit as the Master of the wise. || 5. May precious treasures come to us,—so will I pray. Come to the votary's gift offered with beauteous laud. | Thou art the Lord, as such sit on this holy grass: thy vessels are inviolate as Law commands. || 6. Far went our earliest invocations of the Gods, and won us glories that can never be surpassed. | They who could not ascend the ship of sacrifice sink down in desolation, trembling with alarm. || 7. So be the others, evil-hearted, far away, whose horses difficult to harness have been yoked. | Here in advance man stand anear to offer gifts,

by whom full many a work that brings reward is done. || 8. He firmly fixed the plains and mountains as they shook. Dyaus thundered forth and made the air's mid-region quake. | He stays apart the two confronting bowls; he sings lauds in the potent Soma's joy when he hath drunk. || 9. I bear this deftly-fashioned goad of thine wherewith thou, Maghavan, shalt break the strikers with the hoof. | At the libation mayst thou be well satisfied. Partake the juice, partake the banquet, Bounteous Lord. || 10. O Much-invoked, may we subdue all famine and evil want with store of grain and cattle. | May we allied, as first in rank, with princes, obtain possessions by our own exertions. || 11. Bṛihaspati protect us from the rearward, and from above, and from below, from sinners! | May Indra from the front and from the centre, as friend to friends, vouchsafe us room and freedom.

Hymn 20:95.

1. From the three jars the Great and Strong hath drunk drink blent with meal. With Vishṇu hath he quaffed the flowing Soma juice, all that he would. | That hath so heightened him the Great, the Vast, to do his mighty work. | So may the God attend the God, true Indu Indra who is true. || 2. Sing strength to Indra that shall set his chariot in the foremost place. | Giver of room in closest fight, slayer of foes in shock of war, be thou our great encourager. Let the weak bowstrings break upon the bows of feeble enemies. || 3. Thou didst destroy the Dragon: thou sentest the rivers down to earth. | Foeless, O Indra, wast thou born. Thou tendest well each choicest thing. Therefore we draw us close to thee. Let the weak bowstrings break upon the bows of feeble enemies. || 4. Destroyed be all malignities and all our enemy's designs. | Thy bolt thou castest at the foe, O Indra, who would smite us dead: thy liberal bounty gives us wealth. Let the weak bow-strings break upon the bows of feeble enemies.

Hymn 20:96.

1. Taste this strong draught that gives thee vital vigour: with all thy chariot here unyoke thy coursers. | Let not those other sacrificers stay thee, Indra: these juices shed for thee are ready. || 2. Thine is the juice effused, thine are the juices yet to be pressed: our resonant songs invite thee. | O Indra, pleased today with this libation, come, thou who knowest all, and drink the Soma. || 3. Whoso, devoted to the God, effuses Soma for him with yearning heart and spirit, | Never doth Indra give away his cattle: for him he makes the lovely Soma famous. || 4. He looks with loving favour on the mortal who, like a rich man, pours for him the Soma. | Maghavan in his bended arm supports him: he slays, unasked, the men who hate devotion. || 5. We call on thee to come to us, desirous of booty, and of cattle, and of horses. | For thy new love and favour are we present: let us invoke thee, Indra, as our welfare. || 6. For life I set thee free by this oblation from the unknown decline and from consumption; | Or, if the grasping demon have possessed him, free him from her, O Indra, thou and Agni. || 7. Be his days ended, be he how departed, be he brought very near to death already, | Out of Destruction's lap again I bring him, save him for life to last a hundred autumns. || 8. With thousand-eyed oblation, hundred-autumned, bringing a hundred lives, have I restored him. | That Indra for a hundred years may lead him safe to the farther shore of all misfortune. || 9. Live waxing in thy strength a hundred autumns, live through a hundred springs, a hundred winters. | Through hundred-lived oblation Indra, Agni, Bṛihaspati, Savitar yield him for a hundred! || 10. So have I found and rescued thee: thou hast returned with youth renewed. | Whole in thy members! I have found whole sight and all thy life for thee. || 11. May Agni yielding to our prayer, the Rakshas-killer, drive away. | The malady of evil name that hath beset thy labouring womb. || 12. Agni, concurring in the prayer, drive off the eater of thy flesh, | The malady of evil name that hath attacked thy babe and womb. || 13. That which destroys the sinking germ, the settled, moving embryo, | That which would kill the babe at birth, even this will we drive far away. || 14. That which divides thy legs that it may lie between the married pair, | That penetrates and licks thy side, even this will we exterminate. || 15. What rests by thee in borrowed form of brother, lover, or of lord, | And would destroyed the progeny,—even this will we exterminate. || 16. That which through sleep or darkness hath deceived thee and lies down by thee, | And will destroy thy progeny,—even this will we exterminate. || 17. From both thy nostrils, from thine eyes, from both thine ears and from thy chin, | Forth from thy head and brain and tongue I drive thy malady away. || 18. From the neck-tendons and the neck, from the breast-bones and from the spine, | From shoulders, upper, lower arms, I drive thy malady away. || 19. From viscera and all within, forth from the rectum, from the heart, | From kidneys, liver and from spleen, I drive thy malady away. || 20. From thighs, from knee-caps, and from heels, and from the forepart of the feet, | From hips, from stomach, and from groin, I drive thy malady away. || 21. From what is voided from within, and from thy hair, and from thy nails, | From all thyself, from top to toe, I drive thy malady away. || 22. From every member, every hair, disease that comes in every joint, | From all thyself, from top to toe, I drive thy malady away. || 23. Avaunt, thou Master of the Mind, I Depart and vanish far away. | Look on Destruction far from us. The live man's mind is manifold.

Hymn 20:97.

1. Here verily yesterday we let the Thunder-wielder drink his fill. | So in like manner, offer him the juice to day. Now range you. by the Glorious One. || 2. Even the wolf, the savage beast that rends the sheep, follows the path of his decrees. | So, India, graciously accepting this our praise, with wondrous. thought come forth to us. || 3. What manly deed of vigour now remains that Indra hath not done? | Who hath not heard his glorious title and his fame, the Vṛitra-slayer from his birth?

Hymn 20:98.

1. That we may win us wealth and spoil we poets verily call on thee. | In war men call on thee, Indra, the hero's Lord, in the steed's, race-course call on thee. || 2. As such, O Wonderful whose hand holds thunder, praised as mighty, Caster of the Stone. | Pour on us boldly, Indra, kine and chariot-steeds, ever to be the conqueror's strength.

Hymn 20:99.

1. Men with their lauds are urging thee, Indra, to drink the Soma first. | The Ṛibhus in accord have lifted up their voice and Rudras. sung thee as the First. || 2. Indra increased his manly strength at sacrifice, in the wild rapture of this juice; | And living men today, even as of old, sing forth their praises to his majesty.

Hymn 20:100.

1. Now have we, Indra, Friend of Song, sent our great wishes forth to thee. | Coming like floods that follow floods. || 2. As rivers swell the ocean, so, Hero, our prayers increase thy might, | Though of thyself, O Thunderer, waxing day by day. || 3. With holy song they bind to the broad wide-yoked car the bay steeds of the rapid God, | Bearers of India, yoked by prayer.

Hymn 20:101.

1. Agni we choose, the messenger, the herald, master of all wealth, | Well skilled in this our sacrifice. || 2. With calls they ever invocate Agni, Agni, Lord of the House, | Oblation-bearer, much-beloved. || 3. Bring the Gods hither, Agni, born for him who strews the sacred grass. | Thou art our herald, meet for praise.

Hymn 20:102.

1. Meet to be lauded and adored, showing in beauty through the dark, | Agni the Bull is kindled well, || 2. Agni is kindled as a Bull, like a horse bearer of the Gods; | Men with oblations worship him. || 3. Thee will we kindle as a Bull, we who are bulls ourselves, O Bull, | Thee, Agni, shining mightily.

Hymn 20:103.

1. Solicit with your hymns, for aid, Agni the God with piercing flame, | For riches famous Agni, Purumīlha and ye men, Agni to light our dwelling well. || 2. Agni, come hither with thy fires: we choose thee as our Hotar-priest | Let the extended ladle full of oil balm thee, best priest, to sit on sacred grass. || 3. For unto thee, O Aṅgiras, O Son of Strength, move ladles in the sacrifice, | To Agni, Child of Force, whose locks drop oil, we seek, fore-most in sacrificial rites.

Hymn 20:104.

1. May these my songs of praise exalt thee, Lord who hast abundant wealth. | Men skilled in holy hymns, bright with the hues of fire, have sung them with their lauds to thee. || 2. He with his might enhanced by Ṛishis thousand-fold, hath like an ocean spread himself. | His majesty is praised as true at solemn rites, his power where holy singers rule || 3. May Indra, who in every fight must be invoked, be near to us. | May the most mighty Vṛitra-slayer, meet for praise, come to libations and to hymns. || 4. Thou

art the best of all in sending bounteous gifts, true art thou, lordly in thine act. | We claim alliance with the very Glorious One, yea, with the-mighty Son of Strength.

Hymn 20:105.

1. Thou in the battles, Indra, art subduer of all hostile bands. | Father art thou, all-conquering, cancelling the curse, thou victor of the vanquisher. || 2. The earth, and heaven cling close to thy victorious might, as sire and mother to their child. | When thou attackest Vṛitra all the hostile bands shrink and faint, Indra at thy wrath. || 3. Bring to your aid the Eternal One, who shoots and none may shoot at him, | Inciter, swift, victorious, best of charioteers, Tugrya's unvanquished strengthener.

Hymn 20:106.

1. That lofty energy of thine, thy strength and thine intelligence, | Thy thunderbolt for which we long, our wish makes keen. || 2. O Indra, heaven and earth augment thy manly power and thy renown, | The waters and the mountains stir and urge thee on. || 3. Vishṇu, the lofty Ruling Power, Varuṇa, Mitra sing thy praise: | In thee the Marutas' company hath great delight.

Hymn 20:107.

1. Before his hot displeasure all the peoples, all the men bow down, | As rivers bend them to the sea. || 2. This power of his shone brightly forth when Indra brought together like | A skin the worlds of earth and heaven. || 3. The fiercely-moving Vṛitra's head he severed with his thunder-bolt, | His hundred-knotted thunderbolt. || 4. In all the worlds That was the best and highest whence sprang the mighty God, of splendid valour. | As soon as born he overcomes his foemen, he in whom all who lend him aid are joyful. || 5. Grown mighty in his strength, with ample vigour, he as a foe strikes fear into the Dāsa, | Eager to win the breathing and the breathless. All sang thy praise at banquet and oblation. || 6. All concentrate on thee their mental vigour, what time these, twice or thrice, are thine assistants. | Blend what is sweeter than the sweet with sweetness: win quickly with our meath that meath in battle. || 7. Therefore in thee too, thou who winnest riches, at every banquet are the sages joyful | With mightier power, bold God, extend thy firmness: let not malignant Yātudhānas harm thee. || 8. Proudly we put our trust in thee in battles, when we behold great wealth the prize of combat. | I with my words impel thy weapons onward, and sharpen with my prayer thy vital vigour. || 9. Worthy of praises many-shaped, most skilful, most energetic, Āptya of the Āptyas: | He with his might destroys the seven Dānus, subduing many who were deemed his equals. || 10. Thou in that house which thy protection guardeth bestowest wealth, the higher and the lower. | Thou establishest the two much-wandering Mothers, and bringest many deeds to their completion. || 11. Bṛihaddiva, the foremost of light-winners, repeats these holy prayers, this strength to Indra. | He rules the great self-luminous fold of cattle, and all the doors of light hath he thrown open. || 12. Thou hath Bṛihaddiva the great Atharvan, spoken to Indra as himself in person. | The Mātaribhvarīs, the spotless sisters, with power exalt him and impel him onward. || 13. Bright, Presence of the Gods, the luminous herald, Sūrya hath mounted the celestial regions. | Day's maker, he hath shone away the darkness, and radiant passed o'er places hard to traverse. || 14. The brilliant Presence of the Gods hath risen, the eye of Mitra, Varuṇa, and Agni. | The soul of all that moveth not or moveth, Sūrya hath filled the earth and air and heaven. || 15. Even as a lover followeth a maiden, so doth the Sun the Dawn, refulgent Goddess: | Where pious men extend their generations before the Gracious One for happy fortune.

Hymn 20:108.

1. O Indra, bring great strength to us, bring valour, Śatakratu, thou most active, bring. | A hero conquering in war. || 2. For, gracious Śatakratu, thou hast ever been a mother and a sire to us, | So now for bliss we pray to thee. || 3. To thee, Strong, Much-invoked who showest forth thy strength, | O Śatakratu, do I speak: So grant thou us heroic might.

Hymn 20:109.

1. The juice of Soma thus diffused, sweet to the taste, the bright Cows drink, | Who for the sake of splendour close to mighty Indra's side rejoice, good in their own supremacy. || 2. Craving his touch the dappled Kine mingle the Soma with their milk. | The milch-kine dear to Indra send forth his death-dealing thunderbolt, good in their own supremacy. || 3. With veneration, passing wise, honouring his victorious might, | They follow close his many laws to win them due preeminence, good in their own supremacy.

Hymn 20:110.

1. For Indra, lover of carouse, loud be our songs about the juice: | Let poets sing the hymn of praise. || 2. We summon Indra to the draught, in whom all glories rest, in whom | The seven communities rejoice. || 3. By the three Soma jars the Gods span sacrifice that stirs the mind: | Let our songs aid and prosper it.

Hymn 20:111.

1. If, Indra, thou drink Soma by Vishṇu's or Trita Āptya's side, | Or with the Marutas take delight in flowing drops; || 2. Or, Śakra, if thou gladden thee afar or in the sea of air, | Rejoice thee in this juice of ours, in flowing drops. || 3. Or, Lord of Heroes, if thou aid the worshipper who sheds the juice, | Or him whose laud delights thee, and his flowing drops.

Hymn 20:112.

1. Whatever, Vṛitra-slayer! thou Sūrya, hast risen upon today, | That, Indra, all is in thy power. || 2. When, Mighty One, Lord of the Brave, thou thinkest, I shall never die, | That thought of thine is true indeed. || 3. Thou, Indra, goest unto all Soma libations shed for thee, | Both far away and near at hand.

Hymn 20:113.

1. Both boons—may Indra hitherward turned, listen to this, prayer of ours, | And, mightiest Maghavan with thought inclined to us come nigh to drink the Soma juice. || 2. For him, strong independent Ruler, Heaven and Earth have fashioned forth for power and might. | Thou seatest thee as first among thy peers in place, for thy soul longs for Soma juice.

Hymn 20:114.

1. O Indra, from all ancient time rivalless ever and companionless art thou: | In war thou seekest comradeship. || 2. Thou findest not the wealthy man to be thy friend: those scorn thee who are flown with wine. | What time thou thunderest and gatherest, then thou, even as a father, art invoked.

Hymn 20:115.

1. I from my Father have received deep knowledge of the holy Law: | I was born like unto the Sun. || 2. After the lore of ancient time I make, like Kaṇva, beauteous songs, | And Indra's self gains strength thereby. || 3. Whatever Ṛishis have not praised thee, Indra, or have lauded thee, | By me exalted wax thou strong.

Hymn 20:116.

1. Never may we be cast aside and strangers, as it were to thee. | We, Thunder-wielding Indra, count ourselves as trees rejected and unfit to burn. || 2. O Vṛitra slayer, we were thought slow and unready for the fray: | Yet once in thy great bounty may we have delight, O Hero, after praising thee.

Hymn 20:117.

1. Drink Soma, Lord of Bays, and let it cheer thee: Indra, the stone, like a well-guided courser, | Directed by the presser's arms hath pressed it. || 2. So let the draught of joy, thy dear companion, by which, O Lord of Bays, thou slayest foemen, | Delight thee, Indra, Lord of princely treasures. || 3. Mark closely, Maghavan; the words I utter, this eulogy recited by Vasishṭha: | Accept the prayers I offer at thy banquet.

Hymn 20:118.

1. Indra with all thy saving helps give us assistance, Lord of Power: | For after thee we follow even as glorious bliss, thee, Hero, finder-out of wealth. || 2. Increaser of our steeds and multiplying kine, a golden well, O God, art thou; | For no one may impair the gifts laid up in thee, Bring me what-ever thing I ask. || 3. Indra for worship of the Gods, Indra while sacrifice proceeds, | Indra as warriors in the battle-shock we call, Indra that we may win the spoil. || 4. With might hath Indra spread out heaven and earth, with power hath Indra lighted up the Sun. | In Indra are all creatures closely held; in him meet the distilling Soma drops.

Hymn 20:119.

1. An ancient praise-song hath been sung: to Indra have ye said the prayer. | They have sung many a Bṛihatī of sacrifice, poured forth the worshipper's

many thoughts. || 2. In zealous haste the singers have sung forth a song distilling oil and rich in sweets. | Riches have spread among us, and heroic strength; with us are flowing Soma drops.

Hymn 20:120.

1. Though, Indra, thou art called by men eastward and westward, north and south, | Thou chiefly art with Anava and Turvaśa, brave Champion! urged by men to come. || 2. Or, Indra, when with Ruma, Ruśama, Śyāvaka, and Kṛipa thou rejoicest thee, | Still do the Kaṇvas bring praises, with their prayers, O Indra, draw thee hither: come.

Hymn 20:121.

1. Over the three great distances, past the Five Peoples go thy way, | O Indra, noticing our voice. || 2. Send forth thy ray like Sūrya: let my songs attract thee hither-ward. | Like waters gathering to the vale.

Hymn 20:122.

1. With Indra splendid feasts be ours enriched with ample spoil, wherewith, | Wealthy in food, we may rejoice. || 2. Like thee, thyself, the singers' friend, thou movest as it were, besought, | Bold One, the axle of the car. || 3. That, Śatakratu, thou to grace and please thy praisers, as it were, | Stirrest the axle with thy strength.

Hymn 20:123.

1. This is the Godhead, this the might of Sūrya: he hath with-drawn what spread o'er work unfinished. | When he hath loosed his horses from their station, straight over all night spreadeth out her garment. || 2. In the sky's lap the Sun this form assumeth for Mitra and for Varuṇa to look on. | His bay steeds well maintain his power eternal, at one time bright and darksome at another.

Hymn 20:124.

1. With what help will he come to us, wonderful, ever-waxing Friend, | With what most mighty company? || 2. What genuine and most liberal draught will spirit thee with juice to burst. | Open e'en strongly-guarded wealth? || 3. Do thou who art protector us thy friends who praise thee | With hundred aids approach us. || 4. We will, with Indra and all Gods to help us, bring these existing worlds into subjection. | Our sacrifice, our bodies, and our offspring shall Indra form together with the Ādityas. || 5. With the Ādityas, with the band of Marutas, may Indra be protector of our bodies. | As when the Gods came after they had slaughtered the Asuras, keeping safe their Godlike nature, || 6. Brought the Sun hitherward with mighty powers, and looked about them on their vigorous Godhead. | With this may we obtain strength God-appointed, and joy with brave sons through a hundred winters.

Hymn 20:125.

1. Drive all our enemies away, O Indra, the western, mighty Conqueror, and the eastern, | Hero, drive off our northern foes and southern, that we in thy wide shelter may be joyful. || 2. What then? As men whose fields are full of barley reap the ripe corn removing it in order, | So bring the food of those men, bring it hither, who come not to prepare the grass for worship. || 3. Men come not with one horse at sacred seasons; thus they obtain no honour in assemblies. | Sages desiring herds of kine and horses strengthen the mighty Indra for his friendship. || 4. Ye, Aśvins, Lords of Splendour, drank full draughts of grateful Soma juice, | And aided Indra in his work with Namuchi of Asura birth. || 5. As parents aid a son, both Aśvins, Indra, aided thee with their wondrous powers and wisdom | When thou, with might, hadst drunk the draught that gladdens, Sarasvatī, O Maghavan refreshed thee. || 6. Indra is strong to save, rich in assistance: may he, possessing all, be kind and gracious. | May he disperse our foes and give us safety, and may we be the lords of hero vigour. || 7. May we enjoy his favour, his the holy: may we enjoy his blessed loving-kindness. | May this rich Indra, as our good protector, drive off and keep afar all those who hate us.

Hymn 20:126.

1. Men have abstained from pouring juice; nor counted Indra as a God. | Where at the votary's store my friend Vṛishākapi hath drunk his fill. Supreme is Indra over all. || 2. Thou, Indra, heedless passest by the ill Vṛishākapi hath wrought; | Yet nowhere else thou findest place wherein to drink the Soma juice. Supreme is Indra over all. || 3. What hath he done to injure thee, this tawny beast Vṛishākapi, | With whom thou art so angry now? What is the votary's foodful store? Supreme is Indra over all. || 4. Soon may the hound who hunts the boar seize him and bite him in the ear, | O Indra, that Vṛishākapi whom thou protectest as a friend. Supreme is Indra over all. || 5. Kapi hath marred the beauteous things, all deftly wrought, that were my joy. | In pieces will I rend his head; the sinner's portion shall be woe. Supreme is Indra over all. || 6. No dame hath ampler charms than I, or greater wealth of love's delights. | None with more ardour offers all her beauty to her lord's embrace. Supreme is Indra over all. || 7. Mother whose love is quickly won, I say what verily will be, | My breast, O mother, and my head and both my hips seem quivering Supreme is Indra over all. || 8. Dame with the lovely hands and arms, with broad hair-plaits and ample hips, | Why, O thou hero's wife, art thou angry with our Vṛishākapi? Supreme is Indra over all. || 9. This noxious creature looks on me as one bereft of hero's love. | Yet heroes for my sons have I, the Marutas' friend and Indra's Queen Supreme is Indra over all. || 10. From olden time the matron goes to feast and general sacrifice. | Mother of heroes, Indra's Queen, the rite's ordainer is extolled. Supreme is Indra over all. || 11. So have I heard Indrāṇī called most fortunate among these dames, | For never shall her Consort die in future time through length of days. Supreme is Indra over all. || 12. Never, Indrāṇī have I joyed without my friend Vṛishākapi, | Whose welcome offering here, made pure with water, goeth to the Gods. Supreme is Indra over all. || 13. Wealthy Vṛishākapāyi, blest with sons and consorts of thy sons, | Indra will eat thy bulls, thy dear oblation that effecteth much. Supreme is Indra over all. || 14. Fifteen in number, then, for me a score of bullocks they prepare. | And I devour the fat thereof: they fill my belly full with food. Supreme is Indra over all. || 15. Like as a bull with pointed horn, loud bellowing amid the herds, | Sweet to thine heart, O Indra, is the brew which she who tends thee pours. Supreme is Indra over all. || 16. Indrāṇī speaks. Non ille fortis (ad Venerem) est cujus mentula laxe inter femora dependet; fortis vero estille cujus, quum sederit, membrum pilosum se extendit. Super omnia est Indra. || 17. Indra speaks. Non fortis est ille cujus, quum sederit, membrum pilosum se extendit: fortis vero est ille cujus mentula laxe inter femora dependet. Super omnia est Indra. || 18. O Indra, this Vṛishākapi hath found a slain wild animal, | Dresser, and new-made pan, and knife, and wagon with a load of wood. Supreme is Indra over all. || 19. Distinguishing the Dāsa and the Ārya, viewing all, I go. | I look upon the wise, and drink the simple votary's Soma juice. Supreme is Indra over all. || 20. The desert plains and steep descents, how many leagues in length they spread! | Go to the nearest houses, go unto thine home, Vṛishākapi Supreme is Indra over all. || 21. Turn thee again Vṛishākapi; we twain will bring thee happiness. | Thou goest homeward on thy way along this path which leads to sleep. Supreme is Indra over all. || 22. When, Indra and Vṛishākapi, ye travelled upward to your home, | Where was that noisome beast, to whom went it, the beast that troubles man? Supreme is Indra over all. || 23. Daughter of Manu, Parśu bare a score of children at a birth. | Her portion verily was bliss although her burthen caused her grief.

The Kuntāpa Section.

Hymn 20:127.

1. Listen to this, ye men, a laud of glorious bounty shall be sung. | Thousands sixty, and ninety we, O Kaurama, among the Ruśamas have received. || 2. Camels twice-ten that draw the car, with females by their side, he gave. | Fain would the chariot's top bow down escaping from the stroke of heaven. || 3. A hundred chains of gold, ten wreaths, upon thee Ṛishi he bestowed, | And thrice-a-hundred mettled steeds, ten-times-a-thousand cows he gave. || 4. Glut thee, O Singer, glut thee like a bird on a ripe-fruited tree. | Thy lips and tongue move swiftly like the sharp blades of a pair of shears. || 5. Quickly and willingly like kine forth come the singers and their hymns: | Their little maidens are at home, at home they wait upon the cows. || 6. O Singer, bring thou forth the hymn that findeth cattle, findeth: wealth. | Even as an archer aims his shaft address this prayer unto the Gods. || 7. List to Parikṣhit's eulogy, the sovereign whom all people love, | The King who ruleth over all, excelling mortals as a God. || 8. 'Mounting his throne, Parikṣhit, best of all, hath given us peace and rest,' | Saith a Kauravya to his wife as he is ordering his house. || 9. 'Which shall I set before thee, curds, gruel of milk, or barley-brew?' | Thus the wife asks her husband in the realm which King Parikṣhit rules. || 10. Up as it were to

heavenly light springs the ripe corn above the cleft. | Happily thrive the people in the land where King Parikṣhit reigns. || 11. Indra hath waked the bard and said, Rise, wander singing here and there. | Praise me, the strong: each pious man will give thee riches in return, || 12. Here, cows! increase and multiply, here ye, O horses, here, O men. | Here, with a thousand rich rewards, doth Pūṣhan also seat himself. || 13. O Indra, let these cows be safe, their master free from injury. | Let not the hostile-hearted or the robber have control of them. || 14. Oft and again we glorify the hero with our hymn of praise, with prayer, with our auspicious prayer. | Take pleasure in the songs we sing: let evil never fall on us.

Hymn 20:128.

1. The worshipper who pours the juice, for gathering and assembly fit, | And yonder foe-destroying Sun,—these have the Gods designed of old. || 2. He who defiles a sister, he who willingly would harm a friend, | The fool who slights his elder, these, they say, must suffer down. below. || 3. Whenever any good man's son becometh bold and spirited, | Then hath the wise Gandharva said this pleasant upward-pointing word. || 4. The most unprofitable churl, the wealthy men who brings no gift, | These, verily, as we have heard, are cast away by all the wise. || 5. But they who have adored the Gods, and they who have bestowed their gifts, | Those liberal lords are filled with wealth like Sūrya risen up to heaven. || 6. With unanointed eyes and limbs, wearing no gem or ring of gold. | No priest, no Brahman's son is he: these things are ordered in the rules. || 7. With well-anointed limbs and eyes, wearing fair gem and golden, ring, | Good priest is he, the Brahman's son; these things are ordered in the rules. || 8. Pools with no place for drinking, and the wealthy man who. giveth naught, | The pretty girl you may not touch, these things are ordered in the rules. || 9. Pools with good drinking places, and the wealthy man who freely gives, | The pretty girl who may be touched, these things are ordered in the rules. || 10. The favourite wife neglected, and the man who safely shuns the fight, | A sluggish horse whom none may guide, these things are ordered in the rules. || 11. The favourite wife most dearly loved, the man who safely goes to war, | The fleet steed who obeys the rein, these things are ordered in the rules. || 12. When, Indra, thou, as no man could, didst plunge into the Ten Kings' fight, | That was a guard for every man: for he is formed to stay disease. || 13. Easily conquering Maghavan, thou, Hero, bentest Ravi down, | Rentest asunder Rauhiṇa, clavest in pieces Vṛitra's head. || 14. Thou who didst separate the clouds and penetrate the water-floods, | To thee, great slayer of the foe, be glory, Indra, yea, to thee! || 15. They said to Auchchaiḥśravasa running as side-horse of the Bays, | Safely to victory, O Steed, bear Indra with the beauteous wreath. || 16. They yoke the white mares, on the Bay's right harness Auchchaiḥśravasa. | He joyeth as he carrieth Indra the foremost of the Gods.

Hymn 20:129.

1-2. These mares come springing forward to Pratīpa Prātisutvana. || 3-4. One of them is Hariknikā. Hariknikā, what seekest thou? || 5-6. The excellent, the golden son: where now hast thou abandoned him? || 7-8. There where around those distant trees, three Sisus that are standing there, || 9-10. Three adders, breathing angrily, are blowing loud the threatening horn. || 11-12. Hither hath come a stallion: he is known by droppings on his way, || 13-14. As by their dung the course of kine. What wouldst thou in the home of men? || 15-16. Barley and ripened rice I seek. On rice and barley hast thou fed, || 17-18. As the big serpent feeds on sheep. Cow's hoof and horse's tail hast thou, || 19-20. Winged with a falcon's pinion is that harmless swelling of thy tongue.

Hymn 20:130.

1-2. Who carried off these stores of milk? Who took the dark cow's milk away? || 3-4. Who took away the white cow's milk? Who took the black cow's milk away? || 5-6. Question this man, Where do I ask? Where, whom that knoweth do I ask? || 7-8. Not to the belly comes the grain. The patient ones are angry now. || 9-10. Undecked with gems, and decked with gems: deity rivalling the Sun. || 11-12. Dapple, Hariknikā, and Bay ran forward to the liberal gifts. || 13-14. When the horn's blast hath sounded forth let not our friend discover thee. || 15-16. Hither to the cow's son they come. Libation hath rejoiced the God. || 17-18. Then cried they. Here he is, and, Here; again the cry was. Here is he. || 19-20. Then not defective be our steeds! A splinter so diminutive!

Hymn 20:131.

1-2. He minishes, he splits in twain: crush it and let it be destroyed. || 3-4. Varuṇa with the Vasus goes: the Wind-God hath a hundred reins. || 5-6. A hundred golden steeds hath he, a hundred chariots wrought of gold. || 7-8. A hundred bits of golden bronze, a hundred golden necklaces. || 9-10. Lover of Kuśa grass, Unploughed! Fat is not reckoned in the hoof. || 11-12. The ladle doth not hold apart the entrails and the clotted blood. || 13-14. This O Maṇḍūrikā, is mine. Thy trees are standing in a clump. || 15-16. The plain domestic sacrifice, the sacrifice with burning dung. || 17-18. Aśvattha, Dhava, Khadira, leaf taken from the Aratu. || 19-20. The man pervaded thoroughly lies on the ground as he were slain. || 21-22. The biestings only have they milked: one-and-a half of the wild ass, || 23. And two hides of an elephant.

Hymn 20:132.

1-2. Then too the single bottle-gourd, the bottle-gourd dug from the earth, || 3-4. The lute dug up from out the ground: this the wind stirs and agitates. || 5-6. Let him prepare a nest, they say: he shall obtain it strong and stretched. || 7-8. He shall not gain it unspread out. Who among these will touch the lute? || 9-10. Who among these will beat the drum? How, if he beat it, will he beat? || 11-12. Where beating will the Goddess beat again again about the house? || 13-14. Three are the names the camel bears, Golden is one of them, he said. || 15-16. Glory and power, these are two. He with black tufts of hair shall strike.

Hymn 20:133.

1. Two rays of light are lengthened out, and the man gently touches them with the two beatings on the drum. | Maiden, it truly is not so as thou, O maiden, fanciest. | Two are thy mother's rays of light: the skin is guarded from the man.

Hymn 20:134.

1. Here are we sitting east and west and north and south, with waters. Bottle-gourd vessels. || 2. Here east and west and north and south sit the calves sprinkling Curds and oil. || 3. Here east and west and north and south the offering of rice clings on. The leaf of the Aśvattha tree. || 4. Here east and west and north and south adheres when touched. That water-drop. || 5. Here east and west and north and south in iron mayst thou not be caught. The cup. || 6. Here east and west and north and south fain would it clasp what would not clasp. Emmet hole.

Hymn 20:135.

1. Bang! here he is. A dog, || 2. Swish! it is gone. Falling of leaves. || 3. Crunch! it is trodden on. A cow's hoof. || 4. These Gods have gone astray. Do thou, Adhvaryu, quickly do thy work. || 5. There is good resting for the cows. Take thy delight. || 6. O singer, the Ādityas brought rich guerdon to the Aṅgirasas. | Singer, they went not near to it. Singer, they did not take the gift. || 7. Singer, they went not near to that; but, singer, they accepted this: | That days may not be indistinct, nor sacrifices leaderless. || 8. And quickly Both he fly away, the White Horse swiftest on his feet, | And swiftly fills his measure up. || 9. Ādityas, Rudras, Vasus, all pay worship unto thee. Accept this liberal gift, O Aṅgiras, | This bounty excellent and rich, this ample bounty spreading far. || 10. The Gods shall give the precious boon: let it be pleasant to your hearts. | Let it be with you every day: accept our offerings in return. || 11. Vouchsafe us shelter, Indra, thou to be invoked from far away. | Bring treasure hither to reward the far-famed bard who praises thee. || 12. Thou, Indra, to the trembling dove whose pinions had been rent and torn. | Gayest ripe grain and Pīlu fruit, gavest him water when athirst. || 13. The ready praiser loudly speaks though fastened triply with a strap. | Yea, he commends the freshening draught, deprecates languor of disease.

End of Kuntāpa Section

Hymn 20:136.

1. Si quis in hujus tenui rima praeditae feminae augustias fascinum intromittit, vaccae ungularum et Sakula. rum piscium more pudenda ejus agitantur. || 2. Quum magno pene parvula ejus pudenda vir percutit, huc et illuc ilia increscunt veluti duo asini in solo arenoso. || 3. Quum parvum, admodum parvum, Ziziphi Jujubae quasi granum in eam incidit, ventris ejus partes interiores, velut verno tempore arundo, extentae videntur. || 4. Si Dii mentulae intumescenti faverunt, cum femoribus suis se: ostentat

femina tanquam vero testi. || 5. Magnopere delectata est arnica: ut equns solutus adveniens vocem edidit: Vaginam juvenis! pene percute: medium. femur paratum est. || 6. Arnica, pilam superans, dixit: Ut tua, Arbor, I (verbera) pinsunt, sic etiam nunc (hic me permolit). || 7. Arnica eum alloquitur: Tum etiam tu defecisti. Ut tua. Arbor! (verbera) Pinsunt, sic etiam nunc (me permole). || 8. Arnica eum alloquitur: Tum etiam tu defceisti. Ut silvae ignis. inflammatur, sic ardent mea membra. || 9. Arnica eum alloquitur: Fauste infixus est penis; arboris fructu celeriter fruamur. || 10. Arnica cum fuste gallum circumcurrit. Nos nescimus quae bestia pudendum muliebre in capite gerat. || 11. Arnica post currentem amatorem currit: Has ejus boves custodi tu. Me futue: coctam oryzam ede. || 12. Fortunatus, Arnica, te opprimit. Bona est magni viri fututio, Macrum pinguis. femina obtineat. Futue me, etc. || 13. Sine digito mulcta vacca *vanankaram* producit, Magna et bona est Aegle Marmelos. Futue me, etc. || 14. Infelix, Amice, te opprimit. Bona est magni viri fututio. Flava puollula, opere suo perfecto, procurrit. || 15. Magna certe et bona est Aegle Marmelos. Bona est magna Ficus Glomerata. Magnus vir ubique opprimit. Bona est magni viri fututio. || 16. Quem macrum factum puella flava pinguisque capiat sicut pollicem ex olei cado fossorem ilium extrahat.

Hymn 20:137.

1. When, foul with secret spot and stain, ye hastened onward to the breast. | All Indra's enemies were slain and passed away like froth and foam. || 2. Indra is he, O men, who gives us happiness: sport, urge the giver of delight to win the spoil. | Bring quickly down, O priests, hither to give us aid, to drink the Soma, Indra son of Nishṭigrī. || 3. So have I glorified with praise strong Dadhikrāvan, conquering steed. | Sweet may he make our mouths; may he prolong the days we have to live. || 4. The Somas very rich in sweets, for which the sieve is destined, flow, | Effused, the source of Indra's joy. May your strong juices reach the Gods. || 5. Indu flows on for Indra's sake—thus have the deities declared. | The Lord of Speech exerts himself, ruler of all, because of might. || 6. Inciter of the voice of song, with thousand streams the ocean flows, | Even Soma, Lord of Opulence, the friend of Indra, day by day. || 7. The black drop sank in Aṃśumatī's bosom, advancing with ten thousand round about it. | Indra with might longed for it as it panted: the hero-hearted laid aside his weapons. || 8. I saw the drop in the far distance moving, on the slope bank of Aṃśumatī's river, | Like a black cloud that sank into the water. Heroes. I send you forth. Go, fight in battle. || 9. And then the drop in Aṃśumatī's bosom, splendid with light, assumed its proper body; | And Indra with Brihaspati to aid him, conquered the godless tribes that came against him. || 10. Then, at thy birth, thou wast the foeman, Indra, of those the seven who ne'er had met a rival. | The hidden pair, the heaven and earth, thou foundest, and to the mighty worlds thou gavest pleasure. || 11. So, Thunder-armed! thou with thy bolt of thunder didst boldly smite that power which none might equal; | With weapons broughtest low the might of Śushṇa, and, Indra, foundest by thy strength the cattle. || 12. We make this Indra very strong to strike the mighty Vṛitra dead: | A vigorous Hero shall he be. || 13. Indra was made for giving, set, most mighty, o'er the joyous draught, | Bright, meet for Soma, famed in song. || 14. By song, as 'twere, the powerful bolt which none may parry was prepared: | Lofty, invincible he grew.

Hymn 20:138.

1. Indra, great in his power and might and, like Parjanya, rich in rain, | Is magnified by Vatsa's lauds, || 2. When the priests, strengthening the Son of holy Law, present their gifts, | Singers with Order's hymn of praise. || 3. Since Kaṇvas with their lauds have made Indra complete the sacrifice, | Words are their own appropriate arms.

Hymn 20:139.

1. To help and favour Vatsa now, O Aśvins, come ye hitherward. | Bestow on him a dwelling spacious and secure, and keep malignites afar. || 2. All manliness that is in heaven, with the Five Tribes, or in mid-air, | Bestow, ye Aśvins, upon us. || 3. Remember Kaṇva first of all among the singers,, Aśvins, who | Have thought upon your wondrous deeds. || 4. Aśvins, for you with song of praise this hot oblation is effused, | This your sweet Soma juice, ye Lords of wealth and spoil, through which ye think upon the foe. || 5. Whatever ye have done in floods, in the tree, Wonder-workers, and in growing plants, | Therewith, O Aśvins, succour me.

Hymn 20:140.

1. What force, Nāsatyas, ye exert, whatever, Gods, ye tend and heal, | This your own Vatsa gains not by his hymns alone: ye visit him who offers gifts. || 2. Now hath the Ṛishi splendidly thought out the Aśvins' hymn of praise. | Let the Atharvan pour the warm oblation forth, and Soma very rich in sweets. || 3. Ye Aśvins, now ascend your car that lightly rolls upon its way. | May these my praises make you speed hitherward like a cloud of heaven. || 4. When, O Nāsatyas, we this day make you speed hither with our hymns, | Or, Aśvins, with our songs of praise, remember Kaṇva specially. || 5. As erst Kakshīvant and the Ṛishi Vyaśva, as erst Dīrghatamas invoked your presence, | Or, in the sacrificial chambers, Vainya Pṛithi, so be ye mindful of us here, O Aśvins

Hymn 20:141.

1. Come as home-guardians, saving us from foemen, guarding our living creatures and our bodies, | Come to the house to give us seed and offspring: || 2. Whatever with Indra ye be faring, Aśvins, or resting in one dwelling-place with Vāyu, | In concord with the Ṛibhus or Ādityas, or standing still in Vishṇu's striding-places. || 3. When I, O Aśvins, call on you today that I may gather strength, | Or as all-conquering might in war, be that the Aśvins' noblest grace. || 4. Now come, ye Aśvins, hitherward: here are oblations set for you; | These Soma draughts to aid Yadu and Turvaśa, these offered you mid Kaṇva's sons. || 5. Whatever healing balm is yours, Nāsatyas near or far away, | Therewith, great Sages, grant a home to Vatsa and to Vimada

Hymn 20:142.

1. Together with the Goddess, with the Aśvins' Speech have I awoke. | Thou, Goddess, hast disclosed the hymn and holy gift from mortal men. || 2. Awake the Aśvins, Goddess Dawn! Up, mighty Lady of Sweet Strains! | Rise straightway, priest of sacrifice! High glory to the gladdening draught! || 3. Thou, Dawn, approaching with thy light, shinest together with the Sun, | And to this man-protecting home the chariot of the Aśvins comes. || 4. When yellow stalks give forth the juice as cows from udders pour their milk, | And voices sound the song of praise, the Aśvins' worshippers show first. || 5. Forward for glory and for strength, protection that shall conquer men, | And power and skill, most sapient Ones! || 6. When, Aśvins worthy of our lauds, ye seat you in the father's house. | With wisdom or the bliss ye bring.

Hymn 20:143.

1. We invocate this day your car, far-spreading, O Aśvins, even the gathering of the sunlight, | Car praised in hymns, most ample, rich in treasure, fitted with seats, the car that beareth Sūrya || 2. Aśvins, ye gained that glory by your Godhead, ye Sons of Heaven, by your own might and power. | Food followeth close upon your bright appearing when stately horses in your chariot draw you. || 3. Who bringeth you today for help with offered oblations, or with hymns to drink the juices? | Who, for the sacrifice's ancient lover, turneth you hither, Aśvins, offering homage? || 4. Borne on your golden car, ye omnipresent! come to this sacrifice of ours, Nāsatyas. | Drink of the pleasant liquor of the Soma: give riches to the people who adore you. || 5. Come hitherward to us from earth, from heaven, borne on your golden chariot rolling lightly. | Suffer not other worshippers to stay you: here are ye bound by earlier bonds of friendship. || 6. Now for us both, mete out, O Wonder-Workers, riches exceeding great with store of heroes, | Because the men have sent you praise, O Aśvins, and Ajamīlhas come to the laudation. || 7. Whene'er I gratified you here together, your grace was given us, O ye rich in booty. | Protect, ye twain, the singer of your praises: to you, Nāsatyas, is my wish directed. || 8. Sweet be the plants for us, the heavens, the waters, and full of sweets for us be air's mid-region! | May the Field's Lord for us be full of sweetness, and may we follow after him uninjured. || 9. Aśvins, that work of yours deserves our wonder, the Bull of firmament and earth and heaven; | Yes, and your thousand promises in battle. Come near to all these men and drink beside us.

The End of the Veda Saṃhitās

Made in United States
Troutdale, OR
05/08/2024

19702056R10277